DANCE ON THE HORIZON

DANCE ON THE HORIZON
1994

Caroline Sullivan, Editor

THE NATIONAL LIBRARY OF POETRY

Dance on the Horizon

Library of Congress
Cataloging in Publication Data

ISBN 1-56167-251-3

Proudly manufactured in the United States of America by
Watermark Press
11419 Cronridge Dr., Suite 10
Owings Mills, MD 21117

Editor's Note

As editor of **Dance on the Horizon**, I am happy to present this fine collection of poetic works. Through our North American Open Poetry Contest, we at **The National Library of Poetry** strive to discover and publish both new and established artists -- not only from the United States, but from around the world. It is you, the artists, who keep us, the literary world, and the public aware of both the changing literary trends and of the changing global community.

As evident by the size of this book, we were clearly inundated with outstanding submissions that ranged from traditional subjects and poetic forms to more unconventional topics and free verse. This particular volume of poetry features works on such poignant subjects as the Serbian-Bosnian war, child molestation, racism, feminism, abortion. Also represented are uplifting works conveying universal ideas of love, family, relationships, and faith. Grudgingly, we had to narrow this group of semi-finalists to only 70 prize winners. All the poems presented are praiseworthy, however there are a few poets I believe merit special recognition.

Two of our prize recipients employ poetic forms. Mildred Cavallo uses the villanelle in her "I Think I'll Melt My Mask." The originality of images and ideas are a fresh juxtaposition to this traditional form. In "Sonnet on the Exeter Class of 1942," Charles Van Doren chooses the Petrarchan sonnet. Particularly noteworthy in its command of the English language is the closing sestet.

John Getman's "Studio Light" caught my attention through his unique use of metaphor. He writes of the light that "silks across a rough and dark-scarred wooded chest." Very original. "The Fall" by Edith Kalish flows with grand allusions that reverberate with "Camus-esque" ideas.

Ultimately, however, it was "Echoes from a Winter Grave" by William Howard Thomas which captivated all the judges' attentions. Like the aforementioned works, this piece exudes original images that trickle through subtle rhymes and weave ideas that are profound yet apprehensible.

Unfortunately, I do not have the space to give each poem the critique that it deserves. I congratulate all of you featured in this anthology and sincerely hope you enjoy reading **Dance on the Horizon.**

Caroline Sullivan, Editor

Acknowledgements

The publication **Dance on the Horizon** is a culmination of the efforts of many individuals. Judges, editors, assistant editors, typesetters, computer operators, graphic artists, layout artists, paste-up artists and office administrators have all brought their respective talents to bear on this project. The editors are grateful for the contributions of these fine people:

Lisa Della, Chrystal Eldridge, Jeffrey Franz, Ardie L. Freeman, Hope Goodwin Freeman, Julian Friedman, Diane Mills, Eric Mueck, John J. Purcell III, Jacqueline Spiwak, Cynthia Stevens, Ira Westreich, and Margaret Zirn.

Howard Ely, Managing Editor

Grand Prize Winner

William Howard Thomas

Second Prize Winners

Audrie Bennett

David Chase

William Davenport

Stephen John Eyre

John Getman

Edith Kalish

Dan R. Kiely

M. Scott Myers

Parikshit Singh

Devon Knight Svarda

Third Prize Winners

Rex E. Alford

Darren Bates

Bill Britton

Lyman Brownfield

Mildred Cavallo

Donnis Coffey

Grace Conlon

V. Cottrill

Michel Dinan

Denise Domergue

Timothy J. Duffy

Britt East

David Eaton-Messer

Jo-Anna L. Edwards

Joshua Eisenstien

Francisco E. Feito

Jack Fullbeck

Christine V. Grupp

Jean Hull Herman

Helen Hilbert

Rose Mary Hooper

Susan E. Hughey

Sarah Elzbieta Kanouse

Thomas Kochman

Clifford Neil Krentz

Konstantinos Lardas

Rosamond Leadbetter

Heather Lieberman

Stanley Linder

J. Robert Maruyama

Jennifer Robin McConnell

Ronald Moore

Josephine Mosdell

Gretchen Mullin

Maria Marosek Naylor

John J. O'Brien

Marian Ford Park

Samuel Penny

T.M. Pride

Peggy Rambo

Justine C. Reily

Jerry L. Richards

Maurice E. Robinson

Ferdinand A. Ruplin

C.G. Schmelter

Mildred Shaver, S.C.

Laura G. Simon

Sid Sisco

Theresa Stickley

Verla Swanson

John H. Thaden

Christine Tibbles

Mary Tiffney

Sabrina Valo

Charles N. Van Doren

Michele Willowtrout

Christie Winter

Alice Wojewoda

Edith Stein Zelig

Congratulations also to our Editor's Choice Winners.

Grand Prize Winner

Echoes From A Winter Grave

When winter death obliterates the sun, or darkness comes,
  or brittle bier enfolds a former beauty,
  or what was once is not;
   then memory serves as text.

The perfumed breath of spring conspires to melt a frigid frown,
  and summer breeze drifts by to rustle silken gown,
  while autumn art drips gold on brown;
   when memory serves as text.

Clutched close in fright, a timid candle makes the night
  less light, and black; but held upright,
  thrust high, its fire becomes the sun;
   if memory serves as text.

Thus winter death can not unknot nor ever start to sever
  this magic thread; instead, remembered warmth
  weaves a velvet cloak:
   vibrations of and echoes from
    another time
     another place
      another world,
  when memory serves as text.

—William Howard Thomas

Rock Hounds Glory

My friends and I made our way up the Hill,
with a little cloth bag, we're hoping to fill.
Our tools and our lunch, made a very big part,
of the few hours ahead, tucked in our heart.
Slipping and sliding, our shoes filled with dirt,
we set out in earnest, as we went to work.
Amid all the noise, and the wiping of sweat,
a rock hounds glory, we'll never forget.
With the sun going down, and our breath getting short,
we started our trek, back to our port
The bag held so tight, with our treasure inside,
we're on our way, our eyes glowing with pride.

  —*Beulah Norton*

Spring's Renewal

Spring air vibrant with rebirth
Wind blowing pleasantly pungent perfumes -
Fragrant soil, buds bursting
Gaining strength through spring's warm sun.

Last night's rain now prisms
Of sparkling crystal dew drops,
Rainbows of colour
Washing away the traces of winter.

Greening grass, freshly sprouted
Flecked with snow drops delicately white,
Strings of unstrung pearls
Spilt over verdant carpets.

Showy crocus, pallets of colour
Splattered on warmed dark humus,
Scattered sun bouquets
Splashed among a copse of trees.

White socked pussy willows
Thrust into azure skies
Pollen energizing bees
Escaping winter's unconsciousness

  —*Ann Vanderhoek*

Letter To T.S. Eliot In the Crossroads

One can accept that the Thames
widens its settled clay
towards the harsh-sounding walls of the banks
and can listen to T.S.
saying heavenly inundations.

The warm timber of his name bowed towards the dew
and the sea gull.
His voice sprouted from the blank verse to signify the psalm
and befall the loaf of bread and the dove..

He waited the disappearance at the edge of himself
with a look of broken astonishment.
Attentive, shining attentive to the heedless absence
that so often he observed in the dead.

He departed as one who turns to a friendly face
and knows that he has to repeat the first sob,
conceal the last tear, and understand
the lonely removal of oneself
in that only instance of the whole soul.

  —*Francisco E. Feito*

Studio Light

Subdued, Toledo's evening light obliquely
whispers through the window panes and silks
across a rough and dark-scarred wooded chest,
topped by deep red damask, ink horn, drawing pen;
ordered work bench in El Greco's studio.

Cross-hatched ochre floor tiles catch surface
shimmers from the failing light, patina'd
footfalls, silent echoes from long gone days.
Leather-backed, a tired sagging chair
sits by the window, fetching light for sketching.

Dusk mood harkens to the fervid vision
many hundred years ago, last embers ebbing
in the fireplace, where still there is
a lingering glow, suffused through timelessness
of art that saw beyond his time, time itself.

Sit there now and be with him,
the warmth is not the light alone.

  —*John L. Getman*

Sunday Afternoon

You drive me out of hollows, out of brooks
Where jealous deer protect their tenuous broods,
And leave me wandering with a string of books,
In marble labyrinths, securing woods.
I visit stores that aimless devils built
Vacationing from the world's oppressive hours,
When God's bright workmen danced beyond their guilt
And trees retracted retrospective flowers.
I look at neon signs prostituting goods,
And wonder at the merriment in their greed.
I hear the sounds of music of inner moods
And feel no relief from my deepest need.
I dream a misalliance with the birds,
The hungry craftsmen with no sacred day,
But, victim of a gathering cloud of words,
I spill their dewy porridge when I pray.
I sway at the edge of cauldrons blind,
Yet, as running children bow, I hold my rage.
I am still searching for that peace of mind,
While you, strong Casanova, rest in your parrot's cage.

  —*Peggy Rambo*

The Sea

I know a rock-bound, rock-ribbed coast,
Where a grey and sullen sea
Breaks with a roaring, re-echoing boast
Of a nameless savagery.

Out from the sea swept, storm lashed rock
A hidden reef extends,
Sinking each way-worn, weary cock
Which the current shoreward sends.

O'er all a bleached-white bone dust lies,
And the mist from angry waves
Covers the time-worn, timber ties
Which number those unknown graves.

Oft in a blood-red, berserk moon
The sea folk far and near
List to the ghostly, ghoul-like croon
Of the souls lying captive there.

  —*Lyman Brownfield*

The Lasting Kiss

Did you e'er taste the atmosphere of love?
When passion hangs in heavy scents around the room,
Where silk'n lips like luscious peaches beckon,
Intense desire your mind and body doth consume.

Hands touch gently first to warn of fever,
Dallying kisses round her swanlike neck begin,
Blood runs fast as fondling grows the firmer,
Who can sense the longing, bursting from within?

Light streams through window pane 'cross covers all around,
Disturbed so much as each embrace would make them both as one,
Those cheeks so fair shine like a velvet, sunlit, meadow,
Where kisses must be gathered ere sets the sinking sun.

As daylight fades the kissing still relentless
Dispels all thought of food or mundane fare,
Though evening shadows haunt the room with darkness,
This passion knows no time or temporal care.

For ages it would seem, affection flows unhindered,
Conveyed to worlds of sensual bliss,
Could this be yours, I know you would embrace it,
Experience sublime, the lasting kiss!

—*Henry Gibson*

Oh Ancient Bristlecone

Oh lonely gnarled Bristlecone tree,
  What tales of life can you tell me?
Nude - wretched, but still standing tall
  The most magnificent tree of all.

What ancient peoples have you seen
  When younger in your dress of green
You stood upon that regal perch
  As though a preacher in a church?

How was the world, what were the climes?
  What roamed your view in older times?
Did people love, and was there peace?
  Did strife abound, or had it cease?

Did birds make nests upon your limbs?
  Did running water and carving winds
Wear away the valley floor?
  Above your head, did eagles soar?

Oh how I wish that you could talk
  From your grand view upon that rock.
What tales you'd tell of things you see.
  What insights into history.

—*David R. Martindale*

Undertow

Embers of the fire cool from red to grey,
waves erase lovers' imprints and the ash.
A kiss, a touch, a card, and a bouquet,
burn brilliantly, briefly, like a struck match.
She enjoyed the time they spent together,
with emphasis on past tense. A rose dropped
red and wilting onto the sand, forever
caught in the froth of waves that never stop
churning. Dragged out by the ocean's tide
to sink in the depths, the octopus' lair.
Somewhere, unheard, lovers plead how they tried.
But birth flows from brief tide pools and prayers.
Lovers drown in dreams of sunken towers;
everything begins with killing flowers.

—*F.S. Rohrer*

August Landscape

The sweet corn and cotton and cantaloupe die:
Vivid sturdy stalks unyielding now,
Brittled leaves crumble in what passes for a breeze;
Tanned, cracked ground gasps
Spurning sinister heat eternal
(The worms tunnel ever deeper
If they can slither at all in parched earth).
Shrivelled grasses - mostly baked browns;
Vistas of yellow fallowing fields
Visited by sunbroiling savagery
And grey, gritty, dusty eddies revolt,
Dancing sinfully through aborted crops.
And no small relief springs
From an unrelenting Sun:
His charring, saffron tyranny
Withers green and green
To sparkless umber.

—*Justine C. Reilly*

Morning Reader

Oil of lavender warming on the lamp augmenting the reader's
vision, provides olfactory stimulation to encourage revelation.
Reason, like clouds greying the golden dawn, threatens the
confidence of dreams but Prophecy whispers comfort.

The Man on Moore sees hidden danger in The Hero and The
Steeple-Jack. Moore describes a seaside town in action;
enchanting and inviting. Benign printing on the steeple-jack
sign is the only Danger! there. Courageous owl of integrity
speaks of stylish independence as the brave observer wields
precision. Marianne's the Hero here. The adoring buffoon
biographer tracking animal excreta through another's rich
imagination turns her garden into compost.

Unadorned breakfast berry in the bowl lends substantiation
as the message of the morning forming urges, "Fear not. Just
be yourself. A driving sense of purpose births achievement."

Jesus by submission, Hamlet feigning madness, Jonathon through
soaring, and Moore's independent spirit, all clearly give
permission to the reader to be free.

—*Jo-Anna L. Edwards*

As Rivers Meet

With no small flow of trickling down come I
Through bough and rock, so swift my tumultuous quest,
As yet alone, my life within me cries
To merge course of kin and play crest on crest;
From diverse place the mighty rivers yearn
Their soulful paths to others intertwine,
And so do I; from them I hope to learn
Such wellsprings proffer nourishment divine;
Praise! Leap, as now another river meets
With me, we join our foam and brine to ride,
Forever vowed, for now we wave replete
To journey on towards sea, our crowning pride;
  And bounds as one, our fluid lives refreshed,
  Two rivers swirl, confluent lines enmeshed.

—*Rae Bruno*

Real Tears

I have often wondered all these years
How actors could just "turn on the tears";
But now I have finally realized
That their mothers must have died.

—*June O'Mohundro Studdert*

Oh Little One

Oh little One, upon my knee, with questions never ending,
this world I paint is bright you see, with love and truth unbending.
For all the love within my heart, and all the hope I know
have mixed the paint, and moved the brush, and built the glow,
    and eased the woe
or as much as love, and hope, and wishes can ever make it so.

Your world of kings and queens and castles, and royal armies
    battle scenes
has heroes winning over evil, in baseball caps and old blue jeans.
You have your bad men dressed in black, for all the world to see,
and men are judged ... by simple things, like honesty, integrity,
and right is right, and wrong is wrong, and which is which all
    men agree.

Oh little one, upon my knee, your questions are deserving
of so much more sincerity, in all I've been reserving.
You ask for truth in what you see, but I paint pictures wishfully,
although I know... you soon will learn... of jealousy, dishonesty,
and find the world I've painted, is not the one you see.

        —*C. G. Schmelter*

The Forgiving Womb

Oh, this womb of discontent;
    This womb that spat out the first threads
    of life, with dreams of tomorrow shattered
    forever in some cold and watery grave;
This womb that now cries out for recompense.

How can I make amends to a womb that weeps;
    Too shriveled, too barren, too old to
    ever nourish another life toward that
    mystical moment of birth
When womb relinquishes her treasure to world?

I will cradle the children as I find them;
    Pull their tousled heads to my heart of
    compassion; listen to their need for comfort;
    and firmly press them to my womb, now nothing
    more than the lap of contentment.....
And bask in the warm, forgiving wisdom of womb.

        —*Dorothy West Elkerton*

Apostrophe To Amour

He will forget the lust. He will remember
This fleeting beauty, that minute delight—
After the fire dies, and the last ember
Sends a lone spark crusading into night.

He will recall, out of a holocaust
Of thin-veiled passions, the solitary tear
That brimmed and fell, the countenance austere
At fancied wrong, the touch—all else is lost.

Days in the sun beside her, where salt waves
Spilled in a frolic on a grainy shore;
Music, and moments that the memory saves,
Hypnotized once, impotent evermore.

Now is a time for summary. The scars
Acknowledged with the memories, and worn
Like proud medallions on a heart forlorn,
He writes his wonder to the constant stars.

This is a requiem for loveliness—
A moment to sing and bury it. And after...
Only chance meetings of the eyes caress.
And no more bitterness. And no more laughter.

        —*Jack Fulbeck*

Downside Of Motherhood

Indeed they are killing me
They suck me dry (with their needing)
They even wring and squeeze
the last few drops of youth and joy from me
until, exhausted, I hang limp and lifeless
withered....
I am flat and nothing (I am dying)
They batter at me with their words; their voices
beat at me, pounding and slapping (I cringe before them)
The onslaught drains me and I am empty; I echo
My eyes are dead
Yet they reach out to me and they want
They always want to touch me
They need the closeness, to be near me (I cannot breathe)
and they need to talk to me; I have to listen
My ears are full of the sounds
And they berate me because none of it is enough
I am certainly not enough (I am not perfect you see)
I am only their mother and I was dying anyway

        —*Donna Anne Irving*

The Winter Muse

a cold wind blows the leaves,
they fall,
leaving a dry remembrance of a tree.

it is this time when the cold cracks my soul,
freezing the warmth
of hopes and dreams.

it is when conversations with my fears
help me to sleep at night.
the past repeats in such a manner
that i expect yet unexpecting i still feel.

it is a time when
i walk through the graveyard of my past
and find a blank tombstone.

the time in which i feel the worst
i can't help but love the most.
for it is now that inspires my quill,
when death spawns life.
she is the cold air that leaves surrender to.
she is the season i look forward to.
she is the muse my written voice goes out to.

        —*Mike Ruzicka*

Moriarty's Violin

Sir Arthur Conan Doyle says that spirits are benign.
    They do not stay.
    It is only the surface that stays,
    Beautiful, "a search for the Holy Grail," benign.
My mother's surface was torn off in bloody chunks.
"Here," she says as she holds out her heart in her hands
As we escape from burning buildings before they crash.
    And Sherlock Holmes is not benign.
Wherever you got him, it is the whole creature,
    Torn sleepless, his eyes blazing.
"You meaner beauties of the night...
    What are you when the moon shall rise?"
What forest of Bohemia have you torn him from?
    What unfulfilled city he can dream?
What London that recreates itself in the Eastern Desert,
    Red, the color of dreams?
"Ships, domes, theatres, towers, temples lie."

His hands are not a lover's hands but claws.
And Prospero walks Westminster Bridge at dawn.

        —*Rita LaForce*

Sonnet on the Exeter Class of 1942

When we reflect on how our lives were spent
These fifty years since leaving P.E.A.:
The memories of World War II that stay
Of tragic sacrifice and rare dissent;
Foreshortened college years, and all they meant;
Careers pursued, and friendships, modes of play;
Our courting, weddings, break-ups, and the way
They yielded families or discontent —

We realize how much we owe this place
That honed our minds, helped shape our attitudes,
And made us relish excellence and work,
Listen and read for meaning, write with grace,
And speak out plainly, not in platitudes.
It kindled fires that in our souls did lurk!

    —Charles N. Van Doren

Follower In My Footsteps

Through wooded path I walked alone with sentries at my side;
their arms outstretched, their branches bent, beneath a sunset sky.
With naked step I broke the backs of determined blades of grass.
My footprints lingered for an instant, then the forest let me pass.
I became the breathing leaves and I became the wind.
I met the water running free... and I became his friend.
The only trace that I was not born a child of this place,
was betrayed within those grassy marks that took my foot embrace.
Yet glad was I that those marks held my passing on their ground,
for circling back upon my path was another footprint found.
The step was placed within my own but was lighter and more kind.
It knew the things I had come to know as it followed from behind.
I held my breath and turned around, but no stranger did I see...
I saw wind and grace and God's embrace looking back at me.
She had become the same as I; the water, leaves and wind,
a follower within my steps, a traveller and a friend.
I journey forth to walk once more and mark my passing on the
    land,
but a friend now trusts her step in mine, where silent sentries
    stand.

    —Clifford Neil Krentz

The Touch Of Rain

Drought! The terrible lip gnawing dryness!
The throat thirsting pain of no water
I have known!...in body and mind.
Like dark stretched bark, flat against a tree,
broken and shattered, my spirit could find
no comfort. It screamed across the years
In dust and hotness.
It burned in my cracked clay, and buried its
face in the emptiness of space.

Then...one day...I heard it!
The gentle pounding wetness on my window pane.
The shaking thunder and lightning flash
that pushed me out, where I stumbled about,
so dry...with wet eyes, in the rain.
Oh! Could you guess how soaked were the shining
drops? And as new years flew by,
Again and again, I stepped onto the walk
And stood, all wet, with dry eyes, in the rain.

    —Theresa Stickley

Sans Souci

In plush pajamas made to cover little chilly feet
the television flickers as my eyelids slowly meet
gently he carries me to bed so lovingly and sweet
covers tucked and forehead kissed nestled warm and safe as can
    be....
    Sans souci
A favorite fairy tale slips me into silent repose
she smiles at the slumber lulled by familiar fading prose
and offs the light for I am asleep the tiptoer knows
while I sleep my dreams drift free....
    Sans souci
Settled in the backseat for the long ride home
the headlights catch the raindrops as they dance upon the chrome
and on the rippled road the rolling wheels drone
secure in the driver's knowing hands my idle head grows heavy....
    Sans souci
Alone now in the twilight I lament the quiescent past
a fool to think such moments might last
for in youth we feast; as adults we fast
curse the restless tosses for they will not grant me...
    Sans souci

    —Sabrina Valvo

First Connection

The night cracked, spilling flame o'er the seas;
The 'rise lit the spire of the trees,
    A grey dawn starved the mountain's sheen
And I raised myself from a quilted frame
Dingy and warm, are not all tombs the same?

Cool breezes slid down my throat like rain;
My existence is free, soul and brain.
    Yet another virgin beneath the sun,
I danced the dragonfly-wing stream
Kissing the remnants of my quilted dream.

Here now, the sugar-clouds billowed bright
I wanted to sing- but what tune is right
    For the only September I am thirteen?
Silent, I let the day drape me well
With garments of wind and earthy smells.

Why had the Lord sent breath to this day?
No evils were conquered, no truth found my way...
    As evening's living candlelight blazed,
I reread my day's poem, to see
And remember the beauty I shared with thee.

    —Heather Lieberman

This time 'round
the revolution is being televised.
Red fire flows like fresh wound blood
from a nation's charred conscience.
Black smoke hovers like a guilt ridden hangover
on a Monday morning after a three day binge.
Rock video news reels jiz image after image
in numb orgasm.

This is L.A. burning.
This is my country
smoking itself on British tele'.

They're having a grand time
sipping their tea and drinking their pints of ale,
thinking we're all sitting on front porches
with shirtless beer bellies
drinking Pabst Blue Ribbon
cleaning our guns
and saying nigger.

but what is there for me to say
as I watch with them?

    —David Chase

Aetherlogue

Deep in interstellar hyperspace the stars glow pale as ghosts,
the Galaxy shines, a luminous fog, in all the colors of the rainbow
  and more,
and feigning flight faster than light our mighty starship coasts
toward an alien sun, far from home, and worlds for us to explore.
But it's not the destination that compels us, not the end toward
  which we reach.
It's the going and not the arriving that satisfies our need.
It's the voyaging itself we crave, for the Void has secrets to teach,
but only after we come to it, from worldly concerns been freed.

Across the endless vacuum, lightyears wide we've ranged,
listening for aetherial whispers of that from which we're estranged.
And in that awful silence we feel a deep forlorn,
the sense of something we should have gained but lost when we
  were born.
An inexpressible yearning, much more felt than heard,
is a quiet voice that speaks to us, though it utters not a word.
But if that tantalizing other should touch our lonely soul,
we know beyond a doubt the touching would make us whole.
And so we trek among the stars in hyperdriven flight.
Passing vast luminous nebulae, the Galaxy we roam,
seeking the touch of the untouchable throughout eternal night,
exploring, learning, refining our souls 'til Death comes to take
  us home.

—*Dennis Anthony*

Astronomy

The invention of life is genesis,
  the extent of the contrivance of life is the world
The planet rotates around as the foundation
  of ether, and the galaxy is but unknown.
We are the only ones hurled
  into a desolate section where we are prone.
From infinity and beings that are curled
  into the corner of the universe.
We look out from our home
  through instruments that see light reversed.
The stars are dead and moons alone.
  All watch and wait for the ship;
the ship that comes unrehearsed.
  It glides calmly and does a flip.
Over the moons and through the stars it cursed.
  Making room for the dorsal to spread.
The ship was able to dip
  below the earth's great bed,
But the only thing that it was able to clip
  was our mere curiosity.

—*John Lee*

Saverio Sr. In 1930

They said it was pneumonia
that caused your death
but we both know
that January morning you left
in the windowless pick-up
to meet the vegetable truck
your ticker wasn't tockin'
and you weren't returning to five kids
The victrola would never sing along with you
and the kitchen once filled with men in
Calabrese conversations
cards strewn about the table
contained women cooking dinner
for condolence visitors
a wreath hung low on the door
signaling the news a widow is born
And you would never know
your youngest son lay awake
in her womb taking his first breath
of life and your name

—*Laura Orella*

Self-Satisfaction

Clattering combines have come and gone,
Taking with them this year's harvest of ripened wheat...
Six A.M. finds "Fearless Freddy" with shoulders hunched
against October's nippy wind,
ragged raiment glistening with early-Autumn rime.
Stiffly he stands,
like some   solitary   sentry,
surveying a ravaged kingdom of golden stubble...
How foolish he looks! — Charlie Chaplin on stilts:
Baggy balloon-pants, puffed like pregnant parachutes;
dilapidated derby tilted jauntily;
disdainfully he glances at yesterday's bird-droppings,
crusted on his shoulder...
Then of a sudden, with only semi-suppressed smirk,
like some praying pontiff he extends his straw-stuffed sleeves,
and in derelict derision
jeers his mocking welcome to the skies:
"Here it is, you black-feathered scavengers —
Come and get it!
Ha! Ha! Ha! Ha! Ha! ..."

—*Paul R. Houlahan*

Untitled

you wake me in the predawn dark
swimming up my spine, blindly;
a salmon, upstream to spawn
thrusting against the current
sleek and utterly silent, dreaming
under the surface. You are asleep.
I don't open my eyes. i listen
to the dreaming water, the constancy;
flow and ripple and murmur, i move against you
dreaming dark, wet and tidal
something finned and slippery, slick
between us and suddenly
gone

—*T. M. Pride*

Prairie

This flat-faced stormy land, its horizon
stretching like the dawn of time;
Its small rock pinnacles looking west to
the mountains with envy and regret;
Gazing at the mother mountains
rising like great breasts to the west;
Baby rivers, little gullies, small arroyos
try to nurture this sky-eagled land;
Nurture this land of chalk cliffs and boulders;
that has cactus on its chest, scoured by
the ever-blowing dust and winds of time;
With no more tomorrow's thought than
yesterday's wishes. Or does it, too, yearn
for honored days of buffalo and untamed grass,
prairie-rose days silent as the raptor's wing,
before the birth of man, his plow and gun.
  end

—*Irma Wyhs*

Untitled

Last night a
grain
of infatuation
slipped between the years
unnoticed
and turned up in my bed
making me uncomfortable and comfortable
tossing and turning
memories
until now and then blended into one
and tumbled through the hourglass together

—*V. Cottrill*

7

Ode To Autumn

Trees have shed their beauteous raiment,
    Stretch naked arms in helpless pain,
With patience bear their inner torment
    Waiting spring's green brush again.

Above us wild geese are flying,
    Obeying calls to warmer climes:
The chipmunk in his nest is hiding
    Seeds and nuts for harsher times.

When winter's wild winds are blowing
    They'll spread white flakes o'er browne'd earth;
They'll hide the dross, join rivers flowing,
    Emptying into narrow firth.

We mortals dwelling on this sphere
    Must build a fence of trust each year;
Look not beyond the fence to borrow
    Troubles for the day or morrow.
Trust in God; He'll help us bear
    Whatever comes of joy or sorrow.

    —*M. Louise Rudkin*

American Laughter

He knew I was American.
Sounds vibrate within the nose, not the throat
Quinn O'Brien told me...
Holding his bitter. Hearing me laugh

Strumming a guitar. Cracked tactile pads;
skin curling over nails from potato farming outside of Galway.

Went west, last year
to the crossroad
where the cliffs of Ireland
meet the frothed sea.

In between splinters of stone
his boot pounds silently
into wind...
Voice loud, unheard, curdling.
His back towards the isle,
singing.

His face into the mist of the Atlantic
looking over the dissonant ocean

For Heroes.

    —*Karen E. Birch*

A Perfect Day

This morn I 'rose long 'ere the sun had
    Shown its silvery crest upon the blue.
With carbine, pack, and fishing gear I
    Mounted my buckskin - cayuse; we coursed the ridge.
A pleasant ride through yellow pine and velvet grass,
    Then up the long, hard climb through Eagle Pass
    And on into the valley.

'Twas high noon when Rapid Creek gave trout
    to pan, and when consumed we followed
Where it ran; we followed to the Forks.
Then, due north a spell and into Hidden Bowl-
    An earthly paradise to any living soul.

In Sylvan scene I dined, this eve', on grouse;
Then, by the fire I bedded down, to end a perfect day.
And from my lips, as Heavenward I gaze
Come these few words - as only poets pray:
"How bright the moon shines from the sky;
    A silver jewel, set in blue.
How light the clouds go drifting by;
    A spotless army, in revue."

    —*John H. Thaden*

Best Laid Plans

It was one-forty-five in a two o'clock bar.
She sat near the jukebox; I watched from afar.
I looked at her, she looked back at me,
And I knew where we'd be at a quarter-to-three.

I sat near her seat. She didn't complain.
My words had design, like an oncoming train.
My moves were so perfect - I wanted to play.
Then I looked in her eyes and my life changed that day.

The talk turned to Thoreau, Bob Dylan, Ayn Rand;
To that bondage called marriage and castles of sand;
For whom the bell tolls and why and why not;
And whether tis nobler to be or be not.

I was drunk with her thoughts and the shape of her hips,
Her ideas and ideals and her breasts and her lips.
Her "I's" and her eyes touched me places so new
Sir Lust stood his ground — but Sir Love stood there too.

It was one-forty-five in a two o'clock bar,
She sat near the jukebox, but swung from a star.
And only she knew, when she looked back at me,
Where we might be at a quarter-to-three.

    —*Dan R. Kiely*

The Question (Is It The Year 2000 Yet?)

Old Scientific Death Camps
scream their insults in God's face.
New "Neo-Nazi" slugs squirm out from
rocks of our disgrace.
The question begged, for mercy,
as a gasp gropes for God's Grace:
    A Doomsday Book bestseller for the last,
    the new millennium approaches, fast.
    Which road? The one less-traveled,
    or what sells?
    With Frost, or freezing,
    Poe-like, banging bells?
To tintinabulate us
    straight to hell?
And lose the human race
by hair,
baton-drop of God's gracious dare?

We either have a soul, apiece,
or may as well be hogs, released,
    like Circe's charm transposed.

    —*William P. Davenport*

Saudi Arabia Remembered

These are my memories of this ancient and alien land,
Saudi Arabia, peninsula time-etched by sand.
Eastbound by Persian Gulf, some days lapis-lazuli blue—
(The sapphire of the ancients). Tomorrow its hue may
Ribbon coast with band of turquoise bright
Or aquamarine. How sombre is that Gulf at night
With color gone - there must be burning copper sun
To fire beauty a semi-precious one.
The seasons change and elements now violent and cold clutch
This ancient land with bitter and relentless touch.
Yes, here indeed are few of spring's sweet halcyon days,
And brief and rare fall's gentle smokey haze.
Most constant are the blazing summer skies,
The scorching desert heat that lies
Across this land seems but a long and enervating jest,
And time, like any mirage, eludes this stranger and this guest.

    —*Rosamond Leadbetter*

Dame Witch Doctors

Little men who talk with God play an exclusive game,
    restricted to a select few, and certainly not a dame!
Players in witchcraft robes, to denote an august station,
    flaunt awesome credentials for effecting man's salvation.

Never mind that no one knows from what one must be saved;
    witch doctors are empowered by sheep — folklore enslaved.
Mankind's advanced wisdom embraces gender parity,
    but witch doctor preference is a God who stands to pee.

The deity they envision has balls and a chest to bare;
    a deity couldn't be godly with breasts and a patch of hair.
No doubt their heavenly father has a voice that's deep bassoon
    — not a heavenly mother with a woman's gentle croon.

Do they fear a female cleric might lead their god astray,
    to neglect his holy duties — to tarry awhile and play?
By uttering mumbo-jumbo which none can understand
    they confer a male advantage in touching the holy hand.

Some timid enlightened clerics are willing to change the rules,
    but yield to strident protests from their tribalistic fools.
As stronger men become leaders in these spiritual games,
    they'll invent a tolerant deity who will also talk to dames.

    —*M. Scott Myers*

Love Beyond Comprehension

I think, as I take the emblems of un-leaven bread and wine
representing the body and blood of Jesus, our Savior so divine;
the bitterness of the cup He drank; His death upon the tree;
His pain, and His humiliation, through eyes of faith I see.
I compare the pleasant taste of the emblems that we use
to commemorate His memory to the hostility of His abuse.
He suffered so severely from those who did not understand
the meanings of His teachings and how they applied to man.
Today, as I think of Jesus, and try to comprehend
just what He actually did for us, to save us from our sin;
how anyone could love so much to such a vast degree
is beyond the comprehension of mortals like you and me.
As I pray God's forgiveness for excuses that I give
for all of my shortcomings as this earthly life I live,
as I recall the blood He shed upon Golgotha's hill,
I pray for daily guidance to help me do His will.
I know I make mistakes and oft forget to pray
but I thank God for blessings He gives us every day.
And as I take these emblems in my mind's eye I can see
a picture of Christ and hear Him say, "This do, in memory of Me."

    —*Gertha S. Cox*

Gottschalk's "Souvenir de Porto Rico"

Louis Moreau Gottschalk is a name
Puerto Porto Rico is a name
And he calls it a march

Tread silence tread
Step dream-space step
Tread song-dance tread
Step tread step tread

All the in-betweens
Sneaked-in epiphanies

Joy song simple beauty
A braid over the shoulder
Disruptive build-up syncopation
Build-up of svelte downslidings
Cascades waterfalls fountains
Emeralds diamonds pyrotechnic shooting stars
Broad banging swinging laughing
Music-hall vulgarity
An ever-insistent build-up
Shimmying shaking winding down

Tread silence tread

    —*Francis Paar*

Llais Llanddulas

Cruckle of sea-harrowed stones, the green swell under,
Pied peculiar tapestry across an inlet spread
Lifts in the creaming hem of the shoreline thunder,
Oystercatchers settle again, the wide wave fled.

Shouting round the headland a swollen river's hurling
Its cargoes of upland snows, tumbled icily,
Headlong on its muddy crest, bucketing and swirling,
Driftwood batters over the rocks into the boiling sea.

Tide and river clashing send the spray high, dashing
Diamond droplets on the air from veils of vapour flung,
Sudden clamour overhead, grey-goose necks spread,
Trailing echoes in their wake of ululating song.

    —*Shirley R. George*

Christmas On The R

A young bull
paws the winter pond mist,
contemplating his beauty and his strength.

A wild dog
salivates upon the cold open range,
hungry for a newborn calf to eat.

A prodigal cowboy
gores his old man with a pick,
and hides out in the snow.

It is Christmas on the Rocking R Ranch,
a time of celebration and dance.

Little children huddle beneath blankets,
the women drink alone.

And while ranchers
sharpen the blades of an instrument
to deform the Holy Child,

    the beasts lie
    beneath a whitened willow tree,
    and spy
                the icy stars.

    —*Chuck Adams*

Back Bay Morning

Red brick and iron fretted railings
Pattern the quiet streets as darkness wanes
Flashes of polished fittings in the sun
Compete with rows of shining windowpanes

White curtains flare beneath an open sash
A solitary cat ignores their lacy edge
And keeps its standard early morning watch
Surveying silence from the marble ledge

A sweeper probes the gutter with her broom
Scouring the river dampness from its face
Scrubbing again the rugged cobblestones
Whose roughness time and traffic can't erase

A tugboat pushes barges toward the pier
And from the river, morning sounds drift in
Pile drivers pound the earth relentlessly
And noisy first construction shifts begin

A city wakens to another day
A Boston eager to promote its worth
While pockets of gentility endure in sleep
And dream serenely of its cultured birth

    —*Grace Conlon*

Heavy Metal Dreamer

Great cosmic engines rev and they softly wait for you;
past the sun through shining stars they will go.
A silver studded super ship makes music to your ears;
as it speeds to a bright and shiny glow.

Lost in cold, deep space among the silence of the stars;
a dreamer dreams a dream ever colder.
From frozen wisps of nothing comes a heavy metal gleam;
and the music of a legend even bolder.

It sings in the starlight bringing rapture from the gods;
in the light of a never-ending dawn.
Its thunder clapping music can make heaven out of hell;
while its tall, crystal kingdom sparkles on.

And in the blackness of space it travels far away;
the dream with tunes will live until the skies.
It will always be remembered no matter where it goes;
for heaven's heavy metal dreamer never dies.

—Brad Frazier

The Enchanted Corridor

Splattering haze obscures a long plexiglass window.
Pale eyes light on gem-colored machines
gently rocking down a double track. How lovely
the spun warm wax twinkling down the cars,
asleep as they ride through the enchanted corridor.
Little gales billow, clouds hover round the exhausted
metal servants, midget tornadoes eddy and swirl.
A motion at one end persists.
Through the fog a light reflects off dark rubber.
A human! Five of them, flying hands swathed
in soapy towels, leather aproned backs piston-spined.
Black hair is pitted with wet diamonds.
Gold drops weep down Mayan masks, jagged cheeks;
misty faces of Toltecs, Aztecs. Royal faces.
Toreadors brandishing chamois mitts.
Into sparkling sun cars emerge, proud and new.
Women in cotton shorts stand above bent youths,
mastery, blind, in their minds. Trunks are inspected.
Mats must be re-vacuumed. Quarters flash from hand to hand.
A silent Toltec ghost shuts the gleaming chariot door.

—Christine Tibbles

Why Do They Leave?

They come into your life so unexpected
You're so glad they came!
They bring you joy and happiness that you've never known
You're so glad they came!
They show you a good time and give gifts you treasure
You're so glad they came!
They show that they care and their feelings are sincere
You're so glad they came!
Then the joy and happiness you knew goes into hiding
Why do they leave?
The good times become memories
Why do they leave?
The good times become shadows
Why do they leave?
Their caring goes away and the love is broken
Why do they leave?
Now you are left wondering
Why do they leave?

—Tamra Crenwelge

Fog

Stealthily in the darkness,
On slippered, silent feet,
A fog stole in from seaward
And spread her mystic sheet.

She made each gleaming ball of light
A phosphorescent gem,
That might festoon the crescent moon
In a glowing diadem.

She wrapped the leaves of sleeping trees
In wedding veils of white—
Then wafting high into the sky,
Crept onward through the night.

But morning guessed that she had passed,
For glistening far and near,
The fog had left on each fair thing
The traces of a tear.

—Rex E. Alford

The Return

In the warm, sleepy-green silence
of love's first stirring,
I turn away from myself -
and find you.

You who once yearned,
once burned,
to learn my heart's wet language;
you who once sighed
(once cried)
when my moon-drunk eyes
spoke only of tulips,
and dying.

Had you begun to fear you might
have lost this moment forever?
Did you really doubt - even to be proud -
that I would sing again to you of the
way rain hangs
on summer leaves at midnight,

or of the time you were a child
and dreamt you were a cloud?

—Darren Bates

The Stone-Gray Spanish Steppes

Cobblestone steppes caressed the feet
Of lovers walking history's street.
A gentle tear fell for fearless gladiators
Who fought for Fatima's hand.
Above the lion-cage smiled Helen,
Waiting for her wooden wish
That stole silently through the night
Moving toward the fair-faced maiden
Sighing love-songs.

Praise be to Keats
Who from envy called Endymion's name
On the stone-gray Spanish steppes.
On her finger he placed the ivy leaf
To celebrate their union.
Clinging to the flesh,
It took root and grew
And, as many ivy leaves do,
Became a part of time and heartbeat.

—Marion Hart Houston

Out Of Schizophrenic Darkness

The child both predisposed and most bereft
of consolation learns that to not need
brings lesser desolation than to feed
upon hopes for needs fulfilled and to be left
alone, without. To cope the child learns theft:
of joy, of hope, of gentle care. The seeds
of darkness in False self mock True, who needs.
The two like tares and wheat grow mixed. Contempt
of False for True increases; both know guilt;
both hurt. But False, by "happiness" survives
enslaving True until the True says, "halt,"
and through the Name of Jesus claims the lives
of True and False as one, "I am." The vault
of Spirit's joy in love, in light, revives.

—*Susan E. Hughey*

The Dead Farm

Standing here I reach the window sill of the second floor.
    No panes. Just shards, of course.
And the broken door. Ajar. Held with wooden pegs.

And that was the place where Frank picked up the horse.
    From the ditch. Because the horse
Wouldn't come out that far out of fear for its forelegs.

And there's the chicken coop without the roof.
    Torn in by force of snow.
I guess the boys won't be there anymore, pickin' eggs.

The outhouse is on its side from some sport.
    Sprouting from its gaping hole some wild,
Leafy rhubarb. Tepid lake. Hey, boys! No more leeches on
    your legs.

Worm-eaten, sickly trees in the orchard across the lake.
    The grass is coarse from minus forty
And summer heat. And the lake is full of mosquito eggs.

The hill is gone, there's landfill on the shore.
    The fence with gaping teeth is down.
No one lives there anymore. The boys have moved to town.

    —*Ferdinand A. Ruplin*

Disinfectant Trademarks (TM)

"Cleansing," echoes a fork on a frying pan,
    nails on blackboards and in coffins,
    and on coffins, not even coffins,
    lime, running through their fingers
    like so much Comet (TM)

I want to scream, not even scream,
    to screech, to say the first ten
    meaningless words I think;
Anything to rid my mind of
    Yugoslavs and Soft Scrub (TM)

Read the trademark signs because
    you'll find no swastikas here;
Only dying and death, more dead
    than Lysol could ever disinfect
(oh yes, and on Lysol and swastika -) (TM)

    —*Joshua Eisenstein*

October

There is so much more to autumn than pungent crispy air,
More than riotous colors and a glimpse of green swampfire,
A chilly mist and silent, paints frosty shadows in the sand,
A gauzy mantle flung haphazardly across the land.

An owl hoots eerily and fulfills its gruesome flight,
A whip-o-will sings out its heart at twilight,
A moon of frosted silver drifts in majesty across the midnight
    skies,
As if by magic, a million stars come out to see it rise.

Star studded and scintillating through diamond spangled nights,
Vying for the firmament of heaven with breathtaking northern
    lights,
There is more than rainbow beauty where morning glories climb,
Now a ghostly mist caresses one blossom at a time.

Could one ask for more in autumn than a glowing harvest moon,
Where winter's icy winds soon must hum a chilling tune?
As October fades in frozen limbo, its past much with us still,
November's frosty breath tingles like iced champagne,
And a zephyr breeze becomes a howling gale upon the hill.

    —*Louise Devereaux*

The Navigator

Now, this hoary image reflects back on his past life
    like a weather-beaten, battered ketch —
    remembering the tyrannic tempest of turbulent storms,
    buffeting from the tidal waves that beset his craft,
    knowing, not at times, what lay before him.

The fatalistic shifts of swift currents
    drift and pound against the purpose of his goal.
The devoted design did not always fit the scheme of things;
    yet, utilizing his capabilities was a challenge
    to his dedicated will, motivated by creative desire.

He charted its changeable course by his mind's eye —
    no matter what the uncertainties might be,
    to steer through the straits of strife —
    to persevere over adversity of circumstances.

This was perceived when looking back on his deeds,
    where he sowed to harvest the enrichments of this life,
    as the serene sea gull swoops over the scintillant sea
    to the splendent shore to attain its fruitful fulfillment.

    —*Don Bard Widoff*

Moods

The roaring waters rush ever forward
lashing against the rocky face,
where stands the lone sentinel pine
watching the waves never ending chase.

They climb ever higher, reaching
for the crest guarded by the sentinel pine.
Pushed onward by the furious winds
the thunderous waves forever grind.

Exhausted they rest,
lapping the battered rocky face,
a lover's gentle caress; waters
receding leaving a foamy lace.

The sentinel pine stands alone
forever watching the never ending race.
Waves running, dancing, leaping
always enchanting in their grace.

    —*Constance J. Deakin*

Without

Juxtapose yourself with this color of twine
knowing without inspiration a cause of cause
edify someone's creation without sheltering its voice
engaging stage varieties; does not two clones know
flesh? Findings are ours to extend without serious
nomenclature…extravagant dress matching our
flagellant azure…baptized without disgracing
tiara tempered thought inside of belly theory
nystagmus…envy we they must secure loathsome
esteem for without granulure motive it's only just a
dream realm…of power to which we can not
exist…without

   —*Barry Schroeder*

Loaf

The intensity could be a lot of things.
It could be love. It could be blood.
It could be two hands dancing
Over paper. It could be two hands
Held together, parchment-thin.

It could be death looking out at you
Like a well-baked loaf from an oven.
It could be fortune. It could be death
Glinting like a dim eye from ashes.

There are two gold bands.
One is for the way you tie your hair
One is for the way you tie my hands.
Here there are the small clicking bones
In my spine, and a blue ceramic jug.

It could be two crows dancing
It could be the new soup. Mistress of shadows,
Littlest doubter. Teach me to drink, and forget.
Teach me to be small, and not to care.
Teach me to know what surrounds me:
The water. The jug. This silence.

   —*Laura G. Simon*

Untitled

What will it be, oh man who pleases man?
Is not your conscience seared by your own hand?
And what of all the high and moralistic dreams?
Yes! from your conscience came a light, a beam,
But twisted for convenience sake, reduced to naught,
Then turned and railed, accuser of your thought,
And where with all and what and if and how?
Without your God… life's journey now??

   —*Georgia Sanderson*

On Some Ultimate Reunion

If all those hopes that come close to the heart,
If all our dreams break on some rock-bound shore,
If we have been afraid again to start
Along the road that leads perhaps once more
To somber heartbreak ere we reach its end,
If we forget that life on God's love feeds,
If we disdain you, God, how shall we mend
Or quench the anguish of the soul that needs
So very, very much the happiness,
The love and will and help that we confess
You offer us from holy fingertips?
If we forget, God grant we'll pass retests
Albeit by repentance in our breasts,
Albeit by the gall still on our lips.

   —*Samuel Penny*

Outside FA 338

Tripping,
Intoxicated with Boredom
through Institutional hall
freshly mirroring Speckled ground
plateaus like Universal Love into
the interminable hell of never End.

Lightboxes buzz with cold energy,
lit but not illuminating
the confusion fog
my head turns and Moans in.
Distortion, hyperdimension, Supercontortion
shadows flirting with the precipice
gaping beneath-beside distant brick wall.

Far way, sheltered from Anaemic light,
insomniac window struggles against
cheese cutter wires
strangling it crisscross.
me at 3 A.M. shaking
speedy coffee, sugar all I need
sobering the haze of universal love.

   —*Sarah Elzbieta Kanouse*

The Pealing Of The Bell

(To Mother, on drinking red wine)

Through the winter night air it sounded,
Intent on making its crystalline way
Through the misting snow, an edge of laughter
Harkening, echoing in the darkness,
Cutting a curtain to light the black storm.

Its full-throated song resounded notes
of the past joys recalled over wine,
Stories of long-dead lovers and warm
folk of childhood whose tones blended
With the harmony of the moment.

The pealing floated into the night.
Finding a place in the shifting forces
of winter, atoms of all generations past,
a return of once-lived stories now present
again in her resounding laughter.

   —*Nancy Owen Nelson*

Seed

Speaking to me
inside and privately —
(internal album spinning backwards, needle
skipping over deeply-carven grooves, repeating
that other woman I am
whom no one knows anything of, speaks
(they think it is me is not me not me):
Mara says
"I'd name my baby Kristin if that were her name"
and the faceless tiny seed stirs faintly,
figurative life, only breathing in dreams—
(achingly achingly
turning over, under sheets,
I long for another face of me,
long for a heart outside my body)
Mara wakes up and with her I am —
we awake to the life I did not ask for —
(little girls should want to live should want to be
should want to grow up)

   —*Leslie Nuby*

Dear Diary,

To turn the dates flying year by year,
I witness claims, tears and true joy,
I wonder their reality, was it all in coy?
In eighty-four, curved letters of self-centered here,
Two months later, all a blackened smear,
Eighty-seven was of promise, golden, sparkling toys,
When I met the dark, smooth, enchanting boy.
Marriage dreams, buttered content suddenly all appear.
Then irony visits unveiling the suffocated I.
An eighty-nine looped with blossoming pain,
Ninety of denial, charmed smiles and am I sane?
More trips, distractions, obsessions and sharp whys.
Here in ninety-three, sistering ninety-four, a pause, a choke,
Half-hearts, half-I's, I speak, I spoke.

    —Gretchen Mullin

Club Scene

Multiple personalities.
I think that I'm becoming twins.
Or maybe I'll be triplets,
oh what chaos I am in.
It's the knowing, or not knowing
which one I am or who I've been;
am I uptown? Am I slumtown?
Did I go out or just come in?
Multiples of plenty - multiples of me.
Multiples so empty - with facade identities.
Is it criminal to be identical
inside this body built for one.
Let's all get out and do some damage
We all deserve a bit of fun.
Inside my head, a dozen voices
are you you, or just another me.
It's a question of many choices,
Like "to be" or are we not to be.
Multiples of plenty - multiples of me.
Multiples so empty - with no personality.

    —Maria Marosek Naylor

Armor

I saw the thread of steel hanging from your stainless suit.
I suppose the suit had snagged in a long and dead pursuit
Of some high and valiant value lost on some forgotten shore,
Abandoned in the wind when chilling rain began to pour.

But when I looked more closely through the glistening metal weave
I saw the sturdy rivets that were holding fast your sleeve
Had been loosened from the inside till they nearly fell away,
Saw the ocean hadn't harmed you with its sand or fuming spray.

I touched your hand to hold you. The sleeve fell off your arm.
You didn't seem to worry nor think that I would do you harm.
You smiled then and thanked me for helping you get out
Of the thing that held you captive to your loneliness and doubt.

Then I noticed there were buttons where before were steel bolts
And you stripped away your armor like a butterfly that molts.
At last I saw your color, saw your beauty, saw your face
And I wanted to be with you, to be naked in that place.

I was grateful for your courage to let me see your smile
To bare yourself with me there and be free a little while.
I left my suit behind me, after struggling to get out,
To be free with you a while from my loneliness and doubt.

    —David Eaton-Messer

Asters

With the lumbering step of a noisy giant,
I snapped fallen twigs and crushed grasses pliant
And plowed through crowds of sugar pine.
My march stopped short when up my spine
A shiver shot and my heart beat faster
As lo, I beheld a field of aster.

Illumined in the clearing's light,
The flowers on stems erect and slight,
Did in a sunward arabesque extend
And thrilling to breezes, bow and bend.
A percussion of bees abuzz and flickery
Enlivened the winds scored by Terpischore.

Starched violet tutus their array,
The golden coifed corps de ballet
Performed for all the trees and me
In perfect synchronicity.
On tiptoe fleetly on I hastened
By ars naturae inspired and chastened.

    —Denise Domergue

Transfiguration

Pebbles on the beach transfigured in the wet
huddled against the wave crash
sing shining splendor between each splash.

Bared feet hug sand soft spots.
Eyes search every shade and hue
drinking in pattern hoping a clue.
Whence comes such clean beauty? How did it start?

Pebbles in a pocket treasures plucked for tomorrow
clink against my movements.
Fingers caress the smooth, the round caring not
the cold, the hard, remembering the wetshine.

Pebbles on the porch lined up on the rail.
Sun-baked.
Wetshine yesterday's wealth today.
  DRY STONES!

Still, the memory's treasured and pyretic pebbles dream
  the next wave crash
  hoping wetshine
  awaiting transfiguration!

    —Mary Trinity, O.P.

Melted Mythologies

Weeping her private mythology,
Heart pounding in motel room cage.
Slender veins lashed by frenzied blood
Seeking eruption - explosion - escape.
Spitting fire through the feline gaze
Where tears, in weary flow.
Meet trickles of sweat.

Lucid flesh riding near, pulling close,
Inviting tears to enter the flow
Of his own waterfall mythology.

Colors spatter, run together,
Melt to a common myth.
Splashing water-play passes to air,
Sense of time fading with the spray.
The conversation begins - as in any room.

    —John Edward Jones

The Professor Of Logic Demonstrates Breakfast

Professor B. was trying to make a point.
He set out a small milk bottle
on his writing table
and a large ink bottle beside it.
He turned off the light.
Both bottles were shaped alike.
Both were cold with night.

"I can feel the color of milk
and the color of ink," he wrote
in cream in the blue notebook
taking a swig of India ink
before going to bed.

"I get it," I told him
in the morning
as he licked a soft-boiled egg
with his blue tongue.

—*P. G. Fay*

Early Morning

Spingle, spangled, sparkling morning
Glimmer, shimmer, drops of dew,
Fresh spun lacy pattern cobwebs
Diamond gleaming, rainbow hue.

Frothy, foaming Queen Anne's Lace
Creamy white on grasses green,
Surging over meadows bank
Pausing by a hurried stream.

Down where the pale green beeches,
Shafted in sun's early beam,
The fragrant scented primrose cluster
Open petaled waiting to be seen.

Over by the blue-belled spinny,
Through the lifting lazy haze,
A vixen fox trots back to earth
Under rabbit's startled gaze.

And there beside the silver birches
The blackbird sings his morning song
Pure the music as he voices
Singing gladly, singing on.

—*Rose Mary Hooper*

Released

One ring, twelve miles, we find an empty room
Fourth floor—he's moved, but can we enter in
 Three codes defibrillate again...resumes
 This life of diseased lung and ashen skin.

Next day brain dead, decisions to be made
Decrease supports and let him go in peace
If there's no hope then death we'll take in trade
 As he would want it done by this release.

Supports decreased yet he remains alive
There are no words to diagnose this change
 Is it his wife or children who survive
 Or was it love his family exchanged?

Ten days pass by, the end is near to be
 Bye dad, we'll see you in eternity.

—*Barb Luick*

After The Longest War

(for Binh Minh, far from Vietnam)
I look at this photo and what do I see?
A black and white snapshot of you and of me.
A sweet song of youth, a shared mystery
of all that has been and of all that's to be.

You're the one full of wonder, full of what, who and where,
pointing here, pointing there- "bird," "beard," "baby," "chair"-
dancing free as a butterfly in a garden of flowers,
joy and beauty to ponder for ten thousand hours.

I'm the one creased with wonder at our place in this scene,
searching and sifting for times and for spaces unseen,
the debris of a world so often heartless and mean
(my thoughts, like my hair, swept up in the air by the breeze):
Yet enchanted I marvel, as I hold you with ease,
at the soul of a child filled with trust, love and peace.

Don't cease, point the way, with your sweet, guileless smile:
I know you are transforming the world all the while.
Your soft song of truth will keep casting its spell.
And how can it fail to transform me as well?

—*Rubén G. Rumbaut*

We Did Not Lose Our President

I think I can hear the voice of the turtle
Even in the midst of this deafening din.
I think I can hear it already above the sorrow and sin.
It throbs in my heart like a promise.
A song that is long past due
It fills my soul with gladness.
An Easter dawning anew.
For Heroes have walked here among us.
Heroes are working still.
Though all we may see of them during the night
Are flames on a silent hill.
I'm glad the flames are there through the winter
For the winter, indeed, is cold
And timid poets who listen for songs
Are not like the heroes bold
Who will lead the song when it does resound
From every voice and quill
To the God who sent us the heroes
To make the din grow still.

Peace!

—*Mary Beth Royer*

The Accident

Marvelled at, struck there, at bone's
edge, perimeter blow that ails
the body lying within coned-
off asphalt the rain fails
to dissolve with its assailing,
under a blanket of the paramedic team,

the victim dreamed aloud sections of "Howl,"
consumer of the parasitic dream
on the way home to his soul.

He lives out his groans;
at the hydrant a mock dance
of crippled man coming down the street;
somewhere, unheard, plumbing chants
unison pieced together in the dark.
Police lights flash through the ambulance.

Someone waits for him in the park,
alone, cold and stoned.

—*J. Robert Maruyama*

Epilogue

Long years roll back their thousands days or more
each one unique in its implicity.
The first of these a fine and feeble thread
of waking consciousness and trust,
leading on to sturdier strands
of baubles bright or crushed.
Each day a jewel of radiance or disease
interwoven into unchartered chains
crafted to fabricate a cold cold shroud.
The everlasting twist so frail and slight
like spider's web with hidden strength
forging a link into the unknown.

 —Margaret John

The Witch's Song

Your song is a caldron of melody, bubbling,
Doubly troubling all who hear,
Brewing, renewing the spell you are casting,
It's witchcraft outlasting the notes soft and clear.

Your song is a spider web, thread you are spinning,
Winningly pinning each victim in place,
Daringly snaring each unwary listener,
Winding him, blinded, with musical lace.

I hear you: I fear you are fast mesmerizing me,
Sitting, unwittingly lulled by your song.
I'm dangling, tangling into your melody,
No longer caring what's right and what's wrong.

Just a glance, not by chance, sent me instantly reeling,
Bass notes and grace notes bombard me and then
I'm slowing, I'm going, the spell's working faster now,
Hearing the thread of your song once again.

It's tragic, this magical spell that you've woven
It holds me in place like your odalisque smile,
But some lyrical miracle holds you beside me,
Though I'm yours, you are mine for a while, for a while.

 —Helen Hilbert

Gods

Where are these high immortal gods, for whom time holds no fear,
Despite proclaimed omnipotence, their fallacy is clear.
The temples of Olympus have crumbled into dust,
No more in Zeus and Hercules do trembling mortals trust.
The rainbow bridge has fallen, which led to Asgard's door,
We do not fear the hammer of the once almight Thor.
No place for the savage will of Mars in human warfare now,
And no more do young lovers to the goddess Venus bow.
We know that Neptune's trident can never sink our ships,
And no longer does the fate of man rest on Odin's lips.
By logic and by sanity were the ancient gods disposed,
Now the portals off Valhalla shall ever more be closed.
Yet man's quest for divinity still must lay unfulfilled,
For in his heart the seed of awe is stubbornly instilled.
Tis true, our endless universe is wondrous to behold,
But no more made by modern gods than made by gods of old.
Why must some formless deity be worshipped by mankind,
When the only true messiah is the power of the mind.
Cast off this humble mantle, let destiny be slave,
The future belongs not to gods, but to the children of the brave.
Have faith not in untangible force or some predestined plan,
Instead believe in wisdom and the dynasty of man.

 —Stephen John Eyre

The Fall

How have the innocent eyes been hooded
By the fabled Fall!
How have the black garbed wiseacres lied
Doryphori masked as oracles
Dancing a dosados of sapience,
Cloaking the pristine grace of creation
Behind a phylite gloss of guilt
To deflect consciousness from the truth
Of Man's Terrible Fall.

For eve's innocence was despoiled by nudeness
Not by the body's nakedness to love,
But to the worms of decay.
For in the fall
Fell the animal security of endless continuity,
And to Man's anguished eye dawned
The knowledge of the pythian night
Into which all must fall.

 —Edith Kalish

Black: The Man Is Called...

I am a man called black,
but, in my heart the call is "longing",
longing for home-the place where I belong.

My cry is "need",
the universal need of the human heart for life,
for love, ah!, and, for peace!
My struggle is to be free,
free to be all that I know
I can be!
My hope is for happiness,
happiness which is the result of loving
genuinely and fully,
in openness and wonder at all
that is beautiful and good
and deserving of reverence and love.

 —Cletus Watson, T.O.R. Franciscan

Old Woman Moaning

The beast devoured my man, my love, my life.
But first, I spilled out my blood, my guts
in a weird marriage of futility —
eerie dance of ashtrays clinking in the sink
garbage swollen with filthy remains
rooms full of things steeped in the acrid stench,
the man - the partner - only a fantasy -
the grotesque hacking reality
a wheezing red bloated hulk spouting phlegm,
my babies malevolently entangled
their little lungs filling with black tar
as the foul tobacco smoke smothered them.

"Ah-ah, damned monster weed so huge and brawny,
I gouge you with picks, knives, saws, axes.
Still, your flames dart maliciously at me."
Do I hear at last the welcome death rattle?
"N-nah-ah!" I smell the curs ed fumes.
"Now you gorge on my son!" I'm left to m-mo-oa- oan-n
——— on and on to m-mo-oa-oa-oa-oan-n

 —Verla Swanson

Love To Lambert

Deep in the heart of my Appalachian family tree,
Buried beneath Black Mountain in Cumberland, Kentucky,
A ribbon of steep, red concrete leads to Granny Rena's cellar.

I descend, just as my Grandpa Lambert descended
for 20 years into the black Hell of the Harlan County Coal Mine.
This cellar reminds me of him; Although, I never met him.

The opportunity that was going to pull families from the
talons of poverty sucked the life right out of the mountain
people just for breathing.

So I come here, wondering at age 8, what he was like.
Mason jars of plump, zippered green beans, Earthy-smelling
potatoes, mealy onions and bags of rich, organic topsoil comfort me.

I stay here. Breathing in. Exhaling. Wooden, red Coca-Cola
crates, sticky with the residue of last night's family picnic
sit on the floor, dangerously close to the black coal stove,

with its incessant hunger, its incessant hiss,
Licking the shiny silver latch with a flamed fork tongue,
Burning all memories of the past.

—*Michele Willowtrout*

A Tribute to My Uncle

Black capped Jessie is crippled now.
Brown, ugly shoes shuffle down the street.

They do what they want too; curl in, turn out.
Brown thick soles sloping in so old Jessie looks like
he's being towed in after a long, hard race.

Black capped crippled Jessie roots for the Yanks,
and felt up a girl once in Ebbetts Field.
He played stick ball at Prospect Park when all the kids were
white; he hates 'niggers' worse than tea, and shot 'craps' in
Paris on 'D Day'.

The don't walk sign sees Jessie coming......
"Come on old man-push my colors hard. Feel me like that girl.
(the whore from Prospect Park), before your legs made you turns
and started sliding brittle soft like straw.
Before you lost your hair. Before you won the war.
Tired old broom! Your face is pushing air.
Your cap carves out your size, and no one doesn't care."

Old Black Capped Jessie. A soldier in the war,
who shot 'craps' and other men and felt the breasts of a
Brooklyn whore. Did you hear? He's crippled now.

—*Dolores Edwards Sullivan*

Dream And Memory

I know the Atlantic from childhood memories
As well as adolescent midnight fantasies.
I celebrated our Nation's freedom
In the Summer of Seventy-six —
A five year old child's naif wisdom —
Crafting shelters out of sea-grass sticks.
I dreamed I walked her shore with native soles.
My people loved her shore with native souls.

Memories of a Sixteenth birthday,
Of my isolation, far away
From the fields and forests of my home.
Through dreams, in my blue jeep I roam,
Racing slate grey thunder in the sky,
The waves breaking, the tide running high...
I dreamed the clouded chalkboard sky,
The chaos sea gulls, racing by...

I dreamed of steel blue breakers,
And of seafoam Unicorns.

—*Zachary B. Dietrich*

Tinnitus Aural

Yank the bell rope; pull the crank; you'll hear a timid clank.
Bring the rope down hard; you'll hear a ding.
Clank becomes a solid clang with ev'ry clapper spank.
Swing the pond'rous thing; let's hear it sing.
Fling the sound around; make ear drums ring!
Think of all bells you've heard: a cowbell's friendly clink,
Clang of fire engines: Dang, Dang, Dang!
Tinkle of the telephone; it's made the whole world shrink.
Jangling alarm clocks woke us with a bang.
Dangling sleigh bells glistened as they rang.
Train bells, farm bells, old school-marm bells stung our ears
with pain. Strong arms hammered on a Chinese gong.
Chain bells, charm bells, burglar alarm bells rang and rang in
    vain.
Long have funeral bells tolled their sad song.
Long have bells been rung to right a wrong.
Weak or feeble bells don't tell the world they toll for thee.
Swung with brawn, bell tones are thrown far flung.
We the people prize one bell that proclaimed liberty.
Among all lands where free men's songs are sung,
Among all bells no finer e'er has rung.

—*John G. Sprung*

Forest Dawn

Amid the towering trees a shaft of heaven's ray
Breaks through the feathered tracery, and night transforms to day.
An isolated sparrow's song begins this tranquil morn,
The creatures realm becomes astir with forest sounds reborn.
The windless night was still and cool, air from the ground was
    warm,
And there upon all leaf and blade the jeweled droplets form.
Atop a mighty pine appears the glow of sunrise gold
Descending slowly to the ground, its glory to behold.
The forest floor was laden fast with night etched deep and dark
But now we see the green of fern, and moss, and embossed bark.
A gentle breeze begins to sway the fragile branches high,
A sort of music permeates, an eerie, tonal sigh.
Alas! the day is fleeting by. The sun, it starts to fall
And shadows on the tall trees rise till darkness covers all.
Again the cycle is complete, another day has drawn,
The forest now will sleep once more....until the forest dawn.

—*Raymond E. Schenke*

Wind On Grass

Wind on the lea
Bending the long fine grasses..
Pale lights flee
Fleet as a shoal of minnows
In a light green sea.

The wind is a pack of hounds that I cannot see
Coursing the lea
With long light nose bending the grass as they run
Swift in the sun.

—*Harriette Bruen Davis*

The Block

It's a solid brick wall, a thick sheet of metal,
a safe with an endless combination. Nothing can
break this powerful barrier, no one, not even Superman
can see through it. It can't be burnt down, chopped down, or
bulldozed. It's indestructible. The only force in the world
that can break it is your mind.

—*Julia Bratz*

Eros At Sea

You have the quick and all of me
As I grow quickly all with you
Not partly some and sometimes part
Not half with all and slow to hot
But ready all and quickly able
Stiff to point and head to slot.

You have the quick and all of me
The hard of play that spills me still
The spore of work that cores my will...

You have the stuff stiff dreams are made of
You have the song that sings me sweet
You have the strong sweat scent of love
that pours the drink that pores me deep.

I scent the sense and curl the crease
Parsing the pulse to lobe and lip
I sense the sweat that stirs my swirl
Probing to prove, bent knee to hip.

Love is life and life is all
Quickening spring, slowing fall,
Full to feeling, furl to flowing
Sense and sweat, quench and wet.

—*Thomas Kochman*

hiding in hands rumble click...
angles change knuckle-fabric-ending color
phrases of a rapid-dispersal dandelion cloud.

pain permeates from miles away
split warts only postulate bleeding...

twisted-neck monotonously poses;
rapid transit staccato hands tingle.
Facial surface resembles the cork door opens-
cranberries, breakfast, life and depth.

can't you feel the tremors?

West Bank clay...

Jerusalem spheres...
twenty three dollar bills will whirlpool
upwardistraction.

tolerance-bent batch
communication needle threads nine fingertips...
the smell of everything i own,
pine sap and bark throughout
your hair feels warm motion.
squeaky mosquitoes dragged by itchy flesh flowers.

—*Steven Blue Lambert*

Lies Empty The Stage

This falseness, this mask, this macabre of lies
And the actor just smiles as the curtain comes down
The flowers lay wilted beneath the beret
And through the white gauze lies his gaudy made face
His lips fall from arcing and tremble but once
And the dream in one tear shatters cold on the floor
Standing stark still as surroundings collapse
Without motion or feeling; such comical ire
One moment false life and the next a true death
So close to the shield his cheek against velvet
His eyes see the darkness his hands feel the gate
Hesitation, then boldness, he opens the closed
Assault by the baldness of ugly and real
No cry from his throat it is not in the script
But open no more only closed as his mind
A bow to not one his top hat askew
He retreats to the shadows; lies empty the stage.

—*Kerry Jo Lee*

The Cherry Tree

A heedless child, I dreamed my dreams beneath a cherry tree
and time, my friend, in measured pace made dreams reality.
In spring love blossomed with the tree as child grew into man.
In step with time my love and I seemed part of nature's plan.

The cherry bloomed - my love grew pale. My heart was filled with
    fear.
A lifetime's hopes and dreams and plans will vanish in a year!

Beneath the blossom - laden boughs my love and I would lie
As falling petals kissed her brow so softly she would sigh.
I long to stay the hand of time to make this moment last
Forever more, in perfect love. Alas! time moves so fast.

I, too, would tether time to ease my breaking heart.
Before the cherry blooms again, my love and I must part.

The cherry blossoms once again and falls as former years;
The dew drops limpid from the leaves to mingle with my tears.
Beneath a pall of petals pale my lost love slumbers on
while I live out my weary days from dawn to dreary dawn.

As time limps on with leaden tread I long to meet my end.
When time runs out and sets me free I'll own that time is friend.
Beneath the cherry tree we'll lie through all eternity
and blossom every spring will fall in perpetuity.

—*Mary Tiffney*

Untitled

The sultry crimson sun flowed through the dew
and slowly soaked the air and earth to day
as velvet violets floating in your small soft palms
were bleached gray with in broken screams of sight
beyond the fading sheets of petals rose
your eyes, a symphony of whispered whims
without myself (I was so close to you)
remembering that, which, I've never known
I, swathed in silence, (like the moon in day
behind the lonely skies of whiteless rice)
my eyes of waxing witless tears, will wipe
with waning hopes of holding your gray eyes
I softly, shy of strength, again regret
my eyes not meeting, you, with the sunset

—*Devon Knight Svarda*

The End Of Indian Summer

When north wind gnaws the corners of the eaves
And night birds etch the dusk upon a wire
Then sunset burns the old cathedral spire
And makes an offering of crimson leaves.
The autumn twilight hesitates and cleaves
A silent moment at the funeral pyre
As glowing embers flicker and expire
And ghosts of yesterday remain to grieve.

I won't reflect, nor dare to stop and think
Of other Indian summers I have known...
My days with you of love and happiness
Have disappeared as swiftly as a blink
Of just one eye, and now I have been shown
The vast totality of loneliness.

—*Marian Ford Park*

I Think I'll Melt My Mask

I think I'll melt my mask and set me free
and let my brain run loose to spurt and stray
Perhaps the world will choose to censor me.

I'll drink my wine from crispy cups of tea
and sleep in rocking rainbows night and day
I think I'll melt my mask and set me free.

I'll eat an onion dressed in bumblebee
dance naked down a church's aisle in May
Perhaps the world will choose to censor me.

I feel that God will giggle loud with glee
He too is tired of my patterned way
I think I'll melt my mask and set me free.

I'll shred each euphemism that I see
and slice the earth wide open while I pray -
Perhaps the world will choose to censor me.

I know that I have found the master key
my ice blue brain has thawed and dripped away
I think I'll melt my mask and set me free
Perhaps the world will choose to censor me.

    —Mildred B. Cavallo

Muse On Spring

Snow had fallen, then the rain,
And cold had helped increase the pain
of broken hearts and shattered hopes
of happy kids and married folks.
The winter rose by frozen stream
conceals the truth that spring's a dream!
A sound is heard - a sudden sound!
He feels the flower on the ground.
Relief, at last! So long in wait
For spring to break the winter state.
Warm he feels
in fetal pose.
No pain or hurt
does sleep disclose!
Call not to life
you winter rose!
In sweet contentment let him doze.
For should he wake, he still would find
that spring is just a state of mind.

    —Tonnie Rushing

Genesis Of Distinction

I have read what poets long have writ
And ache to pen such words upon the pad,
To paint a picture of such dazzling script,
The beauty of which would drive men mad.

But childish scrawl and mental maunderings
Fall, to shame the written efforts therein.
Desire does not bring forth pungent ponderings,
And will does not consign wit to the pen.

Shakespeare's words came before his pen stroke,
Chaucer's flowed from forth his quill
Keats wrote in blood from heart that broke,
Coleridge dotted lines with sedated will.

My heart has broken, healed, and broke again.
My wit has peaked and fallen low to rise,
And I stand at the oasis in the desert of pain,
But still my pen falls short to moving sighs.

    —Audrie Bennett

Superwoman

Her dreams lay ladder-bound
   against a wall
   papered with hateful hankerings,
Sandwiched between
   guilt-ridden unfulfillment and
   staccato tears.
Outcries of explosive verbiage
   ignite sustaining sparks,
   fuel for love's forgiveness,
   bonding unpredictable, positive patterns.
So was fashioned this amazonian beauty!
Hands, herculean hands
   lift newly visioned longings,
   bucket-brigade,
   through perfumed ladder-angels
   towards a distant OSCAR
   resting on a congratulatory mat,
   placed upon the ace-high ladder step.

Academy Award for courage!
    —Mildrid Shaver, S.C.

Union Street

Braced against our youth delight
Across brown roads for car hood riding
Flee from confine sabbaths bath of guilt
To chase for border wine
And run with cigarettes to cough our lunch
On black top streets with spite
Whisky at one forty plus
Passed oaks and elms in nervous sweat
High on snake stick smoke immobile
Lives in cars with floorboard bugs
Embraced in green reflective springtime
Bite the fish the sad dead fish
Spitting scales and poison teeth
And drop out twenty five juice dripped
Early morning scissors close
To slice our failing thin belief
With sounds like sheets to whisper
On the quiet line of gowns we've torn
And for the road that crepitates
In mimic of our time to come

    —Sid Sisco

The Old Bayman

The old bayman hauls another load up from the bay bottom.
A stew of muddied clams and empty shells
Rumbles onto the deck:
A regiment of silent warriors and their shields
Decorated with badges of barnacles.

Eyes like shiny buttons squint from wrinkled buttonholes
Stitched in skin creased by wind and spray:
Eyes that have seen too many suns
Repeated by the endless play of mirrors
Riding on the backs of waves.

Quick hands cull salty gems from their nurseries of mud
Fooling those who picture clams
Playing in watery sandboxes.
A mouth worked in cracked leather
Grins at this thought.

    —Bill Britton

Morning Song

I make of an unheard music
A matins song on the ordinary trumpet,
No thrilling crescendo that wakens dogs
But a few silver notes I can scatter -
They sparkle like dew in spiders' webs
Any breezy morning you travel down
The long road to the boring town
With the bells mute in the tower.

Where the old have hung up their harps
Children daze through streets like dreamers
Murmuring in mysterious sleep
Of stirrings rumored of the deep
Woods they cannot recover...
Unnatural to me unless
I try to make of an unheard music
Their dreams, my cries of happiness.

 —*R. E. Miller*

From The Grave

I used to fear a phantom grim,
A dark, dank spectre from the grave,
Who bore his shrieking victims straight
To stygian darkness for his slave.

But then the phantom came to me,
So infinitely sweet and kind,
He eases pain and brings sweet rest
As o'er your soul he draws a blind.

So speed the phantom, go thou way
Through darkened hills from door to door,
And with thy gentle fingers touch
Tired eyes and they shall see no more

 —*William P. Gillespie*

Prairie Homage

A lonely hill. A crimson swirl of sunset clouds, a star.
 A changing and yet changeless world with nothing here to mar
The prairie's matchless solitude at dusk and as I quest
 Within this quiet interlude to still my heart's unrest
I search my disillusioned soul for what might justify
 A shattered faith that once was whole and question "why
must I, here in this magic, breathless scene feels doubt and
 turmoil rage? Is there no peace? What does it mean?"
Then somewhere in the sage I hear a meadow lark, his prayer
 a simple, perfect thing. A rhapsody to One whose care
sustains and guides his wings. And suddenly my blind heart
 sees the Way of Life and then, as I, too, pray, the
prairie breeze whispers low "Amen!"

 —*Lawrence Schjodt*

Bird Of Paradise

Somewhere in the moist, dark forest,
A bird of paradise, with tail
Whirring like a child's toy, there flies,
Living out its coma; its gaze
Fixed on the dream-ridden branches,
Its own intentions forgotten.

Like the presence of a comet,
Its whiteness flashes through the leaves,
Perfect, weighted to a feather,
Set in constant mysticism
In creation's deep pool, its flight
flawless with instinctual aim.

Ambushed whilst on some errand bent,
Robbed of memory and detained,
When cognizance could reawake,
Whither the true route would summon?

 —*George Claessen*

The Lost Life

Against the woods so thick,
A boy is caught in a maze.
He is lost.
Running in pain and anger, scared and cold.
Hopeless to find his willing loved ones.
He is lost.
Running, running away from his confusion,
But only becoming trapped in the
thick trees of his lost life.
He is lost.
He closes his eyes, hoping to find contentment,
But his broken heart stays with him forever.
He is lost
Day crashes into night.
Where to go? What to do?
Still running away, sore and bewildered.
Giving a boy a life he didn't deserve.

 —*Kate Imwalle*

Hell, Man, Beauty

The Pains of Hell delve deep within to beckon thoughts of God.
A calling from the unsure core to live a life, oh free.
The separation pains thy breath as voices tilt to chaos.
A calling from the boyish root clings to father's Err.
The conscience stings the memory of times that could be changed.
Once again an interior cry reaches to forewarn the awaiting fall.
The extension releases the enormity of the soul's sadistic sins.
The cry of the central being is to Triumph over false beliefs.
The intensity brews beneath the torment seen by armies.
This everlasting flight of voice yearns to Recreate the life once
 given thee.
Maybe to an eternity of fire and flame but in its bowels of heat
 and death.
The essence of a single heart will not be forever damned.
If the Beauty of thy art and words are held together, whole.
The harmony of all will bring a man away from hellish pains.
The beauty of this human soul transforms fire into truthful
 radiance.

(In response to "A Portrait of an Artist" by James Joyce.)
 —*Kim Jones*

What Is A Canadian?

A Canadian is someone just like you or me.
A Canadian is always free.
A Canadian is never alone
Because he can use the telephone.

A Canadian is someone who speaks out loud,
And is usually very proud.
A Canadian can be black, brown, white, yellow or blue,
It doesn't matters as long as he's true.

A Canadian can speak his mind,
And is usually very kind.
A Canadian is not always right.
A Canadian can start a fight.

A Canadian is from here or there
And may or may not be very fair
But it doesn't matter, cause in the end,
A Canadian is always a friend.

 —*Alysa E. Spark*

Autumn In The Country

The chill is in the morning air,
A cool breeze reaches the nostrils,
Out to work amidst the fog,
Look down to see the markings,
Lightly it lifts the veil comes up,
The sun is peeking over the horizon,
Opening the way for a new day.
Yellows, oranges, reds in the array.
Spray across the fields amuck.
Oh, it's great to be alive!
Out to the west - the mountains stand.
Clear to view and getting snow cover.
Majestic - they are lust oh
I love the flat prairie,
Lots of sky and flowing grains
Blowing to and fro in the wind.
Trees are turning - glorious colors
Your mind can wander away,
Away from your problems.
Oh, it's great to be alive.

—*Maryanne Carter*

Be The King Of Her Dream

Listen closely; it's the dream women will always have —
A cry in the dark that few men ever hear.

She longs to be the Queen of your heart —
The treasure you'll guard until the end of time.

Exalt and praise her in front of your peers.
Make her feel special and always remembered.

Put her first, serve her, cherish her,
Hold her tight and whisper, "I love you".

Speak of her beauty, the sparkle in her eyes.
Search deep within her very being, until you speak to her soul.

Take time to listen to her thoughts and feelings.
Be forever committed to her loyal friendship.

Live in the light - no shame, guilt or fear of lost innocence;
Remember the focus of your lives - Jesus of Nazareth.

Then, she'll truly know...love is your guide (Eph. 5:2).
She can be herself, make mistakes and enjoy life with you.

After all, she reigns Queen in your heart.

When she no longer doubts that...
Then you'll be crowned a true King!!!

—*Kevin G. Paterson*

A Dove Is A Beautiful Creation

A dove is a beautiful bird.
A dove flies high above the clouds.
Little kids wave goodbye as the Dove flies by.
A Dove bends its wings as the wind blows harder
Perhaps you have seen a Dove fling high above the trees
during the summers breeze.
Or perhaps you have seen the Dove's white wings
flapping with all their might.
The Dove stands for peace and love across the world.
The Dove stands for caring and friendship across this nation.
The Dove stands for sharing through out the USA
Kids shout with glee as they see this beautiful creature.

—*Kristalin McClintock*

Dad

What is father? Well... to me
A father is love, and it's plain to see
That I've had my share and much, much more.
Is it any wonder then, that I adore
My dad. Who assisted me into this world
And guided me tenderly as my life "unfurled".
I made my mistakes, more than a few
But dad, I knew I could count on you
To see me through each crisis in life
When my world seemed torn with trouble and strife.
I could always depend on your steadying hand
When nothing, it seemed, turned out as I planned.
You taught me to dream - and to look ahead.
To follow my dreams just to see where they led.
To face life with courage, showing no fear
And to be true to myself and all I hold dear.
You've given so much, how can I repay?
I can't, and I know it, but I just want to say
I love you dad! More than words can express.
To me a father is....happiness!

—*Lillian Andersen*

A Lesson In Life

Growing and showing and certainly knowing
a hope that I can see it through,

A gentle kindness a helpless blindness
of a shared and wanted view,

The beautiful things you can always bring
to the heart of a learned soul

Like a gentle breeze that caresses the trees
and tickles the morning dew

All things will come to those who wait
and always see things through.

—*Kevin K. Leier*

The Atlantis

Beneath the ocean, there lies
(A labyrinth of seaweed is its disguise)
Remains of an ancient culture, that rose long ago,
Left untouched for centuries, it can't prosper or grow.
Ancient column fall, crumbling to dust,
While metal statues of Gods remained rust.
It one day vanished, without a trace.
Because of the constant undersea quakes.
The ancients said the God's were mad, but that's not what
I'd say;
The glaciers melted, leaving its ruins in decay.
Oh, what a terrible place it would've been,
To have never seen the sunlight's beam.

—*Kristin A. Masters*

Joining Of Hearts

Two loves brought together by fate
A marriage that just could not wait
They were destined to meet
A smile of joy, an intense heat
Happy are the groom and bride
As they walk together side by side
To acknowledge their love and say "I do"
An exchange of rings to be forever true
Romantic dances in the spotlight
Moonlight kisses in the calm night
A joyous occasion of love so sweet
Two souls, two hearts to join and meet
Their passion of love, their breath of life
To finally come home now as husband and wife.

—*Michele Bosa*

The Song Of Jane Eyre

As I descend the steps to the great hall
A mask of blackness envelopes me
In the stilly, stark silence
I perceive the scent of a magnificent tea

A minds delight of mystery unfolds
As I trudge stoically from room to room
My solitary companion a lackey's keys

My dear I'm dressed in the best white chiffon
To got to a haunting play
In a deep dark cellar very far away

The suffering mirror signal a commence
To my breaking the locks of secrecy
On solitary doors
Now finally entered
But after this never more
—*Alison Piwowar*

North Country

We moved up here a short time ago and never have I seen
a more bustling community, yet so quiet and serene.
Tis fall and we have a beauty pageant all our own,
The trees are its contestants but the winner is unknown.
Don't say they don't have talents, I'm positive they do,
You've heard them groan and swing and sway and drop
their leaves for you.
Our yard is a runway, but not for noisy jets,
the squirrels have priority, they are our woodland pets.
Have you ever had a dream of living where wildlife runs free,
Where time means nothing and wonders to see.
Have you ever seen a wild turkey feeding in your yard,
The only ones I had seen before were pictures on a card.
The air is not polluted, it has the scent of pine,
And everything is molded into an intricate design.
We find the people friendly and willing to do a favor,
It seems that other places we lived, we hardly knew our
neighbor.
We came to stay and hope we can,
Unless some unknown destiny thwarts our plan.

—*Joyce Tester*

Mother

As I grow older, I realize what the word Mother means to me.
A mother is always there to care for you when you're hurt.
She is a friend, advisor, and listener, but most of all is full
of love for her children.
There are no sacrifices too small or too big for the sake of
her family.

She is always caring and loving even when she punishes.
The old saying, "This is going to hurt me more than it hurts
you", is oh so very correct.
Being a mother is the toughest job on earth. There
is no manual on how to be a mother, so she does the best she can.
Even when mistakes are made she never loses her love,
confidence, or pride in her family.

When that little baby is laid in her arms for the first time,
she knows no other feeling to compare. She will
go to any length to protect the child, even with her life.
Mother's are the strongest, most loving people that we will
ever know. The most precious gift is that of a Mother.
Thanks, Mom, for being my Mother.

I love you very much.
—*Judith A.Farley*

Like No Other

A deep and dreamy ocean reaching to the clouds.
A never ending river refusing to sun dry.
An over flowing chalice pouring out to me.
The love which flows from a mother's heart
is like no other.
Let me dive deep into those arms,
Where once my tiny form found safety.
Let me listen to that voice
that lulled my weary eyes to rest.
Your picture I still see so clearly
Through those childlike eyes.
For it remains unaltered.
The world and all its ways
Will never taint the beauty of my mother's face.
Her love is like no other.
—*Kim Ging*

Untitled

You are so beautiful to me,
A person so innocent that causes so much trouble.
When we walk on the shore of the sea,
I watch as you walk. It's like a wobble.
You have let me do everything for you,
For you are dependent on everyone
And I am dependent on you too.
Let us watch the rising sun.
I am amazed at how everything makes you smile.
You already learned that smiles are free, so you don't save
them.
You give them out a million a mile.
I am surprised at how you give smiles out. You hardly know how
they work, let alone how to use them.
Baby, child, adult, where are you hidden? Now she cries,
You are my miracle child and I still can't believe my eyes!
—*Kelly Jean*

The Good Ole Days

Was there such a time or place as the good ole days, or was it
a pipe dream of some kind of joke or old wives tale? Did
people get up before dawn and work late like the old folks say?
Yes, I'm afraid it's all true, the work day began at dawn
without fail. There were chores to do, cooking, cleaning and
planting the crops. You walked most everywhere near and far as
there were few cars. The weeds grew fast, the bugs increased,
not much time to stop. On rare occasions you could go fishing
if the creek wasn't far. Times were tough just as they say and
a nickel would buy a lot. Not many people had a nickel to
spend in them good ole days. The one room schools taught us
well, the necessary things we never forgot. At recess the boys
rolled marbles while the girls jumped rope just like they say.
How do I know about these days? I live them and hold them
dear. I was taught to obey, love God and respect my fellowman.
My parents set the example by living right and teaching others
who were near. I yearn for the same kind of respect and honor
to once again come to our land.
—*Kathleen S. Davis*

Music

Deft be thy fingers across the piano keys
Across the piano keys
Across the cloudy seas
Through the billowing clouds
Through green pastures deep as shrouds
A sun
A moon
A flash across the sky
Deft by thy fingers across the piano keys
—*Farrah Sime*

Muse Of Seuss

Today was a sad day for every boy and girl.
　a sad say for everyone around the world.
For there was a proclamation on this day,
　that everyone's friend had gone away.
He had been with us for a long time,
　teaching us through words of rhyme.
The stories seemed to never end,
　as they flowed from our friend.
There was the cat in the hat,
　or yertle the turtle.
His creativity was such that,
　I wish mine were so fertile.
Now we must learn on our own,
　to see the world he'd shown.
It shan't be too hard to do,
　we learned from Dr. Seuss.
What we will find,
　a world so kind.
When we look, in the book.
　The muse, of Seuss.

　　　—*Kevin Louis Meany*

Old Homeplace

Blue morning glories wrapped around
　a sagging garden gate,
Clothes line dragging from wet sheets
　and heavy laundry weight.
New lambs bouncing over pastures green,
　welcome to their hoofs,
Painted sheds with tattered shingles,
　hanging crookedly from roofs.
Cool trees full of leaves and wearing robins
　on each tender branch.
Porch swing gliding, then returning,
　but empty on second glance.
Cows mooing— red barn gleaming
　new mown hay smell in the air,
Ripe wheat swaying in the field,
　like a wig of golden hair.
All these things mean home to me
　but none are welcome more,
Than the sight of one of my family,
　swinging wide the kitchen door.

　　　—*Judith Crouch*

I Wish I Were Sixteen Again

Violets in the rain I seem to hear you call my name
A sound of cheer that heals the pain what else remains
What price fame?
It seems to be constant fight for whatever time allows
A wonderful life but much to short the years, not easy
To explain just how it goes - I wish I were sixteen again.

Golden Daffodils, a daisy chain such gentle outlines so
interwoven in one's teen's until illness comes along and
causes pain, but not for long recovery is assured
nothing wrong, soon everything is cured
Dreams renewed again - but never truer words were spoken
"youth is wasted on the young"

Crocus in the snow, red cheeks all aglow waiting for others
to join them on the ice below, trainers for a few - I seem to
have missed out on things I hoped to do - sure I had plans
in mind now left behind reality taking over, broken dreams
remain untried unspoken, by the same token I wish I were
sixteen again.

　　　—*Kathleen Lewis*

Where The Rivers Run

Back in the forest, where the rivers run,
A speck of sunshine, from the sun,
Shines down upon a tiny seed,

A tree will come, perhaps one day,
For a child to laugh and play,
And frolic in the branches,

A tiny bird, will lay its eggs,
Then keep them warm, beneath its legs,
And hope for future life,

A caterpillar will sit tall,
Then curl itself into a ball,
And fly away come spring,

Then night will fall, over the greens,
Hide then away, from unseen things,
Until tomorrow morn'.

　　　—*Kristin Skarbovig*

Winter, Cape God

Whistling winds calling out a tune, forever needing words to sing.
A stillness lying within the pines, awaiting Spring with the
promise of new life. Pompous grass reaching high over frozen
marsh toward the endless grey of sky.

Beaches ever-changing with the tide, swallowing footsteps of the
last beachcombers heading for the warmth of home.
Terns and gulls banking on an ocean's breeze, darting through
the thickening mist in an endless pursuit of prey.
Docks and pilings bent and twisted with age, hold an
ever-tightening grip on scallopers and their catch.

Empty slips and moorings, idle, abandoned in haste by pleasure
seekers forever seeking.
Endless acres of bogs, their sheds and shacks empty after the
harvest, anxiously await a new season. Lonely roads winding
through windswept dunes, spilling over in an attempt to block
any passage. Weatherbeaten owners of weatherbeaten shops close
the doors on another season, as the calendar hanging unnoticed
on the door slowly makes its way on.

　　　—*Kevin B. McCarthy*

Life In A Beer Glass

I gaze into a glass of beer, I see the amber liquid clear,
A thousand other things I also see,
I see the dark, I see the light, I see romance, I see a fight,
and a vision of what man would like to be.

I take a sip from out the glass, and right away I'm in a class
where friendship, love, and hate are all a brew,
careless words and friendships broken, new friends made with
few words spoken and reality takes a totally different view.

I'm near the middle of the drink, it's getting hard to stop and think,
I'll tell the world at large I'm ten feet high
why should I quivel with the rest? I'm equal to the very best,
so I'll have another drink, and pass them by.
I'm near the bottom of the glass, reality has come to pass,
another sip, and the glass of life is dry,
I live to drink, I drink to live, I have nothing in this life to give,
so it's time I cashed my chips and said goodbye.

And whether two or twenty years of whisky, brandy, gin or beers
my glass of life cannot be filled anew,
Like me, it now is cast aside, devoid of honour, use or pride,
both victims of an alcoholic brew.

　　　—*Evan Farley*

A Christmas Poem ...

At last Christmas time is here,
a time for love and holiday cheer!

A time for peace and goodwill on earth,
when all God's children share in his mirth.

Trimming the tree with family and friends,
wishing that Christmas time would never end.

Baking our favorite holiday sweets,
is only one of many splendid treats!

Building the man created by snow,
with a corn cob pipe and a button nose.

Snuggling with loved ones by a toasty fire,
sipping hot cocoa as we conspire.

Serenading the neighbors with carols of joy,
spreading God's love from door to door.

Presents to be wrapped and soon shared,
placed under the tree with pleasure and care.

Anticipating the arrival of Santa and crew,
trusting that he's good to yours and to you!

—*Kimberly L. Wilhelm*

The Legacy

Freddie shone with brilliance right to the end,
A voice so skillful nothing will transcend.
Movement vibrant love of life expressed,
Illness hidden - but everyone guessed.
A star so great will never be surpassed,
Though gone from sight his talent will last.
And thanks to modern innovation,
His music and vision still hold domination.
He left a heritage to allay the cost.
For others less fortunate, suffering and lost.
Friends felt his pain they cared a lot,
This attacking affliction - KILLS - does it not?
Spreading the world this dreadful plague,
Knowledge is needed a discovery made.
All must be made aware of this monstrous fact,
People are dying everyone must act.
Those with the virus know what's involved,
The body defenceless, it must be resolved.
Complacency is out - there is much to achieve,
A cure can be found, we have to believe.

"Sadly, Freddie Mercury died on the 24th of November 1991."

—*M. E. Jackson*

Mission In A Rainbow

My mission is like a rainbow,
Adding colour to everyone's picture of life,
  Blue for the beautiful sky,
  Yellow for the glorious sun upon it,
  White clouds to represent the heavens,
  Red to add conflict,
  Pink for the friendships,
  Green for the grass at our feet,
  Purple for all of our daily smiles,
  And orange to give us energy to live on,
This rainbow will spread in my travels,
To let everyone see the joy of life,
To let them learn to live life to the fullest,
and to the best of their abilities,
My mission is in the form of a rainbow,
  Colours to lighten up life...

—*Lisa Feser*

The Lost Dream

The dream was but a shadow now
A wisp deep within the hearth of the imagination
A spark in the great fire of the subconscious
Now just cold ash in the deep, black gloom.

Dreams are the stuff of kings and peasants
Of glory and evil, of might and triviality, of fame and
notoriety
A single idea blossomed into a river of images and meaning
A story that has not been told before
A tale filled with fresh, new notions and thoughts unheard of.

In the cold, black realm of the mind
Imagination forms a rich carpet
Where the seeds of dreams are sown.

Upon the fertile earth of the imagination
The rains of inspiration fall down
And new growth of thought and idea
Is enmeshed into the great forest of a story.

When twilight breaks through the clouds
The forest of images dissolve
And the dream fades away.

—*Rene Datta*

Value

Beyond the barrier, I see a world of freedom,
A world of serenity and security.
It lays there forever,
Until the right person comes along.
Soon enough, a girl discovers this world of peace.
She is pure of heart and mind.
This world is now hers.
Unselfishly, she invites a guest to share the magic kingdom.
Her friend sees no value in this mystical, carefree land.
Though the birds sing there and bright flowers bloom there.
The girl's guest decides to leave and return to her mansion.
She is rich, spoiled and knows not the definition of value.
The other girl, believing that her friend knows better,
leaves also.
Once again the mystical valley is empty.
And it will remain that way,
Until another time.

—*Melissa Philpott*

A Pondering

Rising golden in the sun the late blooming mum
absorbing warmth — life.

While I lying in the grass
Pondering insect kingdom pass
Watching a bee
the bee watchful of me.

Wary of an outside threat
Buzzing...a fluttering of wings
Laboring toward goal, slowly ascending stem.

Just short of his goal
I moved my arm...no threat at all.
The bee flew away. Nectar unattained.

Does man do that
Just short of his goal
Let an unknown force, by an unexpected movement
Sweep him away?
Straining against
Circumstance.
Needing to continue
Absorbing the nectar of life.

—*Katherine Woodell*

Stoop And Scoop

Stoop and scoop is the law of our town
Aesthetically pleasing - we'll clean up the ground.
Tuck all of our pet's compostable litter
Into non-destructible plastic. Now isn't that better?

But wait! Our children's grandchildren will sicken at play
On the landfill sites we're creating today,
With biodegradable litter carefully interred
In green plastic bags. Ecology served?

—*Elizabeth Maine Smith*

Second Wedding

Beyond the reach of yesterday's regrets,
Against potential future loneliness,
I pledge my love, my strength, my life's endeavor.
To meet your fears, I bring the certainty
Of growing trust that these past months have planted
In us. Toward your joy, I reach with eager,
Willing hands — to share, to build for us
A shield against whatever cause for grief
Might threaten us from time to time. To you
I freely open all my hours, my dreams,
My talents, promising to give your love
A fervent, lasting, nurturing response.
In hope we found each other. Now, in growing,
Loving confidence we go to live
Not only with but by and for each other.
Joyfully I welcome that commitment!

—*Jim Doherty*

Unseen

For years I battled the Beast, never to win
Against treachery, no sword can hold its edge
Each breath and cry in anger smothered
To end the war to end the deception.

Sky so blue, my heart still troubled
The booming sound of war drums echo.
Darkness falls without sunset's warning
Trapped by despair my fate now at Its hand.

Plea's and threats, had no meaning or strength
My life being taken and choked before me, It laughs.
There is no more fight, my world crumbles laid to ruin
Why a tear was shed may never be known.

The words from voices I could no longer remember
A heart once strong now cold and black
Through eyes unfocused seeing the trembling hand,
Touch the face of the reflection in wax.

That is now a day which holds special memory,
When the road of conflict, met the path to be free.

—*Dean C. Littleton*

A Thought

If I had a place to go, there you would find me. But it
all depends of the people there, if they are filled with love.
So here I am dreaming of a place to go. Somewhere, something
there I would find. But that's just a dream. I place that
does not exists. The real world lays ahead, even when it isn't
wanted or expected. Many times you can not understand its
power or why it's there. No matter how hard you try, it keeps
on flowing like the waves caused by wind, down an unknown
stream. There are people in pain, in distress, begging
pleading for help, but they are not heard, ignored, forgotten
in this mixed up place. This people spend their entire life
trying to find to light. This light is the light of hope,
laughter and love!

—*Lise Mabon*

Contemplation

Were it not within my control what would others represent?
Against whom shall I transgress? Or to whom shall I repent?
Would solitude yield some ills? Or would joy cause these to
flee? Could there be a concept of vanity, if, in my world,
there was just me. Are the others outside of myself or, in my

perception somehow? Are they awaiting the orders from me?
Would I command so that they will all bow? How interpret the
things that I see? And what about the words that I hear? Much
unfolds in front of me now, is it best I remain unaware? Those
kindly deeds and such gentle words, what then should these now

mean to me? They enrich me. So, when they do come flowing
from those who are free, spontaneous in expression void of
dress, quickly they yield the need to possess whilst
considering others' acts and words are they avenues to
awareness? What of seasons and elements? Should one try to
adjust these? But how? After what patterns shall he direct

their courses so that in winter he proceeds to plough? Alas!
It's encumbering now to contemplate much like the wiles of
others I see. But of whom shall these questions be asked if,
in my world they were just.... me?

—*Joseph Earle*

Time

The old woman sits motionless
All alone in the highbacked wooden rocker,
On the slanted porch of her aged farmhouse,
Surrounded by the remnants of a time gone by
Held in the grip of a mind vision of yesteryear.

Her wispy white hair fights to escape the bun at the nape of her
        neck
Wire rim glasses perch on her nose.
Her back shows the years of work in its curve
Wrinkles parade across her face
Testifying to the passage of time.

She sits, head supported by a gnarled hand
Gazing out across the yard.
Eyes roaming from the worn path
Across to the winding bramble of roses on the wooden fence,
To the old tire swing hanging motionlessly in the towering oak
        tree.

Voices, voices from the past echo through her head.
Giggles, gasps, calls to look
As would be acrobats ply their art
All gone now, all flown with the migration of family
The old woman is alone, with the old swing and her memories.

—*Kathy Herrick*

Posterity

I watched him working there so near to me
An aged man planting a seedling tree.
His hair gleamed white. Patterned facial lines
It seemed so futile, his planting a tree
He would never live it's full growth to see.
He paused and heaved a deep and weary sigh
Turning, appraised me with his piercing eye.
"Young man, you wonder why I plant a tree.
We both know it will live beyond my time.
Will grow and spread its verdant shade when I'm
Gone. But, my son, men who lived before me
Saw fit to plant shade my shelter to be
And so for you who follow after me
I build for the future, and so plant this tree."

—*Katherine Kline Sibrel*

The End Or The Beginning

The noise, the voices
all around me and yet beyond me
I caught glimpses of them
and yet was unable to move or speak

What had happened?
What were they doing?
In a brief moment of reality
I realized they were speaking to me.
Why didn't I answer them...
What was going on?

I tried to clear my head to remember
there was so much noise, voices, confusion.
I began to cry,
as everything came into focus
and I understood what I had done

What a terrible mistake I had made
and yet I felt so empty inside
and so alone...

That's how it all ended
but when did it all begin.

— *Lorraine Farmer*

Iberian Woman

All raise now for the death of his English eligibility.
All hold together now for the dark sullen seasonal skies,
and behold the awakening,
and behold the resurrection of the previously born.
Clasp him and envelope yourself around him, accept him
into your world for he lost his through death and loss.

You are the world of the new born.
The new light, the one who he at last feels at one with.
The woman who he wishes to caress and live for.
The one who changed his once sunken soul.
The harbinger of life, the embodiment of all that is good.
You are simply the one he loves,
you hold his love, his soul, his heart in your eternal bowl.
The Hispanic woman of love, the most beautiful one of all.

Come cool maiden of the deep. Come kiss his hand and light the
sand. Run with him along the breaking shore. Run together with
clasping hands and make your bodies meet. Your hair reflects
the sun with purple hues. Your body glistens in the beauty of
the twilight. You have the beach to yourselves at daybreak, only
loneliness you will lose. I'll see you both behind the sun.

— *Martin West*

The First Lady

There is a lady I know and she is a lady indeed;
All made up of love, lace, cotton dresses, and shiny
beads.

This lady of such elegance has no arrogance for
she knows not what special qualities she
possesses;
In the darkest of times she is that beam of light
that brings forth the best of those sometimes
horrible messes.

This lady I know has hands of gold and her
fingers are of delicate pearls;
Yet she spares them no comfort as they endlessly
labor, still finding time to perfect her daughter's
curls.

There are many ways to describe the First Lady,
but one befits her unlike any other;
This first lady of love is my beautiful,
hard-working, lovely mother.

— *Janet Scott*

Mother Theresa

Who is this lady in white
All the world over is talking about?
Love all Love

No other can compare
Dedicated, to all human beings
Babies and children, are her delight
Rich, poor, beggards on the street
Men, Ladies of the night.
No one is slighted.
We are all God's children.

Softly and swiftly she walks
on to giving a helping hand.
Compassion and love
that is what the lady in white is all about.
"True Christianity"
In every sense of the word.
If I, ever given the chance
Would love to walk beside
The Lady in white.

— *JoAnna Williams*

The Winds Of Nature

We cannot see the winds of nature when it blows
all we know sometimes it brings disaster to the ocean
towering waves in motion - anyways no matter what
it conveys the winds of nature scatters information
maybe a revolution, nobody really knows we can only
feel the change.

North, South, East or West, the winds of nature
never rest. On sunny days we do not feel the
stormy blast the seas are calm before a storm,
the skies no tell-tale clouds inform, the birds
stay happy in their nest.
The children play, they do not care if raindrops fall
and fill the air. They do not see the darkening
sky, they do not hear the winds of nature rushing by
telling them beware we are on the way.
At times the wind brings a gentle breeze, the trees
wave a welcome with their leaves.
The cloak of winter disappear, we cannot see but
only hear, come spring, summer or golden fall and
the winds of nature covers all. Winters squall

— *Kathleen Kay Lewis*

If I Were Me

If I were me, I'd tell it true
Alone I stand, if not for you
Your eyes, your heart, they do belong
Not to me, I wish I were wrong

If I were me, I'd never quit
Together we share, but not a bit
Our eyes, our hearts, at times do meet
Not for me, for us, it's a treat

If I were me, I'd say I care
Alone I'm filled, but with despair
My thoughts of you I wish to say
Not 'cause of me, but 'cause I pray

If I were me, I'd tell it true
Together we stand, for me and you
My feelings are pure, I will not soil
This field of kindness, for you I'll toil

— *Joe Servais*

Little Girl Lost

Sweet little girl lost in time
an innocent victim stuck in my mind
driven by pain all these years
filled with hate because of my fears

I was as hurt but couldn't run away
since I was the strongest I had to stay
now for so long I've been all alone
please dear child it's time to come home

Ever so often I see your face
peeking at me from your hiding place
I beg you to join me come out to play
I promise to love you please trust what I say

I know you need me for I see your yearning
it's become so clear with all that I'm learning
believe in me as I make this commitment
follow your heart and release your resentment

—*Kelley Lee McDonald*

Gene

A man springs to life, from a tiny seed.
An oak tree does the same.
   An acorn falls upon the earth
   Kissed by the gentle rain.
They both grow tall and strong
and share their strength,
with all who may pass by.
   The man is building treasures.
   The oak is reaching for the sky.
The man takes the oak within his hands,
That acting like a mold
   Creates the treasures left behind,
   For all of us to hold.
And like the carpenter called Jesus,
He has not died in vain.
   For when we see those treasures,
   In our hearts, he lives again!

—*Joseph Tennyson*

Untitled

I am a ship on the ocean
An ocean of ever changing tides
Where the wind and the rain abuses me
And there's no place to hide.
But I sail on into this stormy wind of life
Though battered and bruised I may be
And I keep on looking forward
To new horizons ahead of me.
My crew have abandoned me
In lifeboats the sailed away
And then they watched in fear
Expecting me to fade away.
Though I have holes and bruises
I did not sink to the ocean's floor
I stayed on course, though alone
For that was what I was made for.
The dolphins swim alongside me
All the whales are my friends
And as the sun smiles down upon me
I know that this isn't the end.

—*Aliesha DeLacy*

Can You Swim?

An overflowing river, I see in your eyes…
An ocean of tears you're trying to hide.
A whirlpool of life, slowly dragging you down.
I hope you can swim!
Or you're going to drown.

Troubles pull you under, your air disappears.
Stealing your breath, releasing your fears.
As your eyelids grow heavy, and your body grows weak.
A nightmare is waiting.
Waiting for you to sleep!

Darkness surrounds you, as the lonely night falls.
The tide rolls in rhythm, with the hearts of us all.
Capturing your soul, hypnotizing your mind.
Your memories all forgotten, your dreams left behind.

Break free from this cruel, underwater world of pain.
Reach for the real world, where life's not a game.
No more drowning in sorrow, no more sinking in lies.
No more falling asleep to the sounds of your cries.

Like a lost helpless child, you stand all alone.
While the water keeps rising, your heart turns to stone.

—*Janet Ellis & Tracy McInroy*

Isolated Incident

I thought the thought of you would be enough. Having had you.
An unsound phrase. Just the once. Quite sufficient. "We must not make commitments". You said that is a trice. Now imagination will suffice.

I thought the thought of you would be enough. Having seen you. With as they say the naked eye. Spilling over my naked shaking self. Not once but twice. Now imagination must suffice.

I thought the thought of you would be enough. I have your photo, I've read your card. I have carefully reduced the risk of attaching any value, or setting any price, on. Imagination WILL suffice.

I thought the thought of you would be enough. I thought we might try and turn it into Good Solid Friendship. I thought. Screw thinking! It's you I want.

—*Sally Cline*

My Wonderful Memories

I remember the happiness.
And a few of my cries.
I remember the night that we said goodbye.

I remember that walk.
Along with his smart way of thinking.
I remember the fish and his sly way of winking.

I remember his laughter.
But never a cry.
But how well I remember his crystal blue eyes.

I wait to see him return from work every day.
But he'll not return he's gone away.

It was to many yesterdays when I saw him last.
Oh how well I know yesterdays are of the past.

I shall not find him.
For I know that he really can't be found.
But please, please let me just look around.

I remember the happiness.
And a few of my cries.
I remember my Daddy.
and the night he died.

—*Karen June Rice Pollizzi*

My Hopes And Aspirations

Every day I watch the rising sun of my hopes
and aspirations ascending the throne of sky.
Only to find it drowning in the sea of reality.
And darkness engulfs my whole being.

But the sun of my hopes and aspiration
is not a mere slave to the sea of reality,
on the contrary it is ever living ever rising and
ever lasting, and will always rise to touch the
realm of the sky.

My only prayer is let them sun of my hopes and
aspirations, rise, ever rise, rise again and again.

—*Supriya Banerjee*

The Lord Is Present

Have you ever looked in another's eyes
    And at that moment you realize
The Lord is real, the Lord is true
    And the Lord is present inside of you.

Have you ever seen a babe's sweet smile
    That makes all life seem so worthwhile,
And at that moment, it came to you
    The Lord is present inside of you.

Have you ever watched a waterfall
    Or listened to the wild goose call,
And understood what nature knew
    The Lord is present inside of you.

Have you ever stood by a babbling brook
    And to its incessant chatter took
The time to hear what it was telling you
    The Lord is present inside of you.

Have you ever thought as night came down
    Of the Man long ago Who wore the thorn crown,
The message He came to spread the world through
    Is the Lord is present inside of you.

—*Elaine Baskey-Hales*

Nature's Best

Is it by chance that I am here
And be touched by your beauty so rare
Is it magic of love that I truly feel
Stronger it grows as I stare.

Oh Nature's beauty so radiant, so blest
What comfort you give in time of distress
What hope you give when weakness appears
What calmness you give in time of despair.

A thousand days
    A million years
        As I leave this life in sadness
I simply could not bear
Oh Nature's beauty
    by what magic,
        you will still be here
Touching the lives of those who stare.
A magnificent creation in life's best
    far reaching
        far knowing.

—*Felicitas B. Gonzaga*

Early Morning Thoughts

Quite often I wake up real early
    And before I turn on the light
I walk down the hall to my kitchen
    Just to look out at the night.
I see no lights in our neighborhood.
    Am I the only fortunate one
To see silhouettes of mountains and trees?
    All the beautiful things God has done?

But "just wait a minute" I tell myself
    Maybe all up and down my street
My neighbors are standing at their windows, too
    In their pajamas and bare feet.
Wouldn't it be funny if all of a sudden
    He turned spotlights on us all?
Can't you imagine all the scrambling we'd do
    To get back down the hall?

We'd jump into our slippers and robes
    And probably brush our hair
But for admiring His beauty, dressed or not,
    I really don't think God would care!

—*Joyce E. Jones*

Aftermath For The Innocent

Shaken by her need to forgive
And by her mistakenly lain guilt
She requests to be forgiven
And tearful in my need to have
No more suffering I said,
    I am who I am by the pain
    By the struggle, by the sadness.
    So, like Elizabeth's destiny
    Declared her to be powerful and
    Strong in the shadow of her mother's
    Supposed shame, I am me and
    My destiny helps me to be strong
    And push on and on, in spite or......because.
    I could be so much less if not for the battle.
    You have not met the same dragons
    But we all have our own and
    Slay or love them they are ours
    And make us, us.
    Without, our strength batters at our insides
    And then in truth we are torn.

—*Jacalyn Young*

Yugoslavia

Dark crows and black ravens circle over their head;
And, caring no longer for the stench of the dead.
They are dismembering what was once an Empire.
At the time, established near a nest of vampires.
Hung at each other's throats
They call themselves Croats,
or Bosnians, or Serbs, who are so much akin,
Three centuries ago being each other kin.
Their dark mountains echo the thunder of the gun
And a billowing smoke is obscuring the sun
As if wanting to hide from God and all others
The despair of their wives and the cries of mothers

Oh, man?....

—*Jean-Pierre Fenoll*

He Is God

When shadows lengthen in the early evening
and clouds sail by in many shades of grey...
We think-

When the Maple sheds its burnished leaves
and the Sumac paints the scene in brilliant crimson...
We pause-

When the last Rose of summer toils to display
it's final sweet and delicate splendor...
We smile-

When winter's snow transforms our tainted world
in glorious spotless beauty...
We wait-

And when we wait and smile and pause and think
We can be still and know...
That He is God.

—*Christina Schotsman*

Without Title

I've gone astray the norms and rules
and crept outside the walls enclosing
I fumbled into the open and stood, I cherished
my lost dimensions saw regained that have
been perished and retained.

Life inside my dear walls does still
appeal and gives me pleasure
I realised nevertheless it's bittersweet
to indulge in an outside treasure.

My life has been lately streamed into two parts solely
that of the plentiful past and the barren present
the former feeds the last, let alone future
in the hands of fate and heaven.

I long for a while to get only the last
and be deprived of the ghosts of past
and live my new dimensioned life
away from the shadows of the impeding musts
I led you stealthily into my soul's archive.

—*Tina Kitantzi*

I Remember

Running through the cold ripples of rapid water,
and dying in the fields of golden sun.
Stretching above the hot, drying earth, as the
swaying grasses cool us.

The pale corn sky, filled with lovely passing clouds,
that carry our dreams of innocent needs.
We close our eye's and let the sun blind our whole
bodies, that one rich and bronzed.

Suddenly, we are full of play, in search of new
emotions, has we run through the cooling water,
into another golden gate of pure fantasy. Reaching
out to the sky, hiding secrets never to be told.

This, is our childhood of innocent games and burning
wants. Has the sun turns into solid night; we
race home, engulfed in our holidays of youth.
Dirty hands and faces, covered with a broad smile.

I remember... My youth.

—*Tracy Jones*

Cry For Help

The USA's infected, this disease it's worse than AIDS
And everybody's fuming, with this violence and this rage
1860's...1960's..., doesn't do a thing
Fighting for a cause, but the answer lies within
You can't begin to fix it, when the problem's just begun
Riots, burning and looting, it's the new way; it's just fun
Nobody's dealing, with the issues at hand
Instead we want to destroy, this beautiful land
Doing right and working hard, it's like a foreign tongue
And if you spread this message, then you're the racist one
Everybody's losing, in this terrible mess
And everybody's wrong, but no one will confess
The only way to change it, is to change the state of mind
I'd be nice to you, and to me, you'd be kind

—*Kevin J. Forman*

Sonnet

When I behold the pain behind your eyes
And feel the burn of holding back my tears,
I want to keep you from your deepest fears
That ours was just a love filled up with lies.

You did not know that all those heartfelt cries
for honesty, and loving warmth were dear
to me; you laughed and hoped that I would near
Your deepest self, the one that holds the prize.

Your eyes meet mine and know I cannot hold
my self from wanting you. My grasp is torn;
With every touch we peel away the mold
That years have wrapped around, and we are born.
A living feeling person has unfold
And we are one, from time and place we're torn.

—*James E. Prest*

It Is Here On Earth

A mirror was placed in a monkey's cage,
and he sought the fellow behind it,
   much like a scientist or a sage
who searches but cannot find it.
   He left a particle on the shelf,
   if only he could find his self,
where he hid it and he shrined it.
   To seek it in another place
he stares and wonders into space,
   though here's the world we should embrace.

A mirror was placed in a satellite,
and the telescope was connected,
   to search for life in the starry height,
where it ought to be detected.
   Into this problem the scientist delves,
   though he might find it among ourselves,
and it must not be neglected.
   Life is a mighty seldom thing,
a precious note which the Lord made sing,
right from the keyboard's superstring.

—*Kaj Garbar*

It Only Takes

It only takes one person to change the world,
And if that person can do it
Many others can follow.
A change of attitude can gain many friends.
If everyone in the world could be friends
Hunger, War, and Destruction
Can be demolished.
Then there are those who can't see
Past colour, race, or sex.
They are the ones who need help,
Not everyone else.

—*Terri Stonehouse*

My Dear Mother

When I was a child, you used to say "No".
And how I hated to hear it from you.
But soon I learned that you love me so.
That is why you used to say "No".

Yes, when I was happy I usually forgot you.
But when I got problems, I ran to you.
My dear mother, now you are gone. . .
I now miss your caring hands and "No".

Now I realize your motherly love
  could not be matched by anyone's.
How I wish you were still here . .
  to guide me through with your caring hands.

It is now late to say "I love you".
But I know you love me so much, so you understand.
Thank you so much for guiding me still . .
Through other friendly people's hands.

　　　—Julio B. Castillo

Our Elders Are Flowers

The flowers are falling off the trees
And I can see them dancing in the breeze

They have a beauty all of their own
And really don't mind being left alone

Unlike our elders that we see each day
Who some feel that they are in our way

Just like the flowers that bloom on the trees
They are so full of life and dance in the breeze

So many things live and so many things die
But ours is not to ever question why

Enjoy the beauty and the grace
Of each little flower and elderly face.

While they're still here we should all feel blessed
Because just like a flower how many days do they have left

Let us all watch the flowers on the trees
And enjoy them dancing in the breeze...

　　　—Kimberly Barrett

Searching For My Wonderchild

　　　　I awoke in a whimsical mood today
　And I coaxed my Inner Child to come out to play.
　　Let's ascend to the heavens upon a swing
　　Or marvel at a delicate butterfly wing.
　The trees are all turning, there's frost in the air
　The day's simply magic...come with me...let's share.

　　A sad little voice murmured deep from within
　I've been so scared and lonely - just where have you been
When I've needed your comfort, your nurture, your love...
　　My Wonderchild's lost...I don't know how to share
　　Feelings and laughter... adventure and fun.

Someone deserted me soon after birth, Poor little orphan
　　I still roam the earth, searching for someone
To please rescue me from my prison of loneliness, sad destiny.

　　So you awoke in a whimsical mood today...
　　After all these years you would like to play...
　　Where have you been when I need you so much
　My heart has been starved..we've been so out of touch...
I long to reach out to you... capture and share, lost laughter
　　　and secrets...　But NOBODY'S there.

　　　—M. Mickey Turnbull

Your Name

I don't want a mob,
And I don't want a God,
And I don't want to look up
Just to get a blinding nod.

I don't want a word-game,
And I don't want a war-blame,
And neither will a thump in the ear,
Cause me to condone your name.

Are you a total human being?
Or are you just the sound of your name?
And anything that rhymes with it?
Or anything merely in some way, the same?

Your spirit is your living breath,
Without it you meet your breathless death,
And any sound is a moving spirit,
So remember it. You're more than your name.

　　　—Peter J. Dutton

Our Springwater

She dreamed on through the lonely night
And in sorrow watched the break of light.
Sometimes the pain was hard to bear, for no one came nor did
they care. And then one day the doors did open wide,
As hurried footsteps came inside. They scrubbed and cleaned
and made things bright, then footsteps faded into the night.
She wondered then what all this meant, but standing there she
was content. And then once more the door did open wide
And throngs of people came inside. She thought a miracle had
taken place, for she knew each one and knew each face.
And when loving hands did touch each wall,
She cried aloud, "They've grown so tall."
Soon sounds of music filled the air,
And couples danced without a care.
And when the time had come to pray,
They knelt to think him for each perfect day.
Once more the door was shut real tight.
But for her future seemed so bright.
For now she knew she had their love,
And gave her thanks to Him above.

　　　—Gertrude Avramenko

The Survivor

I am a survivor, a survivor that goes here and there
and keeps going;
A survivor that is lonely and doesn't know where to go;
A survivor that doesn't know when darkness is going to
get here, or if daylight will ever come;
A survivor that hopes for something good to happen;
A survivor that doesn't know when her life will end;
A survivor that hopes her dreams will find her, or
that she will find them;
A survivor that hopes everything will come out alright;
A survivor that is like the river, going places she has
never been;
A survivor that is scared and alone;
A survivor that doesn't know who to turn to, or who to
look up to;
I am a survivor, a survivor that is like the wind.

　　　—Janice Thompson

The Song Of Life

Sing me the song of life
and let me be nature's listener
I want not a song to madly drum mine ear
Nor one to intoxicate my senses and leave me dim
when the last strain is pulled.
I want me a song to linger
like the whistling wind.
The song of life is nature's wine
being drunk in small doses or by gulps
impairs not the senses
but enlivens the spirit to move.
My song of life is a song of hope
the someday the world may not collapse
sing the world, the song of life
that will smelt men's
steely valour for war and bloodshed;
Sing the world, the song of life
That somehow, somewhere, someday
Man shall be closer to his brother
The world needs the song of life.

—*Hugh Todd*

How Great Thou Art, Lord!

Abba! Father, have mercy on our poor souls
and let us hear thee good Lord.
Thank you, Christ Jesus, our Lord and our
God.
O Spirit of Christ, O God the Holy Spirit,
kindly stay always in our hearts and bless us.
Merciful God, our Heavenly Father, we love
thee Lord!

O Spirit of the Lord God.
O Spirit of the Father of our Lord and
Savior Jesus Christ, thy only begotten Son.
O almighty God! The Holy Spirit, Jesus and
the Father being one.
We love thee good Lord, the triune God!

Glory to the name of the almighty Heavenly
Father, His Son, the almighty Jesus Christ and
His Spirit, the almighty Holy Spirit.
The great one, the almighty Christian God.
The one and only true God.
The almighty - holy, holy - spirit God!

—*Orlando A. Varilla*

The Circus Ride

Oh, my love took me for a very long ride
And my heart was claimed by him.
He took me on a circus ride,
Then left me on a limb.

He never loved me that's plain to see,
But he made my heart glow.
Now that he's deserted me
My heart is cold as the snow.

The ride is fun if you can make it last
But this ride ends way too fast.
It's very clear the cost is too dear
And I never learn from the past.

My heart is sore, I shed a tear,
I no longer want him near,
But a broken heart, a love one can't hide
Is a token for a circus ride,
But the cost is way too dear!

—*Lady Sady Rue*

My Verse

One sullen day for sadness felt my words began to flow.
And on page, in perfect ink, my feelings true did show.

Trivial it was to me this verse, with it I was content
Until a friend embraced my thoughts and read them with consent.

She spoke no words although she told of how she was impressed
By saving words of mine to hang inside her place of rest.

Today, I met this friend again and with her words I wept.
My heart was touched for after many years my verse she'd kept.

—*Michelle Szabo*

Angel Hearts

Who paints the flowers purple and gold
and red and blue and white

Who cuddles the sparrows when they're cold
in the darkness of the night

Who coaxes the ivy to grow so green
Or raindrops to fall so the leaves are clean

Who sprinkles rose petals on the garden bench
Who weaves the morning glories on the fence

Who raises each tiny bud to the sun
Or tickles our fancy to make life fun
-only Angel Hearts can-

—*Catherine Simpson*

Wind And Water

Silver moon beams break through clouds
And spill across a darkened lake
Wind strokes water sending shivers towards shore
Water laps slowly and carefully at the sandy edge
Each lap caressing the shore like gentle kisses lovers share
Shivers move to waves of passion
Wind and water crash toward rocks and reunited in a misty spray
Winds touch fades gently from water
And shivers melt into a peaceful calm
Silver moon beams break through clouds
And spill across a darkened lake

—*Lesa Nordick*

Beyond

When we relinquish life on earth
And spiritually rise,
To meet our Maker face to face,
Beyond eternal skies.
What joy awaits, or even pain
Can be our just reward.
For how we've lived in every way
Will measure our eternity.

On contemplation of these thoughts,
I hesitate to guess,
How many people on God's earth,
Have walked with Him, and so been blessed
With His own promises and yet,
Still the hope that one day we,
Will live with Him, eternally.

—*Margaret Chandler*

Karma

Where the horizons hide as the white clouds roll,
  And the mountain tops fade into azure blue.
While God has forsaken my reckless soul,
  Or perhaps I'm one whom He never knew.

The restless wind and the blazing sun,
  Beckons me hither, I know not where.
To the arms of nature, I always run,
  When the boredom drives me away from here.

It may be adventure or enchantment perhaps,
  That excites my heart and even my mind,
And I cover the distance in seven league laps.
  For I'll never be aught but the roving kind.

Should destiny be the end of the trail,
  And only mirages account want and need.
I shall with glee go forth into the gale,
  And that shall be the honor of my breed.
    —*James Szatkowski*

Untitled

As the hallowed darkness rips through my soul
And the wild wind whips through my hair
The night becomes something new
It is no longer a peaceful awakening
It is a dreary force of unwanted hatred and unused love

I shed my skin of the old life and wear the skin of the new

My eyes are open but makes no sense
The wicked wind is howling
The dying dog is whimpering
The old lady is crying out … for me
I walk away in fear of losing sight

My hair is messy, clothes are torn
I wish the man would leave me alone
The barren darkness calls me … I must go
The lonely lady is weeping
I cannot see her, for I am blind
    —*Jennifer Cottell*

a heart for any fate (to: Andy Summers)

a sigh for those who love me; a smile for those who hate
and whatever skies above me; here's a heart for any fate

a sigh for those who love you, a tear for those who care
  a feeling of tenderness surrounds us
  a feeling we've yet to share

your smile makes me wonder, your expressions make me think
  your actions make me ponder, if there's any link

    when i listen to you play
  pressing your fingers to certain chords
  you could probably play them many ways
  but the uncertain principle billed the boards

    a time of sentiment, a piece of art
  when I listen to you, i feel your heart

    and on this 'edge' that you live
    you make my life competitive
    not of who but of fate
    it exists but so does hate

a smile for those who hate; a sigh for those who love
and may all the skies above; touch our hearts with fate
    —*Leila Winters*

Untitled

A man was reading a paper and came across an ad,
and when he finally read it it made him very glad

The National Library of Poetry was holding a contest,
and thought his wife could write one and match up with the best

He tore the ad out, went to work, and later brought it home,
then gave it to his wife for her a write a poem,

All entries had to be received by October 31st,
and she began thinking about each little verse

She wrote a poem to enter in the contest, for just a little fun,
and if by chance she won some cash she'd buy something for her
  son

She finished with her poem just 8 lines shy of twenty,
and if she is a winner she owes thanks to her honey.
    —*Karol Heneghan*

Brown Trout, Brown Whiskey

He wasn't far from the river,
And when the sirens told the
Dam to release the deep, chilled
Waters, he would sometimes cast a
Flat stone toward the rapids from
His cabin door. There was a time.
Twenty years ago when it would have
Been an easy throw. Or maybe it's
Because the sirens always come in
The morning, when he feels the warm,
Amber whiskey from the night before.
On siren days the fishing was bad,
And the whiskey was all that was good.
But soon he would again feel the grinding
Drag of his old fly rod, and see the
Grizzled shadow of his nymph
As it drifted back toward him. The
trout he caught were never kept; it
Only seemed fitting — there was no one
Left to feed but himself.
    —*John David Harrill III*

Waiting At the Edge Of Time

Why can't I, touch the rainbows?
And why can't I reach the farthest star?
And why can't I, fall in love?
I hope you find your knight,
I hope you find your way…to distant galaxies!
I know it!….because I felt it….
In your eyes, last night!

I can control the destiny!
and make my dreams reality…
Through the twisted sarcasm
Of the subliminal life you see.
I'll take you away from suburban.! Misery!
I will break the barriers! To the parallel world!

I'm trapped inside the dream world,
Waiting at, the edge of time…
I'm drifting endlessly through time…
Waiting for my soul, to leave…
But if the winds of change don't come,
I'll be waiting there with you…
I will be waiting at, the edge of time….
    —*Jam Grinder*

Cancer

Critical
Annoying
Needless
Ceaseless
Enemy
Rid of it please

It tears and spreads through your body like acid,
It's there to cause a great deal of pain,
It is certainly not placid,
And it leaves a distraughtful stain.

It can cause damage to the lung, liver and breast,
People can die from such a thing,
You feel uncomfortable and not at rest,
And life is the only thing to cling.

There's no need for an introduction of this terrible pest,
It's definitely not a prankster,
You're going through a difficult test,
And that test is all about cancer.

—*Vilia Amerthil*

The Dawn

Another dawn has broken
Another day begun,
And God knows what we'll make of it,
For He's the only one
To guide us in the right way,
To do what He'd like done,
But maybe we'll not listen
But go on doing wrong
Until perhaps a choice must come,
And we must then decide
To do God's will, or go our way,
Hoping that perhaps some day
We'll find it easier to say
God's will be done!
But maybe that will be too late,
For God might leave us to our fate.

—*Phidelia E. Lemon*

No Mourning After

In writings of love and life, relentlessly I sought
Answers to questions and questions to answers of myself,
Briefly interrupted by—I do not remember her name.

My magnetic eyes easily hypnotized her;
Craving arms embraced my comely body,
Hungry lips sought my ornamental nipples,
Her body responding feverishly to my overwhelming masculinity.
When my succulent lips kissed her, like countless others
She became sick with love, agonizing for fulfillment.

She spoke of this love as a thing worthy of mention;
My laughter—cruel as the grave—silenced her,
This misfit who could believe her love would have meaning to me,
One who has made so many feel blessed to be women.

Had God made her beautiful or more deserving, she might still
    live;
Gladly would I have welcomed her within my harem of friends.
There is no place for love in my world.
My frantic search for meaning is over—the bull has shown the
    way.
He cares not which cows are in heat; he fucks and is content.
There is no mourning; I sing my songs. Herds of virgins await.

—*Irena Nicholson*

Goodbye

Love's blinkers are gone now I see
Any love there was; you have lost for me,
For some years we have drifted along
Blindly I hoped, that I was wrong.

Now I look closely at our relationship
I realize for you; it was just an ego trip,
Your pretence at love really had me fooled
But, now my ardour has finally cooled.

You used me as you would an old door mat
On my aspirations you constantly sat,
In front of acquaintances you pampered and fussed
In private each one was derided and cussed!

As a leach would cling, you took all I gave
I can't stay any longer as your 'love slave',
How I tried to please you, all in vain
My heart is numb with anguish and pain.

I'm saying goodbye to all my wasted years
Without intention of shedding lonely tears,
No more your ego to inflate will I try
I'm glad to see the back of you so… Goodbye!

—*Sue Jackson*

Never

Never will my baby be
Anything but a memory to me
For I will never get to count his tiny fingers and toes
Never get to see his cute little button nose
Never hold him in my arms
Never see him use his charms
Never wipe away his tears
Never chase away his fears
Never get to hear him talk
Never get to see him walk
Never get to see him grow strong and tall
Never get to see him again at all
And now my baby is dead and gone
And I know I must carry on
But the thing I find so hard to bear
Is that drunk driver didn't even care
He killed my baby, my shining light
When he decided to drive drunk that fateful night
The thing that makes it so very sad
Is my baby was killed by his own dad.

—*Joyce Reid*

Advertising

Now advertising is a cinch
Anything goes in a pinch.
Out of the closet are personal adds.
Most of the articles are just fads.

When I was young and eager,
Sex talk was very meager.
A friend may whisper on the sly
A dirty joke or saying just whizzed by.

Now on TV, telephone or the air
Most commercials would embarrass Fred Astaire,
And Don Ameche would take flight.
The words now uttered on the phone are a sight.

It's strange how all the flower smells
Are used from toilet bowls to ——Well!
You can guess—must I say more.
Those parts are not private now for sure.

Today grandma's must take heed.
All privacy is gone—yes indeed!
Old fashioned her ideas are proclaimed.
And with this her spirit is maimed.

—*Jessie Thomas*

Hiroshima and Chernobyl, Mon Amour

While warm, caressing May-winds
Are arriving from the Eastern shore,
We do not know, as yet,
What Spring has in its store.
This year, we learn, too soon,
of cesium and becquerel:
The dearest price of Hiroshima and the Chernobyl.
We are reminded as we watch
our Nature's Horn of Plenty
gingerly unfold,
That man and creature surely share
A common destiny - untold -
- The wisdom man may care to
grudgingly elicit,
On his way up from the ape,
May be the difference - explicit -
Of no return, of no escape.
- A Hiroshima, a Chernobyl, Mon Amour -

    —*Birgit Thelin-McDonald*

Solitude

The ancient rocks and whispering trees
Are calling now to me,
To travel far from the city sounds -
"Come, like us be free!"

I wander the surf beaten shore line,
Midst driftwood, fossils and shells,
Soon lost in dreams I ponder -
"What legends could they tell?"

The gull's cry echoes through mist so dense.
The lighthouse guides my way.
God's beauty so rare have I seen today,
Never, from here, will I stray.

    —*Florence Eugene Wilson*

Ashes To Ashes

We were all standing around you,
Are clothes getting damp by the rain.
I watched as they lowered your coffin.
It symboled the end of your pain.

Your mother was there with her hanky,
Your father too, with his hat.
And your friends had all gathered around me,
Every one of them dressed in black.

I have got you a large grey headstone,
With your name, and the date you did die.
I bought it from all of are savings,
For the new car we never did buy.

One by one all your fiends are leaving,
Everyone with a tear in there eye.
Ashes to ashes, dust to dust,
Sleep tight my love, goodbye.

    —*Robert E. Main*

Blue Bell

I am a bluebell,
As blue as the bluest sea.
I wait all day in the morning grass,
Until I am awaken by a bee.
It is boring being a flower,
Although flowers do not tell lies.
But one good thing about flowers,
Is that they get kissed by butterflies.
One day I got old and I died from the cold,
But the butterfly who weeped and cried,
Kissed me one last time,
And said good-bye.

    —*Amber Goodman*

In My Little World

I live in the North, in the land of plenty. Where hardships
are few, and the pleasures are many. There are Moose and Deer
and Elk and of course Bear. Should you decide to go out
wandering there. Their are scenic views which are a daily
treasure. Fishing in 3000 miles of lakes, of various measure.
Where little creatures and birds of many species.
Are roaming the North, their survival never ceases.
The sunsets are fantastic, and the haunting sounds of the loons.
Serenade us in the twilight, this is an appreciated boon.
There are lumber mills and pulp mills, to employ the people.
There are tourists traveling roads, camping and fishing and
    meeting.
Many old friends met on previous journeys. Lots of tourists
travel back year after year. Seeing new scenic wonders, and
usually a Deer. Now some like haunting, and some like fishing.
Mother nature provides, to each and everyone's pleasure.
Being happy and fulfilled, is each and everyone's endeavor.
So visit a part of the world, created with splendor.
In my little world, which is the North, where I meander.

    —*Jessie Panrucker*

I'll Tell You If You're Right

Can you tell me the colour of my true love eyes
Are they brown like a cornflower, or blue as the sky
Are they green like the sea, or dark as night
If you tell me the colour then I'll tell you if your right

Can you tell me the colour of my true love hair
Is it fair as a flaxen, or black as night
Is it red like the sunset, or golden bright,
If you tell me the colour then I'll tell you if your right

Can you tell me the colour of my true love skin
Is it fair as porcelain, and cool to the touch
Or dark as a bunny, and hot from within
Is it pink like a rosebud, with iridescent light
If you tell me the colour, then I'll tell you if your right

    —*Al Breton*

Bobby And Baby

The wind is not whistling its normal tune.
As Bobby is wrestling to sleep,
Instead it's playing a sweet lullaby as the
trees tap out the rhythm in the window pane,
And the shutters acting like the drums.
Then as the wind ends its sweet song.
Bobby drifts off to dreamland and
dreams one of the sweetest dreams.
Slowly the moon moves to another little
child who needs to go to sleep. The
lights of day rises over the hills and
the birds are doing the singing, Bobby
yawns and stretches his body, as he
slowly wakens. Reaching over gives his
baby sister a hug and kiss, then
Hugs and Kisses for Mom. He then makes
breakfast for himself
and his baby sister happily humming a
strange tune that sounds like the wind.

    —*Kathy Waters*

The Roses

The old man was filled with guilt,
as he watched her flowers slowly wilt.
In his age old heart he thought
They could never be apart.
In the moments before her death,
under her shallow, soundless breath,
he held her tiny, withered hand,
as she spoke to him one last demand:
"I have always loved you, loved you true,
so please do this last thing I ask of you."
He listened closely, holding back tears,
simply remembering their wonderful years.
"Remember my roses, by beautiful flowers,
I beg of you in these final sweet hours."
"Tend to them, water them daily,"
Her grip was not tight, just holding on fraily.
"Love my flowers as you've loved me,
and in our hearts, together forever we will be."
And in that moment, away he watched her spirit fly,
And within a flash, he was back to reality, just sitting,
watching her roses die...

—*Karen Langley*

Ode To The Olde Elm Tree

Down she had to come, more progress had begun.
As I glanced through my window, one bright morning in June.
I thought to myself, "Ye Olde Elm Tree" will be cut down soon.

Just a few leaves blossomed on her side, as she struggled
to survive, but in all her glory, she stood stately reaching
to the sky.

Now, 'tis July and from my window, what do I see, but workmen
who have cut down "Ye Olde Elm Tree" she seemed to be a part
of me.

For many long years I watched her grow, getting warmth from
the sunshine, and glistening in the ice and snow, many birds
graced her boughs, squirrels played around and around, now,
"Ye Olde Elm Tree" lies cut on the ground.

—*Dorothy Manuel*

The Way Out

Days are long, nights run cold,
As I go down this lonely road.
I seek anew, a place to hide
And someone with whom, to confide.

And now my days are bleak and dead,
Though I still lie on this rough bed,
With rocks below and stars above,
My mind is crowded with great love.

Melancholy are now my days,
Time in which to change my ways.
The path of which I must take to travel
Is twisting and winding, all covered with gravel.

Yet I still seek out this new place,
And still I find that I am in a race,
With time, with love and with loneliness.
And I still can not find the way to go
As my days are long, and my nights run cold.

—*Virginia L. Wiebe*

Another Year Holding The Candle

Yeah yeah...
here we go...
Another bloody Christmas alone,
standing on the sidelines,
watching the couples go by.
About this time of the year I get anxious,
envisaging how foolish I will feel
when that New Year clock strikes midnight
and I have to wait for everyone to finish kissing their
partners before they shake my awkward hand.
Honestly.
I just couldn't be fucked anymore.
playing the masquerade of social banter,
smiling insincerely,
my head whirling with wishful wonder
of how it may be like
if ever, one refreshing year
I actually had somebody
who wanted to be there.

—*Steve Cavallo*

Purple Trojans

Now time itself has diminished
as I hear Echoes come closer...
Souls are wells within wells.
Eternal fires are reflected deep in their depths.
Thoughts like sand, sift through subconscious layers,
slowly take shape,
Life.
Beating mystic hearts
under Rivers of Ancient ice
rushing imperceptibly...
Purple Trojans on silver crests.
Stars burning bright
like hell's fires on medieval mountainsides.
Lizards turn the pages of history,
the carnage of petals,
our other lives and deaths...

—*Kenneth David Munro*

First Winter's Snow

It was snowing in that quiet and easy way,
As I stood and looked out my window and watched the
children play
Large white snow flakes were falling lazily
casting a mysterious spell on my mountain home.

As I watched the snow falling down the mountain side,
My heart was filled with much contentment and great pride
I felt pity for others who couldn't see this lovely sight,
For I know if they did they would feel such great delight.

Tucked in the side of the mountain this home of mine Faces a
tiny lake, like a miniature shrine. The peace and serenity I
find here, I will always hold dear, dear to my heart and soul
To spend the rest of my life here, I have made my goal And in
the years that come and go I'll always remember that first
winter's snow And when the time comes for my soul to depart, I
want to be carried by horse and cart To the bottom of the
mountain to my lake To rest in peace there, is what I won't
forsake To lie in peace there and watch the seasons come and go
Makes me not afraid of dying, I'll rest peacefully and wait for
that first winter's snow.

—*Karen Minler*

Untitled

If only I could see what I remember.
As I walk along side of the river, no longer would it feel
like before. Only now it wouldn't be for granted.
The fresh breeze and rustle of the leaves, only
brought back tears of the fond memories, of a
child running on top of stones. The echo of cow
bells in the distance opened up the emptiness
part of a heart thought to be healed. I was
overcome when I stumbled only to remind myself
that I had overstepped my white cane.

—*Shirley Evans*

Shadow

He is my shadow
As I walk along the bridge
I am alone, although he is there
Waiting,
Waiting to take my hand
and lead me down
Down into the cold and unknown waters
And I, I flirt with my shadow
Taking my risks, soon to commit
Only my shadow knows all there is to know
and only my shadow knows the time
For my shadow is what makes my life precious
and no one knows it, until....
Until my hand goes out for his
And we begin our journey
This is my shadow
And that, that is yours.

—*Lori Rakowski*

The Wind's Tales

The wind is blowing across the hills,
As it has done since our time began;
I know if I listen to its song,
It will tell tales of my fellow man.

I know the world has sorrow somewhere,
When the wind moans and there is no mirth;
For death is knocking at someone's door,
And soon they'll rest in the quiet earth.

Again I listen and I can tell,
That the wind is warm and feeling gay;
So a wedding for some bride and groom,
Will be full of joy this happy day.

Then the wind softens as it whispers,
And somehow I know as it goes by,
I can hear the wind quietly say,
That soon a new born baby will cry.

So as the wind blows, we should listen,
And maybe take some time to ponder;
Always knowing the world has sadness,
Yet has its share of love and wonder.

—*O. Lillie Randa*

Death

When someone dies, reactions change
as you look on face to face;
Listening to the sad whispers of everyone's voice;
as tears drip down endlessly;
Not knowing what to say, or how to feel
But trying someway, somehow to make it through the day;
And then never forgetting, but starting over to a
Whole new brighter day....

—*Kristi Taylor*

A World Painted Black

Screams of silence echo in the wind
As molting currents of radiation flow
No time to think-no time to run
A man made demon-as vicious as they come
Bright flashes of colour striking our eyes
Colours we can't describe
Pain we can't feel
Because there's not enough time
Our shadows imprinted on the ground
Will lye lonely for centuries
As our silent screams echo in the wind.

—*Vicki Jurkovic*

The Bookworm

I know a little bookworm,
As pretty as can be.
She's always in the books, of the library.
Of course she likes to read, that's how she
   got her name.
But as I know she likes to glow, with the spirits of
  Mrs. Riddell!

—*Katie Szilagyi*

Untitled

The wind blew her long blonde hair,
as she sat on the old porch swing,
and as it blew through the open window,
the screen seemed to make it sing.

The wind whistled through the windchimes,
as they dangles so soft and free,
and it blew the swing on which she sat,
as it moaned and creaked with glee.

It made the waters ripple softly,
still blowing her soft blonde hair
it had the faint smell of rainfall,
blowing in the soft spring air.

As she slowly got off the porch swing,
went inside and closed the door,
the beautiful serenading wind,
soothed her and sang no more.

—*Trina Klatt*

Time Does Not Heal All Wounds

I look into her eyes and witness the panic there,
As she tries and succeeds in hiding it well.
But, I can see through the attempted spell,
A tortured animals eyes within the stare.

Holding herself responsible for a past,
Unable to save the innocent child,
Who was not quite beguiled,
By an adults love which held her hard and fast.

Drowning in a bottle, aids and abets the forgetting,
The only solace of comfort and peace,
From the endless excuses, her only release.
Never has a greater tragedy afforded such a setting.

Believing the disease to be part of the cure,
She embraces failure in an obscene dance,
Flirting with disaster through a manipulative glance,
Knowing that satisfaction is something she'll never deserve.

The battle is over and over again won,
As she slowly comes hopelessly undone.

—*Kim Rossi*

The Era

Yonder day drifts off to night,
As the sun fades beyond the mesa.
Shadows creep,
While children sleep.
Indeed, it is the era.
The rendezvous takes place - alas!
They dance amidst the darkness of the night
Vagrant in their thirst for life.
Fear not. Be still.
Await the silence of the kill.
It is out of love,
Not out of hate;
Your gift of life that they await.
The life of the dead —
For the dead stand alive,
With passion sweet.
Pulsating crimson with vigorous drive,
As they take the life that makes the dead heart thrive.
We softly weep.

—*Andy Stuart*

The Gift

The trees reach helplessly up to the sky,
As the sun looks down on them with pity,
While the man-made machines go speeding by.

Soiled snow melts in the dirty rivers;
Nature stained by human industry;
Underneath the trash, the weak brush shivers.

The rocks are the tombstones of dying plants
In a losing war against the powerful.
The wind gives branches a last chance to dance.

News of death is the cry of the black crow;
As the destruction of the earth grows.

—*Patsy Gervais*

Love And Living

I wander where the grasses and the nodding flowers bend
As they whisper to the breezes while they blow,
From far across the sea they come, across the plains to send
A stirring and a rustling to and fro.

Where fallen bark so crunchy as it crushes 'neath my feet,
Reminds me that the Summer's here once more,
And moist earth as it shelters in the shade of Summers' heat,
Will nurture little creatures on its floor.

And as I wander further on the hillside of our home
To the gully where the tallest timbers grow,
I feel a real belonging and no longer need to roam,
As I hear the sounds of nature high and low.

So come with me when morning sparkles dew drops by the way,
And share unspoken thoughts of love and living,
And of beauty that surrounds me, let us share this Summer's day
With thankfulness, because the Lord is giving.

He gave to us the morning, and the dew drops by the way,
He gave us the Summer and the Spring,
He gave us the song birds, and the Sun to shine by day,
But best of all, He gave us "A King."

—*Mary Johnson*

It Is There To Love

That feeling of togetherness that one feels
as those that survived the mowing
bullets of oppressors tow away with
solemnity the caskets of those that
succumbed to the temptation of
freedom.

That melancholy that diffuses the air
as comrades chant the blues of this
tormenting tribulation of life.

That undying zeal that emerges
down from the hearts which are
black with vengeance as they, those
oppressed join hands to topple over
the sinister minds that perpetuate
their suffering.

—*David Molapo Setsomi*

A Single Tear I Cry For You

A single tear I cry for you,
As we say good-bye.
This single tear I cry for you,
Knowing it was the truth you couldn't deny.
Those words you spoke so gently,
Seemingly from the heart,
Were nothing to you, but a bunch of words,
That's what drove us apart.
Another tear I cry for you,
Hoping you will soon find,
You don't have an obligation,
To her emotional state of mind.
You have to learn to let her go,
No matter how much it hurts.
Love is an everlasting feeling,
It doesn't come in spurts.
One last tear I cry for you,
As the smile on your face slips away,
All we can do is cry another tear,
Hoping to re-unite one day.

—*Jennifer Russell*

The Flight To Freedom

I know it was your courage that kept you day and night
as you fought against the enemy and freedom was your plight.
The battle left you many wounds as you marched without a sound,
for you understood the purpose that a soldier carrier on.
The battlefield lay open as you braced against the storm,
and your honour never left you as you fell upon the ground.
Another soldier stooped that day amongst the dust and ruins,
and the then he wept so softly as he gently lifted you.
And all around saluted as you breathed a heavy sigh,
a bugler played his horn from somewhere in the sky.
Although there are no medals to grace you as you rest,
today you earned your wings, you were carried by the best.

—*Debbie Palahniuk*

Nature's Fate

The tear drops into my hand
Becoming a mountain
Part of this land
As forests beg for mercy
At our continuing demand
When shall we stop at last?
When the heart of nature breaks like glass?
Then, see nature's wrath
Feeding upon the rot of shame
And so the tears of rain
Can never wash away the remaining pain.

—*Annette Jung*

Winter Time

Winter can be a beautiful scene
As you walk through a forest of evergreens.
Trees that are laden with new fallen snow
All the little snow birds flying to and fro.
Roads that are winding in a ribbon of white
For the snow is glistening ever so bright.
The sun is shining high in the heavens above
One can only feel peace and love.
This scene can change so fast it seems
That it will shatter all your beautiful dreams.
The sky gets dark, and looks real bad
For the wind starts howling like it was mad.
There's not a light left in the sky
Only dark clouds rolling by.
The sun is hidden out of sight
For it has suddenly turned to night.

  —*Dorothy F. Fowler*

The Change

"For perfection is not reality, but a word of false intentions"
ask me for who I am and I will say me, ask me for who you want
and I shall say nothing. Love me for who I am, and not what
you can perceive as change as I have done on to you. Try, and
I will try but to succeed, I can not promise see I fear not the
attempt in my own mind, But more the fear of failure in yours.
My change has brought me pride, but it is pride of silent
support. And when released in your vision, patience is not a
virtue but foreseen again is the chamber of disappointment.
It's not the words of hatred or criticism, but the words of
love and support that enables one to forgive and forget. And
it's not the hand that scolds, but the hand that holds that
secures the room for a second change.

  —*Daniel Brady*

Teatime

   "Is he faithful?"
Asked the contortionist's non-conformist wife.
  "Oh yes, yes, - faithful,"
vowed Mildred, her fez at an awkward angle.
  The two women hesitated to sip
  the coffee watered down with gin.
  "Only liquor in the house,"
  the non-conformist said earlier.
  "Oh gin, my absolute favorite,"
vowed Mildred, her lips devoid of color as they touched the
     brim.
  The two women lingered to eat
  the crackers stale from the wet weather.
  "Is he gone long?"
asked the contortionist's non-conformist wife.
  "Oh no, no, - not long,"
vowed Mildred, her voice as flat and bitter
  as the crackers and coffee.
  "Oh yes, yes, - faithful."

  —*Kathleen Dunn*

And, The Wind Blew

As I look out my window tonight, the stars are shining
bright. The wind hums us a love song. I say it's right,
you say it's wrong. How can it be, when we're made for
one another? All I'm asking is for you to be my lover.

And, the wind blew helpless and hopeless all through
the night. Standing alone shivering in the moonlight.
You've left me so hurt and defenseless. To make it up just
give me that sweet, special kiss.

  —*Kristan Riley*

Promise Me

Promise me that you will take time to look
at a clear blue sky,
watch while clouds go rolling by.
See them take form into birds, bears and clowns
and prance till the rain comes down.
Promise me that you will stand still
and listen to the warble of the Whippoorwill,
then quietly turn an ear
as the wind whispers through the trees,
and feel your cheeks blush
in an Autumn breeze.
Promise me that you will watch
the sun rise over deep blue water.
See the rays scatter diamonds and pearls
on shimmery waves
as they flow quietly
to dancing feet in the sand.

  —*Juanita Moore White*

Little Miss Destiny

Music floated smoothly down the warm long hall.
At its end, rain urgently pelted a peeling window pane.
There sat little Missy curled into some feline ball of sweaters.
Before her misty eyes, a dark wind rose from the north;
to snuggle with tall, proud trees in Yorkshire.
Then pass the blackened corpse.

Before midnight could come, her struggle was suddenly done.
She went to lick the father
Went and kissed the son
Packed her tired soul... walked away
into early evening sun.

Bemused had tried
Only to fail
This one tried so long and hard to hide
From what she had become:
That the wretched soul locked deep inside
Would never completely die

  —*Joseph L. Perdue*

The Sea

As I look out at the big sounding sea,
At the wonderful world and its beauty
As the moon glistens and shines,
I think, what a great country of mine.
As I walk along the soft brown sand,
I lean down and run some through my hand.
I think to myself, this is freedom that will always last,
Unlike the unfortunate past.
History runs through the sandy grains,
Always there through washes, winds, and many rains.
How fortunate am I to be alive today,
Not having to fight in wars that lasted days upon many days.
I am very thankful to be as free as the sea,
And to all the men and women who died for me.

  —*Karrah Shea Orders*

Keep On Trying

Everyone seeks happiness and success in life,
but only a few attain it with all the strife.
The road is long and difficult to travel,
with many obstacles in the paths to battle.
To reach the goals that we must set,
will require a lot of determination and sweat.
We must keep on trying and not give up or stop,
and we might be among the few that make it to the top.

  —*Kaufman Fischer*

A New Era In S. A.

That humid, cloudy, dark weather's setting which covered love,
authentic gift, freedom, and peace
with tears of lost relatives fighting for life,
   is lifting now.
The tears are being washed now by streams of love and peace.

A new dawn is about to rise in South Africa.
Mountains and rivers are sparkling with humorous stories
of past gone times.
Struggle for human rights
Miseries of oppression, injustice, anxiety-
like morning mists are lifting now,

People feel a sense of freedom as reasonable, sensible
compromise of conflicting parties takes place.
This is bound to be of use to the community.
The political parties are jointly working for resolutions.

S.A is entering a new stage of democracy.
Where there will be confluence of ideologies;
Wealth shared for the affluence of every individual,
   and peace,
Peace is coming soon.

   —*Sifiso Nzama*

A Lost Atom

Stifling thoughts and little dreams
Awake the past and what it means
Parents pressed on from distant shores
To meet and love upon these shores
Their dreams
               Atlantic to Pacific, oceans - crests, troughs,
                           waves and calm.
One would escape from grind and chores
And maybe find that glint of gold or better still
A lonely soul who shared with you, still another goal
To bear up, West Tradition high - and not a tear drop in his eye
But later on your family grew, moved on with better things to do
All was then within your grasp till fingers
Frail released their grasp
And now you wonder who you are, and why you really came so
   far
A hall of fame affirms some pasts but atrophy a shadow curls
To one more dream and the will to stand.
Before memory fades and all life has past.

   —*Dora W. Lequesne*

The Serial Killer

He rises to the sound of the setting sun,
      awakened by the nightfall.
His clothes are dark, as is his mind,
his intentions camouflaged by smiles, he prepares himself for
      the night.
Nobody understands his acts, nobody understands why,
      he moves like shadows through the trees,
         eyeing everyone he sees.
He marks his spot and patiently awaits,
      waiting patiently for any type of prey,
hoping she will be beautiful and hopefully come his way.
He traps her and helps himself, beginning only with a kiss,
      to him she is only one more mark added to his list.
He covers his tracks, and tries to make it home before the dawn
he has no recollection, no guilt, no shame at all of what evil
      he has done.
To him his acts were pure enjoyment, as he calls himself a
      thriller, but he is dark, he is evil, and inhuman,
         he is the serial killer.

   —*Toni Digiovine*

Our Dilemmas And Predicaments

Humanity leaned forward in manners lax,
Bags of plans to hang on racks,
But upright he stood and erect,
To make manifest the intended effects:
The dredged sea-bed of frustrations and regrets,
Furnishing sediments and dregs of wrecked events,
And to our pent-up resentments, giving vents.

Thus the bags' carefully contrived contents,
Like contemplations and visions beset by rents,
Go sublime and clean-clear out of reach.
Blending difficulty and ease, that none could breach
As the human knee, and his forearm's reach,
Which leaning, with ease brings within reach,
But shoots beyond reach, when erect to preach.

   —*Adebayo Olabisi*

Desert Storm

Once a silent, sandy desert
bare, naked and uninhabited.
Now, a crawling mass of life,
Tracks are everywhere,
A blanket of metal covers the once bare earth.
Tanks and jeeps,
Guns, guns and yet more guns.
Soldiers in desert camouflage
sweat and pant in the scorching desert heat.
They march on to face:
"The Mother of All Battles."
They are headed for Kuwait.
To free those held hostage
by the tyrancy of the Iraqi soldiers.
All these soldiers volunteered to lay down their lives,
to free a country
ravaged by hate and greed.
They are the heroes of today and tomorrow,
And will be remembered and praised,
Now, and till the end of time.

   —*Janeen Dugmore*

I's Still A Nigga

I's had called myself becoming aware of the things I's should
   be aware of
I's thought an edumacation is the way to be free of stereotypes
I's even tried to be a part of a multicultural thang
but I's kept finding that no's matter what I's tried...

I's Still a Nigga
I's still a Nigga, but not because I's be blacker, you's be
   whiter, or any skin tones
I's still a Nigga, but not because you's be richer or I's be
   poorer
I's still a Nigga, but not because of what I's know...but
I's still a Nigga because of what you's don't

   —*Khan LaVal Mitchell*

A Hero's Last Mile (President J.F. Kennedy)

As the slow roll of many a drum,
Beat sadly in the heart of the throng.
As a church bell in the distance rang,
Four wheels onward did clang,
Carrying a hero though his lips were sealed,
His life for his country had been spilled.
Onward, now nearer, there, just below a little crest,
A great man will soon be put to rest,
And for his many troubles and heartbreaks lot,
Lullabyed over by cannon and rifle shot.
Yet, may the eternal flame burning there by his side
Forever remind, that unto justice and unity he meant
The world to guide.

   —*Leon Bieganowski*

But Life...

If Apocalypse came knocking, I would repulse its might
because death would be interesting

but life....

Death is a cold black slate with no chalk
but life....
Death is cool, calm, collected and silent
but life....
Death is the flip side
but life....
is golden

Not a perfect coin, but like all golden coins
worth holding on to
if just for sentimentality
but never for greed.

—*Anthony Hiron*

Land Of The Giants

Canada - land of many peoples
Before the beginning of the white man on our land
Feather and laughing wooden mask hides our eyes
No one will see the end
For the winter wind changes our sight
How can I tell my braves?
Are their Gods stronger than ours or are they the Gods?
Are we walking toward our graves?

Canada - land of many peoples
We ask you a question -
Whatever the answer
You and I, my friend
Shall die and let the white man be on our land.

—*Alain Boisseau*

Because Of You

Oh why do we wait so long "Lord"
before we come to you our life has flown
so quickly by and our days are nearly through
Forgive us for in anger, hurtful words to
others we have said and pray they in return, will
forgive us for words you truly would never have fed
You have given us so many things in our years and they
were always free but we didn't keep our eyes open long
enough to notice, even thou we could see it wasn't food
for our table "Lord" we desperately needed the most
You are the one we must serve first as you are our
heavenly host "Thank you" for letting me tell others
the way I feel
"Forgive me," as only in kindness you want me to say
Everything from the heart, only when it's real
For this love you have put within me
is to pass to others to
and it's given so easily, and freely to all "Lord"

"Because of you"

—*Eleanor Leng*

Untitled

We seen you walk and talk and grow,
But little did anyone know.
That you would only be with us for awhile,
To hear you talk and see you smile.
You shocked the world and all your friends,
When you left us suddenly, never to return again.

You went to God, where there is no pain,
No work or struggle for worldly gain.
One day we'll meet again, my son,
To laugh and play and have some fun.

—*Claudia C. C. Sali*

Shadows

As the blazing afternoon sun
Begins to set,
Shadows are cast about the land.
Taking on frightening forms of a different world.

A world where the sun does not shine.
A place where creatures of the dark side emerge,
And play their hideous games of crime.

It is in this world where terror awaits you.
Watching every move you make,
Waiting for the right time to attack.

They cannot attack.
For things such as these only happen in dreams,
Or so you think.

These horrors are so true, so alive.
You feel their eyes watching you as you walk down a dark street
They are coming closer,
So close you can feel them.

But they are only shadows.
Taking on frightening forms,
Of a world way beyond our knowledge.

—*Crystal Lucki*

Silent Tears

Behind the silence
Behind those eyes that speak of grief, hidden sorrow, unspoken
     torment

Lies a shattered broken life.
So young yet so much heartache.
Fear cries out
Yet no man hears
For there, for all to see,
The countenance
That would belie the tortured spirit.
The forced smile.
That would attempt to hide the sadness deep inside
That would cover up the multitude of endless nights,
When beneath the veil of darkness, no sleep will come
To help obliterate the endless days
Days washed with secret tears.
From eyes yearning,
Longing, crying out.
Silent tears,
But no man hears.

—*Christine Field-Davies*

Up And Down

How many times have I been
between the devil and the deep blue sea
and I have known the right from wrong ever since
but not once have I tried to turn a deaf ear to the Lord
summoning me to stand back from the worldly things
wavered, he has comforted
tempted, he has strengthened my soul
failed he has forgiven.

How many times has he lectured me
through those lean years
divided between happiness and sorrow
gentleness and brutality
generosity and greed
prejudice and compassion

How many times through the ups and downs
I have faced days of hopeless drudgery
known moments of soaring adventures.
But above all and what's more
he has taught me to choose the common blessings
to all human beings.

—*Kalunga Makengele*

The Rose

Ah the rose has such beauty
beyond meaning, it lives with me
year after year, it dies in the
winter, and blooms in the spring.
Its meaning is of love, as it starts out, it's
so beautiful, but as it dies it sticks
your heart with prickly thorns. The rose
Does not live forever, as love can't, but as we
look at the rose fading away in the winter, once
again to bloom in the spring.

—*Janet Jorge*

Sick

Sitting on the window sill I see the world go by,
Big people, small tots, old people, lots and lots.
What wonderful life, so busy, so gay,
Everyone is running to work or to play.
Sunshine through clouds and through trees alike,
A young boy rides quickly on a new bike.
Cars are coming, a truck, a bus,
Around the corner approaches neatly a whole school class.
The mailman, the baker, a newspaper boy,
A mother and child with an old toy.
The postman brings a pile of mail,
And puts it in the box over the pail.
Then hurries on, to fulfill his round,
And slowly fall some leaves to the ground.
O, Lord, help me get back on my feet,
So I'll be able to join in the city beat.

—*Ilse Sante*

Summer Scene

A little stream trills a melody, to another sunny day
Birds sing sweetly in the trees, in vibrant symphony,
Butterflies and bees, flit gracefully on wing,
And painted in bright colours, the hedgrows flowering.
New mown hay and meadow-sweet, scent the summer air
Orchards warming in the sun, ripens apples, plums, and pear,
Gardens rich with colour, where the flowers bloom and grow,
It's like a picture from a story book in days of long ago.

—*Margaret Robertson.*

Invictus

Out of the night that covers me,
    Black as the pit from pole to pole,
I thank whatever gods may be
    For my unconquerable soul.

In the fell clutch of circumstance
    I have not winced nor cried aloud,
Under the bludgeonings of chance
    My blood is bloody, but unbowed.

Beyond this place of wrath and tears
    Looms but the horror of the shade
And yet the menace of the years
    Finds, and shall find me, unafraid.

It matters not how strait the gate,
    How charged with punishments he scroll,
I am the master of my fate;
I am the captain of my soul.

—*Adepoju Olabisi*

Untitled

Why do we need friends? Why do we need the air that we
breathe? For, oxygen only allows our hearts to keep pumping
and maintains the efficiency of our bodies; whereas with
friends or no friends - do our hearts still survive?

Where oxygen is concerned, it proves our interdependency and
chemical-physiological connection with the Earth. As far as to
say, with another human life, we embrace our bodily temples
with our duty and responsibility as off-spring of our Mother
Earth. We undoubtedly play as manual and human pillars for
those people whom share our Earth as brothers and sisters. Our
friends from the same oil feed from our earthly breath, word,
touch, laughter, - and above all, mind-communion.

The cosmic Miracle that keeps the millions of chemical
reactions of our Earth and private bodies to function - there,
in the same place, the level of understanding we give a
fellow-friend is somehow eternally buried in our Earth's soul,
heart's soul, and universal soul and blooms with new love, just
the same, everyday.

—*Jennifer A. Lee*

His Secret

The bared quill threatens to be inspired.
Bring forth the savage beast, he sits ready.
Yet he hardly notices as the words develop on the page.
It could be prophesy, although it resembles closely the
thoughts in constant motion, of a poet, as the sun sets.
His eyes show experience and consternation.
His visage is clearly troubled, but of what?
A world in turmoil? A dying planet?
Simpler.
Simplicity is his success and so the problem is alleviated
with a toothpick.
He laughs and mumbles to himself,
"Poor venerable flesh, don't you know?"
This statement he makes,
"The sun will set tonight and rise again tomorrow."
He died in his sleep smiling,
And he was right.

—*Lawrence Wegwitz*

Momentum

Relentless momentum of change
Builds in me again.
    Restless nights - sleep is light
        Dreams take flight . . . into the future

Uncompromising motion
    Like the ocean - pushes me into tomorrow,
    My soul speaks - I listen and move forward,
        to where I've been in another
            place and time.

    I recognize the signs.
Billboards of undirected thought
Green lights of unidentified emotion
    One-ways in different directions
        There are no stops.

I will lead and I will follow; and move willingly
    towards tomorrow - wondering where I'll be
        when I get there.

Sometimes a compulsion; always an obsession
    Life must be lived, everyday, in a way
        That satisfies.

—*Kalei Sherlin*

The Last Laugh

he struggled under his
burden
     reaching our for our help...
beads of sweat formed
    and r o s e
and flitted away
with s p r e a d i n g
wings: born
on these wings were the despairing
colors of desolation; his gutted
misery whined our ears in circles...
he always the origin of agony.
his broken voice demanded justice —
our justice demanded his broken voice...
tortured, he bleated for mercy, and
    like feathered rays it
tickled our lives: and we grinned.
he breathed softly   he died
and we laughed.
now he laughs last.

    —*Katherine J. Artishon*

Time And Time Again

Time passes slowly when we are apart
But goes quickly when we are together.
And each precious moment I spend with you
Are the only ones I remember.
"Always and forever," we often say
With stars shining bright from our eyes,
Yet that's not enough time to let our love grow
And it's already as big as the sky.
So when this time ends, life lost in dreams,
Another new time will begin.
A new world or place,
A new name or face,
I will find you
And I will love you again.

    —*Kevin L. Stackhouse*

Quadripeat

I really don't like to watch you
But I can't help it
I have lots of things to do
But I always dig it

You are covered by free TV and radio
And I can't stop following you
But when you are covered by paid cable
It is such a consolation as I am a fan without cable

But some people will talk about you
And I'll be glued listening for something new
I've never been to your basketball game
For your ticket is hard to gain

I have lots of works to do
But I always find time to favor you
Even if I missed you at broadcast night
There's always the newspapers in sight

How can I miss you Chicago Bulls?
As you build a dynasty 'round your walls
With your fourth try this year
As Pippen and company are ready quadripeat is very handy

    —*Joseph G. Lariosa*

Woman

She seems like the simplest creature,
But if you take a much closer look,
You'll see that you have been mistaken,
By the cover of a curious book.

For inside of her feminine body,
Is a heart that's so gentle and kind,
It sits like a beautiful oyster,
And the pearl is her love and her pride.

Give her warmth, give her love, give her friendship,
And show her that you understand,
And slowly her oyster will open,
And her pearl will now sit in your hand.

But be warned don't ever deceive her,
Or treat her like some kind of fool,
For that pearl will turn into a spider,
And its bite can be deadly and cruel.

So next time you look at a woman,
Your mother - your sister - your wife,
Remember this interesting poem,
And use it as a guide in your life.

    —*Chanel Charnley*

Praise To Donahue

Donahue's on our TV screen early morning
    but I'll be too tired to wait
So I'll just have to record it
    I think I will put it on tape

When his smiling face comes on, I'm delighted
    he is brilliant with all his debates
Such wonderful entertainment, he's worth every
    dollar he makes

The studios packed with its audience
    participants there, every one
There's all kinds to make up the party
    I think it is going to be fun

How I love all these open discussions
    Everyone has a problem it seems
There's a marriage gone wrong or a sex change
    It's all there on our screens

It's certainly controversial, with the
    participants there to be seen
And when Donahue talks to the people
    he charms them all when he beams

    —*Gladys E. Weaver*

Me - Me

I'm crawling for the toy
But I'm already there.
I go for my dinner,
I'm already sitting in my chair.
I cry from here,
I hear it over there.
When I look at me,
I get a stare.
When playing with my toes,
How can it be I see me exploring my nose?
I call mama, she turns around holding me -
The hair, the clothes, the same pink bows.
Mama now has picked me up -
I smile and touch...
I love me very much.

    —*Hope McNabb*

Take Me Back ——— Please

It's high speed, high tech, and turmoil
But I'll still reach age ninety or so
If I don't get blasted by a Captain Kirk
Or get nabbed by a U.F.O.

I was never dented by a one-speed bike
Nor crashed by a runaway horse,
But when driving or crossing our roads today
I'm on a perilous, adventurous course.

The Babe, the Gipper, Laurel, Hardy,
Just to mention some oldies by name,
Had talent and pride, not the aura of gold,
To gain seats in the hall of fame.

It's topless, bottomless, and singles bars
And even outrageous TV in the morning,
Riots, murders, inflation and strikes,
And incurable ills with their warning.

I can't agree with this lifestyle
So don't consider me a quack
When I say where's my ice box and radio
And please . . . please take me back.

  —Neil Horn

Remembrance Day

It brings peace to my heart, knowing they did not die in haste
But instead passed away victoriously
Young men just barely grown out of childhood, sacrificed their
 lives
Making freedom a simpler cause
Lying in ditches the cold water freezes right through to the bone.
To have to hide under a dying friend's body
to save their own lives, to keep warm, and for protection from
 the bullets.
Living their lives in the blindness of their blood covered
eyes, and the deafness of wartime melodies of orders to kill.
When times of war and death come into our present,
we should be reminded of the echoing gunshots
that continued long after the war was over.

  —Alexis Reid

Always Friends

It's time for us to say "farewell"
But it must not be forever,
We'll meet again, I promise you
Our friendship will not sever.

We've done things together, through thick and thin
We've never been apart
But, although we've been friends for several years
It's time to make a fresh start

You'll be going away and meeting new friends
You'll continue your life in a new place
But I promise that if you come visit me
I'll always welcome your smiling face.

It's going to be hard on both of us
But maybe it's for the best
Our friendship will not be forgotten
But given a "little rest."

  —Carrie Freer

Feelings

A thing of substance it is not
But more times over it is sought
To hold one's feelings in your hand
But really never beginning to understand
Feelings is only just a word
One's actions making them seen and heard
Feelings are just like the air
A presents around us everywhere
They get hurt, walked on and pushed aside
Showing anger, horror and one's pride
We know them no stabler than a cloud.
They are only what we make them now
Blown in the wind of life never solid
A mere word for something controlled by "you"
But that's another word

  —Larry Watters

My Walk With God

I wake up every morning with a smile upon my face.
But people always ask me, "What are you smiling for today?"
I say it's because I'm happy, just to be alive.
I feel the sun.
I smell the flowers.
And I see the clear blue sky.

"But how," they ask,
"Can you always walk with a smile upon your face?"
"It's easy to smile," I say to them.
"When God holds my hand,
So I won't get lost,
And leads me all the way."

"Is that why you smile every day,
In spite of what goes wrong?"
"Yes," that is why I can always smile,
As I go from day to day.
I put my faith in God.
He walks with me each day.

  —Judy Carris

In The Future

In hoping things will be serene and peaceful as in my dreams
but reality changes that theory so it seems
The bubbles in water that used to be blue
are now full of chemicals and none are safe to consume
We destroy each other anyway so fit with no regret's
given warning and never taken head
handing ourselves or our seeds of death and act blind and not
see, save of us glorified what we see on T.V.
in person it's totally the opposite and seems like we're trapped
Yet death is the only way out of a situation out of control and
 free!
I hope in the future my little cousins, nephews and
 nieces do see
That being good and follow what's right and no mortal man unless
 in need.
Die for a purpose not just because it was due
Live and have fun, enjoy the beauty of the world as I have to,
In this I pray the world will stay safe forever and a million
 days in the future....
  in the future I say!

  —Kevin Mitchuer

K And K

To be deep into your own troubles is one thing,
but to watch a friend in theirs is way too worse.
It feels like the advice you give doesn't work,
and even just being there isn't enough.

Relating or listening, all in all, I guess it's all the same.
If you've got something that has to be said,
I'll be there for you, cuz I'm you're friend.
Maybe it won't help, but it never hurts to try.

Don't mistake me for Superman, however.
I haven't seen enough to say what I think
the way I see the world is, therefore my words of wisdom
may not always ring true.

I do care enough for you, though,
that if you draw me into your problems
I'll go down in flames with you knowing that
I fell with a friend by my side.

    —Keven Miller

We Phobics

Folks may think we are cowards
But we're braver than most
We have to have courage
But we can't boast
We simply plug on from day to day
And enjoy our achievements come what may

About our achievements,
They don't know for sure,
About our trip, to the corner store
And what was even more braver then that
When we walked six steps from our house and back

If we had somewhere to turn
When it all started first
It wouldn't have gone, from bad to worst
Like a snowball it escalated,
To say the least we were very frustrated.

Now I'm recovered, and it's all a bit hazy
Looking back on it now, it seems a bit crazy
A bit of credit we secretly crave.
For making such effort, for being so brave.

    —Eva J. Clarke

Love Remains

They say love at first sight doesn't exist,
But when I first saw you
I knew I would forever yearn for you to be in my midst.
They say love is blind,
But up 'til now
My love for you has stood the test of time.
Because of love they say the heart aches,
But sometimes things happen for love's sake.
Although we both caused great pain toward each other,
Perhaps it is love in the end
That will bring us back together.
Although weaknesses have gotten in the way
For selfish gain,
Regardless what they say about love,
Love does remain.

    —Keith A. Paris

Summer Son

Running in fields of buttercups and sunshine,
butterflies whisper love is mine,
A kiss can be bliss,
An emotional train, a musical myth

Sing songs of love
Songs of peace

Let your mind take you to places unseen,
Criss cross skies of blue and green,
Where the trees breathe and hatred leaves

We will play like children,
We will return to beautiful memories,
Kiss the night,
Kiss me,
I love it,
Peace

    —Robbie MacMillan

To My Parents

My childhood was safe and protected
By caring parents who loved me.
They weren't voted on and elected,
They are parents because they chose to be!

It takes a lot to gain your kids' love;
Discipline, courage and hair pulling.
Kids aren't something you can just get rid of.
Being a parent can be grueling!

That's why I wrote this poem for you.
Your strengths and advice have carried me.
I won't take for granted how much I love you
This is one child of yours who is glad to be!

    —Kathy Beardsley

Amplitude Of Distress

I am constantly amazed
By the amplitude of distress
Which smothers me like a cocoon.
Every time I manage any forward progression
It seems to get overlapped by waves of despair.
This constant ebb and flow of the tides
Keeps beaching me with regularity
Leaving me floundering helplessly
On the rocks of frustration.
I pray for an alteration of the cycle
To allow me an interlude of peace
From the oppressive pounding of the surf
Before I am indelibly mutated by its force.

    —Jan Sutherland

Grass

It catches my eye a glittering
carpet of tears over fear of darkness?
lightness of day dries the grass
like the sun dries my tears over darkness
does the grass cry every night after
a day full of footsteps?
Gentle is the grace of grass
cut off, dug in, stepped on
the grace of the grass grows tall and green.

    —K. Smith

Twentieth Century Grandmas

"Don't call me Grandma," I heard her say.
"Call me Helen, Marion, Kate or Mae."
"Grandma means old and I'm not, you see."
"Don't pin a name like that on me."

No! Grandma means love, affection and poise
Symbolic of families to all girls and boys.
A link for the future with days that are past.
Without the word Grandma, some things cannot last.
Soon Mom and Dad other names will choose,
We'll have Bobs and Dorothys, Johns and Sues.
Respect and honor are lost in the game for
Such rewards are harmonious with the name.
If grown-ups are weak and can't bear their load,
Should we wonder why juveniles detour from the road
Of truth and honesty, faith and pride, when we
Have failed our role as guide.
The, "Don't Call Me Grandmas", I hope are few.
I'm not in this number, I wonder, are you?

—*June H. Van Ness*

Gloria

It was Feb. 10, 1993 that you, Larry and I came to be! As I
can see; I know it was meant to be! In my heart I wondered if
dreams really do come true! It is now unbelievingly true there
is Larry, I and you! The weeks and weeks of anticipation of
where you could be! Larry and I talked it over and over you
see! We had to find you as time was running out! The union
had to be the three of us with out a doubt! We were down to
days and then within a few hours! Oh Gloria, Oh Gloria, Am I
not going to be able to bring flowers! I had lived this dream
all my life, Oh can it be true! I have to keep pinching myself
have we really found you! Yes it just has to be, it has to be real!
And it turned out to be the most exciting feeling one can ever
feel! Can you believe it Gloria, Larry and I! The whole world
could have caved in, even the sky! I was on cloud nine that
day it was April 29th! Where do you start; so many people to
be thanked! I will never forget that first day, hour and
minute we met! Oh what lovely memories that will always be
kept! That day; Oh that day you opened your front door!
Larry and I were waiting with Love to pour! I stood with red
roses, Oh can this be real!

—*Jack W. Beamish*

Troubled World

All over this world are troubles galore
Can we survive very much more
The politicians make promises oh so bold
The outcomes of which makes our blood run cold
Tsars rulers dictators and kings
Have been the cause of some terrible things

The poor working folk and many we know
Slave for very long times with little to show
The rich never seem to care
Their cupboards are never ever bare
To prosper today to crime people turn
Then most of them find they have money to burn

Many also say religion is to blame
Thoughts like so are a terrible shame
The children today have something to face
The world is a shocking disgrace
These nuclear bombs may solve it all
Then we will have no troubles at all

—*Ken Dutton*

Can You Stop The World From Crying?

Can you stop the world from crying?
Can you help the nations dying?
Can you touch their pain and sorrow;
Promise them a new tomorrow?

Can you give to them salvation;
Bring the healing to each nation?
Can you speak to them with gentleness;
Show to all of them, God's tenderness?

Can you open up their eyes to see
Love and joy and peace eternally?
Can you wash away their guilt and sin?
Let them ask the Saviour to come in!

Can you open up their ears to hear?
Can you wipe away each little tear?
Can you give to them God's Holy Word,
So that each one has the message heard?

Can you let them know that God is near,
And that His love casts out every fear?
Can you stop the world from crying?
Are you really even trying?

—*W. Diane Van Zwol*

A Little Child's Wish

Oh I wish I had someone to play with
"Cause I'm tired of playing alone;
Oh I wish I had someone to share with,
My play time that I play alone.

It's so nice to have my own room
With all of my games on the shelf;
Oh I wish I had someone to share with,
My time, when I'm here by myself.

You can't know how lonely it is
With no friend to be at my side;
At a time when the sun sinks low,
And my thoughts run far and wide.

Is there someone out there who will listen
And be the friend that I need;
To share some fun and laughter,
And make me feel happy indeed.

—*Clarence Fountain*

Why Is Man So Cruel?

He who developed and shaped the earth, is he who is harming and
causing such hurt. He who is callous, feeling no pain,
destroying our planet, with nothing to gain. Killing our
wildlife, our water, our trees, killing each other, and yet, we
are he. This planet was kind, it let us survive, so why are we
killing it, tell me why? We are children of children,
grandchildren of kids, one day we'll have children, please
heaven forbid. Don't let them look at pictures in books, then
ask what they see don't let us have to tell them, 'that's an
elephant, that's a tree. Please people, please help us, from
explaining to them, that we destroyed our planet, without
thinking of them. that we exterminated the beauty, that this
planet holds, to clothe and to feed us, to furnish our homes.
That soon we will have taken every advantage there was, and
used up the little and finally lost. That terminal day on the
calendar past. We will live quite normally, it will be our
planets last.

—*Anne Thwaite*

Dead Apologies

We're sorry for the world today
Change is what we'd bring about
if all would be our way.
But we're long gone, far in the past,
With spiders crawling in our ears
and through our eyes back out.
Should we have known in those days,
something grand would have been done.
But none to much listen to ones
that have continued on their way.
Yes son, we're sorry for your world today.

　　—*Erinn Graham*

Christopher John

Child of the desert, reborn in the night.
Child of the desert, eagle take flight.
Fly on the mountains, forests, and seas.
Conquer those mountains, follow you dreams.
Christopher John fly free.
Sand on the dunes, blown on the times
Fill up the hollows, level the mind
Christopher John fly on.
Eagle of the mountain fly with the wind.
King of God's country, magnificent
Shine like the sun not too bold.
Clothe not your body but dress up your soul.
Dust on the mountain is not but the gold.
Search for the riches buried in soul.
Fly on the mountains, forests and seas.
Meadow below you search there for me.
Christopher John fly free.

　　—*Gloria J. Bryce*

Put The Guns Down

Lay down the guns you carry in your hands today,
children are hungry in Somalia, and Ireland
and in East LA,

Hands are far more beautiful carrying other tools,
like hammers and hoes or books for schools,

Enough children have died from hands carrying guns,
while mothers round the world mourn lost sons,

If we stop the violence we can do more good,
build more houses and lives and grow more food,

What good is the killing anyway?
They're still hungry in Somalia, and Ireland and in East LA.

Fine

　　—*Jerry A. Martin*

Count Conclusion

Please let me go with a lasting
close embrace　a sleepy sigh as you turn
around to slip away with
three whispered words of love
to fill my thoughts

And wrap me in the tender
beating of your heart so that I know
that parting could never be complete

for this earthly
one
could never again be
two

　　—*Marguerite Enslin*

The Things That I Dream Of

Laughter, lifting faces toward the sun.
Children in the rain just having fun.
These are the things that I dream of.

Mother's soft embrace on my bad days.
Father's face all creased with smiles of age.
Memories of youth drift through my mind.

Tears of joy and sorrow blend in time
like the changing faces of a mime.
These are the treasures I'm saving.

Electric eyes I met across the room.
The tingling magic of my favorite tune.
Inside my heart a blush that never fades.

The piercing cries of children in the night.
The peace that comes from knowing they're all right.
But fear for them goes on, and on, and on...

The soothing consolation of a prayer.
The warm and trusted friend who's always there.
These are the things that I dream of.

　　—*Joyce Holland*

How Can I Tell You?

Dear Children, How can I tell you that I love you between...
clean up your room, pick up your jacket and empty glass...
I love you, I love your so, children; how can you ever hear
the important words mid scoldings of, put on your boots,
turn off the nintendo, wipe your mud prints off the floor...
You forgot your lunch these again! Did you know these are
words of love? They say, tho quite ineptly, "I truly care"
How then, that you might understand, can I tell you how
very much I do love you, each of you... during the trifles of
day... How can you hear me over the running water,
the rattle of the dishes and pans, the doorbell
ringing, the T.V. blaring over the raucous music on the
stereo... Perhaps with patience you'll be able to hear
the quiet murmur of my heart... Sometime, Someday.

　　—*Kathleen LeCompte*

Forever

O sweet pain
come taketh me
and engulf my presence in thy grasp
of untold bliss.

No more would I wish
than for you to caress me
with your spines of hate
and I shall feed your everlasting hunger.

I am unworthy to feel such joy
but I beg of you
to release mine soul of dire cause
from this world of sick beauty
and allow me to grip thy gnarled hand
as I write my own epitaph.

I endow to you; my spirit,
and kneel forever in thy debt.
Forever....

　　—*Kristjan Jurgen Ehrenreich*

Earth Tremor

Earth Mother turning in your sleep,
Couched in the stygian darkness.
Lifting the massive pillars of the rocks
hollowed in crystal cave and labyrinth river.
Your stirrings rock this bed
as a great hand might lift to soothe me.
I hear you sighing in a thousand motions
through house and tree and hill.
Disquiet me no further with your reaching.
Hush. Peaceful be our separate sleeping.
Life's days are luminous in love's safe keeping.
I shall come in my own good time.

—*Anne Royle*

Labelled

He looks just like all the others.
Covered entirely in the hide of a cow.
Tangled locks beat his back with each progressing step.
Painted symbols of life cover his arms.
A familiar symbol etched on dyed cotton.
Tinted glass hides the gateway to his soul.
If only they knew.
People step out of his way and look at him with scorn:
    stereotyping his character.
Bum! Drifter! Vagrant! Less than human!
If only they knew.
In his heart is warmth.
A compassion for everything that breathes.
Gentle and caring.
He rides off on his steel horse.
They don't deserve to know the real person
behind the image.

—*Jeff Mayer*

Our First Snow

Our first snow it snowed the night before
covering everything pure and white.
It was so fresh and beautiful.
As we walked through the snow
holding hands. My heart beat faster
knowing this was a new beginning for
our new love to grow as one.
As we walked holding hands through
the snow it was like we were the
only two people in the world
in love. People would stop and stare
at us and we would laugh at them
knowing they thought we were crazy
for being in love out in the cold snow.
Because they never saw two people
kissing, hugging, and laughing and
playing in the snow like us
on the coldest day of winter.
I will always remember that
special day. I love you more than ever.

—*Julie J. Arrazola*

The Place Where We Live

This world has so much beauty that people
destroy every day.
We've got to stop destroying the world
and live in it day by day.
For tomorrow we'll regret we did not do
something today.

—*Kelly Myers*

The Spectre Of Hatred

Have you seen the skeletons in your closet
Cradling rotten teeth like pearls
The beat inside your spotless shirt
Choristers of the uncharted world

You have kindled the wicking of their eyes
Dwelt under their jingoistic skin
They bereaved chessboards of their kings
For this terra incognita to begin

You have set their Stygian tongues wagging
Moulded out of tellurian flesh
Hear the calls of this deceiver bird
Cantatas of an earth unblessed

Have you fathomed the well of their spring
Bearing fruit inside a maculate womb
Is it not the breath of all these things
For which peoples have been entombed

—*John Kramer*

Aids

Constantly going through anguish and pain
Cries of helplessness still remains
Immediately in despair I rush to his side,
praying that he won't relinquish himself to die
I patiently await for him to slowly fall asleep,
knowing that it is hard for him to relax because
his body is so frail and weak.
His eyes are like marbles, so big and round.
They tend to stand out all on their on.
His face is so thin all that can be seen is skin and bone.
Even though his body changes so drastically,
he constantly prays and keeps the faith.
For someday, some way someone would find a cure
and stop thinking that this disease is to be ignored.

—*Karla D. Baker*

The Day Of Remembrance

Why my strong but sensitive
Culture people
Sent our brave soldier into battle
For their countryman
To witness the distorted facts
Of a cruel insensitive war
For reasons unfounded
For mankind weep
Soldiers defeated helplessly
Loss vehicles
Man of battle hemorrhage from weapons
Our soldiers rigorously write phrases of file
On mount for one person
But on the gigantic wall
Tangible experience the loss for love
Yearning for compassion.

—*Shirley Rogers*

Secrets Of Janice

Secret by secret I eagerly explore the
delights of your beauty.
Each secret, new and old, brings us mutual pleasure.
My lips mark the secret places so I'll return to
each of them with ease.
As our secrets grow so does my passion — and my love.

—*Joe Toy*

Dandelion Magic

Dandelion magic... you know what I mean...
Dandelions bloom for the gypsy queen...
In the summer grasses,
Along the summer lanes,
The dandelions beckoning the gypsies once again.
Dandelion magic... you know what I mean...
Dandelion perfume for the gypsy queen...
Soon the shiny wagons
Will rattle down the roads,
Coming to our village with their swinging, tinkling loads.
Dandelion magic... made for you and me...
Bringing in a summertime full of mystery...
Warm enchanted evenings,
With fireflies aglow...
Following in our dreams along the roads the gypsies go.

    —*David Mathias*

Sunset

The red of the sun is as deep as a rose.
Darkening a jetstream into shades of crimson
Waves and wind orchestra soft, soothing sounds,
Creating romance - a stage of error.

There is no sorrow nor earth's deadly pains,
Suffering is oblivious for those on the sand
The sun sets the mood for the two at that moment.
Urging them on to things out of hand.

The sun will go down but passion goes on
Lovers for now, let the hourglass go.
If only they'd look past this intimate moment
Look at the future - see through the lies.

Feelings between people shift like the sands
Memories of past moments ache for relief.
Promises shattered - hearts broken
A moment of paradise ... All fetime of reality.

A consequence of one careless moment.
A child conceived - a lover gone.
The error of choice, a fate of romance.
In the heat of the moment - the red of the sun.

    —*David Roberts*

Friendship

It's funny to see how people walk in and out of our lives,
Day after day.
It's funny to see how close we can become,
Without really knowing how close at all.
And seeing how people grow up and change,
Yet still being the same person we've known all along.
No matter the miles,
The memories of friendship are never forgotten.
If we keep in touch,
We will never walk away.
We only realize how much more meaningful our time spent
    together will be.
Saying good-bye is never easy,
Yet I smile, still shedding a tear,
Remembering all the memories,
As you walked into my life.

    —*Julie Sturzenegger*

On His Passing

Grief. It weighs upon you like the skin of some long dead thing
Decaying your mind, defying all healing,
Stifling, smothering, any hope of joy in the life that remains
Without him.
He was the centre of all being,
The world turned, the sun, the moon, the stars were there.
Only by his presence on this earth.
Yet, though he is gone,
It is certain that the same sun will rise and set
Day will become night, the same stars appear
Could it be that he is now a part of them?
That this ritual continues to the end of infinity
Only because his soul, and all the others, from time unspoken
Have given them their powers,
The awesome power of death?
If, for just a moment, I could see his face in the midnight sky
Perhaps this sorrow that secludes my being
Would fall away
And I could learn to live again,
Without him.

    —*Elinor Orvis*

Culverted

I've walked the run of buried rivers
deep river, dark river, river underground.
No surface thing, this proserpine dream
a willing traveller of this Acheron stream
I rise to the occasion and navigate down.

The Cerberus flood snaps wet and wide
to discourage those seeking entry inside
I throw my sweet courage into the maw
my feet seek stability on a water-bound floor
I slip into the dark, into the dark I'll hide.

But everything reverses and stumbles
my light glows dim and the world turns wrong
I must find a new direction, for my orientation has gone
who's that? Who's there? Who am I?
Confusion becomes my element, armed such, I press on.

A monster from the void may bear my name
Cobwebbed and dirty I become the deamon of my drain
Salvation comes with the break of concrete night
Around the final corner I'll be granted back my sight
Embraced by a forgiving sun, and returned back to life.

    —*C. L. McKenna*

Woman

What else besides a body and a soul,
Did God insert into that mixing bowl?
To make what man feels goes beyond the norm,
That hides itself beneath the female form.

What marvel is a woman to behold,
As she grows, her mysteries unfold.
One moment, loving, thoughtful, kind and nice,
The next, a snarling vixen, cold, like ice

Her moods change here and there, just like the wind,
One moment she's o.k. and then you're pinned,
Against the wall, her tongue like steel, it whips,
The next she's in your arms; caressing lips.

peculiar as they are, the world could not,
Exist if God had womenkind forgot.
There's nothing else like them upon this earth,
And nothing is worth more than they are worth.

    —*L. A. Wells*

Moving On

The things he said about me, I heard them yesterday,
Did he really think he'd get away with all he had to say?
Is he so insecure that for a moment's false applause
To get someone's attention, rumours were his cause?
I can't believe he'd hurt me, I thought he was my friend.
I had the greatest trust in him; to him it was pretend.
When you believe in someone like I believed in him
It's hard to think of having faith in friends again.
The things she said about me, I heard them just today.
Did she know I'd hear the praises that she sent my way?
Does she think so much of friendship she'd pass the good along?
It could not have come at a better time, it helped to make me
    strong.
And though I was hurt by the false things my other friend had said,
The compliments she gave to me took away the dread.
It helped me learn that friendship, though sometimes may betray,
There's enough good folks to take a chance and welcome them my
    way.
I'm not in control of the good or bad that people speak of me,
But I am in charge of what I tell, so careful I will be.
It's a terrible thing to hurt someone through what we say and do.
Since life is short, then we should try to be a friend that's true.

— *Marilyn Edge*

Near Union

We approached each other
Did our best, ran as fast as we could
Used all means of transport
Traversed thousands of miles of ocean and land
Across nations, cultures, and time
Paved new roads, built bridges
Learned to fly over rough terrain
Dug tunnels under impassable reaches

We were drawing so close
It was dark, the territory unknown
Was our compass broken
Was the marriage doomed by design
I could hear you calling my name
I could feel your heart beating
But our roads never crossed
Our tunnels just missed within inches
We never met

— *Haim D. Heilprin*

Ode To Humanity

To the multitudes of hungry waiting to be fed
Does it matter what the language or what is said,
Or the colour of the skin upon the hand that brings the bread?
Do they care?

To the homeless and the hopeless that roam the streets at night
Does it make a difference in what language come the words
to soothe the fright.
Do they care?

To the silent ones upon the Hill, with epitaphs on stone.
Regardless of the language, the final rest is home.
No more will they roam.
Do they care?

To those who care enough to share their abundance with fellow
    man.
Or care whether their neighbour needs a helping hand.
The language is LOVE.
Yes, we care!

— *A. M. Klaus*

Quarrel With Me

Quarrel with me
Don't slide beside me.
I need an itch,
Be a rough board.

Quarrel with me
So we can carry the bowl together,
The fruits of knowledge above our heads
Never knowing the truth
But pondering on the quality.

Agreement solves nothing the mysteries of life
Murmur your true ideas
And the road will be shorter
And the house may be haunted.

Don't necessarily believe every word I say.
I could be wrong
    or lying.

— *Vic Farrell*

For Jeff

In any case I find myself
drowned within your eyes -

If there was a place where I could walk
I could surely learn to fly.

If I could dance with solemn praise
I would learn each step, as not to harm
Your soul my friend, Is something that
I sometimes seem to forget.

Crystal dreams elude my heart, although I
listen to your words, to my ears and to
my soul they are the most beautiful
that I have heard.

Yes, my friend, the end is near, but
never say goodbye because someday when
there is room to walk, you will surely
learn to fly.

— *Kristin Hogner*

Heartfelt Whispers

Whispers from the heavens echo in your mind
Dusted by the angel's wings a peace you want to find
Haunted by sweet memories of a love taken away
Shadows creep inside your mind a darkness seems to stay
A wish to join the lost love drifts on through your heart
You question higher beings you do not want to part
The sun beats down upon your face a tear falls from your eye
You gaze up to the heavens to ask the reason why
Surrounded by a living love that tries to ease your pain
Your heart still feels wounded the tears of grief still stain
A sacrificial dreamland has become your living state
Do stormy clouds of emotion paint the picture of your fate
Can you not awaken from the pain so deep inside
Rise above the hurtful memories you've tried so hard to hide
You must treasure every moment and keep the good times in your
    mind
Let your feelings guide you and what you seek you will find
Believe in those who love you and take their helping hand
Together they will guide you back to the living land.

— *Karen Bielecki*

...Yet They Let Their Leaves Wave In Honor

Agonizing screams of a now barren path
Dwell in a place where their rings were of many.

The others look on, as their cries meet the wind,
While indescribable anguish fills the untamed air.

Malady-stricken roots replaced their majestic appearance,
Yet they let their leaves wave in honor.

All was pacific, 'til the slayer came roaring,
Taking their lives down as well as their glory.

Afflicted with agony, their leaves, they did cry
In melancholy harmony as the wind whistled by.

...And yet, they let their leaves wave in honor.

Compassion shown by a small, blameless child
Imagines the cruelty that was performed by Man.
With rare understanding, he felt their sorrow and pain.
He noticed their splendor as the leaves ruffled about.

He then turned away in grief and in heartache,
Yet looked back, only to find their leaves still waving in honor.

...Then the wind died down, and so did the trees...

— *Kiersten Wells*

My True Love

The longing for love when a teenage.
Each boy, one meets! I wonder?
He's handsome! Can this be he? But, I'm told, you know,
without a doubt, when true love comes.
Oh! the anguish, the fears, the longing, the despair
will he never come? I had my photo taken
brought it home for mother to see. So excited was I.
To my surprise a young man was there tall and fair.
Mother introduced us. Electricity was in the air.
He wrote to mother, asking could he court me?
Oh! the excitement the bliss, really is this true?
Have I really met my heart's desire? Who sets my heart on fire.
A smile, a touch, makes me all aglow. Morning noon and night,
he's in my mind. Oh! To be with him all the time.
Such ecstacy, two hearts entwine the gentle caresses,
endearing words of love. Sets my heart pounding
Oh! yes! I know.
This is my true love.

— *Gladys Davenport*

The Beauty Of Harmony

Myriads of tiny prisms — raindrops sparkling in the sun —
Each refracting, each dispersing sunlight's ray — and yet as one
They're reflecting all the colors of the spectrum in the bow,
Brilliant in its appearance to the human eye below:

Seven bands of awesome splendor set in heavenly array —
Each depending on the angle formed by raindrops and the ray;
Each within its range of wave lengths, although none is seen
  alone —
Blending into one another so the spectrum can be shown.

Wisdom is revealed in nature — all the raindrops harmonize,
Yielded wholly to their function as they beautify the skies;
None is seeking recognition, none desiring its own way,
All unite in corporate beauty sunlight's glory to display.

Oh, that we could be as yielded as the raindrops in the sun —
Though a multi-cultured people — as a nation we be one;
Still respecting one another's unique heritage in life,
Blend in harmony together, void of tension and of strife.

As we lift our visions higher, to the Maker up above,
We can look at one another as the objects of His love
Who are fashioned in His image, after His own likeness made,
To reflect His holy nature in our corporate accolade.

— *Agatha Ratzlaff,*

Shadow

I am but a shadow of pain, I roam the
Earth along side my face of joy. I ask
for no sympathy and non I'll give. I carry
my legacy deep with in. I see a smile and I
give a grin.

I'm but a shadow of joy, I roam the
Earth along side my face of anger. I
seek no comfort and show no love. I beg
for no forgiveness and I'll die with my face
and live by a "shadow"...

— *Julie Vasquez*

Who Is He?

Anger...stretched taut like a rubber band
  edges are fraying

my heart is unsure
  love has turned to fear

Snap, snap, snap ......
  the band is dissolving

Fist slamming against walls, fists against palms
  shoulders heaving with frustration

helpless and scared ... I don't know you
  a stranger roams my halls

silence or shouting, where's all the laughter?
  life's becoming a wicked game

I want to tell you don't fight me, "Don't give up"
  "Fight back against despair"

but I'm so tired ... and I'm not sure I can care.

— *Marlene Lapointe*

Eleventh Hour

Eleventh month
Eleventh day
Eleventh hour

Trenches left unwanted souls laid wasted
Crosses standing alone wreaths are laid

Flags at half mass poppies close to the heart
Only metals shine for the lucky ones
Remembering blood in fields
The lost ones what was yield

Crippled lost limbs
Telegrams to next of kin
Deadful sacrifice to win

Eleventh month
Eleventh month day
Eleventh hour

— *Guy Chambers*

Fallen Angel

A look of despair, gives a sign of uncertainty
Falling short of our hopes and a step behind our future
You reach as high as you can, only to retrieve a cloud
A cloud leaves you thinking with nothing secure to grab on to
You fight through the fog to find a place to start
A touch of a hand leads to a clearing of the mist
Ahead is a beauty, a body of lust
Behind is the past, the reference of which we want none
The coming together, brings the body of one
The glistening about is the spark of our affection
And the road to our beginning leads to the sky of our no end

— *Kenneth D. Grune*

Picture

A paper, upon which reside two figures, hangs upon my wall,
embroidered with but a simple wooden encasement.
What is seemingly two dimensional, for myself,
reaches far beyond a limited realm.
Not emotion, nor object, nor spirit but an indescribable,
mysterious being stretches out from inside the print
and softly, with gentle fingertips touches my soul.
Of the two present, one stands boldly ahead of the other,
with an emanating confidence, an apparent pride and selfless
concern for what stands behind.
She is the unconditional protector.
Firm in her stance for all eternity.
The other - unshaken, innocent form clasps her hand in
uncertainty for what she senses lies before her.
The observer of that portrait, I now long for that comforting hand
to guide me through the path of a bitter, indifferent world.
A common box reaches out with the same gentle fingertips
revealing that what was once thought of a past life
is yet attainable in struggle, in ease in life.
Eternally I retain the protector - my loving sister.

—Kimberley Thom

Sojourn's End

Once stopped and no longer looking, I came to the end of my
searching...

For all my life I have been lost in the looking, saddened by the
endless searching, grown so tired in my heart's travelling,
my heart's yearning, worn so by my soul's wanderings.
Trekking through wanton desire and longing lust, losing sight of
what, in my mind, I knew I must...to find one of love of I, one
of I to love.
Left frustrated in the "why" of "not I"; left empty in my endeavors
but persistent in my pursuits; on my knees, the numbing pain of
my begging fall, brought me to surrender my sojourn.

Resigned and resolute to refrain from this folly, to live loveless,
honestly lonely, to bide my time hopefully confident
that love would reveal its hiding and find me out.

Once stopped and no longer looking, I came to the end of my
searching,
stumbled over and fell into the love of you...your loving of me.

Oh to live now, loved and honestly loving, to hold you as my
treasure and our lives as an endless adventure...oh the journey of
our endeavors...the pursuits of our joys and pleasures...the
vision and direction in the loving of you, your loving of
me...hand in hand, stride in stride, as one, building a rainbow of
memories on which to ride, to its glittering end.

—Jonathan Lawrence

Empty Circle

Empty circle spinning;
endless turns colliding with nothing.
With each turn fear eats away at my heart,
spilling love and desire from its core.

With each turn reality slashes me,
tearing away the mask that once hid and protected a love.
A love so pure that it allowed the depths of my soul to
bear its secrets and show its true face.

Spinning faster and faster no control, no limits
just a void where dreams come to die and love is forbidden.
Closer and closer with each turn,
strangling that hidden lust that can never show but a pulse.

The grasp upon my heart now tightens,
squeezing out the love that I can no longer hold onto.
Setting this captive love free.
Empty circle endless spinning.

—Jennifer L. Hale

Today We Become One

Throughout life we have been two separate
entities. Walking in our own paths, weathering
our own storms, jubilating in our own victories,
and always looking toward the future.

Today which was once our future has now
become a reality.

We shall now and forever more walk our paths
together, make the sun shine where there is rain
and excite in the victory of having done it all
together.

For today we shall no longer be two separate
entities but become as one.

—Kim C. Curry

Sadness

Sadness like an invisible silken mantle
envelops me and its frigid fibres
fill my soul with a shivering emptiness.

Not the warmth of the sun,
nor the beauty of a spring day
could take all this misery away.

Not the peaceful emerald meadow,
nor the sapphire sky
could make such a feeling die.

Not the caress of a gentle breeze,
nor the calmness of the seas
could bring laughter instead of tears.

Not a million years
could erase
the memory of your face.

—Rita Quadrini

Solid Like Rock

A rock is the Lord in contemplative form,
Eroded by fire, water, and storm,
Hard to the touch, cool to the feel,
Infinite in wisdom of what it deems real,
Peaceful and solemn, impervious to pain,
Life will thrive on it, again and again,
It exists through the ages, asks naught in return,
Touched by a constant lack of concern,
Eventually it withers to a small grain of sand,
Destined to accept its fate at hand,
Countless and infinite as the sand of the sea,
No limit to its levels of increasing hierarchy,
Continuing decline, growth in reverse,
The rock comes full circle, in the same universe.

—Glen H. Isaacs

Why I Love My Mom...

Mom's are special to a 'girl' like me,
Especially when you're 60 and she's 83.
She has never said "I" -
She has always said "We".
Her kids and grandkids dine there still;
They love it because it's homecooking and no bill.
Chocolate chip cookies are the ones she makes well;
They give her home a really great smell!
She's shared her wealth and love and not complained,
Even when she herself has suffered great pain -
We're a very lucky family to be blessed, you can see,
With a Mom who never says "I" but always says "we".
Happy Mother's Day, Mom!!

—Judy Othmer

Mother

The tender cares and whisper sweet,
eternal look of care when our eyes meet.
From first step taken to this day,
I drained her youth and turned her gray.

With undaunting spirit she braved the task,
never showing but a cheerful mask.
My pains and troubles she bore these too,
but always brought my faith anew.

She asked for naught and gained little more,
my needs came first, foremost and before.
The sweat, the toil, tears and grief,
she managed these with firm belief.

No gift, no gold that I've attained
can bring back the essence that I've drained.

She'd welcome back this task anew,
help me and mine, yours and you.

She slipped quietly from this life to the other,
this silent soldier was my mother
　　—Jerome F. Anderson

The Girl Inside

You say that you still love me
Even after all these years
You tell me you are sorry
And you've cried a million tears.

After all this time I wonder
If what you say is true
There was a time, as we both know,
I thought the world of you.

So many things have happened
To change the both of us
I wonder if it would have worked
If we'd tried hard enough?

You got tired of waiting for me to just grow up.
My very best of loving you was never quite enough.

Too bad it only happened the day you said "Good-bye"
You knew full well that when you left I'd only sit and cry.

Now the girl's become a woman and the tears have long been
dried. But sometimes when I see you -
I'm still that girl inside!
　　—Norma Peters

Wanda

　　　She always smiled,
　　　Even in the hardest times,
　　　Love was what she lived on,
　　　Not on gifts, Nor on money,
　　All she wanted was to be loved,
　　With Wanda it was give and take,
　　But more giving than taking,
　　　Wanda was taken from us,
　　She was grasped by the clutches of death,
　　But was also given no boundaries,
　　　　She is free,
　　　In the world of infinity,
　　　She has no worries,
　　She was too good for this evil world,
　But Wanda has a place in all of our hearts,
　　A special place in everyone,
　　We will see Wanda again,
When we are grasped from the clutches of our loved ones
　　　We will meet Wanda.
　　　On the road to ETERNITY.

—Susan Bissonnette

My Soul

My Angel, my Treasure, you have no idea how much I miss you
… every second is an eternity …

I long to see you, to hear your voice, to hold you in my arms,
to marry you… I have prayed so hard for the most wonderful
relationship between a man and a woman… that you would be my
friend, sister, companion and spouse… I long for the moment
when we will be one and our souls will be united…

I hate every centimetre which separates us… and yet, we are
together… neither time, distance, nor any physical obstacle
can come between us… I thought I had loved, but I never knew
I could love so intensely… to the very depths of my being…

From the first moment I saw you, I was captivated by your
delicate, ethereal femininity— your tall, elegant figure,
green eyes, blonde hair, and your sweetness, innocence, grace
and serenity— reflecting your inner spiritual beauty…

The more I saw you, the more I loved, respected and admired
you and now I know that, despite my unworthiness, we were made
for each other, my soul.
　　—N. G. Mazhar

One Last Kiss

The crowd grew silent when he appeared,
Everyone stood and stared at his tears.
No one ever thought they would see him cry,
But now thousands of tears filled his eyes.

No one dared to breath a word,
Nothing… not a thing was heard.
He bent over to give her one last kiss,
There was no one as dear to him that he would ever miss.

He loved her with all his heart,
But now he knew it was time to part
And as the cold wind began to blow,
He watched her casket lower into the snow.
　　—Sherry Jardine

Stillness In The World

The world in a sense, is of a gossamer kind
Everything in it, even man crumbles-
Everything that arises passes away,
The hatred, the anger, the conceit
Which, too, is but fleeting!
Though this infirmity has the world
In a grip of turmoil and strife,
And has inevitably robbed man of the vision
That otherwise would make for stillness of heart and mind
And make him shine with lustre and thereby view the world
With so much radiance, serenity
And perception, and so hearken to
It and its myriad beings, as one should,
(And as wise men of yore had entreated!)
With love's nobility in one's heart
That makes for compassion for all that lives!
And in this boundless happy mindfulness,
The world will stand still!
　　—Mahendra Siriwardene

Seasons Of Life

The spring of life begins at birth
Everything is new and joy abounds
One is dependent on others for every need
Home - food - warmth and loving care.

Summer comes and new doors have opened
Starting to school and preparing for the future
Bringing its rewards and times of anxiety
Some days bring mountain top experiences.

Autumn is a time to spread your wings
To plan for the future and reach for the stars
Life is enriched when true love is true -
Searching and finding happiness and success!

Winter arrives too soon!
Years have been rewarding in many ways -
A special time to reflect on the seasons past
The season of giving thanks - to God be the glory!

—*JoAnn Porter Cagle*

Thoughts On Bosnia

Midst sounds of warfare people run the gauntlet of the warring
faction. Neighbours lay dead, why? Fetching water was their
innocent action. Children in hospital, their eyes and limbs
missing, how pitiful their cry. The unanswerable call from a
mother now forever in that home in the sky. They all need to
stay fresh, more clothing is wanted, the conditions so torrid.
Discomforting skin sores and lice, oh it's really quite horrid.
In the darkness of night can be heard many cries of pain. Only
explosive flashes light up the mud and the rain. Forcibly
confined bereaved families hungry and dejected become weaker by
the day. Soon no food and no water at best they can pray.
News of Convoys always coming yet still held up down the road.
Would be a uplift of spirit to view the U.N. unload. Hurry
politicians can you sit there in ease? While around lay the
dead and the wounded and those yet to die from disease.
Families turned out of their homes, see the dehumanised faces.
Looking back at the burning, now just a memory of life with no
traces. Each face tells a story with lines so gaunt and
harrow. Most left with no transport how precious the wheel
  barrow.

—*V. Allsop*

Time Spot

Cool winter breezes embrace me—
Fade the creak of a rusty fence.
The sky above me—
A giant blue face with no expression.
Blades of grass dance like a
million crazy elves in garments of green
around a tree, a father figure,
above me with swaying hands.
Here I sit alone in time,
Billions of faces pass unnoticed
Hidden by ignorant eyes, condemned
Only to know a few.
News created every second
Things to know and understand
To live by, appreciate, respect!
People to honor, cherish, deeply love,
Laws to obey, a God to be worshipped!
Yet, here I sit
Alone in time—
The rusty fence still creaking.

—*Jeremy Herring*

Yesterday

Yesterday was a terrible mistake, I wish I could have
fallen asleep to wake up and find that it was all a dream.
But I didn't fall asleep and it wasn't a dream.
My dark, dreading life has disappeared since I met you on that
cold, windy night in August.
My feelings for you grow and grow, although you only considered
me as a friend or as a sister that you never had.
Lying in bed at night and listening to the music float throw
the room was a wonderful feeling, but it was not the same
without us sharing the feeling together.
Without you by my side, I feel heartbroken and lonely.
And now your love has grow into me like it was a part of me,
that no one could ever break the love I feel for you.
If I should leave you, upon your wake, forgive me.
So If we are separated we'll always be together,
in our love that we may cherish forever.
Now, today I'm feeling proud enough to say, "I love you!"

—*Kristy Dozar*

America For Me

It's fine to see the Old World and travel up and down among the
famous Palaces and Cities of renown, to admire the crumbly
castles and the statues of the kings.

But now I think I've had enough of antiquated things, so it's
home again America for me.

My heart is turning home again and there I long to be in the
land of youth and freedom beyond the ocean bar where's the air
is full of sunshine and the flag is full of stars.

Oh, London is a man's town there's power in the air, and Paris
is a Woman' town with flowers in her hair, and it's sweet to
dream in Venues and it's great to study Rome, but when it comes
to living there no place like home.

So it's home again, home again, America for me, America for me,
we love our land for what she is and what she used to be.

—*Helen Ramirez*

The Wolf

Branches rustle,
Fangs glisten in the moonlight
A furry body streaks through the leaves
The deer become tense
The elk sense something evil
The moose are nervous
As they all stand still as statues
The hunter approaches

He strikes!!
As the deer scatter
Two get stuck in the deep snow
Then it comes...

The howl, the fearful howl
The howl to dread
The howl that calls the pack

Stuck deer become dead deer
A feast for these ferocious hunters
The hunters that haven't eaten for days
Lean ribs showing
The pack settles down to feast upon their kill

—*Rick Anderson*

The Old Religion

Moving life trees,
feet slow and holy —
alive like breath that disappears on the wind,
unseen but sure in its existence.
Reborn like the tide out of death,
so innocently expressed
licking the feet of the old women
weaving the sand into winter.
That is the old religion
flying like the sun silvered,
a child's toy.
They believe
the Earth speaks in native tongue —
ears and fingers pressed to the ground,
the new forest of words runs like a lynx.
With hands closing like whispers the hymn is lost,
those books of shadows,
feasts of eyes creating names
from absences of light.

    —*Wendy C. Foster*

Life

Life's passing moments become memories

Behold the world around us
filled with the unforeseen
coming, like silence in the night
vanishing quickly before our eyes

The sandy shores have no consciousness
of what lies ahead
the waves rear up, and
the cadence of the water abuses the shore

We all have red lights within our lives
dormant becomes the wheels of our mind
our memory is absent of thought

Exposure of the green light
activates our minds
therefore, life becomes a challenge,
unknown before the world

    —*Joanne Jackson*

Extracts From "Summer's Song":

Sprung from a million sunsets
Flew the dove on feathered wings
Down to a driftwood forest
Where the nightingale still sings
Dreams you cherished forever
Where the silent waters flow
On the other side of this mountain
Grew a lover's dream.

You are my reason to begin again
In you I've found my self
Now there can be no end
You've turned my nights to bright new days
In you I see my self
Now there's a better way

Treasures lost
And treasures found
How our dreams abound
Through sleepless nights
And endless days
We have found our way.

    —*H. Pistorius*

Dreamers

Dreamers are the envy of all. The rose petals on life's garden
floor. They are clairvoyants that dance to a different beat.
Trying to right the worlds wrongs, through pens and pretty
words. Cloud watchers ever looking for that silver lining.
With witty pseudonyms and rose coloured glasses, to protect
their naive innocent ways. They make fantasies, mixed with
reality. We the readers, hunger for their works and escape.
Escape to never never land, ruled by unicorns and daisies.
That brings the would be, wanta be, to the isle of sane.
Stories of magical mystery, and miracles by little gnomes,
seems to draw the days strain out as a bread an mild poultice.
Dreamers are here to stimulate the young, with wonder stories.
To accelerate middle age, and keep it from going mad. And
rejuvenate the old, showing they still have worth. A breed
unto themselves providing the elixir of laughter. Opening
the minds door to invaluable awareness of life. Speak to a
dreamer, listen intensely, read with the utmost absorbency, and
know you are better for it.

    —*Jonny C. Tryon*

Hip Hop

Mutha Africa.
Flowing beats.
Hearts and soul into one's verse.
Way you talk, walk, and even dress.
Hip Hop is universal and showing no shorts toward racism.
Divided into many types of music (Jazz, R&B, Rock, Funk).
Slang poetry, a black man's constitution.
Kickin lyrics that excite and make a crowd jump.
Total devotion to Ghetto cultures.
A desperate cry for the man's ears to listen.
Getting at societies own doings.
Fills an empty space which education can't give us.
Hip Hop in rap is like putting the sugar in the Kool-aid.
'Coz when you taste it, it's so sweet.
The speaking of the mic...
The scratches of the turntables...
Rap artists are the Malcolm X's and Martin L King's of
today's generation.
Word Up!

    —*Jamal Sampson*

Belize

Oh land of multiple rivers
Flowing towards the sea
Of frolicking boats of laughter
As far as the eye can see

Oh land of beautiful women
Of races, colour and creed
United in that bond of fellowship
the Creator has decreed

Oh land so blessed and bountiful
Where fishes and boats abound
There is happiness, yet the danger
That lurk in deep dark waters there

Oh land of wonderful birds and flowers
Exotic fruits so rare
Of creatures not seen by the eyes
Of animals even that fleetfooted deer

What more could man desire
Beneath the clear blue skies
To set his heart on fire
In this land they call Belize

    —*Verna Coombs*

Dreams

The dream of a crystal voyager was
flying through my mind,
Visions of the wordless kind,
Colours that have no name,
Fires dancing with no flame,
Friends they were not people,
Nor smiles upon your face,
Invisible they were, no colour, form or race,
No boundaries to hold me,
Nobody to caress, nor arms to enfold me,
Laughing, crying, living, dying,
Whirling in a maze,
Wandering in a haze.
Drifting through the sky,
Never wondering why,
Always flying high,
Knowing the answer to every question,
So never asking anything,
Just passing time dancing with the king.

—*Julie Cliett*

Love's Quest

To find oneself on a quest of self discovery, a thousand
fold easier than to find love.
To find an angel of the moment to inspire me is as easy
as to lift a feather compared to finding love.
To set sail in a tinny ship on a mighty sea has no risk
compared to the risk I take to find love.
Book of love I'm not yet written on your pages, sea of
life I'm not yet upon your shore.
Storm of desire pushes me onward through the ages, sea
of fire surging through my soul.
A few fleeting visions pass before my eyes, indigo clouds
laced in cobalt skies.
Fading dreams no longer lead me to despair, Love is in
my heart seems strange to find it there.

—*Jeffrey W. Ford*

I Could Kick Myself

I could kick myself, really kick myself
    For giving you all those phoney lines
Had I known how it's really being oneself
    I'd never have put on that false act
I'll never forget the day you left
    Said you were tired of my cold shoulder
I've never stopped feeling so bereft
    Of the one deep down I really loved

I could kick myself, really kick myself
    For the self sufficient image I held
Often one brings troubles on oneself
    So I have learnt the hard way I guess
For since you went I'm always sad
    For me life is no longer worth living
And only one thing can make me glad
    If you could once more come back to me.

—*Suprosa Martha Achieng*

The Sirens' Song

The Sirens' song, I held it in my hands
for just a brief, oh such a brief moment in time
then it was gone, I felt it brush
against my skin, my face, my neck
untouched though touching.

I shuddered, cold sweat retraced
the movements of the song
and "help" I stammered, "help me",
not knowing what I meant,
touched but still not understanding.

I held it in my hands, the Sirens' Song
and its dark powers hugged me close
for just one moment while it lingered on my skin
with it was gone the danger and the fear
and then I understood —

Sometimes the hollow echo of the Sirens' song
touches my heart and so brings back
just one brief moment of my life
that held a promise and a light -
and all is gone.

—*Beate Jones*

To Find A Dream

To find a dream
for that is what we're really after.
To find a future
in which we can explore and grow and share.
To find a life
that is peaceful, yet a challenge.
To find the questions that lead us to the answers.
To prioritize and choose that which to commit our very soul.
To give our lives to a destiny where our potential never dies.
To close our eyes after looking in every corner.
To find a dream
in which we all could live.

—*Kimberly Smith*

Our Wedding Day

Our love is here to stay;
    for this is our wedding day.
We will be joined together;
    like two birds of a feather.
There is nothing like our love;
    pure and simple like that of a dove.
God, family, and friends give their blessings;
    for this unity and love that is everlasting.
My heart is yours and yours is mine;
    we will be together til the end of time.
We promise our love til death do us part;
    for we have each other's heart.
Our love goes deep within our souls;
    our love will be cherished and continue to grow.
Our love is here to stay;
    for this is our wedding day!

—*Katie Stewart*

The Stallion

His eyes are big and filled with hatred
His long gracious ears are flat against his head
Like a mountain that eroded away.
His name is like lumps of coal sitting in a straight line
While his small delicate head
Is held sooo close to his chest.
His nose twitches at the sent of man
His mouth foaming, while waiting
— ready to charge.

—*Jessica Hrigora*

Untitled

Her soul rides solemnly to the sky,
For today she will die.
The Angels of mercy are close at hand.
She is sure to obey their every command.

But I must cross the river Styx instead,
For "I" was the evil in her head.
With a grin on my face I made her insane,
I smiled and laughed as she endured the pain.

So, for this hellish deed I must pay,
With my life?..... I can not say.
I shall roam for eternity here,
And I'll drown for ever in her bitter tear.

—*Joann Hamrick*

A Voice In The Past

I cannot touch you, I cannot reach you,
For you are now but a voice in the past;
Your words have been taped in the cassette
Of my mind. Yet I see you in the things I do,
In the tears I shed, in the dreams I dream.

Oftentimes in the midst of work
I stop and reflect upon your words.
Their meanings now have changed.
I see you now in a different light.
I understand you now and because of this
My tears come rolling down, unashamed.

Sometimes your words are the very essence
Of wisdom - the wisdom of the ancients.
You who loved me now bequeathing to me
To pass on to posterity this wisdom,
Let me share your secret - was there also a voice
In the past whose words were taped in the cassette of your mind?

But there are still the dreams to dream,
The loves to love, and I will meet you again
In the future they call eternity.

—*Goon Fatt Chee*

Neglect

The graveyard stands deserted and forlorn,
Forgotten midst the ravages of time,
The tombstones tumbled awkwardly askew,
The weeds in riotous profusion climb,
Invading sacred places stealthily.
The rampant tendrils smothering embrace
Enfolds the long neglected crumbling stones
And softens them with cool protective grace.
The long lank prickle seeded yellow grass
Grows thickly round the lonely rotting tombs,
Encroaching deep into the private past
Of long dead sleepers in their silent rooms.
And silence reigns, no bird song fills the air,
No visitors to bring the touch of love,
Only pathetic scripts in flaking words
And here and there a cracked symbolic dove.
But these were loved ones once, alive with life,
Bursting with hope, spreading their wings to fly.
Why do they lie forgotten and alone
Whilst selfish, thoughtless people pass them by?

—*Dick Hyam*

Productions

To create a life a seed is sown
    forming an animal, babe or flower
Beauty and elegance eventually shown
    a little seed with so much power.

So small to produce a flower display
    and vegetable gardens so green,
Tomatoes and fruit trees in grand array
    tended by gardeners so keen.

An animal born tiny and wee
    from a little seed to gigantic sizes
Hard to imagine when roaming free
    beholding Leopards, Panthers and Tigers.

A tiny babe from a seed to be born
    leaves the night to enter the day
As from his haven he is torn
    to make an entrance only his way.

These productions grown each from a seed
    so minute with magical intent
How sad that one cannot be found
    to give us a peaceful continent.

—*Irene Duggleby*

Delicate Crystal

My life has been like delicate crystal
Fragile yet beautiful inside
I've been harmed and almost shattered
Though I have kept my composure and pride

People have touched me in many ways
They've hurt me often too
I've remained in my destined nature
Though sometimes tinted red, sometimes very blue

I often feel as though I'll crumble
Fall apart to an early grave
My life is like delicate crystal
Easily broken, easily saved

—*Karri A. Hujus*

Listen, Canada, I Am Your Heart!

The Native in me cries out from the dust!

Listen, Canada. I was here to welcome you. I married the
Frenchman, I bore his children. Our daughter loved the
man from Britain. Their marriage produced many happy children.

The French in me cries out from the dust!

Listen, Canada. We appreciated the differences in the family.
We celebrated our festivals together. We spoke kind words
to each other.

The British in me cries out from the dust!

Listen, Canada. I speak to my daughter. You remember, my
child... it was not easy for me to express my love to your
mother, but you knew she was so much a part of me that to lose
her would kill me. Tell them my daughter, though I do not
speak with their emotion, I love them, deeply.

Listen, Canada, I speak now!

I who am Native and French and British. I do not war with
myself! Do you hear those who speak from the dust? Do you
feel the presence of the Spirit who created us?

Listen, Canada.

—*J. Maria*

Mr. Bachelor

Right now you're trying to run
from love and what it means.
You don't want commitment
You can't even share your dreams.

You keep playing Mr. Bachelor
"I'll never get married you know"
Of course you still want lovin'
That's the only time you love me so.

You say you really miss me
Even though we spend weeks apart.
How can you miss someone you never see?
And you say I hold the key to your heart!

Well Mr. Bachelor you'd better go play
Cause this girls heart wants someone true.
Commitment, marriage and family
All the things that don't suit you.

Go now, still scared and immature
For you'll be sorry in the end
'Cause when you grow up and want true love.
You and I will just be friends.

—*T. Cleghorn*

The Romance Of Fall

As the sun takes the morning
frost of the earth.
It shines a beautiful light on
the golden fall trees.
The day rustles the leaves from
tree top, to the ground.
People walking through the piles of
leaves, listening to the crunching sound.
Another beautiful fall day gone by.

The evening clouds all roll away
as the sun sets for another day.
The dancing lights in the North,
make even the coldest nights seem warm.
The stars above shine so bright
I close my eyes and say good night.

Another romantic fall passes up by,
soon the winter is in our eyes.

—*Geraldine Stang*

We Settle

Examine your life from a distance, and question the
fulfillment. As life passes ever so quickly, the ability to
achieve your personal goals becomes a race against time. And
for whatever reason, it appears that father time is so far
ahead, that you find yourself in a continuous struggle to
catch him. And thus the introduction of the conflict. Your
mind gives you the reassurance of your past achievements, but
your heart sends to you the feeling of failure.
And as father time continues to stay ahead, your goals now
change, from the sometimes unthinkable, unbelievable, dreams of
a boy, to the more subtle, conservative, attainable desires of
a man. And with no regard to the fulfillment of our childhood
dreams, as all men eventually do, we settle...!

—*Julian Pere*

Father Of Mine

Father of mine, feelings of rejection has appeared, for you
gave us none of your time, leaving us glassy eyed and teared,
you have not filled the "fatherly role," for years, I set you
high on a pedestal, but it was I who felt like a fool,
waiting for you to come around, you took away our smiles, that
left the frowns, I missed out on those special moments between
a father and son, how those six years have passed and went, you
are not miles away, as you have entered my thoughts each day, I
do not understand, and probably never will, a broken sidewalk,
with indentation footprints of my father, to which I will not
repeat nor fill, father of mine, years have passed, and so has
time, for the stone, I will not cast, fingers will not point
for the quilt or blame, nor heads held low, in the darkness of
shame, for I am your son, your eldest child, and not the only
one, as I speak from my sister and I your role is never ending,
so lets tie the knot together, and give it a try, my sister,
you and I - father of mine!

—*Cindy Glover*

Agoraphobia

At random moments you can hear her pacing, pacing on panes of
glass. Like a bewildered felon of a lost colony - pacing
lightly, tensely, endlessly: You may have met her in the 70's
when disco dazzled and she was the shimmering one. Moving with
abandon - dancing with the prettiest men, laughing, rippling in
white silk. [And] when the party was dying, she was still the
stylus for jimmying and jamming, sipping light fruity wines
with serious minded Europeans; being both artist and canvas.
Something or someone slept too harshly with her - mentally and
physically she eased down. Some say she had such promise,
success in sweeping segues, her hair up in lights. Others say
she was in 5 auto accidents - shattered glass and blood in her
hair. Life that she had grasped at so furiously for began to
threaten her. She came home. And began to try and piece back
the fragments with Freud, paste and glue. Now she sees no one.
The essence of her fires has withdrawn and chilled. Neighbors
hear her typing, typing late into the night. Some say she's a
writer. Others say she writes to her one true love.

—*Joy M. Nitta*

Untitled

Falling silently
Glistening moisture rolling down the face,
The salty taste of tears
Plays on the mouth,
And the heart is broken.

An aching throb deep within,
A sadness needing release,
A pain that seems never ending.
For when the heart breaks,
The soul shatters.

An unexpected happiness
Erases the pain,
Releases the sorrow,
And pieces the soul back together.

A smile brightens the face,
The tears have dried.
For when love appears
Nothing else matters!

—*Kimberly A. Charboneau*

The Rape Of Melissa -15 Year Old

Her footsteps echoed on the stones, the street was darkened
gloom The shuttered windows here and there, just slivered
light, no moon. Her heartbeats quickened, a gasped surprise
at each and every noise "no harm can come, I'm not afraid, my
home's beyond that rise. I know it well each crack and rail,
I'll laugh at this with friends" but silently she raised a
prayer, as ghostly mist descends. On cushioned soles he leaped
behind, her throat was squeezed, arms held His eyes glowed red
as he tore her dress sweet nakedness revealed. He licked her
face her eyes her breast his hands dug flesh, so gruesome
Intent upon his loathsome quest, the savagery was awesome. The
pain that tore her loins her legs the brutal way he hit her
His teeth sank into softest flesh her body just got weaker.
She struggled with her last resource her legs just free, she
lunged His strength prepared, his lust aflame her strangled
breath expunged. He strapped her fast, his thrusts went deep
his breath was foul and grey Her tortured gaze in muted plea,
stones pierced her as she lay. His sated torso learned aside,
a knife flashed deep then shallow Her bruised flesh, blood,
mud, collide she will not rise tomorrow.

  —Ruth Cruz

Letter One

These are trying times my children.
Gone are those days when I, your provider
felt no fear for food
now, I fear, my children, you inherit my fear.
My children these are hard times
When the lines for food are as sure as day.
New days bring new hopes
But food lines bring resentment and frustration.
These are despairing times my children
when 'guns' mean more than food.
This is the price we pay!
These are trying times my children
When hunger caresses stomachs.
My children, these are times
to fashion in you, courage
to live and see new days,
to shun fear and despair.
Remember my children
New days bring new hopes

  —Hugh Todd

Big Island Mother:

Thoughts upon viewing Kilauea Volcano at Kalapana, Hawaii

The Greeks called her Gaea, the great Mother Earth
 gone away, some thought, in the twilight of the gods
  but here she floats, face up upon the sea
the long white mounds of her breasts
 bold and naked 'neath the sky
  neither hidden nor dead
 living and breathing
  trembling and bleeding, in constant labor
recreating herself, birthing new land
 black and viscous, red hot
  birth blood hisses and steams
in the moist hands of the midwife
 billowing announcements of nativity
  to mortals
 who know only death
  and do not understand
   destruction of the temporary
    is creation
     of the infinite

 —J. M. Malinowski

Jesus

I was born in a stable, lived humbly,
graciously, yet you glorify the rich and the greedy.
My skin was dark, my eyes were black, yet you
paint my skin white and my eyes blue.
Prejudice runs even in your paintings of me.
Religion was to bring you together, not apart.
Everyone is welcome in the church of God.
The greatest gift is the priceless gift of love,
Yet you materialize the true meaning of
Christmas so much.
You wear the cross on your necklace,
But do you carry my words in your heart?
I was crucified on the cross,
but you crucify me again when
there is hate in your heart.

  —Renee D. Parsons

Grandma's Place

The best times of my life, were the ones I had spent with
Grandma. The fondest memories of her, were the ones we spent
in pender Harbour. From her quaint little cottage we could
see, the whales jumping and playing out in the sea. We spent
hours and hours, just talking beached combed the beach, while
we were walking. We swam in the ocean, fished from the wharf,
and watched the ships move slowly in motion. As we watched
from the shore, the waves dancing in the sun, I remember them
looking like thousands of diamonds. It's hard for me to
believe, that it was over twenty eight years ago. And now my
Grandma, has lost her glow. Her memory is going,
and so is most of her hair, and now she just sits, in her old,
old chair. My love for her will never die. For at times, when
i think of her, I would just like to sit and cry. For in my
heart, I have this lonely space, and I have named it "Grandma's
 Place"

 —Debbie Otway

The Wind

The wind in the past
had no cries nor lies.
The present wind brings terrible frightening cries
with drops of blood and lies...
lies of race and hatred.

This wind carries blood from the frightful cries.
How do I know? I've seen the blood.
It's left behind, and one day I know the wind
I know the wind will show up with cries
and terrible lies.

I will be in its path every day...the terrible wind
brings terrible cries and frightening lies.
Will the wind ever let up and the sun shine
brightly upon us?

I hope the future winds bring sounds
of laughter and peace.
For life is not worth taking—
but is worth living.

 —Kevin Everett

The Eternal Light

As we walk along the river bank. The breeze blows through her
hair. The sun shines a path of light through her heart. Her
hand in mine, I can feel the warmth of her Soul flow through
me. We sit on the warm sand.
She lay beside me. I roll over and press my chest against
hers. As I gaze into her eyes, I see the wild winds of love
blowing the dust of fear out into the purity of the air that
circles around us. My lips touching hers I taste the sweet
incense of her smile. In her mouth the Valley of words that
want to be said. Hushed by the aaah of welcoming love.
As her legs reach for the sky, our bodies leave the earths
sandy surface. The clouds whirling around us. The clashes of
thunder echoes within us! Her heart beats wild with Passion.
For she knows I am her light! There is a sudden rush then
all grows quiet. The darkness surrounds us, and all is
peaceful, for the love inside us protects us from evil. There
will be no scratch or brake, for we posses the eternal light.
For that, the quest is made, there will be no end!

— *Jeremy T. Girtz*

Silent Tears

The way life has been for me
Has left my soul a desolate place
To ponder about what it must feel to see a smiling face
The hurt I endure can never be seen
For as I look in the mirror
It's plain to see
The pain I have endured for all these years
Is slowly killing me with these silent tears
I wish to be happy like everyone else
Yet I can't for I can't see myself
As the darkness sets in and I fall asleep
A deep sleep filled with dreams
And once again as darkness nears
No one can hear my silent tears
For there will be a day when the pain will end
To fall asleep and never wake again
The misery suffered throughout all those years
And nobody heard those silent tears

— *Joe Gonzales*

Needing A Friend

Everyone needs a friend and I hope you'll be mine
You're that special kind of friend who lights up the darkness of
time
Without someone like you I don't know where I would be
Somewhere out in the depths of the deep blue sea
Once I had many, but now they are few
Where are they when I need them is all that I knew
I wish I had met you in days long gone
I wouldn't be here for what I have done wrong
Remembering the day spent with you, laughing and playing in the
park
When it was over I was left standing there in the dark
Wishing I could reach out to those memories of days past
Bringing joy and happiness to my heart that will last.

— *Michael Morales*

From Either End

Read this poem from either end to
have some fun with words that blend.
Take the words down, out, and under,
and place them with frown, pout, and wonder.
Now you can continue this wordy game
with lots of words that sound the same,
but with paper this short and space so little

If I continue this pace, I'll lose the middle.
with lots of words that sound the same,
Now you can continue this wordy game
and place them with frown, pout, and wonder.
Take the words down, out, and under
to have some fun with words that blend.
Read this poem from either end

— *Judith Baker*

College Bound

You're leaving us tomorrow and we've never been so scared.
Have we given you the things you need to always be prepared?
To say no to things that are not right and yes to those that
  are good
To know the things you shouldn't do and do the things you
  should
We've had eighteen years to mold you, but have we done enough?
Will you be gentle when you need to be and strong when life
  gets tough?
Have we shown you by example the righteous way to live?
To take what life has to offer, but be kind enough to give?
As parents we can only hope that we have always shown
The way to live a moral life now that you're on your own.
We love you more than life itself and have always cared.
Is it now our own self-doubts that make us feel so scared?
Be an individual and don't give into the crowd.
Conduct yourself in a manner that will always make you proud.
Live life to the fullest and be the best that you can be.
Although we hate to see you go, we must now set you free!

— *Judy Schmidt*

Homeless Man

Things were good, for a while
he had reason to laugh and smile

But times got tough
and things went bad
he lost everything
that he ever had

Lost his job at the local mill
said he was too old, said he was over the hill

Owed some money to a shark
lived his life in the dark
on the road with no place to stay
people wouldn't give him the time of day

Had no home, slept in the gutter
got so cold it made him shudder
ate the food that he'd found
lying there on the ground

As time passed on so did he
forgotten by society
All he had to leave behind
were the empty dreams of a homeless man

— *Michael Adams*

The Lost Memory

Walking past her room,
    he hears her call his name
He doesn't stop to see her,
    because he knows she's not the same

She can remember his name,
    but not remember his face
The illness, took her mind,
    and left without a trace

She never will remember
    the love that she once knew
But it doesn't really matter,
    because there's nothing the doctors can do.

He knows she won't improve
    she'll be this way until she dies.
And while he can't believe it,
    he won't fill his heart with lies.

So although it breaks his heart,
    her room he will pass by
    —*Kelly Armstrong*

Here But Gone

I speak his name,
He knows me not.
His face is here
His eyes are gone.
His mouth speaks words of nonsense
to this modern era.
Are thoughts in his mind
the ones that I hear?
Who snatched away the pieces
that forms the foundation?
Does this jumble make sense to him?
Only self-conversation is his fulfillment now.
There is no key,
and there is no tear;
except for mine.
His world is his.

    —*Ida Donovan*

One Smile

The girl and her baby, sat alone on the bus;
    he looked so..content, with no signs of a fuss.
His eyes...were closed tightly; and he didn't realize,
    his mother holding him closely, held back tears
within her eyes.
Did she wonder where his father was? and if he even cared?
    Does he know the warmth, and tenderness...
these two bonded...people shared?
I think he is not man enough, to come forth for his child;
    he needs his freedom in this world, to go on being wild.
Does she know that I am watching them, with warmth and
    understanding? I see the love she gives to him, that is
so..undemanding. She looks at me, and then looks away, as a
    smile grows on her face; and I know the smile I had for
    her....was in its rightful place.
As I get up to leave the bus, and these people...I'll see no
more, I know in my heart...she'll be happy in life,
    with this child...I have watched her..adore...

All it took was a smile...from a person who dared,
    All it took..was a smile..to show that someone cared.....
    —*Michele Green*

God

God is the one that created us all
He made us short he made us tall,
He made us look different but some the same
We even have our very own name.

He made animals such as a dog
In the sky he made the fog,
He made the birds that fly in the sky
And water on the earth so it's not so dry.

God made the earth as green as can be
And blue which must be the seas,
He was as careful as he could be
And put everything where it should, like me.
    —*Katina Rice*

Don't Quit

Stand firm when the enemy is at his best.
He seeks to destroy you and will not rest.
At that time you are weak,
And like a babe you seek
Comfort in another's breast,
But, just use your super wit, and don't quit.
The cost-of-living gets you down.
You often fuss and wear a frown.
Sometimes you wonder what's going on
Since there are those singing a different song.
The dollars slips by, and you want to sit
But stand on your feet, and don't quit.
All around you seem dark
The street, the alley, and the park.
There's no ray of light
Where you can plant your feet and fight.
Day and night come with the same plight
But, somewhere, there's a useful kit,
So, use it wisely, and don't quit.

    —*Josephine Lamont*

Class

The predator glides into the room
He waits, waits for his prey
Prey that is not as gifted
Gifted in vicious humor

He strikes
Holding the remains of life
The life that was his victim
His helpless prey

The caretaker looks on
Sitting in her cushy chair
Does she try and stop the slaughter
No, she is too busy drowning in her own rancid apathy

The prey tosses and turns,
Trying to escape this nightmarish hell
With ignorant comments smashing
Smashing away the life

The prey lays lifeless
Lifeless from the hurt
The hurt, the pain and the torment
His work is done.
    —*Karen Elizabeth Cash*

The Halo

Oh! My goodness what will I do,
Headaches galore, oh! It's sore,
"Go to the doctors," he said to me,
When I told him of the halo I'd seen.

Glaucoma the doctor said to me,
Take this letter to casualty,
Tests were given, drops installed,
Acute glaucoma if I'm not so bold.

As time wore on, my head it ached,
I'm sorry to say, you will go blind,
Operations are best to help your case,
Oh! My goodness I'm going blind.

A year gone by, and I can see,
Oh! Thank heaven for the emergency
Operations given by the consultant for me,
and now I can carry on writing for thee.

—*Mary Josephine West*

The Fall Of Romance

Standing below the night,
    hearing the prophecies.
Loneliness
    is only what you make it.

Raindrops,
    surrounding you,
only get you wet if you
    want them to.
The wind,
    shooting through you,
only makes you cold if you
    let it.

See,
    this is Mother Nature.
Embrace the rain and
    wind.
Be one.
Then kiss them...
    full on the mouth.

—*Susan Garnier*

Enchantments

This forest does hold many wondrous sights;
Heaven beholds its splendid creatures
I can walk through here; eyes wide, spirits high
awaiting their secrets to be told to me; to enchant me
I am breathless as a dove whispers in my ear;
her golden feathers sparkling in the sun
A winged horse is soaring above the clouds;
he is swift and strong, yet graceful
A deer grazing in lush green grass kissed with dew
looks up at me with her soft brown eyes;
welcoming me to her home
Spread your love through this ancient land, glorious creatures
Show me how to believe in this magic that surrounds me;
Show me and I will always remember, in my dreams

—*Chanine Honor Pederick*

Though I May Not Come Back

My love - I must answer the "Bugle Call" -
Hence able bodied youth must go and all;
Sigh not but pray for me to our maker,
That I may come back one piece and sooner.

Our Motherland calling defend her shores not alone with many
many in the same shores; all response willingly without murmur,
Though enemies - raring for slaughter.

Our duty to defend Democracy - Japs, may soon attack
us without mercy; youth will go for the initial battle ...
Well engage them for prolonged struggle.

Though friendly troops - ten thousand miles away - Do our
able best to hold them at bay; God willing our action we'll
be able to disrupt their well prepared time table.

Be consoled - love you as our native land but the call to
duty is now at hand; defend Democracy - second to none...
Matters not for her sake I shall be done.

Ill equipped and trained but we've got to go - more than
willing though life I might forego; Motherland in need may
soon be attacked. Don't cry be brave though I may not come
    back.

—*Antonino E. Najera, Sr.*

The Sorrowing World

The world stands upon a brooding precipice
Her eyes with sorrow filled
Her hands pluck at the strings of peace
Her arms hold countless killed

Her fingers caress the sodden mounds
Graves too innumerable to count
And even as she ponders
The cost in humans mounts

Her ears throb from the pounding guns
Evil hovers where once lived joy
Her feet wade in rivers of blood
Tentacles reach out to destroy

Her habitations desolate
Her seas suck foulest air
Protestations silenced by command
Leave her heart in spasms of despair

Oh world, I weep at your destruction
Man sees your loss as gain
But I see a day of retribution
A night of endless pain

—*Anthea Elizabeth Leah*

Untitled

I guess this is the best way for me to say good-bye,
for the pain that is in my heart and the tears are in my eyes.

I just can't handle the pain that you make me feel,
so I must leave your life and hope that it will heal.
Don't think I didn't love you or even didn't care,
for this feeling I feel inside was hard for me to share.
Sometimes I wish I told you how I felt inside,
then this day would not have been a total suicide.
So I must now let you go and hope that you will see,
that the reason for my pain is just because of me.
I will always remember the special years that we have spent
together, you will always be in my heart and in my mind forever.

—*Gary Everitt*

This Little Girl

Here is the girl with no future ahead
Here is the girl who doesn't sleep in a bed
She lives in the cold streets of London near the docks
This poor little child lives in a box

Abandoned when only a babe in arms
This little girl has no skin on her palms
Worn away by the frost and the cold
This little girl looks twenty years too old

Only four stone and losing weight fast
It doesn't look as if she will last
A meal for her is some drunks wasted curry
This little girl will eat anything and not worry

Have you ten pence please she is often heard to say
But no one ever answers, they just walk away
Only yesterday this little girl saw a pound in the gutter
And she was heard to give an excited mutter
But this little girl crossed the road when the man was red
This little girl is now dead.

—*Darren Haines*

High Calling

"Peace on Earth" is already established in the
   High Calling of ME -
Within ourselves - we find Peace to be!
And if we want to live in this priceless Peace -
There must first be inner Peace!

And if we want freedom in the world -
   there must also be Peace in oneself.
Peace - as a spiritual idea -
   contains all Spiritual Principles in itself -
It carries out the High Calling for Peace!
Then - the warfare in people's minds must cease!

And when each individual establishes Peace
   in their own consciousness -
The infinite Nature of Peace succeeds
   over human selfishness! -
The cry for Freedom on Earth pushes us
   into Spiritual Maturity -
Let it be established - firmly -
   in the Twentieth Century!

—*Ingeborg Heitmann*

A Brother's Last Journey

He watched, listened and waited, life slowly draining out of
him. Smiling tiredly at a far-off vision he alone could
conceive... Understanding that he had achieved that measure
allotted to him Son, brother, father, friend, confident, a gem
to many who knew him. It was almost finished, pearly drops
clouding his vision. In a kaleidoscope his life unfolded
before him... Most of all the tender infancy, the happy
carefree laughter. Frolicking blissfully in the verdant fields
and endless greens. Looking for small exotic fish in the
untamed streams of the clay filled valley. Learning to swim in
those same waters... Torrential rain, songs, laughter and
splashes in the muddy pools. Then growing up, achievements and
fateful mistakes... It was time to move on to those far
distant horizons of light and mystery. Joy and perfect peace
and boundless happiness... He smiled, burdens uplifted by the
one who had summoned him. Sensing His nearness, yearning for
His infinite mercifulness... His last breath springing him,
soaring towards lofty mountains... Morn found him still, a
smile of utmost peace on his countenance. He had conquered,
being released to traverse the other worlds...

—*Judy Cottet-Senoga*

So Young

So young, so innocent, so sweet,
His life, yet so incomplete,
Only 17 years of age,
Never knew there would soon be an outrage,
Tuesday, April 19th of 1992,
Eric, why did it happen to you?

He was shot down,
Now he's six feet under the ground,
Shot in the chest,
With one last breathe,
Immediately he was laid to rest.

We all wish they had lied,
When they said he had died,
Now it's been two years,
We'll never forget all those tears.

—*Jennifer Luffman*

Fallen From Grace

When I was a little girl I would sit on Daddy's shoulders
His little princess on her throne
I was safe...secure...loved...
He said the world was created for me. A magical place where
Fairies danced in the grass and the Man-in-the-Moon winked.
If I sat on his shoulders I could touch the stars...
He said he loved me. In his eyes I was perfect.

Now I am grown up and I have to stand on my own two feet
The throne is empty, abandoned long ago
I am scared...sad...alone...
The world is hard and cruel sometimes, the magic disappeared
The reality of life has set in.
The fairies have vanished and the Man-in-the-Moon is blind.
I can't touch the stars...
We have grown apart because I am not perfect anymore.
I have fallen from grace.
I feel lost and so out of synch.
Please help me to find my way back.
Daddy, could I sit on your shoulders again?

—*Kelly Lynch*

Dawn

With dishevelled hair Dawn rose in the East
Holding promise in her hand;
The rose-tinted sky sent its fragrance
Across the earth's fields and Forests;
Her jingling anklets
Waked the million-threated birds
To sweet ecstasy
Which stirred the mighty heart of the world;
Her soft tread on the margin of the sky
Put the million starts to flight;
And the lingering darkness slowly faded;
Gently she descended into the ocean depths,
Making it a vast sheet of shimmering waters.

—*Venkata Rao Nemani*

Merging

Wisps of souls come hither forth,
I am in need of consultation and report.
So alone I have felt to-date,
To join the multitude, I await.

I wish to know who I am, was and will be.
They say, that I have parallel selves, all free.
I don't understand, nor do I wish to debate.
To join kindred spirits, I await.

—*Sylvia O'Callaghan-Brown*

Tito's Lament

Witness my hand is absent from our test,
Homes are tombs, that is where we rest,
Yet forever all moisten-glazed eyes will see,
My place of sleep still, not be it free.

Uttered memories of ways we were, before late,
Shamed souls we be now, at our death's gate.
Those prayers are not now for us, as the tears are but war,
Thoughts of seeing sunlight, be it us, your tears are not for.

Hold sparkled jewels, soon sorrow our hearts reveal,
Our names are not yet etched upon our seal,
Up here, crescenting moons will rise to pass,
Dropping winds scattered seed will size, as the past.

Oh, worry not our loves one day we will show,
The rains of fire will open all below,
Healing through drifting mists, we will circle as white doves,
Is then once forgiven, we rest in a still, quiet place,
Some call, Thou's sweet heaven.

—*Peter R. Ewen*

The Sunshine And The Shadow

How can I see the source of my struggle
How can I know the conflict of my pain
Why do I do all things of involvement
Out of my fears increasing pace
Why do I live in the darkness made
Why do I fall not to get up again
Why do the tears flowing cease
Why am I afraid of this changing day
That covers the earth yet my soul responds...

A living thing unlocked to say
Upon a scroll rolled in fate
And from within a smile begins
A loving deed, a leaf in place
A sharing thought all trust all faith
I can go on to meet and face
The sunshine and the shadow.

—*Joan M. Griffin*

How Can I Swim?

How can I swim when you are not there to hold me if I sink?
How can I run when you are not there to help me if I fall?
How can I walk now that you have left me here to stumble on alone?
How can I smile? - I smile only for you, and you are gone.

Who is there now to wipe away my tears?
Who is there now to comfort me if I fall?
How can I cry when what is left is but an ache?
How can I feel, when what I feel is you, and you are gone?

How can I talk when my tongue is dead?
How can I see when the sun is black?
How can I touch when my touch is no longer for you?
How can I? How do I? How would I? - For you are gone.

How can I fly when it was you who gave me my wings?
How can I leap when it was you who gave me the spring?
How can I sleep, for you have taken away my dreams?
How can I live? - I lived for love,
    and love is gone.

—*Charlotte Cameron-Beaumont*

How Can We Give Up

How can we give up what we have found?
How can we give in? We stand on new ground.
This love that we cherish is not in vain.
It will give us new hope again and again.

So let it grow from strength to strength,
All our weak areas it will mend.
How can we give up a love that's true,
When others are longing to fall in love too?

Why must we give up because others say "No",
When we feel in our hearts that our love is sure?
Why must we give in due to jealousy,
That others are feeling for you and me?

How can we give up? We've come a long way,
Overcoming obstacles as we fast and pray.
How can we give in, we're seeking the Lord?
For he has the answer, and the very last word.

Above all, we desire God's will in our lives.
As from our hearts all fears it will drive.
How can we give up when we know God is leading?
How can we give in, when the answer's in seeking?

—*Liz Bett*

The Prisoner

A prisoner am I, here for all time
How did I get here, I remember no crime.
A prisoner am I, I was born in this cell
Sometimes it's heaven and sometimes it's hell.

A prisoner am I and I want to be free
I call for my judge "not guilty" my plea
He said, what's the problem you know you can't leave
Your in there for life, there is no reprieve.
You have eyes to see and ears to listen
Destiny is your jailer, flesh and blood is your prison.

A prisoner am I but now I can see
I know there are thousands worse off than me
A prisoner am I and no ones to blame
I'll be set free when the Lord calls my name.

—*J. Ellis*

Coping With Grief

How do you cope with the loss of a child? How do you handle the pain?
How do you turn your emotions back on and learn to live life again?
In a sense I've been grieving for Brendan from the moment that he was born,
grieving the loss of potential even more so now that he's gone.
I turned off my own thoughts and feelings, and centred on Brendan instead,
to give him the greatest chance possible of finding his own way ahead.
I directed my strength and my love towards Brendan, all I could give;
and the power of positive energy reinforced his strong will to live.
He had strength of his own in abundance, a power that came from within,
Strength that was drained from him slowly in a battle that he could not win.
I know that the love that I gave him was felt, and moreover, returned
as the innocent love of a child, in a way that can never be learned.
Brendan may not have been able to show that he cared very much,
but the feelings were always present in that greatest of senses — touch.
I wish that I could have held him a little longer the day that he died,
he waited until I could cuddle him, but there was no time to say our goodbye.

—*Victoria Blair*

A Long Time Ago

How does it feel to be strong and tall?
How does it feel to be giddy and small?
How does it feel to be called a twirp?
How does it feel to be covered in dirt?
How does it feel to wear pretty clothes?
How does it feel to wrinkle your toes?
These few things, are ones I'll never know
Cause mommy gave me up, a long time ago
I know mommy misses me I know at times she cries
For the baby that she gave up, I would've had her big blue eyes
I love you mommy and I miss you just as much
But sometimes I wonder, why did you give me up?
I wish you would've wanted me, I hate being so alone
But I guess you didn't want, a baby to call your own
Mommy you would've loved me, I would've been
    your pride and joy.
I would've made a good baby, if I was a girl or a boy
I could've made you love me, I know I could've done it
But it's too late now it was a long time ago
    and abortion is what they called it...
    —*Kristi Oaks*

The Wonder Of You

Every time I look at you I wonder in surprise,
how I ever managed to capture such a prize.
I wish that I could tell you about the love I feel,
it fills me with such happiness; it is so very real.

I love you with such passion, it gets stronger every day,
the love just grows in my heart, it shall never go away,
to think of you puts a smile on my face,
to have you in my arms, makes me feel there is no better place.

My eyes sparkle when you are near,
my heart skips a beat and I hope I will never have to fear;
that one day my darling you won't be near.

Yet now the days are short, and yet so very long,
they took you away from me, and now I must be brave, I must be
strong. There is a place I know, where all dead souls do go.

I live alone now, and my darling I still do miss you so.
I will never see your smile, your face or your arms will never
go around me again. Please stay with me until the very end.

They say that time heals all wounds and that is what I need,
just a little more time, and it will ease from my mind.
    —*Terri Giosia*

Derisive Dream

So you think I sleep. . . (ha ha),
How wrongly mistaken you are,
I could trick you if I wanted —
I could close my eyes and breath heavily,
And you'd be none the wiser.

But, please... explain to me the reason for my
insomniac tendencies.
Look into my lusterless, squinted eyes and tell me what
secrets you see buried in the pained pupils.
I need to know.
When others are snoring and exploring the twisted corridors
of their subconscious, I lie in a dazed, horizontal position,
trying to lure my hyper cerebrum into oblivion.
But, no, I am forced to review my life in such detail
that the happy moments become tedious, monotonous periods
which I suddenly loathe and blame for my restless,
writhing state of mind.
Condemned as I am, a small flint of desperate hope eternally
thrives for the day when forever more I can close my lids
to find darkness...
    —*Lori McMillan*

Two Woodland Gentlemen

Dear friend, though we are very different
How much we are as one
For now we are both old and gnarled
And our journey is almost done.

Our children grow around us
They are our glimpse into tomorrow
We see it in their searching eyes
We look, but dare not borrow

At times the world closed in on me
My life was filled with dread
When nothing else could comfort me
Your strong arms were always spread.

We talk with lips unmoved
Your hidden voice stirs my very being
And though your self feels part of me
Your face I am deprived of seeing

The distant call grows stronger
I feel the answer stir within me
Though I will miss all my hearts true loves
None more than you my beloved chestnut tree.
    —*Stan F. Harrison*

Sierra Rose Vernon

Sierra Rose, our sweet desert flower,
how we've waited eagerly for you to come this hour.

And now our hearts fill with joyful pride
to meet you at last and gaze into your beautiful eyes.

Your Mom and Dad love you so much,
and you have three big brothers to add a loving touch.

That's not all, you're blessed with much more,
Aunts, Uncles, Grandparents, and cousins by the score!

Sierra dear little one, you'll always know you're loved
as you look into the faces smiling at you from above.

Just one more thing our sweet desert rose,
We're all so happy you're here
WELCOME HOME SIERRA ROSE!
    —*Katrina Whittington*

Dear Dad

If the Lord would only grant us one more chance to let you know
How you've shaped our lives with values - "Yes" was "Yes" and
"No" was "No" All your guidance and your wisdom helped us
make the proper choice Though you've left us, when we stumble
we will always hear your voice.

You have raised us with a firmness - iron hand in velvet glove
Teaching morals, setting guidelines, ruling home with sense and
love You've instilled in us a backbone, strong and straight and
proud and true Be a "Caissie", do it justice, in each of us -
a piece of you.

If sweet Jesus would but grant us one more moment, one more day
All the words we left unspoken - all the things we didn't say
Would be shouted from the rooftops to be sure that you would
hear You are loved by all you daughters - you're so precious,
daddy dear.

Oh dear God, we were not ready when you took our dad away
Keep him safe within your bosom - warm his spirit when we pray
Let him know how much we miss him, in our hearts and minds,
he's here Rest in peace our precious daddy - rest in peace our
daddy dear.
    —*Michelle Caissie*

On The Wings Of A Prayer

On the wings of a prayer
Humanity is destined to hover
Hoping for an end to aggression
And soon to recover
From the nightmare of global starvation
We long for peace
So that we can love one another
Join hands to help
Those displaced from homelands, and others
Seeking a safer place
To live out their destiny
Let us hold to virtue
To fight to porn and drug culture
Aspire to clean the environment
And stay closer to nature
On the wings of a prayer

—*Dolores English*

Nostalgia

When I first came to this country,
I always cried.
I cried when it snowed
I cried when it shined
I cried in the bad times
I cried in the good times
Because my family, my relatives, and my friends were left behind
Then years passed by,
I got a degree; I got a job; I got a house; I got a family
I was so satisfied that I no longer cried
But today, deep in my sad eyes
I find a nostalgia
That I was too preoccupied
To notice.
That foremost nostalgia
Always stays in my sad eyes.

—*Thuc Cong*

Unstoppable AIDS

Too hot my home the bed
I am down, cornered by Aids
Finally in a death trap
I spread the gospel to the four corners of the earth
A love champion and a fun fan
Now face to face with the tireless one
Running up and down my entire body
To turn the taps of diarrhoea
That graduation of my love
The endless coughing of soot

Determined to wipe laughter off the face of the earth
Bully that teaches infants grief
Burying husband after wife
Charming sons and daughters from one womb
Clean them off the face of the earth
Destroy silently and secretly, from door to door, estate
to estate
If possessing power enough to create, power enough to beget
Your hand would forever be full

—*Frederick Owino*

World Gone Insane

This world gone insane,
  I am lonely crying in vain,
It's poverty and relentless pain,
  No water, but hunger strain,
On one side - it's technology and fame,
  On the other - it's disaster and shame,
Even God cannot tame,
  The beast within, will have no claim,
No love down the lane.
  Black or white - it's all the same,
No value for moral and brain,
  No philosophy can withstand the drain,
It's sheer need for power, that's part of the game,
  And money - is its name.
This world gone insane,
  I am lonely crying in vain.

—*D. N. Ravi Shankar*

I Am Made Of Sand

I am made of sand.
I am shaped by the wind.
My fate is written by the footprints
of the wandering caravan.
The sand is like me.
And I am bathed in the morning light.
And I breathe heavy and light under its touch.
The tongue of the Bedouin girl caresses my soul.

—*Dirk Klimant*

Remember Me Oh Lord This day

As you hung on the cross Oh Lord, You bled and died for me
I ask Oh Lord you would remember me in your Kingdom
Just as the thief on the cross asked you to remember him
I pray Oh Lord this day to give me peace in my heart
Remember me and strengthen me Lord for your glory
Put to rest all of my temptations that I may have against you
Bring me back Oh Lord, to your loving arms, I pray
I pray Oh Lord, you will take this sin from my heart
and wash me white as snow
Remember me Oh Lord, as I talk to you this day

—*Raymond John Price*

The Knight Orchestra

The sky was filled with stars so bright
  I can reach and hold on tight.
The orchestra of meteors
  was meant for me to see this sight.
I look beside me, you were there
  it was meant for me to share.
A stolen moment exchanging smiles
  A breath of fresh air engaged in desire.
Turning back, the night sky waits
  Instrumenting another fate.
A shooting star, the music played,
  I drifted, I dreamt,
    The knight away

—*M. Ellen Montgomery*

To Emy

I saw you in a dream.

Your eyes brushed me with a kiss

And in a whisper I understood.

—*Olav Ramstad Thelle*

Who Are You Following?

A genie in a magic jar,
A black and white superstar,
A soft, silky picture,
Of an old fashioned culture.

A rich-smelling dream-maker,
In the world of the stockbroker,
A house-owning paragon,
Who you can put money on.

A twisting, swaying idol,
Exposed through a video,
Thrown on a rostrum,
No matter what it cost them.

A crushed, dying leader,
Twisted for our freedom,
Risen for his children,
The renegades are forgiven.

—*Terry Hotchkiss*

Untitled

A brand new mother, just fourteen
A brand new baby, fresh and clean
She longs to hold her to her breast
And give her baby girl the best
Into her baby's face she peers
Dad hears the news, he disappears.
A special babe, a name so fine
Mellissa, I'm so glad you're mine
But Mell my girl, we have to part
I love you so, it breaks my heart
Her face is sad, she starts to weep
Her baby girl, she cannot keep
Her babe she has to give away
They'll be here soon, they'll come today
Although you do not understand
In my dreams Mell, I'll hold your hand
In my dreams Mell, I'll watch you grow
And always love you, that I know.

—*Catherine Alderdice*

A Whisper in the Wind

A whisper in the wind
A breeze in my ear
These are the things
I feel when you're near
A heart full of gold
You wear on your sleeve
I'll treat it with love
and pray you don't leave
The love that we've known
so precious and true
while together we've grown
but apart we are blue
Together forever, the pain that we bare
with me sitting here, and you over there
A love that is true
two hearts that are blue
And together we'll cry
Til all the tears have run dry
Together, forever
I'll always love you.

—*Cherryl Smart*

Small Town Living

The day dawns bright in small town
splendor
A careless light unfolds;
People, cats and dogs and all
Each, the day beholds.

The children rise with sleepy eyes
And trudge their way to stand
By gate post in the frosty morn
Books and lunch in hand.

The town begins to move with life
A shout or bark is heard
The beauty of the scene awakes
My inner thoughts to word.

A city it shall never be
But city look about
You lack the love and life that's here
The strength of, life without.

—*Pamela J. Gazdewich*

The Mystic Entities

What beauty lies in a face?
 a face of so long ago,
Whose eyes that have seen
 the changing of time,
 and the advancement of age,
Whose lips that hold the
 secrets of the past,
 and the mysteries of the future,
Whose cheeks that have been
 touched by the heavens,
 and colored by the milky-way,
Whose nose that was shaped
 by the angels,
 and formed by the Gods,
Whose hair that was stranded
 by the golden flames,
 and caressed by the wind,
Whose face not only symbolizes beauty,
 but of eternal love.

—*Kim Byers*

In The Moment

 "Look,
A flash of lightning!"
 "Where?"
 —*Les Montanjees*

The Broken Dream

From an abyss arises
A strangled, mangled moan.
A crippled heart quivers and whimpers;
Remnants of a soul.

Malicious shadows lurk;
They ravage and they maul
The carcass of a bond,
Oblivious of all.

The tears, they do not wet
The fire and the flame.
Two halves are not a whole at all,
But just a broken dream.

—*Nicola McKinney*

Untitled

A hand to hold,
A gentle touch,
Am I asking
For too much?

Should I be content,
In this my cage,
That society considers
A marriage?

You challenge me
To see beyond,
The powerful grip,
Of this bond.

To reach for the stars,
Achieve a new height,
Come out of the dark,
And see the light.

Can I meet the challenge?
Be all I can?
Or is this who
I really am?

—*Kathy Sauer*

When Will It End

It's a gift
A gift of love
The love of a new child
Brought in this world with no hate
So why is there hate
Where did it come from
When will it end
The wars and anger
Please let it end
For we can have peace
Teach your children
No hate
But love

—*Katrina Shellito*

My Prayer For The Day

Oh Lord, when there is -
A raging storm,
Deep inside of me
Lord calm the raging sea.

But guide my vessel -
Home, safely once again.

And when the thunder
Starts to roar,
And I'm lost
Alone and afraid,

Lord just take me
In your circle of love.
Keep me safe until -
I'm calm again.

For this is my prayer,
For always,
That you keep me safe,
Out of harm's way
Until I'm calm again.

—*Ione Dunbar*

Theory Of Relativity

Like dusky green ribbon
a river stretches across
earth's gently curving brow
and disappears into horizon haze.
As it gradually vanishes behind
the airplane's wing, finger-shaped
ridges from a distant mountain
roll past in single file, only to
join the river's slow retreat.
In turn, contoured farmlands
create impressionistic patterns
under endless moving shadows.
Earth revolves ponderously,
taking its features with it.
In farm houses, hours progress
as usual, without variation,
while in the plane above, we
race backward into time through
a different frame of reference.

—*Joyce G. Bradshaw*

The Artist

A little piece of ocean
A small touch of sky
A tiny bit of earth
Just enough to fill the eye.

The painting on the canvas
Is not as simple as it seems
The soft sound of the rivers
The murmur of the streams.

The rays of gleaming sunlight
Weaving through the trees
The smell of salt and sand
Drifting from the seas.

The magic of the artist
His senses are so real
He makes his own reality
That only he can feel.

—*James Crout*

Forbidden

You looked down when we first met
A special day, I shan't forget.
Deep emerald eyes
They hypnotize.
Surroundings disappear
When you are near.
It's your smile; the way you speak
You make me strong; you make me weak.
I will come to you. I have no choice
Enchanted by your compelling voice.
We are so different and yet the same
Powerful emotions, I dare not name
A tender place inside my heart
Feeling empty when we're apart
But I must never feel your touch
Though I care for you very much
Wanting to be with you every day
Loving you more than words can say.
If only our story was mine to write
We would share each moment; every day,
every night.

—*Patsyanne Garrity*

The Accident

A distant shadow
A sudden flash
An urge of silence
A batted lash

A stranger's presence
A familiar red
The sense of fear
The smell of dead

A wooden door
An uneasy knock
A shattered roar
Turned into shock

A stone faced crowd
A six foot hole
A bouquet of memories
And an endless soul.

—*Laura Predan*

Remember When?

Memory
A treasure untouched by time
an echo in the mind
bringing smiles and tears,
joys and sorrows
I am for people who dream of tomorrow
no memory fades fast
I am a looking glass into
that which has
gone by
I am a window into the minds' eye.

—*J C Poet*

Life

Life: An enigmatic puzzle
 A vision quest
  grasping for revelations.

Each piece
 uniquely formed
Individually viewed
 solitude
Fragmented knowledge
Curious to the mind.

In unity
 harmoniously blended
Mysteriously unfolding, piece by piece
Disclosing leisurely
 answers segmented
 occasionally apparent
 mostly ambiguous
Yet a modicum of wisdom.

Upon completion
 clarity, understanding
The individual's telos.

—*A. M. Lawson*

After Midnight

From this wind swept mountain top,
 a voice calls out in the night.
Down in the valley the dew drops,
While icy forms creep on the height.
 I seek the wind to hear the hail
 and with frozen ears so I go,
 tonight as I stand on the hill
 and all the ghosts come to know.

—*John Okrasa*

Lonely World

I'm living in a lonely world
A world of my own,
No one to really talk to
Except for my loved ones at home.

I'm so sad and depressed
I just wanna cry,
But, it wouldn't do me any good
Because no one would even ask why.

I just wish I had someone to talk to,
Or even tell a joke,
But, in this lonely world, it's
too much to ask for.

So, I sit here alone in my cell,
Wishing my life could be
a lot happier,
Instead, of being alone,
In this lonely world.

—*Josette Julian*

Across Land

Whose voice was first to be heard?
Across land flooded with golden light
Whose people were the first to cry?
Across land where the moon shines bright
Who overcame and pushed aside?
Whose promises were denied?
These questions still echo inside
Yet the answers come from those who lied
What future is there for mankind
If the human spirits cannot bind?

—*Sam J. May*

'And Will You Be Charging This, Sir?'

Financially yours,
Ah will be your destruction.
Your reduction.
Sorry, no redemption…
This ain't no double coupon day.
They don't take Visa where your headed.
What did you think…
 money grew on trees?
Well then, ah guess it's prunin' time!
So order now.
No money down.
(You'll be payin' the rest o' your life).
Operators are standin' by.

—*Richard Avery Creed*

Paisley Shawl

Is life like a Paisley Shawl?
All those slug-like patterns
could be a pouch for a foetus
the beginning seed of life
a bag of worms, a satchel for hunting
a future garden of Eden
seeds for thought
future rain
a bag of nails
an apostrophe.
This beautiful homespun cloth
a classic of today.
I shall keep this old old wrap
its secrets woven in
to keep me safe from cold.

—*Jean Mahaffey*

Broken Dreams

A beautiful home
All furnished with care
With matching colours
Done with flair.

Their yard is alive
With green, mauve, pink, and yellow
A lot of work
For one fellow.

The atmosphere bespeaks
Of some happy times, but more of sad
But where is the love
That they once had.

The heartache tells true the story
Of groping for dominance
Or is it prominence sought
Thereby not living happily ever naught.

—*L. J. Chaykowski*

Of God

I am of God
All the good in me, the pure, the real
      and the true

The will to live each day perfectly and
      individually
To appreciate the birds, the bees the
      flowers and trees
The tiniest most hidden ray of light
Shining through this dense humanity

As each bud brings forth a flower
Each cocoon a butterfly
So should each thought bring forth a
      Prayer
Creative and divine

To live my life
Discriminating between the real and the
      unreal
Abiding by the Light of the Path
And treading in the Footsteps of the Master

—*Olga Graham*

My Grandfather

My Grandfather was a loving man
Always willing to lend a helping hand
Whether it be for one of his own
Or somebody that he's never known

He was tall and strong and full of love
I know that he prayed to God above
Each and every day you see-
He worked hard to raise his family

One by one his children left
Straying not far from his nest
They lived and loved the way each should
The way my Grandfather knew they would

His family grew in leaps and bounds
Sixty-three grandchildren all around
My Grandfather was very proud you see-
He started this little family

Yes, this man was full of love
But now his home is up above
And I know in my heart one day we'll be
Together again as one family

—*Karen M. Chapman*

Till We Meet Again

Unlike the sun has the clouds
and the moon has the stars
in the darkness I stand alone.

Like the shivering chill that hangs
in the night air,
the anguish thoughts my heart does bear.

But to one day know,
that I'll see you again
keeps the faith and hope alive
and no longer will I pretend.

—*Stephen Ricketts*

A Soldier Forgotten

Out there we've walked,
amongst a world of irreverence,
a game of roulette
by which innocence fell...
To all I have loved,
I have fought and not won,
the war of the worlds,
and by the opposing sword shall I die,
for no other place could be hell,
one last time, I shed a silent tear,
and eternal peace embraced my soul...

—*Kristin Kurtz*

Casual Recognition

On the train tonight
An empty can
Rolls across the aisle

I look out the window
And see neon lights passing by
Over the reflection of my face

This place called the Universe,
It's where I thought it wasn't

—*Jon Scott Harp*

Eternal Question

Love is not always
An instant melding,
Although it can be.
It is sometimes
A complete and thorough
Understanding of the person
Over the years;
A sharing
Of their victories
And their defeats
And an admiration
For their courage.
It is looking at things
Through their eyes
Until you get
A mirror image;
Until you are a part
Of their hopes and aspirations,
And until they become
The greater part of you.

—*Frances Gillard Harvey*

The Angels Wedding

The marrying of an angel
an occasion of wonder and grace

A ring above her head
the molten gold
of a rare and precious soul.

The halo glows and pulsate
soft rhythms of delicate heart.

Her full, slender wings
of finely arranged feathers
dazzled, in wondrous unfolding,

capturing the prismatic colours
in a brilliant display.

The disarranged rainbows
glistened and shimmered
rippling through near transparent wings

that quivered,
when I kissed her at the alter.

—*Brian Keane*

Untitled

With eyes which are misting freely
And a soul ready to break
I watch a small hand reach
Gently, but thin and shaking
For food, compassion and hope
That which will never come
I watch a mother holding
Her fondling gently in death
That which has not come with a sigh
But with a silent never ending cry
On thin of legs she stands
And with a whisper of a sigh
She gently kneels, a bowed head
Like when you pray, swaying
Falls slowly to one side
Returning to the earth whence she came
With a heavy broken heart
I kneel with bent of head
And I ask myself "why?"
Silence only answers -

—*Bruce E. H. Strand*

Beauty

Beauty is within the soul,
And as God shows his hand,
There's beauty to be found
All throughout our great land

There is beauty in the raindrops
As the rain comes teeming down
As it patters on the roof top
To the heart it brings a calm

In the spring there is a carpet of green
Flowers in full array.
The winds, the rain, the sunshine
In part will make our day.

There is beauty in a child at play
Or a workman at his chore.
There is a place for every one
No matter what the score

Beauty lives within the soul,
Of those who wish to find it
God made all things beautiful,
It's only we who soil it.

—*Eva Woodland*

Yes I Remember

How fortunate one truly is,
And blest they have to be
To call this lovely land their home
Where the heart and soul are free.

The grand old flag once graced the mast
Could feats of glory tell
It rallied us in time of need
And eased us out of hell.

Ah' the emblem now adorns the mast
Knows not the battle cry
With trust in God and love of peace
The dogs of war shall die.

Canada' You've battled hard,
Yes, honor this lingering break,
But stay alert' be on your guard
For freedom is the stake!

—*Edward Keenan*

Courage

Courage, when you are low,
    And feel things should not be so,
Courage for the faint heart,
    Spurs you on to a new start.

Courage to clear away the gloom,
    And any cobweb that may loom,
Courage for that furrowed brow,
    And thoughts that trouble you now.

Courage will bring new light,
    To any seeming slight,
Courage will shine through,
    To bring hope to renew.

Courage can be called to mind,
    At the must unlikely time,
Courage is always there,
    If you just remember where.

—*Mary E. Guy-Shea*

Just Call On Me

When life feels tough
and gets real rough
don't be down and don't you frown,
If you need a friend I'll be around
If down you've been
then up you'll be
I'm a friend
Just call on me
If you cry tears
Cause of your fears
If you have a doubt
I'll knock it about
Just call on me
There I'll be

—*Jennifer Zebley*

Untitled

I kissed you goodbye
And turned to walk into the darkness
And as I crossed the line that separates
The light from the shadows
I felt the darkness cover my soul
Bring with it the fear of the night
And the fear of being alone
Again

—*Steve Amos*

From Kristen - To My Friends

I am the sky,
    and I am forever...
For I have no beginning
    and I have no end.

I am the gentle breeze
    that warms your soul.

I am the wind
on which the eagle soars.

I am the sun
    that lights your way.

I am the flowers of spring
    which give hope
    of a new beginning.

Be still... and know
    that I am with God...
    for I am these,
    and many more.

—*Pete Juhlke*

No Matter The Label

I am a senior citizen they say,
And I don't mind.
There are others though
Who decry that label.
Not me.
The realization that I made it
To this age
    self-sustaining
    fully ambulatory
    reasonably sane—
Now a part of history,
Having traveled through the pain of
    infancy
    childhood
        adolescence
    womanhood
    wifehood
        motherhood, grannyhood
Leaves me speechless, awed, delighted,
No matter the label.

—*Dorothy Liverpool*

I Wish

I wish I was the moon
And I would look down on everyone
I wish I was a mousetrap
And I would kill
I wish I was destiny
And I would change my life
I wish I was in control
And I would not give in

—*Chrystal Preece*

Dreamland

Close your eyes my love
and see the floating white dove,

Reach out your delicate hand
and capture the fuzzy rimmed
dreamland.

Open up your imagination
and let your soul run free.

Close your eyes....
and dream only of me.

—*Julie F. Wilson*

Old Boat's Song

My days are done
and now I lie
beached upon the shore.
My paint is blistered
in the sun,
and ebb tides rot my floor.
No more my anchor
weighs at dawn
to catch a turning tide!
I chart my memories
in the stars
and log their course
with pride!
No master's hand
controls my wheel!
No cargo fills my hold!
But, Stranger,
sigh no sighs for me,
there's peace
in growing old. . .

—*Sheila FitzGerald McKenna*

Sunflower

Bright noon,
and, oh, I see
a giant flower of the sun,

and it is like a lanky father
leaning on a fence
his face not sunwards turned
but bent and brooding
to this darting son
as if to kiss his eyes,—

the son's face, open,
beams.

—*Konstantinos Lardas*

Untitled

I stood high on a mountainside
And roared a lioness' roar
For I was closer to my destiny
Than I had been before

Thunder crashed about me
And lightning flashed so bright
The ground churned beneath my feet
And a path came into sight

—*Antonia Schiavone*

Kay Bell

She pumps up the volume,
And runs down the court;
She feels the rhythm,
Pumping in her heart.

"C" makes the pass,
"J" misses the three;
Then they did something new
They passed it to me!

I took a step back,
I was behind the line,
I hit the three, and
I knew I had done fine.

I did really great,
I felt it down deep,
It must have been fate,
Now I've got something I can keep!

—*Jennifer Robertson*

The Understanding Heart

When my troubles get so heavy
And seem so hard to bear
That's when I turn to You O' Lord,
I know You're always there.

After I spend a while with You
It seems my burdens lift,
My heavy heart is lighter now
My troubles all a drift.

Oh, Lord, do not forsake me
Make me strong enough to bear
My cross, what e're Thou givest me
As long as You are there.

I think of a time long ago
Thou suffered so hard for me,
So now I offer my love in return,
For that day on Calvery.

Let my troubles turn into roses
The color of bright-blood red,
I'll weave them into a Crown
To place on my Savior's Head.

—*Joyce Marchiondo*

My Mother, My Friend

My mother is always there,
And she shows how much she cares.

She is there to dry my tears,
And their to calm my fears.

She is the best,
She will always be very special to me.

She is my mother but not just that,
because she's a friend just like that.

Someone to talk to,
Someone who listens,
Someone who answers,
Someone who cares.

She has been around for many years,
She knows everything
So, she can answer any question I ask.

But I love her and she loves
me and that's how mothers and daughters
are supposed to be.

—*Kristi Martin*

My Eyes

Look into my eyes
And tell me what you see.
They are clear as the sky
But there is trouble underneath.
There is a reservoir.
That fills up periodically.
And in an instant
It can be drained.

A blink is as good as a dam.

The clever and the intelligent
can only see
That behind the eyes
Are lonely tears.

—*Jen Mai*

The Quake

When the world rumbles
and the ground roars
when the earth crumbles
and nature soars

Waiting for the aftershocks
to finally diminish
will mother nature knock
or is she finally finished

Never knowing when
the shaking could begin
never knowing when
the world could end

Is there a message
behind it all
is there some passage
that we must recall

I put my faith in Him
and everyday I pray
forgive me for my sins
so I may walk His way.

—*Kristine Gilpin*

Ecstasy

Damn the emotions
and the responsibility that
comes with them.

Curse the unbearable ecstasy
as the body separates itself from
mind as if playing some
sadistic game.

Logic must supersede emotion
yet emotion tears apart
logical thinking.

Yesterday I had no feelings.
Today I have so many.

Ego - and the ecstasy surrenders.
Control - and logic has won.

—*Hilary A. Virtue*

A White Rose

   The red rose whispers passion,
And the white rose breathe of
love;
Oh, the red rose is a falcon
And the white rose is a
dove,
But I send you a cream white
rose bud,
with a flush on its petals
tips;
For the love that is purest
and sweetest
Has a kiss of desire on
the tips.

—*Katrina Coleman*

Four Seasons

Autumn days start so bold
And their nights are deep
The sun seems so cold
And the moon begins to sleep

Winter days lose their glow
As their nights grow longer
Cloudy skies are filled with snow
Their chilly winds get stronger

Spring days have their painted flowers
Their nights are made to sing
The sky is filled with its showers
And robins take to wing

Summer days are in their glory
Their nights are truly free
Now begins a whole new story
For their stars belong to me

—*Judith Arterburn*

A Quick Smell Of Her

Sometimes I can smell you.
And then I remember
Your pasta bianca
pasta e patata
Your shoes haven't taken
one step
for almost two years.
I miss you, grandma,
when I'm home
when I cook
when I sleep
but I know you
are with me,
inside of me,
and my mother.
To visit you
in my heart and mind
is what I hope for, for the rest of my life.
To give you to others as you have given
yourself to us.

—*Karen Ann Bagnini*

Someone Behind Me

Silent Jesus, at me you stare,
And then you gently ask,
"The shadows; are they still there?"
What shadows be, I thought awhile
And in that moment He began to smile,
Not knowing, just hoping I would care
To free those shadows?
To make them be not there?
Silently He trembled.
Then I would do my best -
But did you know
Those shadows left
When I knew that you had cared.

—*Diane L. Olsen*

Untitled

The love is gone
And those who shared the loved are gone
Those who laughed and cried with me,
   those who knew not their fate or
   destiny in God's eyes are gone and I
   am left to live and die without them.
Those who shared the love are gone.
And the love is gone.

—*Kerri Weckler*

Life

And they told me it did not matter
And they told me they loved me.
And they told me I was beautiful.
And they told me I was smart.
And they told me to be good.
And they told me it was our secret.
And they told me to laugh with them.
And they told me Life was easy.
And they told me to be grown up.
And they told me death wasn't the end.
And they told me to let it be.
And they told me what to wear.
And they told me whom to be.
And they told me to smile and shine.
And they told me not to care.
And they told me they loved me...

And I told them it did not matter.

—*Janette Lynn*

Unborn Thoughts...

His warm arms thrown around you
And tightly you embraced,
His soft hands pulled you closer
Your heart-beat quickened pace
His lips much more than wine
His fingers through your hair,
Could it be that you were blinded
or did you really care?

For now I'm cold and lonely
My mouth forever dumb,
My thoughts will never be expressed
I cannot go or come,
I could have made somebody proud
I'd like to think it so,
I could have been a dream come true
But now, we'll never know!

—*Nova L. Blake*

D. T.'s Aspiration

I got fired yesterday
And today I drove the
Twilight when I pulled over
To see a sky so rare that

I longed for an easel
And the gift to commit it
To canvass: this black on white
White on black, with the sun

Just over someone's rooftop
Oh, the fame it would bring
Me, this duplication of
Nature's finest in

Positive/negative pose
It hurled my emotions
Beyond our center in
Sagittarius, this encompassing

Elation of fulfillment that
Drives the sun and the stars
And the cars to work...
Which I have not

—*Timothy J. Duffy*

Denial

The night's cold
and unyielding.
I leave
the door ajar.
In the backyard
the gnarled branches,
black against the deep
blue sky, twist
and bend: knots
curling into scaly
scarred knolls.
Snowflakes flutter
with the brisk
December wind,
scurrying to cover,
no, masquerade
my colossal oak.

—*Dr. Gayle F. Arrowood*

God's Land

I journeyed into the forest,
and was overwhelmed with calmness.

The sweet sounding music of birds,
was very distinctively heard.

As I continued on my way,
all thoughts suddenly went astray.

Nature's aroma in the air,
was certainly beyond compare.

Wild flowers displayed such charm,
in their habitat, near and far.

Completely undisturbed by man,
the natural forest, God's land.

—*Maria Di Renzo*

Stars

I sit in my room at night...
And watch the stars so bright
They glow and gleam,
Like they're going to scream
But don't because they're stars.

Every star means something
Some are fun things...
But some are dumb things
So watch the stars sometime.

—*Jennifer Burke*

Untitled

I am sitting in a gilded cage
and watching the TV world in passing
Life is just a stage
full of dead thoughts not everlasting
just as lifeless as dead wood
and my empty heart understood
that my gilded cage was really false
and I stopped dancing the valse.

The year was sad and bitter
without the least bit of glitter
the poet sulked and wept
without a pillow he slept
The dreams had gone
now he had turned to stone.

—*Anne B. Kiaerland*

Learn To Love

You taught me how to love
and what it's of

You never said too much
but still you showed me the way

Nobody could ever know
the part of me I can't let go

I would give anything I own
my life,
my heart,
my home,
just to have you once again

So if there's someone you know
and your loving them so

Remember this

You may loose them one day
someone takes them away
and they'll never hear the words
you long to say.

—*Kevin Kassinger*

The Rose

It lay wilted
And withered,
On a golden,
Bed of sand.

A sign of love
It once was in demand.
Was given to a lover
As a sign of togetherness,
Now it lay dead
A sign of sadness.

The abstract petals
Depart with great forgiveness,
From the once full of life stem.
Falls to the ground
With a soft, booming thud.

That is the end
Of the rose.

—*Christy Elsner*

I Feel The Pain

I am different,
and yet I am the same,
I have feeling,
I feel the pain.

In my chest,
where my beating heart lies,
broken to pieces,
painfully it dies.

Running away,
away from my fears,
never in my life
have I had such tears.

—*Guinevere Janet Vanderveen*

Untitled

I write of love and hope and dreams,
And yet I have no cause, it seems.

I have no one to love, not now.
I goofed again, I don't know how.

I lived and hoped and dreamed of you,
I don't know what I'm gonna do.

My dreams are gone, they went with you,
My love and hope are both gone too.

You left me all alone, and yet
I'll always love you, you can bet.

I'll never love like this again,
Because it causes too much pain.

—*Kim Marie Colby*

Untitled

You are noisy
And you are loud
But you are gentle
And you are so proud
You are the sunshine
That starts my day
You're the cuddler
Who makes the
Aches go away
You are the father
Of our clan
But most of all
You are my man

—*Dolores Stinson*

A Dawning Love

Looking into her brown eyes
And you see where her beauty lies,
Her hair a river of auburn brown
In her presence one begins to drown,
The sparkle of her glorious smile
One can feel its warm glow for a mile,
Voice as sweet as a dove
Turning one's thoughts to love,
From those lips to have but a kiss
Would leave one in eternal bliss.

—*Keith N. West*

Evelinda Mine
Anytime is fine,
with your soul divine,
and your body sublime.

Please stay on my case
just keep up the pace.
This world we'll face
And all its joys embrace.

For we must serve this universe,
together, alone, and free.
We'll work at it now, you'll tell me how,
so simple, if you love me.

—*E.A. Butterworth*

Couple

Here we are walking
arms around waists.
Arms so long,
waists so small,
we feel like the empty box
wrapped with enormous ribbon.
It has all been said now.
The wind begins to
blow like a waterfall.
We dare not open our mouths
and eyes we dare not close.
Straight towards that tree.
Gazes are now reflecting the gazer.
You are now me.

—*Tracy Gibbons*

Searching

Many, many years ago,
As a child in my youth.
Like ocean currents I would flow,
Always searching for the truth.
Although I knew not where to look,
Or what that I may find.
I've searched each cranny and nook,
For a contented peace of mind.
And yes I've looked behind each door,
Upon each cluttered shelf.
The truth and peace of mind I search for,
Is deep within myself.

—*Jim Radmore*

United Flight

The horse,
As ancient as man
    himself
Together in life,
    in war, and
    in peace
In sport and
    in leisure
        Together
    We will fly

—*Annette Fehr*

Divorced Child...

The air was stale and silent
As Disaster did grow near
A storm approached my family
Awakening all my fears

    Love was an Insufficient link
    To the chain I cherished so
    The pain concealed inside me
    I'm sure they didn't know

The storm struck with a Vengeance
It spun me round and round
I hoped deep inside of me
I never would be found

    It must have been an Omen
    for suddenly I knew
        There would be no Restoration
        My family split in two...

    I lived through this Catastrophe
    And bravely faced the morn
        But it left me with Emotions
        Of always being torn...

—*Laurie Bottomley*

Ode To My Brother In Africa

Dear Lord:
As I drink this sweet nectar
So familiar to us here
In this land of plenty,
Please, let one dying soul
Who never has known
The taste of apple, grape, or
cherry,
Drink with me,
If only in his mind.
Let it be a balm
As to the dust he lies
His body down
    to die....
"Man's inhumanity to man"
How can I reach out the cup?
Someday, surely there will be
More equality.....hopefully.

—*Louise G. Howes*

Song Of The Fish Fly

We rise from the mud below the water,
As if in a dream, until we fly;
After brief ecstasy, a mortal day,
We die.

Our useless crackling bodies then
Are swept up, batted away,
Broomed off screens and bricks
Down into the ignominious gutters.
Our God of Death awaits us,
Antennae majestically still
Above closed wings.

—*Jean Hull Herman*

Night Chips

glimmering chips in the sky
as the night tip-toes by
twink-a-ling in the air
dang-a-ling without a care
dipper big
dipper little
shimmering
in the middle
of the vastness
fading blackness
stay the day?
no they may
not be seized
as enveloped with ease
by the tentacle rays
of the yawning sun's gaze
so they scamper in haste
all the magic erased
from the once speckled sky
as they now wave —— goodbye!!

—*Alice Wojewoda*

Autumn

Iteaphylla.
Autumn flotilla.
Zeric beacons of feldspathic sirens
Now signal a boreal truth.

—*Damien Mugavin*

Winter Days

Those winter days are cold and blue,
    At least in some people's eyes,
    But I think winter days are nice,
    Because the snowflake flies.

    It flutters down so gently,
    And melts right on your nose,
    And if you walk right though it,
    It will freeze your toes.

    The evergreens are heavy laden,
    With the fallen snow,
    An avalanche will come tumbling down,
    If the wind should blow.

    The icicles hang gracefully,
    And shrink each coming minute,
    The sun leaves prisms on the snow,
    With magical images in it.

Those winter days aren't cold and blue,
    They're beautiful and bright,
    The sunlight gleaming on the snow,
    Makes everything seem all right.

—*Bernice Later*

Ode To A Lustful Sunday Morning

Not a breath of wind
attended her rising
as the great awakener
laid lavender silks of ice
on her thighs

She is a tender, silent thing
crawling towards me
with interested eyes

Between us
silent foggy shapes
the mist of unknown
and a flash of a moist c__t

Violent, black purple
is the west
as her veil spreads
onto me
in a great, golden oral copulation.

—*Glenn Douglas*

To Those Invoking The Muse

Write of ecstasy, not excrement;
Avoid thistles,
    but scatter soft roseblooms.
Greenness can flourish on stony deserts
    where no trees shed leaves.
Above flood plains, when rain falls,
    a rainbow may arch in triumph,
And look for promise metaphors
as sun transfigures ice and snow
    under a winterblue sky.

Now, a harvest moon invests our land
    in a glow of evening light;
Stars in clarity are winking
    wonder through the dark;
Forget, awhile, terrors of these times
Sing beyond holocaust and hurricane
    of beauty, ever-springing,
        of truths that shall endure.

—*Pat Austin*

The Pain Of AIDS

Thomas Decker twenty eight,
Baby of the family;
Was it cruel or was it kind,
To take you away from me.

You suffered much yet went too fast,
Your life has only begun,
It kills so young this dreaded disease;
When will it all be done.

Your dreams, your hopes and growing up,
Well.. they'll no longer be;
Why in the world must I accept,
That you were taken from me.

I only hope, you are well,
In this world beyond;
And I can help, the fight on earth,
To rid us of this bond.

Won't you come, join my voice,
Shout it from your heart;
Lets cure this AIDS, and save our loves,
It's not too late to start

—*Kathleen Magrini*

Beauty

Beauty I see in all living things
Beauty in song as we sing
Beautiful aromas that we smell
Beautiful stories that we tell
Beauty in colour of different shades
Beauty in what man has made
Beauty in the sky each coming morn
Beauty in babies newly born
Beauty in everything, take time to see
Beauty in everyone, in you and me
Beauty we feel of the skin
But the greatest beauty is from within

—*Malcolm Pearson*

Because

Because you're you and I am me,
Because I held you on my knee,
Because I watched you walk and play
Because I wiped your tears away,
Because I watched you smile with joy
When you were just a little boy
Because you are now a man, but
still you like to hold my hand,
Because now your too big to sit
upon my knee,
I still love you and you love me,
Because your my son and
I am your ever loving Mom.

—*June Holguin*

Death Of A Soldier

We saw him die. Helpless he lay there,
    bleeding, torn,
His every breath can agonizing pain
Yet dying, softly whispering your name.

Death washed his face, erasing every
    line of care
Tending him as only death could know
And we stood helpless by and
    watched them go.

—*Margaret Schneider*

Made To Be

Sometimes I fight the system's flow
because where it leads, I will not go.
It could end good, but I don't know;
I live a day to learn and grow.
What I see, I do not chance,
Society's evil conga dance.
In a line you cannot see
who the leader may or may not be.
Why be them when I am me?
Why follow them and not be free?
Walk against it, take a stand!
Don't stick your head deep in the sand.
You're made to be, no to be made.
Reveal your soul and it won'd fade.
So take my hand and we'll be proud.
We'll walk against the social crowd.

—*Mae Childe*

Skylarking

Flowers of thought
befitting Chakras' head
grow enchanted
beneath the tulips' flowerbed.
Stifling in the dry morning air
makes it seem so unfair
that I should depend
on a depressed existence
through words of songs
undanced
dress
in winged silence;
shower warm smiles of deliverance
on you darling,
among the sweet rosebuds braided.

—*Julie Walters*

Soul And Drum

The drum beat
begins deep in the expressive
soul, slowly slowly it
emerges to release itself through
strokes made by the strong, worked,
perceptive hands
on a skin bound to a cylinder of
comfortable shape and size
to fit the body
making sensual spirit sounds
from deep in the belly
for generations of ears to hear
as if called to flow
as leaves in the wind
drifting wherever they are moved to go
communicating meaning
to celebrate life
to speak to our ancestors
to speak to those who come after us
carrying sounds forever in time.

—*Christine Siarka Bassett*

Untitled

I have grown as I have today
Blossoming love in my heart
Never knowing the hands I'll hold

My one true love
Will he ever know
How much I've loved him?

—*Daisy K. Chand*

Anger

Spitting needles
Betrayals
Fueled by a spirit within
Wrathful and volcanic.

Spite slanders
Spearing, scarring
Revealing my inadequacies
Fears and faults.

Like a wound
Grotesque and painful.
The onslaught thickens
Bursting from my brain
As I pound walls and floors
In desperate release of fury.

The phone rings
For all of my hate
I am still loved
And the anger wilts
As we talk.

—*Barbara Rempel*

Africa Child

Fat but hungry
Big bellied and angry
Big head, thin legs

Rags collected
makes a bed
For an African child.

Stop AIDS
Condition AIDS
But a real African child
Continues suffering.

The fate wornes non
From the president
His cabinet
Members of parliament
Executives
Beggars
And the common man
Of whom all are their for the African child.

—*Obonyo George*

Far From Home

In the cool dark night
Black distance, infinity
Obscure all around
Eternal sleep overcomes
I stare at his wan face,
Death.

—*Julianne Seibel*

Broken Glass

There he lay upon the dirt.
Broken, and shattered like a window,
which had a rock thrown through it.
The suffering is not
out of pain, but out of anger.
Try to join the love,
and grow stronger.
Now, just pray, for which it
will surely dawn that day.
Do not stop
or we will end the same way,
like the man who died,
yesterday.

—*Aaron J. Gowanlock*

Moon Light Stroll...

As we walk along the sand,
Both in love and hand in hand.
Close to each other never to part,
Deep inside I feel my heart.
Every time I see your face,
Faster it gets, I am running a race.
Gently you hold my hand,
Holding hands across the sand.
I never thought that it could be,
Joy and happiness for me.
Kept in your deceitful heart,
More I thought we'd never part.
Never did I ever know,
O'just how you could let met go...

—*Caroline Gayle Kiehne*

Nature, Love, And Life

Ice is like friendship;
Both will support you
But are easily broken

Laughter is like a clown;
Both make you feel good
But with every clown there is a tear

Love is like a rainbow;
Both are beautiful
But a little rain must fall

Lovers are like flowers;
Both are precious
But only a precious few survive.

Life is like a lake
Both are clear and pure
Until they are polluted

—*Nadine R. Fairchild*

The Sorrows Of Love

When someone we love
Breaks our heart
The sorrows of love
Are given to us

When someone we love
Mends our heart
The sorrows of love
Are taken from us

—*Jennifer Kooser*

Morning

Breath of morning,
    breath of May
With your jest of yesterday
    And crisp, balmy
    freshness, smite
    Our old hearts with
youth's delight. Tilt the
    cap of boyhood, yea,
    Where no "forelack"
        waves, today,
    Stroke it with the old
    caress. Let us see as
we have seen, where all paths
        are deevey-green,
    and all humankind are kin,
    Let us be as we have been!

—*Julie Chaney*

Visions of Colors

Many colors around some how
brightens my day.
    All rainbow colors are my
favorite,
    They add happiness
to my day,
    I feel as if I want
to reach the other end.
    To see what's really there,
Perhaps a pot of gold,
    But what I really see
is a beautiful countryside.
    With animals,
To waterfalls,
    And even a few
fantasies appearing.
    A type of illusion
I would love living in,
    Everyday when I need
to get away.

—*Karen M. Boling*

Future Near

The earth, while pregnant once again
Bring forth a prophet (who's not slain).
No castle's roof nor fancy chrome
will we be calling this man's home.

No word, no phrase, will show a slur
for no one's peace will even stir.
And purest love is poured about
The soil rejoiceth with a shout.

And yes my sisters and my brethren
will feel a racial bond together
This victory, this mystery
withstands the storms of history.

The principle of hope and right
will all the unjust doings smite.
From Salem onward to the end
Its message and its orders blend

While ev'ry man includes his kin
This generation's power shall win
Then time indeed shall be no more
We've entered the celestial shore.

—*John Amsterdam*

A Change Of Heart

Living life behind the walls
Built there to protect the heart
Sheltered there with your emotions
And of yourself, sharing only part

But then one day, true love came calling
And you weren't prepared
It climbed over your walls
Catching you off guard and bared

You are scared of trusting it
Wanting it, but rejecting it in part
Such undealt with feelings
Could lead to a change of heart....

—*Kendrell N. Thomas*

The Risk

No brilliance
bursting from her paintings
can unflounder
the beached fish she is.

In her studio, watching,
her peers and critics
are the first to marvel
how she risks
her paintings to conclusion.

In her private life
you could kick her.
For every little turn and move
she freezes, cannot opt...
"Time, I need time,
this is not a painting"...

As if there were no correlation,
life not art,
that insight follows
rather than foreshadows.

—*Stanley Linder*

Shallow Grave

If I die sometime soon
bury me in a shallow grave
where the moon might warn me
of approaching decay.

A shallow grave, yes,
since the deeper one's bones are
the more likely memories
will be that deep too.

Deep bones are hard to find
with shovel or pick or story even.
A shallow grave sets the stage
for discovery.

Two boys pretending to be scouts
or explorers or something of the sort
trip over a clump of dirt with marigolds
blooming from its heart.

The boys will dance then
and kick up the dirt and discover
even more.
Maybe a name even.

—*Joseph F. Nassal*

Daydreams

I am dreaming,
But I am awake.
How is this possible?
'Cause this day was a fake.
In my mind somewhere,
I know I am alive.
But I feel dead inside.

I feel like I'm flying overhead,
Even though I think I'm dead.
I dreaming of dreams,
No one has dreamt before.
Oh, that's not a dream,
I just fell on the floor.

Now I'm unconscious,
Probably die.
Why bother? Why cry?
All hope is lost,
And so am I,
But I have no fear;
I am not afraid to die.

—*Kai Pantin*

To A Lover Far Away

I wake to greet the sunrise,
but it doesn't feel as warm.
And the bed is somewhat bigger,
as I face a solo dawn.

No one to say "Goodbye" to,
as I leave my empty home.
I think of her throughout my day,
and then return alone.

At night I make my dinner,
and I set an empty place.
Then imagine while I eat alone,
that I can see her face.

For my other half is distant,
in a place I cannot be.
And I feel a need to be back with,
the other half of me.

I remember the old poem that says,
"If you love something set it free,"
And I burn a candle in my heart,
that'll bring her home to me.

—*Adam Babidge*

Reason To Be The Sea

I stopped to talk to the deep blue sea
but the sea merely smiled
while the waves lapped my feet.

"Why do you smile?" I asked
"Why do you ask?" It laughed
"Then why do you laugh!" say I.
"If you were I and I were you,
Would you not be laughing too?"
"If I were you and you were me,
I would be the deep blue sea
and carry boats upon my back
With cargoes exotic, eastern spice
to the very edges of this world
and people would stand in awe of me."
"Then you see!" laughed the sea.

—*James Dimond*

Searching

I hear my name in the distance
But they're not calling me
They're searching the past gone
For what I used to be.

I understand my changes
And the pain they have cost
I feel closer to myself than ever
And the same time so lost.

What am I searching for
If not someone of the same
Is it the past that I've lost
Or just the meaning of my name.

I'm wandering in shadows
For in the distance I see the light
The light holds all the answers
But getting there is a fight.

—*Daina Majer*

Canoe

Canoe slide quietly.
Canoe slide peacefully.
Let your only obstruction,
Be your own ripples.
And may your destination, be found.

—*Tim Groenendyk*

How Can You Hear When You Don't Listen?

I cried out to you
But you wouldn't listen.

I begged you
But you wouldn't hear.

I pleaded with you
But you ignored me

Now I am dead
Can you hear me now?

—*Jean Romano*

Heartache

How much hurt
can a heart endure?
I've thought about that often

A child who is yelled at,
ignored or abused
Is that child at fault if
he feels he's been used
as a whipping post, or
just totally ignored?

Oh, how I feel
for that little one
Who doesn't deserve it
no way under the sun

—*Kathleen Dunn McKinney*

Fire

Wax trickles down a pure, white
candle, onto my pale skin.

The hot, melting wax is now my
soul within.

Innocence has turned to sin.

The passionate flame climbing
the burning wick.

Only painful memories seem to stick,
stick to my brain and drive me insane.

Now, my heart is filled with pain.
Thoughts of sadness start to linger.
the heart of fire is filled with anger.

Once my soul was filled with desire,
but now it burns deep in the fire.

—*Keri Rosen*

One More Time

Oh, for the laughter
caught on the lavender moor,
the explosion of stars
that kissed the dream
into oblivion
and celebrated
a fragment of eternity
before winter's nuptial
veils the ground
in a cold embrace.

—*Alice P. Smith*

Downpour In A Mess

Across the veld lay
Carcasses of beasts

Landowner wept like a monkey
Smashed with turpentine in the eyes

The chaff in the villages
Sunk into despair

Beguiled with thirst
As greyhound buried her puppies

When the clouds deepened
In the stillness of darkness

Rain poured like mangoes
Struck by nagging winds

Farmers sung hymns of praises
But my father sung a requiem

For the family dwelling
Was floating in the floods

And our village become another ghost town.

—*Benus Adu Poku*

Untitled

Subway shelter solemn and still
Cocooning herself against Autumn's chill
Dismal dusk, dark and dreary
Awake although tired and weary
Faltering footsteps echo around
Stalking silence, an eerie sound
Pale and pallid, sore from infection
Battered and bruised by rejection
Concrete and cardboard, a
make-shift bed
Despairing, apathetic and underfed
Twisted emotions, tattered and torn
Yesterday's clothing, ill-fitting and worn
Prematurely pushed into maturity
Yet strong shackled by insecurity
As Mum and boyfriend set up home
She tenaciously struggles alone

Life is grim, a daily chore
No roses for Kim, around her door

—*Laura McKinlay*

A Quite Walk On A Winter Night

As we walked home on a
cold winter night the
moon was glowing very
bright.

The night was cold and clear
we could see the stars shining
above and the white snow
sparkling on the ground.

And as we walked he
held me tight and
slowly kissed me goodnight.

—*Grace DeAngelis*

Glide With Me

Come and Glide with me
Come and feel free,
Away from the darkened city
A city with such pity,
Come into the sky
Come let us fly,
The sun and the clouds
Above all the crowds,
Over the tree tops
Over the fields,
Fly, fly around
Without any sound,
Just like a bird
Flying in a whirl,
How wonderful to be free,
Come and glide with me.

—*Jean Atkinson*

Willy In Israel (The Lover In Me)

When will you come home, my darling?
Come from far across the sea:
its blue waves, soft and curly,
now drown the lover in me.

To hold you close and forever;
to be freed from nostalgia;
to smuggle you into my laughter,
to wake the lover in me.

Beware of the sun, lest it scorch
your fresh heart, dearest, you see.
Raindrops trickle down my window,
limp lays the lover in me.

Come back warmer, taller, happier,
if more you can ever be,
but bring me your beauty unchanged
to heal the lover in me.

—*Laura Chalar*

Untitled

Great big leaf,
conspiracy.
Full furry beautiful brown
tall veins,
long.
Others essentially smooth
I got two compliments on you;
do tell
he slipped, he fell
walking through sprinklers on an
autumn day
a lovely girl in his way -
he remembers times:
diving in leaves,
uninvented trees,
when he was younger and she
wasn't there -
but now she's here,
and he loves his leaf;
and he loves her.

—*Joshua Peterson*

Light In The Well

Indigo pearl's
Cosmic dance in a trance
Mesmerised in midnight well
Refractions of the phoenix shell
On sunset's horizontal plate
Sinking fast through western gate
This ancient veil of moon'scape
Silver garment of the One
Shades of rays from golden sun
Amoebic dot of an I's eye
In black ecliptic aperture
Showing well's magnetic lure
Languid in the dawning light
Opens up a second sight
Aegis of eternal rite

—*Winifred Wahlberg*

One

If in my single life span
Could write only one poem
And it make one lasting impression
upon one particular human

The One message flamingly contagious
Quickly spread to one other
the single effort would be worth it
the tale would become outrageous

So the thought gives me courage
And I think "for once" I'll try it;
here's the message! Are you the person?
"Jesus is the answer' Be encouraged!"

—*Jane Scribner*

Dawn In Ireland

Dawn arrives, her silken steps
    covered by the gentle sound
of the mist, as it flows through
    the light at the beginning
of a new day.
    Dew moistened meadows glisten
as if blanketed in a tapestry
    of gems, and the morning breeze
extends a welcome both bracing
    and refreshing.
Oh, to wander this land that
    comforts and protects,
to exult in its radiance,
    one yearns to exclaim to all,
"Pay heed, Erin has awakened!!"

—*Kevin P. O'Sullivan*

Tombstone

Silence is tacked on the stone -
Creating the scenery of fear;
Nurturing the game called peace;
Maturing the ages into fame;
Then life recycles in heaven.

Addendum never runs dry;
Caveat reminds security;
Adios conquers bigotry;
Alleluia greets a holy;
Immortal lives with infinity.

Today a friend have achieved:
Praising the footmarks of journey;
Clipping the mundane of joy or agony;
Serving the jury of man.
Standing pebble is a witness.

—*Angelito Cantillas*

Untitled

Silvery chains, like tinsel
dances on water.
Bejewelled skies, are its ornaments.
Glowing, languishing, luring...
Love nights of music and perfume

Here the light and water dance,
hand in hand.
From the dawn of Day
to the mystic wine of Night.
Incredible calm no thought of time.

Just a tourist in paradise
dreaming of far off stars
and trips to Mars
I'm just a tourist in paradise

Sailing with the wind
Birds gliding on their wings
Enticing sensual desires.
Today, already a memory
Tomorrow, I'll say farewell,
or maybe I'll only whisper...

—*Monique Lengacher*

Prairie Skies

Have you watched a prairie sunrise
Darkness fading with the dawn.
Watched the sun rise slowly upward
Shed its rays on field and lawn.
From pearly grey to rose and gold
Across the sky, the dawn unfold.
See the sky light up with splendor
Turns the world a rosy hue
As the waking birds soar upward
Through the early morning dew.

Sleigh bells ringing, voices singing
Hearts beat fast with eyes aglow
See a winter world of magic
On a sleigh ride through the snow.
Above, the stars, like fairy lights
Sparkle softly in the night.
A glowing moon lights up the darkness
Makes the night as bright as day
While northern lights, like phantom shapes
Dance around the milky way.

—*Kathleen Schnurr*

Time

Slowly it ticks by,
  day
    by
     day,
  month
    by
     month,
  year
    by
     year.
Speedily it goes by,
  second by second,
    minute by minute,
     hour by hour.
Sometimes fast,
  yet sometimes slow.
Now it is going so
fast I can't
finish this.....

—*Belinda Dengler*

In Relation

Beyond bitterness, beyond hurt
deep, deep down
   in the hiddenness
a wealth
  pulses
    seeks expression
.... you bring me joy

Words like a startle
pull back
plunge into, awkwardness
    falls
like nightfall returning into place
.... you bring me joy

Rich, ripe, roundness
flows across the paper,
leaves a feeling
of more to come
   and aching to be,

Then, constant in acceptance
.... you bring me joy

—*Grace Burt*

Destiny Of Man

To be born on this earth is the
destiny of man.
Parochial is our earth
so life on it a triviality...
The value for which
we struggle are a flash in the pan
Let's have a global outlook......
A global feeling for the betterment
of mankind.....
Increase our agricultural
yield so hunger and
starvation will he healed.....
Halt the exploitation
for profit....
And conserve our environment and
prevent destruction.
Our earth has grown
too small soon
she can't sustain us all......
Control population explosion.

—*Simon Leong Choy Yin*

Inevitable Journey

Do not despair my lovely
Don't grip your heart in fear
Life will always give so much
And take it back in time.
We struggled for our first breath
Then worked to stay alive.
Between the termini of life
Waste no time on petty strife
Drain your cup of life's sweet brew
It is your gift
It is your due.

—*Alan Fleet*

I'm Here For You

Listen to me, I'm here for you
Don't shut me out - I need you too.
I can't ignore the way you feel,
I share your pain, I'll help you heal.

No-one should live their life alone,
It's not a crime to need someone.
You're always there to bring me through
So please, let me be here for you.

—*Nicola Elliott*

Climb To The Sky

Yonder on the thermals
Doth the hawks do fly
Gracefully gliding over
Crevice and crag
How simple it looks
So simple the dream
Climb to the sky
Climb to the sky
With rope and carabiners
Harness and shoes
Hand over hand
Every bump every bruise
Talon like fingers clinging to rock
Taking you up and over the top
You stand and look at the hawk
And mutter,
"I should have taken up hang gliding."

—*David Little*

Sadness

Sadness drips, dribbles, drops
     down
 into the gutters and sewers
    of my heart.
Slipping, sliding, slowly
    into pools that
collect in veins and arteries
to be carried through all of me
    To my brain
  until it reaches my toes.
Bathed in sadness,
   surrounded.
   I am
    trapped.

—*Julia Fragias*

Dead In A Book

The blood dripped red
down the page
I was writing my story
my memoir of rage
my pen was dipped
in poison and pain
making me relive
the torture again
the words stumbled forward
ran speeding through mind
the release of my spirit
onto paper unkind

The phrases unravel
the story unwinds
the plot leaves me shaking
and bleeding behind
I thought when it climaxed
my whole world it shook
and now I lay silent
and dead in a book

—*Joe Peretic*

The Disease That Burnt Down My Life

A raging fire,
Driven by a life and furor of its own,
Divesting a body and a spirit of a then,
Leaving a soul to wither and die.

A world of dreams and strength,
In powdery ashes lies,
But born anew a budding spirit and body,
And a world of a now.

Existing, uncomprehended, unaccepted,
For after the crushing fall of death,
So much effort for a weakened hand,
To invite a sun's warmth into a heart,
And the healing raindrops sliding down
A charred breast and thigh.

With a sigh,
I bow to this, a new life,
Fearing its hand, not yet ready to accept its
terms,
Amazed at its awesomeness grace and
strength,
To have overcome the flames.

—*Anita Belliveau*

I'll Remember

A single rose,
dying in the vase
that's all that's left,
of you and me.
I keep this rose,
so I can remember,
how much we were once in love.
I know one day,
The rose will be gone,
but I want to hold on.
Just a little bit longer.
Maybe someday,
we'll again be together,
'til then I'll remember.

—*Stephanie Goods*

Desire

I want to have whole of the world,
Each and every thing.
I don't want even to work for it,
Just aspire for it.
Is there any key,
To make it possible.
Yes, yes.
Really.
Oh, yes.
Only he can make it possible.
Who
The owner of the whole world.
How
Very easy,
Pray Him,
How
Chant His name.
How many times,
You chant it honestly,
He will count it.
And then aspire for any thing in the world.

—*Jagdish Israni*

The Poet

With a book he sits,
Embers glowing bright,
Tempting visions of shadows,
With the fire at its last click
He scribbles;
On love or loss?
His is but to ponder,
To feel and declare undying devotion,
As his mind spills
And heart fills with emotion,
At any point of desire or theme;
He is a thief,
A philanderer,
An artist of words and song,
His passion is but to create,
Bringing tears to the eye
Or a smile to the cheek,
He's a master of utterance
A genius with pretence,
He is a poet.

—*Karl Woolley*

Alone

Without direction in time
emptiness sorrows the
will of man.

Pain understands the bond
of rhythmic energy and a
tear journeys on where
darkness has no courage.

Search the essence of
dreams for perfection,
then blossom into
existence by her silent
embrace.

—*Kenneth Carver III*

The Coliseum

A lyric poem of stones was formed
Exquisitely arrayed in place
This beauty mark that once adorned
The Roman Empire's classic face.

Its curves of elegance and grace
Compel the eye to read the lines
Antiquity has left this trace
A masterpiece of ancient times.

Where people who once gave commands
And fought to make an empire spread
Were entertained in crowded stands
Watched blood turn an arena red.

Great circled verse of grand design
Engraved with massive stones to last
The poem says on the bottom line
The legacy to kill stands fast.

—*Tony Gorman*

Water Lamb

Your infant coat soft and white,
Eyes and nose dark as night.
On the snowy winters land,
Rest my baby water lamb
Don't cry baby, I am near,
Rest, sleep, still your fears.

—*Julie Knight*

Unexpected

Two chairs we sat in
face to face
two adults
mother and son

Two chairs we sat in
face to face
sharing our thoughts
mother and son

Two chairs we sat in
face to face
no future could be told
mother and son

One chair now empty
no longer face to face
but always
mother and son

—*Jackie Polizzi*

Autumn Leaves

I watched a golden leaf
Fall a-flutter to the ground,
Then did fall another
Without an utter sound.

And when my eyes searched to the far
Beyond the naked trees,
Twas then I found my world around
Was full of Autumn leaves.

—*Mitchell John Wilson*

Lichgate

Wish you had divine power
Fan living breath in the coffin
Sending all souls muted violently
"Go back! Go back! Go back!"
Your time's not yet expired!

"Go back! Go back! Go back!
The wells on your kins' faces
miraging with glee
"Go back! Go back! Go back!"
Right of admission strictly reserved

Lichgate...only for the living
To light candles for departed
already in my bosom
"Go back! Go back! Go back!"
Death isn't palatable - live is!
"Go back! Go back! Go back!"

—*Martin P. Monareng*

The Seasons

January, snowing
February, rain
March, the winds a blowing
April, sun again
May, a world of flowers
June, dancing leaves
July, lazy hours
August, golden sheaths
September, apples redden
October, winter is here
November, skies are foggy
December, end of the year.

—*Elsie D. Young*

Untitled

The logs burn slowly
Flames swirl up high
The smoke rises up
Far into the sky

Away in the distance
The sun has set
The moon slowly rises
And is silently met

Met by the shadows
Which fall on lakes
And by the darkness
Which quietly wakes

The stars up above
Shine down on the waves
The summer is over
It's fall at the lakes.

—*David A. Sali (October 2, 1969 -*
October 7, 1988)

Snowflakes

Soft white snowflakes
float to the ground,
Watch them flutter all around
Most of them swirl,
as others twirl.
They dance and prance.
What a show!
As in the moonlight they sparkle
and glow.
Hours later they still
dance in peace,
Each one falling without a crease.
Look out the window, see
what you can find,
All the little snowflakes,
All of its own kind.

—*Nicole Solonenko*

Untitled

I close my eyes
Floating in a liquid state
I smile to myself
Sitting where I am
My legs stir in front of me
Looking at my toes, feet
Map of roads, map of places
Where I drove myself
Around me all is darkness
Nothing else
Sitting where I am
I stretch my arms up watching my hands
I can feel people I touched
Things I made
But why are you here
Why today
There is nowhere to go
Kumba
Nowhere to go

—*Charles Imeme*

Flowers

Flowers grow as tall as towers.
Flowers look nice, and
smell like sugar and spice.
Flowers grow from seeds
and don't look like weeds
Flowers have powers.

—*Kimberly Dykes*

Language

Words, a pauper's wrappings are
For conveying thought;
Simile and metaphor,
Far better they are yet.

Experience pours, will not be caught,
Detained e'en by such traps.
But ebbs her way, we know where not,
A river drained and passed.

Those words rent forth with many sounds,
Or written so to say,
But esoteric babblings bound,
Their meaning's passed away.

If two beside cannot e'en walk
If they do not agree,
What manner discourse is their talk?
'Tis but cacophony.

So with language and her bits,
Soul's substance to convey,
Can but dance in awkward fits
'Less moved by harmony.

—*Bud Lipscomb*

Backward

but conventions are such a Bore.
for now and evermore,

when they see the ground,
and many frown
whose seeds are sown
But life is like this poem,

Awkward.
Backward,
Something eloquent,
Something different,

A different offering.
I am writing
for why in this season,
There is no particular reason,

—*Andrew Campbell*

The Gun

I see the gun as power,
For some it is the messiah,
But only some has the desire,
To let out that fire,
When will they retire?

I see very little hope,
Because some shoot for dope,
And I just cannot cope,
But some think it's a joke,
To kill and see smoke,

Pow, pow somebody is slain,
She was walking a cane,
That family is in anguish pain,
And there is no sweet reframe,
So as a result, no one gain

They shoot for a dollar,
Gun users are of all colour,
From age three and four and older.
I wish the world had a big computer,
To record all the gun murder.

—*Janie M. Villaruel*

My Fantasy Creature

I'll sell my soul
For the heaven I yearn,
  desire for.
I dream of the non existent,
  the unlikely.
Wishing for the stars,
  alone.
I endure hopeless joy,
Yet any love remains within.
Thinking about and caring
  For what doesn't exist.
and cannot be aware of me,
all because my heart belongs to
  a fantasy creature.

—*Tanya McIntosh*

Love Thyself

Love thyself!
  For there is Goodness in Everyman;
Open up your Heart
  And let the Sun shine in;
Its warm rays will pour forth,
  Enveloping those around you,
And, in turn, be reflected back
  In the form of a Love Everlasting.

—*Sarah Martin*

Memories

The memories are all I have
For when you loved me.
I remember you
I remember that night
That night was so bright
It was bright because of you
I remember I loved you
I now realize I still do
But memories are all I have of you, us
I may have lost your love
And those bright nights
But one thing I still have
Are my memories,
And not anyone nor anything
May take my memories
My memories of you
The remembrance of us.

—*Jenny Legault*

Trust In Me

Trust in me, for I am the truth.
For your questions, I am
  your answers,
For your problems, I am
  your solutions.
Trust in me,
For I am the truth.
Never anything to hide,
Never anything to deny
Trust in me,
For I am the truth.

—*Melanie Balcom*

Triangles

Three points in time
Forming together
Conjuring up images
Of ancient stony tombs
Hiding their mysteries
In the ageless desert

Pyramids open your doors
Let us enter
To search your inner soul
For secrets hidden
In the hollow empty chambers
Of your heart

If we stay forever
Within your walls
Shall we find eternity
Amongst the dust
Where proud kings once ruled
Over a different world

—*Peter Hodgson*

Our Oldest Book

'Tis 1600 years old,
found in a grave in Cairo,
serving as death-bed pillow
for a Copt girl.

Composed of four hundred and ninety
pages of parchment, elegantly
filled with dark-brown bamboo script
altho' in obscure dialect,
bound 'twixt wooden covers
and stitched with leather:
'twas her parents' precious psalter —
and, now, our oldest book extant.

For the one recovered, how many
worthy texts have vanished forever.
decayed dust?
faggots for bigotry?
And will a bent computer-virus
trigger a renascent Dark Age?

—*Jagadish Manrakhan*

Insignificance

Imprisoned on this island globe
From all that endless space,
A speck upon a spot am I
And all the human race.

One grain of sand upon a beach
Unknown, completely lost
The universe beyond my reach,
By shifting winds I'm toss 't.

Though insignificant my lot
And ignored is my existence,
I cling to life with just one thought;
What causes this persistence?

—*T. L. Hanlon*

Young Love

I see a face, through the mist,
He's the first one, I've ever kissed.
The first time, he held my hand,
my heart felt like, a marching band.
Side by side, we walked along,
as he sang, my favorite song.
It's my favorite song because,
he wrote it for me, he is my love.

—*Laura Aube*

euthanasia

give me ether
from this emotional implosion
senses in shock
after tremors rack the frame
i wander
in the forest of cacophonic cries
a headless form reeling
i have lost my way
effluence of volcanic activity
seeps out through the cracks
a trail of charring heat

searing
i writhe
i need euthanasia from this state
can i bear the other lifeless state
i do not know

—*annapoorna sitaram*

Come Down

Come down
   from your tower of offices and see.
      Come down to my place
         where you are planning for me
            to deface!

Come down
   from your plane
      come inside, push aside
         those aerial pictures
            before you decide.

Touch down
   to my place, walk on the ground.
      Hear, smell, feel
         the living things that
            I have found.

Come down
   from your position up there on high
      executioner-prisoner, meet eye-to-eye.
         Is it so easy now to justify
            taking Earths last acre from them,
you or I?

—*Kris Yon*

The Road Eternal

On a lonesome road
full of mocking faces

While walking alone
in once familiar places

Is burning desire
and frigid unrest

And haunting dreams
though I never guessed

That the road never ends
but exists at best

And happiness is dying
on your lover's breast.

—*Jay D. Root*

Hockey Heaven

He shoots!
He scores!
and all such wrought,
and through it all... they fought.

—*Ernest E. Paterson*

Untitled

Naked
full of screams
as I began at birth
I walked through time.

Then I returned
   to my present
to accomplish
   my destiny.

Life
is the true home
of a designed death.

—*Alicia Ghiragossian*

The Temptation

Soft moon glowing,
Hanging in the pale sunset sky;
Dark silhouette of pine trees
Blocking moonbeams;
Wind, like a sigh,
Rushes through branches.
My soul longs to gaze for hours -
Let the beauty
Sink into deep recesses;
Let the stillness
Pervade my hurried spirit;
Let the wonder
Refresh my tired mind.

—*Elizabeth Lescheid*

Duty Of Justice

Now that everything
has been discovered,
A wise thing
Not senseless
Will be that well praised
to remit
without hesitation
the claims of conscience
to true Justice
to inquire into
and make a judgement!
And truly
was formulated
a warrant
in which was warned:
if you defend yourself
you accuse yourself
and if you accuse yourself
you defend yourself!

—*D. Mercurio*

Untitled

Jump you little birdie
Hear your mother sing.
Fly you little birdie
Spread your little wings.

You're so very little
And the tree so tall
Oh! I tremble birdie
If you get a fall.

Look! He's flying safely.
He never thinks of fear.
For a little birdie
He knows his mother sneers.

—*Trevor Nicolas Jailall*

"Promise" Me A Smile!

Why must people
Hate before they love?
For then no honor is given
To "The man above"!

This world was not
Made to find its fault
But, to be used as
A "chance" to take a "needed" vault!

Don't let the negativity
Get into your soul
For the "power of positivity"
"makes" your life rock with a "roll"!

Go into each day
With a smile in your heart
And things such as friendship,
Love and "luscious" life will start!

I'm not saying
You can't grieve once and a while
But, after the
Grieving— "promise" me a smile!

—*Karen Priger*

Hope

Yesterday and today
Have already gone
The sun has risen
The moon has shone

The hope for tomorrow
Is in the past
The hope for now
Will no longer last

Here today
Gone tomorrow
Wipe away
Your pain and sorrow

It's not easy
Being me
And it's not easy
Being you.

—*Natasha Hnidy*

Seven Year Revolt

How come the laws of nature
 Have kids turn into teens,
When they go from being angels,
 Into wearing ragged jeans.

They toss rules out the window
 And always disagree,
Mister Hyde and Doctor Jeckel,
 Describes them to a tee.

Their minds are always scheming,
 It's a time we must be strong.
For seven years you wonder,
 If your rules are right or wrong.

Authority they balk at,
 Regulations aren't for them,
But then you find they're twenty,
 And they've turned into a gem.

So don't get disillusioned,
 Your parents felt the same.
Remember that for seven years
 You also played the game.

—*Koreann Kylo*

A Man And His Hammer

A man entered my life awhile ago
He brought with him a hammer
He came upon the walls of my heart
And set to work with vigour

He worked away with love and care
At the mortar between each brick
A happy smile or warm embrace
The tools with which he worked

And with each day, the bricks came down
Till no trace of the wall remained
My love, released, flew out to the man
To the gentle man and his hammer.

—*Chris Warden*

Dark Moon Rising

Last night, it happened again
He came to my room
His hand,
Touching me.
He told me I was Daddy's little girl
He told me he loved me.

She looks at me with accusing eyes.
Betrayal. Sharp. Swift. Stabbing.
Bewilderment.
Shame.

He's not my Daddy!
He's not!
It happened again, last night.

—*Christine Guihot*

Untitled

He comes from the night
He fights with a sword
He dances in shorts
Long blond hair and
deep blue eyes
see through you the things you disguise
With a wink of an eye
and a smirk on his lips
he leans into you
until your hip to hip
Stands on his table
strong and erect
you watch his moves
you crave his touch
and before the song is over
it is already too much
Weak in the knees
and light in the head
He leaves you there
with nothing to dread

—*Laurel Beath*

Lynsey

The Lord looked down upon the earth
He said, "What can I do
For Robert and Elizabeth
To make them happy too
I'll give to them this cherished child
And make their lives complete."
No fairer flower ever bloomed
No star will brighter shine
Than on this day sweet Lynsey dear
God's blessing you will find.

—*James Lawrence Maunder*

God Has No Strangers

God knows no strangers,
 He loves us all,
 The poor the rich,
 The great the small,
 He is a friend,
 Who is always there,
To share our troubles,
 And lessen our care,
No one is a stranger,
 In God's sight,
 For God is love,
 And in his light,
 May we too try,
 In our small way,
To make new friends,
 From day to day,
So pass no stranger,
 With an unseeing eye,
For God may be sending,
 A new friend by.

—*Brian Webster*

The Angel At Your Side

When God created angels....
he made them meek and mild,
then sent them on a mission
to guide each human child.

He gave each one, a gift of love,
of peace, goodwill and joy...
then told them to bestow each gift,
on every girl and boy!

He told them to protect each child
and keep them from harms way,
watch over them throughout the night
and every waking day.

To be their strength, their refuge;
throughout life's rocky road -
to soothe their pain and sorrow,
to share the heavy load!

...Take comfort in this knowledge,
believe your not alone,
the angel at your side
will lift you up!... and take you home!

—*J. A. Hosken*

Easter Morn

 In love and obedience
 He shed His Blood
To save all sinners like me,
 Christ suffered
betrayal, mockery and pain,
 And died at Calvary.

 This Easter Morn Victory!
 No grave, no stone,
Eternal hope to rejoice,
 We see a bright Throne
Christ reigns supreme,
 A Loving King
Death conquered,
 no longer
has the power to sting!

—*Beverly Peaver*

The Lightness

It is as if there was a gate:
heavy
iron clasped
oaken
mounted alone in the midst
of the endless flowered plain;
no wall
only a gate…

And I
standing resolutely
chin up, back to the timbers

And you
the perfumed wind
all around me.

—*D. M. Dusty Gruver*

The Baggage Man

Look out for the baggage man
here he comes again
bearing his problems attempting
to load some onto others yet
wearing others like a fine new coat
Letting everyone into his world
but never crossing the bridge out

Three hours listening time
a generous donation never appreciated
a generous donation never appreciated
and no change

The situation repeats
over and over again

Does he want that on to his inabilities
and what choice inflicting his misery
on others on a wife on children innocent

Your hand over your memories
and your addictions you take no control
The past is your mistress

—*Jennifer Susan Blackwood*

My Little Boy - "Snooks"

Well Snooks what can I say…?
Here I am and there you lay…
I hear the gulls…
They seem to say…
"Leave him alone
and let us play."

I suppose it seems right…
Seems only fair
to think this way
…this way being not clear.

But there you are…
My poor little dear
free of all worry…
to me you appear.

Beneath the soil
On which most children play
There you lay
In an eternal day.

—*Kevin Harrity*

My Coming Of Age

All alone in desolation,
Here I battle with frustration.
Overcome by heat and fire,
Taunt with temptation and desire.
All is lost my ship is sinking,
While I sit here slowly drinking.
All who once have known my joy,
Have misplaced it like a toy.

Now, alcohol's my only friend,
It's my truth so I'll pretend.
All my aspirations lost,
All my goals have long been tossed.
Now all the innocents I had in youth,
Has been lost in this new truth.
Now all my dreams are quickly dying,
Forever now I shall be crying.

What is my part, where is my goal,
I'll give my life, my heart, my soul.

—*Doru Vicol*

The Tattered Teddy

Who could love this bear?
He's tattered and torn,
And his once shaggy fur
is very worn.

Who could love this bear?
His eyes no longer match,
And on his tummy,
he wears a big patch.

Who could love this bear?
On his paw he has a small dent,
And one of his ears
is slightly bent.

Who could love this bear?
He never had any toes,
And now he has a button
in place of a nose.

Who could love this bear?
A child who hugs Teddy tight,
And carries him off to bed
night after night.

—*Judith K. Scheuerman*

Threnody

The old man was prayed out.
His gnarled hands were
As worn as his prayer beads.
Long ago the Holy Mysteries
Had impressed the wax of his heart.
Even his dying was stately
Like the elms outside his window.
His old violin sat silently
On the rocker next to the bed.

The old man was prayed out.
His final breath was handed over
To the Christ he had put on
As naturally as the pines
Put on winter.
When he died,
His spirit was lifted up
On reverent birches
Which stood at attention.

—*John J. O'Brien*

Faith Of An Alcoholic's Wife

Though his world has fallen apart,
his life disaster from the start.
Responsibility he does fear,
and advice he will not hear.
He is totally guilt-ridden
with secrets he has hidden.
The truth he cannot tell,
and his lies are polished well,
He is my husband just the same,
and I proudly wear his name.
On the promises I stand,
the Lord Jesus holds my hand.
In faith I see a vision,
God has made his decisions.
My husband will be well,
set free from chains of hell.
My burdens are made lighter,
our futures' getting brighter.
Through his mercy and his grace,
he will indeed honor my faith.

—*Juanita Molpus*

Spain

Oh, travelers!
How beautiful and joyful,
Yes, so magnificent
Is Spain!
Land of blue heavens -
There are fountains!
There are gardens,
Always filled with songs,
Of little birds hiding
In the shadows
Of flowers,
Where old persons and young
Are always laughing!
There are mountains covered
With snow,
Gleaming toward the sun!
While I,
With my writing book,
Dream happily,
Beneath a pine tree.

—*June Allegra Elliott*

Untitled

Like a monkey at the zoo
how playful are you

in the park
on a swing
climb a tree

all to soon we forget
the child in thee

Watching you brings back
those sweet memories
to me.

—*J. P. Benzing*

Whispers In The Wind

Through the night we move like thieves,
Hiding shadows among the trees.
Your crystal tears reflect the moon,
And deadly flowers are in bloom.
You'll never know my greatest sin,
Although it whispers in the wind.

—*Kerry Seeley*

Back To Genesis

I am walking
I am talking
to my friend

give me your hand
let's go
years ago
we lost us
we never met us
in between.

Now it's time
the sun is shine
let's walk into future
create a new culture

let's talk
let's walk
let's do and create
let's relax and be happy
and be very straight

let's have a lot's fun
let's walk to the sun
let's play a new game
the old was insane

let's look into that endless space
and find there only lovely grace
in our heart certainty
the goal is named eternity

—*Peter Hoffmann*

Untitled

Love is purple
I am violet
You are blue
We together
Are one!
The world
Is
Ours
We glow
In The
Vision
Of what
We
Are

—*Joyce Newton*

Farewell

When I think of you
I begin to cry
as if there were no tomorrow.
I remember your smiling face,
so tan from all the years of labor.
You were always around
to lend a helping hand
and when you were near me,
tears were never shed.
My life was safe,
in a wonderland.
Now you are gone
taken away
when you were needed most.
I stand up.
One last farewell.
I stand up.

—*Katharine Anne Karageorge*

Untitled

Walking by an empty yard
I can see but not too far
In my mind the shadows grow
from a time not long ago

Was it you or was it me
sailing 'cross that emerald sea
In a land too far away
one of us was forced to stay

In the silence I begin
through the darkness once again
slowly 'til I see the light
you were wrong, I was right

—*Jennifer Shaw*

My Love

My love
I cannot wait another day
Since you are only a breath away

My love
How I long for your gentle touch
I miss your loving so very much

My love
I miss your soft and gentle kiss
You are the one I want to be with

My love
Without you life is misery
So please, hurry home to me

My love
I love you without a lie
This love for you will never die
I truly want us to be together
From this day until forever

I love you
My love.

—*Jody Vaillancourt*

The Brook

I'm found beneath a limestone ledge
I curl through mounded snow
Originating from a spring
With many miles to go.

I'm just a babbling little brook
Without the thought of day
No rush to where I'm going to
Just on my merry way.

At times I'm lifted from my course
In palm of thirsty hand
I taste refreshing clear and cold
The purest in the land.

I chatter as I flow along
Sharing time in motion
To meet the brimming river bed
Then the mighty ocean.

—*Ruth Mathews*

Comfort

Do you believe in a love at first sight?
I do, I do; I believe I might....
Carry a torch for someone like you...
Someone special, someone true.
This love we have is never spent....
But always is, heaven sent...
To comfort our souls in this life...
Forever keeping us from the strife...
That easily besets us, on this earth...
Right from day one, right from birth.
So if you need a friend who cares....
Trust in Jesus...He always shares...
The secrets of our soul...
The spirit within, the coal.

—*James Snyder*

Untitled

I felt my life was floating by in sounds
I don't know why
His music in its fast cadence
Revealed to me that inner sense
That destiny was on my heels
That something somewhere spurred me on
Left me no time to linger on
Except to pass the time of day with
Friends I met along the way
With feeling wonder at God's work
The beauty of this earth and all that is
That I might once again belong to this
Enjoy the fruits, the seeds which sprout
Anew each early spring
Sustained by dew which moistens all
Before the sun brings light and warmth
The day's begun.

—*Rjemlije Rjemkje*

He Never Returned Home Again

Life was so treacherous;
I felt dismayed and afraid,
Longing for your return:
What a fool I was.
But now I remember —
Life is but a breath of wind;
He shall never again;
See good days here:
I wilt behold him no more.

Under my very eyes he disappeared:
As clouds break and disperse,
So he that goes down to the grave
Never return back;
My Father —
Never returned home again:
And his place
Will know him no more.

—*Tony El-Buraimoh*

Untitled

There's a child deep within me
I keep hidden though she calls
But the mask will surely melt
When lonely teardrops start to fall
It's the Girl inside the Woman
Still believing dreams come true
Fairy tales have happy endings
She's saving all her love, for you
But the Woman fears the truth
Always watching what the Girl never sees
So the mask is easily mended
forever hiding who she should be

—*Kathryn M. Smith*

To The Man I Love The Most

To the man I love the most
I have a gift to give
There is no charge
There is no fee
This gift of love is his
For free
It knows no bounds
It has no end
To him this precious gift
I send
To the man I love the most
For the sharing, the caring
And the bearing of each other woes
To him this special feeling goes
On and on forever
Will I love this man of mine
And share an everlasting bond
Until the end of time.

—*Catherine Roy*

Distance

The space and time between us
I know we can overcome it,
It's just a slight mishap
That brought us to face...
Distance
The journey in which we venture
For the warm embrace
It's such a little...
Distance
That keeps the smile from coming through
But we can overcome it,
It's just a slight mishap
That brought us to face...
Our love,
Which keeps us travelling, the...
Distance.

—*Lisa Holness*

Listen Friend

Listen friend,
I must say
you've been there for me everyday
you call me up on the phone
you always try not to leave me alone
you bring me up when I'm feeling down
and to make me laugh
you act like a clown
when I'm sad or feeling bad
you cheer me up and act like a Dad
your deep cares I can feel
all of my wounds you can heal
so this poem
I write for you
remember this
our friendship is true.

—*Joyce Anderson*

Untitled

In these quiet, lonely moments
I offer myself to you
Without rest,
Without pause,
Hoping to say the magical phrase
To make you stop
And cast a thought my way.
This sad little game I play
Gives me pleasure.
Hope pours down on me
Like a summer rain
That will not stay,
But lasts long enough
To wash away
My tears.

—*Christine Shaw*

States And Miles Away

The night I saw you,
I right away knew,
I wanted to be the girl for you,
But, you seemed so far away,
I wanted you more throughout the day,
Now you are miles and states away.
   The water may of been deep and cold,
But, you were ever so handsome and bold,
The movie was thrilling and neat,
While you were charming and sweet,
The games we would play,
I wished for that special day,
Now, you're miles and states away.
   As night grows long,
We heard no song,
But, on the radio today,
All I do is pray,
That we'll met again someday,
But, right now you are miles and states
away.

—*Katherine Stoughton*

Solitude

A penny for your thoughts, my dear,
I said to him one day
Your sitting there so solemnly
In such a quiet way
My heart is aching for your thoughts
Be they sad or filled with pain
I lend my ears to you my dear
Your heart and soul will gain
A better understanding
That I stand by you in time
Please, open up your thoughts to me,
Then peace will fill your mind
You seem to think you stand alone
You need no one but you
But stop, and look, time does slip by.
Years left are very few...
The time did come I stood alone
And shed a tear or two
And remembered all the times I sat
Alone not needing you

—*Carole Simard*

Untitled

In my rear view mirror
I saw the setting sun
Burn a hole in the sky
And start the clouds on fire.

The intensity of the blazing orange
Blinded me in splendor
And I longed for a color of paint
That could have that much impact.

The clouds smoldered
In deep purple piles of ashes.
And as the fire slowly died
And the sun bid farewell
I realized I was still alive.

The only real relief from
Pain is Beauty,
And Beauty hides in the
in-be-tweens
Which are easily overlooked.

—*Jay B. Jones*

Wasted Love

As the waves roll into the cliff,
I see my dream come true.
I'll fall into the water
just like I fell in love with you.
The sky is dark with anger
and my heart is weak with pain.
Though the tears roll down my cheeks,
they're hidden by the rain.
My day is dark with you away
and my heart is torn in two.
For the love that grows within me
is a wasted love for you.

—*Joy Kyla Richey*

The Windy Day

The windy day is nice and gay outside.
   I sleep deep into the night
   Then I wake into the morning light.
   I can feel the wind in my soul
   The breeze is nice and cold.
   The trees are tall and green
My feet are bare and my hair is loose.
   I get on my knees and pray
      For another windy day.

—*Keyona Harris*

The Winter Before Pollution

As I walk through the snow,
I stop to hear,
The prancing and prodding
of a lonely cold deer.
With the white on his tail,
and the black of his nose,
he ponders and sniffs
for any close foes.
I cast my attention to
something else new;
A bluejay chirping says,
Winter is nearly through.
I cough and I shiver from
the cold gust of wind,
I knew this one day
would soon come to an end.

—*Krista Mitchell*

You Can Be Superior

You can think that you are superior, you can feel superior.
I do not care for your exaggerated pretenses.
But never try to become superior on my expenses.
I tell you straight and truly, without mystery.
Never try to be superior by somebody else misery.
I am not amused by your fancy stories.
I am not amused by your battles and victories.
I am not interested in your army and armaments.
That to me are just foolish ornaments,
which you think are great; but that stupidity!
Not ask me to recognise your superiority.
Never placate me by long speeches - I like brevity.
I am not too excited by your classy stands.
You are not superior, but you have superior guns.
But I knew already very long time ago, that some bank robbers
had superior guns also, then should I, recognise bank robber as
superiors? Since I refused to do so; you are inferior!
You want to be superior, abandon grandiose idea of single
nation nationality- do something good for all humanity; then I
  recognise your superiority!

  —*Stanley Michalik*

Untitled

Some people look for happiness in material things
I don't ask for much, for my happiness lies with you.
I don't have too much to say when I'm with you
to be with you is happiness.
All I ask is for you to let me share your sorrow.
Let me ease the pain if I can.
Let me share my happiness with you.
I don't have much, but what little I do have.
I'd like it to be yours.
If some day you choose to move on.
Well, I won't hold you for you belong to yourself
I will be happy to have had the time I've had with you.
And if some day you want to return, I will be here.
If neither of us have other ties we can once again
share our lives.

  —*Randy B. Nicholas*

My Worthy Love...

When dawn draws on, and not quite as dim,
I eagerly await to see you, Kim.

You lovely perk from BNA,
I'd fly away, with you today.

When I'm around and in the dark,
Seeing you is like aspark.

Your the kind of girl, that I'd have in my life,
the sort of women to be my wife.

When I've seen you and on my way,
I wish I had time, to stop and stay.

Your personality, lights up my life,
desire for you pangs me like a knife.

As I move on quite nimbly,
I think your the one for me, Kimberly.

Together, we could be like Anthony and Cleo,
I'm sure you're the one for me my fellow Leo.

I, the poet Kim, you'll find a clue,
Who greatly admires and worships you.

I wish I had the guts to ask you out
this is love, that's what it's all about!

  —*A. S. Manning*

Dedication To Aunt Eva

The taste of life forever ingrained on my tongue,
I embellish the thought of it.
My heart pounding, my eyes seek for eternity,
but I can not see it.
My nimble fingers feel all that is material,
but I can not physically reach for it.
The scent of life whispers to me,
I can feel it all around me, yet I can not smell it.
I know what it is to laugh,
the precious memories of my life smile at me.
I know what it is to cry,
for there must be sadness to truly experience happiness.
The sparks of my being light up my heart in a glorious flame,
the heat of my love to envelope those that weep. The strength
of my soul will lead me to the unknown and that which my senses
can not grasp is simply the faith that I feel streaming through
my trapped body lighting the path to my eternity.

  —*Kelli McLean*

Dad, The Man I Love

You make me smile, when you look at me.
I feel so fantastic because I love you, you see.
You lift me high above the clouds so blue.
You are my life, I will always love you.

You're the man I love, you're the man I truly respect.
to know you is to love you, because you are the best
My love is so strong, more stronger than the sea
You are my life, I'll love you tenderly.

You are so special, you are so unique
No one can top you because you are so sweet.
You are a big man, you stand tall and so proud,
you are my life, I'll lift you high above the crowd

When you conceive it, you believe and achieve it too
a man of your promise, the world needs a man like you
You are so honest so fair and charitable
you are my life, you're so lovable.

  —*"Blossom" Joyce Faye Kiefer-Krugler*

I Am A Lion In A Zoo

I am a lion in a zoo
I feel so sad and lonely
I have a few acres to roam around
To hunt for my supper they've deprived me
Oh I do have a mate
But she is just as sad as me
Even to mate we have lost the urge
I go for a walk so she won't see my tears
Oh how I long to be free
but for now we just dream for the life that could have been

  —*Rose Dyck*

Goodbye

As my tears run down my cheek,
I feel the thunder of my heart.
I cannot see what lies, as my eyes are full of fright.
Life has reached its end of the joy and laughter.

We leave this world so bitter and torn,
We leave behind not the material kind
But the thoughts in peoples minds.
But only when, people forget, is when we truly die.

  —*Fidel Martin-Samos*

West Maui Kahuna Eyes

Gazing toward the West Mauis one day from Haleakala;
Another's presence took its hold of me, and I wondered at the thought.
Then from Mauis' mountain folds, in those magic-filled skies —
Arose there a Hawaiian face, looking back from watchful eyes.
Oh, verdant Kahuna eyes,
Why has your paradise so surely changed with time?
Ageless one, vigilant son...
Why is your future here, still yet to be won?
It was then I felt many years had keened, beneath this ancient gaze;
And that he'd been there always, with events sailing on age to age.
From pacific whale watching boys to more helicopter noise —
His jewel never goes unwatched, even filled with rich men's tarp.
Oh, verdant Kahuna eyes,
Can the mana left defend these reefs and skies?
Ageless son, vigilant one,
Or is your future here, as yet to be won?
Maui, Maui, forget me not,
For paradise no longer mirrors the heaven you once sought;
Maui, mai poina oe lau*
Gather as one to make paradise our heaven now.

*Mai poina oe lau is Hawaiian for "Forget me not."
   —*Kimberly C. Wade*

My Magnificat

You have known me since the beginning of time,
I have been the apple of your eye,
And I hold a special place in your universe.

You have guided me,
Protected me,
Inspired me,
Forgiven me,
And have inspired me to try to do your will in
   all things.

I have witnessed your power,
And I have been sobered by your justice;
I fear your full strength,
But I have confidence in your mercy.

Though I feel special, I know a kinship with my ancestors;
You have made us the circle unbroken,
As we acknowledge your overwhelming goodness,
Dear God, our Father.
   —*Kathleen K. Williams*

Dying

Think about me, think about me being free.
I have died many times, but only in my dreams,
When the time comes, don't worry,
For I have lived, what life has offered.
Loved for love...

Now it has come, for me not to receive,
but give.
Give away the life,
Give away the hope,
Gave away everything I've got.
To be me,
To be free.
   —*Ruheyma Akbay*

The Truth That Lies Within

I have walked the highways of the world
I have sought the byways of the world

Searching for the answers that abound
And yet, outside myself they can't be found.

I have sought the wisdom of the world.
I have heard the sages words unfurled.

Then the answers finally came to me
When I sought the man of Galilee!

When you seek for truth you'll surely find
It's not the computation of your mind.

Searching for the answers, from the start
You must find the answers in your heart.

I have crossed the threshold of my mind.
God has touched my heart strings, now I find

Every earnest seeker must begin
Seeking for the truth that lies within!
   —*Joy Linn*

Kinship

Disturbed in dark sleep
I hear the mingled voices
Of yapping coyotes and baying dogs,
Each distinct, yet attuned,
Calling to each other from some distant past;
One yet free, the other fettered by domestication,
But sensing his memory-stirring kinship.
Am I not also bound by this domestication
That intuitively understands the howling paradox?
My voice joins the coyotes' chorus.
   —*Janet E. Graebner*

Hello My Friend

Hello my friend, I see tears in your eyes
I hear the softness of your cries
You've been standing still
Frozen with fear
You cannot cope and have no hope
So come with me just give me your hand
And let me lead you into Gods land

Just see the lush green meadows here
Amidst the beauty of the deer
Just listen to the sounds of birds
And feel the richness of the earth
Just marvel at the colour scheme
And smell the sweetness of Jasmine

Hello my friend, I see no more tears
Forgotten are those empty years
You took my hand into God's land
There is no more fear, but lots of hope
You see my friend now you can cope.
   —*Marga Eich-Collins*

King of Hearts

Everyday that we're away,
I look forward to brighter days.
To laugh and come together as one.
We share what others don't know as fun.
The king of hearts has many,
and with understanding love won't be demanding.
Free as a bird flying away,
Only to come back where it's safe to stay.
So whenever the King feels with his heart,
   he remembers the days of Darts.
   —*Joy Lee*

Nan

Lined face of countless days stared wistfully at me,
I imagined wondering what those dulled eyes could see.

They seemed to stare no farther than the paper's print,
But I knew she was watching me, although I saw no glint.

Wars had ended wars begun, she had seen them all,
Yet she stared no farther than the paper on the wall.

She spoke of nothing more to me than she said last time,
And still I could not decipher her aged riddled rime.

Her youthful thoughts had disappeared into life's melting
    dreams,
And fantasy had merged away into reality's woven seams.

Would I sit so solemn still when life had cheated me,
And then stare no farther than the paper's imagery?

Would I sit so solemn still with but a riddle rhyme,
Or tell my youthful companion be wary of losing time?

   —La Vie En Rose

My Last Goodbyes

I stood by your bedside and wanted to die,
I kissed your cheek and started to cry.
Sitting back and watching you die,
All these months I've been living a lie.
I stood by your bedside day after day,
Watching you die and wither away.
God could not help you, neither could I,
Looking at you lie there I could only cry.
Now that you're gone it tears me inside,
to think of what you went through, taking it in stride.
Now the days has come to put you at rest.
I love you a lot, you'll always be the best.

   —Cara Matijon

Our Children

Looking down at the little hand in mine
I know that there is a responsibility
I give it a squeeze - press it against me
As to give it more accountability

I also feel a hopelessness
Not to be able to protect
When the need might me there
In the future - someday - somewhere

Looking ahead - at the far horizon
I see the storm clouds of warfare
Destruction - pain and hunger may be
It does not at all seem fair

What can I do besides holdings on tight
I know one day the hand will slip out of sight
The child will be on its own

Then I remember when I was that small
And looked up to the one who was so tall
It was overpowering

I wanted to be free
Now I see myself in the little one

   —Joanne I. Lussier

Untitled

I long to die.
I long to die
whenever I see a beautiful landscape,
see the moon or the stars appear,
hear the lone bird crooning again and again
from some far seclusion,
or am surprised with the strange beauty of
a stranger face
whose smile is from other lives and other
loves than now and here.
Who wishes to live
ravished with beauty
and with a blind feel that in the dark recess
of his heart
is a lyre, ready,
with all its strings attuned to tune
and murmuring to every chance-comer of a breeze

.....who wishes to live
when the musician may await us
on the other side of the tomb?

   —Pangkat Harahap

A Cry For Freedom

I want to be heard and truly l listened to.
I need to be loved yet given room to grow.
I yearn to be respected for the many decisions I will make.
I hope for your support when it becomes time to let go.
I, like yourself need room to grow and mature.
I will learn from my mistakes and also learn to correct them.
I need your silent love and support to help me through.
I would like to be respected for the things I say and do.
During my childhood my heart was dedicated solely to you my
    parents.
My heart has grown to make room for the many others I will
    learn to love.
Yet my love will always have room for you.
Please understand my longing to grow and pursue a life of my
    own.
I will always need the love from you,
to help me make it through.

   —Jennifer Wingrove

Heartbeat

As I walked past the garbage bin,
I observed a man eating food he had found within,
And I thought:
In a land that's so rich and free,
Difficult it is for me to see;
People so hungry that they take their hands,
And search through the rubbish of trash cans.
To eat morsels of food thrown away,
So that they can live another day.
One would really be in need,
To use such tactics as these.
For those of us who have plenty of food;
Sometimes look with disgust and say, "How crude!"
Of the man hastily eating,
To keep his heart steadily beating.
Our city must take a stand,
To feed this hungry man.
Homeless, he was, I could see,
What if it were you or me?

   —Karen Hardin

Recollection

Why did you come that evening?
I opened the door
And felt something I couldn't explain
Even to myself

You were so different from your letters
I wish you hadn't been
The next days were like a dream
I didn't want to wake you up
I had to

A wooden shoe is standing on my table
I don't need that to remember.

—*Dorota Davidsen*

A Tribute To The Head Start

Seven or so months ago,
I placed within your hands
One of my most treasured possessions -
My precious little man.

It hurt a bit, to let him go -
That wee small part of me;
What I didn't know, in teaching him,
That you'd be teaching me.

I've watched you giving of yourselves -
The caring that you show
You planted the seed of knowledge within
And I have watched it grow.

My son sparkles, where once he merely shined;
Like a new baby bird who's flown;
Under your guidance and care each child has thrived
And come safely back to home.

I can never truly thank you enough
For everything you have done
But I thank God I placed within your hands
My life - my love - my son.

—*Karen Sibley*

My Prayer

Now I lay me down to sleep,
I pray thee Lord to see,
When dealing with my lowly soul,
Be as merciful as you can be.

If I should die before I wake,
How lucky I have been,
To have a family as loving as mine,
Not many men have seen.

God bless my family, keep them safe,
Through all their earthly years,
Be there to guide them through their strive,
And quiet all their fears.

And when their days on earth are done,
And you have called them home,
Unite us all together Lord,
No more to ever roam.

Amen.

—*Peter J. Lyle*

Thoughts Of You

I think of you often now that your gone
I remember the times we shared together
You didn't care what I was like
Nor I of you
We only cared that our thoughts could meet each other
We had Friendship that could last a lifetime
Or so we thought
I think of you often now that you're gone
This will never bring you back
I will always cherish what we once had together

—*Kathleen Mowrer*

Untitled

Max talked to me the other day (a wild man in his time)
I said "You're gorgeous, Max, but I'm not here to stay."
He said I was a wide-eyed girl and did I know what that means?
He grinned and said for the seventh time "The Edge of Reality!
Why won't you marry me?"
Then Juliette snapped "Oh shut up, Max! I need to do my charts!
Just shut up Max, just leave the girl alone!"
She didn't even look at him, and he stared at the floor,
and when I searched to share his pain, he was standing at the door.
He smiled and gave his "thumbs-up" sign and I did the same;
Max went; Juliette worked on her charts; for her a silence reigned.

And next day Max was back again - he sat down over there -
"Pretty Woman, tell me why I have no scars,
and why I feel no pain."
I said, "Max, ask The Man Upstairs, when you meet one day."
He said he would.
The someone played an LP of the King...
We all heard Elvis sing: The Edge of Reality
and I looked across to see Mad Max crying in his chair.

—*Mavis Stucci*

A Beautiful Picture

I went into a little shop one day and to my surprise,
I saw a picture so beautiful that I couldn't believe my eyes!
"How much is this beautiful picture?" I asked of him.
When he told me the cost, I asked again,
"How much is the final cost?" I asked again,
"How much?" I had not enough, the cost was too high.
When I had to walk away, tears filled my eyes.
I thought as I neared the little shops door,
I could buy the picture, If I only had a few cents more.
Just then I heard someone say,
"Please wrap it for me, and have it delivered today."
I was so sad that night when I went to bed,
memories of the beautiful picture still in my head.
I dreamed I was standing before the Lord, and it was Judgment
day. I had failed to do my best and God had turned me away.
"Almost is not enough, I gave my son for you,
You cannot enter through the gates, You know what you must do!"
I thought of how much I wanted the picture that day,
and how I came short of the cost.
and again, I walked sadly away.

—*Katherine Lucille Gravely*

Untitled

I wrote the bonds
I tore from my depths
the very essence of my art;
which is,
        in fact,
the savagery of my torment seeking release
And thus I gained a reputation
and a responsibility to hone my skill
I am the poet
I wrote the bonds

—*Arnholz*

Secret Child

Little brown girl -
I see your feet flashing past,
A vision swiftly running joyful
Leaping like a jungle gazelle
Heals nothing to the rhythm of my heart.

Bare feet brazen
Beckoning like a drumbeat.
Do you think you can win my heart
By tossing raven hair?

I see a frangipani, soft behind your ear
Whispering of passions unrevealed
And weeping white the blood of purity.

Little brown feet caressing mine
Secret child, to whom do you run?
Lost for a time in the fragrance of the frangipani,
Crushed by some careless hand.

Heat shimmering, fractures your face
Until the shade of sacred words restores your beauty.

—*L. Devindisch*

I Set at the Table Near a Window

I set at the table near a window today
I set there, ate lunch and prayed
Thank you Lord for the happy sounds
I usually don't hear this much laughter
from where I am

The bay is so beautiful, the water and
skies so blue
It makes me feel alive, I loose the blues

Looking around you would not know our nation
is at war
It helps my spirit soar
To know peace can abound
Thank you today for the happy sounds
The sands are so white, the waters so clear
Thank you Lord for being here

—*Joyce K. Nielsen*

"Taunts From The Vanquished"

Come forward ye murderous swine, the second best ever seen
I shall be to your first;
My sabre blood drenched, a few more this day to the Devil will
  perish
For I am already dead, but for thee 'tis a gamble;
'Who will hold my head in hand and cry Victory?'
Blood poureth from my body but here I still stand;
A smile on my face you despair and woe,
I know my fate but which of thee will go to Hell's Gate?
Terror in thine eyes I see, ponder you Fools at this.
Impatient I grow to wait your next move,
Your language I do not understand but your fear I feel,
Tis like the sweat on my brow not knowing which way to go;
Like confused children you surround me and cannot ignore,
So easy to turn away, your battle already won;
But my taunts you despise, my pride all admire -
You knowest many more like me will follow to destroy your
  bloodthirst.

—*David Bonomi*

Fall On My Cheek Tonight

When
I spend my life with you,
There is just only tears.
Because I love you.

When
I tell my love,
There's always the truth,
In our love.

Our laughs are in our hearts,
Our cries are in our eyes.
The tears are falling down from our eyes.
They're falling on our cheek tonight.

Because
Tears are full of lies,
The ones that fall on our cheek tonight.

They look like rain drops falling from the sky.
When the rain drops fall on my cheek tonight.
When the rain is falling from the sky.

It looks like my tears
Falling from my eyes in the night time sky.

—*Joseph M. Terry*

Reflecting

When I remember the warm days
I think of smiling faces
dirty hands, friendly eyes
and wrinkled clothes
When I remember laughter
I think of happy children
big toothy grins, undone laces
and gritty chins
When I remember you
I think of all the fun
we had when
we were together then.

—*Trish Robertson*

Untitled

The house is quiet, I sit alone
I think of the times my kids were home
Their laughter rang all through the house
As the kids would play, sing and shout
Our home was filled with dogs and toys
Dolls and bikes for girls and boys
Guitars they played and they all sang
Their musics sketched upon my brain
Their hugs, their love they gave free
I hope they know what they mean to me
Our house was filled with all of their friends
And it seemed the noise would never end
But all to soon the house is quiet
No more laughter, no more riots
No more guitars ring out their songs
because kids grow up and now their gone
and so I sit here all alone
and think of the days the kids were home

—*Mona Bochar*

To My Brother In Yugoslavia

By the time the white lilacs turned to rust
I thought you would have come to your senses,
But you haven't.

Remember, you always liked to smell the lilacs in our back yard

Remember, Mom used to say;
"He who likes flowers can't be bad."

So why are you bad?

Why are you shooting children, women, old folks,
someone's girlfriend. (Like the way somebody shot yours.)

Have you lost your mind?

    When you come to Canada, as I hope you will-
-you'll see how we get along here.

    But when you come, brother,
leave your history book at home.
Better still burn all your history books Now!

And perhaps
by the time the white lilacs turn rusty again
I'll see you back "home" and we'll vacation
by the Adriatic sea in Rijeka.

—*Charles E. Jambor*

Beach Wear

I touch you; your skin feels strange
I trace you, from your feet to your face
From the curl of your toes
To the electricity of your hair
I kiss you, and fall asleep somewhere
I'm dreaming that you and I are making love
I'm floating, you are high, but I am above
Feeling, the warmth of your every touch
Reeling, I've never known affection so much
My eyes open to see the darkness of the sky
We're still kissing, I can't breathe but I can't die
It seemed forever, reality turned it into a few hours
A heart unsevered, to this day I still feel your power
So long, farewell, take care
To think of you, I just fall asleep somewhere.

—*Darren Paul Wainwright*

I Sit Alone

I sit here alone because we are apart.
I try to deal with the pain in my heart.
I think of you always as I imagine your smile.
But how my arms hurts to hold you now.
I think of your kiss and your gentle touch.
I know that it's you and your love that
    I need and miss so very very much.
When we talk, your sweet voice eases the pain.
But when you say the last I love you, I
    again feel the pain.
When we are together, time just doesn't seem real.
But when we are apart, time stops and stands still.
I know many times you've seen that I've
    had to walk out of our door;
But I long for the day that I'll leave you no more!

—*Joseph B. Porche {COBRA P.}*

A Friend Like You

Life sometimes can be so confusing
I try to win but I keep losing
Sometimes it is a battle to find a way
To have a smile on my face through the day
When I feel down and out, I sit in my room and sigh
Thinking of how bad the day is, as I begin to cry
But with a friend like you, I can't be sad for long
You are there to pick me up and help me along
You give me encouragement whenever I ask
For you know I'll get it done whatever the task
When I couldn't find love and there was no hope
Your shoulder was there to lean on so I could cope
If there is one thing I have learned from you
It is that our special friendship is true
There will be times that I will fall and drop
But with you, I'll find a way back to the top
I can never repay you for what you have done
But if you ever need a friend, I am the one
So when the skies are gray, the sun will still shine through
For it can't be dark for long with a friend like you.

—*Kenneth B. Cruz*

The Amazon Hand

Now I have been touched by the Amazon Hand
I want to run, run into the forest
the air thick with the earth's breath
deep with green thoughts.
Let me get lost there
and do not come to find me
for all that will hold me back
is a tangle of lianas
suckling from the earth's rich breast.
Let me leave you with your thoughts of normality
and go where the trees drop diamonds
and thoughts are dwarfed
by orchids and mushrooms and canopies.
Let me go to the sloths and the monkeys
and beg them to accept me,
or else let me drown there -
deep in watery mysteries.
Let me be washed to the Atlantic
past tapirs and frogs and scarlet ibisis,
happy to be home.

—*Fiona Melrose*

One Small Dream

I want to see Australia and feel her red earth in my hands.
I want to walk for miles across her wide and untamed lands.
I'd like to see America, from sea to shining sea,
And watch the Stars n' Stripes wave in the winds of Liberty.
I dream of going to China, to Hong Kong and Japan,
Of the low veldt of the Africas, of Venice and Milan.
I want to ride a stormy sea, to know her strength and swells,
But the loudest voice of all calls me to the land where the Thistle
    dwells.

I yearn to see an Eagle swoop and fly through clean Scot's air.
I long to walk the Highlands and feel the heart that's beating there.
I need to feast my eyes upon a real life Scottish Stag,
And to hear the music in the air when all the Scots' tongues wag.
I want to stand beneath her towers and watch her flag unfurl;
And to see them dance a Highland Fling, and see their kilts a-twirl.
And how my heart would sing for joy — and no more would I
    roam
To hear a Scotman play the pipes on the soil he calls his home.
To scent the Heather on the wind and to know that peace is mine,
When I stand deep in her forest lands and smell that sweet Scots
    Pine.
Sorrowful, my heart indeed, that I be English born and bred.
My soul is filled with one small dream — to see Scotland before
    I'm dead.

—*Susan Watson*

Night Thoughts

In the endless light of day I think of her.
  I wonder where she is
  what she's doing
  what she's thinking
At night, in the dark and lonely place I sleep
a place she once illuminated and enlivened.
  I wonder where she is
  what she's doing
  what she's thinking
And as days become months, and months
become years I realize that I will be alone.
In life and death. Like a recurring nightmare
I try not to embrace my destiny, still believing
that she may return.
  I wonder where she is
  what she's doing
  what she's thinking.
    —*Joseph J. Fishella*

My Holiday

I'm going across the ocean wide, to home so far away,
I wonder who will still be there, and what they all will say.

There's sure to be some changes there, for time does not stand
still. The people in the town may change, but the mountains
  never will.

I long to visit all my friends, the places that I knew. The
quiet church I learnt to love, and learnt to worship too.

I hear my brothers' grown up now, mother's hair is growing
grey, but I love them just as much, and more, as the day I
  sailed away.

I'm happy here, I like my job, and people have been kind, but,
all the same, I often think of folks I've left behind.

I've been to parties, dull, and gay, I've met all kinds of men,
oh! Yes! I've had a lot of fun, no doubt I shall again!

But oh! I'm looking forward so, to leave, for just a while,
The bustle of the city life, and see my mother's smile.

For summertime is almost here, the skies no longer grey,
There's swimming, dancing, everything, to hasten on the day.

The day when I shall board that plane, and fly across the sea,
To see again the folks back home, who mean so much to me.
    —*Catharine Mary Noble*

If Yesterday Were Today

If yesterday were today I would apologize to you.
I would tell you that you're special to me and
that you've always been, but instead of being nice
to you I was cold and mean.

I would tell you that it was the sound of your
voice, the friendliness of your eyes and the warmth
of your smile that kept me going all day long.
I would tell you that you were my solid
foundation on which I built my life daily, and
that it was your reassuring words that gave me
strength when I needed it most.
I did not admit it yesterday but I do today,
and it's too late, because today you went
away and there is nothing for me to say or do.
If yesterday were today I would tell you I love you.
    —*Yomanda Benjamin*

If I Were

If I were sinead o'connor,
I'd grow some hair,
If I were Madonna, I wouldn't go
So bare.

If I were Jaleel White I'd have a
better role,
If I were Jack Nicholas,
It would be one shot and in the hole.

If I were Guns 'N Roses, I'd just quit
If I were Carl Winslow, I wouldn't have
a fit
    —*Jenna Furtado*

Untitled

If Daddy's were chosen and not by luck of the draw,
I'd have to say mine was the best by far.
Glad am I God gave him to me,
There's none other I'd want you see,
His heart is honest and true,
And men like My Dad are few.
He loves me no matter how dumb I get,
You see he knows too, life isn't through with me yet.
He gives the best hugs of anyone I know,
They make me feel safe and special and helped me to grow.
Of all the earthly fathers I've ever met,
Mine can't be topped, I've not met one yet!
He is the perfect daddy for me,
For through it all, he is mine you see.
Words can't begin to explain how I feel,
But I do know his love for me is real.
  I love you daddy!!!!
    —*Julie Sheppard*

'Flashback'

Only twelve years of age they place a gun in his hand.
"If anyone comes…Shoot!"
She he sits on a sand bag and waits
The tears clouded his vision
The pain of longing, for true freedom leaves him exhausted
yet loyalty keeps him there -
Blanking out the memories that could only do him harm
Faint footsteps echo nearer, he bolts upright … tense
Like an electric current the motion carries through his arm
Skeleton fingers pull the trigger
No!
The shadow falls
He sleeps while another takes his position
The morning sun wakes him
Overwhelmed with curiosity he approaches last night's shadow
He cries, a cry of anger…despair
Empty and bewildered he falls to the ground clasping the body
close to his the familiar shadow
The stranger in the night…His Father
    —*Rosalind Wilson*

Diamonds

Diamonds, diamonds, they grow in the ground.
If you pick'em, you'll get a mound.
Rubies, rubies, they're in the trees,
Farmers say, "Just like peas."
And as you sit with a diamond in hand,
You say, "I want a peach!"
    —*Kevin Bell*

Leaving

It's cool yet warm outside, in the sun that is,
If I don't get cold I can stay.
Christmas is early this year.
They said I'd never see it, they were wrong.
The trees are all decorated with such care.
He painted the leaves, once more, just so I could see.
The colors blend and sparkle, Through water,
I bet He knew that.
There's a fragrance on the breeze, it's the flowers in the field.
They're not really wild you know, he planted them.
He put the grass there too, even the weeds,
He's such a rascal.
I saw a little girl smile today.
I didn't know her, but I recognized the twinkle in her eyes.
It was Him, He's wherever I turn.
I had hoped He would go with me, I've been afraid,
But now I'm not so sure.
I think maybe He should stay
For the trees, the sun, the flowers, the fields,
And the little girl's eyes. I'll find my way.

—*Kenneth W. Aucoin*

No One Understands

No one seems to understand just how serious I am.
If I had the chance, I would leave without feeling any grief.

Parents don't seem to care or let me live my life like a dare.
They just don't understand that they don't have to hold my hand.

If they would just let go, there is so much for me to know.
If they would stand back and let me grow, there would be so much I could show.

That I am able to do things on my own, even if no one has shown me wrong from right,
I will always find a path leading to the light.

The one you think you can trust, he always has a must.
Even he doesn't understand that sometimes you just can't take a stand.

If he really loves me for who I am, then he would really give a damn, that even if I want to go, there is someone who will always say no.

If people knew me for who I am, then maybe they would understand.

—*Sherri Hodgkins*

The Pain Of Love!

Turning the point of our love
if not the dream
the truth is so much sweeter
when combined with life, passion and a kiss.
To seal our souls
in a space so alone
that one could drive for miles and not arrive
but cruise to the border of ecstasy.
This will be such torture
I won't return
but soak my body in the experience
upon a touch
it will decide my fate.
For love is but a reminder
why we exist.

—*Priscella Engall*

Control The Future

There is a light at the end of road.
If you behave like you've always been told,
behold a great reward
the golden chord
of harmony.

It is the light of eternal life.
The warm embrace of your expecting wife.
A child in the womb,
the flowers bloom
with humanity.

We are the ones to make our lives work.
The gorgeous sunsets and the planet Earth,
the vast of the land
are but deaf commands
in reality.

Do you believe in what you've promised me
golden fields as far as the eyes can see.
Life's grains of sand
sift through my hands
with serenity.

—*Kevin Ostroske*

To Be Me

One day I will write a book from start to end
I'll even put in my imaginative friend
Now I can remember how it all began
Talking to myself, oh I wish I had a friend

I was full of fear, even though I felt it
I'd just try to get along
And hope maybe one day it'll all be gone
At times I would live each day to the best I knew
But something came over me
And the pain it grew and grew

I was living my life pretending I had someone with me too
Days were like nights and the nights were so long
I'd lay in my bed and wonder, how will I ever be strong
I know I can't cry 'cause no one can hear me inside
Years still went by, alone and hurting deeper this time

Then with a change my needs were not wrong
That little heart in me was singing
It's alright now, it's time to move on
With that in my mind I'll give it my best
And I'll always cherish the joy of love and happiness

—*Gisele Lariviere*

Home Is A State Of Being

And the where of our world is our reality - Separated by
illusion - expectation and fantasy - Bring it by home!
And the whole of our souls are being constantly challenged-
Incensed by prejudice, starvation and unbalance-
Bring it all home!
   And the why of it all goes unrecognized - Because we
didn't visualize the truth - That believing in love is the
answer- but we trivialize Love as an excuse - Bring it to home!
   So we try to have fun as our reasons - to forget all the
suffering and pain - What is right? What is proper? What is
moral? We ponder questions unsure of our gain!!! Bring
it back home!
   We have to believe in the Truth - when the end comes around
again - And we know truths are our perceptions - Answers just our
questions in reverse - Living for love and our passions-
The only absolute in this world of our thirsts;
We remember living and dying are but moments in time-
from the realities that remain in our thoughts - Bring it to me!

—*Karen Blaine*

Thinking Of You Joey

Of you I'm going to speak,
I'm finding you very unique,
Inspired from above,
You give your love,
To find you in my heart I seek...

With a sexy look in your eyes,
You're making my blood pressure rise,
You show off your body in ways that are naughty,
While others stare on with deep sighs...

You are the only one for me.
Take that thought and put it in the back of your mind.

When you need to think of me,
Open up your heart and I will be waiting for you always.
From the start and always remain yours forever and for life.

—*Kimberly Grigsby*

The Song Of The Soul

If I could trace a melody of Mozart to its source,
I'm sure that I would find my own soul.
Of what Utopia does Mozart speak?
He turns me into a dreamer of golden dreams
That reach out to the very universe itself,
Joining my heart with the very stars,
Bringing ecstasy to my senses,
Blinding my eyes to the manifold tragedy of life.
For what is the darker side of life
Compared to the song of Mozart's soul?
Vital, like the very breath of life itself,
He triumphs over sadness and despair.
Mozart helps me see a future
Touched by beauty and perfection,
Unlimited in pure potential,
The dream of music that tears, however bitter,
Can never wash away...
I listen to Mozart's melody as I never listened before,
And I feel my own soul sing
As it never has sung before.

—*Daniel Mergler*

The Night Shift

The clock has just struck four
I'm tired, so very, very tired
The lids of my eyes are becoming heavy
And I can barely keep them open
My breathing is slower, deep and even
The rhythmic cadence is drawing me
Nearer to the brink of obscurity
I am slowly sinking into a black abyss
From which there is no return
My nodding head begs to be laid to rest
It is increasingly difficult to function
But function I must for I have work to do
And responsibilities that are mine alone
I must not succumb to nature's bidding
But oblivion threatens to overtake me
It's quiet, so very, very quiet
My hold on reality is slipping
I'm falling into the downward spiral
Deeper and deeper
I....zzz...zzz....

—*Linda L. Dowd*

A Wrapper With A Present In

I've got a wrapper with a present in
I'm very glad to get-
Hope it's something I've been waiting for
Upon which my heart is set,
It's wrapped up tight
With strings and tape
I really can not wait -
To open up and look inside
Bet it's something really great!

I've got a wrapper with a present in
I get one twice a year,
At Christmas time and birthday time
From someone close and dear,
I get a thrill
I'll always feel
So happy when I'm bought -
A wrapper with a present in
Perhaps, it's just the thought!

—*Clive Kirsch*

Life And Death

Identities scathed away,
Images sucked dry,
Distant onlookers searching
    Lending an unhelpful hand,
Time starts ticking,
Paving the way for all to be lost,
What is uninvited cannot be avoided.

Identities no longer withheld,
Images once again resurrected,
A distant enemy
    Scorches a not so distant shield,
Any sense of time fades away,
And just when the beating begins to bear its mark
    The path is revealed,
And all that is invited will not be avoided.

—*Dustin K. Rainey*

My Everlasting Love

Out of all the people in the world this individual stands out
in a crowd.
He's one in a million in my life.
He makes me feel wanted and special.
The thirst of love was quenched before I got to know him well.
Yet this love is so abundant I want more and more of it each day.
I have truly everything I desire with him alone.
I cannot see my future without him.
This person is oh, so real to me.
My love for him is more like a promise that I base my life upon.
He is always there for me whenever I need him.
He understands my thoughts and overall situations.
He is strong, and mighty enough to take a chance to know that
I have found love.
I do not mind living for the love of him since he gave the very
best he had for me.
Yet I wish others will look-up for love but when your blind
in sin it's the one thing that you can't see.

—*Keena C. Rimson*

Tears

As she sits alone with tears running down her face and sorrow
in her soul, memories of a childhood filled with fear...and
mother struggling to establish peace where there was none...a
place where footsteps were never sure.
She is but a reflection of her tears...no innerpeace...no
confidence...no harmony...no love.
She does not know when it will end, for to her it seems there
will be none. The torment...the pity...the regret...the pain,
this is what she feels as she sits alone drowning in her tears.

—*Joyce A. Palmer*

Tomorrow's Song

Who seeks the light in the darkness
In a world blinded with you and me
Where does love hide in the fading light?
In the boundless folds of eternity

We've left our hand prints on the clouds,
Our footprints deep in the planet's soil:
We've hacked down mighty forests,
In the name of bread and toil.

Have we forgotten our ancient vow?
Sharing with those that walk and fly
Caring for those who cannot speak,
Shrieking their anguish to the sky.

Let love be a treasured gift
To give and receive with tender care.
Endless as the stars that wink,
And glimmer in the evening air.

This world's on loan to all of us
Look, deep, sincere and true
O world of gentle loving hearts
This is my prayer, my song to you.

—*Terry Lee Erickson*

One Day in the Woods

Walking in the woods one day
In and out of the trees
The wind was whispering
Walking in and out of the trees
Squirrels were scampering
In and out of the trees
I held Daddy's hand talking
In and out of the trees
He laughed I started to sing then played a game
In and out of the trees
Leaves were falling on our heads
It got cold we blew in our hands
The sun went in snow fell to the ground
We ran to the car both scrambling in
Warming our selves from toes to chin
I will always remember that day with him
One day we will do it again
Walking in and out of the trees

—*Ashley Whybrow*

A Lonely Child

There is a little child, his age is of three.
In his soul he can see
his mom and dad not being free.
So now his heart is torn apart
He feels his life has no start.
For he's been left in the dark,
This lonely child, at the age of three.
Who has no family.
He wishes for his mom to see, his love for her and me.
For in his heart he feels the pain
He is alone again.
In his eyes there's a tear.
In his heart there is fear.
In my soul I feel his pain,
of him losing his family again.
With his love for her and me.
His tears drop, forming a sea.
He only wants what used to be
This is called a family.
This lonely child, at the age of three.

—*Dale Birchard, Jr.*

Destiny's Child

She conceived in the colonial tradition,
    in liberty she trusted,
    to bring forth the destined child,
    She patiently waited.

She exalted in her belly of expansion,
    imparting Her great wisdom,
    protecting Her young child,
    within the womb of colonialism.

She provided costly blood to cleanse,
    the native and French infections,
    that threatened Her growing child.

The labor pains began with the taxation of Her body.
She was weary of Her ever-increasing
    struggle for supremacy,
    the time was near, unable to halt destiny's child.

A gradual, painful American birth ensued,
    confusion for the British mother,
    the umbilical cord decisively severed,
    the agonizing birth was finally over.

—*Janell Reyes*

Forgetfulness

Man is apt to forget the contrasts
In nature and life, and all that they mean
In his spiritual growth. Perchance his mind
Is so absorbed in what he sees,
That he doubts the vast realities
He does not see. The present makes
Him blind to the past and to the future
Fooled by glory, he fears not a fall
And baulked in disaster he gives up hope
And sometimes faith.

O' man look at your dominion or
The beasts of the field, or your glorious canopy
of stars, or the eternal hills that feed
your streams, or the wide expanse of mother
earth that nurtures you, and see the
ordered plan of your creator
To him you came and unto him shall you return
O' men, then, learn your lesson and live!

—*Kevin Clay Hughbanks*

Vivian

Her head bent low rocking back and forth
            in slow depression
        shadows blanketing her fragileness
            but not hiding it
            for it is too plain to see
            for everyone who is passing by
the rain-warped cardboard box that she calls home
        She gave her body to men
        and sold her soul to Satan
to still have her dreams shattered to millions
    of sympathetic splinters
        smiling pitifully at her as they
    walk hurriedly by as far away as possible
        believing that they are protected
            from what has damned
        that poor young form that rocks with
            quiet desperation
    and avoids the burning stares of those
            who think that they are
            better than her.

—*Jennifer L. Halpenny*

The Restless Nights

The wind blows strong and steady 'cross the fields,
In the blackness, the white moon yields,
To the pitch black clouds which blot the sky,
The leaves rustle up, oh, so high.
The night is quiet, except for the sound,
Of the nervous birds and the baying hound.
The tall, massive tree trunks sway oh, so slightly,
And deep voice of thunder rumbles ever so lightly.
Across the field a doe runs from the thick brush,
Only to feel the great, swift rush,
Of the howling wind, so sad, yet so lush,
Against the pane of my window, all covered with glass.
Slowly, yet quickly, it comes to pass.
The branches of the trees rustle with the leaves,
A papery nest now silent, with lack of the buzzing bees.
So, the cold, dark night turns to a soft, sweet morn,
As the pearly blue sky begins to take form.

—*Kelly Hayman*

Didn't Hear Your Cries?

After that year you wrote goodbye,
in the darkness I stood to cry,
betraying your promise to love me so,
but away in the darkness alone you did go,
where are you now I honestly ask?
In my life you neglected your task,
for you to nourish support me well,
I'm your daughter you did not tell,
why did you jump from that building so high?
I'm asking, asking please I cry,
I now look into your cold blue eyes,
it's all my fault didn't hear your cries,
now a flower laid on your chest,
putting your soul down to rest,
so now my world is terribly cold,
without my father for me to hold.

—*Cara Diakiw*

The Hummingbird

A little bird, scarce bigger than a bee,
Indeed, a mere speck high in the air,
Descends from out the blue, lights in a tree
Surveys the glorious garden blooming there.
Then, swift as light, he darts down to a flower,
His beak probes deep into its honeyed heart;
To sip sweet nectar 'neath a leafy bower
What ecstasy doth to his breast impart!
As he dips into each flower one by one,
His wings give forth a vibrant humming note;
His iridescent feathers glint in the sun,
A splash of crimson stains his tiny throat …
But lo! A feline form comes into view.
And the hummingbird flies off into the blue!

—*Elsie Mitchell*

Awakening

Praise! soul of the dawn
integrated
of beauty alone, aware

Sweetness of sleep, beginning and end
all perfection becoming visible
pleasures now less rare
mysteries forgotten with "I am, you are"
monuments gone   new strength
waterfalls everywhere, without illusion
golden and glorious sun
praise!

—*Judith Edson*

The Looking Glass

The cold floor shoots icy darts
into my soft, worn feet.
But soon my toes nestle safely
between the blackish cracks in the tile.

I allow my bright orange towel
to float effortlessly to the floor.
It settles around my bare feet
forming an island, my platform.

Twisting both arms so that palms
are turned upward,
my elbows lock and become
tiny stilts supporting my shoulders.
I lunge forward into the looking glass.

I smile and so does she.
She looks like me but appears to be
only a flat image, an empty mirage.
Trapped in her own smile.

—*Kathryn Strickland*

Bridges

Into the darkness, or into the light,
Into the distance, or right out of sight,
Carrying people, or carrying hope,
Bridges of Iron or bridges of rope.
Bridges of hatred, fear and despair,
Bridges between us but nobody cares,
Bridges across life's inevitable gap,
Life's bridges halt us, lap after lap.
Bridges can help us, carry our load,
A bridge to continue life's treacherous road,
Build up your bridges! Don't let them burn!
They're harder to cross in remorseful return.
Build them with honour. Build them to stay!
A bridge for the crossing. A friend for the way.

—*M. J. Stirling*

A Poem For The Bereaved

Slow but sure, we all must pass
into the final good-night.
Quietly or loudly, slow or fast,
into God's cleansing light.
Clean and pure, into our Father's embrace,
hopefully to become renewed,
and stand before His beautiful face.
Like babies awakened by the sun,
and running to our Father's arms.
Knowing that our work is done,
free and now refreshed
and happy to be one
with our Creator.
Forgiven, not forlorn;
and so, to become reborn
in the true image of light and love.

—*Joseph Terzic*

Destructive World

Ugliness invades me, haunts me and,
is unrelentless in its power.
I feel its scaly hands upon me
smothering me in darkness.
The lifelessness of the distant future
lies heavily upon my thoughts.
No air to breathe, no children playing,
the laden recklessness gone bad.
A barren world of mans creation
lingers in the solitude of absolute destruction.

—*Amber Greenlee*

The Gift Of Family

The kindred body of the family
is but, the variation of life's longing
a part of you will stay within them
a part of you, may then, live on.

All you seek from them, will ever ground you
for, in their cradle, you'll find yourself
you seek encouragement and find it empty
you seek a haven and find a stone.

But their stone becomes your gift
for, it will shape you of your own likeness
and in the contrast of your differences
they will reveal your deepest colour.

They'll throw you back upon your very need
like a friend, who once remembers
how you asked them, to help you walk
and not be carried.

You seek their love but know not, its language
for, its language is about being.

And you can't leave them, for you are ever bound
by life's longing to love itself.

—*Kari Brown*

In the Darkness of the Night

In the darkness of the night I write alone.
Is my face pale? I don't know!
For in the darkness of the night I write alone.

In the darkness of night the shadows have fallen.
Is my face dark? I don't know!
All I see is the page before me, the pen in my hand.
As I write alone in the darkness of the night.

In the darkness of the night I clash with my two lives.
The real and the dreaming, the black and the white.
But in the darkness of the night there is no colour, no sound.
So in the dark space that is night I write alone."

—*Yukiko M. Bailey*

The Bumblebee

I hear the humble bumblebee
    is not equipped to fly.
But yet he manages each day
    this problem to defy.
It seems his wing-weight ratio
    is absolutely wrong.
In spite of this the bumblebee
    goes buzzing right along.

Should someone say "it can't be done"
    think of the bumblebee.
He overcomes his handicap
    and flies just fancy free.
So should you hear discouragement
    just set your sights on high.
Make up your mind and spread your wings
    and get out there and fly!

—*James Stuart Richardson*

Farewell

The cold wind blows as we gather this morning.
It brushes the cheek, so bitter, so scorning.
The memories painfully creep through the mind,
The dreams of the life in a land left behind.

The trumpets are sounding, the march has begun.
After so many years, it is all said and done.
My grandpa before me in his own Sunday best,
Beginning eternal and heavenly rest.

—*Kipp Peppel*

Heaven Or Hell

What the mumbling, meaning masses do not see,
Is that God isn't someone else,
It is in you and me.
What the crying, laughing masses do not know.
Is that heaven is full of infidels
that could not trust themselves below.
What the cynical, callous masses do not hear,
is that while they dream of future splendour
the here and now is at war.
What the ignorant, knowing masses do not feel,
Is that in their strive for glory,
they crush everyone under their heel.
What the greedy, jealous masses do not taste,
Is the polluting of their power
In their god-awful haste.
What the broken bloody masses do not smell,
is the burning of their bridges
on the way to hell.

—*Lija Bickis*

We Write Of Life

The grandest work to me I know
Is that slow song written, with pain
Sadly sang with lyrics to show
The musicians heart was slain

The hidden life of poet is true
When his poetic ways are poorly cried
And he knows the world is threw
Yet listens for the mermaid in the tide

Art from paint and hand from heart
Slowly brushed with deadly truth
With every stroke he falls apart
Still beauty can somehow sooth

The actors life is not his own
For every play in every script
His greatest treasure to see we've grown
The scales of reality are sometimes tipped

Words of writers, books from shelves
Stories told of long days lost
Mother goose and the tiny green elves
We write of life at any cost

—*Etienne Vaillancourt*

Beauty - Elicits Jaundice

The beauty in the tree
Is the home it was meant to be.
The beauty in the rippling fields of golden grain.
If seeing it loaded in the box cars of the train.
The beauty in the rolling hills
To seeing the birds, sliding door and taking spills.
The beauty of the rose
Is its fragrance up the nose.
The beauty of a cut of flower.
Is the grace it gives my lady's take for an hour.
The beauty of a sun catcher cut from gloss
Is that it won't wilt when exposed to methane goes.

—*Gene Kristol*

Summer's End

Ah, summer's end,
it is here again...
Now winter and the cold
Will peek around each corner
Just waiting for the chance to begin... again!
And so it goes...
Back to school - vacations are over -
You'll look forward to winter's end... again!

—*Kate DeMarco*

Let's Protect Our Forest

One of the forest's most important feature
Is the wonderful sights and sounds of nature,
Animals depend on the forest for their home
So to carelessness do not be prone.

A match is a tiny small flame
Which is most often to blame,
A small spark from this short stick
Can reduce forests to ashes real quick.

Forests that burn are such a disgrace
Because it takes many years to replace,
Nothing is left but black scorched ground
Where nothing grows and nothing is found.

It seems man has been somewhat careless
With chainsaw and axe they're not fearless,
Do not destroy thousands of acres of land
Because nature and forests go hand in hand.

Let's keep our beautiful forests alive
Something so precious yet so fragile,
Let's protect this most beautiful treasure
Which offers us life beauty and pleasures.

　　—*Monique Ledoux*

Heaven Separate Us

Down to the winds, empty seclusion
It bothers little, sometimes nothing more;
Behold! What else have thee got - the corruption
Needle pins on loose lemon heads, mercy-killing blind-binded
　　yore;
Bottle necks, witchcraft, deadless desolation, sleepless aches
Perhaps, leave it at the end.

Heaven separate us, when the whole world is lost
Family mishap, subtle gestures, idol-headed features;
Devil worship, untrue ablutions, ill-worth superstitious cost
Star powers, spendthrifts, juvenile delinquency, ghostly creatures;
Mind-blowing conceits, sable money despots, sacrilegious fakes
Whom do thee belong, O man!

Selfish endeavours, stunt prejudices, breaking shells-it's a right
　　way to hell
Impostors, arbitrary lives, interpolations, flockless cheats;
Bloody killings, naked griefs, dirty tricks, politics dwell
Pick pockets, dead cruelty, broken skulls, tight rope monkey feats;
Behold, be thine own self be truest, O thee the heaven hand make
Whom, the earth's bosom protect, O Man.

　　—*Savio E. Vaz*

My Love

My love for you is like a flower
It continues to blossom
Through harsh winters the flower shrivels
Inside me dying without your love, compassion
On warm sunny days the buds open
Absorbing the warmth
Of you my sun
When your with another
It is like my sun is blocked
Clouds form around my world
Yet again the flower
My heart slowly dies

　　—*Kelly Beringer*

Walk With Horses

In middle years I've found a new delight.
It gladdens me- the timing's right.
Walk with horses on a moonlight night.
The meadows glisten like a silver sea.
The real world's gone- there's mystery.
With moonstruck horses, that's where I'll be.
If you have a chestnut with flaxen mane,
A shiny hide, a heart that's tame,
She follows framed in haloes and likes this game.
If you have a black horse, you trace the spot...
The shadow horse - you see what's not,
Delegate of nighttime.. a wake up trot.
And if, by happy chance, you have a grey,
A shining, shimmering beacon will light your way,
An image cast of beauty that lasts for days.
There's something gently magical about moonlight.
It cleans your soul- the eye takes flight.
Walk with horses on a moonlit night.

　　—*Kathleen Buck Swain*

Life

Life is so brief it must be lived fast.
It goes as fast as a crisp, new twenty dollar bill.
The hot summer days,
The clear, cool fall nights,
The fun of it all.
The snowy, winter mornings,
The birth of spring,
The enjoyment of the cycle of life,
Where did it all go,
All the dreams...
Yesterday, thinking about tomorrow,
Whatever happened to those dreams,
Were they realistic,
Were they worthwhile,
Or were they just wasting yesterday?
It's over, the living is complete.
Now it's time to wait for the life to end.
Was it worthwhile or was it just being there?

　　—*Kevin Donovan*

This Golden Land

This golden land, this golden land Oh!
It has devoured my people.
Day after day Xhosa fight with Zulu,
For this golden land.
Week after week Boers fight with Zulu,
For this golden land.
This golden land Oh!

This golden land, this golden land Oh!
It has devoured my people.
Month after month blacks fight with whites,
For this golden land.
Year after year whites fight with whites,
For this golden land.
This golden land Oh!

Yet this golden land, I have given,
To provide provisions for all my people.
On the table they have to divide it and its fruits.
But this golden land Oh!
It has devoured my people.

　　—*Stephen Opira*

Rejoice

There once was an incredible beast who was free.
It rolled about nude on my carpet one day,
It screamed and giggled from the top of a tree,
But then man came and took it all away.
There once was a person who led their own life.
Looking around and learning so much,
Knowing themself so free of strife
How did we become so out of touch?
Who are you who has made all of my decisions,
And decided what I believe and should know?
Into freedom you've made an immoral incision,
And I am buried in solidifying snow.
The blood of my oppression flows and fills the snow.
Can you smell it when you walk on me?
Why won't I ever be free? Is it hard for you to feel so proud
When you must reply that I'm not allowed?
I think tomorrow I will light you on fire
And laugh hysterically until I have no voice.
Perhaps I'm crazy, but you're the liar
I really have no other choice... Rejoice.

—*Olivia Ashbee*

The Ocean

The ocean whispers little secrets to me
It tells me its deepest thoughts,
By casting its treasures upon the shore
Inviting me to understand the way it feels
It expresses its feelings of anger
By roaring its rhythmic voice
It shows me its power and strength
By sending its waves crashing upon the helpless rocks
It shows me its happiness
By gayly dancing about
It conveys its need for compassion
By gently creeping towards me
It lets me feel its loneliness
By withholding any sound or movement
Then it shows me its need for solitude
By slowly drifting away.

—*Leslie Ann Harris*

Dinner for Two

One day I cooked dinner for a friend and me,
it turned out to be a catastrophe.
Thank goodness my date was a person with money
And took me to dine out on a spareribs and honey.

—*E. J. Jester*

Roses In October

Beautiful red roses, blooming in my garden
It's a miracle this time of the year,
Cause soon the snow will be coming down
And November will soon be here.
The leaves on the trees, have all turned red
But no patches of brown on the lawn.
The flowers are blooming like wild flowers
Just as if summer, had never gone.
The calendar says that it's nearly November
Today the temperature's ninety-three,
And in the garden the roses are blooming
An extra gift from Heaven, for you and me.
Yes, roses blooming here in late October
And somewhere the snow's falling down,
The Lord, gave us some extra summer
With green grass and flowers all around.

—*A. C. Tillett*

Wicked Game

He liked to show them what he was made of.
It was a wicked game he played.
He had a mind of his own to survive from.
One that would not be erased.

He would lay his cards on the table,
And play everyone else the fool.
He was the love'em and leave'em type of guy
That used every girls heart as a tool.

Their fondness of him grew disrevealed.
And his presence soon became vague.
His aggravation worked on their ignorance.
His appearance, they presumed as a plague.

Yet his mind would not quit that easily,
And his heart was still in the game.
All this crazy boy had ever wanted
Was his own type of fortune and fame.

But the dawn after darkness turned a mishap.
One shown to his disregard.
He opened his soul for the whole world to see,
Pulled the trigger, and was blown into shards.

—*Nancy Psiurski*

The Poetry

My heart was so full it was close to breaking,
It was becoming a threat to my spirit's awaking.
I had to express what I felt come what may;
Then spirit gave me the right words to say.

They came from my heart and flowed through my pen;
When I thought I was done they started again!
All the feelings inside me so long repressed,
Were right there before me, I felt I'd been blessed.

Like a child who suddenly finds she can see
All the beauty in life, I found that in me!
In place of the sad and sorrowful things
My feelings once were, at last they had wings!

Wings that would carry me so high above
To that wonderful jet stream I now call love!
Through spirit and love I've discovered the light;
Those warm gentle feelings now brighten my night.

Today when I feel that my love's unrequited
I know it's okay and I just get excited,
For that once unknown joy within me so true
Lifts up my spirit and creates me anew!

—*Kathleen Jarman*

Alien's Dreams

I have started on an unusual journey
it was on a morning at a gloomy daybreak
with no boots on and no hood in rain
just in one nightshirt and barefoot
how I founded it I don't know
moonlight guided me I guess
straight in the middle of happenings and fictions
confabulated by night
and I looked into the other side
found a lost talisman
where an attic of the time behind the mirror
an old chest with children's stories
among feathers and sleeping butterflies
was a picture of mine in a white dress
she went out the frames for a while
I mean the girl to hold her by the hands
I didn't like her all my life
and I'm sorry
I won't hurt her anymore

—*Ilona Wenek-Ziemba*

My Poem

My poem has no voice ergo,
It will not sing for you.
My poem has no form hence,
It will not dance for you.
My poem has nothing but a story to tell
A story locked up so long.
My poem has just been waiting, hoping and wondering.
When would its story be told?
Now that my poem's story has been told,
What is my poem - but a lifeless piece of paper.
So people go on living and falling in love,
Murdering their fellow man.
Taking things out and putting them back,
Waiting for their big moment,
Never changing or so they think.
For with each mistake, it's a new beginning marked
But my poem will never change.
And as the wild grow wilder
And as we bury our past in concrete and skyscrapers
My poem's story at last has been told.

  —Kristen M. Dare

Giving

It's more blessed to give then to receive.
It's done a lot on Christmas Eve.

Giving is sharing your love with others.
Giving is loving our sisters and brothers.

Giving is sacrificing your time,
Giving is sharing with others and don't mind.

Giving is going out to the poor,
Giving is witnessing from door to door.

Giving is supporting the work of God,
Giving is laboring in the vineyard.

Giving is spending time in the word,
Giving is going out and preaching what you heard.

Giving is being fully committed to the Lord,
Giving is walking with Jesus on one accord.

  —Joanne Taylor

May Day Greetings

Hooray! Hooray! It's the 1st of May.
It's time to gather wildflowers and play,
To hear the bird's song and give a shout,
because the warming, spring sun is finally out.
It's time for friends to get together
to discuss the wonderful changes in the weather,
to linger over coffee and to sit and chatter
over some things important and some that don't matter.
To remember friends who aren't with us today-
Especially our friends of the 1st of May.
My friends, even tho I cannot be with you
I send you may love and have something for you to do.
Go outside in the morning sun and with a holler let loose,
(It doesn't matter if the neighbors think you are a silly goose!)
Because it is only God who we want to hear us
Thanking Him for this season that always cheers us!

  —Janet Pleger

Fighting Irish

Your heart is pained, your mouth is dry
It's too hard to sound the battle cry

You are so tiny, small and frail
Your body weak, your face too pale

It's not easy for you alone
To try and fight your way back home

So you stopped to rest for awhile
To dream of things that made you smile

You walked through a field of flowers
Drank in their scent, and felt its power

And found a place where there is no rain
No more sorrow, no more pain

How could we all have known
This time you would not make it home

Though on this day my sorrow is great
I know for me you will wait

And one day I will follow you
Through your field of flowers and sky of blue

Today, my heart is pained, my mouth dry
There is no need to sound the battle cry

  —Mary-Lou Craig

In Order To Make The World A Better Place!

Why must some of us
judge people by the colour of their skin?

It is a "root of evil" that some of us sin.

We all love,
we all feel the same pain,
by being prejudice there is nothing to gain.

All of us are alike,
we cry, we bleed,
just a little bit of love and understanding
is what we need.

We are the same in body, the same in soul,
making the world a better place
making peace and love must be our goal.

We must look beyond the colours of our skin,
and look deep inside the colours of our hearts,
deep within,

Let us all join together and join the same race,
and let the prejudice rest in peace forever,
let us not disgrace.

  —Frankie Blanchette

The China Doll

She sits in a corner, not to be found
Lays there lifeless making no sound
She's dressed in rags, has tears in her eyes
Even with tears she lets out no cries
A China Dolls face drawn so right
Beautiful is she to everyone's sight
Although to one she is loved no more
One little girl she was always there for
But the girl is too old for her to play
So now and forever the corner she'll stay.

  —Melissa Miller

Untitled

There was a little girl that loved to swim
Just half a mile away there was a like very clean
She would always go there with her Mom or Dad
The place made her happy when she was sad
She swam in the clear blue water that matched the sky
She observed the happy birds that fly
She would always listen to the sound of waves
The place added joy to her childhood years
Now the little girl is grown up and has a son
Like every child he wants to have fun
Once on a sunny day
She took him to the place where she used to play
He wants to swim and dive
But she says no, even when he starts to cry
"Mom why are you being so unfair?"
"I'm not, don't you know how much I care?"
"But this is what you used to do"
"And your said your parents cared about you to"
"It wasn't the same"
"Can't you see the garbage in the lake"

—*Anna Skalka*

Winter in My Heart

Night, it feels like dark will never end
Just laying alone, without a friend
I wonder if the ship you sail, is your love
Then to drown all the ships at sea
And send my sailor back home to me
For the love that somewhere must be
A finger free, a place for a golden band
It seemed so great my happiness, for a few moments or less
Never gave all the heart for love, was hardly worth thinking of
Dews drop slowly, whilst dreams still gather
Among pale eye-lids heavy with sleep
Anguished by defeated visions, so profound,
Awakened to vitality, no greater joy I have found
Though leaves are many the root is one
I sprayed my flowers to bloom in the sun
I try now not to be a stranger, the pain separating us longer
How can I foretell but someday, when there's nothing left to say.
Now that autumn has turned to snow
The leaves have browned and fell
And the winter in my heart will not go

—*Shaku Aswani*

Fairy

Fairy, fairy fluttering by,
Just like a butterfly,
You look so very, very nice,
Your wings glitter just like ice,
Your wand is gold, and so is your crown,
You live in a tree trunk very, very, brown,
Your bed is made of nice soft petals,
Your kettle is made of very hard metal,
Your blanket is made of a maple leaf,
At sunset you sit on a rocky reef,
And watch the sun go down, and down,
Then you fly home to put on your gown,
Then off you rush to fairy town,
You hope you're not late for the fairy ball,
You dance and dine at city hall,
At last when tired and sleepy,
You fly home very groggy,
"Oh no don't crash into that wall,"
You reach home and into bed you fall.

—*Kashmala M. Qureshi*

King Sun

Soft flush of pinky haze along horizon
Kaleidoscope of blue-green-yellow-orange
Melts softly into one another
Sets the stage for rising star KING SUN.

Brilliant blaze of yellow-gold drifts softly
Upward through the Heavenly mist
And reaching zenith
Throws back head in lusty laughter
At poor mortals down below
Who dare not lift their eyes
To gaze upon the beauty
Of KING SUN.

The Regal One surveys his tiny
Kingdom from above
And satisfied with court
Prepares for glorious exit.

Blazing ball of brilliant red
Sinks slowly through pink-purple mist
In grand finale disappears
Below the inky black horizon.

—*Mickey Ford*

Untitled

As a child I always wanted to be invisible. Being invisible, I knew my parents couldn't tell where I was...hiding. I strove to be very small. That way they couldn't punish me for everything gone awry or imagined slights...rebellions. Imagine now, if I could fly, be light and free, I can spin in the wind...up...outa sight with the autumn leaves, I swirl and dance, I am so light. Leave behind me the fear, all the fear, and double the pain. Riding high on the winds, I need ne'er feel all that yet again. As a child I had no-one to go to, to love me, to come to aid me in my search for self, today...it's why my shrink is paid. Fin'ly now, I've learned to make myself

small enou' to hide midst the leaves...the biggest pile. And on the morrow, when the winds gust strong I can spin in my toe shoes and swirl right along, as the winds twirl you so high o'er the ground up and Up...higher...dancing, swirling all around and as you fall, lightly, silent as each old leaf, I sink to the ground, midst the pungent rotting smell in belief that on the morrow, a much better, cleaner, windier day and with its wind gusts, I can escape...dancing and twirling away.

—*Carolyn J. Barrass-Stuart*

Civilization On Trial

Oh! What bewildering discoveries, and what explosion of knowledge. Like cloud bursts giving new vistas of light with each downpour; the secrets of the atom laid bare, travel into space bringing stellar regions nearer home. The computer know how helping to solve the most complex riddles. And power to recreate life no longer confined to the womb of secrecy; is man on the way to become a super being? Is earth getting turned into a paradise? Alas! The brutal reality gives a picture of abysmal delusion. Man is still as far away from being human as he was before, his bigotry and terrorism, and the ethnic cleansing he practises. Are no whit less appalling than the medieval horrors of human devilry; with aids, scud missiles and acid rain added to his grand armoury for self - destruction. And ghettos continuing to be what they have been through centuries. Shelters of misery and squalor for the millions, is man anywhere near to the millennium, his found hope and dream? Or is he getting tuned to sing the song of death with one big bang? Alas! Civilization is on trial, and the planet is in the red as never before. And no mantra can save man till he learns to adhere to nature's laws.

—*Rebbapragada Suryanarayana Murthy*

Come Sit Down Here Beside Me

Come sit down here beside me and let's share a laugh or two,
Or maybe share some secrets, that's something we could do.
We could solve each others problems or maybe just
    chat for awhile,
And greet all those who pass us with a hello and a smile.

Let's introduce ourselves to others asking for their names,
Overlooking not a single one, let's treat them all the same.
Let us not shun the others while being partial to just a few,
Nor pretend to be one's true friend unless it's really true.

Let us never harm ones feelings, nor cast a single stone,
Upon the name of others for we should leave their pride alone.
So come sit down her beside me and let's share a laugh or two,
I'll bet we make some new friends before this day is through.

—*John D. Jones*

Untitled

I want to be forever moving. Fluid. To venture new lands.
Learn of new gods, kill them and reap their fortunes. I want
to be a wicked, beatnik gypsy. Hair so thick about the head
and shoulders that only two cold, blue diamonds shine through.
Hideous. My skin should be dark tanned and covered with scars.
I want to live just outside of madness. In a small adobe made
of dried mud and diarrhea. The Great Spirit will be scheduled for
tea after my mid-evening masturbation break. We'll take turns
tattooing each other and have long, wonderful discussions on
poetry and politics. He'll try to seduce me with his
slide-of-hand intellect. His brain will squirm under the
weight of my revelations. With the sudden, awkwardness of
inebriation, his rage will have killed a working mother in Ohio
and a few stray dogs in Poland.

—*Kiley Jon Clark*

Dragon's Lair

An untamed land, in a time within a time
lies waiting a beast of great strength and solitude.
The beast lies asleep, resting on a fine line
of tranquility, but for hunger it will soon awake.

Stretching its limbs, its wings unfurl.
It takes a long, dry, dusty breath.
Scanning its glistening body, its tail curls
in anticipation, for the hunt brings death.
Soaring under the clouds, it scans the ground
for food, its hunger is insatisfiable.
Eagle eyes, its appetizer is found. Silently
it drops, towards its prey without a sound.

Unleashing its talons, they sink deep
into flesh, a wailing cry pieces the silence.
A rush of air as wings compensate
for the extra weight as the prey's blood begins to seep.

Towards his burrow; a cave in the mountainside he flies with
his catch as he cries. A warning to any trespasser to beware.
For if they linger, like his meal they will die. And become
                        desert.

—*Kris Page*

I Never Said Goodbye To You

I knew that you were weary and sad at heart - the luster of
    life was through—
I knew how much - you missed the one who meant the world to
    you.
Oh, how you fought life's battles you didn't deserve them at all
But you were there with a caring heart when family troubles
    called.
My heart ached when your steps came slowly - your labored lungs
    were tired too.
But strength was there, you made it so, a tired soldier that was
    you.
Your not gone. No, not at all as long as spring follows winter
    snow.
And birds sing in all there glory for us on Earth below.
Your with me still in every way, remembering happy days.
For beautiful memories never wear out, never fade away.
Your at peace and happy now my heart is lighter too.
I'll say "so long" we'll meet again. I never said goodbye to you.

—*Julia F. Prince*

Our Life

Come with me, take my hand, let's see where our
life will go;
    not to watch as spectators, but actors in God's
created show.
Please love me unconditionally when bad times
may arise,
    find the strength within yourself by looking in
my eyes.
Let's live each day with fullness, rich in love
and laughter,
    let's never look back, or wish to change,
only live happily after.
Have children with me and we'll watch them grow,
    we'll teach them what we've learned, and everything
we know.
Grow old with me and love me, even when my hair
turns gray;
    take my hand on our path to heaven and tell me it
was worth every day.

—*Kimberly King*

It Is God's Will

He came to me the other night, showing me his special
light, for I was chosen to stand before the world, for
            peace and tranquility.

"Why oh why do they still die?" Oh those blasted
fire arms, battles are for no reason "Why oh why those
            wasted lands?"

Look at the beauty that surrounds us all. We must stand
tall, create civilization, do not mutilate, lead our young
            away from those battle grounds.

Build rather than destroy, so our children can freely roam,
    take a look at the grace, the elegance and the charm,
    Before you decide to fire, those wicked fire arms.

            As one we will stand,
            But if divided we shall fall,
            Peace to us all, it is God's will.

—*Dianne Poole*

Darkness

Darkness encloses me
Like a cocoon encloses a butterfly
Before it spreads its wings
For the first time
And flies away.
It is darkness that
At this moment
Frightens me and
As the darkness grows darker
Also comforts me
Because I know that
When I see the light
It will be more magnificent
And brilliant.
It is this darkness that my mind escapes to
When I don't want to face today's realities.
It is this darkness that holds me close
And no matter how hard I try to get rid of it
This darkness.
Stays.

  —Jason Woodward

Summer Days

As the scarlet sun beats upon you,
Like a drum in an orchestra.
You feel your freshly washed clothes,
Seal to your hot sweaty body.
Droplets of sweat trickle down,
Tasting the salt in your dry cracking mouth.
The sprinklers pulse icy arrows of water attacking your body,
Soaking you for evermore.
Now you are frigid and exhausted,
So you look at the pointed needle forest green grass.
You feel their blades go into your spine,
Crushing under your limp body.
The emeralds that now surround you,
Make you feel like a queen.
You see a rainbow full of birds,
Floating like balloons in the air,
Gracefully soaring through the ocean blue sky.
The suns flavorful colors slip away into the night,
Saying a sleepy good-bye as it falls over the horizon.
Good night until another summer day.

  —Kelly Giles

Come Back

Lonely lonely lonely in the crushed alleys
like a fish in the vast sea among the big rallies
Separation torments me through chilly nights
when I dream your sights
Now life is like a scent stinking to taste
I am repent for my haste
Your absence makes me mad
everything looks flimsy to me
unable to sleep till the night deep
Come back! Come back! to slake the thirst of reunion
for gathering stranded life stretches
To give me a new hand take me again to the fairyland
for getting me out of gloomed breaths
life will then become bedecked.

  —Zalid Farroq Butt

Brigitta

When our tongues met
Like lash on snaking lash
When our breath was a shuddering sponge
Sucking at the Du!

Brigitta!

Why did your eyes so suddenly sad?
Why did you become
The sum of all women in one?
And I the primitive enemy,
The flame, that eats away the candle for its game?

Believe me, Brigitta, it was you and I,
And our pure nakedness and the sky.
And do not ask if Freud knew
Why you and I had this screw!

  —Anthony Lobo

Naked In My Head

…And so you walk into my dreams,
Like on the cat-walks in the films.
Every camera angle changes,
Yet at this moment we feel like strangers.
Naked in my head we dance,
Mesmerized in forbidden romance.
I turn and try to glimpse your face,
And suddenly another takes your place.
They warn us everything is wrong,
But something makes us carry on.
Then I'm caught on your bangle with my hair,
The crowd lets out a vicious stare.
The picture fades, the world turns grey.
You walk away. "Don't go" I say.
My eyes won't open, I refuse to see.
As in vain I try to keep this dream with me.
They change the channel, I wake up blind.
And leave you dancing in my mind.

  —Matthew Kirk

Against The Flow

Marvel at the birth of Swamp Gum Creek
lined by guardians of giant Eucalyptus obliqua
and ancient man ferns.

Fresh water crays crawl under its grassy banks
while leaches loop along the foliage
with a radar for warm blood.

Scampering past tidy farms
rainbow trout explore playful rapids
as the creek rages from the recent rain.

By Williams Road it joins the Lachlan river
to be initiated by a sharp undertow
and mugged by a diesel pump.

Passing under a moaning wooden bridge
reeking of rubber and rank ideals
litter laps its fringes.

The only escape is a beckoning eddy
time to plan a rebellion
and ponder the laws of gravity.

  —Robyn Ready

So Much To Remember

Summer sun shines like gold.
Lingering thoughts to hold, the call of the land
takes me back to the mountains and trees,
and the whistle of the train in the valley.
The echo of the sounds of the day,
kept perfect harmony.
September sun shines across the sky.
the days are passing by;
the wind blows, the leaves fall, soon will come the snow,
Remembering good times and stories of long ago.
The season changes once again, bringing warm wind and rain
Mother nature has control. Summer sun shines like gold.
There's so much to remember.
From summer through September,
like walking and talking of nature on the move.
Beautiful you call it, to touch it's like velvet.
So timid and tame, little fawn is its name.
Thought's and clearing the mind of what's right or wrong.
Holding onto a tree limb and laughing in the wind.
So thoughtful and thankful of natures game.

—*Bernice Newcomb*

Transitions

Does ice remember water, remember the
liquid ceaseless slip and slide,
the brief moment of the raindrop and
the immortal surge of the wave?

Do glaciers think nostalgically of snowflakes,
and the wild freedom of the very thin air
that pulls the crystal's order out
of the chaos of the cloud?

I like to think yes, that the water
pouring endlessly in deep caverns,
slowly wearing at the roots of mountains,
carries some molecular memory of sunshine
and of being intimate with rainbows;

That the steam screaming madly from the geyser
must be longing for the blue peace at the heart
of the winter snowfall;
and that the salt-flecked tear is still
yearning for the drift of huge seaweeds,
for continuing an old love affair with the moon.

—*Paul Strube*

The Night

Look out the window, there is nothing there,
Listen during night-time, moonlit shadows can scare.
Chills up your spine, eyes shifting from corner to corner,
Imaginary noises, trees rustling, beware.
Turn out the lights, tip toe to the door,
Lock it quick, then take a glance once more.
All alone, imagination runs wild,
Trembling hands, helpless like a child.
Wind whistling down the chimney, your body starts to stir,
Ears pick up on every little sound, sounds that aren't even there.
The ticking of the clock, the creaking of the floor,
The motionless body you control, turns to where it can be unborn.
Lids get heavy, eyes begin to close,
Sleep looms near, consciousness is what you chose.
Unfocused eyes on the wall, finally relaxed and calm,
Slowly you begin to fall, into a sleep that for hours has called.
Suddenly, sensing something nearby, you awaken with a cry,
Looking out the window, you see daybreak, birds fly.
There's a feeling of contentment, laughter's in your eyes,
Laughter now, but never in the night.

—*Mike Bieganowski*

Window-Leaves

I sat in class today, passively
Listening to lectures on poetry and nature
As I stared out the window
At the campus beyond-obscured by trees.
I noticed, as the wind rippled those familiar leaves,
Blocking the view of harried students rushing to their next
building, how several had turned yellow
Which I was sure had been green during our last class
About plays and the theme of loss.
But I guess it is getting on toward fall
So it should be no surprise - a yellow leaf here or there-
A tree slightly more bare than it was Tuesday.
And then the sun peeked out from behind its cloud.
I could tell because my window-leaves
Began to reflect light back toward our class
And the grey overtone to the day scurried away.
The professor continued to speak about
Adjectives and sunny brooks, but...
What about today?
Did I miss the point?

—*Karlynn Herman*

The Song Of Life

I walked the path of life for long
Listing to cloud pacotis sing its song
The song of Indians on ancient burial grounds
And all life's treasure not yet found
The song of an eagle flying in breeze
And silent unseen creatures
In mute nostrial agony
Until one day the eagle fell out of sight
And went were we all must go
After we play the game of life
A place of fiery pits
Or clouds above
One filled so with love
The other with hate
So listen to the shaman
They just opened the gates

—*Jeremy Jones*

Little Ants

I look out of the window and what do I see,
little ants creeping along, one, two and three.

Creeping along the path they go,
Oh, no Dad's going to mow!

I am a hero to the rescue of the ants.
No, don't go up my underpants!

He, He, He, Ha, Ha, Ha,
Dad has stopped, Harrah, Harrah, Harrah.

—*Jane FitzGerald*

Allie

Softly she comes on tiny little feet,
looking left to right softly she creeps,
to Mommie and Daddy's bed she runs holding
her blanket and sucking her thumb.
Face of an angel, eyes of blue, Allie's her
name and she's just over two.
I feel her as she slips into bed, she grabs
up the blanket and covers her head.
I tell her there she can't stay.
But it's close to midnight and she wants
to play.
Oh! Whatever am I going to do?
With my little girl named Allie whose just
over two.

—*Kathy Starks*

Cabin By The River

By the banks of the river that goes slowly drifting by
Lives an old man in a cabin with a twinkle in his eye
He has climbed the highest mountain and fished the many streams
Now he sits there in the evening and reflects upon his dreams

He remembers days of long ago when he was a lad
Running through the fields and hunting with his Dad
He recalls the tender moments when he had a wife
And the babies born from their love that came into his life

Of the time when war was over and he came back home again
To the little house by the river where his happiness began
There were logs by the fire and lamps by their heads
And the music from his old guitar helped pass the winter's dread

He forgets the worried look on his wife that time
When their baby almost died and they nearly lost their minds
He remembers only good things that happened long ago
When life was beautiful and not full of woe

Now the dear old Fella lives all alone and stays
In the same little cabin where his memory sways
Back through the pages of his life from many moons ago
When the world was full of love in his happy home

    —Elda Myers

Portrait And Prayer

You are older than I and have,
locked in your soul,
all the secrets to my future.

You've journeyed a road
I am only beginning.
You can map the way, but I cannot
walk in your footsteps.
I must find my own path my own way.
I need your guidance.

You have the wisdom and
knowledge only experience can bring,
and courage only love can give.

Your hair is graying, lightened by laughter.
The lines in your face are rivulets from tears.
I love you Mother, please teach me to be a woman.

    —Kathleen W. England

Bi-Polar Suicide

Weave down the tread of a spiral -
look for logical rhyme.
You will find a maze of rejection,
that will last till the end of all time.

The myriad paths that encumber,
the mind of one so endowed,
Doom the appellant to bedlam,
whilst his peers excel in the crowd.

The mob that yields to the order,
that diligence and conventional thought bring,
Turns on the maverick exponent
of that which is far harder to sing.

So pack all your luggage and chattels,
if any remain so to stow,
And retire to the island of quiet,
where nobody else can go.

    —Peter A. Birch

Black Bird

The blackbird flies overhead
Looking for a safe tree bed,
Knowing its life is soon to end.

It's lived a life upon the wing,
Looking for a place to rest,
It's had to suffer a life of hate,
Because of its colour; its family trait.

It found no peace upon the ground,
Its nature is to be skyward bound,
Without fear, without hate,
Which has sealed the blackbird's fate.

All too soon it found its goal,
A small, welcoming, peaceful nest,
Where it can finally lay down to rest.

As it sits, wings folded, laid back,
The blackbird sees a small egg crack,
And as it watches; life begins,
The blackbird's eyes begin to dim,
The egg opens; life starts a new,
As a young blackbird comes into view.

    —William Adams

The Single Red Rose

The snow is falling from the sky
Looking out the window, I wonder why
Despite the emptiness I felt and the tears I had shed
All the memories of us together still swam in my head.
Our parents and many friends thought we were the perfect pair
But now you've gone away, and it's just not fair.
For you possessed the power to turn my life into a dream
Sharing all the ups and downs and the feelings in between.
At the flourist I went to this morning
It was a single red rose I bought
Because today is your birthday, but you're not here;
I was thinking of you a lot.
I really bought the rose in hopes
That it would bring you back
But when I put it on your grave
I knew there was no chance of that.

    —Karen Baufeldt

Untitled

My own little island
Looks cozy and warm
When seas are not raging
From a hurricane storm.
On my little island there's no one around,
For I am the only one who makes a sound.
I hunt my own food, and store lots of water.
Why am I prepared?
for when the season get's hotter.
I sit down and day dream
If I only had a friend.
Would all my sadness come to an end?
In the heat of the sun,
I lay in the sand,
I listen to the breeze.
For this is my land

    —Kellie O'Hanlon

Eloise

Every time I look at you,
love pours from thy heart.
O' how proud a father I stand before you,
I pray only death do make us part,
Silently I worship you, with every step that's trod.
Ever more shalt I yearn for you,
Cometh the moment that you're gone,
O' from the moment I held you,
O' from a babe in arms,
Kindness and the love I take with thee,
        When my life is done.
    —Adam Cook

Learning

Every step proclaims her total innocence
marching and skipping
in imitation of all around her
The way she bends to smell a flower
and then another, and another
And her utter surprise, and care,
to avoid a honey bee
She backs away with exaggerated steps
only to be caught off guard
by an approaching sprinkler
and is brought to squeals of great delight
And as she runs
is absorbed in the erratic flight of a swallow
which she too becomes,
but only for an instant
For a guiding hand awaits
and a mother's patient steps.
    —Pete Leithead

Friends

Could I please help you with that thought
Maybe sift away the lint
Possibly make it clearer
Exactly what you think

Not wanting to pursue this
Is natural dear friend
And I'm not interfering
Forgive, if I offend

Take my hand and walk with me
Let our minds surpass expression
With gentle caring loving need
We'll both explore the lesson

As twilight fades their minds dismiss
The clutter that prevails
The sentiment that passed their lips
Resolved and never fails

Thank you kind and gentle soul
For being here today
To share and to encourage
My thoughts, not my dismay
    —C. V. LaCroix

Growing With Each New Day

Take my life, unused and willing
mold me like soft day
shape me to be all of your wildest dreams
and I will take flight.

Dream of flowers, purple and new
Fragrant and aromatic thoughts of you
Don't forget our day so fair,
Of love in bloom, a dream we share.
    —Kristal Emmitt

My Own Happening

You can't imagine what it's like.
Me and my hunger in a big fight.
Just sitting there staring at food
You have to be able to bear it all
Or better yet, not let the pieces of your life fall
I didn't care, it was something I had to do
Every time I ate, I puked in the loo,
I didn't want to show myself in a bikini
I was scared of what he'd think of me
I had to be slim before I could wear that dress
It got worse and worse till I had to confess
I'm being treated in a mental hospital
Before my psychiatric disease would make things fatal
I met others with the same problem I had
Gourmet dinners also made them mad
Now I'm in group therapy
As if it's going to help me
I don't think I want it to
There's too much pain an eating disorder can do.
    —Yasmine Moussi

Wednesday, Muriel - Thursday, Don

First Wednesday's sad news, then Thursday's shocker:
"Memorial service for Muriel and Don".
At the front of the chapel, surrounded by flowers
This framed picture of Muriel and Don.

Images forever in my memory
Aunt and uncle now gone.
How hard it is to accept
Yet friends gathered that morn.

Images: forever her wrinkled face and smiling eyes,
And he with that baritone voice!

    Not old - both sixty-four.
    Dad's twin sister.
How hard it will be for him losing both -
    Sister and brother-in-law.
Now all that is, is the print of husband and wife
This framed picture of Muriel and Don,
At the front of the chapel surrounded by flowers.

Images forever remain, from the service that day,
    "Memorial for Muriel and Don."
    —Linda Donnelly

Cold/Harsh

Her pleas go unheard,
Misunderstood, or so it would seem,
Like her screams ignored,
Whilst her deep dark sorrowful eyes,
Stunned by surprise,
Look on pitifully as the club thuds against her head.

For the third time in succession,
This time splitting her skull and crushing her soul,
As her last breath is breathed,
Cut short halfway,
With barely a murmur of a scream,
And less than a sigh.

Have you ever heard a seals cry,
Or seen the stains where she once lie,
Where the salt of her tears,
Mingled with the warmth of her blood,
And melted the ice,
But not her attackers heart.
    —Danny Holdstock

The Jungle Burns

While the jungle goes up in flame,
Money, power, and greed are to blame.
Because of ignorance the jungle burns.
　Too many ashes to fill one urn.
　The people engage in useless toil;
　No good for farming is the soil.
　What will come of fruitless gains?
　　Surely not the jungle rains.
　　If you let the jungle burn
　For everyday the mother turns,
　You will never see the rains,
　　Chased away by human flames.
While the jungle goes up in flames,
Money, power, and greed are to blame.
　The people cut for a better life.
　Only to create increasing strife.
　The smoke from fires mar the sky;
Adding to the odds that all will die.
　For everyday the Mother turns,
Ten thousand acres of the jungle burns.

　　—John W. Geyer Jr.

Life

In this life that was given to you and given to me
Most of the things are all for free
There is the sun in the sky the sand and the sea
They were put there for a reason, Someday we will see why
There is a tree in the meadow with a stream flowing by
The cows are in the meadow enjoying the grass
The lambs just frolic about and let people pass
In the night sky is the moon and the stars
When I look up I say to myself
I wonder where is this place that we call Mars
We see the birds on the wing the flowers on the land
Someday we will all learn to understand
Why we were given such a wonderful land
My opinion for what it is worth
We were put here to work to reap and to sow
Be good and kind to others for as long as we go
One day just wait and see
Yes there will be you and I hope there will be me
We will all be taken by the hand to the place we are
told is the promised land

　　—Betty Addinall

From A Weekend In Vermont

Peaceful as a silent river the blades of grass sway calmly in
mother natures gentle breath. Laughing gaily, freely, hearts
oblivious to pain like innocent children; strangers to danger
or fear. White fluff like snow gathers in our flowing hair -
spinning, flying up into a cloudless blue expanse as fragile
fingers release the delicate shells of milkweeds. Lilypads
lounge lazily in a crystal pond and the earth's creatures buzz
joyfully about - life is apparent in everything. A mild breeze
carries musical notes of delight. Best friends enjoying each
others company. From one precious weekend a glorious
friendship grows stronger never to be broken - by anything.
Days to months to years - open ears hear heartache and quiet
voices comfort. Friendship like no other; united,
understanding, kindred spirits. As our journey through
childhood draws slowly to a close, however, you venture down
a different path. I am left behind - bitterness, anger and
pain. Memories like blades - my laughter fades - I must face
the world alone.

　　—Kris Cornwall

Just Me That's There

You watch the wind from the mountain's
moving flower's here and there
As though searching for a special one
hidden some where
And leave's will rustle in the cool night air
But worry not, just me that's there.

Later looking out you watch the wind driven snow
And wonder if what's neath it will ever grow
Sadness seems to be every where
But worry not, just me that's there.

As the year's pass by and you older grow
There will be day's that tear's from your eyes will flow
Yet love will seem around you every where
But worry not, just me that's there.

When God calls you to the land of comfort
and beauty to share
Loved ones gather close to show they care
Then some one puts a flower in your hair
But worry not, just me that's there.

　　—Morris Erickson

A Christmas Wish

I remember who stayed away for years with his sleigh of dreams,
My letters wrote with feeble hand…perhaps he could not read.

This year my writing has improved, of that there is no doubt,
I've learned to spell my needs and wants…and how to write
　them out.

Will you be thinking of me this year and leave a toy or two?
A game of snakes and ladders, or checkers, draughts will do!

As the day got closer, a promise to Santa I made,
On Christmas Day, I'll frolic and play, and thank him for
　decades.

That was not to be…
The mailman came to our third floor with a letter addressed to me.

Your letter I received, well written by your hand,
My letter to you dear Joey, will be hard to understand.

No game or toys on Christmas Day, for Casey on my list.
O'Briens, the Murphys, and O'Hares, I'll also have to miss.
"A Dream Died."

　　—Joseph C. Casey

To My Children

To my children of whom I cherish,
my love for you will never perish.
From late at night until early dawn,
I will be sad when you are gone.

You're too young to wonder why,
Mommy and Daddy said good-bye.
And why we always seem to fight,
there should be peace in a child's night.

You wish you may, you wish you might,
keep us together and make it right.
But grown ups just don't see the light,
no matter how many stars so bright.

And when you go away, I must stay,
and though you will be so far away,
our love for each other will never stray,
for we will be together another day.

　　—John R. Pulver

Shutdown

I wish to swoon quickly, float out and away, waiting.
My night breeze soon comes, gently touching my hair,
Softly pushing in sweet breaths - then crisp bites, burning.
Chills, then warm waves swell on my skin and leave a cloak,
A cloak for safety not warmth, to hold, to remember.
Silence, almost, only the resting sounds of a life force.
Darkness, only a lighthouse is left, pale in the distance.
No more words, only being - peace, love, beauty.
Solitude.

　　—Jo Ann Watkins

To The Little Flowers Of Waterloo

Sweet scented flowers in springtime blooming
Myriads of colors on meadows growing
Touched by the sun, with the wind you're swaying,
Freshen with dew; your smell is inviting.

Oh dainty flowers with petals open
Like lovely maids gazing towards heaven,
From stems that stretch out and prayers spoken
That love to sad hearts be truly given.

Dear little flowers are you souls reborn
Of those men who fought and whose flesh was torn?
If yes, go spread your seeds to lands now known
For war and hatred and let peace be sown.

Flowers in spring you're full of youthfulness
Bending with rhythm in untitled dances
Children of the Earth with glowing faces,
Safe and contented with nature's caress.

Blossoms of hope coming from Gaia's nest
Showers of joy listen to my request:
Throughout this life I've struggled for the best,
Adorn my grave when I am laid to rest.

　　—Antonio E. Lim, Jr.

Greed And Destruction

U nfortunately, the destiny I now foresee
N egates hospitality, encourages brutality
I nevitably, competition breeds insecurity
V irtually destroying guardian conscience
E ventually, "winning" is all that counts
R egardless of the "price" that's wagered
S ingularly, there seems to be no problem
A utonomous entities will be restructured
L udicrously, each "power" will be undone
I ntentionally one by one, not noticeably
T heoretically, superiority will rule all
Y esterdays can't stop destructive greed!

　　—Kathleen Acker

Defeat

Left again at the starting line.
No chance of catching up and now.
Everyone has always ran ahead of me...
The seem to enjoy laughing at me from the finish line.

When I stumbled and fell, scarring my face,
I began to tremble and cry.
I slowly looked up,
with blood dripping into my eyes,
and glanced among all those grinning faces.
Some I knew, some I did not.
Then, my heart quietly shattered
as I saw the one person
I always thought I could trust,
laughing, I saw you.

　　—Cecilia Marie Aers

Ugliosis

Ugliosis, a state of ugliness,
Nastiness turned inwards,
The growing products of hate,
Contempt for others.

Too soon unsheltered saplings face the storms;
Too often our innocent are risked;
Too fast we blame;
Too seldom we praise;
Too slow we forgive.
Too soon, too often, too fast, too seldom, too slow
We set the serpent of our discontent to work.

Gnawing its stealthy way into our souls
The serpent strikes,
Feeds on life, on bright eyes, keen minds,
The very blood of our own,
Consuming all. Desolation.
Confidence, optimism, the Light, all go.
And left?
The mirror of the chaff: ugliosis.

　　—Ruth C. MacKay

Crayole Sky

A sunset .... a look of
　　natural, unknown beauty.
Mixing the colors from a box of crayons
　　to produce unique combinations.
Changing considerably until dusk
　　draws near,
Leaving the color of black over the earth
With silver, sparkling stars that give
The night a polka-dotted look from afar.
Not even a sunset can be matched
　　whether a sunset after each day,

　　—Kelly Jasinski

The Unborn Child

Millions of babies will die
　　Never to see the light of day.
Dear Lord, the life you have created
　　They have taken away.
A small hand will never reach out,
Never know what life is all about.
Small feet will never walk or run,
Golden curls will never glisten beneath the sun.
Little Johnny will never bounce upon a knee.
Little Susie's beautiful blue eyes will
　　never see,
And little Ronnie will never climb a tree,
　　Because you see...
They have taken away their right to live...
And we must stand up and fight to give...
　　It back.
We allow unborn children to be killed
　　Willingly...
And yet we call this land, the land...
　　Of the free.

　　—Kaye Grogan

To Love Again

Oh world besieged by wickedness, so angered by deeds,
Oh world full of angry ones, growing as quickly as weeds,
To prune your garden would let the flowers bloom again,

　　—Kathleen Carno

The Mare and Foal

She looked so weary, and stood all alone
Next to her foal, that was cut to the bone.
In his gray little body, there was no life.
With gashes and cuts, as if done with a knife.
The wolves came running, with all of their might,
She stood to protect him, with out any fright.
They grabbed at the foal, and spun him around,
Knocking the bay mare, quick to the ground.
Her wounds were on fire, and in constant pain,
Draining her blood, from a very large vein.
The mare is now weakened, and hanging her head.
In a few short minutes, she will be dead.
Two lifeless bodies, we found the next day,
A little gray foal, and a pretty red bay.
We knew without doubt, she could not compete
With eight hungry wolves, and their razor sharp teeth.
We took them away, the mare and the gray,
And buried them deep,
It took us all day.

— *Julie L. Whipple*

To A Grain Elevator

'Tis true you boast of no enticing lines,
No graceful curve, no architecture grand.
Quite commonplace your structure has become,
For there are thousands like you in the land.

Your outline, rather, speaks of rugged strength,
Of usefulness, solidity, and power,
As 'mid the winter's blast and summer's gale,
Above the village roofs you nobly tower.

I've seen you through the haze of autumn fog,
A dim, grey outline like a shadow high,
And now, I see your form in outline clear
Against the blueness of the soft spring sky.

You are, at dawn, the first to greet the day,
The last, at eve, to bid the sun goodbye,
And, when no longer bathed in sunset's glow,
A silhouette against the purple sky.

Thus, morning, night, and all year round you stand-
A symbol of great tracts of waving grain-
Serving to lift our thoughts in humble thanks
To Him who gives the sunshine and the rain.

— *Joy Merchant*

Unfold

Death I've told you once or twice, I am not your current type.
No longer young and not yet old, early middle content and bold.
Resting between acknowledgment bouts, in complacent times
   devoid.
Past merryments and tempers boiled, first loves forever spoiled.
All the glory I behold, becomes more precious
as I see your wondering gaze unfold.

Though we have met many times before, in friends and loved ones
I've adored. You always leave them just before they come to
know you well. In your desertion, I've learned to hold some
small control. To keep my temper from raging out as a blind
and battered hollow soul. But oh, cruel death I've seen you
cold, deep in the eyes of the ones I can't hold. Though I've
tried and tried to deny, and joked about you willingly. I've
seen first hand your slow and gentle slide, into those I cannot
hide. I've tried to find them from outside in, but even blind
you always win. Then there's those for whom I fear, they
haven't fallen yet know your sneer. For these I've wondered
long and hard, and in the end have always found; My own sweet
life, and you're not around.

— *Juliana M. Yim*

My New Life

My life is full of empty dreams
no memories of times gone by, endless nights alone
wishing for a better life,
stuck in my own world, endlessly my mind churns up
thoughts of death, depression and hate
how can I make this a better life for me?

I can't, I have tried
I've taken my pills and drink, I feel myself falling
as I lay on my death bed waiting to die
doctors's and nurse's rush about in a mindless frenzy
people come and go bringing good cheer.

The life is drifting out of my body
my soul lifts and I am dead,
I'm floating, floating towards a bright light at the end
of the tunnel
I feel calm, freedom and happiness,
my hearing becomes faint from the world I have left behind.

I am there, my new life
my new home, at ease with myself and others.

— *Robert Morris*

Children

Children are one of a kind
No one goes through life without first experiencing it
We develop as our own individual
An individual that will soon generate our own flesh and blood
A creation of our very own

Let there be life
A lifetime of experience, one of jubilee
The child is as sweet as a sugar dandy
It will learn from you
You will be its awakening eyes

Watch as your child grows
laugh with it, let the child know who you are
Take time to be there, for it does need you
You are its provider
It lives because of and for you

Let the childhood memories remain with it
Teach and learn from it
These moments will reflect back upon you
Let the child reflect back in much the same way
Just as his child will

— *Dion R. Burry*

Growing Old

How sad it is when you grow old
No one to talk to, or take a stroll.

I walk alone among the trees
I look around, and no one I see.

The only ones that wave goodbye
Are the leaves of the trees as I go by.

The breeze that refreshes my mortal soul
It must be You my Dear Lord.

Sometimes I love to be alone
Refresh my thoughts of things I've done.

I am not perfect, I'll never be
But it will help me, Lord, if you walk with me.

Help me, O Lord, along the way
Before I fall and go astray.

I look above beyond that cloud
I cannot see you Lord. Where do you hide?

I have the hope the day I die
That You my Lord be at my side.

— *Julian Gonzalez*

Whisper In The Night

The night was calm and dark,
No stars in the heaven to light me,
I was alone and in reverie,
Couching my lonely heart to sleep.

The consolation I got,
Is the cold breeze of the night,
Giving me a little relieve,
Refreshing my broken relieve,
Until it goes to sleep.

Oh! God how can a person being hurt,
With all the things she has done,
Is this just a trials in life?
Oh! God it is just too hurting to impart.

I gave everything to you my God,
Relieve me a little and console my heart,
If this is a part of my suffering,
I'll accept it, for trials is a
part of your love.

—Socorro Ch. V. Trinidad

Remembering

It was a dark, quiet, solemn morning.
Not a word was spoken.
Many nods, many tears.
Remembering that day,
I only remember the blackness,
sadness and mourning.
I was only twelve when she died.
It was beyond my understanding why everyone wept.
I loved her,
her laugh, her smile, and her beauty.

She always talked of heaven,
how beautiful it was going to be.
Why would everyone cry when they knew she would
be living forever in such a beautiful place?
She's watching me from up there,
I feel her gentle eyes protecting me.
As I look up at the sky now,
all these years later,
I remember her.
I'll always remember her.

—Jennie Elg

Untitled

You must not weep, you must not cry. I am not asleep, I did
not die. When storms will rage across your land, just reach
out and take my hand.

When you ache and hurt, too much pain to bear call my name I
will be there. When all around may let you down, and you walk
about with a weary frown, with a heavy heart, faith so weak,
remember I'm here just seek.

When your lost and troubled far from love think of me as a pure
white dove. When your mind is burdened with a heavy load,
remember together we can walk the road.

Think of me as pure clean snow, the morning sun with its
warming glow. Think of me where ever you go. Think of me as
refreshing rain, designed by God to ease the pain. Think of me
as a feather bed a comforting place to lay your head. Look
closely at the one you love for in their eyes you may see that
dove. Like a child you must come to me. I'll comfort you upon
my knee so please don't weep and please don't cry. I will not
sleep I will not die.

—D. Thorpe

Untitled

The days keep passing,
nothing stops,
Your letters, late to come, grow old;
How can I stay with you
Who never shall know age?
And what of after life - how different then
Will three score ten from twenty be?

I must go on - in trust - with God -
Blind faith some call it.
It is a gamble wherein I stake my all,
(I really take no chance at all)
I know I shall meet you again.

The love that comes to many not at all.
Came to us while we were young;
The love that comes but once,
Was ours - but not for long.

Lines written after a telegram of Feb. 15, 1945
informing me of the plane crash of a young airman friend,
Douglas Guest, in Germany.

—Enid Blume

Memories

I remember looking into your eyes,
Now all I hear is my heart's silent cries.
Now that your are gone.
All that's left is the memory of how much I loved you.

I will never forget the time we shared,
I will miss you forever
I'll always remember how much you cared.

Even though you are with me no longer,
Everyday, my love for you grows stronger.

I feel so alone, so empty without you,
To fill my life with happiness and joy.
Why did you have to go?

If you could only hold me in your arms one more time,
Maybe it would ease the pain,
Of letting go, of the one I love.

Down my face falls one final tear.
As I realize, losing you was my only fear

As I fall into a dreamless sleep,
I promise myself, that my love for you,
Will always run deep.

—Nichole Winters

Self Portrait

A mold of sand or clay
Numerous castings along the way
When will it be in final stage
Sorties into the unknown
Before returning to the home
Embarking on the target journey
An extended period of thrust
Concentrating efforts on what you must
A look backwards, the reflection
To what avail upon this ride
Things accomplished and viewed with pride
What now, a time for a new course
Man's struggle and unending strife
The breath of new things in life

—Kenneth W. Scott

The Legacy You Left Behind

Once a major part of my life,
Now all of a sudden you're gone.
I can't express the sadness I felt
When you left me all alone.

You left me with the uncertainty
Of how my life will go.
What kind of mother, what kind of wife,
Where do I turn when I need to know?

I have to trust my instincts
And the values that you taught.
To try and do my very best
In my life and in my heart.

Oh Mom, how I'll miss the special way
You used to smile and hold me tight.
When everyone else had let me down,
It was you who made everything right.

So now all I have left of the mother you were,
Are the memories in my mind.
Your spirit will live on forever,
In the legacy you left behind.
    —*Jennifer Kay Roan*

Mother Nature

M - Maple leaves turn brown and gold,
O - Oceans wash up shells.
T - The wind destroys when angry,
H - Hail tinkles on the rooftop like silver bells.
E - Earthquakes destroy with split-second speed,
R - Raindrops do their "puddle-y" deed.

N - Nectarines flourish sweetly on branches,
A - Air swirls throughout the land.
T - Tornadoes feast on houses and cars,
U - Unctuous soil falls victim to the farmer's hand.
R - Roses proudly display their blood red petals,
E - Everywhere Mother Nature lends a beautiful hand.

    —*Judi Nitcy*

Thanks

Tis time to render thanks to you,
O person that unlatches the very thought of another,
Releasing words from the ices of the mind that has kept
unspoilingly the treasures of a soul. Who are you?
Such tenderness of spirit, causing the ringing of liberty
to gently urge ones deepest expression.
Are you an instrument of He who knew you in your Mother's
womb;
who called you to whisper loudly to an unconscious world?
Behold the interest of yourself and give the riches
of your being left unspent, for shame.
Come and give that others too will live.
Thanks for the refreshment of chat and the magnificence
of your interpretation; Thanks much, O Father child.
Gratitude defines as a feeling of thankfulness.
I say a kiss on the face with a heavenly gesture.
Ah ha, a smile I do receive.
WE HAVE TOUCHED...
    —*Joyce Horsey Smallwood*

Of Dreams

Of all the dreams that one would dream
    of all things two might share
    no poem would rhyme, no song would end
    with no one there to care
No heart would beat a quicker pace
    no beast would swell with pride
    no soul would hold a memory
    shelved fondly deep inside
The path that one might travel
    would seem too steep to climb, the seasons that would be our
    lives would be but endless time
The Spring would pass without the rose
    without the robbins' song
    the chilling dread of winter would last all summer long
And Autumn's mystic colors
    would fade and turn to grey, the clouds would bring an ebon
    night to mask the light of day
Yes, all these things would be my fate
    but I may boast with pride, for I but dream of peaceful
    dreams with you there by my side.
    —*Kirk White*

Autumn Spectre

Autumn has donned her new pretty dresses
Of burnt orange, burgundy and rust,
Green recesses midst amber caresses.
Came on overnite with a thrust!

Do not mourn the passing of summer days.
Nature replaced them with these displays.
Enjoy each color of precious change
That blankets each hill and mountain range,

Paint brush nor pen can't mimic the drama
(No artist could copy this panorama)
Poet's mere words can never capture
The designs or scenes of this festive rapture!
    —*June Elizabeth Geisler Mihaly*

Our Work

I look to the great sea.

Reflections in the waves spark long old memories
Of childhood fun and games;
Of security, and hope for the future.

No more is the day so long,
    but short and hard.
We work till sweat comes no more...
When it is replaced with blood, we may rest.
But our work is never done!
For eternity we must toil,
    in the dirt and glut.

The fifth angel has passed on the key,
    the key to the bottomless pit.
The door remains ajar.
Our life's work is to close it.

We must learn to drink the fruit of the vine.
Then, and only then, may the toil end.
May our mortal bodies give to Him what
    belongs to Him.
May God keep our souls.
    —*Gilad Moll*

City Lights And The Virgin Girl

A little girl giggles puberty and starts sleeping on the pillow
of dreams. Besides, she also likes to hug a cuddly bear of
dreams on her way to the lap of sleep. After a few pleasant

nights of this sweetly hesitant routine A delicate desire
becomes her bed mate to caress her a suggestive whisper: 'Let
discover; get discovered.' Whispers are always fateful; they

change the texture of an Intimate moment; squeezing the
distance between two souls, They let fuse two desires to a
satisfying discovery. The girl (no more little) yawns a valor;

opening the windows of A room where her virgin solitude is in
slumber; to have a view of the fascinating city lights flashing
and winking invitations out in the street. Discovery is
awareness that comes through fascination or haunt: which Both

have a matching shape, however, differ in taste; as ravish and
rape. She fixes her gaze of curiosity on the view of the
lights and gets haunted. Scared, though, she dares to close
the window of anxiety as she has conceived the haunt of the
lights which have penetrated into her through the vulnerable
window panes of her innocence. Her heart is heavy, she feels a

nausea, a light reflects from her eyes.

—*Arsched Hossain Bhatti*

Garden Of Soul

A bleak night invites the lovers to finally seal their destiny
of eternal togetherness.
She lies in a ballet of weeds, dancing gracefully, surrounding
her vacant body.
He rests in a stripped bed, his tired eyes shut to the rancid
sight of mankind, head hung on a silent chest.
Gliding over every tragic case of humanity, separated they swim
in an eternal demise.
Each gropes through Utopia, desperate to feel the depths of
their ocean souls flow as one.
Now, only with still bodies can they know the other's reality.
Stolen lives now live so true.
Entwined lovers linger above the garden of stone;
the garden of souls.

—*Kerrie Lynn Schnake*

The Dreamer

Upon this log I sit and dream
of far far away lands of Kings and Queens
of shining armor and a pure white steed
I am here for my people in their hour of need.

Today I have two dragons to slay.
Then I'll board my ship and sail away
to rid the seas of greed and sin
those pirates are mad they cannot win.

Damsels I've rescued from tall stone towers
stories are told of my marvelous powers
alas, Mom is calling, I really must run
for I'm in big trouble, my chores aren't dare.

—*Catherine Annett McRae*

Sadness

Sadness is the death of a red rose,
Or a sunset of liquid gold fading into dusk
Behind the Blue Ridge Mountains.

Sadness contains the peacefulness of a night in Spring,
Without the fragrance of the blooming dogwoods.

It comes with a hurricane of confusion;
As the fear of a matador in a bullfight,
Without the time to make a final wave
Of his red blanket to the oncoming bull.

—*Katina G. Brown*

Entreaty

How poor, how weak are words to tell
Of how deep, I truly love thee;
My sweet and gentle Marie, hark me well,
I beseech you, with kind eyes look on me.

Long have I wooed thee, every day and night,
Come take heed, my deep devotion now;
For I, as belted knight, to you my lady bright,
Was never more true, this I solemnly vow.

Should a love so strong, and true as mine
Remain within your thoughts of doubt, unrewarded be?
Oh fill my chalice, with life's gladdest wine,
And to its very brim, fill it full and free.

That I may drink, and the saddest memories, quite forget,
Of the anguish, that caused my heart to ache,
Which I, for a long time have borne, and suffer yet,
For you my sweetest lady, and only for thy sake.

Be kind as thou art fair, my dearest love!
And with your angelic face, sweetly smile on me,
For all that's holy held, by the saints above,
Never would I think it twice, but die for the love of thee.

—*K. Bembnista*

My Dwelling Place

Deep within me is a dwelling place
of joy, dawn-hued…
where soft tints unfold
butterfly-light, and these gentle rays
expand into the distant
fields of consciousness…
until there bursts forth
a crescendo of joyous
light… and sound.

Shadow and sorrow lurk within
a hidden inner space.
Grief and sorrow meld
and cling zealously
to some native melancholy.
Yet they, too, must yield
and fade…
for joy pervades.
Like bursting spring
it spawns new beauty
to that inner glade.

—*Ruth R. Ford*

Love Lost; Love Found

A hurricane of love blows 'cross the sea;
of loves lost and ones that will never be.
A sea of tears raining down from the sky;
of loves that will not last and soon will die.

A river of sorrow flowing downstream;
of love that is like it's a shattered dream.
A storm of hate rages in the night;
love's bitterness carries on the long fight.

Windows of dreams have shattered away;
the moment he left that cold lonely day.
One ray of sunshine though, shines from above;
one surviving dream of someone's true love.

Fear not, all hope is not lost, there's a chance;
to find that one person and have romance.

—*Kelly Houlihan*

The Tea Pot

Awe, the tea pot, how the memories flow
Of my father's sister in days of long ago.
"Why. Hello! How nice of you to visit.
Come, sit down, make yourself at home.
I'll be with you in a minute,
I'll just put the tea pot down."

I can hear her stoke the fire and
place the pot upon the stove.
"How is all the family?"
As we make small talk through the wall,
"I'll bet they're glad to see you,"
As she scurries down the hall.

The hours pass by quickly, as we sit and chat
Of the past, present, and the future,
And all of this and that.
The time has come to wind this visit down
But first we'll have a second cup
So pass the tea pot 'round.

—*Farrell MacInnis*

The Waiting Poet

The water stains the tiles;
Of my prison wall.
The steam hides the chrome,
So I write what I recall.

Remains of a cheeseburger platter,
Like the one at my right-
It was there on that plate;
Leaving clean porcelain white.

I'm a poet at heart,
And whom loves a great poem.
I write images from the mind;
Of liars lost in honesty alone.

The flashing neon brew pictures reveal;
Whom everybody is to everyone.
The music drowns me in a pitcher of beer,
Before looking for my own fun.

Another free spirited woman;
Who's also a honest beautician-
She tries to break this chaste male,
By believing I'm a musician.

—*Terry Grant Broza*

Another September

As I sit and watch another late September sun, I daydream
    of our fearless yesterdays;
    Our love was fresh and distant as the Spring of each new
    year.
Time sang the days and danced the nights, reeling us forward on
    an eternal flight; now we drift apart in timeless intervals.
    In loneliness I reflect on such extravagance and waste.

At times our eyes meet, you hold me and we unravel ourselves
    back to a long forgotten but cherished place.
Many a hard winter may be seen upon our faces; and at times
    the mirror catches my attention;
It speaks the truth which my heart refuses to mention.

As I sit and warm my face in the fading summer sun, I daydream
    of our countless yesterdays;
    Crisp autumn days lie ahead and my soul stores the harvest
    of all we bear.
    In the face of such realism and a cool evening breeze
    you waltz me through another
        maturing
            September sun.

—*Janet H. Williams*

King David

This is a poem for you, my brother David
of whom I have heard countless tales;
whose marvelling eyes I have studied for hours,
upon the walls of our empty
home.
I have often wondered how your delicate
frame would have felt
snuggled close up to mine.
My life,
I know, would have been different,
if only I could have healed your small scarred body.
It is you, my brother, with whom I
have ached to be
friends
for you are the strongest little boy of whom I have ever
heard
and I believe you would have been King.

—*Laura Harris*

Passionate Certainties

'Tis a world to which we owe nothing
Oh, how culture frets with ancient scroll.
Me thought I heard a voice, cry a something,
Exposing people with whom we stroll.

Pleading, in view I so rise in search,
As the five pre-conditions swing with gravity;
Such complexities, welcomed and organized per se
Hath become of late, one aspect, one reality.

The nightmare explodes, there glares the spirit
Weighed down and toyed for some detail;
What period these be, of new thorny merit
Life transcends, steered as if by chain retail.

Some substitutes flutter into near view
Were such believers, alas, pyrotechnic fools?
Time urges on, calling on the chosen few
As utopia ceases to use utopian tools!

—*Johnnie MacViban*

Untitled

To an Orchid
Oh, marvelous creation, -
absorbing your beauty from the forest floor,
what wonder seeds you there?
To be awed and then no more.
For years you sleep, with other flora on your host
to be not just another flower -
but the one above all the blooms.

A tree am I, of not so great decor.
The chemistry I use to make me spread so tall,
will in turn, from off me, make you fall.
Although it is said that from my flora you spring
You are adorned with splendor fine, I only wish you were mine
But trees will never be so blessed, even in reaching for the clouds
We cannot compare to your first frost color of white and then in
    violet shroud.
So stay oh, Orchid Fair!

—*Elizabeth Frost*

My Favorite Place

A lonely park
On a cool summer day
In the mid-afternoon

Birds chirping
The wind howling
And ducks quacking

I see bright green grass
The clear blue sky

I like lying on the grass
Building sand castles
And going for a walk on the stone path

But only when the sun is high and there's a blue sky
I will be relaxed

—*Julie Simmers*

My Story Of Fred

There once was a boy named Fred. When he was five he fled.
On the ground he lay. In a pile of hay.
When Fred was a big kid. The alley is where he hid.
His food from a trash can. And soon he'd be a young man.
Now Fred is a young teen. And love he hasn't seen.
His heart had only hate. And raw meat is what he ate.
Now Fred lives in a State Penn. For committing a very bad sin.
He shot a man in the head. For merely what the guy said.
Now Fred is out on parole. And played a very big role.
He was all the kids savior. And got commended on good behavior
In his room Fred quietly lies. And soon he will finally die
He turned his whole life around. And now he is heaven bound.
So Fred closes his eyes. And now he calmly dies.
He feels all the children's tears. Because they truly loved him
    dear.
Fred's memory shines from above. As graceful as a white dove.
All the girls and boys. Have their hearts filled with joy.

—*Kenan Fears*

Who Am I?

"Who am I?"
On the night I was conceived
Was there any tenderness or care,
Any love returned, the kind that only two can share?

Did she love me
When she carried me under the heart?
Did she cry out in pain
Seeing me go, knowing it brought her freedom again?

Would he have wanted me
If he had known?
For in the heart of every man
Surely there is a longing for fulfillment, of destiny, of plan.

Strangers wanted me.
Eager arms so warm with love.
A home, a family, and then, the lie
And later on the pain, of wondering, "Who Am I?"

Are they still out there,
Will my prayers be answered?
Will I ever see myself, my children in them?
When they inquire of me, I can say, "I know who I am!"

—*Phyllis S. M. Benner*

Mankind's Loss

Oh, mankind, where is your shame?
Once green pastures, now stretch concrete ribbons,
Can you not see where lies the blame?
Once blue skies, now oft dull grey,
This was not natures way.

Natures varied clothes we need,
Tear, gouge, decimate this earth.
It's time to cease rapacious greed!
For to our children, what will we leave?
Barren wastes, and of animals, a dearth.

Where bluebells and the cowslips bloom,
and the myriad colours of butterflies were seen,
above a babbling brook, all trimmed with emerald green,
natures masterpiece no more, all alone,
one bluebell now remains, the rest, is stone.

Is not mankind now perverse,
to declare a moratorium, but oft leave it worse?
Yet maybe there are some who've seen,
and have the foresight to insure,
This planet can be so pleasant, and so green.

—*T. Vanner*

We Cry With You Jessica

Who thinks about children?
Once more was the proof
They think that it is justice
But I know it is not true.

Children are born with emotion
Like it's supposed to be,
And nobody pays attention
Although they are human beings.

The whole world was crying
When Jessica left her home
And I ask myself this question,
Why don't they leave that child alone?

An advice I want to give
For all the people that cried,
Pray very hard on your knees
And leave everything to God.

—*Juana Carmen V. Gonzalez, M.D.*

Untitled

All is nothing, nothing is all,
once one thing from something is made.
There can be no spring without fall,
nor can it be bright without shade.

Thus love eternal cannot be,
whose flame transcends death's final pyre,
the cold grip of mortality,
will bring to nought the last desire.

Leave me something, something, something,
to the infinite void I pray,
and hear forgotten voices sing,
the purpose of growth is decay.

Yet the lonely and the forlorn,
have an irresistible force,
upon the hopeless current borne,
which wends its way on endless course.

There is nothing, nothing, nothing,
I cry out to the empty sky,
and hear my echo hollow ring,
the purpose of life is to die.

—*George Campbell*

Freedom

Welcome to a place no one cares, where no one cries cause no
one dares. Behind these bars we all seem to change, from
normal to criminally deranged. Imagine the same things day
after day, and never getting your own way. The anger's building
in my veins, must hold back like 'horse and reigns'

Manipulation plays this place, who will lead the convict race?
Pity is non existent here, hold your own or live in fear
On your thoughts we will scan, who's the boy and who's the man?
As k the Go Boy why he ran, listen to his master plan

So many stories I've been told, both from the young, and from
the old. Look into the wise man's eyes stone cold, on to your
sanity you must hold. Here slowly comes the night, watch the
darkness overcome the light. all doors are locked, every
window barred, leaving me forever scarred.

But freedom now is in my sight
Out of the darkness, and into the night.

   —Jeffrey Portelance

Untitled

Day by day it happens
One way or another,
I must ignore it!
But where am I meant to be?

I am not even who they think I am
And yet, it happens
They try to trust me, reshape me
I am surprised I am not yet broken
It is what I am that makes them distinguish
Myself from others
I go mute when I hear them, see them compare
I should not love to disguise
I am not ugly.
Choices are not meant to be plenty
They will always be ground
I must be allowed to speak!
But I am lost in silent hesitation

   —Joy Pobre-Moss

Untitled

With a nervous smile I glanced your way, and saw in you what no
one else did. A man who believes in a world of choices, not
rules. Shyly, I watched you as my feelings grew stronger, but I
protected myself behind a wall of hurt, with only a small
window to see through. As we talked the minutes passed like
hours into the night, and without any warning, I feel in love
with the voice behind the phone. Your gentle ways captured both
my heart and soul. Soon I found myself anxiously awaiting to be
in your presence, and have your soft touch caress me.
Discovering that buried deep beneath your heart filled with
pain, was a man offering the world, in return for just love.
I wanted to fill your heart with love, where the empty tears of
the past were. Offering you a relationship of trust, laughter
and happiness that will grow day by day with our love.
Then that special moment happened when we first shared our love
together. With the midnight sky illuminated by the full moon,
our lips touched in a kiss. As you carefully placed your hand
on my face, our kiss grew more passionate and I yearned for
you. For the first time I felt what true love was and then you
whispered to me three simple words that changed my life,
I love you.

   —Susan S. Achal

At Night

At night, at night, no more light,
only a street lamp shining bright,
I wondered if it was the sun,
but I was mistaken.

At night, at night, my mother told me to go to sleep,
only in bed there were a thousand sheep.
I was just counting to a thousand and one,
Is your insomnia cured?

At night, at night, everywhere is dim,
you are so tired wondering around your dreams,
wandering your way to paradise.
Am I getting this verse's stream?

At night, at night, quietness sets in,
it allows you to think,
whatever you wish, whatever you do.
Then tomorrow, at dawn,

you are told your dream is over.
That is your brand new morning,
give up
your dreams please! (My fellow men and women)

   —Louise Luk Ling Kwan

Daughter Dear

Hi little Fox, Here is a line to you
One I hope pleases, and makes you happy too
It seems you may hurt a little of late
Many cares you have had to face
You have done so with a gentle grace
One thing I have learned of this life
Is, after darkness, comes morning light
So you should go another day
To find the truth in what I say
Another hill you may have to go
Before you realize that this is so
Around the bend your joy may be
To warm your heart, for your eyes to see
Many a man has stopped just short
With his journey's dream just across the court
The stout of heart went another mile
To find life's happiness, to find a smile
So little fox, stay sweet as you are
For the hill you are climbing may be hiding your star

   —Ken Weatherhead

The Magic

I crave a house close by a brook,
Or a lowly gurgling gutter,
A house that holds in cranny and nook,
Some everyday comfortable clutter.
A rattle laying there on the floor,
Within easy reach of the crawler,
A cup on the table, a kettle at hand,
Awaiting the neighbourly caller.
A sweater across the arm of the chair,
Knitting, laid on the back of the sofa,
Newspaper and Bible on a stool nearby,
When the chores of the day are over.
A house that has a lived-in look,
That I'd never exchange for another,
A house that has been transformed to a home,
By the magic of comfortable clutter.

   —Dulcie Lear Spracklin

The Lilac Tree

Will thou sing saddest songs for me,
or humbly shower petals in the dewy
Morn beneath the lilac tree. Plant a seed
In remembrance in June's all sunshine
Weather. When thou weeps raindrops tears,
thou has kissed my palest cheek, for I am
Only sleeping in paradise in heaven.
For the celestial angels keep vigil
At my side, and the candle doth burn
Ever bright. When I walk barefoot
In the heather, this is when I think of thee.
A hundred flowers raise their sprightly
Heads, forever blooming constantly.

—*Lynne Whitehouse*

Time Well Spent

Out on the high seas...
Or taking a walk in a summer breeze.

Flying in a jet plane...
Or riding in a fast train.

Eating turtle, goat or horse...
Being sick and full of remorse.

Meeting people in far away places...
Seeing their bright smiles and friendly faces.

Having our car ransacked and my purse taken...
Was a scary experience that had me shakin'.

Sipping champagne during a starlit night...
On a beach under the bright moonlight.

Some of these stanzas are dreams I hold...
And others are memories that are not so old.

The travels I've had and the places I've been...
My thoughts often drift to the things I've seen.

When school is done and money is in hand...
I'll once again travel to a far off land.

But until then, I'll just have to be content...
To remember these thoughts of time well spent.

—*Loya M. De Clercq*

Do You Care?

Do you care that you throw stones at my heart,
or that I have many feelings?

Do you care that my color doesn't have to say everything,
and in darkness we are both the same?

Do you care that I can talk words,
and do you care that I don't?

Do you care that I sit in a corner and
cry the same tears that you do?

Do you care that I face the same choices
which also approach you?

Do you care that one day I could save your
life and you still wouldn't give me any gratitude?

Well I do care!

Racism: Stop it!

—*Danielle Graham*

Thoughts From Within

There are no external cures for what ails me
Or the parts of my life that have failed me
I must learn to conquer and defeat
And strive to make my life whole and complete
Can I overcome the pains and pressures life encourages?
Or by discovering my inabilities, bring forth my courage
I need the strength to withstand and survive
And appreciate the privilege of being alive
It's often easier to accept defeat
Then get off my butt and attempt the same feat
And yet through struggles with my independence
My strengths are recognized and fought in my defense
I'm not sure how I handle the hurt I feel inside
But I believe I can show my pain and not have it denied
I'll prepare for war with sword and shield in hand
And the battle I must win is to make people understand
They must accept me as a human being
To notice only my wheelchair is rude and demeaning
I want to be accepted by those who pity and stare
And notice the inside of me and not my stupid chair.

—*Joseph Schmitt*

The Magic Moment

From the eyes of this waif like child, through the glint of his tears,
Our erasable memory retraces these long forgotten years.
Days that formed together a link 'tween now and that time past,
A dandelion chain - woven with love, but a moment, does it last.
The patience and wisdom that comes with age is not always - the case
For oft times in the eyes of a child you'll see mirrored another face.
And see a figure as lithe as the willow this entity - that was you
Now entombed by years that have passed away over a horizon of blue.
Still and small and silent, a mixture of sorrow and joy
For behind the being of every man lies the image of this boy.
A boy that could run and laugh in the wind or earn the title of marble king.
A child bestowed with an inquiring mind to make possible - everything.
This - is the magic moment seen through a glistening tear,
When as a man, you've bridged the gap of that long forgotten year.

—*Norah Kierstead Carter Kummel*

A Time To Live And A Time To Love

Now is the time to come together and live
our lives as one.

Now is the time to love one another just as
you would a sister or a brother

Now is the time to spread love and cheer to
those you meet along your way, everyday...
every year.

Now is the time to let your love shine through
and touch someone's heart and soul with
your love so true.

Loving one another is so easy to do...all you
need to do is open your heart and your mind
enough to let a little of your love "light" through.

—*Karen Morris*

Untitled

In Nature the killer survives:
Out-foxes, clean with leaf and ligament,
Nazi-natural, fascist-pure,
Forget compassion. Earth and excrement
And embryo are oneness. Sometimes rich
Is she, a Mother and magician,
Sometimes almost something of a bitch.
Considering the function and mechanics,
Our pity is absorbed by instinct, spent
On cats that claw the birds and mice-
We know the butcher holds the instrument.
What works, she needs to know, and leaves
Disfunction and distraction far behind.
Time is linear: we eat and breathe,
And sleep in skin-shed darkness. No
Human memory-dipping or
Failure-comforting tonight. The moon's scythe
Protects in peace the rapist and the victor.

— *M. J. Corbett*

A Hole In The Ground

A black flag flutters
Over the morbid decay
Inside the spirits stop and stutter
Lost and confused in every way.
The door swings always in
Never once does it turn out.

The moans and screams form a constant din
Never quite overcome by the Overlord's shout.
His voice booms out in a solid note
That fills its listeners with nameless fear
Shrieking out to a blood-red moat
For all within to hear.

The souls try in vain to escape
Keeping themselves in constant flight
Fleeing from the One that has no shape
Who tortures them with all His might.

The torture becomes an unbearable thing
Here in the depths of hell.
The spirits play to a ruthless King
Who entered here when heaven fell.

— *Rob Mead*

The After

The parting is not as
    painful in itself;
It is the 'after' moments
    in the agonising quiet
Of seemingly eternal bleakness
    that the soul falls apart.

Not in the drama of the first crack,
    or the revelation of a deadly truth
The silent insidious disease that creeps unknown.
    It is the AFTER
The coming
    the dawn
        of realization
            the grappling
                the pain of acceptance.
The soul-twisting process that lingers
    long after all that had happened.

— *Lee Lee Nee*

Pandora's Box

Legend has it—many years gone
Pandora's box was opened wide—for all the world to see
I know this fable to be true—for I have seen the results
All around me
    crowding in my face
    shattering my senses!
The lid's long gone, I'm afraid—in a world gone mad
Panic and strife
War and hunger
Sadness and sorrow
    surrounding me
    encircling me
    taking my breath away!
Care to join me for an acorn, sweets?

— *K. Coleman*

Servant That I Am Passing Over

Long the road has been. Yet short for long waited
peace within. I contend this is that road given
freely. Lonely is the servant, for the true longing
is to see the face of His Holiness, the Father's
chosen lamb. The Magnificent Oneness with our
entwined hearts is the closest. I his servant shall
get till I descend towards the heavens in spirit,
longing, waiting, and faithfully believing the Word
of the Precious Son and His Father. Though my feet I
do not know where it shall lead me, you go willingly
because of the growing love He shows me. As I gazed
upon the stars of heaven, God has stars on Earth
that shine brighter because the Aura descends from
the human heart where His Beloved Son is with us.
All the Children of God are brilliant and truly seen
by the eyes of those who take care of the living
soul. The servant that passes-over earthly things
is loved.

— *Kathyann Morse*

Fruits

Lemons and oranges, cherries so round
Peaches, limes and grapefruit abound
Kiwi and breadfruit, colourful and sweet
All kinds of fruit, good to eat
Pears and bananas the colour of corn
Used in the autumn, harvest to adorn
Mangoes and apricots grown in the sun
Grapes by the basket, picked for fun
Ugli and melons with pips inside
Kids in the orchard trying to hide
Blackberries, gooseberries so very green
Shiny red apples just have to be seen
Nature makes fruit all the year round
Come rain or shine they grow from the ground
They grow for the young
And they grow for the old
Then they're picked by the farmer
And sent to be sold

— *Gillian M. Kitching*

The Ocean

For me the ocean is something
people can't fully explore.
I think we ever really find
its utmost core!
Its deepness carries mysteries, so behold!
It also has moods, hot or cold,
or sometimes it changes colours
from blue to green.
You can tell what it's feeling,
though its face is unseen.
It's full of life and wonder,
that fascinates man's eye.
It's full of unfound treasures;
In the darkness they lie.
No matter how hard they try,
there's one thing man cant fully get,
they can't ever empty the ocean's soul
and that's something I don't regret

—*Reem Amber Ali*

The Gardenia

White flowers coated as if with transparent wax.
Petals joined like folded hands in puritanical prayer,
Reaching to the sky, and paying homage.
Their fragrance hangs with heavy scent;
Like perfume splashed in wild abundance.
A milky colour of delicate smoothness
Sways gently
Throwing a multitude of whiteness
Against a sun-drenched wall
Dazzling in the winter glow.

—*Marisa Pongan*

To A Rose

Fairest of flowers, so gracefully blooming;
Petals of velvet so charming in hue.
Kissed by the sun and caressed by the breezes;
Wakened each morning by touch of the dew.
Proudly thy head is raised up to the heavens;
Richly thy scent is spread o'er garden bowers,
Here in thy beauty; calm and serenely;
Reign thou in majesty; queen of the flowers.

Fairest of flowers, so brief is thy splendour;
Soon thy proud head will be drooping and bent;
Bees will forsake thee; sunshine will scorn thee;
Only to earth for a time thou art lent.
When thy fair petals are falling and breaking;
When thou art left in thy last lonely hours.
Then will I only remember thy beauty;
And hold thee in memory; queen of the flowers.

—*Flora M. Bosrock*

A Writer

An artist at conducting words to fall in place were they become
Pictures in ones mind. We become this artist through the true
Founder of words, the real communicator of communication.
There is a place were we go that takes control of the pen
Their are all good and bad things in the world of artistry
The information that is given to us all may be vital in way
We project pictures, some artist write in the way to project
Pictures that can waste vital brain food, some artist conduct
The food of knowledge that can never be wasted.
We all have had pictures at one time or another were we would
Like to be, so indeed the brain food that we absorb will play
A vital role in the picture we will someday be in.

—*Kamiel Wadud*

The Cruel Circus

You are the ringmaster of the cruellest circus on earth,
Preaching your faith for whatever it is worth.
Reaching for a God through self-centred prayers,
Your sins are forgiven, but who really cares?

When you are injecting needles into innocent eyes,
Are you not affected by their pitiful cries?
Driving all sanity from out of their minds,
Striving in your vanity for beauty for mankind.

Locked behind bars so we can stand and stare,
Knowing what they are, they don't want to be there.
But curiosity killed compassion, nothing will be free
In whatever form or fashion we've made freedom out to be.

With the whole farmyard lying dead on your plate,
Your stomach empty but your head full of hate.
It seems we desire much more than the meat,
As life once admired is now covering our feet.

Who ever gave you the right to hunt and chase?
Who said you could smear blood over your face?
If it is the power and the glory that makes you strong,
Then you and your Gods have got it all wrong.

—*Rhiannon Fox*

The Question

Sometimes you have a question which no answer satisfies.
Prevarication, ignorance or comfortable lies
greet your desire to know about the depth or the design
of your existence on this planet, and what it all may mean:
and so you ask a scientist, a man of great renown
whose reputation in his field is second still to none.

A mind like his is capable of grasping many things,
and like the Walrus will apply to cabbages and kings
the same dissecting logic he discerns in all he sees,
that leaps the mental chasm with such well-accustomed ease
that you will find no difficulty sharing his belief
in the why and what and wherefore of everything in life...

The silence lasts so long you'll think he hasn't even heard,
but he has listened carefully and weighed your every word,
and if you wait in patience you will get your answer soon;
and though it takes the best part of a lengthy afternoon
you'll find you have been given such a priceless gift of truth,
that nowhere else in all the world could you have matched its
worth.
For here is what you asked for, here is sense and sanity -
a sure and simple answer that will set your spirit free.

—*Roxane Houston*

To My Friends

Sometimes life seems dark and full of despair
Problems come along and seem more than we can bear.
Just remember all the things we have to be thankful for
Wake up in the morning and see the sun peeping up once more
To see the wonder of a wild flower opening its petals in full
bloom to see a white fluffy cloud in the heavens can take away
gloom a simple smile on the face of a friend
Can lift your heart and help it to mend
Just take time to slow down in this busy hectic life
Think of the many good things, not the hustle and strife
And don't forget the little things along the way
Be thankful for a new start of each new day
It helps to keep a smile on your face
Brush away the tears and put joy in its place,
So my friend, I wish you love, hope and peace
And may all your troubles and worries forever more cease.

—*Kathy Benjamin Davis*

Your Presence

The whisper's of your presence float so gently,
   quietly by me.

The chains of your once professed love I want
   to break free.

The times once we shared are slowly but surely
   passing me by.

The days of laughter we happily spent in time
   eventually will die.

The endless beating of my worn heart wants
   to desperately stop.

The journey I have painfully walked was wise
   and surely for not.

The road I travelled was clearly paved to achieve
   your eluding love.

The reality has become clear to me and so spent,
   I look to above.

The whisper of your presence is known to me,
   left by the blowing wind.

The wind constantly moving and always whispering,
   "Could have been, could have been."
   —Vanessa Nowicki

In

Read not my gaze nor my stare.
Rather, try to interpret what is in.
For what ever is, may be suppressed or altered
So that shame become pride, and sadness joy.
Therefore, try to be in!

Take not my smiles for happiness,
But check beyond that shield of glee
For joy of face, in mind may not be.
Look for my troubles and my sleepless nights
Show me that you want to be in!

Behold not my slowness nor my anger,
rather, ask about my home and what is in.
Halt my anger! help me grow!
Check my parents and a broken home!
Let me see you in!

See not the color of my skin nor my hair.
But, resolve to recognize what is in!
Search it! find it! nurture it! support it!
Come in! be in! stay in! be sincere!
Be proud! rejoice in the children of the universe!
   —Joseph A. Whittington

The Seasons

Is it spring-time in your heart, O child of God?
Rejoice, and give the glory all to Him
Who opened up your life like spring-time flowers,
And saved your life, and set you free from sin.

Is it summer in your heart, O child of God,
With not a cloud to dim the distant sky?
Then praise Him for a life of blissful peace,
It speaks of Heaven that's waiting you on high.

Is it autumn in your heart, O child of God?
Are shadows falling all around your way?
Then pause, and look to Him by faith,
That you may know His grace to face each day.

Is it winter in your heart, O child of God?
The summer birds have gone, there is no song;
Take courage O my child, and dare to say
That spring-time can't be very far along.
   —W. R. Cairns

Lost Angeles

Riotous city'
rebellious hold,
Blood from black and white
running from your crime,
Thousands of your peaceful
hidden in your folded skirt
at that time.

Blood spilled,
voices stilled,
Behold the wasted life
and bitterness of heart,
Behold the blood and strife,
while thousands peaceful in your folded skirt
take no part.

Life resumed,
fire consumed
Ghettos burning in splendid agony
a torch of shame, mansions looking down
on ugly scenes. While thousands in your
folded skirt, take no blame
   —Alexander G. Atkinson

A Crystal-Gazing

Every morning I find a man in the sun
Reciting verses with his luminous voice,
A human joy bursts out laughing
And I utter: Let there be light!
And the poetry of earth
Surpasses the limit of mortality.

The man in the sun, was a king
A king but he had a revolutionary mind,
Disillusioned, daring,
He revolted against his forefather's divinity,
His slogan of revolution: Aton, Aton, my omnipotent.

Every morning I find poet Ikhnaton, sun-clad,
I hear his recitation:
"How manifold are thy works!
They are hidden before men..."

Perhaps he knew inwardly
His dwelling-planet
Being equipped with a universal truth-
Moves round the sun.
Every morning brings a truth: Poetry is for mankind.
   —Kavi Dilwar

A Plea To Nature's Wonder

In her joyless chamber does she lie,
Resting with restlessness,
Her only comfort the cobweb window-
The entrance of a single shaft of sun.

"Confide to me, O Spring, O Sunny Day!
Be deterred not by that mere thistledown portal,
But come, O Sweet Life, O Wondrous Spirit,
Uplift me to thine celestial place,
So that I might be a transfigured soul,
Away from the humours of dewy-dapple-darkness,
As Dear Warmth is mine ally.

Let me be smothered in thine golden splendour,
And if thou wilt not, but call me your Disciple
So that I could be ne'er again Dian's slave,
But a torch of thine costly radiance,
And those who perchance should see me,
Would see me as Sovereign Light's mistress!"

Yet the object of her unrequited love,
Left her to be betrothed
To the ever-constant, lifeless dust.
   —Dennis Low

Is Anybody Out There?

Gunshots ringing out, lives being lost,
Robbery, pollution and poverty reign supreme:
What is our world coming to?

If a starving child cries, does anybody hear?
If that little baby dies, does anybody care?

Rain forests being destroyed,
Ancient spirits dying after all this time,
Life ending for millions of acres,
Of Holy, sacred ground.

If the Gods cry out in pain, does anybody hear?
If eternal slumbers are broken, does anybody care?

And I stand here watching, our beautiful world crumble apart,
I cry out to all those ignorant, unheeding people:
What is all this for?

Right now a starving child cries, but somebody has heard;
Already that little baby is laid to rest, but yes, somebody cares.

Those God's cries have been heard, by me and now by you,
Their eternal slumbers have been cruelly broken, and we have to
find something to do.

—*Jenn L. Winterburn*

To Be Remembered

Together we had the same frustrations,
            same imaginations,
            the same fascinations.
What would life be like, we often wondered.
Our expectations were to be remembered.

            Far back in time,
            when we hadn't a dime,
            didn't we think of turning to crime?
What if we get caught, we thought, then shuddered.
Our horrified faces were to be remembered.

            You got a job,
            I met Bob.
When both ended, we were left with nothing but a sob.
            Was it us who had blundered?
            Our sorrow was to be remembered.

            Waiting on a plate,
            to be gobbled up by fate,
added to our names was a word called 'Late'.
Dreams can sometimes be so easily murdered.
Soon there was nothing left to be remembered.

—*Shazia Hasan*

The House On The Hill

It looks so sad and lonely as it sits on top of a hill. The
sand sifting over the doorstep, the weeds growing up past the
sill. The walls are swaying and tumbling, like a man who has
been on a binge. The windows long ago broken and the door
swings on one rusty hinge. It once stood so proud and stately
like a lass that was so full of pride. Years ago the man that
had built it, brought it to a blushing young bride. As you
stand very still and you listen you imagine a small babies cry.
And then there's the creak of a rocker and a mothers sweet
lullaby. When you think of the many memories this tumbled
down house must of had. Some would be very happy, others so
very sad. Our life goes on as we live it, not like these old
homes in despair. Who are guarding their secrets forever of
the folks who used to live there.

—*Myrtle Norbury*

Untitled

            Quietly floating in and out of the stars
            Savoring each new and pleasant sensation
            Almost a mystery, deep in thought of us
I am consumed into a field of inhuman distortions

            To be the air you breathe must be a sweet inhale
            If I was the air, would I intoxicate you
Send you into a shattering high no one could match
            As always, the conviction purely true

If I could take you into a world where you could be
            Anything worth imagining in your angelic dreams
            And would you take my hand and let me come too
            To be free and experience everything with you

Would you ride on the darkest cloud through a rainstorm
            To be with me if I were on the other side
            Would you feel the pain if I hurt from far away
            Have we yet gone this far... have we hardly tried

I float as a feather would to a soft place in the green grass
            Open my eyes now and turn around
            Watching your stomach pump in and out as you sleep
As you lay, truly existing on this warm day, on the ground

—*Kimberly Kettlewell*

Steps Towards...

The sound of the steps upon the street full of red leaves
Scraping away the cover of the dark foundation
Sliding forward slowly with determination. The purple
color of the sky surrounding the intense atmosphere of truth
The heavy setting of humidity falling upon the lightness of the
  skin

One by one the steps go forward towards the door of the destiny
Distant as may seem the old wooden gate must be passed
The shrieking of the entrance makes its mark. The determined
eyes start losing their color of assurance. The inner fight
between pride and honesty, image or window. The steps

maintain their route upon the now soft ground of grass
The scraping sound has been overpowered with the loud beating
  of the heart
The tips of the fingers have been numbered with the reaction
  of the nerves
The skin is suddenly weighed down by the humidity that has now
  joined
Courage is almost succumbing to the screams of the little
  child inside

—*Marielsa R. Croes*

War

Crash, bang, guns firing
Screams, pleads, people dying
The war has begun
People try to join as one
No help will come how hard you try
There will always be one more to die
Children crying their pain is felt
Priest praying, beside the Church they're knelt
What ever happens nothing will change
All this fighting won't make it rearrange
"Help me please, don't let me die
Help my frightened child, please try"
Why does the sun shine through all the killing
Why can't it be us that is winning
If there was one prayer to pray for
It would be to help end this war
It doesn't make things go away
All this hatred is here to stay
It doesn't matter how hard you try to put things right
There will always be another to start a fight

—*Jacqueline Lill-Hirst*

Never To See

People who live near the ocean
see the waves calm and dangerous on the sea,
But never can you see waves cross the old prairie.

That is not true I say
I see waves everyday
Prairie grass far as the eye can see
rolling, churning, and lapping against each other.

Who needs a dangerous sea,
When you have the old prairie.
that is as safe as safe can be.
　　　—Amanda Kuhn

My Son Chad Or Only Three

Ever wondered what it's like to be
Seeing the world when you're only three?

We've all been there, but forget we had
But I've got another chance in my son called Chad

He pulls at my heartstrings and my pant legs too
To get my attention to show what he can do

He's full of the dickens and can be bad
But that's okay because he's my son Chad

He stops and he squats when he sees a bug
But if he runs and falls down, he wants a hug

I'm never quite sure what catches his eye
Whether it's rocks, weeds, dogs or a neighbor's hi

He comes up with these sayings that can't be beat
And you wonder how, with a face that sweet

At night when we settle down for bed
He brings me the book that he wants read

And some of the happenings that went on here that day
Might find their way out, and so I will stay

And listen to him as he repeats them to me
All the while seeing the world as if I'm only three
　　　—Maureen Mack

Boredom

Boredom! A word that truly sums up. Its drugged sensation
seizes you, the sedate feeling overwhelms you. Its
procrastinating idleness inhabits your sagging body weighing you
with imagined burdens - listing like a scuttled ship you sink
into the perverse depths of forgetfulness. This is boredom!
No direction or goal is revealed. No land is sighted by the
weary crew on the ship of hope. No vim to conquer the origins
of experience fills your breath. The once pleasant tasks
transform themselves into the toils to difficult to achieve.
This is boredom! A lack of incentive and drive is evident.
The refusal of enthusiasm to propel itself to the forefront of
your being is obvious. All motive to commit the perfect crime
is lost buried in yesterday's bliss. Now a feeling to long
gone to recall. This is boredom! The countless hours spent
wandering the expanse of your mind are less than productive.
The smiling face is no longer conducive to a feeling of well
being and security. You resemble a walking vegetable. This is
boredom!

　　　—Stan Baric

Stormy Night

As darkness falls upon the land
Shadows reach out like giant hands
Caressing the earth with silent strokes
Hiding everything with a greyish cloak

Suddenly the wind begins to blow
Stirring grass and trees wherever it goes
In the distance thunder rumbles
A tremendous storm begins to grumble

Lightning flashes across the sky
Making everything visible to the naked eye
Breaking branches with a snap
Waves hit the rocks with a cold hard slap

When night breaks into dawn
The storm decides to calm
A brilliant sunrises over the mountain
Drawing up water like a fountain

The vast sea of grass is greener
The morning air is cleaner
A storm has done its duty
Turned the world to a picture of beauty
　　　—P. McArthur

Untitled

When my heart is torn,
She is always tender and warm.
She has always been there to make the best
Out of my life's mess.
When anger is all I can find,
She is always kind.
She is there to mend
And be a friend.
Stronger then love is our bond.
It will never be gone.
She . . .
Is my Mother.
　　　—Karrieann Grisa

She's A Dreamer

Amidst the mud and rubble,
She sees roses blooming fair,
When the sky is dark and cloudy.
She sees only blue skies there.

When the sea is tossed with white caps,
She sees waters calm and blue,
And in a noisy city street
She sees green hills in the distance too.

When snow drifts are whirling frantic,
Around the door, in winter time,
She sees springtime in the distance,
With flowers of every kind.

When all the world is gloomy,
And the world seems all astray,
She just looks at all the nice things,
That can happen in a day.
　　"She's a dreamer."
　　　—Agnes Pearo

The Weeping Willow

The weeping willow tree cries her lonely tune.
She sways to and fro.
She droops long and low.
I brush her tears from my face.
I push her leaves from my space.
Amongst her sadness I am free.
I am hidden to be what no one can see.
I sit and I stand.
I walk hand in hand
with my imagination
Oh, how grand.
Underneath the weeping willow tree
A boy may be
Isolated from the world.
Peeping through,
only to be seen
by those he chooses to.
Weep my lovely willow tree.
For I am at peace and I am free
only when you are crying on me.

— *Jared Andrew Daniel*

The Ship

She was but a skin of steel
She was in a coat of gray.
She was a mother of the hunt
Searching for her pray.

Within her skin of steel
There lived 200 plus.
Whatever they made her do
She never made a fuss.

She must hold back the force of time
She must hold back the power's that climb.
For this she stand's alone
A symbol of justice fallen behind.

Although her teeth of have fallen
And she's passed many tests.
The test of time
Will lay her to rest.

— *William Snyder*

Captain Fatman

Captain fatman waits, an innocent to prey
Shinny treasures lure, a virgin babe astray
Devils staircase come, though darkened do not fear
Captain's parlor door, just pass the dragon's liar

Enter child fair, deceit is your reward
Naked paper dolls, bind you with unseen cords
Fatman's icy hands, fondle forbidden fruits
Amidst pictured whores, a virgin mind he loots

Little child weep, bitter waters made to taste
Self-condemnation, your soul is sure to waste
Hurry now escape, the place where no one goes
Secret silent screams, sound cries beyond the soul

— *Joseph T. Gallagher*

Gain From The Cross

He had little strength, he had little power, he was dead after just
six hours. The sky grew dark and voices dim. Then the land
began to quake and the people began to shake. Then soldiers
came and took Christ's body from the cross. Mary the mother
thought it was a loss. Mary Magdalene couldn't believe what
she had seen, His body was lifeless, shapeless, and marred and
His hands were nail scarred. He was laid in a borrowed
tomb but not to stay, because in just three days He would be
raised. He died for you and He died for me. It wasn't a loss
that He died on the cross though it was much pain, praise God,
it was a gain.

— *Katie Cooke*

Intrusion

Sitting on the school steps, curls gently ruffled by the wind
Shoes alongside, bare feet dangling
A little girl, a gentle soul contentedly humming
A melody serene and sweet, nameless yet memorable.

Mummy is only a little late
Soon she will be at the school gate... but wait!
A familiar car is stopping
Without shoes she is off and hopping.

A strange man gets out. He approaches her stealthily
Looks around, then offers her candy
Don't talk to strangers! Don't take candy from strangers
Life is complicated, there are grave dangers.

He drags her to his car
She escapes. Does not get very far
He grabs her, carries her, crushing her hand
This I cannot, will not, should not understand.

A pretty girl with soft curls adorns my milk carton
My appetite for milk is gone
Instead I thirst for blood
Justice, Justice, Justice, please dear God.

— *Martin Copilah*

Responsibility

What does it mean to wake up on time?
Should I spend a quarter, and save a dime?
Do I call for a ride from a drinking party?
Must I be at work so early, or can I be tardy?

Shall I go to school or skip?
Am I being smart or a dip?
Is it smart to drink or do drugs?
Or should I stay home and vacuum the rugs?

Why are these decisions so hard to make?
Am I supposed to give or take?
What would our parents say?
It definitely would not make their day

It ain't very easy being a teen
Things aren't the way they used to be
What's the last answer on this lifelong test?
Live for the moment, and screw the rest.

Be smart.
Be responsible.
Have fun.

— *Hailey Harfman*

Buckover Gate

Amidst the brightness and the silence under a perfect azure
sky,
My eyes behold such beauty I am so afraid to die.
But, should my faith, on earth be imaged in just a
trillionth shade of green,
Then in death behold I life of boundless beauty to be seen.
With conceit do I perceive this earth so beautiful I will
not leave,
Yet since my being of years some score
Counted those, who think as I, as few, and on the fingers of
both hands, no more.
I will not surrender my image, depart this world of my own
free will,
Until the ultimate grain of proverbial sand, through my
fingers slips,
The brightness fades, and the silence echoes chill.

— *John Nicholas Beddoes*

A Small Seed's Strivings

Slowly, steadily, slipping surreptitiously sunward,
    slicing soil as easily as a ship sailing southern seas,
    or a silver sickle scything sheaves of wheat.
Still struggling at sunset,
    shooting stars, silhouettes and strips of shadow
    are what the seed seeks.
Still set for the surface, slowly strength is gained -
    until finally, starlight sets upon the slight stalk.
Now witness to the sleeping shores, sluggish sea,
    the stones and storms,
    soil's sanctuary is set aside in its surging quest for the
    sky.
This is the place where everything's better,
    everything's safe.
Sadly those smiles from established sister's are superficial;
    They know,
    The struggle has only just begun.
        —*Crystal van Ryneveld*

Phyllis

Hair of silver, heart of gold a
smile that said it all, you said you lived
your golden years when we were all small

Life without you, doesn't seem real
We miss you so much, it seems like a dream

Hair of silver, heart of gold
That's my mother true, losing you loving you
Has split my heart in two

Mam I know I'm selfish but I wanted
you to stay. I loved you in a very special way

Hair of silver, heart of gold
A smile that said it all
Mam we had the golden years when
we had you
        —*M. Williams*

A Few Words

Give me a few words, when this world goes passing o'er
So all is seen as a stag bounding into woods
Read, when true calm presses against her slumbering store,
The passionate embrace of solitude.
Not so many, so I see my days drop down into a well
Each perfect, a pebble, down to the bottom
Unnoticed, unmarked, where and when it fell
Dare I say, half vaguely missed, half forgotten.
To let the stag run free, unfettered by care
The silent and noisy day slip through fingers of peace
For all at end our calm's, even times of greatest wear
They make her soothing breasts' flow never cease.
        —*Michael G. Meade*

Where Music Breeds Music

Much of the art today
So naked and nowhere and unashamed
That when the dreamers kneel and pray
They find their dreams have washed away

Trying hard so they may leave
Their mark on the world of creativity
Sad burning souls and eternal screams
God is the truth and me knows me

Transient distractions used to ignite
A focussing on the Attainable Light
Whilst losing a handle of what's in sight
Eagles are soaring, sky lost in flight
        —*Steve N. Zafer*

Sadness

Somewhere tonight a lost heart is alone and aching,
So full of passion that its sides are breaking,
As one once believed love to be a chance worth taking...
    but it is not!
for love has lied to me many times before,
it has given me less when it promised me more
as giving your heart away for nothing is always a chore.
while a young girl's head restlessly lies upon a moist pillow,
a young boy soul-searches trudging through deep snow,
Is there truly no sanctuary for lonely hearts to go?
Trust tore down the walls, betraying our fantasy,
Slicing open a wound in our once secure reality,
So I wish for someone for everyone and for me.
while a lonely harmonica screams into the cold midnight air,
a virgin heart trickles frustrated tears
out of a seemingly empty stare,
but does anyone who is embraced in love really care?
There is but one way to escape this merciless agony,
as a million lonely hearts reach out desperately,
and I close my eyes, praying for sleep
to release the pain momentarily.
        —*Dale Truax*

Black Harvest

My crop grew fuller with each fall day
So I fashioned me a scarecrow to keep pests away.
I got me some gloves and an old dirty hat
And stuffed him with straw till he looked good and fat.
I found a pole and hoisted him high—
He looked real good so I dubbed him Eli.
Instead of the crows all a-cawing a riot
Throughout the land there was nothing but quiet.
His ominous form must have filled them with fright—
When I looked to the sky, not a crow was in sight.
As I checked out my corn, I gasped when I found
Mangled bodies of crows all over the ground.
My field was a stage with death and main act—
Each day more crows with their bones all cracked.
Black feathers and blood on his gloves I did see
As his straw-stuffed form reached out toward me.
I tried to cry out, but my body grew numb
"You got me, Eli ... I ... succumb ..."
        —*April Dawn Conlin*

What Happened To The Milky Way?

In my childhood -
so I remember -
in clear nights I looked in awe
into the dark blue vastness of the universe,
enjoying the luster of the stars
and the illuminant Milky Way.
This gave me a feeling of security.
And now in old age
the luster has almost disappeared.
I just see the Orion, the Polar Star,
some others perhaps.
But what happened to the Milky Way?
I am concerned:
Many a man's heart has degenerated
into a Black Hole.
Oh, Almighty Creator!
Please, restore the Milky Way
to the sight of your worshippers.
        —*Konrad Floegel*

The Flavour Of The Day

We have won!
So the Western Industrialist tells me,
Let us help the African ... all the Third Worlders!
No doubt in us ... no need to self-analyse,
The day is ours - we can criticise.

Aaaaahhh ... to see the cynical smiles of the Spirits,
The Spirits of ...
Pericles, announcing the Golden Age to his ...
Pompous Athenians,
Caesar, saluting his ...
Noble Romans, or
The more certain of the clan ...
Adolf, Joseph, Saladin, Rameses and the Khan!

We are sure of our ways and values,
History NEVER repeats itself,
No lessons to be learnt,
Evolution is the name.

There cannot be any other way...
Or dare I say ...
We are simply the Flavour of the Day.
　　　—Erik C. Jorgensen

Time

As the clocks turn back in time yet once again,
so too does the memories of our past.

The days and nights seemingly to take forever,
the quest is yet to be fought only to
be conquered with time!!

The streets blacken in darkness, the hidden
light shows no direction, lost in time!!

Yet with time comes ease, the darkness
turning, slowly, into light, the lossness
turns to recapture the scene as the
direction becomes slowly apparent.

The eye can regain yet once again its
direction into the future.

Yesterday's past is gone, vanished into
　　tomorrow's time!!
　　　—Lisa M. Woods

Touch Of Love

Sigh breeze, sigh, rise high,
soar above the man;
touch gently, sweeping softly
stroke the earth as a hand
would compassionately brush away the cares.
of all humanity

Weep rain, weep, but waste not tears
nor wash away the stains
of man's so desolate greed;
which seems of gentle, finer thoughts,
yet 'neath its surface, hear it weeping?
Fill the cup of man.

For the time will come for man to meet
his final destiny;
to count his deeds and count his loss
for this will surely be
required of man, for the "gift of life"
in a season of continuity.
　　　—Barbara Holland

A Child's Heart

I can take my flight to soar to freedom,
Soar, as many hours as my wings will fly.
I can land on the tallest tree,
Yet, I still perch alone, in this tree, so high.

I can be at any destination night or day,
Not too worry when I must be back home.
I can enjoy the silence lingering in this room,
Yet, I shed my tears, alone.

I can enjoy the happiness of a sunny day,
As the butterflies travel in a flight of beauty.
I can observe for moments.
Yet, alone, I share the happiness with only me.

I can choose to labour any place I desire,
Be the prime minister if I care to.
I can give my love to someone else,
Yet, the only two hearts I love, is you.

You've taught me to cherish, wisdom, and pride,
You've shared the tears, smiles, and fears with me.
Given me something to be so proud to have,
Yet, with you two, my wings still span free.
　　　—Michelle Wulff

Bird Of Peace

Leave bird of peace, for man is coming.
Soar bird of peace be free.
Go bird of peace away from here,
for they have come and taken your trees.
they have poisoned the air with gasses,
polluted the rivers and the seas.
Without care for the things that suffer.
They crush all, in the way of their greed.
So leave my friend for man is coming.
Soar my friend be free.
Go my friend away from here,
or you will never again be seen.
　　　—Alan Brooks

Adam's Awakening

No juxtaposition, no fragmentation
Solid flowing, sense of security
He told us,
　　Do not hurt people; be kind, be caring
　　You must help people; change your ways
His bellowing voice provided certainty,
　　From beyond this space we are all known
　　As I am not forgotten by you
　　You are not forgotten by me
He goes to leave, he is ready
We are left behind, we are unenlightened
I ask him,
　　What lies ahead
　　Salvation, damnation?
I look into his serene eyes, he answers privately,
　　I have found inner peace
As he walks off, we watch in bewilderment
Some will awaken oblivious
I will awaken remembering
He will awaken with contentment
　　　—Kelly C. Lagan

Love's Freedom

My very being was frigid and spent in
    solitary;
Voices from the past and present were
    screaming in my ear with vindictive
    clamor;
I was scared!
A scared child that didn't know which
    end was up.

In the middle of the heartache and the
    fatigue, you came into my life;
Now you give me love, warmth, security,
    and a never-ending appetite for living;
Above all, you give me freedom!!
Freedom to act like a child that doesn't
    know which end is up.

—*James Joseph Florio*

Home

This is my place.
Some will say, a disgrace
But nobody cares.
Only occasional stares
From people looking
Into a world, they don't understand
And cannot command.
I am a man
Stripped of my dignity
Trapped on the brink, by drink.
A social disease
That doesn't ease, the pain
Or stop the rain, from pouring in
And flooding my heart, with more sorrow.
Maybe tomorrow
I'll start again
But then, no one escapes
These cardboard walls
That I call, home.

—*Steven Dickson*

This Lonely World

.....this lonely world needs a lover.
    Someone who will take her hands
    and understands her many needs....
Someone who will walk with her along grassy banks
    and listen - romantically;
Someone who will talk with her in soft and gentle
            tones;
    Endearing, press her to himself and
        Give away his innocent eyes
            and personal heart.

Someone who....will lie with her and woo
    her lovingly - as naked Adam
    first loved his beloved Eve.

    Where can he be found, this
        Innocent Man,
Who's passionate heart is a selfless
        Fire of pure compassion?

            Are you he?

.....this lonely world needs a lover.
        Someone who will....

—*Seamus Byrne*

The Hunter And The Wolf

There is a shadow on the ground,
Something scary lurks around.

There must be something near,
For the hunter feels fear.

The clouds turn black, the sky turns grey,
As the hunter with fear runs away.

As he awoke the very next day,
He returned to the forest, and crossed the bay.

Is that the wolf he sees again?
Yes, but this time he makes a friend.

They journey home, the wolf at side,
As they leave the forest they say goodbye.

When in the house the hunter lies,
The wolf lets out a deep dark cry.

There is a thud on the ground,
The wolf has fallen down.

The animals tail is holding high,
But soon it fell, and slowly died.

—*John Norris*

The Appetites Of Humanity

Casual success yet a string or two attached
Something underlying... furtive... mysterious...
Not quite good, somehow a little evilly mischievous...
Here it comes, a slight hint of its dark and...
    sinister personality...
The darkness builds... and the climax comes... and it is gone...
But not forever... it is slinking around the dark corners...
A shadow behind the house... a shred of the last darkness
    of the fading night...
It's there, in the presence of what could be called God
    that the person is, lives, breathes...
And doesn't breathe...
Death... death, death, death, death...

—*Joshua Fallman*

Why Do You Bother Lord?

Jesus you saved me and set me in the way
Sometimes I fall when the way gets rough;
But you picked me up and carried me,
Why do you bother Lord?

When I was hungry you fed me
Naked, and you clothed me
I was thirsty, very thirsty you gave me drink
Why do you bother Lord?

There is no good in me Lord
Sometimes I even looked back
And thought the sacrifice was too great
Why do you bother Lord?

Remember, I have pushed back the Planets
And came to your world, remember, I
Sweat great drops of blood for you
And then died at Calvary for you.

Gethsemane, Calvary, how could I forget?
There, Your blood poured out for me
I know why you bother Lord, it was Your love,
Thank you Lord for loving me.

—*Lucy James*

Friend

We shared so much, you and I,
Sometimes we were mistaken as brothers.
But we shared something that should never be shared,
Hatred, for each other.

Lies replaced trust, and in time,
All we lived for, was destruction
For the other.

Maybe if we put our desires aside,
And look at what we once were,
Maybe we could be that again,
Maybe we could be brothers.

But now it seems too late,
Night is drawing near.
In darkness we shall wallow,
Preying off each other's fear.

Our desires took control
And destroyed our dreams.
What were inside, what we felt,
Is now gone.
Forever.

— *Todd Miller*

Sunsets

When the sunsets in the peaceful afternoon.
Soon I'll see the bright stars and the moon.
But till then I see purple, orange, and red in the sky.
Standing there feeling warm and safe... At night I cry.
Knowing that moment only stays for awhile.
Knowing these moments should be expressed to a child.
A child is innocent and delicate, their hearts are led by fate.
But we all know their minds are led by hate.
I wish upon a star tonight, hoping the sunset catches a
child's delight.

— *Katie McGarity*

Heart Beats Like A Drum

Can you hear the beat of military drums
sounding throughout the lands not missing
a single beat

The beat is rhythmical marching young men
move in time to the beat of the drums
all in time never out of time

My heart beats like a drum the very first
time I saw your face my heart started beating
in your arms is where I belong

Still I hear the drums beating throughout the land
there're getting louder and louder never missing a single beat
loud and rhythmical young girls falling for those marching men

My heart beats like a drum I could not stand to be here on my
own from the first time I saw you my heart was filled with
glory like all those girls I fell for one of the marching men

Still I can hear the beat of military drums sounding
throughout the lands

— *Karen Gainey*

The Gift Of Grass

On the velvety softness of childhoodgrass, barefootgrass,
sprinkled with spice of the clover.
   The past and the future are nullified, and I stand in a time
that is zero.
   The grass is a part of the peaceful green singing softly on
ancestors' graves, and of pastures that nurture the life to be
born in the barn of my grandfather's home.

— *Karin Storgards-Hatam*

My Ninety Year Old Grandpa

Youth dreams of adventure,
Space and heights
Of gold and glamour
And bright lights.
We look to the future with our hopes a glow
We are young - how little we know.

You have seen and done much more
Than all of us over the years.
You can tell of wonderful times
Filled with happiness and tears.
You are first in a tree of sixty-three,
This makes us one big happy family.

And in decades to come
We will all retell
The many stories we have heard
And learned to love so well.
Now let's have a toast to Grandpa Jim
For none of us would be here if it wasn't for him.

— *Sari de Coninck Smith*

Consider The Season

Winter at breakfast, fall at noon;
Spring and summer time die so soon!
Ev'ning and darkness bring the night:
Time to sleep and be out of sight.

Some think it poison, some meat;
And choices made may make life sweet;
What is there for friends of a thief?
And choices made may make life brief.

O Lord Jesus, you made it all:
The winter, spring, summer, and fall.
Four seasons Christ gives to us;
Glorify God, and in him trus'.

He changeth the times and the seasons (Daniel 2:21).

— *R. James Malo*

Against The Wind

I dreamed I was a wild mustang
   Standing alone on a hill
A silver line against the black of night.

Running
   Wild and free
Each stride bringing me closer to you.

I found you at last
   waiting
Beneath the spot light of our very own star.

You came to me then
   And laid your head on my shoulder.

It was the happiest day of my life.
   Knowing that I could be there
When you needed someone to lean on.

As long as we are together
   We can run forever free

   Even against the wind.

— *Mark Egeland*

124

"Looking Homeward"

Looking homeward, I can almost see my Jesus
standing there. I know my saviour waits,
There's a longing in my heart that just won't leave me
For He's standing just inside the Pearly Gates.

In this world, there's sickness and confusion
And we're burdened down with loads of care,
Looking homeward, I catch a glimpse of heaven
Knowing all is peaceful over there.

Looking homeward, I can hear the angels singing.
As they gather round God's throne,
Oh, the joyful sounds of Glory, Hallelujah,
I'm waiting for the Lord to say, my child come home.

Looking homeward, I see the old ship of Zion,
and the old conductor, as he yells "on board,"
Knowing well I've got my ticket purchased
And I'm on my way be with "Christ my Lord."

— *Josephine Gibson*

The Estranged

The dark reticent night was the sole witness, the palberating
stars dimmed with pity, for the infant barely a few days old!
"Another unwanted mouth to feed!" The father hollered. "Oh
let him be, he's my son!" The mother appealed. But the cock
of the roost had his say. The baby, barely a few days old,
left by the roadside, with the celestial stars, a holy witness
to the unholy deed! He grew. Some lady clothed him. The
dress was torn! He grew. Some gentleman fed him. The bread
was stale! He grew and grew, an orphan, unloved, uncared for!
By the school gates he would stand, watching lads of his age
bloom, while he, he stared with eyes full of rheum, he hated
mankind! He knew not of God, and when he did, he became a
bitter non-believer! He called himself 'Rajah', the king of
the slums! The winner of mud slings, the donator of black
eyes, the thief, the drug-dealer, the rogue! And one day they
caught him. The blame on him was as such - 'A contamination to
the society.' The deliverance. The end! Oh God!
How many Rajahs are there in this world?

— *Mushira Mohsin*

Reject The Hold Of The Beast*

The herds eyes swivel and bovinely observe him,
Stay and then back to their strained concourse,
As the deadly servant reaches for the brimming Ewer,
Mixing delight with pity as he hands him the Chalice,
Slopping over with the heady crop of Baccarus,
And he raises his heavy Shackled Hand,
Like a ship losing its Anchor in a storm,
To the beasts roars and stampedes of triumph,
And hell and damnation beads his tortured brow,
A curse on the environs of Shamalot.
Slayer of Achievement and Ambitious adventure.

The reptilian servant flicks in his tongue,
He leans forward and gleefully hisses.
"Same again Sir. We have not seen you for a while".

Extracted from "Shamalot Series," a series of four poems.

— *D. C. Bond*

Deliverance

Take the reigns.
Steer us, your trusting steeds;
And we shall follow.
Blinkered?
No for we,
The steeds that used to be guided,
Like mice on a treadmill.
Will no longer follow.
We now have the knowledge, the will;
To turn and snatch those reigns.
We shall whip those that whipped.
Not with brutality, but love;
With warmth, with open arms and lively hearts.

— *Darren Hall*

Thoughts Of Words And Words Of

The peculiar sound of understanding, set standing alone.
Stirring imagination and emotions.
Exercising the mental with the physical.
Repeated vocalization produces strange unfamiliarity.
Beginning to end with variations, a commonality
for compresses learning.
Malignancy to angelical. Negative without
positive... Influence with power.
Controlled communication command captivates calliope canoille.
Ponders of an idea without the thoughts of a word.
Conceptions transferred without the thoughts of a word.

— *Stuart Robert Bisenberger*

My Darling Kelly;

Ten years ago two young kids
stood shaking on an alter,

Led word by word in promises
of love to never falter.

How could we have known what was meant
of words so bravely stated,

I guess we had trust in each other's faith
of a journey heaven created.

Along the path we've tripped and fell
never hard enough to hurt,

Your tender words and helping hand
to pull us from the dirt.

You've been my light, my friend in need
the Honour has been mine,

The Love we've built and what we are
I'll Cherish for all time.

These words my vow of undying faith
of a marriage to sustain,

Put your hand in mine, let me ask you now,
Will you marry me . . . again.

— *C.T. Spackman*

The Secret

A portrait of a young woman
that has a secret, a terrible secret to tell.
That she has kept for many years
and will keep for many many more years to come.
For she has long since passed away
without ever telling anyone of the awful secret she hides.
That she has kept hidden and buried...
forever.

— *Jennifer Dunlap*

Taking A Nellie Out On Town

Let's put a gem in your bellybutton and
strut to Vegas
where "queens ain't permitted"
and everyone applauds a drag show
let's toss a feather boa around your neck and
sidle over to Dallas
where "queers ain't tolerated"
and holy rollers cruise gay bars
I wanna put make-up on your 5 o'clock shadow and
let go the Denver
where "faggots should be shot"
and cops are looking for a good blow
let's put a sparkling tiara on your head and
sashay to the city of Angels
Where "everyone loves a homo"
but only if they're gorgeous.

    —Leslie Dietz

Gone Away

Anger, indignation, ire and wrath
Such feelings consume my daily path
When 'ere my thoughts momentarily rove
Through memories of webs you wove-
Heinous ladders, impossible to summit
Coercing me to stumble, then plummet
To depths of sadness, frustration and despair
An emptiness I refuse to bear
Or reveal even to myself alone.

Why can't success be ours eternal,
Forecasting a freshness like the season vernal?
Spring - it's an answer for today.
Things could change, perhaps, come May.
But never the same - you've gone away.

    —Kathleen Sloup

Untitled

Crowds, noise, a scream -
suddenly there is silence,
People frozen where they stand,
On the ground lies a boy -
His pain excruciating,
stabbing through his body like ten thousand acid-tipped needles
As if someone had released a pause button -
People turn their backs as if nothing had happened.

Angry shouts,
People arguing as to who is to blame,
Discussing insurance policies and lawsuits,
The boy -
Thinking about whether he'll ever be able to walk again.

His right knee,
Already swollen to the size of a watermelon -
continually growing,
Sirens cut through the crowd like a scalpel slicing skin.

Men in white suits run towards the fallen boy,
He has a look of apprehension about him.

    —Krishna C. Gidwani

Death By Default

A calm, serene and sacred sadness,
Surrounded by an eerie madness,
I greet the darkness and shun the light
For I am now black and no longer white,
The feelings are strong, but opposed to fate,
They are not of love, but rather of hate.

There where I wandered has left my spirit now dead,
My soul has cried and my heart has bled,
The flashes running through my mind,
There is nothing left to leave behind,
The pitcher has fallen spilling the salt
And the Final judgement: "Death by Default".

The sentence best carried out by the blade
Of which all life's teachings has forbade,
But there is left only one more need,
The need to escape! The need to be freed!

The blood tides away the endless pain,
Removing from me that eternal stain,
And as the blade runs through and deep,
Now only may I in peace forever sleep.

    —Suleman Mansoor

Said

... And I heard her say
take a last look 'cos you'll never be
A lover, a friend, a husband to me
And as I turned she had departed
Goodness me what had she started?
...and I said to myself
'She won't be gone long, least not on her own
I'll make her regret what she's done'
Then all of a sudden a voice in my head
Said don't be so hasty my son
It was the good Lord who pointed the way
The wisest there ever could be
Thoughts of revenge disappeared from my mind
What would I have been but for he?
So now I do not sit on the fence
And God doesn't have to decide
Resisted all evil temptation
I've opted to stay on this side,

    —Steve Taylor

Father To Son

My dear son, I'm supposed to be your father—guiding you,
teaching you, yet—
There have been so many times where you have taught and guided
me.
I never expected to rediscover the joy of touching a dandelion,
Or feeling the roughness of an old oak tree against my fingers,
Caressing every nook and cranny of its tawny frame.

Indeed, seeing you experience the presence of the wind rushing
Against your face, once again, made me stop for just a moment,
To appreciate the genius of God's awesome role as Creator.

To watch you "playing" our old family piano rekindled thoughts
of years long since passed, yet born again with your presence,
Gently, and sometimes not-so-gently, striking each white or
black key, with purposeful precision, resulting in melodious
cacophony, much to my delight.

Yes, again, I look back on these times, knowing that many more
are yet to come,
But, I must thank you, my son,
For in watching you discover your world,
I have rediscovered mine.

    —Julius J. Davis Jr.

You're Loved And You Love

In my Ivory Tower, blocked chances of any happiness.
Tears for failed romances, aching from pure loneliness.
Curtains pulled, playing every sad song I can find.
Sniggering sunshine seems to mock me, making me blind.
Remembering the ones who played with my heart and the ones who stalled.
Feeling the anguish for the ones who never called.
Retaining memories of not being asked to dance.
My heart counting the times he never gave a second glance.
Hearing distant voices saying I'll end up alone.
A painful release from not being called to the phone.
Rushing home, believing he'll be waiting there.
Eyes filling with tired tears, as each time the seat is bare.
Studying the aisle that may never feel my bridal feet.
Conjuring images of the man I'll never meet.
Watching people hating each other, being kicked and shoved.
Unaware that I'd give so much to love and be loved.
Time goes by, scars heal and experience helps me to cope.
I pull back a curtain, and sunshine winks some hope.
'For everybody somebody much more than you've ever dreamed of.
At last it has happened, you're loved and you love!

—*Charlotte Carthy*

Heaven's Fire

Invasion of warmth; softness aglow
Temperature rises; fingertips slow.
Echo of laughter; boldness sets in,
Shortness of breath; softness of skin.

Awakening emotions; passions soar,
Fulfillment of pleasure; craving more.
Delirious senses; the tasting of lips,
Escape through desire; the plunging of hips.

A quiet purr; the satisfaction of sleep,
Climb to the top both breathing deep.
United as one; heaven's fire.
Waver after wave; fulfilled desire.

The tingling of limbs; heaviness of sleep,
Experience of love; our secret to keep.

—*Kathleen A. Rose*

Count on One Hand When Big Sis Call Lil' Sis

The deh my big sistah called to say,
Thanks fo' foldin' up my clothes,
Shachae says y'all gettin' clos'r

Two o' mine,
Shachae an' G
Kids on
No phone
No radio
No T.V.
Sevuhn dehs;
Fo' fightin'

Sistahs need tuh get along,
Testify.
Stay together,
Unify.
Sisters gettin' clos'r like nev'r befoh.

—*Kristen Thomas*

True Friends

Are very special people in your life,
that are willing to stick by your side,
through thick or thin,
accept you for the person you are,
not trying to change you one bit...

They can always brighten up a bad day,
by being there to listen when you need an ear,
to share what's going on,
ask what they think,
and get an honest opinion...

For true friends care about you,
as a human being,
they also give you special honor,
by calling you brother,
by naming their children after you,
or asking you to be his or her Godfather...

—*John Overman*

A Satin Hand

Man was born with a satin hand
That became locked in a gauntlet of steel
Born to touch, to love, to hold
But then taught nevermore to feel

Able to give a silk soft caress
And yearning to receive the same
But we're locked tight within our iron shells
Unable to play in that game

We're armoured full in this steely skin
Head to toe, and hand to heart
Locking us up within ourselves
And from others keeping apart

Oh how do we break this armour we're in?
How can we give once again?
How can we once more touch and love?
We need it to keep ourselves sane

We need to shed this armour
A single piece at a time
To touch and be touched, to love and be loved
To end the darkness, to end this crime.

—*Roy Scafe*

One Voice

I sat there, my mind lost in the meditative sound of the voice that caressed the notes so gently, yet so precisely. The voice that massaged the words with such deep feelings and expressed what so many of us felt, but could not speak. Before me stood the temple from which the voice came. The eyes showed the sincerity with which the mouth sang. The hair, a translucent red, lay soft at the shoulders; the light behind it making it shine so radiantly. The voice, the eyes, the mouth, the hair! All parts of the whole expression of a soul that longed to be heard. The applause, given in love to show appreciation to the voice that gave words to our feelings and unspoken thoughts. I sat and in the silence I thanked God that I knew this voice—this soul, a little bit better today. And as we hugged I looked into those eyes and silently said thank you for making this day a day to remember. At that moment I knew the attraction I had felt for these last several years was real, even though I had kept it well hidden. Not giving myself away nor wanting to be rejected, I had stayed silent and kept my distance. And now as I sit and reflect upon this day, words finally come forth to help me express my feelings.

—*John Pesano*

Trees And Flowers

Would I could flutter like a breeze
That floweth softly through the trees
Like a butterfly midst flowers
Seeking its mate in verdant bowers.

Wouldst we would find a vapor,
A mist, a world, a forest, a foggy tryst,
At least faint trace of some reality
Instead of a bleak and dreary finality,

Does not the sprite of a
favorite garden
Beckon someone in your
    yard then,
The "bleeding hearts" and
    "Love in the mist"
"Columbine" and tendrils
    Reaching for a grip of some
    support,
To lift us all above, a sport,
Far from the soil to touch
    the sky?
        —*James T. Mackey*

The Alcoholic

He never got any affirmatives
That he was special and good,
He never heard praise or felt that he was understood,
He grew up feeling lonely even lonelier in the gang,
He tried to make his mark he tried to make a bang;
But try as he may he never felt that he quite measured up,
He was a husband a boss and a father
Inside he was still a pup;
Booze, wife abuse and child neglect
Became his chosen way;
I ask you all now where is he today?
        —*Sylvia Krane-Morrow*

Kersmack

        "Kersmack," she said
        that is the code word
like crashing cars on the freeway of love
        so Aretha sang to me
        in my sleep

    Then the dog wanted to be let out
        into that killing field
        He was chasing those cars
    and had managed to avoid the
        kersmack
        R-E-S-P-E-C-T
    that's what the dog said to me
    but he liked Whitney Houston
        and his hypocrisy
        was kersmacked

        He was a mere link
    in the chain chain chain
        chain of fools
Aretha behind the wheel of the Cadillac
        Kersmack
        —*Roger Stroop*

Self-Esteem

Why does that child lower his head, he'll never make the team
That kid has a problem that goes down deep, he has no self-esteem
We wonder why the kids' a creep, and other kids don't like him
Well all he does is cause a fuss and always wants to fight them
His grades are nothing you'd ever want, the teachers say he's lazy
You wonder why this kids' a mess, when mother calls him crazy
He was this way day after day, until someone arrived
This person gave him confidence and made him feel alive
They told him he could make it, and showed him how it's done
TLC was what he got, and he became second to none
You see this kid, whose now a man, in the news and on tv
He's made something of himself, for all the world to see
The people really love him now and he's makin lots of green
All because someone special in his life
Gave him self-esteem!!
        —*Judye R. Smiley*

Untitled

    In this world and beyond, there is something,
        that knew, that there was nothing.
    Out of this something, the Universe was shaped,
    We are a part, of this something and its creation,
    There was the love, which created its own life.
    At first through light and sustained it forever.

        We are a ray of thee, your likeness,
    A born part of Thy loving, creative something,
        Always part, never alone, always loved;
        We are blinded, by our own importance and
            lost touch with thee,
    We lost the touch, of what we are told by "The Old Ones",
            in beginning of time.
    We drifted away from Thee, in our own creation, taking this as
    the truth and the world, not remembering our roots anymore,
            Oh, sad ones.

        By surrendering to Thee, we will certain,
        discover Thee again, what was, is and will be forever,
        To discover the joy of Thy love, again in, no time.
            —*John M. Koorn*

Aug. 19, 1942 4 a.m.

It was a green-tinted murder at the end of highway
That leads me to my memory
A simple bedtime terror
That drives us all insane
For a while
Then the moonshine howls
And we forget that we're all brave and young and strong
But we always know
In our mind's eye
That the sun must rise
At the end of highway
Or will it?
Maybe today, the sun will die
And maybe I'll visit that man in the moon
Who always laughed at my cowering, whimpering midnight form
We've read of courage and valour and dying for country
But only mad men truly die
For I am invincible...
Until the moment my life goes away
Like the sun...that is going to die today.
        —*Warren Levy*

Friendship

Friendship is like a golden chain,
that links to hearts together.
And if that chain never breaks,
We'll be good friends forever.

But if theirs a time when the chains unlock
And we do separate, I'll always
have you in my heart, it's you
I'll never hate

So if you have faith in what you believe
I know were always friends.
All our fights and arguments, never
counts, to a friendship that never ends

  —*Courtney White*

Turning "50"

Why do people always think, because my hair is gray
That my mind is on a journey to the great white milky way
They do not see the sparkle in these faded eyes of mine
They do not feel the youthful joy, that I feel all the time
They think when you turn fifty, that all your feeling's gone
That all we have are memories, we remember with a song.

I love to hold a baby close, and take a youngster's hand
I love to laugh and dance and sing and listen to great bands
So even tho my hair is gray, and I'm looking very old
Remember when you see me, your getting closer to the fold
Remember all that's getting old is this body that you see
The minds as young and full of life as a spring day near the sea.

So smile and share the things you have
Cause shortly you will see
They'll stand and look at you my dear
The way you look at me.

  —*Ruby A. Greenlaw*

The Storm

Despairingly gloomy, with an ominous frown,
That mysterious form is lurking around.

Strutting and fretting, now gliding the sky,
Fearfully I watch the cloud loom by.

With loops and scoops, and unforgettably lunges,
It storms and sways making perilous plunges.

Rage and commotion, then perfectly fits
This furious scene of earth's angry blitz.

Thunderous storms, and rain treads the ground,
As this gusty behaviour, tornado's around.

With its passion all spent — calm prevails,
The disturbance is over, and peace serenades.

  —*Heather Y. V. Henning*

She Grows

I feel a happiness inside to see you grow and know
That one day you'll be the same as I
watch you play and hear your laugh
The helpless child I bore is grown
For everyday she grows and away from me she goes
I feel her eyes watching me
Her hands touching me
And know that my baby girl knows
I love her so and she grows.

  —*Giovanna Esposito*

Untitled

Through the screaming metal masses
That only run on putrid gasses
The soot and smoke that is emitted
The worlds welfare is to be fretted
Masses of gangs who try to impair
What do you think, life is a faire?
On with the terrors from other sides.
Now President Reagan's gone for a ride
To what avail, what's the effect
Nuclear fall out from the Soviets?
Always around and back to the same
We're all gonna lose this funny game
If not now, in ten thousand years
I can see it now through hazy tears
All that we've built and molded with care
by creating our future it'll
  no longer be there
   —*Katherine Torrey*

This Place

Take me to 'this place'
that reflects that look upon your face.
Please take me to 'this place'
where all around is veiled in lace.

From torment of the victims eyes
our children sorrows, their hungry sighs.
From humble beast as in agony he cries
to a silence, a peace, our world denies.

This place, a private secret home
to which we all escape, alone.
But do not linger, you must return
to face your fear, your pain and concern.

This place your haven of all desires
is comfort and warm as homes fires.
But no one else can lead you there
they couldn't stay, they wouldn't dare.
Look deep within, and you shall find
for 'this place' it is your mind.

  —*K. Baker*

The Fatal Gift Of Beauty

What is it about the perfect body
that scares me so much,
that makes me want to be someone new?

I look upon you naked in the moonlight
trying to find a blemish upon your creamy skin,
something to match my own imperfections.

I am frightened by my own reality,
frightened now I have reached the rainbows end-
I am frightened by the idyllic beauty

Of you lying by my trembling side
and I, trying not to breath too loud-

I am frightened of waking you up
and having to look into your perfect eyes.

  —*Mark Lewis*

Alone

The lines beneath her eyes tell you of the pain
that she has seen,
   sadness fills her soul.

Timeless years of disappointment have almost
broken her,
   and the taste in her mouth is bitter.

Hungrily she watches the happy people, wondering
where she went wrong,
   blinking back the tears of reality.

She is numbed by the emptiness inside her and
shivers as she feels the cold,
   she stares out into the night...alone.

   —Kimberly L. McArdle

Forever Friend

Life was fine until that day
That tragic day that ran my way
I thought it would help but actually it hurt
Friends and relationships were turned into dirt
But finally you came and brightened my day
I knew when I saw you smile I would get through it anyway
But then I left soon to return
To only find out you had made a new turn
I tried to be friends like before
I supported you through every door
Our friendship had died you had made that change
Now anytime I am around you I really feel strange
I hoped one day you would realize I wanted our friendship to
soar and we could become friends like never before
I wrote this poem so I could say
Just always remember I am behind you all the way
Because you helped me through that tragic day

   —Kristin Reeder

Unexpressed

Within each soul there is a song
That wants to sing tho things go wrong -
The words and music I do not know -
But the song is pure and white as snow.
There's an inner beauty inside of me
That longs to express if I set it free,
But I've kept it locked in a worried pace -
An endless rush in a frantic race.
There seems so many things to do -
Try as I may, I am never through.
But sometimes, the song breaks through a bit
And tells me things that are part of it
Like, beautiful sunsets skies of blue,
Ruby Red Roses, and "I Love You!"
Then, life continues and I go on
Searching in vain for the words to my song.
Sometimes - when I am weary, tired, or blue -
A crescendo of music comes crashing through
And my soul, for a moment in time, is free
To live this life creatively.

   —Ruth V. Johnson

"Falling Tears" Ode To My?

Falling tears and broken dreams
that's all it ever seems.
I'm wondering where you are and
hoping that you're okay.
I can't believe you're gone, but I
guess you wanted it that way.
   They say love is blind.
   I guess it has to be.
   Because if your eyes were open you would see...
That I'm standing here all alone
wondering if you're ever coming home.
It's been days, months and years
All I have left are falling tears
   The thorn has cut too deep
and scars you'll leave behind
   I really cared for you and hope you didn't mind.
But I must go on, I can't wait anymore
However, my heart will be open as it was before.
Waiting, wishing and hoping that you will return
Because my flame for you will always burn.

   —Joyce Kaila

There Is A Secret Side Of Me

There is a secret side of me
   That's like a solitary Dove.
Where all I feel is tranquility,
   And all I know, is love.

There is a secret side of me
   That very few will ever see.
Because I sometimes feel quite frightened,
   Of letting people know, who's me.

There is a secret side of me
   That I wonder why I hide.
Because if I am honest,
   I like what I am inside.

So please don't look and try to judge
   By what at first I appear to be.
Because I'm sure that if you look closely,
   You'll like who's really me.

   —Kirk Van-Beer

A Choice About Life

So many questions are spinning around.
The answers I think will never be found.

Everyone thinks his opinion is right.
We each feel different about this big fight.

Some people are labeled by the name of pro-choice.
They think that women should have their own voice.

Others say problems aren't solved with a knife.
These people go by the name of pro-life.

So many children live with abuse everyday.
Should their lives have been taken away?

A pregnant teen grows up far too soon.
Is her soon to be child destined to doom?

Should the government say just what will be done?
Or should it be said by our daughters or sons?

Religion, a topic most have feelings about,
Says that murder is not the right route.

Can abortion be said to be right or wrong?
Or just how to survive in a world upside-down?

So many questions we need answers to.
But, for now the decision is left up to you.

   —Katie Barclay

You

When all good things come to an end
The bleeding heart will never mend
Something that seemed so far away
Is the reality of today
I don't think I can deal with the loss
The price of you was the cost
It seems as if nothing is real
But the loss of you I can feel
This heart of mine is on the line
The pain will rip me for a long time
The thought of you is on my mind
Is it some kind of a sign
The memory of you will last and last
As if impossible to put it to past
But when I think about what might have been
How our love didn't win
I can only hope someday I can see
That this was one of those things not meant to be

—Jessica Renee Zeno

Preparation For An Eternal Vacation

The vacation is very near, sun-light is golden flare
The breeze is getting mollified with touch of dews
The jasmine shoots odour to touch the sky blue,
As it is some dear ones warm soft touch
Which makes the hearts blood rush.
In the adjacent sky cumulus clouds lazily sigh
And my senile soul the desire to work defies,
And we house-holders vociferously strive to decide
In which holiday-resort we were going to reside
Suddenly found on the reddish laterite road bare
To the slaughter house butchers taking lambs to slaughters
The sound of their fruitless bleated weeping
Seeps into the autumnal sky and it sighs.
Where spaces nihilistic existence lies,
That they were proceeding towards
An eternal vacation how could they realise,
But where they would now reside?

—D. Bonerji

The Swimming Hole

Translated into modern cement,
The circular oasis of a century gone by,
Complete with weeping willow.

"It's a wading pool,"
supplies a nine-year-old
authority on such matters.

Sun-streaked mothers cool their ankles
From perches around the edge,
While babes and children
Cavort in water
As cool and wet as any gone before.

The kiss of summer in a city park,
Where swings pulse to and fro
And little bodies serve to build sand empires.

You can't dig 'till water -
But you sure can fill the hole
And make a most satisfactory mud.

—Carolyn Landry

Spring

Pretty birds in the clear blue sky,
the clouds above is where they fly.
The whispering winds blow through the trees,
the water trickles down to rivers at ease.
The rain pours down, the sun appears,
Shining on water like sudden tears.
The dew stands still in the fresh green earth,
the flowers now bloom like a delicate birth.
The dears come out, the rabbits awake,
swans swim around the beautiful lake.
The air is fresh, smelling strong but sweet,
spring is hear, we finally meet!

—Belinda Lindsay

The Black Rose

The petals so soft
The color so dark
The stem so green
And the thorns so sharp.
Its petals gracefully flutter in the breeze
Dew decorates its petals in the morn
But by night all freeze.
So soft to touch, like silk are the petals
But to touch the stem
Is a regretful sin
To prick a finger,
To bleed by the rose,
To make a new one grown.
To die by the rose is to
give it more power.

—Colette Miller

Guatemala

Mala Sangre Tierra Del Ensueno (Bad Blood in the Land of Illusion)

Nineteen Fifty-four,
The Eagle flew for the Lords
of Miami:
Democracy the victim.
Campesinas the target.

He lay if asleep,
a kerchief masks face now gone.
Peasant blood stains the
earth with jacaranda blooms.
Flame trees reach toward heaven.

Padre' Giron cries
Communal not Communism.
He is their last hope.
Justice is swayed by gold,
faith torn apart by bullets.

—Laraine McClelland

Gateway

Hard time to distinguish reality, imagination.
The gateway into imagination is an obsession.
The path back to reality, is chance.
Easier to picture a new world, enter with past and be present
Than to live a life, hard times, obstacles.
Being lost in your imagination, horrific in conception.
Being lost in your imagination, is you, making a new world.
You're your gateway.

—Dustin Perepelecta

131

Sensations

The falling of the rain and the loud thunder after.
The first cry of a baby and the sound of your laughter.
The voice of a loved one so comforting to the ear.
The echo of footsteps to let you know someone is near.
A guitar in tune and the chirp of a bird,
are the most wonderful things that I have ever heard.

A child picking shells from the edge of a beach.
The stars up above that are way out of reach.
The feel of a raindrop falling down on my head.
The setting of the sun painting the sky orange and red.
Colorful meadows filled with flowers and trees.
Sunny April showers and a warm sudden breeze.
Clear blue skies and warm peaceful days,
are all images that dance through my mind in magnificent ways.

The feel of sand sifting through my fingers.
The softness of your hair through which my hand lingers.
The warm rays of the sun beating down on my face.
The softness of silk, satin and lace.
The touch of your hand reaching out for my own,
are the most incredible sensations to me ever known.

  —Kimberly Trefcer

Superman's Dead!

War, pestilence, and global warming,
The flouting of nature's laws.
Plague, drought and ethnic cleansing;
Whilst acid rains pour.
They're starving and dying in third world countries,
Whilst you and I sit eating our wimpys.

Fascist dictators or a military coup,
Rape and muggings or an air plane crash.
Always the bad things hit the news,
Another murder, a throat is slashed.
A nuclear accident kills the land,
But who is there to lend a hand.

The forests are eroding for monetary gain,
But nothing comes for free.
The earth's being destroyed but who's to blame,
Open your eyes and see.
Saving our planet is a must,
Superman's dead, it's up to us.

  —Warren Galley

The Flight Of Sensation

Endorse yourself, take flight when
 The foundation steams.
Feel the sensation, let go, be free!

 Soar high, as much as you can
  And discover yourself
 Feel the blindness of yourself
  And ponder freely.

 Glide over pastors and cliffs
  That bonds with the ocean!
  Dance colorfully
Against the ocean, land, and sun!

 Let them know you're free,
  So it can last an eternity!
 Let the gracious wind
Satisfy your thoughts and body, be free!

 Feel the flight of sensation
And know that you're worth living.

  —Kreg Daniel Speirs

Untitled

Like the calmness of the lake,
the fury of the sea waves -
his eyes merge the calm and the commanding.
To say the headlands of the coast had magnetism
would be to know that he wears this magnetism
like a black cloak, veiling his pure emotion.

Let our hearts rise past these futile emotions,
of love and hate
let there only be left an understanding
and companionship...
In this we may find solitude
apart forever, yet always together.

We are of the same mind,
knowing that the elements are all powerful,
but lost to man, uncontrolled.
May we go there often together
traveling apart in heart,
letting the "emotional rescue"
be an acceptance and engulfment
of all the beauty and destruction that surround us...

  —Jinx-Julia Lootens

One Moment

In one moment I found peace. A peace that is like no other.
The great burden of life's worries were gone and in its place
a knowledge that my life had true meaning.
Gone were the frustrations, heartaches, tears, and pain that
this world brings upon us all.
It was replaced by a fulfillment of the void in my heart
that has been there so long.
That void was filled with a feeling of freedom from the
imprisoning walls I had built around my heart.
The freedom came from one man who long ago gave his life for
me.
Little by little and year by year he chipped away at the
wall till at last it was weakened and it fell.
It was then that I saw him and all he had done
for me and all he had to offer.
In his hands he held what I had longed for all my life.
The moment I saw his nail scarred hands and
saw the crown of thorns upon his head I knew that
the searching and longing had come to end.
The moment I looked into his caring eyes my search was over.
In that moment I found peace. The moment I found Jesus Christ.

  —Kimberly Ann Smith

A Time For Goodbye

With the coming of the sunset
The heartbroken unhappiness slowly shadows
over every living fibre.
A honey dipped tear of sadness steals away
from the gold fireball of all gold stars.
The droplet dives into
the depths of the ocean blue.
Releasing screams of sorrow,
cloaked as a soft hissing sound.
As the droplet ruins the calmness of the water
the color gold expanses over the scorching, rippling water.
The reoccurring death becomes a
reality.
But with each sunset comes a sunrise.
In its heart of hearts
it knows it will rise again.
And be able to blow its kisses
and gifts of sunlight upon us.

  —Misty Dowsett

Daydreaming

I'm sitting in my garden, watching the world go by,
The humming of the bees and wasps, the buzzing of a fly
A mower whirs a long way off as it cuts each blade of grass,
I'm sitting in my deck chair, summer's here at last.

I know I should be working, slaving hard and long
But the urge to just sit here is very very strong.
The sun is warm and soothing as it gently tans my skin
If my boss should see me, oh what trouble I'd be in

I'd love to be on an island where I didn't have to toil
Where tower blocks and factories were not allowed to spoil
The views of unspoilt beaches and the sea so azure blue
Where ships would sail by daily with a multinational crew.

I know this is all fantasy and soon I will awake
To get myself in motion and work for my own sake
But if I didn't dream and fantasize so much
I'd just be downright miserable and sadly out of touch.

  —Patricia Wesley

The Human Within

The human must be saved for they have the power to rid the
  bondage.
The ignorance of the person will be her own downfall
For she needs the human to survive.
Teach the person to open life to the human.

There is Vikki the Person.
Then there is Vikki the Human.
The human who is strong and meek
Will dispose of the person who is trembling and weak.
The human who is loving and kind,
Will become whole in body, soul and mind.
Exhult! and make away.
Shed the person for the Human within.

  —Vikki Langelier

En Route Cozani

Sometimes when the contours scar the mind,
the lake is static, I ecstatic, then
the white range touches off explosions in the heart -
I think I know the Ulysses in me.

The search then brings the sign -
potential sight, at least;
chimeras of the mind perform their dance:
The taunt of revelation.

Lines merge to give assurance: There is 'form';
green grass becomes "this miracles". The sound
of laughter coursing after prey of spreading joys
alights eve hope - the Lotos-fruit of all.

Here the sharp grasp of beauty seized in thorns
brings anguish - or why else tears?
Would pure geology destroy me so?
But sights invisible, a torment still
play on an old reluctant nerve,
and galvanize the pain of faith
which I had anodyned so well.

  —Brian Williams

Romance

I watched the sun go slowly to sleep,
 The last bit of rays left the sky.
 And tears from my heart did weep,
I heard the poplars echo your goodbye.

Loons swimming on the lake, sang goodnight.
 Crickets answered with surprising glee.
The evening star, the first sparkling light
 Was like a twinkle in your eyes to me.

 The moon shone with fullness above,
 Casting a shadow you called "Romance"
 Bullfrogs played the song of love,
 To which we always had to dance.

 A cool soft breeze kissed my cheek,
 And wrapped itself around my soul.
 To give me all the comfort, I seek.
 Oh! Why did I ever let you go?

A thousand violins, grasshoppers played.
Dark shadows in the forest, threatened and grew.
 It's now that I wished you had stayed.
I know now, that I have always loved you.

  —Eileen Trott

From My Window

From my window I can see,
The little child I used to be.
Safe and secure holding Dad's hand,
Dreaming of Kings and Dragons all over the land.

From my window I can see,
The young man I used to be.
Eager to help but always wanting to play,
Looking forward to weekends and a holiday.

From my window I now see,
The young adult that is now me.
Looking at our world that is hard to understand,
You see this is the hardest part of becoming a man.

  —Jared S. Mullen

Card XXI

Worlds without end, evolving through
the misty divisions across earths
passing through consciousness' tides
till the end of everything,
through logical conclusions, from
flowers to butterflies to butterfly gold,
with no dust, no tragedy of theme,
no aspect of joy will escape you.

Showing Card XXI in a white hand,
all worlds will accept you.
No death, only metamorphosis will touch you.

If I could seek to ask, I would that
no dead cold water wash over you,
and that your wounds turn kind with time
blinded to this bright earth's shores,
so let those tears go, and let them go.
I've made a straight staircase to the slow sun
and it never casts any shadow.

  —Mandi K. Tweedy

Sounds Of Nature

In the hush of the night, the stars shine bright.
The moon makes a glow, on the water below.
Threading a golden path, to our humble little shack.
I sit by my fire, before I retire,
My spirit sails free, as Gods creatures speak to me.
Fish leap and bound, making a joyous sound.
The chirp of a cricket, sounds rather wicked.
Bull frogs give their mating call, to the lady frogs, one and all.
The brave hoot of the owl; the sound of the coyotes mournful
    howl;
Makes the cattle bawl, and the rooster give its warning call.
A beaver swims to shore, looking for one green tree more.
I watch him in awe, as he begins to gnaw.
I give a deep sigh, as the embers of my fire die.
My heart is light, as I say goodnight,
Thank you Lord, for letting me see, all your creatures running
    free.

    —Gertrude Geisler

How Do You Do It?

Hello! Dear friend; how can you be?
The one that gives; like the giving tree?

How do you do it? That is what I ask;
You always take on each and every task.

How can you love it, when it responds in despair?
You are truly the one that always cares.

Why don't you say, "no more," to thee?
For I am the one, that always looks for the tree.

How can you keep going in spite of your times?
How can you reach out to give your last dime?

How do you manage to make it all count?
This is something I will never figure out.

That smile always shines with the brightest of lights;
How do you do it, and keep up the fight?

I love you always, until the end of time;
But, then I will be able to give my last dime?

    —Kevin Eble

Sonnet

My wife, aged fifty, said the cutest thing
the other day. It is my wont to bring
a poem to her for her to comment on it,
something I have written — limerick... sonnet...
verse that has a finite definite form
to which can be applied a final norm
that's applicable, viz. procrustean bed,
or T.S. Eliot's once-or-twicely read.
She said (the treading ox one must not muzzle)
that "a sonnet's like a crossword-puzzle!"
(in that in it every word must fit
the other words which match and cross-hatch it).
I wonder what, exactly, was the Word
that was — in the beginning — said and heard.

    —Aaron Bell

Me

I look; and what I see, amazes me.
The power, the size and the beauty of it,
confines me... unafraid. Strangely.

I look into its eyes; it looks into mine.
I see myself reflected in him and he now sees
himself reflected in me.

The tiger leaps at me. The majesty of it,
awes me.

    —Alex Conradie

Till Then

The sand has washed away...the beach is gone.
The place I spent my childhood is no more...
In Monmouth Beach...along the Jersey shore.
Where has it gone in all these years?
The memories made there bring on smiles and tears.

The sand has washed away...the beach is gone.
I can't imagine just why this could be...
The place where I grew up has washed into the sea.
Each storm that pounded up upon the shore
Stole grains of sand until there were no more.

The sand has washed away...the beach is gone:
I try to think why God would move this beach
Way out to sea...so far from reach.
Each year it seemed to be a little less...
Until the waves lash up upon the steps.

The sand has washed away...the beach is gone.
It's washed away...it is no more.
The ocean's there where once it was the shore.
So when my ashes fall into the sea...
Each grain of sand will be there waiting just for me.

    —Kathleen Ryan

Sonnet To My Mother

Upon the mind and ear sensations crowd;
The rain, in restless spasms flung our way
Is dashed pell-mell against the glass; this day
Will see the spring, newborn and wrapped in cloud.
When you were young you also looked, and dreamed,
And wondered what the downpour's wake would show.
You raised your face and studied drops that streamed
From unseen skies; you saw the currents blow,
And noted beauty where in mist it gleamed.
You had to face life's storms, to feel the pain,
With heart that could not merely watch it rain.
   There comes across the miles a love aglow
   To answer when with thunder earth cries loud,
   Travailing with new birth, with torrent tears;
   I will not wait until the tempest clears,
   But willingly unlock the door, and go.

    —Theo Halladay

The Miracle Called "Melody"

It's the power and the sweetness of your voice
The rich musical choice
The overwhelming impact you made
Your life, career, your fate
The love you gave, your dedication
The millions of fans in love and admiration
Men and women everywhere, and every age
How beautiful and powerful you looked on stage
The memory of your smile
Your fun, your shyness, your own style
The biggest amount of records sold
Your name engraved in solid gold
The sound of the Zarathrusta theme
The yearning for the Impossible Dream
Our deep devotion to you, the "King"
The applause you get, just everything
This special love inside of me
It's one never ending Unchained Melody

    —Tessa Glas

The Perfect Race

The smell of death is in the air,
The rot, decay and burning hair.
The screams of torture, forever echoing.
The sounds of pain and fear never fading.
No mercy for the weak or the ill.
Young and old all sentenced to hell,
For crimes of being born to the wrong race.
It's not fair, but their history we must face.

—*Sarah DeWolfe*

Untitled

Like a water softly falling slowly and indiscreet,
The salt on my face dripping cold and shame to meet,
All the sands of the earth running faster escaping from a sound,
And like a spinning in my head also dashing round and round.
The ground is below my tiresome feet but there is nothing to feel,
Neither in my body only feeling so lonely and shameful and no
    more so real,
Like the harsh wind that thrashes around my body everywhere,
But suddenly emotional it has stopped and is no longer there.
For my power that was once inside
Seems to have lost me all over and makes me hide.
The water stops moving now as my body has nothing vain,
Maybe all uncovered and given up of all the pain.
There is the colours around in the space that myself hold,
And gracefully one day to find before the body will grow old.
The sound is calm and the image is clear to see,
All is mystifying and reflecting and in front there is me.
Beside me is the sand so beige and brown,
And the difference to see has shaped me and grown.
There is one tiny speckled but colourful thing the grain,
And as my face so cold and different my tears will stop like the
    rain.

—*Karen Watson*

The Time

Too many years, three score and ten,
The scourage has plagued this sorry land.
The scourage of hate, the scourge of war,
The scourage of death, of pain, horror.
The land where freedom, had once sprung,
A land where elders, mourn their young.
Where men of sin, invoke their God,
And innocents will shed their blood.
But man, with all his evil hand,
Cannot destroy, God's chosen land.
And then the land, will send the call,
Enough to death! Enough to war!
The time has come, to end the tears,
To end the sorrow, blood and fears.
To men of war, to men of hate,
It says begone, it's much too late.
And beckons in, and knows not how.
The time for peace, the time is now.

—*Meir Zohar*

Glowing Stars

When the moon is on seventh heaven.
The star shines so bright.
With each glowing, and one telling a story behind it.
There is magic in the air.
A warm loving lullaby whispering music throughout the air.
One soft tiny rain drop flowing gently down on the ground.
Then the stars begin to tell a story from old times.
Of a great party of the stars from big to little.
But aflame that always burns,
so each can find a glowing star.

—*Judy Bohannon*

As Seasons Change

The wonders of nature are apparent as
the seasons change,

Reminding us of our own nature and the
need to change.

Change our minds to
look to the Father,

Change our hearts to
love one another,

Change our lives to
live so much better,

Change our hands to
work with each other.

At this season of Christmastide, as nature
changes into white,

Let us make the changes that will lead us
toward the light!

—*Jeanne Fields*

A Grand Canyon

I desperately need a love in my life;
The sort realized only in a wife.
I feel like a vacuum covered with skin;
I'm lost and need rescue from this coffin.
It's a vast abyss that excruciates,
Only a wife that's best friend satiates.
I feel dead and shrivelled, desiccated,
I've no more tears left, I'm dehydrated!

I've a perfect fit for all the details
Your life may carry and all that entails;
But I also need the same and in kind.
Where can you be hiding, have I gone blind?

My love for you is deeper than you know;
But love's not a potent enough word though.
I'd need to have God's vocabulary
To voice fully what's extraordinary.
So it must wait until we're transfigured
For me to be able to put into word
All of my thoughts and feelings towards you.
I beg of you please, please, search for me too!

—*Scott Blain*

Goodbye

I see the beauty in the window
… the stars suspended in the mysterious dark night
I wonder if I'll ever be a part of that world
… If I'll ever have something so beautiful that
    nothing can change it
I long for the feel of your body against mine
… but I know that we're not meant to be
Things may feel good, but that doesn't mean they're right
I know that I must get over this
… but it's hard when your mind doesn't let you forget
I thought that what I did was right,
    but I don't know anymore
I think of memories you and I shared,
    and I don't know how can I give upon us
I see other guys walk by me and feel sure
    that I don't want them
What have you done to me?
Dear God, what have you done to me?

—*Kaiulani Lie*

Too Late

A car hurtles dangerously along the desolate road,
The stillness broken only by his drunken laugh.
His bloodshot eyes see your headlights through the rain,
But he only curses under his foul breath.
The screech of tires,
The sound of metal crushing metal.
Your car upside down in the ditch.
With another raucous laugh,
He drives into the dark.
He doesn't know that moments ago you were in my arms.
Now you lie silent.
Your eyes no longer see,
Your ears hear no more.
Sirens wail in the distance,
But they are too late.
You have spoken your last words,
Dreamed your last dream.
My heart is broken.
My lips soundlessly whisper
"I love you"

　　　—*Lesley How*

Ecstasy Is A Secret

Ecstasy is a secret.
The subtle taste of happiness.
The bittersweet wine,
Wetting mere velvet dreams.
The chosen sacrifice of deepest triumphance.
Crimson perfume on lingering memories.
The hand of choking motion.
Sweet saffron melody.
A sharp stab,
A silver dream
The will to live.
Desperation, numbing your lips.
A black orchestra playing the softest tune.
To touch the velvet breasts of roses.
Unloved, endearing smiles of sadness.
A kiss of fading truth,
Like cancer in a pounding lung.
Whispers of the darkness,
Being told
Ecstasy is a secret.

　　　—*Jove Bailey*

My Time Is My Own Again

The sky is grey today
The sun struggles to break through the clouds
The house has a kind of quiet engulfing all
in its path.
I sit in my living room and contemplate the
up coming weeks.
My time is my own again.

The first day of school has arrived, just as I
thought my time was running thin
My time is my own again
At least until late afternoon.

I feel a sense of freedom and can for a short
time put my favorite slogan on the shelf
I'm here to serve.
My time is my own again
At least until late afternoon.

　　　—*Sandra R. Monteith*

Untitled

As the room turns,
The truth of vision is uncertain.
Your observations; control your thoughts.
Life's truths become nightmares.
While your imagination runs wild.
Reality becomes the unknown.
As you have entered a new world.
Where your imagination dictates.
Your observation becomes unclear,
and you see something that is not there.
Your fear turns your insides,
and sparks a fire.
As it erupts it becomes an uncontrollable burning.
That lashes out, unconsciously.
You've become destructive.
Destroying whatever is in your path.
Trying to protect what is yours,
But eventually destroying it.

　　　—*James Ashley Cuff*

Love's Virtue

True love makes the earth quiver and mountains move
　　the valleys to cry out and the birds to soar
　　　the wind to breathe softly and the heavens to weep with
　　　　joy.

Rivers roar pounding against the heart of the deep
　　filling the hills with its resonance
　　　always beckoning lovers to its presence.

The evening speaks the mysteries of passion
　　and stirs the morning to rise in glory
　　　bringing melodies to lovers by the wings of minstrels.

All of nature hovers over love's preciousness
　　orchestrating its beauty to impassion the lovers
　　　impressing each moment on their hearts for a keepsake.

The earth then relinquishes its secrets with delicate perfumes
　　and lustrous blossoms as a gift from one love to the other
　　　scenting the day with a hush of sweetness.

And as awe and wonder encompass loves' captives
　　they are possessed with the stillness of time
　　　and whispers of eternity.

　　　—*Kathryn Crawford*

I'm Thinking About You Tonight

I'm thinking about you tonight
The way we used to be,
The way you made me feel
Like a bird just let free.

I'm thinking about you tonight
And wish we were together,
If I could float back into your arms,
Just like a light feather.

I'm thinking about you tonight
Wishing we were back together,
Wishing love we once knew, wasn't replaced,
Wishing you were back in my arms to hold.

Only if you could understand
How much I still love you,....
It's more than words could ever say.

　　　—*Kristin C. Kuehl*

Nighttide

When the day closes, and night forcomes the earth;
The world outside grows quiet, and I behold the
moons rebirth.

With the creatures of nighttide abound us; the shadows
come alive. A blanket of stars above us; nighttide
has arrived.

In awe we so journ, as if by magic we are bound;
Nighttide is exquisite, enchantment all around.

Nighttide is fervent; its passion all about.
Nighttide is the guardian; for the creatures
scamper'd out.

Nighttide is mysterious; majesty is its claim.
Nighttide is mythical; a world of lustrous fame.

Nighttide is enchanting; a many splendered thing.
Nighttide is departing; for dawn's on the wing.

—*Kimberly BrownEagle*

Warrior Of The Night

As night gently covers the land in shadows,
there is a mighty warrior who hides in the shallows.
Strong, agile, with a mind of wills,
it is these that wield the blade that kills.

An enemy emerges from the mist of night,
his gleaming blade drawn, ready to fight.
Battle cries ring, loud and clear
and the who falls shall be the one who holds fear.

The two mighty blades meet in the dark,
but it's the warrior's sword that finds its mark.
The enemy falls, never to rise
and the warrior waits for his next adversary to arise.

The warrior fought on through the night
and many fell to his strength and might.
But as the last of the shadows faded away
and the deadly night gave way to day,
the warrior knew he had earned the right,
the right to be known as the warrior of the night.

—*Jeff Holtzlander*

No More Time Left

The time for completeness and final change is now here
There is no more time left to discourage, no more to encourage
  rage
The time has come and we must write a new history page.

No more time for war and confusion and for confrontation
The time now let it be for unity, peace and reconciliation
The time has come, let there be no more destruction.

The time has come and few eyes seem to see the reality
There is little time left for a dying humanity
Man's vast sums of money is spent on vanity
The time for change is come and hatred and anger still burns
But when eternity comes there will be none.

—*Terance Wilson*

Clear Cuts

Their bulking shapes are like spectors of another time
They take on the forms of moose elk and bear
Out of the corner of the eye appear the massive forms
of the proud animals who once roamed
Closer inspection turns these ragged beauties into the stumps
and discards of forgotten trees.

—*Kateri Carroll*

Nature

The sky is blue-
There is peace in the land,
There is a frown on the face of heaven,
Anger is at hand.
The clouds are camped on the mountains-
The forces of Nature are gathering,
Winds rage and howl across the land,
It is a border skirmish.
Sudden squalls bombard the land
War is declared. The battle is joined,
The rumble of thunder like the thunder of guns;
The flashes of lightning like the flashes of bombs,
The gods are locked in combat,
Heaven is in turmoil!
Puny, forlorn, he cowers - Man,
Stupid sinner. He trembles.
He knows his Master - Nature.

—*Editayo Pabs-Garnon*

Confusion Within

Now confusion occupies a place that only time can heal.
  There's an empty, empty space that nothing can fill.
And I cry again at night, unsure of any path to follow.
  Your name is constantly echoed, but the sound is hollow.

Now confusion occupies a space that only you can fill.
  The aching in my heart refuses to be cured by any pill.
The sweet taste of your love that once was ever so present.
  Is a dryness that no drink, no other companion, can quench.

Now confusion occupies a place within that pains me so...
  And each day that goes by it seems to become stronger.
Within my heart it beats steadily and ever unsure.
  It thrives off of pain and lies dormant in liquor.

—*Kendra LaChelle' Walker-Scott*

Daddy's Unmarked Grave

Return home again—impossible.
There's too much left undone—
  there's shame.
An unmarked grave sits abandoned
  reflecting the hurt and pain of childhood.

Can any parent really deserve that—
  the unmarked grave?
Can two daughters really hate or hurt
  that much?

Abandonment to a child is crippling—
  maybe for a lifetime.
Is this then the ultimate control
  and retribution?
He gave his name then left them,
  they gave a place but no name.

Forgiveness, healing, but no commitment
  for there was no root.
In death there was the final decision,
  "he can wait too".

—*Joyce M. Grubbs*

Best Friends

You've been there for me, and me for you.
Through thick and thin we've lasted more than a year or two.
We've tried to set each other up and we've partied together to.
So why do we argue?
Who knows?
But it looks like we'll be together pretty much forever.

—*Joy Hope Toler*

Re-Calling

anthropologists found out that the average relationship
these days is supposed to last 56 days he said

we talked we always talked talking emptiness into being making
silence roar like the horrifying/-fied animal we were

my grandfather used to take me along to his favourite pub

you always start with the eyes make the contours look at
you then its nose mouth ears hair collar spray finished

56 days

hunting swallows break the river surface twice the one so
many years ago did at the brook near the pub

56 days unlikely

beauty marked swatch eyes returning gazes is it eyes that
make a face mirrors that don't reveal a damn thing

language influences thought or was it other way round mind
in the bondage of the tongue or was it words in the chains of
thoughts whose thoughts mine of those others

another stone another city another country another time

56 days huh

if language influences thought and vice versa does that mean
that what we don't name doesn't exist
> —*Michaela Zimmermann*

To Mum

It seems such a little while ago, when you and I had fun
They had called me home because they said, your life would soon
be done

Ten days had passed since I left you there, all tucked up in your
bed
Not knowing that the words you spoke, would be the last to me
you said

On Saturday, December 8th, the dreaded phone call came
"Mum has gone.." Our Margaret said "...she no longer feels the
pain."

If only I could have been with you, when your final breath you
took
But I guess it just wasn't meant to be, not written in the book

As I look out in my garden now, I have come to realize
No longer will you hear the birds, or see flowers through your
eyes

These pleasures you enjoyed so much have for now been put on
hold
Until Jehovah brings you back, in the way he has foretold

This earth, man's home, he will restore into a paradise
At that time, you and Dad and others, will once again arise

With sickness pain and death all gone, it surely will be bliss
Our guarantee is Jesus Christ, who gave his life for this

So now Mum as you rest in sleep, I can only hope and pray
That Alex, Margaret, Jean and I, can be there on that happy day

For now we have our memories, and many photos too
Of a precious smiling Lady, yes dear Mum, that was you
> —*Dorothy Hutchinson*

Friends

We all need friends
They help us when we feel lonely
They are always there to support us in our endeavors.
Without friends we are nowhere
We just have to be cautious
in how we make friends.
Not everyone can be a friend.
Due to such things as attitudes,
And other differences in outlook on life.
Most of all a friend has to be a caring,
and compassionate person.
With today's world we need true
friends as much as we need family
since family don't always want to
be friends with family.
We must however look to a day when we can all be friends.
It may not happen but we can never give up hope.
We must learn to love one another
despite our differences after all
that is what God wanted for us.
> —*Amanda Jill Augustine*

Of Time Gone By

The hands of the clock keep moving around
They never seem to stand still
But if they could talk of all that they've seen
They could talk for hours at will.

Just think of the stories of love and of glory,
Of hatred and of sin,
Of history old when knights were bold,
Of King Arthur and his kin.

Of that wonderful birth of our Saviour
In Bethlehem long ago,
Of the things that He did, starting when just a kid
About the age of 12 or so.

Of peace and of war, of happiness galore,
Of sadness deep down within,
Of triumph and strife, of man and his wife,
Of temptations that led them to sin.

If only the clock could stand up and talk
These stories to tell us at will
But the hands of the clock keep moving around
They just never seem to stand still.
> —*James Mason*

When Demons Delay

Violet, emerald, and dusty rose,
They sleep deep in Dawn's closet;
News of another friend lost
Is nothing new anymore.

She pretends to not mind,
And flaunts her freedom
As if it were a diamond ring.
But secretly she creates scenes
Of whispers into fallen hair
And strong hands at the small of her back.

She turns and they're gone,
But believes that they can't be
Too far away, or so untrue.
Sometimes demons delay angels,
She reasons,
And prays that they may arrive soon,
With friends and whispers and hands.
> —*Kim Purser*

Hoping Dreams Come True

I am sitting here all alone
Thinking and listening to the clock's ticking tone.
I'm wondering what you're doing and if you're thinking too
Wondering what your fate is and hoping dreams come true.

Do you hope your fate brings luck
And lots of happiness too,
Do you dream health for others
Or are you dreaming just for you?

I am wondering when I think of you
If you are thinking of me
Wondering when we'll meet next time
Or thinking of when we'll see.

I hope that when you think of us, you think of us together,
And I hope that when you wish tonight, you wish us happy forever.

Through all my hopes and dreams
You're the one I wish comes true
I hope forever we'll be in love
And to the end always me and you.

I hope that all for dreams come true
But most of all for me, I wish forever to have you!

—*Lori Levesque*

A New Found Fortress

I was shattered - oh yes frazelled.
Thinking of a lacerated heart of my mother,
pulverised by destiny, devoured by cancer,
of a half witted, jilted ridiculed daughter,
My piccadillos, the foibless that evoked sarcastic laughter
Engulfed in impenetrable darkness...with no beam- no gleam.
Twice married but, shunned, thwarted and never looked after,
Obesity, diabetes, I had to encounter this or that disaster,
What had I? an existence lackadaisical, a life of ennui, lack lustre.
But then dawned the moment of truth
My dreams smashed into smithereens on life's altar.
Picked up by my calloused hands were but brickbats and beams
For building up the citadels of poems interwoven
                              stories-so-sought after
I was in my fortress - in my world-the haven of peace-no torture
With still the vestige of health to stroll in the dewy mornings
And rivet my gaze on leafy arrowcarias, sycamores and sweet peas
That idyllic fortress of solitude, giving me moorings, to revel
                              and saunter
Giving me a new touch with God, the Creator, the Master,
Every passing day surreptitiously taking me to my Lord -
                              closer—more closer.

—*Nilofer Sultana*

Distance

I'm wondering through my past,
Thinking of all life's experiences,
Death, birth and living
So what's the difference?
What's the point?
To be inspired by the ones we admire
The truth is plain and clear to see,
But we're all fooled by the distortion that lives
Within our own minds
Fooled, tricked, deceived and presently silent, for
We are all afraid.
Society, is it the end of chaos or the beginning?
We choose to withdraw
Trapped by our own religions and traditions
The truth is right behind you don't turn
Don't turn around too fast, or
It will catch you by surprise.

—*Tina Gagliardi*

Travel

As I pondered about this world
    This vast, vast universe of ours,
I thought how grand it would be
    To travel and to explore.

I thought of places near and far,
    Of people, customs and food galore.
The more I thought the more I yearned
    To travel near and to travel far.

There were the mountains, streams and falls,
    The flat, flat plains and rolling hills.
The vast expanse of earth and sea,
    To travel meant see all of these.

Traveling North to see its splendor
    Meant planning for flies, moose and tundra.
Travel by day on roads not well kept,
    Sleeping at night where wild animals dwelt.

To travel South and see more grandeur
    Meant crossing the line on into the desert.
The further I traveled the more I saw
    Which told me this world was designed by God.

—*Eva C. Eberhart*

Flesh of Glass

The breeze of time gently stirs the world;
    This world of dying grass.
Upon one billion souls, encased in flesh,
Seek loving hands to guard this flesh;
    This flesh of tender glass.

Flawed from the moment of creation,
Flawed from this play; this earthly role.
Cracked in a moment of desperation,
Spreading deeper and deeper, seeking the soul.

The breeze of time gently stirs the world;
Blowing beside us down the path of life,
Winding around us, every move we make;
While this flawed and tender flesh of glass
    Breaks a little more
With every step we take.

—*Mike Ward*

The Keeping Of My Heart

Strange today, from other days, I've failed to come awake,
Tho quite aware, as I lie there, a breath, I can not take.
My eyes refuse to open, I can not see a thing,
I can not hear a sound about, yet somehow, I can think.
What's happened here, I ask myself, as I try hard to speak,
But words can not pass through my lips, the answer that I seek.
My body lies here motionless, I feel I ask in vain,
And suddenly, I realize, I shall not wake again.
Now torn between the panic, and sudden grip of grief,
I feel that what has come to pass, has somehow, brought relief.
Alas, the pains of life are gone, it's sad, the joys are too,
And soon my thoughts, will too be done, as nature takes her due.
And as I leave this mortal life, forever, to depart,
I leave with you, forever dear, the keeping of my heart.
Strange today, from other days.

—*Joseph J. McKaig*

An Aging Society Is Everyone's Business

Once I was a youngster as I remember of spirit,
   those days that are gone now still have merit.

When I believed 40 yrs. of age was old,
   why was it they all seemed so bold.

As I grew, age was a period of knowledge,
   little did I know of the challenge.

Now my age has mellowed,
   my respect is not of those who bellow.

Because with time comes grace,
   we now have become as valuable as 'ole lace'.

The wrinkles do not bother nor worry me,
   for they were meant to be.

Of those who life is in the twilight hour,
   their memories they want to shower.

To those who have so much to learn,
   from the aged comes only concern.

Now I share the times of a past generation,
   to our youngsters of this great nation.

Oh, age, you do not worry me,
   for what was to be, will be!

   —*Keith M. Turnham*

The Wall

The wall stands there so silent and still
though the air is still warm and breezes are calm.
from within I feel a spine tingling chill.

I stand in reverence, erect and also straight
but the wall is ramrod, never twitching, and black as slate
the wall makes grown me sorrowful, and some even cry.
and all along, I reflect and try to think: Why?
some say it should have never been erected
some say it is a reminder of all that should be corrected.

the Wall honors the men that we can not be forgot.
they left us their name, to fell of a war they fought.
the wall shows the boys who left what was home to them,
their friends returned without them, they returned as men.

as I leave, I think of all of us who cried,
of all of those who tried,
and of the thousands who died.

   —*Jake Eby*

Salt Lake City - Bremmer Jail - 1986

Migrating to our Arizona winter home,
Through many American States we did roam.
Left our classic motel one early dark morn,
To avoid impatient motorist airborne.

At six A.M. while Salt Lake City slept,
We were on the road; not quite awake yet.
The honking of geese flying over head,
Escaping cold winter - with dread.

Salt Lake City lights twinkle on canvass flat.
Artist colours dotted all over the mat.
Silent residents cradled in Cascade's arm.
Mormon luminous spires warn jets in alarm.

Suddenly a sign looms up, "Bremmer Jail."
At this thought I grow sand and pale.
"All is not peaceful I fear," it says.
I think - "paying for sinful ways."

"Bremmer Jail" and "Salt Lake City slept",
Conflicting images, I could have wept.
Ivan at Oldsmobile wheel steadily zums on.
Later, my troubled thoughts reflect upon.

   —*Anna Spady Miller*

Royal Seasons

Searching about- reflecting upon the lowering sun, shimmering
through the haze that is now dancing in the languid stillness.
Vibrant shadows of the ending rays, sifting through the limbs-
casting a crimson glow that made the very air seem aflame.
Summer had come about, but she was a temperamental vixen;
warm, lulling breezes, gentle afternoon patter of rain - could
comfort the soul, making one forget the bitter winters. Angry
clash of thunder, cascade of lightening baring down, bringing
with it a torrent of water. She has brought with her the fires
in the night, with uncontrollable yearnings for nature to be
reborn. Flames burning in her heart are banked by the oncoming
winter storms. The regal tempest of the high peaks had a power
that danced off her fingertips leaving the trees glistening in
a golden crown of glory. In a realm of breathtaking splendor
covering of iridescent snowflakes - cradled in the arms of
towering pines. Lustrous light of the moon sent soaring
untoward the sky- to shine in the night, reflecting all of
natures gifts in the newborn sky.

   —*Kimela S. Page*

Creature Corps

Paint your inspiration on the anatomic wall of the dead
tickle but don't disturb, the rain that drains my head
I am cleansed by what the cloud monuments once had
Paint 'til your discouraged by the anatomic wall of the dead

Fly the ground of the wall with your best hallucination
backlash but acknowledge, the rain that pains my salutation
you are cleansed by a second-long nomadic generation
fly a mound into the wall of your best hallucination

Scratch our manipulation of hallucinated dead walls
revolt but contain, the rain that claims my earthly crawl
we are cleansed by showered anvils (they are really balls)
scratch our dead hallucination.
Back to life before it falls.

   —*Al Stewart*

Day

The bright day slipped slowly into sunset
Till the fiery ball and horizon met
And it was gone
Not to be seen until the next daybreak
With the rising of the sun the people will awake

Be brave my son against this day
For before long it will slip away
Lost for time
Face it with all the strength you can
Be not a boy, but a man

And when the day has finished
Your strength has not diminished
Trudge on
Another day has yet to start
Face it with open arms and open hearts

   —*Kim Doney*

Rain

The warm summer rain we've cried for,
   This summer we have got.
We wanted soft water for garden plants,
   The farmers for their crops.
Some people wanted water for washing,
   Dugouts to be filled.
   Our banks are overflowing;
      And now we realize,
   Are we going to have a flood?
   Or will we freeze right into ice!

   —*Wilma Jury*

A Fairy Tale

Sweet, still solitude hovers over my chamber,
Tiny square and oblong, motley angels of pulp and paper
Keep guard in the mellow touch of the setting sun

But won, behold and hark!
The steppenwolf is lurking nearby
Peeping through peaceful windows of innocence,
Growling and howling his solo
With the backing vocals of the roaring wind

Then raving on,
He sweeps
The stiff grizzly-skin drums of the white desert madly,
Like a red-eyed shifting shadow
At larkless wild winter nights
　　　—Laszlo Murakozy

The Best Of Friends Must Part

Now we must say goodbye my dear.
　'Tis sad that we must part.
　　You've been good to me thro' all the years.
　　My best friend from the start.

But the time has come and you must go.
　It's hard to bear the pain.
　　It makes me sad to think that we
　　　will never meet again.

If I'd been kinder to you thro' the years,
　perhaps you'd have stayed (much) longer.
　　If I'd cared for you when we were young,
　　　You might have been much stronger.

But now the parting time has come.
　'Twill pass as did my youth.
　　Now they come to take you out my friend.
　　My one and only tooth!
　　　—Elizabeth K. Wood

Natures Gift

The autumn spills forth oh so many coats of colour, for,
'Tis true the seasons colour our lives, but why.
A present given with grace, favour and kindness,
For all to savour, cherish and treat with respect.
As each day goes by, the shades are forever changing,
So slowly is natures process, the eye cannot see.
When winter appears, a sullen mood she brings,
Frogs still croak, but birds forget to sing.
White with snow, of food there is little,
Often survival is lost, their wings frozen and brittle.
Gradually a thaw, the first chirp is heard, and so
Life returns with the song of the bird.
The trees lie in slumber, awaiting the birth of their leaves.
Healthy buds to fullness reach, burst open at last to
wondrous shades of green.
Heavy grey clouds release their nectar,
Freshness abounds, the earth sups well.
All too often orange rays of heat scorch the land,
Greens turn to brown, as autumn comes round again.
　　　—Carmel Wallace

I've Been There

I've been there
to a place called sadness
And I've had my blackest day
And I've traveled through loneliness
Collected fear along the way
I've cried tears that would fill an ocean
And I've had days full of despair
So do not think that I don't understand
Because I do………. I've been there

But I traveled further down the road
No matter what the burden, or how heavy the load
I found friendliness and laughter
people who love me, people who care,
So come take my hand, I understand
Remember ………. I've been there

My load is not so heavy, I'm smiling so much more
Now every path is leading me to another open door
It hasn't been easy to start again…. To give, to love, to
share, but I carry on with hopes and dreams
Always remembering ……… I've been there.
　　　—Wendy Ann Harrison

Meditation

Close your eyes and come with me
to a place where the soul and spirit are free.
A sunrise realm that dwells within the misty
borders of reality.

Here you need not wings to fly,
but can soar through a rainbow-hued, pastel sky.
Clouds of shimmering silver drift and collide,
as they glide forever by.

You can feel a power here,
though at first its source may not seem to be clear.
If you learn to listen, and persevere,
its origin you will hear.

It is then that you will find
that the power is created in your mind.
Thought forms energy which echoes to remind
that all life is intertwined.

When the journey you must end,
this time of tranquility you must suspend.
To life's reality you now must attend,
till you can return again.
　　　—Elaine Jauniaux

Freedom

What does it mean to be free?
To be alone, or to run and flee?
Freedom flows from the heart,
It takes over your mind and becomes a part.
Running away in the wild.
When you know at home you'd be reconciled.
To end a life.
As to kill with a knife.
Is to end the dream.
At least that's how it seems
For when someone's life is gone.
Because you did something wrong.
Freedom will make you pay.
For everything you say.
Freedom is not to get rid of.
And not to be stashed away and hid.
Freedom is in the mind
To get away and leave everyone behind.
　　　—Keisha G. Harrison

Can You Hear Me?

Can you hear me? Do you know that I am here? Do you want me
to be here? Do your even care? Have you thought about me? Do
you have plans for me? Do you think you can handle me? Will
there be time for me? I want to be with you. I want to grow
to love you, as I hope you could grow to love me. I want you to
teach me. I want to take walks with you. You can talk to me
and I will listen. I want to make you happy. Can you hear me?
I don't want to be here if you don't want me. I don't want to
be a problem. I don't want you to hate me. I don't want to
learn how to hate. I don't want you to teach me wrong or bad
things. I don't want to be unloved. I don't want to be hit
for no reason. I don't want to be emotionally abused. I don't
want to cause fights. I don't want to smoke. I don't want to
go hungry. I don't want to freeze at nights. I just want to
be happy. I want you to be happy. I want us to be together.
I want us to love each other. Please think about what I have
said. Just make sure you are ready for me. I will be waiting
for you always. So please think about me before you decide to
have me. Can you hear me? Mom...Dad...Can you hear me?

—Joseph Estrada

A Teacher's Prayer

Grant me the wisdom each new day Lord,
To better understand; each golden opportunity,
You have placed within my hands:
As I attempt to teach and train,
In an effort to prepare; each child for new tomorrows,
Reach the goals they each desire:
Tho each are similar in size and age;
From one's personality, another's can't be gauged;
For they come from many different walks of life;
Some exposed to violence, some much sorrow, abuse and strife:
Some were born into environments,
where they've known nothing but the best;
Some, well mannered, well dressed, and politely poised,
Yet others were not so blessed:
Then each one comes my way for help, and the task
becomes my own; to discover a formula to achieve results,
In these products from different homes:
So help me to be patient Lord,
With each delicate, priceless mind;
Treat each with thy love and kindness,
As tho each of them were mine:

—Julia McLeymore Mintz

The Sanctity Of Snow

Divinity descends without a sound
To dazzle all the world with splendor fair
With purity she tip-toes on the ground
Her alabaster presence fills the air
The solemn murmur of her sacred vows
Begins to fill the dark with gentle light
Then nature crisply turns its head and bows
To glorify the maker of this rite
Divinity then whirls around with glee
With silken grace she dances through the sky
And gives her warmth to all so tenderly
Til silently the angel turns to fly
And though she slips unnoticed through Night's door
She leaves her magic footprints on Earth's floor

—Kristin Norris

The Light

We come in splendour, at your request,
To ease the burden, your time of test.
Seek to see the glowing orb,
A touch of tingling to absorb.

Your hand outstretched, the coming's now,
Hold tight, hold on, as you know how.
Do not despair, hold spirits high,
Use the positive word, and you can fly.

Fly to the corners of the universe,
Dance in the colours and be totally immersed.
Sway to the music of the tinkling bell.
And know that the rhythm will increase in swell.

The swell of light, love and laughter too,
A panorama, so crisp and blue
Of flickering light, sparkling throughout that time,
A crescendo of immortal sunshine.

Sway in the colours, float in the mist,
Embrace the passion with a gentle kiss.
Love to the full, je t'adore,
The light of love is standing at your door.

—Carole Grainger

The Return (On Revisiting Chester)

Some urge compelled me to return,
To find again the heart of this old city
To learn some lesson from this ancient town,
To piece together memories, and thus once more to find
That half forgotten, yet suspected peace of mind
Which once before I felt and knew
Yet all too soon, alas, outgrew.
Was this then, could this have been perchance the goal
At which subconsciously I aimed
In this enchanting city world famed?
Some notion fine and vast that would outlast
Even the spirit of the past.
Often mid overbearing crowds, and frustrated in despair
I wondered if such peacefulness would still be there
Where once I knew myself quite whole
A living soul.

—Grace Carr

Impossible

I want to fly
To fly away - far away from all this
And feel as free as an eagle,
Just as high & mighty
I want to run
To run away - far away from all this
And feel as carefree as a soap bubble,
Just as light & easy
I want t be indifferent
Just as indifferent as the strong, quiet mountains
To whatever happens around me
I want t smile, and keep it on
Feel happy every hour of the day
For many, many days in a row
Although I know
That it's impossible.

—Lale Nisanoglu

Seafarers Thanks

Thank you Lord for the times I've sailed upon your sea,
to gaze ever skyward above your clouds and deep beneath.

In awe of your infinite wisdom, and unknown mystery,
I place my faith in thee for everything beyond my reach.

Quietly I've slipped away atop your watery wonder, through
delight in sunshine, beyond the fear of angry thunder.

Gently you've cradled me within your power of waves arms,
to peacefully be guided by your mighty winds charm.

Patiently you watch over me Lord as I travel life's course,
traveling here or there, yet nary beyond your force.

You lovingly allow me to be so near while off and afar,
throughout all my triumphs, defeat, and heartaches that scar.

Never Dear Lord shall I forget your love, whom nor that you are
for in life's darkest moments you shine ever so brightly in
each glimmering star.

With love shed abroad in heart, I thank you Dear Lord for the
time I've sailed upon your sea.

For your lasting love, your patience, and time watched over me.

   —Kelly P. Finucane

African Leaders And Their Relation To The Goldenberg Scandal.

This is Kenya where rules are politically right
to hell with accountability
Goldenberg's scandal epitomises
absolute limits of betrayal of public trust
what angers me to destruction is
the fact that this monstrous schemes
to rip off the country
was actually abetted by people who should know better -
African leaders a rare breed don't quit they die
   The Swindle has grown and changed its character
   with unbelievable ease
   is the silence of the one
   who lives and fires them
   an acceptance of them as efficient and able
   put differently is the government sending signals
   that it has confidence in these officials
   I cannot think of a more serious indictment of a system
   than its approval of graft and high-level theft
   African leaders a rare breed don't quit they die

   —Benjamin M. Munyao

The Devil In Liquid Form

To smile was just to say your name.
To look at you was to rekindle the flame.
Now I fear to think of what you have done
And what you have lost instead of won.
You let your mind overrule your heart,
And because of that you have torn apart,
the only thing that gives us joy, you've
destroyed a family by killing their boy.
You raised your arm a little too high
And welcomed the devil in liquid style.
But you'll never hear that relieving sound,
Of move back people he's coming around.
You made the decision late last night
to take the car and drive out of sight.
Now we know what you have done,
You're taken a life by "hit and run."

   —Melinda Jacobs

My Dearest Friend

To have you in my arms again
To love you, touch you, kiss you

It feels so good, your body next to mine
To have you touch me, your lips kissing mine

Oh how I miss you so...
But wherever I go your always with me
in heart and soul

Remembering our last day, I'm watching
you as you had to stroll away
I wanted to run to you, to hold you and kiss you

Just one last time before we had to part
I just couldn't bear us being apart.

I yearn to have you at my side
together to abide

Till we meet again you'll then be all mine

When it's time again dear friend for us to be apart
Please remember, I love you...

I know deep down you always knew, but
I just had to let you know how I truly
love you... All my love

   —Blair Bouchard

Chelsey

To my dear Chelsey King,
To me you mean everything!
The day you came upon this Earth,
I gave thanks at your birth.
God gave me a granddaughter to be proud of,
And very most of all, to love.
When I look at your little curls,
Then my mind just swirls,
To think God could be so good,
I have way more than I should.
I thank him every day,
For my Grand daughter put on earth to play.
Remember, Chelsey King,
You make my heart sing!

   —Joy King

Love Affair

A rosy love in summertime so true,
To rise gallant affair above day-star.
My heart now pit-a-pat upon your hue
Which glisten vigor fondly from afar.

So come amour when angels warble love,
When voices chime in rhyme, into thy night,
And heaven's word of God take wing by dove.
To bathe inamorata midst the light

In heather bells, and dawn thy day awakes
To cheer! Divine and absolute affair
So grand, we ran in hand to hither break,
Upon thy shore of fragrant angel hair.

Enfolded our frames partook in passion lust
Before the morrow, take away in gusts.

   —G. J. Stoneman

A Man I Once Knew

His appearance is epic, he was the essence of divinity.
To see, hear, touch, smell and taste him
was pure ambrosia.
One could sit and drink in his beauty
for all eternity.
And die in a peace of which only the angels know.
He was a man of tenderness
A gladiator in the age of technology.
A man well aware of his beauty,
Who never abandoned his mind to the grossness of reality.

Yet it is this beauty which had become the misery
of his own existence.
The cancer within his soul.
For he watched the world from afar with eyes of blue,
which mirrored his own personal agony.
Which was deep within himself.

—*Tania Josiphine Cassar*

Faded Friends

I need to know what troubles me and need to realise
To see what others see, through teardrops in my eyes
In Pittsfield Massachusetts I sang with Larry Bart
Folksongs lit the campfire and feelings warmed the heart
Faded Friends return to greet me
Singing softly, smiling softly
Faded Friends from years gone by
Share my thoughts before I die

I need to know what vexes me and need to understand
I need to be alone again to touch each grain of sand
In Tema, West Africa, not far from east Accra
Julie Nii-Moi was my Black Star, Childless Mother, Africa!
Faded Friends return to greet me
Drumming softly, drumming quickly,
Friends for life and friends for after
Share my joy of love and laughter.

—*Miller H. Caldwell*

How To Become An Irritation

Some folks will disagree in every incident,
    To show that they are more intelligent,
Their subject knowledge may be mighty slim;
    That matters very little to them.

    They have the floor for all to see,
    With a great display of their stupidity.
They'll argue a point at the drop of a hat.
"You're wrong!" they'll say, and that is that.

    In a friendly crowd others will think,
    "Just let it drop, don't make a stink."
We'll change the subject, and only hope
We don't get an argument out of this dope.

    Carnegie said, "avoid the right angle."
If you don't, you face one hell of a tangle.
Let's take a lesson in friendly conversation
    And speak softly in every situation.

—*Ken McAfee*

Friend

A word that means different things
    To so very many
But the kind of friend you are to me
    There truly isn't any

For you know what we've shared together
    And all that we've been through
Those hard times and long nights
    Were made easier by you

    You are always there for me
    In good times and in bad
    I just want to let you know
    You're the best friend I ever had

Words alone are not enough to express
    What I want to say
    For you truly are my friend
    In every single way

    I want to tell you from my heart
    I am one of the lucky few
    Grateful for a friend I've found
    My dearest friend... that's you

—*Judy Brophy*

My Nurse

Love is but a name to most, and shame
To some. Few take the word and do the act;
Promises made by these are not forgot,
But exercised 'til hurt, and more. They find
And suffer love by facing pain, and worse.

So you do not complain about bedpans,
Ignore the putrid pus, the screams, the smells
Of rot and urination, threat of Aids.
You get small praise, long hours, low pay. You see
The fleeting joy, endure the random curse.

You see more dying in a week than I
In my life, yet you cry for each, concerned
Only about the lack of time to care.
My greatest feat is helping finish yours.
Each day you meet these truths; I but in verse.

The only sanity, love, is expressed
By soothing, taking on another's pain.
Jesus said, treat the sick. All else is vain.
The world is touched by God through us, and he
Is strong in you, my wife, my love, my nurse.

—*Kevin F. Bowen*

The Battle Of Suchumi

Endless queues of weapons and men arrive
    to Suchumi day and night
People are unloading aircrafts with guns
    each hour
Soon they will cover up all Abchasia
I can imagine myself men with beards who
    didn't sleep for weeks

They have arrived from all parts of Russia
A man, who once was great at peace
    tells armed forces how to struggle
But where are we heading
If this battle has its prize, who will pay?

The defenders do have only the endless
    see behind their backs
Young men will loose their lives
    and mothers their sons
Will we just stay aside and watch
    for the sake of the civilized world?

—*Voitto Virta*

Gulf War

Saddam Hussein must have been insane,
To subject his country to so much pain.
He sent ill equipped soldiers to the front lines,
While he was safe below, being wined and dined.

Baghdad was bombed day and night,
Sending his soldiers scattered in utter flight.
His crack army, were not what he said they would be,
As the coalition forces came in behind by sea.

He tried to draw Israel into the fray,
By launching scud missiles by night and day.
But the Israelis persevered and wouldn't fight back,
Although they were willing and prepared to attack.

Thank-you to the other countries who helped as well,
To help keep our troops from going through a fiery hell.
With the cease fire Hussein would fall,
And we pray this is the war to end them all.

Kuwait was liberated after its fall,
And our forces can stand straight and tall.
They received a welcome home they will never forget,
And President Bush will have no regrets.

—*Masie Edith Cavell Jackson*

Blue Sky

A little Indian girl cast a side to die.
To survive would be a miracle. But the prayers of a
Grandmother would be answered.

As she grew stronger every day, they said
"She was a gift from the sky" So they name the
Little girl BLUE SKY

As she got older, she loved to go by the water
Falls she sat there for hours watching the water.
And the little birds flying in and out the trees.

BLUE SKY lived a long and happy life with
Children of her own and Grandchildren.
When she dies she will blend in with the blue sky

—*Olga Taylor*

Beyond Flight

Freed from the chains that bind me
to this world of dream, joyously
my spirit takes to wing

Far past the eagles' flight, through
layered clouds and atmospheric blue
bespeaking earth, I flee.

Swift past the sun and on into the night,
where reigns the moon, midst
twinkling light of stars.

Still on I speed, now through the darkest void
where no light shines, nor seen the
glimmering of far-flung worlds.

Then lo; a star appears, almost beyond
my visions reach, soft glowing
down my path;

And I, in exultation, now direct my flight
to where that beacon marks
my journeys end.

There, enwrapped in love and peace,
my soul is welcomed home.

—*Kathleen Rollings*

Untitled

Why do we destroy the ones we love
To understand, you must look up above
We're only human, weak and scared
But you can find the answers if only you dare
To search out the answers you must open your heart
And believe in His love right from the start
He knows of the problems
We encounter each day
And guides us through them
In the strangest of ways
And to have His assistance
We need only to Pray
He loves us all dearly
And he gave up his life
To help and assist us
Through all kinds of strife
Your eyes will open
If you just look into his face
Perhaps this is the answer
To what is called the Human Race

—*Kenneth Lee Palmer*

Nature's Melody

The voice of spring is calling me
To wander out 'mongst field and tree
And think no more on cares that be,
But list to nature's melody.

The robin with his gladsome lay
Seems to beguile the perfect day
That I in dreaming while away,
Entranced by nature's melody.

The little stream that flows along
Adds to the chorus its murmuring song,
For singers are a thousand strong
That join in nature's melody.

The lofty hills with verdure crowned;
The vale where ferns and flowers abound
And all the trees and rocks around
Re-echo nature's melody.

So I submit to nature's powers
To while away the enchanted hours
And life's as sweet as woodland flowers
When charmed by nature's melody.

—*Irma O'Neal Start*

House For Love

Back through the blackness we take the step
To when our hopes were left unchecked;
Where youth and beauty reign supreme
Still unscathed by shattered dreams;
And love's not lost to foreign lands
Or built on ever-shifting sands.

So we once built a house for love
And trapped it like a captured dove;
Had it and held it, embraced it so tight
- Until one day, the bird took flight.

Then the walls we'd built tumbled down around us
For fear and emptiness returned and found us;
And every brick we'd carefully laid
Became part of the prison we had made.

Left wand'ring lonely through the rubble
We sank into a sea of trouble;
In our boat now so alone
Doomed within our haunted home;
The maze of mind confused and muddled -
Forever trapped inside this human bubble.

—*Gina Mann*

Sleep

When the nighttime comes and the daylight is waning,
to where fate calls, could it be that I'm dreaming,
for a moment I wake then sleep holds me completely,
am I at home, I cannot say,
am I at home, it feels so far away,
as I walk the road I am in shadow,
to another place where no-one can follow,
take me to a stream to where I can cross over,
am I at home, I cannot say,
am I at home, it feels so far away,
am I looking left or right, I cannot tell for a sea of light,
though I fade I must keep believing,
that the time is now, have I lost the real feeling,
I am at home, I know the way,
I am at home, not feeling so far away.

   —*Jim Clark*

Women Of Color

Women of Color, your time is here. When we gather our minds
together, we are a force of strength, we need not fear. The
Lord is imminent, he's our protection, an invisible source of
power. It's not given to the swift nor the strong, but the
ones who endureth; like a beam of sunshine from a guiding light
tower. Yes we have a dream that has now become a reality,
existing is not enough, quantity is least important when it
comes to quality. Sure, we'll be tested to see if we are whom
we say, our consistency is needed every step of the way. We
owe it to ourselves to find our place in the sun. It's time
out for lip service, but it's not over until the victory is
won. Our fight is a constant struggle with the creature
inside; we can dress him up or dress him down; we can control
him... We share that pride. We must continue to strive for
the quality of life, with the hope, faith and charity, but
without malicy and strife. So go ahead, my sister, I dare you
to be all you can be, the sky is the limit; the door is open;
but now ... we hold the key.

   —*Johnnette Washington*

A Key To Happiness

Jealousy is a bug we all seem to possess.
Too often it curses the things we should bless.
When a man through skill, perseverance, and toil,
Has reached the goal no mortal should foil,
Then this bug within us begins to spin,
Reaching a weak spot in fellow man's skin.
We so readily forget it's not easy to win,
But if happiness counts, hit that bug on the chin.

   —*Nels Berggren*

Embrace

Close to you is where I like to be.
Touching you is the greatest feeling to me.
You send over my body a shiver
And when our lips meet, I quiver.
Like a feeling not felt before
You leave me asking for more.
Every moment I treasure
As our noses come together.
And slowly we slide
Until our faces collide.
The touch of your lips are so delicate,
Much more sweeter than chocolate.
The taste of your name on my lips
Leaves my tongue numb and it trips.
I shudder when the edges of our mouth meet,
A feeling no other could beat.

   —*Jeffrey S. Thompson*

Untitled

Fly or cry, scream and die, toleration with exhalation...
Touch me, take me, kiss me, rape me...
Watch me go make me stay.
Travel the road of inconsequential madness.
I will be your friend, I will hold your hand.
See my scars; I have come from a far.
Open my heart, warm yourself on the kindling of my soul.
Experience your birth; witness the salvation.
I am the crucible carrying the waywardness of incompetence
For all to see, for all to judge.
I will lay on your pillow and cover myself with the cool
sheets of indifference.
Find me...find me... I am not hiding; just forever lost.
My disguise is always the same my solitude in vain.
Can the ravaging cyclone be tamed? Or will these words and
deeds remain infinite and lucid only to me.
Your exclusive medicine is ready for the taking; bitter yet
satisfying.
A interesting combination to ease your aching; for me an
exhaustive trip into self-examination.

   —*Kevin S. Chase*

Fading Fears

Thoughts pacing back and forth,
   trapped in the squirrel cage of my mind.
Fears strike like a venomous snake,
   my heart screams for my own attention.
A distance remembering of a childhood pleasure
   brings the cage to a stop,
Trapped thoughts, gripping feelings
   seem to fall rapidly down a
   dark shaft in my mind.
Fears fade as I find my soul playing
   in a brightly lit garden of desires.

   —*Joseph A. Scott*

Sick

Down in my hole shadow dance in my soul,
Trapped in this hell from grace I fell,
Weak my mind racked with pain see myself old and full of shame,
Stares back he's afraid chest hurts skin is flayed,
Change the shape of my heart you and I shall never part,
Look at my hands crumble with time could they commit such
   crime.
Flame burns behind my eyes how the loveless tell lies,
See the real me and your dead please stop this voice in my head
I must do as is told get on your knees let life unfold,
Happiness is a forgotten dream watch the blood from a stream,
Fiery ball from the inside hold my hand I'll be your guide,
Take you to a place you've never been show you wonders
   from a wild dream,
This land is yours free to roam pick my teeth remove skin
   and bone,
Promised you a heaven true,
I think I love you.

   —*Warren Atkinson*

Conch Song

Once a creature of the sea,
the shell echoes the heartbeat
strummed by the waves against
the shore.

Sing out, child, what the ear
hears, the heart feels,
the sea sings once more.

   —*Kevin Edward Kennedy*

Never Forget

I thought I was someone you cared about
I was never scared
I never thought you would hurt me
You said that you would always be there
I loved the way you touched me
You were always so gentle and kind
I will always remember your kiss
Your gentle lips next to mine
I never wanted to leave your arms
You always kept me from harm
You were always different from the rest
You treated me the best
I must of been dreaming when I met you
Someone must of awaken me and now
    my life is blue
Because I am without you!

—*Jody Ann Umlor*

A Place Of Hope

A city by the middle of the sea.
I wish for a place of hope.
A place where the agony
do not exist.
Where a child can look
forward to a world with no pain.
I want my city, by the middle of the sea.
Where the future is promise
and not a dream.
I want my city,
by the middle of the sea.

—*Juan Zayas Jr*

Meltdown

When I look into your eyes,
I wonder if I'm really
there. When I try to read your
mind, I find inside cold and
bare. When I try to hold you
close, I feel you pull away.
When I want to sit and talk,
you have nothing left to say.

Like a candle
in the night, our
love, white hot and
bright, snuffed out by
an unseen wind, ashes
now, where love had been.

—*Sherri Ellen Theilheimer*

If I Were A Kite

If I were a kite,
I would soar through the sunlight
I would soar through the towns,
And even see the circus clowns.

If I fly over the sea,
I wouldn't think that is me.
Above the clouds it is not loud,
But below there are some toys
That are making noise.

There is a lake,
Where swimming lessons you can take,.
I would not fly over the sea,
Because a fish is not me.

Well it is time to say
"Hi and goodbye".
Now I have to leave this height
and save this sight for another night

—*Kalani Nichol Thorpe*

Who Am I

My name is Katanah
I'm 12 years old
I live in Navassa on
Old Mills road.

My favorite hobby
Is riding my bike
But sometimes I
like to go for a hike.

I really love to swim
In a pool but I'll
Let you know I'm
No fool.

It's time for my
Poem to come to
An end farewell
To you all I'll
Write you again.

—*Katanah Green*

Prayer From An Unborn Child

Dear gentle Jesus, help me,
I'm frightened and alone,
You've tucked me under mommy's heart,
But I'm not safe at home.

My mommy doesn't want me,
She's trying to decide,
If I will make her problems worse,
If I should live or die.

Oh patient Jesus, help her,
She really isn't bad,
Her thinking now is all mixed up,
She's angry and she's sad.

She doesn't know I love her,
Please make her understand,
I really need a chance to live,
I'll do the best I can.

Sweet Jesus, keep my mommy safe
And guide her on her way,
I'm just too little now to help, … but
Tomorrow's another day.

—*Karen M. Harvey*

Illusion

I sit at a window
in a cold sweat
The future is uncertain;
filled with events…
they have not happened yet.

No questions are answered, so
I will ask none
No answer to the truth;
Unspoken words…
like father, like son.

I question myself
my thoughts like a web
covering up the outcome;
dissolve this illusion…
this nameless dread.

Tears in the darkness
screaming without end
Never, never, never;
no relief from the horror…
of seeing my dead friend.

—*John Slater*

New Year Poem To My Brother In USA

I wish to try to write to you
in English just a word or two.
How are you dear brother now?
I hope your mood is never low!

In Norway snow is falling down
and soon are snowballs to be thrown.
On ice are children skating fast,
for winter came to them at last.

Now skiing also is a joy
to every girl and every boy.
They skip and jump and make a swing
and never do they fear a thing!

Myself? - I am correcting tests
of pupils' work, between my rests.
And when I finish with my toil
a cup of coffee I shall boil!

So let me wish for you a day
of New Year feast so bright and gay.
Let happiness for ever be
the New Year wish I send to thee!

—*Herfinn Karlsen*

Mother's Prayer

Dear Lord I thank you for this day
In every thought and every way.

You gathered all I love so dear
From far away and very near.

As we sit around this table, Lord
I ask a new request.

That all who gather here today
Will with your love be blessed.

I ask Dear Lord that all the love
I gave them as their Mother

Through all the years that will remain
They give to one another

—*Josephine Jimines*

An Abyss

I was not even -
In love with anyone!
That the raindrops
could turn into diamond,
that a reflection in the mirror
could show ruby red pouting lips
and my eyes sparkling crystal!
My face aglow with wonderment!
Instead I saw - a dreary abyss,
Pallid color, hollow darkness
a nothingness!
Not even - bitchy remarks,
or striking against
evil witchcraft!
It was the loneliest gap
of non-stimulation
of not coping
with dualities
only an enervating
nothingness!

—*Pamela Dutta*

Come Back

You had to leave me,
In my time of despair.
You had to leave us -
You knew we were there.

You needed help
And you could of had lots.
But you didn't want help,
Even though you were lost.

When we were little,
Til when we were big,
That's when you did it,
Six feet is what they'll dig.

You got out so quickly,
So painless and so easy.
But when we found you,
It wasn't so easy.

Why did you do it,
I want you to come back.
I've missed you so much,
I need you to come back.

—*Jacqui Brown*

The Reckoning Of Time

The cloak of time conceals fact
in robes of earthen lime
once stripped by Bede who then attacked
all monks who passed the time

At Jarrow in their abbey lofts
among the books to read
yet claiming stars at night were soft
flames that danced like beads

Above the town its council strong
conviction then was reached
they cursed his theories to be wrong
and moved fast to impeach

For knowledge is a sacred tool
the wise men cried up high
yet time has proven each the fool
through anno Domini

—*Kris A. Jeters*

Smile

I have learnt to smile:
In sorrow and in pain.
I have learnt to smile:
In utter poverty and in sickness.
I have learnt to smile:
In need and in lack
When clouds are red, I smile.
When twisting in the stomach, I smile.
When pierced in the heart, I smile.
In health, I smile.
In joy, I smile.
In peace, I smile.
All my heart knows is none
But to smile
For with Christ in my heart
I can smile at the storm.

—*Evans Bamwesigye Kabateraine*

The Waning

The moon hangs low
in the dawning's sky,
her light wanes slow
as do I.
Faded the beams
of night's icy shine;
gone lover's dreams,
as are mine.
Gone too the mysteries,
the joys and the tears,
the loves and the sorrows
of long lived years.
As the moon bows low
to the sun's warm glow;
so does life to death.
Dark is death's sorrow
there neath the sod,
but bright the soul's hope
that flies fast go God.

—*Phyllis C. Malone*

The Gardens Of Fate

What flowers grow
In the gardens of fate?
I have heard
That there are black roses.
What vines bear the grapes
Of that darkest of wines?
That offers an eternal drunkenness
Lulling us towards sleep.
Vintage after vintage
Distilled in air
And breathed deep.
And who tends to those gardens?
Crushing the grapes,
Drawing from them the attar
On which we stumble even now.
Who walks among the vines
At dusk, alone in thought?
And to whom do the gardens belong?

—*Anthony Doyle*

Hotel Melia Seville 23.05PM

Into the sterile white pool
In the hotel lobby
Some one, perhaps for fun
Had thrown a daisy.
It had yellow petals,
Like the posed fresh oranges
On the glass and travertine marble
Of the opposing tables.
Around the setting were casts
Of plaster. Warm plaster.
Copies of the sun fired remains
Once dotting the nearby landscape.
All around were manicured shrubs
In pots surrounded by scrubbed pebbles.
Bright native yarns spanned
Newly fashionable wrought iron chairs.
But it was the daisy in all the vast clinical
   foyer
That caught me eye, and I wanted to be
home with you.
And all the while, the daisy
Moved gently with the water jets.

—*Beverley ST Vaughan*

Night Hero

Reaching to my side,
in the middle of the night,
comes my love in shining armour,
on a blessed horse of white.

He draws his trusty sword,
to ward away the bad.
He lights his flaming torch,
and asks me why I'm sad.

I whisper to him quietly,
a thanks for being here,
for my deepest hour has withdrawn,
now that he is near.

He rests his large hand,
on my rounded shoulder,
to help bring me comfort,
and help make me bolder.

He lifts me to the saddle,
on his horse of white,
He holds the reins around me,
as we ride into the night.

—*Grace Park*

A Change Of Season

The wind has shifted
In the night and brought
A dusting of fresh snow;
Along the edges of the walk
A ruffle of rusty leaves
Is iced in place, and
A gray squirrel pauses
While blue jays creak
And hop on lifeless branches.

Now the porch rocker
Moves gently to and fro
As if the spirit of winter
Sitting there, surveys the scene
And marks the change,
Then slowly nods, affirming,
"It is time".

—*Kathryn M. Diana*

My Mother

In time of doubt
In time of despair
When in need of some encouragement
This someone is always there.

This someone has held your hand
Through many of your years
To guide and understand you
And wipe away your tears

This person can never be repaid
For all that she has done
But when there are clouds in her day
You can bring the sun.

This person is so special
And can't be replaced by another
I hope my kids think as highly of me.
As I do of "My Mother".

—*Kathleen Tracey*

Horizon

Loving Jesus, gentle lamb,
In your gracious hands I am,
Make me saviour, what you art,
Live thyself within my heart.

Gentle Jesus, meek and mild,
Look upon a little child,
In the kingdom of your grace,
Give a little child a place,

Lamb of God I look to thee,
You shall my example be,
You are gentle meek and mild,
You was once a little child,

Now I would be as you art,
Give me an obedient heart,
You are pitiful and kind,
Let me have your loving mind,

I shall then show all my praise,
And serve you all my happy days,
Then the world shall always see,
Christ the holy child in me.

—*Charles Hanscomb*

Charade

Seize, squeeze love juiceless
Infinity teases, humors
Our insatiable desire for love,
Love lives, smiles, frowns,
Dissects, rejects and dies
While time fingers love's descent
Notching the fleeting continuum of time.
Why, now, yearn for love?
Love is — when it is.
More time you plead, more time
What sense begging for more time
Or what used to be
When what used to be is now?
Capture time's infinity
Seize, squeeze love juiceless
Enjoy life's charade.

—*Millie Tanner*

My Grandmother

My grandma's memory
    is going fast,
She can't remember things
    in the past.

She thinks it's morning
    when it's noon,
She gets a fork when she
    wants a spoon.

She sits by the window
    looking at the yard,
for her family to watch
    is very hard.

Even if she can't always
    remember my name
I love her just the same.

—*Jason Wiesler*

Untitled

I wait and wait...
Is it history
    repeating itself?
Waiting...
for those
who won't keep
their promises.
The heart of a child
torn between
reality and fantasy.
Trying to build
a wall to protect
from the hurt.
    And...
In the mind
of an adult
the insecurity is
forever planted.

—*Shawna Vandenbrink*

Where Did Daddy Go?

Now that daddy's gone,
is it okay to cry?

Would it be okay to say,
I love him and good-by?

Now that daddy's gone,
where did he go?

Tell me mommy please,
I must know?

Has he gone to heaven,
with the angels up above

Or is he flying in the sky
like the great white dove?

—*Melissa Maracle*

Masquerade

The flow of words
is just there
coming from within

What a liberation
a magic moment
a privilege
of human intricacies
of the mind
the tool, adequate communion
of beings

A code between livings
Aware, wishing to share
and understand beyond
falcities, gimmicks
and false mimics

The truth
comes
underneath
the human masquerade

—*Francine LaBerge*

The Wind

The stillness of the air
Is thrashed by a blow
Does it come from above
Does it come from below

The grass bends to the earth
The trees sway to the sky
Do I look upwards or down
As the air rushes by

The force of its strength
The silence of its sound
Like the blades of a windmill
Turning round and round

As fast as it came
It's gone once again
The mysterious force
We call it the wind

—*Kimberly Crosby*

Little Girl

The little girl who I long to be,
is trapped up and shut inside of me,
One day I hope to find a cure, for all
the pain and anger that I endure.
So that no one will ever hurt me
again. They would only want to be my
friend. I have grown up too fast,
with horrible memories that will last,
my heart aches for someone kind, or
for someone who will give me piece of
mind. Without love is the way I've
grown, hate is the only emotion I've
known. There's somebody out there
who wants to help me, and love me
with tenderness to set my heart free
The lord is my friend, and I will wait
for him to help me, until, the end.

—*Kimberlee Germain*

Pretender

My space within the mirror
is usurped
by a sober woman
with a time-worn face,
rimples about the eyes,
a wasted neck,
dilapidated body
with such sagging folds
as I
could never own.

When did she come?
She was not there
when I looked yesterday.

You, with your ravaged self
and staid propriety,
you are not me.
I'm unassailable.

—*Ann Stiles*

Heaven's Soul

The gift of love,
Is what we hold
It is worth much more
Than a treasure of gold
Hold it high
And let it soar
Don't hide it away
For it conquers war
It brings two together
To make them one
And shines so bright
That it shades the sun
Love holds a friendship
In its place
And paints a smile
On the world's face
It was handed down
From up above
It is heavens soul
This gift of love.

—*Carla Michelle Black*

The Feeling

There is a feeling in this world,
It comes on quiet nights,
It creeps in through the windows,
And gives you cold insights.
It silently surrounds you,
And wraps its tangling charms,
Around your heart and feelings,
Around your empty arms.
It feels like it will drown you,
You sink as days go on,
And one day you will wake up
To find all love is gone.
To find that no one knows you,
That no one really cares,
And when you find this feeling,
You'll name it loneliness.

—*Viveka Melki*

Receipt For Happiness

Take a little bit of sunshine, stir
it in a bowl
Throw it over your shoulder, to
a lonely soul
Take a bit moonlight, throw it
in the air
It will land on someone, who is in
despair
Take a bit of stardust, throw it on
the ground
It will be a blessing to all those
around
Mix them all together and add a
little smile
It will touch many hearts and linger
there a while.

—*Juanita Burgo*

The Echo

The echo calling.
Its words carried
on the wind to be heard
Soft as a whisper it
draws closer to say hello,
then says goodbye.

—*Joseph M. Gibson*

Riffa Woods

Through Riffa Woods, I walked today,
It is the seventeenth of May,
The bluebell carpet, that I found,
Covered, almost every inch of ground,
The blue tits, twittered in the pine,
I've never seen a sight so fine,
As Riffa Woods, today!

The sunlight filtered through the trees,
The blackbirds sang sweet melodies,
And bracken fronds, uncurled to leaf,
With blues and greens, beyond belief,
I also flushed a pheasant cock,
He sprang from near the carved rock
In Riffa Woods, today!

—*Brian Haigh*

The Carrousel

The carrousel in silence sleeps
It sleeps, perhaps no more to wake
Beneath the snow that downward sweeps.

Fond memories, the dark night keeps
Tomorrow's day - a heart will break.
The carrousel in silence sleeps.

The wind sighs low among the reeds
That gather on the banks of Central Lake
Beneath the snow that downward sweeps.

The pre-dawn fire that slowly creeps,
Beneath the dark has flames awake.
The carrousel in silence sleeps.

The brightly colored pedigrees
Are silent by their tinseled stake,
Beneath the snow that downward sweeps.

Between the trees - a soft wind weeps
Along the way all dreamers take.
The carrousel in silence sleeps,
Beneath the snow that downward sweeps.

—*Ronald Moore*

No Identity

Threadbare, ragged and torn,
it walks the streets
both day and night,
shunned at day
ignored most time.
Darkness falls and
it walks under the streets
looking for a dry place
it searches through
the alleys and bins
for anything to quench
the sounds of hunger
echoing from its stomach.
Searching next for marches
something to light the fire.
Anything to get through
yet just one more night
and then tomorrow............

—*Janice Martin*

Untitled

Life is a flower.
It's all together at one point
But sooner or later it all seems
to fall apart.

—*Josephine Celetti*

Kathy

If my commitment was a river,
It would never stop flowing.

  If my passion was a rose,
    It would never die.

  If my heart had a voice,
    It would only call your name.

If my love for you was the day,
  There would never be night.

If true love had another name,
  It would be called "us."

—*Dale Harvey*

Our House

This house is old.
Its beams are held
In place by nail and screw.
And what has lived inside for years
Is nothing strange or new.
The oil lamps have long since
Gone, and with them old ideas,
But the love and warmth
That each family felt, have
Prevailed throughout the years.
Inside we find a fireplace,
That warms our winter hands,
A vase of flowers in the
Spring, and satisfaction
For each demand. So as
The years roll quickly by.
And fashions become strange,
The love and warmth
Within our house will
Never ever change.

—*Lila Zuck*

My Little Pig

I have a little pig of mine
It's fat and strong and good to me
Oh how fat it is my little pig.

—*Ganzi Muhanguzi*

What Is Love

What is love
It's like a dove
Just flying free
Pure and clean
Not full of lust
Which is unjust
It's something shared
That's not impaired

It's pull of gladness
And sometimes sadness
Love is sheik
Which ain't cheap
It fills me with joy
And makes me feel like little boy
So I know what love is

—*J. M. Hauptmann*

Until Then

Don't stray too far, my friend
it's not the end
the road is long but I shall return

And when we meet again
just like before
but I shall love you more
and time shall be the shores
on which we'll stroll

Until then, this song's a memory of you
of the things we used to do
the way we used to care
about the moments that we'd share

Until then, this song's memory for you
of the things we used to do
the way we used to care
and the moments that we's share

And when we meet again, just like before
but I shall love you more
and time shall be the shores
on which we'll stroll

—*Jamie Crocket*

To Those I Took Time To Care For..

My days on earth have come and gone,
I've made no impact on anyone.
I've tried so hard to be a friend
Now it must all come to an end.

For those of you, who now shed tears,
Please don't, my dear.
For I was the one to cry
And asked myself why...

Where were you when I
Was the one who'd just cry.
When the pain was too great
You'd just stand there and wait.

Couldn't bear to be lonely...
But I was the only
One there for the other.
And you never did bother.

So go on with your lives
But please remember,
Loneliness, no lies,
I wish to remember.

—*Estelle Montpellier*

Getting Old

Three score and ten I am today.
I've witnessed much along the way.
Happiness and sorrow too
Have filled my cup with a mixed brew.

Happiness I figure sagely
Is a by-product of giving hugely
Of one's self to those in need
Of spiritual help and physical feed.

I think word of faith and not despair
Can better help a weak wayfarer.
That love is better far than hate
To inspire peace within one's gate.

To all those who are still climbing
From youth to age three score and ten
May you reach it still a climbing
Never faltering, always hopeful,
Peace will be yours n the end.

—*Leone Jorde*

Accident Of Birth

Male Caucasian
Just like a woman I...
Let start again

I'm no longer
The dominant gender I...
Let me start again

I did not plan my
Birth, or my legacy...
Let me start again
Maybe I look like
The people who wronged you, but...
Let me start again

I know I'm male and I'm white
But I'm equal to...
Let me start again

Can you forgive me
The sins of my ancestors?
Let me start again.

—*Peter Knox*

Untitled

I was never much of saying
Just what I thought inside,
To have you for my daughter
Makes me shine with pride.

But as you fight your way
Down the lonely path of ill,
I wish you weren't leaving
But there is no magic pill.

There is no wonder cure
For what you have inside,
But you loved life and us
And held yourself with pride.

And now the time is coming
For you to leave this place,
Remember when you leaves us
My love goes with you Stac.

As the years roll by
Some memories will be sad,
But no one loves you as I do
To you from me your Dad.

—*Klemchuk*

Perceptions Of One

a snowball makes its presence
  known to all in its path
  who can not clear the way;

but a single snowflake
drifts silently in the wind
a flickering beauty to behold.

  a snowflake to some
  seems only to fall
  and melt in their hand;

to me it is the beginning
  of an avalanche
  that shakes the earth.

—*Todd Hickey*

The Darkness Of Light

Up down
left right
there is
nothing in
sight.

There is
no darkness
therefore
there is
no light.

There is
nothing in
sight there
never was
and there
never will be.

And that is
what I call
the darkness
of light.

—*Kass Fass*

The Evolution Of Earth

So it begins,
life from lifelessness,
the dawn of evolution.

No more cosmic disarray,
but molecules, air
and gigantic oceans.

Molecules join,
Weaving life as we know it,
to spread upon the land.

There, on the land,
mighty beasts roam, now as extinct
as the shape of their continent.

Brought into life is another beast,
Deadly and skilled in all ways,
They rise to the top and destroy all,
noticing it far too late.

So it ends,
Dreadfully the beasts look on,
diminishing with their ignorant ways,
extinction is emanate...

—*Robert Duhaime*

Life Is What You Lose

No one wins in war
Life is what you lose
Born in strife
Scarred for life
Boys to men
Girls to mothers
Everyone loses in the end
No one wins in war
Life is what you lose
Mothers cry when the children die
World peace is a shallow sigh
The hatred grows
No one wins in war
Life is what you lose

—*Jim Ciarrachi*

To "Rose"

Your life was so short,
like a rose;
picked when just a rosebud,
you were so beautiful,
and never meant to blossom.

—*Janet Moss*

Contemporary Koori Woman

I've been called many things,
  Like Abbo, boong and coon.
And more and more I get angry
And I'm gonna fight back soon!

Cos I'm a contemporary Koori woman
I'm Black'n' proud'n strong!
  I'm becoming more empowered,
  More deadly as time goes on!

  Yes, my nose may be broad,
  And my skin may be brown.
But those who can't deal with this
  Ain't gonna keep me down!

  I want to live in peace
Not ruled by blind perceptions.
  I need to be acknowledged
For my goals and my directions.

  So when I'm lost and confused
And concerned 'bout big decisions
I turn my thoughts and energies
  To my Koori woman visions.

—*Anita Heiss*

Shadow

It precedes me
Like an ominous shadow
I try to look away,
but it surrounds me
My past and future are clouded by it.
What to do?
Just one speck of hope.
Can I reach it?
My hands stretch out
To touch the faith
of those who,
like me
are covered by the same shadow.

—*Michelle Slaney*

People Things

People do all sorts of things,
Like catch the phone when it rings

Or mow up and down the lawn,
Or name their babies' things like John,
Or talk to their friends,
Or drive their cars around bends,

People do so many things,
Like get dinner when the timer dings!
It's hard to say when the list'll stop,
It got so high it's past the top!

—*Arwen Fleming*

She Stood Alone

The rain fell
Like diamonds to the ground
The waves roared, loud as the thunder
The lightning crashed
As the salt ocean among the rocks
Yet she stood alone

The wind whistled
Through the trees
The snow fell
Misting the landscape
The evergreens drooped
With its weight
Yet she stood alone

Across scorching deserts, raging rivers
Thundering oceans, snowcapped peaks
Through all of nature's extremities
She stood alone
With only her thoughts
And for her
That was enough.

—*Jessica Anne Christina Head*

The Poet's Child

Words twist
Like magic sticks
As from her pen they flow

Dark and tumbling
Through the maze
That no one else can know

Shadows dance
And touch her soul
With these the words are fed

A poet's child
With hope is born
To live when being read

—*Kathryn Almey*

Believe, Little Girl

This land is empty,
little girl.
One survivor, reaching
for the sky.
Tears of sadness.
The sun finally
appearing-
for the first time.
Reaching for the sun,
little girl.
The grains in the sand
uproar in the wind.
Reaching for a moonbeam,
little girl.
Victory.
Never let go of your dreams,
little girl.

—*Shanna Blanchard*

Here I Sit

Here I sit alone and reading,
Living in an unreal world.
Watching people living their lives,
Me a witness in my home

Unfamiliar to real life,
Wanting to be real myself.
Knowing what I've got to do,
To be whole once more.

Sitting as I do and thinking,
What's the next thing to be done?
Shall I go and find myself now?
Or wait for the tomorrow that never comes?

—*Sarah Lucy Dunkley*

The Rocking Horse

Sitting rocking from side to side.
Lonely, waiting for a ride.
Remembering times when I shone
Times that are now long gone.

Up in the attic among the dust,
Parts of me begun to rust.
Then out I was taken into the light
Out in the sun, so warm and bright.

The boy who rode me once was small
Now he's a man so tall.
He handles me with loving care
He too has memories we share.

Now with glossy paint that's new
Tail, saddle and reigns are too.
My heart now fills with pride
As I take my prince to save his bride.

We ride off into fantasy
My brave white knight and me.
We ride under blue skies without a care
Me and my lady fair

—*Janet Russell*

Lakeside Ranch

At the ranch by the lakeside,
  Long ago I was born,
and in the willows I would hide,
  That grew along the shore,
I shall ne'er forget if I tried
  The water birds around,
With the melody in sounds of pride,
  In nests on a nearby mound.

Oft when I've sat on the lake shore,
  Listening to the chatter,
Of swimming birds I'd ever adore,
  Their antic leaps in the water.
The pines stand guard by the lake,
  And cast a shadow long
Deep into the waters wake,
  Where the feathered friends belong.
I fondly recall the horses there,
  Rustling through the forest,
Filling the days with fun to share.
  At the ranch away out West.

—*Evelyn Isaacson*

Unmask The Truth

Turn around
Look me in the eye
See the storm approach
That is my storm
(Unmask)
Show me your true feelings
Or I'll forever be caught
In the hurricane
Of doubt
—*Ryan J. Michael Sullivan*

That Last Leaf

A leaf sits alone in a tree,
Losing its color of glee.
Day by day it loses life,
Pain is drawn, sharp like a knife.
It begins to suffer the day it is born,
Just like anything else that mourns.
It's that time of year,
When the greatest feeling is fear.
It can feel its own grip loosening,
Knowing there is no wing
That will keep it protected and warm,
Away from alls harm.
  It begins to fall
But there's no one there at all,
To break the fall softly,
To take it to safety.
It just falls to the ground and dies,
Doesn't even say its good-bye.
  It's not what it used to be between you and me,
  More like that last leaf on a tree.
—*Bonnie Lepp*

Untitled

Loved ones near.
Loved ones dear.
The laughter of days gone by is
echoing in my mind
Like the seasons we have changed.
Blossomed and bloomed from the
storms and the falls.
Like shattered glass the bond
  is broken.
Each piece in its corner
longing to reunite.
As I long to bring the pieces
of our lives
like the happy days of
  yester-year.
—*Shama Shad*

Talvez

Talvez
means maybe yes
maybe no in
Spanish.

It is yin
and yang

It is noncommittal
and I will do it
if
I feel like it.
—*Judith Rich*

Imagination

Strike it hard!
Make it bend;
Forge what is yours and take it!

Grasp the substance
That is life;
Hold it tight,
A grip of unfaltering strength;
And courage;
Yours the true heart.

The spirit's truth lives eternal
Though shoved and battered,
Pushed from view: a tantrumous child.

To stop is to fall,
To fall - die!
Pulled to opaque disaster;
Crucifixion of the soul;
Suicide in pure form.
—*Andrew Mueller*

This Old House I Live In

My old house is filled with
memories, and each day
As I look around-
My hart is singing with
Joy and happiness and
I feel like a circus clown!

I wrap my arms around
me, and raise my head
to God in prayer,
He's made my life so happy,
and oh yes I know He does care!
"This Old House I live in"
—*Josephine M. Hayes*

Into The Night

Throughout the night
mixed with the sound of
dry leaves and twigs of
being crushed under
his feet
there is a sound into the night
a sound of a sighing soul of
being there left alone
from deep inside silent
sighs is giving to the night
bitter tears sliding
down his face
tears no one will ever see
an atrocious pain invades
his whole being
into the night
a name is whispered
and the friendly night
welcomes the sound of
his broken heart
—*Mario Medeiros*

Forever

Yesterday! you were
my future,
Today, you are
my past,
Tomorrow, a memory
forever to last!
—*Karen Koksal*

Mother Doesn't Want A Dog

Mother doesn't want a dog,
Mother says they smell,
And never sit when you say sit
Or even when you yell.
And when you come home late at night,
And there is ice and snow,
You have to go back out again
Cause the dumb dog "has to go".

Mother doesn't want a dog,
Mother says they shed,
And always let the strangers in
And bark at friends instead,
And do disgraceful things on rugs,
And track mud on the floor,
And flop upon your bed at night
And snore their doggy snore.

Mother doesn't want a dog,
She's making a mistake
Because, more than a dog, I think
She will not want this snake!!!!
—*Eileen Foster*

Silence

Undisturbed is the silence
Motionless in the air
Just the beating of my heart
And knowing you're not there

Calm is the silence
Like mist on the sea
Clinging to everything
And smothering me

Dead is the silence
Lifeless and dull
Creeping into empty rooms
Only there to mull

Empty is the silence
With no meaning at all
Having no place
And no port of call

But the silence is broken
And whispers are few
The voices of people
Both of me and of you
—*Margaret Ann Hunter*

River Bend

Slowly, silently.
Moves the water.
From bank to bank.
Coming to river's bend.

In fall, its low banks are gray.
Leaves of all colour, flow as boats,
Coming to river's bend.

In winter, moves much slower.
Beneath crystal clear ice.
Still searching for.
Coming to river's bend.

In spring, melting slow.
Ice getting thin.
Waters risen and thundering.
Moving, rivers bottom bed.
Coming to river's bend.

Summers back, colour too.
No dark shadows, banks are high.
Moving swifter now.
Coming to river's bend.
—*Carl Wikander*

Buoyancy

A warm spot in the water
moving over to contact
amplifies the impact
on tiny pleasure points laved in love

You are a river
I can float on your dreams
All life's fluid streams
eventually to one sea

Being touches me
All your heart has me
I am all heart
All flesh and fluid
However and always the mind lives
on borrowing and lending

A sunspot on the ceiling
Rolling over the pillows
Sheet full-sail
fairly billows.

—*Kerri L. Birks ('85 V: The First Two Weeks)*

My Rendezvous With God

There is a rendezvous that I
Must keep tonight by midnight sky
For if I fail this promise sworn
I shall not see tomorrow morn.

There, shall be my destiny
Down by the calm and silent sea
There, is where I hope to find
A sweet and pleasant peace of mind.

A peaceful solitude is there
I can escape all worldly care
All my fears I thrust away
Though they return at break of day.

This is the rendezvous I keep
There, by the lonely silent deep
In the refuge which God made
Where all my sins and sorrows fade.

When my stay on earth is done
And I see my setting sun
Just before my life is through
I shall keep my rendezvous.

—*Kelly E. Miller*

Untitled

Forlorn I stand for all to see,
My bark stripped bare in the
November air.

Autumn came in a whistling breeze,
and took from me, my silken leaves.

Under its spell they spilled and fell.
My red, my gold, my silken leaves.

My trunk it grieves, my sap it weeps,
my branches howl for lost silken leaves.

From my bough so bared, so barren,
swaying in the wind,
a songbird sweetly sings, are you
so bowed you can not see the
seasons change, to sully your leaves.

And nourish the earth beneath your feet,
So you can stand a strong oak tree.

—*Christine Doyle*

The Soldier Ant

The Soldier Ant came marchin', across
My bed the other night, and he
Had on all his battle gear, and
He was lookin' for a fight!

I swear I could hear the drum roll
As he marched straight up my leg
I must stand my ground and fight him
For I am not about to beg!

A sudden swat and he went sailing
Dead before he hit the floor, so
I flushed him down the toilet, and
Now he is no more!

I dreamed that night, I heard music
Just my imagination perhaps, but
The music got louder and louder
It was some Ant playin' taps!

—*Wayne D. Fry*

Growing Daisy

Like a growing daisy in a field
My heart's unprotected; it has no shield
At any moment of any day
Someone can easily take it away

Take it away and tear it apart
He doesn't care it's only My heart
To him a heart can easily be mended
To me, my world seems to have ended.

Left all alone and insecure
Will I ever love again? I'm unsure.
Like a growing daisy in a field
My heart's unprotected; it has no shield.

—*Lee-Ann Gagne*

Untitled

Think of it this way,
My love, my truth,
Life only happens to lucky souls.
Free me and start me over.
I want to rise up and fall.
So only for a little bit
We'll remember this moment
Lost in the stars,
Searching for worms,
Smelling car exhaust.
I'll be with you always
Forever, except for now.
If you ever go away,
Look me up when you get there,
And write me a short letter.
Just be sure that if you ever forget me,
Sing a song.

—*Julia Starszak*

Thpeech Impairmenth

I come home from thcool,
My Mom asths me if my day wath good.
I thay yeth, but I lie.
The kidth in thcool teath me.
They thay I talk with a lithp.
They thay I can't thay my ethith.
But I can.
Eth eth eth eth eth. Thee?
That thould thow them!

—*Marlo Friesen*

Shooting Star

The river running, clear and blue
my mind racing with thoughts of you,
The sun shinning ever so bright
wishing I could hold you every night.

As the sun fades
Darkness invades,
The moon arises
full and white,
The stars shimmer across
the river bold and bright.

As I look up into the sky
I see a shot of light passing by,
Now, I know my wish has come true
and that's to spend forever with you.

—*Kelly J. Scanlon*

Nothing Can...

No sun can scorch
My tender spirit.
It's long been calloused
By neglect of its pleas.

No river can chill
The passion in my soul.
It's long been frozen
By reality's ruthless blows.

No wind can put out
The fire in my being.
It's long been extinguished
By the blood of my heart.

No scholar can teach me
The art of forgiveness.
I've been taught to remember
And I've learned my lessons well.

No one will ever win
The battles within me
For there are never victors
In an undeclared war.

—*Karis Chi*

Earth Star!

Informants of
Nether world
Demonic baton twirled
In Arc sand
Very pipes worth
In Kerioth! and
Duty acceptable
Under duresse,
All too soon; a

Loony tune, guess
Why the
Swirling, curling breeze
Through the trees
Arced it way to you

Ranus regions so far?
See Alpha Centauri! Earth Star!

—*Dorothy June Hamilton*

Days Gone By

Games to play, songs to sing,
Never knowing, what life may bring.
May we always be, this care-free,
Days gone by, to fast to see.

Hope, laughter, happiness too,
Everyday is bright and new.
Wondering where, life's path will lead,
Days gone by, to fast to see.

Some tears are shed, along the way,
Making us stronger to face each day.
Lasting love, that was meant to be,
Days gone by, to fast to see.

Windows of life, are open wide,
Doors are shut, as we step inside.
Childhood dreams, are lost to me,
Days gone by, to fast to see.

Always looking, where we have been,
trying to bring, yesterday, back again.
The future is here, so let it be,
Days gone by, to fast to see.

—*Karen Johnson*

Untitled

When a child is born
No matter when the month
It's like a day in spring
A new being bringing warmth.

And when you hold your child
No matter what it be.
Your heart just sings out joy
At the wonder you can see

And when your baby cries
No matter what it is
you want to hold them close
And protect then form all ills

But when your baby dies
No reasons you are told
Your soul is ripped apart
Your left empty lost and cold.

And with your child now gone
You live from day to day
The years help heal the pain.
Of the child you lost that way.

—*Patricia Harrison*

Boundless

I want to be boundless.
No strings or ribbons to hold me.

To walk alone, yet never be alone.

To sit at the edge of a long, long river
Watching the water and know the Giver.

Birds are boundless. Rain is boundless.
I want to be boundless.

Like chimes being blown by the wind.
I don't want to break, but can I bend?

What do I give up in search of me?
Of, if I could only look forward and see.

If I break free and soar to the sky,
Will I know then, will I know why?

Will I find me?

—*Kay L. Forbes*

Love's Famous Path Goes On...

Deep in the woods,
Not far from a town,
Lies loves famous path
All graveled and brown,
Many have walked it,
Many have come.
Some couples love it,
Some turn and run.
Alison and Mike now take this
    long walk.
Into destiny unknown.
If that path could talk,
It would tell of the people
Who've stumbled and fell
But also of the married who've
    turned out so well.
May their love last forever,
And their happiness grow,
So the path in the Spring
    will blossom and grow.

—*Denise A. Berry*

Food For Thought

Feed me.
Not with food
But with your dreams.
Feed me your hopes,
Let me dine on your desires.
Serve me an entree
    to nourish me
Place in me a dessert
    to carry me through.
Let me indulge in your fantasies.
I crave as much
    as you can give me,
    as long as it's full
    of your passion.
Let my lips taste your wishes,
Let me swallow your pride.
Share with me your longing
And may we be content
Until it's time to eat again.

—*Tracy Vetzal*

Neglected

The poor child's hair, once so fair.
Now dull, lifeless and bleak.

Her once blue eyes,
with gleaming shines.
Now tired from lack of sleep.

Her dirty skin,
and body thin.
Used to be plump and rosy.

Since Mother left,
for peace and rest.
Nothing again to be cosy.

The cracks through boards,
on windows and doors.
Show a slight glimpse of sun.

But the hurt will stay,
forever and a day.
The neglect battle never to be won.

—*Katie Cooper*

The Love Of Christ

May the love of Christ
O'erwhelm you,
Your thoughts be of him, and of
heaven above.
With new life and with beauty he
has crowned you,
By dying and by rising
out of love.

His message take to
all the world:
That Christ has died and risen
to save each one;
Their faults and sins he does not
hold against them:
The Father loves them, and
Would have them come; and
Be reconciled to him
and to each other
And live their lives in unity and love.

—*Isabel Bray*

The Picnic

The peaceful sound
    Of brushing leaves
Filled the noontime air
    As we found shelter
From the hot summer sun

In the comforting shade
    We bathed in the joy
Of gentle touches -
    And the magic
Of whispered love words

Carefree and content
    On our picnic blanket
We shut out the world
    Laughing and teasing
Like children at play

-This day-
    As walls crumbled
And fears were overcome
    -I surrendered-
To the power of your love

—*Matthew McNeill*

Flamboyant Finale

Autumn is a necklace
    Of goldenrod and dew,
Of flame-tones of sassafras
    And skies of brilliant blue.

Of swinging purple asters
    In fields of sunflower gold —
With days of lazy leaf-smoke
    And nights of bracing cold.

So wear the necklace flashing
    Its sparks of ice and fire —
And swirl a smoky velvet skirt
    Through autumn's funeral pyre.

—*Kathryn Evans McKay*

155

Blind Inquisition

Who barters for this cruel exchange
of light for dark
and dark for light?
Who guides fate's hands
to steal the dawn
forever leaving night?

Who gives permission
to condemn me
a prisoner to four senses?
Who bears eyewitness
to my crimes and
confines me to these fences?

—*Julie M. Beckmann*

Chemistry And Physics

Long looks
of observation,
our bodies deep
in conversation.
A sideways glance,
is there a chance?
Hidden faces in
different places.
Biting nails,
bodies frail
and weak
for each other.
Hands through hair,
this game isn't fair.
What do we mean
to one another?

—*Dawn Saville*

Life After Living

With each passing
Of one known to us
The veil
Between the living
and the dead
Grows thinner
Love removes
another thread
And what was shadow-thin
But never true begins
To fail its task
As we glimpse
the outline
of our victory
through the mask.

—*Kenya Lee Province*

Days

Day by day, I sit and think
of ways to fulfill your every need;
Day by day, I smile at the thought
of sharing our lives with no distraught;
Day by day, I long for your face
your warm embrace
the love you give that fills my heart;

I know not what the future holds
though we shall be strong and bold;
For the day by days you won't be near
the miles away I will have to fear;
I shall look back on these words
and hold you near and dear to my heart

Desperately hoping for all to come true;
For there only be one love for me
'Tis you

—*Konstantina Ioannou*

Sharing

I've never had the best of things
often not enough to share.
Some people seem so rich.
It just really isn't fair.

I'd love to share if I were rich.
I'd try to help everyone.
The poor, the sick, and the tired
to have a little fun.

But wait a second—I am rich
I have something money cannot buy
I have my precious Savior
And a promised home on high.

He is with me every second
And his love is always there.
My Savior is the greatest
And my faith I want to share.

So won't you please accept my Jesus
Let me share his love with you.
He is waiting with hand held out
Won't you share my Jesus too.

—*June Cooksey*

Awareness

The warmth of the sunrise
on a brisk summer morn
the orange in the sky
as a new day is born...

The scent of the rainfall
just as it starts
the sight of the rainbow
as the rain departs...

The sound of a stream
as it flows to its end
the graceful motion
as it rounds the bend...

The sight of an eagle
soaring high overhead
no greater expression
of freedom is said...

These peaceful things
make up the days
that make living so special
in so many ways.

—*Karen Herring*

Street Kids

In old hinterland of Arraias town,
On a green Contagem Brook's shore,
Our Lady of Remedies in her lore
Made a speech at the peep of dawn
Asking us for help to see
That the whole world will be
Sweet home and flowery garden
For all the homeless children.
What's coming? big train
With so many little guys;
They slept under the rain,
Their roof was just the sky.
They are dreaming street kids,
They're wandering street kids.

—*Rosalvo Leomeu*

On The Verge

At times I feel like a volcano
On the verge of eruption.
My blood like lava
Bubbling inside.

At times I feel like a river,
Fast and furious.
Giving to others
Life and energy.

At times I feel like an earthquake,
Strong and powerful.
Energy fighting back
Self destruction.

At times I feel like the ocean,
Always in motion.
High tides and low tides.
Manic - depressive

—*Tina Ray-Wilks*

One In Two

One soul living in two bodies
Once appearing in short stories
Acted at two different places
To amaze all human races
Love and pain and joy and fearing
All were shared and common feeling
Body one knew what to do
From advice of body two
The one in two could as spy
Rule a piece of world or dye

—*Hubert Hug*

Field Of Flowers

I was walking
one day
through a field of flowers
when I heard a voice
Speak to me.
I looked all around
was no one could I find
in that field of flowers with me
I cast my eyes to the sky
and I know it was God
it was God who spoke to me
He was with me there
in this field of flowers
He was there watching over me
Oh come lets walk
Through the field of flowers
That God planted there for you and me
your nearer to God's heart in a field of
    flower
Would you walk
Through the flowers with me

—*Emma E. Boies*

Autumns

Icy winds, silv'ry sun,
red, brown, golden, dry the leaves,
the forest seems on fire.

Summer's work all is done,
shivering the rodent grieves,
she fears the prospect dire.

Lifelong joys on the run,
colours, warmth me fate bereaves,
old beauty turns to mire.

—*Kurt Gjevnoe*

From My Window - Fall

From the window
One sees the leaves in change,
The greens become the yellows
And the reds.
As each fine leaf prepares itself
For oblivion and death,
Its change delights,
For a fleeting moment,
The appreciative eye of man.
And then it falls, leaving its tree
To the iron grip of winter,
But in the mind of each observer
There is a memory of beauty
Unsurpassed.
Ah! But could we all leave
A legacy like that!

—*Michael McKechnie*

Tangled Web

Love and hate
One web
Closely intertwined

Precious children
Often so loving
Sometimes
Frustrating
Infuriating
Mind-threatening

Abuse can sometimes seem justified
Not neglect nor sexual
But emotional and physical
Children
So powerful
Can drive parents to that

Control is a factor
Theirs, and especially yours

But when the mind
Snaps!

The web disintegrates

—*Virgil Goncalves*

Memory Of Fire

Puppy love they think, is-
only a flick of beckon, it-
does not light up a desire
oh' how delirious they are!

Beacon-love' fifteen's or seventeen's
is more than a thin line of quasar
when mind has reached impulses in-
intercommunication, sparkle with thee'
for pen of fire is more than covenant

Come' embrace to cover my naked body
let us be the physical mean of blood
for need of touch I bleed to dead here'
there' in this mythical E beloved havoc
pity on us' threatening distant light

The time has past yet needs have not
the wars of explosions have polyglot
lets run into an international bind
for we met time and time again there'
here' freely' into laser beam stretch

—*Edith Stein Zelig*

Hope

Hope is as big as a mountain peak,
or as small as thee eye.
it's no more than the sadness
or the happiness of a cry.

Hope has the shadows of darkness,
or the rays of the sun;
which brings a radiant glory
to that which is done.

In Hope, that which isn't done
saddens in a way,
although it is still a pretty song
of a lively bluejay.

In Hope's every unknown year,
there are plenty of lies
but for one long day,
this brilliant hope will rise.

—*Amara Masson*

Warrior's Hope

Warriors don't come home again
or don't come home the same.
Strangers in their Homeland;
their demons deep, concealed.
Buried hidden places
Woman may never ever reach.

No matter how she tries,
No matter what she gives,
No matter that she loves,
Every ounce of strength
might not be enough
to reclaim the war lost soul,
to heal a broken man.

But try she will.
For try she must.
His soul is worth her tears;
Tomorrow worth her pain.
A Warrior's Woman surrenders not.
Her courage is called Hope.

—*Judy Carol Collier*

Hu(e)man

Shroud in blackness -
orifices of light
permeate a spirit
obfuscated
by an eternity
of systematic oppression
and neglect.

Enlightened -
the imprisoned soul
focuses inward
with new resolve
to purge from the abyss
of memory
the demons of denial,
deceit and subjugation.

While adversely masked in fear,
ignorance gives credence to hatred -
and hue is the criterion employed
to castigate a man.

—*Maurice E. Robinson*

Dear Friend

'Mummy's with the angels'
Our peggy held the door,
It shocked my little sister,
Dark blood began to pour.
I could hear the others crying
As I listened by the stair,
When no tears came to comfort me
They thought I didn't care.
But oh my grief, my sorrow
Too deep to comprehend,
My childhood dreams were shattered
I'd lost my dearest friend.
We've all had lonely years since then
Life dealt us all hard blows,
We tried to pull each other through
God in his wisdom knows.
And although I have a good man
And our children look to me,
There's still a place in my deepest heart,
A dear friend holds that key.

—*Joan A. Whittle*

Homeless

Oh abandoned one,
outside of heaven
looking in.

Face pressed
against celestial glass,
Tear-stained heavenly panes,
who remembers thee?

—*Karen L. Rohde*

The Walk

Wind
Over wave swept sand
Like loneliness
Stronger than my jacket.

—*Charlotte Verberne-Eshleman*

The Honey And The Sting

The masochist-mystic's
pain is ecstasy,
the two are one,
the sting and the honey.

The bear's tongue often
seeks out agony,
the bee's sting turned
sweeter than honey.

The ascetic's insipid,
fearful and frigid.
He alone is king
who's known the moment's
sheerness of feeling.

Lick them both, says the seeker,
they are same and come together
and he alone is king
who's celebrated the exquisite
pain of the sting.

—*Parikshit Singh, M.D.*

A Glance

Just a glance,
Passion frozen in time.
The moment has past
The spell is broken.

Her heart cries in longing
Wanting the moment to never end
To hold the desire
To embrace that space of time forever.

The obsession
Surrounds her heart,
Overpowers her will,
Captures her soul.

Dreams and fantasies
Bombard her sanity
Distorting her ability
To distinguish make-believe from reality.

Just a glance,
Passion frozen in time.
The moment has past
But the memory will always remain.

—*Michele A. Noordhof*

Prisoners

The men,
perhaps a dozen I think,
black faces pressed
against windows
heads bobbing in perfect cadence
to the rhythm of the inconspicuous van,
brown.

They toil in semicircles
by the side of the walking path.
Rakes in hand,
monotonous raking
fresh small inconsequential
piles of brown pine tree needles.

Bodies shackled.
Glances escape unabashed eyes
leaking essences of light
that swells and recedes,
undaunted and uncaught.

—*Jennifer Robin McConnell*

I Understand Rage

I understand rage
pitted against omissions
of vision, repeated subtractions
from factions who say
they are friends, who
when the chips are down
are nowhere to be found.
Secure - or so they think -
in their empires behind
stockades, they murder millions
as if they are mowing grass
to a uniform, manageable height
pleasing to the sight
of those who distrust
the irregularities of birth and life.

—*Joan Jason*

Honney

I'm grieving in guilt for you,
  Please don't let your life
fade in the dark, gloomy, shadows.
  I watch and wait, hoping
you will revive.
  I see your lifeless body,
and tears began to fall.
  I remember when I first
met you, it seems like only
yesterday.
  Have you ever stopped
to think what's the point of
life?
  I wish I knew!

—*Jennifer A. Heimann*

Mandy's Prayer

Dear God in heaven above
Please hear my mournful plea
Show me through your loving eyes
the things I need to see.

When the world is cruel and hard
take me gently by the hand
and with your loving kindness
lead me through this dreary land.

If I should happen to fall
pick me up in your arms so strong
and tell me in your loving voice
that I did nothing wrong.

But most important of all
If I should wish not to live
Hold me in your loving embrace
and tell me of all that life has to give.

—*Raylean Teierle*

A Tribute

On a battlefield of gray
'Pon the following day
Of the great fight
It was a horrible sight
As the crosses were set in rows
And the survivors took their bows
Before the graves of the boys
Who had left all the joys
Of the Friday evening prizefights
And the warm mid-summer nights
Oh, how hard they fought
Toward the day that they thought
They would go back to these
But the dirty Vietnamese
Had ended it this round
And had put them in the ground
None then cared that they died
But now we honor them with pride
On a wall for all to view
Yes, they died for me and you.

—*A.M. "Gabe" Gabriel*

Poets

Poets drink ink,
Spit out discontent and joy.
Reek of passion,
After a fashion,
Churn out the butter of life,
And compose themselves.

—*Christine V. Grupp*

The Sentence

Say a prayer
Prayer a say
hope it's heard
and turn a whisper to scream
make the darkness turn to light
stop the madness and the fight

Close your eyes
your eyes are closed
spend a minute in deep thought
find there's nothing, loose all hope
find the icicle over your skin
realize is the world that is not clean

Live and dream
dream and live
because one memory don't last
and a life time is so endless
not today nor tomorrow
we're condemned to live in sorrow

The world is empty and yet, full
It's the sentence way too cruel?

—*Mario A. Rodriguez*

Sparring Partners

I listen as your laughter shakes,
  quakes and quivers;
your words flow like silken rivers;
  as your verbs fly high
  like acrobats in flight;
hiss seethe like snakes in a pit;
  spit froth foam
  with electrical charge.

While your nouns crouch, watching,
  with quiet control.

These spurring, sparring sparks
  of voice
  light my fire.

—*Glennis K. Salmon*

Untitled

There are many
Reasons why one
Never stays too long
Always on the run to find
new life and the beginning of one's
Real self... Never doubt the
Reason why one must shy away
Just remember the thought of
a caring Friendship is always
here to stay...the feeling of your pain
will soon begin to fade like the rain
And soon once again
the sun will shine and
you will be happy
with the colors of the rainbow
in the sky.

—*Jody Sprague*

Night

When the sun is out of sight.
That means it's really night.
The moon shines so bright.
And the stars have so much light.

—*Kristin Duer*

Beauty In A Dream

Waves crashing over the rocks
Rolling in towards the land
My eyes drink in the beauty;
I want to hold the ocean in my hand.

The thunderous waves
loud that they may be
Are calling my soul,
come, come, to the sea.

I see people at play
but their voices I don't hear
just the sea calling me,
calling me, to come near.

As I sit on the beach
my mind at peace
watching the waves
in front of me just a few feet

If this is a dream and reality it will never be
Don't wake me up just let me sleep
on and on for eternity.

—Judy Steele

Fool's Mate

Pawns up front
Royalty to the rear.
Every things set
Both player in gear.

A pawn is off
And then the queen.
Next the bishop
And looking mean.

The bishop waits
The queen is gone.
Quickly eaten
The sitting pawn.

A hush is felt
The rebuttle's late.
It is clearly heard
"Check mate."

—Peter Davey

Sailing Ships

Past their time of history.
Sailing ships at hand would be.
Times were hard, or so we're told...
Deck boys, cooks and officers, bold,
Scrubbing decks, raising sail...
Climb the rigging, captains hail...
Lash the cargo, hoist the flag,
Check the lifeboat, pack your bag.
All the crew report to me,
Pacific bound today we be.

Dockside merchants from wool to wood,
Sailors drunk, lay down in mud.
Captain calls the crewmen's names.
Check the cargo list again.
Seaman tales and stories cold.
Tales of monsters and serpents told.

If you stroll the docks today...
Sailing ships, all passed away.
Oceans vast, oceans deep,
Your sailing dreams are yours to keep.

—P K Lockwood

The Affair

Turbulent Rose
Seduced from your secure soil
Draped in thorns
Piercing my heart
I drink in your scent
Your presence attacks my senses.
Twilight's journey of passion
Strips us of purity
Until dawn's storm
Snatches you
Like a thief
Leaving you barren, lonely,
Withering.

—Joanne M. Herrmann

Flavors Of Life

Open your eyes,
See the reality.
Lick your sweet lips,
Taste your mistakes.
Close your saddened eyes
And drown out the reality.
Lick your paled lips,
And taste the emotions.
Open your eyes,
Look in the mirror,
Look into the bloodshot eyes of others.
Lick your lips,
Taste the blood and pain
You have caused.
Lick your lips,
Taste the warmth and comfort
You have brought.
Lick your lips,
There's nothing left to taste —
Are you satisfied now?

—Karen Weiner

After

Silence on the stairwell
Seems to relay a creak!
The wind is gusty—
It's wanting to speak.

The windows are rattling
In the mid of the night.
A bush slaps the house,
Like knocking in fright.

Footstep sounds are 'most heard,
On the old wooden floors.
A whistle sound squeals
Through unfitting doors!

Tones I hear, from my bed
While I rest there at night,
At the old homestead—
God says, "It's alright!"

—Judith A. Obuch

Untitled

Right at this moment
The girl is anything,
Or anyone I choose.
Even in the blatant, overt
Mutual stare, she can be
A slut
Or a saint.
Up close, I am invincible.

—Ed Peterson

I'll Never Be the Same

Kindred spirits, kindred souls.
Separate lives, separate goals.
we're so different yet so much the same.
We were living life like it was a game.
You my friend have made me see,
just how good my life could be.
You've also taught me just how bad
it hurts to lose this love we had.
When you left you opened my eyes.
I finally understood with some surprise,
that in your life I had no part.
Oh bestill my aching heart.

—Kimber Riggs

Take It With You

Find a job
Settle down
   Sell your mortal soul.
      Stocks and bonds
         Buy a beamer
            Money is the only goal.

Conform, sell out
   All your neighbors to impress.
      China silk
         Cashmere, wools
      You can tell a lot about a man
         by the way he's dressed.
            Step on each other
               Reach the top
         When will we ever learn?
            Make it big
               Darkness falls.
From ashes we all came my friend, and to
ashes we return.

—Jill Ann Griffin

Old Woman

She enters the cafeteria
at dinnertime
and says,
"Gosh,
it smells like food."

—Keith Hirata

The Black Swan

A Majestic and unique creature
she floats alone on her sea
surrounded by countless others
that can't compare to her beauty.

Her rare and dynamic soul
covers her in a dark shroud
protecting her from the dangers
that are held by the crowd.

She hides a gentle, tender heart
beneath a vicious visage
looking for the perfect mate
to suit her unequaled image.

Her grace and her elegance
hold true throughout her being
but to the single, wild Black Swan
alone....holds just no meaning.

—Monique Martens

This Tiny Child

I saw a child the other day
she had no words to speak or say,
through her eyes I saw such loss
and then I knew what it had cost?

She sat alone in such a daze
her eyes so clouded with a haze,
is it possible to break through
for the horror she saw or knew?

This tiny child so lost in fright
her tiny mind lost all hopes light,
I cursed whoever put her there
and caused her heart to see such fear.

A tiny child so young yet old
all her trust now turning cold
so I reached out and gave my heart
to give back life part by part.

When I saw her I saw myself
for I had known for horror felt,
to see her fright reminded me
how hope is crushed by cruelty....

—*Brenda Keough*

The Withered Reeds

Through paths divergent
Silence reigns,
And trods upon two withered reeds
That bend,
But do not dare to break-
Their bodies rest upon the leaves.

Through vacant wastelands
Love remains,
And rustles memories of you
To tears,
That shed the words unsaid-
And grants each reed a drop of dew.

—*Nancy Lang*

Sitting Alone

Sitting alone; my brother
Sitting alone cross-legged
I saw him once —
Didn't know it was him.

I made a joke,
Easing the mood.
Understandable;
It wasn't funny
But we laughed —
Uneasily.

Sitting alone; my brother
Sitting alone cross-legged
Unrecognizable —
Didn't know it was him.

My brother was killed
In battle; incomprehensible
Sitting alone; my brother
Sitting alone cross-legged

—*Joshua Crump*

Untitled

The power will get you to first.
The cheering will take you to second.
The quickness will get you to third.
And the endurance will bring you Home!

—*Kelli Davis*

Fall

All the birds look fat and fine
Sitting on the hydroline
Every morning they're more loud
Twittering, "Let's all go south!"
Winter soon is on its way
You are foolish if you stay.
In our maple trees they hoover
Till no leave has been left over.
Everyday there is more noise
Like a stream of girls and boys!
When days get short and nights are long
Winterbirds will sing their song.
They're not as many, that is true.
And they need more care than you.
We'll all promise them some feed
They will look for fat and seed.
Regular! For that's the trick.
To keep them strong and looking slick.
And when spring comes down the track.
Summer birds will all come back.

—*Marge Foster*

Again

Candles of love
so delicate,
shadows of greed
so disliked.
The illusive change of a resolution
when the warmth of the lights
complete with the sun
and never forget the tears
of the lonely nights.
The ambitious challenge of impatience
is melting snow
erasing the memory of promises
scarcely touching pride.

—*Karen Clapton*

Finding Me

I've walked a short path
So far, in my life.
Even though I've become a mother
And a loving, caring wife.

I've walked a long path
Through my many days.
I've felt many different emotions
In many, different ways.

I've walked a crooked path
Over several troubled years.
I've laughed and cried
And shed many, many tears.

I've walked a lonely path,
Wandering aimlessly about.
Not knowing where I'm going
Living a life full of doubt.

When I finally found a path
That led me to love and life,
I followed it constantly,
Knowing that I had gone right.

—*Liz Greenland*

Why

Shine me a light
So I can take up in flight
And in soaring high
Maybe I'll understand why

Why,
The unanswered whys
The earthbound chains
Of being earthly sane

The gift of life
The answered sigh

Let me fly
Where reasons lie
Beyond the sky
The answered why.

—*Sam Jaisingh*

Whispers

Your name is near,
So I never have to fear.
You promise me,
That you will never, ever leave.
Now I can rest,
In the shadow of your soul.
Lay my head down,
On my pillow late at night.
Though all alone,
As far as my eyes can see.
Yet, you are here,
Speaking my name, tenderly.
Before I sleep,
Your whispers cause me to think,
Of all your love,
That will not let go of me.

—*Julie Ann Hessler*

Loneliness

As the sun lowers its head,
So I place myself to bed.
I travel there alone and cold.
If only you were there to hold.

Up to my cuddly toy I roll,
A lonely heart, a lonely soul.
Always thinking about where you are,
Knowing in thought....not so far.

And as the sun breaks anew,
My dreams have all included you.
To bare these memories of warmth and
     love,
I know one day we'll meet like doves.

—*Angie M. Burton*

Silently

Something
Somewhere
Someone....
Something
Some dream
Some die, sometimes...
Some scream
I cry, a tear falls from
my eye, silently...
Something

—*Jessica Charchalis*

A Tribute To Mother

There is a woman
So kind and so fair,
Through thick and thin
She's always there.

Love unconditional
Compassion for all,
She picks me up
Each time that I fall.

Humorous, witty
With tales from the past.
At seventy-three
She's still a blast!

A lady like this
is rare. Hard to find;
Just like a diamond
One of a kind.

This woman I speak of
To me, there's no other;
Who quite compares to
My best friend, my mother.

—*Mary-Ellen Burrows Gormley*

My Name Is Kristina

My name is Kristina
So listen to me
I'm the meanest person
Anyone can ever be

I'll hit you I'll bite you
I'll pull your hair
I'll ignore you
Like you're not even there

I'll punch you, I'll kick you
I'll steal your ball
And I won't get in trouble
Not at all.

—*Kristina Daniels*

The Poet's Game

The secrets of the poets,
So quaint to you and me!
Their sage forever interred
In lyrical homilies.

A simple worldly truth
Is capsulate in verse;
Old axioms are raised anew;
A revelatory rebirth!

Kings and fools alike
Are swayed by poets' rhymes,
Their dazzling cryptic messages,
And elegant verbal designs.

They tantalize in riddles,
They scintillate the mind;
They please you and distress you
For the purposes they find.

Could it be out of folly,
Or homeliness of prose?
Who can reason the poet's game?
None but the poet knows.

—*Anthony Zuba*

The Way To Wholeness

April wonderment, as fuzzy green
   softening naked tree fingers,
had ripened into full-blown scarlet-
   only too soon to blanket the earth.

My spring pondering, seasoned into
   reluctant reckoning
   like apples overdue for harvest -
mocked my meager efforts
   to pluck latent meaning
   from decision's hard choices.

Only an inward meeting-ground
   with All-that-is
   opened the way to wholeness.

—*Ruth M. Davis*

Footprints

Cold grey marble
soldiers erect.
displaying
their
etches

Black withered roses
Bow heads.
Praying
In silence

Embedded footprints
Crackling frost.
leaving powdered
dust

—*Barbara Moyer*

Broken Wings

The weapons conquer the world.
Soldiers paid to sow infected grass.
The upright man loses.
The honest man falls down.
Alone against everybody.
Allied with his own pain.
They lie and stab:
In the dock there's the truth.
The truth is a heavy axe
that cuts everyone's head off.
without exception.
The dissolution is here,
the social awareness rules.
Words.
Soft swords that penetrate the heart.
Lies.
War brings profit.
Soldiers called to tread on the sacred soil.
The cowards conquer the world.

—*Rosaria Trenta*

Human Being

Human being, that strange entity
So prone to platitude,
Like sheep, losing all identity
In common attitude.
Evading truth and practicing deception
Lest someone sees,
And having nursed such predilection,
Believes that he believes.

—*Jean Elphinstone*

I Have To Believe

I have to believe, there is more!-
Something else, beyond this.
Life after death, if you please.
Anything!-
A door through which I can pass,
perchance into eternity-
once more to gaze upon you
with loving adoration.
And have that gaze returned,
in full measure.
I have to believe that your essence,
that which was the real you-
survives in some form-
still remains here with me,
in the home we loved and shared.
I think of you in every room.
I am thinking of you now.
as I sit here alone,
under the rose tree,
in full bloom.

—*Roberta Duxfield*

On Tanya's 12th Birthday

If you listen to the whispers
Spinning softly through your dreams;
   If you let this web of memory
Take you back to where you've been.

You will hear the joy of childhood,
   In a rattle's gentle ring;
Christmas lights and loving faces,
   Fireglow and bells that sing.

Laughter on the lake in sunshine,
   Golden days of fun and friends,
Frosted breath of autumn waiting,
   School days calling yet again.

Winter chill and furry snowboots,
   Melting puddles in the hall;
Learning how to cope with living,
   Growing up and standing tall.

Swift the years that speed you onward,
   Birthdays come and birthdays go.
Who would slow this whirl-wind passage,
   Only those who love you so!

—*Pauline Church*

Spirits In The Wind

We are the Banshee,
Spirits in the wind.
From out Irish home
we do descend.
Skin of a fair maiden
hair of silk
beauty only bread
from pure mothers milk.
Silhouettes in the breeze
a symbol of death
forewarning that a loved one
will soon draw their last breath.
I hope you can see
the sadness in our eyes
feel the pain that we feel
as we echo our lullaby.
We are the Banshee
spirits in the wind,
the choir of death
lost souls from within.

—*Brett J. Power*

Day Dreaming

Sunlight dancing upon a warm
spring like day.
Flowers blooming,
birds invading the skies
like vultures who are waiting
for Romans to die.
Breezes touching my face
like a soft velvet glove.
Everything is alive and glade to be.
The water brings forth all kinds
of life to bathe in the nutrients
of the sun.
Let me be not in haste
or quick to set a pace.
For today is a day to
let the mind wonder
in all its imaginary delights.

—*Kathryn Tolliver*

Untitled

Morning, Shadows, Sunlight invite
Still I shy away.
Rejoice, for a new day begins
But sleep drowns it away.

Love. Where is it?
Is that it?
Don't shy away — it is there
Just need to find it.

Awake!
No hiding will do.
There is work to be done.
No joy in my heart!

I need to give,
I need to connect but not to be drowned.
Twenty-two years of near-drowning:
f l o a t!
water-logged
BUT NOT DEAD

—*Hilda Carmichael*

Forbidden Love

Two lovers
stroll down a street hand-in-hand
they are seen
a woman gasps
jaywalks to other side

They enter a store
but the clerk is
engrossed
in a magazine he's holding
upside down

They enter a subway
and sit next to a man who
stands up
and briskly strides to
opposite end

They enter their apartment
and find an eviction notice
the rent was paid yesterday
they realize the real reason
two grown men embrace and weep

—*Matt Loewen*

Friendship

Friendship is like a garden
Surely everyone must know;
Each bud must seem so different
For each one of them must show;
The strength and all its beauty
That makes the garden glow.

Friendship demands loyalty,
For trustworthy we must be;
It desires respect daily,
For we must be respected too.
Friendship is so unselfish
It hoists forgiveness high;
It's bent on showing kindness
And love's the cord that binds.

—*Frances Seymour Cooper*

The Lion

A mighty roar but silent paws,
Surviving on the jungle laws.

A cry of fear comes with his stare,
Reminding life that danger's there.

His servants bow to his every whim,
By nature's law they fear him.

With silent cunning he hunts his prey,
Whenever he hungers, night or day.

The maze of trees clear him a path,
In trembling fear of his fiery wrath.

For the lion is the king of the jungle.

—*Helena Marie Krobath*

The Signs

Here my friend, take my collection.
Take good care of it.
It means everything to me.
I don't need it any more.

Hello my family.
Are you surprised to hear my voice?
Today everything is just fine.
You will see ... everything will be fine.

I float through this final day.
Floating out of my pain.
Today the world smells alive
For everyone else...lucky everyone else.

This decision is a change of colour.
I do look good in the shades of life.
Today I am fearless...but I fear,
Again in my life, have I decided wrongly?

—*Irene Marie Dorey*

Grade 9

I've heard it said
That "No man is an Island"
But how like an Island
Is my secluded world.
Through chattering
Clanging halls
My ghostly figure
Walks each day
And no one says hello,
Though sometimes
I am bumped.

—*Jenny Tremmel*

A Child Within Our Strength

To find that inner child within,
Take his hand and give him strength.
Reach out and touch the soul with love,
Reach in and let him out.

To see the brightness in the dark,
Build castles in the sand.
Let that child out to play.
There's a lot for us too give.

Get out, get out, the strangers gone.
Join hands with the child to live.
Grow as one and learn to live,
An honest feeling from me to him.

We walk together, a brand new strength.
Sweet relief from no more blame.
No more monsters in the dark,
No one give us shame.

—*Ronald P. MacIntyre*

Prayer

Manitu:
Teach me to love
when anger's arrow wounds my heart,
not to unsheathe vengeance's knife
for a wrong
done unto me.

Manitu:
Teach me patience
when deer and buffalo are gone,
so I may understand
that tomorrow
is today's reward.

Manitu:
Teach me the language of the trees
that I may - like the wind -
live in the tepee
of thy eternity.

Manitu:
Teach me to believe that you created only
goodness,
that no one is my enemy until I tell him so.

—*Leon Meersseman*

Past Eight O'clock (20.03)

Nursery spells 'n smells away
Thank God, the end of a working day
Love 'n passion moulded three
Laughing, crying family tree
Bedtime story book away
Three sleeping cherubs,
There they lay.
"My love, my love, are they
   at rest
Time for the one I love
   the best."
News 'n plans 'n good advice
A fond embrace from a loving
   wife.

—*Eliz Hunter*

The Sea

The sea is a swell of blue
That beckons to you,
It tugs and pulls
And intertwines around
Your legs and arms,
Whispering and calling
And luring you.
You follow the sweet voice
Of the swells and the
Impressive waves pull you under,
To join the land of tides
Forever.

—*Kristi Finkle*

The Blossom

I am like a tender blossom
That in the early spring
Is anxious to bud
But also terrified of frost.
And so it opens slowly
Spreading forth its petals slowly
Wanting to express its beauty
But afraid to do so
For it may be frostbitten
And lose its prettiness
To never be able to come forth again.

—*Elia Edvige Gazzola*

Dream

I dream of a place
That is friendly and safe
Where I can roam free
And really be me

Away from the fear
Caused from this horrible nightmare
It cuts like a knife
This torture called fire

How do I rid of this pain?
How do I stay sane?
Where do I hide
When I feel miserable inside

I'd really like to talk
Or go for a long walk
But I'm scared of what's out there
I don't know how I'd fare

I guess that I'll continue
Going on like I'm used to
Dreaming my Dream
Living my Dream

—*Warren Fay*

Untitled

The batter waits patiently in
the box as the pitcher starts his
wind-up.
The first ball flies by outside.
Slowly the fear gets in, but he is
ready.
The second ball goes by strike one.
Now he is anxious. The pitcher
seems so slow.
Fast ball
crack
home run

—*Kristine Musgrave*

Fear Of Love

It hurts so bad,
that it makes you sad.
When he takes your heart,
And then rips it apart.
You thought you really mattered,
But he left you really shattered.
With time the hurt goes away,
Time used locking your heart away.
You're afraid to try,
Because it hurts to cry.
Then as a surprise,
He is right before your eyes.
He pulls at your heart's door,
Opening your heart a little more.
But the memories of pain,
Send off warnings to the brain.
You want to give your heart away,
But the pain gets in the way.
You try to let go,
But you just don't know!

—*Kimberly Reddick*

Victory

Overcoming mountains
That reach above the sky
Fighting for your dignity,
Fighting for your life.

A force of unknown power
Stands before the glory,
You must reach out to your limits
To deal with its fury.

And they tumble down,
Slowly, and one by one
But if you want your pride
You must get the job done.

Grasp your opponent
And prove who is the best
And leave them with the weak,
And all the war-torn rest....

—*Kendall Fontenot*

Mother, Where Are You?

Of fissured and fragmented thoughts
That ribbon through but come to naught;
Mercurial, and yet just rote,
Piranhas guard this primal moat;
What use to rail when none have ears?
Nor yet to cry, there are no tears;
Incomprehensible such fright,
Horizons wistful, out of sight;
What is it now that garners light,
And changes normal into night;
Will Mendel's law come into play,
Or flames consume me where I lay?
To be excused or indisposed,
Then infiltrate a mind marked closed;
To mark an X and then decide,
This melancholy diatribe.

—*Josephine Mosdell*

Loneliness

Loneliness is a dark blanket
that smothers you in the night
it comes when you're not looking
And it blocks out all the light
It can ruin all your happiness
in one small but deadly bite
Loneliness is a black cat
the evil opposite of white
it rises from the graveyard
and can reach to quite a height
Don't bother looking behind you,
for loneliness is never in sight
But beware of it always,
and do everything that's right
'cause loneliness can kill anyone,
and it wins without a fight.

—*Kelly Rae Berry*

Why Can't Dreams Come True?

Friends,
That's all we'll ever be;
Two people in a big world
Facing life up front.

Friends.
I wish there could be more.
More to life?
No, more to love.

I dream of a day in a far away land,
Of sandy beaches and a rolling surf
With a set of footprints
Off into the sunset:
One of yours and one of mine.

Why can't it be that way?
Why can't there be something?
Dreams, that's all they are.
Just dreams.

Why can't dreams come true?

—*Kristopher Pierce*

The Pencil

I am just a little pencil
That's made of wood and lead.
My head is long and pointed.
My body is smooth and red.

I once was long and handsome
But now I soon must die
I like to write quite nicely
But master does not try.

He treats me very badly
And often shaves my head
He cuts me so unkindly.
That I shall soon be dead.

He sucks me too I hate it.
And put me in the ink.
Have I not cause to grumble?
Just tell me what you think.

—*Jenifer Ann Dianand*

The Beholder

Have you ever noticed
The beauty all around?
The pastels of a rainbow
As it reaches t'ord the ground.

The splendour of a dew drop
Like a diamond shining bright;
All awash in brilliant color
On a rose, in morning light.

The splendid hues of autumn leaves
Before they start to fall;
The majesty of a maple tree
Standing proud and tall.

The gracefulness of birds in flight
As they wing their way along;
They soar a while, then come to rest,
And fill the Earth with song.

The golden glow of sunset
At the end of summer's day;
Sinking slowly out of sight
As day's light fades away.

—*Virginia L. Fevens*

My Love

As I lay beside you enveloped in
    the blanket of darkness
I hear your quiet breathing and feel
    the warmth of your body next to me.

And through the cobwebs that cloud
    my sleepy mind,
I think of tears and laughter, of
    joy and pain shared together.

My heart becomes full and I feel a
    lump in my throat because
You do not feel the depth of my
    love for you.

So I reach out and touch you
    and hope that
The feeling will pass through
    my fingertips into you.

And in your sleep you softly
    sigh and turn
And reach out for me
    and we are truly one.

—*Karen Cote'*

Alone At Last

The festivities are over,
The bride and groom are gone;
The birds are going crazy
Cleaning rice out of the lawn.

The guests, too, have departed,
Leaving chaos in their wake;
Empty glasses on the table,
And a carpet full of cake.

Wilted flowers on the mantle
Slowly fading in the sun;
Like the day that now is ending
Their usefulness is done.

Here stand the sweet bride's parents,
Weary from the day just past;
And like the happy bride and groom
Are heard to sigh, "Alone at last!"

—*June A. Taylor*

Last Episode

The canvas of promises ripped to shreds
the canoe of love — drowned
in the saturnine river
of protesting tears.
The heart's as under
in its glory of pain.
Insentience abounds
blanketing the bed of thoughts
a mantilla of vacuum
eclipses the mind —.
I remember nothing
but my thoughts do, my eyes do
the plangent lips malignant in love
ask - where is he?
a throbbing silence
is the sole response
I'm left a breathing corpse
awaiting clemency
seeking resurrection…in death

—*Rita Malhotra*

Mother's Milk

A bluish bulb
The ceiling floats in the firmament
Harmony suffused contemplation
    a tranquil form
    the transient smile
    my baby
Celestial slumber tinkled
tides of Mother's milk
Adoration pondered
    the marvel of her delicate god
    that roused asleep
    mother's milk

—*Imeyen A. Noah*

The Blessed Event

Even though you never wanted
the child that grows in you.
I know you must be afraid
of what you plan to do.
But, please before you let them
take your child before its time.
Would you hear what is on
this heart of mine?

I am a barren woman
I cannot have a child
I've been a mother only
in my dreams.
And the child that grows
inside of you.
Could fill these empty arms.
So please give this child life
and bring him home to me.

—*Kimberly Kaye Horton*

Child

I kneeled one time in
the fields..
    and with
looking I saw

A child knows more
than I
    for she
sees without
    looking.

—*Karen V. McKenzie Smith*

The Affirmation Through Jurisdiction

They were regarded as
the diamond of contemporary
frost which buried itself
by official sentiment, a dream
of fountains and pools.
In the garden was a remarkable
tree; the ellipse of its flames
was a strength in the
fragments of time, a star.
On the brink of this insidious
century, it cherished
the wind and the rain.
These elements are no longer
the friends who cared for
unfortunate rags at timberline.
The peak is covered with snow.
It is a mountain that recurs in
the course of eternity, the
authority of parks and of flowers.

—*Dr. Joseph A. Uphoff Jr.*

Melpomene

The flesh is skinned. The marrow's sharp
    The end is burned upon the bark.
        the ducts are dry
        The tomb is crammed
        The motive's sunken
            in the ground.

Your skin flows wet against my neck
Your hands are callous with regret.

        Tragedy
        wraps its wreath
        around my breasts
        And lifts.

        My heart-
        from thorns bleeds red.

        And you-
        with your pail
        and Erato eyes blind
        kneel upon the grass
        and let the redness
        slip between your hands.

—*Kim Smiley*

God's World

September is a lovely month
The flowers and trees all know
They can have their last big fling
Before the ice and snow.

The sun shines on, but not as warm
The breeze is becoming cool
The migratory birds are eating more
To give them flying fuel.

Some trees have spectacular colour
Putting on their autumn show
With a wardrobe more vibrant than ever
Each leaf has its own special glow.

We know in our world God is in control
For eons the changes He's wrought
The contentment and peace we are feeling
Can neither be measured nor bought.

—*Ginny Shaw*

a rose

HOLD
the fragile flower
LIFE
wrapped in colorful blossom
PRECIOUS
unique treasure unfolds
FIND
layers of importance, meaning
HOPE
in living beauty

—*Kathryn Barnes*

My Forgotten Baby

It was on the 4th of May the day
the Lord took my baby away, with
arms outstretched as wide as could
be he holds my baby tenderly.
I ask so many times why me?
But I guess this had to be.

I've cried so many times I know,
but will the pain ever go.
I loved this child whatever it
would be, but still why did it happen
to me, maybe it's all for the best so
let my baby be at rest.

—*Peggy Burton*

The Lost Dog

The sky is cloudy,
The market crowdy;
The rain will fall
O'er the home of all.

Palm-tree shall prostrate
Guinea-corn shall jubilate

Enough is good a feast,
To him that is nothing a beast;
And nothing does the call cost
To a dog that is lost.

—*Sola Emmanuel Owonibi*

Untitled

Walking in the sun
the moisture of my breath
leaves a diamond dampness
on my soft black scarf.

Hidden beneath layers of dark wool
my body aches from the winter cold.
One small bead of sweat
travels between my white breasts
as I trudge up the cobblestone street.

In the still blue sky
the clouds above observe
the futility of my human condition
and dance in the wind,
laughing.

—*Kate Buckley*

Merry-Go-Round

Ride with me on my merry-go-round,
The one I built for you.
Fly away with me
Into the moon and the stars above.
The life we make will be our own;
Only if you ride with me.
Would you please,
Look at me
Look with your eyes,
The eyes which I long to look into.
Eyes which I wish could see me;
See inside me.
I'm sorry for everything,
Things I've said,
Things that got lost along the way.
Things that you need, I need
To live a life with you
In my arms, to stay,
On our merry-go-round
The one I built for you.

—*Ryan Petkau*

Elizabeth

Elizabeth of a two day week,
The other five she does not speak.

None could hear her, if she did,
So softly has she locked the lid,

On lost caring,
Of music gone astray,
Of a long-ago lover who drifted away.

What does she say when she talks?
Of the pain she suffers when she walks

And the terror involved in dying.

—*Joan E. Conroy*

A Mother's Son

The days ahead lie behind me now
The past is yet to happen
The present now devoid
Long summers forgotten
Cold winters never recalled
Friends are now strangers
Words spoken, never heard
Sights seen, unfamiliar

Time is made of water and stone
Measured by the shifting of the sand
The weathered rocks, small mountains
Bitter the taste of salt
For one who lives on land

For he who befriends the sea
Shares its moods
Return to earth
If you will

—*Simon J. Keeley*

The Lanterns

As I gazed at the lanterns aglow,
the rays of the sun seemed to be
pouring down at me.
And as I blew the lanterns out,
the entire world seemed to blacken.
As the world blackened out,
the hideous cries of people chilled
my entire body.
I swelled up and gave out a cry,
the world was no longer alive.

—*Judy Ann Bromback*

Heavenly Poetry

Look out beyond
the reams of space,
What do I see?
Stars, sun, moon.
All looking back at me,

Sometimes I feel.
Like a grain
Of insignificant sand,
One is 5 billion.
Scattered across the land.

But then I perceived
There is only one.
Who resembles me
My fingerprints tell
the intricacy.

God created each one
A vision of himself
uniquely to be
A shadow of
heavenly poetry.

—*Judy McKinstry*

Please Let Me Know

Tell me o mighty one
the right way to choose
people try to ban
real faith to use!

No one wants to hear
real words from Bible
changing words they dare
to write they use dibble

I am left alone
with Bible in my hands
I quit the church of stone
my faith is not bend!

Did I choose right way?
to stop going to church
or I should sway
to their lurch!

Through my prayer tell
what is right way-
their urge to quell
or as I am to stay!...

—*Dusan Jovanovic Frulika*

The Roach

The roach went under the table,
The roach climbed up the chair.
The roach went up my back,
And deep into my hair,
He jumped off my forehead,
Into a bowl of stew,
But I don't know where the roach is,
So here's some stew for you!

—*Kari Carswell, 10 years old*

The Second Time Around

What is love like
The second time around
The sweet desire
Unending dreams.

Was it 30 years ago
We loved each other so?
Now we've found each other again
For true love, the second time around.

Your blue eyes twinkle so
That smile I can't forget
I tremble at your touch
The second time around

True love is hard to find
Some times you nearly lose
But destiny is not blind
The second time around

We'll grow old together now
I'll never let you go
For happiness I've found
the second time around.

—*Eva Kennedy*

The Stone

I searched the beach
The shore
Looking for a special stone
A precious agate
To give my brother

I searched with eyes and heart
For this earth-formed gift
To hold in my outstretched hand
A tribute of regard

Many agates lay hidden
In the ancient sand
I found not one
I found only the tears of my heart, and
    a small piece of amber lost long ago
By another sister
Searching vainly along
The beach
For a sea-washed gift
A special stone
To give to her brother

—*Jan Sutherland*

Mountain Twilight

On stealthy silent feline feet
The silver dusk creeps in
To sift between the ghostly pines
Neath which the night begins.

Relentlessly the still air chills,
For sun has bowed farewell
With gold salute to snowy peaks
Above the silent dell.

A nimbused pearl of moon floats up
To shimmer through the mist
In which the alpine meadow veils,
And with new stars to tryst.

Starts whippoorwill an aria
With orchestrated stream,
Sky's purple western footlights dim
For overture to dream.

—*Christie Winter*

Miss You

I miss you in the winter when
the snow is crisp and white.

I miss you in the summer when
the birds are in full flight.

I miss you in the spring-time
when the flowers do abound.

And also in the autumn when
the leaves are on the ground.

—*B. Green*

Problems Of The Future

When the sight is seen,
The solution may be lean.
For we sometimes don't understand
What reasoning is needed at hand.

Given into thought,
We search into what's been taught.
Sometimes attaining miracles,
Otherwise forming icicles.

Uncurving our inner self,
Reluctant as it may be,
Leads into certain answers
Belonging to those who see.

Becoming the present sets the future.
And here you realize your questions
Are the answers to your problems,
Ones that only question you again.

—*Jeffrey L. Holl*

Sadie's Coat

Shadows that dance with
the sun rays on the bottom
    of the forest floor.

—*Kelly Ann Malkowski*

The Truth, My Son

Daddy! What's wrong?
The truth, my son
you're only four
but quite a man.
I cannot lie
to you, my son.
I kept a sum
that wasn't mine.
Special help I need
for my disease.
A mind doctor
will treat me there;
weeks we'll be apart.
In mind and heart
we'll be so close,
our hugs we'll feel.
Our love needn't wait.
A better man
you've made of me.
My debt is to you.

—*Kay Bostrom*

Pictographs

The Ancient Ones have marked
the walls of the cliffs...
testimonial to days long
gone.

Where is the milepost
of my hike?
Where are my handprints,
footprints recorded?

Every ruin
holds up
shards
of previous lives.

The fragments of my life
are contained
within
these broken dreams.

Where is the Archaeologist
willing to dig down
through the layers of time
to reconstruct it?

—*Kathryn McGee*

In The Sky

When I am in the sky
The whole is mine,
Surrounded with peace and beauty
That gives my soul a great joy.

My heart desires to touch and feel
The beauty that is before me.
Why can I not touch
The beauty I see?

Not now, but I will
When I become a spiritual being.

That is my destiny -
To be a spiritual being,
To feel and touch the beauty
Prepared for you and me
By our Creator and Saviour.

—*Done Katsorov*

Teach Me The Way

Teach me the Mystery of Nature,
The wisdom of the ancient sun,
Teach me the way of the dragon,
The path to become one.

The motions of a butterfly,
Gentle as the breeze,
Show me the way of survival,
Teach me the taoist beliefs.

The strength of a fire that burns,
The speed of the dragon fly,
The heart of an explorer,
Not afraid to die.

The musical, poetical soul,
With a smile of a knowing friend,
He, who is my teacher,
He, who has no end.

Teach me the way of the tiger,
Whose courage and strength is true,
Teach me the way,
That will lead me back to you.

—*Rebecca Kopernicky*

Death

Death, what is it, why is it, how is it?
Trapped under walls of brown, creatures freely crawling through.
Wood surrounding you back and front, side to side.
All dressed up in clothes that were once your Sunday's best,
but now they're your forever only.
No tossing, turning, in your deepest sleep,
no sadness, no glory, no crying nor weeps.
For those who once knew you, and for those who didn't,
"It would be hard to believe that that skull had a tongue and once
    could sing."
The only symbol that you had ever lived is a stone engraved with
    your name.
As your relatives come to mourn on your sorrowful piece of gravel
    land,
they wish they could hold your once fleshy hand.
But now you're going to a better life,
a life where no pain, sorrow, anger, grief or hatred can ever be
    endured.

   —Crystal Reid

Cold

"I'm cold Mama," said the baby swan
"Trouble is I've not got enough feathers on."
"You're in luck," said his Mama, "snuggle in here."
So she lifted her wing and her child snuggled in all warm.

"I'm cold Mama," said the American baby
"Oh dear," said his Mama, "my darling, then maybe
I should turn the central heating up more
Since it's vital, my darling, my precious, that you're all warm."

"I'm cold Mama," said the African child,
In the cold desert night, just sand for miles,
His Mama wept "Child, there is nought I can do,
I have no blankets or shelter for you." Still cold.

   —Claire Wolfendale

Truly Blessed I Am

Truly blessed am I when I wake to see the sun.
Truly blessed am I when I see the early dawn
To behold all the perfections you have made
To see the sand or the morning waves, crushing so gently
I think to myself how truly blessed I am

Skies so blue, air crisp from the morning dew
How can one not think that all things are created by you
Birds singing and flying away
Makes me want to shout and say, how blessed I am

If I count my blessing one by one
How can I not thank you for a job well done
And if I should take for granted all these wonderful things
I have no one but myself to blame
For one so blessed as I am, surely can only say
Truly blessed am I

   —Kathy Ramsey

Offering

The heart has its seasons. On this third of summer let us, you

and I, lay bare our secret pains to this season's gods. Let
us, too, burn incense; re-awaken passions now etherized by
time. But eyes must only look; and elbows just brush; and lips

mumble dissonances. Be it so. For eyes must only look; and
elbows just brush; and lips mumble dissonances. So come the
rains to snuff our incense; balm this pain; turn cold this
want; let us offer a libation to a third of summer slowly
shaping other season come full circle only the gods understand.

   —Junette S. Bax

A Special Bond

I feel you move in that dark, sheltered place; innocent and
unaware.
You are blind to the world as I am blinded by my love for you.
The time for waiting is coming to an end.
Soon, you shall see what I see.

Poverty, War, Disease, Persecution, Greed, Pollution, Racism,
Death.
Is it selfish to want to bring you into a world wrought with
such problems?
Will you hate me or love me for it?

But what of life's treasures:
Love, Prosperity, Friendship, Peace, Caring, Harmony, Sharing.
They are what life is worth living for, and yet are they to
few to have value?
Is if selfish to want to love you, take care of you, watch you
grow, despite life's many uncertainties?

Yes, it is selfish and I shall wallow joyously in my
selfishness, for you will bring life, and I shall bring you
love. Together we shall be as one. Mother and child united
by an invisible bond for eternity.

   —Laurie Webb

Grandpa

Grandpas are for hugging.
Unlike Dad who's made for bugging.
Grandpas always deny it.
They'll deny it through and through,
But grandpas have always wanted, to be young like me and you.

   —Joshua Terry

A Friend

How could I know what is meant by pain
until one day its freezing rain came down upon my head.

Drenched and frozen my heart kept on beating
although I felt I was dead.
Although I could not see or hear in this
so lost a state;
slowly the ice began to melt and if
by some strange fate I knew I would not die.

There reaching out to me was a FRIEND,
assuring me this was not the end
for GOD who would not let me go
was present also in rain and snow.

   —June E. Donna

The Road To Turin

Down to the sunny brook they danced;
Velvet soil graced their bare soles;
And into the water clear they glanced,
Into water blue and green with fish in shoals.

A gentle explosion of subtle soft light
Was felt falling from trees all around;
And oncoming dark and oncoming night
Vanishing and fleeing reverie's sensuous sound.

And night creeps silently after day;
It, unannounced, whispers its words;
To sleep en route to Turin in sweet hay,
The day's last sounds are of dreaming birds.

   —Stephen Mangan

Our Fiftieth Anniversary

When the soft velvet of night blankets all things
Usually brain functions quiet, go dormant,
But mine rise from the tiredness of my body
And like a firefly flits over the cycles of our lives.

So many times you have paced
The railroad platform, the steamship pier,
The bus waiting room, the hospital corridor.
Always sure that I would be with you
Returning to the arms of my only girl.

But things have changed these last six months.
With you, lying in the hospital bed,
Our Fiftieth Anniversary has come and gone.
I am the waiting one.

You have embarked on a trip of no return
You are here but not here. You are you but not.
Unlike you, expecting me with certainty,
Your pacing led to that sweet embrace.
I have no place to pace but my heart's corridors
With no comfort to be finally found in your sweet arms,
Only the solace of those marvelous years of ours.

 —*R. John Charles, Jr.*

Twilight

Twilight enters as the gloom
Veils and silences my lonely room
It spreads across the heavenly skies
As day and night meet with a touch and a sigh.

Beauty appears in our lives that way
Blending - then parting - for naught must stay.
A choir of angels - a chorus of gold
Violins play then the day is old.

A touch - a smile - then radiant skies
Twilight, the vagrant, all time belies.
Whatever she touches, she grasps in her fold
And the angels shower a bit of their gold

I close my eyes and reach to my soul
Holding that instant of mirrored gold.
When night descends, no sadness shall be,
Just a moment of twilight for me and for thee.

It is said we portray whatever our truth -
Be it beauty, or sadness, or tears forsooth
So hold fast that rare moment of dusky skies
A memory haloed - in forever - your eyes.

 —*June Hummell*

God's Creation

People die, people cry, our world is in a whirl.
 Vengeance of war, rockets to space,
smoke polluting cars, a hole in the ozone we cannot embrace.
 What is to happen to our race,?
  but all we say is why?

A time bomb in the making, a man we should destroy.
It is our life he would be taking, the nuclear weapon is no toy.
Ira,? who are they?, they will shoot, they will kill night or day,
Northern Ireland has no say, it s the army and they must obey,
  but all we say is why?

Given through birth or heterosexual, dirty needles or
homosexual; a virus of the nineties, a virus of no acceptance.
 Why do we turn our heads and close the doors,?
  do we have no compassion anymore.
 Stop, think and save our world, open your hearts,
  work together and not apart.
 Our children are the future, they came without request,
  so let this be a world and not a mess.
   For there is no why?

 —*Lynn McGeorge*

Homesickness

Grey salt and snow on a New York street
Village Vanguard, Guggenheim, everyone
Seeming rhythmic, pulsing to a blues heart beat
Relentless, like the Australian sun

A wailing saxophone, improvisation
Street musicians know every score
Cheevers, Angelou, Morrison, art of a nation
Where are Williams, Boyd and Livermore?

The New York Times, The Village Voice
Tabloids shout a range of choice
Broadway shows, off Broadway plays
Nowhere, deep blue Jacaranda's haze

A garbage-can fire warms the hands
And faces of street people it reflects
Lights of the yellow cab slowly scans
Night reveals the poverty day rejects

The world's largest city writhes and seethes
Playing luck against life and fate
She touches a bruise on a heart that grieves
For a simple "G'day mate".

 —*Alwyn Lewis*

Untitled

The gentle wind across the seas
Visits around my summer door
Minding manners with a bow
Edging closer to my memories
With a smile she brings the summer scent
To softly cradle the golden grain
As I stand within the plain
Embraced by the gift she offers me
Arms outstretched I welcome her in
Flourishing before her like harlequin
A bouquet of dreams I give her
Nurtured by my silent heart
Before the twilight heralds the night
I take her hand in mine
With more than simple poetry
I whisper her name to the seas
In the span of a single heartbeat
I've taken her into my life

 —*Simeon T. Yap*

The Rocking Horse

The rocking horse stood silent in the dim and quiet light
Waiting for the small ones to claim him from the night
Long ago he'd felt them spring lightly on his back
So cocky and so boisterous as they rode the big black
But since then all had faded only memories to remain
But this year Santa'd promised that they'd ride him once again
So here he was all polished and painted up anew
To greet a Christmas morning with expectant eyes of blue
He snorted softly in the dark and all but stamped his feet
The years had been so lonely his control was hard to keep
But just then he heard footsteps fall gently on the floor
And excited little voices as they opened wide the door
His lonely heart was mended as they spied the gleaming toy
And leapt upon his back to ride once more to cries of joy!

 —*Mary Anne Kloosterboer*

The Beggar

A beggar and his wife every day,
Walk down the street in great dismay;
I see them every morn, in sad mood,
Knocking the doors for some corn food;
They go round the streets of city,
No one looks at them with pity;
They cannot find the happiness in their heart racks,
So they pass in great dismay along their life tracks;
They go to the woods which are dense,
Which is their permanent residence;
They have three kids happy and cheerful,
Though their lives are dreadful;
A little one who has a scar,
Comes to me with a jar;
They have hearts without spot,
So, I love them a lot;
They beg for generations and generations,
For them there are no recreations;
One day these little ones surely will receive,
In this world of cry and defeat "The Kingdom Of God."

—*C. H. Raja Ram*

Chasing The Wind

Down the hot dusty road somewhere,
Walked a pathetic young sinner-girl.
Lost, ragged and so alone,
On a path leading nowhere,
Her soul had no home.

Pleasures called to her thirsting within,
To pity parties with a numbed-out friend,
Couldn't satisfy her search for love (in sin)
So tonight she has to go out again.

No one understands, not even her mirror
What it is that drives and moves her to run.
She doesn't know that her soul is a hearer
Of the voice of god and the call of his son.

So she chases the wind...The pleasures of sin
Until she thinks she has happiness
Then it turns to sorrow, but tonight
"Who cares?" She'll just catch the wind again
As it passes by tomorrow.

—*Shirley J. Hill*

Harmony Divorce

Far in the ocean horizon, comes two huge vessels;
Walking side by side - with harmony in-between them.
What a harmonious moment! Harmony is a beautiful lady
Her beauty is the creator of disagreement between the two;
That; who is to marry harmony?
Harmony laughs at them; because, each one of them —
Powerful or weak, has a right to love and express harmony
The two bull-vessels shake the ocean, causing
A reverberation of waves; a storm in the ocean!

Harmony - as tender as it is, she cannot bear this wave.
Like a swift-bird, harmony flies to the ocean shore; for
The safety of her life. Harmony lands on the peaceful shore -
The shore of peace; peace - her genuine companion

With hunger and anger, the two bulls exchange fists in...
The ocean - with a starved surface; a pig's skin,
A mere membrane; which cannot withstand this turmoil...
Head to head bang, sinking in agony... they abused harmony!

Harmony at the shore, looks frightened; scared stiff
But with no regrets! Hey you, me... them, harmony will soon
divorce us; peace, love and harmony please!

—*Jared Amwayi Memba*

Herald

I looked in my mirror today and there
was a silver hair.
Shining bright among the black.
"Oops" said my head. "You are getting old."
With shaky fingers I plucked it out.
The menace looked so innocent between thumb and finger.
One long silver hair.
A herald of what to come?
A wrinkled face and hair all white.
And glasses too for short sight.
With crippled hands, swollen feet,
and perhaps
no teeth with which to eat.
"Begone bad thoughts,
leave me alone,
for can't you see
I'm not even fully grown."

—*Liz Brook*

Josephine

There was a time when I thought innocence
Was the best time of my life
And all the wonders that I saw
Was all I needed to survive

There was a time when youth was all we had
and we shone like the sun
With hearts as strong as hercules
and fears not known to anyone

But the time I hold so close to me
is that time I cannot forget
And the memory of all that's happened
we look back on regret

What is sad about that moment
and I swear this to be true
Is that the stillness of this shattering world
will never see the wonder of one as beautiful as you

You are as beautiful as truth
and as memorable as the stars
And we will always think of you
to remind us of who we are

—*Jundie Cadiena*

The World

This morning as I listen to the radio,
Watching the cars go to and fro.
The news was bad, full of sadness and strife.
Wishing that I was not part of this life
        looking around the world today.
Did the MASTER really plan it this way?
Wondering if in two thousand and ten...
        will there ever be PEACE again.
Will it continue this killing and bombing of humanity.
until we have all gone too eternity.
This world could be a beautiful land, if humanity
        would only give the MASTER a hand.
Then maybe we could hope in two thousand and ten,
The world would be a greater place to live in.

—*Dorothy Fowler*

The Burning

I take the final swig of vodka feel it burn its
way down my throat hiss at it scorching my tongue
and reach for the bottle to pour myself another.
I think of how my tonsils scream every time I let
the alcohol rape me. Then I look down at my hands -
shaking - holding the glass of poison - and think
of how these were the hands that should have pushed
you away from me. But didn't. And I keep wondering
why I took your hell, took your poison. I remember
how you burned your way through me. You corrupted
me from the inside out, and I kept coming back.
I let you infect me, and now you've burned a hole
through me. I hated it. Now I have to rid myself
of you, and my escape is flowing between the ice
cubes in the glass nestled in my palm. But I have
to drink more. The burning doesn't last as long
as you do.

 —Janet Kuypers

A United World Is The Ultimate Call

We are Asians with tan skins
We are resistant to hot sun's grins
Our white brethren over there
Embrace the sun with bodies bare
With umbrellas and hats we cover our heads
You expose yourselves in windy sea beds
Hot spices in curry with rice
We adore never disguise
Fruits cereals and steamed vegetables
Just the mild ones your edibles
To cover ourselves from neck to toe
Great grand parents advised long ago
White brethren less shy than us
Superficial difference what ever it may
We are all human in structural way
Forget the colour forget the race
No apathy over religion one embrace
A common blood runs through our veins
Wish a United world future reigns the way of life
Results difference in all a united world is the ultimate call.

 —Sowmya Chandrika Samaranayake

Death The Greatest Robber

God gave us life to live on earth,
We can't live longer if we are in poor health.
Do we all know what causes people's dearth?
People's dearth is caused by death.

Gold miners die not because of being unhealthy.
We are told that the mines collapse.
The shaft which hold them up to surface breaks.
They die not because of cold conditions.

God paves our life by making us healthy.
We save our life to prevent death.
But even the brave Hitler gave up his courage to death.
Worldwide we have graves for the brave.

Till now nobody will not die.
Hill dwellers mourn as the rest do.
Still we can't understand why we must die.
Pills are given to the sick but later on others die.
Bills are paid because of death.

 —Justin James Mlomba

Lava

Come with me let us begin,
we control our own time.

Breathe deeply calming your nerves,
erase all thoughts hindering consciousness.

Close your eyes but not your ears,
sweet soft words will control you.

Time no longer has meaning and has stopped,
stopped until we no longer unite.

Join me in a place of harmonious beauty,
where we are washed by warmth.

Sweet scents and beautiful colors inhabit,
a place carved by cautious hands.

You are no longer where you once were,
turned in the direction of life's most precious gift.

Accept my hands as life with yours,
locking together joining us as one.

Feel our heartbeats as we come closer,
relax every muscle in your body.

A night, tonight,
as I kiss your lips soft as rain.

 —Jeffrey A. Herle

Lest We Forget

Isn't it a fact; that not so long ago
We had all joined hands to live together
And had promised to survive every weather
I wonder, what has become of that brotherly pact!
Has it become a victim of a merciless theft
Or has this principle, from our lives been willingly left
But lest we forget; we who acquired limitless greed
Have helped ourselves in that breed
Where only violence and dishonesty groom
And without doubt we'll doom!
How much longer, will the deserving be denied
And the sufferings be defied, but lest we forget;
Truth is a force, which forever can't be tied!
How much more is left of this cruel lust,
but lest we forget; death of every living soul is a must!
The forgotten promise can still be revived
Our conflicts can still be brushed aside
As there's still time left to build a bright and prosperous future!
Or else we'll have ourselves to blame
If we are forgotten by the merciful nature!

 —Kashif J. Chaudhry

The Big Whopper

We're at a mountain lake, our lines cast out,
We start reeling in, hoping to catch a nice fat trout.
We cast and cast, again and again,
But the fish just aren't in our hook's underwater lane.
We just can't get any luck even if we try,
So we go back home with nothing to fry.

The next morning we get up, all cold and wet,
And then we have a wild goose hunt for our fishing net.
We go to the lake again and cast out our lines,
But all we catch are a couple of irritating old vines.
I wearily cast out my line, I think I have a fish!
And it feels like it will make a nice large dish.
I begin reeling in, it puts up quite a fight,
When I see it in the net, it's definitely not light.

We return to camp, I fillet the fish.
Mom fries the fish, mmm this is a scrumptious dish!

 —Wendy Siebold

Love Prayer

Oh, to love, My God, how beautiful a gift hast thou given us.
We humans are but small and often ungrateful
But we all realize, at some time, the need for love.
We want love, but we are stupid.
We put forth not the effort great enough for its survival.
And it dies.
It is smothered beneath the blanket of greed.
It is choked by the weeds of desire and selfishness.
It is drowned by the vastness of our self pity.
We allow it to be killed and become extinct from our lives.
Why? Why, God? Because we are stupid.
Our stupidity blinds us and we can not see.
We can not see how we could be cured.
Cured of the viruses embedded so deeply in our hearts.
Viruses which turn to green molds that spread and soon cover
our bodies.
Molds that suffocate the pores of life and the desire of love.
Help us, God! Oh, help us to wash our bodies clean of his mold!
Help us plant the seeds of love once more in our lives
So we may live. So we may love;
For to love is to understand.
And, God, how much we need to be understood!

— *Karen Arena*

Somebody

I look carefully at Somebody across from me.
We look deep into each other's eyes.
Somebody's eyes reflect pain, loneliness, fear, and
heartbreak.
I see dreams of childhood shattered, gone away, lost
forever.
Deeper, I look into Somebody's eyes the future remains
confused and unclear.
I watch a few minutes longer, wondering how Somebody
feels right now.
Tears fall silently down the pale sunken cheeks.
Determination slowly follows the fears, drowning.
Shaking, I turn from the full length mirror, not wanting
to see more.
Slowly I walk away, not knowing that Somebody was me.

— *Keri Galvin*

Silence

She sits with her face to the window, staring into the
welcoming sounds of silence. Silence, an odyssey of orgasmic
pleasure and exhilaration to some; yet to others it can be a
monotonous gruelling journey through terror.
The sound of a pen tapping on a desk almost as it were
synchronizing with a heartbeat can drive even the most gentle
being to the brink of insanity. Or the tick tock sound of the
tall and dusty grandfather clock (you know the enormous ones
sitting in a corner of a blackwood hall), when you are waiting
for your child, lover or family member to come home; your
adrenalin seems to speed through your veins in tune with every
motion of the pendulum and sounds of the chimes.

Silence, it can be the first rustle of the fallen autumn leaves
or the crickling crackling of a winding creek through a
evergreen forest.

Silence, a welcoming piece of time to which one can relinquish
the enormities of one's life, anger, sadness and emptiness all
cease to remain.
The rebirth of happiness, love and hope can be conceived
through the sounds of silence. She sits with her face to the
window, staring into the welcoming sounds of silence.......

— *Kelly Ellefson*

Caught In The Crossfire

The echo of gunfire, a repeating whine,
We're caught in the crossfire... bleeding, dying.
Unjustly lost, our lives like spent shells,
Who started this madness... this gun-blazing hell?
So easy to buy; so little is said.
Guns are carried to school. So young are the dead.
Have we traveled so far that we fail to heed reason,
Just the blast of a shotgun heard in any season?
"To defend, to protect", our forefathers said.
Could they foresee the future? So many lay dead.
Did they envision drugs, gangs, civil war?
If they rewrote their words, would they add something more?
So many have answers, but so few try to reason.
We're still caught in the crossfire of an open season.

— *Judy A. Helms*

Wee Tears...

Mommy! Daddy!
What have you done?
Why have you done this?
Am I only the product of your drunken,
drug-induced lust?
Must I suffer for your imprudence?
Won't you listen to my tears of pain?
I did not choose to be here.
That was your choice!
And I had no say in what you swallowed, or injected, or sniffed
I could not remind you to down your tiny pink pill, Mother
or to don your rubber hat, Father.
Now I lie here helplessly
In the incubator I call home,
Tubes stuck up my nose
Needles rammed into my tiny, malformed limbs.
Only a few moments in this world
to which you've brought me
And already addicted to your drugs.
Already a junkie.

— *Lynne Fezatte*

Secrets Of Time

Oh this house of mine
what secrets of time.
From the first tender kiss
in our bed of bliss.

To the laughter and joy
of babies footsteps.
The smiles and funny faces
of our babies one to four.
All boys for sure.

As they grow older
the school years took over.
Now they are grown and their lives are unfolding.

Now we are alone as the years go along.
With our last tender kiss we have been blessed.

What secrets of time in this house of mine.
For loving, for crying and joy
for anger and forgiveness.
Oh this house of mine what secrets of time.

The faith and hope of life
are the secrets of time in this house of mine.

— *Arlene Willows*

Ode To Golf

There once was a game called golf
What the hell rhymes with golf?
I don't give a shit, but come to think of it
I just saw a movie with Dolphe.

A wonderful game is that golf
What the hell rhymes with golf?

I took a big swing,
But the problem with the thing
Was I nailed my partner in the bolf,
Then he dropped to his knees. "Hey Dolphe,
What the hell rhymes with golf?"

The nineteenth hole is to be thanked
Cause that's where I got tanked.
After my round, theories abound,
Of why all my shots were shanked.

A frustrating game is that golf
What the hell rhymes with golf?

My poem is now over, and my four-leaf clover
Screwed up my rhyming with "golf."
There "fore" I'll go home by myself.

A wonderful game is that golf
What the hell rhymes with golf?

—*Katherine-Lynn Fehr*

Color Me Grey

There is often much said about the color red
what with sunsets and cherries and brave hearts that have bled.
We are oft reminded by poets waxing mellow
of the panoramic glory of gold and bronze and yellow.
We're taunted with the silver and gossamer and white
for the angels and the clouds and with the black of night.

But nought is heard poetically about the color grey,
save maybe to describe a dull, unsatisfying day
or conjure up a picture of an old hag's hair so dank
or an invalid's complexion or the outside of a bank.

What about the saucy undertip on the proud tail of a squirrel?
or vanilla-licorice ice cream licked into a swirl?
or a winter fox, or the neat trimmed beard on that handsome
older gent? the bedroom carpet, my Mercury or the sweater Aunt
Margaret sent? They are grey... even gray... sometimes
greyish or graying like down on a goose or an old head, bent...
praying. I may barter in brilliants, paint pastels for pay,
describe in neon highlights until my dying day;
but when my time here's finished were I to have my way,
if you talk about me when I'm gone... color me grey!

—*Brenda Firth*

Wonder

I continue to wonder of how it will be,
When I leave behind my high school family.
Some of us will succeed and others will fail.
There will be those who would rather say good-bye
instead of cry.
Thinking about the future makes me sad,
Knowing that we will go our separate ways.
When that day comes to reunite us, I will be there
to help remind us of our happy days.
Watch the sky and find a star, and when you do
you will realize how great and special our friendships
really are.

—*Kiomi Wade*

Ode To Mom

When thoughts rainbow across my mind
When I need serene silence to unwind,
It's good to know someone in this land
Knows me well enough to understand.

When tears relieve hurt, worry and care,
And sometimes when life seems so unfair,
I think of your wisdom, patience and love;
Your belief and faith in God above.

Mother, to know that you are near
No matter the miles, I will not fear.
For it seems to me, no matter how far,
You are as bright, as close, as a guiding star.

I marvel at the harmony, this blending of souls;
As one, as ourselves, we are always whole.
I am humbled to think this vast mutual need.
Began with the life of one tiny seed.

—*Miranda Montgomery*

The Miner

I was lost out in the desert searching for a spot of shade.
When I saw this flop eared burro walking briskly up a grade.
Looking further up the hill I spied his tawny mate.
A healthy looking critter who too was swift of gait.
So I dropped in behind them as the sun began to set.
They were all the hope I had, a dying man's last breath.
By now my feet were dragging, my lips parched and dry.
I stayed close behind them on that road to the sky.
It wasn't too much further when I stumbled to the top.
I was out of breath and weary now, a sorry looking sot.
Then suddenly as a shadow, or as lightning in a dream.
Right there on that mountain top was a deep wide stream.
My needs were downright simple, to drink and then be cool.
So without hesitation, I dove right in that pool.
I guzzled down a gallon when a brilliant flash of light.
Showed a dozen grizzled miners moving into sight.
From out of that crowd stepped my smiling Uncle Dan.
And next to him stood grandpa, a mountain of a man.
That's when I finally realized, I had found the pot of gold.
I had made it up to Jericho, and to the Mother Lode.

—*Jack McGuire*

Promises

If I could see my little girl, would her face be just like mine?
When I'm crying, is she crying, too? Is she fine when I am fine?

Or, when I'm down, would she be up? Could her spirit buoy me?
And, when she is feeling so alone could I lift her, gleefully?

Are we so fused that there's no chance that the strong could help
   the weak?
Must it be that simultaneously burning tears smother each cheek?

When one of us runs playfully, might the weary recoil?
Are we meshed as co-dependently as a root is to the soil?

When I'm plagued by haunting memories must my child suffer the
   pain?
Does she have the power for leading me from such thoughts to
   keep me sane?

Is there a chance that she and I could one day both embrace,
And squander kisses long subdued on one another's face?

Could both of us, for once, be sure the other will not leave?
Will union shared, so close, so long, leave one to deeply grieve?

It seems no matter how I try, I cannot seem to find
Who's the "she", and who's the "I", so total is the bind.

What difference if we're two or one? No need for solemn vows!
Between us fragile humans, life mere promises allows!

—*Joyce A. Poirier*

Nowhere To Hide

I walk there alone in my head
When I'm scared worried, or sad it's dark
Like a cloudy summer night when the moon is full
But masked by the angry, bitter darkness of the night
I stand there all alone
As the creeping fog enters my body
Carelessly leaving from behind
Dispensing a cold chill in me
I feel evil and scary eyes looking at me
My every move and thought I cannot conceal them
For the angry night knows everything
No protection, no where to go
Like a terrified turtle on its back
I see the old, empty buildings around me.
However, I cannot run in there.
I run away, not looking behind I feel the eyes behind me
Coming closer and closer like a pack of hungry wolves
I'm running out of gas
It's no use I stop, close my eyes, and fall on my knees.
Like the end of the day; I give up.

—*John Yaniv Shabtai*

One Thought

One day,
when my heart and soul is on my wishing star
My mind shall run free,
through the meadows,
grass,
and tree's
my mind shall be as free as a bird,
And I shall only be one thought of peace.

—*Jennie Hargrave*

Treasure

Where do you go when the feelings fade?
When the emeralds glow turns to jade?
Do you go inside yourself? Try to disappear?
   Can you paint on a smile and face the
      world as though you have no fear?
   It takes incredible energy to always pretend,
      that your heart is whole, no need to mend.

How can you carry on? Always pretending to be tough, strong.
The outside picture looking complete.
The pitiful creature inside, white as a sheet.
Do you have somewhere you go? Some place that only you know?

Is it peaceful there? Can you breathe fresh air?
Does there blow a gentle breeze?
Gently caressing, tickling the trees? Does it whisper in your
ear, secrets only you can hear?

Where is the path that takes you there? The one you trip down
without a care? The sun must shine and flowers grow, In this
special place you've found to go. Cherish it and keep it safe,
it is a treasure, after which others will chase It is your
soul. Guard it with care, keep it whole.

—*Bridget McCallum*

Saint "Dennis", My Uncle Santa

He has a child's dreams and an old man's face,
With thoughts of grandeur in his embrace,

He lives and dreams far beyond our sight,
But who's to say who's wrong or right.

Let's raise our glasses: he'll raise his too,
For our time together,
"Uncle Dennis" and you.

—*Elaine Grainger*

When Time Was Ours

I was sittin' in the grass watchin' you pass,
When the moment turned into a mist.
Time stood still and was waitin' until,
You and I had finally kissed.

You came over to me so innocently,
As the sun paused over my shoulder,
It was in your eyes like fireflies,
And the moment was growing older.

The clouds departed the broken-hearted,
The moment was sparkling your hair,
Time was in reach as we walked on the beach,
While our magic tingled the air.

Then a nightbird called but the dusk was stalled,
Somewhere over the still ocean,
We were hand-in-hand, but did you understand,
That time still wasn't in motion?

Then under the pier, you and I, my dear,
Snuggling against the cold,
Found our lips embraced and the chill was chased,
And time was released from its hold.

—*Jami Dvorshock*

The Tide

In the movement of the waters
When the moon is full and bright,
And the tide is at its lowest ebb
Ships disappear from sight.

Near the wharf the boat docks with its crew
The days catch fills the hold,
The sailors mend their nets anew
The men who are so bold.

Are the sea gulls really fast asleep
Or just appear to be,
I hear them calling in the night
Soft echoes from the sea.

The diesel hums a lowly sound
Flags flying in the breeze,
The water makes a lapping sound
Fades slowly by degrees.

At last the tide comes rolling in
The shore is now in bliss,
The first wave comes crashing in
To give the shore, a kiss.

—*Walter Chownyk*

Quiet Place

I've never heard such a quiet place
      where even sounds are silent
         where whispers are lost between the moments
         and kisses between the winds

Such a place as this I shall find in your soul
      where the emptiness echoes
      and echoes
         again...
      sounding sweeter and softer than lullabies

And I shall find this silent music
      a comfort in my breath
Solitude will find me
      embracing the sound of you
And you shall melt in my memories
      like promises

—*Jane' Hughes*

The Sistine Ceiling

Hear, said Manitou, of wondrous lands for men, and lakes
Where fishes thrive and feed the lightning paws of bear,
And where the forests halt at cliffs to send their sheltered
Streams tumbling on to rocks below.

Hear, said Manitou, of sun-blazed hills for tents, and plains
Where mustangs roam and rule the sage-brush tracts of space,
And where an eagle rides the windless skies by day to view
Valleys black with buffalo.

They heard, and gathering up their beds and shawls,
Beat a yellow path through dust and stone and sand.
Their toil was long and great of noise, through years
That passed as days, and soon their age was melted in the
Blasts of trial as mind cursed mind, and wars burst out
On tracks their sons would warm.
Yet still the plod, the surge of belief, the sag.
They curled at night like dogs to sleep,
Their limbs angered by the restless drudge.
Some flagged, some turned, some quit.
But strength was there, and most just filed along,
Their faces worn with line and traced with sweat.

    —Paul Bateman

A Grandfather's Love

The little boy waddled up to the chair,
where his grandfather sat with his eyes in a stare,
The three year old giggled and tickled his feet.
The old man lay slumped there without even a peep.
The child climbed into his grandfathers lap
and covered himself with the old light blue wrap.
The babe fell asleep in the arms of his idol.
If only the old gent could see this dear child.

What the grandson did not know, was the old man was dead.
He died in his sleep, yet not in his bed.
The parents came in and smiled at the sight,
Until they saw grandpas' eyes in a glazed sort of light.
They removed the child without causing a scene,
and took care of the old man as if in a dream.
When the child awoke the next morning with a grin,
the parents felt sorrow, for they couldn't begin:
to tell of the awful events of that night,
for the child would never get over this fright.
The loss of a grandfather so dear and so true
should never have happened his whole life through.

    —Tammy Kerekes

The White Rose

In my room; is a single white rose,
Where it came from; nobody knows.
Now white; is very queer to me,
I'm used to red; but now I see.
Across the oceans; across the land.
I will find the reason; to this white rose in my hand.
I had to know what it meant; I had to go and find,
The person who gave me the rose; before I lost my mind.
Then it dawned on me; I didn't have a doubt.
That the person I was looking for; wasn't round about.
It may not be a person; who gave me that rose,
It could have been anything; who really knows.
How strange; this must be sounding to you.
But if I can figure it out; you should be able to.

    —Tamara Strunk

Fool's Paradise

If you can imagine a world in which war is a thing of the past;
Where no tyrant tries to seize power, where only love and peace
   will last;

Then you can imagine a school in which teachers don't need to
   frown.
And you can imagine no crime. The police are not needed in
   town.

And you can also imagine a country that needs no laws;
That people always share with each other, that nobody has any
   flaws.

Though I think I am a peace maker my creativity comes up flat.
Even in my wildest dream, I just can't imagine that.

We'll always have imperfection; we'll always have hate and greed;
We'll always have some tyrants; a deterrent force we'll need.

Until Christ sets up his kingdom on this sinful earth to rule,
In imagining such earthly perfection, I imagine, I'd be a fool.

    —Vernon Penner

The Silk Man

It's a sad, mad world indeed
Where people can't get what they need,
A piece of bread - a cup of milk
Too much to ask the man of silk.

Wrapped in a cloak of wicked illusions
Lost in a world void of solutions.
The man in silk just shakes his head
As he climbs inside his canopied bed.

There he wallows in dirty luxury
Dreaming about his place in history,
But such a happening can't take place
For he himself, he cannot face.

And all the while the hungry die
Closely clutching the question why.
But the whispers of those too sick to weep
Will tip-toe through the silk man's sleep!

    —James S. Baer

Island Of Skye

Once, on a holiday, I visited Skye,
   where the clouds play chase as the wind whistles by.
At the mountains they wait to let their rain drop
   then, one by one fly over the top.

Misty island of magical light
   from the deep green glens to craggy height,
then, when the sun comes out to stay
   Skye puts her beauty on display.

Sparkling waterfalls and sapphire blue lochs,
   purple heather, thistles, gold fern and rocks.
The peace and tranquillity cast their spells
   with pine scented breezes and wild flower smells.

Glittering rivers with waters that tumble
   over pebbles and rocks, washed into a jumble.
Roads that go on a switch back ride
   with a steep, deep drop on either side.

Cloud shadows and sunbeams play over the view
   changing the scene every minute or two.
Then it's time to go with a deep, deep sigh,
   goodbye misty island, magic Island of Skye.

    —Eileen Ling

The End

I have reached that point
Where the end is all that is left.
At departure's door, I thump and scream,
But your hidden soul, truth, and falsities
Are the beginning to our end.

There is no one left I can hold on to.
I am without body or soul.
The rain - cold, falls hard, and I brush it from my eyes.
The day turns to hideous ruin,
And I beg for you to go.

Our souls have no place to hide,
Or to be lost in. There is no hope.
Your sweetness, like a vulture,
I ravage with cruel selfishness,
And remain indifferent.

My love is destructive
As I consume the tenderness you possess.
Yet, here we go again.

Please stop loving me.
I wish I could tell no more lies.

—*Malti Nijhowne*

Your Challenge!!!

Lord, make me an instrument of your peace.
Where there is hatred, let me saw love.
Where there is injury, pardon.
Where there is despair, faith.
Where there is sadness, joy.
O' Divine master, grant that I may not so much
seek to be consoled, as to console
to be understood as to understand
to be loved as to love, for it is in giving that
we receive, it is in pardoning, that we are pardoned
and it is in dying, that we are born to eternal life!

—*Lynne F. Koorn*

City Of Flesh

The dogs run wild in the city of flesh
While distant tarmac turns to water in the heat
The entrails of Angels hang from the sky
as white coated men pluck out their eyes

Your dealer wears a pinstripe suit, and bowler hat
the addict dies, choking on his own juices
We stop only long enough to taste the meat
then shelter while the purple sky rains bile

The night has come, like a curtain of blood
fear fondles our stomachs, thinking and feeling as one
we know the horror of the fragile mind
In the gutter flows a broken hope
a dream abortion

This is the season of madness, heat upon heat
A creature of darkness
you feel the sunlight laser piercing your brain
In the love heat peak faces melt, eyes rupture
Howling your surrender
you crawl through the city of flesh

—*Russell Jackson*

Grissel Bound Bird

Travelling, a short time companion faces southerly,
Whilst my gaze rotates, checking upon a countenance fair for eyes,
Regarded by some with indifferent speculation, however,
On holding to the road we take,
Many a passing thought, verbally, we make,
And if for longer we had known,
I am sure to this conversive pot we may have thrown,
Many a more enchanted note,
Enlivened, even giddy, anecdote.
But this being not the case,
And in company new, no haste,
Rather still to taste afresh, beginning of things which at best,
be lest, moments from the passing glooms,
Of sole occupancy, solitary, on disparate moons,
By facing common passage on a road, on story, narrated faintly
    arose,
a flight from groundings, metaphorically resounding,
A tale of grissel bound bird,
Left a helpless, melded to unsanctified resting place,
One wing left flapping, yearning, for a never to be returned,
Flight, that freeing space.
    —*Victoria Straub*

Untitled

Enough talk you no listen up, to things I man say.
    Who are you anyway?!

Pirates out to pillage and plunder, raid Mother
    Earth of her wonder.
How much longer will this be?
The struggle for true liberty.

We need cooperation; decisions to make
laws of God we shall not break.
Away with poli-tricks and greed,
Our people will be freed.

Fallen Angels controlling creation
a strong vibration needed to wake the nation.
Jah-liffication, Irie-meditation, No-hesitation
to use my sensi-sensation!

The hourglass is almost empty,
a great loss for those who have plenty.
The stage is set for nuclear-warfare.
The beast comes for his share,
    stay away from his snare,

The turtle wins, not the hare!
    —*John A. Babiarz*

What Is A Friend?

A friend should be someone,
who comforts, listens and cares.
A friend should be someone,
    who is always there.
A friend should be someone,
you can tell your secrets to,
A friend should be someone,
    who likes to be with you.
A friend should be someone,
    you can do anything with.
A friend should be someone,
    you can sit and "veg" with.
A friend should be someone,
to help when there is a void to fill.
A friend should be someone,
who can tell you the truth when no one else will.
To have a friend like this,
    I know is hard to do.
But to have a friend like this,
    this has to be you.
    —*JoAnn M. Karr*

The Spirit of Truth

I am the One - from 'before'
who has 'arisen' - for sure
so all now - must heed this pen
that is - the ones by God chosen

In this - last task
to help humanity - the 'dark one' unmask
for this dark one - is very cruel
and over sinners - is now to drool

So - to all men true
yes - I mean you and you
read my book - The Last Prophecy
its infinite wisdom - will set you free

So that all humanity - you can help
as they are 'decimated' by the satanic whelp
for now Compassion and Love divine
must from you - to them entwine

My lovely sisters - so beautiful and true
my lovely brothers - who stand tall too
'tis to you - I now "reach out"
with my book - God's final shout.

—*Terence de Malaherre*

Untitled

I looked up slowly, to see a friend,
Who passed some boys being rude.
They had no friendly words to send,
They had a negative attitude.

She passed on by without a word,
And I thought of all her fears.
It didn't seem as though she'd heard,
But she was fighting many tears.

They hated her 'cause she wasn't white,
I found this quite absurd.
Being prejudice - it isn't right,
I wish there was no such word.

She was used to it and didn't care,
But each word was a stab in the back.
I couldn't see what they thought was fair,
To hate her because she was black.

—*Michelle Hoppe*

The True Tale Of Spitz The Samoyed

This poem tells the tale of a Samoyed called Spitz,
Whose life started out at a home like the Ritz.
He was loved, he was wanted; he was taken for walks,
And soon became known as a subject for talks.

He ate well, he looked well, he hadn't a care
In a world where all loved him - Oh Spitzy beware!
Came the day when our faithful and loving young boy,
Overnight just became an executive toy.

His Daddy preferred his new twenty foot boat,
And his Mummy no more on her Spitzy did dote.
One dark day in April he was feeling quite low
When they packed up his biscuits and poor Spitz had to go.

He couldn't quite figure what he had done wrong,
But gone was the love that had kept him so strong.
Three weeks in strange kennels - how Spitz he did pine,
Now nobody loved him - he started to whine.

Would anyone ever love him again
Or would he just die all alone and in pain?
Then out of the blue came a man and his wife
And our Spitz has now started a happy new life.

—*Janet Storey*

The Break In The Clouds

Why did the faintest sun shine brighter?
Why did the strongest storm blow lighter?
Because this was the day
when the "Break in the Clouds"
arrived from the National Library of Poetry.
With honesty and without exaggeration,
right away the book took my admiration.
A book of shapely size and form
with great efforts this work of art was born,
enriched with charming rhymes and skilled words
written by people all over the world.
A book of quality, indeed,
in it is so much to read.
The Bible and the works by Shakespeare
are the greatest books and forever will be,
but, please, let us add "The Break in the Clouds"
superbly printed by the Owings Mills Library.
I must confess,
there are times when my words cannot express
my gratitude and thankfulness.

—*Ilse Zenke*

Dying Love

Why don't you love me anymore?
Why do you have to go?
This pain that I now feel in my heart
Is the only feeling I know.

Did I do something to hurt you?
Please don't leave me alone to cry.
I never meant to do anything
To make our true love die

Please give me one more chance to show you
You mean everything to me.
I still love you with all my heart
And that's how it always will be.

—*Kelly Arnett*

At Seventy-Five

Now that I am seventy-five I feel like sweet sixteen,
Why, I've just begun to live, and enjoy life to the fullest.
I've heard so many people say "They are glad to just be alive"
But my life just starts at seventy-five.
There are so many things I want to do
That I'm really looking forward to.
I'll travel across the whole countryside
To see all the beauty that God does provide,
I'll pack up and go when they urge arises
To any place that beckons to me.
On weekends I'll go fishing to our many lakes,
The peace and contentment and quiet is there,
I'll climb a good mountain, I'll reach for the sky
I'll tackle anything that catches my eye,
I'll dance up a storm if my heart so desires
A swinging my skirts, my feet like live wires.
I'll get "Old age pension" but that doesn't mean
That I'll live in a "Home" and sit and play cards,
That's not for me, I'll continue to live life to the fullest
Now that I'm seventy-five.

—*Ann Vardon*

Death And Destruction

The death I wish for
  will one day come
    sometime between the moon and the sun.
     Oh God yes, it will be fun
      When I place my hand upon the gun.

     Death and destruction come my way.
    Do you dare come out to play?
   Listen to your evil master,
Wicked one run faster, and faster.

You will look at me, you will run, I will follow.
 You are my other image, and your personality is hollow.
  I hide you deep inside my mind.
   And now that you've been released,
   you will die

    The sharp white fangs of Samson's Son,
   yearn for you, the chosen one.
  Upon the past you shall not dwell.
Your future destiny is to burn in hell.....

    —*Sara Tjostheim*

Memory Of A Moment

Time slips by fast and nothing lasts. With leaves falling and winter calling. Suddenly the mind awakens to watch as life stumbles on. We are all just sands in the glass. Falling, scaping as others roll past. A gentle breeze blows in the window. The radio plays a certain tune, and... Together we fly free, soaring. As time drifts by forever slow, moments blossom. With icy snow of freshness and stabbing pain. So crisp, so alive and fresh. Deep as midnight rain. Oh, to taste the sweet nectar of dawn's gleaming dew, before it passes beyond me and... You fade away forever out of reach. Listen! Sweet sounds arise like a child happily perched atop a staircase. To stay safe, or move and feel the thrill. Unable to safely have what is longed for. Lost at sea amid the raging static and monotony. Trapped without and knowing unkind memories of hope, love, and passion unsought... Passion beyond measure or release. Time marches by without interest as inevitable, batteries slowly fade and die. The glass is replaced with endless dunes. The breeze is forgotten as the rooms rage in a blast furnace of despair. There is no trace of times passing, and free? Free is just a memory of a moment...

    —*Dale L. Snider*

Guardian?

Somewhat dark dirty complexion
Wiry hair and savage instinct
Lacking the intellect of distinction
Good enough to work but not vote
Use me to advance your civilization
  My Guardian?

I'm just boy to you
Though silver age streaks my crown
And I'm your slave, too
Though the free spirits of my fathers
Roamed this wide land through
  Guardian of who?

My soul a piece of African soil
Stands tall this inherited dignity
No more backdoors and mine holes
This citizen is your equal
I don't need a guardian for my soul
The God of Africa has made me whole.

    —*Marc de Chazal*

Untitled

Over looking the times you've hurt me
With a blinded heart.
The sweet things you did and said,
Seemed to make everything better,
But only in my mind.

Sometimes...when I sit and think,
I can still feel the pain and sorrow...
in my heart

You lead me to believe you loved me...
But I can't read between the lines,
I need for you to prove it to me,
I need for you to show me,
You really love me.

    —*Catherine Croteau-Truhn*

Scotland

A bloody history is our past,
With clan fighting clan,
Our own stupidity allowing this,
Killing our kindred man.

Not all our own doing, was our downfall,
The English instigated,
The Scots were kept where they should be,
As citizens second rated.

Our history is too complicated.
Too complex to surmise,
We are the novelties of our time,
In the worlds united eyes.

We have the beauty of our land,
And our voices always loud,
That what we've left of our nation,
Is pride of being proud.

    —*Hugh Cron*

July

Cool grass reaches out, tickling feet
with feathery fingers.
A cornucopia of light summer winds stir,
carrying the heady perfume of lilac to
the noses of those drinking sour lemonade.
around honeyed laburnum blossoms bees buzz lazily and
birds are s-o-a-r-i-n-g,
   dipping,
    floating.
Butterflies drunkenly flit through the arms of the willow who
weeps by the icy stream.
A gentle jingle from bell on the ice cream truck is echoed
by the chime of nickels dropped in haste and the sound of
padded feet on the scorching tarmac.
The sun is melting in a lasagna sky.
Look, here comes August.

    —*Christina Murray*

Poem For The World

If a moth danced a jig at a moth ball
Would a hound hurry home to tell the news?
Would a rattlesnake begin
To agree to lose its skin
If it knew it was for purses belts and shoes?

Could the world really fit into an oyster?
If the grass could really whisper in our ears
If it told us that our race
Might soon lose its home in space
Would we shed only crocodile tears?

    —*Graham M. Wild*

Europe Supine

Europe sprawls like a giant wheel at rest
With its mountainous hub a rocky nest,
While countries radiate from the Alpine core
And gradually slope to the oceans' floor.
The lengthy boundary of the Alpine heart
Contains the Plain of France which becomes a part
Of Belgium and Holland's fields of grain
That merge with Germany's Northern Plain.
The broad, flat stretches expand through Poland
And enter the endless Russian lowland,
Then curve back by the shores of the Black Sea
To follow the Danube to Hungary.
Italy's curving Adriatic shores,
The broad Po River Valley that pours
Through the Italian Plain complete the wheel
Of Europe that is shod by its southern heel.
The friction of her parts causes melting tars,
Leaves her body with perpetual scars
That are mostly caused by a God named Mars
Who does this writing with red hot stars.

—K. Douglas Beakes

What Happened...

What happened to the unicorn,
With shining mane and golden horn?
What happened to the dragon strong,
Whose memory was never wrong?
What happened to the dodo bird,
Whose silly plumage was absurd?
What happened to the dinosaur,
With shining teeth, flesh he tore?
What happened to the country farm
Where work was done by strength of arm?
What happened to our trust in people,
When word was meant in church and steeple?
What happened to the children's laughter,
As in a barn they swung from rafters?
What happened to the story tellers,
Whose tales were better than best-sellers?
What happened to the bright blue sky?
Technology, pollution, man left them all to die.

—Calvin Gardner

In the Dead of the Night

In the dead of the night the lighting crashes,
with the water swirling and whirling against the
rocks it smashes.

When the storm is all over and day finally breaks,
in the early morning everyone wakes.

What is left over of what happened last night,
everyone who saw has had such a fright.

Still there are ships lost out at sea,
people standing on the shore sadly.
Will they come back that we never know,
but last night was a great show.

The water and lightning at every command,
everything works at God's single hand.

—Jodi Macdonell

With You

I can go for a walk, or just sit and talk.
  With you.
I can tell you about my problems, my feelings.
My trust is at its fullest when I'm
  With you.
We laugh together as we sit and talk.
I can have fun and enjoy myself when I'm.
  With you.
I feel special when I'm.
  With you.
My heart skips a beat when you're around.
It's a real treat being.
  With you.
I wouldn't want to do anything, unless I could do it.
  With you.
Your beauty and grace reminds me of a dove.
That's why I fell in love.
  With you.

—George C. Jeckells

At The Crossroads

Friends now we part, perhaps no more to meet
Within our too-brief span of mortal years;
Though this were true, yet one thought still is sweet:
Believers meet beyond the veil of tears.
So many ways to say I wish you well
As from the nest of nearness you must fly!
Too many memories to ever tell
Assail my mind and mar my brave "Good-bye."
Friend, I commend you to the charge of God,
The Bishop and Good Shepherd of our souls;
Though wind and waves may bear you far abroad,
Though hid in darkness' shroud, you sleep in Sheol,
God's hand will lead you safe to heaven's shore,
Where we shall reunite, to part no more.

—Jerome Van Kuiken

Wealth

For as I looked down the path and saw the beauty that was
within; surrounding the mountains, temples gleaming, and the
brilliance of wealth that was surrounding. The path of
destruction lay ahead for those who were not wise. For all
this wealth and glory it will bring only for a short time; how
the superiority, greed, lust could accede one to indulge in
every whim that life has to offer. But, the one thing it
cannot do is fill the emptiness within. For all the gold and
silver cannot fill the emptiness within. Oh yes my son, it
will only for a short time, but when all the wealth has
expired, the emptiness will still be within. It will
camouflage for a short span but when the wealth is gone the
emptiness is still within. My daughter how now asks?! "What
shall I do to fill this void?" You turn to many of your
so-called friends when the wealth was abundant, only to find
they had turned their backs. Left friendless and moniless who
do you turn to? You search the streets only to find yourself,
as one of the many people you had mocked so many times before
in your state of superiority, now, only to find that he has the
most important wealth of all. Peace of mind and love from God.

—Katherine Rose Richley

Death Is Heaven

I do believe there is a God,
within that God there is a heaven.
When life has passed and death reveals,
heaven is what we must face for eternity.
The world of love and feral freedom,
is the place called heaven which is where we will be.
There is a difference between life and death,
but there is no difference between heaven and death.
Life is an object which God hath made,
It is grateful to one who has their dreams.
Death is not bad; death is wonderful,
because heaven is death, death is heaven.
Picture heaven as a place safe from anger,
a place safe from sadness, a place safe from fear.
You must live life till death becomes you,
but be patient with life, cause heaven's for eternity.
Do not be afraid or frightened from death,
because death is not death, death is heaven.

—*Tanya Bowman*

The Real Thing

When we are together I look into your eyes
without being distracted as the world passes us by.
When I spend moments looking at your lovely hair.
I don't have a worry or a care.
Whenever I hear you sing a song,
All my troubles are gone.
The moments I remember and miss,
Are the moments we would hug and kiss,
When I see your smile...
I think about the joy you have brought into my life.
I'm hoping some day you will be my wife.
Some day you will get a diamond ring.
Because my love for you is the real thing.

—*Kenny O'Leary*

Life's Lonely Road

Did you ever walk life's road.
Wondering how life's burden suddenly become a load.
When all of a sudden a friend appears.
To help you through your past years.

Hand in hand we walk through our past.
Probing and digging to make my will last.
We both begin to laugh and cry.
Because we have discovered a natural high.

And then the time comes to depart.
When we both have to break and make a new start.
Yet the memories will always be there.
Because we both found that someone cares.

So goodbye my friend.
But let's not say it's the end.
Instead we will fix our amends.
Who knows someday we may meet again.

—*Jean Fisher*

His Child's Song

I come before God, my father. I love to hear him say yes!
You are my child. I love you, each and every day.

And as his love enfolds me, my spirit in joy does say
I love you, father, son and spirit you are my life,
each and every day.

Through each day you guide me, in your true and loving
way. Keeping me safe from all harm, from being lost in
worldly ways.

Yes! I want your love always, through times of joy or
pain. To feel your breath upon me. I, your child, at
peace again.

—*Daniel MacIsaac*

Risin' Up

There isn't a day goes by that we the people knows that the
world is near. People struggle, people fight, and they only
fight for what's right. They blame it on white man, but the
Lord has to put it in his hands. The white man isn't to blame,
it's really a shame. Blame yourself for the things that came.

Men out there doing drugs, raping, robbing, and stealing but
yet they are the ones who has no feelings. Degree, nor
schooling but yet always ruling. They take from the one's who
is trying to make it, but yet not seeking education.

To better yourself is one step. Wake up people, wake up.
You to can succeed, it's a need indeed. You are only hurting
yourself and without further ado, you all only making us
stronger too. Blacks killing blacks, wake up people, wake up.
ADC is the only thing they think they need, wake up people,
wake up. They live from check to check, babies taking care of
babies.

Do you really know when you are through? Time has come for
all to seek education, not welfare. Wake up people, wake up.
Stop taking and be more giving. Check out the other side who
shows that they're really living too.

—*Kathlene Green*

Cwmpandy

When walking through its fragrant air.
Yet conscious of every footsteps sound.
Suddenly disturbing a resting graceful hare.
Watched it flee to warren ground.
Paused beneath, one lovely foliage tree.
Listening to birds in praiseful song.
Their harmony my mind to please.
Here Melyn Brook keep sparkling on.
Radiant sun within its realm above,
Blue sky not race of any shower
Silent prayer to God with love.
My thankfulness, for this, blissful hour.
Blue bells kissed by another mornings dew.
Winding path, man's right of way.
Joy when seeing a wonderful view
Then making it, my church today.

—*S. G. Jones*

Untitled

Your name is Bruce, we love you so
You came to us five years ago
You were just an infant three months old
Possible adoption, so we were told

Then one day they came to say
"Sorry! But we have to take him away"
The pain was so great
I was not so brave.

In April one day they called to ask
If we would reconsider the task.
When at the door, the joy was so great
Because I had lots of faith.

On Christmas Eve of '86
Our long last dream came true
Never again would we be blue
No more court, no more judge
Could ever take you away

On every Christmas Eve
Is when we are thankful and believe
That you Lord, came our way.

—*Shannon Hagen*

The Last Day Of 1934

Bonnie Parker with blonde hair and big blue eyes
You didn't know what you were getting into.
You met a man named Clyde Barrow
Who only knew how to rob banks and shoot
Little did you know what he had got you into.
On that last sunny day in 1934 you would ever see
Both came the end of your life and Clyde's.
Now people say every eve of that day of 1934
They see the ghosts of Bonnie Parker and Clyde Barrow
driving by once more.

    —Jennifer Spoto

Forever Friends

The experts say you're lucky if just once throughout your life
You find a special friend who shares your joy, your pain, your
   strife.
Now I can be included as one of those lucky few
Because I found a special friend; because I did find you.
Whenever I was hurting, and no one seemed to care,
You'd always stand beside me; you'd always be right there.
Don't ever doubt our friendship cause there's one thing you should
   know,
You're a very special part of me; I'll never let you go.
No matter what the future holds or where our lives may lead us,
We'll always share a special love—the precious bond between us.
Let's make a solemn promise; one never to ignore.
Let's not just cherish memories, let's make a whole lot more.

    —Judi Robinson

In Your Shadow

Tall, sturdy, powerful
You flex your majestic limbs,
Casting great shadow on stunted, weak undergrowth
Awe-stricken by your perfection.

Foolishly, I creep into this alluring shadow
To steal fleeting protection from summer's sun.
Scars from such childish impudence remain —
Leaves without lustre, limbs fractured, growth suffocated.

Snatched without weaning by autumn's foul winds,
Tired leaves plucked and discarded,
I stand alone in shameful nakedness
For the sun to stare and mock.

Death be better than face the light.
Sentenced to life without place to hide, I bend,
Tormented by bolts of lightning, splitting and splitting into sawdust
Struggling against the wind, yet praying to be devoured by it.

Let winter play the devil's game.
In spring, I'll drink from nature's love
And boldly bare new growth to the sun
That I might have shadow.

    —Irena Kohut

Memory Of Mother's Day

Mother your love was so special it can never be replaced.
You gave it so freely as God gave you from above.
For me everyday was Mother's Day, because of that one
special Mother I had!
Together we celebrated one last Mother's Day, but who
would know it was the last
The yearly buying of cards, roses and gifts have now
become the past.
I see signs, I hear advertisement, I see beautiful red
roses and gifts, all for Mother's Day, Mother's Day.
I stand in the store, I read the beautiful cards, but oh!
there is no Mother to buy one for, because last Mother's
Day was the last Mother's Day.
Go to everyone I say live as if everyday is Mother's Day,
because that one special day might be the last Mother's Day.

    —Ivy Cole

Freak Show

The freak show came to our home last night.
You know, the one with all the midgets.
The price of admission was only a porch light

They were dressed from rags to riches. Hobos,
queens, and one in a diaper. Their make-up
was spread with the patience of a child.

They danced on our porch and giggled for us,
the audience. There were many acts, some on
stage before others were through.

My wife and I gave them all tips. We waved
to the barkers in the shadows as they ushered
them to the next show across the street.

    —James M. Myers

My Hidden Love

Looking in your eyes, I see happiness, peace and joy.
You look into mine and see the same.
But deep within those eyes of mine
Holds something you must never find.
It shelters feelings I hide from you;
Feelings of love that's more than true.

Feelings which you must not know;
Feelings we will never share.
For we are friends from long ago;
Our friendship's something I'll never spare.

But deep in my heart,
I want to hold your masculine hands,
But they always seem too occupied;
I dream of snuggling in your strong arms,
But the closest we ever get is walking side by side;
I want to say "I love you" a thousand times,
But talk of nothing rules it out;
I want to tell everyone you're my lover,
But you're just a close friend
And only friends forever we'll be.

    —Linda Mai

The Lighthouse

On sunny days,
You proudly stand on the rocks,
Enjoying the azure deep sea
And the flying white clouds.

In the darkness,
Through the heavy mist,
Your long beams stretching,
Directing the ships
Towards their destinations.

O! A storm is brewing,
Fierce wind is blowing,
Black clouds are rolling in from the horizon;
Though trembling,
You're trying to shine with all your might.

Look! A small boat!
Struggling against the high waves,
Almost breaking,
Suddenly saw your light,
Striving even more vigorously,
Reached a haven at nigh!

    —Katherine S. Lu

Heartbeat Of A Child

Your building blocks lay on the floor, your toys are spread about
You seem to build such things that life can't do without
There is a child who's like a heartbeat, within the winds off love
A tranquil child, shy and kind, given from above

You absorb, wide-eyed and eager when I teach you something new
I try to answer all the "whys" as best as I can do
There is respect for all God's creatures, the smallest, the wise
There are many things I've learned through the mirrors of your
eyes

You fill me with your heart as no one else has done
And when you call your father, I'm proud to be the one
Alone, we are together and stronger we become
As life takes us on her journey of happiness and some

When you sleep I feel an angel poised above your head
I stroke my fingers through your hair as you lie upon your bed
And you whisper dreams forth-coming of all of life ahead
There is a child who's like a heartbeat...

—*R Peter Bouranel*

Grandma, I Can't Survive Your

You raised me, nurtured me, sheltered me, and loved me.
You taught me the difference between wrong and right.
You introduced me to education, and taught me the importance
   of it.
You taught me to love, not to hate.
You taught me to care, not to be careless.
You taught me to forgive, not to hold grudges.
You taught me responsibility, not irresponsibility.
You taught me independence, not dependency
But most of all you taught me the way of life,
   and its up and downs.
You even taught me how to be a survivor,
But why didn't you teach me how to
   survive your death?!

—*Everdene Francis*

Dear War

How can you look yourself in the face?
You took them away and they can't be replaced.
You made them suffer, you made us cry,
They really didn't deserve to die.
They fought for our country, they fought for
our rights,
Their loved ones struggled through the nights.
You pushed them away without a hand,
And their hearts still made them take a stand.
Having to deal with the shameful killing forever,
They still believed in their endeavors.
The stack of bodies you have built,
Will you ever feel the guilt?

—*Kelley Edwards*

Blond

You speak of beauty; your song is heard.
Your face is perfection, body of a God:
One woman worships every word
And seeks a meeting on each thought plane.
She is of Nature's same vein; preordained
By forces you both share, and glimpse
In vivid dreams by day and night;
And that is the clue; please see kind sir,
There is a key to being with her.
Questing for knowledge you chase dark realms,
Looking at amber eyes, touching black hair;
Love's mysteries seeking to unravel there,
While one soul who was born of July's moon
Longs for you, hopes, in a starry northern room:
And I whisper this as I know you care —
Remember your one true lady is fair.

—*Louise Norman*

The Eastern Shore

Once you visit the Eastern Shore
   you'll forget it nevermore.

Just one taste of Bay Blue Crab
makes all the others seem so drab.

While sailing round the Chesapeake
Is nothing short of magnifique.

   And crabbing in the Tred Avon
certainly does turn one on.

In the fall there's Geese to watch
   flying low across the thatch.

There's ducks to see who dip and swirl
and sometimes a deer or occasional squirrel.

   Now when it comes upon November
there's Waterfowl Festival to remember.

As the seasons reach for their predictable cycles
there's much to do in old St. Michael's.

The simple pleasures Springtime brings
   the gentle rain, the whir of wings.

   You'll forget it nevermore
when once you visit the Eastern Shore.

—*Kathleen C. Wendowski*

Reform

I look to you in thunderous light;
your eyes showing me despite
you, a portrait others won't dare to see.
My brief glance a result of a desperate plea.

Without words you reveal your story;
a time line and detailed inventory
of the actions shaping that denying glint.
A tear forms and you whisper a hint.

A cloudy apparition of the past
haunts, hovers and will forever last.
Your tarnished silver I will change to gold;
relief, yours soon to behold.

Tyrannical rains flood the past
and drown them in an ever darkening vast
body of fact and emotion.
Tomorrow is Change with renewed devotion.

—*Kat Dawson*

Heaven's Bright Tomorrow

   Your favorite chair is empty now.
   Your favorite blanket is put away.
I still remember that warm comforting spot
   Where no one else could stay.

   I miss those eager barks,
   The ones you would cry to me,
   And I miss those coaxing rubs
As you pushed your wet nose against my knee.

   I've put away your favorite bowl
And all the things you won't be needing,
Because now there are no anxious cries
   To say it's time for feeding.

   Your time spent with me
Has brought great pleasure and a lasting memory.
   Your departure has brought many tears
   and heart-wrenching sorrow.
   I miss you, my little friend.
I still wish our days together did not end,
   But we will meet again someday
   In heaven's bright tomorrow.

—*Patty Jenkins*

The Little Things

It is the little things that mean so much
Your loving kiss, your gentle touch,
It's your warm smile on a dreary day
And your tender words that wipe my fears away.

It is all the moments we spend together
I wish would somehow last forever,
And the simple beating of my heart
That hurts me so when we're apart.

So if you're worried, just look in my eyes
And you will see there are no lies,
About the way I feel for you
And to let you know what I say is true.

I look forward to each and every day
Knowing you'll be there to lead my way,
Upon a path which we are taking
Of a new life that is in the making.

So can you understand the way I feel
Can you see the bond that is so real,
I hope you know that you are very dear
And I will always love you, every day of the year.

—*Kristen Marie Whittaker*

Silk

Like syllables sifted through silk,
Your siren brew seeps sweetly down,
BON FILTRE falling from afar,
Inciting me to live again.
Like syllables sifted through sleep,
It percolates upon my mind,
Nectar from some remoter star,
Enticing me to give again.
And as I daily drift in and out of dreams buffered by reality,
This gift, it seems, affords tranquillity...

But with returned lucidity,
The sudden, certain irony
Becomes abundant clear to me —
That syllables sifted through sleep,
Sibilant and sibyllate,
Alone in me originate,
In needs perverse and obstinate,
In that relentless circle-eight
Where no new life can generate,
Only syllables sifted through silk.

—*Patricia Falanga*

After We Loved

You sleep,
your skin pulsates, and glows softly
in the silent of the night.

You sleep,
we madly drank ours kisses tonight,
and we whispered secrets without words, sweetly.

And now,
your womb,
your hands,
your brow,
and your eyes are asleep.
Your pulse sounds faintly,
and your song is silent.

Weary and discharged the soul quietens.
Pulsates in the shadows our muffled desire,
and no clues were left since we resembled fire,
and now,
you only sleep.

—*Humberto Claveria*

"Granddaughter"

How I loved you when you were born.
Your soft as peaches skin adorne.
The smiles you gave to me,
reminded me of a cherished gift to see.
When your hair formed into baby curls,
I knew you would send the boys awhirl.
The pitter-patter of your tiny feet,
gave me a joy that could not be beat.
Your hugs and kisses made my day.
I prayed that they would never go away.
Wanting to help me all you could
made me feel like someone good.
Listening to your point of view,
painted a picture of my school days anew.
Seeing you looking out the window through the curtain,
knowing I would be coming to visit for certain.
Even when you were bad,
and made me feel sad.
I still held you deep in my heart,
Attached to you right from the start.

—*Kathleen I. Braz*

Hey Poseidon

Hey poseidon fella, shake a leg!
You're looking kinda glum
You're much to placid to be at all like a sea
I know you're old and seen too much — but dat ain't no excuse.

I'd like to pump you full of pills
Vitamin E for energy,
Then you'd romp and pound the shore, you'd frolic and cajole.
You'd certainly be, if you think on it,
a happier kind of sea.

My thanks young man for concern so deep
It's needed not at all.
I've not forgotten what I am through all these long years.

If you need to know why I'm so still
This is all I'll say:
I've laboured long and toiled very hard
To look so smooth and calm.
No young one I've not forgotten what I am
But am this way and so shall remain
So my beloved man might see,
The man they've lost in them.

—*Gregory Calinikos*

How The Symbol Designating The Ratio Of The Circumference Of A Circle

To Its Diameter Introduces Himself At A Party

I Pi.

—*Andrew Jason Summers*

Mr. Alibi

A deed is committed, that leaves you dimwitted,
a deed of slyness and mischief,
and you are bewildered, dumbfounded and stunned,
at the mishap of having no witness.
Oh who didn't do it and whom didn't do it
and neither did when or how.
So who did do it, and whom did do it,
and when and most certainly how?
Who, whom, when and how, are all of the suspects now,
and each with excuses and all of them sly,
and all of them quotes from
Mr. Alibi.

—*Arthur E. Jefferson*

The Book

Book is like a house,
The words-Bricks arranged and glued
in a meticulous manner,
would look at the end
like a Book-House.

—*Ranvir Singh*

English

English is no fun.
The work is never done.
English is boring
Cause you hear people snoring

—*Kimberly Ellis*

Untitled

I love you, but you know not
The years pass
But you know not
The kids are here
But you know not
I am here
But I am here you know not
I am here
And you acknowledge
But you know not
But I am here
You do not understand

—*Len Weaver*

About Pride

I'll give you an opinion,
then I'll let you decide
The thing that hurts us most in life
is often our own foolish pride.
How many people will argue
just to get the upper hand?
Being right or wrong doesn't matter,
it's taking the tougher stand.

How many friendships are lost
because of some unnecessary fight?
When all it takes is the wisdom
of saying, "I think you're right."

How often do we cheat ourselves
where our knowledge could apply?
Because of a fear of failing,
we never really try.

These things may seem insignificant
but sometimes it's important to know.
You may have to set pride aside,
if you are to continue to grow.

—*John C. Prichard*

The One And Only

I came off no assembly line,
There's only one of me,
Most people say "Thank God for that."
But the trouble is, you see,
There's only me that knows myself,
Others know me not,
They criticise for this and that,
But don't suggest a lot.
Now with myself, I've come this far,
Guess I'll continue to the end,
Just stumble on from day to day,
With me, I'm my best friend.

—*Duncan Callander*

The First Time

On the trodden path
there was a grown blue heron
leaving the first marsh.

Boating fishermen
soon disappeared in the cove
of the distant shore.

A first cast backlashed
over the trestle through cracks
of the railroad tiles.

One, two, three good casts
next to the shore's lily pads
gave a joyful time.

No even a bite
the fishing line soon tangled
as a plane flew by.

Seen was high water
covering the winter reeds
gone for the first time.

—*Pierre A. LeBlanc (1921 -)*

Cry For Life

One fine summer day,
there was a lady,
Who was trying to say,
She is going to have a baby.

Was she very glad
To have this baby?
Or was she sad?
She just replied, "May be."

When the time came,
She was scared,
And didn't feel the same,
Did she really care?

Suddenly, there was a loud cry,
The birth of a new born baby,
Trying to tell us it didn't want to die,
Please love me, dear lady.

There was I upon this earth,
Feeling so great
To have this safe birth,
And to be loved by my mate.

—*Marc Geirnaert*

Daily Thanks

At the beginning of each day
There's many things to do,
First you Thank and Praise the Lord
For the breath He breathed in you.
Then you Thank Him for the Love
He's given you to share
Go out into the world each day
Let people see you care.
Thank Him for the blessings
That He's bestowed on you
Then go about your daily chores
With His Hand guiding you!
Thank Him when your day is done
For you have tried your best
To follow in the path He's shown
and now it's time to rest.

—*Kathy Huntley*

Teenage Love

Everyone thinks they know love.
They think it's like a white dove.
Clear as crystal, thin as ice.
No one uses the word sacrifice.

—*John A. Duffy*

One Nation

They tore down the wall,
They tore down the barbed wire,
They overflowed our towns,
They were laughing, they were free.

We welcomed them,
We gave them bananas,
We gave them money,
We celebrated with them.

They have no work at home,
We don't give them work here,
They live in a dreary environment,
We enjoy our spare time.

They are poor, we are not.
Nothing changes
Though we are one nation.

—*Achim Strass*

My Parents

My parents are really cool.
They try to understand me.
They're just one of us.
They don't hassle or fuss,
much that is.

They aren't like other parents.
They are themselves.
They let me be free,
To find the real me,
most of the time.

They aren't perfect they know.
But they don't try to be.
They help me understand,
As much as I can,
as much that is.

They aren't scared to cry in
front of me.
They show their feelings for me.
And that is what I like to see.
That is all of the time!

—*Jane Talley Shacklette*

Tomorrow

Go, you are free.
They want you to be happy.
So go and be.

Just think of today as tomorrow.
Leave behind the pain,
and leave behind the sorrow.

Just be glad of what you got,
Even though it's not much,
Even though it's not a lot.

Forget how you were always sad.
Forget all that pain,
and just be glad.

And now you are free.
So go and be happy.
So go and be.

—*Kimberly Joy Baumruck*

The Goddess True But Forgotten

Afraid of your tripartite face,
They've banished you away,
Forgetting your true grace.

But we abide your day
And know your form at night.
We watch you grow and die.

Your cycle is the light
Which your son gods deny.
But you ignore this slight.

For the End they all vie;
You calmly say "repeat",
While they rush, run and hie.

They tamp their feet and bleat;
Reborn again, you grow;
Amazes us this feat.

The riddle's in your show
To understand and know
How seamlessly you sew.

—*Kirt Dreher*

Imagination

Imagination is a wonderful
thing.
Without imagination you couldn't
do anything
Imagination is all in our mind.
We use it daily, time after time.
Many inventions are produced by
imagination.
Everyone likes to imagine the
future.
Toddlers imagine the boogie man.
While other kids imagine new
bikes and games.
Parents imagine winning the
lottery.
Don't forget to imagine wonderful
things.
Because with imagination you
can imagine anything.

—*Jovan McClinton*

Lonely Writer

With my pencil in my hand,
Thinking about my man,
I start to wonder who I am.
As time goes slowly by,
Often I find myself starting to cry.
I wonder why my dreams can't fly.
I'm all alone again.
Wish I had a friend.
Help me through these lonely days ahead,
For without your help, I'm surely dead.
I can dream of star dust.
Let memories hold me if they must,
But I'll still miss your touch.
I'll always miss you very much.

—*Judy Ruppert*

Young Flirters

Who loves warmth that flutters
Through a heart that unravels like
A wild flower in the morning?

—*Kathleen Sarce*

Our Heritage

A land full of opportunities
This wonderful heritage of ours
A land full of hope and promise
Requiring no pledges or vows

For this is a land of freedom
Of cities and rich country soil
Waiting to give up a harvest
As a reward to faith and to toil

The mountains, the valleys, the rivers
The beaches, and glistening sand
the wonderful flora and fauna
Make up this beautiful land

And we proudly call it Australia
This land of sunshine and scope
This land full of opportunity
Of happiness, laughter and hope

—*Cecil J. Bowers*

Loving You Forever

We argue, we fight
Through day, and through night
We shout, we yell
We put each other through hell
We swear and we cuss

The day is over
We barely spoke
The day is over
Our hearts are broke
What is happening to us

We hug, we kiss
We're so sorry for this
We make up forever
We will fight again — never

I love you friend
I'm so sorry for my wrong
I love you friend
For being so strong

Loving you forever!

—*Brandi-Marie Bailey*

Autumn Memories

As specks of sunlight trickle down
Through fiery, dancing leaves of gold
My heart goes racing through the years
Back to the memories that I hold

Memories of cold, sharp mornings
When the grass has turned to white
Glistening with the coat of crystals
That softly cloaked it in the night

Memories of woodsmoke in the air
Hanging gently on the noonday wind
Drifting off to the horizon
In a sky that had no end

Memories of thankful farmers
The work of harvest nearly through
Treading slowly, homeward bound
Through the evening fields of dew

These memories are alive and well
My mind can still recall with ease
Sweet images from long ago
My precious autumn memories

—*Jerry L. Richards*

Sacrament

Now -
Time, suspended like
a molten jewel
On the glass of eternity
Trembles
as it slides
and vanishes into
another night.
Spirit
one moment closer
to freedom,
Knows
Sees
Feels ....
Until tomorrow.

—*Angela Kelly*

One Wish

Would you like to come
to Heaven with me.
Stay with me awhile.
If you could come
to Heaven with me,
It would really
make me smile.

I'm not afraid to go
but don't send me
on my own.
If you could come
to Heaven with me
I wouldn't feel so far
from home.

—*Doris LeRoux*

Untitled

Oh my love how I miss you
To hold you to kiss you
To be with you

How I long to be in your arms
Again
To feel your warm sweet breath
And your tender lips on mine

Why can I not find true love
I am so lonely all a lone

No one to love no one to talk to
Care for or to be with

How I wish God would bless me
And send me an angel from heaven
Maybe he did

But because I was not a saint
He send you away

—*K D M Cooper*

Dawn

You and I
together
with the rising
sun
spinning a tale
of light
and heat

—*Miriam Wamwea*

Untitled

Death is known to some as scary,
To others, a place of rest.
To me death is a peaceful state,
Where no one is the best.

Death is a feeling of relaxation,
Where no one puts you down.
Everyone is seen as equal,
In appearance, there is no match.

Inner beauty is what counts in death,
No racism, poverty, or violence.
Happiness plays a big role there,
As sadness here on earth.

For me, I wait to die,
To live for only death.
To devote my life, to serve my time.
On this cruel planet which I reside.

Death is known to some as scary;
To others a place of rest.
To me death is a peaceful state,
For me, I wait to die.

—*Kim Dowdy*

Nature

The blossoms on the trees burst forth
To scent the air with Spring
And in the sky - so clear above
The birds are taking wing.

The sun shines down to kiss the ground
And release it from the cold
And ditches run like rivers deep
Along the country roads

The sun descends the western sky
And a chill will touch the night
But in the morning - once again
The sun will shine so bright

As winter fades and spring arrives
We will look on all things new
And marvel at what nature's done
But how? - we have no clue!

—*Juanita Loonan*

Different!

God made people
to think and choose

God made sure
that we're not the same

God made colours
black and white

God made sexes
Women and men

So if God had
wanted us to be the same

He would have meant it
to be that way.

—*Catherine Margaret O'Hagan*

Q. B. Q.

Life is a play and we act out our part,
To try not to hurt,
That could be a start,
To please where we can,
Enjoy what you do,
To make someone smile,
Before your life is through,
There's no room for hate,
Jealousy or lust,
And love is a feeling of
happiness and trust,
The length of one's life is not
Measured by flight,
But quality before quantity
has got to be right.

—*Colclough*

Today

Today, I walked in a field of glory.
Today, I forgot about my worry.
Today, I walked close by your side
Today, I forgot about my pride
Today, I held your hand in mine
Today, I forgot about that time
Today, I touched your sweet face
Today, I forgot that empty place
Today, I reached and touched your hair
Today, I forgot about despair.
Today, I pressed you to my breast
Today, I know my soul can rest
Today, I whispered I love you
Today, I forgot you made me blue
Today, I reached and held you fast
Today, I forgot about the past
Today, I kissed your lips again
Today, I forgot about the pain
Today, I opened up my heart
Today, I know we'll never part.

—*Evelyn Thompson*

God's Gift

As you go across life's meadow,
toward the setting sun.
Stop and smell the roses,
Enjoy them every one.

Slowly stand and look about,
and see what God has made.
Things for you to see and love,
not for sale or trade.

City's are made by the hand of man,
many things there to see.
But for all our fine builders,
not one can make a tree.

Stand on a lofty mountain,
look across the salty sea.
This is Mother Nature
Gods gift to you and me.

—*Kay Aiello*

Civilized Struggle

Awakened moth from shadowed curtain
    Trapped behind the window pane
Flits from corner to another—
    Grievous struggle done in vain.
Despite the lure of sunlit mansions,
    Seductive width of azure sky;
Fragile wings are no death victor.
    Its last appeal a silent cry.

Consider man—a mortal creature
    History made of cultures past—
Pity not the moths now vanquished,
    But those confined behind the glass.

—*Donnis Coffey*

Katherine

Arid leaf spilt off the
Tree, dust of stars worn still.
A gold seed, gold mined in
Countenance, hers was the
Courser. Maturation
Sparked departure, now clear
Voice, spoken breeze, blue-eyed,
Cleft sown in galaxies,
She dines the hills, tine and
Spoon. A relentless friend,
Slender leaf shot green, gone
Galloping in the spring.

—*Barbara Lund*

Untitled

To be afraid or not be afraid is a
    troubling question guided by
fear of the unknown and an awareness of
        the courage it
        takes to overcome!
    In the midst of such stillness
    and tension, one wonders about
    death and all its ramifications.
    Until the last instant approaches,
    then pleasantly, but unexpectedly,
    one envisions happiness and
everlasting life, thus the question...
        To be afraid or not be
        afraid is answered.
    So, let the battle begin!

—*David G. Greeley*

And

And I walk over the table.
Turning on the electric light
I sit down and begin to read.
The walls disappear
and the furniture melts away.
I sit all alone suspended in air,
then I too vanish.
After tiring of reading
I lay down my book,
put on my sweatshirt
and leaning over the couch
pick up the keys.
While leaving the room
I stumble over the doorstep,
and enter the darkened corridor...

—*John D. Moore*

Null And Void

Shoulders hunched against the cold,
Trying not to grow too old
Too fast too soon
Too late

Stepping closer to the gate
It opens wide,
He steps inside

The burial ground
Receives its daily blood
Expectant, gorged.
Partial shapes gather, to host
A former man
Whose pride has gone

In the face of death's disgrace
Stale flowers hail his last

In the false light of the moon
By its chill, silverous beam
Is formed a mask of stone.

Eyeless in the dewy grass,
Ghosted features curse the morn
        —*Paul Harris*

In Memory

Taken from your suffering world
T'was a blessing in disguise
Your body left behind to mourn
while your spirit soars the skies

Those who use your name in vain
Dare to go where demons delve
For you now live immune to pain
They must answer for themselves

I live on, with conscience clear
In knowing I done my very best
To give, not take, when it need be
As we lay you down to rest
        —*Karen K. Lyon-Pingleton*

Rivers Of Love

        Love is
    Two rivers finally meeting
After an eternity of loneliness
    In a desolate place
        Called "Nowhere."

    Their waters
Swirl and twirl together
'Til they flow as one
        Never to ever
Be totally separate again

    Pieces of one
    Shall always be
    Part of the other.

    And so it is
    With you and I.
    —*Laurie Knight-Davies*

Prologue

I let his hands play on me..
Until he felt the need.
And know man's only claim to paradise,
Is himself in me..

Story
She lays in the grass,
away from the creepers,
away from the night watchman,
who crawls in the dark.
She's painted formally,
her body in pose,
and waits the invasion
of a man made rose...

Epilogue
Creep the incessant flowing of words,
He shakes the wisdom from his crotch
No more looking through rose coloured
glasses.
        —*S. F. Collins*

The Hawk

Soaring graceful in the sky,
        Untouched
        Free.
    Wings gliding softly,
    Through turbulent airs.
        And then
        Suddenly,
    Its prey sighted,
The hawk dives earthward.
        Closer,
        Quietly,
    Not a sound is made
        But a whisper.
        And then
        It is gone,
    To rise once again
And soar triumphantly.
    Faster, higher,
Wings spread once more
    On gentle winds.
    —*Belinda Verhage*

Petals Of Freedom

Love is a flower
unveiling in time
its true form of elegance
transcending the mime

Its peace and serenity
lie dormant for a while
foreseeing the season
to deliver its smile

As each little petal
unfolds in pure grace
we're shown its beauty
through its colorful face

Delicate like silk
magnificence indeed
great promise and balance
the foundation a seed

Discover the garden
and share the delight
that the flower within
will always be right
        —*Robert E. Matte*

A Castle That Is Mine

Up high,
    Up far away,
        In a castle that is mine,
I search for your face,
        your caring words.
Up high,
    Up far away,
        In a castle that is mine,
I search for...
        Us.
        —*Jasmine Morgan*

Night Walk

Pale shadows cast an eerie pall
Upon familiar sights;
Old buildings take on a ghost-like look
while farther down the street
bright lights beckon to the passerby,
offering respite from humdrum solitude.
There are some people nicely dressed
and gesturing wildly,
the heady pulsations
From the open door of a nearby bistro
drowning out their words
and causing them to appear voiceless
from a distance.
Still farther down the street,
I pass once more into the shadows
now heavier
into the tranquility I have sought
Until at last I can surrender to the silence
in the cool still of the darkening night.
        —*Hugh MacPherson*

Waiting

Waiting
Waiting
Waiting
Forever waiting
What for . . . I know not
When for . . . I know not
Just waiting
Waiting waiting
And in my dreams just waiting
All around me grey just grey
A figure in the distance waiting
Watching and waiting
Now moving slowly closer
The grey turns to black
The waiting getting quicker
The black getting thicker
The figure now absorbing me
All gone now
Dead.
        —*Sarita Callender*

Figures

Once we walked hand in hand,
    two figures as one in the horizon.
As the earth rotated and time
    passed, it seems the horizon got
higher and higher.
All that was left was two figures
walking; not hand in hand as
one; but two separate figures
stretching, grasping, reaching to
bring back' that horizon to be as one
        —*Karen J. Steurrys*

I See Us

I see us walking hand in hand,
walking barefoot in the sand.
I see us kissing goodnight,
as we sit in the moonlight.
I see our love begin to grow fast,
I pray that it might last.
I see us dreaming as one,
as we both go out and have fun.
I see us wishing on the stars,
hoping everything will be ours.
I see our dreams unfold,
your love for me is getting old.
I see us drifting apart,
love is like a fading piece of art.
I see us hiding our true feelings,
this time there is no healings.
I see us as two,
separate, apart like the cold morning dew.
I see us as friends,
trying to make amends.

—Judy Kay Balint

You And I

Hand on hand you and I
walking toward the rising sun...
where threads of morning dew spray
the pace of nature on the run.
Leaving whatever it is behind
as true lovers often do.
Embarking up to a distant sky
and float across the blue
changing warm embraces up high.
Traveling lovers lane
of bliss and joy sublime.
Forgetting there is
a thing known as life.
Come hold my hand
and in a passing breeze
lets romance upon a star.
I can see so many of them
right there where you are.
Together you and I will find
the golden gate to paradise.

—Julio J. Perez

Untitled

Heave Ho! Work and Woe!
War for freedom on it goes.
Young me who strive for education,
All their songs od dedication.
Stock market, on it rises,
Then crashes with many surprises.
Innocent babes, born every day,
Problems ahead, for them will lay.
All this work, and all this toil
When the grave is but the goal.

—Janice Poglitsch

Chalkboard

Large green house
With letter people on it.
Who come in bunches or in pair.
They check in and they check out.
They appear in the day and if
They are lucky stay all night.

—Kirsten Jurgensen

Peace Is Best

Peace is peace
War is war
  Let us have peace instead
    All the world will jump for joy.
  not that many will be dead,.
    A silvery song—
      A heartfelt sigh-
        A bouquet and a kiss.
          The world will cheer—
            The tears will stop—
              carnage we must Miss.

  Good-bye to hate—
Good-bye to strife—
    there will be—
      laughter, happiness—
      Love, prayers—happy days

For it is not too late.

—Marilyn B. Rutter

Comrades

When we were boys
we fought our comrades in the sand
beneath the tree that use to stand
outside the school. And then
we laughed, when
  we were boys.

Now we are men.
We fought again, but side by side.
In other lands our comrades died
beside us. And somehow
we wept, now
  we are men.

—David Townley Williams

Untitled

When we were young
We were always together
We'd argue and play
In all kinds of weather
But now we have grown
And have lives on our own
I've never forgot
The love we've both known
My sister dear sister
I love you
Don't say it, I know
That you love me too
We've both grown apart
In so many ways
But together forever
In yesterdays.

—Debby Jean McLeod

Ice Trees

From my office window after dark,
when the sky is Maxfield Parrish blue,
I see the glittering skeletons
the ice storm left, where the
bare trees were.

The desolation of the icy darkness
seeps through desire and memory
and leaves an apprehension
no laughter can dispel.

—Kathleen McLane

Papercut

In just one of your lives,
we were but a small, quick mistake.

The psychic leaned forward,
her long, graceful hands consoling:
The card bore a heart with three swords.

She said you would be my last test.

And so I stood,
like Christ in Gethsemane,
as you (unintentional devil)
smiled across the grass,
painting visions of warmth in your arms.

It took the strength of God
for me to break the silence
of you holding a finger to your lips,
beckoning,
stealing my breath like a cat from a baby.

—Dawn E. Clark

Forever

The gazebo at midnight.
We were to meet for a rendezvous.
Someone would notice a light.
His note read, "Just me and you."
As through the garden I ran
The rain began.
I reached my destination.
Yet to my consternation,
Found my love was not to be seen;
But between
The rail
And stair
A white rose
Of forever
Lying there.

—Kathryn E. Lane

Only You

Only you....
  were always there,
Only you...
  would always care.
Only you...
  knew when I was blue,
Only you...
  could I tell my heart to.
Only you...
  were there when I didn't know why,
Only you...
  were there to help me try.
Only you...
  could ever see-
  everything inside of me.

—Kim M. Pilz

The Hawk

He sails on high
With gallant wing,
His savage cry
It shrieks, it screams.

His form calls death,
And eyes in search,
For earthly prey
And place to perch.

—Kenneth Phillip Jones

Little Joys

A new addition
What a joy
Never seems to matter
Whether a girl or a boy

Sugar and spice
And all things nice
Makes the little things seem
Very special, times twice

At times you may feel
At an end with the world
But just take a few moments
And think of that little girl

A precious little one
To help you both see
All of life's little joys
The way God meant them to be

—*Jackie H. Sparks*

Pennies

When a man's young,
What does he need?
Pennies in his hand
For friends to see.

When a man's older,
What does he need?
Pennies in his pocket
To help him feed.

When a man dies,
What does he need?
Pennies on his eyes
To help him sleep.

—*M. Barkhouse*

His Eyes

My eyes have seen
What his have yet to see
And yet there is so much,
For him to teach me.

He has the eyes of innocence
And I've the eyes of age
My eyes have seen the world
And his are full of grace.

His eyes are filled with a kindness
You don't find just anywhere
To know a few like him
Is so very rare.

He's gentle and caring
His heart is filled with a love
He doesn't mind sharing.

His eyes are filled with excitement
At the things he sees around him
There is a certain wonderment
As the world moves about him.

—*Judy Tiekamp*

Autumn

The leaves fall today,
winter knocks and says he's here,
autumn cries a tear.

—*James Hanson*

Yesterday

Tomorrow I'll do
What I can for mankind,
I'll mend the fences
I tore down...
    yesterday.

I'll fix the broken pieces
Of the life I left behind,
I'll gather up
My memories of...
    yesterday.

Tomorrow I'll do for others
The things I missed today,
I'll correct the mistakes
I made...
    yesterday.

And all the things
I do today
Will be the things
I should have done...
    yesterday.

—*Kathy Becker*

I Aspire

I aspire not to be;
What you'd have me be,
I aspire not to be;
What you'd desire me be,
I aspire not to be;
What you'd make of me,
I aspire not to be;
That which you'd design for me,
I aspire not to be;
Whatever you'd deem me be,
I aspire to be me.

—*Josephine Paris*

Paki!

Paki!
What's that!
That's you!

But I don't walk the walk
or talk the talk.

I don't listen to the music
I don't stay with that clique!

Paki!

Why? I don't wear the clothes
I don't pose the pose

I don't sing their praise
I'm not of that race!
Why?

Paki!

I don't care about your name
I don't care about your game,
Your place of birth
or what you're worth
I don't even care about your kin
All that matters to me...
is the color of your skin.

—*Paul Nazareth*

Sorry Will Suffice

Why do we always say "Sorry"?
When another word should replace.
Something with more regret,
Even emphasizing disgrace.

Yet there it stands waiting,
At the front of the queue.
Bland and seemingly unscripted,
Feebly trying to undo.

Notorious for making worse,
Before the healing can begin.
Creating abusive thoughts,
Repeatedly committing sin.

So why waste our breath,
On this unprincipled word.
Who is next in the queue,
To cool the boiling blood?

—*George Henderson Baxter*

Fatherhood

My child gives me confusion
When he cries at night
What could be wrong?
Is he all right?

He looks kind of sick
He doesn't look well
What's wrong with him?
How can I tell?

I go and seek some help
Got to find a cure
I've got to act fast
This moment is a blur

My child smiles at me
To let me know he's at right
I love my child
He gives me delight

—*Brent Haverkamp*

Sex In A '78 Chevette

I never imagined
when I came to college
and said good-bye to my friends,
my parents
and my 12 yr. old teddy bear
that I would be here
slouched in a silver '78 Chevette
earning an "A"
in your spanish class,
your wedding band
hidden within the darkness.

—*Donna Marie Moriconi*

Spring

I love the springtime
with all its new beginnings
        summer
Is such a beautiful time of year
        fall
Is spectacular with leaves
    in every color
        and Lord
even winter isn't so bad
    If I could only
    see spring again.

—*Kathy Drapeau*

Untitled

It's a constant reminder
When I see that face
Of all my mishaps
And human disgrace

When I see that isle
And that bloody white lace
Amidst bloody white candles
I see that face

Dearly beloved, we are gathered here
To marry this woman
Though she's full of fear

Her face turns to alabaster
As the bridegroom awaits
To take his lovely bride home

To take her in his arms
And squeeze her to death
Do us part

As veins of love and hate
Run right through
Her bloody heart

—*Kelli Bates*

Things That I Hate

I hate the beach
When I'm covered in oil
I hate dirty kids
All covered in soil

I hate tight shoes
That nip my toe's
I hate dirty habits
Like picking your nose

I hate dogs that bark
And wake me up
I hate drinking tea
From a dirty old cup

I hate spending money
Especially my own
I hate aunts and uncles
Who say "Ain't you grown"

There's not much I like
Not much at all
I hate most everything
I hate you all.

—*C. J. Watts*

Ode

Noble is the night
with its inky veils, advancing
to halt the battlegrounds
of day

Bountiful, the night
as the last of golden tufts succumb
to whippoorwills
in rhinestone skies

Generous, the night
as it narrows with its calm
our thoughts
to love, and other graces

—*Joseph Higareda*

Daddy's Hands

My Daddy's hands fixed "Santa's" toys
when they would break from play,
They fixed all things so I'd enjoy
my childhood every day!

My Daddy's hands they are quite strong
from years of toil and strain,
They worked to keep me from all wrong
and save me from all pain!

My Daddy's hands fought in a war
so I could live life free,
They battled odds one can't ignore
for people just like me!

My Daddy's hands with all their might
have done all that I ask,
They've always helped set things aright
no matter what the task!

My Daddy's hands are loved by me
for all that they have done,
I love them more each day you see
with every rising sun!

—*Judy J. Leago*

I Am Still Me

It's times like these,
when things go bad,
People look at me
with thoughts so sad.
If I could only
make them see,
That though I am ill,
I am still ME!
I have a lot to live for,
And lots to do!
So don't you dare
Give up; any of you!
I love you all!
And this you'll see,
That I am not cancer!
I am still ME!

—*Sandra Wickstrom*

Mother

A friend to me she had always been
When things seemed dark and cold within
I think of her now in a different way
And love her more with each new day.

I wonder how she lived her life
When times were hard and full of strife
When I was lost and so unsure
She always made me feel secure.

I only hope she somehow knows
How much her love helped me grow
I see her face and feel her near
And know there is never anything to fear.

She gave a great gift to me
A gift some children never see
She gave her love for so many years
Through happy days and days of tears.

And to my children I hope to be
As special as she was to me
My Mother's love will always be
The greatest strength she gave to me.

—*Karen Renee Newman*

Loss

Why do I live,
When you are gone?
I smile,
Yet behind my eyes
A waterfall of radiant tears
Society dammed.
Why does my heart beat
So fiercely,
While your heart is silent?
How can life go on,
Where there is none in you?
More than life itself,
I loved you.
Yet still I live.
You could have
Taken me.

—*Fi Livings*

An Ode To Rheumatoid Arthritis

You know the pain is dull
When you don't do anything at all
But the ache is still there
When you sit in a chair

You know the pain is light
When it hurts to reach for the light
Or to comb your locks
Or to take off your socks

You know the pain is severe
When you open a beer
And you have to sit
To get over it.

But you know the pain is much more
When you can't open the door
And you sit and curse at your maker
When you can't hold on to the toilet paper.

—*Bruce M. Patterson*

Daughter

How beautiful you was,
When you was born,
But more later,
With God you left.

Lovely daughter,
Which I never will forget.
In which I didn't see but,
With you I will be.

Daughter from my soul
Now you're not here,
Because you left,
With the angel to take a walk,

Lovely daughter
I will never forget you,
Even if you're not here,
My life has to continue.

—*Juan Rivera*

Clocks

Our bodies are like clocks in many ways
with out parts performing many days,
Our bodies are like the well tuned gears,
that move many different years.
Like a clock our bodies are,
shining like the many stars.
The clock with many parts,
ticks diligently like our own hearts.

—*Kenny Howard*

"The Star" Where Have You Gone???

Where is that son I once knew
Where have you gone
What has happened to you?

Love I gave you in abundance
Why have you cast me in asundrance
What have I done,
What did I do,
To deserve the pain
You are putting me through?

No one, but no one
Will ever know
How much I love
And cherish you so

The pain is bitter
My God it's hard to bear
But remember, My Son,
I will always care!

—*Rosemary McKay*

A Wish

There's a cottage by the seaside
Where I wish to live with you;
Here I show you my desires,
And with passion thee I woe.

But my wish is vain and empty
And I call it fantasy;
Golden dream that my heart burdens,
Day and night sorrow to see.

There's a heart that's always sighing,
Planting roses of sweet smell,
But the ground grows only thistles
And it burns like floor of hell.

Oh! my wish is all tormenting
For I know it's but a dream.
This is life, a sweet chimera,
Flash of light, of sorrow beam.

—*Edward Zarb*

God's Love

I see it in the sunset
Where its beauty reaches the sky.
I see it in the gleaming moonlight
Where memories never die.

I see it in the sunrise
As it peaks over the hill.
I hear it in the robins song
Down near the old sawmill.

I see it in the pretty flowers
As they nod in the gentle breeze.
I see it in the high treetops.
As they wave and happily tease.

I see it in the rainbow
And in the mountain stream
I see it in the meadow
Where the sunlight beams.

I see it in life everlasting
When my life on earth is done
A happy reunion with loved ones
For long, who have been gone.

—*Helen Louise McMillan*

The Mountain

I am returned to the mountain
Wherefore I shall find my peace
I have journeyed far and plenty
Almost without cease.

For I have come to the mountain
Where herein lies my truest me
To relate to God in quietness
In a peaceful harmony.

As I am part of the mountain
Akin to flowers and trees
I will seek my blissful solitude
Quietly, in the gentle breeze.

From the inner depths of the mountain
I shall return to him on high
For the wind one day will whisk my soul
To God - 'up in the sky.

—*Joanna Debranski*

Lies

Truth is like a lone petal
Which floats away with the breeze
Like the stars of the twilight
Which fade into the dawn
Like the final goodbyes of the sun
Before it sinks into the horizon
- It is no more -
Tonight I shared
Tonight I felt discouraged
The anger which floweth out of control
Is like that of a swollen river
Forceful for a time, then peaceful again
A faith of teardrops released
A friend wiped away
Yesterday I had belief
Tonight, it vanished
Though I feel pity
Trust shall prevail again

—*Joyce M. Tremethick*

Praises Of The Blessed Virgin Mary

You are the blossoming Rod,
Which is the portal of God.
You are the celestial balm,
Who is the martyrdom's palm.
You are David's high Tower,
Who is girded with power.
You are the Deity's Shrine,
Which is the table divine.
You were to me a fortress,
In the days of my distress.
You are the ark of the new covenant,
For by the holy spirit you were pregnant.

You are the Queen of Heaven,
The elects' eternal rest's haven.
You are God's best and first Steward,
For which he gave you an eternal reward.
You are a Garden of pleasure,
For on earth you knew no leisure.
God made you dwell in his tabernacle,
For you are creation's pinnacle.

—*Godwins Ratlabala*

Tell Me

Indecisions everywhere,
Which way shall we turn.
Does this road lead to happiness?
Does this road lead to ruin?
Did yesterday teach lessons
To help us on our way,
Or do we have to start afresh
With each new day.
Is there a star above us
Showing us the way,
Or do we change our future
Where we decide to stay.
Help us to decipher
The reason for it all,
And thank our lucky stars above
For bringing us this far.

—*Aileen E. Britton*

Echoes

She
  Whispers a scream
  Laughs a cry
  Makes a statement
  Then asks why...

Why She
  Recites in silence
  Dreams awake
  Swims in sand
  But not a lake.

Alone
  When it's crowded
  In this barren room
  With sounds of laughter
  And echoes of doom.

—*Judy M. Joyce*

The Display

Balls of flame and fizzing fire
whizzing past the churches spire
shooting up into the cold night air
golden sparks spiralling every where.

Showers of crimson coloured stars
racing up to planet Mars
fountains of silver droplets
raining down
from catherine wheels
and honey bees crown.

Colours like you've never seen
orange, yellow, red and green
indigo, violet, bright blue and more
exploding rockets and sparklers galore.

Fireworks welcome New Years day
as the old year finally fades away
be sure not to miss this happy scene
when New Year arrives in a glimmer
of green.

—*Tessa Kerbel*

Untitled

A women can cry
  with not a tear in her eye
Yet you come to her heart
  it has fallen apart.

—*Marie Plante*

Knowing

Beautiful man of my heart
Who moves me like no other
You paint love's sweet dream
With colors from my soul
Creating eternity's rainbow
What about you, do I love you so?

We have no limits of time
To make love rhyme
We have been together before
Past lessons learned
Here now to gain strength
Not yet knowing, to what length?

My feelings for you beyond words
Something in the voices of singing birds
Your love to me such a prize
I see forever in your eyes
I surely need no proof
Yet, ask myself for the truth
Why does my soul, scream for you?

—*Kimberley Dicker*

The Thoughts Of A Little Rat

I am a great big rat
who sits on your own door mat
and eat up your lovely coloured mat
The master of the house called Pat
Never seem to like a rat who is fat
I make a terrible note of that
I am not afraid of any big cat
All day long where I sat
Stands the photo of a bat
The rains come pit-a-pat-pat
But I am not afraid of that
I hide behind the tat
In fear of a black bat
Come along you little bat
Who has never spat
On little friends of Master Pat
Tra-la-la I know the cat
Is frightened of my friendly little bat
Oh' goodbye you big black cat.

—*Evelyn Udawatte*

Guardian Angel

I sit upon the edge of a cloud
Wings draped around me
I gaze down at the planet below
My eyes become misty and tears
    begin to flow
Down there is earth and all mankind
Full of racism, greed and sorrow
If I could change the world around
I'd do it before tomorrow
But, who am I to set the pace
    for all mankind and the whole
    human race?
I'm but your guardian angel
I have a mission too
That is to help you cling to your
    hopes and dreams
And set the stage for you,
    Just you.

—*Gloria Peggy Lauzon*

Gift

Kisses of bronzed silk,
wisps of brocaded satin.

The essence of last night clings
to our minds, as we cling to
each other.

How priceless our experience was,
how wonderful those gifts were
that we shared.

Traces of gold cord, and remnants
of love frame this perfect memory.

The new side to us is irreplaceable;
a sentimental happiness, friendship,
and love replaces plain attraction,
and fondness.

We have a part of each other,
No one else shall ever be given
these same gifts.
I Love You!

—*Keely R. Bowen-Jones*

The Earth Shook When They Shook Hands

From afar with a decision
With a great passion they came,
While some in derision
Looked for someone to blame.

So they came from the east
To show the world that love mends
Broken ties with a feast,
When they shook their hands.

To those who denied
Such a wonder with dismay,
Their hearts were terrified
When clouds of war passed away.

While children are crying
For good things that are right,
Wretched men keep on denying
Ways of peace both day and night.

Hear, oh nations of goodwill
Peace; and to war say farewell,
For a courageous one said; "I will
Abide in peace with Israel."

—*Jesse Correia*

West Coast Of B.C.

Pacific Storm, you rage and roar
You dash the boats against the shore
Your very strength I gaze with ore
It chills my blood right to the core
The beauty of your mighty waves
Engulfs my thoughts, I am your slave
What you demand you always get
If your not treated with respect
At times your gentle as a lamb
I can go digging for some clams
I'll climb around the slippery rocks
To watch the flotsam, birds in flocks
They skim along the golden sands
Which I just love, but you command

—*Denys B. McLaughlin*

The Refugee

Wilted...she sits there
With an open stare,
Having walked all day,
Her world without song.

Dejected spirit....
Lying limp,
Like the dead child she left
On war-charred ground.

Myopic skin retracting
From encrusted red eyes,
She gazes upwards
Into a hazy sun.

Faded light absorbs
Into their liquid brown,
And she sighs at a memory
Of a stability she once knew.

With little hope,
She will travel on....
To a new place,
Where her heart doesn't belong.

—*Susan Jahme*

A Special Thanks

A thanks for all the love you shared
with every growing day.
To all the special moments spent
with us in times of play.

With early morning fishing trips
you kept a watchful eye,
and made us feel your comfort
by being by our sides.

When sickness came upon us three
always you were there,
to help us get back on our feet
and showed us that you cared.

Mother we could ask no more
then what you've done for us,
but with this thanks we give to you
we hope to show our love.

—*Evan Griffiths*

Breakout

Bark strapped to the prison-tree
withered branches scrape
scream to escape the light
I know their plight
to be free

Sun devours the waking hours
eats clouds and licks its lips
rainclaws grind
behind a storm powerless
to flee

Not all bend toward the rays but seek
shelter in the cool sane grays
shun the blinding orb of birth
the dearth of heart
love's bed of nails

Night of vengeance, lightning herds
shadows scar the moon
sex-starved tides rape the shore
I soar
above the tomb.

—*Michel Dinan*

Regeneration?

What's a human being
Without illusion
What's wrong
With a birth
Of yourself
—*Joseph Boekholt*

Morning Breeze

The soft sweet morning breeze
Woke the flowers from their dreams.
The warming sun was kissing
The dewdrops from their leaves.

The cherry trees were blooming,
The swallows flying high.
The blossoms were unfolding
Their beauty to the sky.

The air was full of music,
The bees having a ball.
It brought back memories
Of growing up and all.

So I went back in time
To love and darkest night.
The morning breeze then swept
My daydreams into flight.
—*Elizabeth Anasir*

Our Silent Hours

You can't understand it.
Womb to vagina or eons before
placental toe-sipping lakes
the last to light the natal gang's
banter idle as Pavese's sweet sweat
shadowily shaping us into wet
gneiss coenocytic to the
bone. It is an ending;
an autopsy. Gloves a fine white
to your purple measure us end
to end before the bassinet
or stuffed bear or body
bag silly as privates
teaching Melpomene her next
trade. Every year it's the same:
this cheap trick swaddling your
lyric phantasm and shiny new
head before the humdrum
explosion of one hundred
hundred.
—*Britt East*

The Fly

The fly on the wall, so innocent,
yet I hate him so,
is it because I know of germs,
what if I didn't know.
Would I watch the little fly,
whizzing around the room,
would I listen happily,
or still would I seal his doom.
So little fly I beg of you,
find somewhere else to fly,
because if you insist on staying here,
you will surely die.
What right have I to take your life,
why do I feel this way.
I'll open the window wide instead,
so you can fly away!

—*S. J. Browning*

Acknowledgement

Why did I listen to her?
  Would she sing part of my song?
Should I really take care?
  If her decision isn't strong.

She agreed on my saying,
  But her mind was somewhere else.
No attention she was paying,
  She acknowledged me with no sense.

Love they say is reciprocal,
  It is not a sending message,
One way love is too mortal,
  It has perhaps disadvantage.

I don't want to love anybody,
  Found I experience once more.
Echoes in my mind the same melody,
  Because my heart is still sore.

There is a great God I am sure,
  He will give a good judgment.
If my heart got one day cure,
  Wouldn't hear I any acknowledgement?
—*G. Hossein*

Never

Never say never, I said
years of hope and yearning
and then,
They said, never
disbelief, sorrow,.... acceptance
Never, I said

Then, faint stirrings
a wish, a dream, could it be?
Never, I said
They said, yes
months of wonder and anticipation

And then,
you were born
the overwhelming love
for you, of you,... forever
Yes, I said
Never say never
—*Leslie Lloyd*

A Midday Dream (June 12, 1991)

Just traveling along.
Yes you and me
Down the back roads
In our old Chevy.

I knew the day
That I met you
You were the one
To keep me company.

And now our little girl
Which makes us three
Going down the back roads
In our old Chevy.

We are so happy
All the world can see
Just the three of us
In our old Chevy.

You are just great
To her and to me
Going down the back roads
In our old Chevy.
—*Arthur W. Schuman*

My Other

I am torn in two
Yet I am one
And I hold on
For I have another.

And my other
Is so special
So dear,
I cannot lose.

He is near enough to touch
Near to hold
Near to be close to
Near to love.

He is my love
And he pulls me through
When I am torn in two
Yet am only one.
—*Virginia L. Wiebe*

Untitled

They all say the trees can wait
Yet I disagree.
For I do grow upon a branch,
And branches grow on me.

Whiltering away from the roots,
Smiling to hide the pain.
I feel the hurt in your eyes.
Frightened I might be the same.

I'll think of you when you fall,
Leaving without a trace.
You know you need a hero
So look behind your face.

The scream of silence did not wake
My cry falls on deaf ears.
I express my pain in many ways,
But not in human tears.

Nobody feels the way I do
Nobody see's the pain.
All alone on one branch
Nothing to lose or gain.
—*Tracie Olfrey*

Untitled

A man is weak,
yet kills his prey.

A deer is calm,
yet come what may.

The deer is still.
His body shakes.
He has no hope,
still chance he takes.

The man is eager.
The deer and he are one.
His gun is his courage.
His guilt is none.

The deer does die,
innocent and young.

The man is proud.
"A Challenge!" he sung.
—*Simone Lake*

My Sister, My Friend

You are my needs answered
You are the field I sow with love
And reap with thanksgiving

You are my board and my fireside
I come to you with my hunger
And seek you for peace

When you speak your mind, my friend
I fear not the "nay" in my own mind
Nor do I withhold the "aye"

And when you are silent
My heart ceases not
To listen to your heart

For without words in friendship
All thoughts
All desires
All expectations
Are boon
And shared with joy
That is unacclaimed!

—*Yasmin Mawji*

Hillary Jean

Just like a little cherub
You came into our lives.

We all knew we would love you
You flashed your pretty eyes.

Your mommy and your daddy
They gave their heart and soul.

They tried their best to help you
Always ready to console.

Your life was not an easy one
Your trials every day.

You showed us how to love you
And how to have your way.

Our hearts will always wonder
The meaning of it all.

Our faith will be much stronger
We know we gave our all.

And now we must surrender
Our hearts and yes your soul.

You gave us much to hope for
And now you have it all.

—*Kay Rourke*

Love

Love is a wonderful feeling,
You cannot taste, touch, or
see it,
But it's there.
Love is happiness and joy,
Love is a girl and a boy.
Love is everlasting.

—*Karen Taylor*

How Can You?

How (Erica) can
   you (my lover) walk
      out (standing) on
         me, (there) my
            friend (laughing)?

—*Judith Campbell*

Decisions

Decisions must be made
You can't keep running from them.
You know what the first must be.
You have to see yourself as the most
   important person in your life.
So much time has been invested -
   don't waste it.
You have seen the changes.
Don't you want to see what else
   there is inside you?
You like what you now see?
What other wonderful facets have
   not yet emerged?
The fear of what you truly are
   has faded.
Let it disappear.
You're not going to be the thorny
   stem of the rose...
      but its blossom,
Continuously and forever blooming.

—*Kathryn Verbage Lane*

I Realise

I suddenly know what to do.
You give me unexpected incentive
to follow instinct and
reject reliance you await.
Release is instant, thought
my own and air to breath.

I'm finding now a routine
long forgotten. Hidden trust
and strength arising, had
threatened to engulf me.
Now encouraged, muted voices,
don't try to silence them.

—*Helen Waddell*

To Death

Death! You are cruel!
You taught me tears, sorrow and pain
I prayed to God
To give my life to the dead
But God didn't hear my prayer
And I learned
That God has made this world incomplete.
Death! You are cruel!
But you taught me the reality of life.

—*Izumi Abe*

The Milky Way

How I miss decorating
            your
   corridors of power
those hours we spent
defeating the night;
   sailing ship
      becalmed and
         rudderless-
            love's
      heavenly
         shower
      cascading,
   then melting inside
   cairo's loneliest
      valentine....

—*Rene A. Catindig*

Momma

Mamma, where were you when I needed
you? Tell me momma please.

Mamma, why didn't you hold me when I
screamed in the night?

Mamma, why didn't you console me when
I was hurt and confused?

Mamma, why weren't you there to help
me that day when I woke up and found
that I was becoming a woman?

Mamma, why didn't you listen when I
needed to be heard?

Mamma, why didn't you tell me falling
in love would be a painful event?

Mamma, why didn't you prepare me for
all the trials and tribulations that
go with life?

Mamma, why didn't you show me the love
that I deserve?

Momma, please tell me why?

—*Juliet L. Pate*

Phone Call

Hello.
You'll be where?
Tomorrow.
Five hundred miles.
Weekend traffic.
Gas,
Food,
$ $.
Five hundred miles for a hug.

I used to get them every day
from little hands
sticky with peanut butter.
And then, just once
from grown up hands
clutching a white bouquet.

Only five hundred —
Of course I'll be there.
See you Sweetheart.
Take care Dad.

—*Lloyd Kitching (Carman, MB, Canada)*

Maundy Thursday

I saw it tonight, Lord,
Your altar stripped and bare.
It spoke to me
While I knelt in prayer
It told me what life would be
Without you there -
Empty, stark, forsaken.
I felt grieved.
I shed a tear.
Then my soul
Was relieved.
For I recalled
The empty grave,
My soul to save!

—*Elizabeth Burrows*

Narcissistic Reflections

So you got your freedom.
Your freedom to do
Whatever you wanted
Whoever you wanted
Whenever you wanted.

By your choice
You chose
Lust over love
firewater over coffee
one nighters over
lifetime commitment.

Who's perfect?
Not me.
Who loves you so much?
Me.

—*C. Southward*

Sweet Little Daisy

Sweet little daisy open wide,
your petals white and fair.
The world is bright with morning light,
and gentle cool fresh air.

See the gifts the morning brings,
the diamond drops of dew.
The emerald grass is clean and crisp,
it smells so fresh and new.

Sweet little daisy open wide,
display your golden face.
See the rainbow colours bright,
and the spider's web of lace.

Watch the clouds so plump and soft,
They're slowly drifting by.
Each one, in time, will melt into,
the warm blue sapphire sky.

Sweet little daisy open wide,
please share these gifts with me.
So many wonders to be seen,
yet none as fine as thee.

—*Kay Maxwell*

The Mountaineer

Imagine me, my mother dear,
Your son, a mighty mountaineer!

Up and saddling
in the frosty dawn,
Before the sun rises,
down the trail I'll be gone
Riding the high and lonesome places,
Enjoying all of the wide open spaces.

The beauty before me,
As seen with the eye,
Makes my heart soar
And look up to the sky.

The hawk over head,
The call of a raven,
All this and more
Was sent down from heaven.

So think of me
My mother so dear,
And shed no tears
For your son, the mountaineer.

—*Jeffrey M. Blust*

Ode To Pleasure's Abode

Enter eagerly

that pleasure place

which calls sweetly

to your eyes…

for what therein lies

waiting to enfold you

knows how to make you

revel in delight

that you are there

and not elsewhere

in this universe

or any other.

—*Alex Palmer*

An Experience Of Nothingness

—*Chris Schnitzer*

For You, My Friend

Your friendship is like
a breath of fresh air,
calm exhilarating
and always sincere.
Through the days and nights
Will you ever know
the need I have for
our friendship to grow?
Within me a yearning
I could never get enough
Of your laughter, your smiles
and your love.

—*Donna C. Martens*

Gates

The entrance to the garden
A delicate lattice, detailed but strong
Going through is a choice to be
surrounded by the beauty of life
Hope leads you in
Hope to find and live in the shade
of the great tree at the garden's center
To be embraced by its life giving aura
of warmth, strength, comfort
But at times you must leave the garden
Yet have no fear
The gate that once yielded is
anxious to yield again
And though some may be locked
at times, there are many gates
to be found
The key is always hope.

—*Chris Richmond*

Untitled

A CHANGING world
A FAILING society
A CONDEMNED city?

Look around
Retro FLASHBACK into the 60'S.
Policemen
German shepherd guard dogs
THEY control city transportation.
Bull Connor and Martin King
Is that a shadow with a fire hose I see?
Little babies falling out of windows
Pushed or an accident?
Rodney King
Reginald Denny

Justice
Or
JUST US!

—*Dimitria Cook*

A First Love

A first love
A first dream
A first reason to care for another

A first glance can last so long
A first hello can mean so much
But the first goodbye can sink so deep

—*Amanda Baumgarten*

God's Well-Spring

There is within each mortal soul
A lovely secret bower.
Sheltered, shaded, deep therein a
well spring of holy power.
This is the infinite voice of God
that of his holy spirit
That dwells within each finite man
despite his worth or merit.

There are three secrets we must possess
if we would enter here.
To be nourished by this well spring in
God's holy atmosphere.
We must go down the path of love and
through the door of prayer
Which is opened by the key of faith
to blessings rich and rare.

—*Helen Ada Campbell*

Untitled

What a day!
A Mack truck hit my pup,
All that's left, fits in a cup.

—*Jason Kyriacou*

New Life

One dreary day the clouds were rent
A ray of sunshine came and went
It went so fast I breathed a sigh
Would it had stayed for you and I
Yet in that time so brief a span
A spark of life to a seedling ran

That seedling now continues to grow
And by its fruit we all shall know
Why God sent us that ray of sun
Then took it home, its work was done

—*Elizabeth S. Galletly*

Pride And Joy

On June 14, 1983,
A baby girl came to live with me.
Her hair was a beautiful red,
A rare sight in my family, I said.
Turned up nose, and oh so sweet,
She even had the Rabourn feet.
Good as gold and oh so fair,
The light of my life, I was walking on air.
Then when this darling was four,
God gave to us one more.
A three ringed circus could be no more fun,
Than this little boy, by the time he was one.
He stole our hearts - this little Brad,
Now our days are never sad.
Because Traci and Brad are my pride and joy,
A red-haired girl and a blue eyed boy.

　　—*Evelyn Rabourn*

Regrets

Today is July the fourteen.
A big holiday in my country
It was just yesterday I was a teen
So why do I feel so badly?
So many yesterdays went by
Good or bad, they went so quickly,
I never took the time to say goodbye
To my youth, to my friends, to my family
Now it is too late, and I am left alone
With my memories
Some pictures in their frames looking at me.
What were their names? ... I forgot.
I refuse to admit it, but I forget a lot these days...
If I could start all over again
I would enjoy each and every day
Singing, dancing, loving
And every day would be a holiday!

　　—*Helene Hempel*

Life Or Death: A Matter Of Seconds

She drives down the road, deserted and dark.
A bird swoops down and misses its mark.
She breaks and swerves and loses control.
She skids and slides into a water-filled hole.
The car starts to sink. She can't panic now.
She has to get out. She wonders how.
She rolls down the window. The water rushes in.
She unbuckles her belt, praying she'll win.
She slides out the window and swims to the bank.
She climbs through the weeds. Her mind is a blank.
She reaches the road crying and upset.
She walks into town all breathless and wet.
She reaches the police station at eleven at night.
She tells them what happened and says she's all right.
I hear that my sister has been in a wreck.
I feel a tight ball start to form in my neck.
I try not to cry but still the tears come.
What could have happened leaves me numb.
For saving her life, I give praise to God.
He will always protect us. Our paths he does trod.

　　—*Heidi Husnik*

My Love

I went out one night to see my love.
A cloudy sky followed from above.
Down by the ocean I did go.
I waited and waited for my love to show.
Then the stars came out, they shone so bright.
Oh my I thought, what a glorious site.
For there they were, the love of my night.

　　—*Don Thomas*

Baby Girl

Ray and Andrea are pleased to announce
　　a birth with a bounce

To us a baby girl was born
　　and we'd like to toot her horn

As we most all know, she was two weeks late
　　but well worth every minute of the wait

She arrived on a Tuesday just fine
　　January 24, 1989

To us she came as the sun was leaving
　　at 6:37 in the evening

She tipped the scale at 7 pounds on the nose
　　and is 21 inches from her head to her toes

Her hair is blond, her eyes are blue
　　just like daddy and momma too

We named her Jilayne Kaye
　　beauty like flowers in May

Now the Curnow family has another one to run and play
　　and she's giving us pleasure with every new day.

Proud Parents: Ray and Andrea Curnow

Proud Grandparents:
　　Harold and Deane Yurk
　　Bill and Virlena Curnow
Proud Great Grandmothers: Thelma Rill and Jessie Hall

　　—*Andrea Curnow*

Essence

Strange, that just the taste of an apple —
　　A certain kind of an apple —
Can make me see the dappled
　　shade and beauty of a tree
In an enchanted orchard when we
　　were young.

Odd, that just the fragrance of a flower —
　　A certain kind of a flower —
Can bring back visions of a bower
　　made of lilacs and of dreams
In a lovely garden where it seems
　　songs were sung.

Awesome, that in the whisper of a distant chime —
　　A certain movement of a chime —
Will echo from a distant time
　　the ringing sound that tells
Of a church where wedding bells
　　were rung . . .

　　—*Eunice E. Sadler*

Togetherness

A love so beautiful everlasting and true.
A commitment to stand by each other through and through.
To be together through good and bad; to share, to care,
to always be there.
Two people together, their hearts entwined
in a love so serene, so important a find.
May your bonds of love and friendship grow,
with a strength that only you could know.
As time passes, year by year.
Cherish the love you have - it's so dear.
Never let go of the passion that lingers
let it burn like a candle in the night
smiling warmly in love's guiding light.

　　—*Dawn Pyzikiewicz*

A Toast To The Trees

Here's to the tree in shady lane or mountainous park;
A classic magnolia or a simple pine,
We live with you day by day:
Whether it be with the poet who treads the woodland trails,
Or the artist whose brush slowly paints the silvery forests
at night or the master of music blending the superb beauties
of the woodland hills into his compositions,
Or the historian who relates the glorious victories or
overwhelming defeats of the past,
Or with the whir and hum of the busy wheels of industry,
We acknowledge you as an essential part of our lives.
Lacking the gifts of speech, sight, and hearing, but
contributing to the world a natural beauty which
man has been unable to excel.
Having life, but lacking a soul, you have inspired all
artist and have added beauty and comfort to our
everyday living;
Seeing you ever looking upward to God and giving all things,
may we too, look forward to our Father and outward to others.

—Irene Floyd Craig

What Is Love?

For the heart: It may be "A twinge or a twang"
    "A cling or a clang"
    "A stab or a throb"
For the self: It may be "A psychological mood
    or a spiritual food"
  "A sudden fever that takes over
or an sos signal that the ego might disappear"
For the existence: It may be "A wound in being's heart
    from which you never recover
    or the nature's mysterious way
    for two beings to begin to discover"
For the lovers: It may be
  "Where the mystery of their being is hidden
    or the savoring of an ecstatic experience
    which is no more forbidden"
For the life" It may be
  "A unison of two souls who will be equal partners
    in life's sorrows, joys and fights
  or a reminder not to get attached to anything material
    while taking in everyone of world's delights"

—Ashok Malhotra

The Pain

It's different than any I've felt before, it never seems to go away,
A constant reminder of lost dreams, haunting me through night and
    day.
Worse than all physical pain,
Tugging at my heart and brain,
Forcing me to remember again,
When I thought it would end, it only began.
I wish it would stop, it's been so long.
I wish I could be happy, I wish I could be strong.
But how can I give up the memories I hold so dear,
Even when thoughts of him bring more hurt and a tear?
I tell myself I should forget,
But a hand pulls me, a voice says "not yet."
It tells me everything will be okay and I'll be alright,
But I start to think it is a lie,
Forever doubting I'll recover,
From what still makes me cry.

—Jessica R. Knight

Pink House

The beginnings of establishing our foundation,
  A day friendships strengthen
A summer of sacrifice,
  Creations of imaginations came to life
Construction of a sacred place,
  Proved to ourselves there was much at stake
The floor our weakness, walls our strengths,
  A roof, the bind between our fears and fates
Pink a color, full of life,
  The precision of decisions to led through life
Doubts that children could accomplish such,
  A beautiful building stood untouched
Summer's end determined pain,
  blisters and bruises still remained
Fondness of a dream come true,
  A little pink house I once knew
Faded paint, broken door,
  The house has been long adored
Feelings inside, some will ever know,
  For that pink house is apart of my soul

—Elizebeth Chavez

Untitled

Painted sunset fading slowly
  a day's pink vision passing

    sunset's golden strands gleaming
    the afternoon dream descending

      flocks of sea gulls streaming
      fleets of sailboats returning

        afternoon yearning to bring its evening
        envisioning night's black magic presence,

      the world in wait
      to be romanced
        by the light of the moon.

—Jan Froberg Crandall

Will I Ever Know Why?

A door has opened in my mind,
A door to the joys and depth of music.
The beautiful sounds are
Light, delicate, penetrating,
Reaching into my very soul,
Moving me to tears,
Lifting me to heights I've never felt before.

I seem to swell within, in response.
So moving, so overpowering, so mind-boggling,
That I feel I could move mountains,
I'm exhilarated, overwhelmed,
Then I feel sad, deep feelings of loneliness, and I cry.

I ask why? What does this mean?
What is life asking of me?
Where are these deep feelings coming from?
God, what's happening to me?

There's no answer - no reason given, so I wonder.
Then I hear music again, and the feelings all return.
I know I can never stop listening.
Will I ever understand "the why"?

—Betty Pippin

A Dream Of Love

A dream burns in the mind of a single soul looking for love
A dream...
A dream...
A dream which will fade as morning comes near

Songs of love played softly in the evening winds
As a single soul tries to mend for the touch of a lover's lips

A kiss...
A kiss...
A kiss that last for a life time touch the heart once more
Feel the emotion in this beating heart as the stars shine
brightly tonight

Memories...
Memories...
Memories is all that is left as time slowly passes into the
moonlight of another evening

Slowly...
Slowly...
Slowly watch the time fade, as dreams, memories, warm kisses
touch the lips once more for the very last time.

    —Demy D. Spadideas

Lost Dream

A dream that's gone.
A dream so far away.
Unable to catch unable to be found.
A dream that's blowing in the wind.
In a direction so far from where I stand.
I look and search. For that certain special dream.
Without that dream my life is non existent
Without that dream there is still an empty
Space in my heart that needs to be filled.
that dream of Joy and happiness.
that dream of adventure and excitement
I can wait, but I can wait for ever.
For that certain special dream to blow in my direction.
I need to find it so I can go on with my life.
Without it my life will stand at a freeze.
So maybe I'll wait and maybe it will
come or maybe I'll die before finding that lost dream.

    —David L. Finfer

death of a nation

...and this is what I heard:
a faint whistle
from the train drifting
over the rusting tracks
of a late night —
    a slow whine, asking where?
    where are you and why are you going?
    I couldn't answer.
    so I bent my head and asked
    for silence —
and the train slipped on.

...and this is what I saw:
small, golden children
with hollow, wax fingertips frail as robins' eggs,
gently giving birth to Long Ago.
but I couldn't watch
so I bowed my head and walked inside —
and the children went away.

    —Gregory Johnstone

The Man

The man walked down the street
A fellow told him hi
The man took out his gun
And made the fellow die

The man he loved a woman
The woman loved him not
The man went to her house
And fired the fatal shot

The man went to the park
Two lovers were kissing deep
The man then made his mark
And put the couple to sleep

The man then went to church
He confessed of all his sins
He killed the priest and then himself
This man just could not win.

    —Heather Collins

For God Be The Glory

Because of you, Mother's Day should be everyday.

I am grateful that God sent you to be a Mother not for
a few but for many. If all mothers were like you what a
beautiful world it would be, for the love you show for all
the people you know—your family, friends and others too.
Through the laughter and pain, sorrow and rain you are so
kind and sweet you are one Mother, one friend, that can't be
beat, you are special in every way, you are special to me
every day.

You put the (M) in Mother and the (O) because there is no other
    the (T) because of the togetherness that we share.
    the (H) that stands for her and that is you.
    the (E) is for every day God sends to let you know
        that He is blessing you and He
        will always be there beside you.
    the (R) is for that real love and rough times in
        your life.

I want you to know whether you're up or whether you're
down there is still no other Mother I rather be around
and it's no wonder, because you are one of the "sweetest,
sweetest" Mothers in town.

    —Audrey M. Wise

The Garden

Look quickly, at a glance, can you see?
A flash of brilliant color, flowers maybe
I think it is a garden hidden from view
by thorny bushes of neglect and abuse

Showers that come are in the form of tears
the weeds in the garden are guilt and fears
Floral beauty is hidden by handed down pain
if only the showers were sweet, gentle rain

If the garden is tended the flowers are bright
and from that garden you can harvest delight
cut down the bushes, pull all the weeds
let love be the sun and you be the seed

    —Anna Mary Shelton

Hero Of The Humanities

You entered my life, as if in a poem,
a gallant gentleman with a disciplined pose.
You told me to read, to write, and to listen,
you promised us all, never to wane or roam.

You stood tall in front, as the times read by,
like lyrics to a hymn, with eloquence you spoke
of Gilgamesh, of Homer, of Abraham and sons.
Your love for this period, was certainly no lie.

I could hear your voice, enter into a dream,
from the beginning of Rome until the Middle Ages.
Nothing else for the time, could of easily pleased,
reflecting well, the master of your scheme!

Time of transition and Renaissance would appear,
your teachings so intense, a surgeon of culture,
you could open my mind and give me your world.
Immense studies of these, yet you made it so clear.

Now the time of this enlightenment has passed,
your stories will always be treasures in my life.
Just a token for you, with respect, much gratitude,
a poem for my professor, a wish for you to last!

—*Coral Moore*

Hide And Seek Tears

The moon is playing hide and seek with the clouds in the sky.
A gentle breeze caresses my face, drinking the tear that
slipped silently from my eye.
I'm caught up in the memory of me and my guy, another time,
another place. The velvet night whispers, "are you alone, why
oh why"?

With arms open wide, I reach out to enfold a form that eludes
me for there is no one to hold. The hide and seek tears begin
to fall silently again, as they ride away on the crest of the
wind. Our parting was too quickly. There was no time to
share, the way that I love you, the way that I care.

How gently you laid my head on your chest. A pulse throbbing
wildly against my breast. I need to touch you, to nibble your
ear. Look out, here they come again, those hide and seek
tears. May the night winds carry this message to you dear;
should you feel the moisture, it's my hide & seek tears.

—*Bea Casselman*

She'll Never Be Mine

This is the girl I like.
A girl I see in my dreams every night.
        She is lovely,
        she is bright.
I don't know what I feel tonight.
    It's deep inside my heart,
    but the feeling will never stop.
        My life is not right.
        She'll never be mine,
But deep inside she's my love tonight,
    So let me dream tonight,
        because she is mine,
    but only in my dreams.
So the feeling will never stop.
She will always be in my heart.
But I have faced the facts, that,
        She'll never be mine.

—*Jeff Sinclair*

Prima Donna

In all my days I've never heard
A girlish voice quite like your own,
Which sounds to me so fresh, so dear
Its every sound has perfect tone.
Like fine perfume it fills the air,
Softly spilling your soothing song.
Pervasively it floats, it sails;
It smoothly swims and slips along.
Just like the Midas Golden Touch,
Where all that's touched turns into gold,
So too your voice to music sets
All words that from your lips are told.
Sometimes it's shy, sometimes reserved,
Sometimes robust, your voice transforms.
One day it's glad, one day it's blue,
One day it's sad, but always warm.
A most receptive audience,
You'll find your voice has in my ear.
The lullaby I call your voice,
That melody I long to hear.

—*David Cavazos*

The Cornerstone Of Society

A loving family is, I think,
a good foundation, will not sink.
All humans need a good fair start
Honesty and hard work play their part.

Family planning should say when.
The "first born" should enter, then
Mom and Dad should work real hard
to deal this "new born" winning cards

Honesty, fair-play, humor and love
are traits this "new born should keep above
all problems in this world, to fight,
and come out happy, loving, caring. Right?

Mom's been busy, cleaning and cooking.
Dad will treat her like a queen,
and steal a kiss, when she's not looking.
The "newborn living midst all this love,
will be a winner, thank heaven above.

—*Hank Ring*

Acorns Are A Blessing

High on a mountainside - the valley filled with fog-
A grey squirrel scolds in anger - sitting on a log.
An acorn fell from off an oak and hit him in the head.
But does he wisely eat it?
    No, he's scolding it instead!!
Are we like the grey squirrel, our hearts filled with dread?
Do we ignore our blessings and nurse our woes instead?
Let's start right now - take a vow - that we are going to change
Instead of looking for the things
    That to us might have been bad
Let's count our many blessings - the good things that we've had
Let's not count the acorns
    That fall upon our head
But give thanks for the blessings
    That come our way instead!

—*Betty D. Mason*

Who Am I?

I lost my personality, attitude and my life.
A higher power took control of me.
This higher power was drugs and alcohol.
I thought they were my friends and let them rule my life.
I felt I had nothing to lose, for I was a loser anyway.
I realized I was wrong, for I am a person and I am somebody.
A friend should not have that much control over me.
So I decided I want my life back and only I can take it back.
Well I got my nerve and fired my higher power that I called my friends.
I hired a new friend called inner strength.
I am gaining control of my life and I am beginning to feel good about myself.
I am living my life finding out who I am.
Do you know who you are?

—*Brenda Lee Browning*

The Story Worth Repeating

There is a great loss that makes me cry:
A life that is lived only to die
These are the thoughts that make me sad:
Thinking of what men could have had

Many are the tears shed from sadness:
Seeing men's hearts not filled with gladness
As many live their lives filled with pain,
From striving to attain but worldly gain

The useless price is the loss of their soul,
As they, themselves, become but worthless gold
What tears of sadness, when this story is told

Now there is a great gain that brings me joy,
When I see a man come forth, instead of a boy
As I see this man become a pattern of one
Who reflects the image of God's own son

When he then walks and talks like the man from above,
As his life is now filled with peace and love
He then spreads this love to all around,
From the Treasure of Life that he has found

To watch this man, who has now gained his soul,
Become like the Master of Purest Gold
What tears of joy, when this story is told

—*George Anna Griffin Moss*

On Impending Death

In the night I heard a banshee's cry,
A life was done, someone due to die.
So I bowed my head to contemplate prayer,
A soul was going, I knew not where.
Heaven or hell the choice was made,
On earthen clay, the die was cast.
Goodness assured an angels' light,
Malice be damned, fell jackals prey.
Stranger who reads this heed the warning,
Grim reaper is near at this dawning.

—*Frederick Bakowski*

The Visit

As I kneel upon this cold hard earth
A river escapes my swollen eyes
How sad I think it is, to be visiting
one that is loved, but is far from home
How lonely it is to be so far from home
But as before, I will reassure myself
that although you are missed, you have
moved on to the brighter side of life
I kiss the marker, and whisper goodbye.

—*Heather Margaitis*

Aphrodite's Son

The sea today burst forth with child,
A little boy-girl, sweet and wild,
A misplaced angel, born facile,
Naked and wingless and reviled;

  Bathed in the blue ghosts of azure,
  Eyes stained with sadness and rapture,
  A soul not meant to be captured,
  A heart too easily fractured;

Flesh, once dry, too easily beguiled;
Aphrodite yearns for her lost child,

  "Little baby,
  You'll always be my only one,
  Little baby, take me with you,
  Little baby, we'll never have the sun,
  Little baby, at least let's share the moon,
    with all my love."
  —*Elliott Martin*

Rosemary

A Rosemary sin was I to begin
A little laden, a formed caste
The flowers and fresh faces
The seemingly endless euphoric upswell
Of the taintless and friendless...
The Rosemary begin.

It is my soul that will console
If it must, for I shall not
I will unleash all that is part of us all
Not to ponder - nor pleasure
Never asking, never persuading
My heart knows no meaning of sacrifice found.

I had known of Rosemary and shared of her, too
Lovingly lumpfuls and packs of pride
Looking so wondrously, harboring her call
To be perfectly passionate
Yet quite withdrawn
But I take of Rosemary, and that is all.

—*Jeff Bonner*

Devin And Me

You'll always be my baby, You'll always be my boy.
A little slice of heaven, my whole heartfelt joy...

We must go our separate ways, I see you off to school,
Then I quickly leave for work, for we both have busy days.

I look forward to the evening,
When dishes and homework are done.
Our time to snuggle up together,
For our reading time is fun!

You drift off to sleep
With such a look of content,
All cuddled with bunnies and bears.
I tuck you in and kiss you goodnight,
And wish you sweet dreams of merriment.

I look down on your peaceful face all aglow,
While the moonlight beams through your window,
I give you one more kiss...
I tell you one more thing...
And that is: "I love you so."

You'll always be my baby, you'll always be my boy.
A little slice of heaven, my whole heartfelt joy!!!

—*Deborah A. Droll-Lucius*

Homecoming - A Family Reunion

Coming Home
A long awaited journey of the body, heart and soul.
A gathering in celebration of life, hope, and pictured memories
Waiting
Anxiously for the hour of meeting, for warm embraces.
Poignant moments of spirited happiness.

Watching
Barely discernable images, vague from the passing of time
become vibrant familiar faces again
that give way to smiles, laughter and tears
expressing joy at resurrecting memories too long forgotten.

Recognizing
Familial traits behind the radiant varicolored mask
that hold an undeniable history of family and heritage.
Eager to talk, to reminisce, to recall,
bringing back to life images of those
that time, nature and the dust have painfully reclaimed.

Remembering
The roots, powerful and unique, that etch an ongoing record
of what we are, have been, and will be.

 —*Essie Authorlee*

The Black Widow

I find myself alone, as a black sheep cast away,
a lost oasis, an undependable freedom,
a hidden escape to happiness...
My heart died in the killing game,
the only game it ever knew,
it shattered like fallen pieces of crystal
on the cold hard marble floor of reality,
left to die... But as a whole, it belongs
to only the one who diminished my grasp.
My soul stolen from its innocence
without shelter, lost in a desolate pit
never to be found and never cared for
even by the one who possessed it.
My mind caught in permanent gridlock,
an unsolved puzzle with its pieces in life...
The tears enveloped in streams of sorrow
ever flowing with insecurity,
all hope abandoned by society,
left beside myself alone, I am
the Black Widow of life...

 —*Aimie X. Levine*

Heavenly Bodies

A barren star travelling through time
a lost satellite swinging into orbit

renewed life unfolding from tender touches
solar flares nipping the celestial body
warm salty moisture permeating to the surface
a sweet musky cloud rising
defying gravity-a night flight into space

the super nova becomes a black hole
the final transmission
"But I don't love you!"

 —*C. Whitney Clayton, Jr.*

Life Is A Medley

Life is a medley of numerous things.
A lover's caress, a butterfly's wings,

A sunny spring day, a child's quick hug,
A bird in the sky, a tiny green bug,

The rain on the roof, a pansy in bloom,
A dog's welcome bark, the whistle at noon,

The smell of fresh coffee when you wake in the morn,
A greeting from friends on the day you were born.

All add up to pleasures as you journey through life,
They help you forget all the struggle and strife.

 —*Doris E. Bloodgood*

Materials For Praise And Worship

Stacking speakers on stands
A ministry of music, a service in song
Everything taped down before anything breaks loose
The band starts as I hit play
Driving the monitors to
The threshold of feedback,
Seven voices with seven gains
Funneled through six dynamic coils
Mixed into a praise chorus,
And sent out 150 watts by 150 watts
The horns vibrate into the visible spectrum,
Pushing light into the sanctuary
I'm a gaffer, painting the light with
Bass, treble and reverb
We need to flood the place,
Chase away the shadows
Trying to light synapses
Waiting until testimony time
When I can only watch and pray
That the light of the world will make copper, fiber optic

 —*Jonathan Tollerton*

Snow Rabbit

On a cold and grey December morning,
 a mother rabbit scurried down the river's edge.

Reaching out for remnants of delicious grass,
 unaware of pale and hungry eyes beneath the hedge.

Nibbling carelessly and poising for a song,
 she watched a falling waltzing feather from a sparrow.

She heard the acorn fall, the sun was in her eyes,
 a branch moved slightly, exposing a young boy's bow and
 arrow.

The sparrow flew, she turned, and met his gaze,
 their heartbeats one, they stared and waited breathlessly.

She winked, and a tear glistened down his face,
 she hurried off in great haste as he watched her lovingly.

She reached the hollow and fed her hungry brood.
 he let the arrow go and found the mark where she had stood.

Oh, brave he was, and Snow Rabbit was his name,
 but he threw the bow away, and grabbed his knees in shame.

Could the Great Spirit that lives in the heavens; who created all
 things,
who brings the rain, who blows the wind, who shines so bright
 with warmth,
who brings the winter snows, who grows the wild berries, who
 paints summer rainbows,
create such beautiful friends, and have them killed for food?

 —*Ernie Suarez Guzman*

Renewal Of Hope

There seem to be something recently aghast
A new breed of hope surfacing at last
The man chosen to lead the way
Surely must take on a tough task day by day
I don't doubt he won't make his mark
After all he's Bill Clinton
Our mentor, our Clark (superman)

His backup is Al Gore
With Tipper at hand
He'll make his mark, I'm sure
We won't be left crying in demand

People in Washington will love them all
That was obvious from the count on the Mall
We'll make them feel right at home
To find love no where else need they roam

And Chelsey and Socks will fit right in
They'll love the White House
Through thick and thin
So let's settle back for the smooth ride ahead
After all by two good Democrats we're being led————

—*Arlene M. Swilling*

Who Will Teach Me

Each night as I go to sleep
A nightmare I know will come to me.
Hard at work I passed the day,
Hoping something better would come my way.

Each day as I slowly wake
I dream of how it really should be.
Knowing how they didn't teach me,
Recalling it was more important to play.

Daily, activities swirl around me,
And hopelessly I feel left behind.
Is there anyone who cares
There's millions others just like me?

Drifting,I wonder where to turn
To find the means to change my life.
I feel like I'm in a churn
Without an anchor to hold me firm.

Suddenly, in a window I see a light,
And there I find the thing I need.
I know the future can be bright
As I ask who will please teach me to read?

—*Bobby J. Vance (U.S.A.F. Ret.)*

A Part Of Me

I wish the words were in my heart, to tell you how I feel.
A part of me has always cared, I guess it always will.
A part of me can't say good-bye, yet I must turn and go.
How sad that I remember, how I once loved you so.
A part of me has been so hurt, if only time could mend,
All those empty yesterdays, when I needed you so much then.
Now the crossroads where I stand, unsure of where to turn.
Are only highways of a past, I had to walk and learn.
Have we said so long ago, the end is sure to come.
Yet trapped beyond another day, our lives were left undone.
Now that other part of me, confused within itself
Has held on to good memories, until they're all that's left.
So as I try to say good-bye, a part of me holds on,
To another part of you, that I have loved so long.
A part of me is broke into, for all the bitter tears.
While another part of me, has belonged to you for years.
So for the pain that we have known, it's time for me to go.
I'm leaving with these memories, but I still love you so.

—*Dinah Meade*

Shimmering Sea

The sun made a shimmering path on the sea,
A path of light glittering like gold,
Wave after wave across this path did flow,
A beautiful sight it was to behold.

To this path of light the sea did seem life to give,
A seeming endless motion yet captured in time,
About its periphery there was twinkle and dance,
Quite like a night filled with celestial stars.

Across the bay this path did stretch,
Golden, pulsating in all its length and breadth,
But the sun behind a cloud did recede,
That this grandeur, this sight did wax and wane,
But not before it had been seen at Dorchester Bay!

—*Emoro Efetie*

Will There Be?

Will there ever be a place for me,
a place to love, to set my soul free?

To softly float on an ocean of blue,
upon the wings of a breeze so fresh and new.

Sometimes I sit and think aloud,
"Will I ever be able to feel the cloud's?"
One by one they'll go dancing by;
till nothing but dark has set on my sky.

No worries to burden or endless strife,
no obstacles of hatred to shadow my life.
For there I will be, with Jesus my Christ.

—*Annette Robinson*

Friends

A friend is a person whom you can trust.
A pure person without dirt or dust.
A person you can depend on,
A person you can confide in,
A person who's there, that's a friend.

When no one else is ever around,
Somehow a real friend manages to be found.
A friend is there when times are rough,
They are there when times are tough.
They will be there 'till the end.
That special person called a friend.

They are there to make sure you are O.K.
They will always be there for you
    noon, night, and day.
When you need a helping hand,
It's nice to know you have a friend.

When you need a shoulder to lean on -
When all of your faith seems to be gone -
It's good to know a person you can commend
It's pleasant to know you have a friend.

—*Amanda Veazley*

Home

The home is where one lives and loves
    A shelter from life's care and woes
    A place where comes the roving dove
An ending to the winding, turning, turbulent road.

The home is where one's trouble and trials fly,
    A bonfire on which each are piled your many discommodes.
    A shoulder on which each creature can cry
    A platform on which to unburden your massive loads.

The home is a house in which to love,
To love those who come within.

—*Anne L. Biggs*

Night's Quiet Drama

This night is far too beautiful for sleep,
A silver moon smiles softly in the sky,
The lake is molten silver at my feet -
And in this magic world my heart is high.
The crickets' chirping makes the silence hum,
Small moving shadows dart beneath the trees
As little wild creatures, hunting, come-
And larger quiet hunters follow these.
Entranced and still, I watch the moonlit play
As nature's quiet drama sets the scene;
The insect-hunting mole moves on his way,
The rodent-hunting fox leaps high and clean-
He eats the mole, and then with hunger sated
Trots off. A smiling silver moon serene
Looks down on all that nature has created;
While chirping crickets carry on night's theme.

  —Jean B. Martz

The Gift

It was last year today you brought a gift
A small gift for to land a love gone adrift
I remembered I was feeling the color of blue
But a smile came with happy thoughts of you

The gift came with you and your wee one
That was the night my heart you had won
I was sitting alone in a dim lit room
With visions of flowers starting to bloom

You quietly entered and sat down by me
And whispered about a gift from thee
You covered my hand as if to stop time
Then slowly you put your hand under mine

The gift I saw resting in my opened hand
Told me just how much you did understand
Like this coin of silver with a unicorn
A love that was never before felt was born

  —Janita Mayabb

Dedicated To The Blind

I'm sure my ears have never heard; or likely will they hear;
A sound so lovely as a bird, whose notes can bring such cheer.
No music yet devised by man, despite its lovely score;
Can match the sounds made by the sea as waves pound sandy
 shore;
And breezes rustling autumn leaves, or raindrops pelting down.
Is music that never fails to please; their natures own sweet sound.
A poet once said he would never see a poem as lovely as a tree,
And with that man I must agree; and add one thing I've found.
That nature's face is sweet to see; I'm sure that it will always be,
But sweet too is her sound.
There's nothing I know that can quite replace, seeing mother
 nature's lovely face.
I also know that given my choice; number two is always to hear
 her voice.

  —Donald Lee Leach

It Can Always Be a Time for Learning

When I was a child my Lord opened, wide, a door.
"A successful man is made by struggle," my wise,
Successful grandfather told me many a time over.
I thought of my childhood as that time for play.
From schoolwork, my mind very sadly would stray.

Like a great ship sailing with a broken rudder,
Like a great ship sailing with a tattered sail,
Life without proper education is a dismal tale.
I prayed, in the name of the Lord, for new days.
My Lord opened a window on, new, educated ways.

  —John C. Calhoun, III

To Make Room For Another Day

Sometimes when we're least unaware
A strange thing comes to be
We hear a distant echo from buried memories.

Memories of long ago and not so far away
Makes me ask "Why do things so beautiful go away
To make room for another day?"

Family and friends that mean so much,
Raise you and teach you to be who you are.
Only to disappear with the Lord's simple touch.

And then with a heartbeat, it's over in an instant!
Because a strange thing comes to be:
You hear a distant echo from which you turn and see.

Your son hollering "Choo Choo!" as he plays with his trains.
An adoring wife cleaning your daughter's dress stains,
And you realize things are still beautiful
When you make room for another day.

  —Chad Baugus

Storm Of Life

Looking out the window, the storms of life approach,
A tear rolls down the young mans cheek, for he is not without
reproach.

He hears the thunder rolling, lightning strikes a tree,
His shivering body cannot move, he's longing to be free.

The house begins to shake, the wind is bearing down,
Dark storm is now upon him, on his face appears a frown.

Then on the horizon, a light began to glow,
An angel, maybe Gabriel beckoned the man to go.

He dashed from the house, as quick as his frightened legs would
 move,
The house was then swept away, the storms' violence it did prove.

As he lay on the ground, he glanced up and drew a breath,
He sighed, as he realized he had envisioned his own death.

  —Derek Gustafson

A Child's World

This is the time for cheer and joy.
A time for gifts of little boys toys.
Let's not forget our little girls,
We'll give them a doll with cute brown eyes and curls.

It's hard for children to understand,
The problems involved in unfriendly lands.
So we'll tell them now what lies ahead,
Before we tuck them into their beds.

And pray with them before they sleep,
That the world they know, they may always keep.

Let's also pray that it never comes down,
That in war our children's feet must touch their ground.

For whom among us has the courage to choose,
If my child will win or if your child will loose.

As adults might, we finally lay to rest,
All the bombs, missiles, destructive weapons still left to test.

Hell, if nothing more than put these decisions in the hands of
children who care and who still can,
Spread those words of Peace On Earth and Good Will To Man.

  —David G. McBroom

The Simplicity Of Vastness

A simple breeze forms a gentle ripple
A trickle of sound
And whirlpools spinning around

A moment of peace and all will cease
The beginning of sunshine
Ending darkness and its measure of time

They know of no rest living in their nest
And are never lost in loneliness
Just below the everglades in waving blades
Sparkling joyfully as the sun wades

The animals also cry out as they scurry about
On the trail they all know as "happy"
Overwhelmed in green moss is a pile of old brush
That seemed to sit so peacefully

So beautifully strange - the scenes began to change
And happiness is all I could feel
The simplicity of vastness left behind by the masses
Is a place where serenity is real

Amen.

—*Brandon M. Strong*

Tribute To Eric Clapton

With long fingers caressing his guitar,
A white Englishman speaks of blues we all know.
Guitar crying real tears, we feel the anguish.
As he sings with voice and instrument of his woe.

As he expresses pain with his music,
He tells of blues and moods we feel.
His guitar screams the pain in our hearts...
Death of loved ones, lost loves, loneliness real.

Praised and imitated by young guitar players,
He remains humble while always improving his art.
It's said he never wastes a note, nor plays wrong;
Plays as slow as he wants, and always from the heart.

In soaring rifts and chords, recorded or live.
A special gift to the world, Eric Clapton matures
From a teenage guitar genius in English pubs
To an international star whose music enraptures.

Yet that same guitar can send tremors of joy,
Rock and roll with blues still at the core.
Thankful for his shared talents, the world begs
For his voice and fingers to produce more and more.

—*Betty H. Bell*

Enchantment

An image intertwined and beautiful
a world of pleasure filled sighs
Sounds of laughter echo in my mind
and the touch of my love
still warm upon my back
A vision of hearts beating powerfully
to the music of love
And a shroud of hope and caring
protecting me from the dark corners of despair
building bridges over pits of sorrow
I see stars in an once empty night
I give myself completely to the images
Intertwined lovers
forever one in an embrace
and they in the embrace of a world
which knows only happiness and joy

—*Cassandra M. Cruz*

Out In The Cold

Each day I look at how it should be
A world where no one is left alone
Where each day is not a fight
To find your way out of the cold

A cold so deep it eats away at yourself
You, your precious self
A cold as black as death

But, the cold should not captivate us
Instead we should feel the happiness of dawn
And we should warm ourselves by the fire
A fire burning with love

Yet the cold surrounds some
And continues to mold their lives
And they don't see any hope
Where they should be able to survive

To accept your innerself
Is only half the struggle
Others should realize is too and accept you
Because no one should be left
Out in the cold

—*Holly Hogan*

Stairway

Her name is Lillian, a disgrace to her own.
Abandoned by her family, she doesn't have a home.
Living under a stairway
is all that she has;
her two year old son, some newspapers and bags.

During the day she sells what she has
to strangers who come with money in hands.
Rummaging through dumpsters
she collects some food and cans.
The child stays crying with his face buried in his hands.

Evening can be harsh with cold and cruel wind.
She huddles under stairs with the only of her kin.
Warming her small son
in the lining of her trench,
so close to her bosom while sleeping he would clench.

Her love couldn't stop the hate and the crying
of the little boy whose hunger left him dying.
An end to the pain
but who is to blame,
the father that abandoned or the god who they disdain.

—*Denise Vazquez*

Time

Time went by, as in the blink of an eye, and I cried,
About all those things I never tried.
And I had ideas I though would work.
But I, being me, said "No! Your but a jerk."
Time went by, and still I stared at the sky,
And wondered why.
Why is he or she all that they want to be,
And I sit here like a leaf on a tree,
Shaking, and quaking, but not partaking,
Crying, but not trying.

I could have been all that I wanted to be,
But I would have had to make an effort you see.
It just wasn't for me, it wasn't meant to be.
Time it is said waits for no man.
So you must be all that you can.
You have things you want to try?
Full speed ahead! Don't stare up at the sky,
And wonder why.

—*Bernard Schatz*

The Leaf

In the spring of their life, he had written
About her as a lovely leaf leaping away
From the eternal tree which held her,
Fortunately falling into his outstretched hands.
Time had its say, and as they drove along
On this beautiful, endless autumn day,
No longer did the luscious, vibrant leaves
Picture her to him because the mind's glasses
Are gay on the inside and somber on the out.
As they make one of the sharp turns on the hill,
A denuded tree stump with bark withered away
And two bald branches coming from its depths,
Reaching with it to the source of life above,
Stood for her and her eternity in his life,
The leaf having fallen to the dead ground.
The vision was shattered when his hand on
The wheel was propelled forcefully to the left,
Avoiding a deadly drop into the gorge.
"You are my salvation, dearest," he murmured.
"My leaf has still its beauty and its strength."

—*Frank A. Langer*

Shelter Volunteer

I volunteer at the shelter to help women and children who are
abuse. They come to us beat and battered then cast aside like
something that is used. They could be your sister, your
mother, a grandchild or just a friend. Like in the nursery
rhyme, we help put the pieces of their lives back together
again. I volunteer at the shelter because I remember from
where I came. My remembrance of my father was only of his
name. The beatings came daily from stepfathers that numbered
five. Our home was a war zone, each day a battle to survive.
I volunteer for my mother whose memory is still vivid in my
mind. It wonders me with abuse so often, she was still so
loving and kind. A sharecroppers daughter her education was of
grade three. But when I looked into her eyes, I thought all
her love was just for me. Time is a priceless thing and
given by so few. When you give time to the shelter you've gave
the best of you.

—*Bob Ghrist*

Life Without You

Act I... You entered my life... my world
Act II.. I heard your voice... music to my ears
Act III. You touched me... my body trembled
Act IV.. I tasted your sweet lips of desire... magic
Act V... You and I together... wanting you there always

If I choose to live my life without you...
Yes, I would survive... maybe forget how much
I wanted you... how much I loved you...
But why would I ever want a life without you?

—*Janet C. Goodrich*

All I Wanted...

All I wanted was a hug,
All I wanted was a kiss.
All I wanted wanted so badly,
Was him but alas, he didn't want me.
I think, all I wanted was for him to care for me,
to cherish me, and to love me.
Was that to much to ask.
I guess it was.
Doesn't he realize that was all I wanted.
I guess not.
I guess no one realizes what I want.
All I wanted was to feel loved,
cherished, and cared for.

—*Desiree Rogers*

Friendship

The winter is long and cold
Adds gloom to those that are lonely
Somehow they survive
Waiting for spring
To add a ray of hope to their lives again

If you've never been there
Then you won't understand
How much you need someone's love
To know they are there
To put their arms around you
and really care.

The glow it gives from within
Helps ones state of mind
Not necessarily a lover
A true friend that will never
leave you behind

—*Carolyn Seery Dickert*

To Kiss A Needle

When the judgement was over, your bleeding eyes no remorse
after your exit, I examined my wounds
your claws of fury had torn at my feelings, like a ravenous hawk
your words, daggers of hatred, spit out with the quickness
of a viper's kill your monstrous skeleton loomed over me as I
shrank further into the armchair's fabric, the emotions flew like
bats from an opened cavern your inability to explain showed the
coldness of your stone heart the soft, silken love so familiar
to me had been replaced by a rigid, icy, blue abyss
your inconsiderate soles sent the vase first orbiting, then
plummeting to its pitiless death upon the battleground
I attempted equality, but was immediately tossed aside, only to
sever myself on the awaiting shards of glass, with one last
ounce of deranged kindness you grasped the cord with senile
hands, eyes glimmering with insanity, teeth bright like fires
of ice, and for one last time you pulled the plug, here I am
left to perish in the darkness with only a shred of my soul
spared of humiliation to flicker wearily, till my life's send

—*Jennifer Gradian*

Life's Episode

When one poor soul has taken flight.
Alas, another one in the night
So it's been, so it'll always be.
But in the midst there's life
Precious and treasured, despite all strifes.
Strifes, fabricated by a few men's dream
Adhered to by oblivious-or so it seems.

And it's for varied reasons that a newborn cries
Some for joy, for clear is the path they're destined to thread
Some for sorrow, for the dark, turmoil distance which lies ahead
Life's episode is but a mere glance - a floating mirage in the
    distance.

—*Colin Taylor*

More Other Times Than Some Times

Some times I feel empty,
    alone, and just not going anywhere.

The world seems cold,
    cruel, and frightening.

Other times I feel loved,

The world becomes a wonderful place to be.

It's at times like these, that I put my faith in front of me,
    and any doors that are closed, become opened.

—*Gaye Green*

Reality

Walking in footsteps too advanced is what childhood is
all about, now it is time to unlace the strings
pull off the worn shoes, walk freely-without the guidance
of our parents.
    Time to leave our "reality", our parent's fantasy,
time to let go of mommy's legs and daddy's arms
time to wipe our tears on the back of our hands instead of
on mommy's shoulder.
    We must walk alone with only the advice of our
parents for directions, time to give our shoes to our
own children and restrain ourselves from helping when they
fall; we realize why our parents let us feel pain when
our own grab us with tears pouring from their eyes.
    Another generation is growing up so fast it seems,
but to them it was an eternity. They have grown and are
now set free so that the cycle can continue,
hopefully they will finally understand why we raised them
the way we did.

        —*Alysia McLain*

Obsidian

It surrounds us with a creepy silence
All around us it needs no guidance
Blackness drifts in our minds
Tearing us from our kinds
In the dead of the night
Black squeezes with all its might
It stops the heart from working
You never know where it's lurking
Black reflects not orange, red, or green
But from it all colors are seen
Soundless the attack on its prey
As the black hunts in dark array
People smell black everyday
Forever lingering from evil thoughts that
comes our way

        —*Carissa Burns*

Retrospective

I believed, once,
all I had to do was grow up
to be like you—
a dark-haired beauty
challenging the world behind smoldering eyes—
such intelligence, oceans of knowledge
swept from the shores of everywhere,
orchestrating lives of those you loved
to perform symphonies
when at first we played only disconnected
whistle notes.
I thought, then,
your vision and responsible strength
were merely gifts
of surviving years of time.
I did not understand
that you were the seasons without
a winter.

And now, this space and time exists without—
Seclude yourself in frozen sleep.

        —*Evelyn H. Cahoon*

Sometimes

Sometimes your eyes aren't merely enough. Enough to capture
all that surrounds you. Sometimes you have to pay for
something you didn't want to. Sometimes you love too many
people too much. And sometimes you work too hard at trying to
make those people love you. I know. I have all of these.
You might too. I can't describe it. The feeling.
Impenetrable thoughts. That nothing can disturb. Not even
another thought. Why does this happen? Why do I think this?
Sometimes we don't know. Sometimes we wish we knew. And
sometimes we all don't want to know. So I remain silent in
my thoughts. In my world. And I won't speak of such thoughts.
Yet sometimes certain people want to know something.

        —*Cory Boughton*

Son

A son is someone you want to be,
All that you could not be.
Someone to fulfill his goals, so
he will not suffer when he's old.

When he was young and full of fun,
You were proud to say, yes! That's my son.
You want your son to turn out to be,
better than you or me.
To see him laugh, to see him cry,
You hope he'll be that better guy.
So, remember son I'm always there,
In heart and soul, do not despair.

        —*Anthony R. Bonaguro*

A Fraternity Of One

Solitaire! Egalitaire! Fraternitaire!
Alone with nature: alone before God!
Alone in thought: contemplating the past.
Lost in a crowd of memories.
Remembering things as they were...
At home facing challenge!
Relishing victory!
Overcoming defeat!
Surviving life!
Outlasting death!
Leading the charge!
Progress following in the wake...
Facing forward when there was nowhere else to turn!
Apart from the rest!
Life finally done...
Riding into the sunset, alone.
A fraternity of one!

        —*David Colson*

Love Hurts

    You love with your mind and soul,
    Although my heart aches when your not with me.
    Your stone cut eyes reveal a sharp twitch in my side.
The magic that rushes through my body when I rap my arms
around
    you,
        And yours around mine.
    The wounds I bare drizzle blood,
        yet I don't notice.

        —*Courtney Lo Castro*

My Room

My mind is my favorite room.   The furnishing are not
   Always the same it changes minute by minute, both
   Day and night. Most times it's sunny and bright.

Every day I awake in my room and ponder man's lot
   I wonder why some are born rich and some do loath
   Their every day poorness which doesn't seem right.

To wonder and ponder man's plight takes all I got
   Sometimes I fall short, but I'll give you my oath
   To do nothing would be the worst, I pledge my plight.

It's crowded with things of this sort, to let nothing rot
   I sort it all out, finding the good to pledge my troth
   Wish it were easy as to say, most times it's a fight.

   —*Elizabeth Samedi*

Always Rain

             Rain come,

                          then, cold w i n d -
                                       water,
 Always
 Again rain,   f r e e z e
                                       to
                                             ice.
 S K Y
 become
 W A T E R   F i r e come,

   D r y w i n d come.   and

                          I c e melt,

   Then,

                          W a t e r,

          put out fire.
   —*Angela Loporchio Friedlander*

Suffocation

Am I alive or is this a dream?
   Am I really what I seem?
Is it really me sitting here?
   Is it really you sitting there?
When will the room stop turning?
   When will my eyes stop burning?
   When will my stomach stop churning?
I can't think, my head is in a daze.
   I can't see, my eyes are in a haze.
   I can't breathe, my lungs are ablaze.
I want to get up and talk to you.
   I can't, hands are on my neck my face is turning blue.
My head is numb, my body weak.
   The cadaver next to me is starting to reek.
Deadlines, stress, the pressure overwhelms me.
   Destroying my soul, killing me.
I must first finish my task.
   Before in peace I can bask.
But relief is nowhere in sight.
I can't breathe I can't breathe
   —*Dale Patterson*

Questions

What? Where am I? Who am I? Am I here?
Am I there? Does anyone care? I cannot see.
I cannot feel, what am I doing? Is this real?
I cannot talk (to the dark), I cannot walk,
And there is no morning, no evening, and the wind does
not blow! What is this torture, that burdens me so?
Confusion going on in my head, I am alone? Or am I dead?
This world that surrounds me, I cannot touch, O' how I
miss things so much. What was the name of that book?
And how did we look? Were we good? Were we bad? Was
it happy? Was it sad? I don't know, I don't know,!
Am I mad? (suddenly). What was that? Was that a cry?
(that I uttered?) I heard a voice, like a sigh,
Was that ? Clear as can be,
O Master, help me, I can't breathe, O' my I think I
see light. Who are these creatures dressed in white?
All praises to "Him" should I propagate? To the pain of
life should I prostrate? Should the angels of the
earth no longer mourn?
Or should they all rejoice because a child is born?
   —*Ijaaz L. Givens*

Homecoming Dance 1947

I heard stardust on the radio last night
Amid the hip-hop and the chatter
"The nightingale tells his fairy tale
And I am once again with you..."
Those undulating notes strike my auditory nerve
And instantly we dance again together
In the gym, serious and intent we move
Your hand pressing my back, on fire
And like the ducklings who imprint
The first thing that moves
With "mother,"
So you are now and forever imprinted
with "lover."
   —*Eleanor Moye*

Beautiful St. John, Virgin Isle

Narrow paths climb, serenely, to awe-inspiring scenes,
Amongst lush green hills, rising high above tranquil bays,
With white sandy beaches, glistening in brilliant sunshine,
Beside the painted sea of blue and green, with crest of foam on
   waves.
Cool breezes scatter fragrance of radiant tropical flowers;
And palm trees twist magnificent, green branches toward the blue
   skies.
While gorgeous flamboyant vie for superiority in the scene,
Their clusters of deep, red blossoms, flaming, beyond all other
   flowers.
Beautiful canaries sing sweet melodies to the molten sunset,
And ensuing night spreads silence over the solitary plains.
   —*James Latimer*

Spirit Wind

O'Spirit Wind, you have been here for such a long time, the
   ancients heard your voice, the elders hear you and so do I.

Spirit Wind, you come gently filling me with peace and wisdom,
   strong and harsh when I stray and do not listen to you.

You carry the coldness of winter and death, the warmth of spring
   and new birth, the howling wind to remind me of the past,
   lest I forget our ancestors and the ways of our people.

O'Spirit Wind, help me to walk gently upon mother earth, to
   care for her so she will continue to care for me.
   —*JoAnn Kruttlin*

Spirit

I in a moonlit, high lofty place, am still.
An abandoned eagle, young in body.
Soul, searching the ages.
Scars, old wounds slowly healed.
Passing with years as most of existence.
The lost heart torn, but found.
Time, so much wasted on what was.
Eagerly my eyes scan the horizon.
To soar, to once more lift upward and fly!
Solitude conquered loneliness, longing conquered fear.

The heaven's winds and storms come and go.
They, like the rocks far below are as we,
they are and they have always been.
Points of illumination guide our way,
in our passing through these dim ages.
Again I stretch my worn wings and take flight.
Straining ever upward, climbing ever nearer.
On, on towards the sunrise!
Light comes after so dark a night.
Eternity recognizes only love, as history remembers.

—*Gregory W. Rumbles*

My Angel

A Long time ago, God was alone thinking,
And a beautiful thought came to mind.
He wanted to send an angel to earth,
But she had to be an angel of the purest kind.
He said she shall have golden hair,
The kind that would reflect heavens light.
And that soft, warm light would shine,
To warm one's soul through the darkest of night.
Then he said she must have the most beautiful eyes,
So he made them hazel, perfect as could be.
So for when one looked into those eyes,
A vision of heaven is what one would see.
And he wanted her to have a special smile,
One that would make a persons heart glow.
Then for anyone who saw her smile,
From heaven she was sent, that they would know.
And in her voice, he thought.
He wanted to hear the angels sing.
So he picked her up, gave her a kiss,
then sent her to earth on an angels wing.

—*Henry J. Gureski*

The Flowers Of The Field

I strayed, where the waters are flowing,
And all was so peaceful and fair,
The birds in the branches, were swaying
Their songs filled the soft balmy air.

I roamed where the violets were peeping
Where modestly seeking the light,
The lilies, were gracefully floating
On the waters so crystal and bright.

They spoke of the Father's protection,
And told of His wonderful love
That bade us be hopeful and earnest,
And lay up our treasures above.

The flowers of the field,
The birds of the air.
All speak of His love
And His infinite care.

—*Edith L. Hackman*

Whisper

I stood by the ocean and looked out to sea,
and asked God! What can I be?
Whisper to me soft and low, and tell
me which way to go. Listen carefully I was
told, for what's here, is worth more then gold.
So listen to what I say. Listen, listen and listen
some more and keep coming through that door
I was told to be seated, my God I was defeated
You'll get it just your wait, but give it time
you're never to late.

—*James Ronald Arns*

Just A Little Boy

The game of the year is about to be played
And bleachers are packed with 3 fans of each age
This game is important, win, lose or tie
The home team is losing, the score 6 to 5

All bases are loaded, the crowds on its feet
The other team knows that a hit means defeat
The next batter steps up, his bat full of grace
His hands are still shaking as sweat drowns his face

He stands at the plate with his heart pounding fast
The crowds in an uproar, the die has been cast
His parents can't help him, he stands all alone
A hit at this moment would send the team home

The ball meets the plate, amidst boo's and hisses
He swings with great force, but suddenly misses
A thoughtless voice cries, get rid of that bum"
As tears fill his eyes, he finds baseball no fun

So open your heart and give him a break
It's moments like this that a man you can make
Remember this when you hear someone forget
He's just a little boy and not a man yet

—*Jerry L. Roisentul*

Untitled

I lay my head upon my pillow
And close my eyes upon this day
To sleep ... while darkness hides the willow
'Til morrows morning walks this way

I lay my head upon my pillow
To slumber through the mid-night hours
To wake when dawn first touches willow
And prods the dew encrusted flowers

I law my head upon my pillow
To slumber while deep shadows play
Till subtle mist enchants the willow
And silent sun brings forth new day

I lay my head upon my pillow
And...should God choose to take my hand
Should I not wake to see the willow
Nor kiss the dawn as I had planned

Then lay my head upon my pillow
that I might rest more comfortably
And put me there beside the willow
To sleep...till God awakens me.

—*Donald C. Goetzinger*

He Was Something Special

He was something special his mom said as she was crying
and crying and hugging all the people while it was
raining and making me look like i was crying although
I WASN'T CRYING and his mom gave me a hug even though
she didn't know who i was and i told her i was
REALLY SORRY even though I wanted to yell at her
HE HATED YOU AND YOU HATED HIM you wouldn't even
put his pictures up on the living room wall with this brother's and
sister's and you're the reason he is dead and gone
lying there in that box with a scarf wrapped around
his neck trying to hide the scars
you're all the reason all the people leaving
leaving his mom his dad already
left i have to leave i have to get out of the rain
but i heard more crying his girlfriend was standing
there in a green dress crying all alone (she has to
leave we all have to leave) probably thinking he was
something special.

—*Alicia K. Guild*

White Apes

They used to burn us at the stake!
    And drag us through the city streets!
Screaming "faggot" as they beat us with clubs,
    until our bones would break!
Burned alive with the sticks that bore our name!
    Our torture continues as history repeats!

White Ape police now stop your car,
    for trumped-up reasons whoever you are.
Brainless albino gorillas, the town bullies in their youth,
    care not for right or wrong or truth.
Bullies now on a grander scale, are cops making car stops,
    seeing you as a criminal with their criminal minds!
Searching through your most personal
    sacred possessions with impunity.
God help you if you're black,
    worse yet, a white befriending them.
Wake up America! The black man is not your enemy!
Your enemy is the White Ape in the blue uniform.
    He's carrying a club and a gun!
And has a rubber stamp judge behind him!

—*James Paglia*

Fantasy

Were I a little child still
    And dreaming on a starlit hill,
Of places far and distant shore,
    With thoughts as high as eagles soar.

To be a giant in pygmy lands
    And carry fire in my hands.
To see beyond the pale of man
    Way back to where the world began.

Then build it up with not a care,
    Whilst cloud and sun adorn my hair.
Soon would all nature bow and sway
    To loves own harmony, be gay.

—*Charlene M. Christopher*

A Candle

A crying sax alone in the dark.
And I alone at the bar.
Intently watching a candle.
Wanting so desperately to be extinguished.
Yet, wanting so much to shine.

—*Dale Wielechowski*

When I Go To Heaven

When I go to heaven, monkeys will still climb trees
and drop on stuff that's underneath and eat each other's fleas.

When I'm up in Heaven, camels will still spit green
and do the work that others shirk if someone treats 'em mean.

While on the earth below, birds pluck out my aged eyes
to let their young ones feed on them midst loud, impatient
    cries.

From my new home I won't care that ants devour my face
thus sparing old flesh the loneliness of withering in place.

Worn out body serves at last to let the maggots spoil
and trace the ruins of forest blooms within the quickened soil.

For now in Heaven I am soul and freely embrace the joy
of giving wings to a zillion things by being one small boy.

—*Gordie K. Edwards*

Haunted House

    I went inside the Haunted House,
    and everything was quiet as a mouse.

    I walked into a mighty hall,
    not knowing I'd find a crystal ball.

    It showed me what my future was,
    and I'm not telling just because.

    My future, yes, it does look bad,
    it makes me very, very sad.

    It told me to walk behind the pole,
    but little did I know I'd fall in a HOLE!

—*Christine Feller*

A Journey Inward

When I looked inside there was darkness there. I grew disturbed
and extremely scared. I searched and searched and finally
found, a box buried ever so deep and securely bound. With dread
and excitement I started to unlock, the mysteries and
nightmares, as I turned back the clock inserting each key,
removing each lock I laid aside the chains. To remove the bonds
took so much strength, I wept again and again. Then when I
opened the top I awakened inside, a precious child with
sparkling eyes. With upturned face she began to speak, her
voice a forgotten melody, low, soft, and sweet. Her plea was
so simple, I would say She asked may I go free to learn to love,
to finally play. As I lifted her up and held her close to me a
warm light began to glow and helped us both to see. Now when I
look inside I find us together there. We embrace as she begins
to share. I am so glad you finally came, to rescue me from fear
and pain. Now we can live before we die. I experience her joy,
our spirit flies.

—*Barbara Hamilton*

Take Time To Listen

Two little children were playing one day,
And got muddy from head to toe.
As a grandmother I should have understood
But oh! I scolded them so.

Just then a little bird
Way up in the top of a tree,
Began singing its beautiful song,
And filled their hearts with glee.

They listened as the bird sang its song
It was so perfect, no hurry or fuss.
They looked up with innocent eyes
And said, "Listen its singing to us."

—*Boots Billings*

Summer Love

We first met on a sunny summer day
And from the very first moment you stole my heart away
You see my heart longs for my own true love
Someone sent from heaven above

When you kissed me it blew my mind.
Made me leave all my worries behind
You fill me up body and soul
And when I'm with you, I feel whole

When we make love my feelings soar
Shakes me down to the very core
We came together, it happened so fast
It feels so good, I want it to last

My mind is telling me I better slow down
But I look in your eyes and start to drown
You know you have me under your spell
But you're not the kind to kiss and tell

I think you know now how much I care
For if you need me I'll always be there
And if our oneness ever comes apart
Just remember I loved you with all my heart.

—*Cheryl Buehrle*

My Lily

As I sit here in my comfy chair
and gaze about my room,
My eyes tend to focus at my flower
in full bloom.
I gaze at the lily in sheer disbelief.
That such wondrous splendor could be conceived.
Those vivid, bright colors of pure pink and white
I'll try to preserve them with all of my might.
As I gaze at its beauty I soon realize
That only God could make one of these, Oh how we strive,
With gold, apparel, and precious stones
ourselves to beautify, not oft remembering that in our
inner self both beauty lie.
Then a familiar scripture does my mind appease,
"Man in all his glory is not arrayed like one of these"
Oh God, teach me to be humble and wise and let you fashion
me like one of these a pure lily.

—*Edna Beach*

Heart Of Love

Move still O'Heart that beats for love's new seed,
And give her heart the time to know that love,
Released in perfect love from God above;
Gives grace for both to have His will indeed.
Amid the years that grow and time slips by,
Reflect on life, and children come to be;
Enjoy their part in love so brought to thee,
To live God's perfect way is worth the try.
And as the gray falls down upon the hair,
For every year there's change for each to see.
Renew our hearts to greater love and care.
As children's children come to thee and me,
Now keep that heart of love to always share;
Know well, God's Heart of Love, we must agree.

—*Francis G. Vater, Jr.*

Where Have All The Cowboys Gone

This country was tamed by men of true spirit and women of
    patience and grit.
We trace back a heritage of pioneer cowboys who knew not the
    meaning of quit.
Riding tall in their saddles, they roped and they penned, working
    from sunup 'til dark.
The ranges were open, the ranches were vast, the prairie—a
    natural park.
The cities were towns then, and towns were one street with horses
    tied up to a rail.
And Saturday night the towns came alive for a dance, country
    music, and ale.
Life used to be simple—they worked to survive, and neighbors
    helped out where they could.
The family was sacred, each having a part, and kids grew up
    strong, as they should.
I reflect on my history as I sit at my desk in my office ten
    stories high.
As I muse I can almost see them old cowboys galloping swiftly
    across the sky.
My phone rings and someone walks in with a fax, another one asks
    for direction.
There's a meeting—I'm late—and decisions can't wait—in the
    window I see my reflection.
I'm rugged and rowdy and honest as Abe and I'm no longer
    wearing a suit.
My white hat is dusty, my wranglers are blue and my spurs are
    attached to my boots.
While I race to my meeting, reports underarm, wondering "What
    is my chance of exposure?"
No one in the board room suspects I'm a cowboy maintaining
    professional composure.
At six, I head home to my ranch of five acres and saddle my trusty
    steed, "Dancer."
I ride to the pasture to rope a few steers and pretend I'm a real
    old-time rancher.
This country belongs not to cities and streets, nor to cars and
    mass transit that flies.
It belongs to us all who still saddle up horses, and it will 'til
    the last cowboy dies.

—*Del Whittaker*

Your Gentleness

You held your gentleness against me
And I fell far beyond the blue
of your eyes
The instant brought together the
moon and stars in uncensored
phases of love
Then you exploded into my heart
with a sea of warmth that flooded
the crevices of my childhood

The moment was breath taking

I held you without fear
Touched you with only a whisper
I drifted across the wave of your hair
Breezed across the softness of your skin
Each movement in itself, its own splendor
I took no direction to discover you
Only to follow the discovery of myself
And along the way as we revealed
a select courage of the heart
I stopped to adore you

—*Christian Stanicek*

Encore

Twas the night before Sunday
And I just by chance
Was out walking not far away
When I came across the Great Hall of Dance

And I out of curiosity and all
Hearing the music blaring
Peered into the hall
I could not stop staring

To my surprise
My Grandparents were doing the swing
I could not believe my eyes
They were actually dancing to everything

Then Grandma's stockings started to hang
And they just kept on dancing didn't rest
When all of a sudden a bell loudly rang
My Grandparents had actually won the contest

Then all of a sudden a great sound of clatter
My mouth dropped as they started up once more
Still I was stunned but it didn't matter
I got so excited I shouted out loud "Encore"

—Helen M. Gaal

Memories

I miss it when you hold me,
And I miss you in the night.
I wish that you could hold me close to you tonight.

Even though I can not see you, I feel you in the night.
I think of you when a cool breeze blows,
Or when the moon is high above
It reminds me of a night we spent, so many months ago.

The wind was blowing and my heart was racing,
But only when I look at your face
Do I feel my heart beating,
Your eyes are soft and dark,
And your skin is silky smooth

Why is it now I'm scared to say that you may be the one,
To give me what I need,
And show me what to care for.
My tears fall now for only you,
So please don't ever let my memory go.

—Jamie Lynn Warner

And I said,... "Nothing"

"What do you want?"... you asked,
and I said, "Nothing".
My love will never ask for anything.
As long as I can love you from a distance.
As long as I can hold you in my dreams.

My love will never ask that you come forward
and take care of the needs within my heart.
I will be happy just to know you care
to keep me in your thoughts when we are apart.

So, as you see, my love is not demanding,
nor selfish, nor possessive, nor in vain.
It's just a lonely rose growing in a garden
surrounded by the weeds of joy and pain.

—Celeste Escobar

Ode To A Broken Heart

Today has come and gone
and I still wonder what went wrong,
Lonely nights lead to lonely days,
Please make the hurt go away.

Oft I see you proudly standing there,
Laughing and smiling and tossing your hair,
Happily we would romp, laugh, and play,
Please make the hurt go away.

Wedding bells were to gaily ring,
Children were to gather and sing
to celebrate our special day,
Please make the hurt go away.

Being without your loving is the worst,
I feel for sure my heart will burst,
A blast that will leave all in dismay,
Please make the hurt go away.

To end this ode to my broken heart,
Is my way of saying good-by,
For we will meet again some day,
Please make the hurt go away.

—Bill Shrum

I Thank God

I thank God for the mornings,
And I thank Him for the evenings,
And all the days of my life that I'll spend with you.

I thank God for the sunshine,
And I thank Him for the clouds,
With silver linings that look like you.

I thank God for your hand,
Which is placed in mine,
While I hold onto His.

I thank God for this life,
For He's been so good to me.
He made you to be my dear wife,
And He made me for thee.

The future is not in our hands,
We need only let Him lead,
As we walk with Him, hand in hand,
He has everything we need.
And for this,
I thank Him, indeed.

—Gary W. Frazier

With Every Setting Sun...

With every setting sun evening does forth come;
And it would bring darkness to what was light;
Blackness everything would at least bring forth some;
Through the pathway of the ever widening night.

Hindering everything but our undying flame;
Coming of two forever intertwined hearts;
That is much more difficult to tame;
Like we got hit by two of Cupid's darts.

People say our hearts are too young to know
That we are told at each passing of day;
Yet when the forsaken autumn winds blow;
It would tell true loves, young or old, the way.

We are always and forever young and free;
And that we must be till eternity.

—David Waszilycsak

Come Unto Me And Rest

Jesus says, "Come unto Me,
And I will give you rest."
All who are burdened with sin and woe
Must to the saviour go.

He died on the cross for you and for me
Who suffer from sin and stress.
He forgives our sin; makes us free
And gives comfort, peace and rest.

Trust Jesus, the Saviour, He wants you to come
He's waiting your soul to bless.
He loves you, needs you, and wants you
To have this rest — sweet rest.

Without him you perish, the Bible says;
With him you live — complete.
Let him come in and free you from sin;
Have access to mercy's seat.

He knows all about you; He made you, ya' know,
So from him you never can hide.
So confess all your sin; ask him to come in
And allow him to always abide.

—*Chlora Dean Lucas*

When You Were Mine

It's been a long, long time,
And I will never forget when you were mine,
The time that we spent together,
Lord know there never been any better,
Oh yea, it's been a long, long time,
But you continue to be on my mind,
Though we were not together for very long,
The love I feel for you is still so strong,
I dream about you each and every night,
And God how I hate to see the morning light,
For it takes me away from once again,
But not without leaving this empty space within,
Even though it's been a long, long time,
I will never forget when you were mine.

—*John Hofegartner*

Answer In Rain

One day's hard labours brought me to my knees
and in such posture,
I raised my head, as if toasting with wine,
to the sky and beyond the to the great divine
and asked it did I why
all our labours seem so little by themselves
yet are much bigger seen as one.
A voice not speaking answered my call well nigh,
one raindrop fell to the dust by my hand,
swallowed it was by the driest earth
and I puzzled at its significance,
yet puzzle did I not for long
for in a second instance the heavens grew black with rain
In moments I understood
when water up to my ankles swam.

—*Jeffry Buisson*

The Ugly Duckling

An ugly duckling, the world would call you.
And in your troubled spirit, I think you knew
With your frail, lean body and beady eyes,
Lips too full and nose too wide.

But in my eyes you were a thing of beauty,
Strong, handsome and tall,
I loved, cared and needed you,
Oh, how hard did I fall.
Only to discover, you were an ugly duckling after all!

—*Alice Clark*

A Thirty Minute Walk Through The Best Part Of My Mind

I'm going to send my mind on a trip to memories it's never had and it will tell me what it sees:
It is very early morning. I can see the first streaks of dawn sneaking through the thick pines on the mountainside as they drag a lazy sleepy sun into a new day. I can smell the pine needles that cushion my steps into the new day. I smell the pungent odor of decaying wood from an old patriarch of the forest as it give back to mother nature all she has let it borrow to shade, support, and protect her little friends. I have wandered onto the edge of a beautiful lake. I love this quiet time of the morning. The night birds and tree-frogs and crickets have quieted. Their shift is over. Shortly the whip-poor-will and the owl will be replaced by the wood-ducks and the eagles.
Listen! A mother loon calling her little ones to breakfast as the cycle starts over again.

—*James D. Blickenstaff*

Untitled

Life is so short it seems
And it's gone just like a dream.
We find a love so rare
Counting on them to always be there
We wake up and they are gone
How will we survive in this world alone

Drawing from God's strength
Often makes us stop and think
Knowing we couldn't make it without him
When we lose our next of kin
Certainly he feels our pain
He sees our tears from heaven's window pane

Yes he is always there
Letting us know how much he cares
Our real home is in heaven too
She just went before you
To be waiting on Heaven's shore
Where you'll be reunited forever more
Take comfort in this God says to you

—*Joan Shelton*

Three Wishes

If I could have three wishes,
And know that they'd come true
I'd not wish for wealth nor fame
I'd only wish for you
I'd not wish for the stars
I'd not ask for the moon
I'd just wish that each day had 25 hours,
That I could spend with you
My second wish wouldn't be,
To be beautiful or to be strong
I'd just wish that I had eight days
each week, in your arms where I belong
my third and final wish would be
that there were 13 months in each year,
so that I'd have more time with you,
in which to hold you near
but I'll never have three wishes
and I know they'll never come true,
but at least I know I have one life,
one life to spend with you.

—*Brandi Periard*

The Seasons Of Love

As Autumn comes to the world again
and leaves begin to fall
I remember Spring and Summer too
but the greatest joy of all
Is remembering the sharing, the laughter, the caring -
the love you gave to me.
Through rain and snow, though cold winds blow
In good times and in bad
Whatever the season, the time or the reason -
Your love I always had.
And so I say to our very last day -
Our love was meant to be.

—*Dorothy Ney Pichel*

More Than A Pen-Pal

Absence makes the heart grow fonder
And leaves much time for me to ponder
Over the short time you were here -
To remember the handclasp strong-sincere.
I knew I'd always love you - then,
Tho we may never meet again,
Face to face, hand in hand
But we'll be together in memory land.
Tho many miles now separate us
And the years have taken toll,
In my heart there is a longing
That tells me we're not really old.
Strange, I pray that one day again,
I may be blest to hold your hand
And look into your smiling face
And feel again your strong embrace.

—*Jewell Marshall Betsill*

Winter's First Day

These four years, they have passed like a season;
And like a season, they have brought a new day.
The pure white snow of winter's first day,
has become as the darkness of night.
And oh, the bitterness of the cold and windy nights,
biting the flesh and burning through the soul, like a bullet
that has left its chamber.
I shall not another season endure.
And if a new winter shall fast approach,
I shall not taste of the bitterness of the cold nights;
I shall not be as the fool once again.
For, I know that I must fly where it is safe and warm,
until all threat of winter has gone.
And now, the last night before the new day;
I shall not sleep, but ponder the coming of the heat of
Summer;
When I know that I will long for the return of the beauty and
the warmth, in the cold of that winter's first day.

—*Delores G. Weissman*

Untitled

Stop for awhile;
And look at the beauty that's around you
for there are those who cannot see.
Listen for a while to the sounds
that surround you,
for there are those who cannot hear.
Walk for awhile - the earth that's
beneath you,
for there are those who cannot.
But don't feel sorrow or shame
for those who don't seem to be the same,
for they know God is awake
and one day will give them a chance to take.

—*James L. Peoples*

The Whisper Of A Bird...

I sit among the wild grasses
And looked above, the blooming trees.
I noticed a shadow hovering over me
It was the same bird that whispered to me.
The bird flew down and sat with me
Not knowing if I would ever hear it sing.
The whisper of the bird was magnificent and heard
Until it came, and touched my love.
For some reason, I couldn't refuse
To touch the overwhelming bird.
The bird came over and touched me too.
The feel of its feathers was of someone I knew.
The bird that once whispered to me
Turned into a beautiful, warm, loving girl,
She told me to remember everything of the past
Of the words she told me, "Our future will last."

—*Carlos Barnes*

Oh Lord

Oh Lord how I hunger for you, to do
and love what you want me to. I know at
times I still get lost and it leaves me blue,
For I am and have nothing without you, when
I was lost somehow you found me, and for
this I will be eternally grateful to Thee. I
still at times want it my way, please give
me faith, and courage to turn to your will
day by day. I really do not want it any other
way. I do not deserve your loving grace, and
I thank you for never walking away, from me
when I turned from you, so please let me always
remember you, and that you're always there
for me, if I let you be and help me to know the
true meaning of love especially when things
get tough, and help me to be gentle to all I
touch, and let me pass on to others your
undying love.

—*Donna Solitario*

Love's Domain

Love was here long before we ever came
and love will be here when we no longer remain
It has to do entirely with the feeling that we feel
and rules were never set as to who it could appeal
We all see certain rights and wrongs because of how we chose
but whether they are just or not no one really knows
Only one person has the power to say who we may love
and he is Almighty who lives in the Heavens above

—*Julia Anne Strickland*

Life

I've got a hundred and ten milestones to cross,
And many more burden's to share;

A hundred and ten
someday one less
And now a hundred and nine.

Eventually all will perish in time
And new ones will yet arise.

But the hundred and ten
And weekly one less
Strengthens me to survive.

—*Debra L. Brown*

Untitled

Old friends are dear;
And new ones become them when they part,
In the spectrum of time we meet the millions,
And a few we actually know,
My friend I called him that,
And proud am I of that,
Now I walk the lonely mile home,
For it is over and done,
Perhaps I shall never see him again,
Nor know of his where abouts,
But just for the time together makes the hurt worthwhile,
How many times are we afraid to love another,
For good friends do not come from air,
And must be found amongst the rabble,
A good friend is trust and faith,
And so my friend,
If we never meet again,
Thank you for being my friend.

—*Andrew Dorsch*

Owed To Frustration

As I sit down to write I stare at this paper,
  And nothing will enter my mind;
I search all around for a good place to start,
  But I think I'm just wasting my time.

I try to envision a scene to begin,
  This essay that I have to draft;
'Cause in trying to write it's sink or swim,
  So somebody toss me a raft.

Now my head has begun to be filled with frustration,
  No comfort in paper that's bare;
The best part of my life slowly drifts into space,
  While I sit petrified in this chair.

As each stroke of the clock passes seconds away,
  The pressure mounts up on my nerves;
A deadline to meet but with nothing to say,
  Because I lack knowledge of verbs.

But just as I start to lose all composure,
  And give up my writing career;
Written down on this paper miraculously,
  The poem you've read right here.

—*Dustin M. Crayton*

Shannon Jennifer Wess

I rocked your Grandmother and your Mother
  And now I'm rocking you
  Oh, little Shannon
  You are our dream come true.

Down through the years I wiped the tears
  From your Mommy's dear little face
  And watched her grow into the Mother you know
  With love and pride each day.

May God bless you, little one
  And always keep you in His care
    With love and happiness all around
For you, and those you love, to share.

  —*Janet G. Kimbell*

Untitled

Clear your mind of the ignorance of society
And see what I see
To survive as a people
Together we must be.
We all have prejudice in our minds
But our hearts must transcend
And see the souls of ourselves
To bring hatred to an end.

  —*Bercha T. Anderson III*

Perceptions:

True, reality is universal
and people are alike.

But, why are wars perpetual,
and truth, hard to come by?

Well, people come in many shades
and many shadows too- and perceptions
oh, so different - come in pink, or gray, or blue.

Take, for instance, allocation of resources
when they're due, and you think, for sure,
ability is the right and only cue.

You may be right, you may be free
to think and say what's true
but, situations are particular now,
and choices - personal and relative.
So, others see as they shall see
in pink, or gray, or blue.

And one question that could spoil you,
a criteria we all hear,
is the one that's so expansive:

say, are you not, of a different hue?

—*Estrella Besinga-Sybinsky*

Another World

I live in another world, one where there's happiness
And rainbows arch through the bright morning sky.
I live in another world, where there's enough for everyone
And people can always find ways to get by.

I live in another world, where dragons and griffins
Fly through the air of the welkin above.
I live in another world, where for all, there is freedom,
And their lives are filled with laughter and love.

I live in another world, one where there's danger,
And battles are fought with swords, shields, and spells.
I live in another world, where most heroes die young,
And their deaths are mourned with the ringing of bells.

I live in another world, a world filled with music,
Where every living thing has its own song.
I live in another world, where music is magic,
And it can help people find where they belong.

I live in another world, one for dreams and dreamers,
Who open their hearts, and know what they feel.
I live in another world, one of song and story,
Where anything that you believe can be real.

—*Amanda Hayes*

Smells And Smiles

Smells of feedstore grain and molasses, a dolly,
and regimented rows of salt blocks crowd the room.
A blatant mouse celebrates another wonderful day,
as bulging gunny sacks leak their bounty.

Kinda hot fer this early...19 cents fer gas? Ethyl's 22,
eggs ain't worth the feed...Truman's done it ya know!
More than most places this store of goods,
a refuge to grumblers, loafers, and liars.

Not much happenin' around the square,
lots of room to park, even on the shady side.
SALE signs and FREE ICE TEA, bribe the buyers,
more flies come in than folks.

Seed jars are full and ready for warm damp dirt,
noisy and concerned, April chicks persuade knowing smiles.
Nosey roaches climb to the edge of their bins to look,
new life and sounds make today a little special...
    here, for now...

—*Herb L. Karcher*

Bigot

You smile and call me brother
And rob me like a thief in the night
I work the double burden and silently take my pay
While you wallow in your whiteness and recline on down

My children wear the hand-me-downs and politely "thank you"
Yours dress in Neiman Marcus and curse the saleslady.

You march to protect human rights
Yet move away to suburbia when your home turf color changes

You are the boss who pats me on the back
And hates me for knowing more because I am of a darker breed

You are the minister who preaches God's love
And wants only to administer to more than the poor.

You are the politician who rallies for civil rights
And is always politically incorrect

You are the smile, the sweet agreement in my face
Behind my back, I am "those people".

—*Feiruz Shehadi*

The Devoted Trucker

If you were to call me or write me a letter,
And say that you'd left 'cause you didn't know better,
And ask me to come get you now If I could,
I'd say I'd use every way, yes I would.
I'd get in my car and I'd drive like a fiend,
Till I ran out of oil or else gasoline.
I'd be stopped for a moment, but now don't you fuss,
I'd get me a taxi cab or else a bus.
If not one of those, then I'd get on a bike,
And if that was broke down, then I'd even hitchhike.
By wheelbarrow, pogo stick, roller skates, too,
You don't have to worry, I'd come and get you.
If all of these failed, you're still not out of luck,
'Cause I'd cheat on the boss and I'd borrow a truck.
The terrain doesn't matter, why, it's not a factor;
There's no place I can't go with my old Gravely tractor.
But I can't come right now, and I hope you won't laugh,
'Cause you see my dear I'm on time-and-a-half.

—*Charles L. Minnick*

Endings

Days' ends wrap themselves in quieting robes, blued from use
and softened by suspended clouds. The stillness of pastels
arched across the western sky hush the last few frantic moments
clinging to one's overspent mind. Hushing all speech, making
still all frenetic movement, giving comfort to the blisters of
toil and pain — the sky, with the wind and clouds in tow,
bathes its blessing upon one's heart as it whispers its
nocturnal benediction. Motionless, the days slip away from the
tenuous clutches of the forthcoming nights. As each star
resumes its position in the sky, the pastel edges lingering
from the sun dissolve into their blended border of
twilight-graying blue. Evening has come. Its arrival eases
the cooling quiet into the mind and heart, bringing comfort to
the day's stress. Chiseled stars in crisp exactness shout
forth their calming peace which softly drapes the world below
in a mantle of simple sleep. All is done which can be for this
particular day — all else must wait for the recuperative quiet
to once again cease. Upon another day the breaking of this
repose will bring forth new activity, which will in the turn of
its time, resolve into its own peaceful end.

—*Joan B. Shulmistras*

My Own Stream

The soft wind whispers through the trees
And softly, oh so softly, reaches out and touches my face.
It was peaceful there, with the water gurgling below me.
The weather-rough wood of the swinging bridge below me;
The cool shade of oaks and sweet gums above me.

I miss it there, eating the sweet
honey suckle from the vine next to me,
Watching the crystal waters rush beneath my feet;
Not too far off, I hear children playing,
Their voices but a song on the air.

Oh, when will I return,
To the stream that harbors the memories
Of me playing there as a child,
And of me, receiving my first and most beloved kiss,
And most importantly, the stream that
actually bid me farewell.

—*Andrea Frost*

Melinda

Day folded herself in a blanket of Night
And softly warm rain began to fall.
Through a silent mist of half-light,
My thoughts turned backward and you were what I saw.

As a child I observed you with wonder,
Conversations, there were none.
Yet your presence, strong as thunder
Aligned the moon, stars and sun.

I, one of the grandchildren to your score,
From the eleven sons and daughters you bore
Sang each Sunday your unheard song.

You were born, you lived, then ceased to be.
Perhaps you now live in me.

—*Janice C. Aselin*

Prologue

There are such people who pray to their gods,
And such who adore their lovers,
There are old maids who love their cats
And such whose heart beats fast for the dogs.

There are such, believe me, I know,
Who enjoy these pleasures all at once:
For them Gods are the best of all,
Then come to lovers, dogs, and cats.

Where do I express my poor heart's desire?
Whom I am going to kiss? Where to kneel?
My prison cell seems to be on fire,
There is nothing to live for, nor to feel.

And yet, I do strongly believe
That there is truth, and that truth
Lies not only in the stars and the moon,
But also in the Eclipsed sun.

—*Jan K. Kasprzak*

The Shaman Of Autumn

The shaman of autumn extends his staff
And touches the green leaves,
Transmuting them into gold and flame.
But all too soon they turn brittle and brown
For no glory in this world's realm
Is without price.
But even in their dissolution
They renew the land.

—*John M. Doyle*

My Prayer

Good morning, Lord, to you I pray
and thank you for another day,
to be with all the ones I love,
to see the moon and stars above.

You lifted me when I was low,
You sheltered me in times of woe.
You kept me from the Gates of Hell,
You healed my wounds and made me well.

I pray each night that I may see
what plan You have in store for me.
I say the Rosary every night,
so I may see the Golden Light.

Lord, when it's time, please take my hand
and lead me to the Promised Land.

Amen.

—*Alice De Stefano*

To My Son

As I sit alone in the dusk of the day
and the evening hours slowly pass away.
My thoughts go back to the by-gone days
when you were young and life was gay.
The smudges and smears on the window panes
were some of the things of which I complained
the noise and fussing as you grew up,
I learned was a part of life's full cup.
For now as I sit here all alone
it's a quiet place and cold as stone.
For there's no one to cry or smudge or make noise
and I miss the clutter of all your toys.
I'd gladly wipe all those smudges away.
And to hear the noise as in yesterdays.
But time is something we can't retrace
only our memories will live in its place.

—*Florence H. Tollefson*

Beyond

Through the doors
and the fierce gauntlet of emotions
over the clouds
the journey has begun with minds separations

Rising to
a higher level of perception
travel beyond
the simple thought, of simple minds, and learn the truth

Take the hand
that offers this experience
the new way to
feel, to love, to live, is through the open mind

Beyond the
love and fear of this ascension
cherish the sign
of pain and ecstasy, the mark of unity

Wear this mark
in the mind, but for all to see
and be secure
in the faith that the mind and body are now one

—*Andrew S. Hughes*

Benji

First day of nursery school
And the last one to go
Fear, insecurity, an unknown task
Hidden feelings beginning to show.

No tears, just I won't go
I want to stay here,
Mother encouraging, stressing positive things,
Resistance strong, a tiny tear.

I will stay with you this first day,
acceptance attained, "I will give it a try"
arrival at school, soon engulfed in play,
mother leaves, grandma arrives.

First day a success, he learns to adopt.
Later he tells me, "Grandma you stayed, I liked that a lot"
His confidence up, he felt he could say.
To Grandma and all, he would be O.K.

—*Betty Jane Perry*

Waiting Room

Slow, slow grind the wheels of bureaucracy
And the people wait patiently,
Knowing no other way.
Important things are not accomplished rapidly
And their time means nothing
In a government's day
Their empty eyes stare out of dull blank faces
Like robots temporarily shut off
Waiting their turn.
And the important ones move to and fro
With steaming coffee cups
And no concern.

—*Anne Boscia*

Africa!

Africa where the earth is red
and the waters maybe purple black;
Africa where the women are sisters
and the sun is on fire where the earth is red
and the waters maybe purple black;
Africa where sounds and rhythm communicate,
stimulate and pace traditional life
Africa where the moon is gold and watches
over millions of stars
where the earth is red and the waters maybe purple black.
Africa fight for survival, children of innocence
dance sing, drums, heartbeat, pulse, drums
Africa passion celebrating all life
where the earth is red
and the waters maybe purple black
Africa.

—*Ingrid Sertso*

A Star In The Sky

I believe when God takes someone special, then they go up on high.
And with the help of Jesus, there's another star added to the sky.
I look into the heaven and see the stars sparkling with delight.
And I have the warmest feeling when I see that beautiful sight.
All the stars in their place are shining with their silver light.
These are God's ornaments that decorate a night.
God in all his glory and with his added friend.
He puts another star into his heaven; for in his heaven there
   is no end.

In Memory of Someone Special
R.M. & Ellaney T. McBee

—*Faye McBee Henderson*

Moon Song

Tonight I went out.
And the wind tossed me about
Like an ancient leaf on the wind.
It was a cold wind, the kind that really
Gnaws your bones.
Clouds abounded in the starless, Christmaslit night,
And between the wispy shadows of a distant forest
Beyond the abodes of humankind, I saw
Her.
Like an angel shrouded in mysterious brightness,
She drifted across the sky as the earth precariously
Turned on its karmic wheel,
And none of man's pettiness
Seemed to matter.
The cold wind blew onward, and with the seasonal
Orange glow of a thousand screaming trees,
And stars echoing their cry faintly in the distance,
A flicker of hope appeared in the midst of the
Shadowland, and I
Carried on.

—*Eric Yarnell*

Almost

I almost picked up my pen today.

But, then the noisy water called
And there were birds to feed, and
squirrels to befriend.

I watch as the industrious box elder
Insect goes through its mysterious drill,
The handsome drake paddle against
The current, the delicate finch struggle
Through the wind.

As for me, I will not labour;
For the creeks water beckons still
And the birds hunger still and
The squirrel is not yet in my trust.

—*Donna Michaels*

Now

If you see a bunch of violets
    and they make you think of me,
        Give them to me now.
Don't wait till I cannot smell their fragrance
    nor their beauty see.
        Give them to me now.
If you know a deed of kindness
    with love for me you plan to do,
        Do it for me now.
Don't wait till I am past knowing.
    Let me share the joy with you,
        Do it for me now.
If you have a word of comfort
    that might cheer or bring a grin,
        Say it to me now.
When I'm dead I'll never hear you,
    there is no use to say it then,
        Say it to me now.

—*Jean Lancaster*

Untitled

When roses wilt and leaves begin to fall
and trees start to sleep, you and I know
fall is coming in to stay and will leave
when the sun disappears and wind is on his way.

—*Andrea Ferko*

Led By The Master's Hand

As I go through life's trouble and sorrow
And things are uncertain today;
i'm led by the hand of Jesus,
He guides my life all the way.

He leads me through each valley
And upon the mountains I stand.
I am touched by the hand of jesus,
For I'm led by the Master's hand.

Though the clouds seem dark around me,
There's a bright silver lining above.
Jesus takes away all my troubles
And leads me with his love.

If you cast all your cares upon Jesus
And turn your life completely to him,
He will save you and then he will guide you.
You'll be led by the Master's hand.

Yes, Jesus will guide you always
If you live by his command.
You know each day He will guide you
For you're led by the Master's hand.

—*Charlene Paul*

APFR

Used to see you twice a week
and thought it was no big deal.
I saw you again for just one night
It was glances I would steal.
You asked me out and I knew you
would. I had no doubt and you
knew you should. After just two weeks
I was hooked line sinker. Was
this love at first sight may be so.
Who would figure. I sit and wonder even now how
long this love will last given your
so many infatuations and my unstable
past. You know this time it could be
different couldn't it? I know this time
it's special isn't it? Then why the
questions ifs and or buts. We shouldn't
dissect this love. Just take it for
what it is this feeling so full and
true. This love at second sight; I
call it. This knowing I love you.

—*Frances Ann Riviere*

Sunset (In Memoriam - A Teacher)

The golden sun took flecks of white clouds
And thought of playing a game.
Some she tinged with orange bright,
Others with purple, red, and yellow,
Or just a glistening white
All blending into so calm a splendor
That eyes had never seen before
Nor could ever hope to see again.

Upon the earth she sprinkled sunbeams
So warm, so brilliant, so strong
That danced into deepest caverns.
Darkness cracked and opened into light.
On waters blue, shafts of golden rays
Turned placid waters to glistening gems.
Then all nature joined in a soft song
As she sank to rise on the other side.

—*Ena Leyden*

The Spirit Is Willing But The Flesh Is Weak

Saviour could I make amends,
And truly foil the devils ends
If I would spend one sinless hour
At mass each week while demons coward

I know they I'll wait to take my hand,
Life tempts me, I cannot withstand
The loss of all the fierce wild joy
In Dante's hands I am a toy.

I beg to drink this bitter cup;
Don't prick conscience and disrupt
Just let me give one hour to thee
And for the rest just let me be.

No wait! Don't go! Desert me not
Lest hopeless fire should be my a lot
Instead descend and visit me
When I am least expecting thee

And breath into this soul so black
The strength to all these sins attack
Then grateful will I ever be
To feast of Thee eternally.

—*Ada L. Gregg*

Nightmares, Realities and Dreams

We come from different nations which span across the world,
And walls are built that separate, while hatred is unfurled.

The words we use can cut the heart, worse than any blade;
As we argue against each other, like ignorance on parade.

Yet in our time "the wall" was broke, in pieces on the ground
The "Iron Curtain" shattered, and was heard the world around.

"We are the world" reminds us, we can't give up the fight.
Too many have died senselessly, we've got to make it right.

For Lincoln, King, and Kennedy, they shared our distant dreams
A nation built on unity, is closer than it seems.

It's on our flag of colors. Embroidered on each thread,
For each life that is taken, in each blood drop that's shed.

Why can't we see the destruction that prejudice creates,
And live up to our name which there is still time
We the United States.

—*Fred Vena*

Twins Home From College

They came home last night to visit
And watch the game,
Bringing optimism and exuberance
Into a cold, quiet house;
And a box of dirty laundry.

The house suddenly came
Alive and alight
With their electricity and
The electric company's.
It began to look lived in again.

They told of their classes and tests
And of dates with girls.
They inspected the house; the dogs
Were glad to see them.
The refrigerators welcomed them with open doors.

They stayed the night and now they're gone.
The house is again quiet and cold and in order.
They'll stay at the dorm tonight.

I should go outside and work but
It's lonesome out there, too.

—*David J. Nordquist*

Lost In A Fog

I love to go hunting in early morn
And when I tried to move
I learned that I was going round and round
Lost in a fog.

I kept trying to get out,
Yet ending up in the same spot,

I sat down on a log;
The sun came out, and it got real hot,
So I got out of that spot.

Confusion in life is like a fog;
We need to wait on light from the sun,
And then get up quickly
And be on our run.

We need to pray
Three times a day,
And less confusion will
Come our way.

I was lost in a fog,
And I sat on a log
Until I got help from above.

—*Blain Arlington Boling, Sr.*

Ponderments

Where do you think hope goes after it dies?
And where do our tears stay before we cry?
What happens to pain, once you get numb?
How do you know when you're just being dumb?

Why is it people want to push away help?
Where does the sound go after the whelp?
Who knows the reasons inside of God's mind?
Why is it justice really seems to be blind?

Do you think trees mind losing their leaves?
Do you really ever know what someone else sees?
What was His Dad thinking as Jesus Christ died?
Just where are our feelings kept, on the inside?

Shouldn't we have pockets inside of our brains?
Would the sun ever like to go play in the rain?
What if at "next war", we all just stayed home?
What if our true thoughts were in a glass dome?

What does my cat hear when I tell her my secrets?
Will a tempest fit fully inside of God's teapot?
How does a person do all that he needs to?
What are you thinking, now that this poem is through?

—*Charles A. Dorka, Jr.*

Tulip Time Or The Land Of The Wooden Shoe

Across the sea where tulips grow
  And windmills dot the scene
And row on row of tulips
  With carnations in between

Where canals they seem to wander
  Through village and city alike
And tales are told by young and old
  Of the boy who saved the dike.

It's beautiful in winter
  On canals that make the scene
With ice boats swiftly sailing
  And skaters in between.

So if you go a wandering
  On a misty night its true
You well surely get to Holland
  To the land of the wooden shoe.

—*Clifford H. Feeney*

Untitled

She looked down at her sleeping baby
And wondered what kind of future it would have.
She prayed it would not be as hard as her own past—
   her sixteen years of struggle
   her nine months alone
   her dead end job.
She watched it breathe deeply;
her daughter, her joy, her only love.
She knew its life would be hard
It would have to work alone
   to pray alone
   to try too hard alone.
She knew it was almost impossible
   she had done it
She had saved herself.
After only a little more than a short decade and a half
She knew her time would soon be up.
She would end it.
And she knew, just like herself,
her child was just a statistic.

   —Danielle Pignataro

In Love With You!!!

I knew from the beginning you were a flirt
And yet I fell in love with you
Knowing I'd get hurt!
I thought I could tie you down
And make you love just one,
But how could I do something no one else has done?
I know you never loved me
And I've tried not to cry.
For I must find the strength,
To kiss your lips goodbye!
But when you ask for me again
You'll find I won't be there!
I want a love to call my own, not one to share!
So for now I hide my broken heart,
   Beneath my smiling face!
And though it shall seem I never cared,
Just remember one thing,
No one can ever take your place.
You had your chance, I moved on.
Just remember, the woman you once had, is gone!

   —Alisha Wageman

Burdens of Life

When the burdens of this life get you down
and you find that no friend is around
when the burdens of this life seem hard to bear
and it seems like no one even cares
Jesus is the one that always sees you through
Jesus is the one that answers prayers for you

When the burdens of this life brings a frown
And it seems as though no help can be found
When the burden of this life just won't let you be
Just remember Jesus, he has set you free
Jesus is the one that always sees you through
Jesus is the one that answers prayers for you

Just call on Jesus, there's power in his name
Just call on Jesus, he's always the same
Just call on Jesus, the way, truth, and the life
Just call on Jesus He makes everything alright
Just call on Jesus, yes without a doubt
Just call on Jesus He'll bring you out
Just call on Jesus, just wait and see
Just call on Jesus, we have the Victory

   —Claudia E. Green

Teddy Bear Tears

Yesterday an angel came and took you upstairs
And you had just turned sweet sixteen
Thus the powers who choose to rule our world
Trashed my life at twelve fifteen

I use your room like an altar even a shrine
And all your girl treasures are there
As high on a pillow a top your sweet bed
Lies your best buddy, a small brown Teddy Bear.

Oft when I'm hurting, I'll cuddle this Bear
In the same way that you used to do
And since there's always a dampness on that cute
whiskered face
I know that he's crying for you.

Oh yes, Teddy Bear tears do mingle with mine
When great pain is riding me hard
Know that that Bear and I will hold your fair face
In our heart lands of love, little pard.

   —B. H. Mullins

Untitled

   You smile through the pain,
     and you laugh through the tears
that's what you've learned after all these years.
   So you kiss him passionately,
     and you hold him closer than before
because you're so afraid he'll walk out the door.
   So you give him your heart,
     and with it, your soul,
   as you try not to fall into an empty hole.
   You learn you can't make him love you,
     you learn you can't make him care,
   and yet you decide to always be there.
   And as the sun out lasts the rain,
     as the joy outweighs the tears,
so you learn to love, after all these years.

   —Ana M. Freed

Anger

When you feel upset inside
And you think in your heart, there is no pride
Believe it or not, it's just a stage
Filled with pain, discouragement, and rage
You'll get over it, in just a little while
'Cause someone will come along,
And start to make you smile
Thank this person for what they have done
And go on with your plans, and have lots of fun
This feeling comes every now and then
And for many women, you get it towards men
They can be charming and sweet sometimes
But don't you forget the good and bad rhymes
This feeling you'll have, will seem like forever
But if nothing else, never say never
Listen to all the advice I have given
And use it through every day you are livin'
Keep yourself under control every day
And anger will surely travel far away

   —Jessica L. Silye

What Is Black?

Black is sadness and shiny black cats,
anger, death, and vampire bats. Instead
of bright, sunny flowers in May, black is
the clouds on a dark, rainy day. Rats,
rabbits, witches, ink, the deep black
floor of a roller rink. Dogs, eyes, hair,
skin, the pain of when you fail to win.
This is black, all things combined,
This is my poem and only mine.

   —Jenn Arsenault

Life

Life is a game that we play.
And your body is just like clay.
Molding it into whatever you want,
You can even mold it if you are a runt.

Life can have unexpected turns,
And you feel as if you became burned.
But life when you are young is a joyful time,
Reassured by your parents that you don't make a dime.

But by the time you reach ten and six,
You're able to drive something not made of popsicle sticks.
And growing up on your quest for money,
Even if your nose is runny.

And then you reach your mid-life crisis,
Looking and finding all the cheapest prices.
And some skin begins to wrinkle and fall,
And you'll need aerobics and basketball.

And as your life comes to a close,
Hopefully at 100 years or more, but no one knows.
And as you make your final descent,
You'll leave this life without a red cent.

—*John Michael King*

Queens Bound F

Bing Bong - Step lively and make room for the boarding
passengers.
Another Manhattan morning commute on the F line. It's there -
stationary - aluminum - red lights - it's mine. The heat wafts
up the stairs with the monkey-house smells of morning. The
last passengers are now boarding.

The morning DJ warned me - "Wake up you sleepy head" "Roll
over and stretch - you won't feel so dead." Why did I take so long
in the shower and that toast seemed to take an hour

Down the stairs that are mostly slanting, doors still open -
engine panting. Gushing stale air refrigeration. Welcome to
the Church Street Station.

I see my boss with his coffee cup. What's a matter sugar was
it trouble getting up? God help me make that train - 15
minutes - Not late again. Conductor hold those doors - watch
the maniac cross the floor.

Those people on the train look so perky. Oh no - black and
blue pumps - I feel like a turkey. Move in we're all Chock
Full-O-Nuts and slide over I won't make a fuss.

Bing Bong - step lively and watch the closing doors.

—*Jennifer Ryan*

Keys

He sits down at the piano and my heartbeat speeds with
    anticipation before his hands even meet the keys.

He plays and I feel his touch as his hands caress the keys.

He plays a romantic passage and looks my way, knowing I am
    receiving his message from the keys.

He and I exist separate from the audience, joined by the keys.

He alternates powerful chords with light arpeggios and I
    transpose the touch of his hands to my body from their
    place on the keys.

He takes his bow to enthusiastic applause, departs the stage
    and takes my hand in his, reality replacing the keys.

—*Betty J. Hengemuehler*

A Problem From Hell

And with the knell of the bell,
Another perishes.
Death upon Death,
Murder upon murder;
The world shudders and cries
Yet still denies.

Mass rape and torture - systematic,
The world agrees it's oh so tragic.
Yet we sit, make hollow threat
Only thankful it is not we who are met;
with death, rape, and murder.

Orphaned child, widowed mother
How can we allow another?
What we see is reality,
Yet we've displaced our own morality.

Another is raped, another dies,
How we've separated our heart from our eyes.
Where is our heart, where is our soul?
Death once summoned, Death now lingers;
The decrepit bell continues to toll.

—*Allan Jane Pensfield*

For Time Without End

A chaotic existence of ultimate doom, heartfelt misery of
anxiety and gloom, no more of life's pleasures enjoying ones
friends, one person alone for time without end.

An empty room of despair of anguish and woe, the feeling of
loneliness why, and how so? From the time to destroy to the
time that would mend, sheer madness from loneliness for time
without end.

A deeply broken heart with pieces unfound, to lose all trust
from those who are around, with no love to borrow and no love
to lend, a hopeless existence for time without end.

The darkness upon her escaping the day's light, brings
heartfelt emotion in the gloom of the night, a soft still voice
speaks through her eerie scream, "I'm here as you need me,
even when it doesn't seem. My peace I will give you, my love
I will send, my love will be with you for time without end."

—*Donald Coles*

Sleeping Ears

Every morning the first thing I hear
are very loud sounds in my sleeping ears
the puppy is whining
the baby is crying
my two little boys are rudely fighting

The first thing I do is cover my head
but I know what I must do is get out of bed
So I get out of bed and let out the pup
I go get the baby and love her up
I look at my boys and say please shut-up!

At the end of my day I bathe all 3 kids I scrub
them and love them and put them to bed
by this time of night, all I can think of is me
trying to relax by the deep blue sea.

So I jump in the tub and try to relax
because if I don't I may throw in the ax
then I get into bed and the next thing
I hear are very loud sounds in my
sleeping hears.

—*Jackie Wright*

Words

Words in anger, I could have said.
Are words that are better left dead.
Words in anger do no good.
They never hurt the one they should.
A word in kindness will always do
Twice as much for me and you.
so remember, be kind when you speak;
And gather the friends you always seek.
Words are tools for right or wrong.
They can cut and hurt or form a song.
They can make you laugh or want to cry.
They can make you giggle and want to fly.
They can make you feel happy or just plain mad.
But to do the latter is just plain sad.
So remember this good advice
Use only words that are really nice.
Just keep this principle in your mind.
Let it guide you til' the end of time
Words of praise are repeated forever.
Words in anger are repeated never.

—*John E. Pregler*

The Way

Can you see, can you see? Or,
are you a naive little soul searching
the seven seas and lands for a child gifted
but among many wounded in the fierce
darkness of the shadows and moon.

Can you see, can you see? Or, are
you smart beyond intelligent with your
soul locked tightly in your petite yet large
heart. Romping lands over seas for a place to
rest.

Oh how I've found the way
beyond darkness, beyond land and seas.
Up, up, up beyond the blue sky is the way.
Oh please, oh please tell me can you see the
brightly lit way? Yet not too brightly lit to see
the way.

—*Gina Buzzetta*

Temp'rance

(A Cry and Hew for Breathalizer Tests)

Wherefore art thou, temperance?
Are you here among us?
Be it you now at our beck,
No longer awaiting our call?
Yah, wouldst have us pristine pure,
Naying now a beckoning nature need,
Denying, yet, our very seed?
Be this as it may,
Waiting never our very station,
Forever, too, shadow of Carrie Nation.
Hear we now a hush,
Rending us as driven slush.

Written after 25 years of sobriety
followed by a "random" breathalizer test.

—*Glenn Abercrombie*

Flower Garden

The lilies that grow by the waters edge
Are both pure and divine,
The daisies that grow by the bushy hedge
Are as pretty as you will find.

But the violets that grow by the garden rail
Are as radiant and fresh as dew,
And the orchids that grow beside the trail
Will thrill your heart anew.

—*Eldon W. Robnett*

The Gold Sky

Frustrations abound, my emotions tumble
around and around.
Sometimes I smile when deep inside
I wear a frown.
When I'm misunderstood and feel like crying.
My innermost self compels me to
keep on trying.
And look on high toward the golden sky.
Where God almighty watches over me.
Through the storms and trials I
call upon the one divine.
Then peace and calm I find.
My burdens are lifted, he does it for me.
Right up there from the Golden sky
He takes my grief and sends me relief.
When I need him, he's always near.
With lots of mercy and love, he's kind and dear.
All up there from the golden sky.
My God is the loving one who comforts me when I want to cry;
Not far away, he's right up there in the Golden sky.

—*Bernardine McComb*

In Loving Memory Of My Husband Donald J. Roberts

The leaves of golden brown are whirling all
Around, as Donald Roberts does the town.

Going here and going there, making friends
Just everywhere.

He stopped to smell the roses all along the
Way, knowing he was soon going away.

The leaves are crunching under our feet as
Donald goes to his final retreat, God is here,
God is there and now Donald is in his care.

—*Gail Roberts*

Love Whispered... A Cry Of Love

The dawn appeared in the Eastern sky
As a white cloud passed by
Awakened from a love within
Another day has now began
A journey I long to take
Praying for forgiveness of my past mistakes
A whisper of love dries my eyes
A step into the right direction and my guide
Awakened sound and in my right mind
Jesus' love is always on time
The rising sun shining so bright
Reflections of his love out of the guiding light
Up above the world so high
Serving His purpose with no questions why
A day in the life we want to know
Jesus Christ is the way to go
Making it through the morning with all our wants and needs
God has given love... satisfaction guaranteed
As trouble seems to come my way
Love whispers... a cry of love is in our day

—*Charlotte Miller*

Peace

Dark at night the gangs are at fight with few people in site.
As I walk through the streets the homeless people have nothing
to eat teenagers think they're grown babies are being born
mother is at work dad is acting like a jerk the kids are at
school acting like fools brothers hangin' out on the corner
thinkin' he's cool prejudice has begun when will it be done
blacks hate whites can't we talk without a fight children are
being abused there is no excuse for any abuse let's stop being
funny this is more than money let us combine as one let there
be peace on earth!

—*Gabrielle Mayes*

The Greatest Gift

My Christmas list grows smaller each year
As friends and family all disappear
What can I give to those left behind
The wonder of Jesus, forgiving and kind

Our friend in dark hours
When forsaken we pray
He uses his powers
To show us the way

What greater gift
Can my humble heart bring
Than to wrap you in Jesus
Our Lord and our King
  —Florence Pearson

Sorry, Gramps!

We wish we had noticed the feeble old man.
As he labored every day.
He fed the calves and mowed the lawn.
And helped to bale the hay.

When his ancient well went dry,
Down into its innards he went
He quickly repaired the rusty pump
Though his strength was all but spent.

He sat in his chair one sunny day.
And we patted his wrinkled cheek
It was too late, he was too far gone.
They laid him to rest last week.
  —Genevieve McNulty

You, Me and "Quiet"

Well, here it is a Saturday
as I begin another hospital stay
The Admissions girl begins her long task
of endless questions to ask
Each day cards keep arriving - so do the Interns,
nurses and tests
And then the doctor arrives with a twinkle
in his eye
Left behind is some reassurance
Not this month, my love, will you collect my
insurance
Visitors, nurses and patients are gone from
the halls
Hiding their tumors, tonsils and galls
Medication hasn't been passed out yet
but things like that the nurse don't forget
Soon, last pills, some idle chat
The nurse walks to the door and puts out the cat
  —Clarita Comello

Untitled

On a recent trip to California,
as I turned into the narrow lane to a motel
A fast driver from behind, cut me off on my right side
And forced me back on Freeway to avoid an accident.
It was a long drive to Scottsdale being as tired as I was.
I made up a tiny song to keep me awake and alert as follows.

When you're sad, and feel that you're forgotten
And so lonesome, you don't know what to do.
That's the time, when God gets our attention.
Call on Jesus, and He will see you through.

I fitted the words to a tune and arrived home,
very tried, but, safely.
  —Grace Guthrie

Memories

My darling Earl,
As I gaze at what lies before me,
Unfulfilled dreams are my destiny.
We had planned to get lost together,
Instead, I'm drifting around like a feather.

How grateful I am for twenty five years of your smiles;
  of your morning embraces with accompanying,
   "Good Morning, Spots"
  of your good company and delightful humor at mealtime;
  of your calm temperament;
  of the thoroughness with which you did your errands;
  of little things you made to simplify my tasks;
  of your ability to turn downers into uppers;
  of your continual favors that made other people happy;
  of your faithfulness to me and the confidence I could
   place in you;
  of holding hands;
  of the intimacy I shared with you;
  of knowing your forgiveness when I was less than perfect.

Though you are gone,
Memories keep you near!
  —Della E. Pederson

Yesterday

Loneliness begins to fill me
As I stare into your crystal eyes
As thoughts begin to enter my mind
Though fast asleep I'm wide awake
Tenderness has now escaped me
As I walk into the wind, it sighs
Alone, this time by myself, I hear
Your voice in every breath I take

Happiness pretends to feel me
As I glance into the empty hall
But the music no longer plays, will
All of the memories be lost?
Home again, my thoughts betray me
As I wonder why I felt so tall
Thoughts of hopes and doubts and yesterdays
So many times my mind they crossed
  —Bryan A. Ross

She Fills My Heart

  I follow a narrow path. . .
as I walk through the woods alone...
all the sounds are of nature only...
 no television, no cars, no phones.

  I stop and sit against a tree...
to see what nature has to share...
 I begin to think about a lady...
  whose beauty is beyond compare.

  A chirp comes from a branch nearby...
eight little chickadees land in the tree...
all dressed in grey with little black caps....
  thank you for visiting me.

  I hear a sound and turn around...
to see a little fawn and a doe...
 so fragile and so innocent...
  like someone that I know.

  There are so many simple things...
  we never take notice of...
she fills my heart with laughter...
  she fills my heart with love.
  —Brian Yacur

Take Care

A demon once said unto me,
As I walked in his garden;
"Take care where you tread
with your tender bare feet little one.
For you see, the one wicked thing,
That the Devil gave the rose,
Was the thorn."
I just stared at him,
And smiled stupidly.
For I knew not what he meant.
But over time, I've trodden on the roses,
And been pricked by many a thorn.
And hence I have come to understand,
What the demon had said;
"Take care...."

—*Charmon J. Luther*

What's In My Heart

In the midst of the storm
As I wander slowly along,
I think of "Why can't I be with you?"
Inside my heart is torn and blue.

I've known you for oh so long,
Your tender touch causes me no harm.
You cross my mind in many ways,
With you forever I want to stay.

I have thoughts of you everyday,
Whether I am at work, school, or at play.
The pleasure that you give inside,
Is so very obvious I can't hide.

If I could only see you for a while,
Then I'd be happy, I'd even smile.
But since you've gone and left me here,
My mind reminisces without you near.

I miss you when you're not around,
Upon my face there is a frown.
I know that you have things to do,
Couldn't you at least include me too?

—*Darlene R. Hall, R.M.A.*

Alabama Girl

Most folks think of Alabam
As little but grits and country ham,
Cornbread soppin' and collard greens,
Fatback meat topped with butterbeans.
Buddy, you'd better take another look.
There's more there than what they cook.
Just take the time to look around.
You'll see that beauty does abound.
And if your mind might so incline,
You'll find yours as I found mine.
I slowed a bit in life's hectic pace
And found my rose in that very place.
She's all flashing eyes with face so fair,
The prettiest one, I do declare.
I travelled the world and finally found
My caviar girl in a catfish town.

—*John W. Olive*

Untitled

Along the water's edge we roam,
As the waves rush up to meet my feet.
My step, as a drop into water, falls
And disturbs the tranquil glowing sands.
My heart enthralled with nature's beauty
Sings out with love for all the world.
My hand enveloped with strength and power, is
Warmed by his touch, entranced by his love
As I revel in my mind's mirage.

—*Glenda Lynn*

My Prayer To Thee

It matters not to me if I take a girlfriend, nor even a wife
As long as I can be of service to You through my life
I pray, Dear Lord, for a servant's heart
that I may help those afflicted by Satan's dart

That through my times of triumph and those of suffering
may I the lost and hurting to Thee bring
I pray, Loving Father, that I may a good steward be
of all that You so lovingly provide for me

That Your love and kindness overflow my brim
and that Your light through me, be a beacon in the night so dim
Something more I bring to Thee
that every soul Your's forever be

And not one be left for Satan, on this vast earth's floor
that he be not a threat, nevermore
And may I be an instrument of Thy peace
and a lonely soul may I comfort, as a lamb's wool fleece
Now I release my life from my hand to Thee
for whatever Thy will, I want to be. Amen.

—*Bryan Humphrey Penney*

The Fishing Boats

How often I watched the fishing boats,
As the fishermen brought them ashore.
The waves rolled high, wetting their coats,
That was in the days of yore.

In those days the work was seldom for naught,
The fishermen left in the early morn,
They were anxious to see what they'd caught,
All was stillness except for the old fog horn.

Coming in the boats bobbed up and down out of sight,
It could be seen only when it came upon a crest.
The fog was lifting, and it was getting light,
It hadn't been easy, but they'd done their best.

Thousands of sea gulls were beginning to land,
The fishermen threw them the remains of the fish,
As the sea gulls settled down on the sand,
They were hungry and enjoyed their delicious dish.

—*Grace McGowan*

Stuck Or Unstuck

I look at you and I'm filled with emotions that are boundless
as the sea. Rambling, I try to find a way to contain them so
that you can not discover this weakness. Doing and saying
anything to hide my feelings, I realize it is useless. My
heart is filled with juvenile feelings of curiosity,
nervousness, expectation and fear. The sequence of events have
come full circle. With my heart and my mind partaking in a
struggle that only Shakespeare could describe. I have come to
a point where I can do nothing, finally I am stuck! I stare
into the gateway of your soul and hope I see the same conflict
that binds me. The ability to read your thoughts is impossible
due to my own inability to react to mine. As you look away I
tug on your arms in hopes that your eyes will welcome my eager
stare. You turn back to me and once again the battle rages in
me. Finally, my heart has won, destroying all feelings of fear
and hesitation. Now, as our lips meet, my breath is taken away
and my heart feels as though it will explode. Regaining my
consciousness with reality, I find a new pillar of strength in
my life. One made with love and passion, and now I am unstuck!

—*Daniel Lee Thompson*

222

The Leaves

Look at the leaves,
As they fall from the trees.
Red, yellow, brown, and golden
An array of colors,
As they fall swiftly to the ground.
But the viewer does not hear their sound.
The leaves are trampled,
By the foot of man,
As we tread on the land.
That crispy crackling sound of destruction,
As the wind wisp swiftly by.
Oh if we could only feel,
As our head is pointed toward the sky.
The season is changing from day to day,
But we are not astute,
We must find our way.
For the leaves have been brushed
and pushed aside,
And we have lost the universal prize.

—*Deborah Skannal*

Joyce Faye Linker

The boy in me was relinquishing to manhood.
As this phenomena unfolded, so did certain fantasies.
Heroes, I had read, won the hearts of maidens fair.
Thoughts of these damsels brought delightful ecstasies.

One day, unexpectedly, I saw her. From deep within
an inner chasm, my soul ignited the mental fuse;
my heart performed the ritual spasm.

Amidst a crowd, she was, with her friends.
My eyes beheld her profile as the crowd provided sanctity.
She turned, faced towards me, and smiled.
Her image, from that moment, is with me for eternity.

In that instant, the meaning of beautiful became much clearer.
I was mesmerized by her smile, raven black hair, and almond
eyes. Her face was masterfully, delicately freckled and it
radiated warmth. I could not contain from within,
uncontrollable, yearning sighs.

What strange and wonderful feelings were surging through me.
Ne'r had I felt them before; ne'r again will they be the same.
Too heavenly to approach, she was, and beyond my world.
Forever and always, 'My First True Love,' shall be her name.

—*Brian Kuhlman*

Will You Love Me

You love me now, our years are few.
As time goes by, will you remember, "I Do?"

In sickness in health, till death do us part.
Will you remember the words, you felt in your heart?

Time passes by, with the speed of light.
Dark healthy hair, becomes so white.

My walk slows down, I hear not too well.
If I ask something twice, will you smile and tell?

My memory fades, the mind not too keen.
Will you give me your arm, on which to lean?

My eyes may cloud, so hard to see.
But I'll always love you,
Will you love me?

—*John Lindvay*

From North To South

The smell of the damp earth beneath my feet - the smell of pine -
As we perceive time, the moment is fleet, but the moment will
    always be mine.
The smell of my horse as he stands beside -
the feel of the leather as I start to ride.
The feel of the wind upon my face -
it wraps and enfolds me like a lover's embrace.
The colors of greens against the hill - the palette shades one
    into the other unbroken.
The scene is beyond the mere word spoken.
The color of cattle against the greens - red with faces shining
    white,
or others, like the raven's wing, as black as night.
Blue sky, with clouds from white to gray - a flash of fire from
    a sun gold and red.
It changes, and changes so we are led -
from dawn through a day, 'til night's blanket is spread.
The memories remain, tho the moment is past.
We are prisoners of time and nothing can last,
Save that, engraved in the mind and the heart -
sweet memories that shall never depart.

—*Jaylene Sutton*

The Dolls Of Christmas Long Ago And Far Away

Christmas has never been the same my dears
As when I was a child.....
To awake with youthful glee
And see you underneath the Christmas tree
It was the most wonderful time
When life was kind and you were mine
We played all day till dark, then to bed we must depart
Where I would hold you close to my heart
You heard my secrets, my joys and tears
And even all my growing-up fears
You were there through good times and bad
And some that were even very sad
You got me through and now I'm grown
With a son of my very own
Maybe someday he will see
Exactly what you mean to me
You were my childhood light
To brighten up my summer days and winter nights
It seems like looking through a haze
To my youthful childhood days

—*Barbara K. Grgurich*

Moonlight

"O, dear old wise man, what is moonlight?"
asked I.
That old man, he looked at me with a twinkle in his eye.
"Moonlight is a delicate lace that dances in the night,
across the sky."
With his answer I was satisfied, yes, I was
satisfied with his reply.

"O, dear old wise man," I said again, with another
question in mind,
"Why cannot man capture the moonlight and
watch its beauty age with time?"
"Moonlight should never be captured, for it
would surely wither and die;
Then its light would be gone once more,
once more our people would be blind.

For beauty has to float about for all the world to see.
It cannot be confined to one place, like a
common bush or tree.
Now listen to what I say, I tell you, listen to me;
Beauty shall remain forever, as long as it is free.

—*Erin M. Anderson*

Open Your Eyes

The skies are gray, it looks like rain,
at least that's what the weatherman says.
"It's so dark, I can't see, won't you light
a candle so I can see?
The candle's so dim, can I light another one?
"What's wrong with me, why can't I see?
Two candles and I still can't see."
"What's wrong with me? What's going on, why can't I see?"
"Come on, tell me! What's wrong with me?"
"It's time to face the world, open your eyes, look around,
stop hiding behind that cloud.
It's always darker before the light, open your eyes,
face your life!
Open your eyes, open your eyes!
Stop hiding behind that cloud."
"I can't see, I can't see, help me!"
"Open your eyes, face your life, open your eyes,"
"I can see, I can see, I can see!"
"You face your life, now you can see.
Face the world, it's all Yours!"

—Dorothy Jean Barker

Rainy Day

She lay curled in a small bundle, staring out
at the rain. The trees trying to brush away
the clouds heavy with nature's tears, bent
almost to the ground in vain. The leaves
sweeping close to the earth then up to the sky
again and again, only to be beaten back, washed
clean in the splashing sound. Hidden birds
that refused to sing, in water-filled nests
like upside down bells that no longer ring.
The wind joined in the fight, blowing the grey
clouds across the morning sky, as it whispered
to the sun to hurry with its drying light. She
pulled up her warm blanket refusing to cry,
fell asleep just as the sun sent down its rays
of brightness to light up the sky and the earth
to dry.

—Dorothy M. Clark

Memories Of Grandma

To some, she was mother, grandma, or sister, To others; maybe
aunt, neighbor, or friend. Some called her their SCRABBLE
partner; (She loved competing 'til the end).

Folks would love to just stop by To chit-chat friend to friend,
She'd always make them feel welcome And said, "Please come
   back again."

A visitor never came to church; Without her friendly greeting,
Nor did she ever miss a service, Or Ladies Missionary meeting.

As time took her memory, she couldn't always recognize us,
But she never forgot about Howard, and that's when she'd make
   a fuss.
She'd look out of the window, as she sat in her rocking chair,
And then she'd say once again, "When will Howard be here?"

Although we'll surely miss her, we've shared a lot of love,
Time spent with grandma was precious, but grandpa waited above.
She's happier now in Heaven, more than we can know,
Since the day she heard her Savior say, "My child, it's
   time to go."

—Debbie Hauch

The Last Day Of Frances

Silence, overwhelming; mid-afternoon, bright and sunny;
Autumn in Michigan;
Colors, reflections; falling leaves, motions;
Peace and serenity, permeating and filling,
The blue sky, the universe, each cell of my body and my soul.

A visit with Frances,
Dying, waiting, for months in a hospital room.

Silence, overwhelming; elderly blind mother, weeping;
Grownup children, standing in the corner, sobbing;
Husband, ever trying to find a comforting word;
The uncontrollable motions and twitchings of the cachectic body;
The uncontrollable, never-ending waves of emotion;
Each moment, an eternity, filled with thousands of memories;
The panorama of life unfolding at the speed of light.
Suddenly her face lights up, then the mystic smile, then the peace
   and serenity.
O, then the color, the glow and the warmth of love,
Quickly fills up and brightens up the dreary hospital room,
Outshining the brightest color of Michigan autumn.
My heart then knew what she had already known.
Today is the last day after years of gallant fight.

—Hahn J. Lee

Rambling 1

Moving forward delicately balancing between frost and fire.

Writing isn't lonely; you have your memory for companionship.

You leave reality and embrace madness. Sanity seems to slip
away. I don't want to play the game of life this way . . .
this day!!! It circles, skirts, and mocks the burping baby
standards I've known.

The innocent path my mother bundled me up for, held my hand,
and walked me through, no longer applies.

Take the boxing gloves off the demons. Dress them in suits;
they are much easier to deal with that way.

I birth my characters in a bittersweet sauce . . . Reality.
The bond that binds is the arm that reaches from childhood to
present and clutches all of it together.

The winds of greed, hatred and doubt are blowing with little
regard, reverence, or respect for anyone or anything. The
knowledge of hope, promise, and fulfillment, are waging a
mighty war with doubt, weakness, and despair.

I cannot fathom the mind that is shackled by the mundane. I
would claw to open the door braced against discovery.

—Constance F. Knutson

The Better Fly

"So", said the fly, "You're a better fly than I."
   "Aye", he replied, "That is I."
   "Bye, my dear fly", he said with a sigh.
   "And for that you must die!" he cried.
   "Why?" he inquired, "Surely that is a lie."
   "Nigh, fly, you may not fly by my eyes!"
      "My, my, my."
"My, my, my to thy! Now prepare to decry your sly, spy!"
      "I must imply, that I am a flea."
"Thee art a flea? To thy I am no fly, either. I too am a
      flea. And you see to me, to be a flea
      is to be free. We are all fleas, see?"
   "So", said the flea, "You're a better flea than me."

—Barry Schechter

Old War Buddies

Oh where are they now, my comrades at arms
Back at their desks, in their trucks, on their farms

It's been twenty five years since that year overseas
We spent filling sandbags beneath the jungle trees

We were closer than kin, we shared so many things
Though we'd come from all over, from Maine to Rock Springs

Young men of nineteen far away from Dad and Mom
Most of us had not heard of this place, Vietnam

Through fear and the horrors of war we weathered the storm
Thanks to the friendships and the bonds we did form

I wonder quite often how their lives now must be
As I think of them now, do they think of me

What like are their jobs, their families, their wives
How do they look, are they well, still alive

Just to see them once more would do my heart good
We'd reminisce, laugh, drink some pitchers, we would

Oh where are they now my buddies from the war
I'll see them in my memory, for evermore
—*Douglas J. Boyle*

October: Welcome!

October dressed in many colors moved day by day
back into time, while the cool brisk arms of an
early winter came dancing, nimbly prancing to
nature's tune of the falling leaves.

The rising sun spread across the skies above,
while flickers of sunlight bounced to and fro
from the many trees and falling leaves of colors
bright. Some yellow, some green, like snowflakes
floating down to the ground in colors of red.

So, don't become frightened or upset. Halloween
is coming…. but it's not here yet.

Now, if you should hear strange sounds riding on
the wind behind you and there's nothing in sight,
it might be October's leaves tumbling…not
footsteps lurking through the night.

Still, if I were you… and I'm not always right…
I wouldn't take any sounds lightly…if they are
like footsteps in the night.
—*Alfred Jack Northern*

The Melody

The artist gently coaxes a melody from the
battered piano.
The melody fills the room, seeking empty places
and filling them.
The walls vibrate slowly as the melody sings of
love, hope, peace.
Now they shake violently as the melody tells of
war, death, illness.
The chairs nod as the melody sings of healing.
The melody ends on a hopeful note as the
artist leaves the room to dream.
—*Beth Topping*

In The Light

Seeker of the beautiful and wondrous
be content in your dreaming
for their is credence in their being

Conform not
to the images held in the hearts
of those who cannot see with your vision

For in the darkness and gloom
that is made
there gleams a sun for you
still dream and have won
—*Deborah Freilicher*

Retirement

It would be hard for her, she knew it would be. But it would
be worse for him. The very thought of it brought a tight
feeling to her chest, a thrill of dread to her heart. He
wouldn't even talk about it.

This land into which he had poured the strength of his young
manhood! Leave it? No, he would rather die! He could not, he
would not talk about it. It would be hard for her. It would be
much worse for him.

She would have some work to do as usual….cooking, a bit of
fancywork. But he? How could he while away the long, idle
hours? He wasn't much for reading…his slow, old mind was
left far behind by the noisy box in the corner.

The rooms were so small…they had inspected the place. She
said that there would be less word to do. He said nothing at all.

No garden in which to feel the soil if spring should come. No
old familiar trees to caress… Everything seemed so …new.

Hobbies? A foolish word! He had always kept up the place.
The orchard, the fields, the pasture, the yard. Yes, it would

be hard for her. It would be much, much worse for him.
—*Elaine Ray*

The Stilling Of The Tempest

"Awake Him! Awake Him!" 'Tis the cry of disciples on a storm
beaten sea. With faces aghast, and hands upward turned
They grope for the master, who lies fast asleep
At the end of the ship; nor ever does He
Heed the waves splashing o'er Him.
Unconscious is He of the tempest before Him.

The tempest is high and the ship,
As if in defiance of the frantic disciples,
Rocks high on the waves, sending the fresh spray o'er them
and the master
Nor hope to escape from the present disaster.
With quivering lips rouse they Him from His sleep.
"We perish," they cry, 'gainst the noise of the deep.

The Master, an infinite calm pervading His face
Arises, and going to the side of the ship
Outstretches His hand with the comeliest grace.
The wind, wild, doth cease;
The sea, wroth, doth roll in soft billows now.
His followers question, "What manner is He,
Obeyed by even the winds and the sea?"
—*Cora E. Walters*

God's Love For Us

I am living my life peaceful today,
　　Because God has shown me his holy way;
Although at times I get upset and swear,
　　My heavenly father will always be there;
He comforts me when times get hard,
　　And he promises to be my personal guard.

Every night I kneel down to pray,
　　To just give him praise for getting me through another day;
My love for God is deeper than the sea,
　　And the love from God is inside of me;
It is in my heart and in my soul,
　　I will surely have God's love wherever I go.

So if you would like what I have now,
　　Read God's word and it will tell you how;
I ask you please to give God a try,
　　Because his love for us will never die;
God our father is waiting for your call,
　　And he promises to help us if we stumble or fall.

　　　　—Hunter W.K. Jamile

My Heart's Door

As of today I am closing my heart's door
because I just can not love you anymore!
It's wrong to think that you understood;
I would give and you took all you could!

My soul's eyes are open and they can see
that you tried to make a fool out of me!
Yes, you'd make me laugh and I did smile
making our worldly life worth its while.

I have my needs, but simply want to say;
before I turn and start walking this way
I did love you, but all is to be no more
because I've now locked my heart's door!

　　　　—H. Daniel King

Life On The Blessed Road

Life on the blessed road is the one I choose to trod,
Because my Saviour is with me
　　with His tender comforting rod;

To uphold me with His righteousness
When at times I seem to fall;

But never will I be cast down
　　for He's my all and all;

And though the trials of life will come to toss me to and fro.
My Saviour keeps me sound and gives me strength
　　as I leave them at His door;

I must always remember not to worry or fret,
Because my Saviour lightens my load...
　　as I travel on this blessed road!

All I'm saying my Christian friend, is that Christ is by my side;
　　and as I travel on this blessed road,
I have the Saviour as my guide!

　　　　—Betty Gene Wilson

There Is No Love Quite As Lovely As A Motherly Love

When all other love reject you a mother love will always be there
Because there is no love quite as lovely as a mother love
For all of her love ones, and children to share
It is their health and welfare that she is always thinking of

A mother love her children all the time
She is more concern about them, than she is herself
Where they go or maybe they are always on her mind
She really love those little darling in the pictures upon the shelf

No there is no love as lovely as a mother love
For all the things that she have to go through
Sometimes putting up with delinquency kids, sometimes denial of
But from sunset to sunset for her kids her love is always true

So when the job is done and the fight is won

Always think of your mother as number one
Because there is no love quite as lovely as a mother love
Indeed it is one of our greatest blessing from above.

　　　　—Earl Hopkins

Isla De Todos Santos

It's the island where all the saints go and Lord they need them
　　there
Because waves the size of mountains are the island's fare
A rock in the Pacific that arises from deep blue
Northwest swells show their full force to an intrepid surfing crew
I've lived and I have died there my soul I've laid to rest
The times have been the worst and those same times have been the
　　best

Arriving with the vigor of a young boy who needs a date
Only to leave a little wiser having flirted with my fate
Every trip is an adventure camaraderie at its best
But take the time to study because you need to pass this test
Seek those who've gone before you the elders of your tribe
Listen to their words of wisdom the path to follow to survive

The drop will leave you breathless craving a little more
But outside could be the beast that takes you to the ocean floor
One or two will tax your system more than that will shake your
　　core
Further beasts on the horizon and you may wash up on the shore
So plan your journey wisely and sleep well in the night
Because outside the beast prepares to embrace you come daylight

　　　　—Bill Updyke

"We're The Homeless But We're Not Hopeless"

We're the homeless but we're not hopeless
Because we live on the streets
We're just as much apart of your society
When night comes you can find us laying around anywhere
By day we're taking up our personal belongings
As such as they may be
Cardboard boxes you've seen them many of times
For money we'll buy something to eat here and there
As far as the rest of us- it's right from the trash cans
Taking no thought for tomorrow just like the good book says
For the next day it's the same thing all over again
Standing up or on our bended knees, hands out asking
Do you have any spare change please?

In parks on benches just like foxes
Trying to find a hole to call home with our cardboard boxes
We push our carts faithfully everyday so you see
While you're on your way to work having coffee or tea

We're the homeless but we're not hopeless
If given half the chance to function again as we once did
In our society.

　　　　—Arnette M. Flowers

Memories Of You ...

Memories of when you were two and would say "uh-good-licious",
  Because you couldn't pronounce delicious.

        Or when it was time for bed,
You would run and get 'Ultra -Violet Catastrophe' to be read.

When I would drop you off at nursery school,
      you'd wave and say, "see you de later",
or when you would sing the song 'There was a Little Alligator'.

You would not cry when I left you there, but at the end of
        each day,
      You would have so much to say.

I remember when you where four and you would run up to me and
say, "Mama you're my favorite girl in the whole wide world
        today."

      Memories of you will always be sweet,
        Until the next time we meet.
  —Dorothy Revels

Imaginations

I image loving you.
Because you were so special in my life.
Like a falling greenback.
You were the most sweetest man alive.
I image my eyes gazing as you past from time to time.
I image taking you every where to show you off as my king of
  love.
I image teaching you, leading you, explaining to you, how love
  is shown.
I image talking to you in latin.
You whispering to me in spanish.
I image you playing and teasing me with enjoyment.
I image you holding me tight and kissing like wild dogs in
  heat.
I image you and I making love all day and night.
I image you awakening me with a kiss of windsong.
I image you and I together forever.
I image mostly how you loved me in style.
They were all great imaginations.
But that's all they were-
  —Carolyn Spann

Sister

Sister, girl you are my friend.
Been friends from the beginning to the end.

Things lookin up, trouble lookin down
I looked far and near.
No one else came, but you were here.

Then sister I must say.
When you walk tall and how you do achieve
Never is there a time.
I wish that you are me.

When you lost weight,
No problem did I have.
When I gained weight,
You said having a baby was my great fate.

Thanks for your hand on my shoulder
When my mountain looked like a boulder.

Yes, we go back a ways.
Our friendship of family, lets keep it always.
Yes, each and every day.
  —Bobbie Jean Goodall

Black And White Forever

Black formals and white roses will
begin our life together.
As we say, "I do", we can not know,
what the future will bring.
As we begin our family we are filled with joy.
Wondrous are our girl and our boy.
Crumpled like a toy, the car sat motionless.
The call came at three a.m.
The children knew something was amiss.
A drunk driver...your wife...two cars...one driver
    dead...the other alive...is all you heard.
What is wrong with this world?!
A black casket and white roses will end our
life together.
Please, tell them I loved them and kiss them good night.
Black and white forever.
Always remember, I said, "I do" and goodbye with black
and white.

      —Jennifer Mead

"Rage"

The war isn't over yet it's only just
    begun, we feel pain and anger
    of the soldiers in the sun.
Blood between our fellow man and
    killing in the street, leaves our
    world a battered place; a world
    of self defeat.
The self destruction of our peers has
    lessend our own minds, to make us
    think that all our dreams were tossed
    and left behind.
Images of "great white hope" and
    "knights of armor" shine, is not the
    life we live each day but that of hate and crime.
The rage of all the pain we feel is what
    we live each day, the ignorance of
    some of us has made so many pay.
The trials and tribulations of the pain
    out in the street, are those of our
    fellow man and those you tend to meet.
    —Daisy Henderson

Youth

Thank God I'm not fifteen again,
Believe me that's the truth,
Waiting expectantly for some awkward gangling youth
To ring my front doorbell,
And escort the bashful inexperienced girl that once was me,
To some drive-in show, for pizza and a coke.

Each lull in conversation,
My shrill laughter to a corny joke.
The lonely painful silence that each lull in conversation
    brings,
Only to realize that the worse is yet to come —
In my hesitation there is one thought foremost in my mind,

As the evening draws to a close
Will he reach to embrace me,
This gangling youth of mine,
Oh how wonderful to pass this stage you see,
for now that I am middle age
My fears have ceased to be!!!
    —Anne Morrison

227

Reign Of Winter

Arching limbs of pine and fir
Bend low beneath the fallen snow.

A vaulted dome of leaden skies
Looks down approvingly on winter's
Latest mantle of glistening white.

Well-fed bears are in their dens;
Nests of squirrels are full of occupants and store.
Songs of birds are silent now.

Nature sleeps!
Frozen creeks flow but a trickle.
Coyote yips are heard from distant hollows.
Familiar tinkling bells and bleats of sheep
Float far on heavy, crisp, still air.

Faintly heard is one jet high overhead.
Sleigh bells jingle as two thin ribbons
Cut along a curving road.
Children laugh at frosty whiskered stead.
Winter reigns!

—*Dale A. Strawn*

Balcony

The moon is slipping
beneath black clouds. A scant breeze wafts in,
yet still the trees are silent.
From my perch, all I can hear is the rhythmic, graveled crunch
of footsteps, and the punctuative snap of twigs.

Hidden by clouds, the moon now ceases
to exist. There is still some lighting, neither diffuse
nor direct, but seeping quietly from some shy place. It traces
the outline of the trees, and lets me see, but its source is
still a mystery. Now, though, one thing is certain: There
was never any moon, only characters standing for sounds,
sounds which evoked an image.

Moonlight comes, and goes, with the wind.
Never truly clear, either diaphanous
or muted, the moon bobs along, a reflection in the sky
of what lies silent in the puddles below.

The moon tonight, while very bright earlier, is now dark.
The clouds seem eternal. More than muted, the light is not
hiding, but simply gone.

—*Aaron Tieger*

Lady Bug

Does thou travel in the night,
Beneath the stars that shine so bright.
How many spots does thou have, four?
And does thou want to be squashed upon the floor?

Oh, yes I do travel in the night,
Beneath the stars that shine so bright.
Yes, the spots on my back are four,
And I do not want to be squashed upon the floor.

—*Briana Sacco*

A Flag That Waves True

A blowing of the breeze this morn,
Brought to an eye's glance
This flag we oft' do not see,
the awe of its perspective clear,
Now, we close our eyes with no flag there,
'Tis indeed a something that we felt,
After these eyes opened this dawn
My heart attained that new awe,
For the flag that waves so true.

—*Dorothy M. Bearss*

If Only

If only the leaders of this political world could see, from
beyond the windows of their hearts, and not through eyes of greed,
this good earth shall flourish for many more years to come, now
and then witnessing the wrath of elements, should they not
heed. If only they, who say they are truly concerned and fear
what's to come, and are quick to ward off temptation of
personal gain and greed for power, world existence in freedom
and peace becomes reality, instead of foretold warnings of
total devastation, day to day, hour to hour. If only from the
goodness of their hearts, decisions benefiting all were met,
and mutual agreement for peaceful times and nuclear disarmament
did not wane, living humanist, not militarist, sharing wisdom
and knowledge through compassion, death by peace seekers past,
and patriotic many, will not have been in vain. If only they, from
behind closed doors, could hear the myriad cries and pleas, and
for world salvation break from the monolith, in conscience,
never lonely, from all corners of the world, they gather
without barriers of restraint, power and wealth, striving to
live as one, in peace and in harmony, if only…

—*Camille St. Amour*

Untitled

There is no love, just infatuation.
Bitter as I may be I think it's true
Even though in my adolescent years I am
compared to a pendulum, given as much
freedom as a snail with its home cut off,
I am convinced
Unexpecting boys and girls take the
passion of their inseparableness, the
ability to finish each other's sentences
And they take this as proof of the extremity
of their love. In reality, it only confirms the
degree of their preceding
Loneliness and isolation.

—*Erica Lauren DeRosa*

Beyond A Dream

Here comes Mr Death,
black cape with no face,
quietly, gracefully, sneaking up on me.

Being led by Mr. Death,
his slight touch upon my elbow
guiding me beyond the walls of consciousness.

Rising up, higher and higher
away from the living, soon to be
engulfed by blackness.

Waiting hours… days… maybe years,
when a light appears in the form of an angel,
come to guide me to where I now belong.

Beyond a dream;
memory does scream;
recall the past to see your death.....

—*Debra M. Machmer*

We'll Join Jesus In The Air

Moon, moon, big balloon. "Jesus said you will turn
black. On that day when He comes back". (Matt. 24;29)
Jesus will call us all by name. (John 10;3) Nothing
on earth will be the same, when we board that heavenly
plane. (Thess. 4;17) We'll join Jesus in the air. (Thess.
4;17) Our christian friends will be up there. If you want
to come, just say your prayers. When we leave this earth
we won't care. It's so much better where Jesus is. (Psalm
50;2) Moon, moon, big balloon. Jesus Christ is coming soon.

—*Frances Johnson*

Colours

Yellow reminds me of the sun shining in my eyes,
Blue is the color of the bright azure skies,
Grey is the color of the dust way up high,
And black reminds me of people that die.

Green is always special to me, it reminds me of
the flowers and the trees,
Red is the color of the autumn leaves,
And purple is the color of the tapestries,
Still there are the colors so rare,
but yet so beautiful and so fair.

Peach is the color of the skin so light,
and brown is the color of the African tribe.
White is the blend of all known colors,
But gold is a shade for color and for metal.

But the favorite colors of an American true,
are the colors of red, white and blue.

—*Jenna Kahnke*

Untitled

And I have found a new love, a love of a world where there are
blue skies and fluffy marshmallow clouds as white as snow.
There no people exist in my mind. No words are ever spoken for
they would only be forgotten tomorrow. And I am too intrigued
by the sky of blue to notice possible distractions including
even you? Here no one makes promises but no one breaks
promises as
well. But a promise is felt of how you'll never be sad again!
And you're at peace with yourself, but suddenly the song
changes and Tori is not singing of beautiful things anymore.
Instead she begins to sing of how the world really is with
prejudice and selfishness, and how he wouldn't let her go!
Tears! Tears! Tears! She kissed him, but she still said
"No!" And now lips are brushing across mine... I have so much
love inside. Still I have found no one I want to give my love
to so why did I just give my love to you? You cannot hold
the things I give like love to all colors and the life I live.
I hope when I awaken that I don't see him, but see beautiful
fields and horses in a world where everybody is one and there
is so much love that no one can even remember what hate is.

—*Jessica Riebel*

Waterworld Wonderment

It's the best of times while sitting on the edge of the
boardwalk, watching the gulls as they soar as kites upon the
wind, forever chasing and fussing with each other. One stops
and stares at me with a quizzical look of head-cocked
wonderment, cast at the sandwich morsel in my hand that I
brought to share. Later, while on the shore, bucket in hand,
I pause to wriggle toes in the sand, and a lone gull rises
before the crashing wakes, screeching as it goes. I wonder of
the numbers and thoughts of those long ago who have passed
before me on these same sands, and of the recent prints left
behind that I see, all to be quickly washed by the silvery
sheet of shimmering brine, and tumbling, flowing, grains of sand
forever. I round the bend and plod up into the bay where the
high tides come. That's where I see a treasure chest to
explore with time at hand. I wonder of the times when men set
sail upon that crumbling, broken hulk that lies in a final
resting place, as roost and lookout for the hungry horde of
squawking gulls, when traversing on the feeding grounds they
purposefully go day after day. What was the name that graced
that derelict? How did it come by that fate?

—*Clifton C. Phillips*

Another Mother

There I sit with my newborn son,
Born a week before Christmas,
Savoring in his being - caressing his warm, fresh skin,
Teaching me of the greatest love - just by his presence.
I hold him so close, never wanting to let go.

Another mother readies for Christmas,
Presents joyfully wrapped and waiting,
Waiting for her son to arrive home from college.
Home together - for Christmas.
Her son wears a sweater his mother carefully bought,
To keep him warm - and safe.
He boards his plane in Europe,
And suddenly Lockerbie becomes famous.
Unopened presents remain full,
Open arms remain empty.

I hold my son examining his every breath, his every sigh,
Wishing with all my heart this moment would never end.

Another mother sits,
Heart untamably heaving,
Wishing her moment had never begun.

—*Elizabeth McWilliams Piarulli*

Requiem In May

Silence still skipping on violin strings,
Bows gambol on manes of white little horses,
There will be in hearts a graveyard of birches,
Though spring will still come again and again.

Mourning tuxedos forgot how to cheer,
Souls have nightmares of burglarized drawers,
Musical clefs are stretched into lines -
invisible pains tuned to the stars-.

Spring will soon come - a fugue on the staff -
Bows do still gambol on manes of black horses,
His gallop is equal and rhythmically sure -
heartless reminder of cold, winter Mays -.

—*Iolanda Scripca*

The Boy Treated Wrong

Hence, forward it had to be said, there was a
boy who had to be declared dead. With bruises
and cuts from his toes up to his head.

Why o'why was he treated wrong, He looked
out for danger and kept people from harm. But
instead, His heart was shreivered and pricked by
a throng.

He went in the desert a long lost peasant,
When you looked at him he had a glow of fluorescent.

Way out there it was very hot. His feet were bloody
and filled with clots, but when people needed him
he was there on the dot.

Speed in need, nice indeed, besides his brain
his heart made him succeed.

His life came with age, He couldn't be paged.
All he owned was a brush and bush filled
with sage.

After he was made taken a dive, and routed,
"Hark," someone shouted, "He was the noblest
and sweetest thing alive."

—*Harold Buggage, Jr.*

Starry Eyes

For oh so long I use to gaze upon a star that sparkled more
brightly than all the others, when the moon was full yet and
the night cool yet warm. As the shadows from the moon light is
reflected on the walls of my dark room, as darkness hung in the
late hours as the soft night breeze blow in my room I feel the
warmth of the moon. Nights can be eternal as I gaze upon my
star. But one night I gaze above I saw my star fall, as my eyes
saw it fall my heart felt it more than all! For oh so long,
now I wonder in despair, and wonder oh where have my star had
fallen too, others stars are still there but their sparkle give
no signs as to where my star could have fallen to in the
heavens above, I search the sky countless lonely nights now
without hope without dreams I sleep at night wondering oh where
had my star fallen to. Until the day came and I met this girl, so
beautiful that she made love begin to grow in me and others as
well where there was no without a word spoken with out the moon
above with only a look the love there! no love song could be
written to tell the tale of the love that fall upon those who
see her who falls to their knees but rise to love as well, but
when she lifted up her head so slow and opened her eyes, I see my
fallen star and where it had fallen to, for there it was sparkling
in her eye so brightly.

—*Annie M. Averhart*

The Santa Claus Letter

Dear Santa Claus:
Bring me a toy as magical as you are,
so childlike as I am.
A toy that at the end it becomes
so old and so bright as you certainly are.
A very tender toy as my grammy's blue eye.
But wake me when you come, Grampy Claus;
so we will be three if you decide to play with us
to the holy trinity.

—*Jose Rivadeneyra*

Snow Angels ... In Memory of Marilyn

When the season's first snowflakes start drifting through the air.
Bringing laughter, and excitement to children everywhere.

Three smiling little faces pressed to the window glass,
Watch a soft white blanket slowly cover the grass.

The smell of baking cookies filled the house that day.
Setting those aside, she called, "Let's go out and play!"

Shiny, twinkling, dancing eyes were all that you could see.
Bundled up from head to toe, as warm as they could be.

She had a very special plan, into this wonderland they'd go.
And have such fun together, making angels in the snow!

She made a "Mommie Angel" lying down near them to show.
They followed right along beside, her angels in a row.

Later on, their snow suits were hanging by the door.
And six little "cowboy" boots making puddles on the floor.

She gave them all hot chocolate, with the cookies that were done.
How much it came to mean to them when she took time for fun!

"Mommie's" up in Heaven now, they had to say good-bye.
But they still quickly run outside when snow falls from the sky.

Little angels everywhere, lying in a row,
Smiling up at "Mommie", so she won't miss them so!

—*Bobbie McCreary*

Untitled

Knowing someone like you,
    brings a sunrise to my life.

And like sea waves that continue nonstop,
    your name flashes in my mind.

Reasons to live are abundant now,
    for you are my lost golden rainbow.

Like a rainbow in my life,
    for they are not seen very often.

And soon even the deserts will bloom,
    for such joy can not be contained.
    —*Caleb Ramos*

The Watch

This watch, symbol of my life
Broken and torn
Like the soul within me.
The black band,
Which no longer fastens itself
Like the black emptiness
Between my mind and heart.
The face of this watch hides its insides
And all the gears that make it work
As my face hides my feelings
And expresses nothing but that which I wish you to see.
As the buttons are pressed and the gears shift
More faces of the watch are seen
But no one can touch my broken heart
Or attempt to get me to care.
    —*Brian Hoskins*

Never Alone

Soft velvety blackness
Broken with shrieking wheels,
Another midnight madness steals,
Spirits, mysteriously coveting the darkness
Softly fading shadows slipping into secret places,
Hiding the majesty of flickering
movements and expectant faces,
Awed at the stillness of moonlight's sleeping beauty
What is this madness this honorable romance
But a part of each — all peoples —
Shrouded by our most intense desires,
With love, fear and hope.
    —*Berni Page*

Christmas But Once A Year

Christmas comes but once a year a phrase so often said
But could anyone afford the cost and work that lies ahead
For every card, for every wrap, for every gift you must shop
Shop and shop until you're exhausted and about to drop
The baking, the cooking, the cleaning, before and after the big
    event

Work loads that reach the rafter, and Oh the money you have spent
The hopes and prayers that the gifts will fit and that the style
    is just right
That all the recipients just won't cast them out of sight
There still are exchanges it's just inevitable
A size too small, a size too large, wrong color, or wrong label
As everyone I love Christmas with all it signifies
Christmas once a year is quite enough, because time swiftly flies
It takes a year to recuperate, and from gift shopping to refrain
Before you know it, guess what, it's that time of year again.
    —*Jeanette Nodulman*

230

Country Mountain-Aire

The spring time brings real splendor when leaves turn from
brown to green.
It's just about the prettiest sight you think you've ever seen.

Trees are a buddin'. The fruit not far behind. Children laugh
and watch the blossoms grow to see what size and kind.

And there's something really special 'bout that country
mountain-aire.

Mamas' roll and bake the pies. Oh! What the family has in store.
Tiny tots hold up the dish and humbly beg for more.

Today, the flavor is peach. Tomorrow we have cherry.
But, all will be so merry when they get that big strawberry!

Yes, there's something really special 'bout that country
mountain-air.

Honey bees a buzzin' winters gone at last.
Workers clear out the hive to get the job done fast.

Birds in the trees are nesting. Little ones are chirping loud.
At times they're so harmonious one could do without the crowd.

But, there's something really special 'bout that country
mountain-aire.

—*Elma B. Ullman*

Untitled

Starlights
Burn bright
Playing their part
In the universe as
Overseers of earthlings
Who play charades in the night
Defying truth - so they think
Because the sun has turned his back
Yet like a hero in disguise - he has
Dressed the eve in black to chill, and tempt
And tantalize, all - save the blind, and the wise

—*Elizabeth Gowan*

The Bullfight

Blades dancing in the sun, capes billowing
  burning red — daring, screaming crowds;
  hooves thundering forcing the ground to groan.
Dark eyes blazing, stare into the open - arena
  will soon bathe in blood, beast or human; stakes
  are high, throats run dry as game began.
Silence, shrieks, cheers or sigh — capes billows
  in the April sun; red, black... black, red.
  blood foretells death looms ahead; fear has
  no place, the vanquished weep or die.
Blade sinks, smoothly as flesh burst open
  like a ripe melon in the sun. Dark eyes now close
  slowly, growing even darker as twilight draws near.
Viva torrero! but el torro charges again gorging the
  victor to the ground, both falling and dying —
  arena reeks with blood of beast and man.

The empty seats, the empty centrum is now bare
  of multitude screaming for blood. They are
  more beast than beast who kill for game and
  pleasure; the beast kills only to survive.

—*Jay De Leon Mamaradlo*

Divinely Free

A beautiful young child playing in a park
Bursting with laughter and bubbling
Over with endless energy,

The multitude of colors that blaze and
Sway with the thinning trees in the
Crisp smell of an Autumn wind,

A glorious reddish sun rising over a
Smooth blue lake with sailboats
Forming silhouettes on the horizon,

The awe of towering ice capped mountains
Laced with dark green pines and
Wondrous wildlife of every kind,

The serenity of brilliant white clouds
Drifting timelessly through the soothing
Vastness of a peaceful pastel sky,

When I look for Gods Miracle in
Everything including me,
I can truly see,
I am divinely free.

—*James J. Young*

The Language Of Christmas

Merry Christmas — is not a cliche.
But an expression of love — for each passing day.

It has a good sound — as it rings in your ears
It has many voices — I know you have heard.

The meaning's the same — in every language you use
I'll say it in rhyme — I hope you're amused.

Feliz Navidad — the Hispanic will say
A time of rejoicing — on this special day.

Joyous Noel — a Frenchman declares
The joy of Christmas — resounds in the air.

Buon Natale — the Italian will say
Let's worship the Christ child — as He lay in the hay.

Kala Christonyenna — the Greek will attest
We'll kiss all the children and ask to be blessed.

Kristos Rashdnetcya — Russians shout with great glee
For only in Christ — can a Russian be free.

Aye — and a Merry Christmas to ye — the Scotsman will say
Christ gives us our strength — to conquer each day.

But to the Irish and English — and Americans too
We just simply wish — a Merry Christmas to you.

—*James C. Noonan*

A Blanket

I raised my head and saw
  But could not believe,
    All the stars that I could see

From end to end
  They covered me
    A blanket...truly God's tapestry

The vastness of God's love
  In the smallness of my mind
    Evidence only of my humankind

Life's but a whisper on the breath of time
  Lift your mind skyward to see
    None of this belongs to us...
      It's only God's tapestry

—*Gary M. Staggs*

Poor Mom!

Housework is one thing I really do hate,
But for some reason, it has become my fate.
You work and work with your nose to the grind,
And yet you seem only to fall further behind.

You wash and cook and clean the floor,
Only to discover it needs something more.
And cleaning the toilet is really a treat,
Scrubbing the bowl and washing the seat!

Why does my family leave such a great mess?
Can they not see a Mother's distress?
Clothes on the floor, clothes on the bed,
I didn't agree to this the day that I wed!

Do they not understand that I struggle to stay?
Sometimes I want only to run—run away.
With careful maneuvering around all the piles,
I'll go to the mall and check out the styles.

But Look! Someone has taken my car!
They knew that I would not get very far.
Yet another plan that has dashed all my hopes,
So I'll put up my feet, and watch the Soaps!
　　　—*Carol C. Taylor*

Adam's Plight

Woman was made for man that's' true
But for whom was man made I ask of you?
God made man in His own image
And discovered later that He did not finish,
Because man was lacking in his ability to cope
He just sat in the garden all day and moped.

God looked down from heaven and He knew
That there was something He had to do.
He pondered and pondered over the work he had done
Not an animal or fowl had He left all alone.
That's it" said God, "Adam needs a mate"
So I will make one just for his sake.
When darkness came and all was still,
God came and took one of Adam's ribs,
He made the woman and put her beside him
When he awoke the woman beguiled him.
They roamed the garden hand in hand,
She was his help mate in everything.
Woman was made for man that's true
But without the woman what would man do?
　　　—*Annabella D. Bruce*

The Basketball Player

He came from the streets without food or clothes,
But his faith in God and family gave him hope to survive.

He made it through school even though the odds were against him
He owed it to his strong belief that God was watching out for him.

He struggled all his life to make his dreams come true,
Because he knew God would be with him in good times and bad.

He wanted to be someone special, a basketball player, too,
He wanted to achieve these goals, be one of the lucky few.

He became an NBA player working hard day and night,
Even though he became rich and famous,
He never changed his outlook on life.

His faith stayed with him throughout every game,
His love of God showed through in every move he made.

He beat the odds and his dreams came true,
All because of his love of God and the courage to believe in
　　himself.
　　　—*Alison Markow*

I Miss You

I told you I didn't want to be with you anymore
but I didn't have a reason
I said it anyway.

As days and nights went by, I started missing you.
I missed your touch, your soft voice, your smile,
but most of all, I missed not being with you.
I missed the way you used to tease me
and the way you tried to be in control.
I missed the times talking about how we miss home.
I missed being by your side, and the memorable times shared
　　looking in each others eyes.

I missed you more than the world will ever know,
because the love I have for you will be thrown in the snow
There hasn't been a day or night I haven't thought about you
We are meant for each other and no one will tell me different.
I missed you most of all because, you're you..........
　　　—*Jacqeline McIntosh*

Questions

I may not have all the answers,
But I do have a lot of the questions.
How many times do I sit and wonder,
Am I going in the right direction?
Do I keep going on the road I've chosen?
Do I take a chance and make a turn?
Will it be for the better?
Will there be a lesson to learn?
It's hard to get out of bed in the morning,
It's harder to put a smile on my face.
It always feels like there's something missing,
How can I fill the empty space?
I'm always at work or at home.
When people are around me I'm still alone.
Why is my heart so empty?
Why does my body feel so weak?
At least my mind is still going, I have to stop and think.
But if my thoughts keep me sane, why am I confused?
Why am I so frightened?
What have I got to loose?
　　　—*Jennifer L. Griebel*

The Vows

We have not taken the vows publicly,
But I feel them just the same,
For richer or poorer,
Made it through the ups and downs this far.
In sickness or in health,
So many times I have cuddled you in both.
To love and cherish,
For as long as we are together.
Until death do us part,
May our love never die.
So we may live as one,
Past infinity may we never part.
　　　—*Amanda Gorringe*

Letter To The World

Received your letter and left for Amherst,
butterflies, clover, bees and death guide me
down "the path". Where nature's bride behind her
window, witnessed one's immortality.

Your gardens are gone. Evergreens remain —
prairies in the distance — (though seen by few).
Uninvited guests invade that vault once
questioned. They now judge tenderly of you.
　　　—*Elizabeth E. Bliss*

Picture On The Wall

So soon my nights became lonely and long.
But I knew I hadn't done anything wrong.

I became so sad,
I guess, I knew, I could sense, something would happen,
Something really bad.

Soon enough I was proven right,
This would be the last night,
I would turn out our bedroom light.

On the wall hangs a picture of me, so lovingly made.
Now it's collecting dust and soon it will even fade.

Some - one will be the new mistress of my home,
The man I loved won't be alone.

He'll have a new bride and he'll be so full of pride.

She'll be the one you now hold,
While I lay here so cold. For she will be his new wife,
At least till the end, of her life.

No one will ever know, it was you that put the gun to my head,
While I lay sleeping in our bed.

And now I know thinking back about it all, all along,
I was just really a picture that hung on the wall.

　　　—Debra S. Keeling

Epilogue To "Bloom Where You Are Planted"

Well it's surely taken longer,
But I'm finally having fun.
I now stand and bloom real tall here,
And I'll tell you how it's done.

Send out roots in all directions
'Neath the surface of the ground.
It takes time and your attentions.
Still, it's worth it, I have found.

Wrap your roots around some others.
Any other roots will do.
Now pretend you all are brothers.
First love them then they'll love you.

'Cause it's really not the weather,
And it's truly not the ground.
No, the thing that makes you flower
Is the love you pass around.

　　　—Donna Price

It's You

The time has past and we must go on.
But in our hearts it will remain the same.

Together as one and the love we have won.
Always shared with you.
Darling ain't it true?
It's you!
Have you ever felt so wonderful?
Or so fine?
Or so alive?

Your love I've known.
So many ways to know.
So many schemes, so many dreams, that we dreamed.

　　　—Ernest Stephen Ackler

Is Autumn Still...

They are the first cold days from winter,
but in some trees, even remain the leaves,
autumn does not like to go now away,
by thinking that so close, there is a pretty shell.

The wind looks to entwine the enormous solemn oaks,
as the ivy embraces the mute and big walls,
a sadness fills completely my nostalgic soul
too tired in the world, as a lost, small bird.

The silence is sleeping in the beautiful prairies,
is a profound stillness in an infinity peace,
often the air breathing the mountains and woods
in an eternal hug, to be in love again.

And I dream to climb the hillocks and the clouds also,
by roaming through the seas and rivers with no end,
going down the caves and reaching the volcanoes
in a futile intent to go away and flight.

In between, the cold of the winter comes
leaving a few fresh leaves, in the trees still,
autumn does not like going too far away,
by thinking that so close, it sees a pretty shell.

　　　—Esther Ortega-Lage

Mother

To one who knows me better than anyone,
But isn't even paid for a job well done.

To one who made sure my health was good,
Even though sometimes I don't know how you withstood.

To one who was always there to explain things out,
Even though at the time I was filled with a little doubt.

To one who has stood so strong,
And backed me even though I was wrong.

To one who strongly disciplined me,
Even though I tried to beg off on bended knee.

To one I disliked at the time for making me walk the straight
and narrow, no matter what my feelings were then, I thank you
for making me go straight as an arrow.

To one who was there to share my ups and downs,
Even though you looked upon me sometimes with frowns.

To one who has been so sweet and kind,
No matter what day or time.

To you, Mother, I thank you,
And am glad they made you as you are for I love you.

　　　—E. Dian Hagler

Memories

Four years have past since the dreadful day.
But it only seems like yesterday.
It's hard to remember the past.
How long will the memories last.
I see him smoking his cigarettes,
And watching the Braves play the Mets.
He did not think about his health.
He did not care how Grandma felt.
Emphysema had crossed our minds
He did not care, we've soon to find
He was a fool for doing such
Did I love him? Yes, very much.
Why God, why did you take his life.
It caused us all a lot of strife.
At least he is there with you,
starting his life, as if a new
I'm not glad I'm able to say,
I still remember the dreadful day
.....when my grandfather passed away.

　　　—Jeremiah Paradis

Forbidden

There are things acceptable, and things that are not.
But it seems more thrilling to choose the latter.
Consequences pushed aside, all is at risk.
What do we gain if we gamble and lose?

A hand reaching out for what it cannot have.
Searching for something seen only in a dream,
That crumbles to nothing when reality rushes in,
Lost, except for a bittersweet memory.

Anticipated, but never tasted,
Longed for, but never obtained,
Forbidden, but not forgotten.

Why do we want what we should not desire?
I saw, I pursued, I won, I lost.
　　　—J. Kaycee Scott

Once Upon A Summer In New York

I never saw the Hippodrome before the wrecker smashed its
　　stones,
But I've seen Jumbo's pile of bones. It's no mystery.
He's still playing the American Museum of Natural History.
One night a girl and I rode a hansom in the park, horse-powered.
And anther night, in Times Square, I met Noel Coward.
I was a barker for the Astor movie house,
and he was coming toward me faster and faster.
"What time does the show go on?" he asked, at once curt and
　　ingratiating.
"Oh, five minutes, Mr. Coward," I said; "seats on all floors!
Seats without waiting!" The reason I didn't die of fright was that
I'd been repeating that not-too-accurate spiel all summer, every
　　night.
New York, for all the dangers that even then lurked there, could
offer wonderful moments like that to people who worked there.
I married and had children and remarried and went out in
　　New York when I had to,
But finally the streets were so bad I couldn't look at the city,
　　even from my window; it was too sad to,
I've left New York, but I never look back with scorn on it.
How could I? We're related? I was born in it.
　　　—Fred McMorrow

Natasha

Her eyes were like the starry skies I saw yesterday,
But I've seen them once again in a different light.
She made me question all I've known and held dear to me,
She made me compromise what I thought was right.

She can tell you how it feels.
She can tell you how it feels... to be evil.

ahsatan
Ah... Satan.
　　　—David Barnes

My Dear Best Friend

When times were tough I turned to you, to help me through it all.
But since you gone and left that day, my life is bound to fall.

I see you all the time it's true, but things are not the same.
The times we had were awfully fun, our little children games.

The walks we took when days were hot, the talks we always had.
The things we could not tell our moms, when we were really sad.

But now the days are changing, we're growing up real fast.
You'll always be my best friend, no matter what will pass.
　　　—Cecilia Barrera Garcia

The Best Is Yet To Come

The best is yet to come, I hear
But life looks bleak as we stride
We're struggling now, we'll get by somehow
We'll even put away our pride

We moan and groan, but we're not alone
As He guides us through this life
The best is yet to come, I hear
As we face each trial and strife

Then time goes by, we have it all
Our life's work has reaped its reward
The best is yet to come, I hear
If we'll only but give to the Lord

All I have belongs to you Lord
I can only give Glory and Praise
"The best is yet to come," I hear
As He whispers that old familiar phrase
　　　—Cyrilla D. Pecoy

You Say You Don't Believe

You say you don't believe the coming of the end
But look far in a distance, continue to pretend

Pretend that you don't see the raptures thus foretold
The shaking of the mountains, the taking of men's souls

The rising of the rivers upon this troubled land
The frequency of disasters, the moral decline of man

The offspring of the four winds that whips its mighty tail
The ground beneath our feet, is said to harbor Hell

The rise of violent crimes from every color and creed
The rumors of war yet to come, the darkened moon that bleeds

The cesspools of addiction, of every kind and type
Abraham's descendants, from every walk of life

When do we start to see the callous of our ways?
The doctrines of our scholars explaining it away

Religious institutions conscious of their flaws
Exhaulting themselves above our God, thinking to change times
and laws

Foolish are their doctrines, a world out of control
The realm of Satan's Kingdom, his walking to and fro

So take a look around you, tell me what you see
This world is far more too complex, for any man to lead
　　　—James Pillar

Immortality

Immortality is, perhaps, an imaginary reward.
But, most of us think of it, through faith,
As a realistic, celestial, or spiritual gift of God.
It provides a sense of solace that we may, in time,
Dwell in the house of the Lord in comfort and
Pleasure for evermore, and to meet again our loved ones
Who preceded us and know that others are to come.

Yet, there is another form of immortality, though mundane,
That fulfills an innate wish that our name or that of another
Will long live after us, in perpetuity, for all to know.
The reality may depend upon our contributions or
Accomplishments, such as providing funds or scholarships
At colleges or universities or funds for income to a church.

So immortality is a dual goal for which to strive,
Especially that our future is
Assured in heaven with our Lord.
　　　—Arthur F. Peterson

My Essence

One doesn't have to love, I know
But not to love you, I just can't
And that is why after you the love will go
In freezing weather, yellow sun and burning sand.
I didn't stop it-no right to interfere
And suffering I took and never gave
And all my eyes and all my soul were so clear
Until was asked: "Do you want to be my slave?"
Oh, the word was "yes", but the feeling was already gone
In to the corner of the bed.
And suddenly I saw another sun,
It wasn't yellow, it seemed red.
And what was next - I do not care
Because it couldn't be the pleasure of the life.
Suppose it was good-like what we need, like air
Or maybe it was a sin.
Lost... What should I talk to you about
In our world. I don't want my thought to be doubt.
I want Earth to be wider, Moon to be there and Sun to shine
I command myself to start care if I don't have Human Soul.

—Boris Khodorkovsky

Give Of Yourself

Friendship is golden - a coveted thing
But only if sincere and true.
Happiness is always the sharing of joy,
For others need some cheering too.

Moments of sadness can be overcome,
Just knowing you're there to the end.
For life has a way of reversing things,
Then you'll be in need of a friend.

So never more shirk your duty each day,
Have compassion for your fellow man.
A kind word will long be remembered, friend,
And love every barrier will span.

For what is life but the passing of days,
And surely we all must go through it.
You'll benefit more by sharing your love,
Then he who always withdrew it.

—Amy Stoler

Crime: It Doesn't Pay

This day in age there's a crime everywhere,
But try and look for good things
That's the problem I must share.
Just look at any newspaper,
On the front cover there's probably a story about a raper.
Then there's murder or theft...
How much good does this plant have left?
A long, long time ago man used his gun to get food,
But in this age, man kills his friend just to be rude!
It's not that the police aren't doing their job,
It's that more people think they are unstoppable,
When they steal and when they rob.
Let's try to spare lives,
Instead of taking them with knives,
Let's try to work together,
For ever and ever,
So that hardly never,
Shall we read about a raper,
On the front cover of a newspaper.

—Erica Campbell

Children's Pledge To Save Our World

The meek shall inherit the earth they say,
But we will be strong in every way
To make sure that the earth is here to stay
And that it flourishes day by day.

We pledge all energy to conserve
And give it the respect that it deserves.
Whether it be petroleum or solar cell,
Water or electric will do as well.

And we shall never, ever refuse
To recycle, reduce, and reuse.
The cans, bottles, and paper too
Are things with which we're never through.

To ensure earth's splendor will never cease,
Our joint efforts must increase.
We promise that we will do our best
And challenge others to the test.

To save the world is our vow...
Not tomorrow, but right now.
So let's all help out Mother Earth
To let her know just what she's worth.

—Brenda Rogers

My Sasha and Me

You came to the door as a good dog would
But you were only a cat
You rolled on the mat
You awaited my pat
Lying there on your back!

You gave me such joy
I thought you were a toy
Running from room to room.

The joys that we shared
Cannot be compared
After all, you were only a cat!

Something went wrong
And I wish I knew
What made you suddenly do what you did
And caused me to hurt quite a lot!

If only I could have read your thoughts
And transferred them into words
I wouldn't be sitting alone and lost
Writing an ode to my cat!

Sasha! Sasha! Sasha my cat!

—Elsie M. Ryan

Forever Friends

They may be gone,
But you'll be okay,
All you need is another day.
They made you laugh so hard you cried,
But now they're gone,
For they have died.
You thought your friendship would never end;
You thought you'd be forever friends.
Your love for them will always shine bright,
But now they've seen the holy light.
Pray for them with all your heart,
And someday you'll no longer be apart.

—Felicia Leo

Respirator

Dariusz pulled out his respirator tube,
By accident or by design?
Large flakes sank silently,
Snow buried the winter pavements.
A white mist of indecision,
Made clear thoughts impossible.
On morphine to kill pain,
Kill the patient more like.

As thaw arrives I wonder,
Funeral behind us and winter over.
Would it have happened if Spring crocuses,
And sunshine warmed his skin?
Trapped in his white cell of silence,
Cheated of hope.
He pulled out his respirator,
By accident or by design?

—*Emory J. Villines*

Thoughts On A Birthday

Growing old is complicated - true?
By many things, of course. There's health
And will the money last as long
As these old bodies do? And, yes -
We think of death. Will it be soon, or late?
Perhaps we'll even get to 90 some!
I'd rather not, unless you do it, too.
Cranky old lady, I don't want to be -
Or fuzzy-minded. What a dreadful thought!
I would, though, like to see the grandkids wed
Or graduate from high school, anyway.
There's always something more I'd like to do!
People say romance doesn't last. Perhaps.
But my heart's happier when you are near.
I do believe that there's another world
Beyond this one - but even if there's not
What joy - what miracles this life has seen
Even with sadness, and there's been a lot!
So I thank God for giving me this time
On His good earth - and some of it with you.

—*Hazel F. Lindquist*

Alone

Just alone in here, so isolated.
Bystander in life, so fascinated.
The question why, continuously coming up.
Confusion invades, I'm some kind of nut.
I'm so alone, so out of place.
In the human race, the perfect disgrace.
Oh, I don't know-what to do?
Teach me to reach out to you.
Looking out, all that I see.
People blending, so easily.
But, I don't know - how could they all?
Through a view finder I watch, as I sit in withdrawal
Why am I like this? Why can't I change?
Alone in my thoughts, all too deranged.
I must go, but to where who knows.
Is insanity the path, that I have chose?

—*Diana Sanches*

Getting Through The Spines

Getting through the spine of a
cactus is not easy. Threw the eyes
of God an animal watches me getting
through, getting through the spine of a
Cactus is not easy, but God will help me
through, all the troubles, I had been through,
a spine is off me because God helps me
threw.

—*Claudia Lugo*

Harvest Moon

Over the pine trees -
Came the silvery glow,
Of the huge round moon,
As it hung so low.

Bathing the cornpatch
in its ghostly light,
Shining on pumpkins so orangey bright,
Squash all scattered in the moon lit night.

The old dry leaves make an eerie sound,
As they rustled and blew across the ground,
Back in the shadows stood the old scarecrow
With his big straw hat and long red bow.

Watching over this scary scene,
Was a big round owl with eyes so keen,
Perched on a limb with his eyes aglow —
Made this harvest moon a halloween show!

—*Helen Elizabeth Campbell*

Window To My Room

Tossing and turning, desperate for sleep.
Can't seem to drown my eyes,
to end the monotony of the day.
Thoughts begin to circulate to every corner of my mind.
As I lie there in my thoughts,
I ask the Lord for forgiveness for all my sins.
Still, the thoughts are evident.
To efface them from within my mind,
I reach over and switch the radio on.
Song after song,
played over and over again throughout the night.
Melodies I thought I would never hear again,
suddenly bring back memories.
I rise out of my bed and walk over to the window,
and the streetlight on the corner shines right through.
I admire the night as I gaze out the window,
and embrace the breeze as it enters —
the window to my room.

—*Abel Villalobos*

Ageless

Oh wishful tree holding tight your coat of green
Can't you see the beauty of your sister's robes
In their gorgeous yellow and red
There mature beauty is a sight to behold.

The fall season has come — yet with regret
It's hard to see the loss of spring
So cling a little longer — oh green leaf
Have one last youthful fling.

Have one more day of youth
Look with disdain on icy frost
Then another beauty will gain hold
So no regrets — all is not lost.

Beauty is in the eye of the beholder
Whether winter, spring, summer or fall
So green tree have a grand finale
Then joyously enter the new season proud and tall.

—*Inga Rodden*

Family Reunion

On a Wednesday in September 1908,
Carl and Eva had found their mate;
Pleasant Hill was where it began,
Their life together they would plan.

Blessed with children, six in all,
Was like starting a rolling ball;
Families expanding along the way,
One hundred plus, the count today.

If only they were here to see,
The abundance of their family tree;
Their hearts would swell with Pride and Joy,
With love for every girl and boy.

Now—this family, spread so far apart,
Will be together for a heart to heart;
A tribute to a father and mother,
Who taught us all to love one another.

—*Gwen Neese*

Air Borne

Fly on Oh bird of petrol power.
    Carry me across the sea
While I slumber through the darkened hour
    Within the very womb of thee.

Thrust thine whirling blades
    Into the ancient wind
Through which treasures of gold and jade
    Once glided on tiny ships so thin.

From your torso stretch your wings
T'ward the vastness through which you fly
    As though reaching for invisible rings
    To keep your body tethered high.

You soar on, high in Heaven's realm.
    Challenging the speed of Apollo.
    The tiny voices 'round your helm
Against your Herculean throb sound hollow.

Fly on, Oh bird, with earned regality,
    Carry me across the sea.
Cut your way through Heaven's serenity.
    Spill me on new lands to see.

—*Harold J. Hill*

Life's Road

Blindly, I wonder along this winding road,
Carrying upon me, my own heavy load.
What lies before me, is an unknown mystery;
What lies behind me, is now just history.
Throughout this journey, there is much I will meet;
When I have met all, my life will be complete.
Coming are decisions, only I can make,
Their consequences, too, I alone must take.
Thunder, lightening, and the pouring down of rain,
Bring with them hardships and trials of disdain.
But just around the bend, sunshine can be found,
Where laughter and joy are the only heard sound.
The last bend in the road that you take is best,
For your body and mind, can truly now rest.

—*Brenna Phillips*

Missing In Action

You are not at the picnic,
Caught in the gold moment
Of a summer day,
Whose leaf shadow, breeze, and clover scent
We did not know were precious.

You are not in the car, singing
With me as we travel the green miles,
Nor in the high, thin mountains,
With our campfire snapping
And our voices blending with the pines.

You are not in Viet Nam,
Although they sent you there;
You're not among the rows
Of grassy resting spots,
Angeled by a white cross.

But there are times at night,
When the wind sings, and stars
Are tapers, when your young voice
Is clear and strong again.

—*Catherine Corley Anderson*

My Secret Place

The sunbeam filtering through the lush trees,
caught on a spider's web and got lost in its intricate maze
forgetting for the moment where it was headed or why.

The spider paused, then seeming to gather strength
from the ultra violet rays
continued about its business of spinning endless doilies
among the tree branches.

The water below gurgled lazily
washing over the semi precious stones,
polishing them to a smooth lustrous surface
that was as pleasing to the eyes as it was to the touch.

I held my breath for fear
It would all disappear
as a dream at the first light of dawn.
At that very instant, I owned the universe.

—*Corliss Fyfe Whitney*

Those Ole Days

When I haven't got a smile,
Cause I'm feeling down and blue,
And the clouds are so dark,
That the sun can't shine through.
It's a beautiful desire darling, for me just to lay,
My head upon your shoulder, in a loving sort of way.

It makes me feel so childish,
When my teardrops start,
And I feel a small ache,
In the region of my heart.

I don't know quite what to say,
So, I'll make one request of you.
Just allow me to lay,
My head upon your shoulder, in a loving sort of way.

Oh, this world's a cruel place,
But, at least God knew it should be,
So he gave me a piece of heaven,
At least that is what I must say,
When I have my head upon your shoulder,
In a loving sort of way.

—*Connie Lynn Stafford*

The Still Night

Come spirits that control my thoughts.
Change me to a man, and fill me full of hatred
   from my head to my toes.
Make my blood thick so that it will stop me;
   stop me from feeling regret.
So that no sounds shall scare me into stopping.

Let the night be thick and filled with smoke.
Smoke from hell so that my knife will not see
   what I have done.
Nor that others shall see through the mist,
   announcing to all what I've done!
     —Amy E. Clark

....

Life has a cycle from beginning to end
Channeled through cataclysmic paths.
Traversed and traveled ....
To temporary cradles in hospitals.

From institutions of homes
To institutions of learning.
On roads signaled straight ahead
To winding corners, curves, up hills and valleys;
Transition marks the path.

Path-goals and path-roads that tells us:
Slippery when wet.
Those that say: Hazardous!
Pass at your own risk.

Unafraid, one rises to the challenge despite fearful components.
Unafraid, one understands that the ocean in which he or she
   swims is larger than the sea in which one may drown.
"Thy word is a lamp unto my feet, and a light unto my path."
Psalm 119:105.
     —Cedric E. Cooper

Song Of The Birds

   Oh' God, thy birds - they sing and say to me;
Cheer-up, Cheer-up! for can't you see,
   That God lives in the rose, the bush, the trees
and even in me?
   Cheer-up, Cheer-up! and look above,
See God's showering love, in the sunshine,
   the rain, and even in me.
As we sing God's praises in our songs,
   we know only too well,
that God loves us each and every one-
   and provides our every need.
Cheer-up, Cheer-up, man-kind,
   turn your hearts and faces upward,
follow our example true,
   For God loves us, this we know to be
true, but, we also know that he lives in
   and loves you too.
     —Betty Louise Kenyon

Untitled

When you told me you loved me you said it was true.
But then you left me sad and blue.
You left without warning not even a clue was left behind.
I cried everyday and every night.
I was here with nothing to do but wait for you to return.
To tell me you loved me too.
My heart was torn apart down deep inside.
It hurt so bad that I thought I would die.
But now that all my hope is gone
I'll just relive all the good times we had together.
     —Deborah Carvalho

I Can See By Your Knees

You've Been Dancing With Fleas

Tapping, tapping, knock and rapping, on your windowpane.
Cherub fingers. Angel eyes. Faeries chuckling at the wise,
watch and wait with patient sighs. Through the wind and rain.

Giggle, giggle, laugh and wiggle. Mice chase cats all day.
Skunks love roses. Turtles joke - lost on ordinary folk.
It stopped raining, don't you poke! Come out with us and play.

Dancing, dancing, strut and prancing. Red rhinoceros.
Sheep in curlers. Bears with wings. These are all the special
   things.
Upside down the blue pig sings, with a hippopotamus.

Hello! Hello! Banana jello. Can you play my game?
Magic bubbles. Noses cold. Ever young, forever old.
Whoops! The secret's out and told ... Childhood is my name!
     —Donna L. Prentice

Radiance

Following University
Choose from wide diversity.
Permit no diligence recoil;
Constant stoking makes it boil.
Impact of intensive college
Steeps mind with worldly knowledge.
Numbered days are rarely equal;
Use them well, there is no sequel.
Weed the wild, dig deep, plow the course
Take aim, pursue a goal with avid force;
Wise tactics hew the burls;
Standing tall, success unfurls.
Accomplish grace in name of cause
Win special marks amid applause.
     —Alice Helfesrieder

Praise You Dear Jesus

Praise you my dear Jesus...for entering my life, as a single
christian I'd like to be your wife. I can sing you praises,
and worship you all ways, through prayer and the Holy Spirit,
walk with you all my days. Oh dear Jesus...how I love
you...and need to know just how, I may do Your will always, and
daily make that vow. To always follow Your command, and
preach and teach Your word, to minister throughout the lands, so
Your truth can be heard. Dear Jesus is it possible for the likes of
me...to be used to open hearts to you, so they too can see...
that You are their salvation, that You are the Only Way,
Satan's world is a dead end street, all they need is to repent
and pray! Will You use me Jesus...to open up their lives? To
save more souls, to help men love, to see you as the light?
Please use me as Your servant...use me as Your slave...make me
victorious over the devil, make my heart be brave! Use me as
Your soldier, use me as Your friend. Keep my christian heart
aflame, and use me to Your end. Show me where You want me,
let Your words burn bright. Use me where You want me, guide
me day and night. Oh how I love you Jesus, please show me what
You will no matter where You lead me, help me do Thy will!
Amen.
     —Dona Marie Stengl

Perfect World

   Our Lord, a sweet and gentle man,
  Caring and compassionate, lending his hand.
    He created this world a long time ago
  Thinking it was perfect, but he didn't know.
    He loves everything he created so dear,
    And he speaks to us, but we do not hear.
So he sits up there with his fists all curled,
    Knowing this isn't a perfect world.
     —Jared Byerly

Image

Fleecy, as the clouds
clear and brilliant, as the morning dew on
a lotus leaf
She emerges, disappears—
In white, in grey, in that soft soft blue
She comes to inspire me, in her gentle
silence
Suddenly, I feel the cool freshness of the
mountain spring
the warmth of the mid-summer breeze
high above the orchid filled valley
It circles, as a long lost crane
searching in the evening haze
So much I longed for her word of goodbye
Yet I savor the feeling of unknown
Which would remain clear and brilliant as
the lotus morning dew

    —Hsueh-chen Cheng

Vienna 1815

As she peered over the dropping
cliff, she sees the red rose which
she has cast down onto the crashing
rocks, the foaming curl of the sea
washing close upon it, twin tears falling

She began to delve deep inside
her past and she heard a voice
beckoning her view upward to the sky
"does the moon sing to you, its patient
lullaby, does it see you and contentedly sigh

As it passes through the misty night
sky? Does its shine lure you, to the
open sea? Or does it draw you to its light
like a beautiful, floating moth onward
to find its peace, to surrender without fight"

Her white dress fluttered at the rim
she felt the breeze pass her bosom
and for a moment, she caught sight of him
as the sea wells up to claim the rose
and as it swirled upon it, she leapt

    —Christopher Teaters

The Rope

I feel as if I'm holding onto a rope, that others seem to be
clinging.
Can I pull them up? Do I have the strength? Please people
stop that swinging.
It makes it harder for me to hold on, the rope is slipping
through my hands.
The earth is sliding under my feet, I need a better stand.
I hear your needs, your wants, your pleas, don't think I
haven't heard.
But I need time to develop my strength, do you hear my words?
The rope is getting heavier from the weight of the voices
calling.
But I must let go, from the weight of the rope to keep myself
from falling.

    —Arneita Marie Langford

Burden For A Loved One

I lay in the bed with a burden in my heart.
Closed my eyes in wonder why did we have to part.
Six beautiful angels they had appeared.
In all that amazement I got real scared.
They spoke in soft voices and said to me.
We're your guardian angels we've come to set your burden free.
Your loved one's in heaven and she's alright.
She's with her master this very night.
He's pouring her with his blessing.
Filling her with his love.
Showing her the home in heaven he prepared for her above.
She told us to tell you she loved you and to wipe your lonely tears.
That she's with God now and had no more fears.
I lay in the bed without burden in my heart.
Closed my eyes not wondering why we had to part.
Those six beautiful angels opened my eyes to see.
How wonderful God's love is for people like you and me.

    —Foster Franks

A Day In The Mountains

In the majestic mountains where trees stand tall against a blue
cloud ridden sky;
Where babbling brooks rush rapidly over boulders and rocks
nestled deep in its cozy bed;
The grass grows like a plush green carpet
And flowers beautifully defy gravity on the mountain side;
There creatures great and small live in harmonic tranquility
And birds soar to lofty heights.
The snow lies quietly white beneath the giant trees
And the wonders of God are in magnificent array.
Even in my small insignificant state,
God knows that I am
And loves me.

    —Doris D. Holmes

Beyond The Beyond

Beyond the beyond where the sun always shines, and the rain
clouds cease to appear. There where the flowers bloom month
after month, and singing is all you hear. And the laughter of
people ring out through the land, through the green covered
valleys and the white shored sands. Yes beyond the beyond
you'll find me there, singing and laughing with people who
care. But only to often I have to return, to the land of
reality only to learn. That few people stray beyond the
beyond, As I do day after day and live in a world of make
believe, for this is wrong so they say. But they are wrong to
say it is wrong for your stay is much too short, and there I'm
as happy as a sailor would be sailing into port. So people
please listen and heed what I say and visit with me today,
Beyond the beyond where tomorrow land lives and there's never a
yesterday. For there you'll be happy with nary a care and
tears you'll never see, beyond the beyond I'll look for you for
is there that you'll find me. In all its grace and beauty
through all eternity.

    —Brenda Sue Fredline

Dandelion

Swaying in the grass,
confined to a miserable life, calling for help,
the people pass it by so uncaringly.
Never planted or brought in,
neither consoled nor talked to,
the loneliness is overwhelming.
No one cares.
It will soon blow away, however,
and be totally forgotten.
Unknowingly, society treats so many the same,
as the plant world does its children.

    —Andy Detweiler

At Love's Bequest

Watching the sky, behind her window she waits. Looking into the
clouds, she envisions her heart in all its sorrow. Tears fill
her eyes. They fall onto her pillow. Her sky is gone. Its
broken light is draped across her bed. After all her patience
and tears, her spirit too, is broken. Searching her soul; through
her dying faith, she reaches for her heart to endure. Never again
to suffer alone the sorrow of tears. And, so, to an empty glass box
she returns with her heart. There to rest, peacefully; beside her
bed while she whispers softly to the night.

Beside a stream;
his attention flowing along its surface, he sees himself gazing at
pieces of his reflection; broken and distorted. While dwelling
on his future, the stream gradually opens to a river. He
considers then, end-to-end, the flowing of this stream. In
moments, he discovers his fortune is but a dream. And, resting
for precious moments before they dissipate; falling into the
uncertain depths of this widening river, pieces of his dream
appear to shimmer in their own light. At love's bequest, so is
one heart: lost in the clouds of a fallen sky. And is one
another heart; awakened from an uncertain dream...by the sound
of tears upon still waters falling.

—Gerard J. Paulauskas

Lapis Lazuli

Pre-dawn cobalt nebula,
   colors gauzy, indiscernible.
Blue grey intensifies,
   teasing colors, false dawn.

Nightingale, owl hush.
   Breeze barely breathes.
Suddenly, Sun peeks over the horizon,
   burning red all he sees.

Songbirds awaken on the mountaintop
   like an opening music box.
Fog embraces the valleys;
   peaks converted to islands.

Senses overwhelmed, dream world
   uncertainty, complacently disoriented.
From this back drop a figure appears
   and approaching, it could be anyone.

I saw you...
I saw you.

—Andrew Jeremiah Weisner

Our Flag's Destiny

In a distance I see flying o'er the housetops 'gainst the blue
Colors that are never dying, colors of our flag so true.
What a glorious sight unfolding as it waves above the crest
While I stand in awe beholding the great flag I love the best.
Stars and Stripes to you I'm lifting, prayers to keep you o'er
   this land
And to keep mankind from drifting from those ideals for which
   you stand
In challenging times through many years you've inspired the
   souls of men
To answer freedoms' call 'mid tears of sacrifice to find the end
Where hopelessness and tyranny would be no more upon this earth
But peace resounding as a symphony would usher in loves noble
   birth.
Your life reveals one glorious story but you have yet a destiny.
So keep on waving, dear Old Glory, in the sky victoriously.

—Gladys Taft Johnson

Attractions

The night calls out sweetly to you:
"Come into me, my innocent.
Let me caress with my darkest hues,
Surround with my deepest velvet.
I will fold around, envelope,
Pressing luxuriant blackness against you.
Within my arms, let love develop
As secret desires you pursue."

The abyss beckons demurely to you.
Lovingly. Coaxingly.
"Come into me. Take a dive.
Learn to soar eternally.
Experience irreality, alive —
As you join my immortality,
See yourself sinking, floating, dreaming,
Frozen as you pass through my infinity,
In a cinematic view never ending."

—Jaclyn B. Spitzer

For My Future Is My Pass:

Thus saith the Lord, "King of the Jews,"
"Come, stop, listen, and hear this news"
All know my name, but don't know me
I'm life everlasting I'm your family tree.

I'm your future, I'm your pass
I'm Alpha and omega, first and last
The beginning and the end.
It's I who brought Daniel out of the Lions Den.
The wind, and rain which sometimes cause pain
The father of Abel, and don't forget Cain.
I created everything including the Whale
For your future is your pass and
that's no fairy tale.

—Catherine Amos

Untitled

Birds fly, not knowing if there is a cold frost,
Coming to stop the journey.
Fish swim, not knowing if today
Is the day when they are going to be hooked.
A dog plays, not knowing if its
Master has left it forever.
This tells us to have more faith in life even if there is an
unknown,
The future.
Why?
Because today is a sunny day,
The fishermen are at home and the
Master lets his dog in.

—Heidy Laboy

Is This, Then, The Beginning Of The End?

Is it when the price of household gadgets
Concerns us more
than the expenditure of leisure time
for which they were designed?

When ownership of toys
Exceeds in value
the little chuckles for which they were created,
And steel-
Conceived to serve-
Makes slaves of its conceivers
And hides the star beyond?

—Dorothea Gaines Galloway

Untitled

Graduating from high school is a one time affair
Completing a section for those who really care
Twelve years seems like a very long time
When you finish you feel ever so fine
You are now ready to set the world on fire
To keep on learning you must go higher
Enter the college that offers the most
So when you finish you can really boast
Now is the time to decide what your life's career will be
Whether it is teaching flying or sailing on the sea
You get out of life just what you put in
So keep up the good work you will always win
When you think all is in vain
Keep your head high and resist the pain
Keep your nose to the grindstone and resist the worthless fads
You have a proud mom dad sisters grandmamas and granddads
Always look forward and never behind
Treat others with respect and be ever so kind
So in closing we all wish you the very best
The years ahead will be the supreme test

   —Ed Warren

Have You, Your Reward?

Trials in this world,
Complex, they maybe,
The reason, to prepare us,
For the world of eternity,

If from this world, nothing we learn,
the right to live the next,
Most assuredly, we will not earn.

We must try hard, to let his reason be ours,
Without his light to guide us,
Very dim are our powers.

You may think yourself cunning,
Actually a slave to this world,
I prefer to be humble,
A servant to the will of our Lord.

The choice is each of ours,
We need not a dictator,
To think of others, before ourselves,
I believe the reward to be greater.

   —James E. Rankin

CONFLICT

How do you describe conflict
confusion on every side
deep in debt - down at heart
gee I'm all screwed up
fast to think, slow to comprehend
conflict seems to have no
end - from the start to the past I've began to fear
like there is no hope at last
some way - no way there's got to be a conflict
free world for me and one for you
too big a thing - to small an answer conflict has
got to go - I can't stand all this confusion all
in a row - downtown, uptown nowhere to run I'm even a
looking where there is no sun - how far, how
wide must I go inside - stop the pain - stop
the rain for soon I'll stop to exist help me, show me
the road to take conflict has me running a race
big time low time I've got to succeed for I just
realize that I can bring conflict down to its
Knees!!!!!

   —Elizabeth A. Dingle

Baptism

The heavy rain fell like a mist
covering each tree in solitary bliss
as their branches reached up towards heaven,
rejoicing in the presence of this old friend.

The sky was filled with bleak grey clouds,
trapping the earth in an unshakable shroud,
Yet the trees of the forest welcomed its presence,
basking in the coolness and the soft new fragrance.

To them grey was a wonderful sign
that soon they would be free of the dirt and the grime
by baptismal waters that poured from above,
drenching them in a shower of love.

Sadness crept in when the rain began to slow
as the clouds signaled it was time to go,
but this sadness did not last very long
as the sun peaked through the clouds
and the birds began their song.

   —Ann Meredith Nienhuis

My Lost Love

She was so affectionate, she was so sweet, she was a bit
crafty, sometimes and may I include unique she was very
articulate, she was so considerate, but I was irresponsible and
may I include materialistic when it came down to poverty, she
wasn't afraid to say, that she was poor - but I wanted to play
the role of Mr. Rich, cause my pride couldn't take it anymore.

Though I was on the same level she was on, she knew what was
inside my heart. I just felt that we should have had the best
in life right then and there from the very start.
She was kind of like an educator and may I include motivator,
whenever harmful words crossed our paths, we would find
ourselves making up later. She was an enthusiastic lover of
art, she was just too brilliant, but I was too belligerent at
the time and now I hate myself for being ignorant. How we
manage to meet, well it was through God's grace but how we
manage to depart - well, as of yet I cannot trace. She was
perfect image, she was really meant for me, but now that she
flew into the unknown, I miss her dearly. If I ever made
another wish to the man from up above, I'll bow my head faithfully
and ask for the return of my lost love.

   —Andrew Cannon Winstead

If There Were No God

If there were no God then who made the world
Created boy and girl and gave us the wonder of love

If there were no God then who'll make it rain
To water the terrain so food could grow and
 feed our hungry mouths

If there were no God then who gave us the animals
Without we could not survive who often for our sake
 give up their own precious lives

If there were no God then who gave us the air to breathe
And who created its complex machine we call a tree

If there were no God then who gave us the sun
Which not only warms our hearts but tells us
 when another day comes

If there were no God then who gave us life
Whose image were we created in and who delivered Jesus Christ

   —Gregory Paul Michael

Rodeo

An unseen force
created through the symbiotic turnings
of the sun and its moon
is pushing down upon the liquid sea,
sending water roaring out and upon the shore
in all the ten directions.

Against this pre-ordained,
tidal course
the mechanical outboard engine pulls
in opposition
to being-times holy and chosen groove,
contrary to the natural law
of cause and effect
that sweeps effortlessly, relentlessly,
about the bow of my wooden boat.

In evening's light,
illumined in enigma,
I steer defiantly toward home;
a peapod moving upstream,
endlessly bucking the Buddah-tide.

—*Bruce A. Marshall*

Sonnet To A Teacher

The greatness of the world is measured by
creativeness of a school teacher's aim;
as in her spiritual hands the talents lie,
in patient tenderness that she has claim.

With "tid-Bit" knowledge molds the growing mind
to think, to imagine, to find new friends
by reading books, the epic-classic kind.
She stimulates an interest. She leads

the thought. She works through word that
will excite
a mind to grope, to seek for the first rung
of ladder to the wonders out of sight,
which build the soul and spine of very young.
A teacher, man or woman, starts the role
that guides the student to the final goal.

—*Helen Nencka*

Of The Mind

A thunderstorm moves slowly by the paled sky
Crowned by the glow of setting sun
Such goings on inside
Rumbling sounds.

The pillar of rain slanted as it moves
Crackles of light irregular,
Within and striking out to unsuspecting target
Not known to anyone but the billowed soul of it.

All around grows silent in awe of how it was to be
An odor thick and fresh about
Thoughts of what it is, how it is, why it is
— Singling life in mystery.

Then is it of the mind
Within and beyond
To what beginning-what end,
Or —

—*Daniel B. Jeffs*

The Pain In My Heart

My heart cries out to him, but listen he does not
Crushed are my feelings, by he, without a thought
Lost and heartbroken, those feelings seem to dwell
In the nights of sleeplessness called my living hell
Left alone to weep in vain, fear consumes my soul
With every passing minute, I have less control
Every dream left in my heart dies and fades away
As do smiles and happy thoughts every passing day
In hopeless desperation and sad refrain
I try to tell my feelings but find only shame
Lies and games I cannot play, fill my lonely nights
Spent alone in sadness with feelings I cannot fight

—*Ginger Glasscock*

River

A turbulent mountain river,
Crushes against its steep sides.
Suddenly, it disappears into a cave,
As if it hides.

The river follow its narrow path,
The cave is dark and wet.
Then the water comes out the sides,
Like it wants to be bad.

The river comes out the back of the cave.
Then goes down a high waterfall.
It's falling down fast and hard.
It's the most beautiful thing of all.

A river is like a tiger.
Trapped between the shores like in a cage
And it tries to get out the edges,
While hitting the sides in rage.

—*Irina Polonsky*

The Unknown Symphony

My heart is free in the wind, but my soul hears a lonesome cry. The air I breath is magic, but the sweetness I taste soon goes away as an overcast of unhappiness comes along.

When that day of reckoning comes and happiness wins, no longer shall my mind cry tears of a melancholy symphony. Aching to speak its first words, but unable to here the right song so it can play. Instead it's silent and unheard, even though it's as beautiful as an eagle. It becomes as lonely as a flower with no sun and as careless as a breeze flying over the sea, forgetting that destiny's listening, calling her broken heart. Looking for the one who holds the master key.

Please dear God save thee, and my perilous misery shall come to and end, and a new day a dawning will come threw the dark green forest. As the field grows a basket of wild flowers, I shall pick a beautiful bouquet. And remember this happiness that finally came my way, when destiny finally came knocking and the door came open, and love came in.

—*Dahn Sweet*

Death

Death is something that you can not live with.
Death can strike you when you're well or sick.
Death is something that leaves many lives shattered.
Death is like many puzzle pieces scattered.
Death can cause devastation, depression or suicide.
Death makes you lucky to be alive.
Death is mean, nasty and cruel.
Death is for no one, especially fools.
Death is when you go to a funeral to see a loved one buried.
Death is something that is quite scary.
Death will not just go away
Death knocks on your door, to tell you that it's here to stay.

—*Anitra Y. Harrison*

World View

This world of ours, how vast and various.
Cultures and religions
Customs and politicians
Painted the landscape.
Remnants of lives gone away
Yet new ones maintain the beauty of it all.

Happy is the traveler who shares
The experience of God's creation.
In little ways, the world is known.
Faces, out-of-the-way places,
Exotic vases, embroidered laces
Manufactured by hands like mine
And his inspiration permeates it all.

One soul at a time is how it's best viewed.
Without looking, you'll miss
Subtle differences, similar instances
Shifting perspective, and bridging the distances.
Of history known and ignored, we lose out.
Present circumstances move us toward others —
Keep open the mind's eye.

 —Annette Davis

Untitled

Damn you!
 Damn you, damn you, damn you!

Damn you for
 removing my masks
 with something as simple as a smile...

Damn you for
 tearing down my walls
 and showing me
 light, and warmth and love...

Damn you for
 handing me a mirror
 and showing me I'm someone...

Damn you for
 making me stand
 on my own two feet
 and facing life...

And damn you
 for writing me today
 and doing it
 all over again.

 —Dale Cox

Hard Days

Days come,
Days go,
No matter the case,
I work to the bone
I arrive late at home.
And I have to brace myself,
And meet the look of sorrow,
On my children face,
I apologized over and over.
For missing my daughters play,
She just runs away,
She just doesn't realize what I go through everyday
Now to face up to my son
on why I missed his first home run,
All I am able to say sorry hon,
I'm not just a bum,
Am I?
No I work hard to get things done.

 —Erika Nichole Faz

There Is No Beauty In The Grave

There is no beauty in the grave silence by death, is rule by
darkness control by spirits, a clammy squelch own by dust and
worked by ants or worms there is no beauty in the grave. Life
is a thing full of beauties. Creatures and things, good or
evil are full of beauties
From firmaments of Heaven, deeps of ocean, lands are beauties
Created with beauties, life and death are severed by beauties
Friends or strangers, painful is death, sweet are beauties.

Coming from beauties in the Womb, once like a bride, I
paradised in clairvoyance douse and douched like dough in a
dormer snorkelled and nourished, I limboed in doldrums of
do-it-yourself spurting claustrophobicly from squeeze belly,
clattering and clacking-with staccato breath I spuriously
fisticuffs, spooky and spurning with outcry when
outmaneuvered.

Living and growing all in beauties, here in the world I'm
clambering on beauties, dying of beauties, graven to beauties
There is no beauty in the grave. Lifeless and calm, empty and
dry, there's no beauty int the grave.

 —Alex Nwigbo

Abiding Faith

Everyone has a story to tell,
day by day...How is life supposed to Jell?
Deliverance is the compelling ingredient,
Do others listen, or get bored, at the
Trivialities you share expedient.

Some are the greatest stories...you've ever heard.
Others are a trial...with each passing word!!

What would you say, if you were asked to share,
To condense so many years, into a segment of care!

What you do for Him, or what He does for you,
Probably so much more than was ever due!

Oh! what a lopsided episode, we would all hear,
Because Our "loving Heavenly Father," is always near.
We all received so much more, than we give,
We must all focus only on the positive,
To gather material to live!!!!

 —Dorothy Cheever

Untitled

In the dead of winter
Death stalks.
The weak die. The strong birds fight over crumbs.

In the dead the Winter Death walks, leaving no footprints in
the old gray snow piled high in miniature steep crags like
volcano cones.

In the dead of winter
Death talks, keening shrill in the ice clear air
with the odor of old skin warmed by a fire.
And the whispering sound as children
Make snow angels with their arms,
Moving them up and down.

Death walks drifting quietly, furtively away,
Letting us live another day
In the dead of winter.

 —Alys J. Hopwood

Sophie's Song

God has given you a deep heart,
Deem you would be wounded,
rather than lose a beautiful rose to age.
He has infused your sweet soul with grace of heart,
You have learned that beauty, truth, and goodness,
are parts of the same collage.

"A good book is the precious life blood of a master,
Treasured up on purpose to a life beyond life." (Shakespeare)
Through books you have discovered
a kinship with the world.

"Such sweet compulsion doth in music lie."
Harbinger of eternity, like a jeweled butterfly;
Your philosophy is as musical as Apollo's lute,
Your love of music will never make it mute.

Nature is another art known to you,
Violet-embroidered and apricot streaks-
of earth, your senses imbue.
You behold nature and discover,
the music of humanity!

—*Irene George*

If We Were Blind

Under this shell we call a skin,
Deep beneath and well within,
Is this thing . . . our inner being . . .
Food for thought, but not for seeing.

Sometimes I wonder what you would see,
Should you look to know the inner me.
Is there something also in you you want to tell,
Something you safely entomb within your shell?

Should you hate the darkened surface of my skin,
Or I despise your eyes of superficial blue,
When, down inside and deep within,
You are like me, and I am like you?

Try to imagine, if you can, everyone blind.
Wouldn't we all feel each a brother?
Why, then, with seeing eyes and good mind
Must we now so mistreat one another?

Can our shaded skin really matter that much?
If, when we communed and when we signed,
We only could touch,
Because . . . we all were truly blind.

—*David W. Cunyus*

Moved On

I have been sad since you went away,
Deep down I knew you could not stay.
For he wanted you, in the air
I am in complete despair.

Your job was finished here,
So, I keep your picture near.
Although, there is a gain,
I have had much pain.

Yet I have memories that are planted in my head,
It is still hard to accept that you are dead.
You have went to a better place,
Therefore, I can not keep a sad face—

—*Brandy Brown*

Concealed Heart:

Search within until you find, a heart that's hidden down
deep inside. It tries to hide but it's always found, no
way to escape its beating sound.
Disguises are used but they don't last long, for you see
that beating sound in much too strong. Instead of giving
into being found, we keep looking for defenses to silence
the beating sound,
When one has found the perfect defense, it's hard to let
go because it seems so intense. Why let anyone past my
wall, when I see its protection won't let me fall?
It seems so senseless to allow others near, when I know
that their presence I'll eventually fear. The pain some
can cause makes me really scared, I guess that's why I'm
afraid to care.
I know it's a risk everyone must take, but something
inside tells me my heart will break. It's already
severed in different parts, sometimes I wish I never had
a heart.

—*Joan Altmire*

Broken Union Cold Betrayal

Within the valley between two mountains it seeps
Deep into the cold hard core
Of a scarred soul is the fear of pain
That spills from broken hearts
    Harsh words of healing
    Rebuked and demoted
Flowing as a rushing river of sorrow
Dark regrets penetrating the mire
Therein enslaved alone amid cheery masks
Illuminating the shadowed hollowness inside
    Tranquility of soft souls unrest
    Denial and self deception
Disillusioned by dried bones of broken dreams
Dead trees sprouting from poisoned fields
Disdain reviving strife to resentment
Resurrecting hatred for the romance of lust
    Beaten unjustly by kind cruelty
    DIVORCED

—*D. Craig Knowlton*

My Poems, My Children

Just where do my poems all come from?
Deep thoughts...the fruition of daydreams.
They all spin around me on tiptoe
Like children, all dancing on moonbeams.

My poems, you see, are my children;
Each one holds a warm place in my heart.
I've brought them to life e'er these daydreams
Like butterflies, all drift far apart.

One poem's as sad as a storm cloud
On a face that once smiled happily.
Another is one kissed by raindrops
That keep falling to parched earth with glee.

Still others are laughing and flirting
With fond lovers in pure ecstasy,
While several pay tribute to nature
Whose raindrops and bright sunshine are free.

My poems, my children, are precious;
With my dreams and deep thoughts coming true.
When inscribed on this pad of paper,
I am sharing these secrets with you!

—*Helen D. Johnson*

A Poem, A Life

A poem is an adjective of life
descriptions of life's eternity
silent screams in black and white
a spoken song, a melody of love

There's a life behind those lines
emotions shine above them all
the lives, loves, and countless dreams
the kiss of a lover, or the touch of a child

Take a stroll along a sunkissed beach
Kiss the dew of a flame-tipped bud
cry at the depression of a battered mind
revolt against the war of young nations

I can hear the sounds of the seas
Or taste the salt of the tears
I can feel my heart anticipate
or see the graves of the deceased

I can feel the emotions unfold
as the life of the poem is born
revealing the masterpiece letter by letter
every word another kiss, another thought
—*Faithe Leach*

A Wall Versus A Shell

Did I build this wall?
Did I grow this shell?
Can this wall fall down?
Will I shed this shell?

Your wall, who helped you build it,
how long have you had this wall?
Can this shell protect you
if you fall on your back,
or does it expose your heart?

What if I see a heart, as big as a person?
Should I try to surround it?

Is the heart behind a bullet proof vest?
Velcro holds the vest.
What holds the heart?
How can this heart rock this wall?

If I shed this shell, can I grow another?
I want no wall around my heart.
I shed this shell, forever.

I think I know the pain of a heart attack.
I think it happens when a wall falls on your heart.
—*James T. Palmieri*

When The Day Is Done

What have you accomplished when the day is done?
Did you extend a hand to help someone?
Did you count your blessings for all you got?
and did you say a prayer for those who have not?
Was there plenty of food on your table today?
and have you thought of the hungry
and filled their tray?
Did you visit the sick or helped the poor
today?
or did you look the other way?
May your conscience be your guide,
if by the laws of God you did abide
As you face your maker one on one,
when the day is done.
—*Espedito Valli*

My Mama

My mama went away one day.
Didn't even bother to say good-bye,
Didn't even give the world a try.
Maybe it was all to much to bear,
Or maybe she thought no one cared.

Mama left the man she'd vowed.
Felt she couldn't do him proud.
Guess she figured she'd never be missed.
Didn't really need his tender kiss.

Mama, I'm sorry for some things I said.
Mama, I'm sorry you never got to see,
What kind of lady I turned out to be.
Mama, I'm sorry I never got to know you.
Never got to say how much I love you.

Mama. If you're somewhere up there
Listening, please remember, I was only
Age nine, and a child doesn't always
Understand about a delicate mind.

Love, your daughter, age 48
—*Jo Anna Boehmer Eisenbise*

Inner Thoughts

I've been something I didn't know, could I be?
Didn't know anybody could be.
You stop, looking inward, looking young, looking old
You want to talk, not anybody, somebody!
You become most out of the world, to feel you're in the world
Alone or alive?
You could live yourself, find yourself or be yourself
What's stopping you?
You do awful things, those times, sometimes, to people
Unaware but aware.
It was though they aren't real, are they?
You reach for life, empty, other times full
Is it both? Can it be?
You find yourself at the bottom
Sweating, crying, shaking
You smell, stink
You think you will die.
Run, but it follows
You didn't know, you still don't know
Will you know?
—*Gregory P. Costa*

Teach Me

Black is my face
Different, yet the same

Accented features
Red blood through my veins

Look beyond the pigment inhabiting my skin
To the beautiful person living therein

An inquisitive being
From you, knowledge I implore

Teach me, guide me
Like an eagle help me soar

Explore with me, hold my hand
Through literature carry me to extravagant lands

Experiment with science, allow my mind to wonder
Teach me the significance of discovering the thunder

Relinquish the mystery of square roots and signs
Geometry, Algebra, Statistics, I'll shine

Unveil your knowledge, guide me with respect
A contributing citizen a lasting affect.
—*Gail Holloman Holmes*

Eclipse

I reach out into night. Find only stars by distance
diminished. By darkness curtained, hallowed deep. Veiled
beneath her arch-vault I enter night's sarcophogal slope.
Stars vanish and solitude saws its cutting edge. Severing
synthetic skeins of shorn comfort. Bearing heavy blankets of
loss in crowded cradle folds. Like shroud-cover binds or
worm-cocoon winds of Dusty Miller moths. Dense night envelopes
as my chest tries to burst taut bands anguish offers my
breathing. In smothering discords of disastrous song,
"Tomorrow and Tomorrow and Tomorrow". Sing to me no more!
O stringent strings. Sawing back and forth on endless bows!!!
My ears strain to hear only my love, now gone. His
contemplative concourses, his punctual wit. But they are lost,
stolen in night silent longings. Which hold no pretense of
Tomorrow Promised. Night binds me, Lo, with incantations of
sorrow. Yet, the low-banked glow from your eyes pursues.
Perfuming my passage as I travel labyrinths of nocturnal
timeways. On languid rivers that never reach sunrise or flow
into Dawn.

—*Frances P. Abbey*

Lies Upon Me

To my mother, I'm not the daughter hoped to be
Disrespect shown, a family in unharmony
To others, I am the daughter hoped to be
Total respect shown, friends in harmony
… A lie that lies upon me
To the outside world, I act in peace
As if nothing goes wrong with me,
So to them they see, a "perfect child"
On the other side I'm troubled
… A lie that lies upon me
To myself,
I know what I do
I know what I think
I know what I say
But yet I don't know for sure
What I do
What I think
What I say
… A lie that lies upon me

—*Erica Dancel*

A Past Affair

Do I know you
Do I remember you
Do I want to remember you?
No I don't know you, no I don't remember you
No I don't want to remember you
What Was Your Name? Yes, I'll try.
If only for a moment, if only for a time
When there seemed not enough
But, it was different then
Just the thought of you filled every hour.
Just the touch of your hand and the smile on my face
When I knew you were near.
But time moved on as it always does
And those few precious times became what once was.
Now it seems like years and I pass you by
And you stop me and ask through the tears that I hide
Do I know you, do I remember you?
Yes, but I'll ask just the same
What Was Your Name?

—*Helen Gamarsh*

Some Things Stay

A moment lost, a feeling gone,
Do not dishearten; some things stay.

A simple treasure,
A piece of time rarely visited.
A fleeting experience of notable measure;
For a while great joy, but then quickly exited.
Do not dishearten; some things stay.

Private adulation over an accomplishment made.
For it to last but a second more, what would you trade?
So long in the coming, so short in the stay;
That feeling of triumph over the day.
Do not dishearten; some things stay.

So then, in some things that stay?
Be it in truth some complex metaphor?
Perhaps in honesty it could be read that way,
But in simple fact, it's my love forever more.

Please, no longer need you search
For a happiness that will not go away.

Do not dishearten;
It is I that will stay.

—*Edward Bankson*

Who

Who is he that walks beside me, who is she that sits by my side?
Do they know what a marvel they are?
Do they know me when they pass this way?
Their limbs, do they feel them before me?
Do they feel them among crowds, in front of crowds?
Their arms reaching, hands forward.
Do they feel the touching of glass, metal, fabric, skin,
Do they feel the difference at their fingertips, wanting
   to stay and absorb?

Their voices, do they hear it first unheard, then heard?
I sit in crowds or do they sit in me? I feel their applause, I
am filled with them! Do they feel the crowd in me? I feel the
crowd in them and I want to hail their coming sobriety! Who
are they that walk beside me, who sits by my side? Do they
know they carry with them riches, the experience of riches? Do
they know that they have passed the crowd, and having passed
they can leave the crowd behind. I ponder them who are beside
me. Do they know they can give back to the poor, the
experience that was poor, and sit and walk in majesty?

—*Alton Sears*

Travel Of Birds

How far do they travel in flight?
Do they travel both day and night?
Always they rise, into the blue skies.
What do they do when the clouds are black?
I bet their speed gets very slack.
And when it rains, do they find their nest?
Eat food and rest.
What really is their quest?
I know they love to sing.
They make their little voices ring.
But without birds, what would life be?
Not nearly as much to see.
The answer is the Lord, who takes care of
them.
Both day and night,
To lessen their plight.

—*Betty A. Ream*

Mom, What Do You Do All Day?

Mom, what are you doing today?
Do you watch over me at work and play?

How does God keep you occupied
During all the hours that glide?

Do you see the things I do?
And are you pleased with them too?

When I see pretty things of lush
I think God has handed you a paint brush.

When I hear lovely voices ringing
I know you are an angel singing.

When I see the beauty of a rose
I see your face, God knows.

When I see the shape of a flower
I see you in your tower.

When I see the beauty of the sea I see your hands blessing me.
When I think of all my trials, I see your sweet, beautiful
smile. When I rush out in the morning with a tear,
I hear your voice saying, "Allah with you, my dear".

But dear Mom, though I miss you more every day,
I am happy that you are with God to stay.

    —Alice Sanders

Don't Keep Me Down

Please friends, don't keep me down,
  don't make me laugh and later frown.
Don't trample over me and make me fall,
  don't keep me and my world closed in by walls.

I want to view the sun as it sets,
  and photograph a face I have never met.
I want to feel my hand against the sky,
  and watch the sky larks fly by.

I want to capture a piece of the sun's ray,
  and share it with my friends each day.
I want to ride the wings of a dove,
  and find the true meaning of love.

I want to explore my mind,
  and treasure the things I find.
I want to listen to each and every sound,
  so please friends don't keep me down.

    —Gloria Ann Williams

Born On Wings

Cries echo in the night
Dove resting from her flight
Tired wings and weary eyes
Her pain begins to rise. No it's not over...it's just begun

  she's got to fly....

She can fly, she was born on wings
Attached to her there are no strings
If weathers change and storms arise
She won't turn back to compromise.

Throw your mind into time
Chasing dreams ain't a crime
If weather change or storms arise
Don't look back, don't close your eyes. No never...Give it
  a try

Child fly high, you were born on wings
Forget your pain and suffering
Child fly high, you were born to sing
Attached to you there are no strings...

    —Constance E. English

Dear Jesus

Walk with me Jesus
down lives narrow road,
For this, Dear Jesus, is where you reside.
But when there's a
mountain lead me to the other side.
In the night when no ones there.
Stay close to me,
King Jesus, God's hope and heir.
Let me cling to you Savior,
when the world is a mess.
Help me learn from the trials.
Because you know what's best.
Help the lost, see when there's no other way.
To come to you Jesus.
When on bended knees they say...
"I claim the shelter of the sheep fold."
"For dear shepherd, you're always there."
Dear Jesus, King Jesus,
Dear Saviour, dear shepherd.
God's hope and heir.

    —Cheryl Bills

Untitled

It's early morning and it's darn cold
Drank late last night, so I am told
Herd's wait'n and it's time to feed
I was warned about cowboy'n but didn't heed

Built a half mile of fence just yesterday
Irrigated late last night to water grow'n hay
Went to town for fun and a few drinks
I drank too much I think

I'm reach'n up to scratch an aching head
Boy! I wish I could've stayed in bed
Working hard to stay broke
Sometimes I think it's a bad joke

The cattle fed and the fences fixed
A day off! heck, it got mixed
The lower pasture gate post rotted through and fell down
I'll probably never get back to town

    —JJ Malone

Untitled

What is time, but a long span of days
  Drawn together by Friendship and other ways.
What is time, but a passage of the Seasons
  Dark days omitted for varied reasons.
What is time, but a number of years
  When from friends and loved ones he hears.
What is time, when all else seems Mod
  When at Christmas thoughts turn to God.
What is time, but our Lord's way
  to build understanding that will always stay.

    —Al Newman

Nature's Fireworks

The night came swiftly after the long hot day
Deep inky, blue black, with a slight breeze,
Suddenly, out of the blackness came the, "Lantern Carriers."
Tiny, jumping, glowing darts of fire
They laced the oaks with silver threads
The pines became pyramids of diamonds
They drew rainbow patterns on the grass
The kingdom of the Plum Fairy could not compare
With this scene of motion, peace and beauty

    —Annette Geoghegan

Child Of The Times

Child of the times, passing through Life,
Drink deep the simple treasures of the Earth.
Watching the blossoms on the trees, the Robin singing
The child sits upon the swing, swinging and dreaming.

The young man now, passing through seasons
Amid life's chaos, searching for reasons,
He does not see the blossoms now,
Nor hears the Robin's song so clear,
He sits upon the swing and strives to dull the pain and fear.
He has learned to laugh, only to cry,
He has learned to live, only to die.
Why on that fateful morning did you dream
Of taking Life so meekly by the hand
And leading Her to your beloved swing
With one swift, fatal blow to end?

Parents, awaken to your children's cries
They cry for understanding and for Love,
They're crying our for help,
They're crying not to die!

  —Angie Yniquez

Encountering Beethoven

Sunday afternoon in nowhere...nothing is around.
Driving Route 7...mad light and red sumac.
On the radio Beethoven's fifth.

Ahead, something...squat and sturdy
a black bear or what?
Bulging brow furrowed, tormented,
his cocked head shaking off...madness?
No, bees strafe his wiry head and ears.
Nearer now...The exile whirls
shambles back into an orchard.
High loping rhythms shake the ground.
He swats his misery...bellows a tonic chord
over and over...Aggrieved and grieving fortissimo.
Approaching...I see him storm the hive,
claws tear and snatch...snout buries in
And then...I come that close...
music spirals in my ear:
the snap of jaws, the crunch of teeth;
lapping a belly full,
drops stick to glistening fur...dolce, dolce.

  —Geri Radacsi

Storms Of Life

The crystal clear diamond-shaped drops of rain
drizzled down my dry cheeks, leaving a trail of cool, salty
water. The wind screamed as it whipped my coarse hair against
my face, imprinting welts deep into my skin. The Master of
light streaked rays of heat through the fiery, black clouds.

Struggling, grasping for air the smoldering clouds struggled to
separate, escaping the evil mood.

The ocean grew angry, clutching the air with its almighty,
powerful claws. The ocean's jaws gaping open, loosed at the
hinges, swallowing the golden sand, engulfing pebbles of stones
snapping at brisk, bony branches, popping them at the joints.

When all seems to be lost in the hands of destruction and all
hope has gone, the demon of the water recedes, drawing back
into its wings, as though giving up on life, no more a strength
but a weakness. A silver lining, reflecting the light
surrounds the fluffy, cotton-like clouds.

The light overpowers the dark like good conquering evil. The
charcoal black sky transforms into baby blue, calming the
fierce wings and hushing the crashing waves.

  —Denise R. Bahr

Combat Zone

Men of precision,
Drumming out their musical advance,
Dispersing through the combat zone,
Running to and fro,
Into trenches to taste dirt;
Rigid frontiersmen, dressed in forest green,
Kick at sunlight
To camouflage their blood in patches of brier.
Havoc sweeps over the battleground,
Ascends to Heaven in wreathing flames-
Bayonets churning guts,
Madmen at their throats!
Blood spills out
From bullet holes
And mangled brains!
Destroy, destroy, destroy!

And it's all child's play
On a Saturday afternoon.
Made-in-Japan implements,
And helmets from Sears.

  —Jeff Hearn

A Melancholy Memory

As I approached the atrocious gate, I was
 dubious that I could belie an aloof
 demeanor.
As I approached the door, my heart was laden
 with antipathy.
Upon entering the wretched prison, I
 automatically followed the latent superior
 who silently told me to keep walking
 down the path I'd been walking
 down every day for almost five years.
Step after step, I made my way down the
 well worn path in the carpet to
 my cell, euphemistically called my room.
I'd spent countless days and nights, hours
 and minutes in that incorrigible place.
My trepidation of the future debilitated
 me to the point of lethargy.
It seemed so superfluous to deprave
 someone like that.

  —Hilary Ray

A Builder's Lament

Ray - Ray - so they say -
Dug a hole one summer day;
Went to town and bought some blocks
While Brons and Raymond picked up rocks.
Got some cement and some sand
And measured it out with an old tin can.
Cindy managed the mortar box
As Ray dipped in and laid up blocks
Straight and even, without a kink -
Except right here, "where we'll put the sink."
While Cindy's dreaming about kitchens and stuff,
Ray is worrying if there's blocks enough.
Brons is saying, "Won't that be cool?
I'm going to tell all the kids at school."
Raymond can't wait till he gets his own room.
If it happens tomorrow, it won't be too soon.
Cindy says, "Here's my kitchen and there's the bath,
And I'll plant flowers along this path."
While poor old Dad is turning grey
Thinking about how he will pay!

  —Bertha Moore

This Little Ones Loves Thee!

With faith and hope and love I pray.
Each of these gifts I appreciate.

To adore Thee, O Almighty God,
is a privilege given to this little one.

The strength, the desire,
the opportunity to recognize Thy care
are blessed inspirations.

This little one who came to be —
beloved by Thee, the One Who Is!
the One Who always Was!
the One Who always Will Be!

Than Whom there is none greater!
In Whom I place my trust!
For Whom my soul does yearn!

May I live forever with Thee
and will all of Thy beloved!

—*Mary Frances*

Rejoice, But Remember

Rejoice America, our Hostages are free
Each soon will be with their own family.
The yellow ribbons tied across our land
Told everyone just where we stand.
United, we prayed, with hopes held high
As for their release, President Carter did try.
Finally it happened after 444 days.
We should be thankful in so many ways.
But always remember those eight men who died,
In Spring, in Iran's Desert, as they tried
To prepare a rescue of the Hostages held
By Iranian students and leaders as well.
All were volunteers and extremely brave.
They knew the danger: The situation was grave.
But still they went to rescue their brothers;
The operation depended on them and others.
But Fate worked against them on that Spring day,
And eight men were killed in a tragic way.
Remember them always, close in your heart
As the Hostages return for a fresh new start.

—*Frances M. Bauer*

Remember When

Remember when the clouds were lily white?
Each turning to silver when close to night.
The rain would fall so fresh and clean.
Watering God's earth with softened serene.

Remember when the sky was truly blue?
With evenings bringing a mixing hue.
The quietness of a darkened night.
A prayer, then peaceful sleep until daylight.

Remember when real flowers grew?
Each breath of air was always brand new.
With all life's changes, we must realize.
The joy of living, our priceless prize.

Remembering when, with precious memories to last.
Today's a day we move from the past.
Let us release the anxiety of by-gone strife.
Because today's the beginning of the rest of our life!

—*John M. Elkins*

You Can't Buy Your Way Into Heaven

You can't buy your way into heaven you've got to
earn it, my friend. You have to live by the
good book and trust the Lord to the end.

You can't buy your way into heaven money won't buy
back your soul. You have to answer to God,
friend for the free love that your stole.

You can't buy your way into heaven so you had
better repent. Money won't do you no
good there if you could take every cent.

You can't buy your way into heaven
It is a fact you should know. For wicked
sins in our lifetime we go above or below.

You can't buy your way into heaven
All of your wealth stays, my friend.
No one can hide from the good Lord
In this big world without end.

You can't buy your way into heaven
We leave it all when we're gone.
Do good and you'll be rewarded,
Up there we're judged and reborn.

—*Daniel Andrade*

War About The Night

Black horses, march across the heavens,
Echoed with hoofs of thunderous rhythm....
Gallantly about the battle ground,
There's war in heaven again tonight.

Not Fought by mighty men and armors,
But with elements, nature trembles at the sight...
Flashes of spectrum, more powerful than moonlight,
Natures reversed her purpose.

With Sounds of broken glass,
Shades of night become illuminated....
Holy Terror!
Even the windy sea challenges anger,
Neath the powerful hand.....
Of a bolten lightning crash.

White capped waters appear on the horizon,
Captured by winds and gales,....
Fiery snakes become giant monsters,
Striking all about the universe.
The war is over! the nightingale whispers.
Natures wounds shall heal before daybreak.

—*George Wilder Evans*

Solace Of An Old Friend

A lone figure sits hunched on a granite outcropping near the edge of the lake. The wind plays with the tendrils of hair as it quickly passes, but the figure does not seen to notice. Her eyes are turned to the endless expanse of water and the steady rolling, pounding, and crashing of the waves. In a trance-like state, she sits, arms wrapped tightly around her rocking body, but does not see the beauty before her. Only the turbulent churning of the water is felt and taken in. Just as calm, peace, and serenity are missing in the movement in the lake, so

also within the woman. A lone tear slips from her eye and follows a trail down her cheek. Soon it is joined by a rush of others... They, just as the waters of the lake, could not be held in check. When the inner storm has raged and run its course, a fragile calm overtakes the woman. The winds calm as evening approaches; the waves ease their turbulent motion. The

lone figure leaves, raising her hand in a gesture of thanks to an old friend.

—*Jan Stauffenecker*

As We Lay Locked

As we lay locked in this passionate
Embrace, our souls are swept away to a
World that promises a thousand eternities.
As we lay locked, our bodies inter-twined
As one - while we dance the dance that
Only two lovers can do.
As we lay locked, emotions run like rivers
As we search to find the true meaning of
Love from within the total darkness of
Ourselves.

 —Hattie Lathion-Lee

Pulses

There are times
energy flows like liquid gold,
pulses flame, fingers fly,
creativities abound -

There are times
quiet enfolds, peace ebbs and flows,
web and fog surround -

There are times
tears burst forth, knots tie tight and
futilism envelope all around -

There are times
joy leaps out, fulfillment seeks its place.
Self realization bears fruit and is found -

These pulses are life each day all
year round -

 —Beverly Willig

Barstools

Next to her, he sat
engaged in his own nothingness.
His skin, thick and crawly,
aches from a hangover.
Yet his eyes thirst to begin again.
He hardly notices her.

She, on the other hand, is
overcome with thoughts subdued
of faraway places and once upon a time.
A woman, staring into a glass as empty as
her tomorrows.
My God! Someone pour her another drink.

 —Deborah S. Green

Enjoying Inner Travel

Alone but not lonely,
Enjoying my indulgence in self,
Treating my ears to favorite songs,
Treating my tastebuds to fattening favorite foods,
I welcome me to my inner world.
Exploring my friendship with myself,
I entertain myself effervescently.
Could I be relish on a hot dog?
Could I be dew on a spider web?
Enjoying my sense of personal contentment
With who I am and with where I'm going,
I handsomely hug my sense of personal growth.
Could I be someone's smile?
Could I be someone's ticklish laughter?
Knowing and liking myself brings obvious comfort.
Could I be someone's favorite chair?
Could I be someone's warm embrace?
I like sharing me with me.
I promise to visit myself more often!

 —Cosma Stamis

The Harbingers

Cerulean sky, canopy of light,
Enhances reds, yellows and changing green.
Sun-filled day following a frosty night,
Gives clue that leaves must change - then no more seen.

Gone are the bright florid of summer time,
Replaced by crusty pods of darkened brown
Filled with wee seeds to sprout in old begrime
When Mother Earth accepts them in her ground.

Scanning, searching for blue of lakes and ponds,
Noisy geese swoop down to sandy shore line.
They giggle, gaggle—raucous vagabonds—
And swim with grace, at home in the marine.

Then one by one they life into the air,
Rising, honking, higher, higher they go,
To fly in formation with such a flare.
Soon they head for warm lands sans ice and snow.

There they giggle, gaggle and strut around.
Their time in southern warmth too soon is gone.
Air-borne again they leave for northern ground
To land of changing trees and pines enthroned.

 —Annette Lewis

Yesterday

You and I will never learn to
Enjoy the beauty of a
Setting sun or a newly risen moon while it's
There.
Even the rarity of a child's smile or a purple
Rainbow is unseen until tomorrow's
Dawn breaks
And leaves us
Yearning for yesterday's promises.

 —Deborah A. Reading

Memories

I can still hear your footsteps in the hall
Even though I know you're not there at all

I can still see you sittin' in that old tattered chair
Oh Lord how I wished you were still sittin' there

I can still see you drivin' that old tractor and plow
I don't know what kept it going only the Lord knew how

At times when things are so quiet at night
Right after I turn out the light I toss and I turn
For it's you that this old body will always run

I can still see those eyes
I can still feel your touch
Oh how I loved you so much

For memories are all I have left of you
And I'll never, no never let them die.

 —Debbie Peters

Love-N-Life

Life is one of life's greatest miracles
Death is one of life's greatest tragedies
So
To love is to live
To fall out of love is to die
In contrast
You must live and let die

 —Corey Murph

It's Really Over

I wanted to leave this day behind me
Even though it hadn't begun
I'd rather die in my sleep tonight
than live knowing we are done

I can't help but think about the future and the past
The past was so full of memories, I knew it wouldn't last.
But the future is not nearly as bright
as a cloudless, moonless night.
And the thought of living another day
Fills my soul and clings so tight

How can I imagine a life after death,
When my life has just run away.
I hope to see another night with you,
But I won't make it through today.

—*Chad Brookins*

Even... Ode To A Hopeless Love

Even though the sea drys up and the sun stops shining bright,
Even though the wind is rough and blows with all its might,
I will still be there, thinking of you too.
I will always be in love with you!

Love is still a motivating factor in our lives
Love, I think, is the only thing that makes the world turn.
But even if it stopped for awhile and left us standing there
I would always be in love with you.

Every little thing you say and everything you do
And every little thing, you see, it builds my love for you.
So even though the winds may blow, and fate will come my way
I will always be in love with you.

But even though I really must, I can't go on like this.
I'll close this book upon this page, a chapter in such bliss.
Yet I can never really say, goodbye, so long, goodday,
Cause I will always be in love with you!

Please save a little spot for me, way deep down there, inside,
And I will never bother you, I'll try my tears to hide,
So I will go and fade away, give up, give up, you say?
Oh, how can I, when I'm still in love with you!

—*Charlette A. Chatwin*

Be Not Afraid

God has not given us the spirit of fear,
Even when bad times or tragedy is very near.
God has not given us the spirit of fear,
As Christians, our future is plain and clear.

God has not given us the spirit of fear,
But of love' a sound body and mind.
God had not given us the spirit of fear,
Trust Him and sweet peace you will find.

God has not given us the spirit of fear,
But of faith, tested, tried and true.
God had not given us the spirit of fear;
With his protection, there is no need to be blue.

God has not given us the spirit of fear;
His hand reaches out to us in love.
God had not given us the spirit of fear;
Be bold, and dare to trust the one above.

God has not given us the spirit of fear;
Be challenged and think of the Apostle Paul
God has not given us the spirit of fear;
Be brave, and forsake not your sacred call.

—*Iris D. Rice*

My Beloved—America

My country what have we done to you, once you were the envy of every nation. Men fought gallantly and proudly lay down their lives for you to be free. America, when did you fall and lay so broken and hate invade your very shores? You gave so much to everyone and asked for nothing in return. Your waters now smell of corruption and your air filled with poisons of greed. Arms that once beckoned all to come are now filled with lies from politicians. You are bleeding, dying, gasping for your last breath of air in vain, your pain invades my very soul, still, I am helpless to save you. Like a bird shot with an arrow you are quietly but swiftly and surely falling. Falling to your death, your mournful cries do not escape my ears. Forgive us my country! We allowed your deceitful leaders to destroy you. Your day is coming soon my country ——— The day when you will no longer be. Valiantly and bravely you stood alone, how I grieve for you and for me. But through the pain and sorrow I am somehow consoled, for one I knew you. I have such warm, happy memories of you that remain, I hold them close to me. But you! the NEXT GENERATION, you will never have what I hold most dear to me. You will never know this great land filled with love, hope and freedom. You will never remember anything from the ashes that remain of a once proud land. A land that gave its all, my beloved America.

—*Doris Marie Goodrich*

A Music Box Filled With Peace

Oh, the "Fine French Horns" in
every Orchestra and Concert Band,
J. P. Sousa " The March King" of course!
Do you know what S.S.B. by F.S.K. stands
for? If not "Kate Smith" would inform
you our God bless America Lady. How
about M. Wilsons, "Music Man?" Star
and Stripes forever "J.P.S. and G.M.C."
Yankee Doodle Dandee?
Get with it America they all belong
to us just like the "Wonderful Art" of the
Bird's Song and singing from "God's own
Art Dept."
Shout and Boo! whenever one tries to
destroy our Red White and Blue!
Sound your best A - U.S.A.

—*Anna Geck Sr.*

True Friends

What would life be without the love of true friends,
Every road traveled would be a dead end.
Having true friends is such a rarity,
Year after year it brings such serenity.
As days pass by we sometimes take our friends for granted,
We don't realize, someday, their roots will become unplanted.
Opportunities come that they can't pass by,
So they must move on and give it a try.
All those daily phone calls, we never once considered,
That someday we would be waiting for the mailman to deliver.
Our daily trials and tribulations,
Which always caused our great conversations.
It's just not the same when we're so far apart,
But when it's "true friends", they stay close to the heart.
All roads traveled will not be dead ends,
As long as we have the love of true friends.

—*Donna L. Moffett*

Just To Get A Rep

Today's the first day of school
Everyone's dressed fly, decked out real cool
That's why I hate to go to school that first day
Because I hate to hear what all the kids say
I'm tired of it all so I got me a plan
I had an idea how I could be "the man"
First I got a gun, a 9mm is what I choosed
Then I headed to the streets to get me some shoes
I picked out this kid, his shoes were fly
And even better yet they looked like my size
I followed him into an alley I made sure we was alone
Then I reached in my pocket and pulled out my chume
I pulled back my piece and squeezed off my load
Now he's in right in front of me layin in the road
Went for his shoes he started moaning
Please oh please! Not my Air Jordans!
I got to school the next day, I got just what I hoped
People all around saying how I was "Dope"
I guess I'm gonna be "cool" as long as I keep packin
I'm going back out tonight I need a new jacket.

—*Eric Bishop*

Beauty

Just look out your window at all the beautiful things
Everything that is out there are God's little beings.
Big things - little things out there were ever you can see
Were put on this fine earth for you and for me.
But as all the years go by I'm confused by it all
What some people do with it, destroy and make things fall.
Feelings that come through to me are not what others feel
The uncaring people here, is hard for me to deal.
There has to be something that everyone can do
Not just a few of us but for you and me too.
If people would think of what they do each day
They could care about the earth so that the beauty can stay.
Then they might find it easy to reach down in their heart
And pull that special feeling that shouldn't tear apart.
Those special things created from someone great above
The beauty of his planning like the beauty of a dove.

—*Donna Steiner Roberts*

Your Heart

　Your heart is something everyone has,
except is different in everyone.
　Some are full of parties and fun, but
lots are full of love.
　Love of passion, love of money, love of
everything.
　My heart is full of love too, but of
something different, something not everyone
feels.
　It's full of love for the world, for
the problems in the environment, for the
people out on the street.
　But I intend to change that in the
time to come. There are more problems
that I would like to change. For those
are just some.

—*Courtney Kimball*

-Music, Oh, Music -

Music exalts each joy, allays each grief,
Expels diseases, softens every pain,
Subdues the rage of poison and the plaques.

There's music in the sighing of a reed;
There's music in the gushing of a rill;
There's music in all things, if men had ears;
Their earth is but an echo of the spheres.

Therefore by music, minds an equal temper know,
Nor swell too high, nor sink too low;
If in the breast tumultuous joys arise,
Music her soft, assuasive voice applies;
Or, when the soul is press'd with cares,
Exalts her inliv'ning airs.

Because music resembles poetry; in each
are nameless graces which no methods teach,
and which a master hand alone can reach.

—*George R. Morris*

Expressions Of Love

Velvet and lace, ribbons and bows,
Expensive chocolates, a bright red rose.
Huge red hearts, cupid's darts,
A pure white dove, expressions of love.

Candy and flowers, verse and song,
Sweethearts declaring their love all the day long.
Parties and laughter meant to convey,
Undying love on Valentine's Day.

In daytime or nighttime, under moonlight or stars,
In farmhouse, in cabin, on battlefield, behind bars.
Love shines forth on this happy day,
Expressions of love are so easy to say.

The greatest expression of love ever told,
Is recorded in the Bible - the new and the old.
The ultimate love was expressed for you and for me,
On an old rugged cross at Mt. Calvary.

—*Bertha Pittman*

Flood Water

Evacuation, trying to escape, people crying, animals dying, sad faces, lots of tears, haven't had one for years. Flood water.

All that you owned destroyed before your eyes, my what a shocking surprise. Flood water

Dreams and success floating away, nothing but memories to cling to, towing sights, cam cords filming the scenes of condemned disaster areas. Flood water

Sinking bridges, blocked highways, streets and freeways, business loss. Flood water

The horrible smell, the muddy sight, I can image how some people felt. Even the homeless chased away, it was sad to watch them find somewhere else to stay. Flood water

No one knows what God will do, but hold to faith and he will see you through. Just pick up the pieces and start again, and you will see we all survived the great Flood of ninety three.

—*Erma Milton*

Untitled

As this world of hate mills around,
fears of anger run through my brain;
Words of frustration and confusion are found.
The words hurt deep to cause pain.

There isn't anything to smile about,
there is nothing left to live for;
Faith and trust have turned to doubt.
The world needs help, and we hurt it more.

Now is the time to open our eyes,
realize what is being done;
And work together in compromise.
Destroying the world has already begun.

This isn't about trend or being cool,
it's about our lives, and the ones coming in.
We have to do something for this world,
before what we have comes to an end.

Don't do this because you're told,
Don't do this just because you need to,
Do it because you care,
Do it for our future.

—*Angelina Brittain*

Feeding Sparrows

Gray puffs of sparrows flying in at first.
Feeding dirty sparrows at such expense!
I seek the rare exotic bird. I thirst
And long to brag to friends as recompense.

Gray brown puffs surround me and inundate!
Feed bills continue in their upward rise.
Finally, primadonnas come, but late.
Frost of cold winter wind drives out their cries.

Cold with greed exposed and deafening chirpings,
Sparrows on ground and every branch of tree!
The grays and browns, the fat and saucy kings!
Fluffs, with intrinsic personality.

I name each one by mark and unique look.
They come with saucy mien and chippy stance.
There is no need to look them up in book!
I know their names and not a one by chance.

The feed bills are no longer now a curse.
Each puff and fluff now known and come on call.
My hand more eagerly goes to purse.
I brag to all my friends with names for all.

—*Edwin A. Griswold*

Nightmare

A cold sweat starts to cover your body
Feel a shadow creeping up from behind
There's something out there and it knows what you're doing
It's sending chills up and down your spine

Every minute sees the night grow colder
Try to run but there's nowhere to hide
You feel a hand come across your shoulder
Your heart stops, OH!

Endless hours staring out at the darkness
Who knows what evil's waiting outside the door
Try to fight it but there's no way to stop it
Every night you'll be going back for more

—*Charles A. Freeman*

A Christian Prayer

Father in heaven, please help all mankind to
    feel the need to become a born again
Christian.
    Fill our heart with joy and love.
Lord help us appreciate your saving grace.
We pray that we will remember that we are
    created equal regardless of race.
Lord help us treat everyone the way that
    we would like to be treated.
Father help us to read and understand the bible,
    because it is our road map to eternal life.
Father please help us to love and respect each
other because, if we truly love, hate and
fighting will cease,
Father in heaven please help us to be able
    to live in a world of peace.
Father in Jesus name I pray, Amen.

—*Hattie Mae Haynes*

The Changing Seasons

As the seasons begin feeling confused more and more each day,
feelings of different emotions in words to hard to say.
Loneliness of love rendering in heart, to the seasons of love
this is the start. As the seasons begin to change different
emotions flow, spring is the start, a time for a new love to
grow. It's when a life between two strangers, a love that has
begun, like us, two lost dreams now together as one. As the
seasons begin to change different emotions flare, summer is the
warmth and the time of moment so rare. It's when you feel the
passion of love through their special touch, like us living
each day loving one another so very much. As the seasons to
change different emotions leaves you in dismay, autumn is the
change, the time to remember yesterday. It's when two people
decide whether to make a stand, like us holding so tightly the
dream clinched in our hand. As the seasons begin to change
different emotions makes you cold, winter is the pain the time
when nights are lonelier your pride begins to mold. It's when
two lovers feel the most emptiness, hurting to cry, like us,
distant from each other lost in the words of goodbye. As the
seasons finally go by I feel for you much more. I dream for
the future to the day it was before. You were everything to me
more than a friend, so to the seasons of love this is our end.

—*Atsuomi James Yasuo*

Time

Time, momentary reflection, what are you?
Figment of imagination; desire to eternity?
What meaning to our lives, so controlled by thee,
Do you really have? What amount of you is here for me?

By you, quickly passing, my life is run?
Yet you are nothing to be noted, to desire;
My precious gift of life I waste on you;
It is not mine to give, you has'ning flier.

On you I base the hurry of my being?
On you rely to go and do? It seems I must
Alter you to fit what really is,
For not in you, only in God I trust.

Time, fleeting deceiver, thou art naught;
You pass or dwindle, seeming without note;
There can be none as you believe you are.
God is all; you misdirect, misquote.

What importance have you? You cannot stay;
Your length, or depth of sorrow is unknown;
I seek you more, or bid you pass me by,
But you are not - already you have flown.

—*Donna A. Jones*

Are You Listening Lord

People homeless and abandon
Fills our nation's lonely streets
Homeless living in card board boxes
The hungry eating from garbage cans

Government officials keep getting richer
While the poor keep getting poorer
People on welfare and unemployment
Drown their sorrows in another pitcher of beer

The final war keeps getting closer
With each and every passing conflict
Between nations big and small
People just can't get along at all

People fighting about abortions
Some don't think about the life they take
Others stop and wonder why
Who'd want to be born in these times

Oil spills are destroying the ocean's
Homes of every fish and whale
It's our last garden of eden
Before we go straight to hell.

—*Johnny Lee Crawford*

Reflection

Poets with their gift of writing
    Find no problem to begin,
Unfolding tales of things exciting.
    Or sober thoughts that lie within.

But then you'll find some folks like me
    Who haven't really lived, and such
But love most everything they see-
    Though can't express themselves as much

Joyce Kilmer wrote about a tree-
    Exquisitely, in flawless tongue,
Now I love trees, but then well me-
    I have to leave that love unsung.

The call of earth and grass and sky,
    Of leveled earth and rolling plain,
This vastness falling on the eye-
    I want to write, but all in vain.

All these things, they thrill me so,
    I pray that I could but transpose,
But fear I lack poetic flow-
    So shall content myself with prose!

—*Elizabeth Zepernick*

Love

When someone says love what are the
first things that come to your mind? A kiss, a hug,
or a butterfly. When someone says love do you think
of an intimate moment with someone you cherish.

When someone says love the first thing
I think of is you because of the time we spend
talking and sharing our feelings. I think of being
with you not caring what we're doing or who we're
with just as long as your with me.

If you would think about love, you can
compare it to a bunch of little hills and great big
mountains and then there is always that gently
rolling flatland. If you put it all together you get
a very loving couple, you and me. In translation it
means we'll have little fights and big fights, but
there will always be those good times to make
everything else go away.

—*Jennifer Silfies*

By Grace

Many days ago, more schooling I decided I did need. In the
first few days of my tenure, it was by Grace I did learn to
count numbers and arrange them all neatly in a row. It was by
Grace that I arose in the early morning to critique these
numbers because Grace would only accept quality.

Later on it was by Grace I learned to write flowery illustrations
and stories grand. I learned where to put that comma and period,
by Grace. And all the while I would say "I can't," but Grace
would always answer, "You'll see."

Now it is by Grace that I have learned to appreciate poetry and
stories, some so silly I have learned to decipher the strange words
of Poe and understand the meaning of metaphor and soliloquy.
Grace I can even find humor and love in these lines so strange to
me.

Oh, this Grace of ours is a strong one, full of knowledge and
wisdom gained from the strains of life. She has suffered life's
many heart-aches. She has lost love and suffered tragedy, yet she
still laughs.

However, each day, by Grace, this icon to human endurance, this
rose in the thorny garden of humanity, this, our own special Grace,
goes forth into the world to teach and strengthen others,
never wavering in the test of mankind.

Here I not only learned lessons from books, but I have gained
much strength, for I have learned that if this one mighty woman
can face the world with a smile, then I know, by Grace, so can I.

—*Janet D. Kidd*

First June Weekend

Sky so blue with white clouds,
First star in the West.
Bird just flew in front of me.
Moon so big and bright you can see,
before the blue sky becomes black.
My heart aches this lonely night.
I can't share with my love.
I hear a cricket in the back ground.
I hear cars go by.
A year this night my love asked me out.
A year tomorrow we had are first date.
On a star I wished that there were
More nights that are peaceful like this.
When I and my lover can spend it together.
The stars appearing one at a time in the
cool night air of this night.
I hear an airplane flying over head.
I hear kids down the street yelling in
this cool night air having fun.

—*Heather Homer*

Creation

The birds and the bees, once all around,
Flew away, leaving us without a sound.
Boats are no longer on the shore,
Far away lands don't exist anymore.
Trees in the forests, here and everywhere,
Hardly any left as we did not care.
The tracks are silent now, not like before,
When load after load came through and more.
Waters once blue and clear,
A color now nowhere near.
The planes don't arrive late or on time,
Joyful reunions with friends are no longer mine.

All we have left is what we created and
Never knew what it was leading to.

—*Hans Blom*

Symbolizing Awareness

Rushing, flowing in large vivid colors-
Flashing- red, green, oh that beautiful black!

Black - Deep dark specks of brightness during intervals,
swirling in huge colors, the wound opened wide its
huge, ugly mouth. Run continuously, bleed bastard
bleed, still hopelessly, helplessly you fight. Stop,
oh God!

Green - That beautiful, wonderful place, gigantic waiting
patiently, a place of warmth, greatness, and of love.
Isn't that how it ought to be. The color of green
so emphasize: peace, harmony, togetherness, may it be
day or night, don't you wonder? Maybe glorify
in the beauty of the thought.

Black - The most dreadful color, only harm may come to you.
The saddest in mourning draped in black. No! black!
Grateful texture of the mold - blackness shining,
standing out greatly with poise none other so great
prided with inheritage of historic remembrance.

—*Ida DeLois Allen*

A Bucket or a Vase

There was a vase of finest design, a beautiful sight to behold,
Flecked with the purest of silver, and etched in the finest of gold.
It stood in perfection and splendor, displayed in a prominent place,
And the pride in the heart of the matter was easily seen on its face.

There was a well-battered bucket, dented and bruised and old,
But it carried the purest of water, refreshing the body and soul.
Tempered and tried in the furnace, made fit for its master's use.
If you had to be one or the other, I wonder which you would
choose.

Would you rather be an old bucket fit for the hand of the Lord,
Or an elegant vase on a shelf soaking up praise and applause?
Would you be rather be just a vessel fashioned for use every day,
Or a cold and empty idol kept sheltered and out of the way?

It's not such an easy question, but once that comes to us all,
To lay down our lives in service or hide when we hear His call.
He doesn't force our decision, we have to make it ourself,
To pour out our life as a bucket or stand like a vase on the shelf.

—*Betty J. Ross*

Reality

The chain of hope has snapped; the flame of life has
flickered out.
The stricken Earth lies in sorrow, mourning the loss of its
once great bounty:
The winged creatures of the sky, the great beasts of the land,
The fish of the sea, its plants both great and small;
And, noblest of all, Man.

Earth gave Man many chances and gifts, but they were wasted on
him. He wove an intricate and beautiful garment, and then he
strangled himself with it. None of their gods could save them;
their images lie broken on the ground. Man did not hear the
Earth's warnings, nor did he see her wounds. Nor did he think
to stop the wars, the killing, the pollution, the wasting.

Earth will not recover from her wounds; she will not be cured
from her affliction. Her 'air' is no longer clear, but filled
with smoke. Her skin is invisible; it is littered by trash
and rubbish. Dead bodies are thick as tar. Earth is not a
planet. No, it is but one huge trash dump.

—*Christopher P. Benson*

Bananas

You can have your fig & eat it, too. But I'll have my banana
& eat it, too. I will take it & hold it, peel it open, subdue it,
control it. I will make it emotive. I will mold it & mold it &
feel it & know it. I will break it & make it & make it & make
it. I will make that banana mine... With nowhere to hide,
no mystery to it, just the obvious of all aspects to it, this fruit
disappoints, like the male's tee-tee, if released from its skin
too often, too soon, or, else, too late, for then it's spoiled
rotten, soft & mushy, as if dying. And if never opened, then one
of God's little angels, or compost cowed on earth awaiting,
sigh, sigh, sighing. But when fit as a bottle of wine, as fit as
its orbs when picked & primed, then take it, open it, breathe &
bear it to thy lips & drink it-for God's sake, don't sip it!
Insorb, inhaust, imbibe... Take it all. For I will take even
more & make you blubber & titter & drawl. For in my love I
have bared my self, so it is only fair that you bare your self,
if in your love were truth. All's fair. The war then is no
more. So, lay open the sluice & if you cry I will drink those
tears & then you will know; Nichts verboten, meine liebe,
diene liebe. And then you will know & know love.

—*I. Buenaventura*

Child With Child

In the bloom of youth I erred.
A beautiful rosebud was I
But my impatient petals
Made me a full blown rose
Much too soon.

It was in the age of moral ambiguity I bloomed.
Entrapped in immodesty and
Immorality I became
Selfish, mundane pleasures I exploited.
Many are the hearts I have saddened.

Now, I have grown weary
From cries of night.
Expressions of love and endearment
Have disenchanted me
My own heart too, has become heavy

Instruct me please, in the way of uprightness
Deliver me from my selfish course.
Lend a sympathetic ear, please
To my earnest plea for forgiveness
For I am but a child — with child.

—*Sadie Watson Carter*

A Better Place

A better place is a bundle of white clouds.
A better place is a place where they open the gates
Of love and forgiveness.
A better place is where they give you wings
And you learn to fly.
A better place is where all your fears
are no more.
A better place is where angels
are perfected.
A better place is more often
referred to as heaven.

—*Tara Eastridge*

Untitled

A new day has begun!
A million "Good Mornings" float
upon the air! Nurses and aides
sing their greetings, waking
patients with an aura of unusual joy.
Carts loaded with trays arrive! Still
the footsteps echo down the hall!
Barely audible, the rubber soles
silence the footsteps, but not
the cheery "Good Morning!"
But nothing can silence
the echo of good morning,
nor the smiles and laughter
that ring so clearly down the hall.

—*Helen Richards*

The Patience of Loving

I feel that I should die tonight,
a night of deep and somber tone.
A hurt buried inside my soul
that cuts me deep, and to the bone.
Of love I speak, my gift to thee,
of tattered heart be true.
Now faint I hear the angels cry,
for one whose heart you slew.
I feel that I should die tonight,
a night to trap the lovelorn buck,
and gild the cage that clutch thy heart,
to know his time has struck.
Be true o' love and never scorn
the passion that may hide,
and keep thy thought forever young
of one whose love has died.

—*Brian Dyer*

Borrowed Time

Not a day goes by I shall not cry
A night shan't follow I will not
wallow, in the grief and in the
sorrow of all the time that we
must borrow, time for breath, and
to live, oh my lord, what must we
give, to stop the death and sin
that bites us, cease your threats
and come to smite us.

—*Ernie Martinez*

The Silent Path

A path traveled by everyone,
A path of cheer, sorrow,
    and memories past.
Things sometimes forgotten,
    yet, memories will last.

As I travel this "Silent Path"
I can see far ahead,
    goals out of sight.
This path holds an enchantment
    of life,
If we look far beyond
    our sight.

At the end of the "Silent Path"
We will leave our past,
    to reach a goal,
That will always last.

—*Janice Rose*

The Winding Road

Life is a winding road
A path we all must follow
We must take our chances
Of finding good or bad ahead
Not everyone's road is the same
Some wind more than others
If we stray from our path
Or give up our journey
We will find ourselves lost
And then we will know
That down in our hearts
Our path was meant for us
So stay on your path
Take it one step at a time
Let your path lead you on
Follow your winding road

—*Allison Podboy*

Ronnie

For years we've been together
A perfect pair from the start;
We laughed, we cried, we argued,
Forever bound at the heart.

As Kids there was nothing
We were afraid to try;
In fact we tried so many things,
All people said was "Why?"

We borrowed cars, we stayed out late,
We drove all over town;
We cracked up cars, got very drunk,
And always fooled around.

The years went by before we knew,
Our lives took different paths;
We stayed in touch, talked every day,
Grew closer with each laugh.

I love this man, and he loves me
Together till the end;
His death won't change my feelings,
I'll always be his friend.

—*Jill McNamara*

Danger At Dusk

As darkness approaches
a primitive band of
marauding invaders
lurks in the uncut grass
their poisonous weapons
prepared for attack

What a strange paradox
I have to rush inside
to protect myself from
a harrowing onslaught
of primeval predators
almost too small to see

—*Dorothy Lauer*

A Tear

See a tear roll down a face
A tear of sadness,
sorrow and disgrace
A tear of happiness,
joy and content
A tear of water means so much
in so little space

—*Dawn Chevrolet*

The Liberty Bell

A bell, a bell, a ringing bell
A ringing bell, what does it tell?
What, means this loud pulsating sound
As it rebounds from sky to ground?

This bell, this bell, this broken bell
This broken bell, what can it tell?
This precious gem of history
Is still proclaiming liberty.

In independence hall it rests
One of our nations great assets.
It is a truly priceless thing.
Oh, how we love to hear it ring.

We should all know its identity
As freedom emblem to you and me.
No other symbol has surpassed.
This cherished relic from our past.

Its message still is clear and loud.
Of this dear bell we should be proud,
And those great men of leadership
That signed that treasured manuscript.

—*Everette E. Jones Sr.*

Slug

A slug
a very slow one
is how I feel today.
a little bit slimy
and a little bit
squishey
if you step on it.
this slug is a nice one.

—*Eleanor Enos*

Mixed Feelings

I have mixed feelings
about a boy. Because this boy
brings me no joy. He's really
cute, he's not real shy, but I
have a problem with him and
I'll tell you why. He's not real
nice, he's immature and that is
why I can't be sure.

—*Grace Davis*

Paradox

Be not concerned
about how long you live
but how well.
There is neither a good
nor a bad time to die;
there is only your time.

Of life, of death,
there is no control;
there is neither yesterday
nor tomorrow,
there is only now.

Now is all there is
and now is enough,
The one most ready to die
is the one most willing
to live.

—*JoAnna O'Keefe*

December's Colors

Dark gray branches stretched
across frozen ponds

Pigeons perched upon
monuments of black rock

Winters brown-carpeting
summers green

Leaves-lifeless, crumpled
on the ground—with
autumn's gold all but
a memory
—*Carlene F. Baum*

What Do We Do

What do we do
After we've done
All the forbidden things?

What do we buy
After we've bought
One of everything?

What do we eat
When we have tried
All the "foreign" foods?

Where do we go
When all we want
Is some solitude?
—*Joan Risley*

Creator

God formed the mountains
all around, he planted the trees
in the ground.

God gave us the beauty of
the flower, he created man and
gave him power.

God formed the rivers and
the sea, then he began to talk
and call to me.

God is my creator, Father from
the heavens above. Oh! how he
gave all this beauty to me and
gave me all his love.
—*Irene Parkerson*

Snow

God made the snow
All beautiful and white
And where the northwinds blow
It makes a beautiful sight
It falls from up in heaven above
And lands on this great earth
And tells us of His wondrous love
And what each soul is worth
God made the snow
So that we on earth could love
The magic of His gentle touch
And know that He's above.
—*Christine Butters*

The World

The world is an upside down place
All the covering on its face
It is hiding from itself
So much like all humans do
We try to clean it up
But instead we scrub it bare
And poison it dirty
No matter what we do
It will always be touched by man
Never will we know if we are
Right side up
Or right side down
Are we right or wrong
All of us are equal in one way
Or another
The possibility is there
—*Barbara Littlefield*

Untitled

What if this Autumn, around Halloween,
all the pumpkins turned bright green?

And trees were purple, blue and pink,
If this happened, what would we think?

If fields of wheat were suddenly red
What color would be our bread?

If one cool, crisp, frosty morn
the grass like silver was adorned?

But Natures' colors are so clever.
We as people could have never,

Thought of yellows, oranges, golds,
blazing leaves of fire. So bold!

Imagination's such a gift.
It's always fun to think, "What If?"
—*Angela Meggs Sanders*

Love

I
Alone
Now and then
May wish, sometimes,
To sit on your lap
Soft as a cloud to me
Each pore absorbing your love.
By only your presence, I feel
A warmth sent from you to me.
Secure, wrapped up in love,
I would laugh and smile
Happy to be
In love with
Always you.
—*Elizabeth S. Fast*

Dreams

I've been a fool for less
And I've been a fool for more
A shot at our dreams
Is worth a little loss of face
As long as the dreams hold true
When they rest in your hands
Some turn bitter, some sweet,
And some worth defeat
Seek your dreams, face reality,
But never stop enjoying
All that life has to offer
—*Cheryl Witman*

The Lonely Rebel

Alone I stand
Alone I will be
Nobody will lend a helping hand
So I have to take care of me
I wander the streets
in search of food
Yes, I feel the defeat
but crying will do no good

I look up in the sky
as it starts to rain
if you look into my eyes
just maybe you can feel my pain.
I long to be home
to feel my parents' embrace
They are probably happy I'm gone
They must think of me as a disgrace.

I have no money
but, I still have my pride
Isn't it funny
how I thought I'd survive.
—*Andrea Smith*

Old Age - The Flip Side

Memory lapse,
Alzheimer disease,
Hope they don't collapse,
From arthritis in the knees.

Arteries clogging,
Heart attacks,
Joints that are locking,
Aching backs.

Thick bifocals,
Annoying blind spots,
Softening vocals,
Hurting blood clots.

Rapid hair loss,
Increasing osteoporosis,
No teeth to floss,
Looking as old as Moses.

High blood pressure,
Upset stomachs that are rough,
Occasionally a seizure,
Old age really sucks.
—*Joel Pavuk*

Untitled

I have no name.
Although some do call me the sandman,
others may call me a demon,
but I prefer a puppeteer.
My eternal fingers knead your mind,
to create your mental state
as you drift off into my world.
I judge your days actions in a word or
on a whim as if I was the Almighty,
then send you to your proper place
in my vast creative world.
So sleep now little one
for the day you can control
but the night times is my time to play.
Do not respect me.
Do not believe in me.
Neither of which I ask of you.
Although one thing I will warn to you,
is do not anger me
for your regret will rest in your dreams.
—*Billy Hopkins*

God's Love

God shows His love in many ways,
Although we do not understand,
He shows us how to see the beauty
Of the creation of His land.

Take time each day to ponder,
On His wondrous love from above.
And as you look about you,
You know it's by God's love.

Spread His love throughout the land.
Reach out to one another.
Peace and joy will fill the soul
Of friends, comrades and brothers.

—*Frances L. Martz*

What Is A Friend

A friend is kind and loving
always greets you with a smile
and willing to help you at
all time.
    What is a friend
someone you love and trust
and always there when you
need them most.
Having a gracious word
will smooth the way,
a joyous word may light the
way, a timely word may
lesson stress,
a loving word may heal and
bless,
So say a kind word to a
friend today.
What is a friend,
God is my best friend,
have you met him today

—*Annie B. Taylor*

My Daughter, Janie Marie

You have a gift of love
an expression that says
I love you Mom .....
forever, not just today!!!

You are, my innerself
in our heart
there's always a smile ...
we touch each other
across every mile.

    My daughter, my only one
so loving and carefree
always so full of fun
filled to the Brim with laughter
regardless of hardships
or disaster, that is forever won-

    A loving heart that grows
with each shedding of a tear
a faith so strong, it over comes
all your fear - when I thinks of you...
Oh, how I miss my pretty priss

—*Jane Cupit*

Poet

With a twist of the brain,
And a flair of the hand,
Comes forth; the writer's command.

—*Amy Riegel*

The Blue Planet

Cruising along
    an open mindless sky

I see an azure glow
    a glow that seems to grow

To grow into
    a huge conglomerate

A conglomerate
    of ever changing hues

And as I hone in
    upon this colorful scene

I wonder
    why so blue

Can it be
    what is being done to you.
        —*ferdinand*

Untitled

When my life seems bitter
and blue, I just get a picture
and think of you.

Your everything to me, then
and now, then I think I see
you, "why and how"?

When you died, I felt so bad,
and didn't realize all the things
we had.

You were a father to me, even
though not my flesh one,
and then the day came, when
your life was done.

Life for you was so short,
but then you move to a heaven
of some sort.

Don't get me wrong, life can
be grand, only when your walking
with your father hand-in-hand.

—*Amber Atteberry*

The War Poem: Soldier's View

Miniature suns burn the land
And cause the earth to shake.
Another's life is in my hand
And there's not much more I can take.

Weapons held in shaking hands
We're scared we won't survive.
Murder's no cause for reprimand
You kill to stay alive.

We journey across the barren waste
Destroyed by burning rain.
All our decisions are made in haste
But there's nothing, really, to gain.

Yet we press on towards our goal
And try to conquer Them.
We realize we've no control
So we can't possibly win.

And in the end when we're sent home
We try to adjust to life.
But it's so different from what we've
    known
We can't adjust to life.

—*Brent Hepner*

The Seed Pod Of Hungary, 1956

Gone is the fruit of the orchard,
And crumbled the leaves of the oak.
Strong are the winds of the line-storm,
And tearing the teeth of the sleet;
Sternly endureth the seed-pod
In guarding the life of the spring.
Cracking like cannon are branches:
Uprooted's the tree and the youth;
The Flame of Hungary falters, fast
Guttering in blood and agony, cruelly
Quenched by a rage without reason;
But proudly defiant the seed-pod
Still cradles its embryo warmly
In guarding its life for the spring.

—*Evelyn Cobb Arthur*

Daily Son

I look up to see the sun
and feel the warmth on my face.
I look up to adore the Son,
His light guards my every pace.

I look up to the sun daily,
for healing rays and plants to grow.
I look up to know the Son,
He guides me to help me grow.

I look up to the sun for light,
as it shines its rays on me.
I look up to praise the Son,
He suffered and died for me.

I look up to the sun for days,
its light separates the day and night.
I look up to know the Son,
for it's Jesus that's the true light.

I look up to the sun and see,
through the mist a rainbow of peace.
I look up to love the Son,
to honor Jesus - Prince of Peace.

—*B. Joyce Hester*

The Sunset

Just let me sit in the evening
    And gaze on the western sky,
It thrills me and sets me dreaming
    Of the God who reigns on high.

With awe and wonder it fills me
    As the colors come and go
A sunset so filled with beauty
    Only He can paint them so.

Ah, long I study the picture
    Of wondrous lights on the sky,
Losing in the colorful mixture
    My sorrows for they are neigh.

I find in God's splendid making
    Joy and love and delight
One may have just for the taking
    Ere it fades away into night.

—*Ida L. Thatcher*

Lord

I reflect upon your goodness
and I see my nothingness.
O Humble Man, Lord of Love and Mercy
Hear my plea and save me.

—*Brenda Lee Gearhart*

The End Of The Road

When you've sinned so long and often,
　And hope fades far from sight
Another nail goes in your coffin
　You'll soon "give up" the fight.
No tears can heal your broken heart,
　No "promise" stops the fears,
The one you love will soon depart
　Regardless, of spent years.
If God is not the one you seek,
　And on your knees you fall,
Your future only can be bleak,
　There's "noone" left the call.

Please help me God,
To you I cry,
Before my life, to "death"
will lie.

　　—*Hildegarde Girard*

"The Real Thing" or Satisfaction

I started with You
　and I'll end up with you,
My Beloved,
　my God, my Lord.
I started with you
　and I'll end up with you:
The only one
　who deserves to be adored.
Oh, yes, I love others,
　but you love them too;
So as long
　as I keep you first,
There's really no problem
　for you'll help them too.
You make me so happy
　my poor heart could burst.

　　—*Dorothy Chaffee*

My One And Only

I pray each day,
and into the night,
May we never part,
You put up a good fight,
I give you my heart.

With you near me,
I know I'm in heaven
May our love always be,
I'm at the top with Kevin,

Not a moment goes by,
That you are not on my mind,
My, my, my,
My very special find,

Now let me end this,
with a very special kiss,
and to let you know
whenever apart,
you are truly missed.

　　—*Jo-Anne Biglov*

Untitled

Jack Frost was out again last night
　and played a prank on me.
He covered with lace my windowpane
　and painted my maple tree.
The lettuce in my garden droops
　and my marigolds look limp.
But I'm used to this for every year
　He does the same! The imp!

　　—*Euretta Jane Rowland*

Leave Me Alone

Why can't people just leave me alone
And let me sit at home and waste
my life away.

Let me feel sorry for my self
if I want to.

Why cant you just go away?
I don't need you around to make me
feel worse.

Because if I wanted you to make me
feel better I would have asked you
FIRST!

　　—*Celia Whitehurst*

Searching

I call to the Father
　and only silence answers
　me
I call to my parents
　but they have no time for
　me
I call to my friends
　but they are all to drunk to hear
　me
I call to Him
　but even He won't answer
　me
I call to myself
　and I see that I have no strength to
　go on

　　—*Jason Makoutz*

The Beach

　Suzy went down to the beach,
And saw an ugly leech.
　She sat on a log,
And interviewed a frog.
　She picked up a sea shell,
And threw it down a well.
　She went for a swim,
And jumped off a limb.
　She jumped from the sky,
And when she landed she died.

　　—*Andrew Gronewold*

Meeting

We walked together, not together,
And spoke in bitter silences
And words wrung out by habit's hand,
Barren and heavy, meaningless.
Our hooded sightless eyes said aye
To the sea gulls shrieking rip across
Our leaden silence, stiller yet
For this unmeaning explication.
Hand brushed hand, sand, sand and broken
Shells were in the touch, not love,
Not felt, too deep the pain, the stone
Indifference of loving lost,
Calcified, denied, too deep
To feel, to turn away, betray,
Betrayed.
We parted, unstarted, unmet,
Unsaid; and dreary clouds hung low
Above a sullen silken sea.

　　—*Eleanor Johnson*

What The Shadow Knows

The Shadow speeds above the air
And sits in every vacant chair.
He's in the plush and everywhere,
Distilling justice from the air.

"I'm going to the deathhouse now
To visit Dan and show him how
To judge himself and make his vow.
I'm going to the deathhouse now."

"Dan's gift is a solemn, secret fact,
Acquired by silence and by tact;
By stealth he looked and saw the act.
Dan's gift is a solemn, secret fact."

Dan Malley wrings his bloody hands.
He sometimes sits; he sometimes stands;
He wears a brace of electric bands.
Dan Malley wrings his bloody hands.

The Shadow catches his ascending thought
On wings of conscience where blind souls
　are caught
Before they plummet into thinking not.
The Shadow catches his ascending thought.

　　—*John Pilkey*

Breaking

I feel my heart breaking,
And stare at the flowers you gave me.
Is this a bump we're going over,
Or just a phase of reality?

I've tried so hard,
To keep what we had alive.
But just like the flowers,
We've withered away... to die.

　　—*Heidi Okada*

Just A Dream

In the twilight of the evening,
and sun is sinking low.
That's when I miss you darling,
Why did you have to go?

I hear your voice in the breeze,
I see you standing near.
I realize it's just a dream,
of the one you loved so dear.

The years we spent together,
was years of perfect bliss.
You'll never know my darling,
How very much your missed.

I hear the lonely whistle blow.
I hear your voice as you go,
It beckons me-I too must go
Into that world we do not know.

　　—*Bonnie Branum*

Word Weaver

He spoke in a voice
Ambered and rich
As the late summer's honey.

And I; I was caught.
Caged with those measured tones
As a bird trapped in hand.

Reassuring and calm,
Yet ever his voice thrills.
A willing captive, I.

　　—*Elizabeth Kowols*

Untitled

The candle starts to flicker
And sweet music fills the air
As we're lying in each other's arms
We have nothing to despair.

As I feel your body heat so warm
With passion that's so true
I pull you closer in my arms
As I whisper, "I love you."

As the night goes by
The candle dims
Sweet music starts to fade
I turn to see the glow in your eyes
From the love that we just made

We still hold on all through the night
Never to let go, you see
For love will always be kept in sight
Inside both you and me.

—*Cheryl Shulkusky*

Together

Please close your eyes
And take my hand.
We'll go off together
To a far away land.

Where no one makes war
And everyone cares.
Where nobody hates
And everybody shares.

The best part of all
Is the love all around.
You need never worry.
It can always be found.

How long can we stay?
We can stay there forever.

As long as our eyes remain closed
And our hands stay together.

—*Jonathan Moses*

Lost Love

Here we sat
And talked
And there
'Cross frozen fields
In silence walked,
And now, alone,
I see them,
Every one.
Shared scenes
Forever done,
Tears?
Foolhardy
Would they be
Since forever
You are lost to me.

—*Beverly M. Post*

Midnight Horrors

Midnight horrors
Are midnight dreams
When you shut your eyes
To see goblins
And ghouls
In every corner
Breathing out fear
As you walk through the corridor

—*Jessica D. Glidden*

Life

When the sun comes up in the morning
And the clouds are gone from the sky
Then I, like the green grass, springeth
Up from the bed where I lie.

For there are things to accomplish
Before the rain starts to fall
And we lift our heads to the heavens
To the one who cares for us all.

When the day grows ever so dreary
And it seems the sun cannot shine
There's always a clear light shining
It comes from our Lord divine.

Don't wait until life's ray fadeth
And the sun seems to sink quite low
Accept Christ in your life real early
He will give your life a bright glow.

When you look through the mirror darkly
And life's rains begin to fall
Remember each cloud has a silver lining
God watches and cares for us all.

—*Dorothy R. Watkins*

"The Good Old Days"

The good old days
And the good old ways,
That Mom and Dad
Had always had,
The work was rough,
But we were tough,
He rattled on, and he rattled on

We went fishing and swimming everyday,
In the creek behind the bales of hay,
Licorice candy after church,
And when Tommy was lost
The whole town searched.
Ah! That was the life,
He rattled on and he rattled on.

But the days grow short
And his breath grows weak,
It's hard to move and so hard to speak,
And now today with his last breath gone
How I wish for times
He rattled on.

—*Debra Abohosh*

Night Wind

Last night the wind went out abroad,
And with the land made free.
He whistled low at my attic eaves,
And danced with the old plum tree.

He caused the stately pine to sway,
And hum a doleful tune;
Then up he went, to help the clouds
Play peek-a-boo with the moon.

He swung upon the back yard gate
That shrieked in loud dismay,
While maple leaves on branches high,
Skipped up and down in play.

He wandered down the garden path,
And kissed each flower's head;
Till tired with so much roistering,
He drifted home to bed.

—*Eleanor F. McGraw*

Untitled

Sometimes the mountains seem low
And the river seems slow
The day is long

My heart is strong
I listen to the lions roar
The woman who walks through the jungle
Walks through trees caught by vines
But at no time is she
Subdued by the jungle wine
I would walk through the jungle myself
Walking tall and full of stealth
Perhaps meet the jungle boar
And acquire some wealth

Yes I would walk under the wonderful sky
Under the wonderful canopy of the trees
To understand better the birds and the bees
To move myself next to
The flowers and the trees
And walk through the jungle and meet
The lady who is a boar

—*Eddie Smith*

No Secrets Allowed

Above the hills
And through the valleys,
Across the lakes
And throughout the forests,
Down the highways
And into the nights—
We see.

—*Eudocia Turner*

Nature's Love

As nature calls the sun falls
and up comes the moon. As I
look into your eyes I could
hear the cries of the moon as the
clouds covered it. As I stare into
the eyes of fear I can almost
hear you call my name. I look
away and watch a dove the
symbol of love fly over the
lagoon and on it shines the
moon. Such a beautiful night.
I look up at the sky I want to
cry.

—*Jolene Kruusi*

Desert Sand

At seventeen, he raised his hand
And with a solemn vow he swore,
   to defend the shores
Of this great land.

From misty morn 'til darkest night
He trained with all his manly might

Those weeks were lengthened into months
Before they called him to the front.

For God and country he would be,
   a hero brave for liberty.
In a barren land he made his stand
   now dreams eternally in desert sand.

—*Claude Satterfield Sr.*

No Door, No Star

Every door was open.
And yet, every door was closed
in front of me.

Every star was shining.
Though I saw no ray
of light around me.

Then I trod briefly
upon the sands of time,
and realized there were no doors.

When I raised my head
toward the universe,
there was no darkness.
Only the sun was shining.
Thus, no star was visible.

When I perched my lips
to kiss the cosmic awareness
I realized that the limitations
existed only within.

—*Dorothy F. Davies*

Feel My Dream

Your dreams are your feelings,
and your feelings are your dreams.

If you try to dream of how I,
feel I can feel what it means,

Our spirits will understand,
just what our bodies never knew,

Like the instinct of hard,
passion that comes from me to you,

Deeply moving our souls as,
are minds drift back away,

As communication between,
us is open vastly with no delay.

Emotions rush pumping through,
our veins like a feeling so real,

I've dreamed of this moment,
can you see how this dream feels,

Open to me your dreams with,
no fear and no type of commotion,

The day that you express your
dreams is the day you find your emotions

—*Bart Sweeney*

To My Daughter

May your days be full of glory
and your nights with shining light,
you deserve the love and laughter
that change life from dark to bright!

There were times when I had feelings
of despair.....or losing all!
You were there when I stumbled
and you never let me fall!

May the blue be in your horizon,
with nice flowers from spring.
May God bless you my good daughter
with the best that life can bring!

—*Elena U. Kabrick*

Aerial Melody

Demon of my mind or
Angel of my thought,
Thine ethereal notes sublime
Whirlest me from site and time.

Thy spinning o'er the ebony keys
Thy twirling on the purened notes
Are like unto a billion eyes to me
Gliding past all memory.

The strength of thy unfailing mind
The power within thy fingers nimble
Didst make the animate to find
Inanimate, possessor of life and rhyme.

With dew drops and with thunder
The two did journey on
So fast they didn't even wonder
Why the past perpetuated blunder.

But suddenly the music stopped
The spell broken all around
The silence sifted moments 'till they
dropped
The soldier rose. The concert stopped.

—*A. B. Nimmo*

Crossing

The regions I've invested in
    are a conglomeration of confusion,
    confidence and wistful dreams.
Fragments of the lost and restored
    As testament to my own evolution.

My propensity for a difference
    may emulate a new beginning.
Unfolding the tendrils of the past,
    shedding old petals for truth-
I've found a land and passed the fence.

Take me to the land of unknown
    I find comfort and shelter there.
I don't believe in Utopia,
    only ground that is yet to be sown.

I know of pain- like shards of glass
    They cut the soil/sever the mind
Leaving portions/remnants that never pass.

Transcending toward light for the warmth
    of my sun-
Crossing the boundaries of time
I breach my own space beyond false sight-
as I'm crossing.

—*Jamie D. Cooper*

The Essence of Love

True love is as fragile
    as a flower,
as pure as that first
    breath of spring,
in order for it to
    flourish and
carry its essence
    forth,
love must be respected
    and seeded first,
from within!

—*Brenda Kimball*

Twilight

Power transcends,
as a prelude to the night begins.

Sunsets of power
in multi-colored hues,

anoints the knowing spirits
with its power that ensues.

It's the inbetween
of day and night,

resulting in the beauty
of mystical twilight.

—*Ann Clenard*

A Kiss, A Kiss

Her lips pursed pink
    as an early rose
        fragile, sensual.
And as her lips
    met mine, once, then....
exploding! as the first
    ray of sun, shooting ore
        the horizon
to pass my way,
    ...to simply disappear,
leaving a wake of warmth and light.
Ahhh......A kiss, a kiss.

—*Jeffery I. Grubbs*

Words That Mean Nothing

A tear rolls down my face,
As I remember how it used to be.
The tenderness we once shared,
Has vanished from existence.
I feel... I don't know you.
What happened to the person I once knew?
Could it be I never knew you?
I came to you over and over again.
Trying to get you to see.
What you were doing to me.
Yet, my words seemed to mean nothing.
If you'd only taken a moment,
And gazed into my eyes,
You would have seen all the pain.
I tried to be a true friend,
But always fell short of your expectations.
I knew I'd never be as pretty as Mariah
    Carey,
Or have the superb personality of Jen,
But I'd always hoped that you'd accept me,
For who I am.

—*Barbara Maranka*

Listen, Women! Listen, Men!

This came to me right out of the blue
As I slept my night away;

It brought new meaning to the alphabet,
And it gave me something to say.

As I explain, or elaborate,
Please listen, hear, and then tell;
And practice it in your daily life,
And teach it to your children well,

Other than H and I in our alphabet
That come together a word to spell,
Are the 14th and 15th for all to use.
Now, use them often and well
N O!

—*Angie R. Robbins*

Untitled

Last night
    as I walked down my lonesome highway,
    I glanced up to see a falling star,
        to show my concern,
        I gently picked her up
            and held her in my arms;

I knew she cared,
    for she turned to me,
        and lit the night sky
            for the rest of my journey...
—*Alexander C. Patuzzi*

That Dark Night

Into that dark night we slip carelessly
    as if we were right not to see,
    a path so well-worn and travelled.
    Our course goes unnoticed...down.
        Our life-line unraveled,
    till our souls we found we missed.

Too late the realization occurs
    of something lost long.
    The journey backward infers,
    the turns twisting, turning wrong,
    and to all true fate belong.

—*Christine J. Strickland*

Knowledge

Do you know truth?

Have you seen light
as it exists to itself?
Have you felt the peace
of the dreamy newborn fawn?
Have you heard the wind
playing joyously in the woods?
Have you smelled death
with its sweet promise of rebirth?
Have you tasted purity
in the pristine snow?
Do you understand
that man is the beast
who will kill eternity?

—*Benjamin J. Wilkinson*

As I Sit In My Swing

I want to smell the 'lectric spark
As lightning splits the sky;
I want to hear the tramp of feet
As ants go marching by.

I want to watch a leaf break forth
And turn from green to gold;
I want to hold a budding rose
And see each part unfold.

I want to taste the breeze that blows
And touch the heart of a tree;
I want to soar as my blood flows
Through every part of me.

I want to see a new star arrive
As I sit in my swing;
I want to know that I'm alive
And never miss a thing.

—*Hymie Samuelson*

Age

It comes without much notice
    as most do stand in awe,
For it passes fast upon us
    through moments we never saw.

It records on us time's history
    with memories from the past,
Even though our minds are very set
    that youth will ever last.

But, lo, it's to the rest of us
    who know that age's the thing,
That gives each one of the best of us
    the character on which to wing

Through time to eventual destiny
    unknown as we did start,
But grown over years within ourselves
    in body, mind and heart.

—*Alfred G. Huber*

Changes

Many people have passed through my life.
As one leaves I call it another chapter,
In my book of life.
I go on to the new chapter.
Meeting new people
But remembering the old.

—*Florence Mead Grover*

Our Night

Crystal waters shimmer,
As our reflection starts to fade.
The moonlight grows dimmer,
Mere promises are made.
The air is filled with whispers.
I gaze in your eyes.
Slowly the night closes in,
As our whispers start to die.
Together we reminisce.
Of times we will forever cherish.
We tenderly share a kiss,
To show our love won't perish.
As we silently gazed at distant stars,
They twinkled in the sky.
The night we shared was only ours
Our love would never die

—*Chessie Lancaster*

Bend As The Willow

I will bend as the willow
As the wind, I will billow.
I will not bring a tear to your pillow.

I will bow as the bough
As the pine, I will sough.
A frown won't crease your brow.

I will sway as the palm
As the lagoon, I will be calm.
To you will come no harm.

—*Jane Pierritz*

Life Is Not Always Fair

When she died I cried
and to me it seemed so unfair,
But then I learned the world still turned
and life's not always fair.

—*Erin Wolfe*

Under The Stars

Together we stand hand in hand,
as we look across the moonlight land.
Gazing into each other's eyes,
the love we share is no surprise.
How strong it is, we'll never know,
all we can do is let it grow.
Our romance is like a storybook,
it's one that's hard to overlook.
Like the stars above, will always shine,
the love we share is yours and mine.

—*Amber Croff*

For You Michael

I guarded corners of sharpness
    As you stumbled, then walked.
Crawling up lawn hills,
    Learning to talk.

Before your trusting, bright eyes
    Toy rattles of rhythm.
No playpen for you,
    Instead, my lap to sit in.

Your 5th Birthday Party,
    Santa's cookies at Christmas,
Tying blue-sneakered laces,
    Bedtime tucking in kisses.

I think of you and miss you,
    Now that you are a man.
More than 1st day of kindergarten...
    Can you understand?

—*Cathi Amann*

Butterflies

To see a butterfly is to look
at God's finished product.

We see the beauty,
He remembers the ugliness of
the worm.

We see the grace,
He recalls the trials of
flight.

We see the freedom,
He reflects on the bondage of
the cocoon.

A butterfly reaches its beauty
and dies.
We reach our beauty and live!

We are God's most precious
"butterflies" in reverse.
We see the ugliness, trials and
bondage,
He sees our grace, freedom and
beauty!

—*DeeMaris McCarty*

Tackle

Textbook tackles consist of,
        Being low,
        Hitting hard,
    Good point of attack,
        Power,
        Strength,
Good insurance wrap up!

—*Jared Kleier*

Way Up In The Sky

Look,
At that thing in the sky.
I can't figure out,
Why it's up so high.
I wonder what's its meaning,
Or purpose for being there.
It's shaped so big and round,
I just had to stare.
I ran with all my might,
To try and catch it.
But I lost my strength,
So I just said, "forget it."

—*Felicia M. Coffee*

Dollar Signs

I try to make the most of it
at work it's why I cannot quit
There never seems to be enough
to purchase all my needed stuff
I like to dream of winning big
and acting like a capitalist pig
I'd buy new stuff that's all for me
and live my life in luxury
To have more money than I need
I scoff at those that call it greed
They only wish that they had more
may ask for some but I ignore
Those louses call me on the phone
At dinner time, they know I'm home
I always give the same reply
"Call again and I'll black your eye"
Yep filthy rich is what I want
so all my neat stuff I could go flaunt
And never worry 'bout my job
Do what I want, and become a snob

—*Donald MacIver*

Untitled

I love a fireplug
  Because it speaks to me
Of rushing mountain torrents
  That started for the sea
But encountered man's restrictions
  And ended up below
The streets of a metropolis -
  A power-pressured flow
That finds its termination
  In bright colored monument
So costly to blind motorists
  Who pay as they repent!

—*Jean Gordon*

Lost Love

Nothing matters without you
Birds lost their songs
Stars don't belong up in the sky that
yields only darkness
Footsteps that once were so light
Tread no more in the night
Since you're gone - nothing matters.
Winds blow empty sighs through naked
  trees
Flowers turn their heads die like the
leaves time stopped - nothing matters
Lips move but have no meaning
Words are hollow sounds that leap
and bound as an echo across mountains
You are gone! You are gone!
Nothing matters

—*Joan N. Lutz*

A Midnight Sky

Fading from my memory,
Becoming a blank page in my past,
Your face becomes an image
  through a cloud
In a midnight sky.
The outline of the clouds
  portray the profile of your face.
The moon shining over you
  brings out the life, which was once
    within your smile.
The clouds overlapping the shining
  moon, become a grayish color,
Just as our love fades away,
  with the brightness of the moon.
Like a love story in a history book,
Our own saga becomes
a fading page of love once alive.
As the moon becomes totally covered,
the darkness which occurs reminds me
  … You're only an image.

—*Anna Maria Gencarelli*

Beauty

Tree spirit
Bird spirit
Bright spirit
Light spirit
Spirit of all nature
Alive and well.

Wild things
Freedom
Like a home to me
Come.

Orderly disorder
Meadows growing
Full of life
Wild beauty
More everlasting
Than any manicured lawn.

—*Anna Hawk*

Today

Today is swirled into a pit
black as the unknown secret
Groping, seeking, pulling at the light.
A ray of hope tries to appear
only to be consumed by the mass;
a mass so thick, it has no boundary.
Is the hope of the day lost?
That's the real question of today;
and also the beauty of the light
cause the light has no secrets.

—*Callie Hunt*

Secret Horse

Trip-trop, clip-clop,
Blaze is his name,
chocolate color
streak of lightning white
on his forehead,
I ride him in the field
of my mind.
Trip-trop, clip-clop.

—*Bridget Joyce*

Red Bird

Graceful and bright,
blazon red through the sky.
  Making a wish as
  hence you fly.
Your song gives pure hope
and joy to this heart,
As God's feathered messenger
  from its vision parts.
You fly into heaven with
  prayers on your wings
May you return to your tree
and more beauty bring.
To wake every morning,
the window dreams tread.
Not to hear your call,
is their only dread.
In summer and winter,
tarrying all year,
Steadfast and constant,
your presence so dear.

—*Alana Morgan*

Apartheid

White, black; black, white
Blite, whack; whack, blite
Blight white; whack black
Blind hate; hail white
Day, night; white hate
White fight; back black
Black fight back white
Fight day, fight night
Fight, fight, fight, fight!
Sound, sight; sight, sound
Dead souls; cold ground
No sun; cold night
Night dark; dark night
Night black; no light
No white; no black
No black; no white
No color; no hate
No hate; don't wait
Stop the hate, stop the hate!
Too late, too late.

—*Jill Y. Gold*

Winds Of Tides

Winds of tides,
  blow to me a new song.
For I have seen the sun set
  from the cliffs of sorrow,
  and seen him rise
  from the valley of grief.
I do not believe in these places alone,
  for the sun exists
  to prove through darkness
    cometh light.....
So there must be the unseen.
  Blow to me a new song.

—*Barrett Welding*

The Eagles

The eagles fly over the water.
Before winter, they fly south.
They catch fish with their feet…
And then the eagles fall in love!

—*Jade Buehler*

My Cat

She is part of me like a piece of
  blueberry pie tasting so good
and sweet in the midst of my eye.
She is loving sweet and caring
as she is peering down the hall
showing confidence and walking tall.
  When I'm sad she makes
  me happy to be alive and
then I know I can survive
  another day.
When I can't talk to no one
I can talk to her because she
won't answer; all she does is purr.
  This is my cat, Samantha, and
she is a big part of my family.

  —*Gregory Hendricks*

Nation Under Seize

Homeless on corners
Boxed
Concealed with debris
Unrecognized
The city breaths
Trains spin
Vultures
Nighttime reigns
Isolated victims
Stalked and condemned
Politics
Hold all bars
Who's the prisoner
Nation under seize

  —*Debbie Lipton*

Johannesburg

Dali designed this town;
Braque built it; Picasso painted it.
Guernica-Soweto
(At a decent remove)
Lies limply, but not
Mutely across the land.
And the boiled white beans
Scuttle to and fro, constructing
More limp watches in
Smothering self destruction.

  —*Edwin S. Segal*

The Color Of Love

The sun coming up 'tween the mountains
Breaking the mist of dawn
Cutting its path of warmth and light
To a day that's newly born

Chasing away nightly shadows
With stars fading into the blue
Warmth and light crescending
Till it blends into a beautiful hue

This is the color of my love
That is born every day for you

  —*Hugh Canning*

Untitled

Your presence
breaks over my being
like dawn
flooding over the land
like daybreak
shattering the darkness
into shadows
that hide
between the cracks
collecting like
cobwebs
in our infinite
persona

  —*Erin Eileen McNamee*

Pencil In Your Thoughts

The sound of a pencil
Breezing flow across its allies face
To pursue the process
Of literary and imaginary thoughts
That portray what so many people
  Are afraid of -
Reality
Because if it is on paper then
The imaginary part of thought
Has become -
Literature
So keep writing dude

  —*Bruce Elliot Coy II*

Change

The rippling of the water
Brings back memories
Of times gone by...
So rich and free.

The only changeless thing
Is "change."
And You, dear God...
You never change.

Where has the time gone
Of days so free...
If we miss this moment
It could mean eternity.

The rippling of the water
Brings back memories
Of days gone by...
So rich and free.

Do you ever wonder of
Another place another time,
What it would have been like
If change hadn't begun?

  —*Bobbie Jones*

Agony And Defeat

Weeping willows cry to me
But I don't even glimpse
I keep my eyes on destiny
Do not let fear overcome you
For no one will hear you whispers
  in agony
She's so helpless it's pitiful
For not a soul loves her

  —*Heather Quass*

Daddy

I love him, but he does not see this.
Broken promises, no calls,
Not even a happy birthday.
I'll be there, then no show.
I'm sorry, next time.
Don't you love me daddy? Well...
I hear this in my head.
I cry at night but you don't
see this.
Why because your not here.
Tending to your problems, new life,
new family.
Forgot the eldest and left for dead.
Well daddy I'm here.
And I want to be known!
I exist, I was first
Don't you remember.
Or did you forget, again.

  —*Elaine Geigel*

The Tree And Me

Chaotic birth
bursting forth in agony
springing into being
tender, delicate, hungry

Vigorous youth
dancing to life's melodies
affording comfort, nourishing
those who dwell there

Autumn arriving
too soon to soon to be prepared
clinging to the perennial
fighting the inevitable

Delay Winter
with its deadly withering
sustaining life's moisture - fading
while the one sadly awaits
the dying time.

  —*America Desiree McKeehan*

Dream Away Days

Dreams are what life is made of,
  but don't get carried away,
  work to make them happen,
  every single day.
  You can't get through life,
  with just a simple dream,
  although it may sound fun,
  it's not as easy as it seems.
  So don't just keep dreaming,
  you have to work hard everyday,
  make your dream a reality,
  don't dream your life away.
  When the days are long and dreary,
  the nights only seem to make one weary,
  dreams and fantasies can be fulfilled,
  give life its strength and will.
  The same dreams that carry people on,
  can cost pain and suffering beyond.
If holding on to a point where they become,
a substitute for the life of days to come.

  —*Florence L. Hemple*

A Silent Diary

You did not plan it I know
but here I'm like a seed sprouting
pushing its mother earth

Cuddled inside the warmth
of your womb, I listen to your
heart's rhythm in my quiet awaking

What names am I called?
an embryo, a fetus, a sperm
why am I made into a term?

Look inside your womb see how
I'm fully formed you'll know
I'm God's masterpiece

Instead you conspire to end
A life begun in you
Wish I understand why

Hastily death's cold hands
tear my frame into pieces
as you lay motionless
My silent cry unheard

—*Akumla Longkumer*

Art or Artifact

I don't know, I try to be neat
But it always seems to end up in a heap.
Junk is the stuff I give away,
And stuff is the junk I keep.

We go to those Antique Shows and Swaps.
It seems there is one a week.
They have one of all I've got.
How come I don't have a boutique?

Oh, sure, some of it's sentimental,
Some of it's pure found gold.
Some of my stuff you say is junk,
But I know I'll never say sold!

This thing here's an artifact-
That one there's an antique-
Those are just old, so I'm told,
But none the less unique.

The pencil of today, my friend,
Will be tomorrow's treasure.
So save that book and crochet hook,
And that one-cup measure.

—*Irmtrud Labant Adams*

Knowing When

Knowing what,
But not knowing when.
Knowing what to say,
But not when to say it.
Knowing what to know,
But not when to know it.
Knowing what to do,
But not when to do it.
Knowing you're going to die,
But not knowing when.
Knowing what to prepare for is easy;
But not knowing when is the hard part.

—*Amy Ayers*

Passages

Yesterday I played,
  but possessed not joy.
Yesterday I was free,
  but possessed not freedom.
Yesterday I knew,
  but possessed not knowledge.

Today I have joy,
  yet do not play.
Today I have freedom,
  yet am not free.
Today I have knowledge,
  yet do not know.

Tomorrow I shall embrace joy,
  and learn how to play.
Tomorrow I shall embrace freedom
  and learn how to be free.
Tomorrow I shall embrace knowledge,
  and learn to understand.

—*Janet M. Seavey*

Watches Over Me

Sometimes I feel nobody cares about me.
But somebody does.
Sometimes I feel no one loves me.
But someone does.
No one here knows my thoughts,
or what I need.
But there is someone up above
who watches over me.
When I am down, he picks me up.
When I am unhappy, he makes me smile.
When I cry, he wipes the
tears from my eyes.
When I feel alone, he is
always by my side.
The one who watches over me,
is my Lord Jesus Christ.

—*Gwen Cooper*

Bliss

There's a state of sweet contentment
But very few have reached that goal,
Where there's peace beyond all measure -
For the maker is in control!
Bereavement comes to bring some doubts,
Stormy waves of disappointment
Rock the once solid foundation,
The Lord Jesus, whom God has sent!
Evidence of God's matchless love
Answers questions that come to mind -
The impossible circumstance
Actually reveals, Christ is kind!
For our adversity may be
Sent so that greatness we achieve,
By yielding all to Jesus Christ
The Saviour, in whom we believe!
With focus on the one above,
Satisfaction is guaranteed -
The reason we are then content
Is because His voice we do heed!

—*Carolyn F. Marquis*

You And I

You and I are human beings,
but we have different tastes
although we have the same needs,
you and I are not the same

I am tall and you are fat,
you are strong and I am not
When you see somebody sad,
you feel sorry, I do not

You don't think the way I think,
I don't talk the way you do
You are shy and I am free
I like red and you like blue

You like music, I like sports,
I love cats and you love dogs
you have faith and pray to God...
I believe in the green dough

You dislike me and my ways,
I don't like the way you are
We can not communicate...
why don't we try to understand?

That you and I are human beings,
but we should be far apart
although we have the same needs
we can not go hand by hand

—*Gladys Pelegrina*

The Only Soldier

I may choose from an army of men,
  but what do I want of these?
I scorn them, but if I could have you
  I'd plead on hands and knees.
All of my love I would compromise
  if you would take my hand
I would not think it a sacrifice
  if beside me you would stand.
But another girl has captured your awe;
  with her you are entranced
With spears of light and daggers of love
  my soldier has been lanced.
Of what worth are meager golden coins?
  I cannot buy your heart.
Oh love, my love, why are you hers
  and not my counter part?
I'll never ask you to turn your face
  to one as low as I
But show your love's full potential
  wherein your heart may lie.

—*Jennifer Field*

The Elf

I was kissed
by an elf
who had a tongue of fire
and eyes to match
I fell in love
with an elf
who knows the
language of trees
they tell him stories
I buried my face
in the neck
of an elf
who whispered words
that sent fire
to my cheeks
and lightning
to my heart

—*Elizabeth Hoover*

Untitled

I own a mantle
called my wife.
She always suits me perfectly.

I try her on every woman I meet.
They look good together... temporarily

Then the stains appear,
the fabric shrinks, a button is lost.

I check the tag:
Warm water only gentle cycle.

Are all guarantees
conditional (if not fully satisfied)
or just mine?

—*Bill Harroff*

Is Anyone Listening

Is anyone listening?
Can anyone hear?
Do you see my anger?
Can you feel my fear?
Betrayed by friend
And shunned by foe
Disloyalty and hatred
Is all that I know.
Friendship is phony
And friends are so fake.
Why do I have trouble
With the decisions I make?
Life can be so cruel,
It can be so mean.
If you've done what I've done
And seen what I've seen.
Finding truth and love
Is a moment so rare.
Is anyone listening?
Does anyone care?

—*Amanda Ludwin*

Untitled

A little bit of happiness
Can help me through all strife
For when I'm with you darling,
You are my hope, my life

To talk with you is all I need
To mend my weary heart
To hold your hand and at that time,
Know you won't depart

The little time we have together
Is all my heart desires
For just your warmth so near to me
Can set my soul on fire

But then the dream is ended
My cherished time consumed
Just like a lonely orphan
For me there is no room

—*Jackie M. Siekerman*

Ode To Old Age

The mirror is easy to deny;
choosing what we want to see
is not that difficult.
It's when the ancient bones,
pleased with the image,
turn to go
to dance to old remembered melodies
that truth sets in.

—*Gladys Bolo*

Why?

A calling bird is calling
Can you hear it?
It's asking you a question
Why is there such racial violence,
crime, and punishment?
People silent about the issues
We endure why it asks?
Can you answer it?
Men and women
Straight and gay
Patriotic and disgraceful days
It asks why? Can you answer it?
Don'ts and do's
Can someone answer it soon?
The calling bird is calling-
Can you hear it?
All the questions - no answers
The calling bird is calling
Can you heart it?
Do you want to?

—*Ann-Jennette Rizzuto*

Homeless

I am prepared for cold winds,
    Cardboard for insolation.
I'll survive this bitter night,
    With pure determination.
I finished off that bottle,
    I found out behind Joe's Bar.
People say I shouldn't drink.
    But it keeps my insides warm.
I collected cans all day,
    I looked for a place to sleep.
I hope for something better,
    But it seems out of my reach.
I don't know how it happened,
    But I'm living on the streets.
I don't know why I'm crying,
    It is only Christmas Eve.
It's starting to rain again,
    I am frightened wet and cold.
But I know I'll be O.K.,
    After all, I'm twelve years old.

—*Darla Fridley*

Peace

A blanket of softly rolling mist,
caresses this quiet land.
    Droplets of dew as diamonds sparkle,
adorn leaf and blade so grand.

    The trees in majesty stand, clothed
in raiments of green.
    Upon the waters not a ripple,
to disrupt this lovely scene.

    The meadow grass covers completely,
the evidence of battles fought.
    The sun peeks gently over the horizon,
glimpsing what God has wrought.

    It matters not what the cause,
nor who was right or wrong.
    Nor how many here now lie,
in answer to the sirens song.

    Wounds have healed, memories faded,
the tempest long has passed.
    It matters only that man is free,
peace reigns supreme at last.

—*James A. Boyd*

Mother

She is so loving and
caring as warm as
her touch.

She is the most beautiful
person in the world
when you look through
a child's eyes.

She always made home
feel warm, comfortable
and safe.

She was very stern and strong.
And helped you work towards
your dreams and build for the
future.

I want to be just like my
mother.

—*Heidi Hydock*

Darkness

The sun sinking behind the trees
carried in a hollow breeze.
Hanging in the corners of a room
bringing sadness and doom.
Lurking throughout the timeless night
what a tremulous fright!
Dancing behind the haunted wood
moving like a riding hood.
Laying in a fitting grave
sailing in a poisoned wave.
Darkness

—*Hillary Laurent*

Our New Beginning

How often we wish for another
Chance to make a fresh new start
A chance to fade out our mistakes
And change failure into winning
It does not take a new year
To make a brand new start,
It only takes a deep desire to
Try with all our hearts
To live a better life and to be
Always forgiving.
Just add a little "sunshine"
To our world and bring a rainbow of your
Own to the world we're living
So never give up in despair
And think you are through
For there is always a tomorrow
And a chance to start a new beginning.

—*Charlotte Hutton*

To Joan (Stepchild)

How I have come to love thee,
    Child of another's womb!
Daily my prayers go steadfastly
    To keep thee from the darkened tomb
Of smoldering thoughts and needless fear.
In full comprehension, let us seek
    Each other's heart
With deep humility,
    That, day by day, week by week,
Thou wilt hear
    My offering to thee
All the knowledge and wisdom
    That is within me.

—*Fredrica A. Meyer*

Bad Mood On An Afternoon Flight

See them scurry to and fro.
Chittering, chattering as they go.
Why they babble no one knows.
As they hurry to and fro.

Fading, fleeting, faceless crowds.
We dare not call their names aloud.
For if just one form assumes a face.
They crowd into our private space.

So let them wander through their days.
Chittering, chattering, in an inane way.
Caring not that trivial words.
Smother the voices that should be heard.

How strange it is that so many find,
Pleasure in echoes from empty minds.
Yet no one listens nor seems to care.
That each echo is fixed with an empty
    stare.

Yet ever onward mankind goes.
Chittering, chattering, to and fro.
Grasping at expression of feeble thought.
Parched mentalities in a timeless drought.

—*Dean L. Lashbrook*

November

Bright and cheery twilight,
    Clear and rosy dawn,
Noontime gay with sunlight,
    All this soon is gone.

Cold and misty mornings,
    Cool and dry by noon —
These are Autumn's warnings
    Winter's coming soon.

All the leaves have vanished
    From the treetops tall,
And from mind is banished
    Summer, spring and fall.

Children seem so happy
    Romping in the snow,
Autumn's air so snappy
    Makes their faces glow.

Why November leaves us
    When we love her so
Is a thought that grieves us
    More than she must know.

—*Henrietta A. Scott*

Night Hawk

Night hawk calling
clear at twilight.
The cry, constant, melodious,
cruel to midnight -
Sleep, weary, o for rest,
or morn to come.
The night cry goes on.

Bird or beast,
night hawk or cougar,
circling, stealthily, on the prowl.
From where does this cry come?
How does it move so?

Come back bird.
Please, cat, go.
Leave me rest this one night.
Leave me peace.

—*Annie L. McClure*

Plight Of The Wolves

Wolves howling, wolves prowling.
    Clever wolves are proud and free.
        Hunting on the wooded hill.
When food is needed, they come to kill.
        Noble beasts of mystery.

    Men talking, men walking.
    Clever men with guns for claws.
    "We are not like wolves," they say.
They kill for sport and not for prey.
Steel traps have replaced their jaws.

    Wolves running, men coming.
    Clever wolves know men mean death.
    Shotguns roar with deafening sound.
    Wolf blood soaks the thirsty ground.
    One more wolf draws one last breath.

    Wolves dying. We're crying
    "Wolves belong in nature too!"
    "Big Bad Wolves" do not kill men.
    Wolves deserve to thrive again.
So strive to find the wolf in you.

—*Andrew H. French*

Courageous Youth

My dear young son with limbs so fine
Climbed the tree of sturdy pine.
Never shall I fall he said
Don't worry Mom about my head.
But alas so brave and free
He came tumbling from the tree,
As I ran to hold him tight
Almost overcome with fright,
He looked at me with cheerful grin
I asked him please don't you
    want to come in?
No thanks mother, not now said he
For I mean to conquer that pine tree.

—*Ivy Shaw Gordon*

The Country Of Symbols

In this country
clocks are synchronized with
slow motion clouds
dotting the sky, moving
with the season.

In this land time
is the clear, clean sound
of water in single streams
rolling over pebbles.

Look, look carefully at
the world as it stretches.

Love here is a vast orchard
at sunset. There is no room
for other voices.
In this country time is sacred.
It is the dimension
where the rose lives with the stone.

—*Artem Haroutiunian*

Little Fishes In The Brook

Little fishes in the brook; Daddy
catch them with a hook; Mama flies
them in a pan; Baby eats them like
a man.

—*Bobby J. Roberts*

Unspoken Love

From the far reaches of sleep
Close upon the wakeful mind,
Visions play, portents mature
Feelings unvoiced swell, endure.

The one that I … know
Has left sorrow and is gone,
And hides from my silent care.
Distance is felt, even when near.

Desperation builds greater
'Til sleeps threshold has been passed,
Yet fear remains by my side
Urging sweat to seeping tide.

Skin disclaims dreamt of absence
As I embrace dozing flesh,
To her waking I whisper,
"I just need to hold you near."

—*David Darryl Lathrop*

Solitary Confinement

Darkness
Closing in
Like a Cage
Locking my Heart away
Beating, Pumping
Trying endlessly to escape
Rattling the Iron Bars of my Mind
Leave me in the Dark
All alone
Talking to myself
Gibberish
Muffled Voices flood my Mind
So distant, yet so near
Rats
Gnawing at my Shoe
I close my Eyes
Bringing the Darkness closer
Closer

—*Christopher J. Dom*

Winter's Child

Dark in spirit.
Cold at heart.
Essence of winter.

Bare earth, frozen earth.
Nothing lives, nothing blooms.
Nothing grows there.

Lacking to contribute,
Cold, cold earth.
She's so cold!

Dark, depressing,
I see shades of grey,
I see hopelessness.
I don't like what I see.
I don't like to look at her.
She's winter's child!

—*Debra Choate Gisler*

An Advocate With The Father

We are not sinless,
    but we do sin less.
We are not fault free,
    but we are set free.
We have an advocate with the Father
    when we do wrong,
to stand in our behalf and say,
    Father, I've paid for it all.

—*Celia Wilson*

Goodbye

When the time has
come upon us.
In my heart, you will
not know
Goodbyes will be
unspoken.
When I spread my
wings and go.

When the time is
finally here
The pain you will not
feel. Our parting will
be sorrowful. But
the feelings are sincere.

The time is now my
friend. For me to say, Goodbye
Our laughter may
have stopped
But the memories
will not die.

—*Brandi Nocchi*

The Spiritual Fetus

Out of the old man
comes forth the new
within the outer man
grows the inner too

The inner man
is the fetus in man
which will be birthed
the son of man

The new man within
resurrecting within man
suddenly manifesting
the son of man

The mounting stresses
upon mother earth
the early pains
of childbirth

The contraction pains
in mother man
the impending labor
and son of man

—*Daniel T. O'Neill*

Untitled

Softly, o'er the hills of my mind
  Comes the voice of the Lord -
  O, so near. . .
Softly, o'er my mountain of sin
  Comes His word
  To my waking ear. . .
Calling me into His presence;
Calling me unto His Son;
Joyfully, o'er the path of His heart
  Into His kingdom I run!

Gently, through trailways and valleys
  Comes the presence of Jesus -
  So clear. . .
Gently, through my joys and trials
  Comes His presence
  To send away fear. . .
Keeping me safe in His presence;
Keeping me safe by His side;
Thankfully, o'er the path of God's heart
  Safe in His love I abide!

—*Dorothy Lake Boyett*

Hush! Did You Hear Something?

If you hear a coughing,
Coming from my coffin,
Please stop, and look inside.

Maybe even a knocking,
Followed by a rocking,
Please stop, and look inside.

Even though it may be shocking,
To reach over and unlock it,
Please, oh please, look inside.

Cause to everyone's surprise,
You just might find,
That I'm still very much alive!

And to prove to all, I'll sit up straight,
I'll stand up tall,
And laugh at fate.

But something I must really do,
Before I actually do die,
Is to find the guy,
Whose job it was -
To bury me alive!

—*James Adduci*

Knowledge And Faith

For all believers of faith
  Confused or not
That dwell on for meaning
  Whose questions may
  Never be asked
Lost in the past
  The knowledge carries
Forth the questions that may
  Be carried from thy past
With thy hopes, dreams and faith
  For all that matters;
Believers, confused or not
  I voice my dreams
  And hopes with
Meanings of questions in
Knowledge and faith......

—*Charles Lambert*

Time

Envelope of evidence.
Containing all we see.
Fourth dimensions measurements.
That shrouds eternity.

With it we can measure space.
Without it nothings clear.
Within it we run life's race.
Outside the realm of fear.

Its presence gives us comfort.
Great sorrow when it's spent.
Though our share be long or short.
We know it heaven sent.

Its essence pure amazement.
Its purpose plain to see.
Each new life to circumvent.
Then set the spirit free.

When time runs its full measure.
Hear that last trumpet sound.
When God reveals His treasure.
Eternity is found.

—*Bill Kail*

My Mother

Soft as the leaves of a
  cool summer's breeze.
  My Mother
Warm as a flower in the
  sun at noon's hour.
  My Mother
Tender as time, fighting
  towards that final chime.
  My Mother
As strong as ever, no matter
  what the cost,
She fought that final battle,
  with dignity and strength,
  and lost.

—*Jill Ileen Keefer*

Sunset

A circle of flaming passion
Cooled by blue stillness
Covered by green loneliness
Accented with pink beauty
And darkened by purples deepness.

—*Erica Richard*

The Perfect Sunset

If only my mind
Could be as peaceful as the waves.
  And if only my heart
Could be as pure as the water.
  Then maybe my life
Would shine as bright as the sun.

—*Calvin Mathis*

Loneliness

A state of being...
Could it be too
A state of mind;
Or separation,
Not a part of,
But apart from.....
A longing to belong,
The need to the
warmth of a friendly
Heart.....
Welling up from
Deep inside, a
Feeling of emptiness!
An aching almost
Physical,
To be a part of
That which one is
Apart from!
That is the state
Of loneliness.

—*Dorothy R. Rovello*

Sparring with Life

He walked into a
dingy smoke filled bar.
Cocked his gangster hat,
and lit up a cigarette.
Took one drag,
fell on the floor and died.
Mourn! Mourn and mourn!

—*Hassan Restum*

Untitled

Slowly a blanket descends.
Covering all, hiding nothing.
Soft waves float down upon
  As rough edges are hewn and
    Sharp corners graceful turns,
      Carrying
High upon the clouds where
Dare not look
  down
Not .... fear of heights
The fear is of losing
The height, so near the
  source.

    —Eric Maynard

Waves Of Wind

Like the butterfly's wing beat,
Dancing days of autumn treat
We who watch leaves gently thinned,
Fluttered down by waves of wind.

Winter gales are sounding strong,
Freshened by cold nights run long.
Air waves rush with seaside roar,
Pounding 'gainst our bolted door.

Surging north with warming sway,
Breaths of spring thaw ice away,
Raising newborn joyful shoots,
Waving, cheering to their roots.

Now comes welcomed summer breeze,
Softly voiced as if to please,
Courting hopefully to win
Smiling sky and our fair grin.

    —Evans Burn

Blood On The Shamrock

Wilted Shamrock at my feet,
Derry's thirteen children lie
bleeding in the street.
There's red on your green,
it can plainly be seen!

St. Patrick is mourning,
and the trinity is scorning
Great Britain's Executioners!

Bloody Sunday! Bloody Sunday!
The stark scarlet terror of
death's pallbearers have
carried off the souls of
Irishmen!

    —Bernie Ryan

Age

Seasons change
  each will too.
The troubled sky
  no longer blue.
Dark green the earth
  all green will die,
First starts the rain
  then snow must fly.
All breath will cease
  we live with grief
Return the Son
  the tree will leaf

    —C. R. McHaney

I Deserve To Know

I have a mind,
  Do I want to know?
I have eyes,
  Do I want to see?
I have a heart,
  Do I want to feel?
I have a soul,
  Do I want to be?
I deserve to know.

Inside there are emotions,
  Do they really show?
Inside I am growing,
  Does it mean there's hope?
Inside there are dreams,
  Do I have to awaken?
Inside a voice is calling,
  Am I asking to be free?
I deserve to know.

    —Erika N. Colin

Love

Do you have me as I love you?
Do you arms enfold me "Love"
Shall my arms enfold you my "Love"
Come embrace me "Love"
As I have embraced you
For you my love, have
made me love "Love"
In complete abandonment
— By loving you completely my "Love"
I know the complete and
unadorned beauty of simply loving you...

    —Elsie F. Waters

Love

Do you see?
Do you hear?
Do you cry?
Do you fear?
Do you know?
Do you care?
Can you feel?
Do you stare?
Do you know who I am?
Do you see where I stand?
Do we see one another,
with a love like no other?

    —Jennifer Bock

Lullaby Lane

Just around the corner
  Down in lullaby lane
That's where the sunshine
  Takes the place of the rain
My darling do you remember
  The first time we met
The smile that you gave me
  I will never forget
Just around the corner
  Where dreams do come true
That's where my darling
  I vowed my love to you
Though we're old and grey dear
  My memories of you are the same
Just around the corner
  With you in lullaby lane.

    —Ivan Slade

Beach Children

Children on the slide
Down the sandy beach
With the merry-go-round they glide
So near, yet far from reach.

Sand blowing in their face
Children swiftly running
Wind just more than a trace
On the sand greatly funning.

Children grow tall
And children grow old.
I remember it all
Children in the sand so bold.

Young become adults grown
But there is nothing as fine
Wild oats they have sown
Acting as Gods, young and divine.

They cover the world, so rich
Being most important to me
Everywhere there is such
The sand and my children by thee.

    —James L. Norwood

Floating

Floating on the sea,
  drinking a cup of tea.
Going to see Meleanie,
in Miami.

Meet her electric eel,
  eat some pie, tell a lie,
eat more pie to tell the truth.

Meet Ruth whose on the roof,
watching horses hoofs.

    —Brandy Crabtree

Catatonic Counterpoint

My sister sits in a corner,
  early, late,
The slightest smile on a
  frozen face.
Her fingers run scales on keys
  we cannot see,
Her lips murmur words
  unheard.

Up, down, she makes her music.
Is it sight with sound, a late
  (or early) movie in her mind,
  a silent song she sings?

She told me once, when little,
  (pointing her finger)
  that I never, ever,
  let her play on
  my piano, up or
  down.

    —Bettylee Elgin

Sourire

My lips will not permit a smile
Despite my best intentions.
My heart cannot suppress its bile
Aroused by love's inventions.

    —Gwynn Hoffman

Colors

Colors, swirling, flashing,
Echoing through my
Otherwise empty mind.
Running, leaping, jumping, spinning,
They yearn to be enjoyed.

Silently I move my pen,
Across the blank white page,
The colors no more in my head,
The paper full ablaze.
—*Angela M. Krysiak*

The Puppet

I awake to a chilling scream
Emanating from an unknown entity.
The hideous voices mock my fear;
My assailants I cannot see.

My attempts to escape are futile
As I await the fate they bring.
I am a puppet with wooden limbs.
My enemies control the strings.

My trembling hands receive their gift
Conceived in the realm below:
The dagger of a thousand lies
With a shimmering, fiery glow.

I have no choice. I must obey.
Their summons I can't deny.
I see my frozen tomb await.
I know that I must die.

I clasp the dagger to my heart.
I kiss its gleaming blade,
And as the blood begins to fall,
The voices begin to fade.
—*Debra M. Shafer*

Imprisioned

Dark, dark, gray walls
enclosing me.
Bars on either sides of me.
Imprisoned, confused
I can't get out.
Trapped! Trapped!
Yelling, pleading, pounding
let me out.
Let my soul run free.
—*Amanda Lehman*

Hands Of Time

You are forever here,
Etched across my soul.
Burning deep within,
Was a fire that's grown cold.

It used to be only you,
That played havoc on my mind.
Now when I look inside,
I see that I left you behind.

If the hands of time would turn,
Back to when I saw only you,
Maybe I could have held on
And kept a love that was true.
—*Heather L. Wolf*

Our Destiny

I found you and you found me,
even though weren't looking
for each other at the time.
It was our destiny, God's
plan for us. He knew what
we needed and how to be
complete. To be together,
forever, as one, as husband
and wife. To have as a
best friend and a lover,
and then later on, he
blessed us with the children
so we could be a father
and a mother. Thank
you Lord, for the planning
of our life, for bringing
us together as husband
and wife.

—*Jeanie Pitner*

Dreams

I wonder, if dreams.
Ever do come true?
I've had a few, I don't want to loose.
The one special dream!
Of the day, I met you.
You glanced my way.
Your eyes seemed to say,
Came take my hand,
And walk with me.
Through this beautiful world.
Of make believe.
This dream was so real,
I looked back, I could see.
This beautiful rainbow.
Then you, and then me.
A love bonded so deeply.
All humans, could see.
A God given love.
For you, and for me.
—*Bea Royal*

The Face Of Friendship

My mask remains with me
Everywhere I go,
Should I need to wear it
So Me doesn't show.
The real Me stays hidden
(I'm afraid of what you'll do!)
Til its removal is bidden.
(I might lose you!)
I'll try to do as you ask-
To let you see Me.
Understand, it's not an easy task.
Close your eyes, be patient;
Its removal will be slow.
There! It's gone!
Oh, how it hurts
To let the real Me show,
I feel naked! Bare! So cold!
Look now-
And if you still love all that you see,
You're my friend, pure as gold.
—*Jean Stoffel*

Summer Song

I am so glad God gave me
Eyes that I might see
The bright, bright blueness of His skies.
The green of distant trees.

The lushness of the growing crops
The gold of harvest grain
The flaming color of wild flowers
On a gently rolling plain.

The brightness of the summer sun
That sinks amid rosy clouds,
The silver whiteness of the moon
To soften night's deep shrouds,

I am so glad God gave me a tongue
That I may proclaim
The wondrous beauty of His works,
And glorify His name!

I thank God for all these gifts
That are mine just for the viewing,
I pray that they may ever be,
Uplifting and renewing.
—*Claire Petersen*

Winter's Gem

Quiet winter's green,
Falling daintily upon
A white snow cushion
From proud boughs above.

Liquid crystal gems,
Sparkle and flash
A promissory ring
Upon a rose's bed.

The virgin carpet,
Soft, deep, and wet,
Here was demarked
By lightly falling feet.

Slender long impressions,
thin, shallow and shapely;
Where she walked alone.
Oh, that she had walked with me.
—*Christopher Hammett Myers*

Family Reunion

Embraces -
Families renewing their love.
Memories shared,
Memories made,
Tears of sadness for those who are gone,
Tears of joy at seeing everyone again.
New members meet the old.
Children enjoying their cousins,
Who said you can't go home again?
—*Heather Wasserman*

Wilderness

In the distance mama bird
feeds her fledgling.
In the distance a swan is
bathing.
In the distance a colt is
nursing
In the distance animals
are birthing
In the city where I live,
There are no animals.
—*Adam Sneek*

The Dying Child

Sitting in silence crying
Feeling the pain so mild.
Seeing someone dying
Knowing it was a child.

In my fear I found
That I was the child indeed.
Knowing that I was bound
This is my only seed.

Tears rolling down my cheek
Touching my small hand
This child once so slender and meek
Is now like a grain of sand

I have lost my childhood
The pain soon would pass
If only I knew I should
Children never last
　　　—*Angela D. McCallister*

Ancient Ruins

Coolest of moonlight
Find her a star
To wish away sad nights
When they grow dark

For I can't love her
Now that I'm gone
Won't you please take over
Where I left off

Grace her distant smile
With tangible faith
Don't let her cry out
yesterday's pain

Heaven has no tears
Though Oh Lord are they brewin'
Through my dim eyes
Of Ancient Ruins.
　　　—*Anthony Gerych*

A Speck Of Sadness

When you leave me a speck of sadness
　　flicks through my mind.
But I know you will be back.
Returning with your warmth and
　　everflowing love.
As days go by my love grows for you.
Your smile rubs off and catches me.
You and I together makes me overwhelmed
　　with happiness.
I hope it lasts forever for you
　　are my life.
　　　—*Charlene L. Holguin*

Questions

Do we grow or does everything else?
Everything we do is it the past?
Are we characters in someone's
dream, and if we are when they
wake up, will we die?
　　　—*Ivy Quihuis*

Fright Night

The falling leaves of red and gold
Float down on Goblins bold.
There's a chill in the air,
Sky's will no longer be fair.

Fright Night is not far away.
Keep Safe that night, I say!
Early out, early in before dark,
Will confuse the Goblins. Hark!

Hark! A candle I see.
In a small one's hands? Oh, Me!!!
Use the light without flame
Or you may never be the same!!!

All around you evil slinks,
Accidents happen, Quick as a wink.
Look before and behind,
Safety conscious people are not blind.
　　　—*Janet Joann Butcher*

Wondering

I see crystal clear water
Flowing over miles of sandy beaches
I stare into the horizon
Wondering what it all was before

I see towering rocks
Stretching out toward heaven
I stare up in awe
Wondering what shall be our destiny

I see endless meadows
Spreading out for all to see
I stare into the grassy fields
Wondering how long we have

I see thousands of stars
Ascending into space
I stare up in admiration
Wondering if it is all a dream

I see extraordinary mountains
Waiting peacefully
I stare out in agony
Wondering why it all has to end
　　　—*Jennifer L. Moore*

Precious Moments

I saw a lovely butterfly
Fly across an azure sky;
The beauty of the moment
Lifted my heart on high.
As it floated in the morning breeze
And nestled in some far-off trees.

Then I heard the song of a bird;
The loneliest melody I have ever heard.
It touched my heart and lifted it high
As the song drifted softly by.
I grabbed that moment and put it away
To save it for another day.

Then I saw a rose
Kissed by the morning dew.
And I thought of all the beauty
God gave to me and you.
So stop and enjoy the moment
As they come your way;
Treasure them forever,
Not just for today.
　　　—*Dorothy S. Watson*

Simply Frankie

In Hazel pools of love
Fools like I swim endlessly
On and on forever endlessly
It's times like this
a simple kiss
can bring simple joys
It's times like these
that men become boys
But worst than this
Emotions become breakable toys
Dreams go on endlessly
On and on forever endlessly,
　　Drowning in dark pink kisses
Encaged in soft pink embraces
Running in emotional marathons
There's no winning or losing
　　These Hazel Races
Only seeing them through
swimming in Hazel pools of love
　　with you.
　　　—*Craig Spriggs*

Reminders

I wear a reminder on my wrist
for everyone to see!
It's plain & simple but is worth
More than gold to me!
it's because of this reminder
That I can never forget, a man
I have never met.
There is another reminder I think
Everyone should see.
It's a wall in Washington D.C.
People will cry and ask why
Did they have to die!
But through the tears it's plain
To see, they died for you & me!
but what it comes down to is this,
All the men we still do miss
So let us not forget, the men who
Are not home yet!!!
　　　—*Deanne Eichburg*

Song Of The Rain

The silence waits outside my door
For footsteps that I hear no more,
And in my heart an empty pain
He will not walk this way again.

We worked the fields, a tiring pace
The sun shone warm upon our face,
And shared a special kind of love
That only comes from God above.

Then children, four in number came
The bonds of love remained the same,
A daughter fair and three sons strong
And in our world there seemed no wrong.

As time flew by on elusive wings
Our life was blessed with many things,
Then he no longer walked with me
And only sadness could I see.

For every thing there is a season
And for each pain an unknown reason,
And often in the falling rain
I hear him softly call my name.
　　　—*Bernadine T. Joyce*

State Of Inner Peace

Let us not tarry upon the road
　for life's adventure is a load.
And the journey that is at hand
　we carry to the promised land.
We are human in the way we feel
　not just entities pursuing an ideal.
To achieve the state of perfect peace
　is something far beyond our reach.
To be distracted by the pains of flesh
　yet know that you have done your best.
To win and lose, to laugh and cry
　the fate of humans who still must try
To reach that state of inner peace
　the journey itself let's us lease.
So tarry not upon this road
　for together we go lightening our load.
On a wonderfully new journey to reach
　that blessed state of inner peace.

　　　　—Bette K. Brown

Unreturned

　　　I live
　　For one thing only
　　　My love
It keeps me striving for another day
　　　I wait
　　For one time only
　　　My life
　　To live is to love
　　To love is to live
　　　Love hurts
　　Life hurts even more
I long for an end of desperation
　　My love is my life
Without love, there's no life
Without life, I'm desperate
　　　For what
My life shatters into smaller pieces
　　　I die
　　And for what
A love just as great, not returned

　　　—Bryn McNichols

So Many

So many stones
For so many deaths
Caused by so many guns.

So many guns
Bought in so much anger
Over so little mistakes
And so many tempers.

So many tempers
For so many loved ones
Caused so many fears
And so many tears.

So many tears
Shed for so many people
And so many fears
Were built up inside

So many people
Have no sorrow
For they don't know
How much so many lives would cost.

　　　—Brooke Miller

The Price One Pays

What price must one pay
for such joy?
It is but fleeting
in the best of times.
What heartaches must
one endure for
a glimpse of heaven?
It is but a momentary
vision amid life's turmoil.
What pain must one feel
for touching another soul?
It is a blessing to be
counted but not kept.
What peace must one forfeit
for such a love?
It is the price one
pays for such joy.

　　　—Beverly Lynne Gray

Dear John Poem

The words are no longer spoken
For the chain of love has been broken
Gone are the nightly talks
For now only the pain stalks
The caring is now gone
The end to a perfect song
Trust no longer lingers
As my feelings flow through my fingers
When one heart stands alone
It truly has the feeling of stone
My life is no longer my own
But for this I have grown
You will never understand what I need
We are not made from the same seed
My heart will never be the same
After this cruel and unusual game
You used to show so much compassion
I guess it's no longer in fashion
Sometimes you must let it go
And with this you will grow

　　　—Barbara Strong

Untitled

Let the children play,
For they turn corners and see cowboys
and arrows shooting towards their hats
They feel tiny nurses tending
their tremendous wounds
And fly airplanes at high altitudes
having a hazardous mission
They see ants as dinosaurs
An empty house
as a haunted castle
Ghosts and goblins appearing
at their will
Puddles of water as disastrous floods
And other children as their peers
Let the children play
for their short time as little people
Is our long time in growing old
Let the children play.

　　　—James Shorette

My House

This old house was once brand new,
For thirty years give or take a few.

Room number one is for Dean and me,
Let's skip over to room number three.

This room we call room number three,
Catches everything from Dean and me.

Room number three is really I clump
We call it the city dump.

In the garage we can't use a card
We call it the junk yard.

The rest of the house, is like these two
We call it the city zoo.

　　　—Billie Hardy

Baby Alexandria

Our love is so great
for this child so small,
our sweet little girl
who can't even crawl.

She came as a surprise
an early one, too,
a baby so small,
and so weak and so new.

A surprise to us all,
for us each to adore,
as the days go by,
we love her more and more.

We laugh and we smile
at each little touch,
such a sweet little girl,
we love her so much.

　　　—Brooke N. Copani

Towels

The towels smell so
　fresh and clean
　sunlight
Contradiction to life
　black
　smelly
Pain and hurt
Never end
　No way out

　I don't want to breathe
　I don't care
　don't want to be.

Let me out
I wish I were a towel

　　　—Jennifer L. Thome

Feelings

Feelings, feelings,
Everyone has feelings.
Happy, fine, excited, glad.
Some feelings are even bad.
Sad, mad, lonely, bad. Don't feel down.

　　　—Jillian Coleman

The Alcoholic

Shallow bravery explodes
from cowardice and weakness
at the sniff
of a drink.

Hollowed fears deplores
for love
and kindness
to be link.

Passionate lust in the
vapor of neon lights
flashes deep fuzzy blues
and screaming whites.

Pricks away at hidden
desires that shatters
like a big male fist
onto his wife.

An evening dampen
by allusions,
an evening hampened
by confusion.

—*Heyward Fulton*

Reawakening

Tonight I felt a stir of passion
from deep within
Where for a long, long time
none had been.

I thought perhaps those special
feelings were to be no more.
I knew this to be all wrong
when you walked me to the door.

I ask myself, do I wish to risk
rekindling of the fire
Or vow to not get hurt and
smolder my desire.

I think that I shall let the
fire grow into a flame
And see, my Dear, if you will
risk the same.

—*Doris Sindle-Pruitt*

Seasons

I thank you, Lord
for the springtime of my life.
I was only seventeen...
when he asked me to be his wife.

The summertime was beautiful -
well blessed with daughters, four.
God gave us health and safety -
and love and faith and more.

I'm living in the autumn
with the man I love so much.
I pray the winter's extra long...
Dear Lord, I need his touch.

—*Eileen C. Blair*

Kindness

I've often thought that this old world
a better place would be
if we'd try a little kindness
after all it still is free.

In the rush of just plain living
the important things slide by
a hand clasp, nod or some kind act
let's give them all a try.

It may be that the smile we give
to someone on the street
will give to him new courage
and lend magic to his feet.

Or maybe just a "thank you"
to a tired weary one
will be the thing that helps him
till all his tasks are done.

So take time out for kindness
you will surely find your pay
in knowing you've spread sunshine
to someone on your way.

—*Violet Tyrrell*

A Sunrise To Death

A sun breaks the horizon
a bird sings its song
everything comes to life
everything that must belong.
But then everything is silent
as scream after scream is heard
from inside those great walls
death is the only word.
Thousands at a time
innocent people they all are
men and women, mostly Jews
and children cooped in a jar.
For years it lasted
the death rate was so high
millions and millions of people
but no one heard their cry.
Stop all the anger
murdering and hate
because the next holocaust
is not going to wait.

—*Tara Sanborn*

Untitled

The stars are shining very bright,
a breeze blows the trees ever so light.

I can see the moon glowing from afar;
I begin to wonder, where you are.

The water is clear and blue;
There will soon be a morning dew.

I watch the sun peeking over the sea;
You were here, in my memory.

—*Sharon L. Wittman*

If I Were

If I were a poet, I'd write for you
a poem of love so strong and true.
If I were a dancer, with you I'd dance
a dance of joy, if given the chance.
If I were a painter, I would create
an image of your face so sweet.
If I were a captain, I'd cross the sea
for just one kiss from you to me.

—*Paul Generes*

A Moment In Time

Life is but a moment in time
A brief and fleeing moment in time
And in this moment I love you
As if that's all there is.

We began our love one springtime
In confiding friendship
Our summer blossomed
To the fullest hue
With autumn came the harvest
And I spend my winters now with you
In an all too brief
moment in time

—*Maxine A. Meitz*

Broken Heart

Broken glass and broken dreams,
A broken heart and broken things.
These all fit together so swell,
like you and I go together so well.
I have had a broken heart before
from someone who hurt me
that I did adore.
I adore you now and forever I will,
and if you ever hurt me
I will have my heart still.
Broken or not it will never leave me
until the day I die it will forever beat.
I hope you never leave me
but if you ever do I'll leave
a piece of my heart with you.

—*Tawnya Merrick*

A Candle In The Dark

A lighted candle in the dark;
A dark so vast, so deep.
And when the candle is put out,
A thousand eyes shall weep.

But who puts this out this candle?
Who blows this candle out?
For the dark is lonely,
You cannot scream, nor shout.

You cannot feel, you cannot see.
You cannot know who's there.
So how does breath escape the lips?
And move across the air.

No one knows, nor will know,
From whence this deadly breath came.
For all candles light is different,
But death is all the same.

—*Nicole Valera*

Where Is The Horizon?

I saw a mountain at the horizon,
A mountain bulging through the sky.

I said I must climb that mountain,
I've never been that high.

But when I reached the mountain,
the horizon already bid goodbye.

And the summit of the hill seemed
A million miles from the sky.

—*Oral O. Thomas*

School

I really like school a bunch there's
a big cafeteria where I eat my lunch.
We do lots of homework, but that doesn't bother me
because I'm going to be all that I can be.
The teachers are nice and sweet,
but all of them tell us to stay in our seat.
I go to Brandon Fletcher Middle School
you're a fool if you don't go to my school.

Pencils, paper, books, and crayons,
don't forget our special school band.

— *Susan Jacobs*

All Is One

"Ho"! The crow flies.
A bird of strength and guidance.
My soul soars within it
And as we fly I feel freedom and a sense of inner power
Freedom from the bondage of the past
I see the world in a different light
The beauty of it all, the great mother
The puma, my power animal whom is always with me to show me
the way is on top of a hill.
He seems to be affirming.
Affirming that I'm heading in the right direction on the
medicine wheel of life.
I feel my spirit guide ever present.
Everyone is with me
The more I soar, the more balanced I become
Coming to great awareness and light
This strange and powerful light enfolds me
Desisting all that is negative
Another protector in an assemblage of many
I know as long as I stay in this spiritual light, and
honor its presence, I will be safe and tranquil
To conquer all I wish to subjugate.
"Ho!"

— *Michelle Davies*

A Desired Love

A desired love I cannot bare.
A bleeding heart I'm scared to share,
from a past that controls my body and mind,
The future you can't see,
for yet it is blind.
To a young love let my heart be true;
for as long as I live I shall always love you.
My passion stirs like a roaring sea;
but when I look at you, you see right through me.
All the pain and suffer I've over looked;
can't you see my dear you've got me hooked.
Just remember when you're sad and blue
all the good times we had.
I shall always love you!

— *Lindsey York*

The Sounds Of City life

I sit alone, but not in solitude.

A baby's cry jars my reverie,
A car door slams and jolts my senses,
A cheering crowd announces victory,
Mozart's genius floats in my consciousness.

Neighbors talking, children playing,
Birds chirping, cars humming.

I sit alone, but not in solitude
As the sounds of city life surround me.

— *Margaret Paul*

Love?

What is love?
A celebration.
Or is it passion?
Or is it romance?
Yes, to all because love is a
celebration of passion and of romance.
Love is a wind of emotion and of life and death.
It can neither be seen nor heard but, is comprehended in
the heart. It manifests itself one to another and teaches the
heart gentleness. Love is the impossible, for who so loves,
believes the impossible. Because love makes the ordinary the
extraordinary. Love covers the faults of ones beloved and
makes them appear as gods and goddesses. A face that is
eternally beautiful and boundless-that is the content of love
in the heart. Love is the gift of oneself; love conquers all,
even hard hearts. There is so much confined in love.
Where it goes, we shall follow and, where it lives,
we shall live and where it ends, we die.

— *Roma Fore*

Kicsit (Little Bit)

There abides in a house not far from me,
  A charming Kisla'ny of old hungary;
She pleasures my eyes, my mind and my heart,
  A joy to be savored this precious up start;
Her sparkling wit and mischievous smile,
  Those flashing green eyes that disarm and beguile;
Born at midnight between scorpion and archer
  The signs of the zodiac do aptly describe her;
Tis said, "Lassies born at this splitting of signs,
  Are three different spirits whose souls must entwine;
  Kiskiralye', kisciga'ny and kicsitboszorka'ny;"
I know that it's true I'm delighted to say,
  We four were together just yesterday;

  Little queen, little gipsy,
  Little bit of witch and I.

— *Richard Tefft Fitzpatrick*

Poodle Talk

I noticed, strolling down the avenue one day
A chic young lady who appeared happy and gay.
Her clothes were a fashion plate, mini-dress and all...
The smile on her face hinted that she was having a ball.

But what caught my eye the most I'm thinking
Was a little poodle that she was walking.
No bigger than a toy, but just as fluffy; full of joy.
With flashing eyes and a prance; mischievous as a boy!

He tugged away at that leash occasionally,
Eager to explore the area completely.
You could tell he had the spark of adventure
As he darted to and fro, up front, then around her.

Occasionally, as she whispered his name
He'd freeze in his tracks, look up...so humane.
You could tell the affection was mutual.
They were a pair, those two...so lovable.

But I guess by now the poodle had enough.
He changed direction headed home, and was getting tough.
His mind was made up, for the moment he was boss.
And to tell just "who was walking who" I'm at a loss.

— *Louis F. Gagniere*

Just Child's Play?

What do you mean just child's play
A child plays with dreams men leave astray.

A child on the beach no matter where he stands
Plays that he's the king of his castle in the sand.

A child in the water swimming through the way
Pretends that he's a whale crashing through the waves.

A child in the dirt to him is a big delight
To become the whole crew of a big construction site.

But a lesson to the learner who says it is just for play:
He can accomplish his goals the very same way.

　　—Steve Abel

A Dying City

Mistruths, destruction, crime,
A city in its decline.
Vacant fields, dilapidated houses,
A city that cares not, if the homeless is without.

Streets filled with potholes,
Houses boarded up,
Politicians perpetrating a role,
While the real causes go untold.

A city, once in its prime
is now victimized by empty promises and lots of lies.

　　—Pamela C. Davis

The Seasons Of Life

Suicide, salvation
A contemplation
The lose of mortal eternity
To loose life is not living,
in the happiness of immortality
Life is change,
not a perennial season
Live life in fall, winter, spring, and summer
And admire the beauty of change
　—On the eve of the Blood Harvest Moon

　　—Vanessa Lee Vincenzini

Suzi

I see you there playing in the sand,
a creation of Gods loving hand
I laugh as a cool wave catches you
by surprise as it glides in around your feet
and catches you on the rise
I smile as you chase a gull bobbing quietly in the shallows,
The wind pulling on its wings and up into the air it follows
I cry as you break into a run speeding down the beach
for it brings to mind the day that you will be out of reach
Running in a place no harm will ever come to you,
a place where the loving hand of God once made you
There to await the time when we can again be together,
never to be apart because it will be forever.

　　—Bill Eardley IV

Untitled

A silent cry falls amongst the spirits again tonight.
A cry hidden under a river of brandy.
It finds its momentary comfort amidst the bright lights
　　and swept floors.
A comfort only to be removed by still ears.
Once again the battle between ignorance and understanding
　　is lost.

　　—Leonora C. Merkel

Feelings

This time of year it's hard to find
A day with sunshine, unclouded mind.
A time when fear creeps into mind
A day when raindrops are hard to find.
Let's walk down paths with feet unshod —
Where swirling winds blow up the sod.
The New Year comes and minds do swirl,
With thoughts of coming things do whirl.
Winds blow on with carefree bliss
Leaving is to bend through this.
This new year has gloom and fears,
Thoughts to live and grow for years,
Let's cast away our fears today
Live life-love carefree and gay.
Say what's in our hearts today.
Hide not the fears of yesterday,
Do the things that we must do
Believe in what we feel anew.

　　—Vivian M. Lawrence

Tiny Headlights In My Yard

As I turn into my driveway after dark,
A dozen tiny headlights appear,
Rushing to meet me as always.

Next morning, this sea of felines
Swirl at my feet, uncountable.
Fighting and running,
Waiting to be fed.

There is Precious, being Grumpy,
　fighting everyone in sight,
Baby, who has kittens everywhere,
Littl'un with the raccoon tail,
Lil' Gray, of the softest shade,
And Mert, who thought she wanted to
　accompany me to work one day.
In the house awaits Cricket, who greets me
At both ends of the day.
At least two dozen
For I have no heart for destroying
　nor the shelter.
I keep feeding and loving
And smiling when met
By these tiny headlights in my yard.

　　—Rose Staggs

Under The Eagle's Wing

Dipping on the surface of sleep,
　a dream forms
My head heavy and my body light
　on the soft pillows
I dream of unicorns with golden horns
　and pegasus with rainbowed wings
The pink and yellow sun setting in the sky
　is just beginning to sparkle with stars
The mermaids, with their tails in the water,
　are brushing the flowing hair, readying for slumber
And the blue-jays are just settling in their nests
A sweet music swirls through and around my head,
　putting me in a tranquil state
The flowers are closing their blossoms,
I lay down, my head under the eagle's wing.

　　—Shaina Guthrie

Frustration

A confused state of being, and unpleasant circumstances,
A feeling of deep depression and anxiety,
A low spirit that dries the bones,
A mental maze and dilemma of the mind,
A mirage that sees water on a dry desert plain,
A soul on ice that needs melting,
It's like lava that's coming from a volcano
   that's out of control,
A boiling pot of water that dries up,
Like help that's coming from a remote place that
   never seems to arrive,
Like a sink that's clogged with grease and dirt,
A mind-bottler,
The question is can you cope?
If not, that's frustration!

    —*Mary L. Bonner*

Our God Is

God is a bird, high in the air,
A fish in the sea,
A honey bee,

He's comfort and wisdom and wondrous power,
He's the mighty trees, and a fragile flower,
He's all around us, and up above,
But most of all, our God is love.

He's sunlight beaming, warm and bright,
He's moonlight streaming, night's cool light,
With all of this, and much much more,
He paves the way to heaven's door.

Rivers flowing deep and wide
Flowers that raise their heads with pride,
Birds that are sailing in skies of blue,
This is all God's glory and it's there for you.

    —*Margie Sopp*

Friends

A friends is a friend from beginning to end
A friend is there to talk, go for a walk
   At times when you feel down
   They can turn your frown upside-down
   Make you laugh even act like a clown
   A friend will never stab you in the back
But if you have a true friend there's nothing you lack
   We all have good times we all have bad times
     But the times with our friends
      We remember best
   We could stay up all night never rest
   We can always find time for laughter
It's not always our own interest we look after
     But those of our friends
      Because we care
   It's our friendship and lives we share
      And that's why
     A friend is a friend
     From beginning to end

  —*Sef Garcia*

Embers Of A Flame

I am the embers of a dying flame.
A man or woman, you can not blame.
For trust is the price our love has cost;
an embryo of a heart;
lies have lost.
If righteousness gave us meaning;
then sorrows' darkness remains beaming.
To let the light from the flame die out,
is worthless;
because love is what life is all about.

    —*Tena N. Cowan*

Who Am I?

Who am I?
A heart, a soul, a feeling,
One small star twinkling in the vast sky
To my parents, Christopher Columbus,
   their first child forging ahead into the unknown
My sister looks upon me as a hero, someone she wants to be
Yet, I hide behind a cloak,
Afraid to fail,
Afraid to fall.
To my friends, I am a fragile structure and they are the
   stone pillars holding me up.
I am made of glass, so sensitive that I could be shattered by
   the slightest disturbance
Yet my inner core is stone, determined to achieve and striving
   to survive the turbulence of adolescence
Who am I?
I am one small chance for the future to succeed,
Pushing for the top, celebrating the gains, weathering and
   mourning the losses.
Living each day as if it were my last
Hoping for just one more chance to make a difference.

    —*Victoria Fallon*

If I Could Be Different

If I could be different, Oh what would I be?
A horse, a cat, or maybe a flea!
A baboon with a face that would make people laugh
Or one of those tall animals known as a giraffe.
A seal all slippery, shiny and sleek
Or maybe a parrot with a very sharp beak.
A bunny would be nice with a fluffy bunny tail,
Or maybe something as large as a whale.
A mouse that could sneak into curious places,
Or a cheetah that could win all kinds of races.
A mule so I could be "stubborn" all day,
Or a lazy old sheep that just likes to eat hay.
A kitten would be nice for kids love them so much,
Or maybe a snake that people don't touch.
But of all the animals on the land or sea,
I've finally decided
I'D RATHER BE ME!!!

    —*Sharon Cowling*

Unseen Love

A life that wasn't meant to be.
A life that could've lived so free.
A life that didn't get a chance.
A life that was taken away by a doctor's glance.
A life that was an illegitimate child,
Because its mother was just too wild.
She went to her last resort,
Rather than hear her parents retort.
She went under the doctor's knife,
And ended her sweet baby's life.
She always said her child would have the best,
But she gave it away, just like the rest.
Who would have thought that from her womb,
Instead of life comes incredible doom?
Now because of her horrible choice,
She'll never hear her child's voice.

    —*Willie Schmelzle*

A Home

A house without love is not a home.
A house without happiness is not a home.
A house without care is not a home.
A house without understanding is not a home.
A house without trust is not a home.
Someday I wish to have a home.

    —*Virginia M. Dubose*

Disclosure

It sits within me like an anchor on my soul,
a mass of words and thoughts waiting to be set free
like a small, young bird
eager to burst forth in flight on a chilly, spring morning.

Aiming for the horizon,
faltering at times, weakly soaring;
frantically landing on a nearby limb
to catch a breath of cold, crisp air.
Ready to start again.

We soar, we fall, we rest, we search.
We leap again toward the horizon.
Clinging to the familiar,
yet longing for distant, open skies
that lie beyond the tangle of branches
and the thickness of the leaves.

So much to navigate; so thick are the trees,
but so beautiful is the sky beyond.

The answers lie not in the destination, but in the journey.
For by the time the tiny bird reaches the majestic skies
it already will know how to fly...

—*Susan M. Scribner*

A Mother Can Be...

A mother can be a nurse, lawyer, bus driver or a truck drive
A mother can be that force that motivates you on
A mother can be your best friend and that's a friend indeed
A mother can be a mother when it's time to be a mother, and
that's all the time.
For whatever reason - a mother can become sad, or glad - a
mother knows how to laugh
A mother can be short or tall - a mother can be an indian,
black, or caucasian,
And all those others too numerous to mention - mothers are
everywhere!
A mother can be a little league coach, an empathizer, and a
friend by a sick friend's bed
Mothers keep this earth replenished with folks
But after all has been said and mother has done -
I'm so glad I can still see my mother, she's sitting over
there, it's her birthday and she's seventy-one.

—*Sylvia Davis*

Buzzards

A hastily hidden smirk, a passing shot,
A nervous giggle followed by a furtive glance,
The embarrassed silent smiles when you enter a room
Which fall like a dagger thrust upon an unprotected, innocent
   breast.

The acid spray from a viper's tongue,
The sudden rebuff from an old friend,
The cold embrace from a cherished love,
It's the barren, broken heart that a few kind words could mend.

It's the vivisection of a bright, lively,
Youthful and willful spirit,
A piece here, a piece there,
Never fatal but dishearteningly painful,
Leading to sleepless nights and battered days.

A just, timely death I've seldom feared.
A quick ending to a now uncherished life.

It's the body sprawled in the street,
Painfully clinging to the fringes of existence
As the vicious scavengers gather for the feast.

It's the picking apart by buzzards I've always feared.

—*William M. Burdick*

Formative Years

Childhood was a battleground or so it seemed to me.
A never ending war waged fiercely,
the combatants unrelenting,
the destruction incalculable.

My war room was a busy place,
the epitome of efficiency,
my defenses always on the ready,
alert to any new stratagem or felt threat to my safety.

The attacks were cruelly savage
coming at any hour, day or night,
offering no respite - nor safe place.
But that's what war is, planned chaos
exhausting the enemies' resources.

And imagine if you can this calamity.
This holocaust was in my mind - a total fiction
causing bewilderment and ruining everything.

Until one day I finally capitulated,
and dressed in full armour I entered the closet,
a temporary haven from the destruction.
Once again captive of my plan.

—*Robert A. Wagner*

Friends

Friend, you are
   a person I can love,
      whom I can share my deepest, darkest secrets.

Friend, you are
   a person who can love me forever,
      and never let me down,
         if and when I am in need...
            and I'll need you always.

Friend, you
   lend me your ears to listen to my woes,
      never once saying "I can't".

Friend, you are
   someone who shares my tears of victory or sorrow,
      who comforts me in my times of depression or loneliness.

Friend,
   forever is short
      but my love for you is everlasting.

—*Nilda Linares*

Love

You're lovely as a star in all its splendor!
A picture sweet as you, so beautiful and neat as you,
Only nature with its nimble touch could render-
A character replete as you, so charming and discrete as you!

Your eyes so mischievous, sparkling and so bright,
dancing and entrancing every element they meet,
Look deeply into mine and obscure all other light,
For the love they bring is brilliant and the sentiment is sweet

Your lips so full of living, beckon unto mine
with a smile so white and ringing, I can almost hear it chime
Such everlasting sweetness, scarce could one opine-
Oh time's inconsequential and nothing's so sublime!

You're a feather in the breeze as you tip toe through the air,
So nimble and so nymph-like in every move you make,
As graceful as a goddess and doubly debonair,
As slim as a silhouette and fleeting as a flake

In other words you're glamorous, you're glimmering
That is to say, you're sparkling as the stars above you
I mean - oh God, you've got me simmering!
You know I want to say-to say I love you!

—*Leo R. Dantona*

Bosnia

All over the world is the Bosnia word,
A pillar of Islam in the Western world.

On map of the world emerges Bosnia forever.
Her courage and valor will be forgotten never.

They are forced into war by the Serbians.
The soldiers that are unarmed are the Bosnians.

But they never bow down in front of their foe,
No matter how much oppression the Serbians show.

Those Serbian beasts who are committed to rape
Of mothers, sisters and girls of young age.

They demolished the mosques and ruined their country
Inhibited hells to quenching the fire of debauchery

For the dawn of freedom, the sun has risen!
So was will of Allah that caused it happen!

She can't be destroyed by the conspiracies of foe.
Islam can't be dissected from the body of Euro.

The green flag of Bosnia will forever flutter!
The darkness of evil its light will shatter!

Heartache, pathos and blood of wishes combined
Shaikh wrote this poem with pearls of tears joined!
—*Rashid Shaikh*

The Switch

Not born as a lesson of life, but one of dreams,
A place of escape and solitude, yet despair shrouds
life's only light.

History's path lay before one so innocent, never before
seeing the ghosts that would invade,
Life like nature knows no forgiveness to one who strays,
Straight in sight, though it would appear, a maze exists-
the Minotaur within me.

An Autumn wind, a sign of the pilgrimage,
An opiate to the senses as to nature,
Counsel sought,
Countenance to be gained,
Fears and trials laid to slumber.

Through the switch (a tunnels end) a shot,
Silence as dreams are shattered,
The lesson life.
—*Walter S. Krasneski, Jr.*

The Urban Society

Dinkins at the helm of an Urban Society,
A place where artistic dreams begin,
A place where beautiful people are ambulating along the
sidewalks.
A place where different ethnic groups are laughing together.
Majestic lights are gleaming in the darkness of the city.
In the darkness, transforms a whole different society.
A society within a society.
In the daytime, a divergent society is leaped upon the
inhabitants. Traffic, Traffic, Traffic!!
A mass of people wresting along the streets and sidewalks.
This is the society where the police are walking their beats.
Sports plays a big part of the society. Two Major League
franchises call it home. The Mets in Queens, the Yankees in
the Bronx. Sports is just the tip of the iceberg. Ethnic
groups share their cultures with each other. Forget about the
negative aspects of the society, just come and share your ideas
with this Urban heaven. The Society is New York, the Big
Apple, one of America's greater Urban Societies!!
—*Nick Teng*

Tori Rae

A year has passed since that great day.
A proud Grandfather, I am, Tori Rae.
You were so beautiful, then, as today.
It is fitting, then, this first birthday,
to say, I love you, Tori Rae.

What a joy it is to see,
those big eyes when you wrinkle your nose,
and make a face at me.

For you can do no wrong, I say today,
As you set out to play.

Your Mommy loves you.
Your Daddy, too.
For you are an angel, come true.

Grandma's, Grandpa's, Aunts, Uncles, they all say,
"What a treasure we have in you, Tori Rae."
—*Marjorie S. Roberts*

Angel In A White Cap

White light gleaming on
A quiet river, caressing the
moon with warm arms

Quiet words spoken like the dust of angels
Resting upon bright
colored leaves

A gentle touch that passes
With the night as soft as
the wings of butterflies.

Feelings of comfort expressed
as tomorrows turns into yesterdays

Work on my angel, healing broken
Hearts and mending wounds that is left
Bare to the world
—*Nancy Lee Wright*

Untitled

An empty feeling swept over me today,
a realization that you are gone away.
You left us so soon,
so unexpectedly.
But while you were here,
you taught us so much.
How to live, how to laugh, how to love.
At this moment in time, sadness clouds the memories.
But as time goes on and the pain lessens,
the happiness will return, and the memories of happy
times will remain with me forever.
—*Laurie Henderson-Phan*

Christ's Return

Flashing as lightning across the eastern sky;
A star is arising in the by and by;
Up above the clouds does lie;
A sword that is quicker than the eye.

He is coming as a thief in eve;
Eye nor ear can be deceived;
Riding upon a snow white stallion;
Leading God's heavenly hosts, the angel battalion.

Valiant spirit's far above all other's;
Qualified beyond what one could dream;
Fighting for the one-none other;
Than "the rose", my Lord, my brother!
—*Nancy Rhoads Pamplin*

Senses

Imagine a place where there is no scent,
a rose's perfume has all been spent,
no smell of burning leaves in the autumn air,
no fragrant shampoo in the silk of her hair.

Imagine a place where one cannot see
a clear blue sky or the waves on the sea,
the growth of a child, a bird's splendid flight,
the goldness of daybreak, the sunset at night.

Imagine a world where one cannot hear
the tea kettle's whistle, the horns at New Year,
a storm's mighty thunder, a lion's great roar,
the beat of a bass drum, or an airliner's soar.

And, imagine a place where one cannot feel
a happy soul laughing, a wounded pride heal,
the joy of remembering, a broken heart's pain,
the feeling of love at the sound of his name.

It would be lonely with no senses alive,
no love, no flowers, no songs, no sky.
Yes, life may be difficult, but God gave us a chance.
The presence of our senses; our lives they enhance!

—*Menka E. Johnson Neal*

Reserved For Parking

I can remember those hectic days
A rush from daylight to dark
My children were always ready for school
For that was always my Golden Rule!

They now call me a Senior citizen
And that really isn't so bad.
After all those years of running the race
Slowing down really isn't that bad!

Those early years of raising the kids
Kept me running just doing my part
But now they are both married and gone
So, I think I will just sit down & park!

My grandchildren come to see me quite often
And that parking sign then comes down
It's let's go here and let's go there
And lets play on the Merry-Go-Round!

I thank the lord for my blessings
and the good things he has let me see
But I thank him most for my children
Who have been so - good to me!

—*Loma Garner*

A Child's Dream

Ever dream of fields and streams
A streams where there's sunshine, but not a drop of rain.
Flowers in blossom, spring always in the air
When day give's into night, stars are everywhere
Never no need for food or sleep
No clock sounding, no time to keep.
Only time for laughing and running in the sand.
Time for sharing, a fresh clean place,
one of a kind land.
Yes a place in our dreams, may our
young ones hearts never despair, when
we dream we have hope and care.
So dream little one's and dream well, they
my come true only time will tell.

—*Paul E. King*

Love

Love is a quiet beach on a cool autumn afternoon or
a sunset with someone you love.
Understanding someone better than they do themselves and
being there when the one you love needs you to be.
Blind, but knows all.
Wonderful, when experienced,
agonizing, when lost.
Right, and when it is you will do anything to defend it.
The best feeling a person can have.

—*Robert M. Elliott II*

Untitled

To whom it concerns I'm just a normal teen...
A tender soul, with a mind to rebel.
To whom it concerns why do I go alone...
The loneliness echoes with time.
To whom it concerns is my life yet to come...
Will there be a time of my life...
To whom it concerns does someone hear my hearts cries...
Rusting with every aching tear.
To whom it concerns will true love come...
Will fate one day deal me an ace.
To whom it concerns why does every door slam in my face...
Every opportunity seems to shatter like glass.
To whom it concerns is this my reality...
Will the meaning of life appear???

—*Melissa Petersen*

Untitled

A tired eye weeps a dry tear
A tense brow hiding fear
First anguish, then pain as confusion sets in
Another chapter in life about to begin

Like nature's seasons which come with splendor
To time and change one must render
One must be strong and be sincere
For the dreams are real and the challenges clear

Run through the sand. Jump over the waves.
Climb the mountains. Explore the caves.
Free the mind, the spirit, the soul
Enjoy life today, for tomorrow may go

—*Richard J. Gaton*

AIDS

It came one eerie cold wet night,
A thief unknown to human site,
A parasite that eats you slow,
Without us even knowing so.
For it is vicious and it is strong,
Discrimination, to it unknown.
It knows no bounds to pain endured,
It slowly takes you on a tour.
Slowly you will implore, you just can't
take it anymore, and as this thief
breaks down your will, with ease you
mouth in passing still—
So cometh death and take me now;
For you can't be worse than what I know now;
That a love, a want, a need, a search
Has come unfounded — and has left unquenched.
I'll never look back tomorrow; - and for once,
tomorrow comes swiftly.

—*Mildred Medina-Pasinkoff*

Book

I think of life as a book
a thing that makes the critics look
but not at themselves
and this is my story with eight pages of photographs.

Then I hear the blandish tones
over airs and telephones
but no one really cares
and my story is being told by he who lived on intimate terms.

I wanted to see what should be there
through all the depth of foggy flair
but who could give a damn
and this story is an authorized biography.

I tell the acts of man on man
and know what has been banned
I can't find what I really want
but they don't know what they have lost
and my story is an abridged edition.

— *Lee A. Hall*

It Looks Like Rain

A time to live,
A time to cry,
A time to love and then goodbye.
To live again with no goodbyes.
You come back again, like the rain
To open the furrows of the past
Sorrow and gladness comes with the clouds
For happiness...the rain, the furrow closes.
Flax green, with spring blossoms blue,
Clouds white with summer wind.
It storms again, you leave, dark clouds
And summer ends
Until you return again.

— *Robert McRae*

Reflections

I looked into a quiet pool and saw reflected there a face with
a vacant stare. The eyes dim with sadness of the past-of
things seen with sorrow and things that did not last.
The mouth though it did not say a word spoke tales of the
heart-tales that had started in the sunlight and that now had
ended in the night. I stood there aching for this image
wondering why life had brought so much sadness to one person,
and then with the uncertainty of a child I reached out to embrace
this image and then to only draw back with the realization that
it was me.

— *Rhonda Brinkman*

Convict

I pace my cubical, alone from the world
A victim of self-imposed strife;
How many times have I condemned myself
Being absent from normal day life;
At rational times Latticed through my thoughts
I have no ill will for man;
Irrational times power-pressures my mind
It's you and society I can damn;
This stone-cold tomb-radiating fear
Loud thoughts pounding, depression severe;
Stripped of my will, naked of respect
So much lost, I think and reflect;
No matter the crime, the evil and all
That's robbed me of family and birth.
It's fantastic what your life is worth;
So hear me God as only you can
Will you redeem and forgive me my fate?
If not my soul is lost and gone
Oh Lord, is it possibly too late?!!

— *Ronald Wm. Kerr*

Untitled

Wandering through old Westbow Forest,
A voice teasing, tourist! tourist!
Looking around, from where came this sound?
Cardinal in tree, no one around.

Who could that be? A scratch to my head,
Here only a Cardinal disguised in red.
Lacking in thought, I turn to my leave,
When I heard a whisper, it is I Steve.

Wondering worried, who could it be?
It was Cardinal, who could believe?
I gazed upon his clever disguise,
Cardinal you really are not wise,
Humans know of trickery and lies.

Deceiver in red, simply flew away,
Left me discouraged, alone in the day.
Ears were saddened, he did not even say,
It was, I, Cardinal who spoke today.

— *William J. Barry, II*

Simplicity

As I sit here my mind begins to burst.
A wanting for knowledge is no longer a thirst.
The only question I have is why?
Why can't people by happy with the sky?

I can tell you how to rebuild a car.
I can tell you the building blocks of a star.
But I ask myself, "What will these things do?"
I ask myself, "Will they bring happiness to you?

I know why the forest is green.
I know about things unseen.
But who really cares
if genes come in pairs.

Now everyone calls for a revolution,
they say it is evolution.
I only give them pity,
and wish myself simplicity.

— *Matthew Mick*

Being Young

A teenager's life is just what it seems,
    A world built of hopes, a world full of dreams.
The ice-cream parlor where everyone goes,
    The little secrets that everyone knows.
The silly jokes, the favorite songs,
    The wonderful feeling that you belong.
The grades you fail, the parties at night
    The hours it takes to say "Goodnight."
It's having a boyfriend and hoping he'll phone,
    It's having the gang in when no one's home.
It's doing the thing you know that is wrong
    The childish crush that lasts too long.
It's movies and cokes and basketball cheers,
    And having a romance ending in tears.
It's laughing and crying and having fun
    But most of all, it's being young.

— *Patricia A. Agrillo*

Fall

Another fall's dropped into town,
    A model in her flaming gown.
Her cool, coy entrance gives her poise
    She comes forth with not a noise.

A joy to watch the colors float down and round
    But now, a breeze!
Then 'tis still, there's not a sound,
    All her clothes lay on the ground.

— *Merle M. Else*

Injustice

I'm fighting to take a stand
About the misconception of truth
and the deceit of man
I'm not fighting with my fists,
But with my pen
To tell the promiscuous ways of man.

Why am I caught in the middle again
Between a sister, brother and a friend
When will this petty confusion come to an end?
This injustice served now and then
Because I'm the friend.

I've alienated myself from family and men
To heal my wounds and start again
I pray this selfishness and coveting will end
And folks stop walking on the hearts of men
Perhaps one day that woman, man or friend
Will say I'm sorry
And this injustice will never happen again.

—*Phyllis L. Raines*

Universal Star

Universal star, my star shining high in the heavens
above. Bright as the flame of a flickering fire.
How bright you glow in your vast erie darkness of
space of a faraway universe many light years away.

The expansion of traveling time within your galaxy
spreads far and wide as if just standing still.

The experience revealed will be a long adventurous
journey. Your travels in this time and dimension will
bring you to a vast and lonely place. Traveling faster
than the blink of an eye to the cosmogony of outer space.

Universal star, my star. My search is for knowledge and
wisdom. As I travel through time my kingdom of mind
will enrich me with things I should know.

You probably don't know I am searching for a way for
the world to love.

Universal star, my star I found with you teachings of knowledge
and wisdom, I traveled far, I found my home of peace, among
your stars, in this dark erie place. Far beyond the reaching
of the moon, here in outer space.

—*Westley Thomas*

My Daughter I Give To Thee

Here's to my daughter, the bride to be may you be blessed
abundantly may happiness follow you down through the years may
your arguments be few, and your babies sweet and dear may your
husband always stay by your side and love continue to grow as
time goes by may the sunshine always shine upon you and yours
and you have family and friends galore, may the Lord keep that
beautiful smile upon your face daughter of mine let no man
erase to my son-in-law, you are more precious than gold to you
I give my daughter to have and to hold take care of her,
protect her with your life go through this land together as
husband and wife name you mean the world to me, to you I give
name please keep your arms wrapped safely around thee, let her
know love like never before close out the world, don't let
gossip in the door go through this world hand in hand you are
bound by God as woman and man there will be many obstacles to
climb but just knowing the two of you, I know you won't mind
Name you have entered my family we welcome you with outstretched hands be good to my baby that is why she chose you as
her man she gives you her heart she gives her soul to God her
mind belongs to her put them all together. Everyone has a part.

—*Muriel Eaton*

The Creek

As I walked through the green swaying meadow, the wind blowing
across my tan face, I picked a long blade of green grass to
chew on. I was heading for the creek, where I used to fish
with my father.

The creek has beautiful blue clear water. As it flows
downstream, the white caps hit the rocks. God made a beautiful
picture to paint. If only I could be an artist with my hands,
I could paint on canvas the lovely visions I see in my head.
You could see the fish jumping and springing over the rocks, as
they were going downstream.

I was born on the Cherokee Indian Reservation, and could see
the Indian maidens doing their laundry at the creek. In my
vision, I could see them catch their fish for supper. After
returning to the reservation, they clean and cook their catch
for the warriors who came in at night fall.

—*Roberta Johnson*

Memories And Hopes

We have struggles down the river of life,
across the rapids of exotic paradise.

We have bridged the crevices of life,
through the use of the book of ancient and Holy knowledge.

We have sat upon the chair of sorrow, only dreaming
of tomorrow.

We have been tempted by exotic dreams,
to some we submitted, others, we omitted.

Our earlier environments, home, school, church and
children, have led us up the stair steps to heaven.

Finally, we reach the sea of contentment, where,
once again, upon the horizon we see clouds of love, rays
of hope, and visions of our life to come.

Oh, sweet life, sweet dreams of tomorrow, what in our
destiny will you show?

Will our lives be happy, or will it be full of
sorrow?

No matter, no matter, today is ours.
Goodbye, goodbye, oh sweet yesterday's flowers.

—*Wallace D. Kuykendall*

Time Warp IV

I was a secret agent licensed to kill
Adventure, money, guns and gadgets for a thrill
But it's a fast life and sometimes too short
Never know who'll shoot you when you file a report
    Any corner I turn could be a time warp in my mind
    A surprise on any street anytime day or night
    Something waiting for me to place me in a bind
    Then it's time warp time or at least get out of sight
I was a mountain man living out in the boondocks
The trees too tough my cabin was made of rocks
I killed my own meat and panned a little gold
But I can't go back there the place has been sold...
...I was a poet for about fourteen of the years
    I was all pen, they thought I was all ears
    I'm still a poet and a dreamer at heart
    Here comes another time warp, what a work of art

—*Stan Thirsk*

A Moment

A breath, a sigh the wink of an eye. A flash of light from
afar; the swiftness of a falling star. All this and so much
more a moment has in-store. Our life is lived without a care,
never to stop and wonder, if you dare, that life, although so
grand, is simply a moment, a moment strand. Like grains of
sand along the shore, strung together for the ocean to pour.
Our time, the same, each moment a grain. Together a beach, to
live through life's pain. The rain, the snow, the sea, all of
us fighting to find the key, the key to life and death the
same; for moment by moment they each have no name. Alas! a
moment and moments of excitement and bliss, you, have brought
about a metamorphosis. One to another the moments they cling;
happiness, joy and elation you bring. As the sands of the hour
glass abate, with child-like expectation I await... The next
moment with you, my key my destiny.

    —Michael Calo

Cancer Dream

We laughed, dined, sang, - waiting for Christmas Eve.
After the dinner cordial, - we toasted, wished in yearn,
had a sudden malady, - put me on Stage, sieve.

New years Eve, I was told, - Active cancer, within
the unfamiliar illness, - Tears flawed, on that Eve;
I was startled, and weary - befuddle, of what bred in.

Received the final right - vague, the want to live
my young life, was ending - yet..., having a beginning.
Heard my father say, - God, see my daughter live.

In this aftermath, the anguish - the dark passage, starting
all festooned with needles; - all torn by wounds, I repair
nature parts, replaced, - by science, are healing.

I ask myself, it's a dream? - Is it real? This cancer Air?
I only lived, a few spring. - I am, at the beginning.
Will I outlive? This dream? - Wilt get out, of this appear?

Epiphany, am well again. - Nature, replacement
I have a price to pay; - but for life, thin payment.
Now: thereafter, the pain ending; - willed, a new beginning.

    —Maria Attilia B. Barra

My Brother's Not Heavy

Love is there for us to take

It's the lion lying down with the lamb.

It's the dove mating with the hawk
After their display of an aerial courtship.

It's roses blooming out of the barrel of a gun
Put there by a flower child with the help of
A riot-geared officer.

It's the white hand clasping the black's shoulder
As he cradles in his arms their infant child.

It's the blood from the finger of a Jew mixing
With that of an Arab's.

It's the protestant and catholic worshiping
together in Belfast while the Irish republican
army disbands and the British Bobby returns home.

In the end - it's the aids quilt
being adopted as the universal symbol
For world peace.
Covering us all with its warmth and humanity.

    —Mary Zilli

We Are Remembering

We are remembering your non-violence teaching
  All along your way,
And the timeless ideals and goals and
  What you had to say,
We are remembering your long journey to
  The top of the mountain,
And the dream that it revealed as you drank
  From heaven's fountain.
We are remembering that we must push
  Forward for equality and peace,
And our struggle against inhuman acts, we
  Will fight until it cease.
We are remembering that you made live and
  Love as part of your quest,
And we shall continue the struggle until
  We, too, are called to rest.

    —Yvonne R. Myrick

Blue

See the little girl sitting there
All eyes and a bunch of hair,
She pats her pup, she is ever so kind
And looks into his eyes to read his mind.
"Your eyes are blue but one is half brown
Some say you're too ugly to take to town.
Your coat is brown and black and grey
But I don't care what people say
And just 'cause you've got a floppy ear
That doesn't mean that you can't hear.
You walk that way 'cause you broke your leg
And who cares if you can't sit and beg.
You've chased enough cows around the farm
So lay there by the fire and keep warm,
It's okay, old fella, named Blue
You snap and bite but I love you!
Just lay there and have a good moan
I'll pat you until I'm all grown."
See the young woman sitting there
All eyes and a bunch of hair.

    —Naomi Babb

Homeless

There was an old man who didn't have shoes.
All he could do was drink booze.

That old man didn't have a shirt,
and all he could do is live in the dirt.

He didn't have food
and he lived in a box all taped and glued.

That old man didn't have a house,
and what's worse than that, he didn't have a spouse.

He didn't have anyone at all who cared.
He thought his life wasn't worth being shared.

So that old man lay on a park bench
and no one even knew he died till they smelled the stench.

    —Terrie Leib

Dark Night

    The night holds no shadows,
      all things are clear.
    Moving through the stillness,
      nothing remains hidden.
      With senses heightened,
you navigate not with eyes but with mind,
      with heart.
Sight does not distract from what you see.

    —Peter Brian Buikema

Dad

When I am sad
All I have to do is call my dad.

He has always been there for me.
Even though my eyes would not see
How much I needed that fatherly love so desperately.

I refused that love for so many years
Till one day it turned into tears.
For my eyes opened and I could see
Just how much his love really meant to me.

I went through life feeling empty and sad
For I could not accept the love from a man who wanted
    to be my dad.

My feelings remained the same for years
Till that day I broke into tears.
For I had learned to face all those fears
That had hid so deeply within my heart.

Upon that day I faced that fear
I realized I wanted to accept that man who wanted to
    be my dad.

    —*Tonja Means*

Ending The Confusion

Nothing but confusion enters the heart,
All of life's pressure poured into the pit of the soul.

Everything in the mind's eye dwindles away,
Nothing remains but empty frustration and total migraine.

It seems that nothing remains of importance,
Though everything revolves around the necessities within.

Every so often a whisper of hope falls upon us,
Then fate tares it away as if it were paper thin around us.

After all the fog of the world's waste clears,
What remains is the refuge of a brutal society at war.

If hope is to remain intact within us,
Then our barbarianism must let go of the hatred inside.

Our hearts must open up and accept failure,
Then search for solutions to a pagan idealism of peace.

Inside the conscious minds of us all,
We must deal with our own deaths so that the world may
    survive in the souls of the children...to end the confusion.

    —*Timothy G. Power*

Doctrine Of The Soul

    Sometime in the near future,
all people will be equal as intended from
    the beginning of time,
We will love one another with our hearts from
    deep within our souls, be free of
    the burden of judgment,
    There will be no war, crime or poverty,
for one hundred lifetimes,
    Disease, man made disasters, will be
banished from the earth, they cannot
exist in an air of pure harmony.
    The sun will shine and warm, just as
the rains will quench the thirst of all that
lives, life will flourish.
    We will all be rich in love, health, wisdom
and peace of mind.

    —*Sharleen C. Hutchins*

Alligators

An alligator can be under your bed.
Alligator live in the water.
Sometimes they can walk faster than people.
Alligators eat people.
Alligators can bite people.
Alligators are green.
Alligators have sharp teeth.
Alligators have scary eyes.
Alligators feel bumpy.
Sometimes they feel slimy.
Alligators have a tail.
Alligators eat butterflies and birds.
Some alligators are white.
Alligators eat ducks.

    —*Mrs. Keller's Kindergarten*

See the Weeping Willow Tree Alone...

See the weeping willow tree
Alone in the meadow where flowers once grew
Where love and sunshine made life anew
Where the stars dance and sing
Rejoiced at everything
Where the water moved along merrily
And white doves spread their wings
See the grass now brown and wilted
Buried beneath two hearts so sad
Saying goodbye to the love they once had
See the water once filled with a bright reflection
Now grey and still... with no direction
Picture my little one
The light shone in her eyes from morning
Till days done
I wish you joy in your meadow anew,
I'll never spend a day without you
Forever you dance in my heart
Whether we are together or apart.

    —*Sheryl Minter*

Heart And Head

My head tells me one thing and my heart tells me something
altogether different.

People tell me to leave you. That you are no good. They say
you will just hurt me again. My head agrees, but my heart
tells me something altogether different.

Sleep don't come easy. My heart wrestles with my head. When
it concerns you my heart wins every time.

There are times when I say I'm going to do something about it
then my heart stops me. I just can't win where you are
concerned.

My head tells me one thing and my heart tells me something
altogether different.

Yes, people call me crazy. They say I'm a fool for staying
with you and taking what I'm taking and I guess they are right.
My head agrees with them, but my heart tells me something
altogether different.

My head tells me one thing and my heart tells me something
altogether different.

    —*Maxine Howell*

Life

Life is much more than we know,
    Always so complicated and trying.
There are many extremes of highs and lows,
    And sometimes nothing stops the crying.

Life is so short and can be sweet,
    Filled with hopes and dreams.
Enjoy the many people you meet,
    Think of their love and not of their schemes.

Life is an expression of happy and sad,
    Looking for approval of what is done.
Always weighing the good and the bad,
    Hoping for the best possible outcome.

Life is always full of wonder and why,
    Spent seeking out answers never to be found.
Occasionally reaching a wonderful high,
    And then realizing you must find ground.

Life is sometimes an unsettling place to be,
    With untold haunts and memories to face.
So your time is spent in search of the key,
    That will release the darkness from every place.

—*Marilyn Simms*

The American Custom

It is the American custom to be free until we die
Always the American custom to hold our head up high.
We are a new born nation but we have a battle cry
To embrace this whole wide world so others do not sigh.

Our pioneers came in numbers from many distant moors
And penetrated to a land that had no bolted doors.
They came to foreign places that were both wild and free
Where with God and freedom their needs would always be.

They saw the changing seasons that gave reason to see more
And yelled a cry of "yonder" to another distant shore.
In wagon trains through miles of plains on horses or on foot
The need was ever onward to a place they could take root.

It took courageous hearts to push on through deserts dry
And over snow capped mountains that nestled clouds to sky.
We owe them honor mention and salute their victory
And pray to God in Heaven we uphold their history.

—*Masella Messenger Rowe*

The Quest

Am I delinquent in my duty as a man?
Am I sure I'm doing all I can?
How can I know my mission here on earth?
In what way can I demonstrate my worth?

These questions are a few of those I ask.
To seek the proper answers is the task.
To start I must no longer go astray.
I'll not relent until I find the WAY.

I've tread the path of knowledge: books and learning.
And with all this my heart continued yearning.
With many facts accrued I'd still decry
That I learned how, but, still, do not know why.

Experiences broadened by perspective;
Many chosen, others not elective.
My knowledge mounted with this new supply.
I know a great deal more, but, still, not why.

I defiantly refuse to court defeat.
There are answers to the questions I entreat.
Through the world of sense I'll never find my goal.
The true Path lies deep - rooted in my soul.

—*Ralph Del Pizzo*

Why Won't You Love Me?

Why won't you love me, too shy or mean,
Am I too young not good enough?
This poem comes from my heart.
I Love You.
Can't you see you fool?
I wish I was never born if I can't be with you.
Without you I'm a shadow in your dreams.
You're two years older, but age doesn't matter to me.
I will always love you, even though you don't love me.
When I asked you out, you said "No."
Now I'm shy around you, I can never face you again.
Can't you see I need you? I Love You!
Why won't you love me?

—*Sabrina A. Tullis*

America

The poet once said
"America is hard to see"
But the girl from Wisconsin confides in me
America sees
the hard and the heartless.

The poet twice said
"America is hard to see"
But the girl from Wisconsin confides in me
America sees
hard and heartless.

Heartless the Poet said
"America is hard to see"
And the girl from Wisconsin confides in me
America sees
Hardly.

Hardly the poet said
"America is hard to see"
But the girl from Wisconsin wonders with me
Does America see?

—*Ursula M. O'Neill*

Freedom

Freedom is precious at any cost
amid this troubled world of wars
at a price of a million slain from coast to coast
none died in vain, yet we beseech no more.

Even now at the break of morn'
as well, we know all pain and scorn
a million, a trillion soldiers has been sworn
hurriedly to defend, homes of sorrow's an' scorn.

—*Lagracella Omran*

Winter Child

I was born in a blizzard
amidst steel and concrete
the snow was cold grey ash
and I was very young

Winter was icy barren beauty
for a few months all life was frozen
and I would feel warm and secure
in the bitter emptiness around me

Now I am older and winter comes again
the season changes and so do I
now there is a warmth inside me
that is frightened and lonely
it finds no solace in the snow
and if feels lost in the cold that surrounds me.

—*Steven M. Gordon*

My Best Friend

My best friend is as sweet as
  An American Beauty rose;
She always thinks of others first,
  Her thoughtfulness really shows.

How I wish she lived next door,
  Or, maybe, across the street!
Then, we would say, "Good Morning," together
  When, each day, we'd be able to meet.

But, we cannot be together just now,
  The next best thing to do
Is just to wait a bit longer
  To see if wishes do come true.
      —*Laura E. Gunby*

Marylou

  A loving mother you've been so long.
  An anxious little girl to grow so strong.

  You named her Rebecca and she was so young.
    Now her songs have all been sung.

  You gave her your love and still it grows deep,
      but now she must sleep.

And though we weep, his open arms called for her,
and there she went, because an angel he had sent.

      Sometimes life can be unfair,
But my dear sister-in-law, your sorrow we share.

      —*Mary Rietta*

The Rainbow

A rainbow is a promise of good things yet to come,
An arch, some say, to bridge the gap from Earth to God's
  kingdom.

When we are young, we hear the rain and wind and thunder roar.
Then it's all o'er, the sun peeks out, and a rainbow we adore.

Of fairy stories, we may hear, of golden treasure hidden form
  sight.
Or is the treasure in the spread of glorious color and shimmery
  light?

God sent his promise in a bow to Noah in the Ark,
That ne'er again for forty days would the Earth be so wet and
  dark.

And now I see the rainbow holds a promise greater still,
For a life that's everlasting, to be together again, at His
  will.

And so, My Love, though I have gone, and we must be apart,
I'll ask God to send an angel to place a rainbow in your heart.
      —*Mary Ellen Hardy Grayot*

The Child Of The Season

Amidst the glitter of the night
  An eastern star appeared in sight
Its brilliance shone with golden worth
  Proclaiming to all, a royal birth
Not Baby Doe did angels tell
  His name was called Immanuel
A special child was born that night
  To take from darkness all men to light
We celebrate with pomp and 'stance
  The birth, the child—"divine romance"
For through His life does God reclaim
  All who will trust in Jesus' name
So my friend, if you believe
  Confess, be saved, and Christ receive

      —*Mel Waters*

Armageddon

Asleep in the willows lies a little bitty babe. Quiet as
an evening breeze does the little one sleep. No cares, no
worries, no fears, but beyond the willows the world lay heavy
sorrow for the babe who's asleep in the willows. Man had
reared its ugly head and brought death to the babe in the
willows. Not swift or kind but slow and steady like the
ticking of a clock. When man lays his heavy hand upon the
ground things never quite recover to what it was, as hunger
stirs the little babe in the willows. More frightened does it
become as hunger form within churns a painful twisted smile.
No mother for the babe who's asleep in the willows. How
swiftly death becomes the end of all creatures. But how has
man done such a terrible thing. And has death then become
such a terrible thing as man as well as the babe in the willow
will someday cease to create its presence known. So as man
struck down the mother of the babe in the willows, so will he
smite himself with his heavy wasteful hand.
      —*Jones*

Family

Somewhere there is a link,
An infinite bond in the chain of things.
Invisible mucilage holds it tight,
And toughens the strength within its rings.

  I see in my daughters' eyes the gleam
  Of a brother's rollicking humor and jest.
  I hear in their voices familiar tones
  I have heard for years in all the rest.

  I start, and glance again at a smile
  I know I have seen on a sister's face,
  And remember a gesture of other hands
  At another time, in another place.

  Our mother's concern for the care of us all,
  Our father's wise words that led us right
  Are echoed again in our children's ways,
  As they follow a path that is still in sight.

And I know that indeed there is a link,
An infinite bond in the chain of things,
And love is the mucilage holding it tight
To toughen the strength within its rings.
      —*Ruby Corley Dewbre*

Prelude To Nicky

  It's hard to know the phrases,
    And all the things to say;
  To such a special granddaughter,
    On this sentimental day.

  But it seems just right somehow,
    To say these things today;
  You're very close in thought and heart,
    Not now and then, but always.

  It's here at last, that day of days,
    And oh! Those wondrous years;
    Seems like a fleeting moment,
    Of laughter, joy and tears.

  You think now of the future,
    And what it holds for you;
    Knowing you'll work extra hard,
    To make your dream come true.

  Be kind to those around you,
    Give help to those in need;
  Have faith in those who love you,
  Trust God, and you'll succeed.
      —*Margaret R. Clark*

Missing You

I'm sitting here thinking of you,
and all the things we used to do.
It's so hard to realize we're done,
No longer are we one.
How many times have we been through this?
This time it won't get better with a kiss.

There isn't any laughter or a warm embrace,
Helping me to get through the day with a smiling face.
I can't help feeling this way.
You always knew just what to say.
Maybe if we just tried to talk things out,
and try not to shout.

I want us together again soon,
So we can sit together under the moon.
And I want it to be like it used to be,
Me always wanting you, and you always wanting me.
Please, lets give us another try,
make it work, and never say good-bye.

—*Lindsay Harshman*

Preview

It's early September
And along the roadsides

Aspen leaves quake,
chatter in brisk breeze.
Purple lupine rolls out royal carpet.
Goldenrod and yarrow spread wealth in fields.
Cat-o'-nine tails
clad in brown suede uniforms
march in close-order drill.
Scarlet sumac crop up
like flag bearers in the parade.

Harbingers of autumn,
they herald, proclaim....
Riot of color to follow.
Vibrant hues on the way.
Cranberry crimson,
pumpkin orange,
burnished copper,
smoky gold
soon on display.

—*Lee Brezina*

Oh Creator!

When the order to my body, to descend it to the grave,
and be given my spirit, and I have to appear before my God,
and go back to that, oh! ground, from all of we were made,
before, I plea, my Lord for mercy, and remember... not in vain,
that I delivered all my works to you, of love and faith!

May I raise my eyes, as of you spiritual converted,
where you live my Lord, to the third heavens,
I will glorify your name, Oh, the universe Creator!
of the life you showed to me, the flowing waters,
and the bleeding of my wounds that you have cured!

To the stone and wood, with human faces I worshipped:
crying, kneeling, begging: they will never listen.
later I understood were you whom my prayers answered!
the light of your word came; before was blindness,
from endless and deep, and dangers paths, you gave the lightness!

You said to me: make treasure, not in here, but yes in heavens!
Where you are living oh! My God, remember me, have mercy!
I am almost at the end of this my life...
from my existence the clock, go back the grades...
then, I beg to you my Lord, stop the appointed hour to the grave!

—*Maria Sui-Qui deBanda*

For Mimi

I dreamt of her last night, I felt her embrace
And breathed in her fragrance.
And as in days of old,
I heard her high toned voice, full of eloquence.
I met her eyes as she spoke to me,
Green and blue, happy Irish eyes,
Full of life, I was entranced.
Roses bloomed in her cheeks
And, crowning that happy face,
A crown of red gold curls for the sun to touch and to sparkle.

So real, so near, and yet so far.
And then me thought, I could not speak, she could not hear
As if an invisible gate separated us.
I could not tell her the things left unsaid
I could not tell her "I loved you".

I could not ask for her blessing.
And I thought, was it because I had never said goodbye
And so, in the red gold sparkle of the morning light,
    I awoke and knew that she was gone.

—*Linda Falzone Barth*

From The Lessons Of Land

I am reminded where the winds cry constantly
and burnt stone sun up to down
lays across the ages of land
that was here before we were anywhere,
or the owl began to sleep away the day;
I am reminded of the wild will of rivers
racing through rock to marry with greater waters,
leaving only their track of gorges
and fossil printed fish where they swam;
I remember because all parts of me were there
and the symbol commemorates in the wind and in the stone;
I am replenished by the scrubgrass left to gaze on
just as the sheep who feed on it now;
signs of the wanderers wind through the hills
but the flats of sage meadow go on and on forward;
I am reminded by baskets of toilers
that the land is to yield if we gather and go;
taking just what our fish mouths can swallow,
leaving the rest for the next living fellow;
I am reminded of all I should know.

—*Ruth S. Agoos Villalovos*

Not Forgotten

We used to stare at the sunflowers
And dream of how it would be
For you to be in love with me.
You never tried to love me, never knew how,
But that is all the past now.
You left one day and never returned,
I hung around with a heart
which was broken and burned.
Still hoping and wanting you to love me,
But knowing all the time
You deserved someone who was above me.
My hair is still as brown as the
chocolate we shared,
My skin as pure as the daisies you
sent to show you cared.
I always loved you and always will, I think,
As I walk, everyday, through the
meadow and over the hill.
To your place, where you lay absent and away.
I cry as I wave, to your angel who sits upon your grave

—*Michele Gerbino*

Dreamer

I dream of the moon
  and dream of the earth
I dream about death
  and dream of birth.
I dream about you
  and dream of me
I dream of things I know
  cannot be.
I dream a lot and maybe that's bad
  but dreaming makes me happy whenever I'm sad.
cause to dream is to live
  and to live is to be.
but with out my dreams
  I just wouldn't be me!
  —*Terie Paige*

A Nice Day Together

I wish we could sit down together
And drink a cup of tea
But since we can't when you drink this...
I hope you think of me
With love to share
And friends who care
And life's finest things are there
For you to bare.
  —*Nettie Katz*

"Dada"

"Dada" was the first name I called from my crib
And everyone knew then that your fate had been sealed
    "Papa" renamed from that day on
The sun rose with your smile and set with you gone
      I would seek your kind face
        Your eyes gave me solace
        Your wise words I absorbed
        They gave my life promise
To just see you smile gave my heart such elation
That I loved you so dearly was my heart's proclamation
  And now you are not here, I wish I could reach you
   They say you are happy, I just want to see you
    Is it such a crime that I do miss you so?
    I cherished you dearly and couldn't let go
  But as time goes by all you were will be me
    For I am determined to still let you be
  And I know you will always remain in my heart
    My "Dada", from us you never will part
  —*Melanie Pitts Martinez*

Unsuppressed

When you've learned to catch a cloud
    and feel the atmosphere
When you've learned to touch a void
  and reach for a handful of dreams
    that you can share

When you've learned to hug the air
  and embrace solidity —
even when there's nothing there
When you've learned to cast aside
  hypocrisy and foolish pride

When you've learned that truth is free
  and peace of mind is honesty
    Only then you'll truly see
    the friend that you can be
    to you and me and humanity.
  —*Phyllis Paul Davis*

I'm Thankful For I Don't Take Time To Thank

I am thankful for family, friends and relatives,
and for their continual love that always lives.
For my fellow students, 10th graders,
and for the earth and moon invaders.
For the air, wind, sea, and sky;
and for me, myself, and I.
For hands, legs, and brain;
and for flurries, snow, and rain
For the three stooges, Larry, Curly and Moe;
and for needle and thread to sew.
For Tom and Jerry,
Joseph and Mary.
For night and day, light and dark,
and for Yellowstone National Park.
For sensation,
and God's creation.
For my finger and toe,
and for Edgar Allen Poe.
For yellow, red, green and blue,
and for Carmen Sandiego's discovering clue.
  —*Reena D. Paul*

Treats of Dr. Zollicoffer

A wonderful doctor lived on our street.
And for youngsters he always had a treat.
Whenever they hear his car make a stop,
They ran to look for a lollipop.

It never seemed to matter how many,
For there would always be a plenty;
To satisfy little desires and taste.
Then away pattered little feet in haste.

You abided by the oath of Hippocrates.
You were sometimes alerted for just a sneeze.
You'd lend attention to our every sob.
A strong dedication you had for your job.

From New England's coast to the Southern Span,
One will never find your kind of a man.
In all kinds of weather we've seen you labor,
To aid a patient and even a neighbor.

Along toward evening about six o'clock,
Thoughts of you linger with kids on the block,
As we lift our hearts in an earnest prayer;
We wonder if you think of lollipops there!
  —*Lois H. Martin*

If

If we could have a spiritual intercourse
  And gain the intimacy we lost
If we could entwine our minds
  And bring forth our souls
If we could touch each other's hearts
  And nurture our love
Then life would be beautiful.

If you could look into my soul
  And see its bleeding wounds
If you could hear my pleas
  And heal my broken heart
If you could see the truth
  And try to understand
Then we would have a happy life.
  —*Nena Aragon Decena*

Pass It On

Since God has washed my sins away
And given me a brighter day
I'll pass it on in some kind way
That others too, may know you Love!

I look around and what I see
Is multitudes that seem to be
so filled with hate and misery,
And act it out - that's plain to see

Now - "The Bible" tells us of a happier way
That really can be lived each day
With faith and trust in One True God
Who sent us "Good News" from above

Angels, spoke and sang of God's Great Love,
Who sent us Jesus from Heaven above
He came to sacrifice His Life for our sins,
So would you open your hearts door
And invite Him to come in!
—*Mabel A. Solheim*

The Revolutionary

I approach the hedgerow
and glare across the open field
where the soldiers look like candles
on a cake in their coats of crimson.
The sweet smell of honeysuckle transcends
my senses until the cloud of soot and smoke
fills the sky.

The musket bucks, the bullet flies.
Its iron tip tears into my flesh and I fall.
The night drops its curtain over the
battlefield which now becomes my graveyard.
The honeysuckle dies.
—*Matthew B. Morrell*

The Dream

Rainbows dance on unicorns backs
And gold can be found in potato sacks.
Wonderful, mystical things happen here,
A place of no sorrow, no pain, and no fear.

All people, all races, all getting along,
Living together in unity, and singing one song.
I listen intently to hear the words of the melody.
They sing about a brotherhood, and solidarity.

They sing a song that's both happy and sad
They sing about the hatred for each other they once had
They sing how they're world almost came to an end because
they could not rise above and transcend, they're hate within.

And as smoke appeared, right before I awoke
I saw a man come close and point at me as he spoke.
He said, "If you don't love all races, your world will end.
It'll be destroyed by your hatred within."

I have pride in myself, I have pride in my race
But people of all colors I'll love and embrace
And maybe one day everyone will love each other
And call everyone of every race, 'my brother'.
—*M. L. W.*

Forever Last

Today I stood before a judge
And got a divorce from up above,
I don't want this, I wanted to scream
You're taking everything away from me.

And yet I knew my love was gone,
He didn't care because he was alone
He didn't mind the nights alone
Or the long lonely days that hurt me so.

He's a loner he says, and seems to like it.
But I remember the nights when I lay in his arms,
And we loved each other until the dawn!
But now he's gone and I miss him so.

This man that I met, not too long ago,
We laughed, we loved and we made plans,
But my world ended today, as the judge said,
Divorce granted, he's not your man!
—*Lavada M. Maples*

Trapped Goose

You were born free with the gift to fly,
and happy to dance with the wind.
Your sky is bluer than ever but you can
only look at it. The other geese
are flying in the sky, they are inciting
you to follow them
but you can only look at them.
What could you see now?
Your eyes are weighed down by the snow,
by the cold. They call you louder and louder
but you can only hear them.
Memories are reminding you of blooming meadows
and blue skies. Your wings are trying to fly again
but you can't dance with the wind any more.
Your body is trapped in the ice.
On the river of the lake I am crying, powerless
and my tears mingle with yours.
—*Palma D'Alessandra Marchesi*

A Thought For Today

Although the road we trod seem sometimes uphill
And hard to climb with weight that's very heavy
That may slow you down but we must not give up

We must press onward toward the mark of our calling
We must not stop or look back at the stumbling
Blocks that has been in our path so long

We must believe that we can achieve and reach our goals
We must never say we can't but always say We Can
We must continue to climb the hill until we reach the top
We must not stop no matter what we are confronted with
No matter what we have to endure

We can succeed and we can overcome the negatives
And learn to be positive I believe we can
We Can! I know we can!
You can

We all can!!
—*Sarah Pines*

288

Undying Love

I was thinking about Mom
and how it used to be
When an angel came from Heaven
to comfort me
She took me by the hand
and in it placed one seed
She said, "Plant this in your heart
for a rose will grow indeed"
Some petals shall blossom with memories
for which you'll hold so dear
Everlasting peace has come to her
so do not shed a tear
The others of pain and sorrow
will eventually wilt away
But all the love you have for your mother
forever it shall stay

—*Linda S. Urbano*

Secret Place

There's a secret place, where I hide at night,
and I cry myself to sleep,
Because the only way I can find myself
is hiding in my dreams
The night is full of reality and fantasy I
long to see,
I can either rejoice in rappiness or
wallow in misery.
A dream I had since I was 5 and
it never gets old,
In fact people reminisce night time
when the story's told,
Any religion, any race my sister
and my brother,
And sex or disability we still love
one another,
My dream is so beautiful or at least
that's now is seems,
wouldn't it be even better if it was
more than just a dream?

—*Modestus Ashes*

True Face

I hide behind my confusion
and I fear the unknown, hoping the pain will leave
when your true face is shown.
Guessing and wondering what your trying to hide
makes me really curious
if there is a true man inside.
Like a small child you lead me down a road
with many street sings
but only one way to go.
Knowing that rejection is not to far away
keeps my feeling inside
and my true heart at bay.
Hiding behind a mask of mirrors
you reflect what I wish to see
while at the same time asking yourself
do I really want this
and could this really be...

—*Shannon Nichols*

My Beach

I walk along the silent beach,
And I feel the sand under my toes.
I sit down and look out at the never ending sea,
And I feel totally isolated.
I hear the echoes of laughter from people long ago
And I hear the weeping for lost loves.
A single tear slowly rolls down my cheek.
At the time between the warmth of noon and the coolness of night,
The sun's rays seemed to have missed me,
The cold wind wraps it icy fingers around me.
The sun slowly slips below horizon,
And the sky turns colors of soft pink, purple, and red.
The sky slowly fades to a warm black,
The first stars peek out from behind a cloud.
The wind dies down,
And all around me people wish upon a star.
As I walk out of the beach,
I pick up my head and straighten my back,
Because I know I won't always be alone.

—*Meg Stone*

Hopi Tale

The sun bled upon our fathers' lands
And I touched the earth with my hands
We went north to the back door.

The earth touched me in her response
We laid down and we wept in the ground
We went north to the back door.

Our prayer will be heard
We will carry the word
The spirits breathe truth in our hearts
Our five clans emerge with the power of the word
We go north to the back door.

Northward, still northward the star led us on
'Till a mountain of snow blocked the sun
We were north at the back door.

Still the door of this fourth world was closed unto us
But the woman said, "Call on your sons
To melt through this back door".

Our prayer will be heard
We will carry the word.

—*Linda Bonavita*

Trouble In The Land

There is trouble in this land, trouble in this land
and if my good Lord don't soon intervene,
we won't be able to stand.

There is crime and murder everywhere you go
and people are hating each other so.
They don't care what they do,
just so they get back to you.

Please, please, dear people out there,
all this crime is getting you no where.
Behind some bars for the crime you have done,
if you were thinking you could have shun.

There are many a person in jail today
who wish they had gone another way.
Being loving and kind with a noble mind
and living the Christ like way.

—*Sadie Allen*

The Golden Keys

Come walk life's road with me
And I'll share with you the golden keys
Than unlock the doors of life's mysteries...
Oh, I promise that they are free.

The first is love, encompassing all,
Reaching out, holding strong...
A binding force that cannot fall,
A knowing that you are not alone.

Service is the second key,
Strong as the first, totally free...
Service to God and our fellow man...
A labor of love in a master plan.

Friendship is the greatest key,
Something given, again it's free.
A gift that returns so much more
Than the giver ever gave before.

Come walk life's road with me.
We'll share whatever is held in store.
We have the precious golden keys...
We've only to use them to unlock the doors.

—*Perry Ann Boyett*

The Melting Man

The haunted man kills the hunter man.
And I'm laughing at the words of the burning man.
For the clocks are melting in that desert and you
need time to fly. But instead you run. For the thorns in that
bush are cutting you and you trail like a perfect path to
the castle on top of the desert. And the resurrection of that
screaming tree, for it breaks and cracks from the lumber
man. And the silence of the sacrifice of the lumber man. And
the tranquility grows in favor of the baby held in that
castle on top of the desert, pulls up a chair as a failing
physician. For you are stunned by the death of the lumber
man and you are singed by the fire of the burning man. And the
dread of the day to come pulling you further and further
away from your ability to reach back and grab what you once had
and pulling you closer and closer to the end. And having
crossed the swords of the peasant boy coughing up blood like a
dripping rose of the deepest red draining from his stomach.
And here's to you and a thousand dark knights the worthless
effort I have accomplished. For this is the melting man
fading away and his arms wrapped tightly to his heart.

—*Tatum M. Moore*

Memories

I remember the first time I looked into your eyes
and in your arms you had held me so tight
We fervently kissed each night away
And our bodies against each other we so longingly pressed
Feelings of passion and lust were being newly born
as we danced together, under the stars that so brightly had shone

I remember the first time I looked into your eyes
and in your arms you had held me so tight
The world around us could crumble and fall
but in your arms I would've still felt safe and secure
Our love and lives have grown apart
We went our own separate ways
A far cry from what we once shared in our hearts
I now look back on the first time I looked into your eyes
and in your arms you had held me so tight
Thinking about it now still makes me want to cry.

—*Samira Abbas*

Echoes Of My World

I reached out to the world
    And it embraced me

I became
    A Sabra planting seeds in barren deserts
I became
    A searching student - in Tiananmen Square
I became
    A worker in Soweto resisting apartheid
I became
    A fisherman in Valdez mourning his poisoned catch

I reached out to the world
    And it embraced me
It gave me
    A new hope for lush green fields
It gave me
    A home, bread and education
It gave me
    A real equality that knew no color
It gave me
    An Exxon-free sound, river and ocean

I reached out to the world
    And it embraced me
While I waited — for its echoes.

—*Shirley Brezenoff*

My Blue Bottle

I have a blue bottle that sits on my shelf
And living inside is a wee little elf.
He comes out to visit me when I'm alone
And takes me to places I never have known.

We run through the mountains and breathe the fresh air;
We swim in the ocean and chase the fish there.
We fly with the eagles and dive like a jet,
But there are still things we haven't done yet!

When it's time to return from our journeys afar,
We jump on the tail of a bright, falling star.
We share our adventures, he knows what I like.
He even agrees that my wheelchair's a bike!

I never have seen him, but I know he is there.
He never has spoken, but I do not care!
He is there when I want him; he's my special friend.
He hasn't a name, so I call him, "Pretend."

—*Marilyn Marnon*

Untitled

As their eyes met
And mine gazed from above,
I knew their passion for one another has been set
So unto each, a shot of my arrows of love.

Determined to follow the course of this event
My duty to have her in his arms is what I have been sent.

Why, his life so complicated?
NO doubt in mind what his feelings are;
A fear within he has created
Is close to being loose yet so far.

The time is close at hand
Only now that he's beginning to understand
That he must let her know;
His feelings for her he must show.

He thinks to himself what she will make of this:
"Let me fade away from your memory
Or let me feel your kiss,
For I shall know my fear has been set free."

For the first time ever with an open heart he is able to speak
To be in that girl's heart eternally is what he tend to seek.

—*Michael Van*

Invitation

-Come to my life- you asked me once
and mine was flowering.

I didn't board your boat, wild one,
I didn't run through your valleys, nor your forests,

in your arms the dawn I didn't see,
nor Vesper in the crimson afternoon.

-Come to my life- you ask me once again,
and with your kisses I now want my redemption.

Of my autumn today I offer you my landscapes
with my skies full of colorful clouds;
on my boat and at dawn we will catch
stars with my net and with your oars.

—Leonora Acuna De Marmolejo

Virtue

If my love fables sublime the sky
and mountains surrounding me;
then the love I feel burning in my heart
like a passion is not mine, for it no doubt
belongs to the full forces of Nature itself.

If my love destroys like dead leaves
consumed by fire everything that is noxious;
then there is in me someone else
that is not me — none other than a superior
being with full power to acquit the soul.

If my love survives and does not give up
to the sudden strikes of storm and winds;
then all of the force of Nature
is nothing but a meek gesture,
in comparison with the Love of God.

And because God has showed me His love,
I have understood in full, after a long journey
through life, which place in this Wonderful creation
is the one allowed for men and women to belong:
the virtuous vara stick of good and evil!

—Maria de la Luz Valenzuela

You'll Grow To Love Me

My tiny heart has started to beat
and my body is starting to grow.
There isn't much to tell yet, because
there isn't much that I know.
When I lie here motionless, I can
always feel that you are near.
Pretty soon you'll find out that there's
a little body growing in here.
You shall feel my tiny hands and feet
when I decide to move about.
I should warn you now, you'll feel
much pain when I come out.
Mommy, there's just one more thing
I'd like to say, "I love you."
I know in my heart, that you will
also grow to love me to.

—Tonya Lee Kitzman

It Rains

It rains
    and I sit, looking out the window
        at the dark, rolling clouds
            the flow of mellow music from the radio
and it rains
    and darkened sky weeps
        covering the earth in its tears
            its cries of anguish clear in the air
and still, it rains

—Tracy Kirkham

Epitaph

With a light heart I ambled 'cross knolls of green grass;
And my eyes quickly swept o'er the headstones I passed.
Not much thought did I give to the mortals who lay,
Nor their souls who, now judged, were in that Endless Day.

Then, decrepit and worn, one stone stopped my quick glance,
For upon it were words which were seen not by chance.
God intended my eyes to upon these words fall,
And no true child of God could turn deaf to their call.

"Mortal men know not when the Almighty may call;
To collect from them souls which He gave to them all.
These gifts were to men given as pure treasures then,
And expected they are without traces of sin."

As I read those words, simple, I knew why I lived;
For my own soul to God I one day must then give.
Since He trusted me with such a trace of Himself,
I must cherish its worth and increase its great wealth.

—Natalee Theriot

Final Sanctuary

Twilight smothers a burning sky
and my guard tumbles to the ground
as I run free
among the dark, twisting branches
of trees as old as creation
as I run free of questions and fears
and expectations and regrets
free of pain and guilt and disapproving eyes
Decaying leaves, once green, rip underfoot
as I flee mindlessly through the winding trees
from the life I left behind
towards the truth that shines ahead
I stop in a wonderful place
soft and inviting
where no eyes watch nor lips laugh
Maybe I will rest in the beautiful emptiness
of this new freedom
for I feel warm and peaceful now
and a long rest may save me.

—Ricky Radley

Apricot

As I lie upon the grass that pricks the skin of my back
    and my legs,
my eyes arise to the summer sun
That beats flushing redness into my burning cheeks,
I open my lips to luxuriantly bite the warmth,
and my hand reaches out in midday lethargy
and plucks a ready-to-fall apricot from the tree.
Lips feeling it in advance, my hand brings it closer to my mouth
And its liquid warmth pours down my arm,
drooling down my chin, on to my chest,
seething with sweet flavor on my tongue,
heat of juice against my already heated teeth;
sucking the saver into my throat,
I let it engulf me for one gloriously fulfilled moment,
till I spit the pit out onto the ground
and the process of the seed begins again.

—Scott Giantvalley

Only Yesterday

I remember...when footsteps would make my ivories shine...
and just a touch sent shivers up and down my spine.....and
a firm stroke expelled ripples of unbridled joy....from the
caressing fingers of girl or boy...but now in this day of
Electronics..TV and VCR'S.....and tiny fingers stroking
the wheels of juiced up cars...I sit in my corner...unused...
unwanted and forlorn....just an old Piano...a toy..whose
day has gone.

—Oliver A. Darden

A Place Of Your Own

Where is there to go, when one wants to be alone?
And once there, what is there to do?
There is a place that I have been shown
Which has so much beauty in its view.

Its name will change, for one person to another;
The decor within, may, also somehow vary.
There is quiet and calm which sometimes smother,
A field and sky so vast they're scary.

There is always the music of a resonating song
In the normal days activities dins stead.
If allowed, we'd linger the whole day long
For this place exists inside your head.

—*Richard Dukes*

Choose Your Steps Wisely

Your future lies before you like a drift of pure white snow,
and only you can decide which direction you will go.
With each step you take you leave an impression behind,
so choose your steps wisely, you never know what you will find.

Life is full of surprises, it's full of ups and downs,
Around every corner new experiences can be found.
The people you will touch will affect your life as well,
so choose your steps wisely, don't be afraid that you will fail.

You have so much to learn yet, so much left to do,
your life is just beginning, your nowhere near through.
So choose your steps wisely, and no matter where you go,
Your future will lie before you like a drift of pure white snow.

—*Stacie L. Sisk*

Does It Matter

Why does it matter if our chair
And other things need some repair,
What do I care if the walls are cracked
And many things our house does lack.

What does it matter if the shades are torn
And our best carpet old and worn,
What matter if we have no light,
Our love makes our house shine bright.

What matter if our house is bare,
We know that a great love dwells there,
Our house doesn't have curtains of lace
But it is still just our little place.

—*Mabel M. Montgomery*

In A Christian World

An unknown person killed a soldier today
and part of our country died
As a member of arm forces, he swore to protect
Will be buried with him as well as his pride.
The battle field he travelled on was no easy game,
His duty to our nation, will bring no fame,
The flag of country will fly at halfmast,
For all of veterans who died in the past.

The enemy who killed him, will suffer no remorse
But the young soldier's family will suffer of course.
His commanding officer will fight for his rights,
while his dear old mother will have sleepless nights.
Many of our people will be killed at the firing line
It could be a friend in your town or mine.
While we sleep in comfort and may think he is fine
Yes it is heroes such as he who puts his life on the line.
Now his spirit walks the street he used to play,
he stops to greet and humbly ask all to pray.

Dear Lord, our God in Your infinite wisdom remove our fears
That this world and all nations will live in peace all of our years.

—*Ralph Merigliano*

Thanksgiving Prayer

Dear Lord I want to thank - you! For all the things I've got,
    and pass along a prayer to those who do have not.

I often sit and think, then pray for things from thee.
I then ask why, you passed me by? Others need more then me!

So why am I possessed, with thoughts of selfish greed?
When you always make a point to give the things I need.

Now, Lord it's thanks I'm giving, for all you give to me.
    This time I hope and pray, for those who really need!
            Amen

—*L. Aryn Sieber*

Tree Of Greed

Now that we have killed Santa Claus
and poisoned the rain,
tomorrow's children will have to
place childhood play on indefinite pause.

They will learn instead the adult games of beg,
borrow, cheat and steal. Winners have the distinction
of one who has won and lost. The reward? They will
plant the seed whence grows the tree that breeds the greed.

The final yield from this harvest might well be bitter,
unpalatable fruit on a withered vine, conceived and
contaminated in toxic time. Man, unlike the beast of
the field and the birds that fly, has failed his test.

The test that lower forms of life passed on the highest
level. For what he's done, (MAN) natures cautions gone
unheeded, broke all the rules for lasting existence. He
violated earth. In so doing, he fouled his own nest.

—*William James Tremper*

My Sheri Jean

Heaven has a double chin, a rosebud mouth with a tooth within,
And pudgy little knees which a sidewalk hasn't scraped,
And deep blue eyes in which sorrow hasn't gaped.
In the beginning an accident of fate,
Months of misery, then a whole life to dedicate,
Heaven hasn't scolded me, or even sought revenge,
For my thoughts in those days of darkness without end.
Heaven wears hand-me-downs, she never seems to care,
She knows my love for her isn't mere cloth to wear,
Don't anyone say or try to demean,
The angel from heaven is my Sheri Jean.

How the years have passed, and now she's fully grown,
She has a little angel from heaven all her own,
That's the way life is, and ever ought to be,
Don't you think that I know that God's been good to me?
Heaven has a double chin, a rosebud mouth with a tooth within,
Her name is Robin, a grandchild supreme,
The ultimate present from my Sheri Jean.

—*Peggie Greuling*

Robin's Egg Blue

I remember that robin's egg blue blouse
And how I felt that spring.
The fragrance of the early blooming shrubs
That nearly burst my being
Never smelled that way before or since.
And nothing ever touched my feeling
Which was raw
In just that way again.
And I do not long for those throbbing, vibrant times.
Make no mistake, I'm glad I had them.
But they are buried in the past
Much too strong, intense, and deep to last.

—*Martha Adams May*

Rome

Ah, sweet Rome, bells forth, ring clear,
And ringing, thus allieve the tear
Of bitter recollections, sweet,
Which both now meet
In your resplendent gardens, villas, streets.
  Recollections: sheltered in the drone noontide,
  Along the walls of Trinity;
  Or by the glossy Tiber side,
  Or in the embracing shade
  To attendant olive branches keep
  To guard the fount, recalling Medici.

Recollections that, like a peeress, lovely damsel,
Presides, and gazing o'er the wall,
Surveys, in silent splendour, her domain:

  The Colosseum, St. Peter's dome,
  And von Campana's fertile plain.

Ah, sweet Rome, once more the mind beholds
Clear bold seraglios, spires cold:
  Stark tribute to the Byzantine.
        —*Ricardo Martel*

Just For You

Just for you, I'd like to take the sun,
and save it for the darker hours
to light the way.

And gather up the moon's smiles, putting them
in a safer place than just the evening's sky.

And knowing all the stars were tucked away
for you to grasp at will - would you waste away the sunny days,
or savor all the love I have to give, the way I give it
just for you.

And just for you, I'd like to make the evenings long and cool
and push all the clouds into someone else's night,
to keep the storms away.

And send gentle rain to wash away all the doubts,
And happy dreams to fill whatever void would be created.

And taking all this goodness for your own,
would you while away the meantime in search for more —
or simply hold me close,
and share the love I have to give,
the way I give it,
just for you.
        —*Susan M. Schlotzhauer*

The Dreamer's Open Prayer

    I sing my song, the dreamer's open prayer
      And sing my song, my lover my only care

  If I could be with you I would share my life
      When willows weep I am your wife

        And as I lay my head to rest
        My heart and soul are at your breast

  So come with me my lover, together we will sing
    To hear the bells toll, their verses an open ring

      A never ending circle, my never ending love
  We will always be one, we will be blessed from above

  Two lives will intertwine, two hearts shall beat as one
    We will live as a single soul, may God's will be done

    So sing with me my lover, our dream has yet begun
Become one with me my lover, until we no longer share the sun

    Hold me tight my sweet love, never shall we stray
    For now we have come together, until our dying day

    Now sing our song, the dreamer's open prayer
      And sing our song, my lover my only care
        —*Lisa Chirigos*

Each Time We Meet

So as each week passes, there are tears of departure
And smiles of arrivals

As we walk I feel your stare.
I turn and there you are, beaming.

I feel unrest,
For your eyes look into me, through me,
To the stars.

I know it's the stars,
Your eyes reflect their glow,
Your heart, their wonder
And your smile, their warmth.

I have never known such surety.
I have always desired it,
So curiosity grows.

You refuse my self doubts and quickly stroke all concerns
I instantly feel your strength.

Time closes in on our senses.
As we speak, words fade into memory as expectations grow.

You arouse my heart and my mind stirs at the thought...
Of being in your depths.
        —*Victor Sabino*

Old Winter Sea

Yesterday you were crystal clear and blue,
And tendered by sweet summer's song.
Yesterday you were warm and young,
And host to the great throng,
Of gentle friends who flew and swam,
Of children who touched your sunlit crests,
And ran along the sloping sand.
But now you're dismal, cold and gray,
And rough hewn by winter's wind.
Now you live alone and in your way,
As if to pay for hidden sins.
Winter sea you froth and foam
And hide behind the sandy dunes,
And probably wonder, in dismay,
If there will come another June,
When once again, you will be
young and gay.
        —*Ronald Sarkis*

Hurt

When someone hurts us we hurt them back.
And that's not healthy for us
because we're always getting hurt
So if someone hurts you, you have three choices.
One choice is to hurt them back.
Choice two is to drop them.
And your last choice is to just keep taking the pain
And don't do anything about it.
And I don't know which one you pick but for some
reason I end up choosing the last choice to do.
But don't keep the pain inside to long because that's worst
them just hurting them back.
So whatever you do, don't keep the pain inside,
get it out by crying, yelling, writing poem about it,
talking about it, or hitting something.
        —*Shanha Stephens, Age 14*

Homestead

The Idaho, Kentucky or Wisconsin grass is knee - high
and the breeze is smooth.
In the freshest dawn there is a woman running through
the field, her arms embracing a love that's all around her.
In her house that resides by the last hill, pancakes are
cooking. The scent floating past children's admiration
up to the heavens. The house stands in the passing of all
time and its generations while its white painted wood
remains cracked. There are no fences on the homestead,
just a big patch of green.
The green of the drifting meadow that stretches on and on.
Through the gentle life of a farmer and the grass that
shakes like a belly dancer in God's whispered wind.

—Shontay Nevels Luna

Only For A Moment

I feel the poverty
and the misery, only for a moment

I feel the loneliness
and unhappiness, only for a moment

If I could feel
for longer than a moment, the wonders I would do

I would erase poverty
and misery

I would eliminate loneliness
and unhappiness

If I could feel
for longer than a moment
the miracles that I would work
the hearts that I would heal

If only for a moment

—Salome Bon

The Wind, The Woman, The Desert, The Sea

The wind blew the sand in circles
and the sun had thirty years aged her.
Her skin wrinkled and dried
and the desert went on living.

The wind blew the water in circles
and raindrops pelted the surface like pearls.
The sky grew dark and the water angry
and the sea went on living.

The wind blew the circle of water
and the circle devoured the land.
The desert and sea had come together
and the circle went on living.

The wind pulled her into the circle
and the rain replenished her youth.
Her skin soft and supple
and she lived for the day.

The wind blew the circle back to the sea
and the circle left her lying in the sand.
The sun hot on her skin
and the desert went on living.

—Tamara O. Heater

Vertex Of Death

I plunged a sharp knife into my womb
and then I did not hear that night
the beating of a fleeing heart any more
which had been a faithful confident
of my confused soul and embittered senses.

I tied over my motionless skull
late afternoons of death
and over my empty bones
a strange solution of wretched ashes.

Maybe the mist has blurred my sight,
maybe the fire has consumed my reason,
and here I am:
Begging you not to forget me
when the vertex of death comes.

Oh, keep my memory alive
and if for lack of time you forget me,
only after that
will I have died completely.

—Roberto Day'Left

The Prisoner

There is an "I' In each of us,
And there is an image of the I,
The I is the prisoner of its image
Crazy, afraid and shy.

I try to break out, image forms a wall
In the innate comprehension of life I become so small.

Like random molecules, I's move around.
Yet like prisoners, Each are gagged and bound
By the image.

Yet, I forms the image,
To take I through its life.
Everyone is aware of this old tale
Yet people are so naive.

Image changes from place to place
I stays inside like a stone,
Like Angelo said to Countessina,
"I must do what I must my feelings are my own"

Imagine there is no ego, no images and all is cool,
I's could have such a wonderful time or do you think
Dalis, Lenons and Dylons are fools?

—Sarbojit Mukherjee

A Ray Of Hope

I'll drive a knife through my arm deeply
And wash away the blood with soap.
I'll even jump a steep cliff.
But isn't there a ray of hope?

I'll sit down on a chair willingly
And tie myself up with thick rope.
I'll even watch myself dying.
But isn't there a ray of hope?

I'll make myself put on a blindfold
And laugh as I try to grope.
You may ask me in the meantime
If there is a ray of hope.

I'll take away my joy and laughter
And try my best to mope.
But even if I do these actions
Isn't there a ray of hope?

I'll watch my life as it gets worse
And I won't even try to cope.
Because in my dreams there is no light.
But is there a ray of hope?

—Vivian Lang

Untitled

I saw love in my dream.
And what did I see.
I saw a little man shooting an arrow at me.
As the arrow moved so swiftly through the wind.
I said to myself could this be the end.
It stuck me directly in my heart.
And then I felt chills of some sort.
And as I was opening just one eye,
I saw my wife lying at my side.
She was looking so beautiful and looking so sweet,
as she laid there so deep in her sleep.
Then I put my arms around her and kissed her gently
on her luscious lips,
As my hand caressed her backside down to her hips.
Her skin felt smooth like a baby's bottom,
and her hips are as soft as freshly bought cotton.
Then I though to myself, oh now I know,
That little man was cupid that shot the arrow.

—Tony Jones

Silent Dead

Fourteen years to this day he lies there in the ground
And when a traveler wanders by, he is to hear no sound
For in the valley of the dead, a graveyard stands alone.
And in this graveyard, silence sits on dirt and sand and stone.
And all the dead ones lie there, in their grounded beds,
And they will lie there always, alone - the silent dead.
For who wants death in a city full of life and joy?
A death that steals indiscriminately, even the youngest boy?
Of course, his parents mourned the loss and cursed the evil one
Who tightly held in his cold hands their one and only son.
They'll always weep and cry for him and sadly bow their heads
And know that their beloved son's soul is yet undead.

—Roy Wright

"Sunup" Or "Viejo Amanecer"

He was "sunup" to all who knew him
And when given his fill of mash
He'd run with his soul like the wind
In the race they called the 100 yard dash

Life was but a game to him
For which he had a knack
He liked to have his belly scratched
And sometimes farther back

So how does one say goodbye
To a friend — of so many years
To think that this friend could die
Would cost too many tears

I pulled the bridle from his ears
And said my last goodbye
Like — thanks for all those years
Better go before I cry

Years have passed my bones are tired
And my hair has turned to gray
But just as a priest remembers his prayers
I'll remember "sunup" today

—Wm. Howard O'Brien

To The Experts (In Comradely Sympathy)

Rankling like hunger when blood-sugar's low,
Anxiety grips us when we do not know;
And spurs us to imagine what might be,
And shield the image when facts disagree;
Better a dressy fiction when one goes
Abroad than flagrantly to wear no clothes;
As to the facts, we judges are, and trustees,
And must not maim for profit, like Procrustes.

—Sam Nelken

Untitled

For now...we are leafs upon his tree,
    and when we have fallen, are gathered and burned
we will be that smell upon his coat
    and be with each other always.
        Tallen

My summer is nearing its end... I can see autumn approach,
    no hope of sharing the things of spring, no hope of capture
    again.
Now, a strong gust of wind nearly blows me from my feet
    and as I brace myself in this gift of an almost forgotten
        spring,
I find this wind begin to blow warmer,
    comforting me against the chill I thought so near,
and a truth slowly joyfully begins to form in my mind....
    Although the moon is red
        light still descends,
    Rivers still flow when shadows deepen,
        perhaps, after all, this is not the end.

—Thomas L. Allen

Solitude

Where are the stars tonight
and where is my love
As the stars are hidden and beyond
my grasp, so, too is this love
If I should scream and pierce the night
with my longing
would this light and gentle breeze bring
the matter to you
If I screamed in my mind would this lay
to rest the desire you've awakened in me.
O desire, why have you cursed me so
And love O love—
A star has appeared, dare I hope
No but it is alone
Shall I sit here under this vast sky
hoping for two, three or thousands
O this night, a single star
    and me!

—Vicki Crystal

The Fighters

Softly first, the North Wind stirs the leaves
And whispers - "Sleeeeeeeep".
The leaves shudder and sigh,
Then float - willingly.
The earth accepts the leaves to blanket the plants
Who doze - peacefully.
Yet the Evergreen shakes his branches
And laughs - haughtily.
"Oh North Wind, give me your bitter cold.
Give me your snow; your icy breath.
I will not sleep - silently.
Blow North Wind;
And I will smile and sing to you
My song - triumphantly!"

—Shelley Lande

Rose

Just outside my window, there's a beautiful fragrated rose;
a little bit of heaven, a gift from God, I suppose.
What really has me puzzled, has my heart really torn,
is how something so fragile can be surrounded by a thorn.
But Jesus wore His thorns for all the world to see,
how could he endure such pain?
Well He did it for you and me - Jesus
survived His thorns, & so will that
beautiful rose, we can survive our thorns,
as long as we remember, He knows!

—Shelia Mitchell

295

Two-Four

With all my heart's strength
And with difficult labor,
I will triumph the spirit of your young heart.

Upon springing these words
To your everlasting soul,
My voice might not be distant or in vain.

I will speak of your beauty,
And those endless eyes
Until this affectionate dream fades and ends.

I will remember your words
And every breath you spoke,
Until my shadow can no longer stand.

I shall struggle and prevail
Unto your young heart,
And envision the day I wish your love forever
—*Peter A. Wong*

Illusion Of Life

Progress we marvel at the electronic wonders,
And yet we can't seem to do anything about hunger.

Information traveling at the speed of light
And yet many of our children can't even read or write.

The SST takes us from here to there in the blink of an eye,
And yet we abandon our old, so relieved when they died.

Magnificent sky scrapers reach for the stars,
And yet our homeless mostly live in broken down cars.

Politicians leave a bad taste in your mouth.
Unemployment is rising and all our jobs are heading south.

Higher education is supposed to insure you a piece of the American
    Dream,
And yet when the cost sky rockets, all you can do is scream.

Urban violence has us afraid to even walk the streets,
Untrusting and leery of anyone you meet.

We Americans, think we are so smart,
This may be true, but we've lost our heart.
—*Rick Roberson*

Christmas Postscript

When the holiday dream has ended
And you sit in the after glow,
While the candles are dimming slowly
And the fire embers burning low,

As the carols fade in the distance
And the snow is melting fast,
And the holly withers and ages
Are you wishing the vision will last?

Hold fast to the beauty that's Christmas
Let it shine through you all the year,
Be as sparkling and bright as the tinsel
Make a heart warm to have you near.

Keep the spirit alive within you
And as the days come and go,
The true meaning of all that is Christmas
Will brighten the after glow.
—*Margaretta Morris*

A Country Morn

The crimson light breaks through the sky,
Announcing clearly that morn is nigh.
With vacuum in hand, Rose begins her work,
Echoing the coffee as it starts to perk.
Farm hands arise and appear in the field
While owners to third cups of coffee yield.
Out of the muddy ditch, with head so sore,
Katt staggers to work as each day before.
From the door the merchant removes the bar.
His first patron now steps out of his car.
Milton the milkman comes dangling along,
Leaving his products and departing in song.
Trailers of cotton are off to the gin,
Ready to be emptied and filled again.
The kids stumble outside, all in a fuss,
Dreading the ride on the big, yellow bus.
Mom sweetly smiles as the chaos is o'er,
Thanking the Lord that it's morn no more.
—*Nancy DeVaney*

Mother

Another newly dug grave,
Another body laid to decay.

Another family dying from hurt,
The men wipe tears on sleeves of their shirts.

The women use tissues, they can be sad.
Funeral directors are the only ones glad.

Everyone dies sooner or later,
Then laid to rest in a six foot crater.

Morning continues for who knows how long,
All they can think is their loved one is gone.

Lives will continue, this much is true,
But my simple question is why was it you?

I remember the day of our "last" meeting.
You left in anger, my heart bleeding.

You only wanted to love me as a mother should,
But due to the situation, you never could.

I wish you could be here today and forever,
We could start to make our lives better.

My memory aches for you to return,
But you're gone for good and sometime I'll learn.
—*Todd Karas*

Personality

Why is it that one person is peaceful & content.
Another gets drunk & abusive to an awful extent.
When people are sober they are more coherent.
The people they bother most is the ones that are related.
I guess it's because you're not using your heart
You're using your mind.
You become more firm not kind.
Try not to get drunk & stay on the straight & narrow.
Start today don't say I'll start tomorrow.
Ask advice and stay in touch.
Don't become a lush.
—*Robert J. Allocca*

The Immigrant

My love has brought me to a distant shore,
another land, so far away from home.
A land quite different from the one I knew,
and yet a land, that I now call my own.

The years have passed. And things that I once knew
are distant now; are memories so old
that they become the stories of the past,
stories, that are to children's children told.

But there are moments that it seems as if
a door has opened, and I see just so
the house and neighborhood, the street and town
where I once lived so happy, long ago.

And then I know, that, what once was, still is,
kept in my heart and in my children's, too.
And all the shores are bound by endless love,
by brotherhood and trust and courage true.

—*Ursula E. Pansini*

Nando's Theme

Another day with destiny, another night's despair
Another thin lonely breath of icy mountain air
Another makeshift funeral, another urgent prayer
Another chance to contemplate the sorrow that we share

Bottle up the melted snow, ration our reserves
Place the dead in icy graves to keep them well preserved
Manipulate the radio, try to keep it tuned
Search the sky for solace, the familiar crystal moon

Give me strength to face the mountains and the bitter cold
I've emerged from this wreckage now sixty days old
I march to save the others, perhaps their last hope
Are my chances as steep as the grade of this slope?

Partaking of our meal, the flesh of our kin
Instincts of survival emerging from within
Outer layers stripped, our soul must endure
Of the promise of rescue we're no longer sure

Give me strength to face the mountains and the bitter cold
I am the survivor the world will behold
The most important lessons in my life are being learned
I must not falter now, I promised I'd return

—*Sean P. Dickson*

Autumn Memory

Driving down a two lane road
Anticipating the splendor of fall
Reminiscing from youth
The size of maples and birches tall

Many years have passed since childhood
Will the brilliance of colors compare
To those etched deep in the heart
Which the mind's eye carried everywhere?

Closer as familiar mountains appeared
Flowing together as two breasted lines
The breathtaking brilliance of yellow and red
Could not my soul confine

A statement of nature with grandeur
As the layers of gold, orange and green
Indelibly imprinted in memory
For future recall of this autumn scene

Shortly the trees will be barren
As the season of winter draws near
Yet the glorious, luminous picture
Will remain in the memory so clear

—*Marcia Waldbillig*

Mark,

I still have the paper people we created together.
Anxious eyes strained to grasp the forms
As we outlined shapes on white, blue-lined paper.
Carefully we gave life to our world with crayons.

We entered a world of make believe
Till our voices were alone in the night's still air.

I marched behind you, as a shadow follows a traveler in
moonlight. But driving forces of diverse waves swept you from
me, dashing your beautiful black body against stones that rose
above the water. You would not stop. You would not die, but
lived on without me, left me standing, searching for a
needle-pierced arm and fiery eyes to stare into.

Mark, my friend and beloved brother,
I see your sullen, black face behind tall gray imprisoning
walls. Where doors slam and keys turn
To lock me out, to lock you in.

Your face is amongst old, yellowed paper people.
They are bent, crumbled and unsmiling.

No voices ring in the night's still air.

—*Tamar E. Woodhouse*

Upon A Night Time Dream

After the sun has fallen down,
appears the dreary night time clouds,
rainbow's hiding behind the hills,
owl's hooting in the wind.
Crow's are circling all around,
doves glisten behind a cloud,
lakes shimmering like silver tinsel.
Crystal dew drops upon the emerald green leaves,
the moon glimmering like a loan candle flickering
in the dreary night.
The wind howling in the skies,
scented flowers fill the air,
upon a night time dream.

—*Lauren MacLaren*

Inner Self

Beauty within itself should not be wasted; fair flowers that
are not gathered in their prime rot and consume themselves in
little time. I see a cloud shaped like a grand piano. Ready
to flood our oceans and sea. To feed the sky again as vapor
from the ocean as a mist that rises so high, it reaches the sky
and form another cloud. Only the rain never tires. One strain
at the skies for miracles, when the sky itself is an illusion
and marvels of atoms and cells and nervous systems. Which make
miracles seem trivial, to look for miracles is like looking for
the end of the rainbow. The rainbow with components by passage
through rain drops. The order of the clouds is red, orange,
yellow, green, blue and violet. The red being bent least and
the blue most. The rainbow is not painted - it is pervasive.
So silent rainbow, one would think a lark. A songbird notes
are in order. Daydreaming usually occur doing a rainbow.
Enjoy your daydreams. Above all make them creative by linking
them to your goals. Time escape, a major factor. Old faithful
yellowstone's most famous geyser erupts fairly regular
intervals of about an hour. During time lapse. Light the
velocity of light which has been measured many times is 186,000

—*Robert Joyner*

Along The Water's Edge

In a dusty room, I found her picture
As a gleam of light shown through.
I caught my memory taking me back
to a place that I once knew.

My eyes could see the sunrise
and the water's mist dancing in the air.
I could feel the chill of the morning
as the wind swept through my hair.

At a glance, I thought I saw her
silhouetted as clear as the day.
I ran to try to catch her
but she had slowly drifted away.

I felt a rebirth of life inside
for now I know I can move on.
She may no longer be standing here with me
but in my heart, she's never gone.

I sat the picture safely in its place
upon the window ledge.
Then I felt her spirit flying
along the water's edge.

—*Terri S. Anderson*

The Ghost

Plastic, protean plasma pulsates
as a Phantom fathomless in panting and
pandering after passion's leisure in pastures
protected from parasitic pain, playing among
the unsheltered shadows where lovers have lain.

Chasing down dreams in coves and meadows,
guardian of the night, orphan of love,
white as midnight is dark, circling certainly
its quarry, like a shark til it wanes in the
dawn, wandering and wondering where his
companion can be, fusing with the other of
light, and not till the next night free.

—*Leonard Warzynski*

That Moment Lost

From out time's vault where dreams are kept,
As bright and poignant now as then,
Undimmed by all the bitter tears I've wept,
That moment lost comes haunting me again.

If given second chance to choose, my dear,
Would heart rule head, with reason flung aside?
Or does that moment only shine in memory clear
Because, that long-gone day, it was denied?

—*Mary N. Moore*

Death, The Sounder Sleep

Weep not for me,
as death approaches and knocks.
While I, unprepared answer.

Am I so wicked to have tasted death
so soon.
The shadow of things to be surround me,
throwing a chill into my dream's aspirations.

I am filled with fury, the struggle,
of my mortal being is now lost.

—*Renata Kacprzyk*

The Most Wonderful Land

The prairie is a sea of grass
As far as sight can carry
The grass rolls along in the wind
It looks like the waves of the sea.

Insects thrive in the prairie soil
No bug repellent to worry about
Worrying about being stepped on, forget it
Just do whatever you want whenever you want.

To the people of the prairie
Land is precious
For it grows the grain
That is used to make the bread they eat.

Buffalo roam on the land
Indians used to shoot them
Not for fun but for survival
The buffalo meant clothing, food, and homes.

The prairie is a wonderful place
Not too far away
Just trust me it's great
The length and the breadth of the prairie.

—*Shannon Duffy*

Child's Fear

The fear from the child's eyes
As he foreseen the future of the world.
The child experienced the love and hate of war.
Between mankind
The child's love is an amazing how the child
love for their own little world.
If the child hates, that child's
would start a war on themselves and others.
As the child see their city
burning brightly in the darkness of the right.
The fear of the child's eyes seeing their world.
Coming to the end of time.

—*McCarthy Susan*

Time To Say Good-Bye

The old man wept silently
As he knelt beside death's bed.
The tears rolled down his pallid cheeks
And pooled onto the old, gray, pillowed head.
She was dying, this crumpled lump of flesh
In whom all hope his life was blessed.
They'd lived sixty years together,
But no one ever said that sixty felt like six.
Now, after the years had passed,
And kids had grown, and teeth were fixed,
And grandkids were married,
It was time for her to let life be.
The man let go of the old frail hand
And longingly gazed down at her.
He thought of all the times and dreams they had
Yet no gold, no frankincense, no myrrh
And he breathed a breath and sighed
And kissed his love good-bye.

—*Tiffany Armocida*

Whispers of the Mind

BORN into corruption, violence, destruction, hatred, and despair.
AS humans it's our legacy for the young, innocent, and caring.
THEIR lives so precious, and full of wonder.
HOW can we watch there twisted faces seeing our insensitive
    horror.
EVERYONE slowly killing each other....friend or foe it doesn't
    matter.

IT'S everyone's fault,
NO one's left unshamed.

TIME has come for us to gather together.
HEAVENLY father, teacher, lover, brother and sister.
EVERYBODY, every single day, in every single way.

LET'S help each other,
INSTEAD of hating one another.
GIVING love from a golden heart freely.
HOLDING back won't help you spiritually.
THE time to spread your wings is now, not tomorrow, or
    yesterday.

OFFER spiritual freedom anyway that you can, to every person.
FOR blessings may come and hardships most surely lesson.

GO for now, you're aware of my pleadings.
ONLY you can decide if you'll hear my call, and help my world,
    and stop her bleeding.
DO let me tell you the answer is in, every first letter of her calling.

BATHE IN THE LIGHT OF GOD!
    —*Romi Lee Bilodeau*

I'm Not So Concerned

I'm not so concerned about the race issue
as I am about the human condition

I'm not so affected by female oppression
as I am by mental suppression

I'm not so moved by economic recession
as I am by learning cessation

I'm not so saddened by the physical death
   of a loved one
as I am by the spiritual demise of the
   same one
    —*Wanda Flowers Peacock*

Soul Mate

Empty vastness filled my restricting soul
as I helplessly watched my love flow down
the drain of rejection and pain once again.

My mind pleaded with my heart to stop the
constant torture but my determined love symbol
smiled and reassured the body that she was out there.

The one angel sent to earth to become one with my
yearning soul was planted in our world somewhere
And we just needed to wait for her to bloom.

She would melt the frosty loneliness that chilled
my spine with her heated passion and inviting
arms of eternal warmth and protection.

The dynamic description of this wonderful person
con-ed my trusting life into following the
risk-taking heart into the unknown but hopeful future.
    —*Michael P. Harlow*

My Departure

One night was spent with rain and thunder
As I lay listening to it talk
Of people, places, spirits and things
That made great kings walk
As I lay in wonder heaving the steps that rain made
And the stomps of the thunder
I became hypnotized and my mind and soul spiritually plundered
Then suddenly the winds grabbed a desperate hold on the waters
And the thunder ceased
While mind and spirit had traveled over waters
Reaching heavens to the highest plane of reality
I became one and my body was laid in peace

    —*Marshelneal O'Neal*

Untitled

They laugh and they mock
As I look at the clock
It reads quarter to two
Nobody knows what I'm going to do
15 minutes before I step out
Into the cold, bitter, endless night
Nobody wakes because nobody cares
As the devil urges me, do you dare
I take the rope and hang it to a tree
A voice says, they won't even miss me
Those last thoughts were on my mind
When I stepped out and slowly died
Now people step out and say they're my friend
To bad when I was alive they hadn't been
But please understand, I'm not mad at you.
People alive need friends to.
    —*Randall Lewis Young*

Crisis

Pangs of pain suffuse each day
as I mourn your death.
Stupefied by sorrow
Confusion envelopes me.
Tangled in tentacles of tension
decisions become impossible.
Adrift in a sea of uncertainty
I remain quiescent
terrified of moving in any direction
fearful that the foundation of my life
constructed on the concept of self-confidence
will collapse and take me with it.
    —*Nettie A. Halpern*

Just

As I make my way I am just a nobody.
As I walk the leave will fall,
As I think the bird will sing for
just is my cause,
And life is passing me by, and
the ending there is no just
reason for I am just a no body.
I am falling deeper, deeper each year,
As I asked question I wonder about the answer
is there just reason for I am just a nobody.
    —*B. Hayes*

As I Walked Down The Street One Sunny Spring Day

A new doll was sitting in a store window display,
As I walked down a street one sunny spring day.
Then I sat down, and I thought, and I wondered,
Why, without any reason, did I think of my mother?

Then it hit me, and I had a wonderful feeling,
And so I would not forget, I wrote it down, for my mind is
sometimes failing. I remembered my doll, her name is Michelle.
I remember telling her secrets that she would not dare to tell.
And as I told her, she looked at me
As we set out our blanket and sipped our tea.
My doll, Michelle, was always there,
Like the time my beautiful pink dress got a tear.
Also like the time my single tear fell.
I did not cry due to her, for life with her is no hell,
It is opposite, it is heaven, even just as grand.
For every time I turn around, there is her hand.

My mother's warmness is there, every single day of every year,
She sees me in all my ways, even through my lakes of tears.
So mom, when you see a new doll in a store window display,
Don't forget I love you, in all of your ways.

  —*Nicole Rosine Mashni*

Flash Back

The cold, crisp wind tingles
As it touches my wet tear stricken face
The hurt lies so deep inside
The memories I cannot erase

Helplessness, overpowers me
The weakness, I begin to feel
In my mind it plays over again
The fear, it is so remarkably real

The jagged ends of the puzzle
Slowly begin to smoothen and connect
Rage begins to overtake me
The tears still endlessly trickle down my neck

My thoughts then became scattered
Like the snow on a cold frosty night
As quickly as remembered, they were forgotten
And left behind once again, anger, frustration
and fright.

  —*Lelia Joy Kinney*

Love

Love came quickly unto me
As lightning in a storm
And love, being as it may be,
Felt for me no sympathy.

I beheld her with a brow-raised eye
Her beauty different from the norm
And yet I gave a heartfelt sigh
To the thought of us together, I said goodbye.

How I wished to be bold
As like I never had
Yet now, I am still cold
The story of "us", forever untold.

Love left quickly from me
I, alone and sad
And love, being as it may be,
Felt for me no sympathy.

  —*Miguel A. Martinez*

Mom (I Love You)

I know I didn't say I love you
As much as I really should
Or sit and spend more time with you
Right now I wish I could

I guess I've taken life for granted
That the ones I love would always be near
Not thinking that maybe tomorrow
I'd wake up and you wouldn't be here

My days are filled with sadness
My heart so filled with pain
To get me through this time of grief
My faith it must remain

For it is he The Lord above
His angels he does choose
He's taken my mom to a land filled with love
With him she can not lose

Until the day we meet again
Pray the Lord He'll choose me too
Listen for my prayers at night mom
These three words I Love You

  —*Michael G. Onorato*

Sky Of Love

Two flowers in the field,
as the breeze blows smooth.
A butterfly twinkles above,
the blue sky surrounded with love.

Far off in a distance a bird flies south,
yet meaning to go north.
Confused in such a way not thought of.
The blue sky surrounded with love.

Twirling in the wind, a leave falls,
yet not sure to go.
The bark on the tree, reaches limits above.
The blue sky surrounded with love.

The thunder roars with a burst,
the clouds roll about.
The hard rain falls upon a dove,
The gray sky surrounded with love

Soon the rainbow of many colors,
extends from sky to earth
As though there has been a birth,
the blue sky surrounded with love.

  —*Nancy R. Wiese*

Rotation

The great spirit inspires a holy tranquility
 as the close of day
changes places with the night guardians.
 A different sensibility reigns.
Nature in the night-wild entertains few
 human intruders. And those who do
trespass the nocturnal forest, do so with
 with great respect and caution.
Daytime bravado is drowned in darkness.
 An innate warning system turns on
the animal alert.
 High noon violators become night prey.
An immanence returns to the natural inhabitors.
 The hierarchy of fear and power changes
places at sundown.

  —*Robin Montgomery*

Love's Fears

Softly I would touch thee
As the sunshine through the day
And on breezes I would whisper
Ere I frighten thee away;
For to frighten thee, my love,
Would be naught but a sin,
For I am but a shadow wafting soft upon the wind,
And calling on the breezes
With quiet words that you can't hear,
Words which ask of you to linger
For a moment, with me here.
But, should you hear me calling
As I slip among the trees, and hear the dreams I whisper
As I drift upon the breeze;
Would thy arms begin to open
And thy finger tips reach out,
To that which now lies hidden
In this heart that's calling out?
Or would thee simply turn and say it cannot be:
For thee are more than heaven; and I am naught but me?

    —D. Jonathan White

Untitled

Leaves falling slowly to the ground,
As they touch they make no sound.
The sky is cloudless shades of gray,
Summer is rapidly fading away.
The mountains are unfriendly and bare,
There is a cool dampness in the air.
The rain beats hard against my window,
The trees bow down as the cruel winds blow.
I sit and think about what lies ahead,
All that I've done and all that I've said.
Life is like the changing season
Passing by with no rhyme or reason.
You wake one morning with the sun
   shining through,
When the night before, the rain clouded
   your view.
You've got to keep living day by day,
You can't let the seasons slip away.

    —Pamela O'Leary

Legendary Lupine

They appear overnight upon the Texas plain
As those pioneer women did, long ago
They came, standing firm and tall,
Sunbonnetted, bringing grace and loveliness
Into a land withered and harsh.

Mothers... daughters... they came
By thousands
Conquering the west
With their silent strength
Pulling life from the earth
They held on
Swaying with the winds

Silent sonnet in beautiful blue
Spring brings the legendary lupine
Swaying in the wind
Holding their sunbonnets high, they whisper
"Remember, remember, we are here to remind you
How the west was won."

    —Laura H. Root

This Isn't The Way It Should Be...

I once said I loved you (many years ago), but you seemed not to
   care
As you drank your evening tea in your dark brown easy chair.

Each day I awake and pray for the revelation of your love for
   me from deep within your heart
Only to end each night in the refuge of my room crying silently
   in the dark.

Every time you walk back into my life, I feel my heart beating
   once more
Only to have you take it with you when you walk back out the
   door.

I fear that this may be my destiny—to touch love like this for
a few fleeting moments, and spend the majority in pain.
Yes, there have been a few others, and who knows what the
   future holds
(yeah, sure), but a life without love like this would be lived
   (loved) in vain.

    —Lynn Effinger

I Am A Tree

I am a tree so don't kill me.
As you hammer and chop, I scream out for help.
But you don't hear me, for all I am to you is tree.
Though my branches may weep and my leaves may fall,
I'm still a tree so don't kill me.
All you care about is your profit and money.
You don't care about me, for all I am to you is,
One lonely tree.

    —Mandy Beyer

Accepting

It never ceases to amaze me, the durability of a tree, it never
asks for one thing audibly. Yet it survives.
It stands tall and its roots dig down deep to plant itself
on firm upper ground. Each branch is carefully designed,
each leaf a thing of beauty, it sways in the breeze so
gracefully, that is it! It is full of God's grace.

It withstands devastating storms; soaks in the sun,
accepts the rain. Full of humility, its branches
droop beneath the load.
In a little while, the sun comes out, its branches
lift again.
As in giving thanks for its struggles and coming
through them.
Again gracefully swaying in the gentle breeze,
"Accepting"

    —Ruthann Santoro

My Prayer

While gazing down on their tousled heads,
Asleep serene in their tumbled beds.
A silent prayer escapes from me
To the quiet forms, my daughters three

Oh God! Grant me wisdom to them impart
Gentle words and a tender heart.
Help me teach them their courage to find,
Honesty, truth, and a wholesome mind.

Give them patience, compassion, let them understand
The blessings of offering a helping hand.
And then above all, from their dawn to their dust
May they place in You all their love and their trust.

    —Lorene Banner

Is This America

I heard somebody shoutin' this evening
At the far end of the road.
If you are born black in this country you gotta
Carry a heavy load

As I turned to face my brother to give
Ear to what he had to say
I told him my own self, all you can do is hope and pray

There's no use in trying to fight the man
Just trust in the Lord and follow his divine plan

For with each wrong, you learn what's
Right, give glory to God and try to see the light

I thought - is this America
I say - is this America

What freedom do we have

The only liberty that we can claim
Is a smile we get from our holy savior
Jesus Christ - our creator is his name

— *Wayne Newsome*

Faith In Yourself

Have Faith in yourself cause your worth it
  At times it seems hard to believe
    Remember that God always loves you
      And knows that you need a reprieve.

He'll test you in handling the bad times
  He knows you can do it with care
    His faith in you reinforces
      What you need so much to hear.

You have what it takes inside you
  To know right from wrong at a glance
    To practice the rule of compassion
      And leave nothing at all to chance.

So believe in yourself cause your worth it
  No one knows this better than you
    Have faith in yourself you can do it
      Once YOU start believing in YOU!!!

— *Sharon Ann Bingert*

Seconds As Thoughts

The bodies on this earth, wither
away like a dried up leaf,
swaying through the air as the
wind carries them.
It's their only power, their only strength.
The force of the wind to one day come an end.
Until that day live a life of wonder,
to be wandering about, closed
in one single room.
Trapped on the inside, not on the outside,
sweat pouring, voices screaming,
trembling and trying.
Using your might, the panther soars out of you,
you've done it, you're through the
dark, over the clouds you now roam.
Stomach no longer cramping,
you've fought the fight.
It's done and over with, others
are left in the dark.
Show your glory.

— *Tammy F. Eby*

The Attic

Full of remembrances, childhood laughter and dreams.
Baby's cradles, infant blankets.
Playpens, bottles, diapers.
Pictures from school, old books and pencils.
Report Cards filled with grades.
Awards, diplomas and honors.
Yearbooks, caps and gowns.
Old trunks with worn-away locks.
Yellow pictures, dirty scrapbooks.
Collections of dolls and stickers.
Old out-of-date clothing.
Toys that broke long ago.
Stuffed animals, faded and thin.
Packed away... and found again,
are treated like new.
Another generation... another era.
When the toys and trunks are old and forgotten,
They will remember you.

— *Lauren Lamonoff*

Life

Life is an ever flowing river, filled with both good times and bad times that flow from the beginning of time to the end of eternity.

Life is the pathway for the struggle and the desire to succeed. It is filled with many milestones and stumbling blocks that often reach out their limbs to trip you when you are about to reach your highest aptitude.

Like is a mountain. It is cold at the top, but when you finally reach your peak you can't help but think of the warmth of the bottom, the feelings that encouraged you to reach the top.

Life is clay. It can be molded into many forms by the sculptor, it can be molded the right way or the wrong way. It can be molded to your satisfaction. A long one is not always guaranteed, so it's up to you to make this the best indeed.

— *Makeba Hayes*

The Night I Lost My Past

How can a love so tender and sweet
be so cold at the turn of one street
I said I'd pull over, so we could talk
afraid if I did you would walk
And much to my reluctance and fear
I looked behind and the police were near
I tried to lose them around the turns
as I think of it now my stomach churns
My thoughts were to lose them and talk it out
but you were going to jump, I had no doubt
Once you were gone - I didn't know what to do
I punched the gas and kept thinking of you
I drove away - lost in thought
Drove to lose them but it was all for naught
They finally pushed me into a car that was stopped
and I knew my chances for us had just been dropped
I sit here today wishing to turn back time
this can't be done, so I look for a sign
My past life is over and this is true
I must go on for me, with or without you....

— *Rick Hussey*

Mothers

For the mother who wipes away the child's tears
   because another hole in a blanket already
     quite worn has appeared.

For the mother who stands by the window and waits,
   for the school bus to deliver her sweet baby
     cakes.

For the mother who tolerates the plunking and plinking
   of young fingers practicing, and possibly
     thinking.

For the mother whose love is so plain to see,
   in her eyes, her pride, and her
     priorities.

For the mother whose courage, strength, and firm hand
   are drawn up for the sake of her
     children.

For the mother whose strategy, hope and simple plan
   is to see that her child has more than
     she ever had.

   —Mary Kay Borsgard

Just One Soul

There is within my heart, a tear,
   because of one lost soul.
And, oh, how I wish I could
   but bring it to God's Heavenly throne.

I pray about it daily
   and ask the Lord God on high
To help, lead and guide me,
   to this very long, lost guy.

I know that he is weary
   and wants a friend so true;
And, oh, how I want to give him
   my Heavenly Friend
To keep him from feeling blue.

I'll pray for this soul forever
   and continue to the end
Until I see him glorified and say,
"Now I've found a 'Friend'!"

Dedicated to Allen McCracken, April 17, 1967

   —Susan Davidson Nickel

The Negro's Nigger

The Negro's Nigger was a black man hired by another black, and because of this he was thought by his employer as his nigger;

The Negro's Nigger's life was worst than hell because he was looked down upon by his own black brother;

The Negro's Nigger was shown no compassion because the Negro forgot that they both came from the same bottom;
The Negro's Nigger was not able to graduate from Nigger to Negro because he was not educated;

The Negro's Nigger made the Negro feel good because the Nigger worked for him;

The Negro's Nigger would rather work for a white because he expected hell from him;

The Negro's Nigger had the ups on him because he knew where the Negro was coming from. He had been around the white man for so long, and now he desired to be like him;

But the Negro's Nigger knew that no matter what in the eyes of the white man they were both just plain Niggers.

   —Sandra McClinton

Ode To My Son

I carried you in my body and fought to hold you by the very
     being of my soul
The love I feel is intermeshed with pride to see the gentleman
     you have become
   The tenderness of your ways fills my heart
   Your spirit is strong and my heart is full
I want for your happiness - my son all the rest of your life.
  As I see you grow with understanding my love grows for you -
     MY SON!

   —Rachel Drewes

The ABC's Of Word Association

  Accept ... believe,
Believe ... credit; Credit ... draft,
Draft ... enlist, Enlist ... fighter,
Fighter ... guerrilla, Guerrilla ... hostility,
Hostility ... insanity,
Insanity ... Jeopardy ... killing,
Killing ... Lethal ... mortal,
Mortal ... natural,
Natural ... ocean,
Ocean ... pacific,
Pacific ... quiet,
Quiet ... rural
Rural ... society,
Society ... today,
Today ... unrest,
Unrest ... violence,
Violence ... war,
War ... xeno,
Xeno... yore,
Yore ... zero......

   —Maria-Victoria Orlando

Untitled

In the stillness of the night there are the dreams of those who believe in the goodness of others; that had never before shown any. Dreamers, lovers, thief's walk on stone slabs, listening to the constant hum of the city with the looks that can read strangers like a book. Kids, drunkards, killers hunt those who dare to cross into their lair; devoured in an instant by salivating chops and burning eyes. The lust of the blood burns in their veins that in time drives them all insane. As fathers, mothers, brothers and sisters cry stale tears of pain, for the loss that was in vein leaving them scared and numb for the rest of their lives. Sometimes under the moonlit night two souls come together in the embrace of a lover, proclaiming there would be no other in this lifetime. Standing alone at the edge of the city out into the sea of tiny lights watching the specters as they float on by me, voiced I'd once known tell of another place another time confused by it all until the fog cleared in my mind that the abyss before me just happened to be mine the window of my soul stood open for me and showed there was still time until I would catch up with it; then eternity.

   —Robert John Lamphere

Tryst

Meet me under the crescent moon
beside the river of gold.
Where angels eyes pierce the sky
through winds that never blow cold.
Amidst the fires of Satyrs that burn
in piles of passionate zest,
we will embrace the night, together as one,
beneath trees of baroquian dress.

   —Melissa Constance Vassel

The World According To Me

I am but a speck of dust amongst thousands,
  billions of other specks of dust.
I am just a small part joined with other small parts
  to fit together into a large puzzle.
A puzzle of time and space, of places unknown.

My heart is true and my eyes are open to others
  and their problems.
If one thing were to change or if one thing had
  changed many years ago.
I may not have existed yesterday, today, or tomorrow.

The world according to me, would never be the way it
  was then, the way it is now, or the way it will be
  in the future.
Without me everything would be different, and nothing
  would be the same.

— *Stephanie Hagler*

Broken Promises

You'll always be there, in the mirrors of my mind
Bittersweet memories of years left behind
What should have been - was not
What could have been - can no longer be
Like a flickering candle casting reflections on my past
I saw promises burning brightly then broken and trashed
A love filled with passion so special from the start
When I needed it most, it was time to part
Your promises I believed, but my trust was betrayed
My knight in shining armor began to fade
Gone now is the pain - and all that remain
Are the memories and tears of twenty eight years.

— *Marilyn R. Wood*

Miner Monday

He is the miner who can see in the dark, shout out if in the
black coal see a nugget. The chap dog whipped off his
billycock-hat, and throw after for the glittering like gold
rat. Hit his head on the upper bed, suffer and howl, behind
the minor car his chum guffaw. All for this responsible first
day of the week, celebrate his Sunday, but he can't stand
Monday. Miner axe get niched, he having liver atrophy.
Alcohol in his blood keep back the muscle. Only one thought
turn round on his mind, chase a rainbow, that call everybody
for saloon. The throat parched, sweat profusely how he
crosscut. Do his job poorly, the pit-prop have a bad limp.
Great time the breakfast, what he don't like. Drink lot of
waters, which in the saloon is poison. When from the dark
flash out the next shift miners, shout with joy and creep in
the drainage ditch. Swallow the chewing-tobacco, care for
nobody, hurry in the gangway, first at the miner cage. His big
hope the rainbow, neighbouring reality. Salary go for the
whisky, the saloon owner happy. From the miner wife eyes
saltless tears over flow, under her heart the future, who
already hate the fate.

— *Laszlo Szuromi*

Only You

It's sunset now, and in the hush I see you
As once you stood outlined against the blue.
Your eyes outshine the colors spread before me;
All else is dwarfed and there is only you.

It's memory, and yet more real you seem
Than daily living, barren now you've gone.
Thank God for dreams that come at eventide
To sweeten loneliness with wine-rich song.

— *Nella Holloway Cole*

Winona

Black hair, brown eyes, red lips, white skin.
Black hair, black as the darkest night,
The blocks out the light of others
So that all I see is her.
Brown eyes, two liquid pools of love
That I swim in, and sink in, and drown in.
Red lips, red as the burning blood that gushes through her veins.
And as they touch me, I am filled with a fire
That is hotter than the hottest sun.
White skin, that surrounds me, and envelops me,
And draws me into her.
And as I enter her body, she enters my soul.
And our souls become one.
So that she is no more, and I am no more.
And there is nothing left but love.
A love as large as the universe, that will last for eternity.
For love never dies.

— *Steve Jakab*

Yellow, Black, Red And White, The Four Winds!

Red granite blew from below to create Paha Sapa,
Black Hills, from the trees so plentiful.
Yellow gold trickles down through every stream,
White snow covers even the pretty white flowers.
Today Black, Yellow, White and Red skins are on every trail.

Before explorers, Sweet Medicine reached for a Vision Quest;
For centuries quests four days long were made to "At'tay".
On Bear Butte many were given 4 arrows, 4 laws, 4 colors,
Wafting Sweet Grass in 4 directions seeking
Life, health, regeneration, prosperity.

Thunder roars down from the north, from White Buffalo Woman.
Far to the east breaks daystar - with black tail deer.
Down south where the summers live are spirits of animals,
While to the west fly the eagles and the misty clouds.
Wakantanka hears prayers as the smoke reaches Him.

All Vision Quests end with prayers up, around and down - yet
Why should Paha Sapa, Bear Butte, fields, even streams
Have fences, dividing what he made in such unity:
The White from Red, the Black from Yellow …
Shall we not all live on His earth together?

— *Richard S. Miller*

Eagles Flight

Engulfed with the freedom to fly,
Blessed with speed and beauty;
I watch you soar higher and higher.

Your wings command the wind,
Bend it, and caress it.
Soothing speed, and creating direction from it.

Grace and agility flow from your every move,
Creating a brilliant combination of flight and art.

Every feather rustled by the wind
Shines with a silkened stroke of the sun.
And every color upon your body
Stretches and blends across the sky,
Leaving only a faint mark of your existence and flight above.

With your commanding beauty and grace
You are the ruler of the sky;
And apart of the wind.
Letting only your eyes search for your destiny.

— *Laura Clement*

Love Must Be

Love must be blind.
Blind to shape and form which always change.
Blind to moods and attitudes that often rearrange.
Blind to dark and crooked perceptions.
Blind to status quo misconceptions.
Love is a bridge as are the eyes.
Eyes - world to mind
Love - soul to mind
Without eyes we cannot understand colors.
Without love we cannot understand ourselves.

—*Meri Kelso-Peacock*

Metamorphosis

From the caterpillars cocoon
blossoms the beautiful butterfly.
Nature smiles and spreads its wings anew.
Born again, it is given the chance to see
the love, grace and beauty of life renewed;
easily adapting to the changes that arise.
This, like you and I, is our new beginning,
just as the butterfly does not question
its new existence, neither shall we;
let us trust this higher source.
So, like the butterfly, fly with me.
The familiar fluttering of your wings
excites the fluttering within my heart,
and makes me realize the beauty of it all.
Let love wrap around us like silk threads
wrapped tightly around the caterpillar,
and may nature work its miracles
once again, on you and me.

—*Wesley Carlton Dennison*

Memories

Time is like the wind
Blowing gently by
As memories of our friendships are created
The good times will never die
Like a leaf in the fall
A memory will fade away
But only to be stored
So it may be remembered in our hearts again someday.

—*Melissa Bakner*

Memories Of Eleven

There were eleven
born to our parents,
and we were not only siblings
but friends, as we grew to adulthood on the farm.

Eight girls and three boys
enjoying the wonders of farm life.
The older children
caring for the younger.

We never needed
someone over to play.
We had each other,
creating our own games and fun.

We grew up together,
learned respect for ourselves and others,
learned to accept our responsibilities,
and the value of a good day's work.

For our mother
widowed at thirty-nine, taught us
to be giving, that family helps family,
and to stick together during the tough times.

—*Vera R. Raasch*

Good Friends

To be with you when I want, to have our first dance,
Boy how I would love a second chance.
A chance to find out just what makes you laugh,
A chance that I might just make you cry, but forever not
Knowing we just had a glance, I would sure like to have
A second chance.
A chance for me to know just what your about, for me to
Be your man skinny but stout.
A chance to show you a really good time,
And not have to worry there is plenty of time.
If there is no second chance then I will never know,
It will be hard enough to just let you go,
But whatever weird way our relationship bends,
I hope we will remain forever good friends.

—*Travis Hallgren*

Depression

In the beginning the sun shines so
bright and everything is so clear.
Slowly, so slowly it withers away
until a haze falls down upon your existence.
Dreams become your wishes,
wishes that are impossible to be reality.
So you sink deeper into darkness,
when only a faint light can save you.
The struggle hurts and death calls.
Reaching for you, its presence is
comforting, but scary.
To fight it wears at you and
the battle is a long and vicious one.
Then by some glorious surprise
the sun shines on you.
It's not as bright as before
but it shines on you, finally,
the warmth and love touches
you once again.

—*Monica A. Ring*

A Ray Of Hope

Smiles on the innocent faces
    brighten one's mood,
Angelic laughs, graceful movements
    overwhelm mothers with happiness...

Children, pillars of hope—
Give them love, encouragement;
Give them time, listen with your heart,
Mold them with values and wisdom!

Toys can be bought,
    dress, video game can be forgotten,
McDonalds, Tacos, Kentucky Fried Chickens
    for the stomach —
How about the hungry mind?

Plant needs nurturing,
    loving hands, caring soul...
How much more humans?
    children most of all!

Let them grow with values, with convictions,
with goals, with determination—
.....because they are the hope, the future!

—*Lourdes M. Arafiles*

Bursting With Color

An aura of colorful bubbles surround their imagination
Brings many faces and expressions of their fantasies
Some sad, some happy, made with lines and designs
Combination of colors, skits and wits brings laughter to the air
Personality and determination brings a touch of love to your heart
The endurance that is meet to shadow out their own identity
Is dedication of their art, deep in their souls
At the end of their day those colorful bubbles burst one by one
Till there's only the remains of their imagination lying upon
the vanity
This is the life of a clown

 —*Shirley Ann Morris*

Celebration

I wonder if the family of the last one to die
Broaching forbidden borders, waging war on the wall
Just days before it collapsed on both sides
If they felt as if freedom were too little, too late

I wonder if the family of the last one to die
Crossing lines in the sand, in the Golan, in Gaza
Just minutes before all sides signed the Treaty
If the family felt Peace were too little too late

And I wonder if my friend of Yaroslovl village,
Who feels lucky to live in the great Russian country
Where the new lines for milk and the new lines for bread
Are shorter than those people face in the city

I wonder if her family will be the last one to die
When she stands there this winter for bread and for life
While Beirut and Berlin line up their bright futures
But her line moves too slowly for too little too late

 —*Linda Selby Larson*

Vagabond

Up, in the gray winter's sky,
Broad wings straining, ever strong,
The silent image moves swiftly long.

Wandering goose, alone you fly
Over the white land, frozen and bleak,
You're very far from the Chesapeake.

Above the pins, beyond their sigh,
Above white lakes and hardened streams
Above this world, beyond its dreams,
Your journey's end, where does it lie?
What far goal do you alone see
And where might all your brethren be?

Neck stretched taut, then comes your cry
It fills my heart, oh, lonely bird,
With the sweetest sadness I've ever heard.

Vagabonds both, you and I:
Far away from those most dear
And the season's end, is far from near.

 —*Mario D. Bartoletti*

Life And Time

Upon first breath of life
Babes spar with passing time -
To gain a life eternal
From that unyielding might.

Youth bursts forth-seeking joy and pleasure
A storm of endless desires -
On invisible wings these mortal treasures
Take flight for Promises higher.

 —*Lois F. Montgomery*

Recalling Thoughts

Blue eyes
Brown hair
Mustache and beard
Grinning face.
I open my eyes and see all this.
In his gentle way he touches my cheek and I too begin to smile...
I stand now at his grave and think of him
Laughing at the way I said all the true things of earth and life,
Silent now to hear me speak no more.
He is silent forever more.
I will no longer see his face mornings.
Woman in love,
You have paid your price.

 —*Laura Trout*

Wake Up, It's Morning!

Dark and heavy chains of power, money, and control
Busy bees, buzzing with monotonously prodigious tasks

Release your heart and inner soul...
To see God's grandeur truly unfold...

 In a joyous, but helpless child's eye
 Free yourself to truly love
 As in God's design

 Vicariously in the womb
 Rejoice with the child's spirit
 And leave your tomb.

 Await the glorious colors of the morning sky
 Breaking through into the light of day
 Enveloping the gift of life, not asking why
 Just shining upon the flowers, and showing the way

 Do not compare the daisy to the rose
 Do not be tempted by the sinister scent in your nose

Awake and free yourself to join in God's plan
The child lets go of the controlling condition of man.

 —*Lisa Weiland*

Alchemy

They said, "In nature you can learn of life."
Busy working in the ground,
 A worm by shovel cut.
Two sparrows built a shining nest,
 The babe fell from the tree.
Lightening came and burnt the branch.
 The rose was broke for all to see.

But then I looked again.
Where the injured lay
 Two lives now played.
Where one was felled
 Two babes flew free.
Where storm had tossed
 Grew new the tree.
And life was passed
 From you to me.

 —*Shirley Samarzia*

Our Love Remains

Caught up in a whirlwind of fanciful dreams,
Awestruck with wonder we planned and we schemed.
Younger days have now passed us by,
But our love remains strong and our hopes and dreams high.
May the future days turn into years,
Growing old together without fears or tears.
And in the end when He calls us home,
May we look back and say we accomplished it all.

 —*Wuanita M. Vikdal*

Remembering

We met..we danced..we soared aloft. Our spirits joined in flight.
But all too soon I turned and saw you vanish in the night.

If life is a play as it seems it must be; then too briefly we took
    to the stage
One moment together unreal and yet real. An instant, an hour, an
    age.

So lovely your face in the candle glow; you sparkle before my
    eyes.
I reach to gently touch your hand but the fleeting vision dies.

Again I hear a soft refrain, recall a distant shore.
Raindrops strike a window pane and you are there once more.

Inquiring how it goes with me and where I wander now,
But sagely knowing I'll return some day, some way, somehow.

For you have captured me. I wear your searing brand.
You fill to overflowing still, the heart that guides this hand.

We met...we danced...we soared aloft. Our spirits joined in flight.
But all too soon I turned and vanish in the night.

—*Sarah Nordwall*

Nuclear War?

The no-nukes say the next big fight, we're all going to hell
But as far as I'm concerned, only time will tell.
If we will be such fools
To go ahead and do it, just because we have the tools.
But the government won't listen
And the hostages can't be free
Just tell me where does that leave you and me.

Why I am feeding the welfare babies
When I can't make the rent?
The homeless want their piece
Too bad my paycheck's already spent.
The government needs more
For departmental policy
Believe me it's not going to open any doors
No bureaucrats got the key.
So can you tell me where's that leave you and me?

Seat belts, smoking, abortions
Everything that the government is trying to tell me to be.
Hey, wait a minute, I thought this was a democracy
So just where does that leave you and me.

—*Lisa M. Rose*

Beauty

Beauty is said to be in the eye of the beholder,
But as I grow older,
I seem to find
That beauty is all in the mind.
There is more to beauty than looks.
You can never find true beauty in books.
If you need a place to start,
Try looking in the heart.
The head is another good place
To find some beautiful space.
Although good looks are nice,
It's a good idea to think twice
And find what's underneath
That pretty sheath,
For it's what's inside
That will take the ride
Through the pages of time,
And help with the climb
In and out of strife
For your entire life.

—*Mike Nielson*

Years Gone By

It's been a long time between now and then
    But certain things never change.
        Your smile, your style,
    Both have softened over the years...
Your intensity and passion have increased.
    I'm glad for the time we shared
    For it adds flavor to my life.
    Sometimes sweet, sometimes bitter
        But never hard to swallow.

From that dark mark on the top of your leg,
    To the hot pink of your tongue,
    The sharp bite of your teeth
And the sparks that flash in your eyes,
    All these things and more
    Are burned forever in my mind...
        And in my heart.

    Where once you were my lover
        Now you are my friend
        I would trade neither...
But for the chance to start over again.

—*Susan Nash*

Your Day

You have had so many roles in life to play.
But coming soon is your day.
You started out being you.
But before long there were others telling you what to do.
You became Daddy's little girl, a student in school, a fiancee'
A bride, a wife and lover.
But where are you? Hiding inside.
You became someone's mother.
Maybe grandmother too.
You became a care-giver of those older than you.
Now you are all alone.
All the others are gone.
Your role playing is over, it's very clear.
Look deep inside and find the happy little girl you once were.
Your day is here.

—*Paddy Walker*

He's Always There

Sometimes life seems so unfair,
but don't forget God is always there.
People may say religion should not be discussed,
but who else can we go to, who else can we trust?
When times are hard and no one seems to care,
just remember God does, and that He's always there.
The loss of a loved one, a child gone astray,
whatever the problem, please take time to pray.
In His infinite wisdom these things come about,
don't despair, He'll always bring you out.
He'll help you through life's problems,
He won't let you down -
He's everything we need, He's always around.
When within your heart you say your prayer,
I promise He'll hear you,
I KNOW that He's there.
And He'll answer you too,
don't give up, just believe.
Be encouraged, He'll help you
because He ALWAYS helps me.

—*Rachelle Warren*

To My Friend

For many men I have little time
But for Dale gladly write a rhyme
He has a strong love for our flag
And his life is not a monotonous drag.
A strong commitment for his friends
And when wrong; will make amends.
He is dearly loved by the old
And will not allow them to get cold
He loves to see their radiant smile
And for their sake go the second mile
Loves his family with all his heart
And with God's help will not soon depart
The one most special; His wife
and will not forsake him in strife
Here's hoping their marriage lasts
a long time
And if it does I will write another
rhyme.

—*Rufus Pierce*

The Swingset

You touch the tip of your realm of belief
but get thrown to the ground
you are a
discard of your dreams
Push yourself back up because
you can't give up
you've come too far
I want to meet you where
our worlds meet.

—*Randee Robichaux*

Memory

It's coming. The light. It filled the sky only seconds before
but has now become a dim twilight. The wine glass. Each bubble
represents an image from the past. A word, a feeling, a tear.
That special person who made cloudy days sunny with a smile or
a touch, or that one phone call which meant so much, but now
means so little. Those three simple words I could never get
him to say. The hate. It turns saints into devils and makes
heaven hell. It's coming.

The thunder rolls, and metal rain makes stone roses melt as it
bruises the ground and petrifies the trees. Another bubble has
burst from inside the wine glass. Another old grudge lost in
the pages of an ancient photo album has been rekindled. Two
people are falling in love. Two people are falling apart.
Someone dies and someone is born. It's coming.

We run to it, and we run from it. We can see it peeking from
behind every corner. We wait patiently from second to minute,
and minute to hour. The tables of time go backwards, then
forwards, then from side to side. The trees throw their fists
in an angry uproar as the wind rushes past us, and above us,
and inside us. It's here.

—*Steffani Smith*

The Divorce

My kids became a nervous wreck,
But I was in love — what the heck

I made up my mind this had to end, that's
When procedures for divorce began

When he found out it was nothing nice
He even threatened to take my life.

For eleven years my life was off track, but,
guess what? I've gotten my life back.

—*Sandra Martin Benton*

Untitled

Sometimes I wish he would speak to me louder,
but he only whispers to me when I'm at the threshold of awareness,
and he speaks to me softly only when I'm about to confess.

He says it's alright to pray at night, and cry in the warmth
of the morning light.
Where there is darkness soon comes the light, and the sun will
rise after tonight, tonight. Ooooh it's alright.

I heard the river he told me to see, and I tasted the sunrise
at the tip of my tongue.
I've never been old but I've always been young,
and my mind won't see his face in this silent place.

Why does God only whisper when there's much for me to see?
Why can't he scream to awaken me?
Why does the darkness blind me with such unnerving peace?
And how is it I'm touching him, when he's only watching me?

I heard him in the silence of a whisper. Yes, and he awakened
me. He closed my eyes and opened my eyes and took me by
surprise in the silence of a whisper.
In the silence of a hush. Only him. In the alacity of a rush.

—*Lisa Thompson*

Prices

Mortgage rates are at record lows,
But houses are not selling.
Why! Why! This terrible crisis?
Prices, prices, prices.

Automobiles, just cost too much,
So they are rented by the month.
Why! Why! This terrible crisis?
Prices, prices, prices.

When the politician, are running for office
They say "Listen and take our advices."
When elected, their pay and taxes go up,
And so do prices, prices, prices.

Postage has gone up, up and up.
But the service gets worse, worse and worse
The national debt, is the highest ever and soon the
Country will burst, prices, prices, prices.

The economy has suffered, so very long,
But if prices came down, it would boom,
So get out of high gear and shift into low,
Low prices cannot come too soon.

—*Robert F. Schneider*

A Thoughtful Good-bye

It is true that you don't think of me everyday.
But I am part of you.
I helped you to break through.
I released you from you.
I am poured in the stone of your new foundation.
Part of you.
I made you go on when you were exhausted.
I watched over you while you were sleeping.
I held you when you were frightened.
Part of you.
We shared the things that can only be between us, forever.
Maybe that is why you hid yourself from me,
As you prepared to go on without me.
And it is true that I was sorry that we fell apart.
Even though you will never see me anymore,
I will always be with you.
You can not lose me or leave me ever again.

—*P. A. Brisendine*

Yes, You Can!!!

Someone said 'No, that can't be done',
But, I flashed with a great smile,
"Why can't it be done?, If you aren't the one,
Step aside! Let another invoke some style!"

"Nothing's `impossible'", I said affirmatively,
"If one invites `God' in for a part,
Just watch what can be done, with style, and with fun,
When He's allowed to build from the heart!"

If you've got a dream, share it with Him,
And if it's worthy, He'll play a key role
For all problems, to He, are easier to move, than the sea,
With a glance of 'His' hand, they shall fold!

Just say a small prayer, to the One who knows where,
All answers lie for you!
And He'll pick you up, with what seems like 'luck',
And soon you'll be moving a-new!

Keep your vision towards the sky; do what is worthy, up high!
And you'll certainly receive His helping hand,
And with Him helping you, there's nothing you can't do,
And what to another was a 'can't' is your 'can'!!!
      —*Phil McLaughlin*

Listen To Their Call

There are some things I don't talk much about,
But I think that now is the time.
A close friend of mine once told me
The fearful thing of life will soon take her away.

I would worry and cry late at night
Because she would trustingly pray
That He will soon come and guide her through that uphill road.
My heart and mind were filled with confusion.
I could not understand what made her think that way.
Then, on one warm, summer night, I received
a little appealing note that asked me to come and visit.
I know that friends are suppose to be supporting and caring.
But when I saw her take those pills one by one,
I tearfully watched my friend die.

So once again I say,
There are things I usually don't talk about. But because of my
self-centered behavior my friend has left those she loved.
So my final word to you in this world called Earth
Listen to what a friend in trouble says,
Listen to that pleading call.
      —*Marissa J. Yabut*

I'm With You

I'm glad I got to know you and for the times you let me near
But I wish you wouldn't keep me quite so far away from here

Cause I hate to see you so alone and trying to work things out
I know you'll see things through somehow for that I have no doubt

Yet every now and then I'll find a phrase or word or two
That might help for you to hear or think - oh, here's one ...I'm
  with you

And if that pulls too hard on you please take another look
For it requires nothing more than a robe upon a hook

You wear it once or twice a day - take it off and hang it there
It's always there when you get cold so you've its warmth to share

Then as each morning rolls around; you wake up fresh and sigh
That same white robe is always there as if to say, "Well Hi!"

I hope this rhyme will make you smile and start this day brand new
And as you're going through this time, just remember ... I'm with
  you
      —*Larry Macdowell*

Strength In Weakness

Sometimes the light gets dim
but I won't let it get dark again.
Sometimes I feel like all hope is gone
but you keep me believing and I carry on.
I realize life doesn't always go the way you plan.
When I fell you catch me and help me stand.
In moments of weakness I find you there,
Someone who understands, Someone who cares.
My patterns of thinking slowly change,
things will never be the same.
For the lessons I've learned let me know
that I'm not strong enough to make it alone.
It's not a sign of weakness to need someone by your side.
No one can make it alone, if they say they can, they lie.
And I'm not weak but rather strong.
Struggling yet moving on.
      —*Michele Fauteux*

Until Then

Many say love will come,
But in three days I shall be twenty-one.

Could it be my looks, or the way I dress
It's funny how love seems to put me to the test.

There are guys I met and think "He's cute"
But shyness holds my tongue and I think what's the use,

I receive love from my mom and dad in large amounts
But in some ways that doesn't really count

I think it's because my friends are saying "I do".
Deep down I think that's what I want too

I guess I'll just have to wait till that day comes
But until then, I'll pray for the perfect one.
      —*Tina A. Maddox*

Understanding One Another

I try to understand the people in my surroundings.
But it is so very hard to do.
I try to make people understand me.
But it is also very hard to do.
I try to make people realize what they are doing to this earth.
But I cannot.
Why?
Must it be so hard?
Why must life be such a struggle?
I look to the people who understand me.
And when I do they are there, with all my answers.
I am but one of the people in this world
who cannot relate to some individuals.
So now, I thank God for giving me someone to count on.
I will try my best from now on
to help people understand one another.
      —*Stephanie Lake*

When The Wind Speaks

For a split second, I thought I heard my name
But it was only the rustling of leaves outside
my open window.
As I lie in my cozy bed,
I once again hear the wind speak
words of peace to my heart.
I am overcome with the words of the winds that
sweetens the air as I fall asleep
      —*Michael A. Brady III*

The Reunion

It was a day that started like any other day
but it would not end that way.

It was a day of making every minute last
but not to forget times past.

Those were times of cookies and playing in the snow.
Tears and pain I did not know.

Those were times of sickness and years being apart.
Mother's love in a son's heart.

Being so young, they would not let me see your face.
Only from a window's lace.

Being so young, they would not let me say goodbye.
Only to wonder how; why.

Gone so long, but there you stand.
Sparkle in your eyes, and into your arms I ran.

So many questions, so much time.
No; we do not have angel's wings or worry about crime.

The same earth and sky are here.
But people now hold and treat each other very dear.

As sure as the rising sun,
We will always be together; as Mom and son.

—*Richard Putman*

St. Charles

St. Charles is but a tiny town,
But just compare it, all around,
To bigger places near and far,
And see if they generally are,
Better than we, from this coal town of Virginia!

From these hills our men have mined,
Coal for a lot of mankind.

Our people here have learned to be,
Unselfish, kind hearted and free.

St. Charles indeed is such a place, Where you can
see a smiling face because of love for one
another, forever, will stand by their brother.

We want to see St. Charles grow, And then
everyone can go, And tell others near and far, how
very important that we are, about our town so very
small And that we matter after all!

Let's build it back to a booming town, And then
the people all around, Can say, "St. Charles the
tiny town, Is once again ON THE REBOUND."

—*Nell Stewart*

Untitled

In sorrow I wandered, my spirit oppressed
but now I am happy, securely I rest.
From morning till evening glad carols I sing
And this is the reason: I walk with the king

For years in the fetters of sin I was bound
the world could not help me; no comfort I found
But now like the birds and the sunbeams of spring
I'm free and rejoicing, I walk with the King

O soul near despair in the lowlands of strife,
Look up and let Jesus come into your life.
The joy of salvation to you He would bring.
Come into the sunlight and walk with the King.

—*Oscar Wright Sr.*

Thoughts Unspoken

I know I don't say this as often as I should,
but no one has put up with me as much as you could.

> You've been beside me like a true friend,
> like a willow branch that will never break, but only bend.

But sometimes weakness would set in, and we'd both be in
corners, slumped over, and painfully curled.
Then you gave me something I thought I could never afford...
you gave me a new world.

> When I would see only darkness, you'd turn on the light.
> Like a special sister,
> you could always make me see that bright light.

Even though we are many miles in between,
it's because of you the future I've seen.

> The future is brighter than you or I could know,
> because I'll always be beside you,
> and I'll never let you go.

So, when darkness has set in, let me be that light within
I'll guide you through dark alleys, and unlit tunnel ways,
to find the way to a brighter day.

—*Linda Y. Hummel*

My Beautiful Reward

It is not a FRIEND that takes care of, or fixes the other,
but one who steps back and allows that person to live their
own life. Through the victories, through the struggles and
through the mistakes.

Not with judgment, abandonment or rejection but RESPECT and
FREEDOM. To let that person know, agree or disagree, they
have a friend.

One person cannot be everything to the other - nor - can we
always be there, but leave the door open for shelter from the
cold.

We all have paths to follow, each in different directions, when
those paths cross and our lives touch, we're never the same.
We take what we want from our friends and gracefully let go
of the rest.

The human spirit is unique...
Allow it to be!

—*Paula Kozak*

Reading, Books, And Me

Now, I love science, and I love math,
But reading and I take the same path,
For I love to read, and I love to write,
I guess I love learning, in day or in night

Now, reading's a subject that can't be ignored
The men who can read are the men who have soared,
You can read about mysteries, or fairy tales,
Or even Prince Madoc, who came from Wales

Reading is what I most enjoy,
It's better then any boring old toy,
For reading's adventure, that's what I like,
It certainly beats riding my bike

When you read you can find whatever you wish,
A striped crocodile, or a polka-dotted fish,
If you want to find something without having to look,
There's only one place, and that's in a book

So, if you want to find something without having to look,
Do what I do, stick your nose in a book!

—*Sarah K. Lanius*

A Letter To My Older Brother

I know we are in different worlds now
but the past cannot be changed.
The times and the memories
No matter how short or long, bitter or sweet,
Are never to be forgotten.
The times we were together as children
Were harsh and painful days.
Now my life is full and I am alive.
The emptiness of not sharing
the good life with you is facing reality.
A visit is but a scoop of ice cream out of a gallon of ice cream.
A scoop is sweet and nice
But a gallon would make you sick.
So it is with us, a visit is nice
But we would with total enlightenment
Be repulsed by the individuality of our personalities.
You are happy in your world and I in mine.
I am happy for you and you are happy for me.
So the emptiness remains
But my love for you remains forever.

—*Roy R. Luepnitz*

Unchanged Feelings

They all come and they all go,
But there's something I just have to know.
Did you come into my life to stay,
Or will you leave this coming May?

You've touched my heart in a special way,
I think about you everyday.
I knew exactly from the very start,
That if you ever left you'd take my heart.

You've stolen away all my fears,
And left me crying with no tears.
There's no doubt in my mind,
I'd ever leave you far behind.

When I look at the stars above,
I'll remember you as my first true love.
And I know I'll keep you high in thought,
Because your too special to be forgot.

But whenever you go,
I want you to know.
There's a place in my heart,
For a brand new start.

—*Tonya D. Smith*

Feelings

Not to be loved,
But to love
Is my great desire.
But to love
I must be loved
Be loved by her.

Over and over I've dreamed dreams of you
Dreamed dreams I hope will someday come true.
Though they are fanciful, oh so sublime,
Why cannot they come true sometime?

Not so much the year gone by
As the year that is to come.
Not so much the memory
As the hopes I welcome.
The year has meant so much
Would the coming have that touch.
The memories are so dear,
Hope seems not so clear.

—*Nicholas Battenburg*

The Heros Cheated

Vietnam was the only black-eye the U.S. military ever got;
 But we all know that is a $500-hammer purchasing rot.

Ya'll be ashamed of no parade for Vietnam Heros;
 But blame U.S. leaders for being zeroes.

The French stood a decade of guard on Vietnam's pike;
 But de Gaul got a $10-Billion gift from President Ike.

White House static continued with Johnson's tall Texan lip;
 But halted with the crash of crook Nixon's slip.

The question of "agent orange" the World Court will decide;
 But unexplained cancers and one-armed babies is a herbicide
 like thialamide.

M.I.A.s must be forgotten for America to buy Vietnam's oil;
 But that makes unexplained-cancer victims' and patriots'
 blood boil.

Vietnam Veterans count on proper care from the Veteran's
 Administration.;
 But what good are doctors willfully giving wrong x-ray
 radiation.

Most countries wish to copy the democracy of our start;
 But freedom is nowhere till Heros get a fair part.

—*Robert John Byanski, Jr.*

Blue Chicago

We were once the jewel of the Midwest
But, we don't shine anymore
Rick folk live in the shadow of the ghetto
Along the Gold Coast shore

Steel towers infest the horizon
The Loop is dark at night
At city hall they consider issues
Spelled out in black and white

The world still thinks of Chicago
As living by Al Capone's rules
But, the real hoodlums and gangsters
Sell coke and crack in our schools

There's the crime of poor education
There are crimes of different names
But, in the crime of apathy
We must all share the blame

At a glance, it's a great looking skyline
It keeps growing each year
But, in the eyes of the Picasso
I swear I saw some tears

—*Wayne Richards*

For Terry

Vulnerability twists my heart and bleeds it dry,
but what I feel is merely an echo of what I see in her eyes.
It shines from under layers upon layers of past hurts,
asking me if I think she is worth loving.
This hits me like a blow, for to me her worth has no measure.
Yes, yes, dear heart. Don't ever believe differently.
But I know she does, and although I cannot fathom what she has
gone through, I can imagine of what it has robbed her; I only
wish I were able to restore it.
Studying her, an indescribable feeling fills me, somewhere
between anger and incredulity. She is so delicate, so fragile!
A man would be a monster to touch her without tenderness.
I feel a sudden desire to cradle her in my arms. Maybe if I
hold her tight enough, I can shield her from any harm in the
 future.
If healing her were that simple, I would gladly hold her forever.

—*Sally Timko*

Nights On The Rooftop

Summer nights are usually warm
But when family disputes occur,
The nights are disturbingly chilly
It is then that Juliet and I quickly disappear to the rooftop.

A soft quilt, a flashlight,
And my journal make up our gear.
We lay here our secrets emerging
The comfort of the pitch black sky secures us
Assuring our secrets will go no further

As I read to her, I carefully choose certain words
To confess to my friend.
I notice the yellow street light,
Casting mysterious shadows,
Creating a bluish outline of her serious silhouette.

The glare of my Shark watch
Urges me to look at the time,
Discovering moments of silence down below
We descend
Disappointing the mosquitoes.

 —*Shelly Bonoan*

Star Dancing

Your extra dimensions heighten my intentions,
But who am I to say what's beyond space and time?
Infinite emotions portray my devotions,
As distant horizons are beckoning to us!

But now let's take this chance with rhythm as we dance,
And rhyme to be written and songs to be sung,
There's mystery in the stars and this magic is ours,
Sharing secrets of our soul-so let's go rock and roll!

Star dancing at midnight!
Star dancing-the time is right!
Star dancing-this hour of romancing,
This treasured time for you and me,
As we try to make the others see-
"We're star dancing!"
You're my very own dreamchild-
We're spinning and driving me wild,
Oh! Clap your hands and tap your feet!
Yes, dig the beat of the band and try to understand,
This vehicle of true expression upon our fantasy flight!
Yes, we're star dancing... we're star dancing...
We're star dancing!

 —*William D. Irwin*

Untitled

I am truly alone
 But writing takes me home
To be among the beloved, me in all my emptiness,
 oh writing says it best
Solidity before my very eyes
And I mean to impose, for it's then I compose what's right
 there in the room upstairs
That attic of the mind that sacred place, precious space in time
Words caress as Mother's nest
and I, a child of manners, mild am comforted
Oh, it soothes me - like Coletrane, moves me
 to a higher ground of altitudes profound
My saviour, rescuer from this cold, dark world
 frightening world
And I know it to be the only remedy towards my salvation
When I'm near to falling to the depths of oceans deep
 I turn around as I hear the sound of words urging me to give
 life them life and in exchange, they'll rearrange my present
state and they'll take me home
 for it is there I so long....to be

 —*Sheila Brown*

No Trace Of Me

I started to shout,
but you did not see my face.
 The lights went out,
and on the earth I had no place.

 My friends were not there,
the world did not know me.
 I had no one to care,
because me, no one could see.

 I vanished in thin air,
no trace of me was found.
 It was too much to bare,
So I tried to take off but I was bound.

 So then I closed my eyes,
because I wasn't ready to see.
 I wanted my chance to say my good-byes,
before they had "No Trace of Me."

 —*Shari Lynn Wrezinski*

Sweet Dreams In Yonder Moonlight

Here I sit, with yonder moonlight, gleaming in my hair.
By brookling streams, the sweet night air I breathe.
The grass, the trees, my new found friends, I suddenly
notice that I can hear them singing their song to me.
Oh how they sing, Let the winds blow, blow your cares away
Oh how beautifully nature sings to me!
Hear the trees sing, sing to me tonight set your soul free!
And as I look up to the moon so bright, he bows his head in
loving approval.
Yes, yes dear missy, let this be the night, for your
dreams to shine bright! the night. Well the night simply comes
only to make room for a change.
To bring another glorious bright filled day in which peoples
goals and dreams can be exchanged.
Oh the blessings and the dreams that the sweet night time
brings. All to the light of day so that these dreams may be
seen. Oh night air blow your song to me.
OH moon light gleam make my path be seen! that I may see a
new day! That people may see all the dreams and promises the
the night has given to me.

 —*Melissa McCoy*

Kissing-Flower

The kissing-flower surrounded
by green and silver garland
hovers overhead.
I give Pissy Randy a nudge, then a push
before hanging my head in shame.
His wet lips, fully puckered, touch mine.
Those furry eyebrows wiggle
up and down, up and down, up and down,
to the rhythm of my fifth-grade classmates' laughter.
Accumulating sweat on Pissy Randy's nose
form droplets, which resemble
kissing-flower bulbs
with furry brows and puckered lips
that taunt me.
The laughter; the lips;
the brows; the red kissing-flower bulbs
all fade into oblivion—
except for the face,
that matches the voice,
that echoes the words, "Merry Christmas".

 —*Shelley Hines*

Bird Brain

To have access to the world
By having liberties of the sky
To have freedom from all man-made laws
By living of self-made decisions
To fly solo or by flock
By responding to what lies ahead
To enjoy the best of many places
By using a bird's brain

Who differentiates the brains
The one who discriminates against the other
The human race is smarter
Maybe not
Who lives without harming others
And believes in self-preservation
Not self-destruction
Never the less must possess more wisdom than all!

—Ruth Smith

Male Maledicted Malefactor

All my looks go unseen
By he who lies beside me.

A lost man I see
Your distance blocks your way within me.

What do you plead?
Are you saying I only compliment a need?

Now with this all in sight
Watch as I turn the light.

Please once again tell me the tale
Your silence spoke this night.

—Simmer Sara'n

Playing Games

Two people playing games
by ignoring each other
just because they're in love
with the beauty of the exterior.
When the fact is they want to intertwine
the reality is the thought of it
won't reach further than their minds.
For their insecurities rise above their wit
and in turn make them blind.
Instead of reaching the inner soul
they only reach the outer rind
whereas to each other they are unknown
and underneath lies secrets of many kinds.

—Stacy Berger

A Prayer At Dawn!

Every little creature scurrying to its nest
By your divine Hand created and blessed
Every fluffy cloud gliding along
Every red breast singing a song
Oh! Lord how I marvel at your beauteous world
As another dawn is gently unfurled
Hear my prayer, as the bitterness disappears
Let me banish my unfounded fears
Let me glory in your compassionate love
As my heart wings to your haven above
How I cherish your caring - you've opened the dove
You've forgiven my errors - peace is in store!
And as I smile, there are tears too
For what could have been
Had I only known You!

—Yola V. D'Aniello

Our Animals

Our animals habitats have been destroyed
    by man
They need their habitats and surroundings
    for their survival
They won't have their habitats and surroundings
    if man doesn't stop developing the land
Like man, our animals need their homes
The birds need the trees, the waterfowl needs
    the wetlands
The water animals need the water areas, our
    animals need the land to roam free
Our animals need room (the land) to grow
At one time our animals were plentiful — there
    were many varieties, many families
Man came along to develop the land-
They destroyed our animals habitats and
    surroundings
Man needs to reconstruct our animals
    habitats and surroundings and to help
    the growth of our animals population

—Sheri Newby

What Special To Me

What's special to me is horseback riding,
By the sea.
What's special to you might be,
If you get a new hair-do.
What's special to me is strolling near the bay,
What's special to you
Might be what you wear that day.
What's special to me is dancing,
On a starlit night.
What's special to you,
Could be which guys are a handsome sight.
What's special to me are God's gorgeous
Creatures,
Not my boyfriend's facial features.
Though the most special thing to me,
Can not be wrapped or bought,
But is something that lies within you,
That in which I've given a lot of thought,
And the answer is life. And I can't wait to see,
What life has in store for me.

—Lauren Anastasi

Prayer For First Born

My heart is like a captured fox.
Caged and bound by heavy locks,
Pacing back and forth each day,
Waiting for someone to say,
She's free - and it's okay.

Paradise is no more,
Never felt like this before.
Beauty around is tainted.
Until we are more acquainted,
With what reality has painted.

Is this the child so happy and bright,
Afflicted with this horrid blight?
Questions pester like gnats - why? If? How?
Give help-relief-please Lord, Now!

—Vivian Kilzer

Paradise II

Our hearts became one in a land
   called Paradise.
Our love soars free now as the eagle
   on the wind,
As we ride through the meadows and
   fields of green without caring
   where our Pegasus shall send.
I have no fears now as I gaze into
   the beauty of your eyes.

We stop now at a bubbling stream, it
   too like our love is forever
   changing, always growing-yet never dies.
Take my hand once again now as we
   wander through the forest;
   through the trees overhead
   soars a snow white dove,
A seal to our Paradise and to our pure love.
Yes my love, I truly bless that day
   my hand you clutched and I
   carried you to Paradise.

     —Vincent Jungenberg

My Dad And I

I can still hear his boisterous voice
calling my name from the bleachers,
behind home plate.
On his back, he carried me to bed.
His strong arms, held me tight.
His soft touch, put me to sleep in church.
And I remember...
Today, I feel the same support.
I have never given up, he always said not to.
He has loved me deep inside himself,
with all his power.
He has never given up, he never would.
When I was wrong,
he disciplined the wrong,
never selfishly...
He never abused my person...
For it is me...
inside himself, where we
my dad and I
share our love...our sanctuary.

     —M. Elaine Hollier

Untitled

   Stand among your painted meadows
     Calling to the wind!
Stand, and hear life; beautiful life,
   pass you by in playful answer.
Let your heart fill with its song,
   and overflow; In joy.

Feel the sun in golden love dance.
Drink its warmth deep into your soul,
Allow your heart to fill with that song,
   and overflow; In joy.

   Now will you find life.
   Now will you find warmth.
   And now, in the excess of the
   Overfull heart will you find;
     In Joy:
     Love.

     —Wesley Craig

Her Sadly Shattered Head And Heart

Someone tried to save her from all harm, but of course, no one can do that for anyone. And for some unknown stroke of fate, she slipped from her spot of safety, and she was so crushed both head and heart. A tear silently fell unnoticed by all who tried to scoop her up. A tear so small that she hardly felt it herself. But it was there, and it burnt, it hurt - it throbbed - it emptied her of emotion of uplifting and purpose. What to do? Can the pieces of porcelain ever be replaced so that she might appear whole ever again? One can try! One can re-glue the fragmented parts, but the cracks will always be there, even if not evident to any eye. Many can try for restoration, but in the final chapter, this tiny doll will have to be loved with all of her cracks and faults. Even if the wig does not conceal all, she must be loved anyway by anyone who sincerely cares. And for the others? Well, everyone has their own cracks and faults, and often badly sadly shattered heads and hearts. They too must be loved for themselves if they, themselves, can overlook their cracks their sadly shattered heads and hearts and try to love themselves!

     —Patricia O. Kopp

The Porcelain Pond

Standing in a bantam boat, balanced there by oars.
Can it be, I'm still afloat, yes, there's all four shores.
What a trip I had, spinning like a top.
It really wasn't all that bad, till the water took a drop.
I'll be ready on my next ride, in the gleaming tank that
   beckons.
Now I know that this old tide, will rise and fall in seconds.
As the water rises up, it slowly takes a hue.
Seeping from a plastic cup, to make a shade of blue.
This job I have is a tidy task, for I do not reach the bowl.
Perhaps I'll just relax and bask, and drop a line to troll.
I have time to sit and wish, there is no need for rushing.
So I'll just pretend to fish, until someone starts flushing.

     —Roy N. Smith

Untitled

Time
   can we ever go back
   turning the hands
   spinning, spinning
   nothing changes except time it goes on.

Accepting fate
   Good or bad future
     yours, ours, theirs
      who's is best
       right or wrong
       who's to say?
Time
   remember when -
   go back to a true friendship
   deep true, easy, safe, comfortable
   like an old shoe...
   a shoe you couldn't live without
   couldn't live without you.

     —Linda M. Bolton

Love Is

Love is a word which is taken so lightly by many,
But, love with you is so deep.
Your love to me is like a rushing river.
This river is always moving, building, but never ending.
The love I have for you is always growing,
Like a pine tree in the forest.
It will continue to grow during cold and warm times.
Love, just a smile, an embrace from you will always
Warm my heart and relieve my mind.

     —Thomas R. ReBant

Around You

Listen!
Can you hear it?

What you say?
Anything, if you may.

Look!
Did you see it?

The morning hours,
Of which the day had devoured.

The hours that have slipped away,
The morning has turned into day.

Smell!
Oh, the smell of spring has come and gone,
Did you miss the beauty after a winter so long?

Feel!
Cold air as it touches your nose.
Mud squishing between your toes.
The softness of the petal of a rose.

Taste!
The beauty of what has been offered you by life.
Or, have you let it pass you by?
        —*Shirley Billingsley*

Mothers

Mothers are made of everything nice
Candy, honey, sugar and spice.

Sometimes they say yes,
Sometimes they say no,
But most of all they spend the dough.

When we go out shopping
I'm right by her side.
She'll say, "Let's hurry! The stores close at five".

After dinner and TV we climb the stairs,
get ready for bed and say our prayers.
"Thank you Lord for a day well done and make us ready for
another setting sun."

My Mom is thoughtful, loving and kind and I thank God she's
mine all mine.

So don't forget Mom, not for one single minute, you didn't grow
under my heart but in it.
        —*Pamela L. Acklin*

Untitled

Is this a dream
Can't be what is seems
You've gone away
Had so much more to say

Our lives will go on
Memories will still be strong
When it thunders I'll feel the pain
Strikes of lightning I'll see the strain

With your life at its end
It's our love that we all send
Don't know what else to say
Deep inside know it's better this way
        —*Todd Srodes*

Can't

Can't is not in my vocabulary
Can't — How often that word is used every day...
I wish people would discontinue that word;
That it would go away...
People always telling people what they can't do,
or you're dreaming' it will never be...
But keep on believin' and dreamin' and you will see
that you can...
The next time somebody tells you it can't be done
because it's never been done before...
You're dreamin' you don't but it will never be...
You tell them: "Look, I don't deal with negative
thoughts or people..."
So dig this, baby;
"Can't is not in my vocabulary."
        —*Tonia Renee' Lee*

Just Cry

You look into my eyes
Can't tell me why I cry
Yet you say you can help me
Give back my sanity
With one tear I shock the world
It's not the fact of being a girl
You always see me smile
But like a jungle inside everything's wild
I am human like all of you
I get hurt like everybody else do
With two tears I reveal the truth
That there's nothing harder than being a youth
To look at "Last" and see such pain
Makes it hard to stay sane
When you feel like you may die
It's all better to just cry
        —*Tanishah L. Chisam*

Innocence

Once in a while, we touched your tiny portrait,
    Caressed your face, with strokes of trembling finger tips.
    We embraced your longingness with visions of images.
    We cuddled your feverish body with sweet lullaby.
Once in a while, we dressed you for the days' happenings,
    And then beckoned, goodbye!!
    We wiped your hurting tears, with inspiring love and hope.
    We dreamt dreams of who you are,
    And reached out for that kindly smile.
Once in awhile, we begged time, for time and time
    Again to re-do the things, we hope we could have done.
    We disappeared within reach, yet so far to seek.
    We built hope, and dreamt change for changes sake.
    We paused, to communicate, and to reflect.
    We counted the steps to your heart.
And.....
    Ever so often, we wonder....
        Are you too, once in a while.
        —*Nysonnet*

Untitled

An individual captured within the illusions of substance;
Carrying on while others have no desire to experience.

To influence, one must have been influenced; which leads
us into a period where we are controlled by the absurdities
of life.

Deception appears in many ways and we are able to prevent the
wicked involved. This illusion is called reality.
        —*Leanne Bedwick*

Untitled

A shadow danced amid my bed
casting players acting out a score
a fools' paradise, aching in my head
no, not knocking at my curious door
no messengers sent to meet my expectation
sculptures of forms so absurd
the disappointment is my own creation
another path taken, again detoured about
the shadow laughs and flickers
knowing I'll cry myself to sleep
sending the players and shadow out
into my paradise I silently creep...

—*Susan M. Urbano*

Christmas Of 1993

We can never return again to Christmas of 1993 as we
   celebrate this day
Let me wish you the joys and peace of God all along the way.
May the Heavens reign with guidance, may it fill your
   soul with love.
The road of life is a one way street that leads to
   heaven above.
Experience life in all its splendor, take the time to see
The path is strewn with gold that's put there for
   You and me.
Gold is the color of sunshine, gold is the light in your eye
Do not live with vision blurred, to worry say goodbye.
For one who celebrates the birth of Christ on this
   Christmas morn
Will know they found the right route and the reason
   they were born
May love be your first priority for it makes all
   dreams come true.
Since it is the greatest power on earth, it is love I
   wish for you.

—*Mildred O'Neill*

I Love Your Eyes (For Sandy)

   When you smile it's like a
      chain reaction . . .

   Your lips slowly slide upwards
      to the stars.

   Then the stars sprinkle sparkles
   into your eyes - and they shine!

   When your eyes are shining into my
      eyes, they warm me all over.

I love your eyes, especially when they are
      looking into mine.

—*Terrie L. Brewer*

Dark Dreams

Dreams of death surround me as I sleep
   but they are just my own thoughts
      plotting against me.
They say to go ahead and end my miserable
   life, that it could all be over with
      just one jagged knife.
One jagged knife deep inside my heart
   would let out all the pain that
      made me fall apart.
With or without me the world will still go on,
   no one would miss me or wonder where
      I've gone.

—*Melisa Montes*

Look At You Now

Look at you now!
Charming me.

All decked out in silk;
Smelling like freshly cut wild flowers,
   lips full, and teasingly painted red.
Well cut and painted nails to match your
   chocolately, velvety skin.

Your mind as sharp as a whip,
Knowing all my thoughts, even before I say them.

To see you walk is like being in a dream
Each movement is so artistically correct.

You overwhelm me with your presence
And, who thought that I could not be charmed by anyone;
I'm supposed to be so cold and unbending in love
Yet in your arms, I melt like molten lava,
   hot and liquidy, under your control completely.

My mind is gone; I can't think beyond thoughts of you.

All in all, you are what I need to make me human again. . .

—*Paul M. Alleyne*

Our Home

Here I sit … so all alone. My windows are boarded, the
children all gone, Even though I set empty, and look so forlorn.
Remember … inside my walls … Twelve healthy children were
   born.
Some think I'm lonely and sad... But really … I'm
contented and glad. I closed my windows and shut my door.
And memories return of children galore. I remember the
gatherings on special days, when the kids came home for short
stays. There was hugging and laughter and plenty of cheer,
Reminiscing and singing and an occasional tear. Please don't look
at me and feel sad. Remember the good times we once had. I'm
not lonely nor blue, as inside my heart I hold memories of all of
you. Come visit me . . . and sit for a spell, as I have plenty of
stories to tell, About mom and dad and kids and things;
grandbabies, great grandbabies, and wedding rings. But . . .
please . . . whatever you do, don't feel sorry for me; as I have
known so much happiness that my walls ring with glee.

—*Norma L. Pellegrin*

A Guy Taking A Shower

Light filtering through fluttering lace curtains,
Chokes abruptly on hot dense steam.
Elusive soap squirts and plunges.

Pulsating streams of water beat down,
Like the drums of a primitive tribe,
Erupting into a frenzy of battle
As they attack, foaming and frothing
Until the enemy is purged.

Wildly scrabbling fingertips
Send cascades of lather down,
Forming images on tightly scrunched features.
Picture Hitler, now Groucho, now Santa Claus.

Moisture-laden lungs expel their tune
As a fish might croon a bubbly love song.

Fresh tropical scents waft through the mist
As the assault subsides.
Groping hands fumble for
Something thirsty for excess moisture.
Hesitant toes venture out.
A rubber ducky suddenly squeaks indignantly!

—*Sue Hoyuela*

Mamma's Quilt

I went through Mamma's clothing
choosing each piece with care,
creating one pile, then another
of the clothes mom used to wear.
I chose the clothes she wore most often,
before she passed away,
thinking I would piece a quilt of Mamma's clothes someday.
Thoughts of Mamma filled my mind
as the year passed swiftly by,
so I took her clothing down to give the quilt a try.
As the scissors cut the pieces for the quilt that was to be,
Mamma and the early years filled my memory.
With every stitch I recalled scenes from long ago,
scenes with all the family that Mamma did love so.
I whispered up a prayer to God and mom above
to guide me as I made a quilt for each of those I loved.
With much help from heaven, I set about my task,
"Let it be just right, dear Lord" was all that I asked.
In time each quilt was finished, there were only three,
A special gift for those I love, from God, our mom and me.

   —Mardi Crutchfield

Artimesia

Saturdays are for seeking nature
Chores done, I ambled along Lake Artimesia
From berwyn heights with an umbrella
For rain had added to the endeavor there was no one else but me
When my friend, little heron, took to a willow tree
And stopped my trip to the lavatory;
Then circling cautiously...Egrets! One...two...three.

But before my two hours stroll was done
I'd met my first great blue heron
And inquisitive thrushes, jays, chickadees and a robin;
A clever swarm of birds bent on having fun

With a two-legged monster determined to change;
Some perched like sentries, the rest out of range,
One or two venturing closer with their sweet refrains
To see if I was a scarecrow or one with brains

On a rain quenched saturday I might have been Francis come out:
Nature was exploding in the lake, on trees, under bushes of rose,
Because we had reserved a lake; the joys make me want to shout!
But wait...when I did reach the restroom, a sign said: Closed.

   —Neil SookDeo

My Brother

As I remember it clear in my "mind"
You've been gone for two years I can't deny.
That night in May you were assigned
to a different mission of another kind.
Having taken your life was very selfish
thing to do you destroyed me, and other people too.
I miss the man who use to say "Hey spaghetti what
a beautiful day!" No one understood the relationship
we had, we were like no others, just a band of a hand.
When you was gone I thought I'll die along with you
(side by side). That morning they put you where you
were to attend, I said goodbye my brother for I knew
this was the end. You took with you a part of me,
for I also took a part of you,
   "I love you my brother
      and
I will agree we'll meet again
      for
   Eternity?"
      —Nancy Torres

Christmas Memories

Making cookies... Baking pies, little children.. Laughing eyes-
Christmas carols... Being sung, lots of tinsel..To be hung.
Jolly Santa... Elves and toys, giant workshop ... Lots of noise-
Little tin soldiers... Teddys of fur skates for him... dolls for her.
Christmas lights... gently blink, neighbors visits... cider to drink-
Cards are sent... full of glad tiding, babe in a manger... love
   abiding
Presents wrapped... bows are tied, gifts of love... tucked inside-
Stocking hung...stories told, Mr Snowman...in the cold.
Silvery moon..new fallen snow, Rudolph's nose..bright red glow-
Christmas Eve..finally here, dreams of Santa...Eight reindeer.

Christmas morning... Children waking, sugary treats... turkey
   baking-
Children enter...on the run, open presents...oh what fun.
Busy day...time for bed, tired children..prayers are said-
Christmas over... memories made, they may grow old... but never
   fade.
Hair turned silver... children grown, days of youth..swiftly flown,
Quiet house..stays too neat,I miss the patter... of little feet.
Open trunk...tattered doll..
Returning memories...when I was small,
Thank goodness for Christmas... and memories old.
Each one precious...worth more than gold.

   —Marlene Gowdy

Pray "Optics"

Enjoy this rhymed "yak"
Clap of nicety this extend salute truly

Am truly challenged so write-

Now hope you enjoy find its ray.
An eager effort so can sight
This proud salute hail this hope may
In our lives poetry is great,
Oh, an ease does give our tension.
Now this fact does help me this date
As my real effort use mention.
Let you now know with others share.

Lines "comb" letter thoughts from my mind.
I am on land, ebbed for care,
Be no more "sea", land steady find.
Real truly send this as salute
And enjoy as my way it say.
Really send to give joy, hope cute,
Yet truly pray enjoy.

   —Ray W. Connor

Things

Gum machines and round submarines-
Clearical, cubical, spherical things.
Bubbles and marbles and Japanese floats,
Fishbowls and agates and glass-bottom boats.
Jellyfish, icicles, droplets of dew,
Waterford, waterfalls, a window with a view.
Paperweights and test tubes, an Erlenmeyer flask,
Snow globes and ice cubes, elevators made of glass.
Lalique and Baccarat, martini glasses,
Emeralds and amethysts, rubies with facets.
Gum machines and round submarines-
Clearical, cubical, spherical—my favorite things!

   —Sara Lea Williamson Lemke

Native Nature

The winds off the mountain, carry my people's laughter,
  Clearly, as if it were not many, many moons after.
     I hear from the whispering tree,
     Prayers of nations on bended knee.
    Then there is the chant, loud and strong,
  At the place where the rivers move rapidly along.
  Warmth from the sun reminds me of the meetings,
Where the tribes gathered yearly for festive greetings,
   In the fields I glimpse the ancients playing.
   Dressed in those animal skins chose for slaying.
  The sky holds the shadows of healers, of holy men,
These are the most obscure, appearing only now and then.
    When I look down at the great mother earth,
    I can see the colours of humanity's birth.
  And as the night approaches, the twinkling lights,
  Keep a check on each of these sounds and sights.
  By responsibility passed on to new generations,
We keep alive the traditions of our separate nations.
   This is the nature of native rituals, even today,
  Times may advance, but the teachings shall not sway.

    —Lynda Winsor (Sha Rosa)

Wind Chimes Of Life

The consistency of the
Cling clang, cling clang mimics my
Pulsating, aggravating, and ever-hating heart
For the prejudice of the painted.
The crayon box of life,
The sight, sound, and touch of individuality.
Cling clang again
The whisper of the wind allows the chimes to
Clash in cadence.
It is for all to hear for they hold
No obligations, and even though they are hollow
They hold heart.
Cling clang, sing the song of equality
Scream it loud, and vibrant, and wild
Let it drip from the cold pipes
So the hate will not drown out
The music.

    —Sabrina Moshtaghi

Passing Friends

We are two ships that pass.
Closely, gently we touch.
Our bodies meet as our sails are extended upward to greet
the prevailing winds that guide us.

We sail forward only resting when profusely exhausted.
The heart of our ship beats forward to aft and quickly we
relax only to set sail again to dock at another port.

We enjoy our time together and spend it wisely too,
for we both cannot be certain if the feelings we have are true.

If we had time to explore the ocean with our ships and set
sail again, we would realize that we could have been more than
just passing friends.

    —Stan McDonald

Remarkable

Lady night took but ten minutes
Changed completely to Lady day
Brushed mascara pinks on a sleepy blue face
Painted light rouge-red on blackened cheeks
And Voila! - had changed herself completely
to give us human beings more time -
more time to move on
and make our own Good Changes.

    —Peter Gross

Spring

Softly warming winds came
Coaxing golden crocus cups.
Too early. Too soon.
Fooled by early
Lenten celebration, they came to join
The joy and found piercing sleet
And silencing snow.

Bird chorus, jubilant in migratory dress,
Huddled against unprepared branches
For shelter from the slash of wind-borne ice,
Bemoaning their southern lair.

Envelope of ice on the deeply sleeping
Lake, honeycombed by low sweeping sun
And drunken breezes, drops tethers to shore
To drift aimlessly, shrinking from contact,
Returning to the redeeming depths.

Mantled with the ludicrous
Masquerade of winter, sheets of ice
Shatter into spiralling shards.

    —Patricia Riccobono

Looking Back

As I turn my head, I catch a glimpse of him.
cold and alone, his eyes bare so much pain
as he looks at me I think, "I should help him."
So I stand there a minute, and debate in my mind
should I help this old man, should I be so kind
as to give the blanket that's keeping me warm?
Why not, I have a dozen others at home.
"But this one's my favorite," I think to myself.
"He'll be all right. He doesn't really need my help."
So I keep on walking, and never look back,
after all God should cut me some slack.
I am cold too. What am I suppose to do?
And then I realize just how selfish I was,
In my decision not to help him because,
I was too concerned for my own well being
That I couldn't help some poor man who was freezing.
And here I am all warm and snug in my bed,
But how can I sleep with all these things in my head?
I had the opportunity to help but instead I just kept
walking, and never looked back.

    —Melissa Beck

Our Dharma

Mystify.
Come, anoint the mother with the one humane and holy object,
Yourself.
Within the very soul of a lost faint, spectral image lies...
The Child.
Beneath the crying November wind exists,
A Smile.
In the dark and drowning lady lake there comes,
A Touch.
The blessed moonman radiates the holy ghosts with..
Love.
The autumn boy pulls down into the cracks of earth and brings
forth,
Forgiveness.
The very essence is a swell of
Laughter

    —Todd Cirillo

Of Tomorrow

Shattered dreams whose time has passed
Come crashing down like panes of glass

A thousand diamonds razor sharp
To blind the eye and pierce the heart

That once beheld within their reign
The joy, the anguish, love and pain

Of thoughts and hopes never expressed
Upon one's soul, eternally impressed

From amongst the scattered dreams, oh smitten!
Those who lifeless lay

We'll find the colors of the rainbow
The sun yet shines today
　　　　—*Mark Steven Freehoff*

Come Here

Come here, come here and sit with me.
Come into my waters.

No, not on top where it's swirling so rapidly.
There's too much chatter on the surface, it moves too fast.

Come, swim deeper into my waters.
Let my whirlpools soothe you, feel their various movements, let
them embrace you. There is no judgment here in the depths of
my waters, no walls to hold you. Free yourself from the
barriers you've confined yourself to.

No, stay, don't let your impulses drive you to the surface so
rapidly they cause vibrations in the undertow. Feel the
gentleness absorbing your body. Snuggle up to its warmth.
Let it release your fears of criticism.

Come here, come here and sit with me.
Come into my waters.
Now talk!
　　　　—*Leslie G. Shepherd*

The Whisperin' Pines

In Cooperstown the pines whispered off the shore of Glimmerglass:
Come see famed bronze faces adorning the walls of the hall,

Read of Leatherstocking Tales and look for the muse
Amidst reds, oranges, and greens of the Sleeping Lion,

Walk through rooms of the Fenimore House and feel the
　frontiersman's frustrations.
Relive your Field of Dreams, devout fans of the all American
　sport,

Watch from rows of splinter-ridden bleachers where children's
　ouches are forgotten
As foul balls fall from the blinding orb in the sky,

Experience whether shoeless, sporting different colored socks, or
　hued a true Kentucky blue,
All braves, twins, and blue jays becoming one on Doubleday Field,

Live the birth of two who are new to the esteemed teams this year
Wearing stripes and solids of teal and white, purple and black,
　one from the land, one from the seas,
Adding Florida and Colorado to the ranks of the major league,

Commemorate a famous Yankee as he rises to his grand day,
　Mr. October enshrined in bronze,
Always to be remembered for success in The House That Ruth
　Built,

Sleep to the music of crickets and a running stream bed
Awaken to the sizzling grill, breakfast in bed at The Whisperin'
　Pines

And remember, no need to lock your doors.
　　　　—*Maria Cassano*

Oh, To Be Able To Sing

Within my thoughts, so many times,
Comes the imagining of tuneful chimes,
And, as the notes begin to sweetly ring,
One wish arises, oh, to be able to sing.

Songs reveal innermost dreams and expressions,
Laying bare countless feelings and confessions;
Being good for the soul, a message they bring,
And the wish continues, oh, to be able to sing.

There is a saying that is well understood,
Some songs can do more harm than good;
But, for the most part, to the good they cling,
Then, the wish goes on, oh, to be able to sing.

For the untold tuneless ones, such as I,
There is great hope that by and by,
The greatest of songs, a hymn, will bring,
A glad chorus that all will be able to sing.
　　　　—*Nalda Morris*

A Teacher's Prayer

A child -
　concerned, considerate, content -
　The Master's special legacy to me,
　A novice teacher.

An adolescent -
　Unconcerned, inconsiderate, discontent -
　A teacher's gift to Thee
　My Master Teacher.

Have I failed along the way?
Hear me, Lord, as I pray.
Make me mindful of this life I mold -
This bit of human clay.
So that at the close of my teaching day
Hours in my classroom spent,
I give him back to you, dear Lord,
Concerned, considerate, content.
　　　　—*Mercedes G. Manieri*

Flight Of Fancy

　How you soar!
Confident, serene, gliding effortlessly
　How I stumble!
Frightened, confused, laboring gracelessly
Would that we could, briefly, change places
　(I'd probably fall out of the sky!)
　But if for a moment, just one, I could
　　Glide, float,
Then perhaps, I'd return with feet of grace and
A Soul that would always remember what it was like to
　Soar—unshackled and unafraid.
　　　　—*Mary A. Aversano*

Seasons

My favorite season of all is fall, the leaves turn
colors, the air smells crisp. The birds fly south, the
Ghouls and ghosts come out. When winter arrives the
cold white snow tickles my nose. Friends and family
gather about to celebrate and sing aloud. Then comes
spring, oh what a beautiful thing. All the beautiful colors
of moms favorite flowers. Butterflies flutter, grasshoppers
hop, kittens run free, and I can climb my favorite tree. Soon
after that the temperature rises, and summers here at last.
There's no more school and no more work, and now we're free to
have a blast.
　　　　—*Mercede Ultey*

I AM

I AM
confused, scared, happy and sad,
quiet, loud, good and bad
intelligent, naive, smart and dumb
awake, asleep, sensitive and numb

I AM
young, old, loving and hating
beautiful, ugly, certain and debating
mean, nice, fake and true
vague, concise, mannered and crude

I AM
weak, strong, funny and serious,
fat, thin, sane and delirious
organized, chaotic, fearful and bold
different, plain, hot and cold

I AM
chosen, rejected, beginning and ending
infatuated, in love, independent and depending
teacher, learner, confined and free
I AM not a lunatic I AM just me!

—*Lois Cae Rockwell*

United In Time

There is an essence surrounding our souls...
Could it be those fabled behavioral patterns of emotion
Some have sought for eons?
These Apocalyptic societies have blemished
our free spirits.

Through strained dedication...
Our minds have met.

Like the fragrance of a flower,
our souls have binded.
And in unity we have orgasmed,
And in this rejoiceful moment of
divine pleasure...

Love, has finally made its presence!

—*Robert W. Hall Jr.*

Charmed Over

Drama is a love-sick female somehow outdone by her male
counterpart her talents white-washed, they swoon over a more
traditional facade the leading role requires strength but
they've never seen Ellisa let loose at the reins
Offering up a non-speaking role with pay weltering her very
spirit determination grew preposterous, along with all Ellisa
achieved a woman fidgeting at the pinnacle of success,
Unnerved men try to inflict upon her a so-called wage freeze,
more over a house arresting limbo, how perplexing aspirations
flaunt haughtily beneath all mankind's sheen
Ellisa's nonplussed voice carries a packed auditorium, a fresh
cleansing like no after-rain has ever brought to attentive
souls Ellisa's the best "man" for a moment in their eyes,
she rules the stage in their awe they are one, with her
performance done she steps down no longer the actress
but the woman Ellisa cast in her most challenging role
which unfortunately, takes the most charming over.

—*Noel K. Johnson*

Black Prince

Powerful body, muscular strength
crouching, wary, excited
Chrysolite eyes smoldering, looking
waiting, the right moment has not come.

A growl deliciously low emits from the night
tensed and ready ebony moves,
a hunter, a warrior, mighty in strength.

Blood rushes!
heart pounds!
Running, oh caught!
Sweet heaven!
The prince and his captive
spinning round and round
a heart exposed, bare and naked.

Black velvet paws, smooth ivory claws
working their magic, ripping,
tearing, blackness surrounds,
the pain is unbearable yet
it is bliss.

—*Rachel Smith*

Night Stalk

The dreams of summer rise midst burning leaves,
Crumbling into smoke, unable to survive
The icewhite blasts of winter
Or the interequinox,
Unless they were to hide
Safe from death within that paradox
Beneath the ground
Where roots and worms abide.

There is a home for all
Within the dark black earth;
A place for living and for dead
Where dreams of spring
Dare delicate beginnings,
And some still presence knows
That in another year there will be
What the trails of smoke foretold:
Rising midst burning leaves
To greet the thorn and rose,
Miraculous marigold.

—*Roger M. Morrell*

Elan Vital

In flawless script the phrase was inscribed,
Cut into the flesh of the tree of life,
An indelible command charged in one universal language
to the fruit that this tree bore.

It found beauty in the music of the thunderstorm's fury
and artistry in the purity of the sea's hued cast of players.

It uttered the human or deal by tongue and cry,
enacted fiery mortal passion through the poetry
of unsated limbs and the zeal of feverish dance,
and it unfurled a decree proclaiming the force created
by all who attempted to taste the triumph of survival.

It unleashed the jubilant freedom of human spirit
and set sail on whimsical possibilities carried by the wind.
It treasured senseless outbursts of ardor for the surrounding
splendor, and it exalted in the deluge of knowledge that
emerged with every dawn.

And I journeyed there to
inhale fresh savory breaths of vigorous living
and relinquish my indifference to the departing winds.

—*Sara Hearne*

Death Of A People

My six pointed heritage
Dangling in the sun.
Hanging on the gallows,
And vaguely calling to me through the wind.
Emblazoned in the hearts of the innocent,
And the minds of the guilty.
A yellow-starred fleck in the eyes of inhumanity.
Unseen, unknown, unloved -
My ashes fall onto his altar of hate.
My soul belittled to a pile of soot
And swept away by his Nazi broom.
Deny my faith, Deny my existence.
And where now is my God?
Locked in an air-tight box -
Sealed with a swastika.
Six million skeletons in the closet.
Never again.

  —*Valerie Daniels*

As One

The day awoke,
 Dawn quietly surrendered to sunshine.
 Animals stirred, nudging life into day;
 Breezes gently engaged chimes into song.

Peace.

The evening quieted,
 Water brushed against the river banks.
 The sky filled with reddish-orange splendor;
 Silhouettes cut into the distant horizon.

Peace.

The night stood still,
 Snow lay in undisturbed cover.
 Moonlight brightened dark edges of evening;
 Trees cast unwavering shadows on the ground.

Peace.

People united,
 Living in harmony, intertwining colors,
 Accepting their differences as natural order,
 Blending hearts, beliefs, caring for each other.

Peace.

  —*Marilyn K. Christensen*

Caretakers

I heard them complain about the sweltering heat,
 Days without rain, the dust chocking and deep.
Several months later the cries just the same,
 Except now, it's so cold, the snow is so deep.
To look at our life as God would have it...
 Be grateful for all, accept that you have it.
We are the caretakers, so go with a smile.
 Take the bad with the good, be thankful for it.
The caretakers need to take our earth's care;
 Planting, cultivating, and to clean up despair.
Wanting ourselves to watch and dispel,
 The grieving and suffering, the things so unfair.
I have no complaints of God's bountiful works...
 Though we deserve not to have it, including the perks.
To make this world a more beautiful place,
 Look at ourselves and see all our works.
So gather up all your tools, lead all the way,
 Change the adversity, attitudes and dismay.
Sure we can do it, if we'd only try...
 God loves his caretakers, He made You and I.

  —*Russell C. Brown*

Oh Death!

Oh death! How could you come and take my love.
Death, how could you separate us. Oh death! How
could you take my heart, my love, my joy, my peace,
my pain. Oh if I could only hurt again, it
would be worth having another moment.

Oh death! How could you leave me alone with only
memories. How could you interfere in my life,
stripping me. Oh death! How dare you take the only
thing that means so much. How could you take my
song, my dance. Now I listen alone and dance with
the steps of tears.

How could death be so cruel, so rude, oh how I hate
him. Thief in the night take my personals, take it
all, leave my heart. Now I look, as he lay, resting
so peaceful, without me, my love, oh how I grieve
for death. Shall I join him and be free or shall I
continue in prison. Lord help me to close this
chapter in my life.

Death, you've won! You have conquered what no
man would dare.

  —*Loreatha Vernon*

Spirits Of The Wind

 Nocturnal tears flow, filling life's rivers
Deliverance manifests but mere condescending emission
Souls seek sanctity, yet vehemently, Death overrules
 Struggling alongside ancient premonitions,
 spirits seek nothing but return to native grounds

Restless spirits deliver visions among Nature's Children
Howling winds churn, grinding acute cries of redemption
 Faithfully resting within Earth's immortal soul,
indigenous agents empirically suffer eternal separation
 The wind dissolves frightful gasps of desperation

 Howling wolves echo nature's sorrowful cries
Winter's frozen sheath tempers Earth's spirituality
Weakened by death's throes, disintegrated, starved
 Nature's Children cry for mercy

  —*Michael Duane Miller*

Life

Life is one big surprise package,
Delivered by God and parents,

Life is one big learning flower, the more
We learn, the more we bloom,

From parent we branch out,
We take all advice and adapt it,
To make our lives.

Life at times has bad packages,
Delivered by our bad people, and ourselves,

Life can shine in our bad times,
to make them small,
Life does this with people like James,

Life in all is just one big merry go round,
With up's, down's, a start and an end,
Life is life we make it our own, special cloud.

Life it's one very large package,
And I for one am glad to have it.

  —*Lesley Wilson*

Imperfect State

There lies a defeated town whose inhabitants have
deserted her for another.

Her total existence has been battered.

Misery and defiance have made themselves
rulers here; and sit in the throne which
once belonged to tranquility and serenity

Woe with his allies bitterness and self pity
is another welcome party that resides here

Together they have arrogantly plagued this
once divine abode of many great ones.

As I journey down there, I hear the restless
cry of a morbid soul.

And the perturbation that lies in a heart so foul.

Indiscreetly aroused by vicious vice; a heart
that seeks, batters and obliterate all acts of justice.

Seduces and rapes various shades of peace.

Knowing not that every action is but a
fine measurement of your sanction
    —Mary Spio

Cinderella Liberated

I sleep with my feet in the fire
destroying the evidence
one glass shoe
melting like butter
both feet black as brickettes
while the prince in a world of questions
searches for an answer

he drinks from the other shoe
champagne and espresso
he has a special pillow for it on his desk
where he places it and in it sees his reflection

it is his talisman his illusion
his astigmatism
let no man touch it
it's all he has left
beside this note
dear sir whenever you see rising from the ashes
a bird its feet blazing like torches
observe closely
it passes for me
    —J. K. McCrea

Untitled

Little old ladies dressed in slacks.
Don't think they are so fragile,
Some pack guns in their sacks.
They may carry canes, but often they aren't lame.
They are just waiting for a mugger before they play their game.
Some of those bodies, lying dead in the gutter,
Are because someone tried to rob a little old grandmother.
Some have notches on their garter belts, too numerous to note.
And some carry a stun gun under their coat.
Think twice before you think "Old" is an easy mark.
They may just plant you six feet under, in the nearest park.
    —Laurel J. Intrieri

Unspecial Delivery

On a frigid gray December's day
Did the detested letter come.
And while I knew so well its contents,
I searched to see whom it was from.

The envelope, brown and heartless,
Bore not the sender's name.
Yet no matter who had mailed it,
Its contents were the same.

The cold and dampness of the season
Had worn the parcel much.
For as I went to open it,
Brittle was it to touch.

The sharp and angular writing overtook each page
Like a lecherous little beast.
It made me wonder to myself,
Could not it have been typed, at least?

But now I had resigned myself
To the awful truth it held.
No longer could I look to future days,
For from that letter was my spirit quelled.
    —Scott F. Heil

How Is It In Heaven, Mother Dear?

How is it in heaven, mother dear?
Did they all meet you with outstretched arms
Or were they each, hard to find

How is it in heaven, mother dear?
Is heaven far, or is it really very near

How is it in heaven mother dear?
Do they wear colors: green, blue, yellow or pink
Or are they all in white, I do not know

How is it in heaven, mother dear?
Do they smile, laugh and grin
Or are they too, sometimes very sad

How is it in heaven, mother dear?
And someday, I too will die
I know I will, I know I must

Please be there to meet me
Your answers to these questions, please share with me
I too will keep them a secret
I know I must, I know I will....Amen
    —Ralph Castillo

Image

I looked in the mirror today,
Differently from the norm;
I traced a line that had appeared,
Wondering what personal history caused it to form.

I touched my hair and lifted a strand,
Differently gazing in the mirror today;
Wondering about my personal history
Taking its toll and turning my hair to gray.

I looked in the mirror today,
Sadly recognizing physical transformation;
Realizing my past was catching up with me,
Revealing too much information.
    —Sandra Merchant

Nightmare To A Stance...

Common sense is the only fence around your mind-

So to find you, I must be kind to you and in line with you-

Do I shun?
Do I have fun?
I have a gun-
Or in the morning do you want to see the sun?

A shiver up your spine-
Potent wine is very kind you see.

The city sleeps tonight... On ecstasy made of this dream
called democracy. You see them- You dream of them- Can
you escape them...

A dream. A scheme. Whose in whose dream.
Suddenly, you wake up in a scream.
So much pleasure in this measure of time.
Time is all it will take for you to think.
So what is it? Am I a link? Or are you?

I know an old lady who lived in a shoe. She cried, Boo-hoo...
Literally....

It's you....
So go now you have to be lewd to a stance or in proclamance...

— *Mark Lynn Ratcliff*

Excuses, Excuses.

What's your excuse for using drugs?
    Do you expect it to solve your problems?
Or if you think your life is boring,
    Expect to break out of the doldrums?

The moment you swallow that chemical,
    You're admitting you're just a slave;
(Do with me what thou wilt, O Master),
    And become candidate for an early grave.

Perhaps it's a religious experience you seek?
    Or better the gift of cosmic consciousness?
Wake up! There are powers only a few souls have,
    That you were never meant to possess.

Whatever you experience, whatever you see,
    Is merely a sign your brain is desperately
Attempting to rid itself of the poison,
    That you have ingested so foolishly.

Maybe you're seeking the peace. My friend,
    That's only found at your final transition;
So, why shorten your days? Let Life turn you on,
    And you'll be thankful you made that decision.

— *Yolanda Marin*

Little Girls

What are little girls made of — do you know?
Dolls' houses, dolls, skates and jump ropes
Singing and dancing and putting on a show
Crayons and pencils on papers in envelopes.

What is one little girl made of — I surely know:
Pandas, raccoons, doggies and ducks
Hugged with tight little arms and a dimpled elbow;
Doll buggies, horses and chickies with "clucks."

This special little girl is made of all good things —
Honey and milk, cookies and steak, and ice cream
Pink cheeks, red lips, white teeth, a mouth that sings
Songs, poems, stories—all woven into one dream.

What are little girls made of — we know!
The best things in life rolled into one.
Soft, cuddly — as we watch our little girl grow —
Shining brightly around us like the rosy sun.

— *Ruth Grossman*

Stand Up America

Stand up America for every star and stripe;
Don't let our standard of God fail in our life;
We believe in freedom, and justice for all;
Liberty comes with responsibility, false pride will fall;
Stand up America to that old renown beckon call;
Stand up America, for in God we trust;
Our values and beliefs are declining for selfish lust;
Cocaine, the white lady, is putting many of us to sleep;
Weakened family ties and apathy evoke a time to weep;
Stand up America and arise from our slumbering sleep;
Stand up America, money will never replace unity and love;
Endless technology, things have replaced our God above;
Children and parents are killing each other without a frown;
Daily younger ones are filling a prison & graves in the ground;
Remember, this is America, the land of the brave;
Stand up America and save our children, do save;
Stand up America, the land of the great melting pot; have we
polluted our lofty esteem with a sorry lot; strong men & women
are weakening as water in a glass; stand up America,
let's recapture some workable values of the past.

— *Rosita Marie Cornish*

Rap Conversation

This is me here with a rap conversation,
Don't start bugging, you don't have an invitation.
And I'm talking to you, you little bum on the street,
Don't talk bum, just have a seat.

Don't be using that stupid white little powder,
Come on everybody just say a little louder.
Don't do drugs they make you mess up;
If you end up alive, it'll be real luck.

You see drugs is a group of things that you get,
You start taking them and they bite you like a pet.
Start taking crack, cocaine, marijuana;
Have some drugs - No, I don't wanna.

Drink and drive and see what you get,
You won't go nowhere, you won't be set.
Don't do drugs they make you mess up;
If you end up alive it'll be real luck.

If you didn't do drugs yet, don't do it ever,
If someone offers you, just say never,
Don't do drugs, they make you mess up;
If you end up alive, it'll be real luck.

— *Matthew J. Singleton and Joshua J. Rogers*

Come, Walk With Me

On a clear, bright day, long, long ago
Down by the sea of Galilee
Passed a stranger who called,
"Come, walk with Me."

The multitudes came. He healed their sick,
Raised their dead, made the blind man see.
And always they heard the same request,
"Come, walk with Me."

Storm clouds gathered, conspiracy grew
Between Rome and a jealous Pharisee.
But still the call was loud and clear,
"Come, walk with Me."

Death could not hold the Son of God,
He returned for all to see.
And to those who would listen softly He called,
"Come, walk with Me."

Two thousand years have come and gone
While others carried on His plea;
As clear today as it was back then,
"Come, walk with Me."

— *Olive Rader*

Silent Thoughts

I see her crying in a corner,
drained of any feeling, as expressionless
as a rag doll, unresponsive to my pleas.
Her eyes wander, darting all around;
vacant.
Silent lips pressed together
scare my ringing ears.
No words to say, no thoughts
to think
only clouds, breezes,
lapping, rushing waves
of darkness, black as the sun drowning
in an abyss deeper than
the soul
never to be seen again always out of touch
running out of time
no time
no breath
  —*Sherrill Berry*

The Sky

Tender moments shared in soft pale light
Drifting clouds of love on a summer night
Azure and lavender sunset on a sky of gold
It is only you I want to hold
A gift from God the sky He painted
Only a gray dark storm of lies will taint it
Warm soft tears of a summer rain
Mingle with my own in vain
Often I wonder what happened and why?
Especially when I gaze at the sky
Night, blue black velvet jewelled starlight
I see only you when I look into the night
Yet again the sky will awake with dawn
Pink rosy hues, but you are still gone
Dancing go the clouds across a sky of blue
Seeing all this beauty I once saw in you
A gift from God the sky He painted
Only a gray dark storm of lies will taint it
  —*Laura M. Fialkowski*

Untitled

I have gone as the wind blows gently
drifting far away
I have tried as spring comes always
once a year
My heart has broken as the rose dies
in the cold of winter
My attempts have failed as the movement of water
when frozen over
So I wander wastefully as does snow
when dropped from above
So I wait for the one as a rock
accenting natures beauty
  —*Scott Shedlock*

Sunrise

Raindrops fall like tears from the dark, sullen sky.
Days of sunshine, happiness, and love have long since passed by
Wind rustles through the trees, scattering leaves into the air
 They drift away into the night, but who knows to where?

I sit alone at my window, staring deep into the night,
Waiting, patiently waiting, for the sun to bring some light.
One last thought of hope glimmers before I finally close my eyes,
 knowing deep in my heart it's only a matter of time
  Before the sun will once again rise.
  —*Suzanne R. Drinnon*

Summer Clouds

Summer spirit drenched in wintry rain
Drink the roots like our searching eyes,
Which light upon clouds that tiptoe,
Then kiss on the run.
Thespian clouds that pause in passing
To present their thousand faced drama,
Then are gone with the rosy, puffed cheeks
Of the infant wind, while dons the world
A grey cloak with a green lining.
We sit wide-eyed, in some inner pocket.

Our moment is like
A string of minute lifetimes
Together linked.
  —*David Gregor*

Ignore The Devil!

When you're going downtown
Eating in a restaurant
Going to church
Or any place
Someone may be rude to you
Try to stab you in your back,
Scandalize your name
Or slam a door in your face.
But instead of getting mad
Or even
Just call on Jesus and pray.
Don't sell your soul to hell I shall say!
Ignore the devil
And continue throughout your day
Depending on Jesus
Because he can make away!
  —*Travis DeWitt Veal*

Home Again

As I plunder the battlefields of my past,
echoes of lost dreams and irreverent loves
beat like a fading rhythm.
Home Again

Memories take flight like a thousand shadows,
ooze from the charnel in my mind
bares putrid shame and moldy secrets.
Home Again

Casting aside the burden of armor I rejoice,
fear stripped of its oppressive flesh
becomes understanding and peace.
Home Again

I open the windows in the bunker of my heart,
tears of forgiveness cleanse my barren soul
purging the dark with breaths of light.
home again
And Free
  —*Linda C. Hall*

Our Common Lot of Pain

We cannot escape our common lot of pain nor someone else's.
Emotionally or physically the pain will always be there, the
pain of losing love, or not achieving something. Try to escape
the pain of death. It's nearly impossible yet you may be able
to drift away but will eventually drift back. You see the pain
of someone else and it may hurt you. Now you have pain too.
It will always be there regarding something, anything.
You cannot escape it.
With time your escape will find reality once again.
  —*Lisa Fey*

The Final Movement

The drums start low and bring to pace, as I watch with an
empty face.
The harpist pulls her strings with refrain, as I sit here,
watching in pain!
The piano plays the heavy song, as I wonder, "what went wrong?"
The trumpets blare fierce and foul, as I release my saddest howl!
The violins sigh the filthy trend, as I stand here mourning
my dead friend.
The drums pick up like shooting shots, as I ponder his final
thoughts.
The chorus sings loud and clear, and all the while I think
"if only I had been there!"
The drums are my heart in strains and fear, as I start to
wipe a falling tear.
Then the coffin is closed upon him, as I argue "it was life
that killed him!"
The saddest of songs had ended now that I've said goodbye
to one I have befriended...

   —DJ Rees

The Old Fashioned Village

The old fashioned village is covered in dust,
Empty from people, empty from lust.
The village is quiet, painfully so,
Yet no other people seem to know.

The old fashioned village lies in despair,
With no one to fix it, no one that cares.
The houses are fragile, wind may blow them down,
No one will notice, not in this deserted town

The windows are eyes searching for life,
Wanting to give up the everlasting strife.
Old memories are stored in decaying attics,
That would awe the biggest antique fanatics.

Although it's forgotten, it is still there,
And the younger generations comes to wander and stare.
For the old fashioned village is, and forever will be,
The home of forgotten old memories.

   —Marissa Putten Vink

Thursday's Dinner

We'd traveled a long, confusing trail
that seemed to have no end.
He led us to a borrowed loft
provided by a friend.

We entered that cool and dusty place
out of the heat of the day.
We ached for rest and refreshment,
but the words he had to say

jolted us from our weariness.
"Choose a seat." A simple request.
But which of us are the well loved friends,
and which of us are the guests?

Like children, we scratched and we scrambled.
He watched as we fought for that seat.
Then he quieted us with his sad, sad eyes,
took his cloak, and began washing our feet.

Then he sat at the table and offered us
a feast of bread and wine.
"This bread is my body, broken for you.
The blood in this cup is mine."

"Love each other now, as I have loved you,"
He offered us unscarred hands.
"Though the darkness is falling, remember,
it is LIFE that the Father has planned."

   —Teri Smith

Be Happy

Put a smile on your face, let your mind and body experience and
enjoy your being happy. Happiness could be found in many ways,
nice things you do for others and for yourself, just about
everything you enjoy doing. Put your troubles and problems and
yes heart aches on hold, so you can take pleasure in each day
you are living. Be part of the beautiful earth and all that
goes on it. Be happy you have what you have and look forward
to each minute of really nice times. Laugh and make others
laugh and see how good it feels to put your worries to the
side. Divert your mind when troubled and start with what you
take pleasure in and see how happiness will flow in you.
Refresh yourselves by being happy as often as you can, you will
receive great benefits. All of us don't have to pay for
happiness it is part of our make up and many times we don't let
it come forward. You don't have to study happiness or look for
it, it is in each and everyone of us and when experienced your
out look on life is much brighter, your problems and stress is
better and you will be so glad to be alive and happy.

   —Sally Buscetto

Dallas

November day in Dallas City, sun was shining all was pretty
Enormous crowds with great big smiles
The streets were thronged for miles and miles,
In Dallas City on that day.

A quick Hello a fleeting Hi! the motorcade moved quickly by
A nod a wave a flashing grin, who knew what horror lay within
Dallas City on that day.

In some dark corner lurked the devil, dressed up in the form
of man sowing seeds of hate around him,
bent only on his gruesome plan from his darkened window high,
looked around with evil eye, waiting there with baited breath,
to cast below his bite of death.

Three shots rang out in quick succession and tore into that
grand procession did this foul deed make him content
when he shot this man, our President. Was this to tear us all
apart, to instill fear within our heart breed contempt within
our nation, this murder done with contemplation.

We go onward as we must, to show the world our faith, our trust
With out leader buried in the sod,
We are still one nation under God..

   —Richard A. Adams

Untitled

Catchers should sacrifice their bodies not worried if there's
enough equipment
To act real tough and have a good attitude
can easily make the other team intimidated by not only you but
your teammates too.
You should also stand-out and prove you run the field!

   —Michele Schiffelbein

Untitled

Two bodies consumed by passion,
Entangled, gripping, moving together.
Oblivious to outsiders,
Lost in their hideaway.
One soul longing, wanting, loving the other.
But the other indifferent to the love,
Wanting only the pleasure of the act.
Both receiving the satisfaction of it.
Parting, one aches for the closeness.
The other never looks back.

   —Marni King

Friends Forever

Moving on is hard to do
Especially if it means saying goodbye to you.
We've been through laughter and the tears.
We've shared all of our hopes and fears.
You've been there during the sorrow and pain
And never looked for anything to gain.
You never wanted anything from me
Just to share to my thoughts and dreams.
I just wanted to say thank you
For being a friend that's true
And for always caring and being there.
I may not have always shown how much I care,
But you're always in my heart
No matter how many miles keep us apart,
Or what the future may bring.
You'll always be special to me and nothing
Will ever break the bond of friendship that we share.
Nothing will ever change how much I care.
Just remember all along the way,
We're friends forever and a day!

  —*Paula Lentz*

Untitled

I'll always look forward to tomorrow
especially if it promises to be like today
 I never have time for pain or sorrow
ever since the day, you came my way.
 A heart once bleak, empty and cold,
has now overflowed with happiness and love
 the future has finally come within my hold
yet the time we share seems never enough.
 I remember when there was a time
When my world seem to come to an end,
 You were there like a ray of sunshine
My one true love, my very best friend.
 Now the days are so much brighter
there's no longer any clouds in my skies,
 when I'm with you, I want to hold you tighter
to make sure you'll never leave my side.
 So if a person wishes, to have a love so true;
where perfection is what they hope to find
 I can only wish they find someone like you
for I'm eternally grateful your mine.

  —*Laurie Pascarella*

Breaking Up

Breaking up is hard to do
Especially when it happens to you.
When the decision is yours and you know it's right
Then you have conquered half the fight.

The idea to leave the person you spend so much time with
Is hard to believe when it's time to split.
When the decision is made and all is said and done
Part of the battle may have been won.

The rest of the battle has to be fought on the inside
Even though we try to deny, this is where we tend to hide.
Somehow, trying to show how we really feel
Without making it such a big deal.

The heart may be in great pain
But outside you may seem as sweet as sugar cane.
When it seems like the pain is always there
There is always a need and much pain to share.

Tell a true friend how you feel
At least someone else knows the pain is real.
When the pain seems to let you be
Then, I say, that you are considered free.

  —*Yekitha Robinson*

Life

Today is part of the expectations of
 eternity;
To-morrow, to-morrow and to-morrow brings
 the last of the final things.
Yesterday is the making of history;
The passing of time; the living today;
 the future to-morrow, makes living
 on borrowed time most gratifying.

  —*Maryida Horn*

Death - Spirit

The loss of a loved one is hard to conceive,
Even with the cards and flowers received.
Out of sight but not out of mind,
The hurt will heal in time.
Little things will continue to appear,
or the reminder of their voice to your ear.
It's not wrong to have your time of grief,
But you know their not in pain but have relief.
With Gods helping hand and loving way,
your loved one will always be with you to stay.

  —*Peggy Porter*

Untitled

I have loved you ever since....
Ever since God created the moon above,
Or the place we live that circles the sun.
Ever since birds have flown the open sky,
Or the mountains that stretch to the stars so high.
Ever since the oceans were blue,
Or the time that flowers and trees were first to bloom.
Ever since creatures on this world started to roam,
Ever since man and woman from children have grown.
Ever since the Lord gave his only son,
So that through him our sins will be undone.
Ever since we were born unto his life we live,
Ever since my eyes were opened to the person you've been.
Ever since we have met,
My heart has been tender.
I have loved you for as long,
As long as I can remember.

  —*Steven Sanders*

Simple Things

The setting sun does lay his head during the twilight,
Ever so slowly,
Dozing, dozing,
Opening his eyes once more to say,
Good night.
The sky mixes her paints during the twilight,
Wondering, thinking,
Am I doing this right?
I sit looking at the half-sunken flaming ball of gold
During the twilight,
Wishing, wanting,
To hear what the sun has to say,
Then...I catch it,
The sun opening his eyes once more to tell,
Indeed,
Everything is all right.

  —*Leela Raju*

A Tragic Notion

A watch, measures, the ticks of time
Every hour, you, will hear a chime.
A scale, weighs, the pounds of weight
But, which is greater? Love or hate.

The greatest emotions, without measure...
One is pain, the other, pleasure
Which is which? You might ask
That may be, the greatest task.

Both, we feel, with all our might.
Which is wrong? Which is right?
Both, consumes, our biggest passions
Seeking each, to greater rations.

Can you tell, the two apart?
One is easy, the other, hard.
How, do you tell the difference?
Both, are foolish, yet both, make sense.

The key to emotion, is first, you feel.
The second, is how you must deal.
Everything else, will soon take place
But, not to feel... is empty space.

　　　—*Mark A. Wise*

I Feel Like Sailing Away

I gaze out over the cabin light
Every morning, and every night
In the serenity of moving tides
I feel like sailing away.

　　Oh, the tiring city heat
　　And hustle and bustle of scurrying feet
　　I've got to run back, to my cabin retreat
　　I feel like sailing away.

Sail away, to an isle of tranquility
Remote from the earthen fire
Free from the din and calamity
Boating is my one desire.

　　Yes, I gaze out over the cabin light
　　Into the briny's enchanting sight
　　With the serenity of moving tides
　　I feel like sailing away.

　　　—*Stan Rose*

This Is My Dream!

I wish
　　Everyone had a home
　　Food on the table
　　And a loving family

I hope
　　Someday color won't matter
　　We'll and be mixed
　　And no one will be ashamed

I believe
　　One day there will be peace
　　No windows barred
　　And no loaded guns under our pillows

I think
　　Soon children will grow-up fearless
　　They will be bold, brave, and full of love
　　And they will rule the world

Martin Luther King,
　　This is my dream!!!
　　　—*Mandy Almoney*

Everyone

Everyone has their own type of style.
Everyone is different from the other.
Everyone is able to anyone how they feel.
Everyone should be able to live a happy life
it's just that "able" is not given to everyone.
Everyone here is free, yet people are imprisoned.
Everyone could say a different meaning but yet all of them still
correct. Everyone should mean what they say or don't say
　　anything.
Everyone has a choice, they just have decide which one they
　　believe.
Everyone can make a decision so be careful and make the right
　　one.
Everyone could always be there for anyone but they're not.
Everyone should please as they do instead of doing as they please.
Everyone should be able to be expressed, instead of being
　　depressed.
Everyone could make their move, but yet they could stay in bed.
Everyone could be in a home that's only if jobs were offered.
Everyone should be able to get a chance in college
yet others don't have the green paper.
Everyone could read and write but yet there still are expenses.
Everyone has a voice and all I ask is that they use it.

　　　—*Sonja Marie Birr*

How To Fix The World

Put a permanent smile on everyone's face, lift the burden from
everyone's soul.
Let the evil in every heart become grace and success be
everyone's goal.
No more rapists, muggers, killers, kidnappers, guerrillas,
psychos or women face slappers, no more racism,
AIDS, child neglect or abuse, birth defects,
hatred or substance (drug) use.
Love would replace hate and happiness sorrow,
we'll be able to look forward to a brighter tomorrow.
Wait! am I going mad this world can't be fixed, not even with
the help of a great magician's trick.
When this world was created it was fair, fresh and new and it
got corrupted by a miserable few, but that few soon grew to a
perplexing degree, till there was nothing could be done by you
or by me. To fix the world,
I surmise, in conclusion and I'm sorry to say to my
disillusion would be to blow this world up to eternal reclusion
and hope it's created again by confusion.

　　　—*Rosemary Cruz*

A Boy's First Bike

A boy's first bike is really neat, it has a license for
everything, it can be a car, or even a plane, you see this
bike, has everything, it can shoot a laser farther than
yours, it can blow up the neighbors, house next door. It
can be a racer, when no ones around, just let a cop catch me
now. It can make any noise I want it to make, it can even
make noises from outer space. It can do anything I tell
it to do, it can jump a house if I want it to, it can win
a race in two seconds flat, and leave a skid up and back,
it can jump any ramp, and no ditch is to wide. My bike
has wings now, it can fly. And God forbid that terrible
sound air stars leaking from the valve. Oh' what will I
do? How will I play? my bike will be down for a couple
of days, I can't sleep at night, my worst fear has come
true, my bike has a flat, what will I do? Call a doctor
or a friend, just get my bike, running again. See to a
boy, it's everything, that bike holds a lot of his
unfulfilled dreams.

　　　—*Vanessa K. Beineke*

327

Life

Once I was a baby
everything was so bright,
I saw something new every day and night.
Then I was a child everything was so clear,
I saw the world as one big cheer.
Then I was a teen I saw everything green,
I didn't realize how the world was so mean.
Now I am a woman I see everything is right,
I notice there's violence day and night.
I try to look up and think everything is mild,
but I remember I can never see the world as a child.
I wonder what the world would be like without any violence,
But then I know, peace and silence.

—*Wendy L. Bailey*

Untitled

It almost happened, he was almost gone
Everything we worked for for so very long,
Things kept building up and we never got to talk,
Cause every time we did one got up and walked,
We can always work things through if we try,
Maybe there'll be a time or two when someone starts to cry,
But if we can work through it,
All the tears and grief would be worth it,
Because I love you and you love me,
And if it works out we were meant to be,
So we've got to try and do our best,
Care about ourselves and think less about the rest.

—*Wendy Vickery*

Wall Of The Dead

Black marble shone dully in reflected light.

Unseen names drifted through the night.

The mourner stood mammothed by the awestruck sight.

Ten agonizing years his tortured soul had journeyed to
experience the somber wall this night.

He stood, he stared, pain-filled tears crept down his
care-worn cheeks.

Some he had saved, but those on the wall he felt had died in
vain.

Suddenly, a gentle yet strong voice said: "Do not grieve for
them my son, they bought eternity through the barrel of a
gun."

The man slowly turned and walked away. He had finally found
peace at the wall of the dead.

—*Tim Phillips*

Gloom

Dispersing itself in all directions, overtaking the
distressed without regard for what heart it tortures.

Penetrating through the soul, and throughout one's entire
being.

Giving its symptoms into the actions of men, as they go about
their daily business.

Causing thoughts to arise which otherwise would have no
bearing.

Creating misty eyes, sick hearts, and wandering memories as
it passes, leaving the soul destitute.

—*Melissa Gray*

Bear's Progress

Dispersed yearlings on the move,
exploring new territory away from
older bears and family.

Ranging far, into settled lands,
following creekbeds, travelling at night.

An occasional sighting,
a raided beehive,
a track in the mud.

Then a mound of black fur
crushed beside the interstate
unrecognizable.

Was it panic, headlight-stricken?
Cloaked in rain, inky night or pre-dawn gloom?

A great shape, a shadow,
transfixed in the glare
shattered.

A roaming, unwelcome bruin
soaring back to its birth haunts,
the beckoning mountains.

—*Scott E. Strasser*

Every time I See Diamonds

I see blue/white sparkle
Eye catchin mind trappin radiance
Status symbol brilliance
When I see diamonds I see red glitter
A bright shiny blood red
A kinda deep down in the ground slave blood red
A fierce midday angry sun red
When I see diamonds I see black
A cold mine tunnel black
A triple dark mine tunnel grave black
A null and void mind black
I see shiny black with big brown eyed brightness
Dulled by bullets
I see a glarin human injustice
When I see diamonds
I see azania, watts, harlem and everywhere greed for shiny
thangs exploit, oppress, murder and imprison
I see, we feed apartheid, jimcrows bastard son
I see a relationship between the diamonds we buy and the
bullets they use

—*Nafis Nabawi*

Why?

He's dead yet he still fills affections
eye, his heart was wise and also kind.
Nobody could deny that the killer should serve
for life. When the angels called for aid
and nature prepared the deathly blow.
The vicious crime replayed the power
of death without the blow.

In misery's darkest cavern known his
useful care was ever bold. The busy day
the peaceful night. All was still,
I wonder why?

His arms were firm, his eyes were bright
I wonder now why didn't he fight? I mean
it's only his life, life.... life.

They took away his 16th year.
They took away a friend.

Now with no pain
no graduations, all went away
Death came and broke the chain.
And freed his soul the nearest way.

—*Soledad Gonzalez*

New England Mayflower

I can't conceive why God, with will divine,
Fashioned this wondrous world to hide for me
Among the deep-shed needles of the pines
Or near some wood brook's moist fertility
A tiny flower whose poignant fragrance steals
Into the roadway where I walk alone,
So I must turn aside 'til search reveals
Its secret beauty hidden near a stone.

He must have known that some day I would need
To cup my hands around its dewy face
And steep my soul in fragrance, and to heed
Its gallant blooming in a wintry place.

The breath of springtime that its presence brings
Heals as by magic every scar I bear.
Life takes new luster, and fresh gladness springs
When I can find a mayflower, anywhere.

—Vileta N. Selchow

Dream

It's me again, though I have no name
Fear me not, for it's you I came
The world outside has drastically changed
All the confusion has left you mentally drained
I'm no stranger, so let me in
I've traveled a distance just to be your friend
Prepare yourself for a pleasurable night
Soon you'll journey a mystical flight
Comfort I seek when you're in pain
Therefore, the depth of me can't be explained

—Yolanda I. Long

Solitude Of The Excalibur

Shadows of the darkness, came to me, making me
feel not to be. Making me feel the loneliness
in my heart, the quietness of my room that whales me apart.
The light of the silent moon, its beams creep
in as the curtain is moved by a cool breeze so
thin. Hence, violently wipes the window trim,
to light the space within. It blows my hair to
teary eyes. I feel the chills, the fire, the sine.
A silvery, gray shade reflects a non-shadowed
starry haze. Its sharpness slender to a dark helve.
For there lies the blade next to me, in all its
devilish crusade. For there lies the excalibur
ready for the taste of crimson, my sight of a
cloudy gaze. For there lies the knife awaiting
the thick stain of serum, my soul to slowly fade.
Smiling as I flout to a dream world up high and
proving them all wrong, as for being humane, and
awaiting to hear my vain and foolish cry, for
now the unloved princes must die. A thought of pain and not
knowing why, for if this were you, you'd feel the same as I.

—Valerie Joy Ray

I

Identity; the experience of sensation, like a newborn child
feeling, sensing life for the first time.
It is not a pleasant time for the child
because there is pain and fear and heat and cold
and so the child cries out for love
In a world where love is hard to find,
like car keys in a mad rush out the door for some trivial task.

—Scott Fentress

This Son Of Ours

Seems I can see you yet, as in the days of yore,
Feet cold and dripping wet, tracking mud upon my floor.
I remember how I'd scold, even threaten to keep you in,
Then your sweet charm would unfold, and nearly always you
  would win.

I would have my windows bright, so shiny they would gleam.
On those chilly winter nights, you'd draw pictures there in steam.
You would let me have my say about that and other things
When I'd turn to walk away, you'd untie my apron strings.

Well, my dear, now I confess, I loved those antics all the while.
Although I seemed so in distress, within my heart I wore a smile.
When you were young and played with toys, I said then, and I still
  do,
I wish I'd had a dozen boys, if they could all have been like you.

—Mary 'Jean' Jameson

Liberation

Most of my fears, like leaves at autumn's end
Fell, were trodden, crushed, till they were no more;
One remained, one I could not comprehend:
It haunted, gored my thoughts and, at last, tore
My soul, I lost what nothing can restore,
Death snatched the one that hushed me at night
And left me angered at his petty spite.

I feared this most; but time has changed my view
Of death and our coming date with its change
Of life, of scenes, of friends, and while it's true
I have no choice of dates—cannot arrange
Our rendezvous, dying seems no more strange
Than migrant birds who wait on some strange lawn
To be fed by unknown hands at dawn.

—Leo Richards

The Charmer

Armor-less he enters the perilous zone of droning squadrons,
fiercely guarding their secured territory.
Exposed arms to elbows, face to neck, equipped only with the
spirit of a Shaman Priest, he penetrates into the menacing whir
Cellophane capes, shielded bodies, bristly legs, lusty
claws, and burning lances surround and envelope the Bewitcher,
who has begun "the seduction." Fearlessly in command, he
mesmerizes, enchants, and transforms the rushing rage.
Soon turbulent tongues are vigorously sucking nectar and
magically shaping wax, submitting their offerings to the master
charmer.
Departing with treasures in tow, skin unscathed,
the Bee Keeper emerges.

—Terri Dalla Valle

The Fruits Of Labor: A Writer's Report

Hour upon hour of labor
finally ends in the ceremonial cutting of the
  umbilical cord.

I lay the pen down,
  sigh,

And submit my child for the approval
of a reluctant, yet hopeful surrogate,
the determined stage mother of only the
most gifted and promising.

This done, I sink back to lick my wounds
and prepare
to conceive again.

—Melissa E. Brooks

Peace On Earth

To create a peace on earth
First allow a space for birth.
Then begin with peace of heart
Not setting minds and souls apart.
Do not form an attitude
Of narrowness and platitude.

Peace is not rigid morality
But an expression of inner personality.
Forget about bias and constraint.
Peace is voices heard, even faint.
Peace is not a problem national or international
But individual insight rational and irrational.

Peace is a level we can not know
If we seek enemies or select foe.
It's not a thing to be won by war
To force a move or settle a score.
It's right and wrong built in our fibers
Without winners or powerful survivors.

Peace is not a gusty game of politics and fame.
Peace is understanding, tranquility and humility.

—*Stephanie A. Smith*

Captors Of The Future

Brown, big brown eyes
Fixed on the wall opposite mine
They stare longingly when I'm not there
When I am, they challenge me to a staring contest,
I never win

Are you staring past me, or am I seeing through you the
fulfillment of my dreams?
Forever they will always be near,
So I hope, to compliment a fragment of life's construction

I have not yet built my grave in this world that I have
been exiled to,
They always stop me - black foreseeing dots
Tell me of a better land
Existence, freedom from solitude - the future

I can hardly see it, it's very far off
From this place I reside within myself
I hope I survive the journey
Will you be my seer as I embark on this voyage of
blindness?

—*Michael Petoh*

Genesis

Exploding light everywhere present,
flashing far-flung distances,
rolling thunder of existence penetrating,
shouting, insisting on its revelation,
everywhere sparking strength;
everywhere melting what wasn't;
everywhere longing for what could be.
It is the moment of moments,
the eternal yes of night rolling away like mist succumbing,
clouds bowing before skies majestic,
an army vanquished by its own power,
routed in its intent to wage its own benefit.
Spiraling currents heat the absence, firing the nothingness,
hot kiln throwing the potter's wheel in chaos,
hot clay thrown to the four winds,
chasing every can't with could,
expanding to fullness the Name above every name,
beyond every light,
the illuminating power of
Holy, Holy.

—*Tom Umbras*

Peace Current Circles Earth

Enough, enough, is the song;
floating high where humans belong.
August thirteen, nineteen ninety-three.
From war on this earth, we are set free.

Touching, sending, powerful waves
of true peace, reaching from earth's graves,
to the blue sky where dwells our same God,
bringing harmony to earth's precious sod.

Biblical addition was written that day.
May it continue we thankfully pray.

—*Mary W. Knoll*

Love So Vast

Love is like the water's tide;
Flowing gently, side to side;
Never making up its mind;
Creeping stealthily close, then lagging hesitantly behind.

Whispers soft run through the trees,
Echoing relentless pleas.
Strangely silent lies the night; holding its breath,
Awaiting next flight, and pondering its present plight.

Where, love questions, hides that elusive tunnel
Leading to that glorious light?
When, love wonders, will mankind realize
That elusive tunnel still lies-buried deep within his soul...

Patiently waiting to be given the chance
To truly enhance his life and make him whole?
At long last, he can forget the hurt and wrong of the past,
In love so vast.

—*Wendi Steel*

Autumnal

Here on this upland meadow
flurries of crisp and crimson leaves
are dancing their adieux
in a scattering wind.

Shortly, they will feed the earth's new growth.
That is their immortality.

So shall it also be mine
(when I shall have spent all my days)
if, haply, there remain
Some gold and ruddy remembrances
to nurture my son
and his sons.

—*Ruth B. Walty*

Thanks Dad

Thank you dad for all the times that we've shared
For being there for me, when it seemed no one cared.

As I grew up you spent special time with me
We could laugh, we could cry and even talk seriously.

Although we've had bad times most times were good
We went fishing and camping like father and son should.

You cheered me on at my football games
I could hear you scream and shout and call out my name.

These memories that we've shared together in our past
Will remain in my heart and forever will last.

—*Ursula Bobo*

Palomino

Father is dying, mother is crying
for a daughter gone astray

Was this neglect or genetic defect?

No means of attention nor cost can revitalize

Antagonized by helplessness, they are the leaves of fall
with their battle with gravity
Guilt spreads faster than flame

Doors close, and beaten down paths rebuild
The branches dragged behind their palomino hide
their whereabouts

Forsaking their lives for another, the struggle between
obligation and survival continues

She watches from afar, but has never been
far away
Sighing in desperation, she rises each morning
Hope remains on the list, but time keeps
moving it further down.

—*Steve Waller*

Full Circle

A single celled bacillus makes a tasty little bite
For a multicelled amoeba with a hearty appetite.
Both in turn succumb to a minnow passing by,
Who promptly gets ingested by a guppy lurking nigh.

A termite wandering aimlessly is by an ant consumed,
And then is eaten by a gnat, who in the end is doomed,
As he falls prey to water bug out looking for a snack,
Who soon is swallowed by a chick in merciless attack.

A baby salamander to a lizard comes too close,
And soon becomes a part of his tissue adipose.
He in turn is seized by a gopher on the prowl,
Who alas becomes the quarry of a hungry screeching owl.

But man in all his arrogance thinks from attack he's free;
That brandishing his armaments his safety guarantees.
Forgetting the tiny predators no guns can keep at bay;
Those single celled bacilli that kill us every day.

—*Milton Schorr*

The Snake Is In Trouble!

Jesus keeps His Word!
For by His Word, He upholds all things in His
conduct of God's affairs.
And, He has said this about Himself and Satan:
"Now is the time for judgment on this world;
now the prince of this world
will be driven out!
But I, when I am lifted up from the earth,
will draw all men to Myself!"

And, in Isaiah regarding this matter, God says:
"I, even I, have spoken; yes, I have
called Him (Jesus).
I will bring Him and He will succeed
in His mission!"

So, the battle between Jesus and Satan is a
winner-take-all situation!
Through faith in Jesus, everyone can conclude:
The snake is in trouble!

—*William H. Colley*

Alone

A man is lonely in his home,
For he is too old to be at the seat of his throne,
They put him away quickly, too quickly away,
Before he could voice his say.
It was because of that minor stroke,
That the family began to provoke.
They argued for days,
What to do with Dad and what were the ways,
Finally they came to peace and the quarreling ceased,
They agreed and slowly said,
"Put dad in a home, where he'll be safe and well fed."
They never thought what his feelings were,
Since everything was in such a blur.
Now that he's taking his dying days in stride,
He does not know whether to live or hide.
He does not feel shame for what they have done
He just wishes the decision was left,
To a certain one.

—*Natalie K. Walker*

Dragon's Night

With haste I strode toward the castle
For I felt a dreadful ache.
I envisioned the greatest of fears.
Castle walls began to shake.
Roars purged silence from Winter's cold morn'.
Barren land felt Danger's quake.

Their Beast held within had risen,
Awakened from a spell's sleep.
It's time to escape bondage was nigh,
Time to return to his keep.

The sharp shackles that had bound him broke.
He erupted through the wall.
Surrounding dungeon guards were frozen,
With terror striking them all.

How would the Dragon's gaze be broken?
Only I could cast that spell.
Master, am I, of that Dragon-Beast,
And together, we must dwell.

So upon mystical magic's might,
We escaped into the night.

—*Scott Young*

Fly Away

Stand aside as I fly away into the east
For I have spread my wings and now am at everlasting peace

Sing praise with great voices to be heard by the glorified Lord
of Lords, my God
Cause forgiveness is what I ask so before Him I shall
kneel and nod

See, I am no longer in your world so empty and cold
For the Lord has blessed me in his warm rays and streets
made of gold

I have done all a man could do and seen all a man could see
and now I must leave the nest for I have been set free

And devil, you tried hard to trap and condemn me
Even though you won a few times, you must now let me be

And as I walk along the quiet river banks looking at the
clouds in the sky
I realize no matter what you take from this world at the end
it win because you must die

So, let me fly away as shimmering tears from my eyes fall to
the ground below
The beautiful fire colored sky fades away, and I know I won't
have to cry no more.

—*Shawn Freeman*

I Should Know

As I sing to you my song, I hope you listen and agree.
For I write you these words, hoping you will share with me
My journey through life and all my goals
For I live in a world of the past that man should always know.
Know how to share, know how to care
For in my world I know no despair.
I know where I am going, I know where I've been.
Having you in my life is hard - I've never let somebody in.
For then it will be the end of my goals, you see.
You completed them.
Oh, someone please see me.

—*Vincent F. Cipolla Jr.*

To Live For A Day

Rise up all ye who are sleeping, waiting for the sun to rise.
For it waits not to be greeted nor do you control the path it flies.
Take hold of today and live it as if tomorrow the world will never turn.
For yesterday is gone forever and never again will it return.
So take hold of this special moment, for the gift is yours for the day.
Take not this gift for granted for your gift may be taken away.
Do not be left ashore just watching as another man's boat sails out to sea.
For that captain has set a course in life and today his spirit sails free.
Today is your chance to soar high above and to live life full of scope.
For to live is not just to survive but to embrace love, faith and hope.
Wait not to dance tomorrow when you are given the chance today.
Now is the time to live your life full and to let go of yesterday.
Remember how precious life really is and never forget how to say —
Thank you God for all your gifts. Thank you for this day.

—*Terry Williams*

What Love Does

Love labors on a bridge - long, tough and high
For just one to cross over - to the safe mountain side

Love never complains - too busy listin' for sheep
One lamb cries out - love's shaking off sleep

Love never spouts off - "Just leave 'em all alone"
Love knows about - hurtin' to your bone

Love won't walk away - in a dragon attack
Love cradles the flock - till the dogs fall back

Love never dwells - on all the scars it bears
Love's giving thanks - that heaven still cares

Love pours in oil - and love pours in wine
Love looks for the sinking - and throws our the line

Love gathers in - and love just won't stop
Keeps on feedin' and leadin' - to the mountain top

Then love'll turn ya loose - in ya' Father's big love heart
Where love first came from - and got its start

For God loved this ol' world in the midnight of sin and heard
his Son volunteer - to come take us in

He's knockin' now for you - ya gotta let 'him know
Yes, I receive your love - Lord Jesus, Let it flow!

—*Shirley L. Bledsoe*

Let Go And Live

God help us—take time to pray
For lives that are shattered into bits each day.
We can't help holding on to the past,
Mourning and grieving while memories last.

It takes a long time to get over the change,
The missing past—different life—makes one feel strange.
But everyone knows that nothing forever will last,
We all have to think of the future and let go of the past.

Please God—help us have something left in our life to give,
To create a new life—be happy and live.
God, I took your advice, you see,
I let go of the past—and discovered me.

—*Peggy Raduziner*

Untitled

Illness, hospital visit after visit,
For me, why is it?
What have I done, throughout my life,
To warrant and justify all my strife?
Through the effort to be a success,
Moving to benefit others, not as blessed.
The pressures that created this physical mess,
I tell myself, don't consider yourself any less.

Hope, for a quiet, peaceful, life,
That escaped me and my ex-wife,
And now there's another, quite possibly out of reach,
Someone I helped, along the way,
Yet never ever had the courage to say,
I love you with all my heart,
Is it possible for us to get a fresh start?
To change what we've both gone through?
Into three powerful words, I Love You.

—*Spencer Shaw*

Oh! My Crazy Heart

Oh! my crazy heart, you wander around like a bee;
Devour a pollen, from all those flowers you see.

Wherever you eye a beauty, you get stuck with her.
How to deal with you, so far, I can not figure.

You want to soar to majestic heights, to view down;
You want, like those happy mountain streams, to flow down.

You want, with every beauty here, to lie down;
Oh! my crazy heart, I don't know how to calm you down.

—*M. Aslan*

Life

Life is like a never-ending story
Day by day playing small parts
It is a story of evil
and a story of laughter
Each person playing a small part

Life is like a winding road
of tunnels
Each separating to make a
different obstacle
All of its victims
Learn valuable lessons
On what each twist and turn
means

—*Rachael Chappell*

It

It thrusts itself upon me
A desperate sigh of gloom
Escapes a mutter from my lips
It emerges tauntingly from its tomb

A cataclysmic cyclops
Old aged beyond our time
It casts its deformed shadow
Only over mine

All my understanding
And all of my unforeseen doubt
Came thrashing through my mind

No more will man be at peace
Nor live nor laugh nor love

It thrusts itself upon me
A pitiful sigh of doom
Escapes from my tortured mind

I am left to die alone
—*Maryann McMahon*

Or The Innocent Child

A family
A few souls
A fight
Anger, bewildered, mastering
The table tipped
A leg broken
The glass shattered
Fluid spilled
But—who's the victim?
Is it the enemy?
Or the innocent child?
Who's looking in
With aching heart
As fear shivers from within
Suffocating her spirit
Sinking her soul
To the dying grave
And she can do
Nothing
But cry.

—*Sitha Som*

Indian Rock

Whispers in the air do tell.
A flowing river gushes by.
The mountain hides what once was there.
Majestic are the trees that tower.
Hidden life of long ago.
Imagination brings them back.
A time when warriors did gather.
Confrontations on the earth.
Remnants of a fire warmed.
Rock of Granite ground the food.
Flint buried under top soil.
A gathering for ceremonies.
A voice, a call, a cry to hear.
Proud, the tribal framework flowed.
Music called the spirits near.
Making medicine to survive and prosper.
Feeling for the land ran deep.
Settlers came in torrents swift.
The push upon ancestral territories.
Evolution let them rest.

—*Stacey D. Broussard*

Return to Nothing

Yesterday I was numb
A foreshadowing feeling of death
I felt so cold and alone
Today my mind is flooded with pain
Why did this happen
What did I do to deserve this?
It hurts so much
This sinking feeling in my body
Now I must turn to you
The catalyst of my pain
To try and ease me
Out of my shell
To make me see life
As something worth living
How I pray for the numbness
To return
—*Michael Mascitti*

New Little Soul

The hall of souls
A heavenly place
Where new souls are born
From heaven's grace
A new little soul
Created for you
Preparing for a journey
To be loved by two
This new little soul
Your child to be
Becomes a new little life
As two become three
—*Timothy Plant*

Please Don't Go

Come sit awhile - oh please don't go,
A little time would mean so much.
Days are so long and nights are too,
A warm embrace, a gentle touch -
Is all that I will ask of you.

Oh yes there is so much to do.
I understand, be on your way;
But promise me before you leave,
That you'll come back another day
To laugh and talk about the things
In all the world that used to be
When I could always lean on you,
And you could always lean on me.

—*Mildred Timms*

Love

A love that binds.
A love that's kind.
That includes each
    Family member,

It bends the knee
    to a low degree
to be a little tender
    to the sick, the weak,
to the offender.
It gives a love
    to render.

The warmth, the glow.
    is needed.
To bring the family
    all together.

—*Virginia Clintsman*

Soul Of A Nation

In a harbor near a city
A mighty lady stands
Tall and proud, head held high
A torch raised in her hand

She stands for freedom of the just
For truth and liberty
She represents those who died
To keep our nation free

On a hill outside a city
An old rugged cross there stands
My savior died thee, head hung low
With nails piercing his hands

He died because he loves us all
And wanted to free our soul
He shed his blood upon that cross
To cleanse and make us whole.

—*Rachel Ross*

A Poem

A 20 liner that could not be finer
A noetry yet poetry
My subject is Atlantis Secrets Revealed
That will not be repealed
This is the 5th line very sublime
The 6th line a rhyme
The 7th a shoot
The 8th a boot
The 9th a toot
The 10th a root
The 11th a moot and out
The 12th a pout
The 13th a route
The 14th a tout
The 15th a run
The 16th a bun
The 17th fun
The 18th a ton
The 19th none
The 20th the Sun and Ancient Symbol.
God Bless You.

—*Michael A. Martin*

Abortion

A part of me is missing
A part I do not feel
A part of me is missing
A part that wasn't real

A part of me was crying
A part that I now mourn
A part of me was saying
Please let me be born

A part of me is missing
A part I didn't know
A part of me was saying
I want to live and grow

A part of me was screaming
A part I would deny
A part of me was saying
I want to live not die

A part of me is missing
A part I want so bad
A part of me is crying
For the child I never had.

—*Muriel T. Rollock*

Untitled

It's not too often you'll find,
A rainbow sliding through the sky.
With awesome colors that shine,
I would love to hold it in my
    arms and call it mine.
With a good friend do stop and stare.
It is an experience to share.
For something that is so rare,
    placed in the sky with care.
Put there with a promise
    of love,
After an olive leaf found
    by a dove.

—*Lori Lawecki-Butler*

A Day In The Desert

A hot summer day in the desert
A red scorpion was hiding.
The pounding sun was
shining on my sweat-filled neck.
I trudged along
in a sea of sand and shrubs
Infinity it seemed
Alas, a water hole.
I looked in my pack for a cup.
There was the friendly scorpion.

—*Mike Moe*

To Steve

Your laugh can lift a heavy load.
A serious heart behind that laugh!
Caring, sensitive spirit, as you
stumble, stride, fumble on the path.
Brother, may the light that's yours
and mine
and all of ours
clarify the steps we need to take.

—*Linda Griggs*

Images In Still Life

A heart filled with dreams.
A soul full of fire.
Images where nothing is real.
Abstract designs woven on a rainbow
Not to see
But to feel.
Doves fly on outstretched wings
O'er the mind's canvas of desperation
Comes an artist's still life of love
Of hope; and all inspiration.

—*Lee Linc Stallings*

Time

Time,
A substance of man,
Always moving,
Sometimes hurtful
    in ways,
Moving fast,
And then slowly,
As every challenge comes,
With time.

—*Matthew McArdle*

Untitled

You're so special - a one of a kind,
a sweet guy like you is so hard to find.

And now that I've found you,
I haven't a clue what I should do.
To hang on or let go,
I hope someday fate will tell me so.

As for now just keep in mind,
I do care for you, and maybe I'm
the one who is blind.

—*Staci Elizabeth Ross*

Trapped In The Loneliness Of Self

Like a raindrop rolling off a leaf,
    a tear escapes my cheek.
        Lonely; like an outcast,
    who has sentenced himself.
A dark cloud hovers over my spirit,
unprotected by even an umbrella:
        In search of companionship;
        in need of affection.
        Trapped because of myself?

Am I destined to wallow in self pity,
        without living life?
    Self-analyzing existence till
        meaning ceases?

    As if by divine intervention,
    my mind snaps out of delusion:
    If never had to be this way;
        It never has to be.....

—*Marc Molino*

St Joseph To Sacramento

The Story Of The Pony Express

As a storm blows in
a ten day run begins
with a bible, a dollar, a pledge
no friends, no family, no loss

Crests form on the wheat
Almost ready to break
sharp peaks stand
Like broken bread
cold crumbs fall
Reload the Colt
tighten the saddle
The sun beats down
Fences live: cowboys die
Wires sing in the wind
As dust blows away a ten day run ends.

—*Laura Lee Anderson*

Wondering

Have you ever wondered,
About your kin of long ago?
Did they know about the Savior,
Are they safe within the fold?

Have you wondered about their character,
And the life they chose to lead?
Did they falter by the wayside,
Or were they good in word and deed?

What were their gifts and talents,
Did I inherit them?
One day I'll know the answer,
When I ask it all from Him.

—*Virginia Cruse*

An Arabian Stallion

Within a damp and dreary stable,
    A tiny foal is born.
He would grow into a grand stallion,
    Of fine Arabian blood.
This he did as gracefully,
    As a rose blossoming.
A coat of silver, mane of satin
    And eyes of shimmering gold.
In his heart he wanted more,
    He wanted to be free.
One evening a storm crept from
    The bosom of the mountains.
The fearful stallion of glowing white
    Leapt from his entrapment.
Freedom was finally his!
If you should see a stallion
    Of glowing white,
Do not try to harness him —
    For his heart will always be free.

—*Meghan E. Higgins*

The Meaning Of

So this is the meaning of
A tortured soul
Emptiness the only friend
Pandemonium life's only reward
Apocalyptic in nature
What does it all mean
Can anyone feel this alone
Immaterial to everything
Irrelevant to nothing
Just want to scream....goodbye
But no one is listening they only hear
Fear of the unknown
The genius of it all

So this the meaning of

—*L. Johnson*

If There Was A Tree That I Could See

If there was a tree a tree
a tree that I could see
I'd see it with all my sight
the sight that once came to me
yes came to me
in the night

If there was that tree
that tree that I could see
I'd climb that tree
not too high
not too low
just in that tree
would be me

Alone
alone in that tree
you'd find me

—*Michele Rossello*

God

God is the goodness
and brightness of my life.
He rises my spirits, hopes and joys,
of my life. He gives me the power
that no one else has earned. He is God,
the powerful spirit.

—*Misteania Dawn LeBlanc*

Truth And Lie

There must be something
A truth in your heart.
Try to release it out,
Because telling the truth is an art.

You should open your eyes
And see what you need.
Both truths and lies
Are always with you indeed.

Maybe for you to feel safe
Lie is a high tower.
But it can't last so long;
Because truth has the real power.

To see the truth
Don't be too late,
Because life is too short
To escape from the fate.

—*A. Alp ICoz*

Dirge For Dying Elms

As the twilight doom descends,
A weird, subdued light penetrates
The spectacle of deadwood
Ladened with shriveled greenery.

The pungency of trees felled and
The soft souls of slaughtered elms
Hover over in requiem,
Enduing men and things with
A veiled transparency.

There is no movement in this display
Which exhibits as one
The anatomy of life and
The structure beyond the grave.

So much sadness is there here
That somehow I have come to feel
That the sorrow I bear
Is not entirely all my own.

—*Ralph R. Gayner*

Bad Wound

Seared open flesh
A whiff of bowel
Spurts of blood
Dabbed up with towels

Big, ugly
Black thing there
Pulsing and living
Tendrils fingering
And penetrating
Other organs

Needles and silk
Whirring through skin
Not much to do
Operation's over

—*Patrick W. Stang*

Cold

Cold
A winter's night
The morning frost
Frozen creek
A wind blown shown drift
A glacier's gloom
A person's stare
A soldiers blade
People
Death

—*Tara Underwood*

Manimal

I'd like to live in
A world where the killing would stop
Where deer and rabbit would hip hop
Into my front yard to eat from my hand
Not afraid of being killed by man
A world with sky's so blue and clear
And water so clean you use as a mirror
And when darkness came
It brought nothing to fear
This is the world I would
leave to my child a place to be free
Full of animals in the wild

—*Tim Lenahan*

The Race Of The Horses

Let me tell you a story
About two horses.
One called Snow,
The other Coal.

These horses' owners
Decided to race.
Snow has won,
But the owners quarrel.

They race again.
Coal won.
The owners bicker and fight
Until one horse dies.

Why can't they tie?
Why aren't they even?
They're both horses
But their color interferes.

—*Lauren Russo*

The Well

On the hill,
 above our valley.
There is an old well,
 so dark and dreary.

Voices (moans and groans)
 rise up from its depths.
So low and haunting,
 it would make you sweat!

We looked into, the old well.
Deep down within, its depths.

Unto our squinting eyes, we see.
Little green glowing eyes,
 looking back at you and me.

Never would you guess,
 what was in its depths.
I'll tell you,
 if you must know.

For in, the depths
 of our well.
Our imaginations dwell!

—*Michelle R Cash*

Nightmare

The cats of black,
again last night,
came to visit me.

Ranked with death,
their bladed teeth,
took what they did see.

Tugging my flesh,
tearing my heart,
movement left me still.

Fading sounds of,
the life I knew,
left with all my will.

To die just once,
is what we're asked,
but dreams bring you back.

To fear the sleep,
that never wakes,
beyond the grasp of black.

—*Lisa M. Erickson*

Waiting

The cabin creaked
against the wind
lights flickered
Please don't go out
She prayed.

She held the baby close
his smell was perfume to her
a baby's smell.

The clock was ticking
he was late
She was worried.

The lights again
her heart skipped a beat.

She looked at her child
She could see his face
Come on through that door
I love you.

—*Regina Hauserman*

Perpetual Advertorials

Pump up your heart,
Air out your mind,
Just do it - here and now!
Bo knows condition's temporare
Word power will avow.

We all use crutches
Day by day
Creator will provide -
And God helps those
Who help themselves,
Revealing other side.

There is the inner self to meet.
Convincingly - get to it!
Values are the goal to set,
Solution - you will do it.

—*Patricia J. Naderer*

Whispers In The Wind

Through the ages mankind has known
All of the arts are here to stay,
Eons have passed, dust has flown,
Reveals a misty yesterday.

We see, we read and learn in time,
In depth we search until the end,
Vaguely we know friends of kind
By gentle 'Whispers in The Wind.'

—*Merry Brown*

Spring

Spring is in the air,
All the birds make up a pair
We forget about ice and snow
And go out and begin to sow
Enjoy the flowers lovely and bright
And longer sparkling daylight

Maybe we should plan our lives
The same as nature does her drive
Forget the hardship and tribulations
Make a new beginning on occasions
Make the most of our given lot
And thank God for what we got!

—*Margaret Ott*

If Only...

If this were a perfect world;
    all would be forgiven, without a
    single doubt.

If this were a perfect world;
    no one to be heard, would have
    to scream or shout.

If this were a perfect world;
    every stranger, we would greet
    as an old friend.

If this were a perfect world;
    true love would last a lifetime,
    not just a passionate weekend.

If this were a perfect world;
    our praises would be to God, and
    his glory for giving us peace of
    mind.

If this were a perfect world.

—*Patricia Ann Shearer*

Fame

Fame, an elusive damsel
Almost within one's grasp
Only to flit coquettishly
Into another's arms
This aggressively sought trophy
Aching for personal display
Is the utmost goal of vanity
For egotistic array
Bless the one who quietly
Without ad blitz or fanfare
By actions of abject humility
Creates acts of time etched virtue
In service to mankind

—*Stanley S. Reyburn*

To My Love

When we were together
Alone that night
When you held me so close,
In the moon's soft light.
The way the rain sounded,
So cold and dangerous outside
The way our hearts beat,
So warm and safe in your arms tonight
Did we mean to let it happen?
Did we mean to let our passion go?
As I lay here watching you breath,
I realize how I need and love you so.

—*Robyn D. Martin*

Love

Israel and the PLO
Although progress has been slow
A new country is on the make
Borders being cut like cake.
United States rolled out the mat
to Rabin and Outlaw Aerofat
There's many facets to explore
But both walked through the open door
All the people of Palestine
Have put out the love peace sign
Rifles traded in for plows
Horses chickens ducks and cow's
There's a great spirit in the air
For this great new born love affair.

—*Sam Chambasian*

Love You Mom

Dear Mom,
    Although you have left
our side today our love will
always be there. Thank you
for showing us all the wonderful
things there is in life. You were
our best friend and no one will
ever replace you. Nothing was
ever too much to ask from you.
For today you have even given
us the strength to endure our
pain.
    Thank you for our lives.

—*Rita McQuay*

A 90's Child

I'm a 90's child
Always smiling
Hiding my fears deep inside
For according to what I see
There is no place for me
To give, to love...
And I think to myself
If only I could find
A grownup sweet and kind
To take me outside
In the fresh air
For I am gasping for breath
Choked with fear
You see, there's no role
Model here.
Oh come, give me hope
Come walk and talk with me
I'm small but can grow
If you remove this fear
And replace it with love.

—*Sherley Owens*

Balance

Keep me next to you,
        Always
Please, don't shut me out.

Hold me within your heart.
        Share
your fears, your aspirations.

    Our souls strengthen
    Pushing and Pulling
    Giving and Receiving.

We are each other's refuge
    Finding Balance
from the world's turmoil.

    You are me, and I you.
        in many ways,
        We Are Truly One
        together.

    Keep me next to you
        Always
Please don't shut me out.

—*Patti C. DeFilippo*

We Both Can Now Feel Sure About This

We both can really live a happy life
Always having bright and shinny eyes;
We both can surely feel very secured
About sustaining, deep love for sure.

We both can every day hold our hands
Going through a very wonderful land;
We both can sustain our togetherness
With very real deep daily tenderness.

We both can also smile, on every day
And sustain happiness on all our way;
We both can show our deep expression
To demonstrate a true love sensation.

We both can protect, all our actions
Always sustaining deep satisfactions;
We both can now surely keep going on
Feeling secured, it will not be gone.

—*Rene Cordero*

A Study In Passing

Your squared jaws stirred something
Amid my ashes I hadn't felt
In a long while
Something reminding
Me I'm still a woman.

Lazily tall and striding like a panther,
Your dreadlocks just as dark
My eyes gave me away
As they always do
You knew it too.

I studied your beautiful body
And you watched me watching
What is Adonis to you?
Your broad shoulders and trim waist
Keys to your kingdom.

From black shining hair
To tight skin on lank legs,
I studied the likes of you
And I understood temptation men find
In younger women.

—*Rita S. Spalding*

My Dream Of An Angel

You were in my dreams when I saw you
An Angel in disguise,
A figure of pure loving sweetness
Descending to earth from the skies.

You were everything expected
And a lot more you surpassed,
But who was I to tell you
You had me way outclassed.

All this and more I noticed
Yet words could not express,
The thoughts as they ran through me
Or the feelings I possessed.

I simply couldn't leave you
But I figured in a way
That I'd be kind of stupid
Standing; watching you all day

Pay-no attention to this
Destroy it - if you will,
Do anything - your heart desires
But I will love you still.

—*Margaret Jones*

The Past

The past touches the spirit
An everlasting want
A memory revealed
A moment left untold
The heart, the mind, the spirit
Uplifted by the soul
That touches all the memories
For the present to unfold

Oh God, to smile and cry and cheer
What can I hold tomorrow
But the essence of my spirit
Not touching any sorrow

—*Norma I. Camacho*

The Statue Of Liberty

The lady with the torch
And a plate in her hand
Tell me dame who are you
What's thy name, O grand.

The first sight by the harbor
'Have fallen love, O hearty
Gate way to America, 'Bedloe's Island'
The shrine-the Statue of Liberty.

Let my poem lies beside you
Bravo 'Bartholdi' and 'Emma'
Myself in 'The Wall of Honor'
People owe to the stemma.

The torch for freedom plate for peace
O America! Thou are shelter that frees.

—*Muhammad Rashidul Kabir Chishty*

The Kiss

I hoped that he would love me,
and he has kissed my mouth.
But, I am like a stricken bird
who cannot reach the south.
For though I know he loves me,
tonight my heart is sad.
His kiss was not so wonderful
as all the dreams I had.

—*Vicki Lovell*

When I Think Of Christmas

When I think of Christmas
    and all its manifestations—
Trees lit up in homes and out
    with lovely house decorations;
Somewhere are sounds of tinkling bells,
    and the jolly Ho-Ho! wherever it
    dwells;
Also the fun with mistletoe,
    following laughter wherever folks go.

I think of Christmas while
    Greeting cards I write,
To all my family and friends,
    I hold dear for life.
But—mainly I think of Christmas
    for the reason that it's here—
To Honor Jesus Christ—
    To keep His Memory bright each year.

—*Louise E. Munding*

"Dear Lord"

Touch my aching heart,
And dry away my tears
Give me strength to go on with my life,
for the coming years.
To be where I'm needed
for the good, and the love
I have with-in me.
Let me share it with those,
who need it.
Thank you dear Lord for the
strength you've given me.
And for the light that guided
me through my trials.
With-out you my Lord
I would be weak and lost
Thank you my dear Lord for
today's blessings
And when tomorrow comes
I'll thank you again

—*Monica Franzese*

The Woes Of Our Children

With eyes that cannot see,
And ears that cannot hear,
The woes of our children,
Fall on dreaded tear.

With arms that never reach,
And feet that never stride,
The woes of our children,
Are swallowed up in pride.

With selfishness and greed,
And hearts that never yield,
The woes of our children,
Are like the barren field.

When change comes from within,
And minds are doors unclosed,
When hearts are filled with love,
The children have no woes.

—*Linda R. Kurtz*

"Heart Of A Captain"

Land ho, and so the captain sees,
And feels the coolness of a breeze.

He knows land is where he should be,
There, with his wife and family.

But his heart will forever stay,
At sea, moving with ev'ry sway.

A storm suddenly hits.
His faithful ship, it splits.

"Ev'ry man for himself." he cries.
Knowing he is the one who'll die.

Ship sinking, he's where he belongs.
At last, Death comes and is too strong.

And sometimes on those foggy nights,
You can see the ship's glowing lights,

Can hear the tolling of a bell,
And know his heart's content.
    Farewell
        —*Melissa Hassell*

Alexander, My Son

Son, I gave you life,
and for no reason,
One lonely day you gave it away,
leaving my poor heart in pain....
When you became to light,
The world went wild, the bells
rang faster, the birds were dancing,
and the starts glittered in the dark,
But son, when your faith was lost,
and you walked out the trace,
Leaving behind the path,
in such a stormy hurry.....
seeking for the unknown
the bells cried lowly,
the birds flied slowly,
the day turned duskily,
my heart broke in pieces,
and the starts never again
twinkle in the night....

—*Rosie Munoz*

Ergonomically Correct

I came in the office today
and found my desk in disarray.
It seems that everything in fact
had to be ergonomically correct.

The chair was lowered to my delight,
now my feet won't have to fight.
They stay right on the floor, stiff
and straight to swing no more.

The computer's face now has shades.
It's not as bright but that's all right.
It sits so straight and tall, eye
level you know and that's not all.

The keyboard now has a neat little
pad to help my hands not be bad.
Hold the hands straight we're told and
don't let that carpal tunnel get a hold.

The desk itself will get a lift.
The left arm part will be raised a bit.
But now don't worry and don't you fret
They haven't been to your desk yet.

—*Pamela Phillips*

The Silent Roar Of Love

As softly as the twilight glows,
And fragile as the fading rose,
Are feelings born on the wind,
In silence, wisped away and gone.

And promise thrust on eagle's wing
To places where the angels sing,
Bear the pledges of the troth
To the altar, and the throne.

As lovers pledge, in ecstacy,
Rapture through eternity,
Beseechingly they realize
Intercession from above.

And only hearts inclined to share
Are among the privileged who hear
The song resounding from the soul,
And the silent roar of love.

—*Loyed L. Arnold*

My Lover

God took twin stars at early morn
   And from them made two eyes.
He took the curve of rainbow light
The soft sea's surge,
The peace of night;
The song of birds,
The glow of sun -
The strength of earth -
   And one by one He fused them,
Until at last from the gleaming whole
He made a rare and radiant soul.

His work was done,
   He called it good.
And then He led me where you stood.
The moment I saw you
That moment I knew -
For my heart spoke loud,
And hearts speak true,
And the thing it cried
   Was a name for you - My lover.

—*Zoila Conan*

Cow Boy Joe

He has big feet,
And his legs are long,
He has great muscles,
And his arms are strong.

He has huge ears,
And a long nose too,
His teeth look funny,
Cause they're new,

He is the kind of person,
You would like to know,
But he walks kinda funny,
Cause his legs are bow.

He has herded a lot of cattle,
And shot a lot of moose,
And has hunted down the bear,
The bob cat and the goose.

His hunting days are over,
Cause he's getting kinda old,
But he still prospects a little,
Up in the hills for gold.

—*Mildred Childers.*

Contentment

The years have come and gone,
And I have lost, not found....

The love, I have always longed for,
A love to call my own.

My dreams go on from day to day
And through the lonely night...

Yet, I have found contentment,
In the solitude of my plight.

I reminisce on all I have had,
In all the years gone by....

For, only then, I can sit back,
To dream, to smile and sigh.

At times I do get lonely
And occasionally shed a tear....

Yet, I do not regret the loneliness,
Of all those past years.

So, do not feel saddened
For you see, I am not alone....

For I have found contentment,
In the arms, of our Lord.

—*Mary Fernandez*

Untitled

If I could make a wish come true,
   And live my life again.
Oh, my, what wondrous things I'd do.
   What glories I'd attain.

What mountains I would conquer.
   What dragons I would slay.
Such admirable valor would
   I constantly display.

What castles I would build, and all
   The oceans would I swim.
The evils of the world I'd fight,
   And every battle win.

And yet on second thought I find,
   I truly must admit,
I am weary with exhaustion
   At the very thought of it.

—*Patricia N. Worsham*

A Spoonful Of Memories

As I leaf through all my recipes,
And many I do own,
They bring back warm, fond memories,
Of all the cooks that I have known.

My mom, my grandmas and my aunts,
Although they all are gone,
When I recreate their specialties,
Memories of them live on.

Many whom I've worked with,
Have added to my cache,
And as I sift and stir and bake,
I recall them in a flash.

Yes, photos fill my albums,
But not often do I look.
Thus my fondest recollections,
Come to me whenever I cook.

—*Louise N. Zuelch*

Goodbye, Again ...
My Dear, Dear Friend

The fogged up window I sit in front of
and look out of for hours
Reminds me of us,
Our relationship.

As the air grows colder and colder
The window cracks,
The window shatters
A million little pieces
Now more clear to see through.

Can it ever be put back together?
It seems impossible,
There are so many missing pieces.

The time has come once again
Whether that window that is us,
That is between us
Just cracks or if it shatters
There'll always be a next time.
So goodbye again...my dear, dear Friend
Goodbye

   —*Linda Roath*

Creation

I love to watch the babbling brook,
   And love to fish without a hook.

I love to hunt without a gun,
   And watch the deer and antelope run.

I love to hear the bluebirds sing,
   And listen to the church bells ring.

I love to feel the morning sun,
   And share its warmth with everyone.

I love to dream and talk to God,
   And watch the clouds, and see him nod.

I love to plant and see life grow,
   A gift that only God can know.

   —*Louis Robert Samuels*

Free

To all my dear friends
   and loved ones I say
   'tis not me you see
lying here in this grave
   'tis only a shell
   in which I did dwell
   until such a time
that my shell had to die
   for me do not mourn
for this shell is not me
   and I am not dead
I'm a spirit roaming free

   —*Lona Kaye Plisek*

My First Kiss

I was a baby in a crib
and my mother was taking
care of me.
She would take me up
and give me a kiss.
This was over 90 years ago.

   —*S. Edgar Calhoun*

My Friend Or My Enemy?

He was my friend,
And my greatest enemy.
He was my love,
But only known to me.
His way was strange.
But his love was strong.
His name said hate,
But his eyes, they said love.
My eyes told me never,
But my heart-beat said always.
My heart ran away with his,
But my mind strayed behind.
Did his heart want mine,
Because mine longed so for his.
He was my everything,
I was his nothing.

—*Rebecca Hocker*

The Most Beautiful Star

I looked up in the sky tonight,
And oh what a magnificent view,
There must have been a billion stars,
Looking down on me and you.

I imagined the stars were angels,
Some had a beautiful hue,
When I saw a pretty bright one,
And it reminded me of you.

For if the stars were angels,
One fell to earth you see,
All the way from heaven,
Just to be with me.

I'll never know why from heaven,
You felt that you must part,
But I know I'll love you always,
And forever, in my heart.

And as I stare up into the heavens,
Just as far as my eyes can see,
I realize that "The Most Beautiful Star",
Is here on earth with me!

—*Roger Davis*

Where The Trees Are Tall

Where the trees are tall
and problems small ...
said the wise one to the other.

Where the rocks are steep
and people don't speak ...
(about anything unimportant)
said the wise one to the other.

Where the stars fill the skies
and friends tell no lies ...
said the wise one to the other.

Where the air is clear
and sometimes there are tears ...
said the wise one to the other.

Where the trees are tall
and problems small ...
said the wise one to the other.

—*Sue Cox*

Friends

You never pointed your finger
    And said, "I told you so"
You ever laughed or made fun
    At the things I didn't know.

You never left me alone
    When I was feeling blue,
You never said I could not be
    All the things I wanted to.

You were always so supportive
    You pushed me gently all the way,
You were always my hidden strength
    Through many a difficult day.

And so my friend, I may not have said
    Or showed in any way -
I've always known you were there
    And I thank God for you each day.

—*E. F. Hawkins*

Sometimes You'll Need Someone

His heart was broken, torn apart,
and scattered on the ground.
His life was shattered, helplessly,
he sank and wished he'd drowned.

He had no reason to go on.
The future lost its light.
He gave into the darkness,
and lost his will to fight.

Into the darkness called a voice,
"Reach out and take my hand.
I promise to be there for you,
and help you understand."

He was this soul who had been lost,
till he looked into her eyes.
That was when he'd found himself,
and when he'd realized.

That life goes on no matter what
the past has done to you.
That sometimes you'll need someone,
who'll help to pull you through.

—*Thomas A. Smith*

Untitled

I've known you for a couple years,
and seen you now and then.
And the one thing that I wish for,
is to be with you again.

To wrap my arms around you and,
to hold on oh so tight.
To hear your words of love that,
get me through the night.

I want to be held close to you,
and look into your eyes.
I want to kiss your tender lips,
that never say good-bye.

But this is just a crazy dream
that never may come true.
And when I dream it's always that,
I want to be with you.

—*Stacy E. Kletter*

What Would I Do?

My sun rises
And sets
In your eyes .
You are my eagle
Soaring
In the skies.
My hopes
And dreams
rest upon you.
Without your love,
What would I do.

When the storm rages
Outside my door,
You are with me,
And I never want more.
You are everything
I need and want,
My life is you.
Without your love,
What would I do.

—*Wanda Faye Baker*

Harriet's Star

A star shining in the night,
And she pointed
And said to the people around
her,
Follow that star to freedom;
That's my star.
Follow that star to food and
clothes.
And she pointed again,
Follow my star
A star shining in the night.

—*Lisa Knorr*

Ulysses in Steel

"A stick in the mud", he smirked
And stalked across the sun swept walk,
Transfixed I stood, immobilized
By sculptured sheets of polished steel
Unfurled against the storied scape
To once again declare to all
The wandering myths in mind of man.

How many voyages I have made
To watch the sun cast linear paths
Across the streamlined seamless sails,
And mirror cells of walled-in-panes
Pointless towers of Idiom
To now declare these rites to all
Of robot roles in bind of man.

Ulysses sailed on through paint and page
Through multi-shapes of real, surreal
To abstract the tract of what has been
To express the stress of what can come.

—*Miriam R. Kossman*

Untitled

Without butter
And not a fly
I really am
A flutter-by

—*Paul Anthony Chadwell*

My Love

You encourage my goals,
And support my dreams.
By loving, accepting,
and believing in me.
You're often quick to praise,
And slow to criticize.
Which is why I feel confident,
Secure and wise.
You're there to share my thoughts,
and feelings to.
I'm always myself, when I'm with you.
It's a relationship
That supposed to be,
one that brings out the best in me.

—*Stephany Jones*

My Heart Stood Still

My heart stood still today
    and teardrops filled my eyes
As fifty years of memories
    brought happiness and sad sighs.

I looked beyond the green high hills
    the ocean waves of blue
And visions of four active babes
    now gone from out of view.

I retraced every step of each
    from infant to maturity.
And smiled at all the happiness
    these treasures brought to me.

So now I travel on the road
    of lonely eternity
And close my eyes and thank my God
    who was so good to me.

—*Terri Kasaba*

Teach Me

Listen,
And tell me what you hear.
Look,
And tell me what you see.
Touch,
And tell me what you feel.
Sniff,
And tell me what you smell.
Taste,
And tell me the flavor there of.
Experience these things.
Learn,
Grow,
And share them with me.
I am hungry for knowledge.

—*Patrick F. Pinckney*

Untitled

As I lay me down to sleep
Ann I want you to know
My heart and soul is yours to keep.
I thought that you would like to know
That my heart goes where you go
That I'll never can forget
The time we first met
That life is brighter and sweeter
For such a sweetheart as you are
And now my constant prayer will be
That God may keep you safe for me
Because I love you baby.
Amen

—*Paul DeVoe*

Aaron

With eyes so blue
And that little hint of green
I love you
Even though at times your mean
I see right through to the real you.

I know you miss your dad
But their isn't a lot I can do
It's not your fault, it's your dad's
Even though you think it's you.

When you are sad
I'm here for you
Even when your bad
No matter what you do.

I've been here from the start
I will never leave you
We will never part
I love you.

—*Shelly Cross*

Untitled

As the sun sets
And the air grows cool
The moods of the night begin
The rustling of leaves
And the chirps of a cricket
Join with the sound of the wind
Out of the shadows
The night ones come
To do what they must do
They squirm and climb
And creep and crawl
You know they're looking for you
Don't look around
Keep moving on
Or else you'll meet your fate
The wind is still…
The air is cold….
My friend, it's now too late!

—*Robert W. Gale Sr.*

Where All Else Originates

Where there's the burden of great hatred
and the silence of great love,
and that of embittered friendship
that has fallen from above.
Where the loneliness of silence
comes down on me and you,
and unspeakable contrition
shows you things you never knew.
Just know that every nighttime
leaves us farther than today,
and the light of someone's friendship
will lead and show the way.
Although the tragedy of time
may find us far apart,
my friend, you'll always have a place
that's special in my heart.

—*Lori Vellutini*

Timeless Kindness

If, I were you
and you were I
sometime, somewhere
in this galaxy.
Then, I could but be
kind to you least
I be cruel to me.

—*Vicki Lee Awalt*

The Song Of The Earth

I feel the pain of the moon and rain
And the sun, shining brightly above.
I blow out stars, I carry cars,
For the oceans, I have love.

I sing a song, but do no wrong,
The universe is my home.
The mountains high where valleys lie
By the plain where the animals roam.

The stormy nights, the morning light,
These feelings give me sway,
But the greatest power is a rampant hour
That turns into a sunny day.

—*Megan Rhodes*

Sanctuary

It was the rocks that saved me
    and the wall at the end
    of the long dark hall

These   not soft   not warm
    spaces   that wrapped me
    round with safety

Taught me to withdraw my essence
from the pain and terror into an
    older   wiser view

Shielded the source of my strength
through all the long years of struggle

Awaiting the day I should reclaim
that which lay hidden   within
    the fastness   of the earth's bones

—*Rebecca Aronson*

Tonight, I Dream

Tonight, I dream of things that were
And things that might have been.
Of thoughts so pure and actions bold
That we both shared so long ago.

Tonight, I dream of magic days
When beauty shone its light
On everything in life we touched;
With love so strong, we had it all.

Tonight, I dream of shattered hopes
That promised once great things,
Then cast us as two empty shells
In a sea of despair and doubt.

Tonight, I dream of starry skies
From where you now look down
Upon me and my loneliness
That weighs so heavy on my heart.

Tonight, I dream of things that were
But more of things to be.
Of hope and love and peace again
In God's great plan for me.

—*Linda M. Yamaki*

The Woman

To have a woman touch my soul,
    and teach me gentle things.
To have her make my life whole,
    would make me feel a king.
To have her stay until I die,
    and consent to be my wife.
For these things I tell you now,
    I'd gladly give my life.

—*Thomas L. Sailers*

The Master Held My Hand

The Master held my hand
And walked with me today,
And as we trod life's pathway
This I heard Him say:

I have strength for every trial,
Grace for every care,
Balm for every heartache,
Help for all you bear.

I'll go along beside you
As each step you take today,
I'll lead you and I'll guide you
All along the Pilgrim way.

So trust in Me, my child,
Lean hard upon My breast,
And I will bear your burden
And give you peace and rest.

—*Mary Giddens*

Line of the Times

The line began at Henry's door
And wandered down the street.
It went 'round several corners
And was walked by many feet.

The line grew longer every day
And sang with louder voice.
The multitudes stayed through the night,
For few had any choice.

Old Henry minded not his toil —
His job was an enjoyment.
At least old Henry had a job—
He worked for unemployment!!

—*William T. Hartwell*

They Passed Him By

Shoulders slumped, he sat
and watched the people pass.
Never once did one speak and ask,
"May I help you, Sir?"
Never once did one give a glance of
sympathy.
Never once did he cry out in pain
as he sat,
shoulders slumped, eyes pleading.
He was deaf, though not dumb,
dying, though not sighing,
and they passed him by.
So did I.

—*Luray R. Powell*

New Years

Years may come,
And years may go.
And this one is special,
I hope you know,
And because your here,
I'm glad to say,
Let's let the new year,
Get on the way,
I know this year,
Will bring the best,
And let's let the last year,
Go with the rest

—*Samantha Trail*

Him

When you feel discouraged
and your pathway lights are dim,
There's one thing you can count on -
you can always turn to Him.

Remember as the days go by,
the sun will brighter shine,
And all your wounds will heal -
just by passing of the time.

He can make the days seem shorter,
He can make you feel quite sure,
And the thing that you can count on is,
He will help you rich or poor.

—*Marion A. Hockman*

Angel To Inmate

Baby boy, as I look at you
angel from heaven with eyes of blue.
Perfect gift sent from above,
Born of parents so in love.

Years fly past and child is grown.
Father dies of cause unknown.
Son is now the man of home.
Money needed, source unknown.

Answers come from dealers hand
Sell my drugs, join my band.
Money for the family made.
Son is trapped, illegal trade.

Son is sharing good and kind.
Not a violent or angry mind.
Starts a family, stops the trade.
Tries to mend mistakes he made.

Arrested, charge? Conspiratory.
Ten years sentence, mandatory.
Son in prison, family in tears.
Angel to inmate in twenty short years......

—*Pam Causey*

Opera Star

She's enchantingly poised and sweet—
Appealingly rich to the eye.
Her manner is graceful and neat
Whenever I see her go by.

And add to her charm her attire;
She has colors that subtly suggest...
Her necklace for all to admire
So jauntily hangs at her breast.

I'm awed by her musical voice
And entranced whenever she trills.
I have no freedom or choice;
She captivates as she wills.

She's fair as the flowers beside her
And the dewdrop that flashes a spark;
She dwells in the grasses that stir
For she's the talented meadow lark.

—*L. Glen Guengerich*

Beautiful Rainbow

Beautiful is the rainbow,
Arching high in the sky,
The rains come down,
To give life to the earth.

The sun shines forth,
Plants sprout and grow,
The flowers bloom in vibrant colors,
To beautify the land.

Beautiful is the rainbow,
'Tis the creation of God's handiwork,
To admire in awesome wonder,
The beauty before us.

—*Leilani S. Andrews*

My Pony

The leaves
are crisp,
the morning
pure,
my pony's
hooves
are quick
and sure.
So early yet
that birds
still nest,
so dark,
as yet,
the farmers rest.
No saddle, bridle, bit
for me,
I grasp my pony's mane,
and we
are one together,
galloping free.

—*Ruth Feder*

Tears Of The Heart

Tears of the heart
are difficult
To quench.
When you hurt
The one you love,
Pain never ceases.
When you lose
The one you love,
Pain increases.
Gold cannot buy
Life's precious gift,
Love!
Treat love with respect
Then the heart will be
Joyous, serene and
Tearless.

—*Mary Goehring*

Today's Children

Today's precious children
are in reality,
tomorrow's emerging angels
and the salvation
of humanity, if,
that is what
we teach them to be.

—*Thomas M. Le Rose*

Thoughts Of You

Thoughts of you
are drowning me inside:

Wondering how you are,
Thinking you are lonely;
Asking if you're alright,
Maybe you need someone
  to love you.
Wondering if you think of me,
Happily remembering the great
  times we spent together and
Regretting decisions made in the past.
Questioning if "true love"
  endures all things.

One thing holds true:
No matter what
How much time passes us by,
What the past holds, or
What the future might bring
Above and beyond all that
  I'll always love you!
　　　—Olga Lozano

Seasons

Summer's decorations
are falling
out of her hair

She's danced long enough
it's time
for her to go home
so fall
can begin his concert

Winter doesn't dance or
play music
he paints
landscapes.
　　　—Linda Scott

Regrets

"I'll love you forever"
are the words that you said,
tears well in my eyes
as your voice storms my head.
I will not forget you,
and I cannot let go,
of all of these feelings
that I never let show.
All the things that I whispered
too soft for you to hear,
all the mistakes that I've made
these last couple of years.
All the memories run through me
like the blood in my veins,
how can I deal
with all of this pain?
I can't bring you back,
it's too late for good-bye,
and I'll never know
why you had to die.
　　　—Lyndee Underbakke

Discovery

It rained last night,
As though you didn't notice.
I saw you at your window
Peeking your eyes out at the world.
　　　—Theodore G. Smith

Illusions

The shadows of yesterday
Are walking besides me
Phantoms in the air
Memories of a lost dream

I reach and want to touch them
But frivolous they run
Teasing my emotions
Leaving me alone.

How long must this loneliness
Keep on haunting me?
I know that you are just shadows
And he was just a dream...
　　　—Olga Lopategui

Why

　I saw you today with her
arm around you.
It made me realize
I don't belong with you.
Are you sad are you mad
that I didn't say yes.
Why can't you see it was
all for the best.
I don't want to lie,
but I can't tell you why.
Seeing you only makes me
cry.
　　　—Melissa Sterk

I Remember

I remember the death of my father,
As bright as winter sun at noon;
I remember the old fashioned hats,
The smell of stale perfume.

I remember the sighs and cries,
The gloom in the crowded room;
I remember polite nods in black,
The day did not end too soon.

I remember the pulling me down,
As though in silent tomb;
I remember my silent good-bye,
Thatched sprays in pastel bloom.

I remember the wrench in my soul,
A feeling that still does loom;
I remember the death of my father,
As bright as winter sun at noon.
　　　—Reed Vernon Lloyd

Timeless

The sun kissed the sky with light
As I kissed my lover's charms.
Heaven seems to marvel at how
You have made my dreams come true.

Darkness wraps the world by night
As I wrap you in my arms.
The stars witness my happy vow
That I will grow old with you.

But I won't speak of twilight
Years; we are far from their harms.
Rather, I will enjoy you now,
While yet our young love is new.
　　　—Thomas J. Walsh

Look Beyond

In the mist of the sunrise
As darkness slip away
Bringing a new dawn to existence
In a subtle kind of way

Look beyond the rainbows
When clouds get in your eyes
Uncover all life's treasures
Forget about the lies

Live in every moment
Value what you've seen
Cherish all life's ups and downs
Not in what "might" have been

Smile when you feel sorrow
To make happiness grow
Be humble in your heart
Let all resentments go

Live towards a better future
Learn from every mistake
Reflect on the good times
And remember...give yourself a break
　　　—Stewart Akana

Lost Treasure

Treasure, treasures where it might be?
As far as my eyes will not see
digging deep, looking high and low
Still, it can't be found
Life's rushing by
Running against the clock of time
I must find this treasure before I die!
So where? Could this treasure be?
I must, search deep within me
I must, quiet my mind
And think, what will I find?
It will probably be of great value
there's no price that can be made
I open my eyes and gaze about
Majestic mountains rise beyond
Skies that are bluer than blue
Delicate petals of blossoms in bloom
Finally my eyes began to see
There's treasures abound, shining bright!
Like diamonds, which is forever more!
　　　—Steven I. Takara

The Running Man

The running man runs
as fast as he can,
from life's pain and despair
and darkness to bear.

The running man runs
to keep a distances pace,
always charging forward
from his inner desolate place.

The running man runs
trying to find the light,
but finding the light
becomes an inner fight.

The running man runs.
If he decides to slow his pace,
he will face his true competitor
and then he will win the race.
　　　—Teresa Krayer

The Star

The star shone in the sky that night
As from his mind he sought respite
For he was making himself depressed
With each thought that he addressed
His loves lost forever more
His heart would just not ignore
And to his eyes tears would brim
For his hopes all seemed so dim
But when he saw the star in the night
Peace and hope came with delight
For like a friend, it shown for him
And it was not large, just a pin
But it made his problems seem so small
That he hardly noticed them at all

—*Phillip Alexander M. Bray*

Cruel Bindings

"Cruel bindings" he said
as he drank.
    The stench of death
mixed in his breath.
    She walked in as if her poet
had died without inspiration.
    Potatoes in ears,
    fish bowl eyes,
    apple peel tongue.
    Never known the front door
to a back door Heaven.
    Never known the wrath
of a backwards Hell.
    She spoke of "Curses and Invocations"
by joining her muse.
    "Cruel Bindings" he said.

—*Tim Carson*

Christmas Morning

It came at dawning
As I lay awake,
The patter of footsteps
As they made the stairs shake.

There was Jenny and David;
There was Liz, Missy, Steve.
"Old Santa has been here!
Oh what did he leave?"

The stockings were turned out
Upon the den floor,
Candy and bracelets,
Toys and much more.

I stood in the door,
And as I beheld them,
I thought what a treasure
The dear Lord has given.

Grandkids together,
Some tall and some small,
Made a glad Christmas morning
Which I love to recall.

—*C. Josephine Haller*

Glimpse Of Serenity

A wise man embraces each day
as if it where a beautiful child
smiling at him.

He breathes the morning air deep
as if each breath was filled
with the rent of fragrant flowers

And he smiles, for he knows that
God is close to his heart.

—*Neil J. McKenna*

Gone

Stronger thoughts of death appear,
As in a sphere of blues and greens
And mists and clouds,
But why they do is not real clear.

No one knows just why or when,
The slice of life that was then,
Is gone my son forever, and
All that was is now together.

Take it all as a joke or start
To live like "old folk" with
Dreams destroyed and "might have beens"
Becoming larger

—*Ron Layer*

Sad

Hearts break so silently
As silently as the stars appear
As softly as snow falls
Upon the frigid earth,
And as quietly as tears
Slip down a woman's cheek

No more heart leaping with gladness
No more pounding with anticipation
Only the quiet pain of despair.
Silently hearts break,
He who thinks silence golden
Knows aught of a breaking heart.

—*Wayne J. Spence*

Joy Lights

As the lilies of the fields grow
As the grass is green
As the waters of the ocean flow
So is the joy of the redeemed.

As the light of a candle shines
As the sun glares very bright
So must our reflection of the divine
Shine as a star studded night.

As the stars are many in the sky
As the mountains stands high
So will your joy flow high
If the Lord, we let be our guide.

—*Thelma L. Connally*

The Warrior And The Battle

Standing tall
As the smoke clears to reveal
The warrior's triumph
In victory - his fate is sealed.

But the winning of a battle
Just makes for a bigger war
And victory becomes so fragile
When every battle breeds one more.

And amidst the smoke and the fire
He sees the new day sun
Looking towards the horizon
he finds he's the only one...

And with the gift of knowledge comes
The gift of wealth
And the battle he's been fighting
Has always been with himself!

—*Sheila Ann Weaver-Sjodin*

Gemini

Walk on the opposite side
As two can lead the way
Harmony in May
Comes by twice each day
As the sun turns its face
Time has no place
Settling upon the earth
Revealing its beams
Many have dare
To tread so high
For it's not the climb
Bewildered clouds form
A life untorn
Swept up into the
Third generation of man kind
Faith has locked its wheels
As time stands still
And taurus embraces
The warm sensitivity of orion.

—*Sandra Estelle*

The Mountain Lies Silent

The mountain lies silent
As we approach its granite hall
A line of blue in the horizon
Gives its beckoning call.

Old as eternity,
Yet ever new,
Forbidding yet inviting,
The magnificent ridge of blue.

History is unraveled,
On your misty peak.
From Indians to settlers
Of the past you speak.

Old settler cabins
Look on the valley below,
A golden touch of memory,
Memories of long ago.

Memories of days,
From the misty past.
Memories of plenty,
Memories to last.

—*Paul K. Horn*

Our Country

Oh, the good old USA
As we hear our people say.
Let's be glad and always true
To our own red, white and blue.

No more hate and greed to flourish
But together we will nourish
Every woman, child and man
Who resides in this great land.

We have reds, we have whites,
We have blacks and yellows too,
Let's forget our racial differences
And start our thoughts anew.

To bring honor to our country
God intended us to care
With no more prejudice to stop us
Let us show justice everywhere.

—*Pauline Brinker*

Be Thou With Us

Be thou with us, oh Lord Jesus
as we travel here below.
Comfort strengthen, and please keep us
until heaven we will go.

Many loved ones have gone before us
to the place you have prepared.
They are in a mansion yonder
all because a Saviour cared.

We are thankful for having known them,
and we laboured hand in hand.
Now their work on earth is finished.
They are rejoicing in that fair land.

Be Thou with us as we serve Thee,
we are weak but Thou art strong.
Be always mindful of our weakness;
Keep in our heart a joyful song.

—*Travis E. Sparks*

By My Side

I can feel your hand in mine
As you gently comfort me.
You are so loving and so kind.
You're everything I need.

This trial of faith has been hard.
But I know I cannot stop,
Because your word has promised me
That I will reach the top.

I can fight this battle and I'll win
Because you're by my side.
And when the storm grows very dim,
In your loving arms I'll hide.

But for now I will keep fighting.
Pressing onward tried and true.
Until the day I finish my battle,
And go home to be with you.

—*Susan Emmons*

Untitled

I love springtime,
best time of year.
New things come up.
That's when I got married
in the springtime.

—*Rose Lopes*

Above The Clouds

Above the clouds the sun is shining.
Ask the pilots, they all know.
Above the clouds the sun is shining
Though it's raining here below.
Here on earth the clouds of darkness,
Sin and sorrow, hate and strife
Can make of us discouraged people
With a warped embittered life.
O, look above ye of God's children
Ask the Pilot you all know.
Above the clouds His love is shining.
It will reach us here below.

—*Margaret M. Swofford*

Light

Bundle of papers and bunch of pens
asks the echo in the heart:
What to write?

Everyday the sun passes from my eyes
But ah...!
There's a curtain around my eyes!
That turns a day into night!
Also keeps me away from the light!

The light which is inside the eyesight
Reflexes: Even you don't write
Remember you always write.
That too not on paper but...in heart.
Not with pen
But with feelings.

What in words?
Nothing but funny!
Yes
Affection is honey.
It inspires the rays in the heart
And makes to write:
The twinkle dreams
And songs of sweet memories.

—*P. B. Patel*

They Say

Time heals all wounds.
At least that's what they say.
But feeling as I do right now,
I know they never walked this way.
They never had their soul divided,
split asunder, torn in two.
They never spoke to ears past hearing
the magic chant, I love you,
and have the essence of that spell
drift off and not return
with words of like, with look and touch
that made the spirit burn.
They never cried past tears and feeling.
They couldn't know the pain
of wishing for the cloak of madness
in the freezing world of sane.
Time heals some wounds.
Those of flesh are easy tended.
Mine, I fear, are with me always,
never, never to be mended.

—*Rae Nell Causseaux*

Pastorale

The Garden of Paradise
awaits us Beloved.
The Garden beckons us-
There we shall sit, shaded
by lofty trees-
Dancing glints of light will
delight us as we kiss.
No one will disturb us in
our sequestered rapture-
For no one has, or ever will
enter our Garden.

—*Paula F. Roga*

Open Thy Eyes

Open thy eyes little one,
    Because life has just begun.
Don't be afraid my dear,
    Because God is always near.
Little one don't be sad, life goes on,
    Even in your eyes, till dusk is dawn.
Now it's time to wipe your eyes,
    To see through God's disguise.
He is here to lend us a hand,
    On working on this dreary land.
Now it's time we must part.
    Just remember me in your heart.

—*Myrtle Sprague*

A Super Hot Day

In summertime it should be hot
    Because this is the season,
But what we've had the last few days
    Goes far beyond all reason.

    The news showed a person cooking,
And to believe it, is really hard.
    But a man was actually cooking
    On the cement in his back yard

Now that has got to be really hot
For a beautiful summer day.
In wintertime we dream of this.
    Now we want it the other way.

    We can't ever just be happy.
    We're spoiled in many ways.
No matter what the weather is,
    We dream of the other days.

—*Lois Ashuckian*

My Best Friend

    Many lines have
    been written
about what you call a friend
    But none come even
Close to the feelings that you lend
    Hope and love and even pain
    These are the things that
    your words caress
I give you my empty heart
    and get it back filled
    That is the way
That God's garden is tilled
    There is so much more
    I should chance to say,
    But will these
word's for your friendship
    repay?
    To all of this,
one more praise to sing;
    don't change a thing

—*Wayne J. Porter*

America, Save Your Children

America, save your children
before it gets too late—
Teach them while they're young enough
to love instead of hate—

Show them all the rights and wrongs
That they will need to know—
To carry them throughout their life
Wherever they may go—

Give them a sense of purpose
keep them ever strong—
Give them courage to meet each day
and, the obstacles that come along—

Help them find the wisdom
to learn to live together—
Once they do, they will see
There's no storm that they can't weather—

  —Tommie Martin

Dance on the Horizon

Sailing, soaring, flying high
being one with the sky.

Over the mountains, I am free
just the wind, the birds and me.

Into the heavens I have soared
earth has become a checkerboard.

Fields of blue, puffs of white,
the sky, a beautiful, glorious site.

Room to romp, room to play,
unspeakable joy, I cannot say

Circling, twirling
twisting, whirling

After my day of play is spent
back to earth I regret,
descent.

  —Stephanie Bonee

Homecoming

Finding little warmth
beside a dying fire
I listen to the wind.
Beyond the rattling window
leaves fall.

Acorns snap beneath your feet
helplessly
as you approach.
In the shadows
you speak.
I cannot understand.

Your words lie
beside my heart.
My arms reach out,
touch nothing.
You came home
to walk out of my life.

  —Patricia L. Palmer

Untitled

Daydreamers were
at one time
the only true thinkers
until time catches
up with them
and reality
passes them by.

  —Nathan McGhee

The Weaver

My life is but a weaving
Between my Lord and me.
I cannot choose the pattern
It's done mysteriously.

Sometimes he weaveth sorrow
And I, in foolish pride
Forget he sees the upper
And I, the underside.

Not till the loom is silent
And the shuttles cease to fly
Shall God unroll the weaving
And explain the reason why.

The dark threads are as needful
In the weavers silent hand'
As the threads of gold and silver
In the pattern he has planned.

  —Viola Seitz

The Stolen Heart

In a little town
Beyond these streets
Around a corner
Destiny meets
Into your eyes
I looked so far
About in my mind
You were my star
Off in a corner
Against your soul
Into the darkness
My heart you stole.

  —Melissa Lunsford

I'm Fine

Bothersome souls
bite at my strengths,
leaving only the skeleton
of my weaknesses,
betraying every ounce
I kept tucked safely
inside my loosely-bolted
mind.

Assuming always
an estranged evil
has opened
and entered my soul,
never assuming
I'm perfectly
fine.

  —Laura Wright

The Tender One

One so small on unsteady legs,
Born not so long ago.

Eyes still closed to the world around,
Not yet knowing about life.

One so tender and innocent,
Born to a world which can find no hope.

Newly born to a changing world,
Never knowing of what lies ahead.

Grown to see the earth dissolved,
Unafraid of what the future holds.

  —Terry Ann Emory

Glorious Salvation

We all think of it as a
blackness of which we cannot
escape but, it's actually not
like that.

It's a new foundation of
golden glorious salvation and a
feeling of joy beyond our thoughts
and imaginations.

It's a fullness of sound,
a newly purified taste and a
smell of the fresh air, for which
brings us ever lasting happiness.

The warm feeling installed
inside we all no longer need
not be afraid, for it truly sets
our spirit free, from the earthly
accumulation of tribulations
that bind us.

  —Terry Stevens

Fallen King

Blackness
blanketed the castle
that
night.
Visions of a king-fallen
whisked
away
in the
wailing red
chariot.
Seen through the eyes
of the anxious child
seeking answers
from behind
crumbling
walls.

  —Shirley D. Lodge

Gathering Place

Rays of light
Bouncing from my favorite tree
Holding my attention
Balancing me
A gathering place
That I know
This special place
Where I can grow
So much beauty, so little time
Who's to say that this is mine
A gathering place for me
Can't you see

  —Richard Nicely

6-5-90

A fire on the beach
Brilliant light is cast forth.
I walk towards it
I shed my mangled uniform onto the sand
Only then am I allowed into the flames.
Peace and love fills my naked soul.
Another man follows
Only to be repelled by it
He is cast into the ocean
and tormented for all eternity.

  —Stephen A. Smith

Desert Exile

You left me here,
Bound me with barbed wire,
Dusted me with fine, grey sand,
Gave me a sagebrush to hold,
And wished that I would die.

Now,
There is no iron left for wires,
The sagebrush,
Proliferous and free,
Chokes the land again.
But each time I breathe,
The fine, grey sand buries your wish
That I should die.

—*Takako Endo*

Untitled

The wind blows through my open window,
Bringing in the coldness of the sky.
The leaves shake with fury and anger,
I listen to the rain wondering, "Why?"
Why is my happiness hidden,
In a strange faraway place?
Does it not have the courage,
To show itself in my face?
It creeps around in the night,
For I remember it being here.
But when I wake in the morning,
Where it went is not too clear.
Happiness, where are you?
Why are you no where to be found?
How come when I call for you,
You won't even make a sound?
Now looking out my window,
I wish upon this star.
I wish for you to call to me,
And tell me where you are.

—*Mary Potter*

April Serenade

Winter has been sad and dreary,
Bringing sickness and death;
Come to me April
With your essence of spring.
Speak to me softly as you bring
Your golden daffodils
Brimming with life.
Bring me a colorful bouquet
With spoonshape petals;
Bring me some dainty pink clouds,
Soft, beautiful sunsets,
Toss in a spring rainbow.
The winter has been long and barren,
My love has flown away;
I need a gay note,
A charmer like you
To inspire my Muse
And awaken me
From my winter lethargy
Of loneliness, sadness and despair.

—*Myrtle Doane*

The Greater Tragedy

No feet, it's said, a cause for tears,
But a greater sorrow seen,
A man without a loving heart
Ah, dead, this man is deemed.

—*Patricia St. Clair*

Politics

Her strength, they say, should be feared.
But, can Hillary be domineered?
    While Billy smokes plants,
    She wears the pants,
And it's said she can even grow beard!

—*G. Ronald Bento*

Love's Reach

Excuse me,
But did I touch you?
This may sound strange,
But I felt a warm hand
Brush my heart.

I'm sorry,
I don't mean to sound crazy.
It's just that I can't remember
Getting that close.

I won't bother you anymore.
I just needed to know
If I touched you;
The way you touched me.

—*Tim Williamson*

Wild At Heart

Some say "Everyone has a hungry heart"
But made me their exception.
They don't know I'm wild at heart
My life, one big deception.
That far beneath this pristine skin,
in my soul's depths, I hid within,
white hot passion, yet unnamed,
Fiery desire, never tamed.

All my life I lived the part
At the cost of my rebel heart.
Time to break those chains that bind,
Don't really know what I might find.
Maybe love, and that's a start,
To freeing the bonds
'round my wild, wild heart.

—*S. M. Berry*

Reflection

Looking inside
But more than
A glare.
Hoping to see
What never is there
Asking why, but
Never an answer
Staring, but without
Comparison.
Looking deeper
And what do I see
A man in the mirror
Who is facing
Me.
The question is
When you look
Inside yourself do
You really see?
If not, don't look
At me.

—*Timothy McFadden*

My Place

I was once there
but now no longer am.
I have grown so far away
from something I once had -
something so dear to me,
something that meant the world to me.

It confuses me,
that I can't seem to understand,
some of the more important things
in this world.

It worries me,
that I can't even begin,
to drain these problems of mine.

If only I could start
from the beginning,
once again.

—*Lisa Glisczinski*

Petals

Tightly budded yesterday
But spreading now
Yellow petals transmit their essence
Into the hallways
Of my memory.

Every bouquet I sent had at least one
Yellow rose
Even in a small town in Minnesota
Where a particular rose
Was hard to come by.
Sometimes I had to settle for
Yellow jonquils
Which gave her almost as much pleasure
Because with her, the thought mattered.

My thoughts weep openly
Transparent petals falling,
Touching the child
The mother no longer
Remembers.

—*Peggy Harbers*

There Was A Time

There was a time, a dream we shared,
But that was long ago.
There was a time we really cared -
We let our feelings go.
There was a time when you were mine,
And I belonged to you.
There was a time the sun did shine,
And in it, our love grew.
But somehow, somewhere along the way
All those dreams became too old-
And there was nothing left to say
When our love had grown cold.
We took a chance and paid the price,
Lord, it should be a crime-
We live with hearts as cold as ice-
But, oh, there was a time...

—*Madeline Couch*

Too Protected

Too protected
behind the walls
for what I yearn to do
too protected
behind the walls
and the walls
are made from ice.

—*Rhonda L. Boyd*

Fulfillment

I stand a bit crooked
but unshamefully tall
my feet anchored with
solid gravitation to the earth

With gentle energy of steely strength
I am charged with an infinite torch
dictating my courage
and a fiery brilliant undying hope
governing my spirit

A rhythmic peace encompasses
my body and mind
and at last I am a person
a whole person
I am glad I am alive

With all this heaven before me
I lift up my life and sing
to glorify the magnificence
and wonderment of the universe
and of all mankind.

—*Peggy P. Hooper*

Of Life And Love

I have no age unless it be of years.
But what are years if only to belie
the youth that lies within my heart,
of which I shan't deny.

I won't allow the burden of my days
to mock the stoutness of my gaze,
or slow the swiftness of my pace,
or doubt the morals I embrace.

Speak not of life to me
unless it is of what's to be.
For what is gone is gone,
and I care not
to dwell among the ruins of life,
or wallow in a desert sea.

Speak with me of years to come
To beauty, let our eyes succumb.
And in some quiet dell we'll dream
of pleasures past,
and cherish mem'ries
of love held fast.

—*Leonard A. Lippel*

My Sunny Day

We have dreams of the future
but where's reality shown?
In a field with the sun
the bees and the shade.
On a cliff that sees everything
with eagles that play.
Reality is what happens
to your beautiful day.
I carry the thoughts
of good times and bad
of wonderful places
and friends that I've had.
My dreams of the future
may no longer be,
but opportunity rises
and that's what I see.
So wish me luck
for tomorrow's not done
there's so much for the future
that hasn't even begun.

—*Sean Doucette*

By Definition

By definition, man.
By definition, woman.
By definition, court.
By definition, hear.
By definition, lead.
By definition, follow.
By definition, logical.
By definition, emotional.
By definition, pragmatic.
By definition, romantic.
By definition, half.
By definition, half.
By definition, you.
By definition, I.
By definition, feminine.
By definition, masculine.
By definition, I;
By definition, you;
By definition, us;
By definition, whole!

—*J. S. Jailawi*

The Sign Of Success

Success can't be weighed
by the company one keeps;
Nor by the riches and wealth
that one reaps.

Success can't be measured
by flashy careers;
Nor by gathering crowds
to applaud us with cheers.

Success is best gauged
in still night, naught a peep,
When my conscience and I
at last day down to sleep.

—*Mary Anne Moresco*

The Metamorphosis Of Charities Daughter

And I listened, and thought it out.
By then, I was gone!
For nothing can inspire a fool's quest.
Indeed, if need be, I will awake
and dream no more.
If love, touched me, long ago?
The memory withered as Autumn left.
Winters chill? No!
The fires still burn, the crackle
of it dances - here, there.
And, as the flame keeps me captive
I remember nothing.
I've pressed my memories between
the pages of a book.

—*Roberta Mandell*

Nature's Fire

I want to feel nature's fire,
By way of your desire.
To be embraced within your heat,
It would be our greatest feat!
Nature's fire is our passion,
Lets explore it in like fashion.
And when our fires have been doused,
Through our love it will be aroused.
For never will this fire die,
Because we keep the flame up high!

—*Pamela Johnson*

Just One Of Life's Little Lessons

Watch your back from so called friends.
They will try to make amends.
Treat you nice to your face.
Invite you in to see their place.
When you're gone words will fly.
Then they begin to lie.
Sometimes life can be unfair.
So pick your friends with utmost care.
Don't open up until you're sure.
Friendships can become a blur.
Use caution, move slow.
In this advice I do know.
One of life's little lessons.
You can save some heartache too.
Remember true friends won't make you
blue.
Why do people act this way?
This is all I can say
It's just one of life's little lessons

—*Tammy Lynne Perryman*

America, The Land Of The Free

Afar from the old world
came different peoples

Peoples of colors,
values and creeds

Peoples in search
for freedom and truth

These are the faces
now called Americas

Yes, like them my forefathers came

Yes, like them my forefathers suffered

Yes, like them my forefathers succeeded

For this is America,
the land of the free

—*J. A. Fabia*

Time

Can't touch it!
Can't hold it!
Can't stop it!
Can't see it!
When we're young,
It's expendable
As years go by,
It becomes dependable
A gauge for plans
A pattern for days
Then age takes over
It becomes precious
We never know,
How much we have
We cherish each day
At night we pray
Thank God for this day
Leaves turn gold,
And winter comes.

—*Margaret Benz*

The Blue Find

Oh how the beauty can only be
captured by vision,
With its courageous movements,
The unpredictable direction of path,

Deep within the oceans reach,
you hide yourself so well,
you tease us giving piece by piece,
we exchange as if to sell.

—*Suzanne J. Holubek*

The Loneliness Of The Night

As the soft, gentle breeze
caresses the leaves on the trees,
the warm air lightly brushes my skin.
The moon plays hide and seek with
the clouds,
as they dance around
in the darkening sky.
In the loneliness of the night,
your memory comes creeping in
bringing tears to my eyes.
In the loneliness of the night
this broken heart cries out!
"Mend me, love me.
Touch me once again with your warmth,
with your gentle ways,
touch me once again with
your love.
For I cannot live like this much longer,
I cannot take the loneliness of the night."

—*Larry Suhrbier*

Kissing

His lips close to mine
Caressing my cheek
Softly he kisses me
His lips on mine
Slowly our tongues meet
The passion fills us
Kissing for what seems forever
We break away panting for air
Then our lips meet again
Needing, wanting, craving more.

—*Tracy L. Wonzer*

The Downs

The tide is moving in,
    carrying times of change;
a new year, a new beginning,
    and nothing is ever the same

It's a time to test strength
    against innocence lost
just live for the future,
    and forget the past.

In this world it's essential
    for life
an innocent adult removed
    of all strife.

People who think that
    all things are neat,
make the world seem
    rosy and sweet.

—*Theresa Wylie*

Rainbow

Colors dreamy in the air.
Catch them!
Catch them!
If you dare.
The heavens dream.
Walk across them.
Promises kept.
Colors soft and sweet.
They speak so loud
But yet they don't say a word.

—*Michelle Spigonardo*

Soaring

Soaring over landscape
Catching thermals to stay aloft,
The silence is so profound
Only air is heard, sounds so soft

Drinking in the vista
Of quilted land below
Spread glorious greens,
The gems that farmers sew

For sailing on the wind
Bestows a joy and peace,
Creating weightless freedom
Of exhilarated release

—*Patricia C. Stuller*

Change

"Many times in life,
Change can cause suffering,
And suffering causes pain,
But often times,
One needs pain to grow."

—*Sandro Finamore*

One Rose

Rich loam through stem ascending
Changing earth to fragile life,
Proof of hope unending,
Beauty, truth, in spite of strife:
Petals safely wrapped in green
Pushing outward, breaking ties,
Ruffling edges of satin sheen,
Coloring faith for human woes.

Young song through spirit blending,
Bringing hope for all who hear,
Pause a moment — answer pending —
Truth, in one brief tear:
Souls immortal, guarded, lone,
Reaching outward, breaking ties,
Thrilling heart of faith serene
Knowing All because One rose!

—*Margaret Ingalls Cowsar*

Charge

People choosing
Children losing
Police are on the chase

People lying
Children crying
What's happened to the place

Help is needed
Fear is feeded
Please change this human race

—*Nikki Linn*

Chicks

Oval cradles burst with life
chirping…
But one is still, too soon
cracking…

Leaving earthly breath
as spirit slips through to
rainbows glowing girth…

No ties on earth can
hold a spirit when it flies
through to rainbow skies,
heaven…

—*Ruth Tausta*

Snow Whispers

Cold,
Clean,
Fresh,
I sometimes hear,
Slowly it comes to me,
Growing, sinking in,
Finding that special place,
All its own,
At peace.
Hunger creeps deep from the pit of me,
Sweeping me away to lost memories,
Still lost.
Remembering nothing,
Something's there,
Unreachable.
Control comes,
Too cold

I walk away.

—*Patty Jo Grewing*

God's Reply

I asked God why I had nothing.
    Closely, I listened for reply;
Yet, around me stillness lingered
    As I gazed at woods and sky.

Well then, God, why can't I see you?
    At least, just tell me this.
        But again no answer came
    While above birds flew in bliss.

Tell me please, why can't I hear you?
    Sweet words He did not send.
Down my head drooped in such sadness
    All I heard was whistling wind.

One last question, do you love me?
    And again his answer plain.
    In the silence I cried softly
My tears mingled with falling rain.

—*Regen Michal Dennis*

Winter

Solid white like the clouds above.
Cold like the nights before.
More beautiful than any song,
so silent but then all is warm again.
Winter ends.

—*Stephanie Vines*

Father

When you died, I grieved.
Cold, uncertain, the last male,
I wept.
And soon it was as before.
We had only talked in banalities,
like a bayou fog,
a palpable barrier between us
the threat of an unseen predator
rendering us quickly hushed.

But we did discuss the fog-
  how thick,
  how wet,
  how cold,
  its chemical composition.

We did discuss the fog.
  —Robert Lawrence

Untitled

Love you, love you
  Come closer dear.
Let me love you,
  Nothing to fear.

Tender caress
  Kisses so sweet;
Feel the passion,
  Feel the heat.

Bodies move,
  Bodies moan
Ecstasy near,
  Be as one.

Blade comes quick,
  Blade cuts sure
Cuts through the heart
  None can endure

Remembering passion
  Still taste desire
Pull back the sheets
  Uncover the liar.
  —Pamela K. Yeaw

Ode To A Fly

  Oh fly upon the window fair
come just a little closer, if you dare.
  Fly away! Fly away!
  Thy time has come.
  You must greet the day
    and kiss the sun.
  As short of breath,
    in time of need,
  you'll find your death
    a faithful steed,
to carry you far beyond this land,
for the morning star is close at hand.
    And if you find,
  the morning dawning,
    to brunch unkind,
  and peasants yawning.
  Fly away! Fly away!
  Your belly's gnawing
    on its empty decay,
  and this morning's dawning.
  —Todd Albertson

Roads

Sometimes along the road of our lives
comes a fork,
and sometimes we don't always
make the right decisions,
but none of us are perfect,
and we all have our share of faults.
We must remember
that God loves us all,
and he will be behind us
each step of our way,
whether we choose the right road,
or not.
  —Ryan Sliger

The Clock

Tick-tock non-stop, the sounds that
comes from a steady clock.

Pleads, cries, laughs, the sounds
that come from all walks of life.

Times are bad, times are good,
times are short, and our time soon dies.

A clock keeps us on schedule, and
deadlines; but clocks never loses their
beat.

Clocks can be replaced, but life just
leaves us with a sacred trace.

Tick-tock non-stop the sounds
that comes from a steady clock.

Ding-dong we will soon be dead,
but time goes on without us,
and that is a sad time we all
dread.
  —Lorinda Long

Untitled

  Out from the darkness,
    comes my black soul,
      beneath my feet,
    are the riches of gold,
of a land I've never touched,
and a people I've never known,
upon the earth my spirit roams,
  I am the Black Woman!
  —Nannette E. Banks

Shine On Me

When the real star
Comes out of his world
A world of danger
The light will be shining on me
The future will show the dream
I will tell you so then
In time you will know
As my talent rises roughly
Some sunny day soon
It's going to be for all to see
I will correct my errors
I will mail all a signature
To all as I believe in me
All will see as I'm set free
The light will snip
The shine explicitly
  —Valerie Mochulski

The Mirror

Catching a predestine glance,
confirms what I know to be true.
Time;
  relentless and unforgiving
  has taken its toll
  and forever turned
  from ally to foe.

I relive a lifetime of memories
with one passing glance.
Did I love?
Was I loved?
Does it matter!?
I don't know!

I'll end it all now...
...Isn't that better?
My shoes grind the broken mirror
into the floor.

Yeah; much better.
  —Thomas S. Bozek

My Mary

A mass of curls all tossed and blown
crown her little face.
No matter how I comb them,
they never stay in place.
And peering out from under bangs
eyes like you've never seen;
they sparkle and dance as in her mind
she plans a mischievous scheme.

A button nose she crinkles
as she bursts into a smile
and even when she's naughty
I love her all the while.

A devil could cause no more trouble,
an angel shed no more delight.
And when I rock her in my arms
and bed her down each night,
I think "No little girl
could ever be this fine."
How can I ever thank you, God,
for making this baby mine?
  —Rhonda Ekstrom

Tough Bein' A Kid

Mom's got a headache,
Dad's in a bad mood.
I looked at my pillow...
The corner's been chewed!

Went up in my tree house
and took off my shoe.
Three toes were dessert
for a fire ant or two!

My friend the black lizard,
he lives in my cart.
When I picked him up,
his tail came apart!

Sometimes late at night,
if I see that lightning,
a pillows' no good
for a noise that's so fright'ning!

My brain is too busy
to wonder what I did.
All I know is...
It's tough bein' a kid!
  —Sue Baisch

Chance Encounter

Colorless gleam of linoleum
daggers across her eyes.
Soundless chatter of gossip
pricks her gauze wrapped ears.
Her cheeks are frozen,
stretched in a Maybelline smile.

Animated and lifeless,
ice drips through her blood
to puddle moatlike at her feet
in black and white tile.

Choppy, she turns her glance
away from the pulsing walls
and is stabbed by familiar eyes.

She tears her feet from the ice
and leaps
to dive into the peacock of his stare.

But he shifts his gaze
and she falls
to smash shuddering on the tiles.

—*Zara Anishanslin*

Northern Lights

Sky blooms in cyan.
Dark oaks mirror their green
Up to the cool citron of the
Aurora borealis.
A north wind collides
With the last heat of summer
As the ecu of God's stars
Blinds us with an echo of light;
And it is Jesus who helps us see
Past the invisible eclipse which
Battles to rob us of vision.
It is always he
It is always he
Who pilots and drives us
Heavenward.

—*N. Marsala Ryan*

Illusion

I tear open a secret door
Darkness prevails
A flashlight reveals skeletons
Prehistoric figures large and small
Cuddled together.
A closer look and soft touch
Shatters the figures instantly
turning into a cloud of dust
settling like a carpet
over a dream.

—*Rose Sidoti*

Untitled

Born from the mistakes of lust,
Cursed by the eyes of God,
Raised with angry hate filled hands,
Cold brown eyes stare into silence
No solutions; no where to run
Endless betrayal, lies and greed
Innocence remains lost, forever more.

—*Michelle Palermo*

Coming Of Summer

When the realization comes
Death is truly forever
I close my eyes in concentration
Trying desperately to remember
Thoughts of you now cloud my mind
Time not having changed
The unforgotten memories
Have only been rearranged
For no longer able to feel the warmth
Of your protection
I've learned with time
To settle with pain
To live only with reflections
Still for years
I've kept you alive
In thought - in mind
In me - forever
and with the coming of Summer
I close my eyes
I remember..........

—*J. Gerardi Carpenter*

Inspiration

Inspiration comes
From far off places
But is experienced
In solitary repose.

Emily's is exemplary
Of a mind
That bounded over hill and vale
While sitting in a New England room.

The lady's learned head
And puritanical practicality
Gave her a world
Most of us are required to travel

To know as she did
And understand
Its hues and subtleties
And variations on a theme;

To know of places
Both on the map
And in the heart,
Glimpsed from her candle-lit room.

—*JoAn Mahaffey*

The Donkey's Triumph

From sea to sea, from pole to pole
    From May until December-
My race has been despised and mocked,
    As long as I remember.

I am not much concerned or grieved
    By critics mean and sour,
Since that grand day, long, long ago,
    When I had my great hour.

Beneath my feet a path of palms;
    By shouting folks surrounded;
Upon my back the Son of Man,
    My joy and pride unbounded.

That hour will live as long as I;
    No ridicule can dim it.
Laugh if you will, joke if you want;
    My patience has no limit.

Since once the Christ chose humble me
    To bear him to the city;
As long as donkeys plod the earth
    They do not need your pity.

—*Albert W. Buck*

Untitled

Take this dagger
    from my heart…
Set me free
    from Satan's dark…
Mend now
    the broken seal…
That I may live
    in eden still…

—*Glenda Messer*

The Picture Within

I am soft to appearance
Gentle to the touch.
But look close,
Look deep,
I am really not there.

Leonardo has the spirit
Of the brush as he paints
The kindness of my soul.

Leonardo didn't just paint me.
He painted a life
Sometimes soft and caressing,
And sometimes rough and jagged,
Harsh and brutal,
Loving and caring,

The softness of music had overcome
My smile to release itself passionately.

The laughter within equaled the
Madness of life
Possessed by the glory of the finished
work.

—*David Cole*

Helpful Tips On Winter

Winter is here, my friend
Get out the sweaters and the muff
Get ready to button up
Cold wind, nipping at your nose
Don't forget your heavy hose
Stir that soup, nice and hot
Careful when you handle that pot
Keep the house toasty warm
And cheer away the weathering storm.

—*Ann Annunziata*

Life's Gardens

Treasures and blessings -
    Gifts from our God -
Like the fresh smell of rain
    And new broken sod
Flowers and blue skies
    Birds in the air.
Gentle sea breezes
    Freedom from care

Sunshine and happiness
    Friends old and new
A new baby's laughter
    Grass kissed with the dew

Mountaintops and valleys
    As we walk through each day
The counsel He gives us
    When we kneel to pray -

But, we must be grateful
    And with our hearts we must show
If He is to help us -
    Life's gardens to grow -

—*Beverly M. Fuller*

Sale Pending

Take the pictures off the wall, leave the windows bare and cold
Flowers withered and forsaken, guess I've just grown too old
Boxes packed by the door, waiting for the van
Advertised as a starter house, this is where it all began

Sale pending, this house is almost sold
Sale pending, guess I've just grown to old

Once my hands were lean and strong, my back straight and tall
Pushed the children on the swing, raked the leaves in the fall
Mixed the mortar for the stone, pounded nails for this home

Children grown, my wife is gone
I've grown weak and frail,
Stop the papers, hold the mail
This house is up for sale

Sale pending, this house is almost sold
Sale pending, guess I've just grown too old

—Anne Penna

Raptures

Two hearts meet
Flowing together
As the waters of the sea.

The magnetism of burning desires surge
Emotions swell longingly,
As the waves of ecstasy mount,
The storm rages fiercely.

The passion of the movement grows,
As the rolling swells of the sea rush unceasingly,
The intense force rams the shores of desire.

Spent of it's fervor
The gentle evening winds return the tide to sea.
And I....
Lay tenderly in the arms of my love.

—Dolly Kijorski

The 'I'Iwi

The red, scarlet 'I'iwi bird
Flutters her wings,
Like ribbons floating in the sighing trees.
Her beauty you see
Her songs she sings
Oh, come listen to me.

With feathers rare,
Of red and black I do share,
For my Kings and Queens, you see;
They make cloaks to cover thee,
And walk so majestically.

My beauty is compared,
To the jewels so fair.
For I give so freely
My feathers rare;
Only one or two
Can it be,
For it takes a long time to see,
My treasures I give so lovingly.

—Alexander L. Akau

Peaceful Flight

On wings of grace
Flying, filling the air with songs of peace
Sailing high, where singing doesn't cease
Watching sun shine on heavenly space

The winds have calmed
Your ruffled feathers, now groomed
Eyes bright as stars, erases gloom
And you're free wherever you roam

Time changes on your side
And there's never a moment of indecision
Occasionally clouds meet in collision
But your faith stays alive

Bravery is born in your eyes
Looking across the waters for your prey
A straight and narrow dive is your surviving way
To muffle the new born's hunger cries

Sitting atop your nesting place,
Alert and threatened under the open sky
Without a worry you protect your family's pride
As a unique boldness is seen in your face

—John D. Jones, Jr.

A Family

What is wrong with our families today?
Folks think nothing of breaking away,
And going on their own with someone else,
And leaving their families to care for themselves.

Remember that vow you promised that day
The day that you said, "I do!"
I'm afraid we don't take it seriously;
"Until death do we part" should influence you.

But the ones who are hurt are the children;
They love both parents so much,
And miss being with them each day
And the hugs and kisses and touch.

Children need both Dad and Mom;
Think what an example you could be,
And the training and care you could give
If you weren't so eager to be free.

A family is a wonderful relationship;
It's rewarding throughout one's whole life;
Mom and Dad and brothers and sisters
It's an institution that is just right.

—Bessie Kerns

Oh Deer

It has come full circle again, that most dreadful time of year
for all of us for legged creatures. Hunting season is upon our
turf for one more depressing week. This is going to be another
sad time for all who are hunted by man, during his so called
"Deer Week." We have been preparing for the slaughter since
the last hunt and the many, many years before this one. People
the world over marvel at how beautiful and statuesque we look
and yet we are still killed for the sport of it. Surely we are
not much in demand for our meat, being wild but we are shot and
killed all the same. Last winter many of us were hurt and
didn't fall victims to your hunting knives. We ended up maimed
for our short lives, some lost limbs, eyes, had skin ripped
from our bodies as we ran for our lives ahead of you hunters,
who were determined to kill us no matter what. And what for?
To boast about another hunt where the big one you shot is now
mounted in your living room or den, for all to see. Does it
really make you feel proud that you shot another creature that
cannot defend itself? And finally, I wonder. Do deer kill
people for the sport of it and amount their heads, so they can be
displayed for all the creatures of the forest to see?

—A. E. Groleau

351

Shed a Tear

Shed a tear for a heart that stopped beating,
For arms waiting for someone to hold.
Shed a tear for a soul that is pleading,
To spread laughter and joy untold,
Shed a tear for the one that will never hear,
The sound of rain against her window,
For the one who was wandering through life,
Now, by the angels, has been led home.

  —Donna Newnum

Thank You

Thank you, God for the planet Earth,
For being able to delight in what is within,
For the micro-universe that is my body,
For being able to see you through what you have created

Thank you, for being my light in the darkness,
For sustaining me during all my falls,
Like a loving father you see no darkness in me,
With love you restore all my injuries
Thank you, for the ideas that germinate in me,
Giving a new path to my life,
Changing my tears and sadness
For cumulus of immense happiness

Thank you, Lord for every new day,
That illuminates the face of those that trust in you
And banishes from my soul of the injuries,
Brings hope, peace, light and harmony

Thank you, for all the universe,
For giving more than what I ask,
For caring for me despite of being foolish,
For being my father and my best friend

  —Fanny Parra

The State I Was In

This past Thursday was a special date
For corrective surgery to my aging prostate
Dr. Shockley didn't seem to mind
For after all, he had seen lots of "behind".

Doctors and nurses were all I could see,
I remember thinking of other places I'd much rather be.
They all smiled as they looked at me
And gone forever was my modesty.

As I laid on the table and I looked at the ceiling
Dressed in this gown that was oh, so revealing!
To my physician, all I could say
"Do you always look at tonsils this way?"

When it was over, to recovery I was sent.
A bloody mess in this gown with a "vent".
With IV, antibiotics and sodium chloride bags
No wonder that I was starting to sag.

And now that it's over and I can return home,
I can relax and once again "go on my own".
But I can't help wonder and to my chagrin
Admit it was all due to the "state" I was in!

  —Albert F. Guretse

Tongue

Naked, I am vulnerable to these words,
for designs of hate are new to my flesh.
And as water cools my open wounds,
you come again with your rapid tongue fire.

Seeing me encased within my fears,
your laughter comes to pierce the sensitive.
And as the release of snakes contemplates my death,
I wish for death.

Not for you,
but for me.

  —Christina R. Corbaci

Black Hole

Watching dear faces with tears
for eyes, flowing like rivers into
a child's casket.
Further now, I look past the present
into a darkened past where a boy
stands by a hospital bed, holding
his mother's bleached hand only to say
"It's okay, Everything will be fine."
His own tears flowing as he realizes
the falsehood in his voice from her own
weak grip
Watching her slip in to a black hole
of the brightest light.
Back to the present, looking up at a
bright midnight sky. Looking at stars;
Looking for mothers and Fathers and
Grandparents and other shining down.
Quietly embraced by a luminescent black
hole somewhere in the night sky.

  —James Barry

The Cherry Orchard

  I beseech you not to chasten,
  for I did not intend to tarry—
but the bells of youth which toll eternal,
  beckoned me to the grove
   where fragrance enticed—
  ablaze with cherry blossoms and
  secret pleasures—intoxicating.

Encompassed roundabout by ethereal splendor and
  mesmerized by its blissful beauty—
  I stood enraptured, drinking deeply,
  oblivious to temporal concerns and
   the lateness of the hour.

  Mundane tangibles fade obligingly
into that which transcends the ordinary,
as I come bearing sweet gifts of nature,
not to appease—but to delight and weave
  the spell of life's magic around you.

  —Alexandria C. Stephenson

Yin And Yang

Give me thy strength, and I'll give thee my warmth,
For in thy strength my security.
I will give thee my fealty,
And we two constant lovers will be
If thou wilt be my shelter strong.

Give me thy strength, and I'll give thee my warmth,
For in my warmth a haven fair.
A cradle to rest from worldly care—
Thy peace to disturb none would dare,
And I will be thy eiderdown.

  —Cherie Martin-McCormick

Kitty

She was named Kaitlin Frances Johnston at birth.
For me she was the sweetest thing on this earth.

She was so tiny, precious, cuddly and pretty.
Her parents decided to call her "Kitty".

As she grew older I loved her so much.
I could get "Mushy" just from her touch.

A sure way for me to get rid of the "Blues"
Is to see my "Kitty" with bells on her shoes!

She tries to repeat all the things I say.
I'm so proud of her in every way.

Now let me tell you, and this isn't a joke!
"Grandpa's Baby" is the first complete phrase she spoke!

On Grandpa's driveway she loves to run!
As long as she doesn't fall, it's really fun!

Everything she sees she wants to touch.
Maybe that's why I worry so much!

Kitty is like the jewel of the "Nile"
When she is around, you can't help but smile.

Kitty's always so sweet and caring, "Never Aloof"!
She will always be welcome under my roof.

—*Alan Owens*

Label X

Dumped into a category, labeled, and dumped upon
for measure,
the sins of a nation have caught us fleeing
from the age of excess...
I did not want these things
forced down my throat —
and no guttural cry will he heard
by those deafened to the sound of falling walls even
when they hold the harnesses of ruin and
push the papers bloated with bureaucracy and
       it all
       trickles
       down
       to me —
       a filter
       for their
       residue

—*Jonathan E. Minton*

My Window

My window is a picture frame
For nature's glory and artistic fame
The morning brings a canvas of beauty and colors bright.
Of flaming golden sky and shafts of brilliant light
Shimmering silver grasses and green bushes too
Was ever an artist so quick and so true?

Noontime brings another facet of nature's ability
My canvas now is a thing of rare beauty
Bright golden sunshine and azure sky
Green bushes and trees, so cool to the eye
Everything aglitter with the clouds riding high
All one can say is "My oh My":

Evening at twilight another canvas unfolds
Misty purple and grey in the dimming light
Outlines of trees and shadows on the horizon. The sky is a
haze of orange and blue and evening light turned on.

How great is the artist with talent divine
My canvas renewed each change of time
My window becomes a gallery of art
For man to enjoy and gladden his heart.

—*Alice R. Lafleur*

A Friend So True

How do I know that your friendship's so true?
For one, you always know when I am blue.
You're able to make me laugh and smile.
And afterward I just think awhile about all
the things we've been through, the good times,
the bad, all with you. I hope that we will be
friends, you see, because you've grown to be
a part of me. With each passing day we open a
new door, to all the things we're looking for...
A future together and much, much more. You
are my friend so true, and I will always care
for you.

—*Debra Werderits*

As We Move

Wandering acres, how long we have searched
For our home and shade and a place to work.
For pastures green where the cattle will roam,
Truly there is no place like home.

We thank you, God, for your constant care
As each day we strove our load to bear.
We pray for strength for the days to come
That we might be pleased with a job well done.

For our neighbors' help, both great and small
We couldn't have made it without you all.
Each firm handshake and friendly smile
Helped us to go that extra mile.

To our dear family, for your sacrifice
We thank you as we rest this night.
Spend time with your family, a gift from above,
Never taking for granted their most precious love.

—*Jean Marie Toombs*

Forgotten

Forgotten, forgotten, oh what a terrible word.
     For someone with it all, some may say unheard!
Yet, as I sit in my room and think... could this word
     possibly have anything to do with me.
Might I find myself still sitting in my room alone...
     watching the most important minutes of my life
         go by...
Is my life the same?
     Are my jackets still made of leather?
     Are my clothes still made of cozy soft cotton?
Well, I guess it all depends... If I'm forgotten.

—*Christopher Zito*

Untitled

Come let the mist fall upon this hallowed ground
For sorrow has fallen upon this heavy heart;
The soul cries out...a silent whisper in the wind,
Blowing fiercely, carrying away the unconquered dream,
The dream of yesterday's future, forever untouched
Forever banished—emotion now devoid of meaning;
In this time, in this world...a world once filled with love,
A love that made us strong, but now weak and empty,
Only the black abyss remains, sucking the very life of
     humanity
From that which was once the source of our existence,
An existence endangered if change is not made,
A change for the better, so that one day
The heart and soul may again rejoice.

—*Brian Gagne*

Thank You God

Thank you God for sky so blue,
For the moon and stars so bright,
For the sunshine's lasting yellow,
For birds singing songs so mellow.

Thank you for white swans in flight,
For the beauty of the night,
For the flowers wet with dew,
For each day we treasure anew.

Thank you for the mountain stream,
For the grass and trees so green,
For the life deep in the sea,
For puffy clouds that smile on me.

Thank you for the gift of life's treasures,
Children's smiles that bring us pleasures,
For friends and family we love so dear,
Blessings we receive when we keep You near.

—*Dorothy Vander Lind*

Grandmother's Lullaby

Hush, little one, do not cry, soften your sobs,
For there is a love lullaby singing softly for your
Tears to dabs.
Cotton soft pillows and soft warm satin sheets
Await your tender body to soothe, not forgetting
your feet.
A mother's warm arms and silken voice, speak
Cooingly to you and you alone.
Always know there is always someone there
To hear your slightest moan.
Hush sweet cherub of heaven's love lair,
No one will ever harm you, nor even dare.
Loads of loving arms are around to hold you and
care.
You baby, are important, so very important,
That heaven and earth, are for you to share.
So hush, little one and off to sleep with you,
For grandmother's near.

—*Adeline Stibbard*

Mother

Mother please forgive them
'for they know not what to do.
All the doctor say its nothing new
'but it feels there's something I should do.

Please let my mother be!

Things circle my head
'like a bird in the sky
Wondering why she'll have to die.

—*Debbie Briggs*

All Alone

Do not feel sorry for me on my 81st birthday
For it was the happiest, saddest, holiest day of my life.
For the man I lived with for 63 years died and I was his wife.
Our son, two daughters, he and I went to church and ate dinner;
The we ate my birthday cake and had ice cream.
We visited the cemetery where our other son is buried.
I'm 82 now - after a year it's still a bad dream.
For he walked over his grave space, our son's, and
  A little further, and fell over and died.
Absence makes the heart grow fonder.
I still miss him, no matter how hard I've tried.

—*Hazel V. Kaser*

1969 Plus

Young, who gives a damn
For those who went to Viet-nam!
We wait for the return only to learn,
A family sobs on the flag draped coffin.
Another died in Vietnam.

Draft dodgers, war protesters.
Strung out, hung out, on the run
Up to Canada, safe houses, home free, what a scam!
Sit-ins, make love not war, four dead in Ohio.

Live for today, to hell with tomorrow
"I" is all "I" need - horse, weed, and LSD
Far out on speed, put away that sorrow
Free, in the mind but hell imprisons the soul
Another died in Vietnam.

Free at last! Today the flag flies proud.
Old wounds run deep, healed, aren't they?
No longer the protesters vile target.
No longer coffins shroud, bereaved crying aloud.
Two black stone walls, names inscribed
To those who died in Vietnam.

—*Jana R. Mora*

Cherish

Cherish the one you're with.
For time together is so swift.
Although we met in a brief moment of time
How I wish forever you'd be mine
Compassion and caring is what I'd give.
To you my heart as long as I live.
I see in you a heart of gold.
How gently your heart I'd hold
Your feelings I'd never hurt
For the fate of losing you I'd never flirt.
Life passes quickly like the waves of the sea
How my heart I'd want you to see.
Friends and lovers can we be one.
Just the touch of your heart is all that
needs done.

—*C. Alston Bailey*

I Know You

I know you
for what you are.
You are a spirit of another kind,
which has come to change my mind.

For you said I will go far, and
in this world become a star.

You told me to run with those on top,
but something within said, stop! stop! stop.

I know you spirit for what you are.
I use to walk with royal folk, ordained
by God to do his will. And these were, they
who obeyed God when he spoke.

He told his disciples to follow him, and Jesus
will make them fishers of men.
That in his kingdom souls may enter in.

Jesus is the light that opens the eyes of
the blind,
This wisdom is from God and has become mine.

Read Daniel 12:3, and you will his truth see,
that Jesus can lead, and make a starlight of me.

—*Helen A. Fisher*

A Special Bond

You built a wall around my heart, forbidding my love
for you to escape.
I placed a mold around your heart to alleviate a break.
With you I have made a bond, a lifelong promise I'll
always keep.
With me you also made a bond, which I treasure
very deep.
This bond is not in writing, it has no signature signed.
It's the kind we have inside our hearts that keeps
our love entwined.
It has no special verse, it's said in many ways
It has no date of maturity, but grows more secure
everyday.
This bond is my love for you, a love that's very dear
It's also the love you have for me which I envision
very clear.
This bond cannot be broken, hence, it will never
need a mend.
It certainly won't expire from now until the end.

—*Diane Gallagher*

Forbidden Love

Forbidden love, it is so sad,
Forbidden love, can drive you mad.
With hair of gold; and lips like wine,
I can never say, that she'll be mine.

The hurt that comes, when we're apart,
The stabbing pain within my heart.
You hate to see the night sky fall,
Because you know, her, you cannot call

With eyes closed, she comes into sight,
So, you lie awake, late into the night.
While you sit thinking, you shed a tear,
Dreading the thought, of another day drawing near.

You need her so badly and want her so,
You know in your heart, you must let her go.
With two children and husband there at her side,
She and her family, you dare not divide.

So you turn to your friends, to get through the day,
Hoping they won't notice; or that they won't say.
As you think to yourself, she's an angel, sent from above,
A voice in your head, says no; she is your.... Forbidden love!

—*Arthur J. Cook*

I'm Power Hungry

My thought's are so consumed for power, but not the kind for
fortune or fame. Nor the temporary power that comes from
money, but I want power to tell others of Jesus name. I want
power to love my brother, even if he doesn't love me. That
same loving power that Jesus showed, when He died on Calvary.
I don't want my name in lights, nor do I want it carved in
stone. I want the power to show compassion, to those who feel
so alone. I want power to fight off satan, when he attacks me
from every way. And the only way to get that power, is to stay
on my knees and pray. I'm power hungry and I can't help it,
that's the way I want to be. I want to tell everyone of Jesus'
love, and about the wonderful things He's done for me. I'm
power hungry, so power hungry, the kind He can only fill.
Because there's only one power that brings happiness, and it
comes only by doing His will. The world judges power by
education, and accumulating earthly things. None of which can
help them, when tragedy comes that life can bring. The world's
power leave you empty, and is only temporary to say the least.
But the power that comes from Christ, will give you everlasting
peace.

—*Gregory Gayden*

The College Application

I sit and I ponder, what should I say?
Four years of high school have come down to this.
Arranging the words in just the right way,
Careful now, leave nothing blank or amiss.

Do not worry they say, "it's not so hard."
Yet decisions are based on what I write.
My credentials become my calling card,
No wonder I sit here all day and night.

Then later on the ideas come to me,
Application finished and the essay complete.
What a challenge the deadline is to meet,
Finally sealed and stamped, at last I'm free.

Wonder if I'll get in? Time will soon tell,
For now, relief, 'cause it's ready to mail.

—*Amy Hiddessen*

Satan's Spell

There's a story to be told, in the depth of the winter, in the
freezing cold, way back in the past where you had to fight
evil then be a hero. Children run and play when dad goes
away. The wife is weary and it's everyday knowing he'll be
back. The fear is a living hell, cause this man is satan's spell.
It's peaceful and cold in the winter, and the deer run free,
oh little ones come cuddle next to me. I'll tell you a story
that will help you sleep. The morning comes fast as we all live
in fear, we know he's gone, we know he's near. What do we
do when the man comes home? I can't even walk, I was just born.
One day we'll leave our cloths we'll pack, mom promised her
children, we won't be back. So we walked a mile with no shoes,
government homes brought us good news. We were well hidden,
so they say, but he found us one terrifying day. He went in our
house, intentions to kill, no one was there to give him this thrill.
The neighbors called the police, they took him to jail,
nature spared us this living hell. One day soon after mom
dreamed of his death, it came to pass my dad found dead in the
woods, in the creek where he fell, that was the end
of satan's spell.

—*Darlene Yvonne Bennett*

African Dream

Began as a child
from a soul just begun.
The love for lions
and the African veld.

Through adolescents and young adulthood
the dream struggled.
Unclear with no focus
but still a desire.

Married life and motherhood
with demands of their own,
Suppress the unclear dreams
of the African child within.

Dreams of the Husband put to rest
with the passing of his soul,
Reawaken dreams no longer at rest
with new focus and direction.

The African dream lives on
still to be fulfilled.
Though the time is not yet present
the sight of the dream is not too distant.

—*Aylea M. Butler*

The Voice Of One Crying In The Wilderness

Now halt your minds and listen to their cry
From northern alters formed of snow and ice
Beneath celestial curtains in their sky
The wolves give evensong of sacrifice.
All creatures stop - transfixed by somber hymns
Which rise from frozen mountains to the stars
And one whose understanding never dims
Who walked with man and also bears the scars.
The howling joins the wind which sweeps the earth.
Angelic zephyrs sing like flute and fife
Reaching the ears of one who from his birth
Has dared deny the sacredness of life.
This man, now trembling, sees upon his wall
A mounted wolf, his trophy - his distress,
That prophet's head brings judgement on us all
Like one who also cried in wilderness.
So listen now- we may not have so long;
Please listen to the crying voice and care,
And pray that we may never end the song
Of wolves and wind that fills the arctic air.

—*John H. Bidwell*

Fidelity

He was a man of many gifts,
From out his finger tips sweet music flowed.
She was an Appalachian lass,
Who drank each note in silent ecstasy.
  But could never make it.

He talked of foreign lands, applauding throngs,
Of marble halls and fountains.
She thought of shady glens, of babbling brooks
Of warbling birds and mountains.
  But never spake it.

They went their separate ways, two kindred souls,
United by a strange, un-touched affinity.
She hears his music still in Heaven's Symphony
His grave a lonely shrine until Eternity.
She lingers on in tedious longevity.
A solitary symbol of Love's Fidelity.

—*Beulah A. Thacker*

Suzi-Q

Blithe little spirit,
Full of the joy of kittenhood,
Trying to encompass the whole world in her being.
Leaping to grasp anything that dangled,
Sinking her sharp little teeth into anything she could impale
  with her needley little claws.
Jumping, frolicking, racing up and down the stairs,
Chasing anything that moved.
Frisky, vivacious, brimming over with vitality,
Coming a-running at the sound of her name,
Loving and lovable, giving so much joy and affection,
And so-o-o curious, constantly seeking to explore
The mysterious caverns behind doors and within drawers.
So fearless, so innocently unaware of the dangers and the hurts
  lurking everywhere — everywhere around her —
Ready to strike, to injure, to snatch her life away
And this was her doom.
Came that fateful moment when the maid started to unload the
  clothes-dryer.
Blithe little spirit, so soon stilled.

—*Estelle G. Friedman*

Folly

Count the stars, call each by name
Gasp, gape, gaze in awe; are they the same?
Colors...name their hues... depth of brightness
can you? Do!
Monitor the sparkles, quickly...add winks, twinkles,
blinks....odds on.
Bright stars! Smart, witty, keen, acute
unfenced, unwalled, unroped, barrier-free...reach!
Select, pluck more than a few.
Rent, sublease, lend and give stars.
Separate stars....the bright ones with glistening
heavenly dew.
Teach your stars, sparkle, blink, wink, twinkle on cue
for you!
Cloudy, deep darkness, starless nights
Winks, blinks, sparkles, twinkles out-of-reach
....out-of-sight.
Smart Stars!!

—*Florence T. Wilson-Mack*

Ten Point Urban Plan

Babies having babies, naive, uneducated; ill-equipped to cope,
generational welfare, learned helplessness. Is there any hope?
Crack, marijuana - called different names; teens pushing dope,
powder cocaine for the upper class. Is there really any hope?
Metal detectors in schools, less money for books, microscopes,
arsenal of weapons designed to destroy. Where is the hope?
Average citizen fearful, carrying guns, on an emotional tightrope,
more jails built, more prisoners to control. Is there any hope?
Break-ins, burglaries, stealing meager check-filled envelopes,
robbing banks, pedestrians, children. Is there really any hope?
Drive-by shootings, innocent victims; for want of the golden rope,
death, poverty, political and moral decay. Where is the hope?
During a similar situation long ago, lived a very wise old man,
who went to the mountain top, prayed; then descended with,
    the ten point urban plan!!!
If faithfully followed and used, mankind will unite, become one,
victorious over the negatives, hardships; any battle easily won.
It will resurrect the people offering a renewed spirit of love, hope,
making this a better place, beyond any real or imaginative scope.

—*Janine Carter*

The Earth Never Rests

The ocean twirls wildly like unkempt hair
getting in your eyes, strengthening you sleepy feeling that
the beach is a warm blanket to be pulled up around your cold
morning, shivering shoulders. The grass between your tired
toes tells you to dig in. Feel its roots tugging at the
wiggling worms.

Dancing beneath you, for the earth, spinning and teeming with
life, never rests. So how can you, merely because it is early?
Well, perhaps, if you're feeling a wisp of laziness
gently curving through your eyelashes
you might pull up some of the dawn's sunshine
and lay your head on that soft pillow;
let sleep take you in its long kiss
feel those delicate lips and know that although
the earth may never rest
it can always wait
while you dream.

—*Eric Yarnell*

To My Mother

Thank you, for all the caring, consideration and support you've
    given me, in my twenty-one years of life.
Thanks for being a friend, a mother and sharing your advice.
You lifted my spirits often when they were down, you gave me
    the strength to go on when there was so many times I wanted
    to fall.
You gave me hope understanding, patience and love in your
    greatest moments.
You helped me when I needed help and picked me up when I fell
You feed me, bathed me and took care of me when I wasn't well
You mothered me in the times when I needed it most
You stood by and watched me grow from a child to an adult
You gave me the strength to look at the world in wonders and as
    a challenge instead of with fear
You gave me the wisdom to help me with the family I call my own
You kept me in your bosom until it was time to let go
    and now I say to you my mother I do love you so
Thanks for the kindness you bestowed to me and I hope my kids
    are as lucky.

    —*Deborah Miller*

Giving Up

Taking that first step even though you are afraid;
Giving of yourself
As someone takes away,
To give someone that special chance,
What you wouldn't give
To see your sacrifice pay off
In the way another lives.

As the days are shorter and your mind is slower,
Remember what you've done.
You've been giving up for someone else
Who needs that special love.
And one fine day you'll realize
How very much you gave
When you see the love that you gave up
Come from another's gaze.

Even in this day and age it still stands very true;
That is a sign of a love
That someone gave up just for you.

    —*Amanda M. Griffin*

Knights In Blue

Here's to the boys in blue
God knows there's only a few
We hardly say thanks for what they do
Yet, they never complain
For the credit they're due
If we only had knowledge
And really knew,
The stress and long hours
That they always do
There's never a better group of men,
Like the ones in blue
So, we say God bless and really thank you
Until the next time I need help
And want to feel safe,
I'll think of you blue knights
Keeping our city and lives secured
From my heart and soul
I say thank you, thank you, thank you

    —*Charles F. Molina*

Don't Worry God's Not Done Yet

To my children from the first to last
God's not done yet.

Don't worry my son's, mother still here,
I'm not going nowhere it's not time
because God's not done yet with me.

Don't worry my daughter I'm here to stay,
So dry your eyes and pray,
mother will be here for you one more day
Don't you know God's not done yet with me.

I lay on my bed and I ask God
what shall I do today,
He tell me to rest for there's lots more
for me to do.

So don't worry my sister's because
God's not done yet with me, he left me
here for you can't you see we will walk
together for a little while, because as
you can see, so stop your worrying
because God's not done yet with me.

    —*Ella M. Sykes*

I

f I Could Give A Gift To The World,

This Is What It Would Be

Here's Hope, with bright bands of courage,
    Good health in a large package, too!
Years full of days filled by gladness,
    With bright family ties glowing through.
Just can't finish love and friendship
    (I'll give you some each time we meet);
A heart that's merry, wisdom, wealth,
    Then, to make this present complete—
        We'd conquer disease;
        And to make it secure,
            I'd wrap it in peace
                That would always endure.

    —*Grace S. Fishlin*

Grant Us Grace

Lord:
    Grant us the grace to stand upright
    in faith, love, trust, and self-righteousness.

    Grant us the grace to face gracefully
    all our endeavors in rich splendidness.

    Grant us the grace of an enlightened spirit
    to forever enrich our minds of God's Worldliness.

    Grand us the grace to mold and successfully
    strive in understanding life in its realness,
    to feel the need, love, trust, and kindness
    among friends with heart warm closeness.

    Grant us the grace of an awareness
    of our presence here in its fullness,
    and acknowledge life's inexpensiveness
    with faith, love, trust and the Grace of God.

    To thee oh Lord I pray.
    —*Gwendolyn C. Miller*

White, Green, Blue, Red, Black, Orange And Yellow

White is like the color of snow,
Green is like the grass that grows.
Blue is like the sky above.
Red is like the sun that glows.
Black is like the night
Orange is like the color of juice,
or an orange that grows on the trees.
Yellow is like the color of a flower,
that blossoms in the spring.
To me, these colors are the color
of things I've seen.
White black, orange, blue,
yellow and the color green.

—*Jerelean Dozier*

Real Stuff, Serene Screams And Package Deals

Sweet sounds gently found
Green on blue and blue on brown
Rushing over, falling down
Timeless, spaceless
Here peace abounds

Tiny crystals in the sun
Shining rainbows they become
Laughing leaves tease jagged cliffs
A patient presence in the mist
Shivering shadows, damp and stark
Behind the beauty lurks the dark

Where there is danger there is peace
Where there are children there are beasts
Where there is truth there is release

Enjoy the moment for it is real
To touch, to love, to risk, to feel

—*George A. Srur*

Lost

I sit here and I stare - I can not focus
Grief and fear grips my body so tightly it hurt to breathe
There is an emptiness so deep nothing breaks through
Darkness engulfs my space - my life has shattered

Just recently I realized I once again saw beauty, I saw life,
I felt alive

Now they are telling me my child - my life is no more
My reason for living, for surviving
My reason for leaving my abusive husband - his father
The reason I could accept welfare
The reason I work two jobs but at the end of a long, long
day can still smile
Now! I have lost it all because somebody else child felt a
gun and bullet was his salvation
Because my son - my only child, passed by at the wrong time

Here I sit, unmoving, unknowing, forlorn - a shell
Oh God! I feel the rage! It dashes itself through me like
waves in an angry sea
The pain! I feel the pain, it tears my soul, if suffocates me
I reach out, I start to rise - I scream

—*Charrie A. Edwards*

Lost

Something died inside of me. It's of infinite possibility.
Grand in its leisure, long in its road.. yet untraveled.
Weak in the heart where the love awaits. Dreams shattered in
front of your faces, now tears fill the empty spaces. Touch
the sky of midnight blue with your mind, let the thunder be
your guide. Let the lightning strike you and accept it with
pride. Take hold the power, for your soul must not die!

—*Cyndi R. Wilson*

To My Very Favorite & Special Kindergarten Teacher

You are my favorite everyday school friend, who looked up at me
and grinned.
In a friendly manner/good cheer, realizing my first big
kindergarten day is here!

A classroom of first-time students, beginning our lessons of basic
rudiments.
You instilled in our treasured little minds the knowledge of
unending power,
Which throughout life, gives us strength in our most difficult or
finest hour!

Our small, but secure little world,
The words 'n ideas/pictures 'n concepts, everlasting in our minds
are hurled!

All we ever needed to know we learned from you in kindergarten:
  *that playful sandbox,
  *those sometimes, but necessary long teacher talks.

You disciplined us with fairness, you taught us well.
In parting, but never from within the fields-of-our-hearts, we bid
you farewell!

Always, I will be able to with just-a-thought, as we depart,
Remember you in that special little reserved place in the corner of
my heart...

So, after-all, we will n-e-v-e-r ever really be so far apart...

Dedicated to: Niece Teona Lee Fagundes,
Sister-in-Law Madeline Lee Fagundes

—*Donna Mello*

A Symphony In Pain

The silence is a deafening cacophony in my ears;
      Growing louder
      And penetrating my soul,
   With the melody of darkness and fear.

   The loneliness is the echo of a violin;
      Plucking the strings
      In the corner of my heart,
   Where hope has grown so dim.

   The emptiness is as the sound of a flute;
      At once so sweet,
      But now a far away laughter
      At a pain I cannot refute.

   The longing is the pounding of a drum;
      Vibrant and strong
      Calling out its urgency,
   For a reprieve that will not come.

   This is the symphony of my anguish.
      So piercing;
      The orchestra of my soul,
   That only you can conduct to the finish.

—*Dana Mink*

Untitled

Remembering the beginning.
Half-concealed shyness, reaching out.
Hesitation, tentativeness,
Overcome by thought, talk and
-time-
revealed unrecognized affection.
A constant awareness prevented meaningless anger.
Unforced understanding
dispersed sometimes separating years
and built the strength that
finally, easily said is
I love you.

—*Elaine Marian Greicius*

Secluded Ball

Withered lips and fingertips
growing old from the lack of touch.
You roll yourself into a secluded ball
using the past as your crutch.

Refusing to venture out again
you feel warm and safe inside,
no one else can touch you there
but it's the worst place you can hide.

For in that place you'll remain
while others pass you by,
not knowing the wonders that live within
they smile while you sit and cry.

You were born to be alone "you say"
from inside of your sphere.
No one knows you're locked inside
except you, and of course your fear.

—*Gil Dickason*

Decay

Wooden rails, broken down,
guard a road with weeds o'grown.
Rusty hinges hold a gate-
now, as then, it seems to wait
for those who play beyond the call
"Come home before the shadows fall."
Missing shingles spill the sun
on stairs once climbed when day was done.
Strips of paper cling to walls
that echoed with the morning's call.
A slide worn rail suggests the way
to sagging floors of brown decay,
past a dusty and idle loom-
quiet vigil in an empty room.
A rusty pump stands alone
in barren garden walled by stone.
Roaming hearts still delay.
A precious heirloom knows decay.

—*Dortha V. Traux*

Girl In The Mirror

Her thoughts are dark and her dreams are secret,
hair blows in the wind, she listens to the birds
but can not hear them.
She is scared and alone but she is not lonely.
She lives in dream only she has the key to open her heart
and to set the dreamers free.
Her heart is willing but her body is weak.
She calls out for help but no one hears
until one day a passer by heard her cry for help.
She opened her window with a little help and all her dark
dreams and secrets fly by.
She is now happy and free and can hear the birds sing
of things to be.

—*Jennifer Peavy*

The Silk Worm

The first time I saw the silk worm,
He was high up in a tree.
I watched all day as he climb down to me.
On a tiny ladder
That only he could make...
Made of the strongest silk so it would not break.

He was very friendly,
Invited me to tea...
So we climbed back up his ladder up in the tree.

—*Betty J. Dupree*

Ode To My Father

He was a shadow of strength, a perfect image of youth, His dark
hardened skin gleaming in the rays of the sun, His hands were
gnarled by unending labor, his muscles were burning. Yet in his
face there was a glow of pride, in his lips an undying smile.
Soon the day is done, the golden sun will kiss the horizon,
it's time to be home in the arms of his loved ones. My
mother's greetings of love, longing for his touch. Our hugs
and kisses, our endless laughter will soothe away the pain. We
were his inspiration to toil the scorched land. Countless days
had passed, we have grown and left the warmth of his nest. To
seek a brighter future and offer him love and comfort in
return. But the road to success was treacherous and destiny was
not in my hand. The glittering lights I thought was guide,
were traps to fall. Triumph was within my sight, never could I
reach it, never could I hold it. His strength was weaning, but
his spirit was full, his tired eyes refuse to close, his
weakened heart refused to stop, he yearned for me who has
failed to return. The time has come to give up his unfulfilled
dreams and eternal love, late I may be, but I knew in his heart
there's a space to be filled. He had passed and all I could give
him was a kiss and a prayer to God.

—*Ana J. Laud*

The Spirit Of Life

The full-fledged believer of our heavenly Father,
    Has faith in His goodness and guidance forever;
For everywhere in life He is surely around,
    Seek Him early or late He will be found!

A message expressed some find Him by prayer,
    Through inspirational music His presence felt there;
With nature His creations not a shred of doubt,
    Since time began He has been about!

The kind, selfless folks who for others care,
    Spreading much love and readily share;
Here at work is the spirit who keeps on creating,
    All souls may tune in, He's patiently waiting!

—*Bertha Fisher*

For Thee I Love With All My Heart

The love I have been longing for
has finally found its way to my door

My faith in God has brought us here
so that we may be happy in ensuing years

God has watched over me, guided me and
has granted me the greatest gift of all,
a love I have never experienced before
for you, I will have, hold and I
    Will always adore

My heart will be open for you at all times
filled with love, open ears and open eyes

As we grow and unite as one
Our hearts will be filled with joy and love

For thee I love with all my heart
My love for thee will never part

—*Angela Catanzaro*

Lanmans Creek

The precious memories of small town folk
has stayed within me of loves pure stroke.
And when I gather these thoughts so complete,
I'll always have this feeling of love that was sweet.
I was so young and innocent with emotions galore
as I think of this young girl that I loved to the core.
We used to meet at our favorite spot -
With a body of water we shared a lot.
And when we watched the sun as it started to fade,
it was like ripples of diamonds that sparkled in the shade.
We sat there emersed with thoughts of a kiss
as we waited for the one who couldn't resist.
The sparks of emotion that aspired for two -
were bourned to be treasured as young love came true.
And when I reached for this memory for a peek,
it was of my first love at "Lanmans Creek".

—*Edward R. Williams*

Montana

Sweet dreams tease my heart and love songs
haunt my memory and make fun of the way I've
been living.
Still, his smile torments me and I can't seem
to get enough as he kicks me in the head
once more for old time's sake.
But I know what's best for me, or so I
am hoping as I toss his old photograph into
my backpack and head toward the mountains.
Here the trees will sing to me and I will
feel love from the sky. The grass will become
my blanket and the only friends I'll need will
be the stars.
I will forget him with his vicious love and
I will embrace the night with a purer heart.
The world will say, "I love you," and then
I'll know it's right.
And I will stay.

—*Decima Danyese Gray*

Untitled

Where's the Black artist? Sculptor? Poet?
Have they all gone to Hollywood?
Or "Gone Hollywood" and don't know it?
There are many who would speak for us
But where are they who would speak to us?
To speak of America...
The Grand, the Absurd
To depict our lives in oil, wood or word
Who will there be to tell our story,
To this new generation that knows nothing of glory?
They've seen no victories in their short time
Only heartache and sorrow
Poverty and crime
Where are the activists? Those concerned groups?
That would talk to us kids hangin' out on the stoops?
When they spoke of our birthright
They'd draw quite a crowd
And we'd all say "Yeah, we Black
And we Proud"

—*Charles Carter*

A Flower

I have searched many hours with all my power
Haven't found anything as beautiful as a flower
A flower in full blossom it's elegant to behold
It's tender leaves, sturdy stem, makes it precious as gold.

It's sweet aroma filling the air, attracting bees from here and
    there
As they gather sweet nectar, to honey with the world to share.
See it weave to and fro by the strong wind that helps it grow
Sometimes sheds a leaf, and pedal down to mother earth below.

It's beautiful in the sunlight, moonlight, or snow
And anywhere in the world it may grow
People pluck a blossom or a leaf
Makes it shed a drop of it's fluid in grief.

Come on agree with me a flower is a beautiful thing to see
Has many colors of the rainbow on it's blossom to show you and
    me
A thing of beauty, a joy forever
I hope nothing will happen to it, no! never.

—*Charles Irvan*

We Are The Giants

We walked into the abdomen of a big bird,
He carried us soaring aloft the earth.
We are now in the endless sky.
Surrounding with various clouds and sunshine.

There are miles and miles of white cotton spreads,
Floating in the mid-air to cover the world's unknown beds.
The crystalline cliffs hang above the snowy carpet,
Hastily the swift cirri like hundreds of horses gallop across it.

The sun shines on the universe eternally,
Its radiance sparkles in the space powerfully.
Our big bird pierces through the celestial bodies.
He is a libertarian fleeing from the earth's gravity.

We seem to fly among the stars and the moon,
There is no other superman coming soon,
We are the Giants in the universe at this moment,
And proud of being as superior human.

—*Diana M. P. Chang*

My Father

Dedicated to my father, Antonio Giovagnoli

My father was a pacifist
He did not believe in wars
He was a soldier in the Italian Army
in the First World War
His rank was the infirmary
I will do all I can to help my fellowmen
I will not go to the front with the rest of my troops.
He said to his commanding officer
You can take my life if you must
I will not take a gun in hand to kill my fellowman.

—*Emily Giovagnoli*

A Broken Heart

You hear him say it, but don't know if you should believe it,
he whispers it one more time, gently in your ear.
You want to believe him and take him in your arms and never let
him go, but a broken heart you know is too, too much to risk.
He looks at you deep into your eyes as you try to fight the
feeling of holding him in your arms once more.
You walk away with your head held high, like it doesn't bother
you and he didn't even pass you by.
As soon as you get home alone, you cry yourself asleep, knowing
today you can live without a single broken heart beat!

—*Brandy Pirc*

Love Thy Neighbor

A friend once told me to love thy neighbor
He did not say love thy neighbor
Because they are white or black
He did not say love thy neighbor
Because they are rich or poor
He said simply love thy neighbor
Be they Christian or Jew
Either way it shouldn't bother you
Be they straight or gay
Don't let your love delay
Now I know what you might say
But if it were you,
Wouldn't you want it this way?
The way it should be,
Love between all humanity!!

—*Chip Jones*

Born in Bosnia

Overture
(He dreamed that he was once again in Sarajevo, on the same
street where he grew up: mother and father sitting in the
garden, and his sister coming out of the house bringing them
coffee and newspaper; then they all looked up at him...)

(Act 1.) As the airplane was ascending over the Atlantic,
four teardrops came out of his closed eyelids.
  One for father.
  One for mother.
  One for sister.
(Act 2.) And one for himself.
(Act 3.) Yes, he has returned to his roots.
To a country, that some people claim, no longer exists.
To a place where no one waited for his return.
  But it was a place where he belonged.
  Like... a shadow of a dream.
  Like someone - born in Bosnia!

    Epilogue
(And no one noticed the lost gaze of his eyes.
  People say: this is just one effect of war.)

—*Brane Jevric*

Left The Range

A friend has gone I had so few
He has gone on as all must do
Yet left behind even for a time
Darkens my life and it's sunshine

He took the care to share my thoughts
And laugh with me about life's costs
Our families too both understood
This friendship brought them only good

He took me as I thought I was
Forgave my faults as a brother does
Listened and let me speak my mind
Tho my logic was often far behind

He gave all of himself in time of need
For friendship was his lifelong creed
And if our worlds had strayed away
He was always there on a rainy day

His death has touched my inner soul
And leaves a space that can't be whole
Tho I have all in life that helps to mend
I can never forget this lifelong friend

—*Elmer Coffey Sr.*

Grandfather

Yes, He has wisdom, strength and virtue.
He is someone to look up to.
He's a leader and a friend
On which the family will depend.

He's seen many days and years,
Endured hardships, sorrows and tears.
Yet like a pillar strong he stands
Reaching out his calloused hands.

Oh yes, those hard worked hands they tell
Of love and labor endured so well.
Out in fields with horse and plow...
Then, it's time to milk the cow.

And though the days were weary and long,
He'd always end it with a song.
And every day he'd say a prayer
That in heaven each child would be there.
God has blessed us with such a man
For he has given all he can.

—*Heidi Klein*

Red Room

The faceless man broke down the door to my red room. Now that
he knows how to break in, he spends many hours there, searching
for me. I don't go there very much anymore, so he is never
able to find me. It's decor, which hides the unpresentable
areas, he throws about and leaves out of place. Any existing
furniture he rearranges, making my room unfamiliar. He
deconstructs every wall that I've worked so hard, for so long,
to build, exposing more than could ever be seen by mere windows.
And I'm the one who has to make all the repairs and clean
everything up. No one ever helps me. Some people offer their
help, but only the ones that don't have the right equipment.
They cannot help. Usually, when he looks for me, I'm hiding in
my gray room. Other times, I am somewhere else, like my blue
room. Sometimes I want him to find me, but he never does.
When I'm in my gray room, I hear him as he is busy in my red
room. The noise he makes causes my ears to bleed. When I'm in
my blue room, I don't always hear him. Sometimes I
can escape the sounds. One day, I'll go back to my
red room, and he will find me there. He will make me look at
him. Only then will he ever be able to claim a face.

—*Jessica Rossiter*

The Old One

The old one raised his head
He looked at me and said
Times never change, there always the same
Been that way, since the white man came
First the land and then the buffalo
All the old ways were sure to go.

The old one kneeled to the earth
He said, son, don't think of this as dirt
It's life, it's blood and full of tears
Wears the scars well from the years
It's a white mans world as far as you can see
Rivers are crying, and mountains are no longer free.

The old one looked at me and smiled
He said, son, let your heart run wild
It's not to late to save this land
It's not to late to teach the white man
All that you are is all that there is
And a truthful heart is bigger than all of this.

—*James W. Sutton*

The Hands Of God

He's there, watching your uncertain smiles.
He looks in you, where things develop and grow.
His hand always take's yours-
And steers your spiritual awareness
In the dank, creeping, dark rooms.
You'll know everything will be fine.
Give your troubles to Him,
He lifts, soothes, guides thoughtfully,
A radiant balloon will devour them
And drift off into oblivion.
Nothing is too hard to accept.
When life leaves your confidence
In the lost forest elsewhere,
Ask Him, He'll answer and help.
He has everything you need,
He has strength, love, and truth.
He is in whatever you do.
My inner peace and deep foundation-
He is my one real escape,
No one else gives that kind of life.

—*Jennifer LaMance*

Jim

I sit side-by-side with my brother Jim,
He looks like me and I look like him.

We eat from one bowl and like to be fed,
He also likes crusts but I like the bread.

When we are finished we like to go play,
We share lots of toys and ride trikes every day.

We get bathed in one tub sitting one behind the other,
We're soaped, washed and rinsed while we splash our mother.

When it is nighttime and we're ready to sleep,
We go to our cribs with our teddy bears to keep.

When the lights are put out and I lie in the dark,
I hear Jim giggle but it's not time for a lark.

I feel pretty sleepy and my eyes won't stay open,
Jim soon seems quiet and he gives up hoping.

Tomorrow we'll start another new day
When my twin and I can frolic and play.

—*D. M. Cole*

New Trail Of Tears

The ancient Cherokee trudges up the winding trail, deep in
    thought.
He recalls a time when the land was his and his ancestors'.
His face is as dark and rough as the granite cliff rising above him.
He has ebony eyes that had once observed beauty.
His woodland path was a cool passage between tall trees.
He now sees a barren path paved with black asphalt.
His spring was full and sweet, clear and sparkling.
He now sees a spring that is small and sluggish, brown and foamy.
His stream was full of life, fish leaping for elusive prey.
He now sees a lifeless stream filled with the broken debris of man.
His azure sky was spotted with white clouds and multicolored
    birds.
He now sees a sky, empty of life, that is yellow with poisonous
    smoke.
His forest was thick and alive, home for countless creatures.
He now sees a forest that is blackened from fire, dying with
    disease.
His mountain was unbroken, tall and majestic.
He now sees a mountain scarred by man's machines.
His valley was vibrant with the reds and yellows of autumn.
He now sees a valley, almost obscured by the orange haze.
He recalls a mountaintop, so high birds flew below.
On his mountaintop, he sit on a discarded tire and weeps.

—*Charles F. Mize*

A Little Boy

A little boy came into my life one summer day,
He touched my heart with his golden ray.

The twinkle in his eye, and the touch of his hand,
Melted my heart, and the feelings only I understand.

If at night he should waken in hurt or scare,
Suddenly, yet quietly, I find my way there.

A keen mind, yet a mischievous boy likewise
He possesses, yet endears to me each day.

We know not what the future holds,
Or the problems life enfolds.

But, in this child, awesome promise I see,
"Please God, take care of him, for me."

—*Alta Adams*

Grandpa

Grandpa was loved in all our hearts,
He was known in so many parts.
And though we all miss him in so many ways,
We know we'll all see him one of these days.
He has finished the course and kept the faith
and given us all an example to look up to.
He talked about Jesus night and day and told
us He was the truth, light and way.
He loved his family with all of his heart
and told us he would soon depart.
He spoke of his mansion bright and fair
that God had for him waiting over there.
I know that he is happy in his new home,
listening to the angels sing victory songs.
Although tomorrow we'll place him in the ground,
we know where his spirit will be found.
I know I'll see him in the sky,
over there in the by and by.
Until the day I see his face
I'll praise the Lord for His mercy and grace.

—*Jana Baskin*

Timeout

Another weekend of miscommunication. He said, she said.
He wasn't really listening
- Or he didn't like what he heard, so he tossed it aside.
She just talked harder,
Then eventually gave up and fell silent.

Some weekends the talk flows a lazy Southern bayou;
Easy, warm,
Moving in no particular direction, in no particular hurry,
Everything connected, smooth.

This weekend's dialogue felt more estuarial:
An incoming tide fighting a river's outward flow,
Foaming and swirling in muddy chaos.
Nothing can be seen through such murky water.

—*Charlotte L. Wilford*

Spring Commands

The mountains issue Spring commands.
Her heart obeys, and muscle strands,
'Till spent and ring'd with drifts she stands.

The rising moon with gentle glow
Smiles more glad on her camp of snow
Than on the city far below.

—*Ginger Pena*

He Who Talked To Walkers

He was a wise young man.
He watched as the elders
Gathered stones. He learned as
They tried to speak to
Spirit of Stones.
Soon, he too, found great old relics,
Stones far more worthy
Than all others.
He talked to the stones, and
They listened wholly.
The rock's spirit told him of their life as walkers.
Soon after, the elders
Awed his etchings of these
Long gone walkers.
The Great Walkers had
Given up their legends to him.
He carved a living niche in the
Proud tribe's life, for
All knew of
He who talked to Walkers.

  —*Jeff. Norris*

A Look Back

We were bandbox neat in salesclerk blue
He worked at sax's or the five and dime
Ladies dress shops or a place to dine
We must for lunch at the local grill
we laughed and talked of fashions and work
or how we handled a certain jerk
we were Jews and Wasps
sharing this hour
talking, laughing-hadn't
we just won a war together?
Time scattered our group
Some to make chili
Others chicken soup
Why can't the world be
like this group
with interesting differences
but one goal in mind
To make life better
For all mankind.

  —*Florence S. Sparks*

Night Angle

Capture it in my heart
Hearing your voice in the dark
And I watered it in fears'
Night and morning with my tear's

You walking in the night
Letting your shadow into the light
I sunned it with smiles
And with soft deceitful wile's

Searching for some past
No trace of what you had
If I can recapture your face
Bring you down to the human race

Suddenly I hear to see you walking in the night
Letting your shadow in my life
There to hear your voice to say
As I watch the angle draft away

I thought it could never be
To have a angle at close to me
As I watch the angle go to the sky
I gave her my last tear to cry

  —*Clifford Sowell*

Hearts And Books

We together, yet miles apart, there's the book and there's the
 heart
A passing of knowledge, a beautiful glow, make people come back
 for more
Do not stop at a crossroad, until each direction has been explored
Send out the book, send out from the heart
Till all is calm, we're no longer apart
Wake up tomorrow, watch a smiling face and know we have put
 them in place
When all is done, we will rest
We have done the best
Don't be surprise if we are called one day, to do it different
 in some way
A fulfill heart, a written book, cause someone to grow.
Nothing can stop them as they go
We laugh, we cry, our hearts beat like drums, there is sun,
 after the storm

  —*Bernice Petty*

Angel Of Death

Today I saw the angel of death knock on a
heart's door and grant a wish to one that was old,
frail and praying to go home. She crept into his sleep
and carried his soul so gently up and through the clouds
to it's eternal rest.

Today I saw the angel of death give peace to one
that was lonely, depressed, and dependent on others.
To one that had been visited so rarely by family
and friends even forgotten by others.

Today I saw the angel of death spread her
wings, smile, and rejoice as another kindred spirit
passed through heaven's gates. Tho his empty bed
will be a reminder, to those of us who cared for
him, that he is gone. I have to smile and remember
today I saw the angel of death and wonder how long
it will be before she returns for me.

  —*Alta Hester*

The Deer

The deer bounded right in front of me,
He'd been concealed behind the great oak tree.
He stared at me with most soulful eyes,
He spoke eloquently, "am I another that dies?"

We stood facing each other for several seconds,
It seemed much longer, as each of us reckons.
I stood quite still, not daring to move,
He stood still, too, his courage to prove.

I'm not a hunter, but would he know?
Would he wonder if I carried either gun or bow?
We wrestled with each other's innermost feelings,
How would life treat us in its absolute dealings?

He made a quick move and crossed the road,
I sighed; I was relieved of a tremendous load.
I watched as he disappeared from view,
Surely, we both had experienced life anew.

There are those who would hunt the deer,
They would shoot and kill without shedding a tear.
I could never do such a thing as this,
That soulful eye, that proud bearing, I would miss.

  —*David M. Armbrister*

Warrior

A warrior stalks this trail alone out of the jungle
hell. Leaving his soul behind

A tortured and lost soul. In his dark jungle hell.
The anguished scream for help. Unable to bear any more pain.
Wildly and blindly searching. For the child 20 years gone.
Crying the tears of fear. Walking on the trail unknown.
The warm embrace, the cold hard stare. The warrior brother
sharing in love, unable to bear my pain.
The sun climbs slowly in the early morning dawn. The
eagle sours free.
As the early morning mist slowly rises out of the river
bottom. So the warrior comes home.

—*Jay R. Whitcomb*

The Camel's Back

The camel's back is broken
He'll tote the load no more
He's walked the line so many times
He's finally learned the score

The load you set so carefully
Each straw in it's place
But one more straw you tried to load
And now you've blown the race

The camel's back is broken
The writings on the wall
Your house of cards is tumbling down
The walls begin to fall

The tide was turned, the wind has changed
My court has the ball
You thought you had your hooks in me
And now you've lost it all

The camel's back is broken
I'll tote your load no more
Too many times I've heard your lines
And finally learned the score

—*David Brandes*

I Changed

Things do not change; we change.
 -Henry David Thoreau
You change when you learn.
 You discover.
After Dallas -
 I discovered
 my faith,
 friendships.
 I began to trust people
I changed.
 I learned.
 The world was still the same polluted world,
 but I started learning and discovering what is in it for me.
I changed.
I discovered what it's like for a friend to move away,
 the emptiness,
 missing him,
 now trusting him.
I changed.

—*Harriet R. Latta*

Amanda

Amanda was loving in every way
Her beautiful smile would light up my day
She had a way of touching your heart
And with this gift she was very smart
I loved my Amanda from day one
But its killing me now to realize she's gone
It breaks my heart that she wasn't around longer
But day by day I feel a little stronger
I just want to say and please understand
I will make it through with Gods helping hand

—*Denise Palmer*

The Final Song

The quilt is drawn up to her chin.
Her eyes go blank.
"Ma ain't that sick," Pete says.
John Michael's still trimmin' at the boards.
Did you know Hattie Mabry is going to die?
I look at her, at her face.
Pa stands bedside the bed and says, "She's gone."
Hattie Mabry is dead.

Nail it?
His shadow stays. Her's gone.
It will be and then it will not be.
Is your Ma...
John Michael drives the last nail.
I done my best.
Looks like more rain.
They had laid her in it.
He promised her. 'Sides, it's too far to quit now.
Pleasant Valley Church 2 miles.
We do not go in.
The song ends.

—*Dayna Lassinger*

Close

The child sighs and shivers at the room,
her father holding her small body close.
This will not be her only glimpse
of the arching heavens with him.
Soon he will tell her of the craters,
Petavius, Gassendi and the Sea of Crises.
Archimedes, Pythagoras and the Ocean of Storms.
Soon she will know the planets
Pluto, Neptune and Uranus,
and see adventure in the shape
of Hercules, intrigue in the arrangement
of the Seven Sisters and wonderment
at the name and namer of long ago
who called them Pleides.

Evenings, waiting for a darkening sky,
she will feel her father's flesh against hers,
the memory breathing a tender sigh.

—*Barbara Stephens*

I Know an Indian Maiden

I know an Indian maiden
Her hair is sparkling black.
She know's how to act.

Her eye's are of gold.
She's not very old,
And her skin glows.

Her cloths are made of doe skin.
And, best of all, she is my next closes kin.

—*Barbara Gullicksen*

Confrontation

She twisted around, shaking in anger.
Her hair was tangled around her face—
confusing her features and hiding her eyes.

The finger that she lifted to my nose
was gaunt, and threw beams of accusations at my soul.

Her voice was marred with passion and rage.
"Don't lie to me!" her lips screamed.

As I faced her I knew that now was my only chance
to taste freedom, to stand up for the truth.

With cheeks ruddy from anger and a controlled, still voice,
I defied her demons cautiously,

Inching along the tightrope of her mind.
"It's the truth. You know I'd never lie to you.
He would. And he did," my steel voice shocked me.

"No!"
Then she whirled around and slammed the door on me
and her world
while I patiently felt my heart breaking.

—*Jennifer Westurn*

When Autumn Came

I was awake this morning, and I knew when Autumn came,
Her morning skies ablaze with plumes of gold and purpled
    smoke —
A maple tree dressed suddenly in shades of crimson flame,
And squirrels stealing acorns from beneath a towering oak.

The river slept beneath a blanket woven from the fog,
The wildlife on her banks ignoring daybreak, sleeping still,
One lonely 'possum ambled back into his hollow log,
To end his nightly search for food, escape the morning's chill.

The quiet village lay in slumber waiting for the sounds
That would bring to life its houses, shops, and streets;
But in the morning stillness there was none to wake the town,
And so it slept, and dreamed within its sleep.

I could not bear that no one else should witness such great peace,
And so I shouted, "Wake! Come out and live, and breathe, and
    be!"
But no one heard my calling, and at last the echo ceased,
And so it was that none encountered Autumn there but me.

I was awake this morning and I knew when Autumn came,
But though I shouted loud and long, no others cared to stir.
Yet now I somehow know my heart will never beat the same,
Since just this once I met, and lived, and walked awhile with her.

—*Brenda Bland White*

The Battle

Her body gets weaker as she starts to grow old.
Her once settled life begins to unfold.
Her bones become brittle, her skin so thin,
Little by little, the changes begin.
I look in her eyes and I see her pain.
But never once did I hear that woman complain.

Her mind is not what it was once before.
She seems to forget things more and more.
Three years ago, her husband past away.
Beside his grave her only child lay.
There is an empty space beside them on the hill,
To lay her body when she becomes still.

The smile on her face impresses me so.
That grey haired lady said she was ready to go.
"I have no fear of dying." she said.
"I believe in God and I know what's ahead.
Life is not over, it has just begun.
This was my battle and I have truly won."

—*Diane K. Dewey*

War Zone

And there she stood in the shadow of death:
her profile etched in pain;
her eyes wandering in vain;
numbed by shell after shell -
Oblivious to the flurry from hell.

and there she stood in the shadow of death:
tormented and teary-eyed;
war-torn and weary-eyed;
lost in a heart-wrenching haze -
as the nights merged into days.

and there she stood in the shadow of death:
amid the debris of a bygone bliss;
clinging to the memory that was his;
a solitary soul-beaten and bereft -
with not a whisper of hope left.

—*Feroza Abbasi*

Meanderings

As her hands extended forward
Her whole body went limp,
She turned pale
    as color seeped away from her face.
With power from somewhere unknown
She felt herself go forward.
Her hair stood on end, body went numb.
She encountered all the forces of the two worlds.
Mists so heavy it felt like rain.
As she gradually emerged from the mists,
She found herself gazing at a world never seen.
Concealed in an unwieldy mist
She felt compelled to move ahead.
Preceding her was a woman
Whose beauty astonished her
As she was led to dimensions unknown,
Incognizant of ever returning again.

—*Colleen Malone*

I'm Here

I'm here for you for the need is there.
Here to help make the waiting easier,
Here for you just to share.
Here because I care;
Not really knowing how you feel,
Here if you want to talk.
Here just to sit; simply because I care.
Truly believing that everything will be alright,
A belief from deep within that all is indeed made right.
I'm here if the need arises,
Here if you need a touch;
I'm here in prayer for you,
Yes, I do care that's why I'm here.

—*Carleen A. Lane*

In The Dark

In the dark and all alone
here we sit away from home.
In the sky we see the stars
on clear nights we see to mars.
Smell the air so crisp and clean
See the trees so spooky and mean.
Hear the frogs crock hear the cricket sing
what a very amazing thing.
As we sit here in the dark
and Armadillo comes to lark.
Up we get and off we go
back to camp here we go.

—*Danielle Goins*

The Ocean

In the ocean is where treasures are found
Hidden among the glittering white sand
The tropical fish all swimming around
And the coral reef so brilliant and grand

The water, how clear, like scintillate glass
And the best secrets are kept inside shells
The winding kelp looks like billowing grass
Where all the mermaids so lovingly dwell

The smell of the salt, the chill of the spray
And the barnacle speckled rocks below
Marine life teaming, a colorful array
Oysters with pearls glimmering like snow

Oh, how I love the beautiful blue sea
The peace, the quiet, the serenity
        —*Christine Valdez*

The Escape

A sad and lonely child escaped into a book
        Hiding from the world outside
        Her feelings of isolation fading
    As the plot wove itself around her
Exposing forbidden ideas, her mind becoming open
Accepting and understanding, some of what lay beyond
Embracing new concepts; feeling power and strength
She pored over each page, drinking in every word
        As if it were the last
        Until the final page
    And the conclusion of her journey
        Then, weary but content
        She sadly closed the book
        And placed it on the shelf
        Ready to rejoin life again
        Knowing that soon enough
Pain and frustration would send her back
    To the solace of the written words
        And a friend she'd never met
        Would provide a little comfort

—*Ann Vetter*

"Out Of Reach"

As the eagle soars, so shall he;
High in the clouds, forever free!

Life is strange, happy or sad;
Sometime tragedy claims a lad;
Who filled a void when he was born;
Now from us, forever torn!

Above the punishments and stress;
Beyond my reach or my caress;
Out of the reign of mortal temptations;
Away from the faults of this nation!

He left this life while in his prime;
I believe this to be society's crime;
Even a Mother's absolute caring;
Made little difference or had any bearing;

On the length of his precious life!
        —*Dorothy Rittenhouse Fuchs*

Snider the Spider

Snider the Spider lived in the church
High up in a lofty perch

Until one Sunday morn
He felt alone and so forlorn

He slid down his silky thread
And landed on a lady's head

But he must not have liked his hairy bed
Cuz the next day, they found the lady dead
"From a spider's bite," the pathologist said.

Snider was never again found
But I think he's still around

Probably underground — in the lady's coffin.
        —*David Vorpahl*

The heavens sunder at his beck and call,
    His countenance spills forth
And vanquishes the darkest foe.
    And the blazons of joy ring forth
From high amongst the trees,
    And stir along the floor.
Beauty shouts its victory call
    In legions of glorious colors,
Life regains anew
    As Nature lays with her lover.
She cradles close to the passion of his breast,
    And pleasures fill her soul.
        —*Douglas S. Picklap*

Dad

A man of peace walked this earth
His dreams not all fulfilled
But we remember all he left
That day that he was gone
No request ever denied, no problem ever too big.
On Tuesday morning with bagels in hand
His warmth entered our home,
Never a time when it was too much
A drive never too long.
Pick me up Grandpa-Dad will you take me?
Sure - I'll be right there.
A promise of hope in everyone's future
A helping hand for all he knew and those he didn't
A legacy of life.
Not a saint-just a man with days of joy and sorrow.
With thankfulness and love we remember him
And in these words we express his life
"I was always there"
        —*Florence Zaccaria*

Mal De Mer

I saw my friend today.
His face green, but not with envy.
The skin was loose, and slipping from the bones.
His eyes were forced open by the current.
Seaweed draped his bloated body.
Suddenly, I longed to hug my friend.
As I lifted his lifeless form,
creatures scurried from beneath him.
Memories flooded my mind,
as rapidly as the sea filled his lungs.
I saw my friend today....and I said goodbye.
        —*Holly Cardinell*

The Eyes Have It

Others just see him old and bent, but all I see are his eyes.
His "git up and go" has got up and went, but it doesn't affect his
    eyes.
No noise around as we quietly sit, but words are still in his eyes.
The spark is there and definitely lit, for I see the light in his
    eyes.
Discomfort by him is obviously felt, still all I can feel are his eyes.
The love I see just makes me melt, as he covers my face with his
    eyes.
He speaks a volume without a word, by each change I see in his
    eyes.
He knows the peace that's found in the Lord, for it shows in the
    depths of his eyes.
Some might think he's just a shell, but there's strength within those
    eyes.
He may not speak but I know well the story he shares with his
    eyes.
The touch of his hand is very weak, but not the touch of his eyes.
And as I kiss him on the cheek, our love is sealed with our eyes.

—*Betty Rill Webster Bishop*

My Grandfather

My grandfather was once here for me to love and hold,
His heart was loving and made of gold.

He was always there to comfort me when sorrow appeared upon
    my face,
He was always there to teach me about a wonderful place.

A place of soft mellow breeze and lightly glowing sun,
The fresh scented flowers that never close, because the day is
    never done.

The pebble path that has no end,
The river flow that turns at bend.

A place where there are no enemies, you are friends with all,
You walk together upon the clouds, but don't be afraid, for you
    shall never fall.

Because you have wings, wings of love,
Wings that shall carry you far up above.

Now that my grandfather has left this earth,
He will enjoy heaven for what is worth.

—*Jill Marie Trombley*

A Walk In The Sand On A Sun Drenched Evening

Whose beach this is, I think I know
His house is in the heavens though
He'll surely see me stopping here
To watch birds fly and sea oats grow

My tameless pup must think it queer
No leash, no pens, no fences here
Between the tide and sand and wind
The most colorful sunset of the year

He gives a sand crab a snap and shake
But it bites back, there's no mistake
And many other sounds break free
The porpoise breath, waves roar and break

The beach is awesome broad and free
I'm in my place and it's in me
Suns will set and there I'll be
With miles of life and God to see
With miles of life and God to see

—*Buddy Goldsmith*

Forever We Will Be

My dearest friend, my life and my love
hold my hand forevermore.
Pull me closer to your love - filled heart
Walk with me along the shore.
The rocks we climb and the holes we find
symbolize hardships we face.
But no matter how rough the shore side
our love cannot be defaced.
Step by step we come closer as one
feeling the pump of our hearts.
Though forces pull us another way
we're deemed never to depart.
As endless as the waves that roll
so our love is just the same.
As a wildfire in the forest deep
our love can never be tame.

—*Charlene Moore*

Hope For Everything, But Expect Nothing

Hope for the day to come, but expect the dark.
Hope for the sparrow to fly, but expect him to fall.
Hope to be carried, but expect to walk.
Hope for sunshine, but expect clouds.
Hope for love, but expect anger.
Hope for peace, but expect war.
Hope for the whole world, but expect only a piece.
Hope for tomorrow, but expect an end.
Hope for forever, but expect time to stop.
Hope for time, but expect finality.
Hope for life, but expect death.
Hope for Everything, but Expect Nothing.

—*Bonnie L. Berzonski*

Untitled

For you, this lovely pink rose.
Hope it tickles you from head to toes.
With it, love and happiness goes.
May it dispel your worries and foes
As it grows.
You shimmer more beautifully than the winter snows
And each part of you glows.
From you, love and happiness flows
So the gate on you, I shall not close.

—*Bob Svoboda*

Seeking Happiness

I go to the window and look towards home
Hoping to catch a glimpse of happiness:
I turn away, knowing it is not there to be found.

The day I left lingers in my thoughts -
I remember it infallibly:
Wistful goodbyes, wishing to have one last word,
Fought back tears.
The air has now turned heavy and regretful:
Wishes of being with true friends and enemies are constant-
Nothing is settled.
The days pass by inconsequentially:
Lulls between excitement are long and thoughtless -
A life full of monotony continues.

And one day a spark of joy strikes -
Should I resist? Joy slowly spreads over me:
Happiness is just around the corner.

I'll find it soon.

—*Jessica A. Reynolds*

How Should I Tell Thee

How do I tell thee,
How beautiful you are?
Or tell you how much I love you,
Without making it come out wrong?

Should I say how your eyes,
Remind me of a soft evening night?
Or your skin is soft,
Like the wings of a butterfly?

Should I tell your laughter,
Is like a breath of spring?
Or your hair is soft as the floating clouds,
Just after an early rain?

Should I tell you, your voice is like,
A chick-a-dee that sings in the early spring?
Or should I say, it's like a soft warm breeze,
Just before a gentle rain?

How should I tell Thee,
I'm in love with you?

—*George F. Allen*

Dearer Esteemed Mother

Oh, my truest, gracious, fascinating mother
how can I dwell for thee with your spoken honey
sweet words, which crush my heart and sweeply
cracks down with all my sweet heart's desires dirt.

Everyday I hear your truest words which slop down
like a river tide, beside my untidy heart
through a splashing earth.

Oh, my life's master you told me those successful
words which I won't flop through your lone post of death.

Oh, divine faithful mother, why did you suddenly
perish from this long untrodden way like judgement day?

That was she, who you were esteemed by your sugar
words, with all the colorful view; like
the early morning hours, sleepy dew.

Oh, my heart's tasty mother I owe you my life
like the goddess brightest sunshine
which flops down in this enormous world like
your esteemed truest significant words.

—*Fahmida Mahmood*

Save Us From Ourselves

Lord my God, can you tell me one thing?
How can you make everything so beautiful,
be destroyed so easily.

You made us in your image,
and spread us across the sea;
to live with one another in peace, love and harmony.

But we couldn't accept this.
No, we had to change everything;
we dropped our pain from the sky and shot our misery,
but it blew up in our faces and it tore at our souls,
and I wonder sometimes if we should have ever been given
control.

Save us from ourselves,
for we know not what we have done.
Everything you have created,
we destroy with our guns.

—*Brian J. Bunt*

The Silent Symphony Of Leaves

Leaves skipping and dancing with the wind...
How do they hear it, how do they blow.......
Skipping and dancing, first fast and then slow.
Whirling and twirling faster and then.......
Stopping and starting all over again.

First to the right and then straight ahead...
Bouncing and twirling up and down...........
Skipping and dancing, not making a sound....
Only to start again, not touching the ground.

Why do the leaves dance, pushing, pulling and jumping
around in a spin....
To dance even higher and then down again.

What makes the leaves love to dance so and bend...
Spinning and turning with precision, as it they had
practiced for years on end.

A silent symphony of leaves in the autumn air...
Spinning and turning without a care............
Just jumping and spinning and going nowhere.

—*Joan O'Latta*

My Lover's Heartbeat Music

My lover's heartbeat music
how mysterious and constant,
even the tempo and tune ever alike,
but each time it plays it — announces —
true balance meaning of life and everlasting love.

Even God's messages (Guardian Angels) are calm,
knowing that his continuous concert;
 can even magically control the
  DEVIL (himself) to rest.

When I receive a private show
I feel a powerful spirit;
teaching my soul the secrets of time.
It's a two way street
 a honor to be shown
 and also the music — itself — lives on forever!
  — dedicated to my Guardian Angel! —

 —*Heather Hodgen*

Life's Road

I thought about my life and noticed,
How things change so fast....
The future I was looking in,
Has now become the past....
It seems to come in phases,
So this story I have told,
"I look at life in this respect....
Its kind of like a road".
There's ruts and curves, and fast lanes too....
There's even warning signs.....
But you must learn to read them see,
Before your out of time,
Cause if you don't....
You could get lost....
And each wrong turn you make will cost,
The way you live your life each day,
Determines how much you must pay....
So choose your exits very wise,
They could be dead-ends in disguise.

—*Connie Brister*

Monsters Within

The monster is feeding upon our souls
hungering, thirsting, for our possessed lucidity

Waiting quietly; pursuing us with thought
Listening closely for our moment's hesitation;

For that very moment, when we all pause
he screams out with madness and begins his song
    reaching out, he guides us with severed claws

Some will be lead blindly through;
to the end of life's road, to pay death's due

The strong will remain behind;
their minds have been ripped out
their thoughts lay motionless drowned in themselves

The monster is still running madly through our streets
his eccentric behavior bleeding; starving for the kill

The monster is dancing in my neighborhood
I stopped him to question his actions

A smile came to the freakish beast's face
He turned and faced me; he made me cry
    for that beast, that horribly awful beast,
        was me, in disguise.
    —Janell Jolley

Going

The notch is carved upon the stone,
    I am feeble, but not yet cold;
Though my story is unknown,
    It is one so often told.
Sometimes I cling to what is young;
    My mind forgets; I sometime wonder
For whom the song is being sung;
    That shakes this soul like violent thunder.
"My flesh, though wrinkled, my head's unbowed;
    My hand makes not the fist I knew."
I'll not cry, or shout aloud,
    Though endless burdens I must subdue.
In this fast decaying mind
    Churns' the scores of thoughts unwanted;
In this whirlpool of intolerable time
    Are stored each moment still unflaunted.
As the pain of going nears,
    Each passing hour I reminisce;
Through the web of dauntless tears, I feel
    So soon forgotten, so seldom missed.
    —Charles H. Norman

Lonely Rose

I am a lonely rose,
I am planted far out in the courtyard,
Now and then someone may glimpse at me,
Through their huge glass window.
They would only see my red luscious petals,
That makes me so excessively sweet,
And my thorns that say keep away,
But never shall they look deep at me,
And find my true beauty.
Never shall they search into my heart,
And find me.
I know though, one day another Rose,
Is going to be planted next to me,
And forever shall we be together,
Never shall I be lonely again,
Never shall we be parted,
We shall bind our ever lasting love,
Forever and ever
Never, will our love nor our souls die.
    —Cindy Rampersad

My Own Little World

Everyday that I fight,
I am pulled deeper into the blackness of night,
Into my own little world,
Where truly nothing can be hurled,
I pull further and further away,
If only I had stopped to stay.

Everyday that I fought,
I was pulled deeper into the blackness of thought,
Into my own little world,
Where truly nothing could've been hurled,
I pulled further and further away,
If only I hadn't been so afraid each day.

I did my own thing,
Where I could be king,
Look where it took me,
So far away I had to plea.
    —Christine Mueller

Untitled

As I close my eyes and the music begins to play. I feel
I am slowly swept somewhere faraway to a place that is warm
with a cool whispering breeze, a place where my heart is
forever free.

There is no one to tell me what to do with my life only the
sand, the sun, and these eternal beaches of white. Here, there
is no use for my dreams anymore. I have all I need beyond this
endless blue shore.

Not for granted. I take each day. No longer do I worry
each moment away.
Confused thoughts, no longer enter twined, each is a thought
one at a time.

Something always shines throughout these vast opaque skies
and with every night comes the passing of the tides. They the
world's immortal ticks on the tocking clock of time and they
the only reminders of what is to be left-behind.
    —April Crider

The Opium Child

You find me a paradox, an angel of the Odd, an imp of perverse
I am the daughter of King Opium and his mistress, Agony
How sad that you must seek the patronage and protection
Of my terrible family
I will spin the helter-skelter dreams to you
From the ends of the Universe
Then I will spin them away
To leave you clutching at a telephone pole - a tattered sleeve
Spilling your guts out over a curb, into a river of filth
That you will wish would carry you also
Into the sewers of oblivion and death
Friendship will try to grasp and hold close
The emptiness of your existence
You will scream inwardly - dance in flames for me
I will forever be with you - to haunt you in your loneliness
I am the Opium Child - Persephone, Death's Queen
    —Jeanna Cooper

My Poem Of Writers

Having the ability to write makes me feel like a knight.
I can go anywhere even to Bel Air,
My friends do it too. Even my brother, Jamie, writes.
He says writing is like sighting a talent.
When I write about a camel, I feel Egyptian.
I'll write a story about a Christian Egyptian.
Culture! Yaa, it's another great thing about writing.
Learning!
    —Chris Love

Choose The Choice

I am the middle child so caught up in despair.
I am the middle child in the middle of the air.
My life has been so tragic, so bitter, and so cold.
The world around me punishes for things I wasn't told.

The path of life that I have chose has only brought me pain.
The wants in life that I have sought bring me closer to the flame.
There is a choice that I can make to rid myself of strife.
There is a choice that I must take in order to live my life.

I am the middle child so caught up in despair.
I am the middle child in the middle of the air.
For half my life upon the earth, I have been deceived.
And now that I have found the man, I can be relieved.

He's watched me stray in every way that leads me to his door.
I walked, I ran, I stumbled then, I woke up on the floor.
I am the middle child in the middle of the air.
I am the middle child, the choice was always there.

  —*John Charles Allen*

This Is Who I Am

I am a woman.
I am the she of the human race.
I am the adhesive that holds lives together.
I have been abused emotionally and the bruises have blackened
my psyche, and I am who I was-no more.
I have been abused physically and the stitches leaves scars on
my children and my children's children.
I am the product of divergent races; yet I belong to no race.
I have been touched by substance abuse and my sorrow breaches
the levees of my soul and floods my body.
I work with no paid vacations and no sick leave; yet I have no
prior work experience.
I have a mother and a stepfather: their distance from my life,
no human may travel.
I have laugh lines that run deep and crease the pains in my
chest.
I am with life in my womb and I wish to see no dusk.
I am a Woman and I am Homeless.

  —*Denise Foster*

Adolescence

The young years have passed, they went so fast
I am young, but yet I am not
Blackness came over me, I noticed things I could not see
Was there a purpose for this treason?
I did not know what was the reason
A bright light tried to break through
Do I see it? Do I want to?
Is this the step that I should take?
My whole self being is at stake
I wish I knew the answers to my problems
It does not help when others try to solve them
Just like the wind I should blow free
To understand things and understand me.

  —*Donna Brown*

Untitled

It's not quite light, but already he's coming,
I can hear that truck's motor just a-humming.
To house after house he quietly creeps
Leaving fresh milk while everyone sleeps.
He's almost to our house; I see him looking this way—
I wonder if there's something special for us today?

Mother told me that he once drove a horse,
And he had to shout "Whoa!" at every stop, of course.
The wagon and its nag rambled clippety, clippety, clop,
And the milk in the bottles had cream on the top.
Old Nellie wore a straw hat, and from it stuck a rose—
What grand time of life that was, I suppose!

  —*Dana Smith*

My Essence

Oh dearest soul,
I believe you have shot deep Eros'
 arrow in my heart, for I bleed
 the pain of love.
I have seen birds fly into the sun
 and exit alive.
I have seen diamonds bounce and tumble
 on the moonlit ocean.
And now God has blessed me with yet another
 wondrous sight.
A field of flowers, in all colors and scents
 could not match your beauty.
The sun could not warm my heart
 as does your smile.
The moon in the fullest,
The stars in the sky,
you are.
You capture my mind, and captivate my soul.
And thus, I stare at the most heavenly creation on Earth.

  —*Brandon Bunker Cook*

Despair

As the sun beat's down upon my roof
I can reflect upon my youth

As I enter a road I've been down a thousand times
Things are so familiar as time

We live in a world where we toil and cry
None can feel the pain of another's despair
Nor does one care

Life is like an endless highway
With all kinds of rest stop, detour's dead ends, and exits
And at the end of the Highway there lies our enemy, death

It's rule seem so unfair, but it is king
Until Christ, the king, bring it to nothing

Who will fare in this way of despair.

  —*Daaiyah Jolly Boyd*

Always Hurt

In your life you always hurt the one you love the most.
I can tell you my life is always hurt, I've been hurt
enough to know the path so well.
The more you love, the more hurt it makes.
My friend and I can tell anyone about hurt,
We know your lives so well,
It hurts to look at what we had and
what we don't have now.
We all can hold it in, but it always comes out on its own.
Whether we like it or not.
Always hurt is like your life falling,
only one person can catch you, whether
it's by the heart or just by the hand.
My life is always hurt, and your life
is what you say it is.

  —*Joanna Young*

Boy

Play! Play! For someday you will say ...
 "I did play"
I was a boy I jumped, I ran, and fell,
 tears I did not show.
Torn pants, patches, holes in shoes,
 No socks were there.
People stopped to stare, I did not care ...
 I was a boy,
For I will say someday, "I was a boy"

  —*Felix A. Garcia*

September Song

Leaves, leaves, do not entice me with your siren song,
I cannot answer your call today.
Their hypnotic cadence rises,
Stirring my senses,
Awakening a primal need.
Come, they whisper, you need us.
Wait for me I cry,
Surely tomorrow will be soon enough.
The wind rises, calling to me.
Today is sacred, there is no tomorrow.
Embrace us, live, and breathe us!
I abandon my plans, led by that primal
feeling to seize the day.
I run through their wind songs
To hold September in my soul,
Before the leaves are mute,
And the wind is hollow with their passing.

　　　—Diana Halliday

Untitled

As I'm approaching the golden years
I can't count the endless tears
I spend my days wishing that the air
We breathe is clean, the water we drink
isn't polluted - People would never grow old
Nor would anyone treat another mean
sitting here, I'm waiting for summer to end
The cold winds will blow, along will come snow.
Then I will count the days till spring.
Hoping for a better season to begin
Can't wait to hear the robins sing.
Hearing the children playing, some loud
Music, a dog barking. The birds larking
My memories start haunting me, I picture
In my mind all the seasons I've survived!
Oh I'm happy I'm alive!

　　　—Betty J. Heflin

Feelings from the Dark

I can't see the trees, I've no eyes
I can't smell the roses, I've no nose
I can't feel the earth, I've no limbs
But, I can hear the sweet, sweet
Music of the song bird singing
So, I finally accept my fate,
I no longer feel the pain and the agony of defeat.
I've carried so much turmoil in this distorted body.
The overwhelming bitterness of being in complete darkness
Where is that gleaming light?
Oh, how I once hated this cruel injustice
That was put upon me
I no longer question the reason,
This decision was from my God from above.

　　　—Dulcenia Price

O Grave, Where Is Your Victory

How glad I am that you outlasted winter!
I could not bear
To leave your fragile form in frozen earth.
But now, thawed by sparkling, sunny days,
And gentle, warming winds,
Once glacial ground is pliant, mellow
A soft and loamy cover for your shriveled shell.
But faith gives this assurance
That you have been transformed,
And have made that veiled transition
To our Father's house.
To the promised place
He has prepared for you.

　　　—Charls Ballard

Life

I felt a pull; I heard a sigh,
I caught a breath; I gave a cry,
A soft voice spoke through tears of joy,
"Is it a girl?" "Is it a boy?" ... I was born!

I felt two arms press me tight
A gentle whisper, "He's all right,"
And as I lay at my mother's breast
The world opened wide; I was blest ... I was welcome!

I started to crawl, I started to run,
I started to school, the world was fun,
The years passed by, they went so fast
And I was tall, a man at last ... I was grown!

Now I'm a father, children all grown,
Oh, my, how those years have flown,
I see my wife with steps so slow,
Our eyes meet softly; there's still a glow ... we are loved!

I reach across — I take her hand,
No words are spoken, we understand,
Our memories live; in silence lie,
For we were born — and we know why ... born to die!

　　　—Helen S. Buffone

Restoration

Laden with cares of my world and its pain,
I come to my quiet place
and enter the stillness of my soul.
I sit numbly listening to the sounds.
A soft wind stirs the trees;
the leaves nudge each other affectionately;
the coolness kisses my face.

I gaze at the vines that have wrapped
their arms around each other
and spill out into pink trumpets.
The roses, glorious in their array, offer their blooms
giving of themselves silently and generously to all.
Their fragrance fills my senses.

The birds fill the air with their songs;
my heart lifts at the sound.
I think of childhood and dream of tomorrow.
The lush grass cushions my bare feet
as I walk through the garden receiving its gifts.
The cares of the day
fall into harmless heaps behind me.

　　　—Gwendolyn Jo Sullivan

Reminiscence...

My hands were busy through the day;
I didn't have much time to play
The little games you asked me to.
I didn't have much time for you.

I'd wash your clothes, I'd sew and cook,
But when you'd bring your picture book
And ask me please to share your fun
I'd say, "A little later Hon."

I'd tuck you in all safe at night
And hear your prayers, turn out the light,
Then tip-toe softly to the door...
I wish I'd stayed a minute more.

For life is short, the years rush past...
My little girls grew up so fast.
No longer are they at my side
Their precious secrets to confide

The picture books are put away;
There are no longer games to play,
No good-night kiss, no prayers to hear...
That all belongs to yester-year.

　　　—Frances F. Phelps

Untitled

When I say, "I'll give him a piece of my mind!"
I do not mean that I will send him
some of my better thoughts and opinions.
It means that I have a chip on my shoulder
and I dare him to try to knock it off.
It means that I will speak out in anger
and inform him that I disagree
vehemently!
It means that I get down to the bottom line
in a hurry!
It means that I would put tacks on his chair
with sharp points up!
Violent words lead to violent deeds.
O peace and love, have we forgotten you?

—*David P. Boyd*

Untitled

I'm stuck in hell
I don't know what I did
The walls are hot as they say my name
I don't know what to say back
Everything is getting closer
The walls are turning into flames
I'm stuck to the wall
Naked as my birth
Give me a knife and cut these rusted chains
Off my body
I never thought it could be this bad
I never knew the torture of pain
I wish I could save my soul from the
Eternal burning
Oh well
The truth is a virus and now I am sick

—*Christy Estep*

Future

Looking back thou out our time together-
I don't recall a memories that didn't start with you
or a yesterday that didn't include the thoughts of you.

My past started the day we meet and ever today after
started and ended with the memories of you.
Regardless of the days and nights-
how well they went the most important thing of the day-
was you- being there.

You was my past- you are each day in between and
together we made a future between us.
Yesterday was the past - as I lay us down to sleep-together.
Today- the dawn will break- as we awaken from yesterday into
tomorrow we will put yesterday in to the past and tomorrow
into the future. And today will remain our future.

—*Crystal Lee*

The Eternal Flame

Lost in the deepest dark of night,
I found no trace of external light,
not a silver beam of moon light,
not even a flicker of star light.
But what I did find, was the light of faith,
in a thought.
In the same instance, I understood
the greatest light of all,
this being, the eternal flame of the Soul.

—*Anthony DePietro*

My Dreams Of Youth

In velvet green fields, and soft moonlit hills,
I dream of my sweet youth.
With forest green trees, sweet honey from bees,
I found some impossible truths.

The fields are all gone, replaced by stone,
Man's concrete beneath my feet,
No more do I roam, the fields are all gone,
lost was nature's retreat

The child I was then, was seen n'er again,
lost in a world of dismay,
No long nature calls as the new twilight falls,
to tempt the young heart so gay.

Sweet impossible dreams, that fill life seams,
days trickling slowly by,
and life has it's pay, with each passing day,
bitter sweet tears do I cry.

But all is not lose, I've considered the cost.
all the might have been's.
With God's sweet relief, I've conquered all grief,
to start each new day again.

—*Connie Popovits*

Papa's Sugar Maple Tree

Perched up high in my papa's favorite tree,
   I dream of the magic that used to be;

To the left, there in view, lies an old rusted bicycle built
for two, papa would pedal, as I would steer,
Down the path we saw rabbits, butterflies and deer;

My memories now lead me to the right,
I see the big pond where the fish used to bite,
Papa dug wiggly red worms for our bait,
On the bank he'd play "captain," and I was "first mate;"

Now looking straight down, you'll find a ladder that leads to
the ground, my papa built it just for me,
He said it led up to "serenity;"

Before I climb down, I wave "good-bye" to papa who now
lives up in the sky.
As the leaves of the sugar maple tree blow freely in the wind,
I wink to my papa, he's still my best friend;

I miss you papa.

—*Betty Lou Doss-Miller*

"My Love Will Come"

I sit, I hope, I wish and wait, my love will come to me;
I dream, the dreams of romance,

I cry love tears in advance,
So my love will come to me;

No, no, I can't let go, of that notion,
No, no, I won't even motion it, for my love will come to me;

My heart being filled with these emotions,
And me believing with all devotion,

That today or tomorrow like a strong potion,
My Love will come to me.

—*Elsie S. Croxton*

Lonely

I feel lonely in the world, like I am the only one.
I feel like there is no one left, and I cannot have fun.

Locked up inside me, like a bubble about to burst.
I feel all alone, just to find it getting worse.

All my worries and frustrations, building up inside my mind.
I should have let it out a long time ago,
and now I wouldn't be so blind.

But now I am lonely, and it is way too late.
So now my heart is lonely, and it is filling up with hate.
Locked up inside me, like a bubble about to burst.
I feel all alone, just to find it getting worse.

Why do I feel lonely?
What did I do?
Why am I all alone?
I'm lonely, alone without you.

—*Bethany Fecho*

All I Do Is Close My Eyes

My memory takes me back to yesterday
I feel you loving me again upon that lovely day
I had all the love I ever wanted
But I slowly let it all just slip away

All I have to do is close my eyes and pretend
And I can feel you loving me again
Lord, I'd give everything I own
If you'd just say come on home
Please say you'll let me stay

Won't you give me one more chance today
All I do is close my eyes and pretend
And I can see you loving me again
You see me getting over you
Would be more than I could ever stand
So let me have just tomorrow

Then I can feel you loving me again
All I do is close my eyes and pretend
And I can feel you loving me again
Yes I can feel you loving me again

—*Bobbie Lee Wilson*

Housewife's Blues

I woke up feeling blue, and the skies were grey,
I figured this'd be a grand old day,
shuffling towards the kitchen, looking for brew,
flipping the daily pages to see what's new,
not much, I surmised as my eyes became unglued,
Just an ordinary everyday day was due.

So I swept up the floors, and put out the cat,
Made all the beds and said, "that's that"
And then I sat.
Time kept a ticklin', as I stewed the chicken,
peeled the onions, pared the 'tatoes,
and sliced up some plump ripe tomatoes.

All along I kept wonderin' how pointless this all was,
Day after day of chasin' dust and fuzz.
But then suddenly my son and husband came in,
hungry and rustling for their scrumptious din,

Made it all seem worthwhile to me.

—*Denise Cantwell*

Watch The Signs

I walk down a road paved with my hands
I find I am nearing the end,
How quickly it came
I should have watched the signs.

The curves I did not feel
not even the bumps,
The marks I took, and those I made
as I laughed toward the incline.

The battles with others
over who should lead,
All have become but one
the signs I should have seen.

The toll impedes my path
His price I omitted from my belongings,
there is no way to go around
I must turn to walk the remnant of forever on this road.

—*Alan Seal*

Dear Daddy

I know you were young when my life had just begun.
I guess you'll never really know what you missed.
Daddy, why wasn't I first on your list?
So many questions I must ask;
Was being a Father such a hard task?
I would have liked having those strong arms embrace me,
When I fall or to guide me when I crawl.
Who will teach me how to play football,
Or show me how to throw a ball?
Daddy, who will give me those long father to son talks,
Or take me for long walks?
Who will take, me on long summer hikes,
Or buy me a bright red bike?
Who will show me how to fly a kite,
Or tuck me in to bed, at night?
Daddy, thanks for the great start but
How will I ever fill the empty space in my heart?
Daddy, I just wanted a minute or two of your time.
It really would have made my little heart shine.
Knowing that I have a Daddy that's all mine.

—*Cassandra Scally*

Memories

I remember when
I had someone to hold me
To share with me my moments of despair
My hour of reflection
Someone some one to care
That one, my only, my dear love
His become a loving memory
And fall of the year for me
I greatly fear
Will always very painful be
When the leaves began to turn
The vanegated color of yellow red and gold
The tear will flow, but I will know
I once had love,
Love, that for me
will never grow old.

—*Jewel Simon*

When I Saw You

At the light I walked across an intersection.
I happened to look into one of the cars. There I saw the most
beautiful woman in the world. Her eyes were brown & glassy.
Her skin was so smooth as if it was made of silk,
but as I looked at her it was more than her outer beauty
that attracted me to her. Something inner like an aura about
her. That made me feel an inner peace & warmth
Over my entire body, as I continued to walk, she made a left,
and honked at me. I walked over to her luxury car nervously.
She asked me why I looked at her that way.
I responded "What way? "Like you knew me from a past life
or something." I responded, "you never know,
but when I saw you. I never had a feeling so powerful
touch me like that off a mere look.
When I saw you a force of beauty & peace overcame me,
when I saw you sweetheart. I wanted to say I love you
I don't even know you and now that I've met you.
I want to be with you eternally. Be with me
And I still can't believe all these feelings
overcame me when I saw you.

—*Ernest F. Green*

The Dance

Have you ever danced the perfect dance...?
I have.
It's about two people hearing the same song
without music-
A similar rhythm
free of restraint and caution.
I have used so much energy
in trying to dance with you, my friend.
But in the brief moments
that we moved like a reflection through
a mirror,
I always found myself
afraid of stepping on your toes
For with you,
the beat is always changing.

—*Carol J. Davis*

Branches

My branches don't sway freely in the mind.
I have emotional branches,
branches that can't get cut down,
can't be broken.
They feed off my life,
off my mistakes and my past.
These branches are in my mind
and they keep growing and growing.
I don't think my branches
are ever going to stop growing,
ever going to be free.

—*Helen Xereas*

Ariana

I have held a child's hand
I have felt their palm and the warmth
that flows from it.
Do we realize how far from childhood we really are.
Innocence is so sweet a pleasure
one wants only to stay within it's grasp
What as such, with age, we do forget
what the meaning be.
And with regret I realize it won't return until the end.
As such, the child's palm does tend to
remind me of the sweetness we will all become once again.

—*Ellen E. Chapman*

... Dreams Of Change

I'd like to think that you have seen this dream,
I have felt, within, in past days.
Here is the coin you touched with your mind, and
now you'll touch it with your skin, as it lays.
Your duty and your quest is to accept this coin, and
keep it with your "CHANGE". some of life's many.
For it's rare and precious, and known as the "Dream Penny".
Remember with this coin, that shines and gleams:
"YOU CAN LOSE THIS PENNY BUT NEVER LOSE YOUR
   DREAMS."
You can lose the pennies and lose your cents, but
if you lose your dreams your life has no sense.
Be assured that there will always be
more change in your life than you'll want to see.
Dreams cause change and change causes dreams.
Live to dream and dream to live.
Now live your dream, and REMEMBER each day, for it
might have been "CHANGE" that changed your way.

—*Bill Zinke*

Dear Lord

When I think of all the endless times
I have pictured in my mind,
The vision of what heaven is like
Praying for some of its perfection in my life

I thought I had seen it all before
But he proved me wrong out on the dance floor,
It feels as though we're dancing on air
I can see that he was created with tender loving care

We have loved and lost others in the past
Preparation for us to be together at last,
You knew it was time and that we were ready
It feels so right and I know our love was meant to be

I thank you for Danny, my heaven on earth
We have been blessed without having to search,
And for giving to us what many only dream of
I'm so thankful that I have him to love

We know that we are not perfect as one
But we're perfect for each other
In the name of our Fathers son,

Amen.

—*Angela G. Hill*

A Sister's Prayer

Dear Lord,
I have seen the dimming of Light within her eyes
I have felt the waning of Strength in her body
I have heard the lack of Laughter in her life
I have shared the Tears that flow from her soul.
   Take from me the blessings you have leant
      And give to her the power she needs;
         Invigorate her spirit
            Heal her body
         Fill her Life with laughter
            Strong and pure-
   Return to me the sister I once knew.

—*Frances Bejarano*

"Ghost Train"

As I listen to the raindrops falling
I hear the ghost train calling,
Calling out its sad, sad song,
And blowing its ghostly whistle loud and long.

Its passengers have long been dead
And I have heard it said,
That nightly now they face their fears
For wrongs done in yesteryears.

Their souls may have no rest
For theirs is a never ending quest.
Traveling over every hill and plain,
Facing an eternity of pain.

—*Hillary Allenbaugh*

Soulmate

You have been with me for, Lo, many years now.
I hear your gentle voice call my name,
whispered in the measured tones of music
or felt as a wisp of breeze against my blushing cheek.

My childhood play was shared with you.
Deeply embedded in the storehouse of my memory,
it speaks of sunshine, field, and flower;
of protective arms around my soul, shielding my youthful nature
against the cold rain which beat against the windows of my heart.

As I journey through this life I have learned to heed your
voice, to open the door of this heart and invite you to enter;
to join with you in love and peace and growth.

And so, today, as the tears of love and joy flow I allow them
to unhindered, because I wish to express what I feel for you;
to inscribe these tears unto paper.

Someday time will remove itself from my eyes
and I will lift the eyes of my spirit to gaze upon you,
to glide with you past the silver clouds and beckoning moon,
to the right....to the light...towards home.

—*Ellen Mueller*

An Appalachian Miner

Into the depths of the earth I go. I travel in silent darkness.
I journey almost without motion.
And yet my thoughts are proportional to the endless molecular
images present within me. I descry! I behold! I envisage!
I am far away from the melodic voices of my loved ones.
I am far away from the sparrow's saccharic song.
And I contemplate. There will be no thrill of a sunburst
Radiating my dark depth of surroundings.
I am deposited into the subterranean passages. There are many
with me. Yet I know I am alone, completely removed from any
semblance of reality.
My driving task is to discover the black magical substance
Hidden in the dark recesses of the earth.
I must remove from the mine face all that is stored within its
depths. My muscles are fueled up to a purpose.
My spirit of obligation drives me onward.
I must find this valuable combustible form of energy.
That is my commitment!
But my greatest mission is to make a hurried return.
To once again be earthbound!

—*Eleanor Slusarczyk*

The Two Of Us

I met her in the mirror the other day
I just stared in amazement not
    knowing what to say
She looked back at me with such sad eyes
She was trying to tell me I was living two lives.

I stared back at her from head to toe
Unsure if I was certain I wanted her to go
she shows up in the mirror every now and then
Reminding me of what has and could have been.

The past in her face, the present a waste
    and the future more her pace.

Sometimes I don't know what she's doing there
We just look at each other with such a stare.
I don't know if she'll ever go away,
Until we're certain and want one way.

And on that day which one of us will stay?

—*Claudette Drieu*

Awakening

When into the darkness I wandered alone completely surrounded
    by sin.
I knew in my heart that the place I was in would soon become a
    "has been."
But how could I turn away from my friends, for friends they said
    they were.
If I left those I knew, to whom could I turn, who could be there
    to care?
I was alone and lost in an unkind world I felt as though I were
    blind.
The world was so dark, so cold and untrue these thoughts raced
    through my mind.

Where is the light I had once before - why did it leave me behind?
Why did it leave me to fend for myself - why was it being unkind?
I then learned a lesson I could never forget - a lesson that would
    help me through life.
I learned that the light that I thought was lost would never leave
    me in strife.
It was always there when I thought it was not, it never left me
    alone.
I only lost sight of the light of His love by the door that I closed
    on my own.

Never again would I shut out His light - a light which filled me
    with love.
The light filled all of the holes in my life, for this light came
    from above.
Now, since I've found that which was lost, I can help others see,
    too.
I will show others what I have learned, the ones that say
    "What can I do?"
I will help those who question their faith, and the ones who are
    seeking the truth.
To all those who wish, I will show them the light and be an
    example of good.

—*Jodi Bills*

The Lottery

I scratch and scratch till time won't end.
I mark those numbers in hopes I'll win.
I have the computer pick for me.
In hopes I'll win the lottery.
Someday I know my time will come.
When I will win that big million.
On that day, the folks will stare.
'Cause I will be a millionaire.

—*Carol A. Sheren*

Boy

The call me David.
I know not of shepherds and slings.
I seek to unravel my untold fears
buried beneath my shattered shell.
The scope of my reality extends your world.
My hopes and dreams confound and distort
The very essence of our lives.
Will the contortions of my twisted twig,
restore itself in that special learning place?
Will love, friendship and respect emerge
from my chaotic pit to abound with
ceaseless joy?
Oh, release and guide my tortured soul!
The peace I sought is in the Psalms.
I now know the meaning of that
six-sided star.
Exalted in peaceful meditation, transformed
and distinguished among mankind,
I have become a giant

—Beatrice Harry

Power Of Living

I feel, but don't know why.
I laugh, even when I must cry.
I talk, when silence would be better.
I want to speak, but end of writing letters.

Listen, if that's all you can't do.
Talk, if that's all you can't say.
Sing, when music overflows you.
And when Satan is beside you, just pray.

Give, and you may be given in return.
Take, it becomes a greater yearn.
Hate, but always forgive.
Love, it's the only way to live.

Protect, when you're feeling insecure.
Rely, when your senses are not sure.
Follow, but learn to be a leader.
Lose, but know you're not a cheater.

Help, those who've fallen in the pit.
Survive, life's worth it.
Believe and prayer will somehow mend.
Confide, and you can be my friend.

—Catherine Rotzien

"It Seems Like Only Yesterday" The Grandchild

It seems like only yesterday
I lay my baby down to play,
The sweet smell of powder and soft skin;
Brings all those memories back again.
Those tiny feet stood up to walk,
And gentle lips began to talk.

It seems like only yesterday
That smiling face and little teeth,
Biting down upon my cheek.
The warm body close to mine,
Holds me to an ageless time.

It seems like only yesterday
And yet, within my arms I hold,
A child of my own grown old.
All those years that whispered by,
Return again with this ones cry.

—Jeanette Marchant Van Cleve

I'm Falling In Love

There we stood in the barn, a place we both loved,
I leaned against the rough wood,
And all I wanted to say was "Kiss me,"
But I didn't, afraid of your reaction,
So instead, I was silent,
As I looked into your soft blue eyes.
I listened to your words;
Your voice is so soft and warm, but also deep and romantic.
I knew then that I was falling in love,
But I thought to myself, "Could he ever love me in return?"
Now here we stand in the barn once again, a place we both love.
We're hand in hand,
As I lean against the rough wood,
Looking into your soft blue eyes.
You softly say "I love you,"
I pull you closer and you reply with a kiss.
I'm still falling in love,
And I realize now that my question has been answered,
You're loving me in return, just as I had once hoped!

—Aimee Lorson

Dreaming Of You

Last night I dreamed I was dead
I lived during your nocturnalness
I watched laugh cry need and grow as a person
I waited for you to come to my heaven
A place where you don't worry and are never lonely
A place where you get is not what you need but what you desire.
After some time I realized that this could not be heaven
It could not be heaven, unless incomplete, without you there
I would love to love you, just to be with you
Heaven is hell without you.

—Chasity Smith

The World As It Is Today

As I start my day with my morning coffee.
I look at the newspaper and my heart
is saddened. When I see that someone has
died needlessly, and too many times
it is one child taking the life of another.

So many times we caught up in our busy
lives we forget to say I care to the ones
we hold so near and dear.

I often wonder how some people can turn
their backs on the ones they say they love so much.
Or how some times we forget to touch.
You know some times a gentle hand or just
a smile can make someone's life worth while.

—Chris Armstrong

Wonder

Small wonder, that wondrous moment of truth
I looked upon that which filled me with ecstasy;
Became the second abandonment of youth
Gave me not a moment of hesitancy
A second chance granted by unknown fate
A reprieve, pardon, redemption from hell
Made this heart of mine open and cast out hate
With a sweeping hand, and all is well
Then emotion responds, released from a jail
Of pent-up obligation, held for so long.
Life's rebirth lets out a healthy wail
Of words once poured out into a song.
Knowing that I am not forced to, but wanting to,
Love; it is a light from heaven
touched from above.

—James Michael Kerst

I Love You

I love you more than anybody else,
I love you more than you know,
I adore you.
I love you like I never love anybody else,
I love those who you love.
How can I prove to you.
But, I feel being rejected
That make me resent on everything,
confusion arises.
But, I love you 'til death do us part.

    —Cherrylin C. Goodman

Wasted Years

I married him because the one I loved said that he loved another,
I married him, he knowing that I loved him only as a brother.

For twenty years we shared the joy and pain that's found
   within this world of men.
For twenty years, all this time, I dreamed, but never
   saw my love again.

Then, last night my old love returned, and with joy did I discover.
That all these years I've loved a dream, but my husband was my
   lover.

    —Claire V. Crain

Love In Harmony

In the silence of a reflective mood
I meditate upon events as we were together.
Music was more than music.
It took on a glow, a restless vibrance
That did the composer proud.
The shadings and nuances were altered
As you smiled, as you sighed,
As you nodded your head in rhythm.
A lovely passage surpassed its intent,
A melancholy phrase was all the lover's tears.
And when we kissed, the music transcended
Our sphere and entered a world where
Only lovers dwelt.
We two together fused in harmony,
Evoked a magical moment.
And all the world did stop.
They listened, but they could not hear.

    —Bernard Hailperin

Lost Friend

She was so special and dear to my heart,
I miss her so,
And it's only the first night since our fight,
So much I would change,
So much to take back,
So many things I wouldn't have said,
Oh, well,
I can't turn back time,
Oh how I wish I could,
I feel so bad,
She's so special,
Like a sister,
I'll never forget her,
Never,
As long as I live,
I will always remember her,
Because she was my best friend.

    —Alisha Hulett

A Seedling Called Love

I planted a seedling so tiny and new
I planted a seedling and it grew and grew
It grew up high, it grew out wide
I planted to seedling and it grew

This seedling is called Love
For love is so true, it never leaves or dies
It is always everlasting and true

A seedling called love? How absurd but, so true
For love can only grow when it is planted by you
A kind little word, an action that is true
For love is a seedling that can be planted by you

Love will grow and grow and grow
For God gave us the means and we need to know
The love comes unconditionally, it comes from the heart
It comes from our knowing how we can play a part
So the next time you are out in the doom and gloom of this world
Plant a little seedling called love and watch it bloom, bloom, bloom

    —Ann Christine Collins

Oh Mommy, Why Me?

I was a part of you, and you a part of me
I really had not a chance just to come to be

I didn't get to see your smile,
Nor your eyes when they cried.
I never got to hold your hand
And kiss you when I died.

I never understood the reasons why I was taken away
I begged, pleaded, cried, and called out to it,
   just to let me stay.
But thing did not hear me,
   nor did you I guess

Because it came and sucked feet, legs, and arms
   Left and came again for the rest............

   All that was left was darkness
A few fragments of the
   "Once going to be"
Echoes and cries of the past piercing the dark
   "Oh Mommy, why me?!"

    —Capretha Jones

Elegy

I'm assigned captain of the ship.
I receive some respect and some lip.
We start our adventure out to sea,
The crew is content, not a hint of mutiny.
When the voyage grows longer,
The crews thinking becomes stronger.
Are the captains decisions right?
For years he's endured turbulent nights.
They feel, I'm not giving them a chance,
Not understanding the protection in, you can't.
After 18 years they leave in their life boat,
I'm hoping their preserver keeps them afloat,
You've done what you could every day,
But now you watch them sail away.
As the sun goes down deep red,
No one knows how much you've bled.
After darkness comes a spark of light,
Perhaps with time I, they will be all right.

    —Burt Cram

Goodbye Blues

As I sit back to forget my blues,
I relive a recent cruise.

I hadn't relaxed in so many years,
The cruise relieved me of my fears.

Basking on the deck with the soft summer breeze,
As the ship gently glides o'er the glistening seas.

No phones, no cars, no traffic jams,
No noise, polluted air or clanging trams.

It's just me and God and good clean air,
As gentle winds blow through my hair.

The stars overhead sparkle so bright,
While the moon casts its image on the water at night.

Now every time I get the blues,
I just sit back and relive my cruise.

—*Diana Sarantis Lardas*

Evening At Grace Ridge

At evening,
I rest my arms awhile on the window sill of Heaven,
And gaze upon the glory of God.
White fluffy clouds are floating across a bright blue sky.

In time, the sun slips down behind the mountains,
Leaving a golden glow. Soon colors begin to join the gold.
First faint, then brilliant - pink, mauve, lilac and blue.
The majestic mountains reach up to absorb the muted tones.

After a while the colors slowly fade, leaving an afterglow.
A new moon appears high in the sky.
It is twilight.
Who but God could create such moving beauty!

—*Elizabeth Walker*

Birth

One night sitting at the top of a hill
I saw a flash of light
A drop of rain fell from the sky
But no clouds were in sight

The droplet fell in front of me
Bursting without sound
From each tiny particle
A plant grew from the ground

The plants grew and entangled
At a very rapid pace
unusually large they grew
to form a human face

They grew even larger
An image come to view
A body arms and legs
that's when I finally knew

The drop was not a drop
It was yet a fertile ray
A ray sent down to earth
From a place so far away

—*Ernest Cecil*

Bill Clinton

I prayed for Clinton to win
I prayed after he got in
I am praying that he will make America sing
I am praying that America again will be King
I am praying that freedom and the American Dream
will spring once again

—*Grace Kirby*

The Weeping Willow

Walking through the forest,
I saw a tree; not an ordinary tree,
but an oak or an evergreen.
This tree still blossoms while others remain bare.
It seems as though everyone
in towns nearby could see its sturdy trunk
and flourishing green leaves.

But as I neared, I realized
the trunk was not so sturdy,
nor the leaves so green.
The branches, long and skinny
drooped forward like a man
who'd bent to pick his fallen hat.

I looked down at the tree and saw a ditch,
filled so high with water that the leaves
turned brown like a bike in rain.

I looked up at the tree once more
and then turned to walk away.
And as I looked back at the tree,
I saw its beauty.

—*Allison Siegel*

Cory's Here

At 2:43 they said, "Cory's here!" All around could tell by my
    cheer.
I screamed and jumped and made such a stir, no one could see me
    except for my blur.
I waited so long to see the sight of one just imagined, but now a
    real life.
I sat, I waited, my foot tapped the floor - your Grandma and
    Grandpa found me all but a bore.
So off to the nursery I went to see this beautiful life that was
    meant to be.
My energy I could curtail no more. Then suddenly as I opened the
    door,
Your Mom's face said it as I wondered awhile could this be the
    one, is this her child?
At first just an image, but now a real life,
Your world just beginning, it'll be a great flight!
I could not believe my eyes when I saw your soft, silky skin and
    limbs so small.
They say you are big, and tall you will be in your long life
    ahead —
    we'll just wait and see.
All of our lives are blessed by your life, especially your Mom's as
    I saw the sight.
A moment so special time could not capture, your precious life has
    your Mom so enraptured.
Such an intruder I felt, when I saw your Mama kiss you and stare
    in awe.
She loves you so much, just remember it's true,
She'll always love you because you're you.

—*Dawn Van Arnum*

Wings

Clear up above the bright, blue skies
    I see a place so far, so high
I reach out, as if to touch
    the feathery clouds I've seen so much
But, alas my arms aren't as long
    to get me to the place where I belong
With my heart, I pray tonight
    so in the morning, I'll start my flight
With the wings I'd held so long, so tight
    and by the whisper from the sky
My wings are able to take me home high

—*Heidi Van Nostrand*

Doctor Law And Doctor Grace

As I walked this road of life, my heart seemed so burdened down.
I searched for some relief, but there was none I found.
I finally called a Doctor, and he said to come on in.
From a brief examination, he found my heart was black with sin.
Doctor Law said that my problem had been growing all my life,
and without an operation, I would surely die.
Doctor Law helped me to see the great need I had inside.
But to perform the operation, he said he did not qualify.
Now who would do the surgery was the question on my mind.
I fumbled and I faltered, I knew I didn't have much time.
Doctor Law just stood there watching, with a stern look on his
   face.
Then he pointed toward the door, and in walked Doctor Grace!
When I looked into his eyes such love in them I saw.
Not at all the same expression that I saw on Doctor Law.
Doctor Grace reached out his hands and I could not resist.
I reached out with both of mine, then I saw the scars on both of
   His.
I knew that Doctor Law had somehow been replaced.
I put all my hopes and fears in the hands of Doctor Grace.
When the surgery was completed my old heard had just been
   changed.
By the greatest of all Doctors, the blessed Doctor, Doctor Grace!

    —Diane Rittenberry

A Walk In Paradise

It is dusk,
I see the blue, darkening sky my ceiling.
Moon and glittering stars my lamps.
Feeling textured carpet of moist, green
Earth under bare feet,
As billowing trees lace walls of infinite space.
Rain in rhythm drumming,
Drenches dust back into Earth
Cool winds breathe sweetened air
While at dawn, the glance of a
Jealous sun polishes all into
Brilliance!

No doors to open, close or lock.
Only our windowed eyes - Seeing
from depth of Soul - INFINITY.

    —Joanne Saraceno

Justin

Mom says our eyes look much the same
I see the sunshine, and you just the rain

See how we both have one pointed ear
The more that I talk, the less that you hear

Look at the way our fists clench when we're mad
Thoughts of me make you run, and of you I get sad

All of the things that I hear, see, and do
Are a constant reminder I'm here 'cuz of you

If I'm not bad won't you please tell me why
When I mention your name Mom starts to cry

And If I'm not bad then help me to know
Why you won't stay, you always just go

Mom tells me all guys won't treat me this way
That somebody, someday will love me and stay

But until that day comes I still need to know
What I did to make you not want me so

Mom says you owe me the truth, please don't lie
Just look at me Daddy, tell your little boy why

    —Alice Hull

Your Eyes

When I look into your eyes,
I see the warm summer sun
and it makes me feel warm inside.
When I look into your eyes,
I can see the hurt
and I want to be the one to tell you
everything's going to be alright
while I am holding you in my loving arms.
When I look into your eyes
and see an ounce of tears,
it wants me to take you to an April shower
and show you how letting a few tears fall
makes two people grow together
as if we were the May flowers.
When I look into your eyes
and see your love and I know that you see the same
in mine and we know that our eyes see it all
and our love will over come anything
that will come towards us.
If we look into each others eyes
and know everything is going to be alright.

    —Cassaundra Kohen

Identity

I should have been a story-teller
I should have been a square dance caller
I should have been a carol:
An old round dance, a prance, with singing,
Circling four hands round with fiddles ringing.

   Instead:

I became a Psychological Person,
I became a Poetical Person,
I became a Philosophical Person,
I became an Authentic Person,
   a Centered Person.
I went into therapy
To work out my Identity.
On every beach, in every Church,
I continued with the Search.
I did time:

But all that time,
I should have been a sales clerk in the
   five and dime.

    —Carol Dinklage

A View Out My Window

Overlooking the parking lot I see many strange things
I sit watching the pulse of the city passing by my window
Engrossed with their own cares and woes, loves and hates
And all striving for a certain niche in their city fare
That sets them free to find a more rewarding quest in life
But all these desires are common to a bustling city life.

However I'm stuck in a corner by chessmen of company games
That keeps me reeling in the same dull ordinary status
While I'm tied down by earthly chores that can't be ignored
And here I sit steadfast with thoughts of extreme jubilation
That someday I would be able to become one of the masses
Who parade up and down, in and out of my small cubicle.

I wish I could break this corporate chain of domination
Which keeps my soul locked up in pain at life's expense
But now I see a ray of hope from my internal dilemma
As I catch a smiling face outside my window with club in hand
Which inspires me to drop everything at this invitation
To break my corporate bonds for a round of golf at the country
   club.

    —Ed T. Kett

Somemore's Dream

Confused and aroused,
I submit myself to the marshmallow machine
It processes my being into an unending flow of sugary sweetness
Where I am packaged into small glass containers
And sold for at a more or less reasonable profit.

inside my mind i saunter sexily to my lovely graham cracker
while the smell of overcooked chocolate invades my nostrils
her hand in mine, we stroll to the unheard beat of the Bee Gees
forevermore nevertheless but moreover.
our laughter carries us higher and higher into the night sky
until we slam into a giant airplane high above.
we land in a small pile of butter, laughing still.
noticing how the smell of the chocolatey chocolate hangs heavy
like the thick beef stew my mother used to make.

Except there is now no more air because of the chocolatey stew
But fear not, brave reader, for I am the marshmallow man
And although I will be at your nearby store at a reduced price
My lovely sugarlips will be there to console me
As the Bee Gees sing "Staying Alive" in a local elevator near you.

—*Gregory Getner*

Without You

When I'm alone, I feel so cold.
I suddenly feel, I want you to hold,
So I may caress your sexy blond hair.
When you're gone, I feel so empty,
And it seems so long, between now,
And when I get to see you again.
I feel so alone, I just can't stand the pain,
Of not being able to see your brown eyes.
If you're ever in silence,
You'd hear my cries.
They are of you, and the pain,
I feel when you're gone.
So deep, so strong, it makes me weak,
It makes me long, for just one more time,
To be in your presence.
I'd give up a lifetime chance,
Just to feel your kiss. I'd give one day,
For you to stay, and hold me,
Love me and never scold me.
I love you and I can't live without you.

—*Joanie Buell*

Doll

In these days of uncertainty,
I think in memory.
Speak your mind, construct your time.

Gazing into your face of moons,
believing kind of soon.
That's your way, hey doll is love, doll is love.

Sometimes I feel unmanly lost,
For life brings forth the cost.
Hear my plea, be good to me.

The timeless search could be over,
take the C from clover.
That's your way, hey doll is love, doll is love.

—*Eugene Woehr Jr.*

Untitled

As I stare out the window, my eyes fill up with tears,
I think of a higher place above that can extinguish all my fears.
Living on hopes and dreams will never get me far,
neither will the endless wishes, wished upon a star.
Faith is my answer, since it can bring us many things,
like a messenger from heaven with extraordinary wings.
I know in my heart there is something special that walks beside of
    me,
for when I feel its presence all my worries are set free.
Perhaps it is my imagination, but the feeling is indescribable,
a feeling of warmth and comfort quite unusual.
The emptiness just fades away, and painful thoughts escape from
    my mind.
Out of faith, I believe an angel I did find.

—*Debra Monaco-Poccia*

Communication

I wondered why it is when we're apart
I think of saying breathless things to you,
Of all the tenderness that fills my heart
And kindles dreams of all our love anew.

So while you were away from me today
I planned and practiced how I would begin
And memorized the words I meant to say,
Then found to my dismayed chagrin,

That when they reached my eager lips
They stopped, just short of saying all
Those lovely words I meant and hands on hips,
I said, "I worried when you didn't call!"

You grinned, my heart shown through my eyes,
Somehow you knew I'd made your favorite,
Fried peach pies!

—*Georgia McRee*

These Little Footprints

These little footprints are mine,
I think of them all the time.
They belong to my wonderful children,
In my arms and heart where I hold them.
Some in my womb before lost for only a short time,
I can vision your smiling faces in my mind.
There's more little footprints in my family tree,
That few people know or can even see.
I wish you were all here with me on earth,
But some of you are with God and His Holy mirth.
Whether here on in Heaven each holiday and season,
Each child gives me a rhyme and reason.
This my poem to send all of you my love,
My special children here and in heaven above.
These little footprints are mine,
They are running through my heart and mind.

—*Christine L. McDaniel*

For The Love Of Dolphins

They swim through the water with such great grace,
It is as if they are challenging us to a fabulous race.
They warm us up with all their charm,
We know they can do no one harm.
They have all the answers if only we would hear,
But we won't take the time to open our ears.
They always have a smile on their face,
Which would brighten up any dark place.
For it is man with his antagonistic fashion,
Who destroys and gives no compassion.
So leave them alone, let them be!
They have the right to be free!

—*Christine F. Spangler*

Wisdom

Wisdom is a treasure,
Given from above,
Kinda like Noah
When he sent out his dove.
We all should seek wisdom,
For it's our best friend.
It will help us,
And guide us,
Even 'til the end.

—*Creshia Cecil*

Gloria

The look that lies on your face
gives me the strength to go on.
Yards of tubes flowing with agents
of life running in and out of my
body, yet you stay by my side
gripping with all your will to hold
on to me as I do with my life.
Tears of remembrance swelling in
our eyes and dissolving within
our flesh. How can I thank you for
all that you have given me?
You gave me everything from love
to the gray hairs that are crowned
on my head. Our hands both the same
in wrinkles, but yours are filled
with warmth and life. I can't go on
any longer for it is too painful.
I must leave, but I'll wait for you.
In heaven is where we will meet and
love for an eternity.

—*Jennifer Villanueva*

My Images

My image of hope brings
gladness to my eye.
My image of dreams shows
gifts with childhood memories
that never were.
My image of love gives
heart and soul to my
gloomy and lonely being.
Through my three
images I have a world that
seems so perfect for me.

—*Erin Cotter*

Still

I kissed you goodnight
Going to my room to make ready
For another night's rest.
A heavy THUD filled me with terror—
A sound unlike all other sounds
I called, then rushed to the kitchen
In time to see you lying prone
As I watched your last breath
Leave your body
And you lay still—cooling—
Finished with an ailing earthly temple
With no way to tell me goodbye.

—*E. L. Moore*

The Eagle King

Through the air the eagle flies,
Golden brown feathers and keen eyes,
And though the eagle may call,
He is not afraid to fall,
Graceful he may be,
But to me,
He is the king of the air.

—*Andrea Denny*

The Virgin And Her Baby

There she stands.
Good posture.
Palid.
Her long tresses hanging
From the cloak she wears.
Her baby in her arms.

Born in a barn,
The baby lay.
The animals trampling about.
Though breezes through the barn,
The baby lays.
He cries not.

The virgin stands in scorn of men.
Her family ready to give her up.
A messenger says:
"Do not be afraid."

Both enamored into crystal——
Forever.

—*Angela Suh*

I Breathed Deeply

Dead grass rises, turns
green in the rainfall.
The daises spring up
between the blades.
Little tulips blossom.
Rivers overflow with
joy and happiness.
Rolling meadows give pleasure.
And red robins chirp,
pecking at seed, filling
their needs.

The sweet and refreshing rainfall.
Clouds fill and darken,
Only to explode and disappear.
A rainbow arched on the horizon.
I breathed deeply and
Sprouted from the soil.
Then I spread my petals.

—*Brian McDowell*

The Sculptor

Words as clay,
hands of thought,
carefully crafted

beauty is wrought.

—*D. Allen Cross*

With Rain

With rain gives grief
grows green grass blade

With rain drops dew
dawns deep dark trade

With rain slips soot
sown seed spreads away

With rain leaves love
loud lust lucid day

With rain beams blue
boughs bend bath pelt

With rain hurls hope
holy heart hold felt

With rain casts care
calm clouds crash down

With rain mute mist
mocks mild minds crown

—*Darryll Holguin*

Cadillac Lady

In her Detroit chariot
Hair-do hive
A queen bee
    and humanity her devoted drones

Husband
A mere shadow of himself
Always turning the wheel
Never the master of destiny
But driven from backseat

"Park it close. There!"

Enter the mall
Shopkeepers bow
Before her green fist
    her delusion maintained

Exiting

A chair-bound vet
Winded from his
Parking lot trek
Leers as she passes

The bees go about their business

—*Brian A. Zipp*

I Love

I love the feel of your soft, brown
hair flowing between my fingers.
I love the ever loving look I see
deep in your beautiful, brown eyes.
I love the softness of your lips
while they're touching mine.
I love the gentleness you show
with each caress.
I love the trembling of my ever
waiting body as I lie next to you.
I love the warmth I feel deep inside
when we make love.
But most of all I love you, my
little bit of paradise, my small piece
of heaven.

—*Dena Bugarin*

Tucked Away

in one of her seldom used drawers
half-remembered, a silly scarf,
remnant of a young man's dream,
tucked away.

in a desk drawer always closed,
he carefully set there in a box
an old coin wrapped in a memory,
tucked away.

in their minds each will carry
echoes of growth, daring, caring,
knowing certain what could have been,
tucked away.

in their hearts each will stow
an uncommon love now passed,
once held, it will never end,
tucked away.

in their souls each will bear
constant ache, somewhat faded,
a longing that will always be,
tucked away.

—*Cliff Elgin*

Hands

Hands are black
Hands are white
Hands are not what makes us fight

Hands are tough
Hands are strong
But hands can never lead you wrong

Hands are thin
Hands are fat
Hands were not made to attack

Hands are tools
Hands are tread
With "His" hands were many fed

Hands are handsome
Hands are cute
For hands' there is no substitute

Now lets put these "Hands" together
Shake them, clap them
Pray, whatever

Pray for me, I pray for you
Pray that minds won't let hands do...evil.

—*Angela D. Edmonds*

I Never Contemplated

I never contemplated
having stardust in my eyes
as rosecolored glasses
painted real life in disguise

I always longed to be with
one who somehow was there after
the little trials and broken dreams
birthed rainbow colored laughter

How seldom stayed were special ones
who leaped in bounds to capture
How quickly all so easily fled
and feared a sincere rapture
I never contemplated

—*Debra E. Fields*

These Things I Hear

Help me, love me,
Have compassion for me.
My future? Some really care.
The core of my being is to be.
Plans, Family, Friends, Thoughts.
My soul is laid bare.

At times I am afraid
But most days lifted up.
A gesture, kind words said.
Others turn away,
With words that cut.

Let my days be full,
Let me face adversity and be strong.
And when in the storm there is a lull,
Let me focus on the rights - not wrongs.

Love brings together
And is sanctioned from above.
Faith, hope, charity,
Words of our Father,
The "Greatest of These is Love."

—*Carolyn Reeves-Wills*

Always And Forever

It's funny how our hopes and dreams
    have finally come to this
It seems like only yesterday
    we made that one small wish
We wished that we could graduate
    and leave the rest behind
But all we seem to do is cry
    while standing in this line
We realize that we will miss
    the good times and the bad
And all the friends and classmates
    that until this point we've had
We realize this is the time
    that we must all let go
To make decisions on our own
    and have the chance to grow
But most of all we realize
    that we will never part
For always and forever we'll hold
    memories in our heart

—*Allison Lindsey Johnson*

Empty

I lie in the blue
haze of morning,
thinking only of you,
despite my effort to
think of nothing,
to let myself be empty
as I know I soon must be,

Alone in the hour of dread,
I see the shape of your mouth
when you spoke the words.
I hear the pitch and turn
of your voice,
and I am drowned
in your pornography of music.

Alone in the house,
alone in my life,
I lie here in the blue haze
until the vast engines of morning
which drive my grief are silent.

—*D. W. McWilliams*

My Jesus

He doctored an old lady back to health
He caused the lame to walk
He caused the blind to see again
He caused the dumb to talk

These are a few of the miracles
My Jesus did perform
Before they placed upon His head
A heavy crown of thorns
And hung Him on a cross to die
Which He did for you and I

He never spoke a word
He never shed a tear
I guess He did it His way
As He hung on the cross that day

—*Doris Tyner*

Seven Years Old

A seven year old's mama dies
He hears, as tears fill his eyes
Cancer,
He say's to himself
I don't know what it is,
And no one, will help.
Cancer,
Can I go with her
I love my mama
Don't leave me alone,
I'm only seven years old.
Cancer,
He thinks to himself
Why did you take,
My mama away

—*Angel Mendez*

On The Death Of My Father

We stood encircling his grave,
He, in the center -
Father,
Grandfather,
Great-grandfather,
Patriarch -
Eloquent in his silence.

We stood encircling his grave,
We, on the periphery -
Children,
Grandchildren,
Great-grandchildren,
Progeny -
Eloquent in our grief.

We stood encircling his grave,
He, in the center,
We, on the periphery,
Generations -
Eloquent in our continuity

Then, now, to be.

—*Jane Seward Pomeroy*

Untitled

Rodeo
Horses bucking
Flying, falling down
Cowboys whooping their cries
Excitement

—*Debora Kan*

Loser

He is the loser.
He is the king.
Just ask him,
Everyone says it's so.

Now he's a boozer,
Shuns Everything,
But I like him,
Even when he feels low.

He didn't conform,
Or give in to Norm,
When told to.
That's when they cast him out.

So now he's a Loser.
You heard him sing?
I didn't think so.
Just go, and leave him alone.

—*Dale McMullin*

Betsy Marie

God gave us little Betsy,
He sent her from above.
He picked a very special family,
Who'd give her lot's of love.

He choose extra special parents,
For this precious little child.
Their reward for many sleepless nights,
Would be in Betsy's smile.

At first we thought He meant her,
To be with us just a day.
But He heard our many prayers,
and decided she could stay.

Please God Bless our little Betsy,
In the rough times take her hand.
For she has brought us closer to you,
I'm sure that was your plan.

—*Helen Robbins-Paratore*

Always There

For every single tear I've cried
He shed a drop of love
For every shameful sin I've done
Fell mercy from above.

In every lonely moment
His spirit was so near
In moments of decision
His "word" would make it clear

In bitter times of grief
His promise gave me hope
The presence of his loving arms
Made way for me to cope

When answers weren't enough
And at his feet I fell
He'd walk the valley with me
And healed my soul so well

Who have I but thee
When troubles will not cease
The King of Kings and Lord of lords
Who gives such perfect peace

—*Cindy Mack*

The Cross

Hung on the cross in a holy light
He shed no tears
And put up no fight.

Of the father, Son, and the holy Ghost
You walk down a path
A sign nailed on a post.

The sign is being rejected
Across a stream of unholy blood
The flaming cut across the mirror
A creation is being reflected.

Coming out of the sky
In a "V" shaped ring
Crucified on the cross
Was our most popular King.

—*Jason R. TenBrook*

The Line Of Truth

As the soldier walked the twisted road,
he walked the line of truth.

On one side lay a field of pain
where he saw his life pass by,
and as he walked, the field grew ripe
with tears his loved ones cried.

On the other side was a golden field
where dreams blossomed and came true,
and there he saw his childhood
and the innocence of youth.

As the soldier walked the twisted road
his head turned left and right,
but never did his footsteps falter
as he journeyed into the night.

—*Brandy Lloyd*

Sol

There he went
He went right through
There where the hippopotami
And the unicorn fly
He flew with the thrush
And the inscrutable roc
The dodecapoli of mighty
Rome and the gardens of
Holy Babalon
As he flew by
High up in
The open sky
A thrush flew through
There where he went by
He flies where none
May fly
High up in
The open sky

—*Brandon Cord Bradshaw*

The Search

As always I'm searching, but for what
    I don't know.

I often wish I could just let go...

Today, tomorrow and nevermore if only
    I could figure out what for.

The answer's within my being yet I
    feel empty inside.

There's not even a place to hide;
    I'm just along for the ride.

—*J. L. Ward*

Little Ones

The patter of small feet
Hear it hurry, to us, to meet.

Life for you and I are here,
The joy of it brings us near.

Soft cry of hunger fills the house,
Can't say he's quiet as a mouse.

Being of breath is now alive,
For this love we strived.

The trouble they cause is just
Because of the thoughts they must.

Curly soft blonde is his hair
As the light refracts from there.

He knows his way around
From the top of the bed to the
    floor he bounds.
Being last to close his eyes,
But early is he to rise.

To play with his mind like a toy,
Only we know the real love and joy!

—*George P. Roese III*

Nature and Love

Trees softly swaying
hearts quietly breaking
Something blows by
    so we sigh
A pretty little kite
and give up the fight
    A branch grabs it
    for a final sit
And holds it for a while
    we try to smile
Then as it lets go
    and try to glow
It rips the kite end to end
    but we cannot bend
And waits for the next to land
    in her strong wind

—*Cory Armantrout*

Sanctuary

Emotions unwinding, legs entwining
Hearts throbbing, passion sobbing
Bodies heaving
Sites and sounds weaving

Creeping time of speeding action
Everlasting feeling, of satisfaction
Mercy cries in that exact moment
Lost in innocence and it's torment

The beads of passion trickle down
As bodies sink slowly to the ground
Rushing blood slows to a walk
Minds still blurred begin to talk

Whispered words from exhausted hearts
Glassy eyed stares from where it starts
Minds and limbs, too heavy to move
Bodies still limp in a sanctuary groove

Feelings euphoric beyond compare
Every time so different that we share
Cleansed away all fears, doubts and pain
And washed our souls pure, from soft love
    reigns

—*James Granahan*

She Laughs

From the twilight she knew,
Her angried soul raven.
From the laughter her voice rouse blue,
While they considered her a heaven.

She calls from the depth to play,
While she sits still of heart.
Embraces those while she lay,
With quickness they are torn apart.

From the twilight of brother moon,
Her nerves are set.
She is a lady until noon,
While a demon, when she is let.

She calls to one and all, have a ball,
For I am at peace.
Struck me with respect, all,
I am to tear you to piece.

From the summons of things,
Her wrathful voice controls.
Every ones tears sings,
While she is not considered, she blows.

—*Barbara Kay Shaw-Hampshire*

Death Of Love

The blood runs down
    her lovely face

She doesn't wipe
    it away

She looks into the face
    of your love

The day he died
    was very hard

The pain she feels
    is too strong

She wonders if the pain
    will ever go away

She wonders if she
    will ever
    love again.

    —*Cindy Ann Balsay*

Always And Again

He moved with
Her motives

She called for
Second chance

A polite agreement for
A particular arrangement

Ironed skirts and
Ignored shirts

Watched over dinner
While on lookers danced

Remembered eyes
Relinquish emotion

Suppressed memories
Surface meticulously

In conversation
Intents converge
And it all starts again

—*Christopher Lee Walter*

Look At Her America!

Look at her America!
    Her stars of gleaming white;
Scattered on a field of blue
    Waving gallantly on high.

With her valiant sons and daughters
    Marching forward to meet the foe,
Shouting their songs of freedom
    As into battle they go.

Look at her America!
    Her heroes of land, air and sea,
Who valiantly gave their lives
    That this nation would be free.

God bless you America!
    May your blessings ever increase,
And over all your sea-girt shores
    Forever fly — the dove of peace.

Yes look at her America!
    Her stars and stripes on high,
With her bright colors waving
    Against the blue of freedom's sky.

—*Eugene L. Cowen*

A Perilous Exchange

This old pear tree shared
her yellow fruit sparingly.
Tough and generously laden,
she dared me on every pass.

The business owners where she lived
motioned me to help myself.
While I prepared with great care
how casually to unburden her,

Bees and coons took their fare.
So finally I climbed her,
displaying an agile flare,
quite rare for 57, but still scary.

I made a pact with her and said,
"Warn me with a wary thump
when we both have had enough." I shook
until we had a tumbling peary rain.

And she, becoming nearly bare,
and I, so worn and weary, felt a bump.
I shinnied down, and thanked her
for a fair, but perilous exchange.

—*Gail M. Cullen*

In Memory Of Rod

How do I live without my Rod?
He's been so much a part of me.
When life is lonely without him,
I turn to friends and family.

Dear people help me through this time.
The emptiness brings so much pain;
But pain is eased when others care,
And I have learned to smile again.

I'm grateful for the times we've had.
Not everyone has 50 years
Of living with the one she loves.
I've much more happiness than tears.

I thank you, Lord, for easing pain
And bringing joy again to me.
And through eternal life with you,
Some day my Rod again I'll see.

—*Dorothy Lynn*

God's Love

God's love is everlasting
His grace is something to behold,
He forgives us when we fall and sin
And makes us pure as gold.

God's love is such a great love.
He gave up his only son,
To die for us on Calvary
And our victory was won.

God's love has redeemed us
From the curse of death and sin,
For he has given to his children
A new life to begin.

God's love is everlasting
Of that we must not doubt,
And we are blessed by his great love
That enfolds us round about.

—*Claudia G. Dillard*

Prayer

I felt his arms around my neck
His hands upon my face

I have this child's love and trust
through God's boundless grace

His little feet carry him my way
To be hugged and kissed
At the end of the day

I remember the boy and
pray for the man

As a teen I felt his fury
like heavy rain
His eyes so sad, I shared his pain
I reached out the child to hold
"Not now mom", "I'm a man"
I was told

The man is still a child
of my heart
Tho miles and time
keep us apart
God remembers the boy and
Answers prayers for the man!

—*Dorothy Steiner-McQuay*

My Love

My love looks into my eyes and
his soul is bared to me.
I see a love there that I never
knew possible.
His caress sends delicious
ripples of pleasure over me
And troubles are forgotten as I
reveal in his gentle touch.
A perfect union of heart, soul,
body, and mind feeling all.
Light and beautiful as a
butterfly on a summer's breeze
Being lifted up, up, and into
oblivion, with no return.
My love, my life, my all
Today, tomorrow, and forever.

—*Celia May*

A Woman's Place?

Her yielded face
His worn out embrace
Their constant chase
Her old spaghetti paste
His bad breath she tastes
Their years of waste
Her can of Mace
His drugs that he laced
Their fights in haste
Her bruised up face
His hands disgraced
Their big court case
Her floor she paced
His deals he aced
Their lawyers race.

Her money spent in waste
Her broken vase
Her beat up face
Her life disgraced
Her hopeless case.

  —Ava Kahn

Your Mother

Your Mother loves you son,
 Hope you ne'er forget.
Mother's love is greater
 Than any yet.

No matter who rears you,
 Or give you their love.
No love will replace
 The love your mother can give.

She may not be near you,
 To her you are dear.
For she always remembers,
 Your caresses and tears.

You will ne'er have another,
 Should God call her away.
No need regretting or fretting
 For your Mother's no more.

So keep loving her son
 And remembering this too.
She loves you and needs you,
 As all mothers do.

  —Catherine M. Karpiak

Golden Girl

Ah - golden girl
How beautiful you were,
so young, so fair . . .
You held the keys to heaven
in your hand.

But ah! You took another road,
the glittering road to hell.

Dancing all night,
diamonds and men,
liquor, smoke and drugs.

Then came the sudden crash
one night,
and the lonely road to the morgue.

  —Colette Nance

My Grandchild's Prayer

Please don't scold me
Hug and hold me
I'm just a little kid you know
Please don't tease me
Pinch or squeeze me
I'm just a little kid you know
In my room
By myself
I talk to all my dollies
Sitting on the shelf
So please love me
lord above me
care for me
And help me grow
Hear me mommy
Hear me daddy
I'm just a little kid you know
 Amen

  —Dorothy Cascio

Hershey

My name is Hershey
I am as cute as can be
long fluffy hair and
my whiskers are free...

My paws are quite big
5 toes in the front
but better to bat with
or maybe bunt....

My mom is Michele
my grandma Jacki
they are my masters
and I am very happy...

I can't go outside
because claws I have none
but I love to play
run and have fun....

I am a spoiled rotten cat
and I love to eat
but the best of all
my favorite is sleep.......

  —Jacki J. Manley

All Alone

 I sit here all alone
  I am so cold
 I shake and tremble
the tears pour down my face
the air fills with my moans
as I sit here crying all alone
 I hear someone calling
but it's not your voice
 I feel naked
 so much pain inside
 why can't I forget you
I see arms reaching for me
but they're not your arms
I feel nothing touching me
 I see others around me
 but they are not you
  I'm all alone
all alone without you
  I am so cold
 so cold...all alone

  —Cheryelona Sanchez

The Dead Bell

Ring the dead-bell now, I say.
I am too tired to stay.
Ring it now, right now!
I want to have my way.

For I am a setting sun,
And my life's no longer fun,
Shadows block my view,
I'm too tired to run.

Life was over when she died,
Keeping on was hard — I tried.
Will she hear that bell?
I want her by my side.

So ring that dead-bell strong.
Ann's been waiting too long.
Ring it loud and clear.
I hear it — so long!

  —Glory Lukacs Johnson

Of Love And Dreams

 Amongst the mist
 I arise from
 Dreams pale cheek
 and echo the
Faint and serene sleep
Carefully dividing it...
 With each color,
 Each thought,
Love's time is not.
 With what voice
 Do we hear?
 And what wind
Beckons to our ears...
If I am to hold myself
 back, I will glide
 Softly through
Higher dominions...

  —Alisa Smith

A Picture Perfect World

I see beauty in a picture
I ask myself, "where is that
beauty in my life"?
Then my reply,"it's not that my
life is so bad, it's just not
the life that I want".
I have some good times
but I want to replace the bad
times.
What do I want?
 Perfection.
How can I make my life
 A picture?
I see beauty in a picture
And I dream a dream that's
good. Then a feeling rushes over
me.
 sadness.
Where and how will I find
 The picture?

  —Barbara Pilarski

The Flag

Our nation's flag waves high and tall,
high and tall on the classroom wall
and it always has a part of my heart.

  —Hugh Anderson

Why Am I Here?

Why am I here,
I ask you, mother dear?
To brighten my world
My wonderful child.

Why am I here,
Father of mine?
To better this world,
When it is time.

Why am I here,
My very best friend?
To give support,
In troubled times.

Why am I here,
Oh Lord above?
To bring to the world,
Much needed love!

—*Carl Ferrel*

Twigs Versus Bricks

Twig by twig
I build my
Fragile
House of dreams.
Friends warn
It's been done
Disastrously.
Bricks are the in thing.
Do I listen? No.
Today it suits me.
I love
The play of sunlight
Stealing through
Lacy tapestry,
Soft warm air
Brushing my face.
Will it last?
A lot depends on
Where the wolf is,
And how hungry.

—*Gladys Lough*

Last Shot

My love for you is so strong,
I cannot stand our distance.
It's hard for me to wait that long.

Yes days travel by so fast
that breaks my heart.
If only we could begin
from the very start.

Every time I see you
I think of everything before
Your a very unique man
And I want you more and more.

This feelings I have inside of me,
tells me how much you mean to me
If only I could tell you I love you
In person it would mean a lot
I want to take that last shot.

—*Abby Ada*

Incomparable!

Shall -
    I compare you with the moon
    Oh no, it will vanish soon
You -
    Will remain like the amaranth
When all else is mortal
As the day passes by
And stars come out in the sky
I -
    Compare their brightness
With your bright eyes
I forget myself
I forget the world
In my mind dwells
Only your radiant smile
You are immaculate
You are incomparable

—*Aminul Islam*

Crying Out For Love

Just a hug, just a smile to feel wanted,
I cry out in the night the tears flow
undaunted.
Come to me, come to me a love I've
yearned for, for so many years,
Just a touch, just a whisper cool
my fears.
Walking along the sea shore on a cool
summer night,
Looking out over the waters as my
heart take flight.
floating over the moonlight, lift me
high in the air,
Touch me love, how I've yearned
year, after year, after year.

—*Johnnie Kirkland*

A Soul

The light was so bright
I did not want to see,
Then I fell.
I got up but the light
Was gone,
And there was hell.

—*Dottie Lawson*

The Spider's Web

On passing by an idle tree
I felt the web I failed to see.
And with me came a spider's home
As well the spider came to roam.

He sped across the clothes I wore
To find himself displaced once more.
Was only just the other day
Another human passed this way.

No blame or guilt did the spider wear
Even though it seemed to be unfair.
Was ignorance of the path by man
But the spider never cursed, just ran.
(Back to build his web again!)

—*Glenn Stuart Smylie*

Lost

Away, away
I find you there alone
Far and deep
Sadness is all you've shown
Left in darkness
Nothing to spare
Like a drowning sparrow
I thought that you would care
Midnight is black
And full of dark desires
Blessings found and thrown away
I see you standing by the flaming fires
You seem to be lost
In a world of your own
Escaping the fears
That have always kept you alone
Silence has become a part of you
That runs in constant motion
I feel like you are the sparrow
That is drowning in the ocean.

—*Blain Anderson*

The Christmas Flu

On a cold Christmas morning,
I got the flu.
I went to the doctor.
But there was nothing he could do.

When I got home no one was there,
and I was left in my socks
and underwear.

So I started a fire,
it made a big blast,
and down fell Santa Claus,
and he started to laugh.
So I ran upstairs to get some clothes,
but as you can see my family took those.

—*Charissa Arneson*

On Modern University Education

With open eyes before the sun,
I greet the day with wish of sleep;
But knowing that I'm grown, yet growing,
Serves to push me to the street;
That I might drive my horseless carriage
To the church on time for marriage
With that Lady, Education
As I master my vocation.

Knowing when I'm done
I shall be competent among
All the masses (and their rashness)
There I'll blend and carry on.
And there happy I will be
As I fit it comfortably
Content to live my dullard's life-
A number in society.

—*Dorian Darroh*

Morning Break

In the morning when I wake,
I look into the morning break.
I see the stillness with my eyes,
The morning dew is still outside.
The stillness of this morning,
Is so beautiful in my mind.

—*Elizabeth Anne Edelmann*

Winter Warmth

Winter is near, the days grow short.
I hear the owl call at dusk.
A chill wind whispers to the trees
And the moss takes on a smell of musk.

I hear your voice call in the wind,
"It's time to gather wood for fire.
Winter's wind will soon grow cold,
We'll fell her temper, sure".

But this year I must go alone
To where the fallen timbers lie.
And build another fire upon the hearth.
And quietly watch as glowing embers die.

—*Edna J. Drye*

Poor Wealth

If only I was born to wealth
I heard the poor man say
I think I would have lived my life
In a satisfying way

I know I would have made my mark
For someone else to see
If only I was born to wealth
The world could learn from me

If only I was born to wealth
I heard him say again
I'd spend much time among the sick
Bringing comfort till the end

And as I slowly walked away
I heard the poor man sigh
Though he became a wealthy man
Life still passed him by

—*Agmen Gill*

My Grandpa

My grandpa is the very best
 I know because he's mine.
We play lots of games together
 And he tells me stories all the time.

So when I'm tucked into my bed
 And I feel a little afraid.
I just think of my grandpa
 And of all the games we've played.

Very soon I'll close my eyes
 And I'll be fast asleep.
'cause my grandpa has sent the sandman
 Just to help me go to sleep.

—*Irene Shatraw*

Memoirs

Oceancrest and hallowsnest
I lay here silently awed.
Dandy luck and wonderstruck
Her beauty my mind it clawed.

Baby eyes and lullabies
Shine sweetly in my mind.
Angelhair and teddybear
Is tender in her bind.

Daddy's near, my sweet dear
My love will always unfurl.
Loving caress and Sunday dress
For she's my little girl.

—*Charles Gallot-Krendall*

Untitled

When I come home at Christmas time
I know just what I'll do
I'll wrap the biggest package
Then I'll label it for you
My heart will ring with laughter
For I'm sure I'll make you guess
What you thought would hide inside
This great big gift of happiness.
It wouldn't be elaborate,
As a gift to queen from king
You couldn't show it to your friends,
They wouldn't see a thing
I'd just chock it full with all my love,
And dreams I hope you'll share.
Won't you heed the Christmas tag?
Handle this with care!

Handle my heart with care,
 handle my heart with care

—*Claire J. Phelan*

My Captain

I'm sailing on a stormy sea,
I know not what life holds for me.
Though tossed about by storms of life,
And on every hand faced with strife.
I know there's no cause for alarm
My captain steers my ship from harm.
He guides me safely on my course
As I travel on life's highway.
And in his safe and loving care
I'm kept each moment of the day.
I have only to call his name
And I know he will be there.
My captains my blessed saviour
Who for me suffered bled and died.
Upon a cross in calvary,
He was unjustly crucified.
I can't begin to repay him
Because for me he gave his all.
But I'll carry on best I can
until I hear my Captain's call.

—*Bonnie Inlow*

Good-Bye Grandma

The picture I look at while
 I lay on my bed.
Is the picture I looked at before
 she was dead.
I remember all the times
 that we shared,
All those times I knew
 that she cared.

I can't face for what
 is now true,
her death is the shadow
 that makes me blue.

Together forever that's what she
 always said,
together forever even though
 she is dead.

I will always have pain
 deep down inside
but I have to live my life
 and say . . . good-bye!

—*Deneen Rae Alexander*

Memories

I wandered back to my home one day
I looked with much surprise.
I found it was all torn down.
I wiped the tears from my eyes.

The lonely path which I once trod
was still along the road.
The footprints, I still could see.
How sad I was no one knows.

The happy days of my childhood
still lingers within my heart.
I could hear my mother calling
come home it's getting dark.

I could hear my father singing
the song he loved so well.
It sounded so sweet and beautiful
oh, no one can really tell.

I turned around and walked away
and wiped away the tears.
But, oh what wonderful memories
still lingers in my heart for years.

—*Addie Combs*

Back In Time

Years ago there was a man
I loved desperately
People called it puppy love,
it was real to me.

What ever happened to this man?
I can't recall his name,
if I could meet this man today,
Would I still feel the same?

They say the minds the first to go
I think this is true,
if my memory should come back,
perhaps it could be you.

After years of wear and tare
and going back in time,
forty years is quite a while,
to cause a troubled mind.

If I could do it over and
this might sound strange,
and if you were the man I met
I wouldn't change a thing.

—*Emogene McGraw*

Life Of Sorrow And Madness

As I walk in the midnight streets
I meet my past of what I feel-
It makes me so mad I want to kill.
The nights seem short and soaked
with the blood of a dead man's
corpse; struggling to control my
angered heart, I feel my life
should make a brand new start,
but the struggle and traumatizing
event that occurred makes my life
seem so damned blurred.
My soul is trying to climb out of
me and seek a new person surrounding
me. For what I am and all I'm worth,
there's nothing for me here but to
head up north. Dark and alone in a
place unknown, I wait for the day...
For the sorrow and madness, to lie
in some dirt covered and buried I
feel no more hurt.

—*Bobbie Flores*

Dove

In the dark I do not dwell
I met a guy I loved so well
He stole my heart away from me
And now he wants to set it free.

He sat a strange girl upon his knee
And told her things he never told me
I ran home to cry on my bed
Not a word to anyone that I said.

My father came home late that night
And looked for me left and right
Then through my door he broke to find
Me hanging on a rope like a vine.

Oh, darling dear, what have you done
You killed yourself for one man's son
And as he was about to cut me down
On my dresser, a note he found . . .

Dig my grave and dig it deep
Cover me with marble from head to feet
And at the top, place a dove
To show that I had died for Love.

—*Christa Dasher*

Seasons

Of spring or summer, winter, all
I must feel loneliest in the fall
It seems life's memories, I recall
Come back to haunt me in the fall

When leaves are dead and dying
I vividly recall what makes me cry
Of other autumns past and gone
When sounds of fall hum their sad song

A warning always in the fall
Of colder days that I recall
The frost upon the sugar cane
The heavier dews, the autumn rain

All speak to me in sounds so clear
Of why the purpose everywhere
Of life and love, present and past
Divine unfolding alone can last

The only hopes and dreams that can
Are unfamiliar to mortal man
We live and love and hope and pray
But can't comprehend for just today

—*Grace Ward*

Why?

I walk on the grass God made,
I pass trees God made,
I see animals God made,
I see rivers, lakes, and oceans God made,
I see the sky and clouds God made,
I see people God made,
I see the land God made,
I see the beauty God made,
Then I see the pollution, we made.

—*Jillian Weber*

Untitled

Unicorn, unicorn, what do you see?
I see a heart looking at me
It's so beautiful for me
I can wear it now I see
I can see the heart on me
Won't you be a heart for me?

—*Alicia A. Saldana*

Gideon

Slowly,
    I picked up my book
    Got hold of my pen.

Gently,
    I scanned my thoughts
    To look and ponder.

Quietly,
    I scribbled a word
    Your name on my poem.

Gladly,
    I did what I have to do
    Penned a poem about you.

—*Arlene Joan Gerochi*

Prayers

I pray the sky not fall on me.
I pray the sun to let me see.
I pray the fields to bloom and grow.
I pray the soil be rich below.
I pray the trees to touch the clouds.
I pray the birds sing sweet, aloud.
I pray the day to quietly pass.
I pray tomorrow come at last.
I pray the wind in trees hum sweetly.
I pray the earth restore completely.
I pray my prayers may be by chance heard.
I pray that none remain unanswered.

—*Jeremy Hooper*

Armageddon Is Near

Now I lay me down to sleep -
I pray whomever my soul to keep.
And if I should die before I wake
I pity the one my soul to take.

Nuclear warfare is our death,
And death is our only friend.
Awakened by screams of pain.
Our leaders now we can trust,
But in the end — we will all be dust.

—*Charlie Petersen*

Pleasure Hunt

As I tip-toe through life's doorway
I search for hidden gold
For we all have inner riches
Least, that's what I've been told

They have naught to do with money
Or cars or rings and things
For riches can be feelings
Such as love and trust can bring

I've felt the warmth and ecstacy
That comes from deep within
When I befriend another
That's when the glow begins

But, ah, because I'm human
I've my share of guilt and sin
The secret, I have found is
Accept and start again

I hold the key right in my hands
T'was always there, you see
My riches are in those I love
And those who care for me

—*Dorothy M. Heinis*

Untitled

The moon is shining bright tonight
    I see its face o'woe
The moon is shining bright tonight
    Lighting the dark with its glow
It shimmers across the water
    And dances like a ballet
It lights a path in the night
    And looks down, its face so grey
Sometimes clouds cover the moon
    See not my hands 'fore my face
Sometimes clowds cover the moon
    And hides its lighted grace
The moon doth shone on many a year
    It has heard life's laughters, trial,
Frustration, and shedding tear
    The moon looks over all
It sees great happiness and fear
    The moon look over all
And will continue when I am no longer
here

—*Benjamin Burch*

Those Eyes

When I look into your eyes
I see . . . well lots of things.
Looking in your eyes is like
a diamond,
It blinds me in my mind...
....I hear nothing but the
    sound of your voice.
I see nothing but you...
...and those eyes,
    those bluish-gray eyes...
...they make me cry.
    Maybe it's love!

Well I can't explain
anything else, but
now you know what
I see.

—*Jami LaClair*

How It Is

    Every moment of the day
    I see you through my mind's eye
        An unrelenting vision
        Of all things beautiful
            In my world.

I hear the sounds, smell the fragrance
        Feel my senses tingle
    All because your portrait
        Is painted on the canvas
            Of my heart.

    Seeing you ignites my soul
    Into a raging inferno of desire
        Burning out of control
        Erupting from the touch
    Of your gentle, silken hand.

        Time moves too slow
        Fore we once again meet
        Still my heart hangs heavy
    Until our eyes and lips engage
        Then another world begins.

—*Joe Campau*

The Gypsy Life

When I was just a little child
I stood in awe, eyes westward bound
And watched the gypsy wagons come
With jangling pans, and happy sound.

A longing deep entered my soul.
Their carefree life aroused in me
A deep desire to see the world
And live like them, a spirit free.

The years went by; the world changed
And people everywhere began
To have that secret wanderlust
To see all corners of our land.

Today, I too, can rove the world
Escaping daily cold and strife.
I've joined the millions in our land
Who've spread their wings in trailer life.

—*Evelyn Sinke*

I Am Alive

I am alive.
I think,
I feel,
I live.
I can see,
and taste,
and touch,
and hear.
People depend on me,
and I depend on people.
Whenever I think
of being alive,
I am overwhelmed
by how much I do,
and think,
and feel.
I am alive.

—*Aimee Hess*

Love

How could it happen?
I tried to resist.
His charm overcame me,
And now here it is.
This thing called love,
So confusing ... Yet desired.
To all who are for it,
It's far worse than fire.
It burns and sparks,
Then like love itself,
Dies down...
Fades out...
Left without help.

That's how it has been.
That's how it will be.

As love continues for all to see.

—*Angela K.R. Whitman*

Elements

Hearts of gold could not be strong
If they never allowed to bend;
For if our hearts were built of stone,
They would sooner grow cold than mend.

—*Jennifer L. Martz*

Untitled

In the quiet of morning
I wake to find
My pillow blessed with your presence

Your face still given
To the solace of slumber
You stir
Slowly
Stretching reaching
Suggesting recognition of
The new born day

I am made warm by your familiarity
Completely engulfed by your being
Like a bird in flight
Against the wind
I find you
Truly beautiful...

—*Bev Cook*

And Now I See

I watched in awe,
I wondered why,
God made you deaf,
Why you, not I?

A mind like yours,
So quick to learn;
It seemed unfair,
Your needs to spurn.

But as I watched,
And saw your drive;
I realized,
You will survive!

He made you strong
Your life to live;
I hope that you
And God forgive—

The thoughts that came
From this small mind;
I was impaired,
Not deaf, but blind.

—*Eleanor M. Achterhof*

To Height's Unknown

If I could hide in 'His' shadow
I would be so safe and sound.
If I could walk in 'His' footsteps.
I know I would never fall down.

If I could only look into 'His' face.
And 'He' would smile at me.
I can't think of any place.
That I would rather be.

If I could hear 'Him' speak
I know 'His' voice would be
Clear and strong and 'He'
Lifts me up spiritually
To greater heights unknown.

I know some enchanted day.
My dreams will all come true
And I will walk and talk with Him
In a world that is
    Brand new

—*Ethelyne Moody*

If I Had Wings

If I had wing's
I would fly away,
Over the mountains,
Across the bay.

Into the clouds,
I would soar around,
Loving the feeling,
Of freedom found!

New area's I'd seek,
Where I could be,
Free as the birds,
That fly around me.

Freedom at last,
To do as I please,
Morning upward and onward,
With every breeze.

No permanent ties
I'd constantly roam
If I had wings-
The "world" would be home!

—*Adeline Fleischer*

The Dream

I had a dream the other night
I'd died and gone to hell
That every pain I did inflict
Became part of me as well
That every heart I'd broken
Was tearing me apart
That every dream I'd shattered
Left me with another scar
Now my eyes are open
And I can see the light
Was it just another dream
Or a warning from the night

—*David C. Shoenfelt*

Pretend Horse

If only I could have a horse
I'd feed and clean her not by force

I'd ride her every other day
and always feed her lots of hay

my horse and me would have such fun
I'd ride on her and she would run

it wouldn't be too much to do
I'd learn her every need and clue

and maybe fences we could jump
as long as I don't get to plump

or could we even win a race?
why then I'd have a smiling face

oh why do horsies cost so much?
a great deal more than I can clutch

Since piles of money are absent
with pretend horse I'll be content

—*Joe Zinobile*

Gifts

If it were mine to give
I'd send you the sun
But it is there for all to see,
So I will bring you fun.

If it were mine to give
I'd present you with all the beauty
But it is owned by no one,
So I will describe it to you in words

If it were mine to give
You would have the privilege of eternity
But I could not leash the immensity,
So I will give you me.

If they were mine to give
I'd collect all the stars from above
But they are far beyond my reach,
So I will give you love.

—*Barbara Strong*

Thoughts Of A Housecat

If I could get out,
    If I could be free,
I'd lay in the sun,
    or I'd climb a tree.

I'd run through the yard,
    or roll in the dirt,
Tease the neighbor's dog,
    Maybe I'll get hurt.

I look out the window,
    at the grass and the trees,
wishing I could get out,
    and do what I please.

If I could only manage,
    to open the door,
I'd leave this place,
    and be trapped no more.

But because I can't,
    I'm trapped in a house,
With nothing to play with,
    not even a mouse.

—*Donald M. Leaden*

Pass Me Bye?!

If I have no pride; I'm not a man
If I have no shame; am I alive?
If I have no love; can I live?
If I have no dreams
Do I dare try?
If I have no feelings
Why do I cry inside?
If you've seen me now
Would you stop to help?
Or just pass me bye?!
If I have no money
Would you still know my name?
If I have no car
Would you offer me a ride?
If my spirit leaves me
Will you acknowledge I'm alive
If my life's in shatters
Will you help me pick up the pieces?
Or just pass me bye?!

—*Erich E. Sirkowski*

The Thought Of Loosing You

What would I do
If I lost you?
I could never forget our time's
We shared, just you and me.
Your new friend
Is coming between
Our love
For another.
What are we to do?
I just hate the thought
Of ever loosing you.

—*David Jones*

A Word To The Wise

You may pass by the garbage.
(If it is in your way).
You may look at the garbage.
You may even touch the garbage
(With gloves on).
You may smell the garbage if you dare.
But do not get IN the garbage
If you get in the garbage
You are garbage

—*Dee Dee Smith*

Homeward Discernment

Let us discern
    if we can
beyond the limits of texts
and materially ingested knowledge
    or that which races
before the viewing screens
    of our eyes for Truth

Laugh-tracks and Pontiacs
    are the cataracts
that govern point-of-ewe
    or have you not herd?

Yet we can plow-sow-deep
        that we too
        fall asleep
to gain access to that
which was new yesterday

And the withered "Tree of Life"
    surrendering to intellect
    loses its natural roots
    to spiritual instinct.

—*C. Thomas Irving*

Untitled

I'm shades of red, green, and blue
I'm love
I'm hate
I'm jealousy too.
I'm one
I'm many, and yet far too few
I'm scared
I'm lonely, and I've a darkside too
I'm young
I'm old
I'm caring, and sometimes cold
I'm all these, and more.
I'm man, and nothing more.

—*Gary Lee Hayworth*

Sister-In-Law

Sister - in - law, stop crying for me.
I'm holding on just fine...
Remember tomorrow is another day;
Another beginning.

Your handsome brother is the
One to be blame.
He left silently....
Leaving me with a broken heart.

As the days pass by,
I try hard-to erase him
Out of my weak heart; all in vain.
My heart still beats for him.

There will be another surprising day
Hopefully, I'll have his strong arm
To protect and guide me into tomorrow;
Where no exist hate, only forgiveness.

Having loving and caring
Sister - In - Law like you,
Makes me realized, I'm not alone,
Tomorrow is another day...

—*Candida Lomba Pina*

Traveler In time

I'm just a traveller in time,
I'm only passing through.
I want to cherish this moment
That I have to share with you.
I've said so long to memories
For yesterday has past.
I can't say about tomorrow,
Today may be my last.
Time will last forever
Like the waters of the sea,
But life is so uncertain
Tomorrow may never be.
Who knows when I'll be leaving
Or when I'll say goodbye?
My life is so uncertain
Any moment I could die.
So today I will hold you
And do all I can for you,
Today I will love you
And be all your dreams come true.

—*Garfield K. McBean*

Graven Images

This God of yours is nothing
Image graven in a book
You think you've found the answer
Will you take another look?

You swear on mythic prophecy
Divine promise from within
Some still kill and need no reason
In this their carnal sin

Look at your stone-carved image
Reflecting all your life
You may pray for soul salvation
All you find brings painful strife

Do not seek for an answer
You may find only your death
Sins will be cast by all men
To ourselves must we repent

Your God is there inside you
Listen now to your true self
You will see the answer
Put this book back on the shelf

—*Grant M. French*

One Perfect Dream

The spring wind blew through the trees,
In a glade by a cool mountain stream.
I heard the buzzing of many bees,
As I began to dream.

I saw my love on a white horse,
Gallop to me at a hurried pace.
I knew he'd come for me, of course.
As he held me in his passionate embrace,

My heart beat for joy.
With tears in my eyes, I wept.
No longer would I pretend to be coy,
For only by him should I be kept.

No one in the world could ever part,
The two of us and our beating hearts.

—*Celeste J. Glaser*

In The Flow

Did you ever think of why
In a storm the birds don't fly
But nestle on the limbs of trees,
Bending to and fro with flexing ease?

All birds know instinctively
The safest place where they should be.
With the flow is nature's way,
Non-resistance, come what may.

If I could learn to live as birds,
Expressing trust instead of words,
I'd flow gratefully through any storm,
Expecting bright days to be born.

It takes a storm to clear the air.
So, let's find appreciation there,
And prepare when warning signs you see.
Storms don't come in without a key.

—*Consuelo Brown*

A Mother

A mother is much needed
In all our lives today,
She pours bundles of love
In numerous of good ways.

The caring that she gives
Is far beyond compare,
She seems to know the heart
Especially when in despair.

She gives the best advice
Makes smart decisions too...
A dear sweet gentle mother
Is the best role model for you!!

She taries about her duties
With a smile on her face,
Knowing she's that person
That only God can replace!!

—*Constance D. Mayers*

Untitled

We animals clothed,
In finely spun robes,
Nurtured on history's milk;

Sing siren songs,
Of things gone wrong,
Neglecting the will to prevent them.

—*Harry T. Roman*

Fall

You fall so gracefully
in green and scarlet splendor
leaf by leaf before my feet,
but we meet in sadness
as summer drifts away
yielding reluctantly to your display.

You fall so gently
in gold and russet splendor
leaf by leaf before my feet,
and we meet in gladness
at the holidays this time of year,
but soon you will disappear.

You fall so silently
in many colored splendor
leaf by leaf before my feet
and, though it is time for you to go,
I shall still remember your glow
as I dream of falling snow.

—*Edna Junemann*

A Mother's Final Farewell

The unshed tears shine
in her eyes, shining like diamonds.
She watches as her flesh
and blood is lowered
down, down into the
dishearten earth.
The one she had borne
is gone, forever.
The rose she grips in
her hand is wilting.
The blood red petals
sparkle with dew, as
her eyes sparkle with
tears.
The thorns cut into her
skin.
She does not care
The one she had borne
is gone, forever.

—*Amanda Hayes*

Quest

On my way to school,
in my endless quest.
Until I get my degree,
I shall never rest.

All my teachers,
seem pretty cool to me.
I've only had,
one bad one,
at that school,
you see.

My persistence
at my quest,
will inspire my children
at best.

Upon completion of my quest,
I will finally
get some rest.

—*John Rowland*

My Red Maple Tree

I have a Red Maple tree,
In my front yard,
I love my Red Maple tree,
And it love me.

When I was hot, it gave me shade,
When it was thirsty, I gave it water,
So you see, we love each other.

I love my Red Maple tree all year-round,
And it love me.

So you asked me,
How could you love a tree?
I told you,
Because, it loved me.

—*Eugenia Grace Marshall*

Reality Check!

So detached am I - unrelated.

You're just a soul's thought
in my mind's eye,
but not real -
An extension of my own -
but unfathomable...
A concept I cannot accept.

But now - today -
the ultra - sound,
Tuned in to MY being
but reflecting YOUR beat!!

Ah, dearest grandchild -
a first, a girl,
Almost here - but not.
My God, you're real!!

Ah, Sarah, Sarah,
could I give my life for you?

"In a heartbeat!!!"
—*Carol Ann Sutton*

The Dove

A river runs
in my soul.
It runs to deep
to ever show.
Next to the river
a candle glows.
For the man I love
only I can know.
The flame glows dim
to dim to see.
His hate for my love
is killing me.
My life goes on
without his love.
All that is left
is the cry of a dove.

—*Anne Poulin*

Thanks Giving Poem

Pilgrims and
Indians were once known
Long ago from
Gods heart to celebrate a
Rare occasion for the
Indians and Pilgrims to rejoice these
Moments in all of are
Sacraments to despair

—*Erika Montemayor*

Patiently

The forest deep and the sea
In the depths, spirit and soul
I am waiting patiently.

Descending sun and evening light
To pause in solemn reverence
As the eve becomes the night.

The sodden quiet in the woods
A quietness that beckons tears
To live a life without the noise.

What is this world, why this pain
Where sensitive and gentle souls
Turn either bitter or insane?

Eyes are deep and the sea
Misty harbor, rising wave
I am waiting patiently.

In quiet walks and to spend
My time in kinder, gentler thought
And converse with kindred friends.

The leaves are whispering in the wind
To be in awe of little things
—*David Skellion*

Untitled

There's a face of a girl
In the mist covered window
She is lonely
Scared

There are ghosts in the closet
Running all over all day
Chasing her
Constantly

There are countless tears
Streaming onto the floor
Making her tired
Weak

There is a still body
Of a troubled girl
Laying by a window
Dead
—*Christine DiDonna*

My World

To close my eyes
    In the shadow of a tree,
And lose my thoughts
    Of things my hands must do
To earn my keep.

To hear a fish, catch a fly
    And feel the earth
With a hand that fell
    From sleepy eyes.

To hear my Father's breath
    That makes leaves dance,
While mother earth plays
    Her stream for me.

To wake and find
    The tree has moved
And the sun is hot.

This is the life for me.
    The world man-made is not!
—*Bill Youngblood*

Solitude

When I walk
In the silence
Of dripping rain
Through field and forests
Apart from man
I feel no hurt
I feel no pain
Of yesterdays
When I stand
In the stillness
Of falling snow
On mountain trails
Where hemlocks grow
I feel no fear
I feel no dread
Of future's woe
Only
Complete serenity
Only
Timeless solitude
—*George R. Stahl*

No Contest

I walk
in the sting of sleet
to your grave.
Evergreens
in this city of stone
help me find my way.
You died one week ago today.
I waited until now
to see you so we could be alone.
I need to know why you took your life.
You never answered the gypsy
I paid twenty-five dollars
to conjure you up.
You never come to me in dreams.
I want an answer
and I am not leaving
though sleet persuades me.
My blanket of anger will keep me warm.
I cannot accept silence as your final word.
—*Heather Miller-Cottom*

Footprints In Snow

Today I think I'll walk
In the woods and leave
Footprints in the snow.

These I shall leave behind but
Only for a moment in time
For my footprints will be quickly
Covered with new fallen snow and
The traces of my having been there
Will be gone forever.
—*David A. Yacobucci*

Summer Time

One last plunge into cool Lake Deadwood.
Indian summer is almost gone.
Dry winds a rustling golden brown
leaves of autumn.
Cold North winds will soon be here,
chilling us all to the marrow.
Visions of summers warm caress
greet us in our dreams.
Deep in slumber summer times here.
—*Brian Nagahama*

The Heart Of A Marriage

I vow to take this man
into my life,
and become not only his friend
but also his devoted wife,
to have and to hold
to life's bitter end,
In health or in sickness
till death as his friend.
I promise to cherish this man,
to share my heart whenever I can
The commitment I offer
is from my heart
together forever,
our souls never to part.
—*Jeanna Zivalich*

Reincarnation Of Life

Snow on the ice of a clear mountain lake
Is a beautiful dream
For no one to fake.
As real as the sun that takes it away
With every warm and radiant ray.

Why, how, who can say!

Soon the ice will melt away,
But for today lets enjoy our stay.
With mother nature we will pray,
Pray for life or snow and ice,
Death in life our final price,
But while we're here we must think twice.
Love your neighbor
Be courteous and nice.
Live with control, don't be cold,
As ice will warm,
Love is not torn,
But carried off to be reborn.
—*Brian McMillen*

The River Of Dreams

The River of Dreams,
Is a place where dreams
are dreamed and stored,
Like water waiting to flow
over a water fall,
Just waiting to be dreamed,
In the River of Dreams,
Dreams become reality
You can feel love, hate,
joy, and sorrow,
You can feel the presence
of loved-ones,
The River of Dreams,
Is a place to forget anger,
A place to relax,
A place to take a break
from daily life,
In the River of Dreams,
Anything is possible.
—*Evan Turner*

The Dark

As the darken shade of night
Is drawn upon the earths fleeting,
Light, a star comes through that,
Darken shade to bring us hope and,
The coming of a bright new day.
—*Girard Cohen*

His Gift

All my love for you thought bright
Is before God a pale light

A true loves heart cannot be won
Until at first you love His son

How this precious gift is known
Is a secret that He has shown

That was the beauty of His plan
When he made woman to be with man

You are the moon and I the sun
And yet our love will make us one

To put our faith and trust in Him
Is to know our love will never end

And when we love to do what's right
It proves our love is His delight

And to us both He has yet to show
How abundantly our love can grow.

—*Andrew James Spence*

Uncertain Affection

A contradiction
Is fiction
Blame
Is shame
Deception
Dimension
It is my implication
To say that
I love you.

—*Bruce Scott Perkins*

Motherchild

So often, the child
is herself, and not me,
as I had planned.
Off she trudges
through the universe,
leaving time to follow.
Her body is a string quartet,
blending rhythm with
every beat she finds.
Her mother dances
in the sun,
turning,
    reaching,
        laughing,
as the music sets her soul free,
soaring high. Together
they are a symphony,
overpowering and
impossible
to ignore.

—*Dianne Strasser-Leslie*

Dress Parade

Did they tell you my costume for life
is quite simple -
a bold front, a kind word, a smile?
For offensive oafs - a frozen mien
a rolled up sleeve, or a shrug.
For the eager, courage - seeking,
ingenious youths, the applause
they need to conclude.
And for the loving, the kind,
and the helpful ones, an
expression of gratitude.

—*Harry J. Kay*

Black

Is it a crime?
Is it be cause the
Color of my skin?
Can't you see there's a
Person inside of me
If I was a book
Would you judge me by my cover?
I have feelings
I laugh
I cry
Judge me by the person I am
Inside not because I'm
Black.

—*Jamarra Render*

Res Roses

Red roses, red roses,
    Is that really what I see?
Hundreds of them, thousands of them
    Shining on a tiny tree.
Like many, many rays of sunlight
    Sent from Heaven to chase the gloom
Yes, for each delicate rosebud
    In my heart I will find room.
Love them, kiss and caress them;
    Let each petal's rosy hue,
Penetrate the days of loneliness
    Like a message loving and true.

—*Eugenie Makinster*

A Rich Man's Advice

To a rich man my advice
is try not to entice
a woman with a price.
It would suffice
to be nice
and not look for vice
or a woman who's like ice,
playing you like dice.
Crawling over you like mice,
alluring you as spice,
so they can use you as a device,
to extract their hefty price,
and destroy you like lice.
And that's to be concise
for a rich man's advice.

—*Abe Friedman*

A Blessing

Such a small frame
It brings much joy
A delicate thing
No bigger than a toy
Depending on arms of warmth
To love and to keep safe
The cry at night
Melody raging for support
Only to snuggle in delight
As mother whispers
"My baby a blessing"
While darkness breaks to daylight

—*Inga Abraham*

Morning Light

The morning light pervades the scene
It comes, so softly, so serene
And I must rally every sense
For constant day cares must commence,
And onward, forward as it must be
The tasks of living are thus upon me
The sun o'ersees the trivial chores,
The daily cleaning, tidying tours,
And every need that one attends
Until delightful dusk descends,
And winding down, but moving ever,
The evening hours still hold endeavor,
And finally night enforcing rest
God ends his ever-wearing test.
Will I, unswerving face that fight
That comes once more with morning light?

—*Carolyn Geraghty*

Straws In The Wind

Something must have happened.
It is too quiet.
I have not seen either of them—
And they seemed happy as larks.

Day in and day out
they rushed to and fro,
he, bringing whatever he could scrounge,
seemingly;
she darting about, too,
but mostly arranging and rearranging.

I watched their springtime labours,
almost as proud as they
at the building of that nest,
which now is desolate.

Luxuriant spring lavishes growth
all around the still nest.
I suspect mindless vandalism
has struck again.

—*Beatrice L. White*

Prisoner Of War Prayer

I met a girl once;
It seems a million years ago.
She smiled as I went to war.
She said, "I'll help you're garden grow.

And so I went across the waves,
To a land way down under.
Where many good men found their graves,
From the cannons rolling thunder

I only cried just once it seemed,
Within the prison cage.
I used to go and see her in my dreams,
To calm the guards cold rage.

The day I died; I saw her face,
Smiling down at me.
I knew that this world and the chase;
And finally we'd be free.

—*Bill Fleming*

Peace Of Mind

Like a leaf on a flowing river,
    It seems nowhere to find
A place to stop and rest awhile
    To have its peace of mind.

I feel like that a lot of times
    Never knowing which way to turn
Trying to hide the feelings I have
    So my heart won't get burned.

My thoughts should be at each days end
    On a peaceful positive tone.
It's most important to share your life
    And never remain alone.

Not one person I have ever seen
    Could be satisfied all the time.
Just try to get through each day
    And maintain your peace of mind.

If you ever find the perfect match
    With whom to share your soul,
These two people are like two halves
    For together they make a whole.

    —*Donna Nix-Byford*

The Mountain Stream

The beauty the wonderful sound as
it travels up, over, under all around
the ground
It has a destination, and nothing
Will change its will
to keep moving to continue day
and night never to cease
its marvelous journey to where
it be bound.

    —*Jean Turpin*

The Memory Of You...

You were taken from us,
    It was all just so sudden.
All that is left to us,
    Is your loving memory and smile.

You always had a big smile,
    No matter how bad you felt.
You had very special friends,
    In their hearts you will always be.

Tears are falling for you,
    It just isn't fair!!
Now, there's a place just for you,
    Somewhere special up there!!!

The tears falling for you show,
    That when you look down on us,
Our hearts and minds will be full
    Of the times filled with love and laughter
That we had with you!!

    —*Angie Marie Claxton Nihart*

Untitled

I ate a pie. . .
It was fried, they said.
Then I died, they said.

But I'm in Havana now,
Eating bananas,
And singing cockadoodledoo
On the beaches
To the strutting gulls...
They pay no attention.

    —*Donald Coughlin*

Sunday Morning

It's as dark as night.
It's as light as day,
It's the end of April,
And the beginning of May.

Birds are soaring,
Oceans are roaring,
As you hear all these wonderful sounds,
All on Sunday morning.

People are waking,
A church bell chimes,
There are little children on the street,
Saying nursery rhymes.

Soon it starts raining,
Birds stop soaring,
Oceans stop roaring,
All on Sunday morning.

    —*Adam Warrenfells*

Shannon Dawn

This feeling runs so deep, so cold,
Its cutting edge grows ever bold.
This tender rage just hape'd upon.
entered now with Shannon Dawn.

I ask you God, do Angels cry,
to see this little life pass by?
I ask you God, do Angels weep
to see this purest soul in sleep?

The silk-spun gold upon her head
moves gently with these winds of dread.
Her life now seems to flutter by
No time to lose, no answers why.

I ask you God, do Angels cure
if pleas of love are ever pure?
I ask you God do Angels sing
when bringing miracles from the king?

As Angels fly, as Doves will soar
My need for strength grows ever more.
My faith in you must never stray,
Although I fear each coming day.

    —*Elizabeth Armstrong*

Realistic

When we get older
    it's hard to fulfill;
All of our dreams
    on blue bird hill.

So, I guess I'll do
    what needs to be did;
For out in the open
    keeps no secret hid.

    —*Clyde W. Jontz*

The Tree

"I had a tree
My friends and me
We played with glee
Under the tree
We ate sugar and pop
Without a drop
Then watched the rain go plop!"

    —*Emily Kaiser*

Remember That I Care

When life brings you change
it's usually for the best,
as you feel worn down
remember to take a rest.

When anger engulfs you
listen to what it's saying,
as you find peace of mind
remember - no denying.

When you've been hurt
take time and feel the pain,
as you learn to rise above
remember the strength you'll gain.

When you need a listening ear
I am here - never despair,
for when your world closes in
remember that I care.

    —*Gerri Kemnetz*

Sunday Morning Sun

    All week long
I've been aching for something.
    The puzzle seems to have
Me spinning toward infinity.

    At last,
It comes striking down on me.
    Surrounding my body,
Exciting me, tingling me, feeling me
    With rays of warmth.

    My eyes creep open,
My neck rolls to the source,
    And my arms extend.
Stretching widely to accept
    Every inch of the light.

    It's here.
It has finally arrived.
    That eternal
Sunda Morning Sun.

    —*Debra Jackson*

It Shall Always Be

For every day I've lived and dreamed,
    I've dreamed of loving you;
And yet our love never quite seemed,
    To be completely true.

You doubted each and every thought,
    That ever crossed my mind;
No matter what the gifts I brought,
    Your actions were unkind.

I tried and tried to comfort you,
    But never with success;
For you were always sad and blue,
    And short on happiness.

I shared my deepest sympathy,
    Yet felt I could do more;
So when you said you needed me,
    I knew what love was for.

No matter what love means to you
    It means one thing to me;
My love for you is finally true,
    And it shall always be.

    —*Bradley S. Baum*

My Darling I'm Sorry

My Darling I'm sorry,
I've hurt you, I know,
Just a slip of the lip
caused the harsh words to flow.
I want to make up
and
hold you real tight.
So please be
My Darling
won't you
Kiss me goodnight.
Darling, I swear
I've tried to be fair.
I sometimes say things
I really don't mean.
So I want to make up
and hold you real tight.
So please be
My Darling
and kiss me goodnight.

—*Raymond Elda Ellyson*

Giving Praise

We should think of our Creator
Jehovah God as a real person
who can see and hear. Especially
when we approach him in prayer.
The most high is without equal,
being infinite in power and wisdom,
wholly just and the personification
of unselfish love. Yes, praise God
in prayer, our heavenly father above.
Give praise to Jehovah God and his
kingdom we will proclaim, till all
people on earth living will honor
his name. At the end of each day to
Jehovah thanks I convey for guidance
on my way. Give praise to Jehovah
in prayers for giving his only begotten
son's life in behalf of ours.

—*Elsie L. Gilliam*

Flower Of You

Standing ever so grand
Joy - take my hand
A touch of morning dew
Sits gently on the flower of you

Rays of shining bright
Faith! see the light
The flower of you to unfold
Courage to be bold

Glistening of the skies
Hope - sparkle in your eyes
The flower of you shines above
Life's ever eternal love

—*Joan Leslie Gullison*

There's Room For You All

There's room for you all
My arms are of endless length
I feel your needs
I hear your calls
Trust me, Kids,
There's room for you all.

—*Carolyn M. Foy*

The Dolphin Wish

The bright blue dolphin
Jumps as he swims.
He is a newborn child playing.
The ocean is his home
And the fish are his friends.
He eats when he is hungry
And sleeps when he is tired.
Oh what fun it would be
To live like a dolphin
So happy and free.

—*Angie Matz*

Zookeeper

God bless your bones,
  Keeper of apes and elephants.
Our limbs, our very marrows mesh;
Transfusions of tigerblood revive me
  While hyenas snap at my heels.
You breathe lifefire into my flesh.
  (Are you dragon-keeper as well?)

Wrapping me in elephant dung and hay,
You offer freedom
  without a breath of air.
I trust you implicitly:
  There are no liars on this planet —
Only inventors of elephants and hyenas.

—*Gretchen Schas*

In Regards To Innocence

One
last
solitary multi-colored flower grows

the rest were wiltedmutilated
by our unrelenting
winters of experience

he (not with out reluctance)
uproots

the last flower
and pleasants its fragility
to the whore

she then
dyes the pedals black, rapes them,
and returns it, bleeding

he clutches it to his own regret
and screams and screams and screams

dine upon my tears
feast upon my regret again

Oh Lord, what a stigma

—*Jason Deeming*

Birth And Beauty

A new child brought
laughter to the silence of pain,
light to the darkness of discontent
and a quiet joy
at the miracle of life
bestowing
experiential knowledge
of the wonder of being human.

—*Hilda M. Stebbins*

Falling

Below the hidden abyss
lays treasure only the brave
know
with the awe and splendidness
of the ocean
you feel you're falling
  falling
  falling

—*Jillian Sauers*

Untitled

I'd like to be a porpoise
leaping in the air,
almost falling.
I'd come up on the beach
to watch the pretty girls go by.
I'd take them for a ride on my back
out to sea.
Being a porpoise feels good
Better than it is now.

—*John Pine*

Home Maid

A maiden in a village
Led a pure and blameless life;
She loved a carpenter and
Had agreed to be his wife.

She had a vision that she would
Bear a wonder working-son;
Though puzzled how 'twould come about,
She declared it should be done.

Her finance' learned about her state
And knew they'd be disgraced;
He also knew, by Jewish law,
The penalty she faced.

But she persisted in her love,
Persuaded him that he
Should be the father of her son
And head the family.

This just man and his virgin bride
Are honored to this day;
For, though they were unready,
They did God's will anyway.

—*Dewyne Anderson*

Lest I Awake

Walk silently with softened tread
  Lest I awake amidst the dead
  And scream in agonies of pain
And fight the whole World War again!

I fought for peace - so let me lie
  For finding peace I had to die,
  No weary form - no matted hair -
Just bones and death are lying here.

Let me forget the fearful sound
  As I lie here beneath the mound -
Of screaming shells, the sudden fear
Of shapeless mass of comrade dear.

Close the wound the shrapnel ripped
Gently wipe the blood flecked lips,
And hush! Oh hush - the mother's cry
  Lest I awake - again to die!

—*Edith S. Hood*

Alfred

Normal in every way.
Let me tell you if I may,
Small and fragile,
but someone I can handle.
Feisty and sweet, and of
course not neat.
Only for me, he's
someone I need.
Always bringing me joy,
he's someone I adore.
Never hurting my feelings,
Letting him go would be a
killing, he's my son
and my love he has
definitely won.

—*Jessica Montgomery*

Let There Be Time

Don't hurry the sunset
Let the mountains be.
Open wide your eyes
Drink deep the sea.
Let there be time oh friend
Let there be time for you and me.

Feel the morning sun
Let its passion rise.
Reach out open hands
Search wide the skies.
Time - oh lovely friend
Time - for you and me.

—*Doug Hedemark*

Take The Time To Heal

Children of war only beget war
Let us all live through the next year
And take the time to ponder
Heal, heal the pain wrought
By the aeons of madness

Let bygones be bygones
Rebound in our own good time.
Learn to believe, tip the scales of
Justice in mediation, appropriate caring.
Learn - to live, love, again care
Appropriately, in our own good time.

Let Libra and Scorpio come together
And let us all be - ourselves
Safe in the knowledge that time
Will again be ours - love, laughter,
joy, true caring.

Again, take our hearts... heal, love, care.

—*Catherine L. Brown*

Untitled

Many children's needs
lie unfulfilled
By mother, who is, herself
a child, still.
A child needs to know
you love him.
Guide him - teach him,
and show him the way.
Soon they are grown, and
what you have taught him
Will carry him through.
Oh! If all these things, I knew!

—*Dorothy Abramson*

Untitled

Beyond the door
Lies treasure unspoken
Beyond the voice
Lies a song unsung
Beyond the eyes
Lies vision uncanny
Beyond the tears
Lies an ocean of dreams
Beyond the pain
Lies a thread of hope
Beyond the impossible
Lies the possibility
Beyond the inaudible
Lies a vast horizon
That horizon I must walk
Though the edge may cut
My feet.

—*Bethanie Yeakle*

The Resurrection Of Jesus

For you and me
Life he laid down
For us to see
God's love for humanity

We drink the cup
Eat the bread
For what he gave up
For us instead

Life laid he down
Received his crown
Now waits our reply
To show the reason why

We shouldn't live right
Fight the good fight
He fought so well
To keep us from hell

Now freed from sin
Prepare to live with him
In heaven together
Gloriously forever

—*Bion E. Smith*

Untitled

Ever-changing, never constant
Life's ups and downs.
Moods changing like a clock
Once brings promising happiness
Next, a plunge into desperation.
The many faces of courage,
Cowardice, physical strength
And weakness.
Living for today, in the past,
Or in a fantasy world.
The feelings and memories will remain
As will the dreams.
The clock keeps ticking.
There is no constant.

—*Danielle Cormier*

Together

Let us walk down the path, together.
Let us endure the pain, together.
Let us make the choices, together.
Let us fight our problems, together.
Let us live our lives, together.
Let us love one another, together.
Let us learn to love our God, together.

—*Bill Hooley*

Untitled

The twinkling
lights of the city
like stars
exploding
into dreams
for you
for me
The horizon
unlimited
The hush
of evening
descends

—*Barbara B. Taber*

Mystery

Western sun
lights the ragged crust
of rocked upward thrust
where wandering dark paths
move upon its eastern face.

There glows a pale mix
of dusky rose,
a streak of orange,
cascade of saffron shades,
a strength of evergreens.

Mountain of mysterious shadows
with mystic lettering
breathes antique messages
to quiet muse.

—*Estelle Jones Langston*

Resist

Stretching the lies
like a new rubber band
at first hard to pull
yet it eases with each try
amusement as it wears and tears
this white lie becomes blacker still
even harder to erase
though you try and try
harm grows and spreads with every trace
and someone will surely suffer
Stretching the lies
like a new rubber band
it kills as it grows
stretching from A to B and on
snapping and stinging just so
stay out of its way
as this deadly whip cracks
let the lie disappear quick
and resist the temptation to
stretch it ever again...

—*Brian J. Donovan*

Late In Life Love

Never thought I'd feel this way again,
Long ago forsaken promises of men
Buried deep, dreams of belonging
Unwilling to tolerate the longing.

Then you appeared upon the scene,
Awakening a long forgotten dream
Healing wounds with your embrace
Kissing smiles upon my face.

Praise to angels up above
Blessing us and this -
Our late in life love

—*Carleen Aviani*

You Bring Me

You bring me a smile to my day,
like the sun to shine on my face.
You bring me tenderness,
you bring me warmth, and with that
you bring me grace.

You send me stars of light,
to brighten even my darkest night sky.
You send me sweet secrets through
the misty night air, that turn to dew,
and make the weeping willows cry.

You make me beautiful clothing and
jewelry from the sea.
You make me a token of our love
that I'll carry forever with me.

You bring me these gifts of love
and faithfulness, such gifts I have
not had before.
You bring me these gifts,
and I thank you, and with that
you bring me more.

—*Adelle Bernard*

Dreams

Thoughts that possess me
    lingering quietly,
Softly reappear, upon
    my pillow nightly;
Dancing as a fairy,
    Darting to and fro...
Etching loves whispers,
    in an enchanting moon glow;
Thought that flee on
    gossamer wings,
Leaving stardust
    memories, in lovely
    peaceful dreams.

—*Ann Bea'ne-Hutchins*

There's A Place

Listen to the trees
Listen while they speak
Hear their song in your soul
Rest and do not seek

Take me away
To that special place of peace
Time is always slipping
One day the time will cease

Got to get down to the waterside
And fill my eyes with willows
The water rushes up to greet me
The leaves become my pillow.

—*Elisha D. Gilliland*

Love Is

Love is grand!
Love is sweet!
It knocks me off my feet!
Can't you hear my heart beat?

Love is a dove,
When it comes from above!
It can not become undone.

Love is blind!
When you find someone kind.
To bring you peace of mind!

—*Jamie Griego*

Nursery Rhyme for God's Children

Today

Hear Little Boy Blue blow his horn.
Little Bo-Peep has lost her sheep.
Their perishing we fear and mourn.
They're Laodicean. They're asleep.
Of the tribulation we'd warn
with "Malachi's Message" to reap
all sheep who Christ's knock do not scorn
and loving truth with fear so deep
at God's word tremble and are torn.
Courage, sheep! To a small flock leap
with hope to serve and be reborn
pillars and jewels, never to weep.

—*Genevieve Stocker*

Freebird

Fly high,
little freebird.
    Let the wind cast
upon your wings.
    Fly high
little freebird.
    Let the wind
be your guide.
    Fly high
little freebird.
    Fly high above the
stormy skies.
    Fly high
little freebird.
    Fly high, till I may
see you,
    again.

Fly high
    Freebird.
        —*C. C. Fox*

Milestones

What a joy as we grow older,
looking back upon the past,
every chapter, every blessing,
memories that will always last.

Many times we've been discouraged -
challenged, met at every turn,
disappointments without measure,
many things we had to learn.

Oh, so often were the stoplights,
signals, warnings, here and there
but the days that were before us,
filled with joys we have to share.

Precious moments, bits and pieces
fill our thoughts with times that pass
like a piece of treasured china,
silver spoons in crystal glass.

As we reach the grand finale,
may our courage never fail,
with our eyes on things eternal,
we can know that all is well.

—*Crayola Dawon Collins*

Seeds of Love

We plant a seed and watch it grow,
More seeds of love we need to sow,
For if more love we would give,
A happier life we would live.

—*Joanne A. Vogelsong*

On Top of the World

Looking out over the world,
looking over the edge.
hear the cries,
sense the tears,
see the fires burning,
feel the heartbeats beating;
know the hope.

Stars fall from the sky,
the moon shines down,
the wind and the clouds
whip around my head.
The ocean moves my soul;
riptides of sanity.
Mountaintops cradle my heart;

on top of the world,

looking over the edge.
        —*Daniel Firth*

What Is Love?

Love, makes life worthwhile.
Love gives it heart, gives it style.

Love is the light that leads us home
Love, can melt a heart of stone.

Love brings smiles of happy content.
Love is truly heaven sent.

Love can give the weary rest.
Love can pass all life's tests

For God is love.
        —*Hazel Quast*

Now Or Never

Your heart was meant to be broken
Love is bound to disappear,
While you're only left with sadness
And a river made of tears.
So why does God gives us a heart
And enable us to feel,
When it will soon be torn apart
And seem it wasn't real.
Maybe he's trying to tell us
That good things don't last forever,
And if we want to be truly happy
We must accept it now or never.

—*Christie Lee Frimml*

Love

Love grows,
Love shows,
Love knows when you are sad.

Love weeps,
Love speaks,
Love seeks to make you glad.

Just suppose you love your foes,
and you love those who make you sad.
Your love will grow and you will know,
that love will show through good and bad.

Love shares,
Love bears,
Love cares when you are down.

Love feels,
Love seals,
Love heals and wears a crown.

—*Betty M. Carr*

The Circle Of Love

One ideal make it strong
make it strong
make it bright
make it right
make it last.

You have one love,
make it sweet.
Give yourself with joy
to the one you love,
and the circle is complete.

—*Courtenaye Weeks Evans*

The Contented Red Cows

Red, red cows, you are; merrily,
merrily munching the grass away
on this most beautiful day
as I was happily a gazing
and you all were a grazing
with no worry at all
whether it be summer, winter,
spring or fall.

—*David L. Fant*

The Day I Turned My Back On Life

The day I turned my back on life,
Misfortune followed me.
She paved a thorny path of strife,
And led me out to sea.

A ship, unchartered and unmanned,
I drifted without aim.
I listed to a foreign land;
A soul without a name.

I wallowed in my self-esteem.
No man could prove me wrong.
Existence without hope or dream;
A sonnet without song.

But life with finite qualities,
Stopped short to give me pause
For time to face realities;
A duty without cause.

If I could but retract my ways,
I'd walk to hell and back;
I'd hasten to recount my days,
And ride a different track.

—*Helen C. Odom*

Could It Be?

Sharing these precious
   moments with you,
Fills a void in my life
   that I can't construe.

Could it be your radiant
   smile or your inquiring
   stare,
Could it be your latent
   sensuality or your
   cultured air.

Why ponder on things
   that the heart oft-times
   decree,
For a man and a woman
   like you and me.

—*Clarence Carter*

Validate

Tell me with your eyes
More than a look
Tell me with words, piercing words
Tell me with a touch
Your hands to mine

Help me erase what has been
Seared into my forehead
Free me from anticipation
Resignation has been my ally

Don't tell me I am beautiful
Don't tell me things that
Hold me in loyalty
To what should be left to go

I know who I am
For ten thousand years
I have known
Yet at this time I cannot
Be sure of what I want
Your answer to be
I keep moaning

—*Alvin K. Upton*

Springtime

Springtime is here.
Most beautiful time of year.
Tulips and daffodils so tall,
I sure do love them all.

Comes planting time again,
I am so anxious to begin,
To plant the seeds and watch them grow,
I sure do love them so.

The days grow long,
Birds sing their song,
Flowers bloom in full array,
I sure do love this day.

The flowers bloom in every hue,
From white to pink, from rose to blue,
I think that I will sing a song,
I sure am glad that I belong.

—*Elsie F. Weis*

Music

Music is played all the time
Music brings you peace of mind
Music bring tears to your eyes
Especially when it come from above

Music softens hard men heart
And it make you want to jump and shout
When you'll burden down it bring you out
Especially when it come from above

It makes you forget the hard times
And it makes happy in the good times
It's created with love
And it sails through the air like a dove

Music created with love
Especially when it come from above

—*Calvin Cooke*

Epitaph

The day has come. The final one.
My deed is done. I served her well,
Mother Earth, and in return she grants
Me peace and rest.
My contributions were great, my research
Valuable for I brought new meaning to
The life of science. The science of
Marine biology - my only love.
Dedication, hard work, and admiration
For the beauty of nature brought me
Recognition so previously unknown.
To the oceans I explored, to the whales
I saved, and to the sharks I betrayed,
My soul and the dust of my body will
Remain with you always - in harmony with
God and the miraculous wonders of the sea.

—*Heather L. Crawford*

My Love

Why is it when I look at you
My heart begins to race?
Why is it when I think of love
I see your handsome face?
Why do I always think of you
No matter glad or blue?
Why do I always fantasize
About my love for you?

Why is it that I smile
When I hear your name?
Why is it that without you here
Nothing's quite the same?

Often when I think of you,
A light goes on inside.
Please, don't let the darkness come.
Be here by my side!

—*Heidi Lyttle*

Man On The Moon

   I'm gazing upon you
   My heart is full
   I call your name
   Silence is my answer.

   The tears fill my eyes
And carve a path down my face.
The wind blows and darkness hides
The loneliness wrapped around me.

Way up high on my lonely hill
   It's just you and me
   Mr. Man on the Moon.
Please come sit with me.

   Time crawls by
And you just sit and shine.
Oh please Mr. Man on the Moon,
Won't you cry a tear for me?

—*Donna Fogle*

Nature's Joy

So far, so faraway, a blackbird's cry:
Morning stillness...
Sound of cooing:
Pigeons huddling on powerline...
Radiant pond:
Echoing in stillness,
A sparrow's voice...
Baritone voices!
Wild geese gliding round pond..
A water fowl's cry
lost in swelling murmur of trees.

—*Edward Nathan Stenbar*

Special

Truly special feelings have been few and far between.
For myself feelings were often cold and hard and mean.
But lady since there's you, they're better now it seems
        And you don't think you're special. . .

I've forgotten how to cry, but remembered all the pain.
Mostly life's been dim and grey, and at the worst of times it's
rained. Oh girl, now I'm feeling strong, instead of feeling
        drained. But no, you're nothing special. . .

After taking all the punches, you have to learn to fight.
Well I did, and it was easy, but it didn't make things right.
Holed up in a darkness, but now there's a little light
        What makes you so special. . .

Never really wanted bad things, I guess I wanted good. Just
got stuck in the in-between and never did the things I should.
Never really mattered, but now with you I think it could.
        You're an angel and one that's special. . .

If all is fair in love and war, this just isn't fair.
To have these feelings and not be able to show how much I care.
I know I'll never have you, it's the one thing I can't bear.
        You're so very special, we'd make a special pair. . .
    —*Mark A. Duckwiler*

Love

For some it comes and for some it goes.
For others, they may never even know.
But then there are those fortunate few,
such as me and you,
who discover that love can be true.

A teardrop.
A soft kiss.
A feeling not quite in the heart,
but also in the soul.
A tender moment.
A burning passion.
A life only for the fortunate few.

That is what I want to share with you.
With this poem I dedicate all of my love,
the love I have learned from you.
    —*Terrance A. Williams*

Happiness Is All I Want

So much pain in my heart,
For someone who doesn't want to
be by my part.

For you feel so lonely, down and out,
That's what my world is all about.

Shattered dreams of that little girl,
I have no means in this world.

You give your heart, your soul, your life,
For someone to cut you like a knife.

So left out like you don't fit,
One more person without a hit.

Life is strange in many ways,
But still we face the night and days.

A chance for happiness in my heart,
Oh Lord's that's all I want.
    —*Nancy Ruiz*

Is There Hope

Will there ever be any hope
For someone who is trying hard to cope

Are you willing to take a chance
On someone who can fill your life with romance

Can you ever forget your heart was broken
Can you hear unconditional love, when it's spoken

Are you ever going to open your heart
And let the happiness and love start

Tomorrow might be to late to decide
For your hopes may just run and hide

And then if you've waited to long
The love of your life may already be gone
    —*Linda Houston*

A Child's Prayer

Thank you God!
For taking, so very good care of me.
    Thank you God!
For everything, and bless my family.
    Thank you God!
For the heaven above, the stars, the earth, the seas.
From all the children of the world we pray this
    prayer to Thee.
God. Bless each child, that was born one day.
God. Bless each child, for their lives we must save.
God. Bless each child, that's with angels up above.
God. Bless each child, that give us joy, that
    give us love.
God. Bless each child, with a spirit so free.
God. Bless each child, for the guidance that
    we need.
God. Bless each child, with an innocent face.
God. Bless each child, from all Human Race.
Amen
    —*Linda C. Waleford*

Fall Review

Fall is such a glorious time of the year,
for the colors are bright and the sky so clear;

There's a nip in the air and a fading sun,
which hold's the promise of things to come;

Like jack-o-lanters and turkey time,
and lacy white snowflakes tumbling in rhyme;

Let's pause and give Mother Nature the respect she has due,
as she changes her costume for our fall review.
    —*Magda Lynn Miskulin*

Forbidden Feelings

As I watched her from afar, my admiration
for the graceful motions of her true beauty grows
beyond heartfelt. Alone and uninhibited she
serenely flows about, unaware of my forbidden
love. I imagine her flowery sensual scent mingling
with my primal and wanton lust. A mere glimpse
of her brings upon a carnal and fervent
arousal of my true self. Her icy blue eyes
ignite a deep and cherished passion in me.
My love is exposed in the tears I shed for the
true love I can never be with; for I live in
a world that shuns love.
    —*Ryan Broussard*

My Happiness Is Over

My happiness is over
  For tonight, I found out
    Where you have been going
     For the past few nights
      So I begin to think of what to do
       So finding my answer
        Ended my marriage with you

I followed you darling
  To see where you had gone
   I know it was a sneaking thing
    But I knew something was wrong
     I just could not let it keep going on
      I saw you tonight love, where you really belonged

With her you looked so happy
  With me you never belonged
   So when our divorce is granted
    She can become your wife
     I could not believe what people said
      I love you so much
       I had to see for my self
        —*Truda M. Little*

To Eternity

Take my hand and walk with me,
For we will find the path to eternity,

In this winding road we must travel,
Will not always smell of sweet roses,
But can be hard and rough as gravel.

The key to happiness lies within the love we share.
To be kept locked, the envy of all,
Is a beauty so true and rare.

In this beauty, we must keep the burning glow alive,
Within our eyes,
For to feed the fire to a never ending true love,
Where a spiritual magic lies,

While always believing in yourself and then me,
There will be nothing unconquered thinking not as one,
But as we.

For to share from the heart the same truth and respect.
Will give us everlasting pleasure, not hurt of neglect.
So......
Take my hand and walk with me, for as one, we will love to
eternity.

    —*Latricia P. O'Hagan*

Leaving

Do not cry for me, not a single tear
For when I am gone, memories will be dear
I'll look at your picture and sadly say,
"Maybe I'll see you again some day"
And somehow, if I do see you
You will remember my face too
We might just smile, and walk away
Or we might stop and talk that day
But inside my heart's a secret room
And it holds a friendship, like a tomb
Within that room will always be
The memories of you and me

    —*Tali Sherman-Hall*

Mother Earth

Gasping... Evil water with snow-tipped fingers of God's strength
forces liquid salt into his air
Deafening pleas, silent to the husky sand-yard savior with lighted
eyes chasing a darkened dream princess

Muscles and spirit exhaust from thronging
Prayer and apology for every lost dream in twenty-seven years

How long can you survive without assist from Mother Earth?
The trees she breeds for air to breathe and food from leaves
kissed by sunlight

Yet, it is Mother Earth, yes, in all her perfected fury
who claims this theft of soul with her lean shattering waves
CONSTANT..... ABSORBING..... CONSUMING...

I see his reflection shine at midnight
    —*Renee White*

Never Deprive Anyone Of Hope

Every now and then something or someone
Forces me to stop what I'm doing, and reflect.
Instantly, a vivid memory comes to life,
On a huge, drive - in movie sized screen in my mind. This has
gone on all my life, and I can't say I'm used to it yet!

The big screen in my mind just replayed a conversation,
That I as a young boy once had with my Dad.
He said "Never deprive anyone of hope my son,
Because hope may be all he or she has".

My father felt strongly that a passionate belief
In a lifelong dream, is precious!
My Dad called it cruel to have hope taken away.
He said that the fulfillment of such dreams was priceless.
I've since learned that heartache is the price you must pay.

I still have high hopes despite life's heartaches,
And for what am I hoping tonight?
That one day a young boy will reflect back on a conversation,
That his Dad once had, with his Dad, who said:
"Never deprive anyone of hope my son,
Because hope may be all he or she has"...

In Memory of Fred Wall
    —*Mike Wall*

In Memory Of My Daughter

Soft fall the snow flakes, covering the ground,
forming a blanket on top of a mound.
Where lies the gift, that God sweetly keeps
safe as the storm rages on as she sleeps
    —*Robert B. Petrick*

Cornering The Paper Market

I am weary of bureaucratic systems,
forms, organizational ghettos of voluminous
memos bereft of meaning - I am
Sick of setting mightily mechanisms
that Shriek at some un Godly hour
and rush me into washing, dressing,
dashing, down filth encrusted tunnels
swarming with multitudes of human
drones plodding toward their cubicles
of disciplined enslavement to earn
daily bread each at appointed hours
return to boxed-in prisons for the
required tune - until the gang starts
the round for another day's survivals!
I would chuck it all to string
bright colored heads and sane
    —*Trieste Kildoyle*

Friends...

Friends until the sun shines no longer upon us.
Friends until the wind blows no more.
Friends until the earth is nowhere to be found.
Friends to be seen, until we depart from earth to heaven.
My friends are me.
My friends are my life.
My friends will always be here until here is no more light.
Friends.

—*Lisa Murphy*

Bouquet

As dusk's pastel curtain falls the melody is light—
frolic and skip in
airy steps with
the gentle rocking of
golden autumn leaves and
slow deliberate spreading of
sanguine petals;

The flower begins to bloom

The dance becomes desperate in night's deep throat—
the music has maddened to
a howling wind
gamboling bodies vibrate and
stretch sweat shiny faces heavenward;

Dew sparkles on the blossom

Dawn drinks away the dark
the tune fades in the light—
going sweetly
falling like spring rain
and a silky snow of talcum powder;

She sleeps in her blanket of foliage

—*Lauren Seidman*

Building A Dream

What makes a dream, from where's it fed;
    from a caring heart or thinking head?

What turns it on, what makes it start.
    How do we then become a part

Of this new vision in our mind
    is it just for me, or all mankind.

I'd like to think it's shared by you
    and not for me or just a few.

Let's dream and plan, day and night
    let's build it strong and make it bright.

A place to worship God, our King
    to learn His word and grandly sing

A church! Our dream for all of you,
    Come help us make the dream come true.

—*Peter Gardner*

Requiem For A Friend

    Your gentle ways and soft approach to me,
gave me confidence, I felt good inside, you see.
    I suddenly felt that I belonged;
part of the team, a friend, not to be wronged.
It wasn't easy for me, to try to be a friend.
I've been hurt before and now it's at an end.
Your untimely departure will leave a void in me.
I shall remember your kindness for all eternity.

—*Lawrence Spirio*

Collection

Oh, how we love to collect things
From cards of the diamond, to diamond rings
Stuff of our fathers, articles of kings
Oh, how we love to collect things

Oh, how we love to collect things
To keep them forever, for the joy that it brings
As the words of a poet, or a tenor that sings
Yes, we love to collect things

Oh, how we love our collections to grow
They pile up quickly, as a brisk winter's snow
Sentiments come, as realities go
But ho, how we love our collections to grow

Oh, how we love to see children grow tall
With rulers and pencils, we mark up the wall
A collection of lines, ever since they were small
No paint in the universe covers them all

Oh, how we treat our old photos with care
A collection of memories, made unaware
We smile at the changes in clothing and hair
And glad the old family camera was there

—*Robert G. McKeag*

The Eyes I See Through

The violence I heard, every sound,
From crying eyes to dying carnals and sisters.
At night my dreams lead me to the lonely eyes
That I seek to meet.
I see two paths, one to hell, one to salvation.
But for these eyes are blind and go ahead living with no
    determination.
What I saw through those eyes was the Barrio, Pachucos,
The Cholas, one in particular named Lagrimas.
Salvation was beautiful holmes.
A life with a holy soul, with nothing to blame.
They had it made easy.
But in that dream I realized those lonely eyes
I sought to meet holmes, they were the eyes of only one
And that was me. I remember being asked by my familia
If I cared whether I lived or died. I said no.
Challe, I think back esa I do care. I guess it's too late,
I guess I'll have to learn the hard way.

—*Lagrimas Healey*

Anonymous

A book of poetry lay in my hands
From distant times and ancient lands
Names of poets who inherited the earth
Their sweetened words of romance did birth
Touched our souls and shared their pain
Their words now eternal their hurt not in vain
But of the poems that touched me so deep
The ones upon my heart I keep
The quotes to bring me strength today
That chase my troubled thoughts away
Were the quiet souls their identity hid
Glory they denounced the fame they rid
Inspired words, not knowing where they came
Their brilliance masked from a secret name
Their only trace of immortality
A single word stealing eternity
A final request of humble sacrifice
Noble intentions with an empty price
A gift to the world, bowing in generous
They signed their poems anonymous.

—*Shannon Gregory*

Slow To Grow, Slow To Die

Of all the flowers in the garden, the rose caught my eye -
From its seed the plant grew, slowly but surely, although it
   seemed to care how fast the others grew.
The rose took in every ray of sun, every drop of water and
   every breath of fresh air.
If you watched closely enough,
   you'd think it was gaining knowledge.
The rose took on its own shape, and at full bloom,
   was as pretty as the other flowers.
But this rose was special!
It has almost a gentleness to it,
   almost a human characteristic.
At winter, when all the flowers had to die,
   The rose, the beautiful rose,
      was the last to give up its life to the harsh death wind!

    —*Sabeen Ann Edwin*

The Plum Tree

I live each year to see the plum tree bloom,
From my room I just saw a blue jay hopping in its branches
It is at its peek today.
Tomorrow it will start snowing white petals
Heralding spring.
I live each your to see the plum tree bloom
Hope springs eternal from
His empty tomb.

    —*Rosemary McMahon*

The Principal People

He was strong and brave, his skin was red.
From natures wealth his people fed.
They lived in places full and green.
The air was pure their water clean.

Their lives were full, their land knew peace.
Time was short; it all would cease.
The civilized intruders came.
Life could never be the same.

The white man brought a better way.
They could not trust the things he'd say.
He took their food, their lives, their land;
And reduced them to a meager band.

Today the sleeping giant wakes;
And trains to find the skills it takes.
We'll see the Indian Phoenix rise,
And soar with eagles in the skies.

    —*Roger Paul Poe*

Resident Robins

Resident Robins are ready to roam
From our yards waving tree tops, snug next, summer home.
We'd watch in the spring days, harried flights as they tried,
Worms dangling from beaks, to fill mouths opened wide.
We'd look for and found broken eggshells, robin blue,
As fledglings left nests for the bigger world too;
Watched puzzled youngsters learning the magical trick
Of listening, listening, then pouncing so quick.
Who's telling our robins the leaves soon will go?
Is it heard in the music of breezes murmured low?
Do they whisper to the youngsters so they too will know
To flee toward the southward, escaping our snow?
Whatever it is I will wish them good flights,
And will miss them and await them during the long winter
nights.

    —*Virginia H. Hurley*

Michigan Weather

The weather in Michigan is subject to change.
From scorching to freezing, indeed the whole range.
One day it's hot, the next day it's cold.
The one thing it's good for is that old common cold.

The weekend is nearing with the relief that we seek.
But the weather has changed, it's the worst of the week.
The temperature's falling and it sure looks like snow.
About all that's left is for that north wind to blow.

A saying in Michigan may seen strange to you,
But, the longer your residence, the more it seems true.
If you don't like the weather, stick around it will change.
As a long time resident, I've seen the whole range.

We listen to the weather before bedding each night.
Then, we lay out our clothes for tomorrow, tonight
But the most accurate and dependable forecaster I know,
Is the aching that occurs in my wife's big toe.

    —*Lynn R. Hawker*

Untitled

He was eighteen, and a handsome young man;
From the way he dressed, to his interesting van.
He came by one day, with a flower in hand;
Asked me to love him, and no other man.
So I gave him my heart, one hundred percent;
And was willing to go wherever he went.
We spent hours together, just laughing and talking;
And most summer nights, on the beach we'd go walking.
A most perfect couple, we did seem to be;
And instead of two, there soon would be three.
But after awhile the spark seemed to die;
We started to fight, and he started to lie.
He was drunk all the time, he was mean and cruel;
It made him do things, he didn't do as a rule.
After sometime, I couldn't take anymore;
I turned on my heals, and walked out the door.
That's the last time I have ever seem him;
I just hope given time, this pain will grow dim.

    —*Michelle M. Reeves*

Steps In Your Mind

As you watch from your seat
from your eyes to their feet
Each one's hair in a bun as they leap one by one
In your mind—in your mind.
They're elegant in pink turn as fast as you blink
Twirl and twist in the night as you watch them take flight
In your mind—in your mind.
They stand firm on their toes
as they strike a graceful pose
Dancing right on the beat
pointing and flexing their feet
In your mind—in your mind.
The steps in your mind drift on and on
Until the show's over and the spotlight is gone.
Encore..........

    —*Lauren Thurm*

The Son's Gift Of The Sun

    The caress of the Sun
  Glides across the enfeebled woman
  As she gratefully accepts its source.
For it is the gossamer radiance of the Son
    Who penetrates the void
    Of the cloistered recluse.

    —*Melinda K. Blade*

Goodbye To Yesterday

Time has kept me still,
    frozen in a world of yesterday.
A world that is no longer mine,
    a world that is no more.
People want to let go of the past,
    I want to keep it alive, forever.
I try to live in a world of today,
    but I can't bear to hear the words;
        Goodbye to yesterday.

Time goes on, yet I still linger in the past.
Hoping that this feeling will not last.
Don't want to let go, though I know that I must.
The memories and pictures will collect all the dust.

Memories will never fade.
Unlike the pictures taken of a brief moment in time.
I hope I shall never forget them.
Throughout all the years, all the memories,
    I have no regrets.
I just don't want to say;
    Goodbye to yesterday.
        —Lisa Ann Hitt

I Call You Lady

A passionate flower an untamed storm,
full of surprises never the norm.

Different as night and day subtle to the touch,
fragrance abound, laughter, nonsense, and such.

    I call you lady
Glue, mortar, cement describes you to a "T",
steadfast and unmovable, with a heart as vast
as the largest sea.

Compelled by your nature down a dark and sometimes
lonely path, with one thousand cycles each as complexed
as the next, some even feel your wrath.

    I call you lady
Concave, smooth, pleasing to the eye,
unmasked beauty in which men vie.

A canvas revealing the colours of all nationalities,
a strong mind to cope even the most taxing of
rationalities. Yet still I call you lady!!!!
    —Nathaniel Rhodes

In The Mind's Eye

The tea I sipped last night was warmer,
fuller than the one the night before,
though each had come from one packet.
I stopped to wonder, as the color was the same,
the cup did not vary, why the taste abruptly changed.
Something in my mind's eye perceived the latter in ways
the former lacked; perhaps it was my daughters growing up,
my wife's coming to grips with things,
or my cat's unwavering trust in master.
Then again, maybe I've simply mellowed.
Staring straight at my cup, once half empty,
now brimming with pride,
I leaned forward and savored every drop.

    —Murray Cohen

The Germ Of My Birth

A dream it was, shadows bursting.
Galaxies far and near,
Embracing universes, suns, unfolding stars.

What was this dream? This rainbow? This blood?
this bone? This crying wound?
No tower small reaches high, or yet spires to the eye,
as one small miracle found in some beating heart.

We cried, I never knew why.
So graceful a shabbiness, grew beyond the stars,
just around the corner, from a broken jar.

It was I, yet many the voice shouting at the edge,
rising high from the ashes, shaping burning lips into eyes.

At last the world Sparkles, cheeks fresh and black,
sprays forth twinkling glass, falling harshly on the earth.

As before, eons, eons, in the mists of forgotten time.
The horn full, nearly bursting,
Spewed forth the germ of my creation.
        —Richard D. Valentine

Mystery Unicorn

Standing still in the forest green,
Gazing upon the moonlit sky,
Seeking a destiny unknown to you,
Curiosity leads you on.

Ground does break beneath your feet,
Startled by the sound,
Soon you arise again,
With feet put back on solid ground.

With a prideful walk you continue the journey
Determined to fulfill your dream.
Truly strong in spirit, you are,
And a leader you shall be.
    —Paula D. Jacobs

Those Lacy Put-Ons

Those lacy put-ons called Valentines
generally have a red background in the shape
of a heart on which is depicted a Cupid
With bow and arrow. Girls receive them with
giggling excitement.
While oohing and ahing they look for the signature.
On seeing the same the recipient knows right
off if it's for real or if it's a "put-on".
The name might cause shimmering tremors of
delight and joyous beating of the heart.
A romance might bloom. There might be an
engagement and a wedding. After that —
well, for birthday or anniversary she
might receive another lacy put-on.
A lacy put-on of a different kind.
They call it lingerie.
    —N. Battenburg

Ghost Travelers

I watch the clouds in sepulchral forms.
Ghost travelers on a grey sea of twilight.
Their destination unknown; possibly
their life short-lived.
Floating as the day turns to night.
Eerily, they pass by my window.
A loneliness sinks into my soul.
Their end is a mystery.
Ghost travelers as on they roll.
    —Sherri Teed-Baker

Significance

"Are you Swiss, French, Irish, Hispanic, Portuguese, Mexican,
German, English, American?" he asked.
"I was born in Indiana," she replied.
"What country is that?" he asked, as he pulled a switch blade
from his pocket. She looked at his age-old black leather jacket
wondering who had previously worn it, what happened to its
sleeves? Did he cut them off at the shoulder with his blade?
she observed that he was wearing black military boots.
his left ear was pierced with a safety pin.
she looked into his black malevolent shifty eyes, she could see
no pupils. He was cutting his finger nails with the knife,
slicing the white part with a great precision,
"what nationality are you?" he yelled.
"I was born in America; the land of freedom, opportunity,
choice." "I did not decide what country to have my birth,
I was just born, no matter." "I do not know we all live under
the same sky, rely on the same sun, romance the same moon,"
she diligently replied, hoping he would not sense her fright.
he put his long jagged knife in his pocket.
not today he thought, no killing today.

—*Susan Kersch*

Untitled

If I had wings, I'd fly through the sky.
Gliding and gliding up the mountains high.
To be free as a bird, without any care
Flying through the clouds, until I get there.
I would not look down, but head straight up,
To where the clouds meet the sky, without disrupt.
I'd fly up too heaven where I could be free,
To see the Lord Jesus, and he could see me.
And would not come down, but glide all day.
And when I was tired I'd stop to pray.
Lord look down on the earth with love and care,
And cover your people everywhere.
So that they all can one day be free,
To glide all day long in the heavens with me.

—*Ruth D. Simpson*

To Sherlock

Red fur edged with gold
Glistening in the sun
Pink nose, white whiskers
Lifted to sniff the breeze

A sudden noise
Startled eyes
It's all right
Just one of his people entering the room

He sits in the window, head held high
Majestic for all the world to see
All he owns is in view

Another noise
It's just a bird alighting on the rail
Breezes ripple his fur

He jumps to the floor
A stop to fling a favorite toy into the air
He leaps like a ballet dance after it

And then, another leap
Back upon the window sill
He will live there, and in my heart, forever

—*Patricia M. Costanzo*

God's Flower

Once God placed a little seed so gently on the ground.
God made the clouds grow dark. He made the rain come down.

God's little seed soaked up the rain and swelled up big and
    round.
It burst into a little plant, all nestled in the ground.

God sent sunshine day after day, upon His little plant.
And reaching for the heavens above, up through the ground it
    went.

Up, up, up, it stretched and stretched, until it got so tall.
Leaves began to blossom. A bud appeared so small.

God richly dressed this little bud in colorful attire.
And in God's time, low and behold, His bud became a flower.

God's flower, dancing in its beauty,
Caught a young child's eye.
She touched and smelled and picked it,
As she went skipping by.

Toward home she ran so swiftly,
So anxious to get there.
She kissed her mother's cheek
And gave God's flower to her.

—*Lorna Minge*

Our Little Lad

Fair of face and freckled nose, flaxen hair that shone like
    gold happy smile and disposition.
        Vivid blue eyes. Surely a picture to behold.
    Little brown body tanned gently from the sun.
        Then when he was eight years old
He said to me, "What did you do in the olden days"?,
        And I said to him, "You mean
    When knights were bold and brave and strong,
        Riding on horses in gay regalia,
    Their ladies resplendent in attire most beautiful,
        Pointed hats with ninon floating from them,
        Handkerchiefs waving in the breeze"?
One day when feeling very tired, I said to him, "I feel like
        the last rose of summer",
    His answer was, it is often the most beautiful.
Another day when I thought my little holly tree would never
        bloom, I bemoaned the thought to him.
I awoke the next day, to a neat little tree, just covered with
    berries, red and bright, what a beautiful sight!
        The poor cotoneaster had lost its fight.

—*Mildred Dickens*

You Wonder Why?

When you sit back and look at your friends that are now
gone and you wonder why you lived so long
    I'll tell you why and you probably already know. It's
because you're blessed. You're a wonderful person never
rehearsing to do the things you do, you're just beautiful being
you.
    You came to keep us when nobody else would, and I know you
did that because you felt you should. You risked your life
when you did that for us and we really love you and in that you
can trust.
    You have so many talents, I remember when you came to our
church and sang, you even recited a poem. And the clothes you
used to make and especially that pie and pound cake.

    I know you're very thankful for your life and I can just bet
you were a wonderful wife. You had nine children and they are
all grown and they have children and their children had some of
their own. So you're not only a mother you're a grandmother,
and a great grandmother, but to me you're the greatest
grandmother. And you wonder why you lived so long? As big as
your heart is you'll always be strong.

—*Sharae Ellis*

Our Past

When I first saw you I thought we were
gonna last forever...

If you see me crying, I wonder if you even
care...

If you see no happiness in me, I wonder if
you even regret it...

As I close my eyes I see you and only you
whispering in my ear, (I will love you no matter what).

I promise myself I would bring back our love,
but it never quite came true...

I sit under the stars with no one since
you were gone...

Every time a star shines I see our past...

As much fun we have then will bring back
memories that will soon fade away...

As soon as you read this I hope you will
say...

Let our past and our love last forever,
"I miss you!"

—*Pang Fang*

I'm Moving On

I tried my best to give you love, all I
got was pushed and shoved.

I thought you were the man for me, but now
I see you didn't want to be.

I gave you my heart and my soul, but to you
I was just another accomplished goal.

I'm not a habit you can pick up or down,
I have feelings also, I may not always be around.

I've done all I can do, and said all I can say,
all you have done was pushed me away.

You said that you loved me, and would stick
by my side, after the sweetness wore off, they
were only sugar coated lies.

I'm tired of singing the same ole song, it's
about time I be moving on.

—*Phyllis Kelly*

The Big Blue Stroller

Kelli is little and Amber is big
Grandma bought them a stroller, oh what a rig
Kelli can lay on a bed in the back
We'll go for a ride while she's taking a nap
Amber can ride in the front, on her seat
We'll go for a ride that will be hard to beat
What a wonderful stroller, it's big and it's blue
I'll bet you just wish you could ride in it too
We'll roll along Dixon and up Third Avenue
Then come back down Main, in a circle we'll go
Going by Uncle Carls foxy will bark
We may see a rabbit if it's getting dark
We'll stop in at Grandma's just to say Hi
Get some ice cream from Grandpa before we say bye
As we roll along in the stroller we'll sing
That big beautiful stroller, what a wonderful thing.

—*Leslie J. Thompson*

The Detroit Pistons

This is a little poem for our Detroit Pistons too, they are a
great basketball team true. Each and the other players are so
very fine, make those baskets each and almost every time.

Boy they are big and very strong and tall, and the baskets they
try to make, each one and all. Their coach and all the players
too, get in to win, and we all cheer for you.

You are in the lead, smiles on your face, go in to win, every
time no one can take your place. A free throw you are up for
true, and the basket is made forever more too.

All your families are there at your game, your wife, daughter,
son are glad they came. You are a great basketball team, and
hear the crowd cheer and scream.

Fast are your plays right under their nose, for your guys are
all great players, of course pros! In the past the
championship you have won, a great team you are loved by your
daughter and son.

Each and every year, you are so very fine, and basket after
basket, make the team I call mine. Be very thankful to God,
and your parents too, and of course your wife and family,
all true and true.

—*Sharon R. Walker*

Shades of Autumn

Many different shades of Autumn
Greens and browns and golden hues
Melt into the sky, a perfect fuse.

Still a few apples hang on the trees
Weeping willows bending their knees.

Bundles of hay neatly stacked in a row
Tractor is warming, all ready to go.

Windmills are turning, a vigorous rate
Turkeys aren't prancing, do they know of their fate?

You feel very thankful, as you look 'cross the field
Maybe the willows, thank God, for the yield.

—*Theodore J. Jahn*

Or

"Be not afraid" - You said. I try.
Grey shoulders of hills are hiding the road
dry and long.
My dead brother,
you are on the road already.
White deer flashed among the old trees,
and stars are flying from its antlers...
Maybe I was not born yet,
or the world had lost me once.

—*Vera Hatcher*

Untitled

Waves run into rocks
Gulls beg to be fed by the sun.

Shells, gagged by Chance
from sharing the secrets of the sea,
sing...
  Pink
  Smooth
  Yellow
  Sharp

Sparkling eyes see the symphony of the world, and dance!

—*Mari Palou*

Dylan's First Birthday

Dylan, today you're turning one year old,
Growing fast and learning quickly - I'm told,
To your family, you're far more precious than gold.

We worried for a while about your rough start,
But to this family, you're a very special part
And you've worked your way into everyone's heart.

During the next twelve months you'll do a lot more,
Walking, running, and falling, and getting sore,
You'll even learn how to open a door.

You'll keep Mom and Dad quite busy - I am sure,
And as they watch your energy level mature
They'll wonder, "How much more of this can we endure"?

There are so many things to look forward to -
Everything you learn will be exciting and new,
Not only to yourself, but for Mom and Dad, too!

There will be many funny things for Mom to record,
Some times should be remembered, some should be ignored,
Either way, into you, lots of love will be poured.

Although you won't remember this special day, today —
And always, we will pray for God to lead you in His way.
   —Lori O'Donnell

When Grandpa Died

W here has he gone?
H eaven up there? He has left the
E arth. Always calling,
N ever falling.

G one to where he can
R un under the sun
A nd sit under a
N earby tree.
D arkness never will
P enetrate the gates of
A beautiful place as heaven.

D eath is not the end.
I n the sky he soars.
E ternity is always there.
D ead he may be, but he is always with me.

   —Rebecca L. Lais

Children

C - Christ, for He made all His children.
H - Heart, sometimes they make us happy or sad, mostly proud.
I - Ideals, they have for their lives and their families.
L - Love, that they give us that fulfill our life.
D - Dreams, watching them grow.
R - Restless nights, at times, as they grew up.
E - Enjoying each child, watching them make their dreams come
   true.
N - Never being to lonely, for they might call or come over,
   saying hi mom and dad!
   —Linda Strick

River Of Tears

   My pain feels like a river flowing
hard and dangerous through my body.
   As I weep, the waterfall of salty
tears cascades down my face and plunges
into a dark emptiness.
   You don't care if my river floods
and soon I will drown in my grief.
   My river is freezing and I am trapped.
You can see me, but you don't try to
break my fragile ice and set me free.
   Maybe when spring arrives I will
thaw and be happy again.

   —Shannon Ryan

Senses Of My Mom

I see her big round blue eyes, I see her big, fluffy brown
   hair. I see her beautiful, pink nail polish.
I see her big lips covered with lipstick, stretched in a happy
   smile. And most of all, I see her pretty face.

I hear her vacuuming right before she leaves her work.
   I hear her pumps on the kitchen floor when she is making my
   breakfast.
I hear the pump of her perfume, the sound of her curlers and
   the sound of her voice when dinner is ready.

I love the taste of her homemade pies and
   the taste of her brownies that make me feel warm all over.
I also love the special Thanksgiving dinners that she makes.

I feel her warm hugs and kisses on cold nights.
   I feel the warm kitchen after she cooks dinner.

I smell her beautiful perfume in the morning. I smell
   her breakfast on the weekends, that drag me out of bed.
I smell her kitchen that smells like all the meals that she
   makes.

All of this reminds me of how much I love her.

Happy Mother's Day!
   —Nicole Anne Thomas

Before The Fall

Green gold of August
hangs hot in the air still
a knowing of crispness

Late season showers
mold clouds in blues and blacks
edged with silent iridescent fireworks
and distant mountain lightning flashes

In the lay of rainlight glow
with fresh wet smell of earth
and grass and pine tree bark
children play kickball in the shiny street
and run the last of their merry mighty races
chasing summer
   —Stephani Pfau

The Journey

The golden sun holding the ebony darkness of a summer night
Happiness of another time another place joining laughter on
   changing winds
Sendings from star ships playing hide and seek with willow the
   wisps of yesterdays and tomorrows
In emerald forests winged messengers lead into shadowy woods
   beyond darkening clouds
The poignant songs of a meadow lark in the distance
Waves merging with footprints into silver sands
An indistinguishable candle flickers changing into a crystal
   brilliance of ruby and jade on a mysterious journey ever
   renewing

Spirits of universal love holding rainbows of many colored
   lights
   Loving, loving beyond the beyond.
   —Ruby M. Burns

A Child

A child lay so innocently in his bed,
Happy, pleasant thoughts, going through
   his head.
"I love you, I love you", his mother said.

Then the little boy, sadly, went away.
His mother knew not where he went that day.
All she could do was pray and pray.

The little boy had been taken from his room;
His mother's life was now full of gloom.
She wondered if her little son was doomed.

Then one day she got a call on the phone;
The police found the boy wandering about alone.
Soon after, they brought him home.

The little boy's mother had gotten such a scare,
Leave his bedroom window unlocked again, she
   did not dare.
She never again wanted to experience such a
   nightmare.

      —*Theresa Williams*

Journey

Journey through love a life time quest,
Has stops and torns subtle highs at best!
Moments of happiness lots of pain,
Desperate tasks searches in vain!

Journey through love the sordid twists,
Visions of love a heart's at risk!
Your tears are plenty in silence you moan,
Heartache to heartbreak often you're alone!

Journey through love a life time quest,
You travel wearily no time for rest!
Journey through love entrapped in its mist,
Hold on to your dream of wedded bliss!

      —*Robert A. Thomas*

Within Love's Garden Wall

The sunlight of your caring has stirred my sleeping heart
Has warmed my mind with sweet sunshine
   and feelings to impart.

The sunlight of your sharing, like warm rays from above
Sends tender roots and fragile shoots
   growing into love.

Slowly our bonds will strengthen with spring rains gentle fall
Give nourishment, encouragement
   within love's garden wall.

The sunlight of your caring, kind words to make roots strong
Brings into flower love's saving power
   strengthening our bond.

The sunlight of your sharing breaks through on cloud-filled
   morns
Through hurricanes and bitter pains
   among life's prickly thorns.

And when our feelings blossom, and turn we to love's call
We'll share the hours 'neath love's sweet bowers
   within love's garden wall.

      —*Paul F. Hernandez*

"This Bleak And Hatred Place"

Take me away from this bleak and hatred place.
For I can stand no more of my heart to ache.
   I can see beyond the path so clear
I reach out to touch but it disappears.
   Why should I stay in this forsaken
Place when all of my fears leak and escape
   Take my hand lead me away from
this bleak and hatred place.

      —*Tracey Parmley*

For My Grandsons, Cameron And Philip

Two little boys so very new
Have entered life's doorway
To learn of you.

Though they have known as one or two
Clasped close to your breast
As one with you.

Now in their bright worldly eyes there appears
Their own Daddy's smile
And their own Mommy's tears.

Soon little fingers sand grains will caress
And squashy pink worms
Their soft toes will press.

At holiday time they'll have fun with the cousins
And as years tumble on
There'll be baseball and "love-ins."

They'll learn how to share and to love and to care
These are your gifts
To our precious pair.

      —*Mary Lauhoff Brecht*

Autumntime

Football games and Halloween fun,
Hayride parties when Autumn's begun.
Wiener roasts and painted leaves.
Birds in flight, swift blowing breeze,
It's Autumntime... Autumntime again!

Blaze in the fireplace, rakes in the yard,
Grass has withered, the lawn mower's retired,
Bonfires burning and frost on the ground,
Dark clouds above, the cool rain's sound,
It's Autumntime... Autumntime again!

Sounds of the river more impatient seems,
Mem'ries of Summer wrapped up in dreams,
Thanksgiving dinners and first snow fall,
Coming of Winter brings shivers from all,
It's Autumntime... Autumntime again!

      —*S. R. Silverman*

Seasons Of Life

Of hopes, and of dreams,
Happiness comes from above you
Like the branches of a tall maple
Bringing forth smiles of shade and comfort
To the green lawn below.
The grass matures through the Summer.
New experiences and new shadows
Cast down upon it until Autumn
As the leaves gently cover
The lawn, it calmly fades.
It becomes dormant in winter.

      —*Marc W. Estes*

Time Passed Him By.

Depression and dust bowl and World War II
He did have troubles, more than a few!
When he hit Normandy Beach in forty four,
His days were numbered, there might be no more,
He did his best like a good soldier should
He then raised a family as well as he could.
He lived with the same wife for fifty two years,
Now she is gone and there is headache and tears,
His only son died at age twenty eight.
His daughter lives in a distant state.
He should have married first love, instead of chasing fame,
And sired five sons to bear his name,
His first love could walk by with never a glance,
Cause these never was a flaming romance.
Too shy as a youth to let it be known,
That he was ready to start a home,
So we bury his now, don't shed any tears!
He lived a total of eighty good years.

—*Russell L. Kelch*

The Giraffe

By heck! but the giraffe, has a long neck.
He eats leaves off trees with ease,
But just think!
He has trouble getting a drink.
He puts his legs in a stance,
That would rip up the seat of his pants,
(If he wore pants)
But be glad that he's wearing a coat
Of orange and black plaid.
And surprise!
There's a brush at the end of his tail,
To shoo off the flies.
With his long legs and ungainly stride,
No one can possibly ride such a beast,
No one has (while I'm looking) at least.

—*Virginia L. Randall*

The Sea Is My Lover

The sea is my lover, he holds me, rocks me.
He gives me the security I need and is my
sanity, my peace of mind.
You have taken All my chances for love away,
but I won't let you take this one.
The sea, is the only one who understands my
loneliness and needs.
The sea, understands and helps me forget
the hurt for awhile.
The sea, cools me with tender touch and lets
me know that with him, I'm need no one.

—*Maxine Mora*

Content In Death

Although I turned my back on death,
He kept pursuing me.
His haunting smile of contempt I felt but did not see.
Like a love untrue, he came to me
In the middle of an unsuspecting night.
I gave him what he wanted; it did no good to fight.
His presence filled my being although I knew he wasn't there.
His absence gave a rarity, a grief I could not bear.
He left me then to wander over whatever hills he might
And bade my mind to ponder on the mysteries of light.
Of all my heart's best feelings, of all my soul's remains;
The content of life is love,
The significance of death the same.

—*Marlene J. Knoll*

Sam Byrd Psalm

Sam Byrd is my Pro, I shall not want.
He maketh me to practice in green pastures;
He keepeth me out of still waters; he restoreth my swing.
He leadeth me in paths of the fairways
For his name sake.

Yea, though I drive through the valley of rough and bunkers,
I will fear no shot.
For thou art with me;
My Putter and my Driver, they comfort me.
Thou preparest my bets before me in the presence of mine
enemies.
Thou annointest my ball with a putter that overflows into the cup.
Surely good days and low scores shall follow me,
All the days of my life, and I shall play on the
Course of the Lord forever.

—*Walker Reynolds, Jr.*

A Little Friend

I let a spider live today, I could net end his life.
He might have had a family, with a sweet and loving wife.

He had crawled across my drawing board, perhaps to view my art.
He may know some would be artist, that was looking for a start.

After all, it takes a talent, to spin a web of beauty.
And something that is functional, to provide a daily booty.

I let this spider live, I don't like to take a life.
Perhaps he wanted to be friend me, and lessen his world of strife.

I thought if I knew him better, he might take me for a spin.
So I asked him where did he reside, he said, "It's Clifton Webb I
  live in."

I told him that in human life, of the tangled webs we weave.
He agreed t'would be a better place, if we dared not to deceive.

We thought we'd talk again real soon, there's so much we've both
  to give.
I made a little friend today, when I let this spider live.

—*Ray Woodward*

The Old Gardener

Rain or sunshine he hobbles around the garden
He passes the dew-covered roses and smiles at their
beauty in the morning sun
Their fragrance reminded him of happy years too
swiftly gone
Youth was a dream it seemed
He looked at his weather-beaten old hands and wondered
if he were ever young
Memories came flooding into his mind
A tear fell as he remembered the outreaching of his
love so many years ago
He picked a faded rose and held it tenderly against
his wet cheek
The young may have their youth but he has his
treasured memories

—*Loretta McClure*

Ode To A Humble Man

For lack of a job and too honest to steal
He was one of the many down at the heel.
Neatly dressed though quite threadbare
(As the worn out cover of a very old chair)
He trudged each day a different route
For the sidewalk pickings of abandoned loot
And earned enough in this humble way
To meet his needs from day to day.

Hats off to you, dear little man
Declining to mooch from Uncle Sam.

—*Rose Loewinger*

Does Jesus Care?

I know my Savior does care!
He sees constantly all my affairs,
Day or night He watches over me
This is what we all can ever see.

He cares in my ills and in my sorrow
He tells me, "My child there's a Tomorrow."
Exercise your patience, as you move, on,
This is my process to prepare you for dawn.

Whenever trouble or tragedy hits you hard
Do not feel ever, living is absurd,
Remember there is sunshine beyond, cloud
Telling me, "Hang on and sing my love aloud."

Suffering of pain is God's chosen method
To remove our scar and our odd,
Purifying us to turn into precious gold
So in time of ease, we shall not be sold.

He cares for me from my blessed birth
Until I say, "Bye" to my family on earth,
He is gone to prepare for me a place
So I may live with him in his grace.

—*Nirmal C. Dewri*

A Long Time Ago

A long time ago in a little town
He was so serious, she was a clown
But there was an attraction, it was strong
He thought it was right, she thought it was wrong
He said it was love, she couldn't see how
He wanted her then, she said not right now
It hurt him so much, and it hurt her too
Because she realized what she put him through
She realized the difference was night and day
But she wanted him, some how and some way
By the time she told him, it was too late
He had moved to somewhere else in the state
That was the hammer that broke her poor heart
No more together, they now were apart
She had to move on, but never forgot
Her heart never healed, she missed him a lot
Those few little moments in her young life
They hit like a rock, and cut like a knife
Now when you ask her, she'll tell it like so
"It was a long time. A long time ago."

—*Lisa J. Angarano*

Lost Love

My love was beautiful.
He was sooo cool.
Beautiful chocolate color skin.
Damn, he was smooth.
I remember those full brown lips.
One kiss from those beauties and they'd make you flip.
I loved that man's walk.
It was smooth sooo smooth the same when he'd talk.
I miss those lovely brown eyes.
The sight of those always soothed my cries.
With him again I want to make love.
In the living room, the kitchen, the bathroom,
shoot all of the above.
Just as long as I could feel the warmth of
my wonderful lost love.

—*Pamela Andrews*

Memory

I have nothing, except my brain and heart.
Heart beats which suggest fear and my brain which feels
grief that are all I have now after I lost you.

My eyes became marbles. My nose forgot your fragrance.
My mouth doesn't say "I love you" any more.

My arms which always hugged you turned into sticks.
My feet which I used going to your house are only used
As I run away from deep grief.

You stole everything from me.
After you went by, I had only sadness and grief.
And one more thing, it was the worst thing you left.

The memory of love with you.
—*Yukihiro Naito*

Echoes of Love

There comes a time when you feel something in your
heart that you just can't explain.
It arrives one day, moving you.
It's all you need, and with each breath, you know it's true.
The power it holds has no boundary.
It captivates you, leaving no room for fear.
You will do everything,
no, you will do anything to hold onto it.
With your arms reaching for the sky you will fall to
the ground and beg for mercy.
Only your alone, and no one hears your screams.
It's too late, your heart has been stolen.
You've been stripped, left naked.
So, you reach down into your soul looking for answers where
there's none, and you pray for guidance, but no one comes.
Once at the end of your rope you whisper the sweet softness
of I love you, but the silence echoes.

—*Stacy Saldana*

Mountains

Shoulders of earth-
held high in haughty grandeur above those plains
that stretch beneath a sea of blue-
and lose themselves-
in billowy waves of summer's golden grains-
'tis your backbone of stone and rooted trees-
that keeps all else from falling into swamps and deep morass-
protecting rich-loamed farms-
from tornadic winds that blow-
and coat your mile high crests-
with a year 'round crown of white-
that sparkles like ten million jewels-
as dawn begins to run along your rim
and dance down shaded glens-
along the gurgling brook that flows-
from springs unseen-
and greens the hem that grows around your feet
far, far removed from where it all began-
in that misty land of Alpine heights-
both a challenge and a boon to man.

—*William E. Mays*

Untitled

She sits there and one can not look away;
her beauty is a magnet to ones eyes.
try as one might to deny this sight,
but give up this fight and enjoy her light;
a glow that overwhelms,
even when one is not near
her presence, her warmth is felt always;
as if nature meant for all to find
safety in her smile, security in her embrace.

—*Samuel A. King*

Summer Sounds

A crow's caw in the distance near
helps wake me to the sounds I hear
  Of chirps and chipes and bluejays' call
oh how I love to hear them all

  Wake little wren and join the fun
can fly so high, can jump and run
  To do this all I wish I could
least I can watch through field and wood

  The meadow lark and chimney sweep
from high above their vigils keep
  The cooing dove makes time standstill
where sits the lonesome whippoorwill?

  The blackbirds blue ones, red ones too
provide the music soft and true
  And species I shall never find
make up this place called summertime!

— *Wayne Slusher*

Untitled

Injecting the needle, stifling a cry, the young girl waits for
her beloved high. Already caught in the drug institution, gets
her drugs from prostitution. She wanders the alleys of the
busy city, getting spare change from people's pity. The girl
continues on her way, but this child doesn't go to play. She's
paying constantly for giving in, to the hated world of crack
and sin. Most people don't understand why, this girl has the
need to get high. Maybe it was the stress she endured, or
maybe by her peers, she was lured. However it happened, this
girl's gonna die, slitting her wrist, she begins to cry.
Here's the shock, the girl's only ten, merely a child, whose
life's going to end. She never got a chance to see, what the
world offers to you and me. Unfortunately, there's many others
like her, nameless statistics, who aren't really sure, of where
they'll get their next drag, where they end up is a body bag.
All that's left of her is spirit and stone, her name printed on
it, and a pile of bones. This girl never had a chance at life,
ending something forever, with the slip of a knife. When it
comes down to it, don't go with the flow, if drugs try to drag
you down, just say no.

— *Megan Moody*

A Mother's "Prayer For Peace" In The Mid-East...

A mother looks at her children;
  Her daughter and her son.
As she sees them playing happily,
  She prays for peace to come.
These are her prayers:

The ways of life, are full of strife;
  Sorrow and woe, wherever we go.
We seem to find, no peace of mind;
In anything we do.
Can it be? That we shall see?
The impossible dream come true!

"Friends," "Let's be friends,"
Let's not wait, 'till it's late, and all ends.
"Friends," "Let's be friends,"
Let's not fight, day and night, for revenge.
Every mother, loves her daughter and her son.
Let's say "peace" "shalom" and the battle is won.
"Friends," "Let's be friends,"
All that matters, is in our very hands.
Peace, love, and understanding in all our lands. "Amen"

— *Ruth Ernstoff*

The Black Woman

She is articulate,
Her ethics are distinct and precise,
She is a woman of integrity and pride,
She is the black woman.

Her struggles are many,
Yet she does not succumb,
Her zealousness is commendable,
She is the black woman.

Her strength surpasses other,
She is real,
She is refine and beautiful together,
She, is the black woman

She strives for good
And not for sinister,
She is a mixture of affability and sweetness,
She's an Esther.

A woman who's black,
Yes, indeed,
She is the black woman.

— *Turkessa Dennis*

Reflection From a Mirror

Looking in a mirror, I saw this childlike girl.
  Her eyes I see, contains too much of sadness,
Born without parents, abused childhood, sadness becomes her.
  Black bags beneath them, ghostly she looks,
    Not much of sleep, nor peaceful days.
    Her hands I see, wrinkled to the bone,
    Hard working days, and working alone.
  Her hair so burned brown, so thin and dull,
    Nowashed and uncared for.
  Her profile is unaware of, she does not even realize,
    But beneath all her outside layer,
      She is abundant in beauty.

— *Thy Tong*

AIDS

A small sigh came from her frail lungs
Her fragile skeleton supported her deteriorating body.
She lays in a crib, all alone,
A jail which will be her death bed.
She makes no noise for she has no tears to cry with,

Everyone has forgotten.
There are no hugs and kisses, for people are afraid,
Afraid of this poor, fragile, girl who could be
a killer.

Her mother never had the intention to kill, to hurt,
to infect.
She gave birth,
Yet it wasn't a birth for life,
It was the beginning of her death.
She is now cursed with the disease to kill, to murder.
There is no cure for her pain and no cure
for this disease.
She is another sad example of an ongoing
tragedy.

— *Stephanie Bebis*

We Miss You Friend

Donna was kind, good, refreshing in her own unique way.
Her gentleness like a warm breeze on a summer day.
She was fun loving, well known for her smiler and laughter.
Like a bouncing, bubbly brook, that runs ever faster.
If there was mischief about, one could often be sure,
That she was part of it, for she believed laughing a cure,
For bad times, sorrow, and even stormy weather.
She was the instigator of many fun loving hours together.
She had a way of making things special, that extra little
touch. That's just one of the things we miss so much.
She was always willing to help others, her talents she'd lend.
Why sometimes she would even volunteer for a friend!
She was close to God in her own quiet way.
From him she drew strength day by day.
What a legacy she has given, what memories to make us smile.
If laughter is good for the soul, then our lives should be
better, because she walked through them for awhile.
And oh, we miss you friend.

—*Mary Lou Schons*

Mother, I Love You

My mother's tender kiss, brings joy to my heart everyday
Her inspiration and encouragement, gives me the will to live
on day after day.

My mother's words of wisdom can never lead me wrong
A mother's pride and joy, is a daughter of her own.

My mother is my best friend, no matter how near or far.
She'll always be here for me, giving her all and all.

My mother's smile is like a flower blooming in the spring,
anything she touches, will be blessed tremendously.

I mourn the day that we must part, I know this has to be,
I dream of the day we'll meet again, this is what keeps me
free.

The love my mother and I share, comes straight from the
heart, my mother and I are as one, nothing can tear us apart.

I'm fortunate to have a mother, whose love is unconditional.
God Bless you mother for loving me from day one.

—*Teresa Rosebud*

BIG "M" THE GIANT AND SUNSHINE SUE

BIG "M" THE GIANT AND SUNSHINE SUE became friends.
Her rays tender and true warmed his heart, melted the iron
and turned his heart to Gold.

Since BIG "M" THE GIANT was a Polish Metal Artist he used
the GOLD FROM HIS HEART like the Duck that Laid the Golden
Egg for really BIG beautiful pieces of art all of pure GOLD to give
back to the world.

"M's" GOLDEN ART, full of heart filled with diamonds and
pearls shone brighter than SUNSHINE SUE'S RAYS traveling
around the world.

Children jumped for joy, Fathers smiled, Mothers danced
the Polka and Mazurka while BIG "M" AND SUNSHINE SUE
KEPT LAUGHING.

—*S. T. Curran (Have a good day everyone...)*

The Old Woman

When he went to visit she didn't know
   her son.

But she looked at him and said,
   "You look like a part of me."

And she smiled as she watched the pigeons
   cooing on the window sill, and softly
   remarked, "they are telling secrets to each other."

And
   we say her mind is gone.

But could it simply be
   a way that nature has of dealing
   with years of pain and loss and illness,
   and aging;

And her mind has just retreated
   to another level of awareness
   where life is bearable....
And
   the birds
   tell secrets to each other...

   —*Suzanne Cogley*

Rose Of America

America the greatest place to live,
Here freedom, love, the good life, they're for real.
Our leadership tries constantly to give,
All men and women a fair and square deal.

With all the beautiful flowers that Earth brings,
God gave us even more the pretty rose.
To symbolize love more than anything.
Let's all stand tall, give three cheers for the rose.

We won freedom and independency,
Both here and abroad, brave men defended
Our country, principles and liberty,
Returned triumphant, as God intended.

And now all cheer for peace throughout the land,
With God's blessing and will, so shall it be.
Our nation's symbol, perfect rose at hand.
Peaceful, but strong our goal for you and me.

Oh rose, rose, rose of America,
You represent perfection and love.
Oh rose, rose, rose of America,
We salute you with God up above.

   —*Y. Parker Gee*

Choosing God

Here is our cause,
   here is our sorrow.
Fathers lead mothers astray,
   and children take their cues from them.
Widows have no shortage of mates,
   children have no shortage of "fathers."
Mothers cannot find a man,
   and men cannot find a wife.
Children have not cause to worry,
   for they have all they "need" in life.
For who cannot find a "father,"
   and who cannot find a "mother?"
Who cannot find a "wife,"
   and who cannot find a "man?"
No these are not the problems we face,
   no, they are just bad solutions to problems.
For I can provide all things,
   even the care of a stable life.

   —*Michael J. Meyer*

411

The Wedding

A darkness shall come to this land so very far away,
here, where kings and queens were crowned and knighthood came
 to stay.
When I shall climb the olden steps of the great church of England
 where marbled angels pray.
And there before them, on hollowed ground, a single rose shall
 lay.
For when you walk down your isle,
I too shall walk down mine, slowly in somber, devoid of smile,
till I come before the great cross of Queen Victoria where I shall
 stand,
just as you and he there, pearl dressed white, hand in hand.
When to him your words of a love forever undefiled,
there shall come to me a quick and fleeting simple smile.
In remembrances of better days when we would pray,
that before this very cross, together, our vows we would say.

Then, before the whole congregation to see,
I shall light one single candle for you and he, one other just for
 me.
And when to him your vows you say, I shall drop to my knees to
 pray,
that my memories of you will fade away,
like the candle's smoke, forever gone far away.

—*Richard Marqua*

God Is Near

God is as near to me as breath
He's not far away and just a myth
He hears me when I call His name
and answers too, "He's" always the same
He forgives and forget when I fail to pray
Reminds me that there'll be another day.
His love is kind even when I'm cross
and keep forgetting He's the Boss
He cares for you as well as me
You won't shed a tear, that He doesn't see
Life would be happier and troubles would go
If Jesus as Saviour we each did know.

—*Pauline G. Adkins*

Child's Play

The unexpected warmth of the January breeze
Hesitantly entered space which for weeks had
Forbidden entry, and then becoming more confident,
Filled and swelled my small, sparse rooms.

Its brazenness unfolded as its fingers lightly
Touched, and then danced upon my shoulders,
Playfully inviting me to join in its merriment of life
As it caressed first my skin, then my heart, with its song.

I rode with it to memories long left unbothered
By the rare energy of this dance;
Of the child who was I and the world so newly seen.
For just a moment escaping this tragically adult mind.

—*Fish Socks*

Untitled

Wicked jish schools to river hends wending
Hooted owl cadences murmur hoot! hoot! hoot!
And I doesth hoot!
I hoot to my cromwellian pursuit

Swilf Fox from the rear guard comes
further thicket to greet
Running bear by the rivers edge they meet
With wicked fish under those paws and feet
A divine treat to be Eton toute suite.

—*Richard McLaren*

To My Glorious Eagle

O' Glorious Eagle; your spirit soars
High above those of us who cannot see
Your dreams, your visions, your aspirations.
Your strength and courage are unsurpassed
And your keen sight is beyond our realm of understanding.
Your spirit is untamed, and thus it should be
For those with your power and energy are the leaders of the
 future.
Hold onto your dreams to make this a better world,
For the torch has been passed from father to son,
And with your strengths go our hope for a better tomorrow.
So spread your mighty wings, my young eagle,
Go forth from my nest and soar to the heavens.
Carry your mother's love, your father's pride...
And that special spirit that makes you...
My son, my hope, my joy....
My Glorious Eagle.

—*Linda Lee Lance*

Jesse

His skin is so pale.
His eyes are filled with knowledge
of such that none should ever know.
Peering into their blueness,
I see a thousand lifetimes fall like fragile snowflakes
that melt before they touch the earth.

His skin is so pale.
How terrifying to watch
the world slip, like silk, through his own tender fingers;
And still, to gasp with fury for each breath of life,
as flame does to open air;
And still, in silence pray to "be" for one moment more.

His skin is so pale.
He is held captive in its prison;
I by its purity and strength.
I see a shadow of darkness surround his aching heart;
Yet, a light emanates from within him;
A brilliance that will forever shine.
I think it is perfect soul dancing in the sun.

His skin is so very pale.

—*Sari Rubin*

Who Is He?

He stepped out of nothing into darkness, and with a wave of
 his hand, it became.
As he looked around at what had become, he smiled and the sun
 did beam.
While admiring it, tears swelled in his eyes and dripped upon
 its substance which caused the waters to part from the land.
Placing his hand upon his chin, he slowly rubbed the seeds of
 life down upon its existence, and beauty grew all through
 the land and seas.
Taking a seat, he thought to himself what else can I create?
Looking upon the earth he whispered, "man."
Just as he spoke gentle winds began to sweep upon the land.
As the breeze ceased, an image stood.
Kneeling to admire it he exhaled sweetly into its nostrils,
 and it became a living soul.
Fading upon the stars he lovingly nodded his head.
 "For it is Good."

—*Lamar Bass Anderson*

God Gives Us Power

God gives us power, that we can live faithfully,
His is the only power, to all eternity.

Power to meditate and pray for all that's ill,
Power to trust and believe in His divine and Holy will.

Power to use our hands to do his work today,
Power to guide our feet in the straight and narrow way.

Power to talk to others and tell them why Jesus died,
Power to channel our minds to know he's right by our side.

Power to focus our eyes to see some good in all,
Power to open our ears to hear his heavenly call.

Power to use our nostrils to breathe his precious air.
Power to stop and think, "that God must really care",

He gives Power! Power! Power!

—*Sewilla K. Grant*

My Duty In Life

My God is strong and fine.
His laws make the universe go round.
Using His laws every time. As a goal in life is sound;
To be attuned to all the time. To God's plan happiness to find.

Future salvation is a nebulous thing
To spend a whole life worrying about,
When "abundant life" Jesus came to bring,
Freedom, happiness, peace is all about
If we'd only give God's laws a fling
And do our part to bring it about.

Jesus in His wisdom taught us the way,
Love your God and your neighbor too. As a motivating force
every day, Do unto others as you'd have them do unto you.
This law works for good or for bad whichever way
You use it in your work or play.
So when the Lord's prayer you say recognize our duty to make
comes true, God's Kingdom on Earth and not it just say
Thinking Jesus will come to do it for you.
The duty is ours to do our part today. Remembering God's laws
are tool to use not pinpricks to make you behave.

—*G. F. Lincks*

Our Special Brave Hero.....Brian

With hair of spun gold and eyes of blue,
His little hands hold the very heart of you.
He loves to fish and be all boy, too,
Yet he takes time out to say "Grandma, I love you".
For ten whole years he has brightened my life,
and his love helped to overcome my strife.
Suddenly without warning a storm appeared red,
My Brian had leukemia the Dr. said.
With medicine, IV'S and mediport in view,
A brave little soldier battling - getting bone marrow, too.

From his hospital bed he smiled, enfolding my hand like a glove
And said "Grandma, I love you" like a gift from above.
He went through hell this 10 year old boy,
He'd given his grandma those years of joy.
But God wouldn't answer our prayer through tears,
To let our Brian live to enjoy future years.
When this little boy died, part of me went too, with rage,
I couldn't see why he should go and me stay at my senior age.
We can't question God's will in things,
He picked a special Angel - with Wind beneath his Wings.

—*Marge Loveridge*

Lodestone

Ever drawing, the fibers of my life.
Homeward bound, through rocky shoals to fight
or bleed in pointless shining light that drains the
marrow from weaker,
striving bones.
Ever drawing, from peaks of noble strife
thrown upward to roar through skies filled with
crashing, deadly hate and cries of screaming pain
and watch strong men vie to die.
Ever drawing, through sharpness like a knife,
Temptation's constant slashing at the bonds
that tie the feeble threads of moral life
and throw wide the open doors of unsated wild desire.
Ever drawing, ever there... my wife.
The unseen beacon,
for only one ship.
Special lit...
So does it light the rocky shoals
and hostile sky to show the way.
So is your love.

—*Robert M. Johnston*

Learning Today How To Cope With Tomorrow

Learning today how to cope with tomorrow brings about joy,
Hope, no sad tomorrow
Not knowing what each day shall bring,
We hope for peace and hostage release;
May they go home with joy, at least.

Fighting for my country, if that's what I have to do,
I'll keep on fighting 'til the war is through.

We understand that you're a man,
Doing the duty of a great command.
Leaving your friends and family behind,
They're all sweet, neat and so kind.

God's got a shield around His child;
Looking at him with a great big smile.
When you kneel and begin to pray,
Just remember what we say;
He'll keep you and He'll be proud
Just to know he had such a great child!

—*Linda Raynor*

Forbidden Word

Working in the dark with your mind far gone
Hopelessly afflicted to finish before dawn
Nine seconds remaining and not a drop on the scroll
Then beginning to wonder while stress blocks your goal
The feeling of sweat as it drops from your face
Falling to the ground while landing in disgrace
Three seconds remaining and you run out of ink
You panic awhile and begin to think
Dashing to the closet in search of another
Finding one in time and begin to wonder
Touching the paper while writing in doubt
Cause now you are aware this pen is also out
Putting down your pen you begin to cry:
"It is all my fault and now they will die...
I brought about this disaster so take me instead..
Because of my failure, I should be dead!"
There the scroll rest in search of a master
The chosen who might end all of this disaster
Meanwhile it is untouched and left to the birds
In hope that another will finish the...Forbidden Word.

—*Yanel Jay LaRoche Jr.*

Greed

I returned to the wilderness- to find my life
Hoping for refuge- in the shelter of the tree
Dreaming of endurance and stability
As displayed by the sturdy rock
And knowing that from earth comes strength
And from the pure streams- the waters of life.

These I sought.
But Man had been before me.

The trees had been hacked.
The rocks had been blasted.
The good soil of the earth
Had been removed or contaminated.
And the pure waters
Had been fouled and tainted.

All this done by the greed of man
Whose desire for power and money
Had ruled his soul.

So I left the wilderness
To wander again- to seek again
And to ponder the heartlessness of Man.

—*Lee Pelton*

For The Love Of A Father

Sometimes she sits by the tree,
hoping he will show.
He abandoned her at the age of three,
but that she doesn't know.
She's never had the love and attention,
that she really needs.
The love of a father I forgot to mention,
but that's not what he heeds.
She doesn't understand where he has gone,
or why he went away.
All she does is sit at home,
and cry every day.
The only person that she loves,
is her dear mother.
Now it's time that she receives,
the love of the other.

—*Rachael Weamer*

Phantom

Looking out endlessly upon this blazing sea;
Horizons like fire on glass look back at me;
Colors bursting, fire rocketing, puddling;
I see a vision of you forming;
Your face is grave, blending storm clouds;
Eyes piercing the darkness like lightning;
Mouth trembling like thunder;
Hail falling, sky flutters;
Feelings mix, intertwine, become interlocked;
Twirling this way and that way, unable to stop;
I reach and reach for your defiant touch;
Your pulling, away, purposely dodging me;
Drifting, fading, creating illusions;
You appear dark then turn light;
My mind has reached its height;
My emotions can envelope no more;
Then the blessed tranquil silence breaks;
I see your face drifting away;
I realize I have phantomed your soul;
Yet knowing your soul makes me whole.

—*Michelle Morris*

My Michigan

I wish that everyone could know about this state we live in,
How beautiful it is to see, from its top down through its "mitten."
There is Lake of the Clouds, a joy to behold, and Brockway
    Mountain Drive,
And the limitless beauty of Taquahmenon Falls that makes you
    come alive.

The lighthouse there on Mackinac Isle beckons one and all
To come and see its loveliness and linger for awhile.
Lake Superior tells many tales, some lovely and some scary,
Of ocean-like storms and sinking ships, and sailors who dare not
    tarry.

The Soo Locks are a sight to see, as the mighty ships go through,
Loaded down with wood or steel as the world's great markets await
    their due.
Back and forth across the Straits the ferries used to go,
Carrying folk to play or work; but that was many years ago.

Then the "Big Mac" came to be, built with awe and majesty,
Its steel and girders hum a song for all to hear as they drive along.
Grand Traverse Bay is a lovely spot, for camping, swimming and
    fishing,
And for skiing when it snows it's great, for all to really
    appreciate.

At Houghton Lake there is Tip-Up-Town, an event that is truly
    world renown
As winter's really great event, attending this is time well spent.
There is all this, and much more too, and I say this with great
    pride,
It's grand to live in Michigan, and here I'll forever reside!

—*Marilyn Kelly*

Letting Go

How can I let go, of someone so special to me?
How can I say goodbye, when I'm not ready?
How can I tell you, I love you, when I know you'll never hear.
How can I tell you, I'll remember you, forever throughout the
years?
How can I let go, of who you used to be?
How can I say goodbye, when you meant so much to me?
When will you know I loved you and I'll always be by your side,
Just the way you were for me, every time that I cried.
All of your advice, all of your kind words,
All of your help, all that you once were.
I appreciate all you've done, but now, you'll never know,
that I'll hold you in my heart, and I'll never let you go.

—*Lori J. Kaiser*

Untitled

Love. What is it? Is there really such a thing?
How could something be real, yet cause so much pain?

Is it possible for something to make someone hurt so bad?
Can something really break so many hearts and cause someone to
be so sad?

Or is it just a cover up, just an excuse,
Just a reason made up to explain someone's heart being bruised?

Love. What is it? Will we ever know?
Should we keep questioning it, or just leave it alone?

Love is a mystery no one can explain.
No one knows exactly what it is, that causes all the pain.

Love is a maze, we all must explore.
If we try - someday we may know more.

Love is full of so many secrets, above, below, and behind,
There for us to discover, for us to find.

—*Natalie Barota*

A Mother's Love

Tomorrow was a lifetime away, now suddenly it's here.
How did it happen so quickly? This wedding drawing so near?
How can I be so happy? How can I act so gay?
When in such a very short time, I'll give my daughter away?
I wish I could grasp a moment, and make the clock stand still,
So I could make my heart catch up, but I know it never will.
All the worries of being a parent, all the battles won,
No one ever warned me about the day the job is done.
Yet, there is another side, where my heart is not as sad.
When I look into my daughters eyes, I can't help but feel
    joyful and glad.
This is the day she's dreamt about for just about all her life.
She's going to be such a beautiful bride, and a loving, caring wife.
I'll stand with the congregation, as my daughter walks down the
    aisle.
And even though there are tears in my eyes, my face will bear a
    smile.
For I know that I was very blessed, when God lent this child to me
To love and care for and nurture, so she would grow up to be
This lovely, bright young woman who tomorrow will be the bride.
And as always, I'll be there, with love at my daughter's side.

—*Linda Jo Lewis*

Artist And Model

How very fair Thou Art,
How like a flower,

And I don't mean any smooth-petal posy either

But a big burgundy-colored hibiscus,
With tough, ribbed petals.

—*Violet Bruner Windell*

It's Just Another Way

Can't let you know just
    how much you mean to me;
    though it's much easier
for you to know without
    my telling you.

    I give you laughs,
and love and tenderness,
    but, yet I don't tell
you what you need to hear.

I know you need to hear,
    I love you and you are
    everything to me. And I
know I need to say it...

It's just that if there's
    some other way I could
        let you know;
    It's just another way
to say I'm loving you.

—*Sharon Finelli*

Deep Inside This Woman

Deep inside this woman, there is a hurting child, a grieving
                hurting child.
        You comfort her, you hug and don't hurt.
Deep inside this woman, there is an angry child, a destructive
                angry child.
        You soothe her, you hug and don't hurt.
Deep inside this woman, there is a frightened child, a fragile
                frightened child.
        You calm her, you hug and don't hurt.
    And because you comfort her, you soothe her, you calm her -
            And you hug and don't hurt.
        Deep inside the woman, there is hope.

—*Peggy Paulin*

Heroes Of The Floods

When the going gets tough, the tough get going.
How those words continued echoing.
As the pride of America's heartland was showing,
While the banks of its rivers were overflowing.

The face of adversity is the truest test
For making Americans perform at their best.
While the floodwaters rose to record crests,
They stood in defiance of their land transgressed.

While his companions were swept to a watery grave,
A Missouri boy survived three days in a cave.
The sheer determination of his life to save,
Is what a man can accomplish when he's resourceful and brave.

The Illinois farmers who sacrificed their land,
So their town would be permitted to stand.
The townspeople who stood at the levees and manned
Their defenses, armed only with bags of sand.

While the damage was beyond human comprehension,
The loss was minimized by the acts of prevention
By all these heroes, too numerous to mention,
Who gave it their all under direst apprehension.

—*Randy C. Meyer*

The Fall

One brisk autumn day the leaves dangled upon their branches,
    hugging, clinging like a newborn, afraid to let go for fear
    of the unknown.

Having bloomed from a mere bud, they transformed quickly
    into a family of supple and simple brothers and sisters,
    slapping against the forces of the elements.

Not rain, nor wind could lift them from their secure bondage,
    each one dancing with its own rhythm, defying nature itself.

Oh, how cruel time can be! Each day becomes more challenging
    to merely survive against Mother Nature's will.

How sad it will be when they have to depart from their security
    blanket, to be thrown against the ground, crumbled against
    the cold, wet floor and become a fragment of time lost.

As these withered, dry tree foliage's mourn their death and
    accept their new resting place, Springtime brings forth a
    seed from the trees above, and uses its plush, fertile
    blanket as nourishment.

Popping their virgin stems from amidst the compost, they yawn
    happily as the bright sun caresses them and Mother Nature
    triumphantly smiles at her never-ending way of restoring life.

—*Maureen Flynn*

My Special Someone

You're the one, special someone to share my life with
I am madly in love with you, we became lovers.
We got pictures and picnics to come.
To remember happy times and we have more good times
to come our way.
To hold you in my arms to kiss you.
To be your wife. To be the woman you like me to be.
To be the one you love to make you happy.
To be true to each other what more could I ask for.
Well for you to be my husband.
My lover, my friend till the end of time.
Never take the love I gave you away
I no longer have to dream for our love affair
came true, Honey I love you.

—*Patricia Colquitt*

Just A Suggestion!

Angels come in various shapes and sizes, not unlike the normal
human being.

It matters not whether they be small, large, fat, thin, or any
of those other superficial adjectives.

The dramatic difference lies within their spirit, their
connection to feelings, places, things and creatures.

Unlike the robot-oriented human, the angel soars upward and
forges ahead.

Stopping only to guide, urge on and heal …. folding his/her
wings around the fallen in times of need.

That is the difference between an angel and an earthly being.

However, take heed, for, as an angel, do not stop too many
times along your own golden path of glory.

For remember, you too have a mission to fulfill to your own
self which will, in turn, guide, aid and inspire others.

Just beware of interferences along your own journey that are
not of major importance or necessity.

    —*W. Elliot Hyland*

Slipping Through The Hands Of Time

Slipping through the hands of time,
I am his and he is mine.
Like the pretty flowers of today,
Yesterday, and tomorrow,
The blooms are beautiful in their style.

There is such color for awhile,
'Til yesterday is somewhat faded,
Though deeply in my heart engraved;
For I am his and he is mine,
Slipping through the hands of time.

Today, for us is brighter, we see clearer.
Like the flowers today, we are brighter too
In our hue, for I am his and he is mine,
Slipping through the hands of time.

Who can tell about tomorrow.
If there'll be trouble, woe, or sorrow.
Who can tell about tomorrow,
Except I am his and he is mine,
Slipping through the hands of time.

    —*Rita Collette Calhoun*

Forever

When I begin to wonder what life has in store for me,
  I am only certain of one thing, you.

I dream of my wedding day, as all girls do, and there
  you are waiting for me to become yours.

I explore even further to find myself as a mother.
  Once again, there you are guiding our children
  with a strong, yet gentle hand to offer love.

I then look to the years of aging, when I yearn to be
  young again, but by my side you still stand telling
  me I'm more beautiful than the day we met.

I can not be sure of every little quirk life will offer
  me, but I know for certain, I can see you in my
  heart, you will be there.

You will forever be my support, my friend, and my
  everlasting love. As I, my darling, will forever
  be yours.

    —*Mary Kay Short*

Untitled

You are my burning desire, my passion.
  I am whole only with you.
    To me you are fulfillment.
    You have become my love.
To taste you on my lips, to penetrate you
  feeling myself slip deep inside you
      is my desire.
    To make love with you wholly
      is my passion.
    Sharing my entirety with you
      is to be whole.
    To breathe life with you
      is my fulfillment.
Through all of this stems the basis
    of my love for you
      You are my love!

    —*Ross C. Reeck*

Adam's Questions

I have been.
I am. Will I be?

Will I be here 'till the end,
To live, because I sin?
Is my punishment for real and not pretend?

Each fruit or failure of my labor
Thorns my side and tears my heart,
A grim reminder of what might have been.

Eden shakes her finger.
Will she ever let me see her?
Will I ever get to walk with her again?

Or may I die and pass the pain?
Am I an infinite refrain?
Is there one to whom my burden I can lend?

I need answers…

    —*Tim Haynes*

Wolf Dog

I am outcast, alienated, run off.
I am without a pack, a mate, another
soul to share the sleeping and hunting grounds.
I howl but with no answer, I bark but with no ferocity.
Separated from the pack for my difference,
attacked for my foreign ways.
The nights are cold, long, empty.
The oneness has reached my soul,
closing my emotion and sealing me up like a vault door,
never to open again.
For my uniqueness, I was valued. For my difference
I was ostracized.
The irony of the event has become as an anvil straining my
legs, chained to my neck as if to impede my progress.
Darwin, your words ring true, I am not the strongest.
Tonight I sleep eternal, forever the wolf dog, never a pure wolf.

    —*S. E. Frost*

On The Fourth Anniversary Of

Even now, I see your blue eyes.
I hear your voice, and see the special,
strutty way you walked. A piece of my
heart is barren - a field that lies
fallow - the only crop verdant memories - and
regret. Silent tears drip steadily
as incessant rain. Because they flood
the inside, no one knows I am drowning.

    —*Violet A. Bahr*

The Other Land

At night while I lay in bed
  I ask God to send an angel above my head,
To take me to another land
  If it be in His Master plan.

The other land would have no bounds
  You could do whatever you wanted without being chased down
  like a hound,
You could sail the sea,
  Bungee jump, or climb a mountain to see what you could see.

You could swim in the sea
  And you wouldn't have to go to school because you knew what
  you wanted to be,
It would be a great land it seems
  But, too bad, it's only a wonderful dream.

  —Ngyhia Randle

The Art Of Living

As I put my past behind, forgetting time wasted.
I base my life on a new beginning. Reaching out
to simple things, taking time to enjoy them.
Placing velvet embers upon memories. This the art of living.
Here lives happiness once again, making love eternal.
Looking for a new obscenity. Running blind no more.
Blocking out the things that could have been.
Making dreams come true. This the art of living.
Knowing the difference of surrendering and giving in.
As I begin once more to live my life.
I find my days and night are content.
Composing love letters to make my world complete.
Looking for the formula for success.
And knowing the true meaning of happiness.
From this day on protecting the satin ribbons
attached to my heart.
Bolting the open door to my feelings.
Falling into a life that will be wonder and gratitude.
This the art of living.

  —Tammy Spurling

When You Were Mine

As I sit back and remember the times we once shared,
I begin to wonder if you really cared.
You said that you loved me,
And at once I believed it was true.
But the harsh things you say,
Are different from the things you do.

Maybe we tried to hard,
Maybe not enough.
But with the way you feel now,
I guess I'm out of luck.

I love you more now,
Much more then I did back when,
The times we shared,
Meant more then our friends.

Now times running short,
Somewhat like our tempers,
But my love still runs deep,
Deeper then the rivers

  —Sarah West

Sand Castles

Don't step on my castle of sand.
I built it with my own two hands.
It's not so big and not too grand.
Don't step on my castle of sand.

Don't cut the string to my kite.
I fly it high and hold it tight.
To touch the clouds, I hope it might.
Oh, don't cut the string to my kite.

Don't throw stones at my paper boat.
I folded it so it would float.
To sail far and free is my only hope.
Please don't throw stones at my paper boat.

The wind has died,
The stream has finally run dry.
The tide came in and ebbed again,
And I stand where my castle had been.

  —Wade Newbrough

Waterfalls

As I was walking in mid-fall,
I came upon a brook so small,
I knew not from where it came,
This brook so small and so untame.

The speed it had was so quick,
Sweeping the ground of brush and stick,
I followed the brook up stream,
When through the bushes shown a gleam.

A waterfall trickled lightly o'er the stone,
Bribing me closer with its bubbling tone,
Its loveliness so intriguingly blue,
When my eyes fell upon not one waterfall but two!

These waterfalls standing side by side,
Their waters soon may be an ocean tide,
But when the time is surely right,
I'll tell of these two, well.. I might.

  —Suzanne St. Pierre

Time Is The Key

I could love you until time ends.
I can, and will make time to hold you, and to listen to
  your story of war and triumph.
I will give you the time that you need to heal a broken
  heart, to make a new start, or to find yourself in
  that never ending quest.
You see, time to me is the only thing that cannot be saved.
You must use it, or have it forever lost.
So, enjoy the time that is yours, share good times with
  friends and loved ones.
Use your time wisely, and take time out to remember that
  I love you so much, that I am willing to give, spend,
  and share valuable time with you.

  —Mubarrak Morris

Listen

Please try and listen, try and understand
  I feel like I'm being stretched like a rubber band
I want to talk, tell you how I feel
  To you my problems are made up, unreal
Please understand why I act the way I do
  You'd act this way if you only knew
Open your ears, look into my eye's
  If you look real close, you'll see my smile lies
I know you tried, it's not your fault
  I just want to tell you put my pain to a halt
I wish you knew what ran through my mind
  Wanting, wishing I could put it all behind

  —LaNise Broyles

Please, Daddy!

"Please, Daddy, I know I haven't ridden a big bike before, but
I can do it! I know I can. I'm a big girl!" When I fell and
skinned both knees you took me in your lap, wiped away my tears
and said, "It's okay. Daddy's here. I'll always be here for
you." "Please, Daddy, I know I've never had a driver's license
before but I'll be careful! I promise! I'm a big girl." When
I wrecked the car and was afraid to tell you, you put your arms
around me, wiped away my tears and said, "It's okay. Daddy's
here. I'll always be here for you." "Please, Daddy, I know
I've never been in love before, but I really love him and we
want to get married. We'll be so happy! I know we will! I'm
a big girl." When he broke my heart and I came to your door, my
little girl in my arms, you took us in and wiped away our tears
and said, "It's okay. Daddy's here. I'll always be here for
you." "Please, Daddy. I know something is wrong. Mom said
you've been ill and the doctor says it's your heart. She says
you have something to tell me. I can handle it. I'm a big
girl." "Please, Daddy. Take me in your arms just one more
time, wipe away my tears and tell me it will be okay. Please
tell me you'll always be here for me!" "Please, Daddy?"

—*Rebecca L. Darling*

Childhood Past

Thinking back on times gone by,
  I cannot help but wish I were
    a child once again.

To abandoned myself to childhood fancies
  instead of the burdens brought on
    by having stepped into adulthood.

Little did I know how different life would be
  once I left innocence, forever behind,
    only to momentarily experience child play myself.

Thank God for the children that help bring out
  that little child we once were
    and makes us mourn for our childhood past.

  —*Teresa Keller*

My Love...

If my love for you were pennies,
I could buy this world at twice the price.

If my love for you were the stars above,
The night would be brighter than the brightest summer day.

If my love for you were grains of sand,
A desert as vast as the Sahara would lie before you.

If my love for you was grain for bread,
Feasts would be born and hunger would end.

My love for you is limitless and beyond the understanding
of mere men, but I share it with you forever more.

  —*Richard Eric Edder*

Two Hours To Kill

Ma's in the service——they split —
I don't need much, ... just a better way to feel:
I guess, you'll never know: you are the boy, I...
Always wished, I'd had!
A woman ... seen, with an empty baby carriage ... at
noon ... did — she —?? Have an instant same day delivery?!
A praying mantis... pops, like stepping on dead locusts!
Only needing Jimmy Carter's ... chocolates' book!
Are you ... y-o-u?? ... really washed in the blood
of the lamb???!
Grasping at charms; ... on a hot afternoon of over-bearing
heat; needs a new — longer term... coachman's
rose-crest ... dream.
Who knows, if, more help at, a little soft ball, etc.
can remove ... north-south... hates... so deeply warred?!

  —*Richard C. Miller*

My Thoughts

The simple things in life
  I crave
  A mind that is pure,
  A heart that is brave
  The things I ask of thee

  A friend to hold my hand in trail
  A book to ease my thoughts a while
  A dog for silent company
  A tree to bring me close to thee!

Because life way side is not a bed of roses.
One by one we wilt a way
To improve our way
One day at a time
Give it your best
With the rest, sister and brother
Mother and father and God's children
The mountains, the rocks and trees.
Birds, flowers, bees better fly
And Buffalo, elephants, deer along
The trail. A beautiful sky and trail
of the mountain.
Good morning.

  —*Lois L. Hereford*

Troubled Family

I heard a cry in the night,
I dare not move because I'm frightened,
I leave for school wondering why,
My mom is bruised and my dad is hyped,
I sit all day confused and mad,
Wondering if mom is sad,
But after school, and I go home,
Mom is there all alone,
She's in the kitchen, and greets
me with a smile,
She sings and laughs until dad arrives,
And now the time has come,
Dad is here, whom we all fear,
Mom greets Dad, and there's no response,
We drop our heads and hold back the tears,
For we all know what is to come,
A moment of silence, for this will tell,
If Dad is happy or if he's mad.

  —*Yolanda E. Blevins*

Where The Flowers Grow

I remember when
I did not know
Where the flowers grow.

Until one day when
One grew in my heart
It filled my lungs with petals
That make my words flow with love.

For where the autumn knows
And the cold Winter runs through my veins
The flower warms the skies above
Of summer dreams, and blends
The thought and the deed.

It is the Golden dawn
That makes the flowers grow
As it breaks through the windows
Of early morning

In that morning I turn
To you and as your lids raise
I see the dawn and your flower
Blooms inside me.

  —*Robert W. Haberkorn*

My Dear Friend

When I heard the news you went away to a better place,
I didn't think that again, I would see your smiling face.
But, sometimes you are in my dreams,
So I have vowed to never again be mean.

Together we always had fun,
Until the day I said I had to run.
But never did I think that day,
That I would never again be able to say,
That you are a good person and a true friend,
And you always will be,
Until the end.

Now my dear friend,
It's time to say good-bye to the past and head towards the
future,
Which I will have to go through,
Without you.

—*Missy McCament*

Innocence

Oh-h-h-h
   I do so much
      want to learn to skate backwards.
I know you are a good skater — backwards and forwards
      And I do so want to learn.
You just glide effortlessly
I enjoy so much just watching you.
You would teach me?
   But I'm so awkward —
      promise to hold both of my hands.
But....
   don't you need to hold
   my waist — you know just kinda
   Wrap me up in your arms?
Oh.... that's after I've learned
   the basics of
      the motions of
   skating backwards.
Oh - kay.

—*Marian LaVerne Perkins*

Plant A Rose Garden, And Never Pick A Rose

It is time that I let you go.
I don't think I ever wanted to hold on to anything so much before.
How did I get so "crazy glued"?

No one could have asked for a better friend.
You constantly lifted me up and helped me to grow,
as well as nurturing the child within me.

The light that was behind your eyes reflected my need to be.
And I became.
Could you really plant a rose garden and never pick a rose?
I became that flower.

Please don't think me a coward, for I did not want to see you wan.
To watch that brilliant light flicker.
To see fear reflect, from who to who?
It was not know, the last time we met.

You cough made me insane.
I know what helpless means.

Hey, you have two stamps and my life in your drawer.
Can you see my heart too?
It's not one that is tied up with ribbons and lace, better than that.
It is real, and pure, and so thankful for the time I so hungrily
   shared with you.
The best gift I ever had.

—*Lisa Richman*

Beginnings

In a land where it all begins.
I feel it is time to win.

Each day you trod along.
Wondering where the time has gone.

Glad that your not alone.
Feeling the higher presence as you go along.

Ever aware of the heavenly realms.
With your feet on solid ground.

In a land it all begins.
Life takes wings and begins to fly.

Suddenly the answers come.
Oh, you definitely know what you must try.

The mission is revealed.
So you proceed with zeal.

Realizing humanity is ready to move.
Beyond the present grip of the negative groove.

Love takes hold and fires you on.
Thank God for the great beyond.

So in a land where it all begins.
You know that you can win.

—*Valdyne J. Johnson*

The Ocean

I watch the ocean, and never say goodbye.
I feel its spray upon my tired face.
I see its beauty dancing in my eyes.

We rest by watching. We never want to die.
I hear the echo sound fade each day.
I watch the ocean and never say goodbye.

Alone, not me, the ocean's at my side.
I read each wave and never think alone.
I see its beauty dancing in my eyes.

The safety of the surf as it collides,
makes me calm and takes away fear.
I watch the ocean and never say goodbye.

The ocean holds the secret of our past.
It also brings our future near.
I never fear what it wants for me.

The sounds of the ocean keeps me free.
This is my friend-forever and a day.
I watch the ocean and never say goodbye.
I see its beauty dancing in my eyes.

—*Ryan Kress*

God's Loving Light

Just look at the stars how they're shining so bright;
I feel so secure in God's loving light.

And look at the moon how it's all aglow
We are so loved God's told us so.

The Heavens above are his temple you see,
And he lights it all up for you and for me.

I can tip toe the stars and slide down a moon beam
And God's loving arms are all that I need.

So look at the stars how they're shining so bright,
And the moon all aglow, that's God's loving light.

Tip toe the stars and slide down a moon beam
Into God's loving arms that's all you will need.

—*Shirley Swedensky*

Untitled

Things are falling in place for me,
I feels free again
Without the help of my daughter "Carolyn"
And my son "Michael"
This shall never passed to be.
God has found his way into my life again,
I have a purpose in life itself,
Take time to pray,
It is the greatest power on earth
Though weekend in body,
My spirit took wings to heights
I never dreamed it could be.

—*Sally Tamburo*

Who Will Hear The Children Cry

When you curled up in my arms today
I felt the pain in your eyes,
How long had he been hurting you
I wondered, "Did anyone hear you cry?"

I wondered how many times
you had to endure his big, cold hands
The way he stole your innocence
I couldn't begin to understand.

I thought how you suffered in silence
and what torment there was inside,
How could he violate this little child
I wondered, "Did anyone hear you cry?"

I wondered how he could look at you
and see right past your pain
Why didn't he stop when you begged him to
and how could he do it again.

Did anyone hear this child cry
when her pain was too much to bear,
and who will hear the other children
When no one else seems to hear.

—*Shirley Huber*

Life's Commitment

Now that I have ridden behind so many hearsts,
I find my life to be so blue.
No more husband, no more parents,
To give me that certain love and joy
That is so needed when I'm so tense.
Now, I must respond to life's ploy
Give of myself to others.
There are the hungry to feed,
The homeless to shelter. Need to read
to those who cannot. Need to lead
Whoever I can through life's ups and downs
So I can eliminate some of life's frowns
And make life happier for at least a few
Than I, myself, will not be so blue.

—*Rosalie B. Andrews*

Star Gazing

Standing silently
I looked upward into the night
My eyes amazed by the dots light throughout the sky
"Such beauty"
I thought to myself
Just one of the many wonderful works of the Lord
What excitement I feel when I behold God's tender creativity

—*Sylvester L. Anderson*

On The Hills

There on the hills that kissed the lofty sky,
I gazed at the untouchable depth of blue.
The doves carry my voice, gently they fly
Across the heavens to bring love to you.
Though you disbelieve what is to me true,
I still recall upon those fields so green
That sweet, warm winds of summer gently blew,
Which left my mind contented and serene.
The soft winds blow the sweet fragrance of love
Across the vast meadows where we did lay
In grasses, lofty so high; I did prove
What felt to me, you would to my heart slay.
And you have departed and left me all alone
To bear forevermore my heart of cold dead stone.

—*Thomas C. McCague*

Brad

When we were kids, special playmates we had
I had one too and his name was BRAD
Each morning I would call him and we would go out to play
We were both so happy, so carefree and gay
I would stay by his side and watch over him
For he wasn't to healthy, he was so frail and thin
In games that we played and he couldn't take part
To see him standing there would tear at my heart
So I gave up my friends and I'm not sorry I did
For he had to have some one he was only a kid
He was grateful to me and he often said so
I would take him with me where ever I'd go
I had chance to travel, many places to see
But I'd rather stay home, just BRAD and me
People said I was foolish, but I didn't mind
He had to have someone BRAD was blind

—*Harold Whelan*

My Secret Wish

I saw the shimmering lights below,
I had seen them there before,
Filled with an illuminating glow,
Amidst the fields, hills and lore.

My eyes followed it with joy and glee,
Up and down the sloping, bumpy road,
Creeping slowing, thinking I should flee,
I could see the lights emitting a code.

Wearily, I walked through the darkness,
Hoping my mission was not in vain,
The lights grew brighter, I could only guess,
I would find the ultimate source sans any pain.

Behold the sight, resembling a huge dish,
Before losing the vision or my grip,
I hastened my pace and began to wish,
Yes, magically, there it was, a space-ship.

—*Sunda A. Hardison*

Untitled

Begging for breadth of resurrected winds on sweated brow,
I lust for life as my soul's desires unfold to fathoms unheard of.

Ah, gallantry and courage of men before me,
whose noble spirits reached heights sought after.

Grant me also the courage to pursue and crystalize
the satisfaction of my every need.

Then will my soul joy in quiet glory, and find rest,
in realizing, its ultimacy.

—*Paraskevi Rollins*

It's The Truth

I have seen your best and worst my son
I have seen your life full of pain
I have seen you looking and seeking
I have seen you trying to gain.

I saw in your youth the pain and abuse
heaped, and poured out on your head
I saw your spirit being crushed like a seed
I was there when you wanted to be dead.

The song you feel now inside you
Will soon replace the pain
Take heart my son, for it's you I do love
My kingdom, in truth, you can gain.

For out of your heart came your true desires
you want released from Satan's hot fires
That time you called me, while on your knees
I heard you, my son, I was touched by your pleas.

I know in your heart you have loved me
I know what you did in your youth
But all that is done and forgotten my son
you're forgiven, you know, it's the truth.

   —*Ron Greenwood*

Baby Chrissy

It is the last day in May.
I have survived a year, it's my birthday.
Granny will bake me a big ole cake,
Sit me in the middle of it, for goodness sakes.
You won't believe how I'm beginning to grow,
Look at my little face, see it glow.
For a while it looked as though I'd never survive,
But mommy is so happy I'm still alive!
I'm starting to grow and do very well now,
I always knew I'd make it some how;
Though things for me weren't going so well,
Jesus was taking care of me I could tell.
It took mommy a while to understand,
Jesus was beside me holding my hand.
Mommy now is starting to believe,
That God's blessings I shall receive;
Soon my second birthday will come around,
Because the love of God my mommy has found.
Things in my life are falling into place,
I know I'm here only by God's Grace.

   —*Robin Hill*

Baby Sister's Sleeping

Good morning, Mr. Bluebird upon my window sill.
I hear your cheerful chirping; it has a lilting trill.
But this I have to tell you, so listen closely, sir,
I have a baby sister, we must not move or stir;
For she is soundly sleeping and surely needs her rest.
My mommy told me this and mommy knows what's best.

Oh, how I'd loved to hold her and kiss her rosy cheek.
But mommy says that I must not for sister's still too weak;
But someday she'll be big like me and we'll go out to play;
We'll laugh and run and romp till mom shall surely say,
Wait until your dad comes home, he'll make you girls behave;
But we'll just laugh and giggle and turn to her and wave.

Our dad is such a creampuff when we look into his eyes;
With two such little angels, how could his anger rise?
But now she just a tiny girl, and really needs her rest.
So she can grow up sound and strong to be her very best,
So just for now dear bluebird tone down your cheerful song,
For baby sister's sleeping and to wake her would be wrong.

   —*William E. Donohoe*

Conversations With Father

I remember all my Daddy taught me, and all he used to do...
I hope she remembers all that I have taught her, especially about
   you.
How he tucked me in at night and showed me eyes of love...
How our father watches her and looks down from above.
What he said about a light shining through the darkness...
What I said about a light when everything looks hopeless.
He always said, "God knows the future," but I feel so all alone.
I always said, "God knows the future," but my faith still hasn't
   grown.
I just want my Daddy's hand to wipe away my tears...
I just want you precious Lord to calm her every fear.
Can't I be safe at home Daddy, in your arms so strong?
Can't she be safe at home Lord, it is where she belongs!
My voice is all I hear tonight without my Daddy near...
Her voice is all I recall tonight, Lord it sounds so very clear.
It's strange that as I talk to no one, I think you hear each word
   I say...
It's strange that I sit here Lord with no one, but I can almost
   hear her pray!

   —*Ruth Elise Torres*

My Son "Brandon"

Your a very bright boy, and a fine young man,
I hope you remember me for the person I am.
The word "Daddy" has a special meaning to me,
For God gave me a son and called him Brandon you see,
With eyes as blue as the ocean that you can see for miles,
Also a heart as good as gold, it shows when you smile.
Your 10 years old and growing up to fast,
Remember I'll always love you, in the future, present and past.
Brandon, I may not see you as often as I like,
But you never leave my mind or even my sight.
As a baby you were such a bundle of joy.
Crawling around the house and playing with your toys.
As you continued to grow soon started school,
Walking, running, jumping and playing in the pool.
You've made lots of friends some special and some not,
We've had our share of problems, me and my little tot.
We've had some special times like going to movies and lunch.
Please don't forget Brandon I love you a whole bunch

   —*Steve Reinsel*

Of Self

I was a drop of rain clinging to a leaf.
I hung there
not ever wanting to fall
my thoughts centered on my own mortality.
If I were to fall I would no longer be.
Absorbed by the earth below
I would become nothing more than a spot
of wetness on the ground.
I hung on tightly, selfishly, relentless,
not willing
to abandon what I was at that moment in time.
The sun tried to dry me
The wind, to push me off
yet I clung to that leaf
vowing to never let go.
How selfish it seems now
for when I looked down
I saw the acorn of a great oak tree
gasping for the waters of my being.
And I let go.

   —*Michael F. Gworek*

Indeed

Twirling, spinning, jumping, kicking
I hurtle toward the refrigerator screaming, entranced in the
rhythm of the dance
The gleaming white door springs open in my hands as if it knows
my purpose
Smiling, I remove the goat cheese sandwich and peel the
shining layers of tinfoil from around its succulent expanse
Ah the sweet aroma, the delicious scent
The first heavenly bite passes between my lips
It is good
The door closes beneath my palm, no longer bright, having
relinquished its prize
The mad gambol begins again
　　—Uzodima Okehi

When I...

When I see your face,
　I just can't look away,
　your touch and your sweet grace,
　makes me want to stay.

When I look into your eyes,
　I fall into a deep, deep sleep,
　my heart jumps out and flies,
　you are something I want to keep.

When I hear your voice,
　I just stop and listen,
　it makes me laugh and rejoice,
　when I'm with you there's nothing I'm missing!

When I walk with you,
　I feel so great!
When I get to talk to you
　I just can't wait!

When I'm with you,
　I feel so good.
Should I love you?
　I think I should!
　　—Shela Stickle

Suicide Note

Excuse my leaving so abruptly;
I just couldn't take it anymore.
So I decided to answer the knock
Of the four horsemen at my door.
I know by seeing me lying on the floor
You are most likely to be in awe;
Trying to figure out why some like me
Acted upon a careless thought.
I admit, I too wonder of it;
But no one was by my side.
No one was there picking up my low spirits;
No one was there to be my guide.
Don't worry about me though,
You all have been set free.
Imagine how the world will be now
Without the petty existence of me.
I don't wish none of you a happy life;
I request calamity for you all.
You are the main reason for this:
My short life, my unhappiness, my fall.
　　—Tynisa Gartmon

Lost Aha's

Hearing the song
I knew
why she left the cake out in the rain.
New Guinea natives live in the now,
without time.
My past, present and future blended.
Ancient Aztecs drink enemy blood,
becoming pure.
I felt a spiritual cleansing.
Einstein's time curves; Heisenberg says thinking
affects all outcomes.
Enlightenment flooded me.
Sometimes for brief moments
I understand the meanings of life.
These heavy thoughts keep running away.
Why can't I keep them tethered?
　　—Marguerite Marler

Cheechako

I was leadin' the life of Riley.
I knew it could never go wrong.
What better way to spend it
Than wine, women and song.

But you've heard of the fool and his money
And Riley, you know, was a joke.
Then nothing is ever funny
When you're cold, sober and broke.

So here I am in Alaska.
I believed all the things I was told;
How easy it was to assemble
A fortune in glittering gold.

But all is not gold that glitters.
The things that they said were untrue,
And even the girls were fictitious like the lady known as Lou.

But I've certainly found a fortune in this land of the driven snow,
And it's not the golden nugget but the life I've come to know.

And now I love this country. I'll stay 'til my days are run.
I'll stay right here forever in the Land of the Midnight Sun.
　　—C. H. Ketcham

Ah, Spring!

The winter night is such a cold, and dark, and dreary thing,
I know just why the poets write about the dawn of spring.
For with spring comes the greening of the valley and the tree,
And nature paints new color on the things that old eyes see.
The grass grows tall, the flowers bloom, and life takes up new
pace,
All creatures great and small join in the reproductive race.
And as the world around me stirs, and Winter's grip is gone,
I see unfold a multitude of things that need be done.
I've rows to hoe, and seeds to sow, and weeds that grow,
unending.
A cart to start to take apart, a rake whose art needs tending.
A coop to scoop, a wheel to hoop, my field to snoop for critters,
A night to fight the ache of blight, then wake with frightful jitters.
I try so hard to get my mind to focus on my chores,
And cabin fever wants to keep my spirit out of doors.
To work is hard when lakes are calm, and waters lay so still,
And I can watch the stars go round, while resting on the hill.
The restless poet fans my soul to try to stoke its flame,
I have no fuel to nurture her, and hide from her shame.
For things that want attention is there no end to be found?
And I can hardly wait until frost is on the ground.
　　—S. E. Bottino

Chimera

I had a dream
I laid down and closed my eyes
In my dream sickness was all around me
I was sick

You came to me
You said I had a nightmare
Yes, it was certainly a sad nightmare
You calmed me

I was dying
I looked at myself and wept
Isolation severed my joy, my hope
I ceded

Anger, despair
Animosity at death
Aimless, you pondered, how I could go now
Ailed by loss

Anyone there
Alone in this lonely world
All we have, each other, no exceptions
And now you

—*Steven Simmons*

Oy, Mein Kinde

As she closed her eyes in final rest
I laid my head, childlike, upon her breast
And from stilled lips—like a whispering wind
I seemed to hear a relieved, "Oy, mein kinde".

Feelings, too deep to spill in tears,
Knowing the battle she fought for years—
I was forgiven—if I had sinned
When I seemed to hear that, "Oy, mein kinde".

I'll always remember—oft to recall
Her look—her deeds—her acceptance by all—
And when I am kissed by a soft spring wind
It will always be Mama's, "Oy, mein kinde".

—*Zelda Denny*

Solstice

Hard as stone and all alone,
I live a life
Although I thought some years ago,
my soul had died

sanely, I'm preserved among my souvenirs
in time of gloom, the rain becomes my tears

emergent in the dark of night,
the moon unveils its face
in isolation, we live a life

self pity and lunar grace

—*Pamela Reitnauer*

The Sound Of Nature

I was awaken this morning by some wonderful sounds.
I look out my window and there were birds all around.
They all were singing such a beautiful tune
So I sat by window and listen until noon
I like the one in the shade of blue and even the others
Were pretty too, and now that the birds have sang.
Their best, they are flying back to take of their nest.
And if you think that this is the end, they will be back
In the morning, to sing again and what you are reading
Is really quite true so I have written this poem for
Someone like you

—*Richard A. Kaiser*

Dusty Dreams

I'm forever dreaming dusty dreams
I look back in the corner and all I see
Is all my Dusty Dreams.
Have you ever wished you could go back
And live five minutes of each dusty dream,
That lies in that old corner.
Have you ever thought that maybe in all those
Dusty Dreams that there is actually
A dream that you have passed up,
That could be the dream your actually searching for.
The last dream that I put in the corner,
To make another dusty dream,
Was the love and the dream of music.
I always thought the dream of music
would pull you through anything
But the dream I had of music caused me to put it
in the corner with the rest of my dusty dreams.
The only dreams I ever have is
Those dreams I'm forever dreaming
    And they are those Dusty Dreams....

—*Shari Valentine*

Rear View Window

Looking out the window just before sunset,
I marvel at the beauty in the trees ahead,
The sun glistens every leaf, and
as it shines on me I feel like one of them,
My time here has ended, I'll miss
the songs of nature.
My favorite view the rear window,
where I watched the seasons change,
and with them so did I, like I was one of them.
The voice of the children in the
back yards of the neighborhood,
laughing, playing; knowing summer
is right around the bend.
It feels so mild, so fresh and so relaxing,
I'll miss my times with nature,
the silence and the sounds,
the Blue Jay's song,
the smells of grass, as it all came back to me,
while enjoying the view of my rear window,
which became a part of me.

—*Maria T. Falcon*

To My Friend

When I am sad, please talk to me..
I may not show it, but I need someone to make
me smile.
When I cry, please don't turn away,
try to comfort me for a while.
Because you see my friend, it's just a game with
my emotions,
    But I can't seem to play it anymore.
So when I get mad and you don't know why -
just remember, sometimes neither do I
and when I get upset, please don't say "cheer up"
sorry but it doesn't work that way
I've needed you before and I need you today.
    Are these things too much to ask
    is it to great a task?
this message to you is all I send.
Be there for me when I need a friend.

—*Mindy Millman*

What The Poet Said To His Muse

So goodbye my dearest friend,
I must say goodbye.
And drift beneath the violent sun,
for now my time is done.
The prose upon the paper,
the white upon the black.
And I shall dance beneath the catacombs,
should they lie me in a deathly tomb.

You my dearest friend, you have been my joy
to frolic with thunder waterfalls
and watch the cobalt sky,
as the angels passed us by.

My dearest joy, my spiritual sun
why do you weep so low?
For here I am to drink the hemlock
the master gave to me,
alone to set me free...

—*Michelle Patricia-Austin Lambert*

School

In school I dream and dream and drool.
I never do my homework, it's not cool.
I like to ride my bike and play.
But school is boring, all day.
I don't know how to multiply, subtract or even add.
All the teachers say I'm bad.
I like to talk.
In music we're studying Bach!
We're studying verbs and nouns.
I guess in life we all have our ups and downs.
There's a boy in school named Matt.
And the cafeteria serves dead rat.
My teacher's name is Mrs Walk.
Most of the day she just talks.
I guess by now you see,
That school is not the place I want to be.

—*Stephanie Dambach*

Hold The Days

Where did it go? Where did it hide?
I never had the chance, to go outside
Yesterday, I was a baby
Playing on my mother's knee,
Today I am old
Barely able to see.
Nothing between the yesterdays and present
Please someone
Hold the days.
So many things I didn't do.
Places I have not gone.
But life never
Promised you it would go on.
When I open my mouth to speak
The words are still in my head.
I open my mind, the words are in My heart.
Please hold the days,
For there is not enough time
To gather all the material
Scattered in my heart and mind.

—*Leontyne Young*

In Memory Of My Mother

Tonight I saw a blue moon
I never thought it would be so soon
My mother passed away this very day.
Listening to what my peers have to say
Why does it have to be this way?
I feel so blue
I think her death was so untrue
I love my mother
And I cannot love no other
My entire family is prejudice!
Is there any justice?
Why must I grieve?
Why don't I believe?
Why can't everyone be color blind?
So I don't have to feel left behind.
All that is left of her is bone
Since she is gone
I will remember the funny things she has done
I love my mother and in my heart she will stay forever more.

—*Shirley L. Rzepka*

Tomorrow

I don't know what I'll be tomorrow
I only know what I am today
Still I fight the sorrow of my mind and its decay
Should we all get to heaven and dance the eternal groove
Side by side with angels trying hard to bust a move
Slipping right or left or straight 'cause up and down's no good
Dropping extra cargo and freight like he knew we would
Backwards isn't the answer either like up and down you'll tire
And living a long and healthy life is every man's desire
But of course men no longer we are for we serve a higher
    purpose
Reaching up and past the stars beyond our fragile surface
And should all and nothing collide head on to remind us of
who we are
That's when we'll howl in unison to be heard both
near and far
I don't know what I'll be tomorrow
I only know what I am today
Still I fight the sorrow of my mind and its decay.

—*Robert Earl Harris*

In Loving Memory Of Veronica Michelle Goncalves

Now I lay you down to sleep
I pray the Lord your soul to keep
If I knew it was your time
I would have asked the Lord to take mine |

—*Mary Joe Goncalves*

Heartache

It hurt to see you leave, although I hated you,
I really loved you inside, with all my heart
I wanted to share my true feelings with you.
The insecurity remained within me, they now
start to fade, but return when your turn your
back on me, the unwanted, unloved feeling returns.
The look you gave me, the hatred I felt, was unbearable.
I ached for your motherly touch.
The love a mother was supposed to give, I never received.
Didn't blame you but myself.
I realize now that it was you hurting me,
I was and still am the child.
You take care of me the best you can
and I've learned to live with that
and love you just the way you are.
Although the heartache returns every now and then,
I love you with all my heart.

—*Rosie Aguilar*

I Know

I have stopped the vicious cycle and killed the cancerous seeds.
I refuse to duplicate the pattern of the abusive deeds.

It pains my heart greatly to know the malevolence you endured.
Through you, though unaware, I am the second child injured.

I know about her foul perversions. I know of her evil wiles.
I know the ire you possess about not being a magical child.

I have created a new pattern of love unconditionally.
I refuse to be a victim of my dysfunctional genealogy.

I experience your sorrow, your hateful insolent ways.
I know your shame and masochism; to me these gifts you gave.

I know you are a victim but you CAN become whole again.
I know how to heal your gaping wound without verdict,
death or blame.

—*Suzanne K. de Spelder*

Lullaby

It is true
I sang a lullaby to the king
When he could not fall asleep
The same song I sing to you every night
but when he heard it
a gentle smile swept over his face
as his eyelids softly shut
he took my hand and told me my voice
Was like that of a small bird singing
of the beautiful, early, summer morning
he told me he saw angels in my eyes
Kissing my inner face
Making it shine
like that of a star
and I sang on
grasping for the words he so generously gave out
Yes, I sang to him
the same lullaby
I sing to you
every night.

—*Rena Siwek*

Son Risen

One Easter morn I wished the sun would rise
I sat and ordered it to ease my sighs
The sun arose, but by its designation
I knew it had by local illumination.
My barn, however, had blocked those rays from me
I turned and cursed that which I could not see

The barn had really served no practical purpose
'Twas empty and things put there had raised a fuss
One day I felt creative- and I built it
Not much to look at- leaning left a bit
Too close to the house and a perfectly wrong color brown
It's probably not surprising I tore it down

The job was easy, and the hardest I'd ever do
In spite of the fact good planks were notably few.
I hauled the lumber a mile away from home.
Its flames soon spread, creating a fiery dome
The planks burned quickly, although they're rotted to the core;
I later enjoyed His son risen immensely more.

—*Robert Lee Grantz*

Their Love

She was preparing the dinner as so often she did
I sat upon the radiator just being a kid
I watched her move around the kitchen with ease
Her grace was that of a warm summer breeze
She was so quiet today seeming not to even notice me there
I wanted to break the silence but I did not dare
The aroma of spaghetti filled the room with sweet love
and I inhaled it as it surrounded me like a well fitting glove
Then daddy came in the house from working all day
And mamma reached for him and they embraced in a tender way
I caught my breath as tears flowed freely from her eyes
They poured just like buckets of rain from the hot summer skies
As he held her I could hear mamma clearly say
"My mother is gone, she died today."
That's when I saw the bond of a man and his wife
That very moment in time has stayed with me all of my life
I think in our silence before he arrived
I played a big part in helping her survive. Until her
husband could come home and feel her despair. And their love
lifted them above the storm clouds as it permeated the air

—*Maryellen Nye*

Flo's Throw Away

Flo, why did you throw it away?
I saw a soft white doggie in the charity store
Long floppy pink lined ears
Black button eyes and nose.
A pink bow for a girl twined round its neck,
The card, like a brand, was still attached.
I was curious to read your message, it said
'To: My wife
From: Your husband
    I love you Flo'
Merry Christmas was crossed out.
Your husband had written
'Happy Birthday Flo',
It was a 'hug-me' collectible.
Flo, who didn't hug you enough?
Flo, I took your doggie home with me.
Your public pain pierced my heart.
Was your husband and the doggie to blame?
Or did they rekindle a childhood flame?

—*E. J. Farrell*

When The Shaman Played His Ancient Drum

When the Shaman played his ancient drum
I saw myself as sitting in a cave
High on the side of a lonely mountain,
An Indian dressed in suede-like pants
An eagle feather tucked in my braided black hair
Facing the sunset, playing my drum.

My drumming was a prayer, welling up in my heart:
Great Spirit, speak to me in Thy mysterious ways;
Speak in the sound of rain falling on stone-hewn steps;
Speak with the voice of rolling thunder
Through the blackened sky;
In lightening, splitting a tree.

Come in the sound of children's feet
Running down the path of the valley
Where the cornstalks rustle in the wind;
Come in the tender touch of my woman
Who lovingly cares for me and our children.

Come in the stillness in my heart after all
Sound ends. Then stay with me, forever.

—*Marion Davis Sallani*

The Ghost Outside My Window Sill

I was sitting by my window sill at night
I saw something flying around outside,
I opened my window.
It was a ghost; it was a she.
Her hair was long and black.
Her eyes were blue like the ocean.
She was wearing a long white dress.
I could hear her chains.
She was yelling help me.
Then she disappeared into the clouds.
Only leaving behind the sound of her chains.

—*Rachel Domenech*

Meaning Of Life

Mazda says the meaning of life is his,
I say the meaning of life are these,
To love and be loved by someone special,
To work at a meaningful job that's real,
To leave this world a better place,
Hopefully to finish the race,
In tune with God and the rest of mankind,
Be remembered by those who are left behind.

—*Melvin E. Kau*

"Sometimes"

Sometimes, when things are rough
  I say to myself, "It won't bother us."
We'll get through this now, take care of that later.
  This is what to do, sometimes.

Sometimes, when I fall apart
  I bite my lip and feel my heart
As if it would break in two
  This is what I do, sometimes.

Sometimes, I want to give up
  I get mad and upset when I feel my cup
Has indeed overflown with trouble and grief.
  I can't do anymore, sometimes.

Sometimes, all is well.
  I say to myself "We're out of this hell."
We've made it through another time.
  We did it again, this time.

—*Linda Susan Doak*

Our Love Is Unconditional

  Our love is unconditional we knew it from the start
I see it in your eyes, and you can feel it from my heart
  You will always be the one who makes my life complete
Because the love you give is so tender and so sweet.
  I hope we can stay the way we are right now
To share in each other's love, like only we know how
  You and I have been through so much together
Always know in your heart that I'll love you forever
  In all the world you'll never find.
A love as true as yours and mine.
  Our love has stood strong, through life's rockiest storm
We have our love for one another to keep us warm
  I cross my heart and make this promise to you
To make all your dreams and wishes come true
  Some say we have the kind of love others only dream of
We know in our hearts that our love is blessed by God above
  Our love for each other, is as pure as pure can be,
For our future is only as far as we can see.
  To our family and friends our love has been educational
We can truly say that our love is unconditional.

—*Sharon Neibert*

Our Love Builds Stronger

Inside your blue eyes full of passion
I see my destiny.
Every time we kiss I feel the love
You give to me.
I feel the passion growing deep inside me.
If the moon and stars should fall,
Our hearts could easily replace them
If I lost the key to open up your heart,
I'd replace it with tender passionate kisses.
If I lift you up to heaven our love would
grow forever more.
If the sun should ever fade away our passion
would be burning to make enough light,
My undying love for you will keep growing.
I'll never walk away from the good love
I have now - if I walked away,
There would be no future for a single soul.
Remember how much I love you.
Look deep in my eyes. And you will
See just how true our love really is.

—*Marcia Johnson*

Beautiful Earth

Earth shows her beauty each special day.
I see the sun, grass and trees as I walk each day.
Beautiful wild flowers, grass and small trees
are along the highway.

People driving cars and buses on the street are sitting
and smiling while in their seats.
People walking on sidewalk
Happily greet friends to talk.

It's a pleasure to walk or ride,
Smell the flowers and see the beautiful earth.

—*Lura L. Sherman*

In Your Eyes

In your eyes
I see warmth, tender love
And your affections towards me

In your eyes
I see you
And us making sweet love to each other

In your eyes
I see your love to me

In your eyes
I see myself

In your eyes
I see how much I love you

With these memories or things I see in your eyes.
I just remember how much I missed you
And I just want to hold you in my arms.
Just be with you forever
And forever until we, both clasped down together!

—*Lisa M. Lussier*

Untitled

August 27, 1993 at residence 1639 Payson Ave Quincy,
I see when our 4 children were small. I was down on
my knees with a brush in my hand I came across,
Gather round me scraps of thread, cracker
crumbs and crusts of bread.
Fuzz and dust can join us too;
Now and then we meet a shoe, baby dishes,
pop gun, toys, that go to make home for
4 girls & two boys.

—*Ruth M. S. Harper*

Silent Love

What are you thinking of my friend, my friend?
  I see you and I look at you
  with memories appearing in my head
  like ghosts from times gone by.

A movie about the moments and words spoken
  during the days, weeks and the months passed.
  Some of which were happy, very little were sad.

Being with you, I feel happy and secure.
  Since the first day I met you,
  I have felt close to you.
Even though I feel closer and closer to you with time,
  I can not find a way to tell you the three words
  that come directly from my heart....
                    I love you...

God help me! What should I do?
  Say it or keep it within myself?
  I know........love you in silence.

    —*Lydia C. Alejandre*

Susan's Flower

I walked alone for all to see,
I sent out my soul in disarray,
I called for nourishment for
  sweet repose, for comfort,
  for hope, for helpful heart.

A gust of wind, sweet fragrance on wing,
A burst of light, color my sight,
Spreading roots tapped to eternal stores,
Soul to soul, a flower in the field.

I drank the nectar of Susan's flower,
I felt the breath of life,
  the strength, the helpful heart.
I had a taste of Susan's flower,
  the cool fragrance and reasons why,
  glimpses of cheer and delicious peace.

Please bloom forever, please be sweet,
Please bloom forever, please be cheered,
Please bloom forever, please share your fruits,
Please bloom forever, Susan's flower.

    —*Michael Kulas*

I Sing To Thee...

From fields of grass and trees of gold
I sing to thee both bright and bold
I sing to thee under cobalt skies
from beside a river that ever cries
  "Why do you sing so lovingly?"
asked a pigeon perched to the side of me
  "I sing to my lover, I sing like a bird
  I sing with hope that I might be heard."
  "But who is your lover, I see not a one?"
inquired the most curious creature under the sun
  "Cannot you see the water? Cannot you see
  those mountains?
  "Cannot you see those dandelions decorating
  those fountains?"
I sing to nature, for she is my lover
I sing so sweetly, for I'd sing to no other.

    —*Nicholas Capanear*

Dreaming

Dreaming under the stars, beneath the moon,
I sit and stare at the entire universe.
Alone, I think of all that is happening,
Eternity orbiting around in space.
All occurring within me now wanders,
Thoughts of you revolve around me,
Inside and outside, coming and going,
But they're always there.
Once set in motion, now circles around all.
The moonlight shines upon the pond
And all life now seems insignificant.
You totally capture the entire realm,
A product of nature, unique and different from the rest.
Qualities of life above all else.
We merely a dot in this universe,
But you are the world to me,
Encompassing my every thought.

    —*C. S. Coppage*

The Rose Of My Life

One morning when I was out walking in the Flower Garden of life,
I spotted a Rose so fragile from being neglected by passer's by.
I stared and thought for a moment, that Rose had once been
    part of my life.
All of a sudden my emotions took over as tears formed in my eyes.
Yes, now I remember long ago when this Rose could have been my
    wife.
I felt the urge to hold this Rose and bring it back to life.
I prayed a prayer to God Almighty to guide me in this flight,
To rekindle the love for this Rose I had forsaken in the Youth
of my life.

    —*William W. Shores*

Dreadfully Thin

In this year of nineteen hundred and eighty,
I start off with a problem a little bit weighty.

The fact that I'm slightly overweight,
Blamed always, of course, on something I ate.

Many muffins and yogurts, and too much bread,
Eating apples and things before going to bed.

Never listening to Kathy saying, Nick, stop!
As into an armchair with cereal I plop!

All of this now I declare is to change,
As I steer clear of refrigerator, oven and range.

No more cheese before bed so I'll have a nice dream,
No more pies, no more cakes, and especially ice cream.

And no matter how hungry, no matter how famished,
With goodies around, from the kitchen I'm banished.

I'll just live on green leafies and water and such,
I've just promised myself not to eat very much.

I'll starve and I'll starve 'till I'm wasting away,
Until pretty soon I bet there'll come a day

When people will say what a terrible sin,
That Nick has now gotten so dreadfully thin!

    —*Nicholas C. Nordine*

Tear Drops

It was a windy night last November,
I looked out and the leaves covered my porch.
As they fell I imagined they were the tear drops
That I had shed for you and I began to weep
Because I knew I still had to rake the damn leaves.

    —*J. D. Brock*

I Love You Daddy

Searching forever
I still haven't found
The love you have for me
Hidden with you underground

Not knowing you
But loving you just the same
And forever in life
I will carry your name

In our Heaven
You are free
With Grandpa and you
I will someday be

I've waited twelve years to see you
I can wait many more
To be with you for the first time since then
Is what I'm dreaming for

Even though you can't hear me say this
I know you understand how I feel
I love you Daddy
And I forever will.

—*Tonya Witte*

Untitled

My life is abstract, yet simple in style.
I talk with my friends and give them a smile.
The way I get noticed and praised by my peers,
is through my small poems, I've wrote them for years.
They express me completely, in all of my ways.
No matter the time, no matter the day.
Whether I'm laughing or crying inside,
a line or a poem soon comes to mind.
Expressing my feelings, either laughter or tears.
Showing my faults, my unshakable fears.
These are all reasons for writing my poems.
They help me accept life and just keep me going.

—*Penny Miranda Green*

The Lonely Grave

Weeping I sat talking to my 13-year old son,
I thought I could tell you when you were older,
But I was too late and now it is all done,
The heavy weight has crashed down like a big boulder.

I've been thinking about the good times we had,
The fun and games we used to play.
All these thoughts are making me sad.
Because of the many things I didn't say.

I know you can't forgive me.
And I can't blame you if you don't
Your suffering now as I can see.
My weeping can't help you and it won't.

The look on your face is what brought tears to my eyes,
I wanted to pick you up and give you lots of hugs.
Oh, how I wish I was more wise,
Instead, you went and filled your body with drugs.

Listen, and don't make the same mistake I did,
Or you will be sitting by a lonely grave.
Don't be afraid to tell your kid,
Tell him everything: tell him to be brave.

—*Jessica Lancaster*

Heaven

As I stared out my window,
I thought of long ago

On a cold winters night,
A little girl with a little candlelight

For she as a little girl had no home,
for nights starving in the cold just roamed and roamed

She was piled with snow from head to toe,
cold as ice but still nowhere to go

Hoping and praying someone, somewhere would find her
and give her a home

Finally she fell asleep
Her wish had come true
someone, somewhere came and gave her a home,
someplace and somewhere that not everyone may roam

—*Janice J. Champine*

Untitled

I thought of death
I thought of others deaths
I thought about her
I thought about death
When her I think of, death is all remembered
Her last images were of life's destruction
Many great memories together we shared
but none remembered
All I can recall of her is death
The ugliness of her struggling to keep life
Then her struggles ended, and then beauty
No longer in pain, no longer with us
Greatly missed, but soon to be forgotten

—*Chad Brimm*

Missing You

I wrote our names on the beach today.
I thought of you the whole time,
Wishing you were here with me.
I need you to hold me.
I need your tender touch.
I have so many things I want you to see:
The way I grew up, the places I used to go,
the things I still treasure.
I'm missing you so much.
As I walk down the hall to my room,
I can smell the faded scent of your cologne.
As I put on your shirt and get into bed,
I hear your voice saying, "I love you".
And I whisper it back.
I doze off to our song on the radio,
hoping the days go by fast.
Why?
Because I'm missing you.

—*Amaia Frandsen*

If I

If I were painted blue, I'd feel the warmth of you.
If I were painted red, I'd feel your love instead.
If I were painted white, you would be my dream in sight.
If I were painted green, my love for you would be seen.

If I were painted gold, I love you is what you'd be told.
If I were painted pink, I would take you in a blink.
If I were painted black, you wouldn't want me to attack!
If I were painted brown, I would move to your same town.

If I were painted gray, I would come in your heart to stay.
If I were painted tan, we could set a date or plan.
If I were painted violet, I would be your lovely co-pilot.
If I were painted yellow, you would be my favorite fellow.

—*Denise Leno*

Words My Only Paintbrush

Words my only paintbrush,
　describing colored shades of light.
I was sprightly primary,
　she was delicate pastel delight.
Many times when I was wrong,
　we both knew she was right.
And as my kite soared through the air,
　her breeze enhanced my flight.

She was my lovely compliment,
　sisters of the soul.
Our personalities opposite,
　having frequently been told.
When she was strong, I was weak.
Where she was meek, I was bold.
Our beings sang in harmony,
　loving mare and youthful foal.

Like precious metals mingled,
　creating lustrous strings which glow.
I was merely silver,
　but she was solid gold.

　　—*Lucy Bernadette Conti*

Untitled

Just because it had been
Didn't mean it
Always would be
I will miss you
But that's only the water
That flows beneath the bridge I burned
So much that I want to say
So little time to say it

I'll never love another
The way that I loved you
But it's all over now
That's one fact
I have to face
Were still friends
For that I'm glad
And even though I know
I'm the one who messed it up
Thank you for forgiving me

　　—*Amera Lynn McCloskey*

Moment in Time

Love,
discovered with the wonder and joy
of finding a delicate, perfect shell
on a deserted beach.

Two people,
tossed by the waves and
yet washed up on the same shore
at the same time.

Marveling,
at the order and plan of the universe
that brought two yearning souls
to their completion,
as a wave meets the shore
and pauses for its moment in time.

　　—*Sarah E. Dieter*

A Flea And Me

It slowly crawled across my desk,
Distracted me from my history test.
I looked at him, he looked at me,
To my surprise it was a flea.

The flea was all of one inch tall,
The biggest flea I ever saw.
And then he said "I'm not a flea,"
And slyly he had smiled at me.

"My name is Mary," I said to him.
"Glad to meet you my name is Tim."
So we talked just him and me,
I a people, him a flea.

He crawled across my candy bar
And then I cried, "You've gone too far!"
My hand just fell on top of him.
Know what happened no more Tim!

Well if you'd like to know the rest;
I never took the history test.
Because I talked to that darn flea
There was no time left for me!

　　—*Mary Rogers*

Reflection

Where am I going
Do I know
What to follow
Nothing to show

Doors open and close
More ways to go
Changes augment the
Burden to know

Out of the past
The closing door
On what we see now
Is not as before

Open the door
To life anew
Up the steps
There are a few

Open your heart
New life to instill
The spirit of love
Yours to fulfill

　　—*Peggie Fenske*

Automaton

Sometimes I feel as if I am a
Droning Automaton
Walking mindlessly
Obeying the signaling bell
Waiting for instructions
Traveling an undesired path
　But alas! I have a soul
　whose chief job is to
　separate me from my automaton
　nature. It allows me to
　splurge in my creative juices
　and gives me the desire to
　explore the world and my
　inner-self.
I pity the soul-less automaton
For he has nothing to live for.

　　—*Paul Aluotto*

Passing Away

To my friends loved ones and family
Do not be sad at my passing away
I did what I came here to do
and now I must move on
Who are we to say that death
is not good
It maybe that death gives all
there is of worth to life
It maybe the closing of one
door and the opening of another
the poor barbarian weeping
above his dead can answer this
question as well as the most
robed and authentic priest
If those we press and strain
against our breast could never
die - perhaps that love would
wither from the earth. So do not
weep and mourn and wish them back -
For life at its every stage is good!

　　—*Lyda Gray*

As You Grow

Hello, my little child.
Do you still know my name?
Do you remember the face before you?
Do I still look the same?

You've grown since I last saw you.
Will you let me hold you tight?
Will you walk with me and hold my hand?
Will you let me kiss you good-night?

Your words seem so mature now.
Will you say I'm still your friend?
Will you tell me that you love me?
Will you remember me 'til the end?

Someday you'll be a woman.
Will you read this when you've grown?
Will you pick up a phone and dial it?
Will you call me when you feel alone?

We have a special friendship.
Will you remember just how deep?
Will you ever stop to think of me,
　at night, before you sleep?

　　—*Nicholas C. Consolino*

Untitled

Time
does not know
the dimension
of existence and parting.
When presents
in distracted life
deliberates the necessity of choice
between now
and uncertain tomorrow,
unexpectedly
draws away
into loneliness.

　　—*Miroslaw Wlodowski*

Pitch In '93

As I go about this world
Doing what I may
As I do a good deed
Love myself and say

I'll pitch in for the world
I'll pitch in for a friend
I'll share with all mankind
Pitch in American

Do a good deed for a friend
Watch your friendship grow
All mankind is your neighbor
If you treat him so

All mankind has a soul
Just like you and I
Our differences make us both great
We'll all meet when we die

I'll pitch in and love the World
I'll pitch in for a friend
I'll forgive my enemies
For I'm American
—*Raymond Schlup*

Man Versus Mosquito

Buzz, buzz, buzz
Don't mess with me
or I'll squash thee!

Buzz, buzz, buzz
I'm warning you, pest,
with me don't you mess!

Buzz, buzz, buzz
whoosh!—buzz, buzz
Hold still, darn it!

Buzz, buzz, buzz
toink—whap! whap!
buzzzzz, Hold still!

Buzz, buzz, buzz
toink—OUCH!!
slurp, slurp-ahhhh!

Buzz, buzz, buzz—
And so it ends.
A man just can't complete
with a mosquito who wants to eat.
—*Ripley Cord, Jr.*

Country Roads

One day I went walking
down a country road.
I was happy as a tadpole
that had turned into a toad;
A flash of light overhead
caught me by surprise?
The sun burst through a cloud
I thought that I had died;
suddenly the sky darkened,
and the rain fell quick and fast.
I scurried under a tree
until the rain had past.
I turned in haste
with sadness upon my face;
So...when I see a teardrop
upon the windowpane:
I'll set my feet countrywise;
and take my walk again.
—*Nethelia Osgood*

A Walk With God

When you walk on misty mornings,
Down among the towering trees;
And you hear the wind whispering
As it gently moves the leaves
Then you know that God is living,
That His great and mighty hand
Has created all this beauty
So be sure to understand,
That you must walk softly on ward
And step lightly, as you trod
Lest you ruin the tender foliage,
Placed there by the hand of God.

—*Vene Holman*

The Tear

Teardrop fell now,
Down the well now,
The well of hope,
The well of dream,

Teardrop fell down,
With a harsh sound,
A sound unheard,
As it flowed downstream,

Teardrop continued on,
Now teardrop is gone,
Over the waterfall,
With a scream,

Now it's washed away,
Down the well today,
The well of hope,
The well of dream.
—*R. M. Hoffman Jr.*

Shame

A woman sits there,
Drove to shame.
A tiny smile of happiness
To hide the pain.
Whispering about her,
The white-collared people smile.
She sits there alone,
And without her child.
They made her like this:
Sad, cerebral.
They created a killer:
Madness, evil.
Now she regrets what she has done:
Hatred, hollowness.
But she sits there alone,
And to them she is meaningless.
—*Melissa E. Lomax*

Life

Life is a rainbow
enjoy the beauty
wonder at its mystery
riding out its arc of dreams
reflecting peacefulness
mirroring the mystery
of our souls
chase the golden illusion
discover the treasure within
a fantasy of colors
to be found only
at the end of your heart
—*Pam Oren*

Untitled

Remember when
Each day you greeted Jesus,
Asking help but giving thanks
As you pledged and loved "Old Glory"
Not for color, creed or rank?

Remember when
You roamed the streets or woodlands
And enjoyed a sunny day,
Never locking doors or windows,
Never thinking of foul play?

Remember when
You owned the place you purchased,
And if things went out of whack,
You had a right to fix them
Without permits on your back?

Remember when
A handshake bound your honor,
When you truly had a friend?
Well, if you do remember,
Let's thank God we lived back then!!
—*Regis P. Tewksbury*

My Heart Is Another Animal

In the forest
each sound echoes
a river flows
animals run
the wind blows
and I,
cautious
of animals,
move about the forest.
There are no strange deaths here.
Deeply,
I breathe in.
Waiting,
I watch the river as it flows away
the wind
riding running animals.
I came
to murder my heart.
—*Mara Squar*

Fantasy Flight

Floating like a kite
eagle in the night,
the wind blows me
up and down the hill side.

Sailor in the sky
wind ship up so high,
carry me to the castle
where you hide your rain.

Like scarlet cardinal bird
songs float through clouds unheard,
travel through the blue
of your vast space.

Forever turning tides of rain
into fathomed depths again,
returning me to earth to walk
the paths of fate once more.
—*Susan Lyon*

Sky Blue

Everyday you are so true
Eagles soar beneath you
Every time that I look your way
It's like the start of a new day
Though clouds sometimes obscure you
I know that your always there
You send down the morning dew
And scatter it almost everywhere
You always give us a clue
As to whenever your going to rain
There is nothing under you that's new
To you it's always one big game
Of how long you are going to last
Long before man was created
You have been around forever
And you always have the upper hand
Yet sometimes you are so unpredictable
For nobody knows what your next move is
Sky Blue Sky Blue

—*Paul Michael Halsey*

Rape

Rape hovers over a woman's life;
even if she is a wife.
The anguish which forces life
is like the pain of a knife.
After the rape, the world ends
no happiness or even a smile;
only sadness without a style.
Rape can not be healed
because the soul has been stealed.
Any signal such as a sigh or whelp,
is a cry for help
The victim can not talk,
for the fear of being stalked.
She can not see
for the fear her soul might flee.
Rape hovers a woman's life.

—*Mona Al Rifai*

Twin Stars (Gemini)

We both, two bright stars
Ever and ever go deep and far,
And hang freely in the sky;
We conserve our love of twin stars.

Hand in hand, we, together.
Cast our eyes further and further
To the warm horizon of hope
And go forward, we, together.

We are care-free from bustle
Despite great changes to the world
Our love is everlasting and firm
Reachable of life's bliss, why disturb?

Our universe is so immense
And our world goes high and far
Among points of lights and planets
We, forever, twin stars.

Up higher and higher
We look at each other
Disregarding obscurity ahead
Our eyes grow brighter.

When you turn to your twenties
My future has just passed
Born on the lucky day of birth
We are both souls of mirth.

—*Le Quang Sinh*

Untitled

Just another lonely day
Ever slipping fast away
Sun goes down
Up comes the moon
Strife misery and gloom

Can thee be another way?
A voice says to me
Rest I have for your soul
Even joy with me
Simply look and see.

—*Stephen W. Howell*

Wedding

Wonderful
Everlasting
Day of
Dither
Ideal for the
Newlywed
Gala

—*Victoria Broekhuizen*

The Coffin

There's a coffin in her mind,
Every time she dares to sleep.
She's too afraid to open it,
afraid of what she'll see.
So slowly it creeps open,
Her eyes begin to see,
She peers into the eerie box,
And reaches desperately.
So quickly it slams shut!
She screams in disbelief!...
With bloody tears upon her face
She drowns in her own grief...
Awakened by the horror,
And all too real, it seems...
The death inside the coffin,
Was of her life and dreams.

—*Regina Lea Dallas*

Silence

Silence, white and pure
Existing as you please
Only whole surrendering
To the tranquilly obscure
Infinity in reach
Silence will endure.

Silence, dark and frightening
Mysterious in its gloom
Searching lonely perils
Of uncourageous thought
In the eyes of the beholder
Silence can't be fought.

—*Richard L. Boxwell, III*

Untitled

A scream for help can be a scream
far away that you can not hear,
A scream for help may be so near
that you may not hear,
A scream that you can't hear may
be so far or so near.

—*Laura Schwartz*

Loss

The accident took it all away.
Expunged in one step.
Time, held not by fate, but the
lack there-of.
Suspension in bipolar decadence;
Though I was self-apologetic,
Regret is now exhaustion.
As I sit here in revery, slowly
Losing the mortar to my inner-wall,
I am crumbling.
Emotions are like a deluge through the
barrier.
Eroding my psyche and digging its mark.
I am on the breech.
Loss of control and liberation.
All from a single step.

—*Mick Frederick*

My Love

My love is like the powerful
extension of fire.
It can't be stopped immediately
while it goes high and higher.

My love is abundant as the
water surrounding the earth.
It's like the waves in the ocean
rejoicing when the mother gives birth.

My love is like the sky giving
the birds freedom to fly.
They come through me from a
very low level to high.

My love is colorful as the
rainbow that gleams after the rain
I come in different colors rising
to ease the pain.

My love is the stars you see at
night that sparkle through your eye.
That's how far I'm away from
you as time passes by.

—*Patrick Carrasco*

The Gentle Man

A gentle man lay on his bed
Eyes filled with tears for he was sad.
No family members for him to care
No one to lean on or to share.
This mans last wishes or his fears
Or notice his eyes filled with tears.
A nurse into his room did enter
The gentle man thought God had sent her.
He asked the nurse his hand to hold
She took his hand and it was cold.
He said the Lord will be here soon
I know He sent you to my room.
Now I won't have to die alone
He closed his eyes and God took him home.

—*Phoebe L. Ex*

Morning Dawned

Snowflakes, glittering snowflakes
Falling from the sky in the dark,
In the blissful night.

Winds were blowing and drifts formed
And then, morning dawned.

—*Mary L. Baron*

Sitting On A Street Corner

Sitting on a street corner -
faces stare -
a flood of life gone at fleeting pace,
choosing oblivion.

Sitting on a street corner -
addictive -
the city infects some, and others
swallowed forever.

Sitting on a street corner -
pale and cold -
the city stamps out the homeless,
and provides no mourners.

—*Win Groseclose*

Dragon

The Dragon sits with leash and chain
Far below the plane of prying eyes.
Above, the sky is blue, sunny and clear
Without a hint of the Dragon.
His anger sleeps.
Gold and swords beneath his feet
As he stirs in slumber
Clink and echo soundly
In the dusty chamber.
Kings above
And kings below
Have reigned o'er the Dragon's head
Waving mortal power
Like a toy in the air to the Dragon.
Eras and eons to the man
Hours and days to the Dragon.
Upset his balance, disturb his sleep
Only rage will satisfy the hunger
That burns within the Dragon.

—*Thomas Coghlan*

City Lights

High atop my mountain,
Far from city strife,
I view in awesome wonder.
The shimmering City Lights.

Spread across the valley floor,
As far as the eye can see.
Twinkling in their majesty.
The City Lights for me.

Come sit atop my mountain
In the quiet of the night.
Hold my hand and talk with me.
Above the City Lights.

Atop my starlit mountain,
Beneath the moon's quiet stare,
Take in the breathless beauty,
Of the City Lights we share.

Then in that peaceful moment,
With silence all around,
Feel God's loving presence,
Far from City Lights and sounds.

—*Mary O. Capriotti*

Empty Places

A soul comprised of elements
fashioned in purest light.
Angelic beings sailed from far
as they stole through the night.
Whispers of silent winds
carried along the sound.
The prayers of lonely men
the kind the light has found.
Carried under the wings secure
on a far more endless flight.
An unconditional love is sought
one seems so far from sight.
An empty place can be fulfilled
when the light begins to glow.
Becoming one with all
a man, love in his soul.

—*Sheryl Simmons*

Please Remain My Energy

At the start of my day
Father I give you praise
I do this right away
I know you are not amazed
I pray to be strong
Oh my journey for you
I pray all day long
For what I must do
I opened my eyes
To a brand new time
And to hear my cries
Is a positive sign
Help me not to frown
At those who have less
I want to be Heaven Bound
I want to stay blessed
At the close of my prayer
You remain beside me
Help me not to compare
And, "Please remain my energy"

—*Maxine Gunnels*

Untitled

Sun shines, blue sky
feel the warm summer breeze
Standing tall beautiful trees
Each branch holds shiny,
green leaves

Plants dangle on the porch
River flows, endless search
Summer days
will soon go away
Flower petals will soon
blow away

Soon to follow
Autumn chill
If time would once stand still.

—*Todd Neal*

Reaching Out

Reaching out to strangers,
family and friends;
As the tree beckons to
the birds, animals and
insects too.

—*Yetta Wolfe Chesner*

Untitled

It's so hard to hide, those
feelings left inside.
He hurt you so bad, now you
feel like you're dead.
First he say's he love's you, then
he just don't know.
All those feelings he had, he's letting
them go.
It's hurting so bad because everyone's
saying that you have to let go.
You say you know but can you
really?
Can you let him love someone
new (not you)?
He knew everything he could
about you.
All you can do now is try and
try and try,
Until you find someone new and
learn to love them too.

—*Michelle Lynn Gruer*

Lily

White lily
field of purple
My heart stands still
Waiting to be revived.

Motionless I walk
without tears.

Standing
crowd of many
Wondering if a single
touch will reach
my form.

Stems of anger
No memories to cloud my eyes.

Opening to embrace dawn
Born to die
alone.
Bitter wind, break my stem.

—*Lori K. Scott*

Untitled

Hills to Buddhist shrine
Filled with growth of bamboo trees
Monastic retreat

Japanese fern fine
Fronds delicate do not touch
Road recesses clear

Stones cover frontier
Single line of beach beyond
Ocean breaks silence

Drifting clouds wander
As seashore journeys over
Newly thatched huts

Rugged natural paths
Preferred by eager bikers
Original thought

Ripe persimmons fall
On lawn of friendly neighbor
Shares fruit of the day

Banks of Boi River
Orchard for banana crop. Edo people rich

—*Ramona Kruse*

Rhapsody

Everyday that goes by
finds me happier
than the day before
do you ever wonder why?
That I love you more.
It seems like just yesterday
that I liked you.
You came into my life
at a very melancholy time
your humor touched my heart
and made me feel alive
you're the sweetest man I know
that has a look of innocence
in his sexy eyes of blue
somehow it all makes sense
to fall in love with you.
You're the flame that burns
a fire in my helpless heart
my very soul yearns.
So be my for-get-me-not.

—*Ruth Oppelt*

First Love

First love is you and I,
First love made me cry.
First love is what we shared,
First love is when you cared.
First love is my first shed of tears,
First love is my first real fears.
First love has long been taken,
First love was my first heartbroken.
First love is you and I,
First love for us will never die.

—*Liz Finan*

Night Flyer

Away... from the ordinary,
    fleeing closer to tomorrow

Up... to be consumed
    by the midnight sky

Alive... amongst neon stars
    and dancing moonbeams

Caught... by her brilliant flame
    my beguiling inamorata

Torn... from her breast
    suddenly alone, cold

Hurling... through my mind
    fleeting visions so far

Apart... from where I began
    down to a cold sea

Darker... where her sounds are fading
    to whispers, softly

Falling... deeper into the abyss,
    her radiance dimming

Never... to soar again
    or touch my beloved

—*Michael James*

Untitled

Our marriage will be
Flowers in vases and gardens
Love gathered not collected
Growing wild in fields
Standing side by side
Held with open arms

—*Laura Christensen*

The Winged Bird

The winged bird
Fluttering its wings
Against the sky.

The winged bird
Flying in great majesty
In our vast world.

The ponder blue sky
With a lonesome white cloud
That disappeared from view
Leaving a lonely powder blue sky behind.

The scenery of Ideal Beach
Makes one have many words to speak
Of its rolling waves
Of its blue blue sky
Of its blue blue waters
Of its flitting sea gulls
Of its peaceful grandeur.

—*Mary Martha Siano*

Butterflies

Four little butterflies
    flying away...
  In July

—*Sarah Sinsabaugh*

The Vulture

Today I saw a vulture,
flying ever so high,
I never thought such a dreadful bird,
Could turn my head to the sky.

He glided so gracefully through the air,
Like a dancer ending a play.
Never in my life did I think.
I'd think of this bird in this way.

He climbed so high in the sky.
Like a pilot controlling his flight.
then, he sailed around, and around,
And, then he flew out of sight.

So whenever you see this bird,
Remember how graceful he flies,
He only acts a buzzard,
When one of Gods creatures dies.

—*Peggy J. Groce*

Yesterday Today Tomorrow

I fear what's ahead
for I can't see
If this land I live in
will always be free
The hatred and jealousy
will always be there
But you'll always find
someone that will care
So live each day
as if it were your last
And don't worry and think
about the past
For the future is a mystery
to everyone of us
Not knowing if tomorrow
will be just

—*Sandra M. Klosowski*

Child's View

I have known you as my father
For many years,
But you are not my own.
The truth is but a lie.

You may buy me things
To win my trust
Only to buy the rage
You have brought against me.

You challenge my knowledge
Thinking you may win
But I am smarter
I know the truth

Your violence may bruise me
But only on the outside
Inside I pray for your death
To arrive soon

You say you are my father
Through marriage and not my blood
My father would not do such things
In his present state.

—*Scott A. Clegg*

Miss Lonely

Don't tell me 'bout loneliness
for my heart is familiar
Yet the heart continues to beat
cause it must carry out major functions
The heart has a job to do
Why don't you disintegrate elsewhere
Miss Lonely
My heart is tired of you

—*Millicent M. Lowe*

When It Rains

When it rains, everyone should listen
for rain signifies the tears shed by God
drizzling means we are one, showers
mean feed the people, and when it
pours mean to wash our sins away,
for God has cried to long, everyone
should listen when it rains.

—*Samejra Wiggins*

A Sad Goodbye

Assumed that I would be prepared
for the eventuality of death.
Unaware that I would feel
his last breath.
I was embraced by the
spiritual presence
of supreme beings; that came
to take him away.
To a world of the once living.
On a warm summer day,
that was gloomy instead.
I whispered a sad goodbye, to the
greatest man that ever lived.
  My dad.

—*Ruth M. Raices*

To Love Within A Dream

I have dreamed myself mad,
For the love I once had.
For my love there is none,
I awoke to find you gone
All around is me is so cold,
There is nothing to behold.
To love within a dream,
But only within a dream.

Here I stand within myself,
With a vision of loves wealth.
I have dreamed once more,
For the land of lore.
And my love was not finished,
Only my hope which had diminished.
I have loved within a dream,
But only within a dream.

—*Olan F. Jackson Jr.*

Someone To Love

God is preparing someone especially
for you, someone to count on and
who will always be true

Someone who will be there through
night and day, someone who won't
leave you but is always home to stay.

Someone who will comfort you in times
of despair, someone who will love you
and always care.

Someone who will love you like I wish
they would, someone who won't hurt you
but treat you like they should.

Someone who is deserving a special
person like you, someone who will care
and love you as much as I do.

—*Tavia Tyler*

My Beautiful Country

Rolling mountains, wide open plains
forests reaching up to the sky,
fresh rivers flowing by the trails.
So much to see from morn to night,
for nature is yet in power -
the harmony be so serene.

Roaming herds of bison awild,
hearing the sun's rising sound
its golden rays enriching all.
So much to see, this our country,
for nature gave us the treasure
miles and miles of endless beauty.

Rearing horses, soaring eagles
lofty high peaks, flowering valleys,
infinitely big are the skies.
So much to see, each time again,
of which the heavens must have blessed
when this great land was created.

—*Mark Migita*

On The Road From Terre Haute

Ebullient red streaks
from a throaty tenor sax
cascading down the dank
October morning treeline

—*Mark D. Winnubst*

Numb Sympathy

Persecuting - tear apart,
Frightened to behold.
Cries of mercy laugh of pain,
Finish finally fold.

Down below the careless talk
Lies the thief retrieved.
Harsh to heartless fire direct,
forgotten once believed.

Words of desolation,
Whispered with a sigh.
Disreguarding sympathy,
Ask yet not to pry.

Twisted sickness - allow within,
Felt as if in vain.
Carol on to self-destruct,
Weep not for past refrain.

—*Sarah Goeller*

My Friend

My friend was sent to me
    from God above
To bring me happiness and
    so much love.
Her precious love will always
    fill my life
And be there to help me
    deal with strife.
It also appears that her role
    as my friend,
Is there to help me meet
    my goals end.
She is so caring and generous,
    my spirit lifts,
My friend, she is one of God's
    most wonderful gifts!

—*Violet Henson Anderson*

A Runaway

A runaway,
From her past,
But,
The memories,
Still,
Do remain,
Deep within her heart,
The pain,
Sometimes fills,
Her days,
Although,
She is unaware,
What really is causing,
Her to feel,
This way,
For she is,
    A runaway.

—*Rebecca S. Dorian*

Gone But Not Forgotten

He is gone but not forgotten
He is loved but not forgotten
He is missed but not forgotten
He is safe but not forgotten
He is happy but very sad and not
forgotten
He will always be loved but will
never, never be forgotten

—*Tracey Hirth*

An Irishman's Dilemma

My friend is Patrick Sullivan,
From Ireland's shores came he.
By some mischance, misfortune
postponed his destiny.

I went to see a wise man,
Along came Pat with me,
The words were few,
No time was lost,
T'was spent between we three.

Said Pat before the kindly man,
How shall I choose my lot?
I've left me job in Canada,
I'm in a dreadful spot.

Tut, tut my friend,
Lets face the facts,
This fear and doubt won't do.
Get confidence and courage
Your future lies with you!

—*Walter J. Reynolds*

Untitled

From where I stand you're so far
from my reach let me hold you in
my arms this I beseech. I've never
felt this before, I've never longed
so much for someone's touch. Every
night I dream of you. Oh how I
wish I didn't love you.
    You've caused me so much pain yet
I can't sustain my feelings toward
you. God forgive me for I love you
beyond words. I only hope it's an
illusion because I don't want to
wallow in this hurt.
    You won't let me love you the
reasons I can't say. I think you feel
the power of what I'm feeling and
you're simply afraid, that this might
mean there's been no other and there
never will be because we were meant
to be with each other for eternity.

—*Sandra E. Rivera*

Untitled

Take pity, and listen loving mother
From our Cuban nation its cry
Break the unbearable chains
Held by the tormenting brother.

The evil in our sibling, Fidel
Usurped from her highness, glory
Should surrender to the Cubans
The mystery of its obscure well.

It was our generous blood
That our Cuban lineage redeemed
Suffering the oppression and violence
Throwing our virtue in the mud.

Your name touches the universe
May your glorious fame and beauty
Fill our hearts with sweetness
Harmonizing with mercy, my verse

—*Mario J. Davidson*

Anniversary Prelude...!

As I watched you grab the clothes
From the line that fell and rose,
Amid the storm;
I was grateful for your care
That you showed going out there,
While I stayed warm....

I'm so thankful to the Lord
For the blessings He has poured
Upon my life.
Giving me a love like you,
That has been a husband true;
To me, your wife!

Almost three years will be passed;
Finally, it seems, that now, at last-
We will be three...!
Wonderful life that God has given,
For us to care for while we're livin';
A future family....

—*Lual O. Krautter*

My Friend

If I live a thousand years
from the time that I was born.
I'll keep the memory of you,
in a vault with precious coins.

I have not the wealth of many
nor the treasures of a few.
Kings will live and die
and not have a friend like you.

I'm not so self inclined
to be weighed down with much fame
My fortunes are more than measured
by the mention of your name.

I've never had the pleasure,
nor the chance for much success.
But I've always had the courage
to acknowledge that you're the best.

To say that you're my friend,
these words are oh so true.
It ranks right up at the Top,
with words like "I Love You."

—*Robert J. Bocage III*

Untitled

Oh yes when I go home and
get into bed I know my tears will
flow all through the night.

P.S. this has been notarized.

When I was small I knew
nothing at all.
When I became grown I
knew only half all.
Now that I'm old and know
just about al, soon will be the
time when the Lord shall call.

—*Madeline Kutsehinski*

Untitled

Lost and alone
Heart made of stone
Alone and lost
Heart made of frost

—*Sarah Newell*

Valley Song

Thunder sounded in the valley
Giant pine trees swayed and broke
Clouds of darkness soft yet strangling
Swathed the sky with an ebon cloak.

Where the dust motes danced in sunlight
Now the raindrops glittered fair,
Changed their tempo to a pounding
As they slithered through the air.

All the valley mute with waiting
Listened for the earth's protest
Like a giant finger pointing
To the storm king's brutalness.

But a woman knows her lover
And the myriad thirsty lips
Of the earth were opened slowly
To receive the rain god's kiss.

—*Ruth Van Heusen*

Give Praises For Ever

Sing along, sing along
  Give praises for ever:
    To God the Father,
    To God the Son,
    To God the Holy Ghost.

  In the morning,
  In the noontime,
  In the setting of the sun.
  Give praises for ever:
    To God the Father,
    To God the Son,
    To God the Holy Ghost.

  When in sorrow,
  When in gladness,
  When in triumph.
    Give praises for ever.
    To God the Father.
    To God the Son,
    To God the Holy Ghost.

  Amen, Amen, Amen.
  —*Steve Rahawi*

Thanksgiving

O God who rules the Universe
Give us strength we pray
To carry on in Thy name
In a thanksgiving way
Grant we may ever hold fast
To the teachings of thy will
That peace, love and harmony
In our hearts will instill
Free from want and care
And guide us by thy might
Help us increase our faith in thee
That we may have favor in thy sight
O God today we do give thanks
For all these and more
For in tomorrow's dawn
The whole world must thee adore

—*Mae Street Kidd*

Precious Gifts

When asked how many children,
God has given me,
I will answer one,
Not three.
But in my heart,
There lives two more,
Who's purpose here,
I've asked what for?
But then I see
The one that lives,
Each day a precious
Gift he gives.
He needs my patience,
Love, and compassion,
I have to feel
That in a fashion,
When he sits
Upon my knee,
He receives the love
From, not one, but three.

—*L. A. Kemling*

The Labyrinth Of Love

Before entering the forbidden land
grab onto my hand.
For together we will go where no
man is ever safe from falling in.
Now if you are ready I will show
you the Labyrinth of love.
Where fantasies are all abound
and happiness is just a step above.
So take a chance and come in deeper.
For together we will soar
into the realms of ecstasy.
And forever the walls of love
will protect us from the
world outside.

—*Linda K. Schmit*

Bright Song

  I reach for the sky,
grasping for bright clouds,
  grasping for hope.
    Bird sings.
  How can hope elude
in the midst of such beauty?

  I reach for the sky,
grasping for bright stars,
  grasping for hope.
    Coyote sings.
  How can hope elude
in the midst of such beauty?

  I reach for the sky,
grasping for bright lightning,
  grasping for hope.
    Rain sings.
  How can hope elude
in the midst of such beauty?

—*Paula McMillion*

XIX

Driving fast in light-splashed darkness
Green smell and nicotine settle
Necessary for life:
Like your fortune and your future,
  the dream of better days,
And your smile as we shout
In unison of a city made myth,
The wasteland of the West.

—*Vilkas*

Four Seasons

In spring life anew.
Green leaves on trees and morning dew.
Easter Sunday not far away.
Warm weather is here to stay.

Summer, summer makes me smile.
Makes me want to walk a mile.
July 4th. oh, what a day.
To bad summer isn't here to stay.

In the fall, pretty trees
Say good-bye to all the bees.
Windblown hair, falling leaves.
Halloween and laughing screams.

In the winter cold and white.
All colors dull, not very bright.
Christmas presents, Christmas tree
That is what winter is to me

Pretty seasons dull to bright
Warm to cold, day to night.
Holidays we look forward to.
It's something all humans must go through.

—*Sandra M. DeBrabant*

Our Glorious Freedoms

Converse confidence respect;
Guide assist protect.
Accomplish work, wishes intertwine
amiable relationships;
Triumph through inevitable tribulations.
Acquire admirable friends, property interest
compassionate
    drive;
Read, learn, instill to survive.
Reminisce, travel around the world.
Conscientiously pray daily God our Lord.
No matter sex, age, politics, religion, rich
    poor, education or race;
Death comes to all God we face.
On earth we strived to preserve heritage,
our glorious
    freedoms;
Deserving souls reap everlasting happiness
and love above in
    His heavenly kingdom.

—*Louise Filippazzo*

Leave It In The Dirt

If you see something
Half buried
In the soil,
    Gleaming.

If you see
The reflected rays
And are curious,

Leave it in the dirt,
    Don't disturb
The earth,
    The object,

Trying to understand
    What undoubtedly
Would have been
    Irrelevant.

—*Martin Dowd*

On The Threshold Of A Dream

The last sun ray
Has just vanished away
To let the dark
Mark the sequence of time.
On the top of the night,
A dream comes.
It comes to console the day;
It comes to make the day more meaningful.
And
It comes to tear everything off.
So that,
A new...
Can be established.

—*Nguyen Van Chanh*

Strength

Life without you
Has made me change.
I was once in order
And now all rearranged.

I still see you
Once in awhile.
Your eyes are empty
- A cold smile.

I still love you
But your heart's full of hate.
I don't understand the reason
Only the happening of fate.

So now it's over
And our love is gone.
I hold my head high
And try to carry on.

You haven't broken me,
I'll be as good as new.
As soon as I can master
    Not loving you.

—*Tesse Wild*

Promiscuity!

Sexual promiscuity...
    has now become reality
Folks keep on with not a care;
    of warnings they seem unaware
They seldom think before the acts;
    of what's been learned by the facts
For every wild oat you sow;
    there are things you should know
Before you "do", please be smart;
    think things through before you start
When you decide please be wise;
    or you may cause your own demise
Protect yourself at all cost;
    it's your life which may be lost
If you choose a partner please be sure;
    that afterward, you won't need cure
Better yet, the fates beware;
    choose a mate with special care
Take them as husband or wife;
    love only them all your life

—*Lynn M. Koppel*

For Us

For us He gave His life;
He died on the cross.

The world will remember him always;
Especially for his loss.

He is my only savior;
For him I'd give my life.

The world will always love him;
His name is Jesus Christ.

—*Sarah Yeager*

Set Me Free

Jesus set me free
He gave His life, on calvary
Drugs took the life
He gave to me.

Divine is gift to thee
Dear Lord don't abandon me

Oh my God I am hearty sorry
For having offended thee
Speak the word
And my soul shall be healed.

At your feet I shall kneel

Jesus died to set me free
Nailed to the cross on calvary

Drugs is the cross that I bear
About this gift it seems
I do not care

Fall to my knees, do I dare
Can you hear me Lord
Are you there?

You must be I am here!!!

—*Rodney Everett Luckie*

Yet Another W.H. Goof

There was a little man, and
he had a little gun, and
off to Mogadishu he
    did run,
He said he was from
    U.N.O.
Here to feed the hungry poor,
But the bush administration
    said this was not enough,
So he sent troops to
Mogadishu,
To quelch, and quence,
The hungry thirst,
of the Bush-Quagle
    Administration,
The stupid bums.

—*Roman Pierre Van Parijs*

Spiritualism

Smile—
exude and dishume
the warmth of celestial self.
Inundate fear and loneliness
with intrepid gregarity.

Sing—
a soulful soliloquy of regeneration
and harmonize
with a universe
of self perpetuation.

—*Nathan K. Slate*

Each Ones Destination

Our God made this universe
He handled it with care:
 He placed life upon it
  With two as a pair.

He placed rules before us
To guide each one through:
 He sits back there waiting
  To see what each shall do.

Each enters into this universe
With two choices to make:
 There is God or Satan
  Which shall you take?

There's God's pathway to heaven
Or Satan's pathway to hell:
 One must be wise
  Their decision shall tell.

God sits on his throne
He awaits there for you
 Will you make the right decision
  Or has Satan blinded you too:
  —*Wanda Lee Leach*

My Dad (The Way He Is)

My dad is from Tennessee
He has a great personality.

He tells great jokes
and drinks a lot of diet coke.

He works real hard
on his Volkswagen cars.

Sometimes he makes me sad
because he is mad.

but it's okay
I love my dad this way.
  —*Susan Hobock*

My Dog

My dog is faithful as can be,
He never gets mad or disgusted at me.
His greatest pleasure is to please
And his only reward,
is a pat and a squeeze.

His golden red coat
Glistens in the sun,
And his almond eyes say
"Let's have some fun."

If only from a dog
A man could learn,
For material things
We should not yearn.

When I look at my dog
My heart feels such pleasure.
A feeling I know.
I will always treasure.

No matter what your tribulation and trial,
If you had my dog
You would always have a smile.
  —*Louise Kochanowski*

Rights Of Laughter

Oh God, I'm laughing
 Hear me laughing
 Thun'drous belly laughs
 Praising won'drous things

Oh God, I'm laughing
 Watch me laughing
 Great rolls of laughter
 For the joy love brings!

Oh God, I'm laughing
 Such grateful laughing
 Impassioned tear-drop laughs
 Landing on dove wings

Oh God, I'm laughing
 Soaring high, I'm laughing
 My never ending laughs
 Loops of eternal rings

Oh God, I'm laughing
 Now you, too, are laughing
These contagious, outrageous laughs
Rights borne of heaven's kings.
  —*Olivia Braida-Chiusano*

Autumn Leaves

Autumn is here, it's plain to see,
Hear the soft rustling of the leaves,
Falling so gently from the trees,

With thoughts of being earthbound,
Floating slowly to the ground,
Then, patiently waiting to be found,

Red, orange, brown and green,
Bright hues of colors drifting down,
A lovely brilliance exciting the scene.

Yes, autumn is here for us to see,
With bright colored gifts for you and me,
Leaves drifting slowly forever free,
  —*Lee V. Cotleur-Steinbrick*

Please Let Me Sleep

Last night I dreamed I was your lover
Held in the arms of the wind,
The surf was our blanket,
The red sky tinted our skin.

There were sea gulls gliding overhead
Circling over the sea,
ev'ry movement, a painting;
You gently took hold of me.

Don't wake me from this dream,
Please, please let me sleep.
If that's the only way I can love you
Please, please let me sleep.
  —*Marie Amedy*

Untitled

Her hair, straight as an arrow
Her face, distinguished
Her skin, smooth as silk
Her actions, gentle as can be
Her appearance, teases all
Her attitude, never bad
Her eyes, like crystal
It's all a dream
  —*Ricky Priemer*

Wanderers

Little girls wander the streets
help screaming out on their faces
Do we hold them dear to us, or walk
in faster paces?

No one bothers to shelter them
from this cruel world of ours
As we drive so quickly by, in our
heated cars.

We leave them there in pain and
tears, no place to call home
They are left out there in the cold,
lonely streets, where forever they
will roam.
  —*Michelle Twining*

Amen

A mother's aching love for
her child's vulnerability.
The child's vulnerability
worn unknowingly.
Can we see the sturdy stuff
of fragile life?
Escapes to freedom,
Truths whispered behind
forbidding walls;
Lifetimes of injured souls
growing toward a light
so far away.

Yet,
the light will become
brighter and larger

for us all someday.

Let us pray.
  —*Elizabeth Bryan*

While She Sleeps

While she sleeps
her mind is far from peaceful.
With knit brow and tensed lids
she braves her fearful dreams.
 Her breath flows smoothly,
  but she is not calm.
 Why won't she ask?
 Why won't she tell?
  Anyone.
 Dreams, thoughts.
  Eyes closed,
  voice silent,
  she sleeps.
No one can wake her from her unrest.
 While she sleeps
 no one hears her dying.
  —*Laura Wallace*

My Husband

My husband is the love of my life.
I am so glad to be his wife.

If it weren't for him,
life would be so dim.

So I have to say and hope you agree.
He is the best man any man could be.
  —*Lisa Walters*

Polly Mae

I had a little parrot
Her name was Polly Mae
Every time I'd speak a word
She'd say what I would say

Her talent was quite admirable
But I could tolerate no more
For the echo of my spoken word
Became something of a bore

I asked myself, "What can I do
to make Polly understand
That her never-ending chatter
Has gotten out of hand"

Then a thought crept in my mind
It was quite a revelation
If I didn't talk so much myself
Polly would end the conversation

We started listening to the radio
And it wasn't very long
Before my little Polly Mae
Learned the words to every song!

—*Terri Jo Eyestone*

Bury Your Sorrow

Bury your sorrow
hide it with care.
Bury it deeply
the world has its share.
Think of it calmly
when alone at night.
Tell it to Jesus
and all will be right.
Tell it to Jesus
He knows your grief.
Tell it to Jesus
He will send you relief.
Bury your sorrow
let others be blessed.
Give them the sunshine
and tell Jesus the rest.

—*Rose Bochniarz*

Teaching Cleveland

The boy sits in
His cage,
Locked between himself
And his hopes.
Far away within
His reach (if he stretches) lies
The key: Some black
Marks on a paper
White as soul,
Some teacher,
White as paper,
Some words, words
Words that just remind him
He is caged.
He does not want to be re-minded,
And so he sits in
His cage, locked
By its key:
Wordless.

—*William A. Clark*

My Father

My father is calling me to him
his calling from far away
My father is calling me home to him
And his calling me home to stay

I think that I will like my home
though I've never been there before
For there are many streets of gold
And mansions with big brass doors

When my father sends for me
When he calls me to his side
I'll go to him with my head held up
And I'll stand by him with pride

When my life has ended
And my soul has carried me away
I'll hear my father's sweet loving voice
And that voice to me will say

Come to me my precious child
And together we will be
For with me you will stay
Through all eternity.

—*Leeda Morton*

At The Flame

Whose grave this is, we all know.
His life was short but ere did glow.
He will not mind us stopping here
To gaze and let the memories flow.

This worried world must think it queer
To lose someone who was so dear.
One man's hand, his life did take
The saddest day of that year.

We now all give our thoughts a shake
And ask, "Is there some mistake?"
The facts are there, we shall recover,
To wish a dream we must forsake.

His words were witty, sharp and clever.
He may be gone, but not altogether.
His memory lives on and on,
His memory will live on forever.

—*Mary Dettinger*

September Rain

The sun is hot
His love wasn't as true as I thought
The day is bright
I tried to hang on with all my might
The night is black
I guess there was something I lacked
The wind is cool
For his love I was made a fool
The fog is dense
Around his heart he built a fence
The moon is dim
For him I went out on a limb
The rain is wet
He was like nobody I ever met
The stars fade
Just like the love we made

—*Teresa L. Marx*

The Arizona Snowbird

Ho! for the boots and saddle
Ho! for the desert land,
Where the mesquite bush is growing
And my hair is full of sand.

Ho! for the days so sunny,
Ho! for the snakes that coil,
Where the rivers are dry and dusty,
And I forgot my suntan oil.

Ho! for the stars and moonlight,
Ho! for the cooling breeze,

Where at night you need a blanket,
(But I think I burned my knees)

Ho! for the mighty mountains,
Ho! for the valleys low,
Where the rain comes down in buckets,
But at least it isn't snow!

—*Marione W. Warren*

Earth

In all its beauty and splendor,
Hot or cold, wet or dry
Flat areas with valleys and mountains
The Earth is green in the spring
And water flows like a fountain.
Beautiful flowers are all around
Birds are making lively sounds,
The hay is stacked in large mounds
Then comes the snow to cover the ground.
Earth what a wonderful place.

—*Martha L. Cooper*

Loving

You know I care
How could I not
Your smile so rare
Which I'm glad to share
But not just your smile
It's your whole lifestyle
So heartwarming and true.
To know that you chose me
Sets me on fire
Your love fulfills my every desire
Sharing it with you
I'd never be blue
Because I'm not only care
But I love you too.

—*Magdalen R. Faulkner*

A Letter To Scott

Why did you?
How could you
Put the gun to your head,
Pull the trigger?
You're dead,
You're gone
Oh God why
Did he have to die?
What could of frightened you,
scared you so damn much?
What caused you all that pain,
to put a bullet
through your brain?
What could you have become?
Will the tears and pain
ever go away?
You pulled the trigger on the gun,
now you are forever young.

—*Sarah Hamby*

Can I Tell You About Jesus

Can I tell you about Jesus
How he died for your sins
I know you don't want to listen
Please can I tell you, I'm a friend.

During our life there are many
Trials and tribulations
But trust the Lord above
He's the father of all nations.

I will not lie, the journey's tough
But God will help you through it
God loves you so. He'll never leave
Unlike satan who can't endure it.

I care about you deeply
A friends love from the heart
But God loves you so much more
Eternal love will never part.

If ever you're feeling lonely
If ever you're feeling blue
Please remember God will help
If you'll only ask him to.

—*Natalie Huber*

Longings

Oh, mamma, my mamma,
How I need you today!
Need to run to your arms
Need to cry my heart out
As I did so often
In the days now long gone.
Oh, mamma - you were always there
So quiet - so understanding.
And how you would listen
And listen
And listen!
And after the raving and tears
Your hug and words of assurance -
It isn't the end of the world
Every cloud has a silver lining
Tomorrow everything will be right.
Oh, mamma, my mamma!
I feel your presence again.
    Thank you
    Thank you! Amen.
    —*Rosalie Morriss Carney*

Untitled

Time is passing, fast and faster -
    How the moments fly!
Nine o'clock comes much too early,
    The night is hardly by.
How we'd like to grasp each moment,
    Hold it, stretch it, tie it fast!
Many tasks we'd then accomplish,
    Then the day would really last.

—*Marie Harris*

Untitled

Kling, kling, kling
I have a thing
On every finger ring
I am the King.

—*Vera Lazdins*

My Father

The distance between us
However near or far
You are my dad
That's who you are
The times that we missed
And the times that we spent
I believe the time lost
Is what I most resent
I was born into your life
As your only child
The youngness in your nature
Kept you running wild
Your absence of time and
Seldom hearing of your voice
Chance made you my dad
I didn't make that choice
In and out of my life
At times you didn't bother
Even through it all
I love you... you're my father
—*Michelle R. Myrick*

Present

I'm happy today
Hurrah!
Because
you're back
your front
your side
you're tops
your bottom's
your rear
your insight
your inside
isn't outside
you're near,
you're here!
    —*Sherrill Watson*

Sadness, Loneliness, And Despair.

The things that
I am starting to feel
Are sadness,
Loneliness, and despair!

I feel these things
Simply because,
All my surroundings,
Are now closed.

My heart is sad,
My mind is in despair,
And last of all my
Loneliness I share.

Two relatives of mine
Are with me no longer,
But they are in my mind,
And I am getting stronger.
    —*Molly E. Sheriff*

My Scar

When I was a little girl
I had a dog named Mikki
And one night I rolled over on her
and she turned around and bit me.
    —*Melissa DiPonziano*

People, Places, Things

All the people that I see,
I ask what they want to be,
They all say as I quote:
"I'd like to walk across the moon,
Or read speeches as famous people do,
Or hike to a distant land,
And be so glad,
When I sing and dance,
On the stage,
You can be happy, sad, or in rage
These are the things I want to do,
How about you?"
    —*Rebecca Aquino*

Jake

Oh babe of mine upon your bed
I bend to kiss your small blond head
I wish you did not have to sleep
These precious hours I want to keep

The doctors say that you will die
A thousand times I've asked them why
There is no hope, nor any way
Lord please give me one more day

Once more to see your smiling face
To hold you tight in my embrace
A million things I have not said
And so I watch you on your bed

Oh Lord my faith is growing thin
I can't believe that you'll take him
There must be others you can take
Spare me please, my little Jake
    —*Phyllis McKenzie*

Mechanisms Of Defense

From a crack in my bedroom door
    I bore witness to
Her mechanisms of defense
    I can still see Mama pacing
Flicking the ashes of a Newport
    On that Oriental rug
She kept the phone off the hook
    So you could not have
The satisfaction of apologizing
    She waxed the kitchen floor a lot
Sometimes she polished her toenails
    But most of her time was spent
In the window seat
    She sobbed
Hugged her knees
    While gently rocking
Back and forth
    Waiting vigilantly
So tell me
    Why did you leave
    —*Ricci Young*

A Tree

It's like being a tree—I'm here,
I have my branches, I have my roots,
But my sap no longer runs. I weep not,
I laugh not, I simply wait.
And if the seasons change I live again,
And if the seasons do not, I die.
    —*Shada Newell*

Home Work

I hate home work,
I cannot lie,
Other people cannot deny,
Home work every day
I wish I didn't have to say
I hate home work
I wish I didn't have to do home work
When I get home from school
I wish I could dive in a pool.
Do dishes
Clean house
"Do you home work",
My aunt and uncle say
I don't have time to play
"Just do your home work every day."
They say.

—*Marie Julius*

Untitled

Like initials on a tree,
I carved your face into my memory.

Like a song one hears a thousand times
I repeated your name over and over
in my heart.

Yet...
How could I know?
That like the leaves falling
on the ground today,
You would be gone with the wind
tomorrow.

—*M. A. Davin-Lane*

Untitled

When at last
I catch a glimpse,
Of this ethereal light.
Breathless wonder,
Sightless blunder,
Into the long dark night.

—*Lynn Squillante*

An Explanation

This very special child
I chose to take and love
and if you want to see her
just pray and look above

I will give you strength and guidance
but the faith you'll have to find
and when you find it my dears
you'll see to you I've been most kind

For this sweet baby is at peace
at a place you do not know
where I keep the best of mankind
and someday you too will go

I promise to protect your babe
and I will love her for you
I can give her the things
the world below just cannot do

I am sorry you have to suffer
for my big mistake
this baby's home could only be heaven
and I realized that too late.

—*Nancy Witter*

Here I Am

Here I am, talking to you.
I close my eyes, and
I want you to know
how I feel inside my
heart.
I try to imagine,
how you are, and
even if I feel you
I can't reach you.
Here I am, crying
hoping that someday
I'll meet you.
But for now, here
I am, talking to you
God, just imagining
You.

—*Maribel Otero*

Untitled

Her eyes run so deep,
I could get lost in their lucidity.
Her beauty,
she does not realize.

I let her in.
Was I smart
to let down my guard?
If I am hurt
it will scar for life,
I fear.

I was led in to
this eternal pit.
This place is more pleasant
than any place I know.

The feeling of a feather bed,
the smell of roses and perfume,
fill my senses with ecstasy.

This hold of feelings I have fallen in,
and speak of now is ... LOVE.

—*Newton Bosworth*

When I Was Young

It's great to have come this far
I couldn't have done it alone,
I wouldn't have known where to start
If you, my love had gone.

Oh what a wonderful feeling
the happiness throughout the years,
help came to us from God above
Our laughters and our tears.

We use to always run and play
having a lot of joy and fun,
now I think about our yesterdays
and good times when I was young.

My eyes glittered like the stars
My smile was the noon day sun,
hair was like the blackest cloud,
This was me, when I was young.

Now that youth has faded away
the gray clouds cover the sun,
I am happy about our yesterday
and memories of when I was young.

—*Minnie Lee Hope*

Time Was

Time was I couldn't lift my head
I couldn't open my eyes
I couldn't face the morning
Nor watch the sun rise.

Time was I couldn't see the sky blue
Nor hear the falling rain
I couldn't feel the morning dew.
Nor hear the birds as they sang.

Time was I couldn't look into your eyes.
Nor hear you say you loved me
I couldn't face the morning
Nor look up at the skies.

I had thrown my life away, you see
All my friends were gone
Then new love, life and hope came to me
Now I'm singing a new song

God was not gone from his Heaven
It was I who was lost
Once again I've found my way.
And wake up smiling everyday.

—*Yvonne C. Ricks*

Not Even A Nibble

It was a piscatory night.
I didn't know what to write
so I was fishing.
I thought of you. It was a
fluke. I didn't mean to.
I wouldn't throw you a worm,
much less a thought,
Because you hooked me and then
you cast me off.

It was a piscatory day.
I didn't know what to say
so I was fishing.
I talked to you. But it was
tripe. I didn't mean to.
I wouldn't throw you a line,
much less the slack,
Because you reeled me in and then
you tossed me back.

It was a piscatory plight
and I was sunk.

—*Stephanie Salkin*

Untitled

I'll use my toothbrush,
I don't play the piano.
I will throw a collection
of pains that dance renewal.

—*Mildred Hope*

Nameless

Naked in God's presence
I feel like an onion,
Layer upon layer peeling off.
The raw wound of my vitiation,
Primordial, ancestral, but mine
Exposed to view
An open sore festering is I.
Alleluia! Alleluia!

—*Robert Angel*

Untitled

I say nothing,
I feel nothing.
I am nothing.
Say hello to a
False front
In a
False world.
Keep on turning through the darkness,
With a
False front
In a
False world.
I know
But I am nothing.
I can see with
Blinded eyes.
I can fly with
Broken wings
But I can't taste
The sweetness of freedom

—Vanessa N. P. Pastore

As I Rise To Face The Day

I pray the blues will fade away.
I feel that if I lay back down
In depression I will drown.
I get to my feet and take the pills,
So I can cope with all my ills.
With breakfast I read the secret place.
It helps me the world to face.
Lots of T.V. and a crochet hook
Knitting needles, a good book
Sewing, some organ practice even less
Painting is sometimes a mess.
Designing things, and planning more.
Starting poems and projects galore.
To finish them all I will have to be,
At least 1 hundred and 43.

—Reita Martin

The Ghost

In a hidden corner of my heart,
I found a tiny seam.
It held, I saw, a tear or two,
and long-forgotten dreams.
"Be gone," I shouted, quite alarmed.
"You have no business here."
And when it would not disappear,
I killed it... out of fear.
I never missed it, never once,
until the stranger came.
He loved me - or he thought he did-
which may be quite the same.
But when we touched, I felt a shiver,
cold against his chest,
And so I sent him from my sight,
believing that was best.
He went and left me standing there...
unmoved, unloved but free.
And then I knew, without a doubt,
I'd killed the soul of me.

—Norma V. Lugar

The Door

Sitting in the shadows dark
I glance upon a door
It seems like someone beckons me
To look and look some more
I look to my surprise I see a face
I wonder how it got in that space
I can't stop now
I see some more
I see a wolf upon the door
I show someone else my find
He says the face seems mighty kind
I move a towel
What do I see
More wonderful things in front of me
I see an eagle
Then one more
That's all I see upon the door

—Susan Morrison

Before I

Before I could love like a woman,
I had to play like a child.
In order to behave conventionally
I took the time to be wild.

How could I stand upright,
if I had not been small?
Locomotion cannot be achieved
without learning first to crawl.

Gaining a greater vision,
does not come to eyes that close.
You cannot float downstream,
on a river that does not flow.

I could have sough you forever,
somehow, you'd not be found.
The natural order of the universe,
is what brought you around.

As endings follow beginnings,
or a trout swims upstream to spawn.
I was born to walk with you
at last I'm where I belong.

—Robin Ratz

The Mighty Mississippi

I am the mighty Mississippi
I have ravaged, and destroyed
I have filled your home's with water
and other things of utter deplore

You can fight me, you can hate me
for the monster I have become
yet, you can't live without me
I'm as needed as the sun.

I know I'm deep and muddy
and I'm filled with trash and filth
but man has made me what I am
and now I must resist.

You have thrown all kinds of trash at me
you have filled me with disgust
now I'm riding high with anger
to face me is a must.

When my anger has subsided
when I'm running calm once more.
Could you treat me kind, and
please decline to trash me, as before.

—Loretta V. Strickler

Thirty One

Today you're thirty one.
I hope you have lots of fun.
Thirty one is not that bad.
Some... thirty one never had.

I have no other gift for you.
These words, are the best I can do.
But I want you to know tonight
God loves you, with all His might.

Blessings He gave you under the sun.
Start counting, the love of your son.
He gave you health to do your duty
and garnished you with great beauty.

So tonight, when you hit the sack
and before you lie on your back
don't forget, get down and pray
thank Him, for all He blessed today.

—Roberto Alago

Feelings

I hate myself for loving you,
I know I shouldn't but I still do.
You make me smile,
then make me cry.
You make me want to live,
then make me want to die.

You're like a gorgeous rose
that's great to see.
But if you touch it,
its thorns might make you bleed.

You're the shooting star
that lightens up my world.
But as you keep on flying,
you take my life with you.

You're all of these things
and a million more.
And even though I try to stop it,
my love for you just grows.

—Olga Camacho

Unspoken Love

I loved you the first day I saw you
I love you now
Your burdens are my burdens
Your tears are my tears
When a smile is on your lips
My heart pounds with joy
You have never said mom
I love you
You probably never will
When God sent you to me
He did not deem it necessary

—Ophelia Thomas

Untitled

Every morning before my day
I make some time so I can pray.
I thank the Lord for what I've got
Even though it's not a lot.
I've made it through these sixteen years
Happiness, hopes, tears, and fears.
I love the Lord with all my heart
And from Him I'll never part.
Like a golfer who needs a club
I need the Lord and all His love.

—Robert Casarez, Jr.

Untitled

My kindergarten teacher is gone.
I miss her.

My mom is gone.
I really miss her!

All my dolls are gone.
I miss them.

The horned toads by the tracks are gone.
Come to think of it, so are the trains.

I suppose someday I'll be gone.
I'll miss me.

—Margaret Poe

Untitled

I am a stagnant creature of this earth,
I move in solemn-disjointed
motions that no one understands,

I breathe, I think, I feel.

The wind blows cold and the snow
drifts; I stay still.

My heart moves but my mind intrudes,
I am free, but captive to my thoughts
and imagination.

My steps outlined, my days numbered.

Through verse I curse and love worse,
I dream,

A beggar to my own fortune and a
reflection of reality.

—Steven Youll

Clouds

Clouds nestle in mountain gaps
I play the circle game...and
Wonder... what this is all about
From where did we come
And to where are we going
Are there answers and a way of knowing

What about those who died so young
We missed the poems
And the songs they sung
Those wondrous ideas
They took to the grave
The effect they had
And the cause they saved

Do those who were never
Get a chance again saved from oblivion
Or cast to the wind

I looked again and
The clouds were undone
Like the questions of life
The answers are none

—Rod Mantor

Jesus Is His Name

There is a man up in the sky
I wonder why, I wonder why?
He saved my soul
And it didn't cost me any gold.
He found me when I was lost
And He died upon the cross...

Jesus is His name.

—Le'Chantier Sheri Smith

Solitude

In solitude
I prepare for winter
Conjugating memories
of a warmer time
I'll dream of the greenness
Of another season
When I'll be planted
In a kinder garden
And tended by God,
Or one who sees
My children
Waiting
To be
Born.

—Patricia B. Murphy

Memories

I remember when you loved me,
I remember when you cared,
And I remember the good times
That we used to share.

I remember when you told me,
I remember when I cried,
And I remember you felt guilty
That you cheated and you lied.

And now at night I sit alone,
My life as dark as ebony;
Love is just a shadow,
And you're just a memory.

—Lauren Quinn

You Are My Dreams

As I sit here thinking of you
I say to myself where were you
when I needed you throughout
all those lonely years feeling
blue. And now I say to you!
You are my life, you are my
dreams without you I'll wander
again through days and nights
lonely and blue. For you bring
out the joy in me and all that
is good. For love is a word,
a word of feelings, compassion,
trust, and the understanding
of each other. So tell me now
the things I want to hear to
comfort me throughout the years
for you are my dreams I'll never
forget throughout my living years.

—Roy Michael Guzman

Real Love

I may be in love with being in love,
I think my love is real.

If it's not love that I'm feeling,
Why is it this way that I feel.

I never told her I loved her,
Sometimes I wish I could.

I can't seem to find the nerve,
Or I think maybe I would.

—Matt Clark

A Little Day Dream

As I sit alone and close my eyes
I see a beautiful dream, just waiting
for me to realize.

It's a warm, sunny day with just
a hint of air moving
Walking along an old mountain road
alone
The quiet is so spooky
I sit down in a warm sunny spot
The warmth so peaceful, so lazy
In a meadow with wild flowers
around me
I sit back closing my eyes and listen
You can hear forever

I picture you here by my side
My eyes give away to you, what I
try to hide
The smell is so warm and clean
"Oh God, what a day dream"

—Mary Wetzel

Alzheimers

My inner landscape is in disarray,
I see the laser-bright September sun
then the wires slip
and my mind is a sand-swept beach
with no footprints.
There are no people here
no tears, no pain.

Demons in the night
make me call out to you.
You are no longer beside me
and I want to go home.
You are home you tell me
but I do not understand.
You are angry.

People greet me. I smile
Are you angry?
I do not know these people
only you.

Don't leave me. I am afraid.

—Peggy Labes

Mama's Tears

When I recall the yesteryears
I still can see my mama's tears;
Tears of pain and tears of sorrow,
Not knowing what would come tomorrow.

A letter from her wayward boy
Would always bring her tears of joy,
An old hymn on the radio
And mama's tears would start to flow.
"Mom" I'd say, "you're acting crazy";
Again her eyes would get all hazy,
Then she'd reach out and touch my hand
And say, "Some day you'll understand".
Well, I grew up, became a wife,
Contented with my blissful life.
A brand-new baby every year-
I had no time to shed a tear.
Then all too soon the years flew by, the
kids are gone and here
am I old and gray and all alone, sitting by
the telephone.
My mind goes back across the years and
my eyes fill with mama's tears.

—Louise Newcomer Davenport

Humidity

I'm sweating quite profusely.
I think I've sprung a leak.
For sweat is rolling down my body
even as I speak.

It's as if I've hit a tidal wave
while sailing the high seas.
It's gushing out of every pore
and cascading off my knees.

And as I tell this shocking tale
I'm become quite befuddled.
For my toes, feet, and ankles are gone,
replaced by a strange puddle.

Now I realize my stupidity,
my problem is too late to solve.
I can no longer fight the humidity
and I continue to dissolve.

If my friends ask where I went,
just tell them that I drowned.
And now I'll say my last good-bye
as I soak into the ground.

—*Sue Barnard*

I Can't Get You Out Of My System

The day that you walked out on me
I thought my heart would break
And many nights I spent alone
Hoping to get over the heart ache

I don't want us to be a part
Or to look far some one new
I want a place there in your heart
And I'll leave mine open for you

I can't get you out of my system
I don't want to get over you
Don't want to be without your love
And I want to know you'll be true

I can't get you out of my system
I don't want to get over you
Don't want to be without your love
And I want to know you'll be true

I can't get you out of my system
I don't want to get over you
Don't want to be without you love
And I want to know you'll be true

—*Uledene Cantly Bean*

Rain I Know It Well

It sat upon my head one day
I thought perhaps it would go away
However, it decided to stay
I left the house and it was there
It followed me everywhere
I saw a girl I tried to flirt
but there was rain on my shirt
I ran home to save the day
but the rain washed my house away
It washed away my car and spouse
It washed away my barn and mouse
and to this day I sit
With the rain upon my chin

—*Michael Herman*

In Case You Didn't Know

In case you didn't know
I want to hold you
near my heart.

In case you didn't know
I love you with all
my heart.

In case you didn't know
I wish you were here
with me, to hold me,
and to keep me company
forever.

I will always love you!

—*Michele Thomas*

Going Home

Going Home! I'm going home
I will never more roam;
Never more walking in circles
For I know I'm Going Home.

Going Home! Such beautiful words
And a beautiful place I'll see.
Just to be with my Master
Will mean so much to me.

When my life comes to an end
And I move into another zone
How happy I will be 'cause
I know I'm Going Home!

—*Virginia D. Davis*

What Do You think, Johnny?

When you look at me,
I wonder what is more beautiful;
The wind in the willow
The clean sting of salt
Moonlight on water
Untouched snow?
Maybe a kitten's down,
A curve in the road.
I like rainbows and blue-bells
Sudden low thunder
A swirl of chiffon,
The color of yellow
A sad saxophone.
Pewter,
Black walnuts,
Love's urgent moan
Tomorrow
When you don't look at me,
It doesn't matter.

—*Priscilla Eberle*

Shoe Laces

Shoe laces, shoe laces,
I would not bring you
on a ship.
   Every time I walk
I always trip.
Shoelaces, oh shoelaces,
you hate my shoe,
I wish you were a
pot of stew.
Shoelaces, oh, shoelaces,
tist, tist, tist!
Shoelaces, shoelaces,
your last on my list!

—*Michael K. Fenech*

Untitled

If I could fly,
I'd soar through the clouds,
Battle the birds,
Burn the sun.
I'd erase all the stars,
And outshine the moon.
I'd find you up there
In heaven's ranks,
And carry you back home
On my wings.

—*Randi Baff*

A Random Poem On Schizophrenia

Say "Hello"? I bellow yellow
If he wants me to fight.
I'm a shallow little fellow
Who wants to get it right.

For some many power towers
Runs a dynamo.
Cursing on my joyous powers
Is what he next did show.

Later, an alligator ate
With a big crocodile.
There went my fish, lure, hook and bait.

Now, I fish for a smile!

—*Roy Carl Ervin*

Untitled

I've been told I am a fool,
If I do not continue with my school,
I really know that I can not run,
From getting a good education.
I have the brains, I have the will,
I don't have cash to pay the bill,
Tuition and books are some of the fees,
But money doesn't grow on trees,
My teacher then gave me the tip,
Of winning my own scholarship,
My poem is the only key
For me to go to a university.

—*Roy L. Williams Jr.*

Red Dawn

Would you miss me,
   if I were dead?
You who were the first
   to stain my body, red.
On a summer's wind in June
   with words left unsaid.
Our bodies silently speaking
   with the earth as our bed.
And you by my side
   laying down your weary head
I was the fool to believe
   the food that you fed
the fawn.........
Paint me red, words unsaid,
weary head, scars unfed, in my bed,
when I'm dead.

—*Lisa C. Mora*

The Candle Burns For You

My child is very beautiful,
If only for my mate and me.
Now he or she is on a milk carton,
For everyone in the world to see.

Come back home to us,
We miss you our dear.
I promise I'll love you,
And never shed another tear.

We sit and gaze through the fire,
Of the candles glow so bright.
To see your picture standing,
With your face relieved of fright.

There was a loud noise,
And I jumped to my feet.
Lord Jesus what a nightmare,
To be robbed of someone so sweet.

—*Preston F. Missey*

Out To Make You Mine . . . .

Out to make you mine
if someone doesn't hold the key,
cause love is truly blind
and I want you to understand me
when I tell you that I've fallen
into the sea too deep,
but I pray you hear my calling
and hope that you don't fall asleep.

Out to make you mine
When I met you that first day
I didn't waste no time
to ask you could you come out and play,
but you would not, so; I came in
and stayed for a long while
just to be a good friend,
and to see your lovely smile
I am willing to take it
one day at a time,
but you better believe I'm
out to make you mine.

—*William Webb*

Him

There he is so peaceful so quiet,
If you ask her if she loves him sure
she's going to deny it,
The perfect couple made from heaven,
But it's too bad she's only seven,
The love for thy is all so strong,
I hear bells in my head and they
go ding dong,
And that is how I feel about Chris,
To live together forever that would
be my only wish.

—*Latonya Landers*

White Rose Slippers

Like a ballerina dances
In a suspended circle
The petals of a white rose
gathers at my feet
In a cascading motion,
a little breeze,
Makes each petal dance
on their toes for one
last performance.

—*Sheila Porter*

How Do You Know

How do you know
If you'll be here tomorrow
If you'll be full of joy
Or filled up with sorrow
If you'll have a good job
And earn a good living
If you'll continue to take
Or finally start giving
If you'll find the right one
The one that you love
If you'll fit good together
Like a hand in a glove
If your life will be full
Your dreams be fulfilled
If you'll die in your sleep
Or if you'll be killed
If you'll have a big family,
That will continue to grow
Somebody please tell me
How do you know

—*Mark A. McGrew*

Sanctuary

Come and take me by the hand.
I'll take you to a different land.
Come along and leave the night.
Experience this soft new light.
It's a fascinating place to be
You'll be glad you came with me.
Things to do and much to see
Climb aboard, you can fly with me.
It's a place to go to clear your head
A place to go to be instead.

Drop your fears open up the door
Free your power to explore.
Use your freedom, lose the chains
You can soar in your domain.
And in your realm you will find
All your troubles left behind.
Who you take is up to you,
No one else can follow you
One more thing along the way
Once we're there you'll want to stay.

—*Larry Dagle*

Dream On

Tick, tock, tick, tock.
I'm looking at the clock.
It's 8th hour,
my substitute is getting sour.
She gave us lots of home work!
The bell rings, I go buzurk!
I wake up.
It's all a dream!
I go to school,
recess is cool.
It's 8th hour.
My sub's sour.
I'm waiting to go home
so I can sit happily alone,
and dream.

—*Nicole S. Meyer*

For My Mother

You are my mother
I'm proud to say
I'm just like you
In lots of ways

Your not only my mother
But also my friend
I know on you
I can always depend

We've had our differences
In my younger years
If only I'd listened
It would've saved me a lot of tears

No matter what
You listened to me
You helped me understand
That some things are meant to be

I love you very much
So Happy Mother's Day
You are a special part of my life
In my heart, you're here to stay

—*Susan Camerer*

Thinking Of You

I'm calling for you
I'm reaching for you
but still you're so far away

You know I want you
You know I need you
You know I want you to stay.

You're on my mind
You're in my heart
and still I await that passionate start.

To kiss you once
is only but a dream
but a dream is all that I have.
So I will wait for that lovely day
when your precious love can be mine
and I will hold you
and I will love you
forever 'til the end of time.

Be Mine.

—*Michael Gallo*

A Day

Sunrise is so beautiful,
In all its wonderful glory.
It is the beginning of a new day —
A day of an untold story.

After a certain time has passed,
And the day is almost through;
You learn all there is about a lie
Of which nothing there is true.

When night has come and gone —
And of a new day you are aware;
You consider each day a package
Stamped — "Handle With Care."

—*Virginia Reedy*

Haiku

White, pillowy, billowy clouds
In an aquamarine sky
Magic carpet for daydreams.

—*Valaria Gibbs*

In God I Trust

A road of task to follow
In God I trust
Nothing of myself but of deed I must
Follow his guidance and his love
Knowing this comes from heaven above
When danger is around each
Broken bend
The Devil, his advocate send
But God knows the devil's intent
So in his love the angels He sent
To let the principalities of darkness see
He is the God that watches over me
So in comfort and in love I must
Put my next step in his trust.

—*Ruthel Johnson*

Untitled

My uncle drowned the other day
In his backyard pool
He's dead, that's what they say
But, I know a secret, It's not for real

Everybody's eyes are teared
Dad—for goodness sake
Mom must know the secret
That this is a big mistake

We see a body all dressed up
It almost looks like him
It seems that everybody but me
Believes that he could not swim

The priest stands on his stage to say
The Lord has His reasons
While I sit on the floor and read
To his three baby orphans

He'll come back, he always does
We'll play as we did before
I know if I wait a little longer
He'll come walking through the door

—*Patricia Memminger*

To Foster Care

He stoops, hands fisted
   in his darkmost shadow,
for charity's pathway is shrouded
   by the hiss of a sigh
howling pain, through eyes
   slitted, tortured and clouded

with the parent, who lied
   to this beautiful child,
leaving him curled, in damp
   darkness alone...

small arms streaked with tears,
   soul weeping no words,
sweet innocence lost,
   with his home.

—*Penrose Hammond Anderson*

Untitled

Standing on the shore
in knee-high water
Looking out
and seeing a surf-tormented sea
wondering if those waves
could ever be me
or I them
being so free

—*Lahela K. Han*

Requiescat In Pace

A frightening disease
In love (?) acquired
Destroyed you
Slowly

And
In the end
Death
Seemed relief

—*Michaela Sczepaniak*

All Love

It comes to us
In many different ways.
As a baby we're held
In loving arms.
As youths we're protected
From daily harms.
Our teens are spent
In loving advice
Making life so very nice.
And then love comes
With sparkling eyes
When you observe
Your lifelong prize.
Your heart beats fast
And soars like a bird.
A gentle touch - a loving word
And life is changed forever.
You're close - you build
A love that leaves your never.

—*Margaret Olson*

The Great Oak

Standing still, but always moving,
In the forest, deep and dark,
stands an oak tree broad and tall,
with strands of ivy on its bark.

The winds may blow, the rain may fall
but that wont hurt the great oak tree
The oak tree stood for many years,
many years for us to see.

—*Shawn D. Swartz*

The Man In My Dreams

I dream of him each night,
In the hopes that he might,
Come and rescue me.

When I look into his eyes,
I see the clearest skies,
And it makes me wanna cry.

Because as soon as I get close to him,
My head begins to spin
And I close my eyes.

When I open them,
He is gone again,
And I've lost the man in my dream

—*Tricia Reed*

Untitled

Webs. Dust. My footsteps;
In the shadowed stable —
   No sounds of horses.

—*A. E. Hendricks*

Untitled

Tell me of Spring
In the language of Flowers

Tell me of Sorrow
In the language of Tears

Tell me of Joy
In the language of Laughter

Tell me of Love
In the language of You

—*Zee Pacifici*

Ole Porch Swing

Remember summer evenings
in the old porch swing?
All the wonderful feelings
childhood memories bring?
The evening shadows
casting shadows on the grass,
and family sat and chatted
to the people strolling past.
There was happy sounds from children
running homeward from their play,
and crickets softly chirping
a summer roundelay,
that's why at twilight
the warm nostalgia it brings,
those sweet and tender moments
spent in the "Ole porch swing".

—*Nora Wolverton*

Not To Touch The Earth

As not to touch your gentle mold
   in this autumn night
I see the fields of wheat and fancy
   of your drawn out mane
And the redolence of your silky vellum
   envelope the air
   over the garden bastion
While your teal-stained stare
   as fair as the calm waters
   and the lucid sky
   remain in rest
You, the daughter of my fair sister
   In self-coercion, I renounce
      careful,
   Not to touch the earth

—*Ryan Pierce*

My Daily Prayer

Lord, let me be a little more giving,
   in this earthly life.
For a little more living
   and less of bitter strife.
Let me reach out to
   some chance passerby and heed,
That certain individual
   with a special need.
Let me be true
   beautiful and fair,
And please God, help me do these things.
   This shall be my daily prayer.

—*Wanda Louise Estes*

Justice

Lost justice, now,
In this world of lies.
Hatred and anger prevail,
Fighting men of larger size.
You'll never win here.
The verdict already clear.
Future down the tubes,
There's no doubt, you lose.

—*Peter Colburn*

Growing Older

It seems these days I'm being told
In very subtle ways I am old
We pause and smile and gently say
Have you found pleasant things today.

If they but let us slowly age
We're at a very graceful stage
It seems I have more time for me
I do not spend it fretfully.

I am out there getting the latest view
If steps are missed I start anew
The tube is off I am on my way
Grandma having fun today.

—*Mildred M. Ziegler*

In A Kiss

In a tear I see your face
In your soul I see a dove
In your eyes I see reflection
In your kiss I feel your love.

In these months of joy eternal
In these days of "you and me,"
We've become a pair,
Whose kisses bear our love as poetry.

On the canvas of perception,
Colors dance and slowly drip.
Feel the vibrancy of colors
As we gently join our lips.

How I love you, oh sweet woman!
How, alone, do you I miss.
How, in love, I still keep yearning
For your soft and sweetest kiss.

—*Peter Daniel Lago*

Untitled

We often look
Inside our minds
To find answers
That cannot be found

We dwell upon
Our failures
And seek
Deeper recesses

That can only
Lead us
Too greater
Remorse

Encompass
A broader vision
And solutions
No longer evade us

—*Marge Edelman*

Who Ever

Hear these words
Inspired from above

Giving you warning
Of things to come

The time is set
There's no returning

Most prophecies complete
The raptures dawning

So heed this word
Read your scripture

Keep the commandments
Pray for repentance

Abstain from sin
In heart and mind

And be of wise
Don't live, just to die.

—*William S. Jones*

Black Skies

As I sit and look off
into the distance —
I listen and hear the
whispers of nothingness!
As I sit and look off
into the distance —
I look and see the stars
that dance and twinkle
like loving eyes staring
down on earth.
As I sit and look off
into the distance —
I see nothing, I see
black, I see night!

—*Mary Claire Pierce*

Untitled

As I walk
into this strange world
of music and love
my mind goes blank.
I'm fascinated
by what these people
are playing.
They are doing a dance
of their heritage.
It is a fast dance
like a cheetah running.
They play a drum
and something like a flute.
It's a soothing feeling
to hear this music and dance.

—*Tierra McCulligh*

I Care

When you know someone you care about
  Is hurting deep inside,
What can you do or say to them,
  Some comfort to provide?
Don't burden them with parallels,
  Advice, or much ado,
Just say: "I care, I'm always there;
  And I will pray for you!"

—*Ruth J. Colella*

Sex Without Love

Sex without love...
Is a rose without fragrance, beauty...
Without nature's own red, pink seal.
Sex without love...
Is a road, a dead-end...
Blind-alley with no horizon.
Sex without love...
Is power, ruthless power, self-consuming.
Sex without love...
Is male without female...
For what is human without love...
As an idea without expression, smothers.
Sex without love...
Is youth...alone, without compromise...
Deprived, never aging, never maturing.
Sex without love...
Is life blossoming wild, solitary...
Seeking, searching, reaching for love...
For love is never alone.

—*Marco Gentile*

Greed

Deep within the heart of man
Is a wish to win the foreign land.
So many have tried,
So many have died,
For besides the wish to win
Greed grows from within.
Greed that causes man to die.
And greed that breaks all family ties.
So don't get caught in the trap,
If you do there's no way out
No matter how you scream and
shout.

—*Sara Whisler*

Everlasting Beauty?

The Earth, you see
Is everlasting to me

It contains the most
  beautiful things;
Flowers, trees, you, and me.

But....the beauty
Is disappearing, you see?

—*Rachel Guagliardo*

Communion

The taste of bread
Is in my mouth
Fresh from the loaf
of His brokenness

The wine is sweet
In the bread entwined
Bringing wholeness and healing
Of body and mind

Blessed Savior
Spirit divine
Dwell in my heart
Spanning eternities time

—*Lena Gibson*

The Weeping Willow

Oh, weeping willow, why do you weep so?
Is it because you've lost a loved one?
Or the birds no longer roost in
your branches?
Or is it for providing shade for
those who work long hours in
the sun?
Or to hide lovers who caress
under your branches?
Do you weep because you know the
secret of the earth and mustn't
tell?
Or is it for birds to find a
home for their young ones?
Is it for the same reason I'm here-
to find peace in the tranquility
of nature?
Oh, weeping willow, why do you
weep so, with your leaves that
almost touch the ground?

—*Sara Saint*

Fall

Fall, is it more than a word,
  is it more than a season.
    Is it a way of life,
    is it another reason.
  We try to take flight,
    and soar to the top.
  We look down at the world,
  and to find it does not stop.
    We warm our faces,
  on the sun's rays of success.
  We find the road leading to home,
and the road of question and guess.
    The warm and safe places,
    a child in the wilderness.
    The arms that embrace you,
    and a place to confess.
    A beginning of life,
    and a meaning to it all.
    To be brave and be true,
    and to rise we must fall.

—*Veronica H. Ahlfeld*

She

The actress beneath me
is playing her favorite part
as the whimsical recipient
of my love force.
Pretending satisfaction
for my satisfaction.
Shall I reap her reward
and jilt her
so she can cry wolf
to her friends
and claim she is a victim?
Or do I kiss her nose
and take her in
only to have my heart broken
when she leaves me for another?

—*Theodore Hayes*

Haiku '93

Photographic art. . .
Is sensing just when to "click"
The camera's film.

—*K. L. Whitcomb*

Lessons

To live life
Is to learn
Who we have become
Who we need to be
What it is we have to offer
What it is we need
When we must be dependable
When on others we must depend
Where our dreams can take us
Where our dreams must end
Why we must stand silently
Why we must have our say
How yesterday lasts forever
How tomorrow steals today

—*R. Andrew Szurgot*

Alone, With Hope

To realize that you are gone
is to start an endless day
of pain and unbearable grief
at not knowing when, if ever,
you will return to me again.

To think that someday you may
is enough to carry me through
but oh, the uncertainly makes me wonder
if I can endure the coming times
until I hold you close again.

I know you will not deceive me
by making my life barren
of your warm and precious love,
for you will return again
and I will thrive on your nearness.

For it is you who makes
the sun shine, the breeze blow
and love bloom in my heart,
and when you once again do return,
my life will begin anew, close to you.

—*Pat Doyle*

Beauty!

"Beauty is as beauty 'does'!"
Is what I was always told,
And no amount of outward beauty,
Can outshine a "beautiful soul"!

External beauty is the "package,"
That nature does provide,
But "internal" handsomeness,
Is what one "develops" inside!

The one with fairest beauty,
No "camera" can convey,
For "beauty" is hidden deep within,
And it will not "decay!"

Outward beauty catches the eye,
Yes, that "may" be a start,
But the one with "inward" beauty,
Is the one that "touches" the heart!!

—*Sandra Justice*

Time

Time,
is what we were waiting for;
  Time,
is what we needed;
  Time,
we never had;
  Time,
could have been right;
  Time,
could have brought us back;
  Time,
could have made us right;
  Time,
could have brought us love;
  Time,
has gone away;
  Time,
will never come back for us;
  Time,
is over for good.

—*Melissa Willms*

Untitled

No red dawning tonight
Isolated with the tumbling waves

Thunder roars with the strike of light
As we pray to the one who saves

Premonition of things to come
The calm before the storm.

—*Vicki Seal*

The Sun Rises, The Sun Falls

And even though, I love you
It doesn't mean. I hate you
we can only be friends
just this once
for which we will part
and , leave only memories behind
which will only hurt us even more.
If we take even one memory away.
  The sun rises
  The sun falls

—*Lori Dill*

Bryce Canyon

The sonic boom was sharp and clear.
It drew our gaze aloft,
and through the silence, following,
all lesser sounds were soft.

We heard the trickle of the sand
as fragments were displaced,
which gave our hearts an erie chill
as minarets defaced.

Sifting down upon our heads,
sand fell beneath our gaze,
into the canyons far below,
to vanish in the haze.

When sonic booms reverberate
within those canyon walls,
all nature shudders, instantly,
while grit and powder falls.

—*Virginia Grosvenor Allee*

The Me You Don't See

Have I not been stifled enough, from birth to this pen?,
I too want love, prosperity, health, and peace within;

You can just turn hurling damnation to burn in hell's fire,
It appears my honesty proves fatal and you would prefer a
    masked liar;

I never spoke untruths, I just never spoke them all,
My conscious is clear, it's your unmasked ignorance that's
    permitting our fall;

I only wanted to clean your window allowing a true glance
    at me,
I stand before you, a freshly scrubbed soul:
    The Me You Don't See.

—*Dwayne D. Erby*

Me And The Seasons

Summer lets me go.
I tumble like a kitten playful and frail.
I glow like a rainbow colorful and rare.
I gleam like the sun warming the earth.
I shoot up like a flower blooming in the sun.
I fly like a tree blowing in the wind.
Now winter has grabbed me.
I am a cat shivering in the bitter cold.
I am dark clouds blackening the sky.
I am white, thick snow freezing the earth.
I am a flower wilted and dead.
Me and the seasons.
We are nearly alike.

—*Ashley Reinier*

A Love Song

Never thought I would find a love as Beautiful as Ours,
I used to spend all my nights staring into the stars.
And then you came to me like a warm and gentle breeze,
and gave me all the things I thought I would never see.
You are my life, my Love, You are everything to me;
Never let me go, never set me free.

—*Danny Joe Poppe*

Aqueous

When I throw my muses,
I usually augment the puddles,
And the mud forms within the dry earth.
Oh, I've felt lonely.
Once in a while, I can saturate the air.
Warmth pervading beautiful haze.
But noon comes after repose,
And the sober dry air expands through my cold cloud.
A few times I've drenched,
Left friends in results of soothing showers,
Comforting is the heat of understandings.
A few other times, I've failed,
Friends covered from the icy rains,
Yes, I feel lonely.
Maybe soon there will be one,
There to imbibe and absorb,
For love and life,
Till death.
Then I could see my loneliness rapid,
Flowing toward the briny sea.

—*Chris Kim*

Lazarus

I live with my two sisters now in darkness
I venture out at night when roads are free.
I cannot bear the curious gaze of people
Who know about the thing that was done to me.

When I look back, was I a man like others
With hopes and fears, desires and sunny days?
A three-day blackness put all that behind me
And cut me off from all the normal ways.

My sisters are my sanity and strength now;
Martha cares for my body, and my soul
Is kept from madness by the love of Mary
Between the two I manage to keep whole.

For who can look upon a dead man risen
Without a furtive horror in his eyes?
I stumbled from a coffin to a prison
And lost my little hope of paradise.

I feel his arms around me, warm and tender,
I feel his burning tears upon my head.
I hear him say, 'Forgive me, little brother,
I kept you from the kindness of the dead.'

—*Elizabeth Harrison*

Daydreaming

The day they placed you in my arms
I vowed to keep you from all harm
To watch you as you grew each day
To supervise your work and play

To teach you of life's ups and downs
To wear a smile and not a frown
To live for today, instead of tomorrow
To help you through your times of sorrow

Right from wrong, truth from lie
Just look at how the time did fly
Now tell me did I hear you say
Someone stole your heart away
Who was that thief who slipped past me
a lucky guy your husband to be

Yes! Yes! now I remember, it's your
wedding day, come this September

—*Catherine Barnette*

To Let You Go

As I gaze into your baby blues,
I want the world to know the news
that you are mine right from the start
But it's you that caused my broken heart.
Because when you leave, I feel the pain
In this affair, what could I gain?
She's the one who's got you by the nose
Isn't that the way that marriage goes?
You have a life away from mine
It's always alone I sit and dine.
I think of you when your not here
of how we'd make the perfect pair.
I'd give the world on a silver platter,
But then again, what would it matter.
I knew at the start you were a flirt
But why the hell does it have to hurt?
I really have to let you go-
To get on with my life, get on with the show.
So when you see my smiling face,
Remember no one could take your place.

—*Cynthia Spooner*

Friend Of Mine

My heart is deeply saddened, Why?
I want to cry, but I can't, Why?
My heart is afraid....Afraid?
that I'm slowly losing my friend

My friend that knows how to make me laugh,
My friend that speaks from the heart....
My friend that really cares for me—
always has from the start.

The thing that I feared has slowly crept upon me
and that's the way it will have to be.

Although I may not ever see my friend
and we may not ever talk, ever again
my friend will Always be my friend,
Always in my heart
till the end

So
if my friend were here today, I would look my friend in the
eyes and say "I love you more than words could ever say."
—*Joan Celeste Smith*

Road Myways

Road... I want to be a road
I want to ride the wind of never-end and be a road and bend
round life's curves swerves lips and dips, I want to ride with
a glide that will never ever die...sigh...high is what I am
when my mind probes the land the sand the grandest of the grand
curling and swirling through life and strife cutting like a
knife through the deep to seep in steep in leap in the grass
of the rolling hill waves saves and delays my heart from the
days when my ways were dead end, deafened - to the beat the
drum the hum for some the call to come and be a road...
a destination an inspiration, a perspiration on the forehead
of time, a deviation from the normality of rhyme, an
invitation to the life of the sublime...Oh the paths I would
follow the miles I would swallow my heights would never fall,
Oh...to flow with the slow and low grow of tempo, I know-
roads like veins strain and drain deeper to the thumping
refrain where the highways are myways and continue for always,
Oh holy road my feet are meant to meet your gravel so unravel,
unravel, before me, after me, for I must let free, set free,
to be a road
—*Abby Susik*

Pocket Change

Once	Now
I was a coin	I am a piece
In your pocket.	of weathered metal.
New.	Old.
Clean.	Dark.
And bright.	And dull.
But	And
I stayed	My face has faded.
In your pocket	So hard to see
Too long.	Who I am
I slowly	Or the value
Wore away.	I once had.

—*Cesar A. Villarreal*

The Spark Of Life

In the depths of my soul there is the agony of realization.
I was not formed for the spectacular.
Neither angelic nor demonic.
Not rapturous beauty nor reviling deformity.
My passing by brings no reaction.
I am a-muck in anonymity.
A monotonous middle ground spreads endlessly before my life
    line.
Not even a "Kil-Roy" to mark my passing.
No glorious victories — no tarnished trophies of strengths now
    gone.
And yet — the spark of life breaths hope in spite of reality.
The mirror and its image seem far less important,
Than the fire burning still with-in my breast.
—*Flo Gonya*

Farewell To A Daughter

Standing here, tears streaming down my face,
I watch her start down that long road,
to find her life and rightfully take her place.
I know that she must carry her own load.

Not so many years ago I held her in my arms,
wiping tears shed for a broken doll.
We all were quite subjected to her many charms;
now suddenly she's grown, it seems so short a while.

Together we laughed, sometimes we cried,
and I remember well her first big date.
I know as now she leaves my loving side,
our parting has been preordained by fate.

She's coming world, please treat her well.
She is so young, yet eager for this start.
She must discover things I couldn't tell,
but with her goes my blessing, and a big piece of my heart.
—*Betty Jo Phillips*

And So I Danced With Orion

In the absence of the moon
I wept for the emptiness of my arms
on this romantic starlit night.

He stepped from the sky hands outstretched,
inviting. I curtsied low.
And so I danced with Orion
on grass brushed with dew
to strains of music far, far away.

Round and round we circled
under stars twinkling in merriment;
more brilliant than diamonds scattered upon velvet.
We drank from the big dipper
then danced again
while waves below, in joy, applauded.

And then he was gone
riding back to the heavens on the tail of a comet.
I blew a kiss in farewell, no longer lonely;
my spirit having been caressed by God.
—*Jeri Chrysong*

I Am God's Instrument

I am God's instrument that plays night and day.
I will play the music that God wanted to hear.
I will play a tune that people will hear and
  know that I have care and love for them.
I will play a tune that would be like saying,
"I Do", in marriage to God.
I will play a lovely tune for God.
I will play a prayer to people who need love and care.
I will play a tune that my elders can hear to be healed.
I will play a tune that poor people can hear to be fed.
I will play a tune that weak people can hear and will be
  strong. This is a song of joy.
This is a song of light.
I will play a song that people can hear to be healed.
I will play a tune that will give more love than money can buy.
I will play a tune that people can hear and
  bring them out of their world that they hate.
I hope I will play a tune that will bring them out of misery.
I hope I play a harmony.
I hope I play the best.

        —*Erin I. Wessling*

Love Is.......

The way you held me tight
I wished you were there day and night
I always dreamed you were here
And I always wake up in fear,
Hoping that we'd never part
I thought something serious would start,
Underneath this clear sky
It hurts deep inside to say good-bye,
I think I'm still in love with you
Even though we agreed we were through,
But, I can't help thinking of you,
I want to describe my love
But, there is no possible way,
Your eyes as blue as the bay
Your sweet, gentle smile kept me up all night,
Your gentle kiss is what I miss
No one could move their lips like you.
When I think of you it makes me blue

        —*Danielle Faulk*

I Am.....

I am a peacemaker and a dreamer.
I wonder if someday there will be peace.
I hear Martin Luther King speak kind words.
I want to create a world of nice people.
I am a peacemaker and a dreamer.
I pretend people share life.
I feel the wind, gush on my face.
I touch velvet.
I worry about people who are poor.
I cry for the world.
I am a peacemaker and a dreamer

I understand that life is not simple.
I say words of laughter
I dream of becoming an actress
I try to be someone special.
I am a peacemaker and a dreamer.

        —*Ashleigh Hurley*

I Am...

I am worried and confused
I wonder why crippled Romanian children are locked up.
    I hear them crying and
    I see them dying.
I want to help them, but I know I can't.
I am worried and confused

I pretend to help them because,
    I feel their anger, and
I touch their skinny disfigured bones.
I worry that their lives will never change. Every time
    I cry, I know they are too.
    I am worried and confused

I understand I can't do everything to save them, but
    I try to; maybe if...
    I say I can, and
I dream I can, I will be able to save them.
    I hope it works because,
    I am worried and confused

        —*Heather Branagan*

My First Poem To Dad

As Mom laid in the lonely hospital bed,
I wondered whether my Dad was dead,
I kicked and screamed and watched Mom look sad,
And I asked Mom where was Dad,
I said Mom, pick up the phone and call,
But the phone only rang off the wall,
I asked Mom what this really mean,
She said your Dad is a human being,
You can ask your Dad what the future bring,
So, we don't have to pick up the phone and listen to it ring,
This I ask of you dear Dad,
I don't like to see my Mom so sad,
Mom used to have a glow on her face,
And now she has slowed her pace,
I don't want Mom worried,
Because I might have to be hurried.

        —*Dorisonia A. Malcolm*

If I Were A Flower

If I were a flower
I would blossom in the warmth of your affection
And whisper into the wind a sweet magnetic fragrance
To call you near...and end your fear

I'd dazzle you with the wild bright colors
Of my passion and awaken forgotten places in your heart
That would only be a start...if I were a flower...

If I were a flower
I would capture you and enrapture you
With a magical mood...erasing from your mind
All that's cold...I would touch your soul

I would help you feel yourself and heal yourself
With me you'd come to know your own inner glow
I'd give you comfort in your pain,
Sunshine after the rain...

And you would pluck me from my place and not be sad
When I, subdued by time, began to fade
For you'd recall the time we had dancing in the glade
If I were a flower

        —*Harvard Jennings*

Grandchildren

I love my grandkids with all of my heart,
I would never sit and pick them apart,
I look for the good in all that they do,
Would you like it, if I criticized you?
Like, you are too heavy, you don't look like me.
How is a grandchild supposed to be?
If you are just kidding, please tell them so.
If not, how in the world are they supposed to know.
Don't forget to tell them you love them, every day.
Actions will show it, but it's still nice to say,
How nice they were today.
If they do a good job, let them know it's true.
How much I love having a grandchild like you.
You don't have to shower them with presents,
But if you want to, that's nice.
I always have cookies or a snack, I don't think twice.
Look for the good, I can't say it more,
If you're looking for love from them, this is the cure.
If criticizing and correcting is what you like to do,
Look in the mirror and who do you see? It's you.

—*Catherine N. Lear*

A Prayer

In this world of anger and strife -
I yearn for peace, for a better life.
To be content - unafraid - secure,
As a newborn child - innocent - immature.
Blanket this world with warm giving love,
With peace, serenity, the faithfulness of the dove.
Rid this world of immorality and abuse,
Teach me love - understanding - and truth.
Filter my thoughts to be clean and pure,
Instill in me strength - my pain to endure.

Lord, let me recognize the good that you've done,
For life - for flowers - the warmth of morning sun.
For family - for friends - for food - for health,
For the privilege of knowing you - this is my wealth.
When my trial comes - facing the eyes of death,
May I know in my heart - I've lived by best.
No longer will I - down these earthly paths trod,
I will now sit - at the right hand of God.
My epitaph written - "A Man, A Friend,
He is now at Peace - Amen. AMEN.

—*Bob Bell*

Across The Barrier

From across the barrier
I yearn to touch you-
As I touched you last evening.
Light glistening in the dew on your skin;
As I touched you today,
Lightly, on a hand just now requited-
To beckon the smile that paints ecstasy
On the canvas that is my soul.

Yet, I think of your message that caused me hesitation:
Do sensations bring you fear of what could be lost
Amid the glory of our pas de deux?
And so, the barrier rises to shield the silver once tarnished
By a thief unknowing of its value.

I won't take any part of your life - I promise
Because it is a design you have fashioned
That stirs me to consider a mural never seen...
And so, I pass across the barrier fragile gifts
That I have never shown
In hopes that they may brighten
The beauty you have crafted.

—*Gregory J. Borden*

Someone Special

If I had someone special
I'd give up all my love to her.
I'd hold her, love her, treat her fragile;
With all I have, I'll always offer.

I simply beg for love and that's all.
Maybe a date, or an everlasting endeavor.
I'd have a reliable hug waiting when sadness falls
Upon life when it is tough to recover!

But most of all, when she does call,
I'll be right there by her side.
Should she take a fall with her back to the wall
I would pull her far from the treacherous tide!

—*Anthony G. Kanzig*

The Book

I found it quite by accident one rainy summer day,
I'd gone up to the attic just to pass some time away.

I'd done this many times before, yet every time seemed new,
Sometimes I'd find a treasure that before escaped my view.

I poured through faded pictures then rummaged through the
trunks, re-read the old love letters and examined bits of junk.

Then suddenly I saw it! By the chimney on the floor,
A dusty leather volume I had never seen before.

I wondered where it came from what chance had left it there,
Who had read these yellowed pages? Who'd kept it all these
years?

And then I saw the writing...one simple purple line,
But time had long since faded the name I'd hoped to find.

I hurried to the window and held it to the light,
But the secret that I longed for had vanished from all sight.

So time had left a mystery, as he so often does...
Just "Merry Christmas son, I love you"...I wonder who he was...?

—*Elizabeth Ritchie*

A Dying Thought

I'd love to have been held in my Daddy's hands.
I'd love to seen my Mother's face,
But there was no time or place for me among
the human race.
Love to have known my brothers and sisters,
And everyday in our yard we could have played.
And as I got older, could've gone to school.
I could've learned the golden rule.
All the scratched up knees, the kiss that would've
made it all better.
Puppies I could've chased.
I don't feel bad for God has a special place,
But I wish I could have been held in my
daddy's hands,
And kissed my mother's face.

—*James R. Gordon*

Chili

Chili is Red, Chili is Green,
If you eat it in bed, it makes you scream.
Is this a nightmare, or is this a dream?

Don't ask if it hurts my tongue,
'cause all I can feel is,
numb, numb, numb.

—*Candice Roach*

Habits

I awoke with a start, the room was bright,
I'd overslept, 'twas no longer night.
I sat up straight and trembled with shock,
Squinted my eyes so I could see the clock.

I threw back the covers and struggled from bed,
And stumbled to the bath, I'm filled with dread.
I pulled on my shorts and socks and shoes
And wondered how much of my wages I'd lose.

I brushed my teach and combed my hair.
And looked at the bed, my wife was still there.
And then I knew I had nothing to fear,
I just remembered I retired this year.

—*Jack E. Kinnebrew*

Only Friends

I wonder often of what could have been,
   if he would have heard me through his den.
Why must he joke at my times of earnestness
   and be so proud, with his cockiness.
I wish he'd explain what he meant of my greenness,
   and if that is truly my only weakness.
Then he must admit, and open his heart,
   for it is not my wish to depart.
Won't you remember me, my one so dear,
   the time is aeons, it is many years.
Perhaps in the future we'll meet again
   then I should love to be best friends.
If only you knew how right you were
   when you revealed my secret and then deterred.
How I fervently wish it could only be,
   that time would stand still for you and me.

—*Elizabeth Kim*

He Told Me

He told me he would not tell
if I told anyone else.
So in my hasty mind I complied,
to understand what he thought and why.
He was here a street of darkness and gloom all around,
and not a friend to be found.
But I wondered why did he,
leave his home so suddenly.
I did not know him a child before,
and I did not know what was in store.
For him crime and dirt, and drugs no doubt.
On the corner so called friends all about.
"Do not go friend, stay with me.
I can help you can't you see!"
"How can you?" he said with anger and hate.
"When you go home the streets are my fate, this is
my life here and there".
Said with a shrug of his shoulders without care.
So alone he went on his way,
And my heart breaks, because,
he needed help yesterday.

—*Debra A. Rioux*

Flower Bud

The flower bud is opening in a long yawning
In every bud the one that sleeps is craving
Till late the skies stays open
Even at night sparks spring on the sleeping branches,
Swinging by in a warm wind
"Wake up" he said touching everything smoothly,
A shoulder or
Slapping a new born baby
Who starts crying right after.

—*John Plesh*

Colorblind

If I'm black then I'm black
If I'm white then I'm white
There's no need to argue
No there's no need to fight

We're all human beings, God's creation
Let us stand tall under one nation
Working together we can be one
Throw down your knives put away your gun

Children are starving, abused everyday
They can't fight back no they don't know the way
All we see is color, we're falling apart
We look at the outside not at the heart

We've all become prisoners, afraid for our lives
Killing each other with double edged knives
Words are spoken that cut so deep
The nightmares so bad they rob our sleep.

Please God I pray make us all color blind
Give us the strength, give us peace of mind
Let us show love, oh please Lord I cry
Don't let another one of us die.

—*Bobbie Jo Sloan*

Baby - Sitting

Baby-sitting can be a lot of fun;
   if it is well and properly done.
Whatever they are having for dinner;
   whether it is pork or bean.
Always make sure when they are through;
   their plate is clean.
Entertainment is as easy as can be;
   they can read a book or watch TV.
Toileting can be a trick;
   but it is worse when a child is sick.
Before bedtime you can read them a story;
   so they can sleep with comfort and without worry.
It is sometimes hard to tell kids "No";
   but the worst part is when they don't want you to go!

—*Amber Steele*

Ocean Wide

Ocean wide, no one can decide
if they can see from side to side.
A thousand miles around the world
over sea under stone, you will find it all alone.
Under all the water top, you will find peace.
Colors of diamonds, crystals and more.
Try to soar in your mind and you will find the ocean kind.
Schools of fish with colors all bright
and fire burning in their sight.
They do not sleep at night.
From the bottom, miles down you can't see any light.
No wars to fight just some sharks that might bite.
It's all like a flying kite.
I know I'm right, go see for yourself. Buried treasure you
may find, maybe a boat from history signed. Seaweed of sorts
many resorts, and structures that no one can define.
As your soaring, can you her the ocean roaring? It is such
a delight to see such a site! But one last comment for this
poem "Ocean Wide Side To Side, no one still can not
decide."

—*Daune' J. Gonsalves*

My Only Love

When I fell in love with you,
I'll always remember that day,
For you my Darling were my very own.
From the moment I heard you say
That you loved me very much too,
The same way that I loved you.

It wasn't too much longer,
Until we met at the alter,
To give our vows to God,
That we would worship each other.

I sincerely hope that our love will last.
And as the years pass by,
I will never forget our past -
And hope that our love never dies.

Our life together has been great,
And our love very sincere.
To you my love I dedicate
This poems for this year.
—*Dale D. Gould*

Missing You

Hundreds of miles from friends and love,
I'll forever wish to the heavens above,
That one day I will return home,
Where I will no longer be alone.

I wish night after night,
That someday I really might,
Go back to where I belong,
It doesn't matter how long.

Uprooted from my old life and placed somewhere new,
No matter how much I try, I cannot forget you,
Even though we are apart,
You'll always be in my heart.

I want to be home and some day I will,
So that my now empty heart will be filled,
My friends are everything to me,
They are my life always will be.

My new life is good and yet
My lonely heart will never forget
—*Jennifer Zorko*

God Who Cares

I love Jesus, hope you can tell,
I'll serve Jesus, I'll serve Him well.

He loves you and He loves me,
I'll be with Him eternally.

He cares for each and everyone,
even after the things we've done.

He wants us to read the Bible and pray
He wants us to do these every day.

If we do these in a cheerful way,
He'll reward us on Judgement Day.

When Jesus descends back to earth again,
He'll take all believers to be with Him.

Now that my poem is said and done,
I hope you will listen and follow the Son.
—*Jennifer Fauver*

What Is A Boy?

You ask, "What is a boy?"
I'll tell you, if you don't know
He's sometimes a pack of mischief,
Wrapped in dirt from head to toe.

Sometimes he's just full of questions,
"Why is this," and "What is that?"
Like "Why do I have to wash my face?"
And "what makes dogs hate cats?"

His appetite equals a pig.
He is perpetual motion in action.
He can climb like a cat, swim like a fish.
And run to a deer's satisfaction.

Sometimes he's as good as can be.
Sometimes he's just aggravation.
But still he's a joy forever,
And the wonderful people of our nation.
—*Elaine D. Johnson*

Letting Go

It's time you finally know
    I'm letting you go
I still love you my dear
    That's why in my eye you see this tear
I think it's best if you stay away
    And I'll get over you day by day
The memories of us I can't forget
    And that's my only regret
Letting go isn't an easy thing to do
    Because of how much I love you
You must realize I also have pain
    But a new life each of us will gain
Sure we'll see each other again
    But that will only be as a friend
Can't you realize by the tear in my eye
    I'm feeling agonizing pain as I tell you good-bye.
—*Deidre Underwood*

Michael

Young and sweet and dear.
I'm so sad that your sweet voice,
Again, I'll never hear.
Your good morning kiss, I must admit,
I'll forever truly miss.
Your sweet smiling face,
No one could ever replace.
You were my precious little boy.
Oh! how you brought me so much joy!
Then, suddenly Jesus took you away,
But in my heart, my precious Michael,
forever you will stay.
Why? Oh why? I cry dear Jesus,
did you have to take my precious Mikey away?
But then, I stop and pray how
wonderful it will be, when dear
Jesus brings us together again, someday!
—*Christy Malaric*

Cold Love

I'm walking the line
   I'm walking the line
treading thin ice time after time.

I go for the best, end up with much less
I need the real thing forget all the rest.

Started out good, working out bad
all the sweet love turned
   sour and sad.

A face and a name, it's always the same
so tired of playing love's foolish games
tell me why, love passes me by.

Cold love, wrong love
whatever happened to that good old love.

   —Eynar Gonzalez

Imagine

Imagine the world without war, without hate.
Imagine the world full of love, full of joy.
Imagine a girl smiling to a boy.
Imagine a fisherman fishing without bait.

Imagine the world without borders, without walls.
Imagine the nations without armies, without guns.
Imagine the children with food by the tons.
Imagine the children playing with cotton balls.

Imagine the world with no differences among the races.
Imagine the world without hunger, without sickness.
Imagine the world without anger, without stress.
Imagine the people holding hands like braces.

   —Joe S. Valente

A Teacher's Life

It all began long, long ago
Imparting knowledge to and fro
Developing intellects great and small
Running the country for us all.

Over the years you've done your part
Providing thousands of students with a good start
Encouraging them to prepare for life
Striving for success without much strife.

If there existed a Teacher's Hall of Fame
We certainly would find your name
You've served your time and done your best
Now you place the responsibility on the rest.

Over the years retirement is a teacher's final goal
It calms the nerves and relaxes the soul
From June 11th on your life is yours to enjoy
There'll be days when you'll say "Boy, Oh, Boy"!

   —Carolyn V. Watson

Miwa En Treis

Magical spent moments, to contemplate, her mystery;
Incomparable Miwa, with no, known rivalry;
Wondrous lady, her name, a constant melody;
Adoring thoughts, for her alone, such blissful ecstasy.

Melodious my heart, were she but, my destiny;
Imagine her, life's center, would I rush devotedly;
Warmhearted I, with loves gift, true fidelity;
Affections given, returned how perfect, heavenly.

Merriment ours, together playful, in spontaneity;
Ideal Miwa, a life of, boundless gaiety;
Whispered secrets, pledges vows, most lovingly;
Ardent moments, to share we two, ours eternally.

   —Gary S. Willard

Drums

The tatoo inside his head should have warned him, of his
impending doom, the beat so steady, night and day and day
and night.

Ringing inside his head, the drums beat an ever-increasing
tempo, building, to the ultimate finality.

The crescendo would finally silence. Deaths curtain would
drape the stage of life, and the drums would be silent,
forever. The beat so steady, night and day and day and night.

Why hadn't he just ignored the drums, and listened to the
melodies in his heart?

The joy of today becomes our memorials. When we walk with
honor, we are remembered with honor.

The drums that I hear, are sometimes overwhelming. Raising
the fear, that now is the time, the curtain of life,
will fall for me.

Those times, are the times I must focus on. The melodies of
the past. Remembering the memories of those, who in my life,
did love me, and will still,
when my drum has fallen silent, and the beat of life moves on.

   The beat so steady, night and day and day and night.

   —D. R. Ostman

In A Memory

Everybody on earth has been written about
in a memory.

Both the sky and the sea, and the ocean breeze
in a memory.

I see now that they all just belong to
the sky. The sky finding earth. To the rainbows
hitting dirt.

To the mountains and the sea and the bird's
living in the tree's, that live within me
today.

And tell me it's okay there's no memory to
pay, but life only today.

Live the moment that is, and never kiss
from afar, just let go of that falling star
in a memory.

   —Denise Boyce

In Memories Of Memories

I sit here among these carolina pines and watch the leaves
in all their splendor, no two colors alike, and realize there
will never be another whisper or secret shared by you and me.
   We once dreamed the dream of lovers, of things to come and
how it would be "when". Fate has robbed us of "when" and now I
have the memories of things past and the hopes of things yet to
come... alone.
   Now I sit beneath these pines, watching the leaves, knowing
and not yet accepting that you are a part of my yesterdays. I
am not bitter, for you gave me those yesterdays and left me
with the courage to face tomorrow on my own.
   My wishes and hopes continue and just as the leaves change
so has my life. For as the earth will be richer for the
passing of these leaves, my life is richer for knowing you, for
loving you, for sharing our whispers, secrets, dreams and life.
   So next time I sit and watch the leaves in all their
splendor or see the reflection of the sun on the wall that now
holds your name, or listen to the laughter of new dreamers, I
will think of you... and smile.

   —Debrah J. Hendrickson

Home Is

Blessing,   We take our home so casually
  In an abstract sort of way.
It just doesn't seem to register
What a blessing it is each day.

Retreat,   It is a retreat in time of trouble,
  A place of rest from our toil of the day.
When the trials of life seem heavy,
In its solitude there is a quiet place to pray.

Springboard,   Love in a home is so precious,
  It makes the cares of the world seem light.
It provides a springboard of hope for tomorrow
And lightens our load every night.

Anchor,   Many things in life are uncertain
  Ever changing like the sands on the beach.
God's word provides the anchor to hold us
In the direction our homes must seek.

Reward,   Dad...Mother...Daughter...Son
  There is a place at home for everyone.
When we are all together in this special place,
Let's each pause to thank God - Face to face.

—*Jim Leverette*

Retirement

Re-runs and the like I'll get to see.
In and out of town and state, my travels will take me.
Everything from give aways to soap opera's, I'll select;
Traveling by car, plane or by bus, I'll make my trek.
Retirement from one plateau of life to another adventure,
Everyday will be lived to its fullest potential.

Many things will catch my fancy, yes working will be
included, so you see,
I'll retire only to another location, can't recline
to that rocking chair, healthy life is activity.

I shall attempt everyday God gives to me;
To share in some small way:
With nature, my family, friends and those who need me.
And noting that sharing is costless, and to my life
It will brighten and my time it will use.
Retirement is only to another plateau.

—*Hattie M. Belcher*

I Smelled Summer

I smelled summer
  In birth of wet-grass morn'
I smelled summer in
  A southern breeze.
I smelled summer in her sunlight as
  rays gave fragrance to glossy green leaves.

I smelled summer
  In the mother's thunder
    That coaxed a drizzle
    That beaded dust.
I smelled summer in fresh-cut melon
  My young heart swelling with wanderlust.

I smelled summer in spicy mimosa,
  sweet magnolia,
    the Dogwood tree.
I smelled summer
  in perfumed mem'rys
    dancing wild within the soul of me.

I smelled summer roses bloom beside me that June day,
I smelled September in the Eastern then I smelled summer .

—*Deanne Kay Farrier*

The Realities Of The Literary Life

The pen is mightier than the sword,
  In every time and nation,
But the thing that's ev'ry where adored-
  My friend, is Reputation.

Once won, and once attained, a height,
  Is held with little trouble,
While those just barely, out of sight,
  Are striving, at-the-double;

How hard acceptance is, and yet,
  How much, the writer pained-
When he observes, when e'er it comes,
  How little, he has gained.

So know the fickleness of fame,
  'Midst all its ebb and flowing,
And see it clearly just the same,
  To know, where you are going.

Remember too, the words you write
  Are seen, but for a day,
And then, ensconced, twixt covers tight,
  Then neatly, stacked away.

—*A. C. Lee*

Beauty Of The Basement

Once a person-poet lived there,
  In great despair; angry at first.
An uncontrollable money situation.
  He was better than a basement!

That was the half-loaf of bread
  I could give to you, son!

As you lie on your bed
Above the river of overflowing spring,
  You felt sadness, anger,
At the stupid, moldy half-loaf I offered you.

Then, suddenly, you knew! You grew!
  From mold grows life!
From hardship's basement-fame.
  Brains are not all.

Rice is China. Basement is my C. J.
You are a Chicago poet of future fame.

Some times below, I hear the ghost of typing.
  I miss you dearly.
    The mold still grows,
    But for an empty purpose.

—*Catherine T. Parker*

In Anguish

I can hear you moaning,
In great pain when you were hanged,
Taunted, tortured, reviled by men,
Every hard blow to your pierced hands,
Manifested man's cruelty to man.
And these are still repeated across centuries,
Every time man damns another,
Verbal, physical, or whatever the torment be.
Your great lessons of yesterday,
'Till now have not touched all humanity-
Lessons of love and forgiveness.
When anguished you cried, "Father, forgive them...."
You bowed your head, ashamed,
For you knew the meanness of men-
This, you redeemed by dying.
But love was deeper, stronger than death,
Leaving yourself in men's hearts,
And when evil persistently prevails, enslaving men,
I hear you moaning again,
Christ! Was giving one's life in vain?

—*Herminia P. Marapao*

Despondency

Lost hopes rolled on
In heavy lead of clouds
Above his silver head.
Waving pitifully cried in despair hopeless mirages.

Not too far away a blackbird sang
Cheerfully admiring God's creation,
The lightness of his voice made
Confused view of the surrounding world adding to its secrecy.

The tragedy, which seemed inevitable,
Was coming from apparently bright happiness.
Erasing contours of reality,
He was dying but through everyday
Living he was catching bits of escaping hope.

And sun was Getting ready to awake new life
The happiness of passing,
United with transformation.
The morning seemed to breathe
With all might of its freshness,
Nobody saw the evolving pain.

   —*Andrew Grabowski*

The Flower Of Life

The eternal splendor captured in time, has only beauty
in its design.
The softness of each pedal, unfolding in the mist, resting
safely on the ground only to exist.
Just for a moment to reach beyond its space, only to leave
the earth with more to take in its place.
All beauty as we know it, that comes from within, to share
in all its mystery time and time again.
If not for the showers, that spreads the earth with flowers
such as life goes on and on.

Dedicated to Dr. John L. Stoker D.O.

   —*Debra Phillips*

US, The Child Within

Who is that child that lives within me?
In my heart I feel she yearns to be free.
She's experienced a lot of hurt and pain.
So, inside me she chooses to remain.
How very afraid and sad she feels.
The secrets within her are too terrifying to reveal.
What happened on that awful day?
That made her slip away,
To hide within a dark place,
The only way she knows how to feel safe.
Come out little girl and take my hand.
For together we'll take a stand.
You do not have to stand alone,
For that secret place is not where you belong.
Come out little girl into the light.
So, we can have a future that's happy and bright.
For no one can hurt you anymore.
No, little girl not like before.
Let's count that battle as done.
So, we can live the rest of our life as one.

   —*Francine Poindexter*

Sacred Angel

In my mind, there is no one else.
In my heart, there is only you.
And in my dreams, that go on forever,
   so shall my love for you.
I have searched through the hills and valleys,
   across the deep blue sea,
but I've never found another, that means so much to me.
And on this day, that we met,
   Oh! so long ago,
I pledged my love to thee, and promised to never let you go.
And through the years, that we have,
   yet to live as one,
I will continue to love you, and cherish you like the sun.
I will hold you, and love you,
   on a pedestal, oh! so high,
      you are my sacred angel,
         and with thee,
      I will continue to fly.

   —*Jim Moore*

Summer Passion

Rain pouring from the sky, water dripping off of the leaves.
In my room, I stand, my body glistening from the shower
I had just taken.
You came in and helped me brush my hair.
Outside we sit, listening to the birds sing their song of love,
waiting for time to pass.
To say I do, is all that you need to put a smile back on your
face.
Negativity coming from my mouth, breaking your heart.
Explanations are yet to be told.
We hold each other close, both crying.
You understand how I feel, just like how I knew that you would.
Promises of giving each other time are once more made.
Evening comes, stars shine so bright.
Our bodies fitting perfectly with one another as we sway
to the soft beat of the music.
Last night spent together this way.
Never to see one another again, until the next year
When we would bond again; underneath the warm blue sky,
Of our island paradise.

   —*Amanda LeDee*

Untitled

An orange moon, as bright as the sun lies overhead
in the blackened sky. Is this fiction or future?
What happened? Why? Could it be society, in a
power driven fit. Or more phenomenon. You see the
story unfold, bit by bit. You fight for your
country, die in the sand. What is so sacred about this land?
There are nuclear weapons, atomic bombs, things that will
hurt you. Is it worth the pain? For the loss of a child
what do you gain? More power. Is that it? It only equals
more struggle, putting up with shit. The world is lost, now,
and can not be helped. It's up to the future generation
to deal with the hand it was dealt. I pray for
peace, I pray for change. It's up to us to end the
rage. Let's stop it, and stop it now. We can do it
and I know how, together.

   —*Brian Ledis*

When I Depart

Guide me how to breathe,
In the choking wilderness
Of perennial separation
And forced alienation,
When I depart from thee.

Guide me how to warm,
In the far flung, distant land
Where clouds of memory are dark
And rains of loneliness drench a lot,
When I depart from thee.

Guide me how to resist,
The wintry storms of life
As I'll be backlashed
By the reins of thy trap,
When I depart from thee.

Guide me how to survive,
Among fields of alien land
Where time plies on opposite sides
And I'll find you not by my side,
When I depart from thee.

—*Eric V. Dutt*

Untitled

all the creases
in the depths of his cheekbones
leave her white dangling Christianity
between the breast of my child
plowing fire fields
dark corralling thoughts of cold winds
through paper houses and paper dolls
never ending lines, lines of the nostril
intakes fear from the spikes of his head
the glory of my red white and blue
dead from the smoke house clay and brachia walls
i see them in a hollow line of steal spoons
curliest growing pumpkins of life
and fields of peculiar pepper plums
sun roofs peeling
sunflower shells printing her love to him
his eyebrows damp from the gloss of her eyes
he folds up his tractor tight
and her tears are peaceful and alone
dark grey buckets singing their song

—*Amy Long*

Personality

Poem #S58112b7 3 lounges back against the rug
In the form of a wooden pipe.
The pipe sits coughing and coughing its smoke.
The smoke laces the guitar,
Winds its way up the fingerboard,
And sends shivers through the one who is
Playing it.
Playing the smoke?
Playing the pattern that is
Crumbling faster than he can
Set it down.
Is this his life rushing by?
Or just another grain in the wood?
The pipe now hugs the carpet, smoke slowing down.
Is this the real thing? It asks itself.
Poem #S58112b7 3 better change its
Personality or else
Face an identity crises.

—*Dave Pierce*

The Hidden Devil

I gazed at the clouds in the sky as I walked along the shore,
In the distance I heard the sea gulls cry against the ocean's roar.

Standing among all God's beauty with the wind blowing through
    my hair,
The clouds seemed dark and threatening, as if to say, "Beware."

I reached out to touch a lonely shell, and it was so fragile in
its beauty that I fail to notice hell as it came upon me.

The shell flew from my hands when I turned with such a start,
Hell seemed curious when I cried, as the shell broke away from
    my heart.

Long ago, Hell was my truest love,
I felt that he was a blessing sent from God above.

But he was the devil in disguise; how could I have known he'd
    break my heart?
How could I have known that the shell would fall apart?

Now it has been years and the devil is home,
Coming true is one of my greatest fears;
My house is where he roams.

This poem is dedicated to my friends and family for their
encouragement and their incredible faith in my abilities
as a writer. Thank You.

—*Dana Catoline*

The Screaming Of The Seraphim

Many voices long to be heard
In the echoing martyrdom
That was once a trusting shelter.
The influence of raptured souls
Has turned its face to the sky.
A seraphim of disbelief,
A revelation In its own capacitated anger-
Enough to send angels screaming into hell.
I no longer wear the face of my element
For the unsettling balance
Of nature has been upheaved and tortured
In a melancholy environment.
I cry to be saved;
But no one answers my calls.
No one sheds their souls.
No one dies for love.
No one trusts the silence
When the danger of association is closer-
Than the pain in my eyes.

—*Jennifer Beard*

Liberty For All

Our liberty bell is ringing exceptionally loud,
In the land of the courageous and proud.
Surviving troops march the last mile home,
Firmly embracing loved ones after being alone.
Upon the ground the fallen lie cold.
They will not be forgotten, our heros so bold.
Bugles solemnly bid farewell, as we lay to rest,
Our dependable soldier, the military's best.
Pray for our captured prisoners of foreign war,
For the lonesome suffering they must endure.
Keep faith they will soon see our countries shore,
Reclaim their lives and be happy once more.
American flag waves proudly on the pole,
Symbol of freedom for all, is our ultimate goal.
Illuminated sky from fireworks on fourth of July,
Most celebrate without understanding why.
Would our country be safe if it were left to you,
To protect American red, white, and blue?
God bless the men and women who serve and fight,
To keep our homes a place we feel safe at night.

—*Christy A. Slone*

457

Dream Land

Through the midnight hour
In the midst of slumber,
Through my mind I often wander.
To a far away castle
Built high above the sea,
Guarded by Knights mounted on mighty steeds.
For honor and glory they protect their queen.
Or perhaps to the dense jungle
Where exotic animals roam
Could this be the place that my heart calls home?
Where savageness and survival are all that is known.
And is there a point
Where these two will meet
To create new adventures that are bitter-sweet?
Well, that is a question for another day,
Because my time grows short and quickly slips away.
For the sun is rising
To the tone of my bell,
So I must bid you good-bye.
Farewell.

—*John P. Holmes*

Star Of The Night

Brilliant the star that reigns
In the night, a sojourners hope
for weary hours when cares of the day
O'er power hearts delight in happiness,
and daily blessings.

Glittering white lights hover, as I behold
Its presence secure in a web
Of Celestial beauty sparkling profusely
With royal radiance, awaiting darkness
And my peaceful slumber.

There must be a secret passageway
That leads to a secluded chamber
Where wishes are granted,
And an invisible trusty ray
Guards my dreams in gentle stillness.

Heavens brightness dims
With early sun; where, in eons of time
It shall rotate perhaps till earth
And heaven are one, and we are drawn
Into the mass with the wind.

—*Anna M. Rohrbaugh*

The Magic Of Winter

Looking through a window,
In the stillness of a winter morn;
The flurry of snowflakes gently dancing
Their way downward,
And dusting the ground below,
With a precision unrivalled by man.
The spectacle of dusted pine trees,
Along a highway in the countryside,
The indomitable freshness of the air
That distinguishes itself from other seasons,
Revealing the brilliance
And the majesty of winter.
Oh man, that thou art so busy,
Missing the beauty of nature,
Take a moment in a somber reflection,
And enjoy the allure of winter,
That by Nature's own law,
Is denied other lands,
And give thanks for the privilege
To behold the miracle of winter.

—*Anthony Kofie*

80 And Over - Remember When??

During the summer, no air conditioners or fans could be seen,
In the winter, the pung carrying the milkman with unhomogenized
milk with caps riding high on frozen cream. Black and white,
silent movies, we thought were great, along with gifts from the
show, Until talkies and color, improved the big screen with
their glow. Clothes took so long to launder and iron till they
looked "just so", Now a trip to the dryer, and you're ready to
go. Men took such pride in building their own crystal sets,
But it wasn't long before all kings of radios, you could get.
If you were lucky and had a "job" to go to. 48 hours, with no
unheard of coffee breaks, you worked through. Folks used to
travel by train, ocean and sea, But today's planes and cruise
ships are the luxury. Electric lights, beautiful bathrooms, so
many improvements to be seen, With so many miracles, it's
almost like a dream. Of all the changes that have come in the
past. Can you really imagine what the future will cast?? Oh
yes, open air cars, and those hard to climb into rumble seats,
Today's models, so complete they make driving and riding a real
treat.

—*Frances McGlue*

This Child

This child, conceived, was nurtured and grown
in the womb.

By an act of love.

This child when born, received the breath of
life with love and promise from our Heavenly
Father.

By an act of love.

This child, welcomed with open arms and hearts
full of hope and dreams for his future.

By an act of love.

—*Helen Brumage*

The Tree

My church is out of doors, on lakes or forest floors,
In valley's low, or on mountain's high,
It's there I find The Tree, a sense of harmony,
It's something you can't see with just your eye.

It's present in the air, a coat of peace I wear,
The name that seems to fit it is The Tree,
It's quiet and it's calm, as good as any psalm,
I come here to its presence to be free.

I see The Tree as hope, a trouble cleansing soap,
I come here and it washes off my care,
I think on many things, my soul stands up and sings,
The peace it brings to me has no compare.

Out here I am content, not something you can rent,
It's what I need to make me feel whole,
More than recreation, or quiet contemplation,
It's what I need to help me cleanse my soul.

And when I get back in, I know you'll see the grin,
That says that I'm at peace inside once more,
I know you'll then agree, that I should seek The Tree,
Whenever I need to let my spirit soar.

—*Erick L. Sokn*

Wintertime, Out My Window

As I look out this starlit night, I see the earth all dressed
in white: I see the trees by moonlight's glow, all glistening
with new fallen snow. And here and there a tiny print where
little creatures came and went. Searching for some food to
store, for it is wintertime once more!

And adding to the magic scene I see the lake, calm and serene.
Awaiting with submissive grace, the icy chill of winter's
face: In silent beauty God will keep both earth and creature's
silent sleep: Until the early morn of spring when every
earthly sleeping thing. In keeping with the master plan,
awakens and then lives again!

As I look on this wondrous sight on this enchanting winter's
night. It comes to mind, perhaps that I shall never ever
really die. But, rather, have my "winter" too and in the
spring will live anew. And in another world so bright I'll
look out on a starlit night. And on that bright and shining
shore, I'll be with God forevermore!!!

  —Geneva Wilson

This Is My Poem

 This is a poem of hate and regret, It hurts down
inside and sometimes it burns....Just thought I'd
mention it to whom it concerns.

 Terrible man who hurt you inside, unselfishy known
he messed up your mind,
Thrown in jail and lost of the key, for hurting you baby
oh sweet mine......oh me!

 Your not a little girl that you've never been
because of a stupid selfish mans sin,
Flash-backs of terror, flash-backs of fright, wish you'd
forget them with all of your might.

 Thought of as jokes never given second thought,
their trust cannot ever and will not be bought.
 Sweet little baby I know of your pain no ones trust
can you ever gain.

 These are my memories these are my thoughts,
sometimes they hurt, sometimes they burn.....Just thought
I'd mention them to whom it concerns.

  —Jahaira Marin

The World Needs A Hug!

A little more time in the practice caring
Instead of just dreaming of blessings in sharing,
Some minutes gave to the sweet cross of giving
Not quite so long on our comfort for living,
We preach how to do - it's great in the saying
We enjoy all we can, if it's someone else paying,
We contemplate wisdom passed down through the ages
We think of our lives as history filled pages.
We judge now ourselves with a great deal of charity
But see others failings, their faults with real clarity,
We should ask, Dear God, as we pray for tomorrow
We cause no one hurt, no heart ache, nor sorrow,
Asking our Father, that we may be the first
To see in each person, their best not their worst,
Then perhaps we'd not in just bragging and blowing
Say now, how the world, it ought to be going,
In the doing its proved, not the saying so smug
By your caring, your sharing, the world gets a hug.

  —Don J. Chambers

Betrayal

Silent whispers blow through the trees,
Intent on destroying everything I believe,
I stand here naked with no defense,
They'll come after me as I grow tense,
How can they look at me like they do,
When I'm forced to lie because of you,
It's the ultimate horror of a different kind,
It burns my soul and it rapes my mind,
I twist, I turn, writhing I die,
No one can face them as well as I,
I scream to myself "this must be the end",
But still life goes on death is only pretend,
Like someone I knew that I never met,
I will always remember this I will never
Forget.

  —Charity Egli

Web Of Life

Life is a silver strand I weave
Into a delicate web with my todays.
My entity woven with joy, bending with sorrow,
Held fast by yesterday's memories.

What designs will I spin in my fine lace?
Only today holds the rhythms of life to unfold,
And my delicate web will show
That I too passed this way.

My patterns of joy brought by sons
Fade into a tear of my heart as they seek their own destiny.
Still I weave my enduring thread into a lasting web
Interlaced with the strength of family.

Sunbeams capture designs of dear friends,
Reflections of love in my silver thread.
Our souls intertwin'd with the song of friendship
That begins and ends in a heart.

My memories enriched with exquisite designs,
Yet, my entity incomplete with desires untold.
Hear my sound of being in song, laughter and tears
For I and the web are one.

  —Fran Ford

Wistful Thoughts

As the gradual clouds re-shape themselves
into another man's daydream,
So does the soul create new avenues of which
the heart has only to choose.

These moments slowly evolve into the
eternal etchings of days past,
Never to reclaim their present glory,
destined to become more faint and fleeting.

In our search for the truth we reach for the
forbidden shadow - which can never be held.
We seek the mountain top beyond the globe's
horizon - which can never be seen.
The pasture is so full of green.

The man whose heart flows within the banks of
his kingdom, is the man who need not drink
from the desert pond.
With a sharp wisp of the wind, his bow
may point towards the sunrise,
and his course may never change.

  —John F. Thomas

Clayton Burdette; First Life

The sun's risen a dime's worth
into the weary sky,
belatedly beating early heat
through the naked pane,
bouncing light rays
through fly crap and dirt,
finger grease and soiled reflections.

His back to the wall,
he hunches around his life,
a wretched miser hoarding his last penny.
His empty stare echoes silence
through the chambers of his past,
desperation captures the future.

Burning its way from hell,
exploding upon his senses,
splattering thoughts against the wall.
With resignation they gather,
then ooze their way down
to mingle with the filth-encrusted
crotch of the floor.

—*David M. Rollins*

One Woman's Prayer

The peace I feel when I get on my knees
Is an unexplained calm that brings me at ease.
It is my assurance that God is still there,
That He has granted this earnest prayer:

Lord, here I am, I'm flying on faith,
Please take my troubles if it's not too late.
Please wrap Your arms around me and hold on tight
Until my head hits the pillow tonight.

Please be with my daughter in school today,
Please surround her with love, be with her in play.
Please give her the sign that she's praying for,
That You're walking with her when she walks out the door.

Please be with my love and fill up his heart,
Please guide him this day in his craft and his art.
Please hold him tight, too, he's not real strong, yet.
Of the things You have shown him, don't let him forget.

And thank You, Lord, for giving to us
Your grace and goodness, a drink from Your cup.
Thank You for melding our three hearts in one -
Just thank You, Lord, thy will be done.

—*Catherine Dietz-Harr*

Who And Where Is God?

Who and where is God in your life?
Is He in the good times as well as the strife?
Is He in the heavens way up high
or is He here right in front of our eyes?
To me, God is a poetic, artistic, and loving being.
Just look at the beauty on this earth to be seen:
in the majestic mountains and the vast seas,
in the flowery meadows and the mighty oak trees.
The big puffy clouds as they float way up high
in the beautifully blue sun lit sky.
He created the animals both big and small,
and the seasons: winter, spring, summer and fall.
He is in the sound of a slow summer rain.
He reaches through us to someone in pain.
You can see Him in a smile shared by two
whether you're feeling happy or feeling blue.
So would you share with me, too,
the who and where God is for you?
Let us take time to put our insights together
so that we can understand God even better.

—*Debbie Deems*

Where Is Heaven

Where is Heaven, I often ask myself,
Is it far away on some high-top shelf
Where I must climb 'till I can climb no more
Then enter into some far Eternal shore?
Is Heaven past some Pearly Gates hidden from my view
Or is Heaven where I'll always be with you?
Could it be beyond these mountains that I love so well?
Could it be beyond these lakes, singing rivers
And wild-flowers lofty smell?
Could it be beyond this valley where peace and joy abound?
Or could it be beyond our cottage door where love
Is all around?
I cannot think I must go far to find that heavenly gate,
I cannot think that I must hurry for fear I might
Be late.
As I look up and see the sun, the moon, and stars galore,
The mountains, lakes, rivers, and the people I adore,
I need not ask—where is this Heaven that is spoken of?
It's right here in this valley, encircled in
God's Holy Love.

—*Ellen Eagar*

A True Love

If everyone in life has a true love where is mine?
Is it just not my time?
Could it be they think I am really neat;
or maybe just kind of sweet.
It couldn't be that I am very pretty;
or even too witty.
Why can't they understand how I really am?
Is it so hard to see;
that I am only me.
Maybe it's just not the right time;
to find a love that could be truly mine.

—*Dawn Murray*

Questions

Why am I alive in this impossible time?
Is it that I might sit at the feet
of this impassioned woman
as she strums her guitar,
sings poignant, melancholy songs,
her face alive with the flow of emotion?

Is it because I was born to live through the century
that has seen great changes, terrible wars,
unlimited technological expansion,
killings of countless forms of life?
How about humankind, hyper-sexed animal
supplied with super-cerebral potential?

Is it to see, with startling clarity,
through the ongoing rush of pollution, depletion,
desolation of wilderness; increased population,
mountains of machinery—: a final debacle,
with radioactive debris and dark clouds
spreading over this good earth?

—*Everett Whealdon*

Thoughts In October

Let me learn the lessons hidden in every leaf and rock, an
Indian prayer implores.
I think, today, I have learned.
The leaves, brilliant and playful as they dance a last round
with the wind, fall smoothly into place among their sisters on
the ground.
There is no remorse as they lay beneath the mother tree,
secure in the wisdom that what they have been is yet to be in
the unfolding of another spring.
Life is eternal; I've learned it from the leaves.

—*Florence L. Koentje*

460

Patchwork Guilt

The patchwork of the hillside as seen from far away,
Is like a quilt of grandma's, pieced in another day.
Bright green of grass, dark green of trees,
  vary in their tint,
The fields of grain are turning gold, you can see the hint.

Tho far away, the split rail fences are as a fine cross-stitch,
And stumps of earlier fences add embroidery, oh so rich;
The graying stones piled carefully, one upon another,
Suggest back-breaking work, while they separate the colors.

The children of the nineties rarely see a patchwork quilt,
But their elders see on the hillside the ones the farmers
  built.

   —Gladys Crittenden Shaff

Family Love

The Complete Love Of A Family,
  Is Like The Never Ending Circle
    Of A Carrousel
      With Everyone Catching The Brass Ring.

   —Eileen Raum

A Tree Of Brown And Green

The prettiest tree I have ever seen
Is one of brown and one of green
A tree alive; and a tree half dead
There is no beauty in that I said
But how much like us; is this two-tone tree
For there's dying and living in you and me.

But it's not our dying, and not our life
That gives us victory over self and strife
It's the death of our Saviour, and
His risen power
That gives us victory hour by hour

How else could the story of Jesus be read?
Not just by the living; not just by the dead
But by those who walk in the light of the word
And bearing the cross of Christ
Find victory over all things, you see
His dying, his living, in you and me.

   —Joe Pullman

Patience

Patience -
is that the mind of a virtued man,
or a fuse for one who loves revenge...

Perhaps a view, perception, or a stand.
Or a monster on a wild rampaging binge.

Some believe it's the dainty float of a butterfly,
but I know it's the claws of an eagle grasping its prey.

Is Patience the honest will to comply,
or a psycho's willingness to wait another day?

Patience is the fall of a floating feather...
Patience is the jaw of an angry shark.
Patience is the time that pulls lonely hearts together...
Patience is an eclipse that changes light to dark.

So begins another day whether if it will be fast or slow,
will patience play a role in deciding which way you will go?

Patiently the sun rises to begin another day...
Will it be the best or worst; who's to say?

   —Charles G. Rouse

The Only Thing Greater Than Yourself

The only thing greater than yourself
Is the beauty that God has created for you to behold.
Behold the universe into which you were born.
Treasure forever the miracle of your birth.

Lie down, spread the flowers
Listen to the heartbeat of the earth.
Feel the power of the land
Understand your worth.

Lift your eyes to the sky
In darkness or in light
Stars, moon, sun, clouds drifting
Behold the miraculous sight!

Sail to the horizon
Let the waves of the ocean touch you.
Return. Tell the story you have learned.
The only thing greater than yourself
Is the beauty that God has created for you to behold.
What God has created, no man can destroy.

   —Antionette M. Davis

Light And Darkness

One of the greatest gifts from the heavens above,
is the dawn of day seen through the eyes of love.
A hint of ghostly light appears upon the horizon,
the birds on the wire have begun harmonizing.
Although the darkness of night fades once more,
the stillness that surrounded it calms like before.
As the September morning dew forms on the grass,
fall becomes apparent, just as clear as glass.
One of the greatest gifts from the heavens above,
is the dawn of day seen through the eyes of love.
Nature's mother has given us the darkness and light,
the day has quietly revolved into the night.
Earth's infinite wisdom is endless, and brightly knowing,
the warmth that she feels is all powerful, and ever growing.
When the flowers bloom in the spring season,
We know that light following darkness is surely the reason.
Electricity sears through the darkness in the sky,
the thunder rolls along, as the clouds begin to cry.
One of the greatest gifts from the heavens above,
is the dawn of day, seen through the eyes of love.

   —David Mastrome

The Rapture Is Coming

If I am blind the first face I'll see
Is the face of my savior that waits for me.
If I am deaf the first sound I'll hear,
Will be the Lord's trumpet calling me near.
Jesus, my savior, is coming back soon,
No one knows when, night time or noon.

Jesus saved me from my sin,
Satan has lost and he can not win.
Jesus wants to save your soul,
That you should die is satan's goal.
You can be saved and live forever,
Just join God's family that satan can't sever.
Soon I'll see Jesus in the clouds,
I pray that I'll see you among the crowds.

   —Howard S. J. Brown

461

Fish In The Sea

Of all the fish in the sea -
Isn't it odd, all those fisherman?
Catch a prize, throw it back in
Always the enjoyable drudgery.

Of all the fish in the sea -
Keep on fishing 'til you catch one
Until one is too large to hold on;
Quite often, however, size is not easy to see.

Of all the fish in the sea -
We continue to put ourselves through pain
It is hard to quite understand why we feign
That is the way it's supposed to be.

So now my reel is set loose
It's a dilemma I can treat,
For the fish that I may eat
Is the very fish which I choose.

—*Carl Hurwitz*

Tears

The dark is secure, it gives me peace,
it blocks the pain from me,
In the dark I feel so strong,
the world is in my hands,
But too soon the dawn comes,
I begin to cry,
I've lost my peace,
I've lost my serenity,
I kneel on the ground and touch the dirt,
my tears form a pattern of hate,
Slowly the tears stop and I sit in silence,
waiting for the sun to set waiting for release,
Awaiting the return of my peaceful world,
waiting for the night to free me.

—*Jennifer Barnett*

For The Loss Of A Love

"IT" is gelid, dark, and drab.
"IT" can be violently tranquil.
"IT" can come in many forms, as distress, loneliness, emptiness,
  heartache, and confusion.

"IT" can come in the form of an evil barren thought of a once
  warm memory.

"IT" can come in the form of a melody - once enjoyed.

"IT" could show its viciousness in the form of a soft breeze,
  carrying a scent, of an unforgettable moment.

"IT" could come to you during a mediocre chore, during a quiet
  drive, or as an anticipating glance at a once common ground.

"IT" can follow you to bed and into your nocturnal consciousness
  as to say there is no domicile of peace, no sanctuary in which
  to run.

"IT" can be especially unforgiving, most unrelenting and
  completely unforeseeable.

"IT" will seem as "IT" is a never ceasing tormentor and relentless
  pursuer.

"IT" can have the tedious passage of time as a confederate.
"IT" has only one remedy - the same tedious passage of time.
"IT" comes only under one very evil self destructive name,
  this unrestrained feeling - this hurt consuming your - this -
  "DEPRESSION."

—*Dennis D. Ward*

Love

Love is free and cannot be bought or sold.
It comes deep from the heart, or from within one's soul.

It's like a spark that ignites a fire,
From deep within a great desire.

Like a mother for her newborn babe,
Or a very young lad and his first big parade.

A very young girl and her kitty cat,
And her older brother with his new ball bat.

It touches both young and old just alike.
It fills the heart and soul with warm delight.

I feel sorrow and remorse for those who have yet to learn
How to receive love and love in return.

—*Charles E. Llewellyn*

Primary Colors

You offer us your straw basket:
it contains small plastic packages of colored powder
each package a single, bright, primary color
yellow, red or blue.

I cannot see your eyes,
shielded by the straw hat with the striped woven cloth tied
about it. But your straight nose like carved wood and dusty
brown lips assess me instead
And mahogany hands hold forth the basket.

We are exuberant.
We chose all three colors
and pull sweaty, crumpled quetzales from our pockets.

You accept the bills
and disappear
into the towering green volcano,
into maize and asucar,
and leave us in a dream.

—*Debbie Abramson*

She's My Home

Paint peeling, windows falling out.
It doesn't matter, I want to shout!
She's my home: U.S.A.

Strangers invaded, we can't keep them out.
It doesn't matter, I want to shout!
She's my home: U.S.A.

Kin folks betraying, we'll find out.
It doesn't matter, I want to shout!
She's my home: U.S.A.

The "haves" forget the "have nots"
The "have nots" fear the "haves".
It could be different, I want to shout!
She's my home: U.S.A.

Is the power in the elite, or do we all own
The ability to make her HOME?
It doesn't matter, I want to shout!
She IS my home: U.S.A.

She's hurting, don't shut her out.
It DOES matter
I want to shout!
She's OUR HOME: U.S.A.

—*Jean Evelyn Durbin*

462

It

It grows pulsing and pounding through our brains
It enters our bodies and makes us move
The lights flash, the music pounds
We move like caged animals longing for freedom
We make wild designs across the floor

Slowing down we wish to stop and rest
But it drags us in, it pulls us back closer to it
Escape is only the glinting golden ring
Our bodies being moved not by us but by it
It leads us on and into the black of the night
— *Elizabeth Wileden*

Greed Creed

Fat is not contagious
It has no color, race, or creed
Most of its owners have placed it there
By a simple act of greed.

Many people frown upon us
The portly people of today
Fat, disgusting, overweight
Are just some of what they say.

But in America's infant days
It mattered not, a mans girth
Our declaration may not have been
If a man's size determined his worth.

When shopping for a car
It's the body that makes the sale
But as the years accumulate
It's the motor that tells the tale.

So though my slimmer sisters
Have your praise and your eyes
It's not the packaging that counts
But what's inside that's the prize.
— *Donna L. Norris*

Untitled

Writing verse is a blessing to me
It has overcome much that in me be
So I write this poem in the Name Of The Lord
Presenting it freely in my walk wide and broad

I pray as it goes on its way
It will bear fruit for the Lord each day
May the blessing of the Lord be on each word
Making the spiritual dead, free as a bird

So hearts may soar to heights beyond comprehension
That will make the world come to attention
So the Lord's plan continue to increase
That the power of the Lord in men never cease
— *Frank W. Entwistle*

Journey To Spring

There is a season in life carried in by the wind.
It is, at best, spontaneous.
It comes from no particular direction...
And whistles down the glen as it hastens away.
Like a winning streak, you can never be sure
when it arrives, how long it will endure, or
how much attention it will require.
It be fragile. Yet everlasting for the moment
It be tenuous yet eventual and even predictable
It be wholesome, while leaving such emptiness
As to compare only unto death.
It be love, and the only way to be certain
It was here, is after it's gone.

— *Blaine Lowe*

Love

Love is a friend that has caught fire.
It is quiet to understanding, mutual confidence,
  sharing and forgiving.
It is loyalty through good and bad.
It is settling for less than perfection and makes
  allowances for human weaknesses.
Love is content with the present; it hopes for
  the future; and it doesn't brood over the past.
It's the day-in and day-out problems, compromises,
  disappointments, victories, and working toward
  common goals.
If you have love in your life, it can make up for
  a great many things you lack.
If you don't have it, no matter what else there is,
  it's not enough.
— *John G. Miller*

Revenge Or Hope!

The earth is not square, flat or rectangular.
It is round like a ball, not at all peculiar.
The United States is a democracy, so they say.
Yet an election is not based on majority vote.
We love our country founded on God's word!
Now it appears He is as stubble and hay.
No! No! This must not be, please note!
God is our creator, our friend, He wrote.
He will avenge, as you may have heard.
But his love overcomes evil,
And we can again be civil.
— *Irene D. Rosales*

My Love

My love for you is like a waterfall
It keeps going and never stops.
My love for you is like an old oak tree
It keeps growing and never stops.
My love for you is like the moon and the stars
It keeps glowing deep down inside my heart.
My love is like the ocean
Filled with never ending devotion.
My love is true love
My love is your love.
— *Barbara Cross*

Young Christmas

The house was all scrubbed, it is shiny and slick
It looks like it is ready for good old St. Nick.
The fire place crackles as it burns the yule log
In front of the fire lies a sleepy old dog
The Christmas tree sparkles a truly beautiful sight
You can tell just by looking this a very special night
The children are in bed but they are unable to sleep
They lie wide awake but they don't make a peep
Time passes from evening to early morn
Now 'tis the day the Christ child was born
The children doze off just as the time draws near
They will not see Santa or his reindeer this year
Mom and Dad are downstairs scurrying around
Hoping all the gifts they've hidden can now be found
Christmas is special for every young child
With all the excitement, their imagination runs wild
They say as you grow older Christmas loses much of its joy
I hope this is not true, but, if it is then I'd rather
  stay a young boy.
— *George E. Ryan, Jr.*

Vision From The Screen

It can't be, but it's there
It lowers you into a stare
It holds you there, you can't break lose
It's like being hung without a noose

You're paralyzed by the sight
It drains your energy, so there's no fight
You're a body without a breathe
You're in a state of living death

As the spell, starts to break
You start to wonder, was it fake?
Real as life, though it seems
But then again, so are dreams

It's hard to tell if it's true
But then again, what can you do
Even though the vision was clear
It's just a spawn of your own fear

  —*Joseph M. Chironno*

Bluebirds

I love to hear the bluebirds sing,
It makes me think of Jesus our King.

They sit upon a fence post high,
And lift their beaks up to the sky.

I love the way they make their nests,
Because they always do their best,

They're always busy with their young,
And while they work a song is sung.

About God's love and for his care,
They're thankful God is always there.

I'm thankful God made the bluebirds to sing.
Let's thank him now for everything.

  —*Crystal Lapp*

Within

I carry a hate inside so strong,
It makes me want to run and hide,
I hate the sight of him each day,
The birth, a painful one for me.

I cry and cry for pain so strong,
His face I wish away each day,
With questions, I cannot answer.

Each day he grows worse than the other,
No matter the cries I cry.
He wonders with each passing minute,
Is this my mother, or is this my friend.
I wonder too, is this my son or a cannibal.

I try to love him, yes I do!
But the hate I feel just surfaces through.
I pray to God for strength and peace,
But the hate just grows, and grows, and grows.
I yell at him I hate you son, wishing you were never born.
A look that startles him and I, and makes my stomach churn and
 churn.

Do I hate him, or do I love him?
God send an angel to carry him home,
Another night I cannot bear.

  —*Ingrid Christopher Sims*

One Red Rose

One red rose that I see, one red rose, what does it mean, could
it mean you are very special, could it mean you are the only
one. One red rose given by a friend.

I speak of one red rose that was sent, a rose that is as lovely
as she, as the rose, she too is very delicate and must be dealt
with loving care, she keeps this rose were everyone can see,
she must be proud of this rose, because she places it close to
me. I want to say something about this rose so red, each time
I look at her, memories dance in my head.

One red rose not a word she spoke a chance at love would be
captured is the only hope. One red rose has opened in my mind,
for you see, this red rose was given, but not by me.

  —*Alton D. Britt*

Love

Love is like a flower when it blooms
It opens the heart with its many rooms
Things are said that were never said before
Like the shifting sand that lies along the shore

It's like the sparkling dew that falls to earth
Just before the early morning sun.
It's like lying down to rest when the day is done.
It's being at peace when there is trouble on every hand.
It's feeling every beat as you listen to the band.

Love is ours to have and to hold.
Something we can't buy and cannot be sold.
Surely God in all his wisdom knew, when He
Put love into the heart of man.
That we as well as others would spread
Love all over the land.

  —*Bobby G. Bunting Sr.*

My Foolish Heartburn

The food of Mexico is hot.
It peels the paint right off the pot!
Though it be chili,
Cold it's not.
I like it!

At certain I simply gotta
Have a fiery enchilada.

Yes,
I confess,
"Me gusto" plenty
Latin dishes "caliente"!

So, fire up! There's no fiasco
When I tackle the tabasco.
And though from hell's own cauldron sprung,
With sauces sure to scorch my tongue,
I still cannot admit to folly,
Because I love a hot tamale...
    by golly!

  —*James Blewer*

At The Edge Of Darkness

Another brilliant sunrise dissolves
into a muted dusk.
I remember the height of the day
when there were no shadows
and the heat was intense.
We stretched the afternoon together
and clung to each other
as swirling colors enveloped the sky.
Now I stand in the twilight
hearing my heart scream for the light,
crying until the first faint shafts of pink
filter through the pines.

  —*Barbara J. Hill*

In That Distant World

I saw a star in the heavens tonight
    it seemed to glow a different light
Amongst those countless stars above
    its brilliance pierced into my heart

I stood out there so mesmerized
    why a star so small could give such light
Oh could it be in that distant world
    a Holy Child has just arrived

Are angels there with their golden harps
    singing their songs on mountain tops
In exaltation of a baby Christ
    oh what a wonderful glorious sight

Are there kings with gifts to honor Him
    and shepherds with their flocks
Kneeling in adoration of a newborn child
    while angels caroled through the night

In the peace and stillness in my heart
    I knelt in prayer to impart
My hope for that distant world and mine
    The best of everything in life
                    —*Harry C. Braff*

Looking Back

Oh how the time is passing
It seems as though it was just yesterday
He rode his stick horse around the house
A young boy, while at play

While now he stands before the mirror
And sees an old man looking back
He is leaning slightly forward
With a hump upon his back

He is looking at the same man
Where time has grasped his youth
He speaks now with a quiver
His hair has faded grey

He stands and looks at this old man
And thinks of only yesterday
And now and then you catch a smile
That shows upon his wrinkled face

He slowly touches the mirror
With a trembling hand of past skill
Then turns and slowly walks away
With only dreams of yesterday
                    —*Itasca Cody Cox*

A Thought

When does all of this hard part of life end
It seems to go on forever in mine, do things
get better or worse.
It's like there's some kind of curse,
Wake up, and if it's not one problem it's another
What do I do as I feel I'm about to smother.
I just go with the flow, and what do you know boom!
another sudden blow! Things have got to get better some how
someday, I swear I'm gonna find a way.

Moving somewhere else where I have no memories of old
friends, and still loved girlfriends. That's some of the hardest
parts, is losing good friends you spent so many of your
younger days with and suddenly don't speak.
Each day you seem to give up more and more to which you
become so very weak. I feel as if I blow up, it will
relieve a lot of stress! But blowing up,
Gosh what a Mess! What else can you do if none of thee
Above, but tell yourself again this is what life is made of.
                    —*Joseph S. Gercone*

Untitled

The beast came swiftly, stealthily on padded paw,
It spied the huddled masses, trembling on beds of straw,
for they had by now seen it and that odious gleam in its eye.
And they knew it meant only one thing,
to spare its life, one of them would die.

It circled round, slowly, methodically
searching for who was right,
and when all was over, the unchosen
moaned rancorously at the sight.

It dragged the chosen to the place,
where the other beasts gathered, waiting for the word.
As it said "Amen", not a tear was shed for the little bird.
                    —*Christie L. King*

Untitled

Death is a darkness full of fear
It traps me in and holds me
It longs to pull me near

Yet, I hold on to tomorrow
And hope it goes away
Free my mind of its music, still it tries to stay
Death has not a home
But the home within your heart
A lonely stranger
Coming in from the cold
Who will pull your world apart

He will haunt you endlessly
Cover you with his cold blanket
Made of dirt
Do not let him fool you, my friend
It will hurt.

I know because he's watching to capture me
Each day becomes
A constant struggle with him
He refuses to set me free.
                    —*Jenney Nelson*

Thieves Of Summer

It was a brisk cold burdensome morning.
It was almost freezing!
It was as if the bleak suffering morning was in labor with
Winter, the cries and pains of frost were all about.
All the trees, bushes, and grass appeared to have had their
lustrous green coats stolen by Autumn, that dreaded thief of
    summer.
Summer was a time of frolicking and picnics, a time of
warmth and joy, a time of life and vitality. It was
one cold frost ridden morning, which one I can't remember,
Autumn that thief of summer came in like a gang of robbers,
raped and pilfered, and plundered my summer wonderland!
All I was left with was a bone chilling cold pregnant day;
which at any moment could give birth to winter.
It was as if all who survived Autumn's rampage and even the
sky, mourned in the heavy gray morning air, awaiting winter's
birth who would come and rob us of all life with his cold
callous frozen hands.
Perhaps we who could escape, might survive to sing the
song of summer. I must hurry; will I see you then? I hope!
                    —*Jesse D. Franklin*

O Word Of God!

O word of God! O word of God!
It will bless you, every nation;
It gives you inspiration.
Let all the people trust His care
Then you with wisdom can prepare.
You'll change from sword to garden tool,
Then you with good thoughts will rule.
The beautiful you will behold,
You will be led right to the fold!

O, come at once all nations!
Receive fruit from your devotions!
There will be no war, as there was before.
With God as your expression,
You will show pure perfection.
That the Bible can teach you, it is clear;
You know God is listening and will always hear.

—*Allison Doeden Boldra*

Beautiful Child

There's this cloud that's been hanging around, seems to me like
it's been trying to get me down! But your smile my beautiful
child, keeps the sun warm within the even though I can't see.
Your innocent laughter is what I'm after: It fills my ears and
my mind, with memories of younger times. The joy you find in
living every day, makes my heart burst with vibrant love in
every way! Your silly little questions that you often ask,
remind me of a child that I knew in the past. When you wake me
deep in the night, when something unknown has given you a
terrible fright! My beautiful child you hold me oh so tight!
Your small body trembles, and your eyes are filled with tears
they seem to wash away, all the grown-up years. I sense the
fear you feel my little one, and I wish at that moment to share
with you, the warmth of the sun! Your smile my beautiful
child, and your silly little ways are what keep me going, on
the cloudiest days! Your smile keeps the sun warm within me
even though I can't see. So please remember my little one as
you grow every day, that you fill me with the warmth of the sun
in every way!

—*Aggie v. St. James*

Soft Light

A lone candle sits on the cherry wood of my mantle,
Its flame weaving back and forth, jumping up and down.
Dancing to the rhythm of the room,
A room once active with much life.

A flash of yesterday enters my soul
To a time when candles would illuminate my being,
Igniting and blazing the love and passion,
That I had for the one who is now but a shadow.

So primitive is the gift of fire; with the dawn of man it came,
Bringing warmth and light, showing direction
To cave dwellers who travelled the hills of the past,
This gift handed on, from one to another.

I stare at its amber and soft yellow glow,
And long for the excitement and anticipation it brought,
Which I have hidden in the deepest recesses of my soul.
But every now and then, the fire will lick at my heart.

How quickly the light can arouse the warmth within me,
Sending quivers of passion through the essence of my being.
I need to share these primeval emotions,
But reality comes rushing through. The candle dies.

—*Dolores Sloat*

The Rose Garden

The rose is more than just a flower.....
Its fragrance and beauty last for hours.
God placed each petal in it's perfect place,
Old fashioned ladies wore them with lace.

Each rose is different, yet magnificent to see
Like a bird that sings in the willow tree.
If I had a rose garden with a pretty rock path,
In the center I would like a charming bird bath.

My garden would have many bright colors,
I would give a red rose to the young lovers.
Each bush would have tender care so true,
And the first one invited to my garden would be you.

—*Gloria Lee Miller*

Listen, Here The Angels Whisper

Here, we are among people with such qualities
It's hard to find the one that most fits you
You are far more than the average person
Because of your deeds

You can hear angels whispering about you
You can almost see the heavens smile as they call your name
And as you hear them whispering
As though a gentle breeze sweeping through the clouds
The sun bursts through gleaming
As though it was smiling upon hearing your name.

O' if you could hear then whisper about you

—*James A. Wiggins, Jr.*

This Tree

This tree is of need to cultivate
Its many strong, directed branches;
Each having a limb to mate
Needs firm ground in life, not chances.

This trees life depends on more than nature
It needs nourishment, pruning, and light,
Thus growing stronger against failure
Giving its branches an equal fight.

This tree needs no chemicals in its seed
Planted firmly in Holy ground...
Upon the soil of truth it feeds,
Nourishing strong branches - heaven bound.

This tree violently scarred through the ages
Having many battles fought and won,
Standing strong through trying stages
Its many branches protected by the Son.

This tree is of great importance
Nature need clearly see,
Without it life has no substance
For this is the Family tree!

—*Creaestia B. Hall*

Sisters

Glad I have a sister
  Just like you.
Ever if we need someone
  Each other we can turn to.
No matter how it all turns out
  Sometimes we know just what to do,
Even with the good and bad
  We always made it through
Although the miles have been long and far
  I hope you always knew
That I'm glad to have a sister
  Just like you!

—*Connie L. Huffman*

The Window

I am looking out the window trying to see,
    It's raining so hard, the street, a river will be.
I see the Paradise Theater, stars in the sky,
    How active the balcony, the boys sure do try.

The Bronx Zoo, animals galore,
    How I loved the giraffe, the monkeys and more.
A peanut for me and one for the bear,
    The elephant and the hippopotamus also will share.

I see the schoolyard, handball against the wall,
    Then an eggcream and halavah at the nearest mall.
The Park Plaza Theater Saturday morn,
    Eleven cartoons and no porn.

The clouds are moving, the sky looks like a sea of blue,
    The sun is shining, everything looks new.
I am looking out the window trying to see,
    It will be a new day for you and me.

—Donald R. Siegel

The Bridge

I'm building a bridge, you somehow gave me the plan,
    It's right in the book I hold in my heart;
    Each page that I read, helps me understand,
        To build on love, and not on hate;
    I'm building a bridge, across the divide,
    I'm building on love, and not on hate;
You somehow gave me the plan I'm following through,
    I'll make it somehow, but how about you?
    Some people I know, can not understand,
    How I can go on, loving you this way,
    It's hard to explain the way that I feel;
    But I'll not complain for you are real.
        I'm building a bridge
        across the divide,
        I'm building on love,
        And not on hate;
    You somehow gave me the plan,
        I'm following through,
        I'll make it somehow,
        But how about you?

—Crissy Anderson

Oh Father

Oh Father, where can you be?
I've searched all of my life.
Oh Father please come back,
you forgotten, you have kids and a wife.
Oh Father, you were always there to make me feel alive.
You ought to know through the good times.
We had that you don't have to hide.
Oh Father, you have no idea how much influence
you had when you were here.
You were always there to lend a hand and
you always had a free ear.
Oh Father, why won't you come home?
There's love can't you see.
Oh Father, please come back
so we can again be a family.

—Danielle N. Nicholas

Believe

There's so much within me that needs to be known.
It swells up within me, it squeezes my soul.
So full of words that need to be said.
I just can't see how I can believe.
Believe in the words that need to be free.

—Alejandra Barbosa

What Humanity Needs

When I'm sad, discouraged and blue,
Jehovah is the one I pray to.
He gave humanity his beloved son.
With blessed tears in his eyes
His hope was for, humanity to survive.
His blessed tears fall upon the earth.
Knowing the world has little hope.
This world is filled with sorrow and pain.
No hope for a better future
Only emptiness remains.
Poverty and hunger rules the world.
Violence overflows this relentless world.
The blood and cries of victims cover the streets.
Hatred and greed fills the deep.
Only brings anger and despair.
No hope for the future, for humanity doesn't care.
My hope is for the world to hear my pleased,
And join me in a prayer on bended knees.

We must ask God to supply our needs,
For peace is what humanity needs.

—Elaine Cotton

Transfiguration

With
        Jesus's appearance,
still
        she is following me,
and
        she would follow me
                        perhaps
                                    forever,
through
        the repeated hallways of a labyrinth
towards
        horrendous dead ends.
        Diane, Jesus, Lion…

—Gorgin Arzemanian

Sweet Hour Of Bliss

The lights of heaven
Jewels … bright gems sparkling
On black velvet cloth
While my soul ponders tomorrow.

And the hole … the tiny hole in
The wall so thick
Brings roaring water
And rushing wind.

I sing inside me for I
Know they exclaim the quenching of my thirst
They speak at last
Of freedom's song.

And from the tower bell it too rings
Now comes my rest
O, sweet hour of bliss
Eternal night of peace.

—Gary T. Muse

Upside Down World

Would you like to hear the story about upside down world?
It's where you carry your horse instead of the horse caring you
And the grass is above you while blue sky is below you.
It's where you walk on the ceiling, and look up to see the
floor, where you wear your boots on your head, and your hats
on your feet. It's where the fish are in the sky, and the
birds are in the sea. Where dogs howl at the sun and sleep in
the moon beams. Have you ever heard of upside down world?
Have you? Have you? Have you?

—Brandie L. Vohwinkle

New York Subway Train

Come along and take a ride, On a New York Subway train
Join the throng to push inside, of the New York Subway train

With a clang clang clang, and a bang bang bang, the trains come
   roaring in
And, above all this din there's pandemonium

Above all these noises, you can hear these voices
Let me in, let me out, what's it all about they shout
And more noises and voices
"Get off my lap, mister," — Can't you squeeze me in sister
"Stop your pushing mister," — I'm only musing you up, sister!

There's a mumble and a rumble, in this vast subway jungle
With no one caring, and everyone daring, all are raring to go

Tempers are flaring it's unbearing the action is not slow
Yes, see the turnstile jumpers, and rowdy crowd bumpers
And a cop at every stop, with a gun to make you drop
Glimpse the pimps, and the dips and the pips

Yes, you may be bold and brash, when your dash toward the train
But, then, it's happened again and again, A crash, and you are
   maimed

And if you are stuck in the door of a moving train you go insane!
You are no more and it's good bye to the N.Y. Subway Train

   —Isidore Elfand

School Journals

As if treasures might fall from pages like blossoms pressed,
Journals open carefully.
There, a personal world rests between bars of blue.
A hidden part set free
Life changes when pen meets paper.
Waking from hibernation,
The ideas reach out,
Navigate the blood,
Flow down arms,
Into hands,
Out through pens, and
Onto empty pages.
Taking a life of their own;
Emerging Athenas full grown.
Chased
From dreams and
Spaces of mind.
Netted butterflies
Caught
Between valued pages.

   —Jacquelyn Hinton

The Anniversary

I sit here
- Just another night, another date -
-Another passing in time -

I do so especially to
Separate myself from you
The void a barren heaviness in my chest
Making me long for your touch even more
For the feel of your lips as they dance with mine
We'd have a delicious time...

I find myself gazing out my window
Hoping you will parade through that door
Take me in your arms
- and hold me -
Make passionate love to me
Till we can't anymore...

I long for your touch
But would welcome the Sandman's
So this wouldn't hurt so much...

   —Heidi Beach

The stillness was loud with no grooms for a bride!

He was quick to battle and his musket!
Just as fleet was his adversary - not one you forget!
With sabres, swords and horse-drawn canon;
They fought in mountains, valleys and canyon.
Through snows and fierce winds that bode ill.
As death lay down its hand until all was still.
Again he was quick to war with his rifle!
His adversary did not relent or try to stifle.
The terrain was reborn and patiently awaited.
Bombs burst, cannonades defiled and men hated!
A large hand raised its scythe and swept all aside!
The stillness was loud with no grooms for a bride!
Death closed over this familiar scene;
Shrouded in black-morbid and obscene.
He was quick to his sabre to rattle!
Zealous for power and others to fight his battle!
Died and reborn with many names and faces.
Battles raged and ravaged with no traces.
A large hand raised its scythe and swept all aside!
The stillness was loud with no grooms for a bride!

   —Bill Bundzak, Sr.

Little Me

Together you walk hand in hand,
just as God has planned.

Soon it's no longer just the two of you,
but someone that will be a part of you.

I'll be a little like mom, and a little like dad —
but I'm all me; I'm sure you're glad.

I'm just a little child,
who will start off meek and mild.

Tiny fingers, tiny toes,
don't worry, mom, I'll grow.

At first you won't feel like a mother, I bet.
But believe me, I haven't started yet.

A screech during the night,
will jump you up with a fright.

Teach me right from wrong,
so my faith is always strong.

I'm one of God's collection,
He designed me to perfection.

I was created with love,
Blessed by Our Lord above.

   —Alison Hamilton

Just Because

Just because you said "No!" to me,
Just because the wind and rain do meet,
Just because of the noise children make,
Just because nerves and sinew break,
Just because.

Just because I said, "I love you!"
Just because the movies are not true,
Just because a rose is a devious hypocrite,
Just because our lives are taboo,
Just because.

Just because love is splendid,
Just because you are missed so much,
Just because you do so much for me,
Just because you care,
"This is why I chose the other woman!"
Just, just, just because.

   —Christopher A. Stevens

Lost Youth

Speak to me o'er rolling hills!
  Just like you ached to before;
When I was a wee tyke-
  and you came knocking at my door,
You, with your shadowy trees,
  teased me with an enchanting chorus,
Until I came out, skipped in your breeze.

Hold me, I command of you!
  Wrap your green blanket around me;
Embrace me o'er majestic land,
  like no other be,
Crave me, you old fool,
  Haunt me with your wind's shrill,
Until I have nothing to will.

Tempt me, I say to you!
  You deluded earth;
My hair almost gray,
  Isn't life but a span?
But ah! What throbs in my memory
  still may.
    —*Donna Sledd*

Is It Too Much To Ask?

Is it too much to ask to have someone to count on to be there
just to hold on to and to show that they care? Is it too much
to ask to have someone show some concern and compassion when
you are down in the dumps and just need a friend to lean on?
Is it too much to ask to have someone to share all the special
moments in time without feeling as though you are committing
some major crime? Is it too much to ask to have someone who
wants to be there and have fun, to play and laugh, spend
quality time with their beautiful daughter and or son? Is it
too much to ask to have someone who takes the time out to show
you what the words love and family are all about? Is it really
too much to ask? Is it...why? That is the question I ask each
day that goes by. Why do so many people let so many things get
in the way of what could be a beautiful and special day? It
doesn't take much time and energy to make a child smile and
that little thing you took the time to do creates a happy
memory that lasts a long, long while. Time is a funny thing,
it keeps on passing, it never stops. One day you will look
back and see that you have missed out on a lot. Don't turn
away because we all need you so much, each and every day!
    —*Debra A. Swearingen*

Sighs From The Seashore

Not so long ago, it was sheer ecstacy
Just to lie by the edge of the gurgling sea.
To escape the mighty steam roller's assault
On my gentle body, with black tar and asphalt.
To escape the never-ending tyrannous reign
Of the ever-speeding truck, tractor and train.

But now, I'm afraid, it's not safe even here,
For I have to stomach the stench, my dear,
Of horrific, blackened death drifting ashore
In the wake of gigantic oil spills, I abhor!

Man, have mercy, a million barrels of oil spills
Torments, tortures and ruthlessly kills
Our flora, our fauna our fabulous fish
Which you have the gall to serve up on a dish!

Back and forth, whether she's high or low,
With gushes she weeps, to and fro.
Her tears I absorb, quickly and quietly,
So no one playing by the sea, may see.
    —*Jameela Alter*

My Love...

There are but two stars up above
Just to remind me of your love;
The mighty breeze, the welcome mist,
Reminds me of the last we kissed.

To count the masses, you count by two,
This brings to mind my love of you;
But don't give up hope, please don't despair,
For soon I'll be with you there.

Soon my love I will be home,
But home to whom? And what? And where?

When these are answered, Oh, my sweet,
Then, perhaps, we shall meet.
    —*Dennis A. Wolfe*

Bluebird Of Tomorrow

Remember to keep smiling when the bluebird lets you down
Keep in mind we all must have our share of ups and downs.

Even though your heart will ache when laden down with sorrow
Don't forget the sun will rise to start a new tomorrow.

The teardrops that fall from your face in all these saddened
  hours
We hope will be as dewdrops that will kiss tomorrow flowers.

So if the song the bluebird sings today is one of sadness
Remember God will lift you up and fill your heart with
  gladness.

Don't forget you are His child and He will see you through
And He is not alone you know because I love you too.
    —*Brenda McDoniel*

Grandma

Quilts pieced together from different patches of cloth,
kept me warm and cozy many nights.
Sewn together with loving finger tips, never store bought.
Baring pieces of material from an old dress my mom had once
  worn.
Feeling safe and secure as an infant new born.
A hug and kiss each and every night expressing emotions of
love, before she cut out the lights.
Grandma has been laid to rest. God you have taken from me
the woman who has guided me from wrong to right.
Please take care of her.
She's the best, and when she comes your way down that tunnel
of light, don't forget when they lay me to rest, to keep the
light burning bright.
    —*Carolyn Dooley*

The Fatal Stairway

Deep digression from
  kindness, sinking slowly
    into a slimy pit, cold and
      dark and feeling useless. Why
        are we even here? Frosted feelings,
          shattered pieces, remnants of a
            bitter time and place. Heartless
          motions with resurrected hatred
        showing nothing but dirt and grime.
      Then comes the last and final step.
    Falling down, no, falling backward
until depression does you in.
    —*Chad E. Wright*

469

To Kiss The Sky

Feel the tender touch of a rainbow
Kiss a fallen star
Taste the moonlight upon your silken lips
Hear the comet speak its wonders
As its tail sails you off to distant lands
You can see the magic of the night
And live its wonders on your winged flight
Let the pegasus lift you away
As the horn of a unicorn spins a web of beauty
Drape your body with the splendors of dawn
As I bathe you with the dew of a mid summer psalm

to Carrie
  —Jonathan Michael Kish

River Of My Dreams

 I sit alone watching the full moon
 kiss you with the light of a million stars

  Your waters hunt about the marsh
  for the mother sea in which to mingle

  Your colors vanish in the lights that
creep along the banks between sundown and darkness

 Your night-song calls to me from everywhere
  it appeals to my sense and soul
   my will to love

 You are the poem and romance of my life
  your song kissed my heart
  your waters passed into my blood
   and I whisper
  SAVANNAH you are my fantasy
   My dream

  —Edward Huguenin

Grandson's Walk

The first grandchild is always eagerly awaited, not quite
knowing what in this world they're fated; brought into the
world as Grandparents ponder, just why their Grandson is way
over yonder. As time slips by as it surely will, Grandson runs
'round the house - never still. While Mom and Grandma stir
pots over cooking; Pawpaw is in the floor playing bear with
Grandson - while no one is looking. The farm is the place to
take the little boy; riding a real horse instead of a toy.
Being bucked off the first time is certainly shocking; afraid
but astride again as Pawpaw is mocking. The tractor was
always a wonderful ride; we kids got to stand next to the wheel
on the side, speeding down dirt roads as fast as we dare... We
didn't know better 'cause Pawpaw was there... He showed us the
past as we watched and we wondered, as he worked with the
engines that pumped as they thundered. The history he taught
us was not from books stored away; we got to see what real life
was like with him every day. The first grandchild is always
eagerly awaited, not quite knowing what they're fated; brought
into the world as Grandparents ponder, just why their Grandson
is way over yonder.

  —Greg Matheny

Just Inside The Gate

When I think of all the souls that Jesus came to free, my heart
leaps with joy that He loves even me.

In heaven in the by and by, where there are joys unknown, I
don't expect a golden crown, I don't expect a throne.

If God would only grant for me just a tiny space. There are
times I feel I don't deserve even that much grace.

My heart is filled with joy, oh that would be just great, to
think that I might rate just a tiny place just inside the gate.

  —Diane Gallegos

Time

Long before fire even knew it was hot, and ice was not yet cold
Knowledge was brewing in seeping poise, for life was about to
 unfold.
Long before there was rhythm and rhyme and nothing was close in
 sight,
The sun not yet a spot in the sky to change the day from night.

Before raw energy exploded to dust and plans had yet to be laid.
Seeing was still a distant truth beneath a foggy shade.
Wind as still as silent reflection and sound could not be heard,
Seconds lasted a million years as whispers longed for words.

When light was as is darkness and no man walked the earth,
Tightness and space were one and the same and value had no
 worth.
The wisdom at hand so unclear of fact, for answers would come
 with age,
The rain as dry as desert sand, as clam threw fits of abandoned
 rage.

Time can't be bought, will never sell out, yet only time will tell.
Time's held all the answers to the secrets it's hidden so well.
Time will come and time will go and has always led the way.
Time with its constant flow has been around for ever and a day.

Fruitless in our searching for another's soul to mend.
Lost in a sea of reality from beginning until all things end.
Time is what it's all about,
Is there still time when time runs out???

  —Greg Harris

Bob:

Early fall of '90 you were put on a high "state of alert",
 Kuwait was being invaded and its people being hurt.
You waited your orders and then they came -
 For you to go to the "land of sand" and Saddam Hussein.
It was on a Sunday you called just to say -
 "The time has come - I'm on my way".
Tears rolled down my cheeks - I cried for a spell
 When Will proudly said "O.K. Bob - go give 'em hell.
We watched and we listened to see you win
 The war - more each night - on the TV news channel CNN.
We called Jill each day to see if she was alright.
 Knowing all along she was - 'cause she heard your voice
 almost every night.
We wrote a few letters and sent a few snacks,
 To you while on your mission in far off Iraq.
Then President Bush ordered all firing be ceased.
 Some of the resolutions were complied with and P.O.W.'s
 released.
We knew then your mission complete,
 You'd soon be home driving the "Charger" down Nantucket St.
  —Charline G. Womack

The Wrong Answer

Tears streak down my haggard face
I've never felt so out of control.
Holding a loaded gun to my head
Ready to end it once and for all.

Crouched in a dark, secluded corner
I feel my throat turn suddenly dry.
My heart pounds faster with every beat
Too miserable to live; too young to die.

A shudder streaks through me and I turn cold
As I await my eerie fate...
I've pulled the trigger and it's all over.
I want to go back, but now it's too late.

  —Amber Ruth Austin Lewis

470

God's Nature

At a cabin on top of a mountain that over looks Gods beautiful land. The trees are so tall and full of leaves and green as green can be. Through leaves of the trees that's over looks Gods hills, the sky shines it beauty. The dew on the leaves makes me think of Gods tears of joy. As I sat on the porch of the cabin I look under the tall trees there is only one tiny red rose between two logs, it makes me think of Christ on the cross between the two men that was crucified. Out from the rose there's a small tree that a fence is surrounding it as if God has his protection around it from harm, as he does his children. On each side of the drive way there are two hedges that are the guards that protects us. The thunder in the heavens lets us know that God is all around, the winds blowing the trees lets us hear his voice whispering. "Don't be afraid my child". The rain drops on the tin roof are like soldiers marching into battle for Christ. The water that runs off the edge of the roof is like the blood that will be shed on the battlefield for his name sake. And as the lighting strikes like a sword so shall his words on that day.

—*Earnestine Parsley*

Untitled

An imaginary ship of pink glow
landed in hush forest of sherwood green..
Creatures came forth
on a thought
seldom spoken...
Showing a book
of written verse
sealed never opened.

"Open it", they whispered
and I did.

Ink tears mixed
with red blood
published by lost souls
with a dedication...

"For you my love
from this world
exiled forever"

Crying alone in a dream
I dreamed
together
never.

—*Aurelia Cleo A. Battle*

Traveling Symbolism

The conductor calls out "Harper's Ferry! Note this historical landmark. John Brown made his final statement here..." Intonations implore that all ears hear the same thing. The place. The person. The absence of a middle name. A message to the world. But this is not a concrete tongue called "Pennsylvania Turn Pike". No predictable rubber humming rhapsody to hypnotize. This is the Amtrak Express, and at this quiet point there is no hurry. The cold steel rails slowly curve, curling past the once bloodied bluffs where the river's throat swelled, satisfying its deep inner longings heard above human syllables, syntax, or phemerisms. This river may have burped at John Brown's going down. It may have rippled in applause. What was his middle name? Did he cry in pain for his beloved, gag as hot lead dug into his vein puffed chest? Did he hear the final conductor call, "all aboard!"? Or whistle through his half-slit throat to catch a wayward Ferryboat? Silver snake tails wheel us past one hundred ghost. Witness, too, the appetites of new waters called rivers tomorrow's historical markers.

—*Aaron Anthony Vessup*

A Phoenix From The Ashes

The tranquil peace of days gone by,
    lay dormant as the clear blue sky..
'Tis deeds of pity though she dread,
    which all too often fall her head.
Into the dark deep abyss she flows,
    where painful memories cease to slow.
With thoughts of laughter, pain and woe,
    to cloud her mind each day she goes.
Down the narrow focused trails,
    speeding, grasping fears bestowed.

'Tis knowing life's trials, though not a few,
    of times gone by she bid adieu.
Again she climbs, the plan thought through,
    directing her path to start anew.
A time will pass, she'll arise and sing,
    the days have come, I feel no sting.
Like a Phoenix from the ashes, she'll spread her wings,
    and soar to heights still yet unknown.
Knowing with grace, she will have shown,
    across her abyss she will have flown.

—*Diane H. Moulton*

The Sands Of Time

The Sands of Time slip through my hands. Falling, falling,
    leaving me, forsaking me. Timing my life like an hourglass.
    They are gone. They have vanished. They have left me all
    alone.
My only company is the dirt around my coffin and the voice of
    the priest, "The Lord is my shepherd I shall not want..."
The shell that held my soul hostage is now beneath mounds of
    earth. And I am free. Now from heaven I watch my sons and
    daughters pick up where I left off.
My grandchild, now aged from time, cups her hand, chanting the
    words I once knew. "The Sands of Time slip through my hands
    Falling, falling..."
Sometime later, her grandchild will gather the Sands of Time
    into her hands-the ones that I used to hold. She will watch
    them slide away into the hands of another child - an unborn
    child the one that needs them the most.
Then, she will sadly retire, leaving her family to pick up the
    pieces.
And she will join me in heaven to give glory to Him, to watch
    her and God's creations, and to forget the Sands of Time.

—*Christy Evans*

Nothing To Live For......

When the rain hits the ground,
Leaving no sound,
The earth seems to rumble,
And my thoughts tremble,
Is there really nothing to live for?
Or is there nothing that I really want more?
Then a key to my own heart,
For this will never bring me apart,
From the person I love or really myself,
But what do I really want in life?
Is it something that is going to pierce my heart like a knife?
Or is it something that can keep me pure as a dove?
Maybe there is something to live for or maybe it's love,
And when the sound of the rain hits the ground.
Deep inside we know it's been found,
We will all know that there is something to live for...

—*Bunnary Sou*

471

Sweet Lips

Sweet lips bites his lower one
leaving puddles of crimson blood on linoleum,
yelling, "No man has ever loved you
the way I do,
but woman, you're insane."
Doors slam.

Tick tock
I threw the clock in the garbage can.
Don't wanna know
how many hours have gone by
since that door shut
and the silence crept in.

Sweet lips, candy-coated,
Why couldn't you be everything—you,
telling me next stop Kenya, then Nepal;
yet always landing me down in Disappointment
where I wake up
from farfetched dreams of paradises
we'll never see.

  —*Debra Machida*

Kid Gavilan

The Hawk that soars above us
left his footprints on the summit
at the top of the world.

If shadows could talk
they would of told him
that the pendulum that swings to the east
will eventually swing to the west
and the scales of life will balance.

The money, the women, the cars
the good times
and even the parasites
are gone forever.

His dignity
undefeated

will last until
the final bell is sounded
and his graceful decent
to the earth
is through.

  —*F. Daniel Somrack*

Passionate Ebony At Lone Mountain

I am warm and white from loss of you.
Let me hold your hesitant black hands!
 Songs of honey and cream
 Burst of serious laugher
Your ebony eyes are moist and full,
 I look away ashamed
 Knowing the closeness we share
Is only as deep as the touch of your soft skin.

 Obsequious songs of social unrest
Strangle strange times of moral conquest
  Never a moment's love
  So shackled by taboo
 While callous subservient glance
Obscures your desperate smile and its chance.

Let me hold your trembling black hands.
 I weep for growing into you.
 To surge beyond the color line
  Moralities ancient choir
Can never douse the lust and fire
  Of a love so fine.

  —*Christopher R. Jennings*

Eagle's Prayer

Oh great spirit allow my wings to open.
Let me spread them and learn to fly.
Please don't let me fall.
 Oh great spirit allow me speed and courage.
Guide me to the sky and watch me glide to the sea.
May the waters part for me and allow me to enter them.
 Oh great spirit allow me grace in my flying.
Let me be free and be beautiful.
May I never lose my way and go with me always so that I may
find peace.
 Oh great spirit allow me wisdom.
The wisdom to find just what I am looking for.
And offer me the strength to continue in hardship.
Amen

  —*Angela Baltes*

Hope

The words scribbled on the boarded up store front
Let the Sun Shine In!
Carefully, cautiously stepping my way along through the squalor.
It was repeated again and again
Let the Sun Shine In!

Determined and boldly was the ghostly hand that writ,
Let the Sun Shine In!
Our souls are soothed, warmed, lighted and cheered by the sun.
Let the Sun Shine In!
Brightening the somber cold pale remnants of life.

Let us wade through odors
that make our senses wilt.
Oh, yes the hope is here,
The hope is here.
Let the Sun Shine In!

  —*Florence A. Navolio*

Thoughts On Top Of Another

Time passes quickly
life carries on indefinitely
like our thoughts
And everything revolves in circular motion

changes
rearrange our lives consistently
as ideas filter into memories
that linger in our minds like the sound of wind chives
It's hard to keep up sometimes

  —*Denise Harpham*

Life's Vision

Life challenges the young and the old
Life develops one to the right or to the left
Does life offer enough?
Or does life bring disappointments?

Without encouragement, life fails us
Without support, life fails us
What vision, therefore, does one see?

Without vision, one loses sight
Without vision, one loses hope
Are we so frail that we allow life to destroy us?
Are we so weak that life disappoints us?

Life is good!
Life is joyous!
With life challenges, it can bring—
 a shine of a new vision
 a strong force
 a new you.

  —*Donna Crawford*

Why

Why do we have spectacular sunrises to start the day?
　　　Life is full of surprises.
　　　　　Yes, that's God's way
　　Why do birds sing, winds blow,
　　Bells ring and roosters crow?
　　Why are some people so wealthy,
　　　while others have so little.
　　Why are some people so healthy
　　while others grow weak and brittle.
　Why do trees dance in the breeze and
　　kites hang in the sky with ease.
　Why all the beautiful colors of flowers
in bloom or why sun beams float in a room.
　　Why do some die so very young
　　while others old and sick live so long.
　Why do raindrops make music on a roof?
It is all to give us proof that God has a plan for
　each of us. He is the one we have to trust,
　　　for there is no guessing,
　　we should thank God for each blessing.

　　　　　—*Gladys White*

I Will Win

I said life, you can't hurt me anymore.
Life said, that's what you think,
There's plenty more in store.
Each day there's more sorrow and pain,
Falling down on me like doomsday rain.
Just when I think I'm on my way up and out,
Guess again, fool, I hear life shout.
I have more troubles and woe in store for you,
To turn your life upside down, and make you blue.
Ah life, one day I'll thwart you and your evil ways,
And I'll find happiness in all of my days.
For I know great strength lies within,
And I will fight you life, and win.

　　　　　—*Geraldine C. Dobry*

Janus

Life with her, remembered,
Life without her, tomorrow's question,
His gnarled fingers re-chisled
"Eternally Yours," into the granite slab.
December winds, aged as he, scourged his leathery face.
Turtling his snow-cropped head into frayed collar,
He counted cadence to a siren's wail, a grim reminder
Of the ride to the hospital with
His sweetheart, his wife, his bride, his sweetheart.
Memories reinforced the oneness of fifty years,
Loyalty, devotion, passion and compassion,
Her smiles and tender scoldings over trivia
Her guilt of fallow womb, no blame for his sterility,
As the reason for an empty cradle.
Years, silent as a panther's paws marauded their lives
Eroding her parchment face, shadowing the lavender peignoir,
His last gift to her.
Unable to share the requiem, he tottered homeward.
Tomorrow, he'd replace linens, hand-monogrammed "ours"
With a bath towel, labeled "his."

　　　　　—*Alma J. Barnes*

Yielded

Lord see through my eyes what is pleasing to you.
Lord speak through my mouth words pure and true.
Lord hear through my ears what you want me to know.
Lord walk with my feet wherever I go.
Enlighten my mind with visions from above
And fill my heart with peace and love.
Lord work with my hands 'til there's nothing to do
For I'll forever be totally yielded to you.

　　　　　—*Dorothy Conner*

Glory

As gentle as the breeze that blows across the channel
lifting the gulls into flight out to sea,
you have softly come upon the wastelands of my life,
and uplifted me.

As serenely as the music of the masters that echoes
off the mountains which surround the Alpine lakes,
you have drifted across the expanse of my consciousness,
reverberating off that thing called me.

As softly as the aged man kisses his granddaughter's
cheek, stooping over with effort and grace,
you have touched my being with kindness, caring, and concern.

As majestic is the sunrise in the mists of dawn that
signals the advent of day,
Your smiles, your glow, have illuminated the darkness
in my life, in this being called me.

And as awesome is the liftoff of the giant rocket that
reaches for the stars.
you have created an explosion of deep love for you in
that person called me.

　　　　　—*Gary R. Joachim*

Untitled

The boy lies awake in a strange place
Light struggling in
Dark pushing out, way out
Change is taking place inside him
Dropping acid in this cold dark place
Something supernatural is about to happen
The other side is near
He is alone in this desolate wilderness
Emptiness in soul, poverty in spirit
　the time has come
Confusion
Disillusion
Hypocrisy
　the time has come
He hears a rhythmic drumming now
Steady throbbing hypnotic rhythm
He enters a soft hazy glow near the roof's edge
The point of no return
　the time has come
He begins to hear the music...

　　　　　—*James Woomer*

The Stranger

You disappear and reappear every now and then;
Like a shadow of darkness.
I've never really gotten to know you;
Never really taken the time to try.
You're a mystery to all that know you;
To all that try.
You come and go as you please.
Nobody seems to have the right keys to open you up.
You keep to yourself, never trusting anyone.
People may try to get to know you, but not succeed.
What do you hide in your head and heart?
What does it take to open you up?
What are you hiding? What are your fears?
Why don't you open up and be a Stranger no more?

　　　　　—*Debra A. Morris*

Pyramid Of Peace

Peace is inner tranquility of the mind,
Like a trinket box simply silver-lined.
Peace comes so softly, like a moccasined toe,
Without primitively alerting the foe.
Leaving lurid traces in a wilderness maze,
Puffing smoke signals by a campfire blaze.
Peace is a covenant of a person's heart,
Beyond earthly splendor — light miles apart.
Utterly abstemious is a start
To get the thorny hate out of one's heart.
Peace is the murmur of a tranquil creek,
Or is compassion for the sick and weak.
Peace is the halo of a baby's smile,
Or the gentle tones of a large base viol.
Peace can be revealed in a poetry book,
Or on a wooden bench in a shady nook.
Peace is instilled by the symphonic, mute, strains
In Johann Strauss waltzes, pulsing one's veins.
Peace may be attained via various ways,
But God has the format, so Him we should praise!!!

— *Alberta N. Williams*

Moment In A Net

Completeness envelopes and caresses me
Like a warm blanket.
My body, heart and mind are one
In tune with the symphony of the universe.

Should I some future day
Lose this delicious time
A vivid memory will succor me
In hours of my dissonance.

— *Eve Holloway*

The End

There's a feeling in my head
Like everything is dead
Life doesn't begin it ends
Never really having friends
Don't understand is why they stare
Lord knows they don't care
When I dream it's in red
Inside of me is already dead
Death creeps up behind my ear
Making me hear things I fear
Icy fingers snatch my life from me
Crumbling to my knee's, could this be
Screams I hear cut me like a knife
Praying to the Lord, first time in my life
Hearing his voice makes me cry
Feeling safe I accept I must die
Peaceful feelings rise into my heart
This is the beginning with the end I shall part

— *Jon Garrett Kelly*

A Day In Slumber

The stock market has crashed
like no room in the inn.
A bankrupt nation, can anybody win?
Beggars poor a-knocking at the door.
Bread-lines form and there's no end in sight.
Millions lost by millions not wrong or right.
A day in slumber. No help to make ends meet.
War on every side, give a grain of wheat.
Banks and piggy banks shiver and shake.
Milk in a baby's bottle is our only goal.
Signs of picket for a nickel or some dough.
A day in slumber, they come all in a row.

— *Diane Ayala*

Silent Secrets

Silent words that hold no meaning drift within my mind,
like tattered clothes worn once to often,
their purpose is left behind.

To talk to you seems useless,
It just isn't worth the tears.
I find it's safer to ache quietly,
than expose to you my fears.

And as I sit in the silence
that has come to know me well,
I share with it my secrets that it will never tell.

So now I hold you close in memories,
though you lay upon my bed,
and I mourn for the man I married,
the man who was my friend.

— *Ann M. Tremblay*

Crystal Hall

A picture of a hallway,
Lit with all its crystal chandeliers,
And windows to let the sunlight in;
Memories of the past,
Come flooding through my mind.
I remembering the two friends I met,
And one old friendship renewed;
A tear comes to my eyes of parting;
But, as long as I have the picture,
The hall of memories will always be there;
In my heart and in my mind.
The crystal hall from some other time,
To remind me of friendships and memories;
Thus, the crystal hall is also,
The hallway of memories.

— *Elsa L. Chase*

With Pain

Granite-hard for me to write these words.
Little I know of you...
Only that we love the same man.

Days and years I called him mine.
Moving next door, you soon found need of him
    To start the mower
    To coax the squirrel from the chimney
    To bring a candle to a storm-blackened house...
    No matter that my lights were out.

With pain I grope
Through dizzying days of change.
Always have I known
A break would come,
Properly,
For mother and son.

— *Joann W. McMaster*

Underground World

Thirty homeless people sleeping by the el...
Living their lives to the fullest on our earth
which is their hell ... Thinking that no one
loves them, wondering, "Does anyone care?"
... Being put down and laughed at by hard
words and cold stares ... It's time we do
something about this, it's about time we face
the facts ... Because someday we may be on
the streets and become members of the pack
    So let's join hearts and hands and voices
and cry out to God above ... To ask him for
strength and courage to give these people our
love.

— *Joan McMullin*

Father's Day

It was just a late Sunday morning pickup baseball game;
Little Leaguers jostled in our front yard.
I watched from my upstairs bedroom window.

My brother hit a hard liner—
Ryan, the neighborhood dreamer, missed the hit
and danced into the street after the ball.

My screams could not make Ryan dance faster,
could not stop the bullet-jeep.
I could only run to his side.

As I knelt by his fetal-drawn body,
I saw his chest move up and down, up and down.
I sprinted to Ryan's house.

"Mr. McCarthy, there's been an accident—
Ryan was hit by a car.
But he'll be all right—he's breathing!"

Ryan's breathing stopped late that afternoon
in the hospital, with his father,
on that brilliantly blue June Sunday.

            —Dianna P. Schmitz

Tribute To A Martyr

Born alone,
Live alone,
Most certainly will die alone.

Involved in so many lives, yet,
A part of none.
Mine is the last house of the Zodiac,
I live in a kingdom of shadows and darkness.

Loneliness is a thin blanket providing little warmth
Against life's icy bitterness.
When I finally do reach out to partake in life's gusto
I'm told the parade was yesterday!

I'm a prisoner!
Locked within the stout walls of my mind.
My nourishment, my repast, has the bloody flavor
Of pure Masochism!

Perhaps one day
I will face the harsh reality that my destiny, in this life
Is not to enjoy .... but to endure,
In the comfortless solitude of my emptiness!

            —Fred Kurtz

"Alone?"

Though there is a singleness about alone, alone is not
      loneliness;
It is akin to solitude, but in no form is it
      sentenced solitary.
Alone is not a state, or condition, but opportunity to
      explore a selfness;
To search one's needs and wants and wishes to the
      point of clarity.
Alone is a virtue. When wisely turned to meet an
      internal need
It is tool to clear the soul of confusion, the
      heart of a burden.
Alone is a time to build on that eternal want, and
      plant a seed.
From which grows life, personalized, ready to share
      with someone!

            —George E. McCullough

Living Memories

So long as the window of memory is unshaded - so
long as the door will open for the passage of memory-
so long as the mind is clear, so long will the past be there.
Only when the mind is destroyed, by whatever means,
will the past be dead.
Only then will the Past be Passed.
There is tragedy as well as beauty with those memories.
The unshaded window and the open door must allow
the ugly and bitter, as well as the lovely and
beautiful to pass through.
Time, fortunately, heals most wounds and allows
the sweet, the lovely and the beautiful to triumph.

            —Harry Morris

Middle-age

Look at me,
Look at me,
Look at me,
Bourgeois, fat, middle-age.
With scars: tonsillectomy, thyroidectomy, mastectomy, bilateral.
With scars: appendectomy, salpingectomy, hysterectomy.
With scars: oophorectomy, prostatectomy, cholecystectomy.
With scars: hemorrhoidectomy, laparotomy, switcheroo-ectomy.
I'm a wreck to me!
Bourgeois, fat, middle-age.

            —Edwynne G. Bradshaw

Day's Gone By

What happened to the love you felt
Look at what life has dealt
You were everything in my eyes
You were the dream that ended in lies
All I ever asked for was a friend
But you used my love in your game of pretend
And here we are talking about day's gone by
I want to believe in those words you cry
Your eyes have nothing else to hide
Just a million tears of the years that passed us by
There is no need for us to pretend
No need for you to play my friend
When I needed you to stay
You were the one to run away
How could I explain what I feel inside
You took all I had for a ride
I can still hear the laughter of many years
But all I hear now is empty words filled with fear
My tears were all I had
You should have been there to be my Dad

            —Florika Zgrda

Remember Me

Look across the fields of wheat, swaying in the breeze,
Look back and see,
And remember me.

Look at the sky, the sea, the clouds,
The blue, the green, the grey,
All into one young pair of eyes
That are so old.

Look away and think of not what is lost,
But of who was found.

Look inside to see who you are,
And where you will go.

Look across once more and see, by the fields of wheat,
By the skies of blue, by the seas of green, by the clouds of grey,
The color of my hair and of my eyes,

Look back and see,
And remember me.

            —Cory Jean Watters

Receive

The day will come when spirits are low —
Look up and say,
"This is what I have to show!"

A smile for a stranger
A card I can send
One more hug
As I part from a friend

See diamonds or crystals
Fall from the rain.
Past the mountains
Is a smoother terrain.
Make each day one where a chance can't go by —
To give or receive a cheerful "hi".
Happily spirits will rise
As we create warmth and joy
In one another's lives.

    —Iris Torres

Dances With Sharks

He prowls the sea night and day
  Looking for some unwary prey.
They come in all sizes and shapes
  Looking as though they're full of hate.
They destroy their food with fury and might
  Crushing its bones bite by bite.
Men catch and destroy them and then boast about their triumph,
But in reality, that's one less fish in the sea to enjoy by you and
  me.
They must use their hunting weapons to find food, you know
  Just as we use the arrow and bow.
Their teeth are like swords that rip through flesh.
  for they always dine on their meals fresh.
They swim gracefully displaying their elegant side
  But to you and me they are killers, and deserve to die.
We scream in terror when we see them near the beach
  Hurrying to get out of the water and out of reach.
Their reputation is overrated
  And they are far outdated.
Let's let them live in peace
  Before their lives have evaporated.

    —Jared English

Silenced

  Sweet and silent laughter quickly sang me to sleep.
    Lost I felt within the depths of white wind.
      Soon I dreamed, I dreamed of magic.
        The power was in my hands.
    The wind I sent was free, it lashed into your mind.
  Left your how I had hoped...gone, but you were still here.
    I try to wake but soon I find that, I am here.
        But I can fly.
      I take flight and run.
      But your memory chases me away.
And so I fly 'cause I want to and I dream 'cause I don't.
    I look at something beautiful, as I fall.
      And I want to fly.
    I fly to the heavens and my life.
    I fly to the emptiness and the light.
    But I flew to close and I burnt myself.
      I am falling.
       I am screaming.
        Am I dying?
      But I am silenced.

   —Cassandra Knight

It Could Have Been Me

It could have been me, sitting over there
Lost in a world of pity and despair
It could have been me, standing in the street
Begging for money and a bite to eat
It could have been me, walking the highway
Selling my body to a couple of strangers today
It could have been me, buying some drugs
Trying to make up for all the lost hugs
It could have been me, sticking a needle into my arm
Blocking out all the memories of yesterday's harm
It could have been me, coming so close
Of becoming another casualty from an overdose
It could have been me, in a mental ward
With my mind completely gone, locked behind bars
It could have been me, committing genocide
Not even thinking twice about the precious innocent lives
That's why I'm never to forget where I came from
I always thank God for what he has done
Because I finally realize without a doubt
That without Jesus, it could have been me, with no way out

    —Cantrice L. Montgomery

Midnight Storm

At midnight, fierce winds began to blow
Loudly shrieking as they banged the doors,
Rattled the window, and shook our farmhouse
Causing echoes, to resound on every floor.

Thunder made a booming entrance;
Shafts of lightning went on display.
Our lights flickered-then went out,
Slowly came on again-then off to stay.

Rain fell in splashing torrents on the windows
As violent explosions of thunder rolled overhead.
Lightning split the sky with jagged bolts of light
While I shook with fear, in my cozy bed.

The rain, the thunderous noises-lightning flashes,
Sounds entered the house with a frightening clarity.
Nearby, pines moaned as winds lifted their swaying boughs
And the howling winds gained in severity.

All night long the storm raged about the farmhouse
Reverberating and quaking-thunder shaking the ground
Followed by lightning's brilliant flashes.
What a rough stormy night-all pierced with sound!

    —Alby A. Velek

Welcome

Barriers broken, chains unloosed!
Love in its grandeur, with willingness flies to its roost.
Seeing all things through its all loving eyes.
and freeing the Spirit in human disguise.

Love conquers all, overpowers is more clear.
Its strength is in caring and patience to bear
the waiting, the watching, the pain as we test
our humankind frailties - not loving, not blest.

Yet Love's there for the fullness of spirit to claim
when asked - Ah, the waiting, the long waiting game.
It will be, and is, and was far before.
yet now - is the time to open the door.

Yes - open the door, that's all that it takes to welcome the
Spirit as slowly we wake to the world as it is -
Love's perfection in phase,
all movement and stillness wrapped up in a gaze
of loving and living, of spirit and flesh -
Yes, clearly perfection
God's love at its best!

    —Jolene Larson-Gardner

Love Is. . .

Love is something a women feels for a man.
Love is something a man feels for a woman.
Love is something when a man and women are joined as one.
When they become husband and wife.
Love is something a husband and wife share for their children.
Love is something a brother and a sister share.
Love is something when a parent becomes a grandparent.
Love is family.
Love is special for a friend.
Love is something a small child has for their favorite toy.
Love is a way of sending your loved ones a special greeting from
  afar.
Love is for lovers on a hot summer night.
Love is for telling someone you love them.
Love is for Jesus, because he was the one who died for all of our
  sins.
Love is never having to say I'm sorry.
Love is to share from me to you.

    —*Beth A. Chiatello*

Hydra

How many heads has the Hydra?
How many heads want to devour innocent victims?
Innocent victims in Bosnia, Israel, South Africa....
Innocent victims in hundreds of places
Innocent victims in hatred,
Innocent victims of racial persecution all over the world.
When will mankind have cut off the hundred heads of the Hydra?
When will mankind have the humanity to kill the Hydra for ever?
When will all men be human?

    —*Egon Strauss*

Untitled

When I think about you
It makes me smile,
And it reminds me of how lucky I am.
Don't go red when I tell you
How special you are to me.
And don't feel flattered
When I tell you how much I love you,
Because it isn't hard falling for someone like you.
Someone who is caring, loving, and thoughtful.
So baby, you have no worries tonight,
Because I only have eyes for you
And my heart only loves that heart of yours.
And if you ever see any doubt in my eyes,
Just remember you must be dreaming
Because nothing is going to change
the way I feel for you.

    —*Kelsey Duncan*

In Due Season

The wind is churning the pile of leaves
Left swept underneath the dripping eaves
While dancing drops of winter rain
Start a lively ballet of spatters again
Spouting up dust in the restless mound
Then seeping quietly in the thirsty ground.

The leaves lie laden in damp despair
Absorbing the sun from the rain drenched air
And thoughts of new leaves green from the rain
Say winter will go and spring come again.

    —*Doris Barton*

Slaves

There in the land of ever green.
There is the land of the rich.
They get their riches from slaves.
He stands wiping off the sweat from his forehead,
While his master sits under the tent watching his slaves
Working, his pleasure is in the money he will receive from the
hard work of his slaves.

All he thinks of is the freedom he wish to have and the friends
he lost from the beatings they had. The master would give a
command to his guards to beat slaves if they don't work hard,
Money comes from hard work the master would say to his slaves.

They work wearing nothing on their feet and hands, their feet
cracked, their rough like a diamond nearly finished on a
diamond cutters table.
As he would escape he would be hunted with dogs and guns,
there would be a reward for his capture to the one who caught him.
The life of a slave is the same as a life of a prisoner of war.

    —*Gladwin Dijoe*

Untitled

The sparkling of the snow,
the burning of the candles.
The bright lights of the tree,
the shining of the wrappers on the presents,
and the dying of the carolers
as they go home for the rest of Christmas.

It is now the day of Christmas,
the crunched up parts of snow,
which were left behind from the carolers.
The melted wax of candles, sitting on the sill.
and the ripped up wrappers from the presents,
are lying under the still beautiful Christmas tree.

    —*Julie Ladik*

Looking Glass

    Twilight comes much, too fast
When you're going through the looking glass
    Darkness falls against, the wall
  Like the shadow falling, far too tall

    Emptiness consumes the masses
    Lonely stares from hollow glasses
  With no warm heart behind those eyes
They don't know why, love they despise

    Cheer heart now go, with no return
    A pot prepare, a crucible to burn
    Dare we step beyond the door
Beyond the looking glass, if there be a floor

    —*A. Melinda New*

Marriage Of Sincerity

Let sincerity talk frankly
lest his story will never be told:
Once in the human Kingdom
he went out in search of a wife:
he cooed to Frank in her frank-chair,
but he thought:
why must I let her take my hand in marriage?
He hissed and walked by.
Later she saw insincerity sit at the end of the road;
her beauty shot out radiance of joy.
He stopped and thought out loud:
"She would make a good match,
must I marry from my own kind?"
Sincerity took insincerity as wife.
When they were asleep,
insincerity unmasked of her beauty
and her ugliness choked sincerity to death.

    —*Barine Sanah Ngaage*

In Love...

Soft breath against my cheek...
Do you whisper?

Speak, my heart,
In tongues only those who dare to feel can hear.

I have opened my soul to you;
Crashed down the barriers that imprisoned;
Turned my heart inside out;
Constricted and gave until I ached.

So now, I say again,
Voice your emotions, my heart.

The sweet tenor reaches me not through the ears,
But through my very existence.

Swinging out on a rope overlooking
Rippling velvet; free like a child
Bursting with the purity in life... Vulnerable.

Suddenly my hands are free from the roughness,
And I'm soaring, above the china-like violet sunset,
Above the wispy feather-soft white of the clouds,
In Love....
Though, someday, I know I shall fall.

  —Lisa Manuel

Mother

Of all the mothers in the world
I'm glad God gave me you,
You reached out and touched my life
To last my whole life through.

"Thank you's" are not enough
For the caring home you gave me.
Learning to love unconditionally
Is a mother I aspire to be.

You were always there to comfort me
Through those turbulent teenage years,
Patiently listening to my hopes and dreams
And wiping away my tears.

As time passes and you're growing older
And I've got teenagers of my own,
I'm torn between my gratitude to you
And maintaining a happy home.

If I could make a magic wish
I'd grant you "anything" because of your love,
What you've conveyed to your whole family
I'm sure is blessed from up above.

  —Kay Foreman

Think Of Me

Think of me my dear when I'm away,
Think of me my precious
in every word you say.
When you stop to maybe smell a rose,
or when you gaze out into the open sea,
Surely my love I hope that
you will think of me.
In due time when a song may come to my mind,
As a smile will cross your face,
Keep a strong thought,
And keep a kind heart,
that I'm not so far away as you will see,
that I'm always so near if only you think of me.

  —Frank Mathis

Untitled

Take me, hold me in your arms so close to your heart,
Your voice in the deep recesses of my mind.
Your touch the finest silk on my skin.
Your sweet caresses render me numb with desire.
Passion-filled haze illuminates from my eyes.
The words on my tongue, should they be spoken?
So delicately woven a dream would it not shatter?

I Love You...
  —Dana L. Fewkes

A Cry For Help

Lord I know I am so blessed
so why do I feel so depressed.
Please help me not to despair
because somehow you know my every fear.
I try and try to end my life
I am sick and tired of this stupid strife.
I know I know you hear my prayer,
I know I know I should not despair,
but so strong so strong are my fears
and I cry and pray but no one hears.
I need your strength, your love and guidance,
lots of faith and a million pardons.
Lord, oh Lord I know that I am so blessed,
so why dear Father do I feel so helpless.

  —Alicia Sangster

Hurricane Andrew

Mother Nature, they called him, and yet
Somehow that title seems justly unfit
The thrashing of wind, the pounding of rain,
And who could forget the sound of that train.

Trees that once stood proud and tall
Were left bare and broken if they were left at all.
In that one fearful night our lives torn apart
Our homes and our keepsakes, left shattered, like our hearts.

A generators' hum would lull us to sleep
We prayed the Lord our soul to keep
Months without electric, and few telephones
Everyone's a victim, but still, you feel alone.

With strength from above and pride from within
The rebuilding process would slowly begin
Neighbors helping neighbors, blood, sweat and tears
We tried to ease the children's fears.

Yet - from out of that darkness
A new light burns bright
To think a hurricane lit it
One dark August night.

  —Jill Lori Boone

I Sympathize Daddy

  Dad's fifty-two,
successful, but not monetary wise,
  bucks but only a few.
 His kids are no good he feels,
not good enough they don't kneel.
Nine A.M. to five P.M., six days
 a week another twenty two years,
is that all there is? I think my
  Daddy fears.

  Finally sit home, feed the
 garden, watch T.V. ... die?
 Another twenty two years,
is that all there is I think
  my Daddy fears.
  —Michael Rabinowitz

478

I Cast A Spell

I cast a spell of sorrow
This secret I shall keep beyond tomorrow
Through the valleys and even the heavens
My spell shall lie unspoken

I cast a spell of sadness
So everyone will weep
And silent I shall keep
just thinking of my spell

I cast a spell of despise
Till that day the sun doesn't rise
No more worries no more fears
Yet all I'll ever see is tears

I cast a spell like no other will ever be
Only I
And only me
shall ever be free
—*Julie Hudson*

Tit for Tat

My brother tore my paper.
My brother took my pen.
My mommy's angry with me, but then —
I said, I didn't mean to sit on my brother.
I didn't mean to pull his hair.
Mommy didn't want to hear my why's and wherefore's
Because she was standing right there.

Don't you ever sit on your brother!
Don't you ever pull his hair!
I looked at her and listened
With a pout and a stare.
I thought,
But he had torn my paper.
He took my pen.
If he had done that to you.

I WOULD BET THAT YOU WOULD SIT ON HIM THEN!

"If you like to sit so much —
Over there is a chair — SIT!"
—*Elaine Meli*

Yearly Review

The 80's went by very slow
The 90's are going by fast
The 80's had a mellow year
The 90's got it bad.

The 90's had some causes
From the beating of Rodney King
The 80's had a quiet year
At least that's how it seems.

The 80's were a positive year
The 90's are very strong
The 80's were kinda hype
But the 90's got it going on!
—*Sasha Burns*

One Dozen Roses

I always wanted to receive a dozen roses
I thought it would be so great, but when yours arrived today
Well, I'm afraid they were just too late

Now so much has happened and so many things have changed
They don't have the meaning they should
No matter how beautifully they are arranged

For one rose stands for the way, that you used to care
Two reminds me of all the times, when you were not there
Three stands for the things, that you used to do
Four reminds me, I really no longer know you
Five is for the things, that you used to say
Six reminds me, you chose another one day
Seven is for the trust, that now has gone away
Eight reminds me, there's not much left to say
So, nine must be for the love, that we once had
As ten reminds me of how it all went bad.
But through it all eleven must hold the memories,
That we shared together
As twelve reminds me that memories,
Are something that last forever.
—*Tamara A. Wade*

Follow Your Dream

There I was on my job my eight to five,
I told myself I got to cut out this jive.
I was working hard it didn't seem to matter,
For I was not moving up the corporate ladder.

I had several ideas that I wanted to pursue,
I finally asked myself what should I do?
It doesn't matter how long of a shot it seems,
You are better off if you follow your dreams.

There will be those saying what you can't do,
You should follow your dream and see it through.
The road may be long and the road may be tuff,
It doesn't matter if you got the right stuff.

Times are hard and sometimes they will be rough,
To follow your dream you will have to be tough.
Hard times will come and hard times will go,
Follow your dream you won't be back no mo.
—*William Earl Sims*

Pattern

Every evening as the sun goes down
I trace again a path inside my house.
The northern window in the dining room
And then the west, both of the shades are drawn
Against the night. The living room
Can slow my pace — its windows hold
The last wild brilliance of the sun.

Another room, still west in shade of trees,
And still another west are open wide
As far as the mountains, nothing in between
To shut them out except my reluctant hand,
And all the others, all are shuttered in.

What do I fear of night? Not night itself
Nor dark, but there is some vague thought
That something out there holds a chance of harm
Or danger if I have no shield.

The tags of worry leave when sleep is near;
I open one small shutter and begin
To count the stars. I leave it open, now
It's safe at last to let the nighttime in.

—*Margaret Neff Bosse*

Slowly falling, cascading down,
It falls into a puddle on the ground
Its silence and beauty quenches all
    natures thirst,
Never leaving on anything, some kind
    of curse.
To be held so preciously,
But used so carelessly.
It often makes one wonder why
    when we have something
    we abuse it,
But only when it becomes scarce,
    do we treasure it.
　　　　—Sara K. Davis

Couples With Love

There is this thing called love,
    It flows throughout the air,
Hoping to find the loving couple
    To love each other and care.
Hoping that they last a while,
    To hope and follow through,
To find the day of marriage,
    The truth between me and you.
Our lives will be filled with laughter,
    Feeling, truth, and respect,
To have the feeling of love,
    In life, it is the best.
It's a feeling you can't live without,
    A feeling of happiness and joy,
Shared between a loving couple,
    A blessed girl and boy.
　　　　—Michelle Stickle

Faith Is Personal

Faith is personal and real
It grows big like a mountain
When things go wrong
And your feelings are bruised
It descends upon you instantly
Like an overpowering giant
Spreading its wings about you
Surrounding you, reassuring, serene.

Taste of it and tell someone
It's contagious, it's accessible
As close to you as a prayer
Use it for a small request
Believe and watch it grow
The one who gives you faith
Also gives you hope
What a powerful combination
To enhance your spiritual growth.
　　　　—Suzy Cox

Hands of Time

My mother used to say, "Look at my hand
It's hard to understand
That it's mine
So wrinkled and old"
I didn't want to look—but I'd say
It looked fine
And I shrugged the thought away
The years have passed, and now and then
The thought kept coming back again
Today I looked at my own hand
And I did understand—
I saw my mother's hand.
　　　　—Lorraine Feuer

It is A Puzzlement

It is a pronoun,
It has no sex,
It has no case,
It has no person — It is.

You is a pronoun,
You has no sex,
You has no case,
You has person — You are.

I is a pronoun,
I has no sex,
I has case,
I has person — I am.

You and I are we.
We is a pronoun,
We has no sex,
We has case,
We has person — We are.

But We is plural
and We have sex!
　　　　—L. P. Corbett

Enclosed Insanity

　　First —
　　It hides in darkness
　　Looking for the light.
Intelligence-but with no thought.
　　Second —
　　Dominating its desires.
Success-but with no achievement.
　　Finally —
　　Welcomed-it came.
　　All is now unretainable.
　　Now —
Actions-but with no movements.
　　　　—Pam Dworzynski

Untitled

If it comes natural
    It is good,
If it comes in time
    It is fair,
If it comes at all
    be glad,

If you force it
    It will hurt,
If you clock it
    It will vanish
If you tell it
    It will be stolen

    Trust it
It will be wise

    Forsake it
It will die
    Listen to it you will hear
So,
Run with it and you
    will never fear.
　　　　—Starr Page

Trepihany Fundamaximus

Within my heart there is a tree -
    it knows me not
    it knows very little
At times it doesn't move at all
    when times are cold
    when times are dry
But summer brings the knowledge back
    to reach for water
    earth
    and light
The light it found has helped my eyes
    my eyes have learned much in it
They search for earth and water too
    they helped me build a garden
The garden's brought me even more
    more than beauty
    more than fruit
My gardens brought me other trees
    we stand together
    against the wind
　　　　—Raymond Recco

The Vast And Vast Blue Sea

The vast and vast blue sea!
It makes our heart wide and bright
The sea in the evening sun light.
Fills our heart with rosy glorious light.
The sea in the starry night
Gives wonderful starry present
Into the heart of each of us.
The sea knows everything.
　　　　—Rae Asazuma

Hi Daddy

"Hi Daddy" is a tender phrase
It means so much to me
The kids all said "Hi Daddy"
As they climbed upon my knee

It was "Daddy, will you tuck me in?"
As they tripped off to bed
It was Daddy who fixed all their toys
And kept the family fed

But soon the kids grew older
I then was known as Dad
It lost a little tenderness
That Daddy always had

When teenage years had rolled around
I then was known as Pop
I felt the kids were being cruel
This nonsense had to stop

But years have passed by rapidly
And Pop I'll always be
And that tender phrase "Hi Daddy"
Is a loving memory
　　　　—P. LaRue Teaney

Death And Darkness Toll The Hour

Death and darkness toll the hour,
It shall have you in its power,
It takes humans every hour,
It creeps upon the midnight tower,
It makes many many scream,
It makes you puff into steam,
Death becomes you one dark hour.
　　　　—Robyn Dollins

Love Is A Meadowlark

Love is a meadowlark.
It sings of itself
With sweet insistence.

Love is beside me.
It takes my hand
And leads me to the sun.

Could you tell me
Of your joy
That bounces off my soul
Like springtime rain?

We all leave some day,
So why not love
While we have a chance?

Love is a meadowlark
Singing in the field.
Love is a song without end.

—*Spencer Knox Kendig*

The Ladder Of My Ages

When I was one, I walked a mile.
It stretched so far and wide.
When I was ten, I raced the wind.
It was one fantastic ride.
When I was twenty, I drank the sea.
I grew with every drop.
When I was fifty, I climbed the Alps.
Then I rested at the top.
When I was eighty, I walked again.
Only this time with some grace.
For I spent the rest of my ages,
Breathing heavens space.

—*Lonnie L. Veitch*

Music Without Words

I love music without words
It's soothing and pleasing
To the mind
Like the soft breeze
On a summers' eve
Raindrops on silvery blades
of grass
Rays of sunlight dancing
on the lake

—*Sonia Moodie*

Alone

A perfect night... for emptiness.
It's strange how two people
can lie next to one another
yet be so far apart.
Another time, another night —
perhaps.
But can you really forget
or even understand?
We both know as an evening it failed.
Just one night lost,
but it always seems to hurt more
when it's someone you love.

—*William Borovsky*

Angel of Mercy, Angel of Love

Angel of mercy, Angel of love
Jehovah God, our Father
Showed us His love.

Angel of mercy, Angel of love
Baby Jesus in a manger
The shepherds told of.

Angel of mercy, Angel of love
Holy Spirit descended
Down like a dove.

Angel of mercy, Angel of love
Jesus, our Saviour, on the cross
Shed His own blood.

Angel of mercy, Angel of love
The King of Kings, Lord of all
We'll shout from Above!

—*Sue A. Schrowang*

Choices

In the time of peace and quiet
Jesus speaks unto my soul.
As I often pause to seek Him;
how He longs to make me whole.

Oh, please take the time to know Him
for His peace is beyond compare.
Yes, the joy of really knowing
that He keeps us in His care.

So, my friend, you choose each day
the path that you will walk.
It's by these choices that we know Him
while others they just talk the talk.

It's so very important then,
these many choices that we make.
We will choose to walk with Him,
or we will choose to be a fake.

There is no peace or rest in falsehood
and so my weary friend,
Won't you trust in God today and
He will see you safely to life's end.

—*Roy Bowen*

Autumn And The Apple Tree

The apple tree had leaves up to its top
Just awhile ago.
But winter winds have passed
This way, the leave were kissed
by snow
No cover now
Beneath the bough
To rest within its shade
No sign of green among
The grassy blade
The sun has taken
Leave of earth to
wait the birth
of spring!

—*Mary Ann Davis*

Fruits For Your Labors

"Hope's"
"Joy's"
"Love's"
"Peace's"
"Laugh's"
"Patient's"

—*Mary Walters*

Love Re-Threading

Eyes —
Kaleidoscopic windows
(shimmering incantations
of Pretense and Folly)
Vivify us, one to another,
But shade
our inward suns.

Would we shatter
the polychromatic panes,
shatter the eclipsing smiles
and arachnoid desires.

Still.
Your latticing voice
baffles the hollowed darkness
re-geometrizes the enwebbing glass—
star-stunning mosaics flower—

My soul and yours:
A prismatic bower.

—*Richard D. Lucero*

Attitudes

Treacherous stares from afar
keen looks from the corner of the eye.
Spitballs tossed.
Sneaky chatter.
Hands to mouth.
Naughty boys
and girls
huddled like a football team.
Facial expressions
bodily gestures
implicit plots that conclude
you definitely have it.

—*Sandra R. Kiser*

Grandparents

Grandparents are made from a special
kind of mold, they have away about
them, that can not be told; the
wisdom and love, they've gotten
through the years, is making wrongs
to right, and shedding lots of tears;
mommy and daddy say they love us,
I think that is sweet, I guess that
is why they meet our special needs.
Grandpa's deep voice is gruff like a
bear, but deep down inside, he's
only a teddy bear. Grandma's tender
touch, when I've got a cold, I'd
rather have grandparents than a
pot of gold!

—*Martha Jean Kennedy*

Seeking Love

High above the endless sky,
Lies my heart alone and blue.

So high above to keep it safe and warm,
So hence it would not be harmed.

But now I take a glance at you.
And can not stop loving you.

Now my only wish I do conceal,
Is if you would come and glance at me.

With your stare, if I do acquire,
I'd wish you'd seek some love for me...

—*Vanessa Cortez*

Love's Embrace

You were once but a notion
known only in obscurity
now, you are my reality
and as to my immortal soul
the promise of love eternal

With willful resolve
you stole back my heart
from the pain that
so cruelly enslaved it
enfold me and let me surrender to
your mellifluous renderings of love
and with every heartbeat
bring to light what
only the lonely have known

Though it be oft times mortal
and ever elusive
there remains no better place
than the comfort and warmth
of love's embrace

—*Laura L. Abbott*

Divination

Beyond the horizon
Lake Superior escapes the shore
stealing power from the wind
to rush here with solutions
locked in foam and sound.

The Crone of the Lake
casts her bones of wood
in lots upon the shore
crooning our future in the
hiss of the curl
moaning our sorrows
in the backwash.

Bones of past fore-tellings
litter the shore and dunes
symbols locked in solitude.
Tales heard on the wind
only by the sawgrass
staying the dunes.

—*Patricia E. Thurston*

Love's Spark

Comes another one fine day
Late my eyes open to the sun
They sparkle like its rays
The new day has begun

Like the lucky old sun
There's a spark in my heart
It seems to only see shadows
On the days we're apart

This closeness that we share
Has built a bridge to cross
We meet in the middle
And love shows its gloss

Be mine, walk beside me
Put in mine, your hand
Stroll with me to paradise
Let love sail, through this land

Take in all of the sunshine
That towers way up above
And carry inside its glitter
You know your in love

—*Monte R. Shockley*

Glow Worm

Sun of amber, fury with fire,
leaves a glow-worm full of desire.
As far as the sun can reach,
it can't strike the night.

Man can demand
and man can fight.
Man can kill
for what he thinks right.

We can revolt for change
and blow up buildings,
but isn't it strange

Those who don't know
themselves well
spend a life turning
earth into Hell.

—*Lewis I. Chace*

Who's To Blame

The words you told me as a child
Left heartache and great pain.
You said I'm just a stupid kid
And I'm the one to blame.

I won't amount to anything
I'll always be the same.
I believed in what you said
And now I hang my head in shame.

I lack faith in all I do;
This, forever, will remain.
And the guilt I carry with me
Tells me I'm the one to blame.

I wanted with my heart and soul
To join in every game.
I was convinced I'd never win;
Nor would I feel the fame.

I dream to hold my head erect;
That, once, I may stand proud.
I whisper, NOT, this question;
I ask, who's to blame?, out loud!

—*Lisa Schultz*

My Prayer For Today

No matter what comes my way today,
Let me find a reason to smile.
No matter how rough and rocky the way.
Let me go that extra mile.

Give me the will to do my best
To lighten someone's load.
And help me hold my tongue Dear Lord,
Don't let me tease or goad.

Help me to be a loyal true friend
To someone who's in need.
And stop me quick if I should start
A cruel or thoughtless deed.

Let me be a good example
To my children and their friends.
Let me be remembered fondly,
If today my life should end.

Let me stand and look around me
At the closing of today.
And be thankful for your bounty
In these things for which I pray

—*Margaret Cook*

An Unborn Child's Prayer

Please, please,
Let me live,
If only you could see,
I'm a Human too,
God created me.
Don't take my life,
my breath,
but take the time to see,
That I'm here for a reason,
God created me.
He fashioned me together
To be uniquely me.
So please don't take my life,
But let me live like thee.

—*Tracy L. Carver*

Within The Heart

With in the times that we separate
Let us not drift apart.
Only a strong love like ours could
Remain with in the heart.
And upon the time of return when it's
Down to you and me.
Look deeper within the heart for
there is where you'll always be.

—*Michael Lane*

Intrigue

Come let us dance together
Let your warmth lay upon my skin
Doubt not the joy in my eyes
As I look upon you each morning

Stay with me now for the day is short
And I can't see the flowers in the dark

The birds stop singing,
the doe closes her eyes
Though the stars are intriguing
I long for the light of your heart

—*Michele McCabe*

Is Life A Voyager In The Universe?

If human is not immortal,
Life is a flash on the pan.
If human is not imperfect,
Climbing the Everest becomes a pinnacle.
If human is impure,
Life is an endless struggle.
If life is a navigation full of danger,
Any joy is a climax.
Only if human is imperfect,
Then life is a voyager in the universe.

—*Yung-Feng Chang*

Three Japanese Poems Of Life

Slow down be quiet
Life's meaning is all around
In stillness is God

Broken dreams today
Faith, hope, and love, united
May future bring peace

Teaching one to love
So on each and every day
Showing constant love

—*William Durbin*

Try To Live It...

How will we all bear up to
life over a long period of time-

Maybe with its successful
trials and sorrows-

Maybe the secret is to try to
live only from a day to day, from
a moment to moment-

Do not worry about tomorrow,
for tomorrow will take care of
if its own-

We can have a piece of mind
and strength for every need, if
we live piece meal, from hour to
hour-

So try not to torment ourselves
needlessly, when trying to live
tomorrow today...

—*Lena Gander*

Untitled

Dreams gone,
like a shattered mirror
never to reflect an image again

Time lost,
like a stolen rainbow
never to cast its beauty again

Feelings change,
like the dead awakening
never to see darkness again

Today is now history,
no longer a burden
left to be reviewed later
looked at as a sad past

Thoughts created,
like the imagery in a book
used to amuse the reader

My heart is broken,
like an abandoned toy after Christmas
never to be held again after
that wonderful day

—*Misty Buchanan*

Father's Love

The child that I am trying to raise,
Like any other child,
Has a sweet tooth for praise.

That I listen & hear what he has to say
    may well be the high point
    of his busy day.

But praise without effort is a
    lie being told,
And not making him listen an
    action so cold.

For he needs my input, my
    nagging, my wile...

To develop someday, to a
    man-child with style.

—*Tim Coogan*

The Orchestra

The drums pulse
like blood flowing
through the body.

The strings ring
like a screeching woman in pain

The horns pound,
like an angry husband
pounding, pounding.

The flutes sing
like a ray of hope
drowned out by the sound of harmony.

The orchestra rushes,
moves onward; it's a race.
Pounding.
A silence.
A pause.
Off again, with more fury.
pounding, pounding,
pounding, pounding.
Silence, this time forever.

—*Sarah Reinecke*

Coming Home Pt. One

Leaves trickling down
    like snow
As I walk through the countryside
    again

When did leaves ever
Leave such an impression on me
    So vivid
That I had to pause

And bask in a beauty
I almost forgot existed
Yesterday I would have missed it
But today I just had to visit

To find something that was taken away
Emotions inside I thought ridden
Actually they were hidden
Forbidden until I saw leaves falling along
    The countryside
    Trickling like snow

—*Obiama Iwuoma*

Love....

Love is unique
like the sound of waves
But all seem to seek,
the good looking babes
No one ever dares
to look within
we only seem to care
about the beauty and the sin,
They break your heart
that's all they do
then leave you all the pain
you actually thought
they loved you
But they are all the same
then the day we met
I have came to see
that not everyone
is alike
Some feel the heart
with glee...

—*Summer Jones*

Ghosts

Impatient souls
lingering at eternity's end

A watchful eye,
searching for yesterday
and finding a pool of blood

Day's last light is gone
as quickly as is a wisp
of smoke from an incense burner

An old man sits,
inhaling the
sweet, juicy fatness
of a suckling pig

New York, and
the lights are on
but nobody's home

Life goes on.
    Period.

—*Valerie A. Brinson*

Spring Night

Light cloud, nocturnal, proud,
Lite as concealed lamp, tonight,
Moon softly concealed, as shroud,
Attempting to glimmer so bright,

Earth stars, captured in glance,
Around world seen just here,
Gaping, abounding, light as dance,
Wondrous picture of night so dear,

Moment captured forever in humility,
This becomes absolute picture,
Shedding thought of any futility,
Seeing heavens makes one sure.

—*Thomas N. Cranston*

The Lake

Little boy's swim and swim,
little girl's swim and swim, father's
fishing for supper, mother's clean and
clean, fish for supper father's say,
mother's cook and cook, after supper
children go to bed and mother's and
father's talk and talk.

—*Titan Crawford*

Pastels

I envy those who live their
    lives in pastels
Who find peace in sandstone
    and azure blue
    Whose worlds remain
    unspoiled and clean
Untouched by the vivid splashes
    that spot the canvas
    I exist in

—*Stacia Giunta*

Untitled

When night come
Loneliness say, I can't see
I am afraid!
Who? Can you be.

I lay in the still-ness of the night
hoping and praying
hurry! hurry! hurry daylight.
For when light comes
loneliness vanish out of sight,
and my fear is set free.

For darkness in prison me
being afraid of darkness you see
is like slow death over powering me,
But day comes you see and set me
my loneliness free.

So, I guess known you can agree
darkness and me don't see.

—*Lorriane Murray*

Untitled

Lonely night,
lonely place,
tears falling
from my eyes,
with no one to see
but the lonely moon.
Aye, lonely me.

—*Sendic Veluz*

Poor Kitty

Kitty was sitting up in a tree,
Longing for some company.
She sat and sat, but no one came;
I thought it was a doggone shame
Kitty sang a lullaby
To the moon up in the sky.
Neighbors heard the midnight blues,
So showered her with clocks and shoes.
One boot kissed her on the face,
Robbing her of time and space.
Kitty now has gone to rest,
And daisies grow upon her chest.

—*Mary Barbara Kozul Blazic*

Ode To A Mama Robin

Well there, Mrs. Robin,
Look at how we've grown!
The season is turning
and another has flown.

We are scattered 'round the country
one is down the hall,
But reach down inside your heart
We aren't far at all.

You have done a great job
just look at us now
The world sees us shining
and they know just how.

How that you brought us up
to be faithful and wise,
We love you Mama Robin
You are the star in our eyes.

—*Lisa McUmber*

"Agony Of Honesty"

Whirlwind sacred fires
"Lord, where are You?"
So deep the desire
    so blood-shot the heart:
        Passion and death!
"To whom shall I go?"
How holy and absurd!
Here - there,
No-where - all-where.
Agony of honesty.

—*Malia Wong*

Lost And Found

Lost in thought
    lost in feeling
Cerebral wandering.

A solitary realm
    Alone.
    Within.

Lost in thought. Again.

Discovery
Deeply hidden. Essential.

Sanctuary.
    Oneself.

Found.

—*Sean Patrick Mckenna*

Love Is the Devil

Love is unfair
Love is deadly
like a gun that takes a life
Without even a fight
It takes everything from you
It's out of control
There's nothing you can do

Love is like suicide
Stripping you of everything
including your pride
leaving you with nothing
almost taking your life

Love is the devil
he puts that gun in your hand
tells your mind to pull the trigger
to take you to the neverland
you try to scream and yell
Try to get him out of your head
But your on the road to hell
You loved therefore your soul... is already
dead

—*Stacia Rolston*

Untitled

On the wings of wind and time
lulled by seasons lullaby.
A life,
a line.
That bends, curves,
twists, turns
and ends up where it deserves.
Death comes to all
in either violence or serenity.
But either way, fate is fate
and we all have a destiny.

—*Melisa Spencer*

Reverie

Amidst the darkness of the night,
lying down so restlessly beside
a mysterious, melancholic love.

Bewitched, yet bewildered,
wanting to kiss, however barred
by deep, inexplicable thoughts.

Eyes wide open, visualizing
two souls in love united in harmony;
but ... the night was devoid of warmth
and passion my aching heart desires.
Suddenly entrapped in a sullen mood,
sensitized by the truth clandestinely
kept within the realms of a mystic
nook ... a witness to silent tears.

A misty reverie of an illusioned
romantic, boundless love that
failed to keep its vows -

Marred by the universal perils
of this sinful, ruthless world that
captured our union's sanctity.

—*Yolanda Laurel Merdegia*

The Words Of God

God of heaven and of earth,
Made the skies and gave me birth.
Years have gone and years have past,
And God's love still does last.

God of wisdom and of love,
Once talked to me, while He was above.
God used no words and sang no song,
Yet, spoke to me loud and long.

God of beauty and of joy,
Used nature to talk to me, His boy.
His words were stars and little flowers,
God spoke His awesome powers.

God of wonders and of mysteries,
That day, brought me to my knees,
I saw that almighty God does show
That from everywhere His graces flow.

—*Percy Mamikunian*

Season Of Change

There's the snowman,
made with care.
Carrot nose, such cold toes!
Sunny skies shine upon the fair.
Snow no more, grass is green.

Shooting star across the sky,
way so high, so hard to see.
Maybe I can hitch a ride?
Up above the clouds that storm,
I feel the glow that is so warm.

I know all things must change,
but why so hard, so fast, so cruel?
I will take the time to ride my star,
to slow things down, that is my rule.
I will let the seasons change.
Welcome sun and stormy rage.
Until my star grows dim,
I will appreciate all within.

—*Nancy Seruya*

Choices

Choices
    Make choices
        Making choices.
        Choose!
Take responsibility
Take power
    Empowered!
Control
    Controlling
        Controlled!
Don't choose.
    No choice.
        Not responsible.
        Powerless
Trapped
Victim
Caught!

You choose!

—*Mary Till*

Knowledge

As I journeyed through my mind today
    many things discovered.
In deep abyss, emotional turmoil,
    hypocrisy uncovered.

Idiosyncrasy of the mind
cause innuendoes of the heart.
Fear of acknowledgement
    tearing me apart.

—*Melissa K. Folse*

Purple

I love purple and so do you
maybe black can go with it to, if
only it would go with blue maybe
it would look like you.

—*Quintin Natale Fields*

Heaven

You often dream what heaven
maybe like, look like;
above the clouds; there must
be a wonderful sight.

At night the stars touch;
You often wonder; what they
are spelling out for us.

At day break; you can see
The light watching over us;
Heaven is far; but not
out of reach.

Someday, when you look
up in the sky; at the
sunlight
we may all see that wonderful
place; known as
Heaven.

—*Lora Albright*

Lonely

Their muddled cheers
meet shouts of anger
and cries of encouragement.
Together they drift
through the sweaty air
and my distant ears.

They huddle around
and place their hands
one on top of the other.
All of them belong,
bound by goals of victory
and friendship unknown to me.

Till just one
turns to the sideline
and gives me a genuine smile.
I smile back,
surprised how his simple gesture
pulls me closer to the game.

—*Sheri Watson*

Resting In God

Here, this exhausted body
Melts into the comfort
Of pillows and blankets
Alone with You
And I am blessed
With the warmth
Of Your eternal love.
Here, all things
Confirm the thought
That You are my Provider.
In Your great omnipotence
You have answered every prayer;
And so the indecisions
Of this mind
I place completely
In Your care —
Taking all peaceful slumber.

—*Wanda Lee Porter*

A Friend Gone

In my mind there lives a
memory that time just can't
erase.

It is of many, many friends
with tears streaming down their
faces.

I watched them for a
moment then I knew; so I
turned and walked away.

That was sometime ago, but
I still recall the day.

Now I finally understand,
why God took him away.

—*Tonya Richie*

......As The Barn Crumbles

A chord is struck in my mind
It's hard, harsh, and pitiless
Like the sun settles in the West
By the same degree I am disarmed
This paralytic affection
Idyllic though it was
Has dismembered me

—*Steve Nwaeze*

What Have We Become?

What have we become?
Men with clenched fists,
Instead of open arms?

Are we capable of love,
or does hatred reign?

What have we become?
Children with fear in their hearts,
and blood on their hands?

Is compassion a thing of the past?
gone and forgotten?

What have we become?
People with weapons,
Instead of pens and voices?

If violence is our solution,
What have we become?

—*Tracy Carr*

Lawn Mower

Giant, earth-bound,
Metal bumblebee,
Gorging on green grass
And on an occasional...
Green water hose!

—*La Retha Adams*

The Impact

Glass shatters!
Metal crunches!
The force of the impact!
Then, a quietness.
Strange, I don't feel anything.
What's happened to me?
I don't feel any pain,
But I can see the blood.
My body is crushed
In the twisted, smoking wreckage.
This isn't what I wanted.
I don't want to die.
Please, just let me feel something....
Anything.... anything at all.
Even pain is better than this.
I don't want to die, but I'm slipping away...
I can feel it.
Then peace settles over me...
Like a cloud of dust.
I'm home free now.

—*Nancy Raley*

The Brown Jacket

When we were young, long ago
Michael bought a brown jacket.
And when he tried it on for me,
a handsomer man I will never see,
I told him so.

When twenty years we were wed,
he put it on again. I said,
you have not changed at all my dear,
you are so young and debonair.
I meant it.

Today I take it from the rack
cover it with tears and hang it back.
How I miss him

—*Thelma M. Lasko*

Beyond

A destined passion,
mixed with pure satisfaction...
A burning desire,
for an exclusive fire...
A drop of misery,
for extreme luxury...
A touch of pain,
for a stainless fate...
A glance of rejection,
for absolute perfection...
A kiss of coldness,
Farther than protection...
But for the unforgiven,
It's beyond damnation...
Fore it's eternal liberation...
Fore years of lamentation...

—*Lissette Almanzar*

Depressed

Rain drops falling on the ground.
Mixed with tears, it's a sad, sad sound.

Trying to find my little space.
In what we call the human race.

For I have not accomplished anything.
Only thing I have is an intense pain.

For when I die who will mourn my death
To bad that will be my last deep breath

—*Sabrina Boyce*

To Those Who Have A Dream

I am in love with the dream
    more so than reality.
And to know the reality is
    to break my heart,
Yet the dream remains only a dream
    and my heart remains intact.
But if the dream were to become reality
    my heart would also become a reality
Broken into pieces unrepairable
Because the dream knew reality.

—*Tahira Haseebullah*

Poetry: A Potpourri

Poems rhyme
'Most all the time;
But sometimes don't.
With clear insight,
They can delight;
But often won't.
Poets ponder philosophy,
And frolic in frivolity.
In haste, they may abbreviate.
At ease, they may expatiate.
People and pets,
Antiques and jets,
Landscapes and seascapes,
Scarcely a subject ever escapes
The poet's perspicacious ken,
And the peregrination of his/her pen.
To say it all in summary:
With candor or with subtlety,
With levity or sobriety,
Poems specialize in VARIETY!

—*Teresita A. Ryan*

As Time Passes By:

As time passes by
My ears hear a cry
Of a life that is lost
Where emotions get tossed
A love which was near
Has left in a tear
Where the fun had once been
There's now sadness within
Where a laughter was found
Now memories abound
So share now the time
It ends like a crime
Death breaks a close tie
As time passes by.

—*Toby L. Timberlake*

Too Seldom

        Today
        My heart
    Has reason to smile
        For a while
        Anyway
    In the slow lane
        Too seldom
Surrounded by solitude
And the simplicities
        That
        Too often
    Go unnoticed

—*Martin Morgan*

Rodney King: Reactions

        Microwave
    my heart until it explodes
        like an egg.

        Black eye peas
dancing in the wired dimensions.

    Bushy tail headless leaders
    arranged urgent flight.

        Oh my god
    those colored folks are
        mad as hell tonight.

—*Shirley R. Berry*

Without You

As each day passes
My love for you grows stronger
Without you the night grows longer
Only to fear we'll soon be strangers

As each day passes
Your smile makes no escape
My heart makes no mistake
A touch from you is all it takes

As each day passes
Dreams never lasting
Love songs forever passing
Rainy days forever lasting

—*Steve Snyder*

Bennie

Dreams are life, days like song.
My love for you, I waited so long.
Adored treasures, so far away.
Fantasy dreams, from yesterday.

Locked away, forever it seems.
Starlite nights, sun beams.
Caring emotions, hidden inside.
Love for you, tried to hide.

Miracles happen, dreams come true.
This I know, for me and you.

Real awakening.
Daylight sounds.
Knowing you're mine.
The love I've found.

—*Lois B. Buchanan*

Hands Down

I wish I could coordinate
My powers to perambulate
With a metacarpal gait.
The cultivation of this inclination
Might well effect emaciation
Of my cobbler's large vendation.

—*William L. Walker, Jr.*

Life

        Society
        My prison

        My color
        My downfall

        My sex
        My destruction

        My dreams
        Never reality

        My hopes
        Always fears

    My neighborhood
        My sorrow

        A way out
        Always walled

What do you call this?

        Life.

—*Tiffany Pleshette Jones*

Wildflower

I'm no hot house plant.
My seeds were not dropped in some
rarefied air, nor were they placed
gently in rich, black soil, nourished
by soft spring rains and warm summer sun.

No - my seeds fell on frozen ground.
They felt the icy fingers of winter
and there was no escape from the
heavy boot that crushed them into
the hardened soil - somehow they
flourished - unnoticed.

In the spring look for us. We're
found along every country road
every garden path. Our colors are
many, pink, yellow, blue, gold.
We add beauty to God's world.
He calls us His wildflowers.

—*Margaret Gaffney*

The Edge In Sight

I'm on the inside looking out,
my sight is taken away by doubt.
How do I drain these empty dreams,
while I'm falling apart at the seams.

Wish you could take it away,
this silence,
if not I cannot stay,
I will cleanse... my life.

I have taken it all since youth,
just now that self destruction induced.
All the promise I'd ever shown,
is now muffled to this hollow groan.

Wish you would take it away,
this violence,
if not I will not stay,
I'm past tense... goodbye.

Once I lay in that fatal womb,
already their well constructed tomb.
Stare as their blows had struck me well,
now resulting in that empty shell.

—*Nathanael J. Spann*

Inner Beauty

Don't judge me by my appearance
My treasures are held within
Behold what you might find
And discover what I may send
Absorb my knowledge and hold my beauty
To create a ring of gold
Pleased to quench your desire
To discover what my mind beholds

—*Shaunda M. Betts*

The Horizon

Far away on the horizon
nearing twilight time,
I can see the edge of darkness
begin its long and lazy climb.
Reaching to the heavens this
mysterious gloomy shade
will slowly veil the world and
all the things that God has made.

—*Mary E. Lytton*

At Juvenile Detention

Children on the wayward road,
needing a tender touch
with a firm hand.
Who will give it to them?
The attorney?
Who listens, questions, sympathizes
for 30 minutes?
The Judge?
Who questions for 30 minutes,
then imposes sentence?

Is it a Badge of Courage
to be
part of the crowd?
Is it courage
to pay for mistakes
you've made?
How deep are the emotions?
Who is repentant?
See the mother's cry.

—*Ruby Vernon Stull*

Untitled

She is silent
Nervous thoughts
Wandering eyes
random placement of her hands
toying with hair

She is frightened
No niche to fit
Where does she go?
I don't know
I don't know

She is unknowing
the world has no rank
no segregation
no qualifications

The world is me
The world is we
She has no world

—*Reginald Rodriguez*

Revolutions

Changes always come around
New beginnings
Coming full circle
Revolving through time

Repeating the rhythm
Of birth and death
In and through all things
Of substance and idea

Circles of repetition
Acting on life
As well as inert
Adding conscience to dirt

—*Steve Krucker*

God's Perfect Child

I know she was a perfect child,
No blemish on her could ere be found.
Her sea green eyes, her golden hair,
As bright as sunshine, a child so fair.
So full of life, so full of love.
God gave her to me-from above
I had her for a little while.
It made my life to see her smile.
She was so funny, full of glee.
T'was everything she meant to me.
I prayed each day she would be safe.
As she wandered from place to place.
A perfect child, so close to me,
But she was God's not mine you see.
He took her back and gave her wings.
With angels above and Him she sings.
He opened up His heavenly door.
God's perfect child-forevermore.

—*Marie E. Grant*

Impressions At Vicksbury

Blue skies, still, blue and serene,
No echoes of bugle nor cannon.
Ghosts lie silent and sleeping
Their fears and tears in times keeping
Forgotten the blood, sweat, and fear.
Of what lay ahead, but wasn't clear-
Stones stand where one fell
The message not much to tell
The lad of nineteen, far from home
To end a very short life, a life unknown.

—*Louise Carroll*

Splash Of Color

There was a little spaceship,
No larger than my hand.
On vivid wings of scarlet
I watched it safely land.

I climbed up the mountain;
Went down the other side.
I searched in every crevice,
Where someone small might hide.

My eyes swept the winding valley
Where twisting paths wound.
I listened intensely for
Some whispered sound.

I called, "come out, little one;
Teach me of your ways,"
I quickly turned about and met
His searching gaze.

I couldn't understand him,
But right where we stood,
We clasp our hands in friendship;
And sealed the bond of brotherhood.

—*Tilda S. Akers*

Subpoenaed

I revel in the thought that I am
No longer immortal
Taken for granted, all these years
Especially in the younger days
Tormented by nothing but the sun
Disappearing into the horizon
And the distant ring of the
Black horseshoe chiming through
Autumn air, summoning
The end of play, another
Caustic yet reassuring reminder
Of moments yet to come and the
Subsequent sleep that gives
Reason for waking.

—*William Santos*

Peace

Peace is what we all need,
no matter who we are.
To love one another,
Whether it is near or far.

Peace is a small word,
But it means a lot.
To all of us whatever,
It has brought.

Peace can be beautiful,
If we all get along.
It makes us all happy,
It makes the world strong.

Peace is what we are,
All looking for.
We don't want to
Be in a war.

Peace is all we
Are asking for.
It doesn't matter if,
We are rich or poor.

—*Margaret L. Rodkey*

The Satin Bed

Just knowing you are forever gone
no more on earth to be
has left a space of emptiness
that hovers roundabout me

My cherished mother the sweetest face
a child could ever see
just closed her eyes with one last smile
then died so quietly

I stood beside "the satin bed"
where she lay in final rest
kissed her cheek for one last time
then placed a rose upon her breast

She looked so regal lying there
like a queen, she lay in state
a vision of tranquility
even death could not erase

Tired and weary for life was long
earthly trials here are past
"God" in his infinite mercy and love
gently took her home at last.

—*Wanda E. Pellonini*

Go Through Life

No where to run
No where to hide
About to go crazy
But still I'm alive
Looking both ways
From left to right
Getting my way through
This most beautiful life
It's just like a maze
So find your way through
And once you make it out
Something wonderful
Will be waiting for you!

—*Sally A. Lane*

Guidance At The Light

Sleep softly, whisper not a word,
Not a sound shall escape, not a breath
will seep.
Close thy eyes, those that will never open,
In a dream you shall wake, cloudiness
you will see.
Open arms will greet you, in heaven
you will be.
For dear child I will be near with the
open arms you seek.

—*Teresa Sanderson*

Mood

To think of blues and lovely things
     of heather maybe?
To feel the sun as day begins.

To feel the shade of big old trees
     a soft breeze may be?
It's not only what one sees —

To smell the flowers of perfume
     roses maybe?
It's hard to tell, I just assume.

To hear the fast small bustling flutter
     birds flying maybe?
I could be wrong - it does not matter

—*Mary Van Kuyk*

Never Alone Will Two

Two ships passing in the night
     Not knowing
     Not showing
     Any sound or sight

     Waves crashing
     Heaven's gods clashing
     Fiery white bolts
     Of lightning light

One will find safe haven
But never alone will two
One or both stranded in
     Mournful destiny's rue

Two ships passing in the night
     Not knowing
     Not showing
     It's True

—*Mark A. MacLaughlin*

Wanting To Move On

We went our separate ways
Not my choice to make
I see you now and again
It all seems so fake.

One minute things were fine
The next you shut me out
I still don't understand
What was it all about.

I think I've done quite well
Some nights I feel the hurt
Most nights I think about it
Knowing it could've worked.

I'll never know if you regret it
I'd like to think you do
We had something so special
And now it's through.

—*S. Lewis*

My Mom

Truly my Mom is quite a gal;
Not only a friend but also a pal.
She listens to me when I'm feeling blue;
And she always smiles and lets
     her love through.
In all the world there never will be.
As great a Mom as God gave me.

—*Rachel A. Wallace*

To A White Birch

Hail! to thee O tree of majesty,
Of beauty unsurpassed in all
of arboretum.
Of stately, spiraling branches
looking up to heaven in quest
of answers to all being.

In spring and summer fully
Clothed you are nature's
perfection.
In autumn purest gold adorns
your stately form
In winter bereft all
attire you are still queen of trees
Regal without a crown.

—*Lois M. Riegler*

The Mind Of Poetry

There sings the beauty
of a farther knowledge
There howls the screams
of raw reality

That all of whom create,
as such
and know beneath
of what I speak,
are too, blessed-
of the vision you hold;
And tortured-
of the realities you see.

You inhabit this mind,
You are the poet

... gilden of wisdom,
unaware
of the mind's atrocity.

—*Laura Joy Lustig*

Incoming - Ongoing

At night he still fights battles
     of a now forgotten war.
     He's yesterdays hero,
     not needed anymore.

     Memories that haunt him
     and give him no nights peace.
He drinks the beer and whiskey
     and prays for a release.

     His family has left him;
     his friends there are but few.
     Not too many can stand by him
with the pain he's put them through.

     Why did he survive the death
          so many had to face?
Only to find he's allowed his life
     to fall in such disgrace.

What happened to the proud young boy
     who too soon became a man?
Whose life has never progressed far,
     since the day he left Viet Nam.

—*Sharon H. Hendricks*

Memories Of Woolton Woods

I lay on the hill and hear the drone,
of an aeroplane returning home,
the sun is warm upon my face,
I hear children laughing, having a race.
The grass I lay on smells so sweet,
a bee is buzzing round my feet.
My mother's voice is calling me,
to picnic on sandwiches and tea.
I wish that I could go back then,
when I was just a child of ten.

—*Veronica Joyce Moore*

Firenze

There is a thin line
     of blue haze
     laying on the city.

Ancient Gods would simply
     thread it to a spool
     and wind it up.

—*Luce*

A Friend in Jesus

When the angels pull the curtain
of day and pin them with a star
just remember you have a friend
in Jesus where ever you are.

—*Lela Thurman*

Untitled

Do you know the origin
Of my disease
Can you feel the pain
That makes me drop to my knees
Not a pain so physical
But one so damn real
Can you understand
The way I always feel
Look into my eyes
Tell me what do you see
Do you see the pain
Do you see the real me
I bet you only see
The shallow outer shell
Can you get inside
To my self-inflicted hell
If I were to confide in you
Could you comprehend
Is your mind open enough
To catch the message I'd send

—*Randy K. Stracuzzi*

Bright Or Dark Windows

The eyes are the windows
of the soul: what do
I see through your eyes?
Abiding love on the look
that deceives me.
That look that makes my heart
to pant - my lips to yearn
my eyes to reveal that you are
my hearts desire.
I cannot hide it but can you?
I can't ever deny it but can you?
My eyes are the windows of
my soul, they reflect your own.
Your heart and soul are they
bright or dark windows?
The candles of life and love
often go out, the tragedy is
when one goes before the other.

—*Mary N. Dees*

Thinking

I've been thinking now and then,
Of the time my life began,
  Long ago,
Of the good years that have passed,
And which one will be the last
  That I'll know.

And if I should live so long,
That there's not one note of song,
  In my heart,
Then I hope, without a sigh,
I will smile, and say goodbye,
  And depart.

—*Wilma V. Deyo*

Always On My Mind

Thinking of you just because…
Of the ways you always help me
And the way you're always there
For the little things you do and say
That let me know you care;
For the intimate moments we shared
And the way you held me tight
For the times you took care of me
And made everything alright;
For the times you make me happy
When I am feeling low and blue
For the times you've comforted me
Make me love you the way I do.
These are some of the reasons
I think of you as much as I do.
They are all little reminders
Of how much I really love you.

—*Tina M. Rapczak*

A Farewell Salute

Evoking fond memories
Of your happier times,
This verse reminiscent
To you I present
For all those years when you
Did understand me:
I should not forget —
And so I haven't.

As venture you into
Your retirement years,
Just "bon voyage!", Bob,
Seems not enough. So,
May you "now, voyager,
Sail thou forth to
Seek and find" life's
Most marvelous glow!

—*Peter Brown*

Daddy

Father, I miss you
Oh, can't you see
That while you're gone
Something happens to me.

I cannot explain it
Though you know it to be true
It only happens
When I'm not with you.

Oh, daddy, you should see me now
I know you will find
I have found someone new
And very, very kind.

I still love you
Though you're not around
But your love for me
Was never, ever found.

—*Victoria H. East*

Love Says It All

Love is joy and I have joy today.
Joy is the key to love and love
is the key to life, life is the
key to hope and hope is the
key to love, love is the key to
every door, to keep us together
and happy. That's why love says
it all.

—*Tykari Blackmon*

Good Memory Recall Room

We had them here for a while;
Oh! How great it is to love a child.
  But time moves on,
And too soon they are gone.

We do have something to possess -
Their sweet memories to redness
  Found in pictures of each child,
When we visit for awhile.

We cannot go back in time
Not even to seek a pleasing rhyme;
  But our vision of them is there
For we can see them everywhere.

—*Marshall W. Abernathy*

Love Is Here

Love is here,
Oh just look around you,
And listen to what it's saying

Love is here
It's in every town too,
but not in every man

Dreams, they will never come true
Without that glow of love from you.
For as long as love can do
Then you'll have a chance - want you?

Love is here
Such joy, such power
It's how the world began

Love is here just like a flower
Hold on to heaven's hand

Hold your head up towards the sky
Don't let love just pass you by
Soon, someday we all must die
Until then, give love (life) a try.
…Love is life

—*Willie T. Edmonds*

Rest

In a quiet moment
on a quiet day
Only the clock
was ticking
And this heart
of mine was beating
And I though
of days gone by
Friend I lost
who could not stay
So I tap my fingers
on the desk
And think of those
that are now at rest.

—*Ned Wells*

Nature Prevails

No famous face casts a glow
on frozen snow
No glamour exceeds green hills
and tinkling rills
No greatness lingers near
probation
No finish won by any nation
Time is not found out
Form cannot replace the heart.

—*McNeill Thomas*

You Are My Reason To Live

The floor you walk
on I praise and,
The bed you sleep on
I cherish and,
The kiss you gave me
I will never lose.
For you are my life.
No one can give me what
you have, a reason to live.
You are my inspiration,
You are my life.
Do I not only love being,
your wife.
I love being your lover, and,
your best friend.
You are my life,
You are my reason to live.
I could not of made it with out you,
for you are my friend.

—*Stefanie Miller*

Rainfall And Tears

Rain falls -
On rooftops, trees, plants and flowers.
Rain falls -
Refreshing, cooling, cleansing.

Tears fall from broken spirits -
Are they equal to the tears of heaven?

Certainly -
Washing away sadness and grief,
They are humanity's rainfall.
But please Lord - make them brief.

—*Raymond J. Winieski*

Alone

I said I was sorry
Once before
But you did not listen
You did not care about me
So now I walk alone
Miles away
And am lost without you
Did you forgive me?
I do not know
For I do not see you
Anymore.
From that day on
I could not resist
The feeling
Of running away.

—*Lauren Melso*

A Poet

Poetry the way I see it,
or should I say,
the way I sometimes vision myself.

A poet's mind, wisdom in thought
yet not always understood.
A poet's soul, a silver lining
yet not always recognized.
A poet's heart, full of wealth
knowledge of love and pain.
A poet's body, content
to live life day by day.
A poet's pocket, empty of coins
yet the hope still remains.

—*Lana Tremblay*

Jehovah Dreams

A thought came unto him;
    One of spectacular possibilities.
Where shall this great undertaking
    begin?
He possessed no books or pictures.
Young was he in his knowledge, but
    old was he in his wisdom.
He knew the truths that would be
    laid forth, but what of the
    substance? Where shall it be
    born?
And within his holy words did the
    answer come to be,
    "A grain. A grain shall be my
    my guide; for whomever shall
    know my light, shall know
    my dream."

—*R. G. Rickey*

Nothing

There is nothing,
Only darkness,
There is nothing,
Only fear,
Not knowing what'll happen,
I'm scared when you're not near.
I feel empty,
Something's missing,
When you're gone,
And we're not kissing.
When I'm empty, when you're gone,
I try to figure out what went wrong,
So confused, as alone,
Won't you please just come home.
But then again who wants or needs you?
All you do is fight and fuss!
In response to loving words,
You just shout and pout and cuss!
Let me go, set me free
Won't you please let me be!

—*Liza Fam*

Country Side

Country side
Open fields filled with pride;
Empty sky open wide;
Smell of spring,
Lonely road heads far from home,
Old American cars under the stars
A bird flying that I can see,
This place is a part of me.
The day closes, night approaches
Under the oak tree which I sleep,
The full moon contemplates over me.

—*Melissa Marie Galiga*

What Is A Poet?

Is it someone who repeat a lot
Or changes a thing for their own
liking. What is a poet? A good
speaker or a good writer or is a
poet one who feel all???

—*Min Whitelove*

Shadows

I'm a shadow hear me cry
or my tears will soon die
faded memories faded plights
that's the shadows in my life.

—*Khela Long*

There's A Side Of Me

There's a side of me no one sees
or really knows of.

A side that thinks of wild, thoughtful,
intellectual stuff.

I guess I'm afraid of this side, afraid
of being an intellect.

Or maybe I like this side of
me best, I try not to project.

This side likes romantic films, making
love on the beach.

But then I see the side I am,
and it's so far out of reach...

Maybe someday I can grow into,
and be this side of me.

But until then I have to
keep it hidden, no one must ever see...

—*Shelley Childs*

Moments Beyond

Beyond the shackles of my soul,
    or the chains that bind my mind,
There still are moments in my life
    that no one could match in kind

Beyond the splintered spirit,
    or the body lean and frail,
There still are moments in the world
    that set my life asail

Beyond the fragments of my heart,
    or the loneliness beyond compare,
There still are moments in my life
    that I am proud to wear

Beyond the disappearing passion,
    or belief in myself or man,
There still are moments in my life
    that let me know 'I can'

Beyond the mundane, futile feelings,
    with just one flick of my magic wand,
I am able to enjoy my life. . .
    and forever keep going beyond!

—*Margo Braer*

Margaret

I can't draw, I can't paint
    or write
I need talent to still fear
    in the night
No longer do I try - I think
    I'm too old.
Then I visit Margaret and
    I'm told
She can't write — her hands tremble
She can't paint and can't remember
I sign her cards, I wash her teeth
    and then go home
I'm so talented.

—*Suzanne Christian*

To A Physician

A scientist, the conductor of the
orchestra,
the leader of the flock.
May wisdom and guidance be
companions.
May the Lord be the shepherd.

May the music be of fine precision,
to be read as well as heard.
May the conductor be blessed,
for his task is not as easy as it seems.

—*Sally Hollen*

All My Love Goes To....

All my love goes to my best friend
Our love will never end
She is my heart
She is the start of happiness
She has the kindness of nobody else
But it is bad,
That she hardly ever things of herself.
She is as beautiful as a rainbow
She is so cool yo!
She is like no other,
Did you know
That she is my mother.

—*Nicole Fulmino*

"He Died For Me & He Died For You"

When we think of all the
pain that rips us apart,
Just remember that Jesus Christ
is in our heart.

for Jesus is there to take care
of you,
and add life to a world of blue,

No matter what the hardship or
great the loss,
Just leave your pain at the
foot of the cross

When you think of all the
pain and suffering Jesus went
through,
   Just remember he died for
me and he died for you.

—*Todd Anthony*

Untitled

Empathy for the creator
passion for the poison that
creates the seance.

Your beauty is such a surprise
It anticipates me and moves
me miles.
Your love is my life
- the water that sustains me
- the poison that kills thee.
Experience this vision quest
Ride on virgin senses.
Tingling with anticipation.

I once saw the first time
the Earth was born.
I understand the greatest
Art-piece in progress
A masterpiece in the making.
(Sometimes images are wars of illusion)

—*Michael Christian Rudar*

Close To You

A sweaty razor
Penetrates your defense
On a languid Monday mourning:
The obscure eroticism
Of the lemming blood
Diving into the basin
Stroking impressionism
Upon the flecked formica.

The first stroke fondles
Your erect skin;
Goosepimples, ecstatically shiver
Under the whipping soft caress
Of the lascivious hand
Behind your voyeur's eyes.

—*J. Dylan Beals*

Racial Harmony

Racial harmony is caring for
   people different from you
Racial harmony is loving for
   different kinds of colors too.
Racial harmony is beautiful
   that's why God created me
   and you.
So be in harmony with all
   different colors that's my
   message to you.

—*Luz Michelle Guerra*

Untitled

Pick offs provide outs
Pick offs prevent steals
Pivot creates surprises,
Jump gives pop on the throw,
Pivot-Jump-Surprise

—*Noah Wilson*

Tolerance

If I am black
Please don't stand back

If I am brown
Please let me hang around

Because I am not white
That doesn't make me not right

If I make a mistake
Please forgive me for my sake

I try to do my best
Just like the rest

Just give me a chance
Despite my happen-stance

Judge me by my character
And not by my caricature

—*Nicholas J. Kayganich*

Rain

Pennies from heaven.
Rain is good for the grass,
the lawns
and good for the gardens
vegetable or flower.
Rain brings the flowers up.

—*Robert Ewing*

Happiness

Home is where the heart is,
Poets have always told us so.
It's where our hearts are happy.
And contentment rules our souls.

Happiness isn't lovely mansions
Or palaces in Spain.
It can be a small apartment
With dusty window panes.
Happiness we carry with us.
It cannot be bought or sold.
It comes with years of caring
For another, young or old.

So, if you search for happiness,
It's not found in silver or gold.
Help some needy person,
It's sure to heal your soul.

Happiness lies within us.
Loving others is the seed that grows.
Giving and loving and caring,
Bring happiness to two souls.

—*Mary Parks*

Dissolving Revolving

Poverty, war, poverty-score.
Preordained, foreordained-re-ciprocal
unto Rain-drops on-
she roof-top-falling-falling-
into everlasting-dream-through-
she clouds-from-Africa-to-
Russia and Kingdoms far-
away pain remains to stay -
Disconling, revolving, in
our-lives-through-out-
the day. Cry's that stain
the brain, frowns on-the
Somilian face by year-to-
year we live to see -
the disgrace. Poverty -
war and conflict

—*Lamar K. Mallery*

Old Secrets

Leaves fly over the porch
Pushed lightly by the wind
It whistles through the floor
Whispering stories of old friends

The wood is still strong
On this old porch
The night is cool
The wood no longer scorched

Because this house
Is very old
It holds the stories
of love untold

It knows of babies
Born beneath its roof
The love that was shared
the living proof

And though these secrets
May never be told
You can feel them
Deep in your own soul

—*Shay Crocker*

Ashes To Ashes

The wind blows softly around me,
Pushing, ruffling, sniffing but
Doesn't recognize me as the
Woman it passed many years ago.

I have aged and mellowed.
I am ripe and fragrant,
Rejecting subterfuge and lies,
Refusing pettiness and deceit.

Aware that my life is better.
Travelling light, I jettison
Anything that is not desperately
Needed for the time.

My body has a thousand wrinkles,
All of them channels and valleys of
Thoughts, images, sorrows and laughter
I have allowed to come through my skin.

I have come to grips with life.
Realizing finally that our sadnesses,
Joys and everything in between
Are what makes us who we are.

—*Lita Trent Dorman*

The Dawn Of Reality

Not long before where answers were,
Questions run throughout my mind.
Dissatisfactions' embers stir,
Contentment lost, I cannot find.
Illusionary visions cleared,
from dewy eyed naivete.
Where reality, desperately feared,
was gently touched by truth today.
A tempting suggestion,
a turmoil within.
A well thought out question,
the way to begin.
What was once so uncluttered,
will be again.
With windows unshuttered
the light can come in.
The forever night ending,
a new dawn is breaking.
A life of pretending,
from slumber, awakening.

—*Linda Romano-Colepaugh*

Eastward Breeze

The eastward breeze blows
    quickly through the trees
And gently but firmly
    awakens all it sees
Alone in the green, green valley
    a young woman her lover awaits
The night comes, ever silently,
    and she wonders about the fates
Granting her a love so true
    yet she wonders if he feels it too
"I only have one question, dear,
    do you love me, as I love you?"

Waiting for him here all alone
    there is so much she finally sees
And she is quietly awakened
    by the eastward breeze.

—*Nancy D. Simpson*

Worm Massacre

Soft crashing
rain and slimy-slink
drown human ears with
springtime pleasure.

Seeping from drenched dirt homes
attacking the shining
asphalt desert.

Smiling away their hearty
lives in the instant
of suffocation.

Squished by the
sole of
thoughtless human
supremacy.

Squirmers have
ten hearts.
Humans one.

—*Susan Sarvis*

Under The Lion's Paw

Shade drawn as one empty raincoat
Against weeping waves of heat;
Crawling, suffer not simply we
The acid past of our day of days
Pressed onward, steamed,
Set vast the sails for keeps.
Under the sun
Without raunch and breakfast,
To paw, teeming frets and nails,
Immune behind a grill of irony
Unknown beneath a consuming
    roar.

—*SC Seatter*

Untitled

Ever growing older
Reaching towards the heavens
Weathering life's storms
Battling life's wars
Still standing after it's over
We grow stronger through it all
That is what life is.

—*Lori Schneider*

Another Day

Dawn, the sky is fire all aglow
Reddish orange-purple and blue
Birds flying across the horizon low
The grass glistens with sparkling dew

A cool breeze caresses the skin
Aromas of nature impress the nose
The leaves of autumn slowly bend
The pleasures of life surely grows

Say sky, sun, and breeze if you can
Oh the joy, no illusions or dismay
Completeness of nature is at hand
The cycle of life for another day

Greeted by the lights of early morn
The value of life passes my way
Uneasiness within no longer scorn
Thankfulness abound for another day

—*Lawrence R. Boswell*

Untitled

Sun immense and red
Reflecting on the Gulf's calm
Spreads silent shadows.

—*Sally G. Cook*

The Leaf And The Rose

A cloudless day with sunny sky
Reminds me of the day gone by,
When hand in hand we strolled the park
And felt like children on a lark.

A five star leaf fell to the ground,
You picked it up and turned around
And placed it in my hand to see,
I held it very tenderly.

I brought it home and placed it right
Inside a book and closed it tight,
For if our love was not to be,
I'd have a cherished memory.

Today I looked inside and saw
The golden leaf without a flaw,
And gently, so the book would close,
Beside it, I had placed a rose.

—*Mary Teska*

The Statue In The Park

Warm summer moonlight
    rests on her cold marble breasts
    flaming ancient love.

Soft rain at daybreak
    drips from trees and tranquil tears
    fill her hollow eyes.

—*Sunny Rivera-Reyes*

Autumn's Fantasy

The breeze is gentle and kind
Rich colors from yellow to wine
    Enjoy me.
May there be a reflection of me
    in your wardrobe

On canvass paint me, then my beauty
    will not be lost.
In your song, sing about me
    There, sentiment is felt.

In your sleep, dream of me
That on waking, your thoughts
    are refreshed...
    Time is fleeting,
    I am only here for
    a little while.
So with tenderness,
    Embrace me.

—*Mattie H. Thompson*

Life Reigns

I once had a sister -
she once had me

Through her eyes, I saw
through mine, saw she

Life took away -
what life gave to me

I once had a sister -
She once had me

—*Rhonda R. Bennett*

Brothers Killing Brothers

Brothers killing brothers
Right and left
Each day there's another
Unfortunate death
Brothers killing brothers
With each passing time
There would never be another
Another of their kind
Brothers killing brothers
With no concern at heart
Not even considering
The other being apart
Brothers killing brothers
With no shame or guilt
Just taking lives of others
Not thinking of the lives they built
Hoping to win
We kill one another
When will we put an end
To brothers killing brothers

—*Shakira Jones*

Forsaken Freedom

I have seen my freedom dying
Right before my very eyes
I've heard politician's lying
While the homeless baby cries

And wandering the gang filled streets
The youth that make tomorrow
Gather where the drug lords meet
Despite their mother's sorrow

And nothing just one soul can do
To make it all be better
No remedies like cold or flu
Or putting on a sweater

We have to find a better way
Before it is too late
To stop this social mind decay
That turns love into hate

One thing we should remember
As we stand to face the night
Our freedom's burning embers
Are worth just one more fight

—*Renee Rowley Breedlove*

Heart To Heart

Lord, I feel so alone when I can't hear,
Rise up, my child, Jesus said,
Receive my word, and be fed,
Listen to your heart instead.

Listen to your heart, dear child,
Jesus, your Savior, on you has smiled,
On the cross your name has been filed
Thus, by Satan be not beguiled.

Lord, speak to my heart, I need Thee so,
More of Thee I long to know;
Jesus speaks in cadence low and clear,
"I am the way, and I am near."

—*Minnie Herman*

The Mighty River

See her scream and dance near the
river.
It rushes so violently,
filled with eternal passion,
see that in her eyes.
She is I, wanting to joint the river.
Desire to dive.
Yet stopped, by gentle hand.
He pulls me close as I fall
in arms of heaven,
down to the earth.
Laughter echoes on the banks,
hear the mighty river.

—*Tisha Anne Caruso*

My Child

Little girl with flying feet
Running swiftly down life's street
If your progress I could stay
Keep you happy here at play
Oh I wonder, would you be
Content to always stay with me
Would your active restless mind
Always ample solace find
In a mother grown old and gray
Or yearn for youths joy
At a too late day

—*Mary E. Moreland*

1972

A midnight walk down the country road
    ruts made deep by the jeep
    horses hoofs and people's feet
        and I place one foot
        in front of the other
        walking, not disturbing
    the sleeping deer or the colts
        nursing from the mares
    all of nature is in balance
        as I stop and sit
    in a horse trough to watch
        the moon become full
    and scorpius chase his tail
        not looking back I rise
        and walk further down
        the country road, waiting
    for tomorrow and the beginning
        of the Summer Solstice
    as all of nature is in balance.

—*Mark Walters*

Untitled

    Be mine, mine I say.
    Say is mine. Do you say?
Let go of my thinks they say
    can you believe?!
    Be mine mine I say -
    Do this if you are mine
        say say-
        let me go
        be mine
            or
        Die doing so.
    e say e say.

—*Maria Daigle*

Forlorned

Forlorned, the body turned away
Saddened by the city worker's
Destroying his meager belongings
Hollow cheeks
Below his sunken eyes
His stomach rumbled
With hunger pains
The body shivered
As the night winds blew
He shoved his hands into his pockets
Heading in an unknown direction
He walked for hours in the cold
Suddenly like an omen from heaven
He saw the church on the corner
As he trodded up the steps
Leading to its opened doors
His hopes surmounted
As his bare feet touched its wooden floors
Times can only get better
He had been told, many times before.

—*Norma E. White*

Moon Rise

Behind the towering
    sandstone cliff
    rises an ashen moon
Massaging the landscape
    while I doze

Moon shadows
    blanket me with swirling
    sand and grit
The desert floor absorbs
    my weariness

Ears listening
    for the heartbeat
    of earth and time
As a sandy pillow comforts
    my heaviness

Fatigue, abraded by dust,
    erupts past soaring
    canyon walls
Adding polish
    to the moon

—*Linda Van Wagenen*

Wicked In The Garden

Something wicked
Scarlet darkness
The dark camellias
Waxen
Dark grass, and burly boxwood
Something wicked
Crepe myrtles kissing
Hollyhock so tender
Dark and moving shadows
Slick and serpent blackness
A figure in the darkness
His eyes they blaze like forge
Soul a depthless Quagmire
Something surely wicked
Can't you feel the darkness growing
Slowly tis' your blood to flowing
He is all around you
Here's the heart of Hell
Here in his perdition
Here the garden swells

—*Richard J. Mann*

Me And The National Deficit

So many things aren't working,
seems we're in a terrible spot.
So many things take millions
   and billions of dollars
      we haven't got.
   Somebody do something,
      do it quick!
   Balance the budget,
      cut programs.
   Which? Take your pick,
      just don't touch
      the one I guard
   with my voting stick.
Solve the problem otherwise,
don't ask me to economize.
   Things could change
with an economic plan, sir,
   just don't count on me
to be part of the answer.

    —*Velma Cozzutto*

Reflections

All is very quiet here peaceful and serene
Another day has ended time now to dream
To dream of children far away brings
sadness to the heart
To dream of parents so long gone who
loved us from the start
Ah life what is your message
Are we here for naught
The passing time will have the answer
To all the questions sought

    —*Loretta De Rosso*

Miss Daisy

When Miss Daisy gets her pay
she goes to the horse races
every week-end in May
She bets all her money
on "Johnny eats hay"
One day her horse will win
and she will buy a diamond or two
or a big yellow hat to wear to the zoo
Today is Sunday and Church has begun
but you won't find her there
she's having too much fun
betting on a horse that's #1

    —*Lorelie Nedevick*

Missing You

Although it's been a while
Since I last made you smile
You must believe it's true
That I truly care for you
Although it's been sometime
Since we last shared love
I thank my stars above
For someone as true as you
You came into my life
Without hesitation
We got to know each other
through crazy communication
I wouldn't doubt
as sure as I can be
That you I can't live without.

    —*Phyllis R. Ware*

Lost Ophelia

Ophelia was a good daughter.
She lost her lover.
I weep for her.

Lovely maid Ophelia,
Dreaming through the misty waters,
Singing your little song
To the drooping branches
That reach out
To drown you
In your singing.
I weep for you.

I lost an Ophelia once,
Only daughter, began in love
But never finished.
Somewhere do you wander
In the mists of time?
Singing and making flower wreaths
And floating down the stream.
I weep for you.

    —*Norma Aletha Adams*

His Prize

I want to write the perfect poem,
she said one day to me,
It has to be a special poem
for all the world to see.

It has to cheer the weary,
and it has to dry sad eyes,
It just can't be any poem,
This poem must take the prize.

She sat down so pensively,
and with her pen in hand,
She knew the words would come to her,
they'd be at her command.

Her hand moved with inspiration,
feeling guidance from above,
"The only perfect poems, dear child,
are in my Book of Love.

As a poet I will guide you,
With words divine and true,
Perfection cannot be obtained,
but I will walk with you."

    —*Ruth A. Patrick*

21201

I didn't think I'd like her
She was the least attractive
   in the neighborhood
Neat inside and dependable
   but outside
Not looking the way she should.

Coming home to her on cold days
Was a joy to behold
This was what I could expect
Even when she was getting old.

Finally, she was left with others
And suffered horrible abuse
Trying to repair the damage
Just seemed of little use.

Now she has a new owner
Is he treating her just fine?
I really worry about her-
This house that I called mine.

    —*Roellen Stoerr*

Exile

Tears
shed and shed
not even a single death
what a miserable life
in exile
if
blood spilled
perhaps many men killed
but
they're definitely worth while.

    —*Thanh Nguyen (Houston, TX)*

The Star of Bethlehem

The star of Bethlehem
   shining above
Leading men so wise
   to Eternal Love;
And those of long ago
   heard a voice from within
Saying, follow the Star
   to One, born free of sin.

This Star guiding all
   who follow their lead
Find the Way to their
   own Eternal Love seed.
Jesus is born this day
   in the hearts of all mankind.
And we, too, find the Star
   searching the heavens of our mind.

    —*Paul D. Gray*

Best Friends

Best friends
Shouldn't copy your trends
They should be
true to you

They should try to understand
What you're going through
They should never steal
A guy from you
They should be nice to you

They should try
to stick with you
no matter what you say or do
they should be honest
with you

They should trust you
no matter what you do
or what they're going through

    —*Rani Goldsborough*

Fun In The Sun

Lying in the sun
   Sipping rum
Oh boy! am I having fun.

Crowded beaches
   Sandy feet
Beach ball dodgers
   Lots of laughters
Oh beautiful island in the sun
   Sipping of rum
Oh boy, am I having fun

    —*Suhailah Beyah*

U.S. Applebyrm

Uriah Sam Applebyrm ran a mile,
    showered down,
    ate some bran,
    went to town.

Uriah Sam had a date,
    strings, white wine, cherry flambe',
    bussed her adieu,
    then puffed some hay.

Went to church on Sunday morn,
    croaked out a chorus,
    canned a prayer,
    cocked an eye at Boris.

U.S. Applebyrm clocked in next day,
    straight into the bowels of belly-el,
    now he jogs in molten pitch
    and gnashes his teeth like hell.
            —*Richard Hoover*

Some Tomorrow

Slowly, the housing called my body
    sighed deeply and ceased to be.
That which was me, transformed
    into a free floating entity.
The galaxies are my stepping stones.

I use the moon as a ball
    to play jacks with the stars,
I swirl with the vapors of the universe,
    like once on earth.

On clear nights you have only
    to look up to feel me,
I'm all around you - can't you see?
    like once on earth,
I enter you each time you breath,
    now I am forever.
            —*Rosemary T. Robinson*

Imagine That...

We have been friends
since I was eight;
They were my comfort
and even my fate;

When reality was tough
They were my only escape;
A world of my own,
then things started to take shape;

I needed them in the morning
When I first wake;
I needed them in the evening
because I started to shake;

They warmed and soothed me
like I knew they would;
No more pain no more worry
even though I knew, that I should;

I would have been sixteen
If understanding hadn't lack;
Your friends are your worst enemy
Imagine that...
            —*Liza Desir*

Dead Art

Tumbled stones dead spider webs
skeleton bones surround our heads
it has many faces
some of tin
Crunched and bent with its mangled grin
wrapped around a lamp post
embracing brick walls
Guts that kiss pavement
after a fatal fall
journey bound for sites unseen
slapped from reality or a movie reel
dream
A spine embraces cement as its maker
as brains flow down a sewer drain
still knowing of its own taker
            —*Michael Recco*

Wild Things

Did you know that a lizard
sleeps with its head up!

It's neat how a Giant
Sequoia starts from a little
seed to a big tree!

It's neat how pretty birds chirp!

It's really neat how your body
works inside!

I wonder how God makes
Blue Bonnets!
It's neat how the ducks at
the pond don't run away when
I feed them!
It's nice how life is!
            —*Marie Nicole Fjordholm*

Harmonized Bliss

From first ray of light, til twilights
    slumber dreams.

My world is enriched through Gods
    blessed gifts.

Each moment filled with harmonized
    bliss, each hour kept in memory.

Each season stored in victory of
    wondrous love embracing me.

As gentle hands guide me from
    this mortal land.

My seasons shall be victories, as
    shall my moments kept in memory.

Simple faith, and answered prayers
    give me proof of eternal care.

Being a child of God, I am born
    again in everlasting life.

And More Harmonized Bliss.
            —*Pamela Sears Mitchell*

Space Placed at Center's Edge

A signature signed
small on the line space
small character tall.
As the hours glass sand sifts
life as a gift God
character tall.

The thoughts of Lola
            —*Lola Hansell*

Sweet Song

So sweet the morning song.
So bright the light within.
This is how the melody
Of each day will begin.

Let the words flow.
Be swept from shore to shore.
Let the music carry you
Until you're sad no more.

Find the peace that's offered.
Find the eternal friend.
Don't let trouble overcome you.
Don't let the music end.

Take hold the tie that binds.
Let your sorrow go.
Place your feet on firm ground,
And let the music grow.
            —*Lucy Barnett*

Dream

My dream day, the animals
so gay, will dance about their
merrily way.
    The sky is clear, I rain
a tender tear. So happy, so bright,
no darkness, no fear.
    Sunlight glares down on
me, flowers bloom under
an old twisted tree.
    The breeze is soft, a
herd of deer prances by. The
red birds nest, and the
eagles fly.
    Pure crystal water
rushes down a stream. I
wish it would last...
....But it's only a dream.
            —*Natasha Curtis*

At Seventy-two

Wisdom comes with age they say,
    So I should know more and more
But as the years go by I find
    The less I know for sure.

I envy some who firmly state
    Their opinion as final word,
But some of the things I used to know
    I now find quite absurd.

I suppose I'll sit in my rocking chair
    If I live to be a hundred and four
Still wondering about so many things
    With questions and questions galore.
            —*Marian T. Johnson*

Thoughts

The wind that blow's
So sweet through the leaves
Whispers, thou art with us.
The flowers that bloom.
Their order is like spring
They are always with us.
The sun that shines,
Smiles on us showing us the
ways of life.
And then the moon comes
Out at night to tell us,
God is right.
            —*Lee Searcey*

For That Is The Way

We fall to rise
So it is said
So do not terry
Get out of your bed

The failure of yesterday
Is experience for today
So don't let despair
Lead you astray

You fail today
So you can succeed tomorrow
But only if you don't give in
To heart break and sorrow

A loss, a win, is
One in the same
One step after another
To finish the game

Listen to what I say
We fall to rise
For that is the way

—*Wanda Simpson*

Deception

Deception
So sweet,
So dangerous,
So tantalizing,
Delightful.

How long will it last?

Dreaming,
Scheming,
Laughing.

Does it have to end?

Deception.

Deception,
A circle
Which symbolizes
The gold wedding band
Around my finger.

—*Sonja Ann Keserica*

Motives

You wish to be impressive
So to others you are good.
Goodness is my sole intent
no motives understood.

These actions find the same result
each person well refined.
Both modes of kindness seem sincere
but goodness is goodness defined.

Affairs can be so falsely judged
in acts which meet one goal.
For truth lies in one's character
Where motives reveal the soul.

—*Patricia Ann Buckelew*

Unanswered Prayers

Ungranted prayers - they haunt us
    So we pray in utter fear
In hopes that He is listening
    With an eager open ear.
It seems that we do call on God
    In our selfish time of need
We expect Him to be listening
    To what we pray and plead
You must share with Him every day
    Of every give year
If you want Him to cleanse your soul
    And every shedded tear.
Though prayers they go unanswered
    In times of deep despair
It's because we don't have faith
    And know He's always there.

—*Rhonda S. Bailey*

Soldier Of Stone

You bravely marched to battle
Soldier of stone
But one in a herd of cattle
Yet all alone

And as the wounded lay around you
You heard them not
Nor did you hear the sound to retreat
Nor the bullets that you bought

Now your remains lay in a field
A million miles from home
Where bullets soon will fly no more
And grazing sheep will roam

But your loved ones had already lost you
Now they pray without a grave
Never to know the hell you suffered
the courage you displayed.

—*Raymond Maxwell*

Shelter

Let my soul find shelter elsewhere,
Some place where it needn't hide
Behind this mask of a body
Behind this facade of a mind.

Let my soul find shelter elsewhere,
Where all possible dreams come true
Where my body language isn't
Interpreted as orange or as blue

Let my soul find shelter elsewhere,
Amidst the future or the past
The present leaves it empty
Or more simply, leaves it aghast.

Let my soul find shelter elsewhere,
It's weary of this plane
A shelter where I can explore
Other probabilities without feeling insane.

Let my soul find shelter elsewhere,
With no more need to roam
It longs for its true companions
It longs for the quiet of its home.

—*Tracy Causey-Jeffery*

One And Only Heart

I need a heart to call my own
    Someone loyal and true
Someone who will stand by me
    Cheer me when I'm blue.

Give me strength to see life through
    With a smile and a hug
Believe in me and all I do
    Though outsiders may pull and tug.

I've tried in vein to find that heart
    That to me alone belongs
My life is passing quickly
    Soon I will be gone

When my maker I do see
    He'll take me in his arms
"Dear child for all your life
    This heart was yours to take
I waited and hoped
    It was your decision to make
Now we are together, never to part
Aren't you glad to finally find, that one and
only heart?"

—*Wendy Moritz*

Paradox

We were looking for a hero;
    Someone who could win the fight.
Finally, he came to us,
    and filled our hearts with light.

He taught us much
    For we were eager to learn.
We followed where he led
    and watched the pages turn.

Yet we sent him to his death
    For we lacked the vision.
We saved and damned ourselves
    With one swift decision.

We've spent many years in sorrow
    and pure regret.
Teaching others to remember
    While we tried to forget.

Our past was dark,
    But the future's still grim
'Cause after two thousand years,
    We're still shouting, "Crucify Him!"

—*Shaunathon Davids*

Memory

You are gone
    So far away
It seems you were
    here the other day
    Some knew you barely
And some knew you well
    A lot hurt right now
And a lot you can't tell
    You taught us a lot
About the person inside
    You showed us the person
With nothing to hide
Even though your face
    Never will we see
In each of our hearts
    Is your memory

—*Sharon Slade*

A Love That Never Goes Cold

We seem not to let each other go
Something strong holds us together
Love in each of us
Love that seems to last forever

Even though your not around
You end up in my dreams
My heart you make pound
My mind you make scream

I'm dead without you
I seem to be lost
You are the road to truth
I will have you at all cost

Some say it's not to be
What do they know
As sure as the sun rises in the east
So does our love grow

Your beauty overwhelms my eyes
Your spirit invades my soul
Your love for me a surprise
A love that never goes cold

—*Xavier Ovalle*

The Blues

The blues came knocking at my door
I tried to tell them, "I don't live here anymore"
But they just kept knocking at my door

We're just the blues, we won't stay long
We promise we won't do anything wrong
We'll stay awhile and then we'll be gone

So I opened the door and let them in
Okay, I said I guess you win
So slowly but surely those blues came in

When they entered my problems seemed to multiply
All I did was sit and cry
Everything's so awful, I don't know why

The blues decided to hang around all day
Wherever I went they got in my way
Didn't know what they wanted, they wouldn't say

As I sat in despair and looked at the hour
And seemed to wallow in my sorrow
I decided they could stay but they must go tomorrow

—*Ruth Nagy*

I Try To Remember

As my hands shake and my headaches,
      I try to remember
When my lips speak of tales,
      I try to remember
My legs stagger no where,
      I try to remember
My eyes are red, did they see the truth?
      I try to remember
My ears hear nothing,
      I try to remember
My heart is heavy, did I say those words?
      I try to remember
As I look at the bottle I cannot remember
Please, take my hand and cradle my head,
      And please God help REMEMBER.

—*Madelyn Brown*

True Friend

I cast a faint smile and lowered my eyes
I turned to walk away but to my surprise
I heard a soft, "hello," so I turned around
My eyes are no longer looking at the ground
We both reached out with a lonely hand to lend
Standing face to face we feel we have found a "true friend"

Hand in hand down the path our faces aglow
First we quicken our step then we go slow
Giggling girls looking for something to do
My friend kicks a pebble so I kick one too
We promise our friendship to the very end
Hand in hand we know we have found a "true friend"

To school, to parties we are together every day
Not once do we think of looking far away
Into the future into our life
When someday each of us will become a wife
With children of our own to care for and tend
And pray in their life they will find a "true friend"

—*Marylee Buerkle*

Awareness

I look at the tree. The brain brings the word, I remember...
I used to see a tree just like this as a girl in school. Now
the heart starts pounding, there is pain and anguish; The tree
no more there; there is only thought, and this feeling fear.
If I see the tree, and no word is there; no thought, and no
image recalling the past. Then I am all there; no pain and no
sorrow appear. But who is aware? Just the tree; no one. Can
I look today at that one who hurt me last week; and just see
his face, and do not remember the hurt? Then I look anew. His
face, and the tree are just there. Then I am aware, I can
really see. But I well remember the hurt of the past; and
looking at him note only my hurt; and although nearby, he is no
longer there; there is only anger, and pain. And who is this
one in front of the mirror? The sum of all memories from all
yesterdays. And that looks at life, the birds and the
prairies; and sees only images of long, long gone days. Could
I ever look at that which is here, and when thought arises,
just observe the thought: Watch how subtly rises, bringing
sorrow and fear, and see that this image is a shadow, a ghost..
And if I persist in watching the image each time it appears.

—*Olga Diner*

Memories

As I sit and watch the sun drift out of view,
I usually cry, and think of you,
I'm not embarrassed to show I cared,
About the friendship that we shared.
You were the best friend I've ever had,
A friend who helped,
Through good times, and bad.
You are a special friend,
We share a friendship I know will never end,
Because, although we've been pulled apart,
We both have a special place in each other's heart.

—*Liliana Mary Cabrera*

The Baseball Gardener

Yes dear, wait a minute, I'll do the outside work,
I want to watch our pitcher first, throw one past this "jerk."
Why does my wife's poor memory seem to remember better
All those jobs for me to do when there's a double-header?
No "ifs", "ands" or "buts", once she's made her decision
It doesn't matter a bit that the game's on television.
If only she would realize that knocking off the Cubs
Might be more important than trimming those darn shrubs.
Some day I may surprise her, she won't know what to think;
I'll pitch right in but won't tell her the TV's on the blink.

—*Robert E. Brazell, Ph.D.*

Grandma Can You Hear Me?

Tuesday night, ICU.
I.V.s beeping. Monitors alarming.
I love you Gram.
"I love you too."
Wednesday morning, stroke.
I love you Gram.
Silence.
I love you Gram, can you hear me?
The rise and fall of your chest tells me you can.
Monday afternoon, the call.
I love you Gram, can you hear me?
Your absolute breathlessness leaves me uncertain.
Raw pain, tears, rage.
Please come back to me.
An impossibility.
You are on the other side of the night sky,
A lifetime away - my lifetime away.
I love you Gram.
Can you hear me?

    —*Margie Boyle*

Tenderness, Love And Devotion

I want to be your only one
I want to feel what your feeling
When you fall down I want to be
there with my hand held out helping you.
I want tenderness, love, and devotion.
I want to caress and stroke your tights gently
I want to give you a warm peck on the cheek
To let you know I care.
I want to walk right beside you, never
Behind you because I cannot compliment your beauty
I want to wake up in your arms with a
Safe and secure feeling
I want tenderness, love, and devotion
I want you to never feel you owe me anything
I want to love loving you
I want tenderness, love, and devotion...

    —*Lynette Roberts*

But The Best Thing Of All

As I walked outside on a nice spring day
I was awakened by the sound of birds
Chirping and bees buzzing by.
Everything in sight was full of bloom:
The flowers, trees, and warm grass at my feet.
As I looked up into the sky
The sun's hot rays felt warm on my skin
But the best thing of all are the butterflies
They look so pretty as they fly around
   through the air,
so gracefully, without making a sound.

    —*Michelle Weber*

As I Continue To Dream

As I lie here
I wish you were near
I can't believe you're gone
As I continue to dream on...

I wonder if our feelings are the same
An I hope we never forget each others name
You are the best thing that's ever happened to me
As I continue to dream free...

I hope our love for one another never dies
Similar to that a bird never forgetting how he flies
An in our hearts we will always be together
As I continue to dream forever...

    —*Richie John Eggers*

To An Unknown Friend

I rode on his strong shoulders into the surf.
   I was no more than eight or nine.
     He carried me lightly into unbounded euphoria.

From my perch, I could see the coastline reaching to
   forever. My chest expanded with excitement.
     A high adventure - unspoken friendship -
     laughing without words.

I cried when we were back in the family car,
   ready to leave Daytona.
     Deep, uncontrolled tears for a companion
     whose name is lost to me now.

My father told me to be quiet.
   I choked back pain and tried to breathe
     and pretend that I was OK.
     But part of me had gone away with him.

I was alone. As alone as I could ever remember.

And then I cried once more.
   This time, quiet inner tears for a friend
    that I would never see again.

    —*Terry Emerson Ward*

Baby Cries

I was the shadow, the shape of darkness in her heart.
I was the bad memory that she never forgot.
It was so long ago, and I painfully heard her sigh,
so today I visited my mother.

It was the beginning of November
the beginning of my life years ago.
The days passed on and in her womb,
I began to grow.

She didn't understand I suppose, that I now had a heart.
I had feelings by now and fingers, hands, and toes.
My brain developed and I could make a fist.
I felt so grand, for I began to expand.

When all in one day
It was taken away.
The wonderful feeling I had.
I felt such pain, and I began to slowly shrivel away.

My angel came and took me home,
to where I now lay
looking upon this person who is called
my mother, my murderer, who took my joy away.

    —*Michele Cabana*

My Brother

My brother is a total dork,
I wish I could stab him with a fork.
He always starts to whine,
He'll have to learn to pay the fine.
He is a total brat you see,
'Cause he's always trying to hit me.
We disagree in every way,
We fight and argue every day.
He steals the remote control from me,
When I'm trying to watch T.V.
He is an ugly, dirty rat,
I'd like to hit him with a baseball bat.
My brother is a royal pain,
He locks me outside when it's pouring rain.
If he's not bothering me,
He's stuffing his face and watching T.V.

    —*Nicki Moore*

Indifferences

"You engender indifference"
  I was told that once...

"You belabor the obvious"
  I was told that once...

"You make psychological judgments you're not qualified to make"
  I was told that once...

"I love you"
  I was told that once...

But the world is different now
and, we don't live in that reality anymore.
and, although you may
    or may not be pre-eminent in my thoughts,
    allow me the leeway to move on!

No fantasies recycled
No memories revisited
It all pre-dates current affairs
The end justifies the means, so let's not "press-to-test!"

That was then!
This is now!
  —*Sylvia Elaine Jones*

I Hate The Word Tiny

I loathe the people who call me tiny,
I wish that I could kick their hiny.
  My mother tells me not to care.
    But being called tiny,
  Is something I cannot bear.
If the people who call me that are rolling
        with laughter
  They are the ones that I am after.
  I don't think that it's very funny,
After all, they don't get paid any money.
    I am not tiny.
    Why can't they see?
I just wish they knew what it's like to be
        me.
  —*Thanh Giang*

The Garden Of Flowers

I am a girl who loves flowers
I wonder if I can have my own lovely garden
I hear the rain hitting on the purple feather hyacinths
I see the colorful roses, tulips, and daffodils
I want them to grow tall, strong, and healthy
I am a girl who loves flowers

I pretend I am walking through a field of yellow daisies
I feel the soft petals brushing against my skin
I touch the slippery, wet sunrays after it rains
I worry when the beautiful pink buttercups die
I cry when people destroy red and white marilyns
I am a girl who loves flowers

I understand why people use flowers for decorating
I say let the wild flowers grow!
I dream of the magnificent red firecrackers when I go to sleep
I try to water the blue grape hyacinths regularly
I hope I can have my own exquisite greenhouse
I am a girl who loves flowers
  —*Sojah Hurt*

One Girl's Dream

I am a girl who likes football
I wonder if the officials will ever let a girl play for the
    Redskins
I hear the wind whistling through my bright red helmet
I see the ball in the hands of the opposing team
I want to tackle the front line
I am a girl who likes football
I pretend I am quarterback and do nothing but make touchdowns
I feel the impact of the Steelers' quarterback
I touch the ball with my foot as I make the punt
I worry that I will break my arm
I cry out to the Steelers, "You lost!"
I am a girl who likes football
I understand how women are afraid to play football
I try to change the minds of women who don't like football
I dream that I will play in the Superbowl
I am a girl who likes football
  —*Tedeidra Zickefoose*

In Memory Of Alvin Lock

As I set and watch my life inspirer,
I wonder what has happened to our cowboy;
The one whose strong hands helped us saddle up the horses,
Time seems to go by so fast.

Even tho we see them once a year - it seems a lifetime.
To watch a loved one age, fills me with sorrow - it don't seem
fair - no doubt he's lived a great life,
But life should go on forever.

To watch his lady busy in the kitchen is touching to everyone's
eyes. She shows of her love all minutes of the day.
We will take care of her when in need
And will have the right touch to handle her with.

My thoughts grow deep, as I watch them together,
And I pray I will be just as they.
My dear Uncle, you give a gift as no one I have ever known.
You encourage me, and help me understand.

My love for you is strong,
And will grow deeper ever day
May God be with you-
Always.
  —*Susan Welch*

I Am Her Granddaughter

I am her granddaughter.
I wonder what she's thinking,
I hear her mumble words that have no meaning.
I see her in my heart from when I was little,
I want so much for her to get better.
I am her granddaughter.

I pretend at times that she is okay.
I feel her love.
I touch her hand.
I worry what will happen to her.
I am her granddaughter.

I understand that she has Alzheimer's disease.
I say I love her.
I dream of the day that she will understand,
I try to let her know by holding her hand.
I hope and pray that God is with her.
I am her granddaughter.

Dedicated to my Grandmother, Lucy Russell.
  —*Peggy Golis Sayad*

Desert Storm

I walk along, the desert's hot and dry.
I wonder who's been here before and why?
How many battles have been fought here, too
And ask how many soldiers yet must die?

In swirling sands the leaders give commands,
And soldiers fight with bloody hands.
They're told to jump, but not how high
While plodding on to save their lands.

Why do men have to fight anew?
Have they no other work to do?
I fear I never will know why.
Someone must stop this — WHY NOT YOU?

—*Marie Regina Van Doren*

The Lovers

If I was asked how to make love last
I would say "search your heart and your deep dark past"
For it lies in you - and in you alone
so come to truth with yourself
And you will unlock the unknown
Reach out for true love with all of your might
never give up - 'til the end of the fight
For if there need be true love
Then so shall it be
For when you find your true love
you will have found me

—*Michael French*

I'd Like And I'd Hate

I'd like to remember the things we shared
I'd like to think that you really cared
I'd like to remember that nice strong kiss
I'd hate to remember that I got dissed!

I'd like to remember the things we did
I'd like to know why you acted like such a kid
I'd like to think you didn't want anything but sex
I'd hate to think you now tell people I'm your ex!

I'd like to cherish every memory
I'd like to be with you for eternity
I'd like to know where I stand
I'd hate to see you holding another girls hand!

I'd like you to touch me all over
I'd like to have a wish on a 4-leaf clover
I'd like to tell you that you are fine
I'd hate to say that you ain't mine!

I'd like to have a new beginning
I'd like to see my whole world spinning
I'd like to hear "A new relationship we will begin,"
I'd hate to hear you say "Never again!"

—*Michelle Eramian*

When I'm Wrong

You'd think, I'd stuck a dagger, in the middle of your heart.
  I'd need to say I'm sorry, and I would if I was smart.
    Things get kinda crazy, when battle lines are drawn.
      And it's hard to say I'm sorry, when I'm wrong.

We can be, down right vicious, in the middle of a fight.
Every now and then, it seems, the flames of hate burn bright.
  Soon before you know it, words are said that don't belong.
    But, it's hard to say I'm sorry, when I'm wrong.

You'd think, I'd shot an arrow, through the center of your soul.
  I wish I could explain to you, just why I lose control.
There's, two sides to every story, and my love for you is strong.
    But, it's hard to say I'm sorry, when I'm wrong.

—*Thomas K. Porter*

Loving Hearts

What a bare world this would be
  if each day we failed to see
    a lovely flower-green grass- a tree.

Our Heavenly Father knew our need,
  and so - He started with a seed
    that's nourished through His loving care
      whose final beauty all can share.

But so much more He cares for us
  He wants to see us grow
    to develop full potential
      with an inner beauty glow.

And so He planted loving hearts
  around us - everywhere
    to nourish us - through sharing
      of their tender, loving care.

—*Lillian Lins Ulsh*

What Would Christ Say?

What would Christ say,
  if he walked the earth today?
Would he turn and walk away,
  or would he destroy it that very day?
Would he be pleased
  with the way you treat your mother,
    or would he cry at the way we treat each other?
What would he say about the way we sin?
Would he reach out his hand,
  or would he raise them up and
    say just let it all come to an end?
Would he hang his head in shame,
  and say no one knows my name?
What would he say, if he walked the earth today?

—*Thelma Jean Bryant*

Time

Oh time, where do you go, so quickly?

Why don't you linger or stand still?

Time doesn't wait for anyone
If I stand still time goes on
I must keep up with time; else time will slip by.

Time is oh so precious
If I take advantage of time, it will bring me many things
But, yet, if I linger knowing time does not, I will waste
precious time.

Time is not an object that can be felt
Neither is it a ruler that can be measured, but many
accomplishments can be reached in time.

Time past, time present, and time in the future
These three parts of time let us know that every moment that
has been or ever will be, is time.

Oh time, keep on going, do not linger
For if you did, we would not value time.

—*Martha McAfee*

Kieran

How I wish to hold you tight,
In my arms throughout the night.
To lay my head upon your chest,
Would ensure a goodnight's rest.
For never farther than a fingertip away,
Is where I always want to stay.
To be kept safe and secure in your love,
Is as precious to me as a Morning's Dove.
Our love together will forever be,
Especially when two become three.

—*Pamela Johnson*

A Near Encounter

Round a curve there stalked a Griffin, just a youngster, not as
  if in his adulthood, he was yet a fearsome beast from ancient
      and long-hidden lore.
Toward him crawled a feathered Dragon, young as he, large as a
wagon, proudly noble, brazen, strong, and fierce right to her
  very core. In canyon bleak and snout to beak, they met upon
      the rocky floor. Met and stared and nothing more.

Now, dear reader, please remember, it was in a past December
That these creatures with their kin, vowed ages of unending war
  Both youngsters knew their families' strife must be upheld,
      should it cost life,
Or at least they'd send the foe a-running for a distant shore.
Each would prevail and could not fail to discharge this scared
      chore. So each prepared a mighty roar.

As if one beast, they voiced their cry, so loud was it that
      they did fly
Quite far away, each promising to ne'er return to stroll upon
      that canyon floor.
Into that canyon they would venture, claimed the children,
      "Nevermore!"

    —*Susan Helton*

For My Love

Even though he is only a few miles away
If our hands do not interlock I feel astray.
His smile, his laugh, his tone of voice
Make all my worries seem rejoiced.
I know one day we will have to part
But right now it is only the start.
Because of all the trust we have built
Never will one of us experience guilt.
All his feelings he will never hide
In me he always can confide.
Ways to help he tries to find
When many troubles cross my mind.
Something mysterious brought us together
Like a child and its most valuable treasure.
I'd be willing to pay the most expensive price
To be with this man for the rest of my life.
But times will change over the years
And he'll be the man for whom I shed my tears.
So maybe it sounds a great big old myth,
But this is the man who I am in love with.

    —*Nisha Gonsalves*

The Original

    In my basket, I bare fruit,
  If someone eats from it becomes loot,
    should someone paint it must change,
  For no two descriptions are the same.

    In my basket, contents past ripe,
  Slowly becoming a most hideous sight,
  Not to mention the odor from where,
  A different vision of fruit does appear.

    Inevitably, all things will change,
When it's impossible to identify the remains,
    Only those who before were to see,
Could attempt to describe the original to me.

    —*Vincent D. Ince*

Pregnancy

She went down town to see,
If there was a pregnancy,
The harsh reality, of deciding what will be,
Comes crashing down around me.

She holds me close and leans to me for strength,
Asking for nothing more than my confidence,
Believing in me, she follows my lead,
My decision, of never my baby to see.

The pain won't subside in me,
Of those dark days now history,
Of what my child might now be,
But was a victim of my insanity.

I can't change what now was,
But I keep wondering how it might have been,
If I hadn't been young and weak,
I might now be holding my son, next to my cheek
Sharing a love which now seems incomplete

Love, I can't ask for forgiveness, for I can't forgive myself,
I just try to live with the doubt and work it out,
Though I'll never be the same within or without.

    —*Randolph V. Schmotzer*

Mentor

I often wonder who I would be
If you had not given of yourself to me.
Potential was dwelling in dreams in the dark
But it found its life with your special spark.

When anyone gives to me acclaim,
You are the mentor that I will name.
And I will be working all of my days
Until that sweet debt can be repaid.

My fondest hope
Is that proud you will be
When you look on the person
That I grew to be.

    —*Terri W. Jerkins*

Think Twice

You will change your life
If you hit that pipe
Never in your life have you seen such power
It will keep you up for hours and hours
You think you slick gett-n dem kicks
But it ain't kool
Being a fool
Think twice or you just might end up on ice

Eyes glisten
But something's missen
Disturbed and hurt
Lying in dirt
Body in lock
On a mental ward in a state of shock

His name is coke
This ain't no joke
Listen up folks
He'll take you for a high ride
Then give you the low dive
Think twice or you just might end up on ice

    —*Virginia Lee James*

Earthenware Urn

Gathered from the four corners, usher sands that stir.
I'll form myself into an earthenware urn.
Inside lit with a molten glow.
So I feel what the earth must know.
Now I'm not easily broken, hardened by fire.
    Sunbaked countenance, with futile desire. (This makes even
    laughter smile).

Literally, land of my birth.
I've been kneaded from pure earth.

Can I enclose the spark from the Thunderbird's gaze?
It supplies the heart that lusters my glaze.

I cry, (it resounds to grounds' root).
    "Liberty fields once formed me, now their use is underfoot."

I'm kept, captured a sad vessel.
    Reflecting setting sun light.
My land is an offering, not a sacrifice of sight.

Anticipate your fire, it brings re-birth O'Phoenix.
I cry your name, too late. My world has been crushed,
I return to dust from whence I came.

Alas earthenware run, when will we ever learn?
    —*P.J. Miller*

I'll Love You For Forever

I'll love you through the laughter.
I'll love you through the tears.
I'll forgive you when there's anger
and comfort when there's fear.
I'll be your shoulder to cry on,
and give advice when its due.
I'll trust you when I have my doubts,
and hope you'll tell the truth.
I'll promise you tomorrow, if that's what you wish.
I'll share your every hope and dream
and let you know you're missed.
I'll think of you on sleepless nights,
and long to feel you near.
I'll sit next to you and hold you close
and whisper in your ear.
I'll love you for forever, every week, and everyday.
I'll love you through those little misunderstandings,
and I'll love you in every way.

    —*Robin Elizabeth Knisley*

Dreamer

If this is a dream then don't let it end
I'm happy this way just picturing you
Could you really be as perfect as this image in my mind?
No one else can see you the way I do.
So I've never talked to you
But we've exchanged a million words in my mind
More than that
Because I've memorized each line, each touch
Every movement of your lips on mine
And I've grown used to the thrill
of being close to you
Sliding my fingers through your hair
And savoring the feel of your arms wrapped about me
But I'm dreaming, dreaming, dreaming
Still once in a while I catch your glance
Surely you must see these dreams in my eyes
If dreams are made to become real; to be true
Then my own dream tonight is only of you.

    —*Rosie Valentino*

"Mommie Dearest"

I thank you Mom for choosing me to come and live with you.
I'm just about the sweetest thing, but I want your attention!

You see, I'm very small and I know more than most.
I'll tell you when it's time to start a brand new day if you'll
give me your attention.

I don't want you to work so hard, don't cook without my
permission.
Just sit down, Mom, and hold me tight, brush my hair, wash my
clothes, tickle my toes, and rub my nose so I can go to sleep.

When I awake, I've planned a trip for only you and me - to
Mamaw's house we'll go,
For I'm her pride and joy. Pappa Dodd, he loves me too, but I
have got him fooled.
I'm only his Great Big Dollar Bill.

I'm ready now to go home, now, to live with you and dad on
Millionaire Street, there to make our life complete,
Where faith, joy, peace and love abide,
our life will be so sweet.
    —*Zelma Sumerel*

My Husband, My Love

A thoughtful look, the loving touch
I'm privileged to received each day

And when I'm sad, who is there to make me smile,
He'll find a way.

A voice so kind and comforting,
There are none to compare.

Support when I need it, is there a chance
That he walks on air?

The days may come and go, I know
But I won't soon forget

The richness I've experienced
Being married to my Ed.
    —*Linda Brady*

Untitled

Can somebody help me?
I'm sitting here in a world full of people yet I still alone.
Can this be possible? I have so many people that give me
companionship, but I feel they're not enough. Is it that I'm
jaded and all I need to do is be satisfied with what I have?
I'm always leaping and shooting for the stars, but my feet
never actually leave the ground. Is what I want sitting here
in my face? Do I even know what I want? I think the only
thing that I want is love, not just the word love, not someone
just saying it to me, but someone feeling if for me as I feel
it for them. Am I alone in a world were I have so much that
amounts to so little?

    —*Michele Millard*

Prejudice

What is prejudice? Prejudice is denial,
immaturity, guilt and negatively. It
describes one as looking at the color of
one's skin and judging on that, and that
alone. Prejudice is fear. Fear of not
knowing. Not knowing right from wrong.
Good from bad. No one should be judged
on the color of one's skin, but by things
much deeper. By attitude, by intelligence,
and personality. Prejudice is not an
image. Prejudice is a reality. Prejudice
will never die, it's here to stay. It is
up to us, to change that.

502
    —*Renee Teresa Robles*

A Veteran Reminiscing

Yes, I am a veteran
I'm that little scalawag
Who climbed the fences - jumped over hedges
Swung on the gate - teased the dog
Scared the cat and annoyed the neighbors
Constantly whistling "Olde Black Joe"

Yes, I'm that little so and so
Who tossed daily paper up on porch
Just missing a plate glass window
Causing many folks to scratch their heads
And rub their chins murmuring
If only I could lay my hands on that little so and so

Today I'm proud to be that veteran
While on brow of a hill
Looking out over the horizon
At my feet lay my buddies
Row upon row
Who in their youth and their dreams
And Love of Life - gave for you
Gave for you - gave for me
  Their lives
    —*Mary Agnes Moran*

Untitled

To the heavens minds will soar, past mountains through
impenetrable walls. They will, they will take stride.
Unstoppable as they go, untouchable their pride. Cannons can
sound not stopping this flow. To the heavens the minds will go.

People understand their lives this day and age but are lost to
their purpose. For each is given a place to find but stray
from the path that leads their way. The unlucky few find it
someday.

Their lives are so clear and they see that of others but the
world is so cold and minds are so cluttered. Can we change our
path through the clouds or do we hit the walls and cry aloud.

I tell you mine is all too clear. Yours my dear friends, well
look beyond your fears. For I am here to tell you, your mind
will prevail. If your heart lets it follow its winding trail.

Remember this because it is true. Follow your heart, follow
your mind, follow your path, follow through. To the heavens
minds will sour, past mountains, through impenetrable walls
to the heavens minds will go.
    —*Ronnie Boals*

A Forest Rain

A dark rain falls
in a forest glen.
Trees blow
as lightning brightens the sky.
The light flashes again,
but the black blanket covers
the sky, once again.
Like tear drops from heaven,
the rain continues to fall.
The dark clouds lower and the rain thickens.
Just as this fury climbs to its peak,
a great rush of light fills the air,
a great sphere of glory stops in midair,
it shines brighter than King Midas's gold.
Then the cold rush turns to warmth,
like a loving hold on it all.
Then a stream of color crosses the sky
with a glow of happiness,
to add to the glow of light already smiling
across the sky.

    —*Melissa Koch*

Premonition

A man no more than fifty-five, casually dressed
  in California's best,
Disturbed my view today.
He lived here but a month or two, with a bride
  of twenty-two.
I waved, I smiled, as he passed by.
My gaze was open, his was ominous.
I recoiled in fear that eyes so blue,
  could never drown my tears.
Besides, he never before was impolite.

The sightless evening came and lulled me asleep.
My dreams abridged, by a knock on my door.

She stood before me like a waif,
  wrapped in grief and sorrow.
"Pete is dead" she said to me.
A widow now, to cry with pain.
Life is brief, grief is deep, her eyes said to me.
    —*Millicent Sen*

Glory of the East

Minarets and Pagodas of the East
In domes of gold the people feast
They feast with hearts so light and gay
Yet in those temples the people pray.

Beautiful mosques with their big round domes
Beautiful buildings and castles and homes
Golden temples of the Orient
On the worship of Idols some people are bent.

Pillars, columns and pyramids will never, never die
For their beauty will give ideas to the modern man's eye.
    —*Phyllis S. Freedman*

Just Believe

I believe...
  in fairy tales and love stories.
I believe...
  in honesty, truth and friendship.
I believe...
  in picnics in the park.
I believe...
  in walks along the beach.
I also believe...
  there is someone for everyone.
I believe...
  in time, for time holds the future.
I believe...
  it takes time to find the right prince.

It may not be tomorrow,
  it may not be next week.
It may even take a month or more,
  but believe in it, it's worth waiting for.
So keep your chin up, live for tomorrow.
  but most important of all, just believe.
    —*Pam Swenson*

Angels

In the mist of Angels: A small child in a hospital bed is healing.
In the mist of Angels: A teenage girl is alone with no one to care.
In the mist of Angels: A young mother is crying for her child is
  gone.
In the mist of Angels: An old lady is wondering who she is.
In the mist of Angels: A small child, a teenage girl, a young
mother and an old lady are laid to rest to never suffer again.
In the mist of Angels: My mother walked into heaven to live
with God who loved and took care of her, as she walked her path
  of life.
    —*Shirley Gillum*

Untitled

Uncle Funky Bar Malone carries greasy chicken bones
In leather sacks hangin' close besides his wallet.
Likes to share them all around with lonely dogs down on the
   ground,
Canine picnic's what he'd probably call it.

He's got followers you see,
Hangers on and two or three cats show
Sunday evenings for community affairs.

Over chicken bones the town comes quiet,
Funky Bar averts a riot,
Dogs and cats reign serene
On the civil civic side,
Gaily submarining on grease jowled contentment,
Chicken calories spent on raising Monday's sun.

   —J. Nelson

Landscape #1

Behind the heather there was a bee's hive,
in moldering boards, through which dripped
a stream of honey once carried by diligent wings.
Under the sun and into buzzing silence
I heard their thoughts, quietly sailing on the landscape.
I bid them hello with a smile when they returned, tired
from a field, somewhere, far from here, absorbed by fatigue.
Among the flowers one stopped, weary.
Sitting between the clover it told a sleepy story
with a hoarse voice.
There was a place for me, lulled to sleep near a sweet
stream, into whose hands my head escaped into thickening worlds
vanished beyond the hill,
disappearing in an increasing croak of garrulous frogs,
escaping into darkness with stormy responses of animal desires,
which tore the quiet dream hammered by a blacksmith's arm,
like an old cart's axle, like a hoop perfect in form,
boasting on art along traveled villages,
the quiet rumble measured.

   —Marek Nej

My Town Is Made Of Concrete

   My town is made of concrete and it's not just in the street.
In my town, concrete begins and ends where both horizons meet.
My town is made of concrete, the school, the churches, and the
store, all are made of concrete, there is concrete galore. Go to the
concrete hospital when you become ill, on your way out stop by
the concrete office to pay your bill.
   Every house is also made of concrete, the walls, ceiling, and
the floor; just step out your door and you will see the concrete,
there is much, much more. Walk down the concrete sidewalk past
the concrete town hall. Mail a letter at the concrete post office
which is in the concrete mall. Park your car in the concrete
garage or fill it up at the concrete gas station. It is safe to say in
this town there will never be a concrete ration.
   Walk up the concrete stairs into the concrete bank where you
put your money. If you think about it, there is so much concrete
it's really kind of funny. Trains speed over the concrete bridge
along the track; here in Morgan Park concrete we do not lack.
   There is a concrete police station and concrete fire department
as well, although in Morgan Park you will never hear a fire bell.
You see, the fire-fighters soon did learn, concrete simply will not
burn.
   You would think that Morgan Park being made entirely of
concrete would have concrete weather, and we do. It snows
concrete every night; stop by some time and you will see it too. If
you don't believe my town is made of concrete, you think it just
can't, I would suggest that you talk to the workers at the nearby
concrete plant.

   —Mike L. Flaherty

Your Pain — God's Gain

   The beauty of the Lord is seen
  In persons who've been tested and tried.
And have realized that to God they must cling,
  For adversity happens so that He'll be
    glorified.
  Their hearts become soft and tender.
They've learned to see life differently.
  God, the Great Character Builder,
  Has taught them the principles
  They need to live Victoriously.
  The Holy Bible becomes their guide.
  The Old Testament becomes alive.
For answers, explanations, and insights
  Have come through this at night.

   With Jesus as their friend,
   They've got great joy within,
  Inner peace and great fortitude,
But most importantly a new attitude!

   —Marilyne St. Louis

Dance Of The Atoms

Finally escaping the storm waves of mind,
in pure nudity stripped of thought activity,
ego and desire
can we serenely dive to the depth of being
where, in the fountain of life, we are honored
to witness the miracle dance of the atoms.

Infinitesimal atoms...myriads...
their swirling energies ever alert.
Each atom—a thinking and feeling entity—
though placed in pattern, is free in its individuality.
At the slightest signal from another,
they harmonize with the whole—
like improvising musicians.

Dancing in light, joy and majesty...
they emanate ecstasy.

   —Margaret Bowen Deitz

Reflections Of The Fire

Thoughts spin through my head,
in quiet reflections before the dawn,
of things that have been and could be,
of lives that have lived but now are gone.
In silent solitude I sit with my shadow,
with muffled resistance I watch my life pass.
Through the fields of my childhood my mind races,
Till it meets with the blackness of my passing youth.
Sometimes, on the edge of remembrance I'll linger,
just long enough to catch a smile or feel the sun.
Never knowing if tomorrow will bring sadness or elation,
it's the battlefields of my mind where no wars are won.
If by some divine grace I awake on the morrow,
to find the stopwatch of the day has begun again.
I will remember the night that I sat by the fire,
and sifted through the ashes of my memories and thoughts,
and I will live my life not so much by the words that are
spoken, but by the action I take when they are spoken to me.

   —Shawn F. Graham

Contemporary Lexicon

The Dumbest words of which I know
In the chatter of the day,
Is for one to interrupt his thoughts
With just two words and say, "You know."

He knows at once that you don't know
Of all that's to be said,
But still he interrupts himself
And you are being led with; "You know".

Exasperating? yes it is, you wonder what comes next,
Just what the hell he's saying
And you're completely vexed with; "You know."

It's not that he is asking if you really truly know,
Just what conclusion he will reach,
And then go on and blow with; "You know."

It cannot be a guessing game, or think you're just a jerk,
Perhaps he thinks you're stupid
Or have a mental quirk, with: "You know."

I'll tell you what should temper it, and really make it pay,
Just interrupt with — "Yes, I know",
And slowly walk away.

—*B. B. Hutchinson*

A Peak At The Real Me

I empty my burdens and brighten scarlet skies.

And see the tears I have shed silently,
in the darkness of my fear

Anger strikes me weak from the hammering of the
lustful hands that I forbid to touch my feelings

I grow leery of my defensiveness that frame my loveable
self that desires to be loved and touched gently

I look into your eyes and become yours
melting into your warm embrace

As I peak at the real me

I manifest the emptiness of my soul
And yearn to have it filled with your love

My heart is lonely and my mind's eye trembles scared
yet drawn, Again and Again

To peak at the real me
—*Stephen Crutchfield*

Angel With A Broken Wing

She strolls down the long, shaded hollow
In the fields, she lives with the flowers
In need to fly, high in the sky
But lost all her powers
All dressed in white with golden hair
Ready to take flight on a road to anywhere
Upon the highest hill carrying her load
Hoping for another rainbow
so she can take the colorful road
Wondering where it will lead
She waits in pain while her lonely heart bleeds
Making so many plans
Her dreaming never ends
And it will take time for her broken wing to mend
A curse has her hanging by a string
No stairway to get home
An angel with a broken wing
Left on earth to roam.

—*Stephanie Johnston*

The Paths of Yesterday

Yesterday is lost forever
In the forever memories of what might have been
The what ifs and the why nots
Will never be answered now
Let it go
The paths we take
The directions we head
As if traveling in total darkness
Only to be surprised
Tomorrow
What might have been
If only
Yesterday
Would the other path have been brighter
Would the joy have been more
Would the love have been stronger
If only
We will never know
Let it go
—*Linda Gomez*

Nightfall

Nightfall has taken over another day, as lighting-bugs dance
in the glow of our headlights along the highway, all the while,
our eighteen wheels keep on turning, we slowly approach
another town, with quiet looking streets and dogs roaming
around, surrounded in the darkness comes all my thoughts,
staring out the window at the silhouettes of the tree tops,
I watch as the lights of the houses appear, and silently
wonder what everyone's doing in there, with the hum of the
engines beneath our feet, I look out at the town, are they all
fast asleep?, we are so far from the place we call home, all
the while our eighteen wheels keep on turning as we continue
to roam, the bill-board signs fill my mind, I'm still reading
them through the rear view mirror as we leave them far behind,
Wishing for a truck stop with an open space, as we persist on
our run at this governed pace, as yet another town slowly
disappears, all the while our eighteen wheels are shifting
gears, into the night, into the quiet night, and I glance at
the man I love driving our truck, all the while our eighteen
wheels keep on turning.
—*Susan Mary Twarog, Higgins*

Untitled

Walk with me,
in the land of the frozen spirits,
where the mighty oak is frozen and lonely,
the wind will rattle your soul,
as it does the few brittle skeletons,
still clinging to that frozen tree.
    The spirits talk,
they whine and moan in the vicious violence
that howls through the frozen land,
when spring comes,
the spirits of the forest will be released,
in billowing, breathtaking shades of green,
the land will be free,
free from the biting wind that blows by me.
—*Thomas P. Chapman*

Untitled

There was a little fellow, all so black and white
Innocence and sweetness were all his very might
We nourished, we cared for him, as if our little boy
And he in turn grabbed hold our hearts and gave us simple joy
Our home was his domain, and he loved to browse about
But a certain something in our cat said Lord, I must get out
Days went by, we searched and watched, kept running to the door
And then we knew in our aching hearts we'd see our cat no more
An emptiness prevails now, all through the day and night
For that little fellow's gone who was so black and white

—*Natalie Buzil*

The Hollywood Sunset Machine

O brother, can you spare me a glimpse of the world,
In the light of the video screen,
Where the dreams of the people are superbly unfurled,
On the Hollywood Sunset machine.

Where Jackie and Lucy and Aunt Bea still reign,
With Alda and Dansen and Sheen.
And Snoopy is following Spock's missing brain,
On the Hollywood Sunset machine.

The children all learn from the Big Bird and Ernie,
And their elders from Roger and Gene.
News and the arts are discovered in turn,
On the Hollywood Sunset machine.

Arrangements are made and debuts are played
In the contest for Almighty Green.
Commercialized, cable-ized, advertised trade,
On the Hollywood Sunsent machine.

O brother, can you spare me a glimpse of the world,
In the light of the video screen,
Where the dreams of the people are superbly unfurled,
On the Hollywood Sunsent machine.

—Robert M. Wallace

Being There

Where are you when your babies cry
    in the middle of the night?
When thunder roars and lightning strikes,
    making such a fright?
Huddling for a hug; or just needing to be near;
Spilling out their little hearts,
    to someone who will hear.
Where are you when these fleeting things are met -
    with each 'Kid day'?
-when laughter pierces the quiet air
    with impulsive play;
-capturing a moment, to praise a deed
    or comforting a doubt;
-chasing butterflies and lightning bugs; roly polies in ajar-
Finding the big dipper, or answering a-why;
Where are you, Mom/Dad - My child?
A tear or shrug cannot undo or mend-
Where will we be, when days are gone-
Who will be left to tend?

—Mona Gonzalez

Today

Today all the knots have been tied
in the proverbial rope. I've depleted all
the reserves from my fountain of hope.

I've a need to expel all the poison within.
I've journeyed inside and had a talk with a friend.

Today, I sent out a summons, for spiritual fortitude.
I'm exhausted and need a higher court to change my attitude.

The light I bask in, says open your spirit,
for that's where I live.
Reach out your hands, through you I give.

Today, trust in me, I am the way.
The force, that guides you, through many.
Today, today, and today...

—Luthenia Gould

Daytime Soap Opera

She tells me this woman and man
in the serial we watch,
grope for each other day after day:

They eat, talk, kiss and fade in
to her sitting on his lap.

Truly,
the script needs some well-meaning neighbor
to advise the handsome, young man,
"Go back to work
before it's too late."

I personally would caution
the beautiful, boring ingenue,
"Wash your dishes,
and more than that, get a life!"

The issue is not really illusion,
but 'Daytime Digest.'

—Marilyn Hochheiser

Overwhelmed By The Darkness

The beauty of the day surrenders to the majesty of the night.
In the stillness of a darkened room my soul has time to rest.
I cry in the empty room. Oh Lord, how much longer can I last.
The quiet walls return the echo of my plea. Now even they cry
    for me.
The strength of the day has flown from my body just as the joy
    has fled my heart.
The humid air is broken by the fresh cool breeze of the
    approaching storm.
I hear the gentle rain as it embraces my window.
I silently start to pray. Oh God, My God. I've stood another
    day.
From where the strength came and went I know not whence.
How will I stand again. The days have weakened my heart.
The tears stream from my defeated face.
I feel a warmth that causes my body to glow.
The radiant love of my Father has changed the ebb and flow.
The power of His love has given me back my hope.
The quiet reassuring voice of the Most High has a word for me
    tonight. "The strength of today is the hope for tomorrow"

—Ron Levi

The Lady Of The Sea

On a boat out to sea, sails a lady like me.....

Her dreams of adventure and beautiful cascades while bathing
in the sun and daring escapades. Sailing the islands,
her sails full of wind, with a broken heart that would never
mend.

On a boat out to sea, sails a lady like me......

A handsome rich gentleman in her life once appeared, gave
promises of grandeur and passions that seared. Her love flowed
freely, her heart given completely. But alas, his love
could not be acquired, for his riches it was believed she
admired. His family, of high social standing, a poor
girl he would not be banding.

On a boat out to sea, sails a lady like me......

From port to port, over oceans and seas, for her true loves
heart she still grieves. Alone with the wind, the dawn of a
new day, her riches are boundless as she sails away.

On a boat out to sea, sails a lady like me.......

—Linda Wesley

Michael Jordan

Michael Jordan you're one of a kind, and we know you're hurting
In your heart, and mind, but Jesus Christ son of God above, will
Heal your pain, by blessing you with the gift of your fathers
Spiritual love, and like your father, you are captivating, most
Definitely stimulating, not to mention vigorating, and when you
Are performing your magnificent game of basketball, you never
Let your audience down with a fall, because you're always on time
With the right shot in mind, so son, always remember, you're one
Wonderfully bless young man, for Jesus Christ son of God, bless
Your parents with you born in their nest, which express, that
Your parents with you born in their nest, which express, that
You're apart of each parent's best.

Who could ask for anything more?
God Bless You!!
Michael Jordan

—LaVerne D. Nixon

Willow

Oh! Weeping willow,
  In your long tresses that hang to the ground,
Reminds me of a love lost and never found.
  Oh! Weeping willow, as the wind blows you sway,
I listen for whispers, to here what you say.

You tell me, "man can save face,
  Then try to help the human race.
The way they are going is a shame,
  And have only themselves to blame."

Oh! Weeping willow,
  Let me borrow your Salicin, to ease my pain.
Then maybe,
  I won't feel so drained.

Sometimes life can get so tough,
  And things can get really rough.
Oh! Weeping willow, as time goes on,
  I hope we can learn to sing a song.
To get along with one another; to love our sisters and
  brothers.

—Patricia Purdy

Word Play (II)

"As you wish!" I said; yet wished myself to be
In your wish, as you, in mine,
Are mover prime and, yet, not moved to magic
  (Our birthright, we two, we too, we to be...)
For in this darkest hour of night,
  (The day, without you, is as dark)
The Incubi and Succubi come by-the-bye,
And buy, with fearsome currency,
That P(eace,iece) of mind(ful,less) Dreamscence, Dream Screen
Play in which I once played all parts....
The audience of one, for which this was rehearsed
  (On, endlessly, and yawn, sometime,)
Is, all too jury-like, not in:
The curtain cannot rise, the lights not struck, and
Cue-less, the actors, too, two (now,) to
  (For the audience plays as well
  In this theatrical mirror)
Wait, wonder, prepare, despair, repair,
In anxious anticipation of the performance
Of their lives, too, two, to ————— ?

—Max Middleton

Beautiful Child Of Mine

You once were a part of me.
Inside my womb you grew
You grew to be a precious child
One day, that great day -
You were born.
Your eyes were as blue as the crystal sea
Your cheeks became rose -
When you smiled with me.
Your mother, you knew I was.
You cuddled with me
As if to share a time of love.
You yawned and snuggled
Close to my heart ...
Secretly telling me. - we will never part.
That was the moment of true light
That was the moment God made you right.
In God's eyes you are beautiful ...
In my eyes you are -
My world, my heart
Beautiful child of mine, I love you always.

—Ralna Lynae Rowan

Hypatia, A True Story

It is written that she was very beautiful; born in 370 and most
  intelligent in science
she was the last to work in that library so full of knowledge,
our planet's promise for advance
a mathematician, astronomer, physicist, neoplatonic philosopher,
a rebel in her time, when men owned women, she chose freedom.
Her name in history is whispered softly in the hall corner;
even today in the age of information, equality, and wisdom,
for her story embarrasses faith in our civilization, our religion
  and vision.
A time when the Ptolemys built the greatest city of learning and
  creating,
Rarely has a state promoted so much evolution of human
  understanding;
Sophocles, Aeschylus and Euripides, all published in this book
  capital of mind
where Euclid wrote his geometry, later rediscovered by Kepler,
  Newton, and Einstein
where citizens of the globe came to live, trade, learn and invent
  the word cosmopolitan
for the Cosmos was discovered here and here became known to
man and then forgotten for one thousand years of Dark Ages, lost
  from Alexandria,
city for the elite, where many suitors wooed her, this lady called
  Hypatia;
close friend to the Roman governor, well connected, a symbol of
  freedom,
but to the rising mob, the Christians, she was a mere wealthy
  pagan
the fanatical mob of parishioners shredded her with abalone shells;
  she was Cyril's enemy.
The library, most of its memory, died with her and the city built
  by slavery.

—Mark Biskeborn

Intimacy

Intimacy comes in all shapes and sizes,
Intimacy comes in all disguises,
Intimacy is listening to the Robin sing,
Intimacy is waiting for the phone to ring,
Intimacy is a kind word, a dream or two,
Intimacy can cheer you up when you're blue,
Intimacy can take you and make you a star,
Intimacy a wonder, a closeness from afar,
Intimacy is love, is trust in you and me,
Intimacy is wishing to be free.

—Shirley Yan

David Stone Sheffield

Double diamond, double daring, darling David, legs churning,
intent on the horizon, you drove your big wheel with abandon, a
tiny world explorer, who, in your wide-ranging voyages,
transported your parents to a state of worried pride. When
sides were chosen, you were first-drafted, quick and fast, you
transformed a soccer field into a Land of Opportunity and
claimed it for your team. Above the curve of your triple-treat
smile (shy, amused and secret), and behind the windows of your
eyes, your thoughts flickered tantalizingly, but usually
remained unspoken, and, ultimately, your own. Careful of
others and careless of self, you skied mountains and waters,
picked, rolled, passed and took it to the hoop. Racing time,
you were first to break the tape. When earth could no longer
contain your venturesome spirit, you carved a bright trail to
some new place where there are flesh slopes to test and
challenges to meet. Out of our sight, you remain in our
hearts, deft and graceful, so at ease in your body, your
luminous memory serves as a brilliant beacon for those who will
follow when you lead.

   —Trish Cole

A Flower Blooms

A seed is planted and starts to grow,
Into a world that consists of chaos
To whom things are unknown.
It's fertilized with religion and watered
With a loving care.
A whisper in the wind to let me know
God is there.
As a harsh winter approaches, it snows
Sin and thunderstorms temptation.
Still, a flower grows past every thorn of
speculation.
Spring appears and everything is anew.
A flower is blooming, a warm soft rose,
Also some things I still do not know,
But with wisdom of others and the
guidance from God,
Just as a flower,
I shall continue to blossom and grow.

   —LaTonya Simmons

The End?

Where will I go when life is gone
Into the blue or out beyond
Or deep within the changing earth
To silently wait for my rebirth

Or will I just relive again
The same sweet life that I did then
Who knows I may just roam this land
Trying to touch a friendly hand

Or lurk in shadows eerie and black
To send cold shivers up mortal backs
Perhaps I'll return as a siamese cat
With a knowing look when humans chat

I hate to think that when we've died
And there's nothing left of our human hide
But ashes and insignificant dust
That that's the final end of us

   —Patricia A. Ashforth

Untitled

A hawk descends through my vision, through my eyes,
into the paths of my direction,
swooping me up on its wings where my soul lies.
It flies dangerously close and dangerously low
into the valleys of perception,
and out of the duality of confusion.
I am a Sinbad, a pirate, roving the sea of skies in search of
logic.
I will steal it and hide it
under my overcoat of feathers.
I will return it to man, through the hawk,
through the sky,
through my soul which lies naked on the wings of fear,
exposed to the rays of the sun and wings of morrow.
We, who drift on the trade winds of life,
can only touch the tranquility of man's destiny
before we eat the seeds of our inevitable demise
and fade into the sun which is our home.

   —Muriel Wolfson

Un-Union

I took the war to paper 'cause I couldn't stand the noise:
   inward, propaganda; outward, calm and poise.
I think the change of venue was a strategy of self.
I didn't give permission,
I don't think I agreed.
I moved the thing to paper so my ownness could secede.

   —Pamela R. Burkland

The Art Of Living

The art of living, so hard to learn.
Is filled with many a twist and turn;
Lessons lost, never to be learned,
Passions empty, emotions burned.
Guilt and shame bring doubts unfounded;
My sails are empty and my craft grounded.
Learning to share, care and trust,
Basics yes, but for all a must!
With the basics you then can find love,
Granted and guided as if from above.
Understanding, tenderness and deep emotion,
With trust and loyalty comes devotion.
The art of living, a skill divine,
With determination may come to all in time.

   —E. "Shadow" Maddox R.A.

Morning-Mourning Time

Birds chattering in the wind
Is it already daybreak again?
The safety and insanity of night has
left me and mourning time returns.

Why is morning so hard without you
Oh yes! Our breakfast calls, our morning talks
Now a blur of mourning tears as the
Months roll by and fade to a year.

Gone-Dead-Away-Forever-Never-
Your form-your presence! Present but
Not in the usual way.
So I awaken to face another day.

   —PhiloMena Mudd

Shakespeare's Cottage

To see it from the outside, Shakespeare's home
is like its pictures, neat and primly built.
But go inside! Our first reaction is
surprise to see how low the ceilings are.
A six foot man would have to watch his head
lest he might bang against the portals there.

Their rooms are small, as though they huddle close
together from some fear of parting soon.
The floor is laid with wooden puncheons that
in places squeak. Though ancient flooring, this
still holds the hordes of visitors who come
to see the bard's first home. The open hearths
are big, as well they might be when you think
their fires were used for warmth and cooked as well.

This place is proud. Though men were not as tall
in stature then, here lived a mighty man.

—*Mildred Fielder*

The Unknown

The fears I face in my dreams
Is much more than a cold stone scream
They are the pictures of life and death
That lead me onward to an unknowing path
Frightened of what I'll see and not
But relieved to see the pleasures I've got
Try to achieve all that is right
Without betraying in the middle of the night
For I am human that's plain to see
Still frightened of what's become of me
My fear is great of the unknown
And what He has yet to me be shown
Clutching at life and the love for tomorrow
And hoping I'll see her never in sorrow
I think so hard that this is impossibly real
But it must be, for I have a soul and it can feel
So I'll watch my life blow past like a breeze
Until I can see my fate in the trees
And on that day then I will know
What is yet to be seen and called The Unknown

—*Michelle E. Rogers*

Winter Song

Oh, one of the noteworthy songs, I have heard
Is the clear winter call, of the crimson redbird
High in a tree, the first month of the year
It's a pretty, pretty, pretty, and a cheer, cheer, cheer

It's a beautiful song, from high in a tree
Trumpeting happiness, for you and for me
He bugles his clarion call, far and near
On ice covered branches, he sings without fear

He's plainly intent, on declaring one thing
Bursting forth boldly, the coming of spring
Hoping his concert, will bring it along
He gladdens our hearts, with cheer in his song

With snow on the ground, and ice in the trees
No attention is paid, to either of these
Yes, one of the praise worthy hymns, I have heard
Is the clear winter call, of a flaming red bird

—*Ruth Hall*

Under The Spell Of A Leprechaun

Under the spell of Leprechauns in their green,
is the only way they are able to be seen.

In the mist of Erin they dance and they sing so bold.
While the song's of the Celts are told.

Clovers unfold, with a touch of a kiss, and
gently they become four leaves in the mist.

As Leprechauns paint an aurora of hues in the sky,
in the sun rise of morning it will catch your eye.

A rainbow of hues, on which you can wish,
dreams and schemes for Leprechauns have told you,
at the end of a rainbow is your pot of gold.

And if you stand under its hue you'll love the view.
For the Leprechauns wish will come true.

And the pot of gold will be for you,
if you believe the Leprechauns tale,
then it is there for all to avail.

—*Roxanne Mosher*

Soft Mad Children

Is there a place for me here?
Is there a place for my words?
Where can a faithful heart turn?
Where are the dreamers?
As I reflect now, on those days of doubt
I see faded photos of a lost generation of an age
I can't envision of an age
I don't recall
Is there a place for us?
For our words?

—*Stacy D. Sells*

Sweet Woodruff Reeve

What is this heavenly white point?
Is this my fortune star, or is this my anoint?
Oh, can this be a holiday.
A shorebird or just a snipe - at bay.

Her affection has filled my cup.
All that sweetness has ruffed me up.

What does this provost dove have to woo this mist.
Can potent bravery solar charm this fair
Fragrant perennial kiss.

How can this whist partner migrate from capitol to perch?
Perhaps this is not a shorebird.
But a pigeon, a pheasant or a grouse.
Something in a birch.

Has the sight failed the solar?
Where is the pathway into the grove?
No! This wood, has she to rove.

Be this the primrose path and is she.
What at bath? Is this the reeve?
Oh look a lovely bird of paradise
No! It is the sweet fair perennial kiss mist.

—*Sonny Trost*

Poem

Although these word's are not much of a poem
It is all I could muster from deep in my bones.

Phrases may match words may rhyme
Yet it's a simple thought spinning round my mind.

But still I conspired to put it on paper
For some contemplation sooner or later.

—*Robert J. Delahanty*

Hand In Hand

The time of day I love the best,
Is when the sun has gone to rest,
When the moon is coming up real bright,
And a strange bird calls into the night.
The sound of a wolf in the distance is heard,
Again there comes the cry of a bird,
As a blanket of peace settles over the land,
We walk together hand in hand.
We walk beside a little stream.
In which the tiny pebbles gleam.
We then sit down upon a rock.
Where we can have a quiet talk.
You ask me then if I love you.
Although of course you know I do.
And then with hearts that are aglow.
Hand in hand back home we go.

—*Twila Weisenberger*

My Sister

She's seventy today, that's no big deal
It all depends on how you feel.

Her step is light, her mind is bright,
She still can give you a darn good fight

Her fingers move nimbly as she knits,
Sometimes, really, the sweater fits.

She challenges drivers on the road,
As she proceeds in a reckless mode.

Her shopping sprees are most historic
As through the malls she will frolic

Her husband attends to her every whim,
Where did she get a guy like him?

Her children are the joy of her life,
Some more joy, some more strife.

But when needed, she always there,
To acknowledge this is only fair.

The number of grandkids increased to eight
With the arrival of "Kiss me Kate".

She's seventy today, that's no big deal
It all depends on how you feel.

—*Rose Mellie*

Tonight I Feel Forgotten

Whenever we spend time together
It always feels so right.
We laugh, we tease each other, we open our hearts!
We never yell or fight.

But it's now so rare that we're together
And for weeks I've been feeling rotten.
I've called, I've written, with no reply.
And frankly, tonight I feel forgotten.

My head advises "This too shall pass, it always does",
As it mentally prepares for "No Reply".
But for my poor heart tonight's been rough, very rough.
To say it's not, is a lie.

Your phone message, "I'll call you tomorrow" revived my heart,
But that was twenty nine long days and nights ago.
Are you OK? I have no way of knowing,
But if you miss me, it sure doesn't show.

Each time I see you I fall in love,
So on August 18th my heart was hoppin'.
But it's now September 16th, and I'm again way out of touch,
And so, tonight I feel forgotten...

—*Robert Berardi*

A Quiet Vacation

If there is an answer in this crazy world of ours, where might
it be? The city has lights and bars, skyscrapers and sports
arenas, yet where in the city can I relax and think— of the
ocean, a sea of blue expanding far, into the listless horizon,
yet how can I concentrate with such monotony in plain view— of
a desert with its warm breeze and cool shade, yet how can I
comprehend with no human life around me, as I dream of the
plains, and smell the fresh vegetables, yes the plains are a
land of freedom, yet what obstacle must I overcome, to walk
along the flat terrain— so as I sit here on nature's doorstep,
I decide to breathe the air and hear the animals, while feeling
the breeze of the rolling hills, I notice two lights in the
distance, the first reassures me, the second relaxes me, so
maybe there is an answer in this crazy world of ours, perhaps
you should just see the elk, or smell a rosebud, drive a sports
car, or wish upon a star, but in the hills you can realize
variety, just let the answer come to you, as the rest of the
world passes by, like a newly formed butterfly, peace, love,
happiness, thank you. And one more thing, I suggest you
decide.

—*Michael Alan Scott*

Remembering Dad

There is an empty chair in the circle of my heart;
   It belonged to my Dad, but God set him apart.
In mansions of Glory, in heaven so bright,
   I know he is singing in endless delight,
With the light of Glory on his face
   He is singing now God's Amazing grace.

Each time through the years when we gathered there,
   We worshipped the Lord in song and in prayer.
"Throw out the life line across the dark wave,
   There is a brother whom someone should save;"
"How firm a foundation" we sang at his pace
   Then lifted our voices in "Amazing Grace."

I wish there was room to write all the songs;
   To tell of Christ's love to whom he belonged;
To repeat all the scriptures he read to us there;
   To show us God's love and infinite care.
With the circle complete, as around him we face
   Hallelujah! We'll sing "His amazing grace."

—*Wilma Jones*

Untitled

Yes it's been a long hard road.
It could of been easy, it could of been sold.
How sad it is not to want to grow old.
This time is given to us for free, although
all through life we have to pay, our maps we
make from day to day.
Some are unfortunate and may not get lead,
while some souls are starving and not get fed.
There are many questions that have yet to be asked.
To reveal the answers, uncover the mask.
We do the footwork and the unknown does the rest.
He passes out the problems, we do the test.
Failing the course, we then learn the lesson.
Experiencing the pain, fighting back the aggression.
Yes, I have witnessed the evil, and deep in my heart
have felt the good.
One day I'll meet the creator.
One night I'll walk within the man in the hood.

—*Sheri Tucker*

Night Shades

Hark! What in yonder woodpile lies?,
It dares not move; it does not cry.
    Could it be a watersnake?; crawled in there
from yonder lake;
    Or perhaps a startled loon, seeking refuge
from the moon.
    Me thinks! It is a little fawn seeking shelter
until dawn.
    A closer look reveals to me, a mooncast
shadow from a tree.

    —*Paul H. Schwan*

A New Star In Heaven

    She was a frail little girl, and she suffered so
It eased her pain when God called her. We had to let her go.
Tho, she wasn't with us long - The years just numbered three
    We know for now and forever she will be pain free.

    There must be toys in heaven, and other children too
    And with new life she'll play, just like the others do
    The agony is over, of waiting for that fateful call
    For now she is in Heaven with the greatest Healer of all

    These are times that try the soul, of us here on earth
For we loved Samantha and cared for her since her birth,
    We must not feel cheated tho, as we shed our tears
    Because of the hugs and kisses of the past three years

    Whenever she is thought of, Samantha isn't too far
Because, if we look to the Heavens we'll find a brand new star
Behind this window of Heaven is this child with good health,
And tho she is with God now, He gave us more than any wealth

    —*Robert H. Watkins*

Past

The cool refreshment soothed my throat
it filled a need in me so deep.
It entered me and worked its miracle
and penetrated me to my innermost keep.

You cradled it with your flawless hands
you let it run down your face.
You held it above me, poured it softly
as we were lost in the pleasure of inner space.

We rejoiced in what we shared
joined with fleshy bonds.
Experienced all that was new, together
we swam in the sensual, lush ponds.

The forest held new treasures for us,
we searched and touched and left all bare.
So consumed with the experimentation
and went beyond what we shouldn't dare.

We continued moving, traveling
from green, plentiful trees
ferns, the copious lush of the forest and came
to a place where there was no peace.

    —*L. Renee*

Farewell Fear

All alone when fear is around,
it stalks me then hunts me down
an evil prince, a deadly villain,
it has come here on a mission
I feel as though this is the end
but wait, laying quietly is my best friend
a strong warrior clothed in black
always ready and on the attack
he protects me from all evilness
my favorite dog "Guinness."

    —*Michael Savage*

Love

Love is a beautiful thing,
It fills you up with happiness,
You feel like you're flying and spreading
your wings.
Love makes you feel great,
It can happen any month like June, December,
or May.
It can happen any minute of any given day.
You can't think of anything else, except
the one you love.
To you, they're special, wonderful, funny,
and perfect in every way.
You hear songs on the radio and think
about him or her.
Whenever you hear their name, your heart fills
with joy and begins to flutter.
Sometimes it's hard to explain what your mouth
cannot utter, but love is a beautiful thing.

    —*Shannon Andrews*

The Promise of Better Times

The land laid parched and dry.
It had not seen water for quite sometime.
But the hint of rains to come echoed in the distance.
Once more the ground would swell with moisture
Brought by the laden clouds.
It would be soaked up by the barren soil.
Again the ground would become green and fertile
With renewed strength and hope that the water would remain
Leaving the land afresh with abundant life
And the promise of better times.

But the hint of rains to come,
Once more, is one of false hope.
And so, for yet another year the plains will remain desolate
Without the much needed water essential
To foster new life, and hope.
Allowing no chance to know what might have developed.
Growing and exploring all the possibilities existence can bring
Thus, like in the past, life will remain obscure and unattainable.
And the promise of better times, like the land,
Will remain empty and unfulfilled.

    —*Linda Rubio*

Lois

Such a warm - yet unfamiliar feeling,
It happened from the start;

This gentle-yet powerful yearning,
Steadily pulling at my heart...

These strange - yet comfortable sensations
That are churning from within;

Are signs of much deeper feelings
Than from just being friends...

Also, these feelings seem to be growing
with each passing day;

And I've been longing for your tenderness
Every moment since I've been away.

So I've come to realize,
In these few days apart;

These yearning and comfortable feelings,
Must have been "Love" from the start...

    —*Scott*

About A Parting

You ask me how I feel about losing him
It is like standing over a perilous cliff
Staring into the depths, seeing nothing but feeling
darkness seizing air from my lungs
sensing underfoot
the division of land and nothingness
in my mind
the blood in my head pounding thunderous
sweat bleeding from my face mingled with
burning tears from the wells of my eyes

The water evaporates, leaving me with words forming
from cracked lips dry as desert

I love you
is sucked from my lips into nothing
I scream, my love and pain unheard
My love, I only want to touch you one more time.

    —*Mary A. Reavis*

Divine Love

What is the most precious commodity that can be ours?
It is our speck of that same Divine Love that powers
planets, moons, and stars.
Without it we are poor regardless of how much material
success has been achieved in our name.
The richness it imparts to our lives is much superior
to great, wealth and fame.
This super, magnetic, power is guaranteed to heal
everything that is wrong.
Keeping it forever alive in our hearts helps us to
always sing a happy song.
Being filled with this highest form of love will
enable us to be open and receptive to everyone's needs.
No longer will we be selfishly focusing all attention
on ourself because it will be others we want to please.

    —*Marion Cureton*

This Thing Called Life

The wait is over and the egg cracks open
It is the beginning of new life and old work
Mother feeds her young without knife or fork
And father stands guard, a proud old stork

The time is spring and before long summer
Up close the change seems ever so slight
But in reflection it is a powerful might
This thing called life and one's first flight

Nature calls and refuses to be ignored
The first try may look like a mistake
The falls are many and all the bones ache
But the will is strong and does not break

Parents look on with growing expectation
Their guidance proceeded by words of criticism
Because each sees life through a different prism
And many times appear the only victim

Despite their rebellion many lessons are learned
Like the prodigal son they cease to sponger
The young soon mature and the gap is no longer
For with each other's love the bond grows stronger

    —*Melanie Winters*

Heartland

I peered into the window of my child's heart;
it is there he sometimes goes. A quiet place,
his refuge from a world that doesn't always play fair.
A place he slips into and out of silently-where others cannot
    invade.
Scattered about are his favorite things:
his teddy bear, a ball, his bicycle.
They are all reminders that this heartland is his very own.
In his heart he is free. He expresses who he is and
how he feels, and it is always okay.
He scribbles messages on the walls of his heart.
He draws happy faces and sad faces, friendly ones and mad ones.
He knows them well. They are all him at one time or another.
Sometimes, he runs carefree and happy
through golden meadows filling the air with laughter;
his aches and cares tossed away like old, forgotten toys.
Other times, he nestles in a corner seeking security and
    reassurance,
snuggling his raggedy blanket, clinging to it tightly
as if it holds all his hopes and dreams in its threads.
Today he saw me peeking in at him.
He looked out at me and smiled, then he invited me in.

    —*Sharon Warren Coberly*

True Love Is Forever

True love is like a fan revolving.
It must keep on turning to be alive
If it stops it will surely die.
True love is something forever.

The love we shared was such True Love.
A few bad times crept in to tempt us,
But happiness was never far away,
Because True Love is a thing forever.

The love we shared was a quite love.
For us to show the way we really felt,
Thrills and excitement were never needed,
Because True Love has a voice of its own.

Even though he's no longer at my side,
I still love him just as much as ever.
For me he'll always be here with me,
Because True Love can never be denied.

Once again some day we'll be together,
Hand in hand to stroll the fields of clover.
Never more shall we be apart because,
True Love is something forever.

    —*Marie Davis*

Time

Time is such a priceless thing,
    It passes us so swiftly by,
This is our moment to live and do,
    For some of us, perchance, to die.

But while we live, let's fill it full
    Of worthy things and true,
Of words that count and deeds that bless,
    To lift another's hope anew.

And when that bright tomorrow comes
    For which we all have prayed,
We'll look into the face of God
    Alone, perhaps, but not afraid.

    —*Velma Kienel*

Inertia/City Dweller

I sat and I heard what seemed like a pounding thunder;
It roared; It clapped; It rapped; It moved over and under.
"Maybe," I uttered. "It's a passing storm or a rare sonic boom ."
"What a noise!" I thought. As it moved through the room.

Alone in my space, as it moved through the house.
So, I crept to my window to peep-out, tippy-toeing quiet as mouse.
Although, the sun was bright; the sky was clear.
I heard the rapping of thunder coming. It was very near.

The clock in my house struck twelve o'clock
Tick-Tock, Tick-Tock
Along strolled a Brother, on his shoulder was a loud rapping
boom box.

—*Rae McBride*

Family:

Why do you argue, cuss and fight
It seems to happen almost every night
Have you ever took the time to discuss
That we are tired of Satan leading us
Family look at me
Don't you see it's time to be free
People don't you see the enemy is so vile
Just take out one minute to smile
Our children are not very amused
Look on their faces they are totally confused
Mom and Dad stop flirting
Don't you see your children are hurting
It must not be a fable
We never sit at the table
Are someone going to ever say
Can we hold hands and pray

—*Roy Chambers*

Three Key's

Arise my son from your place of rest, though the day is young,
it soon will pass, reach for the top, your goal to excel, climb
to new height's never yet held.

For desire and ambition are simply the key's to open vast
treasures of secrets and dreams. Let faith be your strength
yield not unto doubt, for great ideas are born, from within
ones self.

The strength of a person as measured by time, is not physical
strength, but power of mind. For the power of knowledge, put
in motion by deed, is the greatest weapon the world has yet
seen. So seek after knowledge, for then you shall see, you
will hold in your hand the master key.

Knowledge, desire and ambition indeed, are all that is needed
for one to succeed. The door to success, though closed it may
be, will surly be opened by these Three Key's.

—*Michael Dawson*

Preservation - Luke 17:33

A rose will bloom forth from the broken ground
Its petals embrace life without a sound
The aroma will not linger from its earthen bed
The sweetest scent comes after the flower's crushed and dead
From the brokenness of man came another tender shoot
Some only saw the surface, very few the root
A man of sorrow, acquainted with pain
He was crushed as petals, under the strain
From the weight of the world He bore it all
That we may live and know our call
Like a rose, crushed and dead
So he may reign in us instead

—*Monica Kittleson*

Separate Pieces

Who is or what is
    it that keeps me
from myself -

that keeps me out of
    c o n n e c t i o n s ?

Who claims and proclaims
    my unworthiness!

I cuddle in the arms of the angel;

Crying out of separateness
        severed, scattered, dispersed among the cosmos!

Will those particles come
together? What is this
frantic force which

    Spins the winds of divisions?

My anger burns an
    empty spot.
Coals of longing are left.

Alone - Because

I am not with MYSELF

Devastated on the brink of possibilities.

—*Penny Schricker*

The Ghosts Of The Sea

The ghosts of the sunken ships remember the fog,
It was like the danger of a wild, mad dog.

Hidden in the darkness it came into the night,
Everyone aboard the sailing ship became affright.

They lost their way in that thick cloud as they felt the
rhythm of the waves,
They could hear the water as it crashed against the shore
and caves.

Before the sailors knew it they were in the sea among the
rolling, foaming crests,
The deep sea was calling them as the waves broke across
their breasts.

The high seas had taken another ship as it lay battered
among the rocks, moving slowly with the tide,
Softly they could hear the whispering of the fog as it
spoke to the ocean wide.

The ghosts of the sea beckon as the ocean becomes a sheet
of glass,
The fog has lifted and the ghosts of the deep invite the
ships who would dare pass.

—*Ronald K. Dawson*

Expression Of Love

How do I express my love?
It's so pure, it's like a Dove.
The only way I know, is to write instead of show.
The love for my father so handsome and strong
The love for my mother, how could I go wrong.
All the years I was there, they showed nothing but care.
Through all the hard times, we heard the music chimes.
God gave me to you because only he knew
That I needed tough love so I could battle and shove
My life has been hard and I've also been barred
from taking the easy way out.
Thank you my father, thank you my mother
For wiping my tears along with my fears.

—*Martha Brocho*

A Blade Of Grass Grows In Berlin

A blade of grass grows in Berlin.
It was watered by tears and blood and fertilized with
The frustration and helplessness of a living city.
"Stop - Freedom ends here" ordered one hundred miles of
　concrete.
Courage

A green field flourishes in Berlin on once-barren land.
Runners creep across east-west lines where tanks stood firm.
Fresh growth melds the divided city into one field,
One plot of unification.
Freedom

A tree grows in Berlin in no-man's land.
The Wall is gone; the Iron Curtain destroyed.
Oh roots of peace grow deep; Oh limbs stretch toward Heaven
And leaves, touch the land of God.
Peace

A blade of grass grows in Berlin.

　　　—Lana Robertson Hayes

Sadness

Sadness is in everyone's heart
It will make you weak
Sadness takes part of your soul
It is part of your life
Sadness can turn to joy
But joy can turn to sadness
If you lost someone or something
Sadness will be there in a second
As long as there is happiness
There is sadness
Sadness makes you hurt, cry and feel empty
For sadness is loneliness
no one can replace
When there is happy feelings
There are sad feelings
And when there is sad feelings
Something or someone can
Brighten your day

　　　—N. Eldred

After The Womb

My mothers love has made a darkened stop,
It will not give what is want or need.
A deep want for feeling, to find I know not were.
I look to find my gift to share,
I look to find offering and know it never there.
The clues have been dropped over many many years.
I pay no mind, I reason her behavior.
I stop to worry, could this be wrong?
Finding only pain, anger, confusion in my life,
To her a life, that is gone.
Only she holds the key, should the lock be picked?
To try for her love and live once again.
I could wait longer for the key in her heart,
I need her gift of freedom, will it
come to my door? My heart beats sadly,
All I want is her love. For now I sit and wait,
I hope for Mom with nothing close to hate.
For I also hold a key, it is to my open door,
To this I tell you I love you and forgive you even more.
I love you Mom...I will wait...

　　　—Tina Burrus

The Special Living Doll

Katie Doll is her name - K. D. for short,
It would be meaningful to describe her,
The special living doll on mother earth.

She has blonde-curly hair and big blue eyes,
She stands two feet and seven inches tall,
And she weighs practically within her size.

Katie Doll has clothes like an ordinary girl wears,
Short, T-shirts, caps and sun glasses for summer,
Skirts, blouses and long dresses for winter.

Katie Doll is charming and exceptionally lovable,
She is tender, gracious and extremely beautiful,
She has a magnetic personality that attracts a human soul.

Katie Doll has the family's uppermost support,
To place her name on the honor roll list,
For the special living doll on mother earth.

　　　—Philip Muldez

Changing Winds

The wind blows in my direction.
It's a gentle wind not a gusty wind.
When it's peaceful, the wind whistles;
When it's angry the wind becomes turbulent,
Like the thunder and lightning from a rainstorm.
The wind has inner strength like the human soul.
The fortitude to grow like from a tiny baby to an adult,
or to blossom like the flowers do in Spring.
There is a winter wind that is like the Almighty
and scares the gallant and bravest type of people.
The Summer doesn't have much of a strong wind.
It's rather calm with a touch of a breeze.
The Summer's almost over and the fall will take its place with
the colorful leaves falling to the ground without making a
single sound.
I love the fall. It's a beginning for adventure.
Just grab a light jacket and walk along the scenic view of the
country, and enjoy life's little treasures.
And soon the wind will start howling
and then we know Winter is here with a vengeance.

　　　—Susan Simon

Prejudice

It's a black thing
It's a white thing
It's a human thing to me
and I don't understand why people don't leave it alone
It is a thing that is not of any importance.
There are a lot of things that the world should think about
not the stupid things as Prejudice.
If everyone in the world minded their own business,
we would not have this problem.
There a lot of things that people do that you dislike,
but why linger on it???
Just let it be and forget about it. . .
The world has become a place of hatred, violence, and of no
Love whatsoever. .

Why has it become a place like that? ? ?
In the beginning it was okay,
but now look at it. . .
Go on and do the things that are wrong if you like,
but don't bring me into it. . .
Sincerely, unhappy...

　　　—Stephanie Ijames

Happiness

Happiness is something wonderful.
It's all over the place.
A rose in bloom with beautiful red color.
The policeman on the corner tooting his whistle,
Tipping his hat to me as I cross the street.
A doorman saying good morning to me with a big
    smile on his face.
The chocolate on a child's face as his tongue tries
    to lick it off.
Happiness is the newspaper man asking me, "where
    have you been, stranger?"

So you see, it doesn't take much for me to find
    happiness.
All I have to do is look all around me.
Up at the sky with the birds flying above,
The trees swaying in the breeze,
The sweet aromas coming from the bakery shop.

But most of all, you see happiness is something
I don't have to buy, for it's waiting there for me.

—Rosette Mines

An Ode To A Mango

It was sitting there
Its awesome presence and luscious covering captivated my entire
    being
Its bulged skin depicted the unending nectar to be sucked from
    its fruit
I stared at it
My eyes began to roll
My mouth began to dribble like a leaky faucet
drip.. drip.. drip
I took it up
Slowly…
I placed it under my nose
I inhaled its delicate aroma
It was intoxicating
Its skin felt smooth
I could taste it
My teeth wanted to sink into its beauty
And my mouth wanted to bring its taste to life.

—Lorna Grant

Untitled

I see a light shining far away.
Its glimmer gives hope of a better today.
The darkness holds my prayers
And like the sun, they too, will rise again at
the start of the day.

Angry children fight on the streets.
With their guns and their gangs their future looks bleak.
But they are us … a side we don't see.
They hold our future and they put it at our feet.

There's more than the nightly news or the papers can do.
It's up to each of us to help pull this world through.
By reaching out to a troubled soul
We can make today grow into a better tomorrow.

It won't be easy … the pain will be great.
But if our heart is true then we know what we must do.
So reach out to someone in pain. Show them that you care.
We have a better world to prepare.

—Tirana Blok

Dionysian

The sun rises and sets day after day-
Its light beaming with brightness and reason.
Like a photograph it seems, and seeks,
to stop time.

Clouds sometimes beckon the horizon-
Airy and moving they flow, provoking our deepest emotions.
Like a musical composition they can be
associated with many different arrangements:
Rain; Lightning; Thunder;
in a Dionysian atmosphere.

The sun, with its light and reason,
is the symbol of our present-day culture
in which man comprehends the earth from afar.

The clouds, with their moving depths,
are characteristic of tribal times —
Times when women ran into the darkness,
unencumbered by domesticity and reason,
searching for their god, Dionysus.

—Lisa Heffernan

A Mother's Wish

It's not the fancy gifts you give to me at certain times.
It's not the colorful cards you buy with pretty words and
    rhymes
It's not a big show of affection or acts of love pretended
It's not of promises made and promises rescinded.
I'll tell you what it's all about, it's simple and it's free
It's a pat on the back, a little hug and a wink especially
    for me.
It's now, you're special, Mom you look pretty
Or something silly like that
But oh it's all those little things that make my heart pit-pat.
If I had but this one wish to make my dream come true.
It wouldn't be on expensive gift
Just a quiet mother I love you.

—Marilyn H. Welch

It's So Hard

There comes a day that we all must cry;
it's the day we say good-bye. You try to
hold back all your tears, but you can't
because the love you shared through
the years. It hurt so bad to lose the one
you had come to love so much; because
her spirit had a golden touch.
Nevertheless you can rest your tears;
because an angel of God has appeared.
She now can put her soul to rest; for
we all know that God knows what's best.
Although we know we'll never see her
face, deep in our heart we know she's
going to a better place.

—Roy Bogan, III

Got The Cyrus Virus

Well I got the cyrus virus
It told it on the Rido
Just sit and listening at him
and they ant nothing to take for
it cause it ant like the flu
I even went and seen him in Dalton, Georgia,
and Knoxville and it just keeps getting worse
and worse every day,
well it's just hard to get rid of it

—Star Elaine Mambur

Listen

To speak is easy, to listen is not
It's what we must learn to move from this spot
To listen to words or the wind or a song
Can shorten the way that we fear is too long
By listening we learn most of what's known
It's let us progress, it's how we have grown
What we've attained, the seeds that we've sown
Are from what we've heard, not we on our own
The tools of the present, come from the past
We've listened and learned how they can last
How can we learn what others are feeling
Listen and learn their words are revealing
In order that speech be a means for sharing
With what we teach we must be caring
To show that we care we must be attuned
That the tree of this knowledge be carefully pruned
It has often been said that knowledge is power
To listen's the water than makes its seed flower
Listen and learn so that we might gain
By what we have learned, what we've attained

—*Matthew DiMinno*

My Dad

When trying to make a decision, I throw in the dice.
It's you, my darling Father, I come to for advice.
When life seems to become unfair, tears fall from my eyes.
It's your compassion, Dad, that separates truth from all those lies.
And if someone asks, "Who is that lad?"
My heart swells and I reply, "Why, that's my Dad!"
When money continues to rule this world, sometimes I fall in the ditches.
It's with you, my loving Father, I know of true riches.
When God's forests come rumbling down, the world seems so small.
It's your knowledge and achievements, Dad, rebuilding structures tall.
And if someone asks, "Who is that lad?"
My pride sweeps and I reply, "Why, that's my Dad!"
When other men have dropped their seed, and forgot their sons and daughters wept,
It is through your goodness and unselfishness, Dad, our bond is stronger kept.
When the day comes when fate may pull us apart,
It's you, my sweet Father, who will be forever in my heart.
And if an angel asks, "Who is that lad?"
My prayers will shout, "Why it's my Dad!"

—*Patricia Sommers Barnett*

Columbia River Communion

I've been acquainted with the river.
I've felt its presence, wet and deep.
In empathy I've visited
The fishes where they sleep.

Sliding only a foot below
The deck on which I stroll,
The voice of the river calls me
From the swells that, endless, roll.

The river's knowledge of the past;
Its prescience of time to come,
And the power of its continuum
Commands me, "Come, come home!"

I back away with trembling breath
And steady my eager tread
Determined to resist the river's pull,
And to savor life instead.

The moment is gone and I turn away,
But with ecstasy aquiver
Knowing I have been, in a mystic way,
Acquainted with the river.

—*Mary B. Hurley*

Lost Love

Although you and I had to part,
   I've never gotten you out of my heart.
I think of times we used to share,
   how nice it felt to have you there.
And when I sleep it always seems,
   memories of you are in my dreams.
I miss you more than you'll ever know.
   my love for you burns deep in my soul.
Because you see I love you still,
   and as long as I live I always will...

—*William C. Woodson*

In A Corner Of My Mind

In a corner of my mind,
   I've tried to block the memory,
To protect me from the pain.
   Pretend I never knew you,
And never heard your name.
   But the walls I built aren't strong enough,
And though I fight my tears in vain,
   The feelings still come creeping through,
And the hurt is still the same.
   I wish that I could forget you,
Or make you disappear.
   I thought I could trust you,
But somehow I was wrong.
   How you could do this is beyond me.
The pain may go away,
   And the tears may pause.
But the painful memories will exist forever
   In a corner of my mind.

—*Tabitha Rice*

It's Easter Time Again

Hooray, Hooray, it's Easter once more,
Jesus has risen and opened the door,
For spring to warm us and greet us
And light the way;
The darkness of winter has passed away.

It's Easter time with renewed hope and love,
The blessings have come from Heaven above.
Again and again, every year we awake
To new life and a chance
To renounce all our hate.

So cherish these luscious days of Spring,
With robins and flowers and everything.
The sunshine, the clouds,
The gentle rain, that bless us all
Over and over again.

—*Mary Lucci*

A Poem

Why, is a poem called a poem. Is it meant to rhyme, form a jingle or create a song, but to me a poem is words of love and thought ..... a thing of beauty to be sought.

—*Tommie Lee Watkins*

The Flower

Rain drops fall to the ground
Later to from a stream
Suddenly a flower grew not knowing
Where it came from or how it came
It is the most beautiful thing you've ever seen
The only thing more beautiful is you

—*Mark Saleeby*

Joy Of My Life

Early one fall before the morning sun, a new
Joy entered my life. So tiny, so warm, so full
of life. The agony and pain was well worth it.
You are so unlike any other. You make my day,
when it has been dark and gray. You are the love
of my life. Your big brown eyes are the mirrors
of the world, for in them you I see all that could
be and I see me. Many a day I stand and watch you
and shed a tear. A tear of pain and a tear of joy.
I wonder what life holds in store for you.

Will you be happy? My motto to you my son,
"Stand tall and never fall. Be a man, the very best
that you can." As I enter the fall of my life and
you enter the early spring of your life, I wish you
all the very best that life has to offer. You are the
Joy of my life, My son.
　　　　—Sam H. Hughes

Who Will Step Forward?

How far have we come
Just a few more steps it may seem
Then who will step forward
And say we have reached the dream
How far must we go
Just a few more years it may seem
Then who will declare we have reached the dream
Equality, dignity, self-esteem and pride
Who will analyze the dream before it's put aside
How long will it last
How far must it go
What man or woman will step forward and say
I know!
　　　　—Wendell S. Hawkins

Happy Little Christmas Tree

I'm a happy little Christmas tree
just come and take a look at me
In the summer I'm bright and green
In the winter I'm snowy white
But I'm the prettiest of all at Christmas
Just you wait and see.
When I'll be red, green and blue and maybe silver too.
At Christmas that's me.
Yes, I'm a happy little Christmas tree
At Christmas I'll have a front row seat
to see Santa Claus
And he'll be dressed in his Christmas best
With a big bag of toys. And all the kids are full of joy
Now you see why I'm a happy little Christmas tree.
Then I see under my decorated feet all the presents
Wrapped so neat. Waiting for the kids to get a treat.
There's Mom and Dad with their faces lit up like mine.
Waiting for the kids to have a good time.
Now you can see why I'm a happy little Christmas tree.
　　　　—Robert C. Allen

It Hurts

It hurts to be mad
It hurts to be sad
But it really hurts when you're not there
Or when you don't say you care
It hurts when you break my heart
It hurts when we are apart
It hurts to know you may not come back
It hurts to think it might be a fact
It really hurts when you don't say I love you
　　　　—Mary Livesay

Loves Sweet Reality

Come walk with me my darling. You'll be amazed by what you'll
　　find.
Just take my hand and open your heart to the wonders of my mind.
Come explore these precious feelings and the love I have to give.
Come see this joyous world in which your love gave me to live.
The beauty and the wonder. Vast elation you've made known,
Are in my mind for you to see. Just ask and you'll be shown.
The peace that has engulfed me since you surrounded me with
　　love,
Is not for words for most know not the peace I do speak of.
That tranquil easy feeling when true love has been found.
Given pure and naturally from the heart without a sound.
So experience all these feelings whose depths with you I share.
Come fly with me into the clouds and walk with me on air.
And as we soar up through the clouds setting our love free,
Our two make one, this dreams becomes love's sweet reality.
　　　　—Severn

Untitled

Is love just another four letter word? Something people say
just to hurt others. Because as soon as you use it you let
down your guard and soon the pain comes, the pain of which this
word brings? What is love? To some people it's just a word,
something they say because they think it's the right thing to
do, but is love something that you can just think up, or is it
an emotion, something that you feel. People mistake thoughts
and feelings it's easy to do they both come from inside ones
inner self, but one is down low in your heart and isn't always
easy to get to. Love is something someone gives to someone
else to show how much they care. Love is a special gift that
is given to you, but like a drug people abuse it, think they
can casually use it, take it in stride, but sooner or later
someone gets hooked and they are all caught up in something
they don't understand. Love is a two way street but for some
people this street ends up in nothing more than a dead end.
Love to me is getting to know someone while they get to know
you. Sharing feelings with someone and not being embarrassed
to have them. To respect one another. To care for one
another.
　　　　—Sara Arreola

Sweet Surprises

Dainty white lace curtains; pastel pink from wall to wall,
Just waiting for a baby girl, so precious and so small.
I anticipate the moment I can hold her in my arms
And brag as all good parents do about her many charms.

Later when she's toddling, as mothers do with girls,
I'll dress her up with pearls and lace and fix her hair in curls.
Someday we'll share our secrets as we snuggle up in bed
And watch a scary movie while we paint our toenails red.

We'll shop until we drop—I'll buy her everything in sight!
We'll be the best of friends and we will never, ever fight.
When she's older we'll put makeup on, my grown-up girl and I.
And I'll have all the answers every time she asks me why.

I feel it in my heart that she will soon be on her way.
The doctor says that he suspects it might be any day.
And then I'll have the one thing that will make my dreams come
true,
A darling daughter all my own, so beautiful and new.

I check the nursery one last time and close the door real slow.
Then I wake my husband gently, telling him it's time to go.
The baby's born, and I confess I never felt such joy
When I became the mother of a bouncing baby boy.
　　　　—Linda J. Knaus

Retirement Is Bliss

In the office I sat, day after day
  Keeping books, there was no other way.
Some day, old enough I would be,
  To retire and come home, you see.

We flew to Jamaica, what a beautiful scene!
  Ninety degrees weather in January, I mean.
Mini vacations are what we have now,
  New places, new friends and how!

No, I wasn't anxious to get old.
  I'm younger than 10 years ago.
Magazines - time to read all of mine.
  Many books I've read every line.

Ceramics, doll making, crafts of all kinds.
  Time for volunteer works I find.
Take grand-children to the beach for fun.
  They all like games (even if I've won).

New and old recipes and times to bake.
  No alarm clocks startle me awake.
Aquatic exercises begin at 10:00,
  Bored?   This I don't intend.
    —Mary Barnes

Drugs

Drugs is one of the problems that plagues our society today;
Killing, maiming and robbing us of our safety in every way.

Whether it be on the streets or behind a closed door;
Drugs are causing grief and pain and much, much more.

There are some things that Drugs can cause you to do;
Like being cruel, irresponsible and dishonest too;

Drugs cause greed and violence in nearly every community;
Clearing a path a devastation at any given opportunity.

Adults and children alike are innocent victims of crime;
No one utters a word, fearing it may be them the next time.

Dealers use our children for cover-up, profits and greed;
Destroying the minds of our future and planting a bad seed.

Deformities present at birth occurs from Drugs effects;
The ending result is death or children becoming rejects.

Drugs give you the illusion that your totally in control;
Deceiving you into destroying your mind, body and soul.

So stop, look and see what Drugs are causing around you;
Drugs are surely the last thing you'll ever want to do.

Get your education, reach your goals, leave behind the rest;
Say No To Drugs and your on your way to achieving your best.
    —Stephanie S. Wallace

Clowns

Clowns are supposed to make you laugh, but not cry,
Laughter is good as gold, tears are dross,
Behind a clown's make-up, there can be pathos,
Pagliacci hid behind his make-up, a broken heart.

Cupid's arrow had pierced too deep,
He did nothing but sing, and once off stage, did weep,
Sunshine and rain mixed together,
Can produce a rainbow,
With streams of light in tow,
So it follows suit, that life is made up of ups and downs,
One day wearing a frown,
The next a crown, a halo of happiness.
    —Sylvia Ashley

Giving New Love A Chance

Caring, sharing, trusting is...
Laborious, frustrating, perplexing ...
Difficult to do
When love has hurt so much
Leaving the heart ...
Barren, unyielding, fruitless
Love's defeats leaves a doubting,
Questioning state of mind
Too cynical, skeptical to try again
That's when one needs to give new love a chance

New love is a refreshing breath of air
Scented like the smell of grass cut on a sunny day
Aromatically rich as a rose
New love, a perfumed bouquet of spring flowers
The essence bringing one's heart alive
Deeply breathing in the fragrant joys

Sweet and pure is the fruit of a bountiful new love ...
  Abundant in its caring ...plentiful in its sharing ...
    Natural, fertile and rich flavored like vintage wine
      —Terri L. Johnson

His Game's Name Was Love

One warm February day in Richmond, VA, beside his mother was
laid to rest, a quietly gentle prince of humble birth.
Whose color denied him playing tennis on most public courts
of clay or dirt. His close knit family prioritized academics
first, then pursued his dream, wielding a racquet across planet
Earth. Championships at Forest Hills and Wimbledon, broke
barriers, setting the pace. Sharing personally in South Africa's
struggle, helped bring justice to his race. Took our three young
children to see him practice on the Davis Cup Team. Years later,
as symphony receptions, guest of honor, autographed my napkin
with his name. Heart problems, in his life's prime, caused great
concern, noting from competition, his exceptional courage taught
many youths to learn. To play life's game rules on the court,
rather than breaking them and landing in court. Life's greatest
challenge, he wasn't able to back, when media headlined his
illness, medical science has yet to defeat. His grace, strength and
dignity helped erase much stigma, giving hope for the AIDS cause.
Funeral celebrations of his life was interjected with loud applause.
Wife, Jeannie, and daughter, camera, should be proud of loving
tributes.
    —Laura Crowder

City Of Angels

I live in the City of Angels,
Land where only demons survive.
Home of the fallen angels.
Where innocence comes when it's willing to die.
I'd begun to give into temptations,
My will to survive, gave into the fight.
My virtues devoured by wicked sensations,
Of being who kept me away from the light.
Then on mystical day, out of the blue.
Fate decided to bring me to you.
Presenting me with wings anew,
You made me feel your love was true.
Now your gone, I'm here alone,
I fight to keep away my fear,
And evil deeds of which I'm prone.
Oh how I wish that you were here,
With me, in the City of Angels.
    —Nicole Rhea Hansen

Free Your Mind...

Free your mind,
Learn how to be color blind.
Don't judge people by the way they look,
Just like you don't judge the cover of a book.
Don't think the kid on the back
Seat can't read and write, just because he's black.
Don't be afraid to say hello
To the new girl in your class, just because her skin is yellow.
Don't think the boy named Pablo
Is naive and less ambitious, just because he's from down below.
Don't assume that all whites are snotty
And that they have no respect for minority.
C'mon, you know we're all human beings,
let's not hurt each other's feelings.
Instead, let's accept one another,
And join our hands in unity together.

—Maria Ailen Borromeo-Dolatre

Missing Feather

This is the way, walking by myself
  learning to love
Smiling, head up and arms back
  The pain wasn't too heavy til I met
You, experienced liar with a graceful sway
  My, I, rebellious heart drown in tears of your say.
Tripping over my mindless soul,
  What is see-through?
Music, laughter and claps of approval
  While into the passage, my flowers bud blossom,
Reformational soul and spirit as my feet ferment
Walking along with the sunlight,
  blind by the dark trees as you watch
the sadness aroma swifts by me.
    I'm walking by myself learning to love;
   You for what, I sing softly with the birds,
   While flying away from the prey. Turn around
and looked, learned and love as I save my day.

—Stephanie Woodall Jawaid

The Storm

Proud men and women were sent to the storm,
Leaving behind their families and babies unborn.
I had my doubts and I had my fears,
Praying each night as my eyes filled with tears.

Fighting for our country scared as can be,
Wondering if another day they will ever see.
Barely getting their rest and losing sleep,
Praying to God their soul he will keep.

Yellow ribbons displayed and flags flying high,
Mourning families cried as they said their final goodbye.
I never thought this country would be in a war,
Don't our leaders give a care anymore.

Watching the evening news for the latest,
Bush & Hussein competing to be the greatest.
Lives being lost over oil prices,
I wish they had the heart to end this crisis.

Prisoners of war want to be set free,
Hoping that the two leaders would soon agree.
Brave soldiers fighting in a country far away,
Asking God for world peace is what I pray.

—Yolanda Joiner

Human Spirit

The rain washes over my face
leaving not a trace of tears
scars from the fears of years passed by
and yet... I still want to try

To begin again and again
a true survivor from the wars
of circumstances and lies
and yet ... I still want to try

I feel an ocean of beauty within me
to come forth upon this planet earth
a new beginning - a rebirth
from all the evil and the cries
and yet ... I still want to try

If you ever get lonely, need a true friend
if the road seems too weary, and you cannot bend
call to me - I will come
and listen to your sorrows
of the days gone by
and yet... I know
you will still want to try

—Nancy E. Keeler

The Loss

Death steals away the ones you love,
Leaving you to face life on your own.
You temporarily stop believing in God up above,
And no one calls you on the phone.
You walk around for a while in a daze,
And your friends are there now to help you again
You're feeling better in so many ways,
Even though it still hurts every now and then.
Eventually the hurt and anger become a dull ache,
And you've put your memories away in your heart on a shelf.
  You've learned that life is never a piece of cake,
and the strength to get through this . . .
lies within yourself.

—Sharon L. Torres

A Prayer For Life

If I am to drown,
let it be in the North Sea
where the water's cold can numb
me past caring for the world.

If I am to die by fire,
let it be while rescuing a stranger's child
from that crackling anger.

If I am to be a traffic fatality,
let me swerve to avoid a deer
scrambling across an unnatural path
we have cut across her land.

If I am to be claimed by AIDS,
let me be counted among the many
while taking no one with me,
and let my obituary not mince words.

If my heart stops short,
let someone else see with my eyes,
let me help even at the end.

But if I am to live
let it be with you.

—P. Dean Pearson

Black Unity

Let B stand for B eauteous, not for B ullets
Let L stand for L earning, not for L ooting
Let A stand for A chieving, not for A rson
Let C stand for C ultivate, not for C rack
Let K stand for K indness, not for K illing

Let U stand for U pright, not for U ptight
Let N stand for N otable, not for N otoriety
Let I stand for I nsight, not for I ndifference
Let T stand for T hrifty, not for T houghtless
Yes Y ou be all Y ou can, develop Y ourselves.

  —Yvonne Pamela Shepherd-Marshall

Silent Night

Silent night, how sweet the sound, that saved a wretch like me
Let there be peace on Earth, and let it begin with me.
Hallowing cries from youths mislead. Misleading. James, 4 and
10. Hiding his face, hiding his soul, and mounting the steps
to number 411. And silenced from the roar of media, and shut
away for correction. A trigger's flash, a stray
thought...mislead. Dust blown tears echo from the belly of
abysses unseen. Mislearned. Mary, 12 years. Raking her
mother's purse for one more moment of rainbow-drenched
spirals...strobe stars...and choruses of pretty lights. Laying
on this satin pillow, her eyes wide with greedy expectation.
As her mother lowers the enameled handles over her still form.
Mislearned. Carrie, age 13, and not yet a woman; again enters
the sheets which envelope her pain. everyday challenges
becoming a war, thanks to the solution she found. Seeping
depression...sanity ajar...Screams capsulated in her tears as
he again forces himself upon her. Muted. Misloved. Peace on
Earth! Goodwill toward men... One thousand, nine hundred and
ninety-three years have yielded. How long? How long until
another, Silent Night?

  —Susan Hassell

Oh, Israel, Promised Land Of The Bible

Oh, Israel, promised land of the Bible,
Let us cultivate your deserts
Into blooming orchards and fertile fields.
Let us build foundations for the future
On the history of the past
With a firm grasp on the present.
Let your land be a land of peace
And sanctuary for all people.
Let us live in the warmth of the sun
That extends into our hearts.
May the land of milk and honey of the Bible
Again give forth the sweet fruits of loving labor
And dream for peace.
But if we must fight for our cherished land,
Give us the strength to preserve the laws of the Torah
And remember that while the land rests with the people,
Our hearts belong to God.

  —Shirley Cheifetz Silverburg

Going Crazy

  Going crazy, want to come?
  Let's leave reality behind
   Let's take our thoughts
 And burn them beyond recognition
 Let's take our sorrows to the extreme
And shelter our souls from the rest of the world
 Let's take everything we've ever learned
  And disregard it from our heads
 Let's create a paradise of passion
  To ignite the flames of hell
   That live inside our hearts
   Going crazy, want to come?
   Just turn on your t.v. set

—Mark Rosier

Rockport Memories

The morning call of a raucous crow
Lets me know it's time to be up, on the go,
As with Orff-like pattern and precision
It announces town-wide a personal decision
To enjoy a God-given day in Rockport.

Then the Town Clock follows with its message
In tones round and resonant, announcing the hour
Reminding all: "Make the most of this day!"
It's a special spot, this beautiful place...
Whether off to work or just to play, in Rockport.

If the beach calls, waves lapping beige damp sand,
Add footprints with terns, gulls and town pigeons
That land, sociably sharing the beach
But always just out of reach, on a balmy day
Left from summer's display, in Rockport

From a pond on the hill, beachward running,
A fresh-water rill travels down over rocks,
Its sparkling flow all birds welcome and know
As they happily drink near the ocean's brink
On a bright end-of-summer day in Rockport.

  —K. Helena R. Laramee

Every Day Is s Piece of Gold!

Every day is a piece of gold.
Letters lining up to enter my brain.
News waits me to read.
Politicians, sociologists, naturalist, artists face me
on T.V., newspapers, and books.
What do I lack?
My God!
You do love me in our color world.

Every day is a piece of gold.
Birds wait me to sing in chorus.
Trees have contest with me, oh, who grow up faster?
Flowers smile to me, oh, who win more appreciations?
on air, ground, and hearts.
What do I need?
My God!
You do love me in our cold world.

Every day is a piece of gold.
I put it in a furnace, to build pure human faces.

  —Millie Lee

Reminiscence

At the ripe old age of eighty-seven
Life has not all been hell
Nor has it all been heaven
With the fine young son to take my place
And a beautiful grandson to join the race
A loving wife, who is a fine cook
Who, at any time reads me like a book
I think of the young man who liked to play
Chasing the girls night and day
Now I walk down the street with cane in hand
And wish I were back where it all began
I see pretty girls with their skirts in the wind
Gosh, it would be great to be only Eighty again.

If we could see the same girls 30 years hence
With added weight that make the scales wince
With blue and grey hair and a wrinkle or two
Ask them their age, they lie about that, too
With too much red on cheek and lips
Their skirts no longer fly in the wind
'Cause it can't get 'em over their hips.

  —Les Ferguson

520

Singing Is Living

No matter what might be wrong,
    Life is better with a song.
Sing, even when you are flat;
    Trying harder will overcome that.

Now, some people like to whistle.
    But, sometimes, this causes a bristle.
Whistling, particularly in dark,
    Will, generally, make dogs bark.

Always be happy, when you sing.
    Clean fun, this probably will bring.
Others will know you are feeling fine,
    Although, the old grouches will sometimes whine.

Singing will keep you at your best.
    Surely you can sing without much rest.
It will help you breathe, deep and strong.
    Time will pass, and it won't take long.

Please sing softly to those who are ill.
    Remember, they won't listen against their will.
Show you care and love them very much.
    Smile, when you give that friendly touch.

    —*Raymond A. Wells*

Life's Not The Same

I'm writing these words through tears and pain,
Life is so empty it's hard to stay sane.
Some say Soul Mates is what we were.
Being in your presence could make me purr,
Like a cute small kitten being held in your arms,
And your smiling blue eyes were a part of your charms.
I'll never forget when you went away,
I begged and pleaded to get you to stay.
You left not only me, but all our friends too,
You were so unique, we all loved you.
Life is not the same, it never will be.
The night that you died Sonny, you took part of me.
People tell me to get on with my life,
But living to me was being your wife.
How do I turn this love off, that I have for you?
I can't think of my future, I don't know what to do.
I'm told that in time the pain will go away,
It's been two and a half years, my pains here to stay.
I'll keep on existing, and of course I will cry,
But my Darling Sonny, I cannot say Good-Bye.

    —*Sue Simmons*

Me Myself And I

    Intelligence. Intelligence is being able to understand
life. Thee eternal quality of God. Intelligence is being
able to take hold of racism and reverse the cycle. Able to be
among evil doers and not let it effect a real being. Creating
a path for others to follow.

    Being able to obtain life riches without losing my soul,
my youth, my pride. It takes intelligence to acquire and apply
one's lore. I am inspired to write, to tell a story of a proud
Black woman. Who has much to share.

    Shortly, after Leanetha, got married for the first time,
she realized people she had known and people she had not. Were
people to be like an ostrich with his head buried in the sand.

    She would listen and observe. She felt people were living
empty lives. For following someone else to dictate. She did
not want this for herself. She set out on a quest for the
truth. What she uncovered was the ultimate truth.

    Life is a gift judge not unless you are willing to be judged
love is the key
We are our brothers keeper

    —*Leanetha Smith-Darby*

Dawn

I love to see dawn come
Lifting a curtain from the hills
Exposing a glimmer of azure sky

Branches and foliage reaching upward
Blossoms defining them with color
A kaleidoscope of nature's diversity

Light sifting through a leafy canopy
Shimmering reflections of early morn
The orange glow of a rising sun

Hills quilted with abundant vegetation
Fragrant aromas wafted by a gentle breeze
Honeysuckle, wisteria and chamomile

I love to see dawn come
Bringing a radiant new day
Overflowing with the joie de vivre'

    —*Maxine B. Mayer*

First Space Launch

Straight the spaceship stands, proud and eager,
Lightly held to earth. Through a night,
A day, and another floodlit night
The countdown ticks away.

Behind the barricade watchers gather,
Quietly talking, choosing their positions.

In the rose-gold dawn its sleek white skin
Glows shiny pink as living flesh.
Movement, around its base and up its sides.

The crowd presses forward; eager,
Leaning into the final seconds.
Chanting the count in urgent voice...

...five...four...three...two...one...
LIFTOFF!!

Straight and true it rises,
Thundering upwards to pierce the vault of heaven
And carry Man beyond his skies.

    —*Vida Louise Marks*

Guilt Be Gone...

For the dark shadows of guilt lays upon us,
    Like a blanket, covers the cold;
For the guilt becomes our nightmares,
    For words unspoken, words untold;
The living get questioned,
    The dead get acquitted;
For crimes of silence,
    Unconsciously committed;
For the simple words of "I Love You"
    Often forgotten to be said;
Could have eased the minds of the living,
    And added peace to the dead....

    —*Vickie Lynn Lang*

A Dream

        A dream is a wish,
    like something from the wilderness.
It's wild with fear, and gushes with hope.
It's something from deep down in our hearts,
        we feel it can not be sold.
    A dream can soar above the mountains,
        it can swim beneath the sea,
    it can gallop across the prairie,
        and it's inside of you and me.

    —*Lindsey Ann Mattson*

Yeu

It creeps upon the midnight hour,
  Like a thief in the night.
No warnings and no delays.
  It searches for the soul within,
For within the soul is the heart.
  And within the heart are found many things,
Things that are kept hidden.
  When Yeu finds its destiny,
Things will be made known
  For all the world to see,
For all the world to see.
  That's what is caused by Yeu:
The searcher of the soul,
  The searcher of the weak.
    —*Lizadia Melendez*

Weaver

Birds, flowers, blue indigo; this old man sits and weaves
Like a withered mannequin glued to a wooden chair;
His eyes flutter as blue butterflies.
Bobbins go in and out of the heavy wool;
Not one thread falls to floor. His colors are memories
of brilliant leaves fallen in enchanted gardens
He knew once long before; nobody dares speak to him
As his fingers twine up the rows of calendulus
Into the ivy vines; this old man nobody knows;
Each morning in the same grey chair, he brings the poppy
threads to bear; his flowers are never quite the same
In glory of their flame.
He dares not to speak for fear, death calls his name
And all the orange and amber petals suddenly disappear
Into his lap like withered April madrigals.
Birds, flowers, blue indigo; this old man sits and weaves;
His shuttle is a book of ancient memories.
The aspen trees stand very tall guarding the wooden chair
Where the weaver weaves. I dare not make a sound or call
For fear his poppy petals fall.
    —*W. Edwin VerBecke*

The Poet

I'm a poet who plays with words of light
Like an artisan I build bridges of rhythms in the night
My fingers run through brushing the ink like tinsel
My words inspire confidence and hope in a soft whisper
As a poet my destiny is to inspire
All those who read with passion and desire
With rhythm and music in my writings you will find
A key that will open the doors of your mind
Letting me scope a place in your soul
that only a poet can grasp and behold
    —*Luis A. Molina*

Living

  Living is something we all must do
  Like it or not the statement is true
  Sometimes it seems so hard to achieve
  Living this life full of broken dreams
  You often wish, for things to come true
Like having someone there, who truly loves you
  Living to survive isn't living at all
It's really just making it trying not to fall
  Living to achieve is what you must do
  Gaining from knowledge and prosperity too
Once this is accomplished living isn't so bad
You're learning from your mistakes and correcting
    the ones that you've had.
    —*Lamarr D. Wimberly*

"I Am An Old Woman"

I am an old woman with lines on my face,
Like roads I have travelled that can't be erased.
Searching for something to do till I die,
Pondering the choices on which to rely.

My memory fails me, my vision grows dim,
I fear if I fall, my bones may not mend.
I am still the same person I once was, inside,
Helplessly trapped in a slow-shrinking hide.

Like fallen rose petals and butterfly wings,
Moldy leaves uncovered by spring,
Caught up in a whirlwind and then tossed aside,
Alone in a corner as if trying to hide.

I am an old woman, where is my place?
No prized possession, just taking up space.
With memories that haunt me, disturbing my rest,
I am an intruder, no longer a guest.

Come, sit here beside me, my friend, and converse,
Not mindful of riches or empty purse,
Master or servant, we survived the strife
And are given God's wisdom in the twilight of life.
    —*Sylvia A. Gould*

Travel Dreams

There are so many places I've longed to go
Like Spain, Rio and Ole Mexico.
I've dreamed of Alaska and felt cold winds blow
And thought I saw huskies run in the snow.
I've yearned to see Switzerland and look far below
From the Alps up above - while in my Chateau.
I'd love to see Egypt and said down the Nile
Just like Cleopatra - I'd do it with style.
My friends have all toured-both England and France
When they spoke of their travels - I went into a trance
I've been seen at airports and boat docks as well
Waving to my friends as they'd fly or they'd sail.
I've said "Bon Voyage" and "Goodbye" when we'd part
They've said "You'll be with us in spirit and heart."
I will not be sailing or taking a jet
My fear of the dangers have me too upset.
I don't feel I'm destined to go very far
Unless I can get there by train or by car.
    —*Sandra Phillips*

The Spice And Soul Of Life

Like the pages of a novel once read - then quickly turned.
Like the ending of a chapter in the book of life we've learned.
To reflect the many years that passed and to savor moments dear
do we really know the gist of life as year succeeds to year?
"Those were the days that men were men" so goes the song of old,
lest we tend to forget the past we watch the times unfold.
Then indeed the world we knew was in a frightful state,
Pearl Harbor jolted us to war and tried to seal our fate.
As stars hung in the window panes of homes throughout the land,
they told of men and women who so bravely took a stand.
Shouldn't we recall that hate breeds fear and fear leads to
mistrust, the lesson to be learned again past history now a
must. The future holds for each of us an unknown scene ahead,
with faithful trust and steady steps we journey now instead
of looking back with sad regret we live each day with care,
and bring to others renewed strength that only hope can dare.
If knowledge is the spice of life then music is the soul,
to listen to a classic tune is to be completely whole. The
secret now of staying young is to keep an active pace, you may
not reap a rich reward but you'll receive God's fullest grace.
    —*Van Wunderlich*

Clouds

I see the soft, white lace of them
like the gate to heaven in crystal blue
soft steam rolling in purity
the sun shines through
golden amber and silver white
bright like the light of God
and I can fly
I spread my wings
see through the spirit eagle's eyes
I climb and climb
until I'm so high
the earth spins beneath me
and I soar on astral winds
I touch the edge of the starry black night
it is the face of my only true friend
the emptiness of galactic space
here I am whole
and know I have arrived
—*William A. Norman*

To The Republic For Whatever It Stands!

One by one the Anti-Anxious soldiers
lined the battlefield...
With bodies clothed in green cloth they
marched and bellowed out a sad croon...
"Hey!" "Hip!" "Hop!" "Ho." One two, three,
do you know what's in store for you and
me?...
Their eyes full of tears, their minds
full of wonder...
The cannons and grenades roared like
thunder...
Human flesh sailed through the air...
Eyes, cheeks arms, legs, heads, internal
organs... Do you really care!
Hearts, ears, toes, even some fingers...
Time please pass... How long must they linger?...
One by one the Anti-Anxious soldiers
lined the battlefield...
And two by two in Star-spangled boxes
they returned home...
—*Levada Overton*

The Voice

He looked out with eyes unseeing,
Listening through the crowd for a voice,
A voice unlike any other he had ever heard,
A voice that had authority,
But was gentle and full of love and understanding,
A voice that commanded the elements to obey,
But yet a voice that loved the unlovable,
As the voice grew nearer, he knew that this was the time,
He had only one chance,
"Master" he cried "Master have mercy",
And the voice stopped, and turned,
The same voice that brought sight to the blind,
Hearing to the deaf, children to the barren,
Brings hope to us,
This is the time to cry out,
It may be our only chance.
—*Ruth A. Grubb*

The Little Ones

I look around the world and I see
little children looking at me

Their eyes show the pain, the ache of abuse,
with wounded hearts that say, "what's the use?"

Their souls are disfigured and mangled
by the perversions of man,
their innocence has been taken
by the devil's evil plan

Their cries churn deep from a broken heart
and echo without end into every part

Are there those who will listen?
Are there those who will hear
this symphony of anguish,
of torment,
of fear?

I look around the world and I see,
I look around my city and I see,
I look around my neighborhood and I see

Those little ones are looking at me.
—*Sylvia Clemons*

The Loving Saints

In the realm of the king of kings
Lives the greatest army that's ever been seen
With tremendous power the roam the stares
Demanding glory for the almighty Lord
For all goodness is why they fight
For Gods love they do what's right
In his presence the saints shall sing
In his name they do all great things
They honor his word each day and night
They give him thanks for love and life
In their greatness satan shall fall
They will destroy all evil great and small
Heaven shall descend and take its place
Then the Lord shall dwell with his loving saints
—*Ronald E. Spell Jr.*

She's Crying In The Dark

She's crying in the dark.
Long gone are the days of insult and abandonment.
She's crying in the dark.
No more unwelcomed touches as fear and guilt find a home.

She's crying in the dark.
Loneliness and desire walk hand in hand.
A soul weak and trembling beneath a toughened exterior.

She's crying in the dark.
Hidden are the feelings of sadness.
Buried are the emotions of truth.
She's left crying in the dark.
—*Vickie B. Miller*

So Many Tears...

Hasn't she cried a thousand tears
Losing her son was her only fear.
You took him from her one raining night.
You've darken her world - it's no longer bright.
The death of her husband was just the start.
Of the pain that would soon rack her heart.
As she grew stronger with each passing day.
A disease developed that was here to stay.
She had to survive - she had to fight.
But she lost the will on that rainy night.
—*Marie T. Patrick*

Ode To A Lightpole: Our Urban Metal Sentinel

(An Anti-Graffiti Poem)

Oh, Lightpole, so stately and tall,
Looked up to for guidance by one and all,
We can find our paths with your light.
You safeguard our way, in the darkness of night.

Oh, Lightpole, how with dirt did you get so smeared?
For you, obviously, some citizens had no fear!
They marred your grace with scribblings in black,
Knowing you could not answer back.
Upon you they stuck paper messages of housing and jobs,
Not caring that from you, your grace and dignity they robbed.

Oh, Lightpole, we will try to keep you clean,
So that your beautiful shapes can be seen.
We'll restore your function to give us light,
And not demean you into an urban blight.

> —*Rosalind Pinto*

Untitled

The moon searches over a sullen sky,
Looking for clouds to rest on and sigh.
Dreaming of lost loves - of mouchlens so fair,
Or of finding a prince who would really care
The water ripples in moonlight or gloom.
And the moon frames a halo around a lone loon.
the night shivers with fear at his eerie cry.
And loneliness fills the land and the sky.
Soon the darkness will pale,
Night doffs her clock and prepares to leave
Her work is done.
There is a still before the oncoming sun
Stirs the dormant sky awake
As he prepares to span the heavens on his daily run

> —*Rose Harkins*

The Little Mouse

Through a crack in the wall, out came a mouse,
    looking for some cheese.
  No one was home, in the big old house,
    So the mouse did what he pleased.

    Into the kitchen, he did scurry,
      To see what he could find.
    He knew that he would have to hurry,
      'Cause he didn't have much time.

    On the counter, there sat a cake,
      Oh, it looked so yummy.
    He gathered up the crumbs to take,
      And filled his little tummy.

  The door did slam, the family is back,
    But don't be filled with sorrow.
  The mouse ran back, into the crack,
    And will be back tomorrow!

> —*Rosemary Ingram*

The Reality Of Things

Peeling off the layers of self deception,
Looking for the truth about myself.
Fighting off the waves of accusation,
And oppositions of those who would oppose.
Digging through all this verbiage,
Looking for the truth; about God, about,
The reality of things.

> —*Robert A. O'Brien*

Sea Travelers

As I was sitting on the sandy shore,
Looking out across the sea,
Wondering if the ships I saw,
Were looking back at me,
I wondered if the people there
Were happy and content,
Or were they just pretending,
Was it really what they meant?
And I wondered if their travels,
Would take them to distant shores,
To London Town, or Singapore, or even Zanzibar.
I wondered what it'd be like,
To just sit and talk awhile,
About where they went and what they saw,
Or just to see them smile,
And when they'd remember back again,
At all the things they did,
I bet that they'd be ready,
To travel the seas again.

> —*Nora Wright*

No Pain

Alone in my room tears in my eyes.
Looking out the window at the pretty blue skies.
Thinking to myself why always me?
Wondering why, I'm as sad as can be.
But of course there is no pain.
No not for me.
Crying away with no were to go.
Alone in my world with no sense to show.
Don't understand why my family argues, and fights
But of course there is no pain, for me tonight.
No not for me.
Don't know why it had to be I.
I get so sad I start to cry.
Don't want to go, but I must say bye.
Now I must go no tears to show.
With no pain, no pain for me.

> —*Tandinika Smith*

Lest We Forget

From the moment of your anxiously awaited birth
Love and favors have been lavished on you.
To your mother and daddy you were the dearest thing on earth.
To brothers and sisters you were extra special too.

Life is so wonderful it is not our desire to forfeit one day.
YOU are YOU - because mother and daddy passed life your way.
You owe them lots of love they were always there for you.
Are your payments up to date or are you overdue?

Your life could have been rough - for all around you to see.
Had mother and daddy not met your needs and lovingly bounced
  you on their knee.
They met your needs because they loved you - their precious child.
Your smiles and laughs pleased them so - your tears drove them
  wild.

It matters not how old we are or where on the road of life we
  might be.
If its happiness you are seeking - then love is the key.
Besides mother and daddy, and brothers and sisters, many others
  will bring love into your life.
I thank God for my precious children and a wonderful loving wife.

Go to a cemetery and notice all the beautiful flowers you see.
All trying to say, "I love you" to someone that used to be.
Let us show our love while the precious gift of life is ours.
Don't wait too late and have to say it with beautiful flowers.

> —*Leon Griffith*

First Love Sign

It came a time in life; where the present became the past
Love came and went as a reality, and you wondered if the world
would last. You began living one day at a time. Not looking
ahead nor looking behind. But you were always wondering.
With just one thing on thy mind... Love, love, love, love, love
For it had hit you for the first time.
You were excited, but you were scared. It took you awhile to
see the first sign. Because the signs are not all the same.
For it can be a kiss or a stare; As that love grows stronger,
That sign will always be there.
One morning you might awake and your relationship is gone.
But the love never stops, your memories will always be there
of what you've done. Sure it will hurt for a long time; and
there'll be times it hurts more;
But that's only because you're thinking...thinking of all the
times before. There's no need to look ahead
Because with an attitude like that your love will soon be dead!

—*Sara Bartels*

Love

How do you tell it apart.
Love has to come from the heart.

Just when you think you've found a new start
Love can tear you apart.

One person can come and one can go.
But the time it takes to learn love no one will know.

It just happens in day or night
Love can come from hindsight

But learning love is the biggest test of all
Whether in the spring, summer, winter, or fall

When you find someone you love take care
If you do, their love will always be there

If everyone loves one another
There will be peace, happiness to our sister and brother.
Love what's your meaning.

—*William Robert Davis*

My Wife

Here's this woman in my life,
    Love her so she's my wife.
Anything I need she's always there,
    No other love to compare.
When I'm sick she'll understand.
    Treats me like a baby, I'm a man.
Have a problem that I can't solve.
    Never one bad enough, she can't resolve.
She's always with me, body, soul and mind.
    Never says no, never declines.
Explores my questions, and tells me what's right.
    Always there to hold me tight.
I've never been this close before.
    To this woman that I adore.
Love this lady love her so,
    Hope to God, she never let's me go.
Can't say enough about this girl.
    All I got, all I got in the world.

—*Leslie G. Kimble*

The Greatest Is Love

Love that is self-sacrificing - Love that is so dear.
Love that bears all things; it cast out fear.

Love covers transgressions - forgiveness and hopes for the best.
Never keep account of injury — endures the most severe test.

Love rejoices with truth and never fails —
It is long-suffering when trying situations prevail.

Love is an expression of caring and sharing for those in need.
Never expecting or looking for returns for unselfish deeds.

Love looks for opportunities to uplift troubled hearts and minds.

To brighten and bring smiles to those unhappy faces because
this wonderful emotion of love is so compassionate and kind.

—*Sandra L. Hollinger*

Love And Sex And Marriage

Sex and love were not equated
Love was special sex x-rated.

Love and marriage would someday arrive
Sex was happenstance it satisfied a drive.

But if sex and love are not equated
Then sex and marriage might be overrated

Now, love and sex and marriage were never the same for me
I should bring them altogether but I'm having some difficulty.

To bring all three into harmony is more than just a yearning
If they're to work including me I must change my early learning

—*Sol Tannebaum*

Caught By Surprise

I loved a man so much...before...
Loved and trusted him with all my life
One day...he just got up and took his love away..
I often ask myself, is it something I did?
I often pray to God he'd show me and not keep it hid

The pain so often stays...
The memory of it all will never go away...

Some time has passed now...
The pain has lessened...
A little stronger I'm sure sometimes insecure...

"Know that I love you"
"Believe in me"...
"Know that I'll always be here for you"...
Are familiar quoted words

Laid my heart out on the line...
Caught by surprise another time.

—*Whittonia M. Hobson*

Each Of Us

Each of us with our secret gifts,
Magic potions, lovely notions,
Wanting to be shared. Waiting to be aired.
Each of us a half, a whole,
A mind, a soul, a heart and yet
A part of a better, richer more
Looking for the door, the key, the you, the me.
I'd always dreamed and never seen
Always tried and never been.
Always thought but never knew.
Until at last, I discovered that the gift I
always sought was you.

—*Renee A. Goggans*

Alone

How does it feel to be alone? When nobody
loves you, when nobody cares. You find yourself
just being nobody to talk to, nobody to stare.
No one to say hi or goodbye. No one to tell you
they care. Some will say I care but down inside
they don't care. At those times everyday you
wish you had a person your own age down by your
side. When you look no one is there. At those
times you wonder why. Why was I born? Then you
say why no one knows you're alive. Why live no
one to do it for. But then I guess that's the
way I was to be, I was born alone, so - I'll stay
alone, be alone, play alone, talk alone. Someone
would say why you're alone you would say because
the word alone is more than a word. The word
alone describe my life.
     That's what it feels to be alone!

— *Lissette Padilla*

Freedom

Look at that bright light in my eyes
Ma'am it is pretty
Ain't it freedom?

It's love in a gentle bit,
Not master throwing his whip
Ain't it freedom?

Running through streams, meadow and mottons
Not in the hot fields picking cotton
Ain't it freedom?

Moses is coming soon tonight then everything
gonna be alright

The star from the north is going to take
us home
With God help we'll never be alone
     That Freedom!

— *Natalie R. Arnold*

Thoughts

          You are what you think you are:
               Maybe a bum, maybe a star

          You are what you think you are:
               For thoughts are living things
          Thoughts can bury you deep in the mud,
               Or help you soar with wings

          You are what you think you are:
               For thoughts are living things
          Everything you see, is a thought:
          Manifest, with the luggage it brings

          You are what you think you are:
               So think your own success
          Born to go far, you may shine like a star
          If your thought life won't settle for less

          Cultivate your thought life well:
               For thoughts are like your garden
          Weeds will come, and weeds will grow,
          And choke at your heart till it hardens

Thoughts seek expression so there lies the lesson:
          Think of the luggage they bring

— *Michael P. Garnes*

The Flagpole

During early school years, it shadowed and drew me like a
magnet, until one day, urged on by two taunting high school
companions, I shed shoes and socks to begin the assault on a
benign enemy. The first few feet are easy.

With height, caution increases and speed slips away.
Past twenty feet, toes touch toes on narrowing widths.
Perspiring hands use trousers as towels.
Wind velocity increases sway with the next pole length.
Would the pole drop me like the young sapling years ago?
I hesitate; the pole wavers, yet seems to imprint
"Proceed cautiously" on my clammy hands.
Adversary becomes friend, steadying me, urging me upward.

Finally, triumph! Suspended in mid air, I caress the cold cap.
The exposed view past trees and rooftops turns fearsome
as I glance down at gaping mouths and unforgiving cement.
A few quick breaths, an inner calm; a moment to savor.
A rapid descent blisters hands and feet to a burning red.
Friends stand in awe as my eyes and heart salute
that fragile friend—
Etched forever in warm memories of steel.

— *Wesley A. Edwards*

Blackwater Refuge, Maryland

Magenta skyline lays the day to rest.
Majestic heron steps his stately way.
Heraldic eagle swoops across his bay.
Busy muskrat paddles to his nest.
This is their refuge: here the weariest
Worldly creature comes to feed and stay,
Footloose and fed, a month, a week, a day.
Refuge—a vital need most manifest.

Those who enjoy such respite in their flight
And happily rebuild their strength anew,
Regardless of their species, size or hue
(And this of course is every creature's right)
I'd sorely envy, save that I delight
In one sweet, joyous, lasting refuge — you.

— *E. Donald Davis*

Strictly Confidential

What could I give that would
     make his eyes shine

This dear little, sweet little
     son of mine?

So we visited Santa Claus today
And be whispered his hopes in the age old way.

"What did you ask from Santa, dear?
You talked so low that I couldn't hear.

Then with a wise little nod
     of his wise little head

And a wise little smile
"You'll see"! he said.

— *Rachel L. Sykora*

Love

Love is what brings two people together, to
love one another, care for one another, and to
be with one another. It is a wishing well, to
wish that you can spend your time and love
with someone who you care for very much. It
can bring tears to your eyes, sorrow to your
heart, and it can bring thoughts to your
mind. So love is a precious thing to two
people who care and love one another.

— *Susan A. Stephens*

Emotional Scars

So many feelings more than one thought, spinning round my head
making dizzy my heart. My feelings and thoughts of love for
you have run true, spinning round and round, but feelings and
thoughts of hate are there too spinning round and round.
Triumph to the one who wins your heart, God knows I've tried.
Once I believed I had it, but you tore it from my hands. You
cut me with cruel and desperate words and left me bleeding of
pain alone. Emotional scars run deep. You told me once your
heart was mine forever, but I guess to you our forever ended
yesterday. You told me give up now and let things alone, we
weren't destined to be together and we were never carved in
stone. Emotional scars run deep. Love and hate spinning
round and round is what I feel for you, spinning round my teary
soul crying love and hate because of you. Need I say?
Emotional scars run deep.

—*Story Earlene Tylor Hofstetter*

Memories, Memories

Memories, memories, what great joys they hold,
Making room for the new yet keeping the old.
With this precious gift, God did bless,
All mankind, so that we might possess,
The power to keep forever in our mind,
All the love and happiness in life we find.
It keeps the "old, so young and alive,
Remembering when they were twenty five."
Imagine not remembering the childhood you knew,
All your hopes, all your dreams, that came true.
Or not remembering the happiest day of your life,
Or the love of your parents, children, husband or wife,
Their faces, their smiles, and their tears,
Their everyday courage, their everyday fears.
Or the love of friends that you have known,
All their kindness, the love they've shown.
Memories grow and grow, they have no end,
They are truly "man's greatest friend,"
For without them all of life's joy and sorrow,
Would be lost and today "be just like tomorrow."

—*Philomena Notaro*

Alaskan Old Town Road

Skating at the Lily pond, was so much fun,
many games were won... Walking to windmill hill,
along the way red fireweed, bloomed in early may...
Passing the harbor, with many boats painted with
colors, of bright coats... Reaching a place called,
the willow tree many friends, there I would see...
The sky so pure and crystal clean many people have
not seen... Following the road, to old woodriver
a chill in the air, gave me a shiver... Across the
tundra, I could see the town around the bend, as I
look down... Spruce trees are grown and so fair
wild salmon berries, scent the air... A ptarmigan
bird, gently flies above my head giving me a message
as if he said this land is full of beauty from above
given to us, with so much love...

—*Linda Nicholson, Forrester*

Forever In My Mind

Oh, how the years pass,
  may happy memories -
  forever last.

Hold on to those feelings wherever you are,
  let it help you reach that shining star.

The happy moments we share in time,
  will remain forever in my mind.

—*Sherrie B. Barkhurst*

"A Memorial Day Salute"

When I saw this old flag cast aside I thought of how
many men had died, and the hardships the living still
had to bear to keep this old flag flying high in the air.
  A flag so pretty should never fall, but instead put in
a place of Honor on your wall.
  And when your eyes gaze upon the Old Stars and Stripes
just keep in mind how everything is so precise.
  Each star reminds me of the soldiers in my platoon.
All covered down and dressed right too.
  So let me reveal to you some of my innermost thoughts.
  I see four squads of stars with twelve men to each.
  I can call their names right off to you, there's Kermer,
De Gregory and Sgt. Paul he was the best soldier of us all.
  They are all stars in heaven this very day, for didn't
they give their lives that we might stay.
  Just as that man died on a hill called Calvary.
  They say as you grow older your mind does regress,
your body dies, and your soul goes to eternal rest.
  This may worry some, but not me in the least. For I know
I'm going to join my buddies and make my squad complete.

—*Ray O'Neil Sr.*

Environmentalists' Song

Dead deer in the back of my truck
Maybe next season I'll kill me a duck
No respect for nature or land
I feel manly with a gun in my hand
Pass the beer, chauvinists delight
there to rape the forest at night
An owl's call foretells death is near
Head hunters do not hear
The earth is crying her last few tears
Bulldozers mow down its mist of years
Majestic mountains crumble in shame
Oh mighty dollar they call your name
Powerful seas sludge with black
Exotic birds that won't be back
Trophy hunters gather round
Search for truth it can be found
Mans mentality is all but lost
But in the end, who will pay the final cost?

—*Cheyenne Autumn*

Time

Time continues to fly by, what does it really
mean anyway?

From stop watch's to sundials, we all go
About our way with a confused smile.

Since the beginning we have all wanted to
try and measure this - time. Fitting everything
into this frame we have given ourselves.

From minutes, to seconds, to eons. We carry
On in hopes of experiencing, growing to our
full potential, and gaining knowledge.

Live now, in the moment. Look at the past
for memories, the future for dreams. God for
the highest - after all, we still have time

—*Stacie Moniz*

The Painter

On the soiled walls of use and tear, of white splattered
memories; moved his hands that adorned the song color of a
brand new melody. And ever so silently she stood, softly
trembling at the fancy of his touch; of the same polish and
vigilance he used, that intrigued her such. They conversed as
he dared not turn to behold her face, and she never prompted him
to do so, while the words coursed with ease and conveyed a
fragment of the untamed and unknown. A smile formed in the way
he spoke and forced its way down the ladder to her, and needfully
she embraced what they held, but proceeded to laugh at what they
were. How she loved this painter of ambiguous talents, of his
hands and of her heart, and longed to be the walls of white
that stood unyielding to keep them apart. It was as if they
too were alive and required him more than she and so maintained
to mock her with ripples of imperfections that he would surely see.
And as she turned to conclude her pain, the ladder creaked on
each step down, and he was there in front of her, hearing her
breathe, savoring its sound. "My lady I seem to have completed
here and shall be parting soon; for once more I paint the colors
of the heart, yet the solemn secluded colors of the moon."

—*Tiffany Jobe*

Untitled

From the time we met
Memories of you and me I will never forget
You'd put me down and act real cool
But still I go back to you like a fool
You stayed out with your friends and partied all night
While I sat at home and knew it wasn't right
I still sit here thinking of you while you're out
hitting the booze I would call you on the phone
But someone there would say, Delbert is not home
We'd make love and things would be alright
then days later we'd be in a fight I gave things up
so we could be together but things still don't seem to
get any better I really loved you Delbert, so very much
But there were things you couldn't give up
I listen to the radio and think of you
But when our song comes on, I get to feeling blue.
You call me stupid, dingy and dumb
When I went on thinking you were no. 1.
I still go on hoping everything will be fine
But I finally realized you were just feeding me a line.

—*Sandra Kinser*

A L'Ombre

Have you seen humility's ravages lately?
Millions of crushed skulls
Bobbing on postures erect
Fate laconically interjects:
"The diet of pathos is essentially sedative"
"Tragedy's food is excessively masochistic"
What good is your parasol
at the bottom of a rabid cliff?
The invisible avalanche is a jealous patriarch
Why "humble thyself"?
Commit abstract patricide instead
—get a hologram of King Hamlet's Ghost—
Many murders need tending
The threshold of this blood inspires
the totality of everything desired
here we are both victim and God
"be ready to cast off everything"
"prepare to move"
"walk naked beneath the sun"
—(all quotes from the deceased Danish throne)

—*Susie Weir*

To My Sister

Tis once again Thanksgiving time, and as the day draws near,
Memories revived once more, a favorite time of year.

Remembering our childhood days, and dreams that we once
    shared,
Telling secrets, scratching backs, to show we really cared.

A birthday lunch, a phone call, a letter long past due,
Little things, that mean so much, when they have come from you.

Through all the smiles and laughter, amid sadness and the tears,
You have stood beside me, to banish all my fears.

Your kindness to all you meet, your ever gentle way,
Brings gladness into all their lives, and sunshine to each day.

The miles that separate us will never change the fact,
Of the special bond between us, that will always be intact.

May blue skies surround you, calm waters soothe your soul,
You have a certain quality that has made you truly whole.

The inner strength that you have found, from your faith in God,
Will lead you on to greater paths, no matter where you trod.

And now at this Thanksgiving time, when I sit down to pray,
I'll thank the good Lord above for giving us this day,

And for a sisters precious love, so warm, true, and sincere,
May His blessings shine upon you throughout each coming year.

—*Shirley M. Houser*

Untitled

A woman standing in her bedroom in front of a full length
mirror with tears in her eyes she unbuttons her blouse
and caresses her left breast, and this what she says: "For
tomorrow a cut of cold steal will take you away from me,
For tomorrow I will not longer be a whole woman.
For I remember the first day you started to form. For I
was only twelve years old, when you first became a part of me.
For from the first day you came, my life started to
change. For my grandmother used to look at me, and say,
you're becoming a little woman. And now tomorrow I'll
once again become a little girl. I also remember the first
time that I made love, you were there. For he caressed
and kissed you just as much as me. Now tomorrow I'll be a
virgin again. I also remember how you fed my hungry
baby with your milk. Now after tomorrow my next baby
will starve. Oh well, I guess this is goodbye, for tomorrow
you will be removed so I will live longer, but also
tomorrow a part of my womanhood will die."

—*Ronald Smith*

Feelings Come As Fall Sets In

Long ago when you were here
missing you - wishing you near
Leaving things so unclear
makes me think and cry a tear

When you talked that night long ago
you said your heart wanted me so
but mind and heart don't mix you know
'cause it was that night we let each other go

Years have past, now your far away
two lives lived apart, living day to day
why then now, in Fall I may say
the feelings still come, yet in a strange way

Remember those times wherever you are
To cherish the memories so dear to my heart
When the fall comes, I will start
To hold those past memories, 'cause we're forever apart

—*Michelle P. Raccosta*

Winter Moment

Barren trees are cracks in soft gray skies;
mist dripping from their branches,
the sky is shattered...leaking.

Shivering, sat huddled at the window,
the tracery of trees
plays in my memories.

My eye sees nature's golden child
in sunspots on the ground,
in brightness all around.

Whispering, your softness speaks to me,
becomes your windy smile...
I'll stay with you a while.

Memories have brought you here in sunlight,
while this misty day
I find a different way,

Pondering the patterns in my mind,
to look through magic eyes
at ancient winter skies.

—*Lily Gebhart*

Kismet

Daylight brings the cry of birth
Morning surprised us as the
cold November air tightened round the heart
The chill of winter never thaws.

Sahara fire on the frozen tundra of my brain
Cold moon over Babylon, Great Harlot of our time
surrounded by mushrooms, running like a watercolor
in the rain.

Solitary passerby, reaches out to a
fleeting companion, but she's never there
Long haired madonna in a tincan town
Empty pulchritude, punishable by time.

The night is endless
The gleaming whites of my eyes
a sorry indication of life
There is no need to tell the children so.

—*Nirmal Velayudhan*

My Brother

It's been three years since you died,
Most of my tears have dried.
When you left I was ripped apart,
Now you give me strength for a new start.

You were so young,
Your life had just begun.
No one can change the past,
But I can live each day like it was my last.

I want you to live through me,
Use my eyes to see.
You're gone forever,
But I'll always have my memories to treasure,
All the great times we had,
Who knew it would end so sad.

Do not fret,
You have helped me more than you know,
Having had you in my life made me grow,
Try and try I must,
I'm doing my best for both of us,
I love you my brother,
For you see, Matthew, I will never have another.

—*Tiffany Graves*

The Mortal Enemies Of Peace

If one can not become the tallest tree on top of a high
mountain, then, be contented with just being the tallest shrub
on top of a molehill; for everyone's fate had already been
destined before being born by a mother, for every womb, pocket
and tomb have limits to any prince, king or ruler. So, be
happy and contented of what you are and shall be, without
lament or remorse for having none of ephemeral wealth and
luxury; for what you lack today shall be compensated and
rewarded someday, GOD in His infallible wisdom can not forget
to give anyone a bountiful mercy. The very root causes of a
country's tribulations, misfortunes, distress and miseries, are
the unquenchable greed and pride of "some" local and national
leaders; though they already have abundance in life to bequeath
to their generations, yet they still grab some more wealth
regardless of any means of acquisitions. Everyone's ambitions
may surely reach a CROSSROAD of "TO BE", or "NOT TO BE",
to rise and fight against OPPRESSION, TYRANNY,
IGNORANCE, POVERTY and DYNASTY; for in politics are
rampant GREED, PRIDE, DISHONESTY, BRIBERY and
HYPOCRISY, causing SOCIAL CANCERS and
poor people POORER down to the PIT of INFERNALITY.

—*San M. Luna*

Atmosphere

The moon and the earth coincide.
The pull of gravity, the mountainside.

Tons of weight floating in space.
Light as a feather, lifted by grace.

Clear summer night on top of a hill.
The stars shine bright, flooding the sky, until...

Morning sun rises above, invading night with day.
Lifting the darkness, watching children play.

The leaves fall into the tall green grass.
The seasons of time all come to pass.

The fresh water stream, carving through stone.
Changing through time, the loveliness shown.

Far away places, reaching out.
Beyond the world's realm, shadows of doubt.

Creation is evidence, there is more to the story.
Believing in God, all his glory.

The voice of his command, created by his hand.
Separating light from dark, water and land.

Creating man, beast, heaven and earth, in just six days.
A work of art, a reason to praise.

—*Lori Hollenbeck*

Untitled

Some say America is bad
My childhood was very sad
But I looked to America,
that I could prepared myself for what I
never had.
I haven't had a normal life in beautiful America.
For I had no education record,
To give back to America.
I'm three score and ten
I still don't believe it's too late to win
I pray to the Lord day and night
Before my end come, let me be discovered in the lights
This would be the joy of my whole life.
I'm mother, and have been a wife,
There was no joy day or night.
I thank God for Jesus in my life.

—*Maxine Whitaker*

My Illusive Dream

I drifted off to sleep last night and then I had a dream.
Mr. Right appeared before me with beautiful eyes of green.

He stood by a babbling brook and then he reached for me.
I knew I should resist this man because I am not free.

He stood alone upon a hill, so handsome was he.
Somehow I knew his true desire was really only me.

The longer I stood, the more I stared-how vivid he became.
I knew just then this man was meant to be all mine to claim.

His hair was really dark, his muscles well defined,
This vision of beauty I could never leave behind.

And then he turned and looked at me and smiled a little smile.
His gaze caught mine and time stood still as we stood there for
   awhile.

He gently pulled me to him; the blood began to flow.
The tenderness between us I could feel from head to toe.

We loved and laughed and loved again as I lay there in his arms.
Feeling his touch I knew to me would never come any harm.

Cool rain drops started falling, I don't know for how long.
But when they stopped I looked around and noticed he was gone.

I woke up then-it was only a dream-my Mr. Right still very
   illusive.
Suddenly I know the man beside me is Mr. Right-it's very
   conclusive.

   —*Marilyn Schuelke*

Exterior Inverse

Body aching,
muscles stretched to
the point of no return,
legs twisted and forced
in impossible directions,
feet maimed beyond belief,
arms graceful as a blowing scarf
on a summer's night,
sweat dripping down the concaves
of her neck,
her hungry body wants to do more,
has to be more,
her mind is in knowing confusion,
her body in patient waiting of what's to come.
Why does she push? Push herself to her last stem
of stamina,
to her last ounce of strength?
Why does she make herself do everything to her highest limit,
then beyond?
Why can't she give in?

   —*Nicole Romano*

Haunting Past

My past haunts me night and day
My dreams call me home to stay.
"No!" I cry "Let me be," I say
I awake to find I have not left
Filled with relief I try to go back to sleep...
But my mind of memories will not keep
For the haunting past of mine is deep
My soul is naked exposed to life,
Living in another's strife.
My dreams of past be oppressed,
Leave me be memories, I pray in silent quest,
Jesus put my thoughts to rest.
Please don't haunt me anymore my past
Remind me not of my fading memories to last
But of my future my life.
   Now in its beginning...

   —*Veronica Last*

To You I Pronounce....

Through the endless days, I think of you.
My concentration is lost completely.
Through the darkest nights, I dream of you.
And the love you give so sweetly.

In the desert sand, I thirst for you.
With your oasis, I hope to meet.
In the tundra ice, I freeze for you.
And beg for your thawing heat.

On hot summer days, I play for you.
Waiting patiently to win the game.
On cold winter nights, I cry for you.
And slowly drive myself insane.

In all my experiences, you are wanted.
Everyday of my life to you I'd give.
And if you'd believe me when I speak my heart
You'd notice for only you I live.

   —*Susana Gutierrez*

Cold And Distant

I talked with her and disclosed
My deepest feelings.

She wouldn't pay me any
Attention or listen to my revealings.

I told her of my deepest emotions.
She laughed mockingly and said, "Oh, what sadness."

Her words seared my ears and burned a whole in
My heart. I became stricken with madness.

I pleaded with her to love me.
And told her that there could be no other.

She just looked at me frivolously
And said, "Oh brother."

It was then that I decided to give up and
End this quest for love.

And to this day, I still cry out
To the heavens above.

Some times I go and sit with her
In the orchard under the apple boughs.

I talk to her there, but only the trees
Seem to listen, for she is very cold and distant.

   —*Michael C. Winkler*

What's In A Name?

Someone mentioned your name today
My eyes clouded over as the sky turned to gray
As if both the sun and I had suddenly lost our way
And like the waves that thunder in the bay
The syllables crashed against my heart in betray
Someone mentioned your name today

Someone mentioned your name today
Outwardly, no emotion did I display
Inwardly, my world collapsed in disarray
And the ache returned like a contrite stray
The sound invoked my soul back to life inveigh
Someone mentioned your name today

Someone mentioned your name today
After a lifetime spent pulling myself out of the fray
One word and I find myself right back amid the game we play
And in reply to them, I didn't know what to say
The conversation ended; they quickly walked away
Someone mentioned your name today

   —*Rae M. Zweber*

The Difference

I speak at night,
    My family draws near.
We're illusive and shy,
    You need not fear.
Some things of yours we take to live.
    You took our home,
What did you give?
    These in the pack,
I care for them.
    Is there a difference 'tween wolves and men?
We hate and love,
    Feel joy and shed tears.
We fear hunger,
    You hunger fear.
Our carnivorous ways you can't abide,
    While destroying the helpless,
Just for the hide.
    We live our lives,
Not guilty of sin.
    Is there a difference 'tween wolves and men?

    —*Timothy Gause*

Cancer

    I've waited for this day to arrive,
My friends all thought it was just a lie.
Well, I couldn't believe it myself, you know;
    But it's here and pretty soon I'll go.
        I think my life has only been,
    A small part and I'm about to begin.
    I ache and the pain's so strong,
But pretty soon I'll be where I belong.
    All this started so tiny,
    And it just grew, and grew entirely.
You know... I'm young, very young you see,
    Not a day over twenty-three.
    And they say the young must also go,
So, I wait...The time will come I know.
    "Oh God, I beg and ask to thee;
I know you are to choose the time to be,
    But could you hurry it, just for me?
        The pain gets worse, you see."

    —*E. Isabel Herrera*

Longing Made Manifest

Come to me now my love
My God is jealously alive
Alluring, taking pleasure in my endeavor to achieve
Burning from within, consuming love like a hungry beast
Devouring, feeding, feasting, dancing, singing
Celebrating the love of life
Ever wanting, ever stalking
Prowling the face of the earth
To touch your essence with conception
Joy within desire, the purest of passion
Flourishing toward the completion of evolution
Taste of me, drink of me
Feast upon me for I am what you seek
My soul cries for the light of your touch
The radiance of our union
I partake in the divine flame dance
Aligning the secret chamber of soul to the compounds of
    existence
Be swift my love, time awaits no one

    —*Roxanna Mason*

Dear John

    I understand where your grief is and I realize your pain.
    My great concern in leaving you is to show you what you've
        gained.

    I know you hurt inside and your pain seems great to bear,
    Your happiness is soon to come, it's waiting for you somewhere.

    You were lost in happiness you thought would last forever
    You blinked the eye of eternity and suddenly it was over.

        I understand. I've been there too.
    And that's why I made sure that I was there for you.

        Lean on me, depend on me, ask me why.
    And dear sweet friend - never be afraid to cry!
    —*Sarah L. Pinkston*

It Ain't Over.....

My eyes don't see so well
My hands don't work as good;
It takes a little longer to get around,
Sometimes I shake a little more than I should.

I can still make out smiles on faces and feel hugs that I receive
Some of us can still sew, and cut and glue, would you believe?

We play Bingo and Dominoes have dances and sing alongs;
Movies and Popcorn, exercise to make us strong.

Nursing homes are not what they have been thought of
A place to waste away; they are instead you see,
A place to make the most of every day.

It's like a motel you know
With dinning room's and T.V.;
Only with added medical care and entertainment,
People to share my days with me.

It ain't over till it's over
And until that day comes;
You can be sure my time is spent,
With companionship, love, and fun.

    —*Rachelle Vogelsang*

I Am One

The Loneliness of being one; empty
My heart full of love and
My arms ready to embrace.

But there's no one here; alone.

Moments spent wondering if
Time will pass with a void.
Nothing to fulfill me, oh yes;
the parents, the friends, the family...

But where is love?
No children? No love?....ever?

Shout to me love,
My inner soul shall be the recipient of fulfillment
And my heart, the giver of passion.

I will find my being, I will laugh, I will live!

I shall be free to give however I choose.

For I am one.

    —*Robin Kittrell*

The Can Man

We see them everywhere on the streets,
My heart goes out to them,
Some have signs, "I am homeless"
And I always think of him.

My son, the oldest of three,
He is one of the homeless ones,
Educated, but also addicted
To alcohol, maybe "crack" he has done.

His trade was that of a carpenter,
He lived here with us for awhile,
Moved out while he was still working,
Said we treated him like a child.

I see him on the streets with a cart,
It is filled with recyclable cans.
I ask him how he is doing,
He answers, "Mom, I am a man!"

My heart breaks, I give him some money,
Drive away with tears in my eyes,
And a fear that someday he won't make it,
And I ask, "Why, my son, why?"

　　　—*Vivian Boyd*

Wisdom

I'm young, I respect the old
My heart is warm and yet, so cold
For I love, but have my hates
I'm human, I make mistakes
The old speak and I listen with a smile
My friends laugh and whisper senile
But as the years go by, they'll realize
For it's no surprise, - that the old are wise
They've seen a lot through their dying eyes
They made many mistakes, I will too
But perhaps I'll prevent one or two
An old man once told me to love
He said; "Love God up above"
"And don't hate, - have faith"
I thank God, - that it's not too late
For now I can accept and prevent one mistake

　　　—*Robert Karpie*

Bleeding Heart

You told me you cared for me,
My heart rose.
You told me you loved me,
My spirits flew.
You told me you'd protect me and always hold me,
I believed this to be true.
Then you told me we would never work,
Your words formed hands and ripped out my heart.
You held my heart in front of me,
You told me we could never be.
Now as I write this I'm all torn apart,
For all you left was a bleeding heart.

　　　—*Mary Jo McCann*

Ocean

　The smell of sea breezes blow through the air,
　　Misting fog that covers the water afar,
　Sea gulls effortlessly gliding with the wind,
　　Rolling waves with colors of green and blue,
Crashing in upon the rocks, with a thunderous roar,
　　Foaming water that races across the sand,
　　Small creatures of life inhabit this land,
　As you cast your eyes back toward the sea.
　　Feel your spirit as it is set free.

　　　—*Paul W. Stevens*

My Everything

　　My love, my life
　　　my hopes, my dreams
these were all the things you were to me.

　　My future, my past
　　　my present, my goals
or at least that's how it used to be.

　　My lover, my friend,
　　　my mentor, my advisor
is what you used to mean.

Why did you leave the way you did?
　Why did you have to go?
Why didn't you just try to listen?
　Why did you hurt me so?

　You used to be my everything.
　　　—*Michele Hoebink*

The Jade Carving

I've carved in wood, in stone, in bone.
My lack of skill has kept me humble,
But, I did see depth, form and the beauty
Of some materials like polished wood and stone.
And then I, or we, my wife and I, discovered jade,
The beauty of aged, oriental carvings.
I read "Jade, Stone of Heaven" by Richard Gump
of Gumps Department Store.
We searched for jade in San Francisco galleries.
We found an ancient carving of a doe and fawn.
The gentle beauty of this family group,
The skill of unknown craftsmen,
The centuries this piece has lived in beauty,
Held and loved by people, priests
(and emperors, perhaps).
Fascinate and talk to me.
(Sometimes I think I mumble back)
I think about those ancient craftsmen
And thank them for this poem in stone.

　　　—*Roy Patterson*

My Thoughts

My thoughts charged with vigor and vim,
　My mind may grow weary, but my thoughts will never grow
　　dim.
I have thoughts even though sometimes I ought not.
　Thoughts of treachery, devious things,
Negatives thoughts; mischievous beings.
　I don't know where they may lead me,
But I hope these will not deceive me.
　Why do I have these thoughts?
Because they are mine and mine alone
　I try to express them
Sometimes I wished I could caress them.
　Thoughts of love and peace
Someday I know they will lead my feet,
　They are positive thoughts,
Not ones that will be bought or taught, because they are mine
　　and mine only,
　And no one can take them from me!!!!!

　　　—*Timothy Johnson*

Perplexed Experiences

One day when only four years old,
My mother took me by surprise.
She grabbed each one of my shoulders,
Then she looked straight into my eyes.

What she said that long ago day,
Never, ever, will I forget.
Was "I want you to remember,
Some things you've hardly known, as yet."

Puzzled by what I was hearing,
What all was she trying to say?
Experiences are my teachers?
For everyone - along life's way?

Still perplexed at her stern message.
Dumb founded - or so it would seem.
"Could I ask this question, Mama?
What does this — experience — mean?"

She laughed as she tried to explain —
"Life's situations you go through,
Is almost like you are in school,
So — Master — everything you do."

　　　　　—*Wilma O. McCarter*

My Mother

In The Temple

I remember when I was young
My mother's voice filling the temple
Resonant and strong; gentle and clear
Her voice alone all could hear.
It was for God most came to pray
And my mother's voice led the way.

In The Home

I remember when I was young
Strong smells of chicken and onion
Of carrots and corn and tomatoes and spices.
I remember a kitchen warm and cozy and a
Smile even warmer and tastes before supper
And oh how we ate and ate and ate.
I can't remember the living room.

Singing

I remember when I was young, weddings,
and "O Promise Me", "Because" and
"Ah Sweet Mystery of Life"
And how people cried when my mother sang
I also remember the food
But that's another poem.

　　　　　—*Morris Salamon*

My Body

My hair is molasses that keeps on flowing;
My eyes are the color of a light brown bear;
My nose is hose that keeps on dripping;
My ears are airplane wings sticking out far;
My legs are train wheels that keep on chugging;
My feet are rotten eggs, P.U.;
My knees are rounded rocks bleached white;
My fingers are Eric Clapton's when it comes to guitaring;
My arms are cranes that never let go;
My body is a battery that never dies out.

　　　　　—*Nicholas J. Della Cerra*

The Goodbye Fax

It's time I leave my customer service desk
my password has been deleted
Although it caused me lots of stress
I know I haven't been defeated
I learned the meaning of hard work
and how to form a file
I learned proper telephone manners
and how to say "*!?X" you with style
I have pushed hundreds of keys and taken hundreds of calls
All the songs were the same, to the tune of "It wasn't my fault!"
Many times I denounced the customers as spoiled
and I resented burning that midnight oil
But I must admit there were good things too
Especially letters from people who said "we like you"
I'll even have to say the job was sometimes gratifying
But if I said I loved it all - we'd both know I was lying
I'd like to thank those who gave an occasional smile
which let me know you noticed, and acknowledged my "extra
　　mile"
It was your attitude which made it all worthwhile!

　　　　　—*Michelle Duffy*

A Marriage Made In Heaven

When a man and woman decide to marry
My recommendation is that they tarry.
Ephesians 5 will tell them what to do,
If they only take time and read it through.

"Submit yourselves one to the other,"
In the fear of God, not one another.
"Wives, submit to your own husband as unto the Lord,"
Then your relationship can be on one accord.

Christ loved the church and gave His life.
Husbands, love likewise unto your wife.
Continue to read until you see the light,
Use all you have of your Godly insight.

So how can we without help from above,
Supply our families with the Master's love?
We must be of one accord
To raise our children as unto the Lord.

What if the man does not love like Christ,
And the woman doesn't submit herself as a wife?
Go to each other, confide and confess—
Only then can the problem be addressed.

　　　　　—*Ruby L. Boston*

A Different Place

　A different place to think to
my self in the hallway, remembering
memories from last's August
to May.
　Lonely after three-fifteen, but
crowded before eight, open books
and loud bells that everyone
may hate.
　Events that cause happiness,
with parties and dances, remembering
holding hands and last
years romances.
　A different place to share a
tear, remembering with friends
what happened yesteryear. This
place is school.

　　　　　—*Leslie Rocha*

And I Proclaim..."How Great You

In my aloneness I walk in the rain...there no one will notice
my tears, the sky is so dark...that it is a reflection of my
soul this very moment, the clouds in hurried motion, like my
thoughts, are without order, going to and fro, like autumn
leaves played by the wind.
And I call on my angels to take all this bundle to you...oh
Lord... for you understand all my fears...you that sees all
my tomorrows...the only one that cares when the unbearable
pain...that overwhelming hurt creeps in and smothers my heart.
Then...I hear...that unspoken voice...that ruffling of angels'
wings deep in my heart...in that perfect moment it seems to be
quoting verses that speak directly to my sadness and are needed
so badly...and full of awe... I wonder...where or when...did
I learn those truths that tenderly are guiding me through the
path...or is it you oh Lord...holding me close to your heart
once again? I know you will make a way once more, but you leave
me free to choose, many times unwisely, to stumble over and
    over...
but as I stand before you...my Saviour dear, with a grateful
heart...I proclaim...how great you are!.

    —*Ligia Zeledon Lloyd*

Ashamed

Enclosed in a secret world all my own
My thoughts are deep and personal; to no one else they're known
The others try to pry beneath my outer shell
But no one will discover my dark burning hell
I crouch in a corner of a room with no door
No windows or air leaking through a single pore
Out pour tears of sadness for I hate myself so
I am my worst enemy; my worst hated foe
My fists punch the walls so many times until my knuckles bleed
My soul leaks of guilt and bitterness for my self-contained greed
My heart screams for love and tenderness for the one that I have
    lost
Curdling of skin and hair standing on end is caused by all that
    have double-crossed
The others; they stare through the bars of my zoo
They snicker; poke fun at me, are so very cruel
I don't try to stop them; I just curl up so small
the few crumbs they throw me I quietly gnaw
My eyes slowly start to shut; Relief is so near
I can now sleep eternally and diminish my fear
I crumble into ashes such as a dry crackling leaf
And the wind forever blows away my never-ending grief

    —*Rachel Worcel*

Untitled

Sitting in my lonely room, thoughts of you begin to bloom.
My thoughts of you flow through my head,
While I lay sleepless in my bed.
Visions of you stay in my mind,
When I think of you time after time.
I lay awake at night, hoping you'll soon be in my sight,
for me to hug you, to love you, and show you I care.
These are my feelings I'd like to share
Your touch is so gentle, your voice is so sweet,
You show me you care when our eyes meet.
When I touch your skin, my feelings, begin to grow
higher and higher it's your love I desire.
The times we shared I keep close to my heart
To remind me you love me while we're apart.

    —*Wendy Roman*

Scanning A Dream

Am I dead or is it a dream
My thoughts run naked through the night
My vision is lightning often touching the ground
My hearing is keen picking up a faint scream
My sense of touch and smell an ambrosia of fright
Death is but a door, time is but a window with pain
End of the day beginning of the night
Flying with silver fire in the sky
To whiten their hair a scream of fright
Mummy dust to age skin and clothes
A human skull and loves first kiss
On a mountain of stone I sat on a throne of bone
Inside four walls of pain
What was will be, what is will be no more
Bed to the light today is merely history
Don't be afraid of what you do not understand
For I am just someone scanning a dream

    —*D. Warner*

Morning Dew

Her morning run gets shorter,
Needing rest, she stops, leans against a tree.
This is quiet time, her time,
The world sleeps, responsibilities still in bed.
Movement in the branches,
There, a robin just above her head.
Its beak filled with breakfast.
Breakfast, she must go now,
Must outrun the sun.
Quiet time goes away,
Like morning dew, erased by the heat of the day.

    —*Mike Epps*

We Saw A Baby Soldier At The Airport...

He had a cheek so soft that if a rose petal brushed it,
neither would have felt the difference.
His neck was so whitely vulnerable that
the moist print of his mother's kiss
could still be seen.

Hi shoulders trembled under the weight of
an oversized khaki trench coat
(they did not, you see, make coats small enough
for his delicate frame).
Looking hardly old enough to be out alone,
his eyes were glazed with his effort to be drunk
his lonely tears barely withheld.

We stopped laughing, stopped celebrating ourselves
stopped to wonder how he could anyone's
enemy when even his girl was a virgin.

    —*Susan Maxson Smith*

Everlasting

We met through that boy of yours,
No one could seem to keep
God gave to me a friend,
More than "just the mother of" he
He, that boy of yours, and I,
We lasted just over three
Three years of time that still left me you.

Thank God you still remain with me,
I care more than time will ever take
Never take this friend I have of you,
I need you longer than he.

    —*Lorraine Lewis*

Power

Never again! No matter how beckoned
Never again will I go second.
I am parched with incurable thirst,
I want to be the one who goes first.

Never again will I follow the crowd
You'll find me up front standing tall and proud.
It's not my style to wait on the side
If I can be the one to preside.

You'll not find me at the back of the stage
I want that spotlight! Is that an outrage?
You need someone to speak, sing or dance?
Call on me! I refuse no chance.

Just stand me near a microphone
And I have Power! (Though you may moan.)
And who is that leading the major parade?
Good grief! It's me, the renegade.

From whence did it come, this confidence
That makes me in love with the audience?
Never again will I quiver with fear.
I'm the best there is. Do you hear? Is that clear?

—*Muriel Roth Kulwin*

Fleeting Moments

....And so I sat,
Never closing my eyes.
For time is wasted
On those who choose to see the world
Behind nature's sunglasses.

....And so I watched
As shadows cloaked my face.
For time passes too quickly
For wristwatches and clocks
Made by technology's hands.

....And so I listened
As the wind's breath caressed my ears.
For time is gentle;
Creating sounds of wonder
Instead of drumbeats that quake the ground.

And so I dreamed
As time passed by.
For as long as reality remains,
Fantasy awaits occupancy.

—*Merrie B. Donehoo*

Dreams

Only the dreams that are never dreamed
   Never come true
Only the thoughts that are never said
   Go unsaid
Only the deeds left neglected
   Go undone
Only the "heart" never touched, never loved
   Feels no sorrow.

But the dreams that are dreamed
   are forever remembered
A kind word of love is well
   worth being said
The deed if only to offer a shoulder
   To cry on - is done
And A "heart" that sheds sorrow finds joy
   In knowing - that you're loved.

—*Melinda Martin*

A Mother's Prayer

May your flame
Never lessen
May springs of peace
Spew forth from your heart
May your bones never weary
And the veins of your wrists and ankles
Like iron bands ever be
May your life be
The salt of remembrance
To those whose lives you touch
And may the laughter of children
Ring joyously in your yard
May that man in your life be a morning, ever renewed
In a love eternally blessed
May his face shine for you always
As surely as day follows night
And may the Lord's life be mirrored in yours
For my child, you are
Deserving of all that's good.

—*Mercy John-Ekanem Umoh*

Enclosing Bubble

Never seen, never heard,
      never touched,
as if a bubble were enclosing my thoughts.
   Never questioned, never noticed,
         never bothered.
   As if they weren't even important so
    I never spoke, never touched.
      Never listened to anything
         but my thoughts.
   In this miserable state of life
            never a friend
            but the friend.
      That was in my thoughts
         and not even then
did he see, hear, touch, question, notice
   or even bother to understand
   my enclosed bubble of thoughts.
   In this miserable state of life
         I'm left all alone
         with nothing in my heart!

—*Tswana Sewell*

Climbing The Ladder To Success

Waking up everyday, just to see a brand
   new day, starting fresh, starting clean
   trying not to forget the dream.

Competing against the outer world, stumbling
   over stupid quarrels, being yourself
   everyday is what's going to keep you on
   the runway.

Pausing at a route, is meant for you to pout
   you've got to keep going to continue your
   way about.

To live easy means to die easy, to live for a
   challenge means to create and get a balance.

Waking up, doing what you have to do to make it
   in life, is it a meaning? Yes. Live a life,
   live a good life, live it at the best ability
   of all the strength you've got inside. If this
   process is being done, you will then see the
   meaning of life.

Life is short, so grab what you want, for you will
   see, to succeed is life's creed.

—*Latoya Evans*

Fate Of Mankind

As I lay awake in a lonely bed, I long to hear a heart beating
next to mine. As I lay twisting away in a tormented mind
Could I ever hope for a future for all of mankind
Can anyone hear our sullen cries
Come back to reality and hear more lies
People are dying and paying in bloodshed
We're embarking on a new age, but yet why are our children like
walking dead gone from their homes and left to die
Where are the empty arms and souls to embrace them?
Is this a cold glimpse of the future where we're just a number
in line; dare we not laugh or be sent away
Where have the sweet flowers gone, even they are now recycled
Is there hope for mankind in the future?
We no longer can be dehumanized as machines take away our jobs
As the inner cities take our youths and turn them into killing
machines, we are slowly destroying ourselves and the earth
Let's stop and become whole again with faith and trust
in the One above us all, our inner worth!

    —Laura Collins

A Mother's Prayer

Thank you Jesus, for my son
Next to You, he is the one
To touch my heart, to hug my soul
Oh Dear Lord, never let him go

Hold him in Your loving hand
Help him Lord to become a good man
For he is my love, my life, my joy
My bouncing bundle of baby boy

Oh Dear Father in heaven above
Help others to know, the joy of this love
To see in his eyes all the love that they miss
When he reaches to me for a hug and a kiss

Someday in the future, we'll look back to the past
And know that our lives are gone much to fast
So for now precious Jesus, my prayer will be
That you lead and guide him safely for me

    —N. L. N. R.

Food For Our Soul

To survive we must forever partake of our victuals
No matter how much or how little
All of us must consume our delectable
Whether with, or without a table

Many eat to live day to day
While the very fortunate live to masticate
All the treasures of their palate
Their prime rib, lobster, and caesar salad

But, despite whatever exotic, or simple sustenance
It definitely makes no difference
For we must feed our stomach no matter what
To remain alive to continue to do our part

While some struggle daily to breathe
Many sometimes forget to feed
Their heart and soul with their grub
The one and only provision is love

Love is the food for our soul
The only prerequisite for abundant growth
Bringing forth our very own truth
So as to truly see, and appreciate, our meat, drink, and fruit

    —Vanessa Hart

Empty Room

There's an empty room in my house tonight,
no more my son will I see.
Oh God, why did he have to die, why couldn't it have been me.
Last night he came home late from school,
so I wouldn't let him play.
I spanked him and made him go to bed without a chance to say,
I stopped off for your birthday present Dad,
I didn't think it would take much time,
It isn't much of a present Dad, for I only had a dime.
he cried himself to sleep last night and when I went to bed,
I saw there were still teardrops, on his new bedspread.
The next day, when I came home from work,
he seen me across the street,
He had completely forgiven me, and to me he ran to meet.
I hollered stop, but out he ran, that big car hit my little
man. I ran up to him and I heard him say,
Forgive me Dad, for yesterday.
Yes, there's an empty room in my house tonight,
No more my son will I see, Oh God, why did he have to die,
Why couldn't it have been me.

    —Larry E. Lindgren

Put Love For God And Country Above Those Of 1776

Love for God and Country in 1776 was great that year
No one had any great need of fears
They all laboured in love for their country
With God to back then everybody
They knew with God as their leader He's show them the way

In 1994, put love for God and Country above these of 1776
Put your maker number one on your list
Let love for God and Country be your guide
You will never need to make a tight first
Love will truly lead you on
Let love for God and Country keep you in tone.

Upon your maker, make your call today
Ask God the right step to take get upon your knees and pray
Ask God the right step to take then 1994 will be a great year
In every year, now and everyday.

Everyone, small, large, old, young, short and tall
In 1776, they called upon their maker to lead them on
The love of God and Country was what made them a tone
In love they laboured and served so that freedom will ring
So let's all with joy turn with love sing.

    —Mary Matlock

No One Home for Christmas

With no one home for Christmas, should I decorate this year?
(No one here to share the happiness, or demonstrate good cheer.)
Should I get the wreaths and manger out, and trim the Christmas
    tree?
It seems like such a waste of time to do it just for me.

But in this busy hectic life we cannot live apart.
We'll let His good and steadfast love shine through us from the
    heart.
And I must nevermore forget, He said; "All men are brothers,"
And; "Go ye into all the world to bring my love to others".

I'll not forget the Christ Child, who did so much for me.
I'll put candles in the window for everyone to see.
Ah yes! I'm not a hermit living in a world apart,
And I must show to others I keep Christmas in my heart.

And so I'll decorate with care,
In memory of the Babe so fair
And place the wreaths for all to see
My love for Him, who came for me.

    —Ruth V. Roushey

Unfulfilled Dreams

He stood apart from all the others
No one wanted him around.
He seemed lost in a sea of fish
just waiting for a shark to devour him.
He didn't give a damn about me.
He even hurt me beyond repair.
I will get rid of my visible bruises,
but I will always have the scars.
His voice alone hit me like a leather belt across the face.
I want to rip his heart out,
like he ripped mine out,
then turn my back on him when he's bleeding,
just like he did to me.
But now when I see him, I weep.
I weep over his cold, dead, rigid body.
Maybe he hurt me but that was all he knew.
Neither of us knew what love stood for.
I make a silent vow over his corpse to never be like him
as hot, salty tears drip on all his unfulfilled dreams.

—*Melissa Arbaugh*

The Disbeliever

If end of time, be upon us, it must be a far, for I have seen,
No signs, coming, of this strange happening, that you, tell me
of. For I hear, no rumble, of clouds, falling away all I see,
is the sun, in the sky, shining, what a beautiful, glorious,
day. If you say, that this be so, why then, would I not know?
Everyone, would know, wouldn't they? Why do I fear if I
disbelieve?

Did, He say, He would come again? Did He really go? Can you
show me, that this will be? For I really want to know. You
say, The Bible, has told us lo, I am with you always, where, is
He today? If this time, be upon us!

What is that rumbling of thunder? I hear up there? And clouds
moving so swiftly, past us, in the air. I see, three angels,
I hear their voices, calling out - the names of those, on
earth, down here.

My God! Thou has forsaken me! As I fall down, humbly on my
knees. Why was I so blind? All this time. Why did I
disbelieve? He is leaving me, He is leaving me, with all the
other, disbelievers down here .....

—*Ruth Rogers*

Whisper In The Night

The night was calm and dark,
No stars in the heaven to light me,
I was alone and in reverie,
Couching my lonely heart to sleep.

The consolation I got,
Is the cold breeze of the night,
Giving me a little relieve,
Refreshing my broken heart,
Until it goes to sleep.

Oh! God how can a person being hurt,
With all the things she has done,
Is this just a trials in life?
Oh! God it is just too hurting to impart.

I gave everything to you my God,
Relieve me a little and console my heart,
If this is a part of my suffering,
I'll accept it, for trials is a
part of your love.

—*Socorro Ch. V. Trinidad*

Untitled

Blessed be the Lord, my children dry your eyes
Non-believers crucified me, but I did arise
My Father sacrificed me for everyone's sin
All you have to do is let me in
I've built many mansions in heaven for you
This wouldn't have been said if it wasn't true
Sometimes my followers, the battle seems long
But that's how I decipher the weak from the strong
And no matter what hardship, I'll be by your side
For my love goes deep, and my heart is wide
So trust in me and don't find these words odd
I am Jesus Christ, the true Son of God

—*A. Gardner*

Untitled

Life is of the essence, but some perspectives are
not as bright,
Though some people are successful, others have given
up the fight.
They may wish upon stars but to no avail, and the
moon may light their way,
Only to find they are heading in the wrong direction,
with nothing more to say.
The sun creates radiant clouds, only to see that
there are shadows inside,
And as the mist clears from the window, there are
less people in whom to confide.

—*Sharon Neumann*

I Saw Death

I saw death today.
Not in the sight of one who had succumbed.
Not in the specter of events that would cause it.
Not in the written words that would describe it.
Not on a stage or screen as authors would portray it.
Nor in picture images that would preserve it for eternity.
It was revealed in the middle of a routine ordinary day.
Quietly and quickly and then it went away.
Yet, I am left forever in its sway.
I saw it in the eyes of a tormented young soul.
One filled with demons for which there was no control.
In a murderous rage and I was the victim.
I could not rely upon his mercy at this stage for he has none.
I must rely on the mighty one in whom I believe.
He alone can grant a reprieve from my swiftly meeting my
final destiny.
I saw death today and briefly felt its sting.
But I did not die.

—*Lita Duke Holmes*

Flower Daughter

We sowed our seed carefully.
Nursing roots in fertile ground,
We worshiped each petal of the blossom we found.

We flaunted our flower proudly.
We sought possession, not to borrow,
Because she belonged to us today and tomorrow.

We lived her life fully.
When our bloom suffered, crying teardrops of rain,
We wept along with her to soften the pain.

Winter wind slaps our faces, commands without mercy:
"Leave your garden, shut the door!
Your flower is full grown now — she needs you no more!"

—*Louise Bronoski*

Pictures In A Still Mind

The profound silence of the still mind. . .
Not like the blowing of the wind,
But more like the wind that you can't see,
A silence of the eyes.

Picture:

The naked branches of winter
Shaking with snow,
And no sound accompanies the wind
That blows them. . .
The dark trees with their
Scrawny fingers stretched out
In the air,
Tracing arcs and circles
Over the almost frozen lake. . .

Picture:
The bald hill,
Across whose green grasses
The edged wind blows.
The low clouds
Brush the plain's horizon.

— *Robert M. Baker*

Hate The Battle's Won

Another day you curse.
Not satisfied with what others do,
People can only give their best and the rest is up to you,
So, do not be angry when your day isn't going right,
But, let it serve as a reminder there is no darkness
found in light,
You can't expect others to live and walk in your shadow,
Each person has a mind and heart of their own.
Life is a series of choices.
But, the ones who are strengthened know they don't walk alone.
The race isn't always to the swift,
But to those who continue to run,
When we're living for the thrill of victory
Instead of mere survival hate the battle's won.

— *Terry Lowery*

China Dolls

Women are fragile
not to be tousled and tossed about.
We are the ornaments of life
while we are hollowed out
left empty with solid facades

Much the same as china dolls

Placed atop mantels
we become ornaments of beauty, of life
becoming more precious and fragile with age
If you break us we're yours so we fear your touch

You adorn us in gold and jewels
If we keep quiet and don't tell your secrets

Much like a shattered china doll
reassembly is difficult
We gaze helplessly, hopelessly
as we long to be given life again

You many posses us but the price is high
The price is our lives and souls so look
but make your touch gentle
Once reassembled your touch is what we fear the most

— *Lucy Fritz*

O Christmas Tree

O Christmas Tree, O Christmas Tree, you're such a fire hazard.
O Christmas Tree, O Christmas Tree, you're such a fire hazard.
Your bulbs are loose, your wires are bare,
Your needles dry, fall everywhere.
O Christmas Tree, O Christmas Tree, you're such a fire hazard.

O Christmas Tree, O Christmas Tree, when can I take you down?
O Christmas Tree, O Christmas Tree, when can I take you down?
You take up all my living space,
I'd like you in the fireplace.
O Christmas Tree, O Christmas Tree, when can I take you down?

O Christmas Tree, O Christmas Tree, another year is ending.
O Christmas Tree, O Christmas Tree, another year is ending.
Though your lights will be in a box,
I'll still find needles in my socks.
O Christmas Tree, O Christmas Tree, another year is ending.

— *William H. Shontz*

Morning Exultation

Let's see what You brought me this morning,
O Magic of Magics!
Gossamer ribbons of spider webs, traced by the dew.
Arachnids of uncounted thousands were summoned to spin them;
then You woke me in time just to harvest the view.

What was it You gave to me yesterday,
Worker of Wonders?
All orange-yellow brilliance is all I remember.
Oh yes! Bittersweet cups opened wide by the frost
of September.
And I feasted my eyes; then I knew
that the Giver was You.

What gift will You proffer tomorrow,
O Dispeller of Dis'ease?
What gift to bedazzle, discover,
to play with, or simply to shine?
For the world's still all Yours
As You make it all, gradually, mine.

— *Shirley M. Steinman*

The Old Sailor's Last Voyage

Shimmering, silken wings of water dance their way across the ocean to an appointed destiny with the beach. Conducted by the hands of God, they rise and fall as if orchestrated to a melody from heaven. The old sailor stands statue-like on the shore, staring out, his eyes reflecting visions of days long past.
His heart aches as he remembers bold, adventurous days aboard the mighty sailing ships. Deep inside his nautical soul, he longs to stand watching the sun rise and set on the ocean from the deck of a peaceful ship, its luminescence splashing across the water. Bewildered, the old man closes his eyes blinking in disbelief. The ship had magically appeared through clouds of golden mist, a young sailor standing at her helm...the old sailor knew he was not alone. Turning, he looked upon his youthful image.
He no longer felt the icy sting from the wind around him. The young sailor reached out his arms beckoning the old man to him. Together, hands clasped, their footprints on the sand disappeared. Only the young sailor remained, his commanding figure now stood alone upon the majestic ship as it drifted out from the shore. On a course mapped out and navigated by the Creator of all seas, the sailor turned the ship's wheel toward eternity.

— *Melinda Miller*

Dolphin's Song

I have watched dolphins move swift and graceful through deepest
    oceans.
Their bodies tracing delicate curves beneath waves of dark
Indigos and blues.
As I saw them move, together alongside my ship, I smiled:
To think that the one leaping was the souls echo of the one
    swimming.
Reaching to leap above the liquid horizon, again and again.
In playful mastery of motion without effort, almost silent.
Complete in the rhythm of air, water, and time.

    —Richard Clay Smothers

The Resurrection

Waiting impatiently for the resurrection
    Of a dear friend
    Of a lost life
    Of a last hope

In an unending dress rehearsal
    For what life could be
    For what life should be

Going through the motions in a meaningless existence
    Through a twisted and distorted maze
    Totally ignorant of the cost
    To rekindle the spirit

But with full knowledge of the price to be paid
    If myself,

I could
    Never
    Again
    Find.

    —Roslyn Clear

The Mirror's Reflection

A piece of glass reflects the tainted past
Of a frightened child who may not last.
A distorted image with secrets to hold,
The child is torn as the story unfolds.

One man beat her, another used her,
Not one loved her, but all abused her.
The faces hazy, the damage clear,
The fear surrounds her, yet she look in the mirror.

Faces of people who truly did care
Not one did she trust for love, to her, was rare.
As she stands at the mirror continuing to peer,
The haziness leaves and a stranger appears.

    —Laurel Bundy

Grammy

When I sit and think of memories long past
of a life that I loved which would be gone too fast

I remember sitting feeling such pride
Knowing you loved me as I sat by your side

A dime under my pillow, a surprise by my plate
the tooth fairy, a friend and always my playmate

A grandmothers love, a hug and her smile
The twinkle in her eye, are so important to a child

When I sit and think of memories long past
of a life that I loved which would be gone too fast

I love you and miss you, as I'm sure you can see
but somehow I know you're still watching over me

I love you grammy...

    —Susan E. Duguay

Us

US! For most a statement of fact
Of a love that gives; and love given back.
Two loving and giving, dedication and trust
Which must be; if there is to be an US.

US! To me the question which lack
The answer of only your love given back.
For love can live alone if it must,
But it is better with two. Better, with US.

US. Is it possible that my love should find
Love in return or is my love blind.
My happiness can never be a must
But sadness can be lifted only by US.

US. Love is the one force that never dies,
But without an US, love's heart cries
With sorrow and loneliness, an absolute must
Unless replaced by love, replaced by US.

US? Love's true answer to giving and trust
Must be answered with the answer US.
Is there an US? I'm afraid your heart does show
For US there is an answer, the answer is NO.

    —Michael L. Hofacket

Spiritual Stairway

To find our own place in the sun, and to help release our minds
of all limiting mental shackles, and bring to birth, the God
that is within. To succeed you must pray, have faith, be
patient, work hard, be honest; if you cannot do all that you
desire, you will have the satisfaction of knowing that you've
done your best. You must put forth energy determination
because it's, not what we have, but what we use, not what we
see, but what we choose.
    These are the things that make or break the sum of human
happiness. The things nearby, not the things afar, not what we
dream, but what we are. These are the things, that make or
break that give the heart its, joy or ache. Not what seems
fair, but what is true, what we dream; but what we do, these
are the things that shine like gems; not as we pray, but as we live.
    These are the things that make for peace. Both now and
after time shall cease:

    "I pray as never sure to pray again, and as a
    dying man to dying men"

    —Willie Brown

Becoming Real

Life is a struggle against the unknown. Buried beneath fears
of being alone. Turning from pain and hiding your will to find
happiness - taking a lifetime to fill. A child will sense
needs and learn to relate to the world in a way so secure in
his fate. Trying to fill those he loves with his soul while
hiding his tears as he acts out his role. Time marches on
passing innocently and a child is hurting but no one can see.
Venting the pain through substitute means. Expressing an anger
that lives through extremes. What does it mean to be without
sadness after years as a prisoner in a world full of madness?
Yearning for love and on one to rely. Searching for truth
through living a lie. How do you open your heart and accept
the love that got caught in the anger you've kept? Being slave
to that anger and the need to be real. Which has led to
perfecting a way not to feel. Be strong as the emptiness
drains confidence. Gearing your strength to fight pain so
intense. Taking that stand can relinquish your role and head
you toward peace with your mind and your soul. Deep in our
hearts we all hold the key to live out our destiny confidently.
Believe in your love, accept with care. For patience will show
you that loved ones are there.

    —Lisa A. Stancati

Lily Of The Fields

A wreath of daisies resting on her sunlit head
  of flowing golden tresses.
Emerald eyes and lips of red
  upon her nature blesses.
With purple heather as her heady scented bed
  she is beauty beyond compare.
No one remotely aware
  of the silent tears she has shed
  among the dew stained grass of dawn.
Many long to touch her face of alabaster fair.
  None seek to stir her soul
Nor merge her heart within their own.
  She cries out for love yet finds it not.
Reaching for understanding - emptiness returns.
They call her lily of the fields
  She roams a sea of wildflowers and swaying grass.
With wind dancing in her hair
  among the fields she stands alone, still as though glass.
She stands alone among the flower spotted fields
  the fairest of the garden.

    —Sheri Marie Boyd

Writer's Pledge

Come, let us seek the light, the truer light
of literature, the inner light of life -
quelling the darkness of ungodly night,
setting aside all struggle, stress and strife
conquering hate through love, declaring war
on war, creating grace from ugliness.
We do not wrong but right; we do not mar
But make; we writers do not curse but bless:
For we building ever-new empires
of wisdom, where revenge is folly, where
forgiveness is law, where deceased desires
are born delights, and where our only care
is the discovery of our destiny
in our awareness of divinity.

    —R. M. Challa

Who Am I

"Who am I" is the hue and cry
Of multitudes questioning before they die
You must know yourself as well as you can
Else you'll ne'er understand any other man (woman)

If you allow others to run your life
In a vain attempt to escape any strife
In that freedom from hassle, you must pay a price
By foregoing the pie and settling for a slice.

Those that talk behind another's back
Have a life as exciting as a burlap sack
If they can influence in untold ways
Maybe it's time to self appraise.

No one can hurt you without your consent
To really know that, you must pay the rent
There might come a time to show that world your face
And lead yourself to your proper place.

The choice is yours, you must decide
If it's important to find out what's inside
And answer the question "Who am I?"
Then proceed to the next one - "Why?"

    —Maurice Levy

Life

When time has healed the wounded sole
of one that has been so strong
Will another's eyes gaze upon
the one I loved for oh so long
So just live on in gentle love
and gather strength from up above
Remember times of long ago
when weeks were long and slow
But as you age and years go by,
like shadows on winter's snow
Don't look back on life with pain
remember the sunshine not the rain
so live your life with love and care
For you know I will be waiting, for you,
Up there.

    —Tim W. Green

Sin

I feast on the bones, in the shade
Of the grave, in the eve
By the light of the moon;
The pale moon, white like the bones which I chew;
And tear at the gristle of each sinew.
I gorge on the bones, and feast
On the meat, aah what a treat
So sweet to eat the flesh that hangs on the bones.
Oh how I love the crack, and the snap, and the sound
Of each tendon that pops, as I pull
The fleshy curtain from its skeletal rod,
To peer in the window of each man's soul.
And snack on his flesh as I go.
What pleasure I find when nothing is there
Though this is common to find
For something I rare. The darker the soul
The fuller the feast, and best is the man
Who lives like a beast, for his flesh is so tender form
Indulgent behavior and his heart is unseasoned
By salt of the saviour.

    —Michael Schellman

Painting The Music

As you listen to the beautiful sounds
Of the music that is heard
A picture is forming in your mind
Just waiting to be transferred

You may not have the artistic talent
To make the picture look great
But all one needs is to look at your eyes
And they know you don't have to illustrate

Your face shows all the expression
Of how wonderful your pictures look
The music is your paintbrush
And minutes was all it took

They won't find your pictures in a gallery
Nor will they find them on the wall
But to the lucky one who reads you well
Will see the greatest masterpieces of all

    —Randy Woody

Lovers

Love beckons with silent longing eyes.
Offers with warm lingering hands.
Voices with yearn aching lips.
Entices with shy trembling smiles.
Returns with close craving arms.
Surrenders with passion suffering bodies.

    —Sammie Edmondson

The Hand on the Sand

(Omaha Beach, Normandy, France - 1944)

A Tribute to an Unknown Soldier on the 50th Anniversary
of the Normandy Invasion of June 1944

Wet from the sea I stepped ashore
And moved over the sandy beach,

My eyes looked down and there I saw
A hand from the sand upward reach.

A man had walked this way before
On Omaha beach he had died,

His palm was all I saw that day
Proclaiming to all he had tried.

"Carry on" his plea in silence
Summoned us passing from the sea,

I paused a moment, then moved on
Wondering who this man might be.

Upon this sand so many died
To gain a foothold on this land.

But on Normandy's shore that day
Etched on my mind was this one hand.

Two score and ten have passed away
That hand in mind does still remain,

I pray this death was not in vain
A gift for peace to one day reign.

—*Lynn A. White*

Compensation For Date With The Devil

Lingering

Like the acrid stench
of whiskey on your breath.

Last night's touch

Sandpaper-fingers brushing,
scouring, course against the grain.

Your bulbous lips
Suckling, like those of hungry babes
clutching at their mothers' empty pitchers.

Wiry bristles
trace the aura of your sardonic grin—
I shut my eyes to slip away,

But

The sable gargoyle
dances in my head.

—*Sabrina Profili*

Webster's Reversal

When we are young we are confused.
Often we are suicidal.
As we grow up we do not know which way to go.
Sometimes we pick the wrong road and people get hurt.
We are hated by people we do not know.
We are discriminated against constantly.
There is little protection for us under the law.
If we are lucky enough to find love, we can't marry.
Some of us are beaten — fatally.
When we die, nobody cares.
Isn't it funny that once upon a time being gay meant that you
were happy.

—*Michael E. Coleman*

Senseless But Endless

Where do all the young men go?
Off to war on orders to destroy some other's hated foe.
Why do these young soldiers go?
To kill a distant someone for reasons they do not know.

To remote places these soldiers go with rifles held high,
Battling for a moment; only to fall, struggling to rise.
Bullets sent from an unknown someone, whining through the air,
Striking down all these young soldiers in an unknown somewhere.

Blood drains from their young bodies to stain the far away ground.
Their foreheads crease in a bewildered, eternal frown.

The world does not care to know their names.
They died playing someone else's game.
Where do we place the discomfort of blame?
We, ourselves, avoid any sense of shame.

Though we share in their anonymous deaths,
We seldom look to our own souls in quest.
We pass our guilt to any and all the rest.

—*R. W. Reynolds*

Where Is Glynis?

"Where's Glynis?" You asked.
Oh she just went inside. Herself.
She had a few things she needed to do,
To clean up, to clear up
And try to undo.

Is she returning? I suppose
When she's through learning
About she, her and most of all me.
But don't worry
I
Am here to answer anything you may need.
Is she alright? Sure.
She's just fine.

She had to go inside. Herself.
To reorganize, reshape, redecorate her fate.
Lie around and recline in the mysteries of her mind.

Where Glynis?
Oh she just went inside. Herself.

—*G. A. Freeman*

Intrigue

Oh the happiness of the moment
Oh the thrill of the fight
Oh the excitement that rushes through you
Telling you the time is right
Oh the joy of victory. The days after
are so sweet will excite you, will amaze
you, will intrigue you, endlessly.

When you know that you have made good
After you have toiled so hard.
On a project for your public.
It took you so long to start. It
amazes you it intrigues you. Knowing
you have come so far.

Now you're all done and the verdicts
in and now you're a shinning star.
Shinning so bright in your public eyes
And intrigued is what you are.

—*Mabel Edith Briscoe*

Rain Child

Rain child, I linger in your undying splendor,
oh Venus, for you walk the humbling earth in garb
of crescent moons.
Deliver me from the angry eye that is the sun
where vultures soar in silhouette in the desert of my
blighted hope.
I hold reverence for you such with piety through
nuances of electric scenarios in which we might indulge.
Tears of divinity cascade from the blue empyrean
and through this haze of falling water you smile.
Pigeons abound at your feet like tiny soldiers marching
into battle as we who fear seek shelter in the bowels
of our twisted creations.
For you Rain child are the Phoenix rising from the
pyre of man's defeat.

—Matthew Aaron Gorman

Mom

I dream't of you, last night.
Oh' what a beautiful sight
You stood on a long bridge made of stone
I 'could tell by your eyes, you were not alone
As you were smiling down on me
There were two small children clinging
Their arms around your knees
Pink, blue, yellow colors were in the sky
And clear blue water, I watched flow by
If I could have a dream come true
It would be the one I had of you
Oh' how happy you seemed to be
No more, sadness, sickness or misery
Joyful and happiness were the
Expression on your face. I know it
Must be heaven, oh' what a beautiful place

—Sharon Weaver Keller

Buried Down Deep

Chemicals, cans, bottles and diapers,
Old rubber tires and windshield wipers,
Possessions we purchased but just couldn't keep,
So it came upon us to hide them down deep.
Our neighbors have cancers and no one has answers.
So could it be the toxic waste
That somehow was just misplaced?
Is it in our water or the food that we eat?
That was raised upon the soil of what we buried down deep?

—Shelley Halzel

Tiny Little Stranger

He came to us one Saturday morn,
On agonizing wings of pain.
His coming filled our hearts with joy!
Like glorious sunshine after rain!!

A tiny little stranger sent to us,
From God to care for and to adore;
We all loved him so very much,
But God must have loved him more!!

On angel wings he silently departed,
Leaving heartbreak and tears to beguile;
He's gone, but he'll ne'er be forgotten,
Though he stayed for such a little while!!

—Pauline A. Turner

Keeper Of The Lighthouse

While sailing on a stormy sea,
On a dark and lonely night,
A sailor searched most desperately
For a guiding lighthouse light.

He searched until he thought
He could not search anymore,
When at last he finally saw
The light shining from the shore.

The light's warmth was an invitation
As the sailor opened all of the ship's sails.
His heart was pounding in his chest
As he fought the tempestuous gales.

When, at last, he reached the lighthouse,
His heart was filled with a joyous song,
For the Keeper of the Lighthouse
Had kept the light shining strong.

The gracious sailor soon realized
The Keeper was from heaven above.
The light that shone so brilliantly
Was God's undying love.

—Lynda S. Mitchell

Fleeting Beauty

Huge spheres of fragrant beauty
On a long slender stem — each one,
Standing erect and majestic,
With pride, they bask in the sun.
Raindrops descend in a torrent;
Destruction and sadness abound;
Stems broken-and blossoms all muddy,
In humility - my peonies lie flat on the ground.

—Lylah Casper

The Judgment

With her hour glass figure, and her diamond mink coat,
On a scale of one to ten, she is a ten.

Watching her dine at the dinner table,
She uses each fork for just the right use, and she of course,
Has a napkin in her lap.

She is oh so polite, and laughs, just so.
The others at the table, linger on her every word.

Her hair is long and straight, not a strand out of place,
And she wears no make-up, having a naturally beautiful face.

Her nails are perfect,
Which of coarse, means she is kept.
Can you image having to sit next to her, and bare this.
Let me tell you, it is awful.

As if all that isn't enough, she now, just has to get up and
Take a stroll, or something.

I have a headache, my heart is in my lap,
Just maybe, if I'm lucky, she'll fall down.

As she slides back her chair from the table, her escort hurries
to help. I am, I am, I am ashamed, for she only has one leg.

I judged and convicted her without even a second thought.
I hope my judge isn't, me.

—Tewonia L. Bradley

Desert Monsoon

Cotton-candy clouds slide flat-bottomed
on glass supported by hilltops
flickering out like light bulbs

A dustdevil lifts her thin wide skirt
and flees
squinting out the sun
Color seeps back up plants
bleached by the glare

The skeletal trees bow to the wind
bushes giggle and the saguaros join in
with their song of whistles
The clouds grumble under their own weight
and the glass cracks
parting the heavy heat
and filling the air with the smell of dirt

Lightning throws broken chalk
growling across the blackboard sky
—*Larry Samson*

My Hand

An x-rayed jellybean sitting lifeless
on my finger,
A wrinkled old lady that does nothing but linger,
Worms slipping and sliding all over the place,
Lasagna still in its microwavable case,
A mass of string all tied in knots,
Whirlpools swishing in pans in pots,
Fields of tall green grass that reaches forever....

Rolling hills that really roll if you flick the lever,
And last but not least a bucket or prunes, that reach all over
my knuckly dunes.
—*Lindsay Eve Ellis*

The Wait

The days roll by as the minutes we see
On the face of the clock seem an eternity
To hold on to the faith, the trust, the memory
Of the one the promise was made 'cause of fate
Makes it easy to deal with the pain of the wait

Though some days are tougher than others to get through
As the loneliness sets in when we're thinking of two
We gather much strength in our words so true
That we smile again and can stand up straight
And without any doubts we believe in the wait

The wait itself we'll happily endure
As its meaning is a symbol of all that is pure
In our hearts as we both are so positively sure
That in our lives this union could never come too late
And that adds value to the price of the wait

There's none more respected, none better the name
Than we who have withstood and have victory to claim
In this battle of loneliness, we understand it's no game
'Cause there's none more beautiful, there's none more great
Than the Sunshine I love, completing the wait
—*Larry Dean Powell*

Falling Leaves

I watched a maple after a sudden freeze.
One after another the falling leaves
Raced each other to the earth.
The breeze that set them free
Also seemed to blow through me
To prepare my soul for a spring re-birth.
—*Rosella Virginia Wood*

Anastasia

I always wondered why I saw the lady
on the grassy rise,
her dress wind pressed against her thighs.

The breeze blowing her hair around
With only a glow for a crown.

But the crown that she knew was in
her heart,
Life to her had become an art.

And on this windy stretch of ground
In the breeze, her vibrations found...

Carried her thoughts up to the sky,
What is this world will live or die.

To her aloneness she now succumbs
as closer her years come.

The pictures in her mind made clear
as decisions from a far come near.
—*Nancy B. Lovell*

A Friend

A friend is someone special to me,
One I often like to see.

A friend is someone who brightens my day,
Even when it's cloudy and gray.

A friend is someone I enjoy talking to,
About the things we like to do.

A friend is always there when I call,
Winter, summer, spring, or fall.

A friend is someone who truly cares,
Gives of their time and always shares.

A friend is what I've found in you,
I'm glad you are my friend so true.
—*Sharon B. Word*

Faces

In two different faces does happiness shine,
One questions the future, one reflects on past time.

One vision young, full of wonder, full of fun,
Growing, unstoppable, like the fires of the sun.

The other image careworn, scars of past years,
One who's felt pain, smelled the fresh scent of tears.

Two common threads weave these two souls together,
Joy and freedom like an eagle, no storm they can't weather.

They're content just to be, to live, never quit,
Like silence, like winter, on your days it does sit.

In two different faces does happiness shine,
Silent as night, yet priceless as time.
—*Sarah E. Ungerer*

Autum's Dance

I saw what could have been a picture today
Of a little boy who was out in play
with his arms raised high in sheer delight
"Look at me momma!"
as he spun round and round to dance with the
leaves before they hit the ground.

Leaves of yellow, brown and gold
swirled about him in their dance of flight
and nature and the child become as one
then the wind dies down and their dance is done.
—*Nancy R. Torres*

Trust

The same, the same, peacock politicians cannot tame
One self-respecting dame
And homeless children roam the streets
Without a parent's claim.
The same, the same, phony prophets all overuse His name
Boat loads of Chinese immigrants are lost at sea
And any mutilated Bosnian could be you or me.
The same, the same, though nameless terror lurks everywhere
The sun and the stars are still there
The birds in the sky still fly high
That baby pilot whale's been cured
And soon will be let out to sea
To be free, even as you and, hopefully, me.

    —*Solomon Pogarsky*

God's Salvation Plan

Jesus made His earthly journey,
One which He did not have to make;
But through His love and compassion,
He took the journey for man's sake.

All men were sinners lost and doomed,
But God 'fore knew the ways of man
And loving as only He could,
He provided salvation's plan.

Jesus willingly stepped from Glory
Knowing the price He had to pay,
Dying the death—the sinners' due;
This He knew was the only way.

The cold, dark tomb could not hold Him;
No power could thwart God's redemptive plan.
He arose the Supreme Victor,
Jesus Christ the Saviour of man.

Saviour of all who trust in Him,
Believing He's God's sinless Son,
Who paid our sin debt on the cross
And for us the victory won.

    —*Rudolph Townsend*

To A Cinder Cone

The last time we were together there was no bridge between us,
Only a footpath leading to the top of a wind-swept cinder cone
  mountain,
Where violence of weather twists Union Pines and the Hopi
  mesas
Stacked up the horizon all the way to Colorado

We huddled together on the Lee Slope whispering
I had found vocabulary made quiet to describe my feelings,
You seemed stiff and bound-up tightly in your muffler and
  mittens,
So we turned away from each other and found fossils within the
  Limestone.

Together we carried our heavy silence back down the trail,
Each with our separate load, a fossil in each pocket
And a catch in our throats where the tears were frozen,
The artifacts of our hearts buried like treasures unremembered.

    —*Lori Goldberg*

Questions

Oh, how it hurts to know that you no longer care
  Or —— did you ever?
So many years since we were wed and now you say you must be
  free, free of me?
What happened to a marriage so happy? Or so I thought ——
  But was it ever?
I just don't know, I just don't know
  Now will I ever!

    —*Marie A. Van Wagner*

To Be Perchance A Randolph Or A Lee

To be born in the South for us was meant to be.

Not hardly ever are we considered provincial, but
  only Southern, or not at all.

Possibly because of the way we pronounce Atlanta,
  Georgia, Carter, garbage, house and oil.

If only we could say, "nuclear."

As to manners we are thoroughly schooled and
  unselfconscious.

Our heavy silver-plate tureens are instantaneously
  transformed into luscious candied yams, and

Gentlemen stand before ladies at table as well as
  in the parlor, where in Richmond and Baltimore
  the word rolls mellifluously off proper lips.

If only hats would come back all the way (preferably
  grey), so that we could tip and doff.

If only the General had been younger, smarter,
  victorious...or had known when to quit.

Much of this one-hundred and twenty five years ago.

But the good times there cannot be forgotten,
  nor should we ever look away...

    —*William Buchanan*

Esoteric Thought

Running to see who the winner will be
  only to find
  it's not me.
So I'm pedaling my new bike
  faster than the wind
  then I fall.
Swimming underwater racing the sea nymphs
  only to breathe better
  no more air.
Quiet inside around is not a sound
  but a faint beating heart beating
  and running water barely running.
So to become all these wonderful things
  that I thought would make me immortal
  would be foolish
  for I am not.

    —*Sara Hiller*

Transformation

A miracle: That sometimes life simply opens up —
Opens to me like a flower shimmers and glows,
And as little daily things come, it shows
Me richness all around, without measure.

I know these late, lovely days of summer
Are but a last, exuberant bloom before dreary
Days of winter come, and then I'm weary
And hemmed in by the world's demands.

But this season, it's different, and my heart
Seems to have expanded in the golden days,
So that I see beauty in a thousand ways;
My soul filled with the wonder of joy.

I received a message, one day beside a waterfall,
Words from a Spirit, clothed in a mantle of peace,
And that happening has given me release
From the doubts and pain of "before."

"When the heart is ready, the learning will come"
Echoes the teaching someone gave to me;
I only know it is wonderful to be free
And to trust in all the tomorrows.

    —*Rosalind Caryl*

My Flight

If I could soar with wings as the mighty eagle
or even the smallest sparrow

I would climb to heights that can only be imagined

I would touch the clouds with my finger tips and
catch the raindrops on my tongue

I would look down on the highest mountains and behold
their majesty and also on the valley to marvel in its beauty

I would drift across the deepest sea and across the deserts sand

I would look down upon my family, loved ones and friends and
blow them a kiss from the brightest star just to say I love you

I would whisper the deepest feelings in my heart, to be taken
by the wind and be scattered about to those who love me, to
those who care

I would say I'm sorry to those I've disappointed or hurt, and
let my tears fall from heaven to ask their forgiveness

Reaching heights that could not be spoken in word, I would
climb higher and higher until I would be in His presence.

    —Theresa Shepherd

A Choir Director's Lament

Oh why do people say "yes" and then don't.
Or faithfully say that "I will" and then won't.
And never a word or a sign do they give
That the promises made always leak like a sieve.

When we practice at eight, it is style to be late.
They sing a few notes and then leave for a date.
So the few that are faithful still plug right along
On the louds and the softs 'till they make it a song.

It's fun and it's work and discouraging too
To enroll so many that end up so few.
But somehow we manage by means to aspire
And bring in on Sunday a pretty good choir.

Of this we are sure, that the sun will arise.
The clouds will disperse to show the blue skies.
And Gabriel's trumpet will sound the last call,
There will only be seats for the few—not the all.

    —Sidney R. Sonnichsen

Seeking Restful Sleep

Just think of things that never were,
Or gold and frankincense and myrrh,
Or things that baa and coo and purr,
Or beds as soft as rabbit fur.

Or think of sultry ladies fair,
With black or red or flaxen hair.
Their realm's a place you'd like to share.
They gently take you in their care.

If sleep eludes you, think of how
Your life got from past tense to now,
Or how to milk or how to plow,
Or why cows moo and cats meow.

Relax your mind by thoughts of things
Like pirate ships or poet kings,
Or lovely girls with angel's wings,
Who say they'll be your underlings.

Then contemplate the ways of Zen,
Or why the sun darkens your skin,
Or all the things that might have been,
If men were gods and gods were men.

    —Richard Danner

Ordinary Men

Once these men were heroes marching proudly in review;
ordinary men doing what the ordinary do.

Left behind their country and familial love they knew;
ordinary men doing what the ordinary do.

Faced uncertainty, horror, wrenching sorrow, terror too;
ordinary men doing what the ordinary do.

Youthful innocence lost to the wretchedness in view;
ordinary men doing what the ordinary do.

Home at last, they found who was and wasn't true;
ordinary men doing what the ordinary do.

Sleepless nights, haunting memories, nocturnal tears like dew;
ordinary men doing what the ordinary do.

Many nights have passed now, men's numbers dwindling to a few;
ordinary men doing what the ordinary do.

Old men, old memories, old comrades who;
as ordinary men, did what the extraordinary do.

    —Mike Morton

Do Unto Others

The adage I heard in a whisper once was to consider someone
   other than me. This secret broke in verse it spoke
for my actions would be the key. I dispatch invitation to this
   grand orchestration and I'd like it to start with me.
I'll make tender effort to be kind to those in which I share
   the planet, Earth. I'll yield to others feelings for I
may not get a second chance, to restore, my own self-worth. A
   gesture of kindness can bring full-circle round, those
with doubts, that harbor fear. Still, we can't know the cross
   that one man bears if his shoes we do not wear.
Assess your actions, are they to model, to this you do believe?
   Therefore, you've done unto others as you've seen fit
as well as you would like to receive.

    —Maria Christine Fritz

Home In Miami

Preface: In years to come, we will remember
our home in Miami, circa 1993.

Our homes have become our prisons,
It's just like being in jail.
Our inept system has failed us.
We feel like we're held, without bail,
Outside bullets are flying,
Our air is full of lead,
Be just a little unlucky,
In a moment — you could be dead,
Steel bars cover our windows,
Six sturdy locks on the door,
You become afraid of your shadow,
For outside, there rages a war,
Our leaders wring their hands,
They are helpless,
Our spirits, once high.
Will soon break,
How much more, must we suffer?
How much more, can we take?

    —Larry London

Untitled

I guess your concrete fashions are fading out,
or at least I tried to notice that in your eyes.

Don't become, just be.

    —Rui Miguel Saramago

January

January—stark, lonely, flash-back scenes of holiday festivities;
outdoor landscapes of greys, whites, ice blues and dark greens;
finding and dreaming of self and past loves

A time for beef stews, homemade yeasty breads, crusty chicken
pies, thick vegetable soups, apple cobblers, hot chocolate with
marshmallows and lightly salted buttery popcorn

Glowing warmth from the fireplace allowing the fire within to
rest and the mind uncluttered for crossword puzzles, painting
in pastels, sketching pictures to while away your time in many
poses

Reading a classic or a book enjoyed as a child, planning and
designing the garden for spring planting from delicate Baby's
Breath to peach-colored roses

All the while music surrounds you from the jazz of Kenton to
the lilt of Chopin—and best of all—a billowing quilt envelops
you from eve 'til morn

Remember—don't venture out 'till you're dressed in layers from
head to toe with those hard-working, story-telling hands
snuggled in fleece-lined gloves

    —Lorraine E. Lant

An Ode To The Forest

Majestic wonders tower into the heavens; arms
outspread: Protecting territory and inhabitants
from the glaring fireball above them.

Moss carpeted, soft and green, I lay; dreamily
Peering upward into the blue and cloud free sky.

Blotches of sunlight creep through their swaying
Arms, tickling; warming; chilling my presence.

Onward through dancing shadows; alone - but not lonely

Sound everywhere: Some echoing in the distance; and
The compelling flow of water makes its way through the riverbed

A whisper; a quiet roar: Flowing; rushing; falling

A plunge into the pond: A swim

Rejuvenating falls shower my near nakedness:
Numbing cold; then soothing warmth

A rest on the rocks; and then returning

Satisfaction: Finally finding the time to
make this trip; a few hours; a day; memories
to last a lifetime!!!

Next time, I'll share it with someone!
Want to come along?

    —Ronald Antone

My Life Without Love

As a child I grew up asking myself one question
over and over. Does anyone love me?
I often sat by the window watching the children play
Hoping and praying I would get a chance to go outside today.
Oh...another day goes by and again
I don't get a chance to play outside.
I would just sit by the window staring at the sky
Asking myself with a sigh...does anyone love me.
Trying to convince myself without disbelief
The stay in this foster home would be brief.
But another day goes by, no mom, no dad
They said they would be back I guess again they lied.
The question I keep repeating must really be
I don't understand why nobody loves me.
Now at whatever age I may be
I realize if nobody else cares
I love me...

    —Patricia L. Rice-Diggs

Lost Love

Once upon a summer's day, as the clouds turned a dulling gray,
Over many a suffering months of care, the end was slowly coming
near, as I watched, my heart felt sad, of the times we could
not have. Sweet memories of him, soft whispers in my ear, all
the things I held so dear.
The future without him, my biggest fear, is slowly becoming all
too clear— nothing left; only a tear.

Some years ago when our love began, laughing and gently holding
his hand, on that dreamy fun-filled night, the stars were
shining extremely bright, I was staring at him—it was love at
first sight. Over many a years his heart he would send, all
of his love to me in the end.
Thinking of what it could've been, knowing that I'll never see
him again—it was almost the end.

Looking back it seemed so fine, walking along his hand in
mine, but now he's gone, there's nothing to say, in the world
he cannot stay. The smile on his face, the twinkle in his eye,
why oh Lord does he have to die? My tears fell on the bed
where he lay, hoping for a miracle that day in May, while I
cried, I began to pray—as the memories fade away.

    —Tammy Henderson

Another Day

The sun rises another day
Parents are at work, kids at play
While along side my bed I pray
Can I make it another day?

Another day of hatred and crime
While so many lives ran out of time
Another day and night of food, beer,
T.V. and fright, another day another fight.

Another day of poverty, or will it
come to be, another phone call, or
Refusal for peace, another country
goes to war, rich get richer, poor stay poor.

Another day of wishing for a blind man eyes
Only left to hear the world cries
Never to see suffering of the young or old,
treated so badly and sometimes even cold, or
even unjust, yet there is nothing being done.

Another day as night seems to fall
I finally made it through it all
Will I miss anything, if I don't wake at all.
    —Taneka D. Beckman

Birth Of A Season

Clouds in rambling silence float,
  Pastures grazed by beef and goat.
Oak trees stretch in languished green,
  Flowers waving to be seen.
Screen doors open for cool breeze pleasure,
  Carriages transport newborn treasures.
Gardens sprouting lettuce and beets,
  Barbecues rotate succulent treats.
Swimming pools filled with mountain water,
  Tractors plow under last years fodder.
Cherry trees bloom, or are they peach?
  Newly-weds stroll on moonlit beach.
Toddlers with bruises from sidewalk falls,
  Violets for one we love most of all.
Mailman exchanges his longs for his shorts,
  Lawyers seek settlements instead of courts.
Bees and mosquitos appear from nowhere,
  Bicyclists in helmets fixing a spare.
Awnings are hung to shield from the sun,
  Cold winter has vanished, spring has come.
    —Mary Moline

Gods Dream

Peace - A distant dream it seems
Peace - A rippling stream
Peace - A battle field silent
Peace - Only God can grant it
Peace - Not all men seek it
Peace - Mans greed won't get it
Peace - Women and children seek it
Peace - God wants it
Peace - The humble spirit prays for it
Peace - God is waiting for all men to ask for it
Peace - Free for the taking for God is ever living
Peace - Guns and money can't buy it
Peace - Won't be granted to unchanged spirits
Peace - Given by the man from Galilee
Peace - The wish of God living
Peace - Is love driven from God in heaven

　　—Sidney Lee Phelps Sr.

Untitled

Whatever happened to our beautiful earth?
People are too worried about what the land's worth.
Just make lots of money, and get much richer.
If the land gets cut then we'll just stitch her.
Where's all the animals who used to graze and roam?
I don't know, I guess we just sort of took their home.
Just better yourself, who cares about the rest.
But look what we've created, oh what a mess.
It's time for the world to open its eyes.
Face reality and forget all the lies.
Were will we be in another ten years?
That's the problem, nobody really cares.

　　—Tammy Wroble

Street Action

The action in the street is getting very fast
People just stare and refuse to blink
Could it be their living in the past
Or maybe search for the missing link

They leave their hearts at the door
To put on a protective face
which will frown when it sees the poor
And smile when it sees a pretty face

If all those eyes could look into the skies
they would see we're made of the same material
and not a high paid player in a daytime serial
So lets stop this high speed pace
Or else we'll end up like the rest of the human race

　　—William Duke Davis

A Way Of Life

I watched him today, all tattered and torn, while he was at
play, it was just early morn.
He tugged at his trousers, that kept slipping away, they were
just a bit large, the knees they did fray.
Tin cans went in this bag, bottles in that, he gathered them
up, while ignoring the rat's.
He spied me watching, then gave me a grin, said "how ya doin'
lady, got any tin?"
"Well no," I replied, "not with me," I said, "Oh well," he
then smiled, "we can do without bread."
I thought for a moment, then realized, with pain, from these
bottles and cans, he had so much to gain.
For what he does, he does not for play, he searches and
gathers, to eat once a day.

　　—Lori E. Collins

The Day We Met

Do you remember the day we met?
Personally it's a day I'll never forget,
We acted as if we'd always be together,
But somehow I knew it wouldn't last forever.

I often times wonder, how it could be;
How such a special love could happen to me?
During the times we spent as one
I prayed that day would never come.

That day when I would say good-bye,
My heart would ache and just ask why?
That last day came and went by
And you were strong and didn't cry.

This poem isn't meant to make you shed tears
Or fill your loving heart with fears,
It's just to let you know
Away from your love I will never go.
I'll always love you with all my heart
I won't let anything tear us apart,
Before you know; I'll be home
And never again will I leave you alone!

　　—Steven J. Flores

When I Need You

The jukebox sat silent in the corner,
Play some American music you said,
The jukebox played a happy tune of trombones,
blues, an instrumental song.
Let's dance - dance to the music,
You can not dance to that you said
I reached for you and you took my hands
And your arms encircled my waist
Swirling to the music, dancing, gliding like on air,
And, the jukebox played on...
My eyes met yours, yours hazel, mine brown,
The music filled the air and we swirled on a small dance floor,
Swirling to the music, oblivious to others,
The music filling our ears. Happy in each other's arms
Our hearts and thoughts were one. The music played on
You swirled me once more and our hearts met
And I will remember the dance and the
music you and I danced to and you and I became soul partners
　forever
When I need you all I have to do is close my eyes
and you and I are dancing...

　　—Sandra Kay Temple

Three Men And A Stove

　Three men sat round a pot-belly stove
Playing checkers and reminiscing about times long ago.
　In younger days, each man was brave and strong
Now their advice and wisdom is never wrong.
　Each wear Fedoras low on their brow
Their style and grace make their grandchildren proud.
　If you listen and do not rush
You will hear stories that make the whole room hush.
　Adventure and courage and all that is right
Three wise old men tell their tales tonight.

　　—Vicki Ledesma

Winging It

An airline passenger out for a fling,
Peers across the aisle and observes -
"Why you folks still have your wing!"
And thereby set atingle a tangle of nerves!

　　—Leonard Pigott

Don't Go

Please don't go
Please don't go for I want you to stay.
You have taught me so much from life to death.
You have even taught me that I should pray.
You have showed me that I need not walk alone,
and should never be afraid.
For you said I would never be alone even when I betrayed.
For if you do go, I don't know what I
would do without you helping me along the way.
Please don't go I beg
Please don't go I want you to stay...

—*Nikki L. Price*

Untitled

On a cold wintry night in a land far away
Poor Joseph and Mary had nowhere to stay,
At the Inn they were turned away from the door,
So in a stable so lowly our Saviour she bore...

On the hillside the shepherds were watching their sheep,
While roundabout villagers all were asleep..
When up in the sky came a wondrous sight,
It gave off a glow and lit up the night...

So fearful were they, they fell to the ground
While the Glory of God shone all around...
An angel appeared and told of the birth
Of the One who was sent to bring hope to the Earth.

The Star guided their steps to where the Babe lay
In peaceful slumber in a manger of hay.
They knelt to give Honor and show Him their love;
They knew He was sent from the Father above.

They brought to Him gifts of silver and gold,
And things of great value I have been told...
So what can I bring when the Manger I see?
Since I have no riches I'll just bring Him .... Me.

—*Ollis L. Beach*

Origins

Somewhere in the depths of the soul
pops a tiny spark, formless as the fire
that fuels it. The spark then flashes forth
burning a swath through the aging images
of the hemispheres, right and left,
to let the one picture shine brightest
among the multitude of paling shadows
engulfing the creator and the creature,
in addition to itself.

Now the ball picks up momentum
in an everlasting spin where
nothing matters. The flames spread
every which way, cleansing all they touch,
imploding in self-sustaining fragments
of utter illumination. There is no return
from the blinding blaze in whose wake
lies the artifact in its fresh-minted glory,
like an old truth retold.

—*I. S. Madugula*

Melanie Faith

Today we met sweet Melanie Faith—
Our baby great-granddaughter, so precious and dear
As I held her close, she stole my heart.
Her big blue eyes, so bright and clear,
Spoke lovingly to me—we'll never really be apart.
I pray to God to keep her healthy and strong
Our first great-grandchild—in our hearts she'll always belong.

—*Sarah L. Greer*

A Portrait

If I were an artist or a poet
Possessing their great gifts
To capture the candor and contours of life,
I'd paint the prose
Or write the ode
That speaks of splendor of sea and sky.

My pallet and brush would
Dab only the hues of love
And of beauty.
In rhyme, there'd be no time
But the enchanting ecstasy of eternity.

Though we pass but briefly
Through this puzzling plan,
We see what we wish to see,
Hear what we wish to hear;
And when our visit is ending,
The pastels fading,
Will we be ready to
Become a part of that grandeur
Of which we paint and write?

—*Philip W. Rothman*

Soulfully Pretending

I'm very good at pretending
Pretending that you're here
But "yet" in actuality
Your love has never been near.

I'm very good at forgiving...
Forgiving all that is done
While I was afraid of losing your love!
I found you had none.

I do not blame you
For what could not be.
I only wish for your happiness
Although it's not with me.

"Dear God" let him help me
Help me to descend
Descend from being her lover,
To just being a friend.

I'm good at pretending we're as happy as can be!
But by pretending, I found reality!!...
The only person in love, you see
The only person in love, was me.

—*Nate Rutledge*

Pride

Pride is not something you're able to give
Pride is a feeling that shows as you live.
Through words and actions you're able to show
What you hold close and what you let go.
Pride is a word that makes you stick out
Standards you have that others won't doubt
Values you set a long time ago...
That help you decide what's a yes or a no.
Pride lets you hold your head up high
You take life at a steady course.
You go the extra mile, and you don't do it by force
You're willing and ready, you try not to fall
You give all you've got or you try not at all!
You seek the right path on the journey you walk
You smile at put downs and petty talk.
You hold your hand out to help another.
Yes, if you've got pride, your like no other.

—*Mandy Mosley*

The Truth

Slavery, instituted in the Black race. Being sold like
property, such a disgrace. Serving, cooking, and cleaning for
the white man. Not only that, also cultivating the land.

The white man who stood tall and proud to own a Black slave.
Whipping and punishing them if they didn't behave. How
disappointed the white man must be, when the Black slave
suddenly became free.

Yes, freedom! How sweet the sound. No more of being pushed
around. Freedom didn't come overnight. It was a long hard
struggle, and a difficult fight.

Although slavery isn't in existence any longer. Everyday
racism and prejudice is getting stronger. Since Blacks didn't
ask to come to America anyway. It's time to realize that
blacks and whites are here to stay.

In order to make our lives better. The black race must join
together. Let's show each other that we care. Get rid of the
attitudes and beware of the negative feelings of the white man.
There's no way that he can understand the problems and hatred
that we've been through. He's just on the outside looking in,
not having a clue.

　　　—Zabrina Miranda Grisby

Runaway

I find my self thinking about it a lot,
Question is what will happen if I get caught.
It seems so easy to just get up and run,
I just need the courage and it will all be done
I've tried everything else and I still feel blue,
In my head this seems to be the best thing to do.
I've wanted to do it for quite some time now,
But I just really wasn't sure how.
Eventually I'll get rid of these feelings someday,
But for now I just want to runaway.

　　　—Mindi McCallum

Steps Of Quiet

Quiet steps of patience, when there was never time.
Quiet steps of kindness, so very hard to find.
Quiet steps of whispers, when shouting reigned supreme.
Quiet steps of gentleness, today so rarely seen.
Quiet steps of lend an ear to what we had to tell.
Quiet steps of give advice.
Quiet steps of wish us well.

Quiet steps we hear no more, your gentleness is gone.
In each of us in some small way, your memory lives on.

So quickly Mike you left us.
You were taken from our midst.

We weren't ready...
You had to go...
If only we had had more time...
If only...
To tell you
How we loved your
Quiet steps

　　　—Patricia J. Dugan

World Tears

I can see a mountain peak and the sun with its rays bursting
out the last sparks of warmth for the night. I can feel a cool
breeze as it passes. Echoes of animals call me. I can hear
children's laughter as they are called in from the night air.
Memories are keeping me alive. It hurts to see the oceans, the
air, and the land cry. I am the world, treated with hate, but
loved because you live with me and on me...

　　　—Lisa Blacksmith

The Quilting Room

My grandma Maime stitched her
quilting pieces for hours on end.
In a room reserved for ladies only,
sewing, gossiping and mending.

The movement of needles, back and forth;
stopping only briefly to stretch
her aging hands, racked with pain.

As I watched the orchestration of
skillfully crafting works of art
in the company of family and friends,
creating priceless things to pass down
again and again, I knew I would never know the
camaraderie of working side by side,
at the quilting table, chatting all day long;
keeping time with the rhythm, like a favorite song.

　　　—Pamela Kaufman

Do You See What I See?

In a world of unforgiving people with unreconcilable differences
Racist views, sexist choices, discriminating voices,

Unreasonable arguments, unsatisfying lives, abortioned girls
who will never be wives, men who cheat and lie,
women who listen and buy, all that is told to them.

Animal testing, helpless deer people digesting, blind men
who don't want to see, if for he one day you could be.

Singing voices in a mind that turn into screams. It's
a trap, I wish I had a map, to life that is. It isn't easy.

Do you think I'm a feminist? I gave this ending a nice
little twist.

After reading this should you be crying? No. You should start
Helping the dying. This world that is.

　　　—Shalan Marie Restum

What I Dream...

A forest of pure crystal glints with the paint of a
　　rainbow sunset.
The mimicking images of the friendly star beckon
　　saying, "Come, dance."
I join it, and am pulled into a world of nothing but color.
I then spent all night dancing with the darkness,
　　and the mysterious secrets that it held.
Then, once again, the befriending star came to play
　　and with it the dawn of a colorful new world.
"Stay," the colors said, "We have so many things to share."
And with that, I left the heavens and joined the
　　rainbow of crystal forests and misting mountain
　　　streams.

　　　—Suzanne C. Myers

The Education

What is education? It is knowledge
Road to better things in life
It needs discipline and sacrifice
That we do not like to feel or see
It will determine what you are going to be
The time it short when we are young
It quickly passes us by, we can't be weak
We got to be strong, challenge in life is
Nothing new to be prepared will get you through
Lets keep on learning all we can
And have some fund now and then
When we receive our degree we will be traveling
First class in deed

　　　—Rudy Slomiany

Reading

Reading is here,
Reading is there,
Reading is everywhere,
All though your life,
You might need to know about the amount,
need to buy a pair of shoes,
or buy a T.V. to listen to news,
or maybe you need a new house,
or exterminator to get rid of a mouse,
Reading is here,
Reading is there.
Reading is everywhere,
Reading is important because you may,
need to know what the computer displays,
So read as many books as you can.
Read about how Christopher Columbus journey began,
Read books while you are young.
Or read about how opera is sung.
So don't delay if you like books say hooray.
And let your imagination take you away,

—Valerie Pagel

Cleansed

The living waters of the sea refresh you, rejuvenate me;
Reconstitute our spirits, renew our zeal;
Reorder our lives, reevaluate the deal;
Restore our sanity; reaffirm our faith in eternity.

Reissue the card which says.....
"You are now entitled to rejoin the ranks of those
considered intelligent enough to be called the brotherhood,
the sisterhood - the Great Humanity."

—Lorna Doone Lover

We Are One

We met each other many years ago, you weren't your every day
regular John or Joe.
I love you anyway and think the world should know.

Being a unique couple on display in society's eyes most every
day.
We receive looks of damnation in the most racial way.
We pray, My Lord for strength, let not our thoughts go a stray
from the two who made December 31 their wedding day.

Our trials and tribulations keep our thoughts on the Lords way.
We as husband and wife refuse to live in society's betray
which has forced us to look the other way.
Showering each other with memorable thoughts of how much we
have loved day after day in the most romantic way.
Always saying "I love you" and stressing
"You are missed while you are away."
Taking an oath to be joined as one was not taken lightly and not for
fun.
Please Lord, remember if you are calling we are still as one
and have created a bond that shall remain undone.

—Sondra L. Russell

Summer

Summer creeps up stealthily,
Rushes in with spring rains.
Rivers over flow their banks.
Suddenly floral beauty floods the countryside.
Sweet pungent fumes tickle the nostrils.
Brilliant colors blaze the hills and valleys.
Relax and enjoy the lazy days of summer.
Their number is few,
Without warning they steal away.

—Lois A. Pratte

Expressing Yourself

Expressing yourself is very real
Relating thoughts on how you feel
Expressing yourself from your mind
Relieves the heart from inside
Expressing yourself makes stress less
Allowing yourself to do your best
Expressing yourself lets out tension
Resolving the problems you haven't mentioned
Expressing yourself makes things clear
No questions asked and nothing to fear
Expressing yourself committing no crimes
Creates a peace and happier times
Expressing yourself with a smile
Makes roads smoother with shorter miles
Expressing yourself with a touch of love
Brings you blessings from up above
Expressing yourself while you learn
Showing others you are concerned
Expressing yourself in a positive way
Will bring success your way someday

—Virginia G. Melvin

The Eagle

Deep within the regions of my mind is a
remembrance of when I was an eagle in your mind and in
your eye.
Oh, how I soared, up, up, like the wind I could fly.
Over the mountains and rivers we would go, soaring
and flying, then just for fun glide along ever so slow.
We would dance on the wind and truly enjoy every breeze.
Hold in special meaning, the gaiety and beauty of the
flowers singing their love songs down in the meadows
and the glades.
We enjoyed life to its fullest, giving no thought
to its end.
Then one day, returning to earth in the shape of man,
I hurt you my love, and fly no more even though I
try as hard as I can.
The hurt I have done to you has clipped my wings,
and no more can I fly.

—Rex Heisler

Marlene Keys - 1962

I kissed the nipples of your firm breasts
Revealing nectar tongue never did taste
White-hot pain burning deep in my chest
Ripping holes in my heart
Where sorrow did rest
Where pain was the patron of waste
And dormant emotions lay sleeping in disgrace
Mired in the mulch of old memories
Loss loves and empty dreams
In your ebony eyes I saw your soul
And found my goal
Your love is greater than my pain
Emanating from your being
Is the passionate poetry of all loss souls
Merging with sorrows of yesterday
And our dreams of tomorrow
Only true love sings a song of happiness
Tinged with sonnets of sorrow

—Leroy L. Moses

The Black Veil

        The mediocrity of life seems to fade from day
    Right into night; the tasks at hand, routine at least,
            And in my mind there is no end in sight.
        My life is such a mix of puzzle parts, so mingled
    That no picture can be made. I hold the realness of my life
        At bay until the time when truth can e'er be said.
        And when things seem, at least, to be routinely well,
    Some foolish word is heard that turns my world to black
        [A mundane word, a phrase with meaning none, by
            Some "no one"] from which I can't come back.
        The feeling, like a tomb, above me lurks and holds me
            So I cannot seem to breathe. And then I know
        That sometime soon, someone will place upon my head
    A funeral wreath. I try to grip to something real and solid
            And hold on tight, and, yes, my view is clearer now.
    Thank God, I made it back this time as I have in the past,
    And then my head I bow, "Dear God," I pray, "please show me
        How to stay within your light and love; save me from
            The blackness and hold me from above.

                                    —*Patricia Patterson*

When I Think Of You

When I think of you thy oceans glisten with beautiful waves and
ripples of luscious beauty and purity, my heart pounds like the
thunder of thy storm clouds when I think of you. As day turneth
to night, thy moon and stars are bright, the smooth cool
tropical breeze of thy night so light while thy feeling is all
so right with my dear embrace of love over you so tight when I
think of you. As thy storm ends, thy clouds moveth across the
sky and thy sun peaketh through thy clouds to reveal the
precious you when I think of you. My burning heart of fire
melts so deep with thy mystical passion of light beyond thy
depths of pure exquisite desires to shower you with all the
forbidden essence of my treasurable precious love when I think
of you. Love is true, so are you, thy things of love I'd do for
you, my love for you is yours to keep as your love for me is
mines to treasure, like the beauty of a tropical sunset,
thy sweet smell of roses, thy precious sound of
chimes and thy wet sound of raindrops forever falling when I
think of you. Every passing day of my life, my precious love
for you is forever eternal, my love for you is forever more, nor
will it ever die as I do still forever love you everyday of my
dear precious life when I think of you.

                                    —*Novarro Ramon Washington Jr*

Why

Why are trucks made in Japan
    rolling all over our fruited plains
why are soup kitchens boomin'
    in our troubled land
whatever happened to the American

why is crazy horse now a beer
    I thought he was a man who knew no fear
why is love lost in sex
    when then lonely are crying
why is everything still o.k.

why does the media have such a hold
    that makes our children grow old
why do stars shine in the sky
    why should we build a station in space
when there is destruction of the human race

why are killers doin' time
    it is just enough to blow your mind
I may be wrong to wonder why
    I may be wrong to give a damn
didn't Christ start living as a man?

                                    —*Timothy Clark*

Poverty Cul De Sac

A cracked mirror reflecting a face etched by chronic failure.
Rough hands creatively carving potato peel spirals destined
to swell the trash heap after the boiled potatoes are gone.
Chipped plates, seated in cold water, passively enduring the
soapless ritual recognizing the souls' need to wage battle
against filth.

A wealth of children held in a sagging mattress,
bare of all except stain. Totally unaware as yet,
their unique contribution to society is the clinging odor of
urine. Mercifully deaf for a few hours to the destructive
bitterness of parents doomed to failure.

One closet entrusted with the generosity of christians giving
their all to the poor; all they would be ashamed to offer friends.
A black dress for the mature figure, pinstripe trousers complete
with safety pin where once a zipper proudly rolled. Awkward,
uncared for garments, to be hung on thin bodies, adjusted to size
and borne down endless halls, into classrooms bulging with
LEVIS's
on carefully turned backs. Unendurable classrooms spilling another
wave of underachievers into the world of eager job hunters.
Ever pursuing the dream of equal opportunity,
ever finding a closed door.

                                    —*Sandy Miller*

The Murder Of My Tear

                        It
                    sapped
                  my strength
            and weakened my
        muscle It walked all
        over me as I idly rustled.
    Jaded perceptions of life flashed
    by, splashes of rain clouded my eye
    thunderous pains barged into my heart I
was a bulls-eye for a venomous dart. It kicked
up Its feet, made Itself at home. Though no one
made It feel welcome It started to roam. My umbrella
turned outward, pelting rain made me numb I kept
    praying and wondering would there ever be some
    consolation for this murder now taking place would
    anyone recognize Its ugly face. Then it was over
        and It had won. My tear had died, the deed
            was done. I had nothing, I couldn't
                fight. It was cancer that took
                    my sister's life.

                                    —*Nancy M. S. Wright*

The Master Painter

Have you ever wandered through galleries of art and
saw paintings of beauty both great and small that it didn't
bring changes to your heart and make you wander about the
greatest artist of all? Who with his paint brush, turned
waters to blue the mountains to gray and the hill side to
green the sky with its vastness to unchangeable hues and gave
beauty to flowers beyond ones fondest dreams.

The violet small, in the twinkling dew he painted it the
deepest, blue not one of the flowers did the masters hand
leave untouched with beauty in the vast expanse and unto the
lily, by the garden wall so gently he brushed it least it fall
then holding it up to the full sunlight he painted it, the
purest white.

The rainbow too, up in the sky who could do it justice, surely
not you or I he painted them all with paints from above then
enfolded them all in his wondrous love how short have we
fallen, from the master piece there in our fondest paintings
when we try to compare what we lack, he has got and has more
to spare the beast artist by far, the master painter up there.

                                    —*Josephine Redmond*

Tears On The Alter

Just minutes before I heard the preacher
Say "expect and you shall receive"
So I dropped to my knees at the alter
Saying, dear Lord, I expect, I believe

When I dropped to my knees at the alter
My tears flowed in sweet relief
Just to know that the blood of Jesus
Would mend my heart filled with grief

Those marks on the alter's not water
They're from the tears that fell from my eyes
Those marks are there to remind you
Of the burden of my heart as it cries

I left my tears on the alter for you, dear Lord
I left them on the alter for you
When you see them there please remember my prayer
I left my tears on the alter for you
    —Pat Miller

One Day He Will Laugh

Cold winter days snow all around kids at play I am all alone
Say not what you feel given your soul though the emperor has
    no clothes
As far as he knew sun would soon shine no morning dew though
    it did arrive
Time seemed still the hummingbird cried his heart couldn't feel
    the pain in his eyes
A price he pays no less a tragedy now out of time he'd never be
Take the day it will come and go clock in the sky the pain
    never shows
Silk stockings in which he walked promises made if pictures
    could talk
The strike was swift forgiveness as quick
Out of the ashes his body would lift
Imaginary lines never to cross beyond the bee hive his kingdom
    lied
His body was trapped the imaginary lines. In his fragile heart
the boy could fly. Looking back at his tragic tale. Hearts
don't lie they only fail. All those years all that time. One
day he will laugh. In the garden of sunshine.
    —Matthew Smaciarz

School Days

Why do we remember the Yesterdays
School yard swings and children at play,
Some racing and tagging to the wire fence
Others laughing and some crying to other events.
All too soon, the shadows of night fall,
As the sun sinks low in the western sky.
Scurrying foot-steps hurry home.....
Dreams begin of the next sunrise.
ALIVENESS is their name.
    —Margaret Hyatt Brown

My Precious Time

Day by day as the clock ticks on and on;
Seconds and minutes are completely gone,
Hours I wish they were still here,
Somehow I let them go so they disappeared.

Why wasn't time meant to come again?
To make a new start only to push it to the end;
Will there be another chance?
To make this precious time really last.

Why did I drive away this precious time?
When I knew that this was mine;
All I can say is that before I die;
Please let me enjoy my precious time.
    —Linda M. Barreto

Cosmos

Man spies, on steel he flies; journey past the skies.
Searching folds, for unknown gold; hoping he'd never die.
Wisdom tooth, but where's the truth? Flickers a distant light.
Exit fast, the time won't last; taking another bite.

I don't wanna know what you've seen. I don't wanna know what it
    means.
I don't wanna go for the ride. But open up and let me inside.

Man finds, an open mind, journey past the edge.
Nothing but night, no end in sight; over the whirlpool ledge.
Cruising the stars, but where's the bars? Won't you step right in.
Exit slow, the time won't know; come on back again.

I don't wanna know who they are. I don't wanna know how far.
I don't wanna go for the ride. But open up and let me inside.

Man lost, forever tossed; a weight within the black.
The truth was tied, the wisdom lied; now there's no turning back.
Time was done, no man could run; the tic had fled the tocs.
The walls are tall, we're very small; living inside God's box.

I don't wanna know where you've flown.
I don't wanna know what you've known.
I don't wanna know how it ends.
I think I'll stay right here, my friend.
    —Steven K. Peer

Memories Of Our Past

Wandering the streets, seeking for that familiar face.
Searching, only to run across a very familiar place.

Memories of the past come back to my mind,
of the love we had, the passion and the time.

Gone are those times, when we shared and we loved.
"But it is all a memory of our past" I said.

Our eyes meet again, and the feeling is the same.
The love still there, but commitments we have made.

Memories of our past, are very much alive!
But, what shall we do? Do we cheat, deceive and lie?
    —Nancy Torres

My Daddy

Was your Daddy, as strict as mine
see I was his only daughter
the boy I loved come after me six times
I thought I'd never get to go
but on the sixth time
Oh; yea, I got to go with my bow.

And now I'm proud my daddy was strict
with me. Cause it seem's now that girls are
to young and wild and free.

I can blame some things on parent's and
teachers too.
because some things they see and are taught
Aren't the right things to do.

This is one of my songs, I'm trying to write
but I thought I've let you have a peek, for spite
I don't won't to let it go to someone else
so could you send it back to myself.
    —Vada Henderson

Can I...

Can I, hold you in my arms, and tell you how good it was to
see you again,
Can I, look into your eyes and see the reluctant woman who
wouldn't release her heart to me,
Can I, see deep into your soul, and discover the woman who
now welcomes me with open arms,
Can I, rediscover the softness of your body and excite your
mind,
Can I, open the flood gates of romantic interlude and drown
you with passion... Can I...?
Can I stop dreaming how it would be to have you mind,
body, soul,
Can I stop wondering how it could have been,
Can I say, and you admit, the chemistry, the mystery,
the intrigue, the fire between us is still there after all
these years...

Shall I, will I, can I?
—*LaMont Kidd*

The Weaver

He crept into my night, my other reality.
Seeking in the darkness any unstable emotion.
He finds the love which I've guarded so well
behind my wall of fear.

He recognizes in his search for the one
the discovery of the other.
He embraces these emotions, holding them ever so gently.
Forcing that which hid - even from the self,
The passion.

With care and delicacy he goes about his task,
weaving with an element of pride.
Experienced in his craft - he moves.
Delighted by his touch - he soothes me.
Confused by his presence - I tremble.
Secure in his expertise - he excites me.

I fight as he sets me free and drown as he gives me life.
The weaver of love, fear and passion
works through the night,
he weaves deep within.
Come morning, he is now a part of me.

—*Nadine Royster*

Alone With God

I went to the mountains alone,
Seeking rest for my tired weary soul;
And God met my soul in the mountains;
With His spirit He again made me whole.

He told me that others had sought him,
Out there in the mountains alone;
They had come to the wild mountain fastness,
To make an appeal to his throne.

There was Jesus and Paul and Moses;
All these had sought Him alone;
And they went from the wilds of the mountain,
With a strength and a zeal not their own.

He had met them there in the mountains,
He had met their soul's deepest need;
He had sent them back to their fellows;
To bless them in word and in deed.

Friend, you have a need of the mountains;
You have a need all your own.
Fear not to go forth to the mountains -
And to meet your God all alone.

—*Thomas T. May*

Loving Twilight Years

Too little too late our dying hearts' fate
Seems our young lives have faded
Into our twilight years now belated
All times we shared when we were younger
Now lights our fires to our hunger
Our eyes still glow as we both know beloved
Long hours of memories now gone by
Flood our minds as days grow nye
When our lives have passed away we say
Old man, old women you are now at rest,
You can't play, don't try to stay
Let our memories stay now to be
Shared with other's who cared for thee
Bring us peace an say at last
It's time for sleep
Now love has passed
—*Sandra Lee O'Farrell*

The Little Dogie

Kickin' through the dirt, the end of the day,
Seems this tough life has always been.
But next mornin'll send the night away.
That keeps me draggin' back again.

There must be somethin' under this big sky
That everyone missed but me.
'Cause it's tough out here, they'll tell you why,
Every day's a fight, come you'll see.

God's open spaces have a place for everyone.
No question, looks like the best.
Seems forgotten though, the little ones,
Like this little dogie at my breast.

Morrow's sun'll pull in the stars once more,
Sort of bringin' them home for the day.
It could be as simple in the bigger world.
We could all come together that way.

—*Richard W. Myers*

Father

Oh Blessed Father of Creation, Father, of life and love.
Send to me, Your words of Righteousness,
Through Your Mighty Voice. Above.

Allow me, to write for You, to become Your Mighty Pen.
So that, through Your words, we may be assured,
of Your Everlasting Love, again.

You gave to us, Your only Son, to perish for our souls,
and Preserve, Our home, called Earth.
We know, we had become tarnished in Sin,
You gracefully cleansed us, granting us, new Birth.

We view Your Masterpieces, everyday, in both,
the Earth, and in the Heavens.
We stand in awe, of Your beautiful, Workmanship,
We marvel, at the Brilliance, of Your imagination.

Oh Father of Glory, Father of Creation.
Our Father of Love and Life.
We seek Your Forgiveness, Your Wisdom, and Strength,
And allowance, to walk, in Your Light.

—*Michael Speers*

A Friend Behind, A Foe Beside

A poem relating to the betrayal and mistrust of a friend in
SEPARATE PEACE

When we were apart, it didn't cross my mind,
Only when we were together could I see the difference.

He was an optimist, I, a pessimist,
He stood out, while I stood behind.
I longed to be like him, to stand beside him and not behind.
And one day I was like him,
I did stand beside and not behind.
I was so close to being like him
That for a moment I thought I could be him.
I thought I could be carefree, witty, and charming,
I came to find out it wasn't so.
If I could turn back time and we could meet again,
I would not be envious, I would be his friend.

  —*Qiana Spraggins*

The Veiled Horizon

A blanket of clouds
Set on the horizon their shrouds
The sun plummets into the west
Immersing into their midst
Making of time a jest

Yet the true horizon
Beneath the fleecy cover
Would never portray that sinking orb
To the eye of the beholder

How many times in this life of ours
With its sweets and sours
Is a distant vision hidden
Underlying the surface - waitin til bidden
To emerge in the glory of its flight
Just for an instant of sight

  —*Richard D. Cagg*

A Country Hayride

Today is the day for the thrilling ride,
Setting all past cares aside.

Children playing and yelling from the hayloft,
Others, below - feeding baby chicks - giggling soft.

The sheep are in the meadow - cows in the corn,
Horses neigh from the barn.

The backyard dinner bell ringing -
Calling one and all for an evening meal,
Outside - the wagon stands still on its wheel.

Anxious children, ready to climb up the side,
Of the waiting wagon - loaded with straw deep and wide.
A glorious setting sun - funtime for everyone.

The tractor hums down the dusty road -
tree-lined, all burnished with red and gold
carrying the joyful load - singing and stories being told.

Dusk succumbs to night,
The silver dollar full moon comes into sight.

The tractor lights glow as it slows around the last bend,
This has surely been a perfect days end.

  —*Ruth Ann Burris*

Angel At The Gate

An angel stands at the gate, amidst
Shadows of graying-blue, and Whispers
Hope to lonely children,_me and you.

An Angel stands by our bed, as we cry,
And bury our faces into pillows of
Shame. Crescent-Moons, and beveled-
Glass-stars, the guardian remembers our
Names, whether close, or light-years
Far.

My Angel is dark and beautiful
To see, though he is a candle, a lighted
And Brilliant-Sea!

Touch the allies of violet-skies, Say
A last goodbye, to that mournful and
Empty place_where no one little, had a
Face. Waiting for the coming of the
Midnight-Sun, with glistening droplets of
Rain, that paint, and water become.

Gypsy-Moon, yellow-roses bloomed, in my
Garden, quietly, one winter's afternoon.

  —*Thea Cooper*

Faded Memories, Shades Of Black

Faded memories shades of black and white,
Shades that cannot be replaced;
Leave behind fragments the imagination has seen.
Still now remembering past moments.

Faded memories..shaded black and white,
Reaching out for yesterday,
The very depth of time will pass,
Looking for tomorrow will draw back a forsaken dream..

Faded memories shades of black and white
Made almost out of make-believe,
Leaves behind a mirage,
Softly as the swift of the breeze passing by.
Recapturing all that has gone by.

Faded memories shades of black and white,
Rekindle all things we have touched;
They leave behind our tranquil state of mind,
For the memories will not be faded,
But just remain black and white.

  —*Linda M. Kret*

Trust

My heart seems to jump
Sharing the emotions
Letting memories remind me
How strong the hold can be.
Love left behind yet
Never truly gone.
Emotions rekindled, feelings acknowledged
Brought through with a look
A word or a song.
The surprise in your heart
To find this to be true
Leaves questions and dreams
Deep in your mind.
Content and happy in your life now
You wonder why it is
This can be.
Accept and enjoy
God is smiling
Sharing in this time
His love and protection.

  —*Sherlene Berry*

Worthless Stone

I slashed my sword onto a tree of gold,
Shattering branches which were once so bold,
My horse jumped back with his head held high,
As the thunder pounded his voice did cry,
Louder and louder until the rains filled his nose,
And as I fell forward his eyes began to close,
So I grabbed his saddle to ease his pain,
Throwing it swiftly in the turbulent rain,
The mud sucked his hooves up to his knees,
I was crawling to save him and crying out "Please,
Spare my steed and you may have back your precious stone,
For I do not wish to be in this forest all alone."
I grabbed my medallion which I received from the king,
Flinged it at the sycamore which began to sing,
"Choose to leave this forest without your sword or steed,"
"I will leave my sword for which I have no need."
The rain began to cease and the mud to dry,
And I saw a glimpse of sunlight way up high,
My horse regained his footing, shivering from the cold
And for me, I shall never ride by that tree of gold.

—*Thomas C. Sepe*

Hers Gone And Kept

Seething with heartfelt passion
          she falls silently,
twirling in and out of a dream, like a wispy cloud,
          lands soundlessly on bent knee.
     The colors change on the brim of her eye.
          But real sleep comes so seldom.
Grasping like a blind beggar for spare change
     she gropes for the keys to sleeps kingdom.
Ever so slowly the lock to the gate turns.
          Only to find emptiness within.
     Frozen in pose like a plastic statue,
          plastic frame, rubber grin.
          Thoughts are a burden to life
               with spirituality swept away.
Out of a daze her young bones creak like a hags.
     Swollen eyes open to bright of day.
     The burning heat of winter sun melts
               away the puffy lids.
     Trepid is, trepid is, her way to live,
          her way to die, trepid eyes.

—*Sean Barney*

The Unekes

Man, that was Paula Sue's favorite word for awhile.
She is a member of The Unekes.
Paula May goes to college and stocks an aisle;
Day and night she works.
She is also a' uneke' person.
Mikey is the only male.
When his head a box falls on
His face oft' turns pale.
There is one person I forgot to mention.
She is the last member of The Unekes
But she is not, by far, the least.
E'en though she is short in stature,
She is a vital member.
If one is a Uneke,
There is one thing one must remember:
"Lean on me."
Remember that and no one gets hurt!
Smile, it's Tina Bean, the last,
But not the least.
Member of The Unekes.

—*Tina L. Cooper*

Dawn

She is like the dawn when it first awakes from its deep sleep.
She is bright, happy, and o so sweet.
She is just a baby, like the new dawn of each day, starting
life anew in a bright and shining way.
Bringing sunshine to our lives, and everything we do.
     Dawn is her name, the start of a new day, a new life, a new
     way.
Dawn is God's way of showing us that each day is worth living.
     My Dawn is the symbol of love and new beginnings here on
earth, she came to show us the way.

     —*Leona Kelley*

Identity

Born into a world of pink and lace,
She is raised to be a delicate blossom.
Too pretty and soft to tackle life's harshness,
she stays nestled within the family who names her.

She emerges long enough to attract a mate
who promises to shield this fragile flower.
She assumes the name of her new partner
and returns to her quiet, unassuming world.

Abandoned by her sworn protector,
she confronts life's battles alone.
Too strong now to be a delicate flower,
She searches for a new name, but finds none.

She believes that she now inhabits a superior world
and strives to imitate the men around her.
She must discard all traces of softness and delicacy
in order to find her new name.

Realizing the new world is incomplete without softness,
she joyfully embraces her former world
and celebrates its equal necessity.
She recognizes her true name.

—*Nancy Magee*

Nickasourous Hippopotamus

Dear Alyssa,

Yesterday I met someone you should know about.
She is wide and broad in opportunity,
tall and long in understanding.
Her hair is spun from a golden fleece,
and gleeful dolphins play in her heart.
Skin is made of ginger,
and her touch of sugar.
Eyes created from such a crystal blue,
I swear I could see the future.
And when she speaks,
a mystical whimsical wind fills the sky.
I am to meet her tonight,
spinning and whirling,
on the mystical purple dancing reefs of utopia.

—*Michael Jerud Swinney*

European Travel

Lovers observe nocturnal diversions overseas, nightly.
Pairs amorously roam inner streets.
Meanwhile aloof, desolate rogues incur dejection,
Veering into empty, naked niches alone.
Likewise I stray, balefully observing national
Ruins of medieval Europe.

—*Thomas Pitchford*

Best Friends

She was a best friend
She loved, cared, and comforted; or so I thought.
When I went through troubles or pains she wasn't there
When I cried because someone broke my heart
She wasn't next to me, comforting me.
Then when I lost my grandmother
She just told me it would be okay; like she didn't care.
She was the most important person in my life
But I wasn't in hers.
She always told me we were best friends
But she didn't mean it
For her true best friend lived right across the road.
She was always with him
Telling him she loved him and that he
    was the most important person.
She once got mad at me for what others told her
Not asking me about it;
That is when I knew we would never
    truly be....Best Friends!

    —Sharon Edwards

Our Cat, Fuzz-Ball

A lovable feline is fuzz-ball, our cat.
She relishes being cuddled, she really likes that.
This feline, we adore her, our cat of eleven years.
The canines in our neighborhood, they are her greatest fears.
Her eyes are black and greenish, her color, charcoal grey.
Except her tail, it's slightly striped, yes it is made that way.
Sometimes she goes a hunting, and she chases squirrels and birds.
But our cat, she is not vicious, it's just a trait of hers.
Her felicitous presence is a comfort where we stay.
At times she's very quiet and sleeps most of the day.
Then she comes into my bedroom and wakes me from my sleep.
To let me know she's hungry and it's time for her to eat.
For eating is her special joy, she savors tasty treats.
She also likes to lay on shoes, I often wonder why.
But she will do it every time, she cannot pass them by.
With a burst of ardent energy, she gallops down the hall.
Temperamental, calm and gentle, is our cat, Fuzz-Ball.

    —Parinella M. Smith

Black Teddy Bear

As the clouds move away from the moon a gleam of moonlight
Shines down on a young girl shivering
In a cold, dark alley fear and sadness
Overcome this young girl but loneliness
Pours into her heart for she has no family.
Just a black teddy bear that is
Full of warmth and kindness!

    —Rachel Cox

Blessed Is The Good Step-Father

Blessed is the good step-father, for he is truly of God's
making.

Blessed is the good step-father who can see past his own
vanity. He knows that children are also of God's making.

Blessed am I my husband for God in his strength and wisdom
has brought you to me with your strength and wisdom of family
life and love for all children.

And last but not least, blessed are your stepchildren; may
they always love and respect you as much as they do today,
for in the fast pace of life they receive comfort knowing
they have a step-father who unconditionally loves and cares
for them.

    —Dee Shay

A Love Poem About Rachel

What have we done? Just a hopeful future thought. Just a
loving desire. Look what we've done. Born the other day,
small, red, and tiny. So fragile like a dream. Joins us to
eternity. A continuity from spontaneity. What have we done?
Just a hopeful future thought. Just a loving desire. Look
what we've done. Walking and talking, thinking and feeling, a
person, a child, a miracle. Just the other day we sat
wondering about which crib, and today watching her play dress
up with friends. Who will she be, who can she be. Just a baby
a moment ago. What have we done? Just a hopeful future
thought. Just a loving desire. Look what we've done.
Climbing the tree but back, building forts, dressing Barbie her
life is full. School, religion, family are the focus of her
life. An adult via blessing, yet still my little girl. What
have we done? Just a hopeful future thought. Just a loving
desire. Look what we've done. Standing at the mirror curling
her hair thinking about boys. With license to drive and a
constantly ringing phone she is growing, dreaming,
contemplating her future. What have we done? Just a hopeful
future thought. Just a loving desire. Look what we've done.

    —Alan J. Schneider

A Mother Cries

    BOOM! BAM! to a favorite rhythm
    Lyrics for dancing with ideas of killing
the Uzi and AK-47 have become the chosen weapons
Replacing simplistic toys as childhood possessions.
      Shots ring out and a young son dies
      Yet all we hear is a mother's cries

    Abandoned buildings amidst homelessness
Streetwalkers searching through endless hopelessness
      Some old friend, now a drug addict
      No one cares to help the derelict
    And in a dark alley on a very cold night
    For another John Doe a Mother cries

On the busy street corner sits a school building
      Children abound but learn nothing
    In the city, while the rich are striving
    The poor are on trash strewn avenues dying.
Each night upon a worn bed her aching body lies
A Mother remembers her child's plight and she cries.

    —Curwyn Bootman

The Wanderer

Only water for the wanderer. Oh, flowers fill your garden.
Magic on my mind, I'll make a wish for you. There is water
for the mountain, look upon and wave goodbye. No sorrow, just
stronger. I could not of touched the sun, and not cried
lonely, so go the words, does the morning, painted colors, so
lily on the coals. Sometimes we just like the shade, still
the grass is green. A run in the mind, it becomes a question,
it became a change. Listen all the night, just to wonder of
the mindstakes. The sandpipers run around and around, when the
water goes away, it will leave a line. Finding the forest,
the body is wrapped in a daydream. Turtles teach love, when
the sun comes up, some will worship idols, once only, the
tongue could tickle the mind, make it wet and want. No ladders
find the ceiling for those who played with dolls. The rain is
heard play slowly on youths. A white mane, teased in motions
the sand. In paradise. Where no questions fill the senses of
a gentle creature guarding his nature. If you reached so far
to a raindrop, you would break the beauty. The stones gather
at the window. It seems easy, next to thunder. Slide against
the lightening. Only water for the wanderer.

    —Jeffrey D. Gregory

Words

Words spoken are
    sometimes
Like dandelion seeds
    blown.
With no thought to
    where they land.
Your blown words have
    covered me
With grief and regret
I wonder if you gave
    a thought
To where and how
    your words
Might sprout?
—*Rowena M. Forde*

Morning's Reflection

Misty morning sings to me
songs to celebrate
autumn leaves.

As you lift the day begins
reflecting on the water's end
in shades of red and orange
burnt.
Your leaves provide a pleated skirt.

Misty morning celebrate
another day—I can hardly wait
to cast my boat onto your pond
to inhale the beauty of your song.
—*Sherril A. Willis*

Changes

Flowers in bloom,
soon fade into
the pale fall sky.
The air is chilly,
the sun refuses
to shine.
And the fall leaves
fall one by one
on a forgotten
summer.
—*Melanie Mullen*

Death To Me Is...

Sadness
Sorrow
Grief
Anger
Remorse
And
Hell

It is...
A part of life we
Learn to
Deal
With
Painfully
But
With
Hope.

—*Sarah Yeager*

Jungle

Walking away
sounds of the jungle
entwined with city noises
beckoning to me.

Walking faster
sounds of scraping claws
trying frantically
to rip apart my morality

Running now
Away from darken memories
of hot molten lava
coursing through my veins

Running faster
towards the approval
of my fellow man
away from the narcotics jungle

Fearful that someday
the jungle will
engulf my life
and you won't hear my scream's
—*Linda J. Phinney*

To Nancee B

Warm and charming
Spirited and smiling
Sometimes bubbling,
Like a mountain brook,
Yet always, with that caring look,
In this sea of flowing humanity,
Oh! who, could this wonder be,
If you really looked,
You will see,
It is the gentle soul
Of Nancee B.

—*Raj Singh Dosanjh*

race

golden sunshine
splash on my face
swiftest footfall
    win the race

fortune cookie
tell me no lie
    richest piper
tell me goodbye

foolish wisdom
don't make me cry
    windy morning
help me to fly

    onyx angel
heaven has sent
reckless danger
    crying lament

    wanton woman
i have become
longest races
    i have won
—*Liz Albano*

The Woman

As I looked at her lonely body
    standing on the beach
I could see her hair
    the color of the night
    her body as frail as fine china

The breeze that was blowing
    was tossing her hair
She walked with such grace
    I was reluctant to stare

As I stood watching her
    from the bluff above
I know what I felt must
    be true love.

—*Meghan Meredith*

The Night Ocean

High in moon-bright brilliance,
Star-burst, black-night sky—
Bows in humble radiance
To the onrushing ocean tide.

Breaking shattering, moon path,
Crystalline shimmering light,
Dancing, spun-light, moon kiss
Swirls in, swirls out of sight.

Scattering, bright-rays, moon beam
Wash endlessly to the shore.
Majestic, gentle, night dreams
Hold close forever more.

—*Lois E. Myers*

Vision

Eyes of wondering enchantment;
    Stars of brilliant hue
Shine with light so very blinding!
    All they see is you.

Spheres of radiant inspiration;
    Suns of dazzling light
Glare in very long duration
    When you're in their sight.

Mirrors of blind adoration-
    Visual images.
Twin balls of deep veneration,
    Your presence raises.

Fires burning with emotion;
    Jewels sparkling bright.
Pearls colored by heightened passion-
    Golden glow...love's light!
—*Laredo F. Velasco*

Glimpses

Golden reform
Subtle exchange
Endless abandon
Artfully dodging
Arrows of anger
Asking reasons
For meanings I never question;
Ignorant armies
Fight themselves
Into fallout shelters
of hopelessness;
Gifted angels rise above
the junkyard
Grabbing candy
in the streets of glass.

—*Todd Gilleland*

Eternal Slumber

Eternal slumber
Such a peaceful dream
Angels on white clouds
Golden gates
Beautiful music
No wars, no hates
Crystal clear lakes
Foaming waterfalls
With grassy banks
And clean cave walls
Eternal slumber
Such a peaceful dream.

—*Monique Samuel*

The Sounds Of Music

Is it magic, or just sleight of hand?
 Such things I scarce can understand
  I'm just a tiny bit of clay
  Who came to life, the other day
  My cradle was my mother's womb
  'Twas quiet as a silent tomb
  My chariot was so cloudy soft
  As soft as cotton borne aloft
 The sounds of life, a muffled beat
No trumpets, drums, or marching feet
 Such music set my world apart
The thump, thump of my mother's heart
Her measured breathing warm and deep
 Would soothe and cradle me to sleep
 New changing sounds I hear at morn
 Are different now that I am born
 The sounds of my prenatal life
Are gentler far than sounds of strife
I'll hence forth live amongst the din
 Since mortal life, I now begin.

—*Ulric Hudson Francis*

Twenty Four Hours

    Pearl gray sky of dawn,
Sun breaks through, the fog retreats,
    Day of man begins.

    Cerulean sky,
Smog below hides man-made snarls,
    A scream is muffled.

    Apricot sunset,
Silver star and sliver moon,
    My heart also glows.

    Midnight sky above,
A bird sings to moon's farewell,
    Until the dawn, peace.

—*Phyllis O'Neil*

Why Cry

Smoke fills the air from my cigarette
Tears flow down all warm and wet.
Why cry, why cry, why cry
30 years is not enough
As I take another puff,
I could have said enough's enough
Turn around another puff,
Why cry, why cry, why cry
As I lie here in this bed
My body's tired and almost dead,
When I pass please don't grieve
Another puff is what killed me
Why cry, why cry, why cry

—*Larry D. Porter*

Waste

Shallowness surrounds me -
superficial beach I tread
- sea of foolishness approaches
with oncoming tide,
another wave crashes down
leaving nothing behind
- but emptiness
and morals swept away
in the undertow.

I put my foot down
but my impression is only
temporary, soon lost.
Once met by the crashing wave
it gets taken in,
washed clean from the slate
- as if it were never there,
or meant anything
at all!

—*Trevorr C. DiMeo*

Alone

A silent dream
suppressed by society
burning on hope
alone.

A child's tear
banished by pride
feeding on every untold
fear.

A soothing whisper of love
hushed by commitment
tearing deep into ones
soul.

One world, slowly corrupted
by the burning, feeding, and tearing
of man, dies in your hand
alone.

—*Melissa A. Burdick*

Neither Here Nor There

I sit here in my house
Surrounded by things I should love,
but yet these things do not fill
the emptiness and boredom that I feel.

I have family, friends, pets
all these things I should love,
but yet these things do not lift
me off this chair and use my gifts.

I have talents, some to admire;
all these things I should love,
but yet these things do not move
me to show people what I need to prove.

There is a place in this world for me.
When I determine that place
The whole world will see!

—*Sue A. Henry*

Make Today Count

Life is so short
 take nothing for granted
For one is here today
 and may be gone today

Always count your blessings
 enumerate them one by one
and you will be amazed
 at what the Lord has done

Take care of each other
 always respect your mother
Show love for your brother
 and concern for one another

Take time to count your blessings
 though they be many or few
One can always be thankful
 for something old or something new

—*Willie Ann Price*

Tide Of Memories

Little waves retreat, advance
Teasing ripplets bob and dance
A gentle swish gains in pitch
The volume of the faint low moan
Becomes a hammering monotone
The silent yammering of the sea
Speaks to me tormentedly.

Tiny rills churn and twist
To a briny, foamy fury
Dash themselves to tiny bits
Do it very thoroughly
Like the tide comes in
Recedes and comes again
Creeps up the beach
Slips back to sea
My memories come and go
Wash over me.

—*I. Stroebel*

Of My Own Making

Worlds spin. The sky is full.
Tell me.
 Tell me.
of desert nights
of restless water
of endless days.

Show me.
 Show me.
the sight of passion
the eyes of fire
the eclipse of minds.

Take me.
 Take me.
to the Virgin Isles
to the North Pole
to bed.

Leave me.
 Leave me.
a memory of you
a dollar cab fare
alone.

—*Mary Meier*

Letters

Letters written
Telling of his love
Are scattered all over
My bedroom floor.

No more letters come.
He has been set free
From his commitment
To love me.

He is gone.
No longer here.
Only a memory
A sad, lonely memory.

I wait with anxiety
For more of the letters
But as each day passes
No letters come.

Then I realize what I knew.
He is gone, no longer here
Only a memory in my heart
A sad, sweet memory.

—*Lynn Turnbull*

Time

She watches the clock,
ten, eleven, twelve. . .
Her time is running out,
the love is running out. . .
The dreams all shattered,
the hopes all condemned. . .
She waits, she watches. . .
she dies.

—*Tiffany Cone*

Request

I'm looking for the little birds
That always tell my Mom
About the naughty things I do
And tasks I haven't done.

For one whole hour I laid beneath
Our oldest apple tree
I hardly even breathed a breath
But no birds came to me.

Mommy doesn't keep so quiet
She sings and whistles too
Yet birdies seem to come to her
And tell her all I do.

Oh, I'm really not complaining
But, gosh I think I should
As you tell her when I'm naughty
Can't you tell her when I'm good?

—*Ruth E. Grewe*

Babies

Babies are little treasures,
That are buried for a while.
They're more precious than a jewel,
On the top of any pile.
They're as beautiful as the box,
The treasure might be in.
The box is what protects them
And keeps them safe within.
But when the box is opened
And the treasure is there to see
It shines and glows with love.
As it looks up at me.

—*Rhonda Melton*

Spring

We cannot count the raindrops
That bring us April showers
We cannot touch the rainbow
Yet the "dot of gold" is ours.

We cannot know the minute
When, lulled by a gentle breeze,
Each tiny budlet opens
And new leaflets grace the trees.

Under ground is under orders
To burst forth with life anew
With beauty, and with fragrance
Bejeweled by morning dew.

We cannot know the sufferings
Of Jesus Christ our Lord
But we know we'll rise to Glory
If we keep in step with God.

—*Kathy Goldthwait*

Circle Of Love

The circle of love
that drapes from my neck
Will never be surrendered
as I will protect

This chain of gold
from any real danger
Never will it fall
in the hands of a stranger

I remember the moment
that torrid day in May
Around my neck he clasped it
and it remains there today

The delicate touch
the sensitive sight
It never parts from me
not even at night

I'm never afraid
I've got nothing to fear
As this circle of love
is forever so near

—*Rebecca Wert Anderson*

I Wish I Knew

I wish I knew a pretty song,
that I could sing for you.
Some special words
of love and joy,
so we could start a new
I wish I knew a story
to tell you every night,
a sweet romantic story
to make you heart feel light.
I wish I knew a poem
a verse to make you see
that you mean more than all
the world & all it holds for me
I wish I knew what to say
or knew what to do?
to make you feel the love
for me that I've always felt for you

—*Raymond Parsons*

Memories

There is a time, there is a place,
That no one knows but me.
A place far away from here,
Yet very near and dear to me.

There are people there, in this place,
From a time that is no more.
People I have loved and still love.
People I keep longing for.

This place of mine is special,
If only just to me.
It holds all my cherished treasures,
And past dreams of what could be.

I go there every chance I get.
But I can never really be,
In this place I love so well,
For it is only just my memory.

—*Rebecca E. Stucks*

Untitled

Those precious blue eyes,
that stare into mine.
The warmth of your touch,
that shows me the classical sign.

Your defiant glances,
that reveal your male pride.
But by looking into your eyes,
I can see what's really inside.

When in your arms,
I'm hoping that you love me.
For if you do not,
I know nothing could ever be.

But if what I hope is there,
then I will always be in your heart.
Then we shall be together,
'till death do us part.

—*Nichole Alons*

Untitled

There's part of me you'll never know
That's hidden deep where tempests blow.

For I have walked in ecstasy.
I've walked a hidden maze.

You'll never, never know me
In a hundred different ways.

I wish it were not so.

—*Virginia Meek*

Autumn Leaves

Winter is setting in;
The air is getting cold;
Leaves are changing color,
Yellow, orange, red and gold.

Color-soaked gliders
Drifting, floating by;
These sparks of brilliant color
Are dazzling to the eye.

Awe-inspiring blazes
That never seem to last;
They are God's crayoned creations
Telling us that summer's past.

—*Lara McMaster*

Passages

What happened to the dreams,
The ambitions, the thoughts,
The joy of ideas,
That came in reams?

What happened to the love,
The well being and happiness,
The things promised,
As all else above?

What happened?
As in tales twice told,
What happened?
Why my children,
We got old.

—*Virginia Salcido*

Mayday

It's seven o'clock in the mornin
The baby starts ta cry
Wife gets up yawnin
Chillin start ta lie.

It's eight o'clock in the mornin
I'm on my way ta work
This towns fulla rummies
The streets fulla jerks.

It's nine o'clock in the mornin
I arrive their on the line
Boss saids "boy you late again"
Docks my pay one mo time.

It's twelve o'clock in the aftanoon now
Everythins goin great
But wait, hold it I spoke ta soon
Here comes enemy Bates.

It's five o'clock in the evenin
I made it thu the day
Don't think I'll take another one like it
for the same amouna pay.

—*Romel Ellis*

Cave Shadows

These words must suggest
The beginning, then and now
But void of poetic expressions

These mirrors are reflections
To the world, no sign in
No exit out
The walls do not create two worlds

There is space, but no enclosure
There is feeling, glimmering
Around an open wound
Each word is a link
In the chain, clothed in mystery
Stripped bare
Naked at the door

No cave, shadows
The realm of light at the bottom
The soul is the light
That shines, up
Through the eyes.

—*Miles Devereux*

Mystic Bird

The first day
The bird came at nine.
Through each dawn's gray,
It came on time.
It sang a song within one line,
Four doubles, single music rime,
Like a p.m. a.m. chapel chime.
  Why it came, I never knew.
  The ninth day, away it flew.

—*Ora M. Lewis*

The Bridge Of Time

Throughout a life time we must cross
  The bridges that we build
As well as those not built by us
  Until our life is stilled
Our journey takes a multitude
  Of highways o'er the ridge
And leads us to the pathways of
  Each chasm we must bridge
Sometimes we feel we trod alone
  Where no one passed before
Or find the range of obstacles
  Far more than bargained for
But as we cross succeeding gaps
  We listen and we learn
That many have preceded us
  And wait beyond the turn
Our final bridge approaches when
  We can no longer climb
'Tis then our soul will lift us up
  Across the bridge of time

—*Melvin E. Olson*

Untitled

  The dark wolf's howling
The bright, yellow moon's glowing
  The silent forest
—*Michael C. Grant*

The Seasons Of Life

A new green pale and growing
the buds of flowers yet to bloom.
A new love lush and flowing.
becomes the future bride and groom.

Two lives meld together
like summer hot with passion,
become accustomed to the weather,
and pass lazy days in this fashion.

Children bring the cozy winter day
complete with occasional storm.
A time some poor spouses stray,
to never again feel warm.

Colors breathtaking to behold,
the nest is empty, and it's fall.
Though you are certain to feel old,
think young, this time is best of all.

Life is dormant again to be born,
although all seems brown and dry.
Eternal life to us is sworn,
with faith, not the question why.

—*Lisa Lynn Imperante*

I Really Do Love You

The gentle ripples flowed down the river
The calmness was in the air
Bass swam by so gracefully
God, I wish you were here.

My heart feels so empty now
My life seemed to change
I wish I could have you back
And stop all this pain.

I felt the coldness in the wind
Or maybe it's the coldness in my heart
The clouds flowed so meek and calm
Why must we be apart?

One tear feel down my face
My eyes are now filled with tears
I really do love you, oh so much
through out the rest of my years.

I can understand you need your freedom
But don't you need me too?
This is going to be the last time I say
I really do love you.

—*Michelle Orduna*

Life

Who of us want to confront
The currents on the sea of life.
The undertow or maelstrom
The giant waves or
The winds of change that
Bring the choppy seas?

We want a quiet cove
With sandy beach and
Gentle lapping waves.
Think twice! Think thrice!
This is where mold, moth
And decay take over.

—*Verna Felkel Ondrey*

Anticipation

Wondering when it'll be the day
the day I wait for is soon
Am anxious for it to happen
on the night of the full moon?

It won't be easy
it never was in the past
anticipation drives you nuts
but it soon won't last.

Every time it's different
but it always feels the same
try to keep a happy outlook
no sense to complain

Can I handle it?
I have no choice
What's done is done
Have nothing else to voice

If you haven't guessed by now
In a moment you'll see
it's the hopes of wellness
for a mother and new baby to be.

—*Linda L. Koziatek*

The Weaver

The sun's bright rays do catch
the dew holding back the night.
The weaver spins its tiny threads
among the milkweed stalks.

The dew it clings and shimmers round
like crystals in the light.
Oh tiny weaver do you know.
What joy you bring to all those who
cannot have your sight?

The crystals shine, the crystals gleam,
as round and round on threads
they cling to decorate the night.

The day is gone, the night has come,
and though the night enfolds you,
you'll still be there on scented air,
your mystery to hold you.

—*Nancy J. Myers*

It's A Boy

"It's a boy"
the doctor said.
No cries to be heard. No first breaths.
"Would you like to hold him?"
"I think you should," he said.
(this can't be happening to me)
The swaddled bundle of stillness
in my arms
flowering a perfect porcelain face.
I unwrap God's gift
to hold the tiniest fingers
Too beautiful to look.
Seven years have gone by
and every day my personal sunrise
is his face.

—*Maureen Reddy-Osgood*

The Fool

Cry not for me,
The fallen fool of life.
Weep for others,
Those who died valiantly,
For they lived life.
Mourn more the hero,
For his last breath
Was given for another.
We both die early.
And yet, I need no tears
For my death was choice of mind;
The martyr's was choice of heart.

—*Peter I. Knauer*

The Rescue And The Consequences

It was radiant and beautiful
The flower I picked,
Downtown in the middle of traffic.
The flower had stood still
Until I saved it from the
Hard looking sole that stepped forward.
It was trembling in the wind,
Until I took it for my own.
And now it sits in my window sill.
It sunbathes in the window until
The moon comes up.
Then it closes its petals
And seals itself up.
But now I think it's dying,
Slowly but still,
Right up here on my window sill.

—*Lisa McAfee*

You Went Away

You went away and now I'm sad
The greatest love I ever had

Just ten good years you used to tell
I hoped and prayed I'd do as well

You left your job to golf and love
I took up golf to golf and love
The first year came, we're riding high
Life was great as the months flew bye
We laughed and loved and then the crash
You left me dear, in just a flash
Now you're gone, life's not the same
It never will be and fate's to blame
I loved your smile, I loved your jokes
All those nights I loved the most
The smiles I had have turned to tears
But knowing you has calmed my fears
We'll meet again, no matter where
I can hardly wait to see you there

You went away and now I'm sad
I'll never forget the love we had.

—*Patricia Havican*

Daddy's Hand

The hand that used to cradle me
The hand that held me tight
The hand that sat me straight
and taught me wrong from right

The hand that used to lead me
The hand that nursed me well
The hand that gently pulled me up
each and every time I fell

The hand that had to disagree
The hand that had to let go
The hand that waived good-bye
to me, yet never felt it so

The hand that I'm still holding
in every single prayer
The hand that I still reach for
and always find it there!

—*Sandra Trammell Martin*

It Grows

Inside this girl,
the hatred grows
and the anger grows
and it grows in her,
she doesn't know it there,
it just grows
scarred by her past, it grows
Blocking out help,
the only fortress
she can find from this thing
that grows in her is salvation
through death.

—*Susan Cho*

Express Rider

No heroes just kids doing man's work
  Station to station the horse rest
   Horse to horse the rider rush
Rider to rider the pouch is exchanged
  Miles after miles along the trail
   Town to town on long dusty days
    All to see that you have mail.

—*Lori Pierce*

Hands

Hands are part of us we say
The impression they make
are shown in many a may!

Some are pointed in and out
some are placed over the heart
To get our point across
there is no doubt!

Hands tell the old story
of how we've aged in life
dark spots we see before our eyes
purple veins rise and fall
and the wrinkled hand becomes small

Hands tell our history too
and all we've been through.
From rocking cradle, washing dishes.
Raking yards, cleaning house.
Typing bills, hammering on a board on sill!

Hands can be pretty too
When we fold them deep in prayer
and our Saviour knows we care.

—*Marguerite Erickson*

In Dawns Light

I have found
the light of dawn
clears the path
so conclusions are drawn
not in darkness
of emotional unrest
but with replenished thought
things get rightly assessed.

—*Maili Rohner*

Never Alone

Whenever upon
The lonely sea,
And the tides of decision
Seems pulling thee
Along the waves
You're not want to be

Know the waves will calm,
And the tide subside,
And you'll be stronger
For having tried,
And ready, more ready
For the next high tide.

And you'll know,
You'll know
I'll be helping you row.

—*Lorin C. Saunders*

A Day

Tendrils caressing
    supple pain,
Slippery finger nervously gliding
        gloriously
    Through amber nerves
        stretched inward
        covering silent
    sentimental screams
        of weeping rage.

—*Scott Handren*

Untitled

On this special Easter day
The Lord came and took you away
It seems like only days you were here
I still shed many a tear
But knowing your happy where you are
I just feel your not so far
I look at the trees blowing
Is that you I see waving
I hear the birds chirping
Is that you I hear singing?
Mom I know you're in a happier place
I just miss seeing your smiling face
I know you'll be watching over me
As I look up and see a blowing tree

—*Pamela Williams*

Untitled

As I wept in bed
The memories of you
Came back to me.
It's been a day
Since that awful time
When I was told
That you've gone on.
I was sad and scared
And I hope you didn't suffer
Though I do wish the guy
Who did this to you does.
As everyone walks
Around in a daze
I just can't believe
The awful time
In Dozier Middle School's
Parking lot.

—*Linda Carson*

In Your Arms

Tonight the stars are bright and
The moon is smiling down
And everywhere there is an air
Of happiness in town
At least it seems that way to me
And I am very happy, too
Because I gazed into your eyes
And fell in love with you
And now I know the sun will shine
The flowers fair will bloom
And there will be no loneliness
And never any gloom
I do not need a calendar
Or any clock to chime
For in your loving arms I want
To lose all track of time
I want to let the world go by
And hold you close to me
Today, tonight, tomorrow and
For all eternity.

—*Maryruth R. Burbank*

Untitled

I gave you my heart
thinking you'd never part
I loved you sew
Wishing you'd never let go
Whenever I'd look your way
You'd pass like the next day
I try to think of where I went wrong
I honesty believe that we do belong.

—*Lynn Furman*

One Day

One day you were there,
the next day I was scared.
Then the next day came and
you weren't there.
My tears flowing as your leaving.
My Mom has left me for good.
Not only did my heart break, but
I hadn't understood.
You didn't leave me.
You are just waiting for me to come
and be taken under your hood.
For you see everything in heaven
is never misunderstood.

—*Tammy Evans*

The Winter Ocean

As the waves rush
the night is full,
through the sand the
wind of winter,
you can see the moon
rushes threw the water,
clearly the snow hits
the ground,
the ocean still have
sound,
day by day it's
getting colder

—*Rosetta Orr*

Love...

The one I love is all I need.
The one I love is part of me.
The one I love responds to me.
The one I love can support me,
from any kind of danger.
The one I love can forgive me
for what I have done badly.
The one I love can invite me
into his house.
The one I love can tell me
that he loves me too.
The one I love can tell me
he will be with me at every place.
The one I love can share with me.
The one I love can trust me.
The one I love is full of passion,
my spirits can be renewed.
The one I love is you . . . !

—*Rose Thomas*

Reaching The Moon

Could I ever reach the moon?
The stars around it shimmer in my eyes.
On the beach, a public room
darkened space lay in the sky.

Stretch my branches towards the sphere
with sand clutched in my fists
wonder, hope, and childish fear
secure me by my wrists.

Satin sheets surround my soul
I have landed

—*Maureen Kubik*

Untitled

My love, my life, my everything
the one I love the most;
the one who shrinks my laundry,
the one who burns my toast.

That very special someone
who brightens up my day;
who hurts my ear when singing,
as I go on my way.

An irreplaceable person that holds
a big part of my heart;
that one that makes my lemonade too
sweet and my kool-aid too tart.

For this wonderful darlin' of mine,
I have but one thing to say;
Despite all the odd things you do,
"I Love You Anyway".

—*LaNita Chanel Pollard*

The Wonders Of The World

Have you ever looked upon
The passing day or starting dawn,
A flower as it blooms in spring,
An eagle as it spreads its wings?

Did you ever want to know
What could cause the wind to blow,
Why an eagle has such an eye
He spots his prey from way up high?

Did you ever want to learn
What could cause a forest to burn,
Why some species or extinct,
Why these things to man are linked?

These things bring wonder and delight
But we may never see the light,
Cause we don't even understand
How the Lord God made man.

God created Earth for us to enjoy
Not for any man to destroy,
A paradise like no other
For us to live in harmony with each other.

—*Lucinda Stowe*

The Pleasure Is His Company

I know an Exorcist.
The pleasure is all mine.
In his presence,
I let go of:
my yellow greed,
my red anger,
my green envy,
my purple hatred.

He keenly senses,
He experiences me and mine.

He knows my blackest color.

In his safe silence,
He heals.

He forgives and gives grace.
He lets me own my feelings.

I know an Exorcist.
The pleasure is all time.

—*Mary Ann Malitz*

Ruby Sea

A heart bleeds a ruby sea
The razor of hope on the ground
It has a grave, yet no stone
Where a casket of dreams can be found

Fly caught in a web
His love was her only chance
'though Mozart filled the corridor
He only asked for one dance

I do not eat the blossoms
For they shadow poison so rare
and murder in the meadow
are why the daisies gather there

So now he tells his story
With velvet smile, cookies and tea
and the woman he once knew
Her heart just bleeds a ruby sea...

—*Melissa Mae Whitney*

The Endless Prairie

The endless prairie
the rolling sea
it stretches as far as the eye can see
the endless prairie.
It waves in the wind to you,
and the sweet smell of grass
the endless prairie.
The bugs hop or crawl,
and chirp a little jig
the endless prairie.
The fox pauses as it sees its dinner
then pounces and has a nice snack
the endless prairie.
The snake glides along the ground
because it has no legs
while other reptiles look for bed
the endless prairie.
The birds fly above
and sing a pleasant little tune
the endless prairie.

—*Michael Rose*

In The Mist Of A Summer Night

The Moon Cast shadows across the
the sea,

Glistening stars in the sky,

When it's warm and in the
mist of a summer night,
The moon is full and shining
fearlessly,

Silence fills the claim misty
night,
A foamy sea,
In a dark gloomy surrounding,
Fog creeping upon the foamy,
nippy sea,

When you glimpse back up in
the sky,
You see an astonishing fallen
star that catches your eyes.

—*Regina Medford*

Old Brickfaced Building

Old brickfaced building,
The sooty dirt smell of time.

The sounding
of uneven
single board floors.

Shallow door way
Narrow staircase
My steps resounding,
The floor its speaker.

Firm old mattress
Familiar
restful sleep;
Home.

—*Richard J. Porter*

Caroline's Gift

Caroline is a song to sing
The sound it has a special ring
Beauty that's beyond compare
Something for us all to share
Smiles that light up any place
Brightening up that empty space
Hands that have a special touch
A heart that loves us very much
Life that was a gift of love
Only comes from up above
Caroline is a song to sing
The sound it has a special ring

—*Lori Anderson*

The Design

The form appears
The spirit over - powers,
And design emerges
The bird sings, and
In the skies leaves its sign
And in the heart within.
The form disappears,
Not the design
Some day, somewhere
They meet again.

—*Prodipto Banerjee*

The Challenge

There they stood awaiting me
The stallions and the mares
And one would think to see me
That I hadn't any cares

They pranced around defying me
Each one in procession
Sweat beaded on my forehead
But I didn't show expression

I saw him then - a thoroughbred
The challenge had begun
I walked to him and took the rein
I wasn't going to run
He gave a winch, I almost fell
The fear began to rise
And then that nauseous feeling
Took me by surprise

Defeated once again I thought
I soon was homeward bound
I doubt if I can ever ride
That darn old merry-go-round!

—*Mary Billig*

My Love

In your arms,
the strength of touch
prevails over fear.

Breathless passion explodes,
into an overwhelming
exhilaration from the moment,

The excitement of touch,
The sensuality of a kiss,
The gentle joy of closeness,
The simple pounding heart,

Into the depths of powerlessness
a fullness swells within
all from your touch.

—*Patricia A. Perras*

America

Oh the flag, how it may fly,
The strong soldiers in battle,
How they die.
The earth plagued by fallen men
never to see,
Their precious country again

War stained the land red
Reminding us of forgotten men,
who bled

Freedom was their inspiration.
United they fought,
with hard determination

The Liberty bell rang out clear
Freedom at last, at last is here.

Our national anthem
So strong and true,
Reminding us,
We are the red, white, and blue

—*Marilyn Pedigo*

Hope

A garden of flowers, a gentle rain,
The sun high up in the sky
The song of a bird, the rustle of trees
These things keep my spirits up high.

When troubles come and stay awhile,
I see only a long dark path
Then comes the greatest sound on earth
The sound of a child's laugh.

No matter how dark things may appear
How meaningless life may seem,
Something always restores my faith
In the good things of which I dream.

Every night I thank the Lord
For giving me another day
To be the best that I can be
And for showing me the way.

—*Peggy Newton*

Untitled

As you speed down the field, hoping
the ball is thrown your way.
As you cradle the football,
the referee gives the Touchdown signal.

—*Trent Dean*

Can't Deny

Doesn't matter if you're not here but,
The thought of you will always be near
Doesn't matter if you're not fine but,
I'll always want you to be mine
Doesn't matter what people say
Because I'm not afraid
Can't say what I feel, because
What I feel I can't say
Can't you see it can't die
Because to you I'll never lie
Time can do so much
I just wish we would touch
Don't you see this love I have for you
Is not just some kind of flu.

—*Sandra Payes*

Summer

Summers gone and winters near.
The time has flown, like every year.
But, it's been great to share this fun
With someone special in the sun.

We started late, but found a beach.
We both enjoyed, not hard to reach.
We got our tans, had time to rest.
This summer was my very best.

—*William J. Feminella*

Your Jacket

The coast clear, I bent low from
the waist and breathed in.
Two times I did this silly,
irresistible thing.

It smelled of you.

I thought to make off with it.
Take it home. Wrap it round my pillow.
Rest my head as one might rest
upon a lover's breast.

I resisted the impulse, of course,
as any sensible person would.
Then I sighed with a kind of vague
yearning and turned away.

—*Mary Jordan*

Let Me Be An Instrument

Like the still small voice of
the wind in the trees
Give me the words to say
So that someone's pain I can ease

In this world of pain and sorrow
Help me bring a little joy
Help me be a lamp shining brightly
and touch a heart ever so lightly

I sometimes stray away
But, Lord, hear me when I pray
And in answer to my prayer
Let me be an instrument

Your will is my will
My all to you I owe
Your will is my will
My all to you I give
Let me be an instrument for you.

—*Laura Washington*

Can You Remember?

In the night
The wind moves the solace of the air
And everything dances.
The disturbance is silence
And the frame of life constant.
The light glimmers upon you
As the moon sits and stares
And that which is ever told
Is heard in the dark
And that is never said is felt.
The moment seems just right;
Isn't that weird?
It's rare that these moments ever come.
And in some other setting
We can feel the wind
And smell the breeze
And realize how precious these moments
are —

We're at peace.

—*Priya Bhukan*

If

If my lips could echo
The words my heart has said
If my eyes could show
The dreams within my head
If my hand on yours
Could make you feel as I
If my tongue could taste
How sweet you are inside
If my tears could wash
Your image from my mind
If I could ignore
This love that makes me blind
If I could deny
Myself this urge I feel
Then wounds would maybe heal,
But love seems not that real.

—*Atreyu*

A Prison No More

Once a child, so scare and alone,
The years has pass, and I am grown.
My body has grew tall,
My hair some shades of gray,
My heart still scare,
My memory a fade,
One day I'll be lay to peace,
All my fear I will release.
Fear will hold me, a prison no more.
For death is my key,
To another world, I hope will be,
Kinder to me.

—*Nancy Richardson*

Loneliness Of The Devastation

Somehow,
Though cloaked in its contour
I'm clinched in reality's
fists of certainty.

Discomfort pleases,
for love is a fool's minion.
And though how I fight
its gravity,
it finds me.

—*Walter Abbott*

Liken To The Honeybee

I've watched the bees gather honey
Then fly on their way
Watched the squirrels storing nuts
For a leaner day
I've watched the ants go marching by
Carrying crumbs somewhere to hide
Watched my lady friends, in turn
Show their cupboards with great pride
They had been as busy as the bees
Canning goods for winter treats
I too, have been a busy bee
Saving my own kind of sweets
I gather sweet love along the way
And store it in my watchful heart
On a memory shelf
And then some sad and lonely day
I'll open up and pour sweet love
All over my lonely self.

—*Mona Hood*

Love Game

You said that you loved me
then leave me again
Stop playing these love games
where I never win
I thought when I met you
your feelings were true.
You said, that you loved me
If I only knew.
'Cause loves not a game
where the winner is you.
Love is an emotion
shared between two:

—*Shannon M. Alonso*

The Hummingbird's Song

Family and friends were
There in the end
As we said goodbye
To a very dear friend

A gentle breeze was
Good to feel
As we realized that
It was God's will

A dainty hummingbird
Lit on a flower
To let us know that
God's still got power

Softly fluttering
Her tiny wings
As if new hope
She was there to bring

Like a message from God
For all to see
That forever with the Lord
Our loved one will be

—*Sandra Reynolds*

Untitled

Soar over the mountains
through the valleys
across the plains

Spread your wings
take one more look across
the land of the free.

—*Melissa Fleming*

Going Home: The Play

In rehearsing the next appearance,
there is confidence in one self.
There is a sense of achievement
and success.
And that first step seems all
too easy.
During the final rehearsal,
there are flaws.
Trying so hard to concentrate,
unable to finger the underlying problem.
Now there is a chill that runs up
and down the spine.
A shadow emerges,
it begins to move.
It follows the movements made.
The eerie feelings, the scent,
it all adds up to what was left behind.
Why the run was initiated.
The performance never begins.

—Linda M. Piazza

In A Prejudice World

In a prejudice world
There is fighting
We can't be friends
We aren't brothers or sisters
Sooner of later everyone will be dead
Our colors stick out
There is no right or wrong
No one cares about you
There is no love for anyone
There are no clothes to cover us
There is no food to be eaten
There is no shelter
We are not weak or strong
We're costing our own lives
There's no music to listen to
There's no help if you get shot
There's no hope, no glory to
become what you want to become
There's nothing but a blackout world
Why must our world end like this?

—Tamara Nick

Brand New

As you mount me,
there is no fear.
Inexplicably I'm drawn to
your eyes. Unblinking
you look back at me
with the same kind of curious
surprise that mine are showing
you.
Just for a moment, I'm speechless,
as I drink in your features.
I reach out to smooth your hair.
A simple gesture, and yet alive with
meaning.
My hand strokes and then stills,
somehow finally falling away,
as my eyes never leave your face.
As much as I know you
this is brand new.
And I like
very much.

—Margaret Kilgore

Us . They

And what of us
They
Will we remember
Petty moments. Family
They
(Us. They) Flowers and music
Did They. Like we
Remind themselves
Trees can red at night
But what about them
Us
Did they remember
Simple shapes. Wooden homes
Us
(Them. Us) Grasses and art
Will we. As them
Remember ourselves
DAD can I have a buck
To go the store

—Pi

Benediction

There is a thing about angels:
they are stronger than demons,
and because they can love
they bring love. Who has had
an angel for a friend
has known this to be so...
which is a special glory.

God rest you, my friend,
and keep you well.

—Thomas M. Beck

To My Prince

The angels danced when you were born,
They filled the sky with stars,
So you could watch them winking,
at Jupiter and Mars.

The world was laid out at your feet,
So you could run and play,
And laugh at all the wondrous things,
You'd find along life's way.

A Prince among the people,
That is your destiny,
And I the chosen, privileged one,
Who is your bride to be!

—Lorna Marshall Kuwada

Give Us One More Law!

There are laws, and laws, and laws-
They make your head just swim.
Some are good, and some are bad-
A legislative whim!
Let us all remember,
back in the good old days-
We spent less time and cash
And still had means and ways!
We go deeper in debt —
with every new chore
Assets become much less,
Liabilities soar!
Is there a remedy?
Just take a good long look.
Don't spend what you don't have!
Add this law to the book!

—Ruth V. Marshall

They Marred My Rembrandt

They marred my Rembrandt;
  They scarred its wit,
A dripping art work,
  Yield and submit.

The degenerate multitude
  Cast their stone.
My Rembrandt lay empty,
  But not alone.

Again, with fear
  The strike was hard.
The framework shuddered.
  The soul was God.

—Paul Fucaloro

Obliteration

Unwanted, cold and hungry,
  they stood alone.
Exhausted from the long chase,
  and no longer able
On the edge of starvation,
  the wild children die.
Men destroyed buffalo for hide,
  while the meat decayed.
Winter cold almost completes the task,
  of the last of the Cheyenne.

—Nancy Holt

Beware

I haven't slept for days
Thinking about being immortal.

In your eyes I can see the
Beautiful skies and fluffy clouds
They are still. My veins
For I'm not breathing heavy.

I don't want you to hear me...

Sneaking up on you.

—Vance Vizcarrondo

This Feeling Within

Such a wonderful feeling
This feeling within
From the tips of my toes
Clear up past my chin

Just a wisp of a thing
That's how it began
But a moment thereafter
My heart felt its brand

An engulfing sensation
A tempestuous flame
Ever-burning within me
Too torrid to tame

At last consummation
It has now reached its peak
With an ecstatic explosion
That has left me so weak

A miraculous feeling
That stays with me yet
A rapturous emotion
I will never forget

—Terry F. Tisdale

Dogs

Within this pit,
This stomach,
This bitch hound wincing,
Heat omitting,
The fiery verbs,
Rolling,
From canine tongues,

Upon the four legs,
Pedestals of fur,
Panting like perverts,
Feed them plenty,

These breathing rugs,
Stepping clear,
Let us not wake them,
Pet them gently,
Let them sleep.

—*Scott Allen Ronald*

The Ukulele Girls

Listen! Do you hear them,
those girls of yesteryear,
harmonizing in the parlor,
their voices sweet and clear?

Attired in pastel finery,
hair marcelled or set in curls,
merrily they dubbed themselves
The Ukulele Girls.

Drawn close in friendly circles
on summer afternoons,
deftly strumming ukuleles,
they provided lively tunes.

Hark to "Camptown Races"
and "Yankee Doodle Boy."
Sing along to "Blue-Tail Fly,"
as hearts are filled with joy.

Vibrant, glowing, pretty,
like a string of lovely pearls,
they pluck at memory's heartstrings —
The Ukulele Girls.

—*Lois V. Denson*

Through the Eyes of a Child

Oh, to see life once again
Through a child's eyes.
Each night, a feat of magic,
Each day, a new surprise.

What energy to spend!
Imagination without end.
A love for all things, great, and small,
No hypocrisy at all.

If I had but one wish,
In this world so wide,
T'would be to see life once again
Through the eyes of a child.

—*Rebecca Deason*

Beauty

Beauty stretched its arms
Towards the sun at day
And the moon at night,
The form of yellow flowers
Of fragile petals of sweetness
Over stems strong and secure.
The sum of light and dark,
Fragility and strength was beauty.

—*Patricia Weinberg*

Simple Hearted Soul

The ocean draws me forward
Through the blackened smoke
It leads me to a sailboat
Tied upon a choke

Into the boat I step
Without a heavy heart
A simple cry or a regret
From the deepest part

I find the boat is worthy
Of a simple hearted soul
A soul not soft enough for a simple cry
And a soul that is not bold

Once I am out of the harbor
I breathe an enormous sigh
A sigh that tells me life's too short
For a simple guy

As soon as I set sail
I know I will have no regrets
Of fast approaching decisions
Or life's constant threats

—*Mark Harnetiaux*

Memories

I walk alone
Through the corridors in my mind
Things only to me known
Things I've left behind
Never to be thought of again
Memories are select
No one's the same
As on them we reflect
Emotions swarm our hearts
Surprise, shame & guilt
Friends grown apart
And the lives we've built
People we once loved
People we used to hate
Shedding of tears & blood
Things we used to anticipate.

—*Rich Stacy*

A Friend Like You

I was your friend,
through thick and thin.
You were my friend,
up 'til then.
All of a sudden,
You didn't need me.
You didn't care.
And I got scared.
Oh how I've missed,
those days we've shared.
I loved you like a brother,
but now I'm not so sure.
Why did you leave?
Please tell me what for.
I will never love again,
the way I loved you.
How could you leave?
A friend like you.

—*Suna Kocak*

Together

Together we walk
through wide and narrow paths
together we have known
the mysteries of life.

Together we travel
by air and by land
together we have seen
the greatness of the skies.

Together we have joy
together we have sorrow
but always looking forward
to a brighter tomorrow.

Together we miss
the beauty of our land
together we worship
the same God, the same flag.

So — if you have someone
walking with you side by side
consider yourself lucky
and — together walk with pride.

—*Maria L. Negron*

Star Light

A small boy holds a star,
tightly in his hand.
Perhaps it came from Heaven,
to help us understand,
that God's still up there
watching over all the land.

He reminds us of another child,
who grew into a man,
and became our own Lord Jesus,
according to God's plan.

Christmas brings such memories,
of times we all have shared.
Of Christmas Carols and little ones,
and lost loved ones, for whom we cared.

It's important that we celebrate,
that tiny infants birth.
But even more to celebrate,
the time He spent on earth.
For in His light we'll find the way,
to celebrate this Christmas Day.

—*Nada Wager*

Geremy Flies Low

Students of a rhythmic age,
Time sequence another page,
Lonely souls drifter rage,
Green valley or sandy sage,
Came along a cornerstone,
Searching out his truth to hone,
Etched his name into a stone,
Bringing forth new social tone,
Alone so lonely he did pass,
Spoke of endearments in mass,
Seen his name eked name to pass,
Of yearned for secrets in a flash,
Truly he would rise to splendor,
Upon his intent true and tender,
Only fell to death and folly,
All the while content and jolly

—*Leland Culliton (a.k.a. I.T.
Bell)*

Darkened Man

I see you only at night and the
tip of your long black cloak jumping
in the wind leaves me with a
questioning look on my face. Why
have you chosen me to cry
silently in my bed at night?
Why do the moonbeams softly
dance around you, but not on
you? I know it is a power, but
what kind? And then you are gone,
but you will come again
and sadden my soul.
"Go away,"
I want to tell him, but I know
him and he will come again.

—Sarah Schmidt

How Do You Say Goodbye

How do you say goodbye,
to a friend that you hold dear?
How do your lips still smile,
while in your eye there lies a tear?

How do you live today,
for it will never come again?
How do you deal with knowing,
that tomorrow it all could end?

How do you still smile,
from deep within your heart?
While all that I can think of,
is soon we'll be apart.

I know you think you're lucky
for the years that you have had,
but when you're young and in your prime,
to me I think it's sad.

You want me to understand,
and I tell you I will try.
But still I sit here pondering,
How do you say goodbye?

—Mary Ann Ott

Ba'Hoghan'Go'Deya Chin'Dii

Hoghan

Going home
  to a haunted house -
Open the door,
  no one's there -
What's this borne
  on air's subtle breath?
Perfumed aroma
  of one I know.
Across the table
  a face I see -
Fleeting, gone -
  perfume and face.
Very real
  days on end -
Haunted house -
  better than one empty.

—Walter W. Snyder

Only The Strong Survive

Only the strong survive
To belong
You have to be strong
In a world like today
We have poverty, drugs,
Crime and every thing going on.

You have to be strong
We must keep the focus on our lives
And keep moving on
Do right not wrong.
We can reach as high or as low.
But, on the bottom there nothing below
Look start ahead there's more
It's not like before

For only the strong survive
To belong
You have to be strong

—Lisa Robinson

October Most Fair

October has come again
To break the hearts of men
With the splendor of red-gold leaves
Drifting softly from laden trees

Long singing golden days
Touched with wood-smoke haze
An azure clear cloudless sky
Flocks of birds winging high

And all the sun comes glistening
And crisp cool winds come whistling
Down leaf-strewn country lanes
Tapping gently on window panes

Flickering shadows-pale moonlight
A hint of frost through the night
A lovely secret wooded glade
Where October memories never fade

October walks the land
With beauty hand in hand
Like a shimmering golden sphere
This is October most fair

—Patricia O'Connell

Life's Way

I'm looking forward to days of new;
To bring new joys and sorrows.
No person knows what lies ahead;
But I'm remembering always you.

I'm looking back at memories;
The silly things we fought over.
And the times we got along.
We were like the best of friends;
And then it'd go all wrong.

I'm looking at today,
And longing for the past.
Then I think of future things;
The friendships that will last.
Then remember I'm wasting today,
And hurry along life's narrow way.

—Lacey Boss

Free To Be

Would you ask the mighty oak
To change its bright autumnal cloak?
A maple, beautiful to see,
How strange were it a Christmas tree.

The graceful eagle up so high,
Would you ask it not to fly?
Plant only weeds with no perfume
To turn the commonplace to bloom?

Let the willow branches bend,
So, too, the pathway of each friend.
Unique is Nature's artistry,
Her handiwork: variety.

—Louise Carmack

Reality

Knowing it's his time
  to fly
Knowing he has to continue his journey
  toward maturity
Knowing I can no longer smooth
  the rough spots
Knowing he will have to work things out
  on his own
Knowing he has the ability
  to do just that
Knowing all these things eases my mind
  in his absence.
Knowing that accepting his absence
  will make my heart ache!
Knowing that the ache of absence
  will heal
Knowing that the healing will fill me
  with love and strength.

—Margaret Hollenberger

The Butterfly

I've spent my life dreaming butterflies
  to have and to hold
Now that I've finally caught one
  I must let her go

She floats in the breeze
  on her gossamer wings
When mine eyes behold her
  my heart and soul sing

On the breeze she was born
  on the wing she must live
For the love that I hold her
  her freedom I give

So I wait here alone
  with my feet on the ground
But each night with sweet memories
  my head will abound

At the dawn of tomorrow
  or the dusk of day's past
Has true love flown steady,
  or have my lips kissed love's last?

—Steve Hasstedt

Labor Of Love

I gave my life
  to my father above,
A living sacrifice
  a labor of love.

I lost my mind,
  couldn't find my way,
I lost my spine
  became a lump of clay.

I gave him my fear
  gave him my loss,
I gave him my tears
  he gave me his cross.

To brace my back
  to shoulder my arm,
To carry my lack
  to keep me from harm.

I received new life
  from my father above,
A living sacrifice
  a labor of love.

—*Susan Schoff*

Short Ballads

I sing short ballads
  to my little ones
Soothing the souls,
  of my little ones
Covey, thus complications created
  I'm their mama, and I know
  save my little ones

Short ballads, soothing souls of
  all the little ones
  Close your eyes now
The world will turn, and slip away
  I'm your mama and I know

Short ballads
for all the little ones

—*Sonia St. James*

The Rose

To wonder the greatest of dreams
To offer the most fashionable things
To reach out to you with all my heart
Could this one rose by a start?
I have no treasures stored with bliss
If to share more - then, I may miss
The source of true simpleness
That is to fill a heart with happiness.
The rose pedals so sweet and tender
With beauty more than all the splendor
The aroma of the softest touch
The rose is a gift that says so much.
Take this rose I give to you.
Accept it from a heart that's true.
Let it be known it's given with love
The rose will be just enough.
Let the rose pedals drift with the wind
To know where love starts to never end.
Of, but to offer you more than you know
Would be my very best gift, the rose.

—*Mildred Allison*

Untitled

To you I give my heart
To open gently, to let love flow out
To envelope your being, Not to break.

To you I give my mind to sit in
To learn from, to teach
Not to destroy.

To you I give my soul
To protect your essence
To bond with yours through an eternity
Not to tear to pieces.

To you I give my body which contains
My heart, my mind, my soul
A superficial cover
To touch
To satisfy
To play all physical roles
Not to leave broken, alienated.

—*Wayne J. George*

Aspirations

Waiting so long
To see your skin,
Smooth, finger sliding
'Cross the bridge of your nose,
Beneath your glowing eyes
Anticipation builds like trust
If only, if only, our life —
One home, one purpose, spirit,
Late-night groping for tenderness
Like tooth-brushing, dishes, and hugs
Sometimes I look at you quizzically,
As if to ask, "Who are you?"
For, indeed, sometimes I wonder
Yet, even if I do not know you,
Like a well-worn book or phone number,
I do know who you are to me
You are to me, my destiny

—*Melissa E. Zalle*

Winter's End

She looked beyond the frosted pane
  to snowy fields and foliage white
With mind's escaping thoughts that life
  should culminate at such a sight

And then beyond the snowy fields
  beyond the foliage white
She looked into the winter's depth
  and then at winter's night

With eyes agazing all around
  aglow with winter glow
Gave a shudder not at season's cold
  but at thought of melting snow

—*Marie S. Patusky*

Hummingbird

Hummingbird, o minuscule!
Tiny haunt of blossoms bright,
Creature-elf, and sight so rare,
Green ruby wonder,
Ceaseless flight.

There among the flowers flitting,
Here, now there,
Now gone - oh dear!
Back again - oh, thank my stars,
The tiny minuscule's here!

—*Sharon Henderson*

Treasures We Can Share

A welcome greeting
To start the day
Can make the difference
In ones work or play.

A word of praise
Can dispel great fear
Help build confidence
And bring good cheer.

Encouraging words
In time of despair
Lightens the burden
That one has to bear.

A pleasant smile
Can ripple afar
And return again
Like a shining star.

The treasures are many
And easy to give
To help another
A better life to live.

—*Laura Belle Martin*

Timeless

In our deepest hour we all want to die
  to take the fear and the pain away
There is no tomorrow, there's only today,
  if tomorrow comes
We close our eyes and wonder will we
  ever see the sun again
What's waiting for us around the corner
A life that no one will know of
  until tomorrow never comes
We take for granted all that we have
  once it's gone, we all think and cry
Love today, don't regret yesterday
  hope for tomorrow
No one's here to stay.

—*Miko Dudley*

Mourning A Family Member

An Indian lost his finger
To the cemetery he went,
  To ponder, and to linger.
He mourned his loss.
  He mourned his loss.
Death of his bodily member
  His daily, daily cross.
His finger, his lands—they are no more.
  Empty words on worthless paper...
What treachery the great white fathers
  For the Indian had in store.

—*Patrick Gilbert de Toledo*

The Web

Like the spider who lays a plan
  to trap a insect in his hand
  sticky webs of life we spin
that hold our hopes and dreams within

And as an insect thus is bound
  our webs of life do hold us down
  the more we struggle to escape
  the strands that bind do not break

And in the end we cease our fight
except the life that is our plight
  and in so doing we start to die
  just like that insect by and by

—*Susan Gail English*

My Destiny

I faintly glimpse the beacon,
To which my compass dials;
It's far across the ocean,
Yet I'll reach through trials.

Many hearts quite true and bold,
A noble start indeed have made;
But left to me rare things untold,
That dreams of duty must invade.

Not with sword nor any javelin,
Will I that ruffled main o'rcome;
But faith in hand and heart within,
I'll crown and roam its lofty run.

Then guided by a "Hand-Unseen",
Omnipotent to trust;
Intrusted by a voice serene,
Fulfill my destiny I must.

And when in the cold, cold depths I be;
Of this vast eternal plain;
Yet I'll live posterity,
In the sanctuary of the "Main".

— *G. W. Plummer*

To My Wife From The Man Of Your Life

In this life there can be fears
Toils troubles, and strife can
   can even cause tears.
But in the midst of life
God gives one called a wife.
Being with you I've understood
Why the creator called women good.
Though there are times when were sad.
There are also many times were glad.
But know that when I pray
that I can always say,
Thank you Good Lord above,
For giving me Karen to love!

— *Ted Herrera*

Tomorrow Is Late

Tomorrow holds my future
Tomorrow is why I wait
Tomorrow will end my sorrow
Tomorrow holds my fate

Yesterday was not tomorrow
Today, I'll try to explain
Yesterday put me in misery
Tomorrow will ease the pain

Everyday I see tomorrow
In my dreams, it's that way
Everyday is someone's tomorrow
Tomorrow may be my day

I write of things gone by
I write when I have something to say
Today I write of tomorrow
Tomorrow I won't write of today

Tomorrow my heart will be in it
Today my mind's in a fog
Tomorrow will put a light on my thinking
Tomorrow is late, I'm in the dark

— *Valentine Benson*

Today

Today we see our day,
Tomorrow it has gone away.
Never, never to return,
This we will never learn.

To grasp each moment,
To hold for enjoyment.
Today is a day of our living,
Our love is for giving.

So keep it for this day,
Let it be here today,
Here to stay,
In every way!

— *Mary Wilson*

Walk Among The Homeless

Walk among the homeless, reach out
   touch and feel their despair.
Look on a child, as it searches for
   a place to lay its head.
The knowing of hunger, the need for
   warmth to its small body, a place
   to call home.
Walk again among the homeless, reach
   out, touch and feel their despair.
Can we as a person, a community or
   nation not stop, look, and care?
Walk among the homeless, but can we
   stop there?
No, as long as there is one homeless
   person, we must share our wealth in
   food and shelter and show them that
   we really care.

— *Sara Hans Hannahs*

Kalliste

Late night precious time
   traveling far within my mind,
A dreamer called to distant shores;
   the "Atlantis" of Plato's lore.

"Kalliste" the Most Beautiful,
   the ancient's great delight,
Transformed by the earth to "Fear";
   shrouded from mere mortals' sight.

Marinatos, Doumas, Pellegrino
   tell her catastrophic tale.
Their's a fascinating quest
   to lift time's ashen veil.

Kalliste will see the dawn again;
   her beauty grace the Kosmos.
Even Poseidon will smile then
   "clear weather"

Someday the dreamer will return
   to taste the sparkling sea and air,
"Santorini", "Thera", or "Kalliste",
   her countenance twill be most fair.

— *Rosalind J. Young*

Crumpled Camel

Near the glass
tray
with its desert
of ash
on the formica
dinner table

a crumpled Camel
pack
it is empty

a half-drunk
white porcelain
cup
of chilling
milk-brown
coffee

red lipstick
still moist
along the rim.

— *Michael Dellert*

20 Years At Wilson Hill

Up before dawn
Try to get my long-johns on
Going to Wilson hill
To get in on the kill
It is wet and cold
I think I'm getting old
Then the geese started honking
My knee's began knocking
I tore my wader's on a snag
While picking up my bag
The water sure is cold
You can tell I'm getting old
Boy, I'm having fun
Almost dropped my gun
Boy what a thrill
20 year's at Wilson hill

— *Rodney T. O'Donnell*

One Day Soon

One day soon

   I'll patch up this old heart
   Try to put the pieces back
   Soon let down my guard

One day soon

   I'll dust off this old pain
   For love was never meant to be
   based on loss or gain

One day soon

   I might unlock that door
   That often kept me tied to
   the sadness that I wore

One day soon

   I'll soon release the fear
   That somehow seems to find its way
   whenever you are near

One day soon

   I just might let you in
   And hope that love will take me
   to a place I've never been

— *Pola Christoforou*

Seeds Of Love

So many of our near defeats;
Turn out to be our gain,
For we are looking for the sun
But what God sends is rain.

We ponder over a tiny seed
That's planted out of season,
And pray that it will sprout and grow;
When God cultivates a reason.

We must keep a steady hand,
Held firmly on the plow,
And not look back to mourn the seed,
That missed it goal some how.

So never feel your goal is lost,
If God's will you did import;
For you have planted a seed of love;
In someone's lonely heart.

—*Phyllis J. Burch*

Construction, Destruction,

Civilization, like a Mobius strip,
Turns in its eternal trip.
A regressive wood age,
Stone age, next stage,
Technology advances
With gambling and chances.
Spear turns to lance,
Hop turns to prance.
Walk turns to run,
Lance turns to gun.
Speech is now writing,
Peace is now fighting.
Tempers become hot,
About who has fought.
One last shove,
Fire from above,
Turning a curve, back grows wood,
Climate is cold, fire is good.
Civilization returns to sun,
When the wood age has begun.

—*Luke Hampton*

A Dream Within A Dream

As mighty as the notion seemed,
'Twas but a dream within a dream.
Starry angel, bright moonbeams,
Beautiful as a flowing stream.
Great matters made of great ideals,
Fantasy of such strong appeal!

Revealed in sight, emotion compound,
My inner joy did so resound!
A dream within a dream it was,
The fog and mist, a shroud of love.
And in event, love's fire was spent,
The dream was there, and then it went!

—*Timothy R. Kirkpatrick*

Us

Us is two.
Us is me.
Us is you.

Us needs love.
Us needs happiness.
Us needs you.

Us is love.

—*Sherida Egan*

Baby

Hoping... disappointed
unexpected... surprised
nausea... saltine crackers
bigger breasts... bigger thighs
flutters... butterflies
rolling... waves
kicks... during jeopardy
counting... the days
bright lights... people hurry
sudden quiet... quiet pause
tiny cry... deep sighs
new mom and dad... new baby boy

—*Toni L. Fowler*

Illusive Dream

I once reached out into the
Universe with great expectations
Out, out I felt into the vast
Endless splendor of space.
Everything in tune with the
Universe, then with one
Fleeting touch all the
Twinkling stars came
Shimmering down one by one
With all the hopes and dreams
Of mankind into a sea
Of darkness and infinity.

—*Ruth I. Kuchko*

Out Of Biafra: An Ode

I came back from that hell,
Unscathed by the fiery shell.
I came out with tales to tell,
Hoping that all will be well.

Oh no; death dropped in so bold,
From the darkness so cold,
To claim a sixteen-year-old:
Handsome, suave and brass-bold.

I have thought so hard and long.
I still sing that moonlight song,
But it has not made me strong
To understand what went wrong.

Sleep in peace, dearest Kevin.
It is not whether we will ever win,
It's when and how we will give in
To this war of senseless livin'.

—*Maurice Ene*

Untitled

Hearts are colors all wrapped
up in one, to make a beautiful
rainbow right next to the sun.
I love you so true; that I'll
wrap up my colors and give them
to you.

—*Lorri Freedman*

Poet Elijah-El

A poet sat solemn
upon a hill...
Solace God gives ...
He sat upon a hill, poet Elijah-el...

—*P. Elijah-El*

Hurting

Why must these salty tears be shed
Upon my pillow soft,
And anguished memories flood my head
With thee, my love now lost?

Why must my torn and tattered heart
Be beaten ever more,
Reminded yet how far thou art,
Across forever's shore?

Does there exist one who can wrench
This dagger out my soul;
And heal again the bleeding trench
To make me again whole?

If only on my hopeless pleas
One gentle word were spent.
Alas, I'm left to drift on seas
Of desolate torment.

I am in need of that which can
Come only from Above.
But on this wretched earth no man
Could lend such endless love.

—*Stephanie Oldham*

The Dying Tree

She tried to lift her limbs
Upward toward the sky
Then she bowed her head
And spoke to the river running by.

"My days are all spent
and I am going to die,
Won't you murmur for me gently
As you go passing by?"

The river answered back
"Don't be sad dear one,
I'll be waiting for you here
When one day you'll return."

"You'll be gone for a while
and go back to the earth
To nourish the soil
And bring forth new birth."

"Then one day you'll re-appear
in fresh and queenly clothes,
As the freshness of a lily
Or as the beauty of a rose."

—*Yolanda Cohen*

Musical Note

Chopin played it
Verdi did the score
Schumann dreamed the melody
A great inheritance and more....

Joplin ragtimed rhythm
Ellington sophisticated jazz,
Hoagy "stardusted" our world,
Nat added class.....

A smorgasbord of music,
Dancing with melodic measures,
A lifetime standing ovation,
For brilliant gem-filled treasures.

—*Phyllis Louise Golec*

I'm Waiting

I'm but a dreamer
Waiting to see,
My dreams become
Reality,

I'm but a lover
Waiting to see,
My love become
Reality,

I'm but a sinner
Waiting to see,
My sins become
Reality,

I'm but a shepherd
Waiting to see,
My flock become
Reality,

I'm but a Christian
Waiting to see.....

—*Sherman Hunt*

Oh! Man!

Oh! Man, oh! Man,
Wake up oh! Man
And bury your pride,
Like the flower and the rock
You come and go,
Like the sound and the light
You only flash,
Like the dream and the love.
You live to die.

You are no more
Than the dust of universe,
Like the bird in the cage
Like the life in the womb
Like the thief in the cell
You are a prisoner.
of nature.

Oh! Man Oh! man
Wake up Oh! man
You aren't special creature!

—*J. Paulo Gomes*

The Prom

She's the dream I've always
wanted to have.
But I didn't
have the courage.

I saw her everyday in the hallways.
And every night in my mind.

Rehearsing the perfect lines.
Wishful thinking
her replies.

She's the dance I've always
wanted to have.
And I finally
got the courage.

But she said-
No...

—*Thomas M. Ryan*

"Like" And "Goes"

Remember when "like"
Was an endearment or praise,
And "like" meant a comparison
In a few different ways,

As in "I sure like you," or
"She looks like her Mom,"
Now it's "like he was walking,"
Where did it come from?

Was he walking or not?
If it's hard to recall,
Then maybe he wasn't
Really walking at all!

And the word "goes" meant leave,
As in "She goes away."
Now it's—"He goes, 'I'm hungry',"
Does he eat, go, or stay?

It's all so confusing,
How "like" and "goes" fit,
Like she goes — "say what!"
Wow! I think I've got it!

—*Marlene J. Vallen*

Mom

Chocolate macaroon cookies - what
was that recipe?
    I'll call Mom, she'll know.

If that mocking bird don't sing - how
does the rest of that song go?
    I'll call Mom, she'll know.

Aunt Ruth's birthday is coming - was
that the 18th?
    I'll call Mom, she'll know.

Stabbing pain in my heart - is this
from Mom's death?
    Who will I call? I don't know.

—*Sandy Gentile*

Whispering Willow

Whispering willow in the sun
Watching the leaves soar
With waves of the wind.

Look at the kite
Way up in the height
The stars glowing bright at night
May that kite be my guide
To my willow in the night.

Imagine that sight
Might the moonlight show the way
In the morning the sun will shine.
It will show my willow's proud branches.
The willow will whisper and grow
When it is gone it will be so pretty
Imagine that willow
It will be a great sight.

—*Melissa Mytty*

Of Deer Hunting

We talk about the deer a lot.
We learn their ways and plot a lot.
We watch them rule the range a lot.
We learn to stop them by a shot.

—*Marie Tschumperlin*

You Are Not A Failure

So you are going through rough times.
We all do.
They seem to bring out the best in you.
No matter how dim the future may seem,
You must never lose sight of your dream.
knowing you has been my pleasure,
Because I know you are not a failure.

—*Larry D. O'Neal*

Lord Almighty God And King

Lord Almighty God and King.
We always praise you as we sing.
We pray to you each day and night,
And hope to see you in heavenly light.

As we go to church each day.
We kneel down and start to pray.
My dearest God we love you so,
And hope you'll be with us where
ever we go.

—*Linda Kaukeano-Smith*

Fall Is Here

Summer over fall is here
We can hear the bugs loud and clear
A little cool and sometimes warm
Fall is here
Trees starting to shed their leaves
Weeds turning brown
We know the first frost
Will soon be here
Birds heading South
Ducks make a show
All the Animals know where to go
Squirrels bury nuts or whatever they can
Ready for the season to end
Fall is here
Out in the gardens and fields we gather
Pumpkins for Halloweens, pie or whatever
Now the time is getting close
For all the goblins and little ghost
Fall is here!

—*B. Harfman*

The Answer

We look to man to get our answer.
We look for money to be our answer.
We look for clothes, homes, and
things to be our answer. We are
Constantly looking for the answer
But, only through the blood, and the
righteousness of Jesus Christ, will
we get the answer too the quest we
have on the inside of us.

—*Marlene Smith-Hughes*

Forever

Looking on a sunny hillside
Up to golden evening sky,
Wind in trees seemed like a whisper:
"Hush, my darling, don't you cry.
If you look at natures beauty,
And can see it with your heart,
We are closer now then ever.
Not one cloud keeps us apart."

—*Lisa Caspari*

Peace On The Way

Now that peace is on the way
We must all pray
That all Nations stay that way
For it is God's will
As He alone created the Earth
Its beauty is unsurpassed
The duty of man
Is to make it last

For without Peace
The Earth will disappear
Just as the Dinosaurs
This many a year
All who do not desire Peace
Cannot on this Earth,
Expect a peaceful Rebirth

—*Rose Mary Gerlach*

Seat Of Passion

Between the vehemence and the storm,
We seem to supervene what we feel.
Take each day as it comes,
For life can be considered ethereal.

To commit an iniquity,
You must feel immodest within your life,
Feel so uncomfortable,
Yet feet still firm on solid ground.

The seat of passion,
Is what we all know as the heart.
We wait incessantly for it to speak,
When we condemned it from the start.

—*Robert Kubacki*

Epitaph

When I die, I don't want marble -
What a hell: To bear that cold
    weight for eternity.
And I don't want hollow words that ring
    With the senseless persistence of
Dinner music in a surgical ward.
What I want I don't know.
What I need is a God
    Who will open the door
    And take me back in,
Just as he closed the door behind me
To see where I would go.

—*C. F. Schneider*

Slave Freedom

Freedom, oh precious freedom
    What a joyful word in a
        song of praise
Freedom, oh precious freedom
    How I wish for you while
        working on those hot
            sunny days,
Freedom, oh precious freedom
    Will I get you before
        I'm buried in
            my grave.

—*Thembi Michelle Terrell*

Untitled

Burning light of time
What time are you from?
Music box, collecting dust,
Song waiting to be sung.
Fossil to be treasured
life unsettled,
voice constrained.
Burning light,
life is waiting.
Walk on.

—*Lucy E. Cavazos*

In A Courtyard, Sitting.

In the cool and calm of the evening,
When gentle breezes clear the smog
The scents of lavender and roses prevail,
The splashing of the fountain
Like tinkling bells of a far off land.
Twinkling stars in a jet black sky
Foil, to shy moonbeams flitting
Through the whispering maple leaves.
And thus we sit, with hands entwined,
In love encompassed,
Heedless not what the morrow bring.

—*Norman H. Noel*

Untitled Number Two

How startled I become
when I become undone over
unspoken words in your mouth
that chews the food
that feeds your body and soul
in silence
absorbing my love
like water on a sponge
swelling with moisture
enriching a need
too deep of which to speak
of sorrow and pain
unguided in a desert of flowers
grown by the moon and sun
from skies unknown.

—*Mary Pillot*

A Star Wish

I wished upon a star one night
When I was feeling low.
I wished that there would be
More happiness for me.

I wished upon a star one night
When I was all alone.
I wished that I had
Someone to hold.

I wished upon a star one night
With tears in my eyes.
I wished that I had
Someone to make me smile.

I wished upon a star one night
That all my dreams would come true.
That last star I wished upon,
Sent me you.

—*Laura Lewand*

Lord Of Everything

Why is just a question
When is just a time
Where is just a place
But I am God, sublime.

Who is just a person
What is just a thing
It is just an object
But I am God, your everything.

Many is just a number
Some is just a few
Small is just a stature
But I am God, who's here for you.

Blue is just a color
Eight is just a size
Left is just direction
But I am God, all wise.

Tree and train, bird and dew
Country, king and flea
Rain, family, bee and government
Everything depends on me.

—*Nancy M. Garver*

I Think About You

In the still of the moments
When my surroundings are few
    Then - my dearest -
    I think about you.

I think of the times
That I shared with you.
Our moments together
    That were so few.

It was sometime ago
That you came my way.
    But in my heart
    It seems like yesterday.

Even though - time has passed us by
    I remember our moments
        That were so few.
    Your still in my heart.
    I think about you.

—*Ruth Hollimon Jones*

Forever Gone

What happens to dreams
When not fulfilled.
Do they flitter away
Lost in the mist,
of nowhere.

Can they be called back,
When days are filled with joy,
To reach out and grasp
In clutching fingers
To be renewed.

Or have they taken off
On a wisp of the wind,
To be gone forever
Filtering dreams,
Into nothingness.

—*Marjorie Quirion*

From The Garden Of Friendship

A friend is someone to turn to
When one's spirits need a lift,
A friend is someone we treasure
For true friendship is a gift.

A friend is someone we laugh with
Over little personal things,
A friend is someone we're serious with
In facing whatever life brings.

A friend is someone who fills our lives
With beauty, joy and grace,
And makes the world that we live in
A better and happier place.

In the garden of life's blessings
There are flowers sweet and fair,
And among them bright with beauty
Is the friendship that we share.

—*Mary Therese Quinn*

Untitled

What do you do
When someone you love
Dies
And you can't bring yourself
To mourn?

How do you explain
To family members who think you
Brave
And family friends who think you
Cold
That you are, in truth, neither?

But because you witnessed
Over months of time
The transformation of a vital person
Who loved music, painting and laughter
Into a dour, silent, chair-bound prisoner
Of the illness that ultimately stopped her
    heart,
You know her life ended long before her
    death
And you cannot look at the frail shell in the
    hospital bed
And mourn what was lost long before.

—*Scott Nesmith*

Burning Candle

In a long forgotten era
When the shadows fell at night,
Pioneers lighted little candles
In their windows gleaming bright.

Through the darkness, a wayfarer
Traveling tired and alone
Found the warmth of friend and fireside
Guided by the light that shown.

Through the years that separate us
And the miles we are apart,
I still keep a candle burning
In the window of my heart.

Praying that its feeble flicker
Brightly burning you will see.
Through the darkness it may guide you
Swiftly, gladly home to me.

—*Stella D. Colebank*

The Button

How will I know...
    When the wind will blow,
    When the sky will glow,
    When life will go,

How will I know...
    When they will say no,
    And make the mistake,
    Of playing the game,
    Or taking the dive,
    Of pushing the button,
    And saying good-bye.

—*Tammy Hosmer*

Hope

Where there is life, there's hope
When there's hope, life begins anew.
We who love wandered from the fold,
Return and henceforth are true.

True to the things that are worthwhile
To the God, who has seen us through
The storm and made the sun, come faith.
And gave us that heavenly view
Of the things that are to come to us,
If we live and love as He taught.
Hope He has given, to lead us on
To live and love as we ought.

—*Marguerite J. Bears Wyant*

Fellowship

Fellowship with a man
When they both work with
their hands
Is beautiful.
A moment in the busy day
to pray.
They search and wonder and praise,
They have found peace in
the study of the word.
All barriers down, nothing
they lack,
Didn't I tell you?
One is white and one is black.

—*Ruth Wrightam*

Senior's Plea

O gracious God, forsake us not
    when we are old and gray;
that unto those who follow us
    we may Thy care display.

Thou who hast sent so many griefs
    once more our souls restore,
and out of sorrow's lowest depths
    O bring us forth once more.

O turn again and comfort us,
    our waning strength increase
and for Thy faithfulness, O God,
    our praise shall never cease.

—*Miles Jerome Jones*

Please, Quit The Habit

Oh, my dear Sonny,
when you are going to learn,
to say "no" to this habit
that could make you insane,
something that hurt you
in and outside,
You've been hurting your family
for a very long time.
Don't you think is time,
for you to stop,
to open your eyes
and be more strong,
make your children proud,
do something for them,
I am not talking of money.
I am talking of honor,
and about a clean name.

—*Virginia Lopez*

Mr. Johnnie

He listens to you talk,
when you have nothing to say.
He'll sit by your side,
through the night and the day.
He opens your eyes,
and shows you what's right.
In the blackest dark,
he brings light.
In his mind,
there is so much bliss.
With his thoughts,
there is so much to give.
To think of him, will brighten your day.
With the thoughts of his words,
your worries will stray.
He is the one,
you should never betray.
For if you don't,
he'll always stay.

—*Michelle Rogers*

Do I Love You
or Am I in Love with You

Do I love you or am I in love with you?
When you love someone, you're always
happy to see them walk in the door.
When I see you my heart soars.
Almost like an eagle in the sky.
But only my love will never die.
When you come by I seem to light
up and glow.
I almost feel like a strong river
    flow......
The time we had seems like a
    dream...
But now we are at least a team.
So, am I in love with you???
    I don't know!!!!
Everything leads to love.
But I must fly like a dove...........

—*Paula J. Brown*

Untitled

Don't do the schottische
    when it's hottische.
It's coola
    to hula.

—*Patti Garrity*

Reflections from a Hospital Bed

At the end of the track
When you're flat on your back
And you think, "Maybe here's
    where it ends" -
In this darkest hour
Not money nor power
Can equal the blessing of friends.

—*Raymond H. Lyon, Ph.D.*

Request

I want your garden of laughter
Where anything is normal
And nobody cares - because nobody knows
Where fairies dance in blank hallways
And in the heads of relost souls
Where moans are symphonies
Recharging the abyss
Where I drink my food
And flies are swapped off my face
Onto my lap
Where I am the specimen looking up
Into the raging chrome
That cuts in
and feeds me death
Slowly.

—*Yadira V. Gonzalez*

Our Place In The Sun

In a far away place
Where dreams roam free,
there is a love,
that waits for me.

With no explanations,
no reason or rhyme,
this love remains
untouched by time.

Consoling my mind,
and consuming my soul,
It is my foundation
and what makes me whole.

Two hearts connected
and strengthened by trust,
bounded by innocence,
not perverted by lust.

Someday I will journey
to this place in the sun,
Where we both shall be
together as one.

—*Vita Bonanno*

Home

There is a place I want to go
Where everyone feels free
No one is ever alone
Where there is happiness
No one is ever sad
Where there is love
No one is ever mad
Where can I find this place
At home with you in my arms

—*Roma R. Rose*

Our Country

Beauty graces this wondrous land,
Where God has blessed every man.
Freedom to assemble, worship and speak,
Privileges which others still seek.
Natural resources so vast and plenty,
Used and wasted by so many.
An unseen future with a glorious past,
One day living together at last.

—*Meredith Carter*

First Snowfall

O'er I walk the padded floor,
where others walked a time before,
Tells a tale of who walked there,
a squirrel a fox a timid hare.

The snow is deep and falling still,
Covers the twig the branch and hill.
What wonders wrought this winter day
as I ramble on my way.

Snowflakes whisper as they fall,
sitting pretty on my shawl.
Roadside fence posts in a row,
wearing caps of pure white snow.

Blue joys scolding in the pine,
where I walk … is theirs … not mine.

So around the bend I go…
homeward bound … walking slow,
Dusk is falling as it will,
snow is deep and falling still.

—*Virginia Smetak*

Secret Dance

Dance by the secret moon.
Where tulips sleep the morning blues.
Where crickets and bugs hide away
to wait for spring to begin to play.
Where winter dreams pass on by
and spring rolls in side by side.
Where the world begins to hear a tune
that turns the scene from gray to blue.
Where secured buds wait to bloom
to shake the chill of winter's gloom.
Where birds call for morning glory
and plants welcome the dew of morning.
When the moon's dance
comes to an end.
The tune is picked up by a friend
where the secret dance begins again.

—*Michael Horan Jr.*

It's My Life

A land so beautiful
Where we only laugh
and smile
And in the game of love
There are no pain or tears
It's just us two
and
You are always mine
Yes
I can dream and I
always will.

—*Lisa Samuels*

Love's Ache

Where is it now,
Where was it then
Where has it gone
Will it come again?

When did it end,
When did I fail.
When can I hope
Will it come again?

Why must I sigh so
Why must I cry.
Why must I die?
Will it come again.

Love's come and gone
Yet - love lingers on
Drifting away into the night
Why has it gone - deep into flight?

Love's never tame
Am I to blame,
This is my shame
Losing the game.

—*Thomas M. Kennedy*

Love Lorn

If I am waiting there for you
Where we used to rendezvous;
    Pretend not to notice me.

If we should meet face to face
And I attempt a quick embrace;
    Turn away, don't notice me.

Voice trembling when I speak
Or tears are running down my cheek,
    Pretend not to notice me.

If we were walking down a street
And almost certainly, we'd meet;
    Turn away, don't notice me.

If you attempt to bring me cheer
To wipe away my pain and fear
    I will not notice you.

—*Ronald G. Farwell*

Born Wild

Restless soul,
where will you go?
Danger;
Dying inside.
Broken heart,
no one knows.
Or do they?
There is hope.

—*Sheila Kolb*

Remember

Wherever you are;
wherever you go;
I will follow you
Not with my body
With my heart and soul
For I know that we cannot be;
But; I shall remember you
As you do me until one day we can.

—*Linda Betti*

Teenage Suicide

Lost in a sea of familiar faces
While cunning eyes stealthily yank
The raft from under me.

The angelic face of a child
Turns bitter with rage,
And she pushes me further yet
Under the tyrant tides of humanity.

Fear flows from my eyes
Not wanting to meet death,
But I greet him with a smile.
His eyes laugh as he is drawn near me.

His hand reach greedily for my soul.
I only wanted to be loved,
But was pushed aside
By my many loved ones.

Pleading, I reach for their folded hands.
Their arms are just out of reach, crying.
Too young to leave, but choosing to go.

A teenage suicide. The forever grief
It turns a love misread into an endless
    sleep.

    —*Rachel Welty*

Suicide

Phi Beta Kappa Key swinging,
While seeking high-yellowing,
    Finds it too exciting,
    Polished-brass stinging,
    Real-gold winning.

    —*Viveca V. Roberts*

Miles Across The Sea

    Miles across the sea
Whispers on the ocean breeze
Dancing on countless waves
Natures passion swells,
Entwined within itself
Only knowing its heart longing
    To find its way to shore.
Two hearts drawn by destiny
Swaying to the rhythmic sound
Enchanted by the sands of time
    Miles across the sea.

    —*Rhonda J. Yawn*

Thinking Of Thought

    Today you don't know,
what the next day will bring
Tomorrow might come and will
    make you a king.
Forever and ever you'll be
    thinking along
    then forever will stop
and you'll know you did wrong

    —*Ronald Caporelli*

Comparison

A thousand times it hath been said
My love is like a rose.
A thousand bards have likened lips
To cherries warm and red—
For ever thus the poet sings
My love is like all lovely things.
And shall I, in the age old way,
Thus praise my love? Ah! no —
If I comparison would make,
'Tis nearer truth to say
A rose is like my love, but such
Would praise the fairest rose too much.

    —*Eric G. Clark*

Dove

My silence sings
my love sprouted wings
became the sun
flew into a fuse
because my blood is fire
the gulf is empty
my tears became the rain
my thoughts the air
dissolved in earth
still rooted there
my simple fears
turned into fretted thorns
the bougainvillaea climbs
a trellis to this solitude
my legacy: A drafty garret
my laughter all became the clouds
my need changed from stars
into some angry cup of ashes
my smile became a coffin shroud
my questions: All the answers

    —*Eric Priestley*

Untitled

My spirit, ascending.
My shadow... No more.
My footprints in sand
Along some distant shore.

Now I shall live
In the presence of Grace.
No sorrow,
No suffering.
Oh, heavenly place

Down golden paths
Where Glory once passed.
And I'll travel with Him,
An angel at last.

    —*Jo Ann Eichelberger*

The Rose Garden

The breath of nature caresses my senses.
Nature's perfumes intoxicate me.
My soul relishes in this new found,
but incredibly fragile bliss.
Roses are as this bliss.
soft, beautiful, fragile-yet,
surrounded by thorns.
These thorns protect its innocence,
its blissfulness.

    —*Brian P. Wirtefeld*

Winged Odyssey

The old man dying lay
'neath towering oak
Those closest gather
Bid farewell to man
And legend

Olympian from foreign climes
Established realm this forgotten
Region established justice where
None had been stretched to foreign land
Across the river

A gentle spring eve
Children's chirps waft 'crost yard
Elders murmuring softly then
Red tailed hawk dives screeching o'er

Rising feebly eyes aglow
Old man points falling back
His last gasp and hawk
Both gone forever

    —*Joseph Reid Davis Jr*

Timeless Mystery

A book in the Hollywood library
next day headed north
not time to lose
when bold spirit rushes forth

Dirt roads into the mountains
dense forest all you can see
eerie in the daytime
what lie ahead for me

A long way from nowhere
see what you came to see
the call of the unknown
A timeless mystery

The lake in brilliant moonlight
could you see it through
only three more hours
the adventurer comes to you

Leaning against the bar
talking to some friends
elbow raised high
time to get amends

    —*Edward J. Phillips*

Untitled

It was the moon I saw that
night - so full, so big, so round
and when I reached to touch
the top my dreams fell to the
ground. I looked back up and
wondered why, why so hard
to try and as I turned to
walk away a tear fell from
my eye.
When I look back on that
night so many years ago,
as I was busy reaching,
I missed the things below.

    —*Elizabeth Barry*

Man

Like the birds of the glowing and dark night,
Man circles and swoops, searching for light.
While their entombed souls, in despair,
Fight to shudder free from an unlightened air.

Forced by gravity onto a clutching earth,
They beat their protesting arms with senseless mirth.
Wrung and deflated in a kind and brutal world,
Most seem caught in a black, downward whirl.

At times, unexpected and like a flash of atomic rays,
Hope flares a fresh, and pierces conscience in true ways,
Cain against Abel, were ever true,
Men will only find righteous from the hovering heavenly blue.

Like a streaking star, the crowned King with holy might,
Will descent, reclaiming His earth, with victorious right.
Terror and joy will mingle with awe aflame,
While earth will shatter, never to be the same.

For a thousand years Eden will burst in bloom,
While men live on earth's harmonious room.
All nature will sing like a heavenly choir,
And rocks break their silence, in a lulla-bye.

—*Eugenia R. Murray*

Memory Lane

We two were young and gay, dear
    many years ago.
I remember the day, dear
    you said I love you so.
Oh, how I cherish the memory
    of the things you used to do.
You made me the happiest one in the world.
    I hope I did likewise for you.
The years have passed and gone dear,
    we both are growing old.
Our hair has turned to silver
    our hearts are solid gold
Life is growing shorter.
    There is nothing left to do … only
Thank you for making me happy …
    I hope I did likewise for you.

—*Anna I. Kelly*

Early Autumn Evening

Red roses long faded, the asters still bright,
marigold turn their colors toward fast fading light,

Soft gentle breezes still warm from the sun
lightly rustle the corn stalk dried and well done,

Swamp maples are crowned with gold shimmering gloss,
with a slight touch of red from a timid Jack Frost,

Wild grapevine still clinging amid wild cherry and oak
stripped bare of all foliage, purple fruit tinged with smoke,

A wispy thin fog wafts upward and beyond,
the reeds and plumed cattailed that still rim the pond,

Whose waters murky shallow will disappear all too soon
yet with still enough presence to reflect a glint from the
moon, tho not at full harvest with no halo or crown,
just a bright slice of silver from evening sky to the ground,

Early autumn evening drifts on toward night,
putting out all the embers of daytime's last light,

A weary nod from the sun as it fades through the seam
enter darkness and solitude, creators of dream.

—*George Stahl (Albion, MI)*

In The Comfort Of Absence

Silence, makes me shift uneasy
Martyr's glory is my immaturity
When colors blink a blinding pattern
darkness weaves a somber melody

Translucent phrases of so much interest
Watching innocence slip into obscurity
Waiting for my chance at truth
I enter a devouring, angst ridden void

Delivering hope into a cavern
of darkened corners and lurking wonders
Who knows what lamps have lit this ground
once tread upon with lighter steps

Wrought iron ramparts block my procession
A medieval birth of crafted devotion
Observe wild animals from safe distance
Precaution seems to inhibit conclusion

Carving shadows on paper thin walls
Imagination drives a stake throughout
A flash and appearance, held up to the sun
cannot see stars in the comfort of absence

—*Devin Booth*

Suicide

A bang rings out, though selfish it may be
Massive in size and crippling in emotion
A red river flows to the floor
Brittle rocks collide as they ricochet off white walls
One last beat before the end

Silence grips the room and the cold harsh reality of death is near
A shocked mother, a shocked father, a shocked sister, and a
shocked brother enter
Another river begins to flow, but not a river of hate not a
river of fear
A river of sorrow a river of questions a river of despair
Why? It is unknown

Gone are the times spent cradled in the arms of a mother
Gone are days spent walking along the beach with a loving friend
Gone are the moments of joy and triumph

Held only as memories, for wherever they may take you
Left behind is a mother a father a sister and a brother
yearning for answers

—*Christopher Sheehan*

Lacitenerf

The questions come tomorrow, the answers yesterday,
Mecca's on the Gaza trip and Hito's gone away.
I'd give what I have given if I could have it back,
and Christ's reincarnated and this time she is black.

Her daughter was my nephew, his son my favorite niece,
the only thing worth fighting for is never ending peace.
I stood still at breakneck speed but then slowed down to move
and what I'd thought entrenchment I found to be my groove.

I gave birth to mother and she gave birth to me,
God's grace gave the cotton gin and Judas went scot free.
The last supper was a nickel, Mary Magdeline a dime,
my lifesaver's orange and I really wanted lime.

I saw a book upon the shelf, the shelf upon the wall,
the wall was on page two nineteen. It's a small world after
all. The questions come tomorrow, the answers yesterday,
my shadow shunned this silly verse and went on out to play.

—*Dennis Q. Murphy*

Still Life

Oh, I wander down the years, the years of my life
Meeting people of and on the street, people I have liked
And I do not look to tomorrow, to fill my empty hole
I am just a human being, but I am quite whole

I see my mother, and I see my father too
They have known me longest, since I was brand new
Their blindness of my independence, always frightens me
They do not wish to look around, they do not wish to see

My family struggles with my thoughts and my views
Thinking only of themselves and what they'd like me to do
But I cannot conform, I am not a puppet doll
The time has come for me to say, good bye to you all

What has become quite clear to me, in my thirty-third year
It's not the calm that cures you, it is always the fear
And the fear keeps me going, going on the road
My back is not always burdened, by a heavy load

So I travel down empty streets, looking for a sign
To tell me everything's ok, everything is fine
And I beg of you when you hear this, please do not laugh
We are all living, and dancing the last dance

—*Heather Gallas*

The Returning

I returned to that well-acquainted setting and
Memories sparkled alive and renewed.

Walking down a worn dusty path, I met with a small barefoot
child.

Her sing-song voice laughed while her eyes were wide and
innocent;
Her soft hair tangled from an entire day of play.

A friendly pond came in sight and a vision of sneaking bread
crumbs to satisfy ducks, who had long since flown away,
Darted among my remembrances.

Turning-a quaint gazebo filled the next space and just beyond
an elderly tree silently sheltered an empty swing.

A tear slipped down my cheek because my tender childhood had
reappeared.

Once broken-hearted over leaving a place so fond,
I now understood that I had not abandoned it, but,
Preserved it within me and in time, these trusting
memories blossomed into a sophisticated individual.

—*Amy Jo Howard*

The Faded Picture

Lots of things grow better with time, the trees, some people,
memories, wine, the songs we sing from ages past, the things that
will forever last.

Tonight I thought of you my dear sleeping in the bedroom near.
My sight has dimmed, but still I see the tender love you have
for me.

The faded picture on the wall mimics life deep in the fall.
With winter near, all things must end, but life anew will soon
begin.

When I have gone the final mile, I hope you think of me and
smile. My love for you will never die, remember this and do
not cry.

As long as I am in your heart, we're only physically apart.
Our spirit lives forever more, beyond the closing of life's
door.

—*Jerry L. Clark*

The Tribe

I have found a place to come face to face with myself and other
men.
Where it is gentle and kind and I can lose my mind.

With nothing to prove, where there's no win or lose
and no women or booze to determine my mood.

What's burning inside is to return to my tribe,
to laugh and to cry, share the truth eye to eye.

I feel complete here, nourished and whole, I found a place to
free up my soul:
to rest, regroup, cry out and be heard, or listen quietly
without a word.
I love this place and the men who share it,
there is a bond of courage and faith,
I just can't compare it.

I am grateful to each of you for your part in the play.
I've come home to my tribe, I've come home to stay.

—*Fred Wolinsky*

Betta You Can Learn A Lesson From a Fish

Fins of indigo and magenta flare vigorously at the magnified
mirror image on the tiny tank wall. Frantically leaping at a
fictitious and hateful foe, the foolish Betta, alias Siamese
Fighting Fish, senselessly (yet unknowingly) battles himself.
Flaunting its supposed dominance so as to tease the threatening
mirage, the confident enraged assailant protects his territory
by lunging fiercely against the glass. As would be expected,
its opponent attacks simultaneously in a path directly opposite
the one taken by the real aggressor. Imitating the ritual
performance of two male cats competing for a female, both fish
stalk each other angrily to get the weak fish to back down.
Neither fish gives in. Did Sybil ever summit to herself— thus
having one personality fight another and win? What would Freud
say if a human displayed such bizarre behavior? Helpless, just
like the Betta, is nature in the hands of man. Our earth has
been continually tortured by wars and substances which poison
our atmosphere. Man is an ever-present mirror. When will we
lay down our weapons and stop annihilating ourselves?

—*Ange Steigert: October, 1988*

My Prayer Poem:

Dear Lord, forgive me for my sins, I pray,
Mold me like a peace of clay.
Wash me white, and make me clean,
Give my countenance a brighter sheen.
Cause the people around to know,
That I am yours, and make it show.

Bless the ones I love today,
Direct their paths, and light their way.
Hold them firm, and make them feel,
The love we share for them, is real.
Bless the sick and afflicted too,
Touch them, and help them to lean on you.

Bless the rich, the poor, the weak,
Cause us all to read and seek.
The words in the Bible, from our Father above,
Proving His forgiveness, guidance and love,
Now bless our president and show him the way
To lead our country safely through another day.

—*Fran E. Vlaeminck*

Since You've Been Gone

What seems like a million years, started the
moment you left me, because a day had never passed in
my life, without the opportunity to greet you early
in the morning.

Everything I say, everywhere I go, and everything
I do reminds me of a time in life I've spent with you.

Even though we did things quite differently in
most cases, the bond between us caused to have
so much in common.

Although informally, I've learned so many simple
things from you. Things that I'll remember and value.
Things that I'll use as strategies, to help me through
the hard and seemingly impossible times. I haven't
forgotten the secret pact for eternal life that we
made with each other years and years ago.

With my Saviour's help, I'll always keep my promise
to you.

So wait for me. Look for me. Pray for me.
It's been a long time, since you've been gone.

—*Edna McDonald*

Decisions

I'm sitting here a seed waiting to grow. In a couple of
months I will begin to show. A seed that is causing
heartache and pain. A thought that is driving everyone insane.
She is making a decision that is hard to make. In bed at
night the crying keeps her awake. He wants the seed but does
not know what to do. Tells her he loves her the decision is
up to you. Decisions that are hard to make. When a life is at
stake. Decisions that are hard to do. Will always affect you
decisions. She has made a decision she does not agree. Her
point of view he tries hard to see. She is just seventeen her
life has just begun. She is not ready to raise a daughter of a
son. He loves her he will back her one hundred percent. A
decision he has made no matter how hers went. Waiting is the
hardest part like they always say. This is just the beginning
of a horrible day. Decisions that are hard to make. When a
life is at stake. Decisions that are hard to do. Will always
affect you decisions.

—*Dimas Hernandez*

Mother

Mother is soft, gentle, and strong
Mother is kind, loving, and warm
Mother can be cruel, tough, and irate
But Mother's love is strong towards her children

Mother is large, colorful, and full of life
Mother is comforting, safe, and beautiful
Mother can be ugly, severe, and damaging
But Mother's love is strong towards her children

Mother is surprising, scary, and pleasant
Mother is protecting, security, and home
Mother can be wise, telling truths, or misgivings
But Mother's love is strong towards her children

Mother can be furious, treacherous, dangerous
Mother can be the center of all
Mother can be calm, life giving, and nurturing
But Mother's love is strong towards her children

Mother's love is strong
Mother's love is strong
Mother's love is strong

—*Catherine F. Lander*

The Spirit Of The Cardinal

Silently I watch autumn leaves fall
Moving through the air like soft blown rain
A sign that summer's gone once more
Only memories will sustain

All the birds have flown south
Everything is dead and gone
All except for the bold little cardinal
Who's spirit is so strong

He sits upon his branch
Looking out onto the snow
Never caring, always challenging
The center of the show

And I think there's nothing I admire more
than that little red bird
Whose the symbol of eternity and memories;
Forgotten times and songs unheard

He's the promise of spring's return
Singing songs of hope, that with eyes never gone
Staying there when the going gets rough
Keeping me company all winter long

—*Dawn Bates*

House For Sale (Stone)

Yesterday
Mr._____wore a cardinal red jogging suit...
Rooted between the blades of his Chem-green lawn,
he waved a barnacled white hand to his neighbor,
Mrs._____every five black years.

today
Mr._____wore a Royal Blue jogging suit...
Statued between the Blades of his Chem green lawn
he stooped to double-knot his high-top Reeboks
and broke his lower back.

—*Beverly Hierholzer*

A Journey

Thoughts moving through sometimes tear the fabric of life...so
much strife...
Mazes of emotions ranging in our mind...
Varying life's color, patterns, and time.

I walked a small stream on a summers' day
and with a light wind scurrying all around...
They asked me to stay...to join in...
Shh...now listen to the blue jay...

To stay and become one...the clouds, the trees
Even the redtails circling over me...
Stay...but another place called so it would not, could not be.

Soon will be the time though...
The journey won't be far...
It's just a short walk to cross the bar.

Sw wait for me my friends...for a summers' day with light,
restless winds...
Beside a small stream where we can cross the rocks and...listen
It's just the wind and the sound of the friendly stream...
Where we can become one
Where life's fabric can color me and join what is...

With what can be...with what will be.

—*Gary M. Staggs*

My Blessings

I woke up this morning. Cheerful
music I did hear. It was just the little
birds chirping in the pine trees that stood
near.
   As the day was slowly passing and the
sunshine shone so bright I thanked
God in heaven for seeing me safe through
another night.
   Then I looked out my kitchen window,
a little butterfly I've seen, then
flowers, grass and small wild animals
came in sight. I thought how pretty
and serene.
   A few friends came by to visit
or simply say "Hi! how are you today?"
Sunset quickly comes I've had a busy day.
But the blessings I like most is
Jesus and the friends God has sent my way.

    —Dollie Eversoll

Sonnet To Music

Music, purest and sweetest of our joys!
Music, the ambrosial balm of the soul,
Whose Apollonian melody holds us in thrall;
Who lifts us out of the dungeon of our days.
Whose celestial harmony continues to amaze,
And rivals in brilliance the rolling ball
Of fire that lights the earth; whose gentle moments lull
The soul to sleep, whose fervent moments set it ablaze!
Music, fill the air with your sonorous tones!
Play on! Play on! We can never have enough of you!
Bear our souls to heaven on your golden wings,
Where a choir of angels so sweetly sings,
That the holy streams cease to flow,
And God sits spellbound on His throne.

    —Ivan Douglas Bellow

Dragon's Throne

I sit upon my golden throne, I tower up here all alone
    My booty taken under my once keen eyes
    My scales are withered old and cracked
    My wings torn and ripped
    And my tongue flames no more

I sit upon my golden throne, I tower up here all alone
I shall stand and wait for the darkness to engrope me
    Yet my legs will not support me
    I shall die alone
    And my tongue flames no more

I sit upon my golden throne, I tower up here all alone
    Memories come back to me
    Of knights and maidens and treasures of old
I reach out to grasp and yet they sift through my fingers
    And my tongue flames no more

I sit upon my golden throne, I tower up here all alone
    A voice calls to me:
      fly away!
      fly away dragon!
    I drift away to infinite sleep

    —Dan Ochse

Down Memory Lane

Today, I took a stroll down memory lane, Visiting the place of
my childhood again. I saw a loving Mother, who was so dear,
with broom in hand, standing very near.

She looked at me with eyes full of love, that seem to say, "My
Child, Heavens Above!" "How Proud I Am, you've become a
  man!"
"Those things I taught, you now understand."

My journey took me back through the trees, where I saw two
oaks, flowing in the breeze. It was here, a home-made ferris
wheel was built, Where as a child, more than once I was spilt.

I moved down the street where my home once stood, And saw
vacant lots, filled with debris and wood. Tears filled my
eyes, as memories filled my thoughts, seeing the things,
so-called "progress" had wrought.,

Next, came the place of my childhood school. It was here, I was
taught "The Golden Rule." We read the Bible, and teachers with
us prayed, and the things I was taught, have with me stayed.

The church of my childhood still stands today, sharing God's
love, and pointing the way. Memories of God's Saints, who took
time to love, Still flood my soul, as I think of them above.

    —Henry T. Davis Jr.

Dark Clouds And Hazy Rainbows

Around the mysterious corners of life
My days are filled with happiness and strife

I look at the clock suspended in time
My soul on a shelf with no reason or rhyme.

I gaze at the sunbeams through the light as it flows
But, all I see are dark clouds and hazy rainbows.

My moments now all pass into days,
And nothing in life ever lingers or stays.

I look to discover things to entertain
Yet, all of my efforts are in vain.

Still, brightness shines from heaven above
For my true happiness lies with you, my love.

And when we must part, as the saying goes,
Until you return, I see dark clouds and hazy rainbows.

    —Cynthia Annette Moore

Jesus, My Comforter

Jesus, my comforter, be with me each day, guide my actions,
  my every thought.

Help me to understand what is happening and be able to accept
  things that are beyond my comprehension.

Dear sweet Jesus, help me to prepare my loved ones for things
  that are beyond our control, to let them know that no
  matter what, I am in the most loving and caring hands, that
  I am in a win/win situation. If I am allowed a little
  more time with my family, then I win. If I am taken
  tomorrow,
then I am with my Father in Heaven and I win. Either way I
  can not lose.

Sweet Jesus, if I go home to be with you and my Heavenly Father
  tomorrow, please be with my family and friends and let them
  know that they haven't lost me, that I have only gone on
  ahead of them and will be waiting for them.

I will not say goodbye, but instead, I will say goodnight, for
  I will see my loved ones in the morning when we awake.

    —Alice Moseley

D.I.S.A.

I was conceived by lies and bred with the plague.
My existence was denied, and all minds were vague.
I was molested by hate and raped by death.
Then abused by deception and all of the rest.
A glass test tube my crib, and a lab was my home.
For years I was tested, and then began to roam.
And I found my way into many a home.
For in the eyes of many fools I am beautiful but one injection, you
    will I kill.
So come, while you make love to me, if you think you can still.
For I will gladly, on my bed of death, spread you lay you down.
And all of your perverted fantasies come true as your genitals spin
    around.
Then you will leave with a pathetic smile on your face.
For many have been spread and lain upon my bed.
And my "love" has infected their that pumps red.
Thus those have felt a pain, and died a death like no other.
But now it is too late, for they lay bleeding under the cover.
So mortals, get drunk and high; have your unsafe sex in many
    years.
But be warned fools;
I will rape and do the dance of death with you, for I am A.I.D.S.

—*Brian K. Barnette*

Untitled

Darkness here so thick and heavy,
    My eyes cannot pierce this forever night.
    I cannot see to know from whence comes
This stench of evil that grips my mind with fear.

The sounds which surround me are
    The sounds that lies make
As they echo in your soul when you've trusted—
    Only to find you've been deceived.

This darkness drives me to panic's edge—
    But I don't think I want to see.
    I taste a bitterness in my mouth
That dances around my brain with vague recognition.

Oh—what horrible place can this be?
    All exits lead to the center
Of unknowable wickedness and filth.
    Must I, can I face such evil?

Oh God of mercy help me!
    Shine your light!
    Forgive me Father!
    This place is my heart!

—*Amy J. Zenner*

The Beauty Of Antiquity

The day was bright yet crisp.
My feet cried out to rest.
Then I heard it; yesterday's music
And yesterday's youth were swirling and twirling
On there faces the map of life pressed deep.
I paused to watch and rest.
Soon I saw the beauty of their life,
For what I once found ugly
In bodies bent and twisted,
I saw beneath the wrinkles
The twinkle in their eyes,
That rises from deep within the sole
That only living life so long
could paint a picture of such beauty.
The story that was told is not of age,
But of life as it is lived.

—*Adelia Arias*

Tears In August

In the month of August I shed a tear, for what I believed was
my greatest fear. The passing of a man so loved by all,
saddening the coming of fall. The man who carried me when I
couldn't walk; the man who talked to me when I couldn't talk,
was the same man I carried in my arms as if he was the baby
starting a new life. He was a father to his children and a
husband to his wife. A man strong and robust: the man I cried
for, Tears in August. Winter is here and the family draws near
for the years first snow. So clear. So white. Reminding us
how his grey hair would glisten in the moonlight. A cool
breeze passes through and I stand back and sigh, could that be
his spirit passing by? Is it really you? The emptiness
remains. I still feel the pain. So deep is the sorrow. When
I pray all I can say is, "Will he be here tomorrow?" It is now
a year since my greatest fear became reality. Although he's
still not here the sadness is no longer a part of me. For I
come to realize the light in heaven is much more pleasing to his
eyes. For what is comforting to me the most are the friends he's
made: The Father, Son and the Holy Ghost.

—*Dhanraj Ramsaran*

A Special Child

I was born two months early on a bright day in July.
My hair was blonde and curly and eyes as blue as the sky,
I was a beautiful little baby though very small in size,
I also wondered why they'd put patches on my eyes,
I had wires and tubes in my chest and one to help me breathe,
I guess the doctor's knew what was best but when would I ever
leave, months and months passed by until they let me go,
I had even started a little to grow.
I finally went home only to find,
The ties to my family would never quite bind.
I wasn't ever able to crawl or to walk,
Or sit up by myself or even talk
My parents didn't want me they left me alone,
So some nice lady said she'd find me a home.
I have a wheelchair and some braces too,
I can't walk or talk like other kids do,
But my new family loves me, no matter what I can't do.
Maybe being born early was not so grand, but perhaps it was
part of a bigger plan to give me a life that is rewarding and
grand, and a family that accepts me just as I am.

—*Catherine Lutz*

Standing To Pass

At last I'm standing to pass.
My heart is broken, flown lightly
to be blown a kiss somewhere I'm
lost. Laughing, singing, casting doubts
upon one's self. The sounds build up
the bottoms dropping off. Voices carry my
heart aloft. Deep well from bed rock
the passage is sweet to taste.
The mountain stream rushes at feet.
Follow the sparkle 'til you're thoroughly
refreshed. Dying flowers, closing
windows. This summer has past.

—*Albert F. Carol III*

Tears

Tears fall, why I don't know.
Maybe I'm happy, maybe sad, could have been from last
week or from a minute ago.
I just saw a new life and it touched me,
or grieved me for a loved one from long ago.
Tears help to bring us closer to our souls and feelings,
and help us to remain sensitive and not get cold and dried out.
But sometimes I feel I could drown in my tears, then the sun
comes out and takes away the puddles of our lives,
then his love can flood our hearts.

—*Ernestine M. Michell*

My Heritage; My Roots

Sometimes I sit and wonder just how it all began;
My heritage and blood line, in some strange foreign land.

I like to think my kinfolk were creative, could invent;
How to teach, to grow things, on life's journey as they went

Along the path they may have traveled, carving out their own
Mold, with nerves of steel, with courage, enough pride to take
Their fold

Into a life of grandeur, down a river wide and deep,
Before they left a legacy, before their long and final sleep.

Could some folk in my lineage write poetry just like me?
Perhaps they authored stories telling tales of he and thee.
Then thoughts that come to mind at times portray a sadder note.
The visions that I see those days could rock a captain's boat.

The idea that my roots were nestled in the blood of some
Buffoon, like the idiotic circus freak that shrivels like a prune.

That's when my thinking changes course to head another way.
My brains begin to rumble, now it's later in the day.

But then to myself I say, 'Whoever my seed may be,
They could never top the life I live, as plain old simple Me.

—Ike Burroughs

My Jeep, Myself

Outside,
my jeep is nearly spotless,
save for a few nicks in the paint,
that make it look rugged.
In the depths of its glossy finish,
you can see yourself, reflected clearly,
just the way you'd expect.

Inside, entropy is the order.
The grey and black interior,
is a menagerie of collected rubbish:
a bright yellow candy wrapper,
split three ways at the end,
a few text books, ashes on the rug.
Some are tiny grey cylinders, others are dust
and a full ashtray (I get twenty miles to a butt).

Rodney, the white stuffed Gorilla, hangs by a thread from the
visor, grinning his secret grin.

There's a fuzzbuster to see what lays ahead,
and a broken rear view mirror to see
what's been left behind.

—David Martina

My Dear Friend

My friend that stands besides me.
My knight of armor, he holds me up,
guards me like a young child,
my cold heart, filled with nothing,
he fills it with something, at least love.
And his blackness that wraps
me in his blanket of care
I sit there waiting he'll calm my tears
my knight of armor my friend of strength
my blanket of warmth and
caring, never leave watch my sake and
my small tender heart.
And keep me sheltered in the dark.
The dark you keep, the love you give,
my friend that stands beside me.
my knight of armor. My God of truth.
My strength of power. My friend.
Watch me till the aching end.
My dear friend.

—Brandy M. Hilton

Her Words Mean Comfort

Mama is such a simple word
My Mama as I always called her
means so very much to me,
First she give me life
and she was always there when I needed her;
Her words meant comfort no matter what you had done;
Now that I have been a mother for thirty five years;
I know what it means to be a mother;
My mother means more to me with each passing day;
I thank God for giving me a Mother such as mime;
Even though she has to spread love between
her fourteen children she always had time for me
and I love her very much, God Bless You Mama.......

—Estelle Johnson

Escape

How do I escape my mind?
my memories?
I close my eyes and I can see you,
feel you.
The tears, the fears,
they're still so real.
I stay awake because you're with me when I sleep,
in my dreams.
I cannot tell when the nightmare ends
and my day begins.
Behind every corner,
you are there.
Behind every grin,
you are there.
I move towards the door,
to close it once and for all.
But I am weak.
My body is weighted down with fear,
with pain,
with you.

—Ana Maria Perez

Untitled

Hey, this isn't as easy as I had thought
My mind is blank and my imagination is fraught
This could be an exercise in humble futility
As I search for a theme and some appropriate vocabulary.

I should tell you I have a touch of 'old timers'
That is a mild form of that affliction called Alzheimers
'Old Timers' is indeed a very strange malady
If you're old enough you have become ancient history.

Yes, wrinkled people with silver hair can miss the point
Their conversation and action can get out of joint
But they are full of love and they wear a smile
Even if they seem to get lost once in a while.

But they realize they are near to the end of the race
And they are trying to earn a little extra grace
They continue to enjoy life but patiently wait
For God's call to report to His Golden Gate.

—Bernard Beach

Let Us Walk

May the wind walk with me, may the stars guide me,
May the sun love me, may the rain beat me,
And may the moon rise above all, to share me,
For I am a gift to all that I know, and to all
that know me.

Let us walk in the wind, let us caress the stars,
Let us carry the sun, let us pacify the rain,
And let us thank the moon for being compassionate,
For we are the gift to all that we know, and to all
that know us.

—Heather Coleman

Lois

I remember waking up to the sound of singing,
my mother's voice chasing my sleep away.
For years I thought that it was her voice
that caused the sun to rise each day.

When I would return from school
I'd find my mother always there,
working on one of her many projects
while her humming filled the air.

At night she would sing lullabies
that could warm the coldest heart.
Each day would end with her song in my ear,
and that's how each day would start.

Not many knew of her talents,
she never achieved fortune or fame.
But she filled our home with music and love,
and she brought the sun up, just the same.

—*Angela K. Black*

Dull

Dull, dull, dull, oh my face is so very dull!
My nose is so boring, people fall into a deep, soundless lull.
My big, clumsy ears stick out miles apart!
My eyes could be pretty, without unshaped glasses so smart.
My mouth is a line like the equator so,
My hair is straight like tree stumps in the glittery white snow.
Oh how I wish I had -
Eyes that were magnificent blue
bright red hair with gorgeous curls too!
My cheeks would be powdery, soft, and pink,
My ears would not be big and they'd twich when I think!
My lips would be like a great movie star,
and my nose would be small and dainty like ladies are!
And my, and my ding dong!!!
"Hello, can grace come out to play?"
Well for right now I might not be as gorgeous as a doll
But still, let me catch that baseball!!!

—*Jessica Serafin*

Almost Free

I grab a knife so sharp and nice,
My one way ticket to paradise.
I raise it up high, my arms wide apart,
I take steady aim, right for my heart.

I lower it slowly and take a deep breath,
It shines with such brilliance, my instrument of death.
It feels like a bullet tearing my insides apart,
I hold in my hand what once was my heart.

My world is now darkness, a world of the night,
But away in the distance is a shimmering light.
I close my eyes hoping the light will escape,
I open to the light which has taken a shape.

The shape is the knife, the realness so sober,
It attacks with full force, stabbing me over and over...
A noise cracks my skull so unbearably loud,
My alarm has gone off, time to face the crowd.

I search for the knife, did I have a death tool?
Mom walks in the room, it's time for school.
I step out of bed into a world causing blue,
I wonder if dreams ever come true?

—*Cathy Lynch*

Grandma's Wish

Goodness me it's quiet now
My place is spic and span
Anyone can be welcome
The house is just so clean
But only just a while ago my Grandchild came to stay
And oh the noise was hectic
Her laughter oh so loud
Oh the little one could really make a scene
The toys were all over, and the house became a wreck
I did complain and wished her Mom would come and take her back
Well now she's back at her home again
I scrubbed and cleaned and then
When everything was put in place
I sat and took it in
Goodness me it's quiet now
My place is spic and span
There is no laughter, no noise, no childish chatter or lively
sound oh how I wish my place a mess
With a little child around.

—*Anastasia Rodia*

Lament

Pleading, crying, alone
My prison, my past
Iniquitous memories
Exploding in the darkness
How I covet the innocence
that Youth once gifted me with.
To laugh at life's insatiable desires
I don't want to reminisce of what once was.

My anguish will only depart
When my only friend arrives
Death
Once so afraid
Now I implore your embrace
I will find comfort in your shroud of darkness
In your thin cold arms, in your breathless kiss
Take me as a lover would
End my solitude

—*Haydee Alvarado*

Fire Command

As I lie here warm and dreaming
My sleep interrupted by a siren screaming
Fire Call! Fire Call! The operator's voice is speaking
On go the socks, pants, and shirt without even thinking

We pull up in front of a house that's ablaze
Survivors are standing there half in a daze
I call to my men to drop the equipment they need
An aggressive attack is what's called for indeed

Hitting the ceiling with a blast of fine spray
The book says to dissipate gases that way
You can't see two feet in front of your mask
Dear Lord why must we have the impossible task

Making a retreat that's been professionally tested
All I can think of is getting my men rested
Standing on the sidewalk reminiscent of Nero
A woman is calling all of my men heros

The baby is safe in the arms of its mother
Tonight it was this way, tomorrow another
Looking around and seeing everyone's frozen
This is the answer why we are God's chosen.

—*Arthur Heredia*

Last Call

It's two a.m. at the Penn Monroe.
My sleeve clings briefly,
To a dried splash on the bar.

A cloud hangs heavy on the bulkhead,
As if it would rain,
And dampen the spirits of this congregation.

From my lofty corner bar stool,
I may sit and judge.
I've been keeping watch for hours,
Sipping my wine in disgust and loathing.
How they revel, lost in the haze,
Of their favored liquid savior.

Peter gives last call.
The flock begins to diminish.
Each passes me to the door,
Into the darkness beyond.

I rise to follow the exodus,
Knowing, we shall come again.

—*John P. Washington*

The Stone Wall

I feel inside myself the wall building around
my soul. On each side a stone is placed upon
my heart. I want to be strong, but the force is
overpowering. Where do
I belong? One side the stones could reach the sky —
on this side
I'd never cry. One is built
halfway, each time you hurt me
another stone is placed on top.
I used to envy those who've been hurt
I thought they were strong, but they were only
weighed down by the weight of so many
stones upon their heart — it hid the soul.
I want my heart wide open, to feel and touch everything
the wall hides.
I want my soul to be free.
To love and feel and touch, but never and always,
to see.

—*Amy Rebecca Ryan*

Untitled

Shall I hide my love in the volume of my heart.
My soul would burst if I contained my love.
Are the eyes of love blind. Shall the shadows
suddenly flee. Curtains are not upon mine window.
I shall reach for thy grapes and squeeze my chalice
full and we shall drink till our parched lips desire
no more.
Let the morning dew wet thy brow and never let the music
cease.

—*Eric Wm. B. vonAnderseck*

I Was Wrong?

"Sally done said her throat felt tight."
My teacher done said my sentence weren't right,
So I took out tight, so it wasn't so long,
But my teacher done said my sentence was wrong,
So I decided to change the action and the name,
"Bob done said let's play a game."
But my teacher persisted,
And still she insisted,
My sentence weren't up to par,
"Kim done said I want a car."
"Joe done said let's walk down the lane."
I done drove my teacher insane!

—*Beth Faller*

The Light Ahead

A light in the distance is casting its radiant shadow upon
my travelling heart, beckoning me in the midst of the dark
night I had so lost myself in what seems like decades ago.

Oh light, shine bright,
as I complete these last steps in my weary plight,
so that I might paint this picture white.

Imminent partnership in love, closing journey of this lone
dove. Shining stars illuminate a pathway to my destination
ahead, the heavens open to resurrect my life once dead.

Oh light, shine bright,
as I complete these last steps in my weary plight,
so that I might paint this picture white.

I will reach the field of roses and wallow in their love-laced
aroma, to be so untouched by the thorns of wrought emotional
pain that had me imprisoned in a lifeless coma.

Oh light, shine bright,
as I complete these last steps in my weary plight,
so that I might paint this picture white.

Oh, the dawn has come upon me, soon I shall be free. Awaken my
life once dead. Lord, I'm coming, coming to the light ahead.

—*David N. Ayoub*

A Feeling

I come to you as a whisper in the night...
My voice is calming and gentle as flight.
Your troubled sleep seems to subside
As I lay down beside you and hold you tight.

When I touch you, your passion will rise,
Feeding the fire of love and delight.
Your response is all I need
To make my love strong and complete.

As we lay in the afterglow feeling the warmth of our souls
Close your eyes my love, for a restful sleep.
I am here always as I said I would be.

Good night my dear and sleep tight.
You know, my love for you cannot be denied.

Think again the words I spoke, as my hand touched
Your face and throat.
A kiss on your forehead as I arose, a gentle I love you
Was all I spoke

—*Franklin D. Gray*

Casper

It was last summer when these two met
My wife and her 79 Corvette
When she first saw him, her eyes became bright
And it was certainly love at first sight
Then we purchased this little jasper
And he was given the name of Casper
She is a girl who smiles the most
Driving around in her little ghost
She's proud of Casper, and wants the world to see
His license plate reads, "DI's RV."
It's the neatest thing I've ever seen by far
Her attachment to that little car
When she feels bad, and has had a bad day
Driving Casper chases her blues away
Whenever she looks in Casper's direction
You can see the love and affection
He's the car she's wanted all her life
And I know that I have a happy wife
Make your wife as happy as she can get
Just go buy her a Chevy Corvette

—*John R. Jensen*

Untitled

I respected you as my queen, and like a king I respected
myself. I raised by children, cared for my elders, my family
was my wealth. I was a warrior/provider, and being hungry was
not a fear, for the store, that was the jungle and for my money
that was my spear. I was a man with much dignity and could
stand up for what I say. But after being captured and
shackled, like a wild animal my dignity was taken away. 400
years, 400 long years of mental and physical pain, and though
the bruises on my body has healed, my mentality is still the
same. After slavery I still felt enslaved, and towards you I
channeled my abuse, but you were enslaved just as I, therefore
I could never j justify that excuse. I'm sorry, I am sorry for
what I did and for what I have not done, for not being that
warrior/provider, for not taking care of my elders nor my
young. As for the black child that I helped produce, create
then abandon, let me explain. I did what I saw the older
version of me do and this older version did the same. You see
as an older black man I don't teach young black men, to
strengthen them as they grow. And as a young black man I don't
listen to older black men, for there is nothing I don't know.

—*Charles J. Ennols Jr*

Storm Of Love

As the dark, mysterious clouds rolled in as he came
near, lighting struck in the air. The thunder ramping
and raving in the savage untamed heart, with the sound
of the wind blowing and the rain beating against the
window, igniting the fire of their passion. As the storm
passes the shimmering sunlight glazing through the
window upon her face. As their hands touched, the storm
of love began again.

—*Christina Marie Cromling*

Lura

Later, is what you'd say to me.
Never good-bye, for that was Eternity.
Farewell or so long is how we stood.
But never good-bye, for that meant for good.

You're smiling face captured many in your stride.
As you took the time to be patient with all mankind.
You're remembered now, from all you've touched.
As you would tell anyone, "Is a smile too much?"

You're with me always in my heart and soul.
I love you, Lura...
You're now God's precious gold.

I love you always,
Your sister, Kay.

—*Gwendolyn Kay Newton*

My Cat Is Queen

My cat is queen of her domain
No one dares challenge her right to reign.
Her coat is white and as soft as silk,
She daintily sips from her bowl of milk.
She preens and struts like she owns the place,
No queen ever reigned with more beauty and grace.
"Her Highness," you'll see, has a mind of her own,
Though I sometimes question her right to the throne.
Like when she sleeps in my favorite chair,
And I bravely confront her right to be there.
But she purrs with contentment and she looks so sweet.
So I pat her head as I slowly retreat.
She has captured my heart with her winning way,
So I'll let her believe that she's queen for today.

—*Beatrice L. Smith*

Angels Never Die

I've been down this dusty trail before,
    Never have I seen the same thing twice
It reminds me of the pain I have caused,
    Now the time has come to pay the price

I've seen star-dust in the eyes of babes,
    While fantasies slowly turn to tears
Broken promises can steal your soul,
    And nothing can buy back those stolen years

I've seen mortals who have died of broken hearts,
    And others who were blind to the pain
Loneliness can take away your will to live
    While memories can drive a man insane

Dancing with the devil in your dreams,
    Never can your back turn on—true love
The shadows of the past come closing in,
    Another tear of blood falls from above

Flying through life with stolen youth,
    Mortals who have learned to love, and lost
Anger in the eyes of the betrayed,
    Never realizing what the cost...

—*Edward R. K. Thompson*

In God's House

The day was cold and dreary. I stood
Next to the ancient green heater to
Warm my hands. The parking lot was
Empty and my parents were no where
In sight. Waiting, wondering when
They would come to get me? I began
To get worried and scared. I had
Only been alive for six brief years
And I did not know where to go or
What to do. I felt so very alone.
I did not understand how I could be
Standing in the house of God and still
Be so afraid. People said God was
Good and he would help people, then
How could he let my tiny soul become
So filled with fear? They said that
You are nearest to God in his house.
Then why when I was standing in his
House did he not lift a finger in my
Attempt to comfort me?

—*Douglas e. Surdenik*

The Late Autumn Rain

Mother nature cried last night... Yes, mother nature cried last
night... All through the night, and all through the next day.
Yesterday so forlorn, and sad, was she. The sky dull and gray,
the wind cold and fierce, foretold the future.
She knew that her favorite gown, her beautiful autumn gown,
was a short prelude before her winter nakedness.
No, her clothing is no longer hers to nurture. She envelopes
her dress about her with the greatest tenacity, begging for
strength she may borrow.
Alas, the wind is relentless, as the well realizes.
Tears from his eyes, she sighs ... There, in the late autumn
rain, lies his gown, scattered about her feet,
covering the ground.
Her beauty now gone, naked and wet with her sorrow.
Yes, mother nature cried last night... Long into the night,
and all through the next day.

—*Grace Castell*

Roses In The Snow

That December, dreams had gone from me.
No hope of direction could I see.
I asked God to give me one more chance,
Then on my window I heard raindrops dance.
I left my room, wondering what this meant.
All of my goals, were they spent?
I muddled alone, all through the night,
Until day burrowed through with light.
I opened the door, snow glistened white.
Icicle fingers shattered with ease.
My heart leaped, as though it would cease.
I lowered my head, where my eyes longed to go,
To see three rosebuds trembling in the snow.
I dropped to my knees, thanking Him,
Who once wore a crown of thorns,
    blood trickling down His chin.
The word came to life in me that day,
Pushing me forward, paving the way.

—*Betty M. Erb*

A Soul Divided

No chains can ever bind, like the ties of heart and mind;
no locks can ever hold, like bonds upon a soul.

A half a soul for you, a half a soul for me;
and neither one, from either half, ever can be free.

Apart, we are two halves, together, we are one;
this, we cannot change, nothing can be done.

We couldn't be completely happy, if we were apart;
for no one can be happy, with only half a heart.

We must always be together, so our souls are joined as one;
if we both try hard to do it, then I know it can be done.
You can't do it without help, any more than I;
if we want to make it work, then we both must try;

It will be worth the effort, to work toward this goal;
for we'll no longer be two halves, but one United Whole!

—*Barbara J. Benson*

First Child

My dear mother is many, many states away
No longer can we laugh, cry together or play

But love goes on regardless of distance
My thoughts are with her each and every instant

The bed making, room cleaning or whatever it may be
Is no longer done by her but is done by me.

Appreciation of pass doings never entered my mind
Until I stood alone and realized my find

Of many, many things I should have said "Thank You" for
But never tried to understand and always asked for more.

As children mature we think of these things
Hoping it's not too late to bring forth a ring

And cry of praise and Thank You Dear Lord
For a Mother of highest esteem who has scored

A mark of perfection in my heart and mind
And to be mine forever here on earth or in God's kind

Of a world where may I someday show her a way
Of kindness and thanks all through the day.

—*Darlene Horsman*

She Devil

No locks to keep this beast at bay.
No mercy shown on me her prey.
The old, the young, the middle-aged
are stars for whom the set is staged.
Unanswered cries and empty rooms,
the uninvited monster looms.
A voracious appetite this evil beast
for the minds and hearts on which she feasts.
Daggered teeth that have no mind,
I must use mine and leave behind...
The fear and heartache of the past;
I'll host no more. This meal's her last.
I'll not be victim, she'll not have me
to sit and suffer hopelessly.
Bolted doors and chains that bind
An answer near yet undefined.
She-devil, loneliness...whichever name,
go away, I'll not play your game.

—*Ella Jordan Sharpe*

Peace In Tears

Death would be so easy!
No more pain, no more trying, no more failing, but most of all,
no more tears!
It would be so much easier.
Please, understand!
There would be peace, quiet, serenity, calm, coolness,
no pain,
no tears.

It would be giving up, I won't let you do that.
Don't despair, dearest child,
For I am here!
Turn to me, trust in me!
Life would not be life without pain,
no more trying,
no more failing,
and most of all no more tears.
Life's more important lessons are found in each tear
that falls.
Never give up, never stop trying, because I won't let you!

—*Anissa L. Johnson*

Home

I just returned from a house, not too long did I stay;
    no need to linger there too long since the owner moved away.

Down the lane, across the meadow we would go to romp and play;
    but there's no reason to go back 'cause the owner moved
    away.

It used to be a lovely place; I still recall the day;
    of flowers blooming everywhere before the owner moved away.

Several families have moved there; not too long did they stay;
    no one really seems to care since the owner moved away.

The weeds have grown so tall; the white paint has turned gray;
    nothing's like it used to be before the owner moved away.

No wonder I don't want to go back, the house isn't happy and
    gay; like it was in days gone by 'cause my Mother moved
    away.

Now the farm has been sold; no longer can I roam
    over the fields and meadow and through the house I used to
    call home.

—*Doris E. Chambers*

The Prisoner

Within my heart, within my home there is a prisoner.
No sentence is more cruel than the one that this confers.
She sits in a small corner of a room that teems with life,
Loved deeply as a mother but forgotten as a wife.
Head bent in silent penance as the memories slowly die,
And now and then some fleeting thought
Will make her start to cry.
Here was a lilting laughter that filled the very air
And on my fevered brow her wrinkled hand would care.
Now keeper of those precious times,
For none now can be bought,
I'm left to serve my own time
With the lessons she has taught.
So now the night has settled;
My soul falls to its knees;
Humbly I ask the heavens
Why Alzheimer's Disease?

—*Edith Parekh*

To A World Of People In Pain

There is a full moon shinning on a heavy heart
No tears to ease the pain
In this old world, in every part, there is sun
And hope and rain

There is joy for the heart that feels sad and weak
There is courage for the heart that feels lonely and meek
There is hope for the heart that feels hopeless and blue
Yes, yes there is something for me and you

See the stars in the sky, so tiny and bright, they all
Mean something good
We should all live with joy and die with hope
If only, only, only we could

Now, I'm not a soul who figures I'm lost but sometimes
I lose my way
Down on my knees is as far as I fall and for strength
Is all that I pray

—*Helen Mary Korsgaden*

Autumn's Dress Parade

I've raced through life with flying feet
No time to enjoy Autumn's Dress Parade
Now entranced I look and find it sweet
Oh wonders of nature, be slow to fade.

I gaze upwards in awe at our sweet gum tree
Where green star-shaped leaves held sway
Now rust-brown, golden and scarlet I see
Fade slowly, that I may see another day.

Saucy bluejays in her branches still play
Below, fall flowers flaunt their brilliant hues
Pleasant drone of summer bees is far away
Sparkle of butterfly wings lost from view.

I'll waste little time idly counting hours
Summer's over, colorful fall must have her day
Spring will bring blossoms again with showers
Bird songs my chimes, neath her boughs I pray.

God of Nature, preserve my church spire tree
Let my soul soar with autumn's bold display
These falling leaves reveal your plan to me
"Another generation cometh, one passeth away."

—*Dorothy Manley*

The Power

Strong pulsating beats growing stronger,
Noise all around me, yet I hear nothing.
Time races before my eyes.
Loud streaks of red light stare at me
Surrounded by many yet alone without a
sense of belonging.
Boxed in with a barrier of fear.

And then, the barrier is shattered.
No longer boxed in, but surrounded by peace.

Shaking - with a new, unknown fear, alive now.
New dimensions invade the private soul.
A heaven created within your own thoughts.
No body. No sound. No touch, No fear.
Eyes, which are no longer physical witness the birth of
Everlasting stillness.
Precious time, distilled within
One master, one importance, one light, much love.
One power. Reach out and it is yours
Forever.

—*Diana Zito*

Life's Silver Linings

Count not the piling years as weights of stone,
Nor as some scourge that hound you down the way;
Count them as precious gems upon a crown,
That you should wear with pride and dignity.

Count not the silver threads as bane of time,
Nor as grim portents of the final day;
Count them as token of mellowed wisdom,
Gleaned and pooled over time along the way.

All the pains and sorrows that you must face,
Count them not as afflictions of your life;
Count them only for their renewing grace,
That mount you up on wings in any strife.

Life, then, needs not be a tragic story,
A trail of woe, of regrets, and pinings,
If one must seek ever so constantly,
The magic balm of life's silver linings.

—*Eufemia B. Dacayanan*

Eleven

when i was eleven i used to swing and play
not a care in the world, until i had to learn
the hard way, it was sixth grade
and we had moved, new areas and different kids
many new styles, i was new
someone to pick-on another new face
another different style
i was full of attitude
because my mother was dying
i hung out with the other kids
we were a group, it helped me escape from reality
and not believe what was happening
but all of a sudden
we moved again, my mother was dying
i couldn't help her
what was happening,
she was slipping away
and i went with my aunt and uncle
and now that's where i stay
i hated eleven and the years to follow

—*Jessica Franklin*

The Words Come...

The words come,
Not from the Language...

Like Michelangelo's David,
    the Work lurks for release
    standing poised, ready to Pounce,
    out of the Marble's heart...

The Words come,
from the paper...

    leaping from the Papyrus,
    like an Asp.
    sinking its Corrupt fangs,
    into the Breast of its Victim...
    leaving him without a choice:
    to write or he ruptured without a voice.

The Words come,
    from the soul...
    the collective Essence, of all mankind....
    Coalescing in its depths,
    screaming for release, and finally...
    Finally, breaking Free...
        —*Bejeir D. Brooks*

Knyghte

I'm a cat, how 'bout that.
Not just any cat, for I'm not fat.
I'm not made of tin, I'm just thin.
Hair of white, I catch lots of mice.
Some are brown, lots are round.
I crouch on my belly, the mice are like a deli.
I pounce on their bones, I never throw stones,
They squirm and try to run, oh, such fun.
After my lunch, I see a bunch,
A bunch of people, man, they're evil.
They always try to catch me,
And take me for their pet.
But I never fret, and I never fight.
When they think I'll always stay, I'll run away.

I'll go back to catching mice, oh, how nice.
So leave me alone you nasty, nasty people.
For next time, I'll run to that place with a steeple.
They'll love me, and strub me.
Never will they try to keep me,
    Can't you see I want to be free?
        —*Jennie Ann E. Farrough*

Realizing

Realizing how much I care about you
Not knowing what to do
Realizing things aren't the same
But your not to blame
Realizing we seemed to drift apart
Not knowing it in our heart
Realizing we're starting to go different ways
Now my life is like a maze
Realizing you want someone new
Which makes me blue
Realizing I should try and let you go
Is something I know will be hard to do
Because I still love you
Realizing it's for the best
And now I have to put my heart to the test
To see if I can make it through
Without being too blue
Realizing it will make me cry
And I'll want to die
But I have to test if our love is best
        —*Dawn Wheeler*

Interpretation Of My Dreams

If only I could live out my dreams
Nothing around me would be as it seemed
The grass would really be green and the sky really blue
I could look into your eyes and see right through you
The problems of my world would seem to vanish into thin air
Anger, frustration, confusion, and the pain would be gone
    and I wouldn't care
Every cloud would really have its silver lining and every heart
    its touch of gold
No shyness would ever be and no one ever too bold
All we can do is dream, because my life's no piece of cake
All the chaos in my world is gone...till the very second I awake!
        —*Jessyca Rodriguez*

Untitled

Stirring emotions in the wind of the past.
    Nothing I have is as certain to last
as memories I've gained from the times that I've had.
    I'm matching up more now as I go along
though the feelings I get while I'm doing aren't as strong
    as the way that I feel when I know what I've done.
Some day I'll look back and see this was all fun.
    When I think about how I once had it made
I was then out of focus with my mind in the shade
    and I didn't consider that it would all fade.
One day I'll look back on the life that I made.
    Will I be content with the efforts I gave?
Will I want to go back so I can be more?
    Will I think about things unconsidered before?
Whatever I do from now on I can't stay
    on the surface of earth here forever to play
as part of reality, living out this big game
    along with these humans which I am, the same.
And slowly but surely it will all be too late.
    Our chances are endless, so why do we wait?
        —*Jerry Harvey*

I Put Here Down A Simple Lay

I put here down a simple lay,
Nothing pretentious or daring
Just a few words put into lines
That my heart has want for sharing.

There's a time for hello and a time for goodbye,
A time for a bow and a curtsy.
A time for distance and modesty,
And praise be, a time for lifting the skirtsy!

There's a time to be cloistered in solitude,
And a time to drink full with companions.
There's a time with Endymion to muse on a mountain,
Or with St. Anthony to weep in a canyon.

There's the warming sun; the lulling moon,
A feast or just bread and water.
But of all these things what sets me on wings
Is to gaze at your mothers daughter.

For as Galileo yearned at night,
To touch the orbs in his view,
So by night on my bed I wish to be near,
The glory and grace that is you.
        —*John Kinsey*

587

Do You See....

Do you see we've grown together,
Now that changes have been made.
The wall between us collapses,
To the strength of our crusade.

Do you see we've grown together,
Now that trust has lead our hearts.
We've changed through understanding
And watch the distance break apart.

Do you see we've grown together,
Now that compromise comes first.
We're talking through the differences,
Knowing silence only hurts.

Do you see we've grown together,
Through all that we have learned.
We embrace our future with open arms
And to the past, our backs have turned.

—*Heather R. Burton*

Fall

Colored leaves drift downward, fallen from the nearby tree.
Now the tree is bare, no beautiful leaves to shade us.
And when the wind blows there will be no sound, just quietness.

The bleakness of fall is the naked trees, showing knots,
curves, and holes of the year before. Sometimes the branches
break because of no protection from its leaves.

The slight crispness of fall notifies the birds to migrate
for the winter, bears to eat food. Enough to let them sleep
through the coldest of seasons. And for squirrels and other
animals to get enough food to survive this scarce time.

Amidst the harshness of the fall season also lies its
beauties, the lovely ways that the green leaves slowly change
their color, and the many new sounds of birds, groundhogs, and
many others.

Fall, with its exquisite beauty.

—*Erika Engstrom*

When Tomorrow Comes

What will you do when you're seventy-two?
Now, while you're young, do you care?
For when you grow older, you'll need someone's shoulder,
and not just a bed and a chair.

Now, while you're young, there are songs to be sung,
and your future seems so far away;
but don't be surprised if you open your eyes
to find tomorrow is now yesterday!

It just isn't right to give up the fight
for the ones who have served us so well.
So now it's your turn to listen and learn
from the people who really can tell.

So if you do care, then please, won't you share
your thoughts of the needs of next year.
For if you do wait, it may be too late....
You'll find that it's already here!

—*Christine Clish*

The Future Of My Life

The future that is now is not like before,
My stepmother who's name is Jennifer I adore,
One thing I know Jennifer is a woman who is strong;
When I kiss her or talk to her it comes from my heart,
When I am with her I feel really close,
Jennifer is one of the people I love the most.

—*Luis Castro*

My World

Tucked into the deep green wood,
O I'd love to be there, if I could.
There it lies, the majestic spring,
How it sparkles, like an emerald ring.

All of the fishies are ready to be fished,
When I cast my line and tug and lift.
I took around at the rained on clover,
While frying in garlic my fileted dover.

There the water is crystal clear,
And the waterfall's sound is crisp and near.
the nearest town is miles away,
An O.K. place in a tiny bay.

In this place all is mine,
There is no crime for everything's fine.
All this is, is a fascination,
Nothing but a figment of my imagination.

—*Brocke Weir*

Sunset Hour

The Golden sun was slowly setting
O'er the distant rolling hills,
Through the clouds its rays were shining,
Filling those who saw, with thrills.

Far in the distance one could hear
The barking of a shepherd dog,
Who, sensing that the night was near,
Was gathering his herd from field and bog.

From a farm house chimney in the valley below,
There rose in graceful bands,
The smoke of a fire's warming glow
A welcome home to tired hands.

The day's work done and rest now due,
At the twilight of an autumn day.
What better could be offered to
A weary traveler of life's way?

—*John H. Ives*

Letting Go

Let go
 - of all your hurtful memories and emotions.
Be happy and content
 - with what you have.

Letting go releases you from the pain of the past.
It's often very hard to do
But well worth your effort.

Letting go allows you to be at peace with yourself.
Be willing to share with others.
You'll gain much in return.

—*James C. Cullen*

It Might Have Been

There is a flavor, yes, a taste
Of how life might have been, which I may savor,
Take how I loved, to file away forever
And wisely discard all the nothingness and never.

It's hard to bury, so I now accept
Its periodic surge and quell the urge
To feed and let it grow, well-kept.

I crush it back and smile at some new flower.
I think of many who have known love maybe for an hour,
Maybe a minute - maybe not at all;
So for myself not one more tear shall fall!

—*Alice E. Johnson*

The Knight

I often wish I could behold, the great and wondrous sight,
Of man and beast together, crashing through a moonlit night.

The man would be, I perceive, tall and dark and strong,
While though he be a knave at heart, he ne're would do wrong.

He'd rush to save the ladies fair, and dragons throats he'd
    slit,
Then dash away to unknown lands upon his wind swept ship.

Neglect he'd not his vast estates, and manor on the hill,
At night's he'd dream of the lady whom would all his dreams
    fulfill.

And soon shall come this lady fair to steal his roughish heart,
And he will love her always, letting nothing keep them 'part.

This man I fear though, rides no more, except upon my mind,
Which travels back to ride the moors, searching for something I
    shan't ne're find.

For with the fall of castles, with the rule of kings and queens
Went the domineering knight who rides and conquers all my
    dreams.

   —*Alecia Wagner*

Impressions Of A Dream

Walking toward an empty shelf of life unknown.
Of reflecting on memories that you've kept to yourself.
And with a photogenic impression of people
from the past longing to lead towards home.

You've cherish a lifetime of unspoken hopes
and mystical dreams.
Of magic unicorns and rainbows that
flow into a diminished beams.

Of a land where flowers bloom and
the lives combined within a waterfall
stream.
As the sun shines endlessly with the beauty
though time, last into eternity.

   —*Gina Thomas*

A "Chance" Meeting

Old wounds had settled to a numb, lack of feeling while seasons
of second hands blessed my soul's healing. Although rejection
robbed my spirit of belief in myself; new breezes blow dust from
my heart, left on a shelf. Infatuation sends tingles,
restoring rested senses inside while I wonder how calmly these
feelings I'll hide. For I'm fumbling as I stutter for the
right words to say, and anticipation breathes possibilities in
the air today. Why try to make sense of it if there's no
reason or rhyme, I guess I simply just met you in the right
place in time. This may be foolish attraction, but what a
beautiful-view I'm discovering a newness in me in hopes of
discovering you. We tell children of stories where dreams will
all come true then the world steals their simple faith
demanding what's due. Reality drills away to a steady,
responsible course you seem so very charming could it be you
ride a white horse? But if by chance I just only met you, and
nothing's meant to be I'll take this chance to just thank you
for arousing sparks in me. But I'll hold on to believing that
life brings to us this chance to hope for those fairy tales of
"Love at a first, single glance!"

   —*Carolyn June Derrig*

Proverbs Of Feeling Love

Love will softly touch, and know the healing
of that feeling.
Needs of love
should not except strokes without feeling,
for vulnerability is for all misleading.

Honest love will shine in you like that brightest star.
Dishonest love will eventually fade,
and cast a shadow on the heart,
leaving one without feelings of love,
a reason to doubt.

If one searches the need to love
one should know love searches love effortlessly
like the stare of the bright eyed cat
find in the heart what is there and the perspective of that

Giving love is the ultimate mystery
for one who has not received,
it's cold, it's distant, it's unknown
yet softly touch, and from healing of that feeling,
one will comprehend a true meaning

of feeling,
Love.

   —*Donna Bradley*

Untitled

The air is filled with anticipation
    Of the coming Joyous Days,
When we await the Christmas Season
    In so many different ways.

When a child, our eyes are wide open
    Awaiting Santa's arrival in his sleigh,
With a pack of goodies in his bag
    For all good children along the way.

We soon outgrew that childhood stage,
    But oh my! - wasn't it great
To look forward to Ole Santa's visit?
    It was really hard - that long wait!

And then came the adulthood stage
    When we understood our Savior's birth!
Bringing Joy, Peace - and, yes, much Love
    To all of us - o'er all the earth.

May the wonder of this Gift of Love
    That God sent that first Christmas Day
Be born in each of us anew
    Fill us with Hope and Peace to stay.

   —*Bernadine B. Drumright*

Is There In Life Left No Love

   Why are so many of us alone...lonely? Is it because
of the fear of love, or the fear of the pain that often follows
love? Love is not a possession, but a feeling. So fragile
and sensitive that it must be handled with trust and care.
Love is an opportunity. It may come your way when you are not
looking for it, and therefore be overlooked. Yet again, it
may come your way and you simply let it pass on by. Alone
you can only think... and learn. You cannot change what will
not be changed. You cannot go where you are forbidden to go.
You cannot be accepted for what is considered unacceptable.
And you cannot be with who you need to be with.
The pain must stop somewhere! Sometime!
When love comes your way again you must grasp it with your
heart and never let it go.
I know in my heart that the next time love approaches me I will
accept it gladly!
I can only hope that you, whoever you are, will be able to love
me as much as I will love you.

   —*Ben Smith*

I'm A Happy Recipient Of "Our World's Favorite Poems"

Take a good look I'm a happy recipient
Of the new poem book,
"Our world's favorite poems."

Verses to read and enjoy.
Oh! Boy! What a joy!
I won't stop reading, until it's over.
Reading the poem book from cover to cover.

Poets here, there and everywhere.
Poets in every nation
Write poems of thoughtful and meaningful creation.

May I make mention the poets writings
Are of great satisfaction.
Poems of inner feelings and extreme perfection.

Reflecting a clear picture
About the character of the writer
In poems of deep expression and impression.
Read and enjoy.
Oh! Boy!
Great Poetry
Of the highest priority.

  —Carmen J. Smith

Last Remarks

As I sit down I hear the Beast's majestic roar under the feet
of the unborn and I listen it cries out words of wisdom and
lashes out great warnings to the children who will grow.
As I look around I see the white pillows in the sky I create
the images and I dream. They resemble flowers from the heavens
white petals in the night for the people to admire.
As I sing my song undistinguished notes blend together in
Harmony.
As I write my poem the words begin to flow and I watch them
fall into place.
As I paint my picture great colors appear shades I have never
seen bold new creations are formed.
As I end my life I reminisce the times I have enjoyed are gone
In place come promises of a new day tomorrow will flourish
like yesterday.

  —Heidi Mueller

Picture Perfect

I hold this picture in my head
of the way a father should be,
And in my heart I have a hole
because you were never that kind of father to me.

When, at school, the talk of "daddies" would come
I had nothing to say so I'd leave the room,
Hoping one day, that you'll come back
and I'll be able to talk of "my daddy" too.

But years have past, time has changed
And I see that you're not coming back,
And, in my life, the "picture perfect daddy"
I guess, I'll just have to lack.

  —Cynthea T. Oberg

Mother

Memories of days long past,
Of treasured moments I hoped would last.
Times we shared together and talks we had,
How I wish sometimes I could go back.
Everything you did, made me what I am today.
Remembering you helps me along life's way.
Love to you always.

  —Arlene A. DiRocco

The Secret Of The Weeping Willow Tree

If you listen intently to the rhythmic sway of the willowy arms
of the weeping willow tree, you can hear it's secrets. It whispers
of romance embarrassed by the passion shared by lovers.
The beauty of the willow tree, knows not only of external desires,
but the desires that captivate the heart and soul. In the
silhouette of the moonlight, visions of a blanket has been
placed below me enraptured by two lovers. I feel the coldness
felt by a young woman that has been thawed by the desires of a
man starved for love and to love. The sensation of the cold
ground is interceded by the warmth of their love. My spirit
embraces this woman, never possessed by such desire for
another. Although this man is vexed with confusion, he seeks
to free himself from an existence that has left him ravenous in
a quest for one that would surrender her soul to and for him.
Enlivened, stimulated by these overpowering sensations the soil
that feeds my roots are vitalized; I feel I have the strength
and vigor of the mighty sequoia that will live forever.
Drought nor flood can suppress the splendor that has befallen
me this wondrous nightfall; man nor God can take away the
immortality of my presence, the shadows of my arms, the heart
of my core for I have experienced true, pure and complete love.

  —Janet Susan McDonough

Prisoners Of Influence

How dare the politicians lie, with smiles from prompted script,
Of values so important and our dreams that still exist.
Our minds are still our property, our conscience for who we are,
And not the toys of officers from life removed afar.

Religions we thought would lessons teach, of value, order and
life, so why then do we hear of church, involved in war and
strife. Is this the role of priesthood, from which our young
should hear, of which interpretation, should win the greatest
fear. The law books set the guidelines, by which we're called
to task, How many times mush we forgive, what money still can
mask. With ticket books and uniforms and badges pinned to chest
Our force of law and order, choose not to co-exist.

Our schools are given challenge, to teach our children well,
With books and words and influence, to keep them out of hell.
Outside the gates the drug lords wait, their pawns are primed
to pray, on anyone without support, so ripe to go astray.

And so the seasons come and go, each day still full of hope,
With who we choose to guide us through, we find a way to cope.
On values not for sale or rent, but things we can effect,
If nothing else, the bad will change with heartfelt self-respect.

  —Alexander Wilson

Thinking

You spend a lot of time thinking
of who you will marry or if you will.
You spend a lot of time thinking
if you will have kids and what they will be like.
You spend a lot of time thinking
if you'll make it to college or graduate.
You spend a lot of time thinking
about what will happen tomorrow
and the days to come.
You spend a lot of time thinking
of what happened yesterday and the days before.
You spend a lot of time thinking
what am I here for?

  —Danielle Chernis

Yesterday

Remember no more the bitter memories
of yesterday, my friend,
Today is in the making and the
tears of yesterday are gone.
We often go through rough situations
and the hurt remains,
No more should you feel the pain
or torment from the memories of yesterday,
Time seems to help in many ways
but we must forgive ourselves.
We may sometimes help others
through trying times and reach them
with the words they need to hear.
Tomorrow will come and we must
know that the past is the past.
Don't ever forget that yesterday
is over, today is at hand,
and there is hope for a better
tomorrow.

—Beth Vincent

In Touch, Can't Touch

In touch, can't touch the tenderness
of your body, the passion of your heart, the
moisture of your warmth, the treasures of your
spirit.
In touch, and can't touch the curious of
your questful nature, the aura of your faith,
the texture of your smile.
In touch, can't touch the spark of your
life security, the well of beauty you display
in everything you do and say.
In touch and can't touch the understanding
of your mind an all the reasons I want you to
be mine; I hope and pray in time we'll touch
and fasten this bond that feelings have won,
a touch of love has begun.

—Benjamin Paul

Friend

I saw a rainbow at midnight, out over the ocean blue.
Oft' times I think of that rainbow,
And it reminds me of you.

All the colors were shining like diamonds,
so bright and vividly clear,
They reflected my heart in its pining,
And its secrets I had to forebear.

God in his infinite wisdom,
Has the answers to all things below.
By chance there's nothing that happens,
Therefore our friendship will grow.

Anytime we may come to our cross-roads,
And forget all the things we know now.
So let's store up good thoughts for our assets,
Any bad ones we must disavow.

When our patience has gone a full circle,
And our nerves are standing on end.
There's always one thing we can count on,
The understanding of one we call friend.

—Herman Saltzman

Trust God

Trials and tribulations we face in life
　　Often times puts our faith to the test

Rarely do we always understand why
　　But remember God knows and does what's best.

Unprepared for life's adversities
　　Which often take us by surprise

Strengthens to bring us closer to God
　　And can be blessings in disguise.

Take things in life one day at a time
　　Knowing the Lord will see you through-

God specializes in whatever we need
　　And He will take care of you.

Only trust Him and be patient
　　Just ahead are brighter days

Don't give up, we have God's assurance
　　That trouble won't last always!!!

　　　Be encouraged!!!
　　　—Ilene Rowser

Spring

The fields and woods are filled snow,
Oh! how the frost does snap and sting.
I wish that the winter were over now,
Giving place for he beautiful spring.

The spring is the time when our hopes revive,
And pour forth from their winter's den.
They are much like the bees in a great beehive,
Coming forth to a flower decked glen.

In the spring we plow and harrow the fields,
To prepare them for the planting of grain.
We think, then, only of the harvest yields,
Not of a probable loss, but of gain.

In the spring we open the cowshed door,
And to the green pastures, drive the herd.
With the streams that from their milk wells pour,
We make golden butter and sweet curd.

In the spring we plant many pretty flowers,
Mow and trim the level green sod.
Our lives are as bright as a starlit night,
And in our hearts we hold pledges to God.

　　　—Lloyd Connors
　　　—Amy Hooper, Grandaughter

Mack

If you should go and I remain
oh, the tears may blur,
but then, I shall slay your dragons,
build paths free from pain.

If I should go and you remain,
have no fear of Mack,
and then, you can sing my praises,
bear no truths to feign.

To the light.
Whose radiance has shone in lives past gone.
To the throne.
Sweet puffs of perfumed mists dull thy senses.
To the veil.
Lift your heart and you'll find a sweet, sweet soul,
clothing thee.

　　　—Charles H. Fleming

Willow:

Like a babies cry in the middle of the night,
old willow sighs.

I've trained my ears to hear her creaking bones.

An old house or abandon church,
this woman was not forgotten by one man.

A leaf.
A seed.
Call me what you will, but I am an offspring
of this weeping tree.

Old willow,
bent by the hands of time.
Drowning in her rain of tears.

She could not forget one man.

I am their leaf and willow was a strong tree.
Stronger than I will ever be.

—*Donna M. Woods*

First Impressions

First impressions are like a door
On hinges, that suspend it;
To give it movement to or fro,
To reach momentum high or low.
Which ever way; impressions may go.

A first impression
Linger's long, once the mind receives it,
To open or close,
This hinge hung door, that movement
Commence; as first impressions grow.

—*Dante Devon Gibson*

In The Ocean Of Your Eyes

Long grass sweeping in the wind,
On the hill where you stand... looking out to sea...
Can you, feel me?

I'm the part inside of you, swirling with the wind,
Playing with your hair...to take you where...
You can fly! And feel alive! Awake the woman longing for...
The passion that is yours...above the crashing shores...
There you glide with strength and pride
The love that I once knew,

If only I had spoken then...in the ocean of your eyes,
I would not have lost...the beauty that is you...
The wind caresses empty fields looking everywhere for you,
The long grass tells the wind...she...is gone...

I was your life or hope to be..
In the ocean of your eyes, Now am I free? Did I wish to be?...

Or did I only once exist...in the ocean of your eyes...
In the caressing of your hair...in your feelings waiting where.
You can fly! And feel alive! Awake the woman longing for...
The passion, that is yours...if only...
I could have been much more...

—*the Dream Seer*

Our Dreams

When we are small we dream
of little simple things, like having a bike
or lots of toys or your own swing.
When we are bigger we dream of
being handsome or pretty and having lots
of dates, of becoming an adult, we can
hardly wait.
When we are all grown up
then we look on our dreams fulfilled
and wonder what's ahead for us still.

—*Bobbie J. Mackerl*

The Parent's Saga

On all fours, with observant ears, the little king looked out
on the vastness and saw the silence and heard the emptiness-
it, the cub and heir of the graceful lioness.

The storm clouds threatened and birds of prey circled high
above. Yet, it waited; waiting ever so patiently as rain
began to pour and the drops frolicked around his eyes on unto
his noble nose and feet.
Still, on that very spot it endured with curious, confused
eyes that scanned the extent of the horizontal abyss of tall,
arrogant grass and nothing more.

It remembered watching the sober rain from under his mother's
frame, her warmth and the enormity of her assuring breath
Child no more and not yet ready to be king, it waited.
This was its brave instinct and this was its fate
To stand and linger of days-disappointed with every hopeful
glance.
Move on it must, and forget is mama and her warmth
The stoic mother who obeyed nature without a second thought
For it was not the human parent-the delicate negotiator,
Whose children would always be its babies.

—*George Thomas*

Do It Yourself Kit

Arthritic knees will be a thing of the past
One can see a new trend blooming fast
New parts are used, to replace the old
Modern surgery is like going for the gold
Before you know it, you can shop for parts
Adds fun to the sales, as you place them in your cart
The next thing to do, is to take a crash course
And learn how to install them with no remorse
I'm sure our surgeons will shout with glee
When they set out to collect their fee
Because we forgot, to use a part
That was necessary, from the start

—*Angelina Valentino*

Somewhere Better

Well she is somewhere a whole lot better.
One day I hope to join her there.
It is a place where the sun always shines
and everyone is always happy to see you.
There is never a dull moment because
everyday is filled with something to enjoy.
She will be at the gates waiting
to meet me when I arrive.
I don't know when that will be,
but I sure hope it is soon.
Because I miss her.

—*Anthony Perez, Jr.*

Death Doesn't Ask

Death doesn't ask: "When or why do you want to die?"
Often, there is no time to say goodbye.
Other times death lets you know:
"Prepare, it's time to go."
Don't be surprised if he plays with you.
Like your shadow he will follow you.
He doesn't ask: "Are you rich, are you poor?"
One day he will come, that is sure.
Once he has thrown his dice,
there is no compromise.

—*Annemarie Mulder*

Me

I love to travel near and far
One day to the moon and stars
I'm very newsy and love to listen
Being bad, feeling sad and always cooking something
Working hard and thinking of the future
Soon it will be here and I'll start working

God has kept me alive and well
I fell real good, you can tell
I'm twelve years old, pray I
make it to 112
The streets are no longer safe for
children to walk on

I have a goal in my life
To pursue my education, to win the fight
To win the fight over drugs and violence
To keep the peace, to end the silence
To have a family who doesn't fear
getting hurt or shedding tears.

   —Amani Bright

For The Little One Soon To Be Here

 For the little one soon to be here
One that will bring you happiness and cheer
 One that will make you cry now and then
 Be mischievous and naughty again and again
One who will need all your strength and care
 That God will send through your prayer
  One that will keep you on the go
  No matter how old he may grow
 But you will bless the happy day
This precious little one came to stay

   —Edna Zukowski

When Etta Mooney Sang

At this time, we pause in memory of one whose heart was love. One who did her duty as a christian, and now resting in the heaven above. She was blessed with many talents, one of them was a gift to sing. She used that gift to praise the Lord and oh how her voice did ring. She had so many favorite hymns, too numerous to recall but with her dedicated voice, heaven knows she sang them all. Whenever she raised her voice in song, oh how the joy bells rang, the program just was not complete until Etta Mooney sang. She went to a church one Sunday not feeling very well. Oh why would Etta sing? They said she is weak, for I can tell. She sang because she was happy, she sang because she was free. His eye is on the sparrow, and I know He watches me. They came to her with great applause, arms stretched out to embrace. No, no, not yet, until I sing of God's amazing grace. Through the years she kept on toiling, always trying to do her best, but our Father is too wise to make mistakes, for He knows when His child needs rest. She grew tired of the load she was carrying. Her engagements she rocks His little one to sleep. But she left some precious memories, although she is passed and gone her footprint's on the sand of time.

   —Catherine Shorter Lewis

Untitled

Nobody knows the words I sew
Only I know the pain that grows
Each stitch is a day that grows longer
Each day another one to ponder.

I've been alone times before
Now I feel this is not a home anymore
Before I wasn't lonely, now I am
I've been changed, I'm not the same man.

   —Andrew B. Clapp

Shades of Gray

Is it always black and white?
Or are there shades of gray?

Two men walk side by side down a crowded street.
Both men see a young girl crying at an old man's feet.

They stop to watch, curious and thoughtful.
They hear the young girl begging forgiveness for
 something awful.

The old man looks at the girl with disgust in his eyes,
She says that she is sorry for telling him so many lies.

The old man kicks and hits her and calls her a whore,
She looks at him through tear filled eyes and
 says, "Papa, please no more!"

The old man turns his back on his pregnant daughter
 as she sits cold and unnerved.
One of the men observing turns his back and walks away
 thinking she got what she deserved.
The other observer rushes over to help the young girl stand.
He asks if he can somehow offer her a helping hand.
Two different men, two different minds, two different reactions

I is always black and white? Or are there shades of gray?

   —Heather Roderick

There's A Gorilla In My Garage

There's a gorilla in my garage,
Or, is it just a mirage?
But, I see him sitting in the car
Eating peanuts out of a jar!

There's a polar bear sitting in my favorite chair
I can't imagine how he got there.
He may have come from the North Pole,
But now he's eating cereal in my bowl!

Do you see the llamas wearing my pajamas,
Sleeping in my bed?
And the hamsters in the hamper
Waiting to be fed?

There's a Brontosaurus singing in a chorus
With a lion and a hen.
And a Triceratops wearing hi-tops
Running through my den!

Imagine that all wild animals
Could live in our house without fear.
But, be careful for now,
'Cause it's just a jungle in here!

   —Elizabeth Teich

Unspoken Love

Whenever birds forget to sing to me
Or sing a song I do not recognize,
I rush outdoors to look for thunder clouds
That interrupt a mockingbird's disguise.
And so it is with love.

I know so well your footsteps,
Your mellow voice which penetrates the hush,
Your whistle that dispels oppressive gloom.
Yet I, lost in my world, forget to speak
The outer words of love, forget to show
How much I care, how much I feel.
But, oh, how terribly I miss you when you're gone.

   —Cecile Cottman

Shadows

Shadows or the wall, never represent your all,
or the person that you are or want to be.
Shadows on the wall, will never tell what you are,
Only what they see and what you seem to be.
You'll never be able to tell, if they've seen heaven or hell,
by the shadow on the wall that you see.
Nor, if they have a troubled mind,
or, if they find truths hard to find,
or, if their soul needs to be set free.
The only thing you can tell, is if their body is fit and well.
Never further than that can the eye see.
So take a little time, it isn't such a crime,
to take the shadow from the man, and set him free.

— *Anita Kay Bonafice*

The Unknown Graves of 1945/E. Europe

Will we ever forget, no matter how much we try,
Or will we remember until we die?
The crying, the dying, the dead,
The graves in the garden or park,
Among the beautiful flowers,
Or in the shade where it's dark.
At the seaside or the far end,
Where the children used to play in the sand. Among
the forest trees, or in the orchard, not far from the bees.

We buried them everywhere, without a casket or a priest,
Because there was no time for last rights or a feast.
The tiny baby, that used to play and never cry all day,
This baby died, because there was no milk and nothing to eat,
It became so weak, that it couldn't lift its feet.

How the mother did nothing but weep,
Because at first she thought the baby had gone to sleep.
We buried it in the garden, under the lilac tree.
The mother went there the next day again the spot to see.
Out of two sticks we made a cross
And covered the small grave with a little moss.

— *Helena M. Jones*

Lists

Lists, and a list of lists he carried
  Organized, numbered, methodic.
What an odd pair we did make
  My life was always chaotic.

In shirt pocket, jeans or wallet
  These lists were filed so neat,
One quick glance and he would know
  What deadlines we had to meet.

He crossed off items, added and checked
  Then reshuffled by new priority,
He took the time to track it all
  From major to minority.

I found some lists not long ago
  Amended, noted, addended.
He's gone. The lists remains here still,
  Along with our dreams lamented.

The lists and list of lists he carried
  Had our life categorized to a "T",
He forgot one item that should have been first,
  He forgot Himself — for me.

— *Felice C. Perkins*

Just Say No!

You are not alone in the syndrome you feel,
others are plagued with it too.
It's atrocious to think you've to go it alone,
no ones traveling this road with you.
You've experienced things that made you feel life was hell.
Your rounds now over and they've sounded the bell.
You've seen a man give his life to be free.
Lots of others are dying but they're not across the sea.
Sure it's going to leave a terrible scar,
but it's reality and wherever it is, it's par.
While quietly thinking all you do is reminisce.
Think of those who'd give their lives for just this.
Faith has brought you from a mighty long way.
And it's going to save at least 5,000 today.
And if faith brought you through toil and strife,
It alone can save the rest of your life.

— *Andrea Burrell*

Words Of Hope

There is a time in our lives when all need to join hands together
Our children may never see what it is like to live forever
In the path of sickness and destruction of war
Their tears will seek hope forever more
Never living their life of fun
Or to see the light of tomorrow's sun
Time has come to mend this forgotten earth
Not to deny our children of what they are really worth
Take away the shame and heal the pain
Open up your hearts, and lets all take an important part
Through the mirrors of life our children look and see
The world with many faces reflects love upon you and me
In dreams of sleep they set themselves free
Minds filled with laughter and joyous smiles of tender glee
A glimmer from a star above is a feeling there is time
Lets hold our hands together and make this world divine
Through tears of hope, through cries of pain, open up your heart
Let the sunshine breathe light through their smiles again.

— *Debra Souter*

Don't Believe Everything You Hear!

Who in his right mind would ever have thought
Our daughter, who is a teacher,
Would claim her father is a hooker,
And, what's more, her mother, a stripper?

Now, before you collapse in shock,
I must explain her sense of "humor."
You see, neither of us is either,
And thus prefer this not start a rumor.

Her father has enjoyed rug hooking,
Making several quite beautiful designs;
While I buy furniture that is terrible looking
To strip, refinish, and improve on its lines.

So you see, the names for us are perfect,
Yet are not at all what everyone must think.
I ask, please be understanding when you reflect
On what is said by our daughter with a "wink".

— *Arlene G. Ponitz*

Old Glory

Old glory is precious that we all know
  or is it an illusion of something aglow
    we died for it we suffered in pain
  and sometimes I wonder if we have made a gain
for the way of all flesh is the way of the world
but there's sure to be peace where old glory unfold
old glory the flag with the red, white and blue
  is the symbol of peace for me and for you
so let us all do our part to keep it that way
  the home of the brave, the good old USA

594   — *Carl L. Hill*

Symphony

Friendship is a symphony.
Our lives are chords, blending to produce
melodies fit for a Heavenly choir.
We, as friends, give to this world a song
varied with sharps and flats,
added to the already-existing notes.
When discord strikes,
and it surely will,
it is only because
we must live our separate lives, be ourselves.
This is not an end, only a rest.
And, after a time, we will continue, as a musician progresses
with a symphony,
never losing a note.
The symphony goes from measure to measure;
we go from day to day,
filling the days of our friendship with cherished memories,
which recur in our minds, a sweet refrain.
So we can share in that which, through life, we have
written: OUR FRIENDSHIP SYMPHONY.

—Gayle Anne Wagaman

Time

Time, a calm delicacy - the most important facet of
our lives. When treated with respect, can provide
us with the greatest joy of all, the pleasure,
to know ourselves.

—Jennifer Michelle Weston

Untitled

You. Me.
Our Love.
My love for you expands to fill every crevice of the spacious
universe.
I sometimes reach out to touch it to make sure it is real.
Then other times I shrink back in fear that its reality may
turn to fantasy.
I've loved before.
And I've loved on purpose.
But your love crept upon me,
like a silent thief in the night.
And for a while I was scared of it,
yet at the same time intrigued.
I want your love to engulf me and fill my soul.
I want to breathe all the love that you can fill me with.
And when I am no more, then let my last breath be filled with
your love.
Let the last words that I speak be, "I love you."
And let my last body movement embrace you...
In one final effort to tell you I care for you now and always.

—Dagnee McKinney

On The Differential

Some of us there are who don't fit.
Our pegs are neither round nor square
but some obtuse form-immeasurable.
The different drum to which we march
is muffled beyond the ken.
We watch with mysterious aloofness
the ebbs and tides-detached from the current.

Yet concern yourself not with the difference.
Disregard the ache of isolation.
For in our solitude we hear the silence.
We sense a cadence hidden to most.
And in our stillness-we know.

—Jane Shadid

A Deviant View

Perhaps someday I'll understand just why
Our reading tries to find some sense in verse
Each word, we think, for deep meaning must vie
To poetry there is no greater curse

Read a poem with your heart and not your mind
Yet feeling's also not among your chores
Suppose not that a meaning you must find
How can you judge a poem that's not yours?

Oft times a poems merely states a thought
Uttered by the mind, shaped by the heart
Language adorned is what is to be sought
Damn us if we tear beauty apart

Not once has any poem on any page
Offered readers just what the felt
The fool sees not the same tree as the sage
More numerous than the stars are readings dealt

Each poem's written with a poet's past
And with a reader's past are poems read
New visions sees each reader to the last
Beware not new ideas, rejoice instead

Unless poet and reader be the same
Their images are bound to be distinct
Both try to understand the other's game
Each poem serves as but a common link

—David M. Roomes

A Play Of What Has Been Is "The Future"

On the threshold of a dream I am, I cry
out to the father. This dream has been
developed from the days of the future
past, the future, present, and the future
itself! Of rust are the days of the past.
Are diamonds of the days of futures.
Past, only moments more to go for my dreams.
Only moments more to go, in his grand plan.

—John R. Holderread

The Thousand And One Goals

How often man must find himself,
Outside the home his labor keeps,
I see him tilling now within the field.
The best for him is always,
What his hardest effort reaps,
And what beyond the crops have yet to yield.
And what beyond , to delve this pond,
Could verily break his shallow soul,
If he were but an insect in a hole,
If under, now, some farmer's plow,
Scuttled in rows on little peaks,
For all the lesser ones to see,
Just what beyond the crops have yet to yield.

And what beyond, to delve this pond,
Will tow us out, and to the shore
From out the pond into the ocean, evermore?
Beneath the depth find freer breath,
In a valley of purpose below,
To diminish this filter of life and evolve,
Within any size space that we know.

—James Rizvani

Bringing It Home

I've seen this scene
outside the simple threshold
on Beverly, the strangers gathered
with pockets full of tightened fists
concealing personalities,
the aged balancing on neighbor walls and
some children milling,

a woman denim jeaned, my age,
like me except I'm full and she
is waiting patiently for groceries anonymously bagged,
the line beginning there, on
a sidewalk, with the others,

I've seen this scene,
but now my shocks run heavy
along this pavement.

—*Craig Miller*

Mom-Moms

Memories come and flood my mind
Over the times spent so kind
My childhood days in strawberry patches

Muddy walks in deep running thatches
Oh, catching so many frogs, crayfish and tadpoles
My small feet getting stuck in cow field holes

I remember smelling the house of cabbage and potatoes
Learning to love the taste of those yucky red tomatoes
Oh sleeping in the attic in the big kings bed
Verily filled with cousins while Mom-Mom prayed
Eternal memories of my Mom-Mom so dear

Years could never erase, always clear
On lonely nights many times I dwell
Unto family memories at Mom-Moms so well.

—**Hugh Downey**

Just Slightly Out Of Control

Thoughts of you froth in my mind
Overflowing into spaces where they do not belong.

Like waves tugging at the shoreline,
Smoothing sharp and jagged edges,
Yet poking long fingers deep inside
Clawing at the firmness of the earth.

Thoughts of you. Just slightly out of control.

My life demands so much of me — rushing, writing, cleansing,
Giving loving, stopping the fighting.

Sometimes I feel that I shall be washed away by one might wave:
A mermaid carried too far out to sea,
Unable to sparkle in the sun.

My life's demands. Just slightly out of control.

Then your presence gives me buoyancy
The power of my emotion pulses through me.

New energy causes my countenance to rise.
My skin glows, my eyes shine, my lips part.
Caring heals the heart and strength returns,
Responding to you like the incoming tide.

Yet your presence leaves me just slightly out of control.

—**Gail F. Blanchard**

Who's Knocking

There was a man begging for only a dime; you walked fast and paid him no mind. There was a blind woman so gentle and sweet; you would not even help her across the street. There was a young boy who had gone astray; he came to you but you sent him away. You continued to live for selfish gain; but then your sunshine turned to rain. You never thought of your transgressions so you lost your material possessions. Then as a last resort you began to pray. Lord come into my life; I can't live this way. You had a worried look upon your face; asking...when are you coming Lord to bless me with your Holy Grace? Then the Lord began to speak... I came and asked for a dime... You paid me no mind. I came as a blind woman needing a guide for my feet; you hurried away, leaving me alone in the street. As a young boy I came for help one day; you would not listen but sent me away. You need to be a Christian and extend your love to everyone; because you do not know in what form I may come. So do not ask when I am coming or where I have been; for I kept knocking but you would not let me in.

—*Corrine F. Young*

Unsighted Love

Words fade from my lips
Pain embraces my heart
Happiness overwhelmed by fear,
Do you taste my salty tears?
Compulsive thoughts unknown to all
Blocked in by what seems a wall.
Voices screaming soundless nothings
as loud as reality.
Watch and you will hear the fear in my eyes.
Been waiting forever it seems
for what now is only a mirage in my heart.
Every time I get close enough,
You pull away with such vibrance
my heart feels the impact.
I dream of us together, wishing it
reality and my pain-an image in my mind.
I'm more than you only see, looks deceive.
For there is so much more to me.

—*Jackie Martin*

The Cave

Trapped in an unexplored cave without a light
Panic fuels the search for a way out
Fear shields the eyes vital for finding the exit
Loneliness is snuffing out the will to fight.

Struggling against unseen walls
Searching aimlessly for any faint sign..
Here, hope is not unlike the light,
Darkness thwarts me towards the inevitable fall.

Falling has now become the greatest of all fears.
Time is of no particular importance—
Survival is all that matters.
Must defeat the cave, even if it takes years.

I only know this from experience.
This "cave" is not a part of the land;
In fact, the strangest part is,
the cave is not much bigger than your hand.

—*Joe Forquer*

The Hunter

Moving through the woods like a black
 panther stalking its prey. The
deafening sound of silence was broken
 by a sudden snap of a twig which
screamed through the forest. His
 disguise exposed with great disappointment
 and anger. Every move he makes,
every breath he takes is now apparent
 in the wind. The hunter now becomes
the deer.
 Is The Hunter Now The Hunted?

 —Jon Sakoda

The River

Time is like a torrent of water swirling by,
Passing onward toward the distant future.
Suddenly, we plunge over the edge.
We lose power as we aimlessly drift,
Seeking a purpose for the endless pushing.

Something causes us to strike a rock.
In our momentary contact with the rock,
There is peace and silence.
Motion ceases.

Desperately we cling to that rock
Who is Christ our Lord.
However, this world continues to push us away.
With new strength and purpose, we move on.

White, the living water plunges forward.
We swirl past life's ups and downs.
Continuing forward, always forward.
We must swirl onward trusting in God to guide and protect us.
Only our maker knows where life's twists and turns will lead us

There is no need to fear, little leaf,
God holds us secure.

 —Becka Johnson

The Master

The Master lifted my soul from the deep, dark depths of sin.
Paved my path with hope and peace.
Clothed my body with happiness.
Filled my heart with love and enriched
my spirit with honor and glory forever.

 —Evelyn Block

Love

A beautiful flower...
Perched upon a slender stem...
Inclines in the gentle breeze...
Sweet nature unfolds...
A sight to behold.
A sparrow...
Soars effortlessly through the clear blue skies...
Tracing the path to the comfort of her nest
An aerodynamic exhibition.
A newborn!
Lies atop its mother's breast
The splendor of innocence personified
Beauty of love's gift to man
Destiny has her lite in its hand
A man! A woman,
Meet by chance
Friendship develops
Blossoms into love.
Two hearts become one
Never to be set apart.

 —George F. Braithwaite

Conversations

As I'm walking through the forest, stately oaks contain the breeze.
Pearlized shafts of light as swords pierce through the dark.
Trailing vines are hanging from the laden branches of the trees.
While each pinnacle homeward beckons for the larks.

Bluish shadows softly wake vibrant colors from their sleep
Gentle breaths of air help dry the morning dew
Fragile silence interrupted, dawning sounds through marshes seep.
Day is breaking forth as tender pastel hues

As I walk and talk with Him in the coolness, so refreshed
Mind alert and spirit yearning for His voice
Tranquil eloquence He displays, for His mastery I have wished
As poetic phrases mirror words of choice

He reveals to me His thoughts, inner groanings and desires
About everything I've ever thought to ask
Keeping nothing in reserve, as closest friend do I aspire
I can tell Him things, He won't take me to task

There's no way I can describe our relationship, mere words
Seem so faltering, and my friends don't seem to care
All they see are my shortcomings and annoying little quirks
They can't understand a depth of love so rare

 —Danny M. Musick

Ode To A Novice Punter

A gambling craze is sweeping the land
People are taking a chance on any game at hand.
Money is used that should pay the rent,
And it won't be long before some are sleeping in tents.

The time is short and the reaper is near,
Before long, their tears will drip into their beer.
So waste not time and purchase this pamphlet,
For it may help you when returning from a gambling gambit,
To quiet the fears of a waiting spouse,
And, maybe then, she might let you back in the house.

 —Frank Kraus

Mama And I Remember

My Daddy, a tribute to you, the Harry O. Cartier, that few
people knew. A special man in so very many ways, who always
remembered the holidays. A flower at Easter and on Mother's
Day, and you always appreciated our praise. You tried to act
tough and then carefree at times, but your love for your
family was always sublime. I can see you up there with a
butterscotch in hand, standing before the Lord, in the promised
land. "Thanks for coming, Harry Jr., my son, my race on this
earth is finally done." No more pain or grief you will have to
bear, but our memories of you, we will always share. So there
you are with a smile on your face, before heavenly Father,
listening to mama sing "Amazing Grace". I know you are happy
with our family and friends, and us left behind, with our
hearts left to mend. But one day we will be together soon, you
see, as an eternal family in heaven we will be. And there
again, my song you will hear. Oh, how sweet it will sound as
it falls on your ear. My heart cries out for the daddy I miss,
but at heaven's gate you will give me a kiss. Come in my
daughter, I have been waiting for you. We must hurry, we have
plenty of work here to do.

 —Beverly Cartier-Kirby

Anthesis

Sere winds blow unceasingly through dry, cracking membranes
Outwardly manifested by thin, scar-like lines and flaccid
 folds of skin
Inwardly unchanged; loving life, eagerly reaching out
Age drapes itself over me and like a veiled statue
I wait for the sure pull of an unseen hand
To reveal the fresh luster untouched by time.

 —Betsy Dickson

Lending A Hand

As the summer fades away,
People stop to remember
The things that have happened around them
To change their lives forever.

The powerful hands of nature
Altered the lives of many.
Some pieced things back together
With help from friends and family.

Homes were pulled from foundations;
Combines were thrown across fields.
Trees were leveled to the ground,
And crops promised very low yields.

Streams turned into rivers
Closing all roads in their path.
Floodwaters filled many basements
Leaving a bleak aftermath.

Through tornado, flood, and thunderstorm,
One thing stayed the same —
Neighbors were there lending a hand.
In rural life pride remained.

—*Jessica Peterson*

Renewal

Sometimes when I'm quiet,
People think there's something wrong.
I admit sometimes there is,
But mostly I am contemplating life around me.
I let my eyes observe,
And my soul drink in what's seen.
I see the sparkle in someone's eye,
The lines of worry on another's forehead.
I see the child in someone old.
I wonder who will emerge
from those I see who are young.
The world around me's like a canvas brought to life
By the artist hand of God,
Who took such loving thought to detail when creating
The kaleidoscope of colors to please the eye,
The orchestra of sounds to please the ear.
In my solemnness I have let my spirit wander,
To be one with what's around me.
So when I bring it back, to be myself again
I am renewed.

—*Elizabeth O. Harris*

Nameless

So you want a peek into my soul. Ok, I'll give you one.
Picture this: You're standing on a school playground
Surrounded by laughing kids, but the laughter is not fun.
It's cold, cruel, mocking laughter that
Picks at your soul like a raven's beak.
These "kids" then reveal their true form as jackals
As they drag you down, rending flesh from bone
As you lie there wishing to die, just to make the pain stop.
But they go on, as though saying "You can't escape.
We'll be with you always." On and on
Til you can't take it anymore.
Then you explode into a fountain of rage: Pure, cleansing
Hatred bursting forth with each swing of your fist.
The laughter gets louder as the jackals/kids
Get what they want. Rage turns to tears
As you bolt for your favorite hiding place,
Tears flowing like a warm summer rainstorm,
Til the recess bell rings.
Still you sit in the earthy darkness
Until a teacher asks what's wrong? "Nothing, nothing. . . . "

—*Dave Cunningham*

End Of A Rainbow

My feelings are like the colors in the sky,
Pink when I'm happy, gray when I cry.
Yellow when I'm curious and wonder what's there,
Purple when I'm lonely and need someone to care.
Blue shows my love for miles around,
And white clouds tell my thoughts without making a sound.
A sunrise shows pictures of the day yet to come,
And a sunset tells my prayers when all the day is done.
Raindrops on roses are like tears rolling down my face,
And the darkness of night shows my fears hiding the day
without a trace,
The stars show my dreams and wishes throughout the night,
Until the darkness fades away leaving a rainbow as the first
sign of light.

—*Jacqueline Clinger*

Rage, Therapeutic

forgetting the stimuli- snakes all around - and inside of me
pity and fear for the kicking one. Victimless, rubber things
fail to comply with the slithering, nightmarish visions of
she. Nothing is moving but eyes-dart and nostrils-flare.
"Will not fall prey to the Evil - it wants me to ... scamper,
and fingertips, toetips, little bits, scittering, coaxing
the slitherthings, 'Prey.'" me and other, she and the
multitudes, motionless, fooling her, set for the kill. When
she goes (but I won't), ingested all everything- deserting
me here with the sneaky red, brown green and black yellow
masses, with forktongues and scalyscales, wet to the touch,
yellow pink on the inside. Where are the monsters with
clipboard and cloaks, where are the powerful punishing devils,
who locked me and left me and watch me and note. Why did they
leave me? Where is the Subject? Where is the subject?
Damn it the subject!? The stimuli! Hel-

—*Andrew S. Ganzekaufer*

Love, I John 4:8

I felt God's Love in the cones of the conifer as a dear friend
placed them in my hand; again in the sea shells tossed by the
high tide when a darling child found them in the sand. Merry
hearts displayed His love as I danced with joy, clasping hands
with my friend, when an ailing child was touched by God
through our prayers that seemed never to end.

His love blossomed forth in the happy whispers of my flowers
swaying in the ocean breeze, and in the rain gently dripping
upon my window pane from the flailing branches of the graceful
trees. His presence is felt in the lofty mountains with
towering peaks reaching toward the sky, and in the eyes of His
precious creatures, for He knows and hears their every sigh.

His love is in the hearts and gentle spirit of my fellow
Christians as we meet and pass; sharing our joys and sorrows,
knowing that only the things of Jesus Christ will last. God's
love softens our grief when loving friends care for us and
pray. So let us thank and praise our Almighty God for His
love that flows through each of us today.

—*Evelyn M. Poitevin*

A Dove For Peace

Could the world but live by the "Golden Rule"
Plus what we were taught in Sunday School
Our nations would overflow with caring!
There would be less violence, a lot more sharing-

The population would not suffer, from prejudice or hunger
Our longevity would be safe, no reason to put asunder...
Perhaps, with all this faith and effort
God would smile down on us, from above

He will know that we are trying and,
"Oh, look there goes a Dove"

—*Florence Thompson*

My Father's Favorite Yankee

My father in his yesteryear
Played baseball night and day
He was always in gear
Come what may.

From his position in left field
Where he always played chipper
He ran and areeled
Just like "The Yankee Clipper"

He thought Joe was cream of the crop
I guess we all do that
Look up to someone, who has made it to the top
In this case, an idol swinging a bat

In later years, when the old timers met
He would watch them on tv
When Joe came on the set
There were tears for all to see

My father passed on two years ago
Watching a hockey game
Someday, maybe so,
He'll meet Joe, in God's "Baseball Hall of Fame"
—*Corrine Howells*

Utopia

I can remember — though three and half decades have passed —
playing in the sunshine,
basking in the peace of solitude,
communing with nature,
and
talking to God.

Though three and a half decades have passed — maybe a year
or two more —
for I was only four,
but
I still can remember:
playing in the sunshine, looking at the big azure sky,
basking in the peace of being alone,
communing with nature,
and
talking with God.
—
        Gwen Woods Millender

The Tiny Cries From Darkness

The darkness... so dark... so cold
Please help me! Get me out of here!
I shouldn't be here, help me!
No once cared, no one listen
Oh the darkness... so dark... so cold
I'm just a child! Someone help me!
Why? Why did you send me here
I don't like this hole
The darkness... so dark... so cold
I screamed... no one would listen
It hurts, it hurts so much
Don't hit me! Please don't hurt me anymore!
I have friends to play with here...creepy crawlers
The darkness... so dark... so cold
No place for a child... the grave
I can't be abused anymore
The light... so light... so warm
Whose loving arms are these who hold me?
The light... so light... so warm
—*Alice Faye Rutherford*

Why Does Thou Stay And Ponder The Moment

Why does thou stay and ponder the moment,
Ponder the thoughts of memories that will never be forgiven,
Don't success smell sweet like the fresh grown mint,
And as pure the feeling like believing there's a heaven.

Look as high as the birds can fly and look up at the clouds
beyonder,
Look at the fields of wheat that sways with the new morning wind,
Or is success like the beauty of all nature's wonders,
Or as free flowing as our dreams or ocean currents.

We are all seeds God has planted,
Some of us blessed and planted on fertile soil,
Doomed the ones being planted on barren sand, what Satan wanted
Haunted by endless horror, endless turmoil.

But you my friend are the good seeds I am talking,
Don't let bad seeds make fools of you,
Only the blessed ones are the ones who are succeeding.

Success is as grand as the mighty evergreen,
And as vast as the true deep blue Texas skies,
Success comes the envy who bears the color green,
And success comes from the Man upstairs, the Man who never
lies.
—*David L. Cantrell*

Let It Be

There are times when there's no room for words and silence does
prevail. It seems as though the human race has stopped dead in
their trail. A time does come when life appears to become
unbearable, when all the world has turned into a disaster fairy
tale. These are times when I stop all that I do. I listen for
my timing, I listen for my cue. I try to hear the words that
are spoken unto me. I listen very hard, the words are let it
be. A song that comes to mind, the words aren't hard to find.
Just listen unto me, the words are let it be. She said the
time had come for all to hear and see. She also said it's time
for all to be free. She spoke the words again, those words
were let it be. They started softly, those words of wisdom,
those words let it be. I can hear them in my head, they're
calling out to me. An answered prayer had come true. The
answer she said, it's for all of you. It got even louder, and
a figure did appear. I knew who it was, so I put aside my
fear. It was Mother Mary, she came to me. She spoke the words
of wisdom, she whispered let it be.
—*Cindy Anderson*

My Golden Years

Living through the younger years....
Proud, unattached, and no great fears...
Finally met the man in my life...
Lived, loved and tried to be the perfect wife...
My perfect mate, with good looks and charm...
City bred, you didn't care if you lived on a farm...
The years we had together, were full of love
and sharing...
Our thoughts, our hopes and dreams, always caring...
But although we were just two years short
of our golden year...
I go along with loving thoughts,
As though he was still here....
—*Carmela M. Siciliano*

Stray Bullets

The sun showers down golden rays of light
Puffy white clouds float aimlessly above
Blues skies and butterflies dance to the rhythm of the wind
Birds sings and laughter rolls as children welcome in a
fresh new Spring

Pop, pop! Bang, bang! Laughter turns to screams
Pop, pop! Bang, bang! Gunfire shatters dreams

Blue skies turns dark
white clouds turn gray as sorrow and anger pave the way

Pop, pop! Bang, bang! Our children are dying
Pop, pop! Bang, bang! Our mothers are crying

Crying from grief
Crying from fear
Crying from loss of loved ones so dear
Pop, pop! Bang, bang!
No more Jessica
Pop, pop! Bang, bang!
No more Erica
No more Sally, no more Sue
No more Johnny see what Stray Bullets do
> —*Furman M. Simmons*

Aurora Borealis

Men pay to see an awe inspiring show,
Put on by those who make plenty of dough.

But I admire the drama God creates
Each evening for everyone without rates.

The many stars, like suns, give forth their light;
Making a beautiful majestic sight.

One act of the great drama I had not seen
Aurora Borealis was only a dream.

I beheld this awesome scene the other night,
The shimmering brilliancy of the Northern Lights.

The dome of the heavens were streaked with light,
Shining and dancing in the autumn night.

Men continue to marvel at this wondrous drama,
The Aurora Borealis, God's panorama.
> —*Howard F. Wolf*

An Ode To The Night Stage Light

Naked, but warm
Radiating dominance in the darkened theatre,
Protagonist without greasepaint or script
Keeping vigilance in solitude,
Making me glow inside.

Hours before
Forgotten, insignificant, pushed into the wings
While kings and clowns,
Characters, masked and unmasked
"Strutted their hour" on these very boards.

Why do you mesmerize me
As I behold your meager light?
'Tis surely because you guard
The domicile of my happiness
When created dreams move men to laugh, to cry.

Tomorrow, at rehearsal beginning
Struck carelessly offstage
While velour curtains rise and fall.
Forever watching, waiting thy cue
When thou again will reign on center stage.
> —*Connie Dillow*

One Last Tear

I smell the smoke before it is time.
Raising my eyes to the foggy signals,
A lonely tear slowly runs down my parched face.
Trying desperately to prepare myself for the coming moment,
I squeeze my lids shut and imagine a peaceful place.
With my heart racing, I see no pain,
When I breathe I feel no pain, I know it will be over soon.
The tears are burning my eyes, trying to escape their captor
   with no avail.
I am strong, too strong. I will not let another tear fall.
I look down on the hospital and see my lonely shell.
I smell the cleanliness and wish for better.
I am aware now, that I am better as a subconscious, for
   my conscious body allowed one last tear fall unnoticed and
   uncared for.
> —*Eileen Hill*

Autumn Night

Far out on the horizon
rays of sun, give a glimpse of day.
A chill sneaking in
while the day slips away.

Golden leaves of autumn
brown and red. A brilliance, oh so bold
begin to fall, spreading o'er the ground.
Like a brilliant blanket, there unfold.

Darkness creeping in, even darker.
The trees a shadow to the sky.
Till their leaves, look like lacy things
against the clouds up high.

Then as I take another peek
all, has disappeared from sight.
A quietness and serenity
on this autumn night.
> —*Anna M. Allison*

Shadows

As a child I listened to stories of old,
Read storybooks with tales of unknown lands
   and forgotten cities
   that now sit in dust and mold.
I remember the quests of courage
And the power possessed in a kiss,
The enchantment of the forests
And the granting of a wish.
I was also told stories of phantoms,
And the mischief of countless ghosts,
When I sat alone and thought they were there
I only had to close my eyes and dream them all away.
But the ghost that haunts me now,
He is faceless - he has no name,
Brings me nothing but shadows from my past
And the memories that still remain.
No matter how hard I try to forget,
Or how long I shut my eyes,
He still lingers in my memory
And follows me through time.
> —*Jennifer Lemmons*

Rachel

In a circle we stand holding hands with Rachel like soldiers
ready for battle. Silently the war rages within, devouring
strength and will. No mercy has this killer who feeds on
hopes and dreams. Childhood follies shatter and laughter is
replaced by tears and suffering. Each new day brings a promise
of pain and tomorrow never comes.
We are the chain and she is the link that holds us together.
There is so much love here, but will it be enough?
As the prayers are said I feel the tears sting my cheeks.
I am transfixed in the moment.
With quizzical eyes she watches; sunken eyes peering out.
Her smooth hairless head turns to watch each of us as we pray.
What is this child thinking so pale and frail?
Do her eyes seek our release or does she plead for our support
to stay? As she looks from one to another she locks her
gaze with mine. In that moment I know the answer. You have
fought the good fight Rachel. Go in peace.

—*Beth O'Connor*

Black Flight

Stars blink for shame
Red clouds scurry and break for the plain
While the peeping moon snatches a glimpse
of the impending pain.
Nature hums a bitter refrain,
Tears splatter the sky
While thunderbolts scream a questioning why?
Fallen souls leap like gigantic flies
Surpassing their numbness with their shrieking cries.
Get ye back Satan, you cannot cross the eternal
bounds where you must forever lie!

—*Gilbert M. Lane*

War

The sound of boots on muddy earth, a killing field which
regrets birth it stalks its prey like a hungry beast
A demon with fire who cares not of peace, in peace time it's
foul, yet now it's fair
to kill and demolish and leave the earth bare
With pre-sunken graves, which are dug with a shell
A hole in the earth, a passage to hell
Although hell sounds bad and eternal waste, nothing could be as
bad as this place
For up on the surface and not down below, the bodies are
stacked high, "who's arm?...I don't know"
But soon it is silent, the bodies are gone
A bright flash of light, no, it's not the dawn
A feeling of peace, the silence is back, the sun disappears,
the world is now black
As the burning snow falls from the sky, with each passing
moment, a human would die
Frozen like x-rays in the heat of the snow, there's no time
for dog tags, no Jane or John Doe no casualties, no sympathy
felt for satan's the dealer and your cards were dealt.

—*Anthony Lo Gerfo*

Two Wings

Two birds glittered through noon
scoping lively wooden rendezvous of hundreds
where on high then higher they glided
to where aerial laws carried all fliers afloat
naturally

When one unpassioned outgrew its feathers for wormling hunger
then wings of two broke to three
which in gale threw one to dive in miss of Moments pair
mindlessly

—*Edwin Quinabo*

Silent Circle

Floater, caring, semi-significant in the heart
replaced or replacing someone else
complete the circle
perform the rites
something begun
will become as cold and dark as the middle of the night
a clammy sick sticky

The set up
The evening, the breeze, the flirtatious ease
the beauty of it all
The ghostly feeling, eerie aura
as the spirits of past lovers walk around in your sacred space
and their words fall from this person's lips
the deja-vu
is this really happening to you - did you just step into a dream?
a mystical world you were once consumed by

A glass room - shattered bit by bit, until finally there is
nothing left but broken glass surrounding you amid the seedless
flowers

and silence pervades

—*Jana Murphy*

Simple Truth

If we kept a simple faith -
Respected the soul and not the flesh -
Balanced commitment with freedom -
Allowed ego and reason to mesh.

If we expected fathers to be Dad's -
Mothers to honor substance not style -
Brothers and sisters to share their hearts -
Individual lusts to be shelved for a while.

To reign in the hatred in our streets -
Protect little ones from the circle of abuse -
Love the planet that nurtures our existence -
Bind up our perversions and turn decency loose.

Respect each other as kindred spirits -
Follow the commandments and the golden rule -
Realize all men have the same needs -
Polish our character like a fine jewel.

God be with you one and all -
Have a nice day with someone who cares -
Improve yourself a little each day -
If I fall - maybe you will be there.

—*Fred Van Orsdol*

The Triangle Of My Life

The triple Rs, Job Responsibilities, Educational
Responsibilities and Family Responsibilities. Aren't these
triple Rs important in every family's life? Raising six kids
as a single parent has no much choice. Except to work harder
and achieve something everyday and every minute of my life. To
set an educational goal and look forward into the bright
future of my children. Training, family guidance, supervision
and self-discipline of growing kids need to start at home sweet
home. Teamwork, diligence, patience perseverance, strong
determination and fighting spirit are all the ingredients of our
accomplishments in our lives. Thanks God for blessing us
enough strength to cope with all these trials of life. Mom and
children are now professionals as I designed them all. We're
now planning to organize and established a family non- profit
organization. M and M Twins National Scholarship Foundation of
U.S.A. Its objectives to help, mold, guide and support young
scholars and future leaders of our nation. Ask not what your
country can do for your family but ask what your family can do for
your country.

—*Dollie Soriano*

Driftwood

Driftwood on the water, tossed by tide, wind and sand
restless waifs of forest, doomed to wander distant lands.
Some will drift forever, victims of the tempest breath
while others rest on lonely beaches, awaiting times rigid test.
Crumbling, cracking, bleaching, breaking, gone forever in
the night
some becomes the treasure, of some frugal searchers sight.

Ghostly shapes by moonlight, erie songs sung by wind
cold and callous feeling, like broken souls of men.
Like a million shapeless tear drops, cried for dreams that
don't come true
scattered over countless beaches, changing shape in days
first hues.
Then some caring hand caresses, a gnarled shape of the night
while the relic of abandonment, becomes a work of sheer
delight.

  —*Gene Sword*

Reunion

Eight long-parted brothers and sisters
 Reunited for a brief time...
Laughter, memory-sharing, eating
 Games, hugs, picture albums
Ninety-year-old Mom there,
 On leave from her nursing home
Sorrowful parting again after three days
Highpoints:
 Mom leading the Doxology in her yet-strong alto voice
  As all stood hand in hand around the food-laden table
 Words to all verses of all hymns still etched in Mom's
  memory
 Though she couldn't recall her own son's name
Mom, upon awaking the first morning,
 With a twinkle in her aged eye -
"Life is worth living after all!"

  —*Dottie Clark*

Our Lives

Not so sweet mysteries of our own human life,
Reveal far less love and joy than strife,
We go with thoughts cutting like a knife;

On-ward society moves much to rapidly along,
Giving some people a feeling they don't belong,
Riches hoarded by a few leaving many forlorn;

With speed and greed a common thing among us,
We dwell too often on sex with great lust,
With hurried tension leading us into discuss;

So little time we take for our self to see,
What makes you so very different than me,
Or even how much good was made by humanity;

Shouldn't we be in touch with our selves?
Shouldn't we get to know our inner selves well?
Weather it be cool or hot as the fires of hell;

Then once we see the realistic sight, you and I could
Get courage to act not just let the world go by.
Will we shape OUR LIVES? Or will OUR LIVES shape us?

  —*Gerald Al LeBlanc, Sr.*

A Walk

  Walk with me a way through life.
  Share with me your dreams and mine.
 And if our paths be separated let us part friends.
Let us look back on our walk and see that it was good.

  —*Henry J. Lawton*

God Manifest

A priest is standing in the temple; people in
robes and people in tatters file past,
muttering prayers and giving alms.
This is Religion.

A man is talking to a beggar; he is a friend
of people he has never seen;
He is poor.
This is Jesus.

A king lives on the street; he provides food where
there is nothing to eat and life
where there is only existence.
This is God.

  —*Henry Scholberg*

Sometimes

Like the rain that falls, such a trance it casts,
 rolling in on the tides of time.
Or the breeze that blows, whispered secrets gone past,
 breathing memories in the air.

Leaving no trace of the pastel hues of dusk,
 let the magnetic orb arise.
Embers at night, bore through an ebony sky,
 hallucinations of mystical powers.

With the rippling of leaves, the wind on the water,
 the droning hum of gods.
Tales told by mountains, cast in silence,
 the shroud of night unveiled.

I have lived all this, in a thousand dark nights,
 the thread woven in my words.
Like waves in the surf, the silence of the night,
 a song of unsung words.

  —*John Swertner Jr*

Racing

I don't stand a chance against beauty.
Running a race I know I can't win.
 Running fast and hard to the heart.
Knowing I'm too slow, only maybe one
 competitor at my heels.
Compassion haunting every step taken toward
 a love of understanding.
I don't stand a chance against him,
Against my own love.
 Taken too far into hopeful thoughts
 Meaning more to me then he can imagine.
Leaving me at the starting line
Beauty and age race so far ahead of my eyes.
 My hopeful heart leaps toward him with such
 force it hurts.
But to be asked to race with the highest rankers is an
 honor, even though he knows I shall lose to excellence.
I know I will never see him at the finish line.
But I can always hope for a miracle that comes
 from within the heart of love.

  —*Elizabeth W. Walsh*

Loving Thoughts

Tears fall down one by one as the day fades to night.
Searching for my love, I see you holding me tight.
Your gentle lips touch mine, that's when the sun begins to shine.
I must begin a new day so I may start to dream of you again.
My mind never rest as long as we are apart.
Till we next meet, I will hold loving thoughts in my heart!!

  —*Amy Sue Butler*

The Ghost Of My Childhood

Do you feel my childhood ghost?
Running through the meadows of home?
Is it finding its way?
Or is it looking at all?
I know that it is still there running through the woods and
fields of green.
Exploring all the secret thinking places only known to me.
Do you hear it calling to the wind or singing to the rain?
Or laughing gently to the song of the night birds as they sang?
Did you happen to catch from the corner of your eye, a shadow
of a child in the woods beneath the shade of the summer trees?
Or maybe you saw her dreaming lazily watching the clouds
pass softly by.
Why can't we go back to happier times
When things were simple and summer was long
Even though the road from childhood has left its loves behind
I feel as thought the road back there is helplessly entwined
With pain and joy the road is paved. And often I recall the
Simplicity in knowing the way the seasons fall.
To a child's young mind the way seemed so simple.
But finding the way back is not.

—*Ann Butts*

Where Once A Peaceful Garden Grew

A coming storm whispered warnings in the night;
Rustled restless shrubs and trees.
Flights of falcons, swift blown leaves and runaway dreams,
Like high kites, battled toward even loftier heights.
All revolved into spiraling dross;
Tossed down, down, down on the losing dice and lost
The rollicking wind let loose again.
Wantons and whirleys tousled the tallest trees;
Enjoined by choruses of lamenting spirits
Whaling nature's ageless rites.
Enormous billows of sanguine grey shrouded earth and sky.
Yet, equalling the mighty scapes cry
Was my weak child's silent sigh.
There where once the verdant earth and prism sky,
Whispered death's hello, goodbye,
A precious blossom huddled nigh.

—*Dorina Lynn Costa*

Easter Tribute To Momma:

Sad yes sad on this Easter day
sadness in our hearts cause Momma's gone away
First it was Thanksgiving and Christmas too
Easter is no better if there is no Momma for you

Next was her birthday so hard to let go
The Forth of July a day we all know
A day to remember from one year to the next
God gave Momma life now he is letting her rest

The love from her family love from us all
Momma was happy with our love she was tall
The love in our hearts from her children so dear
Love that won't die even though God took her from here

Now after one year the holidays have gone by
The memories in our hearts shall never die
So you show your mothers all the love in your heart
Cause God gave us our mothers from the very start

Now on October the sixth a day we shall all recall
The day that God took Momma away from us all
Holidays will be lonely cause Momma won't be there
With our love and memories of Momma we all can share

—*Barbara Fairchild*

I Am, I Said

I am my own! I am, I said, because I exist within the
sanctuary of my own free will.

If I error or make a mistake, it is because I have chosen
unwisely, not because another has led me astray!

When I succeed or fail, it is because I have made the right
or wrong choice.

I am, I said, my own! But, with my will, I can give myself to
anyone or anything, because I choose to.

I am my own until I give myself away, Even then, I can control
my own actions, limiting them to the course which I have chosen
the purpose there to be served.

The will to be good or evil, right or wrong, loving or hateful,
are within my power and control.

But when I met Him, I suddenly found direction, strength and
purpose. When I met Him, the loneliness and dark of night
became fleeing shadows in the brightness of his marvelous light

I am His, I said. His will to accomplish, His task to
complete. Now, I have chosen wisely. To sit at Jesus feet!

—*David Evans*

Isolation

In my moment of isolation
Saw your face in the corner of the room
Time stood still as my senses assess the aura of your being
Dismissing stirrings in my heart
Dark eyes consume me
Walk away don't hesitate
Too soon your presence invade my space
Mind reeling no escape
Anticipation rack my soul
Melodic music ripple from your voice
Two hearts beating to a mystery tune
Lost in this crowded room
Linger for awhile, seem like tomorrow
A stranger maybe a lover a friend

—*Deborah A. Xavier*

Human Rights

We here in the States
Say we believe in Rights. Throughout the World,
And like time, days and nights!

When the sun comes up/goes down
Small groups roam the streets.
Then cultures and in homes preach hate accomplished by feats!

Many use the Bible and interpret the meaning their way!
A history that happened years ago
But values and ethnics, they never say!

Why, oh why, do we hate?
But then, why oh why, do we love?
The word extreme is the block. Extreme prejudice.

Feeling strongly about an issue
Is your business, you see.
But when you want to pass a law
You are pushing your problem on ME!

Let us clean our own backyard
First, before we tell the world
About human rights and freedom!
Here, in America, the flag has not unfurled.

—*Jean K. Mathis*

Listen To The Message To Day

When I was asleep one night a voice came to me
saying, "Wake up and write!"

You must seek and praise God today. He's
coming back, oh yes, he's on his way! We're in
our last days. Matthew 4:7,8 says, "For nations
shall rise against nations, kingdom against
kingdom, and there shall be famines and
pestilence and earthquakes in divers places."
All of these are the beginning of sorrow.

Just listen to this message today. The Lord is
on his way, so get your house in order. He's
coming back, I'll promise you that! Matthew
24:44 says, "Therefore be ye also ready for such
an hour as ye think not the son of man cometh."

Just sit down and listen to your heart read your
bible each and every day. Try "God" in your life. You
don't have to go astray. Let go of that fast life.
Repent thyself and pray unto "God" for that
everlasting life. We should thank "God" in every
thing that we do, not just me but all of you.

—*Janice Franklin*

The Other Side

It is a war that surpasses all understanding
Searching for an explanation can take your mind for a ride
The solution screams out from behind bars of pride and pain
How can we ever see the light of the other side?

It is about color, it is about power, it is about difference
The battle belongs to no man, no victor, we all lose
Two opposing forces, one small division, one big unity
Still the dragon runs wild as each knight draws his sword to accuse

Animosity and ignorance infect our bloodlines
Leaving hopes and dreams of future generations denied
With vision impaired the children eat and drink from tables of fear
Will they ever see the light of the other side?

There is a truth that is sharper than the liar's tongue
There is a love that runs deeper than hatred's bite
There is a hope that calls louder than fear's scream
Grab His outstretched arm and hold on tight

See the truth, feel the love, hear the hope
Discover the variations of light through this kaleidoscope

—*Jason Taylor Stern*

Old Cherokee Chief

Rugged old man with your dark, weathered skin, I bet you have
secrets hidden from my view. You alone know the truth about
how it was back then; you know things that are known by only a
few. Tell me, great chief, all of the secrets you know. If
only you tell me I'll be able to understand things that only
you and I will ever know. Tell me of your people who once
roamed this land. Please let me in on the ways of the Cherokee
tribes. Share with me the victories of your days. Let me
understand a little about your lives. Tell me how it was when
you followed the old ways. Feeble old man who once stood tall
and proud, tell me just a little about the old days. Don't
keep your secrets hidden behind a cloud, tell me, great chief,
so I'll understand your ways. Tell me about the great chiefs
of old. Let me relive the life you led when you were younger.
Tell me of days when your braves went and stole, to keep you
from grieving over pangs of hunger. Tell me, O' Chief, for the
Great Spirit is near. Quickly, old man, tell me of your tribe
fate. Let go of your secrets for the Spirit is here. Never
mind now, old one, for it is too late. Now you can go where
you'll always belong, roaming forever on the vast grassy plain.

—*Brandi Lynn Nelson*

Talk

The tongue can be hurtful and very, very cruel.
Seems most of us have difficulty living by The Golden Rule.
Do unto others as you would have them do to you.
Is this really so difficult a concept to chew?

Seems some folk are insecure at their own game,
they derive a twisted comfort and pleasure from this shame -
the shame of not focusing on where their own faults lie.
They'd rather keep busy plucking specks from others' eyes.

That unkindness like this can exist is so sad.
That human nature isn't more evolved by now is too bad.
We hurt not only others, but a great deal we miss
by closed-up ears and busy tongues,
and by our close-mindedness.

When will we wake up and start to realize
how much beauty exists in all our varied lives?
Not much hope would I give for this world if, in fact,
we continue to refuse on The Golden Rule to act.

—*Christine Marie Riehman*

The Sea Gull Shrieks A Lonesome Cry

The roaring ocean is rough and blue,
sending fierce messages all through you.

The sea gull shrieks a lonesome cry

The sky has turned a dark, dark gray,
and all the birds have flown away.

The sea gull shrieks a lonesome cry

Everyone has gone inside, even the
mice have gone to hide.

The sea gull shrieks a lonesome cry

You shiver and shake and wish it'll go away,
then all of a sudden there is no more gray.

The sea gull shrieks a lonesome cry

The sun peeks out smiling again, and
all the birds come out from around the bend.

The sea gull shrieks a lonesome cry

The storm has gone away once more,
but it will be back for sure, for sure.

—*Dale Epstein*

Sunset Soliloquy

Scarlet sun, slowly sinking,
Sends smoldering spires streaming skyward;
Symbolizing spiritual splendor.

Seared scorched sea sighs softly,
Swallowing subdued sunset.

Swelling surf, scrolling shore ward, somersaults-
Sweeping sandy shoals.

Swirling sea salt sings, soul-stirring songs;
Scattered shells, sealed secrets spawn.

Somber shades soon still spangled sky.
Shifting shadows silently screen solemn scenes.

Sculptured silhouette simulates saintly ship;
Serenely sailing, scanning sea,
Sounding, searching, saving souls so seems.

Soulfully surveying stewardship; seeing sinful self,
Spirit's sharp sword swiftly strikes;
Severing self-sufficiency, slaying shielded stubbornness.

Scripture's salvation story simple signifies,
Saviour's supreme sacrifice solely satisfies.
Secured saints shall see sunrise.

—*Burton L. Goodrich*

New Life

One man, one woman embraced in love,
Sent a seed from up above.
Two people not knowing what the future
    will hold,
Not knowing the life they soon will mold.

One man, one woman together they pray,
Hoping to be good parents some day.
Planning and caring for a life which
    is near,
Their hearts filled with love,
    a little with fear.

One man, one woman always together,
In the form of a child forever and ever
His eyes, her nose each little part,
Blessed by the Lord, right from the start.
    —*Douglas W. Tatro*

Untitled

Two sparks wandering the night,
Separate but same, they struggle against darkness
Floating on breezes, adrift in the wind,
    Perchance to meet and cause fire!

At first only ember,
    Small and easily snuffed
    By the jealous wind.
Time as fuel, the glow gets brighter.

The forces of fear and insecurity
    Bring wind and rain
    To quench the blaze,
But fall like trees to the heat.

More fuel for the ember, more tiny sparks
    Causes the blaze to double.
    Strength in unity, power as one
    In them blazes divine light.

Log after log placed on the fire,
    Yet no chance of its dying
All consumed by the intense heat,
The burning love for one another.
    —*James Filmont*

The Unwanted Need

Walking lifeless among animated characters
Serrated from soul fed emotions
Venomous creature of foregone matters
Suppressing amorous thoughts into malignant
Reflexes of pain
Cupids target transformed into impenetrable muscle
The solidified organ becomes unable to be
Impregnated with the unwanted feelings of love
Cacophonous screams of loneliness are its only flaw
Guised as healthy it lies safe from harm
Safe from the evils of what could have been
Ritualistic acts of caring
Reflexes of the mind given without feeling
Traveling from one to the next, searching
Nothing to impede progression but the screams
The unwanted need
The hunger satisfied by reasons end
A choice between torments eternal
Chance a second impalement of love's pain
Or feign stoicism.
    —*Curt W. Groff*

I Love The Shore

So many hours I have spent walking its beaches.
Sharing my thoughts with the gulls and waves
And sometimes no thoughts in my head at all,
Just suspended in beautiful peace.
Walking under the blue winter sky
With just a trace of heat from the sun.
To hear the waves lapping up on the shore
And then receding to form the strength
To once again come rolling in.
Bringing with each wave a treasure from the sea.
A bleached white shell, small or large.
A piece of driftwood all salty and smooth
And sea glass- in many cloudy colors.
While overhead the sea gulls fly
So lovely and so effortlessly.
Most times I never see another person
But I like the shore alone, it's all mine
It gives up the secrets from the deep to me
And I share my deepest secrets with the sea.
It is my friend. I love the shore.
    —*Jean B. Welton*

Dream Girl

She lives half way down the block
She always blushes, when we meet,
With a graceful... Girlish walk
My heart jumps.." and skips a beat"

    Her smile makes me dream of spring
    When nature builds colorful meadows,
    Surely, new hopes the season shell bring
    As the brook swells, gurgles and flows.

To hear her voice, so tender and sweet
My heart jumps.. "and skips a beat"
Is it possible..now-aday to find
A heart so loving, so true and kind?

    I watch the robin, as he chirps and fret
    Perched on her porch..though cold and wet,
    Doesn't he have anything better to do
    Or does he love her ..as much as I do?

"True, she's so bashful ..we hardly talk
Though she greets me, with a smile so sweet,
With that graceful... girlish walk
"""My heart jumps...and skips a beat"""
    —*Emilio Iannuzzi*

She Was Just Three

She was only three when she went away,
She came in June and she left in May,
But she left behind a sweetness here,
And we cherish each thing her touch made dear.

We hold her image close in our minds,
And many a moment there's someone who pines,
For the gay little laugh and the fingers small,
That twined about the hearts of us all.

I can see her yet with her tumbled locks,
And the mud-pie stains an her bright little flocks,
When she'd stand and laugh in baby glee,
On the old worn path 'neath the apple tree.

I remember the races we used to run,
And it seemed just right that she always won,
How her eyes would sparkle and her pink cheeks glow,
As she ran as fast as her legs would go.

But now there'll be no laugh and there'll be no smile
For she only came for a little while,
And all that's left is memory,
For she went away when she was just there.
    —*Florence McIntire*

605

Alzheimer's

Grandma's eyes are lost.
She can't see.
Senile.
Before the disease I remember her
full of love.
The granny who makes cookies, just for me.
Alzheimer's.
She lives in a nursing home.
Not knowing even how to bathe herself.
Helpless.

—*Brie Todd*

Marie

I have a friend that is older than me.
She is elderly, lonely, and afraid to be.
  Eleven years ago her husband died
   And not a day has passed since
    That Marie hasn't cried.

    She lives in a room
   That is exactly the same
As it was when her husband
   Gave her his name.

  And now that her family
  And friends have passed,
  Marie sits and wonders
  How long must she last?

—*Holman Turner, Jr*

My Destiny

She is my Destiny, She is my only need.
She is my life, She is why I breathe.
I am her protector, She will never feel the rain.
I am her best friend, I will ease her pain.
She is my challenge, I will never rest.
She is my motivator, I will always give my best.
I am her partner, together throughout life.
I am her comforter, I keep her from the strife.
She is my only need, with her I am whole.
I am nothing without her, for She controls my soul.
To hear her voice, feel her touch, I will wait forever.
She is my only love, I will leave her never.
My only wish from God above, is for She to be with me.
My search in life is now complete, for I have found my Destiny.

—*Frank Notarnicola*

The Fast End

Don't let it happen to you, what happened to my friend
She thought she'd never die, not until her road came to an end
But when she got infected with HIV Aids
I never knew how much a difference I could have made.
As I sit here now, I think of the times we shared
Back in first and second grade, without make-up and permed hair
I still remember at recess we'd play all sorts of games
And, kidding with the guys, we never meant anything by names
Back then everything and everyone seemed so carefree
We could still be like that; love for mankind is the key
But when we reached Jr. High we turned our separate ways
If only she would have turned with me, I still think today.
After being such close friends, you'd think we'd never be torn
   apart
But she wanted to be "popular", and left me with a
   friend-broken heart
Some blame it on the Lord, that she died at such a young age
But it was the devil who made her feel cornered in a dark cage
Please, young people, don't be like my friend
Whose road of life, too soon, came to a sudden end.

—*Jessica G. Tucker*

Foul Weather Blues

She usta' love me yesterday -
She usta' come outside to play
But sunshine has been turned to night -
And shadows block the mornin' light
And these five words are hard to say -
She usta' love me yesterday.
I usta' be her love, Oh my!
A gleam of light in her eye
But things were just subject to change -
Now all my days are filled with rain.
But frantically I'll search the sky -
For a rainbow painted way up high -
But the colors seem so far away -
She usta' love me yesterday.

—*Frank T. Torpila*

Violet

Violet is my new dog. As happy as can be.
She was already named Vile.
I changed it to Violet, a pretty dog to see
she is shetland sheep dog
as barky as can be.
The first day we walked her
she barked at the trees, the birds,
and the squirrel to see.

Violet will gently climb up in your lap
and lay her little head
gently on your hand.
You really have to hug her
she's as cute as cute can be
her fur so soft and clean to pet,
she'll lick you on your knee.
Someone was mean to her,
she hides a lot today.
But now she's much better
and happier to be
Violet my new dog she is all love to me.

—*Blanche Colombo*

My Baby Sister

I knew her better than anyone knew.
She was my friend, she knew me too.
We knew each other's smiles and tears,
We were so close for so many years.
I think of her now, the way she had been;
And I wish, somehow, I could have seen
The way she was headed, the way things were going.
But, some people say that it's better not knowing.
My baby sister, so loving, naive.
Why couldn't those people just up and leave,
Instead of taking advantage of her.
I had always hoped for "the way we were."
But now, because of her trusting nature,
Her door opened to brutal murder.
Beaten and stomped on her bedroom floor,
I wish I knew to whom she had opened that door.
Two little girls, now with no mother;
Her mom and dad, her sister and brothers.
No, baby sister will never return,
I just wish I could tell her how deeply I yearn.

—*Ginger Duty*

Divine Alchemist

Stepped forth from the droplets of blood,
She was not hatched. Born,
She was not tucked away in the stages
Of the embryo,
Stepped not from the sea.
She came straight away from the death
Of Chronos' manhood.

Spewed forth from desire,
She was created without the
Union of mother and father,
Symmetry through spontaneous
Generation.
No beginnings, out of dust.

She was perfection.
Forever still in stone,
Prisoner in her captured beauty,
Trapped in her look of love.

Her Affaire d'Amour with man, beast, god
Stirred passion in souls,
Turned lead hearts into melted gold.

—*Diana Lee Pao*

My Wife

I met a lady one winters night;
She was young and fair and such a delight.
She was beautiful as all could see;
I still don't know what she saw in me.
I asked her one night to be.
My wife for all eternity.
She answered me, "Yes I will be".
And stood up in front of friends and family.
The preacher asked,
"Will you take this man for your husband to be?"
She answered, "I will, for all eternity."
She gave me two daughters to my delight.
For me she bore all the pain and strife.
She takes care of our every need.
Never once thinking of her own personal needs.
She makes us happy each and every day.
Not once has she asked us to repay.
Her love is unending for you see,
she gave her love for all eternity.

—*Joe Alan Hamblin*

Woman

All alone on a sultry evening
   she weeps alone, but not by herself,
For her memories of bygone days
   Are embracing her with their warmth.

A simpler time without all the worries
   A simpler time without all the pain,
For nothing can turn back the clock
   Or the searing anguish that lies within her heart.

Words of regret, words of anger, escaped
   from her lips in just an instant
But that moment has turned into a lifetime
   filled with emptiness and sorrow.

For that one yesterday, in a twinkling
   of an eye, has become a life of meaningless tomorrows.

She's aching for love to return to her soul
   But she knows it can never be.
So as she slowly shuffles out into the sunset
   She let's the warm breeze consume her
   burning passion and yearnings,
   so she at last can be free...

—*Christine Keeler*

Moon Of The Painted Leaves

She alone, danced to the Harvest Moon
   She, who had waited an eon of time
Dawn, who was fairer than all,
   Danced and bowed alone before her Master
on a hilltop.
Gliding moths came to dance with her on soundless wings
And the wind wizard paused upon his aimless journey
   to dance with her
But she sent him on his way.
And into this pale emerald light
Came swallow tails dipping before the moon
And gilded branches lifted their arms unto Heaven
   Spilling their colors upon the earth
Mingling their whispers with the mauve and green shadows
   And a fragrance wafted from a vineyard
Fell with a winey breath upon the dancers
And of a sudden, a faint glow touched Dawn
She paused, suspended in mid air, shook her murky hair,
And with a swirl of dew spangled garments
   Dawn vanished, on soundless feet.

—*Dorothy Murphy*

To My Granddaughter Karen Marie

Little Karen is so full of love,
She's as soft as an Angels' kiss.
She fills our lives with laughter
This smiling, bubbly little miss.

To hold her hand in mine,
Fills my heart with joy.
To hear her happy eager voice
As she discovers each new toy.

As I watch her, I travel back in time,
To when her Mama was just her size.
It brings to mind so many memories
To see the mischief behind those laughing eyes.

She's very special to Nana,
In her own sweet little way.
With a beautiful smile and big blue eyes,
She's a precious darling, I'm so glad she came to stay.

—*Bea Bon Durant*

My Precious Rose For The Wedding

Rain-drops come it could not hide
Shining sun with glitters of jewels
Drops of rain on velvet petals
Beauty shone with elegant pride
A majestic rose, swaying gracefully, in the
summer breeze
In a garden a treasured beauty.
Can it be reserved for a bride to be?
When June's lustrous blossom is present in time
The stranger saw beauty, he admired what
A joyful secret to keep, with a prize in mind
Bridal party marched in procession
A ceremony of the wedding begun
My precious rose in a bouquet, they praised, I won
with radiant beauty, my precious rose in blossom.
Time, ceremony, marriage proposed Love.
Its magnificence appeared from heaven above.

—*Inez Kobus*

When I Close My Eyes

To close my eyes is to see you there
Shrouded in moonlight, slaying the fear
Your softness searching for long ago knights
When candles danced to passions delights

I sense you haven't been here for sometime
Maybe it isn't what you had in mind
So radiant beneath the smoke filled lights
So perfect in detail, so lost in the night

It's easy to escape to far away places
With golden sunsets, white sand beaches
Gazing into soft pools, full of fire
Quenching the thirst of human desire

I sail away into dreamy delight
Winged on the scent of perfumed lullabies
So softly I'll try and sway this flower
Who haunts my every waking hour

When I close my eyes!

—*Gene Grasso*

Chrysalis

i wait
silently in the shadows
"hold" button firmly pressed
until You
with the lonely desperation of no-one-knows
turn from the cold light; and
find Me.

—*Janel Atwood*

A Child's Cry

A lonely child cries in the night.
Since her mommy's out of sight.
Why do some people think it's best?
Saying her mom is worse than the rest.
Taking her away from her only home.
Now she has no mother. She's all alone.

Another mom tries to take the first one's place.
A different mom's name and a new mom's face.
The child feels guilt, if she loves the new.
Still loving the old, she tries to be true.
Years pass fast, but the confusion stays.
Lost between two moms and love in many ways.
Which mom loves her most? Which mom to call?
But worse, what if neither mom loves her at all?

Now there's a third woman, she's glad she's met.
She wants to call her mom and love her, yet,
so many walls, she has built over the years.
Jealousy and envy have caused so many fears.
Not understanding love, the why and the how?
The lonely adult child, she still cries now.

—*Connie Whitmore*

An Eagle's Flight

An eagle's flight is a beautiful sight.
So peaceful and so calm;
Fly so high in the sky, higher than the eye can see,
Higher than some mountain peaks.
With his wings spread so wide apart.
Brown and white and his white bald head.
The eagle glides along the clouds,
Like an airplane, he soars so gracefully.
How could a person not appreciate this sight?
A sight too beautiful for human eyes!

—*Cheryl Marino*

Why Do We Fight?

Every war which America has fought in we have participated.
Since the beginning of slavery, we knew we would be
    emancipated.
Through all of the floggings and hangings,
We were able to get out of the tanglings.
Slavery was to be abolished in 1808.
We thought this would be great.
But to our dismay we continue to wear the chains.
And our oppressors continue to inflict the pains.
We have no more cheeks to turn.
The sparks in our hearts are beginning to burn.
Our oppressors whip us, day and night.
Our oppressors hang us, day and night.
Our oppressors rape us, day and night.
Our oppressors kill us, day and night.
And you still want to know, why do we fight?

—*DAHCASS*

The Hummingbird

I saw a hummingbird sitting outside my window,
    singular for an active bird.
  It stared steadfastly ahead, then looked up, unheeding of my
    intense gaze.
  I dared not breathe aloud, lest it hear me and fly away,
  It was so tiny - no bigger than my thumb.

I saw the city in the distance,
  Babel towers of glistening steel,
  Fingers jabbing at God's face.
  Window-eyes surveyed the surrounding landscape of man-made
treasures.
  Everywhere men designed, schemed, and cancelled out the
Deity's
    existence.
  "Are we not Gods?
  Cogito ergo sum," they echoed in voices petulant and self-
satisfied.

My eyes fell back on the hummingbird.
  It surprised me to find it still sitting there.
  Almost somberly, it lifted up; gossamer wings beating
    furiously against the unmoving air.
  It flit back and forth, more rapidly now, examining this
    leaf and that, hovering and parading before me,
    glossy, sleek and resplendent in plumage of emerald and black,
    perfection in motion.

Then quite clearly, I heard God cough, stir and laugh.

—*Bella B. Villeza*

Summer Breeze

Sitting out on a warm summers night;
Sipping our coffee is a delight:
The only thing that can possibly compare;
Is the evening breeze of the Gulfs fresh air:
The sound of the locust and the crickets cheep.
Is enough to make me weep;
After years of cancer and my husbands heart disease;
We've learned to see and hear, what will please;
Don't let the sound of a whip-o-will or the lovely blue sky;
Just up and pass you by;
Look and listen and take it from there;
Enjoy everything that God has put here:
Sometimes we take life for granted and turn a deaf ear;
We're brought down, only to live in fear;
Drop to your knees and thank God for all of these;
Rise to your feet and with God's help
    your fears will ease -

—*Fran Cook*

Earth Goddess

Daughter of the sun
Sister to the stars
Mother of Man

She who is the embodiment of beauty
The vessel of strength
And the bearer of life.

I need your support
Your strength
And most of all your love.

Because without you there is no me.
The love you give is my life's energy.

And my life I pledge to you to protect, respect, and love.
Until the earth crumbles away, the moon spins out of orbit,
and the sun disappears from above.

So, oh beautiful Ebony Queen, Goddess of this earth,
Take me as your partner,
And let us rebuild this ravaged universe.

For we who are the firstborn must return together hand in hand
To reclaim the Power, Respect and Prestige we as a couple, once
had at our command.

—*Charles L. Calvin*

Jibbesama

Basking in the darkness of my well lit room,
Sitting in the light of my darkened soul.

Wishing I had someone to hold,
Only finding someone to scold.

Cheerfully thinking of gloom and doom.
(That rhymes with the first line.)

I found my son and daughter in the bedroom.
Both dead, gunshot wound to each of their heads.

Blood all over the bedspreads,
I look at the record player.

The Monkees greatest hits.
Why couldn't it have been slayer?

This is really the shits.
I haven't got a case,

The judge will laugh right in my face.
So I guess I'll go out and get a case.
(Of Millers that is)

—*Chris Benedetto*

My Horse And Buggy

She was just an old nag, so the neighbors said,
Sleepy and slow and easy to catch.
Gramp' Johnson, likewise, was old and slow,
Barely able to get to his tottering feet.
I can scarcely remember the range of the chores
That he would assign to me,
As I attempted to help, without complaint,
And did what I could for free.
Well really not "for free" as occasionally,
He would slip me two-bits or four.
So rich was I when he gave me Nell
And threw in the old buggy, as well.
Earthly possessions of mine were meager.
A twelve-year-old boy don't need many,
So ownership of a horse and rig,
would change my life a plenty-and it did.

—*Chester A. Wilson*

"The Little Clown" In An Art Gallery

Funny little so-sad-clown,
Sitting there upon the ground,
Painted grin; red bulbous nose;
Floppy shoes with painted toes,
Red wig sitting all askew;
Baggy pants; a shirt of blue,
The circus gone; they left you
In this place.

No others wear your white-clowns face,
Your silly grin,
Baggy pants, pulled up to chin.

Will someone come, take you in;
Dry your tears; help find your kin?

If I could, I'd take you down;
Repaint your tears to joyous eyes;
Hush your fears and frightening sighs.

But, Alas, I have no brush;
No way to hush,
The sadness of "The Little Clown".

—*dep campbell*

Wyoming

Haunting open plain tucked beneath majestic mountains
Skyward, waterfalls rush to the river below
Crystal sheets of icy blue - misty water - colored hues
Timeless

Peaceful grazing buffalo roam oblivious to man
Unaware of the struggles their forefathers endured
Braced against the wind - solitude within their world
Ageless

Breathless beauty paints the wilderness below the jagged Tetons
Yellowstone's natural wonders captured on a canvas of soil
Autumn leaves begin to turn - glow of aspen's yellow burn
Changes

Setting sun on the western horizon
Trailing clouds enshroud the last few rays of sunlight
After-glow fires the sky - unparalleled beauty fades to darkness
Turning

Shadows frame the devastation left by man's careless hand
Fertile, verdant forest erased as fire engulfed the land
The strength of mother nature, scars and shapes the future
Passing hands of time

—*Jeffrey A. Sater*

Indigo River

The river slips along, tripping over rocks,
sliding smoothly past submerged Jim Bean bottles —
pausing to suck at the contents — then
rushing on with liquid laughter, splashing,
swirling, to the sea.

The screech of a nosy Kite bird ripples
the quiet. At dips in the river bank, calm pools
mirror trees and sky. Trout come to spawn,
leaving their eggs — like airplanes
that jettison fuel — spread out to be fertilized,
then to hatch.

Wild chives scent the air with onions. Day
slips along with the river, bright blue
changing to indigo. Celestial lights
cast pale halos around a solitary
wild red rose.

—*Dana Qualls*

Holding Hands

Holding hands was the first thing we did when the
slightest of feelings began to develop. Then came the good
night kiss that was as light and gentle as a feather, but, oh
so effective.
Letters zipped back and forth through the mail until
you returned from your long distance job. Then the strangest
thing began happening on sundays as you left for you
journey back to your other world.
I cried. But why? I wondered.
Laying in my bed at night, the essence of your cologne
and your dark smiling eyes filled my long lonely nights.
Even now after these many years of being your wife, I
still do not understand why my heart races just a bit when
you reach for my hand. I wonder will I ever? No, I tell
myself.
It's love and no-one understands love!

—*Imogene Westcott*

Untitled

When I am alone, isolated in my deathly frigid chamber, you
slowly enter my soul and rape my serenity. Soon experiencing a
dearth of control, my head sinks deep into my pillow and I
begin to open. As the sweat beads glide onto my quivering
lips, I could taste my fears. Your painful love continues to
rip through my weak body every second, deeper and deeper.
My will has been annihilated joining my frozen, hollow heart in
the vast caverns of irreversible evil. I can feel an immense
pressure
hovering over my lungs as I gasp for air. The left and right
hemispheres of my brain begin to collide like clock work gone
mad. As you complete your impish deed, I feel a rush of
emptiness as you escape my inoperative body. Laced in the
depths of uncertainty, I remain frightened, yet comforted.

—*Gina Dorak*

Lacy Comes Home

Daughter Marian knows that Mother is lonely at times
so a remedy she sought to find.
The animal shelter was a logical place to search,
she thought.

Lacy licked her hand at first introduction:
Her heart was touched.
Finding all in order for the transfer -
homeward bound she went.

Training for a California trip began, a new owner to inherit.
With ease she learned the basics for a solitary Mobile
Park life. Next, the flight from Texas to California was
accomplished triumphantly. Even finding comfort in the
travel cage secured just for her.

Surrounded by cats and dogs confined to homes like her,
with leashes only allowed for walks sparingly and her security
cage door left open until times left alone she adapted well,
content to be loved and to love in her new home.

If you need a lacy friend to fill the gap - yield to the
gift of love from a caring child and enjoy the relationship you
can have with a pet who needs your love too.

—*Florence Ray Franklin*

My Star

My star shines brightly in the heavens,
　so bold and so true
My star shines brightly in the heavens,
　to remind me of you
My star is so beautiful, it is seen from place to place
It's like the twinkle within your eye upon your innocent face
My star is like an angels tear in the nighttime sky
It helps me remember you when you say good-bye
My star shines brightly in the heavens,
So lovely and full of effervescence.
My star shines brightly in the heavens,
It reminds me of your presence
It looks down on me as to watch over me
I know deep inside that you put it there for my eye to see
For you sweetheart have the power to make them all glow
As they glow they look like a big smile for me from you
They light the path of love and tell me you love me so
My star shines brightly in the heavens,
What makes it special is that it's mine
My star shines brightly in the heavens,
It'll keep us together till the end of time

—*Chris Coulter*

Needed Time

The entire world,
So confused and rushed,
Needs time to reduce the level of noise
And allow the chaos to be gently hushed.

So as I walk alone
The welcomed solitude is uncommonly quiet.
The dusk brings on a soft glow
And I am gratefully calmed by it.

The rust colored leaves flutter around in a circle
As the sweet-smelling air flows by in a breeze.
I feel the troubles as they leave me
And are forgotten with ease.

This space is needed to unravel my thoughts
And is time to think about everything
With help from the nightingales
As they soothingly sing.

The peacefulness is here now
Where I tranquilly lay,
So I go back to my home with it restored once more
And will return as usual, the following day.

—*Alison Palazzolo*

The Sea

So free and open
So deep and blue
With sun light you sparkle
With moon light you shine.
I sit and look at you everyday
Taking you for granted in every way.
You hold such wonders
You astonish me so.
I look at you now
And I wish I could know.
Your fish swim around all night and day
Each and every one hoping they're not a fisherman's next prey.
Your beautiful mammals—seals, dolphins, and whales
About these glorious creatures many sea captains tell tales.
All of your creatures with their little task.
Go about their business no questions they ask.
The ocean so glorious both when it sparkles and shines.
I am breathless when I think all of this is mine!

—*Alayna Lynn Wilson*

Lord: From Three To Five: I Come Alive:

My mind runs like a computer out of control
So fast the words in rhyme 0 are on a roll,
My memory of good and bad are printed on a scroll.
In the early morning hours, before day break
So many lines on a picture mind, like tape to take.
It is like a fresh flowing stream
It is all real, I'm awake, it's not a dream.
For years, I slept to escape the bad,
Now He said, "AWAKE!" and I'm glad.
As in life all things I now must confess
My half closed eyes, I stumbled through the mess.
The Lord, is giving me a new release
With His, ongoing thought power, never to crease.
And so whatever He, now brings to mind
I will take pen in my hand and find,
I my time to rhyme life from behind.
The love and depths of His showing
My answers for the truth knowing.

—*Dorothy I. Brown*

Never Before Was Spring

Never before was spring so beautiful,
So filled with life and song and radiant hue!
Surely, the birds have sung their loveliest notes
Since I met you.

Never before have April rainbows shone
Through every glistening raindrops as they do.
Never, to me, has opening blossom seemed
So sweetly new.

Heaven could tell, perhaps, but I cannot
How you have wrought this miracle of spring.
Angels may know how loving you has made
The whole earth sing!

—*Faith Cornwall*

Passing By

I visited earth; I was just passing by.
So for those who loved me please don't cry.
I'm gone home to rest in peace; thank God almighty my soul
has been released.
For those who knew me and greeted my loving smile, truly
made visiting earth worth my while.
So rejoice my brothers and sisters in Christ; I've seen you
once and I will see you twice.
Only this time it will be a glorious sight; no more hatred sin
or pain, but everlasting life that will remain.
I visited earth but I was just passing by.
So those who loved me please don't cry.
I'm gone home to rest in peace; thank God almighty my soul
has been released.

—*Jackie Wilson*

To A Sick Friend

I awoke this morning, with you on my mind,
So I'm writing these thoughts, because you're so kind.
The lives you have touched, whether great or small
Are fully enriched, by the wonder of it all.
God's love shines through you, like a great beam of light,
And makes the darkness disappear and everything be bright.
He will carry your burden, and he won't let you down,
You'll again wear your smile, and not wear a frown.
Because through his mercy, miracles can be,
Through prayer and meditation, the answer you will see.
God bless you and keep you safe from all harm,
Just trust in him, and he'll keep you in his arms.
We all love you and appreciate everything you do,
With God's blessing, you'll come through this like new.

—*Betty R. Lane*

White Crosses

White crosses stand, row on row,
So I may pause to see, then know
Who it was that gave a life so dear
That I might go on living here.
Their bodies lie beneath the sod
But there souls are at home with God.

As I gaze at those crosses, white,
Which point toward God, both day and night,
I do not ask, nor should I care
What was the color of who lies there.
He gave his life that I might gain.
He fought and died. Did he die in vain?

He did not pause, he did not stop,
He gave his life to reach the top.
He died for me as for his mother;
Should I do less than call him brother?
If he died in vain, I must ask why?
This I must answer; and only I!

—*Francis D. Thomas*

The Flood Of 1993

The rain came down day after day
So the rivers soon filled and rushed along on their way
Rain again and the rivers could hold no more.
And the flooding began as in days of yore.
More rain gradually covered the crops near by
This is more than we can handle the crops gave a sigh
Then the water entered all the towns and cities in its path
It entered peoples homes and businesses with a muddy bath
A song says "How high is the water mama?"
As it rose higher and higher leaving people in trauma,
Homes and possessions and business places were lost
By that powerful force that stops at no cost.
Everyone worked hard helping each other
with sand bagging and cleaning up, oh brother
Hearts go out to everyone who went through this great ordeal
It's hard to believe that all this could be real
All the destruction that was caused by a rain that would not stop.
Now brave people must recover from losing so much, some a
    crop.
May the Lord watch over all as they get back on their feet.

—*Helen Irwin*

What's In A Poem: Websters' Wisdom That's What

There is a special rhythm in printing of a poem
Some do it with others and some do it alone
Poems consist of derivatives formed by 1-2-3
And also letters of alphabet via A-B-C
They further build by idioms sometimes hard to find
And consist of formation of words not always in rhyme

A poem can project a story never yet been told
And lightens up a reader young, mid-age or old
The core of truth in poetry is usually plain to see
For its readers of interest meaning you and me

Some poems are printed mixed with lies
Which readers must determine helping them be wise
A plain and simple poem may be musical in sound
When and if the rhythm of it is found
While reading a poem left to right up to down
People places and things are identified as noun

Sharing letters and words to make a poem
Can be a fun thing while in our home
Poems may also be re-written in a book or song
And we can ascertain whether it's right or wrong.

—*Jay F. Parker*

A Creature's Prayer

O God, creator of us all,
Some think us dumb and most of us are small;
May man hear our urgent call,
Before so many of us fall
Into extinction or, a lab, worst of all;
Protect us from the factory farms,
The puppy mills, the crate,
The shooting arms;
Our hearts are warm and giving
and just like man, we enjoy living
A free and happy life;
Please God relieve us
Of so much stress and strife.

—*Edwina R. Barnes*

Sisters

We were a large family of girls
Some with straight hair, some with curls
Eight of us all in a row. Why was this? Who knows.
Mother sometimes was distraught
Because all her girls had to be taught
To love one another and get along.
We tried to obey but not for long.
Our clothes went down the line and even our shoes
Housing was difficult so we had many moves.
Food was scarce many a time
But mother always managed rather fine.
Taken to tears because of us
We often tried not to make a fuss
As we grew and the years went by
Not very often did mother cry.
We are all married and mother passed away
If she could see us I know she would say
I love my girls for what they are
To me, they are all a star. The years have sped and gone away.
But all our memories are here to stay.

—*Irene Beaulieu*

Hurricane Andrew

Mother Nature, they called him, and yet
Somehow that title seems justly unfit
The thrashing of wind, the pounding of rain,
And who could forget the sound of that train.

Trees that once stood proud and tall
Were left bare and broken if they were left at all.
In that one fearful night our lives torn apart
Our homes and our keepsakes, left shattered, like our hearts.

A generators' hum would lull us to sleep
We prayed the Lord our soul to keep
Months without electric, and few telephones
Everyone's a victim, but still, feel alone.

With strength from above and pride from within
The rebuilding process would slowly begin
Neighbors helping neighbors, blood, sweat and tears
We tried to ease the children's fears.

Yet - from out of that darkness
A new light burns bright
To think a hurricane lit it
One dark August night.

—*Jill Lori Boone*

Something Very Bad

Something is happening, something very bad
Something is happening, and it's making me sad
You may not see it now, or you may not even care,
But someday when I'm gone,
You'll wish that you were there.
You'll wish you could go back,
to replace what we will lack.

But by the time we reach that stage,
you'll be too late in age.
I don't want to lose you,
You're all I've got.
I don't want to lose you,
You're everything I'm not.
So please do something before it's too late,
Let's try to change this horrible fate.

—*Janice Marie Montalvo*

What Does Love Mean To Me

Love is something to be treasured
Something no one person can measure
It is always a true friend
From now until the end
Being there for me and me for you
When we are scared or blue
Love is being honest no matter what
Whether it will hurt or not
It is to be able to trust with all your cares and fears
To cry with my love through all the years
To hold when I need to be held
To kiss when I need to be kissed
Love is true through all you say and do
Love is to share all these feelings with you
This is what love means to me
What does love mean to you?

—*Amy JoAnne Evans (12/8/86)*

Why Did It Have To Be Me?

Why God? Why did it have to be me? How could I receive
something so horrible from thee, I prayed every night in my
head, yet he still came to my bed. He is an adult but he still
doesn't understand the pain, but you do God, are you letting
the angels cry for me in the rain? I try to close my eyes
tight so I don't have to see his face. But it still cannot
hide all the shame and disgrace. The only time I feel safe is
in my dreams, that's where I can be a real princess or a queen.
Yet now even in my dreams there's nowhere to run or hide, for
he still finds a way inside. Please god try to protect me,
can't he realize that he is doing wrong and let me be. I just
want to live my life, but God you have to remove the knife.
From my heart, you see I've never had a chance from the start.
So now I'm doing what has to be done. I'm saying good-bye,
take care of mother and don't let her cry. Tell her I will
never forget thee, but I guess it had to be me.

—*Deanna M. Hicks*

Good Morning Winter Wonderland

Up in the morning outside the glass
Snow has come finally at last.
People laughing and playing,
Jumping, dancing, and down hill sleighing,
Snowball fights, making snow men,
But now mother says it's time to go in.
So good night world so glittering
See you tomorrow when little birds are twittering

—*Jeanette Quibell*

Censorship

Freedom of speech has long been our right,
Something we must protect, even if we must fight.
However, lately it seems to be in jeopardy,
And I find that very frightening to me.

Government telling newspapers what to write,
On the premise it's wartime, and it will protect
   the men who fight.

People losing their jobs, having fines they must pay,
Because others disagree with the things they say.
Punished for freely expressing what they feel.
America - Can this be real?
If that is their crime for expressing their views,
Will we be punished one day for expressing ours?

Wake up America! Take a closer look!
You need not agree with the words to a certain song,
   poem or book.
That is your opinion, and your right, okay?
You can say what you must say.
But to stand in silence at Freedom's door,
We can lose this freedom, and be free no more.

—*Frances Mancuso*

Untitled

Knowing you takes me to the highest highs and the lowest lows,
   Sometimes I think, "Why I care so much- God only knows."

We are two souls joined by an inseparable bond,
   One of Friendship, Love and Something Beyond.

Together we are nurturing and fulfilling,
   Apart - lost and desperately seeking.

Your smile dispels the clouds of gloom and doom,
   Bringing radiant sunshine into the room.

The sound of your laughter chases the demons from my soul,
   And brings warmth where once there was cold.

Your touch makes my mind race with Dreams of Ecstasy,
   Dreams that dance just outside Reality.

You are Part and Parcel of my Life,
   Without you I would know only misery and strife.

As difficult as life sometimes is with you,
   I know it would be worse without you.

So, I offer all - my Friendship, my Heart, my Life and my Soul,
   Keep them safe and don't let them grow cold.

Sift them through your soul, separate the chaff from the wheat,
   And remember, not all loves are nice and neat.

—*Johnny D. May*

Life Of Man

   Life is like an ocean, ever changing ...
   Sometimes turbulent, oft times wrought with
            pain and anguish.
Churning, ever turning, like a ship without a mast,
   Today is present, yesterday is past ...
      Upon life's shore man casts his bread,
         One day follows another ...
As do stitches, sewn evenly with needle and thread.
Yet it is for tomorrow, man must venture once anew,
      Cast out ashes of his yesterdays,
            lest life vanish from
                  his view.

For life is real and life is earnest. Let not mere
            yesterdays
      Set a man nor his life askew

—*C. Lynn Clark*

A Miracle

Miracles come in different shapes and sizes large and small,
sometimes surprises

We don't always know when or where it is going to come, all we
know is that God sends us some

In the early morning or late at night the Lord knows when the
time is right

Each one of us are miracles, but today we're talking about one
miracle the Lord made and with his blood the price he paid

This miracle is our Pastor sent down from above by the hands
of the Master

When we think of what the Lord brought her through and what he
continues to do we realized more and more that she is a miracle

We thank God for her unyielding love and continuous faith, that
encourages our heart in this Christian race

She teaches, preaches, counsels, and prays always instructing
us to do things God's way

It doesn't matter what you need she shares God with you in
word and deed

Yes miracles come in all shapes and sizes large and small, oh
yes she is definitely one of God's surprises. A Miracle!

—*Darlene Cherry*

Master Of The Game

-I am but silent in my dream, a world I reign as king...
-Somewhere balanced in-between, hanging from a string.
-A fragile world as frail as glass, bound by endless skies...
-With rolling hills 'neath shadows cast, by clouds which dancy on
   by.
      -Dreaming... I awake, from my solitary state,
      -And they ask me who am I? to reject the hands of fate...
-I hear but silence in my dream', I'm drifting in-between,
-Embraced within a shroud of screams, changing with each scene.
-Changing patterns in the sky, as rainbows change their hue,
-Alone I sit and wonder why, I feel the way I do.
      -Angered... I refrain, then understand life's but a game.
      -And they ask me why I cry, when we're all so filled with
         shame
-I find but peace within my dream, I'm one in soul and sky,
-I'll journey on to reach the sun, in search of reasons why.
-Within my dream I'm feared by all, yet loved by all the same,
-and here I reign alone in peace, as 'Master of the Game'...
      -And I tell them who I am, in life's never ending plan,
      -And soon I shall awake, to hold the world within my hands....

—*Brian C. Lewis*

Son

Son of outward strength and power.
Son of inward turmoil and pain.
Son of life pulling in all directions.
Son of loneliness and confusion.
Son of pent-up love and emotions.
Son like a volcano ready to erupt.

Son who has traveled to maturity.
Son who has known the toils of life early.
Son who has found inner peace with the Lord.
Son who has experienced the avenues of life.
Son with outward joy and contentment.

—*Carol-Ann Swatling*

You Look Just Fine To Me

You're always asking questions, and ask if I agree,
Son ow I'm going to answer, and tell you what I see.
You say you're getting ugly, and you think you're getting fat,
You ask me if I agree, and what I think of that.

I don't know why you worry, Babe, you look just fine to me.
But then again, I'm getting old, and I can barely see.
Don't I tell you that you're pretty, when we're laying in the
sack, don't I tickle your big tummy, when I roll you on your
back.

So put these feelings in a jar, and keep it on a shelf,
A pig at best in a dress, is how you see yourself.
I've seen you squeeze yourself in jeans, at times I wonder how,
But the girl I see, in front of me, I'm sure is not a sow.

But in due time, my little swine, I'm sure that you will see,
You don't have hoofs, or curly tail,
And you look just fine to me.

Have I answered all your questions,
Did the answers all seem real,
To cut it short, you kind of snort,
But I've never heard you squeal.

—*David Hinson*

Requiem

Not random gunfire nor the solitary
song of a bird praising its heartbeat bears
more than lightly, no decibel
or decay can sustain me, I
who knew the track that was not
parallel, and the path that was not
taken twice, the not
spoken accent, and I
who would perish
to follow you, bear
instead the gift of your naming, into
the speaking desire that was there, into
the noise of the sun's
empty dying, horizons
and wholeness of light I taught you
awaited : always : as my once
wandering mind knew, past freedom, beyond any ugliness
in the northern light of imagining, where to
find you, how to face you across
any meridian.

—*Geraldine Gobi Greig*

Untitled

In front of us
Sorrows and joys,
Being through thick and thin,
Despairs and hopes;
In spite of us who meditate on fears only.

In front of us
Serene days and nights of awe,
Ascents and falls,
Surprises and pains;
In spite of us who want only happiness.

In front of us
Death and life,
War and peace,
Hatred and friendship;
In spite of us who say "nothing can be done."

In front of us
Choosing,
Proving ourselves,
Time, time for every thing and every action;
In spite of us who lack faith, hope, and love.

—*Grzegorz Dobek*

A Society Trapped In The Cupboard Of Reality

They sit like prisoners in darkness, not a movement, not a
sound. Waiting endlessly lacking purpose and fulfillment.
Time passes slowly, very slowly, as they feel the pulsation of
time. One, two, three...the sensation burns inside with each
passing moment. Then suddenly it happens—anxiety fills the
air with anticipation. Who will it be? Who shall be
fulfilled? An eruption of light, but no...a new arrival. A
different style, a new idea, a new light. Not given a chance,
not able to fit in, not given an inch to spare. Pushed out by
those believing that they are superior. Actually...by those
who fear they will be tossed away. Afraid of change another
word for death! The old succeed, the arrival is smashed into a
thousand pieces. Each raw emotion exposed until it's broken
apart completely. Swept away like garbage because it dared to
be different. A crime in itself that did not go unpunished.
Suddenly...Click! Prisoners once again as darkness returns.
Depression fills the stagnant air but now with a sense of
accomplishment. Things will remain as they are, unchanged,
dark, melancholy, never ending. For yet another eternity.

—*Bonnie Goldenberg*

Reflections Outside The City

Quiet and peaceful.
Sounds of people playing in the water.
Watching the sun go down behind the clouds.
Forgetting your cares, relaxing
Away from the noisy city.
No racing to get where you are going.
Carefree, taking the time to enjoy the scenery.
The sky with the burnt sun, peeking through the haze.
At night the stars can be seen.
You never realize in the city that
There are stars in multitudes.
The bonfire blazing heat in the night.
Barefoot dancing in the sand.
Music in the air.
People gathered together in harmony.
Potluck brunch, socializing with neighbours
    and friends.
Smell of the barbeque cooking breakfast.
Water from the rain splashing from the trees.
Time to think and see the wonders.

—*Doris A. Poirier*

Oxford, Mississippi - My Hometown

My hometown has become quite a place — with sparse parking
space! Old friends are few, hardly any of the ones I once knew

It's constantly changing, re-arranging and expanding —
I tell you, life in Oxford has become demanding!!!
New buildings, new businesses, new homes and people galore!!!
Incredibly, this town was once considered such a bore!!!

This one-horsed town is growing in leaps and bounds;
it's clean, quiet, peaceful and serene —
Yet as picturesque as a magazine.
City Hall, First National Bank and Neilsen's are still there —
in what is known as "The Square!"

In 1962, James Meredith made our city ashamed of being
"The Home of Ole Miss", its only acclaim!!!
Newly found fame via National TV, made top ten list
and is now known as a "Retirement Bliss!!"
Who could have imagined or predicted all this??!!

This place where I was born —
once so forlorn has really blossomed and grown.

Summer of 1993, take it from me — Oxford is a wonderful place
to be — where one can find love, peace and tranquility!!

—*Jeanne B. Cottrell*

My Sweet Merilee

Chestnut eyes and dark brown tresses
Sparkle in the summer's glow;
Woolen mittens and bright flannel dresses
Wave as winter winds blow;
Her smile and presence are so blissful,
Her sweet giggle makes me beam;
Though, in parting I am wistful,
I have her next visit to redeem;
Growing up fast, strong, and pure,
Leaving her diapers and kewpie doll curl;
She's no longer a baby, that's for sure!
But, she'll always be daddy's lil' girl.

—*James M. Henley Jr.*

Worlds Without End

A poor lost soul troubled and tossed
Spent hours condemning me
As I hung on the cross
The wizened face empty
All guile and words
With cunning gossip the illusion of good
Talking and appearing kind like a saint
While destroying and sacrificing
The ones that you save
It's a sad chronic show
A cage full of beasts
The dying victims nailed up
Scarred hands and feet
They are carried by temptous
They think only of gain
And they don't need God
They have their own plan.

—*Janet Friedman*

Johnstown, Ohio Is The...

Chill of the cold water on my face as it
    splashes from the outside pump
heat from Grandma's stove as I run into the kitchen
    for breakfast
smoothness of the red checkered oilcloth
    that covers the kitchen table
feeling of being all grown up when Grandma
    lets me make a stitch in her quilt
roughness of the horses's back that I ride
    as he pulls the plow
coolness of the milk house as I fill the
    pitcher from the big crock
heat of the hot dusty road as I scuff my bare
    toes on the way to the creek
feeling of my heart soaring with the music as I pump
    the pedals on the player piano
softness of Grandma's feather bed as she tucks
    me in for the night
quiet sadness of autumn...
    when school starts.

—*Doris P. Branham*

Fairies

I saw the fairies with their iridescent wings
Slithering and sliding amongst the lily ponds;
Heavenly delights of joy and laughter, that clings
To the childish hearts of the merriment of odds.

And the trauma of the delicate broken wings
From accidental interpretation of acts of lust
Tearing ducts from heart broken mystical flings
As the callous winds took them away in gusts.

—*Eydi Gallahan*

Garden Of Life

In my dream last night, I saw a garden of breath taking delight,
    splashes of color spilled across the land with my sight.

From shoot to blossom, and then to seed went the dance,
    as I watched, I realized my dream wasn't by chance.

God's special garden was here for me to view,
    at first everything appeared to be beautiful and new.

I heard a voice say "Look this garden grows as a mirror on life."
    Seeing the garden in another way,
    I saw some grow with ease and some with strife.

There were plants with beautiful blossoms and seeds,
some withered as they began to fade, and others were just weeds.

Watching now the garden continued to change,
    something happened which seemed very strange.

Stricken plants were at random ripped from the soil and sand.
    Vacant unfilled jagged holes spotted the land.

I couldn't help but wonder what was happening to these plants?
    Gathered at random, torn from the soil, was it just chance?

The voice now spoke again as I heard it say,
    "These I've selected to join me this day."

"They now live, transformed into perfection forever."
    As I woke and understood all life to revere.

—*Charles Roberts*

God Plays Dice With The Universe

The chance that CHANCE will fail is slim,
Spoke Max Planck to Einstein,
As in the Cosmos there exists
An order based on that and this,
All tied together, in ways so fine,
By the Lord's morning betting line.

Said Doctor Einstein, in retort,
That's odd, God's hardly such a sport
To mold the world of gambler's clay,
And draft us all into the Devil's pay.

Well, I don't know, snarled Mack the Knife,
Bopping into view.
Bot' of youse
Are right 'n' wrong,
Yuh been thinkin' much too long
Wit' ya minds outta the gutter.
If youse lived on the streets, like me,
Yuh'd know the answer's plain t' see,
'Cause it ain't that things is mysteriously coded:
God does t'row dice—Only t'ing, they're LOADED.

—*Irving Rappaport*

I'm A Survivor

One day I'll fly across the sky...
Spreading my wings for better things.
Our moment was brief in the sun...
The life you gave now is one.

But I'm a survivor, I will go on...
Even though you are gone.
Wings that are fragile, getting stronger...
I know in my heart it won't be much longer.

Soon it will be up to me...
To make my own destiny.
Soaring high up in the sky...
That is where I will fly.

For I'm a survivor, that is me...
Just you wait, you wait and see!!

—*Adrienne Zwirn*

The Unseen Treasures

As we paddle our way up the stream of life
Sprinkled with joy amidst struggle and strife,
Let's be ever alert for so much that's worthwhile
To ease the anguish of all trouble and trial.

Oh!! Where do we find this sweet easing balm?
By asking Him above all fears and hates to calm,
As He maketh us aware of the beauties that abound
Within the hearts and souls of people all around.

But we must look closely to see what's really inside
Not what's on the surface, the selfishness and pride
Of those possessed with wealth and worldly powers
Or with good looks to appeareth as false towers.

No, it is the kindly deed, the ever ready smile
The understanding hearts that maketh it worthwhile,
To remember, 'it's better to give than it is to receive'
Can be our true serenity if we truly do believe.

So now let's all join hands in love and gratitude
As we gently shove aside all selfishness grudge and feud
And let the Divine Shepherd guide us, we His chosen sheep
That we may some day His promised blessings reap.

—*Eddie Schuett*

Portrait Of Hollywood

White stucco houses with roofs of red tile,
Stand on the hillside under clear blue skies
Among cascading bougainvillea and stately palms—
A picture of perfection and peace and calm,
Unnoticed by tourists, cameras in hand,
Who fix their sights on the boulevard below
Where groups of young people in outlandish clothes,
Vie for attention as they strut and pose,
Homeless lost souls, talking to unseen friends,
Forage for food in dirty sidewalk bins,
And street-hardened hustlers, feeling no pain,
Float along in their drug world of dreams,
Creating a scene of confusion and despair,
Sharply focused in the camera's long lens
For a memorable portrait of EXOTIC Hollywood.

—*Clarice D. Durham*

Lost In Eternity

I touch the earth with bottomless fears why?
Standing erect on the face of the world, pale feet and broken
    bones-
the sky, blue spreads out like an uncut virgin breathing the
surface of its kingdom, a glorious kingdom?
I bend down and taste the world with my salted tongue, a voice
of constant echo sings my name lingering through a tunnel of my
unknown fears-
Where the womb of the earth touches the edge of every vivid
picture sketched upon reality I soon envision my death, a form
of philosophy a statue of truth-
Like a serpent rising above the ground in deep heat and passion,
I question this life a never eternal world a never eternal
being never to be found-

—*Dana Flaherty*

Summer Night

Sitting on the front porch,
sweating in the heat, swatting mosquitoes;
  we were happy.
Lying in the grass,
we could forget about tomorrow;
pretend we had no problems
and nothing else to do.

—*Henry L. Wagner*

House Abashed

High upon the hilltop, looking down on scenes below,
stands a house once magniloquent, deemed a mansion long ago.
Mighty columns gleaming, silent sentries guarded,
what lay beyond the doors. Layered and laced in
petticoats, not an ankle showing, flirtatious, ladies
giggling, behind swiftly moving fans, at fine looking
gentleman, wearing pantaloons, hair as white as angels
wings, or newly fallen snow, from all the powder
their shiny wigs could hold.
The parties then were stupendous, some even quiet
pretentious, in the ostentatious house, high upon the
hilltop, looking down on scenes below. Hanging now by
rusted nails, busted shutters bump, when the north
wind blows, spider webs join up in the middle, of
its broken window panes. Brocade drapes dangling,
can no longer conceal, the inside of this house
abashed, high upon the hilltop, looking down on
scenes below.

—*Anna Morine Mattingly*

Riches Of Life

The riches of life,
Start with a man and his wife.
Through their love and happiness,
Comes children born with peacefulness.
The struggles of life cause despair,
But the riches of life make us care.
Put happiness, music and laughter in the air,
The richer the life and it is fair.
If we share our fortunes with all,
Makes it easier to walk than to fall.
Without grandparents and parents in our lives,
There'd be no children, men or wives.
To reach out with love and continue to strive,
Will make us all more wonderful lives.
Oh, how rich I really am,
Without life's riches, I'd be damn.
Lucky me, you bet that's true,
I'm content, how 'bout you.

—*Glenda Richard Leleux*

Pilgrimage Of The Soul

The trapped soul steals in the silence,
Steals out of the body through dreams
Where it can pay homage to the things
That the body normally confines it from doing.
The soul takes pilgrimage and speaks
With dreams as we rest.
Here the soul dances across
The neurons of the brain
While the body lies lifeless.
The soul takes delight
In the vision of the eyes shut
Where all is within its control
Until the body awakens
Where the soul is confined within again
Until next time
The body sleeps.

—*James G. Sides*

Lightning Bugs

Lightning bugs, lightning bugs, all around.
Some in the sky and some on the ground.
Lightning bugs, lightning bugs, here and there.
Lightning bugs, lightning bugs are everywhere!!!
Look at the time, it's five past eight.
Time to go to bed!
The lightning bugs glow....I really appreciate!!!

—*Andrea L. Kuhar*

Resolutions

Come all ye children,
step from the pool of ignorance,
satan's playground of joyful frolics,
Be his toys no more.
In our multivalent world
There are many tribulations, that divide the multitudes.
satan's tools of inducement include,
Destitution, pre-judgment, association,
And the perpetual cry, that,
To express vain regrets for what cannot be recovered nor undone.
Open your eyes and hearts!
Look beyond the pigment of flesh and find the being within.
Pigment, is but color, the beauty of nature, in all things.
May it be God's will to find common ground,
To monopolize a resolution.
Solicitous be, trifling not, be conscious of inward impressions,
Strive for purity in conduct and intentions,
That this charity, Christian love, be prevalent forthright,
And may our adoring Lord give loving blessing upon our deeds.
Amen.

—James H. Howar, Jr.

Reflections

Heart of mirrors, so many reflections —
stories unending, the journey goes on.
Turn to the right to puffy white clouds,
Turn to the left, to a burst of color —
straight a head, a tiny crack! Around
the corner, bright sunshine, down an incline,
a dusty road — up the hill, musical
laughter — right behind you, shattered glass,
and up above, dancing moonbeams. Peeking
low — a river of tears, another right,
smooth and clear — spin around, double
vision. Heart of mirrors, so many
reflections — stories unending, the
journey goes on!

—Jan Savich

The Scrunch

He steps through the portal of our unknown fears,
Striding carelessly unrestrained, he leaves his muddy
footprints, on the depths of our souls.
Reaching with cold, bony, clawing fingers into the secrets we
hide, even from ourselves.
Ripping, tearing them from their well-guarded prisons,
He holds them aloft for all to see.
As he cackles and laughs, we fight to deny ownership,
Of the ungodly scenes he reveals.
He knows the place from where all hate stems, from where all
fears flow, for that is where he thrives.
Living, growing, waiting for the moment he will make his
presence known, & once he arrives your life is never the same.
For gone is the innocence we strive to hold, of who we are,
The peace of what you think you know.
Nowhere to run, nowhere to hide, you can only wait,
For the moment he will appear.
In your dreams, in the night, in the light of day,
Alone or in a crowd, there is no doubt,
He will be there!

—Gordon Daniel

Into the Sails the Wind Races

Into the sails the wind races,
strong and full the sails embrace it.
Carry my ship to the edge of flying
with mast and halyards screaming their agony.
Riding hopes of victory as the line
races towards me, on the wings
of windy treasures I fly.
To victory I cut the water,
those behind they see my spray
and feel defeat that day.
Into the sails the wind races,
strong and full the sails embrace it.

—Jeffrey H. Cox

Struggle

Struggle is a word used on the simple and the poor,
struggle is the way politicians use to get him
in the door
Struggle is a fool on another persons quest,
struggle is what the poor does best
Struggle is the governments rules and regulations,
struggle is confusions handed down
generation to generation
Struggle is telling others to suffer with pride and hope,
struggle is destroying people and communities
with alcohol and dope
Struggle is the innocent being misused for no reason,
struggle is a mother giving birth in a undue season
Struggle may sometimes seem very odd
struggle is giving birth to a child name God
Think about it!

—Jesus Messiah Hamilton

Eyes Of Darkness

For a moment you sit with a thought; and the world
suddenly becomes bright. You hear the tone of the bell,
and jump to your feet. A voice you can't place calls
out to you. Looking around the voice can not be found.
Soon after, you close your lids to see the darkness
once again. Mysteriously you seek to hear the unknown
voice again, but no sound is heard.

—Carrie Diegel

My Brazen Blue

The absence of warmness mastered the day
Suddenly, in a hasten the cold went away

His side spitting manner captured me, yet I was unaware
Caught up in curiosity, seized by his mysterious air

Like a shadow I sleuthed blazed, followed the trail of clues
Intoxicated by discovering this man so alive and possessing
a profusion of moods
Like a speeding train it hit me why in such a relentless
manner this man I pursued

There was a mutual attraction between us and of that fire we
were both aware
And to pass on such a wealth of intensity would prove to be
unjustly, grossly unfair,

The magic between us as predicted manifested and grew
Engulfed in pure rapture, like an eruption sparks flew

A certain blue eyed man offered his love and captured my heart
He cradled me with gentle assurance of never being apart

And because of this delicate yet explosive connection between
us so beautiful, so new, my love for you will be true, strong
and forever, my brazen blue

—Jennie D'Alimonte

S Is For Stephanie

S is for Stephanie, seraph and song;
    Sunlight and starlight to last all year long.

S is for symphony, smashing its strings;
    School bells and sleigh bells with sharply clear rings.

For showers in Spring that scrub off the sky;
    For streams filled with swans that go swimming by.

S is for smells: steamy stew; sizzling soup;
    Stroganoff, salad, seafood from a sloop.

S is for skiing, skimming and splashing;
    The skittering sweep of stones swiftly smashing.

For snow on the summit; silhouettes in steam;
    A simian slinking with shadowy scheme.

S is for Summer; for skirts softly swishing;
    Strawberries, sherbets and stars made for wishing.

The surprise of a seal as it suddenly scatters;
    The sound of a shell as it slips and smatters.

A shy smile, a soft sigh, a schoolgirl sylph
    Sobbing at Christmas in spite of herself.

S is for Stephanie, sure and success;
    Someday, somewhere, sunrise at its best.
        —*Jackie Denman*

Masked Water

Raindrops' feet are countless.
Surprisingly, their steps harmonize
with rusted metal.
through a crystalline wall today,
reality is falsified,
surroundings blurred,
despite faultless optics.
Palm outreached, Nature cleanses;
deeper than surface soil
but not deep enough.
Perfumes from manmade beasts still
infect Her domicile; immolate Her children.
Natural drink cools
and burns tongues.
All babes cry upon baptism.
        —*Alexis Rauff*

Adagio

As I sit reclining in my desk chair,
surrounded by,
the soft melodious notes of Chopin.
The pain of life's direction fills my thoughts,
As I look out my open window at two perfectly formed red roses.
Sitting side by side, at rest on a green leafy bush,
I wonder,
should I clip them for the vase on my piano...?
Suddenly, a breeze begins to stir and the roses sway,
Their slight sweet fragrance drifts past my nose.
Chopin's music, in time with nature, begins to move rapidly,
as if it and the roses are to be felt as one.
I remain seated,
watching,
and the breeze quiets.
A sense of stillness fills the room.
The roses resume sleep on their bed on green leaves.
Chopin whispers from the keyboard.
My vase on the piano remains,
empty.
        —*Gloria Rice*

Okinawa

An Island:
surrounded by liquefied sapphires and emeralds glisten
in the sun.
Water clear as sheet of fine glass.
Beneath the fine glass,
sea forest sprouts with life.
Leafless trees that look like bonsai
Colored ruby, pearl, topaz, and amethyst.
Swimming in the sea forest are stripped, zig-zagged,
dotted, and solid colored schools of fish.

An Island:
Seems to be floating on crumpled sea blue sheets.
Smooth at the southern part and crinkled at the north.
Luscious tropical greenery spreads like a freshly laid carpet.
With numerous mangroves that anchor the land still.
Banyan trees that look like broccoli.
Palm trees that beckon you to the island.
Island full of quirky looking birds in bloodstone,
garnet, aquamarine and jade colors.
The land that King Neptune world build his castle on top.
        —*George T. Miyashiro*

Graveyard Shift

I took a job t'other day, I needed one real bad.
T'aint the one I wanted, t'was the only one they had.
They said to me, "You won't get rich,
    but you can pay your bills
If you just work the graveyard shift over to the mill."

Well, I thought about it for a while, and says,
"I'll give'er a try.
And if I don't like'er I kin quit'er bye and bye."
But nothing 'else has come along, and Joe you know I still
Am working on the graveyard shift over to the mill.

But there's some compensations there some folks don't think
    about.
The nights are mighty purty, when the stars and moon are out.
And every day I watch the sun come up behind the hill
When I'm workin' on the graveyard shift over to the mill.

But when my shift is over, that's the time that I like best.
That's when I can take me home and lay me down to rest.
But then the dammed old phone will ring,
    and I'll wish with all my will,
That I was workin' on the day shift over to the mill.
        —*Charles Pennel*

Hanging The Moon

I'm flying high, caught a ride on a moon beam.
Take me far and so very wide
As far as the eyes can see.
Gonna wait til the dawn wakes up and sings
Gonna make daisy chains with butterflies
Dreams are the magic I hold inside
As you can see, been trippin' the boundries of the astralplanes
Now they've found me (all the fame, fortune and flames)
as I travel in my oz-like state
Overlooking my grand freakdom - it occurs to me
Masturbating my hate
will not lead me to the gates of freedom.
But tell me ye hypocrites of the world
Would you sell a mother's only child down the river?
Would you kill a scapegoat to be a martyr?
And then tell me every things in perfect
working order?
But never mind me, I'll keep on dancing
With this mad songs doom
Cause I'm touching the skies. Trying to hang the moon.
        —*Christopher Lee Schillings*

Car

People use me everyday like I'm nothing;
Take me places I don't want to go;
I am mentally abused sometimes;
People don't appreciate me for what I am;
Take and stick things on me like I was a wall;
I am washed and fed when I don't want to be;
People scratch and wreck my body;
Take advantage of my speed sometimes;
I witness crimes, but can't do anything about them;
People as the years go by, start to hate me;
Take me to places to be sold;
I usually am sold to other people or stacked in piles;
People just don't understand how I help their lives;
Take me serious if they did;
I just want to be loved. . .

—*Joe Hubbard*

Untitled

I'm almost flying, running swiftly through the trees
taking in the clean soft breeze.
Being high within this life
Taking nature as my wife
I'm cleaning out my soul
For I am now whole
I'm far beyond the reach
of the falsities society teach
And I'm spreading my true wings
The voice inside me finally sings
Thankful for this new light
That's given me this insight
To the knowledge in myself
And knowledge and truth shall be my wealth
I picture me the sky-a mind that opens oh so wide and
I'm sheltering my peace-where shadows of clouds cannot reach
Let me orbit towards the sun
My perfect warmth has just begun
And the Earth shall be my hair
To grow the flowers that it shares.

—*Jen Card*

Untitled

The point guard, the captain of the
team
His penetrating dribble like a furious
stream
When you have the ball have quick
feet
throw bump fake and you'll never be
beat
Shoot the ball whoomp there it
is
That's it, that's the game the agony's all
his

—*Cory Smith*

The Beauty Of Autumn

The beauty of autumn, a sight to behold, more precious to me
than diamonds or gold.
Artist nor poet could ever capture its breathtaking beauty,
its splendor, its rapture.
Its color scheme so perfect, truly a sight to behold.
There's yellow and red, there's orange, green and gold.
Let's not take it for granted, this wonderful sight.
It's a Gift from our Father, through his love and his might.
Let's all show our thanks for this;
Let's go out every Autumn - and never miss.
Enjoy its beauty and be glad the he, our heavenly father,
made the tree.

—*Ethel R. Baker*

Dare To Believe

Do I dare believe that which I am
tempted by,
Should I take a chance,
Am I to let myself be hurt,
Or will I experience the unknown joy,
Can I reveal that which has been hidden so long,
Will I in turn be revealed by the same.
Do I let the suppressed happiness out,
Can I let go of my unchained fears.
Will love catch me if I fall
Will it erase those fears
to let the happiness show
Only time can tell me
what I need to know
Is our love strong enough
To last the time, heal the hurt
and chase away the tears?
If it is, I dare to believe!

—*Elisabeth Stallings*

A Mother's Prayer

Thank you God for this little child,
Tender, loving, meek and mild —

Thank you God for these little eyes,
So I can wipe the tears when my child cries —

Thank you God for this little nose,
So I can feel it against my cheeks as my child grows —

Thank you God for the little mouth that says "I love you".
So I can hear those words and say them back, too —

Thank you God for the little ears,
So I can whisper in them and calm my child's fears —

Thank you God for each little hand,
So I can hold it and help my child to understand—

Thank you God for these little feet,
So I can watch them walk and help them across the street —

Thank you God for this little hair,
So I can brush it and comb it and show that I care —

Thank you God for this little face,
Shining, innocent, full of grace —

Thank you God for this gift that can compare to no other,
Thank you God for this gift of being a mother!

—*Barbara Hansen*

A Friend Lent A Shoulder

Why does no one understand
That a woman and a man
Can help each other get their problems solved
Without becoming intimately involved?

Sometimes outsiders can help you see
That your problems are a reality.
Sometimes they're big, sometimes they're small
Sometimes they're not really problems at all.

But until you confide in a good friend who'll listen,
One who can take a neutral position,
You don't know what's right, you don't know what's wrong,
You don't know on which side of the fence you belong.

Meanwhile, gossip abounds in the whole neighborhood
Ruining reputations that have always been good.
No one will listen to the real reasons why
A friend lent a shoulder on which another could cry.

—*Dona Schicker*

Blossoming Beauty

Your eyes that see me through my blue days,
that glitters as the setting sun upon the rippling waves.
Your skin that glows through my open desires
        with every embrace.
Your touch that strikes me with warmth and courage.
Your smile that lit the flame of love which pierces
through my soul, for you, as the echo of a thousand sunsets.
Your voice as soothing and captivating as the shimmers of a
        dew drop on the soft petal of a rose bud.
And the person itself the essence of life and the
priceless gem which is embedded into my heart forever,
        surrounded with the hope of destiny.

—*Darryl Somrah*

No Prayers

There are so many friends with so many needs, so many things
that go unseen.
So many crying that haven't been heard, of the sad and lonely
that live in this world.
Once I was young and now I am old but my heart still cries for
the things that I know.
So much sorrow and too much pain to many suffering from sin
and shame
The hungry are crying without any bread, the lonely are dying
without prayers being said

—*Carolyn Romans Hall*

Evolution

There was a time when I did not see
That infinite created me specifically to be;
Its complete expression and channel of love,
A recipient of gifts and riches from above.

The source and substance of all my needs -
Providence gently, continually leads
Me, along calm waters into pastures lush with green -
Where the face of Infinite now I have seen.

Each moment is flawless, the future bright.
Because I live, move and have my being
As an expression of this light.

As darkness has evolved into soft, gentle dawn,
God and I commune, we have a master plan;
To share with everyone in this Kingdom,
God's abundance, perfection, guidance and wisdom!

—*Jeanne S. Netzley*

The Grandeur Of Night

Oh— the grandeur of night!
That is when nature proves best
For it is serene and tranquil
Unhindered by humanity.

Night is when....
A celestial moon shines ever so bright
When luminous waters embrace immeasurable shorelines
While gentle winds gaily blow
Night is when....
Spangled stars drift high
High above the snowcapped mountains
High above the sleeping forests
Night is when....
Sanguine harmonies enchant curious ears
As once blinded eyes are opened
Opened and in awe at the surrounding beauty

Oh— the grandeur of night!
It rejuvenates a weary mind
And feeds poor starving lungs.
"I bask in its solitude."

—*Jason Edward Murray*

Clare

The soft rain caresses the new grass,
that just grew in.
The rain makes my face wetter,
and mingles with my tears.
I have been standing out here all night,
now the sun is beginning to rise.
It reminds me of your smile,
The one I'm begging to see again.
But you have left me Clare.
So all I can do is leave you these roses,
and wait, until our souls meet, at
the gates of Heaven.

—*Erin Curley*

Sunlight And Shadows

When you see shadows 'neath the trees,
That only means, dear friend:
The sun is up above the leaves
And you'll come to it's full light again.

The road we walk, it often winds:
Sometimes the path is quick and smooth;
Yet again, we'll find confusing signs,
But God hears our prayer, with love he soothes.

If every morning we see its beauty
And listen to the sweet bird's song,
We can find strength to do our duty,
And with God's help, we'll not go wrong.

In his infinite grace He cares for us:
He'll give us wisdom to find the way
To a happier goal in life for us,
God bless you, friend, always I pray.

—*Frances M. Key*

Freedom To Explain What You Believe, To Be Who You Are...

As we know one of freedoms
    that people have as human beings
is the freedom of feelings
    "love," "hatred," "selfishness" etc...
So that's why I would like, to
express what I feel.

After all this day without thinking of you, today you
are back in my mind. Everything reminds of you, I feel sad
and lonely at the same time. How much I wish you were near
me. I don't know where you live, or who you are.
In my mind is only the sweetness of your face, I wish you were
near me, to enjoy my entire life next to you, and never
leave you. Why don't I bring out all the love I feel for
you? Why do I think so many things? Why do I fear so many
of my dreams?
I don't know why?
Why am I so worried? Would you ever find out and suffer as
much as I do? He would blame me without thinking twice that
I'm just a human.

—*Carmen Rivas*

Mary

They say we are one another and equal in life
Taking, giving, sharing to each another day's portion
Sun rays, rain, shine, entwined together even in strife
Bodies close, arms around faces aside, do we hear
The whisper that speaks the love of our devotion
Minds promise to live and love before we die
But then the word spoken is only a sigh — goodbye

—*Benjamin O. Knight*

To Wish Upon A Fallen Star

I wished upon a fallen star,
that seemed so near, while you seem so far.
It flew through the sky, so fast, so clear,
And filled me with hope for the coming years.
It twinkled brightly, as if saying it cared,
And I wished that you had been there.

I wished upon that fallen star,
That flew so fast, that flew so far.
I wished for you to be with me then,
To say you loved me as more then a friend.
I wished for you, and you alone,
And hoped my love for you had finally shone.

To wish upon that fallen star,
Filled my heart with love that reaches so far.
You'll never know how much I love you so.
But maybe one day that star will let you know.
That star that flew inside my heart,
Will twinkle forever when your about.

—*Carol Ann Selby*

Friendship In My Eyes

For me to connect to someone special,
that someone might be pierced by the idea as to how I connect.
It would give me eternity with that special individual.
It's not my own doing.
It's the fate that strikes my eternity.
The pain that is sent is not intentional,
but seems like the only solution for me to connect to
my only friend.
Even though you don't treat me as a friend,
always trying to camouflage me into the darkness,
or wishing I would just disappear,
you'll always be my closest friend.
Letting me share a part of you no one is capable to share.
You could say I'm almost like a scar.
Never letting you forget what happened that night,
and being the only thing that would never leave you.

—*Jill Pua*

Perfect Love

I wished there was some way I could tell you
That the world's treasures meant nothing at all.
If but for a night to me you were true
And had only thoughts of the heart to call.
Cupid's arrow and aphrodite's smile
Would send us blessings from way up above.
The angels, they'd sing and dance all the while.
As we down below rejoiced in our love.
Time would no doubt try to hurry our bliss,
But we'd face him without even a cry.
For great is the strength concealed in a kiss;
Such to shatter time's hourglass in the sky.
    Oh how we wondered what made the stars gleam,
    But like perfect love, t'was part of a dream.

—*Christine Brkic*

Untitled

How can it be when you say you love me so,
that this vast loneliness continues to grow?
How can it be, you said with a smile,
that this yearning has become denial?
Why did not the feeling remain?
Why is there such a conquering pain?
I needed you to be here be my side.
Instead, alone for you I have cried.

—*Jodi Kuhl*

What Will I Tell The Babies?

My God, what will I tell the babies?
That their father lynched a man for being black?
Why didn't you tell me where you were going?
There is a world outside this backwater town
That just fought a war to free his kind.
There's been too much hating already,
Our life's been dark from the seepage.
Where was your strength, your manly pride?
You said we all had a right to a decent life.
So what if he treated Lucy impertinent.
He didn't know she had the mind of a child.
She wasn't hurt, just scared of strangers.
You men always think you gotta punish
Anyone talking to us without your permission.
We did pretty well when you went to war.
I gotta live with you the rest of my life
Hearing his soul crying between us.
Forever ain't enough to hide the truth.
He did nothing 'cept talk to crazy Lucy.
Dear God, is that what I tell our babies?

—*Janet Reaves*

Death In Chicago

"We live until we die." Say those who have never experienced,
that we are born again, after dying alive.

If living is not to have died, what could then have been
that mourning moment, that tough me that I had never lived?

Sometimes I think I am dead, and feel that I am dying alive.
But when dying, I wake up,
and understand that living is dreaming.

Living dying is death, but dying to live is life.
How many deaths would give me life,
and the right to taste death?

Death that who never dies, to come back to life.
Alive that who dies, to win the game of life.

How many times life kills us, to be able to bring us to life,
and we think it is grabbing from us,
our most valuable possession?

Lucky that who died, to be born again,
and who lived the rest of his days,
like a soul grateful to God.

—*Gustavo Velasquez*

Our Talents

Isn't it important that we each have some talent
That we are supposed to do?
God has given each person something different
That only he can do.

Those wonderful musician and composers too,
Well! They need listeners-so there's me and you.
And those famous painters with their brushes grand
Who paint beautiful scenes from somewhere in the land,

And there are famous preachers, evangelists too
They help keep folks saved if their message is true,
And architects, and scientists and world leaders, too
Who like to step forward and show what they can do.

I like to just be homefolk and tend my garden small.
Making world wide decisions would interest me at all.
And so a politician, I never ever can be
Because I like the simple life of just being me.

—*Frances Gordon*

Springtime Ecstasy

What power within the human mind can fully understand
The awakening of dormant life as spring descends upon the land;
The glorious songs of birds penetrating silent down
or the sight of a dew-drenched rosebud unfolding on the lawn?

Who breathed the soft and fragrant breath into early morning
  breeze
it raises up its voice to the majestic whispering trees?
What mystic hand has blanketed the great, vast earthen bed
adorning it with rare beauty, bright hues of yellow, blue and red?

Who placed the golden sun upon skies of azure blue
and downy clouds like doves that gather upon the heavens too.
What caused dark clouds to suddenly form for a springtime
  thundershower,
to quench the thirsty earth below as it bursts into full beauty
  every budding flower?

The mystery unfolds at sundown beside a murmuring stream
as it joins the choir of other wonders to sing of a Power Supreme.
Peace that gently falls upon the earth with the setting of the sun
brings the silent message once again - hope when day at last is
  done.

  —Genevieve Woodhead

On Running

I woke up on that morning and saw a sunny day;
The beauty of creation had made my life so gay.
I walked out of the city into the forest green,
And it was very pretty, a quiet, peaceful scene.
My heart was thrilled from looking at such a peaceful place,
And I desired to quicken my leisure, walking pace.
I ran and ran through nature, excited by its awe;
My soul was so inspired from all that my eyes saw.
As I enjoyed this beauty and I was so inspired,
My legs ran faster, faster, and I began to tire.
And so I slowed to walking out of the woods again,
Back toward the busy city and all its daily din.
I realized that mankind can't run and be inspired
Too long till he grows weary and soon he will get tired.
But throughout all the ages creation runs in place,
Never panting, never tiring in its continuing race.

  —Clarence E. Billheimer

My Favorite Time Of The Day

  The sky is red and violet and the sun is orange.
The birds are flying in patterns in the bright blue sky.
The moon is out ready to take its turn as the sun lays
down to sleep.

  It is dark now, the sun has left.
The stars are out and bright as ever.
As I gaze at the sky I look to the moon for the answer.
A star falls, I make a wish.

  The twinkling lights of the freeway are multi - colored;
orange, yellow, blue, red, and silver like a midnight rainbow.

  Signs of life are everywhere.
People laughing, babies crying, cars honking, music
playing, the world is alive.
Windows are filled with people dancing, kissing, and
celebrating together.

  I find a partner for tonight's last dance and
celebrate the moment with a waltz across the rooftops.

  —Clelia M. Duff

Memories Of A Virginia Storm

The sky was gray and the sun was white
The breeze picked up as day drifted to night
Dark clouds appeared behind trees across the field
The breeze turned to wind and the tree limbs did yield
Then a distant rumble was natures battle cry
The birds took heed and with ruffled feathers they did fly
I sat on my porch as if in a trance
As the clouds great torch performs the beautiful light dance
The wind now twists the oak above me
The sound and the light are now before me
The rain sweeps in like a waterfall
I am filled with the eerie thought that the sky may fall
But soon it leaves and the sky stops weeping
The birds become quiet and prepare for sleeping
And I recall the sweet, strong smell of water on the ground
How it drifted through the air and there was not a sound
And how I sat on my porch in love with the sight
as the sun shut its eye and day became night

  —David M. Skillman

Untitled

I sit upon the sandy beach,
  the bright fiery sun I cannot reach;
The touch of breeze upon my face,
  I see the trees, the children race.

The beauty of life is all around,
  I look to the horizon, there's little sound;
The birds fly by without a peep,
  the ocean blue, the waters deep.

The sun shines bright, a beaming light,
  I see the boats, a plane in flight;
Life is beautiful, life is great,
  I feel so mellow, I feel no hate.

From afar, the flowers grow,
  their spectrum of color seems to show;
Lovely flowers, they stand so tall,
  for us He made it all.

  —Helen P. Marsh

Halloween Night

It is a cold, chilly, spooky night on October 31
The children are home from trick-or-treating
Eating all their goodies
The wind increases every second, every minute, and every hour
The leaves rumble to the dry ground as the wind takes it away
The clock strikes midnight
As the wind increases more than ever
The witches and ghosts soar through the air
  joined by the pumpkins that are coming to life
And the children start to have nightmares about
  the witches and they toss and turn
As sweat is racing down their tiny faces like
cars at a race track
Their little hearts start pounding like drums in a marching band
Soon afterward the children's nightmares start
  floating away and Halloween night soon comes to an end
Till next Halloween night, sweet dreams, says the
  witch as she turns back to plastic on the
  neighbor's front door.
Ha! Ha! Ha! Ha! sweet dreams

  —Ayesha T. Prentice

Changing Times

     Life changes with time
The clock ticks slowly when you're young.
  Now it travels at the speed of light.
    I try desperately to keep up
     And hide my fright.

    Have I accomplished my goals?
    Have I completed God's plans?
    Or simply spinning my wheels
    And being less than I can?

     Life is never finished
   And of course, neither am I.
     Because if I were
   I'd have no reason to try.

   —B. W. Punyko

Sixty And Beyond...

Wondrous milestone birthday.
The cocoon has cracked,
  setting free the butterfly.

Years of responsibility, nurturing others,
may have melted into wisdom, certainly experience;
  times of pain, disappointments,
  have given strength, courage to risk.
    The wings feel strong, ready to soar.

How filled with opportunity life seems to be.
  How alive the creative spirit!

As if winter's tight bud has blossomed
to become summer's lovely bloom,
so the world has opened
before my spreading wings.

At last, it is time to nurture
  those lifelong dreams,
  my hope to weave meaning into words.

My butterfly years
  extend with continuing promise
    at sixty... and beyond...

  —Janet Marie Elliott

Which Path To Choose?

And here we are, lost, confused, and in a mass of black,
The cold hate of the dark one whose knife is to our back.
We know not from what pit he rose, but we shall all fall in,
if we continue to practice in his acts of sin.
In our sadness and hysteria we seek comfort from his hand,
not knowing all we will find is the torture of his land.
Our deeds grow darker, as we give him our belief.
Not knowing that death condemns us to his dark land of grief.
Blind were we to the other path we might have chosen.
The one that is long, dark, hard, cold, and frozen.
Its road is a perilous journey of belief and of rules.
Those who set out believed themselves to be the fools.
But when they reached the end, they saw a glimmering light,
it was the home of the end of unholy, perpetual night.
Though to get here you need not the axe or the sword,
All you need is belief in Jesus Christ, our Lord.

  —Dim Kostic

Sunrise

Night flies on wings of violet, which slowly fade to pink.
The cricket's chirrup is finally silent, as the darkness smears
thin, like ink. The color then brightens from deep maroon,
and a cock crows somewhere far away. The gold-rimmed clouds
shyly peek through as the sun's light welcomes the day. Dew
glistens like precious jewels on the ground and warmth
coaxes timid petals to open. The news quickly spreads and
then come the sounds, by the creatures of the earth it is
spoken. The bird's herald began their symphony then followed
from each feathered throat, come the songs of a common melody
from places unseen and remote. In the stable a whicker is
heard from the mare, in her web, the spider's industrious hum.
Each subtle sound uttered with special care to announce the
morning has begun. The squirrels scamper from roof-top to
tree, and the pond in the meadow awakes. Each world in its
busy harmony begins anew as on the horizon dawn breaks.

  —Holly L. Lorr

A Key To An Illusion

One Friday just like any other,
the crowd was thinning.
Dim lights and an occasional flicker of a candle,
revealed somewhat of a long lasting dream.

A tall stack, who would decide what was to be said.
What should I choose?
It shall decide on the mood,
the time of life.

The usual few was left behind.
I sat and wondered.
My loved ones who gathered and embraced in friendship,
will time show them the way,
not to run or hide, never slip away.

A certain magic in Music will tell the tale,
decide the mood,
the time of life will be revealed
From Jim to Barbara. (said Gargoyle)

Running through his past, deciding on tomorrow with only a
flip of a disc. An unlimited variety, the stacking inspiring
Elton to the Egg Man.

  —Christopher Anthony Wilk

Life Ride

We rise to the top and fail to see,
  The darkness below
    The darkness to be.
A crash into a desperate fall,
Rumors and secrets beckon and call.
  We toss and turn in such despair,
  Anger, confusion all so hard to bear.
Yet within the darkness, there is the light,
As before the day, comes always the night.
Problems are lost and happiness found,
As we start to balance on level ground.
And just as we think our troubles will end,
We rise to the top all over again.

  —Brook Blasen

Untitled

Think... Just how lucky you are -
That you are able to see;
The grass so green, the trees so tall,
And the deep blue-green of the sea.
Some people aren't so lucky;
Yes — some when born are blind;
But it's the people who can't see everything -
That are the best of all mankind.

  —Helen H. Meyers

My New York

The crime is appalling
The dirt in the streets is still falling.
But, the lights how they shine.

The park is quite scary
The bowery is erie
But, the shows are a delight!

The people some say are rude.
Our schools are asbestos full.
But, oh the sights!

You may not want to come here
But, if you decide.
Oh, the wonders you'll find!

—*Frances Bennardo*

Wife Or Widow?

It might have been the eclipse of the sun
The earth ravaged, nothing left or no one!
Time was forever and "waiting" an aeon
As the sign DO NOT ENTER glared in neon.

Though I was outside, on the table lay my life
My future to be determined by a surgeon's knife!
Interminable, waiting has no end
Will he die or might he mend?
I want my life in place, as I arranged it
It's warm and good; I don't want to change it.

The door opens, prayers forgotten, I revert to fright
A figure emerges, tall, imposing, dressed in white.
He smiles - it is the end of time
He's done God's work. "He'll be fine"
he says, but I cannot speak
I cry and place a kiss upon his cheek.

—*Irma Moss*

A Night After The First

It's the end of the night's sweet romance
the end of the days endurance
I see by the light of a single lamp
burning for an hour at most

I can hear not the wind, nor see the tree
But I know they're there not for myself,
not even for themselves

For nature that ever working, ever turning enterprize
which catches dreams in Its hands
and sends them flying on the breeze, for the wind to keep
then takes them and molds them in her own image

It's not and end to life tonight,
nor an end to living, so now I'll sleep
I will sleep and perhaps tomorrow
with the trees I will wake and try to remember, last night's
beauty yours and the wind's

I cannot remember, I cannot forget, I can only leave my dreams
to the breeze for the wind to keep and blow to nature's hands

Let me sleep now, let me forget not my dreams
for nature's hand, like mine, can only open once

—*Jenny Vassili*

Ashes To Ashes

I gathered the twigs then I lit the match
The fire was low and I wanted it so
There is much to throw on - so much good riddance
I will build it with that 'til the flames are so high
It will never come back
I will throw on the past that continues to haunt
The parts that lay deep almost forgotten
Yet ready to pounce when my spirit finds peace
Others so small I struggle along with
Like the fly in the web hopelessly caught
Let me throw them on too

I sit here alone and I watch them burn
Gone gone gone never to return
The fire burns low asking for more
I know it is ready and very near at hand
As over and over it rises to haunt me
why do I keep it - here is my chance
Throw it to the flames - the pain the hurt the anger
It is mine to give or hold.....
Ashes to Ashes

—*Iris G. Howe*

The Cold Of The Night

As the pale light of the moon shows through
the frosted window, I watch as you gently breath
next to me. I finally feel not so alone, able to share,
all that time would not allow. Hold you tight in my arms
to protect me from all that can sometimes be called living,
only to find you're just as scared. And if we're both
afraid then how can it be so safe, unless you're in my arms,
to keep out the cold of the night?

—*G. J. Beck*

War

The dragons below within their dark cave.
The furious beating of wings begin.
They fight to keep their heavy bodies in the air.
Bloodshot eyes scan sea and sky looking for its prey.
With a turn and a dive the dragons descend fire flying from
their mouths.
The houses have burnt and people have clouded the streets.
But the swarm of dragons has just begun to attack.
Spears flying, dragons dying.
Catapults shooting, the war has begun, who will win when the
fighting is done.
The fighting has ended, the dragons lay throughout the fields.
the rest have left to fight another day.
The men are burned, tired, and hungry.
When will the fighting end, now, never, or when all life
has ended?

—*John R. Peck*

Truly A Treasure

God has given man many gifts, the gift of life.
The gift of a mind to better himself.
The gift of a world to live on.
The gift of different types of food.
The gift of different senses to enjoy all these wonderful
things.
But the gift most precious, most beautiful, most dear; and
most often taken for granted, abused, and ignored; is the
gift of a companion (woman).
This gift should be adored, and cherished above all others;
As life itself!
Not just a gift, truly a treasure!

—*Charles F. Auman*

Autumn

I'm getting older now, I can see it around my eyes
The gray replacing blonde, and the sunset in the skies
It doesn't bring any fear to me, not in any way
Growing old gracefully, means just another day

Somewhere in my living, I detached chronological time
Became the night's cool breeze, that blows welcome through the
    chime
Can't vision me old and gray, moving rickety to the porch
Settling into the rocking chair, that's seen years of sun's hot scorch

Maybe laughter from the porch swing, voices calling from grass
    below
"Hey watch this Grandma," as they tumble to and fro
Or getting up and joining them, in a race across the yard
Fourteen steps behind them, and my heart is beating hard

Dancing in the moonlight, 'round the roses' smell so sweet
See the happy lady, dancing lightly in bare feet
My skin may turn to spider's web, and my touch in to soft wind
My tears in to a gentle rain, that's sweet melody on a roof of tin

    —*Carol Kalil*

My Eyes

Of all the gifts God gave to me
The greatest are my eyes to see
The beauty that's surrounding me.

Off in the distance mountains with snows
and clouds high above them gently flow.
There are rivers swiftly passing by
And birds flying high up in the sky.
There is the ocean, far and wide,
With continents on every side.

Fish and animals are everywhere,
Their beauty and food for us to share.
So every night as I pray on my knees,
I thank God I have eyes to see.

    —*Geraldine Davidson*

A Piece Of Wedding Cake

Having a beautiful wedding
The guests are seated and music playing
but what are they waiting for —
A piece of that cake.
To take home or eat
To save someone whom made this with
love for us on our special day
Now, look for yourself, what do you think.
The cake is done let's eat.
From top to bottom
White and pink
This cake will be the memory for us
Everyone looking at this cake
Who made it wondering through there heads
You know and I know who did this for us
One special lady and a very good friend to us...

    —*Cheryl A. Nolan*

Homeless

Sitting on a park bench, no one will sit near him
The expression on his face, stern and grim.
People walk by and look away
This is how he is treated,
This is how he has to pay.

It's not his fault his clothes are withered and torn
Or his hands, rough and worn.
He lies down on his wooden bed,
He lies down, emotionally dead.

    —*Gage Tucker*

Apartment With the Porch

My small apartment with the porch
The happiness might make its approach,
But life is not so easy and simple too
There is always something full of woe.

Something to worry something to wonder,
How come my life is torn asunder,
Why can't I live in peace some more.
In my small apartment with the porch.

There is the time when you need to hark,
When you need the song to fill your heart,
When love your neighbor you desire
But the respond is hard to acquire.

Might change my life for better I hope
And live by the sea on the sandy shore
With no neighbor only my torch
And no apartment with the porch.

    —*Hedy Wolf*

It Could Be Me

On the sidewalks of our cities, won't you look around?
    The homeless and the hungry, are all falling down!
    No candle in the window, not a friend in site!
    Doesn't anybody care? Do we ignore their plight?
When millions go for weapons and more to industry,
We fight to save the animals, we fight to save the trees.
    Yet, we close our eyes to sorrow and to poverty.
    We close our eyes to hunger and a human's needs.
        Don't you know he is your brother?
        It could happen to your Mother!
        Look inside and say, it could be me!
        The road of life is rough and tumbled.
        What if you're the next to stumble?
        Can't you say inside, it could be me!
            Do I hear a baby crying?
        Over there a young man's dying!
        God please help them say, it could be me!
        Her head can't rest upon a pillow.
        She can't sleep beneath my willow!
        Will you ever say, it could be me!

    —*Jeannie Hart*

Infinity

He lyes there — limp — ashen color.
The hospital bed, with all its uniqueness — is not comforting.
It's too late!
You watch his closed eyes, fluttering!
The turmoil of his pain is devastating.
It's apparent he's reminiscing within himself, over his life.
His devoted wife of 63 years, and their 10 children stand vigil.
His eyes open! Perhaps for the last time.
Suddenly- a smile crosses his lips!
With a gesture of love, he reaches out — wanting hands to hold.
First squeezing with strength! then, - all muscles collapse.
Life has left him.
All that was within, is no longer.
But he will live again, in the hearts of his loves.

    —*Eve Westaby*

The Old Drake House

Big Cove Road's eloquent Oak Tree
The Old Drake House stood nearby
Livestock grassed green grass across the road nearby
A hazy mood of suspicion for their eyes to see
Old Big Cove Road startled Mother Nature's Tree

The Horses Honked and the Cows went through phases
"Baby I Lied"
The Old Drake House is a Home to expose those who lied
The Home for those saved by Jesus with phases

    —*John Wesley Miller*

Untitled

Ambiguous... My whole time here has been questionable
The Jews don't believe in Me, the Gentiles disregard Me
I show them the dirt clumps in My unraveling walnut hair
And I swear to them that I died once
That I was poisoned with sex
And erased with a rubber

They say that I'm blasphemous
That they'd rather Me claim to be
The plumber (and unstop all their asses)
But that is My job
I have a plunger and I wear gloves
Because I am the Prophet

And in a dream I was crucified
In a gingham blue bikini
And in a final reproach to My Father
I threw back my head and asked
"Whose idea was this anyway?"
I woke up
And prayed to Myself

  —*Helen Elna*

Growing Up Rural

Growing up Rural was a wonderful thing!
The keen recollection still makes my heart sing!
The warmth of its heart in the people there
Join the smell of integrity ingrained in the air!

Impressions remain so vivid and rare —
Heat shimmering in waves through the hot summer air,
Of hearing the roosters and old guinea hens,
Of lambs baaing softly and pigs grunting in pens.

Oh, how I loved to awake to the cows
Mooing loudly for relief that milking allows.
The horses were ready, too, for a ride
And nuzzled my hand for the apple I hide.

Riding to town on loose gravel roads,
There only were farm trucks with granary loads.
In winter fresh snow would cover the ground,
So tires on the car made a soft, crunchy sound.

Somehow, Rural living seemed so safe and secure,
The people so honest and the environment so pure.
Maybe my memories are the memories of youth;
Yet, I know my heart holds what is real Rural truth!

  —*Janet Myers Harless*

Screen Door

It was an old red, wooden screen door,
The kind you seldom see;
But thinking back upon it,
It was a palace door to me.

There was a glow that shone right through it,
In the good old summertime;
It was the warmth of love,
That made that old door shine.

For if you ever passed by,
In those happy, golden days;
You'd hear the sound of laughter,
Echoing always.

It was an old wooden screen door,
Made of old, red bark;
But now it's just a memory,
Locked up tight and dark.

  —*Arlene La Rocca Maresca*

The Book

My back is sometimes hard, soft, and paper too.
The leaves are thick, and sometimes
there re just a few.
I come in many shapes, colors, sizes, and looks.
It doesn't matter what shape or color, I'm still a book.

You can hold me in your hand, or put me on your shelf.
I'm always available to you, so you
can find me for yourself.
Please open me, and see what's inside.
Flip my pages, read my words, you'll
see your knowledge grow wide.
I am a teaching tool, giving lots of fun.
I live in the library, but you can check out one.
No, not just one but two or more
If I'm not at the library, you can buy me at the store.
So, come and meet me, be my friend.
Me, you, and of course a bookend
Yes, I am a book, and I love to be read.
So read me in school, and before you go to bed.

  —*Barbara Williams*

Let Me Stay

Has our life now lost its meaning? Has the sun gone - - - and the light? Where are the words which we have spoken in the tender of the night? Did we lose the road together in the busy world today? Hold — my love — and cling together! Make our happiness to stay! Do you know the warmth of feeling? Do you know the precious glow in the heart of understanding? In the soul that needs you so? Like the meadows in the springtime, Full of flowers, and so bright, Is the love so warm and tender, only waiting for the light. Just the touch of warmth and growing, and the sun, so warm and strong, make me feel like I be home, Dear, in the arms I left for long. Take me! Love me! Hold me close, Dear, on your heart so tried and true. Listen to the song my heart sings — only let me stay with you!

  —*Elsie Louise Crocker*

There And Back

Though life seems so hard at times, you have to read between the lines. Trials and tests, will come and go, remember always, you reap what you sow. I thought I was wise, an experienced man, until it hit me: The big grand slam! So there I lay, they thought I died, a broken body: On the road side, But by his grace only a visit: to the other side. On the bridge he stood so tall, the Lord of life, The king of all. He told me that I must change my ways, for my life: The debt, he did pay. Then with one gentle touch, his life restored me, From deaths tight clutch. Then instantaneously to my surprise, I awoke and realized, my demise. In intensive care did I lay, so confused and crushed, I knew not the day. I've come so far since that frozen time, so now I read Between the lines. So: from that day forth I'll follow his tracks, Just another soul that went there, and back!

  —*John A. Woodward*

Waiting For You

As the hours grow short, the day grows longer,
The joy of anticipation is battling the loneliness of heart.
The tears are joyful, they shouldn't be at all.
Feelings are strong...
Sometimes when times are good, they are also sad.
The sadness of saying goodbye
Interferes with the joy of saying hello.
But, I promise not to dwell....
For if I didn't experience that sadness,
I would never feel the joy
I know will arrive when I see your smiling face.

  —*Joan Ferraioli*

Starshell

Beyond the sky the marine farm was calling for more.
The luminous heavenly body of Ursa Major
was dominant tonight.
The sky was brilliant-
I couldn't wait for tomorrow.

As I watched the children surround the seashore
I gathered a variety of sea shells in my hand.
'Come look what I have found,
these are shooting stars from the sky.'
Laughter echoed around me.

As I watched the children leave one by one that day
I knew they would feel different.
A strange feeling will enter them that night
when they see their first 'starshell' fall from the sky.
A creation within ones soul.

It's such an obvious fact-
What fools we are.
The endless marine farm will always be calling for more.
It's an honor; one will never feel the same.
How do you think starfish got their name?

    —Erin Paris

Ethiopia

The sky-touching scrapers of Addis Ababa
The luxury accommodation of the Hilton
The enchantment of the Rift Valley Lakes
The Falasha of Gonder
The Stelae of Axum
The Baboons of the Simien National Park
The convenience of Ethiopian Airlines
The caves and mountains of Bale National Park
The 11 rock-hewn churches of Lalibela
The Blue Nile Falls of Bahar Dar
The ethnic markets of Dire Dawa
The Arabian and Ogaden culture of Harer
The excitement of the Addis Ababa-Djibouti Railway
Ethiopia:13 months of sunshine

    —James Konig

Waterways

The mighty Mississippi, the sleepy Shanandoah,
The meandering Missouri, the streams to Minnesota,
The rippling tributaries that emerge in North Dakota,

The trickling creeks of Texas, the creeping Colorado,
Splendid seaways of Alaska, golden pools of El Dorado,
The roaring Rio Grande, the Niagara's famous falls,
The colossal clear Columbia cruising through the canyon walls.

The whispering Willamette, the swiftly slithering Snake,
The sleepy Sacramento, the Klamath's white walled wake,
The boisterous brooks of Boise lilting their melodious voice,
The hustling humid Hudson, the iridescent Illinois,

The chuckling Charleston's chatter, the snow fed Santiam,
The Rogue River's roaring rapids with its white water monogram,
Rivers making monstrous history flooding farms and shifting
   shoals,
Romantic rivers robed in mystery, nostalgic creeks and fishing
   holes,
Rivers running in a frenzy, surging swiftly to the seas.
I sit, watching the McKenzie, and my heart is filled with peace.

    —Grace Cluster

Life

I watched the tide come rolling in and leave a shell behind.
The next wave took it back again - which quickly brought to mind.
How full life is of gifts to us, yet nothing seems to last.
It's so important that we savor before the moments past.
Never can we recapture the things we hold so dear.
Each sunrise is so different - the glowing sunsets disappear.
We take for granted a warm and sunny day.
Often rain will interfere when we want to play.
Spring in all its glory, nature in beauty lifts its head
Colorful fall somehow knows-when it is time to go to bed.
Summer is so alive with anticipation - a time for rest and
   relaxation.
Winter in its splendor - cold all dressed in white
Sparkles like diamonds in the full moonlight.
Try not to let a day go by - no matter what life has to deal,
That you don't stop to be thankful to see and smell and feel.

    —Dotti Turkot

Thine I

The omnipotent eye is irritated by human advancement.
The omnipotent eye, without will weakens, withers.
Irritation pounds limitations. The blinding intensity
of the pupil, diminished, blurred.
Strained sclera; a maze of bulging vessels. Pain.
Odyssey's cyclops decapitated.
The impotent eye closes.

A pinch of light escapes the other side.
Rays repeatedly reflected enable distorted images.

Water, sand, sclera merge.
The abyss is broken by a relentless attack.
Armies in white create a horizon as they
roll forth with a deafening roar.
But the eye intercepts every incursion of the
infinite infantry's interminable invasions.
Slaughtered battalions cry out like a hot pan
scorched by water. Globetrotting coyote.

The infallible eye rises (Brilliant Innocence!)
laughing at stupidity, paranoia.
Wait! White armies.. afloat! Cataracts.

    —Curtis C. Shin

The Patients Lament

Two types of patients in all hospitals we see
The one that's terribly sick and the other one like me.
Get on that light boy, give that nurse a call
She's waiting on that terribly sick one way down the hall
She hurries and hurries and tries not to be late
To see what Old Puny wants in room number eight.

I know she hasn't much to do and starts right on
But half way there, ring! ring! goes that telephone.
After answering a dozen question she's in a plight
But up over number eight, glares Old Puny's light.
She hangs up the receiver and stands up straight.
And heads once again for Puny in room number eight.

Two new comers have silently intervened
And upon her desk they lazily do lean.
"Mr. So and So's our cousin, and with him we must be.
His ma was pa's sister they were born twins yes sir ree."
In detail she points out the room of the cousin to see
And heads once again for Puny, yes, that's me.

    —B.A. Turner

Gift Of Devotion

How often do we think to ask
The one who blesses us instead
To take a second from this day
And place one 'pon His head?
How often do we kneel to pray
For him to take it easy?
Not often do we stop to think
Our lives for Him aren't breezy!
How often do we think to thank
Our God for merely Being?
For ignoring our shortcomings;
Our bestialities, for not seeing?
Since the time's long past for all of us
To give credit that's long over due;
It's with a Prayer and a Gift of Devotion,
Hugs and kisses we God. Bless You!

—*Joanie O. McClinton*

Innocent Victims

I was non-existent in one at first, until that perfect night;
The passion became stronger and stronger, and they did not put
up a fight. At first I sat around for a while contemplating
what I should do; but I didn't have a choice in the matter,
these lovers were messing with taboo. The passion became wild,
as I made my way through; but nothing but sheer pleasure is
what this couple knew. After it was all over, their true love
was put to the test; when they thought they had forever
together, it's now 10 to 12 years at best. Years went past
and they never knew what was expected ahead; the suffering,
the strife, and the anger, and the constant pain they will
dread. If only they could turn back time, and do it all over
again; they wouldn't have second thoughts about holding those
feelings in. But now I must destroy them and torture them day
by day; I'll rid them of the life they lived, I'll take their
breath away. I'll make them hallucinate until they go out of
their minds; and slowly look like skeletons, and must lay in a
bed confined. And let's not forget the sores and the shots of
which they'll have their remaining days; all because of a night
of lust and passion, they now have to deal with AIDS.

—*Dawn Waynetta Stewart*

Why Are Violent Criminals Being Set Free?

It is apparent to me by our justice system we're being robbed.
The people in Washington and congress are not doing their jobs.
Our courts, the ones we have all grown to trust, are now doing
the wrong. Violent criminals are getting less of a sentence
and the non-violent are getting the strong. Jail is for
punishment and to me that's been changed a bit. The convicts
watch television, have radios, stereos and lift weights. When
they get out, they're healthy and physically fit. Most
criminals will tell you, to them jail is like a home. They eat
and sleep free, don't work, get plenty of recreation and get
time of their sentence when not doing any wrong.
Rehabilitation is out of the question and a waste of time and
tax payer's money and has proven to be weak. Most violent
criminals are back to crime as soon as their feet hit the
street. Our justice system does not care for tourist or if our
own public will ever be safe. They keep letting repeat
offenders go and locking up drug dealers for decades. So look
at the message we're sending out to our youth, that it's O.K.
to kill, because if someone does not find a better way to run
the justice system, the jails will continue to over fill.

—*Charles Patterson*

The Mighty Ocean

The white sandy shore,
the powerful waves
and sea gulls flying gracefully above.

The seaweed that drifts upon the sand
as white as the delicate dove.

Snails peek out of their tiny home
while the mighty shark surrounds the sea.

I put my ear to the ocean shell
and hear the waves roaring at me.

When night sets in
and the ocean is still,
the waves are gentle and calm.

Beneath that deep blue ocean
lie so many wonders around!

—*Cherryl Nadine Sanfilippo*

Rag Picker

Any rags, bottles, bones today
The rag picker repeated in a melancholy way
This figure was slight beneath baggy clothes
He wore large black shoes turned up at the toes...
Gloved hands with stocking, like lace
Pulled down hat hiding his weather beaten face
Though in his heart laid a piercing pain
Destined for the rest of his life to remain.
Any rags, bottles, bones today
The rag picker repeated in a melancholy way
The horse's two pointed ears sticking through the hat toward
heaven. His ponderous gait slowly lumbering craven
He was ready to roll that golden wagon in the sky,
And kiss the rag paddler and his wagon goodbye.
The large wheeled wagon sagging under weight
Of happy children riding as far as the gate
The children's chatter swelled the rag pickers chest.
It lessened the pain and put it to rest
Any rags, bottles, bones today
The rag picker repeated in a melancholy way.

—*Anna Mueller*

The Wind

There are memories echoing in the wind
the reminder of who I am and where I am from
divine birds singing - mimicking the end.
Life so fragile it beckons the wind to come.

A burning sensation to fly away
a yearning in my soul to free the truth
temptations and trials - come what may
as the struggle with wisdom betrays my youth

Soft gentle breezes caress my face
as time slowly comes to a distant end
for age and knowledge have set the pace
as I release my spirit and become one
 - with the wind...

—*Jennifer Oland*

Daydream

A drop of dew suspended from a wooden fence
the sun shines through and makes it into
a star glistening while caught on a branch
in its tiny circumference a whole world exists
the local surroundings inverted in its reflection
the larger earth captured in a drop of dew
suspended magically from a wooden fence

—*Jen Dean*

An Anniversary Gift

Congratulations on the First Anniversary of your wedding
The right direction you both are heading
Together your journeys you must plan
So you arrive safely, hand in hand
Along the way here are things you must do
To avoid divorce, which are one in two
When expressing opinions, ask your partner to repeat
In their own words, what they thought was the meat
Respect for each other, all of the time
And to each always be kind
Listen to what I say and you both will see
This poem on your fiftieth anniversary

  —Charles Henry

Somber Reality

As flows the crystal stream
The road does fall before our feet
As the leaves flicker from the trees
So does the choices of life fall before us
What port shall we dock at in the future
Only the past will know for sure
For as the paradox of the universe unfolds
We see all of life in its infinite glory
As the viscous circle which it is
The roads we travel we have traveled
before so stop and revel at the scenery.

  —Christopher Lynn Ketron

Life's New Meaning

On life's journey, all through the years,
The road has been bumpy with many tears
With many a heartache, many a pain
So much I've strived for has seemed in vain.

I've tried to grasp and hold on tight
But I grabbed the darkness, not the light
Life's greatest meaning that I thought could be
Was floundering on in a murky sea.

I wish that then I could have known
I need never face anything all alone
Right then I did not understand
What it would mean to take Jesus by the hand.

To let His spirit lead me o'er life's sea
To have His presence there with me
To be assured that He's always there
To allay my fears, to give His care

All in the world I had to do
Was to open my heart and let Him through
And when at last I did, oh happy day.
Down in my heart, He's come to stay.

  —Clarice Overstreet

To Forget

Summer is waning away my love,
The roses are fading in their bowers,
Soon you'll be gone from me my love,
I'll have only the memory of these precious hours-

You will return to your kind of life,
I will return to mine,
To go onward will be struggle and strife,
To forget the love we have left behind-

If it must be, then it will be
Perhaps again somewhere our paths will meet,
I'll smile at you and you'll nod to me,
And all will be lost and forgotten in the
crowds of a busy street-

  —Eve Cooper

Falling From A Rising Star

It was love at first sight.
The second he smiled,
I know in my heart he was right.
He came and swept me off my feet.
I never knew I would fall so deep.
Then he said the words I would never forget.
It cuts me right to the heart,
and all I could do is fall apart.
I fell and I fell so fast.
I loved him and I still do,
My heart will always long to stay true.

  —Cheryl Hodge

Madly in Love

 The autumn breeze left the fragrance of a forbidden kiss.
The seeds of innocence will shatter with the drizzles of a
morning spring. Those rose petals will finally release the
pollen of love. How can I stop from being amazed at such a
beauty? How can I express the magnifying bliss of this human
soul.
 The rose will fade, but this stunned look will remain so
that the growing bud can offer, to the young couple in love,
a moment of remembrance. The scent of passion will fill their
hearts through that flower that was given to her by a young man
who fell madly in love.

  —Joselis Saldana

Never Say Goodbye

Though I can't ever know if love was what we had,
The sentiment of a dance and you were gone.
The only sentiment of a chance to tell you had gone wrong.
So hard to hold you, but so easy to love you.
To hold, because I couldn't tell you how I feel
To love, because I know you are real.
Word's were said and memories were made
And I'll never forget what I said as we sway.
Let me talk don't say a word, what I must say is not easy for me
Love is like a candle, it shines bright when light.
Love is like a child, always sorry for anything he did.
But as a candle the light will turn out, as a child the boy will
grow up, but love will never leave just fade.
All love needs is to color in what remains. My love is this, it is
this way for you. When darkness sets on your heart love will
pull you through. What I've said is all I have to tell
Except to say I love you, the dance is gone but my love has
stayed the same please tell me after these years you feel the way.
As I remember the last thing I said that lonely night.
It must has been to Never Say Goodbye.

  —Cesario Martinez

Where Are You

I miss:
The smile you gave me so graciously.

I miss:
Seeing your eyes that sparkle with laughter.

I miss:
Your sense of humor that makes me glad.

I miss:
The conversations we shared so many time.

I miss:
Being happy just spending time with you.

I miss:
The warmth of such a great friendship.

I miss you!!

  —Evelyn Marchant

To My Granddaughter

A corner of heaven I saw today
The smile you had, a glowing sun ray.
Sweet innocent eyes, looked back at me
While holding you close, there on my knees.
Precious and cuddly, feeling so grand
Patting me softly, with two little hands.
Straying gold sunbeams, made lights in your hair
And with rays on your face, nothing compared.
You reached for shadows, that fell in the room
They vanished quickly, with movement too soon.
May you grow healthy, with spirited mind
Giving to others, of the strength you find.
May life treat you kindly, in all you do
And you will be happy, your whole life through.

  —Eva Orr

Pearls

Pearls are tears of angels when they cry
The soft breezes of spring are when they sigh
Flowers are seeds of angels that they sow
For when they grow and bloom and grow
It lightens our burdens when we are low
A beautiful place to be with a heavenly glow
A promise from God so that we may see
How beautiful that this world can be

  —John D. McBride

Life's Beautiful Things

A gentle touch from a precious love one,
The soothing warmth from the morning sun

The joyous sound of a Newborn's cry -
The soft white clouds against a clear blue sky

The cool breeze from the distant wind
An unexpected call from a longtime friend;

A budding rose glistened by the morning dew
The dawning of another day - all anew!

The fresh clean smell after April showers,
The savory fragrance of a garden of flowers;

The sweet lyrics of the birds that sing
These are a few of Life's Beautiful Things!

  —Andrea G. Clark

Untitled

Sirens blaring in the night,
the sounds of things not going right.
A robbery here, a killing there,
no one left to love or care.

We need a world of people who,
cares what their children say and do.

Fifty three years have passed and for what?
We're still, in the same segregation rut.

Prejudice continues to rear its ugly head,
if we don't change, this world is dead.

We go to Church we say "Amen",
but we leave at home our children and kin.

The people of the world will still want and thirst,

Unless we learn to put God First".

  —Jamie M. Wilson

The Troubled Planet...

The Earth is a sphere that floats around space,
The stars in the heavens will argue this case.
It twirls and it spins as it moves round the sun,
This world as we know it has only begun.
With traffic pollution, and killer acid rain,
Our little world has got nothing to gain.
People are dying and animals are sick,
We need a solution times running out quick.
If nothing is done then we're all going to die,
And when everyone's gone there'll be no time for goodbye.
So do something now while we all have the time,
Because if we don't it could be a crime!

  —Carrie-Anne Cooper

The Unicorn

As dawn kisses the morning sky
The sun's rays touch the ground
The air tingles with mystic life
Of nature's magic all around

It's a calm and beautiful day
As soft steps can be heard
A shimmering white moves through the trees
To be announced by their silent word

It stops to listen to the birds' songs
Their cheerful melodies echo through the wood
Its beauty is revered and ever present
Bestowing its benevolent majesty as it should

Its silvery silken hair dances in the breeze
As its clear blue eyes sparkle in the light
Its tail twitches gently without care
As the ivory luster of its hide gleams white

It has one unique feature though
A feature full of magic it's been said
This creature is a rare one indeed
For it carries a single horn upon its head.

  —David M. Maynard

Revenge

Mississippi Slaves and Emmett Till,
The third seal was opened a black horse.
A Black Man sat upon him, a pair of balances in hand.
He was praying for equal rights, for you to love him,
And to treat him like a human being.
We were the instrument of labor, hatred, degrading,
Rape, murder, auctioned off like cattle when too sick to work.
Beaten and thrown in the Mississippi River.

Missouri River came down from North Dakota,
Bringing the souls of the Indians and White Man.
The fourth seal was opened, the beast said come and see,
A pale horse, a white man sat upon him, was death and hell.
Power was given to him over the fourth part of the earth,
To kill with sword, hunger, death, and the beast of the earth.

The souls met at the fork of the River crying for revenge.
You can't stop us now, our decayed bodies will leave a stink,
In your homes, yards, streets. It's a reminder of how you
Killed our bodies but not our Souls.
Old Man River just keep rolling along.

  —Ethel L. Latta

Harmony

Ego what is that? Confidence in mind;
The thought to have or stay behind.

Humbleness, it has to be for those
who have helped constantly.

Empathy, is hard to display when security
is threatened everyday.

Security, is warm the cold is coming in;
Begone the storm brewing the anchors within.

Love and sacrifice have lived for years;
with a bit of happiness and a bit of tears.

Advice is something hard to take;
When it is coming from someone filled with hate

Respect is something that has to be earned;
It comes in life at every turn.

The big "I" is frightening in so many ways;
The "WE" is important to fill in our days.

Life is a team wherever it may be:
with each little molecule in Gods harmony.

 —Ardis Marie Sich

Mother's Awaiting

Mother is awaiting
 The tinkle of your laughter
 The twinkle of your eyes
Mother is awaiting
 The joy of your presence
 Your heart warming cries
Mother is awaiting
 To sing you to sleep with soft lullabies
But
There'll be
 No tinkling laughter
 No twinkling eyes
 No joy in your presence,
 No soft lullabies,
 No hugs,
 No kisses
But plenty of cries and sighs
For you've left mother awaiting
Left before you'd fully arrived

 —Darlene P. Marsh

The Traveler

Through the thick evening mist, the dense evening mist, walks
the traveler. The traveler is blind, though he still can see.
He walks slow but his destination isn't far. The mist dampens
his face and the wind beckons him to stop, but the traveler keeps
moving, slowly as if he were on his death march, but keeps on
moving. He climbed many mountains, crossed many deserts,
ventured many oceans. Even a few times he was rewarded for
over-coming his trials. His trials were often difficult, but
he managed to move through them, never around them. He felt
joy on his journey, he felt hate and distrust. There were
disappointments on his failures. This never made the traveler
stop. Humbleness on his victories made him travel faster.
When the traveler was to vain, or told lies to accomplish his
journey, he would stray of the path into darkness, the demons
would tear at his heart. Although he is blind, the traveler
knows where he is going, He knows where he is going because he
keeps his heart true, his soul cleansed. The path that the
traveler walks is life. It is the same path that we all walk
now. We are all blind, but we must stay on the path. The
traveler has reached his destination, his journey is complete.

 —John C. Dickerson

One Day At A Time

One day at a time, is mine to behold,
The view from my window, is stories untold.
The ducks and the Pelicans that fly to and fro,
Reflecting contentment, brings peace to my soul.
The sun on the water, makes diamonds here and there,
Just makes me realize, God is everywhere.
Moonbeams on the water, looks like magic at night,
I know! God sends them as a beautiful sight.
But on this earth, as long as I remain
Gods beautiful creations, will live long in my brain.
The greenlays and the redbirds, sing such beautiful songs,
But that still doesn't correct on this earth all the wrongs.
There's one thing I know, God's creative hand,
Can lake care of all things across our great land.
So I'll close this poem, knowing things are alright,
And with God's help, we'll all see the light.
The path coming up, we'll try and walk straight,
As when heavens doors open, we don't want to be late.
So God bless you all, and hold you close.

 —Dot Haught

The Time Maker

Somewhere in the great expand, among the still quietness,
 the voice of the Time Maker is echoed through the speckled
   paths of space.
 Where highways and roads emerge of hands unseen
 in the midst of vast tunnel's to heavens unknown.

Behold, the stars of stars that orbit them given unto motion
by who, a foundation never seen belonging to the Time Maker.
A world within a universe and a universe within another world.
 who can measure its depths or lengths.

We are complete to numbers as time is to the Time Maker.
This green world resting just east of infinity sitting on an
   apex of nothingness.
 Living in a world who's maker was time, its genius
 unknown who's ways pass finding out. Where is its

 end, who has known its beginning? As I sit here
gazing up through an ocean of stars, I see the knowledge
of him transcending light unto this little planet of ours.

 Gateways not known to men such as we have seen,
 time to him is but a twinkle of the eye. The keeper
of all that dwell's nearby, for time beheld the Time Maker.

 —George Jenkins

Nature

I see the wind pushing the water
the water as it comes on shore.
Does every single man watch this
'tis so beautiful words can not describe it.
As the fish come to feed that is nature.
'tis so beautiful words can not describe it.
As the crickets chirp with so much
anxiety because they are nature!
tis so beautiful words can not describe it.
As a butterfly glides flittery,
fluttery, go little butterfly that
is nature 'tis so beautiful words
can not describe it.
As you sit on the shore feeling
the sand between your toes
that is nature. 'Tis so beautiful
words can not describe it
'Tis I! I think, why do
they destroy it? 'Tis so
beautiful words can not describe it.

 —Amie Wcisel

Dreaming

The sun sinks to sleep
The water gently caressing the rocks
I drift away into relaxation so deep
And all the doors seem to unlock
I guess I'm dreaming
The most beautiful girl stands to my right
To my left a peaceful haven
She fills my life with light
For this girl, so long have I been craven
One thing, it's too early to start redeeming
I must keep on living a fantasy
And move from town to town
To stay away from life's catastrophes
I gotta keep spinning round and round
It's a good time to start screaming
My friends are not real
There just from my mind
Our thoughts we trade and deal
My true life, no one will ever find
I'll never stop dreaming

—Joe Laronga

The Earth's Revolution

I just can't understand it, how people can be so blind
The way they treat this earth is so unkind
Why can't they see, why can't they see what they've done
What they've done to this earth, to our mother
And it's such a damn shame, because nobody wants to take the
    blame
For the earth's condition
We need to save the earth, it's our mission
It's time now for the earth's revolution
People do you really think there's a solution?
Even though there's so much pollution
And it just keeps on happening, oh will it ever stop?
Why do they keep on destroying, oh can it ever stop?
We need to do something, but where do we start?
Come on peoples of the earth, we need to show what it's worth
Stop destroying and desecrating our mother
Can there ever be a rebirth
                of life
                    for our children, for our people
                    for future generations
                    for our mother, the earth????

—Heidi J. Brewer

Shame

Worn as an old penny tossed aside on life's road,
The wild drifter brooded not far from my path.
Fear gripped my heart, my jaw, and settled in my eyes.
Watch, watch each other and anticipate surprise.

From a distance, I've spied him many times before.
This was his spot, his territory, his home.
I can't avoid this passing, now a breath away.
Would he demand money, food, or maybe my life?
Watch, watch each other and anticipate surprise.

A word, a sentence, his utterance stopped me dead.
"Ma'am, what's the time?" his gaze ashamed to meet mine.
"Five after seven" my words splayed out precisely.
I tensed every muscle and waited for more.
"The store's open now," he said in innocent plea.

I stood there alone awhile as the man walked on.
Stunned, I realized I caused this stranger such shame,
Leaving him with need to explain himself to me.
Our fears were equal, each masks of today's society.
Watch, watch each other and never see what's inside.

—Anna J. Tynsky

The Wind Was June

The experience of a lifetime! She came to me...
The wind blew through my head, and out to sea...
    The wind was June... the wind was June...

    The wind was June... she gave me a day...
I'll never forget... she gave me a day...
        I couldn't hold on to...
    The wind was June... the wind was June...

Searching endlessly inside her... never finding much,
    No matter how hard I tried ... I always lost.
    The wind was june, she gave me a day ...
        I'll never forget...
    She blew right through me ... and into, the west!

        Do you know what freedom is?
    She was something I thought I had ...
        Come now ... and come again,
    I don't know ... if I'll ever be ready ...
    The wind was June ... the wind was June ...

—Bob Syd

Untitled

While sitting on the edge of my bed, I began to stare out of
the window.
The image of other windows fades as I think about the strongest
thoughts in my sub-conscience.
She has attached an unknown force upon my soul, which compels
my reflection on her inane manner to provoke happiness within
myself.
Her physical self is not in my presence; yet I feel her company
within the innards of my heart.
The world erodes permanent structures, yet her mark defies the
laws of nature by not decomposing, rather, ever still growing.
The buildings are shadows in the distance a grey blur of the
tangible macrocosm that my feet pound on in daily life.
This overwhelming, quick paced, densely substantive world has
less of an impact on my constantly thinking soul than her
abstract presence which induces my brain in a strong fashion,
to yearn for remembrances...

—Jason A. Savlov

Lost Love

Open your heart, let me come inside
The world is a cold place, just a Merry-Go-Round ride
Spinning round and round, one face then another
Confusion sets in, why won't you be my lover?

I give my love freely, but to the chosen one
Who can make my world happy, with each rising sun
Your arms like the rays of sun, kept me warm
Yes dear, it's you, my heart yearns for!

My everyday is gray now, since you said "good-bye!"
Every love song I hear, makes my heart want to cry
This must be a dream, surely it can't be true
Everything felt so good, now I'm losing you!

I know right now, you're a little unsure
So many wheels spinning, no room for one more
Don't want to give you stress, or be in your way
Just by your side, heart to heart each day!

So, if your world feels empty, without me around
And you miss my smile and care that you found
Don't be afraid, to bring your heart back
To the one who really cares, no questions asked!!

—Deborah Marie

The Gifts

Give us the gift of a safe haven to where our spirits will be free
The world we have come to know is getting too dark for us to see
Give us the gift of longer lives
Let us rise harmoniously with the brilliant sunrise
For to be awakened to another day has become a surprise
Give us the gift of those children who are determined to succeed
To counteract the negative forces will cultivate a new breed
Give us the gift of brotherly love to sanitize the earth
And create perfection in our new birth
Give us the gift of a triumphant song
To celebrate our new land
Harmonize our voice with the dancing wind
Freedom Freedom together we shall sing
Give us the gift

—Dana Dunn Smith

From The Heart

The tears rolled down my cheeks
The years went by like weeks
Only memories left
From my childhood, up until the death

Now their house, that was made with love
Is also going to go
I say goodbye, shed a tear, a hurtful kiss I blow

All those years went by so fast
I sometimes wish I could go back.
Games to play with Nana, books to read with Grampa

So many good times went by so fast
I'm grateful for the times I had.

I'll never forget them, they were the best
I hope in peace, they both rest.

I hurt but I'm happy
I try to smile
Goodbye Nana and Grampa
I'll see you in a while.

—Jenny Baxter

The Peace Bell Rings

In the midst of a war-torn nation,
Their leaders engage in peaceful conversation.
Enemies for generations do not attack but,
They come together to sign a pact.
Oh, the impact it brings!
All around the world, the sound, of the peace bell rings.

A reformed government all for the people,
A world religion under one steeple.
A new world order full of peace and tranquility,
Or, is it just a false sense of security?
Oh, the delusions it will bring!
When the world hears, the sound, of the peace bell ring.

—Joann Dana

A Poem To Martin Luther King Junior

This is a poem to Martin Luther King Jr.
The man that made black history ring
Through out the American scene.
He is the man that made the victory bell ring
He was praised by all, when he wrote,
"I had a dream".
The theme that all men embrace that dream
So I sing the praise to Martin Luther King.
It is a shame we can't erase that racial
Thing, and call each other brother no
matter the color of any other.
Keep the faith and stand up for what you think
And do your thing for Martin Luther King.

—James De Stefano

Boredom

One second goes by...
then a minute...
Slowly, time drags on and on, and
your mind searches for freedom;
freedom to live, escaping such torture.

I look around my enclosed surroundings
for the key to freedom.
Nothing; no key.
Is my mind going to be locked forever in this state?
Then, a thought struck me.
No, I assured myself.
Once I get out of here my mind will be free again,
There will be no black and white vision anymore,
Everything will be in full color.
I'll have a smile on my face, and
my surroundings will have no boundaries,
I'll be able to live again.
I'll be so happy, I'll be so, so free.

—Carol Christian

If

If I could just once understand your problems
then I could not discriminate against you

If I could just once listen to what you have to say
then I could not judge you

If I could just once be your friend then I could
not dislike you

If I could just once love you for who you are and not
what I want you to be then I could stand by you

If I could just once remember that you have feelings
too then I could not be eager to hurt you

If I could just once let you cry on my shoulder or give
you a hug or kiss, if I could just once say I love you, If I
could just once be the friend that I should be then we
would not be living in pain.

If....It's such a meaningful word. If I
could just once know the (if's) then I'd be living
in a world full of love and not hate!
  If!

—Debra E. Bratcher

Trick Or Treat

T'was a cold dark night and all was so still,
then I heard an owl hoot and it gave me a chill.
I glanced out the window and to my surprise,
I was looking right into two round, beady eyes.

I heard a cat yowl and a whistle so shrill,
just as the moon came up over the bill.
The thing I saw was surely a sight,
a witch on her broom all set for a flight.

It's hard to believe, but I tell you it's true,
her face looked like she'd been drinking her brew.
A ghost floated by and I shook with fright,
then I remembered, it's Halloween Night!

I went right over and opened the door,
there were pirates and clowns, a dozen or more.
False faces and costumes, they all looked so sweet,
then they all shouted "OK Trick or Treat!"

—Darwin M. Rinkenberger

African American History Curriculum

Give me a place I can call my own
Then my mind will cease to roam
Here, there, everywhere,
Sometimes I feel I just don't care

Then something inside makes me stop and think
Just in time before I sink.

They must have been strong. They had to have been great
For those of us to have survived such a fate

These thoughts keep me going. They keep me alive
For in unknown memories is where I'd often hide.

But what about the others, my brothers?
Will they find strength in this, or the other?

Pulling myself up by my strong mind and will,
I realize now, I've a quest to fulfill.

They've cried and experienced the emptiness of not belonging,
They've been sadden terribly by just not knowing

Now is the time for them to know from whence they've come
Now is the time for an African American History Curriculum.

—*Florence Wherry Gilmore*

Age

I never thought age would conquer me
Then, when I turned seventy
With crippled foot and arthritic knee
I learned there was no magic key
To health, or wealth, or memory.

My days are filled with "might have been"
A long list of "remember when'
And wishing I could live again
To remedy mistakes of tongue and pen.

I never thought that I would see
The image that now looks back at me
With mirrored wrinkles that time felt free
To bestow on a face that needed charity.

I really don't appreciate
How much of me screams "deteriorate"
But meekly I'll accept my fate
'Cause the alternate choice is not so great.

—*Berenice Scringer*

Going Along

Whenever you look it's never there
Then you close your tired eyes allowing it to happen.
By the time you open up and glance around,
You see it's magically emerged.

Maybe you're not even sure what it is,
All you know is that it wasn't there before.
And then you thank God, or your higher power, or Mother Earth,
Or whatever it is you think blessed you so.

But what no one seems to realize
Is that you really need to just thank yourself
For letting it all happen and
Going along.

—*Amy Deutsch*

The Earth

The wind was speaking to God, "Help us, please."
The trees were yelling to the world, "Don't kill us!"
The sky was crying for the future because it was polluted.
The lake was mourning for the past that was gone.
The leaves were screaming to the children, "Save us."
For the people were poisoning the Earth and its treasures.

—*Jessica Henson*

Yesterday Was Graduation

I stopped by the house where you once lived...you were not
there.
And I thought about the days you spent that I did not share,
the times you were alone, the small daily tasks performed,
when I was not here.

I thought about the flowers your tried to grow, but I could not
see your small world when you were here
without me.

The time is past, it is too late to be part of your life here.
Bound by work and a thousand miles I could not come,
and it bears heavy on me.

I am sad but also proud, for you carried on well and achieved
you goal and left to open another door.
This chapter's done, the page has turned and somehow
I've lost again the time, and only I
stand here now.

—*Gerald D. Ross*

Time Is Gone

Life is too short to take for granted,
There are so many special moments to cherish.
When time is gone, you'll wonder
Where did it go, it's gone.
Along with the people and the places that you once knew.
You'll look back on the promises you've made,
To yourself and to others,
Did you do the right thing or the wrong.
No one knows but the future and that's where you are,
so you tell me...

—*Jennifer F. Hendricks*

Children Of God

The other evening as I watched the T.V. screen
There came upon it this heart warming scene
It was of two beautiful children, each one a star
Doing what our creator would bless them for
One was pushing, for she could not see but could walk
The other was riding, for she could see but could not walk
When I saw them, by definition, I was prompted to say a prayer
For this was a true version of two showing their love and care
You see what I mean when I say this in part
They were doing something that truly came from their heart
May the Good Lord smile on them from heaven above
And always bless them with His tender and sincerest love.

—*Bill Schwartz, Sr.*

City Streets

These city streets,
There for me.
Discipline is what I need.
Gunshot's sound,
Who can be,
Another death,
Another lesson learned.
Sometimes they are scary,
I have learned,
Sometimes they are scary,
Arson smelt,
Someone's burned.
It is just one of the lessons,
The City Streets are now about to be turned.
Another warn,
Word has it another menace is being born.
City Streets, and is in the shape of a object
It's just a game, so be quiet, sit down, or go home

—*Alex Isaacson*

When A Crumb Falls

One silent cry of agony,
No ears to hear its pain.
One of several others
Long forgotten.
One number amongst infinity,
Its value shall be looked upon as trivial.
One falls, and the universe is not fazed.
Pain is universal,
Yet empathy is difficult to find.
Silence, and one doesn't exist.
No one is significant to all;
Only to a few.
Time continues, people laugh,
And little appears lost.
One voice is silenced
And the chorus of the universe continues.
What significance is one's existence?
Show a person disregard,
And that person will show the universe
death.

—*Brian Bradley*

He Holds My Hand

Sometimes the road seems so long
No end in sight
He holds my hand and says
Don't be sad, things will be alright
Life feels so cruel
With things I can't bare
He holds my hand and says
It's okay I'll always be there.
Then there are days I feel
like just maybe I can
He comes up beside me
And just holds my hand.

—*Cindy Little*

Wild Flowers

You left us with
          no love
Like wild flowers growing alone
          living off the rain
Receiving warmth from
          only the sun
Rejected wild flowers with
          starving eyes
In desperate need
          for a home
Searched for you it was
          too late
You were lost our
          Mother has gone
Leaving the wild flowers
          to bloom alone
Never did they die............

—*Christina M. Tangjian*

Stillness

The stillness of an early morn,
no movement, oh what joy,
The beauty of the plants and trees,
The bees and buds to do their job,
prepare the day for all to see,
The cars go by, the stillness
gone,
The moments great to dream
or hold,
What beauty God has designed
our day unfolds.

—*Darlene A. Rhinehart*

Then Who You Love The Most

No matter how much money you make,
No matter what you own,
Can make you feel happier,
then who you love the most.

No matter where you live,
No matter where you go,
Can make you feel happier,
then who you love the most.

No matter who you meet,
No matter who you know,
Can make you feel happier,
then who you love the most.

—*April McCullough*

You Are My Rose

Love is a beautiful flower
no matter where it grows
Though there are many flowers alive,
you are my rose.

Your petals are gentle
just like your heart
Your fragrance is sweet
and your thorns are sharp.

Where I'd be without you
only God knows
You are the flower of my life,
you are my rose.

You've been with me through it all
through the highs and the lows
You are my everything,
you are my rose.

I could've picked another
but it was you that I chose
You're the best thing that ever happened to
me,
because you are my rose.

—*Curtis Kaanapu*

I Am Content

Death cometh soon, I am content
No more sorrow, no more pain
Only memories are left, of a
Life well-filled and long
Only tears for those bereft.

So many griefs to overcome
So many loved ones gone
Why am I still here?
Must I live on alone?
Death my release, I am content.

—*Evelyn L. Valenti*

The Questions

I have some questions that
no one can answer. If love is
the feeling everyone's after why is
it so hard to capture. How can you
love someone with all your heart
and soul only to be told it's grown
kind of old. What happens to, that
moment of fate when you realize you've
found your true lifetime mate. The
questions I'm asking are truly a mystery
I've searched through my history and
found what I thought no one can
answer the questions I've got.

—*Jeff A. Sparks*

Hands Of The Heart

The hands of a clock keep on ticking
    no one can stop it.
everybody around keeps on kicking
    but no one cares one bit.

Wait, I know some one who cares and
    will always be there
No matter how many people stare or
    even if my heart feels bare.

Someday I will be with the one that
    I admire so much.
I won't have to wait for anybody to come
    because you will be at a close touch.

Please do not ever leave because
    I won't be able to depart.
For you see, you touched my heart.
    So I come to you today just
        To say "I love you"!

—*Crystal Reece*

A Grain Of Sand

By myself I'm unimportant,
No one sees or notices me.
    I get tossed and thrown
        As if I'm no one.

I see love, but never feel it.
    Taken for granted
That I'll be there tomorrow,
    Left as if not important.

    No one knows how lonely
    This grain of sand is,
    Unless you're like me,
        A grain of sand.

—*Cindy K. Sensenich*

Sparks

To me you are the Heaven above,
No other could ever match your love.
We are together constantly,
Although it's just in dreams you see,
The ocean-skies, and seas apart,
There is just you, within my heart.

He made you just for me you see,
That's why I always know you'll be,
Safe from troubles, sickness and pain,
Returning to me, just the same.

God brought us together, always to be,
That's why I know you'll be safe, for me,
But someday soon the clouds will pass,
And you'll be home with me, at last.

—*Jean Voeltz*

The Golden Wedding

They said, it won't last,
Now the future has become the past
Here comes the bride, age 65
Here comes the groom at 75
The best man is their son
The matron of honor their daughter
The ushers are their grandsons
The bridesmaids their granddaughters
They are blessed on this glorious day,
Guess what? There's a great
    grandchild on the way.

—*Helen Book*

First You Must Know Jesus

You cannot go through Heaven's Portals,
    nor claim the Great Reward,
    nor join the Holy Wedding Feast,
without knowing Christ, the Lord.

Nor will you sing with Angel Choirs
    when they their voices raise
    to honor God, the Mighty King
with reverence and praise.

You cannot walk the Streets of Gold
    nor in any way take part
    of Living in God's Mansion
unless Christ dwells within your heart.

You must follow Jesus' teachings
    if you want God to speak to you
    for He has said that 'if you know me,
then you know my Father too'

Even tho the Bible tells us
    that the two are really one
    you cannot know the Father
unless first you know His Son.

    —*Charlotte E. Reinicker (Mikki)*

Liberty

I've never been to Valley forge,
    Nor have I seen Bunker hill.
But when I read our history,
    I always get a thrill.

When I think of the brave men who died,
    That we might have liberty,
It causes me to thank the Lord,
    We live in a land that's free.

Let us all be very thankful.
    For this country that we love,
And help to keep it just as free
    As a soaring white winged dove.

We should all look up to God,
    And hold our colors high,
For without our precious liberty,
    Our freedom would surely die.

So, on this Independence Day,
    Let us all give thanks,
That we live in America,
    Where freedom highly ranks.

    —*Helen Ruth Ashton*

Nightmares

The night was dark and gruesome
Not a bright star could be seen
The witches and goblins had a party
For it was Halloween

Creatures of every kind and color
Came out of their hiding place
Even the little children
Wore a mask upon their face

The haunted house came alive
With dangling chains and screams
Ghosts roamed freely 'through the halls
And the bats were really mean

With the bewitching hour of midnight
The whole world shook with fright
It certainly is a big relief
That Halloween lasts only but a night.

    —*Geneva Guy*

One Life

Whether ever to live a life
of a hundred and twenty
or a life of ten
we all still go as dust in the wind
To ever live a life
And be forgotten in discourse or disgust
a taker of lives and user of lusts
It is hell indeed forgotten utmost
But to live a life as
there is only one
And to be remembered for
the good that you have done
That is heaven indeed
For love you have won
And then so the remembrance of you
shall go on and on and on.

    —*Chris Schweitzer*

Valley

In the clear vase
of a mountain valley
my thoughts were gathered

Small buds of silence
threaded deep
among bright blooms
of solitude
a spray of joy
unexpected
in its heavy scent

A bouquet of contemplation
gathered and held
in the clear vase
of a mountain valley.

    —*Jane Elliot Granberry*

Jesus, The Reason

On this season
Of Christmas cheer,
Let us not forget
Why we are here.

For a baby was born
On this wonderful night,
Shone up above was
A star so bright.

He is the reason
For this joyous time,
For the stairs to heaven
He did climb.

He died on a cross
For the world to see,
Then he slipped off
To eternity.

For he was the one
Who paid the cost,
For all of us,
His life He lost.

    —*Angela McDonald*

Too Pooped To Whoop

I'm a member of a little group
Of folks that I enjoy.
They're people that I really like,
Two girlfriends and a boy.

We went out last night together
And painted this old town red.
We really did kick up our heels
Before we went to bed.

When I woke up this morning
I sure felt like a jerk.
Because I faced the reality
That today I had to work.

When I got home from work today
My tail was really draggin'.
And I decided it would be best
If I go on the wagon.

So, the next thing that I did
Was phone the rest of my group.
I said, "I can't go out tonight
'Cause I'm too pooped to whoop."

    —*Byron C. Casey*

Today I See What You Mean To Me

I've been so full
Of my own self
I seldom thought of you
And my first thought
Has always been
My very own thing to do
I never even made a pause
To see you as you are
Or that you mean
Much more to me
Than anyone by far
Today I see I am very small
In the shadow of your glow
I decided, dear, to take the time
Today to tell you so

    —*Gloria P. Long*

Anguish

Today there's a familiar look
Of sadness in your eyes
A look I once concealed
Behind a faltering disguise

The fear of being fragile
To break apart midflight
Can lead one to disparity
Pushing hard until it's right

You've kept your distance long enough
Let someone hold your hand
Turn away from what was once
And know that you can stand

Your pain seems insurmountable
And time heals hurts too slow
But I swear there's life past anguish
When you choose to let it go

    —*Angela Reis*

Feeling Senses

When open, the center
of the eye feeds
the center of the mind.

When closed, the center
of the mind feeds
the imagination

Intensifying the inner
heart felt emotions
that one senses,

As they're consciousness
visualizes and amplifies
the sensation of one's imagination,

Creating the power
to express ones
sense of feelings.

—*Colleen Stowe*

Wrinkles

A trail of vapor is all that's seen
of the jet, up in the sky.
So it is with the works of our life,
in the years that are long gone by.

Some people see only old age
in the wrinkles of my skin.
But I see only well beaten paths
of where it is I've been.

Hard lessons learned are etched there
upon my wrinkled face.
I never would have made it
without my Saviour's grace.

The hair on my head is peppered,
mixing gray amongst the brown.
My movements are much slower,
nor do I sleep so sound.

But my heart is full of great feelings
for the family I have raised.
So you see, they are not wrinkles,
only trails that I have blazed.

—*Barbara A. Dack*

The Feather

The feather was a watch dog
  Of things I should not touch;
It guarded Grandma's sewing
  And that was rather much.

The feather was a keeper
  Of treasures on the shelf,
For I would go no closer
  When I was by myself.

The feather was a helper
  To the ink upon the desk.
Many letters they were written
  And I was not a pest.

The feather was a comfort
  Pillows stuffed with many more;
They were wonderful to sleep on
  But the clean up was a chore.

The feather was a duster
  Of any trifle mess,
But it kept me out of trouble
  Of this I do confess.

—*Carlin V. Hounshell*

Country Store

They sit and talk
  of yesteryears
Old men with hope
  and fear

Of politics
  and civil rights
Taxes
  and farmer's plight

They solve each one
  with words of grace
Satisfied
  they saved the race

They bid farewell
  and go their way
With lighter hearts
  at end of day

—*Jestine Birlson*

Summer's Melody

Oh cynical music man
off so far
with your flute
and guitar
to keep you by.
sing me a memory,
play me a warm summer
night sort of melody
let your flute be the stars
and your guitar be her eyes
set in my mind so far,
but play with not a smile
for these of us
uncertain of our sin
and wear no grin
for those of rest
who have no guitar
to hold to his chest.

—*Casey Snyder*

The Fan's Prayer

Bless our Favorites,
  Oh Lord, we pray.
Bid your angels to guard them,
  By night and day.
Increase their desire,
  To give us their best.
And bestow on us - patience,
  When they need a rest.
Prevent them from becoming annoyed,
  When besieged by the demons,
Of paparazzi and tabloid!
  Put in their paths,
Some time to play.
  To smell the coffee and flowers,
Throughout the day.
  Thus, when they think
To slow and pause,
  They'll feel thy embrace,
In our applause...

—*Cathy Cormany*

Ode To A Peeping Tom

Oh, Peeping Tom
Oh, Peeping Tom
Oh, unseen visitor in the gloom
Who brings adventure to some room
Of each domestic domicile
Where you peek
And, mayhap, smile.

What housewife ever feels alone
When you are peeking in her home?
A footfall tells her you are prowling
Then she hears a canine growling.

Are there times when you feel hated?
Lone and unappreciated?
Leap o'er the wall
And lightly hop.
Someone soon will call a cop!

—*Helen Blank*

Secrets Of St. Johns

I visited you, St. Johns,
on a balmy spring day.
Your swamplands invited me for
a noisy airboat ride through backwaters
of primeval beauty.
I saw white ibis wading in your marshes
and alligators camouflaged on the banks
of your dark waters.
I know your secrets of war and slavery,
a history as real as raccoons
that now patrol your river like bandits.
I admire your silent non-conformity
as you flow northward
through the belly of Florida.
Your subtropical landscapes renew
my winter-weary spirit
like a drink from
the Fountain of Youth.

—*Janet O. Maddix*

Untitled

In an abandoned house
on a bare counter top
sits an
empty glass

and

somewhere
there is water

and

somewhere
there is an empty hand.

—*Elissa Schoening*

Wrestling

Quickness.
Of the whistle
grab his leg with a quick hand
my timing shows that
my hard head hits
his knee.
With the strength
of the collision he
falls to the mat.

—*John Blosser*

He Is There

As the sun breaks through the clouds
On a dark and dreary day
Jesus comes with sweet assurance
He is there to show the way.

When the way is hard to follow
And it seems you're all alone
He steps in to give directions,
"Fear not child, we're headed home."

Oh to know His blessed abiding
Glory in His matchless grace
Steal away, be still and listen
There's a precious hiding place.

Father help me meet tomorrow
With a faith and love that's true
I am weak and often falter
My hope, my strength is all in You.

Welcome as the rain on deserts
As the calm on stormy seas
As the lost child to its mother
Lord, Thou art welcome here with me.

—Eula Peele

Handshake

History was made
On a handshake this week
From two great giants
Seeking world peace

People and rejoicing
And shaking hands
For two bitter enemies
Who became friends

The world is watching
For these heads of state
To maintain peace
With just a handshake

Mothers need not cry
Families must stay put
As we extend our hands
And be friends as we should

The pen is mighty
And words are cold
But just a handshake
Could save our souls.

—Edilberto Bermudez

Flamenco Dancer

She is dancing
on a red dimly lit stage
every part of her body is alive
with sensuality oozing
but it stays within her

A guitar player is singing
a soulful song
there are people below stage
strange, faceless

But to her they are not important
she is selfish when she dances
forgetting everything around her
but her own body

I wish she was I
and not a dream.

—Aida Ophelia Saldana

Miles Away

Cold is the night
On a summers day
When I look in your eyes
And your miles away

Lost in thought
Or perhaps a place unknown
How I hate when you go
And leave me all alone

Please let me in
To this place that you play
Please don't ever leave me
Miles away

—Cynthia A. Diaz

Pioneer Poem

We're going West,
On a wagon train,
There's lots of danger,
And lots of pain

The rivers are deep,
The mountains are high,
And some of our animals,
Are starting to die

The Indians are coming,
Ready to attack,
We have to keep going,
We can't turn back.

The West will be great,
It's not as cold,
There's more opportunity,
We might find gold

The West,
We're here at last,
We'll start new lives,
But remember the past.

—Alysia Piffero

Time Enough For Tea

One bright afternoon
on my porch I sat alone.
I had come here for some peace
no neighbors and no phone.

But in a short time it grew old,
that blasted loneliness you see,
until the day which I'll relate
about this woman and our Tea.

I was watching the Chesapeake
when she came my way
We said hello and started talking
and talked right through the day.

I had not seen her for a while.
"Have you time enough for tea?"
She reached out and touched my hand
"How wonderful that would be."

I had not felt her touch for ages
since she had vanished from my life
So I wait and she still visits,
this spectre of my wife.

—David E. Nettles

Blue Horizon

I've seen the sun rise
on perfect beaches caressed
by the breath of God.
The endless tide comes and goes
like the vapor of life;
here but for a moment
then sinking into the emptiness
of an endless sea.

I've felt the warm tropical winds
caress my soul
the way a mother's kiss
touches her newborn child.
Soft and gentle they carry me
along on my journey across time.

I've watched the settling moon
filling the ocean with diamonds,
perfect and beautiful.
Each day brings a new beginning,
each night a deferent ending,
as I sail toward my blue horizon.

—Charles Stanford

An Honest Man

A truant gaily was skipping
On the mossy bank of a brook,
Over his shoulder a fish pole,
Stuck in his cap was a hook.
Another lad walked on the highway,
He envied the kid by the pool,
But, alas, he must stay on the highway
As this one was going to school.
For a moment I watched the two fellows
From the shady cool of a tree.
Then to myself put the question
Which one of those kids would you be?
Well, shucks! I'm rarely a liar
To be such could shrivel my soul,
So I'd swear by the conscience within me
I'd be the kid with the pole.

—Alfred E. Moyer

Home From The Beach

Here I am
Once again beyond the call
Of ancient sea.

The late summer night
Hums and sizzles sadly
Through the air,

With agonizing absence
Of that hushed pulse
Of throbbing surf.

I know this same moon
Somewhere slips its silvery sheen
Upon those waves,

Where last night a gull
Posed upon an aged piling
For my entertainment.

He may be there now,
Gazing out over rippling foam and sand...
But I am here.

—Janet Howard

And Birds That Sing

The morning walk
One Sunday morn.
Trees that rustle,
Winds that blow,
And birds that sing.

Elation of the anatomy.
Fresh stimulating thoughts
Of trees, rivers, fountains,
The new life, the old promises,
And birds that sing.

Green though the buds,
Water flowing free.
A sudden wind,
Snowflakes in flight
Cover buds of green on twig.

Eyes are lifted.
Ears strain to listen
Though clouded by white
At buds peeping through,
And birds that sing.

—*Albert Friscia*

Names

A legacy of time
Or part of it
Is in your name.
It helps us trace
The bearers of
Those finite genes
That make us all
Most what we are
When we're deprived
Of social spheres.

But halved and halved again,
One half retained
And coupled with another half
By parents now united,
The other never to remain
In any one of us,
We take our own identity.
So look for names and find
Bearers of the genes
That make your kind.

—*Elsie Hornbacher*

I Don't Want To Care

I don't want to care
Or see you—sitting there
In that, his favorite chair.

I don't want strange lips on mine
Nor new love too quick to find
No one near to remind
Me—of the loneliness and pain
Were all of him that would remain.

I don't want to share with you
My gloomy moods, so sad and blue,
You understand, have lost love too.

I fought you off as best I could,
You conquered me—I knew you would!
Yet memories remain—as they should.

I don't want to care for you
But—God help me—I find I do!

—*Doris Kang*

Who Knows?

Who knows about this thing called love?
Our destiny known only from above
For some of us we choose with gain
For others we loose with pain.
Thinking the future grass was green
Then too late to return, with grief.

Discoveries we learn today
With memories from yesterday
That what we had surpassed
The life that is now at last.
Face the future today with reflections
One day at a time with connections.

Someday with a tear and a smile
We may look at each other awhile
And say "I've loved you still
And perhaps always will."
True love only hearts can show
The question remains "Who knows?"

—*Cullen D. Silva*

Life... What A Price

In our world today
Our life is but a price.
A price many pay
Without thinking twice.

It is a price paid for love
For selfishness or for greed.
For a purpose or for none
Is all of this killing,
Really that much fun?

Life is used as a weapon
A bribe or a cost.
A way of getting what you want
And a way of making sure,
Your purpose will never be lost.

—*Derek Warlum*

Eyes Closed Listening

Eyes closed, listening
Outside - cars rushing by
Splashing through puddles
A truck rumbles
A steady, even rain creates
Harmony.
Heavy drops
Drip off the ends of bare branches
And plunk into puddles below.
Inside - guitar in your lap
sings
cries
sighs
As you strum the song in your head.
Strong fingers on tight strings
Softly, gently
Eyes closed, listening

—*Heather Noel Holub*

Untitled

With heart
of matters
important I
wish to replace
try with all-
ow,let feathers
come to me

—*Chris Marano*

The Butterfly

Effervescent, scintillating
Outward reaching, inward folding
 Wings, like petals
Reach and folding, reach again for Light
 Embracing and embraced.

Effervescent, scintillating
Outward reaching, inward folding
 Wings that flutter
To unseen themes, rhythms of spirit
 Elusive, unseen.

Effervescent, scintillating
Outward reaching, inward folding
 Color cartwheel, new spring miracle
Heralds its joy to be
 Born again!

—*Carolyn Barrett Powell*

The Auction House

Dishes, books, and faded flowers,
Packed in boxes, stored for years
In some long forgotten attic,
Lost in time and space and tears.

Patchwork quilts and tarnished silver,
Necklaces of jade and glass,
Treasures from another era,
Tempt the bidders as they pass.

Sturdy tables hold the memories
Of those days beyond recall,
Hold what once to others dear was,
Hold old paintings from the walls.

When my memories grace that table
In the center of the room,
And the auctioneer is chanting,
Let there be no stifling gloom.

For the God who gives me sunshine
And the fullness of His love,
Spreads His table, filled with glory,
In my father's house above.

—*Edward Randall*

Untitled

A silhouette of darkness
 passes my footsteps
as my delicate feet
 cross a crusade
of shallow waters
 which wonder throughout
the deepness of life!

—*Anthony J. Dunn*

You And Me

We are like strangers in the dark.
Passing each other by night.
Never looking at one another.
Not knowing each other's names.
Afraid to look the other in the eyes.
Afraid of what could be.
But, why I ask myself?
What is it we're afraid of?
Are we afraid of one another or
just ourselves?

—*Erica Lee*

Of Disability Retirement

Over the hill against my will,
Past my prime before my time.
Nearing the grave with one foot in,
Praying the lord my sin forgive.
Oh, the blissful thought of heaven,
Making worthwhile this earthly leaven.

—*Clifford L. Halford*

Dear One

A poem I shall begin
    perhaps a song I will attempt
        not of duty, but of want
            for you my dear, for you

The heavens may claim
    that I took you away
        though they cry for your return
            my angel, I beg you stay

Soon the sky will darken
    and thundering rain abound
        but together we will be
            o wonderful day, o wonderful day

—*Elpidio Tablit, Jr.*

Will They Remember Me?

This too t'was not meant to be
Perhaps sometimes my class-mates
They, will think of me.

The warm winds o'er my grave doth blow
But life goes on,
It must, you know.

It t'was not meant to be
That I should live to see,
All the things I dreamed of
would not be happening.

My graduation has come and gone
And all my friends are marching on.
This too t'was not meant to be
Perhaps my classmates,
Will think of me.

The girl whose hand I use to hold
has found another, with whom she strolls
Through the long years that lie ahead
I hope, they will not think of me, as dead.

—*Agnes Walker*

The Boy With A Blue Face

It all started out with a single
Piece of a star. It was a falling star
that a boy saw when he was walking
through the woods. He touched the
star. Then he started turning
into a monster. There was another
boy with him and the boy shot
him with a gun. The boy got
a blue face because he shot the
monster with a blue face—never
to come off.

—*Adam Warren*

Untitled

Feel the breezes
pile up under
the stars.

—*Charlotte Worden*

Why The Sky

Why the sky
Please answer me
For I have yet to know
The color of blue
And moving clouds too
Well, where do they all go
The stars at night
The moon so bright
I wonder what to say
Oh, why the sky
Yes, I know why
It holds the night and day

—*Amy Lynn Watson*

Untitled

Give me another chance
Please! Please! Please!
Give me another chance
For total absolution and forgiveness
And guide me on the proper path
To better my ways
And to live better days.

Let me be
A better me
No matter where;
On an aircraft
High in the air,
Or at any geographic location
On land,
Or anywhere
On or near the sea;
Teach me to be
A better me.

—*Isak Boruchin*

Pillar Of Doubt

Lock the door,
Pocket the key.
Here I am
Leaving for Limbo.

The letters have
All been burned
And the ashes
Carefully swept away.

The new tenant
Must never learn
Of love's demise
Beneath this roof.

The hearth is cold,
The curtains pulled.
Go swiftly now
And don't look back.

But wait! Return I must.
I left some THOUGHTS
Lying about.

—*B. L. Snedeker*

Snowflake Meditation

I can see the snowflakes falling,
O'er on yonder hill
As they make their journey earthward
To this land that's white and still.

And I wonder, Oh I wonder,
When the sun comes shining through,
Will they fall again in heaven,
As they melt and fade from view?

—*Clarence Baker*

Ode to House Selling

Sure, visit at five.
Postpone till seven.
So vacuum once more
View by eleven.

Doorbell still ringing
More people have looked.
We gave it our all.
Sure hope they get hooked.

Comparison shop.
But then please, come back.
The house hunting's fine.
But we wish to pack.

The move West must wait.
Still not into gear.
Oh, six months have gone.
Stretch it not a year!

House on the market
So sad is a friend.
The sign's on the lawn.
Will this ever end?

—*Anna Rhoades*

Found

I found rose petals
Pressed and dried
Between book leaves
I cried...
I found memories
I could not overlook...
I left them there
and gently closed the book.

—*Elaine E. Peters*

Poetaster

Once this poetaster wished to be,
published for all the world to see,
but no words that rhyme were found,
in the lines he had written down.

With words he toiled and strained,
until his head became very pained,
still he composed no poem or prose,
just words as the old saying goes.

—*John H. Arney*

The Habit

He,
Puff - Puff
He,
Puff - Puff
Burn - Burn, It Burn - Burn
It,
Again - Again
Eat,
Again
Sleep he
Puff - Puff
It
Burn - Burn
Again He -
No more -
It -
He - Free
Sleepppp.

—*Adam T. Sands*

Friend

Beauty,
pure and true,
that's what you are.
Always brightening my day
by blowing the clouds
of gloom away.
Your cheerful smile
could make even
the saddest hearts
shine with joy.
You are the sunshine
that makes everything grow.
And best of all,
you are my friend.

—*Jeffrey Warren Janisch*

from ancestry

unknown, newborn
purest form of ourselves
innocent forbearer of tomorrows
have compassion for all our frailties

small child caress the wind
inherit its wisdom from many ages
small child hear nature's song
solemn is its dance of life
small child touch our hands
love flows through to your soul

daughter from today
wed yourself to the universe
dwell in the consciousness
prevailing in space beyond
remember your humble beginning
naked of clothes and thought
remember our teachings

give of yourself

—*Barry Michael Rosenfeld*

Sanctuary

Angry rain
rages
at our sanctuary.
Cuddled close
like silken kittens
softly purring
in each other's arms
we are oblivious
to all
but
the other's attentions,
and
all around us
angry rain
rages
at our sanctuary.

—*Dana B. Hanefeld*

Honeycomb

Death is quiet,
return to dust, silent.
The sun warms weeds on stones
   heady perfume.
Time trapped in still heat
   presses on sorrow.
Earth accepts and friends forget
the bees commune, pollinating as always
seduced, the hesitant flowers bloom.

—*Joseph Benstock*

Autumn

I love the woods especially in Autumn
Rainbow trees
Red yellow purple tan gold and brown
Kaleidoscope trees
Til leaves fall to the ground

Colors fade to nondescript shades
Crackly crinkly crunchy crumbly
Soggy spongy leaves on the ground

Sadly I stare at the compost there
Close my eyes
Sigh
Then smile
Remembering colors

—*Caroline L. Smith*

Widow

Woman, you're never
         Really Alone

Every time
         You see a Bird or Flower
            Young Lovers
               a Sunset or a Smile

Your Man,
walks beside
and his spirit guides you
Till you meet Again.....

—*Frank Cagno*

Your Memory

As I look around me,
remembrances of you are al I see.
   Your memory is everywhere,
and I pretend that I don't care,
but there isn't a place,
that I don't see your face.
Over is our sour love,
and I know it wasn't sent from above.
There could be no love in your heart.
I should've known that from the start.
It's over, that I know,
Yet my love I must show.
Your face in my memory I keep,
I see it when I go to sleep.
So, for now I'll think of the past,
Hoping to get over you and find a
love that lasts.

—*Jenny Anderson*

The Wild Mustangs

The leader, a fast large stallion
   running free,
Never stopping for a breath,
Caring for and fighting for his
   herd, protecting them.
If ever danger risking his life,
Young colts watching him.
All running free in the WILD!

—*Andrea Haas*

World Peace

Peace in this world
Requires a united effort
By all races and creeds
Of various religions.

   Peace of mind
   Can be obtained
   By eliminating
Hunger, pestilence and strife,
   In order to survive.

   Nations on this planet
   Need the head of a state
   To understand
   The need for peace,
Also, the love for each other.
   Be he white, black,
   That is understanding
   For world peace.

—*Ben Rubin*

Untitled

When
   Sails are down as is the sun
And the
   Sea
   From which thee floats slows down
Do not
   Allow the music of the sweet waters
   Escape thee and the glimmer
of it all
   Lose its shining hope
Hold on...
   to your soul
as do ships on running waters
   stirrings of joy will reap you
   when light is
again near
   and
the rocky
   waters
   have succumbed.

—*Cindy Sanderson*

Prayer For Healing

We bring our crushed hopes
   scattered by thundering words
fractured goals pillowed
   in scalding tears
and our foaming energy
   freighted with spears.

Lord, quiet the wars
   of our minds
pull away the fences
   of our deafness
in the night of our vision
   show Your way.

Teach us to unbend the fist
   from its clench
the pain in our hands
   given to you
Creator of all mankind,
   rebuild anew.

—*John P. Keith*

On The Lake

Lights across the water
  Seeming very near
Sending out a welcome beam
  Wilder there, narrow here.

Lights across the water
  Red, and green and white
Suggesting habitation somewhere
  Tho' it's vacant here tonight.

Light across the water
  Rather a puffy chain
Linking the other shore to this
  Until broken by the rain.

Lights across the water
  A mystery what they're for
One imagines lots of things
  Another imagines more.

Lights across the water
  Lets hope they're always present
They make every lake inviting
  "Come out, don't be reticent."

—*Harriet Schaeffer*

An Octave Higher

Yesterday I was a middle C
Separating highs from lows
Standing very still
I am changing like notes on a scale
I am beginning to learn more and more
Thinking differently
Climbing higher
Valuing life and the soft words
Spoken so sweetly before her death

Today I am an octave higher
Practicing to be the best
Half a step, whole step,
Flat and sharp
Teaching others
Until the song is done.

—*Hillary Zablocki*

Dream's Of Love

  As I awake in the eve of the night
shadows fill the room I am frightened
I wrap my arm about you not wanting
to awaken you from the sleep your in
I know your there for me. But as this
was only a dream. I am missing you as
I cry myself back to sleep I know
my dream will come and fill this room
once again

—*Jennie Mae Shade*

Someone

I lost the someone whom I love
She is the only one
Just my someone
I lost the one I need
Someone greater than the sky up above
She is the someone whom I lost

—*Gary Martin*

She's Not Telling Anymore

She's not telling anymore
she stands so quiet by the door
and where it leads
or if she'll stay
if there's some price I have to pay?
She's not saying, not a word
just watching, waiting
my gyrating
it's up to me to find some fun
please help me, be my guide
together is a word two must decide
and if the choice is only mine
if ever myself in her I find
to be alone would be more kind.

—*Jason Ives*

Asaycia Tess Clayton

A smile, a little giggle
She's there for you to see
A frown and wrinkled brow
Young promises yet to be
Catch her when she's precious
Include her in your heart
And she'll touch you with her sweetness
  whether you like it, or not

Tickle her fancy
Encourage her curiosity
Sail to the corners of her voyage
Show her a place called paradise

Clever little antics
Like the ladies from her past
Always there to tease you
You wonder, will it last
Touch her with an interest
Obeyer of her schemes
Nothing else matters, but the pleasures
  of her dreams

—*Danny Haynes*

Laughter Beyond

Dust in the sky,
sickness in the air,
sounds of screams heard everywhere.
Beyond my feet,
I'm wondering where,
the laughters are I need to hear.

—*Christina M. Sutton*

Rainfall

  The rain drops fall
  silently to the earth.
Tears shed from the Gods.
  Lightening flashes
  and thunder rolls
angrily across black skies.

  Silence.

The only sound is the
faint rumbling of thunder.
  The sound of the Gods
  pounding their fists
  in the Heavens.

—*Jennifer L. Hill*

The Cuspidor

The old cuspidor
Sits silent and meek;
Recalling the days
of his Master's mystique.

Those were the days
of gun fights and water disputes;
His Master related to friends,
cattlemen and strangers of ill repute!

Now, they walk by
with a sidely glance
at the Old Cuspidor
and his wisdom by chance.

Being a helper,
to his Master each day;
brings back memories
of an Un-Godly way.

Now! I get scrubbed everyday,
with gentler hands
God made of clay!

—*John R. Cherokee Culley, Sr.*

Miracles

Blue cloudless sky above,
Sitting by a quiet stream,
Golden sunflowers
Dancing in the summer breeze,
Peaceful blissful solitude.

Distant mountain peaks,
Rock formations touched by sun,
Flapping wings of birds
Building nests with twigs and leaves,
Mother nature's miracles.

—*Gwen W. Sampson*

Untitled

           Diamond
      small, beautiful
shimmering, shining, sparkling
ring, necklace, earrings, pins
  wearing, holding, showing
         red, dark
      shimmering Ruby

—*Jennifer Marie Richardson*

Beginnings

Our eyes met.
Smiles spread upon our lips.
Time froze.
Stood there in a time zone.
Caught up in a black hole.
The earth shook.
Mesmerized by your looks.
When you spoke,
My heart throbbed in my throat.
Sweat poured down my hands.
My smile spread wide again.
I thought I saw Heaven's face.
My words sputtered without grace.
Gushing like a waterfall.
Sounding out a mating call.

—*Airetta Myrick*

Fantasy

Oh, give me a huge silver spoon,
Smooth and long-handled, please,
To reach this July sky
And swirl these stars around.

I would scoop the Milky Way,
Ladle the Little Dipper,
And blend these bright cool jewels
To a dizzy incandescence.

First, I might drip a few,
Yellow-white or pale sapphire,
Upon this lonely reach
Of beach
And sprinkle me a twinkle-path
To anywhere.

Oh, let me tiptoe stretch
To twirl nocturnal heavens
With that tool;
One would do well
To be a star-stirrer.

—*Jeanie Mortensen*

Transformation

Glistening
smooth, icy crunch
of caked snow drifted
over daffodils, melting
pooling, running in
rivulets, revealing
spring

—*Gaye Meyer*

Anticipation

Through the corridor I pass,
so dark and unattended.
Unknowing of my destiny,
yet free and unoffended.
My sheltered berth hath given way,
my security unfolded.
All strength cannot protect me,
from God's time tested power.
What life has yet in store for me,
won't know for still an hour.
And all that I have yet to see,
might never come to be,
Had both of you decided not,
to love and cherish me.

—*James R. Taksas*

The World

The world is steeped
So deep in sin
The word of God
Will never win,
The answer
To this earthly mess
Of humanity
In distress
The greed of nature
Devours the soul
The devil has put them
In a wicked hole,
The cry is lowed
But no one hears
Those with help
Are dread with fear,
So on we go
To the final day
When God decides
We've got to pay.

—*George Barden*

Be Happy For Me

I am home with God
So don't worry or cry
Your sadness will pass
as time goes by.
All my sins I have repented
Just know my soul is at peace
and very contented
On this earth I had my share of
worries, pain and fears.
Believe in Christ Jesus
Be faithful and true,
In heaven we'll be together,
And God and I will be glad to
see and welcome you.

—*Irma Groves*

Who's To Blame?

The world stopped turning
so how do you feel?
Do you know where to go
now that time's standing still?

The choices you made
are now set in stone,
And there's no one to blame
'cause they've all been your own.

—*David Kaltenbach*

Under The Night Lamp

I've pad and pen beside my bed
So I can add a line,
When lilting things pop in my head,
Such thoughts that come in rhyme,

I've often thought, beside my bed,
A red rose bud would be,
A better tool of guidance
To domesticity.

Perhaps, if my thoughts stayed right here
Upon the length of sheets,
The nail that caused my dress to tear,
The vitamins in beets,
My life would be more orderly;
A flowing rich routine,
A scheduled sedateness,
Unruffled, quite serene.

Yet, I've the pad beside my bed,
My joy no limit knows,
For I have warmth within me that
Won't wither like the rose.

—*Frances S. Jacobs*

Sisters

Sisters are the best, when they're
so much older than you.

They are someone you can talk to
when your really feeling blue.

They are all so very special
even in there own little way,
cause in your heart they will
never go away.

So when you are feeling blue,
talk to a sister that is
so much older than you.

Just like I could always do.

—*JoEllen Baker*

Simple Things

As we live our lives from day to day
So much we do stays the same
Caught up in our daily routine
We forget from life what we gain
To feel a bright breezy morning
The wind blowing through the trees
While the sun shines so brightly
Its light dances on green leaves
To watch a flock of birds in flight
To see a laughing child run
Is to know with each new sunrise
Your life has just begun
Stop and smell the roses
Watch today's clouds against the blue
When night falls and we close our eyes
Yesterday is through

—*Diane Kay Gates*

Traveling

Traveling gets you places,
so you can meet new faces.
When you reach your destination,
you'll have plenty of relaxation.
You'll be having fun,
under the beautiful summer sun.
Take your last look,
snuggle up with a book.
Time to go now,
Somewhere, somehow.

—*Jennifer Kandle*

My Children/Your Children/G-d's Children

Some are slow children,
Some are fast children,
Some are sad children,
Some are happy children.

Some are weak children,
Some are strong children,
Some are crying children,
Some are smiling children.

Some are overfed children,
Some are underfed children,
Some are poor children,
Some are rich children.

But, to me,
They are simply pure children,
No labels, no deals,
Just children in childhood.

I pray for my pure children,
My staff loves and cares for children,
G-d watches and blesses our children,
Sweet, happy, growing children.

—*Rabbi Eli Hecht*

After Life?

Some say you see a light
Some say you touch the sky
Some say there's a guiding hand
But no one really knows,
What it is that goes on
When you die...

—*Barry W. Higgins*

Shepherd Of W. 4th St.

Dressed in black,
some sit and stare:
A funny beret and turtleneck
don't answer their questions.
His white socks
seem shocking,
and they look for a funeral.

Damn tourists.

I think he's beautiful
    —*Glyn Gamab*

Envy

You envy a lot of people,
some that you don't know,
You envy how they act,
and places they might go.
You think that they are heroes,
they seem to have it all.
It seems they never stumble,
And surely never fall.
And when some trouble comes,
They know just what to say,
But you don't have the courage,
all you do is pray.
It may not show to you,
but it really hurts inside,
Instead of acting tough,
they would have rather cried.
So envy all you want,
Whatever gets you through.
But just remember the ones you love,
they may envy you.

    —*Cynthia Lyn Smell*

Escape

Peace is a figment of
Someone's color washed dream.
It's something we draw and write about,
But it can never be;
People ever fight for it.
"Peace truly does exits", they'll say.
This is something I doubt,
Yet why do I pray.....?

Peace(s) mixed up spells escape.
    —*Dana R. Brown*

Cities Life

The brilliant night
stretched out an icy hand
stroked her cheek
with the touch of death
a shrill scream
interrupts the icy dead silence
as a body falls
the city is alive
all its evils
all its hate
formed together to make one
cold dark form
of ruthless hate
merciless to pain and cries
no compassion, no remorse.
no end to bloody reign
    —*Jill Dawn Layton*

Life is Cruel

Life is cruel, without a doubt,
Sometimes in people's lives.
It takes the things that we hold dear
and hurts, as though with knives.

Life deals us misery, grief and pain,
along with stress and strife.
It even took my precious boys
...they live with my ex-wife.

I long to fill each of their days
with love, and peace and happiness.
And each day they're away from me
my heart is filled with sadness.

My love for them will never fall,
it towers beyond the sky.
To make them happy is all I want
each day until I die.

Life is cruel, without a doubt,
sometimes in people's lives.
But if I have my children's love
.... I think I can survive.
    —*Ivan Tritch*

Feelings

When you feel empty and out of state
Sometimes you can call on your mate
If he does not want to hear
Say okay then dear

I'll call someone else who does
That is God up above
He is always near
And is also in good cheer

He answers your every call
Because you see he is on the fall
Summer, winter, spring or fall
It doesn't matter to him at all

He's my master and my friend
Even unto the very end
Be it small or large.
It doesn't matter what the charge

"Amazing Grace" what a song
It has been around so very long
And it can be just right
Even in the middle of the night
    —*Jane N. Bice*

Untitled

Mother Earth is a planet that
spews forth with life

She gives all she can but
retracts with revenge

She'll level great cities
She'll flood away sins

When her children grow selfish
her tide washes in

Plain respect for our mother
it has to be great

Because if we turn our backs
we've all sealed our fate.
    —*Bill Cleary*

The Whistler

Come whistle at my window
Spectres of the past.
Of continents lost, Egyptians kings,
Of worlds that couldn't last.
Then whistle next of kingdoms
That have left but single clue.
Of how they lived, how they died,
The things they tried to do.
Whistle winds of desperation
And long forgotten schemes.
Vanished cities, battles waged,
Only half remembered dreams.
Roman legions, golden Gods
Forever lost behind
Remembrances of mysteries
Sealed deep within the mind.
Then as the tune is ended
And our ways have all gone,
Who will be the next in line?
As the whistler passes on.
    —*Edward A. Collins*

To Anyone

Saddened by the words: "I love you"
    spoken to another.
Alone, here I stand -
    possessive of no lover
            except
    in a
            dream.

Arms wrapped tightly about me,
    lips grazing mine own.
"Everything will be just fine -
    I am here
    Do not fear."

My lips draw up in a smile
    and all the while
    the sound of singing
            so sweet
    fills my ears.
compensating for all the years
    of bitter
            Loneliness
    —*Diana Maria Gonzales-Jun*

Summer Solstice

With great pomp and ceremony
    spring ushers in
the Camelot season of Summer.
    June attends the coronation
        crowned by the sun
    and robed in emerald splendor.
Bird song, children's laughter
and the vibration of cicadas provide
        a chorus in full voice.
    Blue and gold days
    framed by the living green
    of leaf, tree and grass.
Summer gives to her subjects
    a benediction of hope
        and benevolence.
....The mountains and hills
    shall burst forth before you
        into singing.
And all the trees of the field
    shall clap their hands.
    —*Beverly A. Casey*

Wild Flowers

'Tis only the bloom on the
stalk of life that fulfills
   one's dreams.
Wild as the flowers that
erupt in a dance of color;
this - yes this brings our
   crescendo to be.

   —*Ann L. Fitzgerald*

Lying Awake At Night

Sometimes I lay awake at night
Staring at books, ideas take flight.
Shall I read them, I might.

Thurber, Steinbeck, Poe,
Sitting in a row.
Cannery Row, The Raven, The Wonderful
   O.

I study them sitting there,
Gathering dust, and wear
Buddies on the shelf they share.

   —*Alexis Grey Butera*

Composer Of Pain

   Trembling quill of thy hand
   Stiff feather of thy mind

   Trembling quill in thy hand
      A rotting feather
         How kind

      So many answers
      So few questions

      A quivering voice
Of a man who loved the world too much

   He gave his only begotten life

   A concerto of my imagination
Is loved by those who are not alone
For it reminds them of who they aren't
   And shows them not of who they are

   A symphony of my passion
Is loved by those who are not loved
   For it shows them someone who is

         As they are
      —*Stephen Fenner*

Untitled

Some say life it is a hassle
striving endlessly for things

Some say life has more to offer
if your soul to pleasure clings

Some say life is pain and sorrow
always yearning for relief

I say life it is a treasure which
we share in deep belief
that the sun will rise tomorrow and
will bring an end to grief.

   —*Erdmuthe B. Stoker*

You Are My Crutch

Strong,
   Sturdy,
      Supportive.

When I feel weak
You are there.
Always holding me up.
Never letting me down.
Dependable.
Yet unlike a healed wound
No longer needing support
I'll always need you.
For you are my crutch.
My life.
Without you . . .
I'll fall.

   —*Donna L. Moss*

Change

Spring must keep its promise,
Summer's surely nigh,
Winter's day has long since past
Yet something's gone awry.
Perhaps it's nature's fancy,
Capricious though it be,
To keep her guardians in a state
Of instability.

Within all change is challenge,
To meet or to deny,
And every time the test is posed
Conflicting forces vie.
Vagaries in the weather,
Another proof to me,
That though God's world is ordered,
It shuns complacency.

   —*Harold F. Damon, Jr*

Cherished Memories

It's a Sunday afternoon and the
sun is setting and the sky is gray,
and I think of you so very far away,
as I walk in the park
between the trees,
I hear the shuffling of the
squirrels and the crinkling
of the brown leaves,
suddenly I stop to take a
ride on an empty swing,
never realizing what It
might bring,
It brought cherished memories
of times in the past,
Something that will always last,
For you realize that time
brings a lot of changes and
we both know that this is true,
But one thing never changes
and that's my love for you

   —*Carol Pesich*

Unreal

See the person stand before
strip away all that they have
strip away all that they are
leaving only an empty husk
even strip away what little remains
leaving behind only an unreal image

   —*Christopher Zanko*

Her Eyes

Dirt
Surrounding the casket completely.
Almost the same color as her eyes.
What a waste for such
Young,
Vibrant eyes
To be placed so deeply into the ground,
Hidden,
From all they used to love to see,
Saddened,
By the eerie presence of a new place,
Never
to be removed from again,
And
Too young
To understand
Why?

   —*Darlene M. Cleaver*

The Icicle

   Lonely icicle
Suspended from a tree's arm,
   Its solemn face shows.

   It sheds a frail tear
Down its cheek, it gently rolls
   And falls below it.

   Day ends; night begins
Jewels adorn the vast, black sky
   It's still undisturbed.

   Thick fog surrounds it,
Obscuring it from my view,
   Keeping it preserved.

   It stares below it
Where a section of ice lies
   Reflecting its grace.

   —*Amy Gordon*

In My Room

My room bespeaks me

In my room are...
symbols of my greatest treasure

reflections of my mental and
spiritual strivings

evidence of my labor and
my values

In my room...
   my potential speaks,
   my future waits,
   my destiny unfolds.

Desiring you have knowledge
of me... I invite you...

In my room.

   —*Allean T. Moore*

Awakening

In the end shall we be like the tugs
That leave only a wake behind?
A gathering of bodies
to heave a final sigh,
Like a stone dropped in a pond
That waves a circular goodbye.

   —*Joan Russo*

Rainbow

O rainbow of a summer's day
Take my heart on your colorful way
A circle you are
But you are not far
From every farmhouse and field

You spread out your joy
For all girls and boys
To run hand in hand and to feel

The touch of your dream
Above a country stream
Before they go off to meal

And when they have grown
They surely have known
Your magical way
O rainbow of a summer's day.

—*Gene Evers*

The Pride Of The Black Woman

I am an African Queen
 ten thousand years old.

I am an African Slave
 whose story has never been told.

I am the pride of the earth
 to be inherited by the meek.

I am the jewel of the nile
 that every man seeks.

I am the soul of the black man
 that encourages him on his way.

I am the beautiful black woman
 and forever here to stay.

So to all you strong black men
 who need a helping hand,

Look to your proud black woman
 for by your side she will stand.

—*Jamie L. Overton-Steele*

Holiday Of Being Poor

Being poor never vexed me more
than an open sore.

No more than the sea is deep.
No more felt than tears
I've wept.

Being poor forever more
Only leaves tears on an
impoverished face.

To flow to your lips with a
salty taste.
Poor!

—*James Anderson*

The Seasons Of Life

The seasons come for a reason
Spring is birth
Life's first days
Summer is life's open blossoms
Autumn comes with golden age
And then comes ghostly winter
Life comes gliding in
And then goes quietly out
And only ghost are left
And yet the beauty lasts through each

—*Amber Vires*

My Space

Each night I lock the door
thankful for my bare subsistence.
No soul mounts the lofty walls
no one feasts on my priceless
treasures.
In this space of mine,
this fathomless celestial sphere
yet frightfully small,
this Temple,
this priceless Museum of mine,
this Pyramid,
this Delphi,
in this sacred crypt,
my stately walls
drip silence.
Solitude, impregnable,
a Medusa, clings like ivy
on every tiny chink.
And I,
A refugee of the Sun!

—*Eleni Paidoussi*

That "Child" Whose "Child"

That child with the starry eyes.
That child with the wondering mind.
 Whose child?

That child with no home.
That child who doesn't belong.
 Whose child?

That child with motivation.
That child with hesitation.
 Whose child?

That child with great expectation.
That child with little appreciation.
 Whose child?

That child with dreams.
That child with no means.
 Whose child?

That child with dope.
That child with no hope. Whose child?

That child could be your child...
That child could be my child. Whose
child?

 Whose child.

—*Edith Smith*

Eternal Decision

My time in life has come to
 That fork in the road
 Where an eternal decision
 Will be made in my honor.

Setting forth a proposal
 Of everlasting shadows
 Leading to the illuminating
 Glow of another domain.

There again I will walk
 With the thoughts and feelings
 Of one who is now immortal
 Free to wander in rapture.

—*Frank J. Tarazewich*

A Simple Thought

A tear is a tear
that falls from our eyes
Small misty drops
that never seem to lie

A natural emotion
as it's defined
look beneath that definition
and ask ourselves
Is it all in our minds?

Some are of joy
Some are of pain
on a cloudy dark day
the light of a rainbow
shines through
the light must of the rain

Why all the tears?
Is something on the mind?
Is it denial or betrayal
or something we choose to leave behind.

—*Bobbi Cook*

There Is A Mighty River

There is a mighty river
That flows down to the sea
And when conditions make it flood
It shows what it can be.

The water closes over dreams
Built slowly day by day
And clears the land of all that's there
While raging on its way.

A little dog with frightened eyes
Is rescued from a roof
And though there may have been a farm
Right now there is no proof.

So when we choose to change the land
And live where'er we please
Though man may build the dams and locks
The river holds the keys.

—*Donna Lee Ladd*

ID

There seems to be a part of me,
 That I don't like so well.
It lives way down inside myself,
 The part of me called "Hell".

It's a part of me that slumbers,
 When it should be wide awake.
 Or is it vise-versa,
 This unpredictable drake.

He doesn't always let me do,
 Or think or be what I should.
He forces me naughty and evil,
 When really I should be good.

I've done so much to be rid or him.
You'd never believe all the plots.
 Yet there he remains like a devil
 Holding the prime time slots.

 Maybe in the long run,
 The best thing I could do
Would be to learn to live with him
 As other people do.

—*Donna Leone*

Heather

She smiles a special smile
that I know is only for me.
It lights her face and dances
merrily in her warm brown eyes.
In three or four running steps,
and a leap, she is in my arms.
Her hug is tight and warm
The memory of her arms
will remain with me forever.
It is time to part,
our tears flow freely.
Though we must say
goodbye for now
our hearts will always
share a special bond.
The love of a child is
...forever.

—*Benny H. Hamilton*

Recognition

I feel sorry for you for all the nights
that I leave you alone to go and
get some energy in order for you
to move around.

I have to leave you to get some
knowledge in order for you to get
wisdom.
Oh! It hurts to know that someday
I will have to go for ever and
I won't be able to do anything
else for you,
When you have done so much for me.

You have allowed me to live in you.
You have allowed me to know your world.
You have allowed me to get sick and well
You have allowed me to give life through
you....
And one day I will have to say good bye...
And leave you at the mercy of time
Which will turn you into dust.....

—*Elizabeth Cepeda*

"Our Best Revealed"

Let's go 'in' to find,
That place that is divine;
Wherein we brightly shine,
And our best is revealed.

I go there everyday.
In silence I do pray.
The highest calls my name;
I'll never be the same,
And my best is revealed.

No more anger, no more pain,
By faith alone I am changed.

No matter long this lonesome road,
Now tired my body feels,
I will rise and lift the load
With my best revealed!

With gossamer wings
in selfless flight
We can become
The radiant light!
And so...we are revealed!

—*Charlotte Bruce and Jay Roosa*

Fear

You see things go scooting by
That really are not there.
The mind is in an awful state
Without the proper care.

The troubles in life are there
But we hide them with a cover.
What we need is to listen deep
If we are to discover.

We need love and sometimes help
To get us through this life.
But fear is one four letter word
That only leads to strife.

Don't be afraid to share your love,
That's what we need today;
To set your spirit free at last
Like a butterfly in May.

Don't be afraid of ghosts and goblins
For you know they're not real.
Believe in something that will last
Like the love for you I feel.

—*Gene Bearer*

The Man Who Loved You

In knew that man,
that today battles,
with death, who is relentless,
and cold, that makes eternal repose.

You who loved him,
till his last breath,
with of any reproach,
with out a gaze that would hurt.

That pride of man,
who feels wounded an ever,
near death!
The one who toast's his last smile.

That one who leave,
you with a reminder of precedence,
the fruit of his love,
that son so lovable.

That tomorrow will grow up,
conserving then it his memory...

—*Albert Campa*

Life Is A Gift

Life is a gift,
That we take for granted.

We use and abuse it,
This wonderful gift we have.

Big or small,
We have a right to life.

Nobody has a right,
To take my life away.

Life is a gift,

Life...
Don't take it for granted.

—*Alba lupia*

The Gift Of Love

From beyond the starry heavens He came -
That wonderful gift from above;
He came to redeem his people from sin,
And bring us God's gift of love.

Jesus our Lord and Savior and King
Came that we all might have life -
Abundant, eternal, unending bliss,
In contrast to this world of strife.

It cost Him his throne in Heaven;
It cost Him his life on earth;
That was the price of love He paid
To come by miraculous Birth.

The gift of love can be yours today
If you will but trust in God's "Word."
He bids you now; He knocks at your door;
Receive Him as your Savior and Lord.

—*Jerry B. Fleenor*

St. Patrick's Day

St. Patrick's day only comes one a year,
That's the time when everybody cheers.
We watch the Leprechauns from the rear,
When we turn he is not near.

They dance and they prance,
They put you in a wondrous trance.
But, you really have to glance,
Or than away they certainly will dance.

They have lots of tender gold,
That in a tankard they tightly hold.
Some people might have slipped and told,
Where they hide all their precious gold.

—*Chantille Reppert*

Christmas

Christmas is a time
that's very cool,
When you get a vacation
from work and school,
It's fun to say we're
on the go, when we make
a snowman in the snow!
I like Christmas. It's
very nice, especially when
I feast on sugar and spice.
Do you like Christmas?
I hope you do, 'cause I wrote
this poem just for you.

—*Amanda Eppes*

There's A Poem In The Air

There's a poem in
the air,
I can feel it there.
It's in the wind,
singing its song.
It's been in the earth
all along.
It's in the sunlight
bright and clear.
It's in the water
far and near.
There's a poem in
the air.

—*Jill Dumbauld*

Everything Shall Come Again

Can you hear it?
The armies of hours like waves
voices of a grateful dead
rise from their water graves

As pain is the daughter of pleasure
Pleasure is the daughter of pain
Like the subtle sound of seasons
everything shall come again

Can you feel it?
The rhythm of days like rain
Voices of a grateful dead
fall to their water graves

As pain is the daughter of pleasure
pleasure is the daughter of pain
Like the subtle song of seasons
Everything shall come again

—*Jeffrey Bruce Lea*

A Soul

A soul is born and it's
  the birth of beauty
A soul is nourished and
  knowledge is formed,
A soul is cradled and love
  appears,
A soul is clothed and wisdom
  is here.
A soul is fed and the meat
  of kindness is digested
A soul is taught and the love
  of God Almighty is in it.
A soul is sleep, for time and
  eternity keeps it,
The soul of man is here

—*Harrietta McReynolds*

Along Life's Road

The peace of heaven on earth I seek,
The breath of God upon my cheek.
I stand beside a babbling brook-
And there with anxious eyes I look.
I see the wheat stalks softly sway,
By gentle winds as if to pray.
Laughing waters and rippling spring,
Of Thy great glories ever sing.
The mighty pines in reverence stand,
Like priestly figures at God's command.
Along life's road I'll follow Thee -
Ever watching constantly.
O'er rocks and crags my footsteps guide,
Be Thou forever by my side.
Along the narrow mountain way -
I journey on 'till end of day,
And then at the end, my journey done -
I look to the glorious setting sun.
Then into Eternity and on through space -
Grant me one thing Lord - to see Thy Face.

—*Ida R. May*

Darkness

Has I peer down the lonely street,
The darkness is all around.
I see nothing but the shadows,
Of objects no longer found.
I feel my heart start sinking,
I see my soul go down,
for the emptiness all around me,
Is the darkness of no sound.

—*Gale A. McMahon*

Remembrances

The past, with fondness I recall:
The children's games and races,
The jacks and hop-scotch on the walk,
And parents' happy faces.

The violets that once did bloom
So bold! They asked no pardon,
And buttercups that spaced themselves
Between, in nature's garden.

The narrow lane that led to fields
Where hare and chipmunk darted,
The little brook that swam between
The banks that it had parted.

The watercress grew crisp and green
Along its tributaries,
And there, I chanced one day upon
A spring, danced 'round by fairies.

Tho miles and years divide me now
From childhood's gay romancing,
Have others wandered down that lane
And seen the fairies dancing?

—*Helen Boyer Johnson*

When The Sun Goes Down

When the sun goes down,
  The colors in the sky
    begins to change;

Like a rainbow that appears
  when it begins to rain.

When the sun goes down,
the colors continues, and seems
to disappear as the day goes by.

When the sun goes down,
a sun of another kind, the moon,
  begins to shine.

Then a single color
  starts to set in.

The sky turns dark;
Stars start to illuminate,
  it is night.

—*Brandie Imai*

The Mendicant Man

Pressed for power,
The dearth is great
That leads.
Whether 'tis bent
Or rumored,
Is worse hated
Than you.

The people are
Mutinous
Who lead you to
The final preparation.
To be considered.
For it most likely
Could be you,
Your old enemy
The mendicant man.

—*John J. Moore*

Judgment

Kaleidescoping, multi-blend,
The different colors of our skin,
Entwine to form a patchwork quilt.
Born to sin, we live in guilt.

In each of us some battle boils,
And to the victor go the spoils.
What is right, what is wrong?
History tells what we've done.

From the cradle to the grave,
The spirit trapped within the slave;
Here is sorrow, here is joy;
And in the old man, is the boy.

Love and change are spirit tools
Bound in chains by all the rules
Of the cultures we have formed
Enslaving children yet unborn.

First an entrance, then an exit;
We shed the skin to free the spirit.
Where is heaven, where is hell?
In death we know, but cannot tell.

—*Carol Frazer Wilson*

Heather

Little baby go to sleep
The dreams you have are yours to keep
When morning comes don't ever fear
When you awake I'll still be here
You are my child and this is true
It is a joy just watching you
I'll help you walk, I'll help you run
Reach for the sky, reach for the sun
Just turn to me when you feel blue
I'll do my best to comfort you
And when you're glad in all you do
Just look for me, I'll be there too
I'll care for you, keep you from harm
Watch over you and keep you warm
I'll be the one till I grow old
That you can trust and love and hold
Little baby go to sleep
The dreams you have are yours to keep
When morning comes don't ever fear
When you awake I'll still be here

—*Charles Larocchia*

If Only For A Moment

In a spark of flame
the fleeting vision came,
its power undulant,
if only for a moment.

In the children's laugh
I knew its path,
time so quickly spent,
if only for a moment.

In her deep brown eyes,
a deeper presence undenied,
more than passion let,
if only for a moment.

For its embrace I ache,
its power to remake
the me that was always meant,
if only for a moment.

The laugh, the flame, the eyes, the ache,
in these all eternity quakes,
a gift of the Mystery present,
if only for a moment.

—*J. Christopher Roberts*

Fall Is Near

Autumn's chill is comin'
The furnace came on last night
The sky is lookin dreary
Summer has took its flight.

The northern geese flew over
When I arose this morn
No more fields of clover
The flowers sure look forlorn.

The leaves are tinged with colors
Red-orange, yellows and brown
Dreams of popcorn and apples
I'll keep the windows down.

Has the furnace got clean filters
I really couldn't say
Forgot to check them in the spring
I'll do that right away.

When winter winds start blowin
And everything is froze
I'll tell you how cold it is
By the feelin of my nose.

    —Harold M. Merrell
    (Crawfordsville, IN)

The Immigrant

Good bye my rio bravo
The grande river sand,
I'm an immigrant
That few understand.

  I was a little child
  Born in Tennessee,
  My Dad was Mexicano
  What do you think of me.

I recognize my mother
The statue of liberty,
I'm proud being Mexicano
She's also proud of me

  I like to speak Spanish
  My father told me so,
  I love the Blonde ladies
  I like the Honky Tonk.

No matter if it's "charro"
The style of hat I wear,
I'm an immigrant
Forever anywhere!

    —Jesus Moron Villarreal (Zvazva
    Nuevo Leon)

A Request Of A Stranger

    Stranger as you enter
  That old house upon the hill,
  Please respect the owners,
They are gone but present still.

  Though it may look abandoned,
  With its empty rooms inside,
  It's truly filled with memories,
  And built with special pride.

So please respect the sacredness,
  Of those who live no more,
And please remember when you leave,
  Reach back and close the door.

    —James W. Stafford

A Haunted Heart

  Pain is real in body and soul!
  The hurt must be born inside!
The lasting agony in the mind to roll!
  A haunted heart I hide!

I strain to give this life some peace;
  A haunted heart still aches!
I pray the torment to somehow cease!
  Waive the throbbing for my sake!

A life of distress should never be;
  Anguish should be cast away!
A haunted heart does torture me;
  "Give me solace and peace", I say!

Hope, I know, is one clear trail;
  Faith will gain the goal!
A haunted heart with no travail,
  Gives a salve for my Soul!

    —Hugh Phillips, Jr.

Cover Girls

Beauty within a woman's breast
the internal
the instinct
the strong insightful soul
not shown on the front cover
Cover girls squeezed into tiny dresses
synthetic breasts forced to
bulge like round loaves of bread
Cover girls faces smooth,
defects removed
by the stroke of the brush
Perfected then perfect
they kiss the camera with silicone lips
But Beauty
within a woman's breast
the strength
the emotion
the knowledge
not shown on the front cover

    —Joni Thissen

To One I Love As A Mother

Dear Father, who Thyself has known
the joy of a mother's tender care,
Hover close and lend Thine ear
while for one, to me a mother dear,
I make this humble prayer.

Protect her life each hour, I pray
who devotes herself to mine.
Smile upon her, hold her close
and give her of Thy Joy Divine.
I know I cannot pay the debt
for the tender love she's given.
But God, Love's Lord, pray don't forget
to bless her doubly in Heaven!

    —Hazelle M. Ingmire

Tear

A glisten in the eye
The lonely tear begins to glide
On its one way silent ride
No secrets left unlied
Leaving a trail across the lips
A taste of salt
A tender sip
Down across the chin it flows
Low tide
Over it goes

    —Anne McMichaels

A Country Holiday

Driving along route 206
The land begins to roll
Crimson trees and wildflowers
Decorate every knoll.

Corn is being harvested
The growing season done
Farmers working in the fields
Enjoying the autumn sun.

A horse and buggy crossed our path
With Amish folk inside
Don't stare, just take a peek
They're a people of great pride.

They live a hard, but simple life
The kind we wish we could
Working hard both day and night
To make life rich and good.

The sun's last rays are fading
The sky is turning gray
Memories we will cherish
Of our country holiday.

    —Carol J. Szymanski

My Living Will

Medical science keeps lengthening
The lives of the human race.
That's no favor to the elderly
Since in this world we have no place.

We may have spent a life time
Working and caring for others
But nobody wants the responsibility
Of caring for us fathers and mothers.

So just "bug off" medical science
And let us die with grace.
If our body organs wear out,
Please don't try to replace.

We don't want a bunch of tubes
Nor to be hooked to your machines.
Life under those conditions
Ain't worth a hill of beans.

There's more to life than just breathing,
Such as love, laughter and glee,
So if you can't guarantee those things,
Then don't mess around with me.

    —Evelyn Schleifer

The Invisible Man

No one knew from where he came,
The man who walked right down the lane,
With the man whose car broke down,
Right in the wildest part of town.
He followed him 'round every bend,
On this man you could depend.
No one saw him, no not one,
Not even the man with whom he'd come;
But the mobsters in the street,
Saw the man they planned to beat.
And then they saw an armed man too,
So they turned around and flew.
And then the armed man disappeared.
Everyone, they scoffed and jeered
At the mobsters who said it was so.
Then they laughed and scoffed, "Ho! Ho!"
No one saw to where he went;
It must have been an angel God had sent.

    —Jathan Pfeifle

649

Lucy

Lucy must hide
the marks of

black and blue,
with sweaters that

are two sizes too big,
and so her back will

not hurt when she sits
in class, and how
she wishes her father would
realize, no matter what,

it's the inside that really
hurts you.

—*Jorge Rodriguez*

Memories

That night -
The memory
Still lingers
In my mind.
It's not only that night
I remember,
It's the times we've spent
Together.
I love you.
You're gone -
I'll never see you again.
All I want is all four of you back.
But all I got left with was
The memories
And good times
We had.

—*Dawn E. Dimeo*

Remembrance

When we are gone love,
The morning Sun will still reclaim
The dampness left by night,
The Chickadee still filch seed,
And Deer browse near,
Perhaps to look and wonder
If we're merely out of sight.

There, in secret,
A simple mark may be,
To let the world know,
That we were here,
And loved.

—*Eugene Bowers*

Time

Time is something,
That never stands still,
For no one, nobody and nothing.

It's a continual machine,
With a mind of its own,
Never stopping, never slowing
Always constant, always there.

It was their when we were born
It'll be their when we die,
No matter what anyone does,
It will keep on ticking,
I wonder why?

—*Jennifer C. Webb*

God Take Care

God take care of the one we love.
The one who has gone to Heaven above.
God take care for we love him still,
And Lord, we realize that it was thy will.

Be with his family in their sorrow,
And I pray, thee God, bring a bright
tomorrow.
For in that bright tomorrow, they may
find joy.
But God only knows, how they will miss
their boy.

Yes, God, take care of "Our Dear John."
and we shall see him afar and
beyond.

—*Chris Kannmacher*

The Sky Falls With Sorrow

The sky falls with sorrow
The river flows with blood
Each day is hope for tomorrow
Tears, dark as mud.
Mountains peak up to see beyond
Oceans being drawn to earth
Try to distinguish mystery or con
You'll die before your birth.
Let go of what is gone
Go on with what is there
Strengthen with bond
Be weak with care.

—*Calista J. Winnett*

Time

Take the time to smell
the roses and you will surely see.

That all the things upon this
earth are here for you and me,

We're only here for a short
time so be all that you can be.

For time passes quickly as
you will surely see.

From young to old, you
never know when your time
no longer will be.

So, take the time to smell the roses
For time is short you see.

—*Cheryl Jilek*

The Winds Of The Tropics

The compassion and warmth
the sharing and caring.
The clear film of bubbly water
you spread over my sand.

The impressions on the grains.
The footsteps of the heart.
The flicker of moon beams
as we hold each other tight.

Powerful is that emotion,
amazing and care free.
I miss you winds of the tropics.
I miss you life by the sea.

—*Jose F. Morillo*

On The Cross

Suddenly the crushing weight,
The sins of the whole world
Warring against His soul.
The agony.
When purity and holiness
Became sin personified.
He poured out His soul unto death,
Shed His priceless cleansing blood,
And it was finished.

Jesus gave up Himself
Died a double death
On the cross
Because His great love
Would not give up on us.

—*Celeste Rhea*

Stormy Sea

The wind is blowing,
The sky is black,
My blood is boiling,
Though I can't turn back.

The waves are crashing,
The cliffs are jagged,
My anger is raw,
Tattered and ragged.

The rain is torrential,
All starfish are drowned,
My senses are lost,
The undertow's strong.

The rock face falls,
A scream is let out,
My heart pounds faster,
I chose the wrong route.

I fall to my knees,
The storm rages on,
My eyes fill with tears,
My lifeforce is gone.

—*Brandon Aguirre*

Black

An empty space
The summer's night sky
A thoughtless mind
The color of death and
of the evil eye

Black

—*Amanda Veon*

Morbid Sun

The sun is a demon,
The sun is a threat,
And the clouds come a long
To act as my net.
Saving me from it's hot,
Morbid rays,
I dance in the night,
And hide from the days.
The sun burns my heart,
And withers my soul,
Scorching my eyes
Till they've turned black as coal
As the sun; it goes down,
And the day fades away,
I'll roam through the stars,
Till the sun does decay.

—*Jane Lee James*

The Sun

When
the sun peeks
through the mountains,
it gives the world a light
to follow, a heat to keep
us warm. It give the birds
something to chirp about. It also
gives everyone something to wake
up to, when the sun peeks
through the mountains.

—*Anna Krantz*

Lord's Sword

Oh the sword comes down
The sword comes down
All of Gods children
Make it move around

Never a drop of blood it takes
Never a law of God it breaks
It smites the beast
to the ground by virtue
of its my T sound

And every word it sings to me
is psalms of music and poetry
Swords word, words sword.

—*Charles R. Cox*

Gone

The smiles no longer on my face
The tears have dimmed my eyes.
You took the laughter from my heart
When we said our last good-bye.

The sun just doesn't shine as bright
As once it use to do.
The moon and stars have lost their gleam
My dear, since I lost you.

Now I must bear my aching heart
And try to quell my yearning
And keep my faith forever strong
To wait for your returning.

And if, you don't return my love
Through all the years to be
I want you just to know one thing
You took a part of me.

—*Elaine J.*

A Poem

Oh the times we've had,
the times we've cried,
we've had lots of chances,
but I think we've lost our pride.

Love is one thing,
that we cannot understand,
but we'll come out of the heartbreaks,
holding hand in hand.

We are stepping into a world,
that we know nothing about,
but we have to go through it,
and walk right passed the doubt.

It will come out alright in the end,
and we'll be okay,
we'll have new chances,
and be together again... Someday.

—*Jamie Mitchell*

Time

Born in the wrong time
The universe could be mine
Who knows the answered
Time and spirit transfer

All life is the same
If it could only remain
If it is to be destroyed
from where was it deployed?

Humanity has its limit-yet
Eternity remains within it
Some things are unexplainable
Yet will always be attainable

—*Bev Whittle*

Dry My Tears

It seems to be very strange
The way our lives will be disarrange
The love ones that we'll leave behind
Not knowing the matter of day or time
It frightens me so very much
To know that I'll be gone as such
I'm sure that when my numbers called
I will be amongst them all
Death is waiting there for me
Someday until eternity
My mortal life will leave my soul
And He, I praise I'll see behold
But no one knows the time or day
When they shall then be called away
So these questions I now do fear
With answers that will
   "Dry My Tears".

—*Dhannyn L. Joyner*

Nature's Meaning

   Have you ever listened to
the whistle of the wind? The roar
of the sea? The singing of
sea gulls flying so free?

   Have you ever felt the sifting
of sand beneath your feet?
Against the warm salty water,
that makes natures meaning
so neat.

   Nature is maris quideur
of beauty, and freedom.
   And for all, man will
know "Nature's Meaning"

—*David D. Adams*

The Tree

A willow is crying in
   the wind.
As I do when my
   emotions bend.
I cry for you, me,
   the world.
We are born to die;
But now we need to
   live and breathe.
Let our crying emotions sing;
So we will never more be
   like that willow in
   the wind.

—*Jennifer Floyd*

Mother Nature

The birds chirp,
the wind blows,
as angels sprout their
wings below,
as the world begins
to spin,
mother nature kicks in
again,
down comes rain,
out comes sun,
mother nature's having fun

—*Jenny Francis*

Once

The flame is still burning,
The winter is cold.
She longs for his body,
To reach for and hold.
She sits by the fire,
That soon starts to dim.
He's holding another,
Where once she had been.

—*Donna D. Palmieri*

The Season For Love

When spring's in the air,
The world makes a new start,
And it makes you aware,
There's a song in your heart.

When springtime bursts out,
With a touch from above,
Then without any doubt,
It's the season for love.

If you don't believe,
Take a look all around,
And the things you'll perceive,
Could just make your heart pound.

Without any strife,
But a touch from above,
It's the springtime of life,
And the season for love.

—*Gladys Claus*

Dahlias

Oh these flowers of summer,
Their brilliance, their colors, their hues.
Their details are exquisitely fashioned.
Each petal minutely disclosed.

A bouquet of dahlias is special.
One thinks, "How could it be so?"
Such gorgeous splashes of color
Cause wonder and excitement to glow.

—*Helen Lager Konyha*

Them And Me

   I wanted to be like Them
Their walk, their talk, their dress.
   But then I looked inside myself
And saw I liked Me best!

—*Alretta Miller*

When Angels Light

When angels light upon this earth
Their wings encircle all
Gentle children, pure in heart
Gliding with the wind at dawn.

Cleansed by love their world appears
beautiful and bright
They touch our hearts with gentle peace
to guide us towards the light.

They dance between the raindrops
to wash our fears away;
and give us strength to face the world
by lighting each new day.

To lift us when our knees are weak
In God we all stand tall.
On a quite hill they hold our hands
to lift us when we fall.

In the silent comfort of a prayer
They hear our hearts despair;
and whisper simply "Do not fear
My Love is always there."

—*Dawna Lee Holloway*

Shine On

I clean my house from stem to stern
  Then fix my hair
  And sit and yearn
For someone to come by and see
  My shining house,
  My sparkling me.

Not one lone soul will stop to chat
  Nor one foot cross
  My welcome mat.
I sit among the settling dusts;
  My hair goes limp;
  My shine all rusts.

If I ignore the dust and clutter
  And let my hair
  Hang in disorder,
Then, you can bet, all day there'll be
  A constant stream
  Of company!

—*Helen E. Waters*

Three Little Girls

  At first there were two,
  then one more later on,
  three daughters had you,
your peace and quiet were gone.

  The first two were charming,
  one was messy, the other neat.
They were sometimes quite alarming,
  but were always very sweet.

  The third was a surprise,
  her blond hair in curls,
  with her daddy's blue eyes.
  You now had three girls.

  But your family grew apart,
  and changes were made.
The first two had a new start,
  but the memories never fade.

  Now all three are gone,
  leaving mom and dad behind,
  they continue on,
their own lives they must find.

—*Curtis Smith*

Treasures

In our old people's home
There are treasures galore
Beloved by their owners
Who keep them in store.
Old letters written
By writers now dead
Books cherished in childhood,
Though now seldom read
Bits of cracked china
More precious than gold
Photos depicting
The young grown old.
A useless collection
Of rubbish you say
But we haven't the heart
Just to throw them away

—*Hilary Akers*

Exile

Exile, to live and die alone,
There can be more,
Lives unfulfilled once lived before,
How can there be?
But, yes there must be more.
With out love, a life wasted,
Sweet flavor of victory,
Never tasted.
Is there?
Yes, something is in store?
Fear, never felt
In your hands my mind melts.
What can there be,
Nothing but love.
Exiled, you and me.

—*Brandon F. Renken*

Help Out A Friend Of Mine

Once upon a horrid time,
There was a friend of mine.

I could see it in his eyes,
It was drugs he did despise

A cry, whimper and a tear,
I could see that he had nothing but fear.

Please help me dear friend of mine,
I have committed a serious crime.

I would if I could confess,
But all I am right now is in stress!

I would if, I could stop,
But, I don't understand the feeling,
I feel like a mop.

Let me help you dear friend,
We shall fight the battle to the end.

Until we show the world that drugs
are a problem and a battle to the end,
So let's take care of ourselves from
drugs, and in case, help out a friend.

—*David Scarpitta*

The Desk

Under the desk
there is an empty waste paper basket
full of rejected ideas
also an empty beer can
another rejected idea

What makes procrastination so easy
is the fact that it never works
for there are in infinite amount of ways
of never avoiding everything

And this poem is no better,
than the beer
both have kept my mind off
what's on top of the desk

—*John Schoenemann*

I Think About The Children

I think about the children
Who are hurting and alone,
The children who are suffering
The children with no home.
I think about how much it matters
That parents take the time
To teach their children carefully,
And with an open mind.
I think about the children
And the patience that they need,
How with love and understanding
Their future we can feed.
I think about the children
So innocent from the start,
And how with just a little love,
We can fill a child's heart.

—*Rhonda O'Brien*

Barkley And Pepsi

I have two cats Barkley and Pepsi.
who can do things so very remarkably.
They're so very playful,
especially huggable,
and one thing for sure they're adorable.
They bounce off the walls,
climb up your overalls,
and scatter about on the floors.
They watch TV with me,
when I play the flute they meow with me.
They love to do tricks,
give a whole lot of licks,
especially when they like you.
I have two cats Barkley and Pepsi,
and to me they're the best in the world.

—*Vanessa Acevedo*

Forgotten

They lay behind me,
willowed among the trees.
Misplaced thoughts, fell
beneath the sheets.
The moon lay on the clouds,
dancing with dim stars.
Even though they were just behind me,
I still felt far, I will take my
place, beyond the realities which
control my mind. They shall never
remember me, the one they left behind.

—*Robin Humphries*

Gratitude

To my former Publisher,
who published my first poems.
"Growing old" and "Trees"
You were so helpful and always
tried to please.

Our parting of the way came soon
after we met. The New Orleans
Convention, how could any poet
forget?

A.P.A. memories will last a life
time, although they are no more.
For poets starting out like me,
they opened the door.

For this I send my thanks to you
for helping me.
I am now a "life time member of
I.S.P.", they are as special as
A.S.A. was before, but I can't
forget A.P.A.. They opened the
door.

—*Mamie Hodge*

The Eagle

You were born to be as the eagle
Who rules and reigns the sky;
To overcome all evil
With courage in your eye.

The eagle must search ground and hills
Each and every day,
And sharpen all his hunting skills
Until he has his prey.

Driven by a hunger that burns,
He leaves his nest with zeal;
To work and hunt and never returns
Until he has his meal.

You can choose to be a parrot
Who works not for his wage;
Although free food he inherits
He lives within a cage.

So go my child and carry your task;
Find your talents and fly,
I will be here, just simply ask
And I'll help you rule the sky.

—*J. Kenneth Gallacher*

Knowledge

What knowledge is to him
   who understands,
He can travel the world
   with just a book in his hand.
He can see far off places
In all their splendor,
From the top of Mt. Everest
   to a Venice vendor.
He can know the feeling
   of life's many worths,
And understand the beauty
   of God's glorious earth.
He can see the aura
   around those he meets,
And know that the mighty
   are no better than the meek.
He who has knowledge
   has the world in his hand.
He can enter the door of learning,
   And emerge a better man.

—*Marguerite Lancione*

A Father Is

A father is a special friend
Who's strong and unafraid
One who gives encouragement
And never ending aid

A father knows just what to say
To change the course of fear
He rids me of my sadness
And takes away my tears

Today's my day to thank you
For strength and for your peace
For love and understanding
Which never seems to cease

May God today walk with you
And grant to you His love
And grant to you His guidance
Sent down from Heaven above.

—*Lance G. Arnold*

A Maiden's Love

Today I met a Lady so fair,
Whose heart was full of despair
Somehow she saw a gleam in my eye,
And I could not tell her a lie.

But then she confided in me,
That she was an Indian; Cherokee.
She is a maiden so pure and fair,
With her shining coal black hair.

A lonesome look I did see,
As she stopped and turned to me.
And all her love I did seek,
As we climbed the highest peak.

It was then I asked her for her hand,
I sensed she wanted her own man.
Now we both want to be free,
Just me and my Indian; Cherokee.

—*Samuel C. Knotts Jr.*

Too Late

Where are you going my friend?
Why are you running so fast?
Turn around and look at me.
Slow down-listen to me.
Is it really worth all the running?

Please, my friend, slow down.
These days will soon be gone.
You can't get back lost time.
You can't be young again!

When I finally stopped running
   it was too late...
I stood looking in the mirror at an
   old, tired face.
I can't go back and be young.
I'm too tired to run any more.
Where was I going?

—*Michelle Haley*

Little Angels

As I lay her in my bed,
With little angels above my head,
Shining light so I can see,
This beautiful lady lying next to me,
When she's lying next tome,
I'm as happy as I can be,
This lady was made just for me,
To share my love with for eternity.

—*Terrance Potts*

The Bluejay

O Bluejay in the dogwood tree,
Why are you so unfriendly?
When I come near, you fly away.
Why do you not wish to stay?

You seem so loving and so kind.
Why don't you have a trusting mind?
Why not on my shoulder stand,
And talk to me as bird to man?

You look so soft - I'd love to touch
If you were friendly, I'd love you much.
But you don't trust me when I'm near.
My very presence, you seem to fear.

Other animals know me well.
My two dogs come and tell
Me at the gate when I come home,
That I am missed when they're alone.

O Bluejay! O Bluejay! Tell me why,
That when I plead, you pass me by?
You fly away to a distant shore,
Where I will see you never more.

—*Martin M. Romine*

Why

I wonder why.
Why do I have to try?
Why do I have to cry?
Why is there so much sadness?
Why couldn't we have just gladness?
Why so much badness?
Why is there hate?
Why is there bad fate?
Why do we have to wait?
Why do we have to wait for joy?
Why do some people use you like a toy?
Why do some people like to annoy?
Why do we ache?
Why do our hearts break?
Why is there always so much at stake?
Why is there pain?
Why are some goals so hard to attain?
Why am I asking why again?

—*Lexi Ridder*

Grandma??!!

I'm too young to be a grandma...
Why, my hair's not even gray!
You're just a child yourself, girl...
Or you were just yesterday.

Why couldn't you have waited?
You have so much life ahead;
I'm too young to be grandma,
That's what I've always said.

You stand there in defiant youth
And tell me you're full grown;
I'm too young to be a grandma...
Too bad...the seed is sown.

I watch you bloom and start to bulge
As the summer months progress...
I'm too young to be a grandma...
But I'll get used to it, I guess.

My flesh, my blood inside you
Is my heritage, you see...
So I'll be the "bestest" grandma...
Like my grandma was to me.

—*Rebecca S. Seefeldt*

Child With Child

She's sixteen and pregnant,
will be keeping the kid.
Her youth will be gone
the day of delivery.
No proms to attend,
just diaper to change.
No more slumber parties,
No more Friday night dances.
No all night phone calls,
just 2 a.m. feedings.
Her baby will cry mama
as the days turn to months.
She'll crawl, then she'll walk
then she'll run through the years.
As her mama seats back
with eyes full of tears.
Because her child is now
a teenager and pregnant.

—*Leslie S. King*

Time Shall Pass

The magic of lunacy
Will come to all
Who correctly
Answers the question
Of faith.

However when you do
Faith will be no more.

It will ironically
Overcome the powers
Of tranquility.
To make time pass
More frequently

Which makes dementia
Linger on forever
Forever
Forever
Forever...

—*Thomas Austin Mungovan*

Gathering

Watch her) a budding rose
will never want or need
to know her beauty
could only implode into
reason creating an
answer—love
and I by nature am
subdued to a gasp of
unknown exaltations

In my mind
her petals wrap around me
a solitary bee gathering
as much life dust as I can carry

The flower understands,
I cannot turn away, so (I

—*F. Gavin Zeff*

You Were There

When I needed a helping hand,
Your hand was always there.
When I needed a shoulder to lean on
And that could bear my tears,
Your shoulder was always near.
When I needed someone to talk to,
You always listened.
You were there.

—*Sarah Tarango*

Fall Fantasy

Please, little leaves
will you play with me?
You are my friends
you grew on my tree;
I watched you this summer
waving at me.

You're all dressed up
in your prettiest clothes
and you dance all around
as the fall breeze blows.
Where will you go
when it's cold and it snows?

You'll cover the flowers
asleep in their beds
or whirl in the cold winds
that blow 'round our heads,
then rest in the blanket
the snow fairy spreads.

—*Marjorie Harrison*

Season

A
wind comes up
whirling summer away
tree dancing whine
whip the pale sky
a dark cerulean shudder
strokes the matted light
birds clatter
debating the squall
butterflies hang
hang on the bluster
life's debris scuttles
scrapes along dusting
asphalt grime and pebble
the first noise of winter
before the silent night.

—*Penny Weeks*

Untitled

The hush of death is silence
Wind the wings of prayer
Time deceiving eternity
As the mask belies the king
In a transition of dimension
Outside a fading dream
Two lives encountered fleeing
This heart of clouded times
I sit within this moment
Traveling through the ages
Outside the realms of time
No past no futures
No distance no nears
Within this time of sadness
Suspended as a tear.

—*Terence D. Mylet*

Angel Love

You're up on high
With friends of light
Your special smile
And winning ways
Your helping hand
From another place
Will remain with me always
I love you Dad

—*Marsha Hart*

A Man In Blue

There was a man all dressed in blue,
With a big Red S upon his chest.
Truth, justice, and liberty for all,
This man in blue stood very tall.
Friend or foe, it all depend on
Which side of the law you was my friend.
He was my hero, he was my friend
He was superman to the end.
Superman is dead, knocked off with a
Pencil of lead.
But we the people, all demand bring
Back our hero superman!

—*Shirley Phillips*

The Game

The visions that flash
with colors so bright,
Come into my dreams
as I sleep at night.
Of roads untraveled
and hearts untouched.
I watch with desire
wanting ever so much.
Cursed are the cards
that fate does play.
As I sit and I wait
and watch with dismay.
He lays them out,
one at a time.
Keeping me away
from what I deem, mine.
The pain of despair
makes my eyes grow wetter,
For the devil himself
could deal no better.

—*Wendy Borgmann*

Sandcastle

I can see it slipping,
With each passing tide.
My sandcastle is falling.
There is nowhere to hide.

The sea is much too deep.
Its waves much too strong,
For my castle to keep.
It will not last for long.

I stand and watch it helplessly
As it struggles to remain.
I stand and watch it hoping
That I can stand the pain.

And as the warm sun settles,
The sea I could not cry,
Now ebbs away my castle,
And I watch it slowly died.

Its pain is in its silence,
As the moon brings in the sea.
It steals away my castle,
There is no one left but me.

—*Yvonne E. Flores*

To My Son

The excitement of a moment shared
With friends and those for whom you care
Becomes a glistening memory...
A golden leaf upon the tree
Of life.

The words you speak, the time you spend,
To cultivate a new-found friend
Become the pages of a book...
A novel through which all can look
At love.

The smiles you give to passers-by
Without them ever knowing why,
Become the stars in heavens' blue...
The lights which show direction to
Happiness.

The way you say just what you're worth
Is the way you spend your life on earth.
So do the best you can my son...
And when life's over, you'll be one
With God.

—*Sharon K. Huxtable*

Untitled

I entered the night,
with my heart, body and soul.
My spirits soared with the wind,
My tears slipped with the rain.

I ran as one with the moon,
trying to escape from the sun.
The stars shone with their brilliance,
whispering to me, I had none.

I listened to the silence,
the strict hush of the night.
the only sound that was heard,
was the whisper of my cries.

The night mocked my agony,
betraying my trust.
Laughing at my stupidity,
and turning my happiness to dust.

Where do you go when the sun shows you
the reality you
don't wish to see?
And the night shows you the horror only
the darkness can see?

—*Laurie Rodriguez*

Memories

Sitting here with my thoughts
With the memories that can't be bought
Memories dancing in my head
As I lay here in my bed
Memories that seem to be so true
As I lay here thinking of you
As the past seems to fade away
Forgetting what I wanted to say
I don't know if it should come so close
These scary things they call ghosts
Don't know what else I should do
I'm sitting here without you
Wishing you were by my side
But I don't understand why you died
So won't you come back to me
That way I could see
What you say is so true
When you say "I'm here for you"

—*Sean Ian Cassidy*

The Road of Life

I walk down the Road of Life
  With my Jesus at my side.
    He guides me,
      Carries me,
  Shelters me from the storm.

I walk down the Road of Life
  With my friends at my side.
  They are my advice, my opinions.
      What they are,
    I am not, I am myself.

I walk down the Road of Life
  With my parents at my side.
    They are my models,
      My true friends,
      They guide me,
    They show me the way.

All three I walk down this road with.
    Some I will follow,
    Others I will pass,
  Down this long, long, Road of Life.

—*Mildred Scher*

Quiet Times

A quiet place all alone,
with no problem but,
your own, to think of
the world you left
behind and come to
the other side.
To look and see what
nature brings to me,
but quiet times and
lonely dreams. To see
the sky all shaded
in blue and to find
that this part of the
world is here for you.

—*Theresa Perry*

Untitled

I can cry no longer,
  with open running
    tears for you.

Only my heart swells
  full of pain.

To see you and hold you,
  are more to just
    my dreams.

Holding on to my hopes,
  has no loving gain.

—*Troy M. Houin*

All Animals Running Free

All animals running free
with the wind blowing through the trees
running, running down a hill
running, running past a mill
In the water, pretty & small
past a mountain, big & tall
with the sun shining so bright
& climb a mountain with all your night

—*Melissa Barz*

Petal Soft Pride

A lone rose,
with withering edges
and tumbling petals;
stands upright and proud
in its hour of death.

Its leaves still green
and thorns still firm;
dare a soul
to prick its pride.

—*Lyn R. Garcia*

Hearts Beating

There is a very special place
  Within my heart for you,
Where only love light shines,
  And skies are always blue,
A kingdom of joyful songs
  The king and princess rule,
Where spring times always rich
  With the sent of flowers bloom,
You are my princess "I Love You"
  Your Daddy is always there,
For it's as if I never left
  Our bond is loving care

—*Tonya Stone*

One Moment

One moment has a special place,
Within the heart of me;
It occurred when a birdie chased,
An unsuspecting bee.

The trees stood tall with solemn grace,
And squirrels sped on grass;
The day was like a virgin chaste,
And you, my pretty lass.

Your hand in mine, and mine in yours,
Two lovers passing by;
And then it came, as moon arose,
In fading blue of sky.

The passing of these many years,
Has brought me endless bliss;
But Oh, my heart still remembers,
Our first enchanting kiss!

—*Rosario D'Souza*

Thy Heart

  Tis it thy heart I hear beating
within thy mighty chest?
  And tis it a butterfly fluttering
in my breast.
  Sweetened air of love blowing
from the west.
  It is thy heart which pounds as
fiercely as a lions.
  It is thy love which keeps the
flame of faith from dying.
  For our love shall last for an
eternity. With the gulls cries
echoing against the crashing seas.

—*Laura C. Del Prete*

Fantasy Man

Deeper, deeper in I fall,
Without a word I hear your call.
Drowning in those quicksand eyes
I lose my grip, don't realize —
No longer earth beneath my feet,
On wings of love I go to meet
My destiny; your heart's desire
Is my command — bathe in the fire.
All will is lost within a kiss
Fantasy man I can't resist.

In the arms of sweet illusion
I'm hypnotized into confusion.
You smile at me and say, "Believe"
Oh tell me now you'll never leave.
Promises whispered in my ears
I let you in, erase my fears.
Romancing me all through the night
You fade away in morning's light:
And in my dream you disappear...
Let me awake to find you here.

—*Michelle Adkins*

Songs Of Yesterday

Living my life alone
Without you by my side,

Silent tears wiped away
Replaced by happy memories.

A quiet walk alone
In the park where once we played.

Songs of birds
Happy cries of children;

They make me think of you
And our songs of yesterday.

People change as time moves on
But friendship still remains.

I see the old bench where he sat;
The old man who told us stories.

How wise and true those stories were
If only you had listened.

No more trace is left behind
Of the child I once was.

Time may take what it wants
Except our songs of yesterday.

—*Lisa E. Dressler*

Searching

Wondering where my place in life is,
  wondering why I'm so confused.
  Looking for an answer when you
are using an excuse afraid to face
the truth, knowing nothing in life
  prospers without initiative and
      lots of care.
So believe and trust faithfully in the
  man up stair and all of your
  confusion will eventually disappear.

—*Lisa M. Henderson*

Ribbons Of Red

Ribbons of red
Won't you wear for me
So all the world can see?
A ribbon of red
For a tear has been shed
Just a name on a quilt I'll be.
Ribbons of red
A ray of hope
For all those who remain.
A ribbon of red
For all the blood has been shed
Will there be a light for me?
So won't you wear
A ribbon of red
So more and more will know?
A ribbon of red
For the road ahead
Has still so far to go.

—*Martina H. Kulak*

A Disciples's Prayer

Good morning holy spirit.
Would you speak to me today?
And give me ears that I might hear
Just what you have to say.

Make my eyes that I might see
Thy perfect will for me,
And give me courage, the desire
The strength to accept it gratefully.

Give me a heart full of joy and love
That I might share today,
With some lost soul that I might meet
Along life's lost highway.

Let me sow some holy seed
That they might spring up soon,
Or water others already sown
That they not wilt with the heat of noon.

Oh, Lord, let me eat of that sweet rich fruit
Of the harvest so bountiful and grand
Of another lost soul as it is plucked
Out of satin's destroying hand.

—*Mark Lowery*

Untitled

Just a bee I need to search
Yes, I am compelled
You're the flower of my love
Your fragrance I have smelled

When I awoke my work I know
And it must be complete
It's to you I must return
To drink your nectar sweet

And al the time I think of you
My heart soars high aloft
I always will remember when
I touched your petals soft

—*Randall Landquist*

Alone

The world is a forest
  Yet we stand alone
For each tree is different
  And each tree its own.

—*Michael R. Karpie*

The Surprise

I don't even know you.
yet already you bring me joy.
  Are you my precious little girl?
or my darling little boy?

Soon I'll get to hold you,
touch your fingers and your toes.
  I'll wash you and I'll dress you,
in your brand new baby clothes.

And then we'll sit down quietly,
I'll hold you close to me.
  And I'll sing to you a mother's song
of love eternally.

You don't know me yet,
but someday soon, the time will come.
  I'll say, "I love you honey"
you'll say, "I love you mom."

—*Phyllis J. McClure*

O' How Great Is Our Lord

O' how great is our Lord Jesus
Yet He is always the same
We know our toils and labor
Will not be in vain.

Let us look forward
To a much brighter day
Jesus with His heavenly power
Will roll all dark clouds away.

One day He saved us
And made us truly whole
That some day we may walk
The very streets of gold.

Though at times the way maybe rugged
Yet we shall have no fear
Because of His loving grace
We can fill His presence near.

Let us keep praying
And try to do our best
When life's trials are over
We shall have eternal rest.

—*Rebecca G. Gray*

Your Narcissistic World

I could please you,
Yet I merely tease you;
C_nt that I am.

—*Jill*

Why?

You made me laugh -
You made me cry!
Now I ask why?
Knowing the answer
  is not to be.
For in the state of
  confusion-
All is but an illusion.
Knowing infatuation is
  only a mirage,
For loves's absence
leaves only dreams...
  And they to—
    will soon be gone!!
You made me laugh-
You made me cry.

—*L. Marie Glidden*

You And Me

I simply adore you in every way
You made my life wonderful,
What can I say.
You taught me kindness,
You taught me love,
You taught me peace and joy.
You're my best friend and my love too
What I see is in you.
For I dreamed of this day you see,
Of it just being me and you.
I want you to know how great you are,
And how you make me feel.
Because you're special so special to me,
Cause you showed what's in me.
And I will say. I'm so glad you're mine,
And no time will be without you.
For you're in me and I in you,
We are created as one.

—*Lesa Peterson*

Untitled

Dear children
you question why

why are there wars
why is there famine
why do we suffer
why do we die

not all birds live together
some fish devour others
weeds destroy the flowers
mommy and daddy are not forever

Dear children
I have no answer.

—*Micki Grossman*

Reflections

If in your love's reflection
you see a broken calm,
Be kind and understanding; for
you know which side their on.
It differs from their natural state,
but one should never doubt:
True love's daily feelings come
from within - never from without.
Sometimes a situation arise, that
pushes and pulls and shouts;
So, look back through - into that pool
and see that love renewed, for
true loves daily feelings come
from within - never from a doubt.

—*Paul V. Tymchyn*

Well-Beloved One

My well-beloved one,
Your smile is like the
midday sun;
How radiant, how brilliant,
how resonant, how pleasant,
it is to behold;
My well-beloved one,
You're like a star,
Always glowing, always gleaming,
Always sparkling, always shining,
   My well-beloved one;
My well-beloved one,
My well-beloved one........

—*Reginald Gentry*

The Gift

I hold in my hand a gift for
   you, something warm and
   treasured,
a gift that will always be
   true.
See how it fits so comfortably
   in your mind;
like a memory that you hold
   so dear, a friend true and kind.
Take this gift gently and
   hold it close;
don't treat it wrong, for it is
   what we all need most.
Hold it close, feel its softness,
   not at all hard.
For you see, once it was mine-
   now - it is your heart.

—*Sandy Moffett Zellner*

My Sandman

All my life I should have known,
You would be the first to go
You filled my life with hopes and
tears and took away my childhood fears
When you tucked me in at
night I would scream
"Leave on the light"
To my bedside you would come with
stories to make my dreams more fun
with spaceships that went as far
as Mars,
and little elves that lived on shelves.
Because of AIDS I'll never
again touch your face, hear your
voice, or hold your hand,
but in my heart you will always
stand, my brother the
"Sandman".

—*Noreen Curtis Griffith*

Untitled

If I were of chocolate
You would hold me in your mouth
Caress me with your tongue
Bite me gently
And savor me as a milky treasure
and a dark secret.

I could linger in your mouth
Melt in your warmth
Be swallowed by you
Move through your veins as a
nourishing sweetness
Know the recesses of you

And you would want more of me.
And I would fill you.

—*Laura E. Gosheff*

Autumn

Autumn is so colorful,
With color that is very full.
The leaves that quiver,
Down to the river.
The birds begin to fly south,
Towards the river's mouth.
And bees and bug go away,
Until the next warm spring day.

—*Lisa Haverkorn*

Amber Eyes

In dreams I most remember you
your dancing smile, electric energy
the salty taste of your skin
the lyrical notes of your voice
and those amber eyes hypnotizing me
hypnotized others too
the tall blonde I found you in bed with
Gina, my best friend at Rose's party.

Ten years the perfect marriage
I worked two jobs, took care of you
you went to school and f__ked around
with drugs and other women
they looked at me with pity
I walked out and you cried.

I saw your wife the other day.
Your son has amber eyes.

—*Mary R. Brandt*

Love

When you really love someone
your love must be true,
because you should never lie
about the words "I love you."

Love is something that comes
straight from the heart,
therefore you must begin
at the very start.

If you truly love someone
let them know your sincere,
by telling them that your
love for them will always
live right here,
in your heart.

—*Megan Nicole Liska*

Shasta County

Shasta county,
your mountains are pretty
With the buck brush growing
In your black lava flow.

Shasta county,
Your mountains surround me,
Hold me like a mother,
You warm and you comfort
My wandering soul.

Shasta county,
I love your manzanita,
And the red bud blooming
In the spring in the snow.

Shasta county,
To walk through your valleys,
Your hills and your mountains,
Are memories to treasure
More precious than gold.
Shasta county.

—*C. W. Vance*

Little Dallas

Little Dallas, my honey-pie
You're the apple of my eye.
I hug you, I hold you,
I squeeze you, I kiss you,
But all you do is
Cry, cry, cry...

—*Vickie C. Darnell*

Untitled

Even though our time has ended
There is a beginning in sight
Of a deeper understanding
Guiding us to a light
A light of pure love
No pain or sorrow there to find
With patience and tenderness
We will achieve a greater peace of mind
There are no demands on us
To be people we are not
The new found strength of our convictions
Are worth the battles we have fought
Those battles saved our love
From a sure and painful death
Our love evolves to new dimensions
Because we have given it life's breath
Do not fear the future - our paths together will cross
Forever in each others hearts - please feel no sense of loss
These words have come easily because they are one and all true
And my deepest desire is to share them with you

　　—Dolores Rubalcaba

True Love

Where there is love
There is also a friend.
When the heart's broken
There present to mend.
Someone who'll be there
In good or in bad,
Listening when there's anger,
And comforting when there's sad.
So what becomes old what was once new
The cherished ones are the ones that are true.

　　—Aysha Leefe

God?

　　　I have no God to pray to
There is no rhythm or rhyme in this world,
　　And reason is a creation of men.

　　　There is no God to pray to
There is no balm or salvation in this world,
　　And death is the fate of men.

　　　We have a God to pray to
There are hope and peace in this world,
　　And love is the life of men.

　　—Erika Dale Garvin

Today

Today is the day that the Lord has made
This is the positive attitude that I am acquiring
Every circumstance comes for a reason
Each day has its obstacle
Each day has its obscurity
Each day is a surprise
Each moment is mine
Each conversation is continued
Each second builds on to a minute
No one shall call a day a day of doom
That is a foolish thought
Doom is negatively based
Reason to create and experiment are part of
　　each day
The rough, raged, tormented moments blend with
　　the subliminal, placid ones
You and I make each day beautiful

　　—Ann Marie Wolfe

Our Future

Look at the world today,
There is something very wrong.
Why do people act this way,
When our lives can last for so long?

People run around with guns and knives,
While children are trying to learn.
Next thing you know, an accident happens,
A child's dream may be burned.

Why don't we do something with this world,
Instead of watching it rot.
Because our children are our future,
They need to have good thoughts.

When they are older,
They will need a place to stay,
Where there aren't as many crimes,
As there are today.

Why don't we get together,
And try to like one another,
To make tomorrow a better day?
Why Do People Act This Way?

　　—Imelda Lynn Hill

Abused

I am lonely, standing deep-rooted, by myself.
There isn't another soul as far as the eye
can see from my planted spot.
No one similar to visit or to wave, except of
course my children, young saplings.

The wind - the unrelenting, pushing, shoving complaining
omnipresent blowing us until we're bent
and feeling old and dry to the heart.

He says we're bad to hold him back!
We're in his way, this stormy fellow,
pushing, shoving, complaining, pounding, criticizing

I try to keep my foothold and my pride
I image myself straight and tall
He says I'm stubborn, hard, set in my ways.

I am, I'm hard, hard as a board.
My exterior is rough, rough as bark,
my God, he's right! I'm stubborn, hard,
Set in my way..so I give in... now I'm
　　firewood!

　　—Ingrid Neel

Raindrop

Surrounded by others,
there seems to be no more room.
But spaces gives way, my space,
closer, closer.
Some can stay no longer, letting
go of the only comfort they know.
Others like myself have been there before.
We have experienced the journey afar
whose perils are unknown.
Our safety is fleeting though,
like pebbles in a mountain stream.
Anyone in our midst could be chosen
at any time, for a reason,
or maybe not.
Only the whim of our
gray master protects us.

　　—Bill Patty

A Mysterious Old Lady

As I walked down the street,
there was an old lady I did meet.
Her face was hidden by the shadow of a cloth hat,
yet I could still see the worn away look created by three
scratches-that of a cat.
Her silvery hair shone bright in the sun,
and her mouth lacked teeth, more than one.
Her mouth was held back in a crooked kind of smile,
one much like a crocodile.
Dried and cracked were her lips,
Bony and slim were her finger tips.
Her fingernails long and twisted too,
and in the wind her long, black cape blew.
Her shoeless feet reveal her bony, cracking toes.
And as she walks the street all day,
you might hear her cackle in a funny old way.
As you watch her with surprise,
she's watching you with her wicked, grey eyes.

—Briar Kerver

Seasons

Where did the time go? — I don't know.
There were many seasons of springs
    summer, fall, and winter snow.
Fall with its changing leaves and nip in the air,
The leaves tumbling down, the wind ruffling my hair.
Winter is so very cold — with its sleet, its snow, its ice.
Wouldn't some hot chestnuts be very very nice?
And then, ah yes!! comes spring
With its rebirth of flowers and trees and birds on the wing.
I love the sand, the sun, and the oceans mighty roar.
The mountains high — the tall majestic trees,
Who could ask for more
And the skies are oh so lovely, be it morning, noon or night,
The stars, the sun, the moon - all shine so very bright
It has been so magnificent, I forgot that time passed by me —
For on the twenty ninth of December,
I'll be a young at heart seventy.

—Grace H. Auman

Summer In Belgium 1932

In Belgium it was the grass,
there's no beach like over here.
I never go on vacation in Belgium.
Where I come from I wouldn't say there were poor people,
but they were mining people.
They worked all the time.
In summer we went in the cellar where it was cool.
There was a patch of grass we sat on.
All around the house was coal mine.
From fourteen years old they worked in a coal mine.
Mine sister worked in a coal mine.
When I was fourteen I worked in a factory,
then a doctor's office, there I learned my French.
We spoke Wallon, a dialect.
I received people who wait for the doctor.
My family spoke just Wallon.
Then I worked in a bakery.
Every Saturday we did a big clean.
Scrubbed the floor with soap and water and took a good bath
in a big tub to get cleaned up for Sunday.

—Bertha Oliver

Christmas

Tiny little baby, lying on his bed
There's no satin sheets, no pillow for his head
He has no fancy booties, or gown made of lace
Neither was he born in a stately place

But, in a lowly stable, where sheep and cattle stay
Upon a bed of straw, the tiny baby lay
In love, He came, carried on an angels wing
A star announced His birth, while Heavenly choirs sang.

Wise men came to worship Him.
And brought Him gifts of worth
Angels were even with Him from the moment of His birth.

Angels hovered over Him
He was always in their sight
For indeed, the King of Heaven is born to us this night

Blessed Babe of Bethlehem we rest in peace and joy
For we have eternal life in Mary's baby boy.

—Betty L. Makris

Share Your Rainbows

Share your rainbows:
They are moments of you
Caught up with fragile, fleeting beauty.

Share your rainbows, if you will,
Because you cannot keep them for yourself,
Except in memory.

Open my minds eye,
Touching my view of the world
With rainbows retold
In the fervor of your wonderment.
Recreate their mystery
Anyway you can to keep the splendor vital.

Paint your rainbows,
Stitch them,
Make a poem,
Catch them on a film.
But please share your rainbows with me,
And I will try to sing them back to you.

—Janiece Avery Petersen

Ode To Two Friends

They met on the eve of three years past.
They became friends and time went fast.
He came and went and came and went.
Alas, she missed him much,
But she always believed she still could...
Feel his touch...
Hear his laughter...
Feel his warmth...
For he had the most unique style.

She walked with grace and beauty,
Head high, dreams intact,
Keeping her secret, controlling her,
For she knew it would never occur.
He had captured a part of her heart and she his.
A smile when he was absent...
A memory of a sweet embrace...

The silent love of two endures all tribulations
That life seems to throw their way,
For love is not of body,
But of soul and mind.

—Cheryl P. Hodges

Each Star

Each star twinkles all night
They dance so merrily in the sky
But for every star, there
Must be a dozen more we can't see

Each star reminds me of you
Shining all night, until morn comes
As I stand there, watching those stars
I'm thinking, knowing, realizing

That you are watching those same stars
I dearly, miss you and wish
I could have you by my side
But we are like each star

We shine all night
Do our best to stay bright
But in the morning we are gone
Into the real world
   —Jared Lee

Along Came Two Bees

Along came two bees, buzzz, buzZZ, bUZZ, BUZZZ
They flew on the baby's knees, buzzz, buzZZ, buZZZ, BUZZZ
They walked up his body, to his face, to his head,
They saw no hair, so they flew in the air
Then the bees fled, buzzz, buzZZ, buZZZ, BUZZZ
   —Janice Colon

Dreams

My dreams are my hope for the future...
They guide me and give me strength...
When I think I won't see tomorrow,
I try to remember times well spent.
But having a happy spirit isn't easy with
all that's happening in the world...
Sometimes it gets so hard to overcome
the widespread turmoil
Then when I gaze upon the sunset, or see
love birds perched in a tree, the wonder
of the sight gives me the strength to
think positively.
The desire to accomplish my dreams is renewed
once in a while...
With them in mind, I go through my days with
a smile
   —Angela Walker

The Old Shack

Once there was a man and a women who lived in an old shack.
They had pots on the floor from the dripping roof and they
slept on a cold damp and smelling couch bed that they founding
in a abandon house down the street. They did not have any
running water. They had two chicken wings, a slice of bread
which they found behind Kentucky Fried Chicken. One day the
man was on his way to the Kentucky Fried Chicken place when he
found 50$ dollars W*O*W was he happy he spent 25 on food 25
on clothing. The next week he went for a job interview and got a
job as a boy at the warehouse putting boxes in people cars but
that did not satisfy him. He went for a another making screens
at a screen factory so all together he was making about 450 a
week. That money went straight in the bank after he finished
his business around his house he was at work the women was at
home making sure the furniture men came and the plumber, car
painter, painter, and the exterminator. The man begin saving
his and her money in the bank.
   —Jessie Matthews

The "Tenderloin"

When you entered their homeland with ease and alone,
 they knew the young writer as one of their own;
You respected their distance but shared in the pain
 of the child from indifference that will always remain:

The longing for passage the youth never shows
 as she drifts through the nightfields where her destiny
 knows...
The singer whose verse gently falls to the ground
 where its echoes are muted by the ironweed's sound;
When the time jester's dance by illusion withholds
 the fate of the image that the traveller unfolds;
And the mime of the teacher as his gestures portend
 of the giant stone listeners and the dreams they defend.

The Tenderloin children still say your name —
 these souls who stay huddled in the doorways of shame,
For they saw their reflection in the gift of your mind
 when you wrote of their poetry the world left behind.
    ... for Mark
   —Ginny Snyder

Friends Are Forever

Friends should be there, through bad and good times,
They know they should.
If you're a friend you should be one that is good.
Friends hold tight through day and night.
They even understand by the way you act.
Friends are always there, they even share.
If you're not a friend, then that's the end.
Please take care,
I want to be there!!!
   —Amanda Evans

Beyond Us

I watch the leaves from my window.
They loose their mooring from the tree.
Yet, somehow their destiny is not their own.
They twist and swirl, dance and fly and play together.
Still, all their movement is at the hands of another power
Beyond them, around them, but outside their design.

Their multi-colors seem to make them rich,
And declare that all their movements are happy ones.
But, such is not the case.
Sometimes, on their way to the cold ground, they touch and talk,
And, it would appear, by the will of the wind,
Their antics will last forever.

Then mercilessly, they are pulled apart.
Perhaps, forever, to end their lives.

Such it is for us.
   —G. Douglas Routledge

Eulogy For The Flowers

Grieve for the wondrous inhabitants of my emerald garden.
They sprout from tiny seeds to embrace their new world.
They inspire beauty and love to all who surround them.
They bring fragrance and color and ask for so little in return.
They provide warmth and shelter to both the birds and the bees.
And through the harshness of reality and cruelty of time.
They are plucked from their world before they flourish and
 prosper.
Do you grieve for my dying children?
Do you weep when you see their petals wither and fall?
All things must come to an end, that I do see.
But tragedy strikes the hearts of those who do not understand..
   —Aaron Killat

A Birthday Gift

Wisemen with your expensive gifts of myrrh, frankincense and
gold.
They're much too heavy for baby hands to hold.
Could they thoughtfully be packed away
And then re-given on a future day?
If I had been there, my gift too
Would have been offered with much love and care.
I would have given Him a Teddy Bear.
His tiny hands could feel its softness,
And maybe His eyes would smile.
Then I would let my Lord enjoy His babyhood
For just a little while.

—*Carolyn Burnett*

The Wolves

Have you ever looked at the eyes of a wolf
    they're searching and hungry
        lonely and scared.

Where will the next meal come from
    they howl to the moon
    will we have something
or have to survive without.

Will you provide for us
will we starve for want
    the moon shines brightly
as they appear fragile and gaunt.

    They are a hunter
      a survivor too
    they will not die
    for lack of food.

    They will howl and cry
in the night for us to hear
but they will become stronger
    there is no more fear.

—*Ali Michele Crofts*

Wild Lonely People

Wild lonely people walking alone
They've got not friends they've got no homes
They just shuffle their feet through every street
And they read the reviews of last year's old news
And they wear cardboard boxes instead of real shoes.
Wild lonely people walking alone
They've got no friends they've got no homes.
Through darkened alleys past dusk in the rain
Missing the good times missing again.
Wild lonely people wild lonely crowds
Wild little kids crying out loud:
Into the cold into the dark
They make themselves at home in the park.
Wild lonely people walking alone
Wild lonely people they can never go home.

—*Gail Pamela Munz*

Maze

Yes, I do remember the Summer that I don't. Oh, like a
thief it was, creeping past and taking all that I had left.
We would drink for today, drink for tomorrow, hell we'd even
drink for yesterday. "You did what?... Really?... I'll drink
to that!" This ritual slowly, but surely grew into a practice,
and this practice slowly, but surely turned into a way of life.
It was so incredibly cruel to me, yet I nurtured this vice, as
though it was my son. It dawned to me that this maze had only
an entrance.

—*Andrew M. Loos*

Sent From Above

God looked around and said, who shall I send to look over
this child. Who will love her, teach her to love as I do.
Direct her in the right way to go. Some one who will teach her
to trust in me and obey me. A mother who is kind, loving, full
of joy, "A God fearing woman"

A woman who's beauty that shines out more beautiful than the
rays from the sun.

Someone who's love will blossom as a flower does in the
spring time. Someone who's joy will sing out like a canary.
Who's trust will never die, as in the things of this life.
Someone who "Faith is like the wheat of the fields, "That just
grow and grow".

Someone who can with stand the waves of life "that
sometimes toss us to and fro".

Then God reach down and put me in your arms. "Saying" this
is the right one, so full of grace and charm. I know you will
be well cared for, and shown plenty of love, "Because, you see
my Child" the mother that I'm sending you has been, "SENT
FROM ABOVE."

—*Deborah Kay Winston*

The Last Rose

    I fell in love the day we met.
  This part of my life, I'll not forget.
Each day that past, my love grew stronger.
  A love that will last so much longer.
  Though from my life, he did depart.
  In his last rose, I enclose my heart.

—*Carol M. Brown*

The Grim Reaper

He stalks the earth by night, by day,
This Reaper of the souls of men,
Caring naught for He we kneel to pray,
Nor whom or how, nor where or when,
His great reward is the souls of men

A fisherman, drifting slowly in his small, row boat,
Is suddenly alarmed, it well no longer float,
It sinks from the surface to water below,
While the Reaper waits in the undertow,
He fears, he struggles, strong currents roll,
The Reaper harvests another soul.

Little fawn, don't stray so far from your mother's side,
In the stalking lion the Reaper hides.
He cares naught for man nor beast,
Your mother will weep as the lion feasts.
Go back! Go prance among the trees,
And hear the rustle of Autumn leaves.
Go! drink cool water from the rippling stream,
For in the eyes of the Reaper is an evil gleam.
He waits, he gloats, he beams, another victorious scheme.

—*Jessie Beuchert*

Peace

Whence comes the peace the world has sought?
Though there are some who think it can be bought;
Rather to sow it in the hearts of man
Than place false hope in international plan.

He writes, "I love my fellow man" upon the sand,
Then goes his way, bends not to give a helping hand,
While seeking wealth and power with trumpet blare,
Forgetting that he has a heart to share.

When troubled eyes see war and strife increase
Soon may they look to God for everlasting peace.

—*Audrey H. Hunter*

Rest For The Weary

Through many dangerous tests and trials,
This strong woman has already come,
Courageously determined to run every mile,
She knows there is more work to be done.
Reflecting, thinking and looking at life,
Why does there seem to be so much despair?
All around there is suffering and strife,
Still knowing that God will surely answer prayer.
As the heavenly sun shines from above,
Flowers bloom; the eagle stirs its nest,
Hope runs eternal; there is always God's love,
Towards the end of the journey, she will find rest.
Keep on striving and holding onto your faith,
Victoriously running; always stay in the race.

—Dorothy Morgan

Institution Of Marriage

To those of you, that made it through
This world of toil and strife
keeping with you that same partner
You chose to share your life

The institution of marriage,
Most sadly in neglect
By most of the world it's treated
With little or no respect

Pride in my parents, teamed as one
I offer thanks and praise
These are the times we talk about
Referent to "Good Ole' Days"

Fifty six years .. troubles and woes
Struggling to make ends meet
Raised three children and watched them grow
Making their life complete

All in all, with ups and downs and
Some bitter with some sweet
Parents and children know its worth...
There's pride in non-defeat

—Arlene Hartman

Rockin Chair

Rockin chair that old rockin chair
Though I never had a cradle
Mom was always there
In that old rockin chair
During the day that chair would never rock
Only time for cooking and mendin daddy's socks
I often wondered what made momma cry
So many times so late at night
I guess mom knew back then
She wasn't long for this life
Just continued to be
Mother and a wife.
Now I stand in her room
By the fires light
All I can do is stare
Wipe a teary eye
It's just sitting there
That was momma's
Rocking chair

—Bob Towry

Eulogy To A Friend

I spoke at the funeral of an old friend,
Though I saw him die so long ago.
Internment was but a welcome process.
He lived not to be great nor known.
He was a shell tossed about by the storm.
I saw in his eyes, his pain and sorrow.
Each new conquest was for someone else
For he could never capture the essence
Of the moment, whatever it held for him.
He yearned to be in some other place;
Some other time, and now he is.
I could not speak to him of what I saw.
He knew my thoughts; he read my eyes.
I knew there could be no other choice.
He seemed, finally, to be at peace.

—Eleno H. Robles

Blind Obsession

Intelligent and beautiful was she.
Though she must have left it in the country.
Oh what a grave error on her part.
I hope he doesn't break her heart.

Graduating at the top of her class.
Her parents proud, though it would not last.
She had an idea in her head.
Though, no matter that the man was wed.

Her and her possessions in L.A.
Her parents hoped she would not stay.
Six months pass, family and friends long forgotten.
A married man is what she's wantin'.

Moral values pushed aside.
She'd do anything to be his bride.
Conformed to what he desires.
Her blind "love" for him will not expire.

Said I'd be a maid of honor
Black lace dress represents death and horror
Intelligence blinded by love
I pray guidance for her from above.

—Alexis Harper

Jigsaw

Crumbs, pieces, fragments
Thoughts I can't sweep under the carpet.
It clogs my mind. I can't clear it up.
It comes like a cloud, blocking.
I like being needed,
can I borrow your mind for a moment?
Is it clear? Free! Free! Free thoughts!
No road blocks to bump into.
Can I be a kid again?
Growing up sucks!
I want to sit in the bathtub and watch my toes
play hide and seek in the suds.
Is there time?
The arm of the clock scares me.
I wish I had a stopwatch to pause.............
now and then,
and put the pieces back together
and not to be so puzzled.
Here is a piece,
grab a stopwatch and join me.

—Derrick Brown

The Pleasure Of Light

Timeless light seeking shelter, through-
Thoughts of yesterday's years gone by...
I stopped for a brief moment, not to deny.
I ran from the enter darkness like rain,
Falling forever downward, was my pain.
Seeking that which is far away,
But never knowing night or day.
Morning, night, the difference only;
Seen by naked eyes.
To many longtime goodbyes.
Windows opening and closing to endless.
Passages of time.
Thoughts enter in and out, as one comes to mind.
Rivers of tears, some happy, other's sad
But only for a while, a little mad.
This road in the shade, a lot has passed by,
The sun now shines, no more to cry.

 —*Fred Isaac*

Untold Love

A lovely lady stood by me 28 years,
Through a lot of sacrifice, scares and tears.
We've had a lot of grief, and blessings come our way,
And I learned to take things day by day.
Her brown eyes still sparkle,
Though her hair has a little gray.
I don't tell her often enough,
But I love her more each day.

 —*Earl E. Hart*

A Child Of Imperfection

This child of mine, she sees the world
Through different eyes; her mind distorted,
Not perfect, they said; a useless strain.
The anger from within is a cry of pain,
For her world is now shadowed with ennui;
But my love for her will forever be!

Despair has now become my companion,
Yet I try to hope, knowing there's none.
The hope that dies leaves a life unfulfilled;
The dreams that died leave feelings of guilt.
Yet through it all, expectations I see;
My child of imperfection is perfect to me!

 —*Joan Heinkel*

A Litany Of Love

Timeless Adam seeking Eve
through love's veil of sweet illusion
torn asunder in their youth.
Seductive passions for Nature's procreation
and secret underlying truth.
Fruit of love bearing life
giving meaning to a life span.
Bond of love ultimate to the marriage union
between a woman and a man.
Sexes yolked together
complimentary to each other,
close as kin, yet both a lover.
Intimately fused as one
by fulfillment to become parental
a father and a mother.
To be loved man's yearning hunger
at life's beginning
stretching to the end of time.
In all its forms love brings perfection
God's greatest gift to mankind.

 —*Barbara Lawrence*

The Friend

He's always there for me
Through rain, snow, or hail
He's at my side when I need him
For his love will never fail

To him I tell all my worries
All my sorrows, all my pains
He'll never take advantage of me
For he knows there's nothing to gain

I stare into his deep brown eyes
As I spill out all my griefs
Like an ocean spills out waves
From the shores to the reefs

He'll be there behind me
Like behind the rain shines the sun
And that dear reader, is the kind of friendship
That can never be undone

 —*Divya Rao*

The Journey

They journey on the beat of the Taun-Taun.
Through tears they shed, I suffered with them.
They were apart, but came together
To save the princess of hope and their own hearts.
Their cause was noble, but they risked sinking in the swamp
If they lost their faith.

He, who walks the sky, knew the terror caused by the
Flowing black armor of unresolved pain and hatred.
Yet he fought on, for their love.
They found friends among enemies,
Who helped them fight the imperial forces of death.

And now he walks on hands alone no more.
As the falcon flies unhindered through the millennia,
So does their faith.
And the shriveled emperor of pain and suffering is no more.

For they have won the right to be free
And to love.
And they rejoice and reflect on
Wisdom gained through puppet's Oz.
Celebrate the love.

 —*Deborah Lynn Sears*

Reach Out

Reach out
Through the endless mirror
Confront your nemesis
Connect with your ideal
   Reach out
   To the little one's hand
   Teach him to stand
   Help him to fly
Reach out
To the ignorant debutante
Control her narcissism
Defeat her insecurities
   Reach out
   For the java man
   Remember his wisdom
   Search for its meaning
Reach out
Beyond all confinements
Stretch your mind
Free your soul

 —*Anissa Umbaugh*

Thirty Three

The yelling and the screaming from the stands,
through the Garden was heard;
When all at once stood a man,
the one and only Larry Bird.

Larry Bird did many wonders,
especially when he was hot;
The crowd began to sound like thunder,
when Larry hit that three point shot.

When the Celtics were hopeless,
and trying to stay alive;
The other team would be in aweness,
when Larry went to drive.

Larry is a big part,
of Celtics shamrock green;
And when the Celtics are in your heart,
Think of number Thrity Three.

    —Justin F. Dornhoffer

Dance Of Life

Take me dancing
Through the milky-way, round the moon
Stardust flying from our heels
As we dance the dance of life

Hold my hands tightly, as we leap over the clouds
Our feet bouncing gracefully on the wind currents
Our bodies rolling with the motion of the ocean waves
Swirling and dipping to the rhythm of the universe

Teach me to dance the dance of life joyfully
Let my laughter spring forth like rain
Refreshing the earth and its creatures

Too long have I sat in darkness
Seeing only shadows, feeling hurt and blue
Help me throw off the chains of depression
Which are weighing down my spirit
Fill me with light open my eyes and heart
Show me the beauty and wonder all around me
Open my ears to the music of the universe
So I can dance
The dance of life

    —Carolyn R. Vaden

Who Am I?

Wandering through the pathways of life,
through the oceans of thought,
carrying on his shoulders
the burden of uncommitted sins,
sins that crush the innocence of youth
before it blossoms,
man has always been searching;
either through happiness or the depths of despair
always searching, always asking himself:
who am I?
Hopes are lost, hopes are found:
today is not just another day
it is the eternal day,
to gaze at nature's wonders,
to build new hopes,
to cry over shattered dreams,
to look at all the cultures, all the colors,
all the disasters that man has brought upon himself
out of ignorance, out of pride,
and will ask himself again: WHO AM I?

    —Andreas G. Kodros

Alteridem-A Conscious Conflict Between the Ego and Alter Ego

Who are you my wicked-looking friends, the ruler from dusk
till the night's end?
  I am the keeper of dreams and the knower of things.
  My fears and desires are revealed when I sleep, why is it
these secrets you forever keep?
  I am the keeper of dreams and the knower of things.
  You haunt and tease until you are through, I know not what
else I can do.
  You have ruled me from beginning to end. You made me what I
am, my wicked looking friend.

    —Ashley Channing Knox

Female To Male

We're from the same state the same
timber of colorful leaves.
Into this universe we sprouted call it future existence.
It's female to male a special thing.
A closeness to which we're bonded.
And you've always been a glisten for... you've
made me laugh and even cry and once
again you have made me discover what I had once buried.
Anyway I think it's fantastic that you and I
have stepped on the same stones again
or was it meant to be...
A part of my life, my male, you'll always be
apart of me in every way.

    —Bertha Garrett

Spirits From Above

The hardest thing of life - the conquest not of
time and space, but of ourselves, of our stupidity
and inertia, of our greediness and touching's of
our fear and intolerant wrongs. Every time you
give another a "piece of your mind" you add to your
          own vacuum.

God never make us conscious of our weakness except
          to give us of his strength.

A mistake is evidence that someone has tried to
          do something.

Life is 10% what you make it and 90% of how you
take it. Take it the way you want it, don't
          hesitate.

Do not be disturbed at being misunderstood.
    Disturbed only at not understanding.

The Lord sometimes takes us into troubled waters
Not to drown us but to cleanse us, and to awaken
Our souls to the things available in the lights
        from above that is free.

    —Betty Mincey

Time

Time stops, for their is no tomorrow.
Time stops, for their is no time to play.
Time stops, for it seems the world no longer
can move.
Time stops, bringing quiet and silence to a
world full of noise and hatred.
Time stops, for there is no one left.
Time stops, for life just seems to quit.
But over all time stops for your beauty,
for it is like no one else's, making the
world stop at your command.

    —Edward A. Martinez

Of Time And Space

Suspended! Somewhere in time and space.
Time must be moving forward; I am not aware.
Space..I gaze into it dreamily, with clouded eyes
And wait. For tomorrow? No, I do not dare!

Such happiness! For a time so brief,
Has slowly slipped away into the mist
Of unforgotten dreams and disenchanted hope,
And left me..a faded rose the sun once kissed.

O precious time! With all your many faces,
Why have you turned them all away from me?
In protest of my foolish whims and wishes,
Or anger that I grasped not this opportunity?

And endless space! How can you be so cold?
Could you not see that I would weep, alone?
In memory of two minds that meet in understanding
And gently touch in passing, then are gone.

Suspended? Yes! In time and space eternal.
Time moves not forward, yet cannot repeat.
And space..overwhelming in its vastness,
Cannot remove the taste of first discovery sweet.

—*Barbara Kenney*

Untitled

"Where have you been you say my friend?"
To a mystical land and back again.
"Where have you been you say my friend?"
Go there yourself and never ask again.

This is the age of contradictions
People say we will survive
I don't see them really try.
And when they still pollute the air
I don't think they truly care.

Admit it, when we turn on the news
Another dream is... just "another"
And no one really thinks
Of the father and mother.

Pollution and violence is a common thing
And when I say "common" a bell should ring.
Our planet can't continue this way
If we want to see that future day.

—*Carolyn Duncan*

Untitled

I know you needed the time; just for you
To be with those you care about the most.
But hoped you took the care to not get lost
Within their pain that you already knew.

What you have done - was it hard to do?
To throw yourself open, and to unfold?
To love so much; and yet to be so bold?
You know they love. Can they understand too?

This task of yours so much upon my thought.
So easy for me to live within the rule
Of fear, so much, that I may be the fool
Who lends himself to pain. I have not fought!

I'm glad you gave yourself this time at last.
I pray I do the same before it's passed.

—*Daniel Brinkley*

Ode To Eating Disorders

Food: Someone's delight - another's dread
To become emaciated or look overfed.

A necessary task - a drudge everyday
Or likened to a vintage flask -
life's welcomed way.

Feeding a compulsion - rewarding a deed
Or hiding away some deep fearful need.

Be there no end to life's enslaved
    necessities?
Only tomorrows - no yesterdays?

Come, look into the past -
for therein lies the future
to view life's harvest as its
intended nurture.

—*Betty Yerkes*

Happy Anniversary

Happy anniversary wishes and much ado,
To both of you are certainly due;
Nineteen years of love and success,
Is some achievement I must confess;
At a time when vows are made but not meant,
Lots of congratulations to your home are sent.

But you'll certainly agree, that not alone to you,
Are these congratulatory wishes due,
For the mercies of God we must remember,
And render him praises in September.

Through the years you have been showered,
With blessings in a relationship that has flowered,
Wonderful children to love and nourish,
And a caring family to sustain and cherish.

Now on your anniversary we wish you both:
Love that will be abundant in growth,
Store-baskets that'll forever overflow,
Tolerance that you'll never outgrow,
Happiness as lasting as Isaac and Rebekah,
And the bliss of heaven when Jesus comes back.

—*Bertram L. Melbourne*

Little One Lost

People walk by not noticing the tears.
To busy with life to see her fears.

Just a grain of sand in piles of rock.
No ones spends time to ever take stock.

How can they not see the pain in those eyes.
Despair on her face, they're not telling lies.

She's hoping someday someone will see.
No longer lost this little one would be.

For now she's faceless, lost in the world.
Cries of sadness, not being heard.

People walk by not noticing the tears.
Little one lost in everyone's fears.

—*Beth Bader*

Insomnia

What time is it? I turn once more
To check the lighted bedside clock,
A greenish glimmer in the dark.
4:34. Too early yet —
The house too cold — to start my day;
Too late to hope for sleep again.
I punch my pillow, shift my weight
To find a hollow for my hips,
And lie here waiting for the dawn.
"Try not to think," I tell myself.
As well hold back the surging sea!
Ten thousand thoughts race through my brain:
Kaleidoscopic memories...
Fragments of forgotten dreams...
Regrets for things I left undone,
And worries that beset me now;
And all the while, I yearn to feel
Your loving arms around me still.
This bed's too big for me alone.

—*Jean M. Williams*

Nature's Nightmare

In the midst of the dark I lay awake to a nightmare and pray
to close my eyes to a dream, the nightmare is real yet to me
is fantasy. I lay awake immobile and plead for help, but I
become mute and you become deaf. I wash my face with tears and
beat myself with words, I feel confined within a beast, myself.
What others perceive as the sullen beauty of the rose is only
the thorn that pricks. I am that thorn, painful and ugly, but
to others I am tender and beautiful like the rose. Perhaps I
am that rose but I can only be seen, to be touched I can't, my
thorns enthrall me. I am like nature, but not the rose I am snow,
pretty to see, so easily played with, tintelating to the eye
but painfully cold to the touch. I can no longer feel, I am
what others mold with my word last. And then you come along
saying you're not like the others, and you're not in
trivialities, but once you feel the cold and prick your finger
on the thorn, you become as the rest... Take a petal and leave.

—*Helen Stamatakos*

I Ain't Over You......

Playing a cheerful role,...I act,
to comfort my aching heart,
knowing deep within-I want you back,
but you chose to stay apart.

Acting is not what I chose to do,
but you leave me no other choice,
I try to speak my hearts' true love,
but you ignore my crying voice.

In detrimental supplication,
I endorse my hurting soul,
for as a candle without wick-I'm only half,
needing you to make me whole.

With you, my life was colorful,
but now,...there's only blue,
In a cold, dark world is where I live,
because,.......
　　"I ain't over you"......

—*Jerry Lee Parker*

The Coming Of Autumn

Hot summer days shall soon give way
To cool and frosty mornings,
With colored leaves and longer sleeves...
When school starts without warning.

The days grow short and guns report,
As hunters take the field.
With crops laid by, tired farmers sigh
And marvel at their yield.

The wild geese fly so far and high
In perfect v-formation.
They demonstrate their prowess great:
To rise above any nation.

We now draw near in the slow waning year
To a season not lacking in spirit.
When Autumn arrives, her strange beauty revives.
For three seasons she's had to conceal it.

—*George F. Horne*

Silent Cry

I long to love the child I have
to embrace, to nurture, teach, talk
but there are so many walls up she cannot be reached
walls of anger, pain, fear
fear of love
to see her laugh, to share
the pain I feel is immense
the void
the emptiness in my heart is like a crater, a bottomless
pit, tearing at my soul, crying out in agony
she cannot be reached
She's right in front of me but she cannot see
the words I say cannot be heard
is she deaf and blind? No
she is a rock
a rock of ice, very cold, but it can be melted
when the sun's out, glimpses of the vulnerable child are
seen.

—*Cindy Rittle*

My Forever Angel

Nights of crying feeling all alone nights of ghosts and fears
To free myself I'd fly to the heavens and live there with my
　　forever angel
Forever angels are like 'split-aparts', searching for their
　　mates
Waiting to be joined, evermore sealing their fates
I've searched for love and you I've found
Unspoken 'forever' the only sound
No more having to fly to the Heavens I just
　　turn over in the night and hold your hand
I kiss you softly and hear you murmur you love me
My forever angel you are a gentle man with
　　a wondrous smile, eyes of constant change
A heart as big as the sun
I feel you'll carry me with you to the
　　Heavens and leave no dream undone.

—*Jackie Price*

Blind

Blinded by fear, unable to see clear,
Too worried about hating the black race,
To think about loving the human race,
Looking only at the color of their skin,
Never knowing their souls, passing judgements,
Without knowing them as individuals,
Instead of learning from them,
You frown down upon them,
Thinking your smart, while only having a cold heart

—*Christy L. Spray*

A Look At Life

To look back is to long for a love never felt,
To hear cries in the night,
To fear each moment of the day,
To build a wall of silence,
To live in torture and shame.

But to look forward is a chance
To experience a fresh new beginning,
To be the child you never were,
To hear laughter among friends,
To see vivid colors once grayed,
To have hope for tomorrow,
To grow old without regrets.

—*Anna Bruning*

Introspection

I too, attended church today
To hear God's word and also pray
That I might do the best I can
To serve my Lord and fellow man:
To hear the sermon and the choir
Praising God, and to inspire
Me to live a better life
Among the hatred and the strife
That makes this world a questionable place
For humans of this and every race:
So let's all start by doing our part;
The change occurs within the heart.
Just do it!

—*Geo E. Pittwood*

Voices

Listen, to the sound,
   to hear it, you must be profound,
The sound is so placid and complex,
   to feel its vibes, your mind and heart
   must you flex.

The trees make music, and are green,
   this sound is, to be seen,
It is spotted through the lush colored leaves,
   mostly in a gentle breeze.

The wind whistles through the flowers,
   sometimes whispering sagely for many hours,
It is hard for shallow people to hear,
   for they attempt to listen by the human ear.

It is a sound that comes from within,
   a voice to us God has given,
It is mostly heard when around His natural
   creation,
To destroy a rain forest, to destroy a nation.

—*Elizabeth Durand*

To Robert Schumann

What is it like, to live a carnival for years?
To hide within the strangest, enigmatic faces,
Behind confetti, velvet, paint? And never to come near
the obvious, and leave not traces?
How is it, to be followed by the smell of rain,
To be Pierrot, and Arlequin - as one?
For joy to be a pleasure-filling pain,
To never view a single thing as "done"?
Why look at life from far and only try to guess
What is behind that glossy broken door?
One did, one knew. Before...
The door collapsed - and so did he
At mere attempt to life inside.
Where could he hide?

—*Inna Faliks*

Longing

I long to touch what I cannot grasp
To hold her close is all I ask
An image so pure within my mind
I long to seek what I cannot find

A beauty that's only hers to hold
A ray of warmth to thaw the cold
Her portrait is love perfectly sketched
I continue to search what I long to possess

For one chance of luck to guide the way
That I may surely find her someday
If this be true I thank God above
For I have found my one true love

—*John J. Takala*

Children

The Bible says "Lo, children are an heritage from the Lord"
To hurt, abuse, misuse them, the world cannot afford
You love them, rear them, and nurture them with the Word of God
With the preparation of the gospel of peace their feet will be shod
They grow from being a baby into a mature adult
Responsible and independent you want to be the result
But as you see this happening, inside it begins to hurt
Their thoughts, plans and ideas they now want to exert
We have to stop and remember, "my children are only on loan"
From our wonderful Heavenly Father who's as close as the
telephone
Move out, get married, start a family they one day may choose
One thing you can be assured, though, their love you will never
lose

—*Denisa Y. Gilchrist*

Amen

When it's me your voice is calling, to reveal to me your plan,
to keep my life from falling, into the enemy's hand,
and I don't understand your purpose,
teach me to say "Amen".

When the sun's no longer shining, and the clouds, all dark, are
   forming,
when trouble comes my way, and my laughter turns to mourning,
no matter what you ask of me, teach me to say "Amen".

I can't explain the things that you always seem to do,
to keep my feet on solid ground, my paths leading back to you.

I see through a "glass darkly", for you it's always clear,
the problems that keep coming my way, you soon make disappear.

Your ways are higher than my ways, your thoughts, "who can
discern?"
But just to say "yes" to your will, is what I want to learn.

I guess what I am trying to say,
no matter what trials come my way,
teach me to trust you and obey,
by saying the word, "Amen".

—*Diane Williams*

Nothing To Love

Trapped in a world with nothing
To love and everything to hate

Constant denial of people who care
Realization of how life's unfair

The joy's and sorrows of today
The mysterious happenings of tomorrow

The cruelties of life ring through our ears
Just to remind us all of our fears.

—*Jennifer K. Cascante*

Eternal Flame

Why do poets need pain
to make them stronger,
for their words to have meaning.
I've dealt with so much in my short time.
I've loved and lost
people near and very dear to me.
Sometimes I wonder if its worth it.
Is it worth the heartache,
just so words can pour out of my soul.
Maybe that's how I heal,
the words on paper soothe the pain of my broken heart.
Maybe I'm a candle
and the wax is the pain
that slowly melts away,
and in the end my flame will burn
so bright and strong that all will see
how much my poetry means to me.
In turn they too will see they're not alone,
and that someone once felt the same.

—*Ann Ahlfeld*

What's It Like

To see a miracle happen - when there are so few -
To see the sunshine - when there used to be dew -
To see a life worth nothing - when all you need is love -
To see a heart be blessed - from the great one above -
The elixir or recipe as follows:
Delicious days -
Savory nights -
Morning of glory -
With afternoon of delight -
Mix them all together - in a shaker of gold -
Then drink to a love that will never grow old -

—*Bernard L. Horowitz*

A Christmas Tree's Thoughts

"I'm proud to be a Christmas tree,
To spread some cheer on earth,
To help in my own humble way,
Extol the Savior's birth.
For years I've grown under skies of blue,
The heavens sent me rain,
The sun and moon have shown on me,
I'm from a mighty strain.
How proud I was when the woodsman came,
And singled me out from the rest,
I knew by the way that he handled me,
That I was one of the best.
It's Christmas now and I'm all aglow,
I'm radiant and bright,
My branches are so heavy,
But my heart is very light.
There are children all about me,
They clap their hands with glee,
And I am the proudest thing on earth.
For I'm their Christmas tree."

—*Edith C. Broseman*

A Mother's Tribute To Jessica And Samantha

My daughters were sent from above
to adore, cherish and love.
There's nothing as special or as tender
as the love that these children surrender.
Each day I feel such bliss
especially when I receive a wee kiss.
There's nothing quite like their embrace,
or the innocence on each little face.
My daughters, you see, are the pride of my heart.
May God keep us, till death do us part.

—*Janice M. Spangenburg*

Ethereal Maiden

From the heights of heaven
To the depths of despair,
There are none who compare.
The feelings you evoke,
Fill my being with boundless joy.
It takes nothing more
Than the sight of you there,
The diminished light in your hair,
How it seems almost to glow.
Or the way you incline your head just so.
The seductive glint in your eye,
Or the special way you say Hi.
With your simple, effortless art,
You never cease to stir my heart.

—*Brian L. A. Wess*

Reflections

I have walked upon these sandy shores and whispered
to the sea.
expelling away my secrets, set my spirit free.
Allowing mother nature to cure me of my fears,
that have followed me like shadows, throughout
my youthful years.
By gone days of nevermore, to you I spread my wings,
to travel to a palace, filled with many splendid things.
And upon my cloud-like throne I'll wisp away my hair,
allowing it to billow. As a sail upon the air.
The songs of harp laden angels, will guide my blooming
thoughts
for the palace in Gods kingdom is what I truly sought.
The tears of men will swell into a river upon the sky
and the carpet of his majesty will soak the river dry.
As I upon the angels back gaze down upon the land and
remember days when I was young and walked upon the sand.

—*Christina Doelitzsch*

Friend Always

From the time we met in the sixth grade
  to the time we fell in love in the seventh;

The person I knew I could always count on,
  for a good, brain-scrambling,
  pointless conversation,
  or a deep, serious talk on dreams of the future;

Together or apart,
  you were always there for me.

From the time I left in the summer of 1990,
  to the time I returned in the summer of 1992;

Though our young love couldn't outlast the distance,
  our friendship never died.

From the time I leave this summer,
  to the time of summers of eternity;

I want you to know that I will always be your friend.

No matter what may try to break our friendship apart,
  I will always be here for you.

I will always love you,
  my first love.

—*Jennifer Toles*

Son

I will do my very best,
To write a poem at your request,
But you must really understand,
'Tis quite a task I take in hand.
Poems are not from hands and heart,
Alone they give you only part,
Your soul appears upon the page,
Some love and sorrow, fear and rage.
Meant for someone for whom care,
Someone whose life you want to share,
Memories bind us through and through.
We've shared love and laughter, anger too,
But each time we have to part,
You stay with me inside my heart,
Time goes by as does the weather,
Once again we come together.
Is it a rainbow, bright and true,
No, it's that I'm again with you,
From your cradle we've been one,
You will always be my golden son.

—*Berta Bell*

To Baron Prancer, Our Majestic German Shepherd

How do you say goodbye,
To your most trusting, loyal friend.
Or stop praying for miracles, until the very end.

I have no ready answer,
The hurting goes too deep.
We're glad that we were with you,
In your last and final sleep.

Now the rug on which you laid,
Looks so empty and so bear,
Sometimes in evening shadows,
I still think I see you there.

You were but a wiggly pup,
When first you came to us.
The balls and frisbees that you loved,
Now all have gathered dust.

No more happy, wagging tail, to greet us at the door.
The love and trust within your eyes,
Will be seen by us no more.

But the memories our hearts hold dear,
Will keep you with us — ever near.

—*Barbara J. Yocum*

Color

Red, black, white or green, mix them
together the color supreme.
God doesn't look at the color of skin,
it is what is in your heart that he
looks at.
Follow your dreams, what ever they
may be, and help all people that they
may be free.
Let's make this world a wonderful place,
where all people are happy regardless
of race.
God made different colors for all mankind
to see, the beauty of creation
and for all to live in harmony..

—*Gertrude Peperoni*

Hell-blessed Tears

Maybe they'll discover a cure...
Tomorrow.
Today, aloneness is so very lonely.
Those insidious reminders...
I cough blood.
I hate to be alone, thinking always.
Yet I recoil from people. They all know.
Furtive sideways glances look away from
This gray-white-blue cadaver
And wheezing bones, flesh-covered bones.
I cry unheard, unseen
My hell-blessed tears.
Maybe they'll discover a cure...
Tomorrow.

—*Deborah Anne Cotter*

Then Into Heaven

I am forever hidden behind the mask.
Too many times I have tasted the bitterness of defeat.
Yet, I stay here — a captive of my thoughts,
forever shackled to loss.
Will my friends help, or is it better alone?
For them to never see my scarred face,
it is scarred with hardships and bruised with darkness.
Could I destroy these depression-
or must I endure this pain forever?
Emotions rage wild within me,
trying to destroy all that I have ever loved.
Now I find myself in the darkness,
hidden from the world
and kept in the shadows of evil.
Now the rage breaks free, tearing at my flesh,
blood spilling from every pore!
For now, comes the light—
I am free!
Free at last of the mask and the shackles.
Now I live and breath in the light.

—*Adam C. Davis*

How Do I Say Goodbye?

How do I say goodbye?
Too young to understand how his life came to an end.
Too young to know he will never return again.
They witnessed his funeral and gave their respects.
They got to say goodbye.
But how do I say goodbye?
Too young to realize that with his death a part of me died
too.
Too young to say goodbye and know it meant forever,
Too young to retain memories of my own to treasure.
How do I say goodbye?
Old enough, now, to comprehend that my life must exist on
without him.
But still, as I gaze down at his tombstone,
My heart and soul feel terribly alone.
How does the child left behind say goodbye?
If I could speak to him for just one moment in time,
I know exactly what I would vocalize:
"Father, I love you."
and "Goodbye."

—*Jennifer Byrd*

My Story

I was a little girl, about the age of three
Tootsie was my playmate - she lived across from me
In her backyard, there was a shed
And in that shed Tootsie had her potty
When I told Mom, my mother said, that was not good,
It was really naughty.
So I grew up and went to Boulder
Where CU was and I was much older
In Romance Languages I got my degree.
I don't know why they gave one to me
There were words and verbs, but as one expects
Not one language included that naughty word, sex
Now I'm old and gray, had a good life and lots of play
The world has gone crazy, and one expects
Every TV program to talk about sex
But I can remember what the world thinks
Sex is a word which really stinks
Yes, it belongs in everyone's potty
I still believe when Mom said, "It's naughty."

—*Betty Westhaver McKeen*

Utopia?

The time has come when people feel safe and secure;
Tranquillity reigns over cities and towns;
Home or work place neither danger nor risk exists;
There is quiet, there is peace.

Rivers and seas abound with fishes;
The fields are filled with grain;
Tables are laden with tasty dishes;
There's abundance, there is peace.

Communities are trouble-free;
Workers just devote their time to duty;
To society no one is a menace;
There is order, there is peace.

The nation is a 'land of milk and honey';
Citizens contribute to the economy;
Leaders' concern are the people's well-being and happiness;
There's commitment, there is peace.

The world is one nation people are proud to belong;
There's respect for one's culture, color or religion;
National boundaries have been erased;
There's unity, there is peace.

—*Federico J. Burgos*

Friends Forever

Years go by as if on a breeze
traveling through the halls of time,
Seventy years of joy and pain
Spin like a whirlwind in my mind.
I'm taken back to freshman year
what changes I faced then,
I meandered through the labyrinth of halls
facing more aliens then friends.
So many strangers; too much to learn,
could I ever manage to cope?
But with old friends I found my courage
and with new friends there came hope.
One new friends is prominent in my mind
she was smart, sincere, and sweet,
always concerned with saving the earth,
a person whose ideas were concrete.
Always contemplating every thought
backing up every belief she would say,
that's why, now when I am seventy years old
I know forever friends we have stayed.

—*Jamie Shepherd*

An Answer To A Question

Look around, you can see the simplicity. Look closer at the tree so big and strong. It illuminates itself beneath the mountains who illuminate themselves beneath the sun. Listen to the animals sing in harmony around the river. Thanking it for bringing its water of necessity. Do not utter words, for they are futile. For there is no need to explain it. Merely humble its power, by feeling its harmony. This is Knowledge.

You see when you are young, things seem so hard. But as you grow, the same things once hard become easy. Look at the tree again. When it was young it had to grow, withstanding the wind and rain. And now it stands in simplicity, beneath the sky, with strength enough to root abreast the mountain; strength enough for itself and others, while it gives homes to the birds and shades the tiny flowers as well. This is Understanding.

The two together is where the answer lies. You must see and listen while you grow. Receive stature, and know everything has a purpose, which works together with all things, in goodness and harmony. This is Wisdom.

—*Dave W. Macias*

The Lighthouse

I view a long, narrow road that is rugged,
    treacherous, and somewhat dangerous:

My heart pounds rapidly like a thousand moths
    dancing around a huge, glowing bonfire;
My pulse races like an eagle that takes to
    flight over a high mountaintop,
    But I feel no harm.

My face tightens; my neck is stiff, but I feel no
    pain.

One step closer to the end I am; I am relieved,
    and not scared.

I hear a voice; I stop, but I am not nervous.

I look upward to view the sky; but all I see is a
    single, bright, peaceful light coming from
    the lighthouse. And as I enter it, I know my
work here is done.

—*Jason Bolton*

Stay In School

I went to school, didn't want to be no fool,
tried very hard to learn the golden rule.
But things got tough and I dropped out, I should have
stayed and there's no doubt, learned the three R's
but that didn't stick, that's reading, riting and old rithmetic
I got a job and worked all day, with long hours and short pay.
People who dropout think it's cool, take it from me stay in
school. You'll get a job but you don't know where, these are
my words it's a jungle out there. Day in, day out, the same
old stuff, until finally you've had enough.

You've taken all that you can stand, you stoop to living
anyway you can. Really now you are a fool, I tried to tell you
to stay in school. If you had it all to do again,
I'm sure this time you'd be a man.

A man handles responsibility, I'm sure now that you'll agree.
Don't let our friends talk over your head,
without education your mind is dead,
so around here there's one strict rule,
Buckle down and stay in school.

—*James H. Tucker, Sr.*

Symphony Garden

Flute soprano of lone luminescent Larch
Trills her golden measures over solid autumn Red Oaks
Whose dark limbs lace beyond with a violin bass.

Burr Oaks thrust tenor saxophone limbs up, up,
Belying the weight their charcoal substance suggests,
Tenor melody undulating in harmonious
Victory over arrogant counterparts.
Reaching. Free, into weary grey skies.
Sun, like an offstage cymbal clangs her way through cloud's
gauzy curtain, waiting to burst on stage.

Evergreen all alone, completes this orchestra with velvet
Alto cello. Soon, Concert Master will raise his baton
commanding winter's movement to begin.
Other performers will take their rest, but she will continue.
Frost and snow will visit her as sweet piccolo descant.
Her limbs will duet as both mellowness of cello
And sweetness of piccolo.

Each differs, all contrast,
Together is harmony.
Alone, together, I am blessed.

—Elinor Morris Jackson

The Charge

A long straight line of gallant young men, mounted on chargers,
trusty steeds, good friends. A standard waves with wind it
finds, a general barks orders down the line. A command is
shouted, a bugle sounds, on the field the foe is found. Points
of sabers cut the air, tongues of flame pistols flare. Their
spirited charge meets its end, blood flows forth, there is met
no friend. Smoke hangs thick as cannons thunder, men have
horses shot from under. Cloth turns red as flesh buries lead,
dashing attire is reduced to shreds. The boldest of men fall
to the ground, crying for mothers there not found. As battle's
grisly din fills the air, a dead man's eyes peacefully stare. Young
men find war's romance in error, as brave expressions become
ones of terror. The battle crescendos, and seems to be drawn,
when the hand of fate closes, the enemies luck gone. The enemy
line falters, their courage shaken, as their leader cries
"steady men, regain what is taken". But the enemy is beaten,
the battle at end, as they ride in retreat their wounds to
mend. And though some are borne by living's end, the spirit
lives on to charge again.

—Alan M. Borne

"No" Means "No"

What is meant to be love
turns to shame when force is used.

When I believe in sharing feelings
and you have lost control and fallen into lust.

What chance have we to stay together
unless we touch gently, both body and spirit?

What can the future be
if suddenly fear steps in?

Stop now and listen to your soul.
Was it worth it, the temporary satisfaction?

Is it enough, a moment's physical calm,
when the fragile structure of love lies shattered?

I can be held in love with butterfly's touch,
but I will fly away in fear from chains of force.

"No" does mean "No", even against a background of love...
Listen, next time, with your heart.

—Bonnie Keifner

The Black Hole

As a child I looked to the stars
Twinkle, twinkle, wish and you will go far
All the world is the stage
The world is yours for the asking
Such I was told if you wish on the stars.

Those stars, so far away, were as the end of my life.
Bright and full of promise,
Young, I jumped to catch them, but I fell to the ground
Youthful, I picked myself up and propelled myself more
    exuberantly.
Always never quite reaching, but the stars continued to burn
    bright.

Now, the stage curtain has turned from velvet into cheesecloth.
I can no longer jump, I fall to my knees, but cannot rise.
The world is not mine, I asked, but it was deaf, no one
answered my dreams and wishes.
Stars have dimmed, I am now in blackness.
My life has descended into the abyss of the black hole.

—Gini Gay Grace

Memories

Away in a tiny little house
Two happy people sat rocking away
He with his News and she with her Soaps
Rain or shine whatever the weather
The man and the woman are happy together
Rocking away each in their rocking chair
He would sit and rock while she'd
    chatter and talk
In their bed they would lay -
    there goes another day

Once he looked down and cried in French
    "Ah je vous adore"
She smiled and cried "You adorable bore!"
And you are a Leo that loves to roar
"Ah - but with me you are never bored!"

The years went by as the years they will
Until came a day - a very sad day
The rocker no longer rocks, all talk and chatter stops
For what is a home when one is alone
And what is a chair when no one sits there.

—Augusta Biel

Her Hands

Her hands were drawing, one spontaneously curling -
Unbearable to see, because I remember
How fast they used to be.
Her hands on the typewriter moved quickly -
Like a light feather flying in the wind
With a definite direction.

Later, on the computer she wrote
Hoping to tell how without speeding hands
She had soared, walked, and not fainted.

Since I am away and she is there
I can remember the beauty of her hands -
The speed, the accuracy, the determination
To finish on time. The perfection.

Still writing - though slower and scant -
She writes. Her hands still useful,
Still writing, now floating heavenly.
Yet, she writes, she thinks.
She tells a beautiful story with her hands.

—Betty J. LeClair

671

Love

Two islands stand...proud, independent, self-sufficient
Two islands stand...isolated, unprotected, needy

Intrigue is peaked as a reflection glimmers off the sun-drenched
    sea.
Another land, a new world shrouded in mystery
Perhaps...but is it for me?

Now building slowly piece by piece
Up from each island, out over their sea.

But the welcoming waters turn as does the moon
Once splashing and playful
Once cold and turbulent, thrashing at the fledgling foundation
Until finally the connection is made and suddenly the storms give
    way
To a calm rising up majestically in unison with the bridge now
    complete.

This bridge is not the end, no, no...
This bridge is the means.
For this is only the beginning and this road will be well travelled.

Trust, friendship, respect - these form the foundation
Compromise, sacrifice, hard work - these form the road
Dreams, aspirations, desires - these form the vehicle
Happiness, fulfillment - this is the destination

Two islands stand...together.

—*Bill Albert*

A Perfect Remedy

S oothing rays
U nleashed by a golden sun
N urture all life.
S pirits sigh with comfort.
H eartbroken souls mend.
I nstantly they smile,
N eglecting whatever caused the break,
E xtolling Apollo for this grand remedy, they sing

—*David C. DeSomer*

Again

Gazing deeply out the window one day;
Unburdened birth, free from doubt and dismay,
I saw the madman.
Again.

The bloody field we walked through perished pale.
Leading me down the darkened path to jail,
I was betrayed.
Again.

Crying amidst the voices tempting death,
I suffered painful wounds gasping for breath.
The dream became clear.
Again.

Provoking mistaken judgment in hell,
An unjust miscarriage when mankind fell;
Nobody heard me.
Again.

Sad notes of hopelessness never to save.
No chance at truth for an eternal slave.
I was crucified.
Again.

—*Clinton S. Sabom*

Feminine Wiles

I touch your hand,
Uncertainly at first, lest you object.
Using one finger, I may trace its strength,
Going back and forth
From tip to wrist,
Slowly, of course,
For fear you may desist.
But you remain,
Quietly smoking your pipe,
Leaving your hand within my reach.
Thus, we sit together.
You, making smoke rings for my pleasure.
I, content, beyond all measure.

—*Isabel A. Woodward*

The Song Of The Old Oak Tree

Your foot-steps meant so much to me
    under the archway of the old oak tree.
Sunlight was streaming through the boughs
    and tender leaves.
The sky kissed the earth that day
    with gentle sunlit rays.
Oh, wonder of wonders! Oh, day of days!
For your foot-steps meant so much to me
    under the archway of the old oak tree.

In the midst of beautiful trees, abloom with blossoms
    and a quiet breeze.
Your foot-steps meant so much to me.
Tranquility and delight in the spring of memory
    forever will be
Under the archway of the old oak tree.

Now oak leaves blanket the earth with its moisture sweet.
Autumn has arrived with incredible peace.
A precious treasure, to cherish, the old oak leaf.
For your foot-steps meant so much to me
    under the archway of the old oak tree.

—*Joan Davis*

Untitled

I wish you had seen the things I've seen. Maybe then you'd
understand why I stare, a glare on my face, almost as if a
mannequin. I wish you'd been the places I've been. May be
then you'll understand why I sit and cry tears with no emotion
to my face.

I wish you'd experience the things I experience, maybe ten
you'd understand, why I tremble at the little things about
and in the air.

I should've had the Ace of Hearts from the fortune-teller's
cards and not that other one that told of my life as it
proceeded on.....

I know you understand, so I take back all the bad luck I
wished on you, just for my own selfishness.
I want you to see me, not seeing me vaguely, but for two
I am....

—*Ama Ansaah Apau*

Slumber

While everyone else sleeps, I am awake
    tossing to and fro in my recollections.
While everyone else is awake, I am asleep,
    tossing to and fro in my tomorrows.

At what time does the present present itself
    In my waking hours alert
And the realization of the future as unknown
    Come to comfort my sleeping hours?

—*Barbara Ann Gantt Lezette*

The Hand That Pulls The Bow

There is no dream worth dreaming
Unless it feeds the soul.
There is no race worth running
Without a chosen goal.

The rain is for naught without the sun
For the plant that strives to grow.
The wind must search the billows
To find a sail to blow.

There is no task completed
Without a well laid plan.
There is no life worth living
Unless it makes the man.

The book to the mind is speechless
Without a will to know.
It's not so much the fiddle that counts;
It's the hand that pulls the bow.

　　—*Cullen Black*

The Old Cold Barn

When I was small, the barn loomed so tall,
Unpainted, roof sagging, not noticed at all -
For to me the barn became a magical place,
Always fun to discover some unexplored space,
It was there that I found the first lamb in May
And ran to the house, too breathless to say!

Spring, Summer, Fall - happy and carefree- three seasons spent-
In winter the barn was a place where I never went.
When the North Wind blew all swirling with snow
Each day to the cold barn my Father would go.
My Father is gone now - fifty years - come December -
I was left with the barn and the winters I remember.

Years come and go and life has its changes;
Much time I have spent in scholarly ranges;
But my most valuable time in learning of living
Of life fundamentals, soul scarring and giving,
Or just about ways to keep courage from shrinking
Was the time I spent in those hours thinking
How to cope with it all-
In the barn old and cold but still looming tall.

　　—*Janean S. Hoffman*

Unforeseen Future

Unforeseen future nested somewhere in time.
　　Unsuspecting victims no warning no signs.
　　Judgement day, the second coming arrives,
　　before you see the light you must die.

Unforeseen future nested somewhere in time.
　　Rising dead appointing to valid extremities.
　　Haunting the on-coming world of life,
　　while the angel of death uses her fatal touch.

Unforeseen future nested somewhere in time.
Confiding victims are being tortured by the Army of
Darkness.
Agony of pain and suffering slays in sorrow.

Unforeseen future nested somewhere in time.
　　Another dimension arrives once again
　　to massacre the existence of the nonliving.
　　History sets the day of time!

　　—*James P. Smith Jr.*

Broken Wing

A poor lonely little sparrow began to soar and felt he had
　　everything,
Until he hit a strong wind which broke his little wing.
He fell to the earth where he felt empty, sad and all alone,
For he thought he would never soar again and earth would always
　　be his home.
How he missed his friends who seemed to understand his every
　　care.
He looked around, but he could not find them anywhere.
They did not see him fall, so they kept flying and now were far
　　away.
Oh, if he could feel their closeness just one more day.
But his wing was now broken and it was impossible to soar against
　　the wind.
So he sat upon the earth alone and feeling he would never fly
　　again.
Then to his amazement, there were friends gathering to his
　　surprise.
They began to help him go against every obstacle, they were
　　coming from far and wide.
The wind began to beat vehemently upon his breast,
while his friends pushed him high never stopping to rest.
They were determined to make him soar against the wind,
and it did not matter how long it took, they would do it over and
　　over again.
When all of a sudden, to his surprise, the wind began lifting him
　　into the sky.
He spread his wings and with great effort, began to fly.
What faith is taught by God's creatures so small.
We, too, can make it when we stumble and fall.

　　—*Dorothy M. Batts*

Untitled

Slowly we grow close
Until you are my very best friend
　　and a part of my very own soul.
Slowly, for it takes time
To learn the love that means so much.
Listen to your heart-
For it makes you smile,
And it makes you laugh,
And it makes you cry,
And it may even break in half.
Yet it knows when you have found the true love.
For the heart is so vulnerable,
Causing love to be so fragile.
Slowly, ever so slowly,
So as not to break the heart.
When the time has come to tell the special person 'I love you',
Remember - time is of no essence.
It is how happy your heart is that matters.

　　—*Heather Hall*

The Trellis

Standing alone in a yard, is an old trellis I know
Upon its screen wire, fine roses still grow
My granddad built it and then he told her
"Grandmother, now plant what you've been longing for"
She planted those roses, red, white, and yellow
And as they bloomed, she smiled at the old fellow
"Granddad they are perfect, and just like you
I'm really so happy, I don't know what I would do
If someday that wonderful trellis falls down
And all my roses just die and turn brown"
So he bought some iron and screen wire
And built a trellis to withstand wind and fire
And just like their love, the roses kept growing
Now, when I miss them, I find myself going
To that old trellis standing in the yard all alone
With the roses still blooming even after they're gone

　　—*Allison Ja'ne*

The Eagle

It's born with its innocence, its freedom and glory.
Untouched by guilt it learns to fly
It hasn't yet heard temptations story
And when confronted with sin it passes it by.

As it grows and matures it learns to decide.
And temptation's still there, lingering inside.

And finally one day the wrong choice is made
And the eagle's innocence lost.
In the waters of sin he begins to wade.
And his heart is glazed with frost.

Almost too late his soul gains sight.
It sees the ignorance of what he has done,
And his heart is filled with fright.

So he changes his ways and flies once again with pride.
Believing what's felt in his heart.
He realized from the truth no longer he can hide.
And the beauty shines through his courage and love
That he's had from the very start.

  —*Jason Woolley*

Unwanted

Unwanted, where can I go?
Unwanted, who wants to know?

Cast out and put aside, because no one even tried, to love me.
I felt unwanted, I had this feeling to be dead you see.

I could of long ago been gone, fools said.
But no, I'm not, finished yet.
Yes, I am still alive, because some did try, to love me.
Now I feel wanted, no longer, have this feeling to be free.

For now, I know, that I love me, and God He loves me too,
and that other people, care about what I do.
So for the rest of my life, I'll help others with this strife,
those that feel, unwanted.

So this is not the end, cause there is hope my friend,
with love you can survive, yes even stay alive, those that feel
unwanted.

  —*Eileen Powell*

Midnight

I stand between choices here and there,
Upon a precipice in time.
To finish up my current woes,
What greater bothers find?
What is the prize, the process or reason?
To know, to own to feel?
I sense the end of my youth's season,
I wonder what will be real.

  —*Ann Ober*

My Fathers Intent

I've longed for death from time begun
Wanting to be with the father and son
Wanting the sweetness I know is his
For life on earth had none of this

Is it's no wonder I struggle so hard
To find the desire to survive so marred
But struggle I do as a salmon up stream
To find that light that might make me dream
Of a life on earth full of joy and living
So that I might be a part of the giving

And live my life to the fullest extent
That I might fulfill my fathers intent

  —*Barbara Beyea*

Valley Drums And Ton-Ton MaCoute

The canyon walls whisper seductive greetings,
Urging you forward. Bliss is promised.
Do you believe them? Should you not trust these strange
 voices?
Ton-ton, Ton-ton - Panting sounds which mimic those drums
 nearby.
You look over your left shoulder. Was that for real or was
 it not?
The warm breeze suddenly turns into a blast furnace near your
 cheeks.
The surge of blood and adrenalin paralyze you for a moment.
Then the senses go to work. Ton-ton, Ton-ton.
What could that be?!
Could it be the ancient warrior's battle cry?
Or perhaps a lusty woman's beckoning?
My breathing is yours. The valley wants to consume you.
Movement! That was for real.
A wild boar? No, much larger the ears and eyes determine.
Running now! There, in that direction...
Valley Drums and Ton-ton MaCoute

  —*G. A. Vick*

Imbibe In Death

Sip your J+B you conceal in your coat pocket.
Walking canted, not feeling the wind that strikes his face.
Hell, it can't thrash him down.

The sparrows sing in the trees
They glimpse at him, then fly in the breeze.
His breath has ended their song:
Halt! take another sip of your J+B.

O where can he be...
Hiding his pain in the closet of numbness:
Lest he wakes and feels the rush.

Like a mouse scrounging for food, he rifles through the next
bottle of booze.
Blindness has defeated him, and now imbibe another drink of J+B
It has extirpated the wall of his very soul.

A deceased spouse, and this sordid life he has had enough of...
Make this the last quaff of J+B.

O how I dread this dispirited moment:
He has fallen in the trenches of death...
Imbibe no more.

"Shall I indulge a sip of your J+B, Father!

  —*Francesca Tooley*

What Once Was June

June, a month of delight
Warm and fresh and flowers so bright.
Showers occur and clear the air,
Yards are green with proper care.
Days are long and much to do,
Children play, all out of school.
Songbirds sing their melodic calls,
Creeping vines along the walls.
An easy time, this time of year,
Baseball games for which to cheer,
Picnic, hikes, and vacations to,
Much to life, but to share with who?

A better time in life for me,
Was when my love was here you see.
Alone now, lonely and what to do?
What once was June left here with you.

  —*James T. Smith*

My Grandma - Special Role Model In My Life

My Grandma always had a smile for me.
Warm sunlight and sweet smelling flowers,
That warms my heart.
This is how I remember her.

My Grandma always had time for me.
She taught me to laugh, cry, sing, and pray.
I look to the sky and smile.
My Grandma will always have a special,
Place in my heart forever.

—*Amanda Babler*

All Over The World

It's sad to see the way man has turned from God
Warnings from God's preachers and singers seems to do no good
The penalty for sin is death, but nobody seems to care
Wickedness and evil's getting worse around us everywhere.

Some believe in doctrines which deny God's son
Choosing to believe that when we're dead we're done
Well, people are dying all over the world.

Stop blaming God for all your trials and your pain
Within your heart you'll find the reason for your fate
Since God is love how can you say that he's to blame
When you hate your brother, won't help one another without shame.

If we will learn the meaning of true liberty
We must live the meaning of our God's charity
And show love to our brothers all over the world.

Don't you know that poverty, heartaches and strife
All the ills of society are affecting our lives
Stop tearing down your brother, my friend
Why don't you give him a helping hand
And pray someone will do the same thing
To our brothers in other lands, all over the world.

—*Betty Huntington*

Woodworking

Rough as the day it was taken from the tree,
Warped and bent from mother nature's cynical touch,
It is made to be broken and honed by the craftsman's hand.
A splinter enters his hand and for a brief moment craftsman
and craft fuse. But with love and care it takes on the
intended shape and with love it is polished to perfection.
Its eyes blankly staring at the world around it.
Again the craftsman has won the fight against what nature
intended. It is given away with love and blessings to sit on
a wall and dream of the days when it was a tree.

—*Donna Marie Yager*

The Garden Of Eden

A sight of beauty greater than ever perceived
Was the glorious shimmering Garden of Eden.
When the eye of evil saw, a burning
Envy in its bosom arose
And when the moon's face behind clouds was hidden
Slithered into Eden's Gate, though forbidden
And with smoldering fury, by kindness disguised
Convinced the inhabitants to become its allies
Heaven, in sadness grieved and frowned
And soon the Garden of Eden slowly withered
Into barren ground.

—*Elizabeth Shapiro*

My Feathered Friend

The hanging flower basket
Was swaying gently in the breeze.
Atop a branch with blossom's splendor,
A tiny bird enjoyed wind's tease.

The little finch with rosy head
Seemed to adore this blooming spread,
For every time I opened the door,
My feathered friend was there once more.

A curious hole in the flower bunch
Made me wonder - I had a hunch:
The tiny finch did not just roam,
She actually made this spot her home.

Carefully I peeked into the flower'd abode,
And surely, the smallest nest I not'd.
A nest so round and skillfully woven,
A wond'rous creation by nature driven.

Three tiny eggs lay unattended
Awaiting the warmth of the little hen.
Their success on quiet realm dependent,
I hope to hear the chirps of the tiny brood.

—*Ilse Wissner*

The Last Goodbye

The wind blows gently through the last evergreen tree that
was swaying with the rhythmic breeze of the gusty air. But
were you really there? Everyone told us to wish upon a star
and that our love would go far. Like sand dollars through
time my love for you will never fade with the passing of
time. You are my hopes and dreams such with the sway of the
light breeze. Your tender lips pressed closely to mine, you
tell me you love me from now until the end of time.
Sometimes I think back to that day when everything was so
tragic and the last pill was spilled. Although you said I
would understand on the last day as you grabbed my hand, it
was the last I saw of you. Three years passing since our
last goodbye, three years passing since my long hard cry, and
three years passing since I last got to tell you i love you
and always will. The color of the leaves change from a summer
green to deep autumn red, and I shall always remain by your
graveside with regret.

—*Chrissy Bloomingdale*

Profile Of A Dead Juvenile

I was sent to school to learn the golden rule, but the teacher
was treating me like a fool.

What he was teaching was bull you see, so I decided school
ain't for me.

I went out on a foot loose adventure but on the street death is
out to get ya.

Put you down in a deep dark hole, you realize you didn't
achieve your goal.

To make it big in a world of fools, on the street you got to
pay your dues.

Now as a hustler, you claim you get much respect,
but here's one main factor that you always forget.

You got to have smarts and a lot of heart,
If that ain't in check the streets will rip you apart.

It goes back to the days of old, when on the street to
survive you had to be bold. Now everything is all different.

You have to wear a bullet proof vest but it only protects your
chest. Last week a brother got shot in the head he lay dead
while the criminal fled. You say man that ain't my style,
profile of a dead juvenile.

—*Billy Williams*

The Last Breath You Took

The last breath you took, the one while I sat at home and
   watched TV, where the rest of the family stood by and
   watched you pass, did you know when you died?
Or did you feel nothing, just as you had felt nothing for the
   last two years of your life, when you lived at one time and
   loved and lost it all, until you could barely speak or even
   think, did it hurt when you died?
You were fed with a spoon every morning by one who was not
   even blood, who loved you more than your blood, more than
   me, when you would hug and kiss and cry, when you worried
   and mourned and I watched TV, did you know when you died?
When I looked at your empty eyes, even while you lived, and the
   smell of flowers and wet grass, the cold white rock that I
   haven't seen since that day, and the cold ground and blue
   sky turning gray and back to blue again, while I watched TV
   did you know we cried when you died?

    —Brian Thomas

Gordon's Last Ride

One day cousin Gordon took an afternoon ride,
Watching the snowflakes as they whitened the streets
Wearing cowboy hat and boots, and a gun at his side
He gazed at the scene from his saddle seat.

With his horses's head high it soon paced back home.
There he climbed up the stairs where lights were turned low.
He became shocked, then angry when he looked in his room
While he listened to music from his radio.

What he saw made the teardrops fall down his cheek.
His son was in bed with Gordon's new wife.
He was so upset that he started to shake
He thought he'd go out and end his own life.

Gordon felt for his gun and to his wife's surprise
Said, "I'm going out to shoot the goat for dinner".
But time went by and daylight brightened the sky,
And the goat came back alone. It was the winner.

Gordon's wife had waited for the morning light
To roast the goat meat and bake the bread.
But Gordon himself had on that dark night,
In the place of the goat, killed himself, instead.

    —Eva A. Sampson

Untitled

I close my eyes and I see an ocean of green grass
waving in a cool fall's breeze.
I am standing in front of you, holding your hands in mine,
arms relaxed, gently resting at our sides.
I'm gazing into an abyss of blue. An abyss that captures my
soul and holds it for ransom; your abyss, your eyes of blue.
A shimmering chain of gold laurel envelopes our right hands.
Slowly, you let go of my hand, careful not to break the laurel.
You turn and walk away. My heart races to capture you,
to bring you back to the magic, but my feet do not move.
My mouth opens to call you, but there are no words,
just the crashing of the waves of green grass upon the breeze.
I stand and watch you walk away;
walking away with a portion of my soul.
I hear the rage of a river behind me.
I see you in front of me.
My soul speaks to my body. It leads me to the river.
Will I find you there? Only if you desire to hear the rage
of the river. Only, if you listen to your soul.
Another adventure begins ...

    —Elesabeth Bacherta

Before There Was A Dad There Was A Daughter

   Daughters are special in their own special
way, but fathers can know so much of their
heartfelt thoughts through their unspoken
conversations.
   When a father has lost a tear it is often
a daughter who knows where it can be found.
   It is knowing that daughters can become
mothers that gives great hope to all of us,
especially a dad that wants to hear the silent
song of a daughter for whom he has so much love.

    —Bob Piper

The Changing Clock

As the earth turns and spins and whines,
We all turn our clocks to standard time.
Then the nights get long and the days are cold,
And winter grabs us with a vicious hold.
Ah, but spring is not far away,
And soon the radio man will say,
Must change your clocks, It's that time again,
It's so irritating, you just can't win.
It's for our own good that's what they say,
Gives us more time to work and play.
Looks like the Lord didn't know what was right,
For us poor humans living day and night.
So here we go confusing the nation,
And continuing on in our own frustration.

    —Dick O. Henry

Untitled

People are like flowers.
We bloom in our own unique way.
It doesn't matter our color, shape
or form, for we all have something to say.
Let's take a seed and plant it in
somebody else's life.
It maybe when that person's heart
is filled with pain and strife.
Then they will take their seed
to spread on someone else's lawn.
And pretty soon, we're not just one;
but twenty million strong!
Your seed can be a simple phrase
like "I care" or "How are you"
Just plant that one seed everyday
and watch the flowers bloom.
This is what God intended.

    —Amy V. DeLyons

Reflections

   Remember back then...when our love was brand new?
We discovered reflections; you saw in me what I saw in you.
   You wouldn't speak of it and neither would I.
   We didn't know it then but reflections don't lie.

   We tested the waters each in our own way
   And the reflections remained day after day.
Now we face life together; we laugh and we cry.
We can handle it all; reflections don't lie.

When I can't see your face and the love that it brings
   I can see the reflections in this gold ring.
But the love that is there when I do look in your eyes
Takes my breath from me. Reflections don't lie.

    —Darlene Scott Gontarek

Our 50th

There are days in married life
We can forget old times of strife.
One dwells on memories sweet

Back when our kids were both small watching as
They each grew tall life was such a treat

We loved them each a different way
I loved you more and more each day
I mused on when it started

As time went on the years passed by the boys
Grew up and had to fly we still were happy hearted

No show of words did we need we proved our love
By quiet deed things were not quite like before

With simple things that mean so much we said our
Love with quiet touch we moved at slower bore

These later years with fewer tears the season
The season turns to fall

If some think 50 is the end with my lover
And good friend no way - we want it all

And so I say with love in heart this is only just
The start the rest should be a ball

    —*Aloysius Hoffman*

Withered Vines

We come full circle each time
We contemplate the seasons.
Cool air, days shorter, nights longer;
Feel the tug of fall and mourn summer's passing.
Withered vines sagged, gnarled almost lifeless
Would soon die. Are we the spindly twigs cast off,
Strewn around? Witness before winter looms leaves
Turn green to golden brown to gray.
Time sweeps like the artist's brush mindful
Of these rites: All buds burst forth
From springs of life, white crocuses bloom,
What groundhogs presage will, ants wend their way
To the picnic ground.
Vines rooted now grow luxuriantly branching,
Inching sunward. Only in the mind's eye do young
Vines rise from dead twigs! Tree after tree
Tendrils hold fast unhindered but not for long.
Must this fact of nature fade in those
Withered vines? Summer, once more, comes around.

    —*Evan Balanon*

Times' Serenity

Between dawn and dusk
we create the alpha and omega of being,
only to end in the silent inference
of nature's transgression
where the soul shall hunger not
and the hearts' rich harvest
will lie in silent repose;............death.

Observe the baton that directs the rhythm of life;
the beat that sets the mind in motion;
it is this correlation of filiation
that lavishes and subordinates
the protective armor of the soul.

Feel the vibrations of life that hover!
Rise in exultation of the grandeur!
'Tis this that assures the patients for constant change.
The meaning of dawn and dusk......the interim in which
to create life's bondages.....while time creates our tomb.

    —*Ellen Louise Nixx*

Shadow With Hues

With many roads to choose from and all forever unclear
We follow the simplest path to an open door
Though choices and decisions intertwined with fear
We adhere to our strengths, yet yearn to be more.

Wandering through time behind glimpses and glares
Never believing in ourselves or all we should be
Accepting our own fate beneath critical stares
We fail to realize that our dreams can still see.

Inflicting our ignorance, we start our own plague
Laying judgmental eyes on all colors and creeds
Destroying the innocent with our visions so vague
Killing our young with our poisonous seeds.

A horizon exists beyond doors never found
A place we can share our admissions of pain
A moment in time where love is not bound
by the chains we create for societies gain.

When the past leaves footprints on your heart
And the future you ponder holds no clues
Bask in the present and make a start
By realizing that life is a shadow of hues.....

    —*Daniel Hester*

A Lifetime Lead

Between our birth and before our death
We have a life to lead
Be it but a moment, a minute, or a day
Or just years and years of living
We must all remember, life is just on loan
We will never know just what this time
Given to us means
Until that final call of death
Our life well just unfold
A moment is a lifetime, a hundred years is too
Each one has a meaning - A purpose we'll
    never know
But since it's all just loaned to us
Time itself will always be
So be careful how we use today
For we must some day give it back
In memories of a lifetime lived
As we report to God, when we go to Him anew

    —*Helen L. Casavant*

Steps Toward Peace

Today - Nine/Thirteen/Ninety-three
    we have to all, great news released-
We're gaining ground, in Steps Toward Peace
    in terror ridden Middle East.
It now should, no longer matter
    what be one's religion or race
What is, of the most importance
    is now on Earth. All - this embrace.
For it no longer matters where
    on this globe, might be man's estate.
Now he and all can lay aside
    all anger bred, of greed and hate.
To henceforth, with a sincere love
    live with stranger and with neighbor
Thereby to, with true just respect
    to all mankind, their rights restore.
Let this event in Israel
    in others be, a will to cease
Their upheavals and calm create
    then this Our Globe, will know - true peace!

    —*George P. Derr*

Untitled

'Though we have never met,
We know each other well.
'Though we are miles apart,
We are closer than two grains of sand on the beach.
'Though we may never be together,
We will always be together.
We are two,
Yet one in the same.
Sharing the same thoughts, the same dreams, the same lives.
I can close my eyes and see her,
And hear her voice.
Her laughter is magical,
Transporting me far from worry.
She fills my thoughts, my dreams, my life.
But underlying the happiness
Is sadness.
For every minute that we are apart seems like years,
Every day, like an eternity.
How I long to be with her,
To hold her in my arms, Forever.

—*George A. Bracy*

Down Sierra Way

Down Sierra way, not two minutes from home
We saw, as we drove, many animals which roam.
Amazingly enough, they're next to congested spots,
But how they enjoy their menial ways to a man's rich lots.

To list them takes time - so please prepare,
For it's unusual to have types so rare:
First, a white donkey under a shade tree
With a billy goat that, as America, is free.

Yes, there are horses, cows and a hog
All in one pasture lying by a log.
And last, but not least, near the road—not in the kitchen
Bringing our jingle to a close was a big, fat chicken.

—*Bernice Foster*

Season Of Change

Standing on cliffs up quite high,
We see yet we can not,
The clouds get in our eyes,
During this time in the world,
Changes in far off lands,
Communism deep in decline,
Walls come crumbling down,
As we enter this season of change,

Humming hymns very old,
Till the sound is deep in your thoughts,
Mozarts sonata in Cee,
A time of court and spark,
All sing a song of freedom,
Watching the old times become the new,
To every time there is a season,
From where I stand it's a marvelous view,

—*Alan Bard*

We Don't Care

We don't care about the birds and the trees
We don't care what the new day brings
All we care about are those material things.
We don't care about the stars in the sky
We don't care about the flowers that will soon die.
We don't care about the people we hurt all
We do is judge them by the clothes they wear
Or by how they do their hair - if we just
take the time and look inside we'll
see what's really there.

—*Carlisa Bellia*

The Widow

He was my husband, I was his wife.
We shared each other, throughout his life.
We never quarreled, or did we fight.
We slept in each other's arms all night.

Suddenly he became ill, and died.
It hurts to know he's not by my side,
And when I lay down, and try to sleep,
My eyes fill with tears, and I start to weep.

My daughter asks, "Where did daddy go?"
The tears in her eyes, make my tears flow.
How can I say, "Your daddy is dead.
From this life, daddy has fled."

I forget and make breakfast for two,
Now that he is gone, what can I do.
I miss him so with all of my heart.
It's hard to live, now that we're apart.

He was my lover, and my good friend.
My love story has come to an end.
In my dreams his loving face I see;
I awake, wishing he'd be there with me.

—*Ervin H. Chase*

Farewell, But Not Forever

A month ago, sitting at the table,
We talked as close friends
Little did we know
Things were coming to an end
Now I stand before you
As you lie in your casket
You're just as I remember you
At your side is your beer and cigarettes
I reflect on the last time I said good-bye
I wish I could do it again a thousand times
And see your grin and the bristles on your chin
But this time I'd concentrate on the fact
That there is still life within
Farewell, but not forever
I'll visit you again someday
Someday not too soon
But someday not too far away
We can talk again
And fill each other in on what is old and new
You can call be Buddy, like you did before
And to hear that again, a million times I'd thank you.

In Loving Memory of Edgar Carlson
—*Erik J. Borne*

A Mother's Love

We take our mothers for granted sometimes we do not care,
we think a mother is forever someday she will not be there.
A mothers love comes only once we have to take it all in,
we have to show her how much we care and never put shame to
sin. We never realize just how much a mother means to us till
after she is gone, all we have is her memory and that will live
on and on. We never listen we never say, how much we love her
day to day. We never call we never write, to us our mother's
out of sight.
A mother knows just what you do she has you on her mind,
a mother will always love you no matter how bad or how kind.
A mothers love is always there whenever you're in need,
a mother will always protect you and say you did a good deed.
A mother is not something that you buy a mother is not
for sale, you have to show her that she's cherished and not
let her be stale. A mother will always guide you a mother
knows right from wrong, you have to give her your shoulder and
tell her that you are strong. A mother is only for a little
while a mother is not forever, you have to show her that she's
loved and you will leave her never.

—*Elaine Helene Shanker*

A Letter From Mom And Dad

As we look down on our loved ones today. We have a few things
we would like to say. We are happy to be where we are above.
No pain, no sorrow, just laughter and love. Our friends and
family are with us here. And we get loud and spread some
cheer. We found a good fishing spot over the mountain. And
good cold water from an underground fountain. Mom Paiva
makes bread and good lemon pies. And we have cook outs and big
fish fries. Dottie and I take care of the flowers. Sis paints
pictures for many of hours. Dad and his brothers, and my
brother Ed. Had the best garden, so everyone said. We don't
sleep here for we never tire. God gives us our each and every
desire. The children here are always singing and dancing. The
family pets all running and prancing. When you come to our
graves to show love and respect. Don't shed your tears, take
time to reflect. On all the happiness and love you could be
giving. Not to the world of Dead, but the world of living.

—*Charlene D. Mikrut*

The Developer

A friendly man, tho' short of hair
We'd see him working here and there
Around this mountain we call home
In summertime.

His smile was warm, his words were kind,
If things would break, he'd never mind
But fix them, and go on his way,
Then come home late.

We learned to love this special man
But knew not what fate had planned
That he would leave so soon.

So let's all make this our fervent pledge:
Keep mountains green and lakes just pure not to hedge
But, this to be a tribute to this beloved friend
May he rest in peace.

—*Emily A. Rathjens*

Up To Grandma's

Listen to the applause of the river,
Welcoming its children back home.
Its waters washed away the years
As memories flood their minds
Of the time spent here as a child,
Reflections of youth, memories of love.

This old river provided
Saturday night baths, fish for the table,
And a lullaby written by God Himself
To sing small children to sleep.

A home where the words, "Up to Grandma's,"
Sent children squealing
And now grown children's eyes
Mist with the thoughts of yesterday.

I never knew this river as home,
I never walked here as a child,
But my memories are stirred as I see these sights,
Reliving my mother's stories
Of the days of her childhood
Spent here on these banks of home.

—*Beth Gade*

Silent Cries

When daddy gets home he looks at me as if I
were mommy when I went to bed last night
daddy came in my room to say goodnight
he kissed me on my mouth, he put his tongue
into my mouth it was wet and yucky;
As he reenters my room I lay as quiet as
possible so that he, and nobody else can hear
my silent cries I want to scream but he hushes me
he starts breathing hard as he pushes his thing
in me hard, tears run down my cheeks my
private hurts so bad when he finishes he said
mommy told him to do it;
The pain in my private has stopped so I guess I'll
ask mommy why she told daddy to hurt me
and why she told daddy to put his thing in me
and hurt me, she told me to stop lying so I guess
no one will ever believe me or hear my
silent cries after all who's going to believe a
seven year old or want to hear a seven year
old's silent cries

—*Brianna Twine*

Imbalance

This is not yet a war, just a timely debate.
We've got to take action before it's too late.
I know we don't all see eye to eye.
But the cause is too great now for us to lose sight.

Our solution isn't easy to define.
But we've turned away for too long a time.
We're destroying ourselves, open your eyes and see.
Would you begin by helping to save a tree?
Otherwise, there won't be anymore guarantees.

Stop thinking only of ourselves.
Listen to the dolphins, listen to the whales.
They're also crying out for our help.

The imbalance is our own creation, from money, greed, and
neglect. It's up to us to stop the abuse, otherwise what can
we expect? Before we arrived, our world was perfect.

Help mother earth give birth to a new fertile ground.
We can breathe life into the air.
We can regenerate the land.
We can purify the oceans.
It's time we finally took a stand.

—*Deborah L. Reis*

My Journey

As I drove through the mountains,
what a sight did I see.
The trees in all their splendor were
smiling at me.
The colors were awesome, I could
hardly believe, that God could paint
them so perfectly.
Nature was there too, running
to and fro, acting as if they
knew where to go.
The rain was coming down, no sun did we
see, but that's ok, because I knew it
had to be.
The fog was really thick and the clouds
hung low, but perhaps beyond all this was
a beautiful rainbow.
Life has its sorrows, its clouds and tears.
But if we'll trust God, He'll always be near.

—*Jean O. Watson*

Why

Oh Mother, cried the little child,
what are these things I've read?
Of clean fresh air and clear blue skies.
Were the sunsets really red?

Could you really see the mountain tops
piled high with glistening snow?
Could you really see the birds in flight?
Please tell me I must know...

If all these things were really here,
for everyone to see.
Why then did man pollute the air,
and dirty up the sea?

My world is filled with dirtiness
no fresh air to be found.
I've never seen a green field,
or watched the clouds move round...

I really feel so sad, Mom
for those that had these things
Then with their bombs and big machines
they changed "Our" destiny.

—*Diane de Bourguignon*

Please Hold My Hand

I am dying,
What can you say to me?
You can tell me that yo love me,
And hold my hand for a little while.

I am dying,
Please touch me the way my parents did
when I was a child.
My hair is coarse and thin
and my hands are withered and dry,
But I need you to put your arms around me.

I am dying,
I was once as alert and strong as you,
Please stay with me and let me reminisce
about the old days.

I am dying,
I need your strength and love - please
touch me.

I am dying,
Please tell me that you love me,
and hold my hand for a little while.

—*Joanne D. Mahnken*

What Is "Black"?

Black, what is it?
What does black mean?
We as people call and called that 11,000 times a day,
It's on applications, bill boards, and books,
What are we?
Just black people and most of us know nothing,
Well not me?
Do I look black? Do I look as if I know nothing?
I don't think so because here is my meaning of black,
Black is a color...a crayon color,
I am Afro American...a light brown Afro-American,
I'm not a monkey or a nigger,
I'm a light brown Afro-American,
You are to call me Christina but to describe...,
You're best to say a tall Afro-American chick,
Cause if you don't...I'll set your ass straight,
That's right...without a second thought,
So your best to chill...because mama don't raise no fools.

—*Christina James*

Crying For My Daddy

My heart is filled with words, words I need to tell of 1946 and
what I call, "Atomic Hell". Radiation filled the air,
mutilated human cells, every time I think about it, the pain in
my heart swells. My daddy he cried silently. His voice could
reach no ears. Afraid to talk, afraid to tell, to proud to
show his tears. Abused and used by the government, he lived
with pain and fears, suffering a slow death, most of his living
years. My daddy died, not long ago. His smile was never
whole. Deterioration of his body was mild next to the damage
done his soul. His fight was long and now he's gone, he'll
never hear the truth his heart did know. He lost more then
half his life to the Atomic Bombs in Bikini Atoll. I stood at
his bedside and watched him die, there was nothing I could do but
hand on to each gasp of breath, while my heart it broke in two.
His eyes were empty, his spirit removed, and yet somehow I
knew, he heard me say inside myself, "Daddy.... I'll cry
for you. I'm not afraid to raise my voice, to say what's on my
mind, to fulfill the dream of a precious man, who was treated
so unkind. I'm crying for you Daddy. I'm crying all the time.
Your spirit entered into me and now your fight is mine.

—*Cindy L. Colucci*

Words From The Heart

I write these poems to express my feelings,
What I write comes from the heart,
what I say I do mean,
If I should share my poems with another,
I ask but only one favor,
these words that I write are my feelings,
please handle them with care,
for I have a heart of glass.
Please understand what I am saying,
my mind has been through hell,
and my heart will brake.
If it's not handled with care,
these are my words, this is my poem,
these are my feelings,
and this is my heart.

—*Elizabeth Rodriguez*

When A Friend Moves Away

A salty tear runs down my cheek as I remember
what is about to fade from my life.

The laughter I once knew
is now quieted with dread anticipation.

The spirit-filled hymns of praise, then boldly sung,
are now softened with despair.

Our walks, once populated with talk and questions,
now remain silent.

Every memory is darkened
by the thought of our separation.

Hours of distance become years.
All hope of future joy is lost.

Or is it?

My friends's wise words echo in my mind-
Softly, carefully, teaching me.

The truth of his words speak of another
from whom I must now seek guidance.

The wisdom of his speech moves me,
and I seek out this Great Comforter, my Lord,

Jesus Christ.

—*Felicia Plekes*

A Vote For The Poor

For all of you who chose to do
What love, compassion, and mercy told you to,
In giving the poor what they must need;
Some food, some clothes, a bed, a seed
Of hope, a joy, a temporary reprieve
From the plight of pain, sorrow not yet freed;
In giving the children a promise of tomorrow, not greed,
Will make their hearts to joy and not remember to grieve
Who gave to the mother and father a reason not to bleed.

A moment of time when love and justice are conceived,
I thank thee now on bended knees,
And pray to God that he meets all your needs.
For truly in the heart of God, he hears our pleas.
And as you have joined the course
To meet the pain of life's remorse,
Your vote for them has assured us all a steady source
Of love justified in Heavenly courts.

For through the eyes of humanity you have seen
The pain of all flowing through the same stream.
And so the joy of love must have been in your blood.
So my prayer for you is that God gives you an ark
To protect you from all of life's floods.

    —Donald B. Lindsey, Sr.

Do You Dare Dream?

Guns, drugs, AIDS, suicides, homicides,
What manner of life, my child!
Where are those tomorrows that
    Grandma spoke about?
Have your hopes been dimmed...destroyed?
Do you dare dream?

Fire's flame, police sirens, fast cars, screeching tires!
Will there be a future?
Will you see old age?
Must you hold your thoughts, postpone your plans?
When....where is the end?
Do you dare dream?

Hurricanes, earthquakes, tornadoes, floods,
The very works of God wreaking havoc!
Will they distort or blur your visions?
Is life so fragile an existence?
A young voice is silenced without a
moment's notice.
Do you dare dream?

    —Bernadine J. Wilson

"Lover's Prayer"

You have made a commitment, you have said I do,
What once was one, has joined to be two.
You have started a circle as you both can see,
What joined to be two, has turned into three.

Be kind to each other for heaven sake,
And always remember to communicate.
Always see each other as they really are,
Never let your love drift away very far.

Don't go to bed angry, don't go to work mad,
Resolve the problem and you won't feel so sad.
When you hit a wall, learn to compromise,
A much stronger relationship will be your prize.

The road ahead is uncertain and long,
It's the forks in the road where you must be strong.
I know that you both will never part,
As long as you always keep love in your hearts.

    —Christine D. Marx

The Silent Trees

If trees could speak and messages convey,
What stories they could tell to us of old.
But as it is they all will go untold,
These incidences of another day.

The years go by and now the trees are grown;
The branches and the leaves above entwine
In harmony and form their own design,
Creating shade for man who has thus known—

He can depend upon the sturdy tree,
If cared for when the roots are growing strong;
Although the winters may be cold and long,
Depriving branches of their finery.

But in the spring when snow begins to melt,
And even though the trees still look quite bare,
There is a touch of drama in the air
When Mother Nature's hand can now be felt.

For she caresses every living thing
And gives it strength to push forth ardently:
As tiny buds unfolded on the tree —
As baby birds first flight seen on the wing!

    —Hildegard Corona

The Future Ahead

The future is among us, we think of the past we've led, but
what we must worry about is our life in the future ahead. We
think of the people we have loved who are now among the dead,
but what we must do is carry on with our lives in the future
ahead. The thought of loneliness and sadness run through our
heads, but we must understand that things will change in the
future ahead. Things we regret and our mixed-emotions, that
sleeps with us in the sheets of our bed, but we must always
remember what lies in the future ahead. We need to understand
different people and acknowledge the books we've read, for that
can also determine what lies in the future ahead. We must
advance our skills keep our minds as sharp as a lead, and that
will surely pay off in the future ahead. Think of things more
important than a new car the color of red, instead we can
consider building our family and friends in the future ahead.
But the most important thing we will know about the past we've
led, is that God will be with us every step of the way in the
future ahead.

    —Clyde Alleyne

Bargains

Nature's wonders for barter are;
What will you give for the evening star?
Just turn your gaze toward the sky's deep blue,
And she will give the star to you.

Would you like to buy a woodland trail?
Many of these she has for sale.
All you give is a step or two,
And part of the trail belongs to you.

Another thing she will sell to you,
The broad expanse of a mountain view.
Just give a second of your time,
To own a picture so sublime.

Her handwork too is being sold;
It is very lovely and very old.
If under a tree you'll take your place,
You may walk on moonlight shadow lace.

Nature is selling her valleys and hills;
But not for gold or dollar bills.
The price, I am ashamed to mention,
She simply asks a moment's attention.

    —Jane G. Greenlee

A Subtle Murder

Murder is committed in the subtlest of ways,
when a child is born, and when they play.
Stripped of their true personality,
by the obsessed parents ruled by society.
Children of God is what we are,
to believe any different would be bizarre.
To understand what I'm saying you must first
hear me,
then open your mind, only then you'll believe.
What I'm saying to be the truth,
to change your ways takes some cooth.
We're all raised in a sick society.
that damns the question of authority.
Murder is committed in the subtlest of ways,
by the brain surgeon parents whom wish to
mold and scathe,
the untamed heart, and mind so new,
keep looking over your shoulder, because
their coming after you!

—*Andy Harrison*

A Burglar Named Smee

'Tis the tale of a young burglar named Smee.
When asked about his job, so glibly said he,
"Anything beats honest labor, you see."
This moonlit night, the end was near,
Smee, slightly gladdened by his beer,
Was dared by a young ruffian named Bill,
To steal the jewel from the house on the hill.
Indeed he did agree, 'tho ghosts were rumored in the house to be
Up the hill did he prowl; his only company, the hoot of the owl.
He stole through the door and heard and awful squeak.
He'd trampled a mouse; was too shocked to speak.
Jolted so, Smee's mammoth cowardice began to show.
Ever forward did he march; to be held in high esteem he did
dream.
As he drew closer he was affright; just ahead he spied a light.
From the jewel came a glow and to that rock Smee's hand did go.
Out from the gem a hideous ghost did appear!
Smee retreated out of fear; reconsidering this career.
"Good grief", he said "I need a beer."
Smee returned from the house on the hill
And took a seat at the bar with his good friend Bill.

—*Georgianna J. Daugherty*

Untitled

Please, please listen, oh mother to be
When ever your child calls, hear their plea,

Listen to their faintest cry..............
Their cough, their moan, their passing sigh!

No mother can be perfect, not you, not me
We'll make some mistakes, but hear your child's plea,

Motherhood is a happy and wonderful time
It's beyond compare, it's a state of mind!

Those little ones laughing, and crying, and holding you tight
But knowing with you they're secure, and everything all right....

Oh so many joys in motherhood!! You'll see!
Just be all the mother to your child you can be!

Your children, they'll watch you, and mimic the things you do
The precious eyes of a child, so honest, so true,

So we teach them with love, the best we can
How to become that good woman or man

The experience of motherhood is about to begin
And once it has, it will never end!!!
Good Luck Sherri!

—*Carolyn Green*

God's Riches

Where can I find the blue skies
When everything looks so gray
Where is the clouds silver lining
I need so desperately today

The cool, clear waters and green mountains
Now muddy or covered with snow
Beautiful fields of sweet flowers
Where did all of this go

I awoke from a frightful dream
And found the sky so blue
A drifting cloud came floating by
It had a silver lining too

Thank God for the cool clear water
Breezes blowing through valleys fair
Fields of flowers and mountains so green
Can be found most anywhere

God in his infinite mercy
Has loving gifts to bestow
To all who reach out in faith
To natures riches he left us below

—*Etta C. Long*

Ore

I hear my voice best
when I am alone in my room
or praying to my maker
in the yellow spray of morning.
Yet sometimes, I see it dance
in the dark night when I lift the shade
of loneliness — that barrier—
which separates me from
the orange glow of the moon.
Then the outside quivers in me wake
stretching from their sleepy shadows.
But most of all, I feel the words of this gentle voice
aching to breathe and become itself
— into the ore —
like the sun begging to set on the earth's edge
when the whispering sea brushes into the silent sky.

—*Jennifer Anne Ingle*

What I Cannot See

When I look out my eyes
When I look down at me
What I see is not I
For I am something no-one can see
A soul who won't rest and spirit that won't die
This body I carry
This body that's mine
Is nothing but a package that I will
wear for a short time
Yet unlike a cat I have more lives than nine
I feel I'll live forever
And always forget my past
I shall be born and die many a time
For just one body cannot last
What I have to accomplish I still do not know
Before this question can be answered
Again, I'll have to go

—*Amanda J. Haddock*

You

I am in a quiet and soothing mood;
When I think of you;
There is no sorrow, there is no pain;
You walked, oh so softly by,
in memories;
With a smile, a smile of such pleasantries;
Oh! how I wish to gain, to retain again;
The joy of touch,
The smells of perfumes;
Eyes, beholding beauty;
Speak, speak to me, please speak to me;
Let soft words thrill me again
For in a quiet and gentle mood;
I am again with the world;
I am again with me;
I am again with you.

—*Jose M. Merle*

I Recall

I recall one special night;
When "I thought never again will I ever feel right"
I recall feeling loved one minute in the presence of light;
and the next I was fighting all that could happen in the
out-cry of night
I recall hiding behind the darkness;
for without it I'll only be less
I recall the feelings I felt;
as their deafness caused my inside to melt
Even thou I lost my might;
I carried out my will to fight
I recall my yesterdays and todays yearning for the darkest
black cape;
to protect me for I've suffered the pain and heartache
of Gang rape.

—*Angela Finnette*

Thankfulness

There came a time in my daily life
When it seemed to me that there would be strife.
A bout with pneumonia, then finding cancer
At that time I'd like to have had an answer.
I had no choice but to take chemotherapy
And then entered the doors of Margaret S. Parmly.
Decisions, adjustments and physical therapy
And then there were activities to keep me happy.
So I put my hand in God's healing hand.
Prayers were said and hope he'd understand
That I needed a shepherd to help me along,
To give me courage and make me strong.
Five times to the clinic I went
The doses of chemo through my body was sent.
So at first I felt sadness, By the grace of God I now feel
gladness.
Thank you, Lord, for giving me Hope.
Thank you, Lord, for my faith in thee.
Thank you, Lord, for your love to me.

—*Dorothy C. Larson*

Change

The time's have changed, have reached their peak.
We have applied variety, speed and dollars
now we find ourselves with nothing much left to change.
So where do we go from here?
Back to square one?
Back to the traditional?
After all the exaggerated!
The cycle starts all over again.
Life!
Is it just a circle?
Or is it a circus?

—*Dolly E. Valentin*

The Colorful Web

All they teach is a colorful web!
When letters and words are but silken snare
That lull, lure and capture their prey.
Your art and craft do us blind
For we are scholars unwilling to be timed.

Like a spider's network of webs,
You are a treacherous nest of ropes
That dismembers a tree from its roots.
Your victims are soldiers of fortune
Whose heroic quest only do time unturn.

Though the cultures are willing to accept
Your apparent promises and sense of hope,
Yet your cost in time is more than hype
For he who enjoys your slight contact
Often rejects a detour as fact.

The victim's head is infested with a strange remedy.
So, since the man is unfit for the work back home,
He pitches his tent in a land not his own.
And while the world reaps his gains,
Aloof, the man feels the pain.

—*Jones A. Okeke*

No Longer

What is a tear? A tear is what I shed
when my love was no longer.
At first drops slid down my face with slow, smooth ease.
Then they fell in an uncontrollable flood.
Flowing no longer with ease, but with an
almost jagged roughness.
The torrent of emotions that was surging through me
was great and strong.
Since my love was no longer it seemed as
though my life was not as it was.
No more carefree love, tender caresses,
or gentle kisses.
All that was there now was an uncontrollable hatred.
Not hatred of things beautiful or of love itself,
but of the love that was shared.
That love is no longer.
Gone with the wind, lost at sea.
It blew away like dust.
Or maybe it went away like that tear,
flowing uncontrollably until it is wiped away.

—*Janae Hayes*

My Dog

My dog is very black.
When she runs away I hope she will come back.
She has a curly tail
and likes to go in the garbage pail.
She chews up all my toys
and makes a lot of noise.
She likes to ride in the car
and hopes we take her very far.
She likes to dig big holes
and in these holes she puts our soles.
Now that you know my dog
I think I'll go for a jog!

—*Beth Crowell*

Untitled

Why are we on this planet?
What are we doing to this place?
These questions need answers before there is no human race.
Kindness, love and forgiveness seem to have been forgotten.
By a world where prejudice has rotted our minds.
To quick to find fault sometimes are we.
What this world needs is understanding and peace.

—*Claudia R. Briggs*

Autumn's Symphony

There is a sadness in the air
   when summer's face has disappeared.
For now is the time to say goodbye
   to all our favorites in summer's eye.

You see, autumn is that time of year
   when matchless beauty does appear.
From the symphonies of golden colors
   and the brilliancy of reds it offers,

To tapestries that do reside
   from the jewels of a mountain side.
The awesome wonder of the painted scene
   of the reflection at a lake serene.

So come with me to that season's gate
   and walk on through with eyes awake.
Because autumn is here and it's alright
   just look around and absorb the sights.

        —Barbara Farr

Silent Running

In the beginning
When the now rushing river, curling over moss-robed stones
Was a trickling stream among rocks, then broken and barren
There was no majesty.
No great, green cliffs, encrusted and crowned
With the jewels of existence and age.
Just a stream and rocks, unaware that time had affixed them there.
Forever, as it passed by.

We are not unlike them; each the rock, each the stream.
Our dreams locked within.
Small movements in the breeze; or just a trickle.
Part of life's never-ending landscape.
But silent running.
Always...silent.

        —Bud Light

Questions Of A Troubled Time

Why do we try to live lives of others,
when the one we live is hard enough?
Why do we try to make lite of things that are not running
smooth, when even a blind man can see the road is rough?

How can you tell someone to stay
in a place they feel they no longer belong?
Why can't you just accept them with open arms,
when their feeling all alone?

Why do people believe they are better than someone else,
because of the skin on their face?
Why do have to label someone just because of their race?

People of all color walk the face of the earth
and color is only skin deep,
we all breath air, and bleed red blood,
and walk upright on our feet!

        —Harriet Simpson

Pray

When you pray you're sa' post to feel special,
when you pray you're sa' post to feel like a chosen vessel,
a vessel being used by God up above,
a vessel being used by God with love.

        —Jessica Hooper

The Autumn I Know

On an Autumn day in October,
When the sun is not so bright,
And I stand and look to the south out my window in the light,
Delighted in its warming glow;

Then thoughts begin to flow,
Remembering treasured friends and stories old,
That come to join me,
In memories made in gold.

I recall the experience,
I remember each face,
I treasure the moments,
That I can now embrace.

Remember the autumn that I know,
Remember the friends and stories old,
That will never grow old,
For this is the autumn I know.

        —Joseph Catalano

Your Love

The moon hung low on that mid-autumn night
When two hearts full of love took flight
Forbidden love like a fantasy flew
At the very moment my eyes met you

Your love is like a pair of wings
That fly me away as my heart sings
To the heights of the purest happiness
And beyond to love's eternal bliss

I pray to God you'll forever be
The one and only love for me
The one with whom I'll travel life's road
While shouldering your every load

I'll keep your love under lock and key
That's how love should always be
As the years go slowly by I'll know
That our love will continue to grow

This is the promise I make to you
That my love will be unspeakably true
I'll shout it from a mountain high
When I stop loving you, I'll lay down and die

        —Jackie W. Walker

The Whistling Water Boy

I remember long ago, in the hayfield making hay,
   When we heard the water boy, it made us all feel gay.

Just a whistling up a storm, when he was around,
   You could hear him far away, with his happy whistling sound.

In his old straw hat and overalls and sneakers full of holes,
   He would pass the water jug, as sweat ran off our nose.

Clear cold water from the spring, when the days were hot,
   There was something 'bout that water boy, I never have forgot.

Gotta git um all a drink, that is all he said,
   Quite a bashful little man, with his freckled face so red.

Then he'd wave his hand goodbye, as he went down the hill,
   In the distance you could hear his whistling, loud and shrill.

So it was long ago, in the summer sun,
   For our thirst he brought relief, until the day was done.

The water boy is resting now, he won't be 'round no more,
   Just a sleeping 'neath the sod, his whistling days are o'er.

Yet when the days grow long and hot, it seems that I can hear,
   The whistle of the water boy, when summer days draw near.

        —Carroll R. Buffum Sr.

Remember The Old Times Together

Remember the old times together
When we would hold each other and say I love you
We had laughter and shared a shoulder to cry on when times
    were bad

Remember the old times together
When we needed each other to hold and never to let go
Walking arm and arm, talking of future plans

Remember the old times together
With disagreements between us
We talked out our problems and shared our feelings together
Our love overpowered all

Remember the old times together
That day, our last day
For our love could now only be "the best of friends"
But I will always
Remember the old times together.

    —*Dana Hess*

Tanya

    She's a real cutie, this exotic beauty
        When you make her smile
    But if you cross her, or try to boss her
        She'll snap, like a croc-O-dile.

    So a word to the wise, those big brown eyes
        Will burn a hole right through you.
    While all the while, her seductive smile
        Like a spell, will gently woo you.

So don't play with fire, she's a real live wire
        That is sure to light a spark.
Then you'll fall in love, with that little dove
    And then, she'll break your heart.

    And your only gain, will be a pain
        That'll haunt your mem-O-ry.
It'll drag you down, like a sad face clown
        And never set you free

    So heed my word, that gentle bird
        Hides the talons of an eagle
    She'll tear you down, then turn around
    And walk away, so proud and regal.

    —*Donald Dean Shelley*

Smile

Don't expect a smile of those you meet,
When you walk looking down at your feet.

You won't find sunshine with your face turned down,
Or hope to be happy with your face in a frown.

Change everyone's life, try out a smile,
It's one thing that's never out of style.

Give a smile and it will make you glow,
Give one to everyone wherever you go.

Give one to neighbor, friends, and foes,
A happy smile, some friendly "Hello's."

Smile at the aged, and those who have less,
Not just the ones you want to impress.

No one is better, the short or the tall,
Smile and make some happiness for all.

Smile at the lonely, who need an uplifting,
The crippled, weak, and those who are drifting.

Look each in the eye, have a happy face,
Greet life with a smile, in every place.

Give to all our best and warmest smile,
It costs nothing, and makes life worthwhile.

    —*Dorothy Matulunas*

The Prize Rose

Dearest Anna, do you recall
When you were a wee thing just three feet tall,
You plucked from my garden my prize scarlet rose
Then tenderly held it under my nose?

The love in your eyes as you glowed with pride
At the gift you offered, turned my anger aside.
My heart saw your love through a Mother's eyes;
Though the flower faded it still won first prize.

Among the treasures I hold most dear,
Locked away in a box for all these years,
Is the scarlet rose, now faded and dry,
Worth more than gold as the years flowed by.

And my heart remembers the blush on your cheek,
So much love in your eyes that I could not speak
The love in my heart, dear Anna, my child,
As you held out the rose, looked up and smiled.

    —*Candy Anderson*

Friends

Friends are people you lean on,
    when your boyfriends not around.
Friends are people you count on
    when your feeling down.
Friends are people who care,
    for you and you should care for them too.
Friends are also people who should,
    be treated the way that they treat you.
Friends will always be your friends,
    no matter what you go through.
Friends sometimes might put you down,
    or just might down right make you frown.
Friends may also tell a lie,
    or just every once in awhile not say hi.
Friends may start a fight here and there,
    But deep down inside they really care.
Friends you see are bad and good,
    so please keep your friends if you would.

    —*Chrissy Knapp*

Expression Of Feeling

How do you explain how you feel
When your feelings are too intense for words?
The only words to say, have been used so many times before.
The word love is often spoken,
Yet seldom is it really felt.
So the lucky ones who experience love.
Are now searching for a way to express it.

How do you tell someone how much you feel
When spoken language is so much more limited,
Than language of art and experience
If a picture is worth a thousand words.
A thousand intense, meaningful words
How many is a feeling worth?

To say I love you would not be enough
And to show you, well I just don't know how
This is my way of expressing myself,
When a few words just won't do
Please read this and ponder awhile
And I hope the revelation will be
That you realize how much you mean to me.

    —*Jensena Lynne*

Libraries Can Give Your Life A Special Start

Libraries can give your life a special start,
Whenever there's an idea or philosophy you need to impart!
Come visit them whenever you have a special need,
There's something in them that will help you plant the seed!
Whether it be gardening, home repairs, or something in art,
When you know how to do research you already have a head start!
Printed word, magazines, videos, puzzles and more,
There's so much available that it's hard to keep score!
When was the last time you gave yourself a special treat?
By using a library collection that's really neat!
There's one in your neighborhood and probably nearby,
Finding it will probably be easy as pie!
Use the yellow pages or ask a dear friend,
To begin a special journey that has no end!
Come to the library and find out for certain,
The many lives of Elizabeth Taylor Burton!
If this doesn't please you, something else will,
And in most cases there isn't even a bill!
The welcome mat's out, there are books waiting for you,
Bring a friend with you for an experience that's altogether new

—*Allen P. Rothlisberg*

Love Song

Tired legs moving tired body to tired chair
    where all of me sits.
Overloaded brain sorts, classifying, overloading
    memory space allocated.
Tentative whistles, chirps,
A series of musical notes entering consciousness.
Rise and walk to the cage.
Sharp nails and beaks quickly climb cage wires to
    the top, where freedom awaits.
Tired hands open the cage.
Tentative notes turn to high pitched peals of joy.
Rejuvenated finger offered for a perch
    chirping cockatiels scamper quickly to shoulders
    stealing a kiss,
    nuzzling,
    singing me their song of love.

—*Cyndy Woods*

Retired

I still can't believe it
Where have they gone
The years that were young are moving along
The things that were important are not so anymore
The children are grown and grandchildren are appearing
The leaves are dropping from the trees so much more rapidly
The days are getting faster and faster
Why is everything moving so quickly
If I could only have a calm at this stage of my life and God
    grants me some time to enjoy my family and wife
Where have they gone
I still can't believe it
But, I'm not through yet
There are so many things to do and see before I leave for a new
    eternity

—*James D. Anglin*

A Poet's Prison

A poet's prison is in his mind.
Where his thoughts and his dreams are intertwined
Each line is a thought symbolic in his life.
Explaining many things from a boyhood dream to
The woman he wanted for his wife.
And each line on paper fulfills a need;
For it is an entangled thought finally freed.
Free to touch another soul in some way.
And capture someone else's mind, if only for a day.

—*Annie Norris Stone*

Untitled

My favorite dreams are the ones
where I get to walk around naked in public
and nobody notices
at first it was embarrassing to be
riding on the subway with yuppie commuters
only to realize I hadn't got dressed that morning
but then I came to see that nobody noticed
and then I saw that I wasn't the only one
walking around naked in the crowds
I saw lots of people dreaming they were naked
like it was some sort of fashion statement
some of us go shopping nude
some of us attend board room meetings in the buff
some of us like to take showers on the sidewalks
but people have begun noticing lately
in the office hallways, a sudden stare from a colleague
uh, am I mistaken, or are you naked?
and occasionally, I get this painful, swollen erection
right in front of everybody - it's a bit embarrassing
I guess I'll have to start getting dressed for bed

—*Gregory K. H. Bryant*

The Secret Garden (Dedicated to my Dad)

There is a place hidden deep in the canyon.
Where no one goes, and no one knows the
    magic of this place.
A Secret Garden.
It is sad the people there are not aware of
    the beauty it once had. His beauty,
    when we were all once together.
The roses blossomed in his joy
Carnations grew with the sound of his laughter.
And the sun shown down as bright as the
    love he felt for us all was strong.
But then one day he was not there.
The flowers died without his care.
Now I am the one who must bring this
    garden back, for he is a part of it.
And I know he'll always be in my heart
For we shall never be apart but
    together in our garden.

—*Caitlin Bernstein*

Radiant World

There is a place beyond the clouds
where the air hangs just so.

Where the streams don't rustle violently,
but sway in a gentle flow.

Where sadness is unthinkable and happiness
is everlasting.

Where the pain of your past life
will be forever fasting.

Where you can endure all your dreams
and master all your fears.

Where the gentle wind around you dries
your soaking tears.

Where the border between life and death is
quickly disappearing.

Where you wonder how you can be in
this place you've so been fearing.

Anything is possible in this world beyond the sky.
in this place, this special place is called heaven.

—*Bethanne Harrington*

The Leaves Of Fall

Oh, the woods were warm and soft and wet
Where the seasons song and deftly met
To exchange in a dance I knew so well
As the flaming leaves of the mountains fell
To spread a cloak of gold and green
Near a hidden brook-where the portridae preen
Or a fawn might drink in her graceful ease
While the mother watched from a shield of trees.
When the dance had ended my summer stood bore
Stripped of her warmth and its glowing flare.
She bowed to the role her partner would play,
As a shadow at down she melted away.

—*Charlotte Galusha*

The Dawn Treader

I walk on golden crystal shores,
where there is peace and no bloody wars.
There, I find a longing serene beauty,
where everyone has his own graceful duty.
There is no bloodshed or fallen tears,
and everything goes away, even your fears.
The shimmering sun slowly lifts,
the icy waves are covered with golden rifts.
The sand moves under my pale feet.
This is a place where no one can cheat.
But, I keep on gliding, walking, running.
I am scared, but filled with cunning.
Scared of what, I riskily ask,
but I can't see I am covered by a mask.
My fears come together, a hunter!
He hunts a bird, no!
Running, I keep on running!
I am the bird, and I am falling, plunging,
diving, lunging.
A shock, water, cold, death.

—*Helen Findley*

Turtles

A turtle is a curious thing.
Wherever he goes his house he will bring.
He can't dance or cut any rugs.
But wherever he goes he eats all the bugs.
He sleeps all winter in hibernation.
In spring he visits the plantation.
He eats up all the lettuce he can.
Then into his shell for the next day he will plan.
He can't go fast or run any track meets.
But if you don't watch your garden, he'll eat all your beets.
On his face is neither a smile or a frown.
Some turtles have pretty shells, some are just brown.
He can't say hello, or talk whatsoever.
He doesn't smoke or drink, no, no, never.
He is peaceful and friendly, he can be your pal.
Unless of course someday, he finds him a gal.
Their stumpy legs are strong to hold them up.
But their not warm and cuddly like a pup.
They are nice to watch for a while on a sunny day.
Then we can go off with a smile to play.

—*John Needham*

Daddy

When there's a lot of things to do, we call on Daddy.
Whether the chores are many or few, we call on Daddy.

Whether it's calling the dog or catching a mouse
Chasing the cat or painting the house.
Mother says he's a very good spouse, that's my Daddy.

When the flowers are blooming, and grass is high,
The weeds are reaching up for the sky,
Whose that pushing our lawn mower by?
That's my Daddy.

He's the fellow who keeps our home going,
Keeps us together and keeps us growing,
Even when he has his good side showing, that's my Daddy.

If you have a Daddy who does those things,
Makes you happy when he works and sings,
Even though he doesn't sound like Bing
Then that's a Daddy.
And now we have a day that's here,
That honors our Daddy at least once a year,
It's a day that really deserves a cheer,
These are our Daddies.

—*Charles P. Marriott*

Nur's Life

I close my eyes to awake within a new world, a new life, one in which I'm in control, a heart, mind and living soul in my dreams, pain's real, your able to love, hate, and even kill. I manifested my feelings through words that couldn't be altered or changed in any way. I took control of a dying world and expanded its boundaries form sea to sea. As far as an eye could possibly see. I infatuated a society of fools with a false hope and a tainted lie. I took a place, an inferno and made a kingdom of crystal seas and golden shrubbery. I took erratic people and made them keepers of souls. In my dreams I have three powers the first power is transfiguration by which I changed shapes and facial figures in order to expand on my inward being. The many that form together to create the clairvoyant lad that's left. The second power that I obtain in my dreamstate is domination over all animals. By controlling the beast I control man. The final power I have is immortality. While holding the keys of tomorrow the dreams of today are mine.

—*Jamie D. Emery*

When I Die I'm Gone

Death is something without a trace
    which is left in anyone's heart
My forgotten face

Someone there to take my place
Put in my grave with quiet haste

And I leave this place, like I left those back then
The same places I left, without any friends

I will be gone at the end
At the end of life's journey

Without so much as a friend
I will die with no one to remember me

—*Jerrod Williams*

Baby's First Request

Treat me gently, love me grand.
Show me that you understand.

Teach me 'bout life, it's ups and downs.
Surround me with loving sights and sounds.

Give me approval, encouragement and praise,
And I'll learn to appreciate, and have confident ways.

Take hold of my hand, and help me feel secure,
So I will have faith, and love life even more.

Let me live with tolerance and teach me to be fair,
And I'll learn to be patient and how to share.

Don't shame, don't ridicule or criticize me,
and I won't condemn, be shy, or feel guilty.

Guard me from hostility, so I won't have to fight,
teach me acceptance, friendship and all that's right.

But my most important request of all ...
Never stop loving me.

—Phyrn Liebsch

My Friend

The window pane so clear,
Showed me a scene so dear.
A child, snowman, bent and weak,
The tears were flowing down her cheek.
She wiped away, yet more tears shone,
She said, my friend, how come?
For he had been so tall, but now
it seemed his legs were gone
as his belt began to fall.
Where could they run. How could they go?
I'll miss you Sir, she let him know.
We'll try again, you'll see next year,
and make you taller,
Can you hear?

—Lea Calderone

Teach Them To Swim

It seems like ages,
   since you did this last.
But you finish your paper work,
   and go meet your class.

The kids look at you with fear and hope,
but the parents look at you as if you're a dope.

It's magic parents expect,
   when you take the kids inside.
Yet the kids haven't change much,
   when you tell them good-bye.

Olympic swimmers is what parents want to see,
but that's asking a lot when the kid is only three.

So you try your best,
   to teach them to have some fun.
For it's a long day's work,
   when the day is finally done.

—Matthew Calder

The Flag In The Church

They won the war at whose loss?
Slain heroes worshiped, now honored dead:
Abraham, James and John of fiery fame,
Benjamin rose from those who had been men,
Andrew and Thomas in faith not the same,
Hiram's grant of words so underly read—
all sleep in blood filled furrows.

Light fell as snow drops of milk
dressing earth in an ermine fur;
a still life mantle once pure this, no longer spotless
field I saw never even was idle if
(the past reflected in a mirror)
it could but return to life those fallen bodies.

One life must them be given —
seven times; seven then must be so;
let there be light in those eyes that shone
as stars ascending to highest heaven,
the azure footstool of God's royal throne,
whence freedom and justice is driven
to all creatures here below.

—Ryan Allyn

The Hustler

Here I stand, bare chested in the autumn sun
Slowly strutting near my corner
Pausing, turning, stretching
Under my tousled hair
Glancing at men passing by
On foot or in their cars
Staring as they wait to cross the street
Or turn into traffic
Uncertain if their hesitation
Is an invitation
To discuss my fee and manly talents
But they walk on and turn into traffic
Hour after hour after hour
While I stroll and crouch and look and stretch
Hoping to sell the caress of my youthful body
Or some passionate moments
Or some pretense of caring
To those who will give me
What I want.

—Roy Bishop

Great Grandmother

I watch your fragile body as it moves,
Slowly you seem to fade away.
Do you know that I love you? Do you know that I care?
Do you really know who I am?
Your tired, wrinkled face, has worn many smiles.
Your fading eyes have seen many things,
Your mind has learned many lessons that I have yet to learn.
You have felt much heartache and sorrow in that big heart of
   yours.
You have gone through so much more than anyone that I know.
War, depression, violence, anger, hatred, love, happiness, and
   sorrow.
You've seen the deaths of your friends, relatives, husband,
   and daughter.
Do you wish you could be with them now?
You've closed your eyes now,
So I shall leave you to sleep.
I'll return to see you once again.
Peace to you, my Great Grandmother.
May God watch over you with loving eyes. Sleep well.

—Renee L. Kvasnicka

Northern Lights Hit Small Ohio Town

Wide swatches of purple, scarlet, green
smeared densely and courageously on the horizon,
perfectly suspended—pulsing with half frozen bits of light.

Breath white, air thick with cold
we stand in front of the church,
heads like dead puppets,
relishing the lights' macabre vitality,
wanting to pull the luminescence into our guts.

A grey-brown cat slips its thin, soft frame
against our bare hands as we think of light
where it cannot be.

  —Rebecca A. Hamilton

Julia

She is the Sun's rays in the Spring,
Smiling as bright as the sky,
Making me feel happy and full of life
Like an open Tulip absorbing the sun's warmth.

She is the warm breeze in summer,
Touching my face softly with her gentle hand,
Caressing my skin and warming me deep inside.

Her personality is like the brightly colored leaves in Autumn,
Outgoing and generous,
Giving me all that I need,
Covering the ground with a blanket;
Covering me with affection.

Her eyes are like the stars in the winters night,
Sparkling and glistening through the darkness,
Reaching for my soul,
Chipping the cold ice away from my heart.

Without her there would be no sunny skies,
No gentle breeze in the autumn air
No diamonds in the snow.
Without her there is no rain or soil to make my spirit grow.

  —Scott Patrick Smith

Tough Love

I've got a Tough Love for you and myself
So fulfilling I wouldn't share it with anyone else;
Such a committed romance where we still feel free
With a mutual respect evinced even when we disagree;
An unconditional giving where both of us procure gain,
A powerful force between us that we must try and sustain;
We've both let down our guards and are proud of the very fact
That this understanding we share makes us think before we react;
Unselfishly we take from each other with sincerity and a special
 care
Willingly we always give to one another because we have so much
 to share;
The genuine tenderness in the words we use is almost hard to
 believe
Even the trust we have between us in too intricate for others to
 conceive;
Kindness is reciprocated and not easily understood
Complimenting one another just as true friends should;
At times it's somewhat scary this high level of respect we have in
 place
Hoping this eminent sense of security will forever be warmly
 embraced;
Don't misunderstand this unique love by the things I might say
It's an indistinguishable, involved bond which put others in dismay;
What makes this such a Tough Love which I would never deny,
If need be I can let it go and even say good-bye.

  —Vivian B. Washington Carwell

The Book

I heard your word, was in the good book
So I turned the flap, for to have a look.
 I read the pages just to see,
And found the truth, happiness, and glee.
 Your words of love, shined so bright
Now I read for you every night.
 The verses made me feel warm inside,
So now your book, stays by my side.
 We all need the word, I am here to say,
Just pick up his book and, read some today.
 It won't hurt to read just a bit,
I have been pulled from hell's fiery pit.
 God, loves us one and all
So just reach out, and give him a call.
 Read some today, some of his verse
It won't hurt, it could be much worse.
 His words will help you, when you are sad
In a few lines, you can feel happy and glad.
 I will now leave you, with this line
Just pick up the good book, and give it some time.

  —Paul David Bamford

The Grey Lady Spider

The grey lady spider, spins her lacy web,
So many threads, old and new,
It takes her not long, to make her home,
So beautiful, with dew,
Drops of water, lay on her, she does not mind,
For her fury, back, is made so fine,
Even water will not her bind,
She spins and spins her pretty web
To catch her food this day,
In, comes a fly, now food for lady grey,
Over the trees, she does creep,
Into crevices, dark and deep,
These are her favorite, places, to sleep,
She wakes, by night, with first one eye,
The day time, she prefers to lye,
Asleep, so sound, so cozy, deep,
Nights are my time says, lady grey,
To spin and bite, then crawl away.

  —Nancy L. Brouillette

Right Here And Now

Right now you're not here,
So nothing is moving,
Everything is still,
Time isn't flying,
Clocks aren't ticking,
And you're not here,
Tears coming down my face,
As I look at the dried roses on my ledge,
and only one thing is wrong,
You're still not here.

  —Michelle Miller

You

You said that you loved me, but you couldn't commit.
So one day you decided you would just call it quits.
You pushed me aside cause you needed your space.
You promised to call, but you got caught up in the race.
You shared your life with me, your ups and your downs.
But now that I need you, you won't come around.
Someday when you're older and you're lonely and blue
I will smile when you say, "What the hell did I do."

  —Sharon Friesen

The Spark

A small child's hand reaches from within
so small, innocent, vulnerable and naive
his world is full of smiles and tears,
dump trucks, candy and fears
His small wondrous hands reaches
for those who care knowing inside
there is someone there

The world's hands and light reach from without
A plaything so big, so blinding with nothing to fear
For us to grasp is way too deep
Nothing known about the lighthouse keep
The hands so huge, they engulf all-
Have hope, have faith, have cheer

The two hands reach far and wide
Only to touch and spark and make something special aside
What is left is a special gift inside and out-
It is me without a doubt!

   —*Todd Davis*

Last Words

Leave the casket open
So that I can remember romance
In the sight of the flames.
So that I may breath the air
Of the fresh mountain snow.
For this is where my ashes will lay.

Not forget the wind
That shapes the petals.
That cries the turns for leaves,
The curled; open to bring a new

Not forget the moon
That govern a shadows light
Upon the sea like broken beads
From a pearl necklace bringing the waves,
Breaking into smiles across the shore.
To see sand-piper tracks stitched in the wet sand.

Someday a child born again
Who goes in moods, from smiles to pout
Water colors splashed upon the window pane
Then laughs to grab the sand and watch it fall.

   —*Selisa D. R. Maahs*

Oh Beautiful Mountain

Oh beautiful mountain what a sight I saw
So very far away I can't touch thee
I will look and wonder how far you are away.
And at your trees so tall and green as they sway and sway.
I would like to climb you mountain
and be there where you are.
I'd feel so close to heaven. I could touch a star.

I'd feel your gentle breeze as the wind comes blowing through
I'd reach out and touch your branches, yes that's what I'll do
I would sing a little song with the birds that live with you
and I would watch the deer, as he comes swiftly through

catch a pretty leaf as it falls to the ground.
And I'd play with all the animals
as they come around.

Oh yes beautiful mountain
You have so much to give
May your beauty last forever
And long long may you live

   —*Lola Head*

Untitled

The eagle lives in the high country
Soaring in the warm currents from the valley
Wings out stretched, shimmering in the sunlight.
Silence unbroken, he dives into the river below.
Soaring again with a fish in talons of bone.

The people who live in the valley
Look like me, but, I feel of the eagle.
Soaring to heights they have only dreamed
I dive into the river of life and bring forth
Ideas in my talons of reason.

The few who live in the high country
Soaring in the warm currents from the valley
We are the spirit of mankind longing to be free
But we just gather from the valley of mankind
Prejudices in talons of dust.

   —*Robert L. Anderson*

Into The Night

Listen, as the sound grows from a distance.
Softly, yet bold, it creeps into the night.
 Come close, one may feel the crisp
  clear sounds of solitude.
But wait! Be patient, stand in silence.
Hear the whisper rake through the night.
  Somewhere, off in a distance,
No sight, though sound, loneliness creeps in.
 One chamber to another, the sound,
  bouncing off the walls of emptiness.
 A pain created, only sorrow follows.
Watch! The healing begins, a scar sets in.
 A moment has grown, that from within.
But wait! Be patient. Stand in silence.
Loneliness is captured - into the night....

   —*Robert J. Lingenfelter*

Nostalgia

Like a ribbon
Some distant perfume
Twines through the cells of my nose
Piercing memory.
A forgotten melody circles the shell of my ear
Whispering "child...child...child"
In the dusk the hour-glass
Drips steadily its sands of amethyst
And I am not free to turn it around
Or stop the siren singing in my brain.

   —*Patricia C. Lee*

I Hear The Light

 Look, can you see it penetrate the dark
so far away it resembles not much more than a spark
 I've come too far to turn back now
toward a place I'm proud I left...
 I traveled such a distance on faith
toward a promise we've all heard
 That light at the end of the tunnel,
dear Lord you've kept your word.
 So many times in darkness,
I thought I searched in vain.
 But now I hear it clearly Lord,
it's followed by a train.

   —*R. G. Welch*

The Magic Playground

They say there's playground in everyone's mind
Some enjoy it but others would rather hide
They seem afraid to follow the voice that's inside

Won't you come to the playground? It's just over there
Come let your child join us - free from worry and care

There are swings in the playground
There are ladders and slides
There are stairs you can climb on that reach to the sky

It's a magical kingdom where fairy tales are spun
It beckons all children to come and have fun
Just look for the magic that's inside of you
And when you find it - you'll know what to do

You'll find in this playground there's nothing to fear
The laughter of angels is all that you hear
Angels are playing in this magical place
And every little cherub has a smile on its face

Yes I know there's a playground and it's a magical one
It's there just for the asking - full of magic and fun
So come to the playground, just open your heart
That's all it takes, so why not start

—*Wayne Wilde*

Friendship

Some say friendship is a river that puts life in a tender reed.
Some say friendship is a razor that leaves the fights behind.
Some say friendship is a hunger a waiting aching need.
I say friendship is a flower and friends its only seed.
It's the tear afraid of pouring that never learns to let go.
It's the dream afraid of waking that never takes the chance.
It's the friend that won't be taken who can not seem to give.
And the afraid of losing that friends learn to trust.
When the time has been too lonely and the road has been too long.
And you think that friendship is only for the lucky and the strong.
Just remember the times together and the times that weren't so
  great.
Though we came through them with one another's strength,
That's why we've all become best friends.

—*Lorraine Aboughanam*

War Wounds

    Whistling bullets fly past my head
  Some soldiers say you're better off dead.
  Wide eyes at night are filled with fright
    For thinking of home or dying I might.
  Anguish and pain scream down like the rain
It's thoughts of my country that help me keep sane.
  The light of each sunrise brings hope to my eyes
  That the war will be over, thank God for G.I.'s.

—*Michael G. Kopke*

This Is Known As Life

There is a process in life known as sanctification.
Some will surrender under it and others will go on their way.
The key is staying surrendered.
A state of being surrendered is to be maintained each moment of
each day.
The choice is one's own and only one's own.
What will you do?
What will I do?
Oh, please help me to stay surrendered each moment of each day.
I cannot do it on my own.
I need help.
The choice is my own and only my own.
Oh, please help!!!

—*Melissa Lynn Ollendieck*

Somebody

Somebody's heart is broken today,
Somebody's eyes are filled with tears.
It takes but a second to get a wound,
The healing takes many long years.
Somebody's lips have forgotten to smile,
One day they will change, but it'll be a long, long
  while.
Somebody's heart has a scar now so great,
Hope it doesn't turn all her love into hate.
Somebody's trying so hard now to win,
To prove that life is worth living again.
Somebody didn't really want to be free,
I'll tell you a secret, that "Somebody" is me.

—*Mildred L. McDonough*

Testimony

As the songsters took their place today,
Someone came to the pulpit to say.
Life is a journey and long is the road,
It sure gets heavy beneath this load.

Bogged down today with so much care,
I took it to the Lord in prayer.
He walked with me as the day passed by,
It was evening and the moon was high.

As I looked at the Lord with a sigh,
He looked back at me eye to eye.
It was nice walking today with Thee,
Thanks, He said, for asking me.

—*Wilma Brocksieck*

Blue Me

I feel lonely today - oh, were there someone to talk to -
    Someone with patience, for I have so much to say
  Someone with understanding, for I need to be understood.
      I sneak away and try to shake the feeling
    But, like hunger, it continues to nudge me -
    Keeps reminding me of the emptiness I feel
    Keeps stirring up the recesses of my mind
        Forcing me to remember back when -
  When sharing was common place and vision had distance
    And tomorrow promised that love would abound -
I am lonely today - wishing to shed the shackles of distrust
  And open my heart to experience unconditional love -
  Love that expresses confidence, patience, permanence
    Individuality, respect and is void of pretense.
  Oh, I'm sooo lonely today, quite aware of those around me
      Who fulfill my everyday common needs,
      But my heart begs for a special border -
One who shares my vision and seeks patience and understanding
    too - One with an intent to stay a spell.
        Oh, I'm sooo lonely today.

—*Tobitha R. Moran*

Mood And Attitudes

Sometimes I look up to see if someone's really watching over me.
Sometimes I turn around to see if I have cast a shadow on the
  ground.
Sometimes I react to see if I can still respond.
Sometimes I'll say nothing so as to appreciate the silence.
Sometimes I'll smile so that someone else will smile back.
Sometimes I'll give in so that someone else will win.
Sometimes I'll work hard so that I do not become effortless.
Sometimes I'll try these actions so that I'll always have
Something to do.

—*Stephney Webb*

Love's Endurance

In all relationships
sometimes things go wrong
but love has a strength in its self
that can make what is weak very strong
but in order to achieve its strength
You should know this secret of time
truth and an open heart
is what keeps all love alive
In every relationship some tears have to be shed
because of certain paths that have to be tread
because of certain paves that have to be laid
because of certain dues
that have to be paid
Love's journey is the rose
and its petals
but also the stem and thorns
guaranteed both hearts
will get stuck and bleed
but each petal
makes it worth to endure

—*Shannon Maria Lane*

There's No Hope In Dope

Drugs will make you feel real high
Sometimes you think that you can fly
It temporarily takes away your troubles
It often makes you speak in bubbles
That kind of junk isn't good for you or me
And if you quit you sure will be free
There's only two places that you could go
Either in jail or six foot in a hole
I guess it's not easy for anyone to see
That when you're doing drugs you'll never be free
It's time right now to put drugs in its place
And get it out of our poor children's face.

—*Rusty J. Sylva*

Raped

Violet eyes shun dim,
    Somewhat grayish, almost hoary.
I pondered to find the root of the stem,
    Which would unveil her sacred story.

Those eyes! Those eyes!
    How they prisoned such a gruesome tale.
Now it was of no surprise
    Why she laid there weak and frail.

Reaching out and resting on one knee
    I held her oh so tight.
Whispering softly my beg and plea,
    "Do not leave me alone tonight!"

Tears of heartache now began to show.
    Parading down her face.
Now I felt her soul let go
    And knew it was her fate.

Screaming out to the heavens above
    I cried, "Why are we so existential?"
To sacrifice another love
    Watching her drown in her potential.

—*Phillip Van Every*

The Other Side

Soon we will be there.
Soon we will travel to that place, that time.
The sun reaches for you,
Calling your name, guiding your warmth.
The angel's arc crosses over your head
And touches you from behind.
The sky bespeckled by graying clouds;
Not here but there.
A hand reaches from the other side
Seeking the unwanteds, grabbing those
ready to go to the next.

Soon we will be guided, glided, sent forth to.
We will cross the yellow tiled road to touch
The weeping grass that westward wind blows.
A daffodil laughs as a beacon to guide you
On to that lamp at the end
Which is calling,
Soon.

—*M. H. Floyd*

Untitled

Post-passion pain is present and painful,
Sorrow still felt but showing its shameful,
Denial is trial at some peace of mind,
Acceptance too much, black vision, stay blind,
Lonely and lost and leaning much lower,
If only the cost of love could be over,
Oblivious obsession for joy was inside,
Sadly it ceased, seeping out when I cried,
Clinging to chapters of a book incomplete,
Pages stopped turning, too late to retreat,
Too much of my heart from the start in the trap,
Rips when I pull, still cuts when relaxed,
If I yank it away, the pain will subside,
That's what I'll do, I still have my pride,
Along with my love, my caring, and hope,
Heart still in pain but I'm sane so I'll cope,
The shadow of the present still blocks out the past,
Tomorrow is coming, this bad time can't last,
Too hurt to be bitter, deeds done are done.
Tomorrow, tomorrow, tomorrow please come.

—*Reginald Lee*

Jigsaw Puzzle

Scatter the pieces on to the table,
Sort by color or shape if you're able

Find the ones that build the frame,
You're on your own playing this game

Be prepared to make mistakes,
There are many that are fakes

With your heart you're tempted to choose,
But be careful, with this one you'll lose

For it was not what it appeared to be,
Tricked again by the similarity

Don't get discouraged, hold back the tears,
You've only been a puzzler for thirty two years

Consider yourself lucky in that respect,
There are many much older, I suspect

Just a few more pieces to assemble in place,
You'll be done in no time if you keep up the pace

At last you hold in the palm of your hand,
The final one to complete as planned

You set it down with a triumphant cheer,
Sensing that something is still not quite clear

—*Phyllis Sheridan*

Reflections

Thousands of eyes of gleaming wonder, peering forever inside my
    soul,
The urge to find the mystery of those things I can not control.

A treasure conceived in wonder, in thoughts a sea of blue,
A wondrous gift to carefully be opened, to discover what beliefs
    are true.

In a time of little conscious, from life forever torn,
It is a balance between power, and knowledge waiting to be born.

Part of a world now built with prejudice, set in a time where
    all is unkind.

Now that we are all free, it is time to free our minds.
Grow beyond that which is given, but do not strive to take,
Find the answers to the questions that are locked within your mind,
Yet take care, make no mistake.

The choices will not always be clear, and the paths may wonder
    far.
Still forever hold what you learn dear, for this is who you are.

—*Mark Woodall*

The Planted Seed

A spark had been ignited, somewhere within the soul
Spreading warmth to the planted seed and helping it to grow.

The seed required love as substance for its roots,
and patience filled the water can, giving moisture to the fruit

Time became its sunshine, absorbing each ray of light
and compassion was its protector from the harshness of the night.

Stretching out to gain more space for the knowledge it would store,
The flower pot that held it tight would contain its roots no more.

Pushing free of its restraints, breathing deep the air
embraced by the touch of the gardeners hand, and knowing she
    was there.

Only the heart can tell you true, there could really be no other,
such a precious gift of love and life, is that of a
    child and its mother!

—*Linda M. Jones*

Spring Rain

Walking down the lane one day, there came upon me a sudden
spring rain. I paused a moment, with my hands outstretched, as
also was my head and neck. I felt its coolness upon my face,
this feeling I desire never to be erased. As must the flowers
and the trees, take a shower of their leaves, embarking upon
them, came a gentle breeze, just I have if you please. The
dancing droplets lited gently on their veins, this refreshing,
they could hardly contain. The precious aroma of fresh wet
earth, was comparable to a brand new birth. The joy of the two
is like the morning dew. Let me not stand alone on this view.
What is this I see? Far off in the sky, I see a mixture of
colors that pleasures my eyes. Oh my! I think the painter of
the sky has much more talent than even I. When he painted the
beautiful rainbow in the sky, with its special glow, it even
surpasses Michael Angelo. Writing about the consumption of
this treasure, was a great, great, great pleasure!

—*Susan M. Redfern*

Teardrops

Teardrops full of melancholy sorrow
Sprinkling on roses from yesterday's love
A flood of tears feeding the rivers
As an uncaught fish swims free
Its scales glistening in victory
Sobs of regret quivering off the tongue
As an apology long due is expressed
A mysterious smile suppressing the lips
To discover the rose unfurled in bloom
The river high and fish a plenty
And the contentment of being forgiven

—*Sara Kim*

Jesus Did

Would you leave an ivory palace,
Step down from a throne of gold,
To be nailed upon a cross of wood? Well, Jesus did!
Would you free your heart of malice,
Though your sufferings were untold,
And return for evil only good? Well, Jesus did!

Would you gladly bear the heavy load,
Of all of mankind's sin,
Would you work until the task was done? Well, Jesus did!
Had you helped them all along life's road,
Then crucified by men,
Would you love them each and every one? Well, Jesus did!

Would you walk through town and city,
Helping all the blind to see,
Would you answer every hopeless call? Well, Jesus did!
If they placed you without pity,
On the cross of calvary,
Would you still say, "God, forgive them all"? Well, Jesus did!

—*Ramsey Arrington*

The Dawning

She is like the hour before dawn,
Still kissed by the cool of the evening,
Full of stars and dew and the sometime song
Of the first of the birds in the morning.
The moon hangs ripe and westering,
Clear in the blue and brightening air
And in the pastel eastern offing
The sun is coming, and daylight's cares,
But the moment hangs still; unhurried,
As one orb rises and another one sets
Like the scene of a play before actors' fury
She is full of a promise of newness, and yet
Limitless possible days stretch ahead
Here at the beginning. Blue fades the night.
Morning is broken and she turns her head
As a single ray of risen sunlight
Fires her eyes with the reckless chance
of days and years: a Lifetime's Glance,
As though this is where she's always belonged.
O she is so like the hour before dawn!

—*Timothy Smith*

A Roman Ruin

As the haughty are humbled by ancient tombs,
So awe enshrouds me.
Your severed hand stands two meters -
And lifeless flesh pulsates!
With single finger jutting heavenward,
Destiny is denounced.

What desperate search of lost counterparts
Is in your set scheme?
What buried tales of centuries past
Can sculptured stone unearth?

—*Rebecca S. Strand*

17 North Towards Gloucester With Car Television

Sonnet

The sun's reflections on a summer afternoon
Stipple our undulating highway reverie,
Spray on a side of barn or crenelated ruin,
Thoughts of green fields and the spreading tree.

Then angel forms from infancy stand fast,
As Oswald, dancing flowers, the early day
Of lively motion sprung from dots and lines — at last,
After patient vigil and, yes, awe at patterns' play.

Stop, unrelenting silence! Such gold, such silver coin
No white horsed Indian warrior knew, nor could
We, black with care, the fleeting time purloin
When run unseen the reels in our bright wood.

The films and mists, the lantern shows of fall, let be:
Better we run before, where all roads run, and free.

—*Wilson F. Engel*

Funeral For A Friend

There's a place covered with tears
Stock in your soul trying to get free.
There's some friends quiet and sad,
Honest hugs and false words without sense.
And others so cold, and somebody feeling real pain with no
Words, memories from yesterday today so close
An empty body causing curiosity and confusion
Among the people, or may be the last chance
To forgive and forget, or to feel his presence
And to pay last respects.
A wooden box covered with flowers
Crowns and crosses, the most elegant bed that a
Man ever had, words of wisdom from a priest
Wife, friends, and kids, washing the floors with tears,
And a death friend crying from heaven.
And a man looks for the last time at a grave,
At the end with cool steps turns around
And continues again his road.
Without crying but sad,
Living behind the funeral of a friend.

—*Roberto Garcia*

Beach Of Eternity

Life is but a grain of sand
Strewn on the Beach of Eternity
And as grains of sand our life will end we know not when
But as we live each day we must be a friend to all man
Color has no meaning on the Beach of Eternity
Soon all the grains will mix
God sees no difference in each grain of sand
All of the grains of sand that lie on this special beach
Is but a mixture that one cannot see
In the end we will all be together as it was planned
When God created his Miracles here on Earth

—*Lucille E. Hines*

Lacen Air

Snowflake so exquisite and true,
Six points of beauty make up your pure white gown -
Dusted with starlight as you dance to the ground.

Your beauty is so indescribable as I watch your lacen air.
The most precious jewel can't compare.
Oh! To know your mission beyond to adorn and to sooth.

All I can do is recognize the master's unmistakable hand.
As an artist no man can compare.
Oh! To be blessed!
To have Heavenly snowflakes adorning my hair.

—*Sammye Jo Harvey*

Brown Eyes

There is a little brown-eyed girl I know, who's laughter brings
   such delight.
But what you can't see, her little heart is full of fright.
She was her mama's one true love, the one who made her whole.
But mama's gone now high above, her life the devil stole.
Who's going to tell brown eyes she is special, show her the way?
Who will be here for brown eyes, her mama's gone away.
Is there anyone who sees, or anyone who cares,
does any one stop and wonder, when brown eyes drifts away and
   stares.
Brown eyes looks like any other child, an angel when she
sleeps; but the sunshine is gone from her smile,
safe in her heart Mama she keeps.
Still there is no one to hold brown eyes,
she sets alone and weeps!
So she sits.

—*Susan Lisenbee*

Dear Holy Dove, Thank You!

Long-dark night!
Suddenly, we heard "lovely music" in the air!
Listen;
Heavy rain stopped its cry!
Strong wind hold its anger!
Look;
Silver moon is smiling in saying "Hi"!
Beautiful dove is flying above the Mideast sky!

Dear Holy Dove, we thank you!
You having cure our heart pain!
You having lead our safety way!
You are the flower of love!
You are the fruit of care!

Please continue your Holy journey!
Flying above all the land:
middle, side, far and near!
Flying toward all direction:
North, south, west, and east!
Flying to all people; at each corner, in every where!
Please let us hear your "lovely music" again!!

—*Ruby Young*

The Hitchhiker

Standing with thumb out beside the road,
Suffering some sorrow of life untold.
What has happened that seems so bad,
Pretty young lady with eyes so sad?

The traffic zips by with hardly a glance,
beware of the girl in the black stretch pants.
Is this a young girl run away from her Dad?
Pretty young lady with eyes so sad.

We try to pretend your really not there.
It wouldn't be safe to show that we care,
by stopping for a girl in a red blouse clad.
Pretty young lady with eyes so sad.

What lies ahead on your journey so bold?
Are better times waiting for you to behold?
Your eyes reflect the pain that you've had.
Pretty young lady with eyes so sad.

Though we don't pick you up, we really do care.
Your suffering and sorrow we surely will share.
We didn't dare stop and we feel real bad.
Pretty young lady with eyes so sad.

—*H. Doc Doubleday*

The Moment Of Truth

Lies are always wrapped around the truth
  suffocating what is real
    breeding what is false
so that you can't trust it

  Convincing your heart
    that he will change
      scared that he won't
you stay wise to his game

  You turn your cheek
    like mother taught
    and learn to live
with different thoughts

  He preaches of honesty
    which he betrays
    you want to change
so you walk away

There are times he sends the roses
conflicting aromas of each different past
  both reminders of false proposes
  like clip stems that never last.
  —*Tarra Davis*

I Like

A walk on the beach .... an early morning walk to watch the
sunrise, to watch the sea gull's flight, to listen to the
ocean's roar and to feel one with the Infinite. A late evening
stroll to feel the night air blowing through my hair, the sand
between my toes, to gaze into the darkened night sky and see
the twinkle of every bright star and know I am not alone in the
universe. A symphony, one note higher than I've heard before.
A climb to a mountain top to take in all the beauty that
surrounds me and to know I am a part of this great creation.
Solitude, peace and quite, a time to be in touch, a time to put
things in perspective, a time to listen to my own inner voice.
I need .... a time to heal, so I can again enjoy a
candlelight dinner for two, a slow dance in which we move as
one, a hand to hold as we walk the water's edge, a helping
hand as we climb the mountain top, ... another's heart in
tune with mine!
  —*May D. McFalls*

With Me

I stood upon the stones where we once were
Surrounded by the great mass of water which
Swallow the rocks like grains of salt

The air was chilled from the lakes cool breeze
Which somewhat blanketed me with warmth

Darkness covered all in its path

Across the waters shined a brilliance of light
Which danced upon the currents.
There was a shadow within the waters and an
Echo in the air, a whisper so low it could
Hardly be heard

I spoke aloud, saying I do, I do love you
I know you were there I saw you in the waters
I felt you in the air, I heard you whisper
Something, you I love as well.
  —*Roger W. Grant*

A Mother's Love

A mother's love unfolds like the petals of a rose,
Surrounding, sheltering, enfolding
In the softness of her voice and eyes,
The body and the spirit
  of her child.
A mother's love erupts like the crash of thunder,
Stormy, frightening, intense
In the strength of her hands and heart,
  to guide and protect her child.
A mother's love encircles like the peaceful heavens,
Consoling, calming, easing
With the wisdom of her mind and years,
The anxieties and the misconceptions
  of her child.
A mother's love is YOU.
  —*Rosemary Lucky*

Brief Babe

  Soft as rose petals,
  Sweet as sugar candy;
  My baby lies upon my breast,
Nestled in the warmth and drowsiness of feeding.

  Tiny life that ebbed inside;
  Tickled, thrilled and touched my heart,
  (even before I knew who you were).

Oh, stay the course of time that rushes on so fast,
  so swift, so sure.

  Time will always surge ahead,
  and moments of great measure will slip away.

  Rest safe while you can,
  cleaved to my chest.
  Hold fast to our time and union.

Too soon will my baby be stolen away by the natural course of
  time.
  —*Lynn Marie Kleinfelter*

Untitled

Bitter the pill in my mouth
sweet coating worn away
to a nasty center.
Nothing to do but swallow fast-
avoid the harsh core in waiting too long.
The membrane that keeps pain away is a thin one.
It erodes.
It is delicate.
Preservation and redirection.
Swallow the pill before it tastes too bad...
and you spit it out on impulse
and end up taking two tomorrow.
  —*L. O. Bazini*

Miracles To Me

Things not understood yet liked by me,
such as planets floating in space which we barely see;
The days sun, warming, lighting our planet,
The nights moon which brilliantly lights the night;
Fire with flames showing the way
as the heat warms our souls;
Sleeping to rest as we get away from everyday life,
and the dreams in which we go to get away;
Birds flying on a spring day,
Winter with ice and blinding snow,
Summer with its flowers array,
Fall with pretty colors galore,
For these are miracles to me.
  —*Michael Cravener*

Sweet Sleep

Slow and calm on the island of my eyes
Sweet sleep on the waves of my thoughts
Enter in each of my veins
And take me so high
In the valley of colors
Where I see I touch I feel
Flowery dreams, beautiful songs, lovely drinks
Where I feel
Peace of my eyes
And rest of my hearts
Where all my worries, wrongs and doubts
All are lost
In a hole of dark
Until the sunrise
On the island of my eyes
At the end of each night

—*Syed Mohammad Hassan*

Another Gift

Tall serene, independent, yet reaching out
Symbolizing the yearning within.
Every limb, every branch. Every leaf,
Expressing and vibrating with life.
Resisting the onslaught of the elements
While embracing the nutrients and the melody
Of nature's harmony.
Sheltering friends, nurturing soil, shading
The weary traveler.
A gift, a gift to man and beast of field.
A gift of nature's love revealed.
A tree.

—*Peggy Rose*

I, The Earth

I, the earth am full of such beauty,
    take the time to care for me
    and you'll haven't a worry.
        Soil bears food
        Air supplies breath
        Sun generates heat
    Ozone provides protection
        Water endows life
My natural reserves are all that's needed
to a never ending supply of both Food and Beauty.
    Yet, in order for any of this to be
    and life to continue as you perceive,
        Don't forego - Stop and Bestow.
        Otherwise, if you forsake,
        You'll encounter a fatal mistake!

—*Robyn L. Caseria*

Proof Of Our Love

It's been hard the past two years, the hurt the sorrow, so many tears. Those long lonely nights in my bed, sometimes wishing I was dead. Thoughts of never seeing you again, hurt so much I hate the pain. Knowing you were happier with her, didn't make life any easier. Time has finally come to face the truth, you are gone for ever she's the proof. As days went by long and slow, it's time I give up and let you go. Just when I thought I was over you, I get a phone call out of the blue. When I heard your voice my heart jumped for joy, my body trembling out of control. You said you loved me and wanted me back, excitement sent goose bumps up my neck. I knew in my heart your love for me is true, I hope you know I never stop loving you. The days to come won't be so long, our love for each other is very strong. Counting the hours till I'm in your arms, remembering how your smile made me warm. Thank you so much for giving us another chance, it's proof of our love it only makes sense.

—*Pam Avoledo*

Ecology

Eyes can be blue, brown, gray, green, hazel and I've heard tell there are violet ones too.

They are set in so many kinds and colors of faces;
yet, all are capable of seeing trees, flowers, puppies, kittens, lofty mountains, babies, tall, short, fat, thin, black, brown, red, white, and yellow people.

Isn't it amazing that so many different kinds of eyes can see the same identical objects?......But,
sadly, through existing social erosions, magnitudes of beauty and enrichments are defiled, wasted, bereaved.
Is there some way we can preserve our human ecology?

—*Lucille A. Taylor*

Untitled

Time time ticking away toward my life
telling me tales that torment me daily

Sands silently seeping slowly away
sending sounds sailing in my direction

Fear from far fetched places arrive
fetching forgotten fears I once had

Running rampidly round and around
praying people place peace in my mind

For forgotten fears sailing slowly toward my ear
running 'round people and places to forget fear and find peace.

—*Michael J. Behr, II*

I Think I Can See

Softly I felt her heart beneath her breast
Tenderly it beat within my palm
Easily it comforted my sorrow
Let not this gentle thing be harmed

Sadly I release it....and wait
Eagerly to experience it once again

So sincerely it spoke words I've never felt before
Do these words frighten me...no...it's not fear
And it's not words per-se it spoke
But a sensitive touch back...to let me know
It's responding and it's there

I gazed into the night and ask God why
We see with our eyes, but...not with our heart
Something touch me as if he said
Sight comes not from the eyes, but from within

And those that truly see
Simply do
See with the heart.

—*Ron Bolton*

Heaven's Child

Fair of face, with a nimble mind,
    Surely he is Heaven's Child.
Gifted and agile with pen, pic, or brush.
    Stealthily, the envy of the God's encroached.
How can it be that one such as this
    Be allowed to continue amongst those who live?
Happy laughter, sweetest music, lofty goals,
    Too good for Earth, too good for mortals,
Open wide the spectral portals.
    Begin his homecoming, prepare his crown,
So that heaven-glow may filter down
    Upon the many he was destined to touch;
And upon those of us he loves so much,
    For truly he is Heaven's Child.

—*Mary A. Campo*

Through The Eyes Of A Child

Come shining through the eyes of a child is a love purer than
glittering gold
Not even the tallest mountain or the widest sea can become a
blocking blindfold

Peeping through the eyes of a child, a little love can be brightly
seen
Even in a house of ill will where the light of love seldom turns
green

Unsightly patterns of wild growing weeds or a very dangerous
specie of the wild
Still reflects a sampling of beauty when looking through the
eyes of a child

Little children don't feel, or relate too inner sensitivity
reflecting unjust hate
Their unadulterated emotions are much too busy caring to find
time for malice traits

Come glaring from the eyes of a child is the love that could
unite human kind
Once it finds a way to travel straight from childhood to the
full-grown mind

   —J. D. Horne

America's The Greatest Land

Thank God for America, the greatest land,
Thank God for America, where we can
walk hand and hand,
You can build a future, at your own pace,
And the U.S.A., is the greatest place,
It's a place where people, can walk proud,
And people voice's, are spoken out loud,
You can live fast, or you can take your time,
There's every opportunity here, to improve
your mind,
Thank God for America, the greatest land,
Where you can do anything, as best you can,
America is a giving place, of all man kind
and every race,
There's no place free, I'd rather be,
America's the place,
Thank God for America, it's the greatest land.
Where people care about the U.S.A., by
walking hand and hand.

   —Thomas Ciavirelli

Our Parents

Thanks for being there to wipe our tears.
Thanks for being there to comfort our fears.
You taught us about the world and the Lord,
And to trust in Him when times get hard.
As time went by we grew strong,
You told us to have faith, and we'll never be alone.
You said that if we get off track and stray away,
To remember we're not promised another day.
You told us to live right day by day,
There would be someone standing there to hear every word we say
Thank you for being our parent and friend,
Loving us even when we had sin.
During the times when we messed up,
We knew you were still there to love us,
During these times we saw what you did,
Now we know how to lead our kids.
We know you care, and you taught us well,
You taught us about Jesus now we know we can't fail.
We're blessed to have you both for our Mother and Father,
We want to say we love you, Frank and Betty Carter.

   —Sherry Ratcliff

Thanksgiving In America

Thanksgiving is... A day of fun and feast. A day called
"Thanksgiving" when prayers of thanks should never cease. Here
in a country of peace and love ... Let us all give thanks to
our God above. For food that's abundant and taken for granted
when others die starving where food can't be planted. And let
us be thankful that no war soils our land... for freedom to
worship under your guiding hand. For freedoms to question and
to voice our opinion on whatever we feel without fear of
repression. For the freedom to work in a place of our choice,
for America, we all should rejoice... It's a place where many
have been blessed for years with a steady income throughout
their careers. A place that's known for Pride and success,
and... a country whose cause is to provide us the best. Our
benefit package, the best in the land, Protects us and our
loved ones like his holy hand. We have much to be thankful,
not just for today, But for all of God's blessings coming our
way. Let's echo together this America prayer, our words of
Thanksgiving ... the reasons we care. We have much to be
thankful, on this we'll agree, for all that we have ... our
thanks go to Thee!

   —Leatha Teverbaugh

Twenty Minutes After Eleven

  When I become too tired and weary
    that,
 I think I can no longer reach out to help another.
  When I become trapped in my own desires
    that,
 I feel I can no longer respond to the needs of others.
 When I become guilty of the lack of my resolution
    then,
   I know it's time to step back,
    take time to reflect
    then let go, and
  permit the Universe to utilize me.

    For in all Light
    there is darkness
    and in all darkness
     there is hope.
  Fear can no longer entice me,
   for as I awaken each morning
    I place,
 the white Light of Christ around me.

   —Patricia Caccavale

Take Time

I know of nothing at Christmas time,
 That brings more joy, more feelings divine,
Than a far-away message from family or friends —
 The miles fade away, my spirit transcends
To the one who authored the words that I read,
 And my heart is moved by the warmth indeed.

Now some folks grumble at the price of a stamp,
 I purchase one gladly for it serves as a lamp
To brighten my day, to envision anew
 A loved one or friend I formerly knew;
While distance separates and keeps us apart,
 A little reminder goes straight to the heart.

No eloquent style is needed to cheer,
 Just a little time and a message that's clear.
Why a postage stamp has the wings of a dove!
 It travels through space to someone you love!
It can "make your day" - a friendship renew,
 With just a little love and a touch from you.

   —Ruby N. Reed

My Friend

There is a breed of special human being,
That crosses your path, rarely, in a lifetime,
Who seems to know, instinctively, what you are,
And accepts you, at face value, come what may.

Sensitive, he knows without your asking,
What pain you have, the insecurities you feel.
He gives understanding, assurance, even real support,
Unselfishly, without a single thought,
Regarding possible reward or personal risk.

Surprisingly, such relationships improve with time;
As wisdom comes with age, gratitude increases with each victory
And mutual dependence grows, with genuine respect,
Until, at last, you both can look each other in the eye.
Embrace, and really know the meaning of the words,
"My friend"

    —Thomas G. Baffes

Inside - Outside

There's a person inside of me
   that has a need to be free
With so many thoughts deep within
that just won't blow away like the wind....
I have wishes of things that could come true
And, fantasies of things I wish I could do,
Inside of me there's a person that needs to
sometimes cry, but chooses to hide...
Outside of me there's a person that has need to be a clown,
and bring joy to all who need a smile
   when she's in town...
Hey! does anyone out there know
that I'm really feeling down...
Outside of me I'm as happy as can be,
Inside of me!
       there's sill the need.

    —Mildred Torres

Caged

It's from the shipwrecks of life
That I am tired.
I want to be the one, in charge of the rudder,
For good or for evil,
And scratch destiny in the face!

    —Sergio R. Gonzalez

Our Mother (Dedicated in the memory of Mrs. Virginia Kelly)

Our Mother's love will never die,
   That is why it's hard to say goodbye.
Goodbye to a person you have grown to love,
   As her soul ascends to the home above.
It's not for us to wonder why,
   But we plainly saw the Heaven's cry.

The tears are falling from up high,
   It comforts us in knowing that God is nearby.
The children's hearts was heavy with sadness and tears
   In their eyes, 'cause it's hard to see your mother go.

The love you taught will always apply,
   Go on to be with the one you love.
We will see you again in our home above,
   As you soar through the skies,
Your presence will dry all the tears.

So dear Mother, as we say goodbye,
   We will see you one day soon.

    —Liz Swift

You Make It Happen

In my world a man may say
   That men are small and have no play
In world events or making times;
   But if one hears, he hears the chimes
For men of past and recent life
   Who changed the world through toil and strife
To make the world a better place
   For those who, in the future, face
The toughest problems of the will
   The ones that fall for changes — still
To changes of our precious past
   The ones that made the future last.

    —L. Frank Wear

Unbottled Kindness

Kindness is a virtue
That only few possess
If we put it in a bottle
It would suffocate us to death

But if we release it on our brothers
It will stand the test of time
It will give us what is needed
In order for us to love mankind.

Love is cautious and love is kind,
Love is forgiving and it can also be blind.
Love is patient and love is sublime,
But more importantly-
It can be given in our own sweet time.

    —Warren H. Phelps

Waiting Patiently

I searched for love in an empty oyster,
that, some one else has the pearl.
Dreams of being with you, has become my
shadow, since, I have known you.
How can I leave my shadow?
You are like a geode with beautiful crystals inside.
But, she can't see, you can't see.
Let me find the diamond in rough,
let me find you, and nourish you,
So, you're beauty could shine through.
Don't doubt my love,
my love for you is like a tamed bird in open air.
She sees freedom but she doesn't want to fly away, then,
then, you ask me if I wait for you?
Does a star waits for the night?
Does a star pray for the clouds to go away?
Does she waits so patiently for the clear skies
so, she could shine
you ask me if I wait for you? Wait for you patiently.

    —Shari Moraffah

On Flying Kites

Ingenious design for rigging kites
That they should fly together from two lines,
Adjoined yet never touching, synchronized.
A jonquil yellow and a royal blue.
Upon the hill she stood and held one line.
He pulled the cord that made the kits ascend.
A gust would spin them circling through the air
Until a higher gale should take control.
And then aloft they soared to stretch the twine
That held them anchored - higher not to go.
She leaned to him and let him hold both lines.
They stood together closer than the kites.
A perfect blend of color they became;
His yellow cap - her jacket royal blue.

    —Nancy L. VanDenburgh

Untitled

As the days creep away so does my mind, slowly moving toward that star in the sky the world will end and our souls will be free. Through galaxies we roam, never being able to call anything home. As our minds long for our once abused bodies, cursing every thought I cry, wondering why did that world have to die? To give up our havens so safe forgotten amongst the greed. Creatures calling themselves humans wonder for days trying to get out of the maze they call reality. Straining to hear the church bell ring clear through the screams of those so dear. Smog getting thicker than the fog behind your eyes. The sun is our punishment, God has sent it to fry, the evil boils over and congratulations arise. For those who survived, have sold their souls, fearing the results of being froze from lack of love and meaningful things. Never hearing again the sound, when the church bell rings.

—*Trish Barrow*

Downfall

Happiness shines when there are two.
That surely happens with me and you.
Men and women were created for the same.
What should come is fortune and fame.

When apart the body stretches.
All that brings is plenty of messes.
Strength can keep them in hand,
As though still in high demand.

When life takes its toll,
One may fall out of the bowl.
Unfair it seems when a heart is smashed.
Even if we didn't mean to throw out the trash.

People may guess what will come.
Who really knows when all is said and done.
Sadness may come is what was found.
Just like a puppy being brought to the pound.

—*Russ Brown*

Down Below

Walking slowly soaking up the heat
    that surrounds my body
feeling the glistening sweat run down
    my hot rosy cheeks.
I search desperately for one drop of
    cool refreshing water.
Knowing my search will last forever.
    The worn prints
in the burning sand are those of my own
    blistering feet
that will become raw meatless bone before
    my job is done.
Dreams of heaven dance in my head washing
    out the evil that
put me in this devilish place.

—*Susan Mitchell*

How Magical

Sometimes I wish I could own all animals,
    so I would never be alone.
    I would cuddle with all of them.
    I would watch the birds and eagles.
        How magical!
    The birds fly high, high in the sky.
The lions would awaken me and see the beautiful
        stars.
    Oh, the zebras running in grace!
    How I wish to ride them.

—*Sean Richey*

Why Should It Be?

Why is it, in this world of ours
    That turmoil reigns supreme
And men of good and honest faith
    Are tested to extreme

With countries locked in ardent fight
    The reasons oft' obscure
And children from the cradle grow
    Their future insecure

And stones are thrown and clubs are raised
    In hands confused with hate
While leaders talk incessantly
    'bout actions they berate

But as they converse constantly
    The carnage stays intact
And more do die upon the streets
    A simple horrid fact

Where do we stop this crazy act
    Of animosity
And put within God's complex plan
    Sense not stupidity

—*Ronald W. Mealing*

The Little Boy

It's hard to say in these few words, so you will understand,
that very special feeling, when the little boy takes my hand.
With unsaid words he talks to me, as I hold him near,
a language God and grampaws, are the only ones can hear.

Nothing can be better, a million words can't say,
the joy a grampaw feels, when the little boy comes to stay.
Usually for a short time, just an hour or so,
time flies by so fast, and then he has to go.

The little boy is leaving, two times he told me by,
don't let anyone see, the tear that's in your eye.
Now I hear no laughter, or see no bouncing ball.
his toy's look so lonely, stacked there against the wall.

Silence is not golden, that's what grampaws feel,
Little boy's toys, never ever should be still.
His cars and trucks have quit running, stillness over all his
things, old rocky horse just sits there, on its silver springs.

They seem to know what I am thinking, they look at me as if to
say, were just resting up a bit, that boy sure does like to
play. Don't put us in the closet, or take the train off the
track, because before you know it, that little boy will be back

—*Max Watkins*

To Karen - One Year Old

Who would have thought, a year ago,
That your father I would stand by your crib
Just watching you sleep.
The soft light casting shadows of your long lashes
On to your rosy cheeks.
Blond hair curling at your neck,
Plump little arms, either flung wide,
Or clutching a soft toy.

Sometimes you smile, as if in the midst of a happy dream.
You sleep, dear first born, as only a baby can,
With all the peace and innocence of your age.
The little worries and frustrations of the day
Are all forgotten - in your sleep.

And in the morning, when you wake,
Your smile and outstretched arms
Greet us and melt our hearts.
Making the start of another day
A bright, new experience for us all.

—*Mary Westoby*

Fall To Spring

Autumn is a beautiful time of year -
The air seems to carry a sense of good cheer.
If feels so fresh and crisp and great -
The greens look so pretty through
    the swinging gate.
But soon the flowers will fade away
They won't be back 'til one Spring day.
The snow will fall and cover all
Sometimes it mounts way too tall.
It's hard months ahead so get out your sled
Might as well have some fun -
It's not so bad when there's the sun
But when it's cold, so very cold, you'd
    rather be inside.
There nothing like a nice warm house
    to cuddle in and hide.
When it's all over we'll have the Spring.
We'll see the wonders of everything —
Waking up and coming alive
Watching our gardens grow and thrive.

—*Patricia L. McPherson*

Long Ago

When I was young, the wind blew free.
The air was as clean as it could be.
Smog was a dirty four letter word,
That no one had ever heard.
It was safe to walk at night,
No bad guys around to cause you fright.
There was only one cop in town;
But who needs cops, when there are no crooks around,
He could usually be found
In the little show in my hometown.
This may surprise a few, but you see,
There was nothing else for him to do.
Most people did not lock their door, day or night,
To not trust people, "just wasn't right,"
When dope was mentioned, it produced a grin,
It meant you were not too bright,
Not hooked within.
I have pleasant memories of days so dear,
Every time I read about the latest car-jacking or
drive by shooting here.

—*H. P. McWilliams*

Thanksgiving

The Turkey is in the oven
The aroma fills the air
Pumpkin pies are cooling on the rack
There's excitement everywhere.

The family is arriving
Dressed warmly for the day
Grandma's house is nice and warm
It has always been that way.

We used to go to grandma's house
And enjoy the holiday treat
Now we are the grandma
And now at our house we meet.

Mashed potatoes, mince pies, giblet gravy
Stacked high upon the platters
Sliced turkey and candied yams
And everything that matters.

The food is good, we stuff ourselves
Retire to the parlor so cozy
We're all together once again
And everything is rosy.

—*Rex H. Marks*

Blood Stained Battlefields

A nation divided by civil war,
The battlefield's pungent smell of death.
Pain frozen on a poor man's face,
Breathing his last aching breath.
One grim President mournfully stands,
Then delivers his famous address.
The crowd stands in awesome silence,
His words on their minds impress.
Their sorrowful, solemn-faced President,
Standing tall and strong,
Studies the blood stained battlefield,
Knowing these memories will last long.
The crowd still stands in utter silence,
His words run through each head.
Every heart painfully mourning,
Their never forgotten dead.
A silent whisper runs through the crowd,
Forever loud, never pausing to slow,
My forefathers died for your freedom,
"Four score and seven years ago…"

—*Melissa Schlea*

The Wonder Of It All

Each glorious day brings forth to me,
The beauty of creations and landscapes to see.
The awesome wonder of it all.
Will have a lasting impression
large and small.
If a tribulation has forbidden
me to see or say,
I will cherish the memories
of precious yesterdays.

—*Ruth Champion Morris*

The Seasons Circle

Crocus and buttercups are the first signs of Spring
The beauty of these flowers make your heart want to sing.
    Yellows, purples, blues, and reds
Are brilliantly displayed in their flower beds.
    When we see these flowers, we think of the sun,
Of playing outside, having lots of fun.
    Spring won't last very long, you know,
The sun will get hotter and the grass will grow,
    Then it'll be time to go out and mow,
To work in the garden, to chop and to hoe.
    When harvest-time is over and Summer's gone by,
The trees will show their leaves, high up in the sky.
    Yellow, orange, red and brown,
The leaves fall off and flutter to the ground.
    Now we know Autumn's over and Winter's near
The snow and cold days will soon be here.
    The snow flakes seem to dance all around
As they fall from the sky and land on the ground.
    Then the snow will melt as the days warm up,
And pushing through the ground if that little buttercup.

—*Tommie S. Birge*

Nighttime

    The whistling wind whispers to the night sky.
The bending breeze tugs at the hair of the solitary man,
        who gazes upon the vast firmament -
        the tiny specks of light in the far distance,
            galaxies away,
        but seemingly within reach of human hand.
The lonely figure follows the flight of a falling star,
        the flashing brilliance is momentary -
    The imaginary string holding it in place snaps
            the star disappears.
    The night continues, with the wind whispering
            softly to the night sky.

—*Timothy Crouse*

700

Likeness

God open my eyes that I may see
The beauty of Your love as it surrounds me

God open my ears that I may hear
Your gentle voice as you linger near

God open my mind that I might know
Your wisdom and your will where I shall go

God give me strength that I may stand
Tall unafraid in an evil land

God give me a gentle heart that I might care
For my neighbor who labors there

God hold my hand when I'm unsure
Cleanse my life and make it pure

Forevermore let me be
A "Likeness" of Thee!

Amen

—*Sandra Joyce Brown*

Tears Of Yesterday

I looked beyond the tears of yesterday.
The blood, the joys, sacrifices of today.
I wonder if he feels the same way?

Heard the cries of unborn still
the willows crying in the hills
the laughter gone from children mouths
the grasshopper doesn't jump anymore

The tears of yesterday not enough to dim
the hope of peace so far away
mothers, fathers, daughters no longer
exist or could ever cry the tears of yesterday

Love, love where are your sounds? So distant,
so longing for the tears of yesterday
I wonder if he feels the same way?

They say give peace a chance
I say no to the tears of yesterday.
The hope aspires to chagrin of other men today

I wonder if they all feel that way
about the tears of yesterday.
I wonder if he feels that way?

—*Mahlon Reynolds*

The Lot

Jagged soft green leaves of a dandelion nestle,
The blossom, golden yellow, recreates the sun.
The fuzzy wishing flower stands erect and straight,
Its strands, brown tipped and white,
Separate and fly,
To spread their fertile seeds.

Jagged glass, rusty cans in mounds surround it,
Newspaper, old and yellow, spews from black plastic.
The fuzzy stuffing creeps from a legless seat,
Its strands, grey and ragged,
Tangle and cling,
To spread a grimy veil.

—*Marilyn Hametz*

On The Forest Floor

Crimson crisp with a tinge of orange the maple leaves play in
    the breeze.
The forest floor is laid ready for its new layer of blanketed
    color.
The pine trees send out their sweet tart aroma as they, one by
    one let go of their cones to lace the roots of their fir.
The aspen, yellow and waving send forth spurts of golden leaves
    that make a tapestry of patterns on the forest floor.
Old majestic oaks turn brown and join the gallery of hues
    clustered deep within the land.
Autumn is mother natures royal robe before she sleeps in white.
    Her trees stand like sentinels, glorious and proud.
As the breezes caress the barren branches so soon laced with
    iced pinafores and skirts the forest floor.
Frost outlines each leaf as the first snowfall touches each
    path and knoll.
For soon there will be a twinkling of diamond snow abound to
    cover the hues of autumn and good-bye to a year well
    seasoned.
    T'was autumn on the forest floor.

Tribute to a precious family, relatives and friends,
plus growing up in Northern Michigan, Lower Peninsula.
God Bless you all! Amen!

—*Lu Ann Axelson*

As The Flowers Bloom

Now that the seeds are planted, can we start to grow?
The bud has to now open, and feel the first wind blow
As the cold breeze brings out life, in such a lonely world
You know the time is right, to talk to that little girl
Yes the one inside you, that you know so well
The one you kept picking up, every time she fell
Just like the flower, that has just started to bloom
You have now grown up, and feel it's much to soon
But as that summer wind, starts bringing back the past
Forever you can feel young, and together it will last
So each day as the garden grows, stronger with each rain
You can now feel peace again, for there's finally no more pain
Mistakes made in the past, are lessons you learned from
There are no more tear drops, you realize life is just to fun
Every time you feel as though, your gonna slip and fall
You remember the garden seeds, and how they'd stand so tall
And when you look into the mirror, and see that little girl
You realize she hasn't gone, she's left you with the world!

—*Lori-Jean Ferrante*

You Are Mine

Shh! Be quiet, know that I am me.
The builder, the breaker
Souls created and set free.

Be still! And listen to the beating of your heart
To the miracle that is you,
To the perfect work of art.

Keep silent. Close your eyes and in darkness stand,
Alone and uncertain,
Until I reach out my hand.

You're feeling alone and worthless and small,
And in darkest despair
See no point in it all.

But child you are precious!
You're my love carved in flesh.
You are beauty and goodness,
My child you are blessed!

—*Stephanie Del Regno*

In My Home Town

In my home town,
the children roamed the streets,
begging for food because they had none to eat.
In my home town,
the little old ladies rummaged through the dumps,
searching for mateless shoes to cover their feet.
In my home town,
no one owned a car. There was no need for one.
When everyone knew, you wouldn't get very far.
In my home town,
most of the children never knew their father.
He left as soon as the woman got pregnant,
and went on welfare, so why bother?
In my home town,
we were happy to live on simple means, said our prayers every
night and thanked our God for corn bread and green beans,
In my home town,
where I dreamed of dreams that were never meant to be,
and cried alone so that no one could see, abounds, a truth
very clear to me, I am apart of my home town, and my home town
dwells within the corners of my childhood memories.

—*Mitzi C. Townsend*

City Of Angels

I tried to leave, but I can't say good-bye;
The City of Angels has me hypnotized.
City of Angels, my heart beat of sound-
The strength is in numbers - just look around.

The memories to cherish, the stories to tell
Of Hollywood hopes could fill a wishing well.
The stars on the walk way never go away,
And the Hollywood sign is here to stay.

I tried to leave but I can't say good-bye,
O' A'S got me hypnotized -
I remember the magic on Angels flight.
Little Tokyo, China Town at night.

Olvera Street, Exposition Park,
The Sunset Strip after dark.
If you want to see why I get so high -
Just like a Bonaveture ride to the top.

Oh City of Angels you light up the sky-
Los Angeles - I'll never say good-bye!

—*Paul Carmello*

One Brief Journey

When first we met we knew that we were meant to be.
The costs were high and maybe too severe.
The need was met, the pattern set,
A new beginning yet.

Intertwining tears and fears joined our years
And after many stops and starts
We always picked up where we last left off.
Our way through life was much too brief
Even though much of it held grief.

We missed the early blossomings of youth
And strove to sift and sort our tangled vines with trust and truth
When painful trials intruded and our elusive dreams with drew.

Uncertainties loomed heavily and they were met without regret,
Our finest hours but a prelude to expire
With only quiet valor kept
To help erase the sorrows and the tears

—*Mary Phillips*

The Hidden Factor

Nothing scares me more than the treachery of man.
The dark of the night with its most
uncertain consequences does not frighten me.
The night with its eerie and uncontestably
brilliant sounds does not frighten me.
It is almost welcome in its utter stillness
and patterned plight.
It is calming in a way that cannot be
understood by experiencing only the
hustle and hustle of the ever-moving
unfeeling day.
I am not frightened by the night for to
me it is an old friend.
It comforts me in my time of question
and uncertainty.
I am able to commune with nature
and with out most beloved creator.
Night time is a melodrama of re-examining
and replenishing of the mind and soul
of the most inner plateaus of my being.

—*Yvonne G. Engel Davis*

An Easter Dream

Tread lightly, the savior sleeps;
The dawn will soon be breaking.
The torturous hours are gone.
No more, the cries and the weeping.
It's silent. The cross stands alone.
Calvary's hill is dark.
Soon, the light of day will cast an even pleasant tone
Over the spot where yesterday, Christ hung alone.

Ah, there's a faint light on the hill,
Dawn breaks, let us hurry on
To kneel outside the tomb,
And pray that Christ knows that we have come.

What have we here? The stone is rolled away.
Where have they taken Him, who died but yesterday?
Hear!!! The angel of the Lord speaks low,
"He is risen and is gone."
The day breaks in all its glory,
The sun shines on Calvary's hill.
The world rejoices! It lives again.
Christ lives, He's with us still.

—*Shirley M. McQuade*

The Sky

Look at all the wonders God has created for us.
The dawn with its dark to light effect.
White clouds with dark gray bottoms.
Splashes of orange from the up coming sun.
Turning the clouds into islands, the sky into a sea.
Or, a clear blue day with its white fluffy clouds.
So perfectly placed it seems as if God made them just
    so the angels would have somewhere to sleep.

The dusk with its light to dark effect.
Different shades of orange, red and purple.
Colors streaking across the sky, blending together,
    changing, becoming one.
Turning the sky into one giant kaleidoscope.
As the sun goes down and the moon comes up.

Midnight the darkest of night with a full, half or quarter moon
lighting the way. An unlimited amount of stars on a velvet
midnight sky. Or, out of the darkness flashes of lighting.
Thunder so frightening it sounds as if God himself is ripping
the sky apart. There are no visible stars on this night only
majestic beauty. Thank God for it all.

—*Phyllis Wilmore*

Now, Not Later!

The day grows cold and old with no light
The day is gone from what we knew
To remember a time when all was bright
Cheering green rolling through moist dew

The rains have opened the earth apart
Exchanging fluids to replenish the new
The blood of the living is now dead at heart
Changes have ceased for seasons, in lieu

The brown leaves never again to fall
The rivers flow in whatever direction they can
Birds have ceased to wake a morning call
Animals now roam to die where they land

People could have helped all of this life
If only they would have cared to have known
Waiting and wondering digs deep to a knife
The last seeds of the flowers never to be sewn

I wake to the call of the wild wind's cries
I look around and know that I have dreamt
The birds, the trees, the life not yet dies
I know now that these visions, they were sent

—*Nancy Lawson*

My Day Self Preservation

Today is the day that happens to be
The day that I intend to see to it
That I do something for me
Not for you, not for them,
Not for my family, acquaintance, or friend,
Just for me, just for myself.
I awoke this morning the day was new,
I thought of some others, but then I knew
This day was mine, God gave it to me,
And I intend to be free to love, to give,
With all of my heart and mind to live,
And to be exactly what God meant me to be,
Not for you, for me.

—*Thelma Wilson Matthews*

Autumn

The stage is set for autumn's show,
   The days are cool and mellow.
      Fall is nature's softening time,
         Turning trees to gold and yellow.

With brilliant hues of red and amber,
   Are browns and shades of heather.
      Gracing the hardwoods and sturdy oaks,
         Embracing the autumn weather.

The awesome sight of all the colors,
   Painted for us to behold.
      Standing against a brilliant sky,
         Are trees of shining gold.

And then one day the trees respond,
   To natures mysterious call,
      Shedding their dying foliage,
         The leaves begin to fall.

When last the leaves have all come down,
   And the branches are clean and clear.
      Autumn lies resting upon the ground,
         To be born again next year.

—*Nelson O. Ottenhausen*

A Lonely Man

It's a lonely life, this life I have
The days come and go like the wind
And the highways that life lays before me are lone and hard
But I walk them. All of them alone. All alone.
I've got everything a man could want
All the things needed to make him great
I only wish I had someone to share it with
But there's no one, just me and no one else.
Some nights I wake and wish for someone to hold
Just to hold tight in my arms and share my world and its dreams
Darkness prevails
Only it and its cold, empty feelings that it brings.
When I leave this world, I should like to think someone will be
   here
Mourning for my lost soul
But there shall be no one
Only the feeling of loneliness that shall be left behind to haunt
   another.
It's a lonely life, this life I have
The days come and go like the wind
And the highways that life lays before me are long and hard
But I walk them. All of them alone. All alone.

—*Monty Fox*

The Mortal's Tale

Battered dreams and broken wings and visions of unholy things,
The dragon, he wakes, and to me brings a crystal ball and shiny
   things.

Into this ball I do gaze with memories of the golden days,
spirits screaming, screaming shouts of praise But into this
   ball I still do gaze.

The ball, it glows, and shines so bright into the room a fiery light,
The shiny things, they do take flight and disappear into the night.

I sit and stare and gaze and wonder, for with this ball I
should make no blunder. I touch the ball...it cracks!

With magic spells and whispered sin, the dragon, he does wake
again. He sees the ball and screams in pain, then disappears
   and leaves a stain.

Of red blood, all on the floor; there was a knock upon the
door. Into my presence, I do see, a sorcerer who comes to warn
me. Of deadly spells and conjured things; the sorcerer now has
broken dreams. I've done wrong, an immortal thing, to kill the
dragon and break his wings.

—*S. D. Wisniewski*

Almost 16

I can't wait till I'm 16
the dream is almost here
The saying goes sweet 16
and never been kissed
I wander what I've missed!

It's hard to be a teenager
there are so many rules
someone's always yelling
pull in your stomach and stand up straight
I feel just like a fool.

When I'm 16 I plan to be a lady
Then I'll stand up straight dressed in lace
And hope to attract the fellows maybe!
I'll dance all night and never slow my pace.
Like Cinderella, my dream will start.
I'll begin to date, but I can't stay out too late.

—*Winona M. Adams*

Something To Keep You Warm On A Cold Winter Night

It's warm, warm like a pair of pajamas you've just taken out of the dryer

It's strong, like arms of a body builder, hard yet smooth like a baby's bottom

It's irreplaceable, like those old pair of jeans that fit so right, but have more holes in it then a golf course

Its touch is soothing, and relaxing, like a hot bubble bath, where the steam slowly rises from the water. And with every burst of bubbles to soothe and caress those aching parts, puts me in a comatose sleep

As I sleep, I begin to dream of a world, a world without the stain of blood on the streets or empty valves from the drug users who could not wait to inhale death into their bodies, or the scream of a victim's voice in the middle of the night

If you are lucky, you will have this to keep you warm on a cold winter night

Someone who is very near to my heart like the blood that runs through my body that keeps my heart beating the sounds of love

—*Mirlene Cadichon*

The Cowboy

The rodeo had ended mere hours before
The dusk was now settling in
Reclaiming, it seems, an arena where dreams
Were once consumed by the din

There were victors, of course, sometimes man, sometimes horse
Yet I couldn't help but recall
That cowboy astride, the most fearsome ride
Aware he was destined to fall

He was thrown from his seat, but quickly rose to his feet
As if he, not the stallion, prevailed
With raised head he strode, his spirit unbowed
Not the visage of someone who failed

My son, you remember that cowboy
And don't ever be afraid to compete
It's the dreamers who dare, to try, who may stare
Square into the eyes of defeat

And with pride swelled chest, that you've done your best
Though bruised, perhaps eye moist with tear
You then will find out, again never to doubt
There is nothing to fear, except fear!

—*W. Gregory Doolin*

God's Honest Truth

Hypocrisy or democracy...
    The evangelists have raved.
Christ is the way, the truth, and the life.
    Will you be saved?
If you do not believe in truth.
    You cannot believe in Christ.
In this pleasure seeking world.
    Have you been enticed?
The time has come to embrace the truth.
    Or have we fallen still.
The question is... will you be saved?
    It's a matter of free will.

—*Mark Andrew Holland*

Bilk

This child of light.
The fear of the night.
Given the right,
to cause his fight.

The conscious illumination,
to his enlightened soul.
An immaculate elucidation,
to live to strive.

A joyous day, a pitiable night,
his newfound forgotten love to fear.
One needs the might and right to bring the light,
the situated ethic on his shelf.

—*Michael Russell*

My Little Guardian Angel

Five days after my second birthday, my baby brother was born.
The first boy in the family, everybody was so happy.
Though I was a baby then too, I received a message that day.
God told me that Gerry, Jr.,
known as "Little Gerry", was very special.
He was my parents little boy.
He was my little brother.
I had to look out for him as he got older.
I had to keep an eye on him.
Just about two months after that day,
I found out just how special "Little Gerry" was -
when God took him away from me.
I know in my heart that I'll always love my little brother
that I never knew.
But I also know that he was so special that God chose him
for a reason-he was to come to heaven,
and to look down at us and keep an eye on us.
Til this day - I still listen to
"My Little Guardian Angel".

—*Nancy Miller*

Remembering Eddie

I come two places to see his face.
The first one is his resting place
More quiet than his memory, yet
Suitable for the cause.

The hills roll green and the trees guard
So his youth may be protected.
And I, the older for the ware,
Smile at the peace by visiting there.
But only once a year.

The other place is more our home.
The playing fields, we used to roam,
And measure time in Seasons.
Where strife and trouble stayed away
And it was always Saturday.
Youth served as it must be.

Life and Death, two places I must be
The first a waltz of circumstance,
The later reality.

—*J. T. Smith*

Well Preserved

One hundred years old, and more alone,
than Lewis Carroll's dead dog's bone,
his thirst finally quenched, the martyr egghead,
like Humpty Dumpty, and the life that he lead,
had spent all the money, that made his nose runny,
and got his toe tagged much too soon the poor rummy.

—*Michael Krause*

Wish For Good-Bye

If I had three wishes
  the first would be
    to hold you in my arms so tenderly.
To give you the love
  my heart holds dear,
    to ask you once more, "come close, without fear".

The second, I think,
  would have to be this,
    hold me so gentle, say goodnight with your kiss.
Hold me 'til slumber
  leaves open the door,
    for me to pass on, 'til my breath is no more.

Finally the third,
  may I wish it for you.
    erase all memory of me through and through.
You've set me free,
  don't be angry or sad.
    my soul is at peace now, we must all be glad.

        —*Pamela Clark*

Joy

Powerful; symbolic of strength and freedom, Soaring High
The forest over which I pass will have another vantage point
Another story to tell

Choice of: words sounds
Reality being of the voices creation
And your interpretation

Father mother sister brother sharing secret sins
Never the same flavor of thought or deed?
Reality is in
The artist's brush
  words are her paint, the paper her easel
  the world is her instrument, the voice her trumpet

A superealist attempting to impart to you from the vantage
point, of wherever chosen the mysteries of life and death

The preachers cross heavy upon his shoulders
held the weight of salvation
or did it?

Sometimes when I come to you it is through experience and
incident other times I let a stranger speak

I am the story. You hear my voice

        —*Lyn Dera*

Rapture

  She was dragged by the hair, body banging against
the grass. Her legs cracking and snapping sharp twigs,
skidding along scattered branches as if a wild animal,
kicking in the burning beams of moonlight like ducks
screeching to flashing claws in an outpour of blood.

  A decrescendo spread over the cemetery when shrieks
grew fainter...fainter...fainter. The tomb's crusty,
cold cement moaned shut. The pounding had resumed but,
who would hear? Who could care less?

  After all, it was night, and the slug, her slug, was
busy ravaging the delicate, crimson roses.

  Now, oxygen was scarce and the brain began to boil
from movement. She wondered if it was even really worth
all this, trying to go back to food hungry roaches and
rat droppings forever piling. In that silence, one last
scream - "Thou hath come, my Saviours!"
The gods replied, "Jesus, get the jewels, let's go!"

        —*Pauline*

The Wonders Of Nature

The birds are singing a lovely song,
  The grass is wet with dew;
  The sun is rising in the east,
    The day begins anew.
The flowers start to open up,
  Their colors they're proud to show;
  The air is perfumed,
    as they bow to the breeze,
And the bees stop to say, "Hello",
  Have you ever looked at
    the wonders of nature,
As you walked in the morn of the day?
The breath-taking beauty that you will see,
  Makes you want to stop and pray.
"Thank you, Lord, for this glorious sight,
  Thanks for the birds and the bees.
Thank you, Lord, for the flowers' perfume
And thanks, for the grass and the trees!"

        —*Myldred Slesinski*

Friendship Re-claimed

With eyes wide open I fail to see,
  The greatest things in front of me.
My friends are the people around me daily.
  I take most for granted so carelessly.
Friendship is that marvelous act.
  I forget to preserve nearest my heart.
Considering past experience with new,
  I still regret a thing or two.
Practice makes perfect is what they say,
  And patience helps in a loving way.
Friends are wonderful every moment in time,
  for so that reason I reclaim you mine!

        —*Sylvia Manriquez*

High Flight

The world's more lovely, I have found, when viewed from high
  above the ground.
Life's problems seem so far away when aircraft wings will let me
  stray
above the busy city throngs, to where my airborne heart belongs.

Why does high flight bring such a thrill? After years of flight
  my heart is still
drawn to the sky for joy, for strength; I go up where my soul can
  think.

All pilots know the magic way a flight can change a dismal day
and make it sparkle, make it shine, like a gem of quality so fine.

If you ask a pilot why he goes up where the clouds lie rows on
  rows,
his eyes will sparkle, his heart will dance; he'll try to tell you
  of romance.
He'll try to tell you of the thrill — but words will falter, then
  be still.
He'll shake his head and realize that you must see it through your
  own eyes.

The world's more lovely I have found when viewed from high
  above the ground.
But you must taste your own high flight. I cannot tell you why
  it's so right
for me to fly on silver wings, and feel the magic high flight brings.

        —*Theran Balmain*

Untitled

The farther away you've gone from the shore,
The harder you've had to swim

The currents are rough on the rivers you've crossed,
In waters that run murky and dim.

Venturing too far
Falling into the rocks,
Plotting a course as uncertain as you are.

As your rivers run to the oceans, you will run from me,
With a greater distance between us, I wish you a calmer sea.
When the tide pulls you out and the waves drag you under,
Through the storm, the torrent and thunder,

Look for my beam on the horizon, like a lighthouse on the shore
A compass to safely guide you, back from the ocean's roar.

—*Margie Garcia-Burnell*

The Romeo Heart

I believe in the Romeo heart
The heart that pumps such jealous blood
Blood more green than an emerald forest
A forest so thick no woodsman can chart

This face of grace with leaves of hair
Hair of browns and reds and golds
Gold hands in a mind of urning vision
A vision faint in a cavernous lair

Can you see her skin of olive hue
A hue which smells of Adriatic sand
Sands in the dreaded hour glass
Of time long past now emotions blue

As human I fell but once in love
Love achieved through a broken guard
The guard of societies sightless standards
Standards that blacken the whitest dove

My own green hands did break the knot
The knot which lured me to such a torturous hell
A hell of unconditional love and affection
Affection now spent on a vacuous lot

—*Russell Hellstern*

Stars On Heaven

The glow of stars twinkle through heaven that shines on earth.
The heaven of beautiful white stars that glows through outer space.
The heaven of stars are created by God in the beautiful Universes.
The shooting stars flies through heaven while the earth glows
    with star light.
The Universe of beautiful white stars that twinkle with the
    glow of heaven.
The sun shines on the beautiful white stars that glows through
the great Universe of heaven.
The beautiful white stars glow with the moon light of heaven to
earth.
The Universe of planets glow with the stars of heaven.
The milky way is a group of stars that glows in heaven.

—*Scott H. Swing*

Summer Love

The soft summer breeze kissed my cheeks
The hot summer sun made me weak.
As I lay on the warm white sand.
He sat up and took my hand.
My heart is pounding in my chest.
As I think of the one I love best.
A romantic shadow came from above.
The warm summer air was filled with love.

—*Lisa Viniglia, Errin Shoop,*

--*Jessica Morgan, Tammy Scherer*

A Smile, A Simple Smile

A smile, a simple smile
    The impish grin of a three year old
Expression of contentment
    The lined face of one growing old
Seal of satisfaction
    Parents at a college graduation
Joy of approval
    A delivered mother's salutation
Mark of testimony
    Long night's vigil at death's door is over
Exclamation of success
    Little leaguer's first home run
Renunciation of yesterday
    Wayward child returning home at last
Medal of honor
    True success in a final breath

—*Michael E. Crawford*

Poem

"Because it is there!"
The intrepid adventurer seeks out the highest mountain top
The dazzling pinnacle from which his undisputed boast my arise.
"I have conquered!"

The "chosen" tread softly on the holy ascent
The pinnacle from which a clear view of the valley is achieved
To survey the treacherous landscape which must be traveled
"Because He is there"
And having set his face toward that unknown territory
Speaks the calm words of assurance
"I have been conquered."

—*Robert Morley*

False Love

As I sit here and recollect on thee
the joyful memories of you shine through
You unlocked my heart with your special key
and showed me a love that was o so true
The times we shared were beyond compare
and if they got rough our ties never broke
You were there for me when I needed care
and taught me how I could believe and hope
A genuine man who had time for all,
you lent a helping hand with pleasure
But as the days grew old you formed a wall
and our unforgettable love was severed
Now in misery I sit here and sigh
thinking of how I can pass the time by

—*Margaret Lepore*

Reverie

Today....
The kind of March day one thinks about
    all winter through
A day when the winds stir across the tree tops
    and kites soar high above the fields.
Blue skies without a cloud, and I hope
    that all the kites stay high and
ride their glory through the blue.
Some do not, and the remains hand bedraggled
    on wires man made and trees God made high.
Shredded by the wind and rain, with strings
    limply snarled into branches.
Later the birds will welcome these
    bits and pieces of lost flown glories
as they begin their venture toward nesting.
And all has not been lost nor committed to the winds of
    futility

—*Polly Lambert*

Jesus Is The Light On The Cross

The morning star is He,
The light of the world we see-
Shining out like the sun his love;
More precious than stars above.

Twas in this light of love he saw
As he pressed onward toward calvary,
While throngs of grieving women took pity.

With great humility and pain he bore
His suffering wounds on a wooden cross.
Alas! Beside him pined
His mother's look of loss.

For truly it is the son we see
When we think of the cross and Jesus—
How sinners are forgiven and he loves us.

Oh! Not alone the stars at dawning
Do harmonize hymns to the risen King;
Tis every loving heart unto him we do bring.

    —Marie Rodriguez

The Little Girl Inside

I looked in the mirror and saw what I didn't like:
The little girl that could never find
    approval in her mother's eyes.
This is how it was when she cried:
A broken water glass or spilt milk,
This is what brought a slap on the face
    from the mother she feared.
Low self-esteem with a constant wish for death.
This is the life the little girl led.
Never knowing what mommy's mood
    would be...loving or angry.
This created emotional instability.
Always wishing that mommy would die
So that she could have a peaceful life.
This and more was how it was when she cried.
I looked in the mirror and saw what I didn't like...
The little girl that lives in my heart and mind.

    —Maribel Santana-Shlichtman

A Child's Gift

As you grow and live and learn, soon your wonder it will earn.
The living woods, the fields and streams,
all enwrapped in nature's scheme.
The birds and deer and trees and man,
each is part of God's great plan.
Taste this sweetness, see and feel,
hear the creatures' gentle peal.
Embrace this bounty with special savor,
and keep it always in your favor.
When you are sad and if there's trouble,
seek to hear the brook's soft bubble.
The river's long and cool deep run,
will surely help you find the sun.
The only thing she needs of you, is care, respect and your
love too. So with the spirit of this duty,
hold and cherish nature's beauty.
Someday a child of tender feelings,
will need himself to have some healing.
Show him all of nature's glory,
and share with him this precious story.

    —D. Randall DiBella

Untitled

A poem is like music, drifting through the air.
Telling tales of magic, of princesses so fair.
A poem can be gleeful, a poem can be sad.
A poem can be the most fun you have ever had.

    —Rebecca T. Freeman

His Hands

As I stand and watch the sun set over the bay
    the Lord takes my hand to lead the way,
his way, the path of love truth and peace
    I'm his child! My hand he will never release.

I'm as a baby again, the first time learning to walk
    he just holds my hand talking encouraging talk,
he teaches me to see things I've never seen before
    in such a gentle way I want to see more!

With loving hands, teaches me right from wrong
    in hopes of making me graceful but strong,
While holding his hand I'll never know fear
    for as a father he'll always be near.

As I, you too can his love can receive
    all you have to do is accept Christ and believe.

    —Nora J. Dickerson

I Cry Alone...

When the moments right and I have to fight,
The lump within my throat.

When I hold it in and act "as if",
Nothing can get my goat.

When my eyes form clouds of watery tears,
When I turn away to wipe my fears,

When I can't be honest and say I hurt,
I only cry alone.

When my friends come near to ask what's wrong?
And I turn and smile and say I'm fine,
But inside I cry and don't know why,
I know I cry alone.

For I should have taken that friendly hand,
Or that hug that held me to no end,
Or that smile that said I'll be your friend,

If only you'll let me in.....

    —Monica A. Sanabria

My Secret Love

There it is in all its glory . . my ocean
The magistrate of all the oceans of the world:
    The beautiful Pacific
O' for the time when I can see you for more than a few
days in August....
I long to thrust my feet in your cool waters and to
gaze upon the sun, half-submerged beneath your arms...
Waves pounding upon the rocks and washing over the
sand bringing ethereal harmony to my soul....
Beautiful on the grayest of days when the sun cannot
break through the fog....
Riveted in my memory until I see you again.

    —Rose Ann Modesti

Remember

Take from me what I have offered, let not
the moment be forgotten, our time we share
will be remembered, understand for now so
our hearts stay together.

If our paths, no longer cross, will
hold our love with tender thoughts, through
eternity we will travel with warmth and kindness
from knowing one another, and with whom
we give compassion to, will be the beginning
of me and you.

    —Wanda Solland

Reality

As I walk along I see
The many lives that used to be
Some are loved and some are missed
Some have stones and some have sticks
Some are seen, some forgotten
Still life goes on for those begotten

This peaceful place is where it ends
We must remember to enjoy till then
So many words are left unsaid
And some have felt this was their biggest regret

So many have forgotten how
To show their feelings and to cry out loud
It only takes a deeper look and a place like this
To appreciate the good

So take each day and make it be
The happiest moments you'll ever see
For soon enough we all will be
In this peaceful place called REALITY

—*Susan Marie Caruso*

The Master Painter

'Tis morn' in California
The Master Craftsman sets his easel
On ageless rolling sun-tanned hills.
He paints. From His pallet flows a myriad of colors.
I gaze transfixed by his artistry.
The Heavens glow at His touch.
Crimson hues burn through light pastelled bluish hues.
He brushes in full puffy clouds, that sail the sky
Like phantom storm-lashed ships.
At last, His masterpiece complete
The Master lays aside his brush.
Rembrandt-like, the panoramic scene
Glows in perfection for all the world to see.
A reflection of heaven - our Paradise to be.
Look up, you storm-tossed human souls!
See what art our Lord portrays
In His celestial gallery.
Here is the promise, yes, the hope;
The final salvation, for all who dwell
In earth-bound misery.

—*Ray Weirmack*

A Lovelorn Task

She was a fashion of embellished grace, that love of mine. Soft as
the morning snow, ubiquity of beauty, so gentle and so bold.
Yet since that morning of ages past, the winds of change have
come to blow. Those sparkling eyes of brown and gold, have
drifted off and left me cold. Oh, how your eyes shown with
love, and made the sparrows sing in the valleys high and low.
The robins weep and the doves search far and wide, for the one
whose touch made them spry.

Now the blustering breeze chills the air, as my love lies down
beneath the ground. Laughter and sun relinquished to gloom,
for the one so fair evanesced too soon. November rains and
December snows strike the ground in search of her. Forever
futile are their chores, for the one we love hears no more.

So here I am laden in sorrow, to explain the calamity to the
robins, doves, and sparrows. Our fair young love has gone and
passed, and amorous serenades shall forever be our lovelorn
task.

—*Robert A. Golen*

Extinction

The clouds tower above us.
The mountains gaze down upon our lives.
They watch over us.
In the beginning we quivered under mother nature's greatness.
Now she has lost her glory.
The mountains are leveled.
The forests are gone.
The rivers and oceans have dried up.
We have not only destroyed nature,
We have destroyed mankind.
We have the knowledge of what has occurred.
The vast extinction and constant destruction.
We think our lives are everlasting.
But in the end, nature will have her revenge.
And we shall become the extinct.

—*Mikele Cayton*

I Am What I Am

I am what I am
The myriad images of my chocolate hue
Bear witness to all I come from
But point not to my journey's end

I am what I am
Caged by the inequities of an unseemly fate
I strain to take flight to a just perch
From where I can exhale within

I am what I am
I make no apology for my common air
Nor laud my unique abilities
Often presented to offend

I am what I am
With subtle determination of reviving force
I bravely maintain the pride which lies
Within the darkness of my skin

—*Sybil Irby*

Jade

Beautiful that you are for all to see
The name of peace that brings wonders unto
you and me.
Out of times past, I gaze at you. Longing
to behold you again. Nearest to the heart
and mind, you talk to me. Again, you are a
wondrous sight. The love that you bring,
gives me a joyful delight.

—*Scott R. Holden*

What's It All About

It's about life, living, loving and sense of togetherness
The need to hear, to be heard, to love and be loved,
not settling for anything less.
It's about our faith in God, He alone will
Judge as he puts us through the test.
He gave us eyes to see with, a mouth to speak
with, a brain to think with, use them wisely
and he will do the rest.
To stand by our own, to be near when needed.
to have an open mind, whether right or wrong
To extend our arms with an understanding heart
never to be apart, never to doubt
that's what it's all about.

—*Marguerite De Francesco*

One Last Wish

Picture this you and me, under the stars on a white sand beach.
The night is ours not a soul around, splashing waves are the
only sound. The sand is still warm from the afternoon sun, as
we watch the stars falling one by one. Holding you in my arms
it feels so right, from dusk till dawn night after night. When
you look at me with your angel eyes, I know in this whole world
there is no prettier sight. With a strong heart and a
willing hand, God has sent me an angel from the promise land.
Heaven is only a step away nothing can tear our world apart,
you and I together as one following our dreams listening to our
hearts. With all your love and all of mine, my one last wish
us together till the end of time.

    —Matt Jamieson

Father's Day From Above

On Father's day let us not forget our Father Divine,
The one from above who has been there before time
To show us the way that we may live
In harmony through joys and happiness we can give
This was made possible through our Lord Jesus Christ
He gave us parents even though he paid the price
Let us follow the rule he has given to us
So that someday we may join him is a must.

    —Margaret Coudrey

Solitude

Into the woods I wander, for silence is what I seek,
The peace and quiet of solitude, and utter restful sleep.
I will not close my eyes though, for there's too much to see,
The trees and birds and animals, are wonderment to me.
A mist is falling from the sky, as silently I walk,
It's pleasant to be lost in thought, and not hear any talk.
An acorn falls from a Pin Oak tree, a squirrel scurries fast,
A young doe deer so silently, dines on the repast.
The rays of morning sunshine, come creeping from the east,
The things I saw this morning, to my eyes were a feast.
Now from the woods I travel, but I'd really rather stay,
But I will go and leave no trace, to come another day.

    —Terry D. Wyman

One

The power of one, to see and do.
The power of one, this one is you.
The power of one, is all it takes.
The power of one, what a difference it makes.
The power of one, is all we need.
The power of one, someone to lead.
The power of one, can turn us around.
The power of one, is not easily found.

    —Lisa Padowitz

A Frosty Fall Morning

A frosty fall morning is a beautiful thing,
the promise of winter, the colors of spring.
A cold wind blows and it rustles the leaves,
but the rays of the sun will warm the cool breeze.
The frost coated grass crunches under my feet,
as I walk through the yard to get to the street.
I can see my breath rise in front of my face,
While the red leaves dance with a new found grace.
The sparkling frost that blankets the lawn,
has the appearance of diamonds in the new dawn.
The sweet tasting apples, fresh from the trees,
are as crisp as the dew that decided to freeze.
Nothing compares to a frosty fall morning,
soon winter will come without further warning.

    —Luetta A. Summy

Now ... Is Yesterday

That which is not yet ... is tomorrow
the realized or unrealized dream,
the merit of the idea,
the result, the progress

that which we see, feel, hear, love, hate is... today
the ones we meet, the things we do, the sights we see

the urgency for satisfaction, the immediacy of the next,
the craving is... now
now... is yesterday
what of... tomorrow, son?

    —Marilyn Schlain

Music

Music, the uncelebrated future of life,
The reign of power over mind and matter,
Chords of vim,
Unilluminated minors cross boundaries into bleak,
    desolate obscurity,
Blazing minors ignite the soul with a rhapsody of fire.
Syncopated rhythms pestle visions of laughing children,
Moonlit sonatas captivate the hearts with romantic
    rendezvous in the Paris streets.
Electrifying saxophones blare the dolor of the jazz and
    blues composer.
Entrance yourself in the music around you,
Live with dreams of lofty mountains filled with the sound
    of music.
Snare your enemies with a song instead on unharmonic trickery,
Break all barriers with a simple note of melody,
Praise your friends with a lifted octave of thanks,
And live in harmony with those around you like the keys
    of the piano: Black and white.

    —Margaret Marie Cottrell

Angel

When first I saw you sitting there,
the room grew dark and soft sweet music filled the air,
like the whispering of crystal chimes in a gentle breeze,
your voice enchanted me, making my heart beg, please;
Who is this Angel sitting there?

When first I saw you sitting there,
a glow appeared, soft yet brilliant, which was beyond compare,
a glow, warmer and brighter than the sunniest summers day,
your smile, so warm and charming, making my heart wilt and say.
Who is this Angel sitting there?

When first I saw you sitting there,
my eyes were held by the shimmering brilliance in a pair,
of liquid, golden pools of life, which shown with wisdom and
compassion,
your eyes flowing softly, melting my heart, making it plead with
passion;
Who is this Angel sitting there?

When I first I saw you sitting there,
I lost my heart and all that I could do was say a prayer,
that it would be found and held lovingly in silken hands as soft as
snow,
your hands, I prayed, so soft to touch, to hold my heart and let it
know:
You are the Angel sitting there!

    —Mark R. Thompson

The Rose

The Rose that crumbles after bloom its colors soon will fade
The Rose that years from now will hold you close and dear to
  me I pray,
Fragrance once in days gone by those dreamy days I cannot forget.
Broken crumbled like the Rose my heart will not forget.

When autumn leaves have fallen all the trees are cold and bare
This faded Rose may bring me your and I'll be waiting there
And if the tide of life and fate should drift us two apart
Just take this Rose of ours with this Rose I give my heart.

    —Marge Akana

Untitled

They always say it's so hard to say good-bye,
The sadness it brings makes me wonder why,
Anyone has to leave anywhere
It's just something else that doesn't seem fair.

But as you go you realize there is a plan for you,
A whole world out there with things for only you to do.
Personal mountains to climb and treasures to dig,
It's scary at first, it seems like so much and so big.

You remember it was so hard to leave your family,
They told you to go and you had to agree.
And now they're still there through it all,
Pushing you ahead, but there when you fall.

And you make it to the top and look out across the world,
You see now that you've made it and new things have unfurled.
New races for you to finish with pride,
And new dreams you have burning inside.

You smile as you look back and see what you've done,
Especially when you realize it's only just begun.

    —Robyn Burquest

Birthday Candles

The first candle stands for life,
the second candle stands for adventure,
the third candle stands for understanding,
and the fourth for excitement.

Each candle that we light stands
for a year that has past. A
year of memories, hopes and dreams.

Each shinning light from each
candle is very special because
it all represents the sign of
life and fulfilling years of happiness.

So no matter if it's your first
or your 40th Birthday remember
each day of every week of every
month of every year is very
special because it holds the
gift of life, and the light of
the candles are what leads
you to where your path
may take you.

    —Pristeen Grooms

End And The Beginning

Eternal stillness fills the void of endless time;
the shadow and the light emerging to combine
the sound of silence beating rhythm without rhyme,
as wingless birds fall victims to a senseless crime.

The oceans crest, a droplet on the parching sand,
the dancing tongues of fire frozen as they stand;
the mighty swirling wind with broken hand,
sets free the soul in flight, above the dying land.

    —Stanley R. Manvydas

The Haying

The freshly dried green grass lay in windrows.
  The shining sun cast an immortal radiance upon the meadows
That lay below the rugged and jagged Flat Top Mountains.
  Golden trees in the distance swayed with the breeze.
The wind whipped across the field, swirling anything in its path.
  The last days of a short fall were ebbing away.
Pickup trucks were parked together in the field signaling the
  pow-wow in progress;
Bring in the hay, reap this season's bounty.
  The rancher, with every season of his life etched upon his
smiling face, lightening behind his blue eyes, a floppy hat
  pulled low over his head;
The ranch hands in their brightly colored bandannas,
  and all the ranch dogs joined in to bring in the season's harvest.
The baler churns away like an old riverboat as it follows
  the tractor rake with its smokestack puffing and clanking in
  time.
The procession moves back and forth across the field, deep and
  wide, until the sun sets upon the land.
Another day is done...

    —Sue Ann Kelso

A Backward Glance For Future Reference

Somewhere in our minds we can recall
The smallest detail of one particular day in fall,
We smile with sweet remembrance and we sigh,
Why did those carefree days so quickly go by?

Then in our rushed and hurried days,
Our children grew swiftly to their youth; and where was ours,
Caught up in happy days and Christmas smiles?
Sewn in with those happy days, were nights that never seemed to
end days and nights of sorrow, as we headed round life's bend.

And although the bend is behind us now, it's still not all
downhill, there's the children with their children and so we
  worry still,
Of all the days and nights our years have seen,
It's sad to see we wasted some just worrying.

Worrying never resolved a single thing,
So why did we let it rob us of our time?
Today we have, we love, and always will,
Tomorrow, perhaps we may have waited too long,
Then our hearts and our hands may be still.

    —Maureen Shea

Untitled

Love is like a rose,
The soft touch on your nose,

Just take one smell,
and you're under a spell,

Slow but for sure,
you think it's pure,

One at a time the petals drop,
but there's no way to make it stop,

Before you know it they're all on the ground,
without your noticing without a sound,

Then the wind carries it away,
nothing you can do nothing you can say,

You pick up the stem and get pricked by the thorn,
now your finger is bleeding and torn,

You think you're going insane,
because you turned the gentle touch into pain,

But without a doubt,
a new one will soon sprout.

    —Laurie McOrmond

A Photograph

A photograph can not show,
The softness of your heart.
A photograph can not duplicate,
Your smile, that I love so dearly.
A photograph can not make me feel,
The way I do in your arms.
A photograph can not yet close,
The way you do.
A photograph just reminds me
Of all the good times we share and
Most of all reminds me of how much I love you.
—*Lisa M. Colclough*

Our Seven Star Voyagers - The Challenger 7

No more shall we see
the sparkle in their eyes,
America's seven brave astronauts
who perished in the skies.

This wasn't the first,
but we hope the last;
in all now, ten Americans
have died for their task.

The dreams that they had,
they don't have now.
They left us with the questions,
what happened and how?

We must find the key
to unlock the door,
to pursue our dreams,
to continue to explore.

We will always remember
that flash in the sky;
but even death can't stop
those with the courage to try!
—*Serena Andrizzi*

Starting Over

I'm waiting for AAA to come and charge my battery as I sit on
the stool at the kitchen counter. The counter is made of
butcher block and needs a good sanding and recoating. I need
a good sanding and recoating myself. I would start with a
light bond and slowly rub myself in little circles. Starting
with the bottoms of my feet, sanding with the paper wrapped
around one of those small wooden sanding blocks, I'd sand the
dead cells, the ones that serve no purpose in my life. Like
the regrets over my past.

When I was 14, Mother asked me to go to the beach with her on
impulse to watch the sunset. I don't remember what kept me
from going only that I didn't and she did without me.
Returning after dark, she looked refreshed and liberated from
going. The many young men asked for my phone number, when I
was the asking age, to whom I responded with the Hollywood
Police Station's phone number, maybe refusing up front would
have been the considerate thing to do. The time I slept with
the boy cousin I adored and nothing happened. All I remember
is that I wished something had and when he died in a car
accident at 19 alone I wanted to die with him. The time my
best friend called me in despair about losing her husband, her
child, and her mind. I never went to see her until her funeral.

My body hurts from the sandpaper, but it gives me a way to
begin new cell growth and once again...start over.
—*Linda Rader Overman*

Rain On A Summer Day

As the rain quietly falls to earth
The stream rises from the hot cement
The cars have the windshield wipers on
But yet have the windows down
The air is warm
The rain is cold

People are walking around, in their shorts
Carrying umbrellas
Puddles begin along the streets
And the children come out to play
The air is warm
The rain is cold
—*Leah C. Miller*

My Senses Survive

I walk so quickly because I'm so scared, the night is spooky,
the streets empty. The fog, it's so thick, so full of danger,
it surrounds me. Darkness, a shroud in which I cannot see.
Invisible demons dance through the atmosphere, calling their
taunts like coyotes and silently slithering like snakes, either
may choose to attack. My leaden feet, anchored onto the
pavement because of my fear, I cannot flee. What, I wonder,
will become of me? Glaring red eyes, full of violence, search
me. Hateful bruising hands beat me. Tongues loll out,
panting, through rancid, blade-like teeth. The demons gyrate
on legs of two, four, or as it seems, they're quivering in
mid-air, tearing into my flesh, wanting more. They glory in
the power as they torture, feeding on my blood, my agony. I
scream, they laugh, I fight back, they invade me. My life was
once so joyful, now it's all horror and pain. I have become a
victim, will I ever be the same? Tears and anger can never
take away the memory or the shame. Please, anyone out there,
if you've ever been in my place, know you're not alone, for too
many victims they've claimed.
—*Sherry L. Havercamp*

Dusk

I came too late
The sun has set
Blood is scattered on the sky.

I am alone
I am afraid
Of you and of I.

Bleeding fragments of withered feeling remain
on the grey battlefield of separation
I thought our love was like the sun
and would not wane
Poking at the dying embers of a fire
to kindle it again
and call it eternal.

Like cracked and broken flames
We twist together
in brilliant flares
then shrivel apart.

I said I knew.
I said I loved you.
—*T. V. Padma*

Sparrow

In the thickest mud a beautiful flower grows.
The smallest sparrow sings the sweetest song.
The skinniest tree bears the juiciest fruit.
The frailest woman is strong as steel.
In all these we see the face of God as we do with you,
and of you only, God caress more than I do.
—*Steven Willard*

Work Day

The night is over, the moon is down,
the sun is up and the day has begun,
alarm clocks wake people out of their sleep,
alarm clocks get broken all over town,
people eat breakfast and then they run,
for a new day has begun.

Bumper to bumper all over town people are going,
going, going, gone.
The boss walks in and everyone looks busy,
or the boss will have a fissy.
Around noon the day at its peak,
people go out for a treat.
Lunch!

Rush hour, the time to go home from work,
to their families or to an empty home.
Dinner is eaten,
TV is watched, people go to bed to start all over again.
The night is long,
The night is calm.

  —*Michael D'Ausilio*

Somber Mood

Melancholy dunes sway with blowing sands,
The sun's harsh warmth belays the fear of death.

Drained of embedded cold, our bones ache no more.
The heat is life, breathed to our soul.

The need to love outshines despair,
To be touched to touch to hold,
We know not why fear evaporates,
To shun the gleam of Death's icy gates.

Liquid sky caress the pane,
Against the walk falls summer rain.

The night wears on as silken cloak,
Envelops the body to dash all hope.

To love, we knew not to use its fate,
Sprawled on the ground not love but hate.

  —*Paul Bunnell*

The Message

One morning I woke to the song of a bird,
the sweetest melody I ever heard.
Each note was so perfect,
Each note was so clear,
My heart filled with gladness and so much good cheer.

Life is so precious, he seemed to say,
God has given us one more special day.
Take it and live it, each moment so rare.
Share it with others, let them know that we care.

A friendly smile to the lonely at heart.
A cheerful word to a friend miles apart.
A helping hand where feeble steps tread.
We can share with the hungry, our loaf of bread.

And then in a moment the little bird flew,
leaving his message so loving and true.
It does make a difference,
It may change a life,
as we live in this world of struggle and strife.

  —*Maxine Thomas*

An Elderly Barn

A lone barn stands there in that vast expanse of field.
The tall grasses speak of days of long ago. Years pass and the
barn comes down a shingle at a time, leaving a bald roof.
A board falls here or there as the walls atrophy from unuse.
The arthritic and weak doors lean on each other for strength.
The windows shed water through each pane, crying over the
disregard of their barn; their sight now dim as they peer
through the cataracts of cobwebs. Liver colored spots appear.
The paint wrinkles, dries out and chips with age.
The back walls stoop forward pushing the front over with them.
A tremor sometimes over-takes the barn as beams shrink.
Progress progresses and the old barn is forgotten.
Ashes to ashes, no one hears its last sigh.
The grasses grow over it.
A lone stone now stands where once a grand barn stood.
May it rest in peace.

  —*Lori Michelle Stahl*

Invisible Monsters

The jewels of night fill the sky
The tiger expresses his angry cry
As the maiden of the garden walks away
Songs of tears steal the day.

As passion in the sea turns to waves
The spirit of the dead leave their graves
The jewels disappear, the night is black
The tiger cowardly steps back
Pain is created by her screams
Her terror is now a daughter of her dreams

  —*Sarah Kuhn*

A Tribute To Baba

Baba, you have left this earth to be with God,
The time came when He gave you the nod;

You had so many plans you wanted to fulfill,
But your body no longer had the will;

Yet, for those of us who truly love you,
Your unique spirit will forever remain in view;

For we who are left behind,
Locating one with such priceless qualities will be impossible to
 find;

It is for this and numerous other reasons you will be sorely
 missed,
Since the lives you touched were so pleasantly kissed;

We will all remember your love for life,
Especially in your pride and devotion for being a Baba, a mother
 and loving wife;

Even the home and garden you devoutly nurtured,
Reflect the reverence felt toward things that protected and cured;

And, of course, babies and children were so dear to your heart,
Since they represented a new life that is due to start;

Yes, Baba will be greatly missed by many of us,
But you know she would not want family and friends to raise a
 fuss;

Simply recall the things that made her so rare,
and realize that she is still among us to share.

  —*Walter Kaptanowsky*

This - My Life

Life is evolved from love - even before
   the time of birth, through life and
   unto death, and even after death.

There is a definite time in each life that a
   very special love appears.
Through the years there are facsimiles of
   this love - parent love, brotherly love,
   love of God, love of children, love of nature
   and animals, etc.

But this one love is different from all the others.
This love brings you moments of magical
   happiness, moments of despair, moments
   of worry, and the moments, even when
   alone, when you are aware of a presence
   other then God's and those around you.
This love comes to some very early in life,
   others are blessed later in the autumn
   years and some in the golden years.
In these, my autumn years, has this love come to me.

    —*Shirley Ann Hirth*

I Do

How can I compare you to all the wondrous summers?
The time of life's beautiful, sensual carefree days,
Wafting of cooling breezes borne on scented flower leis.

How can I compare you to the colorful radiance of fall?
Scenic beauty whose wrappings enfold the rich hues,
the bounties of nature,
Displaying to all, its foliage of glorious natural
chromatic stature.

How can I compare you the sudden silent mood
of majesty winter?
The calm that becomes the after thought, the splendor
of the season past,
To perform again with snowy mantle preparing for spring.
The die is cast.

How can I compare you to the purifying,
bathing gentle rains of spring?
Awakening earth with splashes green when life begins a new,
For giving the past, rejoicing in song, awaiting the
spectacular approach of summer,
but Kristin, I can and I do.

    —*Nick Mayser*

A River Trip

    To the water I have endured.
      The time was a vision.
    A wide bodied river of anticipation.
    The anticipation only found by four.
A group formed to provide excellence in the wild.
Of the four I was found for this trip of the unexplainable.
    A man of change and adaptation to all.
   For those who know him unpredictable; but yet
love and passion run like a river through his veins.
A love for those around him and the fixation to survive.
May the river flow for all who itinerate, as did the river
      for me.

    —*Russell B. Foss*

X'mas

I've been told throughout this year
The very same thing I was told last year:
"Unless you're a good little tike
You won't get your train or doll or bike."

They say Santa visits only those kids who
Do what they are told to do.
Now, what I want to know is this:
How do I manage to stay on his list?

'Cause I can tell you in all honesty
I've done everything but throw down our tree.
My mom threatened and ranted and raved
That Santa knew how I had behaved.

She said that for such a human tornado
She'd ask Santa to leave only a rotten potato.
Yet, this X'mas, just like all the others
Santa read my letter and not my mother's.

    —*Lita Mennucci*

The L In Old Means Lonely

I set alone in this lonesome place
The warmth of tears upon my face
Thinking of friends, family and kin
Of a heart opening up to let me in

Why must the L in old mean lonely
If only to hear laughter - if only
If only they'd remember I'm not dead
To know that love will give me life instead

    —*Mary Ann Smith*

Untitled

She gazes out into the greyness of the water;
The waves lap gently onto the sand.
She wraps her coat tightly around her,
As the biting wind whips at her fragile form.

The beach is deserted - even the sea gulls are absent.
A tear rolls softly down her beautiful, pale cheek -
And with one elegant move, she brushes it away.

"It's better to of loved and lost, than never to of loved at all."
She recalls the phrase - and disputes it.
Her heart was breaking right now, and nothing
   could heal the hurt.

She considered her options.
The waves looked inviting; a fitting end to a woman
   who adored the sea.
Yet, somehow, she felt there was more -
though her pain was unbearable, she felt there was more.

As she gazed out into the greyness of the water,
She felt someone join her.
A little further along the beach, stood a man -
And with one gentle movement, he brushed a tear from his cheek

    —*Vanessa Anne Lake*

Change

The sea inside of me is at rest today.
The waves no longer violently collide.
   The wind is in a state of repose.
Oh! The sweetness of a resting place.
How quiet, peaceful. The storm subsides.

   But life is composed of motion.
   The turbulent sea will form again.
   I may rest here for only a while.
   Tomorrow the wind and waves return.
There is no permanent rest. No end.

    —*Loretta Jividen*

I Love

See through my eyes, that you may understand.
the way I think, the way I am.

I love, is my name and as young as I know,
I lived by my name wherever I'd go.

Until one day I met my fate,
I met my match, I met, I hate.
A great battle followed of joy and of pain.
It seemed to me I was loving in vain.
But as I started to cry,
I hate, cried too,
When he saw through my eyes
How my love shown through.
   —*Marlene J. Tears*

Stephanie

 Stephanie, you mean the world to me
  the way you walk, the way you talk
   the way you laugh with glee
 I love you, my daughter Stephanie.
   The words that you say
    to take care of me
 I love you my daughter Stephanie.
  If I didn't love you with the love
   from a parent unconditionally,
  I would really like you for the
person you've grown to be, my daughter Stephanie.
   And now on graduation day
  I know whatever path you take
happiness will come from the decisions you make.
   I'm so happy I'm here to see
   this new passage in your life
    and all it will be.
 I love you with all my heart and soul
   my daughter Stephanie.
   —*Rick Chasin*

Winter Beauty

The snow on the ground, that sparks like light,
the white puffy cotton, that glows in the night.
The crunch of the foot steps,
outside my back door,
reminds me of christmas and all of its lore.
The sounding of sleigh bells,
That ring in the street,
The screaming of children, in snowball defeat.
The smell of the kitchen,
with all its delights,
the glow of the stars,
in the still of the night.
   —*Lisa Berks*

Wonder

Omnipotent God, whose power the universe has shown
The winds of subterfuge have blown;
Bare-souled, the Psyche face-to-face with guilt
Trembles behind the fallen barricade it built
In quiet terror waits the vengeful stroke
Of punishment for the Holy Canon that it broke.
But strangely down the corridors of love
Comes a gentle whisper from above,
"Fear not, my child, I know how weak the will
I saw your pretense from the start and I love you still.
   —*Leola Davis*

Only The Lonely Are Alone

And when she was born,
the world was not ready.
And when she looked up at the stars for guidance,
They looked back and smiled knowing her light had
made them shine.
And when she whispered in the air to know if
anyone could hear her.
The wind blew and whispered back that she was not alone.
And when she reached inside to feel,
Everyone around her felt her warmth.
And when she graduated from the first step,
She took another

Her story continues
Her day continues
Her life continues

No one looks at what she sees,
No one feels what she does touch.
No one thinks with her mind,
No one answers her questions...
God heard her ask!
   —*Rachel Rosenberg*

The Artistic Heart

My heart is a canvas awaiting paint.
The years gave me only background gray.
After all these years, what can I say?
What I want from life is what it ain't.
Did I choose to become a saint?
I think not. What I really feel today
Is that I no longer like this gray;
I want color to flow without restraint.
But for that, I need an artist —
Someone to render me as art
That the whole world could discover.
Moreover, hear what else I've wished:
That you could render this gray, blank heart
Into the artistic heart of a lover.
   —*Philip G. Haynes*

A Sulky Race

See them glide around the track, a wonder to behold;
Their clamouring hooves, shoes slashing down,
The night, flared nostrils blow.
I watch in splendid admiration, their sulkies tightly drawn;
Along the track at full a pace,
Their trots near gallop gone.

The riders hold taut leather thongs, a purse about their lips;
Wheels spin faster, dust billows high,
Their powerful charges grip.
The back stretch looms, whips rise and fall—a rider
Clucks his tongue;
Against the rail, now eye to eye,
The race is almost done.

The end is close at hand, and then, instantly 'tis over;
A race of splendid horsepower done,
And blankets backs do cover.
But for me the race will long be run, a greater distance gone;
For the first may best but all are steel,
Despite which may have won.
   —*Shane K. Gramling*

Be Still

Be still, and listen to the birds.
Their song is sweeter than any symphony
created by man.
They speak of matters of consequence.

Be still, and listen to the trees.
Their choir is accompanied by the gentle wind.
Leaves dance gracefully, as if they had
an audience.

Be still, and listen to the flowers.
Their beauty and aroma sends a song to the heart.
They speak to us in silence, knowing we can see
their elegant performance.

Be still, and listen to the night.
An orchestra plays the music of nature.
Thousands of musicians harmonize until dawn,
their lullaby of peace.

Be still, and listen to your heart.
It, also plays a song.
We are a part of everything God has created,
and united with the music of all living things.

—*Marlene J. Cochran*

When You Are Lonely

I remember Junior High and all the years that have gone by.
Then came our senior year, but still my memory had not been
        cleared.
Then came the day when we had to say good bye, but I knew our
        friendship would never die.

So when you are lonely and all full of tears, nobody's with you
and your filled with fears, you can just call me! I'll always
        be here and if I'm not with you I'll always be near.

—*Melissa Anderson*

Love Is Love

I will give you as much as I can
    Then I will give more.
I can only give as much as you need
    To receive or allow me to give.
If you take all I can give, then my
    Love is endless and fulfilling.
If you receive a portion of my love,
    Then I will give the balance to others
I am capable of giving love in great
    amounts.
I must give all that I have
    Love for others is what I am

—*Mary E. Moore*

Cloud Of A Dove

I lie on the beach, I'm mesmerized by clouds which fill the sky,
then mysteries engulf my mind and fantasies soar high.
Some clouds quickly merge together, forming the figure of a dove,
symbolic of Gods' steadfast hand, symbolic of Gods' love.
I hear a choir of angels singing hallelujahs from above,
praising God in all His glory for His everlasting love.
There's no more lust or hunger, no jealousy or hate,
the world had turned to worship God before it was too late.
It becomes so very clear to me, the reason for our birth,
was to care for one another and find peace upon His earth.
Suddenly I'm distracted and the vision fades away,
I'm back in the reality of our sad and bitter day.
Then I realize much to clearly t'was an illusion of my mind,
but yet I find much comfort in the dreams I left behind.
For a voice reassures me of the "Lion and the Lamb".
"These things, my child, shall someday be,
I always have been and I am".

—*Shirley James Bonahoom*

My Bird Feeder

I had a little bird feeder, but no birds,
Then one day the wind blew,
And oh my word.
Seeds were scattered to and fro,
There they rested till spring brought the showers,
My goodness, I had a passel of sunflowers.
They grew quite tall and made a splashy show,
And what do you know?
Some little yellow birds
Flew in to feed,
I guess that's the kind of feeder they need.

—*Pauline Dewey*

It Amazes Me

God made the many different stars,
    then pushed them into place.
He also pulled the mountains up,
    and assigned each one a space.

Then He gathered up the waters
    and set them with a tide;
but then He set a limit on
    how far they all could ride.

He gathered space and made a sky,
    so birds could stretch their wings.
Then placed a song within their hearts,
    and taught them how to sing.

God even blew the atmosphere,
    creating wind to race;
this breath of God, this gentle wind,
    that touches on my face.

Amazing as it all may seem,
    but oh so true I have to say,
this great creator, this mighty God,
    is the same Almighty that hears me pray.

—*Mary M. Barton*

Family

If love is to hate
Then you surely live to berate.
If hate is to love
Then you surely don't have a dove.

To have a family that dotes
Is to have a family that turns coats.
To have a family that is in constant debates.

Pleasure is in knowing loving arms
And knowing you will never be harmed.
Love is in knowing you will never be in chains
And knowing all of your banes.

But when your heart is black
You have all the world to lack.
And when your soul is empty
That is all the more to pity.

That is why when your heart is pure
All the world is most surely yours.
And when your soul is filled
It's reason all the more to just be silly.

—*Luann Anderson*

Best Friends

A team we were, you and I
Then you were taken, I wondered why.

No more closeness, no more fun
The two had parted, leaving one.

Even though you I cannot see,
You remembrance is always here with me.

The special times that we once knew
The joy I had of knowing you.

It was hard on your parents, sure that's true
But being your best friend, it was hard on me too.

While on Earth you spread your love
Now doing the same from up above.

—*Linda L. Snyder*

When You've Hope In Your Heart

There are dreams to be dreamed,
There are new ventures to start,
There are new songs to sing -

When you've hope in your heart!

For a wee bit of hope
Makes a mighty bright spark,
Chasing away shadows
Where the corners are dark!

It brings clearly in sight the joys, tears
may have blurred;
It brings answers to prayers that
you may think no one's heard!

So why grump in the dark
Seeing only despair -
Why not give up thinking God
Isn't hearing your - prayers?

For there are so many new
things that can start -

When you've hope in your heart!
—*Stephanie Selvidge*

A Mother's Love

What are mother's suppose to be?
There are so many in are family tree.
A mother's love is a special work of art.
Those feeling's are deep within your heart.
A mother's love is the sound of pitter-pattering feet.
Those sound's are so dear and sweet.
A mother's love is the little grabbing hand's.
Sometime's they don't really understand.
A mother's love is sometime's hard to see.
It's only shared between my child and me.
A mother's love is a precious kind of thing.
To keep them safe and under your wing.
A mother's love can not be given or bought.
It come's naturally, it can not be taught.
So if you are ever in need or despair.
Come to me, I will always be there.

I love you! Mom
—*Sherri Tiller*

There Is A Man...

  There is a man, a man of continuous criticism.
There is a man, a man who leads a secret life.
There is a man, a man who is the subject of social dogma.
The man I speak of is the gay man. Don't hate the unknown!
—*Matthew Cummings*

Laura

There's a sigh among the tree tops as the hills echo her name.
There is a sadness all around the mining claim,
For the sun shines no more around my lonely cabin door,
Where the silvery Colorado wends its way.
I met her in the spring time in the lovely month of May.
She was a beauty to behold, so young and fair.
She became my bride in her gingham dress and long blonde hair.
My love for her was a hundred fold.
I lost her one day in winter, the flu had come our way.
My heart became a frozen lake.
Now the sun shines no more around my lonely cabin door,
Where the silvery Colorado wends its way.
I saw two fawns at play on a lovely day in May.
The sun seemed to come inside and I found myself smiling.
God has taken the hurt away as I watched those little ones play.
With all her goodness and sweetness he had put it in a crystal jar.
He placed it on a distant star.
He has preserved it all for a future day.
Now the sun shines once more around my mountain cabin door,
Where the silvery Colorado wends its way.

—*Mary Margaret Morrison*

Untitled

I feel so lost and mystified
There is no place to hide
I am at the wind's mercy and whim
The bright spring sun now is autumn dim
Once green and vibrant I flourished with the help of my tree
But now I am on my own, my survival and happiness depend on
  me
Others marvel at the beauty in my aging
This sets my insides raging
I dizzy when I think of what will pass me by before I am browned
My friend and foe is the gale's whistling sound
To let it continue is to have no control
To have it stop is to lose my soul
The colors change and the leaves are set free
Yet so many fall right next to their tree.

Were they afraid to take a chance?
Were they happy letting the wind sweep them by?
What would they have said?
Who knows? They're dead.

I continued to ponder this as I swept the foliage from it deathbed.
—*Scott Lieberman*

Chapel On A Hill

Small lonely white church, silent sentinel, keeping watch.
There it awaits . . . the arrival of worshiping occupants.
Chapel steeple pointing up through the clouds to God.
See upon the base of the cliff twisted gnarled trees,
wind resistant, storm knocked, attacking rocks and boulders,
resisting all assaults, digging roots into the sod,
Trusting their creator, thankful just to be there.
So do pilgrims struggle, resisting the rocky path to our
salvation. The boulders resist the assault of the determined
trees. An unbelieving populace resists the Christian Faith, as
they assault its covenants daily.
—*Violet Crumpler*

God's Gift

Once upon a time in the land of love
There lived two people, and the man up above
They fought, they bickered, they hemmed and they cried
But God in His wisdom, put all that aside

The times they face are filled with woe
But the path they must travel, is the way they must go
It's lonely and painful, it sorrows their soul
But that's the struggle to reach their goal

God persisted and opened their hearts full of pain
And replaced the storms with a sweet gentle rain
He taught them to trust in the person they married
And with it came ease, for the burden they carried

Alone they survive, together they grow
And in spite of the heartaches, they continue to show
The love, the spirit, the flame in their heart
And bound to each other, and never to part

Sooner or later the tide has to turn
And when it does, a lesson they'll learn
Forgive, forget, let go of the strife
There's love to be had, and it's called our life!

—*Marion Machado*

Promises Soar Away In The Wind

"But you promised me," I cried
There was no reply
It was then I knew the solitude of silence
It was then I understood
Promises could just soar away in the wind,
If you let them.
Promises are spoken and meant
At that particular time
With such deep, believable sincerity
But then changes occur
What was promised, no longer is remembered
No longer is paramount, no longer will be honored
For the one who promised,
Let it soar away in the wind.
The believer of the promise, waits for its fruition
Believes and anticipates, believes and hopes
"But you promised me "I whispered softly
There was still no reply and then I knew
What this deafening silence meant
Promises just soar away in the wind.

—*Phyllis Weiss*

If I Could've Been Gene Kelly

There were really only two,
There were Kelly and Astaire,
And I floated in the darkness as they floated through the air.
I could feel my body lifting from my movie theater chair.
And they said Astaire was better, but it didn't mean a thing.
In my adolescent maleness, Gene Kelly was the king.
'Cause his dancing just exploded and it satisfied my need.
I could burst out of my body, I could feel my body freed
From that heavy self-awareness I was feeling every day
As I watched him turn a dance into games that I could play,
Leaping here, zipping there, as he'd shoot across a room,
And his joy shot through my nerves, through my adolescent gloom
I moved step-for-step beside him as I dreamed how life could be
If I could've been Gene Kelly, instead of being me.

—*Robert Engel*

All The People In The World

If all the people in the world would love each other more
There'd be no need for all our young to ever fight a war
If we would take the time to listen to each other
And love one another as sister and brother
If all the people in the world show how much they care
Extend a hand across the land and all be willing to share
There'd be no tears there'd be no fears
All flags would wave unfurled
For all the people in the world.

—*Mary Bruss*

Behind The Scene

Behind the scene
There's a different human being
The one in the front wants to be heard very loud
But in the back her voice is heard very mild
One that is always in between
One that no one knows behind the scene
One who likes good surprises
Or one who just rather hide it
One who is a little different from the rest
Different, but not the best
The one who tries to act like herself
The one who knows that she doesn't have to act like a star
The one who wants to go in this world far

P. S. The person that you see on see on the outside
   Is not always the person that is on the inside
—*Michelle E. K. Warren*

The Promises

Someday not so far away
There's a place that's promises
if we only believe.
Someday the promises of the Lord will be,
Then we shall know that His love
was greater than our thoughts.
Someday the dark clouds will all
pass away then our eyes will be
open to see, for then we shall see the
light and the light shall brighten our way.
Someday not so far away the promises will be ours.

—*Michael Mannino*

Autumn

The leaves slowly are all turning brown
There's a slight chill in the air, around our town
You can see it, you can feel it, in the atmosphere
Hello, Mr. Autumn, you're welcome here

Tho the sun's no longer nearly as hot
It still shines on the earth, in all the right spots
But the rain, yes the rain keeps falling, keep coming down
Flooding our cities and ruining our towns

But listen, be quiet, listen real good
Flowers for autumn are still blooming, as they should
Birds still singing, high in the air
Ants and squirrels busy, doing their share

Folks working hard, planting autumn gardens
All getting ready for a great winter harvest
All of God's creatures, busy as can be
Even the little fish that swim in the sea

Welcome Mr. Autumn, come on in
You're a nice season, kind of in-between
I think you're the best time of them all
But could your real name, be Mr. Fall?

—*Vernell Black*

Cabot Street

Cabot Street it's a little one way street that's not very wide.
There's only one way in, and one way out. There are nine
houses on the block, and eight of those houses are occupied,
but oh, what stories those houses would tell if they could talk.

Cabot Street where the neighbors come in all shapes and sizes,
from the newborn to the very old. From middle class to very
poor. Where children and adults laugh and play together as
one. And neighbors respect each others right to live a
peaceful existence with man and beast.

Cabot Street where neighbors believe in sharing and looking out
for one another. Were life is viewed as being very precious
and the sound of children laughing warms the heart. How I wish
that every street was like this one. For in my heart Cabot
Street will always live.

—*Sharon T. Myrick*

My Tribute To Mr. Lincoln

I'm never tired of looking at your picture, Mr. Lincoln.
There's something in your face and eyes.
That always gets me thinking
How wonderful you really were.
So strong and good in heart
I hold you in such great esteem
And, feel, I am a part
Of all you'd want us all to be
Good Americans and true
Forever holding high to fly
Our own "red, white and blue".
So, Mr. Lincoln, I am proud
To look upon your face
For honor, truth and mercy, too.
Was yours, by Gods own grace.
I feel still, you are a part
Of all that's "right and good"
So may our pride for you alone
Promote better brotherhood.

—*Marguerite E. Reynolds*

The Touch Of Time

When I look at my hands, I see yours
These hands of yours, my inheritance from you.

When my child places his hand in mine, for guidance and comfort
you will be touching your grandson.

When my arms embrace my children, the hands that hold them
    closely to my heart
will be yours.

When my son swims to me from underwater, grasping my hands
    with a squeal of delight
he will know, and I will remember,
that you once did that for me.

On my hand, my wedding ring, a band of family, commitment and
    love.
On the hand that looks like yours, this promise of the future.

We're all intertwined, a tinkertoy connection of rod to moving
    wheel to rod.
We add to the structure slowly and carefully, removing no pieces,
shifting older parts to the center, creating a core,
a foundation on which we all cling.

With these hands, so much like yours, I nurture, soothe, create and
    I love.
Through my hands, my children will remember you.
Through their love, the structure will continue.
And these hands of mine, so much like yours, will appear again.

—*Linda Stoddard-Leonard*

Untitled

It's mighty cold, in the winter time, in
These hills, and it's pretty hot, in the summer-time,
in these fields, but whether or not, it's
burning hot, or a winter chill, what I love is
living here in these Tennessee Hills.

Now the grass seems greener here, greener
than I've seen, and the flowers they grow
wild here, you should see them in the
spring, and the moon is so bright here,
you can see the fish in the streams,
but that's not, why I'm living here, in
these Tennessee Hills.

She had lived, all her life here, in these
hills, she made me forget, those big city
thrills, I'll thank the Lord, tonight dear,
for letting me live here, cause what I
love is living here, in these Tennessee Hills.

—*William N. Davis*

A Time For Healing

Too long have they suffered through horrors of war,
These neighbors in the historic Middle East,
Where anger and selfish interests have prevailed.
Their compassionate God, whose teachings appear
In the Torah, the Koran, and the Bible,
Has endowed them with intelligence and skills
To build a commonwealth in the Holy Land
That would be worthy of universal praise.
Only when leaders face responsibilities,
And their people agree to cooperate -
Tired of the killing and intense hatred -
Can there be tranquillity and lasting peace.
There are problems of self-determination,
Security, and deadly terrorism.
Once resolved, rich resources can be channeled
Into economic growth and social change.
The never-ending strife, through the many years,
Has been the concern of nations round the world;
"There can be no assured peace...for any nation,
Except as it is achieved for all nations".

—*M. Elisabeth Steiner*

Children

Children are one of God's greatest gifts and love.
They all are special, unique and different, from him above!

A Mother can feel her child growing inside of her, moving
about. Children are very curious, wise, intelligent and have a
mind of their own, without any doubt!

We should teach and train them always, in the way they should
go. When they get older, their teaching they will always
remember and know.

They are innocent and must be instructed, on what's right.
We must take "time" with them always, day and night!

Children are precious, eager, dear and ambitious too.
Children have feelings, opinions, questions and problems, that
we should help them through. They are full of energy, and
are so very great and dear! We must give them our full
support forever, always year after year.

Jesus loves children, and they are special even to him.
He gave children to us, and gave us to them!

"Children", we love you! We want you to know, we do care.
The things, we have experienced as children with you we want to
    share!

—*Nadine Cuyler*

Dedication To The Vietnam Vets

These thoughts I dedicate to the Vietnam Vet,
They all wanted to live to see another sunset.
Many years have come, many years have gone.
Even a new name was given Saigon.

They went and fought, brave and true,
They were protecting our red, white and blue.
South Vietnam needed, needed our help too.
They asked Americans, "come to our rescue".

Fire fight, day or night, nobody really knew.
Would your buddies come back, or would you?
This Vietnam war ended many years ago.
The Vietnam Vet, respect we must show.

When the fighting was over, we have not forgot,
We the Vietnam Vets we gave it our best shot.
Our buddies who paid the ultimate price,
It was for freedom they sacrificed!

What I don't know, and never will,
Why it took so long, to build a memorial.
I cry for the families who lost loved ones.
I cry for the mothers, fathers, for their sons.

    —Rennis G. Garigin

Untitled

Food lion is the best in town
They always have the best food around

Their meat is good and their cheese is old
And their bread is always full of mold

The fish and turkey are soaked in bleach
So when you go you get a little of each

And when your going down that isle
Look at them roaches with those great big smiles.

Rats and gnats here and their
Some are bald and some with hair

Rice pudding is my favorite thing
Them maggots give it a little zing

The meat is fresh right from the deli
It's really fresh and kind of smelly

Their produce is a little absurd
And I think their milk is starting to curd

They wipe the dates with finger nail polish
And from their bugs their food is demolished

Food lion has the lowest price in town
And it has the best food around.

    —Nicolette Reynolds

What's A True Friend

A true friendship is a life long adventure.
They are more precious than the rarest gem,
True friends posses a special gift
The ears that hear your silent screams,
A loving heart.
The tender hands that wipe your hidden
    tears away,
A gentle touch that heal the scars from
    the past.
Eyes that caress your shaken soul
A smile that lights a dreary path
Laughter that sets the saddest soul in flight
True friends go hand in hand through life.
When ones weak the other is their wings in flight.
True friends cannot be separated by death or peerless
It lasts an eternity that's one of the great gifts to be
    given a true friend....

    —Vicky Ellise Stover

Autumn Leaves

In Autumn when the leaves fall down
They change from red to a golden brown
Covering the earth, like a leafy bed
Crackerling under your feet as you tread.

As the cooler wind blows, they twirl in the air
Soon the trees will be quite empty and bare
Natures at work, and she is never done
She knows we no longer need their shade,
from the hot summer sun.

It's time for the trees to be nourished and rest
So into my book the leaves are gently pressed
To hold onto their beauty a little while longer
Before they are gone, as the winds grow stronger.

Blossoming and budding, your breath they will take
As springtime arrives, and the trees all awake
The leaves will be green again and bolder than before
So protect the beauty of a tree, so it may shed its
leaves once more.

    —Marie Bornemann

Birds

I wonder where the birds go when
They die.
I wonder if it is far up in the
Sky.
I wonder if they have golden
nest.
I wonder if it is beyond golden
Crest.
I wonder why the birds never say
Good-by.
I wonder where the birds go when they die.
I wonder if birds have eternal
flight.
I wonder if it is beyond the stars
so bright.
I wonder when I see a feather fall.
I wonder if the birds are trying to
call.
I wonder, yes I wonder where the birds go
when they die.

    —Roy Oscar Frease

Angels With Dirty Faces

Little boys are devilish creatures sure
They plague you, hound you, agitate and more
If you're not careful they'll steal your tie
They've even been known to utter a wee, small lie
Mom's bright shiny floor with dirt they tramp
Your only flashlight they make their lamp
Sneakers they go through by the score
Jackets they hang on the nearest floor
Brush their teeth, wash their ears, if you hover 'round
Otherwise they're outward bound
Yet with it all, I'd like to relate
Tired and hungry as the car pulls through the gate
A blue eyed knight with a mop of unruly hair
Charges headlong to greet you, no second to spare
"Hi Dad" he says, and sticks out his hand
All at once you feel young, and the feeling is grand.

    —William R. Farquharson

A Dad's Prayer

I have two daughters that I love.
They were given to me from God above.
One is a brunette one is a blonde.
Both are real sweet just like their Mom.

Yet I know I can't always stay.
For someday God will take me away.
When I go I have a special prayer.
That I will see my loved ones up there.

For God so loved the world he gave His only begotten Son.
So just ask Him to forgive you and join me in Heaven for the fun.
But if you wait or you're to late.
God will leave you in this world of hate.

Do not cry but only cheer.
Judgment days are very near.
If you die before you wake.
I pray you've ask Jesus your soul to take.

    —*Richard A. Hendrickson*

Two Little Children

Two little children, a girl and a boy.
They were seated by the old church door,
Both of their clothes were all tattered and torn,
And they both were hungry and cold.
As I opened the old church door,
This is the words they did say.

We want to go to heaven where mama is,
That's why we came here to pray.
She often told us that if we'd be good,
We could see her in heaven some day.

We're all alone in this old cold world,
Since Jesus took mama away,
And that's the reason we came here today,
To ask God to take us away.
God in heaven answered their prayers,
And he took them to heaven that day.

Now they're in heaven above,
Where there's no sorrow or pain.
And they are with their mama they love,
And I know they are happy again.

    —*Mildred B. Wooley*

God's Children

Children are a wonderful thing
  they're full of life and love.
They truly are in every sense
  a gift from up above.
This year, however, there are some kids
  with love but without life.
For Somalia's kids are starving to death
  because of their country's strife.
Warlords have taken all the food
  with no regard for the children
The U.S.A. has sent troops in
  to restore the faith in them.
It's sad to see in all the news
  the sick and dying there.
What can we do to help these people
  who don't even know we care.
Our troops can only do so much
  and funds are slowly received.
We can only pray for these poor kids
  that Somalia's pain is relieved.

    —*Linda Arnejo*

They Change

Like fall turns to winter, they change,
They're the children of tomorrow and they do change,
Their beliefs and their feelings grow stronger, as they change,
As a blanket of snow changes to a bed of flowers, they change,
Their minds will get larger and their questions longer, while
  they change,
As the clouds unearth the sun, they unearth their spirits and
  change,
Mankind watches skeptically as they, their future, change,
For the children change like autumn leaves, they become more
colorful, more beautiful, and they become an individual,
Everything about them changes except, their inquisitive souls,
imaginative minds, and loving hearts.

    —*Shannon L. Davis*

My Make Believe Friends

My make believe friends all come to sit and have tea.
They're true and honest and don't hurt me.

We talk and play and I have no fears
Because whatever happens I know they're near.

In my little library all of the books are sitting out
on the shelf.
I say, "welcome my friends - come help yourself"

My mother hears me as she works in the next room
But little do we know that danger looms.

Here comes Pop Pop and he wants to play
But it's not a nice game in any way.

I call to my friends to come with me
for they know I'm in trouble -
That they can see.

He starts to play but I didn't like his game.
I knew in my heart I would never be the same.

When he was all done and had gone away
For they had been with me right from the start.

I've survived all of this and I feel they were the key.
That's why my make believe friends are so very special to me.

    —*Nancy A. Waters*

I Love Those British Boys

I love those british boys,
They've filled my soul with joy.
George, Elton and Rod has sung with the queen,
Aretha, you all know who I mean.

What Paul McCartney and John Lennon have done,
They made music serious yet sweet and so fun.
Paul still gives us music by the ton,
Do you remember band on the run?

I love those British boys,
Billy Idol gives us rock with naughty toys.
The Rolling Stones shows us no matter how old we've grown,
Youth can be eternal and one can hold his own.

Who better than the who,
Man! I just love what they do.
Led Zeppelin keeps me stepping,
Ramble on the stair-way to Heaven.

George Michael, Rod Stewart, Elton John all voices of Gold,
I loved, "Knew you were waiting" with the Queen of Soul
You all are handsome bundles of joy,
Yes we the world, love those British boys.

    —*Lee Evans*

A Time Of Sorrow

When loves name thy lips do touch
  Thine eyes the world do light
      Tho memories past
    Burden thy mournful nights
   And days of sunless beauty
  Gleams of light soon shall light
      Thy daily paths
And thy voice shall bend into music sweet
   And roses about thee will bloom
      Into fragrance rare
       To match thy beauty
    That nature alone can match.
   Dwell not in anguish deep
    For that which the earth
    In solemnity hath covered
    Less love that awaits thee
     Elude they tender soul.
  For when eyes of love thee doth behold
     Let storms of yesteryear
   Like the wind into eternity go!
      —*Serge York (Oslo, Norway)*

Age

Growing old can be lots of fun;
Think of all those years you worked;
And now your work is done.
Think of all that cold, snow ice and rains;
And waiting for those long overdue
buses that nearly drove you insane;
You can now lie in bed until
way past eight;
And not having to worry ever
about being late.
You forever thank God for
letting you see this day;
For letting you now rest, and
still get your pay.
      —*Ruby H. El-Amin*

Untitled

The brain is caught in sweet delight
Thinking of autumn on a hot summer night
The heart is in pain amidst ecstasy
Longing for the day you'll discover me

Holding to the memories that seem so dear
Let curiosity grab you to release your fear
The ups and downs were quite a thrill
Imagine the dreams that are surreal

The quest has ended as I find the dove
The place it takes me is to true love
You want to stay but you have to go
We'll meet again in a life or so

I'll reach to you with a friendly hand
Together we'll find the hallowed land
So these are the thoughts I pose to you
Look for the rainbow with a hundred hues
      —*Rick Forth*

My Soul Speaks

I dream where I cannot go.
  To be where I cannot live.
To do what I will never be able to do.
  To have what I never have.
To live where I will never live.
  To love whom I will never love.

Oh, my soul, please stop yearning.
Oh, my soul, your voice is much too loud.
Oh, my soul, what will it take to satisfy you?
      —*Sheryl L. Chubb*

Suffering From Loneliness

I suffer from loneliness - and feel restless day and night.
Thinking of you inflames me "Why don't you give me delight"

Days of our companionship - it seems to me, you forgot!
You consider them as null - but in them, much joy we got!

You left me in weariness - how nasty to be alone!
Were you faithful to eat me - as meat then throw me as a bone?

But if you return to me - my anger will fade away!
Insist to abandon me - surely, you have gone astray!

To put an end to my pain - door is open to return,
come to settle all disputes - then decide which way yo turn.

Thence, you can cut relations - I shall not care anymore!
There are many who love me - whose kindness I could explore!

From the water of the sea - a net brings fish, odd and strange!
So people are many kinds - oh, kick out false friends and change.

As long as the earth rotates - you will find singles groaning,
suffering from loneliness - waiting a brighter morning.
      —*Rizkalla Girgis*

Last Days

What is this malady that ails me,
This disease that can't be cured;
My body and soul scream out in pain,
But my suffering must be endured.

The illness grips my weakening heart,
It threatens my life to steal;
Nothing and no one can help me now,
For I shall never heal.

The last glowing coal of hope is crushed,
Its light will not shine again;
I want to run away and hide,
But there's no escape from the end.

The silent killer stalks his prey,
He feels no pity or sorrow;
I must live all my life today,
For I'll not see tomorrow.
      —*Lorilei Johnson*

Our Symbol Of Freedom, Liberty and Peace

Fly forth oh flag of freedom, fly proudly in the breeze.
  This flag is our country's symbol of freedom,
liberty and peace.

With freedom there also is a responsibility to help
  preserve the meaning of what our country stands
for, and to honor the thousands who have died for the
  Red, white and blue.

Do not burn or deface it, but be proud of the history
  behind it and as citizens enjoying free movement
throughout this great land of ours.

Our country is showing the world what it is to be free,
  so Americans protect the stars and stripes by each
citizen being aware of what is wrong and what is right.

So take heed and have pride in your banner. Look
  around the world and you will see how lucky you
are here in the land where the opportunities are
  boundless at your right hand.

Therefore, let our banner proudly fly in the breeze as
  it stands for our freedom, liberty and peace!
      —*Sylvia A. Vayda*

Timeless

I love you;
This I have chosen to do.
You make my life complete, we are one. THE SAME.
The things I feel, we are the center of this union.
All to be affected by this.
Our children, our parents, our friends.
To be touched in some common or remote way.
Lives to be changed never to be the same again.
Destination changed by the gathering of two lives.
Coming together as one. Yet with separate identity.
The thought of one connects, the thought of the other.
The flourish of our paths, entwined with the passion of life.
Fast is the process, of our mind connected to the heart.
Blessed is the union of two souls, connected by the spirit,
Engraved by the heart, conceived in the mind.
God all mighty has been the author of the two lives united.
Only for us to obey the will of God, being as one.
You I have chosen...... To by my love......
With the passage of time, timeless together, ONE.....

　　—Sheri Bergquist

Lord's Jail House Dream

The night is cool, the day is hot,
This jail house I should be not.
But as I set here hopes are high.
But I often won't to cry.
But as I cry and whimper in the night.
I know the Lord has my soul in sight.
As I feel his presence in my heart.
I know this jail house I will depart,
because the Lord has promised me a brand new start,
for the Lord and I will never part.

　　—Teddy Ross

Game World

Where have we been and where are we going.
This life is getting sick.
Some of our people no longer do what is right.
They thrive on lying, telling things they know
will not come about.
What has happened to this good American way of life.
Where have we failed. God knows it all.
I hope it's not too late to save of our American way
of life.

　　—Ramona E. Hamric

The Last Word

Give us this day - sufficient prayer
This premonitory day to prepare
To eradicate me from her past,
And she from all future time amassed.
The very tubes which sustained her life
Struck her speechless, increased her strife
To speak of thoughts, of words unsaid
Through half a century heedless sped.
So much unsaid of priceless worth
To those still tenured to the earth;
Too much unsaid—too little time
To span the gulf by pantomime.
And I made mute by desperation
To express a lifetime's aspiration
Between her laboring, terminal breath,
And her impending, certain death.
She reached out to me in her affliction,
Pain savaged hand, in benediction.

　　—T. A. Landrith

Conflicts Of The Mind

They've only been allowed to roam
those conflicts of the mind
to introduce destructive moods
to suppress the loving kind

Denying hope in weakened dreams
they refuse the strong to stand
their purpose is against the light
their will is of the land

Corrupting hearts — a favored tool
with promises of lies
they steal away the precious truth
and shield it from our eyes

Its paths are strewn with broken souls
for whom there is no rest
they are the conflict of the mind
they are a painful test

I sorrow for their conquest's
those choosing to be blind
for one day those who choose to see
will see beyond those conflicts of the mind.

　　—Michael Paras

A Parting Question

A staggered breath drawing to close
Those fleeting thoughts so near repose.
That final breath expelled by breast:
Soul seeking flight with parting sigh.
Charon beckoning, calling nigh
That gentle soul to bring to rest.
Make they their final bed, faith lost,
When doctrines revealed as naught but dross?

Seek all that come their sins to purge;
So God might call to self and merge
Those faithful souls absolved of sin.
Asking are those still spared this fate,
What lies beyond immortal gate?
Does tortured soul, new life begin,
As God does soul to life commend?
Or harbor we false hope; life's end?

　　—Timothy W. Cole

Love Is Never Fair

The nights we spent together
Those times I cherished so
I thought we had forever
But love you didn't show

I trusted you, I trusted love
But these feelings weren't returned
I should have known the flame I saw
Would mean I'd just get burned

I loved you more than life itself
I'd have loved you forever more
But you broke my heart, you took the trust
the night you shut the door

I wish that we could still be friends
despite the feelings now
But with the cold heart that you've shown
I really don't see how

Through all that we have been through
I must say that I still care
But the cold, hard fact of life is
Love is never fair

　　—Nichole Luman

Adam

His name is Adam, and he makes me feel as
though I am Eve, and in his arms it is truly paradise.
    When I look into his dark eyes, they twinkle so
bright like the midnight stars, and my head becomes
swimmingly dizzy with a yearning passion for him
to quench my desires. As his warm lips press softly
against mine, I feel a fire that neither of us can no
longer smolder.
    Then his strong arms pull me closer and closer, until
the flames of passion began searing our bodies, which
are pressed ever so tightly together. As he holds me firm
against his rock hard body, the heat intensifies so, that
it will surely end in an explosive ball of flaming desire.
    His big strong hands, yet gentle and soft, roam my
body freely, and I melt slowly under his touch. But
I know tonight we will not reach total ecstasy, for
we have never yet been completely fulfilled.
    And this man named Adam, will keep me here in
his Garden of Eden, until the day I truly become
his Eve.

—*Tamie Pucek*

Stronger By The Minute

I'm growing stronger by the minute
   though I can't say why that's true
Do I know something others do not know?
Am I crazy or is it you?

There's a baby
I do not know her name
I have not met her yet,
   but she is coming
There's a new life
Continuation of an old life
Breathe in the new life
Think for a minute…

You know the story…
When you get older
   you think about the things you've held in your hands
   and the things you've let slip away
But these days
   nothing can bother me
   and my once unsteady hand
   has found a constant

—*Tom Kenna*

Loving And Living

"Loving and living" - what power they hold!
Though simple in essence - deep thoughts they unfold.

To love is to live - it is truly grand.
Yes, loving and living go hand in hand.

Life's not just living with problems which surmount us,
Life is loving and living with people all around us.

Show love to your neighbor, your friends and your kin.
Put some meaning in life - now's the time to begin.

A little goes far when one cries in need,
So heed the call - be a friend indeed!

Extend a friendly pat or consoling embrace,
Or just a heartfelt smile on a kindly face.

You'll be happier by far for all your caring,
Blessed beyond words for your selfless sharing.

"Loving and Living" - what a tremendous pair -
For you and me and all the world to share!

—*Sophie Bochan*

The Tea Party

We had tea together;
Though there was nothing in our cups.
White dishes with pink buds
Were all she set.

Tousling long dark curls,
Two large brown eyes held mine
   intensely.
And as she chatted to me of her plans.
Her porcelain-faced friend keenly
   listened in.

We lingered till the hour was late,
Talking of her friends, her books,
   herself.
And as she poured enchantment from the
   tiny plastic pot.
I knew I'd be forever in her spell.

—*Rochelle Simons*

We Are Never Ready To Say Goodbye

We are never ready to say goodbye
Though we know that each of us must one day leave this
And enter into the unknown realm of the hereafter
We still are not prepared to lose a friend or loved one.

We remember the face, the eyes, the smile, the laugh,
And the pleasure of just being around a special person.
We yearn for the camaraderie and the warmth
Of being in the company of one who meant so much.

We wish that we had stated our affection more openly
And perhaps held the embrace a bit longer the last time.
We wonder if our sincere feelings really showed through
And our deep and unconditional love was truly understood.

We cry for the loss and the void left in our lives,
We will miss the companionship, the fun and the caring,
Our hearts will keep sweet memories ever close, ever precious.
We are never ready to say goodbye
And so - - - - - we shall not try.

—*Sally Krystopchuk*

Sherry

This old gal knows a lovely girl,
Thoughtful, loving and sweet.
My memories of her so dear,
they can't be beat.
She is far away, but thought of much,
Hopefully we will never be out of touch.
I miss this girl from the bottom of my heart,
When I look at her pictures, the tears do start.
The precious hours we've been together, will always be,
Treasures of love, my Granddaughter,
forever to me.

—*Margueritte Mitchell*

Missing You

I awake with the dawning of each day,
Thoughts of you roaming through my mind.
Tormented by such deep loneliness
That my very soul cries out for you.

Each night I lay awake for hours,
My heart breaking with sorrow.
When sleep does come at last,
You are there, but only.....in my dreams.

—*Monica E. Stroisch*

Three Words

Three words that will forever ring true
Three words from my heart to you
Three words simply stated
Three words with which your heart is confiscated
Three words which make you mine
three words that have and will exist for all time

Three words that came out of the blue
Three words that best describe you
Three words out in plain view
Three words everyone claims they knew
Three words made real only by a select few

Three words from me...your lover so true
Three words forever from my heart to the girl with whom my
    life continues
Three words that are both old and new
Three words that simply say...everyday
I love you.

—*Samir S. Dave*

Half-Way Wonderings

Recently my thoughts review a life that's more than half-way
through; considering in the light of day, why events and
actions came my way, and questioning what's in store for the
time that I will be no more; at least on earth, for I do
believe there is a better place, above the clouds among the
brilliancy of space; my queries, then, seek to assure, that
though the body's dead; something exists beyond the door based
on the life we led.
And, (Part II or Addendum)

What happens to our memories - the storage of our thoughts? Are
they kept somewhere on tape secure, or in a secret box? Perhaps
transformed to energy, the quintessence of all life; since no
one really knows for sure, this causes me some strife. For,
who will know, our worry, joy and mood, or generation's
leanings? Who will care about our brood or moral underpinnings?
No, I don't fear the thought of dying, it's the way of life,
you see, I just seek to leave behind a little bit of me.

—*Matthew D. Kopetchny*

Mother

As events unfold, within one's life.
Through snares and trials, through pain and strife.
In bleakest days, and darkest nights.
When things seem grim, and shines no light.
When love seems far, and out of sight.
And fears they binge, at future plight.
When the heart sinks low, from life's long tasks.
And the world surrounding, in hatred basks.
When you feel you've trekked, your longest mile.
Retrace your years, for one sweet smile.
You'll find it there, in childhood days.
Those times long past, so far away.
I still recall, my mothers smile.
Her love and kindness, which knew no bile.
It heals me still, as I grow old.
Those special times, and stories told.
How she helped Dad, to see us through.
Turns cloudy days, to skies of blue.
My mothers love, it shines so strong.
Her memory kept, my whole life long...

—*Linda Massey*

Winter Daffodil

Unnoticed years have fled
Through spring wild crocuses of dreams:
Yet are there daffodils beneath these drifts
and faint the scent of lilacs

On golden springshine days
and blue of sky and hyacinth
These cold white petal drifts from heaven still
hide soft beneath the snowdrops

My crocus years are sped
And lily summer's shimmered beams:
But there are daffodils beneath this snow
that coats the gold of autumn

I have each revel spring
rejoiced and banked the lily splash,
the rich of bird song, autumn on the hill
against the call of nightfall

Now in the tulips' blaze
a warm of summer pats my face:
And there are daffodils beneath the chill
to warm the hall of winter

—*Willa Dee Maltby*

Hell Gate

From under the Brooklyn Bridge we sailed,
    Through the East River - thence into the sound,
And even when the day's light failed;
    The scenes were wondrous, grand.

When nearing "Hell Gate" we held our breath,
    And fear lurked in many an eye,
For was it not known that here many'd met death?
    By the "skin of our teeth" we got by.

Still I failed not to note that wonderful work,
    Erected by mere, mortal man,
Which took plenty of brawn and plenty of pluck;
    And the brain work of some mighty man.

The winds rose high and whipped into foam
    The waters about the boat,
And the "white caps" foretold of a storm,
    Which came later and from sleep we awoke

On an on through the waters we sailed,
    Moved by an unseen hand,
And ere the more timid of spirit had quailed;
    We were safe on the firmness of land.

—*Mary Petillo*

Sonnet Of Life

What use holy breath on me awasting,
Thy blessed gift so transient in full season,
A bud before full blown, now hastening,
Erased, a shadow inane of reason.
Minute by minute, day by dragging day,
Life is no lost by its lustful dying;
It flies in the flood of time's heedless way,
Like petals blown by breezes and left lying.
My flower of life hastening to wane,
Benumbed by anguish and despair untold,
Unceasing chaos vexed on mortal pain.
Depart from me in youth, not when I'm old;
In flight to hell I'll go without thy grace,
For flesh is cheap and more will take my place.

—*Patricia Hogan*

Me And The Tree

Oh mighty tree of great brown, branches upward facing
thy heart beneath ground.

Oh mighty tree, do you breathe better when there is a breeze?
Or does the greyness of the pollution wither your leaves?

O tree so mighty do you feel warmth when birds nest in your
limbs or when moths, bees cling to your branches
does it annoy you? And is that a sin?
O tree that is smaller, are you a lot different than he, she
just because of your different species?

Is there a feeling of prejudice against race, color, creed?
And when it snows, do you feel the cold?
Is it better, worst than heat on green leaves?
Are you proud when you bloom in full?
Are you afraid of getting old?
I want to know how it feels to be a tree.

—*Sandra Foley*

Where Have I Been

The feelings in side go by and go by,
Til one time they must stop, a sigh.
Hold on a minute, who is this person?
Where have I been? What have I done?
I survived a war but without a score,
Unless pain and defeat deep to the core
Can be counted for points, I'm a winner.
In some eyes I'm believed to be a sinner.
Pain with me to have and to hold til I die
I suffer inside, as I hold in my cries.
I am trying to cope and live with my blues
Understand that it hurts and it still continues

I'm not to be judged for something I did
I couldn't take time for decisions I bid
Yet some of them came so brief so fast
I have nary a moment to take the task
I loved my country, I honored it true
That was what I felt as my fear grew.
I came home from the war, or did I?

Dedicated to our Veterans of War.

—*Shirley B.*

The Hunter

It's five o'clock, the alarm has sounded.
  time to get up to go where bounded.
No time to eat, wash or shave,
  for a minute too late may cancel my rave.

I'm dressed and ready, eager to get started,
  to begin my quest of the soon "deerly" departed.
I've reached my destination, I'm sitting and waiting,
  the temperature so low I can't stop shaking.

I'm having fun I keep telling myself,
  to much invested to put on the shelf.
I hear a noise, it's him I've been waiting for,
  he stands so proud, not knowing what's in store.

I pick up my rifle, it's shouldered and ready,
  to shoot him down as soon as I steady.
He looks so peaceful, beautiful and pure,
  it was then I decided not to procure.

I picked myself up and off I went,
  back to my lodge where last night I spent.
And so comes to an end this year with deer,
  the same damn outcome every damn year.

—*Salvatore Tribuzio*

The Cycle

It's P.M.S. week again at our home
Time to throw the king from his throne
I shop, scrub, clean, rear children and cook
8 hours, 6 days he works, that's enough in his book

All month long men piss and moan
When it's my time, he wants to be left alone!
When hormones are out of whack and emotions are high
that's when the roof hits the sky

Suddenly the kings castle is turned into a hut
All because once a month he can't keep his mouth shut
You have to realize dear, I don't mind the duty
It's the altered chemicals that make me moody

Things will be better, you'll see tomorrow
Perhaps we'll get through this with little sorrow
When the week is over and I'm feeling like new
I'll count my blessings you love me like you do

Once again he's the king, for 28 days at least
'cause with the next cycle… It's my turn,
once again, to be a P.M.S. beast.

—*Theresa Murray*

"Love Life"

The stream of visions to create reflection of the mind
Time too short for words structural appearance
The mist of passion wants not to be destroyed
Mysterious voyage on the ship with Goddess of Romance

The act of life expressed by surprising plots and games
Addicted to words solved puzzles with the charming touch
Unspoken beauty accepting sophisticated blinks of eye
Is gathering flowers in the garden of eternal love

In the story from the wonderland pure heart wins
  glorifying verse
Gentle posture - a lady manner - soft waves of silk
  under the wind
The words are silent, a subtle tune is on with living fear
  against the dream
Innocent desire on the stage of fantasy and art, cool
  just driven to thrills

—*Pat Kayda*

Romance With Life

Take flight on wings of song
To a far-away place - a long ago time,
Where and when undenied love, promises kept -
Entwined two lives.

The day to day struggle -
Its victories and defeat,
The laughter and tears; sadness and joy
Filled the in-between years.

And then — "not in summer,
Springtime or autumn"
But on our "wedding day"
You were taken away.

Now I pray—
Still this longing; spare the memories
That at long last I may begin
Romancing once more — this time — life.

—*Pacita B. Rysanek*

Being Without You

I try to cover up,
To act like I don't care.
Being without you makes me really scared.
Not having you,
I try to pretend,
For there are so many others who I could care.
It's easy to say that I don't care,
But seeing you makes me quite aware,
That I care for you more than you know,
But you are the one who I mustn't show.
If I was in love
It would be with you,
For you are the one
Who I can talk to.
Take it and love me
Or leave it and tell me
But don't leave me
Like you don't care.
So if I could never see you again
Maybe I could believe, that you were never there.

—*Megan Jones*

To Die For

The rough bark of a big oak tree,
To be drenched by rain in a thunderstorm.
The beautiful leaves that it once grew out,
Fall to the ground because winter is here.
Standing alone by a stream in a field,
a lonely soul shedding a tear.
Lonely for a many of years,
but finally a friend from the ground appears.
Joyfully he see's his friend and dies,
So his stranger friend can live a
full healthy life.

—*Patrick Gallagher*

Trapped

Do you know what it is like to be trapped
To be held prisoner by one's self
The soul aching to get out
Screaming with no one listening
Unable to speak your mind
Wanting to express
Afraid of sharing
Unwilling to take a chance
Keeping all bottled inside
The pressure building
To the point of insanity
To be trapped
Is the pain worth it

—*Marty Nussbaum*

Silent Prayer

I pray for the sun always to rise-
To brighten each and every black lit cloud
And to sparkle in the eyes of all the ones we love,
For in truth we love all,
From the wee legged centipede to the mightiest whale-
Gliding through the crystalline waters in the early lights of
dawn.

I pray to hear the heartbeats of G-d's children eternally-
Rocking open the darkness of his majestic lands
With whiteness-
Shining forever in the souls of all.

Bless this day and the many more to come,
Let us feel the warmth of truth
And the vibration of love.

—*Michelle Katz*

A Walk In The Forest

The musky smell of leaves trodden
To catch a fleeting glimpse of life and beauty
As it struggles to get away from an apparent danger it
recognizes
You as causing.

Huge pillars surround you, choking your cares out of your
body.
You submit to the power of the ancient cloak, surviving
year after year, it has passed from generation to generation
Only to now be thrown away by your many brothers.

You must take them for a walk in your majestic domain.
Let them lose themselves to the beauty and serenity
Let them feel the power of a walk in your, their, everybody's;
Woods.

—*River Hall*

What Is

Feelings of confusion and betrayal for what was
To coincide with a forever answer just because
Attribution and retribution, yearning to hear man's tree is
flourishing and his apples are ripening
Spinning round and round like a child singing "ring around the
rosies"
Wishing for a pocket full of posies distorting his garden
Unconsciously altering his image of a desolate junkyard
Into an Eden to which he blindly sees although his time seems
Incorrigible and self proclaimed
He now obtains a heart that has sadly been tamed
Once the world is through with him as well as mankind, he'll
Remember the best has been saved for last
For now he has the stars to wish upon the moon to dream on
Embarking upon an angelic land of dandelions
Which in the end awaits man's somber.

—*Mark Nessary*

Closing The Gap

They wear long hair, ambitions are few do only what they want
to do Uncaring. They will tell you so though we, of course,
already know. But underneath this lack of pride, in some
clandestine place inside, this blatant travesty of youth from

its own self conceals the truth. For of this world that we
have made, our progeny are just afraid. We built a million
miles of road to gird this earth and for their load, one
hundred million motored cars, whose black exhausts conceal the

stars. The skies we conquered. Sunshine beams we overlaid
with our jet streams. Our scientists, those men of skill,
increased our living years until, this multiplying human race
too soon will suffer lack of space. But we'll keep shouting,

we are brave, and hug our secret to the grave. we'll never
leave the slightest clue to let them know, we're frightened, too.

—*Marita Esche*

That Place

There is a place I love so well
There by the garden wall,
A place so shaded from the summer sun,
yet guarded in the fall.
A place so shielded from the winter winds.
Yet bright in the days of spring,
A place where nature's in control,
A place where the robins sing.
I cherish every moment there
New life I do recall,
There is that place I love so well,
It's there by the garden wall.

—*Raymond H. Knudsen*

A Teacher

I'm here some years before you, I've much inside my mind,
To empty out that you may have, I'm not one of a kind,

My task is to guide you, through dark and dangerous ways,
Through fire, wind, gullies and pits, over mountains and through
    the haze,

I'll answer all your questions, and those you fail to ask,
Prove to you that your today, came from out the past,

Prove to you the world is round, like life, thoughts and deeds,
Show that all things were before, that all supply your needs,

Hear me...let me teach you, hear what all I say,
Store it all inside your mind, and then,...give it away,

May your knowledge last forever, and your learning falter not.
And when teaching all you have learned, give out all you've got

I'll be blessed for teaching you, for learning...you'll be blessed,
And blessed again for teaching others, until your day of rest,
Passing knowledge on to you, has one outstanding feature,
From one another shall we learn, thank God...I Am a Teacher.

—*Muhammed A. Rashid*

To Our Children

We say, yet words have not the power
To express the depth of the love
Which lies within our hearts for you.

It may be seen in eyes dimmed with tears.

Tears that well up from the heart,
And make the eyes sparkle with pride
Over your many accomplishments.
Tears that flow more freely,
Because of the mistakes you make,
Realizing that somehow we failed you.
Tears that come as you leave us,
Yet we know this must happen,
That you must make your own life.

We say, yet words have not the power
To express the depth of the love
Which lies within our hearts for you.

—*V. N. Keyes*

Flowers

Flowers smell great to your nose.
To feed them you need a garden hose.

Flowers feel great to the touch,
To hold one near means so much.

If people see flowers the way I do,
They will have a wonderful flower "point of view".

In closing my poem I would like to add,
That flowers can make you happy, even if you're mad.

If you are feeling unhappy, low or down,
Just look for a flower, you will find one around!

—*Penta M. Stanley*

Out Of Place

   What's wrong with me why don't they like me I try and I try
to make friends but they laugh and walk away why? These are
the questions we ask ourselves when we feel out of place out
of time and out of space. Can't you see how deeply your words and
actions hurt me? Of course you'll never know because I can't
let my feelings show. Finally when you've taken all you can
and things just get out of hand you begin to wonder, what would
it be like to be dead gone to Heaven "Sheer Bliss! yeah and
with one pull of the trigger to your head the gun goes off and
Bang!! your dead.

—*Stacey Hammond*

Someday?

I look at you through tainted eyes
To find myself by my surprise
A figure in white, I see you there
With faded glance by my own stare
To see a thought of once I had
Of twisted hope is all too sad
As my thoughts and dreams of you do pass
So do my hopes of old stained glass
Of which to see through rose filled sight
I look again in hopes I might
The thoughts of which may soon come true
The thought of merely, me and you.

—*Tom Slayer*

Achievers And Poets

Achievers climb the hill of adversity alone
To gain knowledge about doing things.
Scientists extract, change, and use the unknown.
Supplying method, system, and main spring.
Engineers focus on operating traction.
Technical knowledge has its specialists.
Aviators are air captains of known action.
Poets may be achievers and a catalyst
Challenging concepts of the world to come.
A computerized assist so bold
Telling of prophesy with modern input wherefrom.
It leaves most of us out in the cold.
A genius arrives every few hundred or so years
Writing words of wisdom unique
Honored by the world achievers and a few smart seers
Picked on by skeptics and critiqued.
The poets called dreamers fancy love, spirit, and God.
Achievers like verse of action and force.
Ordinary folk respect and reverence the odd.
Good verse hits home as a power resource.

—*Ruth Partridge*

Tranquil Musings In A Country Field at Sunrise

The Daffodil stretches her arms upward
to greet the rising Day's Eye.
The spruce trembles with laughter
as the summer breeze
tickles his viridian quills.
Floating clouds
seem beleaguered by the force of change,
swirling through vacillating designs.
Feathered tribes brightly sing to the dawn
in a voice borne of the wind.
The enchanting aura vibrates
with mother nature's offsprings
celebrating the ceremony of life.
Discord evaporates with the morning dew,
while my imagination hums softly
and tip-toes through quiet dreams.

—*Wilson L. Buchert III*

Cat Hairs In Milk

   What a combination this sight is,
The milk is mine, the cat hairs, his.
   The memory of his lapping tongue,
The fluffy face from which hairs hung.
   He left my side to carry on,
the milk is here, yet, he is gone.
   I knew him only for a day.
And now I miss that hungry stray.
   He simply left me floating hairs,
As a symbol of his life-long cares,
   of being homeless and having to depend,
on unknown people to be his friends.

—*Nancy G. Boussios*

The Rose

I have built a little wall,
To keep the world and I apart.
I won't let anyone close to me
So I don't have to worry about breaking my heart.
When someone comes too close,
I just crawl back into my shell.
I climb back up the podium and say,
"At least I haven't fell."
Maybe this is good, maybe bad.
Nobody really knows.
But the story of my life is truly sad.
For me, there is no rose.

—*Tanya Witkus*

Getting Burnt

When I was twelve years old I had but one desire,
To light the cigarette I stole, but not to start a fire;
'Twas out in the backyard I went to puff and puff a lot,
Then I didn't realize that my body would go to pot.

My social life since then has been wrapped around smoking,
Rejected by a few . . brother, I'm not joking!;
Today it seems that I'm rejected by all because of my habit,
So I advise those who want to smoke, "Before you light up,
   grab it!"

Aside of that, by this addiction, there goes your health,
Heart attack, lung cancer, and even part of your wealth;
You start out spending enough for a cigarette a day,
But before you know it, those extra bucks have gone their way.

You do not intend to smoke daily more than a few,
Yet, in a short time, the money in your wallet blew-
On cigarettes, cigars, pipe tobacco, too,
So take my advice: Do not start smoking
   or those cigarettes will smoke you!

—*Lawrence Rothman*

As Mine Is For You

I wish I could keep your smile in my heart
To light the darkened paths that I tread,
   To keep my days full of brightness,
   And to keep away the fears that I dread.

I wish I could keep your laughter in my ears
   To keep my world full of you
   And to wipe away all my tears.

   I wish that I could know you,
   But the answer I fear and dread.
For that one reason and that reason only,
   I keep my love patiently unsaid.

   For you are the one that I dream of,
   You are the one I want to know and love.
   I hear your voice out of nowhere,
And when I turn, I hear your voice circling around me
   In a mist of flying doves.

Only the truest of hearts knows that wishes are merely dreams
   So I dream of you in the clouds and skies of blue.
      Hopefully, one day your love will be for me
         As mine is for you.

—*Travis Carroll*

Love's Wait

What for to live once love has gone away?
To love again to find another new?
Not I for now there lives no happy day.
No brightness fills me, only that of blue.
Imagine me once filled with such great zest,
Preparing for whom I would have my wife.
No longer to find peace upon her breast,
I say I would much rather take my life.
How can they say 'tis easy to forsake?
When I know well that I have tried in vain.
Oh, how I've tried but still I feel the ache!
The ache which lingers like no other pain,
And leaves me to caress mine own sweet pen
Until the day that she comes back again.

—*Robert A. Laucella*

The PCP Program Pollution Control

Who has the authority to inflict laws on International levels
To make all forms of polluting a serious crime
Everyone in the world must get involved
While there still is time
The planet earth can only rejuvenate herself so much so fast
If we don't act now
The human race will not last
Thousands of species are erased and extinct for progress each
   day
We have to start internationally cleaning up
And begin right away
Or sooner or later mankind will pay
Right now the future is vividly plain to see
Let's all join forces and collaborate
To make our planet pollution free

—*Terence M. Clark*

Heroes Of Latin America

      From Latin America these heroes did come,
To make their mark on History through victories they won.
      Marcus Garvey was a great Pan-Africanist,
   Pedro Albizu Campos Puerto Rican nationalist.

      Toussaint L'Overture Haiti's great general
Jose Marti Cuba's hero/poet with liberation plan.
      Simon Bolivar military genius was he,
   Liberator of Latin America he fought to be.

      For Chile, Peru, Argentina he fought,
   His people's freedom was the goal he sought.
      The land he loved he tried to win,
      Argentina's son - Jose San Martin.

         Father Hidalgo - O' What a Man!
   He rallied the Indians to reclaim the land.
In spite of the fact that his mission did fail,
      His name forever Mexicans will hail.

   These are but few of the leaders of the past,
      About whom fond memories forever will last.
Today to South Florida people of their lands do come,
      Open your hearts and bid them - welcome

—*Lloyd E. Afflick*

Evetime

   Silence. It's so quiet no one dares
to speak. It seems that if you break
the silence, you rip through the very
fibers of time. After what feels like
an eternity, someone speaks, and you're
hurtled off into the pit of oblivion,
parted from your own kind forever. After
a while, you fall into an eternal slumber,
never to awake again. Silence is regained.

—*Shalla Samson*

728

Tomorrow

Yesterday as I crossed the street,
to pick up my afternoon treat.
I wondered what my Lord would say,
about the state of the world today.

Last night as I sat under the stars,
and listened to the sound of passing cars.
I thought about if God were here,
was He far or was He near.

Today as I write this simple poem,
I think that I can really show'em.
that God is living in this land,
so sound the chorus and strike up the band.

Tomorrow, with me as part of His troops,
God will win some new recruits.
I can be an example to others,
and show them how we are all brothers.

—*Steven A. Simons Sr.*

Untitled

Solid tears of rugged anger cling pathetically
to piers of stumbling clarity clouded
by words of hatred spoken by a jewel
of compassion shattered by puppets
of dangling riches displaying their
glory in rings of greed circled by
scorching glares of ignorance.
Embracing the beams of
accomplishment hoarding the attention
of a leader raising a generation of
pride. Confused by the attention
lavished by the leader, a shadow
of despair wails infinite melodies of
helplessness seeking the smile
and the wisdom of a teacher
departing from realms of debt.

—*Maegen Lecheminant*

Thank God It's Monday

Thank God it's Monday, so I can start anew
To put my loving spirit, into practice on a few.

Each week you start by sharing, showing,
   helping
Someone less fortunate than you,
And each day your heart feels lighter
When you do God's work it's true.

By doing things for others
Your own burdens seem far less.
Your weeks and months are brighter
And filled with happiness

Don't thank God for Fridays
if your motive is just selfish,
If it's only for your pleasures
and your comforts all you wish.

Each day should be a blessing,
Cause God gives them fresh and new.
Live life to its fullest.
Seven days a week will do.

—*Pauline Trautman*

Stop And See

We as a society work so hard by the hour
To quench our thirst for unlimited power
Take time out to smell a rose
And try to describe that feeling with prose
Rewards cannot be measured by wealth
But putting it simply it's more important
to have good health
The best things in life are free
So why not take a chance and see
Slow down your hectic pace and
Gratefully enjoy the human race

—*Sandra Glassman*

A Failure Is A Try

Sometimes people hesitate
   to reach out for their dreams,
Because they fear the shame involved
   if they do not succeed.

Afraid of simple failure.
   of making a mistake.
Yet what they do not realize
   is risks you have to take.

You may fail once! You might fail twice!
   and feel like giving in.
But lift your head, be confident,
   and charge ahead again!

For all mistakes will help you learn
   exactly what went wrong.
And each will teach a better choice,
   which makes your judgement strong.

So don't let fear cause you to let
   life's chances pass you by.
For nothing in this world can make
   you fail except a try.

—*Leroy J. Ware, II*

To Live A Life Of Sadness

To live a life of sympathy when what you need is care,
To realize you've lost something that was never there.

To have someone to talk to when you are feeling down,
To feel you need to smile but all you do is frown.

To be caught in the middle not knowing which way to turn.
To do something wrong just when you thought you learned.

To plan out in your lifetime what you want to be,
To live a life of sadness from painful memories.

—*Shannon Blodgett*

Be A Dreamer

To dream, to dream a good dream.
To remember the dream you dream.
Know and to understand it not a joke
Some say a dreamer is a fool that dream of nothing
To see things that will never be.
But to be a dreamer is to get ideal.
To make some plan.
Sometime to see what you want to be
If we could not dream what will fill your mind
It just like a movie that is seen when you are awake
But a dreamer see it as they sleep, go on
And dream a world that is in your mind.
Be a dreamer fill your mind with laughter
And so much more a dreamer is a dreamer
That fill the mind with all kind of dreams to be a
dreamer is to dream.

—*Lela Mae Randall*

Perfect Rose

One perfect rose is all thy need
To show thy love for thee
As the redness blossoms
So does my heart
Flowing with the blood of devotion

If you look deep into the pedals
Imagine the beauty of the perfect rose
The incense so exquisite
The coloring so vivid
All the life it delivers

But a perfect rose is too simple to express
The love thy have for thee
There is no way to relate my thoughts
No way to convey my feelings
No way to reveal how much I care for thee

   —Liliana Soutullo

The Night of the Dancing Rose

Follow me, follow me into the mystical night,
To show you a vision, a vision of such delight.
It happens in moonlit fantasy,
A special time for you and me.
See the moonlight bright, as it shines upon spider's web,
Like a sparkling backdrop above the forest bed.
A breeze so gentle it hardly stirs nature's floor,
A time you will treasure forever, a time forever more.
See the princess of the night
As she dances with such delight.
She bows and lofts her head, dancing all around.
A vision so lovely ... at last, free from ground.
The spectators of the night wonder in awe
As she glides through moonlight near and far.
After this night, as you lay in bed,
A remembrance will stir you ... a vision, a vision in a gown of
 red.
So before you lay to rest, in a state of nightly repose,
Remember my children, and dream ... the night of the dancing
 rose.

   —T. Stephen Tsuboi

To Be A Bird

If there is an animal to be it is the bird
to soar through the sky not having to think
of anybody or anything. Fly away, fly away
anytime you wish not concerned with friends,
family or obligations of sorts.

Only wanting to soar in the clouds to
wherever I wish to go. Pick up and go
not concerned about possessions to carry
along whether it is a long journey or
just a short journey.

Only to be happy and free at all times.
Gliding high and low but not in any rush
to get any place or to see anyone in
particular. Having all the time in the
world to soar by dawn or by twilight
which ever I prefer.

I prefer to soar like a bird if I had
the chance to be any animal I wish
to be.

   —Pamela K. Haskin

The Dew-Drop Sea

Come follow me
To the Dew-Drop Sea.
Come follow me
Over a hill,
Through meadows green,
Landscapes so beautiful,
Prettier than you can dream.

Where the children rest and play,
Through the night and through the day.
Where candy corn grows,
And candied peaches, candied plums,
Where candy goes in mouths instead of thumbs.

Beyond Elf Hill
Is a marvelous thrill,
The Dew-Drop Sea
with sand made of sugar.
The sea is pop,
And all you have to do is flop down on the sand
And watch it shimmery shine.

   —Stephanie Wyler

Note That Says Hello

This is a note to say hello,
To the one girl who is my true love I know.
The day of Thanksgiving is upon us now,
And how I would give anything to be with you somehow.
The thanks this year that comes from within me,
Will be for you my dear who have stood behind me.
Through thick and thin these ten months long,
My love for you has grown awful strong.
I miss you darling so very much you see,
I pray for a united Christmas to be.
If I could just give you that one New Year's kiss,
That would fill completely my whole Christmas list.
These thoughts I send to you are straight from my heart,
In these times while you and I are separated apart.
So if ever there is a time when these thoughts you don't know,
Take out this note that says hello.

   —Zachary Vaught Klotz

In Case I Forget

Before I die, I want to give thanks
To those who brought music into my life.
Composer or orchestra, and those in the ranks
Of musicians and singers who banished my strife
Playing or singing in harmony and melody.

Deep thanks to the artists whose eyes
Let me see a new world of beauty.
Created on canvas with their paint and dyes
Treasures more precious than all pirates booty
Giving much joy and some melancholy.

And thanks for the good fortune I've enjoyed
From the wonderful people who entered my heart.
Changing my life and the way I was destined
From such love and inspiration I never will part
Even when long gone from this cosmology.

   —Robert Duncanson

The Rose

The thorns of mistrust and uncertainty are striped away
to reveal a new start.
Petal by petal, fragrant flowers unfold
to expose my hidden heart.
Leaf by leaf, my fears and doubts fall away
to reveal a growing trust.
The deep red evokes a passion and desire that surpasses lust.
The red rose is a symbol of us.
Its beauty intensifying with time.

   —Lynda L. Woolf

Tapestry

I look at the pieces one by one
To understand who I have become
And realize the rich tapestry of this life
We live through learning and loving
And, yes, eve suffering...
This vast tapestry of playing and
Laughing, hurting and crying,
This vast mosaic of all my desires and pain;
And as I sit by the window and hear
The music of myself, this
Composition of all I am and all I ever want to be,
I remember the poems of yesterday —
Mother's dear hand or father's kind smile —
That wove the fabric of my life
And while I watch my children come and go,
I think about all those things
And know that God above listens to the songs
Of the heart — those simple quiet songs
That paint my world of experience.

—*S. J. Hanley*

From A Dying Daughter

You scream at me to refill the ice trays,
to walk the dog,
turn down the music—
the volume of my life.

Through your rants and raves,
through your quests for empty love:
The world is beating outside.

And mother, I'm dying.
I see monsters,
things in cages,
greeting me each break of dawn.
I wake up to the morning mist and pray the won't be storm.
You believe in calm, dear mother,
You think there should be calm.
When the rain hits, then, and these dogs have gone to bed,
Who will be left with you in your storm?

—*Sheryl Straub*

Solitude

Time to watch the stars sparkle and dance
To watch the cows enjoy a little romance
Time to count the colour blue
In all we see, feel, hear and do

Time to stare at the warm sky above
Time to enjoy the peace of a dove

Time to breathe deeply and feel the soul
Time to finally aim and reach that goal

Time to seek solitude and peace
Where inside the warmth I'll find a release.

—*Sharon Garkawe*

Of Destiny

Rapid footsteps echoing down an empty street,
To what destiny go the sounds soft and fleet?
In the dusk of the day, heralded by a rising star,
Smells of an evening meal drifting from afar.
A reminder that life evolves behind each barren wall
Of a city hushed but for a fading footfall.
Night softly falling and forming drops of dew
That glisten in the lamplight with a soft, yellow hue.
Beckoning to the wanderer in the moist evening air,
Promising warmth and security that really isn't there.
Destroying the foolish moth that hastens to the light,
Impersonal to each death, remaining brilliantly bright.

—*Tannie Meador*

The Rain Demon Of Mississippi

When drifting through trills of this world, one begins
to wonder is this really it? Or where is this all getting to.
One feels the world has actually come to its fold. But it's
just the beginning. This takes us back to the days of Noah.
Where God had told Noah to build an ark because he would
destroy the world. Due to sin which had enveloped the world.

But this isn't it either. This is a whole different concept
altogether. So much trembling and rambling between the
residents of Des Moines, Iowa, St. Louis, Wisconsin and the
Mississippi river. My story begins here. For over three
months, one week and a half ago, the Mississippi river opened
up its jaws and out came the bursting floods which caused a lot
of pain, fears, and damages too. Everyone was forced to
evacuate their homes due to the level of water the flooding
had collected.

Most farmers in the middle South lost a lot of money because their
crops had been swallowed and carried away by the floods. While
different age groups in Des Moines, Iowa were determined,
to block the floods from coming in. There was extensive heat,
going on around New York which felt like the planet sun.

—*Yevonne Ihe*

Wisdom

You call it wisdom - with a mind so strong
To write a book - a poem - or song
But God's wisdom are the things we can see
Like birds and flowers, the sky - a tree.
Like tender grass with blades so green
Like willow trees near a brook are seen
An arching rainbow - that follows rain
And wild flowers growing in a country lane,
The roar of the ocean - the calm of the bay
And the song of the thrush at the break of day.
How painted sky blends with setting sun
And how darkness falls when day is done.
That's wisdom - my friend - with power so strong
To make wind and forest sing together in song
So for wisdom wise and knowledge strong
Just read "His Book" and sing "His Song".

—*Lorraine Michaelis*

A Tribute To Magic Johnson

One, two, three - my God cookie and me
Together we will always be
As one to the other you see
For in the days to come
My strength will depend on thee.

I know that no matter how tall the hoop
My God and Saviour can master that loop
To deliver the finest slam of dunk
We will ever witness by one amazing "hunk".

So all the treasures he has given me
My eyes will no longer see
The world as it stands before me.

I will pray for courage when I'm alone
So that I cannot fear the unknown.
Now, all my friends will assist in my needs
To let me know they're there to do a good deed
And everyone will readily see
That the "game of life" has always been played by my God and me

—*Pearl P. Moore*

Today, Tomorrow, Yesterday

Today is tomorrow and tomorrow is yesterday, but
tomorrow is said to never come, but we depend on
tomorrow for the next setting of the sun.

Today, tomorrow, yesterday

Today we go about our chores and do the things we have
to for tomorrow. Tomorrow is the day you look forward
to, but tomorrow may never come, so just live for today
because tomorrow is not promised to anyone.

Today, tomorrow, yesterday

I do today, what I'm suppose to do tomorrow, but then I
think about that which was done yesterday, because it
doesn't count for what must be done today.

Today, tomorrow and now yesterday.

Today is now, tomorrow I may never see, and yesterday
is gone forever.

—*Vera Jackson*

White

Too light,
Too dark,
Nothing like that...just perfect.
Pretty as perfect could ever be.
So peaceful with no error.
There is no hiding of fear or terror.
Just the cheerfulness of love and
every beautiful thought.
White, it is.
Lovely and gentle with passion for life...
Infinity.
Purity and honesty,
it holds itself up if ever surrounded
by darkness or hate.
Spotless and new, it always looks brand new.
The touch of comfort
The feel of forever in you.

—*Tayde Carrillo*

The World Today

Life in the 90's is ruff.
Too many gangs, drive by shootings and stuff.
Kids getting killed by kids.
Blacks getting killed by whites.
People getting beat by cops.
What is this world coming to?
My guess is to an end.

I recently saw a movie that showed
People getting killed by machines.
The way things are going these days,
People are going to be destroyed by people.

Hard to believe, isn't it.
But it's true.
If we don't turn ourselves around,
People may destroy the human race.

—*Lesley K. Cate*

Requiem

Shall I grow dry and dusty remembering a sun-parched stream,
Trapped in too much loveliness, betrayed by an errant beam,
And mourn recalling Autumn, the last of a red-gold host,
Who mocked with paling brilliance a glory now grown ghost;
Or keep a silent vigil for lovely thoughts unborn,
Or cry aloud in pain that the rose concealed a thorn?
These are trifling sorrows; I nourish a man-sized grief
I weep for a lost illusion whose life was all too brief!

—*Ruth Dokson-Nathanson*

Guardian Angel

Her immaculate innocence, her never seen pain,
Too young to know the hatred, too young to understand.
A world she left too early, given wings before she could fly,
An angel ascended to heaven, a tear in her mother's eye.
She shines with every sunshine, her eyes are the clear
blue skies, she's a gentle breeze that blows through me,
As if she never said good-bye.
So until we meet again, sweet sister, and both of us know
we will, keep on shining, as you would have shone here.
Be with me always, until time stands still.

—*Mindy Hughes*

Why The Children?

Why the children?
Tortured in this world we live in.
Children are black, children are white.
Why is this still a fight?
Children with guns and drugs,
Whatever happened to kisses and hugs?
The children are the key.
Does anybody take the children seriously?
You hear it everyday, children beaten or killed.
Into the children's head that is what is filled.
The children will be stuck with all of this pollution,
Is that has what happened with our evolution?
What happened to mom and dad?
Life without them seems like the latest fad.
If the world could listen to how the children feel,
The children could start to heal.

—*Zachary Thom*

Love

'Love' is like a spell it hits and then it takes
Total control, body and mind, the mind starts making
You lose all control of reality, wanting something
So bad you begin to believe it is true, even though in
The back of your mind you know that it is all just an
Illusion. Gripping hold of reality, you realize that you
Get what you don't want, and you want what you can't
Have. You don't choose who you fall in love with, it just
Happens. It takes one to be in love, but it takes two
To stay in love. People tell you that there is no "one"
Love, well they're wrong, age and outward appearance
Doesn't matter, when you're in love, all that matters
Is that you have the "one" you love by your side
Always, and to trust each other, and to stay
True to your word, each other, and yourself.

—*Rhiana Thomas*

Thigmotropism, Too

A poem can be described as a leaf falling
towards the ground in the middle of a hot summer day.

If you look closely and observe its fall,
you can visualize the pattern of its descent.

You'll perhaps wonder what shook it loose
from its branch in the first place?

Did seasons change before your eyes?
Or, could it be something else?

But, nature's rhythm can't always be timed
by one falling leaf or a climbing vine.

A poet can be described as someone who
shakes a leaf off its branch without touching the tree.

—*Pachinikstons*

Dark Cloud

Dark Cloud walks silently through the forest
totally aware of the surroundings
tall obstacles and icy stares
all alone with starved glares

Feeling the path that lies ahead
so many thoughts of fright and dread
behind the remains and forever the battle
the Dark Cloud still strives...

When shall the rain fall?
the cleansing must start; keep on
not yet, not at all
time is not strong enough

The shine of the mind
an everlasting deity
sends the wind howling,
whips the ground in torment

But until the "seventh snow"
the heart will never know
how the Dark Cloud will get by
if he shall live—or if he shall die!
　　　　—*Linda S. Guzan*

Musings

The country lane meanders over yester-year's deep rutted wagon
　　tracks.
Through trails of mauve and misty haze I start my journey back
Now clearly I see the trees, the well, the house just as it was
　　so many years before.
Suddenly vivid scenes candid, clear, alive transport me back
　　in time through the open door.
Tenderness like a warm embrace wraps gently around me like
　　fragrant silk and lace.
Whispered secrets of love so warm, so earthy, so divine glide
　　quietly through the lighted corners of my mind
Aromas fill the air of bread so freshly baked, of tantalizing
　　nut and apple cake.
Long stilled loving voices echo through the halls of memory
　　lane
I hear them say, "This is your heritage, your page from history
　　to claim."
　　　　—*Pearl N. Sorrels*

Transformation

Suddenly from nowhere silence captured my soul.
Transformation in life had taken control.
Left without speech and vision, I became cold.
But, overflowing rivers through my mind did grow.
My reflections became clearer than ever before.
A triumph and glory never to be told.
What was once my woe was no my flight.
Finally, a dawning from a long bitter night.
Sparkles of hope in dreams of daylight.
Armed fully for battle, I near the fight.
All was in time, balance and rhythm right.
Four seasons, I shall speak and again my sight.
For I have reached the cornerstone in life.
Time to release the past filled with strife.
Oh my emotions, they cut like a knife.
So long in time now they have been my wife.
And of man's emotions 'twas rife.
However, I must now rise to my height.
　　　　—*B. A. Malone*

A Poem For Neil

Come here! This moment to stay, say hello. Not too long to be
transported, au revoir, no adieus....

Carried away on the wind so free. As flowers, each, as
intense, sensual; as you circumvent me, round and round;
Ride the carousel magnificent equus, in circles.

No! In minds, never still, ever searching.
The manner in which I've left should reveal I've never and will
never leave, after all.

Once seen, part of me your soul and you, too, the newness of me
of each moment somewhat older than life itself
always only to be older than life;
Here each to seek an infinitely appealing beginning....
There is only time, without ending;
Only meaning.
To explore deaths and windmills and shibumi.
Knowing....
In the mirror of the mirror;
the scattered tesserae of experience.
You've already arrived. Come here!
　　　　—*Louise*

Phoenix

Fiery Phoenix, soar the skies,
Travel where'er you may,
For where you go, your presence known,
For you shine the light of day.

Intense heat from your body flows,
You're entity of fire,
A symbol of eternal life,
Of power, and desire.

Where is your birth, how long ago,
For you, many eons passes,
And why when you die, by flames consumed,
You're reborn from your ashes

Endless life, is it your curse?
Or a blessing in disguise,
And are you real, are you alive?
Or just a vision in our eyes,

Fiery Phoenix, soar the skies,
And fly where'er you feel,
For where you go, may you always know,
That the gods and mortals kneel.
　　　　—*Shelby Lee Chandler Jr.*

Winter In New England

　　　　Cold winds whistle and bite
　　　　Tree limbs twist and snap
　　　in the turbulence of a nor 'easter.
　　Snow touches down like a silent predator.
　　Daylight slowly changes into grey, then black
as the sun departs and the night gains access to the sky.
　　Man-lights twinkle in the blackness causing
　　　　　　beauty to appear.

　　　　Cold gives the snow a tonality
　　　　that makes the sad heart sing.
　　　Frost appears as words fill the air.
　　Men laugh as nouns and verbs become as steam
　　　　upon the tailor's presses.

New England in the winter is a paradise for the hearty.
　　It is a wonderland of fantasy, as shapes of snow
　　　become whatever child or adult wishes.
　　　　　Slide sleds of children!
　　　　　Glide skates of adults!
　　　Sky down the hills, toboggans of teens.
　　　　　It's winter in New England.
　　　　—*Rob Warren Jaxon*

733

A Love So True

To my heart I must be true
true to me and true to you

I love you more than words could say
A love that's stronger by the day

My only dream if it could be
is to hold you tenderly close to me

I love you Lisa with all my heart
that it hurts me so that we're apart.

I hope and pray that you will see
just how much you mean to me

I pray to God that by his grace
that one day soon I'll caress your face

Lisa you are the most beautiful woman to me
a beauty so rare as one can see

I love you so much I truly do
that one day I hope to marry you.

—*Steve Santos*

A Tribute To Lyle

A tribute to Lyle;
Truly a man with a kind and gentle smile.

A trooper and a family man;
For him, all of life's plan.

He was known as a "cop of cops";
Among Colorado State Troopers, one of the tops.

As a technician and a supervisor;
He left many a trooper much the wiser.

Not many will forget the ill-fated November day;
When Lyle was untimely, taken away.

A memorial service brought hundreds from near and far;
They came by plane, bus and car.

A tribute to Lyle, who touched the heart, soul and mind;
Of all friends and family left behind.

A police memorial now holds his name;
Life for many, will never be the same.

He now patrols the highways of heaven's sky;
With each twinkling star, see him go by!

Gone-but not forgotten-slain trooper-Lyle F. Wohlers
—*Patricia Gross*

Still Not Over

It's still not over, I've rubbed a four leaf clover to
try and stop the pain. Not my heritage, not my way, so
I begin to pray. While you sit in the distance so amazed.

He's still on the beat, I'm out on the street, while you remain
in your seat and stare. I've come to you again and again, but
you say, why do you have to complain, over every little thing
said or done to you? The whole thing is spilling over for the
rest of the world to see.

I mean don't it seem funny, although I hear no laughter, first
it was Harlin, Tyson, now King skipped to Denny; still not over
if you know what I mean. While you sit at a distance continuing
to be amazed.

This story has been told, acted out in many different roles.
Now all has come to center stage, no Grammy, no Oscar for me.
I just want to see liberty and justice that's why God blessed
us, America, oh can't you see? I wait to see for many like me,
it's still not over, not over for me.

—*Randel Horton*

Death Smiles

He tapped music into my thigh and I smiled as death did some
twenty thirty odd years ago,
before my conception,
when I was a doll my child-mother scolded,
fed, and put to bed.
"Yes," I thought, "you may look, love,
and touch with gentle fingers now,
but how will you rise with the ripe old ages?"

—*Samantha Bolanos*

A Silent Romance

A silent romance, that's what it will be, as we walk in the
twilight sky. And as the moon cascades on the lake below, as
we walk and talk a little bit more. As we slowly reach the
balcony plateau and look at the view, I can feel your hand on
my hand, and I was frighten. Never in my life have I been
this frighten before, dreams are mine, are romeo. And he is
looking for me, and not anyone else. And trying to win my
love that is his only sin. Trying to win my heart and start
a secret silent romance that was his dream. For me to be in
his arms, that was his only plan, as we, journey to a silent
romance.

—*Natasha Ikner*

Perfect Relationship

Two hands touching as one,
two hearts together with love.

Nothing could be more strong,
than two people holding on for so long.

The trust they have for one another,
the feelings they have they'll never cover.

The friendship they hold,
is so strong and bold.

The love they show,
will grow and grow.

Together they will forever be,
living as one so happily.

—*Robin Diane Altman*

Ode To A Lost Love

She floats, like a leaf on the breeze,
Unaware of my watchful eyes.
Wandering aimlessly through the trees,
Looking towards the sky.
She is life itself.
Her beauty blinds me with radiant light.
She makes my heart beat faster.
Her hair is golden bright,
Her skin, alabaster.
Beauty personified.
As I watch, she notices me.
She comes towards me with open arms.
Mine will she always be,
Attracted by my charms?
Will my love last?
She disappears, as if only a mirage.
Did this really happen? I don't know.
I never saw her again, my lost love,
But she will stay with me as I grow.
An image undying.

—*Matthew A. Parker*

Paper Land

Dismally trudging, a writers hand,
  undaunted in pace, on a paper land.
Letting not his spirit weep,
  though many times, his mind may sleep.
Thought is not friend or foe,
  yet to some, it will come so slow.
Oh how she taunts and teases,
  still her end there of, truly pleases.
No words or lines come to the door,
  of one who look at self, to adore.
To judge or criticize the style of it,
  enjoying the words of fellow poets.
So run those of you that can,
  catch your dream in a paper land.

—*Stanley F. Buchmiller*

Heavenly Rain

I went off to the woodlands late one night,
under the stars I surveyed my life-
as the moonlight lay on the lake nearby-
off in the distance I heard babies cry-
all I've brought forth is an empty sigh.

at thirty seven,
heaven,
has not sent a child-
but I have not sat in sorrow all the while.
Counting all my have's and my have not's
all of my blessings I have not forgot.
few things happen simply by chance-
certain reason in circumstance-
perhaps master plan designs the dance.
yet,
I,
I've never looked above and bellowed "why?!"
my joyous tears mingle with those from the sky.
never one to despise the rain-
for it brings growth as does one's pain.

—*Victoria Ann Weiland*

The Glimmer And The Glamour Of

The glow of the morning sunrise
Unfolds a soft drama
Moving slowly with color
Shedding the first glimmer
With a beautiful manner

  It awakens the sea gulls
  And the sleepy cranes
  Lights up the sand dunes
  Brightening the lazy seaweeds
  Playing colorful games

    The Jetties emerge
    With a gentle splash
    The waves and rocks have arguments
    Splashing louder and louder
    Adding more sparkle, more enjoyment!

      The wet kisses of the waves
      Upon the lovely sands
      Never stops - round the clock
      A life long romance...
      A scene no one can enhance!

        The glimmer and the glamour
        Comes to a final peak
        With a magnificent sunset
        An extravaganza of light
        Mother Nature's glorious feat.

—*Teresa Alamia*

Sea Shell

I lie in the blue depths of the ocean,
Unmoved by current or wave; I wait...
For a strong tide to wash me to shore.
My world is the rhythmic swaying of flowery anemones,
Of myriads of fish passing me by,
Of crabs making a temporary home of me,
Of a perpetual slow-moving dizziness
That seems to hypnotize the creatures of the deep.
Silky smooth as a rose petal, my body spirals,
Pointing to the surface, and the world I dream of.

My heart is yellow, golden, empty.
It longs for a listening ear,
For I have stories to tell of the ocean
And all of its well-kept secrets,
I long to lay on the warm, sun-baked sand,
To see the sky, the moon, the stars.
But my moon is the iridescent glow of the jellyfish,
My stars are the creeping, grasping starfish,
And my sky is the rippling surface, far above.

—*Laurel Mastnjak*

Souvenirs

He cried again in his sleep last night,
unnatural whimpers from this virile
officer returned from another fight
on foreign soil, where the civilian kill
far outnumbered military lives lost.

He leaves the service soon, with scars on head,
a pension, and a soul bound to the cost
of shots in an Iraqi's back, who bled
on photographs of sons, now fatherless.

The shooters were tried and somehow released
for crimes the Army forgot tot tell us
about. Each night their captain sees the deceased,
snapshots, and pistole removed from his grave
souvenirs from sons in the home of the "brave".

—*Patricia Gray*

Fragments

The door is shut.
Unreachable yet so near.
One step closer to being out of sight,
One step closer to being out of reach.
Hoping that time could linger on forever.

The plane turns slowly onto the runway.
Loneliness strikes so hard it hurts.
Wanting to do something,
Wanting to stop it,
But knowing it impossible.

The silver bird is in the air.
Desperately clutching on to those last few moments
Trying to hold them and
Trying to make them last —
But finding no way.

Watching the red and white lights flashing
Smaller and smaller —
Feeling a void within me,
Feeling as empty as the sky,
Sweet memories flood my mind.

—*Miriam Mayer-Mader*

Grace

I saw a Praying Mantis cling
upon a green stalk, tall,
as on my bended knee I stooped
to sit on garden wall.

Her hands were clasped in prayerful pose,
her head was bent my way.
She watched my every movement
to see if I would stay.

I laughed at her and told her no,
I wouldn't spoil her prayer;
that she could pray in secret
and I would leave her there.

She nodded once, she nodded twice
and in her prayer box seat,
she opened up her praying hands
and an ant began to eat.

—*Marguerite Tweedie*

Unforgotten

Nothing's left. Not even marinated hands of scented oils, that
vibrated with radiant warmth to enhance the pleasure in moods
of a tired soul. Hands once felt can now be masked in the
touch of another. Unlock the doors of intellect and dreams
then see those hands again. And so it begins, the white water
rapid journey of memory. From the high clouded peaks of those
hands to the solemn quiet clear water visions of a face, a
time, a place. Moving down stream. Motivating fierce
emotional currents of undertow running deeper with passion
turns clear water white and foamy. Passing through thoughts of
heated warm summer days tinglings of times once passed make
turbulent the ride of subconscious uncontrolled. Hidden deep
beneath the surface, but not forgotten, lay rocky difference of
opinion and boulders of needs never satisfied. Placed
strategically in the channel of dreams forcing contact with the
solid ground of reality. Driven by a true navigator of
Happiness the chasm seems not pitted at all. With heart
pounding and eyes all a mist.

—*R. Laurence Johnson*

Whispers Of Reality...

WAR.....in the beginning the adrenalin is high. The rush of
victory and might compelling you forward.

Halfway to the battle you address your own insecurities,
morals and the value of your own life.
As you enter the battle the smell of death enters your soul.
Fear overcomes you and the adrenalin pushes you just to survive.

As the battle ends you stand there worn, and torn. Not the
same person who charged into battle with might, and vision of
victory and patriotism. On the contrary you stand alone with
visions of death and destruction, and instead of might you feel
weak and confused, wondering "What brought me here?" and then
a voice cries out "O.K. men lets move it out!" And you
remember that one battle does not win a WAR.

—*Patrick Raymond Sigety*

The Eye Of The Hurricane

Aroused and impassioned we walk directly
 towards The Eye of the Hurricane.
Along our journey we will never
 flinch from our fears.
We will quit the winds,
 we will comfort the weary from amongst us.
Finally, we will speak softly to the clouds.
So that they might bring forth a
 more gentle rain for us.

—*Marvin Pippig*

Silver

The silvery moon glides through the sky,
Viewing her realm as she passes on high.
She sheds her beams on the earth below,
Turning to silver the glistening snow.

She casts her light on farms and trees;
Only a land chill and silent she sees.
The lights are off in each silvery home;
Few on a night such as this care to roam.

A silver mouse goes scampering on.
Reaching his nest, in a wink, he is gone.
A silver night owl's hooting now,
Eyeing the moon from his snow-laden bough.

A lone wolf howls at the silver moon,
Calling his mate with that sad lonesome tune.
A few night creatures here and there,
Slink out for food in that cold silver air.

The moon glides on across the sky,
Gazing below with her silvery eye.
Ah, few have paused to see such a sight
As a silvery world on a cold winter's night.

—*Mildred M. Radebaugh*

Toledo Museum Of Art

Faces beautiful, ugly, happy, tortured,
Views ancient, allegorical, historical
Colors bright, and somber
All fashioned in Italy's magnificent age.

Longhi's pompous musician
Falciatoris' fleeing Joseph
Batoni's bare breasted beauty
Provoke quiet reverence.

Handsome Judith with Holofernes' head
Argus' eyes used by Juno for the peacock's tail
Sophonisba and Thisbe choosing death to life without love
Monti, Balestra, Pellegrini, Benefial, be praised.

For eyes to see the issue of the painters' brush,
For soul to appreciate,
For mind to dance away in lonely speculation,
For friends to share art's feast,
I am grateful

—*Maxine Allen*

Ode To Friendship

My friend we've been through many a year
Waikiki, Happy Hours, and gallons of beer

Shipwrecks, Rigger, Benihana, Annabelles
Just a few of the places where we would dwell

Workdays or weekends we'd stay out till late
Usually winding up at Denny's where breakfast we ate

The many apartments that we two did share
Shenanigans only "Laverne & Shirley" would dare

Acapulco, Vegas and Dallas were great
As were the islands of the Aloha State

We've grown-up together through thick and thin
And couldn't be closer if we were kin

All of these memories and more we'll remember
And maybe I'll see you back here in December

I miss you and want us to keep in touch
In the meantime take care and the best of luck

—*Uta D. Lum Kee*

Stygian Shore

I've lived a silent life, a life I've learned to hate,
Walking on this evil Earth, in search for golden gates;
But choices I have made will send me in reverse,
I will not see the angels fly, when resting in my hearse;
For me, it's down to hell, for reasons I won't say,
I guess there's no where else for me, when being sold on
   judgement day;
It's not that I'll be missed, oh no, that's not the thing,
The only thought that bothers them, would be the guilt
   feeling;
They just don't want to be, the one to take the blame,
For my sudden dissolution, with my suicidal game;
But worried I am not, for my hell is not hot,
No fires, nor an endless pit, my body will not rot;
When my death day comes, no one shall waste their time,
Digging a hole, six feet below, 'cause from the pit I'll climb;
Just struggling to the top, until I reach above,
And then I'll journey to the place, a wasteland with no doves;
When finally I'll arrive; and walk through the big door,
My river set forth destination, the end, Stygian Shore.

   —*Marina Moya-Reyes*

The Hurt

And so they wander like little wind up toys bumping into
walls and each other.
Victims of a time filled with confusion and despair.
Searching, wanting comfort for a gnawing burning at
their souls.
Questioning each other how to tear out the pain that
made them wander,
Bumping, searching, seeking the reason why,
Emptiness, loneliness longs to be overcome with love but
They have become wind up toys and their hearts have turned
to each other,
Etching into the book of time a people desiring a place to
call their own.

   —*Marilyn Brehm*

The Road Back To Me

I wandered down a long dark road, for almost half my life, Not
wanting to know what lay ahead, afraid to see the light. And I
stayed within the darkness, content with what I saw, Until one
day I dared to look, and saw nothing at all. I knew I'd have
to turn around and take another road, Or I'd have been born and
died, and no one would ever know. I looked ahead and saw a
hill, I said "I'll take that way!" But little did I realize
then, the dues I had to pay. My hill became a mountain, that
was so high and wide, The road to get there rough and rocky,
always a black sky. So many times I stopped afraid, the
mountain seemed so far, I knew I'd never make it, it took too
long, it was too hard. I lay awake at night and dreamt of who
I was to be, but every time I reached for it, someone was ahead
of me. Sometimes I yearned for the darkness, tired of fighting
for my dream, but some very special people gave their love, and
it became my beam. They carried my through the pain and
frustration, through the darkest clouds. By believing in me, I
believe in myself, I became strong and proud. And now I've
reached my mountain, I will begin my climb, I'm not afraid, I'm
not alone, I know the world is mine.

   —*Phylis Miller*

War

There stood a woman old and grey
Waiting for her son to return the next day
Was he to return or was he not
She stood waiting, watching, listening,
to the clock
A sudden jerk, a crying sound
and she fell sobbing to the ground
Her son was gone far away
Into heaven where he would stay

   —*Millie Lipshutz*

Suicidal Tendencies

She sits there every night
Wanting to run not wanting to fight
Her past haunts her like a child's dream
She wants to wake up she wants to scream
She knows no words to describe her pain
And if she spoke would she be speaking in vain
It's not a bump that a mother has cleaned and kissed
It's a childhood, a childhood that's missed
So try and push harder to stand and fight
Hold onto the child inside and get through another
nightmare tonight

   —*M. E. Quisenberry*

Self Image

I looked into my mirror today,
Was amazed at what I saw,
The person staring back at me,
I didn't recognize at all,
When did it happen, this change I see,
Where did it all take place,
A metamorphosis of great magnitude
That's happened to this face,
Then I thought, it's not so bad,
I'm sure it could be worse,
They call them "character lines" you know,

The aging process curse,
I do dislike it when they say,
Oh my, you're looking good,
Compared to what, I would reply,
I look the way I should,
So take heart, to you one and all,
Don't fret and start to worry,
It happens oh so gradually
Aging is never in a hurry!!!

   —*Lena Tanilli*

The Busy Bee

Years sixty five to seventy
Was just I like a busy bee.
   What comes to thought I would then plan,
   Then "buzzz" at it I have to scan.

I thought they're good and giants I'll make,
So "buzzz" again each I did take.
   Look what you say in piggery,
   It looks dirty but there's money.

After some months you'll find them, Hey!
Do go like mine it's that easy.
   Why do you think I've to study
   Though I'm now like a busy bee?

'Cause I've to use them in a war,
In quest for dough for which they are.
   If you study you'll fill your brain,
   With fiery gas to search for grain.

This life of mine is storybook,
Which if they're smart they'd take good look.
   What Santos did was plant and reap,
   He worked and worked while they're asleep.

   —*Santos Borbe*

His Name Is Wonderful

I heard about His wonderful Name, of all His love and caring
ways, but none of this did bid me near, for I was but a child
so dear, full of life and cheer.

I heard again of how He counseled man, but none of this did bid
me hear, for I had not yet learned to fear.

I heard once more, He is the Mighty God I need, so to Him now
will I plead, for now you see, life has knock me to my knees,
Yes now I see my need.

And now I know His name to me will always be Wonderful, for
    you see
He's the one who has lifted me up from these weary knees.

His name is Wonderful to me, you see.

  —*J. W. Matlock, Sr*

Partings

Like a bird...
We all fly to another place in time.
Leaving this earth and all our past deeds behind.
We give what we can, without malice of mind.
Some travels are hard, with much to endure.
And as we pass through, we sometimes just soar.
Not knowing what flight to take to the end,
And hoping we cared not to hurt or offend.
Those that we love, we pray they will know,
That life is the trial we pass through to grow
And when all is done, and we've run out of time,
We answer to one, who we know is divine.
So let us not judge, and be generous of heart,
For the day will soon come,
That we too must part!

  —*Laraine Sanfilippo Watts*

Thanksgiving Prayer

Thanksgiving is the time of year
We all thank someone for being here
Thanks to our family and friends, we remember those beneath the
    dust
for they to are honorable tale and forever dwelling dear with us
we set aside the turkey, pie and assorted labels
And look upon the faces seated at our tables
Though a matchless variety we behold
We recognize each other for the essence of the soul
And know that here you always have a special place
While trudging along the lanes of this eternal human race
Then the blessing for this day's delight
Might touch those who's absent on this Thanksgiving night
So we bow our heads to yield to one
Who daily brings the bread we eat and the rising of the sun
For there will come times in life buffets will be a rarity
So thank you now for peace and health and prosperity
Praying love might hover always in our mist
May we live long to sit again together in his internal bliss
Then before we eat and share all parts
The Lord shall remain forever in our hearts
     AMEN

  —*Melvin P. Hunter*

A Time For Reflection

 Yesterday, Today, Tomorrow

Yesterday- Is gone- we cannot bring it back, but how fortunate
    we are, to have so many beautiful memories, that we will
    keep in our hearts forever!
  Always try to maintain an optimistic attitude.
  Reflect upon the positive - not the negative!

Today- Is the first day of the rest of your life.
  How many times have we heard that old cliche?
  Have you ever stopped & thought about how true it really is?
  So we must not take it for granted, but make the most of it.
   Make all our precious moments count-
   When is the last time you "Stopped to smell the Roses?"

Tomorrow- ? Who knows? Our yesterdays & todays will surely
    have an impact on all of our tomorrows. With a positive
    attitude, Faith in God & Love in your heart, I wish you a
    Happy Tomorrow!

  —*K. Waskewicz*

Memories

Life is experiences that turn into memories when done.
We choose to hold onto and cherish the good ones.
From the time we are born, till we can remember no more.
Sometimes lapsing into sadness unable to except what lies before.

Memories can make us feel content or break us apart.
Happiness or sadness flows over us like at the start.
A song, word, picture or feeling stirs our hearts within.
But beware, we can lose sight of where we're going or have been

Why do we have memories, are they a window to our soul,
A help or hinderance to our much needed goals?
Can we learn from experiences and their examples each day,
If we channel our thoughts to the positive along the way?

We all have our memories they compile year after year.
Some we will try to forget, while others we hold dear.
What we need to recall is, "we pass this way but once".
Today's experience will be tomorrow's memories we've won!

  —*Lenora Green*

Mixed-Up-World

In this world, this crazy mixed-up world,
We don't even know what's going on.
In this world, this crazy mixed-up world,
We are no longer safe in our homes.

In this great world of God's,
God our great creator,
Created a man to a lover,
Not to be a hater.

God created all things,
Both the living and dead.
But, some men dislike some of God's creations,
So it has often been said.

We should learn to love everyone
Regardless of their race or color.
Every lady to another should be her sister,
Every man to man a brother

In this world, this crazy mixed-up world,
We don't even know what's going on.
In this world, this crazy mixed-up world,
If we don't get together we will be dead and gone.

  —*Stanley Wheaton*

Carolyn's Compassion

During the course of our lives,
    we incur obstacles that we can't foresee.
This time a year ago,
    it was a war across the sea.

As military members prepared to leave,
    families left behind would surely grieve.
Tears flowed freely as they said good-bye,
    only hours now, till they'd be in the sky.

Spouses and families left behind,
    looked for help it was hard to find.
But you Carolyn, with your compassion and warmth,
    saw a need for a leader, so you stepped forth.

Organize, inform, but mostly console,
    you helped families from losing control.
No one can measure the impact you had,
    and in a way that's kind of sad.

Remember Carolyn, as long as you live,
    thousands were affected by the love you did give.
As a spouse affected in more ways than one,
    thanks from all of us, for everything you've done.

    —Robert Fleissner

You Told Me Once You Loved Me

You told me once you loved me.
We lived together in our own little heaven.
Under the New Year's moon light
You cried, as you might
Exclaiming you were torn between two lovers.
But, something's got hold on me
You told me once you loved me.
Now you're with a new love in a different heaven.
Teenage maternity has made you a woman.
As your once called heaven has turned into a prison
You my broken lady, must wait to be risen.
I'm still looking for the answer
But, something's got a hold on me
You told me once you loved me.
Every word I write says, "I love you"
Because, you told me once, you loved me.

    —Thomas E. Locklier

The Storm

There is a storm coming
We need to prepare
The forecast is not good
Because of lack of care

The air is dirty, the oceans are dying
The forests are shrinking, more each day
Years have passed, no one took notice
We need to decide on a better way

People have been selfish and insensitive
We have confused rights with what is right
A plan must be made, to give something back
To turn back the storm, it will be a fight.

    —Michael Ebe

Tomorrow

Oh love, oh love, where have you gone,
We teach love we preach love,
You are not in the street
You are not in the homes.
Oh love where have you gone.
Just like the sun that hide
Behind the trees we know one day
You will appear all shining and bright,
Oh love take off your armor,
And let me in so I can show you love again.

    —Ruthei Walker

For Lyla On Her 90th Birthday

We've shared a lot of life, dear Lyla, you and I.
We never even realized that years were going by.

We've shared our kids; you used your own. The ones I used were
    out on loan
From 4-H families, schools and such-which helps with sharing very
    much.

We shared the Monroe Mother's Club-a jolly, gossipy bunch,
Who worked so hard to get things done; then stuffed us all with
    lunch.
We shared our losses: mothers, brothers, sisters, husband, girls.
But memory makes of them, tis said, a precious string of pearls.
For many years our paths diverged; I went north, you chose south.
We shared ourselves by "Old Ma Bell" I still could use my mouth!

And now we share our "Golden Years" in very different ways:
Our knees, our hips, our eyes, and things hidden from our gaze.

We share our love of doctors, and naturally, their pills.
Expecting every one, of course, will cure all our ills.
And when, alas, they fail, we'll glance right, left, and blink.
"Do you suppose", we'll whisper, "that we should see a shrink?"
But we've too much upstairs for that, I'm sure we both agree.
So we will go on sharing as long as we can see! Won't we?

    —Olive L. Kutz

Wake Up, Wake Up, Wake Up

We've been sleeping for far too long
We no longer control our society
It controls us.
Wake up! Get up!
Stop sleeping
Because every time you close your eyes
to sleep one of our children are
Closing them for good.
Stop being a society of greed,
Color, falsification, uncertainty
and sin. Wake up before the nightmare
becomes reality. Stop sleeping, stop sitting,
stop talking. Get us off the street, off
dope, off unsafe sex. Help us motivate, graduate,
and overtake our society once again.

    —Zelma A. Blakes

Another Day At The Office

We come to the office in the usual way.
We perform our duties day after day.
We have our bosses that we think are great.
We also have the ones we love to hate.
We plan Bridal and Baby showers,
sometimes we get a bouquet of flowers.
We celebrate our birthdays year after year.
We share our dreams, hopes and fears.
We have been to weddings and divorces too,
somehow we still have strength to get through.
We laugh and we cry, as life's troubles pass us by.
We take a moment to thank God we are still alive.
We see each other start to change,
but there are some things that remain the same.
It is always sad when one of us has to part,
but we wish them well in their new start.
There is only one thing that will never go away,
that is the memories of a new friend, I met yesterday.

    —Vera L. Rogers

Nine Foot

Blessed with nature's wine from the vine
We run through the forest looking for all hunted prey
With the bloody daggers in hand from the last ritual
Flames of fire and from our God
The king's son is sad and his brother wants not to hurt

The forest is filled with creatures of all kinds
They are in fear of the new order of religion in birth of the
    forest.
A nine foot circle in the mist of it all.

This circle seems useless to mortals
Life is one thing to live is another this circle
    is proof of all differences between us and them.

        —*Rusty Heitmann*

Somewhere In Space (In the memory of my son, Brent)

The Universe spreads vastly into unlimited eternity.
We search gently into space, but there's so much more to see.

Have we experienced life before on some mysterious planet?
To think this is all there is! It can't be all, or can it?

Are there other cities, towns, houses, and people just as we,
On a far off planet wondering what is beyond what they see?

Do we travel from star to star in the blink of an eye?
Wouldn't that be more thrilling to think of than just to die?

Are other suns like ours shining brightly on life below?
Or is there too much to grasp, and it's better not to know.

What happens to our souls when our bodies are laid to rest?
Will familiar loving beings guide us as they know best?

Do we journey swiftly from earth when our souls take flight,
Or do we linger for awhile 'til our loved ones are all right?

Do guardian angels watch o'er us throughout our Earthly years?
Why don't they help when we hurt? Don't they see our tears?

Or, are we left to our own choices? Is this the way we grow?
Should we search within, because deep in our souls we know?

Well, on with life, on with learning, they never seem to cease.
Take time to share God's love, and one day we'll find peace.

        —*Marilyn Martin*

People

We ride and rope
We sit and smoke
We're the people of the land
The red rock rims
The sage brush grows to
The river we pan for gold
In the San Miguel
If only it could tell
All the stories this river has seen
About cowboys shiners and hard rock miners
The flumes they built
The rails they split
The families that live on forever
About a land strong and true
Like the men we once knew
The little bitty towns
Where nice people still abound
This is the piece of America I know

        —*Susan Hollingshead*

A Thought

As we wander down life's roads,
We sometimes carry heavy loads.
Some are happy, some are sad,
It would be great, to always be glad.

Relationships can be bought and sold,
The heaviest of burdens, are sometimes untold.
What makes a person always wrong or right,
An unhappy person, is not a pretty sight.

One shouldn't live a life in fear.
You sure can't drown it in booze or beer,
Be unselfish, kind and nice,
That's not asking to big a price.

Try and find happiness in each passing day,
It might even help, to stop and pray.
It helps in life, to find some pleasure,
Along life's way, you'll have memories to treasure.

        —*Lois Mallory*

Untitled

Violence begets violence.
We want restitution not retribution.
Let's break this unhealthy silence,
But make a positive contribution.
A race divided can not stand,
We must come together to have the upper hand.
We must work together towards a common goal.
Everyone cannot be the leader, but each will have a role.
It will be a long and tiresome journey to make,
But one we must take.
I say let's join our voices as one-strong and proud,
We can say what we have to say without being rude and loud.

        —*ReGina Crawford-Martin*

The Reading

It was just after Hillel dinner. Last Hillel dinner of spring.
We went to the reading. I borrowed a pen and wrote on napkin
now tattered and torn. A pen, a hammer, tools of trade, of
toil, it didn't matter. God and I would talk about it at
Atonement after summer. Father barely understanding his
proselyte son. Never feeling more welcomed. The napkin read:
Trans something Na. Onto. Some Russian. Projections.
Harmonic divergence I think. Ni was allowed. Chalk on the
sidewalk reads boys allowed sic added. Infinity something,
cafe au lait something, et the coffeehouse something, barely
able to read the scribbling. Brownian motion. A place to stay
in Izmir. Istanbul's so dirty in the winter. But je t'aime
still lingers in the curling smoke-filled air. hackneyed like
Laurie Anderson says it. A lexicon map for the nighttime
navigation day tripper. My poor man's opulence. Poor Richard
the Lion Hearted. Ellipse written out, e-l-l-i-p-s-e not....
The hieroglyphs only hinting at the moment Half in Hebrew,
Half in Latin. Lost Words. It is probably better that way.
Sir Freeman the Third comes up to me afterward says he's with
the Limbic Society.

        —*Todd McCormick*

Moon Song

Indian maiden hums a melancholy strain,
Weaving histories from strands of wampum shell.
Long nights at this loom, silent eves —
Yet by the light of fire, fingers speak.

Legends strung before the eye
As smoothly as sea paints dry shore —
Each bead a part of sand,
Purple softly washing into white.

Migrations fly, yet still the maiden plies her craft;
Moons never know a finished tapestry —
This art as dear as long, white braids
Which tell a history of their own.

—*Patricia Benstock*

Saturday's Fun!!

Saturday morning... soon there is a knock at the door.
Well look there stands two grandkids ... both under four.

A big hug for each one ...
Gee, their happy faces warm us...like the sun.

To each, we give some cookies and milk ...
Immediately they put right into their golden hair of silk.

Playing games and telling stories ...
Erase all of our yesterday's worries.

It is just so grand when they come to visit ...
They keep these old bodies active every minute.

Upstairs, downstairs, out for a walk ...
Over to the park, or ... just to sit and talk.

The Saturday hours go by so fast ...
And so they go home ... but their memories last.

Grandma and Grandpa sit and smile ...
And just have to rest a while.

Gosh, today was such a happy day ...
Don't fret though ... soon it will again be Saturday!

—*Lois Mallory*

This Is Where I Call Home

To ask where one lives I think is ambiguous at best. For if I
were asked this question my mind would say "Los Angeles" with
all due respect to geographic locale. My spirit however would
feel the urgency to shout from its very depths the need to say
"In The Forest"! It is in the forest where my heart is free to
explore itself and its surroundings without the shackles of
social inhibition. Out here where neither black nor white
rules, only the green of our sibling pines has the final word.
In the forest there are no politics, no corporate ladders to
climb, no greed, no stature. There is no violence, no hatred,
no discrimination, no repression of man's will to be. In the
forest only the will of the wind directs my every thought, my
every emotion, my every action. The three merge into one as it
should be, finding their place in the chorus of the evergreens
continuous melody. In the forest is God's canvas. The paint
from His brush surrounds me underfoot, in the air, across the
horizon. Within this masterpiece I am able to measure my
soul's true worth. The color bleeding into me and I into the
color. In the forest comes life. From the boughs of ancient
cedar my bones, have grown.
And to the ferned meadow I will someday return.
This is where I call home.

—*Scott Leising*

ON The Death Of A Friend

Lord, we're in denial and disbelief and distress.
We're saying "why" and "if only" and "it can't be".
We are suffering inexpressible loss and pain and grief.
We feel diminished, less than whole, incomplete.
We want her back, Lord, alive and vibrant, gracious and good,
Serving you and her family and her friends with unselfish love.
Remind us, Lord, of your words of comfort:
"Precious in the sight of the Lord is the death of his saints."
Help us to comprehend that she is gazing upon your glory,
Face to face, while we still see through the glass dimly.
Help us to remember that she is complete in your glory,
And remind us that we, too, are complete in you —
Even in this dying world.
Help us to let her go and give you thanks — thanks for
Allowing our lives to be touched and enriched by one of your
Most precious saints — Barbara.

—*Virginia R. Burroughs*

The Freedom Lay

So oft in time of grief and gloom doth this my soul pronounce:
What cause have I to ring and writhe and all my state denounce?

For truth it is that in my veins no freer blood doth flow
And ev'ry breathe that I partake is given me to know

My life is mine, at liberty, a blessing with a price:
To honor, use, and keep it dear with noble sacrifice.

So if this weal should break apart and all should come to
naught, then shall I weep as Arthur King o'er fallen Camelot.

When comes that night, the fearful bane, and all from me is
torn, O may I then with valiant heart await the blessed morn!

—*Paul Kartchner*

These Growing Things

Once I thought it surely right

for children and young trees to take what course they might,

their spirits and their branches free to grow

unhampered, and tried by strength of will to have it so.

But as I watched my unchecked saplings grope

and stayed my hand, with what shattering of hope

did I perceive where freedom such as this might lead,

what sad distortion of that once whole, perfect seed.

Small value lies in freedom if the seedling then grows wild.

What good a shapeless future for either tree or child?

And so, for all these growing things by which we set such store,

I've learned that careful pruning is the loving gardener's chore.

—*Lee J. Hendry*

Untitled

The lofty ideals of the fisherman
Were only encumbered by the sea.

Not any terrestrial domain, he felt,
Could hold back his longing for a
Less earth-bound fate.

The dolphins were mercilessly
Chewing at the Star-Bushido
Who knew the oceans waves so well.

But the resolve of the oceans mare, the fisherman,
Would rekindle his faith in the watery air!

—*Marc Wolsky*

In A Cemetery On A Gray Winter Afternoon

Who were these mortals...
   What did they look like...
How did they dress...
   What goals did they reach for?

I don't know
   How well they loved or
How intensely they disliked.

I haven't any way of feeling
   The problems that they knew
Or of sensing the emotions
   That once filled their hearts.

But I do know that they
   loved and hated
   laughed and cried
   toiled and rested
   believed and doubted
   and wondered and worried
   about themselves and their world
And, like myself, once lived.

     —Neal D. Wilfong

Down The Road

I travel down the road to see
   What nature has in store for me.

I sometimes walk, I sometimes bike
   And often I go out at night.

Once on the marsh you see strange things
   Like fiddler crabs that have no strings.

Like alligators that look like logs
   Or maybe see a snoozing dog.

That pelican is mighty large
   But then, oh look, so is that barge.

Quick, look over there - did you see
   That turtle sleeping on that tree?

Was that a snake or just a stick?
   I'd better move on and be quick.

I hear a bird calling in the dark
   I wonder why it hoots - not bark?

As I travel on down the road
   Look where I stopped - right by this toad.

     —Virginia B. Huntington

Those Who Don't

What right do they have their eyes downcast on me
What right do they have to wander my streets
They don't know me or my people
Those in their fancy cars who took a wrong turn
Scared of things they can not see
touch
or understand
So I have dark skin and a small house
So I am wearing old clothes
Does that mean I can not be proud
or hold my head high
Go ahead and be scared
I will not hurt you as you have hurt me
I will not judge you as you have judged me
I will not take your dignity or let you take mine
You need to learn to see with your heart
and not your tainted eyes
If you did
you would see that I am just as good as you.

     —Tracee Fuller

Us

So many times I've lain and wondered,
What will become of Us?
I wanted so much to have what others before me had and kept
But, our paths converged for only a short while.

I sometimes wish that life would change
And bring you back my way
What others threw away so easily
Would be the center of my world

If our paths had converged for only a while longer
I wouldn't be lying here now
Wondering,
What ever happened to us?

     —Michelle Ely

A Birthday Present For My Father

If we could just start over, or make some little change
What would you do different, replay or re-arrange?

I know what I would alter, I know what I would do
I'd go back to my early years and show more love for you.

I'd spend more time just talking, telling you all my fears
Letting you see my feelings, my joy, my sadness, my tears.

Then you could tell me some of what you feel inside
What brings you up or takes you down, things you always hide.

In the years that follow after, we'd be closer day by day
Not like the way it has been, further and further away.

Though actions may not show it, the closeness is really there
I think about you often, though I may not seem to care.

Always remember I love you, Dad, carry it in your heart
Keep it there for always, though we may be miles apart.

     —Phyllis Hallberg

To A Novice Seeker

The mainstream of life is a marketplace where you'll find
whatever you seek, be very sure what you're looking for, and
knowingly pick your streets. Take with you the love we gave
you, set your morals and standards high, be honest in all your
transactions and your limits will reach the sky. At each turn,
with each step you take, you'll meet merchants of all degree,
and the searching that lies behind your eyes will reveal that
nothing comes free. Be sure what you sell to the buyer makes
him glad for the price he paid, and never buy from the sellers
supply, goods where you've nothing to gain. In the traders
mart, be just and alert, so a bargain that's struck is fair,
keep a watchful eye for the thieves at large, or they'll leave
you in deep despair. Be willing to lend a hand to one unable
to pay the cost, you may give back hope to a troubled soul and
save him from being lost. You'll find that prices will rise
and fall, and values will change with time, but barter not with
your conscience, it's there to help keep you in line. At last,
if you're truly the master of your craft in the marketplace,
your accounts will be overflowing with love, and your coffers
all lined with grace.

     —Mabel Langworthy

Eclypse

What is this thunderous sound quickly approaching?
What is this silvery-white emerging in the moon-light?
Now I see his graceful gait, flowing mane, head and tail held
proudly, as he comes into full view.
Then in a few moments, as mysteriously as he came, this
magnificent steed was gone.
As the grace and splendor of the eclipse captures man's gaze,
so it is with the arabian stallion, Eclypse.

     —Linda J. Chapman

Parents

P - Patience with some biting of nails,
   When a kid covers up the tallest of tales.
A - Attention to the school play's bright star,
   Who's playing Martian and is bound to go far.
R - Reason a sense of fair play,
   That kids don't respect till they're grown up someday.
E - Eyes that see only the best,
   In a child whom some people might think is a pest.
N - Nights when the folks walked the floor,
   One eye on the clock, one eye on the door.
T - Thanks for a home filled with care,
   And the loving support that has always been there.
S - Sweethearts a dear Mom and Dad,
   The most wonderful parents any kid ever had.

     —Lacy Banks

I Must

Confused, confessed, so hard, so blessed

You find it hard to hear the confession
When all you do is live in pain.

I see the scars in your secession
and know the wounds were not in vain.

You live each day in your shelter,
I fight you in and out of trust.

I know the fear of life in skelter,
You've got to learn, you really must.

Your love means everything to me,
That, I hope is in your view.

I cry when I think of what it could be
but realize that my fate is not so new.

It's all up to me to lead the way,
I just have to say the words.....

It's hard, it's a mess, I really must confess.

     —Nathanael Harrison

When Did I Fall In Love

When did I fall in love
When did I have time
During the rush and bustle of the world
Did I have time for something so
sweet and innocent

When did I fall in love
When did I have time
When did the intimacies become mine
In the morning, or at night, real late
or would it come that fast, like an earthquake

Did it come slow, in a week, or in many days
That I find myself entwined
By my lover, my love in our bed I lay
I shall never know for love has no time
But between the look of love mirrored
between us you are mine.

     —Tiffany Hughes

Heritage

Some folks worry — or tremble — or gasp —
When genealogists dig up their past!
But, we can never correct or erase —
If there was incest, or crime, or infusion of race!
We've no way to bury the skeletons there.
We're grateful today for the comforts we share.
Let's proudly appreciate strengths of today,—
Move forward with pride. God will show us the way.

     —Louella Allen

Special Anniversary

It seems like just the other day
When down the aisle we made our way
There we stood, side by side
An old groom and an older bride
And beneath pink flowers of varied hues
We nervously exchanged rings and our "I do's"

Through the years we've had our ups and downs
We had our smiles and had our frowns
We had our share of fighting bouts
With the usual amount of screams and shouts
Especially did we really clash
When our money went in the market crash
We've had our sickness and our health
We've had our poorness and some wealth

Our shapes have stood the test of time
What now is scarred, once was prime
Our then smooth and silky faces
Have given way to wrinkled places
But we're lucky and happy we did survive
To our Silver Anniversary, number twenty five!

     —Natalie Epstein

Dem Subway Humans

Dem subway humans, dem interest me.
   When evening comes dem homeward bound.
Some a dem a hustle,
   While some dem struggle.
Humans of all races, from various places
   See dem move, some fa uptown, some fa downtown.

Dem subway humans, dem interest me.
   Check de facial expressions.
No one en laughing, no one en smiling,
   Some a dem sleeping, even snoring.
Ya see mean looks, stressful looks,
   Vex looks, even sexy looks.

Dem subway humans, dem interest me.
   Homeward bound, de ride is long.
Congestion, de stops, interruptions, de beggars, de bums,
   Discomforts, de heat, de odors, de squeezing,
Sometimes even freezing.
   Dem subway humans, dem interest me.

     —Roger Holder

Carrousel No. 4

It's the moment, yet again,
   when I am called to the
   black rotation of the carrousel,
   as it carries my memories
In its tattered bulging case.

Anticipation dries my lips
   as the belt click-clacks
   amidst a sea of travelers
   who wait for their own bags,
A reflection of trips gone past.

Some suitcases are slick and light
   and the luggage of the family
   are the same brand in different sizes;
   mine is heavier then I can lift
And it wears the scars of former journeys.

I reach for my treasured case
   and wonder at the ride
   of other's bags of retrospect,
   where they are headed
And what they collect inside.

     —Stacy Rosenhauer

Untitled

My life changed...
When I saw the world through your eyes.

I saw the images I'd never before seen.
I heard the sounds I'd never before heard.
I felt pleasure like I'd never before felt.
And I laughed harder than I ever dreamed possible.

You opened my eyes to a world I never knew existed.
You found the part of me I had forever been missing.
I can now see the world and what is important.
I can see it through your eyes.

— *LeighAnn Burger*

You Were With Me

You were with me
When I took from the candy store
and watched as I walked out, with conscience sore...

You were with me
in school as I cheated on the exam
and watch as I handed in my paper, feeling half the man...

You were with me
those nights I drank more than I should
and watched as I ran, with those up to no good...

You were with me
all the times I lied to my wife
and watched as I acted out my sordid life...

You were with me
while my business conducted a crooked deal
and watched as I laughed, at the way others feel...

Now you're with me
old and broken at eighty-two
as I ask forgiveness, I wonder, will I be with you...

— *Tony E. Jones*

Once Upon A Wish

When I was young I wished to be able to fly,
When I was young I looked at life through
a whole different perspective,
I would tie a towel around my neck
and shout "I wish I could fly" and then I'd
jump off the couch and skin my knee.

When I was young people always asked me what
I wanted to be when I grew up. I always replied
"Tada, Super boy!!" They just walked away as if at
five they wanted a better answer.

Now that I'm older I think in terms other
than super boy

So now when I see the star of hope I then wish
for love,

Not for some one to love me, but for someone
I can love and get the same spiritual love in return.

— *Nigel Coco*

A Simple Seed

A seed is the beginning of a relationship.
When it starts to grow, the relationship matures.
Once the seed is in full bloom, that is love;
  it is the sight of nature at its best!

— *Peter Okun*

When Monkeys Cry

Make ready the ways of war, and behold, the Mother's weep!
When man walks down his darkest side the earth runs red
Life ebbs upon the shore.
The young with calls to glory cut down in adolescence -
butchered by the altar of an age-sick lore.
When battle's done, tomorrow flees, denied;
Its bright promise but a vapor coupled with the scent of
cordite lingering ghost-like in the air.
And death re-echoes its nauseous laugh for it does not care;
What irony - lowly jungle beasts wisely step aside where nations
Marching in self splendor, exalt the evolution of their
passioned pride. For me now, lie,
The ceaseless grief and wondering what if?
But so it has always been.
A flag and a cause you say? No!!!
The only victor, horror, again too soon forgotten.
Yet will you ever stand and question why
When stage is set once more for youth to die?
Woe to the generations when monkey's cry.

— *William Wayne Gilbert*

To My Brother

Bro, you were my best friend through bad and good,
when no one else would understand I knew that you could.
Through all my silly problems, you always seemed to care,
and every time I turned around, your goofy smile was there.
Bro, I loved you dearly, and yes I still do
I didn't have to tell you daily, through our relationship I'm sure
   you knew.
I think back to when we were kids, and all the wild things we did.
Yeah Mommy always caught us, but we still wanted to do it again.
Bro, it was a special way you always made me feel,
and yeah we got mad at each other, but our bond was still so real.
We were just saying a week ago how funny it is to do something
   when one's gone,
but to let my only big brother slip away, to me that would be
   wrong.
So I'll always remember the fun times, and your pictures you know
   I'll show,
but no matter what I do Bro, I'll never let you go.

— *Tiffany L. Gilbert*

Moods

Immeasurable are the pangs I feel
when oft I think in vain
What is there in this life of mine?
I've all to lose and naught to gain

But then again my spirits soar
Begone O melancholy!
For life is different to me now
It's grand; it's sweet; it's jolly

There are merry times; boring times;
times when I feel no pain
and reveries waft around in my mind
like the strains of a haunting refrain

I've laughed 'till tears ran down my cheeks
at humor beyond belief
I've felt the anguish of a wrenching loss
and shed other tears in grief

Moods, like the weather, keep changing 'tis true
as we experience both good times and strife
But we find that we have an endless supply
to accommodate the challenges of life

— *Virginia R. Murphy*

Full Moon

Beauty abounds us in the middle of the night.
When our minds are unaware
And our bodies sleep tight.

Beneath the window I sit
Not a cloud in sight,
On this very radiant star-filled night.

Bright shiny moons are a treasure from above
They are something
To be thankful for.....just like love.

Whenever you awaken in the middle of the night,
Take heart; look to the moon...
Then sleep tight.

—*Lori O'Neil*

My Wish

I wish there would come a time
when our youth would refrain from crime.
And bring some of their values back
and refuse to sell or buy any crack.
They look at the money but they don't understand;
how can you spend money when you are dead man?

There are many good youths still left in our land today
if they would only take time and let someone show them the way.
How they can work and riches untold and buy what they want even
to gold?
Instead of the street which is like a lion's den
just waiting to take someone's child in.

Come into church and repent for your sins,
Jesus is waiting and will welcome you in.

—*Marsh Marigold*

The Place

Where can you go when blue skies start to grey
When rain falls from the clouds high in the sky.
When weary from walking along the way
Where can you go and be never asked why.
What can put all the wrong back to the right
Make merry your sorrow and chase away blues.
The only path you can take now comes to light
You've known all along what path you should choose.
The closer you get, the gray skies turn blue
The puddles of rain drops are sorrows now glad.
A smiling face, a happy heart, to name just a few
Return to the best of times you've ever had.
Behind the door, once before from which you did roam
It's family, it's love, this place is called home.

—*Maria E. Andrews*

Seasoning

Spring is a lovely time of year
When springtime flowers will appear
They'll peek their heads up through the sod
To remind us again there is a God
All summer long the flowers will bloom
Every hue and color to brighten a room
As it to say "Let's all be gay
Tomorrow will be another day"
Then comes the time when leaves will fall
Again to remind us that we are all
Creatures of God - good or bad
Next comes winter to make us sad
But the blanket of snow will keep plants warm
And the one above will keep us from harm
With each new season springs a new light
To cheer us up and make us feel bright

—*Ruth Dooley*

A Look At Life

What would happen if ever came a day
When the birds sing no more, and no children play.
When no longer lovers stand hand in hand
Along the beach kicking up the sand.

What would happen if flowers bloomed no more
In once green meadows, now yellow to the core.
When the trees have lost all their colorful leaves
To stand alone and naked in the dusty breeze.

What would happen if people grew cold
Not caring for their neighbors, not caring for their soul.
When disease may spread across the land
And no one caring to lend a hand.

What would happen if ever came this day
Where life and death could mean the same.
For there is no life in a world living death
As the world is destroyed, no more to feel its breath.

—*Terry Hamelin*

The Hand I Touch

When I touch the hand I love the world becomes my throne.
When the hand must go away I am left alone.
Though I know it is not right I feel its passion flow.
Though I feel its tenderness my love for it can't grow.
Though I feel the mother's touch I do not know the child.
Though I see the band of gold the touch just drives me wild.
Though I seek the ecstacy I see the karat's shine.
Though I smell the 2-7-3 I know the hand's not mine.
I know our touch could destroy all the hand has built.
I know my feelings of love and joy should be replaced by ones of
guilt.
The hand I touch is beautiful.
Its love for me it's shown.
The hand I touch is wonderful.
The hand is not my own.

—*Robert M. League*

Eternally

When the dawn awakens and the birds begin their songs;
when the soft blush of the sky appears;
when the Lord looks down on us and forgives our wrongs;
when we admit our hopes and fears.

This is the time when our hearts beat fast,
this is the time when our love awakens,
this is the time when no shadows cast,
this is the time we are not forsaken.

I can think of no better way to begin a day.
I can think of no beauty as deep and true.
I can think of no better words to say.
I can think of no other except for you.

Now is my love an everlasting thing.
Now is my love so wondrous a choice
now is my love a forever beckoning.
Now is my love the sound of your voice

—*Michael Gricoski*

Eyes

As I stare deep into the pools of darkness,
What is it I see?
Pain, fear, love, or is it sadness and longing,
Longing for someone to hold and caress?
Someone to love and be loved by?
I'm not really sure!
Or am I?
Could it be depression or possibly anger.
I can't help but stare and wonder...
What is behind such dark and frightening eyes?

—*Lovena Hughes*

Still Waiting

I've known you long before we met...

I saw your smile in smooth, cool waters of Finland lakes
when the wind was calm as my soul, my skin fresh from sauna
and the sun dripped orange on the summer solstice.

The fragrance of your body floated over my flesh as I
stopped in fields of lavender resting easily on English
hillsides during days made hazy with golden lager.

I heard your whispers of warning in willowy breezes winding
along the fortress walls of Pamplona where Spanish bulls
chase down narrow streets on the last day of their life.

The taste of your lips in glacial Swiss streams glided past
mine into content villages, gleeful and caressing as the
crimson geranium garlands necklaced about each home.

I felt your thoughts in long nights of lightless highways
with lonely homes shut tight against strangers traveling
tracks disappearing into the time I'm finally with you.

—*William Bleakney*

The Windows Of God

Eternal Jesus gave us one life
which was lived in full view
of so many nations, in so many times,
yet copied by so few.

The message of that life
was very profound, but plain.
It brought release to believers
from sin's bondage and pain.

His life showed the message from God
that we should strive to embrace
until it becomes our way of life
and we come face to face

with the windows of God and we know
that he is love in purest content.
He gave, he gives, and he will give
until each creation has a chance to repent

and repulse the trappings of worldly things
and realize he gave us all we'll ever need.
Then, in full circle, we care for others and become
The windows of God, in deed.

—*Billie M. Muncy*

Unquenchable Fire

The sunrise peeks above the horizon,
while a sunset falls below in
a different type of town or village.
The sunset sinks to the bottom of the world.
As it descends, the sunset tries to catch a glimpse
of the beautiful sunrise.
But she climbs too fast, he falls too quickly.
A tear falls, a smile brightens.
A man cries; he is frightened.
One Dove starts flight, straight upward, toward a God.
She looks down and frowns upon a problem.
A kiss is blown, a reward and a promise.
They yearn to meet, one and only.
To some a dream, to others a farce.
But a union might be made someday.
Two stars. Two colors. Two people. Two lovers.
Too late to care.
Sunset today. Sunrise tonight.
A beautiful rainbow of light will soon flourish over the land.

—*David P. Garbeil*

The Scarlet Figure

We trudged through the snow,
white as an eagle's extended wings.
A bright full moon reflected itself on the large pine trees.
A bitter wind brushed my face whispering a shy tone.
Only one being broke the silence of night, a blood red creature.
Its feathers struck the snow,
breaking the soft white hue
which had lay quietly throughout the evening.
Suddenly, it extended its wings,
and we watched it alight from a branch, and perch onto another.
Our eyes never left the beautiful scarlet red feathers,
looking as if they were just sheets of red silk.
Tiny obsidian eyes struck us as amazing.
Daddy and I glanced above at the giant trees
which guided us through the night;
there on the top of the pine the scarlet figure was perched,
leading our path.

—*Jordan Ilana Namerow*

The St. Joe Lake Bluff Park

Soft winds blowing, across the blue lake,
White sails inhaling, as much as it takes,
To get to their destiny or nearest port,
Never their pleasure cut quick or stopped short.

Maids of the mist rise tall and excluding,
Fountains of water which are precluding
The coming event, Sunday's concert at three,
A lovely event for you and for me!

People with dogs walk by my park bench,
Proud owners of children, their little hands clenched
On bottles and playthings; great wonders to see,
Of our beautiful lake bluff park, and to be -

A part of the ever - moving scene,
Their sense of the good life is very keen.
How wonderfully proud of this landscape am I!
To be part of this world, as it passes me by.

How often we miss the most precious part,
Of being alive and blessed from the start,
These wonders for us to behold for free,
One greatest of gifts to you and to me!

—*Flora J. Gast*

Chance (For Terence Wilde)

I wonder, lately.
Who came with night, to sip tea?
Immersed in metaphysical belonging
Only to fade into his poetry, migrating
With Vampires breathing sanity's sand,
Where the Vanity restores her outreached hand.
The Wheel of Fortune
journey...

Beware!
Ladies old-fashioned in satire.
Flowered and decayed, where beauty resides

His black hair, becoming.
Loves Daily Tide

I miss the laughter
Veiled eyes enhancing
jugglers, fiddlers
colored lights under parasols
Hoping he will write, a masquerade

—*Century*

746

A Secret

No one knew, not even you
There was a secret, that lived inside
It never peaked, was there to hide
Days to years, the time that passed
All the while, it was there to last
I felt it grow, only I to know
Never once let it show
Till one day, to finally confess
What had been, so long suppressed
I watched your face, as I revealed
My inner thoughts, no longer concealed
An expression, was your only confession
Your eyes grew soft, and seemed to glow
Was only then, you let it show
Now we're together, hand to glove
You've guessed our secret, it was love

—*Barbara Ann Puglisi*

That Road

On the face of a beautiful painting,
There's a road pointing over a hill,
I'd love to know where it's ending,
Is there a chance that ever I will??

In my dreams I see a big city,
Its streets paved with pure gold,
Sunlight blazing in all its glory,
No sorrows, so no one grows old.

Maybe someday I'll find the answer,
Until then in my dreams I'll pretend,
That I know where that road is leading,
And I'll surely some day find the end.

—*Frances A. Espe*

Endings

Left on the shelf
There's no one who cares
My feelings have no significance
My heart has no wares.

I'm lost in my mind
I'm caught in my soul
I'm trapped in this body
This big black hole.

I want to escape
I want to be free
From all this suffering
And what it's doing to me.

The end could be near
The end is not far
I wonder what is left
As I look at this jar.

—*Claire Hiscott*

Learning Love

Children are the gifts of love,
they wonder about
As free as a dove.
It is our duty to bring them up right,
to teach them peace
And never to fight.
If we can do this
we've accomplished our mission;
we've just taught our future
to learn and to listen.

—*Bobbie Pletcher*

Love On Level Ground:

When love is planted on level ground
There's no way it can roll around
Just like a railroad track of rails
There's no way to tip the scales.
No matter whether it's country or town
We'll plant our love on level ground.

We want a love that will last
Not one that will fade or pass
We just want one that will stay
One that will never never go away.
A love that's strong won't fall apart
It has to come from the heart
And not one that's up and down
We'll plant out love on level ground.

Now tomorrow is the great big day
A little more we have to say
We agree to face the future unafraid
For a firm foundation we have laid.
Our slogan true love we have found
We'll plant our love on level ground.

—*Joan H. Walton*

Reflection Of Me

I know not why
There's tears in my eyes
Nor do I know
Why my heart cries.

I only know
It's an awful pain
An empty feeling
I can't explain.

My hands reach out
But, all too soon
To pick that flower
That never blooms.

My eyes keep searching
Far beyond the sea
But, all they find
Is a reflection of me.

A smile on my face
Oh, God it's not true
My happy eyes
If, one but knew.

—*Connie Geurin*

The Movies

What happened to the movies
They use to be such fun
With hop a long cassidy
And Annie get your gun

The old time classics
Like "gone with the wind"
When Rhett left Scarlet
We thought it was a sin.

And what about the comedy
"It happened one night"
Everything was so natural
The casting was just right

What happened to the movies
Is what I like to know
It isn't show business anymore
Now all it is, is show

—*Bernadine Flanagan*

What Is A Friend?

Friends are surely nice to have
They are what God intended
To be a beam of light for us
When we are at times discontented.

A true friend listens to your woes
And lends his willing ear
When we continue to rattle on
By releasing those endless fears.

No matter what our problem
They are agreeable to whatever
And seem to understand us
By helping to ease one's endeavor.

I know God is our eternal friend
But he feels we need one here
That can say, "I know I've had it."
And be that added comfort and cheer.

Kind of hope you are that friend
Who bends an ear to heed.
Thus be a flower in one's garden
And not turn out to be a weed.

—*Elva R. Schleiger*

I Know The Night

I am one with the shadows
They cloak me
make me safe
from prying stares
Ignorance
my enemy
Has no eyes to pierce the blackness
Where I alone stand
And watch the world
I know the night
He is my ally
From hateful words
And cruel stares
The blackness is my shield
For I cannot live like others
They see only my outside and run in fear
Though I have done no harm.
When light drives me from my hiding
place,
I flee, but see the people,
And ask my enemy, ignorance: Why?

—*Jennifer Quail*

A Gift Of Camaraderie

I have a new circle of friends.
They're not people — they are birds.
I started the enterprise
With a few crumbs and kernels of rice.
But now the feathered coterie
Bravely comes flying close to me,
Swooping and gaily chattering.
And, strangely, we don't need any words.

We each share what we have to give.
I offer — they are receptive.
And they in turn bestow on me
Faithful visits, trust and loyalty.

—*Barbara Carr*

Another One

The broken down car in my driveway
          This is good bye
Car was packed full with her belongings
She thanked me for the good times we had
She was sorry it didn't last longer
          I hate this part

She would be moving up north to find
     A new life, a home, a job
There was nothing I could do or say
     To change her mind
To her this was no big deal
          Pick up and leave
     Burn the bridges down
Say good bye and mean it
          Forever
No looking back, no second chance
          No tomorrow
     This truly was the end
     And I love her more now
          Then ever

—*Christian James*

In This Our Evening Land

This is no wasted giving
this new love we dare plant
that bursts like forsythia

in the late sun

We who no longer fear
the whim of the moon

This bright is our nakedness
Beneath the covers our flesh
keeps the smell of slow-baked bread
of life salvaged from decay

I can taste my marrow on your breath
as our tongues savor each other
I wrap my legs around you to
hold tight this miracle that is ours
Involuntary music escapes our lips

Our love the sweeter for the aging
for the awareness of mortality
for the slow taking
for the quiet darkening
In this, our evening land

—*Dorothy Friedman*

Why?

Why oh why must I dream of
this special human, she will never
be mine, why must I always be
last in line.
I am a nice guy but if I were
to die she would not even blink an eye.
She is like a swan beautiful is
not enough to describe her one must
go way beyond, but like a swan she
flies away if I trespass in her pond.
I shall not let her simply pass
me by I will try.

—*David Raymer*

Untitled

A good Strong, accurate
Throw with a decent Spin
will usually give you a Strike

—*Jerah Boyd*

Best Friend And Wife

What a wonderful feeling,
This thing they call life.
And it's all cause of you,
My best friend and wife.
You've captured my heart,
You've entered my soul.
I know for a fact,
Together we'll grow old.
A life of happiness,
That's what you've brought.
I'll do the same,
It's a beautiful thought.
You're a wonderful feeling,
You, who I call life.
You'll always be with me,
You're my best friend my wife.
I love you Sweetheart

—*Jose R. Castro*

Actors And The Show

Friends and co-workers arrive about
Three or more hours to prepare.
Warming up limbs, muscles, and voices
Are just part of the preparation.
As show time draws nearer, make-up
And costumes are readied and applied
The stage manager calls for places,
These same people begin their
Mental preparation and remember
To correct mistakes from previous
Times. Technical staffs ready
Themselves even as the audience
Assembles and takes their
Seats. Then, when the audience and
Players just cannot wait anymore,
The show begins. The crowd is
Different every night. Even if the
Players are just not right, the crowd
Is warm and receptive in the end.

—*Charles Johnson*

Forever

     Forever's not so long when looking
through a doll's eyes;
     Or when you see it sprawled
across a brick wall
     Underneath the dirty glare
of a street light.

—*Jason Booty*

Living Dead

The feeble cry pierced the gloom
Through dampened, cold night air -
The newborn in its live tomb
Of hunger and despair.
Her wizened, helpless mother
Attracted pure disdain.
Each indifferent onlooker
Saw the needle in the vein.

Silent calls for help rang loud
But no one seemed to hear.
The live dead, scoffed by the proud
Who didn't really care.
The shameful, hopeless cycle;
Death in the midst of life
Earmarking a new victim,
Yet ending all the strife.

—*Carl W. Bennett*

Nature's Silence

Nature's silence spread
Through the world's atmosphere.
No birds in the trees
With songs to hear.

No frogs in the meadow
With loud but tender croaks.
Only silence for...
The polluting folks!

No horses eating hay
No dogs chasing cats.
At night no howling wolves
or whispering of bats.

The factories have now grown larger
And buildings are beyond the eye can see.
Nature is now dead
And left silence for you and me...

—*Francisca Marie Solis*

New Challenge

Emotions are unsure,
Time elapse into pain,
When does life begin?
Breathing becomes a strain

The essence of new beauty,
Features are unknown,
Life will be forthcoming
Nurtured seed that was sown

Strength seems to cease,
Hysterics becomes a purr,
Imagination is secretly kept,
Sight still, just a blur

True love engulfs my soul,
My Lord is by my side,
A glimpse of my own likeness,
Hearing her first cry

Sunrise brings a new challenge,
Morning reality becomes real,
Wisdom, knowledge and understanding,
Her life I will instill

—*Jamie Puni*

Autumn's Destiny

Autumning nature with your brush
     tint leaves of every hue.
Mount them against that steel-grey sky
     in panoramic view.
Then quiet peace can steal around
     to set those heartaches free,
Will heal the hurts and calm us down,
     your harvest destiny.

I long for autumn time of year,
     the solitude you bring
while sleeping plants rejuvenate
     waiting return of spring.
May my heart too accept this balm
     and harvesting, burst free
so I can reap this wealth of peace-
     Your Harvest's Destiny

—*Beulah D. McConkie*

A Penniless Man

A penniless man sits on the ground,
tired and wet from the rain.
The cup he holds out still is empty,
the people ignore his pain.

The people don't seem to notice him,
they don't seem to care.
They never gave a thought that, one day,
they might be sitting there.

—*Annemarie Eng*

God's Colors

If God had intended His world,
to be of just one color,
He would not have made trees,
that change their color, with each
new season.

He would not have decorated
His land, with many, different
colors of wild flowers, for all the
world to see.

He would not have made His sky
blue, and clouds that turn gray
with rain.

And, He certainly would not have
made the rainbow, to bless the world,
after the rain.

In the same way that God made
His world in many, different,
beautiful colors,
He also made His people, in
many, different, beautiful colors.

—*Barbara Gage*

Delusions Of Grandeur

What can it mean
To be truly free?
Desperately,
Men kill, and die
To see.

Must one stoop in chains
For another to feel free?
Delusions of Grandeur
Surely!

What can it mean
To be truly free?
When, paradoxically,
The only ones who are,
(Like a bird, or a tree)
Don't need to be.

—*Anne Reynolds Metzger*

Finding Paradise

We search th' world far and wide
To fill a void we have inside

'Cause in a world so full of space
There must be one special place

A place where beauty is at its best
Where we can live 'til day of rest

But when we tire of drift an' roam
We find our paradise was here at home

—*Howard Orem*

Autobio

There comes a time
(To call it mine)

Before we can die
(Or overcome being shy)

A need to tell
(Our progeny as well)

A nice little story
(Will it be hoary?)

Please put to paper
(Our neat little caper)

It will take years
(To express our fears)

To write it down
(Moving town to town)

As we had fun
(Under moon and sun)

One's life experiences known
(Will survive if shown)

Or an atom be
(In sands of sea)

—*Fred Small*

To Be In Love

To capture the wind
To captivate the soul
Is to be in love.

To cure the passion
To elevate the mind
Is to be in love.

To glimpse excellence
To thirst struggle
Is to be in love.

To be in love has no comparison
To feel love has no equal.

—*Allen E. Hopkins Jr.*

Reaching For The Wind

A sailor reaches for the wind
To carry him o'er the seas,
A gusty, northern gale perhaps
Or just a gentle breeze.

Ever watchful at the helm
Master of his craft,
His sails are full as if to please
And all's well fore and aft.

Nowhere on earth would he rather be
Than on his ship 'Tranquility',
His cares and woes are distant now
This haven is reality.

As the sailor reaches for the wind
Man reaches for his goal,
The way may be calm or stormy ahead
But the journey makes him whole.

The wind on the sails and the will to
achieve
They are the powers that be,
Voyagers, chart your course with care
Be masters of your destiny.

—*Estelle Davies*

Reality

Is man so weak
To fear what scares;
To be honest with himself,
And admit that it's there,
Or must he always live
In a never ending lie;
Making bubbles with his laughter
Instead of drowning in a cry?

Insistent upon being in control:
Willing to sacrifice his greatest keep
Just to save the reputation of his mold!

Or may he grow wiser
Before the day he dies,
And see the beauty of emotion
As the tears roll from his eyes?

—*Bradley R. Freeman*

A Friend

A friend to cry with
To grow and to die with,
To play outside with all day long.
A friend you can walk with,
To talk and to shop with,
To listen to your favorite songs.

A friend you go to school with,
And swim in the pool with,
To tell who you like and don't
A friend to share feelings with,
To share all your problems with,
To tell that you will and won't.

While looking for a friend,
To have with you until the end,
Follow the description above.

—*Janelle E. Rucker*

Obstacles

A man may strive, to make his lot,
To have much more, than what he's got,
He'll start out fresh and full of vim,
To conquer worlds and fortunes win,
An then one day in great despair,
He'll give it up and you will hear,
Obstacles, obstacles, here and there,
Obstacles, obstacles, everywhere,
I'll be content with what I've got,
I tried, I failed, I'll accept my lot,
If only we could make him see,
That he can be, what he wants to be,
These obstacles that are all about,
Are within himself; He can cast them out.

—*Joe Meaney*

Untitled

To win, you need steals,
To score, you need steals,
Be fast, get in the lanes and be
Aggressive to steal the ball.
Make eye contact with the ball
Handler and good hands to steal
the ball.
Have traction and be quick to
make a steal. Steal and score,
steal and score and the other
team, to be more.

—*Catherine Ard*

I Found You

Did you ever need someone
to lend a helping hand,
Someone to wipe away the tears,
and take away all your fears,
Someone who would be there
and not just stand and stare,
Someone who could make you smile,
and stay with you all the while,
I have traveled many miles,
and seen many different smiles,
but the one smile I found,
was worth the extra mile,
you see my friend,
I found my someone special,
My friend...
    I found you.

    —*Charlina Vega*

I Wish

I wish I was a scientist
  To someday find a cure,
Awakening those who sleep
In a coma of the impure.

  I wish I was a doctor
To heal the world's pain
  Saving those who suffer
Those that die in vain.

  I wish I was the sun
To brighten the sad and dour
  Warming their cold hearts
To the beauty of a flower.

  I wish I was a man
To lead society towards peace
  Guiding a generation
To a place where wars cease.

  I wish I was a broom
To sweep away the sorrow
  Cleansing the world today
For a perfect day tomorrow.

    —*Jim Shelton*

Peace Atmosphere

Searching for that place called peace,
  To spend some time a way.

  From all the sounds and people
  You encounter from day to day.

Today it seems you need some space,
  To "chill" and take a break,

From things that put you on the edge,
  And keeps you in a mixed up state.

And then from work you take a turn,
  And go to the "battle zone",

To tackle problems your family has,
In the place that's suppose to be home.

Sometimes you say forget this mess,
  I'll put them through a test,

And let them do things on their own,
  And do what I think is best.

    —*Angylin C. Singleton*

Love Madness

A slave I am
To the love I bear you
You are the garden of my life
And the Pain that will bear me away.

Audacious lips! dipped in wine,
Angel of Bachus, and my madness!
Your tongue, a honeyed needle,
The fruit of Paradise.

Your eyes my cruel midnight,
Dark, wicked, spiteful sweetness
That bleeds my soul at its gaze.
Yet I die every moment that I have you.

    —*Edmund Rogers*

Farewell To You

Thinking back
To the memories of you and me
I ask myself
How can this be

I still cannot believe it
How can you be gone
I miss you so very much
What could have gone wrong

You had a way of making me feel special
You seemed to always make me smile
But yet I am left here
With nothing between us but many miles

There was never a time,
A time when you were unhappy
You always had a smile
I just wish right now, that's the way it could
  be

Now you are no longer here
But in my heart, you are with me
The special memories of you
Are here now, and always will be

    —*Eunice Joshevama*

Conventionality

The desert landscape that stretches
to the past horizons
is littered with the decaying corpses
of good intentions,
lost souls desperately seeking
to fit in with conventional wisdom,
clinging onto abstract concepts
of a false, twisted reality,
only to wander aimlessly in circles
until the weight strapped to backs,
tender from the course leather
knifing into soft flesh,
sends them crashing to the ground,
to become dust underfoot,
of those with shaded eyes
and purposeful stride
following the sun

    —*Andy Coughlan*

To You

To you - I love To you - I cry
To you I cherish with you I die.

    —*Desmond Greene*

Tangible Livelihood

Man make of thy way
To the path of the stars
Where the luster, shall glitter
And make its way, onto the open

For the truth shall avail,
Of the breath of the faraway
As it seems so distant
And no escape, of resistance

This livelihood shall fulfill,
Attainment of grand suffice
Where the dreams that seem
And the pen shall write to redeem

Even as time, as we make
Mistakes, in our mind's doubtful state
Where our wake
In the hour of making, shall rise

From the entanglement of the obscure
That shall cross over, into the skies
Where the voice, I hear, knows of reason
Of the degrees of the interchangeable and
tangible

    —*Brian M. Tweed*

Devotion

Have you ever listened
to the silence?
It speaks edifying words to the soul,
sings lulling thoughts
to the heart,
caresses the mind with fingers of fire.
The silence can see you,
protect you
from the maddening cries of the world.
It is everywhere.
Never ceasing,
Ever wise,
Sitting on your shoulder,
straining to grasp you in its peace.

    —*Catherine Frank*

A New Beginning

Across the many miles you've come,
To this great land, to make your home.
With God as your guide; help from a few,
You begin anew, the two of you.

The people, the language, the customs...
So much to adjust to!
Take it slow, you'll learn as you go.
From all of us, to the two of you...

Welcome to America!!

    —*Jane E. Long*

My Love

Mysteriously drawn
To your overwhelming beauty
When I'm with you the others I pity
Luck, love, or faith
What the gods wished to create
I'll change the world to your perfection
I'll do anything for your protection
I am not one to fear
For behind these years I too tear
Just one chance to prove my soul
On the outside I may appear cruel
But with your love I become whole

    —*Aaron M. Yaudes*

He Came To Us From Outer Space

He came to us from outer space,
To try to save the human race.
But he was different, as they could see.
Doomed to a life of slavery.

Time passed by.
Life grew short.
The human race
Would soon be not.

But selfish men,
By money made,
Would soon regret
The price they paid.

With each new bomb
They set a price
That soon would end
The human race.

—*Florence Coyne*

A Mother

She cares and loves her child indeed
To watch it grow and to succeed.
With her warm and loving eyes
She will give her child that cries.
Patients, kindness, meekness too
As it needs its whole life through.
Can it be so much for thee
God will give you strength to see.
All the love within your heart
Never, never let it part.
For this child that you must hold
Never break this mothers mold.

—*Debra Jane Suter*

Take The Time To Love

Take time to smell the flowers,
    to watch the kids at play,
        to enjoy the very simple things,
            and live life day by day.
Do everything you dream of,
    leave nothing left to chance,
        and while you're making memories,
            throw in a little romance.
Find that special someone
    who sets your soul on fire,
        spend lazy days in crazy ways,
            and fulfill your hearts' desire.
Take time to feel happiness,
    to trust and want and care,
        to be devoted to yourself,
            and all the emotions there.
But most importantly of all-
    a message from above-
        take some time out of each day
            and take the time to love!

—*Brenda Marie Botello*

Together

Together we are inseparable,
Together forever and ever to pass.
Nothing can come between us,
We are like a sea and its shore —
Both depend on each other.
Together we stand facing the land,
Hand in hand, neither to demand,
Together... forever... in the sand...

—*Cassidy S. Kemp*

The Dog Walk

Time for you and me
Together, daily walk
Where all can see
Then I go sniffing along;
O! There's a delightsome smell!
But your arm is strong, O well!
And the little dogs I wanted to greet,
To know them better,
They fill me with glee.
What right have you
To change my life?
From running, investigating yon lea?
Is it to be I'm not free?
But comfortable eternally?
To your will must I submit?
To walk stiff and proudly by your side,
My nature captured by your pride?

—*Charlene Crepeau*

Perfect Mixture?

They have gotten
Too close again.
The buildings bind
Themselves up
For winter.
Diseases, disasters, death,
No longer exist.
Challenges, change, creativity,
No longer exist.
They live in
Perfection and sin.
There should be
No such thing.
We must
Start over.

—*Joe Pearson*

Tomorrow Is Mine

In one experimenting moment
Too late, I realize my mistake
My future was forever altered
My dreams all erased.

Lord knows it wasn't easy
Sacrifices more than rewards
I made mistakes out of desperation
While fate dealt the cards.

No more guilt and condemnation
For things out of my control
I want a life of my choosing
No more bowing down and toil.

I am my own person
I deserve the freedom to be me
To put me first in my life
To be what I want to be.

I know I can make it
A future of happiness I can see
If I have the courage to demand
And stand up for me.

—*Deborah Sisson*

Late Winter Sunset

Black-clawed limbs reach out
To grasp
The violet-edged horizon, trying
To retrieve
The warm, gold-splattered day.

—*Jane Ross*

Lose Or Win

What will happen when you die?

If not in Jesus you believe
Torments unknown you shall receive,
In life all was yours to do
After death you'll pay your dues,
If on material things your life depends
You will lose and satan wins!

But,

If in Jesus you confess,
Heavenly robes will be your dress.
Beyond those pearly gates
A promised mansion for you awaits.
To see God the Father and the Son,
Your journey then will be done!

Wouldn't you prefer to win?!

—*Cheryl L. King*

Tahoe

Red and blue
trams and stairs
mountains are everywhere.
Skiing and rolling down slopes is fun,
but, emergency carts aren't #1.
Relax and enjoy,
put work aside.
Heavenly is a fun place to try.
Maybe one day you will see
how much fun skiing can really be!

—*Diana Marchetti*

Nightmare At Trane

Trane is a place where I work,
Trane treats me like a jerk —
By giving me too much work.
The work gives me lots of pain —
That seems to make me quite insane.

My pain is like a nightmare
That drives me crazy.
Every day I'm in pain
And I cannot think clear.

My neck hurts so much —
That I curse and scream like nuts
I get so frustrated and blue —
I just want to feel brand new.

I hope that someday soon —
This pain will leave like
a boom and I will say goodbye
to this nightmare for good.

—*Angela Cicchino*

Butterflies In My Tummy

I get butterflies in my
tummy when I take a hot
bath. When I get them
they wiggle they jiggle and
tickle inside. I giggle I laugh
and I scream but when they
are over I'm relieved, butterflies,
butterflies in my tummy.

—*Jessica M. Hamerly*

To Geometry

Beautiful world
twisting life in seasons
and arbitrary cycles
creating warmth and rivers
with clouds of turbulence
as the chief warrior
and viewer—staring at
the remarkable mysteries
within the spectrum
of flowers and orchids
of grace and majesty
fortitude prevails
in angelic pageantry
whisking molecules
of life to be shaped
geometrically
while erosion takes
its course
in continuity.

—*Brian M. Spradlin*

Dream

Two, entwined in a song,
Two, curled up in love,
Two, walking among
Flowers of mauve.

Two, for a trip,
Two, for a dream.
Two, lost in a smile
Of each other's eyes.

Two, floating toward the stars,
Two, dreaming of new start,
Confident like two sparrows
With no fears for tomorrows.

—*Claire Durieux*

What Price Progress

Everywhere you look in town
Under Construction
Flora, fauna covered grounds
Under Construction

Fields where poppies once were found
Under Construction
Squirrels and rabbits underground
Under Construction

Points of interest and joshua stands
Under Construction
Once calm and peaceful desert land
Under Construction

Belching, smoking earth machines mean
Under Construction
It all goes out in the air we breathe
Just can't keep our houses clean
Headache
Under Construction

—*Claire W. Dougherty*

Blue

Blue is the wind slipping
    under the moon
    on an October
      night.

—*Heather Ann Mitchell*

Not By Bread Alone

Unsatisfied I be, dear Lord,
Upon a diet day by day of bread
alone, for I have fed on fresh,
baking bread... and fragrant roses!

I know the peace of Spirit when Your
Word is read where you said;
"I am the living bread."

I've known the ease of body's hungers
stilled when golden, topaz grain is
milled... and crimson roses wave...
perfume filled.

My famished vital craves some of each
when one or more seems missing from my
reach.

Spirit, body and soul. I'm satisfied
with some of these... The living bread,
Earth's Golden Grains... and fragrant
Roses!

—*Helen Johnson Billings*

Decision

Looking for life, so long for love
Used to be with mommy and daddy
Grew out of that, aged too far
Seeking and needing more and more
Not finding but finally
Found the life needed love

Parents blockade and take all away
Saying "protection and shelter"
"We give you all this today"
"Wise" decisions are made for us
Our ideas by them must be ended
Disowning decisions we ourselves make

Try and end perfection why?
Without each other we both will die
If you want us gone or gone
Persist, continue, please go on
Not speaking for her but as for me
If you part us you say goodbye.

—*Edwardo T. Jaquez, III*

Solitude

Inside the forest the quiet
    waits
For those whose souls must
    life escape

Amid the ferns and mosses
    green
The mind may find its
    peaceful dream

A dream of places as yet
    unseen
To live a life, oh so
    serene

Free of worry, pain and
    stress
Away from life's overwhelming
    press

A hidden sanctuary our
    forest allows
A timeless refuge among
    the boughs.

—*Gloria Loucks*

I Saw...

I saw a better me
Walking
    forward;
      Through a
L o n g   r o o m,
    Over the threshold,
across the carpet.

Apprehension (fear [resignation])
    entering (our) my eyes,
as I prepared to step aside
for the
New!
Improved!
me.

I reached
out
To shake his hand-
and touched glass.

—*Collin Turner*

War

War I hear.
War I see.
My mom.
My dad.
We live in fear,
At night when I hear
My mom,
My dad.
I cry
I want to say
goodbye. When I
wake up in the morning
I hear mom crying.
The pain she has. She's
doing it for me.
Will my war ever
go away?

—*Becky Mattingley*

The Bird I Used To know

The bird I saw the other day,
was not the one I used to know.

He used to be happy and free,
and now he's curious and confused.

He had a way to please me,
I'd open my eyes and he'd be there.

Can anyone help him,
can anyone bring him back to me?

The bird I used to know cared,
the bird I used to know isn't there.
Now we're both unsafe,
I can't bare to see his face.

Together we equaled one.
Apart we equal none.

—*Ita Merles*

I want to wrap myself into him
until I suffocate with curiosity
of knowing, what his touch
can't give me,
isn't needed...

—*Danielle Saladino*

The Day She Moved Away

The day she moved away
was the saddest of my life.
I remember thinking things
could never again be right

I remember the day so clearly,
so vivid in my mind
and I know that as time goes by,
I'll never be able to leave it behind.

I remember holding her
and how I loved her so,
and at that moment I knew
I never wanted to let her go.

She's been gone for a month,
but it seems like it's been years
and I just can't seem to stop
all the painful tears.

In my mind I know
that I'll never forget that day;
the saddest day of my life
the day she moved away.

—Cathleen Mundy

Enough

When survival is the base
we build complications
we build unstable walls
to block us in
It's just a matter of time
before we
crush ourselves
to build again.

—Ewing Clay Parton

World Of Peace

If there were more humor
  we would have richer life.
A little more laughter
  In this land of strife.

If we could unite
  In a world of peace.
It would be a delight
  To see all wars cease.

If we were less greedy
  We would have so much more.
And those who are needy
  Would have abundance galore.

For God made the earth
  He created all man.
To be equal in worth
  And to none gave a ban.

He gave us all breath
  And eternal love,
To life, after death
  In his home above.

—Eunice Wheeler

Foo-Foo & I

Foo-Foo and I will have lots of fun.
We'll go out and play
In the bright shiny sun.
We'll play with a ball,
No matter what type.
We'll pick juicy melons,
As long as they're ripe.
When he's happy, he'll smile.
When he's sad, he'll cry.
Oh! What fun we have,
That's Foo-foo and I!

—Chip Armstrong

Angels Here On Earth

Have you ever seen an angel?
Well I have many times.
Every single day that comes
I wish they all were mine.

These angels that I speak of
Haven't walked through Heavens' doors-
They all walk among us-
They are the children we adore.

Every child on earth to me;
No matter race or sex-
Seems just like an angel
To me in all respects.

No matter if the child is rich
Or poor - they're all the same.
They're made just like God wanted...
The only difference is their name.

I love all children everywhere.
I just wish all people would...
Then maybe they'd not be abused...
Only loved - the way they should.

—Debra Keller Barringer

Untitled

On this as you did see my mother
went away from me, there will be
no more hugs and kisses and no bed
time stories to be told. She wonders
in my mind at nights. I ask the
Lord why her, she was so young at
heart, and full of love to give.
I search to find were she might be
and haven't found her yet. I
need to feel her warm embrace or
she her smiling face. I wish that
I could dream of her, but when I
close my eyes she's no where to
be found. I know that I am older
now with family of my own, I love
them all so very much but, please
Lord I just want her touch.

—Dawn Cole

Colors

Purple, blue, green, yellow
We just wanted to say Hello.

All the colors in the world
Look so pretty when they're swirled.

Like a butterfly in a tree
Colors, colors pretty as can be.

—Jackie Schwartz

Mrs. Bee

The wild buttercup and the Goldenrod
Were dancing in the breeze,
When Mrs. Bee came a-buzzing by,
"I want your nectar, please."

"Well, some of course," said Buttercup.
"But I must save some too
For the Humming Bird and Bumble Bee.
Not all must go to you."

"Oh, dear! Oh, dear!" said Mrs. Bee.
"Whatever will I do?
My family is so large, you see.
Who else can help but you?"

"There's many more, Mrs Honey Bee,"
Said the pretty Buttercup.
"The Lilies have more nectar
Than could ever be used up."

"I thank you kindly, Buttercup,
And you too Goldenrod."
So with a buzz, flew on her way,
As the two flowers gave a nod.

—Grace E. Jones

My Mystery In Disguise

Look at my face,
What do you see?
Look at the moon,
and the trees.

Up in the sky,
far, far away.
Oh, in my heart,
in here today.

From the heavens,
to the end.
In this crisis,
there's a friend.

He is strong,
and very wise.
Even mystical,
in disguise.

I only know him,
my angel so fair.
I've never seen him,
But he's always there.

—Angela Lee

Trick And Treat

Horror of horrors,
What do you see?
Someone has come
And "moan" your lawn,
Can it be?
Oh no, oh no, could it be
the friendly little ghost
inside of me?
Well, oh well, it was such fun
To see a ghost mow lawn
in the warm autumn sun!
So it goes, I guess -
A poet, I'll never be
But trick and treat to you, from me.

—Ann F. Bonnie

Succeed

If I was right, about
What I started to write,
Then day be day, and
Night be night.

If I looked across the
Bridge, that could not be
Cross.
Then try I must, even
If I loss.

If I step up, one step at
A time.
I must not fall, but
Continue to climb.

If I'm to succeed in
this life.
Then I must follow, sound
advice.
An education I must undertake,
And many sacrifices, I must make.

—*Earl Nash*

Lament

Oh but yesterday I gazed upon her
what insanity can this be.
To say that today what was is no more
seems pure insanity to me.

Yesterday smiles that are no more
and feelings never expressed.
Today smiles that never were
and longing for life and breath.

What wispy web has been quickly spun
from which all must hang in peril.
To see it break with a baby's breath
and return to white and sterile.

Oh but yesterday I was so sure
that there would be tomorrow.
Faith with her has left me
replaced by only sorrow.

—*Daniel Tyler Gibson*

Night Owls

You can tell me 'bout your geniuses
  What work way late at night,
And spend a lot-a weary hours
  From de wee hours to the light;
But Ise-a tellin' you one thing
  When de night hab turned to day,
Dese here folks you call so smart
  Ain't ne'er miss hittin' de hay,
And sleep so hard dey ne'er wakes up
  'Til pas' de settin' ob de sun —
Huh child, dey ain't got nothin' on me,
  'Cause Ise-a Night Watchman!

—*Harold James Dudley*

Feelings

Feelings are thoughts
We hide deep inside
We can't let them out
I know, for I've tried.

The anguish we have
Because we can't share
Our inner most feelings
With some one who cares.

—*Carolyn Inman*

"Hello World"

Have you ever thought about
What your future will bring?
With ignorance and laziness
Hardly a thing.

Satisfaction will come with Strife
Knowledge will take a while.
Don't give up just go for it
Tackle it in style.
You can make it, there's no doubt,
Reward will wear a smile.

It will take patience,
Sweat and tears.
Believe it - that's just fine.
Someday you wake up and shout,
Hello World - you're all mine!

—*Johanna Borden*

The Company From Within

Oh, what will I do
When children, family and friends
No longer surround me
As the brightly colored flowers now
On mantle, breakfront and buffet?

When the phone has ceased to ring
And the invitation eludes the letterbox?

Why, I'll set the table of my being
With the heirloom silver of memories,
The delicate china of emotions
Upon the linen fibers of my soul
And entertain the company from within.

—*Donna G. Tallent*

The Heart

The heart has 2 sides,
When it is broken it divides
The sadness is great
The pain just doesn't go away.
What could I do to put it back
The rain on my face on a cloudy day.
Gives me perspective of a sunny day.
There will always be days.
The days we want to disappear and there
are days we have pride we can show
pride to the ones that hurt us.
We show them we are not hurting,
but who are we kidding?
The hurt can not be hidden forever.
Don't let them break the barrier.
Just let it out. Be free.
Free from the love of slavery.
It's not worth it. All the hurt they cause.
Move on. Go fish for some new love.
Cause all will be forgotten at the end of
time.

—*Christine Reich*

Alone

To be alone is to be in the dark
Where shadows conceal my sinister prison
I call out to someone, anyone
Only to hear an echo of the cry I made
I can only wait to see a light.

A speck of light begins to shine
Reaching its loving arms down
To take me from this black abyss
Forever holding my hand.

—*Alisa Hageman*

When We Go A Fishin'

My Dad us just a different man
When we go a-fishin'
He laughs and jokes and calls me pal
And I just keep a-wishin'
That we could fish most every day
And never have a care.
That he could pull my ear and grin
And tousle up my hair.
It just don't seem like he's so old
And I look and look to see
If he's my dad or my old friend,
'Cause he's a little boy like me
When we go a-fishin.

—*Blanche M. Hollingsworth*

Christmas Past

Oh christmas of so long ago
  when we were children small,
Two long black stockings we hung so low
  the cheery fireplace wall.
Although sleep would elude us,
  we were sent to bed
Or else santa wouldn't come
  our sweet mother said.
Then we'd hear santa's ho! ho! ho!
  ran down to see before he'd go
Oh sorrow, oh sadness,
  he handed us a stocking black,
filled with garbage and a torn sack.
  Then he would smile begin to glow,
As the other stocking he held in tow.
  Oh joy oh happiness bright,
They were filled with goodies and delight.
  We must thank him, we turned around
but the merry old gentleman was gone.

—*Angela Augustine*

I Love You

"I love you," I say
When you call me at night
When you kiss me good-bye
When you turn out the light.

"I love you," I say
As you look in my eyes
And you whisper my name
As my hopes start to rise.

"I love you," I say
When you come and you go
My heart tells me yes
But my mind tells me no.

"I love you," I say
As you walk out the door
It used to be true
Now our love is a war.

"I love you," I say
Those words are a crime
As I kiss you good-bye
For the very last time.

—*Dolores D. Assel*

There Is A Place

There is a place for everyone
Where it is I don't know
But I think it is in heaven

Often we grow tired of trying to fit
Instead I grow the way I'm shown,
Keeping my faith.

Knowing know matter how I feel or
What I do there can and will never be
A separation from my God

We just hang on trying to be happy
Making contributions by sharing the
Gifts that have been bestowed upon us

Being the best we can be, continually
Growing to become who we were born to
Be, our best

—*Fred Lanzetta*

Mother Nature

I love the outdoor's life
Where nature is so free,
Seemingly without strife,
Comparing her to me.

The animals are contented
In their kingdom free from care.
Until the air is scented,
By man and then beware!

I love to walk the countryside
In mother nature's home,
Upon her carpet green and wide,
Amid her splendorous dome.

To me the joy of living
Is to gaze upon the land,
And see God's fruitful giving
In mother natures hand.

—*Agnes I. Hortick*

Dreaming Of A Place

I dream of a place not long ago.
Where people of all cultures, joined
    together side by side.

I dream of a place,
No prejudice nor crime,
Where joyful tears were spread
    throughout this land
    of time.

I dream of a place,
Where peace is the key.
The key to unlock the door,
to a whole new world of
    harmony.

  I dream of a place.
A place called Earth,
Where people care for one another,
    and rejoice with every shade of
    color.

—*Anitra Golden*

Cortege

Coming up from Chincoteague
where the back road
like a farmer dressed for church
tidies up for the Interstate
a not-new-nor-unbent hearse
sputters with Cadillac dignity
solitary in the middle lane
its black and solemn driver
claiming last due respect
for his soulless cargo
only now come into company
with the racy tourist class
and close behind
in lonely and correct procession
limps one battered Chevy pickup
whose headlights
squinting through their shroud
of field mud and back road dust
speak the sad allegiance
of one white and solitary mourner

—*Barbara Dwyer Brown*

Steps

There's only cement steps left
Where the house used to be.
Today, I could see poke and goldenrod;
Growing around a few stones
Of the old foundation where once
Grew a profusion of petunias.
Not too long ago, an elderly man
And his wife would be, in summer,
On the porch of a gray clapboard house.
They sat in their wooden rockers;
The woman peeling apples
Or shelling peas on her lap,
Open, genial faces talking away
A long morning, remembering
Lives lived before this present time,
Interesting events that had happened.
There's only these cement steps now.

—*Ella C. Rodgers*

Out Of Time

Come, my Indian Brave
where the tall grasses wave
we will lay by the stream
where we shared a lovely dream

Come, we will walk today
before time fades away
where wild horses did roam
and buffalo had a home

Come, my Indian Brave
come, leave your lonely grave
walk this dream known as time
where you are forever mine

Come, my Indian Brave
where the tall grasses wave
and the winds sing our song
free in the wilds we belong

—*Charlotte Ford*

When Shadows Fall

Out among the trees
Where the wind blows free
The horses roam the hills
The birds nest in the field
The old rooster crows
The flowers grow
The ducks swim in the pond
In the water just beyond
Searching for food
Mother hen protects her brood
The cows are in the barn
Munching on hay and corn
But when shadows fall
The evening calls
The night grows dark
That's when the dogs bark
The deer prowl
And the coyotes howl

—*Artie Toler Hoffpauir*

Life's Clouds

There comes a time in each life
Where there seems to be no sunshine.
But don't despair, for in time
Everything will turn out fine.

There is a secret to life's clouds,
When all seems dark and gloomy.
Find something good about each day,
No matter how small it may be.

To focus on the good in life
Is not a easy thing to do.
But to focus only on the bad,
Robs every ray of sun from you.

No matter the size of life's clouds,
May they be big or may they be small,
Remember the smiles, the laughter
Or someone dear and you'll never fall.

Search for the good, if need be,
In each and every day.
For you have only one life
To capture the sun's rays.

—*Ginny Vetter*

Paper Towel Philosophy

Daily, we tend our kitchen salon,
Where words of wisdom are writ upon,
The paper towels we use to wipe
Spots and spills and odors ripe.
Anxious for empty souls to feed,
Our two-ply inspiration reads,

"The heart that loves is always young.
To have a friend, you must be one.
A smile adds value to your face.
A garden is a special place."

What brilliant insight yet remains,
To be inscribed on the paper panes,
Of Viva, Brawny, Family Scott,
And other sponsors of this rot?
Do they believe— it is supposable—
A human brain is that disposable?

—*Angela B. Waterman*

The Far Horizon Or Journey's End

On the escalating steps of time
which in my daily life I climb,
I pause to view the years behind,
Days of pleasure so deceiving
Times of sorrow left me grieving,
Numb and sore unbelieving.

Time is a thief, it steals my friends
It can never make amends,
I wonder have my journey ends
May my soul with angels guiding
As the early sun is rising,
Reach and touch the far horizon.

Day has ended, when the sun
sin so in the west, nights will come.
Then my soul, its journey done,
Hopeful rises up to heaven
knowing sin can be forgiven
pray my soul will go on living

—*Charlotte L. Smith*

A Cold

My nose feels stuffy
while I lay
doing nothing.

I pick up a book
and try to read,
but my head aches
and sinuses drip cheap.

The body hangs on
till the evening sets in,
before my last cup of tea
I toss and I turn.

Medicine does not help,
while another day goes by.
I always make a daily prayer,
so I'll be back to work on time.

Although it's early March
and Spring is just ahead,
I know that
there will be plenty of time,
to spend my cold in bed.

—*Howard W. Cohen*

Untitled

I've danced in the ring of fire
with the children of the sun.
For many years I've sang
the songs of the islands.
Now I am returning to
teach them to you.

I'm going on a journey.
Will you come with me.
Our minds can be as one and
We can fly away.

Were moving through space,
beyond the realm of time.
I'm teaching you the songs,
And we're dancing through
the fire.

—*Jacqualyn Newell*

Miles

I sit with a stranger
While she's with someone stranger

With many miles in between
I lie thinking thoughts unclean

Just waiting by the phone
I feel so f__king alone

Missing and loving her with all my heart
Even thought it all seems torn apart

Does she ever miss me?
Can you love someone you hardly see?

She hides her feeling se well.
While inside she burns in hill

My heart's an open book
Propped up for her to look

She looks but must read
She's the only one I need

I lie in bed
Broken in the head

I scream, I cry and I curse
But it just makes the pain that much worse.

—*Brian Brown*

The Bermudian Man

There was a man
who loved to live
by the sand
He knew it well
but chose
to leave it
to go to hell

When he returned
he was a broken man
who dreamed
of going to hell

Again.

—*Allison Williams*

No Other Like My Mother

There's no other like my mother
who means so much to me
There's no other like my mother
who has set my soul free
No other like my mother
who gave so much care and love
No other like my mother
except for God above
Of God, protect and bless her,
she's done so much
For there's no other like my mother
and her tender, loving, touch.

—*Flora A. Natterer*

The Last Wish

Cover me in a bed of black roses,
with a Poe book in my hand.
Place my head facing east,
below thy greenery sand.
Allow a silver cross to dangle,
round my olive neck.
To guide me to a place unknown,
beyond the sun's haven of rest.

—*Jennifer Sarrgent*

Disillusioned

Once there was a tooth-fairy.
Who used to leave me fifty cents,
But when I found out it was just my Dad,
I've been a skeptic ever since.

Then there was the Easter bunny.
Who brought an Easter basket.
Now he too is dead and gone,
And lying in his casket.

And yes, there was a Mrs. Stork,
Who dropped me off one early morn.
I bet my folks were quite surprised,
To find me in that patch of corn.

Next comes dear old Santa Claus
Down the chimney as you've heard,
But he never really came at all,
And I believed it, every word!

Now please don't tell me that there is no
    God!
I know this can't be true.
For without Him, there'd be no Christmas,
And no special friends like me and you.

—*Elizabeth L. Emrich*

Where Are The Children?

But where are the children?
Whose laughter shook the stucco walls.
Who ran and played among the elms.
I hear no sound now.
Say, where are the children?

Who are these grown up people?
Who jet across the skies?
Who sit in hidden stake-outs?
Who evaluate young tortured minds?
Who test for oil in lonely places?

No longer hiding in the tree house.
Or dressing up for Halloween.
Or reading books of great adventure.
Or dreaming by the corner tree.
These were my children.

They have homes and children of their
    own.
They hike with back packs over mountain
    trails.
They jet ski on the waters at the bay.
And they love roses and do gardening.
These are still my children!

—*Elsie Amancio*

Make The Best

Life's not fair, as you know.
You pick up pieces as you go.
You make the best of what you've got.
The littlest thing means a lot.
You take a drop and make it a flower.
You take a drop and make it a shower.
As you walk along life's lane,
you pick up pleasure as well as pain.
You try your hardest and do your best
to try to keep up with the rest.
A friendly smile does no danger.
It makes a friend out of a stranger.
If you try hard, you'll always win.
For you get out what you put in.

—*Denise M. Hannon*

He Called All To Be

If without a purpose,
    why did God give us life,
If without a vision,
    why did God give us eyes,
If without a dream,
    why did God give us a brain,
If without love and compassion,
    why did God give us a heart,
If without listening and understanding,
    why did God give us ears,
If without encouragement and praise,
    why did God give us a mouth,
If without hugs and closeness,
    why did God give us arms,
If without actions,
    why did God give us faith.
Can we really do without these things.
Let us not lie to
ourselves, but say no, and wake up from
the night, see God for
his awesome power and love, then become
children of the
light.

—*Christopher Barrett Culbertson*

I Talk To God

I ask the Lord when I pray
why I am still here today.
His answer to me is this:
"You are not next on my list."

Do I still have time to do
all the things you want me to?
"Yes, you're down the list a ways,
you still have quite a few days."

Into a bag I want to cram
what I need to show who I am.
I'm just a mortal, it's true
but I do want to be worthy of you.

Let me hear your voice from above
so I'll know I have your love.
When I'm lost in deep despair
I need to know you'll hear my prayer.

I hear him say "Just know I do care.
I'll always know you're there.
Be kind, loving and true, the best you can
be,
and I will come and bring you home with
me."

—*Edna Copyak*

Satin And Lace

As I sit here listening to the rain,
Wishing how I could be on a plane.
Heading for some unknown place,
Where there's lots of satin and lace.

Now, if there is such a place,
Where there is satin and lace,
That is where I would like to be,
A place just for you and me.

There could even be other things,
Like a golden bell that rings,
At this very special place,
That has lots of satin and lace.

I wish there would even be some silk,
That was smooth and pure like milk,
At this very special place,
That has lots of satin and lace.

—*Esther W. Korfhage*

Alex and Kyle

I look at your tender faces
with a love so intense, so deep-
    as you cuddle together
    and softly fall asleep.

Alex smiles so sweetly snuggled
    next to his big brother
I marvel at how wonderful
    it feels to be a mother.

For it was just yesterday
    the child was I
with my mother watching
    and standing by.

Each day they change and
    as I watch them grow
I wonder what paths
    they will choose to go.

They are already so very special
    I think with a smile
    My beautiful sons-
        Alex and Kyle.

—*Cynthia Boman Thompson*

Summer

I must admit I like warm weather
With all its blessed gifts;
Like the summer sea's far-reaching calm
Where a lazy sailboat drifts.

Or an elusive and seductive breeze
Luring all your cares away;
Stealing fragrant garden scents
From where the flowers lay.

Sweet bird songs form a melody,
A lovely, pleasing sound;
Soaring, floating lazily
From all the trees around.

A gift of love, a summer is,
Its sun, its stars, its gentle rain;
Reluctantly we watch it leave,
Impatient, till it come again.

—*Jane Wright Paul*

Then And Now

As youngsters, we had problems
With baby teeth, and THEN
As we are grown-up people
We have problems once again.

THEN we looked under the pillow!
To see if the tooth fairy came.
To leave a dime or a quarter,
But, THEN, it was a game.

THEN when we got older
The dentist came to be,
Taking those pillowed tokens
Many times, away from me.

NOW, where is that tooth fairy?
I need help with the bill to pay,
I'm paying a thousand dimes and quarters
For that troublesome tooth today.

—*Esther M. Childs*

Autumn

Above the trees the sky is blue,
With clouds of puffy white.
The autumn air feels crisp and new,
And makes one's feet feel light.

The trees wear coats of red and gold,
And some of orange and brown.
Then, when the season's old,
The leaves will tumble down.

The placid lake, a stately blue,
The grass, the hue of wheat.
The grass bent down, then back it flew,
When trodden on by windy feet.

By the lake the big geese stay,
Preparing now for flight.
Yet they linger day by day,
To enjoy the autumn sight.

—*Allison Matthews*

Two Hearts As One

He beheld this maiden fair
With eyes so blue and flowing hair;
He had to meet her
And hopefully soon,
But how? ... Would he dare?

He came to her in her dreams,
Looking as resplendent as a prince;
Kissed her softly on her cheek
And left her with her thought:
"Where is this prince, my one and only?"

The maiden and the prince
Met and kissed,
And ended in wedded bliss
Because I played Cupid,
Shot my arrow ... and made a hit.

—*Irene T. Xavier*

On Behalf Of A Spider

I spied a spider
    with no one to guide her
    concocting a glider
    from a thread inside her.

The art amplified
    formed a snare strong and wide.
She decided to hide
    till her prey was astride.

A fly terrified
    in the net firmly tied
    was soon pacified
    by poison. It died.

With the larder supplied,
    appetite satisfied,
    this insecticide
    was a crime to be tried,
    but a world beautified
    by the art she applied
    made the jury decide
    she was quite justified.

—*Dorothy Forsythe Dale*

We The Children Of The Universe,

We the children of the universe,
with unknown mind and untold purpose,
forever striving to reach our goal,
that somewhere, somehow, makes us
whole.

We live our lives across the times,
each life a lesson, learn our lines,
not always knowing what we seek,
but always searching, afraid to speak.

In darkened days we see a star,
a glimpse, a promise from afar.
Yet, when it's close and seems in reach,
a chasm opens at our feet.

We build a bridge across that dark,
a light then leads us from the heart.
But as we reach out to that light,
a veil comes down across our sight.

Thus, when our eyes can open wide,
and finally see the other side,
we'll know our mind and know the
purpose,
with hearts that see beneath each surface.

—*Constance H. Peacock*

Untitled

You greet us every morning
with your smiling face so bright,
You're more than just our teacher
helping us learn to read and write.

When things seem a little too hard
you show us we can do it,
and when and if we doubt ourselves
you're there to help us through it.

Thank you for helping us
with everything we do,
and with each new task we master
it's all through help from you.

You're a very special person
and when the year comes to an end,
remember you're more than our teacher
you've become a very special friend!

—*Colleen Naylor*

Pink Ballerina, Black Ballerina

Pink ballerina
Won't you twirl
Black ballerina
Give it a swirl
Pink ballerina
Beautiful, of course not dull
Black ballerina
You are so graceful
Pink ballerina,
Black ballerina,
Come together
Share the world forever
No! Don't run away
just stay
It will be okay
Work it out
I hope you two
blend somehow, someday.
Maybe today......

—*Candace Boldon*

Cuddly Kittens

Little kittens in a basket
yellow, black and white and tan
meowing, crawling, pig-piling
balls of fluff and noisy purring
snuggled up to take a nap with mother.

Little kittens out exploring
slipping, sliding across the floor
climbing curtains, climbing couches
chasing shadows and following strings
what adventure each day brings.

Little kittens in the garden
giant flowers and tall, tall grass
butterflies and soaring birds
could they catch one if they try
as they see them flying by.

Little kittens day is done
all the time spent having fun
has exhaust each little head
it is definitely time for bed.
Rest up for your next busy day.

—*Heather Pratt*

A Prayer

Dear Lord,
Yes, it's me.
I'm sorry to bother you
But I have a need.

I'm asking you to guide me,
Show me the way.
Be with me always, starting this day.

My heart is troubled,
I have much stress.
There is great temptation,
My soul cannot rest.

I'm afraid,
Afraid of doing wrong.
It would then haunt me for very long.

I hope with your guidance,
I will make the right choice.
Please talk to me,
I want to hear your voice.

My decision is in good hands.
Better than any man.
In Jesus' name I pray. Amen.

—*Ann Zachar*

The Answer

You question me about my love,
You ask me if I care.
You seem to want some measurement,
Like good or bad or fair.

But, my love is so unbounded,
Completely without rule.
It grows and grows within my heart
Like ripples in a pool.

I don't know where it starts or how.
It warms me like a light,
Like the very brightest star
On the very darkest night.

Yes, my love is like the springtime,
Red forests in the fall.
Just think of all things beautiful.
My love is like them all!

—*Elinor Sharpes*

Morning On Cranberry Ridge

We stood on the rim of the mountain,
you and I...two mortals
invading briefly a timeless world
of cloud and morning mist,
The fog curled itself around us,
touching our faces,
sparkling our hair.

In the hazy distance mountain peaks
rose dimly and were lost again.
Tall trees lifted to the sky,
Lacy silhouettes in the cloud mist.
Far down the mountain a bird called...
Piercing, sweet, lonely...
From nearby the answer came.

There was no other place but this one
wrapped softly in sheer bridal white.
Time held its breath...
and I thought of Adam and Eve,
of their first waking
in the morning of the world.

—*Camille Harper Bratcher*

Silent Expression No. 17

I am only a mother.
You are just seventeen.
Somehow, we were parted
Somewhere in between.

Your heart cries out for freedom.
But, my heart holds onto you,
Because it knows
You aren't quite ready
For the world that's calling you.

Frustration turns into irritation
Hurting us both so much.
Something deeper helps us through it
for the sake of us.

But, someday soon this will subside,
and our hearts will meet again,
when the mother in me will stand aside
to let the woman in you go by.

—*Frances R. Lane*

Who Are You Calling Hoot Owl

Who are you calling hoot owl when
you call who,
It intrigues me so when I listen
to you.
Could it be who is listening to you?
Or is it merely a name this who?

Could who be the guilty liar?
Tell me, tell me I inquire
You ask me the question I give
no name.
Persistently bugging me,
do you feel no shame?
If I tell you an answer could
you hear?
If you could your call would
be "Why?" I fear,
Who are you calling hoot owl when
you call who?
It intrigues me so when I listen to you

—*Jada Brisentine*

The Fondest Gift

There are so many gifts
you can receive...
treasure them always
like a pearl in a ring.
   BUT
one gift you cannot receive
like treasure and gold
to show as a luxury
   IT
is a true friend who
gives you a shoulder to lean on
and
is there to hear you laugh...
that is the kind of
   GIFT
you receive from GOD.

   —*Elizabeth Osorio*

Purple Morning

From 8 PM to 6 AM
you can't see a thing,
but at 6 AM there is a purple morning.

A purple morning fresh and new
A purple morning just for you
A purple morning filled with dew
A purple morning that says,
New, new, new!

   —*Dyanna Lynne Pacheco*

You Inspire Me

Like a flash of lightening,
You entered my soul
Causing a flood of sensations
to bathe my soul.
So refreshing after so many years
To have a man inspire me.
To kiss you would be to die
the sweetest death
To be held by you, would be
to release my soul,
To become one with you, would
be to sore through the
Heaven on passions wings
You Inspire me.

   —*Jessica C. Reid*

His Presence

Oh God, I am struggling
You have led me thus far,
And I have faithfully followed.

Show me where I am heading
In this human tragedy,
And help me with my misunderstandings.

Throw down those who attempt
To control me and my talents,
But use me for thy glorification.

I stand in my present darkness
Supported by your caring arms,
And await your peaceful presence.

   —*Jonathan Stotler*

Happiness

If you want happiness,
  you must think about it.
To experience happiness,
  you must do something about it.

To find your happiness,
  Is not the same for all.
'N having true happiness,
  Isn't just having a ball.

To feel real happiness,
  Someone else must know.
Bring happiness to others,
  And you'll surely know.

'Tis the opposite of happiness,
  That brings on sadness.
So smile with someone else,
  And share a little happiness.

   —*Elmer A. Rasmussen II*

Ships In Transition

Times were different. We were young
you nestled your head on my shoulder
trusting, submitting, supporting
Expecting kindness and protection
in return
This gave me strength and purpose
made me a man
Our union was a ship, a haven
In this tempestuous world
I was captain; you, first mate
performing as a crew

Times changed. You have gained
equal rights and independence
we are both captains now
but on separate ships
still close, and yet...

I miss your trusting head
on my shoulder

   —*Henry Boessl*

Scream

What is that sound from the cave?
You say it is the wind,
I say it is the scream of death.

We enter the cave,
Black as night.
Before us is a deep shaft,
At the bottom, a mangled body.
I now recognize that scream,
For it was my own.

   —*Heather J. Simmons*

A Poem Of Love

You live, I die
You take, I give
You hate, I'll love
You right, I'm wrong
Most of all this poem is of love

   —*Harry Johnson, Sr.*

Progress

Indian Brave so sad
You were not afraid.
The white man came
And the land was not the same.

In time there came acid rain.
Mother earth raped and shamed,
By foolish men with many names.

   —*Jay Moca*

Drifting

If you could read my eyes,
you would see an empty soul.

If you could read my thoughts,
you would hear no more.

If you could read my heart,
you would feel so cold.

If you would just listen,
you would know I'm LOST!

   —*D. Kloppenburg*

Think

Life...
Young, old, middle
When...Where does it start
How long does it tarry...
Smiles, grins, pain
Struggle

It's wonderful, painful...
But
How to control it
When
Forces obvious or hidden
steer or drown
the forceful torrent.

Wisdom...
Where do you lie
in richness or
in poverty?
Awake! Build a dam
lest we perish
richly impoverished.

   —*Isabel Ramos*

What If?

What if
your child
  rarely or never
listened to you,
spoke to you,
  thought of you,
needed you,
thanked you,
  respected you
  obeyed you,
laughed with you,
  loved you?

What kind of a child are you
To your Father-Mother God?

   —*George M. Lagos*

759

Able

You need a cool drink
Your forehead's a sweat
A breeze for cooling the sun
Nothing's done, nor the sun-
—*Jack T. Armstrong*

Inside Out

How long?
Your good intentions
Always precede you.
I pace, waiting
Hoping.
The air, my soul
Has your name on it.
I can feel you and doubt,
Looming.
Is it just my yearning
Turned inside out,
Like yes meaning no
And yin meaning yang
And truth meaning lies
And you and me
Meaning nothing?
As I cancel your image
As I wait for the wish
To evaporate,
You call.
—*Diana Darr*

Accept

Seared by scolding cold glances,
Your hands, glued, frozen
Unmoving, unyielding stayed
By your sides, steadfastly hanging,
Neglecting my need for your touch.

Fear below the surface waiting,
For such a moment to break out.
Love seen into oblivion flying,
The brain, feverishly pondering
Weather love could so easily die.

Your silence slowly killed me.
Barbed steel tips of lances frozen,
That my heart tore, and opened,
Tearing scar tissue healed,
And new wounds exposing to bleed.

Love, does not from such die,
Not, from these wounds inflicted,
But reaches for greater understanding.
Finding none, nor an explanation,
It can, but accept, and love.
—*Carlos Valdes*

Heartache

Feelings of inadequacies surround
Where to go, who to see?
The answers haven't been found
for the Alzheimer care-giver like me.
The sting of an injured look
from the loved one who fails to see
The pain a care-giver buries
while watching the light of life flee.
The feelings of guilt abound
I should do more don't you see!
—*Carolyn S. McNatt*

October Query

Lady, where's your scarecrow?
Your porch is not complete
Something's missing, something's gone
When we trick and treat.

Where's the Jack O'Lantern, too?
Where's the ghostly groan?
Where's the whoo-tu-whoo-tu-whoo?
Where's the owlish moan?

Where are all the boys who grew?
Where is all the fun?
Where's the whistling wind that blew?
Why has autumn run?

Lady, where's your scarecrow
On the steps we climb?
Lady, put it on the porch
Please, just one more time.

Hold on to the summer sun
Guard your yesterday
Wear a mask upon your face
Corn husk feet of clay.
—*Diana Notaro*

Ode To Edna...

Three lonely years have passed
Your room is cold and still
Your cheerful voice is silent
Your laughter no longer heard.

I miss your radiant smile
Your tender loving kiss
The rustle of your silk robe
Your morning wake up call.

Heaven will not be Heaven
If I do not join you there
Father, replenish with thy grace
This longing heart of mine.
—*Chester A. Cave*

Until Today

I see your reflection in my mind.
Your touch is so gentle;
Your words are so kind.
When you pass.
Your smile brings sunshine to me;
Like petals of a rosebud,
A beauty to see.
I love you more than you will ever know,
More than I could ever show.
Never before have I felt this way;
Never before...until to day.
—*Danielle Pelter*

Loving Earth

You're sweet as the wind.
You're graceful as the sun,
And in the sun I see your shine.
Passing it on to another
Child beginning life.

You're nice as the flowers.
You're sweet as the clouds.
You give us shade for a
New beginning, and love
Us so that your heart is
Soft as snow.
—*Alexis N. Lawton*

Dad

You're more than a father,
You're more than a friend,
You're the one that taught me
When to take and when to lend.

You showed me how to care
And taught me to share.
You prayed for me
When I needed a prayer,

You showed me right
When I only knew wrong,
And took trouble away
When it followed me home.

Thanks for the things
You've given to me,
And for being the greatest Dad
Anyone will ever see.
—*Jennifer Whitaker*

Forever and Ever

You're part of my heart
You've helped my life grow.
You moved into my soul,
You've made my life whole.

Hiding within me,
a darkness, a void.
You filled with your love,
a seed that keeps growing.

I'll love you today,
along with tomorrow.
The part that is yours,
no other will borrow.

You're part of my heart,
you live in my soul.
Forever and ever, sweetheart,
I'll love you so -
—*Coyetta Wisk*

You Are The One

You are the one I love true.
You've hurt me and made me blue
I loved you then. I love you still
within my heart I always will.
Separate paths we take but for
you my heart does ache.
I want your path to be strewn with
roses. And the sun to shine everyday
My path may be thorny, my sky's grey
because of the love you threw away
Our roads may cross and we meet
again someday, if we do a friend.
I want to find - because you are the
one who means the world to me - even
tho' you are not mine.
I will love you till the end the time
—*Eunice Cole*

Thinker

We have two ends with a common link
With one we sit
With one we think
Success depends on what we use
Heads we win
Tails we loose.
—*Dillard C. Jackson*

The Message

There came into the world a living soul,
Who graciously set her wings.
And looked out over the mountain top gazing as she sings,
Glory is all mankind whose flowers are in bloom,
Help the needy and give to the poor
but not so you won't be doomed,
Give to all out of love and because they're the same as you,
And shed your light on all mankind
for they know not what they do,
Help the little children who only know what they see,
And keep the fire burning deep inside of thee,
Let me here the music for it fills my heart with joy,
And let us sing with the angels for they hear us making noise,
Keep your hearts open and let all understand for all we are
is children playing in the sand,
Don't begrudge your neighbors for what they say or do,
Just keep your eyes open for the Holy one is due.

    —Byron Robinson

Silent Death

Light only shines in the heart of those
  Who have found love
  Darkness has once again crossed my path.
Others see those bright lights that
  Warm the skin of the loved.
  I've been covered with the blanket of loneliness.
Very much suppressing my need to be wanted,
  I'll look to an even brighter light.
  The light of friendship and friendship only.
Elsewhere. That is one place
  No person looks for comfort.
  The light and dark are just the beginning of the
Silent Death

    —Allen Brown

The Bear And The Bee

There once was a bear,
Who never brushed his hair,
Then along came a bee,
And said, "You'll get stung by me,
Bear said, "What should I care,
It won't hurt you'll get stuck in my hair,
The bee tried to sting,
Then said, "Walla ba bing,
I guess you were right,
Now I'm back to my flight."

    —Amanda Anderson

You

Thou art a rose...
whose blossom is as magnificent as you?
or a gentle breeze...
that entices new life through and through?
Your eyes are works of art,
whose meaning is as deep as your thoughts.
Your smile is like a candle
that warms people's hearts.
Thou art the sun...
whose beauty is too radiant to one's sight?
or perhaps the inspiration...
that causes a poet to write?
The sound of your laugh is like music,
a song for the soul.
The sight of you makes me erratic,
because it's my heart that you stole.

    —Farani Lucero

The Cabal

Who are these men, with blood on their shoes
who've come to tell us that war is good news?

We've heard them before, these prophets of gore
with their cries to arise and buy arms for a war.

They brag about weapons, and scoff at defeat
and tell us of wars that are short and sweet.

If their strikes are clean and their bombs so smart
why do their targets keep breaking our heart?

A stock market fall is cause for alarm
they round up our sons and say we must arm.

But those body bag rows so long and neat
did these boys talk of markets and futures in wheat?

Now third world curs are armed to the teeth
if this one starts, it'll be hellish and brief.

"So how will it end?" I cried to the wind
but no voice came, just a specter that grinned.

Then witches three the green sea did roll
"Your God is dead," they croaked. "You killed him for oil!"

To whom could we turn and who would come
if the last man alive still had a gun?

    —Augustus Chenowth

Why

Why do I let you keep coming back?
Why do I open my heart to attack?
I guess that I look into those eyes,
And hope this time,
it's truth and not lies.
I cautiously open this heart
yet once more,
Only it's broken just as before.
To learn from mistakes,
to suffer heartaches,
To love one so much the hope must go on.
To want someone special
to depend upon.
How many times do you believe those same lies?
As long as there's stars
and clouds in the sky.

    —Darlene Whisnand

Why

Why do I tell you, "No", my child?
Why do I wish that you wouldn't do some
of these things you ask me to do,
Why do I say that you shouldn't?

Why do I tell you "No", my child?
Then try so hard to explain, that some of
these things you want to do,
Will only cause you pain.

Why do I tell you "No", my child?
and try to help you prepare, for the
long hard road you'll have to walk,
Well, you see, I've traveled there.

So when I tell you, "No", my child,
Please remember it's said with love.
Love for a child who was given to me,
to care for, from God above.
So, remember, I say, "No", with Love...

    —Evelyn Jane Spear Lucas

Love Or Hate

Why do people love?
Why do people hate?
It takes so much energy to hate
And it takes so little effort or none to love
Love is so free, natural, warm and giving
Love doesn't come in colors, shapes or sizes
Love is a wonderful and beautiful spirit
When I think of love
I think of God's greatest gift ... love
God says love is his greatest gift
of all, to all
People that hate
Cause a lot of negative things to happen
in their lives. And it takes so much energy to hate.
Hate causes; jealousy, envy and strife also racism
Hate causes sickness, evil and a one track mind
Hate is a mean evil spirit and not of God in heaven
And since I love God
I love to love love love
Are you ready for brotherly love?

—*Cheryl Lee*

Why?

Why is it, Black vs. White?
Why is it, most Black men get killed at night?
    I'm writing this 'cause we must unite in order to fight.

Why is it I get no respect? Why is it most Black people are in
debt? Why is it, we don't know self?
    Maybe the history class needs to teach something else.

Why is it that we don't have any jobs?
    Maybe it 'cause we've been robbed.

Why is it that Black men and Black women fight?
    Maybe, 'cause it's time to unite.

Why is it that most police declare war on Blacks?
    Maybe 'cause race is a fact.

Why is it that America is called the land of the free?
    Maybe 'cause in reality it wasn't meant to be.

Why is it that members of the Klan burn the cross at night?
    Maybe 'cause we have to fight for equal rights.

Why is it most Black babies don't get fed?
    Maybe 'cause that's why Marcus Garvey is dead.

Why ask why?
    "cause it is hard to be black and be alive.

—*Akil Asim Hill*

Jesus Will Come

While lying here wondering and waiting
        why is Jesus taking so long,
    Yet, I know he is still on his throne,
I feel as if I am at the end of my rope with no hope
            and my rope broke.
I had to reach beyond the break because Jesus is never late,
  He gives me strength when I get weak, He is my up keep,
      When I'm feeling down and in despair,
        Jesus said fear not, for I will be there.
        Scientific medicine can do only so much,
        There's nothing like his healing touch.
  So I will not worry, nor will I fret, for Jesus has never
            failed me yet,
  I'll just hold on and I'll hold out because of Jesus love,
            I shall never doubt.
    So when you feel at your lowest and can't go on,
        And the storms keep ragging in your life,
And it's hard to tell your nights from day, don't forget to pray
    if you believe in Jesus, He will show you the way.

—*Elorice Hall*

All In A Night's Work

A fellow once asked me, "What's so great about Mars,
why spend the night freezing just to look at the stars?"
A great many answers swirled around in my brain,
as I thought of our lander on the dusty red plain.
And pulsars that pulsate, and spirals that spin,
and planets that orbit the orbits within.
The novae and veils, and comets with tails,
luminesce and fluoresce like meteor trails.
The Big Dipper points to the Northern-most star,
While the Milky Way sparkles with light from afar.
The moon with its phases, occultations and grazes
Ellipses, eclipses, as the Amateur gazes.
There are too many reasons and so,with despair,
I turned and I told him I look "Cause it's there!"

—*Charles DeLongfield*

Life

The most precious thing we have is life.
Why then is it taken frivolously
Not a single thought is given to waking up, crossing
A street or saying good night to a loved one.
Polish life as you would that new car,
Manicure it as you would your nails or the lawn.
The dividends are beauty, purpose and integrity.
Say hello with a smile, give a hug.
Take time for a child, a mother, a father.
If you think it today do it today.
Really feel the warmth of the sun
Walk in the rain fully aware of each drop
Marvel at the shape of a single snow flake.
Keep wild optimistic imagination vibrantly
Alive everyday, every way
To cruise through the fantastic journey called life
Take with you on this trip, love, forgiveness
Compassion and diplomacy
Cherish each day, embrace every year
For in the twinkling of an eye…

—*Barbara Mercer*

Why Did God Create Me?

Why were we born in different places?
Why were we divided by lands and seas,
Why do we speak thousands of languages,
Why do we use, cherish different custom and cultures
When the world is only one and we're only all human!

Let us unlock the mystery of life and mind.
What made some great, powerful, helpful, wealthy and wise,
While many are cruel, unlawful, unruly and wild?
God created me to learn, observe and think
To feel love and touch the world within.

In my little heart and mind must always be entwined
The peace and love and care for everyone.
Although we may differ in color and appearance,
We were made and created by "Our Almighty One!"
So let us hold hands together with feelings and warmth!

Let us give strength, support, and shelter to unite us in one,
Let us bridge the seas and span the lands, with strength of
minds and lengths of lives, with power of soil, water, mines,
and wealth provide, for this world's for everyone regardless
of why, where, how, and what will come!

—*Gaudencia Compania Hasal*

My Mother, My Daughter And Me

In my head I feel she's looking at me with that look.
Will I ever do it right? I'm like a fish
Caught on her hook. Will she reel me in tonight?
What does she expect? I am just myself.
She's not so perfect......oh, maybe as my judge.
Her time and place are different, like the books
Up on her shelf but we wade together through life's sludge.
I'm part of her. She's part of me not identical, but the same.
We're in a never ending circle dance.
And as I hold on to my mother, my daughter clutches me
And I couldn't pull away, even if I had a chance.
And though I feel her happiness, I also share her shame
Our spirits are connected for eternity
With the deepest love I've ever known
For which I'll gladly take the blame 'cause I have never
Cut the cord of maternity. Is this a hopeless situation
Or a comfort and a joy? I wonder, if I'd be this way
If I were a man or boy?
Oh Mother, how I love you! Oh daughter, understand,
I'm giving you your life, as I release your hand.

—*Beth Eichel*

Meant To Be

What greater pain than to be a seed planted in an empty garden?
Will the buds still be the same, not knowing from whence it
came? Will the rains be too harsh for this seed there alone?
Will it feel like an orphan, there alone on its own? Not knowing
where its roots come from they still grow, but without care. Will
it blossom to flower, have the strength to dare? But wait,
beyond the rain there comes the sun. Its rays feel safe and
warm. Its buds start opening and reaching out, beginning to
take form. There's no telling how long this seed will have
life, how long this blossom will bloom. It may last a day, a
week, til' the end of the year, facing an inevitable doom.
There's always the chance it just may re-seed again, and next
time not alone. It'll give life to other seeds which will grow
by its side, to flourish in the same way. Never again to be
alone will grow stronger in knowing it'll bloom again in a
brighter day. Aren't we all like this seed, don't we all have
a need to look forward to a brighter season? With love this
too for us can be. Caring can give the reason. Growing
stronger every year, knowing we're not alone - we come to know
no matter where we came from, how beautiful life can be.

—*Genevieve Brosnahan*

Understanding And Kindness

What will it be like when your eyes find mine...
Will we smile, will we cry, or will we stop time?
Fear clouds my mind's operation and vision..
What kind of an adventure or decision?

Will we see all there is to behold
The start of a story, as yet untold...
The walls of many years...
Will they fall as silent tears?

God is watching us, as we react to His will
That single thought sends me a chill...
Will we see the beauty unfolding...
Will our hearts reach for the holding?

All remains as yet unknown
Will we both discover a brand new home...
Will we live inside each other's heart
Or will we let "The Fates" keep us part?

—*Harriet Lucas Garnett*

Honest Expectation

Will you learn to hold me with tenderness deep,
   will you hand me a heart, that I can keep?

Will you learn to pass by all the things I do wrong,
   and give back encouragement to make me grow strong?

Will you learn to commit to a bond that is true,
   and live day by day as if it's something new?

Will you learn to reveal all the feelings inside,
   and learn that with me you have nothing to hide?

Will you learn to like all the things I enjoy,
   and smile deep inside as you slowly employ?

Will you learn to trust past the walls that you've built,
   and help me to strengthen it with love and not guilt?

The one thing I wish for the most that you'll do,
   is learn to love me the way I love you.

—*Jennifer Alayne Schmaltz*

April Showers

Oh sudden little April showers,
Will you wake the sweet May flowers?
They have been asleep you know,
And do not know it's time to grow.

Will you wake them very soon,
Before you know it will be June.
And if you do not wake them now,
They will sleep right through somehow.

They should wake up very soon,
Be all dressed the first of June.
With their blossoms shining bright,
Some are red, some are white.

Oh April showers please come today,
And wash the earth so clean for May.
The violets they will be here soon.
It's almost time for them to bloom.

Should they forget to wake up now,
The world would be so dull somehow,
Now I know if you but try,
You can wake them by and by.

—*Dolly Perry*

Jennifer Willis

My name is Jennifer Willis. I am mostly recognized by
"Willis." A cat represents my personality. I can be playful,
loveable, and easy to get along with, but if you push me to far
you just might get scratched. There is a lost map inside my
heart neglecting to show me which way to go. I am just like
a little mouse trying to seek my way out of a maze. The word
"worry" is really getting to me. I love the sound of wood
burning when I stare into the fireplace, as the whole world
disappears. The annoying sounds of big trucks and buses
reminds me of a very hot congested day. I love to walk down
the road and be able to smell the honeysuckles. It relieves
me of all the symptoms of life. I despise the smell of pigs.
Tremendously large sloppy pigs. The afternoon is what I enjoy.
The sun setting while a soft breeze gently blows pass me. As
my hands cry, beg, and plead for me to slow down, and take one
day at a time. I have no time — my time is someone else's.
Oh, how I wish I was at my grannies a young child all over
again. Making mud pies, and playing house as if there wasn't a
worry in the world. I can still recall my papa singing, "You
Are My Sunshine" and granny talking about my little grape eyes.

—*Jennifer Willis*

The Call Of The Undertow

Skies all gray with the appearance of smog,
　　Wind whistling shrill as the soprano's tune,
An unusual mist, a low-lying fog
　　Disperse, revealing to me morn's pale moon.

As my toes tread the cool, muddy beach
　　I hear the sea gulls' long, pensive cry-
Like a moaning dirge seeking to reach
　　Some distant soul lit beyond the sky.

As I stare at the cold, gray sea
　　Blankly, though I cannot see far,
Some strange melancholy bids me
　　Visit a presence at the sandbar.

My shirt, torn off, thrust aside,
　　I wade into the cold, dark sea.
My legs flail, grasped by the tide,
　　Pulled beneath. The current has me.

Alas! I'm drowned! No hope for my poor soul,
　　My lungs are consumed with water. Oh, no!
From high I watch my lifeless body roll
　　In, at last released from the undertow.

　　　　—Benjamin DeGrow

The Traffic Light

As I sit here at the smiling, red traffic light; I look out the
window and see the world spinning all around me.

Faceless people in the sanctuary of their cars, speeding before
me as if they were a flock of wild migrating birds, that
started on their cold, long, rigorous journey south, late for
the winter.

A mother and son scurrying in the exhaust fumes of an old
yellow school bus as it pulls away from the corner of the bus
stop to make it's next scheduled pickup.

A small brown, hairy spider making several attempts to spin a
web off of a yellow fire hydrant with each attempt ending in
mere disappointment as the long silver silky web breaks each time.

A soft spring morning breeze moving through the trees with the
gentle force of the second hand on my wristwatch.
As I sit in my car at this traffic light; my world stands still.

　　　　—Bevly J. McGeorge

The Senior Citizen

Heart in repose he sits in the reclining chair
Wisdom of ages etched in his face and silvered hair.
Each strand, each wrinkle storied sorrow, joy, pain
Of faded dream, and hope - a life lived not in vain!

With unfettered eyes aglow now at future gaze,
And flowered paths borning anew in silent ways.
The waiting, joyous world to be of wonders untold,
The rebirth, the new, forever gone the old!

His lowered head bright eyes raising high,
His thought deep within, soars to the sky,
This man, this body, in truth only a clod
Visions in ecstasy, awake - he's true son of God.!

　　　　—John Pusateri

The End

A time warp of sin devours all done,
with a sick mind of matter the eyes find it fun.
A shadow of pain darkens lights of blue,
with veins of black blood,
the heart feels it's true.
A doubt of evil, grades over thoughts of good,
with ears made of stone, it hears what it should.
A rumble of wrath, summons
our final fall, with lips made of poison
it whispers death for all!

　　　　—Amanda Mills

It Is Lonely Without My Wife

Only fifty years young with a laugh like thunder.
With a smile as bright as the sun.
It's difficult to believe a year has passed.
Since you become the chosen one.

I have lost my soul's companion.
A life linked with my own.
And day by day I miss her more.
As I walk through life alone.

The world seems quite another place.
With out the smile of your beautiful face
Not a day goes by that our memories.
Of you do not stay with us.

Everyday you are sadly missed
With your special strength and love.
You gave us all, we will go on.
You are gone, but not forgotten.

And as dawns another year.
In our lonely hearts of thinking.
Thoughts of you are always near.
Time heals all wounds but for some it seems to get worse.

　　　　—Evelyn J. Tallman

The Little Bird's Song

There was an old man that used to be sick. He hobbled around
with an old pine stick. His face was sad and he was in great
pain; he could hardly get out of a shower of rain.

It seems he came from out of nowhere; the people around didn't
even care. They knew not his name or where he lived. The
clothes on his body were like a sieve.

"Oh," said the man; I will call him John. "Wouldn't it be
great if I wasn't alone. "I know what I'll do, go to the park
And If I hurry, I'll arrive before dark."

He picked up his stick and started to go. He got there so
quickly he hardly did know. He sat on the park bench and was
not there long before a bird on a limb started singing a song.
So inspired was John, he shouted with glee, "That little bird
is singing to me."

"I feel renewed from this life of sin. I am happier now than
I've ever been." Some of the sadness left his face as he
started to hum Amazing Grace. He was revived and never the
same; lived for Jesus and gained great fame.

　　　　—Corinne Brown

Fire Fly's

I love to watch the fire fly's darting in the night
Why did God create this fascinating sight?
To make us stop, look, and wonder?
Like a lightning bolt, or clap of thunder?
Or a falling star, on a summery night.
Perhaps a sunrise full and bright
Beautiful, fascinating, wonderful things.
But I like best of all the lantern with wings!

　　　　—Edna Roberts

echo of sanity

not letting go, keeping my grip
with balance so steady, it's tempting to tip
seeing the visions, yet memories they are
i'm physically here, and yet so far
knowing the ending, yet knowing no start
keeping together, yet falling apart
following darkness, yet seeing the light
doing the wrong, yet knowing what's right
climbing inside, yet exposed to the out
knowing the answers, yet still having doubts
fading with twilight, yet blazing so bright
knowing the way, yet having no light
seeing clouds in the night and the moon in the day
following maps, yet losing your way
when touching the frozen and yet it feels hot
knowing forever, but eternity not
hearing the signal, yet making no move
wanting to win, expecting to lose
holding to faith, yet feeling so weak
screaming forever. . . it echoes, echoes, echoes, echoes. . .

—*cheryl l. baker*

So Like The Diamond

Like a diamond in the rough,
    with frailty and fault.

So like the diamond come from earth.
His surface hard, unyielding, opaque to the light.
His heart protected, hidden from sight.

The diamond has the jeweler's gentle hand.
His infinite care brings fourth its faceted heart.
To polish with love, ever so gently,
    til glittering bright.

The facets of man, with no benefit of gentle hand,
    he alone must stand.
His character chiseled and honed by life,
    and the trial of time.

Brought to the age of wisdom, his heart softens.
His soul becomes a thing of beauty for all to see!
So like the diamond.

—*Amanda Jeffers Cooler*

Flowers

What flowers there in tropic sun
with golden crown and cocoa face?

You mean those weeds on yonder run;
those sparkling blooms of meanest race?

Not mean at all, but full of fun
and dancing coyly in their place!

They're Black-eyed Sues, soon to be gone,
by dry winds blown by ice replaced.

But oh, they're so like Melanie,
with dancing eyes and cocoa face.

—*Eva Bogaardt*

Crystal Love

I sip your love from a fragile glass of tears,
    with no fears.
I take care not to spill a drop
    nor shatter the glass.
They are too precious to me.

But if the cup goes dry and the glass turns to dust,
    it must.
Yet I will savor the drink and will have known
    the beauty of the crystal.

—*Jay K. Neutzler*

Hill Called Scull

On a hill called called scull where Jesus showed us His love
With His life He gave us grace, yes Jesus died in our place
Can't you see His precious hands where they drove the nails in?

"Oh sinners can't you see why Jesus died upon that tree, with
His blood He saved the lost with His life He paid the cost,
Can't you see Him hanging there with blood in His hair?

On a hill called Scull Jesus died for us all with His life He
gave us grace. yes He died in our place, can't you see nail
scarred hands where they drove the nails in?

—*Charlie E. Roberts*

Like A Knife Through The Heart

Challenge I shall gladly ignore
With lonely footsteps behind every deed
Many illusions have haunted these darkened eyes
But now I seek to meet that cheerful pride
For life with my love is simply sorrow I've found.

Now swarms and swarms of desolate grief
Rush like cold water haunting a beach
And from the depth of belief I battle this storm
As destiny calls like the wind of a god
And yes it hurts me my love, like a knife through the heart.

So now I sit and wait amidst the fiery sorrow of life
while her passion of pride stalks that trembling night
And the blues I choose to heighten my sigh
Perhaps someday will force her to see the truth of her crime
Because my trust in her is the same as her leaving
As this life with her is merely a love that won't let go
Oh my lord I ask you, will that someone ever bid farewell
Because she stung me my lord, like a knife through the heart.

—*John Meany*

Life Is A Beach

As I walk along the sand
With my lover hand in hand
I see the ever ebbing tide
Within the ocean vast and wide
The pulsing streams of frothy foam
Within whose bosoms microbes roam
I feel the pounding surf at sea
And sense it's all a part of me
I smell the air the salt is rife
And know it is the stuff of life
I hear the seabirds plaintive cry
And watch them wing against the sky
The endless miles of rocky shore
The coral, the shells, the reef, and more
Spirit and elements of the sea
Is what embodies you and me.

—*Arlene Herron*

Books And Toys

A favorite book has tattered edges
worn from reading after reading,
each time something new discovered,
pages aging so gracefully,
comfort and security cover to cover.

A cherished toy has rounded corners
sculpted by loving playful hands,
new adventures abound with creativity,
never losing sight of its purpose,
fun and laughter with simplicity.

We should live our lives like books and toys.

—*John M. Clough*

Street Lambs

Lost; Alone; like some orphaned waif
With no emotional harbor to call safe.
Running into the darkness of dreams
Selling my body like peaches and cream.
Package it pretty; unwrap it nude
Always men I can count on being crude.
Will survivals price always be outrageously high?
Do men believe respect is something they can buy?
Smile; reveal sensuality as the reality.
Yet;
Hide the broken heart, the lack of tranquility.
Are women doomed to always be toys?
Living; feeling ones for grown-up little boys?
Come play with me honey - for always and a day
Then later; kicked in the teeth, thrown away
Believe in forever! Believe in caring!
Doing so to be left alone, so despairing —
Tell me — who will ever give a damn
About THIS lost little lamb?

—*Anna Frances*

My Brother Norman, The Fallen Warrior

Geared as he was for the monstrous battle
With odds that seemed insurmountable.
He stepped into the fray with full armor
The outcome was one that was unaccountable.

Ill prepared and not fully trained, he stepped forth
He looked but never saw a clear image of the enemy
Arrogant and confident, he pretended not to be afraid
The audience in this arena knew what was his destiny.

Did this quiet man suddenly become a monster with demons?
Obsessed as he was, few people recognized this warrior.
Family and friends wanted the former person to crawl out.
There was no exit. Who felt the sorrier?

It was a lopsided battle with little remorse
Norman fought bravely with determined strength
The outcome seemed in doubt; the devil dragged him down
The enemy cocaine won at last length.

And so the bruising battle is finally over
Maybe, it was always meant to be
The people left the arena in tears
I hope his soul is at peace in his eternity.

—*Ed Rasky*

The Day The Tree Cried

Spring was well on the way in all its glory,
With promise of re-birth and awakening.
The majestic maple was waiting ever so patiently
For the warmth of the sun to bathe her bark.
The winter had been one of long freezing days and dark nights,
And the old maple had shivered with all her might.

Then the right day came and none too soon,
When the first tiny blossom was just about to bloom.
With all she had in her, she felt the big break of her branches
  that reached from her body
When the big saws came to take her down.

Just when the sap was flowing and the birds had chosen
Her for their home... her life was ending.

The flowing sap then turned into tears and ran freely.
Save me... save the forest, cried the maple.
Tomorrow and the next spring will come... but naught for
The majestic maple you see... because there was the
Day she cried... and died.

—*Barbara A. Brown*

My First Love, Precious

Gentle colors of black gray and orange,
with raccoon ring paws filled with life
my leaf, bird and bug catcher was.
Made me a Grandma five times in our life time
spanked her the first time
I caught her across the street.
Rescued her from trees, dogs and blue jays
a time ago.
Now the kitten is gone, her black now silver,
her gray now white, the orange a rust,
the ring paws a little slower,
herself a late riser.
Age has set in, now she rests in the sun and bats
at a fly now and then.
Whatever we are doing, wherever we are going.
We have our health, love and loyalty in each other.

—*Jana Stutzman*

My Loyal Companion

A pleasant walk through open meadowed space,
  With the mist of morning...fresh in the trees,
I'm on my way to my own special place
  My loyal companion goes with me.

We've walked by the hour...
  And shared our private dreams.
He lies right beside me...and sleeps,
  While I fish in mossy streams.

We've shared all the bright sunny days,
  And the sudden thunder-showers as well.
I remember how once we romped in the hay,
  'till we both heard the dinner bell.

Together we've hunted for game...in the woods,
  My loyal companion and I.
I've watched you grow up from puppyhood,
  Having fun...sure makes time fly.

Well old fellow, our life's sure been good,
  We've done just about everything we could.
But our days go by, a little slower now,
  We're just not as young as we use to be.

—*Dorothy Pearl*

America

America is like a fragile piece of crystal
With the proper use and care it will still be valuable in years
to come but with the wrong use it can shatter as fast as a
bullet reaching a target.

America is a work of art that everyone did in different rooms
With different shades and colors, not everything lining up
perfectly but yet a priceless piece of art.

America is the people
Made of everything everyone wants it to be made of
Everyone's feelings, beliefs, thoughts, and emotions

America is change
Changing every second like a child
Growing and changing as it wants, always learning as it does.

America is the hearth of the home
Warm and welcoming to its dwellers
Yet sometimes blazing with anger or confusion.

No matter how you look at America, it is a mother.
loving and open, yet sometimes strict, but always there to fall
back on.
America is me.

—*Amy Aho*

766

The Fallen

A vision against the isthmus, arrayed in streaming white.
With unforgiving countenance, she mourns the coming night.
The valiant and the fallen; a tremor and a sigh.
Veiled upon a whisper, to cloak her strangled cry.
Everlasting sorrow, everlasting pain.
All the world will ponder the secret of the slain.
The dreary night confronts her like an obelisk of pain.
A monolith of stark dimension; its might a crushing strain.
The struggle and travail; acquiescent before the stone.
An aching heart rent asunder; a widow's odyssey alone.
Everlasting suffering, everlasting tears.
All the world is pummeled, to an abyss of empty years.
A veneer of human wreckage, beneath the timid tear-stained sky.
She yields her will to darkness, and falls upon the stone to die.
The valiant and the fallen; peel of thunder and frigid rain.
No pall to eclipse the storm, no tapestry to hide the stain.
Everlasting wither, the affliction of the age.
Alone with desolation, she accepts the reaper's rage.

—*Clinton E. Harris*

When You Were Walking By The Crashing Waves

I saw the waves splash at your bare feet
With violent force, yet gentle touch.
The moon is your only light, your only guide...to her.
She's sitting swan-like..in a tree
Wishing on a meteor...false hopes, false dreams.

Walking on the beach is not so easy anymore.
You have to avoid stepping on dead fish.
He tripped on a sand hill and fell on his face
And remained like that for about an hour, or so it seemed.
Thinking, dreaming...but he could see no stars.

He wanted her, he wanted to kiss her.
But her lips were pale, she never wore lipstick
She never went out, she had no friends.
She'd never known love...or what it could ever be.

Although drenched by the sparkling waves, he wouldn't get up.
The sand welcomed his body
Salty water accepted his lost soul.
He would never get up now
She will never know her true love.

—*Gabriela Rascov*

Our Eagle

There's an eagle in our air
With wide spread wings & beak so rare;
He lends his breadth & Holy heir
To all our land that spans our care.

Lend your support & gaze afar
For this eagle will never mar
The graceful picture he inspires,
To all who heed his mighty cry.

Stand tall, stand firm, we must proclaim
To care for this eagle, confirmed by man;
'Tis Gods' fulfillment He has promised
When we stand tall, & take His stand!

Our eagle, so beautiful & so grand
Is really a prize in God's great land;
So guard this bird of prey, 'til the day
Of God's redemption & the promises He made!

—*Carla Ruth Finke*

Beauty

Oh, my daughter so fair
with your eyes that sparkle and shine,
and your golden locks of hair
that make you look so fine.
You have been blessed with beauty
there is no doubt of that,
but that does not lessen your duty,
of the stations where your at.
For what's on the inside
means just as much.
Where in lies the guide,
that seeks the heart to touch.
For without that inner light
the wisdom would be lost,
Shrinking the might
Oh!— such a cost.
So if you wish to gain
please remember this.
From the inner and the outer—do not wane,
For both joined together—cannot miss.

—*Florence L. Pearson*

Broken Feathers

Hey, big white man,
with your rainbow hair.
Who invited you to the promised land?
You came to take more than bear and deer.
You came and left us with a jagged tear.
You took what was not ours to give,
and shoved us aside, the few that lived.
We lived as one with mother earth,
while you named it, and gave it birth.
We raised your bastard, and you razed yours.
You filled us with bullshit, we licked our sores,
we lived in your bottles we bought in your stores.
You showed us our place. Now, when you look in the
mirror, what is your fate? To us life was peace, to
you it was hate. Our tragedy and suffering you can't
deny. You wrote your history, now live with your lie!
Again you ask what is not ours to give,
maybe this time you'll let none of us live.

—*Darrell K. Bressler*

Heart Of Gold

You're the one I most admire,
With your words that truly inspire.
Telling me of things I never knew,
Reminding me, to do the best that I can do.

"Hold your head high," you would say.
Being there for me night and day.
Giving me the courage, to stand up right,
Believing in me, that I would always shine bright.

Never taking the credit, for all that you've earned,
Just a little thank-you, you want in return.
Sharing, caring and the heart to give.
Making my life easier in the world we live.

I'm so grateful to have a special friend like you
So precious, and rare one in a million too.
Like fire so hot, and snow so cold.
But most of all, your heart of Gold.

—*Geraldine Caple*

Hatred

Most feared, most harmful, most evil, yet most common
  Within the heart where I have too often found her
    Living as a parasite, dominant with confidence
    Mind and soul helpless in her wicked ways.
Unavoidable as death, and most disagreeable for
    The abused and oppressed she spits at.
      She is a force few can fight
    Like poison flowing through the veins
      She will not leave or relent
      To restore the mind and soul;
But apply a tourniquet on the wound like a disease
    Whom only love can conquer, and so I use
  O all my love and all my strength to tell her
    That she will be destroyed - not destroyer.

    —Dawn Nordquist

God's Greatest Call

Being a parent is a difficult task. It's all about giving
without being asked.
Some parents take it lightly, some- not at all.
I personally take it as God's Greatest Call.

It's a job you learn as you go along.
Some things you get right, some you get wrong.
But, all in all, if you stick to priority,
you'll produce good citizens that fit in society.

You shouldn't put on pressure for what You want them to be
they need freedom to choose their own destiny.
Just instill in them - Love, Honesty, and Trust.
And let the rest happen without anger and fuss.

Be there for them, give an encouraging word.
Being a parent is a theme that should forever be heard.
Forever and by far the most precious gift of all
Being a parent is definitely God's Greatest Call.

    —Charlene P. Gause

The Voice

    Adrift
Without the glittering eyes of the night,
    She seeks the Voice.
  She remembers its cool embrace;
    the tingling in her soul;
  And she longs for the reunion.

    She's tired of the heat;
  of the warmth of the endless days,
    binding her eyes to Reality,
    blinding them to the shadows
  that linger on the fringes of Truth,
    burning out the darkness
      where dreams reside;
    where Magic stirs Passion,
    and Hope is conceived...

    Aborting it to Fact.

On the arid sands of Sanity,
    she is a stone,
    weighted to the earth,
  without the chance to fly.

    —Debra M. Kraft

Game Of Love

The streets are empty and so am I
Wondering why as I look to the sky
It starts to rain and I start to cry
The answers elude me but I still try

I see in my mind a picture of you
The longing I feel for you makes me blue
I don't even know you, what am I to do
This familiar feeling is nothing new

Longing in my mind feeds my soul with pain
Your beauty invades me but what is your name
I feel for you, do you feel the same
I'm trapped once again in loves inane game

When I think of you I pray in my mind
That it's possibly me that you're hoping to find
And if that's true, it'll just take some time
I pray once again love won't leave me behind

Love is a strange thing, it's here today
Then something will come and take it away
I have found no solutions to making it stay
I guess loves a game we were just meant to play

    —Gerald Reed

The Friend Of All Friends

She carries me to a land of unspoken
    words.
Bewilders me with her kindness.
She hears me out, listening to every
    word that I have ever spoken.
She pours me a drink for my dry, thirsty lips.
She shows me the sun in her glistening
    eyes.
I lose consciousness, slowly drifting
    away from all interactions.
She casts me a picture, permanently
    embraced in my mind.
No looking back to what is real, for
    she is real, revolving in circles
    around my heart.

    —Charlie Shapiro

Somebody

Early, every morning, she starts in any kind of weather
Working always harder and harder and I hope that this does
Not last forever!
For sure I am not wrong that she is a tiny jewel of human
structure only apparently physically fragile she has the mind
strong, and in this is her brilliant future!
Her hair is not black, blonde or brown!
It, probably, has not the color of its own!
She is entirely gracious when walking and marvelous when
talking! always with a smile in her eyes and lips and I have
seen she likes making tricks!
She has teeth of pearl and lips of ruby, but, finally, who is she?!
That is what is missing, till now, in this poem, but I will
tell who she is to everyone.
She is the young laborer Annette Ruiz a wonderful gem
Schiavone's construction company most precious stone!
Go ahead in your life, Annette, my dear. You have done
everything pretty good but I wish that in the next year you
become a great movie star in hollywood!

    —Henrique De Paula

Shattered Innocence

When the pure and innocent roam the
world it's white. There is no sin this is
innocence. When love is forever and will
never die. Tears flow because of happiness
this is innocence. When there is no sadness
and no fear. You don't have to be scared to live
love and die this innocence.
When the devil invades your heart
and world. There is hatred everywhere you go
this is shattered innocence. When the
devil roams the world with dark angels
along his side, its black. There is all depression
no happiness. Everyone is guilty this is shattered
innocence. When tears of blood
flow. You can't breathe, see, or feel anything
around you. The world is turning
black it's all shattered innocence.

—*Amber Sioux Mayfield*

Does Time Stop

How would we know when time will stop? Will it be when the
world stop turning? Or will it be when the sun stop
shining? We travel in life bending our minds trying to
answer the unanswered. But who knows? Can it be when dreams
become the same. Or when babies are born and call out their
mother's name? It could be when the birds all sing the
same. Giving you a moment of pleasure just to ease the
pain. Many try to hide their shame, but do misery come
without pain?
Even when we try to cover it up, somehow it remain a stain.
But would that make us all a little insane? To believe a
mountain has a brain, If one says, "yes" does that make us
sane? So would you send your child into this world without
a name? We shouldn't believe or disbelieve what we can't
explain.
Would it be wise to call a person dumb just because they
can't spell their name? Or is it just our hatred hidden by
pain that drain us and fill us up until we pop? I tell you
how time don't stop, it only start.

—*Arthur L. Reid, Jr.*

A Perfect World

A perfect world, of which I dream,
   Would be covered with beauty, lands so green.
No hate would exist, nor would war,
   Only generosity and kindness, unlike any before.
The world would have equality, with unlimited happiness,
   Without troubles, problems, or any prejudice.
The people who are hateful, cruel, or abusive to a child,
   Would be sent away, forever exiled.
No disease would exist, to hurt the weak or the young,
   And you'd hear beautiful songs, always being sung.
The most beautiful creatures, would exist only here,
   And everyone would live a life without fear,
Hate, war, and despair would have here no home,
   Only love, truth, and honesty would roam.
The land always green, the skies always light blue,
   The world where only the most gracious birds flew.
The perfect world, of which I dream,
   Would be covered with beauty lands so green.
No hate would exist, nor would war,
   Only generosity and kindness, unlike any before.

—*Brian Matthews*

Whispering Love

I listen to the whisper of our love, from times we thought
would ever last. And I hold a picture in my mind, recalling
that love from the past. There are many lovely reasons, that
only you can know. Of captive things that held my love, that
sometimes didn't show. Tender looks throughout the years, were
mystic words unspoken. Along with binding ties of love, that
still remain unbroken. The feel of your caress, like blossoms
in the spring. Just wanting to return, the pleasure that you
bring. The way you voiced your tender thoughts, like the
cooing of a dove. Cascading hair that danced upon my face,
with the passion of your love. The flutter of my heart, as it
tried to speak for two. To say there's not, but one of us, just
me and you. The sweetness of your scent, as you held me
through the night. For the whispered echoes of our love, still
glow like candle light. The memory is so vivid, I feel that
your here. And I can see ourselves again, like looking in a mirror.

—*Harold Albert*

Memories In This Old House

The memories in this old house
Would fill a book with ease.
Daddy lovingly nailed the boards
Placing windows to catch the breeze.

The only thing that disturbed me
Were Chinaberry trees in the yard.
The flower, the leaf, the berry and stem
Fell each season without regard.

The yard was swept with "brush brooms"
And no grass was allowed to grow.
If the weeds decided to sprout,
They were "the enemy" to Dad and his hoe.

This old house has known sorrow
And happiness through the years
It has stool all kinds of weather
Brought comfort and eased our fears.

This old house is my haven
As it stands weathered and worn
I touch the boards with loving hands
This old house is where I was born.

—*Frances Lunn Odom*

Self-Esteem

Our teacher asked one day in school,
"Would you describe yourself as cool?
Of course each student shook their head,
their faces turned a deep, dark red.

She asked us, "why?"
and in that moment we all became extremely shy.
Then I, the bold one of the thirty,
stood up to answer this question we thought dirty.

I said, "Yes, I think of myself as cool."
Everyone laughed and thought me a fool.
In the mist of the dilemma,
our teacher, Miss Palema, started to applaud.

"This is good, children, don't think it bad.
We should all like ourselves, so we aren't sad.
People who have self-esteem,
can work by themselves or as a team."

"These men and women are happy with themselves and others.
They treat all like fellow brothers.
People like this don't have a golden crown,
even so they see no reason to wear a frown."

—*Deanna McMahon*

Would You?

Would you write me a letter just to say hello?
Would you take long rides with nowhere to go?
Would you let me call you from time to time?
Would you share with me a glass of wine?
Would you take a walk in the moonlight with me?
Would you share a dance at the edge of the sea?
Would you hold my hand as we walk along?
Would you let me sing you a love song?
Would you think of me as the sun is setting low?
Would you greet me in the morning with a sweet hello?
Would you share a picnic under the trees?
Would you answer yes to any of these?
These things and more I would do with you,
Cause it would be a dream come true.

—*Charles A. Medders*

Escape

I snuggle into the darkness
Wrapping it closely about me
My shield,
Shutting out all sorrows.
The enemies that pursue me
Cannot overtake me here.
No evil can penetrate this haven I have found.
I am secure.
For the night spins a gentle cocoon about me,
Hiding me from reality
With its unsurmountable problems.
Its chains that bind me in hopelessness.
Many roads of escape I see.
I cannot take them.
Am I too weak or too strong?
I choose the simple path,
One without pitfalls.
I sink into the cradle of darkness
And I am free.
I sleep

—*Edith Sherman*

Nameless Signature

They gathered in the low of the wood,
Writing and reciting the wisdom they could.
Unidentified and unknown, they are tireless in word.
Only in their circle can the identity of each one be heard.
They collaborate in grand conversation,
Writing words that can mystify a nation.
Bits of wisdom in rhyme contained,
Their work throughout history has remained
A constant presence in great books of knowledge.
Taught in small schools, and in the learned college,
Who are these who write beyond our reach,
And seem autonomous?
I know not, for the signature of their work reads simply,
"Anonymous".

—*H. D. Sauls*

You

You are to me what fingers are to a hand
You are to me what water is to the land
You are to me what light is to day
You are to me what lips cannot say
You are to me what every you want
You are to me oh... so gallant
You are to me what black is to night
You are to me what vision is to sight
You are to me what green is to grass
You are to me what church is to mass
You are to me the stars in the sky
You are to me my very special guy
You are to me the love of my life
and I am to you forever your wife

—*Bernadette Mondry*

The Nursing Home

Curling tendrils from
Yellow roses
Mingle with baby's breath and oxygen tubing
Over beds
Of incubation of death.

Crayon pictures over push-button headboards
Proclaim devotion to one
Whose lap
Once held room for skinny little legs
And arms full of picture books.

The lap has disappeared
Into a curve of carefully placed pillows
Surrounding the essence of one
Who served watermelon
At riverside picnics.

Tenderly enfold, then,
The shell
Of long hours of selfless giving
Lest it slip away
In less than dignity.

—*Cynthia A. Van Blaricom*

Karin And Carmel

It's three o'clock in the morning
   Yet I can see by a light from outside -
      As she sleeps so peacefully here beside me
         The ever lovely face of my bride.

We're here in Carmel by the Sea
   To celebrate her very special day -
      She's entered a new decade of her life
         But a young bride to me she'll stay.

The same as she was when we married
   Those most wonderful years ago -
      Here in Carmel by the Sea
         Where to reminisce, we'll always go.

As we've done on each anniversary
   And on many occasions in between -
      To us it's as close to Heaven
         As we'll find on this earthly scene.

A spot unique and filled with charm
   It holds precious memories for me -
      Little wonder I'll always bring her back
         To Carmel here by the Sea.

—*D. Rhea Johnson*

Influence

Oh, as the influence uttered deeply,
Yet meaningfully to the fate of ashes, an outcome
The fiery phoenix reaches a heat-liquidated sun
   only to reveal ancient ones.

To go back in a once living history -
Ancient Roman soldiers, wooden ships,
The oppression of tired souls laboring
To the beat of a war drum -
   Only to be set free by blind death and face
   victory.

Though influence has many faces -
Like courage, desire and success to motivate
   a viewing eye.
To scrutinize his imagination over a poem

   For a person endeavoring to better his life
      through another man's wisdom, that's
      where it lies.

—*Earl West, III*

The Fifth Season

Our inner city windows overlook a graveyard,
Yet not a single tombstone may be found
We have no need of chiseled granite markers
When mothers know too well that death abounds
The view below is often rank and mirthless
As rendered with a madman's wire brush
Fear drifts like vapor down each cloistered alley
Hope suffocates within the midnight hush
Always it is the eternal fifth season
Now the gameboards all will soon be put away
Too constant stays the deadly fifth season
To lift our vilest nightmares into day
Wheezened young men, checkermaster children
How dare you suppress your anguished screams
You ought to raise your voices to the rooftops
And resonate this canyon with your dreams

     —Dennis Reed

Tick Tock Around The Heart

We are two hands of a clock. Together
yet often separated. Regardless
of the time, we are always bound to one
another by that vital center point.
You the minute hand and I the hour. We
are in unison, keeping the clock in
motion. You the minute hand because the
minute moves the hour, as you do to me.
An encounter is granted to us once
an hour and the intervening minutes
seem endless. The chance to touch you seldom
arrives, and when it's at hand, it is brief.
Our moment is over and just like a
mirage, you disappear, and instantly
become an image lingering about
my mind. I wish the hands were together
now, so we would be with each other. Or
perhaps one day the clock will stop at that
moment the hands overlap and we will
be fixed in that position forever.

     —Candace Nakagawa

Away

You only say you love me when it's time to go away!
Yet, you never tell me.

Through the course of any day, I know you care about me
and show me what to do, support me and believe in me
and help me through and through.

Deep in our hearts, the joy we share grows stronger everyday,
But, you only say you love me when it's time to go away!

It's so wonderful to have you to cherish and to hold.
To put my arms around you, entwined like rings of gold.

I've had so many things go wrong throughout the years,
and you've always been there, to help me with my fears.

Things happen for a reason, it may not be "our" way.
But, you only say you love me when it's time to go away.

Sometimes, we are so hateful, words...they cut like knives.
They can do such awful damage and control our very lives.

It only takes three words, to change a point of view,
to give that other person a hope, to hold on to.
A future lies before us, and the start of a new day,

Please tell me that you love me, before...you go away.

     —Ellen C. Doucette

Poem For October

When the bright symphony plays pizzicato on the
   yielding retina
like the look of love in your eyes,
curled smoke tangs the air
like the heavy wisp of a votive candle
or the perfume of your body,
the gentle sting of sweet-sour cider from the
   mellowed cask,
or the gathered wild-honey from your encircling lips,
the long sound of a passenger train through mist —
these are the crisping days of received beauty,
the sensuous days of gathered love,
long nights of remembered music,
moving along life's cycloid toward December -
and the feel of death's tapestry about the loins.

     —J. Alexander Thorburn

My Best Friend

Whenever I need a friend,
you always seem to be there. You
help me with my problems, and our joys
together we share.

I can't imagine life without a friend
like you once we get together we are
an indivisible two.

All the fun I've shared with you
can never be replaced. Together we've had
many good times and conquered the
problems that we've had to face.

So I want you to know that I am
always here, if ever you need a friend to
make your thoughts clear.

And when I must leave as many
good friends sometimes part, I have you
with good memories and an important
place in my heart.

     —Carolyn Wolpa

I Have Always Been Sarah For You

I met you in the water
You appeared about thirty and you were holding a little girl
And she called you Daddy and I was amazed
By how playful you were with her and you asked my name
And I told you that it was Sarah and I have always been Sarah
For you and we swam in the ocean and built sand castles and
Collected broken shells for the moat only to discover that
The purple ocean goddess has swallowed
Our castle into her belly and her fullness blocked the horizon
And if we blinked and peered around her lavender ear
Could we glimpse the future
Sometimes she would have to rest
But she slept standing up
So we never could know when
Or how the blessing would come
If she stretched her fingers a ray of orange light would escape
Through them and she yawned like an intimate wind
And purple petunias grew out of her toes.
I picked one for you.

     —Beth Conkling

Happy Birthday Daughter

You are my daughter, you are my friend,
You are the best thing God could ever send.

There was a time we didn't get along,
You had to prove your strengths and could never be wrong.

You were so much like me when I was a child,
That is why we bucked, we were both a little wild.

But time has a way of taming each one of us,
We allow it to happen with very little fuss.

You have turned into a lady I am very proud to know,
You give of yourself and set others aglow!

You are a special person and very sincere,
You truly care about others and those you hold dear.

This wish comes your way because today is your birth,
Everyone is blessed because you're here on earth!

—*Barbara W. Legno*

I Love You

I love you from the depth of my soul;
You are the strength that sustains me,
The laughter that enlivens me
And a ray of sunshine in my darkest hour.

I love you because of the faith that propels you,
Because of the intensity of your dreams,
Because of your profound wisdom
And the spirit that indwells you.

I love the gentleness of your touch,
The sound of your voice
Which penetrates my entire being;
You are the catalyst that ignites my passion.

I love you because your compassion is undeniable,
Your humble manner is refreshing,
And your honesty is rare;
You are a blossom among thorns.

I will love you always,
Even beyond this existence;
Yes, it is true
I will love you even after death.

—*Bernice W. Wilson*

Heaven Sent

You must have been sent from heaven above
You came into my life and gave me your love
But I was stupid and to blind to see
That I needed you and you needed me
So here I sit, tears streaming down my face
Regretting things from my past...
Things I should have said....
Things I should have done...
Remembering the good and the bad
In spite of it all, we still had fun
You were always there when I needed a friend
I took you for granted, but you were always true to the end
I was always hurting you and letting you down
Looking for a love that I finally found
But I was afraid and couldn't believe
That someone as wonderful as you
Could love someone as wretched as me

—*Cori Ostrom*

Ronda

A gift from God and heaven above,
You came to me one day.
So tiny and so full of life,
Not knowing how long you'd stay.

The love that I knew, it grew just like you.
Each day that we had together.
Our father above has no greater love,
Than a mother has for her daughter.

Our days were full of sunshine,
And wonders that we'd discover.
Then some how, a cloud approached,
And changed my life forever.

The storm it came, it flooded my heart,
With sorrow, that I'd never known.
My days are now grey, and won't go away,
And life for me - I'm alone.

I've got to believe in the rainbow,
He promised so long ago.
The sun will shine, the sky will clear,
And we'll walk the streets of gold.

—*Claudette J. Taylor*

Grandmas

A Grandma is for telling
    You can tell her anything
She likes to hear of what you do
    And learn all about your good friend Sue
        Yes, Grandma is for telling.

Grandma is for asking
    You can ask her anything
What makes the sun so bright
    And where does it go at night?
How do birds fly
    And what happens when we die?
        Yes, Grandma is for asking.

Grandma is for loving
    She likes to hold and hug you
Especially when you hurt.
    And then the hurt will go away
And you can run again and play.
        Yes, Grandma is for loving.

Do you have a Grandma?

—*Catharine P. Field*

She's Velvet In The Rough

You've been a winner with me from day one
            You cared
Our dependence grew between the seasons; fairy-tale
            together we shared
    We were very young at heart; we're as one
            We dared
We struck at the odds and won in our own special way
            we shared
    We even now find ways unique-not forged-to say
            we cared
You never put on a phony front; speaking your mind
            you dared
You always do more then your share of any task; effortless,
            direct you cared
    Truth! truth, you are truth
    You know the beauty of simple language
        The strength of your voice
    You shared; you dared; you cared.
        Now you know that we both
        Dared to share and care.

—*Jim Daub*

Why You

When you lose the closest person in the world to you
You don't know what to say or what to do
And people try and tell you they know what you're going through
But unless you've been through it how could you have a clue

Hey bro where do I go from here
When everything in life use to be so clear
But now there's no relief not anywhere
Oh man I'm telling you its just not fair

Hey bro I thought you could be the one
To do something about this crazy world that's come all undone
Cause you were never afraid to take the ball and run
But how could God take you before you saw you're son

Hey bro where do I go from here
When everything in life use to be so clear
But now there's no relief not anywhere
Oh man I'm telling you it's just not fair

And even now as the year's go by clicking by
I still ask myself why, why, why
Then your son asks why did my daddy die
Oh Lord I can't help but break down and cry.

　　　　—*Fred Starr*

Missing You

Missing you gets old,
You don't know when to stop.
You're more confused every day.
When you hold sand,
It slides through your fingertips
A fatal attraction that you can't let die
I'll hide in my shell
Or lash out at the rain
When you squeeze too tight.
Dreams become meaningless
In the heat of a cold sweat
You think you love me,
I wish you didn't
My world is losing ground
I don't want to live
In my own shadow...
So I guess this is good-bye,
But I won't be missing you
After all.

　　　　—*Blake M. Billings*

Love Memory

When you lose someone you love, or someone special to you.
You feel sad all the time, or you feel very blue.
It's not a dying loss, or a moving loss, it's a love loss.
It takes away you spirit, and pride.
It makes you just want to go and set in a corner and hide.
Your soul feels empty and lost.
It feels cold, just like the first winter frost.
It doesn't help you think about the memories you had,
even times good or bad.
And then no later you start to cry.
You know inside, no matter how much you lie.
You will never get over your first love.
And then you look up, in the sky above.
And then for know reason why, you suddenly see a love show.
But you know in the future.
Someday you will learn to love, and then letting go.

　　　　—*Betty Joe Johnson*

Eternal Friendship

Have you ever had a friend,
　　you hated to tell, it's the end?

This is what happened to me,
　　and it was not a pretty sight to see.

I lived in a very hot place,
　　now there's wind in my face.

Telling that friend good-bye,
　　really, made me cry.

But, I'll be okay, I know,
　　because where I live, it's going to snow.

Through our cards and letters,
　　our friendship can only get better.

Even though we are far apart,
　　our friendship still grows in our hearts.

　　　　—*Dana Miller*

You Are The One For Me

As I stand looking at the blue sky. Wondering and thinking of you. Hoping that someday not far away, we will be together again. And if that should never be, we will think of each other forever. When and wherever you might be. Remember! You are the one for me.

To think of how we used to share, our thoughts and ideas, to understand, together the joy and sorrow of life. This leaves me with a desire of wanting to be near you. To renew my feeling for one so dear. When and wherever you might be. Remember! You are the one for me.

Although we are miles and miles apart. Let space and time between us be filled with thoughts and remembrances of the pleasures in youth, and be a resemblance of our life together, forever, until the moment that we are separated by death. When and wherever you might be. Remember! You are the one for me.

　　　　—*Frances Allison Harris*

"Lovest Thou Me?"

"Lovest Thou Me?" my Master said, to Simon Peter that day;
　　"You know I do!" was Peter's reply
　　"For you, my Lord, I will gladly die!"
"Then feed my sheep, the little lambs too, there's much
　　work in this world for you to do".

That was THEN and this is NOW, forgive me Lord, I humbly
　　bow;
　　I pray for forgiveness, for sheep unfed, little lambs grow
　　up misled;
Amid the tumult of this hour, calm our nation and grant us
　　power, to place you first in leadership strong,
　　Forgive our neglect and things done wrong.

God's children in ghettos, a dirty slum - the deaf, the
　　blind, the speechless dumb;
The hungry - the cold, in deep despair; they plead for HELP,
　　Doesn't anyone care?

These are our neighbors - God help us obey - befriend them and
　　witness Thy love each day!
"Lovest Thou Me?" this call still rings true
　　Are we feeding His flock as He asked us to do?

　　　　—*Harriett B. Griffin*

To Mellie Talley On Her 80th Birthday

Mellie, Mellie, you're smart as can be.
You made it to 80 without a degree.

You majored in Math it's plain as can be,
Trying to figure out how feed six on $3.33.

Reading was great as you passed the test,
By telling your children the stories they loved best.

In Home Ec. you really did cope.
You made a big bucket of lye for your soap.
On wash days you were literally pooped,
But you smiled and said, "pleased join us for soup."
You knew what to add to flavor it so well;
and the visitors never knew you would tell the kids,
"don't eat too much, save for the guests,
and after they leave, we'll eat the rest."

In Science you got a big A for telling the kids why horses
   do neigh.
And answering questions why the sky is blue and who made the
   wind blow clear through.

We love you Mellie and hope you can be—
as happy as this when reach 93.

   —*Doris E. Kinzel*

Tuesday Afternoon

We sit on Tuesday afternoon,
You rest your eyes, I rest on your curves
And count the lines on your hand
Trying to imagine what it would be like
To live where no limitations are imposed.
You draw me closer
And I watch the way your fingers move
In a slow firm caress the way snow falls
Still at rest in falling
To shine the whole length.
At this moment I do not long
For kings with second class realms
Or the light of old moons.
In ways you can not understand
Your breath rises in comprehension
Of what in me is incomplete.
I need your desire and light filled leaves
But in the times to come
I'll need your arms more.

   —*Gayle Calimese*

True Love

Oh Blue-Bird blue who are you?
You sing and scream to sell your soul.
I've been told that from way above you sing for love.
Low lonely lad don't be so sad your attempts are all but true.
Your chirping chants are of circumstance we don't
believe in you
True love is that of a moth who sacrifices life for it's love
of a flame.
It's just not the same as your loud lucid cries.
The moth flutters to the flame so silently sacred and dies.

   —*Ellie Rahimi*

Hypocrisy

Hypocrisy is a mockery of life itself.
You do one thing, say another, for the sake of wealth.
On the sabbath, you adjoin with others to pray.
The next day comes, you have gone astray.
Not remembering your vows and what they had to teach.
It's a way of life to not practice what you preach.
Hypocrisy is not a sickness nor a disease.
But rather, people just doing what they please.

   —*Dian Aljazi*

Professor

You haunt my dreams.
You taunt my soul.
Haloed white hair
Forecasts your visit.
Dark eyes mesmerize me
With four thousand years of Judaic history.
No Siren's call could be more hypnotic
than the melody of your poetic tongue.
One ethereal touch
to my brow
freezes me with devotion,
burns me with desire.
I wake.
I cry.
You exist.
But for me
Only in my dreams.
Why?

   —*Ava Perzel*

A Cherished Gift

The way to a friend's house is never long
You travel the distance humming a song
For you know when you arrive there
You'll find a warm welcome and love to share.
A true friend is a very special treasure
There when one needs sympathy, understanding or pleasure,
He will stick by one to the very end
With him there are no broken fences to mend.
He likes you as you really are
Whether a nobody or a famous star.
That's why the way to his house is never long
And you depart humming a happy song.
Life can be beautiful, this I don't deny
The gift of a true friend is one reason why.

   —*Beryle Kocial*

Loving You Was Painful

Life was too short for you. It took one short blow and then
you were gone forever. It's been a few years, but it seems
indefinite till we meet again. Memories are just thoughts and
actions are the memories lived. Touching you was the sensation...
as your voice continues to echo in my head. You were so very
rare. Qualities that made you special, no one in the world
could compare. Black and silver are the colors worn, like the
chrome from the stang. When the moonlight sparkles, the stars
glimmer and twinkle. Black, usually for death can be found on
the east side. But for the one I loved, ended in one short
breath. The lights across the city, remind me of beams rushing
by. The dew covering our feet ... mist ... lowering to the
ground. Lights seen in the distance and shadows creeping
behind us. Making it through the hole is where the challenge
remains. Waves crushing against the pier, the storm is not
very far; but you were determined to ride. My dearest
Everette, I love you and ..... good-bye.

   —*Alicia Makison*

Charley Puff - Killed July 28, 1991

You showed us good times, we would never forget.
You'd always help in times of need, never will regret.
We rode through life's ups and downs for many, many years.
Shared the laughter, shared the sorrow, sometimes even tears.
Though words can't say what's in our hearts.
Words just can't say enough.
Our lives are richer for knowing you.
We all love you Charley Puff.

   —*Jim Luongo*

774

The Wind

Today I felt your presence on my face.
You were so gentle that your warmth
was worth the embrace.
I truly enjoyed spending time with
you as you comforted me.
However, my heart is still suddened
and searching for glee.
But, I'll feel you each day as
you blow through my hair.
Life's burdens and trials give me such a scare.
I find so much comfort in the
presence of the trees.
I feel that the only way out
is to drop to my knees.
I've begged, pleaded, prayed and
tried with all my might.
But God, you seem so out of sight.
However, I feel you in the gentleness
of the breeze.
And the swift movement of the trees.

    —Angella Labbie

Hear The Victim's Pleas

Dear Lord, we pray that upon this day
  You will give us the wisdom to learn.
Educate us in the way in which we live
  And the issues of great concern.

Lord, why have we been plagued so?
  By this dreadful disease called AIDS?
Is there not enough pain in your world?
  The word in itself degrades.

Enbed in all of us the knowledge,
  To learn about this disease.
That each day we live responsibility;
  And each night we are on our knees.

We pray unto you, Lord,
  That soon we will find a cure.
But until then, we pray for a miracle
  That this nation once again be pure.

Remember your people, victims and all,
  For they are the reason we are on our knees.
Hear our prayers to you, dear Lord,
  But for Heaven's sake, hear the victim's pleas.

    —Cyndi Strickland

Apart

We part, in strangeness,
You with anticipation to a strange new life
And I, in sorrow, for a dead dream.

We shall not meet for a time,
Our spirits apart.

Leave me now to bury my dreams
That I may empty my thoughts
Of the joyous, golden child I once bore.

We shall not meet for a time,
Our spirits apart.

I cloak my agony with steel
And remember not what I once dreamed
And my heart is as a desert.

We shall not meet for a time,
Our spirits apart.

    —Audrey Youngren

A 50th Anniversary Tribute

Like two trees they stood with
young branches open only to each other reaching
for the sun and their first time-frozen summer together

Fall followed
the months turned to years and their only child came
like a branch from their symmetry.

Some trees wither and die through winters of war
and depression; but these with patches in his pants he
worked a sewn sacrifice for their daughter's schooling and she
a weeping willow of understanding and prayer for better times.

It's spring again when trees and lovers bud,
The wind has bent his trunk old and her branches
gone soft like old wet wood but in their eyes
a season only they can see
for their roots become one
somewhere far beneath the earth
a half century deep.

    —Irving A. Baker

True Love

As I look at you
Your beautiful eyes, your wonderful smile,
I think how much I love you,
and I feel that I must have loved you,
somehow, all my life
somehow, everyday, all my love was
stored, saved up, waiting to be given to you,
somehow knowing that one day our paths
would cross, our eyes would meet,
and our lives would be forever changed
In this sense, I really have loved you all my life,
even though we had never met,
because our love for each other was always
growing and nurturing
Now we can never not be together,
because we always have been together
Our love began before we knew,
and will continue through all

    —Doug Stark

The Game Of Love

Your sweet voice called me from far away
your beautiful face and form make me stay
I really do think that it's time that we play
play the game of love

Not the game played by the young and the spoiled
egotistical fools whose thoughts are all soiled
your plans for real love will never be foiled
when we play the game of love

My rules for the game are simple and few
care for your partner and always stay true
never do anything that might make them blue
as you play the game of love

The pieces are in place, the board is set
I've called in all markers to cover your bet
do you think you're ready to play the game yet
play the game of love

    —Arthur J. Merriweather IV

My Perfect Guy

You hair is black
Your eyes are brown
I feel so great when you're around
You're not like the others
You're cute, gentle, and kind
Your heart will always be right next to mine
You're my perfect guy.

When I first saw you
My mind would not erase the beauty of your face
How you touched my heart with so much of your warmth
You will always remain in my thoughts
Each day as I live.

As time goes by I tend to wonder
Did you feel the same?
Did you sense that attraction
The first time we met?
Or was it a feeling, that I should regret
Just a look at your face, that's all I ask
You will surely be in my heart till the end of time
You're my perfect guy and you always will be.

—*Angelina S. Ramlochan*

Thank You Lord

Thank you Lord for everything you have done
Your love has lifted me
Your glory has surrounded me
Your peace is within me
Your joy has filled me
Thank you Lord for everything you have done

Your fortress protects me
Your blood has washed me
Your word builds me
Your truth fulfills me
Thank you Lord for everything you have done

Your grace has saved me
Your light shines through me
Thank you Lord for everything you have done

Through you I have the Holy Spirit
Through you my sins are forgiven
Through you I am made whole
Through you I can stand bold
Thank you Lord for everything you have done

—*Akilah Freeny*

Untitled

Vibrations of thought surrounds me
Your presence hovers oh so near
You standing so close, I can almost touch you
Excited to know it's our time to be united
Next to you with my heart embracing you
Together at last. Once again, once again

Vibrations of hope surrounds me
Your spirit cries out, calling my name
This time hand in hand; friend beside friend
Excited to know it's our time to be freed
Freed from all past mistakes of choice
Together at last. Once again, once again

Vibrations of peace surrounds me
I gaze upon your smiling face
Volumes of thought pass between us wordlessly
This time we are heart to heart drifting into space
Excited to know our time has finally come
Together at last. Once again, once again

—*Andreia Catherine Wade*

What I Have To Say

I want you to know that
you're on my mind every day
all the time.

My heart is the only place
that never could forget
your face.

I hear myself asking for
any reason why. I see
you turn and leave as I
begin to cry

Times will come and times will go.
But there's still one thing you have to know

When you look back I hope that
You will see that your place
will always be next to me.

—*Amanda Odden*

To You Mom

You've been my mother for oh so long,
You've been my friend through right and wrong!
You've loved, birthed, and raised me.
You've done your best, as far as I can see!

Through all this and so much more,
There's one thing missing something I won't ignore!
I love God and you don't believe.
Your reason I can't possible conceive!

I wish so much that you could feel.
Why my love for Him is so real!
He died for us, both you and me,
His nail-scared hands for us to see!

The thorns in His head, we can't deny,
His love for us is His reason why!
You were raised in this belief so firm and true,
But you have forsaken Him, not Him - you!

His loving arms are open wide,
Waiting for you to step inside!
He has left the other 90 and 9.
In hopes for you His lost sheep to find!

—*Cindy Knapp*

Lynda's Love Song

It's nigh five weeks
you've gone..
my love for you grows
each day
as a child grows up
as a woman grows bold

I feel myself a child in need
of your love
I'm aware of my womanhood
the female necessity to give you
my love
my unconditional love

I lie in bed at night and my heart throbs for you
And...you know what pains
for your touch and torch.

—*Harry Major*

The Beginning

For nine long months you've waited, you've longed for this event.
You've waited for this little girl, that God has specially sent.
The little girl you hold so sweet, her eyes that sparkle bright.
Will make you wonder what she thinks, at morning, noon and
    night.
She looks at you and smiles, you give her back a grin.
She laughs, gurgles and sucks her thumb, you see her love within.
This living beauty that has been born, appears all dressed in pink.
You'll try to teach her many things; to walk, talk, eat and drink.
This child was set in your arms, to lead her on her way.
She needs a guideline for her life, her love will always stay.
She's always full of surprises, she's Daddy's little girl.
To her mother she brings a lot of joy, she'll capture you in her
    world.
As her life progresses onward, the sight that you will see.
Is the growth of the little girl, who once sat upon your knee.
She'll depend on you for many things, one of them is love.
Always remember that this newborn girl, was sent from God
    above.

—*Allison DePue*

Listen To The Earth

When the earth shakes look all around.
When the winds blow, listen to it!
Are the winds gentle and kind, or are they strong!
It's telling us, life can, and will go on.
When the suns rays are beaming bright and hot.
Remember with out the sun, We're not!
When it rains and pours, remember we're getting
the gift of water and life.
With out the water, we can not exist.
Listen to our earth - it's crying out loud.
Remember, man's own work hurt her,
But man's own hand can save it.
Listen to our earth, it cries out t us in every earthly sound.
Like the Indian who cries, high on top of the mountain side.
He doesn't ask the heavens above for material things!
He ask for the seasons to come, just like spring.
So He too can raise a strong and healthy family.
Listen to our earth, for she will cry only a few times more.
We must listen to our earth.
Before we don't have her anymore!

—*Vera Secomski*

Peace

One day there will be peace
    When we all can be at ease
        First within ourselves
For it is there where we must delve
    Deep, deep in the center
It is there where we must enter
It is a journey we each must make
    For all humanity's sake
When we can face our own fear
    Perhaps then we will hear
That all wars are fought within our being
    This seeing will be our freeing
    From all the hate and strife
To at long last.. A peaceful life

—*Trudi Cimino*

Dad And Daughter

You bring laughter inside my soul
when you are around
    You made me look up when I was
looking down
    You listen to me with an open mind
Leaving all your troubles way behind
    You made me be honest and never tell a lie
    You never for once had said good-bye
    You taught me how to fly with the
wind
    Like the eagle, I'm free again

—*Lindsey Richard*

One Inch Between Our Eyes

I have written this poem just for you.
When you finish reading you'll know what to do.
Darlin' when you speak to me softly on the phone,
I wish you were with me and not at home.
And each time I look into your eyes, the fire
In me which had died, is brought to life,
To live again, in you I know I've found a friend.
Oh, Darlin', Darlin' try this on for size
Just one inch between, our eyes.
Though we may hope and dream for more
We must wait for that open door.
And maybe then, we can begin,
With just one inch between our eyes
And pray our friendship never dies.

—*Nick Baller*

A True Friendship...

A true friendship is hard to let go.
When you have a true friend,
Each others secrets you know.
When you have a problem,
They'll always be there.
When you have a problem,
A true friend always cares.
A real true friend will never lie,
But always be honest and fair.
I have a friend like this out there.
We are together through thick and thin,
I hope our friendship never ends.
You can ask anyone you know,
A true friendship like this would be hard to let go.

—*Rachel Enlow*

Have You Seen My Jesus

When you hold that little baby and dry its crying eye.
When you smile and say hello as a neighbor passes by.
When you take undue rebuke so there will be no wars.
When you forgive others' sins as God has forgiven yours.
Then you've seen my Jesus and you've been his love...

When for lost love ones you've cried for so long.
When it seems you walk alone while others go wrong.
When you tell your brothers and sisters to be strong.
When you study God's word so you won't do wrong.
Then you've seen my Jesus and you've seen his love...

When you hear birds sing on a bright sunny day.
When you receive an answer to the prayers you've prayed.
When you look up to the sky and see the colors all anew.
When someone hugs your neck and says "I love you".
Then you've seen my Jesus and you've seen his love...

—*Tonya Lee Rodgers*

Heavenly Dwelling

Once upon a star,
Where God and His angels are.
High in the heavens above,
One day my dwelling to love.
No starving, no sickness, no dying,
Only loving, living, and blissful sighing.
My world above, I yearn to live,
To get there, my body I must give.
It does not really matter, if my body must die,
It'll all be worth it, for my body to soar high in the sky.
Peace, love, and tranquility, I shall find,
For my spirit to my father, God in heaven, I shall bind.
For together, the father and son, I wish to explore,
For only their knowledge, I shall seek more.
The father will teach, the son I will touch,
Because I'm in spirit, I can learn oh so much.
If you believe in God and Jesus Christ too,
Remember, how much he loves you!

  —Nefetoria Mack

The Old Fort

I walk the halls of these old buildings
Where once a multitude of young men roamed.
I shuffle through the leaves of oak and elm,
The red and gold of trees who've known
A hundred twenty autumns.
I wander on a beach where young men dreamed their dreams
Or cast them down in deep despair.
I see a puffin and a loon in waters
Where the waves have crashed upon these shores
A million years or more.

And I am old, and they were young;
And I am here, and where are they?

I look upon the grounds
Where countless lines have formed and halted there,
Saluting in a march of endless cadence.
I tramp through woods
Where young men played their deadly games of war,
I come upon the batteries of cannon long since stilled.

And I am old, and they were young;
And I am here, and they are gone.

  —M. Loretta Lawrence

Heritage

'Dobe walls crumbling—
Where once the wagon-trains
Of early settlers went rumbling
Over the plains.

Indians squatting 'round
The busy thoroughfares,
Scatter before them on the ground
Their hand-made earthen wares.

The Navajo, with his blankets bright
Tries to catch the tourists' eyes
With woven colors—red, black, and white.
No more a warrior—he sits and sighs.

On western mesa, raised so high,
Live Indians; as they did when—
To Acoma—the city of the sky,
Came Coronado with his men.

This is an enchanted land—
Of mesa—canyon—pueblo.
From lofty peak to desert sand,
It's our New Mexico.

  —Rodney V. Phillips

Images

We live in a world with no face
Where personalities disappear without a trace
It's all just an illusion
Some fool's dream of inclusion
I was once warned by a friend
Be yourself, don't ever pretend
That was a price to high to pay
After all, what would the others say
Your not proper, that's not right,
When will you ever see the light
It's too late to brake loose
Our necks are in their noose
Beneath these shallow images we wear
Something so much deeper is there
For this I search, but never find
I've lost myself, so now I'm blind
This world we live in is built on lies
And now at last, so am I

  —Robert Scott

Who Am I?

Down deep in the valley,
Where spirits run free;
Someone has a choice to make
and that someone is me.

In the end, everyone has a story to tell,
they either made their life heaven
or made their life hell.

So who am I, in this place where we live,
should I have something to offer, or better
yet, something to give.

Life or death
I have something to choose,
success or failure,
I have a lot to prove.

I haven't grown my future's yet to be known; to me and all who
aren't blind, but in my heart I will do my best to improve my
body, soul and mind!

Down deep in my soul I've often searched, for a certain
identity; I've thought and I've muttered and I've even
shuttered, but "Who am I?"; it's still uncertain to me!

  —Marisa M. Diaz

Spirits Young - Music Box

Will she ever find me in a stone cold world
Where the mirrors don't reflect the soul
Where all that glitters is not gold
But to grasp that is each one's goal

Will she ever find me in a stone cold world
Will she ever find peace among the war
Will her heart ever mend will it shed the pain
Will the scars heal for once it had tore

Open the box and the music still plays
It's been closed for years and a day
Open the box and the music still plays
Spirits young don't grow old they just stay

Will she ever find love in a stone cold world
See the sand in the glass running out
Is there a love in a stone cold world
Or illusion we just talk about

Here today gone tomorrow to much pain and to much sorrow
Still open the box and the music still plays it's been closed
for years and a day open the box and the music still plays
Spirits young don't grow old they just stay.

  —Sandra Kaye

Take Me

Take me far, far away, to a place full of delight.
Where the waters fall, and the daffodils bloom,
Where the hot summer breeze lifts us to paradise,
And the evenings are sparkled by the stars, and the moon.

Take me into your arms and hold me close,
So I can feel that you will never go astray.
I want to know, that you'll always need me the most,
And will always come to me for comfort in every way.

Take me to rooms where we'll be making love.
Where we can caress each others bodies, filled with ecstasy.
Feel the warmth of my flesh, that you've dreamed of,
And hear my heart that will beat for you until eternity.

—Linda M. Navarro

Ago

Sometimes I want to wrap myself in my fortress of solitude
Where the wind of your love never blows
And the sun of your smile never shines

Somehow I want to live in one moment that never ends
Where time stands still but still goes on
And the evergreen trees flow in the watercolor sky

Somewhere along a little boy's rampart
Lives a girl that I once knew
When roses bloomed through the cracks of the walls
As the bricks of my fortress were lain

—Leeor Neta

A Tribute To Lady

Life goes on in another world
Where troubles are gone, and love is unfurled
No more leashes, no more chains, no more sorrow, no more pain

Lady you're free to romp and to roam,
No more restrictions, you're finally home
God gave you to us to use for awhile, to cheer us up, give us a
    smile.
When times were rough and we were feeling down
You were always their with never a frown. Always waiting
at the gate, whether we were early whether we were late.

You learned so much while you were here, how to love, get rid
of your fear. You learned to care, you learned to abide, always
walking by our side. You were taken from us so suddenly, like a
rapture, you are free.

Lady we will miss you, we want you to know
Our love for you will always flow
With memories of the good old days
The daily walks, when you would romp and play

Yes! life goes on in another world
Where troubles are gone, and love is unfurled. There are no
leashes, there are no chains, only love, there is no pain

—Ron W. Breyfogle

Untitled

Never lose your hope and love
Your reward may be a gift from God
Never close your eyes when you see
That help is needed to set someone free
Never walk away from the cry and sorrow
When you see helpless animals live in horror

—Hanna L. Pape

A Childhood Memory

Our cemetery was down by the big oak tree
Where we would hold a funeral ceremony
We would bury anything dead that we could find
Always being serious, tender and kind
As we put cardboard caskets into the grave
The others stood by trying so hard to be brave
Someone would always say a few words
Words that only God and the children heard
We would sing "Jesus Loves Me" and "The Old Rugged Cross"
Then pray for their soul that they were not lost
But knowing for sure as only children know
That to animal heaven they would certainly go
Wild flowers were placed on the fresh dirt mounds
And crosses we made were hammered into the ground
No matter how we tried, tears would finally flow
As from the graves with heavy hearts we would go.

—Lela Mae Burnette

Friends

One little bird said to the other:
Where's your father and your mother.
The answer was; They left at summer's end.
Then he dropped his head.
And this is what the little bird said
Come and I will be your friend.

My Family left me too,
And at first I was lonely, just like you.
But everything will be alright you'll see
We'll be Friends, you and I.
And we won't ever say goodbye;
Our parents were doing what they
had to do.

We are hungry, let's get something to eat;
Then we'll sit down and warm our feet.
I am so glad you came by,
We're not lonely as before,
And we won't be any more.
Because forever we'll be friends,
You and I.

—Lucy Mason

Causes

I have trouble with causes
which take on a life of their own
and suck us dry of the humanity
that allows us to love each other
as human beings individually.

I have trouble with causes
which call us to
the collective need giving us the excuse
to ignore the feelings of those who care
whether we are lonely or tired or in pain.

I have trouble with causes
which rob us of laughter
and back us into corners like animals
snarling and clawing, doubting each other
taking every careless act and twisting it into
some devious pattern of treachery.

I have trouble with causes
which make our friends
more of a threat than our enemies.
We become no better than them.

—Maggie Gover

Jon-Kai...

You're up there, a zillion miles away.
While I'm down here,
Where I wanted you to stay.
I just sit at home, watching T.V.
While you've got things to do,
And people to see...
    You must think I'm really weird,
Which I am, to a certain extent.
But I'm not the kind of weird,
to want big extravagant gifts.
I'm the kind of weird,
that just wants to be loved,
to feel wanted and needed,
not pushed or shoved...

—*Linda Akatsu*

Nature's Gifts

The sea gulls soar high in the sky;
While the visions of nature pass by,
The flowers and trees sway in the breeze;
As the waves and foam come from the sea,
Cats meow, dogs howl;
The ocean is deep; the pond shallow,
In the night sky found is the moon;
The insects hide, the butterflies cocoon,
While up in space you may set the pace;
For the origins of a different race,
Jupiter, Mercury, Venus, Mars;
When added together we are all stars,
Soil is rich, grass is clean;
All we've seen is blue and green,
As the crops grow high my father sighs;
For he knows on him the bank relies,
As we look around our green earth;
Remember the sight of your birth.

—*Melissa Wagoner*

Rage

Rapid fires rage amid the clear blue sky
While thunder roars in the clouds so high
Fierce waters crush the shores below, as
Hail surrounds us wherever we go.
Children who kill at the blink of an eye
As gangs run rampant, (my, my, my)
No one knows the reasons why
Some think it's Mother Nature, others won't comply.
I believe the answers above, looking down on us
with awesome love.

—*Ruthy Cyrus*

The Attitude This World Has

Why are there some people in this world,
who are so cruel at heart to others?
We can not walk down a street with pride
about ourselves without someone saying
something about us.
Why can't they just except the fact that
"we are what we are", and leave
well enough along, why?
Why are there some people in this world who
try to judge others because of our looks
and our personalities, why?
Will this world ever change the attitude
it has upon us.

—*Theresa Wilder*

Dog Smarts

This poem's dedicated to my new pet
    who faced a serious plight
When his heartless owner abandoned him
    one cold and wintry night.

He wandered into my backyard the next day
    and unbeknownst to me
Lay down upon the cold concrete
    Next to a large pine tree.

Upon discovery, he was pressured to leave
    But refused to go away
    Since I owned a pet already
Why in the world, would I want a stray?

Should I say that this dog played his cards right?
    For we now have a second pet
    And I must admit a more precious dog
    A family couldn't get.

We named him squat; imagine that!!!
    But the name fits him to a tee
For with no "squatters rights", but some dog smarts
    That hound outwitted me!!!!

—*Lois Wilkerson*

Untitled

Little bird - who made you?
Who fashioned your feathers so soft and bright?
Who taught you to fly to such a great height?
Who made your shiny little eyes
that look on the world from far in the skies?
Who taught you to sing your cheery morning song?
and warble, and warble all the day long?

What secrets are yours, O tiny one?
What do you know of the moon and the sun?
And have you flown o'er the mighty sea?
Have you known the powers that be
In the wild west wind? One thing I know, O little bird:
You bring joy where e'er your song is heard.

—*Mary R. McKay*

Remember Mother

Who has brought you into the world,
Who has cleaned you when you were soiled,
Who has wheeled you to and fro,
Mother, of course, how well you should know.

Who has fed you with such tender care,
The growth of your body as it lay bare,
Who has stood by you day after day,
Watching and listening, to each word you may say.

Then you grew up and didn't give a care,
What Mother said, was always unfair,
You knew it all why heed her advice,
Till one fine day you paid the price.

Now, let us pause and remember Mother,
Who knows the true meaning of suffer,
Let us be kind, gentle and good,
To the great glory of Motherhood.

—*Salvatore Baudo*

Country Girl

There once was this girl from the country
Who spoke to the fish in the sea
And who tried to tell us the animals could speak
And who knows, just cause they
haven't spoken to me
A girl from the country
She tries to tell us we should love the land
We just turn our heads and laugh
You see we did not understand
Sometimes I think the girl from the
country is the only one who sees.

  —Margaret Brunea

Stairway To Heaven

There was a special person, right here on earth.
Who taught us to believe, from the time of our birth.
Our Lord Jesus had a choir that sung a mighty song.
They needed a new member, so he wanted mom to come along.
Remember, the stairway to heaven can be a mighty long way.
But God reached out to guide her every step of the way.
We knew when she reached the top, because her smile was a
 sight to behold.
All the Angels reached out to help as her wings began to unfold.
Now, if you listen carefully as the dawn breaks the skies.
There is a voice loudly calling for all to arise.
Mom has not left us, she is the breaking of each new day!
As long as we believe, she will never go away.

  —Vivian Johnson

For You Are The Chosen One

Master, Creator,
 who, you said, "He was
showing only His unconditional love."

At this moment, as we remember your memory,
the love you shared so freely.
Tears come to those eyes who cared,
But I know that you are there;
in the arms of the Lord where you belong,
For you are the chosen one.

For you are the chosen one,
You lived your life beyond the selfishness of others,
no matter what.
For you are the chosen one,
and your spirit will be fulfilled
fully in the presence of the Lord.

Broken hearts and dreams, you always cared
you always had the time for all small prayer.
And right now, at this moment, a chariot waits for you,
and a loved beyond, that will see you through.

  —Robin Hagan

Sweet, Brown Baby

Sweet, brown baby only 5 years old.
Whole life ahead of you, dreams yet untold.

Sweet, brown baby, perfect little smile.
Why don't you go outside and play awhile.

Sweet, brown baby, a casualty of today's world,
A bullet through the chest of daddy's little girl.

Her name was Ashley Johnson, she was playing with her friends.
Then all of a sudden her sweet, little world came to an end.

  —Susie G. Simms

The Old Man And His Book

Old man, wrinkled man,
Whose eyes reflect the ages,
What is in the book you read?
What speaks from within its pages?

Old man, withered man,
You have labored, worked the soil
And with calloused hand, tilled the land,
For what fortune did you toil?

Old man, forgotten man,
Man of so many, troubled years,
What sweet thoughts and memories
Have so possessed you,
That you weep your endless tears?

Old man, quiet man,
I beg you, let me look!
What wisdom have you presumed to pen?
What is written in your book?

  —Robert Hocking

For My Father

Who wears ties to go with his mood on sunny days
Whose hair was like black brambles thick as a forest
Whose smile was like a rainbow running true in my heart
Whose eyes were as clear as the morning after rain
Who promised to watch over me from the clouds in heaven
Who read me nursery rhymes endlessly while the sun slept
Who never forced me to smile in family pictures on my
 frowning days
Whose voice was heard by many, but is now lost in the
 depths of my memory
Whose eyes no longer shine
Whose hair that was once a black cloud awaiting the storm,
 was lost to the ravages of chemotherapy
Who in place of ties wore hospital gowns
Whose rebellious fire burns in me too
Who loved to write and passed the love on to me
Who lost the battle against his death
Who watches me from the clouds as promised
Who will live forever in my heart

  —Nicole Ramos

Awakening

Goodbye to the steel breasted mother,
Whose milk is like the mace in your face carried by the wind.
Goodbye to the iron womb, that contains the wanton passions of
youth.

Goodbye to the young Black man
Cut in half by the surgical motorcycle
Hurling down the highway on alcohol guts.

Enter the book lined windowless space
That fully measured many fairly and left them wanting more.

Goodbye to those whose arms are to short to fight with God,
Yet fight Him as if He were not there.
Goodbye to those who pervert that name into a lance that
strikes at the heart.

I'm drawn into the fertile battle of those friends
Who every day attempt to pour a great cultural mix
Into an empty space that knows not north from south.

This factory's work is mine to keep
Day after day, son after son. On stage to face the world
Enters the portrait painter, the choreographer, the artist,
Whose words fill in those who will listen.

  —Thomas J. Hriciga

A Tribute To An Indian

What has happen to the Indian of yesteryear
Whose very presence once brought with it fear
Though their lives are brand new their customs stay old
But braves without warpaint are not mighty or bold
The lands that we give them are seedy and poor
Land rightfully theirs once upon a time long before
Warriors who stood will stand no more
For Indians were killed off by the score
Buffalo once hunted are nowadays seldom seen
For the whites took their land and their food,
    left their pastures ungreen
Though their tepees are gone, their shabby houses still stand
And it shames me to say, that's how they'll die in this land.

    —Yvonne Madison

Hunter

The Hunter comes in search of hearts-
Who've wandered foolishly from home,
And takes from them the hopes they have-
Then sends them back alone.

The hunter feeds on broken dreams-
The heart's tears its bitter brew,
And clings to those in love's despair-
But still envision a dream come true.

Well, here I stand amidst its grasp-
Hoping that I'll be spared,
I can't believe my heart should bleed-
Just because I cared.

But who am I, just another fool-
Who soon too late will see.
That those who care are sure to share-
The hunter's cup of tea.

So be still my heart and make no sound-
Please hide your feelings well,
For the hunter can only find its prey-
Where love, hopes and dreams dare dwell.

    —Laura M. Arsenault

Please Love Me Mommy!

Don't you know there is a reason God has put me here,
Why can't life, and its true meaning become so very clear?

I am a part of you, you know and you're a part of me,
If you let them take me Mommy, whatever will I be?

A spirit soaring in the wind or something not so good,
Please tell me Mommy, what can I say to make it understood?

Don't I get a chance to see what my life might have in store,
Couldn't you just find some time to try and think some more?

I really want my chance in life to see what living's like,
I want to play with other kids and learn to ride a bike.

I won't be trouble for you Mom, cause you need understanding,
When life has dealt some sorry blows and things seem so
    demanding.
Just remember that I'd like the chance to become part of your
life, And together as a family we can conquer all our strife.

Please love me Mommy, I love you, and if I am to be,
Remember, I'll be there for you if you'll be there for me.

    —Pamela S. Hyatt

Justice Has Been Served

Powell, Bresenio, Wind, and Koon
Why did they take the first trial so smooth?
Is it the fact that they knew they were gonna get off?
Or is it the fact that they knew the jury was prejudged?
In result of the first trail, Los Angeles was demolished!
As people of all races senses got ravaged.
500, 600 fires burning at one time,
Looks of fear on the fireman's faces,
"Are these people out of their minds?"
A year has past and the officers are on trial again.
This time the jury consists of 4 women and 8 men.
During this long week waiting for a verdict,
one of the jurors gets badly afflicted.
Now Judge Davies has a problem, should he bring in the
alternate or wait till tomorrow?
Sgt. Koon-guilty. Off. Powell-guilty
Off. Bresenio-not guilty. Off. Wind-not guilty
Sighs of relief were blown in Los Angeles,
Because peoples now know that justice has finally been served.
It's just so sad that they had to mess up their community first.

    —Michelle V. Middleton

Who Are You?

Who are you?
Why do you keep calling me?
I don't even know you,

But from the man I got my name.
I know you from pictures on the wall.

You were gone before I was even a minuscule thought,
You were young, so was everyone

I know you are somewhere calling me out.
But I don't call back my reason is fright.

You are probably a good man with your candy store and all,
Although I think it is better if;
We never knew each other in person.

In a way it is torture; not knowing.
Wondering what it would be like;
To have you still around.

That's just tough in the way of things;
Sometimes you win and sometimes you have to chance.

Well my neck is tired from looking up at the stars;
The moon and the universe
It's time to say goodbye, so long; grandpa.

    —Nathan Rosler

Love

Why do I never tire of your voice?
Why in your presence do I always rejoice?
Why were you the one of my choice?
    Because I love you.

Why has our marriage never been wrong?
Why has my life been just like a song?
Why am I happy all the day long?
    Because I love you.

Why do I worry when you're tired and worn?
Why when you're gone am I forlorn?
Why when you're hurt is my heart so torn?
    Because I love you.

Why have I stayed with you these many years?
Why when you're sad do I shed many tears?
Why when I'm with you joy erases all fears?
    Because I love you.

    —Violet Eileen Reeb

Have You Ever Wondered

Have you ever wondered,
Why things are like they are?
Why peace is often spoke of,
But it always ends in war.

Why love is only given,
To those who fit your bill.
Why a baby has no choice,
On whether it dies or lives.

Why parents don't stay together,
Even though they took the vows.
Why our country is so rich,
Yet there still are hungry mouths.

Why the gospel is preached throughout the land,
Yet its actions you seldom see.
Have you ever wondered,
Why these things must be.

—*Willie Sparks Jr*

Why

Why won't you love me and show me affection
Why won't you let me in
Why when you hold me you always let go
You always want it to end
Why are you afraid to show me who you are
What do you have to hide
Why, when I put you high on a mantle
You set me and my feelings aside
Why do you run
When you know I love you with all my heart
Why, when we seem to be so close
You always break apart
Why won't you answer my questions
And let me know
Why can't you tell me
If you are going to stay or go?

—*Melanie Authier*

She Died For Love

She died for love, that's what they say
Why'd her life have to end this way?
She had it all, including friends
When she's around, the good time never ends
What had made her take her life
She ended it all with one small knife
They do not know the reason why
I had chose to say goodbye
I died for love, this is true
I died because I could not have you
You left me here, all alone
What is left to be shown?
You were the only reason
I took my life this winter season
This poem she wrote before she died
When I said I didn't love her, I lied
Now she's gone, her I'll miss
My heart won't know the feeling bliss
Her life is gone, her soul is free
While I live alone, knowing it was because of me

—*Natalie Gnall*

Perfect Dreams

I'll wait for you with arms open
  Wide,,, ready to catch you when
You are just dead tired, once your bath done
  I'll massage your brows, as you
Drift into sleep your head on my lap
  I'll kiss each eyelid there to
Place each a perfect dream... These
  Dreams both of you and me
Naked to the world, stripped,
  Totally bare ... Inveigling each
Others lust.. Detailing each to completeness
  I would dance for you under
Moon lite skies a dance that would
  Set your lust afire I would then
Drown your desires with title waves
  Of pleasure... Calming you like
The ocean after a mighty storm... Never
  Wakening but shift slightly to
Experience yet another perfect dream.

—*Paulette Brown*

"The World"

The world now days is never the same
Wild, yet boring, unbelievable and lame
There's problems and troubles which triples & doubles
Adding more & more things which sadness it brings

There's poor & unhappy, rich & real glad
But this world has changed & it's making people sad
There are others who need help in health & education
Some don't even live because of starvation

There are kids who want toys, happiness & love
Help from up there, the God from above
It's people like us living this way
If we don't help, they won't live after today.

It's sad to see others humans in fear,
While children can't sleep without shedding a tear
When a miracle comes with fun, love & hope
Wishing to keep kids alive and stay away from dope

And to thank the Lord today,
For this miracle you swept away
For letting people live,
Their lives in every way!

—*Leilani Gaspar*

Flesh And Iron

The coldest water and the hottest fire
  will shape the finest steel.
If the unstressed iron is comfortable,
  then cancerous rust will eat and peel.

But pounded on an anvil bright
  hammered, stretched, and stressed.
it learns a sterner character
  whose harder edge can stand the test.

Those men who never suffered pain,
  who never felt the burning touch,
of searing torments and eroded hopes
  are not tempered to stand for much.

So, when shadows fall, grit teeth, stand fast, endure.
In fire and flood, let your metal, too, forge pure.

—*L. Ezra Tillotson*

The Best Place To Be

The rolling green waves of wheat
  Will soon turn golden from the heat.
And the smell of new-mown hay
  Hangs heavy and sweet in the breeze today.
Then summer is over and harvest is here.
  The sky is so blue and the air's so clear.
The work is hard; the hours are long,
  But farming the land is where I belong.

My tractor and plow are now quiet in the shed,
  And a flock of geese fly overhead.
The chill in the air warns winter is near,
  And I silently thank God for another good year.
As I sit by the fire and have time to reflect,
  I jot down my values—the things I respect.
Honesty, integrity—they're important to me;
  Along with farming the land and being close to Thee.
When I looked out the window at the soft-falling snow,
  I thought, "If I wasn't a farmer, where would I go?"
But the answer has always been clear to see,
  This is surely and truly the best place to be!

  —*Marjorie A. Rostorfer*

Angel Of Mercy

  There are angels of the day and night
  Willing to reach out with their love.
  To someone in need and with fright
  The angel is sent from above.

  She comforts, cares and listens, too
  When someone is suffering and confused.
 They are hurting inside and don't know what to do.
She gives understanding to the one who has been used.

  With patience and love and caring
  Slowly the person starts to heal.
  Just by listening and sharing
  The patient starts to cope and deal.

  The angel is special and always will be
  She gave of herself and time.
  She will always be special to me
  Because she was there at that time.

  —*Linda Schlup*

Writer's Wish

"Wish me words.
Wish me clear, shattered-crystal words.
Wish me frozen time;
Awaiting the warming mind and eyes of another.
Wish me chips of laughter,
Shards of hope;
Wish me love, and hate, and joy.
All true,
All unexpected.
Wish me the power to singe,
And to freeze.
To make tears flow and anger rise,
And to frighten, if that is what the muses will
have of me tonight.
Wish me the feeling and the sensitivity
To leave just a bit of me,
With people I will never meet.
Don't wish me luck.
Wish me words."

  —*Thomas R. Fisher*

Unfolding

C reate your very own professional image
  with a constant

A wareness of the whole person
  and let your

R espect for that person enrich your research
  so that the
I ndividual in you, will love to celebrate
  the individual in them and
N ursing's gift to humanity through you will be
  the flow of
G iving, renewing, restoring, invigorating the
  Science and the art.

  —*Peggy Moses*

Simpleton

And down in Simpleton, a tortured man.
With a lighter in his hand,
He makes his way down to the grand stands,
Where he sets the world ablaze,
in hopes the flames will encompass his anguish.

A simple house contains the tortured man;
Where the fire starts by itself;
He takes his daddy's favorite belt
And whips his children with a fervor
he's not seen since the days of his childhood.

He raises his voice, and then his hand,
and catches a glimpse in the mirror.
In his children's eyes he sees himself,
and his eyes are those of his father.
He lays down his belt, his children flee;
he goes for the flask in his top drawer.
Can legacies like this be destroyed
as easily as they're created?

And not so simple now is Simpleton.

  —*Paul D. Gutierrez*

How I See Myself

I see myself as a person who care,
with a little love I want to share
not wanting to be mistreated or always
on the last row when it's time to be seated.
Not always good
Not always bad
Not always happy and
Not always sad.
I see myself trying to do the things I can
Always ready to lend a helping hand
A little ugly,
Not so beautiful, but I can be very useful
Always ready to take my stand for or against my
fellow man.
I see myself wanting badly to make the best of life
I sit aside to fight to cope with my struggles
and my strife.
I see myself one day standing proud as well as tall
crying tears today "saying" I fooled you all
That's how I see myself.

  —*Sonjia R. Oliver*

Wise Guy

Here's some things a kid wrote down
with a piece of chalk on the ground:
"Rain ain't ever as good as snow;
you can't take nuttin with you when you go.
My Ma believes in Saints, but there are Elves;
people pay to bore themselves.
If you listen to girls you won't have fun;
Two can't live as cheap as one.
It's good to hear things but better to see;
Someday I will be Tom, and he will be me."

—*Sylvia Berry*

My Pal

A short while back three years ago to be exact, I was blessed
with a radiant little guy, a combination of this and a little of that.
Heavenly blue eyes that sparkle and glows, the smile of an
Angel that everybody knows. Sometimes he's happy and
sometimes he's sad but never once could I say he was bad.
He looks at me with those heavenly eyes and radiant smile a
boy of three or thirty-three a bond was formed between him
and me, his love companionship and loyalty has added a new
chapter in my book of life, I have a pal even if he is only three.

—*Richard L. Underwood, Sr.*

Untitled

Summer's fading fast tis true,
with advent of Fall, there's much to do.
With winter's snows around the corner
is all too soon the need for warmer
homes to batten down the "hatches",
and a well-lit chimney fire with matches.
Washing windows, vacuuming floors,
not to spend much time outdoors
except to view Autumn's paint brush
of lovely colors will bring a "gush"
of pleasure to our lips
awaiting Fall's first nips
of winter close upon the door
and crickets crawling on the floor.
When work is done and you can spend
time with loved ones without end
with God's blessing shining down on us,
we thank and count them and wish to say
our prayers are answered-every day.

—*Marion Millwater*

Just Thinking Of You

Your eyes remind me of the blue ocean
With affection entwined with emotion

Your face reminds me of gentle rain
Throwing out future pain

Your breath reminds me of sweet roses
Blooming in the freshness of eternal life

Your body reminds me of a structural masterpiece
Beautifully proportioned from your head to feet

The way you make me feel
Is happiness revealed

Just thinking of you
Is worth the pain of not having you

—*Ryan Miller*

Sunshine

I watched the sun come up this morning
with brightness the world adorning.
I watched it climb down the hillside,
coming to my house for the day to reside.
First it touched the trees
and chased away the freeze
as all across the valley it strides,
and at my house it now abides.
It chased away all the night's dark fear
and fills all my house with bright cheer.

It is a prayer of mine, perhaps the same as thine,
that we would all let God our hearts refine,
and let Him chase away the chill of hatred
that makes our world with blood run red.
If in our hearts discerning love could get a start
and burning jealousy were allowed to depart;
and if green envy were not allowed to take root,
and all efforts for peace were our main pursuit,
then in God's sunshine we would grow
and abundant life from His blessings would flow.

—*Orien Chafin*

Mother

My mother to me was the best she could be
With four children to love and protect.

There were times when a smile wasn't found for a mile
I thought because of neglect.

Now that I'm older
I know she's my molder and made me to whom I've become.

I am as she and I want her to see
I appreciate all that she's done.

Time swept me away and bring to this day
More than miles of distance between us.

But I know in my heart we'll never be apart
Cause my mother to me is the sweetest.

I wanted to say in some sort of way
That she means more to me than she knows.

All I can do is say "I Love You"
And hope it continues to grow.

—*Lisa J. C. LaBelle*

My Love For You

As I look across this unending ocean
With its beautiful waves of blue,
I pray for you to realize
My unending love for you.

As the waves pass by with unknowing grace
Like the gliding wings of a dove,
So my years pass by in an endless quest
For you to return my love.

If my quest ends in vain
And your love not come my way,
I'll live alone in thought of you
Until my dying day.

But if my quest is victorious
And your love for me gives birth,
Then the rest of my days, I'll consider myself
The happiest man on earth.

To sum it up, there's just one thing
That I would ask of you,
If the day should come to prove your love
Just simple say "I do."

—*Michael H. Loffler*

Sunrise

The morning sun has broken upon me,
with its golden fingers atop the hill,
creeping slowly across the mountains thus,
stealing softly o'er the window sill.
The morning sun creeps in my room,
after sneaking past the lawn;
it dusts the china and chases the gloom,
and then from me demands a yawn.
Oh Sun, where did you go last foggy eve,
and on whose slumb'ring night did you tread;
while people sleep and their dreams they weave,
who will you wake from out their bed
while your warmth beats upon the Earth's cold breast,
and I, this Sunday…stay asleep to rest.

    —Wayne L. Groves

Gone… With No Goodbye

You are gone
With no goodbye
I would have never let you go
If I knew you would die

I envision you
And live in the past
The last time I saw you
I would have never thought it was the last

Your life was ended
On your way to be with me
What I feel inside
No one will ever see

Memories are all I have left of you
And a headstone with your name
Our love will never die
In my heart, it will remain

Flashbacks of your coffin
Make me scared to see
A stone with a name engraved
That meant the world to me….

    —Sophia Kateris

Winter

The streets are now scattered
  with remnants from the storm.
In time they are cleared and forgotten
  until the skies darken once more.
And, like us, are turned to dust
  to be carried by the wind.
Where we all are reunited with the earth
  to begin again.

    —Susie Burkett

Grandma

I see you swaying in a big brown rocking chair,
With sad blue eyes.
Thinking of something in a different world or time

You stop suddenly.

Out on the porch, Rocky your old Bassett hound,
Looks up with sad droopy eyes,
Then he starts to sing into the night sky.

Grandpa is no longer with us.

    —Melissa Joy Evans

Chilly Morning, June 29

The seeds of Fall were sown this morning.
With summer only hours old,
I feel some of October's cold
And autumn leaves a-borning.

As humans do, or creatures lesser,
'Ere attaining final rest,
Each season bears within its breast
The seeds of its successor.

With autumn snow or January thaw,
We get a peek at things to come.
Makes sure our senses aren't numb.
Must be a part of Nature's law.

The late June sun will burn away
This morning's clouds and chill.
Our memories preserving still
The taste of Fall we had today.

    —William W. Wright

Untouchables

Behold, these sacred clusters
  With the burning fires of history,
Leading us back up against the wall,
  Shelved in our generations,
Only our fingertips to research and pry
Questions arise, but the echoes won't surface
  The thoughts of our subconscious,
  Meddling in our visions of time
Alas, we wonder about these truthful haunts
Straight forward, we relinquish a look,
  That passes judgement on sight
Again, we wander, only to sway
Realizing that everything could be . . .
  Secondary to none

    —Richard E. Jetter

Marble

I see their frozen faces,
with the same expression for all of time
Anywhere that you see marble,
Please remember of this rhyme
And look for the faces that I see,
and for their last screams for help that have died
Look into their faces,
You know they say an expression never lies
If you ever see the faces,
Think of how they lived or how they died,
…or how they were killed.

    —Teresa Babula

The King Is Coming

Everyday I wake, and look toward the eastern sky.
Will I see Jesus today? I wonder with a long sigh.
Coming in clouds of glory, with a golden crown on his brow.
Dear Jesus, I get tired of waiting, please come now.
I go to work each day, hoping that it'll be my last day here.
I don't know when you are coming Jesus, but I know it's near.
My soul aches to see you, Jesus in your mighty splendor
I know I'll see you, when heaven open its windows.
Until you come, I'll sing and praise your wonderful name
When you saved my soul, dear Jesus, I've never been the same.

  Come Quickly Lord Jesus
    —Zelle Manning

Broken Hearted Gold

I am so lonely with nothing to do,
with thoughts working over-time thinking of you.
I picked up the newspaper to look at the ads
looking for a job, just anything they had.
Groceries to buy, rent to be paid, no job to be had,
no money to be made.
An ad caught my eye, the letters said GOLD
we're ready to by, if you will say SOLD.
I looked in a box where there were three rings,
a birthstone, friendship, wedding band and things.
I remember my wife so white and so cold
as I slipped from her fingers three rings of GOLD.
I walked to the jeweler put the rings in his hand,
my heart beat so fast when I thought of the band.
He looked at my tears, walked away to the scales,
I stretched out my hand and told him, no sale.
As I walked away I was numb and so cold,
there will never be a sale for my BROKEN HEARTED GOLD.

    —*M. Ross Mitchell*

Land

When it was created, it was full of hope. Now it is filled
with violence and dope.

God created Adam and gave him a life. He took a rib from his
body and made him a wife.

He told them to be fruitful and multiply his land, and then
came the Serpent they ate from his hand.

His name is Satan, also the Devil, he is called. When I think
about him I'm really appalled.

He rules this land, and thinks his is slick, he is why we live
in poverty and get really sick.

We need to fill this land with cleanliness and love that was
sent from the Almighty, our God above.

    —*Tina Marie Stack*

Lorena...

She had steel grey eyes intent upon seeing
   with wisps of white hair that were wild
She took hold of my hand and was bent on believing
   that somehow I must be her child

She spoke only Italian while holding my hand
   yet I knew it was her fervent plea
That once I had finished my visiting
   I'd be certain to take her with me

I tried to explain that I wasn't her kin
   that I'd come here to see my grandfather
But she rambled some words and then kissed my cheek
   so I felt she was really no bother

The staff and her cronies, amused at this play
   insisted she could understand
She just wants you to pack her and take her away
   this was not something that I had planned

"Is that true?" I exclaimed, "You trust me to take you?
   I'm not your relation, you know!"
She took my face in her hands, gave a sly little wink
   And then whispered in English, "Let's go."

    —*Sandra L. Pace*

The Death Of A Lonely Soul

Within life, there is death
Within death, there is life
The two are intertwined
Like a vine inching its way up a tree

A soul can die leaving an empty shell
That was once a man, a living, breathing human being
But now it just rots into dust
That spreads upon the wind

For these, where is life?
Life awaits just out of reach
They strive for life, love and happiness
Yet, they are not quite living and not quite dead

It is a non existence caught in between two worlds
With spiritual barriers to overcome
Struggling to achieve that which is precious
Leaving an empty shell for others to do with as they please

    —*Lee Banning*

A Self-Portrait

"I pray that I shall always be,
Within God's forest, a living tree
  With bark intact and stately might,
That grows in stature from wrong to right.
  A tree that gives protective care
And bears its gifts for all to share.
  A tree that hears the whispering wind
Of God's small voice and follows Him
  A tree that endures the stress and strain
Of life's great storms of grief and pain.
  A tree that spreads its arms from seed
And brings forth blessings to all in need.
  A tree that matures with the fullness of Grace
And lends its beauty to every race.
  A tree that seeks eternal light
In His deep forest of greater height.
  A tree of love with roots so strong
That in His deep forest, I do belong."

    —*Royal E. Meyer*

Freedom's Ring

Freedom is not the right to do as we please,
without regard for the final effect.
Nor is it the right to sit back with ease,
while others must struggle to protect.

Our freedom must not allow us to ignore the downtrodden,
while living lavishly, abusing, polluting, but never renew.
Nor to depend on others like Washington, Lincoln or President
Clinton, to deal the hand, then have to play the cards for us too!

Freedom should not through destructive manipulation,
"All in the name of justice,"
alter the laws making up freedom's foundation;
lest they become the ropes that bind us.

In the name of freedom we deny our youth
needed instruction, administered with caring,
to attain their identity in truth;
not from gangs, peer pressure, or the impossible dreams their
sharing.

True freedom comes only from within;
our heart, our soul, our nurture.
Freedom demands morals and self discipline,
strengths necessary for freedom in the future!

    —*Marilyn Haaker*

My Dad

My Dad stands tall like a tree
withstanding the ravages of storms.
The music of life nourishes his soul
And spreads through his brightly colored leaves.
His seeds drop and a sapling springs up.
It grows taller until it almost reaches his height.
Suddenly, it protects him from bending in the storms.
The sun warms him,
But no leaves are budding.
Winter comes and he is covered with snow,
Aging, his limbs bend downward.
But inwardly his beauty thrives.
Deep in his roots is the music he once gave me.
Soon he will be gone,
And I will stand a little less sturdy.
My saplings will grow to the glory of the world
Absorbing life's pleasures.
They will show the world
There once was a tree....
My Dad.

    —Sheila C. Weiner

Legacy

Snaking over the hills, across the centuries, a great wall
Withstands the seasons, a tribute to a xenophobic past,
The sentiment, the symbol will forever last,
And the echoes of lost architects hauntingly call
From deep within the soul of their creation;
The dead, reminders of a society's fear still.
The cold winds sweep the edges with a voracious will,
To challenge the strength of the once-perfect formation.
Broken sections, the winds of time have succeeded
In opening the barricade to the outsider's threat.
And the storm of foreign invasion has been met
By more walls, as this generation has once more heeded,
The worm vestiges of an old tradition,
Secure in their timeless isolationist condition.

    —Lauren E. Burns

Last Day Of Winter

Sitting here blinded by the snow
Wondering if I'll ever see green again.
I'm so cold no one could know this beautiful soul within.

I hear a voice speak of love, telling me it's time to go-
"Walk along the path you dream of
For you're the only one who knows.
There will come a time when you must decide
Whether or not your soul to wither—
Whether or not you wish to reside on the last day of winter."

Wishing, dreaming, hoping to survive
This bitterness deep within me—
I truly wait for a time to revive and set free my genuine beauty.

I hear that voice speak once more,
telling me my time will come—
"You will live no longer as before
And start anew in your own home.
I have faith beyond imagining
In your ability to remain hither—
You will find the answer gleaming on the last day of winter."

    —Nicole L. Chick

I Am Like Thunder

I am like thunder quiet yet loud
Wondering why people dislike the rain
I hear the whistling of the wind calling
As I see the rain running down the drains
I would also like to see the clouds falling
For I am like thunder quiet yet loud.

I pretend people see me, not the clouds
While feeling sometimes, I can not see
I touch the things that are not conceded
I worry some people don't always here me
So I cry when I feel I am not needed
for I am like thunder quiet yet loud

I understand people would rather see clouds
I say what people want me to say
I dream, someday someone will love me
So I try to take it day by day
Hoping in someway some person will see,
for I am like thunder quiet yet loud

    —Tisha Ross

mortal

A crudely cut
wooden statuette
of an old man
looking out to a distant, unscuplted sea.

His wading pants are
too big and baggy for him.
The yellow sleeves of his raincoat
have chaffed too long over his hands
He wears a foolish hat
with too many hooks and barbs.

A small can of worms
rests at his side on the pier.
Ugly birds circle unseen overhead or
wait beside him, quietly.

    —Ralph Palm

"If I Told You, If I Showed You"

If I told you that I was lost
    would you help me find my way?

If I told you that I just couldn't go on
    would you carry me?

If I told you nothing
    would you ask questions?

If I showed you words
    would you read?

If I showed you wounds
    would you feel?

If I showed you the tears
    would you cry?

If I told you I was unable to love
    would you love me anyway?

If I told you that I wanted to sleep forever
    would you wake me?

If I told you goodbye
    would you miss me?

    —Tina L. Moscato

A Territory Brand New

Tell me, if you look deep in my heart, what
 would you see?
Tell me, if you look directly into my eyes,
 what would they tell you?
Would they be penetrating back inside of you?
Would it be searching for something real that only
 you and I can feel?
So here we are. Let us explore a territory brand new.

See where it takes us; taking the good and bad and
 make something better.
We will climb to the top of the mountain and dare
 anyone to knock us off. There we will explore
 each other, searching high and low, writing a book
 of the two of us in code, that only you and I will know.

We will create a brand new love.
A more complete love, of true honesty and respect.
We will show the world what real love is all about.
          —T. H. Nettles

Untitled

This is for you my dear, my heart
wrapped in crystal for you to gently hold.
Take it from my hands, accept my part
in closeness may it never grow old.
It beats for you in quick anticipation
a look, a kiss; a touch from you oh please
deny it no longer you've glimpsed my devotion.
I give it all to you, you hold the key.
What I feel is so deep, virginal, pure.
This symbol for you to hold. It brings to life
that which is for the touch, soft, and demure
childlike, defenseless, and knowing no strife.
     Open your warm soul time is you knew
     What the heart keeps sheltered is love for you.
          —Nancy Rudolph

The Dream

He lay next to me, our bodies touching
Wrapped in the bonds of love
We moved ever so closer
And for a single solitary moment we were one
As he reached over to kiss me our lips met as though they were
     cooling summer breezes gently brushing on the morning dew
Slowly hesitation filled the room as an innocent thought
     entered
"Is it love or just the simple complexity of a dream?"
It's love, it had to be
A love so perfect, so sweet and glorious it would never die
But as morning approaches
I lay there staring at the almost mesmerizing depths of the
     ceiling above
As I reached over to find him
He was gone...
Where was my handsome lover?
What would I do with out him?
Could it be it was only a dream
And now it is lost forever somewhere in the eternal night?
          —Regina Marie Klopfer

What Is Life?

Without understanding there is no forgiveness.
Without forgiveness there is no love.
Without love, life has no meaning.
          —Robert L. Colbert

Awaited Reunion

Discorporated soul clings to memories —
Wraps them round like a breathable skin.
Immaterial essence, prisoner of gravity,
Rest your earthly eyes. Learn to prescind.

Don't compare the shedding of a single tear
To the burden that's on your mind.
What you recall in loving thoughts,
Others cry they can not find.

To say the time of leaving hurt
less than the time apart,
Means the piercings of perfervid feelings
Are better than a healing heart.

Solitary spirit, search the heavens.
Mark your path and build your nest.
Running — racing, your true love finds you.
This angel will need a place to rest.
          —Renee Craig

Me

Lana Sitterly is my name
Writing short stories is my game.
I was born at 6:25 at night
But my height was just not right.

Listening to music is one of my hobbies
But all of my books would take up a hospital lobby.

I have an Indian doll that my grandmother
     gave to me when I was three
But one time I threw it up and it
     got stuck in a tree.

Now I am fourteen and I know what to do,
I'll get a good education and become a
     successful journalist in ten years or two.
          —Lana Sitterly

The Vine Of Strength

So many years gone by
years of growth and strength
years of bad times and good times

Mother's loving arms and soothing words
wrapped around me, enveloping me,
protecting me from the evils of the world

Father's stable composure and wise words
during hard times, helping my strength
creep and expand into a long, twisting vine
A home with enough love to keep me from
any harm that would come my way

Soon I will be leaving my childhood behind me
venturing out into the world where my
parents arms will not be there to protect me
Instilled inside of me will be everything
my parents gave me and taught me

My vine of strength will continue to
wrap and circle around every obstacle
in its way and the love of father and
mother will linger in my heart forever...
          —Megan A. Gottlieb

Snow

Glancing at the snow falling with the imagery of unity
Yet knowing this imagery is not one of clarity
Closer observation reveals not unity, but an oneness
Though they are together, each stands alone with an uniqueness
Transcending downward, each has a different velocity
Never knowing wherein lies their cosmic similarity
Diversity viewed through a simplicity of our own distortions
Yet seldom applauded for its separate unique representation
Each solidarity flake reaching the end of its journey
In space and season fulfilling the planned destiny

—*Veldeanie Hampton*

Lonely Spring

As winter melts away and spring begins to bloom

I feel a certain loneliness which I can not explain to
you

The snow is now all gone and the flowers begin to steam

I feel the warm sun on my back and my loneliness returns
once again

The airs sweet smell has finally returned once again

The loneliness I realize is from the fact that no one is
here to share with me the wonders of spring unlike the
many years before

—*Michelle Dooley*

For Debbie

You came from eternity then returned home again taking with
you all that you learned.
What of our questions.
We put ourselves through so much pain; so many unanswered
questions.
But when the all consuming sorrow fades, there within lies the gift
you gave. The lesson of love.
I thank God for you.
I'm not sure why you chose the path you did. Perhaps the
why isn't important, but I know the lesson is.
How tenderly we are taught. Your spirit lifted our hearts
like a gentle breeze carries a fallen leaf, spiraling upward
towards heaven.
I find peace in the knowledge that when my lesson to teach
is done, you'll welcome me with open arms.
And to those who I have touched, I pray the seed of love
will grow and fill their hearts as yours did mine.

—*Lisa Michlig*

My Dear Sister

Dear sister of mine even though we are far apart,
You are always in my heart. I think of you everyday.
And I pray that you are in good health, and always
stay that way. You mean so much to me as you know.
You remind me of our dear mother to whom we all loved so.
Whenever I have problem, I know just where to go. You
are always in my heart. I thought, I'd let you know. How
much you mean to me and I love and think of you. Dear
sister of mine, I always think of you.

—*Vesta Louise Black*

Choices

If you deny me the right to make choices,
you deny me the right to exist.

Therefore, I must create my own choices or
become extinct in reality, like in your current mind.

I refuse to! Period...

—*Robert L. Dortch, Jr.*

One Of A Kind

No one can lift me as high as you
You are my love and best friend too
I walked around searching, I didn't
Know what I would find, then you came
Along, you are one of a kind.

No one can lift me as high as you do
My life would be worthless if not for you
My heart would be sad, I would be alone
And so blue
I shudder to think of life without you.

No one can lift me as high as you
Oh, how I thank you, I really do
I think of you often, I will never let you go
For the gift that you gave is worth
More than silver and gold.

—*Ruby Andes*

A Tribute To Our Young Nurses

You are so beautiful—only God could have thought you up!
You are the wisdom of the old with the heart of the young!
The lives you touch are legion—
and as their numbers grow, you grow!

Your shining eyes say so much—
Exasperation and shock at the "mistakes" of us oldsters!
Indignation that we don't know what you KNOW!
Frustration at the load placed on your shoulders!
Tears when your efforts are never enough!
Empathy in the suffering your capable hands ease.
Sorrow when those for whom you care cannot survive.
A twinkle as you spot your new Mustang out in the parking lot
in the midst of your busy shift!
A glisten as you sport your lovely diamond engagement ring!

Who but the young can work all night, sleep all day,
and party in the middle!
Who but the young can be so uplifting in our serious work!

We need you young Nurses; we respect and admire you—
We reminisce with nostalgia in observing your caring and your
loving
for we have been there too!
We look at you and harbor no regrets as we trust to you
our wonderful profession!

—*Marie E. Hammes*

My Typewriter's Broke

I know it upsets you and makes you sore, but I really must tell
you at least once more - and though these words might make you
cross, I must tell you 'cause you're the boss -
My typewriter's broke!

Oh, you tried to fix it (but all in vain) so I must bring up
the matter again. The screwdriver and the pliers have each had
their try to dig in its works and find out why the "Q" skips
and the "R" drops and none of the letters have any tops -
My typewriter's broke!

When you offered us new ones and we said "no" we were just
trying to save you some dough, and new ones now the budget
won't permit, but with work awaiting I can't just sit, so
won't you please see what you can do with it.
My typewriter's broke!

When you read your letters you would think you were dizzy, and
I don't mind it, but when I'm busy I haven't time with the
machine to be toying, and after a while it gets annoying. I
want your work to look real neat, but this contraption's got
me beat! If it were just for me, I wouldn't bother, but it's
all for you Oh Great White Father!

—*Lois E. Cabron*

Untitled

Sometimes in the wind
   you can still hear them call.
Ghosts of the past
   that save some of sorrow.
Words spoken harshly
   to the soul of a broken child.

You're shameless in a sense
   that you cannot see.
Hurtful like a sin
   that bleeds through your veins.

Smokeless nights
   of a psychedelic junction.
What became of the past
   lost its meaning to some through time.

       —Tara Malo

Untitled

I never thought you'd actually do it.
You didn't think I cared.
How could you think that with all the times we had shared.
The note said you were hurting.
But it never really had shown.
I only wish it would have, because then I would have known.
Known you were hurting with pain and with need.
Then I could have tried to stop you from doing that nasty deed.

The note did not explain it all.
Why you took the gun off the wall.
Why you put it to your head.
And why the next morning we found your body by the bed.
As I watched the casket lowered in the ground.
I couldn't believe you'd take away the only friend that
I had found.
You may think suicide took away the pain that no one else could
   see.
But the pain you felt only transferred from you to me.

       —Tanya Kempema

The Love Of A Married Man Is No Love At All

The love of a married man, is no love at all.
You find him sitting at a bar, he tells the story of his life
Including the part about the wife, there not intimate any more
But they share the same house, but nothing more,
His life is an open book to all.
He meets a girl and tells her, he's falling in love
a superficial love, just to fill his manly needs
Un be known to the girl, the lies they pour from dawn to dusk
No commitment of course, I am a married man, you see
But his manly needs he has to meet, the lies they flow, so neat
Covering everything, he thinks he is so discrete
Tired of one, he finds another, un be known to the other
The lies and deceit, they never stop
His life is a lie, from the start of each morning, till the end
of the night
He plays the part, a weekend worrier, is he to the house.
Come Monday to Friday 9-5 he works, evening comes
Then bars and woman, motels short stays of course can't stay
stay out all night. The woman believes, till they see the light
His life consist of lies and cheating, morning, noon and night.

       —Maureen Carrozza-James

You

you enter my thoughts with vibrancy and with warmth
you flag me down with your caring soul
you come upon me in my space of wonderment
you step into my life fulfilling the whole

your presence surrounds, enveloping me in the mist
your color comes upon my eyes clear
your smile illuminates around our world
your mind drugs me and brings the truth near

feelings rush sharply by careening off the walls
feelings come forth so different and so fast
feelings which are felt and harbored
feelings to be shared among the past

you leave me with hope for tomorrow and for today
you send me a bouquet of flowers
you bring me to the brink of ecstasy
you engrave love on my heart with your powers

your touch explodes within my mind and into my soul
your origin creates a helplessness about me
your influence directs all the emotion
your knowledge spreads itself far below the sea

       —Patricia Spaeth

Myself

   To have friends I've been told,
You got to have riches and be bold.
But, I don't want riches, wealth, or gold,
All I want is my comrades to hold.

   I want to be fit for myself to know,
I want it recognize, wherever I go.
To have people say, there a girl, I'd like to know.
Even though, she hasn't got dough.

   I want to be clean, from head to feet,
And be fit for people to meet.
I'd like them to say, Isn't she neat,
And her ways are hard to beat.

   I want habits that are decent and clean,
I don't want to treat people mean.
I want a winning way, that always beams.
And a "smile", that sparkle and "gleam."

   I always want to be "happy and gay."
To help people, day after day,
And make them "happy", along their way.
For it is "love" and faith", that always pays.

       —Winifred Bullard

An Anniversary Thought

All the years you have worked to raise me right.
You have given me such a wonderful life.
There will never be anyone other than you two,
Who could ever be more loving and true.
I know it takes a lot, and you gave it all, you've got.
So now it's my turn to say I love you with all my heart.
I'm glad in my life your love you have shared.
Knowing you gave me so much and you cared.
You may not know how much I care for you.
But deep down inside you know I really do.
I know it took all your love.
With a little help from the Lord above.
Knowing your here for me to hold, your
love will always be more precious than gold.

       —Sherri G. Silkey

Who Are You

You are the present, past and future
You hold 3/4 of this earth with in your heart
You walk day by day with the thirst
Of knowledged to cleanse your mind with serenity
You see reality through the things
You say, the things you do the places you
have been and the people you have seen
You are a source of energy
To the sun above you without a doubt
You are a shadow of faith to
the ground beneath you.
You have the IQ of rainbow that glows
Within you in the still of the night
You have a tight heart when it's coming
To lending your heart to a stranger, but
you are a special person, that needs to be
told how special you are to keep
away the cold wars of the world today
You are a beautiful creation of life and God
All in one and so much more who are you

 —*Victor Beasley*

Through The Eyes Of A Stray

I can't believe you've given me away,
You know I loved you even though I was a stray,
Now, here I am in a strange place,
Can't you see the tears upon my face?
I gave you all the goodness that I possessed,
And now you've laid me here to rest,
If only you could see my broken heart,
Maybe you wouldn't have torn the two of us apart,
I know I'm not that bright,
But does that make giving me away more right?
I thought you were my family all the days of my life,
But here I am again, leading a strays life,
Wondering and hoping if there will ever be an end to this strife.
I wonder if I'll ever have the love and happiness of a family,
Or will I love and lose because no one can handle me?

 —*Lynne Wellman*

Untitled

Do not stand there in indignation.
You know that I meant you no distress.
I will not have you examine my every motion,
And analyze every subject that I address.

Do not force your care and concern.
I know for a fact that it is false.
I would rather make it on my own
Than with someone who feigns their very thoughts.

Do not pretend that you only hear silence
When I am screaming from the depths of my soul.
I will not have you disregard the anguish
That you created from the peace I used to know.

 —*Tammy DeShazo Knauer*

Why?

I often find myself wondering why
Why so many young people must die
Losing their lives in such senseless ways
Unable to live for more sun-filled days
We now must live our lives on guard
Hiding in houses with windows barred
Afraid to venture into the street
Hesitant to speak to those we meet
How much longer can this go on
It is time for a new dawn
A clearer, brighter day
Where violence does not get in the way

 —*Tamara L. Lewis*

Our Special Guy

The time you spent here on earth was brief
You left behind family and friends full of grief
So untimely it's really hard to understand
Why God would call home such a strong young man
He must have special plans for you in Heaven above
To call you away from a family so full of love
The tears we shed come like a springtime rain
Yet not helping ease the sorrow nor the pain
It was your time to go to His Kingdom so grand
As your soul was gently placed in His hands
He'll take care of you as He's always done
As He calls His angels home one by one
He'll guide the loved ones you left behind
Help ease our hurt and troubled minds
There will never be a final farewell or goodbye
Because we all have memories of our special "Guy"

 —*Sherrie Isenhart Wilkinson*

Longing

Grandmother, my dearest
You left so long ago
Yet, I see your peaceful face
As if it were yesterday.

Grandmother, my dearest
You were my friend
And my refuge in moments of doubt,
I remember all of your life's sufferings.

I remember your sky blue eyes,
Thoughtful, serene and entrancing.
I remember well the smile...
Your lips composed melancholically.

I remember our walks together,
Conversations and sound of your voice,
I remember our joys
And sorrows of everyday living.

Grandmother, my dearest
I feel your absence everyday
But when I think of the day we reunite
The heaviness lifts from my heart... I glow.

 —*Lidia Hoxie*

Answer Me Please

There was this questioning young girl like one
you may know now.
She never had her questions answered because
her mother didn't know how.
On t.v. she saw crime, innocents being shot.
She didn't know what was right and what was not.
..... So she asked, why?

In school there were kids who were more bad than good.
She wondered why they didn't act as they should.
..... So she asked, why?

Daddy didn't come home anymore - only visited once a week.
She saw her parents were sad and the two would never speak.
..... So she asked, why?

By now she had too much to handle and asked her mother how.
Her mother would get angry and responded with "not now!"
..... And so she wondered, "why?"

The only answer she gave herself was that she should just die.

Last night I passed through the mourning crowd to say my final
"good-bye". There at the end I saw the mother - and all she
could say was "why?"

 —*Maria Gervasio*

To The Ground Hog

In looking over my animal list
You, Mr. Ground Hog, have been missed.
As in a beauty contest you would not win,
When put in comparison with your other friends.

However, you can rise up, boast and grin,
And hold it all over the heads of them.
For no other animal can stand up and say,
The calendar honored their names with a day.

The weatherman didn't give it to you for nothing,
In return you have to sacrifice something.
Awaken early on that day while other animals sleep,
And come out into the world for a peep.

If a clear day with the sun shining bright,
And you see your shadow appear in sight.
Then back into your hole you creep
Predicting cold weather for six more weeks.

If a cloudy day with no shadow on the ground
Then you are suppose to stay awake and around.
Who knows, do you cheat and go back to sleep,
For on February second you can find very little to eat.

— *Sallie Sue Stipes*

Terrible Two's

She get's into Mommy's things,
You name it, - just everything.

Pots and pans, - when she can.
From drawers to clothes, - utensils galore.
She'll pull your hair and bite you to...
That's why she's a terrible two!

She'll smile at you so pretty and convincing,
But she's up to something real sneaky and menacing.

She'll wreck your house inside out,
Take my word without a doubt.
She's known as tasmanian devil, - so cute
but yet a rebel.

I love her although she's a bugaboo, -
that's why she's "my terrible two."

— *Veronica A. Carmack*

Rhyme And-Or Reason

Poetry is the music of lyric
You see it instead of just hear it
    The song of words
        Are frequently heard
But rhyming
    Keeps your recall in spirit
Fools not wiseman
    Practice this art
While setting in stink tanks
    And smelling the part
Wisemen may read it
    With a frown or a smile
But reason and understanding
    Fill their memory file
When rhyme and reason share the same lines
Then fools and wiseman will both be inclined
Unlikely neighbors of wood and ink
Rhyme and or reason can both make you think
Wisemen and fools may write without rhyme
But when they do not you'll remember that time

— *Ronald Edward Walker*

Demons Of Darkness

Through the darkness as you go,
you see the darkness to and fro.

There's no escaping, there is no hiding
the darkness is always lurking behind you.

Listen to the shadowy depths,
hear the sweeping of its weeping
through the darkness of air.

As you trudge along a path never looking back,
for you do not know what is behind you, lurking around
you, standing beside you.

Understand this now, that the demons of darkness know you,
your withery ways your hideous days.

Hiding places will do you no more than banish you forever
more, but the demons of darkness will be sitting beside
your for always and evermore.

— *Lianne Valerio*

A Time To Hate

When you get into a big horrible fight
You think you are out of sight
No one sees you, no one cares
Not even your Aunt Clair.

You sit on your bed and cry and cry
When you could be out in the clear blue sky.

So please let me go, don't make me stay
Let me go play
With my friend Angela May.

I love you, I love you, x's and o's
You know that I do so why do you hate me so?

I will never do what I did today
Or what I did the other day.
I'll hug you, I'll kiss you, I even miss you.

I'll finish my projects before I go out to play
I'll do what you say all day.

I am all out of emotions, so if you say no I'll be OK
It's only for a day.

There is a time to hate
But I think my parents are still great!!!

— *Sarah Shoemaker*

Letter

My heart is so heavy with longing today so I sat down and wrote
    you today.
My heart was so full of so much to say I wrote five letters and
    still could not say what was on my heart this fine day.
My heart kept telling me to start over this way 'til I could
    make sense of this revelation I had.
My heart felt broken and went every which way until God said to
    write it this way.
My heart felt so light I changed in His way. I could feel His
    laughter and it changed my day.
My heart had said to write a poem some way and I wanted God to
    guide my way.
My heart got too heavy and He brightened my day and soared me
    on to a greater today.

— *Linda Brown*

Good Bye Chief: Andrew R. Poliny, A Great American, Laid to Rest

January 23, 1991

You were the One who taught me Right from Wrong.
You were the One who helped me all along.
You were truly Great.
And now that You are Late,
I miss You more than words can tell.

You taught me Duty.
You taught me Honor.
You taught me Country.
I will always Love Thee.

Life for me continues still, even if it seems all uphill.
And no matter where Life takes me.
Even though this day Breaks me,
I will honor You.
Yes I will.

—*Rest In Peace Dad— Val*

The Old Home

    I gave you shelter from the rain and cold
you were welcomed into the bosom of my soul
here was found comfort and rest from your daily toil
and these memories are all that I now hold.
    I watched your children growing and playing in the yard
I remember the bedtime stories you used to tell
and the day it was decided me you would sell
your children were sad and on yourself it was hard.
    For many years now I have stood alone
my body stoops under the weight of my head
and the ground on which I stood will soon be my bed
the storms have raged and the winds have blown.
    No one was around to keep me going to do the repairs
it has been so long since I heard the sounds of life
I give myself back to the earth I have nothing for which to
fight, I wonder if the people kept their memories or if anyone
cares.

—*Sherry L. Rhodes*

Ode To My Husband

My husband, my dear!
    You whom the Lord gaveth me,
Your presence warms the wintry nights, hon,
    And cools the hot summer's sun;
When I'm perched upon your knee.

The days, how long and lonely,
    When our work days take us apart.
But when the evenings are new,
    and our work days are through;
The nights are, too, short sweetheart.

Oh, how I like to hold your hands,
    And gaze into your eyes,
Knowing your heart understands,
    My frailties, faults and idiosyncrasies;
And will always sympathize.

My husband, my dear!
    You, whom the Lord gaveth me,
Are my friend, confidant and lover;
    My protector, helpmate, pal and provider,
I thank God for you, my gift, forever.

—*Mary L. Liddell*

The Dollar

And what makes you so sure
you'll never have to beg
with your soft hands
reaching out for love or money
or another human being
to share your sorrow?

You turned your head so quickly
from his twisted smile
to ignore the plea, as if a dollar
could have solved his problem.

And I noticed how it bothered you
when I gave him that dollar,
perhaps because you don't yet
understand the delicate balance of your own life.

So please, "My darling daughter",
before you run away to greet
this world with all your innocent beauty,
do remember:

We are all a part of this thin veneer
over that which makes us what we really are.

—*Robert Torgerson*

Falling In Luck

(for Cheryl)

Every time
Your eyes meet mine
I want to celebrate —
The way that you walk,
The way that you talk,
The way you smile at me;
The day we met,
Our first kiss,
And, of course, Leonard Cohen,
For serenading us to the Gates of Ecstacy.
And so many other moments,
Too numerous to mention
(But too precious to forget),
Constantly remind me of you;
Proving, I guess,
That it's really true;
Sometimes, you just get lucky.

—*Lawrence Jeziak*

Daughter

Your hugs were my caffeine in the morn.
Your kisses brought up my sun.
Your laughter brought back my life, and washed the
sleep from my eyes.

    Morning! I'd say to you, with your half awake face.
    Then you'd come and sit between my legs.
    We'd sit together for a while, silent as the
    sun would rise.

Then you would pet your pup, and check out the day.
    Then all of a sudden you where ready to play.
      Then one day, we had to say "Good-bye."
    Be good, I love you, It will be O.K.

Your hugs are gone, but not in my dreams.
Your kisses are only in my heart.
    And your laughter echo's through-out my house.

    Guess what? I miss you.
Without your hugs, and kisses and that laughter
    Until next year, I will be here

—*Laura Lea Bowman*

My Dream Land

Close your eyes, take a deep breath, and imagine
Your sitting in the middle of a field of green grass,
Seeing different things as you look around.
Hills as far as you can see,
A beautiful shining river, a crystal lake,
Trees with ripe, delicious fruit,
Begging to be picked...eaten
Reflected in the lake, looking at you,
Stands a unicorn, shimmering silver in the light.
A million different birds soar
Up in the bright blue sky
As you listen to a red robin sing
Accompanied by the water rushing and the
Crack of hatching eggs.
As you hear the baby birds chirping for their mama,
You look around again and realize
It's only just a dream.
—*Raizel Goldblatt*

Farewell

It is my turn now.
Your thin old hand, with veins as blue as midnight sky,
lies still upon the coverlet.
The silver wisps of hair, once chestnut brown, fan softly
out upon the stark white pillow.
You are asleep.
The feet that once strode gaily through the door at
close of day are quiet now...
For age, with its companion death, has withered the strong
limbs, and made the skin that once glowed from wind and sun -
transparent as a frail moth's wings.
I hold the dear gnarled fingers in my own and wish
that I could lead you to a haven of warmth and safety -
Just as you once led me.
All through the years you were the one to whom I fled in pain
and fear. Big, safe, and strong!
You held my hand and brought me home.
Dear God, I put his hand in thine.
Thou too are a Father.
Please lead my father home. Amen.
—*Marjorier Mix Straub*

A Man In Blue

To the people who see you every day on the street
You're a uniform, badge: an image complete.

You're someone to call when they need some advise
You provide all the answers and are always precise.

You're the guy with the radar and flashing red lights
You handle their accidents and break up their fights.

You're solid and strong-always in control
They feel more secure knowing you're on patrol.

You have to be tough-a man of steel
Any night can quickly become, a long ordeal.

What people don't see is the man inside
The husband, the daddy, your sensitive pride.

You mow lawn, watch ball games like ordinary guys,
Fix dollies, tie ribbons, wipe tears from little eyes.

You're a very special man, God sent from above
To keep peace in his world, and spread His love.

You'll long be remembered for the work that you do,

You're one of the best. . . . .

You're "A man in blue"
—*Rosalie M. Calbow*

The Riverman

At first not wishing to go too far
You're content to simply wade
Near the barren desert shore
Where dying trees can give no shade
But soon, so soon, you want much more
That simple life begins to fade.
So you wander where the water's deep
And go on further, deeper still
Until you take one final leap
And fall 'neath the waves, against your will
Your mouth and lungs are filled with water
And you start to feel Death's icy chill.
That's when the Riverman finds you,
His presence you now welcome and adore.
He lifts you up, up out of the water
And puts you down, down on the shore
All your troubles are over, he says,
But you will swim no more.
—*Patrick Davis*

My Little Girl

Oh, how I miss my little girl.
You're growing up in such a whirl.
Only yesterday it seems you were so dainty and small.
Now you're growing into quite a little lady after all.
Your dolls we had to pack away,
Because with them you did not play.
I used to catch you when you would fall;
Now you play softball and basketball.
You used to tug on my apron strings;
Now you're on the phone every time it rings.
I used to rock you in my chair of wood;
Now I only wish that I could.
You are so good with your little brother;
I know someday you'll be a wonderful Mother.
You are growing up so fast;
I only wish I could make this time last.
Yesterday you were a tiny baby.
Today I only hope that maybe,
As time goes by from year to year,
Our love will grow even more dear.
—*Rhonda J. Bailey*

Is It Love?

Since you've each lost your lover
You're now starting to discover
You were meant for each other
Is It Love?

When your heart goes pitter patter
'Cause the Postman brings a letter
And they just keep getting better,
Is It Love?

When you're old and getting older
And there's an arm around your shoulder
And your heart keeps getting bolder;
Is It Love?

You're alone and feeling lonely
Wondering when he's going to phone me
Saying you're his one and only
Is It Love?

Since you're both past ten times seven
You must look to God in heaven
For His wondrous peace and blessing
If It's Love?
—*LaRue Renneisen Weiss*

795

Death Reflections

If a man reaches out into darkness,
Will he find the light of day?
By way of this barren and forgotten world,
Shall man find a paradise lost beneath?
One man, one world, a billion or more souls,
Individuals all, seeking, wandering,
Lost at various times if not altogether.
The time is now, the place is here,
The man, is brother unto all.

And unto each other,
Must all brothers be.
　　　—*Rauyl Nakayama*

Wish

I was watching you
Across the dimly lit room
How the fading light
Glimmers through your hair
The sparkle in your eyes
Sends shivers
Up and down my spine
Someday maybe tonight
I will tell you how I feel
How I dream of loving
Of being with you
How I dream of you in my arms
Gazing in my eyes without saying a word
You say you love me with a smile
One hand on my chest
The other through my hair
My heart pounding
You whisper my name
Then you give me a kiss
Your love is all I wish
　　　—*L. C. Bradigan*

My Love

Let it be known throughout the land,
That I shall have no other man.

For you alone my heart has kept,
Safe and warm, though tears I've wept.

Tears of sorrow for our lost joy,
Tears of happiness for our first boy.

Through all the happiness, we've shared,
Deep in my heart I still feel scared.

That I'm not worthy of a love so great.
God I pray to set me straight.

Give me strength from up above,
Make me worthy of this love.

For such a love, comes once in time.
You my love, are, my once in time.
　　　—*Mary Yruegas*

Autumn Discovery

Along the winding road we drove,
　　past fields of green where lay,
　　the last new mown hay,

Beside the rushing creek
　　autumn leaves fell and brushed our cheeks,

With air so crisp and clean,
　　it was as though we were in a dream,

The beauty of the sky so blue,
　　my heart filled with love for you,

Upon reaching the crystal lake
　　we knew this was no mistake,

Breathing the air so sweet,
　　wind whirling bright leaves around our feet,
　　we knew our love would keep.
　　　—*Hilda S. Koch*

Why Do You Look So Happy?

Why do you look so happy,
　　Whilst now I feel such fear?
Is there something that you know,
　　Is not the end yet near?
You seem to be so gleeful,
　　Your heart so full of cheer.
He must be in the darkness.
　　Is that why you there peer?
All things seem so far away,
　　Since only we are here.
I know he's out there somewhere,
　　And that he's coming near.
Just now as fear gripped my heart,
　　My soul cried out, in tear.
I gaze into the nighttime,
　　And now I know he's here...
　　　—*Timothy W. Wooten I*

Once In A Lifetime

Once in a lifetime
　　Someone comes along,
　　A very special love
　　That fills your life with song.

Once in a lifetime
　　Your heart finds a home,
　　Where never again
　　Do you feel all alone.

Once in a lifetime
　　Through sunshine or rain,
　　Your love stands securely
　　Through sorrow or in pain.

Once in a lifetime
　　Someone steals your heart,
　　It's right, it's wonderful
　　You know, right from the start!
　　　—*Carol Mae Smith*

Biographies
of
Poets

ABBAS, SAMIRA G.
[b.] January 11, 1978, Pakistan; [p.] Ghulam and Anisa Abbas; [ed.] Studying (GCSE) at Bryon College in Athens Greece; [occ.] Student; [hon.] Some high school certificates, English Language, "First Certificate in English"; [pers.] "With first impressions... things and people are not always what they seem to be". I would like to thank my brother-in-law Asim-R-Mithani and my sister Tasneem A. Mithani, without their encouragement I'd never have the confidence to enter this contest. [a.] Blue Springs, MO.

ABBEY, FRANCES P.
[b.] December 31, Fairport, NY; [ch.] 4 sons, 1 daughter; [ed.] On going; [occ.] Antique Dealer and Appraiser; [memb.] "Pennsylvania" Appraisers Association, founder and member of Trombone Associates, a trombone choir performing throughout New York State; [hon.] Dean's List; [oth. writ.] "Wind Song" and several musical compositions. [pers.] To become a "fragrance felt".

ABERCROMBIE, GLENN
[b.] June 4, 1926, Herman, AR; [p.] John and Lucy Abercrombie; [m.] Divorced; [ed.] Kilgore High School, Kilgore Junior College, North Texas State Teacher's College; [occ.] Retired hot metal printer; [memb.] ACLU, AARP, CWAITU, BDA, DAV-life; [hon.] Editor's Choice Award, Business Mgr. "The Flare", Kilgore Junior College; [oth. writ.] News articles in junior college "The Flare", poems and articles in Veterans Voices; [pers.] U/n odds we trust, financially and socially. [a.] Temple, TX.

ABOHOSH, DEBRA
[pen.] Debra Abohosh; [b.] May 18, 1951, Dallas, TX; [p.] E. P and Joyce Scott Abohosh; [ed.] Thomas Jefferson High, Olan Mills Technical School of Photography, California Coast University; [occ.] Manager and Photographer of Portrait Studio; [memb.] Sheriffs Association of Texas, Department of Public Safety Officers Association; hon.] Hosted and co-produced a T.V. show celebrating women's music; [oth. writ.] Lyrics from several songs published in various local newspaper articles; [pers.] I like to think I have been influenced by my great grandfather's cousin Kahlil Gibran, in a world full of turmoil I find the spirituality of his writings very soothing. [a.] Dallas/Arlington, TX.

ABOUGHANAM, LORRAINE
[b.] February 22, 1980, Brooklyn, NY; [p.] Aliyas and Jannette Aboughanam; [ed.] 8th grade; [occ.] Student at St. Anselm School, 8th grade; [memb.] Teen S.O.Y.O. of St. Nicholas Cathedral in Brooklyn, NY; [hon.] Silver Medal for Photography contest; [pers.] My inspiration is my English teacher and my family, who has influenced me to write or to express my feelings by writing and especially to write poetry in our yearbook. [a.] Brooklyn, NY.

ACEVEDO, VANESSA
[b.] January 14, 1982, Queens, NY; [p.] Haydee Cristancho; [ed.] Elementary School; [a.] Elizabeth, NJ.

ACHAL, SUSAN SHOBINA
[b.] December 6, 1972, Fiji Island; [p.] Bob and Maya Achal; [ed.] Graduated 1992 from White Oaks Secondary School, currently attending final year at Sheridan College (grad 1994) in Early Childhood Education program, September 1994 attending University of Toronto for B.A. in Teaching Education (B.A. Ed.); [occ.] Medical Receptionist (part time) ambition to teach chil-

dren; [oth. writ.] Several poems and short stories; [pers.] Close your eyes and let your soul escape to a place filled with unbound beauty, the world of mother nature. Thanks for the inspiration Moriel and the confidence mom and dad. [a.] Oakville, Ontario Canada.

ACHIENG, SUPROSA MARTHA
[b.] October 18, 1956, Kisu.Uv. Kenya;[p.] Leo and Susan Odero;[ed.] Dominican Convent School, Lusaka, some undergraduate study at The University of Zambia; [occ.] Statistician, Min. of Planning and National Development, Kenya; [memb.] Entered in the Register of The Institute of Statisticians, London as an RSA member in 1980 and as an SSA member in 1981, Councilor at the East Africa Women's League (RAWL); [hon.] Between 1988 and 1992 I won a total of six cups and trophies singlely and two jointly at the Homecrafts Exhibition of the East Africa Women's League (EAWL); [oth. writ.] Song lyrics one of which has been printed set to music and several others which at present have been sent to a certain recording company for consideration, notecard poetry which presently have also been submitted for consideration; [pers.] While keeping in mind the art of poetry, I try to give a message in each of my work. [a.] Nairobi, Kenya.

ACKER, KATHLEEN
[pen.] Kara; [b.] September 4, 1945, Port Jefferson, NY; [p.] Edward and Alice Rusin; [m.] Divorced; [ch.] Sherry Lynn and Wendy Kay; [ed.] A.A.S. Suffolk County Community College, 1965, MC-Karaoke and talent shows; [occ.] Co-Editor F.S.S. News, uniquely create personalized one of a kind poems for all occasions, preparing book of poems for publication; [memb.] Customer Advisory Council, Commack Post Office, NY, International Institute of Reflexology; [hon.] Sang on local radio station WNYG-Xmas 1991, 1st place Hustle Dance contest, 1st place Penn Yan Bowling Tournament during college, Dean's List, Key Club, Phi Delta Chi, head typist college newspaper; [oth. writ.] Created tour descriptions for Tour Guide for Fun Afar Travel, comments published in APMI magazine, Editor of and contributed stories and poems in book "The Colors of God's Love", Vantage Press 1994, Editorials and poems for FSS News, poem for Lorry of Commack Post Office, personnel ads; [pers.] Inquisitive, creative minds are being suppressed by our uncompromising robotic system of education. Talent, like a small seed needs nurturing and love to grow. [a.] Commack, NY.

ACKLER, ERNEST STEPHEN
[b.] March 16, 1952, New Haven, CT; [ed.] High school graduate, Milford High -1971, Milford, CT; [occ.] Counselor; [oth. writ.] 578 exposures on micro-film, copyrighted in 1978, all poetry; [pers.] If you have to stop and think what it is you want to write you're not (writing) doing it. [a.] Denver, Co.

ACKLIN, PAMELA L.
[b.] March 24, 1968, Detroit, MI; [p.] Elbert and Bertha Acklin; [ch.] Chaz Vaton Acklin; [ed.] Wayne State University; [occ.] Second grade teacher, Maya Angelou Elementary School, Detroit, MI; [memb.] Tabernacle Missionary Baptist Church, Michigan Reading Association, Wayne County Reading Council, Big Brother Big Sister Organization; [pers.] I am certainly more encouraged to write now more than ever! [a.] Detroit, MI.

ADAMS, APRIL L.
[b.] July 11, 1981, Dearborn, MI; [p.] Jack L. Adams; [ed.] Carver Elementary, Detroit, MI; [occ.] Student;

[memb.] Awana Clubs, Girl Scouts; [hon.] Various school scholastic awards, President of class, 1st place Read-A-Thon; [oth. writ.] None published as yet; [pers.] I like to bring joy to a person's heart and thought to their mind. [a.] Detroit, MI.

ADAMS, IRMA LABANT
[pen.] Irmtrud Adams; [b.] January 30, 1950, Belgium; [p.] Michael and Marie Labant; [m.] Allen D. Adams II, June 11, 1972; [ch.] Amelia E. Adams age 11 and Bassett named Lola, age 12; [ed.] Carrick High School in Pittsburgh, PA.; [occ.] Retired Flight-Attendant and homemaker; [memb.] PEO, Carson-Tahoe Hospital Auxiliary, Carson City Children's Museum; [oth. writ.] Several poems published in the C-THA newsletter; [pers.] When my non-English speaking parents and I stepped off the plane at Idlewild Airport in the 50's, we never dreamed I'd be living in Nevada and writing poetry. [a.] Carson City, NV.

ADAMS, MICHAEL J.
[b.] July 29, 1969, Buckingham, Quebec Canada; [p.] Milton and Elsie; [sib.] Nathalie; [memb.] Society of Management Accountants of Ontario; [hon.] Graduated with Honors Distinction in Business Algonquin College, 1989; [oth.writ.] Several poems published in local papers as a child, as well as several unpublished songs and poems; [pers.] Mine are poems from the heart, mine are poems from the soul, if they make people think then I've accomplished my goal. [a.] Buckingham, Quebec Canada.

ADAMS, NORMA A.
[b.] Kansas; [p.] Reuben and Octive Wilson Reazin; [m.] David W. Adams, September 14, 1942; [ch.] David Jr., Daniel and Douglas; [ed.] Bachelor of Arts, Arizona State University, Tempe, Arizona; [occ.] Freelance writer, retired teacher, welfare worker; [memb.] Grace Community Church, Tempe, Arizona, ASU Alumni, sang in university and church choirs; [hon.] Top honor in high school graduation, worked for State of Arizona in Welfare Department for about 20 years, Dean's List, winner in BYLINE Magazine's writing contests several times; [oth.writ.] Poems, "The Farmer", "Lone Star Graveyard", "Lost Ophelis", "Day At The Blowouts", "The Bloody Seas", "Tragedy on the Prairie", articles, "Unwanted Concern", 'An Attack by Fire", "The Crying Chair"; [pers.] The joys of my life have been my church, my family, reading, writing, music and painting. Our children are all college graduates, one an attorney. [a.] Mesa, AZ.

ADAMS, WINONA M.
[b.] December 11, 1921, Sioux City, IA; [p.] Arthur and Ethel Stadtman; [m.] William Wallace Adams, June 22, 1940; [ch.] Dr. David W. Adams and Nancy Kay Ghanem; [ed.] San Bernardino High Senior, I also took several courses at S.B. Valley College; [occ.] Retired; [memb.] Charter Member of Girl Scouts, troop 1, San Bernardino, CA., Rialto Historical Society, San Bernardino, Perris Hill Tennis Club, (past) member of Rialto Women's Club; [hon.] American Cancer Society, Tennis Tournament 1975, won "B" doubles; [oth. writ.] I've written several poems and a couple of short stories, also an article which I recently sent to Woman's Day magazine, I haven't heard from them yet; [pers.] I've always admired Edgar A. Guest, readings and poems by Grace E. Easley. I like to portray a sense of humor in my poems, they say, Laugh and the world laughs with you, cry and you cry alone. [a.] Rialto, CA.

ADOUCI, JAMES
[b.] December 7, 1947, Boston; [ed.] High school and 2 1/2 years in prison where I found out that I have some talent; [oth. writ.] More poems, essays and short stories; [pers.] My poems are written for the average person. I feel that if you find yourself rereading and trying to figure out a poem's meaning, then the author has wasted not only his time, but more importantly, your time. [a.] Hull, MA.

ADKINS, PAULINE GOATLEY
[pen.] Polly Pirtse; [b.] August 14, 1912, Valley Hill, KY; [p.] Nancy Della Virgin and J. Ernest Goatley; [m.] Robert Carroll 'Tom" Adkins, May 5, 1936; [ch.] Roberta Ann Nickell, 2 grandsons, Charles Whitney and David Robert Nickell; [ed.] B.S. degree in Home Economics, Eastern University, Richmond, KY, University of Kentucky, Lexington, KY. [occ.] Retired in 1980, still active in school and community; [memb.] Retired Teachers' Association, Baptist Church, Retired Teacher of Carter Co. and State Retired Teachers of Kentucky, member of Site Bason Council Committee, member of Woman's Missionary Union, honorary member of Elliott CO. Woman's Club; [hon.] President of Kentucky Vocational Teachers, President of Kentucky Vocational Association, Honorary Junior, Chapter and State Homemaker degree of Future Homemakers of America, past President of Carter County Retired Teachers Association; [oth. writ.] Numerous other poems, skits, ceremonies for officers of organizations, 3 songs that I sing to my grandchildren and great grandson, I am in the process of putting a book together; [pers.] I believe that the home is the foundation of our nation, but there are many forces making a strong drive to destroy the family as God would have us live. Adults are setting the wrong examples, politicians especially. It is up to the parents to get back to putting God first, family second and other things in their rightful place. Parents also need to get active in school and community affairs so that we can put God 1st in out nation. [a.] Grayson, KY.

AERS, CECILIA MARIE
[b.] November 3, 1975, Chatham, Ontario; [p.] Carole Ann and Gilbert Aers; [oth. writ.] I have never attempted to have any of my work published until now; [pers.] My poetry is straight forward, but most importantly, universal. Everyone can relate to it. I find that people enjoy poems of which they can find a personal message or meaning in them. I believe that this is what makes my poetry special. [a.] Chatham, Ontario Canada.

AFFLICK, LLOYD E.
[b.] Jamaica; [m.] Sherna B. Afflick, August 21, 1971; [ch.] Nneka Loraine Shari Sylvia; [ed.] Mico Teachers Training College, University of The West Indies (teacher of history for 25 years); [occ.] Caribbean Resource Teacher, Multicultural Department; [memb.] Board of Education, Browary County, Florida; [oth. writ.] Book of poems on, The Last 500 Years of History, (soon to be published); [pers.] 'Until each life is given equal worth, there will be no peace on this planet earth. What is legal is not necessarily just, in justice then we should put our trust. If there is no justice, there will be no peace, without peace, life as we know it shall certainly cease". [a.] Sunrise, FL.

AGUILAR, ROSE
[pen.] Rosie Aguilar; [b.] July 22, 1978, Gilroy, CA; [p.] Dolores and Frances Aguilar; [ed.] Westmont High, Campbell Middle, Glen View Elementary; [memb.] Environmental Club, Giaretto Institute Committee, Span-

ish Club, Loaves and Fishes; [hon.] "Nuestra Casa", Giaretto Institute, Campbell Middle School; [pers.] I try to put all my feelings into my writings, although I know I'm young I feel you're never to young to become a true poet. [a.] San Jose, CA.

AKRANA, STEWART
[pen.] Jake, Stew; [b.] June 23, 1953, Waimea, Kauai; [p.] Soloman and Margaret Akana; [m.] Tammy Williams, February 16, 1985; [ch.] Tyrone, Ryle and Jenson; [ed.] Eleele School, Waimea High School; [occ.] Laborer; [oth. writ.] Many poems that I have in a book that has not been published; [pers.] I try to reflect my past experiences from a more productive and positive outlook to inspire my children. [a.] Kappa Kauai, HI.

AKAU, ALEXANDER L.
[b.] October 1, 1965, Honolulu, HI; [p.] Leonard Akau and Elaine Isaacs; [ed.] The Kamehameha Schools, Cannon's Business College; [occ.] Clerk-typist, Hawaii State Government, Department of Human Services; [hon.] Mentioned in Who's Who Among High School Students, graduated with honors from college and named on the Dean's List; [pers.] "Life is like a highway, flowing endlessly, only the driver has the end in sight". [a.] Kailua, HI.

AKBAY, RUHEYMA
[pen.] Rue; [b.] August 20, 1970, Edmonton; [p.] Naif and Remziye Akbay; [ed.] E.C.H.S., Eastern Composite High School; [hon.] No honors, no awards but great sisters and brothers I cherish; [pers.] Tis one life we live, live it to the fullest. [a.] Edmonton, Alberta Canada.

AKERS, HILARY
[b.] January 26, 1902, London, England; [p.] Alex and Alice Smith; [m.] Deceased, November 3, 1923; [ch.] George (67) Miriam (68) and Eozin Ann (56); [ed.] London LCC graduate night school, Clarks College, London, England; [occ.] Retired; [memb.] Eastern Star, Senior Citizens Homemakers, MD.; [hon.] London LCC England essay; [oth. writ.] Reported for The Enterprise, Kent County, Chestertown, MD; [pers.] This is the first time I have ever published any poem, I just do enjoy writing them. [a.] Rock Hall, MD.

ALAMIA, TERESA C.
[pen.] Tersa Chapa Alamia; [b.] October 15, 1918, Edinburg, TX; [p.] Miguel Chapa and Adelina Vela; [m.] Jose R. Alamia, April 18, 1942; [ch.] Leticia Ann, Grace Yvonne and Alicia Adelina; [ed.] High school and Bachelor of Arts degree in Education at Pan American University in 1965; [occ.] Retired teacher, taught school for 26 years; [memb.] Valley By-Liners a group of writers that have published 4 books about Valley History, "Gift of The Rio", "Roots By The River", "Rio Grande Round-Up" and "100 Women"; [hon.] One of her poems was printed in the Congressional Record, she has produced teaching aids that were featured in a National Publication, her poem "That Edinburg" appeared on the front page of the "Daily Review"; [oth. writ.] Poetry is my favorite form of writing, I have written about 100 poems, mostly about history.

ALBERT, BILL
[b.] June 24, 1965, Darby, PA; [p.] James and Patricia Albert; [ed.] BS degree, University of California at Davis; [pers.] Hands on a face? But the present is all we've got. [a.] Martinez, CA.

ALBERTSON, TODD
[b.] August 27, 1967, Belle Fourche, SD; [p.] Dorsey and Phill McHugh; [m.] Ann Margaret, March 13, 1990; [ch.] Tess (3 years); [ed.] Overton High School; [occ.] Chef; [pers.] Life is aware of itself. [a.] Nashville, TN.

ALDERDICE, CATHERINE
[pen.] Catherine Alderdice; [b.] November 8, 1960, Glasgow; [p.] Jessie and William; [ed.] Whitehill Secondary School, Glasgow; [occ.] Operator with Polaroid (U.K.); [pers.] I find it very satisfying to put my deepest thoughts and feelings, on many subjects into rhyme. [a.] Dumbarton, Scotland.

ALLEE, VIRGINIA GROSVERNOR
[b.] January 30, 1923, Price, UT; [p.] Charlotte Camp and Clarence Henry Stevenson, Jr.; [m.] Paul Andrew Allee, August 6, 1943; [ch.] Harold Eugene and Paul Allee Jr.; [ed.] High school and many universities in U.S., no degree; [occ.] Homemaker, artist, poet, songwriter; [memb.] Colonial Dames; [hon.] Art Awards in Colorado; [oth. writ.] Family History, books for family consumption; [pers.] Was greatly influenced by James Russell Ravell, largely self taught, responding enthusiastically to the goodness inherent in mankind as expressed by the christian faith.

ALLEN, IDA DE LOIS
[pen.] Red; [b.] February 12,1954, Louisa Co; [p.] Eva Allen and Lee Harris; [m.] Richard Lewis Arnett, Sr.; [ch.] Richard Lewis Arnett, Jr.; [ed.] Louisa County High School; [occ.] Burn Technician; [hon.] Pride in Practice (cited 3 times) in Nursing Care performance; [pers.] We all are unique in our own way, strive for our goal. [a.] Charlottesville, VA.

ALLISON, ANNA M.
[b.] March 29, 1930, Platteville, WI; [p.] Erich and Eula Kuehl; [m.] Jasper Allison, November 7, 1949; [ch.] Barbara, Daniel, Marjorie, Debra, Kenneth, Alan, Mark and James; [ed.] High school at M.S.T.C.; [occ.] Retired housekeeper, Mead Inn and Riverview Hospital, Wisconsin Rapids, WI; [memb.] Wisconsin Rapids Area Writer's Club, St. Mary's Church; [oth. writ.] Several poems published in the local newspaper; [pers.] I write for pleasure and strive for a goodness in reflection of thought for all mankind. I enjoy poetry, novels and screen play,of past and present. [a.] Wisconsin Rapids, WI.

ALLOCCA, ROBEN T. J.
[pen.] R.J.A.; [b.] October 26, 1959, NJ; [p.] Barbara and Dominick Allocca; [pers.] I dedicate my poems to my mother and grandmother.

ALLSOP, V. T.
[pen.] Jayne Plummer; [b.] February 22, 1932, Hounslow, UK; [p.] Mary and Percy Court; [m.] Alan Allsop, July 11, 1992; [ed.] Primary Secondary Private School for Girls; [occ.] Retired Nurse tutor, now a busy housewife; [memb.] Royal College of Nursing; [hon.] Registered Nurse, Clinical Teacher, Community Nurse Tutor, Nursing Post Graduate; [oth. writ.] Book, "Outcasts", poem included in church news; [pers.] I find writing a medium for expressing my views on many issues in society today especially the underprivileged. I do admire the great writers e.g., Charles Dickens and William Shakespeare and the works of Shelley.

ALTER, JAMEELA
[pen.] Jameela Alter; [b.] November 9, 1946, Calcutta,

India; [p.] Hatim and Amena Sachee; [m.] Steven Robert Alter, December 15, 1980; [ch.] Yasmin and Shirin Alter; [ed.] B.A. University of Calcutta, Montessori Teachers' diploma, London; [occ.] Teacher's Aide; [hon.] 1st place fiction winner, Bowie State University, 1993, story to be published this winter; [oth.writ.] Short story published in 1986; [pers.] People inspire and amuse me, I've met a few-having lived in India, England, Libya, Saudi Arabia and USA. I was brought up a strict Muslim and an now married to an agnostic Catholic! Life continues to be interesting. [a.] Bowie, MD.

ALUOTTO, PAUL
[b.] July 12,1975, Hoboken, NJ; [p.] Angelo and Angela Aluotto; [ed.] Currently attending B.C.C. transferring to Stocken State College in the fall; [hon.] I received a Silver Medal from the Academy of Europe for a short story; [oth. writ.] Academy of Europe will published a short story of mine, meanwhile I'm sending our various Science-Fiction stories and Science related essays to a number of magazines; [pers.] Sometimes the best view is a distorted one. [a.] Fairview, NJ.

AMANCIO, ELSIE
[b.] June 17, 1917, Hamilton Ontario, Canada; [p.] John and Elsa Lemp; [m.] Pedro Amancio, February 8, 1946; [ch.] Peter Amancio, Barbara McClain, Paul Amancio and Nancy Flood; [ed.] Kitchener and Waterloo Collegiate, Nurses training, Hamilton General Hospital, Registered Nurse; [occ.] Retired; [hon.] Veteran World War 2, 1st Lt. Army Air Corps; [oth. writ.] Nonpublished short stories and poems; [pers.] Since my retirement my hobbies include quilting, oil painting and writing. The ideas for my projects are inspired by my love for my husband and my children, grandchildren and great grandchildren. [a.] San Diego, CA.

AMEDY, MARIE
[b.] October 2, 1937, Bridgeport, CT; [p.] Jean Lepone and Richard DeCarlo; [m.] Albert J. Amedy (deceased), March 2, 1965; [ch.] One son and 4 daughters and one grandson; [ed.] Completed 12 years 8/4; [occ.] Lyricist and craftier and poet; [hon.] Won Honorable Mention in the American Song Writers' Festival, some years ago, made Silver and Gold Poet at The World of Poetry; [oth. writ.] "20 Years of Stolen Moments" and 4 more manuscripts waiting to be published, lyrics and songs; [pers.] I'm molding my joys and sorrows to remember thru my tomorrows for poets are sculptors of time and I'm learning how to carve in rhyme. [a.] Waterbury, CT.

AMOS, CATHERINE
[pen.] Cat Amos; [b.] July 4, 1955, Drew, MS; [p.] Jessie Mae and Russell Amos; [ed.] Drew High now Joliet Junior College; [occ.] Part time Sandwich shop, full time White Castle; [oth. writ.] Songs and personal poetry for family and friends; [pers.] I write basically on the things that inspire me or hurt me or the things that makes me happy. I'm very creative in thoughts, I'm inspired by my spiritual ability to know things. [a.] Joliet, IL.

ANASTASI, LAUREN
[b.] October 2, 1980, New York, NY; [p.] Dr. and Mrs. John Anastasi; [ed.] Hollidaysburg Junior High, 8th grade; [memb.] I'm a member of the Altoona Community Theatre; [oth. writ.] I'm always writing, but nothing has ever been published; [pers.] I love to write. "What's Special To ME" is the first thing I've entered in a contest. I'm in the middle of writing a book. [a.] Hollidaysburg, PA.

ANDERSON, BLAIN
[b.] July 25, 1975, Lubbock; [p.] Buddy and Hope Anderson; [ed.] Graduated from high school at Coronado High School in Lubbock, now attending South Plains College in Levelland, major-pre nursing; [occ.] Part-time at Video Express; [memb.] Vice president of the Explore Post 104; [oth. writ.] This is my first publication, I write only poetry and enjoy it more than anything else, my mind seems to operate on. Hopefully I will start a non-fiction book soon? Hopefully. [a.] Lubbock, TX.

ANDERSON, CATHERINE M.
[pen.] Catherine Corley Anderson; [b.] March 21, 1909, Chicago, IL; [p.] Gaynor J. and Anna Corley; [m.] Melvin C. Anderson (deceased), January 15, 1930; [ch.] Charles and Judy Oquist; [ed.] Graduated with honors, School of the Art Institute of Chicago, BAE, studied theater arts at the Goodman School of Drama, Goodman Theater, Chicago, Post graduate work at Chicago University, Northwestern University and St. Xavier University in Psychology and Education; [occ.] Freelance writer, artist, puppeteer; [memb.] Children's Reading Round Table, Chicago, Puppeteers of America, St. Louis Puppet Guild, Women's Federation of Garland, Texas, National Museum of Women in the Arts, charter member, Women's Guild of St. Michael Church, Lone Indian Fellowship, Lone Scouts of America; [hon.] First and second place awards, Catholic Poetry Society, first and second place awards, Poets Club of Chicago, Today's Poets, Chicago Sunday Tribune, awards by National Federation of State Poetry Societies and publication in the Federation Yearbook; [oth. writ.] Five books for middle grade and older children, Officer O'Malley on The Job, Sister Beatrice Goes To Bat, Sister Beatrice Goes West, Sister Beatrice and The Mission Mystery, John F. Kennedy, Young People's President and many short stories, articles, songs, poems, plays for young people; [pers.] In my opinion, every good poem should contain a nugget of eternal truth. It can rhyme or not, according to the need of the poem or the desire of the poet, but cadence is important. Ordinary language can be used in original or even startling ways, and the reader should react thus, "that's to true. Why didn't I ever think of that?"

ANDERSON, LAMAR M.
[pen.] Lamar Bass Anderson; [b.] September 20,1961, Little Rock, AR; [p.] Mr. and Mrs. Nelson Bass; [m.] Mark W. Anderson, Sr., August 1983; [ch.] Mark Jr., Laguar and Jason Alexander; [ed.] High school graduate May 80, also attended Local Capital City Business College, received Associate degree May 90; [occ.] Insurance Representative (ASH); [memb.] Arkansas State Employee Association, First Baptist Church; [hon.] Good Conduct Medal, Sea Service Deployment ribbon (military) (Business College), 4 times Honor Roll, Dean's List; [oth. writ.] Poem, "Brotherly Love", printed in Protestant Church program (military chapel), "The Resting Place" printed in First Baptist Church program; [pers.] My goal is to emphasis to our children the need of a Heavenly Warrior and His name is Jesus! [a.] Little Rock, AR.

ANDERSON, LORI
[b.] July 25, 1956, Great Falls, MT; [p.] Robert and Maria Ranieri; [m.] Lynn W. Anderson, July 19, 1985; [ch.] Nathan Henry, Sarah Maria and Joshua Robert; [ed.] Great Falls High School, Child Development Associate degree; [occ.] Day Care Provider; [oth.writ.[Several stories and poems published in local newspaper; [pers.] I enjoy writing about people and feelings, I hope

to touch people's hearts and show the goodness in us all. [a.] Wake Village, TX.

ANDERSON, LuANN
[b.] March 25, 1965, Dallas, TX; [p.] Jess and Leota Cranmore; [m.] Joseph Anderson, June 8, 1990; [ed.] Turner High, Burneyville, OK; [occ.] Housewife; [oth.writ.] Poem published in high school newspaper by English teacher, 9th grade Marietta, OK., trying to find publisher for current manuscript entitled "Through Tragedy Love Blooms"; [pers.] The honesty of ones feelings and beliefs can be found in the writings of all writers. a[.] Ardmore, OK.

ANDERSON, RICK
[b.] August 18, 1979, Calgary, Alta; [hon.] Won 1st prize with my poem "The Wolf" in grade 8; [oth. writ.] Several poems as school assignments; [pers.] Don't judge people because their skin color is different, every individual deserves equal treatment, regardless of age, skin color, gender or looks. [a.] Cardston, Alberta.

ANDERSON, SALLY SUE
[pen.] Sally Sue Anderson; [b.] April 26, 1933, Salem, MO; [p.] Dema and Irl Whitmire; [m.] Arthur E. Anderson (deceased), August 31, 1951, married 40 years; [ch.] Gary, Mark and Wayne Anderson, four grandchildren; [ed.] Texas Kilgore College and living in numerous states and countries throughout the world and traveling in many more; [occ.] Retired, husband was oil executive, Earth Science Research Prof., I worked for three universities and a variety of volunteer work, working with international students was my favorite; [hon.] Honor student in college; [oth. writ.] Many poems and songs; [pers.] Life is a beach, my interests are floral design, painting flowers, growing flowers and writing songs. [a.] Sarasota, FL.

ANDERSON, TERRI S.
[b.] May 5, 1971, Galesburg, IL; [ed.] Abingdon High School, American Institute of Commerce, Davenport, IA; [occ.] Mgr. Brown Oil Company, St. Augustine, IL; [memb.] Business Prof's of America, Women of the Moose; [hon.] Academic Honors, high school, Dean's List-college, American Legion Citizenship Award; [oth. writ.] Strength , Treasured Poems of America, 1993. [a.] Abingdon, IL.

ANDERSON, VIOLET HENSON
[b.] June 8, 1931, Knoxville, TN; [p.] J. Cline and Lena Henson; [m.] Charles A. Anderson, Jr., August 1953; [ch.] Susie, Nancy and Jimmy; [ed.] B.S. Education, University of TN, 1953; [occ.] Professional Artist with my own business; [memb.] Alpa Delta Kappa, International Education Sorority, Stones River Woman's Club, Delta Zeta Sorority, Tennessee Art League, International Society of Poets; [hon.] Who's Who of Poetry, Golden Poet, Silver Poet, 1993 Poet of Merit, Who's Who of American WOmen, 2000 Notable American Women, International Woman of the Year 92-93, 2nd place award for poem in TN Federation of Woman's Club contest; [oth. writ.] <u>Distinguished Poets of America, Best Poems of the 90's</u>, <u>Best New Poets of 1988</u>, <u>Great Poems of the Western World, Vol. II</u>; [pers.] I love to write poetry, it just seems to flow out of my mind, and each poem touches my heart. [a.] Nashville, TN.

ANDRADE, DANIEL
[b.] September 2, 1919, Taunton, MA; [p.] Mr. and Mrs. Manuel Andrade; [m.] Odessa Seelbach Andrade, June 16, 1952; [ch.] Step-son Donald Keith Burkett, 1 son

Daniel Andrade, Jr., from previous marriage; [ed.] Walker Grammar School, Taunton, MA, graduated, Taunton High School, Taunton, MA., (drop-put); [occ.] Retired poet, artist, musician, songwriter; [hon.] Who's Who in U.S.A., Who's Who in South West, artist, musician, songwriter, all songs Crypto album, R.C.A., affiliate Zal 6482 Album, "A Lonely Stranger", Paris France; [oth. writ.] Numerous published poem in U.S.A., inducted-The Homer Honor Society World of Poetry, Sacramento, CA, poem "Old Age Is Creeping Up On Me", classic World of Poetry, anthology book; [pers.] United we stand as Americans with moral and family values against the atheist, secular humanist of U.S.A. and world, the enemy of all mankind and civilization. In God we trust. [a.] Houston, TX.

ANDREWS, LEILANI
[pen.] Lani Anuenue, Heavenly Rainbow; [p.] Deceased; [m.] Deceased; [ch.] Timothy John; [ed.] Maui High School; [occ.] Companionship, Haiku, Maui; [memb.] AARp, Pukalani Baptist Church, Kaunoa Senior Center; [hon.] Hospice Maui, not a place but a comprehensive program of support and loving care for terminally ill patients and their families; [pers.] I am delighted that my poem was selected in the semi-finalist list. The credibility remains in the real source that inspired the writing of words, God the Almighty and Creator of the universe. Thank You! [a.] Haiku, HI.

ANDREWS, MARIA
[b.] June 27, 1950, Elizabeth, NJ; [p.] Ernest and Elena DeBella; [m.] Steven Andrews; [ch.] Peter, David and Christopher; [ed.] East Brunswick High, St. Leo College; [occ.] Computer operator, technician, Pinellas Park Police Department, FL; [memb.] Florida Women in Government; [oth. writ.] A journal of unpublished poems and 2 unpublished novels; [pers.] My writings reflect my belief that "every path we take in life, no matter how difficult, holds many wonder surprises". [a.] Pinellas Park, FL.

ANDRIZZI, SERENA
[b.] April 5, 1955, Los, Angeles; [p.] Nicholas and Lillian Andrizzi; [ch.] Robert Nicholas; [ed.] Our Lady of Loretto High; [occ.] Office Assistant, Los Angeles Unified School District; [hon.] Piano Scholarship, Golden Poet Award, World of Poetry, Silver Poet Award; [oth. writ.] "Between Life and Death", "My Memories of You", "Farewell"; [pers.] What's in my heart is told in all my poems. My poems are from my heart. [a.] Los Angeles, CA.

ANGEL, ROBERT
[b.] December 4, 1981, Chattanooga, TN; [p.] Joseph and Rose Angel; [ed.] M.A. American History, Catholic, University of America; [occ.] Volunteer at United Acres Foundation; [oth. writ.] House of Pilgrimage (novel), The River Flow Forever (novel), not published, The Day of Reckoning (novel);

ANTHONY, DENNIS
[b.] April 3, 1946, Hollywood, CA; [p.] William and Alice Fitzgerald; [ed.] Redwood High, Visalia, CA., UCLA (B.S. Physics 1969); [occ.] Clerical worker; [memb.] British American Scientific Research Association; [oth. writ.] "Freyja's Gift", an adaptation from Horse Mythology and "A Simple Version of General Relativity", a kinematic alternative to Einstein's geometric vision of space and time; [pers.] The job of art is to interpret the world by touching our souls and joining us into a communion of feeling. [a.] Los Angeles, CA.

ANTONE, RONALD
[b.] May 15, 1949, Hawaii; [p.] Richard and Catherine Antone; [m.] Sharon Antone, October 30, 1991; [ch.] Alika Mark, Moani-Keala Antone, stepson Spence Perkins and stepdaughter, Shanna Perkins; [ed.] St. Joseph's grade school (Maui, HI.), St. Stephen's Seminary (freshman year, Oahu, Hi.), St. Anthony's High School (soph. junior and senior years, Maui, HI.), Mauna Oly College (Maui, HI. freshman and soph. years), University of Hawaii (junior and senior years, Oahu, HI.); [pers.] We must learn to listen and heed to the unspoken words of nature. [a.] Honolulu, HI.

APUA, AMA
[b.]] November 1, 1975, Hospital; [p.] Edna Rae Jones; [ed.] Sullivan High attended McCutcheon and Trumbull; [occ.] Volunteer Recreational Director; [memb.] Youth-N-Care, former Black History Club, former Free Street Teen Street Theatre member, school newspaper member; [hon.] Stanford Youth Seminar 1993, Youth-N-Care Network staff and youth conference; [oth. writ.] Poem published in school newspaper, Free Street, Youth-N-Care Network News, "Voices" is my first play I've written; [pers.] There is no end to life when there is love. Sorrow and pain feeds of the weakness of the heart. [a.] Chicago, IL.

APPLEGATE-TILLOTSON, VICKI
[b.] November 14,1959, Logansport, IN; [p.] Lester and Edith Applegate; [m.] Alan C. Tillotson, August 2, 1980; [ch.] Lauren Lache', Rachel Leigh and Thomas Alan; [ed.] South Houston High, University of Houston-Clear Lake; [occ.] Writer; [hon.] Phi Alpha Theta; [oth. writ.] Articles written for college paper; [pers.] Through humor and love, I try to illustrate those aspects of life that shape and define our lives. [a.] Houston, TX.

ARAFILES, LOURDES M.
[pen.] Lucy; [b.] February 10, 1954, Philippines; [p.] Bonifacio Martin and Lolita Roque; [m.] Catalino P. Arafiles, Jr., December 30, 1981; [ch.] A. Claribell and Clarissa; [ed.] Marine Biology, units in nursing; [occ.] Dental Receptionist; [memb.] Phi Kappa Phi, Honor Society, University of the Philippines, Phil; [oth. writ.] My previous articles are scientific and are published in scientific journals in the Philippines; [pers.] "We only live once, hence, enjoy life and make the most of it, through creative writing. [a.] Fremont, CA.

ARMANTROUT, CORY
[b.] January 9, 1975, Wichita,KS; [p.] Chuch and Carmen Armantrout; [ed.] Senior, Wheat Ridge High School; [pers.] Dum Spiro Spero, "While I breathe I hope". Writing is my escape and in it I hope to find my goal of self reliance. [a.] Denver, CO.

ARMSTRONG, CHRIS
[pen.] Chris Armstrong; [b.] March 27, 1964, Mississippi; [p.] Conn and Christene James; [m.] April 18, 1981-March 25, 1992; [ch.] Aaron and Jeremy Armstrong; [ed.] Forsan High School, Forsan, TX; [occ.] Repossession Butler Towing and Recovery, Ft. Worth, TX; [pers.] I write with feelings from my heart no matter what it is. I look for the good things in life. I hope the ones that read what I write enjoy it, and that maybe it can make someone's day a little better. A special thanks to two very special people in my life for standing by me and giving me the inspiration and the courage not to give up on myself. Jim and Charlene Butler, thank you and I love the two of you with all my heart, and to Larry Holder my boyfriend for all his help too. I love you as

well. [a.] Ft. Worth, TX.

ARMSTRONG, JACK T.
[pen.] Jack Armstrong; [b.] August 31, 1967, Detroit; [p.] Marion E. and Dolores L. Armstrong; [ed.] Graduated Belleville High School 1986, attending Wayne County Community College, student and poet; [occ.] I currently drive a truck for a living, I also sell Mason's Shoes, I am currently writing a novel. [pers.] "I Love poetry, finding it enjoyable relaxing". [a.] Belleville, MI.

ARNEJO, LINDA
[pen.] Linda Lu; [b.] April 12, 1956, San Francisco; [p.] Pauline and Sergio Arnejo; [ch.] 2 daughters, single parent; [ed.] Memorial High, Ohlone College; [occ.] Customer Service Rep., S.W.S. of Northern California; [pers.] It is with conviction that I write to stir awareness in people to help all and harm none. [a.] Newark, CA.

ARNOLD, NATALIE R.
[pen.] Nat; [b.] February 17, 1976, Dayton, OH; [p.] Mr. and Mrs. Willie L. Arnold; [ed.] Presicous Blood School, Chaminode Julienne High School, senior class of 1994; [occ.] Library Aide; [memb.] Delteen, Explorers Aerospace Engineering Program, Mayor's Youth Council, Guild Girls; [oth. writ.] Published in Tabernacle Baptist Church paper; [pers.] I believe that God gives us special talents and you'll never know what they are until you try. [a.] Dayton, OH.

AROCHO, MARTHA
[pen.] Martha Rivera; [b.] September 16,1960, Bayshore, LI; [p.] (Foster) James and Helen Lebron; [ch.] Richard, Orlando and Joseph Arocho; [ed.] Sonderling High, Suffolk Community College; [occ.] Student (adult), single parent; [hon.] Working on Associate Degree in Accounting; [oth. writ.] Christmas Memories, Friendship; [pers.] To my parents, James and Helen Lebron, who's love made me strong. My love for them exceeds any love in existence, to my 3 sons who are my reason for living. [a.] Bellport, NY.

ARONSON, REBECCA
[b.] October 17, 1941, Lima, OH; [p.] Walter Gilbert Everett and Marian Marciel Evans; [m.] Douglas Ira Battenberg, May 19, 1979; [ed.] Bowling Green State University, History major (incomplete); [occ.] Semi-retired, designer; [memb.] An COMUNN UISGE BEATHA (The Whiskey Society), position, An Taoiseach (the leader); [hon.] Who's Who of American Women 1989-present; [oth. writ.] I am currently at work on a series of children's stories based on my experience with wild creatures interactions with myself and my three Burmese Cats; [pers.] I believe that poetry is the voice of the soul, by passing the logical mind to express universal experiences in pictures painted with words and emotions. [a.] Shepherdstown, WV.

ARREOLA, SARA
[pen.] Michele Lee Millard; [b.] December 24, 1977, Klamath, OR; [p.] Donna Preece and Michael Millard; [ed.] John Adams Middle School, now attending Santa Moncia High School as a sophomore; [memb.] Varsity softball at Santa Monica High School; [pers.] I write poetry to free my mind and express myself. [a.] Santa Monica, CA.

ARTISHON, KATHERINE J.
[b.] April 27, Ironwood, MI; [p.] Anton I. (deceased) and Katherine D. Raykovich; [m.] Divorced; [ch.] Katherine Grace (7 years), Eli Anthony George (5 years) and

Victoria Ann (17 months); [ed.] Luther L. Wright High School, Gogebic Community College, Ironwood, MI., Northern Michigan University, Marquette, MI., Hennpin Technical College, Eden Prairie, MN.; [occ.] Being a mom, previous, elementary classroom Educator, Nurse's Aide, State of Minnesota Employee as typesetter, Desk Top Publishing, Acting Editor of Minnesota State Register and clerk/typist; [memb.] City Parents United, Croatian Fraternal Union of America, Women, Work and Welfare, Abundant Life Christian Church of Minneapolis; [oth. writ.] Wrote the play my class performed in 8th grade; [pers.] There is beauty in life, look for the beauty in people as well as the earth. Reach out to help another. All persons walk this world on a journey to another. Where is your next world, and what are you doing to get there? Also, children are more precious than money, love them. Jesus is my greatest influence. [a.] Minneapolis, MN.

ARZEMANIAN, GORGIN
[b.] August 23, 1960, Malham, Iran; [p.] Zaven and Ishkhanouhi Arzemanian; [m.] Elizabeth Grigorian, February 14, 1985; [ed.] Kooshesh High, attending Glendale Community College; [occ.] Electrician; [oth. writ.] "Empurpled" 1980, poetry (American), "At The Intersections" 1984, poetry (American), "Blue Pearl", 1987, collection of poetry (translation Persian), "Ship on The Mountain", fiction (translation Persian); [pers.] I like man and nature, harmony and contrast, evolution and transfiguration of existing phenomenon turning into words behind an untouchable curtain. I also like the fire which burns all these and the Phoenix of poetry. [a.] Glendale, CA.

ASAZUMA, RAE
[b.] September 15, 1982, Tokyo, Japan; [p.] Takashi and Atsuko Asazuma; [ed.] 5th grade, Kinto Grammar School, Nakamura English School, Koriyama, Japan; [occ.] Student; [memb.] Chairperson, Kinto School Committee, contest, National Flute, contest 1992, Tokyo, Japan, special prize; [hon.] Contest, 1990 National Childrens' Painting winner, Tokyo, Japan, winner of the 1990 National (FCT) Television Painting contest, winner of the Koriyama, Japanese Brush Writing contest, Silver Medal 1990, Gold Medal 1991; [oth. writ.] Fukushima Prefecture, poetry prize 1992, Fukushima Prefecture, English Speaking contest, special prize 1993, 1992 Fukushima Prefecture Book Critics Award, Fukushima Prefecture 120th Anniversary composition contest 1993; [per.] I would like to write poetry and play the flute, so that when I become a doctor like my father, I can make my patients feel good. [a.] Moriches, NY.

ASLAN, MUZAFFER
[pen.] Muzaffer Aslan; [b.] February 28, 1923, Civril, Turkey; [p.] Ali Galip and Huriye Ince Aslan; [m.] Rose M. Aslan, November 14, 1953; [ch.] Aliskender (Alex) and Alp Aslan; [ed.] Istanbul University Medical School, Internal Medicine Residency in the Hospitals at New York and Oakland, CA; [occ.] Physician (M.D.), Specialist of Internal Med.; [memb.] American College of Physicians, American Medical Association, California Medical Association; [hon.] 1947 Honor graduate of Istanbul University Medical School, founder member of Lancaster Community Hospital, Lancaster, CA; [oth. writ.] Clinical Research articles in Western Journal of Medicine, Journal of Angiology and writings in other subjects; [pers.] Everybody is my friend until proven otherwise. Everyone of us is ignorant in some field of knowledge, more knowledge of nature we gather, closer we come to belief of a Creator. [a.] Los Angeles, CA.

ASWANI, SHAKU
[b.] November 9, 1964, La-Linea, Spain; [p.] Mr. and Mrs. C.A. Aswani; [ed.] 4 O levels, English Lit, English Language, Spanish Lit., Spanish Language; [occ.] Managing Director, import, export, wholesale; [memb.] Baha'i Faith, Women's Institute; [hon.] Credits in beauty therapy, credits in drama, plan acting, promotion as grade 4 in social work; [oth. writ.] Publication of poem in Gibraltar Chronicle, publication of poem in Baha'I Journal, play, duration 1 hour for drama group in Northern Ireland; [pers.] I was born in Spain but was brought up in Gibraltar. I have traveled all over the world, I speak many languages, my view is entirely that mankind is one therefore the world should be one united in peace. [a.] London-U-Kingdom, UK

ATKINSON, ALEXANDER
[pen.] Alex; [b.] September 8, 1925, Canada; [p.] Deceased; [m.] Ruth Atkinson, April 12, 1967; [occ.] Semi-retired; [oth. writ.] Over the years poetry; [pers.] Love creation in all its forms, especially fond of cats. I have seven of these wonderful creatures. Honor the God who made them. [a.] Vernon BC, Canada.

ATKINSON, JEAN
[pen.] Eileen Atkinson; [b.] July 4, 1940, Nottingham; [p.] Leslie and Daisy Carter; [m.] Brian Atkinson, March 13, 1981; [ch.] Lorraine and Liz; [ed.] Sycamore School for Girls, Nottingham; [occ.] Retired; [oth. writ.] More poems, children's stories and others; [pers.] I have been on local radio reading some of my poems in 1979, I write for enjoyment, if I get any published its an added bonus. [a.] Darwen, Lancs.

ATKINSON, REES WARREN
[b.] March 3, 1973, UK; [p.] Gordon Atkinson and Carol Hackett; [ed.] Woodkirk High School; [occ.] Caravan fitter; [oth. writ.] A handful of unpublished poems and short stories; [pers.] Sickness and sadness come to us all, do not regard these as a disorder, use them for the gift they are and the reward shall cushion you fall. [a.] Leeds, UK.

AUCOIN, KENNETH W.
[b.] March 16, 1946, Morgan City, LA; [p.] Eugene and Enola V. Aucoin; [ch.] Angela, Damian and Tiffany; [occ.] Retired, pursing a degree in Journalism; [oth. writ.] Some poetry published locally with a children's book and a novel in progress; [pers.] Remember yesterdays, live today and believe in tomorrow. [a.] Dry Prong, LA.

AUTHORLEE, ESSIE
[b.] November 27, 1945, Camden, AR; [p.] Otis and Octavia Sams; [ed.] BA University of Arkansas at Pine Bluff, MA University of Missouri at Kansas City; [occ.] English teacher, Westport Business Tech/Communication Magnet High School, Kansas City, MO; [memb.] Phi Delta Kappa, Association of College and University Women, Zion Grove Baptist Church, Thousand Dollar Club and Concerned Citizens Committee; [hon.] Teacher in Excellence Certificate 1989; [pers.] In my writing, I try to create images that touch the soul and emotions, love, grief, joy, pain and inspire the reader to reflect and react. [a.] Grandview, MO.

AVERHART, RUSSELL STARBUCK
[b.] January 13, 1948, Ecorse, MI; [p.] Annie and Henry Averhart; [ed.] Graduate from high school; [occ.] Working on a book of poems, Expressions and Confession From The Bright and Dark Side of A Full Moon; [memb.] Poetry Without Eyes; [hon.] For South Sea Girl; [oth. writ.] The Sea, The Clown, Love and Death, The Clown, Rainbow Love, South Sea Girl, Winter Love; [pers.] My poems speak for me and others. I wanted to write a poem about the sea that would be better than Johne Masefield (being her friend) and I did, I wanted to write a poem better than the greatest Allen Poe and I did with (The Beast Hate When It Awakes).

AVERSANO, MARY A.
[b.] April 29, 1943, Buffalo; [p.] A.P. Aversano; [m.] Joel L. Solomon, February 25, 1992; [ch.] Jeffrey and Meggin; [ed.] Mt. St. Joseph Academy Faith College; [occ.] Freelance writer; [memb.] Himalayan Institute, National Scleroderma Foundation, Hemluck Society; [hon.] Magna Cum Laude, Dean's List; [oth. writ.] Poems published in psychology newsletter and in Diocesan newspaper; [pers.] I long to express what most of us feel. to elicit an emotional response in the reader. [a.] Kenmore, NY.

AWALT, VICKI LEE
[b.] August 12, 1948, Crane, TX; [p.] Selman Cooke and Lee Armstrong; [m.] Robert G. Awalt, March 6, 1982; [ch.] Daniel and Brian Friend; [ed.] Kingman High, student Phoenix College; [occ.] Paralegal; [hon.] Phi Theta Kappa, Dean's List; [pers.] The only things we can take with us when we leave this world is the kindnesses we do and the wisdom we have gained. [a.] Phoenix, AZ.

AYERS, AMY
[b.] November 18, 1974, Honolulu, HI; [p.] Ford and Sandra Ayers; [ed.] 1993 graduate Massillon Christian School, freshman, Wayne College, Orrville, OH; [occ.] Student; [memb.] Dalton Baptist Church; [hon.] Who's Who In American High School, 1991-92, 1992-93. [a.] Dalton, OH.

AYOUB, DAVID N.
[b.] October 17, 1967, Silver Springs, MD; [p.] Naim and Judy Ayoub; [ed.] Graduated Springbrook High School; [occ.] Telecom Assistant for Choice Hotels Headquarters; [hon.] Honorably discharged United States Marine Corps in August of 1990; [oth. writ.] A variety of works unpublished as of yet. [pers.] I write what I feel, I feel what I write. [a.] Kensington, MD.

BABB, NAOMI M.
[b.] March 29, 1961, Billings, Mt; [p.] Bruce Gottlieb Kraft and Frances Carol Kraft; [m.] James D. Babb, January 27, 1990; [ch.] Step-children, James L. and Adam T. Babb; [ed.] Central Acres, SDA Elementary School, Mount Ellis Academy, Eastern Montana College; [occ.] General merchandiser; [oth. writ.] Many, none published; [pers.] The day to day things that people do and we sometimes fail to see are the very things that touch my life and inspire me to write. People are the questions and the answers for me. [a.] Nampa, ID.

BABIARZ, JOHN ADAM
[b.] February 24, 1969, Cocoa Beach, Fl; [p.] Vicki and Frank Babiarz; [ch.] Mike Allen Babiarz; [memb.] Suncoast Optimist Foundation, Optimist Club and director at the Jeff Thompson Youth Center; [oth. writ.] Poetry, short stories, various songs and a novel; [pers.] Greetings to all! In I presence I from coverage of I heights. Love for everyone everywhere. It is known that the co-operation of all colors of people voice the decision of I heights. Free everyone and liberate fully everywhere, one love. [a.] Sarasota, FL.

BABIDGE, ADAM
[pen.] Stix, Adam Corish; [b.] June 12, 1964, Australia;

[ed.] Daws Road High, O'Halloran Hill TAFE (Technical and Futher Education); [occ.] Self employed; [oth. writ.] Some minor publications, several unpublished poems and stories. My greatest writing strength is in getting the message across; [pers.] I believe the conscious individual is the highest value in the universe. My poetry is written to express my deepest emotions to the one I love. I think Edgar Allen Poe's "The Raven" is the greatest poem ever written. [a.] McLaren Vale, South Australia.

BABLER, AMANDA
[b.] November 8, 1982; [p.] Brent and Linda Babler; [ed.] Holy Rosary Grade School; [hon.] This poem won first place in Catholic Daughters of America at Holy Rosary Church, Darlington,. WI; [pers.] I wrote this poem after my grandmother died. She is truly missed by me. [a.] Mineral Point, WI.

BADER, MARY E.
[pen.] Beth Bader; [b.] July 25, 1954, Waukegan, IL; [m.] Michael Bader, February 16, 1974; [ch.] Jason Michael; [ed.] Warren High; [oth. writ.] First time being published; [pers.] My poems are one of the few ways I am able to express the feelings suppressed in childhood. A childhood full of abuse. Since I started to write I have healed a great deal. I still have a long way to go, but I'm hoping someone will read my poems and heal even a little, then the pain wouldn't have been for nothing. [a.] Waukegan, IL.

BAER, JAMES S.
[m.] Donna L. Baer; [ch.] James Michael, Celestine Elizabeth, Janelle Marie; [ed.] Crystal Lake Central, Northern Illinois University, B.S., M.S., C.A.S.; [occ.] Teacher; [oth. writ.] Two articles published in Musings and Marmalade, Northern Illinois University; [pers.] The pauper hunts 4 leaf clovers and skips stones, and he listens to the king and all his moans, but he's a pauper, that's all he wants to be. Skipping stones, looking to the stars, trying to be free. [a.] Crystal Lake, IL.

BAFF, RANDI
[b.] August 31, 1977, Queens, NY; [ed.] Townsend Harris High School at Queens College; [occ.] High school student; [memb.] Arista (National Honor Society), Archon (Service Society), Junior Sciences; [hon.] St. John's University Women in Chemistry Award, New York Times Scholastic Art and Writing Award, April 93 Silver Medal, Maxima Cum Laude for outstanding performance in National Latine exam; [oth. writ.] Personal collection of feelings and thoughts; [pers.] My little book of poetry is my best friend. Losing this book of poetry would be losing myself, it reflects the pain of nostalgia and optimism for the future. [a.] New York, NY.

BAGFFES, THOMAS G.
[b.] April 3, 1923, New Orleans LA; [p.] Gus and Tina; [m.] Mary Lou, February 23, 1958; [ch.] Chrisline, Kathy, Paul and Andrew; [ed.] Tulane School of Medicine, DePaul School of Law; [occ.] Thoracic and Pediatric Surgeon; [memb.] AMA, ABA, ATLA, College of Surgeons, College of Cardiology and others; [hon.] Phi Beta Kappa, Alpha Omega Alpha, T.O.Y.M. (US Chamber of Commerce), listed in Who's Who; [oth. writ.] 55 poems, 12 short stories, 2 books, 130 medical articles, 20 legal articles; [pers.] What I am I owe to the opportunities of being a U.S. citizen; [a.] Chicago, IL.

BAILEY, BRANDI-MARIE
[b.] April 24, 1977, Windsor, Ontario; [p.] Kathleen Roberts; [ed.] Chatham Kent Secondary School, Level 4; [hon.] Physical Education Awards in both Level 1-2; [oth. writ.] I have non-published book of poems, entitled A Book of Poems Reflecting Life Itself; [pers.] Be what you can be, start fresh and work to the top. My poems are influenced by mine and other peoples experiences. I wrote this to poem for my mother to teach us both that fighting isn't the answer. [a.] Chatham, Ontario Canada.

BAILEY, CHAUNCEY A.
[pen.] C. Alston Bailey, III; [b.] April 9, 1954, McKeesport, PA; [p.] Chauncey and Doris Bailey; [ch.] Rachelle, Chauncey, Christian, and two other very special children, Lexie and Matt; [ed.] 1972 McKeesport High School, currently student at Western School of Health, Pittsburgh, PA; [occ.] Retail Assistant Manager; [memb.] McKeesport Optimist Club; [oth. writ.] Several poems written through spiritual inspiration, non-published; [pers.] Poetry, a glorious way to put your heart to words, and to have the freedom to openly express ones love, I dedicated this to the one who inspired me to look forward and upward. Thanks. [a.] McKeesport, PA.

BAILEY, JOVE
[b.] December 27; [p.] Alice and Francis Irving; [m.] Fiance, Justin Beaver; [ed.] Home schooling; [occ.] Writer, dancer and singer; [oth. writ.] Many unpublished poems and stories; [pers.] My writings usually reflect my sensuality. I consider myself a romantic poet, I have been greatly influenced by Shakespears tragic writings. [a.] Rapid City, SD.

BAILEY, WENDY LINNEEN
[pen.] Wendy Bailey; [b.] August 22, 1970, Michigan; [p.] Franklin and Earnesteen Bailey; [ed.] Presentation Our Lady of Victory Middle School (past), St. Martin De Porres High School (present) grade 9; [hon.] I was once awarded a $300.00 college scholarship from the Trinidad and Tobago Association. [a.] Detroit, MI.

BAILEY, YUKIKO M.
[b.] August 5, 1973, Australia; [p.] Kenneth and Aiko Bailey; [ed.] Graduated senior high school (college) 1992, now studying for bachelor degree (Graphic Design), University of Canberra, Australia; [occ.] University student (undergrade); [memb.] University Union; [hon.] None (I have however, achieved several high distinctions and distinctions in design studies and photography at university); [oth. writ.] Several poems and essays for own pleasure; [pers.] I love to immerse myself in all forms of artistic creation including painting, sketching, design, photography, poetry and writing. [a.] Canberra, Australia.

BAKER, ETHEL
[pers.] I was born in Avonmore, PA. on December 17, 1934 to George and Mazie Shannon, we were a family of nine children. I have been married to my first and only husband for 38 years. We have two grown children, both married, 4 grandchildren. I wrote the poem you will read in this book in 1969, the same year I wrote most of my heartfelt poems, just shortly after my father died at age 53, we were buddies. I was overflowing with emotions, grief, love, appreciation of Gods love for us, love for our fellowman, nature, the beauty of our earth, the freedom of our country, etc. I'm 59 years old and I may or may not write again, but I'm glad so many people have enjoyed reading what I have written to this point. My humble thanks for publishing my poem "The Beauty of Autumn". [a.] Saltsbury, PA.

BAKER JR., IRVING A.
[b.] February 22, 1951, New York City; [p.] Irving A. Baker Sr. and Dr. Margaret Baker Green; [m.] Single; [ch.] Tamara Hall; [ed.] A.A.S. and B.F.A. Rochester Institute of Technology and graduate courses at University of Southern California in Los Angeles and Fordham University, Columbia University (masters level courses in film/creative writing; [occ.] Teacher of reading, writing and counsellor; [hon.] M.V.P. (Most Valuable Player) basketball star and coach; [oth. writ.] Film research and film thesis; [pers.] I am committed to the importance of human interaction either on a one to one basis or with inter and intra group relations. I believe that the focus of strength for the positive development of personal relationships, group relations, cultural relativity and the entire process of socialization is kept alive, open and viable through oral and written communication. I am particularly motivated toward any commitment that involves any form of social research, independent study, teaching, field work or community action.

BAKER, Jo-ELLEN
[pen.] Jo; [b.] December 1, 1976, Onaway, MI; [p.] Jeanette Kidder and Douglas Baker Sr.; [ed.] Atlanta Adult and Community Education; [occ.] Student, kitchen help at a restaurant; [pers.] I strive to reflect the loving and caring to mankind, as I found in other poems. We need a lot more loving and caring in this world. [a.] Atlanta, MI.

BAKER, JUDITH A.
[b.] March 2, 1947, Ft. Riley, KS; [p.] Mildred and David Bates; [m.] Jimmy R. Baker Sr., October 8, 1974; [ch.] Jimmy R. Baker Jr.; [ed.] Biloxi High, Draughon Business College, East Central University; [occ.] Nontraditional student at East Central University; [memb.] C.H.U.M.S. Multiple Sclerosis Society; [oth. writ.] Essay published in East Central's "Write On" and poetry published in East Central's Literary anthology, "Originals"; [pers.] Some people write about darkness, I write about lightness. When others write negatively, I write more positively. When some write about defeat, I write about victory, that's what makes me an original, instead of a copy. [a.] Francis, OK.

BAKER, KAY
[b.] September 11, 1961, Marshfield, England; [p.] William and June Savage; [occ.] Mother and housewife; [oth. writ.] I have written and am writing many other poems for personal pleasure, none have been published until now. [a.] Bath Avon, England.

BAKER, ROBERT M.
[b.] January 6, 1966, Florida; [p.] Ronald and Joan Baker; [m.] Leticia Vazquez, December 19, 1991; [ch.] Step-daughter, Jessica Ponce; [ed.] B.A. in liberal Studies from Nova University, Ft. Lauderdale, currently pursuing a masters in Liberal Studies, briefly attended Cambridge University England; [occ.] Musician and teacher; [oth. writ.] Various published and unpublished works of music history and theory, poetry and prose, short fiction as well as a number of writings on art and literature. [a.] Ft. Lauderdale, FL.

BALL, SEYNA
[b.] October 29, 1958, Istanbul, Turkey; [p.] Resban and Perihan Emirhan; [m.] John Martin Ball, September 30, 1985; [ed.] Bilir College, Istanbul, Turkey, Turkish Literature, English Art History and Secretarial College;

[occ.] Sales consultant; [oth. writ.] Several other poems, childhood memoirs and writing a story about a man escaping from the Russian Revolution after losing his family and moving to another country, partly fiction, during 1917 and onwards; [pers.] My poetry reveals of a spiritual and the awareness of a world which to me is the only way to freedom and looses itself to selflessness in a kind of floating sensation which dismisses religion but believes in good. [a.] London, UK Great Britain.

BALMAIN, THERAN L.
[b.] December 28, 1941, Detroit, MI; [p.] Walter and Laural Lane; [m.] Doug Balmain, October 9, 1981; [ed.] Associate of Arts Degree as well as training to receive the following flight ratings, private pilot, instrument pilot, commercial pilot, flight instructor, multi-engine pilot, instrument flight instructor, multi-engine flight instructor; [occ.] Flight instructor and Secretary Treasurer of D.M. Balmain, Inc.; [memb.] Member, Coulterville United Methodist Church, member, United Methodist Women, member, Coulterville Community Club, member, Greeley Hill Community Club, life member, Northern Mariposa County History Center, member, Northside Ambulance Association; [hon.] Phy Beta Kappa, Dean's List, Valentine Queen, Blossom Festival Princess; [oth. writ.] Have written dozens of poems over the years, wrote a monthly column for a flying magazine called "Windward Wanderings"; [pers.] My poems seem to write themselves when I am feeling emotions such as joy, love, appreciation and thanksgiving. [a.] Coulterville, CA.

BALTES, ANGELA A.
[pen.] Ashton Perry, Jassamina Blackwell; [b.] June 29, Fort Wayne, IN; [p.] Joseph and Carol Baltes; [ed.] Purdue University; [hon.] Poetry awards; [oth. writ.] My Piece of The World's Chocolate Cake, collected poems; [pers.] Writing is the best way to leave your mark on the world. [a.] Fort Wayne, IN.

BANERJEE, PRODIPTO
[b.] October 1, 1950, India; [p.] Satyabrata and Nilima Banerjee; [ed.] B.A. in English honors, chartered accountant or C.A.; [occ.] Freelance writer; [hon.] Prizes in English and Accounts in college (from St. Xavires College in Calcutta); [oth. writ.] I write poems and short stories now; [pers.] Poetry of all sorts greatly influenced by early romantic poets and writers. [a.] E. Northport, NJ.

BANERJEE, SUPRIYA
[b.] November 30, 1971, Indore, India; [p.] Elora and Prabir Banerjee; [ed.] Completed Bachelor of Arts degree with History, Political Science, English and Hindi Literature, Nagpur University; [occ.] Studying masters degree in English Literature; [memb.] Student member of Social, Cultural, Elocution and Dramatics Clubs in University; [hon.] Passed 1st year of Indian Music with distinction; [oth. writ.] Poems published in school and college magazines, interview and views published in local newspaper, so far written more that 100 poems; [pers.] My poems reflect my optimism and love for life. I feel that life provides tremendous opportunities for contribution and fulfillment. I try my best to spread love and optimism through my poems and work. [a.] Nagpur, India.

BANKS, NANNETTE
[b.] January 27, 1970, Chicago, IL; [p.] Robbie Banks; [ed.] Aurora University graduate 1992, B.A. Psychology; [occ.] Youth Drug Abuse Prevention Program co-

ordinator; [memb.] Delta Sigma Theta Sorority Inc., Order of the Eastern Star, Progressive Community Church the People's Church; [hon.] Aurora University, freshman of the year (88-89), Community Service Award (89-90, Outstanding Senior Woman (91-92); [pers.] All things are possible if one believes in self. [a.] Chicago, IL.

BANNER, LORENE
[b.] September 28, 1916, Akron, OH; [p.] William and Marie Van Pelt; [m.] Divorced; [ch.] Beverly Koger, Bonita Hill, Cheryl Miller; [ed.] East High School, Hamilton Business College, Comptometor School; [occ.] Retired; [hon.] Golden Poet Award; [oth. writ.] Poems published in local newspaper, Editor of Mova Newsletter, poem published in ARA Newsletter at B.F. Goodrich Co. in Akron, OH.; [pers.] Poem written in the 50's and given as framed gifts to them in the seventies. It expressed my emotions for them. All my poems are about people. [a.] Beaufort, SC.

BARBER, TIFFANY
[ed.] St. Margaret Mary School; [memb.] Harrisburg Gymnastics School and Art Association of Harrisburg; [hon.] Harrisburg Diocese, Houghton Miffin Spelling Bee, St. Margaret Mary Art Festival, 1st place; [oth. writ.] Personal poems. [a.] Harrisburg, PA.

BARBOSA, ALEJANDRA
[pen.] Alex; [b.] May 3, 1967, Guadalajara, Mexico; [p.] Marina and Enriguw Barbosa; [ed.] Holy Family Academy, Wright College; [occ.] Manager; [memb.] Phi Theta Kappa; [hon.] Phi Theta Kappa, National Honor Society; [pers.] Through reading, I discover worlds unknown to me. I hope to one day do the same for others. [a.] Chicago, IL.

BARDEN, GEORGE
[pen.] Peo; [b.] May 15, 1897, Yorkshire, England; [p.] Samuel Barden; [m.] Alice Abbott, my s.p. Violet Grace, July 21, 1921; [ch.] George Philip and John Samuel; [ed.] Grammar school, college engineering; [occ.] Retired, Structural Engineer, A.M.I. Struct. E.; [memb.] A.M.I. Struct. E., International Society of Poets, AARP; [hon.] Outstanding track and field, San Bernardino, olympics medals, Gold, Silver, Bronze, art bronze poetry, publisher, writer one book, poetry by George; [oth. writ.] Own life story title "Alone and Battle The Storm" I'm an artist, watercolor, ceramics, bronze medal; [pers.] My age 97 years, perfectly fit, I walk 5 miles a day. I do my own cooking, etc., generally take care of myself, non-smoker, non-drinker, I do my own shopping, laundry. [a.] San Bernardino, CA.

BARKHURST, SHERRIE BAKER
[b.] December 19, 1959, AK; [p.] Ben and Shirley Baker; [m.] James Barkhurst, February 26, 1983; [ch.] Meredith; [ed.] Shelby High, Lake Land Community College, currently studying at St. Louis Community College for Computer/video imagery; [occ.] Freelance writer and Customs Art Designer; [memb.] St. Louis Kaleidoscope Drama team, Audio/visual Designers for Concord Baptist Church, Administrator of Prodigy Violin Concerts, organizer of Ladies Teas of Seasons, member, Concord Baptist Church; [hon.] Scholastic Writing Award (1st place), numerous Blue Ribbons in art competitions, guest speaker to American Dental Association National meetings, named Miss Congeniality Macoupin County beauty contest; [oth. writ.] Published in local papers and several unpublished children's books;

[pers.] 2 keys to success, having a compassion for others combined with a positive outlook, determination and continuously striving for self improvement. Luke 19:10. [a.] St. Louis, MO.

BARNES, MARY
[b.] January 5, 1923, Norfolk, VA; [p.] Josephine and Robert Fleming; [m.] C. Winston Barnes, June 3, 1944; [ch.] Lee (48), Donna (46), Cathy (44), Cheryl (35), 7 grandchildren, expecting a great grandchild soon; [ed.] 1941 high school graduate, night school shorthand-1979, writing course C.N.U-1992; [occ.] Retired; [memb.] 1st United Methodist Church Woman's Club of Hampton, Pine Cone Garden Club, (Vol) Sentara Hampton General Hospital, Sentara Aquatic Exercise class; [hon.] Received a certificate of merit when P.T.A. President, 6 Golden Poetry Awards from World of Poetry, 1st place roller skating, Skatathon -1982, many blue ribbons for crafts, high school honor graduate; [oth. writ.] Jamaican Holiday (poem), Summer Fantasy (short story), many short stories in writing class at C.N.U., letters to Editor (published); [pers.] I love big band music and dance with my husband at the beach every summer. Like to play cards especially Bridge. [a.] Hampton, VA.

BARNETT, JENNIFER
[b.] August 13, 1980, Ann Arbor, MI; [p.] Gordon and Carol Barnett; [ed.] 8th grade education at Ashley Clague Middle School, Ann Arbor, MI; [occ.] Student; [memb.] Girl Scouts of America, troop 550, University of Michigan Gilbert and Sullivan Society, United Methodist Youth Fellowship; [oth. writ.] None published yet, many other poems; [pers.] Poetry is an art, it's a shame so few see it that way. [a.] Ann Arbor, MI.

BARNETTE, BRIAN KEITH
[pen.] Reality; [b.] September 14, 1976, Richmond, VA; [p.] Terry Lee and Nora Barnette; [ed.] 12th grade high school, not yet a graduate, graduate in June 1994; [occ.] Part-time carpenter, grass cutter, yard cleaning business and student; [memb.] Friendship United Methodist Church, Spanish Club, (secretary); [hon.] 1st place Young Authors in the school, 1st place Young Authors in the county, 1st place Young Authors in Regional, all in one year and all about poetry; [oth. writ.] Short stories for Young Authors, Index To The Imagination (for Young Authors, see honors and awards) Total Domination (novel in the process of writing); [pers.] "It is not I who writes these poems, my child, but the darkness that flows through my being", that is the true author". [a.] Chase City, VA.

BARON, ISRAEL
[b.] April 17, Boston, MA; [p.] Harry A. and Dora Breger; [p.] Phyllis M. Baron (Gilbert), May 23, 1942; [ch.] Myrna Ann and Donald P. Baron; [ed.] Lexington Ma High School, AAF Tech train Command, intensive self education, conducted experimental development receiving tubes-Raytheon, also dialectics; [occ.] Retired; [hon.] Advisory Board for Technical High School, Graphic Arts; [oth. writ.] Anthology entry in Florida Poets Annual, 1993, only two years of writing; [pers.] Awaken each morning with enthusiasm to accept the acceptable and to overcome the non-acceptable, keeping my heart filled with song and love and life. [a.] Lantana, FL.

BAROTA, NATALIE
[b.] November 8, 1979, Burlington, NJ; [p.] Thomas and Lynn Barota; [ed.] Western High School, 9th grade, Parma, MI; [occ.] School student; [memb.] Cadet Choir; [hon.] Honor Roll student. [a.] Jackson, MI.

BARRA, MARI ATTILIA B.
[b.] Avellino, Italy; [p.] Attilio and Concetta Barra; [ed.] Columbia Translation, foreign languages, Spanish, French, Italian, Portuguese, (light German), Juliard School of Music, courses in composition, I am a virtually a self started in music, lyrics and became a lettered by reading a lot; [occ.] Bilingual Secretary, FOP Rifinzi and Sons Inc., Importer of Fine Quality Foods; [oth.writ.] In my lyrics, my chief aim is to give a happy message, a message of hope, messages towards the good and on a huge concourse for all kind of people (possible publication in 1994); [pers.] Knowledge inspires us to fight the impossibilities in life, to hope and raise our inner thoughts to a superior being, like a God. Civilization is with knowledge, with the just, with the good, with the truth, with the light in us and the light in us, is a God. When society becomes anti-culture, anti-God, anti-moral, Caso steps in and the result is disorder. The world was created in a perfect order, when we disrupt this order, it will strike back at us and we fall into the Caso that we have at the present time. With time, we loose our beauty, our youth, and the only thing that will remain with us always to the end is, knowledge. However, knowledge without a God and without the good is not beautiful, knowledge with the good and a God is beautiful. [a.] Merrick, NY.

BARRASS-STUART, CAROLYN J.
[pers.] 40 something years of age, divorced, mother of three, Angela, mid-twenties, Michael, early twenties and Beth age 19. In the past 20 plus years, I have lived from Halifax to Vancouver, and returned to find my home in Toronto once again. Higher education received at McMaster University in Hamilton, Ontario, 1971-1973. Worked for many years in the corporate field reaching the upper middle management status before taking early retirement to stay home and work on several projects... two novels in the works at this time, in addition to which, I plan to collect some of my poetry and verse, penned down through the years, and have them published as well. All my publications are going to be submitted under the pseudonym "Constance Stuart MacMillan". Volunteered in widely diverse areas of particular interest through the years, including and largely in, the Big Sister's organization, providing my shoulder for many to lean on over the past 25 + years. I would most like to be remember as a person of great humanity.... a person who saw the needs of others... and addressed those needs, as were possible, as though they were her own. One must always be ready and amenable to the possibilities of change. for it is the possibilities for change that keeps us going in our worst times, in our set-backs. It is not change itself which is bad, but sometimes the transitions can be very painful. Despite how much control we would like to have over life, it is true that change does not come in the form you might wish. As well, change never happens at a convenient time, it is usually when you are busiest doing something else. Change is inevitable and one must learn to roll with the waves, rather than put up any sort of active resistance and be buffeted about the high seas. So maintain your high moral standards and allow no-one to insist that you compromise even the least of them.

BARRETTO, LINDA MORALES
[b.] December 14, 1973, New York City; [p.] Linda and Robert Kret; [ed.] Washington Irving High School; [occ.] Unemployed due to deep recession; [hon.] N.Y.C.P.D. Award 1990, (Christmas season) for dedication of volunteer work for wrapping and arranging over 2,000 gifts for underprivileged children; [oth. writ.] Poetry that I wrote in the past that was never published;

[pers.]"Sometimes I feel that I wished to be like everyone else, however, I did not grow up to be like others yet to know I might one day rise up from the ashes. [a.] New York, NY.

BARROW, TRISH
[b.] August 9,1978, Nashville, IL; [p.] Patricia J. Barrow; [ed.] Freshman in high school; [oth. writ.] Children's poem published; [pers.] Everything deserves at least one chance. [a.] Bullard, TX.

BARRY, ELIZABETH
[pen.] Elizabeth McLean Barry; [b.] March 10, 1968, Santa Cruz, CA; [p.] Don McLean and Christine Leonard; [m.] Keith J. Barry, December 19, 1987; [ch.] Lauran Annabeth 4 1/2 and Bethany Elizabeth 2; [ed.] Upstate New York High School, San Antonio College; [occ.] Soon to be published poet, homemaker; [memb.] Gideons International, Mayflower Society, Officers Christian Fellowship; [pers.] When we strive to understand people's hearts, then we can strive to help those who really need. [a.] San Antonio, TX.

BARTOLETTI, MARIO D.
[b.] June 21, 1933, Los Angeles, CA; [p.] Prof. Alfio and Rosa Bartoletti; [m.] Lili R. Bartoletti, February 25, 1956; [ch.] Carla Perez, Anne Bartoletti and Allison Fulton; [ed.] A.A. Blackburn College, B.A. University of Connecticut, M.A. University of Connecticut, Ed. D. University of Toronto; [occ.] Mediator Management Consultant; [memb.] Academy of Family Mediators, Ontario Association of Family Mediation, American Mediation Association; [hon.] Professional Leadership Citation, Blackburn College diplomate, Forum of Family Mediation American Medication Association; [oth. writ.] COurtship (book), Family Mediation Handbook; [pers.] Becoming a man has filled my life with challenge and satisfaction. I am still in the act of becoming. [a.] Port Richey, FL.

BARTH, LINDA FALZONE
[b.] May 21, 1959, Washington, DC; [p.] Michael A. and Mary Greenlee Falzone; [m.] Karl Friedrich Barth, August 12, 1978; [ch.] Maria Elena and Stella Angela Barth; [ed.] Marymount, Sacred Heart, Southbridge High; [hon.] French Language certificate, Who's Who Among American High School Students; [pers.] I wrote this poem for "Mimi" my late grandmother, Helen Brogan Greenlee, she was a woman I will always treasure in my heart. [a.] Stoneham, MA.

BATEMAN, PAUL J.
[b.] December 6, 1944, Christchurch, England; [p.] Maurice and Patricia Bateman; [m.] Phyllis Neill, September 20, 1969; [ch.] Jennifer Erin Bateman; [ed.] Central Huron Sec. School, University of Toronto, University of Saskatchewan; [occ.] Teaching Professor, Haileybury School of Mines; [memb.] Geol. Association of Canada, Prof. Engineers of Ontario, Geol. Society of America, Can. Institute of Mining and Metallurgy (CIM), Overtones (church men's choir); [hon.] CIM National student, essay winner in 1968 for Geology Thesis; [oth. writ.] Several locally published articles and contributor to several newsletters; [pers.] Love to travel and have visited 6 out of 7 continents so far, some success as watercolor artist. [a.] Haileybury, Ontario Canada.

BATES, DAWN H.
[b.] May 25, 1967, New Orleans, LA; [p.] Joy Bates and Jason West; [m.] Mikkel McGhee; [ch.] Ember (age 5) and Jason McGhee (age 3); [ed.] High school, GED, 1

year Community College at Chemeketa; [occ.] Mother of two children and environmentalist, I like to write and do art work; [oth. writ.] I have written some short stories, essays and other poems. I am currently finishing up a work called Tetra Tora, which is a system using mathematical and numerical verifaction to reunite by reinstilling, 3 dimensional form (Geometry) into the key Metaphysical Sciences; [pers.] Truth should be expressed as multi-dimensional as possible, that balance of mental, thinking, mind in life with heart, love, feeling, can enable one to grasp the higher sciences, that all art form is in truth an expression of. Emotion is math, as math is emotion. [a.] Portland, OR.

BATES, KELLI
[b.] November 17, 1971, Lufkin, TX; [p.] Delle and Geraldene Bates; [ed.] West Orange Stark High, Lamar University-Orange; [occ.] Marketing Assistant; [oth. writ.] One poem published in Ousting Off Dreams, (Quill Books) coming out in Spring 1994. [a.] Orange, TX.

BATTENBURG, NICHOLAS
[pen.] Nic Battenburg; [b.] December 10, 1906, Chicago, IL; [p.] Deceased; [m.] Marjorie Chase Battenburg, March 31, 1930; [ch.] Craig and William C. (both deceased), Bonnie; [ed.] Pullman School of Man. Trng., Radio Telegraphy School, Philco, Bell Lab School/War Trng., FAA School, Okcy, OK (taught theory and lab); [occ.] Living at University Village Retirement community but still active writing prose and poetry as inspiration and mood dictates; [memb.] Life member IEEE, AARP; [hon.] Life member IEEE, Instructor Laureate, FAA Academy, also cited by the USAF HQ, Washington, DC. for prototype of method for "Tie-down of parked aircraft during strong wind storms", wrote many articles for the University Village monthly newsletter-The Villager; [oth. writ.] From Out The Heart (prose and poetry), some other poems as yet unpublished, lesson plans for FAA Academy classes; [pers.] I seek ways to make a mark in life, to be a good role model and in being persistent in attaining goals. [a.] Tulsa, OK.

BATTLE, AURELIA CLEO A.
[pen.] Cleo Battle; [b.] January 30, 1956, South Carolina; [p.] Waverly and Louise Arrington; [m.] David D. Battle, September 12, 1985; [ch.] David and Taylor Battle; [ed.] Attended University of South Carolina, currently a senior at the University of West Florida; [occ.] U.S. Air Force, Technical Sergeant; [memb.] Gamma Delta Phi; [hon.] Recipient of the John Levitown Award and the Commandant's Award at Lindsey Air Station, Germany; [oth. writ.] Over two hundred unpublished poems; [pers.] To be who you are, you've got to find our first, who am I? [a.] Shalimar, FL.

BATTS, DOROTHY M. (MINISTER)
[pen.] Lois; [b.] December 22, 1942, Elm City, NC; [p.] Russell and Mattie Gear; [m.] Jesse L. Batts, Jr., October 14, 1961; [ch.] Terrence, Timothy, Tonnetta, Tabitha, Travis, (adopted, Renee and Tamatha); [ed.] Booker T. Washington High, Manpower Training at University of Hawaii, Carolina Bible College, Fayetteville Community College, Outreach for Jesus Bible Institute; [occ.] Pastor/teacher at OFJ Bible Institute, conference speaker/author; [memb.] PTA, Disabled American Vets., Outreach for Jesus Advisory Board; [hon.] Schofield Barriacks, Hawaii, outstanding service honor, Schofield Hawaii, award for work with the Chaplain, Ft. Bragg, award for service to military soldiers cert., vol. court counselor, American Red Cross, letters of appreciation for work with child and spouse abuse, homevistor; [oth.

writ.] Several poems, 15 inspirational books, seminar and conference teaching material, Bible College study guides; [pers.] We are living in a time when everyone needs to hear encouraging and inspiring words. My objective, as God allows, is to touch as many as I can throughout the United States and abroad with my writings. Every man, woman, boy and girl needs to know "THERE IS HOPE". [a.] Spring Lake, NC.

BAUDO, SALVATORE A. (83 years)
[pen.] Salvatore Baudo; [b.] September 2, 1910, New York, NY; [p.] Anthony and Vincenza Baudo; [m.] Aurora Baudo, 1946; [ch.] Diana Sarfin; [ed.] Pratt Institute, Brooklyn, NY 1933, Architectural Plan Reading; [occ.] Retired, Ceramic Tile Supt.; [memb.] V.F.W. (Veteran of Foreign Wars), active Senior Citizens Center; [hon.] Five major campaigns in World War II, American can be proud, we represent the real role models of America; [pers.] The recent passing of my wife who was the light of my life, and the joy of my soul. She was a real role model of motherhood. [a.] New York, NY.

BAUM, CARLENE F.
[b.] October 2, 1944, Boston, MA; [p.] Glenda and William Semmer; [ch.] Shamlene P. Kelly; [occ.] Owner, publisher of a weekly and monthly publication; [oth. writ.] I write a column for Homes In Paradise and The Sanibel-Captive Shoppers Guide; [pers.] To be a poet you need to surround yourself with dreamers.[a.] Sanibel Island, FL.

BAUMRUCK, KIMBERLY
[pen.] Kim; [b.] May 15, 1980, Illinois; [p.] Sandra and Scott Baumruck; [ed.] Eight grade at Park Junior High in La Grange Park, IL; [hon.] Honor Roll and Presidential Academic Fitness Award. [a.] Brookfield, IL.

BAUSSIOS, NANCY G.
[b.] November 9, 1975, Toms River, NJ; [p.] Helen and Paul Boussios; [ed.] Current high school senior enrolled in honors courses; [memb.] St. Fransic Congregation; [hon.] Student of the Day; [oth. writ.] Various narratives composed for others to enjoy; [pers.] The epitome of success is believing in one's self. Belief in one's self begets optimum performance which results in untainted happiness. Thank you mom. [a.] Barnegat, NJ.

BAXTER, GEORGE HENDERSON
[b.] December 4, 1968, Lanark, Scotland; [p.] David P. and Marion J. Baxter; [ed.] Larkhall Academy, Scotland; [occ.] Accountant, O. Carter & Coley, Chartered Accountants, Bournemouth, England; [memb.] Association of Accounting Technicians, Friends of Cobnor Activities Center Association, Royal National Lifeboat Institution, Royal Yachting Association, National Blood Transfusion Service; pers.] After discovering poetry, I now realize that life could not be whole without it. Satin Woman, I am eternally grateful. [a.] Poole Dorset, England.

BAXTER, JEAN KAY
[pen.] Carmel Wallace; [b.] February 20, 1942, Putney, London England; [p.] Joan and Sidney Whipp; [m.] Divorced; [ch.] Lee, Russell and Alan Baxter; [ed.] Putney Comprehensive for Girls; [occ.] Housewife; [oth. writ.] Children's novel, almost finished, personal poems from the heart but not submitted; [pers.] I find tranquility in my own little world when putting thoughts into words. [a.] Rochester, Kent England.

BAXTER, GEORGE HENDERSON
[b.] December 4, 1968, Lanark, Scotland; [p.] David P. and Marion J. Baxter; [ed.] Larkhall Academy, Scotland; [occ.] Accountant, O. Carter and Coley, Chartered Accountants, Bournemouth, England; [memb.] Association of Accounting Technicians, Friends of Cobnor Activities Center Association, Royal National Lifeboat Institution, Royal Yachting Association, National Blood Transfusion Service; [pers.] After discovering poetry, I now realize that life could not be whole without it. Satin Woman, I am eternally grateful. [a.] Poole, Dorset England.

BEAKES, K. DOUGLAS (DR.)
[b.] November 17, 1923, Washington, PA; [p.] Edwin A. and Elsie Beakes; [m.] Maria Beakes, October 16, 1954; [ch.] Dr. Douglas E. and Christine Beakes; [ed.] Western Maryland College, University of Paris, Besancon, France (Ph.D.); [occ.] Rector, Liberty University; [memb.] Gamma Beta Chi Fraternity, German-American Club; [hon.] US Department of Defense Air Force, Army Exceptional Service Award; [oth. writ.] "Skiing in Austria", training locations, "∶Moroccan Arabic" un. textbook, "East and West at Stalingrad" (an epic poem-600 pages); [pers.] Verse is the ultimate form of expression to characterize true life of the soul. [a.] Wiesbaden, Germany.

BEALS, J. DYLAN
[b.] September 1, 1971; [p.] Jeffery and Marlene Beals; [pers.] Poetry is the philosophy of writing. [a.] Los Angeles, CA.

BEAMISH, JACK W.
[b.] May 4, 1946, Russell; [p.] Lincoln and Alleyne Beamish; [m.] Married in 1975; [ch.] One son and daughter 8 and 11 years of age; [ed.] High school education with several years of night school while working 15 years as a Power Engineer; [occ.] Grain farmer, gravedigger and agent to sell granite monuments; [memb.] Hamiota United Church, plus several Museum Associations; [oth. writ.] I have written several articles into steam engineer magazines in the U.S., I have loved writing articles since I was in high school and would someday love to write a book on my life and also finding all my biological family; [pers.] I have always been very intrigued with the writers of soap operas and movies. I love to read new poetry to out challenge the poet's writings. I believe the terminology in poetry should be kept simple for every average person to enjoy. [a.] Hamiota, MB.

BEAN, DEVIN
[b.] May 13, 1977, Jacksonville, FL; [p.] Rose; [ed.] Hazelwood West, grade 11; [occ.] Fast Food worker at Arby's; [memb.] Member of the Youth Group of First United Methodist Church of St. Charles; [oth. writ.] Several unpublished poems and short stories; [pers.] My poems reflect my own views and personal feelings of society and what the world is coming to, I hope that my poetry can inspire others to do good and make the world a better place for us all. [a.] Hazelwood, MO.

BEARD, JENNIFER C.
[b.] January 29, 1974, Baton Rouge, LA; [p.] Raymond Beard and Charlene Gibbets; [ch.] Expecting my first child December 25, 1993; [pers.] "The biggest and most powerful influence that has directed me in my writing is the voice of my father. If it weren't for his love for writing, I really believe I would not have this gift". [a.] White Castle, LA.

BEARSS, DOROTHY M.
[m.] Deceased-Edgar; [ch.] Daniel Bearss; [ed.] Oxnard Community College; [occ.] Re-entry homemaker, Community volunteer (12) plus years; [memb.] Fraternal Order of The Eagles and member of their Travel Escort Team, Moose Lodge, VFW and family related organizations; [hon.] Schlafly Eagle Award 1984-(CA), featured local radio and newspapers, regarding Pro-Family Book donations to the local community college and public libraries, books donated to help provide a better balance of another viewpoint about family, women's issues book donations (80); [oth. writ.} Featured,"Focus On The Family Citizen", Pomona, CA. August 88, "How To Get Good Books IN Your Public Library", national distribution, guest columnist, "Homemakers Short Changed On Child Care", September 89, L.A. Daily News, CA; [pers.] Pass military experiences as a family has added endearing and lasting memories forever. Writing often becomes an expression of life's experience that brings unexpected future delights. [a.] Poet Hueneme, CA.

BEBIS, STEPHANIE
[b.] February 25, 1978, New Bedford, MA; [p.] Stephen and Nancy Bebis; [ed.] Coyle and Cassidy High School; [oth. writ.] Many poems which have not yet been published; [pers.] Life is something we all must cherish whether little or big, we must preserve our future and our past. [a.] Lakeville, MA.

BECK, MELISSA
[pen.] Melissa Beck; [b.] September 20, 1978, Utah; [p.] Steve and Linda Beck; [pers.] I dedicate this to the love of my life, he's my inspiration as well as my salvation, JESUS CHRIST. [a.] Kearns, UT.

BECK, THOMAS M.
[b.] December 28, 1909, New York, NY; [p.] Deceased; [ed.] Graduate Johns Hopkins University, Baltimore, MD.; [occ.] Retired; [memb.] Sierra Club; [hon.] Miami Shores, Fl, Fine Arts Commission Awards and certificates, life member National Library of Poetry; [oth. writ.] "Astride The Wind" a volume of my poems; [pers.] We must share the earth with nature. [a.] Miami, FL.

BECKER, KATHY
[pen.] Kathy Newell Becker; [b.] July 12, 1957, Lebanon, MO; [p.] Cecil and Mary Newell; [m.] Michael Becker, March 6, 1992; [ch.] Brandon Waterman; [ed.] Graduated 1980 from Waynesville Vo-Tech School of Practical Nursing, currently attending State Fair Community College, Sedalia, MO for RN degree; [occ.] Licensed Practical Nurse at Lake Ozark General Hospital; [hon.] Poem published in 1988 American Anthology of Midwestern Poetry, Who's Who in Poetry 1990, Golden Poet Award 1989; [oth. writ.] Several poems unpublished waiting to be complied with a book in the future; [pers.] I write from personal experience hoping that whoever reads my poems will receive encouragement to keep trying. [a.] Richland, MO.

BEHR II, MICHAEL J.
[pen.] George Taverner; [b.] March 27, 1974, Cincinnati, OH; [p.] Michael and Robyn Behr; [pers.] Learn by the second, live by the day, love by the hour, but don't forget to start over again. [a.] Cincinnati, OH.

BELCHER, HATTIE M.
[pen.] Hattie Patton Belcher; [b.] September 11, 1917,

Memphis, TN; [p.] Harrison Dewitt and Mary L. Patton; [m.] William E. Belcher (deceased), May 25, 1938; [ch.] William Jr., H. Earl, Robert L. (deceased), Walter F., Freddie H., Harold B. and Dale R. Bechler; [ed.] Cols High School graduate and Business School and Government; [occ.] Retired, volunteer; [memb.] Many service organizations including an Auxiliary to VFW Post 3764, Columbus, Ohio (that I organized in 1971), they are still active , Governor's Coalition on Aging, NARFE; [hon.] Veterans of Foreign Wars, National, State, and Local, American Cancer Awards, Government Awards, P.T.A. Awards, Governor and Mayor Awards,Mbr. Union Grove Baptist Church, was 1st Regional Conference Chairman, Ohio, YWCA (1951) volunteer; [oth. writ.] Several poems published in local newspaper (Columbus Call and Post), my first poem was published in the 1930's; [pers.] I love God and His creation. I believe in sharing with others. [a.] Columbus, OH.

BELL, AARON
[b.] August 25, 1917, Bethlehem, PA; [p.] S. J. Levine and Rose Bell; [m.] Mirja Lavanne, March 6, 1987; [ch.] Susanna Bell; [ed.] B.A. (University of Chicago, 1937); [occ.] Retired from teaching and translating; [memb.] ISCSC (International Society for Comparative Study of Civilizations), ISPP (International Society for Political Psychology), Nordic Association for American Studies; [hon.] President's Fund Grant 1939; [oth. writ.] Poems published in Midstream, reviews published in New York Times, translations of scholarly books and articles from Finnish into English; [pers.] My genres include aphorisms, limericks and sonnets. [a.] Helsinki, Finland.

BELL, BETTY H.
[b.] Prescott, AR; [m.] Wade W. Bell (deceased); [ch.] Susan F. and Alan W. Bell; [ed.] University of Arkansas; [a.] Houston, TX.

BENEDETTO, CHRISTOPHER
[pen.] Bizarro, The Iceman; [b.] March 1, 1973, Brooklyn, NY; [p.] Nancy and Thomas Benedetto; [ed.] G.E.D., Fort Hamilton High School; [occ.] Starving artist; [oth. writ.] Various poems of different topics, I have also written songs, short stories and am currently working on my first novel; [pers.] When times get rough, you have to put pain behind you and responsibility ahead of you. [a.] Brooklyn, NY.

BENJAMIN, YOMANDA
[pen.] Manda; [b.] February 19, 1976, Guyana; [p.] Cheryl Smith; [ed.] Graduated elementary and high school, presently is seeking college education; [occ.] Student at Community College at nights; [pers.] The poem is to my family and my boyfriend Keithley. It was you that helped me conquer the fight of inspiration to write so from the bottom of my heart, thank you. [a.] Tortola, BVI.

BENNER, PHYLLIS (SELENA, MARIE)
[pen.] Selena Benner, Mary; [b.] May 18, 1928, Carling, London Ontario; [p.] Roy Howard and Alveda Wesehoh; [m.] Lorne E. Benner, July 31, 1948; [ch.] Ronald William, Thomas Earl, David Howard, Catherine Ruth and Lori Elizabeth; [ed.] South Collegiate, Beah Technical School; [occ.] Homemaker, wife, mother, grandmother; [oth. writ.] Three poems published in The Annals of Saint Anne De Beaupre; [pers.] Nothing dies completely unless we ourselves are guilty of condemning it to death by forgetting it. Oblivion is the only death. The presence of the past in the present is the only life. [a.] London Ontario, Canada.

BENNETT, DARLENE YVONNE GRANT
[b.] February 24, 1952, Daisy Mountain, TN; [p.] Eugene H. and Carline Fay Grant; [m.] Davie Lawrence Bennett, March 8, 1985; [ch.] Tammy Corrine and Gerald Eugene Hall, grandson, Samuel Clifford Amos, Jr.; [occ.] Housewife, show dogs, breeder of English Bulldogs; [memb.] I am a member of A.S.C.A.P. and have been since June 4, 1991, was with the Voice Inc., Chattanooga, TN, since April 9, 1988 till 1991, my works are published; [oth. writ.] I have been writing songs and poetry some true stories about my past and some about my dreams; [pers.] I am the inspiration from the seeds of songwriters, a gift taught by my mother Fay Penny of Soddy Daisy, TN. [a.] Pensacola, FL.

BENSON, BARBARA JOYCE
[pen.] Barbara J. Benson; [b.] March 5, 1939, Houston, TX; [p.] Johnnie E. and Mable E. Ham; [m.] Steve Allen Benson, January 16, 1963; [ch.] Donald Terry Benson; [ed.] G.E.D. at Alvin Junior College in 1975, attended by Steve and Terry, for moral support; [occ.] Homemaker (not a housewife, I am not married to a house); [hon.] Only those accorded by me by husband and son, friends and family; [oth. writ.] Many poems, three books in progress (none published), one poem published in The Lincoln Electric Stabilizer, (a Weldor's magazine) in 1963; [pers.] I have always been able to best express my feelings in the written word, especially poetry. I inherited that from my mother, and an avid love or reading. [a.] Rosharon, TX.

BENSON, CHRISTOPHER
[b.] September 12, 1980, Alexandria, VA; [p.] Karl T. and MaryLou S. Benson; [ed.] (Grammar and junior high school) Longwood Elementary, Shalimar, FL., Meigs Middle School, Shalimar, FL; [occ.] 8th grade student; [memb.] Meigs Academic Team, Meigs Chorus, Ecumenical Bell Choir and St. Michael's Parish member; [hon.] "A" Honor Roll, 1st place math competition, several Academic Team Awards, 2nd place Piano Sonatina Festival; [oth. writ.] Several unpublished poems; [pers.] I have always thought of myself as a poet at heart. I owe a lot to my mother and my 7th grade English teacher, who helped me realize my poetic talent. [a.] Shalimar, FL.

BENTO, G. RONALD
[pen.] Ron Bento, G. Ron B.; [b.] October 15, 1951, San Antonio, TX; [p.] Alice and Ben Cheaney; [ed.] Antonian High School, San Antonio, TX., Texas A & M University, College Station, TX., University of Texas at San Antonio, San Antonio, TX;.; [occ.] Commercial Real Estate Broker, Nutrition Products Sales, band staging crew; [memb.] San Antonio Livestock Show and Rodeo Board of Directors, Texas A & M University Former Students Association, Sigma Phi Epsibu Fraternity, Sigma Delta Chi, Professional Journalistic Society; [oth. writ.] Was general assignment reporter at San Antonio Light newspaper in 1973 handling breaking news items and human interest features. Currently no publishing. I simply try to find humor in current events and express it in limerick; [pers.] I am a devout American/Christian, but also down to earth practical. I live each day anticipating that day worth waiting for. Daily, I confidently strive and advance despite economic set backs in recent years. I believe in teamwork, partnership and commitment and have been very fortunate with health, friendships and family. [a.] San Antonio, TX.

BENTON, SANDRA
[pen.] San Martin; [b.] May 21, 1960, Dallas; [p.] Bethena Bryant and Willie Young; [m.] Bobby Benton, September 18, 1993; [ed.] Graduate of Lincoln High School, Dallas, TX., El Centro College, Dallas, TX. [a.] Sandra Benton.

BERNARD, ADELLE
[pen.] Adelle De La'Laine; [b.] January 13, 1977; [p.] Lona Habbit and Kenneth J. Bernard; [ed.] Presently a junior at St. Martinville Senior High; [oth. writ.] "Isabella", "There Is A Young Man", "Time", "Song of Love", among other short stories, "The Rose and The Nightingale" and "The Rebirth of Mother Nature"; [pers.] Most of my poetry was written in my youth and my beauty came from youth. I was inspired by almost every new experience I was encountered by. Unfortunately, we all age and the number of unexpected horizons is reduced. As I mature, I'm inspired by less and less which is further proof that nothing gold can stay, hold on to youth because through youth comes beauty. [a.] St. Martinville, LA.

BERNSTEIN, CAITLIN
[b.] June 30, 1980, Santa Monica, CA; [ed.] 8th grade; [pers.] I wrote "The Secret Garden" about my dad, Robert Bernstein, who died last August. In memory of him and the beautiful garden we had at his house.

BERRY, DENISE
[pen.] Denise Berry; [b.] May 20, 1965, England; [p.] Ann and Denis Berry; [m.] Single mother; [ch.] Shane Aaron James and Keaton William Berry; [ed.] University of Western Ontario, B.A./Visual Arts and English, Humber College, Travel and Tourism diploma; [occ.] Recreation Co-ordinator; [memb.] Western University Alumni Association, YMCA; [hon.] Rio Algom Education Award grade 12, Western-Nestle Award, Western-Campbell Award (Bursaries); [oth. writ.] "A Year In The Life of Jenny", I am presently trying to get this manuscript published by Penguin Books Canada Ltd.; [pers.] I write from my senses and my emotions, this poem is dedicated to Billy, Shane and Keaton the men who add color to my life. [a.] London, Ontario.

BERRY, SHERRY M.
[pen.] Melissa Douglas; [b.] January 26, 1965, Tennessee; [p.] Donald and Betty Douglas; [m.] Rick D. Berry, April 21, 1984; [ch.] Holli R. and Chelsea M. Berry; [ed.] Powell Valley High School; [occ.] Day Laborer (sewing machine operator); [hon.] Beta Club (high school, junior and senior year) for Honor Roll students; [oth. writ.] Two completed unpublished contemporary romances one incompleted contemporary romance (also unpublished); [pers.] My work at times seems emotional. Its because I strive to put my whole heart and mind into it. [a.] New Tazewell, TN.

BERRY, SHIRLEY R.
[pen.] "AKU Nzinga Euka"; [b.] May 4, 1951, Milwaukee; [p.] Mr. K. C. and Minnie Butler; [m.] Loudry Berry, Jr., August 30, 1981; [ch.] Shane Maurice Berry; [ed.] BA, Education and MS, Exceptional Education from the University of Wisconsin, Milwaukee; [occ.] Teacher; [memb.] Metropolitan Milwaukee Alliance of Black Educators, Wisconsin Historical Black Museum, LaCausa Community Center, Children Abuse Crisis Center and Wisconsin Poetry Society; [hon.] Most Outstanding Teacher, Wisconsin Bell/Ameitech, 1991-1992, Outstanding High School Teacher of the Year, Metropolitan Milwaukee Alliance of Black School Educators, 1993, nominated for the Jefferson Award in 1992

and 1993 by Mayor John Norquis; [oth. writ.] Child Abuse and Neglect Prevention Strategies, 1990 (2nd edition 1992), Nzinga Untied (a poetry book) in 1992, Cause and Effect, a Black Celebration (a play) in 1993; [pers.] Realizing my temple of familiar as caused me to know that my past, present and future are one bathing with my inner gifts with the mother of all civilizations, Momma Nile! [a.] Milwaukee, WI.

BEYAH, SUHAILAH
[pen.] Q; [b.] South Carolina; [p.] Sam Givens and Bertha Bryant Givens; [ch.] Maya and Khalioh; [ed.] Ivenia Brown Elementary, Colleton High, Pace University, Allen Swartz Institute; [occ.] Housewife; [memb.] Mt. Olive AME Church, Hospice Association of Colleton County; [oth. writ.] Several poems, never entered for publication; [pers.] I strive to let the light of my life shine for the goodness of all. I have been greatly influenced by Maya Angelou and others.

BHATTI, ARSCHED HOSSAIN
[b.] January 17, 1966, Burewala; [p.] Lal Din and Khadijja Bhatti; [m.] Aaliya Safdar, October 14, 1993; [ch.] It is inconceivable to have a kid so soon; [ed.] M. Phil, International Relations, M.Sc. International Relations, Quaid-i-Azam University, Islamabad; [occ.] Civil Servant of the State since November 1989; [memb.] Sports Complex, Islamabad, Alliance Francaise, USIS; [hon.] Stayed for one month at the highest battle ground of the world, Siachin, qualified Barcelona Olympic trials for 100 meter dash; [oth. writ.] Working on a novel (God is Lost), a music album (Off The Track), and a collection of poems (With Best of Grudge) is under publication, regularly contributing a satirical column (pseudonym Ali Baba) in an English weekly Pulse, I also write poems in Punjabi, Urdu and French; [pers.] "When you love, you are a poet, when you are loved, you are a poem". "Nostalgia is memory's wet dream". "Every hesitation has its price, one does not live a chance twice". "It is easy to die with a faith" and "I am the most realy reality to myself". [a.] Islamabad, Pakistan.

BIEGANOWSKI, LEON
[b.] April 5, 1928, Montreal, Canada; [p.] Michael and Mary Bieganowski; [m.] Sophie Grzybala, October 26, 1957; [ch.] Michael, Andrew and James; [ed.] St. Aloysius High, William Lund Tech., Navigation, Planetary Science; [occ.] Retired Sgt. Det., Montreal Police (32 years service); [memb.] W.W. II Veterans Association, Police Veterans Association, Dorval Old Timers Hockey; [hon.] Crime Analysis, honored by news media as "Colombo", Coach of the Year, Oldtimers Hockey; [oth. writ.] Songwriting, short stories, theories of the world; [pers.] The material needs of man grow smaller, as man grows wiser, and learns to replace worldly goods with words. [a.] Dorval, Quebec Canada.

BIEGANOWSKI, MIKE
[b.] October 5, 1958, Montreal, Canada; [p.] Leo and Sophie Bieganowski; [ed.] John XXIII High, Lindsay Place High Tech. School of French and International Cuisine; [memb.] Chess Club; [hon.] Dorval Speed Skating Champion, John XXIII High Chess Champion; [oth. writ.] Songwriting; [pers.] The smartest have been known to be wrong, you need not be the smartest to be right. [a.] Dorval Quebec, Canada.

BIELECKI, KAREN
[b.] March 22, 1957, Bedford, OH; [p.] Joseph and Mary Bielecki; [ed.] Bedford Senior High; [occ.] Technician in a Pharmaceutical Company; [oth. writ.] Several

other unpublished poems; [pers.] My heart flows through a pen. [a.] Bedford, OH.

BIGELOW-WEILAND, LISA
[b.] April 1, 1957, Kansas City, MO; [p.] Donald and Martha Bigelow; [m.] John Weiland, August 1979; [ch.] Diana, Julia, Daniel, Katherine and Michael; [ed.] San Jose State University B.A. English, Religious Studies, minor, CA single subject credential clear; [occ.] High school teacher; [hon.] Dean's List, CCAE "Excellence in Teaching" award in 1992; [oth. writ.] Working on first novel; [pers.] Dedicated to my parents for all their encouragement and support. [a.] San Jose, CA.

BILLHEIMER, CLARENCE E.
[b.] November 22, 1948, Canton, OH; [m.] Samuel and Nancy; [m.] Patsy Mae, December 22, 1979; [ed.] Some college plus 3 year Bible School diploma; [occ.] Defense Finance Center, Accounting Technician; [memb.] Heritage Baptist Church, Canal Winchester, OH.; [hon.] Suggestion awards at work, high honors at Tennessee Temple Bible College; [oth. writ.] Letters to Editors, published various times in newspapers, one poem published in high school booklet, I entitled project poetry, first book The Poetry Project; [pers.] My poetry is mostly inspirational, reflecting what God and my faith mean to me. I have been strongly encouraged by friends to put my poetry in a book. [a.] Columbus, OH.

BILLINGSLEY, SHIRLEY
[b.] September 3, 1953, Center, TX; [p.] Waymon and Vera Mae Billingsley; [m.] Willie L. Skinner, July 18, 1983; [ch.] Melinda Sue Billingsley; [ed.] Timpson, Texas, Gary, Texas, graduated abroad; [occ.] Write, instructor in home based study course; [memb.] "The Craft", Private Community Projects; [hon.] Recently offered membership in American Biographical Institute, opportunity to be featured in Who's Who, '95 ed.; [oth. writ.] "The Dream Factory" (book), "Why Send Your Children Out", numerous small articles for local newspaper, home-study course "The Craft"; [pers.] Through dreams we can learn how to better our lives. [a.] Nacogdoches, TX.

BINGERT, SHARON ANN
[b.] December 23, 1946, Brooklyn, NY; [p.] Nathan and Alice R. Shapiro Bober; [m.] John Joseph Bingert, June 30, 1972; [ch.] I have no children, but have a dog named "Cookie Pie" who is very special to me; [ed.] Graduated Erasmus Hall High School, Brooklyn, NY; [occ.] Secretary (past instructor and course developer) American Telephone and Telegraph Company, Morristown, NJ.; [memb.] Past Co-chairperson of the Membership Committee for the American Society for Training and Development, Mid New Jersey Chapter (ASTD), member, National Association for Female Executives; [oth. writ.] Designed and created a Word Processing course in Wordperfect and presented it to the students for 3 semesters at the Adult Education School in my community, also developed a Programming Course in AT & T and delivered it to upper management; [pers.] My poem reflects my belief which is "If you truly believe in yourself, then nothing will ever be impossible for you to do". Growing up my greatest influence has been my "Mother", she is an excellent writer and has helped me appreciate the art of writing. My husband has also been very inspirational to me in my work. [a.] Edison, NJ.

BIRCH, PETER A.
[b.] January 11, 1957, London, England; [p.] Prof. A.H. Birch, Ph.D. F.R.S.C. and D. M. Birch; [ed.] Exeter

School, England Aston University, England; [memb.] Old Exonian Club, Honorable Artillery Company O.C.A., Exeter R.F.C., The Royal Overseas League, The Royal Commonwealth Society Corkscrew Society; [hon.] Aston University Cobras Clubman of the Year; [pers.] I attempt to raise the public's awareness and understanding of mental illness. [a.] Victoria, British Columbia Canada.

BIRCHARD JR., DALE A.
[b.] July 24, 1961, Victoria, British Columbia; [p.] Dale and Joy Birchard and Penny Birchard; [m.] Charlene K. Henry, engaged to be married; [ch.] Joel Dale, Sabrina Gurina and Khanlee David; [ed.] Grade 10; [occ.] Skidder Operator Logger; [oth.writ.] A Traveled Soul, Lady Dove, As I Walk at Night, these poems I've kept to myself; [pers.] I was inspired to write this poem by putting myself in my son Joel's place. He was without his natural mom and myself for 17 months, my son Joel is now by my sid. He has a new mother, a brother and sister. My message to the people is no matter what problems occur stop and look at your children and never leave them behind. [a.] Vernon, British Columbia Canada.

BISHOP, BETTY RILL WEBSTER
[b.] August 10, 1925, Hambleton, WV; [p.] Hugh and Eunice Webster; [m.] Buck, June 11, 1946; [ch.] Reg, Rod, Rim, Rylie and 7 grandsons, 2 granddaughters; [ed.] High school (Tidioute, PA) and experience; [occ.] Housewife; [memb.] Sunshine Club, J.O.Y. Class Club, involved in all types of doll collecting; [hon.] Third place winner in National Poetry contest, Who's Who in Poetry, Poetic Achievement Award from Amherst Society, nine assorted awards for poems, picture spread (twice) in local newspaper; [oth. writ.] Published in Reader's Digest, Christian Reader, Doll World, Saturday Evening Post, published in Tenor Twelve Writing/Poetry publications, poems requested for local programs; [pers.] My writing comes form the heart, on subjects I'm familiar with. My christian belief, my husband, children and grandchildren are my inspiration and my doll collection and my writing are my added joy. [a.] Hampton, FL.

BISKEBORN, MARK
[b.] March 3, 1957, Oregon; [p.] Norma and Carl; [ed.] M.A. Comparative Lit., M.B.A., University of Oregon, B.A. University of California; [occ.] President of a Multimedia Company; [oth. writ.] Unpublished short stories, writing a novel currently; [pers.] Goals to write songs for popular music and to publish short stories and current novel. [a.] New Haven, CT.

BISSONNETTE, SUSAN
[b.] September 8, 1971, Montreal, Quebec Canada; [p.] Thomas and Jean Morris; [m.] Jason Bissonnette, August 29, 1992; [ed.] Macdonald High School, Secretarial studies at Lindsay Place High School; [occ.] Service Dispatcher for Ricoh Canada; [oth. writ.] Several other poems that have not yet been published; [pers.] Thank yo to my dear friend Wanda Kennedy that encouraged my writing, my first poem is dedicated to her and all hit and run victims in the world. [a.] Montreal Quebec, Canada.

BLACK, VERNELL
[b.] Columbia, SC; [p.] Manuel and Pauline Guaghman; [m.] Marion C. Black, March 10, 1959; [ch.] Anthony Black; [ed.] Booker Washington High, Benedict College; [occ.] Retired; [memb.] South Carolina Foster Parents Association, Astaro, North Main Crime Watchers Committee; [hon.] Letter from President Jimmy Carter; [oth. writ.] Several poems not yet published; [pers.] I try to reflect God in my life as much as possible,

to combine God and nature as the author and finisher of all things. I try hard to express this in my poetry. [a.] Columbia, SC.

BLACKMON, TYKARI
[b.] March 15, 1981, Chicago, IL; [p.] Lawrence Blackman and Mattie Franklin; [ed.] 6th grade; [memb.] The Bread of Life, Del Min Church; [hon.] Saucedo School Astic Academy, Honor Roll 1993; [oth. writ.] A story and received an award by Child's Play Touring Theatre; [pers.]] I live with my grandparents, Mr. Booker T.and Odessa Rodgers, which is very helpful to me, with their love and support. [a.] Chicago, IL.

BLACKWOOD, JENNIFER SUSAN HOOPER
[pen.] Jennifer Webster-Wybar; [b.] May 8, 1946, Cardiff, Wales; [p.] Lucille and Keith Hooper; [m.] Divorced; [ch.] Joshua (age 11) and Tobias (age 9); [ed.] Campbelltown High, Torrens College of Advanced Education, Flinders University; [occ.] Co-ordinator of a Housing Association for persons with an intellectual disability; [memb.] Secretary, Australian Society for the Scientific Study of Intellectual Disability, Secretary for the Board of Community Accommodation for the Intellectually Disabled, secretary, Public Service Association Writer's Group; [hon.] Graduated in Applied Science (Development Disabilities), diploma in Fine Art Photography; [oth. writ.] Poems, photographs and short stories published in local publications; [pers.] Family is very important to me and I am fortunate in having two artistic sons. Together we are attempting every writer's dream, our own book. [a.] Adelaide, South Australia.

BLANCHETTE, FRANKIE AL
[pen.] Fabian Joseph; [b.] July 18, 1973, McBride, BC; [p.] Germain and Gladys Blanchette; [ed.] Graduated from Valemount Secondary High School, pursuing Post Secondary Education in the field of art; [hon.] Grade 12, received Citizenship Award for 92/93; [oth. writ.] Wrote several poems, but none ever published; [pers.] I would like to dedicate my poem "Trying To Make The World A Better Place" to Melanie Neale, my best friend in the whole world. Too truly see beauty, one must not open only one's eyes, but one's heart. [a.] Valemount, BC Canada.

BLAINE, KAREN ELLEN
[b.] October 13, 1958, Los Angeles, CA; [p.] Donald and Harriet Levenson; [m.] David Robert Blaine, December 28,1981; [ch.] Davis Justin, Tristan Davis, Brittara Karen and Whitney Kayla; [ed.] B.A. Speech Communication, California State University, Northridge, Journalism minor, 1st year UC Santa Barbara; [occ.] Singer and author; [memb.] Screen Actors Guild member since 1980, AFTRA (American Federation Television and Radio Artists), Sigma Delta Chi, Society of Professional Journalists; [hon.] Alpha Gamma Sigma Scholastic Honor Society, CSUN; [oth. writ.] Two published non-fiction books, published creative arts magazine (CSUN), books of prose composed of allegories, stories, poetry, etc., two unpublished fiction novels; [pers.] In a world that oftentimes seems incomprehensible, poetry can lift our spirits to believe in the love and beauty that exists universally. [a.] Westlake Village, GA.

BLAIN, SCOTT
[pen.] Robert Scott Bradley Blain; [b.] November 20, 1963, South Porcupine, Ontario; [p.] Emmerson and Sally Blain; [ed.] Roland Michenter Secondary School, Northern College; [memb.] Canadian Diabetes Association, Multiple Sclerosis Society of Canada; [oth. writ.]

About a dozen poems this past year when by accident, I discovered I like poetry and enjoy producing it; [pers.] I spend a lot of time watching and studying people, writing about those who touch my heart, or about how people should live their lives. [a.] London, Ontario.

BLAIR, VICTORIA LEIGH
[b.] April 15, 1958, Lower Hutt, New Zealand; [p.] James and Colleena Blair; [m.] Robert John Steele; [ch.] Brendan Anthony (died June 30, 1992 aged 17 months); [ed.] Horowhenua College, Massey University, University of Waikato; [occ.] Purchasing Officer, University of Waikato, Hamilton, NZ; [memb.] Hamilton Amateur Ballroom Dance Club, River City Rock N Roll Club; [hon.] Bachelor of Science; [oth. writ.] "The Will To Live", personal biography of my son, Brendan Anthony Steele; [pers.] Do not dwell on the past or fear the future, live for the present. [a.] Hamilton, New Zealand.

BLANCHARD, GAIL F.
[b.] February 4, 1950, Libertyville, IL; [p.] Richard and Eleanor Rimmer Stenberg; [ch.] M. Justin Franzke and William Benjamin Blanchard; [ed.] Warren T. High School, Barat College (BA English); [occ.] Associate Editor (Copley owned) Star Newspapers Inc., also nightclub manager and disc jockey, No Bull Inc.; [hon.] Magna Cum Laude, Kappa Gamma Pi, Delta Epsilon Sigma, American Horse Publications Association Awrd recipient; [oth. writ.] Previously served as editor of the Sentinel, Spray (serving the boating and snow skiing industries) and the Horse Digest; [pers.] My personal goals include completion of a novel and to write the COuntry Music Associations song of the year. [a.] McHenry, IL.

BLANCHARD, SHANNA MARIE
[b.] July 17, 1978, Comox, BC; [p.] Pat Thompson and Larry Blanchard; [ed.] Currently completing grade 10, GP Vanier High School; [occ.] Student; [memb.] International Order of Job's Daughters; [pers.] I was 11 years of age when I wrote this poem. [a.] Cumberland, BC Canada.

BLEDSOE, SHIRLEY LANE
[pen.] ShiLee; [b.] May 21, 1935, Olive Branch, MS; [p.] Flander L. Josephine Clark; [m.] Jethroe Bledsoe, (May 3,1919), April 19, 1956; [ch.] Palmer L. Bledsoe Ross, Jethroe Jr., Chyll D., Kim M. Bledsoe; [ed.] Melrose High, Shelby State, Deputy Sheriff Academy, Career Academy in Nursing in Washington, DC; [occ.] I am retired, an a Counselor for small business score administration, security guard, detective an investigation co.; [memb.] Mississippi Boulevard Church, Honorary Deputy Sheriff appointed to the congressional staff of the hon. (8th Congressional District of Tennessee); [oth. writ.] Writing on to books, One The Death of My Little Girl, one about Pvt. Investigation.

BLEVINS, YOLANDA E.
[p.] Florence G. Edwards; [m.] Robert W. Belvins; [ch.] Astin Michelle Belvins; [occ.] Traders Assistant; [oth. writ.] I have various poems, but this is my first to be printed; [pers.] My poems are written about problems and situations of the 90's. Most of them end on a positive note, in hopes that they will offer hope to a unhappy or confused person.

BLEWER, JAMES
[b.] March 7, Oakland, CA; [p.] Jim and Harriet; [m.] Shirley Bishop, July 8, 1962; [ch.] Jimmy and Brian; [ed.] B.S.V.C., Berkeley, 1941; [occ.] Public school

teacher 32 years, now retired; [memb.] In a Coolbirth Circle (poetry), First Church of Christ, Scientist, Alameda, California Retired Teachers Association, Boy Scouts of America, Alameda Council, University of California Alumni Association; [hon.] Bronze Star, Combat Infantry Badge, Presidential Unit Citation, Pacific Theater ribbon, Philippine Liberation Medal, past president East Bay Retired Teachers Association, various Boy Scouts of America Awards; [oth. writ.] Articles for religious publications, In A Coolbirth Circle (poetry); [pers.] Spiritually, put God foremost, humanly seek the highest standards for yourself and others. [a.] Alameda, CA.

BLOCK, ERICS
[b.] April 26, 1966, Chicago, IL; [p.] Dennis and Gwen Block; [ed.] Greenwich High School, U.S. Naval Academy; [occ.] Captain U.S., Marine Corps; [memb.] U.S. Triathlon Federation, U.S. Water Polo Inc., National Parks and Conservation Association; [hon.] Won Oceanside Blade Citizen Christmas Eve story competition; [oth. writ.] Several newspaper articles; [pers.] Even though people around the world are very different, we are closer then we will ever know. We are all searching for the same answers. Love and laughter unite us and will conquer our uncertainty. [a.] Carlsbad, CA.

BLUME, ENID
[b.] April 9, 1922, Simcoe; [p.] Grace and Ernest Williams; [m.] Lewis Edward Blume, June 27, 1945; [ch.] John Edward and Mary Martha; [ed.] Simcoe High School, Robinson Business College, Simcoe; [occ.] Retired newspaper proofreader; [memb.] Norfolk Golf and Country Club; [pers.] These were the only lines of poetry I ever wrote and they came very quickly and helped me over a very sad time. A young R.A.A.F. Pilot died attacking trains in Germany on February 13, 1945. [a.] Simcoe, Ontario.

BOCAGE III, ROBERT J.
[pen.] R. J. Bocage III; [b.] November 8, 1950, New Orleans, LA; [p.] Robert Jr. and Geneva; [m.] Ann Paster Bocage, August 16, 1991; [ch.] Janae' and Robert IV; [ed.] St. Augustine High School, Meadows Draughon College, Community College of Denver; [occ.] Deputy Records Clerk, Federation Courts, Denver, CO; [memb.] Disabled American Veterans, American Bowlers Conference; [oth. writ.] Working on self publication of my 1st book entitled Garden of Love; [pers.] I hope that my writings touch the lives of many people in a positive way, especially our young people. [a.] Aurora, CO.

BOCHAR, MONA
[pen.] Ramona; [b.] February 24, 1935, Kamloops; [p.] Jay and Mollie Houseman; [m.] Walter Bochar, October 1,1971; [ch.] Julie, Debbie, Rick, Dan and Wanda (stepchildren) Linda, Donna and Janice; [ed.] Buffalo Creek School; [occ.] Employee of Vance Creek Hotel (Silver Star); [oth. writ.] Poems in Criboo Observer newspaper; [pers.] The love I feel for my family has inspired me to write the poetry I write. [a.] Vernon, BC Canada.

BOEKHOLT
[pen.] Joseph; [b.] September 3, 1948, Amsterdam; [p.] Mother-71, father-79; [m.] Adri; [ch.] Lea (16) and Kim (14); [ed.] High school; [occ.] Advertising; [hon.] I made one myself; [pers.] Regret, always on time. [a.] Amsterdam, Holland.

BOLANOS, SAMANTHA
[b.] June 16, 1972, Ventura, CA; [p.] Roberta and Marco

Bolanos; [ed.] Chula Vista High School (graduated in 1990), currently attending South Western College, graduate in 1994; [occ.] Student; [oth. writ.] One line poem published in school magazine called "Backstreet Journal" (at this point, any burial ground will do) a compilation of student work. [a.] San Diego, CA.

BOLDON, CANDACE MARIE
[pen.] Candace Boldon; [b.] November 6, 1979, West Palm Beach, FL; [p.] C. James Boldon III and Florencia; [ed.] Grade 8 at Wellington Landings Middle School; [occ.] Student; [memb.] S.A.D.D, (Students Against Drunk Drivers Club); [hon.] Honor Roll, Outstanding Student of Academics, Outstanding Citizenship, P.R.I.D.E. Award; [oth. writ.] Quill books published my poem "Where's The Love These Days"; [pers.] I consume the majority of my time writing poems, stories, and essays about love, peace and mankind. My personal dream is to graduate from college with a degree in journalism and become a successful writer. [a.] Wellington, West Palm Beach, FL.

BOLDRA, ALLISON DOEDEN
[b.] November 24, 1912, Worthington, MN; [p.] Alice and William Doeden; [m.] August 1940; [ed.] Elementary, Worthington, University of Minn. Lowell, Mass masters degree, New England Conservatory; [occ.] Giving music lessons; [hon.] Many small ones; [oth. writ.] Special music book of games for children; [pers.] My idea is never to stop attending educational classes and keeping up to date. [a.] Brooksville, FL.

BOLING SR., REV. BLAINE ARLINGTON
[b.] June 13, 1919, Esmont, VA; [p.] Joseph F. and Mamie Waynes Boling; [m.] Dr. Betty Preston Boling, November 24, 1976; [ch.] Blaine Jr., Lenice, Mamie, Beryl and Sheryl, Joseph, Maude, David and Welborn Preston; [ed.] BT Washington High, Tulsa, OK, Wiley College, Gulfside Pastors' School, Perkins, Prairie View, Southwestern University; [occ.[United Methodist Minister (Ret. 1986), writer; [memb.] Community Liaison for HISD, Chr. Mayor's Ministers Task Force and Executive Board of Ministers Against Crime, Conference Board of Ministerial Training and Worship; [hon.] Honorary Doctor od Divinity Degree, Staff Sgt.-5 Battle stars, recommended for Bronze Medal of honor during Battle of the Bugle for Outstanding Leadership under General George Patton, name on two cornerstones for church building; [oth. writ.] My Autobiography in poetry, From The Narrow Path, Reflections and Emotions (Vantage Press, 1993); [pers.] I believe that all mankind is one family and each is responsible for all the rest. I believe that the long and hard process of cultivating mankind into something far better than the present will be the result of the efforts of church and state working together on all levels. [a.] Houston, TX.

BOLTON, JASON
[b.] September 19, 1977, LaFollette, TN; [p.] Judy Nelson (9/21/53); [ed.] Sophomore at Campbell County High School; [occ.] Student, poet; [oth. writ.] Numerous poems written about a wide variety of subjects; [pers.] I feel that poetry should be free, instead of being closed and incumbered. I also feel that the prettiest and most meaningful poems are written about God and flowers. [a.] LaFollette, TN.

BONAVITA, LINDA ANN
[b.] March 16, 1950, Newark, NJ; [p.] Peter and Ann Bonavita; [ch.] Morgan LeMaitre; [ed.] Good Counsel High, Caldwell College; [occ.] Investment portfolio

manager, First Fidelity Bank; [memb.] Nutley Little Theatre, National Arbor Day Society, Rails to Trails Conservancy; [hon.] National Honor Society; [oth. writ.] Poem published in National Anthology of College Poetry, several songs copyrighted and performed. [a.] Nutley, NJ.

BOND, DAVID CHARLES
[b.] February 26, 1956, Berkhamstead, Herts; [p.] Raymond and Elizabeth Bond; [m.] Lila, December 4, 1989; [ch.] Andres, Lyndsey, Jo-Anne and Hayley; [ed.] Left school at 16 and joined British Army; [occ.] Full time writer/painter and thinker; [memb.] British Legion (ex-serviceman), Lurgan College of Futher Education; [hon.] General service and campaign medal and bar, Northern Ireland Police medal, very relieved to have survived 22 years in Army and Police; [oth. writ.] Numerous poems and two novels completed but nothing submitted, "Shamelot" only the 2nd poem ever submitted to a publisher, 1 poem published in an English work; [pers.] I believe the poet must fight against the materialistic world and show that there is more to life than the latest model of car. [a.] Magheralin.

BON DURANT, BEA
[pen.] Bea Bon Durant; [b.] October 10, 1923, Corbin, KY; [p.] Thomas and Susan Lockard; [m.] Don Bon Durant; [ch.] Elizabeth, Patricia and Teresa Kay, former marriage; [ed.] High school graduate, business and English; [occ.] Retired-manager of Willis Music Co., Cincinnati, Ohio; [hon.] English and Math; [oth.writ.] The Life of The Singing Lockard Sisters, Sylvia, Edna, Gert and Bea.

BONEE, STEPHANIE
[b.] October 26, 1964, Ft. Worth, TX; [p.] G.K. and Lois Burns; [m.] Divorced; [ch.] Kenneth Lee Hayes; [ed.] TCC, Aeronautical/Aerospace Engineering and Business Administration (minor); [occ.] Marketing for Architectural Firm; [hon.] Dean's List 1991 to present, President's List 1991 to present, Phi Kappa Theta Honor Society 1991 to present; [oth. writ.] Many poems, mostly unnamed; [pers.] The experiences of life dictate the poem content. I strive to experience all of life and live it to the fullest, occasionally , this obscures the poem's content almost until the work is completed. [a.] Virginia Beach, VA.

BONNER, MARY L.
[b.] Over 39, Chicago, IL; [p.] Joseph and Alean Bonner; [ed.] 2 1/2 years city colleges of Chicago; [occ.] Barber; [oth. writ.] Mgr./Agt for new author Robert C. Ballard, "Evelyn" (still searching for publisher; [pers.] The greatest honor a person can have is to serve their God and their fellow humans. [a.] Chicago, Il.

BONOAN, SHELLY
[b.] June 23, 1972, Honolulu, HI; [m.] Nancy Daly; [occ.] Writer, part-time fashion model; [oth.writ.] Poems and freelance writing in upcoming anthology for troubled teens; [pers.] For as long as I have my muse, I shall continue writing of love, romance and the beauty of things. [a.] Los Angeles, CA.

BONOMI, DAVID
[b.] March 22, 1953, Bristol, England; [p.] Michele and Giovannina Bonomi; [m.] Pina Bonomi, April 26, 1980; [ch.] Alexander and Andrea; [ed.] Private Junior and Secondary Education in Bristol, attained various Secondary Education examinations and further education qualifications; [occ.] Local government officer; [hon.] The

"Russell Currie" Award for problem solving, issued by the Institute of Management Services in 1983, Russell Currie worked in the USA and became Chair of ICI, and was known as the "Father of work study"; [oth. writ.] A number of unpublished poems with themes based on war and everyday walks of life. The war themes are based on human suffering and portray the futility of war; [pers.] I started writing poems some three years ago on the themes of anti-war and everyday walks of life that effect ordinary people. I am self taught and in the past never read or studied poetry. I now hope to publish these poems. [a.] Bristol, England.

BORBE, SANTOS O.
[pen.] Antoy; [b.] November 1, 1919, Polangui, Albay Philippines; [p.] Ong Dy To and Filiciana Borbe; [m.] Lydia Borbe, November 5, 1941; [ch.] Oscar Borbe, Myrna Borbe Santayana, Santos Borbe Jr., Evelyn Borbe, Marlyn Borbe Buenviaje, Estrella Borbe Saquido; [ed.] Aquinas University, Legaspi City, Philippines, graduate, Bachelor of Science in Business Administration, major in management; [occ.] Employee-Service America Corporation; [memb.] Albay Poultry Swine Farmers Association; [oth. writ.] Autobiography 28 chapters, followed by poem pertaining to Chapter; [pers.] Never be ungrateful, never break a promise, and no summit is too high if you try and try and try. [a.] Jersey City, NJ.

BORNE, ERIK JOSEPH
[b.] June 17, 1976, Harvey, IL; [p.] Keith and Linda Borne; [ed.] Currently a senior at Lockport Township High School; [memb.] Who's Who Among High School Students Association; [hon.] 1st place in Lockport High School annual writing contest (met Gwendolyn Brooks, Poet Laureate of Illinois-1992, 3rd place in Lockport High School annual writing contest 1993; [oth. writ.] 163 other poems and songs seeking approval and publication as lyrics, poems; [pers.] I'm inspired by George Michael and Elton John. I only hope to follow in the footsteps of their success and establish myself as a lyricist, singer. I believe I have the potential and the determination. [a.] Lockport, IL.

BOSA, MICHELE
[b.] September 18, 1966, Vancouver, BC; [p.] Miho and Katica Durkovich; [m.] Fred Bosa, August 31, 1991; [ch.] Ameila Bosa; [ed.] Templeton Secondary School; [occ.] Homemaker; [pers.] Love is the key to everlasting inner happiness. Through my writing I am able to express myself freely, visualizing the beauty that surrounds me. [a.] Burnaby, BC.

BOSCHIERI, HARRY
[pen.] Miles Devereux; [b.] May 14,1946, Natchez, MS; [ed.] Cathedral High School, University of Southern Mississippi, Tulane University; [occ.] Clothing salesman, singer, songwriter, poet; [memb.] American Society of Composers, Authors, Publishers; [hon.] Feature pick Cash Box magazine for debut EP, third place film, Mississippi Arts Festival, poetry published in several literary journals, 5 song EP (TV2ME), articles in local newspapers; [pers.] "A man should stir himself with poetry stand firm in ritual and complete himself with art and music" (the Chinese poet Li Po). [a.] Santa Moncia, CA.

BOSS, LACEY DIANE
[b.] October 5, 1978, Phoenix, AZ; [p.] Peter and Diane Boss; [ed.] Currently a freshman at Baptist Christian High School of Hemet, CA; [occ.] Student and a poet;

[memb.] International Society of Poets (charter lifetime member), and ISP Committee dealing with contest policies and California Scholarship Federation (CSF); [hon.] Editor's Choice Award, International Poet of Merit, $50.00 prize for being semi-finalist in poetry contest, Honorary Storyteller of Ghost Town through Knott's Berry Farm; [oth. writ.] "Homeless" published in Wind In The Night Sky and "The Climb Toward Happiness" published in Outstanding Poets of 1994, writings in school newspaper; [pers.] Trials produce perseverance, character, knowledge and hope. [a.] Hemet, CA.

BOSWELL, LARRY R.
[pen.] Lawrence R. Boswell; [b.] April 10, 1945, Wichita, KS; [m.] Gwendolyn Boswell, October 3, 1970; [ch.] Anthony R. Boswell; [ed.] Los Angeles City College, A.A. St. Mary's College of California B.A.; [occ.] Radiological Technologist; [memb.] America Reg. of Radiology Tech., American Society of Radiology Technology; [oth. writ.] Approx. 100 poems unpublished, five novels unpublished; [pers.] I am inspired by nature and its power. [a.] Woodbridge, VA.

BOSWORTH, NEWTON
[pen.] Neb Bosworth; [b.] August 3, 1977, Baltimore, MD; [p.] David and Julia Bosworth; [ed.] I am a sophomore at Chesapeake High School; [occ.] Student; [oth. writ.] A few poems given to my girlfriend; [pers.] I write my poems because I have no other outlet for the way I feel about the world. Maybe when someone reads my poems they can relate to how I feel. [a.] Pasadena, MD.

BOTTINO, STEVE E.
[b.] June 22, 1943, Newark, NJ; [m.] Shirley J. Bottino; [ch.] James Robert and Michelle Lynn; [ed.] Irvington High, Elmhurst College; [occ.] Manager, S-B Power Tool Company.

BOURANEL, ROBERT PETER
[b.] April 15, 1954, Reykjavik; [ch.] Robert, Gudrun Lara and Lara Michelle; [ed.] Erasmus Hall High School; [occ.] Scandinavian Airlines; [oth. writ.] Assorted short stories and poetry; [pers.] Through my writings and paintings, I portray the keepers of the earth and the meek, for they inherit only that which we leave behind. [a.] Copenhagen, Denmark.

BOWMAN, LAURALEA
[b.] March 31, 1958, Los Angeles; [p.] John T. Bowman and Patricia Jean Duncan; [ch.] Erica Christine Neely; [ed.] Yucca Valley High School, Palm Springs Beauty College, Regional Occupational Program, Computer App. Word Perfect, Yucca Valley High School; [occ.] Office Manager for MuBurk Equipment Dynamic Marketing Desert Engines; [memb.] Morongo Indikan's Foresters, IN; [oth. writ.] Thousands, but "Daughter" is the first to be published, dedicated to my only child, it's to let her know how much she means to me; [pers.] My writing is my way of mental survival. I am influenced by all the poets of past and present. [a.] Joshua Tree, CA.

BOYCE, DENISE
[b.] August 24, 1961, Ann Arbor, MI; [ed.] Culver City High School, Santa Moncia City College; [occ.] Medical Assistant, Los Angeles, CA; [hon.] Department of the Navy, Good Conduct Award; [pers.] I love to dream and I like to write poems about what I dream, and how I feel. I love putting my feelings into the poems that I write. [a.] Los Angeles, CA.

BOYD, JAMES A.
[pen.] James A. Boyd; [b.] December 18, 1934, Northville, MI; [p.] James F. and Emma J. Boyd; [m.] Carolyn K. Boyd, April 1, 1967; [ch.] Jack, Darlene, Caryn and Jamie; [ed.] Assc EE; [occ.] Supervisor, University Michigan, ETCA Ret U.S.C.G.; [memb.] Fraternal; [hon.] Fraternal; [oth. writ.] Fraternal newsletters and other philosophies in rhyme; [pers.] I consider myself an amateur philosopher in rhyme rather than a poet. "Peace" was intended to be personal and timeless, written in the Welsh style. [a.] Lakeland, MI.

BOYD, RHONDA L.
[b.] May 22, 1967, Rochester, NY; [p.] Mabel and Stanley Boyd; [m.] Single; [ed.] Regents diploma in Spanish from high school, Associates degree in Travel and Tourism; [occ.] Currently a dispatcher for a copier company (Eastern Copy Products), was at travel agent for 6 years; [oth. writ.] Short stories and poetry. [a.] Fairport, NY.

BOYETT, DOROTHY LAKE
[b.] October 29, 1925, St. Louis, MO; [p.] Robert H., Boyette, Jr., 1944; [ch.] Two; [memb.] Order of the Eastern Star; [pers.] For God's glory and to bless His children. [a.] Longview, TX.

BOYLE, DOUGLAS JOSEPH
[b.] May 19, 1946, Jersey City, NJ; [p.] Elizabeth and Joseph Boyle; [m.] Maria Boyle, May 24, 1970; [ch.] Gregory and Heather; [ed.] Levittown High School, Levittown, NY., L.I. University/CW Post Campus, B.B.A., 5/80. U.S. Army 1966-69; [occ.] Bank Trust and Estate Officer.

BRADLEY, BRIAN
[pen.] Silence Speaks; [b.] September 23, 1974, Denver, CO; [p.] Fred Bradley; [m.] Single; [ed.] Abraham Lincoln High, Standley Lake High School; [occ.] Student; [memb.] American Diabetes Association, Media Alert Foundation International; [pers.] I have had insulin-dependent (type I) diabetes for over eleven years.

BRADSHAW, BRANDON CORD
[b.] January 23, 1974, Peoria, IL; [p.] Melvin and Patricia Bradshaw; [ed.] Tidehaven High; [occ.] Glass cleaner; [memb.] National Honor Society; [hon.] Presidential Academic Fitness Award; [pers.] One speaks to be heard, one writes to be understood. [a.] Utica, MI.

BRADSHAW, EDWYNNE G.
[b.] October 22, 1922, Arkansas; [p.] Deceased; [m.] Deceased, 1946-1988; [ch.] 1; [ed.] B.A. Public Health; [occ.] Retired Registered Nurse; [memb.] Provident Nurses Alumni, Illinois Nurses Association, inactive; [hon.] Miss Provident of 1944, 6 year Honorary Pin from Visiting Nurses Association of Chicago; [oth. writ.] Numerous short stories; [pers.] Have been writing ever since I could hold a pencil, smile. [a.] Chicago, IL.

BRAER, MARGO
[pen.] Margo; [b.] March 11, 1942, Los Angeles, CA; [p.] Betty and Ben; [sib.] Sandy, nephews and niece, Steve, Sue and Todd, great-nephew, Derek; [ed.] Culver City High, honor roll, Santa Monica College, drama major; [occ.] Previous, Blues singer, legal secretary; [oth. writ.] Countless poems, favorite poet, Edna St. Vincent Millay; [pers.] My poems attempt to show that beyond our fears and limitations, man is capable of anything and that life is the ultimate gift. [a.] Woodland

Hills, CA.

BRAIDA-CHIUSANO, OLIVIA
[b.] March 20, 1948, Manhattan, NY; [p.] Peter and Nelia Braida; [m.] John J. Chiusano, March 26, 1978; [ed.] Walton High, Empire State College; [occ.] Self-employed; [memb.] Foodpatch (People Allied to Combat Hunger) board member, Westchester Association of Women's Business Owners (WAWBO), Women in Communications, Westchester County Chamber of Commerce; [hon.] Small Business of the Year Award (from County Chamber) 1986, 1987, 1988, 1989, 1990, 1991, Entrepreneurial Achievement Award (from WAWBO) 1989; [oth. writ.] Unpublished poems, short stories, children's stories, business writings and advertising copy; [pers.] In poetry I strive to touch upon our hidden spirituality and draw out our sensitivity to the divine, in children's writing I seek to renew our lost wonder and innocence. I am influenced by Eastern Philosophy. [a.] White Plains, NY.

BRAITHWAITE, GEORGE
[b.] July 20, 1953, Bronx, NY; [m.] Annette Braithwaite, March 20, 1984; [ch.] Anwar, Kevin, Jamaal and Jamiah; [ed.] B.A., Criminal Justice from John Jay College, New York City; [occ.] Probation Officer; [oth. writ.] Numerous unpublished poems; [pers.] Each of us could overcome our adversities if we would only reach to our inner strength.

BRANAGAN, HEATHER
[b.] April 7, 1980, Boston, MA; [p.] James and Pam Branagan; [ed.] Currently attending East Bridgewater Middle School; [occ.] Student; [memb.] Winterland ISIA Skating Club and Silver Blades USFSA Skating Club; [hon.] Honor student, VFW essay contest finalist for two years; [pers.] My passion is figure skating and I enjoy writing in my spare time. I am influenced by life and show my feelings through my writing. [a.] East Bridgewater, MA.

BRANDES, DAVID
[b.] October 31, 1956, San Diego, CA; [ed.] Blaine High School, Blaine, WA; [occ.] Taxi Dispatcher. [a.] Phoenix, AZ.

BRANDT, MARY ROBERTA
[pen.] Bobbie Brandt; [b.] November 1, 1950, Baraboo, WI; [p.] Robert L. and Jeanette A. Chamberlain Brandt; [m.] R. Timothy Marton, April 19, 1984; [ed.] Crossland Senior High, University of Maryland, George Mason University, WVU College of Law; [occ.] Attorney at Law; [memb.] ABA, Phi Alpha Delta, WV State Bar, AZ State Bar; [hon.] Alpha Chi, Phi Alpha Theta, Outstanding History Undergraduate Award, Moot Court Board; [oth. writ.] Piles of unpublished poetry; [pers.] We are each of us snowflakes, alike and yet unique. [a.] West Virginia.

BRASWELL, ROBERT C.
[pen.] Atreyv; [b.] March 27, 1973, Brooklyn; [p.] Robert and Andrea Braswell; [ed.] John Dewey High School, Baruch College; [occ.] Student, and freelance philosopher; [hon.] Graduate, Academy of Finance, Regents scholarship recipient; [oth. writ.] Short story "Wolf Among the Sheep. published in Baruch Literary Journal, Encounters; [pers.] I advocate individuality, inner strength, self-knowledge, questioning authority and reality and acceptance of the dark side of humanity within us all. [a.] Brooklyn, NY.

BRAY, PHILLIP ALEXANDER MARTIN
[pen.] Alexander Martin; [b.] January 16, 1960, Batavia; [p.] John William and Alberta Bremiller Bray; [m.] Single; [ed.] Attica Central High; [occ.] Black and White Photographic Paper Product Tester, Eastman Kodak Co., Rochester, NY.; [memb.] Alternate Imaginations Guy Alliance of the Genesee Valley, Attica Landmark Preservation Society, Attica Historical Society, In Touch International; [hon.] Honor Society; [oth. writ.] The Princes of Trilon; [pers.] I write poems that reflect my view of things at the time they happen or as I imagine things. [a.] Batavia, NY.

BRECHT, MARY LAUHOFF
[b.] October 3, 1912, Detroit, MI; [p.] Frank and Mary B. Lauhoff; [m.] Lloyd J. Brecht, July 23, 1935; [ch.] David, John, Paul, Ann, Thomas, Mark and Gregory; [ed.] B.A., Mary Grove College, Detroit, MI. 1934; [occ.] Retired; [memb.] Kappa Gamma Pi, National Catholic College, Honor Society; [pers.] Poems should not only be inspiring but should celebrate life. [a.] Grosse Pointe Farms, MI.

BREEDLOVE, RENEE DEE
[pen.] Renee Rowley Breedlove; [b.] December 18, 1959, Haxtun, CO; [p.] Ronald and Rosalie Rowley; [m.] Steven Earl Breedlove; [ch.] Jason, Steven Ryan and Michelle; [ed.] Bellflower High; [occ.] Mother, educator, poet; [oth. writ.] "On The Spiritual Side", "Forsaken Freedom:, "Ambivalence", collective works; [pers.] My poetry gives voice to things that have greatly influenced my life. People and events I will never forget. [a.] Foresthill, CA.

BRESSLER, DARRELL K.
[pen.] Ted E. Bare; [b.] March 18, 1957, Sunbury, PA; [p.] Henry W. and Betty J. Bressler, Sr.; [m.] Vicki J. Miller-Bressler; [ch.] Kelly Adanah Bressler; [occ.] Student; [hon.] Dean's List in the spring and fall of 1993 at Loch Haven University of PA.; [oth. writ.] (Published) My Walk, published and dedicated to my mother in 1974, (unpublished) Broken Hearted, Hopes, Dreams and Happiness, Loving Heart, March Eighteenth, Sharing Our Dreams; [pers.] It is my goal in life to meet and greet all persons with an open mind, an open heart and a smile on my face the way Professor Virginia Martin and Dr. Karen Elias have greeted me. [a.] Pleasant Gap, PA.

BREWER, HEIDI
[b.] November 7, 1970, Thornton, CO; [p.] Rosetta Traversie and Donald Brewer; [occ.] Preschool teacher; [oth. writ.] Several unpublished poems and songs; [pers.] Someone once said, "If you see someone without a smile, give them yours". If my writing makes at least one person smile for just a moment, that makes me smile. [a.] Phoenix, AZ.

BREWER, TERRIE LUNSFORD
[pen.] Terry Lee; [b.] August 13, 1953, Columbus, GA; [p.] Ed and Jean Lunsford; [m.] John (Sandy) Brewer, March 13,1984; [ch.] Gary and Christie Head, Angela, Cheryl and John Brewer III; [ed.] A.A.-CVCC Junior College, senior, Troy State University; [occ.] Homemaker, student; [memb.] P.T.A., Sherwood Elementary and Central High Schools; [hon.] Gamma Beta Phi, Presidents and Dean's List, Drama Award, English Award, Drama and Academia Scholarships, James B. Allen Award, CVCC; [oth. writ.] I have written many poems. I have never entered any until last year. The National Library of Poetry published my first poem "Poems Are Like Presents" last year 1993; [pers.] I

believe as we travel through life, it is our duty and responsibility (not just to leave things as good as we found it), but to make the world a better place. I am a romantic and have been influenced by romantic poets. [a.] Phenix City, AL.

BREYFOGLE, RON W.
[b.] January 27, 1949, Marshall, MN; [ch.] Jolean Beverly Breyfogle; [ed.] Marshall High School, Victor Valley Junior College; [occ.] Custodian, Victorville Head Start; [oth. writ.] Have written several poems not published, first time I have entered writings, first time ever published; [pers.] Most of my poems are written on impulse, the words come usually after a sad of traumatic event has happened or a joyful event has come about. [a.] Victorville, CA.

BREZINA, LEE (MS.)
[b.] June 13, 1927, Albert Lea, MN; [p.] Fred and Irma Gaffron; [m.] Len, August 28, 1952; [ch.] Ivy Brezina, Jill Hinkley and Wendy Ressler; [ed.] Minnesota and Wisconsin Schools, most recent, UW Center-Fox Valley (creative writing courses); [occ.] Retired from Personnel Assistant position with the Neenah Joint School District; [memb.] Wisconsin Regional Writers' Association, Wisconsin Fellowship of Poets, Wisconsin Association of Educational Office Professionals; hon.] Named 1985 Friend of Education by the Neenah Eduction Association; [oth. writ.] Several poems published in Fox Cry "90, Fox Cry '91, Wisconsin Poets' Calendar '93 and will have a poem in Wisconsin Poets' Calendar '94 and poems published in Capper's; [pers.] A special joy of retirement is having the time to pursue a lifelong ambition to write and to have discovered my voice in poetry. The beauty of nature awes and inspires me. [a.] Neenah, WI.

BRILLO, VANDRA
[b.] September 30, 1971; [p.] Robert and Marilyn Brillo; [ed.] Wood-Ridge High School, American Business Academy, Helma Corp. School of Massage, National Healthcare Services; [occ.] Certified Massage Therapist; [memb.] Member AMTA (American Massage Therapy Association); [pers.] Mom, you always said I'd do it and I did. It makes me so happy to feel the warmth of you smiling down on me from heaven. [a.] Wood-Ridge, NJ.

BRINKER, PAULINE A.
[b.] December 21, 1903, Rock Falls, IL; [p.] Henry and Anna Dehlman (deceased); [m.] Harvey Brinker (deceased); [ch.] Four sons, one daughter; [ed.] Graduated from business school; [occ.] Retired; [memb.] Evangelical Lutheran Church, Ladies Auxiliary of VFW; [oth. writ.] Several poems; [pers.] I have numerous descendants and wish a good life for all young people living in our great land. [a.] Mt. Morris, IL.

BRINKMAN, RHONDA
[b.] March 22, 1959, Nebraska; [p.] Merlin Lange and Sherrill Siefken; [m.] Jonathan Brinkman, August 24, 1986; [ch.] Sarah, Sonya, Justine and Jared; [ed.] Douglas High, Lincoln School of Commerce; [occ.] Administrative Secretary; [oth.writ.] Several poems printed in local magazines; [pers.] Life's memories are the true artists pen. [a.] Palmyra, NE.

BRISCOE, MABEL E.
[pen.] (M.E.B.) Optometrist; [b.] August 10, 1947, Chicago, IL; [p.] Mr. and Mrs. William Hoard; [m.] Divorced; [ch.] Gwendolyn, Sherie, Isaiah Jr., Darryl, Toni, Kevin and Tracie; [ed.] Flower Vocational High, Loop College; [occ.] Writer; [oth. writ.] My work has

just in the past few months been picked up by a publishing company and is being edited for publication, it is children's stories; [pers.] In my writing I try to get across to the reader how nice it is to spread love as opposed to hate, to go for the positive and not the negative. [a.] Chicago, IL.

BRITTAIN, ANGLEINA
[b.] August 22,1977, McHenry; [p.] Kathryn and Thomas Brittain; [oth. writ.] Several poems and several stories, none of which have been published; [pers.] Ray Bradbury opened up my mind, but my nana opened up my heart. [a.] McHenry, IL.

BRITTON, WILLIAM S.
[pen.] Bill Britton; [b.] May 10, 1938, Locust Valley, NY; [p.] Mr. and Mrs. Edward Britton; [m.] Barbara, June 24, 1961; [ch.] Christine, Kurt and John; [ed.] Oyster Bay High School, presently a senior at S.U.N.Y. College at Old Westbury; [occ.] Clam Harvester and full time student; [hon.] All Semester Honors at SUNY. [a.] Bayville, NY.

BROCKSIECK, WILMA L.
b.] Kansas City, MO; [p.] Ruby Starman; [occ.] Youth Counselor; [pers.] Knowing CHrist as my personal Saviour has given me a daily walk in His love. Sharing for the first time some of my writings has been an enjoyable experience. Who knows what blessings are ours from day to day. [a.] Silverdale, WA.

BROOKS, LIZ
[b.] December 19, 1940, New Zealand; [ch.] Ellen and Michael, grandchildren, Billie and Jeffery; [ed.] Hatt Valley High School; [occ.] Journalist farmer; [memb.] NZ Federated Farmers, Black Colonel Sheep Breeders, NZ Log Builders Association; [hon.] Winner of several press photography award in NZ; [oth. writ.] Co-authors "Scenic NZ", co-author "Building With Logs in NZ"; [pers.] Poetry is a hobby, a relaxation from the more serious writing I do every day. [a.] Feilding, NZ.

BROOKINS, CHAD ALAN
[b.] September 8, 1968, Terrell, TX; [p.] Rodney and Sue Brookins; [ed.] Freshman at University of Texas at Arlington; [occ.] Electronics Technician; [memb.] Conservative Youth of America, United States Marine Corps; [oth. writ.] None published; [pers.] I mostly write lyrics for songs. I play guitar and create most of my won atmosphere. I only write poetry when I am deeply moved. [a.] Arlington, TX.

BROPHY, JUDY
[b.] April 20, 1960, Scot Lake, Cape Breton, Nova Scotia; [p.] Lawrence and Mary MacDonald; [m.] Billy Joe Brophy, December 1, 1984; [ch.] Melissa, Winston and Miranda; [oth.writ.] Just for family and friends, this is first publication.

BROSEMAN, EDITH C.
[b.] January 1, 1908, New York City, NY; [p.] Sophie and George W. Ranges; [m.] Kenneth Arentsen Broseman, November 27, 1927; [ch.] Joyce Virginia, Edith Margaret, Kenneth Albert, George Frederick; [ed.] East Rutherford New Jersey High School, Drakes Business College; [occ.] Retired; [memb.] Franklin Lakes Seniors Inc., served on Franklin Lake Board of Education nine years, served on Board of Election 49 years, organized Town Brownies and Girl Scouts; [oth. writ.] Numerous poems published in Morning Call, Paterson, NJ. paper, I composed my Christmas card poems for forty years

until my husband's death in 1970 and my four year old grandson was killed in an accident the same year, now I only write poems for special occasions; [pers.] The Franklin Lakes, NJ United Methodist Church celebrated its 125th birthday in 1950. I composed a poem for the celebration that was set to music in 1980 by Roy Meyers a member. It is sung by the choir each anniversary. [a.] Franklin Lakes, NJ.

BROUSSARD, STACEY

[b.] February 1, 1963, Fowler, CA; [p.] Edward and Maxine Lindley; [m.] Paul Broussard, January 10, 1987; [ch.] Julie, Jennifer and Samuel; [ed.] Spring High School, University of Houston, College of Business Administration; [pers.] The creation of poetry gives us an experience testing our imagination and expressiveness. It can be spontaneous or concentrated but is always a graceful way of conjuring our emotions. [a.] Hanford, CA.

BROWN, ALLEN

[pen.] Jacob Timber; [b.] August 27, 1977, San Antonio, TX; [p.] Willie Brown and Sandra J. Harvey; [m.] Single; [ed.] William Howard Taft, San Antonio, TX; [occ.] Student; [memb.] American Heart Association; [hon.] Highest award in Texas Talent Show; [oth. writ.] Short stories, unpublished; [pers.] My mother always said "Stand strong and carry a big pen".[a.] San Antonio, TX.

BROWN, ANNIE L.

[b.] Over one half century ago, Kansas City, MO; [p.] Felix and Louise Henderson; [m.] Eugene Brown (deceased), January 5, 1944; [ch.] Eugene, William, Dwight, Ronald (deceased), Anita, Angela and Leland; [ed.] Lincoln High, Kansas University (1 year), UMKC-Early Childhood Basic Training, (summer school); [occ.] Para-professional in Early Childhood; [memb.] Centennial U.M. Church, U.M. Women's Group (local church); [hon.] February 1991, guest of honor for the Afro-American Culture Club's tenth annual Gospel Extravaganza (Brookhaven Ntl Lab.), Upton, NY., awards (recognition for volunteer in schools); [oth. writ.] Letters to the Editor published in the opinion section of local newspaper, working on a book including material I've written in the past 25 years; [pers.] Beyond the sadness, the tears and frustrations there is love and an inner peace. So, smile you have a lot going for you. [a.] Kansas City, MO.

BROWN, BARBARA DWYER

[b.] May 15, 1935, Waterbury, CT; [p.] Thomas and Mildred Adams Dwyer; [m.] Robert Zanes Brown, August 16, 1971; [ed.] B.S. Fordham University, MA Middlebury College, MA Teachers College Columbia, M.Phil Columbia University, Ph.D. Columbia University; [occ.] Retired, formerly College Administration, teacher of French and English, presently translating novels of Jules Verne; [memb.] Historic Annapolis Foundation, National Trust for Historic Preservation, Long Island Language Teachers, Philharmonic Symphony Society of New York; [oth. writ.] Poems published in literary magazines, comparative study of James Thomson, "The Four Seasons" and Francois de S. Lambert's "Les Quatre Saisons"; [pers.] Every person has an obligation by virtue of his existence, to be all that he can be, and to make that being work for the good of his world. [a.] Annapolis, MD.

BROWN, BRIAN B.

[b.] January 15, 1979, Detroit, MI; [p.] Peter and

Mariela Brown; [ed.] University Liggett School; [occ.] Student; [hon.] 1st place Detroit Free Press writing contest, poetry division; [oth. writ.] Published in several local papers and publications. [a.] Grosse Pointe Farms, MI.

BROWN, CONSUELO JOY

[pen.] Consuelo Joy Parks; [b.] May 8, New York, NY; [ed.] Father Young's Academy, New York, NY.; [occ.] Volunteer worker at Holy Name Hospital, Teaneck, NJ. and Hackensack Medical Center, Hackensack, NJ.; [memb.] Unity Church of Christ, Teaneck, NJ., currently serving on the Board of Directors; [hon.] Harlem Branch, YMCA of Greater New York, Black Achievers in Industry Award for achieving status in industry as a motivator and pacesetter for Black youth; [oth. writ.] 12 other poems to date, one was included on the cover of the obituary for a friend; [pers.] I asked God to reveal to me my divine gifts, He answered me by working in, through and as me in poetry as one of my many gifts. Amazed and intrigued by others, appreciation of my expressions, I am infinitely grateful for answered prayer. [a.] Teaneck, NJ.

BROWN, JACQUI

[b.] January 13, 1980, Sarnia, Ontario; [p.] Helen and Fred Brown; [ed.] Grade 8 currently at Sacred Heart School; [occ.] Grade 8 student; [memb.] Moore Gymnastic Club, Sacred Heart Youth Ministry, R.C.S.C.C. (Sea Cadets); [hon.] Student of the Month Award, grade 8, October 1993; [oth. writ.] None have been published, but I love to write short stories and poems and I like to draw; [pers.] Try your best no matter what, and always follow your heart, your dreams count. That's what I go by. [a.] Sarnia, Ontario Canada.

BROWN, MARGARET ELLEN

[pen.] Margaret Hyatt Brown; [b.] October 3, 1926, Memphis, TN; [p.] Margaret Barnett and John Hyatt; [m.] Robert Brown, June 23, 1943; [ch.] Patricia and Robert; [ed.] Eight grade, self taught by reading; [occ.] Retired; [memb.] Glenview P.T.A., American Legion, Police Association, A.A.R.P. Retired Association; [hon.] P.T.A., enrolled the whole school parents to subscribe to the California P.T.A. magazine, was given an award, also given award for playground "Mother of the Year", Pacific Telephone and Telegraph Co, five and ten year pin; [oth. writ.] Only poems, one published in the Oakland Tribune, have many more poems; [pers.] Severe depression lead me to writing poems. Very healing in releasing some pain that I suffered at the time and being active with children also healed my feelings. [a.] Castro Valley, CA.

BROWN, PETER

[b.] March 4, 1945, New York, NY; [p.] Trunella Howcott and Oliver Brown; [m.] Rosemarie Brown, April 28, 1981; [ch.] John-Erik; [ed.] Stuyvesant High School, Columbia College, Teachers College, Col. University; [occ.] Math teacher; [oth. writ.] Since college days, satirical verse based on personalities, famous, infamous and little known and situations newsworthy and otherwise. Verse influenced by William S. Gilbert, Cole Porter, Lorenz Hart; [pers.] We are born to accumulate knowledge and experiences for tapping resources, known and unknown, to discover or create throughout eternity solutions that enhance our well-being in the universe! [a.] New York, NY.

BROWN, SANDRA J.

[b.] May 28, 1944, Enid, OK; [p.] Clarence A. and Lilly Mae (Hester) Baggett; [m.] Richard Earl Brown, July 13,

1963; [ch.] Joyce Lynn Brown, lost her in a car wreck October 8, 1986, age 16 1/2; [ed.] High school; [occ.] Secretary; [memb.] Hillsdale Bible Church; [hon.] I have won several first place ribbons for my oil painting in County Fairs, had a poem about the Cherokee Strip Race published in Centennial Book about the Cherokee Strip for Enid and Hillsdale, OK.; [pers.] I feel God has given me my oil painting and poetry to help me have a reason to go on living after the death of my only child. I get closer to God thru my art and praise Him for it. [a.] Hillsdale, OK.

BROWN, SHEILA

[b.] July 20, 1967, Los Angeles, CA; [p.] Pearl and Namon Brown; [ed.] California Institute of the Arts (major, dance), Valencia, CA; [occ.] Administrative Assistant, performer (sing/dance); [memb.] United States Organization (U.S.O.) variety troupe; [hon.] Northrop Business Education, English Literature, numerous talent shows, Gold Seal Bearer, Who's Who Among America's High School Students, Foreign Language (French), California Legislature Assembly; [oth. writ.] A varied collection, pertaining to every aspect, every emotion, every movement in my life, thus far. I'll make it a point that they all get their chances. Influences, Dickinson, Poe, Thoreau and Emerson; [pers.] There's a voice that constantly speaks, particularly amidst the silence. I feel it a duty to let the outside world know what this voice speaks of and why, therefore, I write to set it free. [a.] New York, NY.

BROWN, WILLIE

[pen.] Willie Brown; [b.] March 3, 1946, Birmingham, AL; [p.] Deceased, Willie and Viree Brown; [m.] Single; [sib.] Wilma J. Williams, Orlando, Sidney and Kevin Brown, (grand) Cherlanda, Ashley and Aaron Brown; [ed.] 12th grade, Wenonah High, Birmingham, AL, Automatic Electric Franklin Park, IL; [occ.] Retired steel worker; [memb.] King Solomon's Lodge II, Pythagoras Temple No 1, Commander in Chief of Light of Ohio Consistory No 11, Asst. Baseball Coach at Glenville High School; [hon.] GHS Athletic Department, Bth Sheba Court No 47, LTV Steel Steering Committee, A.A.O.N. of the Mystic Shrine; [oth. writ.] I Am, That I Am, Mystic Three, New Generation (poems); [pers.] I am a believer and not a doubter, I am true to the very best, that is within me, I am that I am. [a.] Cleveland, OH.

BROWNFIELD, LYMAN

[b.] June 6, 1913, Uniontown, PA; [p.] W.W. and Faye Shipman Brownfield; [m.] Charlotte Huddle Brownfield, July 1, 1979; [ch.] By former marriage, Diana McBee and Candace Brownfield; [ed.] West High School, Columbus, OH., Mount Union College, B.A., Duke Law School, LL.A., Judge Advocate Generals School; [occ.] Lawyer, corporation, executive Columbus, OH.; [memb.] American Bar Association, Ohio State Bar Association, Columbus Bar Association, Federal Bar Association, Judge Advocates Association; [hon.] Order of the Coif; [oth. writ.] Law review comments and articles, Duke Bar Journal and Law and Contemporary Problems. [a.] Columbus, OH.

BROWNING, S.J. (MRS.)

[pen.] Sue Browning; [b.] October 22, 1962, Wolverhampton; [p.] Mr. and Mrs. E.A. Randles; [ch.] Nathaniel Iain Poeter (age almost 4 years); [ed.] Woodfield Ave School, Colton Hills School, Aberdare College of F.E., Cardiff Institute of High Education (currently); [occ.] Fulltime student (social work) and mother; [memb.] I.F.A.W., World Wildlife Fund, R.S.P.C.A., Homestart

Crymney Valley, N.S.P.C.C.; [hon.] B'tec National diploma in Social Care (Aberdare College), currently studying BA (Hons) community studies; [oth. writ.] Lots of individual poems, 2 children's poetry books, book of short stories for children; [pers.] I love writing poetry, I write about anything that "moves me" emotionally. I fine poetry very fulfilling and rewarding although some of my writing is very personal and revealing. [a.] Quaker's Yard, South Wales.

BROYLES, LANISE
[b.] May 4, 1975, California; [p.] Starlet and Jerry Broyles; [ch.] Tylar Wayne Lee and Kory Andrew Lewis; [ed.] Catoosa Junior High, I went to 7th grade and am planning to go to college after I get my GED; [occ.] GED classes; [pers.] Writing is my passion. Thanks to everyone for support. Writing has always helped me with my problems, poetry is a wonderful way to express your feelings. [a.] Tulsa, OK.

BROZA, TERRY GRANT
[pen.] Terence Grant; [b.] August 6, 1970, Thompson; [p.] Carol and Ted Broza; [ed.] I graduated from Tec-Voc with a trade in TV and Radio Broadcasting; [occ.] A waiter who has waited; [hon.] The Lilian Lee Bursary; [pers.] As a gay man, I try not to change ones view but rather give someone the chance to their opinion, just like Tennessee Williams. [a.] Winnipeg, MB.

BRUMAGE, HELEN REED STAHL
[b.] May 5, 1933, Marion County, WV; [p.] Pearl Snyder and John Clark Reed; [m.] Divorced; [ch.] Peggy and Keith Stahl; [ed.] West Fairmont High School; [occ.] Bank teller; [oth. writ.] I have nothing else published, but am working on stories about a family pet and his antics; [pers.] There is so much inspiration around us, our loved ones, our friends, our past, our hope for the future, I want to write about these things. [a.] Deltona, FL.

BRUNEA, MARGARET ANN
[pen.] Margie Brunea; [b.] September 16, 1961, Batavia, NY; [p.] William and Irene Brunea; [ed.] Pembroke Central School, Corfu, NY.; [occ.] Certified Nursing Assistant, Genesee County Nursing Home, Batavia, NY.; [hon.] Hobbies, birdwatching, collection of 1,000 4 leaf clovers, flower gardens; [oth. writ.] Several poems; [pers.] Self knowledge is always a good thing, no one else possesses the capacity to know us as well as we know ourselves. It is in the awareness of ourselves that our strength lies and awareness of every aspect of ourselves allows us to become who we are. [a.] Batavia, NY.

BRUNO, MARSHA
[pen.] M. Rae Bruno; [b.] July 1953, CT; [m.] Charles Bruno; [ch.] Marin Johanna (daughter) and Francis Joseph (deceased); [ed.] Three Rivers Community-Tech College, Liberal Arts; [occ.] Nurse, long term care; [memb.] Phi Theta Kappa, Alpha Mu Gamma Chapter; [hon.] Award in Geriatric Nursing, Phi Theta Kappa, Dean's List; [oth. writ.] Short essays, poems, narrative essay published by "The Connecticut Writer"; [pers.] Creativity is the child of adversity and the healer of the soul. [a.] Norwich, CT.

BRUSS, MARY
[pen.] Mary Murolo Bruss; [b.] April 16, Chicago, IL; [p.] Albert and Sue Murolo; [m.] Hillard Bruss (deceased 1985), November 11, 1952; [ed.] Six years of Keyboard Harmony at Christenson School of Music from 1942 to 1948, graduated from Chicago College of Naprathy,

June 9, 1952; [occ.] Homemaker and retired Naprapath Natural Healer; [oth. writ.] I Promise You, So Many Reminders, Mother Nature and Father Time, Dear Lord, The Statue of Liberty, Chicago's The Best in The World, these are poems I wrote and put to music; [pers.] I love making people feel good. I do it with my natural healing skills and with my music. I play the organ. The poem I submitted to you, I put to music, I have written words and music to many songs. [a.] Chicago, IL.

BRYCE, GLORIA JEAN
[pen.] Mary Sims; [b.] March 30, 1944, Melita Man., Canada; [p.] Joseph and Magdelina Gress; [m.] Lorne David Bryce (deceased July 12, 1976), October 12, 1960; [ch.] Leslie David and Sheri Dell Bryce; [ed.] Grade 10, GED 12, Frobisher High, Frobisher Sask. Canada; [occ.] Fashion Consultant, Ladies Wear Store, Laurie Anne's Fashions, Bonnyville, AB; [hon.] Honorable Mention (for Christopher John) Talent Show 1982 for composition, vocal and lyrics; [oth. writ.] I Am, I Am (poem), Soar Like The Sea Gull, Blooms and Thorns (numerous poems unpublished) also oil paint; [pers.] We are so busy digging holes in the ground in search of gold, when we could try gazing into the stream of life where the gold lies waiting to be panned. [a.] Bonnyville, AB Canada.

BUCHERT III, WILSON L.
[b.] September 22, 1954, Reading, PA; [p.] Mr. and Mrs. Wilson L. Buchert Jr.; [m.] Cheryl Ann Buchert, April 29, 1989; [ed.] Muhlenberg High School, Lincoln Technical School; [occ.] Process Analyst for Electronics Firm; [oth. writ.] Besides poetry, I have written short stories and am currently working on a full length novel; [pers.] Most of my work is melancholy, I try to accent on social problems or inner-self struggles to raise awareness in my reader. [a.] Womelsdorf, PA.

BUCKLEY, KATE
[b.] June 25, 1952, Aurora, IL; [p.] William and Darlene Buckley; [ed.] B.A. Aurora University; [occ.] Associate Artistic Director, Shakespeare Repertory Chicago; [memb.] Actors Equity Association, Screen Actors Guild, American Federation of Radio and Television Artists; [oth. writ.] Poems published in other anthologies; [pers.] "Words cannot wield the matter".

BUFFUM SR., CARROLL
[pen.] Buff-The Simple Man; [b.] July 28, 1936, Arlington, VT; [p.] Cecil and Christie Burrum; [m.] Nancy Buffum, March 23, 1957; [ch.] Carroll Buffum, Jr.; [ed.] 10 years; [occ.] Retired from G.E.; [memb.] League of Vermont Writers, Buffum Family Association, N.R.A., Middle Town Springs Alumni, Lifetime Charter member International Society of Poets; [hon.] Silver Tray, G.E. plaque, first place ribbon for Driftwood Art, wood sculpture and my book of poems, The International Poet of Merit Award, $50 cash prize, 2 Editor's Choice Awards; [oth. writ.] Numerous poems and news articles published in local newspapers and Grit Magazine, poetry in one local book and 12 nationally, my book of poems in print, working on second book (Good Old Country Poems); [pers.] I strive to write about nature, the good old days, togetherness, Vermont poetry. I have been greatly influenced by The Raven by Edgar A. Poe, The Old Swimming Hole by James W. Riley. [a.] No. Clarendon, VT.

BUGGAGE JR., HAROLD G.
[pen.] Sonic Avery; [b.] March 8, 1977, Thibodaux; [p.] Harold Gregory and Barbara Carter Buggage, Sr.; [sib.]

Dwayne Darrin and Dawyn Ann Buggage; [ed.] Assumption High School; [occ.] Pipefitter, J. Ray McDermott, National Guard; [hon.] Principal's List, perfect attendance, English Achievement Awrd, Environmental Award, Vacation Bible School summer recreation, spelling award, self discipline, Confirmation (church) Award; [oth. writ.] Stories, Dolphin and The Men, The Were-Turkey, The Halloween Worth Saving, Raindeer Christmas, paragraph, My Philosophy of Technology; [pers.] I want to show how some good people are treated wrong because of their good deeds and the good side of how they are treated. I was inspired by a voice that came to me when I was sad. [a.] Belle Rose, LA.

BUNDY, LAUREL ALYSON
[pen.] Alyson Ashley Hope; [b.] August 31, 1974, Erie; [p.] Richard and Betty; [ed.] Slippery Rock University; [occ.] Student in Community Services, volunteer for U.C.P. and other organizations; [hon.] Who's Who Among American High School Students; [pers.] God has planned each day from the beginning of time to the end, so live each day to His fullest glory. Tis only a fool who dwells on yesterday's mistakes, only to miss out on today. [a.] Erie, PA.

BUNDZAK SR., BILL
[b.] January 8, 1919, New York, NY; [p.] George and Katherine Bundzak; [m.] Edna Bundzak, April 27, 1946; [ch.] Susan, Gary and William Jr.; [ed.] Graduate Pratt-Phoenix School of Design; [occ.] Graphic Designer; [memb.] New York Type Directors Club; [hon.] Graphic Design Awards: A.L.G.A., New York Art Directors Club, Type Directors Club, New Jersey, Philadelphia and Washington, DC. Clubs. Package Design Council and Printing Industries, designs have appeared in graphic annuals; [oth. writ.] Several poems published in local newspapers, copy for many corporate identity manuals of major corporations; [pers.] "Beauty abounds amidst evil, I cannot close my mind to both, I will learn from both and live with hope for all". [a.] Bronxville, NY.

BUNNELL, WILLIAM PAUL
[b.] March 30, 1959, Oakland, CA; [p.] Bill and JoAnn Bunnell; [m.] Dawn M. Bunnell, June 19, 1987; [ch.] William P. Bunnell, III; [ed.] B.S. Finance; [occ.] V.P. Financial Planner; [oth. writ.] Other non-published poems.

BUNTING SR., BOBBY G.
[b.] November 15, 1935, Albemarle, NC; [p.] Edward and Mattie Bunting; [m.] Betty Bunting, June 6, 1959; [ch.] Brigitte Letane, Bobby Jr., Beverly Michelle and Brandon Lee; [ed.] Albemarle High School, Albermarle, NC., also Elizabeth High School, Elizabeth, LA; [occ.] Medical Transportation with Med Express, Melville, LA., also Pentecostal Minister; [memb.] Louisiana District United Pentecostal Church, Tioga, LA.; [oth. writ.] Two songs, God Bless The Red, White and Blue, which my two daughters Brigitte and Beverly and I made a record, a single, Glory Bound Records, also "Bound By His Love" "Religious" and many other songs and poems; [pers.] I believe each poem or song written has played a part in the life of the poet or songwriter. [a.] Pitkin, LA.

BURCH, BENJAMIN W.
[b.] December 21, 1974, Augsburg, Germany; [p.] Herbert W. and Mary P. Burch; [pers.] Life is a struggle in which one must find themselves. It doesn't mean a thing if you spend eternity wandering aimlessly lost. My poem is dedicated to my deceased mother, Bonnie, who

gave me the gift of life.

BURCH, PHYLLIS JOY
[pen.] Phil Joy; [b.] March 6, 1929, Jasonville, IN; [p.] Clarence and Hazel Howser;[m.] Malcom Burch (divorced 1970) October 21, 1950; [ch.] Teresa Kay (Burch) Stevens and Michael Alden Burch; [ed.]Jasonville High School graduate 1948, 10 years music education; [occ.] Certified Home Health Aide, music teacher, private lessons; [memb.] Christian Church, Jasonville, IN.; [hon.] National Typing Award; [oth. writ.] Poems published in high school yearbook, newspapers, Home Health newsletters; [pers.] My poems are divinely inspired, that readers may find hope in our creators steadfast love. [a.] Terre Haute, IN.

BURDICK, WILLIAM MACDONALD
[b.] April 24, 1952, Providence, RI; [p.] Franklin Pierce and Lola Alice (Cook); [ed.] 1975 B.S. (Physics), Indiana, University of PA., 1981 M. Engineer (Bioengineering), Texas A & M University 4 1/2 years (82-86) postgraduate to work in biomedical and mechanical engr. at the University of Texas (Austin); [occ.] Biomedical engineer, Food and Drug Administration; [memb.] Biomedical Engineering Society, International Platform Association, National Multiple Sclerosis Society, Native American Rights Fund, Nature Conservancy Human Society of U.S. Greenpeace; [hon.] Received various athletic awards and academic scholarships, as a government employee have received various government sponsored awards, have been included in various biographical references, Marquis Who's Who, International Biographies and the American Biographical Society; [oth. writ.] Wrote 2 technical articles which appeared in a Department of Defense manual published by and for the DOP. This is the first poetry contest that I have entered; [pers.] I don't constrain my writing to any particular style or subject. I write to express my feelings when greatly affected by a particular experience or thought. I find writing to be both an intellectually stimulating and a cathartic, almost spirited experiences. [a.] Gaithersburg, MD.

BURNS, EVANS
[b.] March 14, 1930, Ridley Park, PA; [p.] Richard and Mary Harvey Burns; [m.] Betsey Cuddy Burn, July 3, 1954; [ch.] Ginger and Jeff; [ed.] Nether Providence High School, PA., Swarthmore College, PA.; [occ.] Retired; [memb.] American Weather Observer Network, Atlantic Coast Observer Network, Society of Meteoritophiles, National Weather Service Cooperative Observer Unofficial Station Network; [oth. writ.] Numerous poems and articles published in the American Weather Observer, a short rhyme in the 1992 Old Farmers Almanac, and an article for Impact; [pers.] I try to express my observations and feelings of weather and the seasons interacting with the life experience. [a.] South Hadley, MA.

BURNELL, MARGIE GARCIA
[pen.] MGB; [b.] May 31, 1950, East Los Angeles, CA; [p.] Max and Benita Garcia; [m.] Randy Burnell, June 6, 1979; [ch.] Vanessa, Trevor and Matthew, granddaughter, Mickenzy; [ed.] Woodrow Wilson High School in East Los Angeles, East Los Angeles College, East L.A., Clark College, Vancouver, Washington; [occ.] Secretary Outpatient Services, Community Drug and Alcohol Center, Vancouver, Washington; [memb.] Educational Office Personnel Association, WA State (WAEOP) Americans with Disabilities Act Advocate (WA State ADA); [hon.] Scholarship 1989, awarded through WAEOP to Clark College, Washington State; [oth. writ.] Editorials in local paper, subjects included, advocating the rights of the physically changed-accessibility for wheelchairs in public places, acceptance and appreciation for the diversity in family structures. My poems and short stories portray a subliminal consciousness -my perceptions of the life experience and the human struggle; [pers.] I began writing poems and short stories in high school. It was a way of expression for me, at a time of emotional conflict. It became a way of sanity for me, even now I find the solace I need when I write. All of my writings come from my heart, sharing my personal experiences, as well as my thoughts and sentiments of events I have shared with my family and friends..... Las palabras de mi corazon, the words of my heart. [a.] Vancouver, WA.

BURRIS, RUTH ANN
[b.] May 12, 1935, Washington, IN; [p.] Paul and Sallie Traylor; [m.] Harold L. Burris, January 19, 1952; [ch.] Paul Burris and Kathy Palmer, granddaughter, Erica Palmer; [ed.] Washington High School; [occ.] Retired bookkeeper; [memb.] First Christian Church; [hon.] Completed elementary school within 7 year period; [oth. writ.] Poems published in local newspapers, Washington Times Herald and Daviess Co. Express; [pers.] I have been writing poems for approximately 7 years in my spare time, as a hobby. I only wish to see my poems in print for others reading pleasure. [a.] Washington, IN.

BURRUS, TINA JOYCE
[b.] August 6, 1970, Princeton, KY; [p.] Joyce Barnes and Gerald Walner; [m.] Terry Wade Burrus, February 14, 1988; [ch.] Theron Ray and Troye Wade; [ed.] Livingston Central Career Community College; [hon.] 6 4-H Awards, 7 Athletic Awards, March of Dimes sponsor award, English Award; [oth. writ.] Horror and Detective books that I am trying to find a publisher for, and many other poems; [pers.] There are no limits to the mind. Therefore we must set goals for ourselves and not give up until each is completed. [a.] Metropolis, IL.

BURTON, HEATHER R.
[b.] August 12, 1972, Hammond, IN; [p.] Rex Allen and Carol Jean Burton; [ed.] Highland High School, Robert Morris College; [occ.] Administrative Assistant; [hon.] Outstanding Creative Writing Achievement Award-1990, Honors List 1989, Speech II 100% Achievement Award 1990, Outstanding G.P.A. Achievement Award 1992; [oth. writ.] Other poems and short stories yet to be submitted for publication; [pers.] My poems reflect the periods and people who have influenced the many aspects of my life. They are expressions of gratitude, repentance, love and sorrow. My family and friends have always been supportive of my efforts, but my greatest inspiration is my love, David.

BUTCHER, JANET JOAN
[pen.] Sylvia Warfield; [b.] September 19, 1939, Tipton, IN; [p.] Dwight D. and Ruth G. Lynas; [m.] Lynn Edward Butcher, Sr., June 28, 1958; [ch.] Dana Lynn Randle, Linda Ann Green and L. E. Jr.; [ed.] Indiana Vocational Technical College-LPN-85, Associate Degree RN, 89-Tipton High-58; [occ.] RN charge nurse geriatrics, Certified nurse aide instructor; [memb.] Order of Eastern Star (OES); [oth. writ.] The Desert;s Highest Born 1992; [pers.] Little children are precious. [a.] Tipton, IN.

BUTERA, ALEXIS GREY
[b.] March 28, 1981, Thousand Oaks, CA; [p.] Gretchen Digman and Roy Thomas Butera; [occ.] Student; [pers.] I am a seventh grade student at Cheat Lake Middle School. I enjoy writing very much and hope to do more of it when I'm older.[a.] Morgantown, WV.

BUTERA PEGGY ANNE
[pen.] Elizabeth Bryan; [b.] January 8, 1949, Detroit, MI; [p.] Bruce and Marjorie Bryan; [m.] Tom Butera, April 10, 1981; [ch.] Mary Elizabeth and Thomas Bryan Butera; [ed.] Bachelor in Ed.; [occ.] Housewife, substitute teacher; [memb.] St. John's Episcopal Church Mission Committee; [oth. writ.] A filing cabinet full; [pers.] Life is most interesting to me at the everyday level. Grocery stores and playgrounds offer the observer an abundance of drama, insight and joy. [a.] Ocean Springs, MS.

BUTLER, AYLEA
[b.] June 4, 1954, Glendale, CA; [p.] Mr. and Mrs. Charles A. Beck; [m.] James K. Butler (deceased November 10, 1992), May 24, 1975; [ch.] Christie and Jason; [ed.] Costa Mesa High, Orange Coast College; [occ.] Residential Trainer; [memb.] Maine Media Women (lived in Maine August 81 -July 93); [pers.] I have only recently started writing poetry, since my husband's illness and death. I have my trip to Africa planned to take place in 1994. [a.] Medford, OR.

BUTT, ZAHID FAROOU
[b.] December 25, 1968, Wah Cantt; [p.] Faroou Ahmed Butt (F); [ed.] F.A.; [hon.] Waiting; [oth. writ.] Poems and informative materials; [pers.] I strive to reflect the realistic aspects of human nature and life and suppressed humanity. [a.] Wah Cantt, Pakistan.

BUTTS, LEAH "ANN" THOMAS
[pen.] Annie B; [b.] October 14, 1957, Marietta, OH; [p.] Brady and Joann Thomas; [m.] Charles Gregory Butts, March 3, 1976; [ch.] Derek Jonathan and Andrea Jonell; [ed.] Warren High School and Washington Joint Vocational School; [occ.] Homemaker and volunteer at North Buncombe Elementary and Middle Schools; [memb.] Church of Christ; [oth. writ.] Presently working on novel, poems and short stories about my childhood; [pers.] Life to me is like a well written novel. As we close one chapter we with great expectation continue on to the next. Anticipating the outcome of words not yet read, or situations not yet lived, but life like a fine novel both eventually come to an ending. I hope, like the North Carolina Motto, which states, "To be rather than to seem" with all earnestness can and will be said about my life.

BYERS, KIMBERLY
[pen.] Katrina Bonaville; [b.] July 23, 1973, South Bend, IN; [p.] Kate and Marion Bodenhamer; [ed.] Avon High School; [occ.] Warehouse worker; [pers.] My aspiration is to reflect beauty in mankind, and nature in my writings. I have been greatly influenced by the romantic poets, and William Shakespeare; [a.] Indianapolis, IN.

BYFORD, DONNA NIX
[b.] June 10, 1959, Yuma, AZ; [p.] Wilburt and Dorothy Nix; [m.] Richard Byford, August 23, 1990; [ed.] Duncan High School; [occ.] Accountant, Whitney-Hunt Inc.; [hon.] Most of my awards are for music, this it the first poetry contest I have ever entered; [oth. writ.] All types, Western, emotional, funny, no limit to what a poem could be about, have written poems since childhood; [pers.] The greatest gift of all in life is to judge a man for what is in his heart not by what he owns. Be true

to others and to yourself and you will never be alone. [a.] Duncan, OK.

BYRNE, SEAMUS CHRISTOPHER
[pen.] Seamus Byrne; [b.] June 17, 1954, Dublin; [p.] Patrick and Hannah Byrne; [ed.] Beneavin College, Dublin; [occ.] Composer and writer with S.O.L. Video/ Audio Productions; [memb.] Servants of Love Catholic Community of Men and Women; [oth. writ.] Poetry published in various religious magazines; [pers.] Always be merciful and you will receive love. [a.] Wicklow Town, Ireland.

CABANA, MICHELE
[b.] February 21, 1978, Holy Family Hospital; [p.] Denise and Glenn Cabana; [ed.] Hood Memorial Junior High, Pinkerton Academy High School; [occ.] Student; [memb.] Active in Religious Education Program, school band clarinetist; [hon.] DAR Citizenship Award, Hood Junior High Student of the Month, Student of the Year; [pers.] In my poem I hope to stress the importance of all human life. [a.] Derry, NH.

CABRERA, LILIANA
[b.] January 4, 1993, Salinas, CA; [p.] Omero and Helena Cabrera; [ed.] Madonna Del Sasso School; [occ.] Student; [memb.] Alisal Center of Fine Arts; [pers.] My energy to write comes from strong feelings. [a.] Salinas, CA.

CADICHON, MIRLENE
[pen.] Mirlene Cadichon; [b.] July 14, 1970, Chicago; [p.] Archange Cadichon and Renee Champagne; [m.] Single; [ed.] Jones Metropolitan High School, Roosevelt University; [occ.] Administrative Assistant, License Appeal Commission; [memb.] Student Union, Executive Member, Student Government Association; [oth. writ.] Several poems and short stories, non-published; [pers.] The words I write expresses my passion, sorrow, anger, strength and love. To write is a way to free my mind. [a.] Chicago, IL.

CAGLE, JoANN PORTER
[b.] September 17, 1934, Moody, TX; [p.] Oscar and LeLa Porter; [m.] Franky L. Cagle, December 31, 1954; [ch.] Lee Ann Cagle Ross and Denise Cagle Petter; [ed.] B.S., University of Mary Hardin Baylor-Belton, TX., M.S.-Baylor University, Waco, TX.; [occ.] Teacher, Jefferson Elementary, Temple, TX.; [memb.] Texas Classroom Teachers Association; [hon.] T.C.T.A. Teacher of the Year, 1982-83, Outstanding Conservation Teacher of Central Texas, given by Temple Kiwanis Club-1980; [oth. writ.] None published.

CAGNO, FRANK
[b.] March 1, 1953, Brooklyn, NY; [p.] Frank and Lucy Cagno; [m.] Susan M. Cagno, January 12, 1991; [ch.] Loren M. Cagno; [ed.] 2 years Community College, NYC., 2 years Technical Medical for Ultra Sound, N.Y.U.; [occ.] Owner, Tri-State Medical Diagnostics, Inc., New York City; [memb.] S.A.G., A.F.T.R.A., BMI; oth. writ.] Children stories, T.V. pilots published, fiction, Harry's Horrorscope and Rocky Gossip both appeared in bi-annual Rock comic magazine, songwriter; [pers.] Reach for the stars for even if you don't get there ya still may touch the moon! [a.] Brooklyn, NY.

CAIRNS, W.R. (REV.)
[pen.] Bill; [b.] January 31, 1923, N. Ireland; [p.] Mr. and Mrs. F. Cairns; [m.] Mary Lou, July 27, 1987; [ch.] Janette Ann Thornton, Peter W. (born profoundly deaf)

and Patricia (also deaf); [ed.] Irish Baptist College, Dublin, Ireland; [occ.] Clergyman; [hon.] Theological diploma with honors; [oth. writ.] Have written several hymns, but have been to modest to have them published. We occasionally use them in our morning worship services; [pers.] He/she who sees the invisible can do the impossible. [a.] Tillsonburg, Ontario.

CALDWELL, MILLER H. (M.A.)
[b.] October 6, 1950, Glasgow; [p.] Rev. James and Marjory B. Caldwell; [m.] Jocelyn Mary Caldwell, July 1, 1978; [ch.] Fiona Helen and Laura Elizabeth Caldwell; [ed.] Glasgow Academy, Moray House College of Education, London University, Jordan Hill College, Glasgow; [occ.] Principal Reporter to the children's panels for Dumfries and Galloway Regional Council; [memb.] Association of Children's Reporters former Presbyterian Missionary of Church of Scotland to Ghana, West Africa 1973-78; [hon.] Master of Arts diploma in Social Work, diploma in Reporters Studies (legal) C.Q.S.W.; [oth. writ.] Articles in New Society, Ghana Association of Social Workers, Medicine Today, Christian Herald; [pers.] I am the great grandson of the poet Robert Burns and feel able to express my sentiments of people and places in song and occasional poetry. The bicentenary of his death is the focus of my current interest in preparing a novel by my father about Burns. [a.] Dumfries, Scotland.

CALHOUN, JOHN C.
[pen.] John C. Calhoun III; [b.] March 31, 1920, Cleveland, OH; [p.] John and Katherine Calhoun; [m.] Rita Collette Calhoun-Poet, Artist-September 17, 1983; [ed.] 2 years Col. Writing Workshops; [occ.] Publicist; [memb.] Poetry Society of America, Pomona Valley Writer's Association; [hon.] First place nonfiction category, Pomona Valley Writer's Association 1991, Portrait of A Pioneer by John C. Calhoun, III; [oth. writ.] Autobiography, Struggle Was The Secret of My Success by John C. Calhoun, III. My work has also appeared in magazines including, Hot Rod, Rod and Custom, Car Craft, Farmstead, Down East, Floor Covering Weekly, Super Service Station, Modern Tire Dealer, Modern Garden Center, Luggage and Leather Goods; [pers.] A better life obtained through optimism, profiting by experience and following the christian way. [a.] Claremont, CA.

CALINIKOS, GREGORY JOHN
[b.] October 8, 1965; [ed.] Freshman, Degree College (American College of Degree); [occ.] Student; [memb.] Secretary, International Friendship Club; [hon.] Dean's List; [oth. writ.] (Unpublished) Poems, short stories, novelettes; [pers.] To expound all things, no-things through the jargon, mirror-me! [a.] Athens, Greece.

CALLANDER, DUNCAN
[b.] February 10, 1951, Yorkshire, England; [p.] Joseph Craig and Rosa Callander; [sib.] Heather, Hazel and Evelyn; [ch.] Glen Craig, Heather Claire and Grant James; [occ.] Marine Pilot; [oth. writ.] Many poems relating to everyday life; [pers.] My poems are influenced by experiences, both good and bad in my life to date, written through humorous eyes! [a.] King's Lynn, Norfolk.

CALLENDER, SARITA
[b.] June 14, 1966, Essex, GB; [p.] Conrad and Christine Callender; [m.] Divorced July 1989, September 1984; [ch.] Portia Leixoes; [ed.] The Harwich County Secondary, Brooklands Adult Education Center, Clacton Tech;

[occ.] Care Assistant; [memb.] Felixstowe Rifle Club, Felixstowe Writers Club, I would dearly love to be a member of the Addams Family Fan Club (if there is one) as I draw a lot of inspiration from them in my daily life; [hon.] A number of athletic awards and medals; [oth. writ.] Many poems on a similar vein, although I am also working on a novel and two screen plays all on the paranormal; [pers.] Being surrounded by death, not only in my work. I try to write objectively about it, that it's sting may be lessened for those who do not understand, that they may come to meet it as a challenge rather than a fear. [a.] Felixstowe, Suffolk.

CAMACHO, NORMA I.
[m.] Widow; [ch.] Michael, John and Christopher Camacho; [ed.] Central Commerical High School, Brooklyn College/Creating Writing, New York University/ Admin. Assistant, Katherine Gibbs School of Excellence; [occ.] Legal Secretary; [memb.] Savings Bank Women Association of New York, United Way volunteer; [hon.] Katherine Gibbs certificate of Excellence, honors in steno and bookkeeping; [oth. writ.] Children's story, not yet published, have recently started writing a novel, have written several poems; [pers.] Writing is most enjoyable to me. I can write about the past and feel young. I can write about the future and feel much energy. I can write about the present and then change it all. [a.] Brooklyn, NY.

CAMILLI, TRACI
[b.] December 29, Ithaca; [p.] Kathy and Robert; [ed.] High school education; [memb.] Basketball, volleyball, Student Council, Drama Club; [hon.] School awards; [oth. writ.] Just A Kid, A Bit Of Hope, The Only One, Appearances, The Party, One Wish Come True, Darkened Forest, Poem For Dad; [pers.] Love is a wonderful thing it's my inspiration, along with my mother. [a.] Freeville, NY.

CAMPANIA, HASAL GAUDENCIA
[pen.] Gina Hasal; [b.] March 11, 1918, Manila, Philippine; [p.] Rosendo, Maria Salud Alumno; [m.] U.S.A. R.E.T. Capt. Diogenes B. Hasal; [ch.] Emmanuel L. Emma H. Francisco, Edna H. Baca; [ed.] Torres High, Philippine School of Business, International Business College, self studies and practical nursing. Pharmacy, Counseling, Psychology, Law, Tutor for students; [occ.] Retired; [memb.] Retired Officers Association, the Retired Officers Foundation, Inc., American Association of Retired Persons, Word For The World, International San Francisco Bay Area; [hon.] Prizes, math and English compositions, honorable first place, twice accelerated, (Manila Philippines) prizes all in cash form; [oth. writ.] Poems, local newspapers in Manila (narrative forms); [pers.] Inspired by all worldwide poets, writers. Boundless love, respect for all laws, cultures, persons, preserve peace and justice for all. I love Operas, ballet, classic music-films. "Hacia Dios Por La Ciencia Y El Amor". (Principle in life) America land of love and opportunities. [a.] Daly City, CA.

CAMPBELL. ANDREW
[b.] June 29, 1974, Perth, Australia; [p.] Neville and Gail Campbell; [ed.] Curtin University of Technology, Perth, Australia; [occ.] Full time student, Curtin University of Technology; [memb.] Institute of Engineers Australia, Institute of Chemical Engineers; [oth. writ.] Articles for a local Christian Youth magazine; [pers.] Poetry is a great way to write about the things that matter to you. My pen and paper are a way to reflect the way I see the world, simply. [a.] Perth, Australia.

CAMPBELL, ERICA MARIE
[b.] May 3, 1983, St. Louis, MO; [p.] Daniel J. and Constance T. Campbell; [ed.] 5th grade student at Carrollton Oak Elementary School and Pattonville Elementary Gifted (P.E.G.) Program;[occ.] Student; [memb.] First Christian Church of Florissant Jr. Jam. Choir, Carrollton Oaks Instrumental Band; [hon.] Honor Roll, Student Council Representative, '93-'94, school newspaper staff '92-'93; [pers.] "Kids can do anything adults can do if they really want to. After, all who's going to be in charge of the world in 30 more years?"

CAMPBELL, GEORGE
[b.] August 3, 1934, Roseburg, OR; [m.] Regina Campbell, December 22, 1962; [ch.] Patty and David; [ed.] BS, MA in Math at University of Washington, Seattle; [occ.] Retired; [oth. writ.] Technical articles in Austrian and German Journals. [a.] Vienna, Australia.

CAMPBELL, HELEN A.
[b.] March 4, 1914, Mechanicville, NY; [p.] Percy and Revia Angle; [m.] Earl E. Campbell, October 6, 1933; [ch.] Ronald Earl, Richard Dean, Garry Wayne and Robert Harold; [ed.] High school, Mechanicville, NY, some nurses training, seminars, social concerns and Spiritual Life studies; [occ.] Retired; [memb.] United Methodist Women, Church Women United, General Electric Women's Club, Charleston, SC, National Federation of Women's Club, Hickory, NC; [hon.] Member of National Honor Society in High School; [oth. writ.] Article published in Guideposts; [pers.] It is my hope and dream, my daily prayer, that God's love will prevail and humankind will be united in love and peace and brotherhood. [a.] Saratoga Springs, NY.

CAMPBELL, JUDITH
[pen.] J.C. Campbell; [b.] March 2,1966, Warren, OH; [p.] Mary Jo Cherry and David Campbell; [ch.] Adam Campbell; [ed.] I graduated with a G.E.D. from Alliance High School, currently applying for a course at Youngstown State University; [occ.] Volunteer teacher's aide for the Head Start Program in Youngstown; [hon.] Literary Achievement Award in high school; [oth.writ.] Two poems published in the Cauldren in high school; [pers.] Emily Dickenson and Edgar A. Poe taught me the passion that can be woven into my own writings and showed me how beautiful poetry can become. [a.] Youngstown, OH.

CAMPOS, JOSE J.
[pen.] Jose J. Campos; [b.] November 23, 1967, Mexico; [p.] Edwardo and Martha Campos; [ed.] Junior College, El Paso Community College, El Paso, TX., major, Data Processing, El Paso High School, El Paso, TX; [occ.] Temporarily disabled due to serious motorcycle accident, poetry writer; [memb.] International Prison Ministry, Chaplain Ray; [hon.] Dean's List; [oth. writ.] Poem published in Alpine Texas Newspaper in 1985; [pers.] My interest in writing poetry came at the age of 16, I never studied the subject. My influence in writing poetry is a part of my success in life and my dear parents. [a.] El Paso, TX.

CANTILLAS, ANGELITO ALBARADO
[b.] November 21, 1941, Surigao City, Philippines; [p.] Restituto Albarado and Cenona Cantillas; [m.] Norita Tatlongmaria, October 4, 1966; [ch.] Angelane, Angelisa, Angelica and Angelott; [ed.] Bachelor of Business Admin at University of the East, Manila Philippines, Business Computer System and Programming at Ryerson Technical Institute, Toronto, Canada; [occ.] Real Estate

Salesman; [memb.] Ontario Real Estate Board; [hon.] Community Service in Sports; [oth. writ.] Book currently being published in New York City, entitled "In Search of New Life"; [pers.] To encourage people to step into the world of enlightenment and acknowledge the presence of God eternally. [a.] Oakville, Ontario Canada.

CANTRELL, DAVID L.
[b.] October 24, 1974, Lunstuhl Air Force Base, Germany; [p.] Mary R. Cantrell; [ed.] Soloman Juneau Business High School; [occ.] Management in Fast Food; [memb.] National Eagle Scouts of America, Boy Scouts of America, Order of the Arrow, Our Lady of Lourdes' Youth Ministry; [hon.] Eagle Scout, high school community service award, EPIC Community Service Award; [oth. writ.] Several poems published in high school paper, Pioneer Press; [pers.] This has been a dream for me that has come true. As a new writer, I am thrilled at the possible new roads that lies ahead and with God's help I know I'll make it. Just like you can too. [a.] Milwaukee, WI.

CAPANEAR, NICHOLAS
[b.] March 6, 1974, Livingston, NJ; [p.]] Anne Marie Giorgio and Jerry Capanear; [ed.] Bloomfield High School currently enrolled at Montclair State College; [occ.] Student; [hon.] Creative Writing Award, first place overall at local visual art contest;[oth. writ.] Assorted poems and short stories (unpublished) and many unwritten lingering ideas; [pers.] Wrote my entry in Introduction to Literature class after reading "The Shepherd's Reply to The Nymph". Favorite authors, Hawthorne, Stoker, Lennon, McCartney. [a.] Bloomfield, NJ.

CAPORELLI, RONALD
[b.] February 19, 1941, Rochester, NY; [m.] Jane Caporelli, May 3, 1964; [ch.] Ronnie and Ricky Caporelli; [ed.] Columbia High School, South Orange, NJ.; [occ.] Contractor; [pers.] This poem was written for my wife, Jane thirty five years ago, whom at that time I was dating. We married and have two sons. I dedicate this to her, together we enjoy traveling and camping around the country. [a.] Parsippany, NJ.

CAPRIOTTI, MARY O.
[pen.] Mary-O; [b.] May 10, 1930, Fresno, CA; [p.] Earl Wellbaum and Frankie Wellbaum Smith; [ch.] Sharon L. McGill, Chris A. Capriotti, grandchildren, Brent, Amanda, Ryan (Chris), Crystal Capriotti and Preston McGill (Sharon); [ed.] Fresno High School 47, Fresno City College, California State University at Fresno; [occ.] Medical Office Manager for Dale L. Merrill, M.D. Inc., Fresno, CA.; and Transcription Service (self-employed); [memb.] Martha Lodge/degree of honor; [hon.] CSF (high school) Biology Scholarship (CSUF); [oth. writ.] Various tender notes and poems about and to people, pets and places I hold dear. None have been published, actually never before submitted for consideration; [pers.] I believe life itself to be the ultimate poem. It constantly requires careful scrutiny and thoughtful writing, revising, editing, crumpling, starting over, rewriting again and again, stanza by stanza, until, after having gone over peaks and through valleys and having reached the summit, we pause and quietly pray that our life's poem will have enriched one soul and thus be acceptable to the Master Printer. [a.] Clovis/Fresno, CA.

CARD, JEN
[b.] January 3, 1975, Mt. Pleasant, MI; [p.] Mary Jay (Hafer) and Jerry L. Card; [ed.] High school graduate;

[occ.] Literary sales; [oth. writ.] A collection of poems and anthologies, publication is forthcoming; [pers.] A third eye could make all the difference. [a.] Mt. Pleasant, MI.

CARNO, KATHLEEN
[pen.] Kathleen Carno; [b.] July 2, 1949, New Hampshire; [p.] Roger and Madelyn Cote; [m.] Lou Carno, March 5, 1988; [ch.] Jason Roger and Jeremy John Pfeiffer; [ed.] Bishop Amat High, Monrovia Beauty College; [occ.] Trichology Technician, owner and operator of the Paddock Hair Salon; [memb.] California Cosmetologist Association; [hon.] Signum Fidei Award, for service to high school students at La Salle High School, Advanced Technology recognition from Redken Labs; [pers.] I write what I feel in my heart, hoping to create a positive thought in the hearts and minds of those who read my poetry. I am greatly influenced by those free-spirited thinkers of the 20th century. [a.] Arcadia, CA.

CARR, BETTY M.
[b.] March 28, 1938, Clinton, NC; [p.] Eula House Merritt; [m.] Delbert Carr, November 16, 1957; [ch.] Delbert Arnold and David Arling; [ed.] High school graduate; [occ.] Service Representative Sprint-Carolina Telephone Company; [pers.] I started writing poetry at the age of 12, most of my poems have been written as gifts to others. Words of cheer and encouragement. My poems and songs have been used in sales promotions where I work. [a.] Clinton, NC.

CARR, TRACY L.
[b.] July 2, 1974, Keene, NH; [p.] Verna and Austin Carr; [ed.] Graduated from Monadnock Regional High School in Swanzey Center in 1992; [hon.] School District Rep. at the N.H. Young Authors Conference 1985, Who's Who Among American High School Students 1991; [pers.] Life is full of problems. How they affect you depends on how you deal with them. [a.] Surry, NH.

CARRIS, JUDY
[b.] March 15, 1947, Colchester, VT; [p.] Lorenzo and Doris Cyr; [m.] Robert Carris, December 24, 1986; [ch.] Robert Piotrowski Jr. and Susan (Piotrowski) Robarge; [ed.] Athol High School, Community College of Vermont; [occ.] Writer, writing poetry, songs and children's stories; [oth. writ.] Poetry and articles in church bulletins and newsletters; [pers.] I write to spread God's love and light to all. [a.] Tucson, AZ.

CARROLL, LOUISE
[b.] April 30, 1911, IL; [p.] Bessie and Garl Bernhardt; [m.] Louis Carroll, January 25, 1940; [ch.] Woody Carroll and Maryam Wade; [ed.] Sandwich Public School, Grace Land College, Iowa Waubonnsee Community College; [occ.] Retired; [memb.] Women's Club, Farm Bureau; [oth. writ.] Essay and poetry and a play. [a.] LeLand, IL.

CARROLL, TRAVIS
[pen.] Will Williamson; [b.] July 14, 1971, Raleigh, NC; [p.] William and Gertrude Carroll; [ed.] Baptist Temple Christian School, Wilson Technical College; [oth. writ.] Poem published in Wilson College newspaper; [pers.] I believe poetry is like goodness. A little can be found in anyone or anything if one looks hard enough. [a.] Zebulon, NC.

CARROZZA, MAUREEN
[b.] August 6, 1945, New York; [p.] Eleanor and Charles

James; [m.] Albert M. Carrozza (divorced 1985), 1964; [ch.] Diane Ellen, Linda Ellen and Albert Kenneth Carrozza; [ed.] Graduated, Star of The Sea Academy, Long Branch, NJ; [occ.] Tele-communication Operator for Long Island RR; [memb.] Transportation Communications Union, St Francis of Assisi Church; [pers.] I like to project the reality of life and have the people be able to relate to my writing and see a large or small part of themselves within my writing. [a.] Medford, NY.

CARTER, CHARLES
[b.] May 6, 1943, New York City; [p.] Alfred and Cornelia Carter; [m.] Geraldine Carter, October 9, 1965; [ch.] Denise Charlene, Charles Anthony and Kimya Malkia Carter; [ed.] Petersons School of Steam Engineering, Boston, MA.; [occ.] Stationary Engineer; [memb.] National Geographic Society and the National Rifle Association; [oth. writ.] Poems and rap lyrics about the black experience that are pro-reading and anti-drug and anti-violence
, unpublished; [pers.] On reading, every written page is a door and whether open to the past or the future can only serve to enhance the present. [a.] Delanson, NY.

CARTER, CLARENCE
[b.] September 21, 1927, Brooklyn, NY; [p.] Clarence and Virginia Carter; [ed.] Boys High School; [occ.] Retired after 30 years with the N.Y.C. H.A.; [memb.] Christian Appalachian Project, Robert Schuller's Eagles Club; [oth. writ.] Various poems; [pers.] In order to achieve, one must believe. [a.] Brooklyn, NY.

CARTER, JAMINE
[pen.] JC; [b.] March 29, 1954, Dayton, OH; [p.] Marjorie and W.J.J. Hathorne; [ch.] Joseph, Kimberly, Janette, Jesse, Karl, Marcus and Kristina; [occ.] Customer Service Engineer; [memb.] hartford Memorial Baptist Church, Adult Usher Board, Christian Poet Society; [hon.] Poet laureate of Hartford Memorial Baptist Church, honored by St. Paul A.M.E. as 100 Outstanding Women for work in community and church; [oth. writ.] Mini-verse of poems, "Peace By Piece", "Breath of Life" art and poetry expos recitals, broadcast on local radio stations featured article in Det. News, published in local newspaper, written poems for Rev. Jesse Jackson, Mayoral-elect Dennie W. Alcher, own business writing personalized poems; [pers.] Must use the gift bestowed to enhance mankind. Just as stars are collectively bound to brighten the darkest skies, people must willingly join together in order for everyone to rise. [a.] Detroit, MI.

CARTER, MARYANNE
[b.] March 27, 1950, Saskatoon, Sask; [p.] Hugh and Louise Carter; [m.] Gordon Waldron, April 1, 1980; [ch.] Gayle Shireen and Ryan Timothy; [ed.] Beatty High, Red Deer College; [occ.] Pharmacy Technician; [memb.] Canadian Association of Pharmacy Technicians, Lion Ladies, Carseland Agriculture Society; [pers.] This poem was written for my mother who loves the prairies as much as I do. [a.] Carseland, Al.

CARTER, MEREDITH
[pen.] Meredith; [b.] August 3, 1981, Louisville, KY; [p.] Bonnie and Paul Carter; [hon.] Honor Roll grades 1-7, Young Authors 5th grade, Spelling Bee runner-up first and fourth grade; [oth. writ.] Wrote "The Out of This World Birthday Party, Young Authors; [pers.] To do the best that I can in whatever I am doing and to prepare myself to lead a meaningful life that will make a difference. [a.] Louisville, KY.

CARTHY, CHARLOTTE
[pen.] Charlotte Carthy; [b.] December 12, 9174, Wexford; [p.] Andrew and Dorothy Carthy; [ed.] Kennedy Park National School, Wexford Vocational School, Secretarial College course; [occ.] Accounts Clerk/secretary; [memb.] Blood Donor Association, Creative Writing classes; [hon.] Scholarship to Irish Gaeltacht in Galway; [oth. writ.] Publications in school magazines; [pers.] I have been influenced by the early romantic poets. My poetry is written in the hope that I may relate to people's emotions and help them through difficult situations in their lives.

CARVER, TRACY LYNNE
[b.] June 13, 1962, Harrisburg, PA; [p.] Pat and Jim Cain; [m.] Michael L. Carver, May 29, 1982; [ch.] Megan Michelle Carver; [ed.] Graduated South Dade Senior High School and taken several classes at Carolina Bible College; [oth. writ.] Poems, That Minister, My Special Mom and A Father's Day poem. I am now working on my second collection of poems; [pers.] All of my poems reflect the goodness of God. [a.] Fayetteville, NC.

CASAVANT, HELEN L.
[b.] July 11, 1923, Boston; [p.] Mabel DeVilliar and Daniel Beaudro; [m.] Robert Kent, September 19, 1941; [ch.] Robert Kent, Beth Virginia, grandchildren, Sean, Kelli, Lynne and Michael; [ed.] High school graduate; [occ.] Housewife; [memb.] SouthShore Antique Auto Club, South Shore Antique Auto Foundation, National Model A Club of Mass. Gold Wing Road Riders Association, Wrentham Senior Citizen Group; [hon.] Too many to even mention from many many organizations and years of various volunteer work; [oth. writ.] "Christmas by Mail", book for ages 10 to 100, many poems published; [pers.] Do unto others as you would do unto yourself. Enjoy every moment of life. [a.] Wrentham, MA.

CASERIA, ROBYN L.
[b.] July 3, 1964, Georgia; [p.] Jean Argentine and Vernon Adams; [m.] John Caseria, May 9, 1986; [sib.] Susan Adams; [ch.] Jonathan Gabriela Peyton Tyler; [ed.] Berkmar High; [occ.] Housewife and mother; [oth. writ.] I am presently co-writing a children's book; [pers.] I started writing when I was 13 years old to help cope with a difficult childhood. Therefore, my poetry reflects my innermost thoughts and emotions and truly comes from the heart. [a.] Norcross, GA.

CASEY, JOEY
[p.] Phillip and Julia Casey; [m.] Maisie, November 23, 1953; [ch.] Joey, Pauline and Lorraine; [ed.] St. Columbus School, Kimmage Dublin Ireland, grade six; [occ.] House painter; [pers.] I strive to reflect honestly the thoughts that float in my mind.

CASSELMAN, BEA
[pen.] Buffa; [b.] September 14, 1932, Oklahoma; [p.] Rueben and Hattie Lairson; [m.] Frank (deceased); [ch.] Ginger, Mark, Sheri and Cam; [ed.] Phoenix Union High School, Phoenix College, Arizona College of Bible Int'l School of Accounting; [occ.] Accountant (retired), volunteer various charities; [memb.] John C. Lincoln Hospital Auxiliary, Desert Mission Society, Desert Christian Fellowship- Prayer Coordinator; [oth. writ.] Devotions for Dieters series; [pers.] Never just settle for anything, keep facing upward while reaching for the highest with love. [a.] Phoenix, AZ.

CASSIDY, SEAN IAN
[b.] April 12, 1977, Montgomery, NY; [p.] Veronica and Neil Cassidy; [ed.] Monsignor Donovan High School, 11th grade; [memb.] NSSA (National Scholastic Surfing Association); [pers.] I am influenced by the way society rolls in such a narrow motion and it creates me to ponder why the questions were never asked. [a.] Brick, NJ.

CASTILLO, JULIO B.
[pen.] Ang Pindy and Charlie Brown; [b.] March 16, 1951, Isidro, Philippines; [p.] Mr. and Mrs. Anselmo Castillo; [m.] Ester Reyes Castillo, November 18, 1973; [ch.] Jonathan, Jemerald, Jay and Lady Cherry Grace; [ed.] Bachelor of Arts (A.B.) and self taught photographer and painter; [occ.] Rugger of Campion Marine, Inc. Canada; [memb.] ABRA Tennis CLub, F.C. Association of Kelowna, BC.; [hon.] Nine honors and awards as Top Salesman of the Phil-American Life Ins. Co. of the Philippines; [oth. writ.] Staff writer, Philam-IAB Newsletter, Photo-journalist, LA Tribune, SN Fernando, Philippines; [pers.] Being small, I take it as a great challenge to attain most of what bigger men can and some of those they can't. [a.] Kelowna, BC Canada.

CASTRO, JOSE R.
[pen.] J.R. Castro; [b.] January 12, 1952, Chula Vista, CA; [p.] Catarino and Elvira Castro; [m.] Veronica Lee Castro, November 21, 1992; [ch.] Jose M., Luis A. and Jennifer L.; [ed.] Castle Park High, Southwestern Junior College, Defense Logistics College; [occ.] Environmentalist, Defense Logistics Agencies U. S. Government; [oth. writ.] The Rose, unpublished; [pers.] My poem "Best Friend and Wife" was made possible by the inspirations of a very special person. It was written especially for her. I love you Veronica, you truly are my best friend and wife forever and a day! [a.] San Diego, CA.

CASTRO, LUIS
[b.] June 21, 1980, Long Island Jewish, Queens; [m.] October 20, 1993; [ch.] Luis Castro; [ed.] 8th grade; [pers.] I like poetry it is my favorite hobby, it expresses my feelings. [a.] E Massepequea, NY.

CATANZARO, ANGELA A.
[B.] January 30, 1963, East Rockaway, NY; [p.] Antonio G. and Anna Maria Romano; [m.] Ernest J. Catanzaro, February 5, 1993; [ed.] Bachelor of Business Administration in accounting, Hofstra University; [occ.] Manager, Financial Services for a Patent and Trademark Law Firm; [pers.] My poem is the expression of my inner most feelings that I experienced when I met my husband. I felt I had to relay these feelings to my friends and family of the true meaning of love and I therefore received permission from the church to read my poem without my husband's knowledge on our wedding day.

CATE, LESLEY K.
[b.] November 12, 1975, Dallas, TX; [p.] Patricia S. and Thomas R. smith; [ed.] Senior at Joshua High School; [occ.] Student; [memb.] Student Council Representative at Joshua High School; [hon.] Who's Who Among American High School Students, two years; [oth. writ.] I have written several other unpublished poems dating back to October 1989; [pers.] My writings reflect my feelings and emotions. My mentor has been Robert Frost since I started writing. [a.] Burleson, TX.

CATINDIG, RENE A.
[b.] December 29, 63, Bayonne, NJ; [p.] Myrna Bobis and Augusto Catindig; [ed.] Fordham University, Lincoln Cte., Political Theory, Comparative Literature; [occ.] University student; [memb.] Amnesty International, New York Philharmonic, Carnegie Hall; [hon.] Two-time award winner of the Robert F. Nettleton/Ully Hirsch poetry competition, published in Excursions magazine; [pers.] It is the task of the poet to illuminate truth about life and love, it is certainly not easy, nothing worthwhile is. [a.] New York, NY.

CAUTHON, DOROTY
[pen.] Dorothy Pearl; [b.] January 1, Muskogee, OK; [p.] Flora Bookout (living); [m.] Charlie Cauthon, Sr.; [ch.] 2 boys 28 and 31 years old, 2 girls 29 and 33 years old, 8 grandchildren; [ed.] Muskogee OK., I am in the Children's Institute of Writing at the present time to be a children's writer; [occ.] Photographic retouching artist; [hon.] For my oil and acrylic paintings in Oklahoma and Arkansas shows, I also teach beginning oil painting from my home; [oth. writ.] A full length 8 to 12 year old mystery book, many short stories and scores of poems; [pers.] I have a deep love of children and for animals. Most of my writing seems to be about them. I try to give humor, love and understanding to all my readers... be they young, or young at heart! I also love to crochet and I am an accomplished Pastry Chef.

CAVE, CHESTER A.
[b.] April 29, 1905, St. Louis, MI; [p.] Charles and Arlie M. Cave; [m.] Edna Smith Cave, January 12, 1929; [ed.] Graduate of St. Louis High School, graduate work, Ann Arbor High School class of 1927, University of Michigan; [occ.] Retired August 1, 1970; [memb.] Phi Gamma Delta Fraternity, Owl Club, U. of M., Westminster Church of Detroit, Michigan Shoe Travelers Club, National Travelers Association; [oth. writ.] Hebrew Christianity, Aging and Acceptance, Potpourri of Life, Bob and Chef, Memorials To My Wife Edna, Spiritual and Emotional Side of Cancer, For Christmas; [pers.] I strive to reflect the goodness of mankind and have been greatly influenced by my beloved wife Edna. [a.] Southfield, MI.

CELETTI, JOSEPHINE
[b.] August 10, 1978, Mt. Vernon; [p.] Antonio and Yolanda Celetti; [ed.] Clarkstown Senior High School South; [memb.] Guardia Lombardi, Studio private; [hon.] Art-English Musical Awards; [oth. writ.] 18 other writing, 1 published in school paper, others including this one no one's ever seen; [pers.] I was hurt many years ago by a death and poetry was the only way to express my true feelings. Poems like my painting show whom I really am. Its amazing how she can express herself in words. [a.] New City, NY.

CEPEDA, ELIZABETH
[b.] May 18, 1955, Dom. Republic; [p.] Aida Aleman and Felix Rodriquez; [m.] Victor A. Cepeda, July 15, 1979; [ch.] Vicely, Vilibeth and Elison O. Cepeda; [ed.] B.A. Liberal Art (Spanish) master degree in Earlychildhood Education; [occ.] Kindergarten/bilingual teacher; [oth. writ.] Several poems.

CHACE, LEWIS I.
[pen.] Lewis I. Chace; [b.] October 19, 1954, Greenwich, CT; [p.] Frederic I. and Katharine I. Chace; [ed.] Bronxville Public School, Bronxville, NY, Northwood School, Lake Placid, NY; [occ.] Unemployed at present; [oth. writ.] Poems published in local Lake Placid newspaper.

CHAFFEE, DOROTHY
[pen.] Did-C; [b.] January 24, 1923, Pennsylvania; [p.] John and Nellie (Franks) Dick; [m.] Gordon J. Chaffee, July 6, 1946; [ch.] Pamela Chaffee Davenport, Gordon, Clifford, Deborah and Leslie John Chaffee; [ed.] BS in Nursing, Cornell University, New York Hospital School of Nursing, February 46; [occ.] Housewife, babysitter, homemaker, otherwise retired; [pers.] I learned of Jesus early on in Sunday School and as I get older realize He really is "the real thing". [a.] Chehalis, WA.

CHAKCHALIS, JESSICA
[pen.] Sweet Leaf; [b.] February 17, 1976; [pers.] Dedicated to Trey Cassidy.

CHALAR, LAURA
[b.]] July 26, 1976, Montevideo, Uruguay; [p.] Julio (48) and Adriana (47); [ed.] Currently doing 6th grade (law) Elbio Fernandez High School, Montevideo, Uruguay; [occ.] Student; [hon.] 1st prize, 1988 National Writing contest, 1st prize, 1991 Elbio Fernancez High School poetry contest; [pers.] There are some very special people I would like to thank. Among these are my mom and dad, Rak, Nati, Rossana, Adriana, Maria Noel and Flo, who always understood me and encouraged me to keep on writing. And Willy, I love you. I'll always love you, no matter what. [a.] Montevideo, Uruguay.

CHAMBERS, DORIS E.
[b.] July 14, 1922, La Rue, OH; [p.] George and Pearl (McGuire) Parker; [m.] Jack Corey Chambers, January 21, 1941; [ch.] Barbara Ellen, Mary Joyce (Jody) and Thomas James; [ed.] Graduated La Rue High School, attended Marion Business School and two years of Elocution Lessons; [occ.] Homemaker, wife, mother, grandmother and great grandmother; [memb.] Director of Poetry Day in Marion Association (PDIMA) for 6 years, New Bloomington United Methodist Church, Worship Committee and Trustee at church, Marion County Extension Home Council, Big Island Community Club, Camping Club, Marion County Senior Citizens; [hon.] Homemaker of the Year-1986, Goodwill Award in (PDIMA)-1990, Poet of the Year in (PDIMA) -1993, 1st place in Marion County and State Poetry Contest in Home Council, 1st place writings in church and local contest for several years; [oth. writ.] Several writings published in various papers each year, also each years publication of our (PDIMA) books and in church literature; [pers.] I hope my writings will inspire and encourage others to take pen in hand and put their thoughts on paper. [a.] New Bloomington, OH.

CHAMP, MARY ANN
[b.] Richmond, VA; [p.] David and Alice J. Greene (deceased); [m.] Alfred Champ, Jr., April 22, 1989; [ch.] Debra and Kimberly Jenkins, stepsons, Anthony and Michael Champ, grandson, Antwan R. Jenkins; [ed.] Maggie L. Walker High School, attended VA Commonwealth University (art); [occ.] Medical Underwriting Support Clerk, Blue Cross and Blue Shield of VA; [memb.] National Conference of Artists; [oth. writ.] Have only written for personal satisfaction; [pers.] Writing is a true reflection of ones inner self. Words that are sometimes difficult to say will blossom in print. It is my desire to uplift those that read my work and stir the imagination. [a.] Richmond, VA.

CHAMPINE, JANICE JEAN
[pen.] Janice Wagoner; [b.] December 30, 1972, Rhinelander, WI; [p.] Milford and Carol Wagoner; [m.]

Bart Champine, June 13, 1992; [ch.] Sierrah Nicok; [occ.] Secretary, Home Comfort Center Crandon, WI; [oth. writ.] I have been writing poetry since a very young age and have yet to reveal another piece; [pers.] In a poem you have the decision of happiness or sadness, with this power you can dream, with dreams we'll always strive to be the best we can be. Without dreams life would have no meaning. [a.] Crandon, WI.

CHAND, DAISY K.
[b.] April 3, 1975, Fiji Islands; [p.] Sri and Manjula Chand; [ed.] John Oliver High School; [pers.] Over the years I have learnt to believe that no matter what happens in life, never give up inside yourself. [a.] Vancouver, BC.

CHANDLER, MARGARET
[b.] October 27, 1938, Leicester, UK; [p.] Alfred and Elizabeth Lewin; [m.] David Chandler, October 11, 1958; [ch.] Philip, Elizabeth, Susan plus six grandchildren; [ed.] Alderman Newton Girls High; [occ.] Housewife; [memb.] International Society of Poets, Sec. St. Vincent DePaul Society, St. Patricks Catholic Church; [hon.] Editors Choice Award from the National Library of Poetry 1993; [oth. writ.] Poem published in A Question of Balance 1992 also in Distinguished Poets of America 1993, children's stories and a short biography of my father "A Gentleman" published in Knights of Da Gama magazine; [pers.] I enjoy writing poems and stories especially for my family. Thanks to God for His gift and to my husband David for encouraging me. [a.] Alberton, Transuaal South Africa.

CHANDLER, JR., SHELBY LEE
[b.] August 7, 1967, Ft. MacArthur, CA; [p.] Shelby Chandler and Anita SanJur; [ed.] Downey High School, Cerritos College, United College of Business; [occ.] Safety Consultant American First Aid; [memb.] Jacque-Yves Cousteau Society, Bikers Against Manslaughter, International Society of Poets, Society for Creative Anachronism, Harp and Sword; [hon.] International Society of Poets 1993, Poet of Merit Award, NLP 1993 Editor's Choice Award, 1988 UCB Class President; [oth. writ.] Several poems published by the Newsletter Harp and Sword, National Library of Poetry, World of Poetry; [pers.] I've always believed that the beings and mystical creatures of mythology are just aspects of each of us. Its cruelty or greatness, light or darkness, is just the reflections of the struggle within each of us, which is after all, where the greatest battles are fought. [a.] Dale City, VA.

CHAPMAN, ELLEN E.
[pen.] Ellen E. Chapman; [b.] May 15, 1958, Union, NJ; [p.] Ellen and Norbert Chapman; [ed.] Union High School; [memb.] Barnes and Noble Poetry Work-shop, Belleville Karate Do-Jo, Greenpeace, supporter World Wildlife Fund, supporter ASPCA; [oth. writ.] This is my first poem ever entered in a contest; [pers.] I believe there is a great place in everyone's heart, we should strive to reach. My way is through poetry and children stories. [a.] Piscataway, NJ.

CHAPMAN, KAREN M.
[b.] February 9, 1954, Marlboro, MA; [p.] Gloria and Peter Moffa Sr.; [m.] Jeff L. Chapman, February 15, 1975; [ch.] Kara (23), Korie (18), Jamie (17) and Katie (10); [ed.] Marlboro High School, class of 70; [occ.] Child Care Provider, Religious Education Teacher; [oth. writ.] One poem published by a New York Firm in 1966; [pers.] The loss of my grandfather Perley Ordway, on

June 4 of this year inspired me to write this poem. He was a very gentle and loving man. Born on the Fourth of July 1902, I miss him dearly. [a.] Marlboro, MA.

CHAPMAN, LINDA J.
[b.] January 21, 1943, Lufkin, TX; [p.] Miriam and Alvin Greenville; [m.] Divorced; [ch.] Karen and Tracie Chapman; [ed.] Brazosport High, North Harris County College, majoring in Real Estate and business related courses; [occ.] Owner of Contracting Company; [memb.] Active in many church and school functions and community work; [oth. writ.] I have written many poems pertaining to people and animals. I love to write about nature, life and love, when I feel inspired, I start writing; [pers.] My writings consist of short stories and poems which gives the reader a sense of understanding and awareness of the subject I am portraying. [a.] Spring, TX.

CHAPPELL, RACHEL
[b.] May 19, 1981, Salt Lake City, UT; [p.] LeeAnn and James Chappell; [ed.] I am now only in the 7th grade and 12 years old; [hon.] I have had one other poem published in the American Academy of Poetry, school Honor Roll, SAT Honor Program; [pers.] I think that whatever a person dreams or wishes is the most important thing in life. Work hard for your goals and they will eventually come true. So set your goals now. [a.] Pearl City, HI.

CHARNLEY, CHANEL
[b.] December 30, 1971, Walthamstow, London; [p.] June and Denis Charnley; [m.] Darren McCullough; [ch.] Jay Darren McCullough; [ed.] Chapel End, Walthamstow School for Girls; [oth. writ.] Currently writing and illustrating children's stories; [pers.] I try hard to accept the things I can't forget and though there's fears and pain and tears I try not to regret. [a.] Walthamstow, London England.

CHASE, ELSA L.
[b.] April 2, 1949, Camden, NJ; [p.] Ervin and Marcella Chase; [ed.] High school diploma, Techinical School for Drafting; [occ.] Machine operator and assembler of brushes, mops and brooms; [memb.] ISP Lifetime; [hon.] Ruby Poet, Poet of Merit; [oth. writ.] Jim, Mother, Sam, Blake, Invisible Tears and Crystal Hall in other books plus others yet to be published; [pers.] Everything as the "dance of lights" in them, it is that special something that makes you pick that one rose in a bunch of roses or that puppy out of a litter, or that one diamond out of a million. [a.] Camden, NJ.

CHASE, ERVIN H.
[b.] October 30, 1915, Burlington, NJ; [p.] Stanley George Chase and Marie F. Baranoff; [m.] Marcella D. Chase (nee Maher), January 1945; [ch.] Marcella, Elsa, Yvonne and Justice; [ed.] 1st year high R.CA-Blue Paint Prod. Assembly Progress Prod. Consult, process development, Clarke Cons. of Music Phila 6 gr piano grad-study under E.S. Blades; occ.] Retired 1958, ill health as production consultant; [memb.] Started club of Universal Knowledge, Los Angeles, CA., retired member UEW Union, ISP Poetry Society; [hon.] From various indust., for work done for them, diploma music, gave over 1000 lectures all fields, insp, science; [oth. writ.] Various newspaper, for various ind. firms, story "The Preying Mantis", Literary Press, Maryland USA, "I Saw A Stranger, Fluffy", National Library of Poetry; [pers.] Words and ideas motivate people to do what they do. I combat ideas that divide people, nature, not people. I studied since 5 years old to learn the knowledge of the

universe and hand it to others to improve themselves and the varver around them. [a.] Camden, NJ.

CHASIN, RICK
[pen.] Rick Chasin; [b.] December 5, 1947, New York City; [p.] David Millie; [m.] Divorced, August 22, 1970; [ch.] Stephanie (11-6-75); [ed.] Manhattan Community College, Pace University; [occ.] Sales rep.; [memb.] West Broward Democratic Club, Parents Without Partners; [oth. writ.] When my daughter was first born, I wrote a poem to her sleeping in her crib. The title was "Sounds A Father Hears", unpublished; [pers.] I've come to realize that life is too short, so my statement also is short, be happy. [a.] Sunrise, FL.

CHAUDHRY, KASHIF JAVED
[pen.] Kashif Javed Chaudhry; [b.] November 15, 1971, Lanore, Pakistan; [p.] Mr. Mohd Javed Chaudhry and Mrs. Zahida Javed Chaudhry; [ed.] Graduate, Punjab University, Lahore-Pakistan; [occ.] Studying in MBA Program at Imperial College of Business Studies, Lahore; [memb.] Fatimid Blood Association; [hon.] Distinction in Art, Distinction in Studies from the International School of Kuwait, this was when I was studying in Kuwait; [oth. writ.[] My book was published in July 1992 by the name of "Fading Hopes' which includes 20 of my best previous poems; [pers.] Unlike my previous poems which were mostly romantic, now I try to write on much more delicate and common subjects concerned with peace and humanity. [a.] Lahore, Pakistan.

CHEE. GOON FATT
[b.] January 8, 1924, China; [p.] Goon Kok Hor and Chin Foong Chee (both deceased); [m.] Phuah Guay Kee, January 12, 1955; [ch.] Goon Meng Liew (daughter) and Goon Meng Soon (son); [ed.] St. Mark's School, Butterworth, Penang Free School, Penang, English Normal Class Teacher-training (Malaysia), University of London (England), University of Arizona, (Tucson); [occ.] Government Pensioner; [memb.] World University Roundtable (USA), World University (USA), World Poetry Society Intercontinental (USA), The Royal Geographical Society (UK), Old Frees' Association (Malaysia), Buddhist Missionary Society (Malaysia), The Otis H. Chidester Scout Museum of Southern Arizona (USA), American Biographical Institute (USA), World Academy of Arts and Culture (USA); [hon.] Woodbadge Award (in scouting) swim award, Fulbright Scholarship, P.K.T., Award, Kelakuan Terpuji, Penang State Honors, poetry prize, I.O.M. (International Order of Merit) awarded by the International Biographical Centre of Cambridge, England; [oth. writ.] Books published, The Role of The Principal in Malaysia, Modern Civics for secondary schools, book 4 Joint Tatarakyat Menengah Baru, several poems published in Poet, Eminent Poets, World of Poetry and the Dawn of A New Era; [pers.] Understanding, tolerance and a strong sense of belonging among members of the family are the firm foundations of a happy, loving and harmonious home. [a.] Kuala Lumpur, Federal Territory.

CHI, KARIS A.
[b.] December 2, 1976, Taipei, Taiwan; [p.] Larry and Hannah Chi; [ed.] Graduate from John A. Rowland High School in June 1994, plans to pursue a M.A. in English; [occ.] Full-time student; [memb.] National Honors Society, California Scholastic Federation; [hon.] 1st place, essay contest, Principle's Honor Roll; [pers.] I believe that "The fear of the Lord is the beginning of knowledge" proverb 1:7, the Lord is my inspiration. [a.] Rowland Heights, CA.

CHILDERS, MILDRED
[b.] October 12, 1912, Young Harris; [p.] Noah L. and R. Dillie Sampson; [m.] Deceased, September 1940; [ch.] 5 (2 deceased); [ed.] Attended public schools at Young Harris and Cassville, GA; [occ.] North Georgia Community Action Agency Aging and Nutrition; [memb.] Glory Baptist Church, Dalton, GA., (active in playing and singing at church and nursing homes, etc.); [oth. writ.] Compose poetry and songs for family and friends; [pers.] Composing poetry and songs is my inspiration and favorite pastime.

CHILDS, SHELLEY
[b.] October 26, 1972, Wayne, MI; [p.] Jim and Pat Childs; [ed.] 1991 Southlyon High School; [occ.] Fileroom assistant, Wisne Design; [pers.] My poetry is myself totally, its like standing in a room of people, bare skinned, and if people get something out of my work, then I'll be an exhibitionist. [a.] Novi, MI.

CHISAM, TANISHAH L.
[pen.] LAS; [b.] July 24, 1976, Brooklyn; [p.] Annette Stroud and Hemsley R. Chisam; [ed.] Edward R. Murrow High School; [occ.] Full time student; [memb.] Black Poets Society; [pers.] Hate is a 4 letter word for another, (fear). People hate what they fear and fear what they don't understand, or what is different. I write not to degrade but to bridge a gap between views. [a.] Brooklyn, NY.

CHISHTY, MUHAMMAD RASHIDUL KABIR
[pen.] Shah Kabir Chishty, Ananda Jeet; [b.] April 1, 1931, Phaka (Bangladesh); [p.] Late Abdul Hakim and Ambia Akhter; [m.] Sajeda Khatun, July 23,1954; [ch.] Asfia Kabir, Ashraful Kabir, Mahmuda Kabir Billah, Parveen Kabir, Ireen Kabi, Masrur Kabir and Anisul Kabir; [ed.] Dhaka Secondary Education Board, Dhaka Jagannath College, Dhaka University (Bangladesh); [occ.] Retired Section Officer, Dhaka University; [memb.] Poetry Nigh Purnima Basar, Dhaka Poetry Forum, Director of the Dhaka University Co-operative Society, Vice-president of Khedmate Khalke Mission in Bangladesh; [hon.] Prize awarded in the 1988 Flood Poetry contest of Bangladesh, by the Writer and Reader Society; [oth. writ.] Novels, poems and short stories including articles were published in Bengali and English newspapers of Bangladesh and New York; [pers.] To picture nature's heavenly beauty in my writing as to derive joy and ecstasy which purifies character for ultimate salvation of mankind. Classical poetry of both English and Bengali delight and inspire me. [a.] Jamaica, NY.

CHRISTENSEN, MARILYN K.
[b.] October 22, 1945, Geneseo, IL; [p.] Robert and Ruby Buechler; [m.] Larry D., November 14, 1964; [ch.] Michael Robert and Gregory Alan; [ed.] High school graduate from Geneseo High School, Geneseo, IL; [occ.] Administrator (19 years), California Copy Products.

CHRISTIAN, SUZANNE
[b.] February 9, 1948, Chicago, IL; [pers.] I am and will remain a very private person and do not wish that this trait diminish any enjoyment of my writing.

CHRISTOPHER, CHARLENE MARTIN
[b.] February 22, 1928, Cleveland, OH; [p.] Michael and Elizabeth Christopher; [ed.] Hathaway Brown School, Cleveland Institute of Art; [occ.] Retired; [hon.] May Show, Cleveland Museum; [oth. writ.] Other

poems;[pers.] Commemortus: Mother, who lovingly revealed the beauty of our world to me, Miss Ada Bruce, English (HBS) who literally drove me to surmount my limitations. I believe that poetry frees the spirit from the conventionalism of its mundane bond. [a.] Chagrin Falls, OH.

CHRYSONG, JERI
[pen.] Jeri Chrysong; [b.] October 21, 1954, Inglewood, CA; [ch.] Luc and Sam (dog, Dudley); [ed.] Orange Coast College, California, Inglewood High; [occ.] Legal Secretary-Newport Beach; [memb.] Church choir, Christian Writer's Fellowship, Huntington Beach; [hon.] 3rd place article of the year 1991, The Christian Communication, 2 times article of the month, semifinalist Biola poetry contest; [oth. writ.] Writer/editor for Inspirations for our church, speaker, poetry readings, Parable of the Talented Writers, I Love Being A Turtle, Writer's Block, Bad, Bad Bible Boys; [pers.] Being a poet is the best part of me. I enjoy viewing the world through different eyes. I love the inner voice. [a.] Huntington Beach, CA.

CHUNG, ANH DAO
[b.] April 19, 1973; [p.] Giai and Quio Chung; [ed.] South Hills High, University of California, Los Angeles; [pers.] Dedication may come from the disciplined mind, dept may originate from the soul, but pure inspiration come straight from the heart.[a.] West Covina, CA.

CHURCH, PAULINE A.
[b.] February 20, 1920, Fort Macleod, Alberta; [p.] Fred and Alice Ferguson;[m.] John M. Church, 1939;[ch.] Michael John (1940) and Darcy Douglas (1959); [ed.] Fort Macleod High; [occ.] Retired; [oth. writ.] Only sent one other poem many years ago, published Lethbridge Herald. Have many others I would like to see published. [a.] Harrison Mills, BC Canada.

CIANCUTTI, RONALD DREW
[pen.] Ronald Drew Ciancutti; [b.] December 27, 1960, Berea,OH; [p.] Ronald and Patricia Ciancutti; [m.] Fiance-Cindy Maddaluno; [ch.] Stepchildren, Shanna, Sheena, Tila and Nicco; [ed.] Bachelor of Science, Business Administration, Bowling Green State University 1983, Bowling Green, OH., Master of Business Degree-Baldwin Wallace College (1993), Berea, OH; [occ.] Purchasing Manager Cleveland Metroparks; [memb.] National Institute of Government Purchasing (NIGP), National Association of Purchasing Mgmt. (NAPM), Ohio Parks and Recreation Association (OPRA); [hon.] Graduate MBA, 1993, Summa Cum Laude honors, Dean's List Scholar during undergrad work at BGSU, Who's Who Among Students in American Colleges and Universities; [oth. writ.] Jazz Critiques for Music and Society, concert reviews for Scene Magazine (Cleveland), many trade publications regarding purchasing techniques. [a.] Berea, OH.

CIARRACHI, JAMES M.
[pen.] J.C. Bopoh; [b.] August 22, 1950, Elmhurst, IL; [p.] Victor and Harriet; [m.] Mary, June 20, 1970; [ch.] Christine and Camille, grandson Nicholaus James;[ed.] Immaculate Conception High School, Elmhurst, IL; [pers.] I have been influenced by the writings of John Lennon. [a.] Woodridge, IL.

CICCHINO, ANGELA
[b.] March 31, 1955, Italy; [p.] Vacca Antonio and Vacca Ida; [ch.] Marisa and Amy Cicchino; [ed.] High school Isernia; [occ.] Assembler; [oth. writ.] Darlind, Faith, Special Friend, Divorce, Misdiagnosed; [pers.]

My poems are written to express my feelings when I am in lots of pain. [a.] Yardville, NJ.

CIRILLO, TODD
[b.] July 20, 1973, Warren, MI; [p.] Michael and Janis Cirillo; [ed.] Currently a student at Ferris State University, Big Rapids, MI; [occ.] Student in college of Social Work, Ferris State University; [hon.] Black Belt in Karate; [oth. writ.] Many unpublished poems, that are in the process of being sent out for possible publication; [pers.] My style on most of my poetry comes from my admiration of the beat writers, whom I owe a great deal to. I hope my poetry reflects on my generation with the same truth and humor as my predecessors. [a.] Romeo, MI.

CLAESSEN, GEORGE
[b.] May 5, 1909, Ceylon, Sai Lanka; [p.] Granville Claessen and Ethel Heyzer; [ch.] Roger Gerard and Esmeralda Johanna; [ed.] St. Joseph's College, Colombo, Ceylon;[occ.] Artist in oil and graphic media, self-taught;[memb.] A founder member of The 43 Group (painters and sculptors) in Ceylon in 1943; [hon.] Won an award for abstract painting in the V Biennial Sau Paulo, Brazil (1959); [oth. writ.] Book of drawings, Ceylon (Jataka Press 1946), Poems of A Painter (Mitre Press-London 1967), Poems About Nothing (Arthur Stockwell Ltd. Devon 1981); [pers.] Perhaps, the creative imagery employed by a pictorial artist differs in a way from that of the essential literary poet and the songwriter. My poems were always the result of occasional urges of expression that had become for reasons unknown, assertive in me. [a.] London, England.

CLARK, ALICE
[pen.] Alice Clark; [b.] March 17, 1940, Virginia; [p.] Wade and Amanda Foster;[ch.] Alicia; [occ.] Writer, part time art craftsman; [oth. writ.] "I've Changed", "I Don't Call", many poems and some essays. [a.] Brentwood, NY.

CLARK, CENNE LYNN
[pen.] C. Lynn Clark; [b.] February 27, 1944, Des Moines; [p.] Ben and Loraine Bennett; [m.] James Clark, September 12, 1962; [ch.] Ginny, Dee-Dee, Jim, Tanya, Jeremy and Brandon; [ed.] High school; [occ.] College student; [memb.] D.P.M.A.; [hon.] President of the Layton Utah Jayceetes in the 1970's, Art Scholarship in elementary school; [oth. writ.] I have written many poems, I have many ideas for writing a novel; [pers.] To live my life to the fullest, to reach our for the goals I set for myself, to spread sunshine to all I meet. [a.] Des Moines, IA.

CLARK, DAWN E.
[b.] March 9, 1963, Perth Amboy, NJ; [p.] Jamie and Sarah Clark; [ed.] Metuchen High, Eau Gallie High School, Melbourne, FL., B.A., University of Tampa, M.A. student, University of South Florida (now); [occ.] Publications Editor, USF Office of Public Affairs; [memb.] American Library Association, Sigma Tau Delta National, English Honor Society, Alpha Chi, Hyde Park Presbyterian Church; [hon.] Graduated U.T. Magna Cum Laude, Outstanding Female graduate, Outstanding Graduate in Writing, Scripps-Howard Foundation grants, Presidential Scholar, Journalism Awards, United Way Communications Award; [oth. writ.] Poems published in college student literary journal, articles in several local newspapers, articles in college recruitment materials and alumni magazines and faculty staff newsletters; [pers.] My poetry reflects man's inhumanity to man, for which

a sense of humor is essential to endure. My inspiration has been Emily Dickinson, Margaret Atwood, Shawn Colvin and Sarah McLachlan. [a.] Tampa, FL.

CLARK, GRETCHEN ROWELL
[b.] Tampa, FL; [p.] E. Hendrix and Sallie B. Rowell; [m.] Harry J. Clark (deceased), July 5, 1945; [ch.] Lonnie D., Phillip G., Jeffrey L., Marshall D. and Ralph O. Clark; [ed.] B.A. double major, English with focus in writing and Political Science, Francis Marion University, Florence, SC, May 1983; [occ.] Administrative Assistant to Realtor Associate, doing public relations; [memb.] Huguenot Society of South Carolina, Society of First Families of South Carolina; [hon.] Sigma Tau Delta, Pi Gamma Mu, Dean's List, Political Science Departmental Award; [oth. writ.] Weekly newspaper column, political campaign press releases, articles and short stories, other poems.[a.] Indian Rocks Beach, FL.

CLARK, JERRY L.
[b.] August 13, 1949, Lacompte, LA; [p.] Garland Clark Jr. and Bobbie Clark; [m.] Susan Clark, January 29, 1991; [ed.] Honor graduate, ITT Tech., Seattle, WA; [occ.] Computer-aided Draftsman; [oth. writ.] Numerous poems, short stories, science articles; [pers.] The poets hand had rendered fine with subtleness and strength of line and in the words, I read the sign tis just your window to my mind. [a.] Longview, TX.

CLARK, KILEY JON
[b.] March 22, 1972, San Antonio, TX; [p.] Richard and Betty (Hester) Clark; [sib.] Chad Clark; [ed.] Runge Elementary School, Floresville High, G.E.D. from San Antonio college, attending Odessa College; [occ.] Roofer, student, starving poet;[oth. writ.] I have a ragged notebook overflowing with poems and short stories waiting to be discovered; [pers.] I lean on God for inspiration. If my work is used as a private sanctuary from grief, it has served its purpose. My poems come from limitless and eclectic ideas. Through a medium or a combination of mediums, I wish to help emancipate the masses.[a.] Crane, TX.

CLARK, MARGARET R.
[b.] March 9, 1918, Detroit,MI; [p.] Henry and Elizabeth Rose; [m.] Tarrert E. Clark, May 21, 1902; [ch.] Jerry, Judy, Jeff and Joan; [ed.] High school graduate from Royal Oak High, Roay Oak, MI, class of January 1937; [occ.] Housewife; [memb.] None anymore, taking care of a blind and handicap husband; [hon.] Some in English Literature and Creative Writing in school; [oth. writ.] Poem which took honors, also one published in the Royal Oak Tribune paper in June of 1946, also poems composed for friends and relatives for special occasions; [pers.] People of all races, regardless of color or religion should be able and willing to live together in harmony and peace. [a.] Dearborn, MI.

CLARK, MATTHEW J.
[b.] November 5, 1972, Moundsville, WV; [p.] Gilbert and Anita Clark; [ed.] John Marshall High School, West Liberty State College; [occ.] Full-time student; [oth. writ.] Several other poems, nothing ever published; [pers.] I write how I feel, I can express myself better on paper than in words. [a.] Moundsville, WV.

CLARK, WILLIAM A. (SJ)
[b.] April 16, 1958, Waterville, ME; [p.] William and Theresa LaFlamne Clark; [religious order] Society of Jesus (Jesuits), (vows) August 24, 1982; [ed.] Lawrence High (Fairfield, ME), Williams College (BA), Loyola

University of Chicago (MA), Weston School of Theology (M.Div.); [occ.] Student and Assistant Parish Priest; [memb.] National Association of Pastoral Musicians, Pax Christi (peace organization), variety of music groups, Jesuit Faith and Justice Fellowship; [hon.] Phi Beta Kappa, BA Magna Cum Laude; [oth. writ.] Various poems published in school journals, unpublished fables and short stories; [pers.] Reading and writing poetry is a form of prayer for me as a Christian. It opens up and brings together the depths of our souls and the heights of the universe. [a.] Dorchester, MA.

CLAVERIA, HUMBERTO BENJAMIN
[pen.] Felipe Paz; [b.] August 9, Santiago, Chile; [p.] Humberto and Lidia Claveria; [m.] Single; [ed.] University of Chile, diploma 1974, Dentistry, Seneca College, Ontario Canada, Electron Microscopy (1993), Laboratory Technology Electron Microscopist; [occ.] Records Co-ordinator, Etobicoke Dental Association; [memb.] Microscopical Society of Canada, Microscopy Society of America, Ontario Dental Nurses and Assistant Association; [hon.] Seneca College Ontario Canada, Dean's List, finalist V Contest of Poetry, Zaga-Radio Rosarno, Italia 1984, finalist Canada, first prize in poetry, Chile, Embassy 1985; [oth. writ.] 12 short stories, over 100 poems not published yet, 16 songs (lyric and music); [pers.] "A poem could be in the simply things in life, nevertheless not everyone can find one". [a.] Etobicoke, Ontario Canada.

CLAXTAN-NIHART, ANGIE MARIE
[b.] September 23, 1976, Germany; [p.] Monika Nihart; [ed.] At the moment I'm a junior in high school and planning on going to Virginia Tech after high school; [occ.] Student; [memb.] School yearbook; [oth. writ.] Several other poems not yet published; [pers.] I have been greatly influenced by my 10th and 11th grade English teachers, Mr. Wolter and Mrs. Weatherington, both give me strength to keep writing and my best friends also are a great part in my writing. [a.] Schweinfurt, Germany.

CLEARY, WILLIAM
[pen.] Bill Cleary; [b.] September 1, 1960, Philadelphia, PA; [p.] Bill and Nancy; [m.] Bridget (fiance) 1995; [ed.] Catholic-Archbishop Ryan High School, Crist The King Grammer; [occ.] Regional Manager, Concorde Trading Co.; [oth. writ.] All unpublished songs, children stories. [a.] Garwood, NJ.

CLEAVER, DARLENE
[b.] August 8, 1976; [p.] Karen and Don Cleaver; [ed.] Kent-Meridian High School, Green River Community College, ABC Teen Talent; [occ.] Still going to school; [oth. writ.] Many still unpublished; [pers.] Don't let your past determine your future, forgive but don't forget. [a.] Kent, WA.

CLEMENTE-REID, JESSICA
[b.] July 21, 1965, Bronx, NY; [p.] Carmen and Ruben Clemente; [m.] Andrew R. Reid, June 14, 1988; [ch.] Ramsey A. Clemente; [ed.] Evander Childs High School, Hunter College, Hostos Community College; [occ.] Social Work Assistant; [hon.] Dean's List, English Award; [oth. writ.] I have many more, I need help in having them published; [pers.] My life has been a constant struggle and I've found much darkness in my world. Through God I found inspiration that brought a light into my soul. This light I try to expose through my poetry. [a.] Bronx, NY.

CLENARD, ANN
[b.] October 6, 1944, Chicago, IL; [p.] Byron and Elsie Buker; [m.] Gary Clenard, August 6, 1964; [ch.] Kimberly; [ed.] Glendale Community College; [occ.] Secretary/bookkeeper; [memb.] National Wildlife Fed., Humane Society of U.S., American Heart Association; [hon.] Top 3%, National Library of Poetry's , The Coming of Dawn; [oth. writ.] National Library of Poetry, The Coming of Dawn, Tears of Fire, Dance on The Horizon; [pers.] I hope to project a positive image in my writing, delving into fascinating truths and amazing connections in this life, both spiritually as well as physically. [a.] Glendale, CA.

CLEVELAND, JENNIFER
[pen.] Modestys Ashes; [b.] November 24, 1980, Virginia; [p.] Mike Cleveland and Kathy Hall; [ed.] 7th grade, Honor Roll 4.0 average; [memb.] YMCA, A group of fan clubs, etc.; [hon.] I'm on Honor Rolls; [oth. writ.] None; [pers.] Writing is a time and place when your dreams and imagination can come true by the wink of any eye, writing makes a person a person. [a.] Tacoma, WA.

CLIFT, ELLEN WHITEHEAD
[b.] October 3, 1920, Chatham, VA; [p.] Dr. and Mrs. T. L. Whitehead; [m.] John CLift, JR., (died July 24, 1993) April 27, 1946; [ch.] John Shepherd Clift, five grandchildren; [ed.] High school, Chatham Virginia, junior college-Montreat, NC. (1 year), Longwood College, Farmville, VA. (3 years), West Chester Teachers College and University, West Chester, PA 1 1/2 years; [occ.] Retired, former elementary teacher 2 years in Virginia Norfolk, Co., and Pittsylvania CO., 5 years in Dargy, PA, substitute work until 1982; [memb.] Writer's CLub of Delaware County Pennsylvania, Bethany Collegiate Presbyterian Church, Longwood College Alumni Association, Montreat College Alumni Association, Pub School Employee's Retirement Association, PA Fed. of Women's Club; [hon.] Honorable mention and publications of poems in Writer's Club's publications of members, etc.; [oth. writ.] "Christmas In My Earliest Youth", story published in the December 1988 issue of Good Old Days, many other unpublished, I started writing after the birth of my baby, my son March 5, 1959 and became an active member of the Writer's Club of Delaware Co. PA.; [pers.] The family of my mother the Honorable H. D. Shepherd and my Aunt Alice raised me in the strict Presbyterian faith studying the Westminister Catechims and memorizing them to the extent of having them become a part of my thinking, a source of strength. I have been indeed fortunate to have know such people of great faith and compassion and I hope to pass it along to my children. [a.] Havertown, PA.

CLINE, SALLY
[b.] January 5, 1938, London, England; [p.] Ablyn Temple Cline and Ada Harris Cline; [ch.] Marmoset Katelyn Adler; [ed.] Henrietta Barnett School London, University of Durham-Ba Honors, University of Lancaster, M. Litt. England; [occ.] Writer and Lecturer in University of Cambridge, England; [memb.] The Writer's Guild, Great Britain, The Society/Authors Great Britain; [hon.] Prizes, awards from The Royal Library Fund, England, The Society of Authors, England, Arts Council, The BBC (British Broadcasting Corp.); [oth. writ.] Books: Reflecting Men at Twice Their Natural Size, (Andre Deutsch 1987, London), Just desserts, Women and Food (Andre Deutsch, London 1990), Breaking Silence, Women's Relationships to Death, short stories published in magazines and anthologies in

Great Britain and Canada. [a.] Cambridge, England.

CLINGER, JACQUELINE PAIGE
[b.] March 26, 1980, Ft. Walton Beach, FL; [sib.] Bradley Clinger; [occ.] Student, Meigs Middle School; [pers.] I want my poetry to be a reflection on the beauty of life. [a.] Shalimar, Fl.

COCO, NIGEL
[b.] August 7, 1980, Methuen, MA; [p.] Cherie and Fred Coco; [ed.] Grades 1,2,4,5,6, South Range School, grade 3, Floyd School, grade 7th and 8th Hood School (I'm only in the 8th grade); [oth. writ.] I have written about 45 poems, for myself, my family and friends; [pers.] I'm only 13 years old and I found out that I can accomplish anything whenever and however I want, if I put my mind to it. [a.] Derry, NH.

COFFEE, FELICIA
[b.] August 21, 1978, Newark, NJ; [p.] Lillie Holland and Earl Sowell; [ed.] University High, Arts High; [memb.] Literacy Campaign, Track Team, Share Program; [hon.] Honorable Mention for artwork, word processing and for the literary magazine; [oth. writ.] Wrote a story called "Lisa" and a poem published in the Literary magazine; [pers.] In my writing I like to express the feelings and views of the society from a positive perspective. [a.] Newark, NJ.

COFFEY, DENNIS CLONTZ
[b.] January 28, 1956, Rutherford, NC; [p.] Hugh and Colleen Clontz; [m.] Richard Dee Coffey, October 25, 1988; [ed.] Rutherford-Spindale Central High, Isothermal Community College; [occ.] Textiles; [hon.] Dean's List, Outstanding Student-1991, Associate of Arts Degree with honors, Associate of Applied Science Degree with honors; [oth. writ.] Several poems published in local newspapers, five poems published in the Anuran, Isothermal Community College's literary magazine, articles publishes in the on-campus newspaper the Patriot; [pers.] I am the great great great niece of Thomas Wolfe. It is better to be a has-been than one who never was. [a.] Forest City, NC.

COGHLAN, THOMAS EDWARD
[pen.] Sigfried Sojourn; [b.] December 28, 1970, New York; [pers.] Thomas Coghlan plans to one day systematically wield the power of God and reign supreme within the universe. [a.] Richmond Hill, NY.

COHEN, HOWARD W.
[b.] February 9, 1956, Brooklyn, NY; [p.] Martin and Toby Cohen; [ch.] Still looking for a wife; [ed.] B.A. Brooklyn College, M.A. Brooklyn College, (my major was Sociology), diploma in Creative Writing, Institute of Children's Literature, certificate in Paralegal Studies; [occ.] Counselor (Health) Jamaica Day Treatment Center; [memb.] American Museum of Natural History-NY, Archaeological Institute of America; [hon.] I have taught ceramic sculpture to award winning artists, trophies and awards for athletics, especially basketball; [oth. writ.] M.A. Thesis, Religious values and the Spirit of Bureaucracy (at Brooklyn College); [pers.] I have lived near the ocean most of my life and I'm a true Aquarian, water is the key to my life, but love is the lock of my soul. [a.] Rockaway Beach, NY.

COHEN, YOLANDA Y.
[b.] February 12, 1931, West Virginia; [p.] Clarence Gallimore and Irene; [m.] James Cohen; [ch.] Paul, Janet and Rhonda; [ed.] Ansted High, Huntington Business

School and Crockett Vocational School of Nursing; [occ.] Productions Manager, Orbit Recording Company; [memb.] AF of M, ASCAP, IPA, Brightmore Tabernacle; [hon.] Many; [oth. writ.] Articles and poetry for many publications, TV scripts, commercials, music, children's stories, passion play and two cantatas; [pers.] I believe that each poem written contains within it's lines the personal philosophy of the poet. [a.] Commerce, MI.

COLE, DAWN MARIE
[b.] November 8, 1954, California; [p.] Donald and Nodene Cole; [ch.] Jennifer Mihal, Joshua Mihal and Shannon Zade; [pers.] This poem was written and is dedicated to my mother Nodene E. Cole, nickname (Penny). [a.] Sacto, CA.

COLE, EUNICE
[b.] November 11, 1941, Georgia; [p.] John "Jim" and Rossie Holt; [m.] William Douglas Cole, March 14, 1981; [ed.] High school diploma, EMT Course, Restaurant Management, Convenience Store Management; [occ.] Business Management, Mo & Jo's, Madionsville, TX; [memb.] Eastern Star, P.M., Rebekah Lodge P.N.G., Baptist Church; [hon.] Worthy Matron OES, 82-83, Worthy Matron OES 86-87, Noble Grand Rebekah Lodge; [pers.] The poem that inspired my life most was "Others" in which I have strived to pattern my life after. My daddy's favorite song A Beautiful Life also set an example for me early in life, teaching me that what we do for others is truly all that matters. [a.] Madisonville, TX.

COLE-WARE, GLORIA
[b.] April 3, 1953, Jackson, TN; [p.] Joseph and Lizzie Cole; [m.] Charles H. Ware, Jr., March 4, 1992; [ch.] Step-children, Charles Ware III and Monique Ware; [ed.] Lincoln Elementary, Merry Junior High School, Jackson Central Merry High School, 2 years Jackson Madison County Vocational School, Health and Business Occupation, 1 1\2 Jackson State Community College; [occ.] License Practical Nurse, 17 years; [hon.] Outstanding Young Women of America, my favorite poet is Maya Angelou; [oth. writ.] Linda, Warfare, Tell The Spirits Hush, There is Something Special About You, Is There Any Mercy In The Church, What?, Just A Man In Church, Rodriquez (the rock), The Church, I have also have written plays, clean humor expresses comfort; [pers.] I purpose to let the world know that there is hope for humanity and that there is joy in whatever state or condition you are in, if you look for it. (motto, Remember to use and enjoy the short precious time God has given us and share it with others). [a.] Wahiawa, HI.

COLE, IVY (RN)
[occ.] Registered Nurse; [hon.] For Case History on Fever Nursing; [oth. writ.] Publish Case History X2 in the English (London) Nursing Mirrow (England).

COLEMAN, MICHAEL
[b.] February 2, 1969, San Diego, CA; [p.] Cheryl Smith (R.N.) and Samuel Coleman (deceased); [m.] Single; [ed.] Gompers Secondary School, University of Hard Living; [occ.] Local Government; [oth. writ.] The Dialogue of Love, Hope and Tears to be published December 1994; [pers.] You too can survive a dysfunctional child if you believe in God and believe in yourself. Never give up hope and love those who hate you. [a.] LaMesa, CA.

COLLINS, ANN CHRISTINE
[b.] August 3, 1963, Yonkers, NY; [p.] Anita and Alfred Treiber; [m.] Ronald Joseph Collins, October 8, 1983;

[ed.] Lincoln High School; [occ.] Office Manager of Swayze Maintenance Corp., West Babylon, NY; [oth. writ.] Several poems published in The National Spiritualist Summit; [pers.] I hope that mankind will learn that we make our own happiness or unhappiness as we obey or disobey God's laws. [a.] North Babylon, Long Island, NY.

COLLINS, CRAYOLA DAWSON
[b.] October 12, 1908, Draper, VA; [p.] Lloyd and Letitia Dawson; [m.] Neal Swanson Collins, October 4, 1925; [ch.] Elizabeth Kathryn Alderman; [ed.] High school McDowell School of Licensing and Practical Nursing, Welch, West Virginia, 1961 graduated; [occ.] Retired; [memb.] Baptist Church, Nursing Licensing in Virginia and West Virginia; [hon.] Some poems published in Virginia World Book of Poetry, American Book of Poetry and World Book of Poetry; [oth. writ.] My latest poems, "Life On A Wing", "Gratitude", "The Soul of Gladness", "Bits and Pieces"; [pers.] My inspiration comes from every day living and daily devotions. I have been writing poetry for 40 years, my favorite poets are Kepling, Longfellow and Poe. [a.] Wytheville, VA.

COLLINS, EDWARD "ABEL" LEE
[pen.] "Abel" Lee Collins; [b.] October 16, 1934, San Diego, CA; [p.] Addie and George Collins; [m.] Single; [ed.] 3 years of college, Biola University, La Mirada, CA., Butte Junior College, Oroville, CA; 1 1/2 years (Mayer Christian Education); [occ.] Retired, volunteer maintenance worker at Community Grace Church Assembly of God; [memb.] St. John The Baptist Catholic Church, Chico, CA, Grace Community Church; [hon.] Editor's Choice Award, National Library of Poetry "93"; [oth. writ.] "Angels and Stars"; [pers.] Live today as "if" it were your last, it well could be! [a.] Fort Bragg, CA.

COLLINS, HEATHER
[b.] October 10, 1978, Geneva, OH; [p.] Donald and Mae Collins; [ed.] Prairie Central High School; [pers.] Deep down inside we are all a little insane fearing the wrath of sanity's beckon. I simply write the world the way I see it. [a.] Fairbury, IL.

COLLINS, LORI E.
[pen.] L.E.C.; [b.] March 26, 1961, Neptune, NJ; [p.] James and Ann Collins; [m.] Divorced; [ch.] Tina Marie and Jessica Ann; [ed.] Freehold Regional High, Lakewood High, Vineland Adult Education Center; [occ.] Novelist (part-time); [hon.] Honorable Mention for "A Way of Life" from the 1993 Iliad Literary Awards program, notation for "Doe, John", accomplishment of merit from Creative Arts and Science Ent.; [oth. writ.] "Doe John" published by Creative Arts and Science Ent. in the anthology "Inspirations in Ink", several fiction novels in progress; [pers.] In a fictional state, I write about people and real life problems to help raise public awareness of how life really is for some people. I do not believe in writing any material that is "self absorbent". [a.] Laurel Lake, NJ.

COMBS, ADDIE F.
[b.] September 1, 1916, Kentucky; [p.] Thomas and Laura Francis; [m.] Cecil Combs, December 15, 1939; [ch.] Wilma Combs Rice and Glen Kash Combs; [ed.] B.S. degree; [occ.] Retired teacher; [memb.] President of Retired Teachers Association; [hon.] Gold Medal from the National Education Association of the U. S.; [oth. writ.] Several poems read at family reunions. [a.] Campton, KY.

CONAN, ZOILA
[b.] July 29, 1903; [ed.] Graduated Phoenix High School 1922, Egan's Drama School, L.A. , 1923-24; [pers.] Motion pictures, Sensation Hunters, Her Bridal Knight, Our Gang, Comedy, Sea Legs, Hearts and Hoofs, Her Bodyguard, Belasco and Curran L.A. theatrical producers, nine plays including West Coast production, The Front Page, Cyrano de Bergerac, The Squall. Only woman stage manager west of Chicago. Ingenue leads Capital Players Sacramento Stock Co., ingenue "Bad Babies" L.A. and S.F. when theatrical production reached low ebb became secretary M.G.M. with Maurine "Chicago" Watkins, Sam Marx and Producer/director William "Wild Bill" Wellman. Went with Wellman to Paramount to make "Men With Wings", then to 20th Century Fox where I remained when Wellman left. Worked with Louis de Rochemont, William Perlberg, Robert Sheriff, Douglas S. Cramer, Chas. FitzSimons, Jon Kubichan. Was story analyst, and later as Exec. Secretary in Fred Meyer's Industrial Relations Department, married the love of my life 1962 and in 1974 retired to devote myself to making a happy home. Mbr. Pacific Pioneer Broadcasters.

CONKLING, BETH
[b.] December 2, 1973, Newport News, VA; [p.] Anne and Bill Conkling; [ed.] Lafayette High School, York County School of the Arts, Hollins College class of 1995; [occ.] Student; [hon.] Dean's Lits, Student Leadership Award; [oth. writ.] Article published in "The Church Herald", several poems published in "The Album" a monthly college journal; [pers.] I have been influenced by many metaphysical poets, modern women writers and social activists. Writing is about sharing a secret and offering a gift, all the while hoping to touch another's soul.

CONLIN, APRIL DAWN
[b.] December 10, 1972, Rosetown, SK Canada; [p.] Donald and Yvonne Conlin; [ed.] Bachelor of Education, University of Saskatchewan; [occ.] Student; [hon.] Saskatchewan Drama Association Award for acting, Saskatchewan Music Festival Vocal Scholarship. [a.] Rosetown, Sask Canada.

CONNALLY, THELMA L.
[pen.] Lea Mannah; [b.] December 19, 1939, Hallsville, TX; [p.] Elmo and Rosetta King, Sr.; [m.] Tommie Lee Connally, September 9, 1963; [ch.] Reginald Todd Connally and Karon Linotte Connally Thorne; [ed.] G.W. Burnett High, Praire View A & M College (not University); [occ.] Clerical Technician; [oth. writ.] Freelance; [pers.] A talent is a most wonderful gift from the heart. I strive to reflect a religious monotone in my poems, also this is a legacy to my grandmother Bricianna Janae Howard. [a.] Aurora, CO.

CONNELLY, SHAWN B.
[pen.] Hans; [b.] June 30, 1973, Union, Nj; [p.] Charles and Mary Connelly; [ed.] Delaware Valley Regional High School, Western New England College; [occ.] Student at Western New England College; [memb.] Delta Sigma Chi, W.N.E.K.; [hon.] Dean's List; [pers.] In my poems I try to convey man's pain and anger from relationships, for without pain we would not know what true love is. [a.] Suffolk, VA.

CONNER, DOROTHY M.
[b.] April 2, 1960, Covington, TN; [p.] Henry W. and Lola M. Sadler Conner; [ed.] Millington Central High School, State Technical Institute at Memphis; [occ.]

Secretary; [oth.writ.] Personal diary of poems and songs.

CONROY, JOAN E.
[b.] October 22, 1928, Oklahoma City; [p.] Mr. and Mrs. John F. Ferguson; [m.] Winslow Conroy, September 30, 1951; [ch.] Todd Arthur, (twins) Kathy and Kelly Conroy; [ed.] N.M. Highlands University, New Mexico, majored in English and minored in music; [occ.] Political activist, retired medical secretary, lifelong poet, starting at age 10; [memb.] Campaign American, ACU, Seniors Coalition, Committee to preserve social security and preserve Medicare, B & W Professional Society, American Life League, National Library of Poetry, International Society of Poetry, etc., etc.; [hon.] Pro-life "Unsung Hero" award, Apostolic Blessing, awards from COPS, HHV, DAV and three poetry awards, many political awards, I worked hard for everything I've ever done, except writing poetry. That's a pleasure; [oth. writ.] Short stories and two chapters top my unfinished humorous novels. I also have to keep current with the Republican Party I work very hard, poetry comes so naturally to me, I truly am a "leaking faucet". On leaving the University I worked for the Raton Range in Raton, NM., as the Society Editor, daily newspaper; [pers.] I feel that no one will ever know the scope of my work until I am dead and gone. My favorite poets are, Edna St. Vincent Millay, Emily Dickinson, Gwendolyn Brooks (contemporary), Langston Hughes, Edgar Allen Poe, Elizabeth Barrett Browning and A. E. Hausman. [a.] Citrus Heights, CA.

CONSOLINO, NICHOLAS CARMEN
[b.] September 11, 1960, Chicago, IL; [p.] Dorothy Karaus and Joseph Consolino; [m.] Tania Laster Consolino; [ch.] Kendra Cathleen; [ed.] Bangor High, Life itself was my biggest inspiration; [occ.] U.S. Navy; [hon.] My biggest honor in life was becoming a Dad!; [oth. writ.] Several poems to be published in Tears of Fire, Poetic Voices of America. My own philosophies on life (It's A Mental Thing) as yet unpublished and a vast collection of my own poems and stories; [pers.] Without feeling pain, we could never experience joy. [a.] Bangor, MI.

COOK, ADAM E. C.
[b.] December 1, 1965, Edgeware; [p.] Richard and Valerie; [m.] Lorraine Jeanette, June 11, 1988; [ch.] Eloise and Elizabeth; [ed.] Whitmore High School, Harrow; [occ.] Greengrower; [oth. writ.] "Paradise" published in A Break In The Cloud; [pers.] My children are my inspiration, in them lie my ambitions, also thank you Lorraine for your support. [a.] Harrow, England.

COOK, BEV
[pen.] bev cook; [b.] June 2, 1950, Lancaster, OH; [p.] Rainy and Doris Cook; [ed.] High school (Lancaster High), Lancaster, OH; [occ.] Nightclub owner; [memb.] Founder and President of the Atlanta Bar Owners Association, member National Association of Female Executives, past president Women's Auxiliary Veterans of Foreign Wars; [hon.] Scholarship to Columbus College of Art and Design, Columbus, OH, biography in Who's Who of American Women 12th edition (1984), Atlanta Female Vocalist of the Year 1986-1990, Atlanta Business Woman of the Year 1990-1991, Omni Award for Women 1991; [oth. writ.] Chap Books of Poetry, Freeverse, songwriter; [pers.] I am currently working on a book of poetry for survivors of childhood abuse from the perspective of the adolescent. My writing is designed to surface emotions hidden in the soul. [a.[Atlanta, GA.

COOK, BRANDON B.
[pen.] Butterfly; [b.] February 17, 1975, Houston, TX; [p.] Jim and Trish Cook; [m.] Single; [ed.] Elsik High School, University of St. Thomas; [occ.] Student; [memb.] Galveston Bay Saluki Club, Sussex Spaniel Club of America, National Eagle Scouts of America; [hon.] Pen dot drawing of Whooping Crane published in the Texas Register, and Chrysalis Eagle Scout, Honors Program at University of St. Thomas; [oth. writ.] Poem, "The Gift" published in issue of American Saluki Association Newsletter; [pers.] Time is like water going down a drain, it is all around you, yet you can't hold on, and eventually its gone. [a.] Houston, TX.

COOK, DIMITRIA
[b.] July 26, 1969, Chicago, IL; [ed.] University of Colorado at Boulder, B.A. English, Creative Writing, B.S. News Editorial Journalism; [pers.] Without peace there is no harmony, without harmony there is no love, with out love there is no self, love thy self and the rest will follow. [a.] Chicago, IL.

COOKE, KATHERINE ALYSSA (KATIE)
[b.] June 16, 1980, Tulsa, OK; [p.] Douglas and Edith Cooke; [ed.] Currently in the 8th grade at Fiske Union School; [memb.] 4-H Club, Fiske Union School Yearbook staff, Fiske Union Assembly of God Church, Church Youth Dept.; [hon.] 1st place, Young Author's contest, 1st place, Bible Verse Memorization contest at church, Kid's Crusade; [pers.] Be all I can be and seek God's help to instruct me and guide me in all that I do. Psalms 32:8. [a.] Oak Grove, LA.

COOLER, AMANDA J.
[pen.] Amanda Jeffers Cooler; [b.] September 27, 1955, Ridgeland, SC; [p.] Julian E. (deceased) and Estelle C. Jeffers; [m.] Jerry E. Cooler, July 14, 1978; [ch.] Jennifer Anne and Neil Alan; [ed.] High school, Maye River Academy, courses in writing, Institute of Children's Literature; [occ.] Housewife, aspiring writer, poet (for the fun of it); [memb.] St. Anthony's Catholic Church, National Writer's Club; [oth. writ.] Book reviews and one feature article for local newspaper; [pers.] "So Like The Diamond", in memory of my father Julian E. Jeffers Jr., a tribute to the man he came to be and to fulfill his first dream, that of becoming a published journalist. [a.] Hardeeville, SC.

COOMBS, VERNA DOROTHY
[b.] May 28, 1913, Kingston, Jamaica; [p.] Ernest and Mable Saunders; [m.] Bryon Coombs (deceased); [ch.] Pam, Richard, Carol (Jommie) Churchill, Gordon and Wayne (Pam, Gordon and Churchill deceased); [pers.] Verna Coombs has been blind and deaf for over thirty years, but was not Milton blind and Beethoven deaf. Verna spews poetry as conversation but was until now unpublished. Known for her creativity, love and sense of humor, she is an unforgettable mother, since being blind she has led a life of prayer and devotion to Jesus Christ her Saviour.

COOPER, CARRIE-ANNE
[pen.] Caz/; [b.] January 26, 1977, Aberdeen, Scotland; [p.] Peter Cooper; [ed.] Albyn School for Girls, Aberdeen Grammar School, Manchester Township High School; [memb.] Church of Scotland, Summer Mission Team, Stampbug Club, Albyn School for Girls Former Pupils Club; [hon.] Lumsden Poetry prize 1992; [oth. writ.] Poems published in school magazines; [pers.] Depression is the key to happiness, my aim is to reflect the horrors of society through my poems. [a.] Aberdeen,

Scotland.

COOPER, CEDRIC E.
[pen.] Bruce W.; [b.] May 27, 1958, Plymouth, Tobago; [p.] Christina A. Cooper; [m.] Rodgricia Y. Straker Cooper; [ch.] Antoinette E. Cooper; [ed.] Boston Trade High School, International Seminary, Plymouth, Florida, Th.B., Th.M.; [occ.] Accounting and Ministry; [oth. writ.] Pending publication, Overcoming Fear and Breaking Down Barriers, Journey Toward Unity and 5% Faith 95% Resources; [pers.] Deep calleth unto deep when authors and poets write. As a Christian, I find it stimulating when from above God gives inspiration that touches the inner man of the heart through Christ Jesus. [a.] Missouri City, TX.

COOPER (BA), FRANCES LENORA SEYMOUR
[b.] August 14, 1958, Old Bight, Cat Island, Nassau, Bahamas; [p.] Walter and Blunethea Seymour; [m.] Rev. Pastor Victor Cooper BA, August 8, 1981; [ch.] Jamaal Oneil, Verkeisha Carolyn, Jesmeika Cooper; [ed.] Old Bight All Age School, College of the Bahamas, College of Saint Benedict MN; [occ.] Primary education teacher, Uriah McPhee Primary School; [memb.] Kemp Road, Nassau, Bahamas After School Programme, New Bethany Baptist Church, Key West, Community Youth Programme Choir Director, Usherboard, New Bethany Baptist Church, NBBC Prayer Band Circle, President, Women's Missionary Circle; [hon.] Certificate from the Moncur Family Foundation for professionalism in my profession, special recognition from the Ministry of Education Bahamas for Outstanding Performances (1992/1993); [oth. writ.] Bahamian Dialect, Bahamina I'll Always Be, Tell Me What's Wrong With All of We; [pers.] Whenever you're about to do something start from the heart. Present the favor you would like to be returned to you and in every negative situation find the positive inspiration. [a.] Nassau, Bahamas.

COOPER, GWEN
[b.] November 11, 1947, Higdon, Al; [m.] David Cooper; [ch.] Jr. Cooper; [ed.] High school graduate; [occ.] Homemaker; [memb.] Higdon Baptist Church; [oth. writ.] Several poems and one song; [pers.] The Lord puts poems in my heart, I put them on paper. I strive to do the Lord's will to the best of my ability. [a.] Higdon, AL.

COPANI, BROOKE NICOLE
[b.] November 24, 1980, Palm Springs, CA; [p.] Jack J. and Victoria E. Copani II; [ed.] Currently 8th grade student at Maryvale Middle School, Cheektowaga, NY; [occ.] Student; [memb.] Vice President Student Council; [hon.] Honor student, school newspaper service award, Presidential Academic Fitness Award (original signature by President George Bush); [pers.] I've always found a creative release in writing. My family and friends have always been a source of encouragement and inspiration to me. [a.] Cheektowaga, NY.

COPILAH, MARTIN
[b.] June 10, 1964, Trinidad; [p.] Harripersad and Vera Copilah; [m.] Shirin Haque-Copilah, July 29, 1987; [ch.] Jehana (girl); [ed.] BSC. (U.W.I.) Social Studies currently pursuing diploma in education at the University of the West Indies (U.W.I.); [occ.] Social Studies teacher, Carapichaima Senior High School; [oth. writ.] Juvenile book, "Tales From Happyville" (1994) in press, Vantage Press; [pers.] The protection of children is the responsibility of man. Denial of that responsibility marginalizes the man. [a.] St. Augustine, Trinidad.

COPPAGE, CHRIS
[b.] December 12,1968, Towson, MD; [ed.] Loyola High School, Towson, MD.; [occ.] Student; [pers.] Thanks to the universe, all living life has a chance to thrive on earth. I have been greatly influenced by nature and everything it has to offer. [a.] Lutherville, MD.

COPYAK, EDNA
[b.] December 13, 1917, Kansas; [p.] Joe and Leona Fedell; [m.] George Copyak, June 11, 1949; [ch.] Dennis, Jody, Fred and George; [ed.] Carbon County High, Price, Utah; [occ.] Retired office clerk; [memb.] National Diabetes Association, Young at Heart Senior, Citizen Center, Tyrolean Trentini of Wyoming; [oth. writ.] Short stories of my life's experiences, several short poems about God and nature; [pers.] I am just an ordinary human being who likes to reflect on the wonders of my life and the beauty of this world that God has given to us, to have and to share. [a.] Rock Springs, Wy.

CORBETT, LONDON P.
[pen.] London P. Corbett; [b.] November 23, 1898, Kansas; [p.] NeoNettie and Bert; [m.] (1) Jessica (2) Jane, (1) 1927, (2) 1984; [ed.] B.A. English Major; [occ.] Retired from being Educator, Hospital Manager, Flight and Space researcher with emphasis on preparing astronauts for trips to the moon; [memb.] The Western-ers, Los Angeles Corral; [hon.] Honored Alumnus Walla Walla College 1986; [oth. writ.] This poem and others were written at age 85 while courting my second wife, in the Spring of '84. This entire poem was composed on my early morning hike around the Pasadena Rose Bowl, except the last four lines, which added themselves when the poem reached the written form; [pers.] Enjoy rich retired social life among my conservative friends. Con-sider Tennyson my ideal poet. [a.] Glendale, CA.

CORDERO, RENE
[b.] March 25, 1958, Arecibo, Puerto Rico; [p.] Miguel A. and Nelly Cordero; [ed.] Commerical High School diploma and 4 1/2 years Comm. University course, Hair Design, graduated, American Airlines Computer Train-ing, graduated; [hon.] Won a prize with a drawing made by me in high school on 1975, one Spanish poem came out published on a Spanish newspaper in New York, and I came out on the same newspaper on another year, have had drawings exhibitions and have sold many, also have 680 Spanish poems now. [oth. writ.] Spanish poems, English written items, Spanish written items;[pers.] Writing is a wonderful and deep expression of happiness, love, hope and anxiety, and I have been doing it since I was very young. [a.] Jamaica, NY.

CORONA, HILDEGARD
[b.] September 16, 1926, San Francisco; [p.] Axel and Erna Falk; [m.] Anthony Corona, July 8, 1949; [ch.] Madelina Corona; [ed.] Mission High School, Heald's Business College; [occ.] Retired; [memb.] Douglas City Fire Belles; [hon.] American Legion Award from Paul Revere Junior High School; [oth. writ.] The Copper Key, Melvin The Meadow Mouse (both books for children); [pers.] I have been writing poetry ever since the tender age of nine. It gives me personal pleasure when people find enjoyment with the story wrapped inside each rhyming verse. [a.] Douglas City, CA.

CORNISH, ROSITA MARIE CURETON
[b.] March 30, 1937, Minden, WV; [p.] Timothy and Rovana Cureton; [m.] January 1952; [ch.] 5 children, 9 grandchildren; [ed.] Bachelor degree in human service; [occ.] Registered Nurse; [memb.] American Red Cross

(CRP), lay Minister, Zion Apostolic Church, Royal Oak MI., University of Detroit, Mercy Alumni; [hon.] Dean's List, 1981, University of Detroit; [oth. writ.] A few, non-published; [pers.] " I am that I am". [a.] Detroit, MI.

CORREIA, JESSE
[b.] April 15, 1948, Azores, Portugal; [p.] Jacinto and Maria Correia; [m.] Adriana Correia, January 22, 1969; [ch.] Laura Lee and Michael Correia; [ed.] Elementary school only in Sao Miguel Island, Azores, Portugal; [occ.] Employee of Coca Cola Beverages, Windsor, Ontario; [oth. writ.] Pearls of the Sea (Portuguese) For Thirty Pieces of Silver (Portuguese) From Toronto to Montreal (English) To A Wonder Friend (English) Illusions of Love (Portuguese) By The Strong Fist of Rome (Portuguese). [a.] Windsor, Ontario Canada.

CORSENTINO, KATHY
[pen.] Corsentino Kathryn; [b.] May 10, 1969, Denver, CO; [p.] Leonard and Marliene Corsentino; [ed.] McQueen High, University Nevada Reno; [occ.] Psy-chology student; [memb.] Partners in Education, Psi Chi; [hon.] Cosmetology license; [oth. writ.] Articles in local newspaper and school newspaper; [pers.] Love has no color, no boundaries, no absolutes. Our time on earth is so limited, so I pray that people fill their hearts with love not hatred. [a.] Reno, NV.

COTE, KAREN
[b.] March 3, 1943, Detroit, MI; [m.] Steven, December 6, 1963; [ed.] Farmington High, Central Michigan University; [hon.] Best Wife Award, 1963 to present from husband. [a.] Livonia, MI.

COTLEUR-STEINBRICK, LEONA VERONICA
[pen.] Lee Cotleur-Steinbrick; [b.] June 16, 1932, N. Olmsted, OH. (in an old farm house); [m.] Robert Charles Steinbrick; [ed.] Associate degree in Liberal Arts and Secondary Education (I graduated with honors and was one of the oldest students in my class of 76) Lorain County Community College; [occ.] Retired from the State of Ohio Department of Taxation; [hon.] Some highlights are, writing as a part time employee for a major area newspaper, writing and art work for booklets on Recycling and Littering (2000 printed and distributed copies) for the Lorain County Commissioners and ODNR, wrote logos and created art work for various news media ads also for the above mentioned, painted portraits of various retiring Commissioners, etc., re-ceived various awards for achievements, but I'm proud-est of the one I received from the Lorain County Commissioners which was a gold-tone County Seal imbedded in a leather case along with a Certificate of Appreciation from the Commissioner; [oth. writ.] Politi-cal speeches for various local candidates. Presently working on a series of children's books; [pers.] When growing up I developed a talent to fantasize and use creative thinking while working hard in the fields of our small farm. It was a great way of making the work more bearable while other children had time for play. But, my first introduction to writing actually began during my high school days when I was elected to write for the school paper. I love it! It was my opportunity to use creative thinking to write humorous fiction for my fellow students. Once, I even won a contest for a lengthy Christmas poem I composed during a study hall. After showing it to a classmate, I tossed it in the waste basket. Later, unknown to me, my friend dug it out and entered it in the contest. Imagine my surprise to learn my discarded poem had won first place. It was this experi-ence that opened my eyes further to the value and creative

side of words. It's another way of painting events of life and sharing them with others. Poetry has played an active and important part in learning to write, and it has proven to be a valuable tool in learning the many different ways of expressing oneself. Now, during my golden years, I feel learning and writing is truly my Fountain of Youth, and I love it. [a.] Cleveland, OH.

COTTER, DEBORAH A.
[b.] March 3, 1948, Indiana; [p.] Robert and Lois Cotter; [m.] August 17, 1968; [ch.] Heidi Britt, Christopher John and Gretchen Page Ginter; [ed.] BA in French, English from Indiana University; [occ.] High school teacher; [memb.] Maryland Writing Project, St. Vincent's Child Abuse Center, Ladies Auxiliary, National Catholic Teacher's Association, Yale Parents Association, U. Va. Parents' Association; [hon.] Indiana University, Dean's List, Teacher Consultant Council Rep., Actress of the Year, (for lead in "A Children's Hour" by Lillian Hellman); [oth. writ.] Short stories for local magazine, Family Magazine; [pers.] I write to learn, and I learn about my world by writing. I also write for my family. When I no longer exist on this earth, my children will still have me with them through my writing. [a.] Cockeysville, MD.

COTTRELL, JEANNE B.
[pen.] DNA; [b.] February 21, Oxford, MS; [p.] Willie and Bessie Buford; [m.] Rev. Curtis L. Cottrell, July 10, 1976; [ch.] Bessie, Belinda and Robert; [ed.] BA/BA Business Administration; [occ.] Second grade teacher, O'Toole Elementary; [memb.] ETA Creative Founda-tion, N.A.A.C.P., Operation Push, Love and Peace Missionary Baptist Church; [oth. writ.] Grandmother's House, Black on Black Crime; [pers.] In all my ways, I acknowledge God and I treat my fellowman as I wish to be treated. I have always liked to write and "jot down" ideas as they appear in my mind. [a.] Chicago, IL.

COTTON, ELAINE
[pen.] Elegance; [b.] August 3, 1970, Rochester; [p.] Bernice Tunson and Clarence Cotton; [ch.] I have no children but I hope to have children in the future; [ed.] I graduated from Josh Lofton High School and attended a year and a half of college at Monroe Community College; [occ.] Student and writer, I'm currently working on my Associate Degree in Law; [memb.] Bethel Full Gospel Church, Christian Singles Group, Stargazers North Street Recreational Center; [hon.] I was honored for my volunteer work in a local hospital, Rochester General Hospital; [oth. writ.] I've had writings published in Youth 93 magazine, Fate Magazine and Perceptions Magazine; [pers.] I feel that my writing is a way to reflect the need for change in the world. I gear my writing towards making a change in myself and the world around me. I only write articles that enrich the mind. [a.] Rochester, NY.

COUGHLIN, DONALD
[b.] Galveston, TX; [p.] Eugene and Celeste Coughlin; [ed.] Kirwin High, Galveston, TX., University of Texas, Austin, BA, MA, Ph.D.; [occ.] Film, video writer, producer, director; [oth. writ.] Numerous film and video scripts, feature articles in local newspapers; [a.] Evanston, IL.

COUNCILMAN, SHARYL
[b.] July 5, 1959, Canadaigua, NY; [p.] Ralph and Martha Schultz; [m.] David M. Councilman, May 3, 1980; [ch.] Sarah Michelle and Kelly Lynn; [ed.] Naples Central School; [occ.] Housewife; [memb.] Cohocton

United Methodist Church, Avoca Central School PTSA; [pers.] My first poem, depicting child abuse, came to me after helping my daughter research the subject for a term paper. [a.] Cohocton, NY.

COWAN, TENA

[pen.] T.J. Pierce; [b.] September 12, 1967, Sacramento, CA; [p.] Master Sergeant Retired U.S. Army, George and Venda Bechdolt; [m.] John Roy Cowan, Jr., November 18, 1988; [ch.] Venda and Julianna Cowan; [ed.] Institute of Children's Literature, graduated 1988; [occ.] Yard care service with husband; [memb.] Benning Hills Baptist Church; [oth. writ.] None published yet; [pers.] I wouldn't have submitted my work without the love of the man I married, or the support of my beloved family. [a.] Fort Mitchell, AL.

COWSAR, MARGARET INGALLS

[b.] November 23, 1920, DeRidder, LA; [p.] Mr. and Mrs. Edmond Ilewellyn Ingalls; [m.] Chester Meredith Cowsar (deceased 1972), May 29, 1940; [ch.] Margaret C. Waid, Ph.d., Donald R. (Ph.D.), Harlon W. and Thomas C. Cowsar; [ed.] B.S. Education (1958) LSU, MA English (LSU 1962); [occ.] Retired teacher; [memb.] American Association University Woman, Phi Kappa Phi, Order of the Eastern Star, Hope Villa # 77 (past Matron); [hon.] Outstanding Teacher Award by Greater Baton Rouge Area Chamber of Commerce 1971, Outstanding Teacher Service in Central High School, EBR, 1963, Who's Who of American Woman 1968-69, Who's Who of South and Southwest 1968, 69,72, 73, LSU Chapter of Phi Kappa Phi; [oth. writ.] "How Does Grammar Mean" English Journal, NCTE 1959, "Teaching David Copperfield to Ninth Grade" English Journal 1960, Connected Thinking, LA English Journal CA 1961; [pers.] God hears our prayers if we praise Him and forgive others, He will dispense the cure for our ills through the pharmacy between our ears. [a.] Baton Rogue, LA.

COX, ITASCA CODY

[b.] October 13, 1914, Marlow, OK; [p.] Aaron and Blanche Cox; [m.] Erma Cox, November 10, 1934; [ch.] Aubra, Carol, Frankine and Debra; [ed.] Grade school to 10th grade; [occ.] Retired, sheet metal worker (40 years); [memb.] Sheetmetal Union, AFF-LCIO (40 years); [hon.] Craftsman's award in sheet metal, (hobbies) also does floral drawings and paintings; [oth. writ.] I have composed over 200 poems, songs and writings; [pers.] My name is Indian (Itasca) meaning "The Beginning" it was given to me by an Indian woman who delivered me. Her pay was the right to give me my name. I weighted 13 1/2 lbs., they weighted me on cotton scales (Cody) was taken from Buffalo Bill Cody. My wife ERma who inspired my every thought and touched my every word. I could never have written such words of love, without knowing her, we will be married 60 years on November 10, 1994. [a.] Zapata, TX.

COX, SUSIE

[pen.] Suzy V.; [b.] August 3, 1935, North Carolina; [p.] Mary Eliza and Benjamin Vines; [ch.] Noel and Pierre Cox; [ed.] Phillips High School, National Business College; [occ.] Recently retired (12-3-93) Federal Government Secretary; [oth. writ.] Several poems, children's book, two-act play (complete and unpublished); [pers.] I strive to reflect in my writing the nourishment, strength and love of my parents and family. [a.] Capitol Heights, MD.

CRAVENER, MICHAEL

[b.] September 30, 1979, Tarnetum; [p.] Paul and Gwen Cravener; [ed.] Currently an 8th grader; [memb.] Is in "Creative Writing CLub", signing and band, also a member of CPS (gifted class); [hon.] Has repeatly been on the Honor Roll; [pers.] Michael likes to ride his bike, lift weights and read. He also loves to play video games, he is a very great gift to his family. [a.] Avonmore, PA.

CRAWFORD, KATHRYN

[pen.] Katrin; [b.] June 23, 1953, Denver, CO; [p.] Robert and Donna Moomaw; [m.] Randy Crawford, August 30, 1984; [ch.] Laurie, Phillip and Scott Juengst; [ed.] Associate Degree Judicial Legal Secretary at Aims Community College; [occ.] Insurance Sales-State Farm; [hon.] Dean's and President's List, Faculty Scholarship and Colorado Scholars Scholarship; [oth. writ.] Nonpublished; [pers.] I believe in love and in its salvation because therein lies the secret to life, my writings reflect this passion. [a.] Fort Collins, CO.

CRAWFORD-MARTIN, REGINA

[b.] August 16, 1967, Wheeling, WV; [p.] Valeria A. and I Gene Crawford; [m.] Garr W. Martin, August 31, 1991; [ch.] Tyra M. Byrd; [ed.] Wheeling Park High, Central State University (Ohio); [occ.] Computer Programmer; [memb.] Vocational Industrial Clubs of America, The Easter Seal Society; [hon.] Presidential Academic Fitness Award Program 1985, Who's Who Among American High School Students 1983-1984, The National Dean's List 1987-1988, United States Achievement Academy All American Year book 1988-1989. [a.] Rochester, NY.

CRAWFORD, TITAN J.

[pen.] Titan Crawford; [b.] February 14, 1984, Portland; [p.] Ted L. and Robin J. Crawford, grandparents, J.L. and Eula Saleea and Lono Crawford; [sib.] Cody and Ashley; [ed.] A Dundee Elementary School student who skipped 3rd grade and studies lessons several years above his current 5th grade level, attends several advanced math, literacy and theatrical workshops a year; [occ.] Student, film, stage and theatrical actor; [memb.] N.O.V.A. membership for talented and gifted students, Student Council, Collegiate Theater member currently in production for Shakespeare's MacBeth spring 94, charter member Krayon Kids Professional Theater, basketball and soccer team member; [hon.] Collegiate Award, writing, directing, editing and acting for 8-11 year old category, local literacy and math awards, Outstanding Student Award, Student of Month Honors, several basketball and track awards, spotlighted by local newspaper; [oth. writ.] Working on a book of poems, sonnets and short stories, composes lyrics, songs and monologues; [pers.] I wish to thank my mom and all the great teachers at Dundee especially my second grade teacher, Mrs. Smith for teaching me to write. Writing is hard, but fun and it makes me happy. [a.] Dundee, OR.

CROCKET, JAMIE

[pen.] Jamie Crocket; [b.] April 7, 1958, Glasgow, Scotland; [p.] James Allan (MD.) and Anna Stuart Crocket; [m.] Karen Norma Jean Crocket, May 16, 1992; [ed.] The high school of Glasgow, Glasgow, Scotland, GB; [occ.] Estate Agent, Crocket Property Services; [oth. writ.] Currently writing my first children's story, "Blueberry Cat and Scruff, The True Adventures", publishing has yet to be arranged. [a.] Glasgow, GB.

CRON, HUGH BLACKWOOD

[b.] September 6, 1967, Scotland; [m.] Gwen Cron, October 3, 1990; [ed.] Mainholm Academy AYR; [occ.] Self employed baker; [hon.] Certificates of Distinction in Biology, Integrated Science, Modern Studies and Accountancy through my education; [oth. writ.] At present working on a book of short stories and a second collection of poems, I also have completed a book of poetry entitled A Chronicle of Perceptions, all unpublished; [pers.] I am inspired by observations of live. People can take what they want from my poetry as I don't preach but wish to inspire thought from within the readers. Poems for the unpoetic perhaps? [a.] Ayr, Ayrshire, Scotland.

CROSBY, KIMBERLY

[b.] July 3, 1980, Mesa, AZ; [p.] Thomas and Jann Crosby; [ed.] I am only in eight grade, Neely Elementary and Gilbert Junior High School; [memb.] Gilbert Junior High, Drama Club, Christ Lutheran Church; [hon.] First place in the Gilbert Fine Arts Association's writing contest (1991), a member of the National Junior Honors Society, a 9 year straight A student; [oth. writ.] Numerous articles in the school newspaper. [a.] Gilbert, AZ.

CROSS, DONALD A.

[pen.] D. Allen Cross; [b.] November 10, 1956, Benton, AR; [p.] Dorothy and A.W. Cross; [m.] Susan Cross, May 28, 1977; [ch.] Christopher, Justin and Sarah; [ed.] B.S. Engineering Physics, University of Arkansas, Little Rock, MBA Alabama A & M University; [occ.] Engineering Manager; [memb.] National Management Association; [hon.] R.E. Lee Wilson Scholarship, Trinity Foundation Scholarship; [oth. writ.] "Shalom" published in Treasured Poems of America; [pers.] The poem "The Sculptor" is dedicated to my wife Susan, the source of all my inspiration. May God bless her always. [a.] Huntsville, AL.

CRUMP, JOSHUA

[b.] May 22, 1974, Cambridge, Ontario; [p.] Jennifer and Ross Crump; [ed.] South Secondary School; [occ.] Student, Huron College, University of Western Ontario, London Ontario; [memb.] Western Waterpolo team, Royal Life Saving Society; [oth. writ.] Nothing published until now, but written numerous poems, short stories; [pers.] I just write what I feel and hope something good comes out of it. [a.] London, Ontario.

CRUSE, VIRGINIA

[pers.] I write poems that express my faith in God, and love for people.

CRUTCHFIELD, STEPHEN

[pen.] Steven; [b.] Late 40's, Freeport, NY; [p.] Charles and Marie Crutchfield; [ch.] Stephen Jr. and Dione Darcel; [ed.] Graduate Freeport High School, South Oak Institute for Alcoholism and Addictive studies, Amityville, NY; [occ.] Credentialed Addictions Counselor; [memb.] Long Island National Black Counselors; [oth. writ.] Book, Faces, A Trilogy; [pers.] This poem and all that I write are dedicated to the sick and suffering that they find the healing within and to those who are in spiritual journey. [a.] Brentwood, NY.

CRYSTAL, VICKI

[pen.] Karen Cross; [b.] June 2, 1952, Eglin AFB; [p.] Mr. and Mrs. Edward Rachal; [m.] Henry R. Crystal; [ch.] Bryant and Alex; [occ.] Beauty Salon owner; [oth. writ.] Poems in local newspaper; [pers.] My heart harbors more than my mind could ever express. Life has been my only teacher. [a.] DeFuniak Springs, FL.

CULBERTSON, CHRISTOPHER B.
[pen.] Barrett; [b.] March 22, 1971, Charleston, SC; [p.] Bud and Evelyn Culbertson; [ed.] Beaufort/Jasper County Career Education Center, Graphic Communications (2 years), U.S. Navy Presidential Honor Guard (2 years), Battery Creek High; [occ.] JJ's Hallmark, Pentagon CIty Mall, Arlington, VA; [memb.] Washington DC Church of Christ, Compassion International; [hon.] Student of the Quarter in Graphic Art class in May and November of 1990, 2nd place poster contest in 1990 for National Career Development Week, Merit Award for poetry in '91, letter of appreciation from Commandant of Navel District Washington, I appeared in Who's Who Among American High School Students for South Carolina 89-90; [pers.] I am inspired to read Amanda Bradley's and Helen Steiner Rice's poetry yet I plan to be more inspirational. God is definitely my strength and my best friend. Anything I might achieve is not to my credit but to God's. [a.] Arlington, VA.

CULLEN, JAMES CURRY
[b.] January 10, 1963, Hartford, CT; [p.] Elizabeth A. and Thomas M. Cullen; [ed.] Conrad High School, West Hartford, CT.; [occ.] Clerk.

CULLITON, LELAND
[pen.] L.T. Bell; [b.] March 13, 1948, Taft, CA; [ch.] M. Sandy and Fern Carrie; [ed.] Attended, but haven't graduated college; [occ.] News circulation (cashier), writer; [memb.] Optimist Club, High School All American (wrestling); [hon.] To be judged valuable enough in merit to have my poem (s) published, to be a human being; [oth. writ.] I plan to submit over a thousand I have completed, this is my first poem submission; [pers.] To write one has a overt sense of collecting metaphysical values and they create a life of their own usually fictitious. [a.] Van Nuys, CA.

CUNYUS, DAVID WAYNE
[b.] December 28, 1935, Bryan, TX; [p.] Colonel Paul A. (U.S. Army retired) and Opal (Shaw) Cunyus; [ed.] Stephenville High, Tarleton and Texas A & M, B.A., 1958, Mississippi State, B.S. 1966, M.A., 1971, Rotary International Foundation Fellowship to the Graduate Institute of International Studies, University of Geneva, Switzerland, 1959-1960, department of Defense Race\Human Relations Institute, Patrick AFB, Florida 1973; [occ.] Captain, U.S. Air Force (ret.) 1958-1977, college and university instructor (ret.) 1966-1972, currently freelance writer, photographer and artist; [memb.] Sigma Tau Delta, Alpha Phi Omega, U.S. Tennis Association (USTA); [hon.] Rotary International Fellowship, YMCA Graduate Assistantship 1965-1966, original artwork in Texas Monthly magazine 1989, original design used as unique, one-of-a-kind U.S. Post Office postmark to commemorate the 1989 Stephenville Centennial, and my original logo design won the competition as official symbol of this celebration, named "Unsung Hero" by hometown newspaper in 1990 Horizons edition of Stephenville Empire Tribune, selected by Texas Legislature as 1990-1991 finalist in Texas State Artist competition, and invited to exhibit my original artwork in the Great Hall of the Senate, Texas State Capitol, Austin; [oth. writ.] "Travel Reports" published in Stephenville Empire Tribune of my experiences in 13 countries in Europe as a Rotary Foundation Fellow, 1959-1960, "Edward Taylor", A Survey of Critical Reaction to His Poetry, 1662-1969, (master's thesis) published by Mississippi State University Press 1971; [pers.] To my grandfather, Walter Cunyus, who lived to 98 and loved reciting poetry aloud from memory, and to

my father Paul, now 89, who recorded daily journals, which he has collected into compelling, page-turning, multi-volume accounts of his WW II experiences, I am greatly indebted. [a.] Stephenville, TX.

CURETON, MARION
[b.] December 30, 1924, St. Louis; [p.] Henry and Gladys Stolle; [m.] F. Paul Cureton, November 27, 1954; [ch.] John David, Mark Henry and Paula Marie; [ed.] 1942 high school graduate of St. Elizabeth Academy and Business School; [occ.] Housewife; [memb.] St. Dominic Savio Catholic Church, The Blue Army of Fatima; [hon.] 1977 I was a guest on two St. Louis radio stations and Channel 4 TV regarding my published book. The Post-dispatch, Religious Editor gave me recognition. I won the Golden Poet Award for my poem; [oth. writ.] "Mary Key of 73" published in Soul Magazine, "Negative Earthlings Exposed" published 1975, unpublished novel Love Came Through could have the potential of becoming a movie. I have already written its theme song; [pers.] May the treasure of Divine Love forever remain in everyone's hearts and souls. Let us begin now to use this affective tool for returning Mother Earth to the paradise our Creator intended it to be. [a.] Affton, MO.

CURRAN, SHIRLEY T.
[pen.] S.T. Curran; [b.] June 9, 1928 (residence, Plymouth, MI.); [ed.] St. Clair Community College, Oakland Community College, Schoolcraft College, Madonna University; [occ.] (Retired) Senior citizen attending college Art and Literature major; [memb.] Phi Theta Kappa, Omicron Iota Chapter, Three Cities Art Club, Plymouth Historical Museum; [hon.] Dean's List in Art Schoolcraft College, Livonia, MI., 1991-1992 Michigan State Fair winner, Clay Sculpture Celebrate Life Art show, several poems in anthologies, won Schoolcraft College English Department Literary Art Award 1992, numerous other art shows, 6 drawings 1993 accepted by Plymouth Historical Museum (pen and ink); [pers.] My hope and dream is to leave as much as possible to humanity through my art and writing. To leave this world a little better place than whence I found it. [a.] Plymouth, MI.

CYRUS, RUTHY
[pen.] Ruthy McAfee; [b.] December 17, 1958, Michigan; [p.] John and Ruth McAfee; [m.] William Cyrus, June 27, 1981; [ch.] William Christopher and Ashley Nicole; [ed.] Eau Claire High School, Fullerton College, Cerritos College; [occ.] Housewife; [memb.] Power Community Church, Brownie Girl Scout Leader; [hon.] Sales Appreciation Award 1990, graduated Eau Claire High School with Honors; [oth. writ.] Several poems not published yet, two children's stories and one novel; [pers.] Enjoy writing poetry, gives me a total sense of freedom. [a.] Fullerton, CA.

DACAYANAN, EUFEMIA B.
[pen.] Femy; [b.] March 20, 1929, Sta. Ignacia, Tarlac Philippines; [p.] Pedro Castillo Balabany and Flaviana B. Santillan; [m.] Dr. Emiliano F. Dacayanan, January 6, 1951; [ch.] Danny, Donna, Bella, Gener, Diana, Gina and Eufie (all finished with their college courses); [ed.] Master of Arts, Early Childhood Education; [occ.] Preschool Director; [memb.] Philippine Public School Teachers Association, Lions International 301-D-1, Catholic Women's League; [hon.] Girl Scout of the Philippines Awardee; [oth. writ.] Features, local publications; [pers.] Life is as wonderful as you see and make it. If clouds and rain come, it is only to make way for the sun. [a.] Los Angeles, CA.

DAGLE, LARRY PAUL
[b.] June 23, 1965, Sunbury, PA; [ch.] Jessica Ann and Nikole Christine; [ed.] Shikellamy High "83; [oth. writ.] Are Lying Dormant; [pers.] Music to me, it the greatest influence. [a.] Northumberland, PA.

DAIGLE, MARIA
[b.] March 10, 1959, Italy; [m.] August 3, 1975; [ch.] Adam (18), Marie (15 and Clustier (7) Daigle; [ed.] Finished 10th grade, went to Academy of Hairdressing called National Academy, graduated; [occ.] I write songs for studio on Ontario Platinum Record; [memb.] Affiliates of Art Association of Planview, CT; [hon.] Prize winner 1974 for art work; [oth. writ.] Yes, currently I am writing songs; [pers.] I strive to for mankind to reflect on my work and my writing to be able to bring forth a new chunk of life. I have been greatly influenced by the early romantic poets. [a.] Planview, CT.

DALLAS, REGINA
[pen.] Regina Lea, Regina; [b.] January 21, 1967, Haleyville, AL; [p.] James Wendell and Dale Ann Humphries; [m.] Kenneth M. Dallas, June 7, 1985; [ch.] James Mikel and Kevin Ray; [ed.] Choctaw High and Winston High, Central Texas College, West Central Alabama Skills Center; [occ.] Nursing Assistant; [oth. writ.] Many other poems songs and stories, left unpublished; [pers.] Life is the greatest influence to any writer. What I write is what I am.. or at least … what I have been. To write is to be free. [a.] Double Springs, AL.

DALY, MARK G.
[pen.] Daethis Jain; [oth. writ.] Unpublished, The Sadness of A One Word Silence (novel), Origin and Meaning (collected poems); [pers.] I strive for personal enlightment. If I have helped one person to see through my work, then I have achieved the ultimate. I write because the words come to me, and sometimes they are all I have. [a.] Park City, UT.

DANCEL, ERICA
[b.] June 23, 1979, Phillipines; [p.] Delfin Y. and Yolinda Dancel; [ed.] I attend Salem High School; [memb.] Salem High School Cheerleading squad; [hon.] Honor student, most school spirited, two poem booklets - 1st place, NSHS, SCA, Spanish Club, cheerleading competition, (team effort), 1st place (then in regionals) 3rd place, qualified for nationals; [oth. writ.] Other poems published in school magazines or newspapers; [pers.] All the poems i've written have to do with my life, when I write my poems its all to express my feelings. [a.] Virginia Beach, VA.

DANIEL, JARED ANDREW
[b.] February 2, 1971, Columbus, OH; [p.] Gardner and Phyllis Daniel; [m.] Debbie Dawn Daniel, September 2, 1992; [ed.] Glasgow High; [occ.] Military Policeman, United States Army; [oth. writ.] Short stories and poetry (none published); [pers.] I thank my Lord Jesus Christ for giving me the gift of words.

DANSBY, MILDRED T.
[pen.] Mildred T. Dansby; [b.] December 16, 1909, Chattanooga, TN; [p.] William W. and Ella May Taylor; [m.] Wade F. Dansby, June 30, 1934; [ch.] Joy D. Aldret and Wade F. Dansby, II; [ed.] Central High School, University of Tennessee; [occ.] Retired teacher; [hon.] Various medals for public speaking, ETD Cup for literary composition; [oth. writ.] Poems and articles in small publications. [a.] Anderson, SC.

DARDEN, OLIVER A.
[pen.] Oliver A. Darden; [b.] Atlantic City, NJ; [p.] Joseph and Blanche C. Darden; [m.] Teresa Hall Darden, August 31, 1969; [ch.] Jai Oliver and Praithe Leone; [ed.] West Virginia State College B.A.-1993, University of Pennsylvania School of Social Work, M.S.W. Degree, doctoral courses, Fordham University; [occ.] Executive Director, Determination Inc., organization for disabled; [memb.] Omega Poi Phi Fraternity, YMCA, Philadelphia Urban Coalition, N.A.S.W. and other social organizations; [hon.] United Negro College Fund, Distinguished Service Citation, Community Service Award, City of Philadelphia Professional Service Award, Crisis Intervention Network, Dept. of Human Service Liberty Bell Award, Heart Award, American Family Institute Community Award, Interested Negroes Four Chaplains Award; [oth. writ.] Several poems published in local newspapers, international training programs for social staff workers, collection of analysis system for human service; [pers.] I can..I will.. I must.. with a little help from my friends. [a.] Philadelphia, PA.

DARR, DIANA
[b.] April 22, 1951, St. Louis, MO; [ed.] University of MO. at Columbia; [occ.] Sales promotion and marketing, freelance writer; [hon.] First place poetry winner Golden Triangle Writers Guild-Texas 1992, poetry finalist for two poems, The Writers Foundation-Syracuse, NY 1993; [oth. writ.] Currently working on a collection of poems, several children's stories and songs, developed advertising materials for various shopping malls and other business, television, radio and print copy; [pers.] I write from the heart, from instinct. My words need to reflect something real... to "know" from the inside out. [a.] St. Louis, MO.

DASANJH, RAJ SINGH
[pen.] Raiu, The Sheepherder; [b.] March 25, 1951, Fiji Islands; [p.] Pritam S. and Susheel K. Dasanjh; [m.] Tarah K. Dasanjh, May 21, 1977; [ch.] Chris Raj, Jessica Susheel and Colin Pritam; [pers.] A mother's love, the most natural thing in the world. Give away as much love as you can, it does not cost you anything--the beauty of it all is you have a never-ending supply of love. [a.] San Mateo, CA.

DASHER, CHRISTA L.
[b.] May 16, 1977, Dunedin, FL; [p.] Linda and Dennis Dasher; [ed.] Tarpan Springs High School; [memb.] Thespian Society and Interact, Law Explorers, Academic team; [oth. writ.] I have written many, one "My Disease" in an artistic book at school. The others I keep to myself; [pers.] "My writing is my life. It is my personal achievements and struggles, not philosophical ideas. No one could possibly match the strength of one's personal life". [a.] Palm Harbor, FL.

DAUB, JAMES R.
[pen.] Jim Daub; [b.] August 18, 1930, Auburn, IN; [p.] Deceased; [m.] Nadine M. Daub, November 25, 1985; [ch.] Cindy and Doody; [ed.] Business Ed.; [oth. writ.] New American Poetry anthology, "The Sea, The Tree and Me", Thoughts, Seeds, My Horizon, Visions of Thoughts and numerous others (a few publicized); [pers.] "Learn to be whatever you are". [a.] harrison, AR.

DAVE, SAMIR S.
[b.] July 29, 1970, New York; [memb.] The United Amateur Press Association of America; [oth. writ.] I have been published in the November 92 issue of the India Tribune, also published in the fall and winter 93 issues of Poets Pen Quarterly; [pers.] It is very hard to balance the two most important aspects of life-happiness and sadness. My poems represent the constant struggle of our lives between the two. I would like to dedicate this poem to my flame of inspiration and love, my france' Manisha. [a.] Rego Park, NY.

DAVENPORT, LOUISE
[b.] July 9, 1926, Virginia; [p.] Harry and Nellie Ward; [m.] Widowed twice; [ch.] Six children and five grandchildren; [ed.] High school graduate, secretarial school and later in life, nursing aide, retired 1990; [occ.] Retired; [memb.] Local senior citizens, Untied Methodist Church where I on occasion play piano; [oth. writ.] Have had several poems published in local newspapers, also a "human interest" article from time to time; [pers.] I am a "people person" and get my inspiration from those I come in contact with, also a nature lover and an avid reader and enjoy word puzzles. [a.] Rockbridge Baths, VA.

DAVIDSEN, DOROTA
[b.] March 2, 1971, Gdansk, Poland; [p.] Stanislaw and Janina Wozniak; [m.] Morten Davidsen, July 11, 1992; [ed.] III Liceum Marynarki Wojennej High School in Poland; [oth. writ.] Other poems which will make a bigger collection as well as short stories; [pers.] The mixture of personal experiences and imagination is the source of my work. I hope to stir other people's feelings rather than their minds. [a.] Klepp Stasjon, Norway.

DAVIDSON, GERALDINE
[pen.] Gerry Davidson; [b.] October 11, 1910, Everett, WA; [ch.] Robert Galbraith; [hon.] 2 former awards; [pers.] Dedicated to my son Robert Galbraith. [a.] Mt. Vernon, WA.

DAVEY, PETER G.
[b.] September 20, 1949, Ontario, Canada; [p.] Helen and Jim Davey; [m.] Patricia Davey, June 13, 1975; [ch.] Lisa Valerie and Erin Racheal; [occ.] Maintenance supervisor; [memb.] B.O.M.A. International F.M.A.; [oth. writ.] Many poems, none published as of yet; [pers.] Poetry is an expression of the soul, and when shared with others can be very uplifting. [a.] Saskatoon, SK., Canada.

DAVIN-LANE, MARY AGNES
[pen.] M.A. Davin-Lane; [b.] November 21, 1959, Brooklyn, NY; [p.] Robert and Margaret Tarpinian; [m.] Edward W. Lane, July 13, 1991; [ed.] Bishop Kearney High School-Brooklyn, St. Francis College-Brooklyn Heights; [occ.] Dental Assistant; [hon.] President Zeta Gamma, President-Trouper Drama Club, President-Senior Class College, Internship at The Actor's Studio under Lee Strasberg, Outstanding College Graduate Registry; [oth. writ.[Several poems published in college papers; [pers.] Take each day as it comes, embrace and enjoy it, for who knows whether tomorrow will ever come? And always expect the unexpected and the songs of life will ring, N. Diamond. [a.] Acra, NY.

DAVIS, ANTIONETTE MARY MAHASON
[pen.] Davis, Antoinette Mary; [b.] July 19, 1943, New York City; [p.] Agnes Antionette and Isaiah Davis; [ch.] God-children, Christopher, Nicole and Jonathan Wallace, Robert L. Payton; [ed.] Washington Irving High School NYC, City University of N.Y., B.S. Education, M.A. Education, M.A. Administration and Supervision in Education; [occ.] Teacher and staff developer of writing,

N.Y. City Public School; [memb.] City University Alumni Association, International Black Writers Conference, Bronx Reading Council; [hon.] First place poetry contest award, New York Public Library, Countee Culleen Branch 1991, PS 161M Parent Association Honor with publication of poem in yearbook; [oth. writ.] Poetry, essays on diversified topics, reading and presentations with music; [pers.] Sailing across time and cultural differences, a poem takes anchor within my soul. [a.] Bronx, NY.

DAVIS JR., JOSEPH R.
[pen.] Joseph R. Davis Jr.; [b.] January 24, 1922, Dolores, TX; [p.] Joseph and Lamar Davis; [m.] Margaret, June 4, 1948; [ch.] Megan, Linvean, Joseph III and Andren; [ed.] St. Edward's University, Austin, TX; [occ.] Retired overseas sales executive; [memb.] US Naval Reserve (retired) Commander, Rotary Club, Harbor Branch Oceanographic Society; [oth. writ.] Unpublished short stories and poems; [pers.] Correct fitting words are golden nuggets of the mind, difficult to find and hopefully satisfying when discovered. [a.] Vero Beach, FL.

DAVIS, KATHLEEN
[b.] January 27, 1924, North Carolina; [p.] Robert M. and Lula C. Sessoms; [m.] Leonard (deceased October 9, 1991), February 19, 1949; [ch.] Len Jr., Vivian, Joy and Calvin; [ed.] White Oak High, Appalachian State, Boone, NC., Troy State, Montgomery, AL., currently working on masters at Bible Seminary in MO; [occ.] Student-retired from employment with the State of Alabama in June 1989; [memb.] Gateway Baptist Church, Fifty Plus Group, Alabama Poetry Society; [hon.] Dean's List, Troy State; [oth. writ.] Senior class poet in high school, several other poems published by contest I entered; [pers.] It is my hope that my poems will reflect my desire to be a positive witness in this world for high morals and Christian values. I have been greatly inspired by Helen Steiner Rice. [a.] Montgomery, AL.

DAVIS, KATHY S.
[pen.] Kathy S. Benjamin Davis; [b.] February 2, 1954, Richmond, IN; [p.] Bertha and Raymond Benjamin; [m.] Charles S. Davis, January 18, 1975; [ch.] Kristy and Charlie; [ed.] Richmond Senior High School, Elizabethtown State Vocational Technical School; [occ.] Licensed Practical Nurse; [oth. writ.] Several poems published in the Meadowview Moments (newsletter where I work) "To My Friends", "True Meaning of Christmas", "Things I Love", and a story of my family "The Benjamin Tradition"; [pers.] I enjoy writing about things that are important to me such as family, friends and nature, and it makes it even more special when other people enjoy what I've wrote. [a.] Louisville, KY.

DAVIS, ROGER
[pen.] R.C. Davis; [b.] march 24, 1958, Pleasanton, TX; [p.] Ruth and Wendell Davis; [m.] Michelle I. Davis, October 4, 1986; [ch.] John Anthoney Davis, Tawnya Kay and Roger Dale; [ed.] Southside High School; [occ.] Local delivery truck driver; [memb.] Supporter of, National Geographic Society, Texas State Troopers Association, San Antonio Jaycees; [oth. writ.] Several unpublished poems that I have written in my spare time; [pers.] I have always believed that one person "CAN" made a difference and strive to show this, in my works. [a.] San Antonio, TX.

DAVIS, SARA K.
[b.] July 13, 1976, Anaheim, CA; [p.] Marilyn and

Jeffrey Davis; [ed.] Arlington High School; [occ.] Student; [oth. writ.] Other poems in 3 school literary magazines and the newspaper "Mane Thing"; [pers.] My writings are of personal feelings and those of close friends. True feelings make the writings more memorable. [a.] Riverside, CA.

DAVIS, SYLVIA
[pen.] "AGAPE"; [b.] August 2, Pensacola, FL; [p.] Theodore J. Johnson and Dettie Burke; [ed.] High school, some college; [occ.] Secretary; [memb.] Word of Faith Christian Center; [hon.] National Honor Society, penmanship certificates (two) from Gregg, (shorthand), received a certificate for correctly spelling one hundred words, most important of all I have received several certificates from my church home, Word of Faith Christian Center; [oth. writ.] Yes, there are other writings; [pers.] "Start off RIGHT and you'll end-up RIGHT". [a.] Sterling Heights, MI.

DAVIS, VIRGINIA D.
[b.] November 22, 1925, Maine; [p.] Harvey and Bessie Clough; [m.] Edgar B. Davis, March 22, 1947; [ch.] Marguerite, Alice, Nanci and Sherry; [ed.] High school; [memb.] Fort Wayne V.F.W. 10006 (Ladies Auxiliary); [hon.] Golden Poet Award 1989, Award of Merit 1991; [pers.] Although I've written a number of non-christian poems, I do enjoy writing christian poems, God has given me this gift and He is my inspiration. [a.] Ft. Wayne, IN.

DAVIS, WILLIAM R.
[pen.] William Davis; [b.] June 6, 1969, Washington, DC; [p.] William and Linda Davis; [ch.] Ryan Zachary; [ed.] Crossland High, University of Maryland, FAA Controller Training School; [occ.] Air Traffic Controller USAF; [pers.] I would someday like to make a difference with my pencil. I love peace, happiness and maybe someone will read my writings and smile. One person can change so much. [a.] McGuire AFB, NJ.

DAVY, DOROTHY
[pen.] Dee Dee Smith; [b.] August 23, 1943, Knoxville, TN; [p.] Lamar and Corinne Smith; [m.] Cuthbert Davy, March 29, 1969; [ch.] Colette Danielle and Christopher Sebastian; [ed.] B.A. Sociology, M.A. Education; [occ.] Teacher; [memb.] Busy Bee Daycare Board, Adventure Club Counselor, Jamaica S.D.A. Church; [hon.] Attendance award, Seward Park High School, Service Award P.T.A. of P.S. 156, NY Service Award for Sabbath School teacher, Jamaica S.D.A. Church Queens, NY; [oth. writ.] Non-published; [pers.] My many years of being with children and caring for them has given me a deep concern for them and their quality of life. [a.] New York, NY.

DAWSON, KATHLEEN
[pen.] Kat Dawson; [b.] November 13, 1975, Miami, FL; [p.] David and Joan Dawson; [ed.] Lake Mary High School, Stetson University; [occ.] Student; [memb.] Phi Alpha Delta, AIESEC, National Forensica League; [hon.] Florida Academic Scholar, Soroptimist Youth Citizen Award, Optimist Leadership Award, Chamber of Commerce scholar, various debating awards; [pers.] I believe that with an optimistic attitude, anything can be accomplished. [a.] Lake Mary, FL.

de BOURGUIGNON, DIANE
[b.] March 12, 1946, Phoenix; [p.] Mary and Adam Tople; [m.] Donald deBourguignon, September 24, 1975; [ch.] Deborah, Scott and Cari; [ed.] High school; [memb.] Rialto United Methodist Church, United Meth-

odist Women Salvation Army Women's Auxiliary, Rialto Woman's Club, Church Women United; [hon.] Honorable Mention Chaparral Poet Society of San Bernardino; [oth. writ.] Poets, short stories (poets written for several funerals, tributes and remembrances; [pers.] I am very spiritual and writing can convey these feelings. My writing is to express myself and bring comfort and joy to those I am writing for. {a.] San Bernardino, CA.

DE CHAZAL, MARC
[b.] May 23, 1969, Empangeni, SA; [p.] Mr. and Mrs. A.D.R. De Chazal; [m.] Jane De Chazal, May 12, 1992; [ed.] Kearsney College, Cape Evangelical Bible Institute; [occ.] Assistant Editor, Christian Living Today magazine; [oth. writ.] Unpublished poems and short stories, articles for "Christian Living Today" magazine, report for Candace L. Brown's "Cape Town Commnet" in Record Searchlight (Redding, CA.); [pers.] My life and writings are inspired by the author of life, Jesus Christ. [a.] Cape Town, South Africa.

DE CLERCQ, LOYA
[b.] December 26, 1965, Hinton, Alberta Canada; [p.] hazel and Adrian Hart; [m.] Kevin De Clercq, July 25, 1992; [ed.] B.Sc. in Home Economics from University of Alberta, B.Ed. from University of Lethbridge; [occ.] Foods teacher; [hon.] University of Lethbridge Scholarship for Academic Achievement and graduated "with distinction"; [oth. writ.] A few poems given as wedding toasts; [pers.] My greatest inspiration is my mom. Her poems tell stories, reflect feelings and stir emotions. I strive for these same qualities in my own poetry. [a.] Fort Macleod, Alberta Canada.

DEFRANCESCO, GISELE LARIVIERE
[b.] March 20, 1949, Noranda; [oth. writ.] I'm writing and have written other poems as well as songs; [pers.] I enjoy writing as a comfort to my heart and soul, and when I think of the love I want to share, I know the world is mine. [a.] Caledon East, Ontario.

DEFRANCESCO, MARGUERITE
[pen.] Lee; [b.] May 7, New York City; [ed.] Theodore Roosevelt High School, Bronx, NY., unable to continue my education due to needs at home; [occ.] Retired from Chase Manhattan Bank, New York City; [memb.] St. Jude Shrine of Baltimore Maryland; [hon.] A poem read on radio station WOR, received gift, also received plaque from another contest on another of my poems; [oth. writ.] Wrote a poem to Jim Jensen of T.V. Channel 2, was sent a letter of appreciation by him, actually I am a novice not a professional writer; [pers.] My thoughts and feelings in every aspect are revealed on paper. Togetherness, communication and love for one another can make this a better world, for UNITED WE MUST STAND. [a.] New York, NY.

DELA GARZA, TINA LOUISE
[pen.] Tina DelaGarza; [b.] October 6, 1978, Port Lavaca, TX; [p.] CIndy DelaGarza; [m.] Hilario Eufracio, November 22, 1985; [ch.] Crystal, Raquel and Kalinda; [ed.] 9th grade, Sterling High School, Baytown, TX; [occ.] Student; [pers.] My poems are not racist and neither am I. I am as human as you are.

DELAHARTY, ROBERT
[b.] October 4, 1962, New York; [occ.] U.S. Soldier; [oth. writ.] My Two Life Lines, Lost By Time, The Fall, Vargray, Vaudeville, Ethos of The Harth; [pers.] The Zenith of man can only be found or seen through his hopes and dreams, for without these nothing is possible.

DELLERT, MICHAEL
[b.] January 28, 1970, Englewood, NJ; [p.] Edward and Jane Dellert; [ed.] Bethany College Bethany WV, 1988-90, Sussex County Community College, Newton, NJ 1993; [occ.] Student, swim coach, writer; [memb.] International Thespian Society, Alpha Psi Omega (theatre honorary), Roundtable Literary Society; [hon.] National Council of Teachers of English Achievement Award in writing (1987), World of Poetry Press Golden Poet Award (1988 and 1989); [oth. writ.] "The Fallen" (poem), Golden Poet Award, 1988 and published in The Golden Treasury of Great Poems, "Dreams of Lazarus" (poem), Golden Poet Award, 1989, short fiction and essays; [pers.] "There is truth in the bottom of ashtrays, in bottomless cups of coffee, in the eyes of children and lovers. The rest is window dressing. [a.] Highland Lakes, NJ.

DeLONGFIELD, CHARLES
[b.] March 22, 1945, Glendale, CA; [p.] Maurice and Marjorie DeLongfield, Sr.; [m.] Pamela DeLongfield; [ch.] Cynthia Michelle, Vincent Charles and Robert Edward; [ed.] North Hollywood High, Valley Junior College, West Valley Occupational Center; [occ.] Retired, California State University, Northridge, CA.; [memb.] Past member, Mensa, Optical Society of America, Photographic Society of America, M.A.R.S.; [hon.] Mechanics Illustrated Golden Hammer Award-Telescope Design, Who's Who of Stereo Photography; [oth. writ.] Articles about light pollution in local news, books on philosophy and theology, several copyrighted songs, poetry and humor, Sci-fi, short stories; [pers.] In all of my stories, poems and music I strive to encourage brotherly love and appreciation for all of God's creations. [a.] Kelseyville, CA.

DEMARCO, KATE
[pen.] Katelyn; [b.] April 24, 1946, London, England; [ed.] 2 years commercial course, high school and course 8 grades in public school; [occ.] Receptionist/secretary; [oth. writ.] I have written a short children's story called "The Penguin and The Flee", it is in the process of being published, also various music articles; [pers.] I also am a freelance photographer, but prefer to write, although my work is published, even in Toronto Life magazine, my dreams is to take a year off from my job to pursue my writing. [a.] Toronto, Ontario Canada.

DENNIS, REGEN MICHAL
[b.] November 28, 1962, Shreveport, LA; [p.] Wayne and Charlotte Dennis; [ed.] C.E. Byrd High School, Louisiana Tech University, Bachelor of Science degree in Nursing from Northwestern State University, Natchitoches, LA; [occ.] R.N. at CPC Brentwood Psychiatric Hospital in Shreveport; [memb.] Order of the Eastern Star; [hon.] Masonic Scholarship, Altrusa Scholarship and Delta Phi Delta Scholarship; [oth. writ.] I've been writing poems and short stories since I was twelve, but I've never had any of them published before. [a.] Shreveport, LA.

DENNISON, WESLEY CARLTON
[b.] October 27, 1954, Eglin AFB, FL; [p.] Warren A. and Kaneyo Dennison; [m.] Martha Cook Dennison, March 21, 1987; [ch.] Scott Wesley and Ryan Martin; [ed.] Oak Ridge High, Valencia Community College; [occ.] Gems and jewelry sales; [memb.] Astara, A.R.E. (Edgar Cayce's); [pers.] I believe that experience, truth and knowledge, like life in never ending...and is a true reflection of our inner reality. [a.] Coconut Creek, Fl.

DENNY, ANDREA
[pen.] Denny Andrea; [b.] October 26, 1981, Binghamton, NY; [p.] Llewellyn E. and Carol A. Denny Jr.; [ed.] Lockhart Middle School, 6th grade; [occ.] Student; [hon.] 4 times Principals Honor Roll, 2nd place Science project; [oth. writ.] Jerry The Ghost; [pers.] I continue to write poems in my spare time. I like to draw animals, especially birds that is where I got the idea for this poem. [a.] Tampa, FL.

DE PARRA, FANNY LAREO
[pen.] Carmen Rey; [b.] June 19, 1938, Colombia; [p.] Bedardo Lareo and Alicia Jaramillo; [m.] Ancizar Parra, May 30, 1963; [ch.] Amparo, Ancizar, Mauricio and Lindayse; [ed.] Sagrado Corazon De Jesus, Instituto Comerical De Palmira; [occ.] Nanny; [hon.] Participated in the International Music contest O.T.I.; [oth. writ.] Member of Columbia's Society of Authors and Composers "SAYCO" and "CISAC", International Society of Author's and Composers, various compositions and song writings; [pers.] Love is the basic of everything created, it is life, it is hope, it has no language, creed, color or frontier, it is given with a hug, a smile, a poem and in a song. [a.] Pleasant Valley, NY.

DE PAULA, HENRIQUE
[pen.] El Brujo (Witche); [b.] December 12, 1928, Sao Paulo, Brazil; [p.] Antonio and Amalia; [m.] Maria Luiza De Castro, May 31, 1958; [ch.] Julio Cesar, Carlos Alberto, Valerie-Celia (in-law); [ed.] Commercial school; [occ.] Construction laborer (in Brazil I was sales manager); [oth. writ.] Many articles published, about sports in the newspaper "Noticias Populares" in Sao Paulo, Brazil; [pers.] I write about everything. In poetry I prefer the romantic and the tragic, I am writing a book titled God, The Outright Lie. [a.] Newark, NJ.

DeROSA, ERICA LAUREN
[b.] April 13, 1977, New Haven, CT; [p.] D. Jack and JoAnn DeRosa II; [ed.] Choate Rosemary Hall, class of 1995; [occ.] Current student at Choate Rosemary Hall; [memb.] town Youth Services Committee, Arts Encouragement Organization, Gold Key Club, Make-A-Wish Foundation; [hon.] 1993 nominee to Washington Journalism Conference, participant in the Connecticut Youth Leadership Conference, Johns Hopkin's Talent Search participant, Who's Who In American High Schools of 1993, Cheshire Jaycee Distinguished Service nominee, Scholar Leader Award; [pers.] Nobody has ever measured, even poets, how much the heart can hold - Zelda Fitzgerald. [a.[Chershire, CT.

DERR, GEORGE P.
[pen.] G. Pharon; [b.] November 4, 1907, Philadelphia, PA; [p.] William Henry and Kathryn Miedel; [m.] Dorothy Majorie, September 24, 1938; [ch.] Carol Ann and David Anthony; [ed.] Brown College Prep., Philadelphia, PA; [occ.] Retired, former Ford Mtr., Bell Telephone, Martin Aircraft, Justice of the Peace; [memb.] Audubon Society, International Society of Poets, Founder and Life Member, The Ambler Stamp Club, B.S.A. National Philatelic Association; [hon.] Golden Poet Awards, 1987-1993, Philatelic Awards, awards by National Society of Poets, recently nominated, Charter Lifetime Member; [oth. writ.] Westminster News, Poets Corner, present compilation "Poems To Live By", eighty five poems; [pers.] My sincere wish that my writings, as a mirror reflect, light where there is darkness-truth, where mendacity prevails, patience, instead of irritation, love, with tolerance and understanding, and last, knowledge, of what life is or can be brought to be,

from within. [a.] Clearwater, FL.

DeSOMER, DAVID
[b.] September 11, 1971, Chicago, IL; [p.] James and Joyce DeSomer; [ed.] Curie High, University of Illinois of Chicago; [occ.] University student; [memb.] Southwest Dodgers Club; [hon.] The Cook County College Teachers Union Book Scholarship Award; [pers.] Nature Incites The Creative Fire, inspired by Neil Peart. [a.] Chicago, IL.

DeSTEFANO, JAMES
[pen.] Jamie Dess; [b.] September 19, 1932, New Haven; [p.] Deceased; [m.] Mary, August 4, 1962; [ch.] Joseph, Susan and Nicky; [ed.] Graduate high school; [occ.] Custodian for Board of Education; [oth. writ.] I have more not published before; [pers.] I try to emulate great poets and to use the times that are current, I am doing this as a hobby. [a.] New Haven, CT.

DeVANEY, NANCY
[b.] July 23, 1953, Huntsville, AL; [p.] H.L. and Jennie DeVaney; [ed.] B.S. Ed. from Athens College, M.S.W. and D.S.W. from University of Alabama, additional study at University of London and Jung Institute in Zurich, Switzerland; [occ.] Psychotherapist; [memb.] National Association of Social Workers, Academy of Certified Social Workers; [oth. writ.] The Playdough Children (book). [a.] Fairhope, AL.

DeVOE III, PAUL GILBERT
[m.] Ann Shirley DeVoe; [pers.] Special thanks to our children, James, Savanna, Paul Jr., Patty, Willi Jr. and Jerry. May God bless you all and keep you safe for us.

DeVORRE, ANN
[pen.] Ande; [b.] June 8, 1946, Lincoln, NE; [p.] Everett and Virginia Hawthorne; [m.] David DeVorre, December 18, 1965; [ch.] Danielle and Janette; [ed.] James Monroe High School, Moorpark College. [a.] Simi Valley, CA.

DEWEY, DIANE K.
[b.] August 24, 1954, Chambersburg, PA; [p.] Berk B. and Mary A. Meredith Jr.; [m.] Robert A. Dewey, July 7, 1991; [ch.] Florence A. Smith and Jennifer F. Gossert; [ed.] Fanner Metal High School; [occ.] Employed at (Textile Mill), Hoffman Mills, Shippensburg, PA.; [memb.] Attend Lutheran Memorial Church, Shippensburg; [oth. writ.] Have written a book entitled Forever Jean, that has not been published yet, it is based on an elderly woman, her thought and feelings that people around her do not understand; [pers.] I feel the elderly are not fully understood, I take great interest in how they may feel or what they may think. [a.] Shippensburg, PA.

DEWEY, PAULINE
[pen.] Poor Polly; [b.] August 13, 1906, Michigan; [p.] Frank and Rose Swift; [m.] Scott, July 14, 1928; [ch.] John and Thomas Dewey; [ed.] BA from MSY of life, certificate from Olivet College Michigan; [occ.] Retired teacher; [oth. writ.] Poem about teachers in Michigan's Pride of America published in 1976, Wellman Press, Lansing, Michigan, poem about "Night Before Xmas" in local paper about '41; [pers.] Most of my poems have been for my own enjoyment this is the first contest I have ever entered. [a.] Charlotte, MI.

DEWITT, MICHELLE ORDUNA
[b.] January 16, 1968, Omaha, NE; [p.] Jose and Agneta

Orduna; [m.] Kevin Dewitt, August 16, 1985; [ch.] Bobbi Li and Devin Scot; [ed.] Dunnellon High; [occ.] Jan's Nursery Inc., part-owner; [memb.] TBN, KCM; [oth. writ.] Several poems and children's stories; [pers.] The most important thing I learned in my life is that Jesus Christ loves you no matter who you are or what you do. He loves you! Let Him live in your life. (Romans 10:9-10). [a.] Dunnellon, FL.

DEWRI, NIRMAL C.
[b.] July 1, 1929, Bangladesh; [p.] Mr. Satish C. Dewri (93 years old); [m.] Priti L. Dewri, June 1954; [ch.] Reena Bagani, Beena, Wycliffe, Reeta Spencer, Raymond and Wayne; [ed.] M. Ed. (secondary) in the Philippines, worked 30 years as a teacher and principal of the boarding schools in Bangladesh; [occ.] Working in the Loma Linda University Library; [memb.] Loma Linda University, Church of The Seventh-Day Adventists, CA; [hon.] Received a letter from Ex-president George Bush and from Mrs. Bush for the following poems, "Troops Come Home", " A Happy Mother's Day"; [oth. writ.] Received a Presidential letter on the poem "Our July 4" (President Bush), some poems have been published in the local paper; [pers.] I try to put a direct message of appeal to the readers, challenging them to view the Promised Land as Pilgrims of this earth. [a.] Redlands, CA.

DIAZ, MARISA M.
[b.] October 11, 1978, Westminster, CA; [p.] Rolando and Rosario Diaz; [sib.] Diego and Christina Diaz; [ed.] I'm a sophomore at Etiwanda High School; [occ.] Student, would like a career in modeling or acting; [memb.] Citizen of the Year; [hon.] Awards from San Bernardino County for writing contest for poems in elementary and middle school; [oth. writ.] I have written several poems and short stories; [pers.] My poems are a mirror of my thoughts and feelings. [a.] Etiwanda, CA.

DiBELLA, D. RANDALL
[b.] May 4, 1953, Danbury, CT; [p.] John (died 1985) and Natalie (alive and well); [m.] Paula (Galasso) DiBella, October 9, 1993; [ch.] (Previous marriage) Shannon (11 years) and David (8 years), step-sons, Brian (21) and Thomas (23); [ed.] B.A. Western Ct., State University 1975, J.D. George Mason University School of Law, 1980; [occ.] Trial Lawyer; [memb.] Connecticut Trial Lawyers Association, Connecticut Bar Association, Virginia Bar Association, Grievance Panel Chairman, Judicial District of Danbury, CT; [hon.] Condon Academic Scholarship, 2nd year of law school, past president New Milford, CT. Bar Association; [oth. writ.] Technical Legal, First Person Essays, light rhyming poem; [pers.[Enjoy Jack London tales. [a.] New Milford, CT.

DICKASON JR., GIL
[b.] February 4, 1955, Los Angeles; [p.] Gil Sr. and Gloria; [m.] Single; [ch.] Vanessa Marie and Gilbert Hamlin Dickason III; [ed.] High school graduate; [occ.] Lithographer/transmission Tec.; [oth. writ.] First time published other than high school papers; [pers.] My goal is to someday have my work put into a book or books that will help various support groups and perhaps give strength and a smile to those that are weak or afraid. [a.] Whittier, CA.

DICKENS, MILDRED
[b.] April 2, 1904, Sheffield, England; [p.] George and Mary Walters; [m.] Charles Roy Dickens, September 30, 1923; [ch.] Charles Richard Dickens; [ed.] Private

school, high school, art school, French, music; [occ.] Retired, but enjoy gardening, painting, cooking, arranging flowers; [hon.] Swimming, medals, certificates, school shield this a joint effort team of four girls age 13 which included life saving and resuscitation, diving, etc.; [oth. writ.] Nothing published, but many sent to friends and relatives for birthdays, etc.; [pers.] Sometime ago, while ill in bed, I couldn't read, write, hear or walk, so I amused myself by trying to remember the poems I once knew by heart, sometimes only remembering the first line, each day remembering a little more. Since then, when unable to sleep instead of counting sheep, I try to compose a little poetry, finally going to sleep. Waking up and refreshed I write down the things I remember. I love poetry, always have and always will. [a.] Stanford, CA.

DICKER, KIMBERLEY
[pen.] Ley Niedt; [b.] November 11, 1958, Oakland, CA; [m.] Philip Collins, since the beginning of time; [ed.] San Lorenzo High, CA; [pers.] Search your heart and know the truth in yourself, because there does exist that one twin soul for everyone. Do not fear and take a look within, there lies God and your destiny. "My, it's been a long, long time". Take my hand Philip, there's a place, somewhere a time and a place for us, because if you truly, truly believe you can make things happen.

DICKERSON, NORA JEAN
[b.] May 7, 1975, Greenville, SC; [p.] David and Nora Burdette; [m.] Billy Dickerson, May 21, 1991; [ch.] Morgan Kae Dickerson; [ed.] Travelers Rest High School; [occ.] Homemaker; [memb.] Parents Magazine, Crosswell Apostolic Church; [hon.] Awards in Christian Child Care; [oth. writ.] Several short stories, some poems, a few published in school newspaper; [pers.] Out of all the poetry I have written and people have read, if one person has been touched I'll be deeply satisfied. [a.] Mauldin, SC.

DICKSON, SEAN P.
[b.] June 7, 1971, New Mexico; [ed.] University High School, California State University, Fullerton; [occ.] Rock Musician/accounting clerk; [oth. writ.] Song lyrics for copyrighted music readings; [pers.] "Nando's Theme" was inspired by the struggle of the Uruguayan plane crash survivors in the Andes Mountain as depicted in the true-life account "Alive" by novelist Piers Paul Reed. [a.] Huntington Beach, CA.

DICKSON, STEVEN
[b.] February 2, 1969, Inverness, Scotland; [p.] Leslie and Agnes Dickson; [m.] Kara Dickson, June 20, 1992; [ed.] James Young High, West Lothian College; [occ.] British Telecom Engineer; [hon.] Higher National certificate in management. [a.] Livingston, UK.

DILLARD, CLAUDIA G.
[b.] July 20, 1939, El Paso, TX; [p.] Charlie and Inabelle Jackson; [m.] Warren Lee Dillard, October 11, 1970; [ch.] Alveta Rochelle, Timothy Lee and Christopher J.A.; [ed.] Berkeley High, Merritt College, Dean's List; [occ.] Homemaker; [oth. writ.] Unsubmitted, non-published religious poems; [pers.] I love the Lord and I want to show His great love and kindness through my poems. [a.] Los Angeles, CA.

DiMEO, DAWN E.
[b.] April 8, 1980, Rhine Beck, NY; [p.] Ralph E. DiMeo; [ch.] My cat "Tickles"; [ed.] Currently in 8th grade at Rhinebeck Central School, wishes to pursue a college education (not sure what field maybe teaching);

[memb.] Belonged to, The Girl Scouts of America and Y.A.B.A.; [oth. writ.] I wrote a series of poems which were published in the "Register Star" newspaper, I have written a few other poems on my feelings; [pers.] The poems that were published in the "Register Star" were written after I lost 2 brothers and 2 sisters in a terrible car accident. I would like to dedicate this poem to them, Jennifer, Rebecca, Brian and Justin DiMeo. [a.] Rhinebeck, NY.

DIMEO, TREVORR C.
[pen.] Trevorr C. DiMeo; [b.] August 23, 1968, Providence, RI; [p.] Frederick and Dennise DiMeo; [ed.] Warwick Veterans Memorial High School, Community College of R.I., (Associates in Liberal Arts), enrolled at R.I. College (Communication Major w/English Minor); [occ.] Custodian and student (Warwick School Department); [oth. writ.] Several, most recently had a poem entitled "R.I.P." published in a book Poetry An American Heritage; [pers.] If you let the past control your present, then you have no future. [a.] Warwick, RI.

DINAN, MICHEL
[b.] May 20, 1952; [memb.] Lambda Legal Defense and Education Fund, National Gay and Lesbian Task Force, Bay Area Folk Society, San Francisco Society for the Prevention of Cruelty to Animals; [hon.] "Chansons de la de'esse" a suite for Celtic harp, made the finals of the "Rencontres Internationales de Harpe Celtique" in France, other awards for voice, music, acting and stand-up comedy; [oth. writ.] Short story published in The Guide To The Gay Northeast, poem published in the Folk Harp Journal, songs and comedy material performed on radio and in cabarets, vignettes published in two gay newsletters, currently finishing autobiography and collection of original music for Celtic Harp; [pers.] Creating is my life, but we, Lesbians and Gays are the only minority that do not grow up among our own kind, and so grow up in total isolation, therefore, even more important to me than my musical or literary works is to leave behind a legacy of gay visibility.

DINER, OLGA
[pen.] Olga Diner; [b.] September 22, 1946, Argentina; [p.] Marcos and Lara Diner; [ed.] MS in Biochemistry; [occ.] Secretary; [oth. writ.] Poems (none published yet); [pers.] The poem "Awareness" that I submitted was inspired in the teachings of J. Knishnamurti. [a.] Los Angeles, CA.

DiROCC, ARLENA A.
[b.] Medford, MA; [p.] Leo and Gertrude Johnson; [m.] Enrico; [ch.] Donna S. DiFabio and Edward M. DiRocco; [ed.] Matignon High School, Northeastern University; [occ.] President, Word Processing Company, former Director Sales and Marketing at a Computer Company; [memb.] Director, Board on Council on Aging, Burlington; [hon.] Dean's List, Northeastern University; [oth. writ.] Memories, Father and The Bride, Father, Mom and The Angels, Guardian Angels, Christmas; [pers.] I write because it allows me to create, to remember and to leave a permanent fixture of my being, what a wonderful legacy to leave to my children and their children. [a.] Burlington, MA.

DOANE, MYRTLE LITCH
[b.] May 19, 1914, Lynn, MA; [m.] Widow-Earl Litch, Alfred Doane (2nd spouse), November 6, 1959; [ch.] Dorothy Litch Jones, (adopted) Leita Hodgdon McKinnon; [ed.] University of N. H. Durham, Bachelor of Arts; [occ.] Retired school teacher; [memb.] Poetry

Fellowship of Maine, Poetry Society of Massachusetts, United Amateur Press Association of America, Brownfield Historical Society Brown, Maien, East Boston Branch Freedoms Foundation at Valley Forge, PA, member Faith Bible Church, Littleton, N.H., Poet in Residence Bethlehem Elementary School; [hon.] 6 Freedoms Foundation Awards, 2 poetry, 2 Editorials, 2 letter to special commendation from former, Gov. John Sununu naming me as Poet Extraordinary, through the years, awards for prose and poetry, Best essay on town meeting, best in state of Arkansas on the Constitution, Poet Laureate of U.A.P.A.A. 1993-94, (United Press Association of America); [oth. writ.] Bittersweet, 15 poetry books, 1 cook book, various anthologies, 40 feature articles in Sat. Lewiston Journal, Lewiston, Maine, articles, No. Conway Reporter, Bridgton News, Bridgton, Maine, Democrat Ad., Norway, Maine, Manchester Union Leader, Maine, N.H., Portland Press Herald, Portland, ME.; [pers.] To me poetry is a window of creation, I enjoy looking through it. [a.] Forge, PA.

DOBEK, GRZEGORZ
[b.] February 22, 1969, Poland; [p.] Piotr and Anna Dobek; [ed.] Catholic University of Lublin, Poland, SS Cyril and Methodist Seminary, MI., University of St. Mary of the Lake, Mundelein Seminary, IL; [occ.] Seminarian, Mundelein Seminary, Mundelein, IL; [memb.] Knights of Columbus; [hon.] National Dean's List; [pers.] I try to express the bright side of human existence and illuminate hope in spite of people's preoccupation with evil in today's world. [a.] Mundelein, IL.

DOELITZSCH, CHRISTINA ELIZABETH
[b.] August 19, 1965, Rochester, NY; [p.] Blanca Colon and Christina Doelitzsch; [m.] Patrick Tennity (fiance) June 25, 1994; [ch.] Three children from previous marriage; [ed.] Went to school at Churchville, Chili, then attended Monroe Community College for two years majoring in Psychology; [occ.] Recently disabled due to a car accident, pursuing writing interests; [memb.] Active interests in Adam Walsh Foundation and other local charities, enjoys volunteer work; [hon.] Various medals and awards in dance, poetry competitions and modeling including pageants, Arthur Murray School of Dance and recognition for poetry; [oth.writ.] Children's stories re: Miss McGillicudy, various poetry works soon to be published. [pers.] I've always tried to write from my heart, so that whenever someone reads one of my works they are experiencing a part of me. [a.] Rochester, NY.

DOM, CHRIS
[pen.] Christopher J. Dom; [b.] September 1, 1973, Lancaster, PA; [p.] Barry and Darlene Dom; [ch.] Zachary James Dom; [ed.] Ephrata Senior High School; [occ.] Security Guard; [oth. writ.] Various unpublished poems and short stories; [pers.] Thanks to my parents, my teachers, my girlfriend and the rest of my family and friends for their recognition of my dark side and my real side and the ability to tell the difference. I love you all. [a.] Newmanstown/Ephrata, PA.

DONEHOO, MERRIE B.
[b.] January 30, 1973, Stafford, TX; [p.] Barbara and Richard Donehoo; [ed.] Cypress Creek High School, Sam Houston State University; [occ.] Student; [memb.] Volunteer at SAAFE House in Huntsville, TX; [pers.] Poetry lets me escape to a world of my own, where my thoughts and feelings are the ink in my pen and creativity is the paper to write on. [a.] Huntsville, TX.

DONOVAN, IDA
[b.] September 6, 1948, Glace Bay, NS; [p.] Louie and Mathilda Detcheverry; [m.] Edwin Donovan, August 5, 1967; [ch.] 4 girls and 4 boys; [ed.] St. Michael's High School, Glace Bay, various college courses at University College of Cape Breton; [occ.] Drama teacher, actress; [memb.] Cape Breton Writers Association, Festival On The Bay and Arts, Cape Breton; [oth. writ.] Numerous songs, plays and skits as well as other articles; [pers.] I have been writing since childhood. I write everyday, I write to touch people's emotional side. I want to make them think, laugh and cry. [a.] Glace Bay, NS.

DOOLEY, CAROLYN LOTT
[pen.] Judy Lane; [b.] May 20, 1953, Russelville, AL; [p.] Carl and Lois Lott; [m.] Phillip Dooley, September 19, 1969; [ch.] Phil Jr., Karen, Carmen and Rodney; [ed.] K.V.C.C., Parchment High School Adult Education, Paralegal, Real Estate Law; [occ.] Medical Transcriptionist, Independent Paralegal; [hon.] Editor's Choice, Excellence in Accounting/bookkeeping; [oth. writ.] "All Mom's Nightmare" published through National Library of Poetry, presently writing novel, Shades of Grey Unmasked, currently having my poems evaluated for publishing; [pers.] Education is so important, computers are not only convenient but a must without them you will be lost in the future to come. [a.] Kalamazoo, WI.

DORKA JR., CHARLES ANTHONY
[pen.] Chuk; [b.] October 16, 1951, Akron, OH; [p.] Emma Jeanne Kuhn and Charles A. Dorka; [m.] (As of June 25, 1994 will be) Rebecca Ann Dorka; [ch.] Abigail Jo and Amy Jo Metzger; [ed.] B.S. Comp. Sp. Ed., University of Akron, continuing education, OSU, BYU, Kent State, M. Ed., the University of Ashland; [occ.] Instructor of Intermediate Gifted Students, Shelby City Schools, Shelby, OH; [memb.] Berean Baptist Church, Shelby Ed. Association, Ohio Ed. Association, National Education Association, Phi Delta Kappa, Mensa, ACLV, National Rife Association, volunteer-Red Cross, Association for Children with Learning Disabilities; [hon.] Runner-up Ohio Teacher of the Year 1979, Ashland Oil Golden Achiever Award 1988, 1990, Martha Holden Jennings Scholarship 1978, Mensa 1986, Phi Delta Kappa 1987, Mensa Teacher of the Year (North Central Ohio) (1989-1990), Who's Who in American Education 1990; [oth. writ.] Textbook for individualized Math Methods System (1987), essays in local papers, pamphlet and brochure work for community organizations, fundraising letters for various organizations; [pers.] My poetry has consistently served as the one, true, honest expression of everything I have inside. I have always hoped it would touch the hearts and souls of others in genuine ways. [a.] Mansfield, OH.

DORSCH, ANDREW
[pen.] Andrew Dorsch; [b.] September 23, 1959, Fall River, MA; [p.] Rowena and Enamuel Dorsch; [m.] Claudia Ellen Dorsch, November 9, 1986; [ch.] Morgan Dale Dorsch; [ed.] University of Pennsylvania, Wharton Business School (BS in Economics); [occ.] Controller; [hon.] Certified Public Accountant-NJ; [pers.] Life is short, make sure you take some time to enjoy it. [a.] Edison, NJ.

DOSS-MILLER, BETTY LOU
[b.] June 15, 1965, Fairbanks, AK. [p.] Jerry R. and Martha Sue Doss; [m.] James C. Miller; [ch.] Brittany Jodawn and Tiffany Kayannlyn; [ed.] Modern Business College, Tri-Cities, WA., and Northwest Arkansas Community College; [occ.] U.S.D.A. Inspector; [memb.]

Parent-Teachers Association, United States Department of Agriculture, United States Women's Slow Pitch Softball Association; [pers.] Protect the innocent child who lives behind your eyes and never let the harshness of the world destroy the beauty this child possesses. [a.] Green Forest, AR.

DOWD, LINDA L.
[b.] July 30, 1949, Niagara Falls, Ontario Canada; [p.] Gerald E. and Patricia M. (nee,Pattison) Herries; [m.] Gerald F. Dowd, August 23, 1969; [ch.] Shannon Lyn and Erin Marie Dowd and grandson Michael Patrick; [ed.] Graduated from the Mack School of Nursing 1970, St. Catharines,, Ontario, Canada, have since taken numerous credit courses in a wide variety of subjects; [occ.] Artist (Pioneer Studios), my watercolor paintings are also available in limited edition prints) Registered Nurse (Psychiatry, Public Health); [memb.] Meadowvale Art group (founder past-president), College of Nurses of Ontario, Mississauga Arts Council, Civic Center Art Galley, Visual Arts Mississauga, Lady of the Knights (Ontario VII), Burce Trail Association; [hon.] Editor;s Choice Award (National Library of Poetry-1993 [oth. writ.] Poetry included in the National Library of Poetry's anthologies A Question of Balance 1992, Distinguished Poets of America 1993, written over one hundred poems and have done public poetry readings, also written over forty songs; [pers.] Life is for the living, so get out there and live it ! [a.] Mississauga, Ontario Canada.

DOWDY, KIMBERLEY ANN
[b.] December 26, 1977; [p.] Jim and Kathy Dowdy; [ed.] Presently in 10th grade at Frank W. Cox High School, Virginia Beach, VA; [occ.] Student; [hon.] Presidential Academic Fitness Award, Honor Roll, Cox High School 1993; [oth. writ.] First place, Mother's Day, essay, local newspaper; [pers.] Everyday of my life is an obstacle that must be overcome and I strive to achieve to the best of my ability, the goal that lies after overcoming those obstacles. [a.] Virginia Beach, VA.

DOWD, MARTIN
[b.] October 25, 1945, Southampton, England; [ed.] Ph.D. Computer Science, University of Toronto; [occ.] Research Associate; [memb.] Society for Industrial and Applied Mathematics; [hon.] Certificates of Appreciation, NASA Outreach Program; [oth. writ.] Textbook "Elementary Mathematics" to appear, several scientific papers and one other poem; [pers.] All men should strive to bring peace to the world.

DOYLE, PATRICK
[pen.] Patrick Doyle; [b.] May 16, 1935, Houston, TX; [p.] Marguarite and Stewart Doyle, Sr.; [m.] Divorced; [ch.] Patrick Jr. and Albert Christopher Doyle; [ed.] Kirwin High, Galveston Alvin Junior and San Jacinto College (both junior colleges); [occ.] Coordinator, Amoco Oil Company, Texas City, TX; [oth. writ.] Have written many poems but never tried to publish any until now; [pers.] Being a romantic, I've always found it easy to write on the beauty of love as well as the tragedy of one with no love or one who has lost love and dreams of finding it again. [a.] League City, TX.

DRIEU, CLAUDETTE
[pen.] Claudette Drieu; [b.] February 18, 1962, Winsor, Canada; [p.] Julien and Christine Drieu; [m.] Brian Hogan, April 28, 1990; [pers.] Dedicated to Julien Drieu, my beloved father who is very much missed and who would be very proud. [a.] Michigan.

DROLL-LUCIUS DEBORAH
[b.] December 5, 1954, Fostoria, OH; [p.] Bernard and Bernice Droll; [m.] Mark Lucias, November 19, 1983; [ch.] Devin M. Lucius; [ed.] St. Wendelin High School, Fostoria, OH; [occ.] Sales; [memb.] St. Michaels Parish, Findlay, OH; [hon.] Honor Roll Student, Intensive Office Education President; [oth. writ.] "We Don't Have Time Anymore"; [pers.] I try to reflect the importance of love for our children and family life in today's busy world. [a.] Findlay, OH.

DUDLEY, HAROLD JAMES
[b.] July 7, 1902, Richmond, VA; [p.] Beverley Roy and Hettie Barlow Dudley; [m.] Avis Fountain Dudley (deceased), October 18, 1929; [ch.] Avis LaFayette Dudley Dew-Johnson; [ed.] Hampden-Sydney College in Virginia, B.A., Union Theological Seminary, Richmond, VA., B.D. and Th. M.; [occ.] Thirty years as Executive Secretary of the N.C. Synod, Presbyterian Church in the U.S., retired July 1 following 66 years preaching; [memb.] Tau Kappa Alpha, Omicron Delta Kappa; [hon.] Honorary D.D. degree conferred in 1945 by Rhodes College, Memphis, TN., Hampden-Sydney College Athletic Hall of Fame 1993; [oth. writ.] Editor North Carolina Presbyterian; [pers.] All things do work together for good to them who love God.

DUHAIME, ROBERT
[pers.] Writing is my love, I try to make people aware of things in my writing. I hope that those with their eyes open will understand and make good. [a.] Edmonton, Alberta.

DUNCAN, CAROLYN MARIE
[b.] August 28, 1980, Los Angeles, CA; [p.] Eileen and Raymond Duncan; [ed.] 8th grade at Los Angeles Center for Enriched Studies a public magnet school (enrolled in 10th grade English); [occ.] Student at Los Angeles Center for Enriched Studies; [memb.] Community and Literary Club; [hon.] Honorable Mention for a Star Trek story entered in L.A.U.S.B.'s "Reflections" contest; [oth. writ.] Bi-monthly Sci-fi newsletter, have been publishing it for a year now; [pers.] I wished to call to attention some problems in today's society through an new perspective a time traveler's. People tend to not listen to a view that's directly environmental so I chose to do it through something they do like, Sci-fi. [a.] Los Angeles, CA.

DUPREE, BETTY J.
[pen.] B.J. or Mama Do; [b.] August 15, 1935, Lauderdale, CO; [p.] G.L. and Esther Sanderson; [m.] Raleigh Dupree (deceased), 1951; [ch.] Five, 3 girls and 2 boys; [ed.] 11th grade; [occ.] Housewife; [hon.] Several Golden and Silver Poet Awards, several of my poems have been published; [oth. writ.] I've been writing since I was 12, all kinds of poems and songs, I love to write for my grandchildren, have written lots for them; [pers.] I believe you can do anything you really want to. Dedicated to my daughter, Ramona who reads all of my poems and my grands, whom I enjoy reading to. [a.] Florence, AL.

DURAND, ELIZABETH
[b.] June 23, 1982, Charlottesville, VA; [p.] Linda Swanson (MD.) and Charles Durand (MD >); [ed.] 6th grade student at Riviera Hall Lutheran School; [occ.] Student; [memb.] Coastline Classics Rhythmics Gymnastic team; [hon.] Honor Roll Student.

DURBIN, JEAN EVELYN (SR.)
[pen.] Margaret Durbin; [b.] April 19, 1929, Sunfish, KY; [p.] John and Eva Durbin; [ed.] BS in Ed., MA in ED., MA in Pastoral Ministry; [occ.] Tutor of elementary students; [memb.] AARP, Vista (Public Relations Specialist for Adult Ed.) Clinton Club, AAA Club; [hon.] Red Cross, Commercial for Kahns, honored by Cinti. Police for work with youth, principal of school, printed in National Anthology; [oth. writ.] "Cappy the Catfish" juvenile book, 1500 copies "Gifting" mena book, (Journal of Teacher Tips-magazine), 500 copies poetry book "Gentle Power", "Dim Is The Dawn", novel not published; [pers.] Loving living is mutual gifting. [a.] Mt. St. Joseph, OH.

DURBIN, JR., WILLIAM DR.
[pen.] Soke; [b.] December 31, 1953, Bardstown, KY; [p.] William and Harvie Durbin; [ed.] Bardstown High School, Campbellsville College, University of Oriental Philosophy; [occ.] Minister, Martial Arts Teacher; [memb.] International Okinawan Martial Arts Union, Juko Kai International, Kosho Shorei Kai, Dai Nippon Seibukan Budo/Bagei Kai, Zen Kokusai Soke Remmei, Christian Martial Arts Association; [hon.] Who's Who in Karate, Who's Who in American Martial Arts, Outstanding Young Men in America, Order of Kentucky Colonels, Presidential Sports Award-Judo, Presidential Sports Award Karate; [oth. writ.] Articles in magazines, Black Belt Magazine, Karate Kung Fu Illustrated, Inside Karate, Indise Kung Fu Presents, Karate International, American Karate, Aikido Today magazine; [pers.] It is my faith in God and my development as Soke, headmaster of Kiyujute Ryu Kempo Bugei, that brings poetry into my life which is full of love and joy. [a.] Frankfort, KY.

DUTT, ERIC
[pen.] Eric Dutt; [b.] April 20, 1963, Batala, India; [p.] Victor J. and Mary J. Nath; [m.] Pamlea P. Gill, November 20, 1986; [ed.] Panjab University, Chandigarh, India, G.N.D. University , Amritsar, India, Baring Union Christian College, Batala, India; [occ.] College English Instructor, Triton College, River Grove, IL; [memb.] Midwest Regional Conference on English, SOuth Asian Christian Church; [hon.] High school honor's list; [oth. writ.] Several poems published in college magazine; [pers.] I try to reflect the painful struggle of humankind to achieve perfection. I have been greatly influenced by post colonial novelists. [a.] Oak Lawn, IL.

DUTTA, PAMELA
[b.] August 20, 1955, Poona, India; [p.] Gopaldas and Santosh Rana; [m.] Pradeep Dutta, December 12, 1989; [ch.] Krun; [ed.] M.A., M.Phil. (English), Goa University; [pers.] Writing poetry elevates the mundane into an aesthetic experience. [a.] Vasco Da Gama, Goa.

DUTTON, PETER JEREMY
[p.] Terrence Dutton and Helen Crow; [ed.] Glen Innes High, Tamworth Tech., Riverina College; [oth. writ.] How to spell "Salivation" in Aramaic, My Eyes Pupils Ain't Black Holes, The Etymology of dowsing is A Human Right, The New Rule and The Neural Functions, The Benefits of Atheotherapy, various other works; [pers.] Humans wait for Anno-ther Domini Armaggedon date time/space finally. [a.] Australia.

DUTY, GINGER LEE
[b.] November 26, 1966, St. Louis, MO; [p.] Richard and Marlene (Vickers) Eckert; [m.] Kenneth Lee Duty, June 23, 1985; [ch.]] Kingsley Lloyd, Marshall Alvie,

Mark Edwin and Isaiah Ivan; [ed.] Chester Community grade K-8, Chester Community High 9-12, Chester, IL, class of '84, CNA John A. Logan College '87; [occ.] Housewife, homemaker, mother; [pers.] This poem is completely true. Family, love and friendship are so important, PLEASE don't let a family feud keep you apart forever, "I'm Sorry" isn't fatal... time is. [a.] Murphysboro, IL.

DUXFIELD, ROBERTA
[pen.] Roberta Leighton Howerd; [p.] Robert and Maura Lynch, stepfather, J.R. Brooks; [m.] James Peter, April 6, 1974; [ed.] Notre Dame College of Education (teacher training), Liver pool, England; [occ.] Early retired due to long illness; [memb.] Women's Royal Voluntary Service (W.R.V.S.), Stroke Foundation (English), helpline organizer in crisis situations, Amateur Operatic's and Dramatic's (before illness); [hon.] R.I.A.M. music certificates (piano), teaching certificate, public speaking certificate (English), highly recommended, also Italic handwriting winner; [oth. writ.] New published English poetry, late starter, by Arrival Press Poetry Now, also local publications; [pers.] If you can help someone, do so, if you need help, say so! [a.] Liverpool, Merseyside.

DYCK, ROSE
[b.] January 22, 1934, Hungary; [p.] John and Elizabeth Mutz; [m.] Abraham Dyck, July 25, 1954; [ch.] Robert and Rudy, 4 grandchildren, son in Hungary and Germany; [occ.] Homemaker; [memb.] Fraternal Order of Eagles 2726, Abbotsford, B.C. Canada (Ladies Auxiliary), local art counselor; [oth. writ.] Never entered before; [pers.] I write to express my personality or leave a meaningful message in my writings. [a.] Abbottsford, BC.

EAGLE, KIMBERLY BROWN
[pen.] Kimberly Brown Eagle; [b.] November 12, 1965, Oak Hill, OH; [p.] Sue Rinehart and Stanley Taylor; [m.] Divorced 12, 1991; [ch.] Rico Jr., Ryann M. and Kyle R.; [oth. writ.] Include, The One Who Stands Alone, Mother's Teachings and Morning, as well as countless others; [pers.] This is for you Rico, I love you! [a.] Columbus, OH.

EATON, MURIEL
[b.] June 11, 1938, Detroit; [p.] Rufus and Jennie Williams; [m.] March 6, 1956; [ch.] Lawana, Chandra, Travis and Roquel; [ed.] Northwestern High, Wayne State University; [occ.] Department of Social Services, Social Worker; [memb.] New Mount Carmel Baptist Church committee; [hon.] All from Social Services; [oth. writ.] Reading and writing personal poems for others. Two songs with country western background; [pers.] My writings are a gift from God. I write what I feel, what I see and what I know, I never run out of words. [a.] Detroit, MI.

EBERLE, PRISCILLA
[b.] May 16, 1927, Hutchison, KS; [p.] Lonnie and Leona Collins; [m.] Dennis Eberle, June 6, 1975; [ch.] Stacey and Lauren; [ed.] MSSC-Joplin MO., 3 1/2 years; [occ.] Retired; [hon.] Best of Show (1st) Ozark Writers Conference for short story"Otto", published poems, "American Collegiate Poets", "College Contemporaries", World of Poetry Anthology; [pers.] Searching for meaning of emotions. [a.] Joplin, MO.

EBY, JACOB
[b.] December 11, 1974, Selma, AL; [p.] Jim and Jane Eby; [ed.] Greater Atlanta Christian High School, David

Lipscomb University; [occ.] Student at David Lipscomb University; [memb.] International Thespian Society; [hon.] Eagle Scout Award recipient; [oth. writ.] One free writing published in The Atlanta Journal and Constitution, one other poem published in a school newsletter; [pers.] I have only God to thank for the talent that I have. I thank Monna Douglas, G.T.R. and Jimmy Jones for encouraging me to write, I have Shane Jackson, Christines Biggie, Darby McKinny and W.T. to thank for often inspiring me and of course my parents. [a.] Nashville, TN.

EDELMANN, ELIZABETH A.
[pen.] Elizabeth A. Edelmann; [b.] February 28, 1963, Fairfax, VA; [p.] Dr. Carole M. Hertz and Richard A., Hodson; [m.] David T. Edelmann, June 6, 1987; [ch.] David Alexander Edelmann; [ed.] Bachelors of Science, University of Maryland; [occ.] Mom; [oth. writ.] Many poems to small or personal to be noticed or published; [pers.] Notice and enjoy all things be they blatant of sublime for I am (we) are only here once to revel in the joy of life. [a.] Charlotte, NC.

EDMONDS, ANGELA D.
[pen.] Denise; [b.] December 10, 1964, Chattanooga, TN; [p.] Arthur Lee and Betty Jean Chambers; [m.] Willie Tyrone Edmonds (poet) July 1, 1991; [ch.] Latoya Nicole Edmonds (1 1/2) and Willie T. Edmonds Jr., (5 years); [ed.] Graduate of Howard High School, June 7, 1983; [occ.] Housewife; [memb.] Stephen's Temple C.P. Church Usher Board; [hon.] 5th of August was the day when I turned my life completely over to my Savior Christ Jesus; [oth. writ.] None at this moment; [pers.] I am inspired by my loving husband and friend (Willie) whom has coached me all along in the basic fundamentals of poetry from the very first word to the very end. [a.] Chattanooga, TN.

EDMONDS, WILLIE TYRONE
[pen.] Tee; [b.] June 30, 1959, Chattanooga, TN; [p.] Sallie B. Edmonds and Willie Fuqua; [m.] Angela Denise Edmonds, July 1, 1991; [ch.] Willie Jr., and Latoya Nicole Edmonds; [ed.] Graduate of Howard High School, Edmondson Community College; [occ.] Retired, U.S. Army and boxing; [memb.] Steven's Temple C.P. Church,. Rev. Ernest Jefferson; [hon.] Army Service Ribbon, Good Conduct Medal, Expert Rifleman, Draftsman certificate of achievement, World of Poetry Golden Award (Today); [oth. writ.] (I Wonder), unpublished (Peace is a Gift) and many more, unpublished; [pers.] I've been writing for more than twenty years, since the age of twelve. I'm inspired by life in general, and a loving mother, I am the 5th of 10 children. [a.] Chattanooga, TN.

EDMONDSON, SAMMIE
[pen.] Sammie Edmondson; [b.] January 16, 1955, Rocky, OK; [p.] Arby and Betty Giblet; [m.] Jackie Edmonson, January 5, 1973; [ch.] Richard Todd and Jackie Chad Edmondson; [ed.] Will have B.S. in Elementary Education May 1994; [occ.] Student, homemaker; [memb.] Southwestern Reading Council, VFW Fort Cobb Post, wife of Veteran of Foreign Wars; [hon.] Kappa Delta Phi, Kappa Sigma Phi, Secretary of Kappa Delta Phi, President's Honor Roll, Dean's Honor Roll, Golden Poet Award; [oth. writ.] American Anthology of Poetry, Golden Poet three years, reporter for Trend College newspaper WSAO; [pers.] My poetry is the emotional reflection of the total human condition. [a.] Cordell, OK.

EDWARDS, JO-ANNA LEE
[pen.] Jo-Anna Livingwell; [b.] May 17, 1946, Lynwood, CA; [p.] Wilhelmina Sidebottom and Willard Eldridge Edwards; [ed.] South Gate High School and varied and colorful life experiences; [occ.] Free Lance writer and property owner; [oth. writ.] Poems and essays published in L.A. Christian Free Press and Southern California Singles News, book in progress, no publisher as yet; [pers.] I write for myself from personal experiences, hoping I may encourage others to continue forward. [a.] South Gate, CA.

EDWARDS, WESLEY A.
[b.] March 29, 1937, Taliaferro County Georgia; [p.] Guss Arnie and Hazel Mae Denard Edwards; [m.] Carol Anne Platt Edwards, September 21, 1963; [ch.] Lyle Allen Edwards (age 25) and Mary Lorene (age 16); [ed.] Public school, Union Point, Georgia, Young Harris Junior College, Georgia, B.A., Mercer University, Macon, Georgia, M.R.E. (Master of Religious Education) at Southern Baptist Theol. Seminary, M.Ed., University of Louisville; [occ.] Language Arts, public school teacher (Barret Traditional Middle School); [memb.] Jefferson County Teachers Association, Kentucky Education Association, National Education Association, Kentucky Middle School Association, Crescent Hill Baptist Church; [hon.] (Paid) Summer reviewer of Kentucky eighth-grade writing portfolios; [oth. writ.] I have written my Christmas verses for over 10 years, a local writers' group is encouraging me to revise and publish several poems and short pieces. I have one poem in one of our booklets, as a previous preschool coordinator, I wrote several articles for the church newsletter; [pers.] I believe in the value, beauty and creativity of both children and adults. I continue to encourage my students to write and publish. I like to view people and nature through a camera's eye and poetry. Everyone has feelings and experiences worth saying that need to be written, read and heard. [a.] Louisville, KY.

EDWIN, SABEEN
[b.] September 23, 1980, New York; [p.] Ernest and Rita Edwin; [sib.] Yasmin Edwin; [ed.] Studying in 8th grade; [occ.] Student at Saint Nicholas of Tolentine; [hon.] Poetry contest at Saint Nicholas of Tolentine School, 1990-4th grade, won 3rd place, 1991-5th grade, won 1st place, 1993-7th grade, won 2nd place. [a.] Jamaica, NY.

EGLI, CHARITY
[b.] September 19, 1976, Redding, CA; [p.] Tim and Cindy Egli; [m.] Fiance', Tom Willcockson; [ed.] Graduated with honors from G.E.D. in August 1993; [oth. writ.] Many poems and stories published in school newsletters and books from different contests (ie. Kaleidoscopes of Poetry); [pers.] I write poetry as a channel that takes my bad experiences and turns them into something good. [a.] Wake Forest, NC.

EHRENREICH, KRISTJAN JURGEN
[b.] February 5, 1976, Deep River, Ontario; [p.] Heidi Ehrenreich; [ed.] 12th year student at Harvey Regional High School; [occ.] Forest Fire Fighter; [hon.] MVP for the Harvey Laker's Soccer team; [oth. writ.] Several poems including "Provider", "Guilt", "Last Stand", "Entrance and Sanctuary"; [pers.] I feel that my work is derived from feelings deep in the hearts of everyone. I enjoy using a great deal of emotion and beauty in life and death. [a.] Prince William, Ontario.

EICHELBERGER, JO
[pen.] Parker Cross; [b.] November 28, 1956, Hagerstown, MD; [p.] Patricia J. Forsythe and Harold E. Eichelberger; [m.] Single; [ed.] Williamsport High School, University of Maryland, Mont Alto Campus Penn State, continuing education courses; [occ.] Laboratory Technician. Colombo Yogurt Inc., Hagerstown, MD; [memb.] Greenpeace; [hon.] North American School for Animal Sciences; [oth. writ.] A "collection" of writings, beginning in 1965; [pers.] I give my works to friends as gifts, it is of my soul. [a.] Hagerstown, MD.

EISTETTER, LESLEY
[pen.] Pinster; [b.] August 2, 1968, Regina, Sask; [p.] Al and Dorothy Eistetter; [m.] Working on that; [ch.] 2 quarter horses, 1 German Shepherd, 2 cats and lots of fish; [ed.] Grade 12,m Lumsden High School, Criminolistics, Granton Technical Institute, Psychology and Emergency Medical Technician; [occ.] Auto processing in insurance, cooperators; [memb.] Every horse club possible, Greenpeace, Regina Humane Society, Canadian Track and Field Association; [hon.] Numerous track and field honors, Equestrian and team sport awards galore; [oth. writ.] Until I Met You, Learning To Live Again, If Only, The Inspiring, Our Future in Today, Committed and others, a book is currently in the works; [pers.] Writing is my way of escaping into another world. My feelings thoughts and words can be forever remembered and rekindled by opening a book. It's a love that will never vanish. [a.] Lumsden, Saskatchewan.

EKANEM-UMOH, MERCY JOHN
[pen.] Merci-Me; [b.] July 3, 1959, Nigeria; [p.] Afiong and Ndarake John Ekanem; [ch.] Edidiong Utuk; [ed.] M.A. (English), B.A. (Theatre Arts); [occ.] Teacher; [memb.] UFT; [oth.writ.] A book of poems yet unpublished, short stories (published and unpublished); [pers.] To touch other's lives positively as our paths cross and not to say behind anyone what I cannot say in front of them. [a.] Brooklyn, NY.

EKSTROM, RHONDA
[b.] October 7, 1941, Belgium; [m.] Carl F. Ekstrom, November 15, 1958; [ch.] Steven and Mary; [ed.] Grade and high school in Chicago, college in Lake County, IL; [occ.] Retired; [oth. writ.] Write children's stories in rhyme and am currently trying to become a published author; [pers.] I love writing for and about children, they will someday glimpse horizons we cannot begin to imagine, giving them a sense of magic and wonder now. Can make them seek out the magic of all their tomorrows.

ELIJAH-EL, PERRY LOVELL
[pen.] P. Elijah-el; [b.] November 22, 1952, Winston Salem, NC; [p.] Catherine and William Elijah; [m.] Single; [ed.] Seminary School; [occ.] Poetry, song writer; [memb.] Moorish Science Temple, Inc., Seventh Day Adventist Church; [oth. writ.] One hundred twenty seven unpublished poems, twenty unpublished Cinquain poems, seven unpublished songs; [pers.] As poets and writers one should always mind the things which help create better ideas and outlook for our world. [a.] Washington, DC.

ELKERTON, DOROTHY WEST
[pen.] Dorothy West Elkerton; [b.] March 18, 1931, Wisconsin; [p.] Walfred J. and Inga West; [m.] Donald Y. Elkerton, October 30, 1953 (40 years ago); [ch.] Daniel West Elkerton (age 38); [ed.] High school, junior college, graduate Realtors Institute (GRI); [occ.] Broker, owner Elkerton and Associates Real Estate; [memb.] East San Diego Board of Realtors, California Association of Realtors, National Association of Realtors, Nation Association of Real Estate Appraisers, Nation Association of Female Executives; [hon.] Miscellaneous music award, miscellaneous leadership awards; [oth. writ.] Notebook and shoe boxes full of miscellaneous writings, nothing previously published (the world may not be ready); [pers.] A sense of humor, a sense of honor commitment to family and profession and love of mankind = success and happiness. [a.] Alpine, CA.

ELKINS, JOHN MERL
[pen.] John M. Elkins; [b.] April 20, 1930, Joliet, IL; [p.] John Marion and Harriet Rose Davison Elkins; [m.] Erna Maye (Huie) Elkins, June 24, 1950; [ch.] Carolyn June, Charla Dianne and Cheryl Elaine; [ed.] Master of Science, Bachelor of Education Southeastern Oklahoma State University Durant, OK., Associate of Fine Arts Grayson County Community College, Sherman-Denison, TX; [occ.] Retired professional Counselor from Grayson County, retired Chief Master Sergeant United States Air Force; [memb.] Phi Delta Kappa, Texas Guard Association, Master Mason Acacia # 452 F & A.M., Hella Shrine, Garland, TX, National So-Journers Chapter # 463, Disabled American Veterans, Grayson County Taxpayers Association, North Texas Taxpayer's League; [hon.] Grayson County Taxpayers Tax Ombudsman 1992, United State Air Force Meritorious Service Medal, USAF Commendation Medal (three times), Korean Presidential Citation, Adjutant General's Individual Award, other military service awards, medals and ribbons; [oth. writ.] Hundreds of letters to the editors, letters to Congressional members of state and national Houses and Senate, most letters to editors have been published and are on topics relating to demands for better government, also do my own greeting cards using my own poems personalized for the recipient of the card; [pers.] In my writings, I attempt to share my opinions, and to encourage readers to make the very best out of our imperfect lives. After all, we are sharing God's most perfect earth. All types of poetry have influenced me from early elementary through graduate school. I have always used verse as a vehicle to aid in reaching difficult avenues of a reader's understanding and to convey my feelings about life as I have experienced it. [a.] Sherman, TX.

ELLIOTT, JANET MARIE
[b.] November 24, 1932, Wenatchee, WA; [p.] Marie Hall and Harlan King Usher; [m.] Oliver C. Elliott, Jr., August 12, 1955; [ch.] Steven Oliver, Douglas Ronald, Linda Marie (Scovel) and Kathryn Louise (Ahrens); [ed.] Whitman College, University of WA., BA., SOT; [occ.] Writer; [memb.] AAUW, PNACL, ELCA; [hon.] Service Award, Phi Alpha Theta; [oth. writ.] Book reviews in Lutheran Libraries, many news articles, children's mysteries, adult short stories, narrative and free verse family history, newsletter editing, poetry; [pers.] I hope to reveal the theology of my life in all that I write. [a.] Medina, WA.

ELLIOTT, NICOLA LOUISE
[b.] April 4, 1969, Devon, England; [p.] Neil Ferguson and Ann Elliott; [ed.] Nottingham University (BA Honors), followed by Manchester University (MA) (both England); [occ.] International NSA Distributor; [hon.] BA in Economics, MA in Economics. [a.] Dunton, Beds UK.

ELLIS, ROMEL
[b.] December 8, 1960, Fort Worth, TX; [p.] Isaac and

Dorothy Ellis; [m.] Brenda Ellis, January 7, 1989; [ch.] Cohen and Darcy Ellis; [ed.] Completed grades 1 thru 14; [memb.] Church of Christ; [pers.] Anticipation can bring you either joy or pain, but the promise of uncertainty is almost always a most welcome friend. [a.] Long Beach, CA.

ELSE, MERLE M.
[b.] December 9, Biwabik, MN; [p.] Axel and Jenny Nordstrom; [m.] Arthur W. Else, June 26, 1941; [ch.] Elizabeth Schmidt, Barbara and Roberta Else; [ed.] Horace Mann High School, Biwabik, MN., Virginia Junior College, Virginia, MN., University of Wisconsin, MN, Madison Wisconsin, Summer Milwaukee; [occ.] Homemaker; [memb.] U. Faculty Wives, McDowell Music Club, Lataoge Adult Learning Institute, Christ King Parish, Legion of Mary; [oth. writ.] Several poems not published; [pers.] We should take time to enjoy the natural glories of God and those are the things I've written most about. [a.] Wauwatosa, WI.

ELSNER, CHRISTY
[b.] March 28, 1978, Fort Saskatchewan, Alberta; [p.] Jack, Cindy Elsner; [ed.] Now a student in grade 10 at Fort Saskatchewan High School; [memb.] Fort Saskatchewan Judo Club and Fort Saskatchewan minor softball; [oth. writ.] A short story published in the local county book Stepping Stones; [pers.] Your dreams can begin to happen at any age, you just have to believe in them.

ELY, MICHELLE
[b.] August 29, 1972, Greenville, OH; [p.] Billy and Linda Ely; [ed.] Riverside High School, Johnson S. Wales University; [occ.] Advertising student; [memb.] Delta Epsilon Chi; [hon.] Dean's List graduated Cum Laude; [pers.] This poem was written for the special man in my life, in hopes that he would realize how much I love him. By sharing this poem, I hope that others will realize as I have how important it is to tell that special someone how much you care. [a.] Ellwood City, PA.

EMERSON, NANCY
[pen.] Josephine Redmond.

EMERY, JAMIE D.
[b.] November 29, 1970, Newport, AR; [p.] Mr. and Mrs. Alvin "Sox" Emery; [m.] Pamela Renee Winfrey Emery, June 29, 1992; [ed.] Tuckerman High School graduate, Hillsdale College graduate; [memb.] First Free Will Baptist Church, Tuckerman, AR; [hon.] Graduate Magna Cum Loda; [oth. writ.] Trials, By Fire, Diary of A Daydreamer, Night Falls; [pers.] My work is based on the cognitive concepts of the mind. I look to the world's pain and make it my own. My purpose is to make you think, feel and even be. [a.] Tuckerman, AR.

EMMANUEL, OWONIBI SOLA
[b.] April 25, 1968; [ed.] Obafemi Awolowo University, Ile-Ifb, BA honors English; [occ.] Lecturer, Laduke Akintola University of Tech.; [hon.] Ife Literary Awards in Drama 1991; [oth. writ.] Several poems published in local newspapers, "Peace By Pieces" a play accepted for publication by University Press PLC; [pers.] Why? Why must the soap dwindle that washes the filth of world, why must honey attract grey hairs to the bees? [a.] Ayetoro Gbedde, Kogil.

EMORY, TERESA ANN
[pen.] Terry Ann Emory; [b.] February 26, 1965, Virginia; [p.] Mr. and Mrs. Walter Emory; [m.] Single;

[ed.] Greenville High, NY; [occ.] Commercial loan processor; [pers.] My words come from my heart.

ENGEL III, WILSON F.
[pen.] Wick; [b.] October 2, 1946, Long Beach, CA; [p.] Wilson F. and Sarah F. Engel, Jr.; [m.] Charlene S. Engel (watercolorist), May 11, 1969; [ch.] Grace E. and Wilson F. Engel IV; [ed.] Maury High School, Old Dominion University, American University, University of Wisconsin, Madison; [occ.] Writer, poet; [memb.] Registered Poet in State of Virginia; [hon.] Phi Kappa Phi Honor Society, Summa Cum Laude B.A., Leverhulme Professor of English Literature, University of Edinburgh, Scotland; [oth. writ.] Two books of poems, Shutter, Napping in The Warm Sand and Knight and Flower, both illustrated by C.S. Engel, a novel Mr. Wellworth and His Marvelous Cleaning Machine, many individual poems and stories and critical articles. [pers.] Poetry is an overheard dialogue of self and soul. [a.] Newport News, VA.

ENGLAND, KATHLEEN W.
[b.] September 10, 1952, New York; [p.] Ed and Bobbe Smith; [m.] Gary, January 2, 1982; [ch.] Jarred (10), Dyan (8) and Alex (6); [ed.] Hillsboro High School, Nashville, TN., Draughon's College, Nashville, TN., Nursing degree, Western Kentucky University, Bowling Green, KY; [occ.] Registered Nurse in Occupational Health Nursing; [memb.] American Association of Occupational Health Nurses; [oth. writ.] This is the first poem I have ever sent in to a contest or publisher. I have been writing for 23 years and have many other poems as yet unpublished; [pers.] This poem is dedicated to my mother for support, understanding and unconditional love throughout the years.

ENGLISH, JARED S.
[b.] July 20, 1979, San Diego, CA; [p.] David and Linda English; [ed.] Freshman at Scottsdale Christian Academy, a college-preparatory high school in Phoenix, AZ; [memb.] National Junior Honor Society; [hon.] Honor Roll each quarter 1991-1992, 1992-1993, 1993-1994, Most Inspirational Player, soccer '92-'92, poetry award 1992-93; [oth. writ.] Author of the book entitled Ocean Moods; [pers.] The ocean has so many treasures that we do not understand. I am sure there is room for one more biologist to discover the mysteries and hidden secrets that the ocean hides behind a curtain of darkness. I plan to be that biologist.

ENNOLS JR., CHARLES J.
[b.] April 3, 1971, Chicago, Il; [p.] Charles and Marla Ennols Sr.; [sib.] Jabari and Jason Ennols; [ed.] Jim Hill High School, Hardy Junior High School, Morrison Elementary; [occ.] Christian; [memb.] New Horizon Baptist Church; [hon.] B.E.T., Poetic Justice, Nationwide Poetry contest winner; [pers.] I write poetry to express the love I have for my God, my race, women and children and to crunch the stereotypical image that this country has on young black men of today. [a.] Jackson, MS.

ERICKSON, LISA MARIE
[pen.] Lisa Westin; [b.] October 9, 1961, Minneapolis, MN; [p.] Jerry and Genny Erickson; [m.] Divorced; [ch.] Jeremy Wayne and Thomas Lee Heinks; [ed.] Princeton High School, CNA, MA, VA, college courses of personal interest; [occ.] Homemaker, secretary; [memb.] Friends of Deep Portage Conservation Reserve, MN Deer Hunters Association; [oth. writ.] Many poems, songs and short stories; [pers.] I thank the Lord

for my writing ability and seek to offer the joy, comfort and understanding to others that I have found through words. [a.] Princeton, MN.

ERICKSON, MORRIS
[b.] February 29, 1924, Westby, MT; [p.] Charles and Mary Erickson; [ch.] Charles Erickson; [occ.] Cowboy horse trainer; [oth. writ.] From Rolling Hills of Childhood, not published, book started Life Memory's. [a.] Acme Alberta, Canada.

ERVIN, ROY CARL
[pen.] Roy E., Roy C. Ervin, Roy Ervin; [b.] January 4, 1951, Monte Sano Hospital; [p.] Robert John and Dorothy; [ed.] Page Military Logan St. Elementary, Pinecrest, Van Nuys Junior High, Notredame High; [occ.] Life Master, U.S. Chess Federation; [memb.] US Chess Federation, Federation International des Echecs; [hon.] Too many; [oth. writ.] "The Best Work of My Life"; [pers.] Eternity passes away, until hope springs eternal, oh what a vile scent. [a.] Red Bluff, CA.

ESTES, MARC W.
[b.] January 18, 1971, Dover, NH; [p.] Fay and Frank Estes; [m.] Single; [ed.] Dover High School, University of New Hampshire English program; [occ.] Student, waiter, writer, substitute teacher and tutor; [memb.] National Eagle Scout Association, Order of the Arrow; [hon.] Eagle Scout, Honor Roll, Dean's List; [oth. writ.] Four Pieces for Power, a novel that I currently trying to get published; [pers.] Although I most enjoy writing fiction, I often like to take a break and work on some poetry. I am currently working on three more novels, "The Crickets of Autumn", "Rekindle the Flame" and "Bloodstains on the Battlefield". [a.] Dover, NH.

ESTES, WANDA LOUISE BROWN
[b.] May 11, 1924, Kansas; [p.] Hiram and Viola Brown; [ch.] 4; [ed.] Grade, high school, Nursing, 3 1/2 years of college in Art; [occ.] Secretary and receptionist of Bucklin Tractor and Implement Store (family store); [memb.] National Honor Society of Phi Theta Kappa, D.A.R. member, Civic Club, Legion Auxiliary Federated Clubs; [hon.] 4.0 grades in school in art, etc., winner for poem "My Daily Prayer"; [pers.] You are never fully dressed until you wear a smile. [a.] Bucklin, KS.

EVANS, AMY JoANNE
[pen.] Me; [b.] June 13, 1970, Dekalb, IL; [p.] Jack Evans and Diane Mongeau; [m.] Kyle Stuart Mattis, (January 7, 1991); [ed.] 11th grade in high school; [occ.] Assistant Supervisor at Creative Calligraphy; [hon.] Miscellaneous medals for band and vocal, I also have trophies (5) for auto racing, one of which is 5 ft. tall; [oth. writ.] I have several other poems that would be neat to have published; [pers.] I am really a tomboy, I love to race cars and work with my father installing floors. I enjoy singing too. My son Kyle is beautiful, I live life to the fullest and enjoy everyday. [a.] Dekalb, IL.

EVANS, DAVID
[pen.] D. Evan Cross; [b.] June 11, 1936, Chicago, IL; [p.] Henry and Melvina Evans; [m.] Edith N. Evans, June 25, 1959; [ch.] Carlos, Patricia, Donnie, Belinda, Micheal, Cynthia and Sandra; [occ.] Maintenance Mechanic/electrician.

EVANS, KABATERAINE
[b.] March 24, 1972, Mbaraga; [p.] Franklin and Ann Kabateraine; [ed.] Makerere High School, Makerere University; [memb.] Alive for Christ, Makerere Chris-

tian Union; [oth. writ.] Shattered Family (play), a number of poems and Ten Fun Days (unfinished novel); [pers.] My cardinal goal in life is to add an iota of happiness to the human race. [a.] Mbarara, Uganda.

EVANS, LaTOYA
[pen.] Toy; [b.] August 29, 1978, California; [p.] Debra Evans; [ed.] Junior in high school; [memb.] Church; [hon;] Grade school, English, Math; [oth. writ.] I like to write poems in my fun time; [pers.] I love not hate, I wish I was in authority to change the world around. [a.] Phoenix, AZ.

EVERETT, CLARITA, L.
[pen.] Clarita N. Lopez; [p.] Gregorio and Maria Lopez; [m.] Edward L. Everett Jr., August 5, 1967; [ch.] Lisa Marie L. Everett; [ed.] University of Santo Tomas, Manila; [occ.] Physician; [pers.] The poem submitted was based on the Haiku, the 17 syllable poem I wrote in Japanese, I am at Los Angeles City College. [a.] Los Angeles, CA.

EVERS, GENE
[pen.] Gene Alexander Evers; [b.] March 26, 1951, Manhattan; [p.] Lee Evers and Pauline Stein; [ed.] Pearl River High School, Stony Brook University; [occ.] Script writer; [hon.] Dean's List; [oth. writ.] Assorted other poems including "Cindy of Mountains" and screenplays, I also write poetic lines to be used for songs; [pers.] My poetic endeavor is to try to touch the sky of eternity, the mud of Mother Earth and to gaze into the eye of a mountain. I have been influenced by Plato and the romantic poets. [a.] Bethpage, NY.

EWEN, PETER RICHARD
[b.] Greymouth, New Zealand; [m.] Rosmary Ann, December 4, 1976; [ch.] John Richard, Natalie Ann, Adam James and Rebecca Rose; [ed.] St. Kevin's College; [occ.] Self-employed. [a.] Rapahoe, Westcoast, New Zealand.

EWIN, GORDON A.
[pen.] Gordon A. Ewin; [b.] November 13, 1933, Cranbrook, BC; [p.] John D. Ewin and Annie Eileen Gray; [m.] July 21, 1959; [ch.] Kim V.E. and Paul Kane Lindgreen; [ed.] B.A. and Electronic Engineering Technologist (Robotics); [occ.] Mining, exploration, arts; [hon.] Awards and scholarships, Banff School of Fine Arts, Notre Dame College, Nelson, BC.; [oth. writ.] Technical publications; [pers.] I am honored by this opportunity, thank you. [a.] Vancouver, BC.

FABIA, JOSE ADRIATICO
[pen.] Jofean; [b.] May 26, 1944, Manila, Philippines; [p.] Aniceto B. Fabia and Pascuacca A. Adriatico; [m.] Milagros L. Bagalso-Fabia, April 20, 1985; [ch.] Hoseph Anthony Jr. and Philip John II; [ed.] Elementary school and high school, San Sebastian College, Philippines, Bachelor of Arts, University of Santo Tomas, Bachelor of Laws, Manila, Philippines, Arellano University, Manila, Philippines; [occ.] Philippine lawyer and businessman; [memb.] Integrated Bar of The Philippines, Holy Name Society, Free and Accepted Masons Kasilawan Lodge No. 77, Philippine Jurisdiction; [hon.] College Scholar, College of Law; [oth. writ.] Legal writings adopted as laws, public rules and policies for the Philippine Bureau of Customs; [pers.] My personal life is greatly influenced by my belief in the divine providence and the thought that all men are created equal. [a.] Culver City, CA.

FADIPE, ANTHONY OLAITAN
[pen.] Tony El-Buraimoh; [b.] January 19, 1961, Lagos, Nigeria; [p.] Yewande Adeniyi-Jones (father deceased); [m.] Emma "Mom" Olu Bunmi Fadipe, March 8, 1985; [ch.] Emmanuella Modupe, Frances Damilola and Emmanuel Oladipo; [ed.] St. Patrick's College, Asaba, Delta State, Nigeria; [occ.] Freelance, commissioned writer; [memb.] Poetry Society of Great Britain (37437); [oth. writ.] Previously published poem in The National Library of Poetry's anthology On The Threshold of A Dream, "There He Laid Forever"; [pers.] I give great thanks to the silent one, who holds the fate of all things. I am thankful for everyday of loving and being loved. I appreciate life, both its good and bad. Dedicated to my family. [a.] London, England.

FAHLGREN, SYLVIA
[pen.] Sylvia Ashley; [b.] June 7, 1929, London, England; [p.] Margaret Madeleine and Arthur Adams; [m.] Robert Fahlgren, June 27, 1964; [ch.] Elaine Dee and Arthur Carl Fahlgren; [ed.] Usual grade school, then boarding school, then a trade school, level same as a college; [occ.] Retired housewife, self taught poet and writer; [memb.] MADD (Mother's Against Drunk Driver), Fraternal Order of Eagles, auxiliary member of International Lion's Club (husband is local president, not a member but take an active part in wildlife and environmental preservation); [hon.] At school was commended for grade A's in speech delivery and all English subjects, no awards yet by hoping; [oth. writ.] Compiled pre-school A,B.C's, collection of children's stories, a book of trivia, song writing, greeting cards, short stories, cook-book, poetry, free-hand artist and amateur photography; [pers.] I write for fun and self-expression, it comes easily and naturally to me, never have "writer's block". My first ambition is to instruct children in the right way to live in a fun way. [a.] Danville, IA.

FAIRCHILD, BARBARA S.
[pen.] Bobbi Fairchild; [b.] October 2, 1940, Clarksberg, WV; [p.] Virginia and Howard Warnick; [ch.] Daiiel Kenneth, Barbara Lynn, Virginia Jane and Robert Shawn Crytser; [ed.] DuBois High, DuBois, PA; [occ.] Retired widow; [oth. writ.] I write poems as they strike me and have many on hand, someday I would like to get them published; [pers.] I am the inventor of the "Fairchild Stepcane" thru American Inventors Corp., the Lord has given me a wonderful talent which I want to share with others. I thank Him everyday. [a.] Brockport, PA.

FALANGA, PATRICIA
[b.] July 22, 1941, Newcastle, Australia; [ed.] B.A., The University of Newcastle; [hon.] 1978 The Helmore prize (shared), 1979 the Gertrude Helmore prize, 1981 the Ernest Helmore prize (shared), 1983 the German Community prize (shared), all three Helmore prizes are in French; [oth. writ.] I write prolifically in several languages, but the work in this anthology is the first I have submitted for publication; [pers.] What I write is what I hope to direct, conversational, smart; inner rhymes arise unbidden, sweet confusions, carelessly hidden, reveal, inspite of me, the stops and starts of a still sentient heart. [a.] Newcastle, N.S.W. Australia.

FALIKS, INNA
[pen.] Inna Faliks; [b.] September 19, 1978, Odessa, Ukraine; [p.] Irene and Simon Faliks; [ed.] Sophomore in Niles North High School, Skokie, IL., studying music at the Music Center of the North Shore; [occ.] Entering many competitions, performing, working to be a concert pianist, National Baldwin MTNA competition, Fischoff

National Chamber Music competition, finalist in Tchaikonsky International competition for young musicians, Moscow 1992, etc.; [oth. writ.] Series of poems published in school newspapers, some prose, two one act plays; [pers.] My writing often reflects the music I play, I try to make my writing a part of what I express at the piano. [a.] Skokie, IL.

FALLMAN, JOSHUA
[pen.] Scott Fenton; [b.] September 3, 1978, Sacramento, CA; [p.] Maryanne Fallman and Don Jackson; [ed.] Del Norte and North Euguen High Schools; [occ.] Student; [memb.] National Forensics League; [oth. writ.] Currently writing "Into The Blackness" with co-author Amy Bardwell, "Into" is a collection of poems which are on the macabre, dark side and have the same tone as the submitted poem; [pers.] My writing is heavily influenced by all forms of art. In my writing, I search for meaning in life that others cannot find or see, and then I show that meaning to others. My own life is lived this way, in a roaming search. [a.] Eugene, OR.

FALLON, VICTORIA
[b.] September 9, 1979, Detroit, MI; [p.] Gregory and Kathleen Fallon; [ed.] Now in ninth grade at Newbury Park High School; [occ.] Student; [memb.] Newbury Park High School Speech team and Mock Trial team; [hon.] Principal's Honor Roll, Student Government Superstar, scholarship awards in English and Science at Sequoia Intermediate School 1993; [oth. writ.] "Who Are We" poem read at eighth grade graduation, June 1993; [pers.] I wrote "Who Am I" in May of 1993 while anticipating heart surgery in June. I strive to make the most of my life "living each day as if it were my last". This poem was inspired by my fear of my heart problem and the impending open heart surgery and is dedicated to Beau Dooley who cherishes life as much as I do and to Zachary Plaut who continues to assure me that there's always tomorrow. [a.] Newbury Park, CA.

FAREBROTHER, RIEMKJE JENSMA
[pen.] Rjemkje; [b.] April 16, 1917, Leeuwarden; [p.] Uilke Jensma and Ariet Valkema; [m.] Lt. Col. F.H. Farebrother (deceased), 1st marriage August 7, 1939; [ch.] Three daughters from this marriage, 2nd marriage October 9, 1966; [ed.] Kindergarten teacher, The Hague on Free Activity Methods and Montessori, Educational Seminar on Rudolf Steiner Ed. Dornach, translaters diploma; [occ.] Retired teacher; [memb.] Member of the Christian Community, founded by Rev. Rittelmeyer of the Anthroposohical Society; [oth. writ.] I have translated Rainer Maria Rilke's Dunino Elegies and some of his poems, and have a large collection of my own poetry, busy with my biography.

FARLEY, JUDITH
[b.] June 6, 1963, Kankakee, IL; [p.] Robert Farley Sr. and Jolene Barber; [ed.] Bradley-Bourbonnais High, Kankakee Community College; [occ.] Property Accounting, General Mills Restaurants, Inc.; [pers.] My writing resulted from a creative urge to express myself. May it reach out and touch others to help them express their feelings. [a.] Orlando, FL.

FARR, BARBARA
[b.] December 5, 1966, Utica, NY; [p.] Wayne and Betty Laribee; [m.] James A. Farr, October 11, 1986; [ch.] Thomas (identical twins) Marissa and Melissa Farr; [ed.] Holland Patent High School, Boces LPN Nursing program, Mohawk Valley Community College, RN Nursing program; [occ.] Mother and homemaker; [memb.]

Word Bible Fellowship, Non-denominational church, Barneveld, NY; [pers.] I desire that my writing would reflect the beauty of ordinary every day things. [a.] Barneveld, NY.

FARRAR, BERNADINE
[pen.] Bernadine McComb; [b.] December 1, 1947, Detroit, MI; [p.] William and Gladys Davis; [m.] Jerome Farrar, November 26, 1991; [ch.] Rodney Davis; [ed.] Highland Park Adult Day, Wayne Community Jordan College; [hon.] Silver Poet, 4 Golden Poets; [oth. writ.] Cassette, dedication to husband, interested in writing greeting card verses; [pers.] All gifts come directly from the Almighty-Eternal God, if talents, gifts are used wrongfully you can lose them, finally I like to write for the good of mankind. [a.] Detroit, MI.

FARRELL, VIC
[b.] September 6, 1967, Brisbane; [ed.] Uni-Dropout Griffith University Environmental Studies; [occ.] Education Officer, NSW National Parks and Wildlife Service; [oth. writ.] Album of songs entitled "Magic and Riley", Earthworks Education show, Lismore; [pers.] I enjoy communicating and working creatively with other people, especially on women's issues and the environment. I like writing letters. [a.] Australia, NSW.

FARROW, JUNE M.
[pen.] J. Maria; [b.] May 23, 1929, Amesbury, MA; [p.] William R. Farrow and Irene M. Graton; [m.] Divorced (I have dual citizenship(; [ch.] Baker, Lawrence Stephen, Alexander Charles, Dennis Mark and Bryan Michael; [ed.] Woburn MA. elementary and high school, Boston, MA., Stratford Finishing School, college and university training in California, teacher training, California, securities, life, health insurance training with Investors Diversified Services in Oregon; [occ.] Owner, manager, Professional Management Consulting; [memb.] Computer Software Instructors Associates, Communication Specialists Associate and Language Instructors Associates; [hon.] There have been some, but I have failed in the recording or remembering of them; [oth. writ.] Poems and philosophy, prose, have not attempted to publish. My first love of writing was set aside to deal with the necessities of life for myself and four sons. They are now men with families of their own. [a.] All men are feet of clay, there are no heroes among us, examine your love for God and neighbor therein lies the measure of character. [a.] Victoria, British Columbia, Canada.

FARWELL, RONALD G.
[pen.] Gilbert Fox; [b.] December 27,1935, St. Louis, MO; [p.] Ethel Fox and Olden Farwell; [m.] December 27, 1953; [ch.] Ronald Jr., Gary, Baron, Sharon, Gerald, Lisa and Garland; [ed.] '74 University Southern California, Bachelor in Public Administration, '78 Masters in Public Administration, California State University; [occ.] Owner, manager All City Management Services, Inc.; [memb.] (No prior literary connections) Life Time-NAACP, Guidance Church of Religious Science; [hon.] 1974 graduated most Outstanding Student from USC School of Public Administration; [pers.] I have been greatly influenced by classical love poems written by poets who reflect the poetry and drama of African Americans in early America.

FAZ, ERIKA NICHOLE
[b.] May 7, 1982, Weslaco, TX; [p.] Raul and Rosalinda Faz; [ed.] Attends 6th grade at Watkins Junior High, Houston, TX; [hon.] All A Honor Roll, Math tutor; [pers.] enjoys a good debate and reading. Aspires to

attending Harvard Law School, granddaughter of Carlos and Andrea Moreno, Paul Faz. [a.] Houston, TX.

FEENEY, CLIFFORD H.
[b.] November 25, 1929, Los Angeles, CA; [p.] Bernice Harnden; [m.] Monja Feeney, (departed) August 28, 1970; [ch.] Mark and Gail Feeney; [occ.] Retired Longshoreman; [pers.] Through my wife and (in good hands) gave me enthusiasm as well as my wonderful mother, both who loved the sample ways of life. As good music beloved poetry belongs on the same esteem, so my gratitude goes out to them both. [a.] South Bend, WA.

FEHR, ANNETTE
[b.] April 28, 1979, Surrey, BC; [p.] Ron and Lianne Fehr; [ed.] Mount Boucherie Secondary School; [occ.] Student, MBSS, Kelowna, BC; [memb.] Westbank Pony Club, Horse Society of British Columbia; [pers.] I try to show the diversity of life in my writings and how important it is to live for the day. Some of my writings are inspired by history. [a.] Kelowna, BC Canada.

FEITO, FRANCISCO E.
[pen.] Francisco E. Feito; [b.] April 6, 1931, Havana, Cuba; [p.] Francisco and Daisy; [m.] Gabriela, June 24, 1983; [ed.] Dr. of Law, University of Havana, Cuba, M.A. in Spanish, Rutgers University, NJ., Ph.D. in Latin American Literature, City University of New York, CUNY; [occ.] Associate Professor, Kean College of New Jersey, Union, NJ; [memb.] American Association of Teachers of Spanish and Portuguese, Institute International de Lit. Iberoamericana, Center for Inter-American Relations; [hon.] Associate Editor Discurso Literario, University of Oklahoma, Stillwater, Editor in Chief Slusa Press, Rutger University, Editorial Coordinator Senda Nveva de Ediciones, New Jersey; [oth. writ.] Una Paz Dificil, (book of poetry), twelve books of literary criticism, forty five published articles and book reviews. Twenty nine formal papers read in major conferences dealing with Spanish American Lit., my field of specialization is Paraguayan Literature, however, I have turned to poetry either in Spanish or English in search of myself. [a.] Elizabeth, NJ.

FERNANDEZ, MARY
[b.] March 21, 1937, Kansas City, KS; [p.] Catalina and Albert Fernandez; [ch.] Gilbert and Ray Anthony Fernandez; [ed.] GED-Licensed Practical Nurse; [occ.] L.P.N., Jackson Country Detention Center; [pers.] I was inspired by the poet Metcalf, whose poems appeared in the K.S. Star newspaper when I was a youth, also by the happiness and disappointments, which inspired me to express my innermost feeling hoping that others will know they are not alone in their feelings and thoughts. [a.] Kansas, KS.

FERREL, CARL G.
[b.] July 29, 1950, Iowa City, IA; [m.] Single; [ed.] Degree in Culinary Art, 1973, studied Real Estate, Economics, Business Law and Communications, 1981, Blackhawk College; [occ.] Chef, meat cutter, Business Consultant, President (record company) Restaurant Manager, Septic Surgeon, General Contractor; [memb.] Florida State Poets Association, Inc., National Federation of State Poetry Societies, Inc., National Arbor Day Foundation, Niabi Zoological Society, National Parks and Conservation Association, National and International Wildlife Federation, World Wildlife Fund, The National Audubon Society, Associate member of The American Museum of Natural History and the Smithsonian Associates, Associate member of the Illinois Sheriffs'

Association, and the Natural Conservancy; [hon.] Golden Poet 1990, 1991, Honorable Mentions (7), Distinguished Leadership 1991; [pers.] I write about a variety of subjects, love, friendship, family, nature, social issues, etc., I would like to see world peace and an end to world hunger, and the formation of an international coalition to protect and preserve the earth and its inhabitants and strive for an ecological balance between man and nature that will allow both to survive and prosper. I would also like to see a return to traditional family values. My advice, seek the truth in all things, be honest, fair and sincere. [a.] Moline, IL.

FERGUSON, LESTER J. "LES"
[pen.] Les Ferguson; [m.] Thelma Hollister, June 12, 1936; [ch.] Lester J. 2nd and Robert Raymond; [ed.] Spent 54 years designing and selling business forms for hand use or type and computer; [occ.] Retired; [memb.] Former President San Antonio Manufacturers Association; [oth. writ.] Memorabilia Of Les Ferguson; [pers.] Do everything you need to do today and that leaves more time for the things to do tomorrow.

FEVRI, JANET IRIS
[ed.] Bachelor of Arts (Comm) NSW Institute of Technology, Sydney, Australia; [occ.] Electric train driver for Cityrail of NSW; [oth. writ.] Mostly comedy and murder mysteries; [pers.] Poetry influenced by Tennyson and T.S. Eliot, comedy by Shakespeare and Oscar Wilde. [a.] Sydney, NSW Australia.

FEY, LISA ANNE
[pen.] Lisa Anne Marie; [p.] May 6, 1976, Ellsworth AFB, SD; [p.] Robert and Janice Fey, Sr.; [ed.] Currently taking classes for GED in Rapid City, SD; [occ.] Kay-Bee Toy Store in the Rushmore Mall; [oth.writ.] Thoughts, The Journey, Long Distance Thought, I have written more but none have been published; [pers.] I never believed I could do anything like this until now. Thanks to the National Library of Poetry, I now know I can go far in life. God bless.[a.] Rapid City, SD.

FEZATTE, LYNNE
[b.] November 12, 1974, Kamloops, BC; [ch.] Morgan Elizabeth Anne; [occ.] Part time student; [oth. writ.] I have written several poems and short stories, none of which have been exposed to the public. These include a few love poems and many that deal with social issues, racism, abuse, etc.; [pers.] Much of my poetry reflects upon and is dedicated to the abandoned, abused and forgotten children of the world. [a.] Surrey, BC.

FIELDS, DEBRA E.
[pen.] Elaine Fields; [b.] April 15, 1956, New York City; [p.] June and John Fields; [ed.] B.A. Psych-1978 Lehman, M.A. Communications-1981, Teachers College Columbia University, M.S. Reading CCNY 1994; [occ.] 2nd grade teacher P.S. 92, Manhattan; [hon.] Dean's List CCNY; [pers.] He that observeth the wind shall now sow and he that regardeth the clouds shall not reap. [a.] New York, NY.

FIELDS, QUINTIN NATALE
[pen.] Daddy Q; [b.] May 27, 1984, Stamford, CT; [p.] Laura and Joseph; [a.] Stamford, CT.

FINAMORE, SANDRO
[pen.] Sammy; [b.] July 12,1957, Rome, Italy; [ed.] Franklin D. Roosevelt High School, John Jay College of Criminal Justice-B.S. 1980; [occ.] NYC Police Department Pilot; [memb.] Variety Children's Charity, St.

Mary's Children's Hospital Volunteer, Cops for Christ-N.Y. Chapter; [hon.] Various Police and athletic awards; [pers.] I try to bring forth words of inspiration and encouragement. I have been greatly influenced by the bible and life's experience. [a.] Brooklyn, NY.

FINELLI, SHARON
[b.] February 20, 1963, Haleyville, AL; [p.] J.P. and Betty Haley; [m.] Henry Finelli, April 19, 1986; [ch.] Anthony Henry Finelli; [ed.] Haleyville High School; [occ.] Mid-South newspapers, mailroom manager; [hon.] The National Beta Club, selected Who's Who Among American High School Students 1979-1980, 1980-1981 edition; [pers.] My writings encourages myself and others to believe in themselves. [a.] Haleyville, AL.

FINFER, DAVID LAURENCE
[pen.] D. London; [b.] April 18, 1975, Philadelphia, PA; [p.] Edward and Janelle Finfer; [ed.] Northeast High School, Gratz College, I currently attend East Stroudsburg University; [occ.] Student and Hebrew and ethics, teach at Temple Israel Hebrew School, Stroudsburg, PA; [memb.] Unite Synagogue Youth, Human Relations; [hon.] 10th grade Rockpoint Creative Writing Award, Aleph Award; [oth. writ.] "Lost in Depression", published in a Burlington Vermont magazine; [pers.] Poetry comes from a person's heart, mind and soul. Using those three everything I write can be something beautiful and meaningful. [a.] Philadelphia, PA.

FINK, GLENDA
[b.] Long Island, NY; [ed.] SUNY College at Buffalo; [occ.] Mortgage Broker, Real Estate Investment; [hon.] Golden Poet Award and Silver Poet Award from World of Poetry; [oth. writ.] Many poems, short stories, essays on love and life; [pers.] For me writing is the completion of thoughts, emotions, ideas and philosophies. [a.] Roslyn Heights, NY.

FIRTH, DANIEL
[b.] June 26, 1957, Worcester, MA; [p.] Russell and Gloria Firth; [ch.] Dylan Bryn and Sean Daniel; [ed.] George Washington High School, Golden West College, Scripps Institute; [occ.] Sales manager, aircraft hardware company in Los Angeles; [oth. writ.] Hundreds and hundreds of pieces in backlog to someday be published in my own compilation; [pers.] I tend to write from an almost tactile viewpoint. At times it seems I can almost feel color, light, emotion. I try to translate these feelings into words and I think because of this, most readers comment on the imagery they perceive in my writing. [a.] Los Angeles, CA.

FISHER, BERTHA
[b.] February 7, 1917, Liverpool, England; [p.] Lily and David Kaufman; [m.] Mark Fisher (deceased 1970), October 23, 1958; [ed.] Commercial High School, Montreal, Canada, Outremont Business College, Montreal, Canada (Quebec Province); [occ.] Retired stenographer, senior citizen now, but feel young; [memb.] Opera Guild, Montreal, Canada (soprano), Music Appreciation Groups, Gilbert and Sullivan Shows, strictly amateur but enjoyable, memberships therein, sang in chorus, of Opera, etc.; [hon.] As stated age 15 years won $5 for article "Beating the Depression", otherwise no payment, local Montreal paper, wrote as amateur "Margaret Currie's Mail", articles to the Montreal Star, teenager then, Silver Poet Award, Golden Poet Award, certificates of merit, Milton Berle Honored; [oth. writ.] "Human Rights", "The Spirit of Life", "An Enlightenment", "Bouquets to Teachers", "The Longevity Goal",

"Pot Power" of many, hobby only, not published ever, in Montreal local paper appeared at age 14 years "The Kindered Spirits", not paid; [pers.] My belief is to bring out the best in others, I'm a lifetime "Optimist" also enjoy classical music and believe Shakespeare and the Bible are still "Best Writings". My husband was a musician on "S.S. Sylvania". Sense of Humor most important also. [a.] Miami Beach, FL.

FISHER, HELEN AGNES WATKINS
[b.] January 17, 1938, Salem, NJ; [p.] Earl and Alice Berry; [m.] Lewis Fisher; [ch.] William Berry, Keith and Micheal Watkins, Faye Taylor; [ed.] Salem High School, GED in 1968, Glassboro State College, 1975-1981, received BA Cumm Liberal Arts degree; [occ.] Senior Center trainee; [memb.] AARP; [oth. writ.] Several poems and a few songs, not published; [pers.] I believe the contest was a way to open the door to give God praise through poetry, and to God be the glory for the things He has done. [a.] Palmdale, CA.

FISHER, JEAN
[b.] March 10, 1943, Eau Claire, WI; [p.] Charles and Marcella Fisher; [ch.] 2; [ed.] 12; [occ.] Homemaker; [oth. writ.] Numerous poems. [a.] Duluth, MN.

FISHLIN, GRACE S.
[b.] May 30, 1915, Washington, DC; [p.] Dr. J.L. and Esther Kuhn; [m.] Herman (deceased), November 7, 1937; [ch.] Barbara Dee Wolk (Chief Nurse of emergency, Columbia Presbyt. Hospital of NY) and Lewis H. Fishlin (Lawyer); [ed.] High school and finishing school; [occ.] Recently retired Executive Legal Secretary, Deloit Touche (then Touche Ross); [memb.] B'nai B'rith Women, President AMC Research Center, Editor of both of their magazines; [hon.] Too many to list, in February 1994 I will be Woman of the Year of BBW; [oth. writ.] Several poems and music presented on radio, a letter to Ladies Home Journal said by them to be one of the finest received; [pers.] I try to write with a cheerful attitude... not the somber, depressing note so common to poets. [a.] Lauderhill, FL.

FITZPATRICK, RICHARD TEFFT
[pen.] Wessub Anon; [b.] March 17, 1925, Seattle, WA; [p.] Nora (Goodrich) and Charles Fitzpatrick; [m.] Olga V. (Smyrnoff) Fitzpatrick, May 12, 1951; [ch.] Denise (Dee Dee), Bryan, Charles and Richard T. Jr; [ed.] J.W. Sexton High School, 2 years college (no degree); [occ.] Retired Automotive Buyer; [memb.] B.p.O.E. # 1945; [hon.] Honorable Discharge U.S. Navy 1942-45, poem published (Kicsit) in Dance On The Horizon; [oth. writ.] Personal notes, letters and poems (none published); [pers.] I hold family, God and country with the same esteem. My creed I sometimes don't question, "Never hurt a friend even in jest", Lansing State Journal (1946). [a.] Canton, MI.

FJORDHOLM, MARIE NICOLE
[b.] October 13, 1983, Miami, FL; [p.] Jann and Jarle Fjordholm; [ed.] Galatas Elementary, presently homeschooling (4th grade); [occ.] Student and gymnastic; [memb.] U.S.G.F. (United States Gymnastic Federation), church choir; [hon.] Competitive gymnastic-level 9, Honor Roll, Outstanding Student, grade 3 at Galatas; [pers.] I don't think we should be taking our planet for granted. If you really thing about all the things God has given us, why can't we give Him something back, like protecting the earth. [a.] The Woodlands, TX.

FLAHERTY, MIKE
[b.] October 24, 1976, Duluth, MN; [ed.] Denfield High School, Morgan Park U.H., TEC Middle School; [memb.] Morgan Park, Good Fellowship Community Club; [oth. writ.] History of Morgan Park, a former company town for the United States Steel Corp.; [pers.] I have done many things in my 17 years, including being in the movie "Iron Will" to operating a streetcar. Beware-history is indeed doomed to repeat itself. [a.] Morgan Park, MN.

FLANAGAN, BURNARDINE;
[pers.] I, Burnardine Flanagan, was born in Key West, FL. My parents migrated to New London when I was four years old. I was the first Afro-American to volunteer for the Army from New London. We were Co. 6888 the first Afro American unit to serve overseas; I was the first Afro American to graduate with an Associate Degree from New London Junior College now Mitchell College. I graduated from William Backus Hospital in 1963 as an L.P.N., I worked at the Sub-Base Medical Center and retired in 1982. I'm a member of the American Legion and help out in the community whenever possible.

FLEMING, BILL
[b.] February 16, 1952, Pigeon, MI; [p.] James and Mildred Fleming; [ed.] Graduate Lakers High School, 3 semesters study Northern Michigan University; [occ.] Disabled; [hon.] Ex Army Sgt., Special Achievement award from Air Force, Honorable Discharge; [oth. writ.] Poems published by the National Library of Poetry; [pers.] If people could see as far ahead as we can behind, we would all be alright. [a.] Bad Axe, MI.

FLORATOU-PAIDOUSSI, ELENI
[pers.] Elin Floratou-Paidoussi was born in Washington, DC. Her family moved to Greece during the depression and returned to the United States after World War II in 1946. Eleni is a social activist, teacher, poet and a prolific writer who writes in Greek and English with equal ease and eloquence. She attended Hunter College and Queens College where she earned a B.A. degree in Sociology, Cum Laude. Eleni continued her graduate study at St. John's University and received a M.S. degree in Education. Working full time as a fourth grade school teacher, a job she enjoys, Ms. Paidoussi manages to devote a great of her boundless energy and talent to her writing and community activities. She co-founded the Greek Cultural Center in Queens and The Greek Writers Guild in America. She also served as president in these organizations. The Queens Borough President, Ms. Claire Shulman presented Eleni with the "Citation of Honor" award for her "outstanding contribution and celebration of Greek Culture and Heritage in Queens". For many years. Many of her poems, articles and lectures have been published in various anthologies, literary journals and magazines in the United States, Greece, Africa, Germany, Canada and Mexico. Ms. Paidoussi has written numerous books in Greek and English that have been published in Greece, France and America. They include The Last Swallow, Selections, Nights in Two Hemispheres, The Children of Kronus, First Person Singular, We, 20 Strophes and Other Poems, Silence of Cycles and Screams, Elegies, A Generation of No Escape, novel following 2 young Greek-American children through World War and German occupation dangers through semi-starvation and bombs.

FLORES, BOBBIE
[pen.] Debbie; [b.] August 19, 1975, Munster, IN; [p.] Beverly and Pedro Flores; [ed.] Highland High School to Michigan CI= Elston High to Calumet High School

then, now attending Portage Adult, goal wanting to become an artist and to publish a book; [hon.] In piano, organ and artistic drawings; [pers.] In writing this poem I was inspired by thoughts and dreams, and artists and poets, and still striving to be the best I can be. [a.] Portage, IN.

FLOWERS, ARNETTE M.
[pen.] Arnette M. Flowers; [b.] January 15, 1958, Beaumont, TX; [p.] Robert and Mary Hamilton, Jr.; [m.] Divorced, February 14, 1981; [ch.] Elijah, Jeremiah, Isaac, Crystal and Matthew Flowers; [ed.] Crenshaw High, Los Angeles City College; [occ.] Records Technician, U.S. Department of Justice, Los Angeles, CA; [memb.] St. Matthew Baptist Church; [hon.] Physical Fitness Award, nomination for Employee of the Month during January 1993; [oth. writ.] A completed poetry book unpublished called Poetry Unlimited, in its final reproduction stage. Also working on a second book called A Heart of Gold both consisting of poems in variety relating to my past life's experiences and the everyday changes; [pers.] Never go through life too serious to the point where you miss out on the little things we tend to take for granted like having just plain fun, and always keep your dreams alive. Take one day at a time and make sure you have peace and joy. [a.] Los Angeles, CA.

FOLEY, SANDRA ANN
[b.] August 6, 1962, Stratford; [p.] Vincent and Helen Kay; [m.] Brian Foley, March 16, 1985; [ch.] Brandon Anthony Foley; [ed.] Nursing, RN AD; [occ.] Registered Nurse; [memb.] Dalmatian Club, American Lung Association, American Heart Association; [pers.] Notice the world around you! It offers creative minds a new experience each and every day. [a.] Southbay, CT.

FOLSE, MELISSA K.
[pen.] Melissa Michael, Kate Folse; [b.] April 16, 1968, Royal Oak, MI; [p.] Dennis and Dorothy Michael; [m.] Melvin P. Folse Jr., July 10, 1992; [ch.] Cody Lee and Mackensey Nicole; [ed.] Fort Payne High; [occ.] Lyric and poetry writer, housewife; [hon.] Who's Who in American High School Students; [oth. writ.] Several poems and song lyrics -unpublished; [pers.] My writings have been influenced by personal experience and dedicated to my husband, who has always loved, supported and believed in me. [a.] Fort Knox, KY.

FORD, M. MICKEY
[b.] Ottawa, Canada; [ch.] Three daughters and six grandchildren; [ed.] St. Clair Community College, Michigan, credits at University of Western Ontario and York University; [occ.] Business Management and Real Estate, retired after automobile accident, I now volunteer as a Group Leader for other chronically injured people as part of my ongoing recovery; [memb.] National Honors Society, Phi Theta Kappa, St. James Cathedral Welcoming Committee, Variety Club, Scarborough Support Services, North American Chronic Pain Association of Canada; [hon.] Dean's List, Magna Cum Laude graduate, three drama scholarships, Certificates of Honor from The Ontario Ministry of Citizenship and Culture and Scarborough Support Services for the Elder, Honors Certificates from the Ministry for community service work; [oth. writ.] Publications in Patterns, Pegasus, National Poetry Press, Foreign Service Newspaper Reporter, Public Relations writing for a multi-lingual, intergenerational Pen Pal Program in the community; [pers.] A severe automobile accident forced me to restructure my life and I began work in the chronic pain field in order

to help others as I struggled with my own recovery. I have much admiration for personal bravery and the challenges which we overcome through our faith and tenacity. Hope and respect for one another brings enrichment and quality to our lives. [a.] Scarborough, Ontario Canada.

FORD, RUTH R.
[pen.] Ruth R. Ford; [b.] February 13, 1926, Battrum, Sask Canada; [p.] William C. and Phenie Smith; [m.] Wallace C. Ford, July 31, 1950; [ch.] Ted (Theodore), Janice, (twins) Larry and Laurel, Dale, David, Maureen, Evelyn, Mick (Michael) and Doug; [ed.] Grades one through twelve and Normal Schooling at Moose Jaw (Sask) Normal School; [occ.] Homemaker; [memb.] Hazel Bluff United Church of Canada, Alberta Lung Association, Big Brothers and Sisters, University Hospitals Foundation in Alberta; [oth. writ.] Many poems, several published in local papers, several published in my book Roots and Wings and a few published through submission to other contests, some articles published in local newspapers; [pers.] My writings reflect my love of nature and simple things, a positive attitude, my belief in the goodness of most people and celebrates beauty in all of the above and my love of God. [a.] Westlock, Alberta, Canada.

FOSTER, BERNICE
[pen.] Bernice Foster; [b.] July 9, 1917, North Liberty, IA; [p.] Deceased; [m.] Deceased, June 18, 1972; [ch.] Sandra and Craig Bailey, my pride and joy; [ed.] Completed 3 years in Liberal Arts at the University of Iowa, Iowa City; [occ.] Retired from Fresno County (California) as Legal steno; [memb.] New Hope Community Church, Clovis, Clovis Senior Center, I've conducted gospel sing-a-longs Friday A.M. for months before the Senior Center hog meals came in, folks hum along even if they've forgotten the words; [hon.] Selected Fresno County's Secretary of the Year in 1965, selected as Graduate Assistant in Dale Carnegie course in 1970; [oth. writ.] I have written poems all of my life and still do... the entire poem coming to me about 3 a.m. and I quickly put it down in shorthand, waiting until morning, it's gone; [pers.] I often sent get well cards, Christmas cards, friendship cards in poetry. Even my 8 year old granddaughter has taken up this hobby a thrill to friends, relatives and me.

FOUNTAIN, CLARENCE (CLARE) EDWARD
[pen.] (Clare) Fountain; [b.] June 11, 1928, Midland Ontario, Canada; [p.] Arthur and Bertha May Fountain; [m.] Helena Ferdinada Fountain, December 24, 1973; [ch.] 4 plus 4 step-children; [ed.] To grade 10 plus electric appliance course, real estate course, quality control corrugated boxes; [occ.] Professional Real Estate Salesperson; [memb.] Islington Evangel Center in Rexdale, Ontario, Canada, involved in some community projects, areas of politics, but no actual membership per say; [hon.] Some awards for community services but a number of them for real estate salesmanship; [oth. writ.] Other than a number of letters to local newspapers I have basically written poems about certain paintings, alcohol abuse, real life happenings, family, christian, past experiences, nature, plus a variety of songs needing music for them; [pers.] I have sung Country Western for many years, I have written much about my childhood. I play guitar but not professionally. Writing became my personal ambition as a sailor on the great lakes in the 1940's until the present day. [a.] Etobicoke, Ontario, Canada.

FOX, RHIANNON CATHERINE RUTH
[b.] April 24, 1967, Nantwich, Cheshire; [p.] Frederick

and Irene Fox; [ch.] Isabelle Ruth Fox; [ed.] Brereton Hall Girls School, Sandbach, Cheshire, Brine Lees County High, Nantwich, Cheshire; [occ.] Student at Dandbank College, Crewe, Cheshire, England (Psychology and Welfare studies); [memb.] Student member, "Institute of Welfare Officers"; [hon.] No educational as yet, but I gained the Queen's Guide Award of the Girl Guide Association; [oth. writ.] A poem entitled "My Future Children" to be published November, December 1993 in an anthology published by Heritage Press, England; [pers.] I write what I feel and try to touch subjects that many of us feel afraid to discuss. I gain inspiration from looking into my own feelings and beliefs and of those close to me. [a.] Crewe, England.

FRANCIS, EVERDENE JOY
[pen.] Denise; [b.] April 28, 1972, Jamaica; [p.] (Guardian) The late Mrs. Beryl Robinson; [ch.] Terell, Christopher, Lee and Chivon, Altheia, Beryl McRae; [ed.] I completed kindergarten to grade 8 at Point Hill All Age School in Jamaica, then attended Kipling C.I. in Toronto, Canada; [occ.] Student and sole support mother; [oth. writ.] I basically write poems when I'm a state of depression or when something of some significance has taken place in my life, I usually keep a diary also; [pers.] I treat people the way I'd like to be treated. My favorite saying is "You reap what you sow", my grandmother Beryl Robinson is my sense of inspiration. This poem was dedicated to her, she passed away in November 1989. My poem is for my grandma who shaped me into the person I am today, she raised me from when I was 7 months until I was fourteen years old, She was born on November 25, 1911.

FRANCIS, JENNIFER RENEE
[b.] December 10, 1982, Canton, OH; [p.] Mark and Teresa Francis; [ed.] Louisville Public School in Louisville, OH; [occ.] Student; [hon.] Honor and merit roll in school system; [pers.] Mother Nature inspired me in my first poem writing. I am waiting for greater opportunities with Mother Nature for more poems to come from my heart. [a.] Louisville, OH.

FRANSEN-OIZ, AMAIA
[pen.] Amaia Frandsen; [b.] September 19, 1978, Reno, NV; [p.] Christy Frandsen-Oiz; [ed.] In high school; [occ.] Student; [hon.] Campfire, piano, Religious Recognition; [oth.writ.] Poem published in The Coming of Dawn; [pers.] I think it is important to succeed and make the best of life. [a.] Sisters, OR.

FRANKLIN, JANICE M.
[b.] September 4, 1964, Houston, TX; [p.] Janie Franklin and Hope Aubrey Jr.; [ed.] G.E.D.; [occ.] Health Care Assistant; [memb.] Garden of Gethsemane Baptist Church; [oth. writ.] Several but has not submitted them to anyone else; [pers.] I love to write poetry, I have been writing every since age 12. Michael Jackson really inspired me a whole lot, I feel poetry captivates your mind so I just sat and write. [a.] Houston, TX.

FRANKLIN, JESSICA NICOLE
[pen.] Nicky; [b.] April 5, 1977, Good Sam, Phoenix, AZ; [p.] Patricia Tringali (deceased); [ed.] K-8, Ironwood High School 9-11; [memb.] Cross Country member of Ironwood, track member of Ironwood, Deca member; [hon.] Varsity letterman for three years, scholar athlete; [pers.] There is a beginning and an end, in the middle is living. [a.] Glendale, AZ.

FRAZIER, BRAD
[b.] May 6, 1960, Anchorage, AK; [p.] Prentiss A. and Mary Frazier; [ch.] Jeremy Frazier; [ed.] High school diploma (Douglas Byrd High School); [oth. writ.] Short stories (Science Fiction); [pers.] A spiral-cord quadriplegic as a result of an auto accident in 1982, I fill many empty hours writing short Science Fiction stories and poems; [a.] Fayetteville, NC.

FRAZIER, GARY
[b.] January 20, 1961, Atlanta, GA; [p.] Lamar Frazier and Sherri Prestwood; [m.] Helen, December 16, 1988; [ed.] Associate in Theology degree, diploma in Funeral Directing/Embalming; [occ.] Office worker, Wassau Insurance Companies; [hon.] Literary Essay contest winner, Clarkston High School, 1979; [pers.] I am deaf, having 120 decibel los in both ears, since I was 10 years old. I am presently studying with the Long Ridge Writer's Group. [a.] Dallas, TX.

FREDERICK, JOANNA
[b.] July 14, 1933, Decatur, IL; [p.] Marjorie Mason and Joseph DeBorse; [m.] Barry Rex Frederick, June 19, 1954; [ch.] Grace Ellen and Hope Elizabeth; [ed.] Hamilton High, Los Angeles City College, National University; [occ.] Housewife, volunteer work; [oth. writ.] Journal and short stories, unpublished, other Haiku; [pers.] I write to understand who I am. [a.] Los Angeles, CA.

FREDERICK, MICK
[b.] July 15, 1974, Gloversville, NY; [p.] Michael and Kacey Frederick; [ed.] Working on an associates degree in Psychology at FMCC, will eventually get a doctorate in Psychiatry; [occ.] House painter, student; [pers.] I have no set form of prose, but artistically it's surreal. [a.] Gloversville, NY.

FREED, ANA M.
[b.] November 22, 1967, Brockton, MA; [p.] Marie and Carlos Fonseca; [m.] Joseph E. Freed, March 27, 1993; [ed.] Cherry Hill High School, East Rutgers University, Douglas College B.A., North Eastern University M.S. in Counseling Psychology; [occ.] Crisis Therapist, Screening Crisis Intervention Program; [pers.] Life, with all its joys and sorrows, has always been the greatest teacher and a tremendous inspiration for my writings. [a.] Medford, NJ.

FREEMAN, BRADLEY R.
[pen.] B. Richard Freeman; [b.] October 25, 1967, March AFB; [m.] Crissa Lianne Freeman, June 27, 1992; [ch.] Candra Jordan Freeman; [ed.] Rim of the World High, Big Bend Community College, University of Maryland (Europe), Military; [occ.] Retail Management, Thrifty's Corporation; [memb.] The Boy of Christ; [hon.] Extensive Military; [oth. writ.] Honorable Mention for poem with Iliad Press, Coastal Sunrise, currently writing a novel (The Future Now); [pers.] God is my inspiration and Jesus of Nazareth is my "Hero", Pour Toujours! [a.] Bakersfield, CA.

FREEMAN, SHAWN
[pen.] King Solomone; [b.] November 22, 1972, Detroit; [p.] Parmlee Freeman; [ed.] Kettering High School, University of Detroit Mercy; [occ.] Full time student; [memb.] PSI Sigma Omegas, Tag Team Players, Black Student Alliance, Vibes Session, Kettering Writing Club; [hon.] Dean's List, Who's Who Among American High School Students 90, 91, Vica Club, Art Club Writing Fair Student 90, 91, 92, Creative Mind Association; [oth. writ.]

Write music, comic books, songs, novels, movies, etc.; [pers.] Look beyond the stars for ability lies in heaven cause when you look in heaven you will find your place among the stars. [a.] Detroit, MI.

FREENY, AKILAH RENAC
[pen.] "Lila"; [b.] January 22, 1979, Detroit, MI; [p.] James and LaVerne Graves Freeny; [sib.] Shajuana Leane' Freeny, 12 years old, 7th grade, Birney Middle School; [ed.] Southfield Lathrup High School, Birney Middle School; [occ.] Student, 9th grader at Southfield Lathrup High School; [hon.] My awards are, Academic Excellence in English, Physical Education, Computer Graphics, Exploring French and Word Processing also an Outstanding Effort Award in Health; [oth. writ.] I've written four other poems expressing God's love and goodness, which are yet to be published; [pers.] I try to reflect God's love by allowing my light to shine, through the writing of my poems. [a.] Southfield, MI.

FRENCH, ANDREW H.
[b.] March 18,1969, Woburn, MA; [p.] George H. and Mary Joan French; [ed.] Emerson College, Woburn High School; [pers.] Wolves have become a controversial symbol of our disappearing wilderness. This poem was written in response to "Wolf Control" programs in Alaska, but it reflects widespread attitudes. I hope it inspires people to learn more about this beautiful animal before it is gone. [a.] Woburn, MA.

FRENCH, MICHAEL DAVID
[b.] April 27, 1972, Long Island, NY; [ed.] Independence High School, Fresno State University; [occ.] Full-time student, drum instructor; [memb.] Santa Clara Vanguard Alumni, Blue Devils Alumni, Blue Devils Hall of Fame; [hon.] Most Valuable Performer, Blue Devils 1993; [pers.] Jennifer Elizabeth French, it is you for whom I wrote this, for only through my love for you does my true being shine. [a.] Fresno, CA.

FRIEDLANDER, ANGELA LOPORCHIO
[pen.] Kyoiku; [b.] Year of the Dog, Long Island; [p.] Leonard V. Loporchio and Margaret Lamphere; [m.] July 4, 1984; [ed.] B.F.A., the Cooper Union School of Art, Queens College M.S. program current study- Linguistics; [occ.] Elementary school educator; [memb.] Soka Gakkai International Culture Department, Educators Division and Arts Division (Rapporteur for N.G.O.U.N.), Fourth World Movement volunteer, Educator for Children of Extreme Poverty; [hon.] Both graduate and undergraduate studies were awarded scholarships based on academic grades and work record; [oth. writ.] This poem represents my first published piece of writing; [pers.] I am an Advocate for Humanistic Education for children. Bodhisahva and Altruist, I devote much of my free time to cultural and art activities dedicated to the cause of World Wide realization of PEACE. I enlighten people to the law of cause and effect in order to remove human suffering and lead people to achieving happiness. [a.] New York, NY.

FRIEDMAN, ABE
[pen.] Abe Hersh; [b.] May 12, 1957, Brooklyn, NY; [ed.] Yeshiva and religious Jewish education; [occ.] Real Estate Tycoon; [memb.] National Rifle Association, Kosho Kavate Dojo, Brooklyn Landlords Association, Jewish Chinese National Coalition; [hon.] Publishers committee of the moral majority 1984; [oth. writ.] Published book Secrets of Success In Attracting the Opposite sex, also coming up, The Ruthless Landlord, No Money No Honey, a golddiggers guide to success;

[pers.] I try to bring a smile to the world with a message that touches the inner soul of every human being. A message that radiates loud and clear. It's great to be alive. [a.] Brooklyn, NY.

FRIEDMAN, ESTELLE GRACE
[b.] May 19, 1919, New York City; [p.] Harry and Clara Lieberman; [m.] Dr. Henry F. Friedman, June 30, 1951; [ch.] Kenneth Lester, Gary Richard and Stanley Bruce; [ed.] Thomas Jefferson High School, Brooklyn, NY., Brooklyn College, B.A., Teacher's College, Columbia University, M.A.; [occ.] Retired teacher of English, Brooklyn and Queens High schools; [memb.] Alumni Associations, The American, and The Untied Federation of Teachers, The American Association of Retired Persons, The Humane Society of The United States, The New Hyde Park Jewish Center and various health organizations and animals shelters; [hon.] High school Latin Medal, Certificate of Appreciation of my oral taped history of the Lower East Side, for The Lower East Side Tenement Museum; [oth. writ.] Several other unpublished poems, a half finished book describing my experiences with homeless cats; [pers.] I have a strong compassion for the victims of injustice and abuse, be they human or animal. [a.] Hicksville, NY.

FRIESEN, MARLO
[pen.] Ygor Marlinski; [b.] November 3, 1979, Altona, MB; [p.] Wilbert and Sharon Friesen; [ed.] Grade 9, W.C. Miller Collegiate; [occ.] Student; [oth. writ.] None published. [a.] Altona, MB Canada.

FRIGARD, ELIZABETH
[pen.] Beth Frigard; [b.] May 26, 1948, Elmira, NY; [p.] Sybil and Carl Edson; [m.] Wayne Frigard, March 6, 1971; [ch.] Aaron, Samuel and Nathan; [ed.] Elmira Free Academy '66, Russell Sage College '70; [occ.] Homemaker for the elderly, substitute teacher Helliston Public School; [memb.] First Congregational Church, Deacon, NAIC Investment Club, church choir; [hon.] Friends of The Library, Holliston Poetry contest-adult winner; [oth. with.] Poems published in local newspaper and church publications; [pers.] People see life more clearly through pictures drawn with words. Through my poems I strive to create those pictures. [a.] Holliston, MA.

FRITZ, LUCY
[b.] December 6, 1957, Salt Lake City, UT; [p.] William L. and Geraldine M. Fritz; [ed.] Judge Memorial High School, Western Mt. College; [occ.] Student, writer and novice potter; [memb.] IGNU, Western MT. College Poetry Club; [hon.] Chance Scholarship, IRB grant; [oth. writ.] Several poems and expansive journals; [pers.] This is my frist published piece, I am working on my Bachelor of Liberal studies degree, this poem is the beginning of my poetic voice development. [a.] Dillon, MT.

FRITZ, MARIA CHRISTINE
[b.] November 24, 1967, Atkinson, NE; [p.] Joseph and Loreen Fritz; [ed.] O'Neill High School, Kearney State College; [occ.] Department Head of Herberger's Department Store in Kearney, NE.; [memb.] Elementary Education Majors Club at K.S.C., Big Friends program at Neman Center Kearney, NE., Rose Board Herberger's Department Store; [oth. writ.] Several poems, one of which is published in a book called All My Tomorrows, two children's stories one of which I fully illustrated and are in the works for possible publication; [pers.] Why only go through the motions when you have the potential

to "LIVE" every moment? As a whole we take far too many things for granted, not realizing what we had until we no longer have it. Life is short start today! [a.] O'Neill, NE.

FRY, WAYNE D.
[b.] April 12, 1942, Saint John, NB Canada; [p.] Cliff and Grace Fry; [sib.] Barbara; [occ.] Security Officer, Harbour Station, Saint John N.B.; [hon.] Golden Poet Award 1988, Silver Poet Award 1990 from World of Poetry, Sacramento, CA.; [oth. writ.] Book, Limericks, by Wayne D. Fry, Saint John N.B., volume one 1986, two dozen or more poems published in local newspapers and Toronto, Ontario, poem, "Kelly Ann" published in the book Raphaelite Summer of 1971; [pers.] Poetry to me is a breath of fresh air, a beautiful gift from God. [a.] Saint John N.B., Canada.

FUCALORO, PAUL
[pen.] Paul Bruno; [b.] December 28,1946, New York City; [p.] Thomas and Josephine Fucaloro; [m.] Melody Harris-Fucaloro; [ch.] Farrah and Erik; [ed.] BBA and MBA from CCNY-Baruch, MA from LIU; [occ.] Professor-LIU and Staff Developer, New York City Public Schools; [memb.] Editor -in-Chief of college literary magazine; [hon.] Awarded Assistantship from CCNY-Baruch, awarded Silver Poets Award; [oth. writ.] "Acting the Part", "Think of Mother", "To A Laborer Dying Young"; [pers.] I have been influenced by romantic poets. I am considered the Quintessential Renaissance Man. [a.] Woodmere, NY.

FULLER, BEVERLY M.
[pen.] Beverly M. Fuller; [b.] October 11, 1946, Augusta, GA; [p.] Thomas and Doris McKinney; [m.] Harry L. Fuller III, May 26, 1984; [ch.] Kimberly DeVore, Natalie Johnson and Ashley Smith; [ed.] Waynesboro High School, Waynesboro, GA. (attended Georgia Southern College, Statesboro, GA.); [occ.] Former banker; [pers.] Writing poetry allows me to express my feelings based on past experiences, a great release.

FULMINO, NICOLE
[b.] June 11, 1982, New Jersey; [p.] Maria and Joseph Fulmino; [ed.] Hillsboro Middle School, (junior high); [occ.] Babysitting; [memb.] Columbia House, Neighborhood Newspapers (Editor and Chief); [hon.] Trophy for piano, poem published in paper; [oth. writ.] For fun, for school, anything I love to write poems and stories, some published in newspaper; [pers.] I wrote this poem to express my feelings about my mom, she is a wonderful person and I think the whole world should know it. I'm influenced by her, she always tells me I can do it. In my spare time I write poems and stories and read books especially romance novels.

GABRIEL-HARRIS, FRANCES
[pen.] Frances Allison; [b.] July 26, 1932, Troutman, NC; [p.] Louis and Mattie Allison; [m.] Lester Harris Jr., September 10, 1993; [ch.] Michael and Kathy Gabriel; [ed.] Unity High, Bennett College; [occ.] Retired Postal Manager, U.S. Postal Service, Cleveland, OH.; [memb.] ETA Phi Beta Sorority, First Missionary Baptist Church Usherboard, American Bridge Association, International Training in Communication (ITC) Great Lakes Region; [hon.] Kappa Phi Organization; [oth. writ.] Several articles written for public speaking; [pers.] I desire to inspire and awaken the dept of my feelings for love, nature and God. [a.] Cleveland Heights, OH.

GAFFNEY, MARGARET
[b.] August 20, 1921, Detroit; [p.] Joseph and Loretta; [occ.] Retired.

GAGLIARDI, TINA
[b.] December 27, 1979, Oshawa Ontario, Canada; [p.] Sharon McMahon and Joe Gagliardi; [ed.] O'Neill Collegiate -grade 9 high school (current); [occ.] Student; [pers.] Everyone is looking for the greatest high, that may be life, that may be death but until you are willing to experience them both, you'll have neither. [a.] Oshawa Ontario, Canada.

GAGNIERE, LOUIS F.
[b.] June 19, 1918, Lowell, MA; [ed.] 2 years, Miami University, Coral Gables, FL., languages, interpreted for US Navy in French, Spanish, Chinese, Japanese and Maori; [occ.] Artist, western art; [hon.] Best of Show and numerous 1st place and others; [oth. writ.]"Introduction to Single Sideband", "Day Sailing to La Paz', in Sea magazine, 1967, several published poems. [a.] Corpus Christi, TX.

GAINEY, KAREN AMANDA
[pen.] Carri Sommers; [b.] June 22, 1969, Gloucester; [p.] Anthony Gainey and Margaret Vallender; [ed.] Rednock Comprehensive; [occ.] Art and Literature student; [oth. writ.] Short stories, songs and lyrical poems over the past two years but have not yet been published; [pers.] I gain great enjoyment out of writing and find it to be a good therapy. [a.] Gloucester,UK.

GALIGA, MELISSA MARIE
[pen.] Jasmine Hopkins; [b.] February 9, 1978; [p.] Roxanne and Nicholas Galiga; [ed.] Foreman High; [oth. writ.] Poems which have not been published; [pers.] Time can heal the pain but will not stop the gain.[a.] Chicago, IL.

GALINDO JR., RICHARD (RICKEY)
[pen.] R. G. Rickey; [b.] December 28, 1967, Del Rio, TX; [p.] Richard and Martha Galindo; [m.] Not married, girlfriend, Rosie Greco; [ed.] Attended Angelo State University for 2 1/2 years, Texas A.& M. University for 1 1/2 years, Southwest Texas Junior College for 1 year; [occ.] Graphics Designer; [hon.] University Interscholastic League Literary Awards in high school and music awards, Academic Achievements in college and football; [oth.writ.] "Porcelain Man", "A Mythical Race" and "A Promise" (all still in the writing process); [pers.] " Hold dear a dream, for in it lies the breath". My breath being my inspiration, my girlfriend Rosie Greco. [a.] Del Rio, TX.

GALLAGHER, DIANE
[b.] August 31, 1965, Scranton, PA; [m.] George Gallagher, May 18, 1990; [occ.] Financial Examiner, Prudential Defined Contribution Services; [hon.] Editor's Choice Award, National Library of Poetry; [oth. writ.] "While You're Not Here", published in the Coming of Dawn by the National Library of Poetry. [a.] Scranton, PA.

GALLAGHER, JOSEPH T.
[b.] March 26, 1957, Newark, NJ; [p.] Frank and Grage Gallagher; [ed.] High school, St. Louis, Hom. Hi.; [oth. writ.] Personal poems written for expressing my heart by pen; [pers.] My poems express the inner man's search for peace of mind through the heart, felt cry to my Lord and Saviour Jesus Christ. [a.] Tulsa, OK.

GALLAHAN, EYDI
[b.] July 2, 1948, Clarksville, TN; [m.] Henry M. Gallahan, August 3, 1990; [ch.] Erica, Edward, Echelle and Roger Rookstool; [occ.] Director of Marketing with Distribution Concepts, Entrepreneur, full time wife and mother; [memb.] International Woman's Writing Guild, American Red Cross, International Society of Poets, ADA member; [hon.] Editor's Choice Award from National Library of Poetry, Special Breed of Woman Award from 5th Special Forces, guest appearance on several television stations and several newspaper articles, book signing at Bookland Bookstore, recognition from Parchment Press, The Stockroom; [oth. writ.] It's Just Me, Erica, poetry book published in 1992, several poems published in local newspapers, also publication in A Break In The Clouds and Whispers In The Wind; [pers.] There is an emptiness that I was challenged to fulfill, poetry is the medicine I choose to fulfill it with. [a.] Oaks Grove, KY.

GALLEY, WARREN
[b.] February 2, 1946, Slough, UK; [p.] John Victor and Joyce Galley; [m.] Iris Galley, March 16, 1968; [ch.] Andrea Jean, Corby and Lee; [occ.] Ex. Bus Driver now invalid; [oth. writ.] Had a few poems published in small U.K. Anthologies and one magazine; [pers.] I like to write emotional rhyming verse using simple everyday language that can be understood by everyone no matter what their social status. [a.] Clovelly, North Devon, England.

GALLO, MICHAEL
[pen.] Rose One; [b.] December 30, 1965, Italy; [p.] Giovanni and Italina Gallo; [ed.] Passaic Valley High School, Seton Hall University; [occ.] Store Detective (Sterns); [memb.] Anthropology Club; [hon.] 8 years Varsity Wrestling, 4 years Captain, 4 years football; [pers.] I write to capture the power of the heart, I write to live, to escape and to love. Open your heart and your poem shall come. [a.] Wayne, NJ.

GALUSHA, CHARLOTTE M.
[b.] September 28, 1922, Bennington, UT; [p.] Horace and Lola Galusha; [ed.] High school, UVM; [occ.] Retired; [hon.] First submission; [oth. writ.] "Woodland Walk", "Courage", "Winter Winds", "Rain", "Beauty of a Blizzard"; [pers.] I have always loved nature being born in the country and realizing this as a gift of God's creation for inspiration, peace, joy, courage reflected into all of life. [a.] Shaftsbury, VT.

GARCIA, CECILIA BARRERA
[b.] January 22, 1980, Modesto, CA; [p.] Tony Garcia and Esther Barrera; [ed.] Fairview Elementary School and Hanshaw Middle School; [occ.] Babysitting for my Aunt Raquel and my mother; [memb.] Brownie Girl Scouts; [hon.] Honor Roll and Renaissance; [pers.] I try to let out my feelings and thoughts through my poetry. [a.] Modesto, CA.

GARCIA, FELIX
[pen.] Felix Amando Garcia; [b.] July 10, 1931, Newton, IA; [m.] Patricia Garcia; [ch.] Rita, Jennifer and Robert Garcia; [ed.] Newton High; [occ.] Retired; [oth. writ.] Several poems published in high school poetry contest, 1st and 2nd prize, Newton, IA; [pers.] I love the beauty of people, animals and nature around us, like artists, poets paint a picture of the soul and hearts to others.[a.] Des Moines, IA.

GARCIA, LYN R.
[pen.] Lyn Garrison Garcia; [b.] February 27, 1958, Washington, DC; [p.] John R. and Patricia F. Garrison; [m.] Carlos A. Garcia, March 22, 1980 (separated); [ch.] Danny (12), Derek (11), Dure (7) and Carlyn (5); [ed.] George C. Marshall High School; [occ.] Homemaker; [oth. writ.] Unpublished poems and children's books; [pers.] I'd like to dedicate this, my first published work to my son Dure, who passed away April 29, 1993. I love you, mommy. [a.] Dale City, VA.

GARDNER, ANITA MAXINE
[pen.] Nita; [b.] October 30, 1951, Springfield, OH; [p.] Mr. and Mrs. Richard Scott; [m.] Joseph Gardner, July 3, 1970; [ch.[Amica Chatawn Gardner; [ed.] Graduate of Springfield South High School; [occ.] Unemployed due to company being sold; [memb.] Member of Jerusalem Second Baptist Church; [hon.] High school diploma, certificate of participation in membership classes of Jerusalem Second Baptist Church; [oth. writ.] I've written many other poems for my church and for close friends; [pers.] My poem writing is a gift from God, without Him my talent would not be possible. [a.] Urbana, OH.

GARNES, MICHAEL P.
[pen.] Michael P. Garnes; [b.] June 27, 1955, Detroit; [p.] Bennie C. and Eleanor Garnes; [ed.] Bachelor of Music Degree (composition), Mary Grove College, Detroit, MI., graduation date 7/94, graduate of College for Recording Arts, San Francisco, CA; [occ.] Student; [memb.] President of United Brotherhood of Mary Grove, also founder, member, Rosedale Park Civic Association and Park Players (actor's guild), Church of Today (member); [oth. writ.] "Poems From Within" (a collection of poetry), War of The Gods (a book of Christianity); [pers.] Mankind must begin to mature, we must realize that we are spirit beings, children of God. There is no difference, except that of awareness. We are at war with our flesh, from which all our foolishness stems, we may achieve whatever we will, lets achieve peace. [a.] Detroit, MI.

GARREN, PATRICIA
[b.] November 24, 1955, Canton, OH; [p.] Bernard and Mary Brown; [m.] Carl Garren, August 18, 1979; [ch.] Amy Lynn and Craig Douglas Garren; [ed.] Canton South High School; [occ.] Dietary Services, Massillon Community Hospital, Massillon, OH; [pers.] A heart's deepest secrets can sometimes be a blessing to ones self and to others, thus I share my soul. [a.] Navarre, OH.

GARRETT, CLIFF
[pen.] Fox Garrett; [b.] September 11, 1923, Pendleton, OR; [p.] Katie Garrett; [m.] Lois J. Ross, July 11, 1950; [ch.] Dennis and Kathy; [ed.] North Idaho J.C., Spokane College, Eastern Wash, Oregon State, Corvallis; [occ.] Retired; [hon.] College degree in Education; [oth. writ.] Songs, 100 are in copyright now; [pers.] I'm a believer in Clinton, a liberal and active Democrat, love music, 2 songs are in Nashville now. [a.] Spokane, WA.

GARRITY, PATRICIA YODER
[pen.] Patti Garrity; [b.] October 8, 1933, Oakland, CA; [p.] Kaethe and Adon Allen Yoder; [m.] Stephen H. Garrity, 1957; [ch.] Lisa, Michael, Dana and Sean; [ed.] Boulder Colorado High School '51, Ottawa University, Kansas '55; [occ.] Creator of Holiday Plum Puddings sold Nationwide, owner of the business, my father was well-known Editor, publisher, author, poet and business-

man in Richmond, VA. and Mt. Morris, IL. in early 1900's; [hon.] Columns, mentions or articles written about me and my business (Patti's Plum Puddings) in books, magazines, newspapers (Food Find, Gourmet Magazine, Los Angeles Times, etc.); [oth. writ.] Dozens of letters to the Editors, printed in Los Angeles Times, Life Magazine, local publications; [pers.] God has blessed me with many talents, writing, cooking, friendship, encouragement, enthusiasm, all used to in turn bless others. [a.] Manhattan Beach, CA.

GARVIN, ERIKA DALE
[pen.] Riki Garvin; [b.] February 1, 1974, California; [p.] Roger and Priscilla Houts Garvin; [ed.] Brea-Olinda High School, currently attending Whittier College; [occ.] Psychology student, mathematics tutor; [memb.] Psi Chi, Hispanic Students Association; [hon.] Psi Chi, National's Dean's List, finalist in Disneyland Creativity Challenge Language Arts Division, National Council of Teachers of English Award in writing; [oth. writ.] Several poems published in high school yearbook, high school newspaper, college literary magazine. [a.] Whittier, CA.

GASPAR, LEILANI G.
[b.] March 26, 1979, Honolulu, HI; [p.] Sulficio and Milagros Gaspar; [ed.] Nanaikapono Elementary and Nanakuli High and Intermediate School (freshman, 9th grade); [memb.] Ike Loa Kulana Club; [hon.] Nanaikapono School Writing Fair 1st place, State of Hawaii Department of Education, The Leeward Art Exhibit, Leeward Hawaiian Leadership opportunity, Leeward District Praise D.O.E., merit of certificate Most Artistic, Principals' List grades 7 and 8. [a.] Waianae, HI.

GATES, DIANE K.
[pen.] Diane Kay; [b.] June 9, 1954, Inglewood, CA; [p.] Douglas and Anne Smith; [m.] Robert D. Gates, May 12, 1979; [ch.] Sarah, Christopher and Kathryn; [ed.] High school, thru 12th grade, some college; [occ.] Homemaker, mom; [oth.writ.] Poetry for myself in journal for close friends, family; [pers.] Music, old rhymes, there's poetry all around us, written or not. A day in our life, poetry is everywhere. [a.] Grass Valley, CA.

GAUSE, TIMOTHY KEITH
[b.] April 29, 1963, Carlsbad, NM; [p.] Joel Gause and Crystal Moran; [ed.] Senior at University of Nevada, Las Vegas, majoring in Animal Biology, graduate of Carlsbad Senior High in Carlsbad, New Mexico; [occ.] University Las Vegas, NV. Chemistry Lab Technician and seasonal Park Ranger at Spring Mountain Ranch State Park, Las Vegas, NV.; [oth.writ.] 4 short stories in a college anthology called The 20 Minute Migraine and one long poem in an employee newsletter; [pers.] Poetry opens a doorway to the mind when the mouth is otherwise shut. [a.] Las Vegas, NV.

GAYDEN, GREGORY
[pen.] Gee; [b.] November 30, 1960, Chicago; [p.] Mose and Helen Gayden; [ed.] Wells High School, Olive Harvey Junior College; [occ.] Mail Clerk for Banca di Roma Bank; [memb.] Providence Baptist Church; [pers.] There are a lot of people struggling with problems, I hope they come to realize that Christ is the only answer.

GAZDEWICH, PAMELA JUNE
[pen.] Pam Gazdewich; [b.] June 6, 1953, Kamsack, SK; [p.] Mike and Teena Hrooshkin; [m.] Brent Gazdewich; [ch.] Tricia Nicole, Kyra Janine and Brandi Rae; [ed.]

Veregin Public School, Kamsack Collegiate Institute, University of Saskatchewan, Saskatoon, SK; [occ.] Teacher, free-lance artist; [pers.] Nature's gifts, my home and the people I share my life with are reflected in my writing. [a.] Norquay Sask, Canada.

GAZZOLA, ELIA EDVIGE
[b.] June 15, 1967, Toronto; [p.] Lino Gazzola and Ida Spagnolo; [ed.] Primary Education in Canada, high school education in Italy; [occ.] Translator/interpreter, English-German Teacher; [oth. writ.] My dream is to publish my novels, I have already written several; [pers.] I like coming home from work, washing up and going racing in the streets. [a.] Riese Pio, Treviso, Italy.

GEARHART, BRENDA LEE
[b.] August 14, 1962, Lansing, MI; [p.] Richard and Sally Barber; [m.] Robert Scott Gearhart, February 14, 1989; [ch.] Rick Paul, Elizabeth Jane and Christina Frances. [a.] Lansing, MI.

GEBHART, LILY
[pen.] Lily Vallerey; [b.] December 19, 1943, Dayton, OH; [p.] Jerry and Mary Gebhart; [m.] Unmarried but in love; [ch.] Derrick Ray Hardman; [ed.] Graduation from San Dieguito High School, Encinitas, CA., Ben Shaw Modeling School, Houston, TX, still attending school of life everywhere; [occ.] PBX/Communications Team Leader, Mercy Med Center Mt. Shasta, CA.; [memb.] International Society for a complete earth, Jefferson Public Radio Listeners' Guild; [oth. writ.] From Seed To Shining Seed, novel, work in progress, Answer Without a Question, collection of quotations, work in progress, unpublished collection of poetry and songs; [pers.] I believe that each of us, through our personal means of creativity can become unified in raising the vibratory level of our planet and through the love that we are, can move on to finer work. Mount Shasta, CA.

GECK, ANNA E. STANGO
[pen.] Anna E. Sr; [b.] March 15, 1922, Cleveland, OH; [p.] Hildegarde Fessler Stango and Emilio Stango (deceased); [m.] Joseph C. Geck, July 26, 1941; [ch.] 3, approx. 12 university degrees between them, U of D, Marygrove, Stanford and U of M; [ed.] I have a high school education from Eastern High, Detroit, MI., torn down now; [occ.] Housewife; [memb.] A few minor organizations during school years and adult years, in sports, spelling, youth groups, etc.; [hon.] None, just had the honor of being born around the fine arts; [oth. writ.] Just Gingles and Cheers while in high school, and once wrote a poem for Anne Campbell of Detroit papers, no record of any; [pers.] I have a hope, love for the fine arts and would really be happier it there was equal time for them such as there is for crime, violence, sports, etc.; [a.] Detroit, MI.

GENTRY, REGINALD L.
[pen.] Reggie G; [b.] December 14, 1962, Gibson County, TN; [p.] Mr. and Mrs. Joe U. Gentry Sr.; [ed.] Middle Tennessee State University, Murfreesboro, TN; [occ.] Sales Associate, Wal-Mart Stores Inc., Huntingdon, TN; [memb.] NAACP, National Association for The Advancement of Colored People, New Reedy Creek Missionary Baptist Church, Minister of Music; [hon.] Merit award, World of Poetry (1991) Golden Poet Award, World of Poetry (1990); [oth. writ.] True Sensation-World of Poetry (1991); [pers.] "God is the supreme being of all time", "faith accomplishes much". [a.] Huntingdon, TN.

GEORGE, IRENE

[pen.] Reene George; [pers.] Four loves have I, love of God, family, all people, music and a life long infatuation with the English language. I am a widow, born in Youngstown, Ohio on July 6, an attack of amnesia prevents me from remembering the year. For a time I lived in the East, which might account for the 'different' way I talk. I am of Romanian ancestry, and I speak this beautiful Romance language. My father spoke six languages, and my lovely mother had an operatic singing voice. My three sisters and I tried to harmonize, but neither Beverly Sills nor the Supremes had cause for worry. I am a high school graduate, have had eighteen years of evening college, journalism, public speaking, creative writing, English and other subjects. As a hobby I employ the medium of watercolor to paint seascapes and landscapes. I studied art at the Canton, Ohio Institute of Art. I am an insatiable reader (I read the dictionary). I was employed by Nationwide Insurance Company, having a tenure of 25 years, I recently retired as church secretary. I was married to Raymond, who became deceased in 1987, I have one married daughter, son-in-law and 2 brilliant grandchildren. I hold memberships in Toastmasters, International American Society for Quality Control, National Authors Registry and Atascocita, Texas United Methodist Church. I enjoy writing essays, short stories and especially poetry. My publications include, "I Am The Sea", Toastmasters 1980, "Angel With Wings", Toastmasters, "Mountains of Life", World of Poetry 1989, "A String of Pearls", World of Poetry 1990, "But The Greatest of These is Love", Poetic Voices of America, Fall 1990, Sparrowgrass Poetry Forum. I've received the following awards, Golden Poet Award-1989-90-91, Who's Who in Poetry-1990, World of Poetry, I carry a press card from the Christian Writers Guild, Hume, California. When I was widowed in 1987, in Ohio, my life changed drastically. I reach up to God for my ideas, my philosophy of life and the world.

GEORGE, SHIRLEY RICHARDSON

[b.] July 14, 1931, Manchester; [p.] Paulina and John Copp; [m.] Edwin George, November 31, 1973; [ed.] Levenshulme High School, Colne Grammar School, Lancashire; [occ.] Retired Parks Administrator; [hon.] First prize winner in Conway (North Wales) Poetry Festival-July 1993, nominated one of North Wales "Women of the Year"-November 1993, led successful campaign against "dumping" on shoreline footpath at Llanddulas (July 1991-November 1993); [oth. writ.] Several poems broadcast by B.B.C. Radio Merseyside; [pers.] Poetry is simply my greatest joy whose pleasure increases with age.[a.] Colwyn Bay, North Wales, United Kingdom.

GERCONE, JOE

[b.] July 11, 1969, Joliet, IL; [p.] Benjamin and Susan Gercone; [ed.] Diploma from Joliet West High School, graduated from Cave Technical School in Lockport in HVAC-R; [occ.] Supervisor at Jet Age Containers; [pers.] Someday I hope to improve or get some more background in writing short stories and actually getting them published also. I have always enjoyed poetry the most cause it really relaxes me as I write. [a.] Joliet, IL.

GEROCHI, ARLENE JOAN

[pen.] Arlene Joan; [b.] July 30, 1968, Philippines; [p.] Renier P. and Frances D. Gerochi; [sib.] Jun-Jun and Jay; [ed.] University of St. La Salle, Bacolod City, Philippines; [occ.] Registered Nurse, Rio Grande Regional Hospital, McAllen, TX; [oth. writ.] Several poems, unpublished; [pers.] I thank the Lord for the gift

of love, and to Gideon V. Svede, I love you for loving me the way you do. [a.] McAllen, TX.

GERYCH, ANTHONY

[pen.] Tony, T-Bone; [b.] September 14, 1972, Bath, NY; [p.] Romona Miller and Andrew Dries; [ed.] Rush-Henrietta Senior High School, Hochstein School of Music; [occ.] Writer for Written Love; [oth. writ.] Poems and songs for Written Love; [pers.] I would like to dedicate "Ancient Ruins" to Brenda Lee Crowe. [a.] Bath, NY.

GHIRAGOSSIAN, ALICIA

[pen.] Alicia Ghiragossian; [b.] July 13, 1936, Argentina; [p.] Jorge Ghiragossian and Knarig Yazmalvian; [m.] 1971 divorced in 1991; [ch.] Cara Jennifer; [ed.] Graduated in 1962 as a Juris Doctor, from the National University of Buenos Aires, Argentina; [occ.] Writer; [memb.] Life time Honorary President of the "Berian-American Writers of U.S.A.", honorary member of the "Modern Poetry Center", L.A., Toastmaster International; [hon.] Only poet alive whose work has been illustrated by the legendary Pablo Picasso, Bronze Bust exhibited at the National Museum of Writers in Yerevan, Armenia; [oth. writ.] Author of 20 books of poems, only poet in history that writes in Spanish, Armenian and English; [pers.] I believe that love is the genius of existence, and its opposite is death and destruction. I dream to see justice done to the Armeninan people. [a.] Glendale, CA.

GHRIST, ROBERT

[b.] December 13, 1941, Hocomo, MO; [p.] Velvie Grist; m.] Robin, June 29, 1963; [ch.] Angela; [ed.] High school; [occ.] Machine operator, Exide Corp; [memb.] YMCA; [oth. writ.] I have other poems mostly about my life growing up in abuse; [pers.] About 10 years ago I became involved with the shelter for battered women and children. Through the years while working with our clients, these thoughts from the past started coming out. It seems to help me cope with them if I write about them. [a.] Burlington, IA.

GIANTVALLEY, SCOTT ARTHUR

[b.] June 25, 1949, San Diego, CA; [p.] Bob and Meredith Giantvalley; [ed.] Point Loma High, Occidental College, BA (English Lit.) 1970, California State University, Northridge, MA. 1975, University of Southern California, Ph.D.-English Lit. 1979; [occ.] Deceased after teaching English in Los Angeles area colleges. Most recent being California State University-Dominguez Hills while expecting tenure, Scott also played as a party pianist, served as managing Editor of Humanities in Society, published by University of Southern California, Center for Humanities; [memb.] Whitman-Brooks Institute, Harvey Milk Lesbian and Gay Democratic Club, National Opera Association, MacGill's Literary Annual, Contributing Reviewer Group; [hon.] The Queen Who Didn't Care, a play selected for production in "The Old Globe One Act Play Tournament" in San Diego; [oth. writ.] Bianca and Her Volkswagen in "The Poets' Workshop" in The Writer 1975, Walt Whitman, 1838-1939, a reference guide 1981, Edward Albee, a reference guide 1987, "Love Song" Poetry of Our Times 1973, "How We Kept Thanksgiving at Old Town", Ideas October 1981, "A New Bel Canto Opera", the Opera Journal Vol IX No 4, 1976, "The Use of Rhyme to Achieve Comedy in the Musical Comedy Lyric", the Comic Spirit 1983, "L.A./A.M.", Mrnya Winter 1988; [pers.] Life after Aids, a one man theatrical piece on video tape expresses Scott's

positive outlook, prior to his death. [a.] San Diego, CA.

GIBSON, DANTE DEVON

[b.] June 14, 1971, San Pedro, CA; [p.] Albert and Clara Gibson Jr.; [m.] Single; [ed.] California State University, Dominguez Hills, BS Chemistry 1994, Pharmacy Student; [occ.] Landscape Maintenance; [memb.] American Chemical Society, CSUDH Science Society, Tabernacle of Faith Baptist Church; [hon.] Principals Honor Roll, Millikan High School 1988, 1989, Dean's List CSUDH; [oth. writ.] Other poems and essays; [pers.] My purpose is to create works that allow the reader to come into touch not with my thoughts, but with his own soul. [a.] Carson, CA.

GIBSON, JOSEPHINE

[b.] March 28, 1932, Chester, WV; [p.] Okey and Elsie Sayre; [m.] George Gibson, July 18, 1953; [ch.] Diane Haines; [ed.] Chester High School; [occ.] Retired; [memb.] Nazarene Church; [oth. writ.] Several religious not published; [pers.] I want to make my community a better place, because I passed by this way. [a.] Chester, WV.

GIDDENS, MARK

[b.] September 21, 1973, Redondo Beach, CA; [p.] Ralph and Mary Giddens; [ed.] Sophomore at Mount San Jacinto Junior College, Mira Costa High School, Manhattan Beach, CA; [occ.] Full time student; [hon.] Dean's List at Mount San Jacinto J.C.; [oth. writ.] Many songs in the folk tradition. [a.] Murrieta, CA.

GIDDENS, MARY RUTH

[b.] March 18, 1935, Pueblo, CO; [p.] Josephine and Bob Elliott; [m.] Ralph Giddens, September 2, 1972; [ch.] Mark and Jon Giddens, Steve and David Hunt and Debbie Crawford; [ed.] High school, East High, Denver Colorado; [occ.] Homemaker and Minister of the Gospel; [oth. writ.] Many poems and songs; [pers.] All my poems and songs are spiritual because my life is centered around Jesus Christ. He is my Saviour and I consider all my poems and songs a gift from God for me to encourage others. [a.] Murrietta, CA.

GIDWANI, KRISHNA C.

[b.] August 28, 1976, Bremerton, WA; [p.] Chaturbhuj and Bulbul Gidwani; [ed.] Wuerzburg American High School, Massachusetts Institute of Technology; [occ.] Student; [memb.] Mensa, The United Nations Association of the United States of America, Society of American Military Engineers, The National PTSA; [hon.] Recognized by the American Chemical Society and by the Chairman of the U.S. National Chemistry Olympiad for Outstanding Achievement in Chemistry, awarded the Bausch and Lomb Science Award in recognition of Outstanding Academic Achievement and superior intellectual promise in the field of science, biography published in Who's Who Among American High School Students, College Board's AP Scholar Award, National Merit finalist, United States Senate Youth Program; [oth.writ.] Several poems published in various literary anthologies; [pers.] Truth will triumph. [a.] APO, AE.

GILBERT, MARJORIE

[b.] December 29, 1900, Buchanan, MI; [p.] Miles E. and Annie Treat Sparks; [m.] Deceased; [ch.] Bil Gilbert and Sue Hubbell; [oth. writ.] Newspaper columbus; [pers.] This poem was written when and because I was serving in the Peace Corps in India. [a.] Fairfield, PA.

GILBERT, WILLAM W.
[pen.] Treblig, W.W.; [b.] September 9, 1949, Darlington Co. SC; [p.] William and Lizzie K. Gilbert Davis; [m.] Widower; [ch.] Yvonne (adopted); [ed.] High school in Richmond, VA., attended college in Albuquerque, NM; [occ.] Writer; [oth. writ.] Novels, completed but yet to be published, "When Monkeys Cry" and "Prairie Fire"; [pers.] I wrote these novels and poem to help overcome (the PTSD) suffered during the time I spent in Viet Nam. [a.] McBee, SC.

GILCHRIST, DENISA Y.
[b.] March 1, 1964, Washington, DC; [p.] Vernard H. (deceased) and Doris E. Turner; [m.] Weldon E. Gilchrist, June 7, 1986; [ed.] Eastern High, University of the District of Columbia, Towson State University, University of Maryland-College Park; [occ.] Accounting Specialist; [memb.] Praise Team, Mass Choir, Deacon Board, Jericho Baptist Church, Washington, CD.; [hon.] 1993 North American Open Poetry contest semi-finalist, National Library of Poetry; [oth. writ.] Several unpublished poems; [pers.] My goal is that God may get the glory out of my life as I continue being a servant for the Lord Jesus Christ, allowing the Holy Spirit to guide my footsteps. [a.] Landover, MD.

GILLESPIE, WILLAIM P.
[pen.] William P. Gillespie; [b.] October 29, 1918, Helena, GA; [p.] Napoleon H. and May Bell Coleman Gillespie; [ed.] Furlow Grammar School, Americus, GA., Americus Georgia High School, Biarritz Americana University, Biarritz, France (Fine Arts), Pasadena Playhouse, Pasadena, CA.; [occ.] Retired, but paint in watercolor and also paint porcelain dolls; [oth. writ.] Several poems published in local newspapers; [pers.] All my writings were influenced by Poe and with the hope of a better world, here and in the hereafter. My thanks to Professor Charles Hale for his encouragement. [a.] Greenville, SC.

GILMORE, FLORENCE WHERRY
[pen.] ebony Black; [b.] July 2, Shelby County; [p.] Mr. and Mrs. Andrew Wherry Jr.; [m.] Rickey DeWade Gilmore, November 11; [ch.] Alecia, Crystin and Alex Gilmore; [ed.] University of Tennessee, Knoxville; [occ.] Teacher of Deaf and Hearing Impaired Students, Tipton County School System, Covington, TN; [memb.] Prayer House of Deliverance Church; [oth. writ.] None published manuscripts, Proud Parents, Andrew and Ruby Wherry of Drummonds, TN; [pers.] "Foundations" are necessary for standing tall and believing in self. Foundations that were built hundreds of years before... are what we are all standing on now! [a.] Atoka, TN.

GING, KIM LOUISE
[b.] May 21, 1970, Ireland; [p.] Olive McComas and Ken ging; [ed.] Glengara Park School, Dublin Trinity College, University of Dublin; [occ.] Physiotherapist; [pers.] I would like to dedicate my first published poem to Matthew Hickmott, for all his encouragement, support and love;

GIOSIA, TERRI
[b.] March 6, 1963, Montreal, Canada; [p.] Pietro and Marion Giosia; [m.] Robert Caverzain (I am a widow); [occ.] Writer, makeup artist, Entrepreneur; [pers.] Dedication, to Robert, who inspires me, give me my ambition and gave me love for so long...

GIRTZ, JEREMY
[pen.] J.T. Girtz; [b.] November 18, 1962, Little Falls,

MN; [p.] Leonard and Kathy Girtz; [m.] (fiance') Teresa Wolff, August 25, 1994; [memb.] St. Johns Catholic Church; [pers.] Sobriety is serenity. [a.] Mankato, MN.

GIVENS, IJAAZ
[b.] 1948, New York City; [p.] Edna Morgan; [m.] Divorced; [ch.] Layea, Latif, Jaliyl and Aloha; [ed.] Midwood High School, UBI Medical Trade School, NYC Medical and Dental and Brooklyn Training Center; [occ.] HIV/AIDS Health Educator/vista volunteer; [memb.] Accorn, North Shore Animal League; [hon.] Certificate of award, Adult Service, Mother's Helping Mothers, certificate of achievement Nutrition Program, certificate of achievement, critical thinking; [oth. writ.] Many, but unknown and unpublished; [pers.] I am wary of the harden hearts of the people and I am hoping to renew the love lost by the message I send. My inspiration comes from the "Most High". [a.] Brooklyn, NY.

GLASER, CELESTE J.
[b.] August 6, 1974, Temple, TX; [p.] Stanley J. and LaVelle Glaser; [ed.] Buckholts High School, Texas A & M University, Temple Junior College; [occ.] Student, Temple Junior College, Temple, TX; [memb.] Hope Lutheran ELCA Women, College Republicans; [hon.] Dean's Honor List, The National Dean's List, VFW Voice of Democracy State Competitor '92, Who's Who Among American High School Students 1988-1992, Miss Texas Universal Teen Top 10 merit finalist, Service and Achievement Award '92; [oth. writ.] Texas Sesquicentennial Essay '86, "I'm Proud of Texas Because" published in county newspapers, broadcast script "Meeting America's Challenge" '92; [pers.] This is my very first attempt at writing poetry. I have been reared with the philosophy that the sky is the limit if one will only do their very best in all endeavors. [a.] Buckholts, TX.

GLASSMAN, SANDRA
[pen.] "Melodee"; [b.] August 27, 1940, Brooklyn, NY; [p.] Joseph and Rae Gruber; [m.] Stewart Glassman, December 27, 1958; [ch.] Lee David and Marrah Ellen; [ed.] Samuel J. Tilden High School, June 1958; [occ.] Music teacher; [memb.] Music Teacher National Association, National Guild of Piano Teachers Division of American College of Musicians, Art of Living Center member, Hempstead, NY; [hon.] Award pins from South Nassau Community Hospital for many years of volunteer service, certificate from Hofstra University Department of Music for completion of the art of piano teaching course, June 1989, poem about The Holocaust is published, this poem is in The Holocaust Library in Washington, DC.; [oth. writ.] Composed 25 songs, one classical composition for author Jacqueline Wolf Novel "Take Care of Josette", this music is at The Holocaust Museum and Library at Washington, DC. along with poem about The Holocaust, also wrote 150 poems and 4 children stories; [pers.] Even though I'm over 50, life for me right now is so nifty, I look forward in every way to the sunrise of each new day along with each days dawning I continue my poetry to create for now I know it's never to late. [a.] Oceanside, NY.

GLOMB, PENNY WEEKS
[pen.] Penny Weeks; [b.] September 9,1937, Erie, PA; [p.] Marjorie Donovan Weeks; [m.] Divorced; [ch.] Chris Fabre and Kevin Gregory; [ed.] St. Agnes Academy, Houston, TX., University of St. Thomas, Houston, TX; [occ.] Clerical; [memb.] Keep Your Day Job Poets Society; [hon.] Juried Poet, Houston Poetry Fest 1991, Houston, Texas sponsored by SLAC/NEA; [oth. writ.] Houston Poetry Fest Anthology 1991 "Thu Le"; [pers.]

Poetry does not have to be obscure. Poetry is freedom. (Rilke, Angelou, Carver, O'Hara).

GLOVER, CINDY LEE
[pen.] Tamara Woodrow Wilson; [b.] April 16, 1959, Canada; [p.] Tom and Joy Sorrell; [m.] Divorced, November 25, 1979; [ch.] Gerry Jr. and Taunya Lee; [ed.] Working towards a B.A. in Psychology in Behavior With Children; [occ.] University student; [memb.] Vice President for "Ladies Maple City Optimist, Chatham Kent Big Sister's Organization"; [hon.] Excellent award for writings skills; [oth. writ.] Several poems, illustrations and story books sent for publication in Canada and U.S.A.; [pers.] As I take that first step into a man's world I leave behind my indentation of footsteps for my children to follow, but not to cast the first stone, only to make a dent into society. [a.] Chatham, Ontario Canada.

GOEHRING, (MRS. RUFUS C.) MARY
[b.] Senior citizen, Millerstown, PA; [p.] Grover and Lillain Stroup; [m.] Dr. Rufus C. Goehring (deceased), February 15, 1943; occ.] Homemaker, hospital and senior citizen volunteer.

GOETZINGER, DONALD C.
[pen.] Donald C. Goetzinger; [b.] December 25, 1926, Detroit, MI; [p.] Albert and Lydia Goetzinger; [m.] Carmen Marie LeBeau (Goetzinger), June 15, 1950; [ch.] Karly Ann, Dennis Charles, Allan Michael and Donna Marie; [ed.] Graduate of South Eastern High; [occ.] Retired from U. S. Postal Service; [memb.] Citizen of the Planet Earth; [oth. writ.] Two books of poems unpublished, some good, some trite, some personal... all mine; [pers.] "Nothing is as profound as the natural order of being, we should show more compassion to that which surrounds us... for we are but one of the species that inhabit this orb.. [a.] Roseville, MI.

GOLDBERG, LORI A.
[b.] June 27, 1970, Booton, NJ; [p.] Eddie Goldberg and Nancy Loeser; [ed.] Riverview High; [occ.] Partner in Business; [oth. writ.] Many others, locale newspaper in Sarasota, FL., and Phoenix, AZ; [pers.] One should always express feelings in a windful way so we can all share them. [a.] Sarasota, FL.

GOLDENBERG, BONNIE
[b.] June 4, 1977, Plainview, NY; [p.] Edwards and Janet Goldenberg; [occ.] Student at Plainview Old Bethpage John F. Kennedy High School; [pers.] I am in the beginning stages of exploring my poetic capabilities. This is my first time being published and I am ecstatic about this opportunity. In my writing, I concentrate mostly on the problems in the world both politically and environmentally. I hope to someday make a difference. [a.] Plainview, NY.

GOLDSMITH II, GEORGE C. (BUDDY)
[pen.] Me; [b.] August 24, 1962, Ann Arbor, MI; [p.] James R. and Theresa C. Goldsmith; [m.] Lisa Marie (Waters) Goldsmith, September 26, 1987; [ch.] No natural, plenty of YMCA teenagers; [ed.] Bachelor of Electrical Engineering, YMCA Fitness Training, YMCA Teen Leadership Training; [occ.] Electronics Engineer, Department of Defense; [memb.] YMCA volunteer with teen programs, Covenant Community Christian Church; [hon.] Munitions System's Division selection for VSAF, nominee for Ten Outstanding Young Americans 1991; [oth. writ.] Several poems, few song lyrics, Engineering Technical papers; [pers.] I write poetry to share with God and friends a reflection of life. I thank Christ for this gift.

[a.] Fort Walton Beach, FL.

GOLEC, PHYLLIS LOUISE
[pen.] Phyllis Louise Golec; [b.] February 5, 1928, Hazel Park, MI; [p.] Dominic J. and Elfrieda L. Damm; [m.] Joseph F. Golec, August 27, 1966; [ch.] Daniel M. Golec; [ed.] Denby High School, Wayne State University (Fine Arts senior); [occ.] Retired Legal Secretary (now watercolor artist); [memb.] Michigan Watercolor Society, Detroit Institute of Arts Founders Society, Art Center, Mt. Clemens; [hon.] Private art showings; [pers.] "Whatever you can do or dream you can begin it for boldness has magic, power and genius in it". [a.] Clinton Township, MI.

GOLEN, ROBERT ALAN
[b.] May 27, 1968, Detroit, MI; [p.] Robert F. and Joanne W. Golen; [ed.] De La Salle Collegiate High School, University of Detroit; [occ.] Stockbroker, Entrepreneur; [memb.] Society for the Advancement of Management, The United States Jaycees; [hon.] The National Dean's List, National Honor Society, University of Detroit Dean's List; [oth. writ.] A collection of poems and a soon to be finished book on how to deal with the loss of a loved one, in memory of my deceased fiancee Melanie Swead; [pers.] Life is much too short to be wasted so we need to hold on dearly to those we love and never let a single moment slip away. [a.] Hamtramck, MI.

GOLIS, MARGARET A.
[pen.] Peggy Ann; [b.] February 24, 1981, Illinois; [p.] Mr. and Mrs. Robert Sayad; [ed.] Currently an eighth grade student at Our Lady of Peace, Darien, IL; [pers.] This poem was inspired by the love and respect I have for my grandmother, Lucille L. Russell, her memory will live in my heart forever.

GOODALL, BOBBIE JEAN
[pen.] Long Jean; [b.] March 14, 1944, Louisville, KY; [p.] Vennie Guest and Willie Long; [m.] Walter Oscar Goodall, April 14, 1963; [ch.] Angela V. and Ladana M. Goodall; [ed.] Central High School, Jefferson Community College, both of Louisville, Associate of Arts; [occ.] Fashion Designer and seamstress, organist; [memb.] Member of International Black Women's Congress, Newark, New Jersey, NAACP, National Organization of WOmen, Calvary Church; [hon.] 1988 winner of Dr. Martin Luther King Jr's essay contest at Jefferson Community College, honored for writing a poem about Maya Angelou, gave it to her in person; [oth. writ.] A book "7th Child Wondering", September 1993, published in Christian Reporter, NAACP Newsletter, National Organization of Women; [pers.] As a person, I am, I can and I will, I did what I set out to do. Return to college in my forties and graduated, became published all in 1993. [a.] Louisville, KY.

GOODMAN, CHERRYLIN C.
[pen.] Cherry; [b.] January 2, 1951, Honolulu; [p.] Ignacio and Angela Cabuslay; [m.] Dwayland Goodman, June 27, 1991; [ed.] University of the East, Manila Philippines, Pre-nursing St. Rita Hospital, Tondo, Manila Philippines, graduate nurse; [occ.] Nursing Assistant, Queens Medical Center, Honolulu, HI. and Straub Hospital, permanent part-time, freelance artist; [memb.] Professional Governance Council, Queens Medical Center Tower 5, heart floor; [pers.] My husband inspired me by writing this poem, I love writing poems and strived hard to get what I want. [a.] Honolulu, HI.

GOMES, JOSE PAULO
[pen.] J. Paulo Gomes; [b.] GOA; [p.] Jose Carlos Sta. Catarina Gomes and Maria L. D'Sa Gomes; [ch.] Maria (M.D.), Linda (M.D.), Flora (DMD), Carlos (B.E.), Josephine (M.D.), Ashoka Benedito and Sushruta Paulo (students); [ed.] M.D. (doctor of medicine) Diplomate American Board of Surgery, Diplomate of College of Physicians and Surgeons, Bombay; [occ.] Practice of surgery; [memb.] Fellow of International College of Surgeons, member of Association of Surgeons, India, member of Freedom Fighters Association of Goa; [hon.] Prizes in Obs.& Gyn, Forensic Medicine, Hygiene-Goa Medical College; [oth. writ.] I started writing to the papers in poetry and prose at the age of seventeen in Portuguese first and in English later. My work was published in papers like "O Heraldo", "Heraldo", "Voz da India", "Navhind Times" and others in Goa, India, I contributed to the Anthology of American Poetry in 1982; [pers.] The aim of my poetry is to catch the beauty of the nature and the lasting aspects of our life, it is the response to inner urge to communicate and express ideas and emotions. [a.] Brooklyn, NY.

GOMEZ, LINDA MARIA
[b.] June 21, 1955, San Jose, CA; [p.] Frank and Josephine Bateman; [m.] Ernesto M. Gomez, M.D., December 29, 1979; [ch.] Tiffany, Krystle, Chad, Ashley, Austin and Hunter; [ed.] San Francisco State University, Andrew Hill High, San Jose, CA; [occ.] Housewife; [memb.] League of Women Voters, Las Rancheras; [pers.] As you live your life today, remember that when you look back at it tomorrow you should like what you see. [a.] Scottsdale, AZ.

GONCALVES, VIRGIL
[b.] January 6, 1952, Port Elizabeth, South Africa; [p.] Mary and Zeca; [m.] Lesley, November 18, 1978; [ch.] Kyle and Ross; [ed.] Bachelor of Journalism (English and Journalism), Rhodes University, South Africa; [occ.] Lecturer; [memb.] Whyalla Writers Group, Rostrum Public Speaking Club; [hon.] National award for Editorial Writing (country newspapers) while Editor of Whyalla News, South Australia, in 1989; [oth. writ.] Whyalla Writers Group Anthology contributions; [pers.] We all have myriad flashes of inspiration. To ensure they are not lost forever, we must pen these fleeting ideas down on paper, even if, initially they are in imperfect form. [a.] Whyalla, South Australia.

GONSALVES, DAUNE
[b.] August 22, 1979, Ocean Side, CA; [p.] Merlyn and Donald Gonsalves; [ed.] Indio High School; [occ.] Student; [hon.] 2nd grade honor student, 7th grade honor student, gymnastics award November 7, 1989, attendance award 1987, Citizenship Award 1989; [oth. writ.] Unpublished writings, Oh Well, Blind Faith, Dowadity, Faces in The Mist; [pers.] I believe that the secret of success won't work unless you do. [a.] Bermuda Dunes, CA.

GONZALES-JUN, DIANA MARIA
[b.] January 22, 1973, New York; [p.] Ignacio and Zoraida Gonzales; [m.] Peter Charles Jun, October 10, 1993; [ed.] Cardinal Spellman High School, Queensborough Community College; [occ.] Secretary, N.W. Ayer Inc.; [memb.] National Wildlife Federation, PETA, ASPCA; [hon.] Dean's List, The National Dean's List; [pers.] It doesn't take much for an idea to form in my mind. Normally, it's everyday living which forms the basis for my writing. I just like to spice it up a bit. [a.] Bronx, NY.

GONZALEZ (M.D.), JUANA CARMEN V.
[b.] Havana, Cuba; [p.] Joqauin and Agustina Valdes; [m.] Divorced, March 25, 1956; [ch.] Carmen J.H. Gonzalez; [ed.] Elementary, secondary, undergraduate, Bachelors in Art and Science Institute of Havana, Medical degree University of Havana, Cuba; [occ.] Medical Doctor specializing in Pediatrics; [memb.] Chicago Medical Society, American Academy of Pediatrics, American Medical Association, Illinois State Medical Society, Chicago Pediatric Society, National Medical Association, Cook County Physicians Associations, Prairie State Medical Society; [hon.] Advisory Committees od City of Chicago Department of Health and Cook County Department of Health, appointment to Blue Ribbon Committee of City of Chicago Department of Children and Family Services; [oth. writ.] Numerous poems in Spanish, several were published in newspapers; [pers.] My poetry reflects my experiences in Cuba and in the United States. My work is influenced by friends, associates and my observations of children in my medical practice. [a.] Chicago, IL.

GONZALEZ, JULIAN
[b.] February 16, 1917, Edinburg, TX; [p.] Lucas and Elena Gonzalez; [m.] Rosa DeRosa, 1950; [ch.] Nancy, Christopher and Lawrence; [ed.] 5th grade, quit during depression to take care of 15 children, brothers and sisters; [occ.] Retired; [memb.] American Legion, D.A.V., fought 2nd WW; [hon.] Recipient of Distinguish Ser-cross Bronze Star, Purple Heart; [oth. writ.] My life as I lived it not finished yet. [a.] San Antonio, TX.

GONZALEZ, SERGIO R.
[b.] November, 11, 1947, Mexico; [ed.] BSBA, Roosevelt U. 1971; [oth. writ.] "Un Bochinche En El Pantano", a short play in Spanish written in 1980. [a.] Chicago, IL.

GONZALEZ, SOLEDAD R.
[pen.] Chole Atzlan; [b.] December 1, 1979, Dallas, TX; [p.] Yolanda and Bernabe Gonzalez; [ed.] 8th grade Strickland Middle School; [occ.] Student; [memb.] Ecology Club, Theatre Club, Newspaper Club; [oth. writ.] Poems, short stories; [pers.] This poem was written based on a true event, in June 93, my friend Jesus Garza was murdered by criminals. This made nationwide news, it was my first encounter with loss by death.[a.] Denton, TX.

GORDON, AMY ELIZABETH
[b.] July 15, 1981, Suffern, NY; [p.] Nancy and Denis Hamlin, Bruce and Patricia Gordon; [ed.] Thiells Elementary School, James A. Farley Middle School; [occ.] Student; [memb.] Farley Environmental Action Team, North Rockland Soccer Association, St. Gregory's CYO Basketball team, National Piano-Playing Auditions member, Farley Middle School band; [hon.] Fire Prevention Essay contest winner, D.A.R.E., essay contest winner, Farley Middle School Poetry contest winner, perfect score-NYS Writing test, award of Excellence in Language Arts; [oth. writ.] Two poems published in "Creative Kids" magazine; [pers.] I have been inspired and encouraged by many people. I would especially like to note Sophia Kase, for whom this poem was written. Her high expectations and constant belief in me help me to strive for my best. [a.] Stony Point, NY.

GORMAN, MATTHEW AARON
[pen.] Matthew Aaron Gorman; [b.] October 21, 1973, Seattle; [p.] Kevin and Susan Gorman; [ed.] Nathan Hale High School (graduated); [occ.] Restaurant worker,

semi-professional music group member. [a.] Seattle, WA.

GORSUCH, SARAH MARIE
[b.] June 5, 1953, Fairburn; [p.] Gilbert and Aleta Scott Overlin; [m.] William Marvin Gorsuch, July 23, 1940; [ch.] Floyd, Marlyn, Constance Marie and Clyde Milton; [ed.] High school; [occ.] Housewife; [memb.] The Fairburn Methodist Church and the United Methodist Women Country Cousins Extension Club; [hon.] 5 trophies for serving at county fair, 30 years work with children and youth in S.S. Youth Fellowship, 35 years church pianist, 5 years 4-H Leader, held offices as president, vice president, secretary, treasurer for local UMW (United Methodist); [oth. writ.] None, Church Women and Extension Club member of the Fairburn United Methodist Church for 47 years; [pers.] The only way to rescue our world and youth from its woes of drugs, abuse, alcoholism, AIDS, teenage pregnancies and whatever else, is a return to God's laws, no matter what religion or sect. [a.] Fairburn, SD.

GOTANCO, LIBRADA B.
[pen.] Betty, LBG; [b.] July 20, 1932, Cebu, Philippines; [p.] Esperidion and Prisca Bugagas; [m.] Benito Castillo Gotanco, July 2, 1955; [ch.] Patricia Georgina, Neda Guia, Neuro Surgeon Sec., Gwendolyn, Merchandizer, Glenn, CPA, Gil, Engr., Gary and Guy student; [ed.] Finished sectrarial course only; [occ.] Homemaker or plain housewife; [memb.] Apostleship of Prayer Crusader of the Holy Face of Jesus, Divine Mercy Devotee, and Honor Guard of the Blessed Virgin Mary; [hon.] Certificates and plaques for religious seminars and activities; [pers.] My first written poetry given to me by the Lord, written on board Amtrack, or my way to a wonderful job as a Nanny to be a 2 1/2 year old boy in Bridgewater, my original poem. [a.] Ginatilan, Cebu, Philippines.

GOULD, DALE D.
[b.] July 19, 1930, Beaverton, MI; [p.] Minnie Smith; [m.] Deceased, September 17, 1955; [ch.] Richard Gould and Susan Walker; [ed.] High school graduate; [occ.] Retired; [hon.] Awarded a certificate for completing 20 years in the United States Air Force and retired from the Air Force in July 1971; [pers.] I hope this poem will touch the hearts of those people who loved their spouse as much as I. This poem was written and dedicated to her by me, she passed away on April 13, 1993 of Cancer at the age of 58. [a.] Beaverton, MI.

GOWAN, ELIZABETH
[b.] November 6, 1958, Bronx, NY; [p.] Gladys and Gerry Gowan; [m.] Andrew Berliner; [ch.] Aaron Jacob and Carmen Elizabeth; [ed.] Valhalla High School, Shenendehowa High School, S.U.N.Y, Cortland; [occ.] Singer, songwriter; [hon.] 1988 winner of KNAC Radio contest with "Crisis" as lead vocalist for 1 of L.A.'s best rock bands; [oth. writ.] Extensive catalogue of poems and songs, copywritten but unpublished; [pers.] It is a blessing and a privilege to be a channel for the written word bringing gifts of wisdom and light to the world. [a.] Los Angels, CA.

GOWANLOCK, AARON J.
[b.] November 9, 1981, Simcoe, Ontario Canada; [p.] Jeff and Donna Gowanlock; [ed.] Public school student; [occ.] Student; [hon.] Placed 2nd in the Royal Canadian Legion Remembrance Day Literary contest, 1992, Simcoe, Ontario, placed 1st in the Royal Canadian Legion Remembrance Day Poster contest, Simcoe,

Ontario 1992; [pers.] I think that, if people would pay more attention to what this world needs, rather than what they want, then what I say in my writing would not happen to this world. (Depending what I say in my writing). [a.] Simcoe, Ontario Canada.

GOWDY, MARIENE
[b.] October 31, 1935, Salt Lake City, UT; [p.] Emery and Dorothy Mitchell; [ch.] Michael Joe and Jeffrey Joe; [ed.] Compton High; [occ.] Disabled; [oth. writ.] Several poems in local newspapers and magazines, also children's stories; [pers.] My writing has been influenced by my life and my faith, I strive to emit the highest moral and spiritual values to the reader. [a.] Las Vegas, NV.

GRAHAM, DANIELLE
[pen.] Danielle Graham; [b.] April 10, 1979, Toronto, Ontario; [p.] Ray and Kathy Graham; [ed.] I am presently a grade nine student at Father James Whelihan in Calgary Alberta; [occ.] Student; [oth. writ.] Several poems in my personal journal; [pers.] I have a seventeen year old sister named Andrea. I would like to dedicate my poem to my Language Arts teacher, Mrs. Tzotzos. [a.] Calgary, Alberta.

GRAHAM, DR. OLGA
[pers.] Born July 27, 1939 to Ivy and William Richards from Cambridgeshire, England. Descendent of Sir John Lawrence and wife, Elizabeth Waller, poet and Sir James Richards. Twenty years executive in mass communications media. Resigned from York University to earn doctorate the Theology and since 1980 has been working as Theologian with three books published and sixteen manuals on the Bible and history. Served on three founding Boards for ten years. Note: "Establish a relationship with your Creator and all else will follow. Time once spent never returns. Do not be intimidated, truth and justice are lonely virtues". [a.] Don Mills, Ontario Canada.

GRAINGER, CAROLE
[b.] November 5, 1951, Kuala Lumpur, Malaysia; [p.] Brenda and Don Johnson (both deceased); [m.] Stuart Grainger, August 26, 1989; [ch.] Jade Marie Carla and Alexander Jonathon; [ed.] Notre Dame High School, Southwark, London, and Kettering Technical College, Northamptonshire; [occ.] Light touch therapist; [memb.] Alternative Light Touch Therapy (A.L.T.T.); [oth.writ.] An extensive range of poetry from funny to sad, romantic to spiritual and themes of philosophical guidance, written over many years for which I'm seeking a creative outlet; [pers.] To encourage the promotion of enlightenment and greater understanding of all mankind on a spiritual and physical level. [a.] South Zeal Okehampton, Devon, England.

GRANT, MICHAEL C.
[b.] January 4, 1980, Myrtle Beach, SC; [p.] Edward G. and Miriam C. Grant; [ed.] 8th grade student at Waccamaw High School, Pawleys Island, SC; [occ.] Student; [memb.] Academic Team for 1992 and 93; [hon.] National Junior Honor Society of Secondary Schools, Duke Talent Identification Program (Duke University). [a.] Murrells Inlet, SC.

GRANT, ROGER W.
[b.] January 19, 1962, Mason, TX; [p.] Nancy A. Grant; [ed.] James H. Bowen High School; [occ.] Merchandiser Federated Distributors, Chicago, IL; [hon.] Honorable Mention, drafting Bowen High School; [oth.writ.] Multiple poems written not published, short stories; [pers.] I

enjoy nature and tend to evolve it within my writings also feelings that occur in my life daily. [a.] Chicago, IL.

GRAZIANO, MIKE
[pen.] Jam Grinder; [b.] November 16, 1960, Santa Monica, CA; [m.] Deana, the 8-'s sometime; [ch.] Ryan; [ed.] Cypress College; [occ.] Expeditor; [memb.] Member of the Psychic Trigic Undercurrent (of the universe); [hon.] Blue ribbon at USO show and a free meal; [oth. writ.] Mutated Farmers in The Fields, several musical albums; [pers.] "When the body's deceased and the soul's enraged, it's infinite power will soon take control then it's time to move on and become whole". [a.] Anaheim, CA.

GREEN, CLAUDIA
[b.] June 14, 1948, Chatham, CO; [p.] Derry and Nora C. Smith; [m.] Elbert L. Green, April 26; [ch.] Bradley Pernell, Elton Vidal and Angel LaDair; [ed.] Horton High School, Madam Deshazor Beauty College, Hank Hanna Beauty School, Central Carolina Community College; [occ.] Cosmetologist; [memb.] Member of Liberty Chapel United Church of Christ, Missionary Circle, L.C. Inspirational Singers, member and organizer of the Community Watch Program, February 1993; [hon.] Miss Jocca 1980, certificate of appreciation for participation in singing in spreading the gospel in songs, Miss Relative Gospel Singer 1979; [pers.] My personal goal is to uplift the spirit of men and women all over the world through my poems. [a.] Moncure, NC.

GREEN, DEBORAH S.
[b.] October 16, 1953, Akron, OH; [p.] Mr. and Mrs. Gerald W. Gump; [ed.] Roosevelt High School, Kent, OH; [occ.] Drug store clerk; [memb.] Western Reserve Girl Scout Council, 15 years. I am in charge of the calendar and cookie sales for the city of Ravenna's Girl Scout troops, (volunteer position); [oth. writ.] I write poems simply for the pleasure of it. (I jokingly, tell my friends that one day I'm going gather up my poems, put them in a book and call it "The Collected Thoughts of A Drugstore Clerk"; [pers.] I believe there's a little bit of poetry and storytelling in all of us. When I read a truly great poem, whether it causes tears or gooseflesh, I compare it to placing my hand upon wet cement. It forever leaves an impression. [a.] Ravenna, OH.

GREEN, ERNEST F.
[pen.] Fonte'; [b.] March 11, 1971, Elizabeth, NJ; [p.] Della and Franklin Green; [m.] Magaly Green, June 2, 1990; [ch.] Jasmine and Ernesto Green; [ed.] High school, some college; [occ.] Stock manager; [oth. writ.] None that I've sent out yet, this is only the beginning; [pers.] I enjoy writing about the things that we all seem to forget about and need more of ... love... we need to express our feelings more, think about it. [a.] Linden, NJ.

GREEN, GAYE K.
[b.] April 17, 1956, Anawalt, WV; [p.] Thorna and John Wilson; [ch.] Mitchell, Tiffany and Chautina; [ed.] Currently attending school; [occ.] Student; [oth.writ.] Several features in local newsletter; [pers.] I've been inspired to write of my beauty, pain, joy and fears. My writing comes from deep within myself. [a.] Freeport, NY.

GREEN, KATHLENE
[pen.] Kitty; [b.] September 5, 1958, Cook County; [p.] Herman Gearld and Jurlene Fedrick; [ch.] Shuntaunia C. Green, Mahone and Russell W. Green, and Shuntee T. J. M. Green; [ed.] GED, license cosmetologist, certified

Nurses Assistant and Computer Science skills as well; [occ.] Clerical, disciplinary hearings; [hon.] 20 various certificates, one plaque award and one $100.00 cash bond award; [oth. writ.] Several poems send out for only my own personnel use, to friends and at one time to my x-husband; [pers.] I stress the fact of having whites, blacks, Hispanic and or no matter of creed nor color to come together in peace and harmony. To stop blaming others for their mistakes as well as their situations. Through poetry I can express myself. [a.] Chicago, IL.

GREEN, MICHELE ELLEN
[b.] October 29, 1964, Toronto, Ontario Canada; [p.] Benjamin D. and Kathleen A. Green; [m.] Divorced; [ch.] Kathleen Amanda; [ed.] Fenelon Falls Secondary Centennial College, Ryerson University, The Ontario College of Art; [occ.] Artist, song-writer, poet; [hon.] National Library of Poetry, Editor's Choice Award 1993 for Outstanding Achievement in Poetry , poem entitled "The Warrior" published in the National Library of Poetry's anthology entitled A Break in The Clouds; [oth. writ.] "Poetry of Essence" a compilation of 200 separate entries of poems and lyrics "What Goes Around, Comes Around" (The story of BeeBop) children's illustrated story book-Educational; [pers.] This poem (song) is dedicated to my MOM who has since passed away. Dear Mom, Thank you for showing me love, and this poem is dedicated to my little girl Kathleen, Dear Kathleen, Thank you for allowing me to show you love... the love my MOM once showed me. "ONE SMILE". [a.] Toronto Ontario, Canada.

GREEN, PENNY M.
[b.] February 7, 1969, Plant City, FL; [p.] Earl and Virgie P. Green; [sib.] Kathy D. Green; [ed.] Plant City High, Hillsborough Community College; [pers.] I strive to share my love of literature with others, if I can share that magic then my work is worthwhile. [a.] Crystal Springs, FL.

GREEN, WILLIAM F.
[pen.] Billy G.; [b.] May 256, 1933, Verdun, Quebec; [p.] Willaim H. Green and Olive Collier; [m.] Divorced, May 21, 1955; [ch.] William Steven, Sandra Joan and Stanley John; [ed.] High school graduate, Montreal, Quebec Canada; [occ.] Currently Sgt. Fire Department Captain, bass drummer; [memb.] Legion Band Royal Canadian Legion, Br. # 14 (RMR) Westmount, Korean Vets Association, Unit # 20, (Montreal); [hon.] 30 years exemplary Service medal with the Cote Luc Fire Department and the Westmount Fire Department, Legion medal, past Honorable Secretary (2 years) past Sgt. at Arms 2 years, current 2nd Vice President, RC Legion, Westmount, Canada, fire department captain 34 years, age 60 years; [pers.] Regarding life itself, "it's not the leaving that bothers me, its the amount of time we are away". [a.] Quebec, Canada.

GREENE, DESMOND
[pen.] Desi; [b.] August 25, 1970, Rhode Island; [p.] Norman and Dorothy Greene; [p.] Patricia Greene, October 10, 1988; [ch.] Devin, Kirsten and Katelyn Greene; [ed.] Polytechnic High School graduate; [occ.] Sheetmetal worker title, Field Foreman; [oth. writ.] Several poems written to my wife; [pers.] I strive to provide a better way of live for my family. [a.] Van Nuys, CA.

GREENLAW, RUBY
[b.] September 11, 1929, Grand Manan Island, Canada; [m.] Eston; [ch.] 6, 4 boys and 2 girls; [occ.] Retired;

[oth. writ.] Stories, artist, oil and acrylic crafts; [pers.] I write what I see and feel and what I've learned from life, I live on the Maine, New Brunswick Border.

GREER, DOROTHY
[pen.] Dorothy Buckalew; [b.] May 17, 1943, Oxford, PA; [p.] J. Samuel and Elizabeth Greer; [m.] William H. Buckalew, October 14, 1961; [ch.] Karen B. Smith, grandchildren, Christopher and William; [ed.] Solanco High School, Willow Street Vo-Tech, Nurses Aide; [occ.] Housewife, part-tie baker-candy maker, work with eggs for Flu Serum; [memb.] Colerain Baptist Church; [hon.] Numerous awards for baking and candy making, award from fire company for Outstanding Support; [oth. writ.] This is my first attempt at writing; [pers.] I have written this poem for my special friend, my sister, to express my love for her. [a.] Oxford, PA.

GREENWOOD, RON
[b.] January 14, 1953, Columbus, OH; [m.] Terry Greenwood, August 12, 1972; [ch.] Tina Nichole, Renee Michelle and Kyle Carter; [ed.] Westfall High School, Columbus Paraprofessional Institute School of Hard Knocks; [occ.] Computer Programmer; [pers.] My writing is a reflection of what I feel and what I have experienced as a human being. I cannot always speak about my feelings, but I have always been able to express myself by writing. [a.] Grove City, OH.

GRIFFIN, JOAN M.
[pen.] Joan M. Griffin; [b.] September 17, 1932, Toronto, Ontario Canada; [p.] Herbert and Sarah Rose; [m.] Donald J. Griffin (deceased), September 29, 1950; [ch.] Donald and Brenda, grandchildren, Shawn, Trevor and Sherisse; [occ.] Retired; [oth. writ.] Book of poetry entitled Thy Nature So Deep; [pers.] I am now in the process of writing a book of poetry and songs, some of which have been sung by me in church, Church of Universal Love who published my first book of poetry; [a.] Toronto, Ontario Canada.

GRIFFITH, LEON
[pen.] Leon Griffith; [b.] November 22, 1918; [p.] Lee and Tee Griffith; [m.] Lillian Gullage Griffith, June 27, 1940; [ch.] Henry, Lynn (deceased) and Fay; [ed.] High school graduate; [occ.] Retired building contractor; [hon.] Golden Poet Award 1991; [oth. writ.] Other poems; [pers.] I try to write my poems so that the readers feel they could have written them. [a.] Eclectic, AL.

GRIFFITHS, EVAN
[b.] February 27, 1960, London, Ontario; [p.] Jacolyn and Arthur Griffiths; [m.] Astrid Griffiths, June 22, 1991; [ed.] Grade 12, Goderich District Collegiate Institute, New Germany High School; [occ.] Labourer; [pers.] With our father dying early in our years, the responsibility to raise us three was left up to our mother. The poem express the love and appreciation my brothers and I felt for all that our mother had done for us. [a.] Bridgewater, Nova Scotia.

GRIGGS, LINDA
[b.] May 21, 1943, New York City; [p.] George Eastman Griggs and Marian Hall Griggs; [ed.] Dover Plains High School, B.S. and M.P.S., State University College of New Paltz, NY, graduate of Institute of Children's Literature; [occ.] Mental Health Counselor and children's writer; [memb.] Attender, New Platz Friends Meeting (Quaker), former secretary and vice-president, New Platz Gardens for Nutrition Inc., National Epilepsy Society; [hon.] National Honor Society, Dover Plains

High School, Regents scholarship; [pers.] I try to express my love of nature and human beings in my writing. [a.] New Platz, NY.

GRISBY, ZABRINA M.
[b.] August 26, 1973, St. Louis, MO; [p.] Richard Grisby Sr. and Willie Mae Williams; [ed.] Washington Middle, Sumner High, Saint Louis University; [occ.] Full-time student and part-time assistant teacher; [memb.] Active member of Lite of Jericho M.B.C. and Black Social Workers Association at SLU; [hon.] Washington book award-Sumner High, Xerox Humanities Award-Sumner High School, Valedictorian-Sumner High School, academic award from SLU SESC; [pers.] It is my sincere desire that young African-American children strive daily to learn the truth about their culture and to pass the knowledge on to others. [a.] Saint Louis, MO.

GROCE, PEGGY J.
[pen.] Peggy J. Groce; [b.] Philipp, MS; [p.] Mr. and Mrs. Tom Sykes; [ed.] Cascilla High School, I am a licensed hairstylist, I enjoy creative art; [occ.] Retired; [memb.] Top Record, Songwriting Association, Nashville, TN; [hon.] I won the best poem for a safety award, for Firestone Tire Co., 1959; [oth. writ.] I have a notebook of poems and songs. I have 4 songs with copyrights, with the music to them, I have only been in songwriting a year; [pers.] Every song or poem I write is true, or my life or someone else's life. [a.] Ferriday, LA.

GROVES, IRMA
[b.] October 21, 1932, Kansas City, MO; [p.] Clarence and Annie Bowman; [m.] Marvin L. Groves (deceased April 16, 1993), January 23, 1951; [ch.] Pastor Darryl L. Groves, Marva L. Runnels, Sharon L. Kelley, Denise L. Canady and Eric L. Groves; [ed.] Graduate of Lincoln High School in 1949, have completed courses of interest in assisting my fellowman, in outreach college classes; [occ.] Retired; [memb.] Quill and Scroll, St. Stephen Baptist Church, Vice President of E.A.C.H. Inc. Housing Development, Church's Housing Committee and Sunday School; [hon.] Quill and Scroll, Perfect Attendance as employee at Northeast Junior High, Board Volunteer of the Year for guiding several activities for youth and seniors at our Housing Development, Sycamore Groves; [oth. writ.] Several poems I am preparing to put into book form; [pers.] "When you start to count your Blessings, You will soon run out of Numbers", "Let's Continue To Make A Positive Difference".

GRUBBS, JEFFERY I.
[b.] December 17, 1959; [p.] Joe and Barbara Grubbs; [ch.] Whitney Michele Grubbs (age 5); [ed.] High school graduate, completed approximately 100 hours of college toward theatre/business degree; [occ.] Independent Insurance Agent and bi-vocational church music director; [memb.] Frederick Jaycees, 1st Baptist Church, Tipton, OK., Chairman of Associated Singles Ministry, Resolutions Committee; [hon.] 4 time state speech champion, Best Actor...Lifeguard pageant, nominated for Irene Ryan Award 1981, nominated for Outstanding Young Businessman's Award, numerous talent awards for speech, music and writing; [oth. writ.] Several local publications, Scriberales 1980, 1981, this particular poem has never been published; [pers.] Poetry seems to provide an avenue, allowing one to be perhaps more honest with themself while allowing them to escape of delusional grandeur. It is a harmony many seek, but few find. [a.] Tipton, OK.

GRUBBS, JOYCE M.
[pen.] Jo Godwin; [b.] February 7, 1943, Okmulgee, OK; [p.] Lloyd and Marguerite Godwin; [m.]H.L. Grubbs, January 28, 1962; [ch.] Trula Dee Ann, Steven Eric and Shannon Rae; [ed.] Coe College, Oklahoma State University, Eastern Iowa; [occ.] Community Developer for Share Iowa; [hon.] 1984 Iowa recipient of The Epsilon Sigma Alpha, International Diana Award; [pers.] I believe in writing from personal experience and what I know best. As a survivor of sexual abuse, an overcomer of cultural prejudices and as a champion of the individual, my works reflect healims. [a.] Oskaloosa, IA.

GRUPP, CHRISTINE V.
[b.] November 27, 1951, Brockport, NY; [p.] Loren and Elise Van Orden; [m.] John C. Grupp, May 6, 1972; [ch.] Kevin Christian Grupp; [ed.] St. Paul Lutheran, Hilton Central High School 2 years at Potsdam State College; [occ.] Housewife; [memb.] North Park Lutheran School, International Society of Poets; [hon.] Golden Poet Award awarded by the World of Poetry; [oth. writ.] About 100 songs including the music; [pers.] My poetic life got better after meeting a famous actor (who was in disguise) at a bus-stop in Buffalo on June 20, 1981. [a.] Tonawanda, NY.

GUENGERICH, L. GLEN
[p.] Elmer and Magdalena Guengerich; [m.] Allie Davison Guengerich; [ch.] Lowell, Elaine, Galen, Annette and Audrey; [ed.] Goshen College, B.A. English, Goshen College B.S. Biology, University of Iowa M.A. Philosophy; [occ.] Retired Educator; [memb.] Our Mennonite Church Committee selected me to write its history, Our Goodly Heritage, 234 pages, hard cover, I've also written feature articles and poetry for church and secular publications, e.g., Gospel Herald and Grit Magazine, etc.; [oth. writ.] The Iowa Poetry Association publishes only winners of its annual poetry contest, nine times I've been published in its annual anthology Lyrical Iowa; [pers.] In writing poetry I seek that combination of words that are memorable for their thought, sound and brevity. I've been influenced by many other writers including those from Elizatethan periods to our contemporary period. [a.] Kalona, IA.

GUERRA, LUZ MICHELLE
[pen.] Shelly; [b.] December 28, 1979, New York City; [p.] Adrian and Luz C. Guerra; [ed.] Aquinas High School, Bronx, New York; [occ.] Student, freshman; [memb.] American Legion, Judo Club; [hon.] Second Honors at Aquinas High School. [a.] Bronx, NY.

GUIHOT, CHRISTINE
[pen.] Marguerite St. John; [b.] July 18, 1972, Australia; [p.] John and Sophia Guihot; ed.] Catherine McCauley College; [occ.] Nurse/third year law student; [oth. writ.] Articles published in Australian Women's magazines; [pers.] In my writing, I can escape day to day pressures and allow my inner turmoil to expurge itself on paper. [a.] Sydney, Australia.

GULLA, PAUL MICHAEL
[b.] April 1, 1962, Phill., PA; [p.] Paul G. and Elaine R. Gulla; [ed.] Waynesboro Area Senior High; [pers.] To Virginia, my wife to be, may the rest of our lives together be as loving as the present. [a.] Waynesboro, PA.

GULLISON, JOAN
[pen.] Joan Leslie; [b.] April 16, 1955, Concord, NH; [p.] Leslie and Dorothy Eaton; [m.] Michael Gullison, May 20, 1978; [ch.] Brandon Fitzgerald; [ed.] Hopkinton

High, Maryville College, St. Louis; [occ.] Co-writer and Editor, Chicago Press newspaper, children's fashion design; [memb.] ASID-Student Chapter 1983-1986, The Mentor Circles of the Women Entrepreneur Network-1992; [oth. writ.] Articles in local newspaper; [pers.] Reflections of the past light of the future is what inspires me to write. [a.] Forest Lake, MN.

GUSTAFSON, DEREK
[b.] December 21, 1971, Modesto, CA; [p.] Stan and Barbara Gustafson; [ed.] Denair High School, Modest Junior College, Sunuma State University graduate in Spring 94; [occ.] Student/landscaper; [memb.] National Parks and Conservation Association; [pers.] My poetry is the way I express my feelings whether they are happy or sad. Edgar Allen Poe is an influence. [a.] Ruhnert Park, CA.

GUTHRIE, SHAINA
[b.] September 16, 1978, Wurzburg, Germany; [p.] Mike and Marsha Guthrie; [ed.] Presently a freshman in high school (9th grade); [memb.] National Junior Honor Society; [hon.] Highest English average for the year of 1992-1993 in the 8th grade; [oth. writ.] Several unpublished poems; [pers.] Never give up hoping and never lose sight of your ray of sunshine, it'll always be there waiting. [a.] Ft. Stewart, GA.

GUTIERREZ, SUSANA
[pen.] Little Susy; [b.] February 20, 1978, Hialeah, Fl; [p.] Miguel and Nancy Gutierrez; [ed.] Tenth grade at Miami Killian Senior High; [memb.] National Honors Society, National Science Honors Society, French Honors Society; [oth. writ.] Personal ones hidden in my room; [pers.] I write when my feelings for something change whether they become weaker or stronger. When I express myself in this way, I gain a better understanding of what I am feeling. [a.] Miami, FL.

GUY, GENEVA MARY
[pen.] Gen Guy; [b.] June 24, 1924, Monror, MI; [p.] Elsie and Ellsworth Smith; [m.] Harley F. Guy, December 18; [ch.] JoAnn, Betty Jane and Paul; [ed.] 12th grade graduate; [occ.] Housewife; [memb.] Arrys; [hon.] Merit certifcate and coffeee mug-1991; [oth. writ.] Nook of "Collected Thougths" 1979; [pers.] Three heart attacks and a pace-maker ended my career as cook and dietary aid at the Lutheran Nursing Home of Monroe, MI. [a.] Erie, MI.

GUY, MARY E.
[pen.] Mia Edge; [b.] November 7, 1931, England; [p.] May and Rex Guy; [m.] Divorced; [ch.] Jennife Shea-Gabriel and granddaughter, Amber Gabriel, Angela Shea (daughter); [ed.] Torquay Girls Grammar School, Devon, England; [occ.] Retired (former government of Canada employee) occupied now as seamstress, creative sewing for dance and theatrics, community work and writing; [oth. writ.] Lyrical nature poems, religious poems and children's poems; [pers.] The countryside and wild and beauty of everchanging nature, I see as a continual poetic flow, this has inspired me to write. [a.] Hull, Quebec Canada.

GUZAN, LINDA S.
[pers.] Dedicated with love, respect and admiration to Joseph Castillo (Apache).

GUZMAN, ROY MICHAEL
[b.] February 10, 1963, Agana, Guam; [p.] Ricardo M. and Rosario P. Guzman; [ed.] Lehua Elementary, Pearl

City, Hawaii, Highlands Intermediate-Pearl City Hawaii, Aguda Junior High, Magnilao-Guam, George Washington Senior High, Magnilao, Guam; [occ.] Optician; [oth. writ.] Several poems not yet published, but soon will be; [pers.] I became interested in poetry while attending high school, studying Shakesphere in one of my English classes. Greatly influenced by friends and family to enter poetry contest. [a.] Carson, CA.

HAAKER, MARILYN
[b.] Willow River, MN; [p.] William and Aggie Hennen; [m.] Ray; [pers.] I wish to dedicate "Freedom's Ring" to Ray and my wonderful family for all their love, faith and influence.

HABERKORN, ROBERT W.
[b.] November 24, 1969, San Bernardino; [p.] Marion and Robert Haberkorn; [ed.] Cajon High School, California State University, San Bernardino, Los Angeles College of Chiropractic, Southern California School of Massage; [occ.] Student at LACC; [memb.] Associated Bodywork and Massage Professionals, American Chiropractic Association, California Chiropractic Association; [hon.] B. S. Biology; [oth. writ.] Short stories and poems on a variety of topics; [pers.] Listen to yourself and trust what you hear. That is the only way to live. [a.] San Bernardino, CA.

HAGAN, ROBIN
[b.] June 20, 1968, Peoria, IL; [p.] Ruth and Leon Hatcher; [m.] William David Hagan, Jr., February 14, 1987, December 16, 1991; [ch.] Kayla Shay Hagan; [ed.] South Cobb High, Carrol Tech College; [occ.] Atlanta Journal Constitution Mail Courier; [memb.] Ewing Road Baptist; [hon.] This one honor by The National Library of Poetry, the honor of publishing it in Dance on The Horizon; [oth.writ.] I have over 200 songs I have written that sometimes begin as poems, or stay as a song or songs, I hope one day for my songs to be seen, heard; [pers.] There is one saying that reflect on my life, God's gift to you is the gift of life, What you do with that life is your gift to God. My husband always had confidence and believe in me, when I had none for myself. [a.] Powder Springs, GA.

HAGLER, STEPHANIE SPRING
[b.] February 7, 1979, West Mephis, AR; [p.] Mary and James Albright; [ed.] Yough Schools, PA. (K-&), Marion Junior High (8-9); [occ.] Student at Marion Junior High School; [memb.] National Junior Honor Society, National Stamp Club, high school band; [hon.] Rating of 2 in solo and ensemble, Honorable Mention in NASA Space contest; [oth. writ.] None that are published; [pers.] I love to write and I have ever since I was small, without poems and stories the world wouldn't be the same. [a.] Marion, AR.

HAILPERIN, BERNARD
[b.] November 26, 1922, Newark, NJ; [p.] Beatrice and Samuel Hailperin; [m.] Alice (deceased), March 22, 1951; [ch.] Roy and Mila Hailperin; [ed.] University of Iowa, B.A., M.A., Seton Hall University; [occ.] English, Drama and Speech Teacher and Coordinator of Forensics; [memb.] National Council of English Teachers, N.E.A., N.J.E.A., N.J. Forensics League, University of Iowa Alumni Association; [hon.] Presidential Citation for Excellence in Environmental Protection 1972, Title I Program cited in Congressional Record 1968, Coach of the Year in Forensics (U. of Penn); [oth. writ.] Published articles in N. J. Schoolmaster, book on Newark's Title I Program, 1967, novel, Children of

Vesuvius, radio play, New Wonder Side Show; [pers.] I write from personal experience in order to share with others my emotions recollected in tranquility. [a.] Livingston, NJ.

HAINES, DARREN
[b.] November 23,1966, England; [p.] Terence J. and Mary V.A. Haines; [m.] Single; [ed.] Milbrook Secondary School, Southampton, England; [occ.] Contracts Manager in cleaning company; [hon.] 7 CSE Passes including French, English language, Science and Mathematics; [oth. writ.] I have written some poems for local newspapers and at present have sent some to national papers; [pers.] I write poems, stories, etc., on any subject, especially animals. I also write song lyrics and enjoy a challenge. [a.] Southampton, England.

HALFORD, REV. CLIFFORD L.
[b.] October 10, 1932, Clermont, FL; [p.] Lee A. and Lillie Youmans Halford, Sr.; [m.] Patricia Murphy Halford, December 29, 1955; [ch.] Clifford A. Halford, Laura Halford Derryberry and William K. Halford; [ed.] Umatilla High, Umatilla, FL., Florida Baptist Theological College, Graceville, FL.; [occ.] Disability Retired; [memb.] Westside Baptist Church, Plant City, FL., National D.A.V.; [hon.] Ordained to the Southern Baptist Church Gospel Ministry in February 1965, Who's Who in American Religion 1975; [oth.writ.] College paper, The Three Directions of Faith Healing, Sermon in Song For Easter, 'One Day" a compilation, wrote and published Hickory Baptist newsletter 5 years, Sharpsville, PA; [pers.] To continue to be useful even though spinal arthritis which began at age 19 while in the U.S. Air Force in Paris, forced disability retirement at age 49. [a.] Plant City, FL.

HALFPENNY, DONNA
[b.] June 23, 1957, Cape Breton; [p.] Lyman and Corinne Halfpenny; [ch.] Rachel (age 16); [ed.] Isle Madame High, Atlantic Men's Hairstyling, Marien Emergency Duties, various nautical courses; [occ.] Fisherman; [oth.writ.] This will be my first published poem and an article for a local newspaper; [pers.] I proudly dedicate my first published poem to the late Lyman Halfpenny and all my people who know me and still love me. [a.] West Arichart, Cape Breton, Canada.

HALL, DARLENE R.
[pen.] Angel; [b.] June 12, 1963, Lincoln Park, MI; [p.] Adam and Beverly White Jr.; [ch.] Brandice A., Jack A., Justin A. and Marcus A. Hall; [ed.] Graduated high school in 1981, currently attending 3rd year at college; [occ.] Word processing/secretary; [memb.] American Medical Association; [hon.] Trophy for essay on "Black History Month"; [oth. writ.] Various romance poems, currently working on a novel; [pers.] If you must believe in someone, believe in God, He won't ever let you down. [a.] Detroit, MI.

HALL, DARREN
[b.] October 15, 1972, England; [m.] Patricia Wood; [occ.] Financial Consultant; [pers.] To bring modern day conflicts into understandable symbolism, making poetry accessible to all. [a.] Atherstone, Warks.

HALL, HEATHER MARIE
[pen.] Heather Hall; [b.] September 12,1975, Rochester, MI; [p.] Don and Sue Hall; [ed.] Clawson High School, Central Michigan University; [occ.] Student; [memb.] Humane Society of the United States; [pers.] Writing has always been my way of expression, I can express my

feelings, thoughts and all into my writing. [a.] Clawson, MI.

HALL, LINDA C.
[m.] E.A. Hall Jr.;[ch.] Hal Henn, Jr.; [ed.] University of Tennessee and University of South Carolina; [occ.] Marketing Consultant and "Professional Daydreamer"; [memb.] North Carolina Poetry Society, The Charlotte Writer's Club; [oth. writ.] "Home Again" (title of poem); [pers.] The human truth is like illusive light shadows, visions, fragments. Poetry is a glimpse of the voice within. Favorite poets, Ezra Pound and Marianne Moore. [a.] Mooresville, NC.

HALL, JR., ROBERT W.
[pen.] Bobby; [b.] May 10, 1960, Garden City, MI; [p.] Robert W. and Doris M. (Rochette) Hall, Sr.; [m.] Mary J. (Kozora) Hall, a Northwest Airlines Flight Attendant; [ch.] None (yet) two German Shepherd dogs, Boss and Dominque, (sib) two brothers and five sisters; [ed.] Garden City West High School, Michigan, Henry Ford College of Michigan; [occ.] System Technician for K-Mart Corporation, owner of The Pine Grove Ranch in Cohoctah Township of Howell, MI; [oth. writ.] A collection of my personal, non-published poetry, currently working on writing a novel; [pers.] I write solely from my life, my experiences, my pain, my joys, my feelings and emotions. I truly appreciate life and enjoy writing about just that. [a.] Howell, MI.

HALLGREN, TRAVIS PROCTOR
[pen.] Silent Poet; [b.] April 7, 1972, Ashtabula, OH; [p.] Larry and Colleen Hallgren; [m.] Amy Ellen Hallgren, July 28, 1990; [ch.] Aundrea Ellen Hallgren; [ed.] College graduate with an Associates Degree in the field of carpentry and construction; [occ.] Carpenter; [hon.] Distinctive Carpenter Award, Dean's List; [oth. writ.] I have several poems written but have not shared yet, that's where my pen name comes from, I do have 2 poems being published in the 1994 edition of Treasured Poems of America; [pers.] It takes a wise man to tell a good lesson, it takes a great man to heed his own words. [a.] Ashtabula, OH.

HALSEY, PAUL MICHAEL
[b.] June 12, 1963, Columbus, OH; [p.] Carl and June Halsey; [ed.] Whetstone High, Columbus Business University; [occ.] Janitor; [hon.] Associate Degree with honors -1983, runner-up, Ohio VICA Regional Calculator competition-1980, Employee of the Month-Dongtos' Pizza, June 1992, Knight Award, Clinton Junior High 1978; [pers.] Hope to write poetry someday of my experiences in mental hospitals, maybe they will rival the works of Edgar Allan Poe. I know, I'm just dreaming! [a.] Columbus, OH.

HAMBLIN, JOE ALAN
[pen.] Joe A. Hamblin; [b.] January 7, 1960, Wellsboro, PA; [p.] Owen and Arlene (Wilbur) Hamblin; [m.] Tinna Marie (Johnson) Hamblin, June 23, 1979; [ch.] Brandi Jo and Haylee Marie; [ed.] High school graduate and approaching completion of Associates degree (Wellsboro High School); [occ.] U.S. Army Military Police Corps; [memb.] Middlebury Baptist Church; [hon.] Several Military Awards and accommodations; [oth. writ.] Several other poems; [pers.] John 3:16, For God so loved the world, that He gave His only begotten Son, that whosoever believeth in HIm should not perish, but have everlasting life. [a.] Middlebury Ctr., PA.

HAMETZ, MARILYN
[b.] November 23, 1940, Passaic, NJ; [ed.] Hofstra University M.S. Education, Queens College CUNY, MA, BA Psychology, Summer Institute, writing project Teachers College Columbia University; [occ.] Elementary school teacher, New York City, P.S. 131Q; [memb.] Kappa Delta Pi, Educational Honor Society, Audubon Historical Society of Massapequa; [oth.writ.] Non-fiction articles in newspapers and magazines, newsletters for Not-For-Profit and governmental organizations. [a.] Massapequa, NY.

HAMILTON, ALISON
[b.] October 17, 1954, Detroit; [p.] Ray and Virginia Longuski; [m.] Christopher Hamilton, September 5, 1979; [ch.] Colin (1982), Jared (1984) and Molly (1986); [ed.] High school and some college; [occ.] Household engineer and sub-custodial worker; [oth.writ.] Unseen stories and poems; [pers.] I'm just an average person and believe what will be will be. I've always enjoyed writing poetry for others. [a.] Dearborn Heights, MI.

HAMILTON, BENNY H.
[b.] September 15, 1962, Hyden, KY; [ed.] Berea College; [occ.] Account; [memb.] NPCA, NRA; [hon.] National Honor Society, Who's Who American High School Students, All American Hall of Fame-Band; [pers.] I work to put strong emotion in my writing, I draw upon personal experience and try to share what I feel. [a.] Wooton, KY.

HAMPTON, LUKE
[b.] July 15, 1975, Mansfield, OH; [p.] Thomas and Jane Hampton; [ed.] Madison Comprehensive High School, Ohio State University; [occ.] Student; [oth.writ.] Various poems, essays and short stories; [pers.] Whether it is read, heard or viewed, art should neither be censored nor abused. [a.] Mansfield, OH.

HAMRIC, RAMONA E.
[b.] October 27, 1929, Georgetown, SC; [p.] Dr. and Mrs. H.A. Farris (deceased); [m.] John White, Hamric (deceased), March 19, 1946; [ch.] Jeffrey John, Allen and Jean Annie; [ed.] High school, Business College, SC; [occ.] Retired, Sterling Faucet Co., Morgantown, WV.; [memb.] American Legion, lifetime member of V.F.W. # 9916, Morgantown, WV., lifetime member A.F.L.C.I.O., member of S.O.A.R., member First Baptist Church, Morgantown, WV; [hon.] The National Library of Poetry, fishing contest, Master's Tournament, Capt. Dick's Murrels Inlet, SC.; [oth. writ.] (Hobbies) fishing, ministry, painting and writing; [pers.] I would hope my sayings would uplift others. [a.] Morgantown, WV.

HANDREN, SCOTT
[pen.] David Scott; [b.] July 31, Brockton, MA; [p.] Richard A. and Patricia A. Handren; [ed.] Bristol Community College, University of Lowell, Purdue University , Coyle and Cassidy Memorial High School; [occ.] In search of; [memb.] Boy Scouts of America, Knights of Columbus; [hon.] Eagle Scout, Student Advocacy; [oth. writ.] Non-published; [pers.] Illegitimus non Carborundum, so keep on keeping on. [a.] Taunton, MA.

HANLEY, SHANNON (PETROVICH)
[b.] December 29, 1968, Paducah, KY; [p.] Ron and Carol Hanely; [m.] Single; [ed.] BA-English, BA-History, Emory University, Atlanta, GA.; [occ.] Writer; [memb.] Phi Beta Kappa, Sigman Tau Epsilon, Phi Alpa

Theta; [hon.] Woodruff Scholar at Emory University; [oth. writ.] Published in The Phoenix, The Lullwater Review; [pers.] I am a hedonist by profession and an epicure by trade. [a.] Lexington, KY.

HANLON, T. L.
[b.] October 17, 1920, Nova Scotia; [p.] Mr. and Mrs. Alfred Hanlon; [m.] Georgette, July 30, 1952; [ed.] B.A., St. Francis Xavier University and University of Ottawa; [occ.] Retired; [memb.] Cystic Fibrosis, sports club, Ottawa Officers, Mess R.C.A.F., International Society of Poets (lifetime); [hon.] CD Canadian Forces Defence Medal, CVSN Canadian volunteer services medal, W.M. War Medal, Govt. of Canada Long and Efficient Services Medal; [oth. writ.] Book of poems entitled Kaleidoscope, poem in Treasured Poems of America (Winter 1994), poem in Expressions, Iliad Press, poem in A Break in The Clouds, The National Library of Poetry.

HANNON-HALL, DENISE M.
[pen.] RIO; [b.] November 9, 1969, Bronx; [p.] Elizabeth and Richard Hannon; [m.] Daniel H. Hall, October 31, 1990; [ch.] Daniel Michael Hall, Jr.; [ed.] Preston High School; [occ.] Mail Operations Associate at Sony Music; [memb.] People For The Ethical Treatment of Animals, The Humane Society, The National Arbor Day Foundation, The World Wildlife Federation and The National Rifle Association;[hon.] Regents scholarship and Regents diploma; [oth.writ.] We Don't Know Each Other Anymore, If I Could See You Again; [pers.] My poetry is often written from my experiences and insights of life. My thoughts and ideas, when captured on paper are the basis of my works. [a.] Bronx, NY.

HANSEN, NICOLE RHEA
[pen.] Nicole Rhea Hansen; [b.] December 18, 1965, Frankfurt, Germany; [p.] Alan Hansen, Sofia Yarbrough, Becky Roser (adoptive mother); [m.] Single; [ed.] Fairview High School, Boulder, Co., 1 semester at North Carolina School of the Arts, Playhouse West, Los Angeles; [occ.] Actress, star of feature film, American Cyborg Steel Warrior; [memb.] Screen Actors Guild; [hon.] 1980 Gold Medal winner of Optimist Oratorical contest in Boulder, CO; [oth. writ.] Several poems with Angelic Themes; [pers.] My poetry reflects the irony, pain and hope I've experienced living and working as an actress in Los Angeles, "The City of Angels". [a.] Beverly Hills, CA.

HARAHAP, PANGKAT
[b.] May 23, 1921, Sumatra; [p.] Mangaraja Soripada (father) and (mother) Djomin; [m.] Sofia Malaon, July 23, 1956; [ch.] Isranja Harapah (lawyer) and Riza Harahap (Drs. Accountant); [ed.] Economics, Accountancy, Tax Consultant, writing school; [occ.] Tax Consultant, free lance writer; [memb.] Association of Indonesian Tax Consultants; [oth. writ.] Articles in magazines/Dailies, 1960 Foreign Correspondent in Vienna, Austria, 1956 Co-editor of the Dutch Encyclopedia Winkler Prins, Amsterdam, 1966-1970 Editor of various magazines in Brunei Darussalam; [pers.] I kindly invite poets/writers from other countries to correspond with me to exchange ideas and views and to enhance international friendship. [a.] Jakarta, Indonesia.

HARDIN, KAREN
[b.] May 3, Northport, AL; [p.] Mary L. Horton and Walter L. Hinton; [m.] Divorced; [ch.] Darrell Dwayne, Derrick Ray, Frank Elston and Anne Marie Hardin; [ed.] Los Angeles Trade Tech. College currently attending Los Angeles Southwest College, pursuing an Associate

Arts degree in Business, will graduate in the spring of 1994; [occ.] Head Clerk in the Department of Health Services, county of Los Angeles; [memb.] Member of the Inspirational Choir of Great Ebenezer Missionary Baptist Church, National Geographic Society; [hon.] Dean's List, Southwest College, Heartbeats is also published in an anthology entitled Expectations, Iliad Press c 1992, also published in the Los Angeles Sentinel, September 23,1993; [oth. writ.] I have a collection of poems in a book entitled Heartbeat that was copyrighted in March 1991, I am putting together another set of poems to be copyrighted; [pers.] My love for people and the desire to touch the lives of others has inspired me to write. My writings are filled with joy, pain, laughter and hope. I thank God for the insight to create words that flow from my heart thru the ink of my pen. I have written many poems, but my ultimate goal is to share the poem "Heartbeat" with as many people as possible (world). We may not be able to eliminate the homeless population, but we can make a difference and decrease the numbers substantially. Thank you for the opportunity to share and become a part of Dance On The Horizon. [a.] Los Angeles, CA.

HARDISON, SUNDA A.
[b.] June 21, 1916, Ashtabula, OH; [p.] Nick and Dolores Martello (deceased); [m.] Widow; [ch.] William J. Hardison; [ed.] Ashtabula High School, Cerritos Junior College (CA); [occ.] Retired former "secretary"; [memb.] Downey Committee on Aging, Downey Recreation Seniors, Firestone Retired Club, Board of Directors-Credit Union; [hon.] California State Senate in honor and recognition of extraordinary service and an unselfish commitment for helping others, received the same award for service from the California Legislature Committee, award for the C.U. newsletter in 1976; [oth.writ.] Newsletter for C.U. newsletter for my Firestone Retired Club, I have always enjoyed writing but have never submitted any writings prior to my poem. [a.] Downey, CA.

HARDY, BILLIE
[b.] December 31, 1933, San Antonio, TX; [m.] Dean Hardy, April 1, 1955; [ch.] Stacey Dawn Shuhan; [ed.] Graduated Aranasa Pass High, Aransas Pass, Texas; [occ.] Security Guard, Pinkerton.

HARGRAVE, JENNIE MELISSA REBECCA
[b.] August 6, 1980, Winipeg, Man; [p.] (Step-father) Robert Burdess and Barb Hargrave (father deceased); [ed.] Grade eight; [occ.] Student; [hon.] Most Improved grade seven; [pers.] I've been doing poetry since grade 4-9 years old, I am most interested in poetry by Robert Service and Robert Frost, and Emily Dickinson. [a.] Berwyn-Alta, Canada.

HARLOW, MICHAEL P.
[b.] February 17, 1975, Kansas City, MO; [p.] Robert K. and Kathleen A. Harlow; [ed.] St. John Francis Regis Grade School, Archbishop O'Hara High School, Creigton University; [occ.] Student, Creighton University; [memb.] B.A.C.C.H.U.S., Student Board of Governors Activity Committee, Teens Encounter Christ Religious Retreats; [oth. writ.] Several short stories and poems published in school publications and in a religious newsletter, Teen Encounter Christ newsletter; [pers.] Most of my work deals with love I've yearned for or lost, but as stated in my poem I will never give up trying to find that one true love out there for me. [a.] Kansas City, MO.

HARRIS III, JAMES GREGORY
[pen.] Greg Harris; [b.] November 28, 1958, Alton, IL; [m.] Pamela; [ch.] Samantha; [ed.] 2 years college; [occ.] Manager Used Car Dealership; [memb.] St. Louis Music Network; [hon.] 1993 St. Louis Music contest placed 2 of my original songs, 1 in the top 5 Blues Jazz category, 1 in the top 10 general category; [oth. writ.] I have an extensive catalog of poems, verse and original songs, as far as the music goes I write, arrange, sing and play on my own recordings; [pers.] My goals are to become a recognized poet and songwriter. [a.] Alton, IL.

HARRIS, KEYONA
[b.] November 16, 1983, Kalamazoo, MI; [p.] Jerry and Amanda Harris; [memb.] National Piano Guild; [hon.] Miss Princess Portage, top ten finisher at East Coast Pageant's regional pageant, Michigan Music Teacher Association Award winner, Superior Rating in International Composition contest, 1993 winner of Kalamazoo Poetry on Buses contest. [a.] Kalamazoo, MI.

HARRIS, LENA H.
[pen.] Afro-American Poet; [b.] December 25, 1926, Forest City, NC; [p.] Austin and Bertha Hamilton; [m.] Johnnie Harris (deceased), August 11, 1955; [ch.] Edward, Ellis and Le Andra; [ed.] Grad Grannard High School, Gaffney, SC, graduated Chicago School of Nursing P.N., attended Afro American Leaders Seminar; [occ.] Retired writer; [memb.] Church, Moores Chapel A.M.E. Zion, NAACP, National Council of Negro Women, Lincoln Arts Council, International Black Writers Conference; [hon.] Appeared on local TV Poetry Reading 1993 also local reading in elementary schools and churches, Mary McLeod Bethune Centennial 1975, NAACP Mother of The Year 1979, Lincoln County Human Relations 1993; [oth.writ.] Exp. published three books of poetry (1-1990), (2-1991), (3-1993); [pers.] This book is dedicated to all people in hope that through it some portion of wisdom will remain to touch us all. [a.] Lincolnton, NC.

HARRIS, MARIE T.
[pen.] Wanderer; [b.] July 13, 1905, Texas; [p.] Virgil H. and Martha A. Taylor; [m.] George F. Harris, January 2, 1926; [ed.] High school and Secretarial course (Vocational College); [occ.] Retired after several office jobs and 21 years in US Department Agriculture in Washington, DC; [memb.] Eastern Star, American Legion Auxiliary, Extension Homemakers, Central Christian Church; [hon.] Never "went public" with any verse or rhyme except a non-competitive "Poetry Corner" in a small town newspaper; [pers.] None submitted for publication except as mentioned, any writings done for my own satisfaction, generally on a nature theme; [pers.] It's a wonderful world that has been given us. Let's enjoy it and be thankful to God for the gift He has given us.

HARRIS, PAUL
[b.] April 24, 1970, Birmingham, England UK; [p.] Keith and Yvonne Harris; [ed.] University of Hertfordshire, Cranfield University; [occ.] Ph.D. student in Turbomachinery; [memb.] Royal Aeronautical Society, Institute of Mechanical Engineers; [hon.] Beng (Hons) Aerospace Engineering. [a.] Kempston, Beds., England UK.

HARRIS, ROBERT J.
[b.] March 6, 1973, Leavenworth, KS; [p.] William and Roberta Harris; [ed.] West Valley High School, Central Texas College; [occ.] United States Marine Landing Support Specialist; [pers.] If one state of mind is kept,

then opportunity remains unchallenged. [a.] Spokane, WA.

HARRISON, ELIZABETH
[b.] April 10, 1921, Kansas; [p.] Dorothy and Mortimer Yotes; [m.] Ralph C. Harrison, September 1953; [ch.] Emily, Cecily and Eleanor; [ed.] B.A. from UCLA; [occ.] Retired; [hon.] Oh, several first prizes from various writing clubs; [oth. writ.] More of the same, Religious Biographical Poetry, The Grand Duchess, a biographical novel, unpublished, Bobby Darling, unpublished Caroline's Child, unpublished; [pers.] This poems and others were printed in our little church newspaper. I have been trying to publish for years, just like everybody else, this is the nearest I've gotten. [a.] Anaheim, CA.

HARRISON, MARJORIE K.
[b.] February 9, 1912, Keystone, SD; [p.] H. A. Lyndoe and Louisa Carter; [m.] Lorin E. Harrison, June 1, 1935; [ch.] Lillian May, Lorine Margot (twins) and Craig Russell; [ed.] Pierre South Dakota Grade School and high school, Sioux Falls College, Sioux Falls, SD; [occ.] Retired; [memb.] United Church of Christ, husband, a retired minister; [oth.writ.] Four other poems, never entered; [pers.] Parents both born in England.[a.] Garrett, IN.

HARRISON, NATHANAEL P.S.
[b.] December 20, 1976, Youngstown, OH; [p.] Walter and Marian Harrison Jr.; [ed.] Sophomore at Schuykill Valley High School; [memb.] Belleman's Lutheran Church, Mohrsville, PA; [hon.] National Junior Honor Society; [pers.] I greatly enjoy art and photography and have only recently tried poetry as a creative art form. I find art to be an important way of expressing emotions. [a.] Breinigsville, PA.

HARRISON, R. ANDREW
[pen.] R. Andrew Harrison; [b.] March 13, 1971; [p.] Ralph and Joan Harrison; [ed.] Graduate of Salisbury State University, Bachelor of Science Degree; [occ.] Student; [oth.writ.] Several other selections not yet released; [pers.] One needs no material rewards to achieve the greatest one of all. Satisfaction! [a.] Salisbury, MD.

HARROFF, WILLIAM
[b.] November 20, 1953, Elkhart, IN; [p.] Walter and Elma Harroff; [ed.] Internationale Sommerakademie fur Bildende Kunst, diploma (1983), Indiana University, M.L.S. (1981), Purdue University, B.A. (1978); [occ.] Artist; [memb.] Center for Book Arts, Artists Book Works, Art St. Louis, Chicago Artist's Coalition and St. Louis Volunteer Lawyers and Accountants for the Arts (board member); [hon.] Art Matters, Inc. Fellowship, grants from Women's Studio Workshop, Regional Artists' Projects, Illinois Arts Council, SIA, Artists Space competition awards from ISBK, Artist's Magazine and Nepenthe Mundi; [oth. writ.] Staff writer for the Art St. Louis Publication, articles in Art Calendar, Art Papers, Chicago Artists' News, Estudio and MCAC Publication, poems in many of the same publications; [pers.] The two continuing influenced in my life are art and books. Together, they provide the motivation to find new methods of combining text and image. [a.] Edwardsville, IL.

HARRY, BEATRICE WELLS
[pen.] Hazel Bea; [b.] New York, NY; [p.] Plummer and Adaline Wells, Sr.; [ed.] Hunter College, New York,

NY, Long Island University, Brooklyn, NY; [occ.] Educational Evaluator, Committee on Special Education, Bronx, NY; [oth. writ.] Have a collection of unpublished poems; [pers.] My writings strive to reflect mankind's educational and spiritual advancement. [a.] New York, NY.

HARTMAN, ARLENE
[b.] September 30, 1938, Lancaster, PA; [p.] William and Elizabeth Hecker; [m.] Divorced; [ch.] Wendell, Bill and twins Karla and Darla; [ed.] Antelope Valley High School, Antelope Valley C.C. in Lancaster California; [occ.] Advisor Tech/Youth Program Worker, Great Oaks Village, Orlando, FL; [memb.] (Hobbies) Poetry, songwriting, singing, guitar, bowling, assorted crafts; [pers.] I consider myself a "people oriented" person. To aide and assist where I can, when I see a good man, I may try to emulate him, when I observe a bad one, I try to remember to search my own heart. [a.] Tavares, FL.

HARTWELL, WILLIAM T.
[b.] September 26, 1965, Spokane, WA; [p.] William G. Hartwell III and Linda Siverts; [m.] Better half, Lisa M. Hooper; [ed.] B.A. (1987), M.A. (1991) Anthropology Texas Tech University, Lubbock, TX; [occ.] Professional Archaeologist, Desert Research Institute, Las Vegas, NV; [memb.] Society of Professional Archaeologists, Society of American Archaeology, Plains Anthropological Society, Nevada Archaeological Association; [hon.] Pi Delta Phi, University Scholars Scholarship, Dean's List, Magna Cum Laude (1987) Academic All-American; [oth. writ.] Several articles dealing with archaeology in local, state, regional, national and international scientific journals; [pers.] Laugh for no apparent reason at least once a day! [a.] Las Vegas, NV.

HARVEY, DALE
[b.] June 10, 1976, Calgary, Alberta; [p.] Dan and Elizabeth Harvey; [ed.] Ladysmith Secondary School (grade 12); [occ.] Student; [oth.writ.] Short stories published in the "LSS Select". [a.] Ladysmith, BC.

HARVEY, SAMMYE JO
[b.] March 3, 1949, Amhurst, TX; [ch.] Jodie Hall, Bruce and Ronny Brown; [occ.] Councilor-Ten School for the Deaf; [oth.writ.] Many poems, virsital and short stories with Indian teachings; [pers.] American Indian decent worked with D.D. for 18 years (D.D, Developmental Disable). I strive to teach each, to find answers within, while seeing more than meet the eye. [a.] Knoxville, TN.

HASAL, GAUDENCIA CAMPANIA
[pen.] Gina Hasal; [b.] March 11, 1918, Manila, Philippine; [p.] Rosendo and Maria Salud Alumno; [m.] U.S.A. Retired Captain Diogenes B. Hasal; [ch.] Emmanuel, Emma H. Francisco and Edna H. Baca; [ed.] Torres High, Philippine School of Business, International Business College, self studies and Practical Nursing, Pharmacy, counseling, Psychology, law tutor for students; [occ.] Retired; [memb.] Retired Officers Association, The Retired Officers Foundation Inc., American Association of Retired Persons, Word For The World, International San Francisco Bay Area; [hon.] Prizes, Math and English compositions, honorable first place twice accelerated, (Manila, Philippines) (prizes all in cash form); [oth. writ.] Poems, local newspapers in Manila (narrative forms); [pers.] Inspired by all worldwide poets, writers, boundless love, respect for all laws, cultures, persons, preserve peace and Justice for All. I love operas, ballet, classic music-films. "Hacia Dios por

La Ciencia Y El Amor", (Principle in Life) America land of love and opportunities. [a.] Daly City, CA.

HASAN, SHAZIA
[b.] September 20, 1968, Karachi, Pakistan; [p.] Imtiaz and Nagina Hasan; [ed.] Karachi Grammar School, Institute of Children's Literature (CT, U.S.A.); [occ.] Free-lance writer; [oth. writ.] Articles published in newspapers; [pers.] I want to touch the hearts of my readers as well as well as awaken them to reality. My parents together with my two brothers and dog "Gypsy" have been greatly influenced in whatever success I have had so far. [a.] Karachi, Pakistan.

HASSELL, SUSAN
[pen.] Susan Hassell; [b.] August 15, 1979, Naples, FL; [p.] Jeff and Laura Lee Hassell; [ed.] The Community School of Naples (Florida); [occ.] Student; [memb.] Naples Players, Drama Club, Model United Nations; [hon.] Maxine Strayer Memorial Award (for leadership and good citizenship) '93, 8th grade Class President '92-'93; [oth. writ.] Write for my school's literary magazine; [pers.] I believe the greatest human virtue is to be true to yourself. [a.] Naples, FL.

HATCHER, VERA
[b.] January 10, 1955, Moscow, Russia; [p.] Ivan and Xenia Kondrachina; [m.] Stephen Hatcher, May 19, 1992; [ch.] Anna and Maria; [ed.] Moscow State University, Department of Philosophy, Department of Journalism; [occ.] Russian Instructor, Diplomatic Language Service, Arlington; [oth.writ.] Several poems and essays published in Russia and Russian newspaper "Novoe Russkoe Slovo" in the U.S.; [pers.] I try to listen to the strange, inaudible call signs, struggling to convert them into human language. I can do so only when I am awake of I think I am, and able to distinguish between "good and "bad" calls. [a.] Locust Grove, VA.

HAUPTMANN, JEAN-MARC
[pen.] J.M. Hauptmann; [b.] August 10, 1963, St. Avoild, France; [p.] Phillipe and Ginette Hauptmann; [ed.] Richlands High, Ipswich Taft College; [occ.] Unemployed; [oth. writ.] Small articles in Reader Forum, People Magazine and Sez You Picture Magazine; [pers.] My poems are based on any thing, topic, event that comes to mind at that time. [a.] Willowbank, Australlia.

HAVERKAMP, BRENT
[b.] December 11, 1964, Portland, OR; [p.] Elanore and Robert Bailey; [m.] Single; [ed.] University of Oregon, Churchill High School; [occ.] English Conversation Instructor (Pusan, Korea); [hon.] The Ben vonHipple Memorial Scholarship; [oth. writ.] Book for Asthmatic Children; [pers.] People have always warned others about the importance of living and feeling alive, seems few listen. Our reality is formed by our attitudes. Live life and conquer your fears before you die. EEE! [a.] Eugene, OR.

HAWKINS, ERNESTINE FEARS
[pen.] Stine; [b.] October 10, 1928, Leesburg, FL; [p.] Ernest D. and Juanita J. Fears; [m.] James Hawkins (div.); [ch.] Anita Elaine Hawkins; [ed.] Flordia A & M High School, Florida A & M University, Tallahassee, FL., Wayne State University, Detroit, MI.; [occ.] Detroit Board of Education (retired); [memb.] St. John's Episcopal Church, FAMU Alumni, ZOB Sorority, RTIN; [oth. writ.] Poems published in booklet "Just Thinking" by Sine for family members. [a.] Orlando, FL.

HAWKINS, WENDELL SEAN
[b.] June 4, 1963, Dallas, TX; [p.] Ruth Hawkins-Allen and John Henry Stevens; [m.] Shirley Smith-Hawkins, September 22, 1990; [ch.] Wendell Sean, Myesha Deriest and Kybron Sean; [ed.] V.T. Institute, Arts Magnet High School, Pearl C. Anderson Junior High, Joseph J. Rhoads Elementary, Paul L. Dunbar Elementary; [occ.] Business owner; [memb.] St. Philips Dad's Club, K-3 Chorus Parent's Committee; [hon.] Merit award 1988, Honorable Mention 1988, 1980 Sophomore Art Award, Pearl C. Anderson Art Student of the Year 1978, 100% Salesman Award; [oth. writ.] Ole, The Crash of 87, As The Day Goes By, As The Week Goes By, all published in 1988; [pers.] My poetry began as an expression of my everyday life. As the years progress, I fine myself writing more about the affects and directions of everyday life. [a.] Dallas, TX.

HAYES, BERTHA M.
[pen.] B. Addison; [b.] October 3, 1945, Glen Allan, MS; [p.] Demus and Amanda Addison; [m.] Ernest Hayes, October 16, 1967; [ch.] Craig D. Hayes and two grands D'ante Hayes and Nitna'ta; [ed.] Normal C'Obannor High, Malcolm X College (1 year), Dawson School (1 year); [occ.] Nursing as a Health Worker.

HAYES, THEODORE
[b.] May 27, 1962; [occ.] Culinarian; [oth. writ.] "Fifth of July" published by El Centro College; [pers.] I express male viewpoints in poetic form as well as highlight awareness of the unawareness that exists in the human condition. [a.] Dallas, TX.

HAYNES, DANNY
[b.] September 21, 1944, El Reno, OK; [p.] Boyd and Doris Haynes; [m.] Camilla Hayes, May 24, 1964; [ch.] Buffy Clayton and Burke Hayes; [ed.] B.S. from Phillips University, Enid, OK; [occ.] Hearing Aid Specialist; [memb.] International Hearing Society, Oklahoma Hearing Aid Association, Board of Directors at Willow Creek Golf and Country Club; [oth. writ.] Poem published in The Coming of Dawn. [a.] Oklahoma City, OK.

HAYNES, HATTIE MAE
[b.] November 24, 1937, Lovett, FL; [p.] JuRutha and Thomas Miller; [m.] The late Ulysses Haynes, September 1954; [ch.] Gwendolyn, Linda and Jacqueline Haynes; [ed.] High School; [occ.] Maid; [memb.] New Canaan Missionary Baptist Church; [pers.] I strive to live a christian life so it will motivate other people to do the same. [a.] Greenville, FL.

HAZI, HELEN MARIE
[pen.] Dazi; [b.] December 20, 1951, Pittsburgh; [p.] Julius Hazi and Helen (Rostosky); [ed.] South Park High School, B.A. (1971) M.Ed. (1975), Ph.D.(1980), University of Pittsburgh; [occ.] Associate Professor of Education Administration, West Virginia University; [memb.] State, National and International Educational Associations (AERA, ASCD, COPIS, WVASA, NOLPE); [hon.] B.A., Cum Laude, University of Pittsburgh, Who's Who of American Women 1983, Visiting Scholar, University of Wisconsin-Madison, National Endowment for the Humanities, 1985; [oth.writ.] 17 articles of chapters in educational journals and books, specializing in legal issues affecting instructional supervision; [pers.] This poem is dedicated to my parents and encouraging friends, like Deborah and Nelson. I promise more will bloom and collect in my bouquet, as they have since 6th grade. [a.] Morgantown, WV.

HEFFERNAN, LISA A.
[b.] August 3, 1970; [p.] D. Varanese and R. Heffernan; [ed.] University of Massachusetts at Amherst and University of Rhode Island; [occ.] Philosopher; [memb.] World Wildlife Fund, Lily Crown Society; [hon.] Golden Key National Honor Society, Phi Kappa Phi; [pers.] Influenced by Friedrich Nietzsche, Milan Kundera and Simone de Beauvoir ("Must We Burn Sade?"). [a.] Portsmouth, RI.

HEIL, SCOTT F.
[pers.] Writing is the greatest tool in the common man's arsenal. Used wisely, it furthers the human cause, used poorly or not at all, it is self-defeating. [a.] Ypsilanti, MI.

HEILPRIN, HAIM D. Ph.D.
[b.] October 2, 1954, Tiberias, Israel; [p.] Mordecay and Bat-Sheva Heilprin; [m.] Bat-Chen, August 11, 1992; [ch.] Shachaf and Moran; [ed.] Ph.D. in Psychology, State University of New York at Stony Brook, 1984; [occ.] Clinical Psychologist; [memb.] Numerous professional affiliations; [pers.] This poem is dedicated to J.N.B. [a.] Rishon Lezion, Israel.

HEIMANN, JENNIFER A.
[pen.] Jenn; [b.] March 25, 1980, Monroe, WI; [p.] Richard and Nancy Heimann; [ed.] 7th grade; [occ.] Student; [memb.] Girl Scouts, band, chorus, art; [hon.] Silver Award Girl Scouts, 2nd year chosen for National Library of Poetry; [oth. writ.] Short stories and other poems and my drawings that I will be showing in the Spring at Platteville Round Tree Gallery; [pers.] I would like to thank my English teacher, Mrs. Savatski and my classmates for helping me choose from all my poems "Honney" was to be my poem submitted. [a.] Darlington, WI.

HEITMANN, INGEBORG
[pen.] Helen ole Grahl; [b.] June 4, 1923, Germany; [p.] Johann and Helene Karl; [m.] Widow (Henry Heitmann), December 30, 1959; [ch.] Ingrid Dietlinde, (I like to say here, that I thank my daughter who types my poems in a rhythmical setting which compliments the rhythm of the universe); [occ.] Writing; [memb.] Member of a Literary Group; [oth. writ.] Poems published in a magazine in Germany, True Experiences, written in the form of short stories, not yet published; [pers.] Up to now, man is looking outside of himself for his good, this will never fulfill the longing of his soul. Only when he discovers that the source of life is within himself, that he is life itself, and discerns the beauty of his soul and knows this is a universal truth. The truth of all mankind, then peace will flood the earth and evil is no more. [a.] Nerang, Queensland, Anstnahia.

HEITMANN, RUSTY
[pen.] Lost Boy/Profit; [b.] September 14, 1977, Texas; [p.] Bobbie G. and James Puckett; [ed.] 10th grader; [memb.] Religion of Pagans; [oth. writ.] 92 different poems and one book all unpublished; [pers.] Life is just a flash don't blink. [a.] Houston, TX.

HELFESRIEDER, ALICE
[pen.] Alice Helfesrieder or A.C. Helfesrieder; [p.] David and Elizabeth Kuhn; [m.] Fred C. Helfesrieder, March 20, 1942; [ed.] Some university, Fine Arts School, Washington University, figure, portraiture, scenic painting and sculpture, accounting and advertising; [occ.] Retired; [memb.] Lifetime member in International Society of Poets, AARP; [hon.] 1993, $100 International Society of Poets; [oth. writ.] My novel,

Flying Quarterback, will be out in 1994 and it contains my poem "Radiance", I have several manuscripts on my desk along with miscellaneous poems; [pers.] Except and respect humanity and worldwide creation. [a.] Florissant, MO.

HELMS, JUDY A.
[b.] March 21, 1948, Greensboro, NC; [m.] Engaged to the most wonderful man in the world; [ed.] Associate Degree in Nursing, 1969 from CPCC; [occ.] Registered Nurse in Neonatal Intensive Care Nursery at Carolinas Medical Center; [oth. writ.] Several poems published in family support magazines and one for Carolina Assoc. of Neonatal Nurses; [pers.] My biggest accomplishment in life is that I am in remission 1 1/2 years after chemotherapy for Leukemia. I started writing poetry after my treatment. I am very proud that I have written work that will be here after I am gone. [a.] Clover, SC.

HELTON, SUSAN
[b.] June 14, 1965, Denver, CO; [p.] Philip and Ruth; [m.] K. Mark Helton, May 22, 1993; [ed.] University of Denver; [memb.] Dobro Slovo-Slavic National Honor Society; [hon.] Phi Beta Kappa; [oth. writ.] I have been writing since high school, this is my first piece to be published.

HEMPEL, HELENE
[b.] December 2, 1935, France, Paris; [p.] Salomon and Blanghe Cynamon; [m.] Divorced; [ch.] Linda Hempel Braun; [ed.] Lycee Charlemagne, Paris, France; [occ.] Tutor of French Language privately; [pers.] I started to write for my own enjoyment, my sensitivity is guiding my pen. [a.] Cedarhurst, NY.

HENDERSON, FAYE McBEE
[pen.] Faye McBee Henderson; [b.] June 4, 1949, Gaffney, SC; [p.] Romeo and Ellaney McBee; [m.] Marshall Henderson, January 20, 1969; [ch.] Mike Henderson (February 1, 1969); [ed.] Graduated Gaffney Senior High 1967; [occ.] Cashier McDonald's Drive-thru, Gaffney, SC; [hon.] Christmas Magic printed in Gaffney Weekly Ledger 1992, published in National Library of Poetry, 1993, poems printed in Weekly Ledger, My Heart Cries in The Night; [oth. writ.] My Ole Cat, Jesus The Good Shepherd, God Doesn't Heal Us All, There's A Road, When God Made Angels; [pers.] Poems come from the heart. Everyone has a poem within them, a poem is very special, a beautiful way to express ourselves. [a.] Gaffney, SC.

HENDERSON, LISA
[pen.] Michel Love; [b.] January 5, 1966, Oklahoma City, OK; [p.] Harrietta Houston; [ch.] Christin and Alisha Pennington; [ed.] Oklahoma Junior College, Computer Science Computer Programmer, A.A.; [occ.] Self-employment; [hon.] Who's Who of American Junior College; [pers.] Writing for me is an enjoyment, my writing comes from my thoughts and feeling from within my heart and mind and in hopes it becomes someone else is enjoyment. [a.] Oklahoma, OK.

HENDERSON, SHARON REE
[b.] August 2, 1951, High Point, NC; [p.] V.F. Linthicum and Evelyn C. Howell; [m.] Divorced; [ch.] James R. Henderson V; [ed.] Graduate Old Dominion University, Norfolk, Virginia an English major; [occ.] Counselor, Adult Day Care Center, Norfolk, VA., prior employment English instructor at National Business College, Bluefield, WV; [memb.] YWCA, Trinity Friends Church, Martinsville, Virginia; [hon.] Won prize in Irene-Leach

Literary contest, Virginia Beach, VA.

HENDERSON, VADA MAE
[b.] April 27, 1942, Marshall, CO.; [p.] John and Bonnie Butler (deceased); [m.] William Owen Henderson, May 4, 1959; [ch.] Owen Randy, Ronda Lavada, Zelda Marvis and Rebecca Faye; [ed.] 8th grade, Aurora School; [occ.] Farmwife; [pers.] I always want to write my poem's funny, but most of the time I do true ones, the ones from my heart, some make you happy and some make you cry. I have written them from a little girl of 7 years old and have also written songs. [a.] Hardin, KY.

HENDRICKS, ANNE E.
[b.] October 1944, Colorado; [occ.] Pen and ink artist, illustrator; [a.] Reading, VT.

HENDERICKS, GREGORY
[b.] October 17, 1979, Brooklyn, NY; [p.] Joseph and Ann Hendricks; [ed.] James Madison High School; [occ.] Student; [memb.] American Youth Soccer Organization (AYSO), North Highway Little League Baseball; [hon.] Parents Association Award for character and worthiness, June 8, 1993, Shell Banks Intermediate School 14, Honor Roll, Shell Bank Intermediate School 14, April 15, 1991; [pers.] My mind works like a rainbow, shades of colors just like shades of thoughts blending to enhance my poetry. [a.] Brooklyn, NY.

HENGEMUEHLER, BETTY
[pen.] Betty Hengemuehler; [b.] October 27, 1939, Kenosha, WI; [p.] Gerald Laughlin (deceased) and Rose Mosse; [m.] Divorced; [ch.] Edward Henry, Julie Ann and Joseph Patrick; [ed.] College of St. Scholastic, Briar Cliff College, Morningside College, University of Missouri, St. Louis; [occ.] Owner/editor, The Platinum Palate, community volunteer; [memb.] Women's Committee, Forest Park Forever, Coro Women in Leadership Alumnae; [hon.] Trustee, Sioux City, IA, Public Library, Trustee, Sioux Trails Girl Scouts Council, Service Award, Missouri Baptist Medical Center, Editor, The Platinum Palate Subscription Series, cookbook in progress; [pers.] The poem keys is dedicated to Jeter Thompson, my best friend and an outstanding jazz pianist and composer. [a.] St. Louis, MO.

HENNIES, VICKI
[b.] July 24, 1949, Lexington, KY; [p.] Mr. and Mrs. Charles Nichols, Jr.; [m.] A. Fred Hennies III, April 10, 1970; [ch.] Mark and Nicholas Hennies; [ed.] Bryan Station High School, University of Kentucky, Lexington, KY; [occ.] Reading Instructor, Watterson Elementary, Louisville, KY; [pers.] My poetry has been influenced by my dad, Charles Nichols, Jr., his appreciation and love of poetry inspired me to write. Through my poetry I have entered a journey of self. [a.] Louisville, KY.

HENNING, HEATHER YVONNE VERONICA
[b.] Banbridge; [p.] John and Florence Henning; [ed.] Banbridge Academy, Stranmillis Teachers Training College, Belfast; [occ.] School teacher and speech and drama teacher; [memb.] Trinity College of Music, Speech and Drama Guild, London; [hon.] Diploma in Education, ATCL (Associate Member of Trinity College, London), HONGSM (Honoary Guild Society member); [oth. writ.] Children's stories, short adult stories and poetry; [pers.] It gives me joy to share life's experiences through a carefully selected choice of words. [a.] Banbridge, N. Ireland.

HENRY, DICK O.
[pen.] Dick O. Henry; [b.] August 17, 1923, Waterloo, IA; [p.] George and Stella Henry; [p.] Gale Louise Oler, July 28, 1983; [ch.] Stella 9, Ben 7, 3 sons by previous marriage, Randy, Michael and Mark; [ed.] Graduated Janesville High in Janesville, IA., went 2 years at ISU, Ames, Iowa; [occ.] I'm a security guard for Pinkerton Guard Service; [hon.] Minor role in the movie "Country" starring Jessica Lang, also in a TV commercial advertising for a newspaper, fought on Iwo Jima in World War II; [oth. writ.] Had a poem published in a magazine called "Reflections"; [pers.] I believe in putting forth my best effort at all times, if a thing is worth doing, its worth doing well. [a.] Parkersburg, IA.

HERMAN, JEAN HULL
[m.] C. William Herman; [occ.] Editor of Mobius, The Poetry Magazine;

HERMAN, MINNIE
[b.] July 18, 1917, Clif, CO; [p.] Deceased; [m.] Deceased (December 10, 1970), December 26, 1940; [ch.] Charles and Geraldine, 3 granddaughters Deborrah, Tamara and Jennifer; [occ.] Retired, travelling; [memb.] Thoman's Aglow Lutheran Church; [oth. writ.] Working on "Miracle" Journal's, God Really Loves To Take Care of Us, but says I Will be "Exalted" the stories are many, but need to be disciplined; [pers.] Travelled to Jerusalem, Holy City etc., where God revealed that He was "Rock" and sets His people on solid rock ground. 1985 China Crusade, Hualien, Hong Kong, Canton, 1988 Russia, Moscow, Volgograd St. Petersburg, mission and now a poem accepted, God is good. [a.] Scottsdale, AZ.

HERNANDEZ, DIMAS
[b.] June 15, 1963, Brooklyn, NY; [p.] Jose Hernandez and Maria Gerena; [m.] Norma I. Vargas, September 28, 1990; [ch.] Inesa Hernandez; [ed.] Eastern District High School, World Trade Institute; [occ.] Occupied with my love for Hashem; [memb.] As Grouch Marx had once said I will not belong to any club that would accept me as a one of its members; [hon.] Honor Hasem, Avinu She'ba Shamayim Awards that I have been given in my life are my loving wife and daughter Inesa, as well as my parents, brothers and Rabbi Avraham Goldstein; [oth. writ.] A family portrait, Happy Land, Welcome to America, En El Barrio, El Morro, La tierra; [pers.] Baruch Hashem.

HERNANDEZ, JENNIFER
[b.] January 18, 1979, Brooklyn, NY; [p.] Jose M. and Digna Hernandez; [sib.] Valerie and Krystal Hernandez; [ed.] St. Mary's Sacred Heart, Central Catholic High School, (freshman); [oth. writ.] Another poem published by Pacific Rim Publications in Quest of A Dream; [pers.] My family and friends feel very good of me that at my age 14, I am honored to have my poems published. I thank you very much. [a.] Allentown, PA.

HERRERA, EUFRACINA ISABEL
[b.] August 20, 1965, Piedras Negras, Coahuila, Mexico; [p.] Maria and Marcos Perez; [m.] Victor C. Herrera, November 10, 1984; [ed.] Reagan High School, Durham Business College; [occ.] Administrative Assistant, Department of Advertising, University of Texas at Austin; [hon.] Golden Poet 1991; [oth. writ.] Poem published in Poets of Our Time; [pers.] Dedicado, con amor, para Papa Carlos y Roly, nunca los olvidaremos. [a.] Austin, TX.

HERRICK, KATHY L.
[b.] October 10, 1951, Lansing, MI; [p.] Paul and Mary Ellen Richards; [m.] Tom, December 21, 1974; [ch.] Richard (1-11-76) twins, Joseph and Benjamin (9-27-80); [ed.] High school, Mason High (MI), BA-Michigan State University, MA-Western Michigan University; [occ.] Teacher, elementary, Douglas Elementary, Saugatuck, MI.; [memb.] First United Meth. Church, Saugatuck Teacher's Association, Ottawa Area School District, Writing Cadre, Holland Area Mother of Twins; [hon.] National Honor Society, BA with honors, won local writing contest, Chairman of Ottawa County's Writing It's Elementary at Hope College; [oth. writ.] Several pieces in local paper; [pers.] Writing has been my therapist, just the cost of a pencil and paper! [a.] Holland, MI.

HERRING, JEREMY SCOTT
[b.] January 3, 1974, Jacksonville, FL; [p.] Mel and Vivian Herring; [ed.] Whiteville High School, now in second year at East Carolina University; [hon.] Several 1st, 2nd, 3rd place awards in Columbus County Art contests, David Bessent Memorial Art Scholarship recipient; [pers.] There is so great the number of possibilities in such a short lifetime. [a.] Whiteville, NC.

HERRON, ARLENE
[b.] October 11, 1937; [m.] Widowed; [ch.] Michael Alan; [occ.] Retired, Los Angeles County Social Services worker; [pers.] I have many profound and beautiful thoughts. At times I am inspired to put them on paper and I am surprised at how they come together as poetry. [a.] Culver City, CA.

HESS, DANA ELAINE
[b.] March 28, 1966, Darby, Delaware Co., Penn; [p.] Raymond J. and Dana E. Hess; [ch.] Destiny Dana Hess, 3 years old; [ed.] High school, Modeling School, John Barth Casting Acting School; [occ.] Writing more poems and I paint watercolors; [hon.] Jo Anderson Charm and Modeling School/Adult Charm and Basic Self Improvement Award, 3 Citizenship Awards, 1 Youthfitness Award, 2nd place ribbon for the 800 Meter Run; [oth. writ.] I have about 12 other poems I wrote myself; [pers.] I have been writing poems since I was 13 years old, I have my health teacher Mr. Keys to thank, he showed me how to write my feelings on paper. [a.] Blackwood, NJ.

HESTER, ALTA
[b.] March 7, 1944, Morrilton, AR; [p.] Dan and Alma Potter; [m.] Wilbur Hester, October 10, 1981; [ch.] Treasa Dunnahoe; [ed.] Dermott High School, Petit Jean Vo-Tech College, licensed Nursing Home Administrator; [occ.] Nurse in Geriatrics; [oth. writ.] True Love and Memories; [pers.] "Angel of Death" my first poem was written from experiences in Geriatric Nursing and in memory of those forgotten elderly. [a.] Danville, AR.

HESTER, BRENDA JOYCE
[pen.] B. Joyce Hester; [pers.] From God comes love, from love comes peace, from peace comes creativity and creativity is God's love in me.

HICKEY, TODD JAMES
[pen.] H.T.J.; [b.] December 16, 1970, Corner Brook, Nfld; [p.] James and Doris Hickey; [ed.] Regina High School, Memorial University of Newfoundland; [occ.] Flight Service Specialist, Transport Canada; [memb.] Canadian Association of Professional Radio Operators, Gander and Area Literacy Coalition; [oth. writ.] Small collection of poems, several poems published in Univer-

sity Newspaper; [pers.] I feel words flow easier on paper than in conversation and carry more meaning. Being a parent is as close being a God as you can get. [a.] Gander, Newfoundland.

HIERHOLZER, BEVERLY
[pen.] Beverly Kay; [b.] September 3, 1948, Sharon, PA; [p.] Margaret and Robert Henning; [m.] James Hierholzer, June 24, 1989; [ch.] Tiffanie, Heidi and John; [ed.] Farrell High , Wright State; [occ.] Library Aide; [memb.] Christ United Methodist Church, Ohio Library Association; [oth. writ.] Feature story, articles published in local newspapers, op-ed articles, authored children's plays for Girl Scouts; [pers.] Aware of the class boundaries that fracture the world and destroy the spirit, I sometimes write humorously sometimes candidly and sometimes inspirationally with the hope of encouraging equally. [a.] Kettering, OH.

HIGAREDA, JOSEPH
[pen.] Joe Higgs Perez; [b.] Weslaco, TX; [p.] Angeline and Joseph Higareda; [ed.] Truman College, National-Louis University; [occ.] Proofreader; [hon.] Phi Theta Kappa, Dean's List; [oth. writ.] Poems, photography, news articles, analyses, commentaries in Alternate Press newspapers and magazines; [pers.] Stop dreaming-DO IT! [a.] Chicago, IL.

HILL, AKIL
[b.] May 18, 1976, Tokyo, Japan; [p.] William and Jacquelyn Hill; [ed.] Santa Barbara High School; [occ.] Karate teacher; [memb.] Black Student Union, United Youth Empower, Omega Boys and Girls Club, S.O.A.R., Students Organize Against Racism, Big Brother, Upward Bound, P.B.M. Positive Black Men; [oth. writ.] Written a couple of Editorials to the newspaper, written in teen newspaper, wrote a play and put it on in front of others; [pers.] "I am you and you are me, life is too short to be uneducated". [a.] Santa Barbara, CA.

HILL, CHRISTINA MARIE
[pen.] Christy Hill; [b.] July 17, 1979, Wolfeboro, NH; [p.] James W. and Dorothy S. Hill; [ed.] Carpenter School (grades K-6), Wolfeboro, NH., Moultonborough Academy (grades 7 & 8) Moultonborough, NH; [memb.] Girl Scouts, Civil Air Patrol, Center Harbor Christian Church; [hon.] President;s Academic Fitness Award (grade 6), Academic Achievement Award for highest grade point average (grade 7); [oth.writ.] Poems and short stories published in school newspapers, poems published in church monthly newsletter, short stories and poems published in youth magazine; [pers.] "Age has nothing to do with talent". [a] Moultonborough, NH.

HILL, EILEEN F.
[b.] May 31, 1967, Rockford, IL; [p.] Mary and Lavell Owen; [m.] Alton R. Hill, April 28, 1986; [ch.] Anna Kathleen, Mary Lynn, Richard Lavell and Kathleen Elizabeth; [ed.] All my education past high school was given to me through the U.S. Army 1985-1991; [occ.] Orthopedic Technician, Resident Assistant; [oth. writ.] I have written 2 books for juveniles that have not yet been published, "Coming Home", "One Last Tear"; [pers.] Without my wonderful husband and 4 beautiful children, I would not have the confidence to write. Without my 2 best friends in the whole world, my sister Bridget and my mama, I would never know how to use that confidence. Thanks to all. [a.] Whites Creek, TN.

HILL, ROBIN
[pen.] Robin Hill; [b.] February 5, 1961, Winston-Salem, NC; [p.] Peggy and Robert Butner; [m.] Randy Hill, June 30, 1990; [ch.] Amanda Christine and Christin Nicole Hill; [ed.] High school (1-12); [occ.] Mother, housewife; [oth. writ.] Several poems written for gospel tracts and for handicapped children; [pers.] I strive to reflect the love of God to all mankind in my writings, some poems I have written have been inspired by my baby daughter, whom God is working a miracle in everyday. [a.] Pilot-Mountain, NC.

HILL, SHIRLEY J.
[pen.] Mercy's Child; [b.] April 21, 1935, Ohsweken, Ontario; [p.] Roy and Frances Hill; [m.] Rev. Donald F. Hill, May 2, 1953; [ch.] Yvonne, Randell, Darryl, Rod, Renee, Vickie and Little Darryl; [ed.] Hutch Tech, Blfo, Brock University St. Cath. Ontario; [occ.] Visual artist; [pers.] I must be true to my own heart and vision as a writer and an artist, most frequently I write from a SPIRITUAL point of view and so I make sure that my feet stay on the ground of Earth's Reality too. My goal is to proclaim Health and Victory. Spiritually, mentally, emotionally and physically... ON GOING with determination with a focus on the weary and hopeless. I like fun too, hope I'm not always too serious.

HILTON, BRANDY
[b.] February 7, 1977, Charlotte, NC; [p.] David and Deborah Hilton; [m.] Single; [ed.] Now attending Independence High School (junior); [oth. writ.] I have a large personal collection of poems I hope to be published in the near future; [pers.] I dedicate all my poems to my friends and family, especially my mom that encouraged me and didn't mind me reading my poems over and over. [a.] Charlotte, NC.

HINSON, DAVID
[b.] May 12, 1957, Augusta, GA; [p.] Donald and Joyce Hinson; [ch.] Jennifer and Vanessa Hinson; [ed.] Gateway High School, Community College of Aurora, Vo-Tech Water Distribution, University of Colorado; [occ.] Heavy Equipment Operator; [oth. writ.] My Best Friend, and Jody, originally written as songs; [pers.] I like to write things that we can all relate to and laugh at and hope it brings enjoyment to someone. I hope to hear my other writings as songs one day. [a.] Aurora, CO.

HINTON, JACQUELYN
[b.] June 10, 1941, San Antonio, TX; [p.] Jack and Juanita Watts; [m.] Gregory Hinton, October 1, 1982; [ch.] Joseph and Jim Harrel, Veronica and Gregory Hinton, Jr.; [ed.] Southwestern University-B.S., National Louis University-M.Ed.; [occ.] Teacher, English, Ramstein Junior High School, Ramstein, Germany; [memb.] National State Teachers of the Year, Kappa Delta Pi, International Honor Society in Education, National Council of Teacher's of English, National Education Association; [hon.] Department of Defense Worldwide Teacher of the Year, 1992; [oth. writ.] Poems and articles in various journals, magazines, anthologies and curriculum guides; [pers.] "Assume a virtue if you have it not"-William Shakespeare. [a.] Ramstein, Germany.

HIRON, ANTHONY
[pen.] Anthony Hiron; [b.] March 13, 1978, Putaruru, NZ; [p.] Mary and Peter Hiron; [ed.] Cambridge St. School Primary (Pututatu), Putaruru Intermediate, Saint Peters School Cambridge, currently Cambridge High School; [occ.] Student; [hon.] 1993 5th form English prize (Cambridge High School); [oth. writ.] Collection of 21 original poems; [pers.] There's a legend in the suburbs of everybodies mind. [a.] Cambridge, NZ.

HIRTH, AMIE
[b.] August 16, 1979, Evanston, IL; [p.] Peggy and the late Bill (William) Hirth; [ed.] Freshman in Good Counsel High School; [occ.] Student/child; [pers.] I wrote this to show people what my dad was like after he died at the age of 42. [a.] Chicago, IL.

HIRTH, SHIRLEY ANN
[b.] March 13, 1992, St. Louis, MO; [p.] Emil W. and Irene M. Hirth; [m.] Divorced from William S. Woodress (now deceased), February 13, 1967; [ed.] Clayton High School, Rubicam Business School and Boedecker Conservatory of Music (graduate Pianist at 14); [occ.] Retired from Nooney Company, R.E. Inv. and PPTY Mgrs. - 1983; [memb.] Past member of Beta Sigma Phi Sorority, attend Kirkwood Christian Science Church, Angel Collector;s Club of America, was very active in the U.S.O. during World War II; [hon.] I won $2550 in a local merchandise contest in 1969 by writing a poem, it was sponsored by the merchants of Clayton and Ladue, suburbs of St. Louis, have won several small contest by writing "Why I Like", etc., recently submitted a letter to out post-dispatch which was printed, no award just the thrill of seeing my article and name in print and many memorable letters during the years; [pers.] I believe I should have seriously pursued writing and had I gone to college, I would have specialized in Journalism. Everyone has told me I should have been a writer. [a.] Kirkwood (St. Louis County), MO.

HIRTH, TRACEY
[b.] January 26, 1982, Evanston, IL; [p.] Peggy and the late Bill Hirth; [ed.] I am in the 6th grade; [occ.] Student/child; [pers.] This poem was written because my father died suddenly at the age of 42, mom wanted us to write our feelings in the form of poetry. This is just one of many. [a.] Chicago, IL.

HNIDY, NATASHA
[pen.] Tasha Lea; [b.] May 23, 1979, Wakaw Hospital, SK; [p.] Glenn and Lorraine Hnidy; [ed.] In grade 9 and charm modeling school; [hon.] Medals for figure skating and provincial volleyball, academic certificates, diploma in charm/modeling school; [oth. writ.] Poems and short stories; [pers.] My poems allow me to experience different worlds without moving anywhere. I write little words with great meaning. [a.] Wakaw, SK.

HOBSON, WHITTONIA MARIA
[pen.] Whitty; [b.] February 18, 1955, St. Louis, MO; [p.] Whittonia Evans; [ed.] Crenshaw High School, Dominquez Hills State University; [occ.] Special Education Reading/Language Instructor; [memb.] Rose of Sharon Baptist Church, Agape Christian Retreat and Conference Center, Future Business Leaders of America; [hon.] Future Business Leaders of America, Toastmasters of America, Debate Teams, Speech Teams; [oth. writ.] Several short plays written and performed, poetry journals; [pers.] In my poetic writings it is my wish to delight, encourage, uplift and inspire my readers. No matter how difficult a time Still I Rise a piece written by my mentor Maya Angelo. [a.] Los Angeles, CA.

HODGEN, HEATHER TERESE
[b.] December 8, 1974, Medina, OH; [p.]] Thomas and Dawn Hodgen; [ed.] Cheyenne Central High School, '93 graduate and a student at Laramie County Community College; [occ.] Full-time student at Laramie County Community College; [memb.] J.R.O.T.C., Girl Scouts

of America, P.E.A.K. Wellness Center; [hon.] Bronze Congressional Award, Gold Leadership/Gold Award Girl Scouts, Who's Who Among American High School Students (3 times), U.S. Recruiting Command's Team-work Award, '93 participant to the Wyoming Game and Fish Youth Conservation Camp, finalist in the Josten's National Leadership Award/scholarship, Wyoming Game Wardens' Scholarship, Wyoming Congress of Parents and Teachers Association Scholarship, Laramie County Community College Student Ambassador Scholarship. [a.] Cheyenne, WY.

HODGINS, SHAMA
[pen.] Shama Shad; [b.] January 14, 1963, Pakistan; [p.] Ikram and Lily Shad; [m.] Dale Hodgins, July 22, 1986; [ch.] Melissa (age 5); [ed.] Mack School of Nursing (St. Catharines, Ontario); [occ.] Nurse; [memb.] Spark Leader, Foster Parent; [oth. writ.] I have a collection of poems that I have written over the years, each poem reflects my own personal experiences; [pers.] To love and be loved is what really counts in this life of yours and mine. [a.] Ladysmith, BC Canada.

HOFFMAN II, DANIEL A.
[pen.] Aloyisuis Hoffman; [b.] March 21, 1914, Phila-delphia, PA; [p.] Daneil A. Sr. and May A. (nee Davis); [m.] Katherine F. Hoffman, November 9, 1940; [ch.] Daniel III and Drew H.; [ed.] MS and 3 years college, 4 years extended math courses; [occ.] Journeyman Industrial Electrician 12 years, Sales Engineer Industrial Pur. Transmission 30 years; [memb.] Toomany, active member Republican Party; [hon.] Married 53 years; [oth. writ.] None published unless letters to the Editor counts; [pers.] ALl delinquent kids are the result of 2 delinquent adults, man should love fellowman first, then God Second, for survival! [a.] Springfield, PA.

HOFFMAN, ILANA
[b.] 1992, Hungary; [p.] Zoltan and Blanka Revesz; [m.] Divorced, 1950; [ch.] Arye (43) and Batsheva (39); [ed.] High school; [occ.] Pensioner; [oth. writ.] Very short, short stories with a twisted end; [pers.] As I divorced after 33 years at the age of 60, I have my award and thank you for asking. [a.] Naharia, Israel.

HOFFMAN, JANOAN S.
[b.] April 29, 1923, Oil City, PA; [m.] Allan V. Hoffman, May 1, 1954; [ch.[Carolee H. Morritt, grandchildren, Genevieve and Robert Morritt; [ed.] Associate B.S., Penn Hall Junior College, courses at Purdue University and Clarion State University; [occ.] Owner of Quo Vadis B & B, Franklin, PA; [pers.] I just express my thoughts and observations. You can do a lot of thinking in a cold barn. [a.] Franklin, PA.

HOFFMAN, PETER
[b.] July 28, 1961, Heidelberg; [p.] Herbert and Irene Hoffman; [ed.] High school Walldorf Trade School, Heidelberg; [occ.] Managing Director, ARC Music Hamburg; [memb.] Who is Who , Germany, IAS, International Association of Scientologist, Citizen Com-mission of Human Rights Germany; [oth. writ.] About 120 poems written not yet published; [pers.] My writing style is from high, aesthetic level down to "bad boy" talking, very simple to understand when you read my poems you know "Thats Life", influenced by Heinz Ehrhardt and Christian Morgenstern. [a.] Hamburh, BRD.

HOFFMAN JR., R. M.
[b.] June 16, 1972, Queens, NY; [p.] R.M. Hoffman Sr. and Patricia Marine; [ed.] John Adams High, Kingsborough Community College; [occ.] Guitar Luthier,

Autobody Repair; [hon.] Frieda T. Gallun Award for French, Greenberg Memorial Art Award, Dean's List; [oth. writ.] Several poems due to be published; [pers.] Life is my greatest source of information. [a.] Ozone Park, NY.

HOFSTETTER, STORY
[b.] January 19, 1978, Pasadena; [p.] Thomas and Jamie Hofstetter; [ed.] Currently in tenth grade at Alief Hastings High; [occ.] Young domestic Goddess; [memb.] Mem-ber of the Alief Hastings Players (theatre); [hon.] 1st place in school poetry contest in 1991, first attempt at showing my poems; [oth. writ.] I have many others but this is my first to be published, I'm real private with my work; [pers.] I believe that everyone has the ability to create meaningful poetry, anyone who has experienced a feeling deeply has created poetry. [a.] Houston, TX.

HOGAN, HOLLY
[b.] August 7, 1980, Bowling Green, OH; [p.] William and Sally Hogan; [ed.] 1993-94 7th and 8th grade at St. Isabella School; [memb.] Volunteer center of Marin's Youth Connection, Yearbook Editor, Student Council, Special Olympics, writer for Fast Forward newspaper; [hon.] President's Youth Service Award, speech tourna-ment (1st, 1st, 3rd), Gold Award winner for Academic Excellence (Redwood Empire Pop Warner); [oth.writ.] Writes Press Releases for Youth Connection, many have been published, writer for Fast Forward newspaper; [pers.] The world is growing colder every minute, don't become part of it. [a.] Rafael, CA.

HOGNER, KRISTIN J.
[pen.] Kristin Richards; [b.] August 2, 1969, Chicago; [p.] Sharon and Pete Munoz; [m.] Eric Hogner, July 30, 1992; [ch.] Cody (1 year); [ed.] Newart Memorial High School, Ohlone College, Fremont, CA.; [occ.] Cashier; [oth. writ.] Several poetry writings, short stories; [pers.] I try to find beauty in the most strangest of places and then in generous spirit give it back to the world to do with it as they wish. [a.] Kings Beach, CA.

HOLDER, ROGER A.
[pen.] Roger A. Holder; [b.] October 17, 1957, Barba-dos; [p.] Muriel Holder and Charles Clark; [ch.] Amanda Holder; [ed.] New York Technical College, NY, Parkinson Secondary, Barbados; [occ.] Clerk; [oth. writ.] Several unpublished poems; [pers.] My poetry is me, it comes from within me. I write what I feel and see and hear. Most people can identify with what I write, reality. I'm a people person. [a.] Brooklyn, NY.

HOLDERREAD, JOHN R.
[b.] June 3, 1943, Springfield, IL; [p.] Fred and Marcella and Cora Holderread; [m.] Divorced; [ch.] Jon, Carrie, Allison, Joe and Amy; [ed.] High school graduate, Vietnam Era Veteran; [occ.] Quality, Productivity Man-agement Consulting; [memb.] Association for Quality Participation; [hon.] Past President/co-founder of the Houston Inventors Association; [oth. writ.] A presenta-tion made on my behalf to President Clinton, Vice President Gore and Ron Brown recommending a change America Foundation be formed in order to do a National Legislative Quality Improvement Program; [pers.] I would like all people on this planet to realize there is no separation from our source... we are spiritual beings, encased in a body, to continue "creation" be it good or bad, our Father gave us, free will, His greatest gift to us. [a.] Houston, TX.

HOLGUIN, JUNE
[b.] May 30, 1926, England; [p.] George and Hilda

Barker; [m.] Victor M. Holguin, March 19, 1947; [ch.] Veron G. and David V. Holguin; [ed.] Educated in England; [occ.] Housewife; [pers.] It is with memories of my sons of which I write, I also love to read. I met my husband at the American Red Cross, where I was a hostess. He was with the 101st U.S. Airborn Division, and we have been married 47 years. I came to America January, 1947. [a.] Houston, TX.

HOLLAND, BARBARA
[b.] August 2, 1934, Sydney; [p.] Ethel East and Samuel Hall; [m.] (Late) Leonard Holland, October 24, 1953; [ch.] Alan Jon (d.1973), Nita Marie (d.1957) and Danuel (d.1981); [ed.] Leonie-Ann and Michael Christian Hornsby High School, Sydney, Australia; [occ.] Re-tired, Credit Manager, interests, antiques, oil painting and researching Aust. early History; [memb.] Leisure Coast Ladies Probus Club Inc. (for retired professional women), Justice of The Peace in the State of New South Wales, Australia; [oth.writ.] Published book ISNB 0-646-16824-X, From The Bay To the Border, a history of ancestor settlers; [pers.] I endeavour to portray those human experiences and emotions that are most heart-felt, rather than discussed openly being comparable to the muse of nature. [a.] Wollongong, Australia.

HOLLAND, MARK ANDREW
[pen.] The Mad Monk; [b.] April 12, 1962, New Hartford, NY; [p.] Ralph Edward and Barbara J.W. Holland; [m.] Single; [ed.] Clear Creek High, San Jacinto Junior College, National Radio Institute; [occ.] CEO/Mad Monk and Associates; [memb.] Phi Theta Kappa, National Honor Fraternity (former), National Radio Institute, Washington, DC., and Worldwide Reg-istry for Who's Who in Business; [hon.] (Former) Phi Theta Kappa member, recipient of numerous achieve-ment awards, (NRI) induction into Worldwide Registry for Who's Who in Business; [oth. writ.] Aspiring author of several unpublished works; [pers.] Aspiring to bring out the best in all of us.... We can overcome the nature of the beast, as darkness falls the differences that divide us become obscured, in the dark we all look the same. [a.] Clear Lake Shores, TX.

HOLMES, LITA
[b.] April 19, 1937, Watonga, OK; [p.] Clarence and Anna Duke; [m.] Orland Holmes, July 29, 1961; [ch.] Stacia Lynn and Douglas Duke; [ed.] B.A. -Sociology, Langston University, M.S.W.-Social Work, University of Illinois; [occ.] Social Work, Administrator, Il., De-partment of Corrections; [pers.] I write to relieve tension and to personally process life experiences. There is usually a notable event for everything I write. [a.] Joliet, IL.

HOLNESS, LISA LEANNE
[b.] April 27, 1965, Victoria, BC; [p.] Arlene and Lionel Smith; [m.] Brian Ronald Holness, December 9, 1989; [ch.] Brent Ronald and Dallas Lawrence and one on the way February 1994; [ed.] Esquimalt Senior Sec.; [occ.] Homemaker, part time Retail Sales Representative; [oth. writ.] I have a personal poetry book of poems dating back to my high school days and was once noted a competition for high school works called "Unicorn Be"; [pers.] I write solely for my won enjoyment or to express to friends and family members my thoughts and feelings for them. [a.] Shawningan Lake, BC.

HOLT, NANCY
[pen.] Nancy Holt; [b.] February 6, 1932, New York St; [p.] Hel and Raymond Hargrove; [m.] John William Holt, October 16, 1951; [ch.] Thomas, John, Dennis

Gary, David and Tracey; [ed.] Through the twelfth grade; [occ.] Customer Service with General Electric Capital; [oth. writ.] I have a column for our company newsletter, it is called Words of Wisdom; [pers.] After raising my family and getting into the outside world a little, I found I loved writing and want to write poetry and everything else that comes to me.

HOLUB, HEATHER NOEL
[b.] December 25, 1973, Bayshore, NY; [p.] John and Linda Holub; [ed.] Earl L. Vandermeulen High School, Virginia Tech; [occ.] College student of Architecture. [a.] Port Jefferson, NY.

HOOPER, AMY BETH
[pen.] Amy Hooper; [b.] April 12, 1980, Portland, ME; [p.] Robert and Ellie Hooper; [ed.] I am an eighth grade student at Falmouth Middle School; [occ.] Junior skating coach; [memb.] I am a member of the USFSA and ISIA Figure Skating Clubs; [hon.] Figure skating medals, (3 gold, 1 silver and 2 fourth place ribbons), basketball and softball; [oth. writ.] A children's book titled The Man On The Side of The Street, I have also written many other poems and stories; [pers.] This poems was submitted in honor of my grandfather who used to tell me stories of when he was a boy. [a.] Falmouth, ME.

HOOPER, JEREMY
[pen.] Jeremiah Green; [b.] March 8, 1977, Racine, WI; [p.] William and Lynn Hooper; [ed.] In high school; [occ.] Student; [memb.] School Environmental Club; [hon.] Honor Roll; [oth. writ.] Several poems, but none published; [pers.] My poems reflect my thoughts and feelings. I've been greatly influenced by John Michael Stipe of R.E.M. and Henry David Thoreau. [a.] Racine, WI.

HOOPER, JESSICA
[pen.] Jessica; [b.] August 6, 1981, Lake Charles; [p.] Paula and Monroe Hooper; [ed.] Lake Charles Christian School (elementary); [hon.] Numerous piano awards and trophies; [oth. writ.] Memories, A Family, Love, Trey (dedicated to my cousin) etc.; [a.] Lake Charles, LA.

HOOPER, PEGGY PERRY
[b.] Chowan Co., Edenton, NC; [p.] Edith and William Perry (deceased); [m.] Divorced; [ch.] Thousands of children and teachers I have taught; [ed.] Life, living is learning, learning is living; [occ.] PLD student at Columbia University (Teacher;s College) New York City; [hon.] National Teacher of Gifted, featured in Scholastic Teacher Journal; [oth. writ.] Published, Journal of Psychology, American Ed. Research Assn., Perceptued Motor Skills, etc., presentations, in NY, NJ,CT, NC, Fla, Illinois, Nebraska, Tenn, GA, etc.; [pers.] Fulfillment is a synthesis of my lifes' experiences as an early childhood teacher and teacher of teachers. It is also a catharsis and transcendence of my struggle as a child sibling of Muscular Dystrophy brothers and both sisters' Muscular Dystrophy children. I try to be an inspiration to the children, the teachers and those around me as one who channels pain into creative production rather than self destruction or destruction of others. [a.] New York, NY.

HOPWOOD, ALYS J.
[b.] August 4, 1932, Asbury Park, NJ; [m.] Joseph E. Hopwood, August 25, 1949; [ch.] Jonathan L. Hopwood; [ed.] Graduated 1950 Aberdeen High School, Aberdeen, MD; [occ.] Medical transcriptionist, Peninsula Regional Medical Center, Salisbury, MD, teacher, Writing Class,

WOR-WIC Tech, Salisbury, MD 1980-85; [oth. writ.] Published, "The Wisteria Forest", Doppelganger IV, 1985, Unknowns Magazine, "The Ghost Office" published 1986, Beacon Review Vol IV # 5, "Mr. Fisid", 1985, Twisted Magazine, Spring 1985 # 1, "Regression", Byline Magazine, August 1985 titled "My Writing Life" (article); [pers.] Although past stories have been Ghoulish, presently writing a Medical Murder Mystery. [a.] Quantico, MD.

HORNBACHER, ELSIE
[b.] March 27, 1918, Rogers City, MI; [p.] Amanda and William Hornbacher; [ed.] Master's degree plus 1 year mostly in the field of Genetics, master's degree in the teaching of Science; [occ.] Retired; [memb.] Alpha Delta Kappa, Honorary Teacher Sorority, Women's Overseas Service Group, Greater Lansing Area Retired School Personnel, Michigan Retired School Personnel, AARP Retired School Personnel, I taught in the dependent schools of Japan, Italy and Austria; [oth. writ.] Publication of a time circle for teaching time around the world, publication of a poem in the Lansing State Journal; [pers.] I aim to make Science understandable in poetry or other writings. Learning something anew each year is important to me. [a.] Lansing, MI.

HORNE, GEORGE F.
[b.] December 2, 1938, Paris, AR; [p.] Roy A. Horne and Clara B. Holzman; [m.] Georgia (Power) Horne, February 11, 1961; [ch.] Mark, Beth, Jan and Jennifer; [ed.] 1956 high school diploma, Clarksville (Ar) High School, 1960-B.A. (Eng.) Tulane University, 1963-MEd (Eng.) Southeastern LA University; [occ.] Ed. Consultant (retired Supt. of Schools); [memb.] LA Association of School Supts., LA Association of School Trans. Officials, National Association for Pupil Trans.; [hon.] Trans. Admin. of The Year 1990, LA Association of School Trans.-Officials Trans. Award 1991, exceptional volunteer, American Red Cross Heart East Jefferson Service 1993; [oth. writ.] Approx. 65 poems, misc. transportation studies, handbooks, etc. [a.] Metairie, LA.

HORNE, J. D.
[pen.] J.D. Horne; [b.] February 7, 1943, Alamo, GA; [p.] Deceased; [m.] Johanna L. Horne, July 21, 1984; [ch.] Tonya, Tammy, Kutrina, Ann and Patrick; [ed.] Associated Degree in Resource Management, completed high school in Hazlehurst, Georgia; [occ.] Retired Air Force CMSAT (E-9); [memb.] Military NCO Clubs; [hon.] Military, four Air Force Meritorious Service Medals, Vietnam Service and Campaign Medals and best Air Force Supply NCO in Europe 1980; [oth. writ.] Wrote plays while in active duty in the Air Force, written many poems on request from others; [pers.] I strive to reflect realism (life) in my poems and not too difficult for the average person to understand. [a.] San Antonio, TX.

HOSMER, TAMMY ANN
[b.] May 28, 1972, Oswego; [p.] Lloyd and Carrie Hosmer; [m.] Thomas H. Lester, November 28, 1993; [ch.] Christopher, Audriania and Trisha Hosmer; [ed.] North Rose Wolcott, K-10, GED; [occ.] Homemaker.

HOTCHKISS, TERRY
[b.] September 16, 1966, Shropshire, England; [p.] Leslie and Vivien Hotchkiss; [m.] Helen Hutchkiss, September 29, 1990; [ed.] Mary Webb School, Shrewsbury College of Arts and Technology; [occ.] Accounts Manager; [memb.] Methodist Church; [oth. writ.] Several poems which have been read locally;

[pers.] I attempt, through my poetry to communicate God to the Modern World. I have been influenced by poets such as Dylan Thomas and Stewart Henderson. [a.] Shrewsbury, England.

HOULAHAN, PAUL R.
[b.] December 28, 1939, Melrose, NB Canada; [p.] Michael and Margaret Houlahan; [m.] Barbara Houlahan, August 10, 1963; [ch.] Colleen Patricia, Catherine Anne, Carolyn Louise, Krista-Lynn Margaret and Timothy Michael Paul; [ed.] St. Clement's High, St. Joseph's University, N.B. Teacher's College, Sir George Williams University, University of Moncton; [occ.] Junior high school, Language Arts teacher, Marshview Middle School, Sackville, NB; [memb.] New Brunswick Teachers' Association, Teachers of English Council, District 2 Grievance Committee, St. Bartholomew's Liturgical, Entertainment and Cemetery Committees; [hon.] No major awards, an honors student throughout elementary, junior, senior and college years; [oth. writ.] Nothing previously submitted for publication, numerous articles upon request (memorials, parodies, etc.) letters to the Editor and articles in local newspapers, Editorials in local news bulletin, plus numerous songs and poems; [pers.] My works deal with the follies of mankind and the beauties of nature. Even my humorous works usually have a message. Robert Frost is one of my favorite poets. [a.] Melrose, NB Canada.

HOUNSHELL, CARLIN V.
[b.] September 24, 1949, Rural Retreat, VA; [p.] Mr. and Mrs. Carl B. Wright; [m.] James F. Hounshell, July 2, 1989; [ch.] Michelle Nucholls; [ed.] Rural Retreat High School, Wytheville Community College, Radford University (B.S. and M.S.); [occ.] Reading Teacher, Westside Elementary School, Roanoke, VA; [memb.] Reading Association (local, state and international), Education Association (local, state and national), Daughters of the American Revolution; [oth. writ.] Poems and a school song; [pers.] My writing is inspired by many wonderful childhood memories and family experiences gathered from growing up in a rural environment.

HOUSE, NAOMI
[pen.] Norm; [b.] November 9, 1973, Wellsboro; [p.] Raymond and Ethel House; [ed.] Liberty High School, Empire Beauty School; [occ.] Cook and hairstylist; [hon.] Student of the Month for Empire Beauty School; [pers.] Live for today, for today is tomorrow. [a.] Morris, PA.

HOUSTON, MARION HART
[pen.] Hart Houston; [b.] September 10, 1945, Pine Bluff; [p.] Charles Hart (deceased) and Marjorie Jones; [m.] Carlin R. Houston; [ch.] Cart Houston and Grace Ann Breshears; [ed.] Gulfpark Junior College and Prep. '62, University of Arkansas at Monticell '73 graduate BA, University of Arkansas at Pinebluff (+ 18 hours); [occ.] English Teacher at Jack Robey Junior High; [memb.] Delta Kappa Gamma, NCTE, BEA, AEA, PBEA, Junior League, AGATE, Jefferson COunty Museum Guild, John McAlmont Chapter, DAR, Mayflower Society; [hon.] Honored by the Governor's School as Outstanding Teacher 1991, Alpha Chi, Cum Laude graduate, Secretary Debate Society; [pers.] Send me no flowers, for before I shall die, I shall know life's fullest image and take with me more bouquets than thy garden has in store. [a.] Pine Bluff, AR.

HOUSTON, ROXANE
[pen.] Roxane Houston; [b.] March 10, 1919, London,

England; [p.] Bertram and Winifred Houston; [m.] Joseph Graham, Senior, December 1, 1957; [ch.] Deborah Pyper and Rupert Senior; [ed.] Kensington High School, London, Downs School, Sussex, Villa Brillantmont, Lausanne, Switzerland, Royal Academy of Music, London; [occ.] Writer, singing teacher; [memb.] Association of Teachers of Singing (founder/member), Suffolk Poetry Society; [hon.] Licentiate of Royal Academy of Music (L.R.A.M.); [oth.writ.] "Reflections of Harmony" (musical autobiography) published 1978, many poems in anthologies, book and lyrics for two musicals, two novels, TV play, Libretti for Cantatas, opera, song cycles; [pers.] Since my retirement from the concert platform I have begun a second career of writing. [a.] Aldebureh-Suffold, England.

HOWELL, MAXINE
[b.] December 10, 1933, Arkansas; [p.] Adopted by Paul Sanders; [m.] Glenn Howell, February 11,1960; [ch.] Glenna-Jo Howell, now married to Tom Gelnett; [ed.] Thur second year high school, 1 year college [occ.] Homemaker; memb.] Baptist Church; [oth.writ.] I wrote a story about The Other Half Of Me, it is about my identical sister, plus I have written other stories and poems; [pers.] I have always wanted to be a writer, I have other stories and poems. I have been influenced by my husband and family, so I took a step forward. [a.] Norfolk, VA.

HOWELL, STEPHEN
[pen.] Stephen Howell; [b.] December 25,1969, Barbados, WI; [p.] Audrey Howell and Hullam Carter; [ed.] George Westinghouse High School, University of Hartford, BS Electrical Engineer Tech May 92; [occ.] Science Teacher, Rikers Island Educational Facility; [memb.] East NY Wesleyn Church, Intervarsity Christian Fellowship; [hon.] John F. Kennedy and Science Awards from J.H.S. IS 292; [oth.writ.] Three other non-published personal poems, a few love letters (not published); [pers.] I believe in one God-shaped universal order and a shared spiritual human experience. Love (never and cannot) fail.

HUFFMAN, PATRICIA J.
[pen.] Pat Huffman; [b.] March 29, 1941, Elmira, NY; [p.] Alice E. and F. John Garbay; [m.] Edward L. Huffman, May 28, 1960; [ch.] Debra Huffman Palmer, Thomas E. and Matthew M. Huffman; [ed.] Thomas A. Edison High School, Corning Community College, Elmira College; [occ.] Accounting Department, Corning Inc.; [memb.] Institute of Management Accountants, Ladies of Charity, International Society of Poets; [hon.] Merit Award, International Society of Poets, Editor's Choice Award, National Library of Poetry, Dean's List; [oth.writ.] Several poems, one published in Where Dream Begin, and one published in Outstanding Poets of 1994; [pers.] My writings are based on my awareness of people's emotions, reactions and reflections. I share my love of poetry by doing poetry presentations in my community. [a.] Horseheads, NY.

HUFMAN, MARY MARGARET
[pen.] Mary M. Morrison; [b.] September 23, 1915, Blanca, CO; [p.] Glen and Rose Hufman; [m.] Bill Morrison, February 26, 1931; [ch.] Billie Margaret and Lon Britt; [ed.] 11th grade; [occ.] Retired; [memb.] Seventh Day Adventist Church; [oth. writ.] Short Stories; [pers.] I strive to reflect my early youthful life spent in the Colorado Rockies. I have been influenced by my family. [a.] Alamosa, CO.

HUG, HUBERT
[b.] March 10, 1959, Freiburg, FRG; [p.] Paul and Agenes Hug; [ed.] University of Freiburg (FRG) and University of Liverpool (UK), study of Biology, University of Zurich (Switzerland), Institute of Molecular, Biology I, Ph.D. Thesis; [occ.] Scientist at the Osaka Bioscience Institute (Japan); [oth. writ.] The Neutra and other stories, Minerva Press (London), 1994 in press, articles in Scientific Journals; [pers.] Two Words. [a.] Suita-Shi, Osaka, Japan.

HUGHBANKS, KEVIN CLAY
[pen.] Kevin Hughbanks Jr.; [b.] June 30, 1967, Ann Arbor, MI; [p.] Michael and Barbara Hughbanks; [ch.] Gabrelle and Kevin Hughbanks; [ed.] GED, from Adult Education of Ann Arbor, Michigan; [memb.] NAACP, Jaycees and Fathers Behind Bars; [hon.] Leadership Award and Public Speaking Award; [oth. writ.] Several poems published in local papers; [pers.] Always have faith in what you believe in and never get discouraged, truth always prevails over falsehood, even though I'm incarcerated I never lose faith, my release date is July 16, 1996. [a.] Ypsilanti, MI.

HUGHES, ANDREW
[pen.] Andrew S. Hughes; [b.] August 7, 1975, Garland, TX; [p.] Sam and Elaine Hughes; [ed.] Callisburg High School, freshman, Stephen F. Austin State University; [occ.] Student; [memb.] Criminal Justice Club; [oth. writ.] Countless other poems, some which have been modified into songs and performed by the bad "Fishmonger"; [pers.] Life is an endless journey and becomes only what one makes it. Expressing one own opinions and having one's own ideas in important also. Standing alone makes one strong. True strength comes from believing in oneself the hard work is always the most beneficial. [a.] Norcogdoches, TX.

HUGHES, MINDY
[pen.] Samantha Wilt; [b.] September 15, 1978, Houston; [p.] Lee L. Hughes and Debra L. Junkin; [ed.] Bellaire Senior High School; [hon.] "Most Talented" for a story "The Last Spring Break" that I wrote; [oth. writ.] All I Want To Do, was published in my school newspaper; [pers.] I like for people to think of life as something beautiful and untouched. [a.] Houston, TX.

HUMMELL, JUNE
[pen.] June Hummell; [b.] June 26, 1927, Iowa; [p.] John and Bertha Bradley; [m.] Carl S. Hummell, November 27, 1947; [ch.] John Sheldon Hummell; [ed.] Formal-plus courses in writing; [occ.] Housewife; [memb.] North Congregational Church, Co-chair, Symphony Day Founders Committee, Pomperaug Valley Garden Club; [hon.] Only from volunteer organizations, National Hospital News Award for writing and editing newsletter; [oth. writ.] Other poems published via newspaper, book critic published by newspaper, essays and a non-fiction story, wrote and edited newsletters; [pers.] Secrets are revealed and mysteries defined by the symbolic language of the poet and with new perspectives it delves into the beauty that enriches all of life. [a.] South Bury, CT.

HUNT, SHERMAN
[pen.] Sherman Hunt; [b.] July 28, 1961, Bridgeport, CT; [p.] John and Nellie Hunt; [ch.] Isiaih T. Jackson; [ed.] South Catholic High School, College of St. Joseph; [occ.] Probation and Parole Office; [memb.] Vermont Army National Guard; [hon.] Dean's List, Outstanding Citizenship Award; [oth. writ.] Several poems in my private collection, I have not had any published, it's a hobby of mine; [pers.] Treat others the way you want to be treated and never lose sight of the Lord. My poems mirror my heart. [a.] Rutland, VT.

HUNTER, MARGARET ANN
[pen.] Maggie/Magz; [b.] March 13, 1965, Gt. Yarmouth; [p.] Alex and Joan Hunter; [ed.] Bankhead Academy, Bucksburn, Aberdeen; [occ.] Lab Technician; [memb.] Scottish National Blood Transfusion Service; [pers.] My inner most feelings are greatly expressed through my poetry and I would like to share my personal emotions with others who have experienced the same. [a.] Aberdeen, Scotland.

HUNTER, MELVIN P.
[b.] May 31, 1950, Washington, DC; [p.] Albert and Bernice Hunter; [ch.] Kimberly and Anthony Hunter; [ed.] LaFayette High School graduate, college education Benia Community College, general diploma; [memb.] Columbia House Video Club, Grolier Gold Club; [hon.] Editor;s Choice Award for Outstanding Achievement in poetry, graduate May 8, 1992, master art diploma International Correspondence Schools; [oth.writ.] Challenger Newspaper article, Read On, Write On and Arithmetic, article local poet is published E.C.C. newspaper 1978, Brother to Sister (school); [pers.] I love art, music and poetry, to wisemen (great) freedom is in my pen. [a.] Buffalo, NY.

HUNTINGTON, BETTY J.
[pen.] Betty J. Huntington; [b.] February 3, 1943, Magnolia, AR; [m.] Winston Huntington, February 12, 1983; [ch.] 3; [occ.] Secretary, Michigan State Government; [oth. writ.] Have written fine plays and several playlets, two have been publicly performed; [pers.] The prevailing theme of my current writings seems to be "The Last Days" it is my desire to share in the efforts of others to warn the world accordingly. [a.] Muskegon Heights, MI.

HUNTINGTON, VIRGINIA B.
[pen.] Gini Huntington; [b.] October 3, 1929, Augusta, ME; [p.] Forrest A. and Florence Agar Barbour; [m.] Leonard A. Huntington, February 11, 1979; [ch.] Joan C. Austin, Liza E. Lidke, Susan A. Johnson and Robert F. Eaton; [ed.] Deering High, Portland, ME, 1947 Real Estate License 1969-1985, Insurance License MI and GA '86 present; [occ.] Receptionist/Girl Friday for husband's insurance office; [memb.] First Congregational Church, UCC Post 184, American Legion Aux., Thunderbolt, GA Marine Country Music Association; [hon.] Barry Dean Award from MCMA Outstanding Service in Country Music 1985, Outstanding Service MCMA 1983; [oth. writ.] Maine Country Music newsletter, church newsletters, high school wrote/directed freshman one act play, senior fashion show script, presently enrolled in writing course, Co-editor "Singles Times" 1975-76, program books for country shows produced with husband; [pers.] I feel that the written word expresses ones innermost feelings more than the spoken word. I try to write some kind of humor into all writings no matter what the subject. [a.] Thunderbolt, GA.

HURLEY, ASHLEIGH MICHELE
[pen.] Ashleigh Michele Hurley; [b.] April 18, 1982, Alton, IL; [p.] Rosalinda Rodriguez Hurley and Michael Hurley; [ed.] Apache Elementary School, Kennedy Middle School; [occ.] Student; [memb.] Victory Love Fellowship; [hon.] Spelling Bee Cluster 1992, top stu-

dent D.A.R.E. 1993; [oth. writ.] Several poems and stories written ion private journal; [pers.] I dedicate this to the homeless. I also hope that someday, people will open their eyes and share with people, especially people with nothing. [a.] Albuquerque, NM.

HURLEY, MARY B.
[pen.] Mary B. Hurley; [b.] October 4, 1924, North Loup, NE; [p.] Albert and Jessie Babcock; [m.] Wilton Hurley, August 6, 1948; [ch.] Carol Solis and Jake Hurley; [ed.] MA; [occ.] Retired English Poetry Teacher, Downey High School, Downey, CA; [memb.] California Chaporral Poets, Apollo and Orpheus Chapters, 4th State Vice President New Horizons Poetry Club; [hon.] Several prizes state CFPC, poems published in several small magazines and newspapers, 2 chap books. [a.] Bellflower, CA.

HUSSEY, RICK
[b.] July 25, 1965, Waterloo; [p.] Paul and Ellen Hussey; [m.] Lori Jean Hussey, August 12, 1991; [ch.] Jessica Lea Hussey, November 16, 1992; [ed.] Associate in Business Administration, Genesec Community College, Batavia, NY; [occ.] Construction; [hon.] Phi Theta Kappa, Dean's List 3.65; [oth. writ.] None published by anyone, but several poems; [pers.] I owe my talent to my grandmother Eleanor Ahola, who has inspired me throughout my life, she is also a poet with several writings. [a.] Waterloo, NY.

HUTCHINS, SHARLEEN C.
[b.] January 28, 1961, Monroe, LA: [p.] Patsy Danhof and John Hutchins; [ch.] Sonja Carol Shambaugh and Christopher John Peterson; [ed.] Snohomish High School; [occ.] Carpet sales, Rubensteins Contract Carpet, Seattle, WA; [hon.] Commanding Officer's Accommodation Award, USN, 1981 and 1982; [oth. writ.] Quill Books, "Listen With Your Heart" and "Dusting Off Dreams"; [pers.] In my personal and professional life, I practice what I believe in, if everyone works together to reach a goal, it will be reached. My life experiences have greatly influenced my writing. [a.] Snohomish, WA.

HUTCHINSON, B.B.
[b.] August 23, 1908, Joplin, MO; [p.] H.S. Hutchinson and Harriet Roysce; [m.] Hazel Elenore, July 27, 1994; [ch.] Kerry Keith; [ed.] University of California at Berkeley; [occ.] Merchandise Manager, Sears Roebuck and Company, 35 years; [memb.] Retired Executives Club, Ambassadors Club, Sears Hall of Fame; [hon.] Bronze Medal; [oth. writ.] Poem, Lake Superiors State College, U.S.C.I. papers.

HUTCHINSON, DOROTHY
[b.] July 20, 1941, Lanarkshire, Scotland; [p.] David and Nancy Gordon; [m.] Peter T.; [occ.] Housewife; [oth.writ.] Several poems unpublished, also, "A Little Dogs Plight" published in Wind in The Night Sky; [pers.] I wrote this poem the day after my dear mum died of Cancer. I had spent 5 weeks with her prior to this and through it all she was a real source of encouragement to everyone. She was a very special lady, and I miss her with all my heart. [a.] Ontario, Canada.

HAYM, DICK
[pen.] Dick Haym; [b.] July 6, 1921, Wallasey, Cheshire UK; [p.] Deceased; [m.] Helmi Hyam, November 29, 1947; [ch.] Richard and Melanie; [ed.] Scottish Higher Learning Certificate, (the high school of Glasgow, Scotland), Glasgow Veterinary College, 3 years in Royal Army Veterinary Lorps, 10 years in Govt. Service, 9 1/

2 years in Northern Rhodesia non Zambia, then in practice in South Africa 22 years; [occ.] Retired, Veterinary (qualified MRCVS 1945) surgeon; [memb.] Capetown Writers' Club; [hon.[Occasional prize from Writers' club; [oth. writ.] Autobiographical novel, Animal Crackers, under pseudonym Richard Kirk (because I was still in practice), published by Collins 1979, a long list of poems and short stories, NB rights to my book now returned to me, working on novel, (Braille and the Angel), Animal Crackers was broadcast as a serial on SABC; [pers.] I have always enjoyed writing ever since school days, I drift in a private land of my own creation and very imagination takes over, news thoughts, new characters and new experiences are born and it is a joy to see them materialize from the point of my pen. [a.] Capetown, Cape R.S.A.

HYATT, PAMELA S.
[b.] June 28, 1950, Saginaw, MI; [p.] Kathryn Grace (Pries) and Kenneth Walter Dark; [m.] James W. Hyatt, January 17, 1968; [ch.] Carolyn (25), Linda (23), Matthew (15) and Margaret (9); [ed.] Graduate of Chesaning Union High School; [occ.] Work at Brideport Elias Brothers Restaurant; [memb.] St. Judes Childrens' Hospital Fund, Hurley Foundation and Muscular Dystrophy Foundation; [oth. writ.] Many poems of children and grandchildren, friends and experiences in my life as well as inspirational works dealing with life, love and the world in general; [pers.] My first poem was written on April 15, 1993 as a mending tool after experiencing the deaths of my mother-in-law, my mother and an infant granddaughter all within a 6 1/2 month period of time, from November '92 to April '93. [a.] Burt, MI.

HYDOCK, HEIDI
[b.] January 29, 1973; [p.] David and Iva Stephens; [ed.] Garfield Heights High, Cuyahoga Valley Vocational School; [occ.] Managing Cosmetologist; [pers.] I was in my pre-teens when I first started writing poems. I wrote them based on my feelings and therefore I would never let anyone read them, until now. [a.] Garfield Heights, OH.

HYLAND, WENDY ELLIOTT
[pen.] Wendy Elliott Hyland; [b.] September 6,1939, Melbourne, Australia; [p.] Maggie and Stanley Amott; [ed.] Masters degree, Melbourne University; [occ.] Writer, film producer; [oth. writ.] Cobwebs on the Dublin Bus (in process), How to Make It In Hollywood, Nelson-Hall, Chicago; [pers.] Fortunately I am not influenced by the masse public of today's society and strive to remain an individual through my own philosophy of my "dream life". [a.] Los Angeles, CA.

IHE, YEVONNE
[pen.] Uves St. Gibson; [b.] January 27, 1969, Nigeria; [p.] C. Gibson and Gladys Ihe; [ed.] High school, Federal Government Girls College Abuloma, Nigeria, Texas College; [occ.] Student, Texas College; [memb.] Texas College Ambassador, Young Adults for Christ, Pre-Alumni Council, Literary Club, Honor's Program, Gospel Choir, Young Women's Christian Association, Texas College newspaper; [hon.] Certificate of Achievement in Excellence for Religious studies, Certificate of Recognition Texas College Ambassador, Certificate of Induction Honor's Program, Certificate best costume "Jewels of The Nile", Certificate - Miss All City Pageant, Certificate of Appreciation Most Friendliest Female; [oth. writ.] A poem for the Literary Club, some works of mine to be published in the Texas College newspaper; [pers.] I will always keep aiming high till I achieve my

goals in life. I have been greatly influenced by my parents. [a.] Tyler, TX.

IMAI, BRANDIE L.
[pen.] Bran, Lei; [b.] November 5, 1982; [p.] Lourdes and Michael Imai; [ed.] Elementary; [occ.] Student; [hon.] JPO Lieutenant, won first place in Science Fair, Honor Roll and Outstanding Achievement Speech Festival. [a.] Kailua, HI.

IMWALLE, KATE
[b.] July 13, 1980, Los Altos, CA; [p.] Donald and Katherine Imwalle; [sib.] Donald, Miles and Joe; [ed.] St. Nicholas Grammar School; [occ.] Student, part-time gardener and babysitter; [memb.] National Charities League; [hon.] Commissioner of Ecology; [oth. writ.] I have done many personal and school writings which are all kept in a shoe box to reflect upon; [pers.] I feel you should let your mind go free, and set your thoughts on paper, never throw your ideas away. [a.] Los Altos, CA.

INGMIRE, HAZELLE M.
[pen.] Hazelle Ingmire; [b.] July 28, 1915, Galatea, OH; [p.] Silas and Bessie Brunk; [m.] Glen H. Ingmire (deceased 6/92), April 9, 1937; [ch.] John-Glen L. Ingmire, Seguin, TX; [ed.] High school, 1 1/2 years college equivalent; [occ.] Retiree, Personnel Manager for Army and Air Force Exchange Service after 27 years, retired June 71 at Ft. Bliss, TX; [memb.] Trinity First UM Church, Heisey Collectors of America, AAFES Retirement Gp (area); [hon.] December 62, award for Hiring the Handicapped from Committee of the President of U.S. Employment of Physically Handicapped also Reporter of the Year for the Exchange Post, worldwide news publication of AAFES; [oth. writ.] Hundreds; [pers.] If I fear anything, it is knowing of the existence of the only human emotion that has to be taught....PREJUDICE. [a.] El Paso, TX.

INLAW, BONNIE LOUISE
[b.] February 7, 1932, Morrow, OH; [p.] Decorise and Dora Inlaw; [m.] Everett Alton Inlaw, June 16, 1950; [ch.] Terry Alton Inlaw, Brenda Joyce Slaughter and Johnny Wayne Inlaw; [ed.] Blanchester High School graduate; [occ.] Retired Custodial worker from Cowan Lake Campground; [memb.] Brown Road Country Church; [oth. writ.] I have several poems and words to songs that I have written over the years, I have never tried to have any published but I have thought about it. [pers.] I strive to honor my blessed Lord and Saviour in my writing. [a.] Cuba, OH.

IRBY, SYBIL
[b.] December 20, 1942, New York, NY; [ed.] George Washington High, CCNY; [occ.] Director, Empire Blue Cross and Blue Shield; [memb.] Briarwood Community Association; [hon.] Black Achiever in Industry 1989, awarded by The Harlem Branch YMCA; [pers.] I truly believe that God works in mysterious ways, His wonders to perform. Experiences we consider negative at the time of occurrence are very often blessings in disguise. [a.] Briarwood, NY.

IRVING, C. THOMAS
[b.] July 9, 1950, Vancouver, BC Canada; [p.] Lawrence H. and Phyllis E. Irving; [ed.] Northwest Institute of Medical Technology; [occ.] Research Writer-health publications; [memb.] Alpha Psi Omega, International Research Expeditions; [hon.] Golden Poet-1989 from World of Poetry, Billy Mitchell Award-Civil Air Patrol, Knight's Cross; [oth. writ.] "Improve Memory and Learning",

"Musket Tel", "Two Tonic Nights" and "Luna-Ticks"; [pers.] "When we individually try to escape the realities of this day, "that" collectively, only intensifies and makes manifest those realities for those around us". I have been inspired by early classical poets, archaeology, faith, exercise and the founding fathers of our United States. [a.] Omaha, NE.

IRWIN, HELEN
[b.] May 8, 1920, South Dakota; [p.] Bertina and Alfred Ofstad; [m.] Deceased, 1953; [ch.] Hugh, Matthew, Hollie, William and Eva; [ed.] Business college; [occ.] Retired; [memb.] Pierson Methodist Church; [hon.] High school honor student, high school queen, Parent of the Year, Morningside College; [oth. writ.] One Lonely Tree, Father's Big Choir. [a.] Pierson, IA.

ISAAC, FRED
[b.] July 21, 1959, Ohio; [p.] Everett and Marie Isaac; [m.] Wendy R. Isaac, October 30, 1986; [ch.] Brandon M. and Derek E. Isaac; [ed.] Morehead State University; [memb.] New Yorker, National Geographic Society; [pers.] "The wind is but a passing memory". In memory of Charles Everett Isaac. [a.] Clearfield, KY.

ISLAM, AMINUL
[pen.] Salim; [b.] October 12, 1963, Pakistan; [p.] Imamul and Mumtaz Islam; [ed.] St. Patrick's High, St. Patrick's College in Pakistan; [occ.] Sales; [pers.] All of my poems relate to an individual or the feelings I have at that particular moment. I have been greatly influenced by the writings of Omar Khayyam and Kiaalil Gibran. [a.] Arcadia, CA.

ISRANI, JAGDISH
[b.] September 26,1954, Varanasi; [p.] Shri Ramchand and Maya; [m.] Veena, October 12, 1982; [ch.] Rachit and Sneha; [ed.] B.Sc. Dip. in Mkgt. Management; [occ.] Business, (Pharmaceutical); [memb.] Indian Institute of Vedic Studies; [oth. writ.] Finalizing two books on human behavior; [pers.] Let there be chanting of God's name in whole or the world. [a.] Lucknow, UP.

IWVOMA, OBIOMA
[b.] August 8, 1973, Los Angeles, CA; [p.] Njoku and Rose Iwvoma;[ed.] Birmingham High (graduate), Los Angeles Trade Tech College; [occ.] L.A.C.C. (Human Service work with disadvantaged children); [hon.] The only honors or awards I received was the happy faces of children receiving Christmas gifts we help passed out; [oth. writ.] Published poem for college newspaper and a local L.A. paper read some of my work at my graduation; [pers.] I laughed to see a blind man walking aimlessly but without my knowing he knew exactly where he was going. (Peace is possible). [a.] Pasadena, CA.

JACKSON, DEBRA
[pen.] Dee Jackson; [b.] June 7, 1964, Texarkana, TX; [p.] Willie Richardson (mother) and Cornell Nash (father); [m.] Darryl Jackson, March 16, 1990; [ch.] Ebony and Maya Jackson; [ed.] Hooks High, Hooks, TX., Prairie View A & M University, Prairie, TX.; [occ.] Software Engineer; [memb.] Delta Sigma Theta Sorority Inc.; [hon.] Dean's List; [pers.] "My heart knows no limits" and I try to reflect that concept in every word that I transcribe. [a.] Grand Prairie, TX.

JACKSON, DILLARD C.
[b.] April 5, 1927, Arkadelphia, Cullman County, AL; [p.] John Chester and Sally Jackson; [m.] Iva Mae Kimbril Jackson, July 30, 1948; [ch.] Sheree Marie Jackson Mitchell, Gregory Lee Jackson, son-in-law, Ralph Q. Mitchell, Jr., grandchild, Jennifer Camille Mitchell, daughter-in-law, Jeannie Jackson; [ed.] Cold Springs High School, Howard College; [occ.] Retired 1987, University of Alabama at Birmingham, Manager, Locksmith Operations; [hon.] Certificate of Ordination, The Gospel Ministry, 1962, 1978-1980, University of Alabama at Birmingham, Personnel Advisory Council, March, 1980, UAB Employee of the Month, Associated Locksmith's of America, Inc., Electro-Mechanical Security Systems, 1982, Resolution of the Board of Trustees of the University of Alabama for 28 years of service, May, 1987; [pers.] Life is a gift from God and if you love God you will love people. [a.] Gardendale, AL.

JACKSON, JOANNE
[b.] November 7,1945, Vancouver, BC; [ed.] Abbotsford Junior Senior High; [hon.] Bowling award; [oth. writ.] Have written other poems and now working on a book; [pers.] My poetry is a reflection of my thoughts in the world. I always have inspiration which has helped me write my very first poem "Mother Nature".

JACKSON, MASIE EDITH CAVELL
[pen.] Masie Edith Cavell Jackson; [b.] November 30, 1917, Glace Bay; [p.] Ben and Frances Barrett; [m.] Alexander R. Jackson (deceased), November 6, 1937; [ch.] Frances K. Parsons; [ed.] Grade eight, due to financial difficulties, as there was five of us going to school; [occ.] Retired; [memb.] I give donations to the War Amps of Canada and to most all charities, my church is St. Marys Angelican of Glace Bay, NS; [oth. writ.] I have written over forty poems and memorials which was published in our town newspapers; [pers.] I get my inspiration around two a.m. to write my poems. My favorite poet was R.L. Stephenson, I believe if you have something you really want to do, go for it, as life has no short cuts.

JACKSON, MERCY ELIZABETH
[b.] September 19,1938; [m.] Horace William Jackson, March 18, 1967; [ch.] Three grown up children and four grandchildren; [ed.] All Saints' Church of England School, St. Peter's Girls High School, Wolverhampton; [occ.] Homemaker, housewife; [pers.] I only have a small amount of writings some 19 poems, most of them used to raise funds for charity (at present I am working with Mercy Missions to send food and aid to Bosnian Refugees in Nagyatad Camp). Others have been used as seasonal hand-outs within my church. Re: Freddie Shone With Brilliance. I have been a great enthusiast of Queens music for a good many years and the poem was written to help with Aids Awareness.

JACKSON, JR., OLAN F.
[b.] February 25, 1965, Reading, PA; [p.] Olan and Inez Jackson; [ed.] Texas Tech University, degree, Landscape Architecture, minor, Architectural Design; [occ.] Captain, US Army Transportation Corps; [memb.] Lambda Chi Alpha Fraternity, National Defense Transportation Association; [hon.] Sigma Lambda Alpha, Golden Key National Honor Society, ASLA Honor Award, Distinguished Military graduate, ROTC Scholarship, Outstanding Student Award; [oth.writ.] Article for freshman English text book; [pers.] I am compelled by early romantic poetry to write about love's very constant lows. [a.] Phillipsburg, NJ.

JOHNSON, R. LAURENCE
[pen.] R. Laurence Johnson; [b.] November 26, 1966, Chicago, IL; [p.] George and Anita Johnson; [ed.] Chicago State University, Howard University Graduate School of Business; [occ.] Sales Representative, Shering-Plough Pharmaceutical; [memb.] Omega Psi Phi Fraternity -TO, Phi Beta Lambda Business Society, National Institute of Cost Analysis and Estimators, Business Laboratory Honors Program; [hon.] Sales performance awards from Pitney Bowes, and Schering Plough Futures Business Executive Award, Chicago State University; [oth. writ.] Man Was Made to Cry, Expressions, Escape Black History; [pers.] Love of words fill my mind, love for life fill my soul, I write in love, in love I write, "I'm done". [a.] Alexandria, VA.

JACKSON, SUSAN ANN
[pen.] Sue Jackson; [b.] July 29, 1952, Lancashire, England; [p.] Orphan; [m.] Frank Maxwell Jackson, June 13, 1992; [ch.] 1 daughter aged 18 years; [ed.] Skerton Girls' Sec. Mod School, until 15 years of age, 1986-1987 1 year at Secretarial College; [occ.] Poet and housewife (unemployed); [memb.] The Poetry Library, South Bank Centre, London; [oth. writ.] Five individual poems published in the last twelve months in various British National Anthologies; [pers.] I have been writing poetry for the past 5 years used as a "Self Therapy". I try to reflect all aspects of life modern and past, including my own experiences. Currently writing a book with a friend. [a.] Merseyside, England.

JAHME, SUSAN
[b.] February 2, 1955, Zimabawe; [p.] Richard and Fay Cook; [m.] Graham Jahme; [ch.] Keren and Taryn Jahme; [ed.] Chisipitie Senior School, Hermes Academy; [occ.] Commercial Artist, book illustrator; [memb.] Zimbabwe Wild Life Society, Zimbabwe National Art Gallery; [hon.] Diploma Scottish International Open Poetry Comp. 92; [oth. writ.] Written a series of children's stories with an African theme and a series of poems, am looking for a publisher; [pers.] Along with the Ancient African Soul and David Livingstone's heart... mine shall be a part of this massive, baked land. [a.] Zimbabwe, Africa.

JAILAWI, JAMAL SALEM
[pen.] J.S. Jailawi; [b.] June 23, 1961, Chicago, IL; [p.] Salem A. and Frances H. Jailawi; [ed.] Stockton Upper Grade Center, Mira Costa College, Morton Community College, Loyola University, Chicago; [occ.] Aspiring author; [hon.] United States Marine Corps Honorable Discharge-JA-1; [oth. writ.] "Longing For The Truth"; [pers.] Being human, I recognize, understand and accept the duality of humanity, and equation balanced by an aggressive "male" history and a female "history". [a.] Chicago, IL.

JAKAB, STEVE
[b.] October 31, 1964, Pheonix, AZ; [p.] Steven and Jean Jakab; [ed.] Jefffersonville High School, Purdue University; [occ.] Software Engineer; [memb.] Amnesty International, Greenpeace, The Nature Conservancy, ACLU, Church of the Subgenius; [pers.] Nothing is true, everything is permitted. This poem was inspired after attending a 3 day Winona Ryder film festival, especially the films Roxy Carmichael and Dracula.

JAMES, LISA
[pen.] Lisa James; [b.] October 1, 1977, Houston, TX; [p.] C.J. and L. James; [ed.] Corpus Christi Catholic School, High School for Health Professions; [occ.] Student at High School for Health Professions; [memb.] National Honor Society, Teens for Transplants, Health Occupational Students of America; [hon.] Honor Roll,

Parent Teacher Organization, Certificate of Merit, Society of Women Engineers, Certificate of Achievement, Perfect Attendance Award, Presidential Academic Fitness Award; [oth. writ.] Short stories and poem that have never been published; [pers.] Life is what you make it. [a.] Houston, TX.

JAMES, VIRGINIA LEE
[b.] Washington, DC; [p.] Shuler and Florence R. James, Jr.; [ed.] Ballou Senior High, Struyers College, (WSS) Washington School for Secretaries; [oth. writ.] When I was 12 years, I entered a contest where I had to write an essay from a picture, I wrote the essay and won. In the 12th grade the 12th grade typing class had to write a Christmas poem, I wrote the Christmas poem and won; [pers.] Writing is an universal communication which allows me to read individuals minds through storytelling and poetry. An opportunity that I've always taken delight in through which I've been inspired by children, current events, my spirituality and personal experiences. [a.] Washington, DC.

JAMESON, MARY GENEVA A
[pen.] Jean or M. Jean Jameson; [b.] February 14, 1927, Greenville, MI; [p.] Lester and Mary House; [m.] Charles C. Jameson, October 27, 1945; [ch.] Doreena Mae, Patricia Lynne and Charles Steven; [ed.] Greenville High School, Greenville, MI.; [occ.] Seamstress until I became disabled 1986; [memb.] Evangelical Methodist Church, Evangelical Methodist Womens' Missionary Society; [hon.] Honored on my song writing, have won several awards on my poems and paintings; [oth. writ.] Several poems published in local newspapers and magazines (both local and national); [pers.] To be creative as a poet, a songwriter and an artist, capturing my heart's desire in verse or on canvas is truly inspiring. I'm ever greatful to our Lord and Creator for giving me these talents. [a.] Marshfield, MO.

JARMAN, KATHLEEN
[b.] August 19, 1956, Chico, CA; [p.] Patricia Cross and Mick Turner; [ch.] Matthew and Alex; [occ.] Computer Consultant; [pers.] I believe we are on this earth to learn love, sometimes our lessons are easy and sometimes they seem impossible, but there are no accidents. All our experiences are steps on the pathway to love. The sooner this is understood the sooner we will find true peace and fulfilment. My poetry helps me to find the love in all my life's lessons. [a.] Columbus, OH.

JASON, JOAN
[b.] New Westminster, BC Canada; [ch.] Karl Dummett Jason; [ed.] University of British Columbia, Trinity College of Music, London, England; [occ.] Print and Broadcast Journalist, host radio show, "Poets off The Page"; [hon.] Top student award, medals and trophies for drama public speaking, singing and swimming; [oth. writ.] Novels, film scripts, plays, short stories, humorous pieces, travel stories, many poems published in small periodicals; [pers.] The equal value of all human beings has always been a deep motivator in the way I live and what I write. I urge poets to sent me their work so they can appear (via phone) on my radio program, reading their poems and being interviewed. [a.] Toronto, Canada.

JEFFERSON, ARTHUR E.
[b.] February 26, 1953, Chicago, IL; [p.] Catherine and Elijah Jefferson; [m.] Vanessa Jefferson, December 9, 1975; [ch.] Namandje', Kasandji, Keleya and Arthur; [ed.] Harrison High, Kennedy-King College, Harold Washington College, University of Chicago; [occ.] V.P.

Development and Public Relations, Garfield Counseling Center, Inc.; [memb.] Associate Minister Friendship Baptist Church, Chicago Urban League, NAACP, President Avers Organization of North Lawndale; [hon.] Man of the Year 1990 F.B.C., National Endowment for Humanities Writing Award, numerous community service and leadership awards, wrote high school graduating class motto, received plaques and trophies in basketball; [oth. writ.] Numerous other poems, essays and short stories, publisher PCER Spectrum Chicago School Reform Newsletter; [pers.] Personal achievements are not complete until they help someone eles. [a.] Chicago, IL.

JENKINS, PATTY-LYNN
[b.] February 9, 1976, Springdale, NF Canada; [p.] Bruce and Florence Jenkins; [ed.] Grade 12, student at Grant Collegiate; [occ.] Student; [memb.] Member of school band and Jazz band; [pers.] I take each piece of work I do and put my full effort into it. If I don't feel confident or at all happy with what I've done, I start everything over again. [a.] Springdale, NF Canada.

JENNIFER
[pen.] Dianand; [b.] October 20, 1959, Guyana; [p.] Mangal; [m.] Dianand, March 27, 1993; [ch.] Romana Dasrath; [ed.] C.P. College of Preceptors, elementary typing, elementary English; [occ.] Housewife.

JENNINGS, CHRISTOPHER R.
[b.] September 28, 1947, New York, NY; [p.] John J. and Jeanne E. Jennings; [ed.] B.A. Philosophy from San Francisco State University; [pers.] Poetry is my catharsis. By threading words through the eye of the muse's needle, I can stitch a unique design on life's fabric. [a.] Honolulu, HI.

JESTER, ELISABETH JOHANNA
[pen.] E. J. Jester; [b.] Vienna, Austria; [ed.] Multi Media Art, Central Technical School, Toronto, Canada; [occ.] Artist; [oth. writ.] Several poems published in local papers. [a.] Toronto, Canada.

JETTER, RICHARD EDWARD
[b.] August 29, 1974, Tonawanda, NY; [p.] Richard S. and Suzanne Jetter; [sib.] Lisa Jetter; [m.] Single; [ed.] 1992 Honors graduate from Kenmore West High School, currently a student of the University at Buffalo as an English major; [occ.] Full time student; [hon.] Numerous achievement awards and recognition for percussion, Niagara-Frontier All Star for tennis; [oth. writ.] Currently in the process of writing a novel for possible publication in the future; [pers.] When looking back on my writing, I see many references to the changing of society and its influence on me through friends, teachers, and even common acquaintances. I hope I can deliver this same influence to others through my writing. [a.] Kenmore, NY.

JEVRIC, BRANISLAV
[pen.] Brane Jevric; [b.] May 3, 1961, Sarajevo, Bosnia; [p.] Milan and Milena Jevric; [m.] Postponed because of war; [ed.] University of Sarajevo, Bachelor of Arts in Comparative Literature, University of Sarajevo, Bachelor of Arts in Philosophy; [occ.] Freelance reporter, writer and fighter for peace; [memb.] Federation of Bosnian Journalist, Professional Journalist of Federation of Sarajevo, Journalist Human Rights Group, Red Cross Group of Bosnia; [hon.] The annual first prize, daily news "Oslobodjenje" (Sarajevo) for reporting from Romania on their war, bronze medal 37th International Congress of Journalists, Crans Montant, Switzerland

(Europe); [oth.writ.] This is ("Born in Bosnia") first poem published in English language, first story in English was "The Dubrovnik Golgotha" in "Why" a peace magazine, numerous articles in newspapers in author;s language; [pers.] The life is wonderful, but peace is better. So, patriotism is no to hate another nationality! That is the stand of my just finished unpublished novel about the war in Bosnia. [a.] San Diego, CA.

JIVIDEN, LORETTA HARPER
[b.] January 30, 1939, Nitro, WV; [p.] M.D. and Marie Allison Harper; [m.] Dr. Gay Melton Jividen, January 30, 1959; [ch.] Jon David and Ann Marie Jividen; [ed.] B.A. in Sociology, North Carolina State University (high honors), M.Ed. curriculum and instruction/gifted education also NCSU; [occ.] Instructional Resource Teacher, Computer Resource Teacher; [memb.] Delta Kappa Gamma, National Council of Teachers of Mathematics, Council for Exceptional Children, Tag Division of CEC, National Association for Gifted Children, NEA, NCAE, North Carolina Association of Gifted and Talented and Page; [hon.] Academically Gifted Teacher of the Year, State Award given by NC Association of Gifted and Talented, finalist Wake County Excellence in Teaching Award, past state President Tag Division of Council for Exceptional Children; [oth. writ.] Write for own enjoyment, have not published; [pers.] I hope to write and illustrate children's books in the future. All children should be exposed to the beauty of poetry and language at an early age. [a.] Raleigh, NC.

JOBE, TIFFANY ANNE
[pen.] Tiffany King; [b.] February 5, 1969, Springfield, TN; [p.] Dan and Ann King; [m.] Trevor Conrad Jobe, May 17, 1991; [ch.] Brittany Anne Jobe (2 years old); [ed.] Watauga Elementary, Ridgetop, TN., Greenbrier High, Greenbrier, TN., Middle Tennessee State University , Murfreesboro, TN.; [occ.] Housewife; [memb.] Alpha Delta Pi Sorority; [hon.] Who's Who Among American People", Honorable Mention from the National Poetry Association; [oth. writ.] "My Gift"; [pers.] "To dream is to live, to write is to live the dream". [a.] Goodlettsville, TN.

JOHN, MARGARET
[b.] June 16, 1918, S. Wales; [p.] David John and Ceridwen Daniel; [ch.] Michael John; [ed.] The Abbey Malvern Wells Royal Academy of Music, University of London; [occ.] Writer; [memb.] Mid Island Welsh Association, British Columbia; [hon.] Doyley Carte Award, Royal Academy of Music; [oth. writ.] Various poems, short stories and libretti; [pers.] My philosophy is influenced by the writings of Emanual Swedenborg. [a.] Gabriola, BC Canada.

JOHNSON, ANISSA L.
[pen.] A. Kristanza; [b.] June 27, 1970, Milaca, MN; [p.] Roger and Sonja Johnson; [m.] Single; [ed.] Ohamia High, Brainerd Community College, College of St. Benedict and St. John's University; [occ.] Full time student; [memb.] Phi Theta Kappa; [oth. writ.] Many poems, short stories and the beginning of a novel, all unpublished. However, I have not submitted any; [pers.] Words are only the descriptions of feelings and emotions, however, they sometimes have a hard time describing the exactness of those feelings and emotions. [a.] Ohamia, MN.

JOHNSON, BETTY JOE
[b.] July 26, 1980, Harlan, CO; [p.] Mr. and Mrs. Billy Joe and Betty Lou Walker; [ed.] Wallins Elementary

School; [hon.] In English comp. 2nd place and most scoring ball play thru 92-93, got 3 trophies, basketball, cheerleading, won several for basketball trophies and awards for best player/support; [oth. writ.] Help write articles on school book called Harlan Co., then and now. [a.] Wallins, KY.

JOHNSON, FRANCES

[pen.] Fransicus Jenice; [b.] May 8, 1933, Norfolk, VA; [p.] Deceased; [m.] Widow; [ch.] 3; [ed.] High school; [occ.] Author; [oth. writ.] Poems published local newspaper, under religion poems put to music soon to be published; [pers.] I am a born again Christian, proclaiming the name of my Lord and Savior in my writing. [a.] Norfolk, VA.

JOHNSON, GENE

[b.] July 18, 1922, Vigo Co, Ind; [m.] Shirley, August 22, 1968; [pers.] When bombs fell on Pearl Harbor, Gene was working in the Panama Canal Zone. He returned to the U.S. and at age 21 became a Marine Corp fighter pilot. Later he was selected to fly in a squadron that was given the F7F Tigercat, the first Navy or Marine Corps squadron to fly a twin engine fighter. Three of Pappy Boyington's black sheep were also in this squadron. At age 329 Gene volunteered to serve for three years during the Korean War. He attained the rank of major. When active in tennis, Gene won three state titles, he did some parachute jumping, he is a former member of Mensa, he has seven years of college credits. Gene is a retired high school English Teacher.

JOHNSON, GLADYS TAFT

[b.] January 29, 1921, Petersburg, VA; [p.] Peter J. and Lula Marshpund Taft; [m.] Glenn E. Johnson (deceased), May 6, 1950; [ch.] Glenda J. Ivie, David G. Johnson, Loreatta Hollowell, Charlotte Johnson and Wayne Johnson; [ed.] Kensington High School, Philadelphia, PA. graduated commerical, Mulvey Institute Tech, Philadelphia, PA. Creative Writing, Dobbins Vocational School Philadelphia, PA., Public Speaking L.D.S. Business College, Salt Lake City, UT., Business English, UT Valley Community College, Orem, UT, word processing; [occ.] Secretary 32 years Penna Railroad, Eastman Kodak Store, J.C. Penny Business Office, Salt Lake City, UT., Miscellaneous Real Estate and Construction Companies in Utah; [memb.] Orem Business Women's Club, Good Sam R.V. Timp. Roadrunners Club, Ut. Valley League Writers, National Library of Poetry, American Arts Association, Sparrowgrass Poetry Forum, Western Poetry Association, World of Poetry, International Society of Poets, National League of American Pen Women; [hon.] Golden Poets Award 1991 and 1988, many Silver Poets Award, World of Poetry, Editor's Choice Award 1993 National Library of Poetry, two certificates of Poetic Accomplishments from International Poetry Anthology; [oth. writ.] The Friend Mag, Christmas Story published 1985, Orem Geneva Times Newspaper, couple poem published Provo Daily Herald Newspaper, Christmas story 1991 New American Poetry Anthology 1988, National Library of Poetry , Wind In The Night Sky, anthology 1993, American Arts Association "Glory To God In The Highest" 1991, Latter-Day Woman's Magazine, poem 1988; [pers.] Poetry has been my life since 9 years of age. I feel God has blessed me with a talent to give of myself thru His love to help mankind by poems, stories, plays and service. [a.] Orem, UT.

JOHNSON, GLORY LUKACS

[pen.] Glory Lukacs Johnson; [b.] May 3, 1927, Perth Amboy, NJ; [p.] Anna and John Rusinak; [m.] Charles E. Johnson, 1977; [ch.] ALexander Lukacs III, Diane Doroba, Paul Lukacs and Charles E. Johnson; [ed.] Rutgers University (major English); [occ.] Retired; [memb.] President, The Heather Garden Club, officer, Church Women United, Slovak Folklore Society, Christian Women's Club, officer, Ways and Means, The Heather; [hon.] Poetry honors; [oth. writ.] Glory I, an autobiography, self published 1978, One Hundred Years, Five Families, self published 1988, Glory, The 60th Year, self published 1989, "Old Girl With New Glasses" American Poetry Roundup 1992, "Woman" Question of Balance 1992, "The Stones Cry Out", Voices of America 1992, "My Home in the Heather" Distinguished Poet of America 1993, "Lacrimare (for Donald)" Poetry An American Heritage 1994, "Fuller's Earth" Desert Sun 1994, "The Dead Bell" Dance On The Horizon 1994, "Baobub" Outstanding Poets of 1994, "Fuller's Earth, Treasured Poems of American 1994. [pers.] Write on!

JOHNSON SR., HARRY H.

[pen.] Harry H. Johnson Sr.; [b.] March 14, 1957, Ferriday, LA; [p.] Evan and Florence Johnson Sr.; [ch.] Ramone, Garbille, Dannielle, Tatyana and Harry Johnson, Jr.; [ed.] Ferriday High; [occ.] Banquet Captain, Holiday Inn; [memb.] Church of Christ; [pers.] I reflect the love of God in all my writing.

JOHNSON, HELEN BOYER

[b.] January 21, 1921, Ridott, IL; [m.] Nels T. Johnson (deceased), September 22, 1945; [ch.] Carolyne Quisenberry; [ed.] Rockford High School, writing course, Oakton Col.; [oth. writ.] Many poems; [pers.] I have read and believe poetry should paint a picture in the mind's eye, be it of a person, a place or a philosophy! [a.] Schaumburg, IL.

JOHNSON, JANET A

[pen.] Janet D. Johnson; [b.] August 30, 1976, Lawton, OK; [p.] Frank and Linda Johnson; [ed.] Konawa High School; [occ.] High school senior; [memb.] Beta, Academic Bowl-Team Captain, Future Business Leaders of America, Seminole National Tribal Youth Council-Treasurer, Senior Class Representative; [hon.] Honor Roll, Who's Who Among American High School Students; [oth.writ.] Article published in local monthly magazine, poem published in state newsletter; [pers.] I feel that thoughts and feelings should be expressed through writing. I choose to write about my own personal experiences and about views affecting my life. [a.] Konawa, OK.

JOHNSON II, LEVAR L.

[pen.] Levar L. Johnson II; [b.] August 24, 1966, Elkhart, IN; [p.] Levar and Nadine Johnson; [ed.] Attended Ball State University, Elkhart Central High School; [occ.] Independent Representative, high school football and track coach; [oth. writ.] Several untitled and unpublished poems. [a.] Elkhart, IN.

JOHNSON, MARY

[pen.] Mary Johnson; [b.] August 7, 1916, Korumburra, Vic Australia; [p.] Alfred and Annie Griffin; [m.] Charles Raymond Johnson (deceased), September 7, 1935; [ch.] Peter and Lynette, grandchildren, Susan and John; [ed.] At Mont Albert Central, Victoria, Australia, Merit Certificate, studied typing, shorthand, represented school, swimming sports, presented with Bronze Medallion for swimming and life-saving; [occ.] Home duties, writing, poetry, painting in oils and water-color, photog-raphy, gardening and wood-craving; [memb.] Surrey Park Swimming Club, Golf Clubs, Mt. Lofty, Mt. Osmond, Grange, S.A. Huntingdale, Victoria Garden Clubs and Flora Art; [hon.] Merit Certificate 1929, won scholarship for business school, learning typing and shorthand, presented with Bronze Medallion by school for life-saving and swimming, club champion, ladies breast stroke 4th in Australia, 220 ladies breast stroke championship, finished 5th, open 3 mile Yarra River swim, attained H'cap of 9 in golf, competed Australian Ladies golf championship, award of merit for photography, Victorian championship for floral art, numerous 1st prizes flowers and floral art; [oth. writ.] Produced book "Poems for Pleasure", 25 poems each with my own art drawings, narration and photography of extensive round the World Travels (30,000 words) Autobiography; [pers.] My numerous achievements have been built on self-determination, without the support, guidance or tuition from coaches in the above fields. Under tuition, I achieved a high standard in wood-carving during 1992. Poetry and writing is a natural outcome of lifes' experiences, it is giving me a great deal of pleasure as I recall happy times, look forward to what comes next, to the tomorrows and contemplate the future. [a.] Adelaide, Sth. Australia.

JOHNSON, ROSLYN

[pen.] Roslyn Clear; [b.] August 29, 1957, New York, NY; [p.] Mr. and Mrs. M.V. Footmon; [ch.] Khabeer Jaleel, Jamie Allen and Jason Alton; [ed.] High School of Performing Arts (New York, NY), dance major 1970-74, C.C.N.Y. (2 1/2 years), Jefferson Parish West Bank Vo-Tech School (Practical Nurse); [occ.] Licensed Practical Nurse-Geriatrics; [oth. writ.] I have written many poems reflecting everyday encounters in life but have not, until now shared my writings publicly; [pers.] If one listens attentively life is music, if one watches closely, life is dance, if on is alive, life is poetry. [a.] New Orleans, LA.

JOHNSON, RUTH VICTORIA

[pen.] Ruth Victoria Johnson Swedish; [b.] Over 55, Canada; [p.] Nils and Christina Johnson; [ed.] High school, a physical and Holistic medical studies for many years, had private pilot's license; [occ.] Retired from International Airline Flying Career; [memb.] British Columbia Country Music Association, Pacific Songwriters, British Columbia, Canada; [hon.] Articles written about me in Vancouver, Toronto, Sweden and Japan regarding Aviation activities in earlier years, had a song played at Expo 86 in Vancouver; [oth. writ.] Many other poems and quite a few songs, some Demo's some not, country, gospel and country gospel; [pers.] " I walk confidently now over the broker dreams of the past, knowing they were only stepping stones to my highest goal. I walk the path in faith, trusting God to lead the way.

JOHNSON, TERRI L.

[pers.] Born April 19, 1953 in Detroit, Michigan. She continues to reside in Detroit with her family where she manages a career as a vocational educational teacher and writer. She attended Murray-Wright High and Henry Ford Community College. A former student of the Upward Bound Program, Wayne State University, she credits this inner city youth program for her appreciation of cultural arts. Terri enjoys active participation with "Creative Xpressions", a poetry reading group promoting local creative talents in literary, musical and artistic skills. She is a member of the National Authors Registry and the American Poetry Society, and has affiliation with the National Library of Poetry. In her second year as a writer, she has achieved publications in several poetry anthologies. "My poetic expression results from interactions with people working their way through ordinary situations. Exchanging ideas on faith, wisdom and love. Her role as a poet in modern times is to reflect the thoughts and emotions as they relate to the life and times of which we live. Terri writes creating easy reading with the purpose of capturing the attentions of readers, holding them to image and feel the ideas being conveyed. Stimulating the senses, creating a new inner-self, transforming the changes to a higher level of awareness and wisdom.

JOHNSON, TIMOTHY
[b.] February 22, 1974, Lexington, MS; [p.] Mr. and Mrs. John L. Parker; [m.] Single; [ed.] Williams-Sullivan High, Holmes Community College; [occ.] Cosmetologist; [memb.] VICA-MIBA; [hon.] Dean's List, 2nd place in Vocational Industrial Clubs of America; [oth. writ.] They Dared to Dream, Love From A Black Man's Point of View, personal poems (not published or submitted to anyone); [pers.] I feel that poetry comes from the heart and my hands speak it out. [a.] Pickens, MS.

JOHNSON, VALDYNE J.
[b.] January 5, 1944, Roswell, NM; [p.] Valdyne T. and Walter W. Johnson; [m.] Divorced; [ch.] Walter Alan Barbee; [ed.] B.S. Elementary Education and Masters in Elementary Education; [occ.] Teacher, 4th grade, Del Notre Elementary, Roswell, New Mexico; [hon.] Dean's List; [oth. writ.] Children stories; [pers.] I let the light and love of God guide my hand across the page to bring enlightenment to humanity. [a.] Roswell, NM.

JOHNSTON, ROBERT MARSHALL COL. USAF RET.
[pen.] R M Johnston; [b.] March 25; [p.] Wilmott W. and Irene N. Johnston; [m.] Doris Elaine Johnston, April 1, 1969; [ch.] Robert M., Kareen Jo, Eve G. and Miles A.; [ed.] Shaler High Carnegie Tech, Art Inst. of Pittsburg, Art Students League of New York; [occ.] Retired; [memb.] Air Force Association, Reserve Officers Association, Penwriters Inc.; [hon.] Golden Quill 1964, Golden Quill 1972-1973, (TV), Penwriters (novel) 1993, short story 1992, AACEPA 1990; [oth. writ.] Unpublished short stories, novels (historical), humor, horror; [pers.] My life has been a plethora of pursuits which I feel compelled to put into words for those who have missed it. [a.] Worthington, PA.

JONES, CAPRETHA EULALIA
[pen.] Capretha; [b.] February 1, 1978, Tyler, TX; [p.] William E. and Brenda K. Jones; [ed.] Overton High School; [occ.] Volunteer Tyler Community Store Front; [memb.] D.F.Y.I.T. (Drug Free Youth In Texas), Spanish Club, Debate team 1991, Computer Club; [hon.] Band, cheerleader, Who's Who Among American High School Students, Honor Student; [oth. writ.] "Tribute to My Grandmother", "Me", "My Mother"; [pers.] I am an avid reader of both fiction and nonfiction. I concentrate my efforts on African American authors. I plan to continue my education and someday be of service to the African American community. [a.] Overton, TX.

JONES, EVERETTE ERNEST
[b.] July 1, 1920, Texas; [p.] McCallo and Lillian Jones; [m.] Grace E. Jones, March 7, 1938; [ch.] Mary, Jean, Patricia, Joel and Everette Jr.; [ed.] High school, Leeds College, 2 years Birmingham Southern College; [occ.] General Contractor; [memb.] First Baptist Church,

American Heart Association, Boy Scouts of American, sustaining membership; [hon.] City of Trussville Councilman 1960-1964, Deacon of Church, poem "Alabama The Beautiful" in Library of Congress; [oth.writ.] Published book of poetry "Ripples of Joy" in 1982 in conjunction with my wife, Grace. Grace did the illustrations, book contained 200 pages; [pers.] My wife Grace and I have 5 children, 12 grandchildren and eleven great grandchildren. We have about 250 additional poems ready to publish at this time. [a.] Trussville, AL.

JONES, F. E.
[b.] June 1, 1965, Topeka, KS; [p.] Forrest and Carole Jones; [m.] Madia Jones, February 2, 1989; [pers.] Poetry is a reflection of life at its worst and its best simply put into words of imagination. [a.] Bannister, MI.

JONES, GRACE E.
[b.] October 23, 1919, Dallas, TX; [p.] Mary and Robert Williams; [m.] Everette E. Jones, March 3, 1938; [ch.] Mary, Jeanie, Patricia, Joel, Everette Jr.; [ed.] Eight Great (formal) Pop-Chorsies at Jefferen, State Art School, California and Ala.; [occ.] Housewife; [memb.] Started Cahawba Art Club Trussville, member Pace Art Birmingham Museum of Art, Birmingham First Baptist Church, Trussville, AL; [hon.] Art, poetry, children's art classes; [oth. writ.] Published, Ripples of Joy in 1982, in conjunction with my husband Everette, illustrations by me, have many more poems and short stories; [pers.] My husband and I enjoy writing poems, and I like to write children's stories. We have five children, twelve grandchildren and eleven great grandchildren. [a.] Trussville, AL.

JONES JR., HARDY
[pen.] Chip Jones; [b.] December 20, 1972, Pensacola, FL; [p.] Hardy and Janell Jones, Sr.; [ed.] DeRidder High School presently attending McNeese State University; [occ.] College student; [oth. writ.] "Hope for The Children", "The Evening News", "Trip to Nirvana", "Stupidity", "Something to Write When I Can't Sleep"; [pers.] We need to help each other to become more spiritual and less material. [a.] DeRidder, LA.

JONES, JEREMY
[b.] January 30, 1981, Easton, MD; [p.] Sandy and Dave Pushkar; [ed.] Attending Centreville Middle School; [memb.] Library, magazines, (guitar's); [hon.] Honor Roll (some); [oth. writ.] Several about two notebooks full, all poems dealing mostly with earth, philosophy and death; [pers.] Walk the ledge of darkness, fight the battle of lies. [a.] Queenstown, MD.

JONES, LINDA ALLEN
[b.] October 10, 1952, Trenton, NJ; [p.] Ernest Allen and Isabella D. Ford; [m.] Robert C. Jones, July 2, 1983; [ed.] Gordon High School (Dillon, SC), Claflin College BA English (Orangeburg, SC), continuing education currently; [occ.] English teacher, Trenton Central High School; [memb.] N.E.A., T.E.A., N.J.E.A., Mt. Sinai Seventh Day Adventists, Joelle Eau De Parfum Inc. (distributor) Mercer County Chorale; [hon.] Dillonite Citation 1993; [oth. writ.] Various poems, plays not yet submitted; [pers.] To be all that you can be, set a goal and work toward it. Don't give up! I strive to reflect feelings, ideas and different concepts or ideas in my writing and I encourage my students to write. Maya Angelou is my inspiration, I read and admire her work. [a.] Trenton, NJ.

JONES, MONIQUE ANNDELOISN
[b.] March 28, 1981, Albany, GA; [p.] Tim and Mary

Ann Dennard; [ed.] School in 6th grade, Wayland School right now; [hon.] Third grade poem contest 1989, 5th place; [a.] Wayland, NY.

JONES, STANLEY GWYN
[pen.] S. Gwyn Jones; [b.] 1912, Neath; [p.] John Gwyn and Bessie Jones; [m.] Rosaline Jones, May 12, 1934; [ch.] Terence, Vivian and Margaret; [ed.] Melyn School, Neath; [occ.] Retired; [hon.] For my poem called the "Royal House of York", received a letter of appreciation from The Duke of York, also the Prince of Wales for my poem called "Royal Wedding Day"; [oth. writ.] Fifty six poems, one named, "Sir Winston Churchill", published by Regency Press, London and New York; [pers.] To me, my poems become a "Pointing in Words".

JONES, STEPHANY
[b.] August 14, 1978, Corona; [p.] Deborah Jones; [ed.] Still in high school; [oth. writ.] I write poems none published, mostly love poems. [a.] Corona, CA.

JONES, SUMMER
[b.] July 10, 1979, Springfield, MO; [p.] Sheila Scoggins and Larry Martin; [ed.] Muenster Public High School; [oth.writ.] Several poems not yet published; [pers.] I strive to show my true emotions in my poems. I have been greatly influenced by my friends and family. [a.] Myra, TX.

JONES, SYLVIA ELAINE
[pen.] Bisa; [b.] August 1, 1952, Anniston, AL; [p.] Rev. Cleveland and Mrs. Ella Jones; [ch.] Christopher, JaKata and Anika; [ed.] Knoxville College, TN., Niles College, AL., Miami-Dade College, FL., and the U.S. Coast Guard; [occ.] Administrative Secretary; [hon.] Vietnam and Gulf War Era Veteran; [oth. writ.] The Rollercoaster Ride, Quiet Fury of Distant Soulmates, A Need to Go by Samaria and The Pre-Madonna Speaks; [pers.] I believe that a good carpenter perfects his work by sharpening his tools.. creative license is mind blowing and above all strive for roots and wings, a blessing above all. [a.] Birmingham, AL.

JONES, TONY E.
[pen.] T.E. Jones; [b.] December 5, 1954, Kentucky; [p.] Mr. and Mrs. Cecil Jones; [m.] Stephanie M. Jones, July 8, 1989; [ed.] Ph.D in life; [occ.] Baggage handler, Delta Airlines, Nashville, TN.; [hon.] I have been awarded the gift of life with a keen sense of it's brevity; [oth. writ.] I've written over 300 songs, and now have 4 published (but no recordings yet), I also write short stories, also I have an on going book titled Observations and Poems of A Common Man; [pers.] I believe all the eternal wisdom, creative thoughts and insights are already floating through the air all around us, and there they will stay until we turn them into words on printed page or turn them into breath when we speak. [a.] Murfreesboro, TN.

JONES, TONY V.
[b.] September 14, 1962, Farmersville, TX; [p.] Melva Jones; [m.] Carmen Jones, October 5, 1985; [ch.] Erin Leigh, Tahnee Laurice, Cameron Vanderbritt; [ed.] Northeast High School, Tulsa Job Corp; [oth. writ.] Nine Days In A Gang (short story), several other poems and songs written, and working on another short story; [pers.] The world would be a better place if everyone would write just one poem. For a poem is the inner thought coming from one's heart, then the goodness in the world would come forth. [a.] Oklahoma, OK.

JONTZ, CLYDE W.
[b.] May 31, 1919, Baxter, IA; [p.] William and Letha Jontz (deceased); [m.] Anita; [ch.] Douglas, Kim, Kristin, David, grandchildren, Jennifer, Rachel, David, Megan, Nickolas; [ed.] Baxter High School; [pers.] I am a WWII Veteran that served on a B-17 as a Radio Gunner in the 15th Air Force throughout the European Theater. I now belong to six Veterans organizations and six Masonic and writing is my hobby while tending the 160 acres my grandfather purchased in the year 1870 and attend our Congregational U.C.C. Church on a regular basis. [a.] Baxter, IA.

JORDE, LEONE
[pen.] Jorde; [b.] December 10, 1913, Cardston; [p.] William and Mary Blackmore; [m.] Melvin Jorde, July 22, 1934; [ch.] Crystal, Garth and Ted; [ed.] Grade 12; [occ.] Retired; [oth.writ.] Several poems and articles published in our local paper, an article in the Vancouver Sun and in Whitehorse Star, Yukon, Canada; [pers.] I promote the fact that life is not a bed of roses. We all have ups and downs, I think we must strive to make the best we can of both. [a.] Vernon, BC Canada.

JORGE, JANET
[b.] October 26, 1971, Gil Roy, CA; [p.] Richard and Shirley Kennedy; [m.] Frank Jorge, April 25, 1992; [ed.] Hoover High School; [occ.] Dairymen and housewife; [oth. writ.] Other poems that have not been published. [a.] Atwater, CA.

JORGENSEN, ERIK
[b.] March 7, 1969, Denmark; [p.] Jorgen and Julia Jorgensen; [ed.] British Schools (around the world), Beng-Mechanical Engineering, Imperial College-London, MSC-Manufacturing Engineering-Cranfield University-England; [occ.] International Staff of Shell (Oil and Gass Explorations and Production); [oth. writ.] Fiction, novel set in Ancient Greece (have not made an effort to publish it yet); [pers.] I strive to make people more aware of history (especially Eurpeans); [a.] Lowestoft, Suffolk England.

JOYCE, BERNADINE
[b.] May 2, 1935, McDermott, OH; [p.] Albert and Mary Montavon; [m.] William Joyce (deceased), August 12, 1961; [ch.] Martin, Daniel, Brian and Mary Ann; [ed.] Notre Dame High School, Shawnee State University; [occ.] Billing Clerk; [memb.] American Legion Auxiliary, St. Columbkille Catholic Church; [hon.] Honor Society; [oth.writ.] Enjoy writing poems and short stories for pleasure and publication; [pers.] I write as a means of self-expression with the desire that others may look beyond the surface of people and reality and see the beauty hidden there. [a.] Wilmington, OH.

JOYCE, BRIDGET E.
[b.] April 30, 1985, Hartford; [p.] Mr. and Mrs. Michael Joyce; [ed.] 3rd grader, St. Mary Star of the Sea School, New London, CT, principal, Sr. Ann Loughery, 3rd grade teacher, Mrs. Cathy Zummo, 4th grade teacher, St. Eleanor O'Neill; [hon.] 2nd place Science Award, Thames Science Center, New London, CT; [oth. writ.] Other poems not yet published; [pers.] Writing poems opens a door to a new world of excitement. [a.] New London, CT.

JOYNER, DHANNYN
[b.] March 22, 1965, West Virginia; [p.] Edward and Delcena Gravely; [ch.] Diamond Miquette Gravely-Miller; [ed.] Glenville High School and Plaza Business

Institute; [occ.] Student-working on my degree in Information Science; [memb.] Corona Congregational Church; [pers.] I believe in striving for the very best life has to offer. Also to respect everyone who I come in contact with and don't let anyone or anything stop me from being happy. [a.] Jamaica Queens, NY.

JOYNER, ROBERT W.
[b.] June 12, 1946; [ed.] Maryland University, Literature, 1963, 1964; [occ.] Main Line Models, worked with Director on script for acting (seminar), Universal casting, auditions, screen tests, resume, head shoot, put in files for future works, shoot with C.M.Y. photographic Easton, MD., Karisma, interview, set up appointment with an instructor with 20 years experience, six week course, casting directory, picture in book, metro models, had a shoot with Pauline Morris, seminar, four hour seminar with Jim Carr on acting, actors reps., audition, on file with actors reps. of Philadelphia.

JULIUS, MARIE
[b.] December 20, 1981, Rockford, IL; [p.] Jean and Richard (deceased) Roger and Jane Alton (Guardian); [ed.] Empire Grade School (K-4), Carol Sandburge (5-6), Freeport, IL, Leaf River Grade School (K-6); [memb.] 4-H. [a.] Leaf River, IL.

JURY, WILMA F.
[pen.] Willy; [b.] June 1, 1938, Ochre River, MB; [p.] Frank and Annie Livingston; [m.] Gorden A. Jury, November 19, 1955; [ch.] Orla Lee, Tanis, Timothy, Lorena, Fiona and 7 grandchildren; [ed.] Grade X; [occ.] Housewife; [hon.] Certificates for drawings in Canada's 125th Coin Design contest; [oth.writ.] Beside "Rain" I have had two other poems printed "Did You" 1992 plus "A Fake" in 1993 in other poetry books; [pers.] I love to write, draw, crochet and bake in my own home. We were foster parents for 10 years. [a.] Ochre River, MB Canada.

KARBICK, ELENA U.
[b.] April 13, 1939, Lima, Peru, South America; [p.] Humberto (deceased) and Helena Urrunaga; [m.] William M. Kabrick, May 25, 1986; [ch.] Mario Barrenechez and Maria Elena Andres (from previous marriage); [ed.] B.A. Liberal Arts, major Psychology, Management and Leadership (AMA), Financial studies; [occ.] Translator, President and owner of "Just Translations" Company; [memb.] American Translators Association (ATA), Delaware Valley Translators Association (DVTA), active member; [oth. writ.] In process of writing a book and publishing a poem book in the future, several inspirational poems and thoughts published in some local bulletins; [pers.] The first step to success is to learn how to recognize our own failures adopting a positive attitude at the same time... bitterness or depression will blur our vision and benumb our mind! [a.] Philadelphia, PA.

KAHL, VERNON T.
[b.] November 19, 1951, Detroit, MI; [p.] Alfred and Beatrice Kahl; [ch.] Amy and Jason; [ed.] Melvindale High School; [occ.] Chef, M & K Custom Express Catering; [memb.] American Society for Quality Control; [oth. writ.] Unpublished personal poetry and journals; [pers.] Writing comes from the heart, experience and observation. It helps if you can spell too! [a.] Allen Park, MI.

KAISER, LORI J.
[b.] May 23, 1976, Park Ridge, IL; [p.] Gerhard and Lydia Kaiser; [ed.] Will graduate from William J.

Howard Taft, June 1994; [occ.] Student. [a.] Chicago, IL.

KAN, DEBORA YEE-MAN
[b.] April 10, 1960, Hong Kong; [p.] Anthony and Angela Kan; [ed.] San Mateo High, UCLA; [occ.] Caterer; [memb.] Chi Alpha Delta. [a.] Los Angeles, CA.

KAPTANOWSKY, WALTER
[b.] October 1, 1953, Detroit, MI; [p.] Michael and Natalie Kaptanowsky; [m.] Cyndi (Ewing) Kaptanowsky, October 1, 1988; [ch.[Scott Ewing, Adam Robert and Erik Walter (Adam and Erik are twins); [ed.] Fordson High, Henry Ford C.C. and Eastern Michigan University; [occ.] Member of Logistics Department with BASF Corp., Detroit, MI; [hon.] I am honored by the fact that God provided me with such a loving, caring family; [oth. writ.] Have composed a number of other poems that have not yet been submitted for possible published; [pers.] I simply attempt to convey, into written words, feelings gained through experiencing, or witnessing, life's myriad of pleasures and pains. [a.] Livonia, MI.

KARLSEN, HERFINN
[pen.] Heyrek Dane/Scrutinizer; [b.] September 1, 1924, Vaagan; [p.] Ragna and Hans Karlsen; [m.] Delia B, Karlsen, May 22, 1985; [ch.] Harald Bjornar and Vigdis Robin and Kris; [ed.] Exam from high school, Ship's Electrician School, Commercial School and Commercial Teacher's certificate examination; [occ.] Retired teacher of 6 commercial subjects; [oth. writ.] Newspaper articles, examination papers and lately "A Jewel In Space", The Watery Planet and Its Manual; [pers.] I am scrutinizing all things, looking for the truth and for a publisher of my manus/book, "A Jewel In Space". [a.] Kongsvinger, Norway.

KARPIE, ROBERT J.
[b.] January 23, 1955, Buffalo, NY; [p.] James and Helen; [m.] Susan, September 30, 1973; [ch.] Brandie Marie (16), Jamie Marie (13) and William James (20, deceased); [occ.] Computer Operator for Buffalo Board of Education; [memb.] American Legion Post 1010, Ex-Marine; [oth. writ.] I write songs; [pers.] Someday, mankind will realize that love is the only answer to world peace, but first, he must turn inward, meditate and listen, only then will he realize that we are all one with God! Amen. [a.] Buffalo, NY.

KARR, JOANN M.
[b.] August 20, 1968, Arco, ID; [p.] Robert and Ann Karr; [occ.] Systems Operations Assistant; [oth. writ.] Article published in the Arco Advertiser (newspaper) in Arco, ID; [pers.] I give thanks to the Lord Jesus Christ for the ability to write. My writings come from the head. I strive to make them truthful and thought provoking. I take the Lord's guidance with each one, knowing that He is the first true poet. [a.] Lemont, IL.

KASABA, TERRI
[b.] Colorado; [m.] Edward, August 10, 1946; [ch.] Eddie, Terri Ann, Marie and Kathy; [ed.] Registered Nurse, scholarship to nurses training, Colorado Springs, CO, BS degree; [occ.] Educator Lompoc and Cabrillo High School; [hon.] Straight A student-Valedictorian at graduation, scholarship; [pers.] Love to read and write for my own pleasure.

KASSINGER, KEVIN
[b.] October 18, 1979, Owensboro, KY; [p.] Loretta and

James Kassinger; [ed.] Still in middle school; [occ.] Student; [memb.] I'm involved in Alateen and A.A. groups in Kentucky, and one day at a time is all we have; [oth. writ.] Several other poems wrote for school paper and local paper; [pers.] Life teaches you one day at a time. [a.] Owensboro, KY.

KATERIS, SOPHIA
[b.] May 20, 1970, Englewood, NJ; [p.] Irene and Spyros Kateris; [ed.] Graduate of Tenafly High School, Business Training Institute, The National Academy of Paralegal studies; [occ.] Legal Secretary; [pers.] I was influenced when I lost my only love August 2, 1989. [a.] Alpine, NJ.

KATSOROV, DONE
[b.] March 3, 1936, Sorovich, Macedonia; [p.] Goce and Fanka Katsorov; [m.] Niki Papaiounou, December 16, 1956; [ch.] Fanny, Robert, Gregory, Nikoula and Gefcann; [ed.] Public school in Macedonia; [occ.] Barber; [memb.] The Highland Fusiliers of Canada, United Macedonians Organization of Canada, Literary Association Brothers Miladinovi, Toronto, International Society of Poets; [hon.] Cambridge Memorial Hospital, Cambridge Multicultural Center, Cambridge Volunteer Bureau, International Society of Poets Award 1993, Founder, Macedonia Canadian Community of Cambridge, Canadian Macedonian Cultural Library Foundation, Canadian Literary Poet Association, president, Cambridge Multicultural Center, Cambridge Macedonian Community, Macedonian Canadian Library Foundation, Macedonian Radio Program ZRAK, Canadian Literary Poets Association; [oth. writ.] "I Search for Truth", "Freedom of Choice", "True Democracy", "There Is a Time To Be Concerned", "Lovers of Liberty" and others; [pers.] If you don't love your homeland, how can you love other lands. My thoughts and love are with you when I am near and far.

KATULSKI, FERDINAND
[pen.] Ferdinand; [b.] February 29, 1916, Detroit, MI; [p.] Mary and Ludwig; [m.] Rossella, July 31, 1937; [ch.] Gloria; [ed.] Completed the 9th grade in 1930 to begin work, attended correspondence and night courses at U. of M. and M.I.T.; [occ.] Retired; [memb.] Cousteau Society, Greenpeace, World Wildlife, Wilderness Society; [oth. writ.] Included is the first poem written at age 72 entitled "Clyde"; [pers.] My poetry may not be of a romantic nature for I have tried to put across the problems that confront the planet earth in a scientific approach. [a.] Big Pine Key, FL.

KAUFMAN, PAMELA
[b.] March 4, 1958, Johnstown, PA; [p.] Kathleen and William Kaufman; [ed.] Graduated Central Dauphin High School, Harrisburg, PA; [occ.] Receptionist, part-time, WHP-TV, Harrisburg, PA; [memb.] AWRT-American Women in Radio and Television; [pers.] Live a clean and healthy life with a positive outlook and never give up on yourself. [a.] Harrisburg, PA.

KAUKEANO-SMITH, LINDA
[b.] May 18, 1962, Honolulu, HI; [m.] William Smith; [ch.] Jessica Lynn Smith; [ed.] Old Dominion University, BS in Bio, Temple University, BSN; [occ.] Registered Nurse, managed care co-ordinator; [oth. writ.] At this moment I am working on a book with a Psychologist, Ph.D. on the dysfunctional aspects of nursing.

KAY, HARRY J.
[b.] November 25, 1919, Chicago, IL; [p.] Abraham J.

and Mary Ellen Kay; [m.] Rose Marie Sheehan Kay, December 29, 19512; [ch.] Harry, Patrick, Frances, Mary-Ann, Christopher, Kevin, James and Jeanine; [ed.] St. Mary's, Loyola University, Loyola Law School; [occ.] Retired; [memb.] 4th degree, Knights of Columbus, Director, Purchasing Management Association, American Legion, past commander, V.F.W. Post 2955, Avocation, teaching-instructor, U.S.A.F., teacher, CCD, St. Columbian's Church, Advisor and staff, Orange Coast College; [hon.] D.F.C. Oak Leaf Cluster, Air Medal, and 3 Oak Leaf Clusters, scholarships-4 years high school and 2 years college, varsity baseball and basketball. [a.] Garden Grove, CA.

KAYDA, SLAWOMIR
[pen.] Pat Kayda; [b.] April 25, 1969, Kielce, Poland; [p.] Barbara and Wieslaw; [ed.] High school, Jagiellonian University; [occ.] Airline Industry, Lax; [oth. writ.] Summaries of everyday for last 5 years for personal and historical purposes; [pers.] My efforts concentrate on catching emotional and daily moments in life adventure. Inspired by Kurt Jonnegut and Jazz music. [a.] Los Angeles, CA.

KAYGANICH, NICHOLAS J.
[b.] November 15, 1923, Dearborn, MI; [p.] Milan and Romana; [m.] May 16, 1953; [ch.] David, Daniel and Daria; [ed.] Fordson High School, Dearborn, MI, Cleveland Institute of Electronics; [occ.] Retired Telephone Technician, Michigan Bell Telephone Co.; [memb.] St. Clement Orthodox Church Sunday School Teacher, Dearborn; [hon.] 3rd place oil painting, Michigan Bell employees art show 1989; [oth. writ.] An article for the Young Life magazine 1983; [pers.] A wish that the people of the world to get along together instead of fighting each other. [a.] Dearborn, MI.

KEANE, BRIAN
[pen.] Brian Keane; [b.] October 17, 1962, Scotland; [p.] Patrick and Margret Keane; [m.] Susan Michelle Keane, October 23, 1985; [ch.] William, Jazne, Bryan and Kirsty; [ed.] Port Glasgow High; [occ.] Sculptor; [memb.] Founder member "Art Works" Studio, Gallery for contemporary art in Inverclyde; [hon.] Higher education awards in art, English, modern studies; [oth. writ.] Several poems published in small book "Reflecting Our Habits"; [pers.] My main concern it to capture the readers imagination with fluent images. I have been influenced by the works of Robert Hardy. [a.] Inverclyde, Scotland.

KEELER, CHRISTINE ANNETTE
[pen.] Annie Mishado; [b.] March 25, 1964, Santa Rosa, CA; [p.] Elizabeth and Philip Keeler; [ed.] Santa Rosa High School, Santa Rosa Junior College, Sonoma State University; [occ.] CSR at Bank of America, piano instructor; [memb.] Education Counselor in the Relief Society of the Church of Jesus Christ of Latter Day Saints, organist in the Redwoods Ward (same church); [hon.] Outstanding Musical Achievement Award from Santa Rosa High School-1982, 3rd runner up in the Miss Sonoma County pageant, 1982; [oth. writ.] First published work; [pers.] The poems I create are a reflection of my personal experiences and are mostly written for close friends. Born into a talented family, they are responsible for encouraging me at an early age to develop my artistic self. Thank you mom and dad. [a.] Santa Rosa, CA.

KEELING, DEBRA S.
[pen.] Debra Hall; [b.] October 9, 1952, Columbus,

OH; [p.] Charles Hall, Royina and Heber Moore; [m.] L. Keeling, November 18, 1978; [ch.] Brandy Dawn, granddaughter, Ashton Barger; [ed.] High school, college classes in Agriculture, Horticulture, Forestry, Animal Science, Scheffieled Interior, design classes; [occ.] Writer, farming, decorating houses; [memb.] National Library of Poetry; [hon.] Silver Poets Awards; [oth. writ.] "Too Late", "Whats Happened To Us", poems published in magazines and poetry books, Picture on The Wall, Our Soldiers; [pers.] Live life to the fullest for we only have this time to do it. [a.] Goreville, IL.

KELLER, SHARON WEAVER
[b.] April 21, 1943, Philadelphia; [p.] Eva and Richard Weaver; [m.] Frank, 1962; [ch.] Frank Jr., Connie, John and Joe, 9 grandchildren; [ed.] 10th grade; [occ.] Housewife; [pers.] To my mom, whose love I never doubted, but because of hardship did not raise me and my sister and brothers, but always I felt she loved each one of us, but was unable to raise us because of her hard life. I wrote this poem to honor her.

KELLEY, AARON PAUL
[b.] March 21, 1974, Bridgeton, NJ; [p.] Paul and Jean Kelley; [ed.] Millville High School, Millville, NJ; [memb.] Cumberland County Historical Society; [oth. writ.] Unpublished poems and short stories; [pers.] I am forever in debt to Jesse Marts and Judy Brett for their education and inspiration. [a.] Bridgeton, NJ.

KELLY, ANGELA
[b.] November 8, 1959, London, England; [p.] John and Mary Bergonzi; [m.] Barry Kelly, July 5, 1983; [ch.] Glenn David and Alexandra Catherine; [ed.] John F. Kennedy Comprehensive School, Nottingham School of Radiography; [occ.] Radiographer, St. Albans City Hospital, Hertfordshire; [memb.] Society of Radiographers, Council for Professions Supplementary to Medicine, Yoga for Health Foundation; [hon.] Diploma of the College of Radiographers; [pers.] I'm an avid reader of all kinds of writing where poetry is concerned, my greatest loves have been Wordsworth, Blake and Donne. [a.] Hemel Hempstead, Herts, England.

KELLY, ANNA
[b.] November 25, 1907, Everett; [p.] Ellen and Homer Morsette; [m.] Michael Charles Kelly, June 16, 1934; [ed.] I was going into the 3rd year of Girls Catholic High School, when I had to leave and help my mother as my father had heart trouble and he was unable to work so I had to help at home; [occ.] I am now retired, I worked for the same company for over 50 happy years Converse Rubble Company in Malden as and inspector; [memb.] Over 60 Club I.C., president of S.S. Girls Club School Day Ran Retreat in New Hampshire and in the Cape area at Miramar, took care of my brother who was deaf, wrote many items for conversations at work; [hon.] I was blessed all my life by having a wonderful home life and I owe it all to my dear mother and father which is the highest honor and awards anyone could receive , it was a home not a house, love and peace for each other. Dance contest-ballroom dance, I won many awards, bowling, skating and swimming; [oth. writ.] Many poems and short stories that I have at home; [pers.] My one ambition was to become a writer but, I never had the opportunity, I write as I feel. My life was made up of smiles and tears but I was always happy. I delivered papers morning and night, I pitched coke, fished ash barrels etc. [a.] Malden, MA.

KELLY-GRANT, SEWILLA
[b.] May 23, 1931, Temple, OK; [p.] Rev. J.C. and Sophia Grant; [m.] Willie James Kelly Sr., February 8, 1953; [ch.] Willie James Jr., Carolyn Denise, Debra Kaye, Le'Roy Gregory and Jocqueline Y.; [ed.] Douglas High School, Cosmetology School, Substance Abuse Counseling; [occ.] Retired, homemaker; [memb.] New Hope M.B. Church, President, Missionary Society, Vice President, United Christian Outreach member, Bible Way Crusade, Ministries; [hon.] Certified Prevention Specialist, Baseline Training I and II; [oth. writ.] Songs, short plays and a collection of poems entitled "God Gives Rhymes for Perilous Times" all unpublished; [pers.] I believe obedience, patience and promptitude can sometimes be a reward on their own. I lost many writings because I did not demonstrate these qualities. At first, a good poem is as refreshing and fulfilling to an open mind as a plate of wholesome food to a hungry stomach. [a.] Chicago, IL.

KELSO-PEACOCK, MERI
[b.] December 9, 1968, Birmingham, Al; [p.] Mac and Linda Kelso; [m.] Daryle W. Peacock, June 13, 1988; [ed.] Hewitt Trussville High, University of Alabama at Birmingham; [occ.] Cell Culture Technician; [memb.] Phi Sigma, UAB Honors Program; [hon.] Golden Key National Honor Society, Dean's List; [pers.] I would like to dedicate this poem to my family which was my greatest inspiration. [a.] Birmingham, AL.

KEMLING, LORI
[pen.] L.A. Kemling; [b.] August 31, 1958, Moorhead, MN; [p.] Arthur and Joanne Wonderlich; [m.] Nathan P. Kemling, August 11, 1986; [ch.] Jared (age 6) and Jesse (age 4); [ed.] BAE, Arizona State University-1984, MED-Arizona State University 1990; [occ.] Special Education Teacher; [hon.] Dean's List, graduated Suma Cum Laude from Arizona State University; [oth. writ.] I have written several children's books and I am currently searching for a publisher; [pers.] I write poetry to express my feelings of joy and loss. It is written mostly for personal reasons, but I also want other people to understand it and connect with it. [a.] Columbia, IL.

KENDIG, SPENCER KNOX
[pen.] Spencer Kendig Knox; [b.] January 11, 1947, Los Angeles, CA. (deceased, November 26, 1990, Fresno, CA); [p.] Kathryn Dye and Albert Christian Kendig; [ed.] Roosevelt High (Fresno, CA), Fresno City College, Fresno State College; [occ.] (past) Teacher's aide, ceramist, historian, poet; [memb.] Most recent, Faith United Methodist Fellowship, in past years, Fresno City and County Historical Society, Sigma Delta Chi (professional journalistic society); [hon.] Editor of the Fresno City College newspaper (The Rampage) while a student at FCC, recognition as historian of the Fresno Water Tower, lecturer at the base of the tower during 1985 Centennial observance, at the request of Fresno's Sister City Committee he donated copies of his poetry book Walk With Me to visiting Sister City delegates from Djambul, Kazakhstan, Spencer's poems are featured in the instructional TV production "Voices of Art" produced by me for the Fresno County Office of Education in 1985, one of Spencer's poems was accepted for publication in a 1993 national anthology titled Treasured Poems of America; [oth. writ.] Including Walk With Me, a total of 48 poetry books, in addition to publishing poetry books, Spencer had many editorials printed in local newspapers about the need to preserve Fresno's historical landmarks, additionally, his research article the history of the Fresno Water Tower is reprinted on the back cover of Walk With Me; [pers.] Spencer's poems generally reflect deep personal feelings. Because of this he has been called a lover. Additionally, many of his poems indicate a strong concern for the preservation of history and our natural environment. [a.] Fresno, CA.

KENNA, TOM
[b.] May 17, 1962, Herkimer, NY; [p.] Charles B. and Catherine M. Kenna; [ed.] State University of New York at Albany, B.A. English/communications (1984); [occ.] Writer/lyricist; [oth. writ.] Extensive unpublished verse; [pers.] " You can't remember the things that you were so worried about last year at this time or perhaps even those you worried about last week..." [a.] Boca Raton, FL.

KENNEDY, EVA MARIE
[b.] May 23, 1943, Edmonton, Alberta Canada; [p.] Lucien and Rachel Laudie; [m.] Eric Kennedy, March 13, 1992; [ch.] 5 boys, 1 girl from previous marriage; [ed.] Grade 12; [occ.] Home Care Aide for nursing home; [oth.writ.] First writing; [pers.] I am the mother of 6 children and grandmother of 7 grandchildren. I wrote this poem for my present husband, who had been my teen-age boyfriend many years ago. We both went separate ways then re-united 30 years later.

KENNEDY, KEVIN E.
[b.] November 15, 1944, Boston, MA; [p.] Arthur L. and Helen Kennedy Sr.; [m.] Single; [ed.] Boston Latin School, Mass, Maryknoll College, ILL; [occ.] Proofreader for an international law firm, freelance copy editor; [memb.] The Dramatist Guild, Polaris Repertory Company, AFTRA, IACI (Irish American Cultural Institute); [hon.] 1st prize for dramatic reading, Suffolk University speech contest; [oth.writ.] A Man Between Twilights, A Portrait of James Agee (2 act play), song for the last act,, A Portrait of Louise Bogan (1 act, a woman play) (both produced: Lincoln Center, NYC., Edinburgh Festival Fringe, Scotland); [pers.] I believe there is poetry within everyone and it is the job of the poet to touch that point of beauty and draw it out. [a.] New York, NY.

KERBEL, JESSA LOUISE
[b.] January 21, 1983, Johannesburg, South Africa; [occ.] Scholar, aspiring actress; [memb.] North Shore Talented Drama Ensemble, L.E.P.S. band, (Lindfield East, Primary School), Sydney, Australia; [pers.] I believe that poetry must reflect my feelings or moods, but doesn't necessarily have to mean anything. I seek all inspiration in natures beauty. [a.] Sydney. NSW.

KESAVA, DR. V.
[pen.] V. Mohan; [b.] July 1, 1988, India; [p.] VNB Chary Lakshmiswaramma; [m.] Dr. Annapurna, July 3, 1988; [ch.] Varun, Himant; [ed.] M.D. (Int. Medicine), (D.M.-Cardiology), P.G.I. Chandigarh; [occ.] Resident Cardiology; [memb.] Association of Physicians of India; [oth. writ.] Few poems in local magazines; [pers.] No amount of evolution in the poetry can bring revolution and elevate the living standards in this country.

KESERICA, SONJA ANN
[b.] December 18, 1969, Chicago, IL; [p.] Frank and Mara Keserica; [ed.] Fairfax High, Santa Monica College; [occ.] Receptionist at Kenneth Leventhal and Co.; [pers.] My writings are based on personal experiences that have had a profound and moving emotional impact in my life. [a.] W. Hollywood, CA.

KEY, FRANCES
[pen.] Maurine Garner Key; [b.] January 13, 1922, Lillian, TX; [p.] Wilburn and Ada Garner; [m.] Edwin Key, October 5, 1940; [ch.] Roy Alvon, Sheila Geneen, Dennis Ray, Rochelle and Jimmy Dane; [ed.] Mansfield High School, Mansfield, Texas, 1939 graduate; [occ.] Homemaker; [memb.] Mansfield Historical Society; [oth. writ.] Family and community stories for Johnson Co. Texas History book, also family stories for my children and their children to enjoy; [pers.] I believe that the written word enriches the lives of others long after the author is gone, just as long as the writing is of an uplifting nature. [a.] Burleson, TX.

KEYS, VIRGIL N.
[b.] May 21., 1914, Vernon, TX; [p.] Mr. and Mrs. J. W. Keys; [b.] Blanche B. Keys, May 21, 1939; [ch.] James R. Robert L., Tom N. and Jo Ann; [ed.] M.A.-Abilene Christian University, Certificate of Prof, Meteorologist, UCLA, MA. Sul Ross State U.; [occ.] Retired high school principal; [memb.] University Church of Christ, Abilene, TX, Texas Retired Teachers Association; [hon.] Have been listed Who's Who in Texas, Personalities in the South, Dictionary of International Biography; [oth. writ.] Some articles published in educational magazines and pamphlets.[a.] Abilene, TX.

KHAN, DILWAR
[pen.] Dilwar, Kavi Dilwar; [p.] Hassan Khan, Rahimunnesa; [m.] Warisa Dilwar, December 1, 1975; [ch.] Shaheen Ibne Kishwarm, Ibne Dilwar, Nahid Islam, Rozina Shiraj, Shazias Rahman, Kamran Ibne Dilwar, Ali Imran Ibne Dilwar and Ridwan Ibne Dilwar; [ed.] Intermediate (arts); [occ.] Free-lance Journalist; [memb.] Founder of Shamashwar Lekhok O Shilpi Shangstha, Ex-president Udihi Shilpi Gosthi; [hon.] Bangla Academy prize in poetry, 1980 (highest literary prize in Bangladesh) Fellow of Bangla Academy (Fellowship No 126) Lions Medal 1988, Abul Mansur Ahmed Literary prize 1986, Dewan Gulam; [oth. writ.] Martuza Memorial prize 1991, Jijnasha (1953), Pubal Hawa (1954), Oaikatan (1964), Udbhinna Ullash (1969), Facing The Music (1975), Swanishtha Sonnet (1979), Rokte Amar Onadi Oshti (1981), Nirbachita Kavita (1987) etc.; [pers.] As a man I am in quest of a "Real" definition of Humankind, the finality of which is "One World". I have been very much inspired by classical literature, music and arts. [a.] Sylhet, Bangladesh.

KIDD, JANET DARLENE
[b.] August 9, 1951, Monticello, KY; [p.] Raymond and Lola Troxtell; [m.] David Lee Kidd, June 6, 1969; [ch.] Susan Michelle Davis and James David Kidd; [ed.] Graduate, Wayne Co. High, Monticello KY, Associate degree Paralegal studies Owensboro Junior College of Business, Owensboro, KY; [occ.] Paralegal, law office, Constance E. Revlett, Calhoun, KY; [memb.] Order of the Eastern Star of Kentucky, member Kentucky Paralegal Association; [hon.] Grand Esther 1986-1987, Grand Chapter Committee member, credentials, 1989-91 Order of the Eastern Star; [oth. writ.] This is my first writing; [pers.] Never, never pass up the opportunity to learn something new.

KIDD, LAMONT C.
[b.] January 1, 1958, Chicago; [p.] William and Claudett Kidd; [ch.] Lynye McKiney Kidd (16 years old); [ed.] A.A. Liberal Arts, Kennedy King College 1979, B.S. Education Chicago State University 1985, Masters in Education National Louis University, 1993; [occ.] Teacher, Washington High School; [memb.] Christian Fellowship, Chicago State University, NU Alpha Gamma, Martial Arts Fraternity, International Black Writers

Association, Special Service Agent, Christian Tabernacle Church; [hon.] American Legion Award, Dean's List, Kennedy King College; [oth. writ.] Through Our Eyes We've Seen, He Was There All The Time, It's Marvelous In Our Eyes; [pers.] The Lord will show up at the show down, put God first and you can't go wrong. [a.] Chicago, IL.

KIDD, MAE STREET
[b.] Milersburg, KY; [p.] Mr. and Mrs. J. W. Taylor; [m.] Horace Leon Street, August 20, 1930; [ed.] Lincoln Institute of Kentucky,, Lincoln Ridge, KY; [occ.] Retired, Representative Kentucky Legislature, 17 years; [memb.] Lincoln Foundation, Louisville Urban League, NAACP, served 17 years House of Representatives, Kentucky Legislature; [hon.] Kentucky Housing Corporation Award given each year in my name, recipient of 96 awards; [oth. writ.] "In The Hills", "Thanksgiving", "What is Your Favorite Season of the Year". [a.] Louisville, KY.

KIEFER-KRUGLER, JOYCE FAYE
[pen.] "Blossom" [b.] February 10, 1964, Lutheran Hospital, Des Moines, IA; [p.] Arden and Sheryl Kiefer; [m.] Michael Dean Krugler, November 23, 1985; [ch.] Eric Michael and Amy Arden Krugler; [ed.] High school, Belmond High School; [occ.] Gift Shop owner of "Country Keepsakes"; [memb.] Evangelical Free Church; [pers.] I wrote this poem in honor of my father, Arden L. Kiefer, to know him is to have loved him, anyone who had crossed his path, was all the better for it. [a.] Belmond, IA.

KILGORE, DAWN M.
[pen.] Dawn; [b.] December 28, 1966, North Carolina; [p.] John and Betty Van Arnum; [m.] Brian T. Kilgore, October 2, 1993; [ed.] Leto High School, Saint Petersburg Junior College; [occ.] Student\waitress; [memb.] Christ Our Redeemer Lutheran Church; [oth. writ.] Some other poems never published. [a.] Tampa, FL.

KIM, ELIZABETH
[b.] July 12, 1978, Seoul, Korea; [p.] Dr. Ku-Jung and Mee-Ja Kim; [ed.] Currently (1993-1994) sophomore at Sylvania Northview High School year of graduate 1996; [occ.] Student; [memb.] 5 year member of Toledo Youth Orchestras, Monday Musical, Interact Volunteer, Korean American Youth, Interlochen Alumnae; [hon.] 5 time violin solo winner Toledo Symphony Women's League Remembrance of Fund Scholarship, Monday Musical Piano Solo Scholarship, 1st Honor Student, varsity tennis, JV Cheerleader, Concert Mistress of Northview Orchestra; [pers.] Write with your heart, not you head. Do not be intimidated by the opinions of others. Hold your head high and be true to yourself. [a.] Toledo, OH.

KIMBLE, LESLIE GRANT
[b.] December 2, 1945, Indianapolis, IN; [m.] Julia M. Cheatham-Kimble, July 7, 1986; [pers.] I was inspired to write poetry by my God and my wife. [a.] Indianapolis, IN.

KING, CHERYL L.
[pen.] Cheryl L. King; [b.] May 9, 1963, Huntsville, AL; [p.] Christine C. Tidwell; [m.] Jackie D. King, March 27, 1986; [ch.] Elizabeth Jacqueline-Diane, Christina Juanita-Lynn and Aleisha Leigh-Ann; [ed.] Brewer High School, Calhoun Community College; [occ.] Housewife and homeschooler; [hon.] Choir awards, Dean's List; [oth. writ.] I have had poems published in Hometown

Press; [pers.] My writings are inspired by my Lord and Saviour Jesus Christ. [a.] Lacey's Spring, AL.

KING, JOHN M.
[pen.] John Michael King; [b.] September 13, 1978, Hawthorne, CA; [p.] Marilyn and Wesley King I; [ed.] Bravo Medical Magnet High School, I am a 10th grader there; [occ.] Student at high school; [memb.] Poetry Club at high school; [oth.writ.] This is my first one, I intended on writing more; [pers.] My main focus in life is to do something right or not to do it at all. I am not a poet, but a writer. My hands write what my mind sees. [a.] Los Angeles, CA.

KING, LESLIE S.
[b.] April 28, 1961, Brooklyn, NY; [p.] Edward and Norma Dolleck; [m.] (Fiance) Russell Jordan; [ed.] Beach Channel High in Far Rockaway New York and Beverly Enterprises in Fresno, CA; [occ.] Certified Nursing Assistant; [oth. writ.] I have written may but never published before; [pers.] A special thanks to my best friend Vixen Yvonne for her encouragement and stubbornness to send in my poem, thank you Vixen. [a.] Fresno, CA.

KING, MARNI
[b.] December 26, 1953, Everett, WA; [p.]] Charles and Margaret Blacker; [m.] James, May 19, 1991; [ch.] Annika, Angelique, Matthew, Nikka and Tashlie; [ed.] Cascade High, Everett College; [occ.] Movie Screener and actor; [memb.] Everett Theatre Society; [hon.] Black Belt Karate; [oth. writ.] Currently working on a novel; [pers.] If I may quote Henry David Thoreau, "If one advances confidently in the direction of his dreams and endeavors to live the life which he has imagined, he will meet with a success unexpected in common hours". [a.] Everett, WA.

KINZEL, DORIS E.
[b.] June 10, 1929, Wenatchee; [p.] Harley and Ruby Moore; [m.] John A. Kinzel, June 10, 1950; [ch.] Jeff, Kurt, Phillip, Todd, Vince and Regina; [ed.] Graduated from Pateros High School; [occ.] Retired after 22 years at Mansfield School as Sec.; [memb.] Holy Apostles Church, Grange # 883, AARP, Senior Citizens Wenatchee-Retired Public Employees Chapter # 27; [hon.] North Central E.S.D. 1988, Excellence Award; [oth. writ.] Just poems for people who got married or retired in our small town; [pers.] Keep it simple. [a.] Wenatchee, WA.

KIRBY, GRACE
[pen.] Gratiana Evans; [b.] December 13, 1932, Hampton, VA; [p.] Hezekiah and Beatrice Kirby; [m.] Single; [ed.] Central Commercial High School, Bernard Baruch Business College; [occ.] Office Typist, Civil Court, New York City; [memb.] Metropolitan Life Insurance Company Retirees Association; [oth. writ.] Nutrition and Cancer article published New York State Tax and Finance newsletter in July 1985; [pers.] CAUTION! Human beings here. Handle with care. I have found great wisdom and the true meaning of life in various quotes over the years. [a.] Brooklyn, NY.

KIRKSEY, CINDY
[b.] August 14, 1956, Dallas; [p.] Mildred and D. A. Kirksey; [m.] Single; [ed.] High school, Mesquite High, college, Eastfield and E.T.S.U., Commerce, TX; [oth. writ.] I have had poems published in high school publications during high school and in the school paper in junior high; [pers.] If my writing ministers to others in

any way, I have achieved my purpose. I have used the gift God has given me as I believe He intended. [a.] Mesquite, TX.

KIRNON, ELLEN
[b.] October 31, 1934, Montserrat, WI; [p.] Grace Osborne; [m.] Joseph Kirnon, July 8, 1987; [ch.] Junie, Jeffrey, Tracey, Yvonne and Thomas; [occ.] Retired; [memb.] AARP, Pentecostal Church of Co-op City New York; [oth. writ.] A book Ellen will be out on March 30, 1994; [pers.] I have a lot of love to give and it reflects on my family, they are the reason for my life. [a.] Bronx, NY.

KITCHING, GILL
[b.] February 23, 1963, England; [p.] John and Lilian Trend; [m.] Richard John, July 16, 1983; [ed.] General education at local Comprehensive School; [occ.] Secretary; [oth. writ.] Published in poetry now London (1994), Winter Ensemble 1992; [pers.] My poems are varied and many, this one is a personal favorite. [a.] London, England.

KITTRELL, ROBIN
[b.] July 5, 1964, Montclair, NJ; [p.] Robert and Janette Kittrell; [ed.] Katharine Gibbs School, Montclair State College; [occ.] Administrative Assistant at a major Wallstreet Brokerage Firm; [memb.] Peta, Humane Society, ASPCA; [pers.] To Skippy, Bizzy, Moon D. and Petey, thanks for the encouragement.

KLEIN, HEIDI H. L.
[b.] June 11, 1977, Colorado; [p.] Leonard and Aldine Klein; [pers.] This poems was written in honor of my grandpa, Albert L.A. Eisenman for his eightieth birthday, May 31, 1993. He is a very healthy, active young man. I write my poems with the acknowledgement of my Creator who has bestowed many blessings and talents on me and my family. "Let love and faithfulness never leave you, bind them around your neck, write them on the tablets of your heart" Prov. 3:3, "Do not be wise in your own eyes, fear the Lord and shun evil". Prov 3:7. [a.[Monroe, WA.

KLEINFELTER, LYNN MARIE
[b.] September 11, 1965, Lebanon, PA; [p.] Janet and Ralph Kleinfelter; [ed.] Eastern Lebanon County High School, BA and BS, Shippensburg University, MA, Villanova University; [occ.] English Teacher; [memb.] Alpha Psi Omega, Gamma Sigma Sigma; [hon.] Alpha Psi Omega, candidate for Irene Ryan Award (1991). [a.] Newmanstown, PA.

KLOOSTERBOER, MARY ANNE
[pen.] Marianne Kerr Symons; [b.] January 24, 1945, Weston, Ontario Canada; [p.] Mary and Arthur Kingdon; [m.] Dirk Kloosterboer, August 7, 1971; [ch.] Two sons; [ed.] Georgetown High, Georgetown Ontario; [occ.] Administrative Assistant, North Halton Association for the Developmentally Handicapped (NHADH), Milton, Ontario Canada; [oth.writ.] Several poems in local newspapers; [pers.] I am a romantic by heart and am greatly influenced by my family. [a.] Milton, Ontario Canada.

KLOSOWSKI, SANDRA M.]
[pen.] "Inner Peace"; [b.] October 11, 1968, Bay City, MI; [p.] Frank and Joan Klosowski; [ed.] Central High School; [occ.] Unemployed; [memb.] Vietnam Veterans of America (associate member); [hon.] 4 years perfect attendance (high school), Home Economics; [oth.writ.]

I have various writings in my personal file. One of my writings was published in the Bay City Times; [pers.] I find it very gratifying to express my inner most feelings in my writing, it gives me great pleasure and peace of mind to make others smile. [a.] Bay City, MI.

KLOTZ, ZACHARY VAUGHT
[b.] July 17, 1964, Longview; [p.] Carol Ann and Chandler L. Klotz; [ed.] White Oak High School, graduated; [occ.] Paramount Packaging Extrusion Technician Assistant; [hon.] This is the first poem that I have gone public with; [pers.] Two characteristics of poetry such as rhyme and rhythm make writing poetry fun for me and quite enjoyable. [a.] Longview, TX.

KNAPP, CINDY LOU
[b.] April 30, 1976, Bay City, MI; [p.] Wanda and Ron Knapp; [ed.] Western High School in Auburn; [occ.] Student, senior in high school; [pers.] My future goal is to teach English. I wish to be as wonderful and as helpful as Mrs. Karen Appold, Ms. Judy Fletcher, Mrs. Mary Moskal and Mrs. Diane Sullivan were to me. They have all added something warm, loving, caring and special to my life as I could only wish to add to the lives of others. [a.] Bay City, MI.

KNIGHT, BENJAMIN O.
[pen.] Gentle Ben; [b.] July 4, 1926, Superior, MT; [p.] Deceased; [m.] Mary Lyan Knight, June 13, 1954; [ch.] Susan, William and Nancy; [ed.] Keithsap High School, Pt. Orchard Washington, University of Maryland (US Agency), Acc., Austin, Texas, University of Austin Texas; [occ.] Retired U.S. Army; [memb.] VFW, DAV, American Legion, National Parks and Com. Association, NRA, Wildlife Defenders; [hon.] Association CRT Judge (retired), Department Army Management, Superior Award; [oth. writ.} Some papers and stories, U.S. Army; [pers.] Be as nice to me as I am to you. [a.] Austin, TX.

KNISLEY, ROBIN ELIZABETH
[b.] April 4, 1978; [p.] Rick and Rhonda Knisley; [m.] Single; [ed.] Sophomore, age 15, Bloom-Carroll High School; [occ.] Student; [memb.] V.I.C.T.O.R.S.; [hon.] Honors classes in high school, class president freshman/sophomore years, secretary of FSA. [a.] Lancaster, OH.

KNOLL, MARLENE
[pen.] Greensleeves; [b.] March 4, 1945, Cleveland, OH; [p.] Albert Joseph and Alvina Ruthenberg; [m.] Mark S. Knoll, September 3,1967; [ch.] Aaron Michael and Laura Kathryn; [ed.] Shaker Heights High School (Ohio), Pomona College, B.A. Philosophy, Boston University, MA., Political Science; [occ.] Writer, Chatelaine; [hon.] A year long honors program in legal theory at Pomona College, teaching fellowship 1st scholarships at Boston University, Chinese language scholarships at Middlebury College; [oth. writ.] Cottonwood Cove and A Lover's Guide to England and France, novels and several volumes of poems (unpublished); [pers.] Writing reflects the psychological, social, moral and political stances of a writer within society, I use humor to plant the limitations of politically correct thought in life. [a.] Freedom, NH.

KNOX, ASHLEY
[pen.] Ashley Knox; [b.] February 10, 1973, Lubbock, TX; [p.] Jay and Mary Knox; [ed.] MacArthur High, Southwest Texas State University, University of Texas at Arlington; [occ.] Futuristic and Exotic Street Car Manufacturer; [oth. writ.] I have yet to have anything pub-

lished, but I have written many poems, two short stories and two novels; [pers.] My main motivation for writing is to give my future readers a chance to read my words, relate to them and thereby gain some insight into their own lives. Life has been my mentor, I have learned well. [a.] Irving, TX.

KNOX, PETER
[b.] April 18, 1949, Sydney, Australia; [p.] Roy Eric and Marion Ethel Knox; [m.] Patricia Giles, Defacto; [ch.] Corinna Deja and Xanthe Karma Knox; [ed.] Yennora Public School, Chester Hill High School, University of Wollongong; [occ.] Musician, Community Worker, Student Representative Council President; [memb.] Actors Equity; [hon.] Intermediate Certificate (1946), Gateway Tertiary Entrance Certificate (1990), Illawarra Credit Union Employment Scholarship (1993); [oth. writ.] A number of short stories published in various Australian Journals, article published in Nation Review newspaper, various poetry magazine publications, arts reviews published in Tertangala University of Wouongong Students newspaper; [pers.] I have been a Rock Musician for far too long, but my creative energy refuses to wane, hence my bachelor of creative arts degree, which has helped channel the energy into other creative areas. [a.] Kiama Heights, NSW Australia.

KNUTSON, CONSTANCE F.
[b.] January 4, 1943;

KOCAK, SUNA MARIE
[pen.] Suna; [b.] June 27, 1982, Watham, MA; [p.] Sitki and Marie Kocak; [ed.] Lincolnville Central School, Lincolnville, Maine (7th grade); [hon.] From grades 5 until now, received honors every term; [oth. writ.] I also have been writing children's short stories and chapter books for young adults; [pers.] I love reading and writing, I hope one day to become an author. [a.] Lincolnville, ME.

KOCHANOWSKI, LOUISE SHARON
[b.] September 15, 1941, Armstrong County, PA; [p.] Peter and Anna Samosky; [m.] Andrew Peter, Patrick Sean and Colleen Louise Kochanowski; [ed.] Point Park College, Pittsburgh, PA; [occ.] Housewife and help care for the sick and elderly; [memb.] Past Assistant in school library, member St. James Church, past member of St. James Rosary Confraternity and past treasurer; [hon.] Mu Sigma Sorority; [oth. writ.] I do a lot of writing for my own personal pleasure and expression; [pers.] I was greatly influenced by my father reading poetry to me when I was a child. I like to help people and reflect my feelings in writings.[a.] Spring Church, PA.

KOCHMAN, THOMAS
[b.] May 19,1936, Berlin, Germany; [p.] Max and Ellen Kochman; [ch.] Adrienne and Svitlana Kochman; [ed.] Ph.D. Linguistics, New York University 1966; [occ.] President Kochman Communications Consultants; [oth. writ.] Author, Black and White Styles in Conflict, University of Chicago Press 1981; [pers.] Be all that you can be, just do it! [a.] Chicago, IL.

KOLB, SHEILA L.
[pen.] Sheila L. Kolb; [b.] October 31, 1960, McKinney, TX; [p.] Bobby and Mary Hill; [m.] Daniel J. Kolb, July 28, 1990; [ch.] Alexandra Cailyn Kolb; [ed.] Newman Smith High, Psychiatric Assisting Institute; [occ.] Housewife; [memb.] M.H.M.R., Mental Health Association, Gift of Life Family Church Prayer Hot Line, American Karate Association; [hon.] Highest honors in psychiatric

assisting, winning essay, subject, mental health, certification in self defense in Chinese Kempo Karate, Yellow belt in Tae Kwon Do; [oth.writ.] Children's books, poems, songs, materials on mental health for counselling purpose; [pers.] It is my intent to disclose ones most hidden emotions and feelings in my writings. When we are able to see and accept our fears, it is then that we can began to chip away the walls that block our true selves. [a.] Princeton, TX.

KOPCSAK JR., GEROGE COLEMAN
[b.] July 7, 1962, Ft. Siil, OK; [p.] Linda Rose Kopcsak; [m.] Kathleen Ellen Kopcsak, December 29, 1987; [ch.] Brittany Kathleen (6) and Michael James (1); [ed.] Stonewall Jackson High, Manassas, VA., Bridgewater College, Bridgewater, VA; [occ.] 8th grade teacher, Chattanooga Valley Middle School; [hon.] Dean's List, Teacher of Promise finalist, CVMS Teacher of the Year. [a.] Chattanooga, TN.

KORFHAGE, ESTHER WHEELER
[b.] July 9, 1947, Whitinsville, MA; [p.] Cecil R. Wheeler and Helen M. Wheeler (deceased); [m.] Walter John Korfhage, July 7,1989; [ed.] 12th grade "class of 1966", Douglas Memorial High School, East Douglas, MA; [occ.] Disabled and unemployed; [hon.] Honorable mention-1985, Golden Poet Award-1985, Silver Poet Award-1986, All for "Satin and Lace" from World of Poetry, Honorable Mention-1990, Golden Poet-1990 all for "Special Friends" from "World of Poetry"; [pers.] I have my Aunt Emily W. Thompson to thank for being a writer, whom I take after, a late friend Peggy White whom I wrote "Special Friends" for, and my husband, John who puts my poems to music. [a.] East Point, GA.

KOSSMAN, MIRIAM R.
[b.] Philadelphia, across the road to Memorial Hall in Fairmount Park where developed affinity for art, nature and museums; [ed.] Public schools, BS in Ed. at Temple University, majors with major in English at U. of Pa., studied at Philadelphia Music Academy, Barnes Foundation, G.B. Seminars at Lake Forest and Colby, certified also to teach English as 2nd language and arts and crafts, shows at camps, playgrounds, etc., studied at Foundation of Architecture Tours, lectures, etc.; [occ.] Monthly columnist for the Weekly Press (formerly the University Press); [memb.] Curtis Institute, GB Foundation, Barnes Foundation, Drama Guild, Plays and Players, Wilma Theatre, Arden Theatre, Performing Arts, MMA, Philadelphia MA. PA. MA., F of Architecture plus Prof. Associations, Rosenbach Library and Museum; [hon.] Graduated Cum Laude from all schools attended, recognition for GBGR, leadership at YWCA, recognition from Penn Center House Apts. for editing publication for ten years, (plaque), recognition for writing show (in verse) at Lake Forest. Thank you notes and some verse on paper. Thank you recognition from White House for feature "Talk of the Teens" in Press Clips column in honor of Chelsea's 13th birthday. [pers.] Indebted to parents who equated books with bread, major commitments, community, culture and creativity.

KOZAK, PAULA
[b.] October 29,1962, Minneapolis, MN; [p.] Beverly and Joseph Kozak; [ch.] Anthony Paul Schultz (4 years old); [ed.] Edison High School, Minneapolis Technical College, Ringling School of Art and Design; [occ.] Full-time student, Ringling School of Art and Design (Computer Animation major); [pers.] My writings are personal reflections of where I have come from, what I have gone through and where I am going. [a.] Minneapolis, MN.

KOZIATEK, LINDA L.
[pen.] Linda L. Manning; [b.] August 18, Mass City, LI; [p.] Lois and Carl Manning; [m.] Edward, June 22, 1980; [ch.] Eddie, Mikie, Kristie and Tommie; [ed.] High school graduate, Fashion Merch graduate Berkeley; [occ.] Homemaker currently, was a bookkeeper; [hon.] Honorable Mentions; [oth.writ.] Juvenile fiction, songwriting, picture books; [pers.] Always treat others the way you would want to be treated. [a.] Syosset, NY.

KRAMER, GERT-JAN
[pen.] John Kramer; [b.] August 13, 1969, Ellemeet; [p.] P.D. Kramer and S. Kramer-De Looff; [ed.] Professor Zeeman High School, Philosophy/English correspondence course; [occ.] English interpreter-translator; [pers.] True poetry equals true feelings. My poem "The Spectre" included in this anthology, warns against the destructive forces of racism. I have been influenced by the realistic poets. [a.] Ellemeet, Netherlands (Europe).

KRAUSE, MICHAEL O.
[b.] November 28, 1949, Fond Du Lac, WI; [p.] Oliver and Melvinia Krause; [ed.] Goodrich High, Wisconsin School of Electronics, Electronic Technical Institute, San Diego, CA; [occ.] Electronic Tech. [memb.] Moose Lodge; [pers.] I like to view people from the inside, not by what they look like or how much money they make. [a.] Sunnyvale, CA.

KRAUTTER, LUAL O.
[b.] August 6, 1955, Port Washington, WI; [p.] Rolf and Irene Fostervold; [m.] Martin S. Krautter, May 12, 1984; [ch.] Joel Grant (12-8-87) and Daniel Scott Krautter (1-10-92); [ed.] American School (out of Chicago by correspondence) while growing up in Paraguay, as a daughter of Christian Missionaries there G.E.E.; [occ.] Wife and homemaker, artist, harpist; [hon.] Nominated in January 1981 to point a portrait of the Governor of Puerto, President Stroessner (now Cindad del Este) in Paraguay S. America, also did a portrait of President Stroessner in May 1980, I've also painted other requested paintings for friends and relatives of personal portraits and/or nature scenes; [oth. writ.] Several poems compiled between ones I've written and ones my husband has written, ready for publication possibly in the near future, (1994-1995?), a tentative book title is A Legacy of Memories; [pers.] I enjoy writing about different events happening around me, trying to capture the mood or feelings of the moments, besides depicting God's leading in my life through ways He has answered prayers and that He gives spiritual peace thru His Son Jesus Christ. [a.] Rock Springs, WY.

KRAYER, TERESA
[b.] July 16, 1962, Fort Worth, TX; [p.] Don and Elaine McDowell; [m.] Keith Krayer, September 26, 1982; [ch.] Kristen Alicia and Brandon Matthew Krayer; [ed.] W.E. Boswell High, Northwest Tarrant County Junior College, Texas Christian University; [occ.] Housewife, volunteer; [memb.] Lockheed Recreation Association; [pers.] Through my writing I hope to make a difference in someone's life. The people I know and love help me to create what I write. [a.] Boyd, TX.

KRET, LINDA M.
[b.] June 19, 1950, New York City; [p.] Grace Catrone and Harry Soo; [m.] Robert John Kret, May 18, 1991; [ch.] Debbie and Linda; [ed.] High school (general diploma); [occ.] N.Y.C. Police Department (Police Administrative Aide); [hon.] Certificate of Merit, Certificate of Accomplishment N.Y.C. Police Foundation,

1990 Award of Excellence; [oth. writ.] Poetry that was never published; [pers.] "Strive through life... succeed and conquer all to the fullest". [a.] New York, NY.

KRISTAL , GENE
[pen.] Archibald Hoggord; [b.] December 21, 1935, Sandy Lake, Mantobia; [p.] Mary and Harry Kristalougeit; [m.] Divorced; [ch.] John, Tom, Robert and Carla Taylor; [ed.] M.Ed. University of Manitoba; [[occ.] Retired high school teacher, St. Patricks High School; [hon.] Inco Scholarship-1963; [oth. writ.] Some letters to Editors published in local papers; [pers.] Life is growth, growth is change at present contributions must be made. This particular poem was inspired by its setting, around Sandy Lakes, MB. [a.] Brights Grove, Ontario.

KROBATH, HELENA MARIE
[pen.] Helena Marie; [b.] April 21, 1981, Clearbrooke; [p.] Linda Colleen and Frank Krobath; [ed.] I am in grade 8, I am homeschooled; [occ.] Babysitter; [hon.] I have received first class honors with distinction on my grade 1 rudiments Royal Conservatory exam; [oth.writ.] "The Lion" is my first published poem, however, I have many poems and stories that I am currently working on; [pers.] Live each day as if it were your last, and stick to the basics of life, and it's what you do that will be remembered, what you had will be buried with you. [a.] Mission, BC Canada.

KUASNICKA, RENEE
[b.] June 29, 1968, Berwyn, IL; [p.] Kenneth and Linda; [ed.] Graduated 1986 from Morton West High School, currently attending Morton College; [occ.] Receptionist at Associated Advertisers of America; [oth. writ.] Currently trying to finish writing a few stories on various topics, when they're finished hopefully I'll be able to get them published; [pers.] I'd like to thank my parents, my sister Denise, my grandma Rosalie, my fiancee Patrick and my best friend Cathi for all of the support they've given me. [a.] Berwyn, IL.

KUBIK, MAUREEN
[b.] March 13, 1974, Hartford, CT; [p.] Donald and Ruth Kubik; [ed.] St. Paul CHS, Bristol, CT., Franklin Pierce College; [hon.] Dean's Honor List; [a.] Avon, CT.

KUEHL, KRISTIN C.
[b.] June 24, 1976, Beaver Dam, WI; [p.] Glenn and Carole Kuehl; [m.] Single; [ed.] Sophmore in high school, Lomira, WI; [oth.writ.] "With You"-poem, "Memories"-poem, "I Want"-poem; [pers.] I love writing for one thing, and I must say that all thought my years so far in school, I'd have to give the credit to my English teachers. Poetry has always found a place in my life, and the main reason I like writing is because most of it comes from the heart. [a.] Theresa, WI.

KUHLMAN, BRIAN
[b.] April 5, 1942, Gothenburg, NE; [p.] Henry and Bessie Kuklman; [ch.] Daniel; [ed.] Gothenburg High, Central Technical Institute, Kansas City; [occ.] Electronic Technician, Eglin Air Force Base, FL; [pers.] When I was young I wanted to amaze people with my writing. Now I'm the one amazed and graciously content, that my written words may please someone. [a.] Santa Rosa Beach, FL.

KUMMEL, NORAH ELIZABETH
[pen.] Kierstead-Carter-Kummel; [b.] September 21,1933, Vancouver, BC; [p.] Stanley and Elsie Kierstead;

[m.] 1st marriage, Roy Carter, November 27, 1932, 2nd marriage, George Kummel, July 27, 1933, April 7, 1951, May 18, 1974 (deceased); [ch.] Steven, Robert, Nancy and Grege Carter, eight grandchildren; [ed.] Grade 12, Chilliwack Senior High; [occ.] Retired; [oth.writ.] As I was married at a very young age I did not have the opportunity to further my education, but have been writing poetry since the age of 15, have never submitted any work prior to this; [pers.] My poetry tends to be philosophical portraying an empathy for reality. I try to reflect the heart that is hidden in mankind. I have been greatly influenced by Tennyson and Longfellow. [a.] Abbotsford, BC.

KUTSCHINSKI, MADELINE C.
[b.] November 13, 1946, Plainfield, NJ; [p.] Walter and Jerldine Kutschinski; [ch.] Ron, Jerry, Sherly, CaraLisa, Judy Christine Joseph-LaBoo; [ed.] 12; [occ.] C.N.A.; [pers.] I write deep with in the sole of only of truth, and all the people who read my letter will think and reconsider. [a.] Tampa, Fl.

KUTZ, KRISTIN
[pen.] Kristin Kutz; [b.] April 16, 1977, South Carolina; [p.] Mr. and Mrs. James L. Kutz; [ed.] Currently L.F. High School, past St. Mary's in L.F., Il, grammar school; [occ.] Student, part time job at a Frame Shop; [memb.] Currently involved with NOTHING except Oddessey of the Mind, an educational creative problem solving club and committee; [hon.] Numerous artistic achievement certificates and writing awards; [oth.writ.] Numerous poems, stories and other literacy works which are yet to be recognized; [pers.] My work was and always will be a reflection of myself as an individual and the study of life as a whole. [a.] Lake Forest, IL.

KURTZ, LINDA R.
[pen.] Linda R. Kurtz; [b.] July 1, 1953, Amherst, OH; [p.] Kenneth and Elizabeth Blanchard; [ch.] Anglea and Jennifer Kurtz; [ed.] So. Amherst High School, Mt. View College, Associates University of Texas, Arlington Bachelors degree in English and Elementary Education; [occ.] Teacher, Rosemont Elementary, Dallas,TX; [memb.] Living Bank, Alliance Teachers Association; [hon.] President's Recognition Award (twice), Phi Theta Kappa Honor Fraternity, Kappa Delta Pi Honor Fraternity, Alpha Chi Education Honor Fraternity; [oth.writ.] Several hundred poems, none of which have been published to date; [pers.] I strive to teach and provide comfort for mankind through my poems. [a.] Dallas, TX.

KURTZ, OLIVE L.
[b.] march 15, 1908, Jefferson County, WI; [p.] Will F. and Elvira (Vira) Kutz; [ed.] Ft. Atkinson, WI High School, U. W. Whitewaler, WI B.E.; [occ.] Retired teacher;[memb.] Honorary member WRTA, AARP, Bark River Woods Historian Society, (past President, Director Emeritus) St. Paul's Lutheran Church (F.T.A.) JCARTA (retired teachers); [hon.] Second prize UWEX Yarns of Yesteryear Winner's Circle. [a.] Ft. Atkinson, VA.

LABBIE, ANGELLA
[pen.] Pun; [b.] March 15, 1965, Rayne Branch Hospital; [p.] Grace and Rodney Labbie; [ed.] 1991 college graduate of McNeese State University, BA in Elementary Education, attended LSU at Eunice and Church Point High; [occ.] Teacher at Our Mother of Peace Elementary; [memb.] PASTA-Parish of a Acadia Science Teachers Association, NCEA-National Catholic

Education Association; [hon.] Teacher of the Year Award, 1993-1994; [oth. writ.] Short stories, plays and poetry. I just enjoy writing; [pers.] Writing is a creative state of mind, words express the true meaning of a person's character. Children need to be educated "wholly" in writing creatively. [a.] Church Point, LA.

LaBELLE, LISA JOSEPHINE CARPENTER
[pen.] Lisa J.C. LaBelle; [b.] June 26, 1962, Detroit, MI; [p.] Warren and Dolly Carpenter; [m.] William J. LaBelle, November 19, 1988; [ch.] Jessica Elizabeth and Joseph Kenneth LaBelle; [ed.] Graduate of Eisenhower High School 1980; [occ.] Housewife and mother; [pers.] I am grateful I have the Lord to guide me, protect me and comfort me. Thy will be done! [a.] Warren, MI.

LABERGE, FRANCINE
[pen.] Francine Laberge; [b.] August 18, 1933, Pointe Claire; [p.] Louis Xyste Laberge and Isabelle Lefebvre; [m.] J. Pierre Gauvreau, February 8, 1954; [ch.] Isbelle, Philippe, Simon, and Sylvie, grandchildren, Charles David, Marie Helene and Ludovick; [ed.] Bachelor of Arts, bachelor of degree in Science of Education; [occ.] Small editor; [memb.] Societe D'Histoire De Sherbrooke, Association Des Auteurs, Des Cantons De L'est, Le Choeur Symphonique De, Sherbrooke -Vice President; [hon.] Second prize in mathematic Province De Quebec 1954, B.A. Universite De Montreal, Quebec Canada; [oth. writ.] Publisher of "Famille Et Societe", writer od the Editorial and interviews, newspaper "Square Tab" on education, art and culture; [pers.] "Life is full of surprises, let's enjoy the goodness and forget the others. [a.] Sherbrooke, Quebec Canada.

LABOY, HEIDY
[pen.] Michelle; [b.] July 26, 1976, Vicenza, Italy; [p.] Maria and Miguel Laboy; [ed.] Currently enrolled in Killeen High School; [occ.] Student; [memb.] Junior Engineering Technical Organization, Junior Classical League Reflections; [hon.] Academic Awards in 9th and 10th grade, honor roll throughout high school; [oth. writ.] This poem was previously published in my high school's literary magazine called Reflections; [pers.] I hope all of the world can look towards the future in optimism. [a.] Killeen, TX.

La CROIX, C.V.
[b.] June 26, 1935, Lebret, Saskatchewan Canada; [p.] Placide and Mary La Croix; [m.] Alice M. La Croix, June 29, 1968; [ch.] Jason (22), Dawn (20) and Jennifer (17); [ed.] University -Early Childhood Education (major) drama (minor); [occ.] Teacher; [hon.] Enjoy The Moment (poem) published in Listen With Your Heart, Quill Books, Harlington, Texas, Honorable Mention Award 1992; [oth. writ.] "Preparatory", (poem) published in Poetic Voices of America, Sparrowgrass Poetry Forum Inc., Sisterville, WV 1994 (spring); [pers.] My poetry lends itself to my upbringing and people who have influenced me in the past while growing up and being educated in rural Saskatchewan, Canada. [a.] Regina, Saskatchewan.

LADD, DONNA LEE
[b.] October 31,1959, Louisville, KY; [p.] Leslie and Geneva Ladd; [ed.] Iroquois High School, University of Louisville (B.S.El.Ed., Med.); [occ.] Grade 5 teacher, Frayser Elementary School, Louisville, KY; [memb.] Kappa Delta Pi, An Honor Society in Education; [hon.] B.S. El. Ed. awarded with high honors; [oth. writ.] A personal collection of unpublished poetry and one poem published by the National Library of Poetry in A Break

In The Clouds; [pers.] In my writing, I try to bring situations into focus, so that the larger picture can be contemplated.[a.] Louisville, KY.

LADD, EDGAR P.
[b.] July 3, 1944, New Haven, CT; [p.] Edgar and Mary Lillian Ladd Sr.; [m.] Ramona Ladd, February 14, 1969; [ch.] Fredrick Brian and Sharon Lee Ladd; [ed.] Del Rio, Texas High School; [occ.] Communications Specialist, Union Pacific Railroad; [memb.] American Legion, North America Fishing Club; [oth. writ.] Numerous short stories and poems in Gulf Coast Connections and Dixie Freepress. [a.] Pearland, TX.

LAFLEUR, ALICE R.
[b.] March 10, 1910, Winchendon, MA; [p.] George and Aurisie Berard; [m.] Edouard E.Lafleur, Sr., April 15, 1929; [ch.] Edouard E. Jr. and Paul Alfred; [ed.] High school and extra courses in Psychology and writing; [occ.] Retired; [memb.] Toastmistress Int., BPW Women's Club, Sweet Adelines; [hon.] Navy Civ. Award for Achievement of special duty, Toastmistress speech contest award; [oth. writ.] School Editorials, short stories, etc.

LAGAN, KELLY C.
[b.] August 17, 1970; [p.] Patrick and Constance Lagan;[ed.] North Babylon High School, Marist College; [memb.] Marist College Reynard 1992, Editor-in-Chief; [hon.] Who's Who Among Students in American Universities and Colleges; [pers.] Some of the nicest people I know are developmentally, physically or mentally challenged, this poem is dedicated to them and their families. [a.] North Babylon, NY.

LAGO, PETER DANIEL
[b.] May 20, 1974, Lynwood, CA;[p.] Peter Leonards and Teresa Lago; [ed.] Loyola Marymount University, St. John Bosco High School; [occ.] Student, LMU; [memb.] Mission Marti, Hispanic Choir member, Our Lady of Perpetual Help Church; [hon.] Certificate of Achievement (Cuban American National Foundation), Cuban American Teacher Association Scholarship, Who's Who Among American High School Students 1991-92; [oth.writ.] High school publications; [pers.] Sometimes you don't get what you asked for in life. It is during those times when your true character evolves. [a.] Downey, CA.

LAKE, SIMONE
[b.] September 9, 1971, Edmonton; [p.] Loretta and Darrell Schacker; [m.] Edward Tizzard; [ch.] Jessica Cyrene and Brittany -Lee Mildred; [oth. writ.] Several poems and one short novel, unpublished; [pers.] I would like to promote kindness, toward both man and animal, by teaching readers to empathize through my work. [a.] Waskatenau, Alberta.

LAMB, MICHELLE
[b.] March 7, 1979, Las Vegas, NV; [p.] Amanda and Joseph Lamb; [ed.] Eldorado High School, 9th grade; [occ.] Student; [memb.] Popwarner cheerleader for 13 years;[hon.] Honor Roll, A & B for 4 years; [oth. writ.] Several poems never published, "More Than Love", "You", "Hearts Mess", "Sights and Sounds", "To A Special Friend" and more; [pers.] Love and happiness usually inspire me to write my poems but this one was inspired by my father Joseph Lamb, Sr. [a.] Las Vegas, NV.

LAMONT, JOSEPHINE
[b.] May 26, 1936, Clarendon, Jamaica; [p.] Zipporah Brown and George Lamont; [ed.] Teacher's diploma, St. Joseph's Teacher's College, B.A. degree, University of the West Indies and M.B.A. candidate, University of Warwick; [occ.] Teaching; [memb.] Optimist Club, St. Joseph's Alumni Association; [hon.] Meritorious Service to St. George's College in the teaching of English and Literature, International Poet of Merit Award (1993); [oth.writ.] An anthology of unpublished poems, songs and short stories; [pers.] Let's be human, not savages. Let's save lives, not destroy them, life's the most precious commodity, but it can't be mined, manufactured or traded. So, let's preserve it, your, mine and ours.

LAMPHERE, ROBERT J.
[b.] June 7, 1959, Monteney, Mexico; [p.] Robert and Bertha Lamphere; [m.] Maureen Lamphere, December 30, 1983; [ch.] Carly, Maureen, Lauren, Michell and John Wesley; [ed.] Samuel Clemens High School, University of California at Los Angeles, Pasadena City College; [occ.] Laser Optics Technical; [memb.] N.R.A., B.A.S.S.; [oth. writ.] The Secret War published by Vantage Press; [pers.] Life is sometimes bittersweet, but it's always your own. [a.] Pasadena, CA.

LANCASTER, JESSICA
[b.] January 26, 1977, York, PA; [p.] Lew and Holly Lancasters; [ed.] Biglerville High School; [pers.] This is my first work of art that has been published. This is a great experience and wonderful adventure for me. [a.] Gettysburg, PA.

LANCASTER, JOSIE LUJEAN
[b.] October 12,1908, Nara Visa, NM; [p.] Joseph and Sudie Asher; [m.] James Ericie Lancaster (d), November 20, 1934; [ed.] High school, junior college; [occ.] Homemaker; [memb.] Worldwide Church of God, AARP, Audubon Society, Eldermed American; [hon.] Embroidery, 1st prize sewing, 1st prize Home Economics; [oth. writ.] Several poems, gave permission to publish one in Religious magazine, in process of having autobiography printed; [pers.] I enjoy life, people and nature. The aim of my poems is to give pleasure and inspiration, to show thankfulness for the miracle of this human body and the awesomeness of this universe. I'm a packrat collector. [a.] West Chester, OH.

LAND, EDWARD CHARLES
[pen.] Edward Charles Land; [b.] August 28, 1955, Chicago, IL; [p.] Quentin and Easter Land; [m.] Carrie Lane, May 16, 1980; [ch.] Karen, Edward Charles Land Jr. and George, grandson, Daurelle Kentre; [ed.] Lindbloom Tech. High School, Ged. obtain from the U.S. Navy Malcom X Community College; [occ.] Musician and writer; [memb.] African American Cultural Coalition, board member; [oth.writ.] I've written one book of Romantic poems, dedicated to my wife, Carrie. I've invented an imaginary character The Civlized Rogue and hundreds of poems and speeches on all types of subjects; [pers.] Our women are masterful compositions, of all that is all essential to the longevity of our very existence. [a.] Chicago, IL.

LANDRY, CAROLYN LOIS
[pen.] Caroly Landry; [b.] November 26, 1943, Toronto, Canada; [p.] Lois and Kager Wightman; [m.] Lou Landry, January 26, 1983; [ch.] Ryan, Emily and Susan; [ed.] B.A., M.A. English, U. of Manchester, England, Ministerial Training; [occ.] Minister, Church of Scientology; [hon.] Ontario Scholar, Dickson Scholar-

ship, Trinity College, Govenor General's Medal, Derwyn Owen prize in English, Province of Ontario Fellowship, Canada Council Fellowship; [oth.writ.] Poetry, articles on education, stories; [pers.] In his Art Series, L. Ron Hubbard, renowned writer, defined art as the "quality of communication". It is the only really workable definition I have found. I am glad to acknowledge his insight and pass it on to you. [a.] Toronto, Ontario, Canada.

LANE, GILBRET M.
[b.] January 27, 1938, New York, NY; [p.] Margaret and Herbert Lane; [m.] Norma G. Lane, August 22, 1970; [ed.] B.A. City College New York City, M.A. in Education, City University of City of New York; [occ.] Language Arts Teacher (retired), CEO Lane and Lane Enterprise; [memb.] United Federation of Teacher, Our Lady of the Nativity Catholic Church; [hon.] Mayoral Citation; [oth. writ.] Additional poems unpublished, several plays and literature textbook unpublished; [pers.] True happiness can only be measured through the joy that we bring to others. [a.] New York, NY.

LANE, KATHRYN VERBAGE
[b.] March 6, 1952, Huntington, WV; [p.] Betty Caverlee Verbage and Thomas J.; [m.] Michael G. Lane, February 23, 1990; [ch.] Rebecca Dawn Lane; [ed.] Marshall University, West Virginia University, West Virginia graduate college; [occ.] Substitute teacher; [memb.] PDK-Phi Delta Kappa (Educ. Fraternity), CEC-Council for Exceptional Children, ACLD-Association for Children with Learning Disabilities, ARC-Association for Retarded Citizens; [hon.] Excellence in Education, Who's Who Among Human Service Professionals, Certificates of Appreciation, Academic Booster of Mercer Co., Mercer Co. Special Education Advisory Council and Parent Organization of Green Acres Regional Center for Retarded Children; [oth. writ.] Poems published in World of Poetry, Quill Books, Poetry Press and The Blue Ridge Tradition (a local paper dedicated to preserving the culture of the Southwestern Region), The Happy Camper (Literary Organization of High and Hospital Ashville, NC); [pers.] I write my poetry from my heart, what I see, feel and hear. [a.] Boones Mills, VA.

LANE, MICHAEL J.
[pen.] An American Poet, A.A.P.; [b.] September 27, 1966, Bronx, NY; [p.] Martin and Irene Lane; [ed.] Christopher Columbus High School; [occ.] Trade-carpenter, company name, Best Finish By Steven Ochs; [hon.] Received, awards of Merit for other poems., such as "The Incredible Flight"; [oth. writ.] Several poems published in local school newspapers; [pers.] Writing has become a link to my soul, and it is through words that I express my happiness, my love, my hurt and fears in the world. I like to thank God for my talent. If my poems could touch even one person, then I'm a success. [a.] Bronx, NY.

LANE, SHANNON MARIA
[b.] September 8, 1968, Philadelphia, PA; [p.] Deborah Lane; [ch.] Marshon Lane (nephew); [ed.] John Bartram High School, Philadelphia, PA, Community College of Philadelphia, Phil, PA; [occ.] United Parcel Service employee; [hon.] This is my greatest honor, actually being published by The National Library of Poetry, God is Wonder; [oth. writ.] I have written many poems on various subjects, and I am currently working on a play called "The Struggle"; [pers.] I know that I am blessed with the gift of writing and with the people of the world I love to share my gift. [a.] Philadelphia, PA.

LANG, VIVIANA MARIEL
[pen.] Vivian, Vivy, Viv; [b.] October 17, 1979, Buenos Aires, Argentina; [p.] Saul and Olga Lang; [ed.] Jefferson Davis Middle School; [occ.] Student; [oth. writ.] None published but several written; [pers.] You can only earn what you've worked hard for. [a.] West Palm Beach, FL.

LANGELIER, VIKKI
[pen.] Vikki Marie Langelier; [b.] March 31, 1972, Ontario; [p.] Charles and Gayle Langelier; [ed.] Graduated '90 from Sir John A MacDonald Secondary School, now attending last of 3 year Sheridan College; [occ.] Student; [memb.] Member of Symphony Hamilton, previously member of the Student Literary Association; [hon.] Achieved honors throughout high school and attained the Alfred Orme Memorial Leadership award for general knowledge; [oth. writ.] I have several books I have written, as well as a book of short stories and children's stories not yet published; [pers.] Always strive to attain balance and place within. [a.] Oakville, Ontario.

LANGFORD, ARNEITA MARIE
[pen.] Arneita M. Langford; [b.] September 27, 1954, Los Angeles, CA; [p.] Charles and Helen Arneita Langford; [sib.] Charles Lamont Langford; [ed.] Crenshaw High School, LACC, American College of Optics, Paramedical Occupational Center with internship-USC (University of So.CA.); [occ.] Claims management-workers' compensation-National Medical Enterprises Inc.; [memb.] Crenshaw Christian Center; [hon.] Various certificates of achievements; [oth. writ.] Various poems; [pers.] Life should be enjoyed not endured, because one day come, one day go. [a.] Los Angeles, CA.

LANGWORTHY, MABEL
[b.] January 24, 1935, Boon, MI; [p.] Deceased, Herbert and Melissa (Davis) Mowrey; [m.] Morris Langworthy, January 31, 1953; [ch.] Morris Jr., Jeanne, Shelly, Teresa, Kenneth and Tracy, 5 grandchildren; [ed.] High school, Mesick and Grant, MI; [occ.] Housewife; [oth. writ.] For the most part, what I've written has been for the pleasure of writing. My children and my husband have urged me to see about having something published, this will be my first other than a couple local items; [pers.] Having experienced the normal feelings of each of my children leaving home, I began to wonder what kind of advice could be given that any young person could relate to on their first solo world adventure into life. My hope was that many might see, read and understand the novice. [a.] LeRoy, MI.

LAMPHIER, GLENN WHITNEY
[pen.] Glenn Whitney Lamphier; [b.] November 26, 1919, Ilion, NY; [p.] Grace and Howard Lamphier; [m.] Helen E. Lamphier, June 19, 1940; [ch.] Robert Glenn; [ed.] Ilion High School and Advanced Economics for Business course, Cornell University; [occ.] Former owner of 2 grocery Super Markets (now retired); [memb.] Have 4 songs published, one recorded by my publisher, member of BMI Nashville, member of Past Kiwanis Presidents National Grocery Association; [hon.] Veterans of Foreign Wars, Loyalty Day Award and dinner for writing the poem "Heritage of Freedom", also Natural Recognition from the U.S. President, State Department, plus local recognition from Civic Leaders and government officials, hundreds of letters from citizens; [oth. writ.] Write poems for Army newspaper overseas, others for local papers etc.; [pers.] I am a late bloomer as a songwriter and aspire to be known as a great songwriter. Have the confidence to believe I can. [a.] Zephyrhills, Fl.

LANZETTA, FREDI
[b.] April 12, 1963, New York City; [ed.] B.S. Northeastern University, Mgr. Marketing, min. communicates, Assoc. The University of Maine, Mgr. Management; [oth. writ.] Two manuscripts in the works, first is a book of poems, prose, short stories, linked together by the process of the coming of age, second is a novel of a man who was murdered and how his past passes on to his loved one's life; [pers.] Any artists work must be brought to life from the heart, otherwise, its not art. Peace. [a.] New York, NY.

LARSON-GARDNER, JOLENE
[b.] September 16, 1944, Emmetsburg, IA; [ed.] B.S. Northwesten University, M.A. Mundelein-Loyal University, doctoral candidate, Union Institute; [memb.] Women of Faith Resource Center (Director), The Focusing Institute (trainer), Reiki II, practitioner, "Workshop Facilitator"; oth.writ.] Include children's poetry, short stories, articles such as "Dreams", "Our Natural Connectors" published in The Folio, The Focusing Journal; [pers.] My writings have been important guides that have enabled me to understand my own sense of self-loss during adolescent, and the need to create programs to help enable adolescent girls to deepen their self-esteem and to empower themselves to take charge of their life's direction and potential. [a.] Chicago, IL.

LASHBROOK, DEAN L.
[pen.] D.L. Lashbrook; [b.] August 18, 1923, Michigan; [p.] Ralph and Estella Lashbrook; [m.] J. Eileen Lashbrook, May 27, 1950; [ch.] Toni Lee, Bradley and Curtis; [ed.] Bachelor of Science, Civil Engineering major, Michigan State University, June 1948; [occ.] Consulting Structural Engineer (P.E.); [memb.] Disabled American Veterans. [a.] Toledo, OH.

LASSINGER, DAYNA
[b.] September 24, 1975, Pittsburgh, PA; [p.] Ron and Elaine Lassinger; [ed.] Giles High, VA Tech; [occ.] Student at VA Tech (junior); [memb.] Math Club/VA Tech; [hon.] Dean's List, one year early admit to university; [pers.] Write everything down with sheer determination, in doing so something worthless could turn out to be priceless. [a.] Pearisburg, VA.

LATIMER, JAMES
[b.] September 4, 1926, St. Croix, Virgin Island; [p.] Deceased; [ed.] BS., MA., Ph.D.; [occ.] Retired; [memb.] International House, NYU Alumni, Columbia T.C. and Convocation London University, Quaker Religion Flushing Meeting; [hon.] Five medals for service in Royal Canadian Army Medical Corp., looking after wounded in WWII, England, Italy, N. Aluza, 5 years; [oth. writ.] Foundations of The Christian Missions in Sp. W.I., Psychology, A Joyous Subject; [pers.] As a Quaker my interest in the globe is foremost and I try to be compassionate. [a.] Flushing, NY.

LATTA, HARRIET
[b.] December 10, 1974, Alexandria, VA; [p.] John W. and Jane S. Latta Jr.; [ed.] Washington-Lee High School; [occ.] Student, freshman at Roanoke College; [memb.] Bacchus (Boosting Alcohol Consciousness Concerning University Students), Habitat for Humanity, St. Mark's Lutheran Church, Synodical Retreat Planning Committees; [hon.] Who's Who Among American High School Students, Presidential Academic Fitness Award, Outstanding Achievement in high school business department, Roanoke College Lutheran Grant, Roanoke College Grant, Commonwealth Award, VATAG, AAL

Scholarship; [oth. writ.] Small writings published in elementary and intermediate schools' literary magazines, words and music for Cherug Choir's Easter song (March 1992); [pers.] I believe that one event/trip can change your life forever depending on the people you're with, sometimes. I wrote, "I Changed" with many friends in mind. [a.] Arlington, VA.

LAUD, DANILA ANA J.
[b.] July 21,1958, Lambunao Iloilo, Phil; [p.] Elvira and Eugenio Laud; [sib.] Ma, Luz, Elsa, Proceso, Joel and Nelson; [ed.] Tubungan Elementary School, Lambunao Voc. School, University of San Augustine, Iloilo City, Philippines; [occ.] Staff Nurse, Kings County Hospital Center, Brooklyn, NY; [memb.] New York State Nurses Association; [oth. writ.] Several unpublished poems; [pers.] This is in memory of my father, who died of Cancer in 1985. I could never pay the things he had done for me. Critics, Training, Maridel, Amie, friends, Aida, Belen, Rose, Finnie, Blan, Agnes, Jossette, Ronnie, Flor, Eileen, Rachel, Marrian, Meridith, Sammy, Jo,Fe, Norrie, Rowena, Trinny, Chu, May and Olive. [a.] Brooklyn, NY.

LAUER, DOROTHY
[pen.] Dorothy Lauer; [b.] march 5, 1923, Seattle, WA; [m.] Robert Lauer, February 8, 1946; [ch.] David and John Lauer, Barbara Carrigan, seven grandchildren; [ed.] Broadway High School, Seattle, Pasadena City College, Pasadena,CA., AA-English, Cal State L.A., Los Angeles, CA;, BA-English; [occ.] Retired Executive Secretary, writer; [memb.] St. Andrew's Episcopal Church, (lay reader), The Honor Society of Phi Kappa Phi; [hon.] BHS Honor Society, 1940, English Honors and Spanish Honors, Pasadena City College, 1973, Dean's List, English Honors Cal State, LA 1976;[pers.] My poetry captures a lifetime of images. The spectrum is broad, including people, places, events, nature, feelings, ideas. It is a pastiche of memories. [a.] Tokeland, WA.

LAUREL-MERDEGIA, YOLANDA
[pen.] Mariyol N. Laurel, Maria Yolanda; [b.] June 26, 1949, Makati, Rizal Philippines; [p.] Serafin T. and Evelny N. Laurel; [m.] Rodolfo F. Merdegia, February 21, 1983;[ch.] Royal Apple, Marc Romelson, Karl Romelius and Troy Romerick; [ed.] BSBA Management, Philippine, Christian University, Manila, currently enrolled at Los Angeles City College, Journalism, Pio del Pilar High, Makati; [occ.] Secretary, Building Industry Credit Association (BICA), LA, CA; [memb.] Los Angeles First Church of the Nazarene, Sing group, Asian Development Bank; [hon.] Gold Medalist, Stenography, Guzman Institute of Secretarial Sciences, Manila; [oth. writ.] Several poems published in a Philippine magazine, the Mod, poems and other articles published in our school and office gazette, including my own column, "Campus Roulette" (also in Philippines); [pers.] I love to write romantic poems, some of my poems, though are spiritual. I'm now trying to create poems about sex, written in a subtle way. Knowledge is my greatest wealth, so I keep on studying to learn new things. I want to become a known writer. [a.] Los Angeles, CA.

LAURENT, HILLARY
[b.] August 25, 1979, Green Bay; [p.] Allan and Debbie Laurent; [ed.] St. Mary's now in Kaukauna High School; [occ.] Student; [memb.] Forensics, cheerleading; [hon.] Four Forensics awards and ribbons, one award for exceptional performance in Readers and Writers Work-

shop, Honor Roll; [oth. writ.] A lot of fiction and poetry done in English, a book (not yet published); [pers.] Don't give up writing. The world has a lot of books but not your book. [a.] Kaukauna, WI.

LAUZON, GLORIA PEGGY
[pen.] Peggy; [b.] March 3, 1943, Hawkesbury, Ontario; [p.] Alice and Robert Bigelow; [ch.] Troy and Terry Lauzon, two precious sons; [occ.] Business; [hon.] Merit Award for Academic Achievement; [oth.writ.] Published poetry in "The World of Poetry Anthology", short stories unpublished; [pers.] Poetry and writing are an extension of my soul which takes me beyond anything tangible. To lose oneself in another dimension is utterly seductive and truly satisfying. [a.] Cornwall, Ontario.

LAWTON, ALEXIS NICOLE
[b.] October 1, 1985, Washington, DC; [p.] William F. Lawton and Cathy Delicia Lawton III; [ed.] 3rd grade student at Saint Michael School, Silver Spring, MD; [occ.] Student; [hon.] Honor Roll student for Academic Achievements, Creativity Award; [memb.] Marva Tots n Teens Gymnastics, Saint Michael School (music-piano); [oth. writ.] Poem published in Our Parish Times newspaper, writes and gives poem as gifts; [pers.] Nature inspires me to write more poems. It puts more feelings into my work. [a.] Wheaton, MD.

LAZDINS, VERA (SECOND MARRIAGE)
[1st marriage] Vera Culs; [b.] March 28, 1904, Latvia; [p.] Peters and Kristine Asars; [m.] Emils Lazdins, Albert Culs, April 17, 1931, October 12, 1968; [ch.] Died-Erics Culs, Lija Keire, Maija Culs; [ed.] Technicum in Lativa; [occ.] Retired; [memb.] Auto Club, Telephone Comp., State Farm Insurance Co., and more, in my life I have been through thick and thin, through World War I and World War 2, I am so old, have been in Lativa in social life affairs; [hon.] Some in Latvia; [oth. writ.] have some publications in Latvia; [pers.] Let and let others to live. I entered the U.S.A. in 1967, made my second marriage in 1968, was very busy to make my social life in this country, but the poems are ringing in my ears often.

LE, SINH QUANG
[pen.] Nhu-Hoa; [b.] May 21,1929, Qaung-Tri, Viet Nam;[p.] Trung Quang Le and Hoanhthi Nguyen; [m.] Vang Thi Troung, March 17, 1957; [ch.] Thu-Trang Thi Le and Tuan Wuang Le; [ed.] Thuan-Hoa High, Sacramento City College, Naval Post Graduate School, Monterey, Hue Military School, The Infantry School, Fort Benning, Command and Staff School, Dalat; [occ.] Former Lieutenant-Colonel of the Army of the Republic of Viet-Nam, Battalion Commander 4th Regiment, 2nd Division, Director of Instruction, Chief of Training Block and Officer Candidate Group Commander, the Infantry School, Thu-Duc; [memb.] Vietnamese Ex-Political Prisoner Association, National Legion of Honors, 5th degree (V.N.), the Army Commendation Medal (US), President's Highest Honors (S.C.C.); [oth. writ.] Several poems published in local newspapers, article for Saigon Times, weekly newspapers, Rosemead, Khong-Quan magazine, San Jose, Luot Song magazine, San Jose, Classmate Magazine, Naval Post Graduate School, Monterey; [pers.] I strive to reflect the genuine love of God, country, parents, friends and family in my writing. Especially the years of detention with hard labor have motivated and inspired me to write about love. [a.] Anaheim, CA.

LEA, JEFFREY BRUCE
[pen.] Idmael Kid Karma; [b.] September 7, 1960, Elgin, IL; [p.] Virginia and Robert B. Lea; [ch.] Andrew Elgin Lea; [ed.] Elgin High School, The American Conservatory of Music in Chicago; [occ.] Mental Health Technician I Student of Surgical Technology, Elgin Community College; [memb.] Association of Surgical Technologists; [oth. writ.] The Science of Defiance and other songs stories (unpublished); [pers.] Akili Ni Mali, Wisdom is wealth. [a.] Belvidere, IL.

LEACH, FAITHE
[pen.] Tikki;[b.] June 15, 1973, Fairless Hills, PA; [p.] Richard and Rose Longo; [m.] Adam Leach, March 27, 1993; [ed.] Pennsbury High School; [occ.] Engraver, Neshamin Mall; [memb.] World of Poetry, American Poetry Association, Independent Order of Foresters; [hon.] Golden Poet, Silver Poet, Poet of Honor, Poet of Merit, Best New Poet 87-90; [oth. writ.] Published in American Poetry Anthology, New American Poetry Anthology, Editor's Choice, a selection of John Frost's Favorite Poets; [pers.] Imagination is the key to my life. What you imagine is real and that is important to me. Everything I write is pure inspiration and is never corrected. Live a poem or die a fool. [a.] Fairless Hills, PA.

LEACH, WANDA LEE
[pen.] Wanda Lee Leach; [b.] March 15, 1927, Indianapolis, IN; [p.] Russell and Sadie S. Jeffers; [m.] Charles Eldo Leach, May 33, 1943; [ch.] Charles R., John L., Robert M. and Michael S. Leach; [ed.] Through the tenth grade; [occ.] Retired now, I still do creative writing. I use to be in interior decorating; [memb.] American Heart Association, United Cerebral Palsy, Easter Seals, M.D. Association, Habit for Humanity, Arthritis Foundation, North Shores (Animal) Paralyzed Veterans, Salesion Mission, Handicapped Artist, Chandler Relief Fund, Chandlerparks, NCPPM, NCPSS-PAO, Little Sisters of the Poor, Billy Graham, Jimmy Swaggert, I am a member to so many organizations that I pay to all of them to show I care; [hon.] A letter from the White House from President Carter (1976), Mayor Harold Washington honored me for my poem I composed for him (4-28-1983), also the Pope (8-7-1991); [oth. writ.] Several poems published in local newspapers, The Evansville Courier and Press back in December (1977), the two poems published were (Christmas Eve) and (Christmas Morning); [pers.] I strive to pass on Gods love to all mankind, in my writings is my thanks to God for His great wisdom He has given to me. [a.] Chandler, IN.

LEADEN, DONALD M.
[pen.] Ducky; [b.] May 2, 1962, Omaha, NE; [p.] Robert F. and Darlene Leaden; [m.] Fiance- K. Heidi Higgins; [ch.] Valarie M. Leaden (30-Nov.-89) cats, Casey and Bob; [ed.] Cathedral High School, Omaha, NE; [occ.] US Air Force, Minot AFB ND; [oth. writ.] Several poems awaiting publication, re; love and personal situations; [pers.] If life was easy then it wouldn't be worth living, so face each of life's challenges with an open mind and look for the positive side of all situations. [a.] Minot, ND.

LEAGUE, ROBERT
[b.] September 5, 1963, Pasadena, MD; [p.] William and Mary League; [ed.] Northeast S.H.S., B.S.E.E., University of Maryland at College Park, currently working on a M.S.E.M.; [occ.] Project Engineer; [memb.] The Institute of Electrical and Electronic Engineers, The

Armed Forces Communications and Electronic Association; [hon.] Dean's List, spring 1985, Honors List, spring 1987, elected Tau Alpha Pi National Honor Society, December 1988; [oth. writ.] Several poems and narratives, none published; [pers.] The main purpose of my writing is self fulfillment/self expression. I like to combine my own thoughts and feelings with creative observations of the world around me. [a.] California, MD.

LEAH, ANTHEA ELIZABETH
[b.] June 7, 1935, Taunton, Somerset England;[p.] Isabel Blackmore and William O'Connor; [m.] Henry D. Leah, November 30, 1957; [ch.] Mark D. and Tania E. Leah;[ed.] North Town Sec. School, Taunton Somerset; [occ.] Housewife, poet; [oth. writ.] Book of poems to be published soon, Poems To Reflect On, by Adelphi Press London; [pers.] My aim is to make people think about this beautiful world we live in and what mankind in his creed is doing to it and its own species. [a.] North Tetherton, Somerset.

LEAR, CATHERINE N.
[pen.] Kate Nadine; [b.] January 22, 1957, Lebanon, PA; [p.] Ralph and Florence Phillips (deceased); [m.] Timothy Lear, January 13,1979; [ch.] Angela and Arlie Lear; [ed.] Graduated Cedar Crest High School in 1974, Army Administrative Specialist course in 1977 (5 week course), Army Computer Operator course in 1979 (7 week course); [occ.] Transportation Clerk Typist, PA Army National Guard-Computer Operator; [memb.] United Zion Mission Church in Lebanon, PA., SSG in the PA Army National Guard, 11 years; [hon.] Army Achievement Medal in 1981; [oth. writ.] 70 poems with one word titles unpublished, True Colors of Animal Friends, children's book, unpublished; [pers.] I enjoy writing stories and poems. I write poems based on my life as a Christian and the way I believe others should be living. [a.] Lebanon, PA.

LeCLAIR, BETTY JO COGDILL
[pen.] Betty J. LeClair; [b.] September 25, 1943, Oklahoma City; [p.] Mark and Elma Cogdill; [m.] Divorced; [ch.] Rebecca LeClair, Joan Thomasson, Charles LeClair III, Laura Summer and Jill LeClair; [ed.] Capitol Hill High, Oklahoma City, BA-Oklahoma Baptist University, MA-Columbia College, Columbia, SC; [occ.] First grade teacher, Pierce Terrace Elementary, Fort Jackson, SC; [memb.] Council for Exceptional Children North Trenholm Baptist Church; [hon.] Teacher of the Year, Pierce Terrace Elementary, 1980 and 1989; [oth. writ.] Few unpublished poems.[a.] Columbia, SC.

LeCOMPTE, KATHLEEN
[b.] March 29, 1939, Aurora, IL; [p.] Charles and Bernice Connolley; [m.] Earl Le Compte, December 20, 1974; [ch.] Kim, Sue, Wendy, Holly by 1st marriage, 6 stepchildren; [ed.] High school, paramedic license (exp) some college; [occ.] Homemaker, artist; [memb.] St. Mary's Altar and Rosary Society, Great Books of Literature Discussion Group; [oth. writ.] Several pieces backed in publication by Edie Cole collections; [pers.] We are all no matter what age just running through life like children, down the path of morning.

LEE, CHERYL
[pen.] Cherra Lee, Rochester, NY; [m.] James E. Lee; [ch.] 5 beautiful children; [ed.] High school graduate; [occ.] Licensed Cosmetologist Salon owner; [memb.] I'm a member at God's Cornerstone Church, non-denomination, we don't sse religion, shapes, colors or sizes, we only see LOVE; [hon.] Top hairstylist in our regions; [oth.writ.] I'm writing a book in which I hope to see on the big screen one day. It has a different twist, that has never been seen on the big screen; [pers.] (Heavenly Father) God first, then everything else will fall in place, # 1st Bible, influenced by Terry McMillain, author, Waiting To Exhale, Disappearing Acts. [a.] Henrietta, NY.

LEE, HAHN, J.
[pen.] Hahn Joong Lee; [b.] July 13, 1940, Korea;[p.] Jungho Lee and Byungsook Chae; [m.] Suk Joo, May 1, 1966; [ch.] Harkmore, Ada and Philmo; [ed.] Seoul National University College of Medicine, Korea, six years training in U.S.A. to become a Cardiologist; [occ.] M.D. Cardiologist in private practice; [memb.] American College of Physicians, American College of Cardiology, American Medical Association; [hon.] Teacher of the Year Award for young physicians in training; [oth.writ.] Some two dozens of poems published in alumni newspapers; [pers.] I strive to catch and describe the experience of satori an ordinary man and woman may experience in their daily struggle. I have been influenced by Buddha, Einstein, Zen Masters and Taoists. [a.] Bloomfield, MI.

LEE, JARED
[b.] March 20, 1979, California; [p.] Russell and Bette Jo Lee; [ed.] Currently enrolled as a freshman and attending local junior high; [memb.] Boy Scouts of America, Order of the Arrow, National Honor Society; [hon.] Eagle Scout, National Honor Society; [oth. writ.] Watch for Me in '94-95; [pers.] I believe that the key to a better future is to change today. [a.] Tulsa, OK.

LEE, JENNIFER A.
[b.] April 14, 1971, California; [p.] Mr. and Mrs. John H. Lee; [ed.] Self-studied, self-taught, L.A. County High School for the Arts; [occ.] Student; [memb.] Association for Humanistic Psychology; [oth. writ.] Currently working on a constitution of children's rights; [pers.] Trouver Espirit. [a.] Camarillo, CA.

LEE-HAWKINS, JOYCE
[pen.] Joy Lee; [b.] December 10, 1951, New York; [p.] Lucille Greene; [m.] Deceased; [ch.] Monique Dionne and Kaprice Joy; [ed.] William H. Maxwell High School; [occ.] Executive Assistant City of New York Commission on Human Rights; [oth. writ.] Non-published, Remy or Not, Desires on the Sacred Heart, Passion Demon, Love Poetry. [a.] Brooklyn, NY.

LEE, REGINALD
[b.] November 1, 1974, Johnson City, NY; [p.] Allen and Esther Lee; [ed.] Graduate of Hamden High School in Hamden, CT., currently a student at North Carolina A & T State University in Greensboro, NC; [memb.] National Society of Black Engineers, at N.C.A. & T; [oth. writ.] Yet to be released; [pers.] I'd like to thank God for the gift, my parents for the guidance and my close friends for a "poetic buffet". To all that doubted the skills, DON'T SLEEP! [a.] Cary, NC.

LEEFE, AYSHA RENEE
[pen.] Aysha R. Leefe; [b.] March 11, 1966, Massapequa; [p.] Bob and Isla Leefe; [ed.] Massapequa High, Farmingdale SUNY; [occ.] Current, none was Home Health Aide; [memb.] PWAC; [pers.] I believe that only in feeling if a person is really a feeling person they should show it and that's what I have done, but I can only do that when I'm inspired. [a.] W. Babylon, NY.

LEIB, TERRIE
[b.] January 12, 1955, Gatesville, TX; [p.] Leo Robertson and Glynda Gladding; [m.] Frank Leib, July 31, 1987; [ch.] Wendy and Candy; [ed.] Attended elementary, junior high and high school in Angleton, TX, 1 year at Lamar University-Beaumont, TX; [occ.] Retail Sales; [memb.] American Quarter Horse Association, Palomino Breeders Association, Morgan Horse Association; [hon.] Awarded high school band jacket, 2nd Lt. Civil Air Patrol; [pers.] Through my poetry I'd like to open people's eyes to their surroundings and hopefully influence people in a positive manner. [a.] Mosinee, WI.

LEIER, KEVIN K.
[b.] February 10, 1963, Germany; [p.] Arthur and Ollie Leier; [m.] Sandra Marie Leier, October 13, 1990; [ch.] Joshua and Kyle Leier; [ed.] Okanagan University College "Business"; [occ.] Self employed business of recycling rubber; [memb.] AMA American Marketing Association, World Vision sponsored children foundation; [hon.] Top 5% in graduating class; [oth. writ.] Short un-published novel, many other poems and songs; [pers.] If you believe in yourself anything is possible. [a.] Vernon, BC Canada.

LEGNO, BARBARA WELLMAN
[pen.] Barbara Wellman Legno; [b.] May 1, 1947, Elmira, NY; [p.] Clarence G. and Helen M. Wellman; [m.] Anthony J. Legno, December 14,1985; [ch.] James H. and Kimberly A. Smith, step-sons, Andrew W. and Christopher A. Legno; [ed.] Southside High, Elmira, NY; [occ.] Accounts Receivable Billing Analyst, The Case-Hoyt Corp., Rochester, NY; [oth. writ.] Written poetry from the age of 12 for personal enjoyment, only recently encouraged by family to submit poetry for review; [pers.] "My Daughter" was written June 93 for my daughter Kimberly. I strive for true-to life experiences in my writing. Many poems have been written for family enjoyment. [a.] Rochester, NY.

LeLEUX, GLENDA RICHARD
[pen.] Glenda Richard LeLeux; [b.] July 4, 1950, Crowley, LA; [p.] Noah J. and Anna Bell Richard; [m.] Elridge J. (E.J.) LeLeux, February 7, 1980; [ed.] 1968 graduate of Crowley High School; [occ.] Full Charge Bookkeeper and Secretary; [hon.] Was awarded a music scholarship to McNeese State College (but due to circumstances did not attend), wrote a poem for my 25 year class reunion and it was put in our little yearbook; [oth.writ.] Several other poems that I've compiled to write a book, as well as poems that I've written for special people in my life, but until now I had never been published; [pers.] My poetry reflects my experiences in life. To write about the joys and sorrows life brings along with the stresses shows the growth of ones-self. I am a romantic by nature and the feelings from within should be expressed. Never be ashamed to show love or feel pain. [a.] Crowley, LA.

LEMKE, SARA L.
[b.] January 10, 1961, Mt. Vernon, WA; [p.] Jay and Martha Williamson; [m.] Scott Lemke, January 18, 1991; [ch.] Skagit Valley Community College; [ed.] B.A. Ed. Western WA University, M.A. Ed. Lesley College; [occ.] 2nd grade teacher, Stanwood Elementary;[pers.] I love languages and all kinds of words, especially in the form of poetry. Poetry to me is intensely personal and precise, poems are the pictures the heart makes. [a.] Mt. Vernon, WA.

LEMON, PHIDELIA
[pers.] I was born March 14, 1909 in Port Royal, Penn.

My father was American and my mother Irish and they were married in 1906 in Pennsylvania. I had a brother who served in the U.S.A. Army, now deceased. I am now residing in Northern Ireland after marrying an Irish man.

LENG, ELEANOR E.
[pen.] Eleanor Elly Leng; [b.] 1930, Kingsville; [p.] Fred and Edith Gale; [m.] Eric Leng (deceased), October 4, 1947; [ch.] Richard, Linda, Terry, Pam, Connie and Penny Tina; [ed.] Grade 8; [occ.] Retired widow, 15 1/2 grandchildren, 3 great; [memb.] Anglican Church, Leamington Hospital, District Memorial, volunteer, also volunteer at Br 188 Legion, Past President for 3 years, 26 years in Auxiliary plus Mens Associate for 15 years; [hon.] Past President, Certificate of Recognition, certificate of Recognition from Christian Blind Mission, volunteer heart and stroke, Cancer, where ever needed; [oth. writ.] Love poetry, tell truth in poems, poems printed in Kingsville Reporter, Essex Free Press, also sent to Chatham, The Family Herald Good News Productions; [pers.] Most poems Christian, also story telling, some humor, enjoy and "Thank God" for bringing within me this gift. Enjoy all others, beautiful poets out there. [a.] Kingsville, Canada.

LENTZ, PAULA M.
[b.] June 20, 1975, York, PA; [p.] Paul F. and Lizzie P. Lentz; [ed.] Dover High, York College of Pennsylvania; [occ.] Current student, freshman; [memb.] National Honor Society; [hon.] Honor Roll, Outstanding Student Award (1993), York Count's Best and Brightest (1993); [oth. writ.] Several poems written for friends and loved ones. Some other ones have been published in other anthologies. A few short stories, I'm currently working on my first novel; [pers.] I use my poetry to express my feelings that I don't know how to say. A special thanks to Scott, my one and only love and to Paul Sue and Tina, my two best friends. Without those three, I would have no inspiration or encouragement to be my best. [a.] Dover, PA.

LeQUESNE, DORA WATSON
[b.] February 20, 1903, Trout Lake, West Rootenay, Laracau District; [p.] Octaveius and Dora Wilkie; [m.] Herbert Frank LeQuesne, September 5, 1939; [ch.] Peter and Robert, Phd with UN Vienna; [ed.] Rn, PHN, BSC, UBC, MA and 6 pls towards Ed.D, NYU; [occ.] Confronting the perils of old age and writing for pleasure; [memb.] Wainvwg; [hon.] Never for efficiency, but right on target for trying like so many of my peers. At 90 years of age I have few competitions now and many more; [oth. writ.] Expressions of an original nature, none of them published and difficult to fully understand or why I love to do; [pers.] I work for the most part with the Victoria Stroke Recovery Club and the Peninsula Club, I am, myself a stroker. The challenge to succeed in whatever you endeavor is always there.

LEVANT, STEPHEN A.
[b.] March 18, 1959, Bronx, NY; [p.] Stephen and Deloris Levant; [ed.] Newton High School, LaGuardia Community College, Brooklyn College; [occ.] Data entry at a weekly newspaper; [memb.] Asia Society of N.Y. Postal Commemorative Society, American Indian Society; [hon.] National Dean's List, Who's Who in American Junior College 1983-84, Transitional Svcs. Comm. Adv. Council Award 1982; [oth. writ.] Film and television reviews for a local paper, I am currently finishing a novel about time travel; [pers.] Every little nice thing we do changes the world and makes it a better

place. The people I love are the inspiration for everything I write. [a.] Jersey City, NJ.

LEVI, WILLIAM R.
[pen.] Ron Levi; [b.] March 26, 1951, Hazlehurst, MS; [p.] Julius and Earnstine Levi-Beacham; [m.] Janet Smit Levi; [ed.] Hales Franciscan High School, Chicago, IL, University of New Orleans, B.S.; [memb.] Apostolic Faith Church Drama Guild, Lifes of Passage, Pace-Prison Ministry; [hon.] State of Illinois Commission Scholarship; [oth. writ.] In addition to poetry I also have songs, plays and prose, to date none have been published; [pers.] The purpose for my writing is that God will be glorified. It is my fervent hope that whether through poetry, prose, plays or songs. The hearts of all who come into contact with them will be affected. [a.] Garland, TX.

LEVIN, DORAYNE M.
[b.] January 15, 1956, Butterworth, Transkei, South Africa; [memb.] International Society of Poets; [pers.] Her goal is to attempt to capture, observed and experienced life occurrences into poetic language and form. [a.] Fort Worth, TX.

LEVINE, AIMIE X.
[b.] December 19, 1978, Pennsylvania; [p.] Maureen Applegate; [ed.] Indiana Area School District; [occ.] Student; [hon.] Reflections Art Award; [oth. writ.] Personal un-published collection; [pers.] I portray the realities of the hardships of life and illustrate man's insanity to mankind. I most admire the writings of Emily Dickenson and Edgar Allen Poe. [a.] Indiana, PA.

LEWIS, ALWYN
[b.] October 18, 1934, New Zealand; [p.] Hula and Dorothy McIlvride; [m.] Laurie Lewis, July 17, 1954; [ch.] Jeffrey Leith and Martin David; [ed.] Sacred Heart College, Lower Hutt, New Zealand; [occ.] Private Secretary; [memb.] NSW Jazz Action Society, Fellowship of Australian Writers; [oth. writ.] Short stories, anthology, 30 plus interviews Cadence magazine, NY, interviews and articles, Jazz Forum, Warsaw, Poland, music in New Zealand, poems, articles and reviews, Education Australia Journal, plus theatre reviews; [pers.] When writing I strive to find ways to illustrate how the infinituality of creativity can uplift the human condition. [a.] Sydney, Austrial, NSW.

LEWIS, AMBER
[pen.] Amber Ruth Austin-Lewis; [b.] December 8, 1974, Portsmouth, OH; [p.] Stephen Austin and Judith Wingo; [m.] John Lewis, December 30, 1992; [ch.] Andrew Xavier; [ed.] Peebles High; [occ.] Homemaker; [memb.] J.R. Beta Club, Beta Club, Pep Band; [hon.] Who's Who Among American High School Students 1991-1992 and 1992 -1993; [pers.] My poetry is a constant endeavor to reflect my innermost emotions, although most of my poems express obscurity and misery, I find that people more often identify with this. There is nothing more satisfying than to touch someone's soul. [a.] Peebles, OH.

LEWIS, ANNETTE F.
[b.] February 14, 1914, Madison, IN; [p.] Dr. and Mrs. Wallace P. Fewell; [m.] Daniel E. Lewis, July 28, 1934; [ch.] Daniel E. Lewis Jr. and Nancy Lewis Haswell; [ed.] Madison High School, Madison, Indiana, B.S Education Valpariso University, Valparalso, Indiana; [occ.] Retired teacher, housewife; [memb.] Presbyterian Church, Ruth Coffeen Poetry Club-Past Chairman, Past

President Women's Literary Society, the Delta Kappa Gamma Society member for 20 years, city of LaPorte, Park and Recreation Board, president 10 years; [hon.] Honored by the city of LaPorte for my service in the work and time expended in development of an outstanding park system for LaPorte, bronze plaque with my name as president on stone located in Kesling Park; [oth. writ.] Short story published in A Western Sampler, poem published in the Delta Kappa Gamma Bulletin, Forest Spring -1992; [pers.] I try to reflect the beauty of nature and man's reaction to this beauty. [a.] LaPorte, IN.

LEWIS, KATHLEEN
[pen.] Kathleen Kay Lewis; [b.] September 26, St. Pancras London England; [p.] Dr. Willian E. Vaughan-Lewis, Mr CS. LRCP Rosalie Dorothy Vallotton-Lewis; [ed.] Catholic High, Yorkshire, Staffordshire, England, sometime in Paris France, Switzerland and Hungary, have gained much from self study; [occ.] Literary and poetry, earlier, student nurse in former Mineral Water Hospital, Bath, Somerset, England; [memb.] DAV Commander's Club, National Association of Police, US Olympic Team, Doris Day Animal League; [hon.] IFAW for Animals (champion), Loyalty Award, Paralyzed Vets of America, Hon Trustee American Relief Council, NIA New York, Art School Minn; [oth. writ.] Self published books of 51 poems, short story factual (subject) Battle of Britain, several poems and articles in local newspaper, NIA Writers Digest (Report Satisfactory) poem to UNICEF; [pers.] There is no doubt, that nature, art and love of life in any description one know what it is all about, I write from my heart and experiences, a lover of all animals, a great admirer of poet Robert Frost. [a.] Newark, NJ.

LEWIS, MARK
[b.] July 13, 1971, Pembroke Dock; [p.] Clive and Mary Lewis; [ed.] Greenhill Secondary School, Tenby, Trinity College, Carmarthen; [memb.] British Diabetic Association; [hon.] Second Class Bachelor of Arts Honors degree in English; [pers.] With influences ranging from Bob Dylan to Tony Marrison, I find that my concern for the human character rests in its dark and complex side and it is these feelings of guilty and inner turmoil I attempt to highlight in my poetry. [a.] Tenby, Dyfed.

LEWIS, TAMARA LYNN
[pen.] T.L. Lewis; [b.] November 29, 1970, Baltimore, MD; [p.] Minnie and William Lewis; [ed.] Western High School, 1988 University of Maryland, Baltimore County, B.A. 1992, Hampton University, M.A. 1994; [occ.] Student and graduate assistant; [memb.] Alpha Kappa Alpha Sorority Inc., Wayland Baptist Church, organization of graduate students; [hon.] Build Commonwealth scholar, delegate scholar, senatorial scholar, Who's Who Among High School Students, Miss United Negro College Fund, Who's Who Among American Colleges and Universities; [oth. writ.] Several poems published in college newsletters and newspapers; [pers.] My writing reflects personal experiences, both triumphs and disappointments. [a.] Baltimore, MD.

LEYDEN, ENA
[b.] Jamaica, West Indies; [p.] Herbert and Adeline Headlam; [m.] Volney R. Leyden; [ed.] Ms Education, Hunter College, NY; [occ.] Teacher, Remedial Reading Specialist, C.S.77, Bronx, NY; [oth. writ.] Christ As The First Advocate of Women's Liberation Church Herald; [pers.] "Poetry is the vehicle of the soul". [a.] E. Elmhurst, NY.

LIDDELL, MARY L. (WOODS)
[b.] March 14, 1931, Daytona Beach, FL; [p.] Fannie Harris Counts and Frank McCloud Jr.; [m.] Edward Liddell, May 28, 1988; [ch.] Anthony and Andrew Liddell; [ed.] BS, Bethune-Cookman College-Daytona Beach, MA, Barry University/Miami Florida, Educational Specialist degree, University of Florida, Jacksonville FL., Computer Specialist, Nora University, Ft. Lauderdale, FL; [occ.] Teacher in the Dade County Public School Systems; [memb.] Transit 2000 of Miami, President Scott Lake Community Association, New Way Fellowship Baptist Church; [hon.] Teacher of the Year nominee, Sigma Gamma Rho's highest award, the Gewn Cherry Award for Most Outstanding Woman, won election to committee woman position 2-terms; [oth.writ.] Platinum at Birth, a story of my early years, My Sister and Me, a poem dedicated to my sister (unpublished), Everyday, "A New Beginning" published in the Coming of Dawn and many other stories and poems (unpublished but used in my teaching position) and for 8 years "Out of The Woods" a news column; [pers.] Life is too short to waste a single moment of it thinking negative things. Besides, negative thinking cost far too much in high blood pressure, stress and various other diseases. It's much more pleasant to think positive thoughts that are healing to the mind and body. They look good on us, too. So think only of the good things that always blow in on the ILL WIND. [a.] Miami, FL.

LIEBERMAN, HEATHER
[b.] April 9, 1980, Boston, MA; [p.] Marc and Linda Lieberman; [ed.] Currently an 8th grade student at Curtis Middle School, Sudbury, MA; [memb.] World Wildlife Fund, National Arbor Day Foundation, United States Holocaust Memorial Museum; [hon.] 1993, Featured School Author, 1992, written and illustrated by National Book contest, 1991 Massachusetts Science Poetry contest; [oth. writ.] Read magazine, issue 17, 1994. [a.] Sudbury, MA.

LIEBERMAN, SCOTT
[b.] July 22, 1976, Bronx, NY; [p.] Judy and Larry Lieberman; [ed.] Bronx High School of Science; [occ.] Student at Bronx High School of Science; [memb.] B'nai B'rith Yough Organization, Junior Academy of Sciences; [hon.] BBYO Chapter President, National Merit Scholarship Letter of Commendation; [pers.] Drowning deep in the ocean green, tangled in the corals, struggling to writhe free and swim with one's own morals. [a.] Bronx.

LIEBSCH, PHYRN M.
[b.] June 15, 1958, Baltimore; [p.] Edward and Francis Thomas; [m.] David E. Liebsch; [ch.] Jason D. and Brian R.; [ed.] Northwest High, ICS-Journalism; [occ.] Writer-poems and songpoems; [memb.] Top Records Songwriters Association; [oth. writ.] "Angels In The Sky", "You There In The Distance" for Top Records. [a.] Pasadena, MD.

LIM, JR., ANTONIO E.
[b.] January 17, 1955, Sta. Fe, Phils; [p.] Mr. and Mrs. Antonio Lim, Sr.; [m.] Lourdes Agner-Lim, June 9, 1984; [ch.] Emmanuel Antonio and Kramer Joseph; [ed.] BS Med-Tech, Divine Word University, Phils., MPH, University of the Phils., DAP and E, Int Med Res, Malaysia, MSc, Vrije University Brussel, Belguim, PhD Vrije University Brussel, Belgium (on-going); [occ.] Senior Instructor and Department Head (on study leave), Divine Word University, Tacloban City, Philippines; [memb.] Phil. Association Med-Techs, Phil. Association

for the Advancement of Science, Phil. Association Schools of Med-Tech, Phil. Soc. Microbiology; [hon.] Cum Laude, BS Med-tech, Distinction, DAP and E, Medical Technologist of the Philippines 1984; [oth. writ.] Co-authors of four manuals in microbiology, several articles on education, public health and biotechnology in local and international papers, five other poems; [pers.] I do something that will outlast my life and is beneficial to mankind. [a.] Tacloban City, Philippines.

LINCKS, G. GRED
[b.] January 10, 1901, Jersey City, NJ; [p.] George Henry and Grace Emma; [m.] Beatrice Lincks, May 29, 1935; [ch.] Tomi Taylor and Patricia Tsien, 2 grandchildren; [ed.] High school Jersey City, NJ, Pratt Institute class of 1920 Electrical Engineering, public speaking Union College; [memb.] Pittsfield Y.M.C.A. 1922 till now, president for 5 years, chaired committees, on Board of Directors for 45 years, Fellow American Institute Electric Engineers, on several committees, International Electronics Commission, Secretary Lightning Arrester Committee, delegate on High Voltage Fuse Committee, Writing International Standards, National Electrical Manufacturers Association, chaired several technical committees, chairman of section, Writing National Standards, Methodist Church, Jersey City, NJ, Schenectady, NY, Pittsfield, MA, took active part; [oth. writ.] 32 articles in electrical trade magazines, numerous papers and discussions American Institute of Electrical Engineers, 2 articles in Rocks and Minerals on mineral locations in Mineralogical Record ditto; [pers.] The poem is my religious thinking, a guiding influence for a rich life of service, vocation and avocation, believe I can leave salvation to God, if I do my part in creating "God's Kingdom on Earth".

LINDGREN, LARRY E.
[b.] May 7, 1931, Esmond, ND; [oth. writ.] Book of poetry for home and family, poems published in local newspaper; [pers.] As a mature man, I've been influenced by everything I see, read and do. I'm an observer of life and I draw my poem writings from personal experiences, experiences observed of joy and sorrow and in between, of yesterday's world and todays. [a.] Minneapolis, MN.

LINDSAY, BELINDA
[pen.] Belinda Davey; [b.] December 12, 1977, Orangeville; [p.] Jo-Anne and Vernon Lindsay; [sib.] Alison Lindsay; [ed.] High school, completion of grade 12; [occ.] Modeling; [hon.] French Honor Award in 1990, Academic in Children's Literature; [oth. writ.] I have had many high achievements in my artwork, such as poems and drawing artistically; [pers.] I dedicate my poem to my mother Jo-Anne, my sister Alison, my dad the Davey and Lindsay family. I reflect materials of nature in my poems and write words down from my heart. [a.] Orangeville, Ontario.

LINN, BABBETTE JOY
[pen.] Joy Linn; [b.] November 8, 1931, California; [p.] Herb and Kay Shuttleworth; [ed.] Lincoln High, Fullerton J.C. and UCLA Fullerton; [occ.] Retired into full time writing; [memb.] American Society of Composers, Authors and Publishers (ASCAP), Pacific Opera Society, Society of Preservation of Native Art; [hon.] Who's Who in California, Who's Who of American Women '92, Woman of the Year '93, International Who's Who of Prof. and Bs. Women '94, International Poet of Merit Award '93, Golden Poet Award '89; [oth. writ.] Story Lady Records, The Star, a Xmas record, Footprints in the

Sand, The Calvary Connection, and The Seeker On Stage, series of one acts for Head Start, music for various college productions, theme music for two movies, "Pathways To Power", a poetry book to be published in '94 by Noble House Publishers, numerous articles and short stories; [pers.] Poetry, more than any other form of writing, is an expression of the heart. My poetry is dedicated to those who, like myself are seeking for the truth with the sure knowledge that only the truth can free us to reach our highest potential.

LIPPEL, LEONARD A.
[b.] February 1, 1924, St. Louis; [m.] Ann (Applebaum) Lippel, October 31, 1943; [ch.] Eileen Warner and Marilyn Baden; [ed.] High school, St. Louis Community College at Meramec, still attending; [occ.] Retired and student; [memb.] St. Louis County Senior Citizens Commission, St. Louis County Older Residents Program, Older Adult Community Action Program; [oth. writ.] St. Louis Community College at Meramec newspaper "The Montage", Older Adult Community Action Program publication quarterly, "The Mainstream", Senior Circuit; [pers.] " I try to be positive in everything I do and keep my thoughts and actions as young as possible. [a.] St. Louis, MO.

LIPSCOMB, DEBORAH
[pen.] Deborah-Marie; [b.] March 14, 1961, Baltimore, MD; [p.] Shirley and Robert Lipscomb; [ed.] Northern High, Baltimore Academy of Acting and Modeling; [occ.] Emergency Dispatcher; [hon.] Finalist in Maryland's 1992 Most Beautiful Eyes contest, extra actress on TV's "Moonlighting" and "Downtown" and movies, "In The Mood", "Running Man", Miss Amity 1981 in Maryland U.S.A. Pageant; [oth. writ.] Lyricist with interests in writing R & B, Rap, Country and Ballards; [pers.] I wish to bring to light the causes and effects of today's society and the need for peace, love and harmony among all people. [a.] Baltimore, MD.

LIPSHUTZ. MILDRED
[pen.] Millie Lipshutz; [b.] May 26, 1927, Philadelphia, PA; [p.] Esther and Max Davis; [m.] Aaron Lipshutz (deceased), November 14, 1948; [ch.] David Marc and Alan Bruce Lipshutz; [ed.] High school graduate, currently attending college, level courses; [occ.] Gagwriter for cartoonist, standup comedienne; [oth. writ.] Several cartoons published in National Examiner, several jokes published in local newspapers; [pers.] Dedicated to my late husband Aaron and my late sister, Jerri, who would both be very proud of me. [a.] Cherry Hill, NJ.

LISENBEE, SUSAN
[b.] April 16, 1964, Dallas, TX; [p.] Mike Lisenbee and Shirley Castleman; [ch.] Michael, Charlie and Sarah; [ed.] Kaufman High School (TX), T.V.C.C. Athens, TX., Trinity Valley Community College; [occ.] Criminal Justice Assistant T.V.C.C.; [memb.] President of Alpha Phi Tau a local chapter of Lambda Alpha Epsilon, American Criminal Justice Association, member Board of Directors Henderson County Teen Court; [hon.] Dean's List, Honor's List, President List (4.0 GPA); [oth. writ.] "Dear Lord" published May 1993 American Colegate Anthology, "What It's All About" May 1993, America Colegate Anthology; [pers.] I strive each day to never lose sight of my dream. My wish is to touch the hearts of all the people I shall meet along the way. [a.] Athens, TX.

LISSETTE, ALMANZAR
[pen.] Liz; [b.] August 13, 1976, New York; [p.] Ramona Almanzar and Rafael A.; [ed.] Harriet Beecher Stowe Junior High School, Manhattan Center for Science and Mathematics High School; [occ.]Back Lab. Technical at Dr. Franklin S. Ward's private office; [memb.] Inwood COmmunity Service, Theatro Hey, Youth Committee, General Electrics Scholars, Columbia Records, BMG Records, etc.; [hon.] Excellence, perfect attendance, mathematics, foreign language, Latin, Science, Social Studies, Technology, Spanish Awards, honors in Math and Science courses; [oth. writ.] In J.H.S. a short story, poem called "Madness"; [pers.] From birth we're embraced with chaos and curiosity, then we grow up believing that we are civilized, but deep inside there's a beast hidden within us and only in certain stages of our life the passion is overwhelmed and the beast is freed proving either good or evil. [a.] New York, NY.

LITTLE, DAVID MICHAEL
[pen.] (alias) Forest Vermin; [b.] September 11, 1966, Hamilton; [ed.] Westmont High School, Lakehead University, Mohawk College; [occ.] Laborer, plastic recycling; [memb.] International Youth Hostel Association; [oth. writ.] Publishing, 1985, Raging Bull, Fanzine 1-4, 1985, The Argus L.U. student newspaper 1986, The Agora 2nd Edition, McMaster University's student paper, 1990 Canadian Connection, 4 issues of local writers 1990, Cerebus High School # B comic book; [pers.] Travel everywhere and often listen, look and learn and when you feel your heart then your pen will burn, moderation in everything, humor is the best medicine. [a.] Barnaby, BC.

LITTLE, TRUDA M.
[b.] September 10, 1927, Kentucky; [m.] Ralph C. Little, December 27, 1993; [ch.] Carol S. Thomas, Darlene Combs, Jerlene Knight, Attris Frank, Gary Lee May, Etta Morris and Bill Randy May; [occ.] I am retired, I am a housewife; [hon.] I have had chances to have my poems recorded but I never did try, I appreciate it very much and thank you; [oth. writ.]] I love to write, I have been writing since early 1950 and love it very much, I have written a good many poems, I always got good reports on my poems; [pers.] I grew up I got married at an early age. Born and raised at Pikeville, Kentucky, I married a cold miner. We had seven children, he's no longer alive, so I remarried the year of 1986. [a.] Supply, NC.

LIVESAY, MARY GRACE
[pen.] Mary Livesay; [b.] June 18, 1980, Philippines; [p.] John and Tina Livesay; [ed.] I am presently in the seventh grade at Russell Middle School and hope to got to Harvard or Yale; [occ.] Student; [memb.] Band member, I play saxophone; [hon.] Honor Roll Student; [pers.] I write many love poems but, this is the first to be published. I express my feelings in my poems. [a.] Auburn, GA.

LLOYD, LESLIE ELLEN
[b.] April 25, 1956, New Westminister, BC Canada; [p.] Gerald and Mary Schenkeveld; [ch.] Christopher Ryan Lloyd; [ed.] Langley Senior Secondary High School; [occ.] Lending Officer, Royal Trust, Kamloops, BC; [memb.] Vice President of the Cariboo Child Care Society; [oth. writ.] Nothing previously published; [pers.] My inspiration is very simple and complex, it is life. [a.] Kamloops, BC.

LLOYD, LIGIA ZELEDON
[pen.] Ligia Zeledon Lloyd; [b.] Nicaragua; [p.] Dr. Benjamin Zeledon and Ofelia Masis; [m.] Widow, David Paul Lloyd, married in New York City; [ch.] Arleen, Maria Ofelia, Xarionsella and David Paul Jr.; [hon.] Honorific Mention in Mexico and other in New York, several poems published in newspapers; [oth. writ.] Mrs. Zeledon Lloyd writes mostly Mystic poetry in Spanish, has a book (not published) called Amor y Plegarias; [a.] Miami, FL.

LOBO, ANTHONY
[b.] September 19,1933, Bombay, India; [p.] Mathew and Amy Lobo; [ed.] St. Vincent High, N. Wadia College, University of Pune, Phil. Theol, Hochschule, Frankfurt/M; [pers.] Influenced by British American and German poetry. [a.] Pune, India.

LoCASTRO, COURTNEY
[pen.] Courtney LoCastro; [b.] December 29,1978, West Palm Beach, FL; [p.] Gary and Karen LoCastro; [ed.] Palm Beach County School of Arts; [occ.] Student; [memb.] First Baptist Church. [a.] Lake Worth, FL.

LOCKLIER, THOMAS E.
[b.] February 25, 1958, Dayton, OH; [p.] Fred and Beverly Locklier; [m.] Faye Walker, October 10, 1981; [ch.] Adam E. and Kara F.; [ed.] Andalusia High School, Andalusia, AL., AS degree, LBW St Jr. College, Andalusia, AL; [occ.] Special Agent, US Army Criminal Investigations Command (CID); [memb.] Gentian Baptist Church, Columbus, GA, CID Association; [hon.] U.S. Army certified Hostage Negotiator, Advance Computer Fraud Investigator, Personal Security Protection, Sex Crimes expert, crime scene profiles; [oth. writ.] Several unpublished poems, short stories and crime reports; [pers.] All my writings are based on true factual incidents. I am inspired by today's youth and actual crime scene examinations and interviews of numerous victims, of persons crime. [a.] Andalusia, AL.

LOCKWOOD, PAUL KURT
[b.] December 8,1953, Neath, South Wales; [p.] Peter and Judy Lockwood; [m.] Sandra Lockwood former Squires, September 7, 1973; [ch.] Kimberley Ann and S. Marie Lockwood; [hon.] I am a descendant of Sir Henry Purcell of Nantch BBA, Sheriff of Montgomeryshire, Wales; [pers.] Look to the future, be as a tree firm in belief, look to your children for they are your wealth, the love you lack yourself give to your children, for they will provide a future of peace and harmony for all mankind.

LOFFLR, MICHAEL H.
[b.] January 5, 1971, Washington, DC; [p.] Andy and Barbara Lofflr; [ed.] Chantilly High School; [occ.] Airborne Express Driver; [memb.] Veterans of Foreign Wars; [hon.] Various medals and ribbons for combat service in Southwest Asia, Turkey and Liberia in 1990-91 while in the U.S. Marine Corps (August 89-August 93); [oth. writ.] Two other poems "Best of Friends" and "Dear Family"; [pers.] All my writings were written either overseas or at sea and reflect my feelings for my dearly missed loved ones at home. [a.] Leesburg, VA.

LOMAX, MELISSA
[pen.] Melissa Ashby; [b.] January 18, Waco, TX; [p.] Lisa and George Trewitt; [oth. writ.] Poems published in other anthologies; [pers.] I attempt to mirror the inner feelings of everyone. I have been influenced by many contemporary poets, including Rod McKuen. [a.] Eddy, TX.

LONG, GLORIA P.
[b.] September 25, 1941, Philadelphia, PA; [p.] Emma F. and Thomas Jordan; [m.] Jerry M. Long, February 21, 1969; [ch.] Joseph Torey Long; [ed.] Dunbar High, Strayer Business College; [occ.] Secretary, U.S. Department of Energy; [memb.] Greeting Committee, Fellowship Hour, Largo Community Church; [hon.] Honorable Mention 1981, Edward A. Fallot Poetry competition; [oth. writ.] Several poems in poetry anthologies, Lyrical Voices, Poetic Treasures, Past and Present, Honey Creek Anthology, Parnassus Magazine Comardes in Poetry, Omega News 1993; [pers.] I strive to see beauty in all things and recognize my blessings and appreciate all of them, great and small. [a.] Mitchellville, MD.

LOONAN, JUANITA S.
[b.] August 6, 1954, Iowa;[p.] Raleigh and Lois Rumbaugh; [m.] James Loonan; [ch.] Jamie Danielle and Brice Joseph Loonan; [ed.] Ballard High School; [occ.] Mother and cook; [memb.] Maxwell Methodist Church, Maxwell Old Settlers Celebration Committee; [oth.writ.] Mostly for my own enjoyment or to bring comfort to a friend who's going through a tough time; [pers.] I write about things that touch my life and my heart, for these are the things that really matter. [a.] Maxwell, IA.

LOOS, ANDREW M.
[pen.] Grog; [b.] February 19, 1975, Lincoln, NE; [p.] Douglas and Dorothy Loos; [ed.] Shawnee Mission North High School, Johnson County Community College; [occ.] Shipping clerk, student; [memb.] Henry Rollins Fan Club; [oth.writ.] Many poems printed in school newspaper; [pers.] I write what I feel, without frilling it up just to make it sound good to others. I am influenced the most by John Keats, my parents and Audrey. I thank you all. [a.] Kansas City, MO.

LOPEZ, VIRGINIA
[b.] September 21, 1927, PR; [p.] Mr. and Mrs. Raymond Gutierrez (deceased); [m.] Jose R. Lopez (deceased), March 13, 1957; [ch.] Nine; [ed.] High school (12); [occ.] Housewife, I work part time in a Recreation Center; [memb.] AARP and Lifestyle Fellowship-Sacred Heart of Jesus; [oth.writ.] Poems, novel, songs, (not published), some lyrics at the Peer Institute; [pers.] Years ago I danced and sing in a club. [a.] Brooklyn, NY.

LORSON, AIMEE
[pen.] Amos, Skeater;[b.] January 23, 1977, Salina, KS; [p.] (s-father) Lynn and Dianne Campbell, (father) Dan Lorson; [ed.] Sophomore at Pflugerville High School in Pflugerville, Texas; [pers.] Thank you to all who have ever inspired me to strive for the best in everything and to those who have my dreams reality. [a.] Austin, TX.

LOUCKS, GLORIA
[b.] October 22,1948, Syracuse, NY; [p.] Eleanor Page and Warren; [ch.] James A. Loucks; [ed.] Graduated Central Technical High School 1966; [occ.] Housewife; [oth. writ.] A few unpublished poems. [a.] Central Square, NY.

LOVE, CHRISTOPHER MICHAEL
[pen.] Chris Love; [b.] October 17, 1984, Washington, DC; [p.] Mary and Edward Love; [ed.] Wesley Nursery School, Saint Barts Catholic School, hope to go to Oxford; [occ.] O.C. books, second president, student, St. Bart's Catholic School; [memb.] Congressional C.C., Saint Bart's Catholic Church, Saint Bart's Drama Club,

Cub Scouts (Bear); [hon.] Golf awards, soccer, basket-ball, to correspond with Bucklingham Palace; [oth. writ.] Hot Rods I-II, Tiny Toons Go To Iraq, Adventures of Sedrick and Charles, Foxes Like Popcorn Too; [pers.] Love to read, write and speak foreign languages, I love the U.K. [a.] Bethesda, MD.

LOVELL, NANCY B.
[b.] Febraury 20,1945, Charleston, WV; [p.] M/M James S. Lovell; [m.] Divorced; [ch.] Charles (Chad) Lovell Bogert; [ed.] U of Charleston, Charleston, WV; [occ.] Real Estate, ski instructor at Breckenridge, massage Therapist plus jewerly designer; [memb.] D.A.R., Colonal Dames; [hon.] T.K.D. (Forensic Honorary); [pers.] My poems have always reflected the deepe thoughts feelings and connections with the universe, which cannot be express as well through any other medium. [a.] Breckenridge, CO.

LOVELL, VICKI
[b.] August 20, 1955, Omaha, NE; [p.] Glenn and Clara Bragg; [m.] Dale Lovell; [ch.] Jeremy Scott and Lacey Leigh; [pers.] The need to put words on paper has been with me always. Being a writer is not what I do, but what I am. [a.] Phoenix, AZ.

LOWE, BLAINE
[pen.] Blaine Lowe; [b.] April 21, 1947, Salmon, ID; [p.] Devar and Afton Lowe; [m.] Ellen Lowe, December 16, 1967; [ch.] Shelley, Lisa and Robyn; [ed.] Perris High School, Compton College; [occ.] Operations Manager, J & V Leasing Inc.; [memb.] Delta Nv Alpha, VFW; [hon.] This is the first of I hope many and indeed it is an honor; [oth. writ.] Several short poems and notions; [pers.] Tis the journey, not the journey's end. [a.] Orange, CA.

LOWE, MILLCIENT M.
[pen.] Millie; [b.] May 5, 1966, Flint, MI; [p.] Geraldine King and Henry Lowe; [ed.] Saint Raymond Academy for Girls, Bronx, NY, Pace University BA '87, Political studies, New York, NY; [occ.] Barneys New York, Madison Avenue (New York, New York) Security; [memb.] Convent Avenue Baptist Church, Naval Reserves; [oth. writ.] My Reality, The Brown Bird (short story), Cease Fire, You Called, The Golden Door (short story), Best Dressed; [pers.] God is good. He has given me oppotunties that I did not deserve. As a result, I feel compelled to share every talent I may or may not have. I just want to thank you Lord because you've been good to me. [a.] Bronx, NY.

LOWERY, MARK D.
[b.] September 6, 1955, Marietta, GA; [p.] S.D. and Annie Lowery; [m.] Angela; [ch.] Matthew, Mesahl and Blake; [oth. writ.] The Walk, The Promise; [pers.] All good and perfect gifts are from God. My desire is to live for and use any God given talents to the glory and honor of Him and Him alone. Praise God. [a.] Glen St. Mary, FL.

LUCAS, EVELYN JANE SPEAR
[pen.] Evelyn Jane Spear Lucas; [b.] February 20, 1934, West Newbury, VT; [p.] Fred and Reta Spear; [m.] Edgar Roger Lucas, February 23, 1952; [ch.] Kenneth Fletcher, Reta Jane and Edward Roger; [ed.] Graduated high school, Newbury High School, Newbury, Vermont; [occ.] Retired from housemother at a Girls School and Health Aide for the elderly in their homes; [memb.] Member of Christs Church, Saxtons River, member of senior center volunteers; [oth. writ.] Some poems pub-

lished in school newslettes and the local newspapers; [pers.] I hae always written poems about everyday life, the struggles and the joys and tried to give thanks to our Lord for His wildlife and beautiful mountains and countryside He has blessed us with here in Vermont. [a.] Saxton River, VT.

LUCE
[occ.] Currently living in Florence, Italy, directing an originally designed theatre and language activity called the Performance Workshop; [oth. writ.] "Photographs Without A Camera", a one woman threatre piece on inner and outer journeys while traveling in Europe; [pers.] Writing has been the door, the way in to my creative and personal development. I so enjoy assisting others across the threshold.

LUCKY, ROSEMARY ANN ROTTMAN
[b.] August 20, 1939, Elk Creek, NE; [p.] Harvey and Helen Rottman; [m.] Divorced; [ch.] Shannon Gregg; [ed.] Table Rock, NE, High, Peru State Teachers College, University of Nebraska at Omaha, masters in Reading, ADM.; [occ.] English Eleven A, Bellevue East Senior High, Bellevue, NE; [memb.] Phi Delta Kappa, Alpha Delta Kappa, National Education Association, Nebraska State Education Association, Bellevue Education Association, Who's Who Among America's Teachers, Nebrasks Coaches Association, National Federation Interscholastic Spirit Association; [hon.] Cooper Foundation Award for Excellence in Teaching, Who's Who Among America's Teachers, Teacher of the Month; [pers.] Poems published in local newspapers, articles in Metroplitan Reading Council publication; [pers.] Human nature, the past, and nature are my inspiration. [a.] Bellevue, NE.

LUEPNITZ, ROY R.
[pen.] Roy R. Lupenitz; [b.] June 3, 1955, Ft. McClellan, AL; [p.] Carl A. and Helen E. Luepnitz; [m.] Mary (Ceci) Luepnitz, December 18, 1981; [ch.] Noel Ashley Luepnitz, Mary D. McGown and George S. Paterson; [ed.] Ph.D. Texas A & M University, MS-University of Southern Mississippi, BA-Southwestern Univesity; [memb.] National Register of Health Service Provider in Psychology, the American Psychological Association, the Texas Psychological Association and the Brazos Valley Psychological Association. [hon.] 1993/94 Who's Who in the South and Southwest, 1992 Who's Who in the Elite Registry of Extaordinary Professionals, 1981 Outstanding Young Men of America; [oth. writ.] Numerous poems not published, Mental Health Minutes; [pers.] Man will be judged by the pain, hurt he inflictes, as wellas the eharling, joy he inspires during his lifetime. [a.] College Station, TX.

LUNA, SAN M.
[pen.] Sun-Moon; [b.] November 1, 1919, Medellin, Cebu, Philippines; [p.] All deceased; [m.] Teofila S. Luna, June 6, 1953; [ch.] Arthur, Danilo, Elroy, Emilio and Grace; [ed.] (BES), Bachelor of Science in Education, major-History, minor-English, this college education was honestly earned at the CEBU Roosevelt Memorial Colleges; [occ.] Agriculturist; [memb.] Past, Municipal Chairman of the National Citizens Movement for Free Elections, and Service Officer of the American Leigon Post No 82, Cebu, Philippines; [hon.] From grade 1 up to VII, Valdictorian, from first year to fourth year high school, Scholar, as a self supporting student in college, it was very hard for me to earn honor; [oth.writ.] Poems, "Saga of Afflictions in Motherland", "The Fraternal and Identical Twins"; [pers.] Srtict adherence

in pratice to the tenets of DEMOCRACY and the TEN COMMANDMENTS of CHRISTIANITY. [a.] Hercules, CA.

LUNA, SHONTAY
[pen.] Tempest Waycool; [b.] August 22, 1969, Chicago, IL; [p.] Thomas Oldham and Tina Nevels; [m.] Jose Jesus Luan Huerta, February 19, 1993; [ed.] Dunbar High, Columbia College, Robert Morris College; [occ.] Cashier, stockperson; [oth. writ.] Several unpublished poems; [pers.] My writing covers a broad range of topics but I always try to show things as they really are (and sometimes the way they should be). Special thanks goes to my brother Maurice, who always makes me feel like I can do anything. [a.] Chicago, IL.

LUNDQUIST, RANDALL
[b.] February 4, 1958, Chicago, IL; [p.] Richard and Roberta; [m.] Divorced; [ch.] Charlene and Melanie; [ed.] Watchtower Society Theocratic Ministry School; [memb.] Villa Park Congregation of Jehovahs Witnesses; [hon.] Accepted to be one of Jehovahs Christian Witnesses; [oth. writ.] Unpublished, all poems inspired by and dedicated to my best friend, our friendship became love, may it last forever; [pers.] My life and love are a result of reading and believing God's word, the Bible. [a.] Elmhurts, IL.

LUSSIER, LISA MARIE
[b.] October 5, 1972, Fall River; [p.] Mr. and Mrs. Paul A. Lussier; [ed.] The Boston School 1979-1993 and Randolph High School 1989-1993; [occ.] Burger King at Silver City GGalleria; [memb.] In school I was a Student Council Representative 1986-1991, Junior Class Secretary 1991-1992 and a Senior Class Treasurer 1992-93; [hon.] Honor Rolls 1985-1993, nominate for Randie Awrds 1993, Senior Class Valedictorian 1993, I received Parent's Association Academic Achievement Award, and Suffolk University Outstanding School Service Award; [oth. writ.] Poems and a short story; [pers.] I put all my feelings from my heart and throughts in to these poems to make people realize love is more beauty then making love and a lot of people I know gave wonderful comments on them, and I thank you to those people who helped and got me there. [a.] Taunton, MA.

LUTHER, CHARMON J.
[pen.] Charmon Horsman; [b.] October 14, 1970, Spring Valley, MN; [p.] Clair and Shirley Horsmon; [m.] Colen C. Luther, December 6, 1991; [ch.] Talisman Chaos; [ed.] Spring Valley High School, RC College; [occ.] Starving artist; [oth. writ.] Several books but none published; [pers.] Love, peace and happiness, illusions or realities? [a.] Penrose, CO.

LYNETTE, CANTRICE
[b.] October 2, 1967, New Orleans, LA; [p.] Ernest Montgomery Sr. and Janice B.; [ch.] Naguell Artiega Montgoy; [ed.] Zachary High School; [occ.] Army Reservist and substitute teacher; [hon.] Completed 5 years in the U.S. Army with a Southwest Asia Svc. MDL, Kuwait, Liberation MDL, Army Commendation MDL, 2-Army Achievement MDL, Good Conduct and National Defense, Svc MDL Army, Svc Ribbon, overseas SVC ribbon, expert markmanship badge, rifle M-16 and an overseas service bar medal; [oth. writ.] Several poems published in different newspapers and 3 books I wrote I'm in the process of trying to get published Army Life is Not The Life For Me, What Comes From The Heart Reaches the Heart, I Will Cry Loud and Spare Not; [pers.] To excel and be the best I can be in every area and

to never forget where I came from and who brought me through. I desire to touch more than a couple of lives through my work. I intend to touch many of all race and creed. [a.] Zachary, LA.

LYON, RAYMOND H.
[b.] April 2, 1914, New York City; [p.] Everard and Celia Lyon; [m.] Alberta M. Lyon, September 24, 1946; [ch.] Miriam, Raymond Jr. and Elizabeth (all by 1st marriage); [ed.] Port Richmond High School (S.I.N.Y.), California State University, L.A., Bachelors and masters degrees, California Coast University Ph.D. (a 75); [occ.] Own sales agency, teach 1 night at college and lead Dixieland Band; [memb.] 32nd degree Mason and Shriner, Downey Hi-12 (past president), Downey Chamber of Commerce, Magician Member of Magic Castle , Hollywood, United States Tennis Association, ASCAP, National Sheet Music Society (president), Rasicrucians; [hon.] Service award-Port Richmond High School, 2 Varsity Letters CSULA (for tennis at ages 54 and 55), Sports Illustrated Magazine trophy, Founder and President Southeast Dixieland Jazz Inc.; [oth. writ.] Songs-Our Eyes Met, The End of Our Dreams, Tell Me Sweetheart, Solamente Para Ti (with Don Swan, composer of Dream a Little Dream of Me), Post-coitis Blues; [pers.] As advocated by my late father, to keep the mental physical, social and spiritual aspects of my life in balance! [a.] Downey, CA.

LYON, SUSAN M.
[b.] July 28, 1952, New York City; [p.] Doris Widmayer-Norman Cherny-gren; [m.] Danile Webster Lyon, March 16, 1990; [ch.] Gerald Paul 12 years old from previous marriage; [ed.] Willowbrook High School, Villa Park, IL., Adelphia University and Queens College, major Cultural Anthropology; [occ.] Security Supervisor-Roosevelt Field Mall, Garden City, NY; [memb.] Karaoke Singers Group of Rosedale, NY; [hon.] Dean's List, 3 year music letter, 4 year music pin; [oth. writ.] I have written a whole anthology of poetry and also lyrics to my own songs. In addition to my own lyrics I also composed all my own melodies, and I play 12 string guitar, flute and recorder and of course I sing my own songs; [pers.] On a personal note, I believe in art for the sake of art, and my ultimate striving would be to be able to express painting, literature and music, ultimately interchangeably. To see the light in a painting, to hear the light in a song and to express the ultimate light, which I feel is love and understanding and truth in literature. [a.] Rosedale, NY.

LYTTON, MARY E.
[pen.] M.E. Lytton; [b.] April 3, 1937, Mexico; [p.] Ramon and Esther Mazon; [m.] Edwin A. Lytton, August 7, 1956; [ch.] Perry Alan, Mary Theresa and Gerald Alan; [occ.] Self-employed with spouse, Mel's Sewing Service; [oth. writ.] Several poems published in local church bulletins; [pers.] It was only when I came to know the Lord Jesus Christ, that I discovered a need to pen things, I read about, heard about, but most importantly things I feel as I pray or study the word of God. [a.] Anaheim, CA.

MacINTYRE, RONALD P.
[pen.] Ronnie; [b.] February 4, 1993, Toronto; [p.] Mr. and Mrs. Edward Hancock; [ch.] Chane Paul, James Paul, Dean Paul, David and Christopher Paul; [ed.] Grade 12 upgrading Child Psychology; [occ.] Part-time Nanny and Volunteer; [memb.] Board member for Communities Against Sexual Abuse, United Way, American Fellowship Church; [hon.] Award of Merit for Make the Future Last; [oth. writ.] Strength Within A Tear,

Make the Future Last; [pers.] I see beauty in a poem, as I feel joy within my heart and soul and may everyone's day feel the happiness in life. [a.] Vernon, B.C.

MacISSAC, DANIEL
[b.] October 22, 1926, Nova Scotia; [p.] Archibald; Jessie; [m.] Mary Judith, October 28, 1947; [ch.] Joy; [occ.] Retired, Sr. Mgr. Mining, Construction and Engineering.

MacPHERSON, HUGH A.
[pen.] Hugh A. MacPherson; [b.] July 26, 1934, Sydney, NS; [p.] William and Ruth MacPherson; [m.] Divorced; [ed.] Sydney Academy; [occ.] Sexton, First Baptist Church; [oth. writ.] Many unpublished; [pers.] No sight is as tragic as that of one who stands on infant emotional legs and stares hopelessly into a spiritual void. [a.] Hampstead, PQ, CAN.

MacVIBAN, JOHNNIE
[b.] July 25, 1955, Nkar, Bui; [p.] Dzekashu Gregory and Lemnyuy Hortensia; [m.] Theresia Yuh Keh, August 15, 1985; [ch.] Charles MacViban; [ed.] University of Yaounde's School of Mass Communication, International Communication Institute, Montreal, CAN; [occ.] Journalist; [memb.] Writer's Club; [oth. writ.] Breaking the Silence (poems) MaKuri Alternative (novel) all still unpublished; [pers.] Never go to bed with a clouded mind. [a.] Yaounde, Cameroon.

McAFEE, LISA CAROLE
[b.] July 16, 1974, Memphis, TN; [p.] Don and Kathleen McAfee; [ed.] Germantown High School, Shelby State Community College, University of Tennessee at Martin; [memb.] Central Church, Ridgeway Country Club, Grace Evangelical Church; [hon.] Cum Laude; [oth. writ.] Many other poems, some were published in my high school's poetry journal "Creative Writing"; [pers.] My poetry sometimes reflects what I see from day to day. Other times, it is written just for fun. As for my philosophical view, everyone has been given certain talents if they would just take the time to discover and develop them. [a.] Germantown, TN.

McAFEE, MARTHA
[pen.] Mart; [b.] December 9, 1952; [p.] Willie, Charliestine Armwood; [m.] Fred Jr., October 18, 1969; [ch.] Fred III. Mary Ann and Philip McAfee; [ed.] GED certificate, Old Main High School; [occ.] Housewife; [memb.] House of Prayer Holiness Church/Community Workers; [oth. writ.] Couple of poems for special occasions, readings and letters of inspiration for an assembly; [pers.] My endeavour is to leave an impression and to inspire in my writing. I have been deeply moved by experiences I've had also that of others. [a.] Robbins, IL.

McARDLE, MATTHEW
[b.] September 25, 1983, Ridgewood, NJ; [p.] Robin and Jerry McArdle; [ed.] Hubbard School 4th grade; [occ.] Student; [memb.] St. Paul RCC; [hon.] GreenBelt - Tai Kwon Do, Soccer and Baseball Star; [pers.] I dedicate this poem to my Uncle Ray whom I love very much and will miss. [a.] Ramsey, NJ.

McARDLE, ROBIN
[b.] September 30, 1955, Teaneck, NJ; [p.] Rica and Raymond Westervelt; [m.] Gerald, July 11, 1976; [ch.] Matthew, Kevin, Kelsey; [ed.] Waldwick High School, Ramapo College; [occ.] Owner, McArdle Communications; [memb.] St. Paul's RCC; [pers.] This poem is

dedicated to my parents who inspired me "to be the best I can be." [a.] Ramsey, NJ.

McBRIDE, JOHN D.
[b.] December 1, 1921, Keysone, OK; [p.] B.B. (deceased) and Ruby E. McBride; [m.] Ruth H., December 12, 1948; [ch.] Two deceased and one living; [ed.] Three years college; [memb.] Reserve Officers Association, Retired Officers Association, Hump Pilots Association, Air Force Association, Air Force Sergeants Association, Burma Star Association, American Legion Post No. 1, Soldier's of Fortune, Shanghai China (in Exile), China Burma India Veterans Association, Paralyzed Veterans Association. [a.] San Juan, PR.

McBRIDE, RENEE'
[pen.] Rae McBride; [b.] June 22, Philadelphia, PA; [p.] Anthony Sr. and Doris; [ch.] Christian McBride; [ed.] West Philadelphia High, LaSalle University; [occ.] Teacher, freelance writer; [memb.] University of PA, Museum Mobile Guides, WEPIC Drama Group, AERho; [hon.] Charlotte W. Newcombe Scholarship, LaSalle University, Student Activity Award, WEPIC Drama; [oth. writ.] Between a rock and a hard place; The Loud Silence, Entertainment Biographies; [pers.] For each day you see a new, give thanks and utilize it with enthusiasm because the hardest part of the day is already over. [a.] Philadelphia, PA.

McBROOM, DAVID GLENN
[b.] August 5, 1956, Holton, KS; [ch.] Cody Shane McBroom; [occ.] Houston Fire Fighter; [memb.] 7th Special Forces Group 1976-79; [hon.] American Legion Fire Fighter of the Year 1992 by Garden Oaks, American Legion Post 560; [oth. writ.] 70-150 poems in personal collection and also published in Normangee Star.

McCALLUM, MINDI
[b.] October 15, 1978, San Bernardino, CA; [p.] David and Julia Thexton; [ed.] 10th grade Temescal Canyon High School; [memb.] Grace Evangelical Free Church; [hon.] Swimming awards; [oth. writ.] Several unpublished poems; [pers.] The only way to write is to write from the heart. [a.] Menifee Valley, CA.

McCLINTON, JOANIE O.
[pen.] Joan McVaughn; [b.] December 3, 1964, Grenada, MS; [p.] John O. and Joyce V. McClinton; [ed.] Germantown High School, Memphis State University, John Casablancas Modeling and Career Centers; [occ.] English/Spanish teacher at Booker T. Washington High; [memb.] Zeta Phi Beta Sorority, National Education Association, Ward Chapel A.M.E. Church; [hon.] Order of Omega, Sigma Delta Pi, Omicron Delta Kappa; [oth. writ.] None submitted for publication; [pers.] Poem dedicated to Jeffrey U. Wilson. [a.] Memphis, TN.

McCLURE, ANNIE
[b.] April 28, 1925, Texas; [p.] J.H. Rivers, Ida Rivers-Williams (deceased); [m.] June 4, 1943; [ch.] Renee'; [ed.] Ennis High, Mountain View College; [occ.] Retired; [hon.] Dean's List, Outstanding Academic Achievement award; [pers.] The use of words hold a special magic. They stir the imagination and cleanse the soul. [a.] Duncanville, TX.

McCONKIE, BEULAH DUVALL
[b.] October 16, 1919, Vernal, UT; [p.] Alva James and Alta Manwaring Duvall; [m.] Lynn L., June 3, 1937; [ch.] Larry J., Carolyn, Eugene, Douglas, and Terry Lynn; [ed.] Uintah High School graduate; [occ.] Retired

1984 as Unit Mgr., School Lunch; [memb.] Uintah Chapter of Utah Poets, Daughters of Utah Pioneers; [hon.] Salutatorian of Graduating Class, Seminary Declamation winner, several 2nd and 3rd place winners in local poetry contests, many poems published in Local Vernal Express, wrote and gave tribute to governor when he visited our town; [oth. writ.] Winning story in my senior year at school, many poems for weddings and church functions, as well as birthdays, was President of Relief Society and MIA taught many classes; [pers.] I enjoyed hand work, flowers, gardening love my family around, love to sing and my 2 sisters and I sang many trios. I love get togethers, to travel, meeting people, in other words I enjoy life. "Laugh" and the world laughs with you. Weep and you weep alone. [a.] Vernal, UT.

McCORMICK, TODD
[b.] June 14, 1962, Salem, OH; [p.] William and Lois McCormick; [ed.] Salem High, Kent State BA; [occ.] Grad student and tutor; [memb.] Kent Sailing, Kent Masters Swim Club, Pi Mu Epsilon; [oth. writ.] A Climber's Guide To Logtown; OH; Between Anhedonia and a Hard Place (in progress); [pers.] I want to increase my awareness of the ordinary and extraordinary in everyday and not so everyday sentient beings. [a.] Kent, OH.

McDANIEL, CHRISTINE L.
[pen.] Chrissie Teenie; [b.] January 27, 1965, Youngstown, OH; [p.] John Burl and Helen L. (Slaton) McDaniel; [ch.] Nathaniel Burl R. McDaniel; [ed.] Carrollton High School, Buckeye Joint Vocational School, South Eastern Academy; [occ.] Homemaker, mother; [hon.] 1982 Most Outstanding Student award, Buckeye JUS Auto Mechanics Class; [oth. writ.] First poem published in "Coming of Dawn" also my own personal book, I've worked on and added to since age 12; [pers.] All my poems reflect back to special times in my life, they help me through the rough times. [a.] Carrollton, OH.

McDONALD, EDNA DIGGS
[b.] January 17, 1952, Rockingham; [p.] Rufus and Edna Pearl Diggs; [m.] Percell, February 12, 1983; [m.] Latoya Diggs and Jessica and Ian McDonald; [ed.] BS Early Childhood Education, AA Executive Secretary; [occ.] Chapter I Reading Teacher-Smarkand Manor School; [memb.] NCAE, NEA, SEANC; [oth. writ.] I have written a complete book of poetry, but this is the first poem I've attempted to have published. I'm searching for avenues through which I might publish a book of poetry; [pers.] Most of my writings reflect my personal feelings about things in life. My spirituality and love of mankind influence most of my writings also.

McDONALD, J. ELAINE
[pen.] June Rose; [occ.] Rehabilitation Nurse; [pers.] Lover of reading and nature. My favorite book is "The Bible".

McDONIEL, BRENDA LYNN
[b.] May 20, 1953, Batesville; [p.] Leonard and Faye Green; [m.] Wallace Gene, August 2, 1970; [ch.] Angela and Brandon; [ed.] Newark High; [occ.] RAises miniature horses; postal clerk; [memb.] Arkansas Miniature Horse Society (AMHS), American Miniature Horse Association; Sulphur Rock Saddle Club. [a.] Newark, AK.

McDONOUGH, JANET S.
[b.] January 19, 1963, Martinez, CA; [p.] Eugene B. McDonough; [ed.] California State University-San Ber-

nardino pursuit of BA and teaching credential, AA degree Liberal Studies 5/93; [hon.] Graduated with honors San Bernardino Valley College; [pers.] Dedicated in memory of my father Eugene McDonough and to Anthony Gutierrez for his encouragement and steadfastness. [a.] San Bernardino, CA.

McGOWAN, GRAYCE ELIZABETH
[b.] March 14, 1904, Monango, ND; [p.] Fred and Minnie Moore; [m.] Owen Louis, July 22, 1927; [ch.] Laverne Louis and Jeanette Mary; [ed.] Ellendale High School, Ellendale Ind. College (2 years), BA University of Wyoming, University of N.D. and University of Pacific; [occ.] Speech Therapy Rt. Tr. helping poor and tutoring - help with phonics; [memb.] 4H Canning Club, Girls Campfire, Delta Society, St. Mark's Episcopal Church, American Legion Auxiliary, Rt. Teachers Association; [hon.] G4H Canning Club, Golden Acorn for work in PTA, National Congress of Parents and Teachers, Scholarship ND Society for Crippled Children; [oth. writ.] Twenty poems for my class at Tacoma, WA, articles for Park River School, articles on "Speech Therapy", articles on County Speech Therapy published by local newspaper; [pers.] I became interested in poetry at an early age due to my mother's interest. She wrote articles and poetry for the Literary Club. I taught 4 years the last 7 years were in grade I children, at this age do well writing. I tried to help each student develop his talents to the utmost. [a.] Mesa, AZ.

McGRAW, EMOGENE
[b.] September 24, 1937, Kenova, WVA; [p.] George and Irene Adkins; [m.] Donald, September 26, 1959; [ch.] Dreama Wolfe, Sandy Paxson, Joyce Hayslip; [ed.] 10th grade; [occ.] Homemaker; [hon.] Editor's Choice; [oth. writ.] Poems published in several books and local newspapers; [pers.] This is my fifteen minutes of fame. [a.] Blue Creek, OH.

McGUIRE, JOHN J.
[pen.] Jack McGuire; [p.] Brooklyn, NY; [p.] Michael and Margaret; [m.] Anne, May 29, 1987; [ch.] John, Lou-Ann, Brian; [ed.] St. Francis Xavier and St. Leonard's Academy; [occ.] Wildlife Assistant; [memb.] United Association of Journeymen of the Plumbing and Pipefitting Industry at the U.S. (AFL-CIO-CFL); [hon.] Mohave Community College, Mohave Desert Scribes, American Legion Poetry Contest; [oth. writ.] Novel-"The Two of Us", screenplay-"Unwelcome Stranger", poem-"Our Land" (American Legion Poetry Contest winner); [pers.] "My Heart is True" as sag the Sioux. [a.] Kingman, AZ.

McINTIRE, FLORENCE
[b.] April 21, 1915, Plainfield, NJ; [p.] Anna G. (deceased) Ackerman and William E. Ackerman; [m.] Robert L. (deceased), November 28, 1934; [ch.] Deceased William and Joan McIntire; [ed.] Completed North Plainfield NJ High School; [occ.] Homebody; [memb.] Jehovah Witness for 53 years; [hon.] Key from National Honor Society 1934; [oth. writ.] Some unpublished poems and one song called Black and Gold Ring, words and music; [pers.] To try to be upbuilding and willing to listen to other people's problems to offer help if I can to never deliberately hurt anyone. [a.] San Diego, CA.

McINTOSH, JACQUELINE
[pen.] Jackie; [b.] October 16, 1970, Jamaica, West Indies; [p.] Clementina Beckford and Wilberelen McIntosh; [ed.] Poughkeepsie HIgh, Edward Waters College; [occ.] Bookkeeper; [pers.] We should all stick to our

dreams, because dreams do become reality. Yes, dream(s) do take time. [a.] Poughkeepsie, NY.

McINTOSH, TANYA
[pen.] Tanya McIntosh; [b.] July 2, 1975, Jamaica; [p.] Lillian and Vincent McIntosh; [ed.] Westwood High School, Knox Community College; [occ.] Student; [hon.] Prefects Trophy for Dietitian, certificate for History; [pers.] I strive to stimulate the minds of my readers through my writing which displays self expression. Writing also gives me the opportunity to make people happy through whatever fulfillment they receive. [a.] Jamaica, W.I.

McKAY, ROSEMARY
[b.] June 30, 1942, Bonnie, Scotland; [p.] Margaret and Thomas McKay; [ch.] Thomas Skewes and Kylie McKay; [ed.] Our Lady of Lourdes, Holyrood Sen. Sec. School; [occ.] Office Manager Eltom Mayo School of Management; [memb.] South Australian Justice Administration Foundation, St. Paul's Centre Christian City Ministry, Australian Executive Women's Network, Australian Institute of Tertiary Education Administrators; Amnesty International, Adelaide Diocesan Justice and Peace Commission, Campaign for an Independent East Timor, Indo-China Refugee Association; [pers.] Belief in the following: Recognition of the inherent dignity and of the equal rights of all members of the human family is the foundation of freedom, justice, and peace in the world; for a "that an 'a' that man to man, the world over shall brothers be, for a that Robert Burns; faith, hope, and charity and the greatest of these is "Love" Jesus Christ. [a.] Adelaide, S. Australia.

McKEAG, ROBERT G.
[pen.] Bob McKeag; [b.] January 17, 1948, Pittsburgh, PA; [p.] William Bruce and Mary Helen (Sabina) McKeag; [m.] Judith Anne; [ch.] Erin, Kristen, Jennifer, Jeffery, and Joshua; [occ.] Life's work - musician; [memb.] ASCAP and American Legion and American Federation of Musicians; [oth. writ.] Songs that were recorded by various artists on Atlantic Records and Big Tree Records and Buddha Records from the late 60's through the early 80's; [pers.] Ours is not to question the length of the road ahead, but merely to be glad to be upon it. [a.] Pittsbugh, PA.

McKEEN, BETTY WESTHAVER
[b.] August 18, 1906, Denver, CO; [p.] Cora Etta Taylor and James Benjamin Westhaver; [m.] Dr. Harold Reid McKeen, Jr., June 8, 1940; [ch.] Elsbeth Brigham, Harold Reid III, Rebecca Westhaver; [ed.] University of Denver, University of Colorado, Manual High School, Oxford College; [occ.] Retired high school teacher; [memb.] Delta Zeta Sorority, Daughters of the American Revolution; [hon.] Delta Kappa Gamma. [a.] Waianae, HI.

MCKENNA, NEIL J.
[pen.] Annmarie Siegle; [b.] July 28, 1972, Ridgewood, NJ; [p.] Joseph and Noreen McKenna; [ed.] Southern Regional High School; [occ.] Security Guard; [memb.] Student of "Kum Sung" martial arts school; [hon.] Awarded the title of Assistant instructor and have received several awards as a tournament competitor; [pers.] The road of spiritual growth may seem long and hard to travel but the rewards are handsome. [a.] Parkertown, NJ.

McKENNA, SEAN PATRICK
[b.] March 21, 1971, Frankfurt, W. Germany; [p.]

Patricia and George (deceased); [ed.] BS Mechanical Engineering Rensselaer Polytechnic Institute; [memb.] American Society of Mechanical Engineers, Society of Naval Architects and Marine Engineers; [hon.] Magna Cum Laude, Tau Beta Pi and Pi Tau Sigma Engineering Honor Societies. [a.] Islip, NY.

MCKENNA, SHEILA FITZGERALD
[b.] Fitzgerald McKenna; [b.] 1920s, London England; [p.] George William Fitzgerald, May Kennedy; [ch.] Mary Rose, Margaret Mary, Pamela Mary, Devon May, AnneMarie; [ed.] Claremont Girls School; [occ.] Writer; [memb.] Royal United Services Institute, Cathedral Choir, Glee Club; [oth. writ.] Poems and prose published This England (Quarterly Magazine), Evergreen, (Quarterly magazine), Island Catholic News, Prairie Messenger, Diocese of Victoria, poem in Synod book and time "Capsule", review of books by and about Canada's Indian first peoples; [pers.] Factual vision: I write from an Irish heart on things I see. My great uncle, Edward Fitzgerald, translated "The Rubaiyat" of Omar Khayam from the Persian, mid 1800s. I grew up in Irish Literary Circles. Deo Gratias! [a.] Victoria BC Canada.

McLEOD, DEBRAH JEAN
[pen.] D.J. McLeod; [b.] January 26, 1953, Simcoe, Ont. CAN; [p.] Madeline McLeod and Gary Lowes; [m.] Divorced; [ch.] Jeanny Lee, Michelle Jean, Randy George; [ed.] Picton Ont. High School; [occ.] Mother, homemaker; [memb.] 10 year associate Royal Canadian Legion; [oth. writ.] Newspapers Toronto Sun-Trentonian Brighton Inteleigineer-North Frontenial News; [pers.] Life is full of feeling sometimes so overwhelming it has to be written down. It's good sharing the feeling in my heart. [a.] Northbrook, Ont. CAN.

McMAHAN, TRACY LYNN
[pen.] Cheyenne Autumn; [b.] September 18, 1970, Tucson, AZ; [p.] David and Linda McMahan; [ed.] Pinson Valley High School, Ballet Rio Dance Conservatory; [occ.] Dancer and model; [memb.] Greenpeace; [oth. writ.] Several poems unpublished; [pers.] As an adult, I am finding great inspiration in my native American heritage. I have found my true spiritual home and invite all to walk the red road of peace love and harmony. [a.] Birmingham, AL.

McMAHON, GALE ALLEN
[b.] January 14, 1954, Weed, CA; [p.] Vernon and Earlene McMahon; [m.] Divorced; [ch.] VErnon Jeffery, Michelle Lynn, Margaret Lee; [ed.] Tulelake High, College of the Siskiyous; [occ.] State Military Security Officer, 114th FS Kingsley Field; [pers.] Most of my work attempts to show and enlighten others to their inhumanities to others. [a.] Tulelake, CA.

McMAHON, ROSEMARY
[b.] June 12, 1931, Kenton, OH; [ed.] Our Lady of Victory Academy, Ohio Northern University, College of St. Mary of the Springs, University of Dayton, Ohio Dominican College, Postgraduate Rosary College; [memb.] Ohio Library Council; [hon.] Meritorious Service as a member of the Columbus Technical Institute Faculty. [a.] Columbus, OH.

McMILLEN, BRIAN P.
[pen.] Brian P. McMillen; [b.] July 25, 1970, Kenosha, WI; [p.] James R. and Mary E. McMillen; [ed.] Salem High School; [occ.] Martial Arts Instructor, VP Karate Masters Inc.; [memb.] Taekwondo America, Amateur Kickboxing Federation, Boxing Association; [hon.] 1990-91 World Champion Taekwondo Silver medalist, 1990 VA State Kickboxing Champion and 1991 Washington, DC Outstanding Kickboxer; [oth. writ.] Walk with the Master Poet. Book: Reflections, published; [pers.] Poetry is much more than writing. It is an escape from harsh realities. Realities we must face, when we've ready. [a.] Chesapeake, VA.

McMORROW, FRED
[pen.] Clark Redfield; [b.] November 29, 1925, New York, NY; [p.] Thomas and Hedwig McMorrow; [m.] Jeanne, January 28, 1989; [ch.] Thomas, Robert, Mary, Fred; [ed.] Adelphi University; [occ.] Retired from New York (Time); [memb.] The Newspaper Guild, American Society of Composer, Author & Publishers, newspapers for 43 years; [hon.] Prizes for Headlines, New York Post, New York Journal - American New York Daily News, New York Times; [oth. writ.] Poem for N>Y. Times, 32 short stories sold to Sat. Eve. Post, Playboy, Good Housekeeping, magazine of fantasy and science fiction, New York Daily News; [pers.] 2 books: "Middlescene, The Dangerous Years", Quadrangle - New York Times Books, 1974, New York -"Jimmy, The Candidacy of Carter, Strawberry Hill, NY.

McMULLIN, DALE R.
[b.] December 7, 1969, Bremerton, WA; [p.] Fred W. and Patricia; [m.] Tammy Jo Becker, October 24, 1992; [ed.] Engineering Degree, Mechanical, Colorado School of Mines - 1992; [occ.] Technical Services Engineer, Bakers Hugh Inteq.; [memb.] Sigma Phi Epsilon Fraternity; [hon.] CSM award for Math and Science, Clifford B. Scott award, Engineering Days Scholarship; [oth. writ.] "The Design" published 1989 in Colorado Springs local newsletter, "Rugville" comic strip published in golden paper —Golden Transcript 1989-1990; [pers.] Emotional response is everything. If I can pull emotions out with my art and writing, I have succeeded. [a.] Houston, TX.

McMULLIN, JOAN
[pen.] Cindy Corbett; [b.] October 7, 1976, Philadelphia, PA; [p.] Eileen and Joseph McMullin; [ed.] Little Flower Catholic High School for Girls; [memb.] Students Against Drunk Driving (SADD); [oth. writ.] Same poem published in Philadelphia Daily News and Literary Garland (annual publication in Little Flower); [pers.] I live by my motto "The past is only worth remembering in the present for the future." [a.] Philadelphia, PA.

McNABB, HOPE
[b.] March 26. 1936, Renown, Saskatchewan; [p.] F.G. and Annie Patrick; [m.] Gordon Francis, November 24, 1953; [ch.] Cynthia Ann, Rocky Gordon and Todd Dolton (grandchildren-Lasha, David, Amberlee, Brittany and Hunter); [ed.] South Stony School, St. Ann's Convent; [occ.] Small Business owner/operator; [hon.] "Dance on the Horizon" is indeed an honour!; [oth. writ.] Self-published anthology in 1992; currently working on second collection of poetry and short stories to be published late 1993; poem published in Mid-Island Co-Operative newsletter Dec. 92; [pers.] I'm inspired by the caring my great family circle. I have the need to share my abundance of love for them through my writing. [a.] Nanaimo, BC.

McNAMEE, ERIN
[b.] September 14, 1977, Anacenda, MT; [p.] Phil and Margaret Reiss; [occ.] Student; [memb.] Speech and Debate Journalism; [pers.] I try to capture raw emotion and pure thought in my work in an attempt to show the true human experience. [a.] Anaconda, MT.

McNULTY, GENEVIEVE S.
[b.] May 16, 1915, Mt. Clemens, MI; [p.] Walter and Sybil Sharrow; [m.] Walter N. (deceased), 1939; [ed.] G.M. Technical Institute; [occ.] Retired; [memb.] Flint Institute of Music, Mothers Against Drunk Driving; [oth. writ.] Several limericks - a poem for Orkin Pest Control - several as a hobby, when I was a child; [pers.] I was an avid gardener until my lung collapsed. Now I garden much less using a linoleum knife, instead of a hoe. I also paint. Never give up. [a.] Flint, MI.

McORMOND, LAURIE
[b.] June 18, 1976, Milford; [p.] Lydia and James McOrmond.

McRAE, ROBERT
[pen.] Dan Templeton; [b.] April 26, 1929, Herington, KS; [p.] David and Mary B. McRae; [ed.] Herington High School, USN Submarine School; [occ.] Retired; [oth. writ.] The Magic Window, Dear Norma; [pers.] Living in Miami since 1950, meeting poets and writers at Gilbert Maxwell's Poetry class. I became interested in writing Tennessee Williams quote "make voyages, attempt them, there's nothing else". A year in Kansas, four season and return to Miami. [a.] Ramona, KS.

McREE, GEORGIA E.
[pen.] Georgia E. McRee; [b.] May 27, 1913, Clinton, OK; [p.] R.C. and Daisy May Dougherty; [m.] Monty M. (deceased), October 4, 1930; [ch.] Richard C. McRee and Kay Charlotte McCasland; [ed.] High school, The University of Life; [occ.] Retired from work; [memb.] Good Samaritan Reformed Church, AARP, TBN, formerly Sweet Adelines International, Gahanna Community Theatre; [hon.] None, many loving friends; [oth. writ.] Several published poems - 45 years ago - magazines and Red Earth of OK; [pers.] The beauty of God's grace and gratitude for living. [a.] Gahanna, OH.

McREYNOLDS, REV. HENRIETTA
[b.] August 20, 1941, K.C., KS; [p.] Henrietta Thomas and Harry McReynolds; [ch.] Barney James Betts; [ed.] Sumner High School; [occ.] Associate Pastor Allen Chapel AME Church; [memb.] Kaw Valley Art Association, Nelson Atkins Museum, AME Ministerial Alliance; [oth. writ.] Written several poems through the years one was published years ago; [pers.] I find tranquility in putting words down on paper of what I feel in my heart. [a.] Kansas City, KS.

MAAHS, SELISA D.R.
[pen.] Rebecca Brakenmore; [b.] July 3, 1970, HI; [p.] Ken and Grace Maahs; [m.] James Joseph Raef II, April 28, 1991; [ch.] Charles Edward Raef II; [ed.] High school graduate; [occ.] Homemaker and writer; [hon.] Silver poetry award. [a.] Los Angeles, CA.

MABRY, ROBERT
[b.] September 6, 1969, Canton, MS; [p.] John and Margaret Mabry; [m.] Divorced; [ch.] William Johnathan, Ryan Nicholas; [ed.] Gautier Junior College; [occ.] None disabled from car accident - head injury; [memb.] Mississippi Head Injury Association, Gautier First Methodist Church; [oth. writ.] Many personal poems and songs, I play drums; [pers.] God is real people, he's the only reason I'm still alive. Think first before you do something dangerous. Due to car accident (May '93) I am a head injury survivor and still receiving therapy. [a.] Gautier, MS.

MACK, MAUREEN
[b.] January 1, 1956, Radville, SASK; [p.] Palmer and Betty Lund; [m.] Duane Mack, August 2, 1975; [ch.] Ashley Laura, Melissa Brandy and Chad Michael; [ed.] Gladmar Regional High School; [occ.] Homemaker; [oth. writ.] Poem published in local newspaper "Strathmore Standard'; [pers.] My poems are written about themselves or others and the world around them. [a.] Strathmore, Alberta.

MADDOX, TINA ARIEL
[b.] September 22, 1972, Barksdale AFB, CA; [p.] Mr. and Mrs. Robert L. Maddox; [ed.] C.E. Byrd Math/ Science Magnet BPCC College; [occ.] Second Assistant Manager, Fabric Outlet; [memb.] Data Processing Management Association, Tri-M; [hon.] Who's Who in Music, Who's Who Among High School Student, United States Achievement Award; [pers.] An order for love to work someone must bring the glue. [a.] Shreveport, LA.

MAGRINI, KATHLEEN DECKER
[b.] February 28, 1954, Brooklyn, NY; [p.] Roy and Joan Decker; [m.] John, August 18, 1979; [ch.] Danielle, John, Kristine and Paul; [ed.] West Islip High School, Associates degree Farmingdale, NY; [occ.] Housewife, homemaker and mother; [memb.] Local community organizations; [oth. writ.] Personal poems and writings; [pers.] To express my deep feelings on things that concern me. And to grow in my writing and my writing to grow in me. [a.] Amityville, NY.

MAHMOOD, FAHMIDA
[b.] February 11, 1961, Karachi; [p.] Ghau-Sal (father) and Monowarig (mother) Hussain; [m.] Iqbal, June 20, 1982; [ch.] Permeeta Mahmood (daughter); [ed.] Early Childhood Education Certificate; [occ.] Student; [oth. writ.] My other poems are "Recession", "The Funny Crystal World, Life", "The Beauty Rose", The Truest Golden Company", "The Gift", etc.; [pers.] Poetry is something precious with which one can enrapture his or her heart like a glittering pearl. [a.] Fullerton, CA.

MAHNKEN, JOANNE D.
[pen.] Joanne Mahnken; [b.] July 11, 1927, New Jersey; [p.] Ruth and Frank Davis; [m.] Walter, April 3, 1948; [ch.] Robert Frederick, William John, Catherine Ann, Karen Ruth; [ed.] Hillside High School, Adult Education classes in Accounting; [occ.] Retired secretary from Phillips Petroleum Company; [memb.] Lutheran Church of the Holy Spirit, William H. Jackson Camera Club; [oth. writ.] Book in progress about Hospice; [pers.] As a volunteer for a Hospice in Denver, I have been inspired to write about the wonderful service they provide for the terminally ill. [a.] Littleton, CO.

MAIN, ROBERT E.
[b.] June 9, 1970, West Germany; [p.] Denis and Ethna Main; [m.] Suzanne, August 1, 1993; [oth. writ.] Many other writings such as, Hard Love, A Young Girl's Puppy and Love in the Mist (unpublished); [pers.] My love for poetry was greatly influenced by the love of my wife. She helped me to write from the heart, not just with my hand. [a.] Warrington, Cheshire, England.

MAJOR, HARRY
[b.] June 28, 1930, Trinidad; [p.] Maria Teresa, August 3, 1961; [ch.] Atheline, Maria, Iraci Alison; [ed.] London, Hons Edinburgh, Madrid; [occ.] Ambassador of Trinidad and Tobago, retired; [memb.] Edinburgh's Graduates Association, Scotland; [hon.] Brazilian Award of 'OCruzeiro do Sul' 1984 India's Award 1988; [oth.

writ.] Doctoral thesis: The theme of charity in the work of Don Benito Perez Galdos. Novels: Love's Altar, 1990; A Perfect Love, 1992; Richer America 1993, several collections of poetry unpublished; [pers.] The concern for human welfare and the awareness of spiritual need have moved me to create dramatic personages striving for social excellence and universal values. [a.] Denver, CO.

MAKINSTER, EUGENIE B.
[pen.] Genie; [b.] November 30, IL; [p.] Deceased; [m.] Ivan D., 1946; [ch.] Esther Beth, Barbara Gene, Christopher Glen; [ed.] High School, U. Chicago Werteen Teacher's - Art Institute, American Conservatory of Music (Chicago); [occ.] Free lance writer, report and publisher; [memb.] St. Jude's Ranch, Navy League and Boliteral Club; [hon.] Two plaques - Chairman Public Affairs, Navy League Convention, taught school 4 years private and gifted school; [oth. writ.] Poem Christmas Moving, Manuscript "Magic of Terror" paperbacks, had "Dine Out" column. Have 2001 Achieves Column, By-lines in local papers, wrote Ravenslocj novel; [pers.] Write about achievements and happy life - "Happiness is Urethra". [a.] Las Vegas, NV.

MAKRIS, BETTY LOU
[b.] November 4, 1938, Virginia; [p.] Samuel and Emma Lou Hedrick; [ch.] Chris and Kevin and daughter Kelly; [ed.] High school and some technical schooling; [occ.] Factory worker; [memb.] Piney Flats Baptist Church; [oth. writ.] Poetry published in newspaper magazine; [pers.] I write poetry as a hobby and as a way of expressing myself. In this particular poem, I wanted to convey the message of why the Christmas celebrations. I hope it brings joy to those who read it. [a.] Piney Falls, TN.

MALHOTRA, ASHOK K.
[b.] April 1, 1940, India; [p.] Vidya (mother) and Nihal (father) Malhotra; [m.] Nina J. (deceased), October 24, 1966; [ch.] Raj K. and Ravi K. (sons); [ed.] University of Rajasthan and University of Hawaii; [occ.] Professor of Philosophy; [memb.][American Philosophical Association, Society for Asian and Comparative Philosophy, Phenomenology and Existential Philosophy, Asian Studies Society, Jean-Paul Sartre Society, Comparative Study of Civilizations; [hon.] Gold medal for getting the highest GPA for MA Exam. East West Center Scholarship to do PhD Excellence in Teaching award, consultant; [oth. writ.] Books: Jean-Paul Sartre's Existentialism, Pathways to Philosophy, Transcreation of the Bhagavad Gita, more than 30 published papers and book reviews; [pers.] The goal of my life is to give people compassion and understanding in my daily encounters. I want to make a positive difference in the lives of people of all ages. When I leave this world, I want to leave in better shape than when I arrived. [a.] Oneonta, NY.

MALITZ, MARY ANN
[b.] December 7, 1946, CA; [p.] Mark and Emily Vecellio; [m.] Ronald Lewis, March 21, 1981; [ch.] Erin S. Malitz; [ed.] La Reine High School, U of MD, PG Community College; [occ.] Office Secretary; [memb.] Hospice Volunteer; [hon.] Awards in Dramatic Arts, Dean's List-PG Community College; [oth. writ.] Many, but none published; [pers.] Following the death of my brother, Mark, in the 1976. I began writing poetry to promote my healing. I love philosophical as well as romantic poetry, and especially fond of Shakespeare. [a.] Davidsonville, MD.

MALO, JAMES
[pen.] Stirringhand-Sittingstone; [b.] April 15, 1938; [m.] Linda (nee Mullen), December 15, 1972; [ch.] Sarahlin Elizabeth, Rachel Anne, Ezra James; [ed.] Lakehead College of Arts, Science and Technology (Lakehead University), University of Manitoba; [occ.] Retired teacher; [oth. writ.] Write poems, letters, and composes songs, my dear wife and I are partners in this; [pers.] It is the intent of my dear wife and I to be a voice in society, and to have an impact on people's lives.

MALINE, BETSY A.
[pen.] Mitzi Malone; [b.] February 4, 1963, Louisa, KY; [p.] Evelyn Banfield; [ed.] Jefferson Community College; [occ.] Full-time student, Part-time automation clerk; [memb.] Dean's list; [hon.] Top Sales Real Estate, Top Listing, Program II Silver Poet award, World of Poetry, Golden Poet award, Award of Merit, Army commendation, Good Conduct Southwest Asia Medal; [pers.] My creed. As you walk in fear of falling, you begin to stumble along. To hesitate while in fear, you know not where you stand. Thus, creating doubt in your heart and hand. Once the path is clear, standing tall and proud you triumphantly express to the world aloud. [a.] Louisville, KY.

MALONE, PHYLLIS C.
[b.] November 23, 1923, Canada; [p.] Evelyn Reilly and John Wright; [m.] Joseph (deceased), April 7, 1951; [ch.] One girl and three sons; [ed.] University Entrance Business College; [occ.] Retired school secretary; [oth. writ.] Articles, children's stories; [pers.] I believe that as one grows older, one should also have grown wiser. That we should never stop growing, intellectually, physically, and spiritually. As to physically we should make do with what is left as best we can. [a.] Victoria, BC, CAN.

MALTNY, WILLA DEE
[pen.] Dee Maltny; [b.] March 14, 1935, Kansas City, MO; [p.] Hollis A. and Arthur G. Loeffler; [m.] Robert E., Jr., May 17, 1955; [ch.] Robert III, Joyce, Mike, Holly and Tom; [ed.] Grad. high school, one year nurses training; [occ.] VP/Treas. of family business, author and homemaker; [memb.] Society of Children's Book Writers and Illustrators; [oth. writ.] A poem -"Spiderplant Mind" published 1992 Chapbook at Bowling Green University for a Woman's conference. Several freelance articles for the Bowling Green Sentinel Tribune about gifted education and learning disabilities; [pers.] In a world with so many problems and very few answers, poetry helps me to at least discover the real questions we need to ask. [a.] Wayne, OH.

MAMAKUNIAN, PERCY
[b.] August 18, 1980; [p.] Mr. and Mrs. Gregg Mamakunian; [ch.] One of 17 children, ten sisters and seven brothers; [ed.] 8th grade entering high school Sept. 1994; [occ.] 8th grade student; [hon.] Semi-finalist 1993 North American Open Poetry Contest; [oth. writ.] Several poems that are not published yet; [pers.] Life is a like canvas that poetry reflects its lives and beauty. [a.] Beverly Hills, CA.

MAMBY, STAR
[b.] December 21, 1959, Dalton, GA; [p.] Richard and Mary C. Stanley; [m.] James, March 13, 1981; [ed.] 8th grade; [oth. writ.] Star Mamby.

MANCUSO, FRANCES
[b.] January 13, 1947, Bronx, NY; [p.] Russ and Lillian Bruno; [m.] Mario A., October 30, 1974; [ch.] Nicholas;

[ed.] Sachem High School, Suffolk County Community College; [occ.] Office manager for display manufacturer; [memb.] Poetry Connection of Shirley, American Poetry Society; [oth. writ.] "Selection of Short Poems" a self-published booklet; [pers.] Open you mind to knowledge - Read . Open your eyes to nature's beauty - open your heart to life's little surprises - love. [a.] Shirley, NY.

MANGAN, STEPHEN
[b.] December 17, 1969, Darlington, England; [p.] Arthur Mangan and Margaret Goulding; [occ.] Disinterested civil servant; [oth. writ.] As yet unpublished short stories; [pers.] The representation of an imperfect environment as perfect is my aim when expressing thought, emotion, and experience through words and poetry. Of course, the greatest poet is still to be born, but Yeats and Blake are close seconds. [a.] Darlington, UK.

MANLEY, DOROTHY
[b.] Iowa; [p.] Josie and Vern Sheppard; [m.] Lorimer (deceased); [ch.] James and Dolores; [ed.] Ankeary IA High School, Des Moines University of Commerce; [occ.] REtired; [memb.] United Methodist Church, Forest Green Women's Club, CA and OR Federation of Woman's Club, General Federation of Woman's Club, Book Study and Poetry Club, Forest Grove Service Center, and Sweet Adelaide Singing Group; [hon.] Many awards through General Federation, CA & OR Federation of Woman's Club in writing, publicity, and drama. Publications in over 18 newspapers and magazines; [oth. writ.] Newspaper articles, short plays, Haiku Inspirational, essay, short stories, Light Verse, love articles, club news and CA newspapers; [pers.] I have always mixed and matched words. Upon retirement I vowed not to "Wilt on the Vine" and I have not! My writings reflect my positive approach to life and my love of God and nature. [a.] Forest Grove, OR.

MANN, GINA
[b.] June 30, 1958, Auckland, New Zealand; [ed.] Lynfield College; [oth. writ.] Several poems for "The Parish Pump" currently writing my own songs both music and lyrics. Previously wrote lyrics for a Sydney Board; [pers.] Being is the question - becoming is the answer. Anything is possible through Jesus. Believe it. [a.] Helensvale, Queensland, Australia.

MANNING, ANDREW STEPHEN
[b.] January 8, 1964, Billerrcay, Essex, CAN; [p.] Leonard and Maureen Manning; [ed.] Barstable Comprehensive & Sixth Form College; [occ.] Postal worker; [memb.] British Labour Part & Cooperative, Local Catholic Church, Labour Campaign for Electoral Reform, National Trust Supporter of Europe of the Regions; [hon.] O Levels and CSE's from English school; [oth. writ.] Writings for local newspapers, written for British Labour Party magazine, written local Suffolk history book (Dunwich) trying to get publisher; [pers.] Dedicated to all romantics who have not the nerve to ask their would be loved ones out. [a.] Basildon, Essex, CAN.

MANNINO, MICHAEL
[pen.] Mick; [b.] June 29, 1928, Westfield; [ed.] 8th grade; [occ.] Pet; [memb.] AARP, Westfield Community Center, 117th Cav Association, retired US Armed Forces; [oth. writ.] A New Day, Loving Thoughts an Silent Tears, Silent Thoughts, Time is But A Moment, I Give Thanks, A Pray of Thanksgiveness; [pers.] I hope this would be of little comfort to those who are hurting.

I know for I've found my inspiration in writing of these poems another way of God allowing me to find comfort in my writings. [a.] Westfield, NJ.

MANRAKHAN, JAGADISH
[b.] December 19, 1937, Mauritius; [p.] Ramden and Lilowee Manrakhan; [m.] Puspawatee, September 26, 1967; [ch.] Shalini Neema, Sanjeev Vinod, Vishal Kiran; [ed.] Royal College, University of Reading (England); [occ.] Professor of Agriculture and Vice-Chancellor University of Mauritius; [memb.] Society of Agricultural Professionals; [hon.] Laureate 1961; [oth. writ.] The Mauritian School for Scientific Agriculture, Campus chorus (1-4), Mystique Mathematical and various poems published locally; [pers.] I try to bridge the widening gap between the "Two Cultures". [a.] Rosehill, Mauritius.

MANSOOR, SULEMAN
[pen.] Solly; [b.] May 4, 1973, Johannesburg; [p.] Miriam and A.K. Mansoor; [m.] To Be-Genevieve (Genna) I Love You; [ed.] From Queens Park Primary all through to Christian Brothers College and currently at The Technikon Witwatersrand; [occ.] Student part-time Experiential Job Opportunities; [hon.] Honors Blazer (Principals List), Matric, Top of course in Technikon; [oth. writ.] Opens Spaces: My Private Collection (a collection of previous poems I have written); [pers.] I try to show the pain and suffering experienced along with the joys and emotions of life in my work. Peace and goodwill to one and all now and forever. [a.] Bloemfontein, S.A.

MANTOR, ROD
[b.] Oregon; [p.] Roger and Dorothy; [m.] Garnet Kalscued; [ch.] Jack, Richard, Theresa, Brian and Jared; [ed.] Philosophy major Santa Barbara, CA; [oth. writ.] 40 poems, working on two volumes Youth Sports and Life's Experience, Sports writer and photographer for local paper (Lehi Free Press); [pers.] Although I believe in many things and the possibility of all things. When it comes to the questions of life. I have no idea. [a.] Lehi, UT.

MANUEL, DOROTHY
[b.] December 28, 1921, Toronto, CAN; [p.] Davie and S.E. Peat; [m.] Norman (deceased), May 22, 1943; [ch.] David, Paul, Ronald and Brian; [ed.] England (Grade 12); [occ.] Homemaker; [memb.] "Silver Threads" Senior Club; [oth. writ.] A few poems: "Ye Olde Elm" published in Toronto (local paper); [pers.] I served with the Eng., Forces, A.T.S. for 2 1/2 years in England was a warbride, married a Canadian and came to Canada in 1944. I seem to write poetry mostly when I am sad, I cried when I wrote "Ye Olde Elm". [a.] Victoria B.C. CAN.

MANUEL, LISA
[b.] June 13, 1977, Boston; [p.] Overton and Patricia Manuel; [pers.] Through my writing I express the deeply emotional side we all possess. I like to fall into a fantasy world of love. If only the real world could be as fulfilling as a poem. [a.] Brockton, MA.

MARACLE, MELISSA MICHELLE
[pen.] Karonhianonhaha - She Minds The Sky; [b.] September 29, 1977, Napanee, Ont.; [p.] Dennys R. and Ruby D. Maracle; [ed.] Moira Secondary School; [pers.] Melissa is a North American Indian and lives on the Tyendinaga Reserve Deseronto Ontario. The reason why I had written this special poem was by the inspiration of my father and his death.
MARAPAO, HERMINIA

[pen.] H.P.M.; [p.] Lino Palomo and Mercedes Sison; [m.] Alfonso A.; [ch.] Jocelyn, Reuel, Junnie; [ed.] Silliman University, certificate in TESL, RELC, Singapore; [hon.] Outstanding award in Education, graduated with honors, elementary and high school; [pers.] In writing of poetry is an urge that seeks expression for fulfillment. [a.] Stockton, CA.

MARESCA, ARLENE LaROCCA
[b.] August 19, 1950, Brooklyn, NY; [p.] Daniel and Lillian LaRocca; [m.] Gerard, December 11, 1976; [ed.] Our Lady of Perpetual Help H.S., Kingsborough Community College; [occ.] Secretary, Social Security Administration; [memb.] The National Italian American Foundation, Arba Sicula (a Sicilian Literary Society); [oth. writ.] Book, "Bread Upon The Water" in publication; [pers.] Much of what I write about is the result of my happy experience of growing up in Brooklyn, NY in the 1950s in close proximity to my Sicilian grandparents. [a.] Ellicott City, MD.

MARCHETTI, DIANA
[b.] February , 1979, San Mateo, CA; [p.] Joseph and Frances Marchetti; [ed.] Our Lady of Angels Elementary, Notre Dame High School; [occ.] Student; [memb.] Sierra Club, St. Vincent de Paul Society, Our Lady of Angels Teen Club; [hon.] '93 Presidential Academic Fitness Award, School Highest Academic Award '93, School Service Award '93, '93 Grand Prize winner of the Sierra Club Vocational Poster Contest; [oth. writ.] Various poems which have been published in three books, also have written the following four children's books in the last three years: Willie Wiggly, My Little Blue Bike, From Rags to Riches and Christmas in the Mountains; [pers.] It matters not how lone we live, but how. [a.] Burlingame, CA.

MARETENS, DONNA C.
[pen.] Donna C. Martens; [b.] September 17, 1968, WA; [p.] Ralph and Laura Evalt; [m.] Douglas, January 18, 1988; [ch.] Jacob Alan, Monica Lynn, and Rebekah Ann; [ed.] Bremerton High School, Kitsap Peninsula Vocational Skills Center, Institute of Children's Literature; [occ.] Mother, homemaker; [pers.] I have been writing poems and stories for family members and friends about six years now. I thoroughly enjoy it and it makes it easier to express my feelings to someone who I care about. [a.] Bremerton, WA.

MARGAITIS, HEATHER
[pen.] Heather Margaitis; [b.] March 22, 1973, Tarrinyton; [p.] Joe and Jean Margaritis; [ed.] Wamoge Regional High School, Mattatuck Community College, Western CT State University; [occ.] Shift manager Bristol Pizza Hut; [oth. writ.] Short story "School Bus" published in the Torrington Voice. [a.] Lakeside, CT.

MARIN, YOLANDA
[b.] December 2, 1913, Bronx, NY; [p.] Sylvester and Theresa Frattalone; [m.] Anthony, April 21, 1948; [ch.] Roger Anthony Marin; [ed.] Public and private schools-Evander Childs High School; [occ.] Retired teacher of English and Foreign Languages; [memb.] American Association of Retired Persons, Roman Catholic Church, Zoological Society of San Diego, National Geographic Society, American Numismatic Association; [hon.] Various-interviewed on TV and documentary taped at home for TV 1968, honor of having taught many notable personalities; [oth. writ.] Written my autobiography all in rhymed verse. Started in Sept. 1992 and have written circa 200 poems or more on topics ranging from A to Z.

Poems in newspaper and catalog; [pers.] I draw the bow and let my arrows fly; if but one solitary heart captures a spark of that fire which in me forever burns - I know I shall have hit the mark. Enjoy all of world's greatest romantic poets. [a.] Vista, CA.

MARLER, MARGUERITE
[b.] June 11, 1918, Washoe, MT; [p.] Deceased; [m.] Divorced; [ch.] Merlon and Jacqueline; [ed.] High school plus 90 units from city college; [occ.] Wallpaper Hanger; [memb.] Non published writers "The Writer's Block"; [oth. writ.] Just starting; [pers.] Thank you. [a.] Long Beach, CA.

MARNON, MARILYN
[b.] May 31, 1932, Lacrosse, WI; [p.] Paul and Gertrude Halloran; [m.] Edward, June 8, 1953; [ch.] Kevin, Paul, Edward, Matthew, Mark, Sean; [ed.] College of St. Teresa; [occ.] Writer and illustrator of children's books; [oth. writ.] The Ditty Books (Library of Congress); [pers.] I have told stories to many children over the years and now have preserved them in print as small poems, stories in verse and songlets. [a.] Memphis, MI.

MARSHALL, BRUCE A.
[pen.] Max P. Swartz; [b.] January 3, 1946, Norfolk, NE; [p.] Jack and Eloise Marshall; [m.] Susan Harris, 1979; [ch.] Ainslee Kathleen; [ed.] Wilson High School, Washington State University, The Kerovac School of the Open Road; [occ.] Paint sales and consulting; [memb.] Christ Episcopal Church, Spirit Fish Zen Center; [oth. writ.] Poems, essays at Washington State. Poems in local magazines, poetry readings, children's books accepted for publication, school district readings; [pers.] I have been seeking the modern myths and the words to communicate them through the study of Mythology and comparative religion. [a.] Tacoma, WA.

MARSHALL, YVONNE P.
[hon.] Cosmetology Teachers License, FCC (Broadcasting) License.

MARTEL, RICARDO
[pen.] Ricardo Martel; [b.] January 9, 1916, Mpls, MN; [ed.] Univ. of Minnesota, Georgetown University; [hon.] BSA—Eagle w/ Bronze Palm; [oth. writ.] Two vols. poetry, A trilogy. [a.] White Plains, NY.

MARTENS, MONIQUE
[pen.] Monique; [b.] November 19, 1965, Winnipeg, MB; [p.] Robert and Evelyn Cote'; [m.] Keith, September 12, 1992; [ed.] Darwin Elementary School, Dakota Collegiate Institute; [pers.] I have been writing since 1979. All my poems and lyrics come from my soul; and from the pain, joy, and heartbreak in my life. Life is nothing if you can not be passionate about it. [a.] Winnipeg, MB, CAN.

MARTIN, ELLIOTT
[b.] July 9, 1968, New York, NY; [ed.] Columbia University; [oth. writ.] Recently completed a major cyclical work of novels and epic poetry, as well as a collection of short stories; about to search for a publisher. [a.] Hyannis, MA.

MARTIN, KRISTI
[b.] December 15, 1979. Utah; [p.] Susan and Rick Martin; [ed.] David Gourly Elementary, Bennion Junior High and Joel P. Jensen Middle School (now 8th grade); [occ.] Student; [memb.] The County Library; [hon.] Healy's Hero award, won third place Reflection contest,

Citizen of the Month; [oth. writ.] Poems and stories in spare time; [pers.] I enjoy writing I love to express my feelings on paper. Whenever I'm alone the first thing I do is reach for a pencil and paper. The poem I create will be done within 10 minutes. [a.] West Jordan, UT.

MARTIN, LAURA BELLE
[b.] November 3, 1915, Jackson Co, MN; [p.] Eugene W. and Mary Martin; [p.] Renville High School, Renville Teachers Training 1935, Mankato State University; [occ.] Retired Elementary Teacher; [memb.] Historic Renville Preservation Commission, American Legion Auxiliary, Warrensbury Writer's Circle; [hon.] Listed in Who's Who of America, Who's Who of the World, Who's Who of International Intellectuals, 2000 Notable American Women Hall of Fame, Five Thousand Personalities of the World Hall of Fame; [oth. writ.] Research articles for Hispanic Renville Preservation Commission and news articles for Renville Town and Country; [pers.] To succeed in whatever we desire to do in life we must be good managers. How we use our time, how well we apply ourselves on the job and how we spend our money will determine the level of success. [a.] Holden, MO.

MARTIN, MELINDA
[b.] May 5, 1960, SC; [p.] Willie and Almenia K. Henderson; [m.] Eddie R. III, May 4, 1990; [ch.] Medina Diane Martin; [ed.] McCrorey-Liston High School, Paralegal diploma ICS, SC Law Enforcement '88; [occ.] Dep. Sheriff-Fairfield Cty.; [oth. writ.] "De Je' Vu", "You"; [pers.] All things if worth having will someday be yours. But these things will take patience, but they're mostly take time. [a.] Winnsboro, SC.

MARTIN, MICHAEL A.
[b.] February 29, 1940, Akron, OH; [p.] Beatrice M. Gorcoff and Albert L. Martin; [ed.] North High/College Prep courses/two educational awards in US Air Force/SAC & USAFE; [occ.] Security Officer; [memb.] Masonic Blue Lodge, 32nd degree Scottish Rite and Shriner, NV. Post #8, American Legion; [hon.] Assigned Presidential security; [oth. writ.] Poem accepted by You People. Author of "Atlantis Secrets Revealed" published by Gorman Graphics; [pers.] Strive for Perfection in all I do; especially to make "Atlantis Secrets Revealed" the most successful of all books. [a.] Las Vegas, NV.

MARTIN, REITA
[b.] October 25, 1917, Canada; [p.] Myron Lambert and Alice Price; [m.] James, 1944 (widowed 1985); [ch.] One daughter, 9 grandchildren, 19 G.G., and 4 G.G.G.; [ed.] 32 school in 8 states, Beauty College 1937; [occ.] Retired; [memb.] G.E. Flex Women's Club, Sand Arts Association, Sand Hills State Park; [hon.] Third place Oil painting many handcraft items.

MARTIN, TOMMIE
[b.] February 16, 1949, Wimauma, FL; [p.] Ray Martin and Myrtle Freeman; [m.] Rose Maria, November 17, 1973; [ch.] John Aaron, Malea Sue; [ed.] Gainesville High School, Chamberlain High; [occ.] Disabled; [oth. writ.] Numerous poems in local newspaper (weekly) several unpublished songs; [pers.] I write from the heart, the good as well as the bad, about America and it's people. I'm motivated to write by personal experiences, and all aspects of life. [a.] Tampa, FL.

MARTZ, FRANCES L.
[pen.] Fran Martz; [b.] March 19, 1916, Adams Co.,; [p.] Mr. and Mrs. John C. Shulley; [m.] Guy W., January 1, 1938 (deceased); [ch.] Reverend George C.

Martz; [ed.] Shippensburg College; [memb.] Past Worthy High Priestess, White Shrine Local Poetry Guild, St. Stephens United Church of Christ, PP York Commanderey Auxiliary, Starlight #508 Order of Eastern Star; [hon.] Three poems published in church newsletters; [oth. writ.] Short children's stories, inspirational poems for all occasions; [pers.] Most of my poetry is based on my faith in my savior and a way of spreading the gospel to others. [a.] York, PA.

MARTZ, JENNIFER
[pen.] J.L. Martz; [b.] September 23, 1973; [p.] David and Gail Martz; [ed.] Pottstown High School, West Chester State University; [occ.] Teacher's Aide for Preschool; [memb.] Honors Society, Tau Beta Sigma; [hon.] Who's Who Music Honors, Honors Society; [oth. writ.] Over 120, published in newspapers and in school anthology. I have seen several published by editors; [pers.] I believe that we must love for today on the event of a brighter tomorrow. My poetry reveals the inner strength that I, otherwise, could not proclaim. [a.] Phoenixville, PA.

MARVYAMA, JAY ROBERT
[b.] May 3, 1960, Tokyo, Japan; [p.] Dr. Donald K. and Harriet H. Marvyama; [ed.] College sophomore drop out; [occ.] Federal Prison Clothing room worker; [oth. writ.] "Blue Verse and Terminal Cool" poems and short fiction. [a.] Honolulu, HI.

MASCITTI, MICHAEL
[b.] October 3, 1968, New York, NY; [p.] Patricia and Bari Mascitti; [ed.] Long Island City High School, Hunter College; [occ.] Student/deposit clerk; [oth. writ.] Lot of unpublished poems; [pers.] All one must do to become a god is to conquer the chaos in their lives. Race, religion and nationality are meaningless, all should be based on intelligence. Thanks: Michael Moorcock, E. LiMandri, Romulans, Pain, Fear, and Misery. [a.] Sunnyside, NY.

MASON, LUCY
[b.] Buena Vista, VA.

MASON, JAMES
[b.] July 10, 1936, Toronto, ON; [p.] Anne and George Mason; [m.] Myrtle, June 2, 1962; [occ.] Slurry truck driver at Highland Valley Copper Mine; [pers.] This poem came to mind when I wan on watch keeping duty on a Canadian ship during my 21 1/2 years in the Royal Canadian Navy. [a.] Ashcroft, BC

MASON, ROXANNA
[b.] April 14, 1959, Auburn, CA; [pers.] I aspire to reflect human nature in my writings as a greater than plutonium precious and rare yet highly toxic depending on how its handled. [a.] Applegate, CA.

MASSON, AMARA
[b.] December 30, 1976, Abbotsford, BC; [p.] Jim and Carol Masson; [ed.] Grade 11, Rick Hanzen Secondary; [hon.] Honor roll student, 2nd prize in BC Forestry Ind., essay contest on the environment; [pers.] Life should be full of hope love and happiness, and I reflect this into my writing. [a.] Matsqui, BC, CAN >

MASTERS (TWEED), BRIAN
[pen.] Brian Masters; [b.] November 10, 1971; [p.] Robert and Barbara Tweed; [occ.] Writer; [memb.] The Thalamic Temple and Order of the Golden Dawn; [oth. writ.] Renaissance - The Power of Mystic, Myth, and

Poetry (Manuscript); [pers.] A growing of a power words of living myriad, for life in passages to sanctify by mystery, our ways to abhor by being reputed. Now shall we seek the Nascency.

MATHEWS, LAURIE ANN
[pen.] Lorelei Nedevich; [b.] March 12, 1962, Santa Monica, CA; [p.] Virginia Weston; [ed.] Hamilton High School and Santa Monica College; [occ.] Child care; [memb.] Poetry club; [hon.] Won first prize in school art fair; [oth. writ.] Planning to publish a children's bookl; [pers.] Many of my poems reflect a spirit of adventure and excitement in American life. I hope to bring these quality out in my readers. [a.] Los Angeles, CA.

MATLOCK, REV. JOHNNIE WAYNE, SR. PHD
[b.] June 23, 1943, Dallas, TX; [p.] E.L. & Marie Matlock, Sr.; [m.] Glenda Faye, September 4, 1962; [ch.] Johnnie Wayne Matlock, Jr., Joe Shane Matlock; [ed.] Dr. of Philosophy in Theology, Southern CA Graduate School of Theology; [occ.] Pastor and President of Central Full Gospel Fellowship; [memb.] Tarrant Masonic Lodge 942; [oth. writ.] Be Fruitful and Multiply, Vantage Press; [pers.] My philosophy for having life at its best is found in MTT 6:33-"But seek ye first the kingdom of God, and his righteousness; and all these things shall be added unto you." KJ version. [a.] Ft. Worth, TX.

MATTINGLY, ANNA M.
[pen.] Ann O'Reilly, Morine; [b.] May 3, Central City, KY; [p.] Elestrail and Lockie King; [m.] James Edward; [ch.] Genene, Tammy, Cathy, Adam; [ed.] Central City High School, Madisonville College; [occ.] Homer Energizer; [hon.] Nine Golden Poet awards, five merit awards and one book award; [oth. writ.] Several poems published in local newspapers, World of Poetry, and other anthologies; [pers.] A mind that is stimulated by the written word, will never grow old. [a.] Madisonville, KY.

MATTSON, LINDSEY ANN
[b.] March 11, 1983, Great Falls, MT; [p.] Gary H. and Merrilyn J. Mattson; [ed.] Lindsey homeschooled and in 5th grade; [occ.] Student; [memb.] Galilee Baptist Church; [pers.] I am ten years old and have developed an interest in writing through the love and encouragement of my friend and neighbor Gertie Holtslag. Writing allows me a way to express my thoughts and feelings. [a.] Loveland, CO.

MAJER, DIANA
[pen.] She Kelsey; [b.] January 9, 1977, Whitecourt; [p.] Linda and Dale Majer; [ch.] Siblings-Shaun, Sheri and Brett; [ed.] High school 11th grade; [oth. writ.] Poetry for myself to express my videos and feelings; [pers.] Let go of the past reach for the future this is the way to life's mystery. [a.] Mayerthorpe, AB, CAN.

MARKES, REIMA A.
[pen.] Reima Markes; [b.] October 17, 1952, Kingston, Jamaica; [p.] Mr. and Mrs. Roy Markes; [ed.] Preparatory High School (St. Hugh's); [occ.] Entertainment Coordinator; [memb.] L.P.T.P. Club; [oth. writ.] Profile-Bob Marley, Colin F (artist) J.A. poem-NY Anthology, 1985; [pers.] Love, God's finest divine commandment, has never failed. And though it has even been used as an excuse to create havoc (crimes of passion). Pure love can certainly glorify God's Plan. For a country to feel so strongly about God, to spell His name on their currency. There must indeed be some love for God. [a.] Kingston, Jamaica.

MAXWELL, KAY ELIZABETH
[b.] March 30, 1973, Aldershot, ENGLAND; [p.] William and Mavis Hubbard; [m.] Jack, May 18, 1993; [ed.] Ash Manor Secondary School, two years training Care Assistant; [occ.] Care Assistant for Elderly; [oth. writ.] Have many other poems never thought of getting them published, my first; [pers.] Most of my poems are written with children in mind. When I write a poem, I show it to my eight year old sister, if she likes it, then I know it's good. [a.] Aldershot, Hampshire, ENG.

MAY, JOHNNY D.
[b.] November 22, 1947, Magee, MS; [p.] Johnny M. May and Mary L. Matthews; [ed.] Magee High School, Kapiolani Community College; [occ.] Office Manager TMA Corp; [pers.] My writings are influenced by the emotions of the moment, whether they deal with romance or the glory of the sun rising out of the ocean. [a.] Honolulu, HI.

MAY, SAMANTHA JANE
[pen.] Sam May; [b.] September 24, 1977, Aberdeen; [p.] Barbara and David May; [ed.] Hatton Primary Peterhead Academy; [occ.] Peterhead Academy; [memb.] School orchestra (plays The Sax) Bawff and Buchan Youth Band, school choir and singing group and local drama group, Vegetarian Society, Elefriends Oxfam; [hon.] Grade Certificate for piano, sax and grade two commended for theatre dance; [oth. writ.] Several poems, as yet unpublished. [a.] Aberdeenshire, Scotland.

MAY, THOMAS T.
[b.] March 26, 1919, Huddy, KY; [p.] Sidney Lee and Pricey Emma (Ball) May; [m.] Bertha Rhodes, July 3, 1938; [ch.] Virginia Lee (Morris), Zella Hope (Spoonamore), John Winston, William Thomas; [ed.] Coal Grove High, Olivet Nazarene College, Kentucky Christian College, Ashury College, Zion Theological Seminary; [occ.] Pastoral Ministry; [memb.] Greater Lexington Minister Fellowship, Evangelical Christian Fellowship, Liberty Road Community Church; [oth. writ.] "People and Poems", newspaper articles:, "Whose Are These?" (short story); [pers.] The best things in life come to those who serve the Lord. [a.] Lexington, KY.

MAYER, JEFF
[b.] March 12, 1973, Canada; [p.] Barb and Wendel Mayer; [ed.] Windsor Secondary School, Capitino College; [occ.] Student/waiter; [memb.] Mt. Olivett Lutheran Church; [hon.] high school honors; [oth. writ.] None published; [pers.] Poetry is a way of being; an acute sense of reality and a gift from God unmatched by those of earth. [a.] North Vancouver, BC.

MAYER-MADER, MIRIAM
[b.] October 29, 1954, Chicago; [m.] Rudolf, October 8, 1987; [ed.] Immaculata High School, Mondelein College; [occ.] American Airlines Agent-International; [pers.] This poem was written in 1971 at age 16. [a.] Chicago, IL.

MAYES, GABRIELLE LOUISE
[pen.] Gabby; [b.] May 25, 1978, Kentucky; [p.] George M. Jr., and Betty J. Mayes; [ed.] Butter Traditional Technical High School, Reed High School, Greenwood Elementary, Foster Elementary, Jacob Elementary, Whitney Young Elementary; [hon.] English Honor (Dr. Helen Barnette) Attendance Award, Math Award, Student of the Month; [oth. writ.] Someone I Admire, A Quiet Place, The Four Seasons of the Year, Love, A Dark Stormy Night, Twas the Day of Homecoming, Autowreck of My Relative, Picasso's Great Picture; [pers.] I strive to increase my self-esteem and getting my feelings out. I talk about my life and everything that is happening in my poems. [a.] Sparks, NV.

MEAD, JENNIFER L.
[pen.] Ivy Rose; [b.] December 9, 1976, North Platte; [p.] Ron and Teresa Mead; [ed.] Paxton Consolidated Schools; [occ.] Student; [memb.] United Methodist Youth Fellowship, United Methodist Youth Corp. and 4-H; [hon.] A' Honor roll.

MEAD, ROB
[pen.] Rob Mead; [b.] May 19, 1960, Bozeman, MT; [p.] Joan Wilson and Bob Mead; [m.] Sandra, June 7, 1986; [ch.] Ben, Alex, and Rachel; [ed.] Belle Fourche High School, Community College of the Air Force, University of Maryland; [occ.] Analyst; [memb.] Phi Kappa Phi, Air TRaffic Central Association; [hon.] Cum Laude BA degree. [a.] Brussels, Belgium.

MEADE, MICHAEL GERARD
[b.] February 21, 1970, London; [p.] Michael and Elizabeth Brennan Meade; [ed.] BA Civil Law diploma in Computer Science; [memb.] Amnesty International; [oth. writ.] Written over 200 poems first to be published; [pers.] How often it comes hot and cold - Irish saying i.e. moods change. [a.] Ballypierce, Charleville, Co. Cork. IRELAND.

MEALING, RONALD W.
[b.] June 18, 1937, Sydney, Australia; [p.] William George (deceased)/Vira Thelma; [m.] Kathleen Anne, Feb. 1966 (divorced 1987); [ch.] John Joseph, Suzanne Louise, Donna Therese, Michelle Linda; [ed.] Christian Brothers High School, Australian Society of Accountants; [occ.] Freelance writer and motto picture (animation) producer; [memb.] Nashville Chamber of Commerce; [hon.] Long Service Award, Royal Regiment of Australian Artillery (Reserve); [oth. writ.] "On Cost & Such Things", 1965 (circa) "Adventures in the Lost Kingdom of Radish", Dec. 1984 publication Australia; [pers.] I believe that children's works should ask of their, intellect and not of their subservience to an adult's interpretation. [a.] Nashville, TN.

MEDDERS, CHARLES ALTON
[pen.] CAM; [b.] November 28, 1949, Madison, FL; [p.] Charles Everette and Nellie Merritt Medders; [ch.] Charles A., Jr., Mandy Lynn and Marsha Kay Medders (twins); [ed.] Madison High School 1967, North Florida Jr. College, graduate U.S. Border Patrol Academy #212; [occ.] Law Enforcement Officer Defense Nuclear Agency/Johnston Atoll; [memb.] Trilby Lodge #141 Free and Accepted Masons Trilby; [hon.] Marksmanship award/basic recruit class, Lake City Comm. College, Marksmanship award U.S. Border Patrol Academy #212.

MEDEIROS, MARLO
[b.] October 10, 1960, Portugal; [p.] Manuel and Maria Medeiros; [ed.] High school; [occ.] Sales; [oth. writ.] Wrote my first poems for The National Library of Poetry and some other personal writing for friend a family; [pers.] I write because writing is a part of me it is a hope I have for my writings and of many others writers to bring some sincerity to this world.

MEDFORD, REGINA MARIE
[pen.] Gina, Regina, Medford; [b.] September 5, 1928, Tarboro; [p.] Reginald and Gladys Medford; [ed.] Tarboro High School; [occ.] Student; [memb.] THS AFJROTC Colorguard; [pers.] I hope to inspire young poets to let there poems be read. Never discouraged if it doesn't come through keep writing. [a.] Tarboro, NC.

MEDINA, MILDRED (AKA PASINKOFF)
[pen.] Mille Passi; [b.] December 4, 1962, NY; [p.] Monserrate and Elena Medina; [m.] David, Aug. 9; [ch.] Erica Pasinkoff; [ed.] Stuyvesant 1984, Cooper Union College, John Jay soon; [occ.] Freelance artist-Portrait Specialty; [memb.] American Veterans Association, Police Athletic League, Children Defects Association; [hon.] Fashion Design Scholarship, award Flemington for company cooperation with Traphagen School of Fashion, Superior Achievement in Medical Illustration, Superior Achievement in Art, Exhibits Fish Library and The American Heritage Museum of Natural History; [pers.] Although I am inspired and admire most earth poets, still I honor the one synonymous with horror, namely, Edgar Allen Poe. Dedicated to my brother Eddie Medina, 5/24/61, who is terminally ill. [a.] New York, NY.

MEITZ, MAXINE A.
[b.] February 20, 1936, Louisville, KY; [p.] Avery and Dorothy Wyatt; [m.] Frank J.; [ch.] Rebecca, Cherly, George, Sondra; [occ.] Office Manager; [memb.] Burnham Pork Yacht Club Past President , Arlington Heights Golf Club President; [pers.] Professional Jazz vocalist 20 years. [a.] Summerland Key, FL.

MELKI, VIVEKA
[pen.] Viveka Melki; [b.] June 2, 1976, The Gambia; [p.] Kamal and Nawal Melki; [ed.] St. Margaret's School, Canada Camosun College; [occ.] Student; [hon.] Citizenship awards - two years running, Deputy head girl; [oth. writ.] Poems published in school magazines/yearbooks, many not yet published; [pers.] It in only because the exceptionally rare occurred that I too was inspired to do the exceptionally rare and believe in myself. [a.] Victoria, BC, CAN.

MELLIE, ROSE
[b.] August 25, 1929, Jersey City; [p.] Paul and Maria Pecoraro; [m.] John, June 23, 1974; [ch.] David Mellie and Chris Ann Sherman; [ed.] Ferris High, State College; [occ.] Property Manager, Manager Christ Hospital; [memb.] Christ Hospital Auxiliary, NJ Hospital Association Council, S.H.A.R.E. Board of Directors, Toastmasters; [hon.] Master Auxilian Award, Toastmasters C.T.M.; [pers.] To live is to love, to love is to serve, to serve is to do God's will. To do God's will is to be happy. [a.] Jersey City, NJ.

MELLO, DONNA LEE
[b.] April 21, 1947; [p.] Clarence and Dolores Fagundes; [ch.] Michael, Frank and Tiffany; [ed.] WEst Hills College-field of education; [occ.] Hanford Adult School; [memb.] International Society of Poets; [hon.] Hills College Algebra Tutor/Certificates; [oth. writ.] A binder full: Ranging From the Roots of My Raising Years, Country, General, Holiday Greetings, A Religious Death, & Forlon Memories; [pers.] Dedicated to my beloved sister-in-law, Madeline Lee Fagundes and her kindergarten daughter, Teona Lee Fagundes and Teona's K-teacher. [a.] Hanford, CA.

MELROSE, IONA
[b.] October 7, 1973, Johannesburg; [p.] Ruth and Alex Melrose; [ed.] Roedean School, Pretoria Girls High School; [occ.] Student University of Witwatersrand; [memb.] Dolphin Action and Protection Group; [pers.] My personal philosophy has been greatly influenced by Simone De Beauvoir and Dr. Martin Luther King. [a.] Johannesburg, SA.

MELSO, LAUREN
[pen.] Lauren Melso; [b.] March 10, 1980, Ridgewood, NJ; [p.] Patricia and Joseph Melso; [ed.] 8th grade Eric S. Smith Middle School; [occ.] Student; [oth. writ.] First submission; [pers.] Have just recently developed a strong interest in poetry, and a desire to write. I like to write about serious matters in my poetry. I love to read poetry on death and also on love. [a.] Ramsey, NJ.

MEMBA, JARED AMWAYI
[b.] June 3, 1972, Bunyore; [p.] Stephen M. and Susie A. Amwayi; [ed.] Menegai High, Undergraduate - Kenyatta University; [occ.] Student; [oth. writ.] Several unpublished poems; [pers.] I see society coming towards me; society armed with an axe: Society splits my head; pours salt into my headwound...! Oh! what a terrible experience that inspires me into writing about society's brutality and ruthlessness!. [a.] Nakuru, Kenya.

MENDEZ, ANGEL
[b.] January 14, 1958, Phoenix, AZ; [p.] Paul A. and Lillian (Lily) Mendez; [m.] Laurie K., February 18, 1985; [ch.] Mario Alex, Paul Adam, Joseph Jullian; [ed.] Miami High, Northern Pioneer College; [occ.] Power Plant Electrician; [memb.] Country Meadows Mens Golf Association; [oth. writ.] Currently writing a biography entitled, "Family" from a young man's heart; [pers.] People wonder why things are the way they are, and lost track that everybody's to blame yet tomorrow is a new day. [a.] Peoria, AZ.

MERCHANT, SANDRA
[b.] July 19, 1945, Washington, NC; [p.] Leonard and Thelma Tinker; [m.] Robert Sr., June 6, 1964; [ch.] Robert Jr., Wesley Merchant; [ed.] John A. Wilkinson High, King's Business College, Carteret Community College; [occ.] Medical Records Technician; [memb.] United Methodist Church, Woodmen of the World; [hon.] Woman of Woodcraft, Civilian of the Quarter; [oth. writ.] Local newspaper published several poems and teen column - Hospital News - paper published several poems and essays; [pers.] Writing soothes the soul and eases the heart. [a.] Newport, NC.

MERGLER, DANIEL
[b.] November 29, 1925, Montreal; [p.] Joseph K. and Rose Mergler; [ed.] McGill University, Julliard School of Music; [occ.] Private piano teacher; [hon.] Piano soloist for the Provincial, National and International Networks of the Canadian Broadcasting Corp., essay on music published in booklet by The Montreal Gazette; [oth. writ.] Freelance writing on musical subjects to local newspapers; [pers.] I believe that the greatest poets and composers strive to convey a message that life, in spite of its barker side, is magnificent and worthy of praise. This optimistic message sustains us in adversity and helps us to live with coverage and determindation. [a.] Montreal, Quebec.

MERLE, JOSE MIGUEL
[b.] January 10, 1928, NYC, NY; [p.] Jenaro and Louise Merle; [m.] Ruth, August 27, 1949; [ch.] Joseph William Merle; [ed.] Brooklyn Automotive NY; [occ.] US Postal Clerk, GPO NYC; [pers.] To be beneficial or pleasing for a moment. [a.] Brooklyn, NY.

MERRICK, TAWNYA JOLENE
[b.] March 20, 1976, OH; [p.] Karl Merrick and Sharon O'Reilly; [ed.] High school; [occ.] Lake Havaso High School student; [memb.] Explorers Club-Lake Havaso Police Department; [oth. writ.] Several poems published in newspaper magazines; [pers.] A poem is an expression of feelings, so read deeper than the words themselves. [a.] Lake Havaso City, AZ.

MERRIWEATHER IV, ARTHUR JAMES
[b.] October 25, 1962, Cleveland, OH; [p.] Theresa and Arthur Merriweather; [m.] Lilli Ann Watson, December 6, 1985; [ch.] Arthur V. and Kiara Monique; [ed.] Collinwood High School, Cuyahoga Community College, various Naval schools; [occ.] Instrument and Controls Technician, former Reactor Operator (US Navy submarine); [hon.] Dean's list, Navy Achievement Medal, various military decorations; [oth. writ.] Numerous other poems and short stories, some distributed among family and friends. Few poems were published in college newspaper; [pers.] Through our poems we share our views of the world and in doing so, parts of ourselves. [a.] Cleveland Hts., OH.

MESERVE, LEOTA
[b.] January 1, 1905, Louisville, KY; [p.] Charles and Viola Ehle; [m.] Edward Askenwall (1st) and Arthur L. Meserve (2nd); [ch.] Viola Belle Aspenwall, Charles Edward, L. Carolyn Lee; [ed.] Ypsilanti Mi Normal School; [occ.] Retired; [memb.] Troy Methodist Church; [oth. writ.] Written several poems when need special emphasis for a meeting or general information, over the years have prepared services for use in church, clubs, camps, etc; [pers.] My husband is now in a nursing home and I am alone after many years of going places and being a part of the action. [a.] Troy, MI.

MESSER, GLENDA BROYHILL
[pen.] Gwenavere; [b.] August 15, 1948, Boone, NC; [p.] Ralph and Marie Broyhill; [m.] Donald H., November 17, 1987; [ch.] Cassandra King; [ed.] Watauga High; [occ.] Self employed; [oth. writ.] Currently working on a novel; [pers.] My interest in poetry began in my teens, but only now have I come full circle. [a.] Travelers Rest., SC.

MEYER, NICOLE
[b.] November 4, 1981, Freeport, IL; [p.] Paul and Linda Meyer; [ed.] 6th grade; [occ.] Student; [oth. writ.] Poems published in "Young Author's Magazine Anthology"; [pers.] I'm only in 6th grade now, and I don't know what I want to do in the future. Maybe I'll be a writer, maybe not. But now I like writing poems and short stories. [a.] Leaf River, IL.

MEYER, RANDY C.
[b.] December 20, 1954, Sturgis, SD; [p.] Russell and Gladys Meyer; [ed.] Mobridge High School, Black Hills State College; [occ.] Lease Analyst, Union Oil Company of California; [oth. writ.] Poetry column in company newsletter titled "A Niche in Rhyme"; [pers.] It is my hope to fully appreciate the gift God has given me by dedicating my writing to inspire others to help make this a better world for all who live here. [a.] Los Angeles, CA.

MEYER, ROYAL E.
[b.] January 9, 1916, Gresham, WI; [p.] W.A. and Lu Meyer; [m.] Iloe D., September 28, 1940; [ch.] Stephen R. Meyer and Jeanne I. Meyer; [ed.] Shawano High School, Whitewater State Teacher's College and Jordan College, Lay Minister-NW Conference United Church of Christ; [occ.] Retired Life Underwriter; [memb.] First Reformed United Church of Christ; [hon.] Man of the Year 1991; [pers.] When you have a clear vision of something that will be or benefit to others, but as an individual, are unable to fulfill this dream and desire - then ask our Creator to help you make it happen. [a.] Manitowoc, WI.

MEYERS, HELEN H.
[b.] November 11, 1942, Westerlo, NY; [p.] John C. LeRoy and Metty M. LeRoy (sister-Virginia C. Vincent); [m.] Howard Keith, October 14, 1972; [ch.] Ginae Nicole Meyers and Keith Charles Meyers; [ed.] Schoharie Central School; [occ.] Cleaning lady Schenectady County Court House; [memb.] Delanson Methodist Church, Delanson Ladies Auxillary; [pers.] In this day of such crimes against our children, poverty, and so much stress; we all have to work harder together and with God - to make this a better world in which to live. [a.] Delanson, NY.

MICHAEL, GREGORY PAUL
[b.] June 3, 1965, Brooklyn, NY; [p.] Walter and Carol Wisolsky; [ed.] Fulton Montgomery College, New York University, Five Towns College; [occ.] Musicianh/lyricist and poet; [memb.] Mary Knoll, BMI, American Heart Association, St. Joseph's Church, Institute for Cognitive Therapy, Agoraphobic & Panic Disorder Foundation; [hon.] Class President Statesmenship Award, Angle Contest winner - Best Song, Five Towns College Winner-Best Poem, Signed Recording Artist; [oth. writ.] You Are Love, Sacred To Me, Here I Am, With You, ect.; [pers.] God's greatest gift to you is life, what you do with it is your greatest gift to God! [a.] Commack, NY.

MICHAELS, DONNA G. DR.
[b.] April 4, 1952, Alexandria, VA; [ed.] BS-University of Southwestern, LA, MSW-University of Nebraska, Ph.D.-Barry University (Miami Beach); [occ.] President-The Micahels Group; [memb.] N.O.W., American Association of University Women (AAUM), League of Women Voters (LWV); [hon.] Omicron Delta Kappa; [oth. writ.] Co-author The Whys of Social Policy, Praeger 1991, contributed chapter on Capital Campaigns in book entitled Long Term Care Administration, Aspen 1993. Numerous other articles in professional publications; [pers.] I strive to achieve impact through the economical use of language. It is my belief that by doing so a writer can provide an opportunity for individual interpretation of meaning, at present I choose to use nature as my subject. [a.] Sedona, AZ.

MICHALIK, STANLEY
[b.] April 22, 1922, Poland; [ed.] 10th grade; [occ.] Retired from Ornamental Horticultrist; [memb.] Canadian Wildlife Federation; [hon.] Best Exotic plants display; [oth. writ.] Amateur in Polish language; [pers.] I am survivor of political prisons and concentration camps of Siberia. Imprisoned by Stalin secret police for noncompliance with communist. I arrived to Canada after war. I consider now Canada and United States are the best countries of the world.

MICK, MATTHEW
[b.] March 17, 1974, Creston, IA; [p.] Steve and Cheryl Mick; [ed.] Bedford High School, University of Northern IA; [occ.] Student; [memb.] Physics Club, Talented and Gifted Program, Medieval Reenactment Society, Interpretative Theatre, Show Choir, Concert Choir, Students of Arts & Drama of Bedford School (SADOBS); [hon.] National Art Award featured in 1992 US Achievement Academy, 2 year letter-chorus, 1 year letter SADBOS, first place Future Problems Solving Drama, District Qualifier-Mock TRial, 3 year letter-football, 3 year letter-track, first place-art competition, #1 rating-mixed couple quartet, many in automotive styling competiton, four year scholarship in Industrial Technology; [pers.] Life is a story with a beginning and an end, and it is not how long it lasts, but how it is remembered." [a.] Bedford, IA.

MIDDLETON, MERLE
[pen.] Max Middleton; [b.] Middlesboro, KY; [p.] M.H. and Lorraine Middleton; [ed.] Hills of Kentucky, streets of Manhattan, bars along I-75, beaches of CA; [occ.] Consumer/solipsist; [memb.] S.D.S., C.F.C. International, AEA, SAS, AFTRA, A.M., A.I.M., R.B.O.; [oth. writ.] "Need to Know" screenplay, assorted poems and lyrics various checks to settle accounts; [pers.] Do nothing, feel everything, love everyone act accordingly. [a.] LA, GA.

MIDDLETON, MICHELLE
[b.] January 12, 1978, Baltimore, MD; [p.] Sylvia Middleton; [ed.] Sophomore at Paramount High School; [occ.] Student; [hon.] Honor student, GPA 3.85, President of Clearwater Intermediate '92. [a.] Paramount, CA.

MILLARD, MICHELE LEE
[pen.] Sara Arreola; [b.] December 24, 1977, Klamath Falls, OR; [p.] Donna Preece and Michael Millard; [ed.] Santa Monica High School, sophomore at John Adams Middle School; [memb.] Varsity Softball for Santa Monica High School; [pers.] I write poetry to free my mind and express myself. [a.] Santa Monica, CA.

MILLER, ANNA (SPADY)
[b.] June 11, 1922, Stony Plain, Alberta, CAN; [p.] Fred and Elizabeth Spady; [m.] Ivan, February 8, 1950; [ch.] Malcolm (Inez) Cindy, Jared, Leanne Chromik (Orest), Desn, Dawn, Denise, Dennel Chromik; [ed.] B.Ed. and graduate diploma; [occ.] Retired school teacher and farmer's wife; [memb.] Life member International Society of Poets, Retired Alberta Teacher's Association, United Church Camrose, Alt., Roadhaven Resort Church Choir, Camrose Art Club, Alberta Edberg Senior Drop-In, Alberta Edberg Home Circle; [hon.] Three trophies-Best All Around Artist, New Sarepto County Fair, 1985 and 1990 Honorable Mention, Semi-finalist poet one of 100 from 1500 published poets from 41 countries, World ISP Symposium Convention Washington DC 1993; [oth. writ.] President of Edberg and Communities Historical Society - "Trails, Trials, and Triumphs" 1981 published book; [pers.] I like to reflect upon the world as is, not so much as it should be. Some of my poems are penned everyday living or to easy the pain of the sorrowing. [a.] Edberg, Alberta, CAN.

MILLER, DANA MARICE
[b.] March 9, 1976, Pensacola, FL; [p.] Michael Miller and Deborah Anderson; [ed.] Home taught, graduated at 16, also courses at Pensacola Junior College; [occ.] Sales Clerk at 93 Gold Company; [pers.] I wrote this poem because I miss my best friend, Linda Cain so very much. [a.] Challis, ID.

MILLER, REV. RICHARD S.
[pen.] Dick Miller; [b.] January 5, 1927, Milwaukee, WI; [p.] George and Inez Miller; [m.] Anita E., May 30, 1953; [ch.] Cynthia, Pamela, Judith, Priscilla, Andrew, Lorna; [ed.] Carroll College, General Theological Seminary, North Dakota State University; [occ.] Episcopal Priest and certified Elementary Education Teacher; [memb.] Order of St. Luke, Healing Ministry, Kiwanis International; [oth. writ.] Twelve Saints take the Twelve Steps, Poor Little Fish; [pers.] God placed us on earth to praise him for all he does. [a.] Idaho Falls, ID.

MILLENDER, GWEN WOODS
[b.] August 30, 1950, Baton Rouge, LA; [p.] Carey and Elnora A. Woods; [m.] Ronald Samuel Sr., July 27, 1974; [ch.] Micheline D. Lynne, Ronald Jr.; [ed.] BS-English Library Science, M.Ed-Mass Communication (Southern University); [occ.] High School Librarian-Scotlandville Magnet; [memb.] LA Association of Librarian, Alpha Kappa Alpha Sorority (Gamma Eta Omega Chapter); [hon.] First place winner Melvin A. Butler Third Annual (Memorial) Black Poetry Festival - Southern University 1974; [oth. writ.] Several poems on love, beauty, and sensitivity; [pers.] Poetry must first be felt and in one's spirit and soul before it can be expressed vividly on paper. [a.] Baton Rouge, LA.

MILLER, DEBORAH
[b.] September 22, 1968, South Bend, IN; [p.] Larry H. and Wilda Miller; [ch.] Tamana Shanta Miller and Ballyn Anthony Miller; [ed.] Washington High School, Ivy Tech; [occ.] Administrative Asst.; [memb.] Girl Scouts of America, NAACP-Hollywood Branch; [hon.] Public Speaking awards; [pers.] I reflect my emotions as well as others emotions into my writing. Sometimes we forget, that others have feelings and we walk all over them. The world should be aware of others around them. [a.] West Hollywood, CA.

MILLER, ESTHER N.
[pen.] Sandy Miller; [b.] November 25, 1933, Douglas, WY; [p.] Theodore and Ella Stolt; [m.] Alvin F., May 5, 1951; [ch.] Harold and Kristen Miller; [ed.] University of Colorado; [memb.] Audubon Society, St. Andrews Bay Resource Management, Pt. Washington Methodist Church; [oth. writ.] Article for the Church Herald. [a.] Panama City Beach, FL.

MILLER, KELLY E.
[b.] March 8, 1931, Sumter, SC; [p.] Eugene and Maserine Miller; [m.] Anna Elizabeth, September 4, 1954; [ch.] Timothy Brown; [ed.] Northeast High School, Antioch University; [occ.] Assistant General Secretary fro Adm. United Methodist Com. of Relief; [memb.] National Freedom Day Association, National Black Staff Forum, Black Methodists for Church Renewal; [hon.] National Freedom Day Service Award, LaSalle University Certificate of Merit, St. John's Settlement House Honors Award for Social Services; [oth. writ.] Poetry book-"FRom Creation to Eternity: One Day in the Life of Man". Several articles on Child Advocacy in local newspapers; [pers.] My professional goal is to achieve a position in life that can be utilized to assist those in need and build networks to bring Church and community closer together. [a.] Philadelphia, PA.

MILLER, MELISSA
[pen.] Melissa Miller; [b.] November 8, 1977, Windsor; [p.] Gail and Grant Miller, Art Lavack; [ed.] Grade 11, St. Anne High School; [occ.] Student; [oth. writ.] Several poems and short stories, unpublished; [pers.]

Poetry allows me to speak my mind and emotions. It also allows my creativity and self expression to run free. [a.] Tecumseh, Ont. CAN.

MILLER, MICHELLE
[b.] December 21, 1977; [p.] David and Andrea Miller; [occ.] Student; [memb.] Kathleen's Dance Center; [hon.] Certificates and trophy for ballet, tap, jazz and lyrical. [a.] Annapolis, MD.

MILLER, NANCY
[b.] December 5, 1974, Trenton, NY; [p.] Kathleen and Gerald Miller; [ed.] McCorristin Catholic High School, freshman at Rider College; [occ.] Part-time Dover Park Florist, summer camp counselor; [memb.] Ladies Auxiliary for VFW 3022; [hon.] National Honor Society, poems published in high school literary magazine and in Merce County Community College's Annual Magazine "Aspiratioins"; [pers.] Enjoy writing poems, lyrics, short stories, and personal essays that reflect my feelings; [pers.] I believe that writing is a form of expression. I use it to reveal my innermost feelings which I often conceal from the world around me. It is my escape. [a.] Lawrenceville, NJ.

MILLER, PAMELA J.
[pen.] PJ Lanker/PJ Miller; [b.] December 14, 1958, Indianapolis, IN; [m.] 1984; [ch.] 4 children; [occ.] Build transistors into electronic circuit boards for Honda (Engine Control Unit); [hon.] Various art displays locally; [oth. writ.] Songwriter, Illustrator, Flutist; [pers.] I attempt to respect nature and reflect legend and love.

MILLER, ROBERT E.
[pen.] R.E. Miller; [b.] New York, NY; [m.] Patricia Masuoka; [ch.] Stephen Noboru; [ed.] Columbia University; [occ.] Taught English NYC high schools-worked as editor, salesman, ghost writer, and film projectionist; [occ.] Now retired; [memb.] Academy of American Poets; [oth. writ.] Poetry, fiction and non-fiction have appealed in lietrary periodicals; [pers.] My chief themes are: nostalgia vs. renewal in life and art; the reality of aging and the unreality of everything else, and the powers of meditation and poetry as well as the other arts in our lives. [a.] New York, NY.

MILLER, RYAN JAMES
[b.] October 25, 1973, Conoga Park; [p.] Ann M. and Edwin H. Miller III; [m.] Tracy Lavelle, December 21, 1992; [ch.] Donovan James Miller; [ed.] Summit High School, Northwest Louisiana Technical Institute; [occ.] Student; [oth. writ.] Many unpublished poems, including a short story called "An Ancient One's Bible of Prophecy"; [pers.] Beneath the margins of my mind, you can see the portrait of my soul. [a.] Ringold, LA.

MILLER, STEFANIE
[b.] August 24, 1976, Dallas, TX; [p.] Clyde and Brenda Miller; [ed.] Oakland High School; [pers.] If you have a dream, follow your heart and go for it.

MILLER, VICKIE B.
[b.] April 23, 1960, Johnson City, TN; [m.] Terry A., September 5, 1981; [ch.] Olivia Green, Abram Alexander; [ed.] University of Tennessee; [occ.] Audiologist; [memb.] American Speech Hearing Association, Jr. Chilhowee Club, Broadway United Methodist Church; [hon.] Who's Who of American High School Students, graduated Cum Laude from University of TN. [a.] Maryville, TN.

MILLMAN, MINDY
[b.] June 27, 1961, New York, NY; [p.] Lee and Artie Millman; [m.] Engaged to Giancarlo Dicrosta in 1994; [ed.] Plainedge High School, Broward Community College; [occ.] Entrepreneur, own Telecommunications Company; [oth. writ.] Wrote greeting card copy for classic cards, working on children's unique personalized birth announcements. [pers.] Have been writing for enjoyment only since 8 years old. When I am sad was written at age 15. Have just begun to reserve this further. I feel so blessed to have a gift that allows me to put my imagination into words. When the pen hits the paper and my imagination soars - I enjoy sharing it with people. [a.] Oakville, CT.

MILLWATER, MARION
[b.] December 6, 1918, Plainfield, NJ; [p.] Reginald and Peggy Ralli; [m.] Harold W., May 30, 1936; [ch.] Shirley Ann and Sandra Lynn; [ed.] High School, Drake Business College, Rutgers Ext. course-Real Estate; [occ.] Housewife; [memb.] Rio Grande Bible Church, Elks Club, Watchung Bowman, R.G. Rescue Squad Aus.; [hon.] Editor's Choice Award, Graduated with highest mark "Distinguished"; [pers.] My favorite poets are Coleridge, "The Ancient Mariner" and Byron, "The Prisoner of Chillon". [a.] Rio Grande, NJ.

MINES, ROSETTE
[b.] April 1, 1929, Brooklyn, NY; [p.] Samuel and Esther; [ed.] Erasmus High School, night course Brooklyn College; [occ.] Own business Customer Service; [memb.] Artist League of Brooklyn, honorable mention; [hon.] National Library of Poetry, Honorable mention in World of Poetry 1991, listed in feelings magazines, religious books, poetic eloquence magazine 1993; [oth. writ.] Feeling Magazine 1993, Editor's Choice award in National Library of Poetry; [pers.] My poems come from things as a lead twirling on the ground or a big hello from the cashier in the subway station. The friendly faces and things all around us seem to create a need deep inside me to be expressed. [a.] Brookly, NY.

MINGE, LORNA D.
[b.] November 11, 1943, Marysville, KS; [p.] FEnton and Enola Kraemer; [ch.] Vernon "Todd", Renee Lynn (Benesh), Deborah Dee; [ed.] Marysville High, School of Cosmetology, certificate LPN and DeskTop Publishing; [occ.] Cosmetologist; [memb.] St. Paul's Lutheran Church; [hon.] Numerous awards in art and music during high school; [oth. writ.] Articles submitted to newspapers for publication for a non-profit agency, several short poems for personal satisfaction (some set to music); [pers.] As a child of God, I particularly delight in writing Bible stories in poetic form suitable for young children. I strive to portray God's almighty power in a colorful, descriptive, and artistic manner attractive to children, yet acceptable for adults also. [a.] Plymouth, NE.

MINK, DANA
[b.] June 2, 1962, Philadelphia, PA; [ch.] Samantha (6); [occ.] Currently working on a novel; [pers.] In our hearts lies the music of our souls, if only we would listen. [a.] Philadelphia, PA.

MINTON, JONATHAN
[b.] December 27, 1971, Boone, NC; [p.] Eddie and Allene Minton; [ed.] Wes Wilkes High, North Carolina State University; [occ.] Student; [memb.] "The Windhover" staff member (NC State's Literary Magazine), The Technician (NC State's Newspaper); [pers.]

My poetry reflects inner awareness and the social realities facing my generation. I have been most influenced by Walt Whitman and Carl Sandburg. [a.] Raleigh, NC.

MINTZ, JULIA McLEYMORE
[pen.] Julia McLeymore Mintz; [b.] October 26, 1949, Shelby, NC; [p.] John H. and Austine C. Moore; [m.] Dr. Sam H.; [ch.] Stephen Dewey, Donna Darlena, William Shane, Jason Elvis; [ed.] Tyron High School; [occ.] VP Gentle Hands Ministries; [oth. writ.] Have written approximately 50 poems that I have dated and filed. However, I have never tried to publish any of these some were done in memory or in honor of a special person who left a positive impression on my life. The poem "A Teacher's Prayer" was written and dedicated to my son Jason fifth grade teacher Mrs. Brenda Stroupe, for her sincere dedication to her students educational and moral future; [pers.] My writings have always been an outlet for expressing my feelings in a way I could never express personally. Whether in life's beauty of the disappointments, joys, and sorrows I share with others. [a.] Gastonia, NC.

MISKULIN, MAGDELINE A.
[pen.] Magda Lynn Miskulin; [b.] November 30, 1926, Duluth, MN; [p.] George and Frances Ujdur; [m.] Edward J., February 3, 1945; [ch.] Michael, Edward, Patrick, Cathleen (twins-John & Jacqueline); [ed.] University of Wis. Parkside 1985, with son John; [occ.] Real Estate Broker; [hon.] Grandmother to Michele, Lisa, Chad, Jennie, Stefanie, Jessica, Steve, and Kaitlin; [oth. writ.] Special occasions, poems for family members; [pers.] In such a violent world, poetry has a special role: It puts us in touch with our innermost emotions; As the rainbow uplifts our spirit after a summer storm; So to do we experience an inner glow after we have savored and perceived the message of a special poem. [a.] Racine, WI.

MISSEY, PRESTON FORREST
[pen.] Preston F. Missey; [b.] July 5, 1955, St. Louis, MO; [p.] Kenneth R. and Ruby L. Missey; [m.] Robin J., November 25, 1978; [ed.] Northwest High School, Air Cargo Specialist Sheppard Air Force Base, TX; [occ.] Westinghouse Engineering Services Technician; [memb.] Former Unted States Air Force Sargeant; [hon.] High school grad., honorable discharge from USAF, poem published; [oth. writ.] "Soldiers of TEN" published in "Break in the Clouds"; [pers.] I am dedicating this poem to Angie Housman of St. Ann, MO. May she sleep with the blessing and prayers of those who care. To parent and children who have suffered due to rape, kidnappings, murder or abuse. LEts remember they are only children wanting to grow. [a.] High Ridge, MO.

MITCHELL, KHAN LAVAL
[b.] July 20, 1969, McKeesport, PA; [p.] Samuel and Cheryl Mitchell; [ch.] Paelar Lo'Relle Mitchell; [ed.] Warrensville Heights High and Slippery Rock University; [occ.] Student; [memb.] NAACP, National Residence Hall Honorary and The Institute of Management Accountants; [hon.] Outstanding Student Leader (SRU ARHS) 1991, Silver Pin CAACHURH) 1991, Outstanding ARHS Committee and Program 1991, Honorable Discharge-Navy 1990, Dean's List Srv. 1993, CCC Honor's List 1991; [oth. writ.] Poem published in Campus Newspaper (African American Newspaper - Review); [pers.] Sensationalism is not the way to end "phobias" and "isms", instead they perpetuate them. The only way to end these problems is through self-examination and faith in God. [a.] Warrensville Hts, OH.

MITCHELLE, MARGUREITE ROSS
[pen.] Ross; [b.] March 3, 1922, VA; [p.] Dora and John Elliott; [m.] James E., July 18, 1956; [ch.] Diane, Marie, John and Marty (deceased); [ed.] High school; [occ.] REtired; [memb.] Fredericksburg Baptist Church, Frances Hudging Missions; [oth. writ.] Now working on my life story. How I rowed a boat a mile to school and walked a mile to catch the bus worked during WWII firing guns to prove the various parts and powder; [pers.] I was raised in King George County on a Penisula, during the great depression. No electricity, no plumbing, no phone, no radio. Daughter of a waterman. [a.] Fredericksburg, VA.

MOE, MICHAEL CHRIS
[b.] December 25, 1954, Crosby, MD; [p.] Donald and Joyce Moe; [ed.] University of ND; [occ.] Farming; [oth. writ.] The Words of Jesus Christ. [a.] Williston, ND.

MOLINA, LUIS A.
[pen.] Luis Antonio; [b.] November 14, 1954, New Jersey; [p.] Manuel Molina and Zoraida Jimenez; [ch.] Frances Zairene Molina; [ed.] BA in Commiunications; [occ.] Medical Clerk; [hon.] Acheivement award in fiction writing, achievement award in music, meeting my creator; [oth. writ.] Unpublished novels: The Phantom from Greenwich Village, Jibaro, pero no... Children's story: Ice Castle City (unpublished); [pers.] We must use the power of words to mold the conscience of our fellow brothers. [a.] Tampa, FL.

MOLINE, MARY
[b.] May 30, 1932, Bretz, WV; [p.] John and Mary Lommovilla; [ch.] David and Dawn; [ed.] WVU, Johns Hopkins University, UCLA; [occ.] Author Director American White Cross; [memb.] IPA, Ford Society, Norman Rockwell Society; [oth. writ.] Author 12 books, 2 screenplays, creator of the Norman Rockwell Character Dolls; [pers.] I am motivated by an inner force to help others. My latest achievement has been the organization of the American White Cross (after-care offered to disaster victims). [a.] Greensboro, PA.

MONARENG, MARTIN P. DR.
[pen.] Manley; [b.] June 30, 1947, Alexandria, S.A.; [p.] Simon and Mary Queen; [m.] Mmabatho Alzina, August 5, 1990 (2nd marriage); [ch.] Maria, Lerato, Tumi, Jacob, Monare; [ed.] Matric; [occ.] Spiritualist, Traditional healer, author, poet; [memb.] Herbal Association of Inyangas, Deacon at church, most senior counselor at The Sowetan Crisis Centre; [hon.] Counselor Skills certification; [oth. writ.] Three unpublished manuscripts, 30+ unpublished poems; still writing one approved by National Library of Poetry; [pers.] Inform and enlighten readers about the unknown esp. spiritual divinity etc., life in general.

MONIZ, STACIE M.
[b.] February 17, 1965, San Jose, CA; [p.] Jacquelyn and Edward Moniz; [ed.] Santa Clara High, Lake Tahoe Community College; [occ.] Management; [oth. writ.] Winter of '93 I was published in "Poetic Voices of America", this is my second publication; [a.] For those who have yet to fly, may you find what you meed to soar. [a.] S. Lake Tahoe, CA.

MONTES, MELISA
[b.] October 11, 1975, Camden, NJ; [p.] Edith and Michael Montes; [ed.] Maple Shade HS, Rutgers University (1st year); [occ.] Student; [memb.] Rutgers Union Estudiantil Puertorriguena (RUEP), VP Drama Club, Student Council and cheerleader (high school); [hon.] Who's Who Among Americas High School Students, National Honor Society, All American Scholar; [oth. writ.] Many other unpublished poems; [pers.] Have confidence in yourself and always fight for what you believe in. [a.] Maple Shade, NJ.

MONTGOMERY, MABEL M.
[pen.] Maxine Hart; [b.] January 21, 1926, Picher, OK; [p.] Frank and Jennie Hart; [m.] Horace R., March 11, 1942 (deceased); [ch.] Dugne Allen (deceased), Gary LeRoy Montgomery, Cheryl Lynnette Gross and Vickie Diane Head; [ed.] High school (writing class at city college); [occ.] Homemaker-widow; [memb.] Grace Baptist Church, VFW Letter Buck Post No. 922 Auxiliary; [oth. writ.] Article for college published newspaper, edited church newspaper, condensed missionary news for my church; [pers.] I have written a number of articles and poems and also have a small book ready and several articles written. [a.] Pendleton, OR.

MONTGOMERY, ROBIN
[pen.] Robin Montgomery; [b.] July 21, 1928, Boise, IA; [p.] Bruce and Grace Montgomery; [m.] Divorced-Lewis Goldberg, June 10, 1956; [ch.] Timothy Duncan Goldberg, Holly Goldberg Sloan and Dandall Monte Goldberg; [ed.] US Navy (4 yrs), University of Michigan, Architecture University of Oregon; [occ.] Living; [hon.] Theta Sigma Phi (Journalism Honorary Society), Daughter, Holly Goldberg Sloan Screenwriter "Made In America" and Angels in the Outfield"; [oth. writ.] Wrote a grant for theatre lighting for the National Endowment for the Arts and was awarded grant money; [pers.] Live, love, grow. Life is a journey into self. A smorgasbord if you please. [a.] Los Angeles, CA.

MOODIE, SONIA W.
[b.] Jamaica, WI; [p.] Alfred G. and Lurline Costa-Moodie; [ch.] Desiree Linn; [ed.] Sudbury School, BMCC, CUNY, Hunter College; [occ.] Registered Nurse, Health Ed Teacher (Julia Richman HS); [memb.] United Federation of Teachers, NYS United Teachers, American Federation of Teachers (AFL-CIO) and American Red Cross; [oth. writ.] Personal collection; [pers.] I want to live for today, and work on ways to survive the unknown tomorrows. [a.] New York, NY.

MOORE, CORAL
[b.] March 14, 1960, CA; occ.] College student, Science major; [pers.] My admiration for teachers, students and friends past and present inspire me to write my affections. [a.] GAinesville, FA.

MOORE, EMILY L.
[b.] December 27, 1913, Deerpark Haddonfield, NJ; [p.] Mr. and Mrs. Joseph E. Lord; [m.] Herberet W. Jr., October 21, 1938; [ch.] Janice R. and Herbert W. III; [ed.] High school, Cooper Hospital, Taylor Business School; [occ.] Housewife, writer, poet, artist, teacher; [memb.] NJ Poetry Society, Leaves of Grass Poetry Chapter; [hon.] Have won many awards with my poetry in a variety of poetry publications - including Lucidity, Poet's Viewpoint, Poet Magazine, Lone Stars and local papers; [pers.] Have had articles in REminisce, Good Old Days, Yesterday's Magazette and local paper; [pers.] Having lost two good husbands, I know it takes great strength and stamina to face this world alone. I thank many friends for their support which has helped me to carry on, to find a degree of happiness. [a.] Medford, NJ.

MOORE, JOHN J.
[ed.] Ph.D.; [occ.] Diabled teacher, counselor, stage director; [oth. writ.] Books, plays, poems. [a.] Prescott, AZ.

MOORE, MARY N.
[b.] Kentucky; [ed.] George Peabody College; pers.] Taught English and Mathematics for 34 years. She is a widow, the mother of two, grandmother of five. Most of her earlied poems were written for friends on some important event in their lives. Only recently has she began to seek publication for her poetry.

MOORE, PEARL P.
[b.] August 18, 1944, Arlington, TN; [p.] Mrs. Lula P. Johnson; [m.] Calvin E., Sr., September 5, 1975; [ch.] Paula Monique, Calvin Eugene, Jr., Caldra Chenelle; [ed.] Hamilton High, Henderson Business, Broward Community College; [occ.] Travel Agent, family book-keeper; [memb.] National Coalition of 100 Black Women, Broward County Urban League, President Pearl's Girls Scholastic and Self-Improvement Club; [hon.] Outstanding Citizens Award, Hero's Award, Mayor's Award, LKS Recreation Dept., First Runner-Up Ms. Broward County 1989; [oth. writ.] Poems written for others with a personal touch; [pers.] I believe that any gift from God should be used to the fullest. I love meeting people and I try to influence our youth today to "think positive", strive to the highest peak of reality and most of set goals that are realistic. [a.] Lauderdale, FL.

MOORE, RONALD
[b.] January 15, 1932, Elmira, NY; [m.] Gloria, February 9, 1952; [ch.] Ronda, Roxanne, Cathrine; [ed.] School of ED, NYU, SUNY at New Paltz, Library Schooil, SUNY at Albany; [occ.] Retired; [memb.] Past member-American Library Association, New York State Library Association; [hon.] Three special mentions American High School Poetry Association, NY Regents Scholarship winner 1952; [oth. writ.] Co-author with wife Margaret Sanger and The Birth Control Movement 1911-84 a bibliography, Scarecrow Press; [pers.] Poets reveal insights into the core of the present and the past. [a.] Saratoga Springs, NY.

MORA, JANA R.
[b.] August 4, 1950, Oneonta, NY; [p.] Dana W. and Ruth N. Banks; [m.] Saturnino F., Jr., November 20, 1982; [ch.] Alexander and Joseph Banks; [ed.] Chenango Forks High School, US Marine Corps 1969-72, US Navy 1973, Jan 1991 (retired); [occ.] Housewife/college student at Oxnard, CA College. [a.] Oxnard, CA.

MORAN, TOBITHA (TOBI) R.
[b.] October 19, 1942, Americus, GA; [p.] Tom and Irene Reddick Moran; [ch.] Solita and Sol Moran; [ed.] Booker T. Washington High, City College of New York; [occ.] Account Manager; [oth. writ.] Contributed short story to 111 Spring, an English Class publication at City College and published a book of poetry, My Poetry, My Heart and Me - Vantage Press; [pers.] Out of imagination and experience come poetry. Much of what I write is about the dark side of experience - pain, hurt, and disappointment, the things many of us do not want to articulate. It allows the reader to know that others have walked similar paths and prevailed. [a.] New York, NY.

MORGAN, ALANA
[b.] October 4, 1967, Panama; [p.] Cheryl Angle; [m.] Robby, August 15, 1987; [ch.] Ashley, Matthew and Michael; [ed.] Writers Digest Writing School, 35 hours

Financial Management; [occ.] Bealls; [memb.] Troop 518 leader Girl Scouts of America; [hon.] Honorable Mention award with Iliade Press for "Marriage on End", semi-finale round with Creative Arts for "Devoted Mommy"; [oth. writ.] "Devoted Mommy" Creative Arts will publish Spring 1994. "Marriage on End" - Iliade Press will publish in Spring '94; [pers.] My poetry has always been a means of therapy for me. They are an insight to my soul. I am very proud that something produced from my pain can be so beautiful. It goes to show that there is a silver lining around every cloud at some point in time. All of my work is dedicated to my grandfather Dale Angle. Whose genes gave me this talent. Maybe rest in peace. [a.] Longview, TX.

MORGAN, JASMINE
[pen.] Jasmine F. Morgan; [b.] April 16, 1980, Torrance, CA; [p.] Martin and Terese Morgan; [ed.] 8th grade, Augsburg American High School (Germany); [oth. writ.] Two writings, one published in Sparks, the other in Sketches Department of Defense American Schools publication; [pers.] Thank you to my family and friends for encouraging me to write and for seeing what I couldn't. [a.] Augsburg, Germany.

MORGAN, JULIANE C.
[pen.] JC Poet; [b.] March 23, 1978, Des Moines, IA; [p.] Ron and Jane Morgan; [ed.] Currently a sophomore at Johnston Senior High School; [occ.] Student; [memb.] Johnston High School Chorus; [hon.] Outstanding Academic Achievement - JHS, Spanish Quiz Bowl, participation award, attendance of the 1993 Drake University Young Writers Conference, Heartland AEA Computer Applications and Programming Finalist; [oth. writ.] Short stories: "The Rabbit", "A Window in Time", "The End", and "The People of Hill County", several poems (unpublished); [pers.] Dreamers: don't ever stop dreaming - because dreams sometimes really do come true - just believe in fairy tales and happy endings too. Never stop reaching for the stars and always strive to achieve your greatest potential. [a.] Johnston, IA.

MORGAN, MARTIN B.
[pen.] Marty Morgan; [b.] October 31, 1965, Mt. Vernon, WA; [p.] Brady and Julia Morgan; [ed.] BS Arizona State University 1990; [occ.] Co-founder and VP of H2Owen Corporation; [oth. writ.] "Untitled" Oakwood 1985, South Dakota State University - Printing Dept. "Winter - Young Author's Magazine: March/ April 1984; [pers.] It is all a frame of mind. Waterstar - The Ultimate Water Source. [a.] Sugar Land, TX.

MORILLO, JOSE F.
[b.] October 6, 1962, Puerto Rico; [p.] Carmen and Francisco Morillo; [m.] Rebecca, June 19, 1993; [ch.] Woody; [ed.] Artilles High, University of Puerto Rico; [occ.] Physical Therapist; [oth. writ.] Several poems; [pers.] I strive to learn something new everyday and to contribute in whatever way possible, to the betterment of mankind. [a.] Bryan, TX.

MORRELL, MATTHEW B.
[b.] March 10, 1971, Huntington, NY; [p.] Matthew and Carol June Mottell, sister-Dawn Marie; [ed.] Harborfields High School, State University of NY College at Fredonia; [occ.] Student; [memb.] Delta Chi Fraternity; [hon.] Order of Omega; [pers.] Every man and woman should seek personal peace and harmony. Through individual productivity, the world in general will be a better place. The individual who lacks harmony negatively affects the peace wround him. [a.] Huntington, NY.

MORRIS, GEORGE A.
[pen.] Tony Morris; [b.] Febryary 12, 1970, Honolulu, HI; [p.] George J. and Trudy Morris; [m.] Marcia Marie Lane Morris, December 7, 1991; [ed.] High school and some college; [hon.] Received a certificate of merit third place in writing contest. Obtained this from Irish Cultural Society; [oth. writ.] Many short stories and poems unpublished; [pers.] We the writers have the power to take out a person's heart, lay it out on a table and patch up all the wounds that it has received. We as creative creators have the responsibility to keep on healing, expanding, and creating old and new bonds that link humanity together. [a.] Hempstead, NY.

MORRIS, MICHELLE
[b.] February 25, 1970, Millville, NJ; [p.] Robert E. Morris Sr. and Lydia M. Ray, siblings-Kim Farrell, Robert E. Morris, Jr.; ed.] Stanahan High SChool; [occ.] Data Entry Operator; [memb.] Good News Church; [pers.] I was born with a birth defect called Spina-bifida which left me without the use of my legs. I believe my talent is God given to help encourage others. I have also written a book of poetry not yet published. I haven't found a publisher.

MORRIS, MICHELLE
[b.] November 16, 1974, Grantsville, WVa; [p.] Bernard and Kathrine Morris; [ed.] Gilmer Co. High, Calhoun-Gilmer Career Center, Glenville State College; [occ.] Student; [memb.] National Honor Society, National Vocational Technical Honor Society, Who's Who Among American High School Students; [hon.] Received many outstanding writer's awards throughout school, many awards for my vocal performances (singing); [oth. writ.] Won a Governor's Writing Contest, write many poems, have had some published; [pers.] We are a race of diverse creative individuals, each blessed in our own unique ways. I think God for giving me the gift of literary expression and song. [a.] Normantown, WV.

MORRIS, MUBARRAK E.
[pen.] M.E. Morris; [b.] February 20, 1956, NJ; [p.] Ruth and William Morris; [m.] Patricia, May 1, 1989; [ch.] Everett, Jason, Tommy, Charlene and Christina; [ed.] Abington High School; [pers.] In this world where one is unsure, I would be the one who can bring some heart felt joy to someone life. [a.] Willow Grove, PA.

MORRIS, ROBERT NATHAN
[b.] January 12, 1970, Chatham; [p.] June and Thomas; [ed.] Secondary Comprehensive, Hundred of Hoo, Kent, England; [occ.] Retail manager; [memb.] RSPCA - National Blood TRansfusion Service, WWF; [oth. writ.] Poetry, The Only Freedom I Know, The Graveyard, For You My Friend; [pers.] Good friends are hard to find, but once found are cheaper than therapy. [a.] Rochester, ENG.

MORRIS, RUTH E.
[b.] August 27, 1931, Terre Haute, IN; [p.] Claude and Elaine Champion; [m.] Henry, August 25, 1951; [ch.] Stephen Jay, Kevin Michael, Susan Elaine Wilder; [ed.] Gerstmeyer Technical High School; [occ.] Retired Reuben H. Donnelley-Data Entry Clerk; [memb.] Prairie Hoosiers Folk Music Society, United Methodist Women, Barbour Avenue U.M. Church; [pers.] Painting with oils and acrylics, playing the piano and singing. Poetry: My first attempt to be able to express into words by writing what is in the heart, mind and soul. Conveying the message to all mankind. [a.] Terre Haute, IN.

MORRIS, SHIRLEY ANN
[pen.] Sam; [b.] March 20, 1952, New Jersey; [ch.] Edmund Jr., Lynn, Michael; [ed.] High school graduate; [occ.] Bartender; [oth. writ.] Yes; [pers.] Poetry us my way to express feelings, thoughts, beliefs, or experiences.

MORRISON, L. ANNE
[pen.] Anne Young Barry; [b.] September 5, 1932, Victory Mills, NY; [p.] Peter and Victoria Young; [m.] Allan F., April 18, 1954; [ch.] Holly, Lorna, Mary Alice, Susan, Allan, Amy, Jennifer; [ed.] Schuylerville High School, Plattsburg State Teachers College, Saratoga-Warren BOCES; [occ.] Retired Nurse; [memb.] Board of Directors of Old Saratoga Historical Society, Past President of Ladies of St. Anne Rosary Society; [oth. writ.] I have written several poems that have never been published. Presently writing a children's historical novel concerning events in the Revelation in this area. I never before submitted anything to be published; [pers.] After raising 7 children I graduated as a Practical Nurse at age 50. At age 54 my doctor retired me due to rheumatoid arthritis. At long last I had fulfilled my dream of charge nurse in a nursing home, but it wasn't to be. [a.] Schulerville, NY.

MORSE, KATHYANN
[pen.] Thee Elected Lady; [b.] April 23, 1960, Detroit, MI; [p.] Cahterine and Norman Thompson; [m.] Richard L., March 26, 1977; [ch.] Robert Anthony, Paul Jerome, Catherine Madonna; [ed.] Self taught public library and Holy Bible; [occ.] Housewife and mother and public servant; [hon.] Acknowledged by Catholic Church as "Thee Saratoga Voice and Thee Elected Lady. Pope John Paul II acknowledged my writings and greetings after many visions I have had; [oth. writ.] Many poems and spiritual insights broom the spiritual mind and awaken thee dead tribes of this generation. I have already begun to menu a book to feed the people these words given to all of the tribes on earth; [pers.] I rise I stand to "Let the People Know", the son of men shall weave back the brotherhood od man. My writings are a reflection of truth found only in one's heart the true spiritual minds eye. [a.] Novi, MI.

MORTON, LEEDA
[b.] January 10, 1969, Whitesburg, KY; [p.] James and Faye Reed; [m.] Matthew, December 21, 1989; [ch.] Sabrina Banks, Cassandra Morton, Randall Morton; [ed.] GED from Southeast Community College; [memb.] Colson Baptist Mission of Colson; [pers.] I try to express how wonderful our Lord Jesus Christ is and my love for him. If one heart is touched by my work, than all the time and effort was worth that one heart. [a.] Whitesburg, KY.

MOSCATO, TINA L.
[pen.] Tina Moscato; [b.] August 28, 1974, Long Island; [p.] Robert and Rosanne Moscato; [ed.] Ward Melvill High School, Suffolk Community College; [occ.] Part-time Data Processor at College; [hon.] Scholarship for Outstanding Academic Achievement in English, Business Honor Society; [oth. writ.] "Alive", "The Grip That Sets You Free"; [pers.] I write from within. [a.] Port Jefferson, NY.

MOSELEY, ALICE
[b.] September 6, 1945, Golf Hammock, FL; [p.] Sebron Clark and Kathy Davis; [m.] Harry E. Jr., December 17, 1965; [ch.] Tina Flinn and Ronnie Moseley; [ed.] Okeechobee High; [occ.] K-mart Employee; [memb.] University Community Baptist Church , K-Mart Good

News Committee, Adult Sunday School Outreach/Evangelism Leader; [hon.] Employee of the Year 1992, Employee of the Month 8/92. [a.] Tampa, FL.

MOSES, PEGGY
[b.] July 1, 1938, Baltimore, MD; [p.] Timothy and Margaret McCarthy; [m.] James C., June 21, 1981; [ed.] National Louis University, Aurora University, Philadelphia Community College; [occ.] Asst. Professor of Nursing; [memb.] National League Nursing, American Nurse Association, Sigma Theta Tau, American Association Holistic Nursing; [hon.] VP Sigma Theta Tau (National Nursing Honor Society), Better World award (Gabriel Richard Ins.), Dean's List; [oth. writ.] "Quality Healthcare: A Gift to the Future", "Journal Long Term Care" 1989, "Caring Incidents: A Gift of Holistic Nursing"; [pers.] I strive to be a role model in implementing the humanities value of caring is a nurse education and care giver. [a.] Parkridge, IL.

MOSHTAGHI, SABRINA
[b.] November 25, 1975; [occ.] Student; [pers.] I feel poetry is the only form of emotion potent enough to break through the surface and gently, but faithfully, touch the heart. [a.] Circleville, OH.

MOSS, GEORGE ANNA
[pen.] George Amm Griffin Moss; [b.] April 23, 1933, Greenville, SC [a.] Ruth Thompson and Porter Augustus Griffin; [m.] James R., December 1950; [ch.] Jim, Dana, Rone, Russell, George and Jon; [ed.] Parker High, Meredith Collge; [occ.] Real Estate; [oth. writ.] Plumbline A Measure: to be published in the Spring 1994. The Lens of the Holy Spirit: to be published; [pers.] I believe these writings to be greatly inspired by the Holy Spirit. I have received, more than 150, over the past four years. I am putting out my first Christmas card this year. This is a new sound in Christian Poetry. [a.] Charlotte, NC.

MOSS, IRMA
[ch.] Two daughters; [ed.] Honor Student teacher; [memb.] Secy Board of Judea, Hofstra Cultural, Adelphi Alumni, Writers - Bryant Library, Macular; [hon.] Won short story contest - published; won poetry contest published; scholastic honor A student; [oth. writ.] Wrote and produced plays for NY City School system, Weekly Kids Kolumn, Godl Coast, Newspaper-Anton Press; [pers.] "Writing" has always been the love of my life - was published in Brooklyn Eagle (age 4) before I could write - dedicated to my mother. Have always been involved in school newspapers and playwriting as a kid.

MOSS, JANET
[b.] April 6, 1968, England; [p.] William and Margaret Lambert; [m. David William, November 7, 1992; [ed.] NYK F. Kathedralskole (Gymnasiet) College, Denmark; [occ.] police Officer, WEst Yorkshire Metro Police; [memb.] The Regent Academy of Fine Arts, London; [pers.] Learn from the past, live for today, look for the future. [a.] Leeds 19, England.

MOULTON, DIANE
[pen.] D.H. White; [b.] May 25, 1943, Boston, MA; [p.] Lillian White Moulton and Warren Moulton; [m.] Divorced, 1960-77; [ch.] Eric Eugene, Kyle Bradley; [ed.] Girls High Boston, Art, Crafts and Real Estate course on jon training in business and restaurant management; [occ.] Commercial residential realtor; [hon.] Achievement awards from various businesses; [oth. writ.] Promotional pamphlets, advertising articles; [pers.] In my

search for the truth of God, man and the universe; everything is the way it is supposed to be, with illness, hardships and pain. It is useless for man to try to change what is. Whether or not this is the only life we have or there is a better one after, for our lives to have any meaning our only job is to love enough to help each other get through it. [a.] Ormond Beach, FL.

MOUSSI, YASMINE
[b.] July 13, 1980, Paris/France; [p.] Baya and Lakhdar Moussi; [ed.] Bahrain Doods Lower Secondary School; [occ.] 8th grade student; [oth. writ.] Shedding - collection of poems unpublished; [pers.] I don't think I would get this far. I am thankful to my parents and friends especially Alex and Amber, for believing in me. [a.] Manama, Bahrain.

MOYER, BARBARA A.
[b.] March 19, 1931, Thunder Bay, ONT.; [p.] Cecil and Violet Partington; [m.] William; [ch.] Five (married); [ed.] Daniel McIntyer College, MIT Business College; [occ.] Self-employed, councellor for the unattached; [memb.] Manitoba Author's Club; [hon.] ICS Journalism also Creative Writing; [oth. writ.] Several poems published in local newspapers also book pending; [pers.] If I can be instrumental in touching one heart re-my pomes or writings, then I've obtained my goal. [a.] Winnipeg, MB.

MOYER, MAGGIE
[b.] July 23, 1980, Santa Monica; [p.] Ann and Dean Moyer; [ed.] 8th grade; [hon.] Two awards in string orchestra academic award. [a.] Westlake Village, CA.

MUDD, PHILOMENA MARIA
[b.] October 10, 1951, Louisville, KY; [p.] Letty Peter-Mudd and Don Mudd; [m.] Michael L. Wohlleb, May 20, 1972; [ed.] Spalding University, University of Louisville; [occ.] Registered Acupressurist; [memb.] American Oriental Bodywork Association, Jin Shin Do Foundation, Peta, Greenpeace; [hon.] Kappa Gamma Pi, Who's Who Among Students in American Colleges and Universities, Cum Laude-Spalding University; [oth. writ.] Short story-courier journal; [pers.] I believe in a wholistic approach to life combining body and mind and spiritual needs to bring us to wholeness. I am an activist for peace, stewardship of the earth, inclusive society and human and animal rights. [a.] Louisville, KY.

MUELLER, ELLEN
[pen.] Ellen Mueller; [b.] July 3, 1945, Kenosha, WI; [p.] Stanley and Ruth Carlsen; [m.] Divorced; [ed.] St. Joseph High School, Dominican College; [occ.] Elementary Teacher; [memb.] Business and Professional Womens Organization - former recording secretary, American Heart Association; [hon.] Interests-sketching, classical music, conversaions with cat; [oth. writ.] Liturgy Committee-St. Mary's Church, handbook on philosophy of education; [pers.] One should not write solely to please the public. One should write sincerely-from within. Such writings are sure to touch the hearts and minds of others. [a.] Riverside, CA.

MUGAVIN, DAMIEN
[b.] 1946, Warrnambool; [m.] Susan Raphael; [ch.] Liam, Jacob, Dominic; [ed.] University of Melbourne; [occ.] University Lecturer; [memb.] Australian Institute of Landscape Architects; [pers.] Keen interest in environment and society. [a.] Joslin, Australia.

MUKHERJEE, SARBOJIT
[pen.] Nowhereman; [b.] January 2, 1960, Calcutta, India; [p.] Chitta Ranjan (father) and Madhobi (mother); [m.] (wife) Minakshi, November '89; [ch.] daughter-Riddhi Shilpi; [ed.] BS Statistics, MS Compter Science; [occ.] Programmer/ Analyst; [oth. writ.] Who is Martin? (movie treatment), Singer without a Song (short story), We Are Just Prisoners of Our Own Device (poetic satire); painter - convert poems into paintings and student of Shao Lin Kung Fu; [pers.] REcognize your true self behind your image. Sstop running blind institutionalized existence and let truth and humanity awake. [a.] Brea, CA.

MULDEZ, PHILIP
[b.] May 26, 1926, Philippines; [p.] Pablo and Teofista Muldez; [m.] Rosa Blanco (deceased), December 17, 1947; [ch.] Francis Arthus, Charles Raymond, Richard Edward, Philip D. Jr., Arlene Rose; [ed.] Miami High, H.S. GED, Norfolk Botanical Gardens Horticulture and Landscape Design School, Tidewater Community College, McGraw-Hill Contemporary Legal Assistant Program (grad.), Wrier's Digest School; [occ.] Retired; [memb.] St. Nicholas Catholic Church, Fleet Reserve Association, Virginia Sheriffs Institute, AARP, National Committee to Preserve Social Security and Medicare; [hon.] Certificate of Distinction - with highest honors, Contemporary Legal Assistant Program, Diploma-NRI Contemporary Legal Assistant Program; [pers.] Me personal view about my God-given talent as a poet is to express my feelings according to the best of my abiliuty for my readers to understand what I'm writing about, and not leave them the task of interpretation. [a.] Virginia Beach, CA.

MULLEN, JARED SCOTT
[pen.] Jared Scott Mullen; [b.] November 7, 1978, Voorhees, NJ; [p.] Patricia and Barry Mullen; [ed.] St. Mary's School, currently St. Augustine Prep High School; [memb.] Monroe Twp Soccer and Basketball, Student Council, Computer Club, Mock Trial, YMCA and junior counselor; [hon.] Monroe Twp. Poetry Award, St. Mary's Christian Award; [oth. writ.] Poems published in local newspapers; [pers.] Since I am pursuing a career in child psychology, I will always make sure the children's voices are heard. [a.] Franklinville, NJ.

MULLIN, GRETCHEN
[b.] February 10, 1964, Pittsburgh, PA; [p.] Mary and James Mullin; [ed.] University of Western Ontario; [occ.] Graduate Student; [memb.] Children's Aid Society; [oth. writ.] Editor of Western Health Watch, several articles; [pers.] Poetry is psychoanalysis; a means to explore the seelf, one's pair and ones pleasures in life's journey of truth. [a.] London, Ontario, CAN.

MUNDING, LOUISE
[b.] August 25, 1931, Cleveland, OH; [p.] Andrew and Margaret Haray; [m.] Marvin, September 18, 1954; [ch.] Susan Louise; [ed.] Western High School; [occ.] Retired 1986 Cleveland Plain Dealer Nerwspaper Publishing Company; [oth. writ.] Although not on the market possible publication, I've written children's fairy tale manuscripts, along with other poems; [pers.] The feelings in poetry expresses mental picutures to the mind. [a.] Ocala, FL.

MUNYAO, BENJAMIN MUTISYA
[pen.] Ben; [b.] May 25, 1969, Kenta; [p.] Gideon Munyao and Josephine Kamene; [ed.] Currently in 3rd year University of Nairobi; [occ.] Student; [memb.] Environmental Club; [hon.] Write poems reflecting on

the mistakes in our society. My country has been under what I may call a dictatorial regime until recently that we adopted a multiparty system. I look forward now to writing more; [oth. writ.] Several poems published in the local newspapers; [pers.] I strive to correct the mistakes in our society. I am greatly inspired by what great statesmen say. Dr. Maya Angelou is also a great inspiration to me. I recently did watch her on CNN Larry King Live Show - she said and I quote "bitterness is like cancer I would rather be angry." [a.] Nairobi, Kenya.

MURAKOZY, LASZLO
[b.] 1951, Debrecen, Hungary; [p.] Tibor Murakozy and Rozsa Strohbach; [ed.] Lajos Kossuth University; [occ.] Free-lance; [pers.] To strive, to seek, to find, and not to yield. [a.] Prince Albert, SASK. CAN.

MURPHY, DENNIS Q.
[b.] November 1, 1944, Seattle, WA; [p.] John and Betty Murphy; [m.] Janet L. Jacobsen, July 17, 1982; [ch.] Doug and Shauna Murphy, Kelly Rogers; [ed.] University of Washington; [occ.] Marketing Research Director; [hon.] Beta Gamma Sigma; [pers.] American Pie never said why not a Ford but a Chevy found the levee was dry. The answer it seems is subtle, sublime, facts are but pebbles in the river of rhyme. [a.] Redwood City, CA.

MURPHY, LISA
[pen.] Eassa; [b.] April 7, 1978, Daleville, AL; [p.] Ken and Lorna Murphy; [ed.] Dumas High School; [occ.] Student; [memb.] High School Choir, Bethel Assembly of God, Spanish II, Health Occupations; [hon.] Top 13 of freshmen class, honor roll, World History and Biology I honors class; [oth. writ.] Poems in "Treasured Poems of America"; [pers.] In life we all need friends. [a.] Dumas, TX.

MURRAY, LORRAINE VIOLETTA
[b.] March 16, 1945, Preston, MD; [p.] Mzrjorie Murray Kelly and Gilbert Murray; [ch.] lorraine and Michael Murray; [ed.] Lockerman High, Salisbury State College; [occ.] Unemployed; [memb.] Mardela Apostalic Faith Church, Sunday School Teacher and Minister of the Gospel of Jesus Christ; [hon.] A certificate from the World of Poetry; [oth. writ.] Entered a short story to Ebony called "Still the Clour"; [pers.] All my life even as a child, I love to write and sing but never had the opportunity to express myself. But I keep on dreaming that one day my work would not be hid from the world - I hope the reader enjoy my poem. [a.] Mardela Springs, MD.

MYERS, JAMES M.
[b.] July 19, 1951, Augusta, GA; [p.] Chester and Mary Myers; [m.] Sherry, August 5, 1972; [ch.] Michael and Tonya; [ed.] Hardin-Simmons Unviersity, T.C.U., West Texas A&M University; [occ.] Instructor of history and government (Frank Phillips College); [memb.] Phi Alpha Theta, International Honor Society in History, Pi Gamma Mu, National Social Science Honor Society, Outstanding Youngmen of America; [oth. writ.] The West Texas Historical Association Handbook 1985 "Prisoners of War at Camp Berkeley", "The Army Come to Abilene", World War II, "Music As A Reflection of Homefront Moral 1941-45. [a.] Borger, TX.

MYRICK, SHARON T.
[b.] April 7, 1952, Philadelphia, PA; [p.] Charles and Clara Yates; [m.] Lawrence W., December 26, 1972; [ch.] Jerel, Lawrence Jr., Helen, Yvonne and Rachael; [ed.] J.W. Hallahan, Community College of Philadel-

phia; [occ.] Contact of Representative for IRS; [hon.] Primerica Promotion to Regional Manager Award, Mason Shoe Marathon Sales Excellence Award, Congressional Certificate of Merit; [oth. writ.] Women Victims of Landlords, published in the Philadelphia Daily News 1993, One Sided Version published in Phila Daily News 1991; [pers.] My writings evolve around the everyday experiences of life's survival. [a.] Phila, PA.

MYRICK, YVONNE R.
[b.] May 3, 1924, Gary, IN; [p.] William E. and Rowena O. Hill; [m.] Joe H. (deceased), November 24, 1949; [ch.] Henry A. (deceased), Yvonne R., Timothy J.; [ed.] Hamtramck High, Detroit Inst. of Commerce, Wayne County Community College, Wayne State University; [occ.] Retired supervisor; [memb.] Wayne State University Alumni, Women of Wayne, NAACP, GAmma Phi Delta Sorority, Women of the Church of God, Goodfellows; [hon.] Unsung heroine-NAACP Wayne County Comm. Coll. Outstanding alumni; [oth. writ.] Editorials for local newspaper, presently writing a book on the history of Black people in the city of Hamtramck; [pers.] I am indeed encoraged to continue writing poetry and to finish writing my book. I hope to inspire my grandchildren and other children of this community. [a.] Hamtramck, MI.

MYTTY, MELISSA
[pen.] Melissa Mytty; [b.] September 1, 1981, Royal Oak, MI; [p.] Sue Bergin and Dan Mytty; [ed.] Power Middle School; [occ.] Student; [hon.] Honor roll, winner in Michigan's Reflections Contest; [pers.] I like to write about how I see the world. I have been encouraged by teachers as well as my parents. [a.] Farmington, MI.

NADERER, PATRICIA J.
[m.] George R. Sr., November 29, 1941; [ch.] Gaynel, George Jr., Gary, Patricia, Michael; [ed.] John Jay High School (Cleveland, OH); [occ.] Home Matriarch; [hon.] All four poems have been published in World's Most Treasured Poems and World's Favorite Poems; [pers.] One day at a time thoughts. Perpetual advertorials inspired by sports ads and media overkill on Bo Johnson - football/basketball - said he'd never play again while on crutches - he's playing for Chicago White Sox to date.

NAGAHAMA, BRIAN H.
[pen.] Simon Berry; [b.] July 22, 1957, Honolulu, HI; [p.] James and Rose Nagahama; [ed.] Honolulu Community College, Hawaii Community College; [occ.] Civil Service, US Navy Pearl Harbor, HI; [oth. writ.] Several unpublished poems; [pers.] The harmonious linking of words that transforms words into poetic elegance. [a.] Honolulu, HI.

NAITO, YUKIHIRO
[b.] March 23, 1970, Japan; [p.] Akira and YTukiko Naito; [ed.] Irvine Valley College; [occ.] Student; [pers.] I've been in the USA for two years and its great experience for me that one of my poem is published in here. I may have been influenced by modern French poets - Bandelaire, etc.

NAJERA, ANTONINO E.
[pen.] Tony & Toning; [b.] May 10, 1915, Agno, Pangasinan, Philippines; [p.] Mariano Norice Najera; [m.] Natalia Espanol, June 1962; [ch.] Antonino Jr., and Manalo Najera; [ed.] Stationary Engineering graduate and Chemical Engineering undergrad; [occ.] Retired; [memb.] American Legion, Canada Chapter Post 21;

[hon.] From International Society of Poets-Poet of the Year, winner $5,000 Grand Prize and book publishing contract, merits of awards from the Poetrygram; [oth. writ.] Five consecutive years having Golden Poet Awardee - 1985-'89; [pers.] On macros - man of the hour on his early days - wild pres, media, defamed him in many ways.

NAKAGAWA, CANDACE T.
[b.] September 28, 1975, Hawaii; [ed.] Iolani High School, Boston College Class of '97.

NAKAYAMA, RAUYL
[b.] July 25, 1943, Honolulu, HI; [ch.] Nera Gay K. and Skye R.S. Nakayama; [ed.] MBA; [occ.] Regional Gen. Mgr. United Motivation Corp.; [pers.] Reaching out into darkness: Written on the accession of the death of my father, Ralph Sakaye Nakayama.

NAMEROW, JORDAN ILANA
[b.] December 4, 1982, Englewood, NJ; [p.] Peri and David Namerow; [ed.] Ridge School; [occ.] Student; [memb.] The Ridge School Environmental Club, Hadassah, The Ridgewood Baseball and Soccer Associations; [hon.] Ridge School Student Council Representative, The Ridgewood Board of Education Art Show, The Valley Hospital Poster Contest; [oth. writ.] Several poems published in The Ridge Raccoon. [a.] Ridgewood, NJ.

NASH, EARL
[p.] Oneda Nash; [ed.] Noxubee County High, Automation Inst.; [occ.] Receiving Clerk (Transtar Ind.); [hon.] Dedicated Service award; [oth. writ.] Several poems published in Lines N' Rhymes and a poem forthcoming in Sparrowgrass Poetry Forum; [pers.] I love writing poetry, and my hope, is that I bring joy to all who reads my work. [a.] Cleveland, OH.

NATTERER, FLORA ANN
[pen.] Flora Natterer; [b.] March 5, 1935, Ocean Side, NY; [p.] Peter and Addie Pappas; [m.] Henry, January 21, 1956; [ch.] Jeffrey, John and Addie Natterer; [ed.] Freeport High School graduate - Brown's Business School, Rockville Center School of Ballet; [occ.] Advertising Rep. for "The Mt. Eagle" Newspaper; [memb.] American Heart Association, Smithsonian Institute; [oth. writ.] Six poems; [pers.] I try to express in my poems, the love, goodness and fellowship of others, and seek an inner peace in my writings. [a.] Gilboa, NY.

NAVARRO, LINDA M.
[pen.] Linda Mae; [b.] February 17, 1964, Brooklyn, NY; [p.] Emilio Navarro, Sr. and Josephine Pagan; [ch.] Frankie A. Manganiello; [ed.] Federation Employment & Guidance Services, National Congress of Neighborhood Women, Dutchess County Boces Technical Center; [occ.] Student; [hon.] Honor Roll, Certificate of Participation for Boces Newsletter; [oth. writ.] Biographical Poetry; [pers.] I reflect my writing to those whom want to express their feelings to other people on stationery. I thank my sister Cynthia M. Pagan for giving me the inspiration. [a.] Beacon, NY.

NAYLOR, MARIA MAROSEK
[b.] May 1, 1953, Elmira, NY; [p.] John F. and Bernadette Lafferty Marosek; [m.] John Earle Naylor III; [ed.] Notre Dame H.S.; [occ.] Professional singer and partner in "Legends Sports Pub" Walkiki; [oth. writ.] Co-wrote, published and recorded songs with my husband John and other band members of "Silver Shadow";

[pers.] Life is short, have lots of fun. [a.] Honolulu, HI.

NEEDHAM, JOHN MARTIN
[b.] March 20, 1960, St. Charles, MO; [p.] Bill and Norma Needham; [m.] Sondra Ann, July 2, 1988; [ch.] Jeremy, Jennifer, Amy; [ed.] Ohara High School; [occ.] Warehouse Supervisor; [oth. writ.] Additional poetry some copywritten; [pers.] Writing my thoughts down on pen and paper is a way in which I can release my feelings and emotions, that otherwise would be vocally difficult for me. [a.] Florissant, MO.

NELSON, BRANDI LYNN
[pen.] Brandi Lynn Nelson; [b.] May 4, 1976, Kingman, AZ; [p.] James and Carolyn Nelson; [ed.] Valentine Elementary School, Kingman High School; [occ.] Student; [memb.] FFA & Rodeo Club; [hon.] Who's Who in American School, First place in Young Writers Conference; [oth. writ.] Several poems and short stories written in high school; [pers.] I have always been interested in writing, my first award was in the third grade. I won first place for the Young Writers Conference. [a.] Peach Springs, AZ.

NELSON, JAMES S.
[pen.] James S. Nelson; [b.] July 23, 1943, Norfolk, VA; [p.] Maleigh and Nancy; [m.] Brenda, July 7, 1976; [ch.] Isaiah, Oak, Persia Ruth; [ed.] University of New Hampshire and Middlebury College; [occ.] Chef-August Lion Rest.; [oth. writ.] Creator and editor of: Mirror of Distinction Journal. [a.] East Randolph, VT.

NELSON, NANCY OWEN
[b.] June 14, 1946; [p.] Nannie B. and Wood Ford/Owen Nelson (deceased); [ch.] Owen W. McCord; [ed.] Birmingham-Southern College, Auburn University; [occ.] College Professor (Henry Ford Community College); [memb.] Western Lit. Association, Community College Humanities Association, AAUW; [hon.] Writing award, Professional Category, Dakota History Conference, Phi Beta Kappa; [oth. writ.] Articles in journals about the American West, book reviews, co-editor of The Selected Letters of Frederick Maufred, 1932-54; [pers.] The subject of poetry is the experience of an ordinary life - simple images come together to make a statement about the human condition. [a.] Dearborn, MI.

NENCKA, HELEN
[pen.] Helen Nencka; [b.] May 1, 1908, Thorp, WI; [m.] Walter S., April 22, 1931; [ch.] Susanne and Walter D.; [hon.] Wrote over 3000 poems, 1500 plus published. 3 books- out of print (To My Love, Island Seed and The Christmas Tree Story), radio program, Reminiscence in Rhyme. Listed in anthologies, 20 years branch historian and 2 years National Historian of the National League of American Pen Women. Branch bicentennial chest in the Pen Arts Building, DC; [memb.] League, Wis. Writers Club, Wis. Fellowship of Poets, Listed Who's Who four categories; [pers.] Spiritual inspirations: My Rosary of Poems, couplet Genesis through Noah, two romances (prose) collaboration with my husband, Walter. Over a thousand poems to my two grandchildren. Commissioned paintings only, painting with poem lettered on it, which the poem inspired. [a.] Hubertus, WI.

NESMITH, SCOTT
[b.] April 22, 1965, Columbus, GA; [ed.] WA Berry High School, Samford University; [occ.] Freelance Writer; [memb.] Sigma Tau Delta, English Honor Society, Samford Communications Associations; [oth. writ.] Numerous articles published in local newspaper,

article published in Epi-Log magazine. [a.] Birmingham, AL.

NETTLES, DAVID
[b.] June 18, 1965, Upland, CA; [p.] Darrell (deceased) and Beverly Nettles; [m.] Diane, May 4, 1990; [ed.] Palo Verde High, Community College of the Air Force; [occ.] Writer/actor; [memb.] World Wildlife Fund; [hon.] Americanism Award; [oth. writ.] Several poems published in local newspapers, screenwriter for "Beyond This Pointe"; [pers.] The spirit of a man will sustain his infirmity; but a wounded spirit who can bear. Prov. 18:14. [a.] Phoenix, AZ.

NETZLEY, JEANNE S.
[b.] May 2, 1935, Burbank, CA; [ch.] Leisha Johanna Ormsbee, Thomas Frederick Netzley; [ed.] Doctoral Candidate, Philosophy Masters - Psychology, BA-Business Administration; [occ.] Administrative Assistant-Cal. Inst. Tech.; [oth. writ.] Doctoral thesis: " What would happen if we listened to infinite knowing infinite has something to tell us?" Entire book of poetry ready for publication; [pers.] We are each the perfect expression of infinite. The challenge of this thing cal;led life is to move out of any learned confinement and express infinite uniquely as each one of us. [a.] Pasadena, CA.

NEUMANN, SHARON
[b.] February 21, 1978, Newport News, VA; [p.] Hubert A. Norton (grandfather); [ed.] Denbigh High; [oth. writ.] This is my first writing published-have written numerous other poems; [pers.] I believe that poetry reflects the writer's experiences. Although the mind plays a role, the significance lies in the heart.

NEWBROUGH, WADE
[b.] November 5, 1962, Smithville, MO; [p.] Carl and Opaldene Newbrough; [ch.] Zakkarya David Newbrough; [ed.] Mexico High School, Moberly Area Community College; [occ.] Musician, partners in a cattle company; [oth. writ.] Poetry, short stories and features in the MACC paper, four copyrighted songs; [pers.] My poetry is the most clear reflection of my soul. My stories are my attempt at realism and my song lyrics are for fun. I like to play with words. I am going to teach Ancient Civilizations and continue writing and playing music. I will someday build a small castle to live in on top a hill surrounded by forest. After I retire I will never cut my hair again. [a.] Mexico, MO.

NEWCOMB, BERNICE
[pen.] Niece; [b.] May 15, 1933, Avonport, NS; [p.] Roy and Jessie Guptill; [m.] Robert Frank, August 21, 1954; [ed.] Grade 8th; [occ.] Housewife; [memb.] Baptist Church.

NEWMAN, ALBERT
[pen.] Silver Fox; [b.] July 21, 1920, Havana, Cuba; [p.] Fred and FAnny Newman; [m.] Virginia Ann (deceased), April 29, 1944; [ch.] Five (all adopted); [ed.] John Swett H.S., several extension courses in Labor-Management Relations at USF, UC; [occ.] Retired; [memb.] Shelton Mason County Historical Society, Peninsula Art Association, Puget Sound Maritime Museum, Northwest Steam Society, Washington Center/Performing Arts, Washington State Historical Society; [pers.] Poetry allows me to record and transmit my emotions that would otherwise be forgotten or forever lost to those they were intended for. I was influenced by Wilber L. Crook's "Flitted Moments", published in 1942. [a.] Shelton, WA.

NEWSOME, WAYNE
[b.] March 30, 1955, Ronceverte, WV; [p.] Russell and Ruth Newsome; [ed.] Union High School; [occ.] Disabled; [hon.] 1973-Sectional AA Basketball All Tournament Team; [oth. writ.] Other poems to be printed in a book later; [pers.] I write poetry to bring inspiration to other peoples hearts and elevate their minds to a new consciousness. Jesus Christ inspires me more than anyone. What is Poetry? Words brought to life. [a.] Union, WV.

NGAAGE, BARINE SANAH
[b.] April 13, 1961, Taabaa; [p.] Leonard and Esther Ngaage; [ed.] Uncial and Uniport; [occ.] Literature lecturer; [memb.] Secretary, Editorial Board, Journal of Pedagogy and Development; [hon.] Post graduate scholarship award; [pers.] My poem "Whispered dream" is my personal statement. [a.] Port Harcourt, Rivers.

NICHOLAS, DANIELLE NICHELLE ELIECE
[b.] March 23, 1978, Maryland; [p.] LaQuita Lanier and James Nicholas, Jr.; [ed.] J.E.B. Stuart Elementary School, Henderson Middle School and John Marshall High School; [occ.] Student; [memb.] Drama Club; [oth. writ.] Several other poems; [pers.] I hope my poetry influences the lives of other people. My everyday life experiences have greatly influenced my writings. [a.] Richmond, VA.

NICHOLAS, RANDY
[b.] October 13, 1954, Atikokan, Ontario, CAN; [p.] Ralph and Alice Nicholas; [m.] Charlotte, June 21, 1980; [ch.] Alicia Mae, Jennifer; [ed.] Atikokan High, Confederation College; [occ.] Sales Representative; [memb.] Knights of Columbus; [oth. writ.] Personal, unpublished book of poetry; [pers.] People should never give up their dreams because without their dreams there would be no life. [a.] Edmonton, Alberta, CAN.

NIELSEN, JOYCE K.
[pen.] Joyce K. Nielsen; [b.] October 1, 1930, Athens, AL; [p.] Addie Bernice Hart and Dewey Hobson Knight; [m.] Ferdinand Berg, 1965; [ch.] James William Barnes, Jr. and Dr. Donna Marie Barnes; [ed.] West End High, Tarrant High, UAB and U of F "School of Life"; [occ.] Retired; [memb.] St. Andrews Ep. Church, Executive Board. American Cancer Association, Spanish Rail GArden Club, Crestview Women's Club, Fed. Republican Women, Concerned Women of America; [oth. writ.] "Turn Around America" news journal and have been writing poetry and songs for approx. 30 years and sharing as an encouragement to friends and associates; [pers.] I like people. I strive to write from the heart for we all as human beings are like a book to read, we each have a story to be told and are like a lovely song to be sung. God Bless! [a.] Crestview, FL.

NISANOGLU, LALE
[b.] July 9, 1975, England; [p.] Erdogan-Shokufe Nisanoglu; [ed.] Tehran International High School; [occ.] Student; [hon.] Superior Achievement Award, several honors and awards for being the director of drama club for five years and playwriting; [oth. writ.] Currently working on a novel; [pers.] The truth is like a mirror, and everyone sees in it his own image. [a.] Tehran, Iran.

NIXON, La VERNE
[b.] February 8, 1946, Northfort, VA; [p.] Pauline and Edward Nixon; [ch.] Kelli, Keith, Silma, Andre' Jones; [ed.] High school; [occ.] Allied Heath Career Aide; [oth. writ.] More poems, non-fiction stories, philosophy, etc.;

[pers.] I would characterize myself as a person since the age of 5 years old realize that Jesus Christ son of God chose me to do a prodigious job for the people of this world, and in any way that I could for their highest good, and what better way to help heal the peoples pain in their lives, than through my writing. [a.] Bronx, NY.

NOAH, IMEYEN A. DR.
[b.] November 20, 1946, Ikotekop; [p.] Mr. Akpan and Unwa Noah; [m.] Pauline Imeyen Noah, November 23, 1980; [ed.] University of Ottawa; [occ.] Lecturer in French; [memb.] Executive Committee of the Linguistics Association of Nigeria, Language Writers Association, Secretary Editorial Board of the Department; [hon.] National Association of Mkpat Enin Students; [oth. writ.] Origin and structure et symbolism des contes, textbooks in French for nursery and primary schools, several articles on literature and methodology, two short stories; [pers.] Man transcends the human. [a.] Calabar, CRS.

NOEL, NORMAN H.
[b.] August 29, 1915, MA; [p.] William and Grace Noel; [m.] Annie Byrd Noel, August 24, 1945; [ch.] Richie; [ed.] College; [occ.] Retired; [pers.] Only other writing in high school many years ago. [a.] Chino, CA.

NORBURY, MYRTLE
[b.] August 23, 1920, McAuley; [p.] Sara and Tom Davidson; [m.] Sid, June 25, 1941; [ch.] Keith, Dennis, Donna, Gary, Rhonda, Karen; [ed.] Grade eight; [occ.] Housewife, mother, grandmother and great grandmother; [hon.] Merit for helping with all community functions; [oth. writ.] This is my first time to enter a poetry contest; [pers.] I like to write poetry and when I vision things in my mind, I enjoy putting it in poetry.

NORDICK, LESA MARIE
[b.] May 1, 1968, The Pas, MB, CAN; [p.] James and Louise Nordick; [ed.] Margaret Barbour Collegiate Institute, The University of Manitoba, The University of Guelph Distance Education; [occ.] Practicum Supervisor, Early Childhood Education; [pers.] Inspired by a special place in my heart. My inspiration for poetry comes from those around me and from within myself. [a.] The Pas, Manitoba, CAN.

NORMAN, CHARLES H.
[pen.] Charles H. Norman; [b.] January 18, 1932, Dyersburg, TN; [p.] William H. and Mary Norman; [m.] Norma Jean, January 7, 1955; [ch.] Marcia Lynnette, Diana Dee, Sheila Jean and Lisa Michelle; [ed.] Lubbock High, Texas Tech., University of Texas; [occ.] Rout Salesman-Amature Songwriter; [memb.] World of Poetry-4th place Poetry Contest 1988, numerous honorable mentions and Golden Poet Awards 1985-90; [hon.] Great poems of Today, World Poetry of Anthology, New American Poetry Anthology, The Golden Treasure of Great Poems, World Treasury of Great Poems, Who's Who In Poetry 1989-92; [oth. writ.] My Children 1985, 101 Poems 1992, 300 or more songs, "Trudy The Long Ear Reindeer" 1992 (short story), "Turning Point" (novel-not yet complete), Poetry published in Our Western World's Most Beautiful Poems and Our Western World's Most Cherished Poems; [pers.] I come to the cross road once more, with two forces to conquer; the will to go forward or the urge to return. [a.] Uvalde, TX.

NORMAN, WILLIAM
[pen.] William A. Norman [b.] January 18, 1952, Arb. NM; [ch.] Four; [ed.] College-Ft. Lewis at Durango CO, Leeward Community and Hilo Community; [occ.] Inmate/Artist/Painter/Sculptor/Musician; [memb.] The

United Together Earthlings, The World Youth Realization, Fellowship Foundation, The Urantia Brotherhood, The Universal Life Church, The Ergot Church, The National Alliance of Drug and Alcohol Users Constitutional Rights Lobby; [hon.] Honorable mention from 1992 Pen America Prisoner Writers Competition for a non-fiction essay "Thomas Jefferson, High on Corporate Power", Archives of the Arts 1993, Nation Anthology, Gingberg Radio Anthology 1992; [oth. writ.] The Together Earthling Fieldguide for Freedom, Lines of Force, Aphrodite Star, 207 page collection of poetry and song lyrics "Swinging on the Edge"; [pers.] I'm driven by social injustice and ecological destruction. [a.] Cap. Cook, HI.

NORRIS, KRISTIN
[b.] October 19, 1967, Rahway, NJ; [p.] William R. Norris and Edwin A. Revack; [m.] Peter, June 27, 1992; [ed.] Pinelands Regional High School, Georgian Court College; [occ.] First grade teacher, George J. Mitchell Elementary; [hon.] Sigma Tau Delta, Sigma Phi Sigma, Kappa Gamma Pi, Dean's List; [oth. writ.] Poem published in The Westcoast Fisherman, several poems and short stories published in Fountainspray literary magazine; [pers.] ...Where I have failed in form, I have not failed in feeling. My words are not ink, but blood-and these are not rhymed but felt, believed, endured...I endeavor to say my mind, to draw my soul. In this, I sense, I succeed. [a.] Tuckerton, NJ.

NOTAINCOLA, FRANK
[pen.] J.T. Riker; [b.] January 27, 1974; [p.] Patricia and Frank; [ed.] Ross H.S., Polytechnic University, State University of New York at Farmingdale; [occ.] Bookkeeper/student; [oth. writ.] Warped (unpublished), several other unpublished poems; [pers.] I think writing should inspire people to better themselves. [a.] Brentwood, NY.

NOTARO, DIANA
[b.] May 20, 1935, Buffalo, NY; [p.] Frances and Anthony Gennuso; [m.] Hon. Peter J., August 29, 1959; [ch.] Thomas, Anthony, Peter, Joseph, and Mark; [ed.] Holy Angels Academy; [occ.] Homemaker; [memb.] Conducted poetry classes in local elementary schools; [oth. writ.] Published regularly by local papers, Saturday Evening Post, St. Joseph's Messenger, Senior Beacon, many smaller publications Niagara Erie Writers; [pers.] I am looking forward to a time when poets will be recognized and perhaps paid for their efforts before they are dear. Until then, I just enjoy writing. [a.] Buffalo, NY.

NOTARO, PHILOMENA
[b.] September 2, 1937, Chicago, IL; [p.] Filomena Gaudio/Ferdinando Gaudio; [m.] Salvatore, September 24, 1966; [ed.] Notre Dame High; [occ.] Homemaker; [oth. writ.] First poem submitted in 1967 entitled THE WAR IN VIETNAM. Written poems for special occasions as birthdays and retirements which my co-workers enjoyed; [pers.] I have been writing poems for many years now, which I truly enjoy doing. My life's dream would be fulfilled if a publisher wanted to put them into publication. My husband, Sal, has encouraged me to keep writing as he feels I have a special talent. He is my greatest fan and inspiration. [a.] Chicago, IL.

NORTHERN, ALFRED J.
[b.] May 5, 1916, Macon, GA; [p.] Alfred and Molly Northern; [m.] Ilda L., May 6, 1949; [ed.] Baldwin Conservatory of Music, Felix Deyo Instr., Carnegie

Hall, Correspondence courses, Institute of Children's Literature, Washington School of Art, Writers Digest School; [occ.] Retired; [memb.] The Watchful Eye Neighborhood Watch of Roosevelt; [hon.] Roosevelt Drug Free award, 1993 Anti-Drug award from Neighborhood Watch efforts; [oth. writ.] Curley Tater, a fictional novel, published Vantage Press, NY 1976, The Three Heavens published in 1978 edition of New Voices in American Poetry, I'm American published in 1990 edition New Voices in American Poetry; [pers.] Achievement has no time limit-unless you receive constructive advice, put on invisible earmuffs, and continue to work toward your goal. This is an interpretation of a poem written by Alfred J. Northern called "The Three Heavens" copy sent to Pres. Reagan in 1985. Acknowledgement received 1/31/85. [a.] Roosevelt, NY.

NOWICKI, VANESSA
[b.] August 13, 1969, WPG, MAN.; [p.] Paul and Jeanne Nowicki; [ed.] Walter Murray Collegiate, Saskatoon Saskatchewan Canada; [occ.] Student; [pers.] I hope someday to have a successful career in writing. In writing my poems, it comes from the heart therefore it reaches the heart of the reader. [a.] Hazelridge, Manitoba, CAN.

NUBY, LESLIE
[b.] May 20, 1971, Birmingham, AL; [p.] Jacqueline and Lester Nuby, Jr.; [ed.] Mountain Brook High School, Birmingham-Southern College; [oth. writ.] Poems published in college literary and arts magazine, Quad, poems printed in school newspaper and one other poem published in Living Jewels. [a.] Birmingham, AL.

O'FARRELL, SANDRA LEE
[pen.] Sandra Lee O'Farrell; [b.] February 9, 1943, New Orleans, LA; [p.] Daisy Bedell Jackson and Paul Alexander Green; [m.] Donald Dean, February 23, 1963; [ch.] Beth Allison Demint and Barton Michel O'Farrell; [ed.] High school, Secretary College; [occ.] Writer; [memb.] Krewe of Columbus (Letter) Girls' Scouts Softball Team; [hon.] Poem published high school poetry anthology, 3 blue- first place ribbons in cooking contest recipes published in cooking-baking book 1966; [oth. writ.] "Mother Dear" 1993, "Karen Sue" 1992, "Robin Red Beast" 1952, "Plight of the Oil Field Worker" 1986, "The Runner" 1987, "Happy Birthday Brother Dear" 1991, "Our Little Girl Dana" 1992; [pers.] I am a director descendant of William Brewster of Christopher Columbus' ship, the Mayflower. I am a free spirit and I love people. I personalize most of my poetry. [a.] Nacarre, FL.

O'NEAL, LARRY D.
[pen.] Larry D. O'Neal; [ed.] Vicksburg High School, Alcorn State University, Michigan University; [memb.] Alpha Phi Alpha; [oth. writ.] Several poems; [pers.] I strive to help others through my writing. I have been gratefully inspired by God. [a.] Aberdeen Proving Ground, MD.

O'NEAL, MARSHELNEAL
[pen.] Whisper; [b.] August 3, 1960, New York; [p.] Catherine and James O'Neal; [occ.] New York City Correction Officer; [pers.] Poetry is not only the grandeur of the mind, but the reality of things unseen. [a.] Jamaica, NY.

O'NEIL, LORI M.
[pen.] M.L. O'Neil; [b.] March 14, 1957, Dearborn, MI; [m.] Rick O'Neil, July 26, 1986; [ch.] Megan

Renee; [ed.] Bishop Borgess High, Associated from Oakland Community College; [memb.] Mac-Group Detroit (Computer DeskTop Publishing user group), Farmington Artist Club; [hon.] Excellence Certificate in Art, Suma Cum Laude at OCC; [oth. writ.] Several poems and songs; [pers.] I love writing about striking people and nature. An idea will just pop into my head and I'll start writing. I will have it all finished in 5 minutes - without effort. An then I get so surprised! [a.] Farmington Hills, MI.

O'NEILL, DANIEL T.
[b.] December 27, 1950, Yonkers, NY; [p.] Charles and Anne O'Neill; [ed.] Indiana University; [occ.] Interior Plants Maintenance; [pers.] "The Spiritual Fetus" was taken from my essay currently in progress, which proposes that the title of Jesus Christ: "The Son of Man", means a New Man coming out of a spiritual evolution which culminates in a super-physical man. [a.] Ojai, CA.

O'NEILL, MILDRED
[b.] Astoria, NY; [p.] Leo and Ethel Hughes; [m.] Donald, August 2, 1952; [ch.] Peggy Conaghan, Donna Porzio, Maureen O'Neill, 6 grandchildren; [ed.] High school; [occ.] Retired high school aide; [hon.] Published in The Coming of Dawn; [oth. writ.] Poems for family and friends currently working on book entitled, "The Power of Love"; [pers.] We can only attain peace within the world through education of the spirit starting with self and spread to others through the Power of Love. Love holds a power unsurpassed by anything else. [a.] Brentwood, NY.

O'SULLIVAN, KEVIN
[b.] September 17, 1964, Fayetteville, NC; [p.] Robert and Bridget O'Sullivan; [m.] Dena, November 21, 1993; [ed.] Regis High School; [occ.] Programmer/Analyst Empire Blue Cross/Blue Shield; [pers.] My aim is not to confuse the issue with hidden meanings or cryptic allusions. I try to describe things as I feel them. [a.] N. Middletown, NJ.

OLABISI, ADEPOJU
[b.] October 25, 1942, Igboho; [p.] Mr. and Mrs. S. Ojo Olabisi; [m.] Mrs. M.A. Olabisi, December 18, 1969; [ch.] Adenike, Adewale, Adeniyi, Adeyimika, Adeyemi and Adetunji; [ed.] University of Ibadan, Ibadan Federal Science School, Lagos Teacher Training College; [occ.] Librarianship; [memb.] International Community Education Association, Nigerian Library Association; [hon.] Federal Government Scholarship, Nigeria 1976; [oth. writ.] Journal articles, Tower Court, The Heart of a Woman, A Slender Woman, A Sophisticated Woman, My Ambition, Peace, Let There Be Peace, newspaper articles; [pers.] I contend to project my imagination into the psychological background of amusing and writing of Africans. Tried to reflect various civilizations of traditional poetry of tribes of West Africa with special reference to Western Nigeria in English of Yoneba folk tales. [a.] Ibadan, Nigeria.

OLAND, JENNIFER A.
[pen.] Jenny Oland; [b.] Sept. 5., Rapid City, SD; [p.] Sherman and Fran Oland; [ed.] Rocky Mountain College-Sports Medicine; [occ.] Activity Director at Parkview Convalescent Care; [pers.] Most people don't know I write. I write for myself when I have an inner conflict. My writings reflect what I am feeling inside or how I perceive the world around me. It gives me an inner peace. [a.] Billings, MT.

OLLENDIECK, MELISSA LYNN
[pen.] Missy; [b.] July 30, 1969, Cresco, IA; [p.] Charles and Dorothy Ollendieck; [ed.] Crestwood High School, North Central Bible College, Continental Bible College, Div. at Assemblies of God Theological Seminary; [occ.] Student; [memb.] Central Assembly of God; [hon.] Nominated and selected to be in Who;s Who Among College and University Students 1993, Silver and Gold honors society in Bible College, chosen as one of two outstanding pastoral majors in graduating class; [oth. writ.] While in Europe wrote article for the Boy Scouts Club; [pers.] Keep improving as a person and "to do justly, to have mercy and to walk humbly with your God." - Micah 6:8 [a.] Cresco, IA.

OLSEN, DIANE L.
[pen.] Poco Ferland; [b.] July 27, 1953, Einsing, Manitoba; [p.] Orvil and Bunny Olsen; [ch.] Simon Olsen; [ed.] Bishops College, Dalhousie University; [occ.] Shop Help; [memb.] Canadian Mental Health Association (CMHA) Board of Directors; [hon.] High school scholarship, won Royal Trust Writing Competition in high school, honored as member of Codco by Nfld. Arts Council with certificate; [pers.] I enjoy writing because am often inspired to do so. Personally inspired by me belief in Christ and the earth. [a.] Swan River, Manitoba, CAN.

OMRAN, JALAL D.
[pen.] Jalal D. Omran; [b.] November 27, 1938, Isreal; [p.] Dib and Arifeh Omran; [m.] Angeleanta Omran, June 8, 1963; [ch.] Jamealdolensiano, Dartiniano, Lagracella and Javondelansor; [ed.] Terra Sancta College, RETS Electronics and Tech. School, So. NV Voc-Tech School and Management Schools; [occ.] Retired; [memb.] 32 Degree Scottish Rite Masonic Order, Past Ill. Potentate Suns of the Desert Shriners Order; [oth. writ.] Two books published by Carlton Press Publishing; "I Love Poems" 1984 and "For the Sake of Humanity" 1985; [pers.] To spread love throughout the world and to reach as many as I can, because only through love we can achieve peace. [a.] Henderson, NV.

OMRAN, LAGRACELLA
[pen.] Lagracella Omran; [b.] December 8, 1968, Las Vegas, NV; [ed.] Chapparal High School, ETTC Tech. School, Hotel Administrator; [occ.] Model, songwriter, singer and dancer; [hon.] Miss Nevada USA 1988, many pageants awards, past Cleopatra at Caesar Palace; [oth. writ.] Numerous writings not published yet; [pers.] I want to make people happy through my singing and dancing and be successful at it. [a.] Las Vegas, NV.

OPPELT, RUTH
[b.] September 30, 1925, Winthrop, CT; [p.] Edward and Agnes Congdon; [m.] Frederick, Sr., May 28, 1949; [ch.] Fred Jr., Raymond, Dennis, Douglas, Diane, Donna; [ed.] High school; [occ.] Assembler and packer at Cramer Co.; [pers.] Think positive and love one day at a time. [a.] Old Lyme, CT.

OPIRA, STEPHEN
[b.] November 28, 1954, Gulu, Uganda; [p.] Pat and Acen Olum; [m.] Helen, February 21, 1982; [ch.] Okello Jimmy, Frank Opira; [ed.] National Teacher's College, Makerere University; [occ.] English Teacher; [oth. writ.] Several poems published in college and university magazines; Nanga and The Makererean; [pers.] I strive to instruct society by ridiculing the follies and evils of some characters or groups. [a.] Tebang, Mafeteng, Lesotho.

OREM, HOWARD
[pen.] Soluna; [b.] March 5, 1914, Arcadia, TX; [p.] Arthur and Alma Orem; [ed.] Arcadia High, International Correspondence School; [occ.] Retired researcher, Developer of Soluna Sanctuary; [oth. writ.] The Orco Report, Country Land, Nature Rhymes, Making The World A Better Place, Too Hot To Handle and Absolute Zero, Is Man An Intelligent Species; [pers.] All of my writings are oriented toward making the world a better place. [a.] Petrolia, CA.

ORLANDO, MARIA-VICTORIA
[b.] November 30, 1963, Buenos Aires, Argentina; [m.] Rosa M. Vega de Orlando and Saverio Orlando; [ed.] St. Bernard High School, Johnson and Wales University; [memb.] National Association of Female Executives; [hon.] Student Honor Roll, Dean's list, Silver Key Honor Society, graduated Cum Laude; [pers.] Life is hope; hope must be reflected in every word we say, every act we commit, every thought which passes through our minds. With this we must always believe where there is a will, there is a way. [a.] New London, CT.

ORTEGA0LAGE, ESTHER
[b.] November 8, Havanna, Cuba; [p.] Pedro Lage and Italicoo Fernandez; [m.] Nicanor Ortega, May 31, 1968; [ed.] Dr. of Philosophy and letters from Havanna University; [occ.] Retiree Board of Education; [memb.] NYY (Teachers Union), "La Nuez" (Art and Literature International Magazine), "Aha" Association of Hispanic Arts, Spanish American Cultural Link, Inc.; [hon.] Diploma, and commendation letters from different education centers; [oth. writ.] My first book of poems "Luz y Sombra" in Spanish; [pers.] Intellectual and introvert person, a deep reader, Spanish specialist. [a.] New York, NY.

OSCHSE, DAN
[b.] August 29, 1979, Chattanooga, TN; [p.] Roger and Ann Ochse; [ed.] Stevens High School; [occ.] Student; [pers.] Welcome to my world, where imagination surpasses physical form, and all that is grim is not necessarily Grimm. [a.] Rapid City, SD.

OSTROSKE, KEVIN
[b.] August 19, 1965, Plainview, NY; [p.] Diane and Walter; [ed.] Irondale High School, Louisiana State University, Nassau Community College, Hofstra University; [occ.] Junior Tournament Administrator; [hon.] Named 1991 "Golden Poet for poem entitled Far Award Fear; [oth. writ.] "The Power of Golf" published Aug. '93 in Metropolitan PGA Journal; [pers.] Poetry writes itself through me. [a.] Uniondale, NY.

OTERO, MARIBEL
[pen.] Maribel Otero Rodriguez; [b.] September 26, 1964, Bronx, NY; [p.] Noemi Cruz/Miguel A. Rodriguez; [m.] Rev. Andes, May 24, 1985; [ch.] Mariely, Andres Jr., Jasmine, Erika; [ed.] Oyster Bay High School, Long Island University; [occ.] An Evangelist and college student; [memb.] United Brethren's in Christ Church; [hon.] Middle school and high school honor list; [oth. writ.] Long Island University Poetry and fiction contest. El Diario La Prensa Newspaper; [pers.] Writing is a talent from God. He give it to us to express what we feel without saying it orally. God is my inspiration. [a.] Brooklyn, NY.

OTWAY, DEBBIE
[b.] July 17, 1953, Vancouver, BC; [p.] Glenice and Bill Hennessey; [m.] Warren Otway, March 19, 1988; [ch.]

Three (two daughters and one son); [ed.] Grade 10; [occ.] Housewife; [pers.] I would like to dedicate this poem to my Grama Hennessy, who gave me the best years of my life. [a.] Jernon BC CAN.

OVERMAN, JOHN
[b.] June 2, 1958, Castro Valley, CA; [p.] Marilyn and Bill Overman, Sr.; [ed.] Miraloma High School; [occ.] Child Care Provider, Operations Asst.; [oth. writ.] Published poem in Rigorous Magazine, working on a book of poetry "Sunshine"; [pers.] Most of my poetry has been inspired by a very special lady my Sunshine. [a.] Hayward, CA.

OVERMAN, LINDA RADER
[b.] April 18, 1951, Hollywood, CA; [p.] William Rader and Henriette Balague; [m.] James, June 23, 1978; [ch.] Michael James and Deva Marie; [ed.] California State University Northridge; [occ.] Returning student; [hon.] Pacific Northwest Writers Conference, finalist in Adult Novel Category 1991, Los Angeles Pierce College Annual Writers Conference, honorable mention in Poetry 1990; [oth. writ.] Other poems and short fiction have appeared in several magazines; [pers.] Writing is like breathing to me. I can't live without it. It keeps me alive. [a.] Encino, CA.

PAAR, FRANCIS
[b.] February 27, 1915, Prescott, AZ; [p.] William and Viva Paar; [m.] Jane Muireal Kavanagh, October 17, 1953; [ch.] Andrea; [ed.] Institut d'Etudes Politiques de Paris (when it was Ecole Libre...); [occ.] Part-time cataloger; [memb.] Institute on Religion in an Age of Science, International Association of Buddhist Studies; [pers.] I feel a kinship with Benjy, the idiot, in Faulkner's The Sound and The Fury. [a.] Rochelle Park, NJ.

PABS-GARNON, EDITAYO
[pen.] Tayo; [b.] March 20, 1974, Freetown; [p.] Mrs. F. Pabs-Garnon; [ed.] Christ Church Primary School, Sierra Leone Grammer School; [occ.] Student, Fourth Bay College University.

PACHECO, DYANNA LYNNE
[pen.] Dy Lynne Pacheco; [b.] April 25, 1980, Nashville, TN; [p.] Phyllip and Charlene Pacheco; [ed.] Northside Elem., Stewart Elm., Crosby Jr. High; [occ.] Student/writer; [memb.] Acteens and Church Choir; [hon.] English award; [oth. writ.] Sparky the Flying Dog, The Hidden Room, and Puppy Love; [pers.] I'm thirteen and am one of four girls. I enjoy school and I feel it has influenced me to write. While everyone else is worried about who wears what, and their boy/girlfriends, I am mainly concerned about my education. Through that, I feel my teachers have influenced me a great deal in all of my writings. [a.] Hitchcock, TX.

PADMAVATHI, T. KAUNDINYA
[pen.] T.V. Padma; [b.] November 13, 1969, Madras, India; [p.] Ambujam and T.A. Venkatraman; [ed.] The School K.F.I., St. Joseph's College, Brockwood Park, The College of William & Mary; [occ.] Graduate student at the Schgool of Marine Science, The College of William and Mary; [oth. writ.] Articles and poems published in India, poem published in the Delhi-London Poetry Quarterly, The United Kingdom. [a.] Gloucester Point, VA.

PAGE, BERNI
[pen.] Biddi; [b.] Bridgeport, NE; [p.] Alma Cochran (father-deceased); [m.] David E. Page; [ch.] My pride

and joy; [ed.] Bridgeport High School, Purdue-Grandview Scottsbluff Jr. College; [occ.] Semi-retired Manager-Caterer-Chef; [hon.] Jr. Dramatics Director 1991-93, World Pork Expo Judge, Secretary ACF; [oth. writ.] Short fiction - Recipes for Cookbooks; [pers.] I write to reflect on the inordinate natural beauty of all entities as a part of each other. [a.] Des Moines, IA.

PAGE, KIMNELA S.
[pen.] K.S. Page; [b.] July 29, 1965, Loveland, CO; [p.] John W. (deceased) and Judith R. Page; [ed.] DHS-Durango, CO; [pers.] Being born and raised in Colorado because of this I try to bring it to life through my dreams and my active imagination. What I see with my senses and feel with my heart and soul I put into words to share with everyone. [a.] Mesa, AZ.

PAGE, KRIS
[b.] February 20, 1971, Toronto, Ont.; [p.] Richard and Julie Page; [m.] (friend) Brenda Auger; [ed.] 7R Leger Alternative School of Studies; [occ.] Cook; [oth. writ.] School Correspondent for the Standard Freeholder (Dec. 90-Feb. '91); [pers.] If life refuses to let you live, then reach out and take back what was yours. [a.] Cornwall, Ontario, CAN.

PAGE, STARR
[b.] July 15, Washington, D.C.; [p.] Sadie Rust and James H. Jones; [ch.] Tanya Dowan and Tomeka Summers; [ed.] Maryland College of Art and Design; [occ.] Illustrator/Graphic Artist; [memb.] The Illustrators Club; [oth. writ.] Windmill, Touch Me, What Is A Cloud?; [pers.] Pick a moment, any moment in time, the moment you pick however will be gone. Therefore we must continue to strive forward. [a.] Chevy Chase, MD.

PAGLIA, JAMES
[b.] July 16, 1940, Philadelphia, PA; [p.] Jenny and Basil Paglia; [ch.] Steven Turner, (grandchildren-Stephanie, Steven Jr., Stacy; [ed.] Rowan College, Temple University, Charles Morris Price Insurance-Rutgers University; [occ.] Retired Teacher; [memb.] American Federation of Teachers, Democratic Party, John Fenwick P.T.A., Salem Middle School PTA, Rowan College Alumni Society, Grandparents Association; [hon.] Extensive Poetry in Pen Point, herald, Forecaster A Treasury of Literature Avant, Catholic Star Herald; [oth. writ.] Summer Ennui a play which enjoyed a two week run at The Wilma Theatre in downtown Philadelphia in the summer of 1981; [pers.] When all discrimination ends, mankind will truly achieve humanity. [a.] Salem, NJ.

PALAHNIUK, DEBRA KIM
[pen.] Debbie Palahnuik; [b.] March 6, 1953, Sioux Lookout, Ont.; [p.] Aldo and Marcia Favot; [m.] Kenneth, August 16, 1975; [ed.] Queen Elizabeth High, University of Manitoba; [occ.] Research Assistant for a Pharmacuetical firm; [memb.] U. of M. Alumni Association; [oth. writ.] Several poems not published yet; [pers.] I believe that everyone in life must face sufficient challenges to realize that he/she is worthy and is an important part of this world. These challenges strengthen us and build our character so that in the end we may realize we have succeeded regardless if we have won or lost. Nothing is a better inspiration than to really live! [a.] Winnipeg, Manitoba, CAN.

PALMER, DENISE
[b.] March 31, 1962, OKC; [p.] Bill and Darlene Bingham; [m.] Donnie, November 4, 1986; [ch.] Jennifer Triplett, Kyle and Krysta Palmer; [ed.] High

school, N.W. Classen; [pers.] With family and friends anyones life can be fulfilling.

PALMER, PATRICIA L.
[b.] November 29, 1945, Miami, FL; [ed.] BA Human Development and Learning, University of North Carolina; [oth. writ.] Published in two university publications: The Humanic Arts Project and The Writing Project. [a.] Charlotte, NC.

PALOU, MARI
[b.] March 11, 1970, MD; [p.] Mike and Evelyn Palou; [occ.] Third year dental student at Baylor College of Dentistry; [memb.] PM League of Dallas, Museum of Art; [hon.] Presidential Scholarship at Texas A&M University; [oth. writ.] Several poems (unpublished) Children's Story (unpublished); [pers.] My goal is to reach the reader through feelings. I wish my poems to spark memories, sensations, and perhaps emotions. [a.] Dallas, TX.

PANSINI, URSULA E.
[b.] February 8, 1928, Germany; [p.] Dr. Konrad and Luise Stevernagel; [m.] Jack J., November 6, 1948; [ch.] Michael, Patrick, Frank, Carl, Joe, Elisabeth; [ed.] Grade school and high school; [occ.] Housewife; [oth. writ.] Children's stories, poems in English and German but none published; [pers.] I never send anything in anywhere. This is my first attempt to get something published. [a.] Littleton, CO >

PARAS, MICHAEL H.
[b.] January 4, 1954, San Francisco, CA; [pers.] I'm just a sinner, saved by the AWESOME GRACE of a merciful God. [a.] Stockton, CA.

PARIS, KEITH A.
[b.] January 5, 1969, Omaha, NE; [p.] Keith A. Bates and Frances A. Paris; [m.] Laurie L., March 25, 1988; [ch.] Antionette, Keith A. II, and Jean-Luc Paris; [ed.] GED; [occ.] Taxi driver/entrepreneur; [oth. writ.] Personal poems; [pers.] I am greatly inspired by the laws and principles of our Creator and do what I can to reflect those laws and principles not just in my writings, but as a way of life also. [a.] Aurora, CO.

PARIS, JOSEPHINE
[pen.] Josie; [b.] February 6, 1947, Alabama; [p.] Joe and Margieree Smith; [ed.] John Farren Elementary, Dunbar Voc. High, Illinois Medical School, Wilson Jr. College, Joilet Jr. College, Kenedy King College; [occ.] United Steel Workers of America (Coke Loader Operator); [memb.] American Cancer Society, St. Jude Vineyard Temple, World Book Club; [oth. writ.] For friends and relatives, Hawkins Family Newsletter; [pers.] Not until you look beyond my physical appearance to see the beauty within the heart, then and only then can we be friends. To be a winner, you must learn to be a loser. [a.] Chicago, IL.

PARK, MARIAN PATRICIA
[pen.] Marian Ford Park; [b.] May 12, 1918, Milwaukee; [p.] Charles E. and Gladys H. Ford; [m.] James D., October 9, 1956; [ch.] Gary D. Waulters; [ed.] High school, Penn State Business School (one semester); [occ.] Free lance writer; [memb.] PA Poetry Society, Kentucky Poetry and National Poetry Society; [hon.] Most Distinguished Poet (Jessee Poet 1986), Poet of the Year (Editors Desk 1986), included among 2000 most noted women in America; [oth. writ.] 14 poetry chapbooks, 2 books of fiction publication regularly in many

poetry journals and short fiction and article publishers.; [pers.] Writing is compulsive... [a.] Harrisburg, PA.

PARKER, CATHERINE T.
[pen.] Cathy Parker; [b.] November 17, 1937, Wilkes-Baare, PA; [p.] Margaret E. and Francis T. Moran; [m.] Lynn, June 7, 1981; [ch.] Five children and three step children; [ed.] High school; [occ.] Purchasing Coordinator; [memb.] St. Marks Church Choir, Irish Club, Fox Valley UBA (Bowling League); [hon.] Several honorable mentions for poetry and writings, poetry "Tree of Life" published Beacon News (Copley Paper) 1989 "Christmas Memories), contest "Soap Scum" scene for soap opera; [oth. writ.] Poem "Glasses" July 1993 from Naperville, IL Writers Group-honorable mention; [pers.] My poetry comes from a deeper place than my body or my soul. My poem is about a real son. [a.] Aurora, IL.

PARKER, DOROTHY ELIZABETH CAMPBELL
[pen.] Dep Campbell; [b.] August 17, 1923, Penna; [p.] William Irving Parker and Ava Campbell; [m.] Charles Semlich; [ch.] Three children; [ed.] Mansfield High/ Brander Mathews, Columbia University; [occ.] Poet/ writer; [memb.] Hi Desert Artists/Antelope Garden Club; [oth. writ.] New: "The Art Gallery" a collection of poems as yet unpublished; [pers.] The echos of the future and past can only be heard if you listen for them. [a.] Chino Valley, AZ.

PARKER, JERRY LEE
[pen.] Capri; [b.] December 23, 1966, Chicago, IL; [p.] Laura Parker; [m.] Sandra Gayle, July 26, 1993; [ch.] Tiffiny LeAnn Parker and Diana Deshawn Parker; [ed.] Ferger High School and Rivercrest High; [occ.] Cartoonist and Freelance Poet; [m,emb.] Church of Jesus Christ; [hon.] Cash prizes... six months paid tuition to attend art college of choice, Art plaques, Art Ring, Poetry Plaques; [oth. writ.] Several poems published in local newspaper and Dance on the Horizon; [pers.] Trust in God and believe in self, and let "I Can" become a part of your daily living... [a.] Haiti, MO.

PARSONS, RAY
[pen.] Jeremia McEntire; [b.] February 14, 1969, NY; [p.] David Dewolf and Darlene Brantis; [m.] Laura O'Bryan, December 24, 1990; [ed.] AA in English Lit; [occ.] Writer; [oth. writ.] Twenty poems want to placed on greeting cards; [pers.] Don't judge a book by the cover.

PARSONS, RENEE
[b.] April 7, 1972, Happy Valley Labrador, CAN; [p.] Rex and Rexine Parsons; [ed.] Musgravetown High School, Eastern Community College; [occ.] Stenography; [hon.] First place award - Provincial Poetry Contest, Certificate of Superior Achievement in Canadian National Mathematics Contest, Music Awards; [pers.] My poems are a reflection of my own life experiences, thoughts and feelings. I try to write about the good and beauty in life and in mankind. [a.] Bloomfield, NFLD, CAN.

PATE, JULIET LASHAWN
[b.] April 23, 1972, Chicago, IL; [p.] Daniel E. and Julie A. Pate, Sr.; [occ.] Manager trainee for Lady Foot Locker; [oth. writ.] Poem published in American Collegiate Poets Anthology; [pers.] I would like to thank my parents Julie and Daniel for their love and guidance. My sisters: Sharon, Felicia, and Donna and brothers John and Daniel Jr. for thier love. Also a very special thank you to Steven Boone, Lynette Roberts and Chris Chambers. [a.] Chicago, IL.

PATERSON, ERNEST E.
[pen.] Ernest E. Paterson; [b.] June 26, 1952, Vancouver, BC, CAN.; [p.] Mr. and Mrs. Fred Paterson; [m.] Gillianne; [ch.] One daughter and one son; [occ.] Freelance writer, correspondent to South Canboo-Thompson newspaper "The Journal"; [oth. writ.] Twenty newspaper articles published. Seventeen photographs currently involved in writing a Christmas book which should be published by June '94; [pers.] Be active, trust God, love you family and do nothing that will cause you guilt. [a.] Logan Lake, BC., CAN.

PATERSON, KEVIN G.
[b.] July 10, 1972, Escondido, CA; [p.] JoKay and Kirk Bednar; [ed.] Valley Christian High School, San Jose State University; [occ.] Mathematics tutor; [memb.] Bethel Church of San Jose; [hon.] Life member CA Scholarship Federation, Bank of America Ach. Award in Math, Distinguished High School Student, Honors at Entrance, SJSU Recipient of NAED Scholarship, Golden Key National Honor Society, Dean Scholar, SJSU; [pers.] I wrote this poem when I was 19 years old, after coming through the tragedy of losing my father, Rev. Tom Paterson, Jr., in a plane crash in Alaska when I was 10 years old, and watching my mother come through the emotional struggles to a happy new marriage seven years later. [a.] San Jose, CA.

PATRICK, MARIE T.
[b.] January 30, 1950; [p.] Helen and Louis Romano; [m.] George S., September 22, 1990; [ch.] Shawn, Andrea, Douglas, William and Thomas; [ed.] Bushwick High School; [occ.] Assistant Accountant; [oth. writ.] Several poems published in various poetry books; [pers.] My aim is to touch ones heart with my poems. And to reach out and comfort. [a.] Valley Stream, NY.

PATRICK, RUTH A.
[pen.] Ruth Carpenter Patrick; [b.] July 10, 1945, Whitewater, WI; [p.] Deceased; [m.] Richard L.; [ch.] Julie R. Davis and Mark R. Patrick (grandchildren Cassie and Amanda Davis); [ed.] B.E. (Secondary), U.W. Whitewater; [occ.] H.S. Teacher; [memb.] United Methodist Women, M.E.A.; [hon.] Editor's Choice Award, D.A.R. award and N.H.S.; [oth. writ.] The National Library of poetry has published some of my poetry in various anthologies; [pers.] The key to a good life is kindness and common sense. [a.] Johnson Creek, WI.

PATTERSON, CHARLES JR.
[pen.] Pat; [b.] July 30, 1965, Orlando; [p.] Mr. and Mrs. Charles Patterson, Sr.; [ch.] Candance Renea, Gabrille; [ed.] Jones High School; [occ.] Warehouse worker, Lifestyle Carpets; [memb.] Trinity Temple Youth Choir, Usher Board; [oth. writ.] Several poems never published Violence, Christmas, A Friend, School, What is A Mother, Family; [pers.] I strive to reflect the things that are breaking this world apart, I look to God as my source, aslo I am influenced by the tragic death of sister's Connie and Jackie Marshall. [a.] Orlando, FL.

PATTERSON, DALE
[b.] November 23, 1973, Heidleberg, Germany; [p.] Ike Patterson and Donna and Time Rohakes; [ed.] Sophomore, Economics major; [occ.] Student; [hon.] Salutatorian; [pers.] Poetry is the emotions felt in a split second captured on paper. [a.] Salisbury, MD.

PATTERSON, M.D., ROY
[b.] April 26, 1926, Ironwood, MI; [m.] Elaine, August 28, 1948; [ch.] David Roy and Thomas Donald; [ed.] BS/Doctor of Medicine; [occ.] Professor of Medicine, Chief, Division of Allergy Immunology, Northwestern University Med. School; [memb.] American College of Physicians, Royal Society of Medicine, American Association of Physicians, American Academy Allergy-Immunology, American Society Clinic Investigation; [hon.] Alpha Omega Alpha, Master of Allergy, Distinguished Physician Award; [oth. writ.] Editor Allergic Diseases: Diagnosis and Management, 300 Medical Scientific papers; [pers.] Enjoy one's work, friendships, poetry, art, music, children, animals and the great outdoors. [a.] Chicago, IL.

PATTY, BILL
[b.] January 31, 1965, Long Beach, CA; [p.] Del and Dolores Abercrombie and C.L. Patty; [m.] Melanie, October 24, 1987; [ch.] Andrea Renee Patty; [ed.] California State University (Early Childhood Development); [occ.] F/T Family man, P/T instructor Fresno City College; [memb.] National Association for the Education of Young Children; [oth. writ.] First published poem, also write children's stories. [a.] Oakhurst, CA.

PATUZZI III, ALEXANDER C.
[b.] August 11, 1965, Bridgeport, CT; [p.] Marian and Alexander; [ed.] Shelton High School. [a.] Shelton, CT >

PAUL, BENJAMIN
[pen.] Benjamin Paul; [b.] January 24, 1949, Dallas, TX; [p.] Deceased; [m.] Mary Elizabeth, November 3, 1990; [ch.] Ramses Neon, Eboni Shalana; [ed.] Booker T. Washington; [occ.] Unemployed; [hon.] Having received acknowledgement from the National Library of Poetry; [oth. writ.] Til the Soil, Focus, No Such Thing, Side Effect of Woman, Betwist and Between, It's, Rescue and I Needed That, Firer Up, Blending of Two, Being Real and Sometimes; [pers.] The human exposer contains an ocean of expressions which the depth of insight tides through the spirit to the pen upon the paper to be seen, felt an used chronically. [a.] Dallas, TX.

PAUL, REENA DAISY
[b.] May 8, 1978, Chicago; [p.] Dr. Regi and Rita Paul; [ed.] Divine Savior Grammar School, currently a sophomore in Resurrection High School; [occ.] Student; [memb.] Clubs at School (Political Science, Math, Science, Students Against Drunk Driving, Campus Ministry, Drama and Student Ambassador); [hon.] 1989 Motts Apple Awards, NASA Participation in naming award, Meritorious service (AAA Chicago Motor Club 1992), Drama, appeared on World News Tonight 1991; [oth. writ.] Former editor for "School Daze" Literary Magazine, Divine Savior Teen - contributing editor and currently working on a play; [pers.] The opportunity to write is the lifetime of honor and dignity. My two influential benefactors are my two parents. [a.] Chicago, IL.

PAULAUSKAS, GERARD J.
[pen.] J.J. Paul; [b.] March 24, 1958, New Haven, CT; [p.] Deceased; [m.] Myong K., August 3, 1983; [ch.] David and Thomas; [occ.] Postal worker; [oth. writ.] "I See Mountains..." published in The National Library of Poetry's anthology: "Tears of Fire"; [pers.] Life is filled with inspiration. We have but to look around us and care that what we are seeing is meaningful. Especially, of hope. Hope is the source (the life) of dreams. I hope my poems will share and express to others the simple beauty of tomorrow. [a.] Lancaster, CA.

PAULINE

[b.] November 12, 1975, Whittier, CA; [occ.] Student - Whittier College; [hon.] The John Greenleaf Whittier Art Talent Award Scholarship; [oth. writ.] Several other unpublished works; [pers.] In all matters of life and death, trust God through Jesus Christ. [a.] Whittier, CA.

PEACOCK, WANDA E.

[pen.] W. Flowers Peacock; [b.] Fax, FL; [p.] Aaron and Eloise Flowers; [m.] Donald, September 26, 1987; [ch.] Ingrid Dawson, Donald, Cecil and Cynthia Peacock; [ed.] Bethune-Cookman College, Florida State University, UCLA; [occ.] Attorney; [memb.] UNCF, SGI_USA, Philadelphia Writer's Organization, Pennsylvania Bar, Bethune-Cookman College Alumni Association; [hon.] Summa Cum Laude graduate, Who's Who American Colleges and Universities, Outstanding Young Woman; [pers.] My poetry is inspired by my deep concern for and interest in the development of people as true human beings. [a.] Voorhees, NJ.

PEAVY, JENNIFER LYNN

[b.] December 24, 1977, Macon, GA; [p.] Neal and Mary Ann Peavy; [ed.] 9th grade in high school; [occ.] Student; [memb.] First Baptist Church, Jones County High SChool Band, Youth Choir-church; [hon.] Jones County High School Band "Rating Superior" plays clarinet; [oth.w rit.] Poems; [pers.] Loves to write for fun and enjoyment. [a.] Gray, GA.

PECK, JOHN R.

[b.] August 14, 1973, Glenwood Springs, CO; [p.] Lena L. Peck; [ed.] Rifle High, National Training Inc.; [occ.] Yard worker, Summit Lumber. [a.] Rifle, CO.

PEAVER, BEV.

[pen.] Bev Smith; [ch.] Deborah, Robert, Michael; [oth. writ.] Have appeared in "Home City" newspaper used by Birthright Organization published own small collection Christian poems in 1992 used in churches in Northern Ont. CAN.; [pers.] My aim in writing is to present Christian poetry centering around the King James Version of biblical Revelations. I trust people will be conforted and benefited from my choice of words. [a.] Woodstock, Ont. CAN.

PECOY, CYRILLA DIANNE

[pen.] Dianne Reome; [b.] October 24, 1943, Malone, NY; [p.] Cyril and Lucille Charland Reome; [m.] James, September 3, 1983; [ch.] Armand Rivers, Sherry Brunelle, Dean Rivers, Lena LaClair; [ed.] Syracuse Central Technical High School; [memb.] St. Mary Star of the Sea Roman Cahtolic church; [hon.] GRaduated from high school on honor roll; [oth. writ.] Songs entitled "What He Has Done For Me" recorded on album entitled "Praising His Heavenly Light" Sunrise Records, Inc.; [pers.] I have a deep faith and I believe my writing tends to reflect that spiritual connection. I sometimes find myself using my own poems or songs as a means of prayer. [a.] Oswego, NY.

PEDERICK, CHANINE HONOR

[b.] June 29, 1972, England; [p.] Eileen and Nigel Pederick; [ed.] Graduated Mission Secondary, University of the Fraser Valley College; [occ.] Sales clerk; [memb.] Community Policing Access Centre; [oth. writ.] Have completed one novel (as yet unpublished) and currently working on a second novel. Written a children's picture book (unpublished); [pers.] I love the world of romantic fantasy and make-believe, attempting to bring it out in my writing. [a.] Mission, BC., CAN.

PEER, STEVEN K.

[b.] April 15, 1961, Carlisle, PA; [p.] Kenneth and Nancy Peer; [m.] Polly Sue, December 12, 1981; [ch.] Michael Steven, Audrey Lynn; [ed.] The Delbarton School; [occ.] Construction Business Owner; [oth. writ.] As yet unpublished: "WiX", a novel and "Ida's Woods" a children's book and a collection of songs; [pers.] Religion and science walk hand in hand. God is the big bang; God is the expanding universe; God is energy discovery and mystery of man. [a.] Hampshire, IL.

PELLEGRIN, NORMA L.

[pen.] Mrs. "P"; [b.] July 20, 1933, Wasta, SD; [p.] Bill and Blanche Schell; [m.] Warren K., June 21, 1975; [ch.] Cheryl, Kay, Ginger, Rick, Tammy, Sam (13 grandchildren, 3 stepchildren and 3 step grand); [ed.] Black Hills State University; [occ.] Elementary Teacher; [memb.] Phi Delta Kappa, Honor Society BHSU; [hon.] Graduated with honors - magna cum laude; [oth. writ.] Some articles in local newspaper; [pers.] I love children and nature. I hope to write children's books when I retire from teaching. [a.] Enning, SD.

PELLONINI, WANDA E.

[pen.] Wanda E. Pellonini-WEP; [b.] June 12, 1937, Bakersfield, CA; [p.] Joe and Gladys A. Cox; [m.] Bob; [ch.] James, Kathryn and Cheryl; [ed.] East Bakersfield High School; [memb.] Church of Christ; [oth. writ.] Writing since 1969 have a large collection of poetry "Last Closing of the Gate"; [pers.] To be able to touch a heart and be invited in to touch ones soul. [a.] Citrus Heights, CA.

PELTON, LEE

[b.] August 6, 1913, Indiana; [p.] Victoria and Joseph Bakas; [m.] Orville, June 8, 1930; [ch.] Donna Lee, Caron Lou, Lonna Dee; [ed.] Cass Tech High School, Detroit Business College, various night school; [occ.] Retired; [hon.] Graduation with highest honors and athletics; [oth. writ.] Newspaper publishments of some poems; [pers.] Believe in trying anything and everything once and everybody is an interesting person. Interested in finding out what they think and do and why. [a.] Truth or Consequences, NH.

PELTIER, DANIELLEN

[pen.] Shadow; [b.] December 17, 1993, VA; [p.] Wanda and Chris Peltier; [ed.] WI Sampson Jr. Sr. High and Hull High School; [occ.] Student; [memb.] SADD, Drama, Barbizon Modeling School; [pers.] I'd like to thank my parents, Wanda and Chris Peltier for encouraging me to always do my best. And I'd like to say hi to my friends Linda Hood and Michelle Parker. [a.] Hull, MA.

PENNER, VERNON

[b.] May 29, 1949, Morris, MB; [m.] Anne, December 23, 1977; [ch.] Michael Vernon, Rachel Diane; [ed.] Bachelor of Pedagogy and Post Baccalaureate certificate - UofM; [occ.] Teacher; [memb.] Altona Evangelical Mennonite Mission Church, Manitoba Association of School Counselors; [hon.] Competent Toastmasters Award; [oth. writ.] Children's stories, plays, speeches, assorted poetry unpublished; [pers.] Being an independent thinker I find illustrating my thoughts in stories and poems more effective and less abrasive than direct telling. I use my writing in teaching and counseling. [a.] Altona, MB, CAN.

PENNY, SAMUEL

[b.] February 28, 1910, Danbury, CT; [p.] Alfred C. and GRace Taylor Penny; [ed.] Grammar and high school, Columbia University, Night School of Norwalk College; [occ.] Writer; memb.] New FAirfield Historical Society, was VP in Press Reporting Synidcate (probably non-existent now); [hon.] Class poet; [oth. writ.] Scores of feature articles published: biblical, historical and biographical. Also some 14 years - a popular newspaper column on American paintings, also some ghost writings and poetry; [pers.] I am convinced that God knows of all human heartache and exploding world trouble and will cure it not so long from now despite all our myriad doubts and fears, all the bewilderment, all the misery and trouble, the terror, tears and despair, and all the other woe that has ever crept or sprung into human hearts. [a.] New Fairfield, CT.

PEPPEL, KIPP FRANKLIN

[b.] February 28, 1975, Manitoba, CAN; [p.] Horst and Judith Peppel; [ed.] Atascadero High School, California Polytechnic University; [occ.] Student; [hon.] Scholar Athlete (football), National Commended Student, First place District Writing; [oth. writ.] "Storytellers", "Isolation", "A Helping Hand", all published in local newspapers and anthologies; [pers.] My goal in life is to be successful, self-sufficient, and complete in my abilities; artistic yet realistic, strong yet sensitive and true to myself and those I care for. [a.] San Luis Obispo, CA.

PEREIRA, ANNIE MONTEIRO

[pen.] Leila Winters; Emmy Somers; M., Annie Monteiro; [b.] June 10, 1964, Kitchener; [ed.] St. Mary's High School, Lougheed Business College, International Business College (presently), Rudiments at the Carol G. Ditner Piano Studio; [occ.] Coordinator/secretary, writer; [memb.] The Waterloo Regional Arts Council; [hon.] Received honors in Preliminary Rudiments, Royal Conservatory of Music, Nominee for the Waterloo Regional Arts Award; [oth. writ.] Shadows of Hope, self publication of dream poetry; poem entitled "Simultaneous Occuranes" publish in "Wind in the Night Sky" published several times in Hastings, UK; ocassional music and art articles in The Changing Times; [pers.] Shadows of hope is dedicated to those who find snakes charming, as they slither across golden wires, they are mysteriously advanced and masked. The barricade between "M" and XYZ is not longer bewitched. [a.] Kitchener, Ont. CAN.

PEREZ, ARIEL T.

[b.] December 31, 1971, Cuba; [p.] Celia Blanco and Tomas Perez; [ed.] Student at Miami Dade Community College; [hon.] Recently won first prize in a Hispanic Heritage Poetry Contest; [oth. writ.] Poems published in three review magazines (The Cathartic, The Bilingual Review, and AIM Quarterly; [pers.] My poems are pictures of the circle that revolves around my environment. [a.] Miami, FL.

PEREZ, JULIO J.

[pen.] Julio Jose Perez; [b.] March 12, 1918, Comerio, PR; [p.] Jose Maha Perez and Josefa Rivera; [m.] Carmenza E. Rueda de Perez, June 20, 1986; [ch.] Julio J. Jr., Luis R. Perez, and Jose' Angel Perez; [ed.] Comerio High School, Fournier Business College, Henry George School of Social Science; [occ.] Retired; [memb.] CEPI (used to be Writers of Poets International Club); [hon.] Certificate of honor by "Catha" for my poem in Spanish "Creo"; [oth. writ.] Used to be Editor Assistant to "La Lucha" weekly newspaper issued in NYC in Spanish; [pers.] Love to write specially poems. I published a book of poems "Salto, Rio Y Represa De Mis

Amores in Spanish. Will publish another soon hopefully. [a.] NYC, NY.

PERIARD, BRANDI
[b.] January 28, 1979, Gloversville, NY; [p.] Cheryl and Ken Periard, Sr.; [ed.] Ninth grade high school; [memb.] J.V. Cheerleader for basketball and football, chorus; [pers.] My mother and friends inspired me to submit my poems. [a.] Johnstown, NY.

PERRYMAN, TAMMY LYNNE
[b.] February 28, 1965, Washburn, WI; [p.] Sandra Nelson and William Ledin; [m.] Gerald, June 16, 1984; [ch.] Jeremy; [ed.] York High School; [occ.] Homemaker; [memb.] York Writer's Guild; [pers.] Anything is possible with a lot of hard work and determination. [a.] York, NE.

PESANO, JOHN
[b.] February 27, 1940, Ohio; [p.] Veto and Jane Pesano; [ch.] Laura, Anna, Sara; [ed.] Business Central Michigan University; [occ.] Sales Rep-Jostens Yearbook Division; [memb.] Schubert Male Chorus of Grand Rapids; [hon.] Jostens Admirals Club for Career Sales Excellance; [oth. writ.] "Christ in Me - My Hope of Glory", spiritual poems self published. [a.] Grand Rapids, MI.

PETERSEN, JANIECE AVERY
[b.] December 20, 1938, Rockford, IL; [p.] Maye and Arthur Avery; [ed.] Illinois Braille and Sight Saving School, Illinois Wesleyan University, Trinity College; [occ.] Resource teacher of visually impaired; [memb.] National President-Friends of Art, Delta Omacron; [hon.] Phi Kappa Phi, Sigma Alphi Iota, National Service Award; [oth. writ.] Published poem Homankind Magazine - "Hoe Down"; [pers.] Poetry is a special linkage of events and concerns, houghts and questions, insights, messages, memories and searching. It is a focus that demands presence, personance, and openess. I wish it were a constant instead of being interfered with. [a.] Washington, DC.

PETERSON, ARTHUR F.
[b.] April 17, 1899, Brainerd, MN; [p.] Toger and Pauline Peterson; [m.] Muriel Beisswanger Peterson, June 17, 1988; [ch.] Vivian P. Wolter, Calvin Beisswanger; [ed.] Valparaiso University, University of Minnesota; [occ.] Retired; [memb.] American Pharma. Association, American Inst. of the History of Pharmacy, American Medical Association, Midwest Healthcare Marketing Assiication, Founders Club Valparaiso University, Presidents Club Valparaiso University, Norsemans-Forbundet, Yorkfield Presby. Church, DuPage Shrine Club, Scottish Rite, AAONMS, Phi Delta Chi, AAII, A.F. and A.M., Phi Delta Chi, Alumni Achievement award; [oth. writ.] Numerous Pharma Selling and Detailing, Pharmaceutical Engineering 1923 and 1949; What Difference Does It Make, Suggestons for New Objectives in Pharmaceutical Education 1947; [pers.] Where music abound, harmony and love prevail. One's openness to music is as natural as the individual's propensity to sing and dance. [a.] Elmhurst, IL.

PETERSON, MIKE
[pen.] Mike Stitzel; [b.] October 16, 1978, CA; [p.] Rick Peterson, Shawn Russie; [occ.] Cook; [pers.] In poetry, as in life, you have to have a balance of body and soul, of heart and mind, if that balance is not there, you have nothing... [a.] Belgrade, MT.

PETRICK, ROBERT BRUCE
[b.] March 18, 1924, Walla Walla, WA; [p.] Herman B. and Vivian Petrick; [m.] Margaret Horter, November 12, 1945; [ch.] Damma Ann (deceased April 2, 1964); [ed.] College; [occ.] Retired-semi-minister; [hon.] PH in Theology; [oth. writ.] Number of poems never published, not for publication.

PHELPS, FRANCES F.
[pen.] F.F. Phelps; [b.] June 6, 1917, OKLA; [p.] Loren and Mae Fullerton - Carla Lair (deceased); [m.] George R. (deceased), January 12, 1936; [ch.] Esta L. Robinson and Barbara S. Lair; [ed.] California State University; [occ.] Retired; [memb.] Baptist Church, NEA, CTA, Book Club; [hon.] Dean's List, State Honor Society, CTA, NEA, Community Church; [oth. writ.] Many, unpublished poems and short stories; [pers.] My writings concern life in general. They help me bring back the happiness, sadness and regrets of the past, the expectations, hopes and dreams of the future and to enjoy the excitement of today more fully. [a.] Colony, OK.

PHILLIPS, DEBRA
[b.] January 8, 1955, Flint, MI; [p.] George and Naomi Peltonen; [m.] Nicholas, November 25, 1971; [ch.] Rachel, Samantha, Tiffany Phillips; [memb.] World of Poetry; [hon.] Honorable mention, Outstanding Achievement in Poetry, award of merit in poetry, three times golden poet award; [oth. writ.] Flint area newspaper also greeting card verses; [pers.] Through life we gain knowledge, with understanding we find love. [a.] Linden, MI.

PHILLIPS, JR., HUGH
[pen.] Sam; [b.] July 2, 1931, Batesville, AR; [p.] Hugh and Hattie Hudson Phillips; [ch.] Twins-Stephen and Susan, and twins-David and Debora, Jonathan; [ed.] Newport High School, University of North Dakota, Aviation Cadel Class 55-D Commissioned Wings; [occ.] Retired USAF major-command pilot; [memb.] Iliad Press The National Author's Registry, American Press, The National Library of Poetry, The American Poetry Society, The Amherst Society, American Poetry Forum, Sparrowgrass Poetry Forum; [hon.] "Golden Dreams" published in Anthology "Celebrations" Spring 1993-honorable mention, Chapbook, "Sundlending", May 1993 Award of Merit, Chapbook, "Wings of the Wind" Aug. 1993-honorable mention, "The Unwanted" Summer 1993-honorable mention, Mar. 1993 Poet's Certificate of Merit, "Strife" published in Anthology "Poetry in Motion" summer 1993, "Life" published in Anthology "A Break in the Clouds" Summer 1993, Charter member 1993, "Decision" March 1993, Poet of Merit, third place-"Lack", "The King", "Worth", "Truth or Consequences", all published in the Anthology "Poetic Visions"; "Peace", summer 1993 published in the Anthology, "American Poetry Annual", certificate of Poetic Achievement; "Thunder Without Rain" Certificate of Poetic Achievement; "Reason" July 1993, "A Good Life", "Onward" June 1993, "The Queen" August 1993; "Today" Fall 1993, published Anthology, "Poetic Voices of America" Fall 1993; [pers.] Enjoy reading the classics, playing the guitar, writing music and poetry and gourmet cooking. I attribute the pleasure I realize from poetic expression to all experiences throughout life. Achievements, failures, losses and the emotions gained from these, serve the inspiration of every thought. I strive to lend the essence each theme deserves. I do not seek poetic expression; it seeks me thankfully. [a.] Denver, CO.

PHILLIPS, RODNEY V.
[b.] September 24, 1912, Woodsboro, TX; [p.] John Isaac and Mattie Phillips; [m.] Edna Huff Phillips (deceased), May 29, 1936; [ch.] Ronald Edward Phillips and Alverne Lowe; [ed.] New Mexico Norma University, Eastern N.M. University, University of New Mexico; [occ.] Accountant (self-employed and semi-retired); [memb.] National Society of Accountants (former), Golden Society of New Mexico Highlands University; [pers.] A poem should paint a picture not with a brush but with words. [a.] Albuquerque, NM.

PHILLIPS, SHIRLEY ANN (TAYLOR)
[b.] December 9, 1943, Los Angeles, CA; [p.] Clarence and Lottie Taylor; [m.] David E., June 19, 1963; [ch.] Paul Thomas, Scott Earl, David Earl, Gena Ann; [ed.] Orestimba High; [occ.] Housewife; [pers.] I think it is wonderful to be able to leave a small piece of my mind that just may touch the heart of a child in years to come. [a.] Sioux Falls, SD.

PHINNEY, LINOA JOICE
[b.] November 7, 1952, Chicago; [p.] William and Alice Frisch; [m.] Maurice Phinney (deceased), March 9, 1979; [ch.] Bill, David, Brian; [ed.] Mozart Elementary, Kelvyn Park High School; [occ.] Domestic Engergie; [memb.] A.P.M.A., L.S.C. - A.P.C.C.- Education Task Force Youth Crime Committee, North River Comm. Church; [oth. writ.] Currently trying to write my first novel about life and people in the inner city; [pers.] I write about what I see in life some of it beautiful some not. But we must see all of a rose to appreciate it even the thorns. [a.] Chicago, IL.

PIERCE, DAVE
[b.] August 2, 1960, Urbana, IL; [p.] Dave and Rita Pierce; [m.] Judy, September 1, 1984; [ch.] Lillian Marie Pierce; [ed.] Ft. Lewis College, Colorado Outward Bound School; [occ.] Owner/operator of Morning Glory Earthcrafts; [oth. writ.] A book of poems, Sun Sits on Cloud/Is The Poem/Of An Egg, is joined in my canon by two novels, some short stories, and several essays. After a stint as columnist for a local Colorado newspaper, I became editor for the Green Lantern, newsletter of the Austin, TX Greens; [pers.] The works of life-artists such as Parmenides, Tolstoy, and Louis Armstrong have taught me to seek the spark of awareness that exists in each of us, and to fan it. [a.] Silverthorne, CO.

PIERCE, KRISTOPHER
[b.] January 21, 1977, Munice, IN; [p.] Michael and Karen Pierce; [ed.] Brandon High School, Hillsborough Community College; [occ.] Student; [memb.] National Honor Society, Sabers Honor Club (JROTC), Veterans of Foreign Wars Award; [hon.] Best Drill Cadet, Sobresaliente Spanish Declamation; [oth. writ.] One poem published in the "Anthology of Youn American Poets" selected poems and a short story published in a high school literary magazine; [pers.] The end only comes when you give up! [a.] Brandon, FL.

PIGNATARO, DANIELLE
[b.] February 12, 1979, Brooklyn, NY; [p.] Sal and Joann Pignataro; [ed.] Bishop Kearney High School; [occ.] Student; [pers.] Thanks R.S., R.D., E.Y., and of course Ed O.A.R. [a.] Brooklyn, NY.

PILARSKI, BARBARA JAY
[b.] January 24, 1975, Tonawanda, NY; [p.] Barbara E. Karas and Robert J. Pilarski; [pers.] Always listen if you want to be heard. Respect how people feel because no

one feels the same way. When we feel pain or sorrow another may feel it then times worse. [a.] Knightdale, NC.

PILLAR, JAMES
[b.] July 29, 1959, Davenport, IA; [p.] James and Dolly Pillar; [ch.] Damenica Ronesha, Ceneca Ramele; [ed.] Central High; [occ.] Nuclear Electrician; [oth. writ.] Several poems written but never attempted to have published; [pers.] Thru my writings, I hope to heighten the awareness of truth. That alot of our earthly problems are the results of a society that turned its back on God. [a.] Rock Island, IL.

PILLOT, MARY
[b.] January 22, 1944, San Antonio, TX; [p.] Lee and Ilse Eickenroht; [m.] Divorced; [ch.] John Christopher and Christiana Pillot; [ed.] BFA with honros, University of Texas at Austin; [occ.] Unemployed/artist paintings and drawings; [memb.] American Council for the Arts now organization; [hon.] Ford Foundation Scholarship; [oth. writ.] Articles written fore the Austin Business Journal while working as Managing Editor; [pers.] I'm inspired by the romantic poets - and through the human spirit effecting the ideas of my work through everyday living in a diverse multicultural environment of people and our lifelong struggles. [a.] Santa Monica, CA.

PINA, CANDIDA LOMBA
[pen.] Candy; [occ.] Working in The University of P.R. Mayaguez Campus; [oth. writ.] Book entitled "Beauty In and Out" published soon; [pers.] Since my love for life is very high, it reflects in my writings all beauty and true feelings of mankind.

PINES, SARAH
[pen.] Sara Pines; [b.] November 8, 1942, Alabama; [p.] Jannie and Cossie Pines; [ed.] High school, Medgar Evers College; [occ.] Student; [hon.] Perform plays and skirts at church and job; [oth. writ.] Collection of poems and plays; [pers.] I plan on writing a book of poems. I am presently working with the youth at my chuirch teaching them how to act and speak. [a.] West NJ, NJ.

PINTO, ROSALIND
[b.] NYC; [p.] Deceased; [m.] Deceased; [ch.] Francine, Gerald, Evelyn; [ed.] Hunter College, High School, Columbia University; [occ.] Substitute teacher; [memb.] Hunter and Columbia Alumni Association, Queens and Central Queens Hist. Association, UFT, NAFE, Municipal ARt Society, Community Bd. G. Beautification Committee; [hon.] Cum Laude, Alpha Chi Alpha, Who's Who in the East, Who's Who in Education, Who's Who in World of Poetry, Municipal Art Society - "Design 2000", honorable mention - International Society of Poetry-Poet of Merit 1993, Editor's Choice Award-National Library of Poetry; [oth. writ.] Chapter in "Competency Press" poems published in anthologies, lesson plans published; [pers.] I celebrate the wonderful people I know and the love I feel for all people, places and things in my poetry. [a.] New York, NY.

PIPER, ROBERT
[pen.] Robert Kent; [b.] June 24, 1940, Los Angeles, CA; [p.] Virginia Haynie; [m.] Karole, July 16, 1983; [ch.] Elizabeth and Virginia Piper and Petrice Emmons; [ed.] John Adams High School; [occ.] Insurance Agent; [memb.] American Philatelic Society, United Staes Naval Institute, Monticello Foundation, Civil Liberties Union; [hon.] Many awards as a public speaker and those associated with my insurance career; [oth. writ.] Per-

sonal journals and articles for insurance industry publication; [pers.] My spiritual philosophy is that the evolution of mankind is directly related to its intellectual ability as it is influenced by its spiritual qualities. I am greatly influenced by historical figures, especially Thomas Jefferson. [a.] Boulder City, NV.

PITNER, JEANIE M.
[b.] June 15, 1962, John Day, OR; [m.] Don, November 14, 1986; [ch.] Leo, Dorian, and Meggan; [occ.] Secretary for own small business and hone school teacher; [oth. writ.] Misc.; [pers.] Trust in Jesus. [a.] Battle Ground, WA.

PLANTE, MARIE
[b.] August 23, 1959, Victoria, BC; [p.] Mary and Leo Cross; [m.] Divorced, August 17, 1979; [ch.] Shannon Marie, Paul Austin, Michael Andrew, Cahterine Victoria; [ed.] Edward Milne Senior Secondary, Camosun College; [occ.] Homemaker; [memb.] Independent Order of Foresters; [pers.] To take someone's hand without really being there, to share that special place, to find some warmth in reality and cover it with grace. [a.] Victoria, BC.

PLEKES, FELICIA A.
[b.] October 27, 1976, Ludington, MI; [p.] Walter and Laura Plekes; [ed.] Ludington High School; [occ.] Student; [memmb.] National Honor Society, church choir, varisty club, American Red Cross Volunteer and Tae Kwon Do; [pers.] Uable to repay the awesome gift given to me by my spiritual family. I try to at least honor my father, the Lord and my brother, the Christ, with every aspect of my life. [a.] Ludington, MI.

PLESH, JOHN
[b.] October 11, 1956, Romania; [p.] Florea and Florica Plesh; [m.] Maryana, June 25, 1987; [ed.] Film Institute (Romania); [occ.] Photographer; [memb.] National Geographic Natural History, American Heart Association, American Family Publishers, Exquisity Corpse; [hon.] In film, only. I never sent my poems to any competition, only to be publish; [oth. writ.] October 27, 1979 Romania in "Luceafarul" with a collection of 9 poems - Bucharest Nov. 1980 "Horizon" 4 poems - Timisoara, 1981 "Almanahul Literar" Romania; [pers.] I wish you to do a complete resurrection of poetry with "Dance on the Horizon". [a.] Glendale, CA.

POBRE, JOY
[b.] March 2, 1973, Manila, Php; [p.] Leroy and Greta Pobre, (siblings-Charmaine Gay, Lionel Clark, and Jessica Anne); [ed.] Second year Queen's University, St. John's High School; [pers.] I pray for acceptance, tolerance, patience, understanding, and peace. Above all, I pray for time so that poeple could practice all these. [a.] kingston, Ont. CAN.

POGARSKY, SOLOMON
[pen.] Solomon Pogarsky; [b.] New York City; [p.] DAvid and Sarah; [m.] Sarah; [ch.] Betty Anne, Edward; [ed.] Seward Park High School, City College of New York, New York University; [occ.] High school English teacher; [memb.] U.F.T., Kappa Delta Pi; [hon.] Two medals New York City Marathons, certificate for being a CPR Instructor from the Red Cross; Editor Kappa Delta Pi Newsletter and Greenwich House Music School Quartertomes. Won second prize in Writers Digest contest; poems, short stories and articles in Green's Magazine, Our Pen, Twisted Midstream, Bronxville Villager, Jewish Currents, Seward Park Almanac; [oth.

writ.] A collection of short stories published by Clover Press of Regina entitled The Little Smul and Other Stories; [pers.] I believe teaching and farming are the noblest professions even though I have a passion for writing, playing the piano and singing, especially in operas. 1992 sung Rudolfo in La Bomeme and in 1993 role of Box in "Cox and Box" by Arthur Sullivan. Acted in wedding scene of Prizzi's Honor directed by John Nuston and vis-vis Mia Farrow in Radio Days directed by Woody Allen. Have three cats: Minkie, Brandy and Josehine, singing buddy Beepo the finch and a lady box turtle named Farfie. [a.] New York, NY.

POINDEXTER, FRANCINE
[pen.] The Survivor; [b.] February 13, 1962, Chicago, IL; [p.] Ruth Poindexter and Eirtis Adams; [ed.] Thornridge High, Prairie State College; [occ.] Student-normally secretary; [oth. writ.] Several poems attempted to have published; [pers.] My poems are a part of me. I've only been writing for one year. I have a great need to put these feelings on paper as poetry. Hoping my poems will touch someone with similar feelings and inspire them. Let them know they're not alone. [a.] Chicago Heights, IL.

POIRIER, JOYCE A.
[pen.] NYM KIM; [b.] October 9, 1938, Peabody, MA; [p.] Joseph E. and Florence E. (Langan) Poirier (both deceased); [ed.] Salem, MA High, College of St. Elizabeth, Fairfield University; [occ.] High School English Teacher; [memb.] National Council of Teachers of English, MA Council Teachers of English, National Education Association, MA Education Association, Beverly TEachers Association, The International Society of Poetry; [hon.] The Ledger Person of the Year, 1991, nominee-MA Teacher of the Year 1991, Who's Who Among American Teachers 1992; [oth. writ.] Published "Last Respects" in National Library of Poetry, Wind In The Night Sky, two copyrighted collectioins of poetry, Revelations One, and Christalized (80 poems) another 65 poems not yet copyrighted and several works in process, published "Fledgling" in National Library of Poetry, The Coming og Dawn; "Retreat" in Outstanding Poets of 1994, "Suspended Animation" in Outstanding Poets of America and Britain; [pers.] As a young child, I collected "words", their power lured me to manipulate them, however not until 2 1/2 years ago, when Chris Bravo inspired me, did I plumb my depths and realize the hidden treasures of my poetry there. The volume Christalized is dedicated to her, as I may never have found my gift without her. [a.] Danvers, MA.

POITEVIN, EVELYN M.
[b.] January 13, 1917, Fertilem IA; [p.] Oscar and Hilda Rholl; [m.] Paul B., December 23, 1962; [ch.] Jacquelyn Ann Dillon and Don D. Finer; [ed.] Mason City IA High School, Golden West College and Chapman College; [occ.] Retired; [memb.] Crystal Cathedral Church; [hon.] First in the state of Iowa to pass shorthand test of 120 wpm for five minutes and transcribe perfectly; [oth. writ.] Poems published in the local Mason City paper and church papers. Have written poems for numerous funerals, weddings, parties and friends; [pers.] My poetry reflects the wonderful love of God and the secure peace of Christian living. [a.] Santa Ana, CA.

POLINY, VALIANT R.W. DR.
[b.] June 2, 1952, Perth Amboy, NJ; [p.] Andrew R. and Julia T. Poliny; [ed.] Rider College, College of William and Mary, Valparaiso University School of Law, University of Illinois; [memb.] American Planning Associa-

tion, American Political Science Association, American Public Works Association, American Society of Quality Control, American Society of Notaries, American Statistical Association, The Federalist Society, Operations Research Society of America; [hon.] Elected Who's Who Worldwide" 1993, "Charter Member" 1992 to "Pi Alpha Alpha", The Naitonal Honor Society for the Field of Public Affairs and Public Administration, elected "Pi Sigma Alpha", The National Political Science Honor Society 1989, "Who's Whop Among Students in American Universities and Colleges" 1987-88, "Phi Kappa Phi" National Honor Society 1987, Author "Honor Paper" in Jurisprudence for 1979-80 at The Valparaiso University School of Law, "Omicron Delta Epsilon" The International Collegiate Honor Society in Economics 1978, Ohi Alpha Delta" The International Professional Legal Fraternity 1977; [oth. writ.] A Public Policy Analysis of the Emerging Victims Rights Movement (1977 and 1994); [pers.] God bless the United States of America. [a.] Chicago, IL.

PONGAN, MARISA

[b.] Sydney, Australia; [occ.] Higher education at Macquarie University; [memb.] Italian Institute of Culture, Beecroft Lapidary Club, Rockdale Opera Company, "Christmas at the Opera Hourse" Choir; [oth. writ.] Several poems published in the "Sydney Mornign Herald", several reports and travel articles published in the "Macquarie University Newsletter"; [pers.] My writing, including children's poetry, reflects the beauty of nature. I strive to capture and explore this through strong imagery and muse inspired metaphors. [a.] Sydney, AUST., NSW.

POOLE, DIANNE

[b.] June 26, 1943, Toronto, CAN; [m.] Harold D., September 28, 1968; [ch.] Barrie and Bradley Poole; [occ.] Activation Assistant in Gerontology; [memb.] The Ladies Auxiliary; [hon.] Volunteer of The Year for 1992 Editor's Choice Award, Award of Merit, Accomplishment Award in Poetry, "Charter Lifetime" member of The International Society of Poets, appointed ISP Lifetime Member Advisory Panel; [oth. writ.] Newspaper article, poetry for special occasions, wrote song for retirement and poetry publihsed in local newspaper; [pers.] I strive to reflect the deepness within my heart when writing poetry. [a.] Orillia, Ont., CAN.

PORTELANCE, JEFFREY HARVEY

[b.] April 23, 1969, Timmins; [p.] Wallace and Joanne Portelance; [ch.] Meaghan Amanda and Arielle Portelance; [ed.] Northern College, Ambassador Bible College, Native Northern College; [occ.] Student, author and poet; [memb.] Revelation Generation Guild of Prophecy Students (founder), Timmins Youth Encounter, The Tree Christian Literature Foundation, member of the Living Body of Jesus Christ; [hon.] Ambassador Bible College diploma, Cursillo Award, Omega Letter Prophecy Bachelor Certificate, Youth Encounter Certificate; [oth. writ.] Author of "Revelation Generation" The Great Apostasy Revealed" currently unpublished, Author of "The Poetic Works of A Survivor", Second Coming Magazine; [pers.] Just pay attention and look around you, Jesus is coming very soon!! "And when you see these things begin to come to pass, then look up, and lift up your heads, for your redemption draweth nigh! (Luke 21:28) "Come Jesus Come! [a.] Timmins, ONT., CAN.

PORTER, LARRY

[b.] September 12, 1963, Logan, W.VA; [p.] Arthur and Gladys Porter; [m.] Fiance' Lori Raper; [ed.] West Tech High, P.T.C.; [occ.] Factory worker (Alabama Limestone); [pers.] Always be honest even the best liar can't fool himself. [a.] Spruce Pine, AL.

PORTER, THOMAS K.

[b.] February 16, 1957, Chicago, IL; [p.] Keith and Nadine Porter; [m.] Ann, Aoril 13, 1991; [ed.] Hinsdale Central High, Northern Illinois University, Kishwaukee College; [occ.] Seismic Data Processor; [pers.] I love to write, but find it very difficult to share my words with others. Most of what I write is for my eyes only, with the included poem being one of rare exception. [a.] Houston, TX.

PORTER, WANDA LEE

[pen.] Wanda Lee; [b.] April 15, 1952, Baltimore, MD; [p.] David R. and June Yung, Sr.; [ch.] Harry and Erik; [ed.] Christiana High; [occ.] Taxi Driver; [oth. writ.] Angels in the Trees (Georgetown Press); [pers.] My life's interest is in promoting the brotherhood of all men in demonstration of the scripture "love one another". [a.] Newark, DE.

POTTER, MARY

[b.] March 29, 1979, Saranac Lake, NY; [p.] David and Sharon Potter; [pers.] Poetry closes the door to reality and lets me live in a word of my own. [a.] Middlebury Ctr., PA.

POWELL, CAROLYN BARRETT

[b.] April 27, 1938, Paris, TX; [p.] Mr. and Mrs. A.L. Barrett; [m.] Dr. James E., July 15, 1961; [ed.] Texas Christian University; [occ.] Professional Artist; [memb.] National League of American Pen Women, AAA Sorority Alumni Association, League of Women Vet. (no longer member); [hon.] Various art awards, effervescent, scintillating; [oth. writ.] The poem "REbirth" came from a group of poems called "Reflections in the Loganitas"; [pers.] Check brochure please. [a.] Albuquerque, NM.

POWELL, EILEEN

[p.] Eileen, Spirit Walker; [b.] January 24, 1941, Jamaica, NY; [p.] Cecelia and Tyril Wilkinson; [m.] Felix L. (deceased), June 1958; [ch.] Felix Leon Henry, Gregory Jerome, Careton Tyril, Vincent Rodney, Joseph Edward Powell, King; (godchildren-Julie, Daryl, Dorothy); [ed.] Bayside High School, NY School of Practical Nursing MMATC, Drake Business School, Manhattan Bible Institute; [occ.] Retired; [memb.] Cambridge Elites, Brooklyn Tabernacle Choir, Christian Life Center Church, Committee for David N. Dinkins, Born Again Christian, member of Body of Christ; [hon.] Drake Business School, NY School of Practical Nursing, Manhatta Institute, Watchers Certificate for Committee for David N. Dinkins, Track Team-Bayside HS, community boards, featured in two different newspaper advertisements; [oth. writ.] Three books in the process of submitting: 1) Enter Loves Forbidden Paradise, 2) Lotteries Children, 3) Spirit Walker also one song and several poems published in church publications; [pers.] I strive to put a smile on every frowning face, and introduce hope and love to take its place. To write not about the cause, but the solution. I'm thankful for God's Word, God's people, God's poets. [a.] Brooklyn, NY.

POWELL, LARRY

[pen.] L.P.; [b.] July 27, 1958, Lyon, France; [p.] George and Thelma Jean Powell; [m.] Fiancee: Jeannette Marie Phillips, April 5, 1995; [ch.] Justin Dean, George Nicholas, Ryan Allen Phillips, Brooker Marie Phillips; [ed.] Fulton Co. High, College of Great Falls; [occ.] US Airforce Security Policeman; [hon.] Numerous service awards; [oth. writ.] Dozens of poems written since first newspaper publication at age 10.; [pers.] My mission in writing as well as in life, is to evoke brotherhood and human kindness through and by my understandings of the teachings of my Lord and Savior, Jesus Christ. [a.] Great Falls, MT.

POWER, BRETT J.

[b.] February 5, 1972, Newcastle, NB; [ed.] High school, graduated Academic College; [hon.] Acieved bronze, silver and gold levels of the Duke of Edinburgh award, dean's list; [oth. writ.] A number of unpublished and unseen poems. [a.] Newxcastle, NB.

PREDAN, LAURA

[pen.] Laura Predan; [b.] February 5, 1967, Quesnel, BC; [ed.] Quesnel Senior Secondary, CCompuCollege; [occ.] Part-time Retail Salesperson/part-time model; [hon.] Fashion Design and Merchandising Diploma and awards; [oth. writ.] Several poems and songs in my personal journal; [pers.] My poems are very spontanious. If I feel emotional about something, my pen just flows and the outcome is true and from my heart. [a.] New Westminster, BC.

PRENTICE, AYESHA

[b.] May 30, 1981, Bay City, TX; [p.] Holwyn and Kathleen Prentice; [ed.] Pumphrey Elementary, George H. Gentry Jr. High School.

PRENTICE, DONNA LYNN

[pen.] D.L. Candield; [b.] October 2, 1947, Pittsburgh, PA; [p.] Betty C. Prentice; [ed.] Cheyenne Mountain High School, Pikes Peak Community College, Life; [occ.] Cook; [memb.] Alcoholics Anonymous; [hon.] Semi-finalist 1993 North American DPW Poetry Contest; [oth. writ.] Poetry, Philosophy, Spiritual Inspirations, currently working on a fantasy book for children who have lived within a dysfunctional family; [pers.] The consummate joy that courses through my being, when I am able to express within a finite form that which infinitely impassions my soul...resists that very attempt at expression. [a.] Grand Canyon, AZ.

PREST, JAMES

[b.] June 29, 1941, Providence, RI; [p.] James and Elizabeth Teehan; [ed.] U. of St. Thomas; [occ.] Univ. Professor; [memb.] American Cultural Association, Catholic Historical Society; [oth. writ.] History Text, articles on American History. [a.] Warwick, RI.

PRESIUSO, JOHN F.

[p.] Pascal and Roberta Preziuso; [m.] Susan, September 11, 1980; [ch.] Elizabeth, John Jr., and Vincent; [occ.] Pizzeria; [pers.] I love write poetry and hope someday to get my work published. [a.] Buffalo, NY.

PRICE, DULCENIA

[b.] August 16, 1959, Chicago, IL; [p.] John and Ursella Sales; [m.] Divorced; [ch.] Darnell J. Price; [ed.] James Wadsworth, Hyde Park Career Academy; [occ.] City of Chicago Traffic Control Aide; [oth. writ.] Several poems written in my spare time, never publish; [pers.] Poetry is an expression of how one feels, when spring turns into summer and summer turns into autumn and autumn turns into winter such rare beauty. [a.] Chicago, IL.

PRICE, REV. RAYMOND JOHN
[b.] July 26, 1941, Toronto, Ont.; [p.] John and Christine Price; [m.] Mildred Ann, May 31, 1975; [cch.] Leslie and Christina; [ed.] Ministry of Education of Ontario Secondary Graduation diploma; [occ.] Minister; [memb.] Loyal Order of Moose Lodge, World Christianship Ministries; [hon.] Secondary school graduation; [pers.] When writing poems I try to bring out the themes from my heart. [a.] Hamilton, Ont. CAN.

PRIEMER, RICKY
[b.] November 28, 1978, Flint, MI; [p.] Richard and Louise Priemer; [ed.] Currently 9th grade high school; [hon.] 1992-93 certificates of achievement for: Outstanding work in Math, Outstanding Effort and Excellent Attitudes in Physical Education; Michigan Education Assessment Program Sciences Test, Computers, honor roll; [pers.] Favorite color: any color ice cream comes in.

PRIESTLEY, ERIC
[pen.] ERic Priestley; [b.] Dece,ber 16, 1943, Los Angeles, CA; [p.] Edward G. Priestley and Jeannette Rachal (both deceased); [m.] Deceased; [ch.] One; [ed.] CSULA, Universty of Gahana, Univ. of Hawaii Manoa; [occ.] Teach literature at UCSD; [memb.] WAtts Writers Workshop, Free Mason; [hon.] Academy of American Poets, Ray Bradbury Literature Award, Culture of Arts for Poetry, Lannon Foundation Flight Great; [oth. writ.] Walking Thunder- Book of Poems 1994, Raw Dog-Novel 1985, Trouble Watch-novel 1990, We Speak As Liberators 1970, What We Must See-Young Black Storytellers; [pers.] The only thing we have any real control over is our own free will. Without love and freedom the quality of life diminishes expo - mentally. [a.] Los Angeles, CA.

PULVER, JOHN R.
[b.] November 2, 1955, Kokomo, IN; [p.] Ada Hensler and Edward Pulver; [ch.] Joel, Stacy, Tommy Pulver; [ed.] Haworth High; [occ.] Fashions Manager K-Mart; [pers.] I hope to bring an understanding to all whom read my work, and let them feel the way I understand the beauty of poetry. [a.] Flat Rock, MI.

PUNYKO, B.W.
[b.] July 13, 1954, Connersville, IN; [p.] Wesley Wells & Jean Wells-Harn; [m.] Michael S., May 29, 1989; [ch.] Michael Brandon; [ed.] Business Administration, AA Social Services and EMTT Trauma Unit Rescue; [occ.] Manager and Social Services Director; [memb.] Hospice, United Way, and "Day of Caring" for the homeless; [hon.] Award of Vision, United Way; [oth. writ.] Family and personal expressions and a monthyl newsletter; [pers.] Children and the elderly have eyes that see into your soul! They are my inspiration. One the eyes of discovery and amazement. The other of wisdom and journeys past. Both make me painfully aware of how fragile life can be. [a.] Dayton, OH.

PURSER, KIM
[b.] October 24, 1970, Jackson, MS; [p.] Rita and Gene Purser; [ed.] Rankin Academy, MS College; [occ.] Graduate assistant at MS College, part-time Sales Associate. [a.] Star, MS.

PUTMAN, RICHARD
[b.] May 16, 1944; [m.] Maybelle Fenwick, May 5, 1973; [ed.] Broadalbin High School, Fulton-Mont. Community College, Navy Electronics School, Navy Flight-Simulator School; [memb.] Jehovah's Witness (23 years); [hon.] Associate of Applied Science degree, Theocratic Ministry School, Kingdon Ministry School; [oth. writ.] Research paper on subject of prime numbers - speeches on public speaking, Bible research and human relationships; [pers.] A wonderful future lies ahead for mankind and the earth but the problems mankind face today are greater than their ability to solve. [a.] Vinton, VA.

PUURULA, TAMARA MARI
[b.] Thunder Bay, Ont. CAN; [ed.] Finishing last year high school, hoping to go to college; [oth. writ.] Numerous unpublished; [pers.] The reason I wrote this poem is because it breaks my heart to know that my human race is destroying the world - stopping this destruction and starting to clean up seems so overwhelming. [a.] Thunder Bay, Ont. CAN.

QUADRINI, RITA
[b.] October 27, 1955, Lazio, Italy; [p.] Antonio, Erminia Colucci; [m.] Robert, July 24, 1976; [ch.] Sonia, Anthony; [ed.] Grade 13 diploma; [occ.] Homemaker, banker; [oth. writ.] Poems: Summer's End, A Lonely Walk, Children's Laughter and Play, September, My Best Friend, Just Another Day, The Gift of Life, People Come and People Go, Time, If, A Promise, Mystery, Lonliness, Struggle To Survive, Christmas Past, A Garden of Memories, two short stories (not published); [pers.] When wishing upon a dream, search deep within your soul and be certain; that this dream is most desired for...dreams do come true! [a.] Woodbridge, Ont. CAN.

QUINABO, EDWIN
[b.] April 4, 1970, Honolulu; [p.] Mr. and Mrs. Leopoldo and Remy Quinabo; [ed.] University of Hawaii; [hon.] Graduated from the University of Hawaii with Distinction, Dean's List, awarded membership to Golden Key, National Honor Society, Phi Kappa Phi Honor Society, Phi Beta Kappa Honor Society; [pers.] Orange grass sways under the green sun's reflection – the fields scream Fertile. [a.] Honolulu, HI.

QUINN, LAUREN
[b.] November 27, 1982, Milwaukee, WI; [p.] Pamela Marquardt and Howard Quinn; [ed.] Cleveland Elementary School; [hon.] OEA Award Oakland Education Association 1991, Live Oak Swim Team Outstanding Swimmer 1993; [oth. writ.] Write stories in spare time; [pers.] When I look into a mirror, I see not myself, but my hopes and dreams. [a.] Oakland, CA.

QUINN, MARY THERESE
[b.] January 30, 1957, Neenah, WI; [p.] Don and Betty Quinn; [m.] Fiance: Dan Vara; [ed.] Neil Armstrong High School, New Hampshire College; [occ.] Data Processor for US Navy; [memb.] Adopt- a school program for Washington Cty; [hon.] Delta Mu Delta, Honorary Mention by being the #1 student in class for Data Processing 1984; [pers.] My emotional drive keeps me alive. KISS (Keep It Safe and Sober). To never think less of myself but to think of myslef less. My poetry reflects my relationships with God, mankind and myself. [a.] East Machias, ME.

QUIRION, MARJORIE (FLETCHER)
[pen.] Marjorie Fletcher; [b.] January 12, Skowhegan; [p.] Forrest and Lillian Fletcher; [m.] Joseph G.L.; [ch.] Four; [ed.] Skowhegan High School, Kents Hill Jr. College and Prep, U oif M (Farmington, ME); [occ.] Writing at home; [memb.] American Legion, Foster's Writing Class; [oth. writ.] Boys and Girls: Junior Life: Scripture Press the Counselor.

QURESHI, KASHMALA
[b.] February 15, 1982, Calgary, Alberta, CAN; [p.] Majeed and Aisha Qureshi; [ed.] Hugh Sutherland School; [occ.] Student; [hon.] Honor student, received Ribbon of Excellence; [ith. writ.] Art work, children stories and poems published in Calgary Herald Newspaper; [pers.] Influenced greatly by living with my grandparents who come from a religious and rural background of N.W.F.P. Pakistan. [a.] Calgary, Alberta, CAN.

RABINOWITZ, MICHAEL
[pen.] Michael Rabinowitz; [b.] June 8, 1959, Manhattan, NY; [p.] Mia and Joseph Rabinowitz; [m.] Jackie, July 15, 1989; [ch.] Danielle Rabinowitz; [ed.] Smithtown High School, Suffolk Community College, Hofstra University; [occ.] Securities Trading; [memb.] Crohn's and Colitis Foundation of America; [oth. writ.] Several poems, but never published; [pers.] Appreciate all the moments of your life. [a.] Old Bethpage, NY.

RADEBAUGH, MILDRED M.
[ch.] Three daughters; [occ.] Former kindergarten teacher, currently an editorial assistant for professional educational journal "Thresholds In Education"; [pers.] Loves to travel and write portey. [a.] DeKalb, IL.

RADLEY, RICKY
[b.] February 2, 1974, Port Arthur; [p.] Ricky and Kathy Radley; Will and Judy Kennard; [ed.] Nederland High School, Texas A&M University; [occ.] Student; [hon.] Sixth grade Science award; [pers.] Angry rebel looking for love. [a.] Nederland, TX.

RAM, CH. RAJA
[b.] April 21, 1978, Hyderabad; [p.] Ch. Narayana and V. Rajeshwari; [ed.] Mani Jermaiah High School, IXth Standard of Raja Jitender Public School (Hyderabad, Andhra Pradesh, India); [oth. writ.] Poems, essays in English and in other language (Telugu). An artist, in my view painting is also a better way of expressing my thoughts; [pers.] I wish to create an awareness in people about suffering, poverty and plight of the poor through my writings. I strive to make my poems more elegant. [a.] Hyderbad, A.P.

RAMBO, PEGGY
[m.] William Anderson, Artist; [ch.] Three sons and three grandchildren; [ed.] University of Georgia and University of Virginia; [occ.] Deputy Court Clerk; [oth. writ.] 20th Century Greatest Poems, American Muse, Lyrical Fiesta, many newspaper articles, short stories. Currently working on a collection just for children; [pers.] In writing what I personally feel I hope I have touched the spirit of the reader in such a way he or she can soar to the highest and know that I have done my best and the message has been properly conveyed. [a.] Atlanta, GA.

RAMIREZ, HELEN
[pen.] Claire; [b.] January 20, 1955, Grand Canyon; [p.] Mrs. Eloise Seyomour and Mr. Edwin Ramirez; [ed.] International College of the Cayman Islands; [occ.] Government-Purchasing Officer; [memb.] Credit Unit of the Cayman Islands; [pers.] this poem was written to illustrate the dedication and love I have for America, the land of the free. [a.] Grand Cayman, British West Indies.

RAMOS, ISABEL
[b.] November 5, 1928, Puerto Rico; [p.] Serafin Ramos and Honorina Osorio; [ch.] Marlene Cintron, Ariel Cintron and Obed Cintron; [ed.] New York University, Hunter College of New York, Florida International University; [occ.] Elementary school teacher; [memb.] United Federation of Teachers, UTD (United Teachers of Dade), and Association for Supervision and Curriculum Development; [hon.] NYU Honorific Mention for academic achievement and Hunter College Dean's List; [oth. writ.] A short story titled New Horizons will soon be published as part of an anthology of works by hispanic women writers; [pers.] In God I find peace and stability, learning and singing give me joy, and teaching has provided me the sense of fulfillment. [a.] Miami, FL.

RAMOS, NICOLE
[pen.] Nikki; [b.] June 8, 1979, New York City; [p.] Albert and Shirley Ramos; [ed.] Freshman high school; [occ.] Student.

RAMSARAN, DHANRAJ
[b.] May 10, 1971, New York; [p.] Danny and Rafaela Ramsaran; [ed.] Brentwood High School, Baruch College; [occ.] Internal Auditor-Dime Savings Bank; [memb.] Beta Alpha Psi, Accounting Society, AD Society; [hon.] Dean's List, Provost Scholarship, Cumme Laude; [pers.] August Tears was written in memory of my grandfather, Jose Palermo, who passed away in August. [a.] Bayshore, NY.

RAMSEY, KATHY
[pen.] Kathy Miles Ramsey; [b.] May 15, 1963, OK; [p.] Jimmy and Dorothy Miles Snoddy; [ed.] South High graduate; [occ.] Nanny; [pers.] Writing for me has always been a great joy to my soul. For me that's where the words I write come from my soul. [a.] Reseda, CA.

RANDALL, EDWARD
[b.] April 22, 1924, Jeffersonville, IN; [p.] Edward and Margaret Randall; [m.] Barbara Tyler Randall, September 20, 1946; [ch.] Susan Marie, Julie Lynn, Philip Edward; [ed.] University of Louisville, South Baptist Theological Seminary; [occ.] American Baptist Minister (retired); [memb.] First Baptist Church, American Heart Association, Community Theatre; [hon.] Clay Co. Focus Award, American Heart Association Outsatanding Volunteer (Indiana); [oth. writ.] Several poems published by Wyndham Hall Press and Indiana Baptist Observer. Music published by Lillena's Publishing Co.; [a.] Brazil, IN.

RANDALL, LELA MAE
[b.] June 9, 1945, Riverdale; [p.] The late Mr. and Mrs. Tommie and Willie Mae Lowe; [m.] Divorced; [ch.] Willie, Sheila, Sharon; [ed.] Companion Nursing-A Home Health Care Technician (17 yrs); [hon.] 1989 Golden Poets Award, 1989 Award of Merit Certificate for Poem "Take Time To Understand Someone", 1990 Who's Who in Poetry Honors; [oth. writ.] Take Time to Understand Someone published in Great Poems of the Western World Vol. II; [pers.] I thank the Lord for the opportunity to share my words that I am inspired to write, inspiration from my daughter and dedicated to the late Mrs. Willie Mae Lowe, my mother. [a.] Atlanta, GA.

RANDLE, NGYHIA MARIE
[pen.] Ngyhiaz; [b.] July 19, 1993, Dallas, TX; [p.] Della Thompson and James Randle; [ed.] Brandon Street Christian Academy, Jefferson Davis Elementary, Maynard H. Jackson Elementary; [occ.] 5D Student;

[memb.] YWCA, Good Street Baptist Church Youth Choir, Girls Scouts, Bonnie Blue Bells TWirler, Maynard H. Jackson "S" Team; [hon.] Academic trophies, medals, certificates, and ribbons, Bonnie Blue Bells Trohpies, metals, and ribbons, both badges and patches in Brownies and Junior Girl Scouts; [oth. writ.] I entered the Allan Paige Essay Competition last year with a paper entitled, "The Future is Mine"; [pers.] In my poems, I try to get people to see things from a kid's point of view. [a.] Dallas, TX.

RANGEL, MARIA IRENE
[b.] January 15, 1965, Cavite, Philippines; [p.] Rene and Natividad Ordonez; [m.] Jesus Rangel, Jr., June 29, 1991; [ed.] Cavite National High School, San Sebastian College, Foremost Computer Computer; [oth. writ.] Book of Inspirational Verses (by Irene), A Collection of Stationary Phrases, Zany Works of Lazibonz for Crazy Folks (note: Private Personal Books of Irene). [a.] El Monte, CA.

RAPPAPORT, IRVING
[b.] Brooklyn, NY; [p.] Samuel and Molly Bergerson Rappaport; [ed.] Brooklyn Tehcnical High School, NYU, Columbia University, Graduate Faculties; [occ.] Writer; [memb.] Associate member, American Musuem of Natural History; [hon.] Phi Beta Kappa/Cum Laude (NYU)/Honors in History (NYU), Pi Sigma Alpha (National Political Science Honor Society), winner of NYC High School Poetry Contest for Aetna on Typhon (poem); [oth. writ.] Poems published in USA and Australia; [pers.] Never argue with a fool, as onlookers won't know who the real fool it. [a.] Brooklyn, NY.

RASHID, MUHAMMED A.
[pen.] Muhammed A. RAshid; [b.] June 14, 1923, Pittsburgh, PA; [p.] Mrs. Florence Johnson; [m.] Divorced; [ch.] Saida A. Rashid; [ed.] LaSalle University; [occ.] Retired; [memb.] Disabled American Veteran; [pers.] I love what I am doing, I help people outside of prison and lecture. I take my 93 year old mother and 12 year daughter on all lectures. Both love it and my daughter is doing fine as results. Wisdom, knowledge and understanding she has. [a.] Brooklyn, NY.

RATCLIFF, MARK LYNN
[pen.] M. Lynn RAtcliff; [b.] July 12, 1973, Oklahoma City, OK; [p.] Calvin and Margaret Ratcliff; [oth. writ.] Several poems unpublished and un-edited to give to the human spirit "True Meaning"; [pers.] Through a diversified way, I try to give meaning and bring new life to each word. My influences are: The Holy Bible, E. Allen Poe and Jim Morrison. [a.] Oklahoma City, OK.

RATLABALA, GODWINS
[b.] July 21, 1937, R.S. Africa; [p.] William and Rachel Ratlabala; [ed.] Pax High School-Matric University of S. Africa, University of the North (Junior Secondary Teachers' Diploma); [occ.] Lecturer in English Language and Literature; [memb.] Afircan Writers Association, Diocesan Pastoral Council, Diocesan Vocation Commission, Catholic Teachers' Executive Member, African National Congress Branch, Chairperson-Secular Franciscan; [oth. writ.] Transcendental Joy and Peace, to be published by Minerva Press in London, Liberation and Freedom, Ringing Bells of Eternity, Delphian Musings, Peace on Earth, Pieces of ADvice, Psychology; [pers.] Christianity, Education and Knowledge minus Integrity are equal to Naught.

RAUFF, ALEXIS
[pen.] A.C. Rauff; [b.] May 6, 1975, Farmingdale, NY; [p.] Lucille and Robert Rauff; [ed.] Farmingdale High School, C.W. Post College; [occ.] Freshman college; [memb.] Honors program, merit fellowship; [hon.] National Choral Award, All County Chorus, Academic Excellence Award; [oth. writ.] Numerous unpublished poems and short stories; [pers.] As written by my inspiration, Kahlil Gibran, "Poetry is a deal of joy and pain and wonder with a dash of the dictionary." [a.] Farmingdale, NY.

RATZ, ROBIN BROWN
[b.] May 5, 1955, Pittsburrgh, PA; [p.] Marge and Dave Ratz; [m.] Fiance' Kevin Brown; [ch.] Matt and Rebekah Zinno; [ed.] High school, one year college; [occ.] Meditation Teacher; [memb.] Psi-Beta; [hon.] Psi Beta Kappa, Dean's List; [oth. writ.] Many other poems and several songs; [pers.] True expression is the union of reality and consciousness. [a.] West Sunbury, PA.

RATZLAFF, AGATHA
[b.] February 26, 1933, Winkler, MAN. CAN; [p.] Cornelius and Maria (Koslowsky) Enns; [m.] Henry (Hank), June 27, 1954; [ch.] Jeannie, karen, Tyler, Howard; [ed.] Chilliwack High School, graduated Senior Matriculation, completed Vancouver Normal School, graduated additonal university course; [occ.] former school teacher - Secretary and co-owner with husband (building construction company); [hon.] Entry of Poem: The Cecilia Lamont Trophy, certificate of Award and monetary award for winning first prize in 1979; entry of a story: certificate of Award for winning honorable mention in Contest 1980; [oth. writ.] Published several family history and genealogy books, some articles in various newspapers and historical periodicals, a column in The Vancouver SUN (one day), and one editorial page feature in local newspaper; [pers.] When I feel very strongly about something, I keep it inside my heart for quite a while. The thought and feeling seems to develop until I finally express it in writing a poem. [a.] Clearbrook, BC., CAN.

RAVISHANKAR, D.N.
[b.] July 28, 1963, Madras; [p.] Bhushanam D.N., and Parijatham D.N.; [m.] D.R. Anvradha, October 14, 1990; [ch.] Prashanth Balaji D.R.; [ed.] College of Engineering, MIT; [occ.] Computer Consultant; [oth. writ.] Poems on various aspects of life; [pers.] My writings touch upon life's realities and fantasies. "Life is unfinished without a mission". [a.] Madras, India.

RAY, HILARY
[pen.] Hilary Ray; [b.] January 23, 1978, Dallas, TX; [ed.] Midlothian High School; [memb.] Key Club, French Club, National Honor Society, Junior American Legion Auxiliary; [hon.] Language Arts Award, Student of the Month, first place in U.I.L. Pictionary Skills, Dallas Times Herald Award, Certificate Newspaper in Education Week, US Achievement Academy, 1992 National Awards; [pers.] I try to use my writing as a magical light for the literary blind. When someone reads my poetry, I want them to see and feel the words that they read. [a.] Midlothian, TX.

RAY, VALERIE JOY
[b.] September 16, 1969, Chicago, IL; [p.] Leon R. and Ernestine Ray; [ed.] Graduate of Benjamin E. May Academy and Kennedy King College; [occ.] Auto Technician; [hon.] Dean's List, Valedictorian, $1900 Scholarship, $600 award and $200 cash award; [oth.

writ.] Many other unpublished poems and short stories; [pers.] I dedicate this poem to my Dad (Leon R. Ray) for he saved me from this even though I couldn't save him from cancer. Thanks, Tears for Fears. [a.] Chicago, IL.

RAYMER, DAVID
[b.] May 10, 1974, Louisville; [p.] Lynda Rayner; [ed.] St. Simon and Jude Iroquios High School; [occ.] Student; [hon.] Sports trophies; [pers.] In order to progress one should not curse their mistakes but use them to better themselves and exceed. [a.] Louisville, KY.

READING, DEBORAH A.
[pen.] Doss Anne; [b.] Binghamton, NY; [p.] Edward and Florence Herling; [ch.] Tessa Ann; [occ.] Office Manager; [pers.] I love my family and my life. I am greatly influenced by my love of flowers and all of nature. I try to never take life and its setbacks too seriously. [a.] Eagleville, PA.

REDFERN, SUSAN MARIE
[b.] June 17, 1931, Waltham, MA; [p.] Carmine and Maria Leone; [m.] Thomas P., November 16, 1952; [ch.] Pamela, Eileen, Karen, Jeffrey John and John Jeffrey (twins); [ed.] F.A. Day Jr. High; [occ.] Housewife; [memb.] Newton Senior Arts; [hon.] Acknowledgement for artwork; [oth. writ.] Several short stories of my childhood; [pers.] I believe, a moral life is the only life that can bring joy and happiness to human life. The gifts which are many in life that are free, are passed by too frequently. I would like to bring the awareness of these free gifts to many. [a.] Waltham, MA.

REED, GERALD
[pen.] Ray Grimly; [b.] March 13, 1961, Canton, OH; [p.] Tom and Donella Daily; [ch.] Kodell Ashton Reed; [ed.] Perry High School; [occ.] Assistant Meat Dept., Manager; [oth. writ.] Tey to be submitted, presently raising funds for publication of my own volume; [pers.] Poetry is my form of therapy. It soothes my soul and keeps me sane. [a.] Jenks, OK.

REEVES, MICHELLE M.
[pen.] Mitch; [b.] May 30, 1969, Kansas City, MO; [p.] Gloria M. Reeves; [m.] Ricky Dwane Burgess, February 5, 1994; [ed.] Omochumnes High School; [occ.] CAshier; [hon.] Drawing awards, CPR certified, Community Services award, ROP Award; [oth. writ.] Sean, My Bar Seen One Knight, Thank You, This Isn't Goodbye, Yesterday, The Auction, Peachers, Friends Forever, Wendy Morsea, What's Love?, Mon Is Forever, Yesterday's Hero; [pers.] I enjoy writing because it comes so easy to me. It's the way I express myself. And the idea of making others happy through my poems is terrific. [a.] North Highlands, CA.

REEVES-WILLS, CAROLYN
[b.] December 26, 1933, Marietta, GA; [p.] Claude B. and Annie Hollingshed Reeves; [m.] Norman K. Wills, May 27, 1989; [ch.] Carol Ragsdale Kidd; [ed.] Acworth High School, Kennesaw College, GA State University; [occ.] Registered Nurse, Certified Family Nurse Part-time and Coordinator of Private Care for HIV/AIDS; [memb.] American Nurses Association, GA Nurse Association, GA Nurse Practitioner Council, Altrusa International; [hon.] Dean's List, Kennesaw College, Employee of the Month (Sept. 1992); [pers.] My writings reflect my experience as a nurse practitioner in caring for AIDS patients and my own growth and maturity as a result of these experiences.

REID, ALEXIS J.
[b.] September 11, 1973, Vancouver, CAN; [p.] Alex and Lorraine Reid; [ed.] Port Moody Senior Sec., Douglas College; [occ.] Student; [hon.] Certificates of Achievements in Creative Writing; [oth. writ.] Short stories and poetry; [pers.] If my readers have enjoyed reading what I have written, I have then accomplished my goal. [a.] Port Moody, B.C., CAN.

REID, ARTHUR L. JR.
[pen.] Tony Reid; [b.] June 3, 1962, Barnesville, GA; [p.] Arthur Lee and Virginia Reid, Sr.; [m.] Marilyn A., July 19, 1986; [ch.] Arcriea, Arthur III and Antonio "A.J."; [ed.] Griffin High School graduate; [pers.] My high influence is the heavenly Father Lord Jesus, my parents and my family. I know there's a lo of pain and suffering in life. I can't change the world so I try to change a little of it with my words. [a.] Brooklyn, NY.

REINICKER, CHARLOTTE ANN EICHFELD
[pen.] mikki; [b.] December 22, 1937, Camden, NJ; [p.] Henry James and Anna Clara Ellinger Eichfield; [m.] James Lawrence, September 6, 1958; [ch.] James Lawrence Jr., Dawn Lizbeth, Michael Lisa, Andrew Lawrence and Tobitha Lin; [ed.] Haddonfield Memorial High School, Moore College of Art and Design; [oth. writ.] Poems published in Garden Island newspaper and in Lihue Lutheran Church newsletter; [pers.] My primary aim is to bring about a greater awareness of the love God has for us thru Jesus Christ, to emphasize his promise of eternal life and to reflect the inner peace I receive from him. I also strive to create a deeper awareness that we are the caretakers of this wonder-filled world we live in. [a.] Princeville, Kauai, HI.

REIS, DEBORAH LYNN VESTAL
[pen.] Sarah Elizabeth Marlowe; [b.] March 18, 1953, Dallas, TX.

REMPEL, BARBARA ANNE
[b.] August 12, 1974, Altona, MB; [ed.] W.C. Miller Collegiate, University of Winnipeg; [occ.] Student; [oth. writ.] Notebook full or poems. [a.] Altona, MB, CAN.

RENKEN, BRANDON FRANCIS
[pen.] Brandon Renken; [b.] October 9, 1980, Sious Falls, SD; [p.] Marilyn and Randy Redken; [ed.] Bleyl Junior Middle School; [occ.] Student 7th grade; [memb.] Cy-Fair Youth Soccer Association, Yearbook Committee; [hon.] Opal Hamilton Award-Outstanding 6th grade student; [oth. writ.] Numerous unpublished poems and stories; [pers.] I believe that everyone deserves a chance to do whatever they want and that neither race or gender should matter. [a.] Houston, TX.

REPPERT, CHANTILLE
[b.] June 23, 1993, Reading, PA; [p.] Alan and Tamra Reppert; [ed.] Albany Elementary School; [occ.] Poet or student; [memb.] Mt. Zion Lutheran Church Youth GRoup; [hon.] Winning contests; [pers.] I hope a lot of children can enter poems in this contest. Hopefully from reading other poems, they can create some of their own poems. [a.] Kempton, PA.

REYES, JANELL MARIE
[b.] June 22, 1965, San Diego, CA; [p.] Karen Penner and Thomas Reyes; [m.] Michael, October 8, 1985; [ch.] Carolina and Joshua Reyes; [ed.] CA State University; [occ.] Western Civilization Instructor (Fresno City College); [memb.] Tokalon, Golden Key National Honor Society; [hon.] Tokalon Scholarship, BA granted Cum

laude, Alfred and Lois Krommer Scholarship; [oth. writ.] Unpublished historical romantic novels: When Magnolias Bloom and Forever Spellbound, also a collection of poetry; [pers.] I believed in bringing history to life through writing about historical figures, culture, and the love of history that I have. [a.] Tulare, CA.

REYNOLDS, MAHLON SR.
[b.] January 15, 1950, Michigan; [p.] Philip and Bertha; [m.] Yvonne, September 23, 1973; [ch.] Carol, Cherita, Semaj, Mahlon III; [ed.] HS graduate, WSU, DEtroit Inst. Commerce Business School; [occ.] Recoupment Specialist; [memb.] Board Education Literary Council, Notary Public; [hon.] Honors for AIDS Expert, Literary tutor, Big Brother Organization, Volunteer Mental Health Mentor; [oth. writ.] Beautiful Flower, Where Are We, What Time Is It?, Being A Parent; [pers.] The gift of poetry is a lifeline of blood to the soul of man. [a.] Detroit, MI.

REYNOLDS, WALKER JR., M.D., M.S.
[pen.] Golf Doctor; [b.] March 30, 1916, Anniston, AL; [p.] Walker and Mary Reynolds; [m.] Helen Garber, March 6, 1943; [ch.] Walker III, Helen, and Alexander; [ed.] Anniston H.S., Tulane University, University of VA, graduate School of Medicine Univ. of Penn; [memb.] Beta Theta Pi, Nu Sigma Nu; [oth. writ.] Book: "Walker Reynolds 1799-1871" selected as best history book in AL by Freedoms Foundation of Valley Forge; [pers.] I believe that God has a plan for everyone. Each plan is tailormade for the individual according to inherited talents. The closer we come to fulfilling that Plan, the quicker you find that "peace which passes all understanding." [a.] Anniston, AL.

REYNOLDS, WALTER J.
[b.] April 16, 1919, Lowell, MA; [p.] Thomas J. and Agnes Parsons Reynolds; [ed.] Parochial school, limited high school and college (credits-Seattle Univ.); [memb.] US Navy (4 yrs), and Merchant Marines (30 yrs); [pers.] Best stated by Henry Wadsworth Longfellow, "The lives of great men all remind us, we can make our lives sublime, and departing leave behind us, footprints in the sands of time." [a.] Seattle, WA.

RHODES, NATHANIEL
[b.] December 23, 1957, Cleveland, OH; [p.] Serless and Nathan Rhodes, Jr.; [occ.] Artist, hair stylist, poet, make-up artist, photographer; [pers.] Life! Nothing but a low death. Live it! [a.] Cleveland Hts., OH.

RICE, GLORIA
[b.] November 9, 1944, Detroit, MI; [p.] Robert and Betty Coon; [m.] John, December 24, 1969; [ch.] Rose, Jeff, and Dan (grandchildren-Tara, Amber, Mathew, Andrew, and Daniel); [ed.] Melvindale High School, Marymount College; [occ.] Property Management Agent; [hon.] Graduated with High Distinction from Marymount College; [oth. writ.] Boxes full; [pers.] When writing I try to reach deep within myself for that moment and truth of profoundly intense awareness and truth that comes so infrequently to us all; thru my poetry I try to make that moment available when it is needed. [a.] Anaheim, CA.

RICE, IRIS D.
[b.] February 6, 1959, Lynchburg, VA; [p.] Mr. and Mrs. Cleveland Rice; [ed.] E.C. Class High School, Radford University, Liberty Home Bible Institute; [occ.] Wesley Theological Serminary, Church Musician; [memb.] Association of Black Seminarians at Wesley

Theological Seminary; [hon.] Award for service as pianist of The Jackson St. UMC Young Adult Choir, Service award for Rivermont Baptist Church Youth Choir, Recognition of dedicated service to Music Dept. at Rivermont Baptist Church; [oth. writ.] Book found acceptable for publication, but not yet published, another poem published in a school newsletter; [pers.] My goal in writing poetry narratives and any other religious material is to simply reveal to people the love of Christ and to reveal the reality of the Gospel. [a.] Washington, DC.

RICHARD, ERICA DANIELLE
[b.] March 9, 1980, Columbus, OH; [p.] Cynthia Johnson and John Richard; [ed.] Emmaus Lutheran School; [occ.] 8th grade student; [hon.] First place awards at National Dance and Baton Competitors; [oth. writ.] Currently unpublished but working; [pers.] I was inspired by my 4th anf 7th grade teachers, Mrs. Hamilton and Mrs. Rousch but mostly by the highwayman as read by Anne of Green Cables. [a.] Bellevue, MI.

RICHARDS, HELEN
[pen.] Helen Richards; [b.] June 8, 1908, Arcadia, MI; [p.] Dr. Samuel and Elnne Howard; [ch.] Nancy Telcot, Charles Bell, John (deceased), Patricia Goodward; [ed.] College two years Registered Nurse; [occ.] Registered Nurse; [memb.] President Resident Council, 2 yersa President Rnsurg Group; [hon.] Written over 2,000 poems; [oth. writ.] Unpublished; [pers.] After many losses in my life starting with parents at 2 young age, losing two husbands, and caring for invalid son twenty four years; poetry and art have been my therapy. [a.] Santa Rosa, CA.

RICHARD, LINDSEY FAYE
[b.] May 9, 1979, Oakland, CA; [p.] Louis Richard and Donna Willson; [ed.] Camarillo High School; [occ.] Student; [oth. writ.] Poem published in Whispers in the Wind; [pers.] The obstruction of truth will bring the destruction of being. [a.] Camarillo, CA.

RICHARDS, JERRY LEE
[b.] February 14, 1959, Potosi, MO; [p.] Stephen J. "Sonny" and Norma Richards; [m.] Carla Jo, December 11, 1993; [ch.] Mallory and Jennifer Richards; [ed.] Southeast Missouri University; [occ.] High school/college Business Teacher and cattle farmer; [memb.] Missouri State Teachers Association, American Motorcyclist Association, Christian Motorcyclist Association; [hon.] National Merit Scholar in High School, graduated Summa Cum Laude from college. [a.] Potosi, MO.

RICHARDS, LEOPOLD
[pen.] Leo Richards; [b.] February 12, 1917, Jamaica, W.I.; [p.] May and James Richards; [m.] Divorced; [ed.] Columbia University, studies poetry under Clement Wood Playwriting - Ornato School of the Modern Theatre; [occ.] Retired; [memb.] Society for Ethical Culture, Schomburg Society for the Preservation of Black Culture; [oth. writ.] Kansas Poetry Magazine VOICES (an anthology of Negro poets), Harlem Quarterly and poems published in local papers; [pers.] One need not remain in the purgatory of remorse, tormented and enchained, if one consciously strives--and sacrifices, if need be--to attain one's desires; be it fame, fortune, material or spiritual wealth. [a.] New York, NY.

RICHARDS, WAYNE
[b.] March 4, 1951, Chicago; [m.] Anna Marie, October 25, 1985; [ch.] Shannon June; [ed.] Niles Township

EAst, Loop College; [occ.] Singer/songwriter; [memb.] Broadcast Music, Inc., Annie Time Music (President, Publishing and Production); [oth. writ.] Composer of original film score and numerous travel videos. Composed, arranged and recorded a single entitled, "MacKinac Dreams"; [pers.] A true writer cannot starve for ideas...for the world is a banquet. [a.] Streamwood, IL.

RICHEY, SEAN PATRICK
[pen.] Sean Patrick Richey; [b.] September 26, 1983, Westlake, OH; [p.] Steven and Maureen Richey; [ed.] Breckenridge Elementary; [occ.] 4th grade student; [memb.] Boy Scouts, Summit Tae Kwon Do, Optimist Soccer, Baseball league; [hon.] Various ribbons in swimming and Tae Kwon Do, first place in school Science Fair '93, Mathematics Achievement and Attendance Certificate '93-'94 school year; [pers.] "TRy to enjoy everyday!" Special thanks to Margaret Wynne, the teacher who first encouraged me to write poetry. [a.] Breckenridge, CO.

RICHLEY, ROSA MARIE DeMARCO
[pen.] katherine Rose; [b.] July 29, 1955, Youngstown, OH; [p.] Phil and Santina DeMarco; [m.] Divorced; [ch.] Jason, Joel, Eric Richley; [hon.] Received honorable mention for the poem "Wealth" by entering the Great Annual Free Poetry Contest, in 1991 was invited to New York to the 7th Annual Poetry Competition for Golden Poets Round Robin Presentation; [oth. writ.] "Sorrow" published by Quill Books titled, "Listen With Your Heart", "Pearls of Life" will be published by Quill Books this coming year. Desire, Innocence, For What Is Love, Destruction, My Love, The Stage; [pers.] The Lord is near to all who call on him, to all who call on hinm in truth. He fulfills the desires of those who fear him, he hears their cry and saves them. Psalm 145:18,19 [a.] Struthers, OH.

RICHMOND, CHRISTOPHER A.
[b.] March 10, 1962, Newport News, VA; [p.] Hank Richmond and Julia Brown; [ed.] Langley High, Mary Washington College; [occ.] Ski Tech; [memb.] Greenpeace; [hon.] First degree Black Belt in Tae Kwon Do; [pers.] There are only two reasons to be alive, to learn, and to have fun. Love is what we must learn about, and honest fun is derived from doing things you love. [a.] Breckenridge, CO.

RICKS, YVONNE C.
[b.] February 22, 1921, Many, LA; [p.] Robert and Mary Chandler; [m.] Clifford A. (deceased), August 5, 1937; [ch.] Sue, Betty, Gene, Janice, Karen; [ed.] Vo-Tech Business; [occ.] Retired School Secretary (31 years); [memb.] Boyce Baptist Church; [pers.] A deep abiding faith in God and country. [a.] Boyce, LA.

RIEGEL, AMY
[b.] October 6, 1980, Reading, PA; [p.] Terry E. and Pamela A. Riegel; [ed.] Mount Penn Elementary, Antietam Jr./Sr. High School; [occ.] 7th grade student; [memb.] Antietam Volunteer Corp., Concert and Marching Band; [hon.] 2nd place in 6th Science Fair runner-up in school, Spelling Bee 6th grade, merit honor society 7th grade; [oth. writ.] Other poems published in the local newspapers; [pers.] On a busy road you can only go as fast as those in front of you but on an open road you can go at your own pace. I like to write about the success of people in my life. [a.] Reading, PA.

RILEY, KRISTAN
[b.] August 23, 1981, Portsmouth, OH; [p.] Larry and

Jeanie Riley; [ed.] Lewis Co. Junior High; [occ.] 7th grade student; [memb.] 4-H club, Lewis Co. Pride; [pers.] I write because it is fun and relaxing. Also, I write to express how I feel. [a.] Vanceburg, KY.

RINKENBERGER, DARWIN M.
[pen.] Rinky, Darwin; [b.] October 23, 1916, Buckely, IL; [p.] Levi and Emily Rinkenberger; [m.] Helen (Hunter) deceased, August 15, 1938; [ch.] Sally Jo, Gary (10 grandchildren and 8 great grands); [ed.] 10th grade, on-job training Lockheed Aircraft, and night school; [occ.] Retired; [memb.] 44 years First United Methodist Church of N. Hollywood, Mens Club, American Legion Aircraft Post 581, Disabled Veterans Commanders Club, Gene Autry Western Heritage Museum, Lo-Fe-Lo (Love, Fellow-Loyalty) Sunday School Class; [hon.] Numerous for production and inspection techniques and record keeping and time saving proposals in aircraft production; [oth. writ.] Many poems and songs in high school, to my wife while in army and for many church occasions which have been published in church paper; [pers.] Summed up by two poems, "The Buildres" by Henry Wadsworth Longfellow and "Opportunity" by Edward Roland Sills. I have always felt that anything I participated in should have the hest effort I have, and to take advantage of knowledge I have to make a better world for others. [a.] N. Hollywood, CA.

RITA, MS
[ed.] University of Delhi, India; [occ.] Lecturer in Mathematics KNC; [memb.] Operational Research Society of India, Alliance Francaise De Delhi; [hon.] Academic Scholarships UPTO Ph.D. level, French Govt. Fellowship for Post-doctoral studies in Mathematics in Paris; [oth. writ.] Published several research papers in Mathematics in journals in India and Aboard and published poems (in English) in local magazine; [pers.] Life is my inspiration. [a.] New Delhi, India.

RITTLE, CYNTHIA
[pen.] Cindy; [b.] OCtober 26, 1961, Norristown, PA; [p.] Robert and Irene Ackerman; [m.] Jeffrey, June 24, 1989; [ch.] Jennifer Lynn; [occ.] Licensed Practical Nurse; [pers.] My writing is an expression of life experiences. A freedom to share, that the love of God may be known through the joy and sorrows of life. [a.] Lebanon, PA.

RIVA, CARMEN
[pen.] Carmen Rivas; [b.] March 1, 1975, Dominican Republic; [p.] Pedro Rivas, (sister-Yovanny Rivas); [ed.] NewTown High School; [occ.] Student; [memb.] Spanish club, Academia Literaria de Newtown (President); [hon.] Outstanding work English 2 years, Perfect attendance, Internship Elmhurst Hospital Center, Spanish Biology, Social Studies, Dean's List; [oth. writ.] Published in Social Studies magazine but Anonymous also Spanish Magazine; [pers.] Poems is one of my ways to express my feelings. I have been greatly influenced by "love" and "romanticisim" reflect it. [a.[Corona, NY.

ROAN, JENNIFER KAY
[b.] February 10, 1967, Houston, TX; [p.] Jim and Kay Cook; [m.] Ronald, June 16, 1990; [ch.] Amanda Kay; [ed.] St. Thomas Episcopal Church and School; [occ.] Dental Assistant; [pers.] I've been expressing my thoughts thru poetry for a long time and if my poems can bring a smile to someone's face, then it is worth it. [a.] Dallas, TX.

ROATH, LINDA K.
[pen.] Linda; [b.] August 31, 1978, Elgin, IL; [p.] Rob and Candy Roath; [pers.] This poem is dedicated to my very best friend Lori Ann Cates. Thanks to my mom and stepdad for supporting my creative writing efforts. [a.] Elgin, IL.

ROBERTS, GAIL A.
[b.] January 26, 1943, Monroe, MI; [p.] Reese and Reba Watkins; [m.] Donald J.; [ch.] Mark A. and Michael A.; [ed.] 12th grade; [occ.] Housewife. [a.] Detroit, MI.

ROBERTS, JAMES CHRISTOPHER
[b.] May 10, 1949, Hartford, CT; [p.] A. William and Audrey H. Roberts; [m.] Dr. Darlinda Shepard, May 30, 1986; [ch.] Jesse Conrad Roberts, Darolyn Alyssa Roberts, Jonathan Christopher Roberts; [ed.] Hampden-Sydney College, Virginia Episcopal Seminary, Duquesne University; [occ.] Epsicopal Priest; [memb.] Association for Foundational Human Formation, Chair of Examining Chaplains, Diocese of W.V., Mem. Diocesan Commission on Ministry; [oth. writ.] Wrote numerous poems and one children's novel - none published; [pers.] My writing is a reflection upon my life experience and is greatly influenced by a sense of a the wonderful unfolding mystery which repeatedly touches my life. I hope to touch each person's capacity for transcending the givens of her/his life. [a.][Triadelphia, WV.

ROBERTS, LYNETTE
[b.] March 23, 1972, Chicago, IL; [p.] Herbert D. (deceased) and Willie B. Roberts; [ed.] George Washington High, Indiana State University; [occ.] Ward Secretary Assistant; [memb.] Ebony Majestic Choir, Afro American Studies Club, Sister II and Black Drama Network; [hon.] Received a plaque for participating in the Miss Ebony Pageant; [oth. writ.] Written several poems some published and some not and I write short stories. I also write comedy, skits and plays; [pers.] I am an indepth writer of reality, therefore I reflect on everyday life. I'd like to thank God for my special talents and dedicate this poem to my mother, deceased father, twin sister, my loving boyfriend, best friend, and other relatives and friends. [a.] Chicago, IL.

ROBERTS, MARJORIE S.
[b.] May 8, 1940, Iowa City, IA; [p.] Carl and Adelaide McCann; [m.] Larry A., December 14, 1985; [ch.] Christine, Rocky (stepson), father of Tori Rae; [ed.] Pleasantville High, City Clerk Institute, Iowa State University; [occ.] City Clerk of Clive, IA; [memb.] International Institute of Municipal Clerks, IA Municipal Finance Officers Association; [pers.] Earned status of Certified Municipal Clerk for lifetime of career by achieving education requirements. I strive for perfection in all I do. Words came easy because our beautiful granddaughter is so special.

ROBERTS-GRANDSON, DAVID G.
[pen.] Bobby J. Roberts; [b.] March 27, 1940, Phoenix, AZ; [p.] Bobby J. Roberts (grandfather); [m.] Separated; [ch.] David G. Roberts (grandson); [ed.] Monte Vista Elementary School; [occ.] Bobby J. Roberts Grandfather - Disabled. [a.] Phoenix, AZ.

ROBERTSON, JENNIFER
[b.] April 25, 1978, Ft. Payne, AL; [p.] Ronnie and Kathy Robertson; [ed.] Valley Head High School; [memb.] Senior Beta Club, Varsity Basketball, Band, FHA, Drama Club, Spanish Club, and Bible Club; [hon.] National Beta Club and Miss Sophomore; [oth. writ.] Poems used in school functions including Senior Send Off Day and basketball games, written 21 poems in past two years; [pers.] Besides my favorite, Mr. Shakespeare, I was influenced by friends, family, and teachers. Most of my poems are about fun things I love, love itself and the humor in life we all search for. [a.] Ft. Payne, AL.

ROBINSON, YOLANDA
[pen.] Yoli, Yoyo; [b.] June 18, 1968, Bronx, NY; [p.] Elaine Robinson and Otis Jordan; [ch.] Andrew S.C. Joseph; [ed.] Hunter College, Pace University, Harry S. Truman High School, I.S. 144; [occ.] Administrative Assistant (Memorial Sloan-Kettering Cancer Center); [memb.] National Association for Female Executives, National Organization for Women, National Council of Negro Women; [hon.] The World Who's Who of Women - Nominated 1993, Two Thousand Notable American Women 1993, Who's Who Among American High School Students for 1985 and 1986, Scholarship to visit Japan; [oth. writ.] Poetry published in "Aphros" a literary publication produced by Pace University, World of Poetry has published two of my poems, Vantage Press offered to publish a book of my poems; [pers.] God has been my inspiration and focus when I write. I try to connect with my spirituality before I connect with the paper and words. [a.] Bronx, NY.

ROBLES, ELENA HERNANDEZ
[b.] February 4, 1943, Piedras Negras, Coah. MX; [p.] Elemo C. Robles and Carolina Rodriquez; [m.] Divorced; [ch.] Victoria Marie, Renee Isabel; [ed.] Colorado State University, University of Southern California; [occ.] Law Office Manager; [memb.] Past member various Spanish organizations throughout the United States and Contracting/Purchasing Association; [oth. writ.] Screenplay - Northern Exposure, being considered at this time, numerous poems (unpublished), technical writings, various feature articles in Aerospace Corporate Publications; [pers.] After a full career in the U.S. Air Force and have developed a style that reflects the Hispanic condition without apologies. In effect, I am a reflection of the Mexican-American in the 21st Century. [a.] Dallas, TX.

ROBLES, RENEE
[pen.] Renee Robles; [b.] May 7, 1979, Oxnard, CA; [p.] Paul and Kathy Robles; [ed.] Hueneme High School; [oth. writ.] Poetry: Prejudice, Feelings, If Ever, Love, Life, hatred, Darkness, Knowledge, Always, Apologies, A Letter to God, Pain, Lost Friendship and Troubles (unpublished); [pers.] Believe in yourself, do as you believe and your questions will be answered and your dreams will one day be fulfilled. [a.] Oxnard, CA.

ROBNETT, ELDON
[b.] January 25, 1913, Klondike, TX; [p.] Robert Bruce, Emma Robnett; [m.] Oleta Knowles Robnet, August 7, 1954; [ch.] Fenton Wayne; [ed.] Klondike Hiugh, Byrne College, Texas A&M University, Universirty of Texas, Southern Methodist University; [occ.] Retired from Mobil Oil Corp; [memb.] Dallas Genealogical Society, Mobil EXClub, Tripple LLL Club, Tannehill Masonic Lodge, honorary life member Texas PTA Mesquite Genealogical Society; [hon.] Valedictorian High School Class; [oth. writ.] Poem published in KINVERSE Magazine Freams crowded with families, An Anthology of Poetry; [pers.] I strain to reflect the beauty of nature and mankind in my writing. I love th e work of the 19th century poets. [a.] Dallas, TX.

ROCKWELL, LOIS CAE
[b.] January 29, 1965, OKC, OK; [p.] Charles and Aloma Cline; [m.] Michael A. Rockwell, August 15, 1987; [ed.] Texas A&M University; [occ.] Research Technician; [oth. writ.] Personal biographical short stories and hundreds of poems - all unpublished; [pers.] I write and read for my own enjoyment and fulfillment. I am influenced by my emotions.

RODRIGUEZ, JORGE
[pen.] Jorge Rodriguez; [b.] February 21, 1973, New York City; [p.] Miguel and Dolores Rodriguez; [ed.] Mable Dean Bacon High, Monroe College, plan to attend Fordham University; [occ.] Intern to Assistant Director (Office of Mayor, Latin Affairs); [memb.] Campus Talk - local school newspaper editor; [hon.] Awarded two year honor certificate in Monroe College for outstanding performances in Business and English. President's List for GPA/Outstanding Certificate of Merit; [oth. writ.] First published work, currently at work on first book of poems; [pers.] I have always loved words because of their power, and carry with me at all times one of my favorite quotes by Cicero which reads, "It has seemed to be more necessary to have regard to the weight of words, rather than to their numbers." [a.] New York City, NY.

RODRIGUEZ, MARIO A.
[b.] September 30, 1974, Managua; [p.] Ligia and Mario Rodriguez; [ed.] Completing grade 13; [occ.] Student; [pers.] Success and money don't mean nothing without the basic feeling of life itself. [a.] Rerdale, Ont., CAN.

RODRIGUEZ, JR., REGINALD
[pen.] Reggie Rodriguez; [b.] December 16, 1975, Montebello, CA; [p.] Reginald Rodriguez; [ed.] Pomona College, Van Nuys High; [occ.] Undergraduate freshman Pomona College; [memb.] Lorguin Entomological Society, Young Entomologists Society, Junior Statesmen of America Alumni; [hon.] National Hispanic Scholar Award Program Semi-Finalist, UC Santa Barbara 1992 Young Scholars Summer Program Graduate; [oth. writ.] Several poems published in Chicago/Latino journal, Alchemy; [pers.] Thanks to Lupe Marie Rodriguez and Mari E. Zellner for inspiration. [a.] Los Angeles, CA.

ROESE, III, GEORGE P.
[pen.] George Roese; [b.] October 11, 1950, Pensacola, FL; [p.] Barbara B. and George P. Roese, Jr.; [m.] Kaloua Ann; [ch.] Amber Nichole Roese; [ed.] Embry Riddle University, Walden University; [occ.] Director of International Sales (Medical Company); [memb.] Chamber of Commerce, Retired Officers U.S. Army, attending Trinity on Hill Methodist Church, President of Homeowners Association, Red Oak Farms; [hon.] Distinguished Military Career, Honor Dean's LisEmbry Riddle University; [oth. writ.] Other poems; [pers.] In order to be successful I believe that others around you must first be successful. Each man must lift up and encourage his fellowman first. I write from the heart inside the heart. [a.] Augusta, GA.

ROGERS, BRENDA L.
[b.] November 24, 1949, Severn, MD; [p.] William and Constance Burley; [m.] Julian M. Rogers, Jr., August 24, 1973; [ch.] Crystal Lateka, Jason Lamar; [ed.] Glen Burnie High School, Morgan State University; [occ.] Fifth grade teacher; [memb.] East Orange Kids Fest and Women's Honor Luncheon Committees, Health Curriculum Writing, Technology (TOPS) Task Force; [hon.] Governor's Teacher Recognition Award, State of NJ,

selected to teach Whole Language workshops, TV program on Whole Language with superintendent; [oth. writ.] Written several poems which have been put in programs, cards, frames, and scrapbooks. I have written historical raps and lyricvs to help my students recall important facts. Have also written two children's books, which I intend to try to get published; [pers.] I have enjoyed writing poetry since I was a child. I like to read it also. I especially like poems that rhyme. I write about a variety of topics, depending on what inspires me. I feel that poetry is a beautiful way of expressing one's thoughts and feelings. [a.] Montclair, NJ.

ROGERS, DESIREE
[pen.] Dizzy Devil; [b.] August 20, 1979, Germany; [p.] Ileen and Earl Rogers; [ed.] Heidelberg High School; [oth. writ.] Short stories and several other poems; [pers.] I feel my poems express the emotions people sometimes have but just can't show. My poems help them "express" themselves. [a.] Heidelberg, Germany.

ROGERS, FRANK
[b.] September 20, 1968, Vancouver B.C.; [p.] Opal and Lynn Rogers; [ed.] GRade 9; [occ.] Plumber; [pers.] In the hope that on the mystical road of life people might read some of the good and bad times, stay strong and play on. [a.] Edmonton, Alberta, CAN.

ROGERS, JOSHUA
[pen.] B2; [b.] May 9, 1983, Staten Island, NY; [p.] Lydia Batson; [ed.] P.S. 44-5th grade; [memb.] Goodhue Basketball Team, Learning Place Music School, School Safety Squad; [hon.] Daily News Spelling Bee Champion, six commendation cards, two student of the week plaques, third place Math bee, Best Handwriting award, first runner up Martin Luther King poem contest; [oth. writ.] Rhythm, Eight is too Late, Happy Birthday; [pers.] Thank you Mom for pushing me to the top. Thank you P.S. 44 for the opportunity to perform, thanks Learning Place Music School for their patience and caring and thank you God. [a.] Staten Island, NY.

ROGERS, MARY
[b.] December 25, 1951, Lancing, MI; [p.] George and Naomi DeYoung; [m.] Raymond S., Debruary 20, 1993; [ch.] Sonya L. Rogers Feger, Raymond O., Wendy Joy; [ed.] Phoenix College; [occ.] Church janitor; [memb.] North Phoenix Church of Nazarene; [oth. writ.] No other published writing at this time; [pers.] I wrote "A Flea and Me" when I was 16 years old, during my history class. My philosophy of life is the same as the apostle Paul who said, "To live is Christ and to die is gain." (Php. 1:21).

ROGERS, RUTH L.
[pen.] Ruth Rogers; [b.] March 12, 1941, Clarksburg, WVA; [p.] Late William H. and Ruby L. Messman; [m.] William C., August 2, 1993 (second); [ch.] Four children and 7 grandchildren and 1 great grandson; [ed.] GED Diploma, attended Washington Irving High School; [occ.] Housewife-worked with mentally retarded children and mentally ill from 1964 to 1992; [memb.] Clarksburg Baptist Church; [hon.] Desert Shielkd and WVA poems displayed at flower shop, during Guld War and Viet Nam poem; [oth. writ.] Have written 38 songs, 3 hymns. My greatest achievement was- Why Vietnam Give Us A Reason - also a poem tribute to Hospice for cancer dedicated to my father in his illness; [pers.] The poems and songs that I have written I feel have been given to me from God to send a message to give peace of mind to those who are suffering from wars, loss of loved ones and to give hope for the future. [a.] Clarksburg, WVA.

ROGERS, SHIRLEY DONNET
[b.] July 12, 1956, Bermuda; [p.] Cynthia Thomas and Edward Dill; [m.] Dean A., April 9, 1983; [ch.] Sharolbi, Deanie, Shawn and Kendra; [ed.] Prospect Primary and Secondary, Hotel College Technology, ICS Correspondent School; [occ.] Entrepreneur Poetress; [memb.] Writers Association, Church St. Paul's A.M.E., List: Third World-Sparrow Grass Poetry - Forum-local newspaper Bermuda Sun; [hon.] Merit-Reading Community Events and school Dellwood Primary; [oth. writ.] Quiet Thoughts (poetry book), Mirror of Our Souls, occasional cards, and songwriter; [pers.] The face of our universe reveals a scientific ingenuity a color graphic information of talents, influenced by Maya Angelou. [a.] Bermuda.

ROHDE, KAREN L.
[b.] March 9, 1942, Chicago, IL; [p.] Elmer and Florette Rohde; [ed.] Columbia College; [occ.] Freelance Photographer. [a.] Mokena, IL.

ROHRBAUGH, ANNA M.
[b.] October 14, 1923, Glen Rock, PA; [p.] James and Lida McCullough; [p.] Paul E., May 4, 1946; [ch.] Dennis Edward; [ed.] Glen Rock High, University of Delaware; [occ.] Retired, formally Counselor; [memb.] Second Baptist Church, Poetry Group, former The Poetry and Wriers Society of Delaware; [oth. writ.] Works published in 1989 The American Poetry Anthology; [pers.] Poetry has been my hobby since high school years. The wanders of nature have always inspired me. I seek constantly to perfect my poems and enjoy reading modern forms of writing. [a.] Wilmington, DE.

ROISENTUL, JERRY LAWRENCE
[b.] August 27, 1968, Santa Monica, CA; [p.] Saul and Ilene Roisentul; [ed.] Venice High School, Santa Monica College; [occ.] Real Estate Financial Consultant; [memb.] Toastmasters, Palm Desert Chamber of Commerce, Network Connection; [hon.] Golden Poet Award 986-88, Silver Poet award 1990, Honorable mention, Billboard Songwriting Contest 1989, 2nd place Toastmasters Speech and Evaluation Contest; [oth. writ.] Over 2 dozen poems, a dozen songs; [pers.] Those who try and fail are much wiser then those who never try for fear of failure. [a.] Rancho Mirage, CA.

ROMAN, HARRY T.
[b.] January 3, 1949, Newark, NJ; [p.] Anna J. and Harry Roman; [m.] Nancy J., November 9, 1979; [ch.] Alisa Marie; [ed.] Barringer High School, Newark College of Engineering; [occ.] Engineer and Evening Graduate Adjunct Faculty; [memb.] Institute of Electrical and Electronic Engineers, American Society of Mechanical Engineers, Robotics International; [hon.] 2 US Patents, recognized Who's Who, EPRI Innovator's Award, RAM Magazine Editorial Award; [oth. writ.] Over 190 technical articles and papers and several books published; [pers.] Find out what your skills and talents are - and then them to serve humanity. [a.] East Orange, NJ.

ROMAN, WENDY
[b.] July 11, 1977, Detroit, MI; [p.] Darlene and Carmelo Roman; [ed.] High school; [occ.] Southwestern High School; [pers.] I dedicate this to my first love, Eric Gafford. [a.] Detroit, MI.

ROMINE, MARTIN M.
[b.] March 1, 1925, Governor, NM; [p.] Floyd and Grace Romine; [m.] Shirley, June 18, 1960; [ch.]

Corynne Romine; [ed.] University of MO.; [occ.] Retired US Dept. of Agri.; [memb.] Alpha Gamma Sigma, Alpha Zeta, Orig. Prof. Employees of Dept. of Agri.; [hon.] Two certificate of merit cash awards during employment; [pers.] I have been influenced by the early American poets, such as Whittier. [a.] Memphis, TN.

RONALD, SCOTT ALLEN
[b.] February 13, 1962, LA, Ca; [occ.] Laborer; [oth. writ.] Two books, "Mindspeak" and "Dark Houses" both unpublished; [pers.] Grew up as sub normal as suburbua allowed. My interests in art began early on, always envisioning my surroundings with a slightly demented, twisted view, later for the mere purpose of retaining some sanity. I began writing my observations and experiences out into the form of poetry or lyrics, or as I simply call, writings. Expression, thru the combinaton of these two medias has become my outlet for release, and apparently has worked so far...Perhaps, neither a victim by chance, nor choice, perhaps, not a victim at all. [a.] Santa Clarita, CA.

ROOMES, DAVID
[b.] March 10, 1970, Toledo, OH; [p.] John and Laverne Roomes; [ed.] Sidney High School, Carnegie Mellon University, Miami University; [memb.] Travellers Elite, Dragon Friends, J-42; [oth. writ.] "Icicle" published in Inklings Magazine; [pers.] For Brad "Howling Mad" Hammitt, who taught me how to see the world. [a.] Sidney, OH.

ROOT, LAURA HAYMOND
[pen.] Laura Haymond Root; [b.] December 11, 1932, Clarksburg, WVA; [p.] Rev. and Mrs. FF Haymond; [m.] Rev. Charles H. Root, September 27, 1950; [ch.] Michelle, Timothy, Sylvia; [ed.] Mississippi College, Tallahassee Community College, FL State University; [occ.] Bible Teacher; [oth. writ.] Poetry and short stories unpublished (former) news columns published; [pers.] Writing seems to be an inherent trait in our family I first became interested by reading my fathers poetry, I wrote my first short story at about ten years of age. [a.] Alamo, TX.

ROSALES, IRENE D.
[b.] March 1, 1925, Staten Island, NY; [p.] (deceased) Carl and Lina Deelwater; [m.] Ramon R. June 10, 1945; [ch.] Joan R. Shaw, Barry Carl, Roy H. Rosaales (deceased), Glen P.; [occ.] Skidmore College (1943-44); [occ.] Retired; [memb.] Women's Aglow Fellowship - Corresponding Secretary at Paumyra, Corresponding Secretary Albuquerque; [pers.] My delight is in the Lord Jesus Christ, my children, grandchildren and great-granddaughter, but my husband us always encouraging me and loving me daily. [a.] Tucson, AZ.

ROSE, KATHLEEN ANNE
[b.] October 24, 1962, Virden, Manitoba; [p.] Robert Douglas Rose; [m.] Paul Shayne Boraski, January 15, 1994; [ch.] Timothy Robert and Trevor Jonathan; [ed.] University of Western Ontario, Simcoe Composite School OAC graduate, Port Rowan Public School; [occ.] Self-employed, co-owner of Bash Intertainment; [memb.] 4-H member and leader, Red Cross Volunteer, United Way Volunteer; [hon.] Honors English degree; [pers.] My favorite poet is Robert Frost, his writings have inspired me to see beauty in all things. Through encouragement from my sons, and my Paul Boraski I have continued to write poetry. [a.] Waterford, Ont. CAN.

ROSE, PEGGY
[b.] December 12, 1925, Indiana; [p.] Max and Esther Covinson; [m.] November 14, 1959; [ch.] 5 girls and 1 boy; [ed.] School of Hard Knocks; [occ.] Vocalist; [memb.] Avoid them; [oth. writ.] Songwriter, musicals, poetry, interviewer and copywriter; [pers.] Life is an experience worth living. [a.] Kaysville, UT.

ROSE, STAN
[pen.] Roseknows; [b.] September 12, 1947, Brooklyn, NY; [p.] David and Anne; [m.] Sheila Renee, June 7, 1969; [ch.] Twins: Melissa and Jason; [ed.] City College of NY; [occ.] Columnist and program analyst; [hon.] "Mu Alpha Theta" award for highest achievement in Mathematics, Kappa Phi Omega Grat at CCNY; [oth. writ.] Published for 10 years now for the Custom Art Press in "Lottery News NY and NJ", staff crossword puzzle maker for TV Guide and various other publications, co-wrote songs with Vince Martell, lead guitarist of famous "Vanilla Fudge" rock group of '60s; [pers.] Iffel that words express the inner soul of human sensuality. When words are set to paper, they make our senses vexate to the emotions, both good and bad. When set to music, the words uplift our senses to make us dance. I love to write. [a.] Hartsdale, NY.

ROSEBUD, TERESA
[b.] June 26, 1964, Evanston, IL; [p.] Lorraine Silas and Norman Dabney; [m.] Robert Jr., April 12, 1987; [ch.] Tiffany Rosebud, Robert Rosebud III; [ed.] Oakland Tech High School, Contra Costa College; [occ.] Unit Assistant-Kaiser Hospital; [memb.] St. John Missionary Baptist Church; [hon.] Dean's List, Talent Roster Certificate of Achievement Academic Performance; [pers.] Have faith and believe that all things are possible. [a.] San Pablo, CA.

ROSEN, KERI
[pen.] Keri Rosen; [b.] October 16, 1979, San Jose; [p.] Barbara Held and Russ Rosen; [ed.] Merril E. West High School; [occ.] Student; [oth. writ.] Personal-I write poems to express my feelings; [pers.] My writings comes straight from my soul...My philosophy on life is to love everybody equally live for love and the happiness of the world. I can't cure the world but I'll die trying. [a.] Tracy, CA.

ROSENFELD, BARRY MICHAEL
[b.] March 19, 1950, Philadelphia, PA; [m.] Jane Lyons Rosenfeld, November 10, 1974; [ch.] Stacey Mallory Rosenfeld and Matthew William Rosenfeld; [ed.] Temple University; [occ.] President, Cefra Travel; [pers.] I write poetry to evoke emotions and provoke thought about the reader's reality. [a.] Scottsdale, AZ.

ROSS, STACI E.
[pen.] Staci E. Ross; [b.] March 23, 1975, Warren, MI; [p.] Bernard and Peggy Ross; [ed.] Student-Oakland University; [occ.] Oakland University/Chiropractic Assistant; [memb.] Thespian Society; [hon.] Who's Who Among High School Students (1991-93); [pers.] In my writings, my inner most feelings are expressed truthfully. [a.] Rochester Hills, MI.

ROSS, TISHA JOLENE
[b.] October 1, 1979, Salem, IL; [p.] Donald Eugene and Debra Jo Boss; [ed.] Freshman North Clay High School; [pers.] The poetry of others has influenced me to express my feelings and create poetry of my own. [a.] Louisville, IL.

ROSTORFER, MARJORIE A.
[b.] July 24, 1954, Lima, OH; [p.] Norbert and Catharine Gerdemann; [m.] Daniel R. Rostorfer, September 12, 1980; [ch.] Carrie, Christie, and Courtnie; [ed.] Delphos St. John High School; [occ.] Citizens Federal Savings & Loan (21 yrs); [memb.] St. John Catholic Church, Delphos Young Farmer/Young Farm Wives Association (12 yrs); [pers.] Raides on a family farm, I know the love, the heartaches, the fun, the disappointments, the education - the privileges that living on a farm provides. All are etched deeply into my heart and are memories I hold dear and choose to write about most often. [a.] Delphos, OH.

ROTHMAN, LAWRENCE
[pen.] Red Roth; [b.] March 25, 1944, Manhattan, NY; [p.] Irving and May Rothman; [m.] Rhea Rothman, February 8, 1981; [ed.] College (2 yrs); [occ.] Clerk; [memb.] Epilepsy Society of Greater New York; [hon.] World of Poetry; [oth. writ.] Prelude to the Sea. [a.] New York, NY.

ROTHMAN, PHILIP W.
[pen.] Philip Tell (occassionally); [b.] September 1, 1924, Brooklyn, NY; [ch.] Ellen Ann and Paul Evan; [ed.] Long Island University and New York University; [occ.] Retired Math Teacher; [memb.] UFT, NYSUT; [oth. writ.] Periodicals while employed, letters to editor of Newsday; [pers.] Inspired by environment, life's experiences, former students, current events, people I've known or read about. I have a deep admiration for people who need an outlet for recognition. [a.] Cedarhurst, NY.

ROWE, MASELLA B.
[b.] Masella Messenger Rowe; [b.] September 2, 1915, OK; [p.] Daniel and Matilda Messenger; [m.] John Donald, November 25, 1933; [ch.] Donald Michael Rowe; [ed.] Stockton High School, College extension courses; [occ.] Retired business woman; [oth. writ.] Article concerning the Illustrated History of our businesses in The Second Centennial Commemorative Book of Los Angeles, A City Apart and articles and poems in newspapers; [pers.] A song must first be a poem and America has always met her struggles with songs of life, liberty and the pursuit of happiness. Her vigilance comes from knowing and knowing must come from the telling. [a.] Mariposa, CA.

ROWLAND, JOHN
[b.] December 15, 1951, NYC; [p.] Raymond and Helen Rowland; [m.] Patricia, September 26, 1975; [ch.] Brandon and Lance; [ed.] St. Francis College (grad 7/94 or 12/94); [occ.] Unemployed disabled veteran; [memb.] Disabled American Veterans; [hon.] Dean's List; [oth. writ.] Variety of papers for many classes; [pers.] The children are the answer to the worlds many problems. People in positions of authority should do everything possible to protect these assets. The problems that are small should not be ignored but corrected "nipped in the bud". [a.] Barwesboro, PA.

ROY, CATHERINE
[b.] November 24, 1962, Cornwall, Ont.; [p.] Denise Roy and James Stapley; [m.] Luc Roy, June 5, 1988; [ch.] Charitee Laura, Christien Luc, Kalon James; [ed.] Char-Lan High, ICS Child Psychology; [occ.] Telephone Operator; [oth. writ.] Poems in locval newspaper (memoriums), greeting cards for family/friends, Christmas poem in workplace newsletter; [pers.] Savor each moment cherish every breathe of air, soak in the raindrops and let the rays of sunshine, touch your soul... It'll warm you heart. [a.] Cornwall, Ont. CAN.

ROYLE, ANNE
[b.] February 12, 1922, Chelsea, Eng.; [ch.] Sven Fay Imelda, Amanda; [ed.] London Oratory School; [occ.] Retired Archial Researcher; [memb.] Nanaimo Museum and Archives, Nanaimo Historical Society VP, Bower Park Seniors-Librarian; [hon.] City of Nanaimo Heritage Honor Award 1992, Nanaimo Musuem Service Award; [oth. writ.] Published poems in BC Newspapers 1960 Historical Papers; [pers.] I am writing my family history so that my grandchildren will have a sense of place, strength and continuity in their lives. [a.] Nanaimo, BC, CAN.

ROYSTER, NADINE
[pen.] Yadi; [b.] July 28, 1955, OH; [p.] Mr. and Mrs. Harry Walker; [ch.] Ray Anthony Royster; [ed.] Cuyahoga Community College, Noyes Cultural Arts Center; [occ.] Manager, Council for Jewish Elderly; [oth. writ.] Currently writing and illustrating a poetic, cultural, philosophical and inspirational book of women of color; [pers.] A dtange man took an 8 year old girl by the hand, taught her to dance and sent her on a trip to fairyland. I've tried to always remember the rhythm of that dance, as I strive to recreate the magic of the man. [a.] Evanston, IL.

RUBIN, BEN
[b.] February 17, 1903, Russia; [p.] Jake Rubin; [m.] Katie; [ch.] Two; [ed.] High school; [pers.] To stay well do not drink, smoke, overeat. Think pleasant thoughts sleep regularly and enjoy life.

RUBIO, LINDA S.
[b.] May 7, 1954, Baltimore, MD; [p.] Charles and Katherine Robertson; [m.] Separated, January 14, 1978; [ch.] Christopher Brandon Douglas and Cassandra Melissa Beth; [ed.] Milford SHS, Catonsville Community College, Towson State University; [occ.] Encoder, Provident Bank; [pers.] I usually write about the feelings I have and the ones I see in the world and people around me. I have been writing poetry since I was in junior high school. [a.] Pikesville, MD.

RUCKER, JANELLE E.
[b.] March 25, 1982, Alexandria, VA; [p.] Debra and Marvin Rucker; [ed.] Woodlawn Elementary School; [occ.] Student; [memb.] Girl Scouts, Mt. Vernon Area Band, "Just Say No" Club, Student Council Association, Babysitters Club, Woodlawn Elementary School Band; [hon.] Woodlawn Elementary Student of the Month; [pers.] When I won the spot of Secretary in the Student Council Association, I knew I could do anything I put my mind to. [a.] Alexandria, VA.

RUDAR, MICHAEL CHRISTIAN
[b.] July 28, 1967, Pittsburgh, PA; [occ.] Student of Philosophy; [pers.] My poetry reflects existential and metaphysical qualities in which the writer and the audience are delivered above and beyond the restricted ways in which they view the world. Major influences are the romantic poets and modern poiets such as James Douglas Morrison. [a.] Venetia, PA.

RUGGIERO, TRUDY
[b.] February 2, 1950, Birmingham, AL; [p.] A.H. and Sadie Lancaster; [ch.] Steven and Jennifer; [ed.] Rhea Co. H.S., Draughon's BS College; [occ.] Executive Secretary; [hon.] Journalism awards in high school and Business college, raising two honor students single-handedly while working two jobs; [oth. writ.] Numerous

poems, short stories; [pers.] Philosophy of life is summed up in a line of one of my poems, "My dreams were created in pencil ...to easily erased." [a.] Soddy Daisy, TN.

RUIZ, NANCY

[b.] June 17, 1968, Manhattan, NY; [p.] Luis A. and Ana Hernandez Ruiz; [m.] Joseph Cruz, (to be '94); [ch.] Wilfred David, Luis Davila, Joseph E. Cruz; [ed.] Studying for GED; [occ.] Cashier; [pers.] I was very excited to hear from you and happy to know that my poem was picked for publication. I feel very lucky for this chance of winning. Thank you. [a.] Lebanon, PA.

RUPLIN, FERDINAND A.

[b.] July 22, 1934, Minneapolis, MN; [p.] Kathryn Hennessey Hallet and Ferdinanc Hallet (step-father F. Warren Ruplin); [m.] Lois L., March 17, 1980; [ch.] Ferdinand, Christopher, Edward, Timothy, Sarah (Ruplin); [ed.] University of Minnesota; [occ.] Associationn of Germanic Studies (Emeritus) SUNY; [memb.] American Council on the Teaching of Foreign Languages, American Association of Teachers of German; [hon.] Several Sabbatical leaves, National Professional Society; [oth. writ.] Several textbooks, CAI materials (German), 11 scholarly articles, text materials in Sindhi, Urdu and Panjabi for US Peace Corps.; [pers.] I have retired in the Adirondacks, reclaiming my roots. I find resonance in the works of Sandburg, Frost and Dickinson. And, of course, in the kind and generous people here. What a great place to write! [a.] Chestertown, NY.

RUSSELL, III, GILBERTO

[pen.] Gil Russell; [b.] February 26, 1973, San Antonio, TX; [p.] Mary and Gilberto Russell, Jr.; [ed.] Ramstein High School; [occ.] Stocker and student; [oth. writ.] One poem published in high school English Newsletter; [pers.] My life is full of pain and confusion, like any one else, so I write what I feel, or how I want to feel. [a.] Ramstein Air Base, Germany.

RUSSELL, JENNIFER

[b.] February 12, 1978, Kamloops, BC; [p.] Ed and Evelyn Russell; [ed.] Currently grade 10 at Golden Secondary School; [hon.] Small scholarship towards university for being one of the top students in my 9th grade year; [pers.] I always seem to bring love into all of my poems. No matter how long or short it is. [a.] Golden, BC, CAN.

RUSSELL, SONDRA LYNN

[b.] February 10, 1963, Maryland; [p.] Howard and Nancy Williams; [m.] Tyrone Stevenson Russell, December 31, 1990; [ch.] Maria Lynn, Devin Jahryell; [ed.] Harbor City; [occ.] Office Assistant for City of Baltimore; [memb.] Health, Happiness and Homemaker Club; [pers.] I dedicate this poem to my loving husband. [a.] Baltimore, MD.

RUZICKA, MIKE

[b.] December 3, 1974, Indianapolis, IN; [p.] Joseph and Marilyn Ruzicka; [ed.] Diamond Bar High School, Fullerton Junior College; [occ.] Student; [hon.] First place in high school division of College Poetry Contest; [oth. writ.] Several unpublished poems, "Los Angeles" published in a local college writers magazine; [pers.] My voice is the only cry of sanity in a world too insane to know. [a.] Diamond Bar, CA.

RYAN, BERNIE

[b.] July 6, 1947, Lockport, NY; [p.] Bernard and Katherine; [m.] Ruby Anne, July 6, 1990; [ed.] High school graduate, Penn State University, Ken Brown's Studio of Calligraphic Art; [occ.] Laborer/Calligrapher/Writer; [memb.] Holy Name Society, Jaycees, Town of Hartland Historical Society, St. Bridget's Parish, Gaelic Legaue, Ancient Order of Hibernians; [hon.] Commonwealth of Pennsylvania Annual Calendar Art Contest, PA Black History Art Contest, Certificates of Commendation: Lockport Public Library, Niagara County Historical Society, Catholic Charities of Philadelphia, Order of Our Lady of Mercy; [oth. writ.] The Celtic Warrior (most recent work); [pers.] Poetry is like an artist's paints; it is the substance of writer's creative thoughts; with it the author dips into his or her mind and renders the inspired colorful eloquence of the beauty of thoughts upon paper...The pen, like the brush, strokers and shapes each author's unique individuality with each flowing verse. [a.] Gasport, NY.

RYAN, ELSIE M.

[b.] February 19, 1931, St. Elizabeth, Jamaica, WI; [p.] Charles and Rose Williams; [m.] Major Matthew J. Ryan (deceased); [ch.] Pauline, Lawrence, Donald and Clay Washington; [ed.] Graduate of St. Thomas Moore Business College; [occ.] Executive Secretary; [memb.] Society of Military Widows, National Association of Uniformed Services Board Member, National Association of Female Executives; [hon.] 1991 and 1991 Golden Poet Awards from World of Poetry; [oth. writ.] Several unpublished poems being prepared for publication, two published in Great Poems of our Time and Our World's Favorite Poems and Who,s Who in Poetry; [pers.] I write from my heart, especially on things that affect my personal life. Most of my poems are influenced by my deep religious beliefs and the people, places and things with which I have had contact. I love travel and meeting people from all walks of life. [a.] Bayside, NY.

RYAN, THOMAS

[pen.] Alec Keegan; [b.] November 19, 1969, St. Paul, MN; [ed.] Como Park Sr.; [occ.] Security Guard; [memb.] MN National Guard; [oth. writ.] A 'Canisters" compilation of poems that has not seen the outside of the notebook covers in which they were written. They like me are very patient; [pers.] I never thought I'd see the day when one of my works would be read by someone other than me. Then again, maybe I won't. Oh well, it's the thought that counts. [a.] Roseville, MN.

RYNEVELD, CRYSTAL VAN

[b.] February 7, 1979, Johannesburg, SA; [p.] Fenella and Romney van Ryneveld; [ed.] Greenside High School; [occ.] Student; [hon.] Won S.A.C.E.E. (South African Council for English Education) Head Girl, Prefect, Mini City Councillor in Primary School, one poem published in newspaper; [oth. writ.] Poem submitted to U.N.E.S.C.O. via Pan Afircan Writers Association - accepted by P.A.W.A. - have yet to hear from U.N.E.S.C.O.; [pers.] All that I am is in my poetry - it is a gift I feel very privileged to have. Even then - it is more than just a gift, it is a friend. [a.] Johannesburg, SA.

SACCO, BRIANA DORE'

[b.] February 12, 1983, Plano, TX; [p.] Thomas and Gwendolyn Sacco; [ed.] Greenhill School; [occ.] Student; [memb.] Ecology Club, Caps For Kids, Bian Fossey Gorilla Fund; [hon.] Greenhill School High Honor Roll. [a.] Dallas, TX.

SAINT, SARA

[b.] April 17, 1978, Taos, NM; [p.] Edward and Linda Saint; [ed.] Cimarron High School; [occ.] Hobbies , writing, horsemanship, sports; [memb.] Red River Riding Club, 4-H; [pers.] A person should write only to please themselves; [a.] Red River, NM.

SALAMON, MORRIS

[b.] August 3, 1926, Brooklyn, NY; [p.] Diana Salamon, Leo Salamon; [m.] Rosalind Salamon, June 24, 1956; [ch.] Ira Lawrence, David Alan; [ed.] New Utrecht High, Brooklyn College, Baruch School Of Business, CUNY; [occ.] Semi-retired market researcher, realtor; [memb.] A.A.R.P., N.C.P.S.S.M., J.W.W., D.A.V., South County Board of Realtors, Former American Marketing Association, Smithsonian; [hon.] N.Y. State Regents War Service Scholarship; [oth. writ.] College Newspaper, many research reports; [pers.] I have reached that time of life when writing it down seems important. Maybe I feel memories should not die-maybe I feel they're a ticket to immortality; [a.] Boynton Beach, FL.

SALDANA, AIDA OPHELIA

[b.] April 2, 1946, Mexico City, NM; [p.] Calvary Colonel Ignacio Saldana and Irene Laiseca; [ch.] Luis E. Saldana, Aida Perla Saldana; [ed.] Columbia College; [occ.] Hair Designer; [oth. writ.] Short stories and poetry; [pers.] I write poetry in English to perhaps form a psychological bridge from my Latin heritage to the world which is my home. I continue my personal exploration through Flamenco dancing, studying foreign languages, travel and lifting weights. [a.] Chicago, IL.

SALDANA, ALICIA ANNE

[b.] October 21, 1988, Upland, CA; [p.] Phillip and Ruth Saldana; [ed.] Ahrens Pre-school currently Smiley Elementary; [occ.] Student-Kindergarten Teacher Mrs. Thies; [pers.] In Alicia's kindergarten class on Wednesday's is Poetry Day. We (her parents) had bought her a red heart shaped balloon w/a unicorn in the center. That's when she was inspired. [a.] Redlands, CA.

SALDANA, JOSELIS

[b.] July 3, 1971, Santo Domingo, Dominican Republic; [p.] Luis and Rosa Saldana (sisters-Marilody and Rosa H., niece-Cindy de la Cruz; [ed.] Baruch College; [occ.] Student; [memb.] Teachers of Tomorrow Club; [hon.] United Federation of Teachers Scholarship, dean's list, certificate of Outstanding Achievement; [pers.] In my writing I try to express the deepest feelings of my heart and soul and in a few sentences capture the essence of true love. [a.] New York, NY.

SALEEBY, MARK CHRISTOPHER

[b.] December 3, 1981, Columbia, SC; [p.] Moneer and May Saleeby; [ed.] Elementary 6th grade; [occ.] Student; [memb.] YMCA Youth Center, Accolyte at St. Bartholomew Episcopal Church; [hon.] Brennen Honor Roll, Carolina Elementary Honor Roll, Brennen Poetry Award, Track and field state award, baseball award minor league; [oth. writ.] Short stories and other poems published at school and in Tears of Fire; [pers.] Pursue my education stay away from drugs. [a.] Hartsville, SC.

SALLANI, MARION DAVIS

[b.] October 9, 1918, Derby, CT; [p.] John Wood Pease, Myrtle Stowe Pease, [m.] Paul Schultze Davis, October 15, 1938 (deceased) and Werner Paul Sallani, May 4, 1991; [ch.] Linda Davis Looney, Robert Paul Davis, Richard Allen Davis; [ed.] University of Bridgeport,

University of CT, School of Social Work; [occ.] Writer, retired psychiatric social worker; [memb.] Great Hill Methodist Church, Association for Research and Enlightenment, Washington Seniors Writers Group, Heritage Village Poetry Group; [hon.] Dean's List, Psychology Honor Society, listed in Who's Who in the World, 1991-92; Who's Who in The East, 1991-92; Who's Who of American Women, 1991-92, 1993 Diplomate Directory, American Board of Examiners in Clinical Social Work; [oth. writ.] "The Courage to Love Again" in The Courage to Grow Old, edited by Phillip L. Berman, Ballentine 1989, articles in local papers and church bulletin; [pers.] I try to emphasize what is hopeful, although sometimes I protest injustice to women or to others. I'm interested in pushing us to our farthest potential, as in this poem, where I believe I was able to recall a past life as an Indian Man, as contrasted to my present life as a WASP woman. [a.] Southbury, CT.

SALTZMAN, HERMAN E
[pen.] John J. Herman; [b.] October 7, 1929, Nebraska; [m.] Marjorie Shepler, August 23, 1958; [ch.] Robbie, Kathleen, Bobby and Martin; [ed.] Two years college; [occ.] Working for the Lord; [oth. writ.] Wrote one book (A Thousand Things Around Us, Yea, Nine Thousand), published 1989; [pers.] God is all things to all things all the time; [a.] Oklahoma City, OK 73115.

SAMPSON, GWEN W
[b.] January 8, 1935, Clarksburg, West Virginia; [p.] Ed and Mary Bethune Wallace; [ch.] Mother of two, grandmother of two; [ed.] Kelly Miller High School, Clarksburg, WV, Northern Virginia Community College (Bus Mgmt) 1973-75; [occ.] Library consultant, Salish Kootenai College, Pablo, MT; [memb.] Business and Professional Women's Club; [a.] Alexandria, VA.

SAMUELS, LISA
[b.] May 27, 1953, Illinois; [p.] Edythe and Everett Karten; [m.] Howard Edward Samuels, June 26, 1987; [ch.] Jessica Ida, Michael Taylor; [ed.] Jericho High School; [occ.] Homemaker; [pers.] This poem was my wish for the world, to keep a dream alive;

SAMUELS, LOUIS ROBERT
[pen.] Bob; [b.] December 1, 1912, New York, NY; [m.] Julia Samuels, March 30, 1989; [ch.] Elaine, Christine, Joe, Irwin, Joseph, Judy, Mike, Karen, Daniel, Kate, Josh, Rayna, Darrah, Lauren. Adam, Craig; [ed.] James Monroe C.C., New york; [occ.] Retired; [memb.] Poets of Palm Beach, Intl Society of Poets, Bonzai Club, Bocci Team, Billiard Club; [hon.] New York City Marathon, poetry awards; [oth. writ.] Articles and poems in Century Village newspapers; [pers.] I write for current love and understanding throughout the world, my family and posterity. Just finished my poetry book: Where Love Begins; [a.] West Palm Beach., FL.

SAMUELSON, HYMIE
[occ.] Still a merchant owner of a small menswear store; [oth. writ.] I have written poems and stories all my life. Nothing has been published. [pers.] At 74 years of age, I have simple guidelines: How I feel is more important than how I look, What I do is more important than what I believe, How I live is more important than how long I live; [a.] Austin, TX.

SANBORN, TARA
[b.] April 22, 1980, Manchester, New Hampshire; [p.] Wesley and Donna; [occ.] Chambermaid/babysitter; [hon.] Young Authors of America, MVP in basketball;

[pers.] I express my feelings through poetry; [a.] Jefferson, NH.

SANCHEZ, CHERYELONA
[pen.] Cherelona Eagle Woman; [p.] Joan Chambers, Joe Graves, Maurice Hebert; [m.] Naresh G. Mirchandani; [ch.] Shannon, Daniel, Katie, Sara, Nanak, Joshua, Michael; [ed.] Life, family, friends, neighbors, strangers, and from the earth; [occ.] Shaman to many people, telephone counselor, spiritual advisor; [hon.] To see the happiness of others reflected back to me when I have been able to touch their heart with my words; [pers.] I strive to become one in heart and spirit to all whom I meet. So that I can experience all that I can in this world. I believe in truth at all cost. I want to learn something about everything. This knowledge I desire to share with all whom wish to learn; [a.] Westminster, MD.

SANDERS, STEVEN R
[b.] January 3, 1966, Muskogee, Oklahoma; [ed.] Fletcher High, Redlands Community College; [occ.] Student; [memb.] National Student Nurses Association; [oth. writ.] Several unpublished poems and short stories; [pers.] I wrote this poem to a person that was once very dear to me. Staci; [a.] Chickasha, OK.

SANDERSON, CINDY
[b.] JUly 5, 1960, Stockton, CA; [p.] John and Jan Yost; [m.] Dave Sanderson, April 12, 1992; [ed.] B.A. in Communications and Theatre Arts, with a minor in Sociology, University of Iowa; [occ.] Office assistant, Jackson Atoll Airport; [pers.] I enjoy writing poetry and hope to catch the effect of visions mirrored through me; [a.] Apo, AP.

SANDERSON, GEORGIA
[b.] August 5, 1939, Chicago, IL; [ch.] Mr. and Mrs. Dexter Woods; [ch.] Channel, Alan, Michael, Thelma; [ed.] 10th grade, 1 year junior college, voice training, art training; [occ.] Servant to those in need, follower of Christ; [memb.] Supportive of many ministries and different denominations; [hon.] Honored by my children and by God. Singing many songs written for them, providing songs which glorify God, and delight people; [oth. writ.] Children's songs, working on operata using Old and New Testament, book not quite finished, poems, articles for newspaper; [pers.] No interest in the greatest earthly prize, No motives to be shrewd or worldly wise, But I will look beyond the things I see, To find solutions to each mystery; [a.] Thousand Palms, CA.

SANDS, ADAM T
[b.] December 5, 1969, Brooklyn, NY; [ed.] New Utrecht High School, Brooklyn College; [memb.] Sigma Alpha Mu fraternity, Mu Upsilon chapter; [pers.] I believe Shakespeare was correct when he wrote, "Life is like a play". Although our society preaches love, I feel there is still too much hatred that surrounds each of us; [a.] Brooklyn, NY.

SANFILIPPO, CHERRYL
[pen.] Cherryl N. Sanfilippo; [b.] May 16, 1960, Middletown, CT; [p.] MIchael and Frances Magnano Jr.; [m.] Carmelo Sanfilippo Jr., May 29, 1982; [ch.] Woodrow Wilson High School; [occ.] Sales Representative; [oth. writ.] Several unpublished poems; [pers.] All my love to my husband, Chiop, and daughter, Nadine, as well as the rest of my family who mean the world to me; [a.] Portland, CT.

SANTE, ILSE
[b.] May 27, 1910, Bad Harzburg, Germany; [p.] Mr. & Mrs. Otto Ihlenborg; [m.] Henry Sante, October 17, 1947; [ch.] Two sons, 2 daughters, 16 grandchildren; [ed.] Elementary, High School, 4 years teachers training in Germany, post-grad studies in Montreal, McGill-BEd; [occ.] Retired teacher; [memb.] Active member of the German Pentecostal Church, Teachers Union, PTA, Homeowners; [oth. writ.] I had nothing published before, but wrote poems and short plays for my own use in class and in church; [pers.] Thank you for choosing my poem. I a thrilled and am looking forward to receiving "Dance on the Horizon"; [a.] Chateauguay, Quebec.

SANTORO, RUTHANN
[pen.] Ruthann; [b.] June 28, 1932, Lambs, MI; [p.] Bill and Gladys Clements; [m.] Joseph Santor, Jr (deceased), February 6, 1950; [ch.] Thomas and William; [ed.] 10th grade Rosarian Academy; [occ.] Homemaker, retired; [memb.] Our Lady Queen of all Saints Church, 1st president of the Alliance for the Mentally Ill, Macomb Co, MI, co-chairman, Fraser Senior Citizens; [hon.] Life; [oth. writ.] "Whisperings", "God's Love", "Hugs", "Happy Hands", "In Thanksgiving", "A Promise", "Miracles", "Love and Joy", church papers, newsletters, newspapers; [pers.[Life and its greatness; [a.] Fraser, MI.

SANTOS, STEVE
[b.] March 27, 1965, Hondo, TX; [p.] Antonio L. Santos and Evangelina M. Guedea; [ed.] Milby High School, International Correspondence Course; [occ.] Locksmith, North Forest ISD; [oth. writ.] Several poems which have never been published; [pers.] My writings are inspired by Lisa Garcia, and I would like to dedicate my first published writing to her. I love you Lisa. [a.] Houston, TX.

SARACENO, JOANNE MARGARET
[b.] January 29, 1942, Chicago, IL; [p.] John B. and Margaret Saraceno; [ch.] Christina Barlette and Stephen John Brown Saraceno; [ed.] St. Anthony's High School, Long Beach City College; [occ.] Executive Secretary; [memb.] Palo Verde Avenue Christian Church; [oth. writ.] Philosophical essays, poetry published in local newspapers; [pers.] The physical universe is constantly reflecting the spiritual, unseen reality and I enjoy expressing this in my writing. Writing, I express my experience of Truth, Beauty and mystery in everyday Life. [a.] Cerritos, CA.

SARAMAGO, RUI M.
[pen.] Nate; [b.] March 15, 1969, Oporto; [m.] Hannah Merrick, October 10, 1953; [ed.] John Hopkins University, Harvard University; [occ.] Math Teacher; [oth. writ.] Transcendentalism - A View, A Craving For Skulls, The Other Son; [pers.] I want to be the least expressive I can and look at things they way they are. I want people to open their eyes and neither love nor hate nobody, just look at things directly. [a.] Buffalo, NY.

SARGENT, JEFFREY E.
[pen.] Jeff and Bear; [b.] February 23, 1956, Bar Harbor, ME; [p.] Lean Sargent; [m.] Thelma M., April 10, 1976; [ch.] Troy Sargent and Jeffrey (J.J.) Sargent II; [ed.] Summer High School, University of Maine, Army Engineering School; [occ.] Disabled Supervisor from Maine Dept. of Transportation; [memb.] Maine Army National Guard, Baseball Card Collectors Club, Maine State Employees, Association for Retired Personnel and American Red Cross Instructor; [hon.] Army Achieve-

ment Medal, Adjudent General's Award, Soldier of the Year Award; [oth. writ.] I have written poetry for years, but only for my wife. This was the first time I ever entered one in competition. But now there will be many more to come; [pers.] I have been disabled for 2 1/2 years and have been searching for something to occupy my idle time, thanks to the Library of Poetry I may have found that something. Everything I write comes from my heart. [a.] East Sullivan, ME.

SASTRI, MADUGULA INDUSEKHARA

[b.] September 26, 1933, Iragavaram, A.P., India; [p.] Seshamma (mother) and Ramabrahma Sastri (father); [m.] Lakshmi (wife), December 26, 1950; [ch.] Ravi (son), Raj (son), Rama (daughter); [ed.] Case Western Reserve University; [occ.] Formerly Association Professional of English, Central Inst. of Eng. and For. Langs.; [hon.] Won gold medal for placing first in BA (hons. Engl.) Andhra Univ.; [oth. writ.] Published many articles on applied English linguistics and stylistics; several poems in college/university magazines and one in the National Anthology of Poetry; a book on the Indian philosopher Sankara; [pers.] I believe that metaphor is the essence of life and literature, and the individual metaphor is but a reflection of one's self. [a.] Naperville, IL.

SATTERFIELD, SR., CLAUDE

[b.] August 13, 1933, Fairmont, WVA; [p.] REv. Raymond and Dorothy Sattlefield; [m.] Virginia Lee Satterfield, August 21, 1958; [ch.] Rickey L. and Claude C. Jr.; [ed.] local schools - East Fairmont High; [occ.] Retired - from self-employed carpet business; [hon.] Honorably Discharged Veteran; [oth. writ.] Several unpublished poems. [a.] Fairmont, WVA.

SAULS, H.D.

[pen.] H.D. Sauls; [b.] October 23, 1969, Atlanta, GA; [p.] R.D. and I.L. Sauls; [m.] Mary Jane Smith (fiancee), October 94; [ed.] Colonial Hills High, self educated; [occ.] Central Station Supervisor, GA Security Systems; [memb.] National Geographic Society, Christian Children's Fund; [oth. writ.] I have a personal book of poetry containing my own works humbering around 160. I had one of the works published in a local newspaper; [pers.] My personal book is called "Ethos". Ethos means "away of thinking particular to a group or individual". I feel individual thoughts and ideas are an art form, and should be painted on the canvess' of as many minds as possible. [a.] College Park, GA.

SAVILLE, DAWN ELIZABETH

[b.] September 22, 1974, Vancouver; [p.] Gary and Carole-Diane Saville; [ed.] Stelly's Secondary High School, University of Victoria - Arts student; [occ.] Student; [hon.] Graduated from high school with honors and French/English bi-lingual status, received Humanities award, B.C. provincial scholarship; [oth. writ.] Columnist for local newspaper; [pers.] Influences include Emmanuel Robles, (atullus and John Donne). Creative writing is the journal of the soul. [a.] Saanichton, B.C.

SCALLEY, CASSANDRA IRENE

[pen.] Cassandra K. Stinson; [b.] November 5, 1969, NC; [p.] Bonnie Stinson; [ed.] High school equivalent; [occ.] Master welder; [hon.] This is my forst honr. IU'm still quite young. THank you![pers.] I represent an excellent role model for all women, as I struggle to develop and share my own capabilities and understanding in the Amity teaching community. I have developed

an intimate understanding of the concept that if we want women to change, we need to change our patterns, and find freedom through change itself; [a.] Tucson, AZ.

SCARPITTA, DAVID F.

[pen.] Davey; [b.] February 21, 1978, Queens, NY; [p.] Rose and Dominick Scarpitta; [ed.] West Babylon High School, Wilson Technological School; [occ.] Student; [memb.] Alter Boys of America; [hon.] Newsday Carrier of the Year Award, Presidential Academic Award; [oth. writ.] Other poems in school newspapers and community contests. An autobiography called "One in a Million"; [pers./] In writing a poem I take personal and real life experiences and turn them into universal meanings in which all can understand and relate their experiences to. [a.] Deer Park, NY.

SCHAAB, HAROLD A.

[pen.] Harold Albert; [b.] May 29, 1931, Youngstown, OH; [p.] Harry and Ethel; [m.] Doris, May 23, 1987; [ch.] 2 step daughters (Lorie and Lainey); [ed.] Youngstown University; [occ.] Retired; [memb.] P.M. William Farr #672, Ft. AM 32 Degree mason, Past patron of Ameranth #22, A.A.O.N.M.S. of Cleveland, R.A.M. 223 Commandery #079, Niles Council #130, EAstern Star 458; [oth. writ.] Poems published in Tri City Writers Booklet also poems, memeorial services and other writings for various lodges and organizations; [pers.] Poems are the visions and memories of one's mind. I wish to have my readers transpose themselves into the realm of my imagination. [a.] Girard, OH.

SCHAEFFER, HARRIET B.

[pen.] Grama Bea; [b.] July 23, 1934, North Platte, NE; [p.] Harry A. and Phoebe (Spence) Potter; [m.] Divorced, September 25, 1955; [ch.] Clinton E. and Jeffrey W. Schaeffer; [ed.] UNL (BS and MA); [occ.] Speech/Language Pathologist; [memb.] NEA, NSEA, LEA, ASHA, Cortland United Church, NSLHA; [oth. writ.] Only poetry published by Quill Books and The House of Enright. Professional writings published in the "Networker"; [pers.] I believe, to be a well-rounded personality, in setting goals in 5-year increments and in several areas, and then facing the challenge of risking to achieve them. [a.] Cortland, NE.

SCHER, MILDRED R.

[pen.] Mildred R. Scher; [b.] November 26, 1978, Atlantic City Hospital; [p.] Nancy and David Scher; [ed.] Mio Ausable High School, National Radio Institute of Technology Home Correspondence; [occ.] Student high school; [memb.] Arts/Crafts Center; [hon.] Honor Roll; [pers.] I have read several books over a period of 6 or 7 years (since 4th grade) and I suppose that's how I made it to this far. [a.] Mio, MJ.

SCHILLINGS, CHRISTOPHER LEE

[pen.] Chris Schillings; [p.] March 28, 1970, Dallas, TX; [p.] Doyleen Kurtz and Bill Schillings; [m.] Jane, February 13, 1991; [ed.] Brookhaven Junior College, Eastern OK State College; [occ.] Free-lance Writer; [memb.] The Writers Underground; [hon.] High school Achievement in Journalism Award; [oth. writ.] Several articles for high school newspaper, unpublished novel and hundreds of poems and short stories that reflect my craving for the written word; [pers.] Published or not, writing will always be a passioin for me. It is my belief that none should view the world in only black and white. Remember this, in evry rainbow roars an enflaming mouth of fire. [a.] Carrollton, TX.

SCHLAIN, MARILYN BRANNER

[b.] June 17, 1925, Detroit, MI; [p.] Rose and Herman Brenner; [m.] Abbott (Bud Schlain), October 2, 1947; [ch.] Robert, Barbara, Jan; [ed.] Central High School, Eayne State University; [memb.] Trustee, Archives of American Art, Smithsonian Institute, Association American Museums, Cranbrook Women's Comm., Detroit Inst. of Arts Founders Society, Detroit Symphony Organization, Boca Ratan Museum, Hospice Association, Salvation Army, Project Hope. [a.] West Bloomfield, MI.

SCHLEIGER, ELVA

[b.] February 25, 1920, Pittsburgh, PA; [p.] Charles and Mathilda Bir; [m.] John (deceased), January 16, 1954; [ch.] Mary Ann Luczko; [ed.] Spring Hill Elementary School, Allegheny High School; [memb.] South Hills Women's Aglow Fellowship, Pittsburgh Observatory Chapter #1435, AARP; [pers.] Any talent revealed through me is accredited to God. I see the world a better place by writing my heart's desires in poetry. Helen Steiner Rice impresses me. [a.] Pittsburgh, PA.

SCHLUP, RAYMOND P.

[pen.] his hands; [b.] February 21, 1927, California, MO; [p.] Chas. A. Katie Farni Schlup; [m.] Lillian gladine West Schlup, July 28, 1952; [ch.] Paul,, Peter, Nancy Burditt, Molly Kohl, Jimmy, John; [ed.] 8th grade, G.E.D., Greer Tec. College; [occ.] Soybean processing; [memb.] Regional Church of Jesus Christ of Latter Day Saints, and United Church of Christ; [oth. writ.] 18 Gospel songs, 6 poems; [pers.] Believe in cycle of God the Father, Son, and Holy Ghost, and that mankind is a part of that cycle; [a.] Mexico, MO.

SCMIDT, ADAM B.

[pen.] Barrett L. Welding; [b.] July 24, 1971, Ft. Lauderdale, FL; [p.] University of New Orleans and University of S. Miss.; [occ.] Actor, singer, musician, student; [memb.] Afternoon Social and Sippin' Club, N.O.L.A. (U.N.O.); [oth. writ.] Working on novella of poetry entitled, "Screaming Stories, and the story goes..." and my first novel: "The Cry of the Gull"; [pers.] Lord help me if I ever truly find myself completely or learn everything there is to learn; then I would have nothing left to strive for in life. [a.] Meraux, LA.

SCHMITT, JOSEPH H.

[b.] April 18, 1963, Kalamazoo, MI; [m.] Lori, October 23, 1992; [occ.] Caregiver to my disabled wife; [memb.] Spina Bifida Association, Michigan Wheelchair Athletic Association; [hon.] Received Volunteer of Year award from Kalamazoo Center for independent living. My biggest honor and award is the marriage with my wife and our puppy "Wriggley"; [oth. writ.] Some 40 unpublished poems; [pers.] My poems show the good, bad, and the confusion that life brings to those of us who work at what we want out of it. [a.] Kalamazoo, MI.

SCHMITZ, DIANNA P.

[b.] October 26, 1954, South Bend, IN; [p.] Edward and Teresa Pilarski; [m.] H. Edward, July 31, 1976; [ch.] Jonathan Edward, Jessica Ann; [ed.] Brandywine High School, Saint Mary's College, University of Notre Dame and National-Lewis University; [occ.] English teacher; [memb.] National Council of Teachers of English, Illinois Council of Teachers of English, Kappa Gamma Pi, Saint Mary's College Alumnae Association; [hon.] Carmel High School, B.V.M. Educator's Scholarship, National-Lewis University-Educator's Scholarship, Saint

Mary's College summa cum laude, Senior English Award, Borden Scholarship, Michigan Scholarship, St. Mary's con,-Kappa Gamma Pi, dean's list; [oth. writ.] Several college publications; [pers.] Writing is a way of preserving and cherishing memories of special people and places in my life. It is also a way to super-impose order and meaning over otherwise confusing experiences. [a.] Vernon Hills, IL.

SCHOLBERG, HENRY
[b.] May 29, 1921, Darjeeling, India; [p.] Henry and Ella Scholberg; [m.] Phyllis, June 16, 1951; [ch.] Andrew David, Daniel Lester, Naomi; [ed.] Woodstock High School, University of Illinois, University of Minnesota; [occ.] Writer; [hon.] 1964, second prize ($100) in nationwide children's play writing contest for The Boy King, 1991, Volunteer of the Year for writing history of the Windsor Green Town House Association; [oth. writ.] Several plays, short stories, bibliographies and novels; [pers.] One should never hide one's light. [a.] New Brighton, MN.

SCHORR, MILTON
[b.] April 2, 1921, Bayonne, NJ; [m.] Dorothy; [ch.] Cliff and Carol; [ed.] Brooklyn College, New York University; [occ.] Professioinal Magician, Teacher of Foreign Languages (retired); [memb.] Society of American Magicians, International Brotherhood of Magicians, United Federation of Teachers; [oth. writ.] Several poems published in various periodicals. Also several original magic tricks published in "Apocalypse" a prestigious magic magazine published monthly by Harry Lorayne, the famed magician and memory expert. [a.] Syosset, NY.

SCHROEDER, JR., BARRY D.
[pen.] B. Dale; [b.] March 27, 1971, Rochester, MN; [p.] Barry Schroeder and Nancy Ribick; [ed.] S.E. Polk High School, Iowa State University, University of North Texas; [occ.] Guest Service Associate Marriott; [oth. writ.] Several poems not yet published currently working on a screenplay; [pers.] You will always want what you don't have but, do you have what you want? [a.] Grapevine, TX.

SCOTT, JANET S.
[b.] January 14, 1970, Lexington, NC; [p.] Harley Ray and Virginia Harmon Smith; [m.] Gene, April 29, 1990; [ch.] Wednesday Nathaniel Scott; [ed.] West Davidson High School; [pers.] This poem is dedicated to my dear mother who is my best friend for life and who possesses those unique qualities I strive to achievement. [a.] Taylorsville, NC.

SCOTT, KENNETH W.
[pen.] Ken Scott; [b.] February 3, 1927, Royal Oak, MI; [p.] Harry and Cora Scott; [ch.] Leeann and Randall Scott; [ed.] Royal Oak High, Wayne State College; [occ.] Safety and Security Director; [memb.] Tuebor Masonic Lodge Scottish Rite and Shrine; [pers.] The poem was a reflection of my own life at a time when I was retiring from one career to start another, but it could apply to any new start. [a.] Chebougan, MI.

SCOTT, LINDA
[pen.] Pearl Moore; [p.] Pearlie and James Moore; [m.] Dr. Phillip D. Scott, September 16, 1984; [oth. writ.] Several children's stories with Native American and ecological themes; [pers.] My family stayed away from television which led to a strong tradition of story telling and poetry reading. I learned to see and appreciate natural beauty. [a.] New Orleans, LA.

SCOTT, ROBERT
[b.] January 23, 1974, Anchorage, AL; [p.] James and Brenda Scott; [ed.] Lincoln High School, Wilma Boyd Career Schools, Inc.; [occ.] U.S. Air Express Customer Service Agent; [hon.] Peer Mentor award; [pers.] Everyone's a poet with a story to tell. Now it's just my turn to tell mine. [a.] Glen Burnie, MD.

SCOTT, TENNYSON GEORGE
[pen.] Nysonnet; [b.] November 12, 1947, Montego Bay, Jamaica, WI; [p.] Elizabeth Waldron and William H. Scott (deceased); [m.] Doreen, February 21, 1976; [ch.] Mario, Nicole, Tennyson II, Shaun, and Dwight; [ed.] North Western Academy, Rockland Community College, Simpson College; [occ.] Self-employed, entrepreneur tax practitioner/small business management counselor; [hon.] Black Students Organization President/Associated Justice Student Court, Student Body Senator award Business scholarship; [oth. writ.] Several unpublished poems; [pers.] In my writings I embraced the visions of place missed. The loneliness of realism and the quest for solitude. [a.] Spring Valley, NY.

SCRIBNER, JANE MRS.
[pen.] Janie Scribner; [b.] February 2, 1940, Abingdon, VA; [p.] Paul and Lucilla Bishop; [m.] Wesley Leroy, January 20, 1958; [ch.] Terry, Andrew, Philip, Dan, and Belynda; [ed.] Hyders GAp School, Berrien Springs High; [occ.] Homemaker, teacher (First Pentecostal Church); [memb.] First Pentecostal Church, American Bible Society, American Lung Association; [hon.] Senior High Chorus, Y.F.C. Club, Full Gospel Fellowship; [oth. writ.] Several poems published in local newspapers, articles for Home Life Magazine, article in Apostolic Newsletter; [pers.] I strive to reflect Christ the hope of glory in my writing. I have been greatly influenced by the writers of Christian Heritage. [a.] Batesville, AR.

SCRIBNER, SUSAN M.
[b.] July 18, 1951, New York; [occ.] Financial and Organizational Consultant for Non Profit Organizations; [oth. writ.] "How to Ask for Money Without Fainting" and "Boards From Hell" books published 1991; [pers.] As I learn more about myself I am stunned by what I already knew..and so much I've yet to learn. [a.] Long Beach, CA.

SCRIPCA, IOLANDA
[b.] Romania; [p.] Gheorghe and Viorica Scripca; [ch.] Christopher Scripca; [ed.] Clear Credential University of CA, Chapman University, University of Bucharest; [occ.] Teacher St. Peter's Academy; [hon.] Published poetry and translations of children's literature, assisted in the preparation of the new edition of the Romanian-Bulgarian dictionary at the University of Bucharest.

SCZEPANIAK, MICHAELA
[b.] April 3, 1964, Trier, Germany; [p.] Karl and Irene Davis; [m.] Daniel C., June 8, 1987; [ch.] Daniel C. Jr.; [ed.] Robert Schuman Realschule and Auguste Victoria Secondary Schoor, Trier University; [occ.] Student, Housewife; [oth. writ.] Sevral poems and essays published in our Unviersities Literary Journal of the English Department of Trier University; [pers.] "The pen is mightier than the sword." I try to catch life and its ups and downs like a photographer, only with words. I am very thankful to my husband for his support and to Robert Kroetsch for putting me into the right direction with my writing. [a.] Trier, West Germany.

SEARCEY, LEE
[pen.] Lee MC; [b.] November 9, 1932, Reedley, CA; [ch.] Ron A. Searcey; [ed.] 12 Grade; [occ.] Building contractor; [oth. writ.] None, have over 40. [a.] Three Rivers, CA.

SEARS, ALTON
[b.] October 16, 1932, New Orleans, LA; [p.] Deceased; [ed.] Learned the rudiments of English at Cal-State College as a special student at age 35; [occ.] Resides and works as Counselor in Southern California; [memb.] Navy Advanced Drug and Alcohol, CA Certified Alcohol & Drug Counselor, Nationally Certified A&D Counselor, National Certified Addiction Counselor II; [oth. writ.] Collection of poems published in book titled "Something of Feeling", 1986 wrote a musical called "I'm Dancing My Way to the Graveyard", recently copyrighted another collection of poems entitled, "Who and Other Poems".

SECOMSKI, VERA A. (FIGUERUA)
[pen.] Elvera or Gypsy; [b.] July 30, 1951, Victorville, CA; [p.] Jose and Jean Figueroa; [m.] Janusz F., July 4, 1971; [ch.] Januszek "J.Z."; [ed.] Washington High School, Travel Beauty School; [occ.] Work for husband's company; [memb.] Team Mom in Englewood Sr. League (Baseball), Pop Warner Football Team Mom, Lemons Bay High School Football; [hon.] At football banquet honored on December 12 by coaches and players and given a plaque, helped at high school internation fair for Mexico and Poland; [oth. writ.] Written poetry since about 8 or 9. Wrote a poem to Dick Van Dyke; [pers.] We travelled many years ago on Ringling Bros. Circus and my brother in law's family show. Met my husband there and many people from all over the world. Married on Ringling, I write my poetry based on things I saw in my travels and people we met, then and now. Life has blessed me with many happy things and yes some sad. But that's ok. Life is still great. [a.] Englewood, FL.

SEEFELDT, REBECCA S.
[b.] April 3, 1946, Lockport, NY; [p.] John and Martha Harvey; [m.] Emory F., August 24, 1971; [ch.] Jeannie Shawn, and John Charles (grandchildren-James Emory and Darren Alexander); [ed.] Royalton-Hartland Central School; [pers.] Most of my poetry is based on personal experiences, emotions, and people who are important to me. [a.] Medina, NY.

SEER, THE DREAM
[b.] Unknown; [p.] "Oh please I've embarrassed them already"; [m.] The Mystery Lady; [ch.] The Human Race; [ed.] Self-taught; [occ.] Playboy (Independently wealthy); [memb.] The Psychic Tragic Undercurrent (of the universe); [oth. writ.] Books: The Twilights Dream, Myths and Legends, The Darkness and The Breeze, The Lives of the Dream Seer. [a.] San Francisco, CA.

SEIBEL, JULIANNE
[b.] March 28, 1979, Ontario; [p.] Melmut and Doris Seibel; [ed.] Currently attending grade 9 at Elmira District Secondary School; [occ.] Part-time job farmers market and babysitting; [memb.] Take dance-tap-jazz-ballet at local studio "Encore", studying Greek lanugage, take classical guitar and piano lessons; [hon.] Youth Appreciation Award, first place in Waterloo County History Fair 1992, Honorable mention, Waterloo County History Fair 1993, Best All Around Student 1992-93, Valedictorian 8th grade; [oth. writ.] Several poems/letters published in local record (newspaper), poem published in Elementary County Anthology 1988; [pers.]

We must all strive to do our best and firmly imprint our footprints in the sands of time. [a.] Ontario, CAN.

SELVIDGE, STEPHANIE PROVINCE
[b.] December 19, 1962, Rolla, MO; [p.] Ed and Carol Province; [m.] Blaine Gardner Selvidge, August 2, 1983; [ed.] Parkway Central High and Meramee College; [occ.] CNA at Brooking Park; [pers.] This poem was written to teach young people if you have hope and faith in yourself you will be alright. [a.] U. City, MO.

SEN, MILLICENT
[ed.] Private schools, primary/secondary and two years college; [occ.] Property Management; [oth. writ.] Unpublished-Wit A Your Fingertips; [pers.] To be able to write as fearlessly as William Shakespeare had. My fervent wish is that "I will not be too weak a prop for heavy a burden." Of great influence in my life. My friend, John Chiarenza, Ovid, Shakespeare, H. Spencer, Mary and Percy Shelley, Bernard Shaw and Goethe. [a.] VAn Nuys, CA.

SENSENICH, CINDY K.
[b.] February 13, 1973, PA; [p.] William and Kathleen Sensenich; [ed.] West Liberty State College; [occ.] Student; [memb.] Volleyball Team, Electric Square member; [hon.] Dean's list, All-Conference Volleyball player, Scholar Athlete award, All-East Region volleyball player; [pers.] I see a challenge, I rise to that challenge, I defeat that challenge, Then I am the challenge; [a.] N. Huntigdon, PA.

SERUYA, NANCY C.
[b.] July 29, 1968, Chicago; [ch.] Michael, Nicholas, Tiffany; [pers.] I want my writing to be enjoyed. [aa.] Niles, IL.

SEVERN, PAMELA
[pen.] Sister Sorrow, P.M.S.; [b.] October 5, 1961, Chicago, IL; [p.] Jack Berman; [ch.] Michael Alan, Bryan Douglas, Jason Clayton; [ed.] Trevor Browne High, Phoenix Community College; [occ.] Business Administrator; [hon.] Neighborhood Mother of the Year; [oth. writ.] Several poems published in other poetry books; [pers.] Only through love and open communication, not material things, can we make todays children tomorrows success. [a.] Peoria, AZ.

SEWELL, TSWANA
[b.] September 11, 1979, Philadelphia, PA; [p.] Joan Sloan and Harry Sewell; [ed.] 9th grade Student, Phoenix Academy; [occ.] Aid in after school program; [memb.] Jack & Jill of America, Inc., National Junior Honor Society, Extended Family Fund, Girl Scouts; [hon.] Delta Sigma Theta Oratorical Contest; [oth. writ.] Tears of Blackness, Crystal Pearls; [pers.] Keep your head up! [a.] Wilmington, DE.

SHABTAI, YANIV
[pen.] John Sahabtai; [b.] August 11, 1974, Isreal; [p.] Argia and Eli Shabtai; [ed.] Graduated from Novato High School, attending Santa Rosa Junior College; [occ.] Sales; [memb.] Marvin Jewish Community Center; [oth. writ.] Currently working on an adventure novel; [pers.] Violence is proof that we, as humans, are still haunted by our primitive past. [a.] Novato, CA.

SHACKLETTE, JANE TALLEY
[pen.] Jane Talley Shacklette; [b.] November 19, 1957, Kingsport, TN; [p.] Dayton Talley and Bettie Hurd; [m.]

James Richard, June 23, 1978; [ch.] Stefanie, Joy, Brittany; [ed.] Florida College of Dental Technology; [oth. writ.] Have written ove 100 poems since 11 years old this was my first; [pers.] With imagination and spirit you can do anything. [a.] Jonesboro, GA.

SHAFER, JENNIFER L.
[b.] April 5, 1980, Sacramento, CA; [p.] Ernest and Yongcha; [ed.] University of Washington, Evergreen Junior High; [occ.] College student; [memb.] National Honor Society-Secondary Schools; [hon.] "Quest" program, Early Entrance Program, "Talent Search" Johns Hopkins Regional Award (for high SAT score); [oth. writ.] Several poems and short stories; [pers.] I wrote my poem in fourth grade. No kidding...it's sometimes hard to get better at writing; practice and love of the art is, I've found the best way. I love writing because it doesn't matter if I'm shy. [a.] Redmond, WA.

SHAFF, GLADYS C.
[b.] January 22, 1904, El Heights, NY; [p.] Claude and Eva Crittenden; [m.] seneca Shaff (deceased), January 20, 1935; [ch.] Nancy Crittenden McCaslin, Terry Paul Shaff; [ed.] Elmira Schools, Elmira College part-time; [occ.] Retired Bank Officer; [memb.] Endwell United Methodist Church, AARP, Western Broome Senior Citizen; [pers.] Enjoy writing, early desire to become a writer.

SHAIKH, RASHID A.
[pen.] Rashid Shaikh; [b.] July 15, 1946, Nagpur, India; [p.] Ibrahim M. Shaikh, Fatima Shaikh; [m.] Zaib Shaikh, May 19, 1979; [ch.] Hasan, Hussain, Hammad, Iram, Anam; [ed.] B.Sc., Karachi, Pakistan, B.S.M.E., M.P.M., Chicago; [occ.] Insurance Business; [memb.] Muslim Community Center, Chicago, Pakistan Federation of America; [hon.] Dean's list. Chairman, LSC, Brenneman Elementary, 1990, chairman/founder, Pakistan Day Parade, Chicago, Asian-American Coalition award, 1991, distinguished and devoted services to Pakistani community of Chicago award by mayor of Chicago, 1990; [oth. writ.] Several Urdu language poems published in Urdu Linkl of Los Angeles and Urdu Times of New York, Ebglish poems and articles in Unity Times of Chicago; [pers.] Illuminate candle of love in the pitch darkness of hatred and grudge!; [a.] Chicago, IL.

SHATRAW, IRENE
[b.] May 17, 1921, Dickenson Center, NY; [p.] Joseph and Ethel Gokey; [m.] Charles, January 8, 1943; [ch.] Philip, Donald, Charles; [ed.] High school; [occ.] Retired.

SHAVER, SISTER MILDRED
[b.] October 11, 1922, Lansing, MI; [p.] Mary and John Shaver; [ed.] Mt. St. Joseph, University of Detroit, Miami University; [occ.] Retired Volunteer Ministry; [pers.] My long time ministry in education and hospital/nursing home chaplaincy has kept me aware of the pain and joy of living. To creatively express this in poetry is a goal for my retirement years. [a.] Clinton Township, MI.

SHEA, MAUREEN MCALEES
[b.] July 13, 1942, Scotland, U.K.; [p.] Ann and Samuel McAlees; [ch.] Kevin Michael Shea; [ed.] Greenock High School, St. Louis Community College; [occ.] Entrepreneur-Home Cottage Crafts; [memb.] Ladies Ancient Order of Hibernians, Phi Theta Kappa; [hon.] United States Achievement Academy 1991, Collegiate Directory Vol. VI, Phi Theta Kappa, Dean's List; [oth.

writ.] "A Conversation with Heather", "A Years Gone By", "Freedom From Fear", 'How Soon We Forget", "Annie"; [pers.] As a survivor of incest and a lone immigrant to the U.S.A. where I've lost 5 children (2 buried) during the course of a 16 year marriage - now ended. I've come to appreciate every precious moment in time and dedicate my life to helping others. [a.] St. Louis, MO.

SHEHADI, FEIRUZ
[b.] December 30, 1947, Jerusalem; [ed.] DePaul University, University of Illinois at Chicago; [hon.] Golden Poet Award 1984 and 1985 from The World of Poetry Press; [oth. writ.] "My Aunt Before She Died", second place winner in Body Electric, a literary journal published by The University of L at Chicago, numerous other poems published in Body Electric; the World of Poetry anthologies and other anthologies and journals; [pers.] My poetry is a reflection of our society - the celebration and condemnation; the humane and inhumane; the beauty and the ugliness; the victories and defeats; of the spirit and the senses. [a.] Chicago, IL.

SHELLITO, KATRINA
[pen.] Katrina Malbon; [b.] January 3, 1979, VA; [p.] Gary, Barbara Malbon; [ed.] Princess Anne Middle School; [hon.] Cheerleader and have received many trophies; [pers.] My seventh grade English teacher is who got me into writing poems. I wrote my poems during Hurricane Emily in 1993. [a.] VA Beach, VA.

SHELTON, JAMES
[b.] January 30, 1975, Philadelphia, PA; [p.] James and Karen Shelton; [ed.] Bodine High School of International Affairs, Temple University. [a.] Philadelphia, PA.

SHEPHERD, JAMIE R.
[b.] June 13, 1978, Joliet, IL; [p.] James and Teresa Shepherd; [ed.] Joliet Catholic Academy; [oth. writ.] 5 poems published in National Library of Poetry books.

SHEPHERD, LESLIE
[b.] July 31, 1958, Trenton, NJ; [p.] Donald and Joyce Shepherd; [ed.] Ewing High School; [occ.] Editor/word processor (New Jersey State House); [memb.] National Burn Victim Foundation; [pers.] My brother, Graig, was electrocuted with 11,000 volts of electricity, he survived. Since 11,000 children a year are elecxtrocuted I am presently doing a presentation for the school boards to make people aware of the problem. I am also working with Texas and in the future other states. [a.] Trenton, NJ.

SHEPHERD, THERESA WILSON
[pen.] Paris Lane; [b.] October 10, 1949, Cartersville, GA; [p.] Ray Lane and Mary M. Wilson; [m.] DAvid Allen, May 22, 1993; [ch.] Mark and Jeana Hardin (grandson-Jesse Ray Hardin) Christopher Ira Shepherd and Christie Renee Shepherd; [occ.] Lockheed Aeronautical Systems; [memb.] Emerson Baptist Church; [pers.] Loving parents and close family ties have inspired my writing and also my faith in God. I dedicate my writing to my family and especially to my father who never gave up the fight, and always believed in my abilities. [a.] Emerson, GA.

SHEPHERD-MARSHALL, YVONNE PAMELA
[pen.] Yvonne Pamela Shepherd-Marshall; [b.] 19th century, planet earth; [p.] Joseph Nathaniel and Glovina T. Shepherd; [m.] Joel Curtis Carrington Marshall; [ch.] Johanna Casandra Marshall-Cordero, Jacqueline Celeste Marshall; [ed.] Unity High, Spanish-American Institute,

Ophelia De Vore, Wilfred Academy of Hair and Beauty Culture, Elizabeth Seton College, Empire State College; [occ.] Cosmetologist; [hon.] Dean's list; [oth. writ.] Articles and poems published in church magazine; [pers.] It is imperative that we cease making distinctions among peoples based on age; creed, gender, nationality and race. With the approach of a new millennium, we should engender harmony. The task is gargantuan; nevertheless, we must strive for peace. [a.] Cambra Heights, NY.

SHERLIN, KALEI T.
[pen.] Tyfani Blerins; [b.] June 6, 1976, Ft. Oglethorpe, GA; [p.] Glenn and B.J. Sherlin; [ed.] Lafayette High School; [occ.] McDonald's Cashier; [hon.] Art awards; [oth. writ.] Several unpublished poems and two unpublished books; [pers.] Art of all forms, poetry or drawing, came from the heart. As the holder of my key to success I have the power of all imagined possibilities. [a.] Lafayette, GA.

SHERMAN, LURA L.
[b.] October 31, 1924, Madisonville; [p.] Ethod and Ethel Wheaton; [m.] Charles E., August 13, 1945; [ch.] Dr. Bernadette Sherman, Charles Sherman; [ed.] St. Paul High, Jarvis Christian College, DePaul Graduate College; [occ.] Reading teacher, retired; [memb.] University Church, serve on World Outreach Committee, WTTW; [hon.] The greatest mother, official cadet on the science ship Antares, several other poems written; [oth. writ.] Wrote a speech and spoke on WTTW Television Sunday Evening Club; [pers.] I was greatly influenced by my descendents who were educators. [a.] Chicago, IL >

SHLICHTMAN, MARIBEL SANTANA
[b.] April 26, 1965, New Jersey; [m.] Steven, September 6, 1987; [ed.] High school graduate; [occ.] Receptionist; [oth. writ.] More poetry. [a.] Anaheim, CA.

SHOEMAKER, SARAH
[b.] August 21, 1983, Laguna Beach, CA; [p.] Rick and Kathy Shoemaker; [ed.] Fifth grade; [hon.] El Morro Elementary School, hold office in student council - student counsil treasurer; [oth. writ.] Sparrowgrass Poetry Contest Semi-finalist (still pending). [a.] Laguna Beach, CA.

SHORT, MARY KAY
[b.] December 15, 1971, Binghamton, NY; [p.] Lois and John Tubangh; [m.] fiance'-Mark LeClair; [ed.] Maine Endwell HIgh School, State University of New York at Potsdam; [occ.] Student; [pers.] My relationship with my fiance' Mark, inspired me to write this poem. I thank him for always being by my side. [a.] Endwell, NY.

SHRUM, WILLIAM R.
[pen.] Shrummy; [b.] May 18, 1947, Crown, PA; [p.] Ethel Gilmore and Late Clarence Shrum; [m.] Divorced; [ch.] Derrek Wayne and Dustin Ray; [ed.] Clarion Area High School, Clarion University of PA; [occ.] Student; [memb.] One of founders of presently forming Classical Music Club of Clarion University; [hon.] Many placques and recognitions of merit for contributions of time helping the youth of the local area; [oth. writ.] Presently compiling an article for Newsweek's "My Turn" column; [pers.] I seem to be able to put into words my inner most feelings. I believe that if everyone could do this, they could help ease their troubling feelings as well as those of others. [a.] Clarion, PA.

SHULMISTRAS, JOAN B.
[b.] June 14, 1951, Laramie, WY; [p.] Walter and Mildred Barnet; [p.] Joseph A. Shulmistras, Jr., January 28, 1978; [ed.] Westmont College, California State University; [occ.] Student and homemaker; [hon.] President's Honor List, Phi Alpha Theta, Natural Sciences Faculty Scholarship; [oth. writ.] Commentary and several poems published in college newspaper; [pers.] As I revel in the beauty of creation, I am mindful of the fact that we are called to worship the Creator, not His creation. [a.] Placentia, CA.

SIBLEY, KAREN
[pen.] Sue Sibley; [b.] April 16, 1956, Boston, MA; [p.] Russell and Betty Sibley; [m.] Deceased; [ch.] Ryan, Christopher, Bobby, Vinny and Matthew; [ed.] Randolph High, Brockton Night School; [occ.] Homemaker, School volunteer; [hon.] Head start school volunteer, Martin Young School volunteer, Tower Hill School volunteer, Donovan School volunteer, North School volunteer; [oth. writ.] Many others unpublished; [pers.] I write about what is close to my heart. My children (5 sons) are my greatest inspiration. They were God's gift to me and they are my gift to the world. [a.] Randolph, MA.

SIEBERM L. ARYN
[pen.] L.A. Sieber; [b.] June 17, 1960, Titysville, FL; [p.] William and Gloria Sieber; [ch.] Jared, Eric, and Ryan; [occ.] New Product Development & Marketing; [oth. writ.] Other poems and songs written none ever submitted in contest. "Carry On", "Dreams", "Aloha Hawaii", "Love & Agony"; [pers.] The key to success is to never loose the key. [a.] Roland Hts., CA.

SIEBOLD, WENDY
[b.] March 10, 1984, Rimbey, Alberta, CAN; [p.] Kim and Harley Siebold; [ed.] Bluffton School (grade 4); [oth. writ.] Poems published locally, "What time is best" and "Nightmares" which also won school contest. Has written several short stories; [pers.] I would like to be an author, poet, and illustrator. [a.] Bluffton, Alberta, CAN.

SIGETY, PATRICK RAYMOND
[b.] February 8, 1961, Rapid City, SD; [p.] Clarence and Sylvania Sigety; [m.] Martha (McQuistion), September 21, 1993; [ch.] Robert W., Joshua R., Angela L., Eric R., Robbie S.; [ed.] Rapid City Central High, (Clearfield Job Corp); [occ.] Restuarant waiter; [memb.] Crow Creek Sioux Tribe; [oth. writ.] Have written around a dozen other works, but as of yet have not been published; [pers.] In my writings I reflect my beliefs, experiences, and fantasies. I hope that people discuss my work bad or good, any less and I haven't given you my best. [a.] Pierre, SD.

SILVA, CULLEN DORIS
[pen.] Judith Charis; [b.] February 5, 1952, Rockville Centre, NY; [p.] James and Joan Cullen Doris; [m.] Joseph Silva, Jr.; [ch.] Six; [ed.] St. Agnes High School, Nassau Community College, State University College of New York at Geneseo, Adelphi University, Hofstra University, Southeastern Massachusetts University, (University of MA at Darmouth), Diocese of FAll-River - Youth Ministry Certificate Program, New England School of Floral Design; [hon.] Dean's list; [occ.] Speech - Language Pathologist, Youth Ministry Volunteer, Free-lance Ministry, Free-lance Floral Designer, Retail Sales Consultant; [oth. writ.] Several poems, prose and articles published in local newspapers; [pers.] My writings are most influenced by using faith to recognize,

accept, and overcome the obstacles that befall us. [a.] Dighton, MA.

SYLVIA, HAYDEE
[pen.] H. Dilva; [b.] January 6, 1950, PR; [p.] Julia and Demetrio Silva; [ch.] Yvonne, Mike, George, Kenny; [ed.] BmCC and looking forward to continue; [occ.] Educational Assistant for Hearing Education Service; [memb.] English, Spanish and Sign Language; [oth. writ.] Thank You, Surprised, Evasive, Found Again, Pocket Size, If You Could See, Stories, Chase, Dream, Understand, Was I Selfish", Upside Down; [pers.] I feel that with my writing people can understand that we all can hurt the same. And by writing there are times it make me feel better that I can communicate with someone else. [a.] Brony, NY.

SIMMERS, JULIE
[b.] June 27, 1981, Anaheim Hills, CA; [p.] John and Margie Simmers; [ed.] 7th grade Manhattan Beach Middle School; [pers.] I enjoy writing about peaceful places and letting my mind flow. [a.] Manhattan Beach, CA.

SIMMONS, DAVID L.
[b.] June 10, 1966, Omaha, NE; [p.] Clarance and Elizabeth Simmons; [occ.] Moving Specialist JHU/APL; [oth. writ.] Other personal writings; [pers.] Special thanks Ann Seymour and Theresa Thomas. I only hope that someone could receive a positive mesage from my writings. [a.] Greenbelt, MD.

SIMMONS, LATONYA
[b.] March 3, 1978, Newport News, VA; [p.] Keith and Carnetta Simmons; [ed.] Ferguson High School; [occ.] Student headed for college; [memb.] Hampton University's Upward Bound, Natural Helpers, Center for H.O.P.E.; [hon.] Third grade Spelling Bee, Young Author's Award, Most Outstanding in Drama and Math, All-City Chorus, Natural Helper; [pers.] Writing on realistics and reality are positive ways of releasing ones frustrations of the world, which seems to be inclosing chaos that destroys us as a people. Writing from the heart is truly self-rewarding. [a.] Newport News, VA.

SIMMONS, SUE
[pen.] Suzi Q; [b.] June 6, 1940, Sand Ford, W.VA; [m.] Jerome "Sonny" (deceased); [ch.] Cheryl and Susie Jones; [ed.] Sutton High School; [memb.] Women of the Moose, The American Legion; [hon.] The best honor in the world are the friends who encourage me to keep writing and urge me to one day have my own book published; [pers.] I have read poetry for as long as I can remember. I only began writing this year. One night I had an urge I couldn't resist, and I began putting my feelings on paper. [a.] Clearwater, FL.

SIMMONS, STZEN W.
[pen.] Zeek Heartland; [b.] March 24, 1970, Wooster, OH; [p.] Wayne and Sheila Simmons; [ed.] West Holmes High School; [occ.] Art Gallery Director; [oth. writ.] Several poems and pro's printed in two high school waiting club publicatioins; [pers.] Love with respect this is the key to life. [a.] San Francisco, CA.

SIMMS-LEWIS, SUSIE
[pen.] Susie Simms; [b.] June 10, 1964, St. Louis, MO; [p.] Carl and Bertha Simms; [m.] James Q. Lewis, Jr., November 20, 1993; [ed.] Criminal Justice Administration, Normandy High School; [occ.] MS State Trooper; [memb.] Central States Trooper Coalition, MS State

Trooper Association, MS Law Enforcement Officer Association; [pers.] Everything I write comes from the heart. The more a subject affects me emotionally the easier the words flow from pen to paper. [a.] Tupelo, MS.

SIMPSON, CATHERINE
[b.] March 7, 1950, Lonton, ONT, CAN; [m.] Donald Simpson, November 25, 1967; [ch.] Shawn William and Christ Anthony; [ed.] Lucas Secondary School; [occ.] Professional Artist-Watercolours of Children and Nature; [hon.] People's Choirce Award-Lambeth Art Festival/Grims By Art FEstival Drawing Award 1985 and W/C Award 1992; [oth. writ.] 15 limited edition prints of artwork; [pers.] In the attic of every grownup's head joyful memories of youth are safely tucked away, waiting to be rediscovered. My art and poetry attempt to light the way. [a.] London, ONT., CAN.

SIMPSON, RUTH
[pen.] La Netta Poo; [b.] March 11, 1949, McCall, MS; [p.] Hazel and A.C. Hilliard; [m.] Tommy, November 1, 1973; [ch.] Kimara and Jason Simpson; [ed.] High school; [occ.] Housewife; [memb.] New Covenant Life Church; [oth. writ.] Several other poems; [pers.] I give God the glory for the poems that I write.

SIMS, INGRID CHRISTOPHER
[pen.] Chris; [b.] April 17, 1958, Christiansted, St. Croix, V.I.; [p.] Ivy E. and Patric A. Christopher; [ch.] David Anthony, Kenneth Lamar, Quianah DaShawn; [ed.] St. Croix Central High School, US Army-Act Travel School, Academy of Health Sciences; [occ.] Customer Service Agent; [hon.] Army Service Ribbon, Army Commendation Medal, Army Good Conduct Medal, Overseas Service Ribbon, NCO Professional Development Ribbon, Honorary Member, Carlton Press, Inc.; [oth. writ.] The Turning Point; [pers.] I try through my writing to bring out what I feel within, so that I can best understand myself, my chidren and my surroundings. I have been greatly influenced by God who is my guide. [a.] Deerfield Beach, FL.

SIMS, WILLIAM EARL
[pen.] William Earl Sims; [b.] October 25, 1935, Dallas, TX; [p.] Will and Geraldine Sims; [ch.] Mirey' Noel Sims; [ed.] College graduate; [occ.] Real Estate Finance; [oth. writ.] Book Code Name Zebra, screen plays, One Last Fling, Sallie Blue, Code Name Zebra & Flight 71; [pers.] On the plains of hesitation bleches the bones of countless millions, who upon the dawm of victory, sat down to rest and resting, they died.

SINCLAIR, JEFFREY ALLEN
[pen.] Jeff Sinclair; [b.] August 22, 1977, Grundy County, TN; [p.] Charles Sinclair and Ada Padilla; [ed.] Rhea County High School; [occ.] Student; [memb.] ROTC; [hon.] Nominated to National Honor Society of Who's Who, ROTC Community Service, Second LT-JROTC, Perfect Attendance award; [pers.] Dedicated to the girl who will never be mine. [a.] Spring City, TN.

SINGLETON, JOHN
[b.] September 18, 1968, Glendale, CA; [p.] WArren and Pauline Singleton; [m.] Tracy, November 6, 1989; [ch.] Ryan Tyler, Justin Robert; [ed.] Mary G. Montgomery High School; [occ.] Bus Operator, LA Metropolitan Transportation Authority. [a.] North Hills, CA.

SINGLETON, MATTHEW J.
[pen.] Mattt, R2; [b.] December 10. 1983, Staten Island, NY; [p.] Daniel Singleton, Nadine Singleton; [ed.] P.S.

44, Staten Island, NY' [occ.] 5th grade student; [memb.] Goodhue Basketball, Richmond County Martial Arts, school safety squad, school color guard; [hon.] Spelling Bee, karate tournaments; [oth. writ.] "Happy Birthday", "Rhythmn", "Eight Is Too Late"; [pers.] Thanks, Mom, Dad, Mr. Quin, Mr. Bruno, and Mrs. Termotto. Your believing in me keeps me believing in myself; [a.] Staten Island, NY.

SINKE, EVELYN
[b.] September 28, 1916, MI; [p.] Beatson and Eva Walkinshaw; [m.] Leonard Sinke, August 20, 1957; [ch.] Dr. Jan Bennett, Diana Keenan, Dr. Suzanne Sinke; [ed.] B.S. Western Mich U, Masters, Michiga State; [occ.] Retired; [memb.] Vintage Jazz Club, West Shore Jazz Club, Hot Alligator Gumbo Society, FL, Michigan Airstream Club, AARP; [hon.] Who's Who in Poetry, 1990; [oth. writ.] Other poems and memoirs; [pers.] A love to honor or advise people in verse or record stories in verse; [a.] Lowell, MI.

SIRIWARDENE, MAHENDRA
[b.] September 24, 1938, Kandy, Sri Lanka; [p.] Morley and Hilda; [m.] Shirani, February 5, 1988; [ed.] High school; [occ.] Correspondent in Toronto for Sri Lanka newspaper The Island; [memb.] Member and editor of Canada-Sri Lanka Association of Toronto, Hon. editor, Toronto Mahavihara (Buddhist Temple); [hon.] Winner of General Knowledge prize in school, General Proficiency prize; [oth. writ.] Contributor of a variety of articles to the Sri Lanka newspapers, one letter to the editor of the Toronto Star, short story to The Toronto Life magazine, publication of book on Buddhist tales in progress; [a.] Mississauga, Ont, Canada.

SISON, ANN
[pen.] A. M. Sison; [b.] October 12, 1974, Essex, England; [p.] Annie and Errol Sispn (deceased); [ed.] Beverly Hills High School, Santa Monica College; [occ.] Student, investor; [pers.] I dedicate this poem to my mother Annie Sison; [a.] Los Angeles, CA.

SITTERLY, LANA
[b.] JUly 9, 1979, Albany, NY; [p.] Brenda and Peter Sitterly Sr.; [ed.] School #16, Blessed Sacrament School; [memb.] Teen Research Gang, Teen Magazine; [hon.] 2nd place in Creative Writing Fair, 7th grade; [oth. writ.] Wrote a short story for Junior Writers Week, 5th grade; [pers.] I would like to thank my 8th grade teacher, Ms. Fortune, because wihtout her this would never have happened; [a.] Albany, NY;

SKANNAL, DEBORAH G.
[b.] April 8, 1959, Shreveport, LA; [p.] John and Catherine Skannal Sr.; [hon.] Editors Choise Award for Outstanding Achievement in Poetry by National Library of Poetry, 1993; [oth. writ] A book of poetry and creative writings; [pers.] My poetry is inspired by God, and He gave me the talent of writing poetry. I feel that I have some understanding of the dynamics of mankind and this is depicted in my writings; [a.] Southfield, MI.

SLANEY, MICHELLE
[b.] September 21, 1971, Nfld, Canada; [p.] Eric and Patricia Slaney; [ed.] Memorial University of Nfld; [occ.] Student; [memb.] Teachers on Wheels, Tuors Unlimited, Association for New Canadians, School for the Deaf; [hon.] Previously published in "A Question of Balance"; [pers.] If life throws you a curveball, swing at it anyway, you never know what might happen; [a.] St. Johns, Canada.

SLATER, JOHN C.
[b.] August 6, 1959, Pontiac, MI; [p.] Richard Slater, Dorothy Slater; [m.] Audrey Slater, September 25, 1982; [ed/] Grayling High School; [occ.] Production team member, Weyerhaeuser, Co.; [hon.] Honor Roll, Grayling High School; [oth. writ.] Numerous poems, short stories, paintings with script and other data; [pers.] I enjoy reading, writing, and painting tremendously. I especially like reading adventure stories and I try to create that type of mood in my writing; [a.] Beaver Creek, MI.

SLINEY, TOMMY
[pen.] Tommy Slayer; [b.] July 17, 1973, [oth. writ.] Poems of various topics. Attempted short stories, scripts, and short books; [pers.] After reading some of J.R.R. Tolkien's works and playing Dungeons and Dragons. I feel that there is more to life than just existing. Dedicated to the damsel in distress; [a.] Bronx, NY.

SLOAN, BOBIE JO
[pen.] Yoei Jordan; [b.] August 24, 1968, Boston, MA; [p.] Robert Sloan, Dorothy Sloan; [ed.] Randolph High School; [pers.] I dedicate my efforts to Carol Perry, my aunt, a woman who has taught me to always believe in myself and my dreams; [a.] Tampa. FL.

SLOAT, DOLORES
[pen.] Dee Sloat; [b.] March 9, 1948, Brooklyn, NY; [p.] Irene Cabrera, Arthur Cabrera; [ch.] Vincent, Brian, Darren Sloat; [ed.] Uniondale High School, Uniondale L.I., NY, Middlesex County College, Edison, NJ; [occ.] Waitress; [memb.] Raritan Bay Poet Association; [pers.] Being the oldest ot nine children, I learned very early how to survive in loving confusion. Those skills enabled me to survive a life which was not always loving. My writings are my statement that dreams are our visions of tomorrow. These visions I place lovingly on paper; [a.] East Brunswick, NJ.

SMALL, FRED A.
[b.] June 8, 1928, Cumberland, MD; [p.] Frederick T. and Mary D. Small; [m.] Midge Murphy Small, January 13, 1951; [ch.] Colleen Tara, Kim Collier, Susan Joy, Dawn Michelle; [ed.] The Park School, Lehigh University, Goddard College, McGill University; [occ.] Research and Development; [memb.] The Explorers Club, Detroit Boy Scout Community Commissioner; [hon.] Several dozen government meritorious awards, listed in Who's Who,; [oth. writ.] Several dozen published books, articles and papers; [pers.] Enjoy reading the "100 Great Books" and solving life's problems through writing. [a.] Boulder, CO.

SMALLWOOD, JOYCE
[pen.] Joyce Horsey Smallwood; [b.] November 20, 1938; [p.] Wilmer N. and Anna Jo Horsey; [m.] Ex, May 17, 1970; [ch.] Verna Victoria, Shirley Denise, (grandchildren-Richard, Phillip Raphael, Veronica, Lynn, Pierre Lemuel; [ed.] Haddon Heights HIgh, MTI Business School; [occ.] Computer Operator; [memb.] Berean Bible Mission, Sanctuart of the Abiding Presence; [oth. writ.] Couple poems published in Gloucester City Times and Courier Post both NJ papers, childrens book "Golden Chips for Jr. Snacking"; [pers.] Endeavoring to make a difference, to add to the flavor of love which is so needed today. Even to prepare lily pads of such that our children and grand-children may tread upon. A bit of heart, hearing and hope.

SMILEY, JUDYE RENEE
[b.] December 10, 1955, Tuskegee, AL; [p.] Theodore

and Ollie Sims; [m.] Bernard Smiley, October 27, 1978; [ch.] Jenipher, Rejena, Robyn; [ed.] B.S. degree, South Carolina State Univ, Masters of Education, Wayne State University; [occ.] Teacher; [hon.] Kappa Omicron Phi, graduated cum laude; [oth. writ.] I have written many poems for our school, friends, and family; [pers.] My inner feelings and thoughts are best shown through my writings; [a.] Detroit, MI.

SMITH, ANDREA
[b.] January 25, 1977, Queens, NY; [p.] Lola Smith, Rosevelt Kerr; [ed.] Immaculate Conception School; Monsignor Scanlan High School; [memb.] Student Council, Scholastic Peer Instructional Network; [pers.] You can be anything you want to be in this lifetime as long as you put your mind to it, there are no limitations; [a.] Bronx, NY.

SMITH, BEN
[pen.] Destinee Kristian; [b.] April 21, 1966, Lexington, KY; [p.] Don and Jean Smith; [occ.] Lab tecnician; [oth. writ.] "Pathways To The Future's Past" is a science fiction novella I recently finished but have not been able to publish as yet ; [pers.] I want to recognize my sisters Laura and Angie for their support. Also my nephews Matthew and Zach for being my inspiration. Much love to you!; [a.] Lexington, KY.

SMITH, BION E.
[b.] January 21, 1904, Syracuse, NY; [p.] Pastor Willis B. Smith; [m.] Christina Schultz, April 28, 1928; [ch.] Patricia Beckett, Robert Smith and Leslie Smith; [ed.] Syracuse Central High, Johnson Bible College; [occ.] Retired; [memb.] Mason, Shriner, past president, High 12 Club, Lake Worth , FL, Boynton Beach Church of Christ; [hon.] Boy Scouts Medal WWI, past president and honorary member, Connecticut Society of Beauty Culture Schools, selectman, Marlborough, CT; [oth. writ.] "Love", "God's Holy Spirit", "Love of God, "Miracles of Jesus", "The Resurrection of Jesus" "If You Trust Jesus", "The Evolution of An Atheist;]pers.] I a m trying to leave the world and its people in a better condition than when I arrived; [a.] Boynton Beach, FL.

SMITH, CLIFFORD
[b.] March 14, 1947, Elgon, TX; [ch.] 3 boys, 1 girl; [oth. writ.] "Our Changing World" (poem); [pers.] I enjoy writing about life and the surroundings. I thank God of heaven for the wisdom entrusted to me; [a.] Madisonville, TX.

SMITH, DANA B. E.
[pen.] Dana Dunn Smith; [b.] March 16, 1947, Jamaica; [p.] Elkanah and Olive Dunn; [ch.] Janet Glaze; [ed.] Moveland Hill Primary School, Northwestern Academy, Medgers Evers College, City College of the New York City University; [occ.] Writer, publisher, public speaking, stage performer; [oth. writ.] Author of two books: Faces In The Sun, and The Nations in Waiting. I also appeared in newspapers, tel;evison and radio talk shows, write article for magazines and newspapers; [pers.] We writers must sincerely fight against the enchantment of evil which often invades our thinking. There is an urgent need for kindness, a freedom that should not be hampered by a greed for recognition. I have recently recognized the overwhelming power which sleeps in the pen and paper, a salvation which can only be awakened by good conscience; [a.] St. Louis, MO.

SMITH, EDDIE BERNARD
[b.] April 6, 1956, Chicago, IL; [m.] Natisa Allen Smith;

[ch.] Angela and Maquilla Smith; [ed.] Marquette University, The University of Wisconsin-Milwaukee; [occ.] Business Proposal Writing; [oth. writ.] Manuscripts in metaphysics and general philosophy; [pers.] Writing is a vehicle for the expression of the human soul, its cultivation is a source of personal fulfillment and satisfaction. [a.] Milwaukee, WS

SMITH, JOAN C.
[b.] January 3, 1961, Washington, DC; [p.] Truman and Lilla Smith; [ch.] Three nephews; [ed.] Journalism Clark College, Suitland Sr. High School, Howard University, Press Book Publishing Institute; [occ.] Assistant Cluster Coordinator/Atlanta Project; [memb.] Board of Directors, Together Atlanta Magazine, Inc., Volunteer Grady Hospital First Steps, Neighborhood Planning Unit Secretary, Community Consultant Adams Park Area; [hon.] HS Honor Society, College Honor Roll, GA Department of Labor essay winner, Howard University essay winner, several communications scholarships; [oth. writ.] Freelanced A&L DAily World, Atlanta Tribune, Atlanta Journal/Constitution, Wash. DC City Hall New Times newspaper; [pers.] I consider myself a "heart person" meaning that what I write comes from the depths of my heart. I try to convey reality to my audience. [a.] Atlanta, GA.

SMITH, KAREN V. MCKENZIE
[b.] June 26, 1953, Mapel Creek, Sask; [m.] Dr. Ross H. McKenzie; [p.] Vivian (Hodgins) Smith, Forest Smith; [m.] Dr. Ross H. McKenzie, June 19, 1976; [ch.] Kyle Hugh, Colin Ross, Christina Karen; [ed.] Maple Creek High, River, Camrose, Ponoka, University of Alberta, University of Lethbridge; [occ.] Muli-faceted engineer, including writing, painting, and illustrating; [memb.] A number of charity volunteer organizations, YMCA board, Stonecroft Christian Business and Professional Women; [hon.] Highest Royal Lifesaving award, graduated from university with distinction, athletic awards, gold medal at the Candian Japanese Mixed Bonspiel in Hokkaido, Japan; [oth. writ.] He Is There, Monster Wallpaper, Cutouts, A Lot To Do About Names, as well as illustrations and paintings; [pers.] Most of what I do write, illustrate or speak about reflects what I grasp from the intensities of life and in turn have an overwhelming desire to give it back, in a life-long ambition to give the best of what ever I can whenever I can; [a.] Lethbriodge, Alberta Canada.

SMITH, KIMBERLY ANN
[b.] September 4, 1973; [p.] Eugene and Judy Smith; [ed.] South River High School, Anne Arundel Community College, Salisbury State University; [memb.] International Thespian Society; [hjon.] Deans List, Best Thespian, 1991, Anne Arundel County Fair Queen contest, South River Ruitan Club Scholarship, Maryland Senatorial Scholarship; {pers.] I thank the Lord in heaven everyday for giving me the ability to serve him through my writing. He is my inspiration and without him I could not write a single word. His love for me is why I write the poems I do; [a.] Edgewater, MD.

SMITH MARY ANN
[b.] August 13, 1942, CA; [p.] Clyde and Gretchen Magers; [ch.] Teresa, Debra, darryl, Angela, Randy, Kenneth; [pers.] Dedicated to mother; [a.] Batesville, AK.

SMITH, RUTH
[b.] October 8, 1965, Morgantown, WV; [p.] Eunice H. and Thomas B. Smith; [ed.] B.A. Elementary Education,

M.A. Reading and Reading Content Specialist Test; [occ.] Reading Specialist; [memb.] PTA, Preston County Reading Council, West Virginia Reading Council, International Reading Association, West Virginia Education Association; [hon.] Teacher of the Year 1991-1992; [oth. writ.] Published Spring 1992, "Sky-Scape" with Broken Streets; [pers.] My writing is directed toward nature and the automaticity of life. I have been greatly influenced by my mother. Also, I am indebted to the teachers who inspired me to do my best; [a.] Bruceton MIlls, WV.

SMITH, SARI DECONINCK
[pen.] Sari; [b.] October 14, 1978, Rosetown, Saskatchewan; [p.] Nancy and Rich deConinck Smith; [ed.] Rosetown Central High School; [occ.] Student; [memb.] American Quarter Horse Association; [oth. writ.] Began penning thoughts in verse from about the age of 14. I find it very easy to express myself in this way; [pers.] Writing poems vents alot of teenage frustrations and unanswered questions. It is very therapeutic to let others know how you feel in a simple poem; [a.] Rosetown, Sask.

SMITH, SUSAN m.
[pen.] Susan M. DeLuney; [b.] April 16, 1957, Minneapolis, MN; [p.] Leo and Marion DeLuney; [m.] Ronald P. Hess; [ch.] Brian Hess, Amy Hess; [ed.] GED, 1975, Anoka Ramsey Community College, Metropolitan State University; [occ.] Student and parent; [hon.] Phi Theta Kappa, dean's list, personal achievemen: recovery from drug and alcohol avuse; [oth. writ.] Many other writings, both poetry and short stories. I hope to get published at some point in my life; [pers.] I have a very simple philosophy which comes from Alcoholics Anonymous. LIve and let live./ What a peaceful place our world would be if evryone would follow this simple statement. My two favorite poets are Emily Dickinson and Robert Frost; [a.] Mprth Beach, MN.

SMITH TANDINIKA
[pen.] Tandi Smith; [b.] July 21, 1979, Wa; [p.] Patricia and Rodney Blumenberg; [ed.] Keller High School; [occ.] Student; [memb.] St. Paul Reform Baptist Church; [hon.] Best reading, JUnior Achievement, Honor Roll, P.E. awards; [oth. writ.] I have a poem book, but no one sees it but me. I am on the school newspaper staff; [pers.] I want to say thank you to my mom, Patrice Blumenberg, my dad, Rodney Blumenberg, Maurice Smith, my grandpa, Andrew Mack, my sis Zenobia Smith, two twin brothers Robert and Ronald Smith, and my grandma, LaVonne Mack. I love y'all; {a.][Ft. Worth, TX.

SMITH, THEODORE (TED) G.
[b.] October 19, 1957, Willowbrook, CA; [p.] Thomas E. Smith, Marilyn G. Rutter; [m.] Kathleen I. Smith, May 27, 1978; [ch.] Melanie Kelly Smith, Melissa Lauren Smith; [ed.] AAS Electronic Engineer, CCCC, NLV, NV, National University, UNLV; [occ.] Disabled; [memb.] /Alpha Kappa Psi, Biblical Archaeology Society; [hon.] Magna cum laude, BBA, Woodrow Wilson Distinguished Scholar; [oth. writ.] Songs, poems published locally in high school and college; [pers.] Only one life, will soon be past only what's done for Christ will last; [a.] Las Vegas, NV.

SMOOT, CASSANDRA T.
[pen.] Cassy; [b.] February 19, 1976, Aylesbury, England; [p.] Wendell and Marina Smoot; [ed.] Patch American High School; [memb.] Parlimentarian of Future Business Leaders of America (FBLA); [hon.]

Outstanding Student in Biology; [oth. writ.] Articles in school newspaper; [pers.] Never doubt your abilities to do something. [a.] Buffalo, NY.

SNEDEKER, B.L.
[b.] October 3, 1925, South Lansing, NY; [m.] William; [ch.] Jan (son) and Karen; [ed.] Ithaca High School, Rider College; [occ.] Retired Journalist; [memb.] Sierra Club, Greenpeace, Defenders of Wildlife; [oth. writ.] Former columnist and news editor, The Sentinel; [pers.] Environmentalist and nature lover. [a.] Lewistown, PA.

SNYDER, JAMES
[pen.] J.D. Booker; [b.] December 12, 1956, Saskatoon, SASK.; [p.] Al and Hazel Snyder; [m.] The Ancient of Days, Rapture; [ch.] Natasha and Bear (dogs); [ed.] Mt. Royal Collegiate, Streets of North America, Central Pentacostal College; [occ.] Oil Painter, pesonalized poem-a-grams-send info-any occasion; [memb.] Canadian Mental Health Association, Crocus Co-op; [oth. writ.] Poetry book - "The Rhyme in my Spine Falls mainly on my Brine"; [pers.] Let every man be a liar and Jesus Christ right. Only Believe! [a.] Hawarden, SASK, CAN.

SNYDER, LINDA L.
[b.] October 14, 1949, Millersburg, PA; [p.] Allen and Pauline Leitzel; [m.] Divorced; [ch.] Michael Paul Sedesse Jr.; [ed.] Millersburg Area High School, Harrisburg Area Community College; [occ.] Office Manager/ Secretary Waddell & Reed Financial Services; [memb.] American Business Women's Association, National Association of Female Executives; [hon.] During a 3 1/2 month study, I received the "Human Relations Award" in the Dale Carnegie course presented by Penn Institute, Inc.; [oth. writ.] Poems published in local newspapers and company Christmas cards; [pers.] I base my poems on personal experiences such as this one that was written after the death of my best friend, Wanda E. Leonard, at age 17 as a result of a traffic accident. [a.] Millersburg, PA.

SNYDER, WILLIAM O.J.
[b.] January 28, 1950, Shoal Lake, Man.; [p.] Cassel W. and Kathleen J. Snyder; [m.] Joan Gloria, July 20, 1991; [occ.] Taxi owner/operator; [memb.] Royalk Canadian Legion; [hon.] Canadian Forces Decoration; [pers.] this poem the ship was written while at sea in the South Pacific on board her majesty's Canadian ship Kootenay. [a.] Mill Bay, B.C.

SOLHEIM, MABEL
[pen.] Mabel Amanda; [b.] May 5, 1908, Goldfield, IA; [p.] John and Martha Luthro; [m.] Olaf, June 22, 1946; [ed.] High school; [occ.] Housewife-caring my husband, little singing; [memb.] Church-choir; [hon.] This from Selection Committee is surprising and lovely; [oth. writ.] Will send 2 copies of Devils Lake Journal editions.

SOLITARIO, DONNA M.
[b.] July 4, 1951, Springfield, MA; [p.] Richard and Cecile Dodds; [ch.] Tracy Dodds and Michael Solitario; [ed.] Trade High School, Holyoke Community College; [occ.] Sub. teacher aide and barber stylist; [oth. writ.] Currently a poem book almost finished, the title is Inspirational Poems; [pers.] I started writing 3 years ago, and I truly love touching the hearts of others. [a.] West Springfield, MA.

SOMMERS-BARNETT, PATRICIA
[pen.] Patricia Sommers-Barnett; [b.] February 27, 1953, Utica, NY; [p.] Walter and Josephine Sommers; [m.] Thomas Barnett, August 18, 1989; [ch.] Amanda, Beau, Tyson, Jason, Tonya; [ed.] Whitesboro High School, Valley Community College, U.S. Air Force; [occ.] Domestic Engineer, retired USAF; [memb.] Veterans of Foreign War Auxiliary; [oth. writ.] "Illumination" published in "Poetic Voices of America" 1991; [pers.] I believe that the best poems come from the heart. My husband encourages me and my parents have influenced me. I write poetry to give a one-of-a-kind dedication gift. [a.] Utica, NY.

SOMRAH, DARRYL
[pen.] Darryl; [b.] March 21, 1968, Trinidad, WI; [p.] Sonny and Grace Somrah; [pers.] And though success only comes with pain it will be forgotten with the threshold of victories. My influence on writing comes from loved ones. [a.] Jamaica Queens, NY.

SONNICHSEN, SIDNEY
[b.] May 3, 1909, Coeur d'Alene, ID; [p.] George W. and Emma M. Sonnichsen; [m.] Charlotte Miller Sonnichsen, August 8, 1935; [ch.] Cynthia, George, Donna; [ed.] St. Olaf College; [occ.] Retired; [memb.] Masonic Lodge Eastern Star Chapter, Methodist Church, American Legion Advisory Committee, Area Agency on Aging and Foster Grandparents; [hon.] Member of famous St. Olaf Choir, Outstanding Senior Citizen of my home county; [oth. writ.] When i was in the army I tried to end every letter home with a verse. Many only 4 lines, others longer. Total about 200. I have them all in a home made book. I write verses for many special events. Nothing has been published, special verse for special occasionsl; [pers.] Too much emphasis on the big "I" people have got to start realizing that life is a 50-50 proposition. GIVE and take. [a.] Princeton, MN.

SORIANO, DOLLIE
[pen.] Dollie Soriano; [b.] September 21, 1935, Manila, Philippines; [p.] Saturnina Gonzalez and Ramiro Soriano, Sr.; [ch.] Elizabeth, Walter, Joseph, Michael and Marty (twins) Soriano-Casuga and Catherine Casuga; [ed.] BS - Business Administration (Major-Accounting and Management); [occ.] Student Services Assistant; [memb.] American Association of Retired People (AARP), La Union Association of Ventura County, Oxnard College Classified Senate; [hon.] Honor student in High School; [oth. writ.] Draft of my Autobiography; [epers.] My creativeness and life experiences are instrumental in my writing with feelings and originality which are influential to my potential change of career or life style in my forthcoming retirement. [a.] Oxnard, CA.

SOUTER, DEBRA
[b.] June 11, 1961, England; [p.] William and Sylvia Farrey; [m.] Keith, August 23, 1980; [ch.] Michelle, Kelley, James; [pers.] This poem is dedicated to all of our children. And a special thank you to my Mom for everything..I love you. [a.] Westminster, CA.

SOUTHWARD, CECIL
[b.] Windsor, CAN; [p.] Cecil and Eva Southward, Sr.; [ed.] University of Windsor, Teachers College, Columbia University; [occ.] Educator, Windsor Board of Education; [pers.] The power of the word enables one to create and share life's experiences.

SPACKMAN, CHARLES THOMAS
[b.] October 18, 1960, Edmonton, Alberta, CAN; [p.] Patrick and Sonja Spackman; [m.] Kelly-Ann, July 17, 1982; [ch.] Jennifer Elizabeth Ann, Ryan Charles; [ed.] Crescent Heights High, Southern Alberta Institute of Technology; [occ.] Electrical Specialist, Syncrude Canada Limited; [pers.] I was inspired to write this poem for my wife Kelly on the occasion of ten beautiful years of marriage, she accepted, again. [a.] Ft. McMurray, Alberta, CAN.

SPADIDEAS, DEMY D.
[pen.] The Kikster; [b.] September 18, 1973, New York; [p.] Coastas and Aglaia Spadideas; [ed.] Cardozo High School, Drake Business School; [occ.] Assistant Manager at Blockbuster Video; [pers.] Look deep into your soul, for there is a poet inside waiting to be expressed. [a.] New York, NY.

SPAGNOLI, MADELINE
[b.] October 13, 1926, Red Lion, PA; [p.] Joseph and Thelma Hildebrand; [m.] Ivan; [ch.] Nine and 17 grandchildren; [ed.] University of PA Physical Therapy School; [occ.] Retired from physical therapy in 1990. Pursuing my second love, writing; [oth. writ.] A book being released in the fall of 1994. It is an autobiography from day one to 65, done entirely in rhymed verse; [pers.] SEveral poems have been published - mostly wash-and-wear theories from a drip-dry mind!

SPALDING, RITA S.
[b.] August 23, 1952, Louisville, KY; [p.] Ora and Nevill Spalding; [ch.] Jason, Tim, Erin; [ed.] Holy Roasary Academy; [occ.] Review Appraiser/Real Estate; [memb.] Louisville Board of Realtors, KY Association of Realtors, National Association of Realtors, Candidate member-Appraisal Institute; [oth. writ.] Published a book, "Abstract Ribbons"; [pers.] Writing is a spiritual extension of our inner healing, our greatest joys, our attitudes! It is a reflection of opportunities and adversites of gaines strength. With the reader, we are woven as one universal soul! [a.] Louisville, KY.

SPANN, CAROLYN
[b.] January 30, 1956, Aiken, SC; [p.] Col. Williams Sr. - Myra Williams; [m.] James E., June 22, 1974; [ch.] Jamie-Ammie-Janie-Jenny-James P.; [ed.] Martha Schofield High; [occ.] Housewife and mother; [oth. writ.] First poem every to be published "Please excuse my Mistakes"; [pers.] I have always had a heart of love and lived a life of fanacies. I can express it thought my poems. [a.] Aiken, SC.

SPANN, NATHANAEL J.
[pen.] Nathanel J. Spann; [b.] February 5, 1973, Ontario, CAN; [p.] Thomas C. Spann and Valli L. Fitzgerald; [ed.] Life's experiences; [occ.] STudnet; [pers.] Search deep inside to find your true self and what you need to nurture your soul. Only then will the world fall into place. [a.] Mission Viejo, CA.

SPEERS, MICHAEL LLOYD
[pen.] Michael Lloyd; [b.] March 7, 1961, IL; [p.] Dennis Speers and Nancy Wurster; [m.] Vicki Lynn, June 19, 1982; [ch.] Leanne Nicole; [ed.] GED State of Arizona; [occ.] Pressmans first assistant Quebecor Printing; [memb.] Seventh Day Adventist Church, First Free Evangelical Church; [oth. writ.] I written poems upon request, for family, friends. I've had one published in the church bulletin, and one in Hometown Paper; [pers.] I write for the Lord. [a.] Mt. Morris, IL.

SPEIRS, KREG DANIEL
[b.] December 3, 1973, Vietnam; [m.] Mrs. and Mrs. Robert Speirs; [ed.] Warren County Vocational Techni-

cal High School, All Saint Regional High School; [occ.] Cook; [hon.] High school award and honored for creative writing, theater and vocal music; [oth. writ.] Other types of poems, short stories and short story plays; [pers.] My poetry is a mirror image of visual understnding of worldly situations. I have been greatly inspired by the action and feelings of society today. [a.] Phillipsburg, NJ.-

SPELL, JR., RONALD EUGENE
[pen.] C.S. Spell; [b.] September 28, 1971, Covington, LA; [p.] Ronald and Hilda Spell; [occ.] Truck Driver; [oth. writ.] First time any of my work has been submitted for public evaluation; [pers.] All of my work is created from emotional events during my life. I would like to give special thanks to NIcole Townsend for inspiring me to write. [a.] Covington, LA.

SPENCE, WAYNE J.
[pen.] Wayne; [b.] December 14, 1924, Willow Springs, MO; [p.] Lyman C. and Charlotte May Spence (both deceased); [ed.] Missouri University, Naval Midshipman School, Columbia University, Navy Postgrad School; [occ.] Retired, Navy Pilot; [memb.] Naval Offivers Retirement Association, Experimental Aircraft Association, Trinity Baptist Church, Willow Springs Golf Country Club, Ozarks Genealogical Society, Rhea County History & Gen. Society; [hon.] Four Air-medals plus numerous other flight medals, numerous awards in Music and Music instruments; [oth.w rit.] "Wayne's World of Verse", a small book of poetry I had printed Nov. 92 for friends. It was a compilation of a life time of short verses put in a file and finally put them all together. I have 65 of my poems in it. "A New Look At Shorts", genealogical histories of mine and other families, several poems published in local newspapers; [pers.] Once a friend of James A. Michener as he lived six weeks with my group of Navy Pilots getting information for the book. "The Bridges of Toko-Ri." He was a poor poker player. Also I flew with Neil Armstrong and shared Ready Rooms and Quarters with him. We travelled some in Japan together phoitographung Japanese families and the Country of Japan. I had a stroke two years ago and all writings must be typed with left hand on my computer. It is slow but very satisfying to be able to write something others might enjoy. Thirty years of flying Fighter Aircraft in three wars makes for many sea stories. I am writing them now.

SPENCER, MELISA ANN
[b.] March 19, 1976, Michigan; [p.] Joe Spencer, Carol Spencer, Linda Cooper; [ed.] Vassar High School, Tuscola Area Skill Center; [occ.] Student. [a.] Vassar, MI.

SPOTO, JENNIFER
[b.] April 18, 1979, Tampa, FL; [p.] Carolyn Spoto; [ed.] Home Education Program; [memb.] Avon Breast Cancer Awareness Association; [hon.] Family of God award for Girl Scouts; [pers.] I try to include the forgotten people of the world in my poems. [a.] Tampa, FL.

SPRAGGINS, QIANA N.
[pen.] Kiki; [b.] October 18, 1976, Pemberton, NJ; [p.] Lil Spraggins; [ed.] Bodine High School for International Affairs; [occ.] Internship at WPEB radio station/student; [memb.] Student Goc't, Urban Journalism Workshop, School Newspaper (The Ambassador) staff writer; [hon.] National Honor Society; [oth. writ.] Article in "Back Talk" (a supplement to the Philadelphia Daily News); [pers.] Never sell yourself short. [a.] Philadelphia, PA.

SPRAGUE, JODY
[b.] December 26, 1968, Norwealk, NY; [p.] Harold and Linda Sprague; [ed.] Oneida High SChool, Onondaga Community College; [occ.] Security Officer for Syracuse; [oth. writ.] Several poems written since high school and college, none of which have not been published; [pers.] Since tenth grade in schoiol, I've always been influenced to writing poems. Writing poems always made me feel better especially during sad times. Every since I've been writing - and will continue to do so. [a.] Clockville, NY.

SPRAGUE, MYRTLE
[pen.] Myrt; [b.] March 13, 1968, Charlevoix, MI; [p.] Janice and Allen Sprague, 4 brothers and 2 sisters; [ed.] Southmont Junior, Senior High School; [occ.] Certified Nurses' Assistant; [hon.] Honored deeply by having a nice family and dear friends; [oth. writ.] Have about 90 other poems that I have written, but am proud that now one is finally published; [pers.] I would like to thank some special people, all my family, Mary Hughey, Lloyd and Jessie Potter and family, and a very special thanks to you all. [a.] Boyne Falls, MI.

SPRAY, CHRISTY L.
[pen.] Destiny; [b.] June 21, 1978, Fay, IN; [p.] Dwain and Wanda Spray; [ed.] 9th grade currently; [occ.] Student; [memb.] Several different wildlife organizations; [hon.] Honor roll student at Fayetteville Junior High. [a.] Fayetteville, TN.

SPRIGGS, CRAIG
[pen.] San Tini; [b.] September 10, 1966, Spokane, WA; [m.] Engaged Frankie Guill; [ed.] Military USMC, college student East Carolina University; [occ.] Cook; [memb.] NRA, VFW; [hon.] Two purple hearts, bronze star; [pers.] Art is the way to express yourself to and for God. He puts poetry in all of us, but only seldom few can draw the force of God and the higher being in words that open the heart or the sky. [a.] Greenville, NC.

SPRUNG, JOHN GEORGE
[b.] March 4, 1913, St. Louis, MO; [p.] John Nicholas and Magdalena Tremel Sprung; [m.] Loa Ruth, April 26, 1947; [ch.] John Leon Sprung and Lori Lee Sprung; [ed.] Northwestern University, Scholarships Art Institute; [occ.] Retired plastic engineer; memb.] Delta Beta Phi, Society of Plastic Engineers; [oth. writ.] Tennis is a Racket, Poetry in Stereo; [pers.] My poems have bilateral symmetry. The first syllable of every line rhymes with the last syllable of the line. I call this truly "Poetry in Stereo". [a.] San Pedro, CA.

SPURLING, TAMMY
[pen.] Tammy Bailey; [b.] March 12, 1960, Snyder, TX; [p.] Mary and Horace Kesterson; [m.] Terry, October 15, 1992; [ch.] Jennifer Gale and Tamra LiTisha; [ed.] DeQueen, Ark.; [occ.] Nurse, enrolled in Writers Institute of America-New York; [memb.] American Heart Association, Welcome New Comers; [hon.] First place bronze medal ever won in Automotive class, graduated Automotive CNA School; [oth. writ.] Old Cars of Yesterday; [pers.] Knowing the true meaning of life, expressing life through my writing. Brininging smiles to others. [a.] Oldsmar, FL.

ST. JAMES, SONIA
[pen.] Sonia St. James; [b.] November 30, 1942, MI; [ch.] Chelly, Scott, Jack, Chris; [ed.] Cultural Landscape of Life and graduate student of International Studies; [pers.] I write with a view to the unspoken

emotions. [a.] Austin, TX.

ST. PIERRE, SUZANNE
[b.] November 12, 1977, Caribou, ME; [p.] Theodore and Sallie St. Pierre, sister-Stacy; [ed.] Caribou High School; [hon.] Young Authors award, Caribou's Writing Contest, honor roll student; [pers.] I strive to make my readers use their imaginations and open their hearts and eyes, to the feelings that I try to convey in my writings. [a.] Caribou, ME.

STACKHOUSE, KEVIN L.
[b.] October 26, 1957, Wilmington, OH; [p.] Frank and Maryann; [m.] Diance-Kathy Craft; [ed.] Wilmington High School; [occ.] Firefighter/EMT; [memb.] BPOE; [oth. writ.] Have written other poems for friends and other personal uses; [pers.] Thanks to Bob Simpson, Tom Lapine and Mellisa Maple for their encouragement. A special thanks to Kathy Craft for her love and inspiration. [a.] Wilmington, OH.

STACY, RICH J.
[pen.] C.T./Iron Horse; [b.] August 26, 1969, St. Louis; [p.] Edgar and Margie Stacy; [m.] Hope C. Lyons; [ch.] Matthew Hawk Stacy; [ed.] High school, life, and the streets; [occ.] Marketing; [oth. writ.] Love's Creations/ Corridors and Pathways/Realities as well as several other poems; [pers.] I am deeply influenced by my native American background as well as my life. In dealing with people I helieve the eyes are a windown to the soul. [a.] St. Louis, MO.

STAFFORD, CONNIE LYNN
[pen.] Chaun Laureen Taylor; [b.] May 15, 1957, Larned, KS; [p.] Rollin and Anna Marie Zimmerman; [ch.] Jerome Victor Ruelas; [ed.] Nickerson High, Friends University, Bryan Institute; [occ.] Medical Tech. in TX at Irving Health Care System; [oth. writ.] As a hobby, I have written 2 books at home- not published. Took creative writing and short story in high school. Poetry written for church newspaper; [pers.] All my writings, vocal music and various talents are dedicated to the Lord and his glory. [a.] Irving, TX.

STAFFORD, JAMES
[b.] September 7, 1967, Almont, MI; [p.] William and Barbara Stafford; [ed.] Oxford High School, Eastern Michigan University, Oakland University; [occ.] Yard Leader, Church's lumber; [hon.] Placed third in the Best of Quill Poetry Contest 1990, with the poem "A Lesson"; [oth. writ.] "Wisdom" published by Rocky Mountain Poetry Magazine and Quill Books; [pers.] Dedicated to my parents in appreciation of their support and to Tiffany and our future happiness together. [a.] Lake Orion, MI.

STANACTI, LISA ANNE
[b.] July 14, 1964, Brooklyn, NY; [p.] Martha and Thomas Stancati; [p.] Martha and Thomas Sancati; [ed.] St. John's University, St. Vincent College; [occ.] Attorney; [memb.] American Bar Association, New York County Lawyer's Association, Association of the Bar; [hon.] Dean's list 1988-92, Notes and Comments Editor, St. John's Law Review; [pers.] I find my creativeness emerges during the rough moments in life when pain followed by personal growth are the only option. My writing reflects my life experiences and the inner strength I've developed as a result. [a.] Bayside, NY.

STANFORD, CHARLES
[b.] October 27, 1959, Mississippi; [m.] Cheri, July 20, 1982; [ch.] Ryan and Lindsay; [ed.] GEorge Co. High,

University of Maryland; [occ.] Computer Specialist USAF; [pers.] Life will never defeat you if you strive to always do your best, set your goals and work to attain them, and never look back or dwell on past failures. [a.] Ellsworth AFB Rapid City, SD.

STANG, PATRICK W. DR.
[b.] March 17, 1961, Victoria, KS; [p.] Albert and Anita Stang; [m.] Cahterine, August 30, 1986; [ch.] John Albert; [ed.] Thomas More Prep High School, Marymount College, University of KS Medical School, University of IA; [occ.] Psychiatrist; [memb.] AMA, American Psychiatric Association; [hon.] Who's Who in the Midwest; [oth. writ.] Write a regular mental health newspaper column. [a.] Great Bend, KS.

START, IRMA GRACE (O'NEAL)
[pen.] Irma O'Neal Start; [b.] October 21, 1911, Nebraska, USA; [p.] Ross and Edna O'Neal; [m.] Wilfred John Norman Start (deceased), April 5, 1934; [ch.] Blanche Leona, Elaine Edna, Harold WEsley, Wilfred Donn Norman, Dolores Suzanne, Joyce Irma Christine; [ed.] Grade IX Fairview High School; [occ.] Retired homemaker, a widow, living in my own home; [memb.] Church of Christ, The Canadian Wildlife Federation, Pro-Life and Alliance for Life and numerous charitable organizations; [oth. writ.] A lifetime hobby, articles for local history books and religious newsletters, numerous unpublished poems, special requests for family and friends; [pers.] Life, bored, boring??—Never— When there is so much beauty around me; glorious music to hear, fascinating books to read, inspiring poems to read or memorize, God's Bible to guide my life and the poor and unfortunante to help in every way I possibly can. [a.] Bengough, Sask, CAN.

STEBBINS, BONNIE
[pen.] Bonnie Ransom Stebbins; [b.] January 20, 1951, Setroit; [p.] Elaine Stuart Stebbins and David Boris Miller; [ch.] Ayrianna Dawn Harris and Shawn Charles Harris; [ed.] University of Detroit Mercy, O.C.C., AD Arts; [occ.] Student; [hon.] Berkley Public Safety and Fire Award for Bravery 1988; [oth. writ.] College papers for Psy. and Eng. Rel. non published writings and poems; [pers.] Everything we learn here on earth we take with us into heaven so knowledge never lost because, we live forever.

STEEL, WENDI
[b.] July 24, 1970, Jamaica, WI; [p.] Jean and Fred Steel/Mike Magnus; [m.] Fiance-Kevin Waterston; [ed.] Eastside High, Kwantlen College; [occ.] Actress/dance choreographer/model; [memb.] Union B.C. Performers, Cast International Artists, Extraordinary Casting, La Femme Impressions, Pure Dance Studios, Class Act Choreography, Fridays Models, Starlite; [hon.] Golden Poet Laurate Award 1992, Miss Black Velvet International Model of 1990, Rookie Actress of the Year Award 1989; [oth. writ.] Several poems published in local newspapers and magazines. Articles for The Georgia Straight, Inc., The Vancouver Sun, The Province, The Leader, The Now and North Shore News; [pers.] I mostly concentrate on personal, yet universal emotion and its profound effect on humanity. Of course, my own vast experiences with different cultures and customs of life play a major part in my writing. [a.] Greer, S.C.

STEINER, NOLAND J.
[b.] January 7, 1940, Smithville, OH; [p.] Vincent and Treva Steiner; [m.] Barbara, October 15, 1962; [ch.] Three; [ed.] Bowling Green State University; [occ.]

Minister; [memb.] Masonic Lodge, 32 degree Mason Bowling Green; [toh. writ.] Masters Thesis published Journal of Crime and Deliquency Spring 1973, Internal vs External Control in Defendants Cosmic Countdown 1989 limited edition Environmental Concerns in Biblical Proportion; [pers.] I write and create poetry on themes of Nature. [a.] Bellville, OH.

STEPHENS. SUSAN AUNDRAE
[pen.] Susan Stephens; [b.] January 7, 1979, Huntington, WVA; [p.] David and Mollie Stephens; [ed.] Wayne High School; [occ.] Student; [memb.] Wayne High School Band; [hon.] Outstanding Student Awards, Honor Student; [oth. writ.] Several other poems and short stories; [pers.] I enjoy reading and writing poems and short stories. I think it is really interesting what people can accomplish by this. [a.] Wayne, W.VA.

STERK, MELISSA
[b.] August 22, 1978, Dubuque, IA; [p.] Susan and Dennis Sterk; [ed.] Columbus High School; [occ.] Student; [hon.] Honor student; [pers.] I don't think of myself as a poet. Just someone who puts her emotions on paper! [a.] Waterloo, IA.

STERN, JASON TAYLOR
[b.] March 23, 1972, Pittsburgh; [p.] William and Karen Stern; [ed.] Grove City College; [occ.] Student; [pers.] In my writing I am inspired by a frail and hurting creation striving toward its sovereign and loving Creator in a faith relationship initiated by the Creator's inexplicable grace. Eph. 3:16-19. [a.] Pittsburgh, PA.

STEURRY'S KAREN J.
[b.] May 29, 1953, Rochester, NY; [p.] Dick and Dana Hicks; [m.] Divorced; [ch.] Joel, Shannon (boy), Adrianna; [ed.] Williamson Central, Sawyer Business School, Monroe County #1 - Cosmetology, Fairport Baptist Homes - CNA, Genesee Region Home Care Home Health Aide; [memb.] Williamson First Baptist Church; [hon.] Regents; [pers.] My writings are derived from my own personal experiences they are taken from my passion for life and my own perspective of how I feel. [a.] Williamson, NY.

STEVENS, CHRISTOPHER A.
[pen.] Christopher A. Stevens; [b.] October 7, 1966, Okemah, OK; [p.] James W. and Winnie M. Stevens Jr.; [ed.] Boley High School, Gordon Cooper Area Vocational Tech. School, Oklahoma State University; [occ.] Financial Aid Administrator, University of Nevada, Las Vegas; [memb.] Alpha Epsilon Rho, Alpha Phi Alpha Fraternity, Inc., Nevada Association of Financial Aid Administration, National Association of Financial Aid Administration; [hon.] Dean's and President's honors; Golden Key, Phi Eta Sigma & Alpha Lambda Delta Honors; [hon.] Numerous poems, songs, and short stories printd in local newspapers; [pers.] Your best is the result of personal confidence, a relaxed mind, and a tuned soul. [a.] Las Vegas, NV.

STEVENS, PAUL WARREN
[b.] October 20, 1953, Minneapolis, MN; [p.] Warren and Althea Stevens; [occ.] Source Inspector for Caere Corp.; [oth. writ.] Many yet unpublished; [pers.] I feel that my writings are a true reflection of the essence of life. [a.] Sunnyvale, CA.

STEWART, MARGARET N.
[pen.] Nell Stewart; [b.] June 14, 1922, Arno, VA; [p.] I.T. and Betty Smith; [m.] L.J. Stewart, September 17,

1944; [ch.] James D. Stewart, Greg Stewart, Carol S. Herron; [ed.] St. Charles High School, Clinch Valley College; [occ.] Retired; [memb.] Pocahontas Lodge, St. Charles Water Authority Board of Directors, Lee County Planning Commission; [hon.] Plaque for 20 years volunteer service to St. Charles Health Clinic; [oth. writ.] Poetry for local group writings and poetry have been in local newspaper; [pers.] I enjoy doing volunteer work in the community "and wish to do unto others as I wish to be done by". [a.] St. Charles, VA.

STIRLING, MARK JAMES
[pen.] James and Mary Stirling; [b.] April 4, 1960, N. Ireland; [m.] Sonia Yvinne Kathleen Stirling, 1983; [ed.] Life; [oth. writ.] Childrens works - poems-magazine articles-novels-short stories-screen plays also Bramblegate (children's story) and others Childrens illustrated poetry; [pers.] I write as the mood finds me. Life has many doors. [a.] Newtownards, Co. Down, NI

STOCKER, GENEVIEVE
[b.] December 7, 1920, Portsmouth, VA; [p.] William and Lillian May; [m.] Robert, March 28, 1944; [ch.] Alice de la Cova; [ed.] Clairton, PA High School, State Teacher's College; [occ.] Retired; [memb.] Philadelphia Church of God; [oth. writ.] Only for personal satisfaction - none previously submitted for publication evaluation; [pers.] Following death of spouse on April 23, 1982, I found comfort and understanding in studying God's word and thus was inspired to write this poem. [a.] Sinnamahoning, PA.

STOFFEL, JEAN
[pen.] Ariel Dean; [b.] April 12, 1958, Providence, RI; [p.] Harry and Jean M. Bogosian; [m.] Michael P., July 14, 1990; [ed.] Mt. Pleasant High, Rhode Island College, Byrant College; [occ.] Assistant Kitchen Manager; [hon.] National and RI Honor Society, Anthony Medal, Dionesian Players; [oth. writ.] Several poems and items of prose. Several sitcom plays and several short stories; [pers.] I thoroughly enjoy all forms of writing. Everything I write has some sort of a positive moral even though I do not moralize. I owe my God given gift to my late parents, who taught me to read and to fly on the wings of my imagination. [a.] Dunedin, FL.

STONE, ANNETTE MORRIS
[pen.] Annie Morris Stone; [b.] December 14, 1968, CA; [p.] Violet and Johnny Norris; [m.] William, April 27, 1992; [ch.] Claranda Stone; [ed.] Western Wyoming Community College; [occ.] Housewife; [hon.] Won a lot awards in school, but nothing really significant; [pers.] I have from an early age been interested in the arts I began to study music at an early age. And I fell in love with poetry as early as I could read. They are my truest passion, but eventually I would like to write nayming childrens books.

STONE, TONYA GALENE
[b.] August 28, 1978, San Diego, CA; [p.] JoLynn; [ed.] North Medford High; [hon.] 2nd place award for a writing contest out of the whole country.

STONEHOUSE, TERRI
[b.] June 1, 1978, Red Deer, Alberta; [p.] Bob and Heather Stonehouse; [ed.] Fort Saskatchewan High School; [occ.] High school student; [memb.] Amateur Radio Club; [oth. writ.] Short stories and other poems not yet published; [pers.] My poems reflect my feelings and life experiences. [a.] Ft. Saskatchewan, Alberta, CAN.

STOUGHTON, KATHERINE VICTORIA
[pen.] Katherine Stoughton; [b.] February 14, 1979, OH; [p.] Andrea and John Stoughton; [ed.] New Albany High School; [occ.] Student; [memb.] Save The Whales; [hon.] Little writing awards in school and N.I.E. (newspaper) writing contest; [oth. writ.] Nothing that has been published, but many other poems; [pers.] When writing just let your feelings fo. "If life looks down on you, look to the stars and learn to fly, high." [a.] Westerville, OH.

STOVER, VICKY ELLISE
[pen.] Vicky Ellise Stover; [b.] July 1, 1954, Georgia; [p.] Raised by grandparents Gene and Evaylin Chase/Bill and Jeannie Edwards (dad and stepmom); [m.] David K., September 20, 1975; [ch.] Snezzy and Thumper (cats) and several fish; [ed.] Centennial High School, [occ.] Freelance photographer, commercial art, abstract, mini set design, poet; [memb.] Photographic Society of America, Columbia Council of Camera Club, Cascade Chapter, Infinity Photo Art Group, Honorary Thespian 1973; [hon.] Top 80 slides of The Columbia Council, Creative Photographer of the Year, Two golden poet awards, print in The United Nation Historical Periodical book, being printed in The National Library of Poetry; [oth. writ.] Wrote two other books one on environment the other friends both poems. Three children books none have been published yet; [pers.] I write my poems from my heart. I live my life the same way. The tears of my heart whether happy or sad are the final touch of each and every poem I write. A photography mentor Alora Johnson Self asked me what friendship meant to me. That's how friendship came about from one friend to another. Thank you Alora and thank you ro my family, friends for molding my heart. Thank you Gene and Evy Chase my grandparents. [a.] Portland, OR.

STOWE, COLLEEN M.
[pen.] Colleen Marie Stowe; [b.] April 22, 1960, Detroit; [p.] Benny and Helen Bysiorek; [m.] Daniel J.; [ch.] Gregory and Danielle STowe; [ed.] Institute of Children's Literature Writing School; [pers.] My thoughts expressed in poetry, come from a secret place inside of me. [a.] Berkley, MI.

STRACK, DON E.
[pen.] Don Thomas; [b.] April 6, 1944, K.C., MO; [p.] Anna and Ignatius Stack; [m.] Divorced, May 13, 1971; [ch.] Margaret, Gary, Joy and David; [ed.] Lillis Hiigh School, Maple Woods Community College; [occ.] Route salesman Wonder Bread; [hon.] No special awards although I have been told that I am the second best Breadman in the K,C. area (everyone else in tied for number one); [oth. writ.] This poems is my first attempt at writing. I am now int eh process of writing a full length novel. Hopeful of someday having it published; [pers.] Just a hope that my poem may bring a little joy to everyone who reads it. [a.] Kansas City, MO.

STRAND, BECKY
[b.] December 5, 1947, Alberta Lea, MN; [p.] Lester and Ione Biesterfeld; [m.] Paul, August 2, 1969; [ch.] Kimberly Sue and Kari Michelle; [ed.] Wells - Easton High School, Gustavus Adolphus College; [occ.] Child care provider, professional singer; [memb.] Bible Presbyterian Church, Choir, and Bible study group, Resort Condominiums International; Love through Adoption; [oth. writ.] Poems published in "Lutheran Digest"; [pers.] As a Christian, I want my writing to reflect a heartfelt belief in the value of all born and unborn human life. [a.] Merrill, WI.

STRASS, ACHIM
[b.] September 18, 1968, Freising, Germany; [p.] Hermonn and Grell Strass; [ed.] Technical University of Munich, Germany; [occ.] Graduate student; [memb.] European Student Organization, Association der Etats Geueraux des Etudiants de e' Europe (AEEGEE); [oth. writ.] Several papers about my field of study (semiconductor lasers) are going to be published, article about the Kennedy Space Center in Florida in a youth magazine, scientific and technical translations and elaborations; [pers.] I was influenced and inspired by reports on the reunification of East and West Germany and the time after everyday in the mass media. [a.] Ottobrunn, Germany, Bavaria.

STRASSER-LESLIE, DIANNE
[pen.] Mountain Flower Given Cherokee Nanne; [b.] July 3, 1955, Duranga, CO; [p.] Arthur and Twila Strasser; [m.] Paul Leslie, November 11, 1989; [ch.] Kassidy Justin; [ed.] Christopher Newport University; [occ.] Self-employed Rocky Mountain Trading Co., Weatable Art; [memb.] Virginia Native American Cultural Center, Smithsonian National Museum of the American Indian, Artists and Craftsmens Exchange; [hon.] Christopher Newport University Student Orientation Leader, Photographic Achievement Award; [oth. writ.] Poetry published in teh Christopher Newport University Literary Magazine, presentations given to schools and organizations on Native American History and Culture; [pers.] My life has taken me to exotic places. My mind has the ability to interpret where others merely see. This is a gift, and I wish to share it with you, and with future generations I have not yet encountered. [a.] Newport News, VA.

STRAWN, DOLE A.
[b.] February 20, 1912, Nevinville, IA; [p.] Mr. and Mrs. Strawn; [m.] Rachelle P. Strawn, JUne, 1967; [ch.] Larry, Darryl, Renee and Joni; [ed.] B.A. in 1937, M.D. in 1945; [occ.] Retired; [memb.] American Society of Abdominal Surgeons; [oth. writ.] Have been published in church papers going to all the world for 25 years; [pers.] I am interested in non-fiction writing. Now taking a course in writing (Reader's Digest);

STRICKLAND, KATHRYN ALYSE
[b.] May 18, 1972, Coronado, CA; [p.] Keith and Marie; [ed.] Leysin American School in Switzerland, Virginia Polytechnic Institute, State University; [occ.] Student; [memb.] Kappa Delta sorority, Women in Communications Inc., Greek Week Committee chairman; [hon.[Dean's list; [oth. writ.] Articles in college newspapers and magazines, poem published in The Poet's Domain; [pers.] My writing has allowed me to explore new territories in my mind, and through poetry I have learned to treasure my unique thoughts and feelings. My loved ones and experiences have been my teachers; [a.] Virginia Beach, VA.

STROEBEL, IRENE T.
[b.] March 22, 1918, NE; [p.] Carl and Mary Steinke; [ed.] 8th grade, received G.E.D. at age 54; [occ.] Retired; [oth. writ.] Many and varied; [pers.] I have always loved "words". I like people, I love children. Life can be exciting or dull, even un your own living room-it's all in your own attitude and/or viewpoint; [a.] Kingman, AZ.

STRONG, BARBARA V.
[b.] April 6, 1938, Ilion, NY; [.] Milton and Marjorie Strong; [ch.] Deborah Herbert, Darlene Catania, Diane Deininger; [ed.] Passaic High School; [occ.] Accounting Assistant Cosmetic Company; [oth. writ.] Several poems, none ever published. [a.] Lincoln Park, NJ.

STUART, ANDY A.
[b.] JUne 2, 1975, Yarmouth, Nova Scotia; [p.] Arthur Stuart, Bertha Brannen; [ed.] Yarmouth Consolidated Memorial High; [occ.] Student; [pers.] The poetry I write is inspired by a desire to express my feelings. Any piece of writing that comes from one's heart and imagination is worth as much as the most precious gift we all share-the ability to express ourselves; [a.] Yarmouth, Nova Scotia, Canada.

STUCCI, MAVIS
[b.] September 16, 1946, Owaka, NZ; [p.] Robert and Marion Miller; [ch.] Marc Stucci; [ed.] Primary: Canada and New Zealand; secondary: New Zealand, tertiary: University of Otago, NZ, University of NSW, Australia; [occ.] Freelance illustrator, personal carer/hostel for the aged; [hon.] High school Dux award, 1991: Associate Diploma of Arts (with distinction) UNSW; [oth. writ.] Poem and shirt story in UNSW compilation 1991, two children's books, currently working on a novel; [pers.] The way people "tick" fascinates me; the way people interrelate, the way we lift each other up, or put each other down is an endless map of our humanity; the gift of empathy or the weapon of self-interest creates our boundaries, our histories, our futures; [a.] Blackheath, NSW, Australia.

STUCKS, REBECCA
[b.] October 7, 1964, OK; [p.] Raymond E. and Wuletta Ferris; [m.] Gregory Stucks, November 3, 1988; [ch.] Hannah Rebecca, Michael Zane, Evan Gregory; [ed.] Verden High School, Verden, Oklahoma; [occ.] HOmemaker; [memb.] Trinity Baptist Church, Chickasha OK; [oth. writ.] Other poems and children's stories in poetry form; [pers.] My ability to write poetry is truly a gift from God. I cannot explain where or why. The words just suddenly start churning around in my head. I am thankful for this gift; [a.] Anadarko, OK.

STUDDERT, JUNE
[pen.] June O'Mohundro Studdert; [b.] February 28, 1936, Oswego, NY; [p.] Col Wiley and Mildren O'Mohundro; [m.] George Michael, November 25, 1955; [ch.] Andrew Paul, Patrick Michael, George Michael and David Donald; [ed.] St. Vincent's High School, Santa Rosa K\Jr. College; [occ.] Retired; [memb.] St. Joseph's Catholic Church, River Island Country Club, Sunland Golf Club; [hon.] Speech Awards in HS; [pers.] Although I did not have a lengthy college education, I believe that my strong faith and understanding of human nature have played a big part in my complete education...I owe so much to my God and to my friends and especially my family. I have been truly blessed. [a.] Sequim, WA.

STULL, RUBY (VERNON)
[pen.] Ruby Vernon Stull; [b.] December 21, 1938, Connellsville, PA; [p.] Deceased faher, mother Sara; [ch.] Yvonne, Christine, Marie, Jonathan; [ed.] High school, Scottsdale PA 1957; [occ.] Grandmother to Louis and Kevin; [memb.] Vanderbilt Nazarene Church; [oth. writ.] Poems of spiritual uplifting, self-retrospect and introspect, observing human nature, and "special day" poems. I've only been writing poetry since Mother's

Day 1993; [pers.] I feel God has given me my poems to help people to know Him and serve Him. It has been a gift that was a complete surprise to me but has helped me serve Him better; [a.] Scottdale, PA.

SUDHEIMER, KIM
[pen.] Kim Rossi; [b.] March 7, 1966, Shakopee, MN; [p.] Darrel and Joan Sudheimer; [ed.] Waconia High School, Normandale Community College, Brown Institute; [occ.] D.J., KMMS-FM, Bozeman, MT; [hon.] National Honor Society, high school and Brown Inst.; [pers.] Never cease to be amazed; [a.] Bozeman, MT.

SUH, ANGELA
[b.] JUne 3, 1975, Cheju-do, Korea; [p.] Bo Young Suh (father), Suk Hee Suh (mother); [ed.] University of California, Irvine, La Canada High School, San Marino High School; [hon.] Publication in local newspaper about Key Club, honorable mention in Reflections contest, essay contest on alcohol effects, Mu Alpha Theta.

SULLIVAN, DOLORES EDWARDS
[pen.] Dolores Edwards Sullivan; [b.] April 2, 1951, Rockville Center, NY; [p.] Mary Ellen Frederick; [m.] Charles F. Sullivan, October 6, 1990; [ch.] Colleen, Keith, Brian, Conall; [ed.] Southside High School, Queens College; [occ.] English teacher/playwright; [memb.] Respect life; [hon.] Third place Teacher as a Writer award, Long Island Language Arts - non-fiction Excellence in Poetry Sparrowgrass Publishers; [oth. writ.] Several poems one play "Look Past the Knees", one novel, "A Toast to the Dead", non-fiction articles regarding homeless "To Be Filled and Fed" and education in New York City; [pers.] As a poet I seek honesty void of any judgment. I look to reflect the human person with all his/her imperfections, "and thus encourage thought as to why they exist. William Shakespeare said it all! He's the Bard of all times. [a.] Port Jervis, NY.

SULLIVAN, RYAN J. MICHAEL
[b.] June 3, 1977, Kitchener, Ont, Canada; [p.] Gail and Tim Sullivan; [ed.] Norwell District Secondary School; [occ.] Student; [a.] Harriston, Ontario Canada.

SUMEREL, ZELMA
[b.] January 13, 1913, Spruce Pine, AL; [p.] Willie and MaryJane L. King; [m.] Ollie Mance Sumerel, August 10, 1932; [ch.] Gladys Marcelene, Faye, Jerry Don, Martha Ann, and Carol Marie; [ed.] 10th grade education; [occ.] Retired, housewife; [pers.] I feel that God gave me this poem about my great-granddaughter, Leigh Ann White, 4 months old; [a.] Bear Creek, AL.

SUMMY, LUETTA A.
[pen.] Luetta Summy; [b.] May 22, 1959, Chester, CA; [p.] Mr. and Mrs. L. E. Towers Jr.; [m.] Steven K. Summy, November 27, 1982; [ch.] Edward R., Phillipsm Shanna L. Phillips, Jennifer A. Summy, and John Russel Lawrence Summy; [ed.] Churchill County High School, Fallon NV; [occ.] Homemaker and Jewelry sales; [memb.] Christ Lutheran Church, past member, Theta-Rho, Alpha Beta chapter; [hon.] Past president of Theta-Ro, Alpha Beta chapter; [oth. writ.] Several unpublished; [pers.] My writing is influenced by the beauties of nature and the love of children; [a.] Evansville, IN.

SUTER, DEBRA JANE
[b.] June 30, 1953, Mt. Pleasant; [p.] Michael and Betty Germock; [m.] Kenneth W. Suter Sr., June 16, 1973; [ch.] Kenneth W. Suter Jr., Brandie J. Zelenka (Suter), grandchildren: Kenneth W. Suter III, Brittany L. Suter,

Troy M. Zelenka Jr.; [ed.] Yough High School; {occ.] Housewife; [memb.] Mendon Baptist Church; [pers.] I enjoy life one day at a time, for tomorrow I know not. God gives me strength to face each day and without him I have nothing. I hope the readers will be touched within their hearts when they read this poem, because you see I wrote this for my daughter, cause I love her very much indeed, and she herself became a mother for the very first time; [a.] Ruffsdale, PA.

SUTHERLAND, JAN
[b.] January 11, 1934, Douglas, AZ; [ch.] Dana, Gail, Leslie, Todd, grandson Maxwell David; [ed.] B.A. UC Berkeley, 1955, M.P.H UC Berkeley, 1966; [occ.] Health promotion specialist; [hon.] Phi Beta Kappa; [oth. writ.] 200 unpublished poems, written over past two years; [pers.] My poetry reflects my ideas and experiences of womanhood, and the power of women in relationships and in society; [a.] Oakland, CA.

SUTTON, CAROL ANN
[pen.] C.A., Vasanti; [b.] October 26, 1946, Chicago, IL; [p.] Edwin E. Sutton (deceased), Eileen A. Powers Sutton; [m.] Roberet A. Skaleski, October 1, 1966, Timothy J. Fitzgerald, August 13, 1976; [ch.] Katherine Mary Skaleski Snow, Margaret Louise Skaleski Kazanow; [ed.] Mt. Assisi Academy, Richard J. Daley Jr. College, Illinois Teachers College, Iona College, Institute of Mental Physics, Dr. Clayton School of Natural Healing, American Holistic College of Nutrition; [occ.] Legal assistant, law office manager, retired; [memb.] World Wildlife Fund, Greenpeace, Sierra Club, Amnesty International, National Anti-Vivisection Society, PETA, Chicago Vegetarian Society, Newberry Library Associate, Natonal Parks and Conservation Assn., American Center for Homeopathy, American Naturopathic Medical Assn, NAIC; [hon.] 4-H awards, National Honor Society, Sheltering Arms Volunteer award, A.A. with honors, Masters Course S.K.Y. ND, former English and ESL tutor, president, New Rochelle Newcomers Club, secretary, New Rochelle Democratic Party, secretary, Westchester County Democrats, treasurer, Committee to elect Thomas J., O'Toole, secretary, FBI Agents Assn.; [oth. writ.] Copyrighted story of present disabilities, a genealogy family book, poetry and other literary works to be published; [pers.] When I receive the B.S. in Nutrition, I hope to become a nutritional consultant using my naturopathic degree practice at home. Reading, learning and spiritual introspection allows me to stamp the pictures in my brain onto paper, Thoreau and Mozart inspire me; [a.] Chicago, IL.

SUTTON, CHRISTINA
[b.] April 20, 1980, Chicago, IL; [p.] Katherine and Steve Sutton; [pers.] My desire to get additional poems published is incredible. Without my mother Katherine Sutton's encouragement, my poems would not be as successful as they are. Thanks, Mom, I will always love you; [a.] Chicago, IL.

SUTTON, JAMES W.
[b.] February 4, 1956, Limestone, ME; [p.] Olin S. and Florence E. Sutton Sr.; [m.] Amy Lyn, December 2, 1989; [ch.] Sara Delaney Sutton; [ed.] Cortez High School; [occ.] House husband/writer; [memb.] VFW; [hon.] United States Navy Awards-Vietnam National Defense Ribbon, Good Conduct Ribbons (2) metitorious Unit Commendation award, honorable discharge - 10 years- 2 letters of commendation; [oth. writ.] 200 unpublished poems and songs; [pers.] Don't try and understand it, live it. [a.] Phoenix, AZ.

SUTTON, JAYLENE
[b.] February 15, 1938, OK; [p.] Lou and Felton Holder; [m.] Wes Sutton, February 2, 1957; [ch.] Brady, Kelly, Becky; [ed.] Richmond Union High, S.F. State; [occ.] Wes Sutton Cutting Horses, business manager; [oth. writ.] Other poems published in local publications; [pers.] My writings either reflect the question of just how man fits into God's vast plan, or they poke a bit of fun at the everyday situations in which we find ourselves; [a.] Queen Creek, AZ.

SWARTZ, SHAWN D.
[b.] August 20, 1971, Kittanning, PA; [p.] David and Barbara Swartz; [ed.] Ford City High School, Indiana University of Pennsylvania, [occ.] Student; [memb.] VFW, Rho Tau Chi, ROTC, NRA, U.S. Army Reserves; [hoon.] Dean's list, IUP honrs program, Rho Tau Chi, Southwest Asia Service Medal, National Defense Medal, ARCAM medal, Desert Storm vet; [oth. writ.] Several poems published in University literary magazine at the Indiana University of Pennsylvania. "Images", articles for the Warrior News, ROTC magazine; [pers.] Poetry is a bright spot in an otherwise dreary day; [a.] Ford City, PA.

SWEDENSKY, SH!RLEY K.
[pen.] k-Sky; [b.] December 15, 1939, WY; [p.] Coy and Dorthey Kiser, step-mom Joyce Snow; [m.] G.W. Swedensky, March 22, 1958; [ch.] Tommy Don, Tammy Dee, Todd Eugene; [ed.] Lincoln High, El Centro College, medication course; [occ.] Retired medication nurse; [oth. writ.] Some poems published in Poet's Pen quarterly; [pers.] I have been inspired by my family and encouraged by my husband and sister-in-law B.J. Swedensky; [a.] Red Oak TX.

SWEENEY, BART
[b.] December 26, 1974, Louisville, KY; [p.] Lester and Janice Sweeney; [ed.] Moore High School; [occ.] Laborer for roofing company; [pers.] I try to catch the feelings which everyone feels but I try to put in a perspective all on its own, from inspiration from my soul; [a.] Louisville, KY.

SWERTNER, JOHN H. JR.
[b.] JUly 25, 1964, Huntington, NY; [p.] John and Carol Swertner; [ch.] Sandra Arlene Swertner; [ed.] Minerva Central School; [occ.] Plumber; [oth. writ.] A wide variety of poems and a recent attempt at a novel in the works. All as yet unpublished; [pers.] I hope my poetry brings even a fraction of the peace I've gained from writing, to all those who love words from the soul. Literary influences-Poe, Hemingway, and my high school English treacher, Gary Ammerman; [a.] Minerva, NY.

SWIFT, LIZ
[b.] July 4, 1947, AK; [p.] Clyde and Viola Howard;l [m.] Bert Swift, May 19, 1989; [ch.] Gilbert, Andy, Dennis, Danny, and Libby and 7 grandchildren; [ed.] 11th grade; [occ.] Resident manager for National Church Residences; [memb.] Bedford Chamber of Commerce; [hon.] I have the Editor's Choice award, You Could Have Heard A Pin Drop and for Goodbye My Love; [oth. writ.] Where Would I Be, Our Mother, My Love; [pers.] I was born in West Ridge, AK. My husband and I work for National Church Residences. It is a retirement apartment for seniors my poems are a gift from God. I thank Him everyday for that gift; [a.] Bedford, TX.

SWING, SCOTT H.
[b.] July 4, 1953, Cincinnati, OH; [p.] Kenneth and Mabel Swing; [ed.] Hamilton Taft HIgh School, Norwood Night School ABE Program; [occ.] Thriftwasy Food and Drug Service clerk; [oth. writ.] I wrote poems and essays and short story, they are not published; [pers.] It is an honor to be published in your book for the first time;

SWORD, GENE
[pen.] Eneg Drows; [b.] April 1, 1928, Pikesville, KY; [p.] Everett and Ocie Sword; [m.] Marie Hughes Sword, March 29, 1975; [ch.] Elizabeth Joan, Evelyn Janine, Eugenia Jenice, Eugene James, Ellen Jamie; [ed.] Scot High School, Blackstone School of Law, University of Maryland, Texas A & M University; [occ.] Retired; [memb.] Association of Former OSI Agents, National Rifle Association, The American Legion, Association of Former Federal Agents, Texas State Troopers Association; {oth. writ.] Numerous poems, short stories official reports and technical manuals, plus teaching sylibus; [pers.] I strive to inject my writings with goodness, love and beauty found in persons and things usually perceived as mundane and ordinary by most. Simple and natural occurances imopress me the most; [a.] Livingston, TX.

SYD, BOB
[b.] September 12, 1963, Lynwood; [p.] Dennis and Karen; [ed.] Western High, Cypress College; [oth. writ.] Dying in Colors, Sophia, Harry the Hopeless; [pers.] "I don't know if I'll ever be ready". Mr. Syd is a man who's life is torment and farkness. The Dream Seer. [a.] Buena Park, CA.

SYKES, ELLA
[b.] November 9, 1944, Jackson, MS; [p.] Raymond and Missiour Lewis; [m.] Harold Sykes, December 9, 1968; [ch.] Bartholomew, Judith, Donna, Mariha, Harold E. Sykes III; [ed.] J.M.D. Brown Elementary School, Huges Quinn Jr. High; [occ.] Housekeeper, babysitter, former nurses aide; [memb.] Mt. Moriah Missionary Baptist Church; [oth. writ.] Yes, but not published yet. It's the Day, Calling Me Home, and Mommy Words. My writing was influenced by my children; [pers.] Love your Mother now that you have her, brcause when she's no more then you will have lost the best friend you've ever had. I want children to know Mother is number one; [a.] San Bernardino, CA.

SYLVA, RUSTY JAYE
[b.] JUly 20, 1959, Kahuka, HI; [p.] Lawrence and Lorraine Sylva; [ch.] Rusty Sylva Jr. Monique K. Sylva; [ed.] Waianae High School; [occ.] Offset press operator; [memb.] Crazy Christians; [hon.] O.C.C.C. Poem Contest winner, 1993; [oth. writ.] Poems printed in some news letters; [pers.] I try to remind our young kids that there's no hope in dope, and to stay drug-free. I'm a newborn Christian, thank the Lord; [a.] Honolulu, HI.

SZUMITA, ODESSA A.
[b.] January 23, 1939, Portland, ME; [m.] Walter J. Szumita, November 22, 1958; [ch.] Five; [ed.] Thornton Academy; [occ.] Disabled. Worked as a supervisor at a manufacturing plant until disabled; [oth. writ.] I have written many poems, but kept them in a notebook. I never had the courage or knowledge of where to send. [pers.] I write from the heart and have written poems for many friends and family members. This is the first time I've sent a poem in sice 1970, because I wrote it for my daughter's friend who is dying of AIDS and I thought it deserved recognition; [a.] Biddeford, ME.

SZURGOT, R. A. II
[pen.] Laszlo Zirak; [b.] July 19, 1959, Sacramento, CA; [pers.] Poetry should illuminate hidden truths rather than obscure simple thoughts;

TAKALA, JOHN J.
[b.] April 7, 1966, Virginia MN; [p.] Gloria Nystrom and John Ritakala; [ed.] Mt. Iron High School, St. John's University; [occ.] Accountant; [pers.] I have always tried to write about the things that I am most passionate about. True love, perhaps one of life's greatest passions is something most everyone longs for, but not everyone finds. For those who do, know that you are truly blessed, for you are the lucky ones. [a.] Mt. Iron, MN.

TALLMAN, EVELYN T.
[b.] November 13, 1922, S. Westevlo; [p.] Mrs. Hazel F. Mabie; [m.] Late Raymond H., January 23, 1940; [ch.] Ralph R. Tallman; [ed.] Greenville High School, National Baking School; [occ.] Retired; [memb.] Social Security Pension; [oth. writ.] Recipes in the Albany Times Union newspaper.

TANGJIAN, CHRISTINA
[pen.] Christina M. Tangjian; [b.] September 13, 1967, Island of Kauai, HI; [p.] Henry L. Tangjian; [pers.] This poem was written for my brothers and my sister Steven, Eddie, Nadine, David, and Kenneth and for all the wildflowers in the world. Never will we die! [a.] Honolulu, HI.

TANISTA, JOHN J.
[b.] June 6, 1969, Towson, MD; [p.] John and Caroline Purcell; [m.] Cindy Zirn, July 4, 1990; [ch.] Howard, Jeff, Pamela, Katie, and baby Ira; [ed.] High school; [occ.] House-husband; [hon.] National Rifle Association; [oth. writ.] Poems, short stories - not yet published; [pers.] I enjoy watching all my children while my wife works. I believe in Women's Liberation. [a.] Mount Airy, MD.

TANNER, MILLIE
[pen.] Mildred Shafer-Tanner; [b.] Detroit, MI; [p.] William Joseph and Susie Shafer; [m.] Harold Edward Tanner; [ch.] Marlene, William and Reginald; [ed.] University of Michigan, U of M (Secondary Education, Guidance & Counseling and Dr. of Philosophy); [occ.] Instructor, writer licensed professional counselor; [memb.] Phi Delta Kappa Fraternity, NAACP, Founder of Society of The Detroit Institute of Arts/U of M Alumni Assn., Certified Social Worker; [hon.] City of Detroit Resolution, Detroit City Council, Gamma Phi Delta, State of MI, US Dept. of Ed., YWCA, Toastmaster's International, National Board of Certified Counselors; [oth. writ.] "The Enigma", "Relationships", "The Last Time", "The Kiss", "The Lover", "The Coming of Age", "Gimme A Piece of Candy, Chile", "And Miles to Go...", "Dignity", "If I Had..."; [pers.] The conquest of dignity soothes my consciousness, immortalizes my existence—a sanctuary in the SELF. [a.] Detroit, MI.

TARAZEWICH, FRANK J.
[b.] November 2, 1935, Saco, ME; [p.] Bronislaw/ Nellie Tarazewich; [m.] Judith Holmes Tarazewich; [ch.] Kelly McVey/Christopher Tarazewich; [ed.] Thornton Academy, University of Maine; [occ.] Elementary Principal; [memb.] Maine Principals Association, Association for Supervision and Curriculum Development (ASCD), Literary Cooperative; [hon.] Two time inductee to Who's Who, Outstanding Community Leaders of America; [oth. writ.] Several poems and short

stories; [pers.] My poetry allows for the emergence of my inner self from the chrysalis of my mind. Robert Frost and particularly Walt Whitman have gretly influenced me and my feelings toward writing poetry. [a.] E. Waterboro, ME.

TATRO, DOUGLAS W.
[pen.] D. Warren Williams; [b.] March 9, 1950, Quincy, MA; [p.] Francis W. Tatro and Marion O'Donnell; [ch.] Kimberly R. and Jonathan D. Tatro; [ed.] Milton High School, Boston University; [occ.] Specialist in Gifted Education; [memb.] Florida Association of Gifted Educators; [hon.] National High School Choral Award, High School All-American Gymnastics Coach; [oth. writ.] Several poems including "The Purple Bumble Bee" and "Line and Friend". The short story "The Ugliest Christmas Tree"; [pers.] I started writing at a young age with the inspiration and encouragement of my grandmother, Ruth W. Bailey; we all called her Ninny. Her maiden name was Ruth Williams, hence with love and appreciation my pen name. [a.] Plant City, FL.

TAYLOR, COLIN
[b.] May 15, 1965, Jamiaca, W.I.; [p.] Manley and Vashti Taylor; [m.] Lorna, March 22, 1986; [ch.] Sean, Shardae, Colin Jr., and Peta Gay Taylor; [ed.] Glenmuir High School; [occ.] Clerk; [pers.] Poetryt draws man closer to himself. There is a bit of poetry in everyone. Poets - those who persue. [a.] West Haverstraw, NY.

TAYLOR, JUNE A.
[pen.] June Taylor; [b.] May 10, 1917, Phoenix, AZ; [p.] Harry and Mae Washart; [m.] J. Leonard "Len", June 10, 1937; [ch.] one son and four daughters and 8 great grandchildren; [ed.] 10th grade; [oth. writ.] Poems published in the Akron Beacon Journal; [pers.] Work with one of my grand daughters who is a graphic artist, creating personalized greeting cards for family and friends. Writing is simply a hobby.

TAYLOR, OLGA ANN
[b.] November 9, 1938, Kamnsak, SASK; [p.] James and Vera Sagenace; [m.] J. Richard, June 4, 1975; [ch.] Karen, Aldie, Don, Chris and Ken; [ed.] Rocford School, George Brown College; [occ.] Seamstress; [pers.] Let not anger depress the heart. As not to see the beauty in life. [a.] Birch River, Man. CAN.

TAYLOR, STEVE
[b.] April 16, 1968, Coventry; [p.] Betty Taylor; [ed.] Foxford Comprehensive School; [occ.] Machine Operator; [oth. writ.] Midland Verse (Thoughts of Night), British Poetry Review (Governed By Another), Poetry Now (Turn Back The Clock), Valleys of Thought (Godfather Tree); [pers.] When I experience a lot it is for myself, when I imagine, it is for us all. My writing is a record of society's happenings today, tomorrows hopes, yesterday's mistakes. [a.] Conventry, England.

TENBROOK, JASON R.
[b.] January 4, 1981, Kokomo, IN; [p.] Daniel and Mary TenBrook; [ed.] Maple Crest School; [occ.] Student 7th grade; [memb.] St. Joan of Arc Church, Jets, Basketball team (Maple Crest Mustangs); [hon.] Academic honors certificate, Midwest Talent Search; [oth. writ.] The Journey, Always, Love Bound - works unpublished. [a.] Kokomo, IN.

TESKA, MARY
[b.] September 7, 1923, Monessen, PA; [ch.] Ernest, Michele, Rebecca; [occ.] Typing services-self employed;

[pers.] Poetry is an inspirational calling from within to express one's innermost feelings. It is not for everyone. It is only for those who have conquered the fear of living and for those who have mastered the art of dying. [a.] Greenwood, SC.

THACKER, BEULAH ARLINE
[b.] March 24, 1907, Belington, WV; [p.] Francis and Roberta Thacker; [ed.] Buckhannon, WV High School, W.V. Wesleyan College, Maryland University and Catholic University in DC; [occ.] Retired teacher; [memb.] Maryland and WV Retired Teachers, Barbour Co. Historical Society, Catholic Church, Secular Franciscan Assumption Fraternity; [oth. writ.] Symphony Hall-Mother's Day Mediation-Resurrection of the Trees, have story for children with a publisher, wholesome nature story and condensed "Hester" to 60 page libretto for opera or musical published at my expense; [pers.] Hope to keep in touch with children by writing nature stories, mostly from personal experience. A hearing loss reduces me to one to one discussions. I can think and wrie as I do traditional and original hand weaving. [a.] Philippi, WV.

THOM, ZACHARY
[b.] January 28, 1987, Southfield, MI; [p.] Mark and Ann Thom; [ed.] Shrine Elementary, Shrine Academy; [occ.] Student; [pers.] My writings are based on events in everyday life and in the world, both good and bad. [a.] Royal Oak, MI.

THOMAS, FRANCIS D.
[pen.] Tommy Thomas; [b.] February 9, 1908, Farwell, MI; [p.] Joseph and Florence Thomas; [m.] Ellen C., February 27, 1929; [ch.] James, Larry, William, Sally, Robert - 14 grandchildren and 6 great great grandchildren; [ed.] BS and MA; [occ.] Retired; [memb.] Phi Delta Kappa; [pers.] Many Christian poems family and personal poems. Programs entitled "God's Wonderful World". Poems and slides now with tapes.

THOMAS, GEORGE
[pen.] Jeremiah Psalms; [b.] January 11, 1977, Kerala, India; [p.] P.V. and Sosamma Thomas; [ed.] Stuyvesant High School; [occ.] Student; [memb.] St. Gregorians Orthodox Church of India, Arista, "Bio-Med Times" Magazine, "Inspiration" magazine; [hon.] Gidd Honor Rollm, Arista Police Commander for a day of NYC 106 precinct, honorary mention in The 53rd NYC Science Fair; [oth. writ.] Several works of poetry, critical essays, scientific articles and a number of plays; [pers.] We are spiritual beings that have brief human experiences. I write not merely as an observer but as a filter which traps and cherishes all things of substance. [a.] Richmond Hill, NY.

THOMAS, KRISTEN
[pen.] Sistah Cinque'; [b.] September 1, 1955, Detroit, MI; [p.] Eli and Winifred Hamilton Jr.,; [m.] Charles E., September 30, 1974; [ch.] Shachaesharone, Gihonna, Sungi; [ed.] Cass Technical School, Michigan State University, San Diego State University, Wayne State University; [occ.] Free-lance consultant; [memb.] Faith Temple Baptist Church, Senior Usher Board, Hartford Head Start Committee Chairperson; [hon.] State of MI Certified Foster Care Parent, MI State University Dean's list; [oth. writ.] Compiling original poetry collections for publication; [pers.] I am inspired to reflect the social consciousness that is manifest in the works of Maya Angelou, Nikki Giovanni and Zora Neale Hurston. [a.] Detroit, MI.

THOMAS, NICOLE
[pen.] Sydney Nicole Thomas; [b.] March 22, 1983, Denver, CO; [p.] Bethanne Thomas; [ed.] 5th grade student; [pers.] I wrote this poem as a gift to my mother for Mother's day. [a.] Kingwood, TX.

THOMAS, RHIANA LIN
[pen.] Rita Mae D.; [b.] June 30, 1978, Lancaster; [p.] Ferris and Sherrie Thomas; [ed.] Antelope Valley High School; [occ.] Student; [memb.] Grace Lutheran Church; [hon.] Peer helping; [oth. writ.] A Three Sided Heart, Roses N Pearls, A Winter Eclipse of the Heart, Mid-Night Shadows, Anything But The Love That Once Was, Why; [pers.] I give great thanks to my mother Sheryl Sawyer (now deceased) and my father Ferris Thomas who is a great inspiration to me. I also thank God for my talent. [a.] Lancaster, CA.

THOMAS, ROSE SANDRA
[b.] July 7, 1971, Port-Au Prince, Haiti; [p.] Nathalie Mirin and Alberto Thomas; [ed.] Andrew Jackson High, Suburban Tech Business School; [occ.] Sales Representative; [memb.] Sacred Heart Church Choir member; [hon.] School awards of attendance and service; [oth. writ.] Wrote several poems and stories I kept in my file. Had published a few of them in old school; [pers.] I've been very excited for my poem had chosen between all of the others. I'm still writing more and hoping to publish another one soon.

THOMAS, WILLIAM H.
[b.] Cromwell, OK; [ed.] University of Oklahoma, East Central State; San Antonio College; Oklahoma City University; [occ.] NY City Police Dept; freelance editor/writer; [memb.] Fraternal Order of Police, Masonic Lodge; [hon.] Wall Street Journal, Newspaper Fund Fellowship, names among top 50 journalism teachers by WSJ, five awards for syndicated newspaper column; [oth. writ.] "Man To Man" syndicated column, numerous magazine articles, features, five non-fiction books, ad copy, press releases; [pers.] Alexander Opoe a major influence, whose imagery in "The Dunciad" was the subject of master's thesis. [a.] NYC, NY.

THOMAS-JONES, LAURA
[b.] November 17, 19035, Mobile, AT; [p.] Walter A. and Ruth I. Thomas (deceased); [m.] Divorced; [ch.] Mary E. Meyer, Martha A. Boyle, John G. Jones, Jr.; [ed.] Elementary and high school, one year college - business certificate - personnel mgt.; [occ.] Retired; [pers.] My religious up bringing has given me a very deep spiritual reflection on life, especially to the people who are close to me., It is through that emotion I am able to put into writing my feelings. [a.] Cockeysville, MD.

THOMPSON, DANIEL L.
[pen.] Daniel L. Thompson; [b.] June 7, 1973, Charleston, WV; [p.] Cameron L. and Betty L. Thompson; [occ.] United States Air Force; [pers.] Life is always going to be hard; if you choose to accept the challenge. A person can either play the game, or sit passively by and have no moments of glorious viuctory, devistating defeat, and nerve racking ties. The person who competes knows the tru joy of life is living. The person who does not compete only knows the side of life that is bound by death. [a.] Hurlburt Fld, FL.

THOMPSON, EVELYN
[b.] October 21, 1944, Targettville, NB; [p.] Kelly and Violet Roberts; [m.] Earl, September 23, 1961; [ch.] Elaine Muriel, Janet Lee, Tony Allan; [pers.] Like to write about the contest between happiness and unhappiness joy and sorrow, mostly about pain. [a.] Bass River, CAN.

THOMPSON, JEFFREY S.
[b.] February 25, 1974, Syracuse; [p.] Charles and Brenda Thompson; [ed.] East Syracuse-Minoa School-Columbia College; [occ.] USAF Air National Guard, Arrowhead Golf Course Maintenance; [pers.] I consider myself as a romantic and find that true love is generated from both the heart and the soul. My poems were inspired by the girls that I truly love. [a.] E. Syracuse, NY.

THOMPSON, MARK R.
[b.] November 14, 1960, Howesdale, PA; [p.] Richard and Norma Thompson; [m.] Bozena Kitlinska Thompson, November 26, 1993; [ed.] Wallenpaupack Area High School, University of Pittsburgh, Florida Institute of Technology, NRI Schools; [occ.] International Technical Services Coordinator; [pers.] If one relaxes and permits the mind to flow freely, then creativity and inspiration shine forth to bring a smile to the face of the world. [a.] Framingham, MA.

THOMSON, MARYELLE
[pen.] Mary Ellen Burrows Gormley; [b.] October 27, 1947, Malton, ONT, CAN; [p.] Ellen and John BUrrows; [ch.] Patricia, Sherry and ason Stephenson, Theresa and granddaughter Amanda Stephenson; [ed.] Elementary and 2 yrs business school; [occ.] Gas Bar Cashier; [memb.] Tony's Terrors Bowling League, Rexdale Sec. Treasurer of Bowling League; [oth. writ.] Have written a poem about the Canadian National Exhibition and my sister Donna-neither published; [pers.] I am a very loving person and prefer to write poems about my family and friends, as well as fond memories. [a.] Downsview, ONT., CAN.

THURSTON, PATRICIA E.
[b.] April 7, 1940, St. Cloud, MN; [ch.] Philene, Natalie, Kelly, Damian, Scot, Raymond; [ed.] University of MN, University of WI; [occ.] Writer; [oth. writ.] Poem published in Poets Who Haven't Moved To Minneapolis, book of poetry Climbing Dreamer, children's books: One Sassy Girls and Christmas Cousins; [pers.] Lake Superior is a strong mystical presence in my life who;s every mood is an active force in our community. [a.] Duluth, MN.

TIEGER, AARON
[b.] 1974, New Hampshire; [ed.] Marlboro College; [occ.] Student; [memb.] Poetry, editor, Erato Literary/Arts Magazine; [hon.] First prize in 1992-93 M.U.S.E. (Movement Uniting Student Expression, poetry contest also honorable mention in same contest; [oth. writ.] Published extensively in school literary magazines; [pers.] Knowledge of, and fluency in, structure and form are essential to writing good poetry. Most of my writings is in strict form, (traditional or otherwise), though "Balcony" is not. The poets to whom I owe the greatest debt are W.S. Merwin, Frank O'Hara and Edna St. Vincent Millay.

TILLER, SHERRI J.
[b.] April 18, 1971, Marion, IN; [p.] Kathy Rhoades and Allen Buck; [m.] David L., July 24; [ch.] KieferTiller; [occ.] Housewife; [oth. writ.] A New Life, Your Daddy, The Firl, My First Love; [pers.] The reason I wrote my poem was because of my son and mother. My moms showed me what a mother is. I wanted people to

understand a mother's love. and how much I love me son. [a.] Union City, IN.

TJOSTHEIM, SARA
[b.] Rocky Mountain, Hse., Ab., CAN.; [pers.] Greatly influenced by the writings of Jim Morrison. [a.] Rocky Mountain House, Alberta, CAN.

TODD, HUGH HILTON
[b.] August 13, 1941, Rose Hall Town; [p.] Louisa Todd and Thomas Williams (deceased); [m.] Claudine Esther, December 26, 1972; [ch.] Jugh (Jr.) and Vanessa; [ed.] Rose Hall High, Teachers Training College; [occ.] Principal; [memb.] Board of Industrial Training and Technical Education Advisory Council; [oth. writ.] Books of poems - "Poet's Song", "A Window of my Mind", several poems published in local newspapers, contributions in "Treasury of Guyanese Poetry" and "Talking Dragline"; [pers.] I strive to unfold the various emotions of man and to hope for a word of peace in my writings. I was influenced by the early romantic poets. [a.] Richmond Hill, Linden Guyana.

TOLES, JENNIFER MARIE
[pen.] Lady Turtle, Stephanie Nichole; [b.] November 26, 1976, Huntsville, AL; [p.] Rhonda Jo Holt and Roger Dale Torres; [ed.] High school, Pikes Peak Community College; [occ.] Typist/proofreader; [oth. writ.] One poem published in Of Diamonds and Rust article published in school newspaper; [pers.] I believe a good writer is born that way. Writing should be of the heart, not of the textbook. [a.] Calhan, CO.

TONKIN, DAVID
[b.] July 5, 1958, Melbourne, Australia; [p.] Dr. Raymond and Patricia Tonkin; [ed.] Xavier College, University of Melbourne; [occ.] Lawyer; [memb.] Law Institute of Victoria/New South Wales, Fellowship of Poetry of Mankind, National Literature Institute; [hon.] Literature award-category open - genral excellence, national short poem award; [oth. writ.] Anthology of Poetry 1973-83 "Let The Shadows Cry" 1989; [pers.] The message of poetry must be a reflection of the upward movement of the human spirit. I seek to reflect the beauty of life through male eyes. [a.] Venice Beach, CA.

TOPPING, BETH
[b.] August 16, 1978, IL; [p.] Jean and Kevin Topping; [ed.] Alabama School of Fine Arts, Glenwood High school; [occ.] Student; [memb.] Varsity basketball team, Math team; [hon.] 1991 Talent Identification Pgm Dulce University, 1993 Summer Math Camp, Joint Enrollment Program; [oth. writ.] Several books and poems under revision; [pers.] "Big whorls have little whorls which feed on their velocity. And little whorls have lesser whorls and so on to viscosity." Lewis F. Richardson. [a.] Smiths, AL.

TORPILA, FRANK T.
[b.] December 21, 1951, NJ; [p.] Frank and Ann; [ed.] St. Raphael, St. Anthony High, Hamilton High West; [occ.] Artist; [hon.] Red Wrapped Rose, Wolf Tales, Like Wow, Rose Marie, La Fornarina published by National Library of Poetry, Editor's Choice awards; [pers.] Passions for painting and painting with words. [a.] Yardville, NJ

TORRES, NANCY
[b.] January 8, 1963, NYC; [p.] Manuel Torres and Felicita Beltrain; [ed.] Eli Whitney Vocational, Brooklyn College; [occ.] Legal Assistant; [hon.] Arista Honor

Student, English Regents Honor Student; [oth. writ.] Private collection of poems and short stories not published; [pers.] Whatever we were put here to accomplish, we should do the best job possible with dignity, and pride; never forgetting where we came from or who put us here. [a.] Woodside, NY.

TOY, JOE
[b.] March 18, 1941, Paducah, KY; [ch.] Bobby and Lee Toy; [ed.] St. Mary's Academy, Christian Brothers College; [memb.] Knights of Columbus, Councils 1055, 544, 4972, 8354, 4th degree; [pers.] FAvorite quote, "Hang in There" fahter Carley Ciacosa founding pastor St. Ignatius if Antioom.

TREMMEL, JENNY LEE
[b.] October 29, 1961, London, Ont.; [p.] Helga and Joseph Tremmel, sister-Barbara Ann Tremmel; [ed.] University of Western Ontario; [occ.] Student, part-time London Natural Gas Fireplaces (sales); [pers.] For giving me the courage to try, I'd like to thank Mom and Dad, Barb, Pete and all of my family and friends. [a.] London, Ont.

TRENTA, ROSARIA
[b.] July 6, 1967, Rome (Italy); [p.] Brizio and Margherita Trenta; [ed.] London International Film school, University of London; [occ.] Screenwriter; [memb.] National Anti-Vivisection Society; [hon.] Several awards for written works as short stories and poetries (four book published); [oth. writ.] Three screenplays; [pers.] I wish the world would show a little respect for Mother Nature and all the beautiful creatures that populate our planet. I believe in ourselves there are all the answers to the mystery of life. We simply need to open our heart. Writing could be a way. As far as I am concerned, it is the only way I know.

TRIBUZIO, SALVATORE
[b.] April 26, 1944, NYC; [p.] Pasquale and Teresa; [m.] Susan Escobar Tribuzio, June 10, 1973; [ch.] Christopher; [ed.] Evander Childs High School; [occ.] Retired NYC Correction Officer; [pers.] I don't consider myself a poet at all. I try to take an almost everyday occurence and put it in writing in a rhyming and humorous fashion.

TRITCH, IVAN
[b.] October 3, 1966, Rockton, IL; [p.] Ervin and Lola Tritch; [m.] Divorced; [ch.] Kenneth Matthew, James Clifton, Lucan Nathaniel; [ed.] Paragould High School, Arkansas State University; [occ.] Manufacturing; [pers.] My inspiration come from my children and from Kathy the wonderful woman in my life. [a.] Jonesbor, AR >

TSCHUMPERLIN, MARIE DOLORES
[pen.] General Ann Mail Bag T; [b.] March 27, 1945, Salinas, CA; [p.] Joseph Dominic and Lilyan Tschumperlin (Riopel); [ed.] Sacred Heart Elementary School, Palma High School, Hartnell Junior College; [occ.] Independent Contractor; [pers.] Although many people claim they are not artistic. I think that every person contributes in some way their inate artistic abilities.

TUCKER, SHERI L.
[b.] October 31, 1961, Salina, KS; [p.] Robert C. and Virginia R. Tucker; [m.] boyfriend-Tom Marks; [ch.] Wesley J. Real; [ed.] Moreno Valley High School, Laconia Technical College; [occ.] Student and Domestic Engineer; [memb.] M. Yost, Story and Poetry Association; [oth. writ.] Biographical stories and poems sharing

experience, strengths and hopes; [pers.] My credit goes solely to my higher power, whom I choose to call God. He has taught me the magical lesson that making the most of what we have turns it into more. [a.] Laconia, NH.

TULLBANE, CHRIS
[b.] December 1, 1976, MD; [p.] Joseph and Joyce Tullbone; [ed.] American School of Madrid; [occ.] Student; [pers.] Poetry has never seemed like work to me. It is more a method of communication reaching out to the world. [a.] Madrid.

TULLIS, SABRINA ANN
[pen.] SAT; [b.] August 13, 1979, Ottamwa, IA; [p.] Sherri and Daniel Tullis; [ed.] Davis County High School; [memb.] Basketball team; [hon.] Honor roll; [oth. writ.] Young Writer's Conference 3 yrs. [a.] Bloomfield, IA.

TURNBULL, M. MICKEY
[b.] Ottawa, CAN; [ch.] Cathy, Carol and Jean six grandchildren-Wesley, Melanie, Joel, Jessica, Mark and Mitchell; [ed.] St. Clair County Community College, University of Western Ontatio and York University; Dean's list, magna cum laude graduate, national honor society, Phi Theta Kappa, Lamda MU; [occ.] Project Procurement Manager; [memb.] St. James Catherdral Welcoming Committee, Variety Club, Royal Ontario Musuem, Art Galley of Ontario, Ontario Science Centre, St. Christopher House; [hon.] Three drama scholarships, certificates of honor from The Ontario Ministry of Citizenship and Culture and Scarborough Support Services for the Elderly; [oth. writ.] Publications Patterns, Pegasus, National Poetry Press, reporter with By-line for The Local, public relations writing for St. Christopher House; [pers.] I strive to reflect the inner struggles of people and their personal capacity to reach for the ultimate within themselves in order to enrich and ennoble their quality of life.

TURNER, CHARLES E.
[pen.] B.N. Free; [b.] December 18, 1956, Pompano, FL; [p.] Talbert and Mary Turner; [m.] Vicki, December 15, 1992; [ch.] Charles E. Turner, Jr, Theodore E. Turner and Charles C. Turner; [ed.] Ft. Laud High School; [occ.] Cook; [pers.] All my poems are about love and heaven above inspired by my second wife Vicki. [a.] Thief River Falls, MN.

TURNER, EUDOCIA
[pers.] Open your mind, unlock the doors, see the possibilities, and seize the knowledge. [a.] Dallas, TX.

TWEEDY, MANDI KRISTSEN
[b.] February 8, 1972, Bristol, UK; [p.] Alan and Pauline Tweedy; [ed.] Clifon High School, University of Wales, College of Cardiff; [oth. writ.] Poems published in various anthologies in England, collection of poetry currently being considered for an award by The Society of Authors in England; [pers.] I believe my poetry is expressionist and reflects subconscious images and emotions. It is an attempt to exptess the unity of both sides of the dividing line between dream states and reality. [a.] Bristol, UK.

TYMCHYN, PAUL VICTOR
[pen.] Tymco; [b.] March 31, 1947, Albany, NY; [p.] Olive and Victor Tymchyn; [m.] Virginia Mae Quay Tymchyn, July 10, 1966; [ch.] Gregory John and Ronelle Marie; [ed.] Guilderland Central High School, University of Miami; [occ.] Director; [memb.] St.

Lucy's Roman Catholic Church, Capital District YMCA; [oth. writ.] Hold patent and trademarks and copyrights on several educational toys and games "Cope" txg. 186-679, "Newsbeat" Pat 5,197,884; Tele*Phobia, ddp 343039; [pers.] FAvorite quote from William Shakespeare "Their is a tide in the affairs of men, which taken at the flood, leads on to fortune; Omitted, all the voyage of their life is bound in shallows and in miseries." [a.] Altamont, NY

TYNER, DORIS
[b.] November 17, 1939, Hartsville, SC; [p.] Harrison and Marion Tyner; [ch.] Dale Tyner; [ed.] Hartsville High School; [memb.] Songwriters Club of America; [hon.] Golden Poet Award, Listed Who's Who in World of Poetry Anthology; [pers.] I always will thank God for my talent because he gave me my words. [a.] hartsville, SC.

ULSH, LILLIAM LINS
[b.] Bedford, PA; [p.] Richard and Ruth Lins; [m.] Lewis Ulsh; [ed.] Bedford High, Dickinson College, Gettysburg College, post-grad courses in sign language for Deaf; [occ.] Retired French and Spanish high school teacher; [hon.] Scholarship for high school essay, high school Valedictorian, McDaniel College Scholarship prize, Rees English Bible prize, Womer English Memorial prize, Phi Beta Kappa, college graduation-first honors; [oth. writ.] I make my own greeting and Christmas cards using the many poems written through our Heavenly Father's encouragement and guidance; [pers.] I am humbly grateful to be able to share with others our Heavenly Father's loving, inspirational thoughts, for messages of love were meant to be shared with each other, frequently. [a.] Waynesboro, PA.

UMBRAS, TOM
[b.] March 2, 1953, Detroit, MI; [p.] Benedict J. Umbras and Loretta K.; [ed.] Divine Word College, Epworth, IA, Catholic Theological Union, Chicago, Loyola University, Chicago; [occ.] I'm a priest working in the electronic media with the Divine Word Missionaries; [memb.] Unda/USA, Association of Catholic Communicators; [hon.] Gabriel Award, "Un Nuevo Dia", New York International Radio Festival, "Un Nuevo Dia", "Contigo", "Cantemos al Mundo la Hermandad", New York International Non-broadcast Video, "Cartas de Dios", Emmy-"Still A Stranger"; [oth. writ.] I am a radio and television scriptwriter in both Spanish and English; [pers.] Everyone is a poet. Everyone has planted within the seed of creativity. That seed will haunt us for either good or ill. No one can escape the gift. We must either wake up and accept the gift or dream of its absence. [a.] Chicago, IL.

UMLOR, JODY
[pen.] Zoda Ulmor; [b.] September 1, 1975, Grand Rapids, MI; [p.] Jo Ann and Marvin Umlor; [ed.] Kenowa Hills High School, Grand Rapids Community College; [occ.] Cosmetic Clerk; [hon.] Spanish and music and Pom Pon awards, two years as captain of the Pom Pon Squad. [oth. writ.] Own personal poems; [pers.] Don't let anyone stand in the way of your dreams. [a.] Walker, MI.

UNGERER, SARAH E.
[b.] March 14, 1978, Syracuse; [p.] Ronald and Christine Ungerer; [ed.] Sophomore at Westhill High School; [occ.] Student; [memb.] French Club, class treasurer, varsity soccer, varsity basketball, chorus, Communica-

tions Club; [hon.] Law Day essay contest winner, N.Y.S. Outdoor Writers Association poetry winner, school's literary magazine, poem cover winner, honor roll; [oth. writ.] "Branches", "Struggle For Justice", "The Greatest Gift of All" (newspaper Christmas story contest winner); [pers.] I write to allow people to think… allow them to feel … to make them realize how special it is just to be. [a.] Syracuse, NY.

UPHOFF JR., JOSEPH A. DR.
[b.] March 15, 1950, Colorado; [p.] Melva C. and Joseph Uphoff; [m.] Single; [ed.] B.A. Fine Arts, U. Co., 1977, Shodan degree (Black Belt), Institute of M.A., 1989, Doctor of Letters, London Institute, for Applied Research, 1993, Doctor of Divinity, Universal Life Church, CA 1993; [occ.] Surrealist; [memb.] National Geographic Society, Fraternal Order of Eagles, Poetry West, Colorado Springs Art Guild, Colorado Springs Fine Arts Center; [hon.] Commemorative Medal of Honor (for lifetime achievement), American Biographical Institute, 1993, Knight, Order of San Ciriaco, Italy, 1993, Baron, Royal Order, Bohemian Crown, 1993, Grand Council, Confederation of Chivalry, Australia 1993, Advisory Council, International Biographical Centre, Cambridge England, 1992; [oth. writ.] Hyperbolic Paraboloids, Differential Logic, Yoga, The Art of Flexibility, Spirits From The Inland Sea; [pers.] The meaning of words, as objects or abstract images, is that of jewels and diatoms. [a.] Colorado Springs, CO.

UPTON, ALVIN K.
[pen.] Al; [b.] August 3, 1926, Sweetwater, TN; [m.] Amy Louise, December 1945; [ch.] Elaine, Al Jr., Greg and Sharon; [ed.] Morristown College; [occ.] Retired; [memb.] AARP, Northeastern Presby. Church; [hon.] Distinguish Alumni Award, Morristown College; [pers.] I want to be a worthy way marker.

URBANO, LINDA S.
[b.] December 29, 1950, Detroit; [p.] Robert L. (deceased(and Rita Bruce; [m.] Gary Urbano, September 9, 1978; [pets.] Dog-Magic, cats (2) called The Meanies; [ed.] St. Philip Neri School; [occ.] Mental Health worker, Macomb County Community Mental Health, Adult Day Treatment Center; [pers.] I am inspired through my poetry to write about life's everyday occurrence. [a.] Oakland, MI.

VALENTINE, SHARI D.
[b.] August 21, 1964, Harrison, AR; [p.] Tina Tabor and Carl Valentine; [ed.] Graduated from Brown-Pyatt in 1983, went to school at Vo-Tech at Harrison and I am a certified automotive technician; [occ.] Self-employed, farming and mechanic work; [hon.] I was awarded "1979" most valuable player in basketball at Mt. View, Ark., private school; [oth. writ.] Yes, I have written several but none has ever been published, lost most of them in a house fire, but I still write poetry; [pers.] Poetry is my favorite hobby. I try to make people feel what I feel when I am writing it. To me writing poetry is a whole new world. I love it, and I owe it to my family at home and friends in California. [a.] Everton, AR.

VALLEN, MARLENE J.
[pen.] Marlene Vallen; [b.] September 15, 1932, Los Angeles; [p.] Pauline and Morris (deceased) Barnett; [m.] Allan Vallen (deceased), October 5, 1952; [ch.] Stephanie Girvan; [ed.] 2 years L.A. City College, major journalism; [occ.] Graphologist/writer; [memb.] So. California Publicists Association, American Handwriting Analysis Foundation; [hon.] Certified Graphologist

A.H.A.F., article published in L.A. Times newspaper (View Section); [oth. writ.] "The Mirror" (poem), "Celebrity Tributes", my personalized Tribute Business, (poems, Speeches, Roast to Toasts); [pers.] I love young people they keep me young at heart. I love America, I love to write about America, young people and the promise for a better world. [a.] Los Angeles, CA.

VALLI, ESPEDITO
[b.] June 21, 1916, Pennsylvania; [p.] Isidoro and Giocanna Valli; [m.] Jennie, March 27, 1940; [ch.] 3; [ed.] 10th grade in Italy 1921-1931; [occ.] Retired Ford worker worked at Ford 39 years.

VAN BEER, KIRK
[b.] November 2, 1961, Takapuna, NZ; [p.] Henry and Audrey Van Beer; [ed.] Brockhill Secondary Douglas College; [occ.] Child Care worker; [oth. writ.] As yet, none; [pers.] Reach for the stars, but keep your feet on the earth and don't let today's dreams become tomorrow's regrets. [a.] Vancouver, BC.

van CLEAVE, KRISTIN
[pen.] Kit van Cleave; [b.] January 9, 1940, Fort Worth, TX; [p.] Henry Shibley van Cleave and Lola Kathryn Wimberley; [ed.] BA, North Texas, Journalism 1961, MA University of Houston, English 1972, DL-London Institute, English 1973; [occ.] Writer and teacher, also professional martial arts instructor; [memb.] National Women's Martial Arts Federation, Pacific Association of Women Martial Artists, Yu Dan Ja Whey (Black Belt Association) of ChaYon-Ryu, International Martial Arts Association; [hon.] Librettist for "Day of Love" a song cycle written with composer Thomas Pasatieri, nominated for the Pulitzer Prize in 1979, it had received its World Premiere at NYC's Lincoln Center, by Mezzo Frederica von Stade, and National Premiere at Kennedy Center, 1979, Mayor's Award for Outstanding Public Service 1985, Sport Host, Tae Kwon Do, US Olympic Festival '86, Houston, TX; [oth. writ.] Books of poems, "Day of Love", "Amourette" and "Laurels" published non-fiction, journalistic, and freelance articles in international, U.S. and local media for many years, hard book anthologies, "They Still Do", was most recent, currently writing textbook on ChaYon-Ryu style of martial arts with Grandmaster Kim Soo, its founder, completing first novel of trilogy on Holy Grail; [pers.] "As a third-degree Black Belt martial arts instructor, and longtime professional writer who has earned a living by the word, I work hard to unite these two activities in the style of the Samurai, who were both physical and spiritual, fiercely courageous and cultured in the arts". [a.] Houston, TX.

VAN CLEVE, JEANETTE
[b.] October 11, 1933, Dallas, TX; [p.] Vernon and Inez Marchant, Sr.; [ch.] Brenda Scarborough, Karan Mixon, Stuart Craig and Stephen Kyle, eight grandchildren Robert, Shawn, Gary, Reece, Evin, Jessica, Amanda and Sam; [occ.] Nurse, pedi and adult patients on life support in home care; [hon.] United States Patent Charter member contributor to the restoration of the Statue of Liberty, Honorary life membership, The Texas Congress of Parents and Teachers; [oth. writ.] A poem put to music as a ballad by an elementary teacher for the seventh grade; [pers.] I'm inspired by love and the beauty of things around me. [a.] Dallas, TX.

VAN DOREN, MARIE R.
[pen.] Marie Van Doren; [b.] December 15, 1967, Washington, DC; [p.] Regina and Charles Van Doren; [ed.] Associates degree in Early Childhood Education

from Endicott College in Beverly, Massachusetts, Human Development degree from Mount Vernon College, Washington, DC; [occ.] Assistant teacher, 2 years old at Sugar Plum Day Nursery; [oth. writ.] Poems, short stories published in high school magazines; [pers.] I have been blessed with the gift which enables me to express what my heart feels. [a.] Washington, DC.

VAN EVERY, PHILLIP
[b.] December 16, 1974, Charlotte, NC; [p.] Phillip Van Stryder, Diana Van Every; [ed.] High school senior at Myers Park High; [pers.] Favorite quote, How can you see with your eyes, if your imagination is cut of focus. Quoted by Mark Twain. [a.] Charlotte, NC.

VAN GRAMBERG, RUTH CURZ
[pen.] Ruth Cruz; [b.] June 22, 1944, Colombo; [p.] Ruby Mary Chippendall; [m.] Arthur James Edwards, February 6, 1962; [ch.] Rowanne, Barry and Richard; [ed.] Holy Family Convent; [occ.] Secretary; [memb.] Various Literary Associations Council of Adult Education; [hon.] Dip. English language, English literature, various literary awards, bronze medal, Festival of Arts, UK; [oth. writ.] "Papers Petals Poems" by Ruth Cruz; [pers.] "We learn more wisdom from failure much more than from success". We often discover what will do by finding out what will not do, and probably he who never made a mistake never made a discovery"-Samuel Smiles. [a.] Melbourne Victoria, Australia.

VAN HEUSEN, RUTH
[b.] September 27, 1924, Milwaukee, WI; [p.] Mr. and Mrs. W.H. St. Thomas; [m.] Horace Van Heusen; [ch.] Terry Van Heusen and Deborah Fallon; [ed.] B.S. U. of Iowa, M.S. U. Of Iowa; [occ.] Retired teacher, Chemistry Genetics Botany; [memb.] National Science Foundation, 10 years trustee of F.M. N. C. College, Johnstown, NY., Trinity Epioscopal Church, Gloversville, NY., Monastery Gulf Club, Magnolia Club.

VAN KUIKEN, JEROME
[b.] April 8, 1974, Philippines; [p.] Jerry and Margaret Van Kuiken; [ed.] Mount Carmel High, Kentucky Mountain Bible College; [occ.] College student; [hon.] Who's Who Among American High School Students, high school class Valedictorian (class of 1992); [oth. writ.] Poem published in a local newspaper; [pers.] I seek to honor a glorious Lord, Jesus Christ, through a glorious language, English. [a.] VanCleve, KY.

VAN NOSTRAND, HEIDI
[pen.] Havena Vanlyn; [b.] January 12, 1979, Claire, MT; [p.] Larry and Ruby Dotson; [ed.] Silver Lake High School; [occ.] Student; [memb.] J H Mathcounts, Literary Guild, MYF; [hon.] Presidential Academic Fitness Awards, Honor Roll, junior high, 9th grade; [oth. writ.] Several poems and short stories; [pers.] I've always believed that to read is to live, to live and not to read is not to live at all. [a.] Bladen, NE.

VAN THANH, NGUYEN
[pen.] Thanh Nguyen, Troi-Dong and Nguoi Xu Thai; [b.] August 25, 1947, Vietnam; [p.] Doc-Cuoc Nguyen Thuc and Soi Pham; [m.] Minh Chau, 1985; [ch.] Hoang Yen and Honga Dan; ed.] Saigon Law School, Vietnam 1970, Tennessee University of Chattanooga 1979; [occ.] Manager, Chief Financial Officer; [hon.] Who's Who in The Southwest (USA) (92-93), Who's Who of the World (93); [oth. writ.] Poems and articles published in Vietnamese magazines, Tu-Do, Van-Nghe, Lang-Van, Tien-Phong, Dep., Dan-Ta. [a.[Houston, TX.

VARDON, ANN
[b.] July 25, 1920, Sugar Lake, BC; [p.] Michael and Selma Ehret; [m.] Colin (deceased), November 6, 1943; [ch.] Sharon Colleen, Kevin Todd and Carlton Daniel (adopted); [ed.] Grade 8 at Medora Creek School, Sugar Lake, BC. (a one roomed log schoolhouse); [occ.] Loving mother and grandmother of six; [hon.] Received an honor roll plus 25 year pin for fostering children in the community; [oth. writ.] Had several poems published in the local newspaper; [pers.] I like to express my zest for life and my love for nature in every shape and form. [a.] Vernon, BC Canada.

VAZ, SAVIO E.
[b.] October 14, 1969, Panjim; [p.] John B. and Anne Rita Vaz; [ed.] Master of Arts (English), Goa University, Bambolim Goa, diploma in hotel management, diploma in music, (violin); [occ.] Student, professional violinist in Western Classical; [memb.] Member of Vanxim Church Youth Association, member of Marathi Classical Music Association, Provorim; [hon.] Proficiency certificate in B.A. Preliminaries, merit certificate in Western Classical (violin) in all India Cultural Exchange Programme, Madras 1993-94; [oth. writ.] Number of poems and articles published in local dailies and college magazines; [pers.] "Man" has gone astray by incorporating in himself the evil means of darkness. The world has lost its meaning. (Materialism gained supremacy). Man forgot his true self the "maker" within. Would there be no difference if man remained true to himself? [a.] Panjim, Goa.

VAZQUEZ, DENISE
[b.] February 24, 1972, Bronx, NY; [p.] Sifredo and Aida Vazquez; [ed.] Preston High School, University of Bridgeport, Vassar College; [occ.] Student; [memb.] Poder Latino; [hon.] Dean's List, Academic Room and Board Scholarship, ACTWU Scholarship; [pers.] Growing up in an area where people die everyday from gunshot wounds, drugs and other such violence, I took to writing. Perhaps it will help to let others know what is going on in neighborhoods people call home. [a.] Bronx, NY.

VEGA, CHARLINA
[b.] August 18, 1977, Lynwood; [p.] Cynthia and Mark Repcik; [ed.] Marina High School; [memb.] Huntington Beach Search and Rescue; [oth. writ.] All kinds of poetry, funny, happy, sad, emotional; [pers.] I write my poetry to express my feelings and to entertain others. [a.] Huntington Beach, CA.

VELASQUEZ, GUSTAVO
[b.] June 13, 1956, Guatemala; [p.] Guillermo Velasquez and Olga Monge; [m.] Alma Rosa Sanchez, September 17, 1979; [ch.] Andrea, Raquel, Ruth, Paula and Gustavo; [ed.] Physician and surgeon (Guatemala), Cardiovascular Technologist and Echocardiographist; [occ.] Anesthesia Technologist, inventor, real estate; [memb.] The Church of Jesus Christ of Latter Day Saints; [hon.] By the city of Los Angeles for humanitarian work for 8 years of service as a Bishop for my church; [oth. writ.] A short theatrical essay based on "Don Quijote de la Mancha" and some editorials in our church paper, many poems about different topics never published; [pers.] "The nut shell that keep us afloat in the storm of life, is love". [a.] Los Angeles, CA.

VELASCO, LAREDO FERNANDEZ
[pen.] Crimson R.V., R.P. Sison; [b.] May 22, 1973, Manila, Philippines; [p.] Florante R. and Perserveranda Velasco; [ed.] Cainta Catholic School, La Salle Green Hills High School, University of the Philippines; [occ.] College student; [memb.] Up Zoological Society, UP Association of Biology majors; [oth. writ.] Several poems and essays published in the LSGH High School paper, 2 notebooks of personal poems, a collection of original songs; [pers.] Love, friendship and faith are the most wonderful things in the world. If I have all three, I'd be happy for the rest of my life. [a.] Los Angeles, CA.

VELLUTINI, LORI MARIE
[pen.] Brigit Cerridwen; [b.] March 2, 1975, Berwyn, IL; [p.] Susan Jones; [ed.] Bradley-Bourbonnais Community High School, University of New Orleans; [occ.] Student; [memb.] Staff member for the U.N.O. Literary magazine The Ellipsis; [hon.] National Junior Beta, Who's Who Among National High School Students; [oth. writ.] Several poems and short fiction pieces published in school literary magazines; [pers.] To me, poetry represents many things, most importantly it allows us to articulate thoughts and feelings that otherwise may never see the light of day. [a.] New Orleans, LA.

VELUZ, SENDIC
[b.] July 31, 1973, Philippines; [p.] Ramon and Sally Veluz. [a.] Glendale, CA.

VER BECKE, W. EDWIN
[b.] July 21, 1913, Sidney, IA; [p.] Dora and Walter Ver Beck; [m.] E. Eugenia Chavesey, July 1945; [ch.] Deceased; [ed.] MA U of Minnesota, private tutors, art literature; [occ.] Painter, poet; [memb.] NY Poetry Forum, American Poetry Society, Universal Church of the Master,
Artist League; [hon.] Many, Vice President CAAA, National Convention Chairman 1994; [oth. writ.] "Poems of The Spirit", "Life of the Virgin Mary", regular stories in Elf magazine; [pers.] Poetry is not manufactured but born of the divine fire of spirit. [a.] New York, NY.

VETZAL, TRACY
[pen.] Jane Doe; [b.] January 8, 1917, Toronto, Ontario; [p.] Patrick and Arlene Vetzal; [ed.] R.A. Sennett P.S., Whitby Senior P.S., Queen's University, B.A.M.; [memb.] Reba McEntire Fan Club; [hon.] Academic and activity award in high school; [oth. writ.] Anthologies compiled during high school writing seminars; [pers.] Influenced by Leonard Cohen. Believe in what you write, but don't necessarily believe in everything you write about! [a.] Whitby, Ontario.

VICOL, DORU
[b.] August 14, 1971, Romania; [p.] Demostene and Ioana Vicol; [ed.] Business student at local college; [oth. writ.] Several poems as of yet unpublished; [pers.] Thanks to Byron who always had faith in me. [a.] Marathon, Ontario.

VILLARREAL, CESAR A.
[b.] January 26, 1944, Rio Grande City, TX; [p.] Atenogenes and Estela Villarreal; [m.] Dora Villarreal, June 15, 1968; [ch.] Esthella Denise and Marissa Mia Villarreal; [ed.] McAllen High School, University of Houston, University of Houston Law Center; [occ.] Lawyer; [memb.] State Bar of Texas. [a.] Houston, TX.

VILLARUEL, JANIE M.
[pen.] Cinda Hutchinson; [b.] January 26, 1952, Trinidad; [p.] Jeremiah and Edna Hutchinson; [m.] John Villaruel, December 26, 1971; [ch.] Jan Tamara Melissa Crystal; [ed.] St. Ann's High School, Ogle Business Institute

Medical and Training School Inc., Hemstead USA; [occ.] Nursing Assistant; [memb.] Our Lady of Good Council Church; [oth. writ.] Other poems, songs, simple motivational phrases, writing articles for the church, at present I am doing my first novel hoping to be published in the spring; [pers.] My greatest strength is the power of my ideas, creating good thoughts on paper to capture my readers. My influences, Charlotte Bronte' and William Shakespeare. [a.] Inwood Long Island, NY.

VILLEZA, BELLA B.
[b.] January 28, 1933, Philippines; [m.] Richard Villeza (deceased), June 16, 1956; [ch.] Four; [ed.] 1953 B.S.E. Cum Laude, U. of Philippines, M.A. in English Language, University of Michigan 1958; [occ.] English teacher, Los Angeles Unified Schools; [memb.] Phi Kappa Phi, Phi Gamma Mu, ECLA; [hon.] Dean's List, graduated Cum Laude 1953, University of the Philippines, Fulbright grantee 1955, USC Writing Project Fellow 1981, junior high school English Teacher of the Year 1987, ECLA; [oth.writ.] Unpublished; [pers.] God's plans are always good. I need only to be surrendered to His will so that they can be realized. [a.] Los Angeles, CA.

VILLINES, EMORY J.
[b.] September 12, 1958, Washington, DC; [m.] Raymond M. Lyall; [ed.] B.S. University of Maryland, M.Ed. Beaver College in Glenside, PA; [hon.] Winner of short story contest in The European, The Garden of Dasrivsz, London , May 1993; [oth. writ.] "The Ichnography of Hieronymus Bosch", work in progress; [pers.] I divide my time between Europe and America. For 12 years I have been living with my companion, a Scottish research doctor struggling with aids. [a.] Lansdale, PA.

VINCENT, SARAH ELIZABETH
[pen.] Beth Vincent; [b.] August 30,1949, Salisbury, MD; [p.] Wallace Vincent, Alice Boyd and step-mother, Sarah Vincent; [ed.] Pocomoke High School, Uni-Tec, WOR-WIC Community College; [occ.] Housekeeping; [memb.] Berlin-Ocean City Church of God; [oth. writ.] Short story published, Pocomoke High School paper The Papoose; [pers.] I owe all my accomplishments and achievements to the most important one in my life, my Lord and Saviour Jesus Christ. [a.] Berlin, MD.

VINCENZINI, VANESSA
[b.] August 15, 1973, PA; [p.] Patricia and Mario Vincenzini; [ed.] Biology major at the University of South Florida; [occ.] Student; [memb.] The Wilderness Society, The American Paint Horse Association, Themis Honor Society; [hon.] Presidential Academic Award; [pers.] I see poetry as the author's interpretation of life, but the reader has the freedom to conclude their own interpretation and specialized meaning. [a.] Lithia, FL.

VINERS, STEPHANIE
[pen.] Kristine Leggert; [b.] December 8, 1979, Jasper, AL; [p.] Starlene Sides; [ed.] Parrish High; [hon.] I once won a spelling bee in school; [oth. writ.] I have written other unpublished poems, 9 others besides "Winter", but none published; [pers.] I enjoy writing, it is my life. [a.] Parrish, AL.

VIRTA, VOITTO TEUVO ILMARI
[pen.] Jimmy Craft; [b.] October 3, 1943, Helsinki; [p.] Vildo and Anna-Lisa Virta; [ed.] Pho, Western Pacific University, 15.10.1992; [occ.] Voluntary, duty holder the II social service center of Kamppi, Helsinki; [pers.]

I feel strongly for the great events of mankind. [a.] Helsinki, Finland.

VIRTUE, HILARY A.
[b.] July 23, 1965, Vancouver, BC; [p.] Yuri Shallan and Heather Virtue; [ed.] Various schools but more importantly various people; [occ.] Bartender/coffee slinger; [memb.] Railway Club, hang-out for the artistically insane; [oth. writ.] Hundreds of compositions since the age of four; [pers.] Words are our friends. [a.] Vancouver, Canada.

VLAEMINCK, FRAN E.
[pen.] Elizabeth Cooper; [b.] March 15, 1924, Niles, MI; [p.] Newberry and Faye Cooper; [m.] February 2,1946; [ch.] Tedd BN Vlaeminck, 4 grandchildren; [ed.] 12th grade graduate, Elkhart High School, Elkhart, IN; [occ.] Retired factory worker; [memb.] Stonelake Church of God, Middlebury, IN., Machinist Union in Elkhart, IN; [hon.] I was an A student in art and English and literature, have several awards in our union for dedication for the welfare of fellow union members; [oth. writ.] About 20 poems, not published yet; [pers.] My inspiration comes from God and very good parents, as well as 14 brothers and sisters. I believe if you believe in God and pray He will help you through any situation.

VOGELSANG, RACHELLE
[pen.] Rachelle; [b.] April 11, 1958, Pasadena, TX; [p.] Ferrol and Betty Angell; [m.] Ben, June 12, 1976; [ch.] Brent, Phillip and Matthew; [ed.] Lic. Activity Director, canvas and mural and fabric painting sub-teacher, art instructor [memb.] Yoe High band booster, Public Relations, member of CBC Cameron, TX; [hon.] Dean's List, Graphite Drawings Awards; [oth. writ.] Unpublished poems and short stories; [pers.] My love and work with children and the elderly has allowed me experiences that enrich both my painting and writing. [a.] Cameron, TX.

VOGELSONG, JOANNE A.
[b.] May 15, 1951, Bath, NY; [p.] Jim Morehouse and Marge Starkweather; [m.] Gary L. Vogelsong, November 17, 1979; [ch.] William John, Joy Ann, Rachel Jill, Matthew James and Jodi Lyn; [ed.] Corning P.P. East High; [occ.] Writer and design homes; [memb.] Plain Congregational Church; [pers.] I have always enjoyed reading and writing poetry. I am greatly influenced by observing every day happenings of my family and friends. My husband is a true inspiration! [a.] Bowling Green, OH.

VONANDERSECK, ERIC W.B.
[b.] August 26, 1951, Detroit, MI; [p.] Donald W. and Jean C. Andersen; [m.] Maria T. Vonanderseck, October 7, 1973; [ch.] David, Samuel, Adina, Jonathan and Shanell; [ed.] Fenton Senior High School, Bible College and Business School; [occ.] Self-employed. [a.] Port Huron, MI.

WADDELL, HELEN
[pen.] Helen Waddell; [b.] February 1, 1973, Haddinton, East Lothian; [p.] Helen and Lindsay Waddell; [ed.] Knox Academy, Galsgow University (2 yrs); [occ.] Freelance reviewer; [oth. writ.] Reviews published in Harpies and Quines (Scottish Feminist Magazine), M8 (Scottish Music Magazine), Young Scot Magazine, and articles in local newspapers. [a.] Glasgow, Scotland.

WADE, ANDREIA CATHERINE
[b.] July 26, 1951, Santa Paula, CA; [p.] Andrew C.

Wade and Elsie M. White; [ch.] Larry Stevens, Donna Stevens, Fitch Rebecca Steven, R. Jason Stevens; [ed.] Fillmore, CA High SChool, Ventura Jr. College; [occ.] Extraordinaire models assistant, Wal-Mart Sales and special projects, actors coach; [memb.] Starlight Foundation, Childrens Miracle Network, I.M.T.A >; [oth. writ.] Short children's stories, several poems published in school and local publications. Co-author of several modern, pop rock, lyrics and music; [pers.] In my writing the message leads itself to the higher levels of awareness we may managened if bravely we listen to the rhythms of love, peace and honor given us at birth. [a.] Bakersfield, CA.

WADE, KIOMI
[b.] November 20, 1974, Henderson, TX; [p.] Harvey and Marie Wade; [ed.] Henderson High School, Stephen F. Austin State University; [occ.] Student; [hon.] Rusk County Poetry Contest; [pers.] Never let anyone tell you what you can and cannot do. [a.] Henderson, TX.

WADUD, KAMIEL
[b.] January 8, 1967, Newark, NJ; [p.] Kareemah Kamiel Wadud; [m.] Tamiko, July 17, 1984; [ch.] Kamiel III, Maunah, Jordan, Aliyah, Maiya; [ed.] Weequahic High School, Essex County College; [occ.] Custom Cabinetmaker, Furniture, General contractor; [memb.] Feed the Homeless programs of Newark and New York from the Jerrahis NY; [hon.] For helping train innercity youths in the field of constuction; [oth. writ.] WCLK of Atlanta, GA Sundays poetry readings - Sunday Night Meditations book in publication stages - with Pir Press; [pers.] Love has no eyes for color race creed or religion. Love loves all for the sake of love. [a.] Newark, NJ.

WAGAMAN, GAYLE ANN
[b.] September 6, 1948, Harrisburg, PA; [p.] George L. Wagaman, Desna P. Wagaman; [ed.] Cedar Cliff High School, Penna Rehabilitation Center; [occ.] Office worker for Commonwealth of Pennsylvania; [memb.] Brookfield Bible Church, Harrisburg, PA, Pennsylvania Poetry Society, Harrisburg Choral Society, Campsite Evangelism; [hon.] Who's Who in American Christian Leadership, 1989, small monetary award for writing lyrics for 1972 Harrisburg, PA Labor Day Kipona celebration entitled, "We Can Beat The Blues"; [oth. writ.] Wrote a book of my original poetry, "A Garden Verse", 1974, many poems published in local newspaper, I'm presently writing articles (boigraphical in nature) for my local curch's weekly bulletin, featuring ministries of various church workers; [pers.] I try to let my writings reflect my personal belief in God. I try to let all my works give Him the glory, for He has given me the talent to express His love to others in this way; [a.] Camp Hill, PA.

WAHLBERG, WINIFRED
[b.] March 13, 1941, New Zealand; [p.] Myra Ellen Nicholls, Eigill Wilhelm Wahlberg; [ch.] Damien and Evon Esam; [ed.] Wilford School, Hunt Valley Memory Technical College, [occ.] Portrait painter and writer; [hon.] Editor's Choice Award (for Outstanding Achievement in Poetry), presented by The National Library of Poetry; [oth. writ.] Author of a book on symbolism, articles, short stories, an essay on "The Soul of Art", more poems; [pers.] I seek to give expression the music images and portray the beauty of soul; [a.] Manly, Australia.

WALKER, AGNES B.
[b.] Philadelphia, PA; [m.] Dennis Walker, December

21, 1946; [ch.] Bernadette Walker, Dennis III, Nelson, Andrew, Patricia; [ed.] St. Joseph High School, La Guardia Community College, Queens College; [occ.] Retired;

WALKER, NATALIE
[b.] August 30, 1980, Mi; [p.] Basil Walker, Debra Walker; [pers.] In memory of Ada Hebert Klub; [a.] Rochester, MI.

WALKER, RONALD EDWARD
[pen.] ZPK (it is Hebrew, and it means lion and souds like "R". "E") [b.] June 29, 1939, Springfield, MO; [p.] Billy Jack anmd Alma Irene Walker; [ed.] G.E.D. [occ.] 18 wheel truck driver; [memb.] U.S. Marine Corp, 1957-1965, Chessnuts, NRA; [hon.] Two honorable discharges, I am a fifth generation trail of tears Cherokee; [oth. writ.] So far unpublished; [pers.] Presidnet Nixon is a good man and was framed by liberal Socialists and that's a fact: I voted for Perot, and Oliver North could be the next President if he only knew how much America loves him; [a.] Augusta, GA.

WALKER, WILLIAM L. JR.
[b.] August 25, 1945, Charleston, SC; [p.] William Law, Janice Jefferson; [m.] Libby Owens, March 21, 1981; [ch.] Janice, Catherine, Cameron, Reid Hanna; [ed.] Woodberry Forest School, Washington and Lee University; [occ.] Writer; [hon.] Associated Press award for Reporting in Depth, 1969, S. C. Press Association award for Best Weekly Newspaper Column, 1977, 3 other S. C. Press Assn. awards; [pers.] My yearning is to paint pictures, not with the brush of the artist, but with the power of words on a page; [a.] Sullivans Island, SC.

WALKER-SCOTT, KENDRA L.
[pen.] Ken; [b.] April 6, 1966; [p.] Gene A. and Ora Lee Walker; [m.] Michael D. Scott, May 27, 1993; [ch.] MarKesha K. Walker; [ed.] MountainView College; [occ.] Office manager; [hon.] Numerous high school awards in poetry; [oth. writ.] Pegasus I and Pegasus II; [pers.] Reach for the stars, you might touch the moon; [a.] Dallas, TX.

WALL, MIKE
[b.] February 16, 1956, Queens, NY; [p.] Fred and Marjorie Wall; [oth. writ.] "Poems Insoired By You", a collection of 47 poems; [pers.] We all have dreams of one kind or another far too often, for whatever reason, our dreams go unfulfilled. To have my poetry published by The National Library of Poetry is very gratifying, and for me, a dream come true; [a.] Lindenhurst, NY.

WALLER, STEVE
[a.] Chanhassen, NY.

WALSH, ELIZABETH WORTHEN
[b.] February 2, 1981, St. Louis, MO; [p.] Mahlon and Carol Walsh; [ed.] Hadley Watts Middle School; [occ.] Student; [memb.] Centerville Sophisticates Drill Team, Girl Scouts; [oth. writ.] Nothing published; [a.] Centerville, OH.

WALSH, THOMAS J.
[b.] February 1, 1951, Philadelphia, PA; [p.] Thomas P. Wilma J.(nee Urso); [m.] Patricia (nee Freeman), May 6, 1972; [ch.] Cynthia Patricia, Thomas Andrew; [ed.] Fr. Judge High, Cabrini College, Heriot-Watt University; [occ.] Specialist-Bell Atlantic Corp.; [hon.] Magna cum laude, Alpha Sigma Lambda, ICCP Certified Computing Professional-Management; [oth. writ.] Short

stories and poems; [pers.] I wrote this poem ("Timeless") in 1972 for Pat, my loving young bride of one month. The feelings are still true today; [a.] Norristown, PA.

WALTERS, CORA E.
[b.] January 15, 1914, Philadelphia, PA; [p.] Charles and Cora Stover; [m.] LeRoy B. Walters (deceased), April 9, 1939; [ch.] LeRoy B. Walters Jr., Charles A. Walters, Mary E. Ebersole, Beth Ann Light, 4 spouses, 9 grands; [ed.] Messiah Academy, Lankenau Hospital; [occ.] Now a visiting volunteer, organist, pianist; [memb.] Brethren in Christ Curch, Brethren in Christ Historical Society; [hon.] Valedictorian, articles for school papers in high school, articles and poem for church paper, poem accepted fpr previous anthology, poem for Messiah Village paper; [oth. writ.] Now writing history of the church of my childhood in Philadelphia for our Brethren in Christ historical publication. Hope to write histories of our 46 years of pastoral service and family next; [pers.] A note on the bulletin board at Messiah College read: "If you want to keep warm get all wrapped up in your work". I feel that way when I write. I love it!; [a.] Mechanicsburg, PA.

WALTERS, LISA
[b.] May 6, 1966, Chicago, Il; [p.] John and Sandy Dubrick; [m.] Steve Walters, May 6, 1989; [pers.] My husband was my inspiration for the poem. He is and always will be my best friend; [a.] Ionia, IA.

WALTERS, MARY A.
[b.] December 2, 1922, Lanes Mills, PA; [p.] Joseph and Sarah Jane Penvose; [m.] Robert H. Walters (deceased), April 24, 1942; [ch.] Dianne E. Long, Robert C. and Sally r. Wojnar; [ed.] Freeport High School, 1940; [occ.] Housewife, grandmother of 7; [memb.] Freeport United Presbyterrian Church-ordained elder; [hon.] This my first. Music played a big part in my life; [oth. writ.] "Love", "A New Beginning", "Wonder of it All", "A Silhouette", "My Granddaughter"; [pers.] I write the words, God gives me the thoughts. Widow for 19-1/2 years, but Bob and I had a 32 year honeymoon; [a.] L:eechburg, PA.

WALTY, RUTH B.
[b.] September 4, 1901, New York NY; [ch.] Lincoln, 3 grandsons, 1 great-grandson; [ed.] Hunter College, Columbia, N.Y.U.; [occ.] Retired from teaching; [memb.] Unitarian Fellowship, gardening, migrant workers, saving and restoring the Earth;

WAMWEA, MIRIAM
[b.] March 22, 1972, Myeri; [p.] Felicity and John Wamwea; [ed.] Nyeri Primary School, Ngandu High School, Moi University College; [occ.] Student; [oth. writ.] Several poems not published; [pers.] With the birth and death of every sun my pen is nourished with tales it must tell to the universe. [a.] Nyeri, Kenya.

WARD, GRACE
[b.] August 28, 1918, NC; [p.] Myra Best Mathews Savage, Charlie Savage; [m.] H. L. Ward Sr. (deceased), June 30, 1936, Jim Iannuzzi, December 9, 1988 (divorced); [ch.] Carolyn Bartoletta, Patricia Grande, H. L. Ward Jr., Dwight M. Ward, Terry Buchanan, Grace Johnson; [ed.] School of hard knocks-still enrolled, G.E.D, 1988; [occ.] Taking care of someone who needs care;[memb.] Federalsburg Senior Center, Harrington DE Senior Center, currently considering becoming a church member; [hon.] Golden Poet, 1990 World of Poetry. "Crickets" is the poem I sent and was published.

I do have a recording comopany who wishes to try recording four poems I wrote; [oth. writ.] I have some 400 poems and other writings. Some I believe to be very good and reflective of my life-sort of biographical; In fifth grade I had one poem in Raleigh News and Observer; [pers.] I always wished to be a journalist and at heart am a poet-tho I have absolutely no training. I think a l;arge percent of our greatest talented people are six feet under or never get a chance; [a.] Ridgely, MD.

WARD, MIKE
[b.] January 19, 1975, Sarnia, Ont.; [p.] David and April Ward; [ed.] Grade 12, Ontario Academic Credits; [memb.] Professional School of Self-Defense; [oth. writ.] Poems and short stories: The Magic Man, The Dream and A Child's Fate; [pers.] My writing is generally focused on the human condition; a blurry focus at the best of times. [a.] Sarnia, Ont. CAN.

WARREN, ADAM
[b.] January 20, 1984; [p.] Jeff and Laura Hanen; [ed.] Washington Elementary; [occ.] Student; [hon.] Writer of the month in school; [pers.] I love to write to express personal beliefs and feelings; [a.] Warren, MI;

WARREN, ED
[pen.] Edw; [b.] February 17, 1923, Waco, TX; [p.] Fate and Clara; [ch.] Three; [ed.] High School; [occ.] Technician; [oth. writ.] I have written many poems mostly about people. I can write on any subject if I have a little background;

WARREN, MICHELLE EBONY KHALILAH
[pen.] Moe; [b.] April 30, 1980, Baltimore, MD; [p.] Floyd and Mary Warren; [ed.] St. Francis de Salles Parochial, Bennett Middle School; [occ.] Student; [memb.] D.A.R.E., Methodist Youth Choir, S.H.O.U.T., Methodist Youth Forum, Wesley Temple U.M. Church, Bennett Middle School Choir; Wico. County Health Dept. Youth Aids Teacher; [hon.] Sammy Davis Jr. Youth Award, 1992, Dr. Martin Luther King Jr. Great Achiever Award, 1st place, 1993, U.M.E.S Star of Tomorrow Award, 1993, Student of the Month; [oth. writ.] Several poems published in school newsletter, one poem selected to be read ar martin Luther King celebration, one poem selected as theme for S.H.O.U.T.; [pers.] I strive for the best, and I speak what's in my heart. I feel that God is a very important part of my life. I was inspired by the movie Malcolm X, and I am searching for who I am, and how Black people relate to their surroundings; [a.] Salisbury, MD.

WARREN, RACHELLE
[b.][July 5, 1960, Detroit, MI; [p.] Olivia M. Warren, Jefferson Warren; [ch.] Osborn HIgh School, Wayne County Community College, University of Detroit Mercy; [occ.] Secretary/stenographer; [oth. writ.] An unpublished book; [a.] Detroit, MI.

WARRENFELLS, ADAM J.
[b.] January 9, 1982, Fort Walton Beach, FL; [p.] Karen abd Stephen Warrenfells; [ed.] Ruckel Middle School; [memb.] Boy Scouts of America; [hon.] Gifted Program of Okaloosa County, FL, honor student-Honor Roll since 1st grade; [oth. writ.] Many personal, noen published; [pers.] I like poetry. I like to read and write it. It holds my feelings. My MOm is a poet, too; [a.] Niceville, FL.

WARRENFELLS, KAREN LEE
[b.] April 24, 1960, Lawrence, MA; [p.] Barbara and

George Taylor Sr.; [m.] Stephen Warrenfells, December 30, 1077; [ch.] Adam Warrenfells, Sara Warrenfells; [ed.] Avionic Systems, certified by Criminal Juatice Dept, as corrections officer; [occ.] Correctional officer; [memb.] Girl Scouts of America, Florida Peace Officers Assoc., Boy Scouts of America, Commission on Crime and Delinquency; [hon.] Dean's list and President's list, 2 Air Force Commendation medals; [oth. writ.] Anabelle Star,1991, Homeless Woman, 1992; [pers.] I've grown up loving the magic of words. I've passed this magic on to my children; [a.] Niceville, FL.

WASHINGTON, JOHN P.
[b.] July 10, 1968, Pittsburg, PA; [m.] Pamela Diane, December 28, 1991; [ch.] Nicolette Diane; [ed.] Gateway Sr. High, Virginia Military Institute, California University of Pennsylvania; [occ.] Student, football coach; [oth. writ.] Several poems, short stories, and a novel that may now find the privilege of the printing press; [pers.] I would like to emphasize the intrinsic, good side of life through my writing; de-emphasizing the material. My influences are unlimited as I attempt to keep an open mind, while also not keeping it so open that my brains fall out; [a.] Monroeville, PA.

WASHINGTON, JOHNNETTE
[pen.] Nesca; [b.] June 5, 1947, Forest City, Ak; [p.] Elnora Hannah, Ennis Richie; [ch.] Eleven, 7 living, Andrea, Clarence, Karen, Paul, Mia, Henry Washington, Brian Washington; [ed.] Pontiac Schools, Pontiac Business Institute, Oakland Community College, Southfield Campus, [occ.] Foster care mother; [memb.] Founder of Grandparents Anonymous & Friends, for grandparents who are caring for grandchildren because their children have some type of major addiction problem; [hon.] Sit on board for pregnant girls on crack, Oakland Fanily Services; [oth. writ.] Through a Child's Eyes, Welcome Home Troops, Fatal Attraction, Gratitude, Friends, How Many Of Us Are One?, Erik the Viking, Mama, Mrs. Dad, Grandma's Pains and Gains, Fault Finder, The Creation, Recipe For Lovers, Dr. Death, plus 13 more; [a.] Detroit, MI.

WASHINGTON, LAURA
[pen.] laura Washington; [b.] October 27, 1943, Louisiana; [p.] Thomas and Ruth Washington; [ch.] Pamela Renee, Gregory Orlando; [ed.] Mossville High School, University of Houston, Houston Bible Institute; [occ.] Real Estate Broker and property manager/self-employed; [memb.] Houston Association of Realtors; [hon.] American Legion award; [oth. writ.] Several poems published in Christian Magazine. Created lyrics for two songs used in a Christian play, lyrics for 50 Christian/inspirational songs; [pers.] Focus is on portraying the love and kindness of God toward man and man's potential for love and kindness toward each other throught Christ's example. [a.] Houston, TX.

WASHINGTON, NOVARRO RAMON JR.
[b.] June 1, 1971, Washington, DC; [p.] Novarro R. Washington Sr., Frances G. Kee, [ed.] Anacostia Senior High; [occ.] Charles E. Smith Co. management and writer; [hon.] 1st place Bowling Prize trophy, 1984, job achievement certificates; [oth. writ.] My writings proclaims two professionally self-written poems to my credit and a variety of horror, action, adult, and romance novels now presently in development for future publication; [pers.] I , as an inspiring poet and book novelist author impeccablizes my assuring strive for the best to my phenomenal will to succeed with the ambitional achievement of approaching my gifted goals as a phenomenal male.

Phenomenal, that's me! Phenomonal.; [a.] Forestville, MD.

WASSIL, ALI
[b.] April 6, 1930, Hyderbad, India; Mir Nohammed Ali Fazil, Fatima Khan; [ed.] St. Georges School, University of Cambridge, Nizam College, Massachusetts Institute of Technology, University of California at Los Angeles; [occ.] Author, lecturer, radio, television; [hon.] Pi Kappa Delta (debate and oratory) with honors; [oth. writ.] Song of the Savior, Rubaiyat of Modern Man, Dear Mr. President (Open Letter to Nixon), contributor to newspapers and national magazines; [pers.] In my lectures around the world (to universities, churches, and clubs), I teach Meditation to understand and improve the quality of our personal lives and the world we live in; [a.] Los Angeles, CA.

WASZILYCSAK, DAVID S.
[b.] May 4, 1968, Edmonton, Alberta, CAN; [p.] Suzanne and George Waszilycsak; [ed.] Northern High, Essex Commuinity College, Towson State University; [occ.] Senior Towson State; [memb.] Trinity Assembly of God, active with youth group hope to be in leadership one day, Statistician 1988-1991 Essex Community College Women's Basketball, Women's Lacrosse; [pers.] I love to write poetry becasue a poem is a masterpiece to be enjoyed down through the generations. Life is but a river, running uncontrollable by the wind of a timeless age. [a.] Baltimore, MD.

WATERS, JOAN BETTY
[pen.] J.B. Waters; [b.] Lakewood, NJ; [p.] James and Edna Waters; [ed.] Lakewood High School, graduate American Academy of Drama, Essex County College; [occ.] After school program Clinton School; [memb.] Essex County Magazine IBID, Phi Theta Kappa; [oth. writ.] One play produced off off Broadway, currently working on a children's book; [pers.] Live everyday like it's the first and last day of your life. "Special thanks to McPherson at ECC and Mr. Reighter at Lakewood High." [a.] East Orange, NJ.

WATERS, MELVIN
[b.] November 26, 1951, Washington, DC; [m.] Betsy, April 4, 1992; [ed.] Chapman University; [occ.] Seminary grad student at Oral Roberts University; [pers.] I write to the glory and honor of God. [a.] Tulsa, OK.

WATKINS, TOMMIE
[b.] November 24, Abilene, TX; [p.] Julia and Tommy Moss; [m.] Converse, June 25, 1965; [ch.] Julian, Patrice, Tony Watkins; [occ.] Medical field-Unit Secretary; [memb.] National Geographic Society, The Kidney Foundation; [hon.] Employee of the Month 1987-1990 Medical Terminology Course; [oth. writ.] Poems not published; [pers.] I love life and nature. I enjoy the mountains amd the sea. And I wish man would take better care of our world. [a.] Arlington, TX.

WATKINS, JOANN
[b.] December 6, 1944, Jackson, MS; [p.] K.F. and Jeffie Wissner; [ch.] Roxanne; [ed.] Flora High, University of MS, Benedictine College; [occ.] Computer Consultant; [hon.] Salutatorian, Dean's list; [oth. writ.] None published; [pers.] I am awed at the ability of many poets to express and translate mood and emotion. I would hope to follow many, expressing deep feelings with a light and luplifting spirit. [a.] Jackson, MS.

WATSON, CAROLYN VERNELL WATTS
[b.] November 26, 1945, Laurens Co; [p.] Late Willie J. and Mrs. Minnie F. Watts; [m.] Timothy, Jr., December 20, 1969; [ch.] Adrian Bernard and Christopher Emanuel Watson; [ed.] Sanders High School, South Carolina State University; [occ.] Oakland Elementary Math teacher; [memb.] New Grove Baptist Church, South Carolina Council of Teachers of Mathematics, United Education Profession; [hon.] Dean's list S.C. State University; [oth. writ.] Several poems published in the Oakland School News, poems written but not published; [pers.] My poems are inspired by personal events, work, and the people in my life. [a.] Greenwood, SC.

WATSON, T.O.R., (PASTOR) CLETUS
[b.] November 3, 1938, Philadelphia, PA; [p.] Claudie B. Bridges Watson and Ernest Samuel Watson Jr. (deceased); [ed.] St. Francis College, La Salle University, St. Charles Seminary; [occ.] Franciscan, TOR-Priest-Educator-Roman Catholic; [memb.] Co-chairman Afro-American Office, National Black Catholic Congress, Presbyteral Council-Diocese of St. Augustine, Catholic charities, Office of Ministry, Advisory Board-HRS One Church/One Child Programs; [hon.] Black History Month Award, Jacksonville Naval Air Stat, African American Ministry-Creative Works: Concept of God and the Afro American, Love and the Human Person, An Ongoing Perspective-published by Brentwood Christian Press. [a.] Jacksonville, FL.

WATSON, KAREN LEIGH
[b.] June 16, 1973. Edinburgh, Scotland; [p.] Anne and George Watson; [ed.] Porto Bello High Secondary School; [occ.] Unemployed; [memb.] League Against Cruel Sports; [hon.] The London Chamber of Commerce and Industry's National Vocational Qualification in Business Administration and Secretarial Skills; [oth. writ.] A book and many other poems with great potential yet to be publihsed; [pers.] I have always had faith in my writing therefore I will always be successful. The world wothout peace is like a tree without roots - it cannot live. [a.] Edinburgh, Scotland.

WATTS, LARAINE SANFILIPPO
[pen.] Laraine Sanfilippo; [b.] June 1, 1944, Brooklyn, NY; [p.] Lawrence and Anne Sanfilippo; [m.] Divorced, April 6, 1968; [ch.] Christopher, Tiffany and Todd Watts; [ed.] High school graduate; [occ.] Retired; [oth. writ.] Several poems published in local newspaper; [pers.] I am usually emotionally touched by someone or something when I create a poem. You might say my heart speaks when I write and if I warm just one soul; then I have created magic. [a.] Fullerton, CA.

WATTS, MARGARET ANN
[pen.] Margaret Ann Watts; [b.] April 17, 1980, Edmonton, Alberta; [p.] Don and Esther Watts; [ed.] Leduc Junior High, Royal Conservatory of Music (piano); [occ.] Student; [memb.] Local Honor Band, Ellerslie Road Baptist Church; [hon.] Honor student, several awards: debate, local annual Music Festival for poetry recitation and piano performance, swimming, basketball, horsemanship and other sports; [oth. writ.] Winner of several Royal Canadian Legion Remembrance Day poem contest, Provincial first prize winner for Alberta Rural Safety essay contest; [pers.] "But those who hope in the Lord will renew their strength. They will soar on wings like eagles, they will run and not grow weary, they will walk and not be faint." Isa. 40:31. [a.] Leduc. Alberta.

WAWERZYNEK, WALTER C.
[pen.] Walter C. Wawrzynek; [b.] October 25, 1921, Hamtramck, MI; [p.] Antionette and Joseph Wawrzynek; [m.] Mary E. Radzilowski, August 9, 1947; [ch.] Carl and Carol; [ed.] High school; [occ.] Retired postal employee; [memb.] Disabled American Vets; [hon.] Air medal - Purple Heart; [oth. writ.] 50 poems published in the Detroit News, poems in the "Alura Quarterly" and church paper; [pers.] I try to be realistic in most of my works. [a.] Shelby Twp., MI.

WEATHERS, CATHY
[pen.] Cate Conell; [b.] March 16, 1954, Houston, TX; [pers.] There are a lot of problems in the world today, absence of religious beliefs is a large one leading to many others. If I can inspire one person long enough to step back and take a look at his/her life, resulting in a change for the better, I have succeeded. [a.] Brazoria, TX.

WEBSTER, BRIAN
[b.] December 31, 1949, Calcutta, IN; [p.] William and Catherine Webster (deceased); [ed.] Lugie J.S. School Dundee College of Education; [occ.] Freelance Photographer; [memb.] Church of L.D.S., Sports Writers Association of Great Britain, International Sports Writers Association, Sports Association for Disable; [hon.] Honorary Citizen of City of Indianapolis; [pers.] I like to make people happy. I like to care and love people around the world. To improve my knowledge in the world, and the gospel. Be able to write and take pictures and see the world. [a.] Dundee, Tayside.

WEGWITZ, LAWRENCE
[b.] March 11, 1972, MooseJaw, SK; [p.] Len and Kathy Wegwitz; [ed.] Central Collegiate Institute and life; [hon.] Missionary for the Church of Jesus Christ of Latter Day Saints; [pers.] When I have a pen in hand and a thought in mind, then I am alive. And if by another pen I am refreshed, then we both have profited. [a.] Warner, Alberta.

WEIR, BROCKE
[b.] August 27, 1979, Edmonton, CAN; [p.] Bryce and Mary Lou Weir; [ed.] Rio Terrace Elementary School, Crestwood Junior High, University of Chicago Lab Schools; [occ.] Student; [hon.] Honor Roll Crestwood Junior High, first place coloring contest age 5; [pers.] A life not lived to the fullest is not a life worth living.

WEIR, SUSIE
[ed.] North Carolina School of the Arts; [occ.] Previously an actor and performance artist; [oth. writ.] Numerous poems, songs, screenplays, theatrical plays, and the beginnings of several novels; [pers.] Illusion is the most authentic form of reality. Immunity to the impotent world of studied acceptance is the first step... [a.] Winston-Salem, NC.

WEIRMACK, RAY
[b.] May 3, 1912, Finland, Europe; [p.] Amanda and Olli; [m.] Poppy, June 26, 1965; [ch.] Shirley Clifford, Richard and Raymond Jr.; [ed.] Cal State Hayward; [occ.] Retired-avocation piano-volunteer; [memb.] Charter member Writers West Cal State-Hayward Alumni, Cal Sons-in-Retirement #30, life member Musician's Union, Cal State Fair Advisory Board, Alameda Art Association Pres. 1992-93; [hon.] Alameda Art-CA Awards and Commissions; [oth. writ.] Alameda Ca-Writers' West articles and short stories, poems and anthologies; [pers.] Life is short, poetry is endless. [a.] Alameda, CA.

WEISSMAN, DELORES G. (NEE) HANSON
[b.] January 8, 1961, Chicago, IL; [p.] Albert Hanson and Eunice Hanson (nee) White; [m.] Allen, September 1, 1990; [ch.] Justin Aaron Weissman; [ed.] Triton College, Northeastern University; [occ.] registered Nurse, Author, Playright; [oth. writ.] "The trials of Goldilocks". "Goldilocks Meets the Seven Dwarfs", "The Trial of the Three Pigs"; [pers.] I can do all things through Christ, which strengthened me." Phip. 4:13. [a.] Chicago, IL.

WEISS, PHYLLIS
[b.] July 21, 1943, Brooklyn, NY; [p.] Sylvia and Charles Weiss; [ed.] Samuel Tilden High School, Brooklyn College, Long Island University; [occ.] Elementary School Teacher-NYC; [memb.] Arista, High School and College Sororities, United Federation of Teachers, Hadassah; [hon.] Outstanding Leadership Federation of Jewish Philanthropies, President-Sigma Chi Omega, President-Bell House Brooklyn College, grant from the New York City Fund for Education, Fund Raiser-Hadassah, Superintendent and New York City Chancellor's Letters of Commendation; [pers.] If through my life's work, and a bit of creativity, I have influenced another's soul - then I've succeeded. [a.] Bayside, NY.

WELCH, MARILYN H.
[b.] March 22, 1936, Somerville, TX; [p.] Kermit and Grace Harper; [m.] Vernon E. (Gene); [ch.] Michael Gene, Bob Allen, Charles Anthony and Wendy Magnuson; [ed.] Somerville High School; [occ.] Housewife; [memb.] Pianist First Baptist Church, pianist for Gospel Express Quartet; [hon.] High school queen, Best all around and F.F.A. Sweet Heart, also a forward on B1 Distrist Basketball champions; [oth. writ.] Various poems for programs at church, family friends and two religious songs. One poem was published in local newspapers; [pers.] My greatest satisfaction comes from serving God, working in my church, doing things for my husband, family and friends. [a.] Somerville, TX.

WELLMAN, LYNNE
[pen.] Lynne Wellman; [b.] July 31, 1960, Oneonta, NY; [p.] Henry W. and Ida C. Bard; [m.] James M., January 31, 1985; [ch.] Adam and Kayla Wellman; [ed.] Richfield Springs Central, Herkimer Co. BOCES, American Sign Language Course; [occ.] House manager/accountant Cherry Valley Home; [hon.] Outstanding Service to Clients for Association for Retarded Citizens; [oth. writ.] Local newspaper; [pers.] I generally write my heartfelt, sentiments in poetry to show the meaning of emotion in life and how important it is to feel what we do and express it. [a.] Cherry Valley, NY.

WELLS, KIERSTEN DAWN
[b.] December 28, 1976, Valdosta, GA; [p.] Don and Vicky Wells; [ed.] Northwest High School; [occ.] Student; [memb.] Clinton First Church of Christ Bible bowl team, Northwest High School French Club; [pers.] I was greatly inspired by William Cullen Bryant and his perception of nature. [a.] Canal Fulton, OH.

WELLS, LESLIE
[b.] March 9, 1947, Maidstone, Kent, England; [p.] Dennis and Winifred Cloake; [m.] Jacqueline Scott, February 23, 1993; [ch.] Haley, Rebecca Scott, Leanne Scott; [ed.] Gordon Boys' School, working open university; [occ.] Labourer in factory; [memb.] Institute of Science Technology, Registered Science Technician; [hon.] Honors degree, physics with engineering, further and adult education teachers' certificate; [oth. writ.] Poems published in school magazine; [pers.] If, after you

have gone, the world was enhanced by your presence, then your life has not been in vain. [a.] Newton Aycliffe, Cty Durham.

WELLS, RAYMOND A.
[b.] March 7, 1922, Elfrida, AZ; [p.] R.G. and Del Wells; [m.] Frances A., August 3, 1962; [ch.] Randall Ray Wells and Sandra May; [ed.] Phoenix College, Arizona State University; [occ.] Retired personnel and labor relations manager; [memb.] Maricopa Safety Council, Phoenix Junior Achievement, Labor Management Grievance Committee, State-wide Management Safety Committee, Phoenix Personnel Board, Glass Industry Health and Welfare Trust Fund; Arizona Lumber Assn.; [hon.] Lumberman of the Year, AZ Lumber Assn., Glass Indusatry Merit Award, State-wide Labor Management Safety Award, Junior Achievement Leadership Award; Presidential award for serving as president of Tempe, AZ Kiwanis Club during 1961, 1962, and other awards; [oth. writ.] Writings were basically limited to Industry in which I was promoting. No poems, My poem re: Singing stems from my youth. Change of voice, ruined it for me; [pers.] I believe that God put us here on earth to make things better, and to help others make things better. When we do this, it good!; [a.] Mesa, AZ.

WENDOWSKI, KATHLEEN C.
[pen.] Wendy; [b.] August 12, 1933, Phila; [p.] William and Eleanor Strain; [m.] Leonard E. Wendowski Sr., June 4, 1955; [ch.] Leonard Jr., Joseph I., Steven P., Thomas L., G.C., Michael, Brian, Alexis, Gillian, Leonard III, Rebecca; [ed.] Philadelphia High School for Girls, Temple University, Jersey City State College, Methodist Epis Hosp; [occ.] Licensed Nursing Home Administrator; [memb.] Soroptimist International of West Essex, American Heart Association, American Lung Assn, group against smoking pollution, Arbor Day Foundation, Nshfa, Society of Nursing Home Adm., St. Thomas More Church; [hon.] Who's Who of Ameican Nursing, 3yrs, President's Scholar, Temple University, summa grad of JCSC, magna cum laud, Girl's High; [oth. writ.] Three poems published in the Arcadia Poetry Anthology, Spring 1993, also in various newsletters; [pers.] I believe when God grants you a talent or an ability it must be shared. My inspirations are often anecdotal events and personalizations of milestones: people's birthdays, retirement, births, etc; [a.] Fairfield, NJ.

WESS, BRIAN L.A.
[b.] February 28, 1967, Orlando, FL; [p.] Rosemary A. Wess; [ed.] Kenmore East S. H.. U.S. Army, SUNY at Buffalo; [occ.] Student, writer, photographer; [memb.] Costeau Society, Environmental Defense Fund, National Parks and Conservation Association, American Red Cross; [hon.] National Honor Society of Secondary Schools, Phi Eta Sigma, Freshman Honr Society, Golden Key National Honor Society, Dean's list; [oth. writ.] In work: History of the 1/1 Cav, American Justice, Personal Poems, and Famous Quotas; [pers.] My writing is greatly influenced by life, love, and reflects my personal ideals, most of all. I want my writing to convey some of myself and meaning to the reader; [a.] Buffalo, NY.

WESSLING, ERIN ILLENE
[b.] October 15, 1982, Glendale, CA; [p.] John and Gerri Wessling, sister Krista; [ed.] Notre Dame Elementary School; [occ.] Student; [hon.] Catholic Daughters Education Contest, Essay Div I, 1st place, May 1992, I Love Dance Statewide Competition, 2nd place Feb 1993, I Love Dance National Competition, 1st place, Jul 1993; [a.] Lakewood, CA.

WEST, MARTIN
[pen.] Mart; [b.] May 22, 1970, Leeds; [p.] Trevor G. West, Jean West; [ed.] Woodkirk HIgh School; [memb.] Student member of The Chartered Institute of Management Accountants.(CIMA); [hon.] 8 'O' levelsa, 3 'A' levels (high school), firststage pass of the CIMA exams; [oth. writ.] Stll striving to publish a collection of poetry called "Love, Death and Little Besides"; [pers.] Poetry should not be subject to analysis, it should be a subjective feeling of life and emotion; [a.] Wakefield, West Yorkshire, England.

WEST, MARY JOSEPHINE
[b.] December 5, 1948, Hastings, England; [p.] Edward C.H. Lawson (1906-1993), Mary B. Lawson; [m.] Frederick G. W. V. West, November 16, 1985; [ch.] Jonathan D.G. West, Tanya B. West, Michael S.H. West; [ed.] Secondfary Modern School, Day Release College, Adult Education(New Horizons); [occ.] Housewife; [hon.] Two Scripture Awards (Church of England), Pitmans Elementary Typing Commerce; [oth. writ.] Letters, poems, local newspapers, poem included in southern England anthology book entitled Taste of the South, poem included in Poetry Now Southeast, 1994 (both in England); [pers.] Being the daughter of a photo process engraver, carpenter, and artist inspired me to take up the brush and pen. But the pen proved mightier; [a.] Hastings, England.

WEST, SARAH C.,
[b.] August 13, 1979, Balto, MD; [p.] Audrey West, Steven West; [ed.] El;ementary Sunset, Pasadena, MD, Arlington High School, NY; [occ.] FUll time student; [memb.] Studio of Performing Arts (acting class); [pers.] I feel writing is a very important aspect of my future and hope to continue my education, and look forward to attending college. My thanks to my mother and English teacher, Mrsd. Bontempo who have influenced and guided me alon this path; [a.] Poughquag, NY.

WEST, EARL RICHARD III
[pen.] Earl of Sandwich; [b.] February 15, 1971, San Antonia, TX; [p.] Earl West, Helen West; [ch.] Karen, Kathy, Kris; [ed.] Holy Cross High School; [occ.] European Massage Therapy student; [hon.] In recogniton of my performance in government, Principal's Service Award, recognition in theatre arts; [oth. writ.] None published at this time, but have recently registered 20 manuscripts of poems in Washingtons copyright office, Richard Faoirbanks enthusiastic over my copies as editor of Vantage Press Publishing Co. I excitedly await proposal; [pers.] Poetry is the beating of my cardiac muscle which luminates with an affinity to sooth peoples emotions, shedding a sigh; [a.] San Antonio, TX.

WESTOBY, MARY
[b.] December 4, 1938, LOndon, England; [p.] W. Frank Gardner, Kay Gardner; [m.] Robert A. Westoby, February 3, 1962; [ch.] Karen Elizabeth, Jennifer Gaylem Pamela Jill; [ed.] Winceby House, Bexhill, Sussex, England; [occ.] Self-employed; [memb.] Missouri Botanical Garden, St. Lous Symphony, St. Louis Zoo, St. Lukes Hospital Auxiliary; [hon.] President, Seven Pines Garden Club, life member, Federated Garden Clubs of Missouri; [oth. writ.] Letters to the editor of several newspapers, compoany newsletter columns; [a.] Creve Coeur, MO.

WHEALDON, EVERETT WHITTIER
[b.] September 5, 1910, Naselle, WA;' [p.] Jos. and Emma Matthews Whealdon; [m.] Marie Swatzky (de-

ceased_), JUne 16, 1935; [ch.] Charlotte Ann Odden, Jenny Patricia Ladd, Joseph A. Whealdon (deceased); [ed.] Williamette U., Salem OR, Nasell, WA and Salem, OR public schools; [occ.] Retired, U.S. Fish and Wildlife Service, beekeeper, gardener, writer; [oth. writ.] Argus Press, Cape Disappointment, Hist. novel The Green Chain, and other stories of the Great Depression, Blanket Hill, stoty poem published by Samisdat, Sunset, Sunrise, pre-historical novel, The Old Codger's Almanac, poem collection, Sagitarius Prewss; [pers.] My novel of the hot sixties, The Dreams Are Dying is currently being published by Dan River Press, POB 123, South Thomaston, Maine,04858. Write to aboe address for book prices and time opf publication; [a.] Port Townsend, WA.

WHIPPLE, JULIE L.
[b.] November 14, 1954, Canandaigua, NY; [p.] A. Dorcas Miller, Joseph Miller; [m.] Leroy Eric Whipple, November 25, 1972; [ch.] Patricia Lee, Tina Aileen, Christopher P, [ed.] 11th grade; [occ.] Herdsperson; [hon.] Physical Fitness award; [oth. writ.] Yes, but only sent in one, The Mare; [pers.] Most ot the poems I wrote is what I experienced in my life; [a.] Rushville, NY.

WHITAKER, MAXINE
[b.] August 6, 1923, Lebanon, TX; [p.] HOuston and Mildred Brooks; [ed.] Formal, no degrees; [occ.] Hairdresser; [pers.] The Holy Spirit is the empowering agent to my writing, and visions I see. All writing is done under the inspiration of the Holy Spirit; [a.] Dallas, TX.

WHITCOMB, JAY R.
[b.] Febvruary 24, 1941, Bristol, TN; [ch.] three; [ed.] B.S.; [occ.] Unemployed; [memb.] DAV, VFW, American Legion, Purple Heart Assn.; [oth. writ.] Along this same theme about Vietnam and the life after for a person with PTSD; [pers.] The real cost of sending a person to war cannot be experienced or described with simple words. For many it ended in divorce, suicide, alcohol or drugs. If only everyone knew the real, total cost. Maybe the would be less war!;

WHITE, BEATRICE L.
[b.] JUly 19, 1906, Garfield, WA; [p.] Edwin B. Lockhart, Jeanette Meredith; [ch.] MNeredith Locjhart Bliss; [ed.] USC, Wiilliamette University; [occ.] Retired; [memb.] AAUW, Pi Beta Phi, Delta Kappa Gamma; [hon.] ONe student of yore wrote (to this effect) If all students had had you for a teacher, it would be a better country. Tjis is the sort of award teachers usually get! Judges Choice in OAHA "The Reunion" short story; [oth. writ.] Reluctant Pioneer, 3rd printing, Not On a Silver Platter, bits through the years; [a.] Forest Grove, OR.

WHITE, BRENDA BLAND
[b.] July 19, 1951, BC; [p.] Isaac and Nell Bland; [m.] Gerald M. White, JUly 26, 1969; [ch.] Heatrher Rebecca White; [ed.] Pittsboro High School, Central Carolina Community College, North Carolina Wesleyan College, University of North Carolina School of Law; [occ.] Practicing and teaching attorney; [memb.] American Bar Association, North Carolina State Bar, North Carolina Bar Association, Hanks Chapel United Church of Christ; [hon.] Magna cum laude, departmental honors from NCWC, highest academic average from CCCC, Best Actress and Outstanding Service in Dramatic Arts from Pittsboro High School; [pers.] My mother read poetry to me when I was a child. I probably wrote my first rhyme at the age of 9 or 10. I seem to find inspiration in nature

and in my own emotions; [a.] Pittsboro, NC.

WHITE, DARWIN DWAIN JONATHAN
[pen.] D. Jonathan White; [b.] Novemver 17, 1942, AZ; [ch.] Shannon, 3 grandchildren; [ed.] BSME; [occ.] Self-employed; [oth. writ.] Poems published in various small local publications; [pers.] I write both poems and short stories. Most of them have been written for pleasur but have been compiled into a book for my grandchildren. It's called "Blossoms From the Vine";

WHITE, JUANITA MOORE
[b.] February 24, 1918, Birmingham, AL; [p.] Daniel and Annie Mary Trimble; [m.] Donald J. White, September 5, 1992; [ch.] Arthur D. Moore, Melinda Moore Lampkin; [ed.] Tuskegee Institute; [occ.] Retired; [memb.] NAACP, AARP, Church, civic and community organizations; [hon.] Church and civic organizations; [oth. writ.] Other poems, short stories, editorials; [pers.] I write for the chidren, to make them smile and laugh and wonder. I hope through my poems and stories that the children will feel the love I have for them; [a.] Detroit, MI.

WHITE, KIRK
[b.] September 12, 1942, Amboy, WV; [p.] Thomas and Pauline White; [m.] Sandra White, October 20, 1962; [ch.] Kimberly Dawn, Douglas Shawn; [ed.] Elm Valley High School, Bliss College; [occ.] Factory worker; [pers.] I try to show the beauty in all those things that touch our lives and in the memories we all hold dear to us. I have been greatly influenced by the poems of my grandmother, the late Mrs. John F. Dixon; [a.] Marion, OH.

WHITE, MELISSA
[b.] December 14, 1978; [p.] Roger White; [occ.] Student; [pers.] Always reach higher and try to grasp what you want because usually you'll get it!;

WHITEHOUSE, LYNNE
[b.] August 25, 1965, England; [p.] Robert Whitehouse, Baenda Whitehouse; [oth. writ.] My first ever poem to be published. One in a collection of many other poetical works I have written; [pers.] "Where there is hope, there is always dreams." I dedicate my poem to my beloved mother, who I cherish most dearly; [a.] Lancashire, England.

WHITELOVE, MINISTER
[occ.] Miniter in unconditional love; [oth. writ.] Spirit given by the Almighty God for the souls feeding and rebuilding in men; [pers.] God Almighty is able to see you through in wahtsoever is needed; [a.] Chicago, IL.

WHITFIELD, TELLY
[b.] April 23, 1974; [p.] Mr. and Mrs. Howard Whitfield; [ed.] Hampton University; [pers.] 350 years ago, our people were brought to this land in chains. Today, we must break these chans through education; [a.] Virginia, Beach VA.

WHITNEY, MELISSA
[b.] May 9, 1963, Riverside, CA; [p.] Richard Whitney II, Elaine Whitney; [m.] JOhn KNight; [ed.] Granada Hills High, Pierce College; [occ.] Accounting Assistant; [oth. writ.] Hope to publish a book in 1994; [pers.] I would like to thank the entire Whitmey family, the Webbs, Laura, Windy, and my husband-to-be, John for all their love and support; [a.] Canyon Country, CA.

WHITTAKER, DELORES
[pen.] Del Whittaker; [b.] January 15, 1950, Rupert, ID; [p.] Cecil and Arpha Noble; [ch.] Jana; [ed.] Minico High School, University of Phoenix; [occ.] Mgr. of Contracts for Intrastate Natural Gas Transmission Company; [memb.] Natuaral Gas Association of OK; [oth. writ.] This is first poem submitted for publication but many poems written for personal enjoyment. [a.] Tulsa, OK.

WHITTINGTON, JOSEPH A.
[b.] September 30, 1944, Guyana; [p.] Neil and Mathilda Whittington; [m.] Mayleen Gajee Whittington, August 21, 1972; [ch.] Ray, Allan, Suzanne, Vanessa; [ewd.] Bach of Phys Ed, MS Ed Admn and Supvsn, PD Ed Admin and Supvsn, advanced doctoral student; [cc.] Teacher; [memb.] ASCD, AERA; [hon.] British Commonwealth Fellowship Award, Government of Guyana Scholarship; [oth. writ.] Poems, The Shell, My Teacher Creed; [pers.] Every child can learn. It is the duty of all persons in the community to help to educate each child; [a.] Brooklyn, NY.

WHITTINGTON, KATRINA
[pen.] Katrina Whittington; [b.] June 29, 1958m Ioaw; [p.] Darrell and Jeanine Whittington; [ed.] Ruskin High School; [occ.] Domestic engineer; [hon.] First Team All Conference Award Volleyball; [oth. writ.] Poems in high school and yearbook, currently working on children's book; [pers.] I hope to leave to my neices and nephews, to my whole family, a legacy of words and thoughts that express all that I am and hope to be. Between the lines of all I write is the heart of me and my love for them. [a.] Austin, TX.

WHITTLE, BEVERLY ANN
[pen.] Bev Whittle; [b.] March 15, 1945, IA; [m.] Larry; [ch.] Suzanne Wilson, Eric Van Vliet, Lea Bushman and Aaron Whittle; [ed.] Waukon High School, NITC Calmar, IA; [occ.] CNA for Long Term Care DD/MR/MI and elderly; [hon.] Golden Poet Award 1991 - published several poems 1193; [oth. writ.] Presently working on biography of life experiences; [pers.] Have moved 18 times; married twice - have one child with epilepsy. Wish to share wisdom learned thru lifde experience and appreciation of life itself. [a.] Decorah, IA.

WHITTLE, JOAN
[b.] October 19, 1944, Compton Berkshire; [p.] May Ellen Victoria and Leslie Frank Simmons; [m.] Frank, June 16, 1962; [ch.] Maria, Frankie, and Steven; [ed.] Compton Church of England School and Newbury College; [occ.] Receptionist/Telephonist; [oth. writ.] Many poems and short stories none offered for publication "Mummey's with the Angels" was first poem offered to competition; [pers.] I am one of eight children brought up in a small village in the south of England. Mums death at the age of 42 - when I was just nine years old - gave me an acute understanding of other people's feelings and sufferings. [a.] Longhborough, Leicester England.

WICKSTROM, SANDRA LEIGH
[pen.] Sandi; [b.] June 6, 1972, Windsor, NS, CAN; [p.] Howard and Doris Wickstrom; [ed.] AT time of Sandra's death she was in graduating year at Wadena Composite High School; [occ.] Sandi died October 2 1989 of Ovarian Cancer (17 yrs old); [memb.] Have enclosed copy of her book of poems "Remember Me". Main concern was "what have I done so I will be remembered?"; [hon.] Was Saskatchewan's 1989 Junior Citizen of the Year and a finalist in 1989 for Canadian Junior Citizen of the year; [oth. writ.] She has written over 200 poems and writings. Her dad and I have put them into a book entitled "Remember Me" as a tribute to her short 17 years.; [pers.] Sandi wrote "I Am Still Me" on the day she was diagnosed with ovarian cancer. She wanted her friends to look "inside" and realize she was still Sandra not the girl with cancer.

WIGGINS, JAMES A. JR.
[pen.] Junie; [b.] March 18, 1965, Cleveland, OH; [p.] Mr. and Mrs. James A. Wiggins, Sr.; [ch.] 9 brothers and two newphews and a niece; [ed.] New Bern Senior High School, Associated Business Careers (ABC), and Dorothy Aristone School for Cage Financing; [occ.] Board of Education in NJ; [memb.] The Camden Afro-American Public Library, The Southern Comfort Sports Club; [hon.] ABC Honor Roll, certificate from the casino school, letter of recommendation fron City of New Bern Council; [oth. writ.] Poem published in The Quill Books of TX, contract with Vantage Press, had poem published in The Philadelphia Tribune entitled "Remember the Confusion" it made me poet of the month; [pers.] I believe in the unity of mankind, I have faith in the brotherhood I hate ignorance, and hate of ones color, the future is all we have left, and we should focus on the children because there's our hope. [a.] Camden, NJ.

WILLARD, STEVEN
[b.] June 10, 1968; [p.] Rachel Willard; [pers.] I want people to look within and love themselves and others. The most unconditional love lies within us. [a.] Charleston, SC.

WILSON, JACKIE
[b.] March 30, 1965, AL; [p.] Ezella and Willie Mack Wilson; [ed.] Charles F. Kettering High School, Cuyahoga Community College; [memb.] C.N.A.; [memb.] Christ Temple Bible Way Brotherhood Association; [hon.] Best Supporting Actor, Best Dramatic Actor, Employee of The Month, Most Caring Personality; [oth. writ.] Victory, Wide Awaking, A Touch of Color, I Am A Black Women and The Forgotten Soldier; [pers.] I try very hard to write from deep inside my soul, so that my readers, can not only hear, but visualize and feel the uniqueness of my work. Someday my dreams will become reality and my talent will shine like the star that lead wisemen to the savior. [a.] Cleveland, OH.

WIKANDER, CARL
[b.] June 23, 1946, Dryden, Ont.; [m.] Denise, September 30, 1971; [ch.] Two boys; [ed.] Chef training hotel restaurant, Culinary Field Sault College; [occ.] Pastry Chef; [memb.] Royal Canadian Legion, Scandinavian Home Society; [hon.] Awards in Culinary Arts; [pers.] I do this as a hobby, but if people like what I write this will inspire me even more. [a.] Thunder Bay, Ont.

WILD, GRAHAM M.
[b.] May 4, 1947, Leeds, England; [p.] Louis anmd Vera; [m.] Sisan, Patricia, June 5, 1978; [ch.] Rachel Katherine; [ed.] Leeds Modern Grammar School; [occ.] Secretary Leeds MS Self-help Group, prematurely retired (due to disablement-multiple sclerosis) previously sales manager; [memb.] Greenpeace; [oth. writ.] Many childrens poems, mostly written for my daughter as yet unpublished- essay Shufflers and Steroids - observations on a hospital confinement; [pers.] The resources of the Earth are finite. It is vitally important to actively conserve them for future generations. [a.] Leeds, England.

WILHELM, KIMBERLY L.
[b.] December 11, 1970, Bethesda, MD; [p.] Lesleigh L. Cook; [ed.] Loudoun Valley High School; [occ.] Administrative Assistant Precision Tune Corp. HQTRs; [hon.] Who's Who Among American Student 1987-88; [oth. writ.] A few selection of love poems, never published; [pers.] My grandmother, Barbara Houchin Evans-Smith, is my inspiration of my poetry writing. [a.] Leesburg, VA.

WILKINS, GLEN
[pen.] Charles Hanscomb; [b.] December 6, 1952, Kent England; [p.] Stan and Marjorie Wilkins; [m.] Susan Ann, May 7, 1980; [ch.] Christopher and Hazel Wilkins; [ed.] Mascalls Secondary School, Nash College; [occ.] Electronics and part-time martial arts teacher; [memb.] Regional director for Wales for the independent martial arts Budo Association, Society of Black Belts, International Martial Arts Federation, Councillor at local church; [hon.] 1978 Club Coach Award for the British Judo Association, 1985 Area Coach for I.M.A.F., 1993 Doshi Award for I.M.A.F., hold 3rd Dan Black Belt Practice Judo, Aikioo, Jujitsu, karate; [pers.] I try to write from the heart, to reach the heart. [a.] Newport Gwent, UK

WILLARD, GARY S.
[b.] January 28, 1944, Chicago, IL; [p.] Owen and Martha (nee Kovash); [m.] Divorced; [ch.] Arianne Noell; [occ.] Airline Administration; [memb.] US Marine Corps Association; [hon.] Past National Director of "VietNow' Citation for service; [oth. writ.] Various short stories and poems, as yet unpublished; [pers.] I view poems as 'gateways' to the inner mind...to the soul...they, touch in the most private way. [a.] Huntley, IL.

WILLIAMS, BARBARA ANN
[b.] June 25, 1944, B'ham, AL; [p.] Maggie Ryan; [m.] Claude E., October 31, 1963; [ch.] Darrell, Derrick, Dale and Danielle Williams; [ed.] Completing education with learning disabilities; [occ.] Educational worker in special ed.; [pers.] I strive to build a bridge that lead children to read. My poems reflect my confidence, concern and care that no matter what the handicap is, all children should be given a chance to learn. [a.] Bronx, NY.

WILLIAMS, ROBERT MICHAEL
[pen.] Mike Williams; [b.] September 21, 1951, Hamilton, OH; [p.] Robert J. and Edith Belle Williams; [m.] Divorced; [ch.] Thomas M., Scott C. and Heather C. Williams; [ed.] Garfield Sr. High, US Navy Schools, Olympic Jr. College; [occ.] Medical technologist; [oth. writ.] Write thoughts and observations, have always done so since young; [pers.] Please try to love one another. As we were meant to do. [a.] Silverdale, WA.

WILLIAMS, TERRANCE A.
[b.] June 20, 1969, Valparaiso, IN; [p.] Barbara Wardell and David Williams, Sr.; [ed.] Crown Point High School, Ball State University, Purdue University; [occ.] Engineer; [memb.] American Foundrymen's Society, Kappa Delta Rho and Foundry Education Foundation; [hon.] Honor roll; [oth. writ.] Several poems which will be published in the future, including "Wishes", "My Love Won't Get Away" and "Troubled Soul"; [pers.] I try to reflect, in my writing, the love and heartaches that everyone experiences through their lives. [a.] Indianapolis, IN.

WILLIAMS, TERRY
[b.] May 2, 1965, Tulsa, OK; [p.] Jerald/Sandy Williams; [ed.] Broken Arrown Public Schools, Oral Roberts University; [occ.] Commercial pilot; [memb.] First Baptist Church, Montana Pilots Association; [hon.] F.A.A. Wings award, music aviation, scuba diving, sports; [oth. writ.] Featured in Flying Magazines, newspapers, articles; [pers.] Dedicated to God and my loving parents. It's better to build bridges so you can rach out. Rathern than digging ditches so as to isolate ones self. [a.] Broken Arrow, OK.

WILLIAMS, THERESA
[pen.] Terry Williams; [b.] March 2, 1955, Brooklyn, NY; [p.] Maria and Frank Viola; [m.] Todd David, July 12, 1986; [ch.] Maria Elizabeth, Brandon Francis and Anthony John Michael; [ed.] 2 yrs college entering 3rd; [occ.] Domino's Pizza Driver; [memb.] PTA; [oth. writ.] A Friend, What Is A Friend, The Sea, Reflections on the Water, Christmas all unpublished; [pers.] I've been writing poetry for 13 years now and plan on taking a poetry course in college. Also plan on writing a book someday. [a.] San Antonio, TX.

WILLIG, BEVERLY
[b.] March 15, 1935, CT; [m.] James O. (deceased), September 11, 1976; [ch.] Rosemarie Harvey, Linda Rodriguez, Leslie Uher, Pam Geppert, Stuart Willig, Daniel R. Harvey III; [ed.] Staples H.S.; [occ.] Retired- Vol. work with N. GA. TECH. Literacy Program for GED.

WILLIS, SHERRIL ANN
[b.] October 7, 1954, Spfld, MA; [ed.] Our Lady of Elms, Westfield State College; [occ.] Elementary Teacher; [oth. writ.] Published seveal single poems in following anthologies: Images, An Anthology of Award Winning Verse and Prose 1990, Poetic Voices of America 1990, The Best Poems of the '90, 1992, Quiet Moments 1990, Sunrise, Sunset, Anthology of Poetry 1990, The American Poetry Anthology 1990, Whispers in the Wind, A Collection of Poetry 1989, Free Focus 1989; [pers.] I've been reading and writing poetry since I was about 10. I remember hiding in the stacks at our neighborhood library in Springfield, MA and reading the poems of Langston Hughes aloud to myself. In college and graduate school, I became very attached to the poems of Nikki Giovanni and Maya Angelou. I enjoy all kinds of verse, but I prefer to write in the less formal free style.

WILSON, ALEXANDER
[b.] March 12, 1949, London, England; [m.] Noelene; [ch.] James, Stuart, and Nicole; [occ.] Senior Executive Computer Industry; [oth. writ.] Collection of writings for private enjoyment. [a.] Naperville, IL.

WILSON, BERNADINE J.
[b.] February 24, 1941, Paris, IL; [p.] Jessie and William Daniel; [ch.] Bruce Andre, Malik Ali; [ed.] Harbord CT, Ypsilanti High, Wilberforce University, Wayne State University; [occ.] Elementary Counselor; [memb.] Oak Grove A.M.E. Church, Guidance Assoc. of Metro Detroit, Alpha Kappa Alpha Sorority, Kiwanius International, Wilberforce Un. Alumni and Wayne State Un. Alumni; [hon.] Booker T. WAshington Educators award, various awards and recognition at local schools as teacher and counselor; [oth. writ.] Poems about children and youth unpublished; [pers.] My poems will relate my concern about children and youth in today's world. Also other topics of interest. [a.] Detroit, MI.

WILSON, MITCHELL
[b.] July 12, 1963, Perth, Australia; [p.] Geoff and Fran Wilson; [m.] Mary Wilson, October 27, 1990; [ed.] Completing final year Bachelor of Nursing; [occ.] State enrolled nurse (p/t); [memb.] Greenpeace; [pers.] A life with no aim is not unimportant, a life with no purpose is. But every life has a hidden purpose and all life is important. [a.] Northcote, Victoria.

WILSON, ROSALIND
[b.] January 23, 1975, Bristol; [p.] Christine Wilson; [ed.] G.C.SE; [occ.] Student (Sociology); [oth. writ.] Short story entitled "Waking Up to Reality" poem anthology entitled It's Our World, also writing a novel; [pers.] I write poetry that reflects the very, very different lives of individuals in todays society in hope of educating people, so eventually, people will make the world a better place. [a.] Yorkshire, Halifax.

WINIESKI, RAYMOND J.
[b.] October 4, 1932, Elmira, NY; [p.] Max M. and Ida Krolak Winieski; [ed.] Mansfield University, Elmira College; [occ.] Teacher; [memb.] Kappa Delta Pi, Polish American Historical Association; [hon.] Correctional Educational Association; [oth. writ.] Elmira's Poles 1986, several articles on Polish-American topics for local periodicals; [pers.] Only in poetry do words really "come alive". [a.] Elmira, NY.

WINNETT, CALISTA JOELL
[b.] May 20, 1970, Hermiston, OR; [p.] Mary and George Workman; [m.] William R., December 23, 1992; [ch.] Jeffrey Scott; [ed.] Hermiston High School; [occ.] Secretary; [oth. writ.] Several other poems published in local school newspaper and local church paper; [pers.] By reading my poetry, your reading my life. [a.] Pendleton, OR.

WINTERS, MELANIE
[b.] July 8, 1967, Hartford, CT; [p.] Harold and Judy Flanagan; [ed.] Windsor High School, Marist College, Trinity and All Saints College; [occ.] Journalist; [oth. writ.] Weekly column entitled "Memories Then and Now. [a.] Windsor, CT.

WITMAN, CHERYL
[b.] December 16, 1971; [occ.] Loan Operation Specialist; [pers.] There is nothing in the world like writing. Your characters are in your control and they can be and do all that you can only dream for your own life. And for everytime you fail in life your characters succeed. It is the best of two worlds: real and imaginary. [a.] East Earl, PA.

WITTE, TONYA M.
[b.] September 6, 1978, Phx., AZ; [p.] Nanette Kenyon and Frederick A. Witte, Sr. (deceased); [ed.] Central High School; [occ.] Student; [memb.] National Junior Honor Society; [hon.] Honor Roll; [oth. writ.] Have written several other poems. My poem "I Love You Daddy" published in local newspaper, in memory of my dad who died May 16, 1993; [pers.] I enjoy writing poems and stories. I use writing as an outlet to express my feelings. [a.] Phoenix, AZ.

WLODOWSKI, MIROSLAW
[b.] May 25, 1957, Zakopane, Poland; [ed.] Central School of Planning and Statistics; [occ.] Financial Assistant; [memb.] FLMI, Polish Friends of the Earth Society, Alpine Society; [oth. writ.] Several poems published in polish-language magazines; [pers.] There are so many ways to celebrate our short presence here, writing is one of them. Writing, to find a link between the unspoken feelings and the unattainable secret of life. [a.] Cicero, IL.

WOLANSKI, LAURA
[b.] February 11, 1968; [m.] Stephen, SSGT, USMC; [ch.] Valerie Katherine, Travis Christian; [occ.] College student, Marine Corps wife, and mother of two. [a.] Okinawa, Japan.

WOLFE, ANN
[b.] May 11, 1961, Staten Island; [p.] Mary Jane and Edward Wolfe; [ed.] College of New Rochelle, Special Education Ursuline School; [occ.] Had surgery now recovering; [memb.] Living Word Fellopwship, Rye Handicap Association; [oth. writ.] Poems published in college and high school literary magazine; [pers.] My reason for writing poetry is to thank God for blessing of beauty in life. Poetry is a reflection of life experience.

WOLFE, DENNIS A.
[b.] April 16, 1948, Akron, OH; [p.] John S. and Mary M. Wolfe; [m.] Divorced; [ch.] John Paul Wolfe; [ed.] University of Detroit, DePaul University; [occ.] Own several small businesses; [memb.] Billard Congress of America, National Association of Realtors, Illinois Restaurant Association, Lincoln Park Chamber of Commerce, Lincoln Park Boulders Club, Chicago Council of Tourism, Willow Creek Community Church, Old Town Triange Association, Magna cum Laude; [pers.] My poems are simply emotions that are in me and come out rhyming. [a.] Chicago, IL.

WONG, PETER A.
[pers.] This poem was written from the soul of my heart to the love of my life. I've lost her forever but, the memory of her touch will burn eternally within me. I miss you. A.L.Y. [a.] Gilbert, AZ.

WOODHOUSE, TAMA ELCENIA
[pen.] T.E. Woodhouse or Tamar; [b.] August 10, Colorado; [p.] Douglas and Delois Woodhouse; [ed.] Temple University; [occ.] Chemist, Counselor for MR adults, freelance writer and teacher; [memb.] American Chemical Society, National Chemistry Honor Society, Delaware Valley Chromatography Forum, The Church of the Lord Jesus Christ of the Apostolic Faith; [hon.] Certificates and plaques for volunteer work, honors for academic excellence throughout University experience; [oth. writ.] Articles in chemical journals, poems in University Honors Journal; [pers.] "I think, therefore I am and since I am, I must express my existence through the language of the heart-poetry!" [a.] Philadelphia, PA.

WOODS, DONNA M.
[pen.] D. Woods; [b.] June 10, 1957, Los Angeles; [p.] Foy C. and Willie Catherian Woods; [ed.] Antioch University, Los Angeles City College; [occ.] Artist, muralist and instructor; [memb.] West Angeles Church of God in Christ, National Water Color Society; [hon.] Outstanding Graphic Design, Outstanding Graphic Artist; [oth. writ.] Collection of poems and short stories, unpublished but registered with the Library of Congress; [pers.] There is salvation in compassion, truth in honest expression. My list of repected writers is long: Poe, Maya Angelou and Walt Whitman. [a.] Los Angeles, CA.

WOODS, KATHY WOULLARD
[pen.] Kathy Woullard; [b.] April 16, 1949, Hattiesburg,

MS; [p.] Lon and Winnie Woullard (deceased); [m.] Deceased; [ch.] Brian and Toya Woods; [ed.] Rhema Biblke Training School; [occ.] Mother and student Oral Roberts University; [pers.] I come forth to present to the world a better view of God in all his glory and splendor. I am in awe of him! And as he wills me to I plan to write what I see and feel. [a.] Tulsa, OK.

WOODS, LISA M.
[b.] May 30, 1967, Kingston, ONT. CAN; [p.] Garfield and RoseMarie Woods; [ed.] Loyalist Collegiate Vocational Institute High School; [occ.] Sales consultant; [pers.] Never completely give up, only strive harder for ones inner self perfections. The reflections of your strengths will not be tainted, remember to always survive as a fighter, continue to reach high for the stars. They're never really too far out to reach. [a.] Kingston, ON. CAN.

WOODSON, WILLIAM SR.
[b.] August 29, 1955, Trenton, NJ; [p.] Leda and Wayne Woodson; [m.] Cathy, December 5, 1992; [ch.] William Jr. and Landon Wayne; [ed.] Fulton High, College of the Sequoias; [occ.] Police officer; [hon.] Dean's list 1979-81, Ventura County Peace Officers Association Medal of Merit 1991; [oth. writ.] Several poems of my own personal collection; [pers.] This is the first poem I have ever submitted for public view, I hope it will be enjoyed by its readers. [a.] Chandler, AZ.

WOODWARD, JOHN ANDREW
[pen.] Lightning; [b.] December 27, 1962, Suffolk, England; [p.] Thomas A. and Theresa A. Woodward; [ch.] Jessica Ann And Theresa Marie Woodward; [ed.] Whetstone High, El Camino College, The Recording Workshop; [occ.] Musician; recording engineer; [oth.w rit.] Many poems, songs and short stories; [pers.] Regardless of what this world tells you, the Lord Jesus Christ is waiting on the other side I know I've been there and back you have only one choice to make choose wisely. [a.] Gahanna, OH.

WOOLERY, NED E.
[b.] September 13, 1935, Hominy, OK; [p.] Paul H. and Connie P. Woolery; [m.] Myrna K., December 24, 1984; [ch.] Lloyd B. Wright, Paul D. Woolery, John T. Woolery; [ed.] High school; [occ.] Director, Administrative Support Services; [memb.] National Association of Superintendents; [oth. writ.] "Memories of a Security Officer" various unpublished poems; [pers.] My writings invariably reflect, at some point, my love and admiration for my wife. [a.] Alea, HI.

WOOMER, JAMES COLVIN
[pen.] James Douglas and Phoebe Woomer; [b.] November 27, 1973, New Kensington, PA; [p.] Deceased; [m.] Jamie Coup, September 22, 1993; [ed.] Valley High School; [occ.] Poet/artist/metaphysician/shaman; [memb.] Spee-D Hill Ghetto; [hon.] American legion award; [oth. writ.] Several unpublished poems and opinion papers and role-playing game; [pers.] My poetry is an attempt to scare people into consciousness through the use of dark symbols and surrealism. I must wake people up. Challenge them on a subconscious level. My greatest influences are Jim Morrison, Dave Letterman, and Rush Limbaugh. [a.] New Kensington, PA.

WRIGHT, CHAD
[b.] August 18, 1974, Fond du Lac; [p.] Steven and Beth Wright; [ed.] Arizona Lutheran Academy (Northwest-

ern College); [occ.] Student; [hon.] James E. Casey award, National Football Foundation and Hall of Fame Scholar-Athlete; [oth. writ.] Several poems published in high school literary fine arts magazine, editorials for high school newspaper; [pers.] I try to understand the diversity of life and capture certain aspects with my poetry. [a.] Watertown, WI.

WRIGHT, NANCY LEE
[b.] July 15, 1951, Georgia; [p.] Sam and Pearlie Lee; [ch.] Kimberly/James; [ed.] Palatka Central High, St. John's River Jr. College, University of Florida correspondence; [occ.] Dietary manager; [memb.] Ebony Women, Black Advisory Council, Parent Teacher Organization; [oth. writ.] Church, family and friends; [pers.] I have a perfect and safe place within my soul. That the world does not belong I only, through my writing is able to reach it. [a.] Palatka, FL.

WRIGHT, NANCY SZOSTAK
[b.] August 2, 1962, Methuen, MA; [p.] Margaret and Charles Szostak; [m.] John Wright, May 8, 1993; [ed.] University of Maine/Orono; [occ.] Senior Copywriter; [memb.] Ad Club of Greater Boston, The Academy of American Poets; [hon.] Several local advertising awards; [pers.] Every person is a color. When the sun shines on you, let it reflect a rainbow of happiness in your heart. [a.] Belmont, WA.

WROBLE, TAMMY L.
[b.] December 12, 1973, Melrose Park, IL; [p.] Jeff and Gail Wroble; [ed.] Streamwood High School, Carroll College; [occ.] Student; [oth. writ.] Poem published in local newspaper. [a.] Streamwood, IL.

XAVIER, DEBORAH A.
[pen.] Xavier; [b.] August 3, Trinidad; [p.] Lucille and Neville Xavier; [ch.] Sanchia Rae, Denzil, Dale; [ed.] Graduate New Jersey Real Estate Institute; [occ.] Mortgage Banker; [memb.] Homebuilder Association, Teague Parent Teacher Associations; [hon.] Award for presentations to first Time Home Buyers; [oth. writ.] Short stories unpublished; [pers.] Today is the first day of the rest of my life. Never forget how to dream avoid toxic relationships. [a.] Altermonte Springs, FL.

XAVIER, IRENE THERESE
[p.] Viriato M. and Maria L. Xavier (nee Barradas); [ed.] St. Mary's School; [occ.] Retired Administrative Secretary; [hon.] Been published in seven poetry anthologies, received honorable mention certificate and golden poet award 1987, along with trophy from World of Poetry; [pers.] Poetry is an art, which evokes sweet sentiments from the heart and soul. [a.] Daly City, CA.

XEREAS, HELEN
[pen.] No1; [b.] January 27, 1980, Fairfax, VA; [p.] Peter and Stella Xereas; [ed.] Swanson Middle School; [occ.] Student; [hon.] Won Writer's Fair Contest two years in row; [pers.] I feel the best wa y to express myself is through my writing, especially through poetry. [a.] Arlington, VA.

YABUT, MARISSA
[b.] September 19, 1976, Los Angeles, CA; [p.] Bernardo and Cresensia Yabut; [ed.] Immaculate Heart High School; [occ.] Student; [pers.] My writings express my personal thoughts and ideas. I want people to understand that I am influenced by love, death and affection. [a.] Baldwin Park, CA.

YCAOBUCCI, DAVID A.
[b.] May 17, 1958, Elyria, OH; [p.] Howard G. Yacobucci and Shirley A. Toman; [m.] Julia C., February 6, 1993; [ed.] Marion L. Steele High School, Bowling Green State University, Law School Capital University, Grad school OSU; [occ.] Self-employed investor; [memb.] American Association of Individual Investors, National Geographic Society, The Planetary Society; [oth. writ.] Numerous other poems including "The Train" previously published in Whispers in the Wind; [pers.] We each owe it to ourselves and to the world to be well-educated. This is best achieved by strict adherence to two rules: Read as much as possible every day and Never violate rule no. 1. [a.] Dublin, OH.

YAMAMOTO, DONNA MAILE
[b.] August 31, 1976, Wailuka, HI; [p.] Daryl and Carol Yamamoto; [ed.] Kamehameha Secondary School; [pers.] Life is a test. [a.] Kahului, HI.

YAN, SHIRLEY
[pen.] Banta; [b.] Nvember 17, 1951, West Indies; [p.] Joyce and Gerald Barthelemy; [ch.] Christina and Tamara Yan; [ed.] St. Francois High School, Pace University; [occ.] Vista Volunteer Bed-Stuy Restoration Corp.; [oth. writ.] Best of Banta Yan Greeting Cards published by Quill Books, poem The Weaver; [pers.] Our success is designed by God, with whom all things are possible. [a.] Brooklyn, NY.

YAP, SIMEON T.
[b.] February 1, 1962, Manila, Phil; [p.] Miguel and Helen Yap; [ed.] Xavier School, University of Philippines; [occ.] Banking; [hon.] Top ten MBA graduates, Phi Kappa Phi, Pi Gamma Mu. [a.] Quezon City, Metro Manile, Php.

YASUO, ATSUOMI
[pen.] At-Chan, Ats, Atsu; [b.] March 30, 1974, Utah, SLC; [p.] Yoichi and Chizuko Yasuo; [ed.] Denker Ave. Elementary, Peary Jr. High, North Torrance High School, El Camino College; [occ.] Student; [memb.] Devine Wind Racing Crew; [hon.] Varsity Track, Diploma Japanese school; [pers.] Life is like going through a maze, you pick your path only to reach a dead end. One after another all there is is an dead end. There's a chance that there might not be anything at the end. But then the one that gives up and stops going through the maze will never again have a chance to know what awaits at the end. [a.] Torrance, CA.

YIM, JULIANA M.
[pen.] Anna Fraser; [b.] September 26, 1964, Anaheim, CA; [p.] Judith Yim; [pers.] "I do not f eel obliged to believe that that same God who has endowed us with sense, reason, and intellect has intended us to forego their use." Galileo. [a.] Mililani, HI.

YORK, LINDSEY R.
[b.] December 26, 1978, Isfaban Iran; [p.] Jonathan and Eva York; [ed.] Edmonson County High; [occ.] Student; [pers.] Write for self, when I finish a poem it makes me feel good in side and its a way to stay sane. [a.] Brownsville, KY.

YOUNG, CORRINE FRAZIER
[pen.] Corrine Frazier Young; [b.] August 29, 1943, Churchview, VA; [p.] Linwood (deceased) and Mary Emma Frazier; [m.] Divorced, June 8, 1963; [ch.] Bryant, Gary, and Jamel Young granddaughters-Ashley and Oshae Young; [ed] St. Clare Walker High School,

Cortez Peters Business College; [occ.] Office Service Specialist VA State Health Department; [memb.] Lebanon Baptist Church; [oth. writ.] Several poems published in local newspapers, have written poems for numerous occasions in the community. Many letters of sympathy written in the form of a poem for family and friends; [pers.] My poems are basically written from spiritual and religious experiences in my life. The poems are written so that all levels of society can understand what God has done and will do. [a.] Urbanna, VA.

YOUNG JACALYN
[b.] August 7, 1955, Saskatchewan, CAN; [p.] William and Gina Ross; [m.] Gilbert T. Doll (common law husband 1990); [ch.] Angela, Allan, Robin, Ian; [ed.] University of Saskatchewan; [occ.] Self-employed preparing student study systems; [pers.] Writing is a way of thinking and sorting through life experiences, a way of exploring ones feelings and putting emotions into perspective. [a.] Sherwood Park, Alberta CAN.

YOUNG, JAMES JOSEPH
[b.] January 27, 1957, Cleveland, OH; [p.] James and Irene Young; [pers.] Spiritually, mentally, and physically imprisoned by the insanity of an alcholic obsession in 1970 and Divinely Freed on September 2, 1989 by a Higher Power, I call God. And after nearly five years of sobriety I have been relieved of the fear, lonliness and pain that I had tried to drown with alcohol. I am now a student of life and truly love and savor every person, place and thing that I come in contact with every moment of every day, and hope and pray that at lifes end, to dance on the horizon. [a.] Dearborn Heights, MI.

YOUNG, ROSALIND
[pen.] Rosalind Young, Roz Young, Rozy; [b.] June 29, 1952, Oakland, CA; [p.] Patricia D. Young; [ed.] Aiea High, University of Hawaii; [occ.] Recreation District Supervisor, Art Glass Designer/artist/instructor; [memb.] Hawaii Park and Recreation Association, Honolulu Zoological Society; [oth. writ.] Many personal writings, not yet published; [pers.] I write from the heart, to express my insights and emotions. I choose words that are meant to elicit a shared response from the reader. [a.] Mililani, HI.

YOUNG, RUBY
[pen.] Snow Chang; [b.] November 16, 1920, Honan, China; [p.] Chung-Shu Chang and Shuan-Tse Duan; [m.] Dick, June 6, 1948; [ch.] Karl Young; [ed.] National Honan University, Southern Illinois University, P/T study at Biblical Seminary; [occ.] Elementary School teacher of NY Institute for Special Education; [memb.] Methodist Church, The Chinese American Academics and Professional Society, Association of Chinese Schools; [hon.] 4th prize National Writing Contest for College Students; awards for 10 years, 20 years and 25 years service from NYISE; [oth. writ.] Several poems and articles published in Chinese newspa-

pers and magazines. Most of them for the United Journal NYC; [pers.] Pen is more powerful than gun! We pray God for leading us by safe paths to a happy, peaceful and joyful world family! [a.] New York City, NY.

ZARB, EDWARD
[b.] November 2, 1927, Malta, Europe; [p.] Joseph Zarb and Emily Rixon; [m.] Gina Mafrici, January 28, 1960; [ch.] Emily Zarb Fisher and Anthony Zarb; [occ.] Retired after 28 years with Canada's Postal Service; [oth. writ.] Several poems published in periodicals, newspapers and books in English, Italian and Maltese; [pers.] Poetry is the expression of a soul. It can also be a sharp sword or inspiration of light in a dark night. [a.] Mississauga, Ont. CAN.

ZELLNER, SANDRA
[pen.] Sandy Moffett; [b.] June 28, 1962, Sandusky, OH; [p.] Robert and Dean Moffett; [m.] Fiancee-Terry Miller, June 10, 1995; [ch.] Chas, Kade, Alex, Jessica, Terry's children-Brad, Theresa and Jason; [ed.] Bellevue Senior High School; [occ.] Homemaker and tutor for illeteracy program; [oth. writ.] A collection of over 200 poems; [pers.] God has given me the talent to express feelings that I believe many other people have, but are unable to put into words. I write poetry to give emotions and feelings a voice! [a.] Bellevue, OH.

ZICKEFOOSE, TEDRIDRA
[pen.] T.D.; [b.] April 3, 1982, Pitts; [p.] Robert and Terry Zickefoose; [ch.] Sisters- Kristen and Melinda; [ed.] Horace Mann Elementary, Allegheny Middle School; [occ.] Student; [memb.] Cheerleading chorus, newspaper, Red Cross Delegate; [hon.] Honor Roll; [pers.] I really put my heart and dreams into this poem. For me this would be a dream come true. [a.] Pitts. PA.

ZIEMBA, ILONA WENEK
[b.] June 25, 1961, Warsaw, Poland; [p.] Janusz and Janina Wenek; [m.] Igor, August 24, 1980; [ch.] Aleksander and Klaudia Emilia, Miriam; [ed.] Economic College of Wausaw, Guest student Fine Art Academy of Warsaw, Institute of Professional Upgrading of Warsaw, Artistic Weaving, Barborg Cleslor Art Studio, Ottawa School of Art; [occ.] Artist; [memb.] Ottawa Valley Weaver's and Spinners Guild, Association of the Friends of Fine Art; [hon.] Solo exhibition: Warsaw-Piaski Community Centre, Paintings and Drawings, collective exhibitions: Westboro Fine Art Festival, Ottawa-Almonte Art Show, Ottawa School of Art "Christmas Exhibition" Beechwood Panel Contest, Poetry readings, 5th anniversary of journal "Zbliieniol; [oth. writ.] Published in journals: "Zblizenia" Dartmund, Germany, "Polonika" Ottawa and in printing "Alien's Dreams"; [pers.] I explore the magical reality of children and the animal world as well as my travellers experience in my works. [a.] Ottawa, Ontario, CAN.

ZIMMERMANN, MICHAELA
[pen.] Mitia Blackman; [b.] June 2, 1967, Bendorf/Rhine; [occ.] Student; [oth. writ.] Several poems published in the Literaty Journal of the University of Trier's English Department; [pers.] In my poems, I try to catch thoughts with my pen. This keeps me well stocked with easy questions - whose answers I find increasingly tricky. This dilemma, as well as the courage to deal eith it, I gratefully owe to Robert Wroetsch. [a.] Trier, Germany.

ZITO, CHRISTOPHER NICHOLAS
[b.] February 5, 1981, Brooklyn, NY; [p.] Louis and Elizabeth Zito; [ed.] I.S. 14 Shellbank 7th grade; [hon.] 1991 received the Community Service award from Gerritsen Beach, Brooklyn; [pers.] I can not help but think that someday my children will read this, therefore I will not be "forgotten". [a.] Brooklyn, NY.

ZITO, DIANA
[b.] March 30, 1974, Washington, DC; [p.] Aldo and Alicia Zito; [ed.] Graduated from Bishop Dennis J. O'Connell, one yeat at University of South Carolina, Virginia Tech; [memb.] Association of Marian Helpers; [oth. writ.] Signs, Friend of Truth, Borrower, The Question of Why, Forever, Poems etc (never published); [pers.] "A true friend is someone who walks in when the whole world walks out." Author Unknown [a.] Arlington, VA.

ZIVALICH, JEANNA M.
[b.] October 9, 1969, Chicago, IL; [p.] Norma and Jean Mucci; [m.] John James, October 27, 1991; [ed.] Loyola University Medical Center, Jones Commercial High School; [occ.] Secretary - Human Resources; [oth. writ.] Poem published several years ago in the Anthology book. Never purchased, name at the time Jeanna Mucci; [pers.] Inspired thoughts come from deep within oneself. Shared for many for their own inspiration. [a.] Elmwood Park, IL.

ZMUDA, NICOLE
[b.] June 26, 1980, Scranton, PA; [p.] Adam and Donna Zmuda; [ed.] Valley View Middle; [occ.] Student; [hon.] Honor Roll; [pers.] I try to write about my ideas, thoughts, and emotions. Sometimes I write about my personal feelings. I wrote this poem because I could find no other way to express how I felt about somebody. [a.][Archbald, PA.

ZOHAR, MEIR
[b.] September 28, 1966, Isreal; [p.] Smicha and Tamar Zohar; [m.] Vered Zohar-Toaff, August 24, 1986; [ch.] Efrat and Ohad; [ed.] Bar Ilan University; [occ.] Customer Support Administration-Software Company; [oth. writ.] Biographic story in The Montreal Gazette, currently in the closing stages of my first novel; [pers.] I wsih to see the prospect of pease become reality in this troubled corner of the earth. [a.] Isreal.

933

INDEX

Grant, Lorna 515
Grant, Marie E. 487
Grant, Michael C. 560
Grant, Roger W. 695
Grant, Sewilla K. 413
Grantz, Robert Lee 425
Grasso, Gene 608
Gravely, Katherine Lucille 87
Graves, Tiffany 529
Gray, Beverly Lynne 272
Gray, Decima Danyese 360
Gray, Franklin D. 583
Gray, Lyda 429
Gray, Melissa 328
Gray, Patricia 735
Gray, Paul D. 494
Gray, Rebecca G. 656
Grayot, Mary Ellen Hardy 285
Greeley, David G. 185
Green, B. 166
Green, Carolyn 682
Green, Claudia E.218
Green, Deborah S. 250
Green, Ernest F. 374
Green, Gaye 204
Green, Katanah 147
Green, Kathlene 179
Green, Lenora 738
Green, Michele 59
Green, Penny Miranda 428
Green, Tim W. 540
Greene, Desmond 750
Greenland, Liz 160
Greenlaw, Roby A. 129
Greenlee, Amber 94
Greenlee, Jane G. 681
Greenwood, Ron 421
Greer, Sarah L. 548
Gregg, Ada L. 217
Gregor, David 324
Gregory, Jeffrey D. 556
Gregory, Shannon 401
Greicius, Elaine Marian 358
Greig, Geraldine Gobi 614
Greuling, Peggie 292
Grewe, Ruth E. 559
Grewing, Patty Jo 348
Grgurich, Barbara K. 223
Gricoski, Michael 745
Griebel, Jennifer L. 232
Griego, Jamie 397
Griffin, Amanda M. 357
Griffin, Harriett B. 773
Griffin, Jill Ann 159
Griffin, Joan M. 62
Griffith, Leon 524
Griffith, Noreen Curtis 657
Griffiths, Evan 191
Griggs, Linda 334
Grinder, Jam 31
Grisa, Karrieann 119
Grisby, Kimberly 92
Grisby, Zabrina Miranda 549
Griswold, Edwin A. 253
Groce, Peggy J. 433
Groenendyk, Tim 74
Groff, Curt W. 605
Grogan, Kaye 106
Groleau, A.E. 351
Gronewold, Andrew 259
Grooms, Pristeen 710
Groseclose, Win 432
Gross, Patricia 734
Gross, Peter 318
Grossman, Mickie 657
Grossman, Ruth 323
Grover, Florence Mead 262
Groves, Irma 643
Groves, Wayne L. 786
Grubb, Ruth A. 523
Grubbs, Jeffery I. 261
Grubbs, Joyce M. 137
Gruer, Michelle Lynn 432
Grune, Kenneth D.49
Grupp, Christine V. 158

Gruver, D.M. Dusty 81
Guagliardo, Rachel 446
Guengerich, L. Glen 341
Guerra, Luz Michelle 491
Guihot, Christine 80 '
Guild, Alicia K. 208
Gullicksen, Barbara 364
Gullison, Joan Leslie 395
Gunby, Laura E. 285
Gunnels, Maxine 432
Gureski, Henry J. 207
Guretse, Albert F. 352
Gustafson, Derek 202
Guthrie, Grace 221
Guthrie, Shaina 275
Gutierrez, Paul D. 784
Gutierrez, Susana 530
Guy, Geneva 636
Guy-Shea, Mary E. 68
Guzan, Linda S. 733
Guzman, Ernie Suarez 200
Guzman, Roy Michael 442
Gworek, Michael F. 421
Haaker, Marilyn 787
Haas, Andrea 641
Haberkorn, Robert W. 418
Hackman, Edith L. 207
Haddock, Amanda J. 682
Hagan, Robin 781
Hageman, Alisa 754
Hagen, Shannon 19
Hagler, E. Dian 233
Hagler, Stephanie 304
Haigh, Brian 150
Hailperin, Bernard 377
Haines, Darren 61
Hale, Jennifer L. 50
Haley, Michelle 653
Halford, Clifford L. 640
Hall Jr., Robert W. 320
Hall R.M.A., Darlene R. 222
Hall, Carolyn Romans 620
Hall, Creaestia B. 466
Hall, Darren 125
Hall, Elorice 762
Hall, Heather 673
Hall, Lee A. 280
Hall, Linda C. 324
Hall, River 726
Hall, Ruth 509
Halladay, Theo 134
Hallberg, Phyllis 742
Haller, C. Josephine 343
Hallgren, Travis 305
Halliday, Diana 371
Halpenny, Jennifer L. 93
Halpern, Nettie A. 299
Halsey, Paul Michael 431
Halzel, Shelley 542
Hamblin, Joe Alan 607
Hamby, Sarah 438
Hamelin, Terry 745
Hamerly, Jessica M. 751
Hametz, Marilyn 701
Hamilton, Alison 468
Hamilton, Barbara 208
Hamilton, Benny H. 647
Hamilton, Dorothy June 154
Hamilton, Jesus Messiah 617
Hamilton, Rebecca A. 689
Hammes, Marie E. 790
Hammond, Stacey 727
Hampton, Luke 570
Hampton, Veldeanie 790
Hamric, Ramona E. 722
Hamrick, Joann 55
Han, Lahela K. 445
Handren, Scott 561
Hanefeld, Dana B. 641
Hanley, S.J. 731
Hanlon, T.L. 79
Hannahs, Sara Hans 569
Hannon, Denise M. 756
Hanscomb, Charles 149
Hansell, Lola 495

Hansen, Barbara 619
Hansen, Nicole Rhea 518
Hanson, James 188
Harahap, Pangkat 86
Harbers, Peggy 346
Hardin, Karen 86
Hardison, Sunda A. 420
Hardy, Billie 272
Harfman, B. 571
Harfman, Hailey 120
Hargrave, Jennie 173
Harkins, Rose 524
Harless, Janet Myers 626
Harlow, Michael P. 299
Harnetiaux, Mark 566
Haroutiunian, Artem 267
Harp, Jon Scott 67
Harper, Alexis 662
Harper, Ruth M.S. 426
Harpham, Denise 472
Harrill III, John David 31
Harrington, Bethanne 686
Harris, Clinton E. 767
Harris, Elizabeth O. 598
Harris, Frances Allison 773
Harris, Greg 570
Harris, Keyona 83
Harris, Laura 111
Harris, Leslie Ann 97
Harris, Marie 439
Harris, Paul 186
Harris, Robert Earl 424
Harrison, Andy 682
Harrison, Anitra Y. 242
Harrison, Elizabeth 448
Harrison, Keisha G.141
Harrison, Marjorie 654
Harrison, Nathanael 743
Harrison, Patricia 155
Harrison, Stan F.63
Harrison, Wendy Ann 141
Harrity, Kevin 81
Harroff, Bill 266
Harry, Beatrice 376
Harshman, Lindsay 286
Hart, Earl E. 663
Hart, Jeannie 625
Hart, Marsha 654
Hart, Vanessa 536
Hartman, Arlene 662
Hartwell, William T. 341
Harvey, Dale 150
Harvey, Frances Gillard 67
Harvey, Jerry 587
Harvey, Karen M. 147
Harvey, Sammye Jo 694
Hasal, Gaudencia Compania 762
Hasan, Shazia 118
Haskin, Pamela K. 730
Hassan, Syed Mohammad 696
Hasseebullah, Tahira 486
Hassell, Melissa 337
Hassell, Susan 520
Hasstedt, Steve 567
Hatcher, Vera 405
Hauch, Debbie 224
Haught, Dot 631
Hauptmann, J.M. 150
Hauserman, Regina 335
Havercamp, Sherry L. 711
Haverkamp, Brent 188
Haverkorn, Lisa 657
Havican, Patricia 561
Hawk, Anna 263
Hawker, Lynn R. 402
Hawkins, E.F. 339
Hawkins, Wendell S. 517
Hayes, Amanda 213
Hayes, Amanda 391
Hayes, B. 299
Hayes, Janae 683
Hayes, Josephine M.153
Hayes, Lana Robertson 514
Hayes, Makeba 302
Hayes, Theodore 447

Hayman, Kelly 94
Haynes, Danny 642
Haynes, Hattie Mae 253
Haynes, Philip G. 714
Haynes, Tim 416
Hayworth, Gary Lee 390
Head, Jessica Anne Christina 152
Head, Lola 690
Healey, Lagrimas 401
Hearn, Jeff 248
Hearne, Sara 320
Heater, Tamara O. 294
Hecht, Rabbi Eli 643
Hedemark, Doug 396
Heffernan, Lisa 515
Heflin, Betty J. 371
Heil, Scott F. 322
Heilprin, Haim D. 48
Heimann, Jennifer A. 158
Heinis, Dorothy M. 388
Heinkel, Joan 663
Heisler, Rex 550
Heiss, Anita 152
Heitmann, Ingeborg 61
Heitmann, Rusty 740
Helfesrieder, Alice 238
Hellstern, Russell 706
Helms, Judy A. 171
Helton, Susan 501
Hempel, Helen 195
Hemple, Florence L. 264
Henderson, Daisy 227
Henderson, Faye McBee 215
Henderson, Lisa M. 656
Henderson, Sharon 568
Henderson, Tammy 546
Henderson, Vada 552
Henderson-Phan, Laurie 278
Hendricks, A.E. 445
Hendricks, Gregory 264
Hendricks, Jennifer F. 634
Hendricks, Sharon H. 488
Hendrickson, Debrah J. 454
Hendrickson, Richard A. 720
Hendry, Lee J. 741
Heneghan, Karol 31
Hengemuehler, Betty J. 219
Henley Jr., James M. 615
Henning, Heather Y.V. 129
Henry, Charles 629
Henry, Dick O. 676
Henry, Sue A. 558
Henson, Jessica 634
Hepner, Brent 258
Heredia, Arthur 582
Hereford, Lois L. 418
Herle, Jeffrey A. 170
Herman, Jean Hull 71
Herman, Karlynn 102
Herman, Michael 443
Herman, Minnie 493
Hernandez, Dimas 578
Hernandez, Paul F. 407
Herrera, E. Isabel 531
Herrera, Ted 569
Herrick, Kathy 24
Herring, Jeremy 52
Herring, Karen 156
Herrmann, Joanne M. 159
Herron, Arlene 765
Hess, Aimee 389
Hess, Dana 685
Hessler, Julie Ann 160
Hester, Alta 363
Hester, B. Joyce 258
Hester, Daniel 677
Hickey, Todd 151
Hicks, Deanna M. 612
Hiddessen, Amy 355
Hierholzer, Beverly 578
Higareda, Joseph 189
Higgins, Barry W. 643
Higgins, Meghan E. 334
Higgins, Susan Mary Twarog 505
Hilbert, Helen 15

Marigold, Marsh 745
Marin, Jahaira 459
Marin, Yolanda 323
Marino, Cheryl 608
Markow, Alison 232
Marks, Rex H. 700
Marks, Vida Louise 521
Marler, Marguerite 422
Marnon, Marilyn 290
Marqua, Richard 412
Marquis, Carolyn F. 265
Marriott, Charles P. 687
Marsh, Darlene P. 631
Marsh, Helen P. 622
Marshall, Bruce A. 242
Marshall, Eugenia Grace 391
Marshall, Ruth V. 565
Martel, Ricardo 293
Martens, Donna C. 194
Martens, Monique 159
Martin, Elliott 199
Martin, Gary 642
Martin, Jackie 596
Martin, Janice 150
Martin, Jerry A. 45
Martin, Kristi 69
Martin, Laura Belle 568
Martin, Lois H. 287
Martin, Marilyn 740
Martin, Melinda 535
Martin, Michael A. 333
Martin, Reita 441
Martin, Robyn D. 336
Martin, Sandra Trammell 561
Martin, Sarah 78
Martin, Tommie 345
Martin-McCormick, Cherie 352
Martin-Samos, Fidel 84
Martina, David 581
Martindale, David R. 4
Martinez, Cesario 629
Martinez, Edward A. 664
Martinez, Ernie 256
Martinez, Melanie Pitts 287
Martinez, Miguel A. 300
Martz, Frances L. 258
Martz, Jean B. 202
Martz, Jennifer L. 389
Maruyama, J. Robert 14
Marx, Christine D. 681
Marx, Teresa L. 438
Mascitti, Michael 333
Mashni, Nicole Rosine 300
Mason, Betty D. 198
Mason, James 138
Mason, Lucy 779
Mason, Roxanna 531
Massey, Linda 724
Masson, Amara 157
Masters, Kristin A. 20
Mastnjak, Laurel 735
Mastrome, David 461
Matheny, Greg 470
Mathews, Ruth 82
Mathias, David 47
Mathis, Calvin 268
Mathis, Frank 478
Mathis, Jean K. 603
Matijon, Cara 86
Matlock, J.W. Sr. 738
Matlock, Mary 536
Matte, Robert E. 186
Matthews, Allison 757
Matthews, Brian 769
Matthews, Jessie 660
Matthews, Thelma Wilson 703
Mattingley, Becky 752
Mattingly, Anna Morine 616
Mattson, Lindsey Ann 521
Matulunas, Dorothy 685
Matz, Angie 395
Maunder, James Lawrence 80
Mawji, Yasmin 193
Maxwell, Kay 194
Maxwell, Raymond 496

May, Celia 384
May, Ida R. 648
May, Johnny D. 613
May, Martha Adams 292
May, Sam J. 66
May, Thomas T. 553
Mayabb, Janita 202
Mayer, Jeff 46
Mayer, Maxine B. 521
Mayer-Mader, Miriam 735
Mayers, Constance D. 391
Mayes, Gabrielle 220
Mayfield, Amber Sioux 769
Maynard, David M. 630
Maynard, Eric 269
Mays, William E. 409
Mayser, Nick 713
Mazhar, N.G. 51
McAfee, Ken 144
McAfee, Lisa 561
McAfee, Martha 500
McArdle, Kimberly L. 130
McArdle, Matthew 334
McArthur, P. 119
McBean, Garfield K. 390
McBride, John D. 630
McBride, Rae 513
McBroom, David G. 202
McCabe, Michele 482
McCague, Thomas C. 420
McCallister, Anglea D. 271
McCallum, Bridget 173
McCallum, Mindi 549
McCament, Missy 419
McCann, Mary Jo 532
McCarter, Wilma O. 533
McCarthy, Kevin B. 22
McCarty, DeeMaris 262
McClelland, Laraine 131
McClintock, Kristalin 20
McClinton, Joanie O. 628
McClinton, Jovan 184
McClinton, Sandra 303
McCloskey, Amera Lynn 429
McClure, Annie L. 267
McClure, Loretta 408
McClure, Phyllis J. 656
McComb, Bernardine 220
McConkie, Beulah D. 748
McConnell, Jennifer Robin 158
McCormick, Todd 740
McCoy, Melissa 312
McCrea, J. K. 322
McCreary, Bobbie 230
McCulligh, Tierra 446
McCullough, April 635
McCullough, George E. 475
McDaniel, Christine L. 380
McDonald, Angela 636
McDonald, Edna 578
McDonald, Kelley Lee 26
McDonald, Stan 318
McDoniel, Brenda 469
McDonough, Janet Susan 590
McDonough, Mildred L. 691
McDowell, Brian 381
McFadden, Timothy 346
McFalls, May D. 695
McGarity, Katie 124
McGee, Kathryn 166
McGeorge, Bevly J. 764
McGeorge, Lynn 168
McGhee, Nathan 345
McGlue, Frances 458
McGowan, Grace 222
McGraw, Eleanor F. 260
McGraw, Emogene 387
McGrew, Mark A. 444
McGuire, Jack 172
McHaney, C.R. 269
McIntire, Florence 605
McIntosh, Jacqeline 232
McIntosh, Tanya 78
McKaig, Joseph J. 139
McKay, Kathryn Evans 155

McKay, Mary R. 780
McKay, Rosemary 190
McKeag, Robert G. 401
McKechnie, Michael 157
McKeehan, America Desiree 264
McKeen, Betty Westhaver 670
McKenna, C.L. 47
McKenna, Neil J. 343
McKenna, Sean Patrick 484
McKenna, Sheila FitzGerald 68
McKenzie, Phyllis 439
McKinlay, Laura 75
McKinney, Dagnee 595
McKinney, Kathleen Dunn 74
McKinney, Nicola 65
McKinstry, Judy 165
McLain, Alysia 205
McLane, Kathleen 187
McLaren, Richard 412
McLaughlin, Denys B. 191
McLaughlin, Phil 309
McLean, Kelli 84
McLeod, Debby Jean 187
McMahon, Deanna 769
McMahon, Gale A. 648
McMahon, Maryann 333
McMahon, Rosemary 402
McMaster, Joann W. 474
McMaster, Lara 559
McMichaels, Anne 649
McMillan, Helen Louise 190
McMillan, Lori 63
McMillen, Brian 392
McMillion, Paula 435
McMorrow, Fred 234
McMullin, Dale 383
McMullin, Joan 474
McNabb, Hope 41
McNamara, Jill 256
McNamee, Erin Eileen 264
McNatt, Carolyn S. 760
McNeill, Matthew 155
McNichols, Bryn 272
McNulty, Genevieve 221
McOrmond, Laurie 710
McPherson, Patricia L. 700
McQuade, Shirley M. 702
McQuay, Rita 336
McRae, Catherine Annett 110
McRae, Robert 280
McRee, Georgia 380
McReynolds, Harrietta 648
McUmber, Lisa 484
McWilliams, D. W. 382
McWilliams, H.P. 700
Mead, Jennifer 227
Mead, Rob 115
Meade, Dinah 201
Meade, Michael G. 121
Meador, Tannie 731
Mealing, Ronald W. 699
Meaney, Joe 749
Means, Tonja 283
Meany, John 765
Meany, Kevin Louis 22
Medders, Charles A. 770
Medeiros, Mario 153
Medford, Regina 563
Medina-Pasinkoff, Mildred 279
Meek, Virginia 559
Meersseman, Leon 162
Meier, Mary 558
Meitz, Maxine A. 273
Melbourne, Bertram L. 665
Melendez, Lizadia 522
Meli, Elaine 479
Melki, Viveka 150
Mellie, Rose 510
Mello, Donna 358
Melrose, Fiona 89
Melso, Lauren 490
Melton, Rhonda 559
Melvin, Virginia G. 550
Memba, Jared Amwayi 169
Memminger, Patricia 445

Mendez, Angel 382
Mennucci, Lita 713
Mercer, Barbara 762
Merchant, Joy 107
Merchant, Sandra 322
Mercurio, D. 79
Merdegia, Yolanda Laurel 484
Meredith, Meghan 557
Mergler, Daniel 92
Merigliano, Ralph 292
Merkel, Leonora C. 275
Merle, Jose M. 683
Merles, Ita 752
Merrell, Harold M. 649
Merrick, Tawnya 273
Merriweather, Arthur J. IV 775
Messer, Glenda 350
Metzger, Anne Reynolds 749
Meyer, Fredrica A. 266
Meyer, Gaye 643
Meyer, Michael J. 411
Meyer, Nicole S. 444
Meyer, Randy C. 415
Meyer, Royal E. 787
Meyers, Helen H. 623
Michael, Gregory Paul 241
Michaelis, Lorraine 731
Michaels, Donna 216
Michalik, Stanley 84
Michell, Ernestine M. 580
Michlig, Lisa 790
Mick, Matthew 280
Middleton, Max 507
Middleton, Michelle V. 782
Migita, Mark 434
Mihaly, June Elizabeth Geisler 109
Mikrut, Charlene D. 679
Millard, Michele 502
Millender, Gwen Woods 599
Miller, Alretta 651
Miller, Anna Spady 140
Miller, Brooke 272
Miller, Charlotte 220
Miller, Colette 131
Miller, Craig 596
Miller, Dana 773
Miller, Deborah 357
Miller, Gloria Lee 466
Miller, Gwendolyn C. 357
Miller, John G. 463
Miller, John Wesley 625
Miller, Kelly E. 154
Miller, Keven 43
Miller, Leah C. 711
Miller, Melinda 538
Miller, Melissa 98
Miller, Michael Duane 321
Miller, Michelle 689
Miller, Nancy 704
Miller, P.J. 502
Miller, Pat 552
Miller, Phylis 737
Miller, R.E. 19
Miller, Richard C. 418
Miller, Richard S. 304
Miller, Ryan 785
Miller, Sandy 551
Miller, Stefanie 490
Miller, Todd 124
Miller, Vickie B. 523
Miller-Cottom, Heather 392
Millman, Mindy 423
Mills, Amanda 764
Millwater, Marion 785
Milton, Erma 252
Mincey, Betty 664
Mines, Rosette 515
Minge, Lorna 404
Mink, Dana 358
Minler, Karen 34
Minnick, Charles L. 214
Minter, Sheryl 283
Minton, Jonathan E. 353
Mintz, Julia McLeymore 142
Miskulin, Magda Lynn 399

Oliver, Sonjia R. 784
Ollendieck, Melissa Lynn 691
Olsen, Diane L. 69
Olson, Margaret 445
Olson, Melvin E. 560
Omran, Lagracella 284
Ondrey, Verna Felkel 560
Onorato, Michael G. 300
Opira, Stephen 96
Oppelt, Ruth 433
Orders, Karrah Shea 37
Orduna, Michelle 560
Orella, Laura 7
Orem, Howard 749
Oren, Pam 430
Orlando, Maria-Victoria 303
Orr, Eva 630
Orr, Rosetta 562
Ortega-Lage, Esther 233
Orvis, Elinor 47
Osgood, Nethelia 430
Osorio, Elizabeth 759
Ostman, D.R. 454
Ostrom, Cori 772
Ostroske, Kevin 91
Otero, Maribel 440
Othmer, Judy 50
Ott, Margaret 336
Ott, Mary Ann 567
Ottenhausen, Nelson O. 703
Otway, Debbie 57
Ovalle, Xavier 497
Overman, John 127
Overman, Linda Rader 711
Overstreet, Clarice 629
Overton, Levada 523
Overton-Steele, Jamie L. 646
Owens, Alan 353
Owens, Sherley 336
Owino, Frederick 64
Owonibi, Sola Emmanuel 165
Paar, Francis 9
Pabs-Garnon, Editayo 137
Pace, Sandra L. 787
Pacheco, Dyanna Lynne 759
Pachinikstons 732
Pacifici, Zee 445
Padilla, Lissette 526
Padma, T.V. 711
Padowitz, Lisa 709
Page, Berni 230
Page, Kimela S. 140
Page, Kris 100
Page, Starr 480
Pagel, Valerie 550
Paglia, James 208
Paidoussi, Eleni 646
Paige, Terie 287
Palahniuk, Debbie 36
Palazzolo, Alison 610
Palermo, Michelle 350
Palm, Ralph 788
Palmer, Denise 364
Palmer, Joyce A. 92
Palmer, Kenneth Lee 145
Palmer, Patricia L. 345
Palmieri, Donna D. 651
Palmieri, James T. 245
Palou, Mari 405
Pamplin, Nancy Rhoads 278
Panrucker, Jessie 33
Pansini, Ursula E. 297
Pantin, Kai 74
Pao, Diana Lee 607
Pape, Hanna L. 779
Paradis, Jeremiah 233
Paras, Michael 722
Parekh, Edith 586
Paris, Erin 627
Paris, Josephine 188
Paris, Keith A. 43
Park, Grace 148
Park, Marian Ford 17
Parker, Catherine T. 455
Parker, Jay F. 611

Parker, Jerry Lee 666
Parker, Matthew A. 734
Parkerson, Irene 257
Parks, Mary 491
Parmley, Tracey 407
Parra, Fanny 352
Parsley, Earnestine 471
Parsons, Raymond 559
Parsons, Renee D. 57
Parton, Ewing Clay 753
Partridge, Ruth 727
Pascarella, Laurie 326
Pastore, Vanessa N.P. 441
Pate, Juliet L. 193
Patel, P.B. 344
Paterson, Ernest E. 79
Paterson, Kevin G. 20
Patrick, Marie T. 523
Patrick, Ruth A. 494
Patterson, Bruce M. 189
Patterson, Charles 628
Patterson, Dale 206
Patterson, Patricia 551
Patterson, Roy 532
Patty, Bill 658
Patusky, Marie S. 568
Patuzzi, Alexander C. 262
Pau, Jill 621
Paul, Benjamin 591
Paul, Charlene 216
Paul, Jane Wright 757
Paul, Margaret 274
Paul, Reena D. 287
Paulauskas, Gerard J. 240
Paulin, Peggy 415
Pauline 705
Pavuk, Joel 257
Payes, Sandra 564
Peacock, Constance H. 758
Peacock, Wanda Flowers 299
Pearl, Dorothy 766
Pearo, Agnes 119
Pearson, Florence 221
Pearson, Florence L. 767
Pearson, Joe 751
Pearson, Malcolm 72
Pearson, P. Dean 519
Peaver, Beverly 80
Peavy, Jennifer 359
Peck, John R. 624
Pecoy, Cyrilla D. 234
Pederick, Chanine Honor 60
Pederson, Della E. 221
Pedigo, Marilyn 563
Peele, Eula 638
Peer, Steven K. 552
Pelegrina, Gladys 265
Pellegrin, Norma L. 316
Pellonini, Wanda E. 488
Pelter, Danielle 760
Pelton, Lee 414
Pena, Ginger 362
Penna, Anne 351
Pennel, Charles 618
Penner, Vernon 174
Penney, Bryan Humphrey 222
Penny, Samuel 12
Pensfield, Allan Jane 219
Peoples, James L. 212
Peperoni, Gertrude 669
Peppel, Kipp 95
Perdue, Joseph L. 37
Pere, Julian 56
Perepelecta, Dustin 131
Peretic, Joe 76
Perez Jr., Anthony 592
Perez, Ana Maria 581
Perez, Julio J. 187
Periard, Brandi 211
Perkins, Bruce Scott 393
Perkins, Felice C. 594
Perkins, Marian LaVerne 419
Perras, Patricia A. 563
Perry, Betty Jane 215
Perry, Dolly 763

Perry, Theresa 655
Perryman, Tammy Lynne 347
Perzel, Ava 774
Pesano, John 127
Pesich, Carol 645
Peters, Debbie 250
Peters, Elaine E. 640
Peters, Norma 51
Petersen, Charlie 388
Petersen, Claire 270
Petersen, Janiece Avery 659
Petersen, Melissa 279
Peterson, Arthur F. 234
Peterson, Ed 159
Peterson, Jessica 598
Peterson, Joshua 75
Peterson, Lesa 657
Petillo, Mary 724
Petkau, Ryan 165
Petoh, Michael 330
Petrick, Robert B. 400
Petty, Bernice 363
Pfau, Stephani 406
Pfeifle, Jathan 649
Phelan, Claire J. 387
Phelps Sr., Sidney Lee 547
Phelps, Frances F. 371
Phelps, Warren H. 698
Phillips Jr., Hugh 649
Phillips, Betty Jo 449
Phillips, Brenna 237
Phillips, Clifton C. 229
Phillips, Debra 456
Phillips, Edward J. 575
Phillips, Mary 702
Phillips, Pamela 337
Phillips, Rodney V. 778
Phillips, Sandra 522
Phillips, Shirley 654
Phillips, Tim 328
Philpott, Melissa 23
Phinney, Linda J. 557
Pi, 565
Piarulli, Elizabeth McWilliams 229
Piazza, Linda M. 565
Pichel, Dorothy Ney 212
Picklap, Douglas S. 366
Pierce, Dave 457
Pierce, Kristopher 163
Pierce, Lori 561
Pierce, Mary Claire 446
Pierce, Rufus 308
Pierce, Ryan 445
Pierritz, Jane 262
Piffero, Alysia 638
Pignataro, Danielle 218
Pigott, Leonard 547
Pilarski, Barbara 385
Pilkey, John 259
Pillar, James 234
Pillot, Mary 572
Pilz, Kim M. 187
Pina, Candida Lomba 390
Pinckney, Patrick F. 340
Pine, John 395
Pines, Sarah 288
Pinkston, Sarah L. 531
Pinto, Rosalind 524
Piper, Bob 676
Pippig, Marvin 736
Pippin, Betty 196
Pirc, Brandy 360
Pistorius, H. 53
Pitchford, Thomas 555
Pitner, Jeanie 270
Pittman, Bertha 252
Pittwood, Geo E. 667
Piwowar, Alison 21
Plamer, Alez 194
Plant, Timothy 333
Plante, Marie 190
Pleger, Janet 98
Plekes, Felicia 680
Plesh, John 452
Pletcher, Bobbie 747

Plisek, Lona Kaye 338
Plummer, G.W. 569
Pobre-Moss, Joy 113
Podboy, Allison 256
Poe, Margaret 442
Poe, Roger Paul 402
Poet, J.C. 66
Pogarsky, Solomon 544
Poglitsch, Janice 187
Poindexter, Francine 456
Poirier, Doris A. 614
Poirier, Joyce A. 172
Poitevin, Evelyn M. 598
Poku, Benus Adu 75
Poliny, Val 794
Polizzi, Jackie 77
Pollard, LaNita Chanel 562
Pollizzi, Karen June Rice 26
Polonsky, Irina 242
Pomeroy, Jane Seward 382
Pongan, Marisa 116
Ponitz, Arlene G. 594
Poole, Dianne 100
Popovits, Connie 372
Poppe, Danny Joe 448
Porche, Joseph B. (Corba P.) 89
Portelance, Jeffrey 113
Porter, Larry D. 558
Porter, Peggy 326
Porter, Richard J. 563
Porter, Sheila 444
Porter, Thomas K. 500
Porter, Wanda Lee 485
Porter, Wayne J. 344
Post, Beverly M. 260
Potter, Mary 346
Potts, Terrance 653
Poulin, Anne 391
Powell, Carolyn Barrett 639
Powell, Eileen 674
Powell, Larry Dean 543
Powell, Luray R. 341
Power, Brett J. 161
Power, Timothy G. 283
Pratt, Heather 758
Pratte, Lois A. 550
Predan, Laura 66
Preece, Chrystal 68
Pregler, John E. 220
Prentice, Ayesha T. 622
Prentice, Donna L. 238
Prest, James E. 28
Price, Donna 233
Price, Dulcenia 371
Price, Jackie 666
Price, Nikki L. 548
Price, Raymond John 64
Price, Willie Ann 558
Prichard, John C. 183
Pride, T.M. 7
Priemer, Ricky 437
Priestley, Eric 575
Priger, Karen 80
Prince, Julia F. 100
Profili, Sabrina 541
Province, Kenya Lee 156
Psiurski, Nancy 97
Pucek, Tamie 723
Puglisi, Barbara Ann 747
Pulver, John R. 105
Puni, Jamie 748
Punyko, B. W. 623
Purdy, Patricia 507
Purser, Kim 138
Pusateri, John 764
Putman, Richard 310
Pyzikiewicz, Dawn 195
Quadrini, Rita 50
Quail, Jennifer 747
Qualls, Dana 609
Quass, Heather 264
Quast, Hazel 397
Quibell, Jeanette 612
Quihuis, Ivy 271
Quinabo, Edwin 601

Sailers, Thomas L. 340
Saint, Sara 447
Sakoda, Jon 597
Saladino, Danielle 752
Salamon, Morris 5533
Salcido, Virginia 560
Saldana, Aida Ophelia 638
Saldana, Alicia A. 388
Saldana, Joselis 629
Saldana, Stacy 409
Saleeby, Mark 516
Sali, Claudia C.C. 39
Sali, David A. 78
Salkin, Stephanie 440
Sallani, Marion Davis 425
Salmon, Glennis K. 158
Saltzman, Herman 591
Samaranayake, Sowmya Chandrika 170
Samarzia, Shirley 306
Samedi, Elizabeth 206
Sampson, Eva A. 676
Sampson, Gwen W. 642
Sampson, Jamal 53
Samson, Larry 543
Samson, Shalla 728
Samuel, Monique 558
Samuels, Lisa 574
Samuels, Louis Robert 338
Samuelson, Hymie 262
Sanabria, Monica A. 707
Sanborn, Tara 273
Sanches, Diana 236
Sanchez, Cheryelona 385
Sanders, Alice 247
Sanders, Angela Meggs 257
Sanders, Steven 326
Sanderson, Cindy 641
Sanderson, Georgia 12
Sanderson, Teresa 488
Sands, Adam T. 640
Sanfilippo, Cherryl Nadine 628
Sangster, Alicia 478
Santana-Shlichtman, Maribel 707
Sante, Ilse 40
Santoro, Ruthann 301
Santos, Steve 734
Santos, William 487
Sara'n, Simmer 313
Saraceno, Joanne 379
Saramago, Rui Miguel 545
Sarce, Kathleen 184
Sarkis, Ronald 293
Sarrgent, Jennifer 756
Sarvis, Susan 492
Sater, Jeffrey A. 609
Satterfield Sr., Claude 260
Sauer, Kathy 65
Sauers, Jillian 395
Sauls, H.D. 770
Saunders, Lorin C. 561
Savage, Michael 511
Savich, Jan 617
Saville, Dawn 156
Savlov, Jason A. 632
Sayad, Peggy Golis 499
Scafe, Roy 127
Scally, Cassandra 373
Scanlon, Kelly J. 154
Scarpitta, David 652
Schaeffer, Harriett 642
Schas, Gretchen 395
Schatz, Bernard 203
Schechter, Barry 224
Schellman, Michael 540
Schenke, Raymond E. 16
Scher, Mildred 655
Scherer, Tammy 706
Scheuerman, Judith K. 81
Schiavone, Antonia 68
Schicker, Dona 619
Schiffelbein, Michele 325
Schillings, Christopher Lee 618
Schjodt, Lawrence 19
Schlain, Marilyn 709
Schlea, Melissa 700

Schleifer, Evelyn 649
Schleiger, Elva R. 747
Schlotzhauer, Susan M. 293
Schlup, Linda 784
Schlup, Raymond 430
Schmaltz, Jennifer Alayne 763
Schmelter, C.G. 5
Schmelzle, Willie 276
Schmidt, Judy 58
Schmidt, Sarah 567
Schmit, Linda K. 435
Schmitt, Joseph 114
Schmitz, Dianna P. 475
Schmotzer, Randolph V. 501
Schnake, Kerrie Lynn 110
Schneider, Alan J. 556
Schneider, C.F. 572
Schneider, Lori 492
Schneider, Margaret 72
Schneider, Robert F. 308
Schnitzer, Chris 194
Schnurr, Kathleen 76
Schoenemann, John 652
Schoening, Elissa 637
Schoff, Susan 568
Scholberg, Henry 602
Schons, Mary Lou 411
Schorr, Milton 331
Schotsman, Christina 28
Schricker, Penny 513
Schroeder, Barry 12
Schrowang, Sue A. 481
Schuelke, Marilyn 530
Schuett, Eddie 616
Schultz, Lisa 482
Schuman, Arthur W. 192
Schwan, Paul H. 511
Schwartz Sr., Bill 634
Schwartz, Jackie 753
Schwartz, Laura 431
Schweitzer, Chris 636
Scott 511
Scott, Henrietta A. 267
Scott, J. Kaycee 234
Scott, Janet 25
Scott, Joseph A. 146
Scott, Kenneth W. 108
Scott, Linda 342
Scott, Lori K. 432
Scott, Michael Alan 510
Scott, Robert 778
Scribner, Jane 75
Scribner, Susan M. 277
Scringer, Berenice 634
Scripca, Iolanda 229
Sczepaniak, Michaela 445
Seal, Alan 373
Seal, Vicki 447
Searcey, Lee 495
Sears, Alton 246
Sears, Deborah Lynn 663
Seatter, SC 492
Seavey, Janet M. 265
Secomski, Vera 777
Seefeldt, Rebecca S. 653
Seeley, Kerry 81
Segal, Edwin S. 264
Seibel, Julianne 73
Seidman, Lauren 401
Seitz, Viola 345
Selby, Carol Ann 621
Selchow, Vileta N. 329
Sells, Stacy D. 509
Selvidge, Stephanie 716
Sen, Millicent 503
Sensenich, Cindy K. 635
Sepe, Thomas C. 555
Serafin, Jessica 582
Sertso, Ingrid 215
Seruya, Nancy 484
Servais, Joe 25
Setsomi, David Molapo 36
Severn 517
Sewell, Tswana 535
Shabtai, John Yaniv 173

Shacklette, Jane Talley 183
Shad, Shama 153
Shade, Jennie Mae 642
Shadid, Jane 595
Shafer, Debra M. 270
Shaff, Gladys Crittenden 461
Shaikh, Rashid 278
Shankar, D. N. Ravi 64
Shanker, Elaine Helene 678
Shapiro, Charlie 768
Shapiro, Elizabeth 675
Sharpe, Ella Jordan 585
Sharpes, Elinor 758
Shatraw, Irene 387
Shaver, Mildrid S.C. 18
Shaw, Christine 83
Shaw, Ginny 164
Shaw, Jennifer 82
Shaw, Spencer 332
Shaw-Hampshire, Barbara Kay 384
Shay, Dee 556
Shea, Maureen 710
Shearer, Patricia Ann 336
Shedlock, Scott 324
Sheehan, Christopher 576
Shehadi, Feiruz 214
Shelley, Donald Dean 685
Shellito, Katrina 65
Shelton, Anna Mary 197
Shelton, Jim 750
Shelton, Joan 211
Shepherd, Jamie 670
Shepherd, Leslie G. 319
Shepherd, Theresa 545
Shepherd-Marshall, Yvonne Pamela 520
Shepphard, Julie 90
Sheren, Carol A. 375
Sheridan, Phyllis 692
Sheriff, Molly E. 439
Sherlin, Kalei 40
Sherman, Edith 770
Sherman, Lura L. 426
Sherman-Hall, Tali 400
Shin, Curtis C. 627
Shockley, Monte R. 482
Shoemaker, Sarah 793
Shoenfelt, David C. 389
Shontz, William H. 538
Shoop, Errin 706
Shores, William W. 427
Shorette, James 272
Short, Mary Kay 416
Shrum, Bill 210
Shulkusky, Cheryl 260
Shulmistras, Joan B. 214
Siano, Mary Martha 433
Sibley, Karen 87
Sibrel, Katherine Kline 24
Sich, Ardis Marie 631
Siciliano, Carmela M. 599
Sides, James G. 616
Sidoti, Rose 350
Sieber, L. Aryn 292
Siebold, Wendy 170
Siegel, Allison 378
Siegel, Donald R. 467
Siekerman, Jackie M. 266
Sigety, Patrick Raymond 736
Silfies, Jennifer 254
Silkey, Sherri G. 791
Silva, Cullen D. 639
Silverburg, Shirley Cheifetz 520
Silverman, S.R. 407
Silye, Jessica L. 218
Simard, Carole 83
Sime, Farrah 21
Simmers, Julie 112
Simmons, Furman M. 600
Simmons, Heather J. 759
Simmons, LaTonya 508
Simmons, Sheryl 432
Simmons, Steven 423
Simmons, Sue 521
Simms, Marilyn 284
Simms, Susie G. 781

Simon, Jewel 373
Simon, Laura G. 12
Simon, Susan 514
Simons, Rochelle 723
Simons, Steven A. Sr. 729
Simpson, Catherine 30
Simpson, Harriet 684
Simpson, Nancy D. 492
Simpson, Ruth D. 404
Simpson, Wanda 496
Sims, Ingrid Christopher 464
Sims, William Earl 479
Sinclair, Jeff 198
Sindle-Pruitt, Doris 273
Singh, M.D., Parikshit 157
Singh, Ranvir 183
Singleton, Angylin C. 750
Singleton, Matthew J. & Rogers, Joshua J. 323
Sinh, Le Quang 431
Sinke, Evelyn 389
Sinsabaugh, Sarah 433
Siriwardene, Mahendra 51
Sirkowski, Erich E. 390
Sisco, Sid 18
Sisk, Stacie L. 292
Sisson, Deborah 751
Sitaram, Annapoorna 79
Sitterly, Lana 789
Siwek, Rena 425
Skalka, Anna 99
Skannal, Deborah 223
Skarbovig, Kristin 22
Skellion, David 392
Skillman, David M. 622
Slade, Ivan 269
Slade, Sharon 496
Slaney, Michelle 152
Slate, Nathan K. 436
Slater, John 147
Slayer, Tom 727
Sledd, Donna 469
Slesinski, Myldred 705
Sliger, Ryan 349
Sloan, Bobbie Jo 452
Sloat, Dolores 466
Slomiany, Rudy 549
Slone, Christy A. 457
Sloup, Kathleen 126
Slusarczyk, Eleanor 375
Slusher, Wayne 410
Smaciarz, Matthew 552
Small, Fred 749
Smallwood, Joyce Horsey 109
Smart, Cherryl 65
Smell, Cynthia Lyn 644
Smetak, Virginia 574
Smiley, Judye R. 128
Smiley, Kim 164
Smith, Alice P. 74
Smith, Alisa 385
Smith, Andrea 257
Smith, Beatrice L. 584
Smith, Ben 589
Smith, Bion E. 396
Smith, Carmen J. 590
Smith, Carol Mae 796
Smith, Caroline L. 641
Smith, Charlotte L. 756
Smith, Chasity 376
Smith, Cory 619
Smith, Curtis 652
Smith, Dana 370
Smith, Dana Dunn 633
Smith, Dee Dee 390
Smith, Eddie 260
Smith, Edith 646
Smith, Elizabeth Maine 24
Smith, J.T. 704
Smith, James P. Jr. 673
Smith, James T. 674
Smith, Joan Celeste 449
Smith, K. 43
Smith, Karen V. McKenzie 164
Smith, Kathryn M. 82

Smith, Kimberly 54
Smith, Kimberly Ann 132
Smith, Le'Chantier Sheri 442
Smith, Mary Ann 713
Smith, Parinella M. 556
Smith, Rachel 320
Smith, Ronald 528
Smith, Roy N. 314
Smith, Ruth 313
Smith, Sari de Coninck 124
Smith, Scott Patrick 689
Smith, Steffani 308
Smith, Stephanie A. 330
Smith, Stephen A. 345
Smith, Susan Maxson 534
Smith, Tandinika 524
Smith, Teri 325
Smith, Theodore G. 342
Smith, Thomas A. 339
Smith, Timothy 693
Smith, Tonya D. 311
Smith-Darby, Leanetha 521
Smith-Hughes, Marlene 571
Smothers, Richard Clay 539
Smylie, Glenn Stuart 386
Snedeker, B. L. 640
Sneek, Adam 270
Snider, Dale L. 177
Snyder, Casey 637
Snyder, Ginny 660
Snyder, James 82
Snyder, Linda L. 716
Snyder, Steve 486
Snyder, Walter W. 567
Snyder, William 120
Socks, Fish 412
Sokn, Erick L. 458
Solheim, Mabel A. 288
Solis, Francisca Marie 748
Solitario, Donna 212
Solland, Wanda 707
Solonenko, Nicole 78
Som, Sitha 333
Somrack, F. Daniel 472
Somrah, Darryl 620
Sonnichsen, Sidney R. 545
SookDeo, Neil 317
Sopp, Margie 276
Soriano, Dollie 601
Sorrels, Pearl N. 733
Sou, Bunnary 471
Souter, Debra 594
Southward, C. 194
Soutullo, Liliana 730
Sowell, Clifford 363
Spackman, C.T. 125
Spadideas, Demy D. 197
Spaeth, Patricia 791
Spalding, Rita S. 336
Spangenburg, Janice M. 668
Spangler, Christine F. 380
Spann, Carolyn 227
Spann, Nathanael J. 487
Spark, Alysa E. 19
Sparks, Florence S. 363
Sparks, Jackie H. 188
Sparks, Jeff A. 635
Sparks, Travis E. 344
Sparks, Willie Jr 783
Speers, Michael 553
Speirs, Kreg Daniel 132
Spell Jr., Ronald E. 523
Spence, Andrew James 393
Spence, Wayne J. 343
Spencer, Melisa 484
Spigonardo, Michelle 348
Spio, Mary 322
Spirio, Lawrence 401
Spitzer, Jaclyn B. 240
Spooner, Cynthia 448
Spoto, Jennifer 180
Spracklin, Dulcie Lear 113
Spradlin, Brian M. 752
Spraggins, Qiana 554
Sprague, Jody 158

Sprague, Myrtle 344
Spray, Christy L. 666
Spriggs, Craig 271
Sprung, John G. 16
Spurling, Tammy 417
Squar, Mara 430
Squillante, Lynn 440
Srodes, Todd 315
Srur, George A.
St. Amour, Camille 228
St. Clair, Patricia 346
St. James, Aggie v. 466
St. James, Sonia 568
St. Pierre, Suzanne 417
Stack, Tina Marie 787
Stackhouse, Kevin L. 41
Stacy, Rich 566
Stafford, Connie Lynn 237
Stafford, James W. 649
Staggs, Gary M. 231
Staggs, Gary M. 578
Staggs, Rose 275
Stahl, George 576
Stahl, George R. 392
Stahl, Lori Michelle 712
Stallings, Elisabeth 619
Stallings, Lee Linc 334
Stamatakos, Helen 666
Stamis, Cosma 250
Stancati, Lisa A. 539
Stanford, Charles 638
Stang, Geraldine 56
Stang, Patrick W. 335
Stanicek, Christian 209
Stanley, Penta M. 727
Stark, Doug 775
Starks, Kathy 102
Starr, Fred 773
Starszak, Julia 154
Start, Irma O'Neal 145
Stauffenecker, Jan 249
Stebbins, Hilda M. 395
Steel, Wendi 330
Steele, Amber 452
Steele, Judy 159
Steigert, Ange 577
Steiner, M. Elisabeth 718
Steiner-McQuay, Dorothy 384
Steinman, Shirley M. 538
Stenbar, Edward Nathan 398
Stengl, Dona Marie 238
Stephens, Barbara 364
Stephens, Shanha 293
Stephens, Susan A. 526
Stephenson, Alexandria C. 352
Sterk, Melissa 342
Stern, Jason Taylor 604
Steurrys, Karen J. 186
Stevens, Christopher A. 468
Stevens, Paul W. 532
Stevens, Terry 345
Stewart, Al 140
Stewart, Dawn Waynetta 628
Stewart, Katie 54
Stewart, Nell 310
Stickle, Michelle 480
Stickle, Shela 422
Stickley, Theresa 6
Stiffard, Adeline 354
Stiles, Ann 149
Stinson, Dolores 71
Stipes, Sallie Sue 793
Stirling, M. J. 94
Stocker, Genevieve 397
Stoddard-Leonard, Linda 718
Stoerr, Roellen 494
Stoffel, Jean 270
Stoker, Erdmuthe B. 645
Stoler, Amy 235
Stone, Annie Norris 686
Stone, Meg 289
Stone, Tonya 655
Stonehouse, Terri 28
Stoneman, G.J. 143
Storey, Janet 176

Storgards-Hatam, Karin 124
Stotler, Jonathan 759
Stoughton, Katherine 83
Stover, Vicky Ellise 719
Stowe, Colleen 637
Stowe, Lucinda 562
Stracuzzi, Randy K. 489
Strand, Bruce E.H. 67
Strand, Rebecca S. 693
Strass, Achim 183
Strasser, Scott E. 328
Strasser-leslie, Dianne 393
Straub, Marjorier Mix 795
Straub, Sheryl 731
Straub, Victoria 175
Strauss, Egon 477
Strawn, Dale A. 228
Street Kidd, Mae 435
Strick, Linda 406
Strickland, Christine J. 262
Strickland, Cyndi 775
Strickland, Julia Anne 212
Strickland, Kathryn 94
Strickler, Loretta V. 441
Stroebel, I. 558
Stroisch, Monica E. 723
Strong, Barbara 272
Strong, Barbara 390
Strong, Brandon M. 203
Stroop, Roger 128
Strube, Paul 102
Strunk, Tamara 174
Stuart, Andy 36
Stucci, Mavis 87
Stucks, Rebecca E. 559
Studdert, June O'Mohundro
Stull, Ruby Vernon 487
Stuller, Patricia C. 348
Sturzenegger, Julie 47
Stutzman, Jana 766
Suh, Angela 381
Suhrbier, Larry 348
Sullivan, Dolores Edwards 16
Sullivan, Gwendolyn Jo 371
Sullivan, Ryan J. Michael 153
Sultana, Nilofer 139
Sumerel, Zelma 502
Summers, Andrew Jason 182
Summy, Luetta A. 709
Surdenik, Douglas e. 584
Susan, McCarthy 298
Susik, Abby 449
Suter, Debra Jane 751
Sutherland, Jan 166
Sutherland, Jan 43
Sutton, Carol Ann 391
Sutton, Christina M. 642
Sutton, James W. 361
Sutton, Jaylene 223
Svarda, Devon Knight 17
Svoboda, Bob 367
Swain, Kathleen Buck 96
Swanson, Verla 15
Swartz, Shawn D. 445
Swatling, Carol-Ann 613
Swearingen, Debra A. 460
Swedensky, Shirley 419
Sweeney, Bart 261
Sweet, Dahn 242
Swenson, Pam 503
Swertner Jr., John 602
Swift, Liz 698
Swilling, Arlene M. 201
Swing, Scott H. 706
Swinney, Michael Jerud 555
Swofford, Margaret M. 344
Sword, Gene 602
Syd, Bob 632
Sykes, Ella M. 357
Sykora, Rachel L. 526
Sylva, Rusty J. 692
Szabo, Michelle 30
Szatkowski, James 31
Szilagyi, Katie 35
Szurgot, R. Andrew 447

Szuromi, Laszlo 304
Szymanski, Carol J. 649
Taber, Barbara B. 396
Tablit Jr., Elpidio 640
Takala, John J. 667
Takata, Steven I. 342
Taksas, James R. 643
Tallent, Donna G. 754
Tallman, Evelyn J. 764
Tamburo, Sally 420
Tangjian, Christina M. 635
Tanilli, Lena 737
Tannenbaum, Sol 525
Tanner, Millie 149
Tarango, Sarah 654
Tarazewich, Frank J. 646
Tatro, Douglas W. 605
Tausta, Ruth 348
Taylor, Annie B. 258
Taylor, Carol C. 232
Taylor, Claudette J. 772
Taylor, Colin 204
Taylor, Joanne 98
Taylor, June A. 164
Taylor, Karen 193
Taylor, Kristi 35
Taylor, Lucille A. 696
Taylor, Olga 145
Taylor, Steve 126
Teaney, P. LaRue 480
Tears, Marlene J. 714
Teaters, Christopher 239
Teed-Baker, Sherri 403
Teich, Elizabeth 593
Teierle, Raylean 158
Temple, Sandra Kay 547
TenBrook, Jason R. 383
Teng, Nick 278
Tennyson, Joseph 26
Terrell, Thembi Michelle 572
Terry, Joseph M. 88
Terry, Joshua 167
Terzic, Joseph 94
Teska, Mary 492
Tester, Joyce 21
Teverbaugh, Leatha 697
Tewksbury, Regis, P. 430
Thacker, Beulah 356
Thaden, John H. 8
Thatche, Ida L. 258
The Dream Seer, 592
Theilheimer, Sherri Ellen 147
Thelin-McDonald, Birgit 33
Thelle, Olav Ramstad 65
Theriot, Natalee 291
Thirsk, Stan 281
Thissen, Joni 649
Thom, Kimberley 50
Thom, Zachary 732
Thomas, Brian 676
Thomas, Don 195
Thomas, Francis D. 611
Thomas, George 592
Thomas, Gina 589
Thomas, Jessie 32
Thomas, John F. 459
Thomas, Kendrell N. 73
Thomas, Kristen 127
Thomas, Maxine 712
Thomas, McNeill 489
Thomas, Michele 443
Thomas, Nicole Anne 406
Thomas, Ophelia 441
Thomas, Oral O. 273
Thomas, Rhiana 732
Thomas, Robert A. 407
Thomas, Rose 562
Thomas, Westley 281
Thomas, William Howard 1
Thome, Jennifer L. 272
Thompson, Cynthia Boman 757
Thompson, Daniel Lee 222
Thompson, Evelyn 185
Thompson, Florence 598
Thompson, Janice 29

Weiner, Sheila C. 788
Weir, Brocke 588
Weir, Susie 528
Weirmack, Ray 708
Weis, Elsie F. 398
Weisenberger, Twila 510
Weisner, Andrew Jeremiah 240
Weiss, LaRue Renneisen 795
Weiss, Phyllis 717
Weissman, Delores G. 211
Welch, Marilyn H. 515
Welch, R.G. 690
Welch, Susan 499
Welding, Barrett 263
Wellman, Lynne 792
Wells, Kiersten 49
Wells, L.A. 47
Wells, Ned 489
Wells, Raymond A. 521
Welton, Jean B. 605
Welty, Rachel 575
Wendowski, Kathleen C. 181
Wenek-Ziemba, Ilona 97
Werderits, Debra 353
Wesley, Linda 506
Wesley, Patricia 133
Wess, Brian L.A. 668
Wessling, Erin I. 450
West, Earl III 770
West, Keith N. 71
West, Martin 25
West, Mary Josephine 60
West, Sarah 417
Westaby, Eve 625
Westcott, Imogene 610
Westoby, Mary 699
Weston, Jennifer Michelle 595
Westurn, Jennifer 365
Wetzel, Mary 442
Whealdon, Everett 460
Wheaton, Stanley 738
Wheeler, Dawn 587
Wheeler, Eunice 753
Whelan, Harold 420
Whipple, Julie L. 107
Whisler, Sara 446
Whisnand, Darlene 761
Whitaker, Jennifer 760
Whitaker, Maxine 529
Whitcomb, Jay R. 364
Whitcomb, K. L. 447
White, Beatrice L. 393
White, Brenda Bland 365
White, Courtney 129
White, D. Jonathan 301
White, Gladys 473
White, Juanita Moore 37
White, Kirk 109
White, Lynn A. 541
White, Norma E. 493
White, Renee 400
Whitehouse, Lynne 114
Whitehurst, Celia 259
Whitelove, Min 490
Whitman, Angela K. R. 389
Whitmore, Connie 608
Whitney, Corliss Fyfe 237
Whitney, Melissa Mae 563
Whittaker, Del 209
Whittaker, Kristen Marie 182
Whittington, Joseph A. 117
Whittington, Katrina 63
Whittle, Bev 651
Whittle, Joan A. 157
Whybrow, Ashley 93
Wickstrom, Sandra 189
Widoff, Don Brad 11
Wiebe, Virginia L. 34
Wielechowski, Dale 208
Wiese, Nancy R. 300
Wiesler, Jason 149
Wiggins Jr., James A. 466
Wiggins, Samejra 433
Wikander, Carl 153
Wild, Graham M. 177

Wild, Tesse 436
Wilde, Wayne 691
Wilder, Theresa 780
Wileden, Elizabeth 463
Wilfong, Neal D. 742
Wilford, Charlotte L. 362
Wilhelm, Kimberly L. 23
Wilk, Christopher Anthony 623
Wilkerson, Lois 780
Wilkinson, Sherrie Isenhart 792
Wilkinsong, Benjamin J. 262
Willard, Gary S. 454
Willard, Steven 711
Williams Jr., Roy L. 443
Williams, Alberta N. 474
Williams, Allison 756
Williams, Barbara 626
Williams, Billy 675
Williams, Brian 133
Williams, David Townley 187
Williams, Diane 667
Williams, Edward R. 360
Williams, Gloria Ann 247
Williams, Janet H. 111
Williams, Jean M. 666
Williams, Jerrod 687
Williams, JoAnna 25
Williams, Katheleen K. 85
Williams, M. 121
Williams, Pamela 562
Williams, Terrance A. 399
Williams, Terry 332
Williams, Theresa 407
Williamson, Tim 346
Willig, Beverly 250
Willis, Jennifer 763
Willis, Sherril A. 557
Willms, Melissa 447
Willows, Arlene 171
Willowtrout, Michele 16
Wilmore, Phyllis 702
Wilson, Alayna 610
Wilson, Alexander 590
Wilson, Bernadine J. 681
Wilson, Bernice W. 772
Wilson, Betty Gene 226
Wilson, Bobbie Lee 373
Wilson, Carol Frazer 648
Wilson, Celia 267
Wilson, Chester A. 609
Wilson, Cyndi R. 358
Wilson, Florence Eugene 33
Wilson, Geneva 459
Wilson, Jackie 611
Wilson, Jamie M. 630
Wilson, Julie F. 68
Wilson, Lesley 321
Wilson, Mary 569
Wilson, Mitchell John 77
Wilson, Noah 491
Wilson, Rosalind 90
Wilson, Terance 137
Wilson-Mack, Florence T. 356
Wimberly, Lamarr D. 522
Windell, Violet Bruner 415
Wingrove, Jennifer 86
Winieski, Raymond J. 490
Winkler, Michael C. 530
Winnett, Calista J. 650
Winnubst, Mark D. 434
Winsor, Lynda (Sha Rosa) 318
Winstead, Andrew Cannon 241
Winston, Deborah Kay 661
Winter, Christie 166
Winterburn, Jenn L. 118
Winters, Leila 31
Winters, Melanie 512
Winters, Nichole 108
Wirtefeld, Brian P. 575
Wise, Audrey M. 197
Wise, Mark A. 327
Wisk, Coyetta 760
Wisniewski, S.D. 703
Wissner, Ilse 675
Witkus, Tanya 728

Witman, Cheryl 257
Witte, Tonya 428
Witter, Nancy 440
Wittman, Sharon L. 273
Wlodowski, Miroslaw 429
Woehr Jr., Eugene 380
Wojewoda, Alice 71
Wolf, Heather L. 270
Wolf, Hedy 625
Wolf, Howard F. 600
Wolfe, Ann Marie 658
Wolfe, Dennis A. 469
Wolfe, Erin 262
Wolfendale, Claire 167
Wolfson, Muriel 508
Wolinsky, Fred 577
Wolpa, Carolyn 771
Wolsky, Marc 741
Wolverton, Nora 445
Womack, Charline G. 470
Wong, Malia 484
Wong, Peter A. 296
Wonzer, Tracy L. 348
Wood, Elizabeth K. 141
Wood, Marilyn R. 304
Wood, Rosella Virginia 543
Woodall, Mark 693
Woodell, Katherine 23
Woodhead, Genevieve 622
Woodhouse, Tamar E. 297
Woodland, Eva 67
Woods, Cyndy 686
Woods, Donna M. 592
Woods, Lisa M. 122
Woodson, William C. 516
Woodward, Isabel A. 672
Woodward, Jason 101
Woodward, John A. 626
Woodward, Ray 408
Woody, Randy 540
Wooley, Mildred B. 720
Woolf, Lynda L. 730
Woolley, Jason 674
Woolley, Karl 77
Woomer, James 473
Wooten, Timothy W. I 796
Worcel, Rachel 534
Word, Sharon B. 543
Worden, Charlotte 640
Worsham, Patricia N. 338
Wrezinski, Shari Lynn 312
Wright Sr., Oscar 310
Wright, Chad E. 469
Wright, Jackie 219
Wright, Laura 345
Wright, Nancy Lee 278
Wright, Nancy M.S. 551
Wright, Nora 524
Wright, Roy 295
Wright, William W. 786
Wrightam, Ruth 573
Wroble, Tammy 547
Wulff, Michelle 122
Wyant, Marguerite J. Bears 573
Wyhs, Irma 7
Wyler, Stephanie 730
Wylie, Theresa 348
Wyman, Terry D. 709
Xavier, Deborah A. 603
Xavier, Irene T. 757
Xereas, Helen 374
Yabut, Marissa J. 309
Yacobucci, David A. 392
Yacur, Brian 221
Yager, Donna Marie 675
Yamaki, Linda M. 340
Yan, Shirley 507
Yap, Simeon T. 168
Yarnell, Eric 216
Yarnell, Eric 356
Yasuo, Atsuomi James 253
Yaudes, Aaron M. 750
Yawn, Rhonda J. 575
Yeager, Sarah 436
Yeager, Sarah 557

Yeakle, Bethanie 396
Yeaw, Pamela K. 349
Yerkes, Betty 665
Yim, Juliana M. 107
Yin, Simon Leong Choy 76
Yniquez, Angie 248
Yocum, Barbara J. 669
Yon, Kris 79
York, Lindsey 274
York, Serge 721
Youll, Steven 442
Young, Corrine F. 596
Young, Elsie D. 77
Young, Jacalyn 27
Young, James J. 231
Young, Joanna 370
Young, Leontyne 424
Young, Randall Lewis 299
Young, Ricci 439
Young, Rosalind J. 569
Young, Ruby 694
Young, Scott 331
Youngblood, Bill 392
Youngren, Audrey 775
Yruegas, Mary 796
Zablocki, Hillary 642
Zaccaria, Florence 366
Zachar, Ann 758
Zafer, Steve N. 121
Zalle, Melissa 568
Zanko, Christopher 645
Zarb, Edward 190
Zayas Jr., Juan 147
Zebley, Jennifer 68
Zeff, F. Gavin 654
Zelig, Edith Stein 157
Zellner, Sandy Moffett 657
Zenke, Ilse 176
Zenner, Amy J. 580
Zeno, Jessica Renee 131
Zepernick, Elizabeth 254
Zgrda, Florika 475
Zickefoose, Tedeidra 499
Ziegler, Mildred M. 446
Zilli, Mary 282
Zimmermann, Michaela 138
Zinke, Bill 374
Zinobile, Joe 389
Zipp, Brian A. 381
Zito, Christopher 353
Zito, Diana 586
Zivalich, Jeanna 392
Zohar, Meir 135
Zorko, Jennifer 453
Zuba, Anthony 161
Zuck, Lila 150
Zuelch, Louise N. 338
Zukowski, Edna 593
Zweber, Rae M. 530
Zwirn, Adrienne 615